INTERNATIONAL ENCYCLOPEDIA OF NATIONAL SYSTEMS OF EDUCATION

SECOND EDITION

Resources in Education

This is a new series of Pergamon one-volume Encyclopedias drawing upon articles in the acclaimed *International Encyclopedia of Education, Second Edition*, with revisions as well as new articles. Each volume in the series is thematically organized and aims to provide a complete and up-to-date coverage on its subject. These Encyclopedias will serve as an invaluable reference source for researchers, faculty members, teacher educators, government officials, educational administrators, and policymakers.

The *International Encyclopedia of National Systems of Education, Second Edition* contains 152 articles on national systems of education. The reviews follow a common structure providing easy access to the following information: general background information; politics and goals of the educational system; the formal structure of education; administrative and supervisory structure; educational finance; personnel; curriculum development; examinations, promotion, and certification; educational assessment, evaluation, and research; review of the major reforms in the 1980s and 1990s; and challenges ahead for the new millenium. A complete bibliography and further reading at the end of each article provide references for further research. An extensive author index is also included.

Other titles in the Series include:

CARNOY (ed.)
International Encyclopedia of Economics of Education, Second Edition

ANDERSON (ed.)
International Encyclopedia of Teaching and Teacher Education, Second Edition

TUIJNMAN (ed.)
International Encyclopedia of Adult and Continuing Education, Second Edition

PLOMP & ELY (eds)
International Encyclopedia of Educational Technology, Second Edition

DeCORTE & WEINERT (eds)
International Encyclopedia of Developmental and Instructional Psychology

INTERNATIONAL ENCYCLOPEDIA OF NATIONAL SYSTEMS OF EDUCATION

SECOND EDITION

Edited by

T. NEVILLE POSTLETHWAITE
University of Hamburg, Germany

PERGAMON

UK   Elsevier Science Ltd, The Boulevard, Langford Lane,
Kidlington, Oxford OX5 1GB, UK

USA   Elsevier Science Inc, 660 White Plains Road, Tarrytown, New
York 10591-5153, USA

JAPAN   Elsevier Science Japan, Tsunashima Building Annex, 3-20-12
Yushima, Bunkyoku, Tokyo 113, Japan

Second edition 1995

Library of Congress Cataloging in Publication Data
International encyclopedia of national systems of
education / edited by T. Neville Postlethwaite. — 2nd ed.
      p.   cm.
    Includes bibliographical references and indexes.
    1. Comparative education—Encyclopedias. 2. School
management and organization—Encyclopedias. 3.
Education and state—Encyclopedias. I. Postlethwaite, T.
Neville. II. Encyclopedia of comparative education and
national systems of education
LB43.I584 1995
370.19'5—dc20   95–34436

British Library Cataloguing in Publication Data
A catalogue record for this book is available from the
British Library.

ISBN 0–08–042302–7

∞™   The paper used in this publication meets the minimum requirements of the
American National Standard for Information Sciences—Permanence of Paper for Printed
Library Materials, ANSI Z39.48–1984.

Printed and bound in Great Britain by Cambridge University Press,
Cambridge, UK.

Contents

v

Contents

Contents

Preface

This Encyclopedia contains overviews of 152 systems of education. All systems are described using the same structure. As shown below, there are 12 sections in each overview. The aim of this Encyclopedia is to provide brief descriptions of many systems of education based on relatively recent data. At the end of each article there is a bibliography for those readers wishing to delve further into specific aspects of the educational system. No cross-system analyses have been undertaken or presented since it was never the intention, when compiling the system overviews, to undertake any form of analysis.

Genesis

In 1985 Pergamon Press published the first edition of *The International Encyclopedia of Education* containing nearly 1,500 articles arranged alphabetically, covering many areas of research and including 159 articles describing that many systems of education. Following the publication of this parent encyclopedia a decision was taken to produce a one-volume thematic encyclopedia containing articles on comparative education and updates of the 159 systems of education descriptions. This publication, *The Encyclopedia of Comparative Education and National Systems of Education* appeared in 1988.

In 1994 Pergamon published *The International Encyclopedia of Education, Second Edition* containing 1,266 articles, most of which were completely new, including 142 descriptions of different Systems of Education. Given that there have been many changes – often radical – in the structure, functioning, and problems in all countries, it was decided to publish these descriptions in this present Encyclopedia. In the first edition there were a mixture of authors. Some were from ministries of education, others were comparative educators, and yet others were students in graduate schools of education. The advantage of having authors from ministries of education is that they know their own systems well and have up-to-date information. The disadvantage is that they are rarely prepared to be critical of their own system. However, outsiders are prepared to be critical in their writing but they often have to rely on other – and sometimes outdated – publications with the result that the entries sometimes do not take account of some important change or some aspects of a system fail to be included. This dilemma was discussed and it was decided that in principle it should be ministries that would be invited to supply authors to write the descriptions according to a given format. In the event that ministries were enable to supply an author, outsiders would be invited to write the entry.

Requests were sent to ministries of education. Some replied. Some even wrote the articles themselves. Others did not reply despite continued attempts. Some countries were experiencing civil war, and that is why, for example, there is no entry on Angola. On the other hand, the author from Afghanistan wrote his entry hurriedly from a war-torn area where only streets away from his apartment shells were exploding. If, after several attempts a ministry did not respond to a request to write, every effort was made to find an author who was a specialist in that particular country's system of education. For the most part such authors were found.

A particular problem of an encyclopedia of this kind where entries come from all parts of the world is that many of the authors are writing in a language which is not their native one. In nearly all cases the entries were written in English by the authors and then edited by me, but there were a few instances where the entries had to be translated from French or Spanish before being edited.

The entries were typically written in 1992–93 and were included in the 1994 *International Encyclopedia of Education, Second Edition.* In early 1994 Pergamon decided to publish this one-volume thematic Encyclopedia containing only the descriptions of the systems of education. By its publication in 1995 it would be seven years since its predecessor was published. Furthermore, other similar works would also be out of date by that time. All authors were requested to update their entries and where it was felt that a particular author should supply more detail on a particular point, he or she was asked to include this information. Nearly all authors acceded to this request, some did not respond at all, while others expanded what they had written for the parent encyclopedia.

Later, it was possible to have entries from a further 10 countries that had been unable to prepare an article for the *International Encyclopedia of Education, Second Edition.* These countries were: Algeria, Bolivia, Brazil, Cambodia, Congo, Czech Republic, Ecuador, Haiti, Slovak Republic, and Western Samoa.

Thus, the descriptive data in the 152 entries in this Encyclopedia are, for the most part, from 1994.

Descriptive Information Requested

A nine-page document was sent to each author indicating the information required and in what sequence. This was accompanied by an example of *Australia: System of Education* which had been kindly prepared by Dr Philip McKenzie of the Australian Council for Educational Research. It was recognized that the information required was not exhaustive and authors were encouraged to add other information about their system that they thought would be of particular interest to an international readership. It had been agreed that the length of each entry should be in the region of 6,000 to 6,500 words (or word equivalent). It was therefore clear that no author could supply all the information requested and that he or she would have to make a judgment on where to include more or less detail on a particular point.

The overall aim, therefore, was to have a short description of a country's system of education which would encapsulate the main features and special aspects such that any reader would gain a good first impression of the total system.

Each entry includes the following 12 sections. These sections were deemed to cover the major aspects of a system of education and serve the purpose of having a first glance at a system. Certain information was requested for each section. The notion was that readers would be able to examine either the entry as a whole or certain sections from each. For example, it might be that a reader is interested only in the structure and enrollments of a number of systems. In this case, he or she would look only at Section 3 in each of the entries. Or, alternatively, the reader's interest might only be in the administrative structure in which case Section 4 would be the appropriate section. It should be noted that there is no Subject Index in this Encyclopedia. This is because each entry has the same structure and each system description, in a sense, stands alone. There is, however, a Name Index.

Section 1 is entitled *General Background.* Specifically, authors were asked to present information about the geographical, political, economic, and social structure factors that had had a significant effect on the development of the system of education over the last 50 years and, at the same time, that have implications for the planning and management of the present system. Several factors were suggested to the authors. These were as follows:

(a) size of the country and its physical features, indicating any problem that they might pose for communications with schools, providing schools in isolated areas, etc.;

(b) size, distribution, and growth rate of the population, including any problems posed by population issues for the provision of education;

(c) number of different ethnic and language groups and the evolution of educational policies for the provision of education in multiethnic and multilanguage societies;

(d) occupational structure of the labor force and the changeover time of the percentage of the labor force employed in the primary (agriculture), secondary (manufacturing), and tertiary (service) sectors and where possible linked to the changes in the curriculum of the school. Where data were available, it was suggested that the educational composition of the labor force be given.

Authors were asked to include those contextual factors that they deemed to be most important for their own system of education.

Section 2 is *Politics and the Goals of the Education System.* The intent of this section was to highlight the importance attached by Government and to indicate the unity and diversity of goals for all pupils, on the one hand, and different groups of pupils, on the other.

Section 3 is *The Formal System of Education.* This section presents a brief overview of the different types of schools from preschool to tertiary education and the proportion of an age group enrolled in formal schooling. One feature of this section is Figure 1 which is a diagrammatic presentation of the school types and the estimated percentage of an age group that is enrolled in school and also in the different school types. This was thought to be an improvement on the UNESCO diagrams which show the different school types but give no idea about how many pupils, as a percentage of the relevant age group in school in a particular grade and also the percentage of other ages in the grade. In each figure there is a line at the foot of the diagram which indicates 100 percent of an age group or, where there was less than 100 percent in school an appropriate figure such as 80 or 50 percent is given. It is hoped that this kind of diagram gives a quick overview of the structure and enrollments of the system.

Where relevant, information was also to be given on enrollment trends in both formal and nonformal education for the period 1950–90; regional or sex differences in enrollment and probable reasons for any disparities; state/private school enrollment, etc. Authors were asked to comment on the flow of pupils through the system where this might not be obvious from the diagram and in particular, to supply information likely to be of interest to the reader. This might include the length of the school day and school year at different points in the school system, average class sizes, pupil–teacher ratios, and the *de jure* and *de facto* years of compulsory schooling.

Within *Section 3* there are also special subsections which follow on from the section on *Primary, Secondary, and Tertiary Education.* These include *Preschool Education, Special Education, Vocational, Technical, and Business Education,* and finally, *Adult and Nonformal Education.* The different types of preschool arrangements together with figures on enrollments were requested as well as any special features. For *Special Education* (handicapped, backward and gifted), the categories of special education programs were requested together with their incidence. Special programs for the transition from school to work for these pupils which were thought to be of general interest to readers were to be reported. Information was requested on the typical organizational and administrative structures employed (pull-out v. in-class service delivery approach, full-time vs. part-time arrangements, regular education settings vs. separate schools). In the section on *Vocational, Technical, and Business Education* information was expected about how vocational education relates to regular schooling, the role of employers in this type of education, the relationship of apprenticeships to state vocational education provision, the sources of financing, the determination of the curriculum, the selection and training of teachers, and the examination and certification procedures. *Adult and Nonformal Education* was also a separate subsection because in those countries undertaking massive literary and/or retraining programs, the amount of the educational budget allocated to nonformal education is considerable. Similarly, adult education activities vary considerably from none at all to some countries where it is said that 60 percent of the adult population is enrolled in some kind of adult education course. Information was sought about the different kinds of programs and their organizational, administrative, and funding aspects. For example, how much depends on voluntary contributions and how much does the state allocate? What are the kinds of courses provided? And so on.

Section 4 is *Administrative and Supervisory Structure and Operation*. The intent was to outline the administrative, supervisory structure of schools, universities, and nonformal education. Of particular interest is the amount of centralization and decentralizatiion and the reasons for it. Authors were asked to comment on the degree of centralization/decentralization (locus of control) for decisions concerning the curriculum, the organizational structure of the system as a whole, the organization within schools, and disciplinary problems. Information on the role of the inspectorate, or their equivalents, at the national and local levels were requested. Where there are both central planning units and regional planning units, the linkages between the levels are especially interesting. Finally, given that ministries have several divisions, each with different responsibilities, it was important to have information on the linkages between these divisions for the overall planning of the quality and quantity of education.

Section 5 is concerned with *Educational Finance*. Information on the various sources of finance of the system were requested together with the allocation of finances to the various levels of education. Where it was difficult to know the aggregate of the various sources, then it was the state budget that was requested. The percentage of total government expenditure allocated to education was requested since this was a proxy measure for the priority awarded by government to education. Where available, the latest data on unit costs for the different levels of education were to be provided. Again data were requested for a series of years and not just for one.

Section 6 is concerned with *Supplying Personnel for the Education System* (including Teacher Education). First, it was important to identify the actual number of teaching and nonteaching personnel in the system and any problems that systems were experiencing in this area. Second, was to identify the methods by which different types of teachers were trained in their initial teacher training, pointing to any particular innovations in that training. Then there was the issue of inservice and onservice education of teachers; for example, how frequently, the type of content of such training, and the costs involved. Finally, there was the problem of how the monitoring and evaluation of teacher training and the training of nonteaching personnel was undertaken.

Section 7 is concerned with *Curriculum Development and Teaching Methodology*. The first aspect to be dealt with concerned whether or not there was a central core curriculum for a given grade or whether it varied according to the different types of school or even for different parts of the country. In particular, it was of interest to know which groups of persons decided the curriculum content, how this was done, and how frequently the curriculum guidelines were revised. Some systems have very detailed curriculum statements and others have more general statements. The second aspect concerned the production of learning materials (e.g., textbooks and modules). Information was requested on how the curriculum guidelines were translated into learning materials. Was this done at a national curriculum center and if so, how? If other mechanisms were employed, what were they? How were the written materials tried out and revised before being entered into the school system? Which criteria were used to distinguish between compulsory subjects and elective subjects? Which criteria were used to determine both the total number of hours of instruction per year and by subject per year? What was the total number of hours of instruction per year? Finally, where applicable, information was sought on how the implementation of the curriculum was ensured and what was/were the links between the national curriculum authority and the national examinations authority/authorities?

Section 8 is *The System of Examinations, Promotions, and Certifications.* Different systems have different policies for promoting pupils from one grade to the next. Some have high amounts of grade repetition and others have a policy of more or less automatic promotion. Information was requested about the policy adopted and the reasons for it. Second, some systems have one or more national examinations at different points in the system. To what extent do such examinations exist and how do they influence what is taught? Does one examination act both for certification purposes and selection to the next level of education, especially between the end of senior secondary school and the university, or are different examinations used? Where the curriculum differs to some extent from region to region within a country, how does the examination system assess the different curricula but yet bring all pupils in the country on to one scale? Finally, what sort of certification process exists and is it accepted by the public and future employers? What problems exist and what steps are being taken to solve them?

Section 9 deals with *Educational Assessment, Evaluation, and Research.* It was thought of interest to know about the types of national, regional, and possibly, district assessment that exists within each system. How is evaluation and research organized, how much funding is given to it (where possible as a percentage of the primary and secondary school national budget), and how seriously is it taken in the sense of being used as input for policy and planning decision-making? Information was requested on the major educational indicators on which data were regularly collected and on examples of major educational research studies in the early 1990s.

Section 10 asked for a brief review of the *Major Reforms in the 1980s and 1990s.* These were primarily reforms about the structure, school organization, curriculum reform, and teacher education.

Section 11 is concerned with the author's perception of the *Major Problems for the Year 2000.* This was not an easy task and it was handled differently by different authors. Some restricted themselves to problems and often proposed actions already identified by the ministries of education while others presented their own personal views. It was clear that in many poor countries the main concern was how sufficient money could be made available to ensure that conditions of schooling did not deteriorate.

The final section on *References* and *Further Reading* aims to provide bibliographical reference to items cited in the text of the entry while pointing readers to additional written sources where they can obtain much more detail on specific points raised in the text.

Problems Encountered

One problem encountered has already been alluded to – that of getting ministers of education to reply to the request to them to nominate one person in the ministry to write the entry. In countries such as Angola and Mozambique it was anticipated that there might not be a reply since they had major civil unrest on their hands. And yet, even though our assumption was correct for Angola, it was the Minister himself in Mozambique who went to a great deal of trouble to write the entry.

A second major problem was that the project to produce the country entries began in 1991 and shortly after that certain countries suddenly became a series of smaller countries. Thus, what had been the USSR suddenly became Armenia, Azerbaijan, Byelorussia, Estonia, Georgia, Kazakhstan, Kirigiziya, Latvia, Lithuania, Moldavia, Russia, Tadzhikistan, Turkmenistan, the Ukraine, and Uzbekhistan. However, it took some time for the emerging countries to stabilize their administrations and hence it was not possible to include descriptions of their systems of education in the parent encyclopedia except for Estonia, Latvia, Lithuania, and Russia. It was also too short a time to include them in this Encyclopedia. There were also the cases of the former

Czechoslovakia and Yugoslavia. Both the Czech and Slovak Republics are included here as well as Slovenia but it was not possible, for obvious reasons, to include the other systems in the former Yugoslavia. A great effort was made to include more systems from the Domaines Outre-Mers of France. Despite several letters (in French) to the French Ministry of Education no reply was received. It did prove possible to have an entry on Guadeloupe and Martinique but not from an author nominated by an official body. In any future editions of this work every effort should be made to include descriptions of these other countries.

A third problem was that of language and this has already been mentioned. It should be added, however, that when entries were written in a different language all efforts were made to render a good translation. It is hoped that the translation reflects truly the intent of the author. The English version was sent back to authors and they declared themselves satisfied.

A fourth problem was that even though most of the entries were updated in the first half of 1994 there will have already been changes in some of the systems since that time that are not reported in this Encyclopedia.

For the Future

Given the rapid changes in systems of education it would be desirable to have an Encyclopedia like this one produced every four or five years. The content would change according to new issues that emerge in education. At the same time it is suggested that the number of words for each entry be extended to allow a more detailed description.

Acknowledgments

It takes a lot of work to produce an Encyclopedia of this kind. Nearly all of the authors are ministry officials and had to undertake this task in addition to their daily work. My thanks to them for writing the entry in the first place and to the further work that I asked of them for supplying extra information or rewriting various passages. My thanks to them.

Finding the addresses of the ministries, keeping a tracking system, and writing again and again until a reply was received, was an onerous task. Rosine Lambin at the University of Hamburg was not only responsible for this but also translated the entries from French to English, checked all of my editing, and even wrote the entry on Cambodia. She did all of this with efficiency and in a friendly manner. My very great thanks to her.

In many cases we, in Hamburg had to draw the Figure 1 from the data supplied. Jedidiah Harris then drew the figures on his Macintosh PC and indeed retyped many of my edited versions of the entries. My thanks to Jed.

Not only did we do the above work in Hamburg but Pergamon had a team of editors who further edited the entries and also a technical drawing team who redrew the figures. My particular thanks go to Angela Greenwell, Lucie Herbertson, and Glenda Pringle of Pergamon.

T. Neville Postlethwaite
University of Hamburg
1995

Afghanistan

F. Haq

1. General Background

The Republic of Afghanistan is a mountainous and landlocked country in southwestern Asia. The area of the country is 652,225 square kilometers and it is bounded on the north by the newly independent countries of Tadzhikistan, Uzbekistan, and Turkmenistan (previously republics of the former Soviet Union), on the west by Iran, on the east and south by Pakistan, and on the northeast by the People's Republic of China. Afghanistan is divided into 32 provinces—204 districts and 90 subdistricts. There are 35,500 villages all over the country. The climate varies considerably, from the subtropical Nangrahar province in the east to the year-round snow-filled Salang Pass in the Hindukush Mountains. Temperatures and rainfall vary. The overall climate is hot and dry in the summer, with cold winters marked by snowfall in the mountains and higher plateaus.

For the establishment of schools, areas in the country are classified into cold, hot, and very cold areas. The school year lasts 9 months in the cold and hot areas and 7 months in the very cold areas. Due to financial constraints, the school buildings are not equipped for summer and winter conditions. When extreme conditions prevail, teaching does not take place. As all of the schools follow the same curriculum, so the different number of school days makes it difficult to complete the approved syllabus.

According to the Ministry of Statistics, the population in 1990 numbered 17.69 million, including 1.5 million nomads. Approximately 13.17 million (or 81.69%) lived in rural areas and 2.95 million (or 18.31%) in urban areas. Some 53 percent of urban inhabitants lived in Kabul, the capital city. Males comprised 51 percent of the population. The annual growth rate is estimated to be 1.92 percent. The growth rate is higher in rural areas than in urban areas.

There are two officially recognized national languages, namely, Pashtu and Dari (Afghan Persian). Over 80 percent of the people speak one or both of these languages, which are Indo–European in origin. There are over 20 other languages and dialects. Up to 1978, school textbooks and teaching materials were written in two official languages. After the events of 1978, textbooks and teaching materials for primary grades were gradually prepared in three other languages: Ozbeki, Turkmany, and Bluchi. It should be mentioned that not all native speakers of one language live in one area. There is a mixture. Thus the language of instruction used in one school is the language spoken by the majority of persons living in the community. This poses a difficult problem.

In 1990–91 the eligible workforce (15–59 years of age) was estimated to be 7.78 million and 79 percent of these formed the active labor force. Some 5 million persons worked in the area of production: 82 percent in agriculture, livestock, and forestry; 8 percent in trading; 5.7 percent in industry; 1.6 percent in construction; and 2.7 percent in transportation and communication. The number of people who worked for the public services (education, public health, information and culture; civil services, government institutions, and other related institutions) was 894,190 people (1990–91). To be employed by the government, employees should have at least a high school certificate. However, the majority of services personnel and workers are illiterate and the government has established literacy and complementary courses in their institutions.

All educational institutions from preschool up to higher education in the system are free and financially supported by the government. The graduates of the school system are typically recruited to governmental and nongovernmental institutions. However, the nongovernmental institutions do not participate in the financing of the education of their personnel.

The Republic of Afghanistan is an Islamic country and has a parliamentary system of government based on the Constitution of the Republic of Afghanistan.

2. Politics and the Goals of the Education System

All educational institutions are planned and run by the state government. In order to train the cadres and personnel at different levels in the economic, social, political, and cultural fields, the Constitution included an article in 1990 stating that:

> All citizens of the Republic of Afghanistan have the right to free education. The state shall adopt necessary measures for the eradication of illiteracy, the generalization of a balanced education, education in the mother tongue, the implementation of compulsory primary education, technical and vocational education and growth in higher education for the training of national cadres. The establishment of private educational institutes is legally permitted to be run by the private sector and by foreigners.

The responsibilities for the implementation of educational policies and objectives are given to various ministries:

(a) The Ministry of Education is responsible for general education (primary, middle, and high schools), teacher education, Islamic education (Grades 1–14), and literacy education.

(b) The Ministry of Higher and Vocational Education is responsible for education in university-level *technicums* (Grades 9–14), and technical, vocational, and professional schools.

(c) The Ministry of Work and Social Affairs is responsible for preschool education. (Until 1990 this was the responsibility of the Ministry of Education.)

(d) The Ministry of Public Health is responsible for running medical institutes and nursing schools. (The responsibility for medical institutes and nursing schools was transferred from the Ministry of Higher and Vocational Education to the Ministry of Public Health in 1981.)

Since the establishment of the modern educational system in 1904, the policy and goals of education have been developed by a group of professionals. After approval by higher authorities, implementation took place without the opinion of educators and other related bodies in the country having been considered. However, in 1990, the policy and goals were written by specialists in various areas and were then published in major newspapers in order to solicit the opinion of the public all over the country.

The key points of the education policy are:

(a) a sound training of children and youth in the light of the principles of the holy religion of Islam;

(b) equal education rights for all citizens irrespective of their nationality, race, sex, religion, social and economic status;

(c) free education in state schools;

(d) provision of educational opportunity for special groups who lack parental care or have economic, physical, or mental problems;

(e) instruction in the mother tongue in primary schools;

(f) student freedom of choice regarding the language of instruction;

(g) uniform education throughout the country;

(i) provision of universal and compulsory primary education;

(j) provision of better educational opportunities and the creation of a sound basis for scientific personalities;

(k) development of teacher-training institutes according to the needs of the country;

(l) the award of educational certificates;

(m) development of Islamic educational schools and colleges;

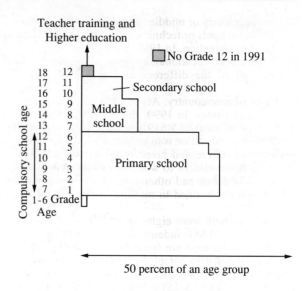

Figure 1
Afghanistan: Structure of the formal education system

(n) expansion of nursery school and kindergarten networks;

(o) continuity of campaigns against illiteracy, expansion of institutions and educational networks for adults, and the initiation of all possible activities to eradicate illiteracy;

(p) continuous adjustment of educational plans to fit with the national economic plan.

3. The Formal System of Education

3.1 Primary, Secondary, and Tertiary Education

The structure of the system of education is preschool (3 years nursery and 3 years kindergarten), general education (6 years primary, 3 years middle, and 3 years secondary), *technicums* from Grades 9–14, teacher-training institutes for preschool and primary teachers from Grades 9–14 and from Grades 13–14, and pedagogical institutes at the university level. Figure 1 presents the structure and enrollments in the system in 1991.

Primary education is free and compulsory for ages 7 to 12. In 1990, first grade enrollment was 132,000 students comprising 28 percent of the total age group. The total primary school enrollment was 700,000, which was also 26 percent of the age group (7–12 years). The ratio of girls to boys was 2:1.

All students who finish primary school may enroll in middle school. Graduates of middle schools can continue in the upper secondary school. Students who complete primary or middle schools and wish to enter vocational schools or technical institutes must take an entrance examination. In 1990, the total enrollment in all 72 technical, vocational, and professional institutes run by all of the different ministries was 16,062 students.

As an Islamic country, Afghanistan also has formal religious institutes. In 1990, there were 22 institutes with an enrollment of 9,519 students. The purpose of this religious education is to train students with Islamic values and culture and prepare them to be religious teachers in schools, or to work as professional cadres in judicial offices and other related areas. Religious cadres are also trained in mosques and some private *madraces*.

In 1990, there were eight universities with a total enrollment of 20,881 students. All sectors of higher and vocational education are financially supported by the state. Students who complete general and vocational schools and wish to continue their studies in institutes (Grades 13–14 or 13–15) or universities must take an entrance examination. This is a national examination arranged by the Ministry of Higher and Vocational Education.

3.2 Preschool Education

The total number of nurseries and kindergartens in 1990 was 282, serving 21,000 children, which was 0.5 percent of the total age group (0–6 years). Parents are required to pay a small annual fee, not exceeding US$2.

3.3 Adult and Nonformal Education

Government formal schools, institutes, and colleges are also available for adult education. Night schools (Grades 7–12) in the national capital provincial centers are established for those who have completed primary school, or any grade of general education, but who have not continued their studies. A graduate of these night schools can enter any higher education institution according to the rules and regulations of higher education.

The inservice training of teachers is provided in teacher-training institutes (Grades 13–14) and pedagogical institutes (Grades 13–16 and 17–18). Teachers who are graduates of Grade 12 are particularly encouraged to attend inservice institutes to strengthen their teaching ability. In 1990, 1,217 students were enrolled in such inservice courses. Kabul University established six further night colleges (Grades 13–16) for working persons wishing to continue their higher education study. The total enrollment in the night colleges in 1990 was 877 students.

Kabul University provides for master and doctoral degrees in different areas and provides inservice support for those wishing to complete the requirements. Students are admitted to master and doctoral degrees under the existing regulations. On-the-job training for adults is conducted in degree courses and seminars (short- and long-term) for the upgrading of their skills. This work is financially supported either by the state or international agencies (UNESCO, UNICEF, WHO, and WFO) in the Republic of Afghanistan.

Of the 2.7 million children aged 7 to 12 years, only 700,000 were in primary school. A further 2 million were not in school. Furthermore, out of every 100 pupils entering primary school, only 65 complete all six grades. It is the Department for Literacy Affairs, under the guidance and control of the Ministry of Education, that is responsible for developing literacy, not only among these 2 million children, but also among adults. The department must also, wherever possible, provide "complementary" education.

The major aims of adult literacy programs are to: (a) establish literacy courses throughout the country; (b) relate the literacy program content to the requirements and demands of the target groups; (c) prepare courses for adults to learn to write and do simple mathematics, and inculcate issues in relation to hygiene, the environment, and nutrition; (d) prepare better and further education to acquaint learners with a basic understanding of the fundamentals of the Islamic religion; and (e) help literacy course graduates toward formal and nonformal education.

The literacy objectives for out-of-school children are to: (a) implement a program which is equivalent to and conforms with that of the general education schools, and (b) mobilize such children to enter the general education schools. Graduates of courses for out-of-school children are recognized as equivalent to the end of Grade 4 in primary school. Depending on their age, they may enter Grade 5 of the formal primary school.

Finally, the objectives of complementary education are to: (a) cover the content of education up to Grade 9 of general schools and provide some vocational skills of interest to the learners, (b) prepare the graduates of such centers for continuing education above Grade 9, and (c) promote and develop complementary education networks up to the intermediate secondary level and higher education.

4. Administrative and Supervisory Structure and Operation

The administration and supervision of general education (Grades 1–12), teacher-training and pedagogical institutes, formal religious institutes, and literacy affairs are the responsibility of the Ministry of Education. There are various departments in the Ministry of Education which are in charge of the implementation of the policies and objectives of education, namely: Administration, Planning and International Relations, Religious Education, General Education, Literacy Education, Physical Education, Teacher Training,

Compilation and Translation, the Institute of Peda-gogical and Psychological Research, the Science Center, Personnel, Inspection, the Education Press, and the Education Construction Unit.

In each province, there is a president of education appointed by the Ministry of Education. The president is in charge of all educational activities related to the Ministry of Education in his or her province. The president of education is also responsible to the governor of the local province in addition to the Ministry of Education. Under the leadership of the provincial presidents, there are the directors of teacher-training institutes, school principals, directors of literacy affairs, supervisors, teachers, and students.

The central structure of the Ministry of Higher and Vocational Education is almost similar to the Ministry of Education. All the universities, technical, vocation-al, and professional schools are actively under the control of the Ministry of Higher and Vocational Edu-cation. Universities have rectors and department heads. Colleges have deans, various department heads, and administrative branches. Each technical, vocational, and professional school has a director, teachers, and administrative branches. The administrative structure of the Medical Institute, nursing, and other vocational schools under the control of the Ministry of Public Health are like the other universities and vocational schools of the Ministry of Higher and Vocational Education.

5. Educational Finance

As previously mentioned, education at all levels of the system is financially supported by the state govern-ment. It is difficult to obtain financial figures from all of the different ministries responsible for various edu-cational sectors. However, the budgets for the Ministry of Education are shown in Table 1.

6. Supplying Personnel for the Education System

The number of personnel employed by the Ministry of Education was 38,723 in 1990. Nearly 60 percent were male; 26,726 were teachers and 11,997 worked in nonteaching positions. The Ministry of Higher and Vocational Education employed 6,879 people in 1991. Of these, 3,554 were male. Just over 1,100 were instructors at universities and 1,300 were teachers at technical, vocational, and professional schools. In 1990, 191 teachers worked in the other ministries' technical and vocational schools, and 4,020 teachers and 2,107 persons in nonteaching positions worked in nursery and kindergarten schools.

Teacher-training institutes, pedagogical institutes, and some colleges in different universities train teach-ers for the system of education. Training also takes place on-the-job for various administrative personnel in the education system with the financial support of the government and international agencies. The preservice and inservice training of teachers was also discussed in Sect. 3.1 above.

7. Curriculum Development and Teaching Methodology

The general objectives of education, as well as the general and specific objectives in each subject area taught in the general school system of education from Grades 1 to 12, should be approved by the government. The last set of objectives of general education was approved by the government in 1990.

The Department of Compilation and Translation at the Ministry of Education is responsible for developing the syllabuses and curriculum for each subject area in line with the policy and general objective of education. According to the syllabuses, different divisions within the department write the textbooks and teachers guides. These must then be approved by the Publications Committee before the books are sent for printing. The allocation time of the weekly periods of instruction in all classes of general education is also arranged by the Department. Table 2 presents the allocation of periods for each grade in 1993. Central supervisors and provincial supervisors control the implementation of the curriculum and instructional material in the schools and submit reports on the relative successes and fail-ures of the teaching–learning process. Lack of school buildings, equipment, textbooks, teaching aids and qualified teachers (particularly in foreign languages,

Table 1
Educational expenditure (in millions of Afs) 1981–90

Year	1981	1982	1983	1984	1985	1986	1987	1988	1989	1990
Ordinary budget	1,912.7	1,677.7	2,238.5	2,285.0	2,120.1	1,941.7	2,790.0	3,069.0	3,375.0	4,450.0
Developmental budget	26.0	107.0	54.3	200.7	150.1	167.0	577.3	500.0	193.0	220.0
Total	1,938.7	1,784.7	2,292.8	2,485.7	2,270.2	2,108.8	3,367.7	3,569.0	3,568.0	4,670.0

mathematics, and physics) are the main problems in the implementation of the curriculum.

8. *The System of Examinations, Promotions, and Certifications*

Oral evaluation of students by the teachers in Grades 1–3 and teacher-made examinations from Grades 4–12 form the basis for determining the promotion of students to the next grade. Certificates are awarded at the end of primary, middle, and high schools. These examinations and the roles they play were briefly described in Section 3.1 above.

9. *Educational Assessment, Evaluation, and Research*

Since the establishment of the modern education system in 1904, the Ministry of Education has not created any specific department for testing, assessment, and evaluation techniques where the results of the work would be used as an indicator for making decisions about the improvement, development, and revision of the curriculum and instructional materials.

The Department of Planning of the Ministry of Education collects information for the following purposes: for compilation of statistical figures in order to obtain correct data from educational situations in general education (Grades 1–12), teacher-training institutions, religious schools, and literacy activities in the country; for analyses of data for designing the short-term and long-term development plan; for compilation into reports to the Ministry of Planning and Ministry of Statistics; for designing financial and budgetary plans of education; and for the determination of indicators for the following year's plan. Finally, all efforts are made to expand the number of indicators for which data are collected.

10. *Major Reforms in the 1980s and 1990s*

After the creation of the Republic of Afghanistan in 1973, the structure of general education was changed from 6:3:3 to 8:4 (8 years primary and 4 years secondary school). Between 1978 and 1990, changes occurred three times in the structure of the system of general education. In 1979, the pattern became 4:3:3; in 1983, it became 5:3:3; and in 1990, it became 6:3:3.

Given that the training of qualified teachers is crucial, the 14 teacher-training schools (Grades 9–12) extended their training period to include grades 13 and 14 in the 1980s. In 1990, five of these teacher-training institutes became institutes of pedagogy, and three other new teacher-training institutes were established.

Table 2
Educational plan of general education schools and periods per week for subjects at each grade level 1993

Subjects	I	II	III	IV	V	VI	VII	VIII	IX	X	XI	XII
			Primary level (1–6)				Middle level (7–9)			Secondary level (10–12)		
Holy Koran	4	4	4	3	3	3	2	2	2	2	2	2
Theology and jurisprudence	3	3	3	3	3	3	3	3	3	3	3	3
Hadis (tradition)	—	—	—	—	—	—	2	2	2	2	2	2
Arabic	—	—	—	2	2	2	2	2	2	2	2	2
Mother tongue (Pashto or Dari)	9	9	9	7	7	7	5	5	5	3	3	3
Second language (Pashto or Dari)	—	—	—	3	3	3	3	3	3	2	2	2
Calligraphy	1	1	1	1	1	1	—	—	—	—	—	—
Foreign language	—	—	—	—	—	—	3	3	3	2	2	2
Mathematics/algebra	5	5	5	5	5	5	3	3	3	3	3	3
Geometry	—	—	—	—	—	—	2	2	2	2	2	2
Trigonometry	—	—	—	—	—	—	—	—	—	—	1	1
Chemistry	—	—	—	—	—	—	2	2	2	3	3	3
Biology	—	—	—	—	—	—	2	2	2	3	3	3
Physics	—	—	—	—	—	—	2	2	2	3	3	3
Science and health	—	—	—	2	2	2	—	—	—	—	—	—
Social studies	—	—	—	2	2	2	—	—	—	—	—	—
History	—	—	—	—	—	—	2	2	2	2	2	2
Geography	—	—	—	—	—	—	2	2	2	2	2	2
Drawing and practical works	1	1	1	1	1	1	—	—	—	—	—	—
Physical education	1	1	1	1	1	1	1	1	1	1	1	1
Refinement	—	—	—	—	—	—	—	—	—	—	—	—
Total number of periods per week	24	24	24	30	30	30	36	36	36	36	36	36

For the training of the qualified cadres according to economic and social needs of the country, there is not only Kabul University, but also five other universities that were established in the 1990s—three of which are in different provinces. In the 1980s and early 1990s, six more colleges were established at Kabul University.

11. Major Problems for the Year 2000

There have been political changes and war in Afghanistan, and the country is poor. How many Afghans will return to the country is not known. Despite the turmoil and incertitude, all efforts must be made to provide good quality education to as many persons as possible.

The major plans for the year 2000 are to expand the number of kindergartens, to enroll all of the school-age population, and to eradicate illiteracy. Only 0.5 percent of the total age group of 0–6 years (which numbers 4.2 million children) was in kindergarten in 1991. There are no proper buildings, equipment, and other needed facilities. They must be provided.

In the year 1990, the population of 7-year old children was 467,000 and only 28 percent were in first grade. Only 26 percent of the 7- to 12-year olds were in school. Or, another way of looking at the immensity of the problem is to point out that only 20 percent of all 7- to 18-year-olds (4.5 million in all) were in school.

Following the events of 1978, large numbers of Afghans left the country. In the period 1978 to 1991,

over 2,000 schools were destroyed, some 2,000 teachers were killed, and another 1,500 left the country or teaching profession for other jobs.

In the year 1990–91, there were 1,401 schools, of these, 548 had their own buildings, 237 were rented, and 616 were schools without buildings. The gradual increase of preschool education and the enrichment of all school-age children requires buildings, equipment, teaching materials, and trained teachers. This will be the major problem.

The slow development of formal education in the past and up to the year 2000 will cause an increase in the number of illiterates. In 1991, about 37 percent of adult males and 9 percent of adult females were literate. Eradicating this illiteracy will also be a major problem. Table 3 presents the educational development plan up to the year 2000 with other statistical data.

Bibliography

Kabul University 1988 *Kabul University During the Last Ten Years (1357–1367) (1978–1988)* Kabul University, Kabul (in Dari)

Ministry of Education 1991 *Education Policy and Objectives. Structure and Curriculum of the Schools and Educational Institutes.* Ministry of Education, Kabul (in Dari)

Ministry of Education n.d. *National Report from the Republic of Afghanistan*, for International Conferences on Education, Forty-Second Session Geneva (3–8 Sept. 1990). Unpublished (in English)

Ministry of Education n.d. *Unpublished Documents* from

Table 3
Educational development plan up to the year 2000[a]

	1990	1991	1992	1993	(1993)[b]	1994	1995	2000
No. of general educational schools	1,400	1,460	1,520	1,600	(2,612)	1,680	1,760	2,260
primary schools (1–6)	560	600	640	680	(1,300)	720	760	960
middle schools (1–9)	490	505	520	550	(827)	580	610	860
secondary schools (1–12)	350	355	360	360	(485)	380	390	440
no. of students enrolled	846,000	889,000	970,000	1,030,000	(1,754,685)	1,093,000	1,191,000	1,706,000
1st grade admission	147,000	166,000	185,000	205,000	(230,000)	226,000	246,000	391,000
% of 7-year olds	40	45	50	55	(63)	60	65	100
no. of teachers	23,000	24,000	25,000	26,500	(49,662)	28,000	29,900	32,300
No. of literacy courses	18,000	18,200	18,400	18,600	(22,854)	18,800	19,000	20,000
no. of students	324,000	327,000	331,000	334,000	(333,000)	338,000	342,000	360,000
No. of pedagogical and teacher-training institutes	16	16	16	17	(18)	17	17	19
no. of students	5,000	5,600	6,400	7,000	(7,500)	7,600	8,500	10,000
no. of teachers	479	500	500	590	(560)	530	540	600
No. of religious schools (madrases)	21	22	22	23	(120)	24	25	26
no. of students	7,400	7,700	7,800	8,000	(15,700)	8,150	8,300	10,000
no. of teachers	400	415	420	430	(780)	450	460	500

a The plan was formulated in 1988–89. Obviously, once the plan is implemented, the numbers may differ
b Actual 1993 figures brought about by educational policy of the new Islamic State Government (established April 1992)

the Literacy Dept., Teachers Education Dept., Administration Dept., Planning Dept., and Compilation and Translation Dept.

Ministry of Education, Department of Planning 1968 *Education in Afghanistan During the Last Fifty Years*. Ministry of Education, Kabul (in English)

Ministry of Education, Department of Planning n.d. *Statistics of Education in the Year 1369 (1990–91)*. Unpublished (in Dari)

Ministry of Planning, Central Statistics Office 1978 *Statistical Information of Afghanistan (1977, 1978)*. Ministry of Planning, Kabul (in Dari)

Ministry of Statistics 1991 *Statistical Yearbook*. Ministry of Statistics, Kabul

Mirza Zada A K, Shafi M, Amaj A M 1990 *The History of Education in Afghanistan (1978–1988)*, Ministry of Education Dept. of Curriculum and Compilation, Educational Press, Kabul, (in Dari)

Yusofzia Aziz Ahmand 1978 The development and direction of the materials testing program of Afghanistan's curriculum and textbook project (1973–1976). Unpublished Doctoral Dissertation, Teachers College, Columbia University, New York

Albania

S. Temo

1. General Background

The Republic of Albania is a state of southeastern Europe, in the west of the Balkan Penninsula, with a long coastline bordering the Ionian and Adriatic Seas. The surface area is 28,748 square kilometres. The population is 3,255,900 (1990) with a natural increase of 19.6 per thousand and the average life expectancy is 72.2 years. The Albanian population consists of workers, peasants, traders, and the intelligentsia. About 36 percent of the population lives in towns and the rest in rural areas (1990).

Albanians are direct descendants of the Illyrians who were created as an autonomous ethnic group in the third millenium on the basis of the ancient population identified with Pellazgo Albans. Present-day Albanian is also a direct descendant of the Pellazgo–Illyrian language and it is spoken by about 9 million Albanians within and outside Albania.

The Illyrians were characterized by a high material and spiritual culture. The beginnings of organized education can be seen in the eleventh to fifth century BC during the time of the creation of enslaving states. Archeological excavations in several Illyrian towns, as well as in other Hellenic colonies in the coastal zone, have discovered remains of educational and cultural institutions such as gymnasia, stadiums, amphitheaters and libraries. The Academy of Apollonia, second century BC, is one of the best known academies in which different sciences, philosophy, and rhetoric were studied.

In the fifteenth century, Albania was invaded by the Ottoman Empire. During a long occupation Albanian national education was developed and based on popular tradition and the right of customs. The schools in the Middle Ages were religious—both Christian and Moslem. The lessons in these schools were given in Greek, Latin, and Arabic. In the seventeenth century, several schools using the Albanian language were opened.

The Academy of Voscopoja (1750) is quite well-known in the Balkans and Europe, functioning as a university in which classical languages, logic, physics, mathematics, and other sciences were taught. This Academy also had a printing press. In the eighteenth and nineteenth centuries, trade and handicraft schools were opened. At the beginning of the nineteenth century the first secular and national schools were opened.

Albania became independent in 1912 but, on the basis of London Conference decisions (1913), the majority of its territories remained outside the mother state. In 1924 the Bourgeois–Democratic Revolution took place, while from 1925–39 Albania became a monarchy.

During the Second World War, Albania was occupied by the Italian fascist army (1939) and later by the German army (1943). Albania was liberated on November 29, 1944. In January 1946 it was proclaimed the People's Republic and in 1976, with the compilation of the new constitution, Albania was proclaimed to be the People's Socialist Republic.

Albania is an agricultural and industrial country with a multibranched economy. For 45 years (1945–90) the country lived under a communist dictatorship, and during this period several changes and reforms of a democratic and socialist character were carried out, such as the Agrarian Reform (1946), collectivization of agriculture, education reform, and so on. The country moved toward modernization through such advances as the development of a centralized and planned economy; land reclamation; electrification of the country; the development of industry, particularly the extracting and processing industry, and light and food industry; progress in culture and the arts; but at the same time the illusion was created that there was movement toward a progressive and just society, the so-called socialist society. It is a fact that this period created many difficulties. The isolation from the civilized world, especially the Western one, the adoption of a rather centralized economic policy, the aggravation of the social class struggle, the universal policy of collectivization, the lack of pluralism, and destruction of democracy led the country toward destruction and misery.

The Democratic Revolution (December 1990) led to the overthrow of the totalitarian power and the establishment of a democratic state. Albania became a republic, with its highest state body being the People's Assembly (the Parliament). The main political forces are the Democratic Party (DP), the Socialist Party (SP), the Social Democratic Party (SDP), the Republican Party (RP), and several other smaller parties. Both private and state ownership exist side by side.

2. Politics and the Goals of the Education System

Prior to the liberation of the country in 1944, an antipopular education policy was followed. Albania was one of the most backward countries of Europe. Between 85 and 90 percent of the adult population was illiterate. There were few schools and no system of higher education. Although compulsory education was established by law (1921–28), only 25 percent of children of school age attended elementary school. In 1945, the right of citizens for free education for both boys and girls was established in the constitution.

The struggle for the abolition of illiteracy up to the age of 40 began. Certain reforms were carried out in the field of education:

(a) The Education Reform of 1946 laid the foundation of a new school system, unique, and compulsory. Schools were separated from the Church, and the right of Greek and Macedonian national minorities to receive education in their own languages was sanctioned.

(b) The Education Reform of 1963 strengthened the polytechnical character of education.

(c) The Education Reform of 1969 further strengthened the political, polytechnical, and professional character of education in order to ensure a better training of the new generation in terms of comprehensive development and socialist ideals.

In the period 1945 to 1990 there was a massive increase in enrollment at all levels of education, but this was not accompanied by an increase in the quality of education. The excessive politicalization of the school, its totalitarian character, the low level and quality of the teaching methods, the formalism, and the pedagogical bureaucracy were some of the features of the socialist education system which seriously damaged education.

The democratic state, which emerged from the elections in March 1992, defined new aims for education in

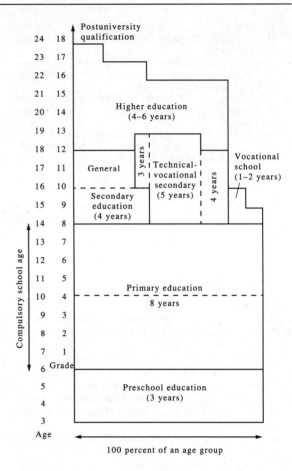

Figure 1
Albania: Structure of the formal education system 1990

the Republic of Albania. They guarantee the complete and free development of the personality of individual students by ensuring, at all education levels, the comprehensive and harmonious development of their mental and moral capacities in order to apply them for the benefit and material progress of society.

3. The Formal System of Education

Figure 1 depicts the structure of the education system and statistical data are provided in Table 1.

3.1 Primary, Secondary, and Tertiary Education

Compulsory school (Grades 1–8) is for children from 6 to 14 years of age. It has two cycles: the elementary cycle (Grades 1–4), and the high cycle (Grades 5–8). The secondary school enrolls pupils from 15 to 18 years

Table 1
Numbers of institutions, students, and teachers at different levels of education (1990)

1 *Preschool education*	
Kindergartens	3,926
Children	130,000
Teachers	5,664
2 *Primary education*	
Schools	1,726
Pupils	557,000
of which Full-time	551,000
Teachers	28,798
3 *Secondary education*	
Schools	513
Pupils	206,000
of which Full-time	145,000
Teachers	9,708
3.1 *Vocational secondary education*	
Schools	466
Pupils	138,000
of which Full-time	89,000
Teachers	7,390
3.2 *General secondary education*	
Schools	47
Pupils	68,000
of which Full-time	56,000
Teachers	2,318
4. *Higher education*	
Higher education institutions	8
Students	27,000
of which Full-time	22,000
Part-time	5,000
Faculty	1,806

of age. Secondary school education is divided into: (a) general secondary school education (*Gymnasium*), and (b) technical and professional secondary education.

General secondary education (*Gymnasium*) lasts for four years, divided into two levels of two years each. The first level, Grades 9 and 10, provides an education to help pupils pursue further studies (at the second level of the gymnasium or in a technical school) or to obtain employment after a certain period of training. The second level, Grades 11 and 12, prepares students for university studies or for specialized professional training.

Technical and professional secondary education includes a diversity of specialties and aims at the professional training of students for different sectors of economy and culture. The number of schools and students attending these schools has increased.

Higher education enrolls students who have completed general secondary school or the longer vocational schools. Studies in higher education last from four to six years. Males and females are equally represented. The institutions include: Tirana University (opened in 1957), Polytechnic University (Tirana), University "Luigj Gurakuqi" (Shkodër), University "Alexander Xhuvani" (Elbasan), University "Eqerem Cabej" (Gjirokastër), Agricultural University "Kamëz" (Tirana), Polytechnic University "Korçë, Academy of Arts" (Tirana), Institute of Physical Culture "Vojo Kushi" (Tirana), the Military Academy of Land Forces (Tirana), and some other military institutions.

Admission is on the basis of the students' results in previous schooling. There is a *numerus clausus* in the Academy of Arts, in the Institute of Physical Culture, and in architecture in Tirana University. In 1993, the admission of new students to all branches of higher education was by competition. However, priority is given to the children of those executed for political reasons.

The following restructuring was undertaken in 1992–93. Institutes were given university status and courses were to last for four years. The Institute of Physical Culture's courses were increased from three to four years. The engineering faculty became a polytechnic university. New faculties were opened in the German language, tourism and statistics, management and business, and hotel management and tourism. A new faculty of social work was created.

3.2 Preschool Education

Preschool education enrolls children from 3 to 6 years of age in 130,000 kindergartens of various types (1990) and in the children's houses.

3.3 Special Education

Special education is organized for handicapped children and for those who have physical, intellectual and emotional difficulties. For children with sight and hearing disabilities there is an institute (founded in 1963) for the blind and deaf. In 1992, there were 248 deaf children and 50 blind children trained by 62 and 16 teachers respectively. There are also special schools (like "Luigj Gurakuqi" in Tirana and Durrës, and also special classes in schools with Grades 1–8 in Vlora, Shkodra, and Elbasan. In these schools in 1992 there were 480 children taught by 120 teachers. However, the number of children needing this kind of education is much larger.

There are schools for children with mild mental retardation in some cities of the country. There are other boarding-type schools for children who are severely mentally retarded, and these schools are under the responsibility of the Ministry of Health.

3.4 Vocational, Technical, and Business Education

Within the framework of the new education reform, agricultural, technical and vocational secondary education will have a structure intended to be more flexible for meeting the needs of a market economy. There will also be a restructuring of special training in hotel management, tourism, business, and computer utilization.

Technical and vocational secondary education will include:

(a) Technical schools of three or five years' duration (Grades 9–13 or 11–13 in the technical streams of the gymnasium) in which the pupils are trained in certain aspects of industry, trade, shipping, tourism, business, and the like.

(b) Art and music schools with courses lasting four to five years. Music schools sometimes extend the length of study depending on the student's specialization.

(c) Foreign language and sports schools with 4-year courses (Grades 9–12).

(d) Teacher-training schools of five years' duration for those having completed eight years of education, or three years' duration for those having completed the first level of gymnasium.

(e) Vocational schools with courses of one or two years' duration for training technicians in areas such as agriculture, shipbuilding, construction, mining, and textiles. The students who complete these vocational courses do not have the right to enter higher education.

3.5 Adult and Nonformal Education

Adult education, which is part-time, involves all young people who are employed. The courses are conducted in the afternoon or by correspondence.

The teaching program and syllabuses are nearly the same as in full-time schools but the length of the courses is one year more. A considerable number of workers are trained in these part-time schools. At the end of the 1980s and beginning of the 1990s the number of pupils in part-time 8-grade schools decreased remarkably but the number in part-time secondary schools increased. In 1990, these schools were attended by 6,000 pupils in the 8-grade school, 6,000 in secondary schools, and 5,000 in higher education.

In the new reform, the further vocational training of workers and technicians will be carried out in centers for vocational training mainly through short-term courses aimed at improving their qualifications as well as requalifying and training those workers who have not worked for a time or who have moved to new jobs.

4. Administrative and Supervisory Structure and Operation

Education in the Republic of Albania is provided and managed by the state. The People's Assembly (Parliament) defines the education policy and approves the basic education laws and the structure of the education system. The Council of Ministers passes legal acts and charges the Ministry of Education or other ministries with the enacting of other legal dispositions.

The Ministry of Education is the highest state body which is responsible for the general organization, management, and control of all categories of schools, kindergartens, and other institutions which are included in the education system.

The new law on education reform allows for the establishment of independent/private education institutions by private persons, foreign organizations or religious centers. They are, however, subject to the legislation passed by the Ministry of Education and they must receive the relevant license from the Ministry of Education.

Universities, academies, and other institutions of higher education enjoy a special status, mainly that of having academic freedom in teaching and scientific research and in the circulation of ideas. They are also independent in creating relations and cooperation with other institutions and foreign scientific research centers.

Education management in districts, municipalities, and communes is undertaken by educational directorates for all preschool institutions, the 8-grade school, and secondary schools. The educational offices in each district work directly with the financial units of education in the district councils. They are responsible for new admissions to schools and for ensuring that the schools meet their obligations with respect to pupils' rights to study, fellowships for pupils and students, teachers' travel, school building construction, and the supply of materials to schools. The administrative units for education belong to the municipalities and communes.

The direct management of teaching and other educational activities in schools and institutions is carried out by their directors and vice-directors. This includes ensuring close cooperation with the pupils' parents.

5. Educational Finance

In 1990 the amount of money allocated to education and culture was 984 million lek, which is equal to 11.6 percent of the state budget. Expenditure per inhabitant increased 11 times from 1950 to 1990.

All the expenses for construction, equipment, supplies, and learning materials are covered by the state. For pupils and students who live in dormitories, a system of fellowships is applied. Nevertheless the financial expenses for education have never been adequate and the material basis is excessively poor. The destruction wrought to the educational system during the transition period by the excommunists in power led to a difficult time for educational finance.

6. Supplying Personnel for the Education System

In 1990, nearly 46,000 teachers were employed in the educational system, 52.8 percent of those being female.

Kindergarten teachers are trained in secondary education teacher-training schools and in former higher education training institutes for three years;

the teachers in the 8-grade school (high cycle) and those in secondary schools receive a 4-year training in higher education teacher-training institutes in education faculties in the universities. Specialists (e.g., engineers, agronomists, etc.) take a special course in education. Personnel for artistic subjects and physical training are trained in relevant high schools.

A differentiated qualification system is organized for teachers according to the level of their training experience. There is also a special course for educational management personnel. Further educational qualifications can be obtained through additional university and postuniversity examinations workshops, courses, and through obtaining a postuniversity academic qualification. In 1990 the number of employees with academic degrees included: 107 professors, 116 doctors of sciences, 226 research fellows, 431 docents, and 1,255 bachelors of sciences.

Essential changes are foreseen in the whole system of teacher training and qualification in order to provide teachers with a sound scientific and pedagogical basis. There will also be an increase in teachers' salaries, especially for those who work in remote areas. Efforts will also be made to reduce the teaching capacity and to regulate teaching norms. Teachers who are regarded as performing successfully will receive titles such as "distinguished teacher", the medal of the "Order Naim Frashëri," classes 1, 2, or 3, and titles such as "merit teacher" and "people's teacher."

7. Curriculum Development and Teaching Methodology

Teaching programs and syllabuses are compiled by specialized groups and are approved by the Ministry of Education. The new experimental programs are developed and followed up by the Institute of Pedagogical Studies in cooperation with the departments of experimental schools.

The curriculum for kindergartens is developed in a differentiated manner according to the age-groups and includes physical training, hygiene and health education, and mental, moral, and aesthetics education.

The teaching syllabi and programs for 8-grade school concentrate on the general education of pupils, and include social courses (44.6 %), mathematics and natural sciences (33.8 %), artistic subjects (7.3 %), physical training (7.3 %), and physical labor (7 %).

In general secondary schools, the curriculum combines general academic training with polytechnic and labor education, and physical training. In order to develop the individual capabilities and interests of the pupils, optional subjects and vocational subjects are planned for the new curriculum in these schools.

The curriculum in higher education is developed by the faculties with the normal combination of theory/practice, lectures/seminars, exercises, and laboratory work.

The new educational reform has resulted in radical changes in the school curriculum. In the 8-grade school the subject of "social" education has been introduced instead of moral and political education. The components of military training and physical labor, as well as the subjects of Marxism–Leninism have been dropped and substituted by other social disciplines. Thus a new subject, "knowledge of society," has been introduced in the general schools. All subjects of a social, humanitarian, economic, juridical, or artistic character have been depoliticized and made ideologically neutral.

The curriculum in mathematics and sciences in both the 8-grade school and secondary school has been changed to make it comparable with the curriculum of advanced countries. The main languages taught in school are: English, French, and Russian; German and Italian have been introduced. All the existing curricula in higher education have undergone improvements and restructuring and some new components have been introduced.

The publication of teaching material is undertaken by state publishing houses: The Publishing House of School Books (established in 1967) and the Publishing House of University Books (established in 1987). Publication is often undertaken in cooperation with foreign institutions and associations, and especially with organizations such as UNESCO, Council of Europe, World Bank, and the Islamic World Organization.

8. The System of Examinations, Promotions, and Certifications

The control and assessment of student achievement is made continuously and individually. The promotion of pupils from one class to the next is made on the basis of their annual progress. Examinations are given only in intermediate classes. At the end of the eighth grade, pupils sit for their "freeing examinations" (Albanian language and mathematics, both oral and written) and when they pass they receive a certificate. At the end of Grade 12, all pupils take four "maturity" examinations, and, if successful, receive the "maturity certificate."

In higher education a special system of assessing requirements such as colloquia, practical duties, and seminars is used. Students take examinations but with no more than nine exams per year. At the end of university studies the student receives a diploma. Students are also awarded honor leaflets, a golden medal, a special diploma for gifted students, and so on.

9. Educational Assessment, Evaluation and Research

The main institution engaged in educational research is the Institute of Pedagogical Studies (IPS, founded in 1969). It carries out studies and experiments concerning curriculum content, teaching methods and processes, and publishes the results. It also conducts studies in the fields of educational psychology and the history of education. The IPS cooperates and coordinates its work with the Academy of Sciences, universities and education directorates in the districts. Furthermore, it publishes the *Pedagogical Review*, bulletins, and pedagogical literature.

The main studies for the period 1991 to 1995 are focused on problems dealing with the implementation and effectiveness of the new education reform, the new legislation on education, the restructuring of the curriculum, the use of technology, and special experimentations concerning new materials in mathematics, Albanian, and foreign languages.

10. Major Reforms in the 1980s and 1990s

In 1982, reform aimed at strengthening the quality of schooling was carried out and was accompanied by some changes in the curriculum and the aims of teaching as well as in teaching methods. However, the reforms were partial and did not lead to the raising of the academic level of students; on the contrary, the formal and bureaucratic aspects of education increased even more.

In 1990, there was reform in secondary and higher education. Compulsory education was to be extended from 8 to 10 years but this reform was never really carried out because of the democratic changes that occured after the overthrow of the communist dictatorship. Reforms planned since the Democratic Revolution, in the areas of vocational education, higher education, teaches education, and curriculum have been referred to in various sections above.

11. Major Problems for the Year 2000

The main problem will be to find means and resources to support the implementations of the new educational reform, especially the restructuring of secondary and higher education, the setting-up of new faculties, branches, and the introduction of modern teaching techniques.

Another important objective will be the implementation of the new programs on an experimental basis for subjects or groups of subjects in order to adapt them to the economic, cultural, and social development conditions.

Finally, there will be problems concerning the differentiation of education, the transformation of a totalitarian education to a democratic culture and education, the creation of new relations among the school, family and society, pupils and teachers, and in higher education between students and faculty members.

Bibliography

Albania 1992 *The Constitution and Regulation of Higher Schools*. Tirana

Gjinushi S On the perfection of the educational system and further qualitative strengthening of school. *Zëri i Popullit* July 7

Mësuesi 1992 Draft law on educational system. October 24

Ministry of Economy 1991 *Statistical Annual of Albania*. Ministry of Economy, Directory of Statistics, Tirana

Misja V, Golemi B 1987 *The Development of High School in Albania*. Tirana

Temo S 1984 *Education in the PSRA*. The Publishing House, Tirana

Temo S 1985 *Education in the People's Socialist Republic of Albania*. The Publishing House, Tirana

Vejsiu Y 1992 The progress of our school in democratic processes. Speech given in the People's Assembly October 15. *Mësuesi* October 17

Algeria

A. Djeflat

1. General Background

Algeria is a North African country bordered on the west by Morocco and Mauritania, on the east by Tunisia and Libya, on the south by Niger and Mali, and to the north its coastline of 1,200 kilometers on the Mediterranean Sea faces Europe. Its frontiers have not changed since the French colonial occupation in the nineteenth century (1830). With a size of 2,381,741 square kilometers (919,352 square miles), it is the second largest country in Africa. Situated at the crossroad of Europe, Africa, and the Arab world, its educational system is influenced by various cultures. There are two distinct geographical regions: the northern part (16%) which is fertile land where the majority of inhabitants are concentrated and the southern part (84%), the Sahara desert, where the population is scattered among oases.

In the north the climate is moderate with temperatures ranging from 4°C in January to 39°C in July and there are four distinct seasons. Rainfall is irregular and concentrated on the center and the east. These geographical and climatic conditions affect both the distribution of educational infrastructures and resource allocation as well as the organization and length of the school year and holidays; thus in the southern regions the heat imposes an early start to the school day and different timing for holidays.

Algeria's largest cities are Algiers the capital, Oran the second largest, Constantine, Annaba, Mostaganem, Skikda, Tlemcen, Guelma, Sidi Bel Abbes, Bejaia, Mascara, Tizi-Ouzou, and Blida. Administratively it is divided into 48 *willayates* (districts). The population annual growth rate was 3.2 percent from 1962 (year of Independence) to 1987 (the last census) when it reached 23,039 million inhabitants, most of whom were concentrated in the north (91%). The urban population represented 49 percent in the mid-1990s while it was essentially a rural population at the beginning of the century.

Algeria has had a long history of occupation by the Spaniards, the Turks, and the French. French colonial occupation was resisted and fought ever since it took place in 1830, the most prestigious fighter during the nineteenth century being Emir Abdelkader. After the Second World War, several political parties were formed (PPA, the MTLD, *l'Etoile Nord Africain*), all with differing views on ending colonial occupation. The FLN (*Front de Liberation Nationale*) which opted for armed struggle, won in the end and Algeria became independent in 1962. While being an Islamic society, Algeria has four major ethnic groups: the Arabs, the Berbers (with the name of Kabyles), the Mozabites, and the Touaregs. The language spoken by the majority of the people is Arabic and it is also the official language of the country followed by the Amazigh spoken by the Kabyles. The policy of assimilation pursued during the 132 years of colonial occupation imposed the French language as the only medium of instruction in schools. Only a minority of children (636,500) had access to schools in the education system run by the French. The rest (about 2.5 million children) pursued their education in Koranic schools in Arabic. The French education system displaced and marginalized the precolonial education system composed of *katabib* (primary), *medersas* (secondary), and *zawiya* (higher education). Although after independence, school teachers who had come from France left the country in large numbers, nonetheless, the French education system (i.e., the education system put in place by the French) was kept with Arabization as one of the major political goals in order to restore Algerian identity.

Massive oil surpluses following the price rise at the beginning of the 1970s helped the government to develop heavy industry during the first three developmental periods (1967–69, 1970–73, and 1974–77). In a new era starting at the beginning of the 1980s, more emphasis was put on agriculture, infrastructure, and social services. In 1992, 9.6 percent of GDP came from agriculture, 33.4 percent from hydrocarbons and industry, and 48.2 percent from construction. The exports of crude oil and gas (96%) are highly dependent on the fluctuation of prices on the world market. This vulnerability is increased by foreign debt, the reimbursement of which cuts into public spending including education and the employment of new graduates and school leavers. The occupational structure shows a relatively strong category of permanent wage-earners (67%), followed by self-employed (20%). After more than 25 years of power monopoly held by the FLN, a new constitution was voted by the people in 1989 signaling a new era of democracy and multiparty systems. Several opposition parties were formed, the most active being the Islamic parties. The government is composed of a prime minister, chosen by the president, and about 26 ministers. After the dissolution of the National Assembly in 1991, the legislative power was given to the government with an appointed council. Due to the lack of long-term planning in the country, needs in terms of educational qualifications were never accurately known throughout the 1960s and 1970s. It was only at the beginning of the 1980s that the development plan (1980–84), started dealing with a real planning policy for education.

2. Politics and the Goals of the Education System

Shortly after independence, the authorities had to pursue several and sometimes conflicting goals, namely, providing free education to every citizen as a result of the socialist option adopted by government, supplying industry with the required qualified manpower, and also replacing the massive exodus of French teachers.

The Constitution and the various political charters stressed Arabization, as a means of reducing the dominant position of French: Algerianization, by substituting local personnel for foreigners and adapting the curricula to local realities and democratization, by giving equal chances for education to all Algerian pupils. The aims of the new system introduced in 1976 were geared toward the satisfaction of people's aspiration for justice and progress and the awakening of the child's consciousness and love of the fatherland. Among the most important principles set out were the right for education and training for every Algerian through a system of free and compulsory education for all. These goals are reflected in both primary and secondary education and constituted the bases for the successive reforms of the education system in the 1970s and 1980s.

3. The Formal System of Education

The educational system has three levels: basic education which includes primary and presecondary education, secondary education, and higher education (see Fig. 1 and Table 1). In 1991 the school age population reached around 31 percent of the total population of the country. The increase in the rate of urbanization, free education for all, and the prospects for an added income to the family budget contribute to explain the rapid increase in enrollment. Girls represent a lower proportion than boys for both cultural and practical reasons.

3.1 Primary, Secondary, and Tertiary Education

In April 1976, Ordinance 7635 introduced the Basic School Cycle which shifted primary education from a ten-year cycle to a nine-year basic education cycle leading to the Basic Education Certificate (BEF). Primary education consists of the first and second stages of the basic education cycle. At the primary level, 50 percent of the pupils are between the ages of 6 and 8 and 42 percent are between the ages of 9 and 11. The gross enrollment ratio for primary education reached 95 percent leading to both high numbers in classes (45 on average) and a high pupil–teacher ratio (28:1 in 1990). Performance wise in 1988, the pass rate in primary education reached 40′ percent, the percentage of repeaters decreased to 6 percent, and the transition rate increased to 81 percent.

Secondary education is designed to receive pupils who have completed their basic education and who can choose to enter secondary general education or secondary technical education. General education is dispensed in about 700 secondary grammar schools (*lycées*) and technical education in *technicums*. After three years of study pupils sit the *baccalauréat* examination with four options: mathematics, natural sciences, Islamic sciences, and arts. The actual length of the studies varies from one to three years depending on one of the 20 specializations chosen. There are two types of *baccalauréat*: the *baccalauréat* of secondary education and the technical *baccalauréat*. The bulk of the pupils (82%) are between the ages of 15 and 18 years representing an average enrollment ratio of 60 percent, but with a lower rate for females. The average pass rate is low (about 25%) while the pupil–teacher ratio is 18:1.

Higher education is conducted in about 54 higher education institutions including universities, high schools, and technological institutes supervised by the Ministry of Higher Education. Other tertiary education institutions are under other ministries called non-university sectors. Access to university requires the possession of a *baccalauréat*. In 1991–92, 87 percent of *baccalauréat* holders of the previous year were registered in higher education institutions where more than one hundred subjects were taught in more than 30 towns and cities. The nonuniversity sectors include 42 institutions for professional training covering a variety of subjects ranging from energy and petrochemicals to social work. There are two types of cycles in higher education: (a) the short cycle (4 to 6 semesters) for training advanced technicians and hence catering more for the needs of industry; and (b) the long cycle (8 semesters) leading to the bachelor's degree (*licence*) and the extra-long cycle (up to 6 years) in certain specializations such as medicine and architecture. Enrollments reached 275,027 in 1993 with an average rate of increase of 12 percent of the total. The majority of those enrolled are in the 20–24 years age group and female students represent about one third of the total. Despite improvements, the efficiency rate remains relatively low (16% on average). Postgraduate studies which began in the mid-seventies usually leading to a master's degree and *Doctorat d'Etat* (state doctorate).

3.2 Preschool Education

Traditionally preschool education was conducted in Koranic schools. Preschool education was formally set up in the July 1976 reform on the principle that it is a noncompulsory preparatory stage for schooling constituting a good back-up and a substitute for a lack of family education. It is dispensed in kindergartens, nursery schools, and children's classes supervised by local councils, primary schools, or even major companies. It is aimed at children aged between 4 and 6 years old. In a recent move, the state allowed preschool institutions to be run privately.

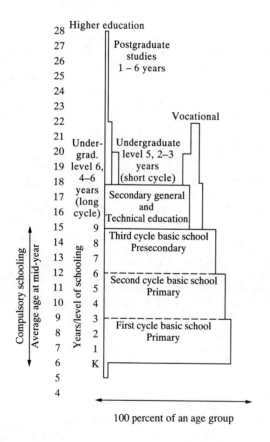

Figure 1
Algeria: Structure of the formal education system

3.3 Special Education

It was only in 1990 that special education received clear objectives in the form of official syllabuses. Special education is provided for the handicapped, and particularly the blind, deaf, and dumb, the motor-deficient, and the mentally retarded children. These schools are centrally run and supervised by the Department of Special Education at the Ministry of Education. In the early 1990s private initiatives through associations were being taken to organize this kind of education. However, reliable statistics are difficult to obtain.

3.4 Vocational, Technical, and Business Education

Vocational training became a necessity in Algeria as a result of the rapid and massive industrialization of the country, a shortage of properly trained people and increasing youth unemployment. Vocational training grew rapidly during the 1980s with the number of trainees enrolled reaching 153,360 in 1990. Two major centers are in charge of vocational training: the Center for Professional and Administrative Training (CFPA) and the National Center for Professional Training. The first one has about 450 training centers covering 17 areas of study and leading to the Professional Certificate (CAP). The second, dealing more with business and domestic subjects, leads to the certificate for professional aptitude (CAP) and the Professional Certificate (*Brevet Professionnel*). Unlike the first one which is state subsidized, the second one is paid for by the trainees themselves. Previously a state monopoly, education and training are being progressively liberalized and private capital is gradually moving into it.

3.5 Adult and Nonformal Education

As a result of the state-run economy and the total control of education by the government, nonformal education existed only at the preschool stage as seen earlier. Campaigns for reducing the rate of illiteracy (43% in 1990) drove the government to organize adult education which is also provided for those who wish to have a professional qualification through distance-learning programs provided in general education centers (CNEG) and in professional training centers (CNEPC). In 1990, about 55,000 fee-paying students were enrolled in basic secondary education and in some other specialized topics in these centers. Adult education is finally provided at the University of Continuous Training (UCT). Three main centers exist to cater for the rapidly increasing demand. In 1993, 3,613 students were registered in short cycles and 9,659 in long ones. Eight subjects in social sciences and nine in exact sciences were taught. Financing is mostly by the state (90%) with a small contributiuon from students (10%).

4. Administrative and Supervisory Structure and Operation

Administration bodies at central level have experi-

Table 1
Enrollments and resources in primary (1st and 2nd cycle), presecondary (3rd cycle), and secondary education Algeria 1980–92

	1980–81	1985–86	1987–88	1989–90	1990–91	1991–92
Pupils						
primary	3,118,827	3,481,288	3,801,651	4,027,612	4,189,152	4,357,352
presecondary	804,621	1,399,890	1,490,863	1,408,622	1,423,316	1,490,324
secondary[a]	211,948	423,502	591,783	754,947	752,264	743,213
Schools						
primary	9,263	11,144	11,843	12,694	13,135	13,461
presecondary	632	1,561	1,929	2,248	2,422	2,498
secondary[a]	230	415	556	758	812	845
Classrooms primary &						
presecondary	56,160	74,361	81,511	90,440	94,177	97,449
Teachers						
primary	88,481	125,034	139,875	144,945	151,262	154,685
presecondary	29,555	60,663	74,031	79,783	82,741	86,610
secondary[a]	10,458	21,555	31,057	40,939	44,283	44,622

a including technical education

enced a variety of changes since independence with sometimes a single ministry for primary, secondary and higher education and research, and at other times a split between two separate ministries. This seems to reflect the constant struggle between the principle of coordination and harmonization versus the principle of specialization. Vocational training has, however, always remained outside the Ministry of Education, being sometimes attached to the Ministry of Labor and at other times a ministry of its own. In essence, the system is highly centralized because of the need to have a single and homogeneous policy at the national level and not a diversified system that might be difficult to coordinate.

The supervisory task is conducted through ministerial departments each with its own specialized functions: human resources, finance, planning and statistics, infrastructure, and procurement. In higher education there are also the Department of Undergraduate Studies, the Department of Postgraduate Studies and Research, and the Department of Grants and International Cooperation. At the provincial level there are two bodies: one is supervisory and the other is operational. The first, which represents the Ministry of Education, is responsible for supervising primary and secondary schools. Attempts were made to introduce supervisory bodies for higher education but these were not successful.

Major decisions concerning education are taken by the Council of Ministers chaired by the prime minister. The Ministry of Education constitutes; in this sense the organ for implementing major government decisions and directions. Universities are run by a rector appointed by the minister and assisted by vice-rectors, a general secretary for daily matters, and a scientific council for important decisions.

5. *Educational Finance*

The prime source of finance for all levels of education remains the state budget. In theory, budgets are allocated by the Ministry of Education on the basis of budget proposals made by various establishments according to their needs. In practice, the budget is always allocated by the central government and in particular by the budget committee of the Ministry of Education on the basis of past budgets plus a percentage increase generally based on the estimated increase in enrollment. Total public expenditure on education grew from 23 percent of the national budget in 1975 to 27 percent in 1989; this represented a jump from 6 percent to 9 percent of GNP. The largest share went to primary and secondary education (from 11% to 21% of the national budget during the same period). This growth results from the implementation of the three major development plans (1967–77), the demographic pressure which required building schools at a relatively high rhythm, and access to oil

revenues following the price increase of 1973. In the following period (1980–90), both capital and current expenditure fell sharply as a result of dwindling oil prices and the economic crisis. The budget allocated to higher education increased at a relatively steady rate indicating not only the importance given by the government to this sector of education, but also the sheer increase of the student population. In 1989, it represented 6 percent of national budget and reached 10 billion dinars (US$244,100,000) by 1992. Unit cost per higher education student reached 45,500 dinars (US$1,110.63) per year, of which only 26 percent was spent on pedagogical activities. The unit cost varies drastically from one discipline to another and from one establishment to another. Thirty-nine percent of the education budget is used to subsidize social expenses: grants, restaurants, transportation, sports, and cultural activities. It is anticipated that the efforts in financing education in the early 1990s will be maintained up to the year 2000. The number of students benefiting from state financing was 116,931 in 1990 which represented nearly 60 percent of all registered students.

6. *Supplying Personnel for the Education System*

Shortly after independence, many categories of teachers of primary and secondary education were recruited—without initial training—among *baccalauréat* and non-*baccalauréat* holders in order to cope with the sudden increase in pupil enrollment. For secondary education, many university dropouts were recruited as well as foreign teachers, essentially from francophone countries and from the Middle East. To cope with the increase in enrollment, teachers were trained at the old *Ecole Normale Superieure* which trained secondary school teachers but in insufficient numbers. Several teacher-training schools for general education (*Institut de Technologie de l'Education*) and for technical education (*Ecole Normale Superieure de l'Enseignement Technique*) were also created. The university also constitutes, both directly and indirectly, a training institution for primary and secondary education teachers. By the mid-1990s, teachers without qualifications from one of these teacher-training schools were not recruited. As a result, the number of primary and secondary school teachers increased rapidly and by 1991 there were 273,286 teachers. Of these 54 percent were in primary education, and 44 percent in secondary general education. The upgrading of teachers at secondary education is usually done through staff development programs organized either locally through staff seminar programs or abroad in specialized centers. Retraining, mostly for nondegree or diploma holders, is undertaken at the university and in summer schools and seminars.

These various policies, although serving the system quantitively, have not resulted in supplying the education system with good quality teachers. This is due to inadequate training and lack of motivation resulting from poor pay and conditions. The evaluation of teacher training is undertaken using traditional exams and on-site evaluation with the help of a body of inspectors. This evaluation leads either to the Certificate of Pedagogical Aptitude of Secondary Education (CAPES) or to the promotion of teachers from one level to the next. Other types of personnel are also provided such as work conductors, administrative and finance personnel, and directors of education. It would appear to be easier to attract administrative personnel than teachers. The relatively high reliance of the Algerian higher education system on foreign personnel decreased rapidly. For example, the proportion of foreign personnel decreased from 40 percent in 1980 to less than 5 percent in 1993. In both secondary and higher educaiton, the Algerianization policy launched by the government at the beginning of the 1970s was relatively successful.

7. Curriculum Development and Teaching Methodology

Primary and secondary school curricula and teaching methodologies are formally developed by the Ministry of Education. Discipline-based commissions work on curricula proposals. These commissions include teachers selected throughout the country on the basis of competence in curriculum matters. The final decision regarding the scope and contents of a particular curriculum remains, however, with the Ministry of Education. Once approved these curricula are nationwide and binding; local or regional variations are not permitted. The implementation of the curricula at primary and secondary education is controlled by a body of inspectors. The proposals made are usually accompanied by proposals for textbooks and handbooks to accompany the syllabuses of studies. All textbooks and handbooks are usually developed by the National Pedagogic Institute. Individual authors can also publish textbooks and handbooks after many years of experience with the relevant curriculum. There are still many problems in curriculum and teaching methods at both primary and secondary schools. For example: (a) the premature teaching of modern mathematics at the expense of some basic yet highly useful arithmetic rules and some sound traditional mathematics; (b) the absence of some key topics and concepts in chemistry in the final grade of secondary school, and in trigonometry in the last year of basic education; and (c) the elimination of modern mathematics in the third-cycle basic education since 1989.

Higher education curricula are centrally developed by the Ministry of Higher Education, through its specialized departments. Commissions consisting of senior members of the teaching staff from various institutions are appointed to do the work. However, these commissions often do not go beyond defining broad outlines of the syllabus leaving the initiative for the details to lecturers and professors. New curricula can also be initiated by the scientific council of a particular institute and then approved by the Ministry. In both cases, they become nationwide and binding. There are elective subjects in the last two years of university studies. Publication and dissemination of most academic books is undertaken by the *Office des Publications Universitaires* (OPU), a state-owned publisher. Foreign languages are taught in the third cycle of basic education and in secondary education. French remains the most popular foreign language, for historical reasons, in spite of the rapid growth of English. In 1993, English became an optional subject holding the same position as French in the fourth year of basic education. Spanish, German, Russian, and Italian are also taught at universities.

8. The System of Examinations, Promotions, and Certifications

In the first two cycles of basic education pupils are automatically promoted by age. Examination-based promotion starts in secondary education where the old system is being progressively abandoned and replaced by a new one which started in 1989. Promotion from lower to upper secondary takes into account both the average of the marks obtained in the last three years plus the average mark obtained in the final examination of basic education. In spite of these improvements, the new system does not appear to be effective in selecting the best pupils: high achievers do not appear to be sufficiently motivated by the system to perform better in order to be promoted to the higher level.

In general, the main qualification required to enter higher education is the *baccalauréat*. However, to enter certain disciplines, the marks obtained by students in the *baccalauréat* are taken into account, except when the applicant had a *baccalauréat* with distinction. Progress throughout the four years of study is done through mid-term and end-of-year examinations where the student must achieve an average mark of at least 10 out of 20 in order to be promoted.

9. Educational Assessment, Evaluation, and Research

Like many other sectors, education did not benefit from formal evaluation until the mid-1980s when it became obvious that the education system was suffering from several failings such as a high dropout rate, a rapid decrease in quality, and increasing graduate unemployment. One of the major concerns remains the high rate of failure in the *baccalauréat*.

Thus, evaluation became a necessity at the various levels of the education system. Several methods were used. Within the system, evaluation was conducted through annual national conferences of inspectors organized by the Ministry of Education where all aspects of the education system are discussed, namely, the adequacy of the system in terms of curricula, pedagogical and teaching methods, and the flow of pupils together with the relationship with employment. At the regional level, evaluation was conducted through periodic conferences and seminars organized by the regional inspectorate and attended by all involved in primary and secondary education: inspectors, school principals, and teachers. Pedagogical matters as well as material problems are debated. Administrative and financial matters are assessed in different seminars and workshops, attended mostly by administrative personnel.

At the higher education level, evaluation is conducted through national pedagogical conferences attended by all parties involved in the system: university rectors, directors of institutes, representatives of administration and the Union, and representatives of students. Regional pedagogical conferences are held periodically to examine specific regional problems. Formally organized research on pedagogical matters is nonexistent except for initiatives by individual members of the staff of the Ministry of Education and by those who are preparing postgraduate degrees and diplomas. More attempts are being made by the National Institute of Education. With what is known as the crisis of the education system, the preamble of the Five-Year Plan (1989–94), for the first time, placed the organization and the development of educational research as one of its important objectives. More and more foreign and local experts from private and public organizations are called in to conduct surveys and assess the efficiency and effectiveness of the system.

10. Major Reforms in the 1980s and 1990s

No major changes were made to the educational system following the reforms of the 1970s. In the 1980s, several measures were taken gradually and reported in the different development plans (1980–84 and 1985–89) mostly to cope with: (a) the problems of the poor quality of education, (b) the overcrowding of classrooms in primary education, and (c) the need to strengthen the technical education option in secondary education. In the 1990s, a new set of reforms are envisaged for primary and secondary education in terms of upgrading the knowledge and the quality of teachers and raising the level of achievement of pupils through better selection and the fostering

of higher pupil motivation. In higher education, reforms in the 1990s are mostly geared toward improving the quality of the output, fighting the ever-increasing unemployment of graduates, improving the pedagogical aspects of instruction which have long been neglected, strengthening the capacity of the university to respond to the needs of the economy, and finally, rationalizing the existing facilities in the face of economic crisis and the shortage of foreign currencies.

11. Major Problems for the Year 2000

Up to the year 2000, the annual rate of increase in enrollments is expected to reach 37 percent meaning that the state has to mobilize more and more resources to cope with such increases with many fewer resources than in the past because of the economic crisis of the country. More and more training institutions will have to compete for limited funds and seek external funding through fee-paying pupils and students. This move will be accentuated by the new event of market economy and liberalization. The high level of inefficiency of the education system (less than 5% of the pupils enrolled in primary education reach higher education) is socially, economically, and politically unacceptable and contributes to social inequality. Major issues include: (a) the rehabilitation of the place and role of the university, (b) the social status of knowledge as a whole, and (c) the balance to be achieved between local Arabo–Islamic culture and values and the requirements of modern society.

Bibliography

Cheriet A 1983 *Opinion sur la politique de l'enseignement et de l'Arabisation*. SNED, Algiers
Djeflat A 1989 Developpement Economique et Developpement Universitaire. *Revue du Centre de Recherche Economique et Social* 100: 35–54
Djeflat A 1993 *Technologie et System Educatif en Algerie*. UNESCO, Cread / Medina / Algiers
Ferroukhi D J 1985 Approche statistique de systeme éducatif. *Statistiques* 9: 17–23
Haddab M 1986 Quelques problemes de l'analyse des changements dans l'enseignement superieur. *Revue Algerienne de Psychologie et de Sciences de l'Education* 2: 59-67
Ministère de l'Enseignement Supérieur 1983–91 *Statistical Yearbook*. Ministère de l'Enseignement Supérieur, Algiers
Ministère de l'Education Nationale 1992–93 *l'Universitaire en chiffres: 1992–93*. Ministère de l'Education Nationale, Algiers
Necib R 1986 *Industrialisation et Systeme Educatif en Algerie*. Office des Publications Universitaires, Algiers
Office National des Statistiques 1987 *Statistical Yearbook of Algeria: 1985–86*, No. 13. Office National des Statistiques, Algiers

American Samoa

R. M. Thomas

1. General Background

American Samoa, also known as Eastern Samoa, is a cluster of seven small islands in the south-central Pacific Ocean, governed since 1900 by the United States of America. Although the system of schooling in American Samoa generally follows the pattern of education found in the United States, the Samoan system warrants separate attention because of the changes that have been effected in the schooling system from the 1960s into the 1990s.

The indigenous people of Samoa are Polynesians whose ancestors came to the islands many centuries ago in ocean-going outrigger canoes to establish a society of clans headed by chieftains. Before Europeans arrived in the early-nineteenth century, education in the islands was of an informal variety. Because Samoans had no written form of their language, children learned the belief system of their culture through a rich store of oral history and proverbs, and they acquired vocational skills by participating with their parents in daily work assignments.

Formal schooling was introduced by pastors of the London Missionary Society who began to establish churches and schools in 1830. The missionaries also developed an orthography for casting the Samoan language into written form so that the Bible and hymns might be printed in the islanders' own tongue. Methodist and Catholic missions soon followed, with the result that within a few decades virtually all Samoans were professed Christians, and a great number were literate. The schools set up by the missionaries were staffed mainly by Samoan pastors and their wives. Classes were held daily in the church or the adjacent residence of the pastor, where children learned reading, writing, arithmetic, Christian doctrine, and some geography and history, all in the Samoan language. The pastors' schools continued to be the principal source of formal education throughout the nineteenth century and far into the twentieth century. Although all children in American Samoa attend either a public or private school conducted in the English language, the traditional pastors' schools still exist, attended by many children in the early morning or late afternoon or during periods of vacation from the secular school.

Beginning in the early 1900s, secular schools were gradually established with English as the medium of instruction, thereby supplementing the Samoan-language pastors' schools. Eventually the public secular schools would become the dominant purveyors of formal education.

Throughout the colonial expansion of European and American nations into the Pacific, Samoan political affairs were often turbulent, with no single high chief able to gain secure control over the entire island territory. As a way to settle political matters, Germany and the United States divided the islands into two sectors separated at 171° longitude, with Germany taking the larger western sector where German commercial interests already owned plantations and the United States taking the eastern sector so as to maintain a coaling station for American ships in Pago Pago Bay.

Under separate Western powers, the two Samoas that exist today—Western and Eastern—began gradually to diverge in their form of schooling. This divergence continued after 1914 when New Zealand took over Western Samoa from Germany during the First World War.

The United States Navy governed American Samoa from 1900 to 1950, while the Department of Interior has been responsible for island affairs since 1950. Prior to 1977 the governor of American Samoa was appointed from the United States capital in Washington. However, since 1977, Samoans have elected their own governor.

The majority of American Samoa's population of around 46,000 live in villages distributed throughout the mountainous islands, with many of them engaged in subsistence farming and fishing. By the early 1990s, the labor force of American Samoa consisted of around 14,000 workers, representing 30 percent of the total population. About one-third of the workers were aliens, mostly from Western Samoa; 32 percent of wage earners were employees of the American Samoa government. As the second largest source of employment, tuna fish canneries on Pago Pago Bay engaged 26 percent of islanders who worked for wages. These two major enterprises were supplemented in the cash economy by tourism and a few other modest businesses.

Although many students in the American Samoan education system have remained in the isalnds after completing their school careers, many others have migrated to Hawaii or to the United States mainland to find employment. Thus, the territory's educational planners face the challenge of preparing youths for more than one occupational setting—the task of arming graduates with skills to succeed in markedly different sociocultural environments.

2. Politics and the Goals of the Education System

The modern era of education in American Samoa began in 1962 as the result of a series of interlinked political events. Throughout the 1900–61 period, schools in the territory were markedly inferior to those of Hawaii and mainland United States in terms of housing, instructional supplies, staff members' salaries, teachers' professional skills, and students' performance on achievement tests. By 1961 the majority of children between the ages of 7 and 15 were enrolled in public or private schools, but attendance was not universal. Some children dropped out after the early primary grades, and many more attended class only erratically.

In 1960, a United States congressional commission arrived in the islands to investigate charges that schools and other social services in Eastern Samoa had for many years suffered serious neglect. The commission reported in 1961 that school buildings were ramshackle affairs, teachers were poorly trained, the curriculum was unsuitable, and the opportunities for secondary education were very meager (Everly 1961). Other social services in the territory were judged equally inadequate.

A second event in 1961 was a *Reader's Digest* article entitled "Samoa: America's Shame in the South Seas" which informed the American public of the sad state of their Polynesian colony. A third event was the upcoming meeting of the South Pacific Commission, scheduled to be held in Eastern Samoa in 1962. The meeting would be attended by representatives of a variety of nations which governed islands in the Pacific.

The political embarrassment stimulated the United States Congress to take immediate steps to correct the deplorable state of social services in Eastern Samoa.

2.1 The Era of Instructional Television

A new governor, H Rex Lee, was appointed to remedy matters. After inspecting the schools, he declared that the best hope for providing quality education lay in establishing a territory-wide educational television system. This decision inaugurated the Samoan experiment with instructional television that would gain worldwide attention over the following two decades.

With millions of dollars supplied by the United States Congress, Governor Lee's staff arranged for the replacement of 50 dilapidated village elementary schools by 24 modern consolidated schools and for the construction of four modern high schools to replace the single high school left over from Navy days. The National Association of Educational Broadcasters from Washington, DC, was hired to design and operate an instructional television facility, so that, by the mid-1960s, the main lesson for each basic elementary school subject was broadcast into all classrooms, Grades 1 through 8, from a central television studio complex. The system's six broadcast channels also enabled educators to send daily lessons into selected secondary school classrooms. By the end of the 1960s, when the television instructional system reached its peak operating level, there were 180 hours of lessons telecast each week. The studio and engineering staff

had grown to 110 people, supplemented by writers and teachers who designed and presented the lessons (Schramm et al. 1981).

However, the trends of the previous decade began to shift in the 1970s. A variety of forces converged to reduce drastically the use of television, so by 1980 the classroom teacher was again the key director of children's learning, and television was used only occasionally as a supplementary medium of instruction, mainly for lessons in oral English. The forces included: (a) a desire of educational leaders to suit instruction more to the individual talents of pupils, (b) an improved system of teacher training, and (c) shortages of funds which caused the virtual elimination of central studio staff members who earlier had produced a wide range of daily televised lessons that the system required. By the early 1980s, the few remaining television programs were nearly all recorded lessons taped several years earlier. The era of the television-centered instructional system had passed (Thomas 1980).

2.2 Goals for Education

Even though television was no longer the dominant medium of instruction, the television interim had wrought changes in public schooling that would become permanent features of the island's educational enterprise. One of these features was the set of aims that schools were expected to achieve.

Over the years from 1900 to 1960, the principal goals of the education system had occasionally changed. Prior to the 1930s, the curriculum emphasized teaching Samoan pupils to be English-speaking Americans. During the progressive education period of the 1930s, efforts were made to focus learning more on life in the islands. Then, following the Second World War, the aims and instructional materials were again drawn from mainland United States, with Samoan language and culture receiving little or no attention in the schools.

However, at the outset of the educational television decades, a dual set of goals was declared. The mission of the schools would be to prepare pupils to function successfully in either traditional Samoan society or modern-day life on the United States mainland. Thus, since the early 1960s, the stated central purpose has been to furnish an elementary and secondary school education that equips each Samoan as "a fluent, literate bilingual in Samoan and English" who will "have respect for Samoan traditions and culture." Schools are to "prepare each individual for a personally satisfying and socially useful life wherever he chooses to live" (Department of Education 1974 p. 5). For Samoan youths who want to advance beyond secondary education, the schools will offer the chance to gain "a sound educational base that will enable them to enter American colleges and universities competitively on a level equal with other American students" (Bronson 1968 p. 9).

Table 2
American Samoa: School enrollment increase 1980–90

	1980[a]	1985[b]	1990[b]	% change 1980–90
Preschool/kindergarten	1,952	1,522	2,869	+47%
Public	1,952	1,522	2,420	+24%
Private	0	0	449	—
Elementary (Grades K-8)	6,892	7,428	8,248	+20%
Public	5,397	6,153	6,825	+28%
Private	1,495	1,275	1,423	−5%
Secondary (Grades 9–12)	2,926	3,262	3,335	+14%
Public	2,427	2,780	2,875	+18%
Private	499	482	460	−8%
Special education (public)	103	50	76	−26%
College (public)	900	758	1,011	+12%
Total	13,973	13,020	15,539	+11%

a Source: Department of Education 1980 p. 11   b Source: Government of American Samoa 1990 p. 38

This ambitious aim of ensuring that youths master both traditional Samoan culture and that of the American mainland has been politically popular with the Samoans who make up the territorial legislature, with the general Samoan public, and with officials of the United States government in both Samoa and Washington. Not only could Samoan tradition be respected and maintained, but Samoans who chose to move to the mainland would be able to compete

Table 1
American Samoa: Public and private school enrollments 1990

	Schools	Students
Preschool total	85	2,869
Public	80	2,420
Private	5	449
Elementary total (Grades K–8)	29	8,248
Public	22	6,825
Private	7	1,423
Secondary total (Grades 9–12)	8	3,335
Public	6	2,875
Private	2	460
Special education (public)	1	76
College (public)	1	1,011
Total	124	15,539

Source: Government of American Samoa 1990 p. 38

successfully for jobs and adapt easily to social conditions. This dual goal has been maintained into the 1990s, despite the fact that progress toward achieving such a formidable aim in practice has proven disappointing. Although Samoan students' success on standardized achievement tests in the English language have improved over the years, the average scores of Samoans have continued to fall markedly below those of students on the United States mainland. Critics of the bicultural goal have estimated that it is beyond the capacity of many students to master the languages and subject matter of both Samoan and United States traditions. Thus, a significant gap has continued to exist between the politically popular bicultural goal and actual student achievement (Thomas 1981).

In 1990, Governor Peter Tali Coleman convened a conference to rejuvenate education in the islands. On that occasion he described properly educated Samoans as being those who: (a) effectively communicate in English and Samoan, (b) have skills for contributing to society, (c) respect the environment and manage natural resources wisely, (d) take responsibility for themselves and for decisions that affect others, (e) recognize the interdependence of all mankind and work well with others, (f) use new complex technologies, (g) resist the temptations of harmful substances, and (h) feel good about themselves and know how to enjoy life (Department of Education 1990 p. 3).

3. The Formal System of Education

Prior to the early 1960s, the public education system consisted of elementary and junior high grades and a single senior high school. During the 1960s and 1970s, the educational ladder was extended downward to provide nursery schools attended by children aged 2, 4, and 5, and extended upward to offer postsecondary education at the American Samoa Community College.

A series of private schools, most of them representing the missionary tradition of the past, has continued to operate in parallel to the public schools. As shown in Table 1, of the 15,539 pupils in the territory's education system, nearly 85 percent were in public institutions by 1990, a ratio that has remained nearly the same in recent decades.

Since the introduction of the educational television system in the early 1960s, the great majority of children of elementary and secondary school age have attended school. By 1990, over 96 percent of those aged 6 through 16 years were enrolled. In 1960 the median number of years of school completed by people over age 15 was 6.5. By 1985 the median had increased to 10.6 years (Government of American Samoa 1990 pp. 38, 46).

Although American Samoa has always experienced a rather high birthrate, the islands' population prior to the mid-1980s did not increase substantially since American Samoans are United States nationals and therefore have open access to migrate to the United States mainland, an option that a great many adopt. An estimated 20,000 Samoans live in Hawaii and 65,000 in the states of California and Washington. This has meant that the population of school-aged children and

youth in the islands has not experienced as rapid an increase as the birthrate might imply. Public school enrollments in the early 1980s remained relatively steady or declined. Notable increases appeared only from the mid-1980s into the 1990s (see Table 2). Because of increasingly rapid population growth of the 1990s, the territory's population of 46,000 in 1990 has been expected to reach 60,000 by the end of the century. Projected attendance figures for all levels of schooling place total student enrollments at 21,310 by 1995 and 24,010 by year 2000.

The percentage of each age group in school by the early 1990s are reflected in Fig. 1. Nearly 85 percent of children aged 3 and 4 attended preschool centers, 98 percent of those aged 5 through 13 were in the eight-grade elementary school, 90 percent of those aged 14 through 17 were in the four-year high school, and an estimated 26 percent aged 18 and 19 were in college (Government of American Samoa 1990 p. 42).

3.1 Primary, Secondary, and Tertiary Education

By the early 1990s, the post-preschool segment of the territory's education system consisted of 29 eight-year elementary schools, 8 four-year secondary schools, and 1 four-year college (see Table 1). The territory's 22 public elementary schools and 7 private schools enrolled nearly 8,300 children in kindergarten through Grade 8. Approximately 83 percent of the pupils attended the public schools. The enrollment in schools located in remote sites had as few as 65 pupils, while attendance at the largest school in the islands' main commercial center exceeded 1,120.

At the secondary level, 86 percent of the 3,335 students were in the 6 public schools. The remaining 14 percent attended 2 private high schools operated by Catholic orders, the Marist Brothers and Marist Sisters. This pair of institutions have traditionally played an important role in the operation of Samoan society, since many of the islands' political, social, and business leaders have been graduates of the Marist schools.

Opportunities for higher education are provided by the American Samoa Community College, an institution started as a two-year college in 1970 and modeled upon junior colleges on the United States mainland. From the beginning, the institution adopted an open-door admission policy. Anyone over age 18 who could profit from the college's programs was welcome to enroll.

The college has provided opportunities for both full-time and part-time study. In 1990, 45 percent of the students attended full-time compared to 48 percent in 1985. Over the 1985–90 period, an increasingly greater proportion of women than men enrolled in the college's programs—52 percent women and 48 percent men in 1985 compared to 58 percent women and 42 percent men in 1990.

The Community College provides programs leading to an associate of arts or science degree or a certifi-

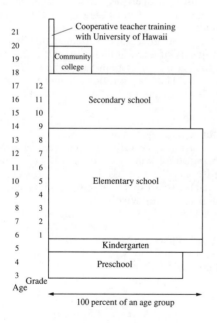

Figure 1
American Samoa: Structure of the formal education system

cate of proficiency in a vocational field. Both liberal arts and vocational studies are available. In 1990, the largest enrollment—48 percent of the student body—was in a newly established English Language Institute designed to prepare students with advanced skills in the field of English. The next most popular program was in liberal arts at 17 percent. Another 15 percent of the students had not yet settled on a major area of emphasis. The remaining 30 percent were divided among such fields as nursing, general business, accounting, administration of justice, secretarial science, allied health service, automotive mechanics, architectural drafting, and personal enrichment. The course in agriculture, which has traditionally been Samoans' main occupational pursuit, drew only three applicants.

The number of students earning a two-year associate degree in the 1980s and early 1990s averaged 100 annually, with around half of them in arts and half in science.

In terms of citizenship, the college's 1990 enrollment of 1,011 students included 614 American Samoans, 193 Western Samoans, 185 United States mainlanders, 7 Tongans, 4 Koreans, 4 Filipinos, and 4 of other nationalities.

Over the modern era of Samoan education, the proportion of the population that has attended college has more than trebled. In 1960 only 5 percent of citizens beyond age 15 had completed one or more years of college. By the mid-1980s, the number had risen to 16 percent.

3.2 Preschool Education

Prior to 1969 there were no kindergartens or nursery schools for Samoan children. In late 1968, at the suggestion of the territorial governor, a child development professor from the mainland, Dr Betty Johnston, teamed up with a Samoan educator, Iutita Savali, to open early childhood education centers throughout the islands. The residents in 40 village locations offered housing and provided volunteers to serve as teachers, who were trained in 10- to 15-week instructional sessions to conduct learning activities in the Samoan language for children aged from 3 to 5. By the 1980s, 5-year olds were being accommodated in newly organized kindergartens attached to the public elementary schools. The early childhood centers were thereafter attended solely by 3- and 4-year olds.

In the early 1990s, the preschool centers operated for 40 weeks during the year, providing 12.5 hours of instruction each week for approximately 1,600 children. In addition, the 4-year olds attended one day a week on a rotation basis for special instruction in English and other content areas. The program covered three general areas—intellectual development, social services, and health services—along with a strong component of parent training and involvement.

3.3 Special Education

The islands' first publicly supported special education program began in 1971 with services for the deaf, hard of hearing, speech impaired, and hospital bound. At its inception it had a staff of 7 who cared for 7 full-time and 35 part-time students. As the program grew over the following years, the types of services were expanded, with a strong effort exerted to keep the handicapped in regular classrooms where they could receive special help but still be with their nonhandicapped agemates.

By 1975 the special education division of the Department of Education was organized into several major project areas. First was a "resource system" designed to identify handicapped children and assess their needs. Second was a speech and hearing project, staffed by two specialists who furnished speech therapy for over 50 children each year. Third was a project for the physically or mentally handicapped who could not learn adequately in regular elementary school classrooms, even with special aid. Thus, they were either assigned to a special education class or were tutored at home. The fourth project was a small on-the-job vocational class on a farm for high school age students. The fifth was a plan for individualizing instruction for children with learning problems.

By the 1990s, children with disabilities that could be adequately accommodated in normal class situations were assigned to regular classrooms, while 75 or 80 of the ones with more serious handicaps were in special education classes.

3.4 Vocational, Technical, and Business Education

Formal vocational education is provided both in the high schools and in the community college. The public high schools, under a new organizational plan inaugurated in 1990, offer vocational studies in business education, home economics, and applied technology. The business education division provides specialist training in accounting, clerical work, and stenographic/secretarial activities. The home economics program is aimed primarily at strengthening the family as the primary unit of Samoan society. An applied technology curriculum in 1988 replaced an existing industrial arts program with studies in drafting, carpentry, plumbing, electricity, small engines, and auto maintenance. For many years a business education program has also been conducted by the girls' high school run by the Marist Sisters.

Advanced vocational courses in a variety of fields are available in the American Samoa Community College. As noted earlier, specialist training is offered in such fields as nursing, teaching, general business practice, accounting, secretarial science, allied health service, the administration of justice, automotive mechanics, architectural drafting, and agriculture.

3.5 Adult and Nonformal Education

Formal adult education is located primarily in the community college. Classes are available for vocational training, academic advancement, and personal growth.

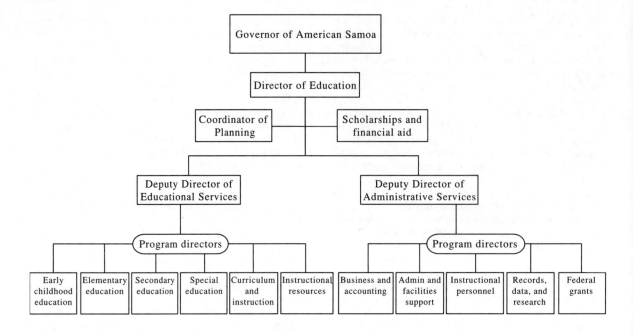

Figure 2
American Samoa: Department of Education administrative structure

In addition, some informal educational opportunities are available on the territory's television channels, which have been dedicated chiefly to commercial programming from the United States mainland since the instructional television system was abandoned in the late 1970s.

4. Administrative and Supervisory Structure and Operation

The conduct of public education in American Samoa is the responsibility of a central Department of Education, the largest department in the American Samoa government. It consists of more than a dozen divisions, approximately 1,500 employees, and a physical plan of more than 300 buildings. The department controls all decisions regarding public schooling. Private schools are obliged to abide by certain general policies established in the department, but are free to select their own staff members, instructional procedures, sources of funds, and details of curricula.

As shown in Figure 2, the ultimate authority for education in the islands is held by the territory's elected governor, who delegates to the director of education the responsibility for administering the school system. The four deputy directors for planning, financial aid, educational services, and administrative services report to the director of education, while 11 program

directors and the teacher certification officer report to the deputy directors.

Since the public school system was founded in 1921, all administrative decisions have been made at the central office. However, beginning in the late 1980s, some control over decisions about matters other than curricula and finance was gradually being delegated to individual school principals.

5. Educational Finance

Public education in American Samoa is financed by funds from both the local government and the United States government. In the early 1990s, the Department of Education's annual budget averaged around US$26 million. Approximately half of the funds came from federal grants. Of the remaining US$13 million, about half came from the United States Department of the Interior and half from Samoan government sources (Department of Education 1992 p. 1). In the territory's public schools, the annual per-pupil expenditure by the early 1990s was US$1,850, nearly 60 percent below the average per-pupil cost for the United States in general.

Private schools finance their operations by means of student fees, donations from local and overseas church groups, and fund-raising activities such as bingo games and other social events.

6. *Supplying Personnel for the Education System*

Prior to the 1960s, the top-level administrators in both public and private school systems were foreigners, whereas most teachers were Samoans, usually with little formal teacher education and a poor command of English. The television era brought scores of United States mainlanders to the islands, not only to staff the curriculum development and television offices, but also as elementary school principals and high school teachers and administrators. However, during the 1970s, as the role of television in the schools diminished, the proportion of non-Samoan educators in the public school system was greatly reduced. Since the 1970s, most top-level administrative and planning posts in the Department of Education have been filled by Samoans. While the bulk of the teaching corps is comprised of Samoans, over recent decades some teachers from the mainland have also been employed, although typically they have not become permanent members of the education system but, rather, move elsewhere after a few years service.

By the 1990s, the principal source of personnel for the public education system was a series of local staff training programs utilizing support activities provided by the University of Hawaii. These sources were supplemented by personnel recruited overseas, principally from the United States mainland.

Two of the local programs have been conducted in cooperation with the American Samoa Community College. The first, entitled the "American Samoa Teacher Education Program," offers an associate of arts curriculum in education and coursework leading to teacher certification. In addition, the college furnishes lower division coursework that can be transferred to four-year colleges overseas as the foundation for a bachelor's degree.

A second training option is the "Territorial Teacher Training Assistance Program," which is conducted cooperatively by the Community College and the University of Hawaii. Regular classes and inservice workshops offer teachers' coursework needed for obtaining certification and degrees. Classes are available both on and off the college campus in the summer and during after-school hours throughout the academic year. Studies are available to four categories of school personnel: (a) teachers who have not yet obtained the two-year associate of arts degree, (b) teachers enrolled in a bachelor-degree program, (c) teachers who have not yet met the Department of Education's certification requirements, and (d) people seeking advanced specialty studies that count toward a graduate degree.

Preschool and kindergarten teachers are prepared in the Talofa Children Project, a program funded by the central United States government, with training support furnished by the Multifunctional Resource Center of Hawaii. The project focuses on preparing pupils of limited English-language proficiency to succeed in their later elementary school studies, which are conducted primarily in English.

Finally, the Department of Education sponsors a program for developing the leadership skills of all administrators in the public school system. The training focuses mainly on curriculum evaluation, the assessment of physical facilities, and personnel administration. Participants engage in local staff development workshops and overseas study under the Hawaii Department of Education's administrator internship program (Department of Education 1992 p. 1).

Enrollment in certain inservice education programs is voluntary, whereas in others it is required. Participation in certificate- and degree-granting programs, although strongly encouraged by the Department of Education, is generally at the particular teacher's or administrator's own volition. However, attendance at school-based upgrading workshops conducted by the principals and by invited consultants is compulsory.

7. *Curriculum Development and Teaching Methodology*

During the 1950s, when the public school curricula focused chiefly on textbooks from the United States mainland, there was almost no attention paid to Samoan language or culture in the public and private secular curriculum schools. Under the television system of the 1960s, Samoan culture continued to be neglected. But with the stimulus of funds from Washington, DC for bicultural education in the mid-1970s, textbooks in the Samoan language and instructional units on Samoan culture were locally produced in greater numbers for use at various grade levels. The bulk of the curriculum, however, has focused on the same subjects studied in United States mainland schools, and the medium of instruction above the lowest primary grades has continued to be English. Since Samoan language and culture play such a small part in the schools' offerings, the maintenance of Samoan traditions remains primarily the responsibility of the home, the church, and the informal social life of the villages.

By the early 1990s, the public elementary school curriculum pursued by each pupil, kindergarten through Grade 8, included the subject matter areas of art, English language and literature, mathematics, Samoan studies, science, social studies, health, and physical education. The public secondary school curriculum has been comprised of both required courses that all students pursue and of electives which students may choose to enrich their education in areas of their choice (Department of Education 1991).

Since the late 1980s, the English program in elementary schools has been organized around basal reading textbooks from the United States mainland that provide experience with all language arts and with literature. At the secondary level, language arts (reading, writing, listening, speaking, literature) are developed around a core of reading that is not tied to specific textbooks. There are three instructional streams available to high school students on the basis of their reading proficiency. The streams are labeled "proficient" (for students reading at their present grade level or one year below grade on United States standardized reading tests), "mainstream" (two or three years below grade), and "remedial" (five or more years below grade).

Textbooks from the United States mainland provide the curriculum content for mathematics at the elementary level. In the secondary schools, students are directed into one of three streams on the basis of their past performance in mathematics. Studies available to the more advanced learners include calculus, probability theory, statistics, and computer programming.

The Samoan studies program introduced in 1985 for all grade levels, kindergarten through 12, is designed to maintain students' command of the Samoan language and to promote their cultural heritage experiences. A core curriculum has been developed by the staff of the Department of Education's curriculum and instruction division, which furnishes teachers' detailed lesson plans and instructional guidebooks.

Science is taught at all grade levels, utilizing textbooks and experiment kits from the United States mainland along with local field trips.

The social studies curriculum for the elementary grades follows an expanding horizons approach, beginning with the environment most familiar to the young child and gradually extending to a global perspective. At the secondary level, all students follow a sequence of four courses—American Samoa history, world history, United States history, and United States/American Samoa government. In addition, six elective classes are available in the areas of geography, legal systems, sociology, and economics.

Health education classes, required of all pupils from kindergarten through high school, focus on nutrition, safety, and disease prevention, including information about drug and alcohol abuse, sexual behavior, and the spread of AIDS (Acquired Immune Deficiency Syndrome).

Art is a required area of study in all elementary grades, but is solely an elective subject in secondary schools.

8. The System of Examinations, Promotions, and Certifications

In recent years, three kinds of examinations have been employed in Samoan public schools: first, standardized achievement tests from the United States mainland, used generally to monitor how the progress of Samoa's students compares with that of mainland students in the fields of English, mathematics, science, and social studies; second, tests that accompany the textbook series and learning kits that form the basic

curriculum materials (such tests are used to measure pupils' progress with specific lessons or units of study); and third, tests created by teachers and members of the Department of Education's curriculum or research divisions for placing students in appropriate mathematics or language streams.

The promotion of students from one grade to another is not based strictly on how adequately individuals master minimum learning objectives for the particular grade level. Rather, more important are a student's levels of social and physical development, diligence, and likely progress if promoted rather than held back to repeat the present grade.

Graduation from secondary school depends both on the number of course credits a student has earned and on the demonstration of certain minimum skills, such as those revealed on a basic mathematics skills test. The diploma that graduates receive entitles them to apply for college entrance, for advanced vocational studies, and for jobs that require the completion of secondary education.

Students finishing coursework at the community college are awarded either an associate or arts or science degree or certification as a specialist in a particular vocational field.

9. Educational Assessment, Evaluation, and Research

Evaluation activities of the Department of Education consist chiefly of monitoring student progress by means of the testing program and periodically assessing the status of the curriculum. The curriculum development division has established a five-year cycle for reviewing all courses in both the elementary and secondary schools. Each year a different set of courses is appraised, with new objectives and new learning materials adopted the following year on the basis of the appraisal (Department of Education 1991 p. 55).

10. Major Reforms in the 1980s and 1990s

Notable improvements in the public education system during the 1980s and early 1990s came mainly in the areas of curriculum and instruction. For example, computer literacy and programming classes were introduced as regular offerings in all high schools. In addition, a variety of annual co-curricular activities were initiated to stimulate pupil interest in academic pursuits. These included a young writer's essay contest, a mathematics in art program, a mental speed and accuracy mathematics contest, science fairs, and a science calendar art contest.

11. Major Problems for the Year 2000

Among the problems that can be foreseen are ones of student achievement, keeping the curriculum up to date, staffing the education system, financing school operations, and maintaining the physical plant.

While student achievement as measured by standardized tests improved during the 1980s, by the close of the decade their average attainment had reached a plateau so that Samoans were still notably behind their counterparts on the United States mainland. By the twenty-first century, the education system will likely still fall short of equipping youths to function equally well in both Samoan and United States mainland cultures.

Changes in the worlds of science, health knowledge, and social living, and in teaching methods and materials over the coming decade will demand frequent improvements in the territory's curricula.

Because salaries of educational personnel in American Samoa are generally lower than in the United States, the Samoan education system will continue to face problems of hiring and keeping talented administrators and teachers who can seek both the higher pay and the opportunities for advanced study available in Hawaii and on the mainland.

The islands' heavy dependence on United States central government for funding educational operations places the Samoan schools in a difficult financial position as a depressed economy on the mainland results in a shrinking of funds from the central government. The financial resources in the islands are not sufficient for making up the loss of federal monies.

By the year 2001, the schools that were newly constructed at the outset of the television era in 1961 will be 40 years old. By the 1990s, many of the buildings were in need of repair, particularly because the devastation wrought by a hurricane in late 1991 damaged facilities so badly that many schools had to suspend classes. Thus, the passage of time and periodic inclement weather in the islands will pose a continuing challenge to the Department of Education's facilities maintenance staff.

References

Bronson V 1968 *A System Manual for the Staff and Faculty of the Department of Education.* Government of American Samoa, Pago Pago
Department of Education 1974, 1980, 1990 *Think Children.* (annual reports of the Department of Education) Government of American Samoa, Pago Pago
Department of Education 1991 *Instructional Program.* Department of Education, Government of American Samoa, Pago Pago
Department of Education 1992 *Briefing Paper: The American Samoa Department of Education.* Department of Education, Pago Pago
Everly H V 1961 Education in American Samoa. In: United States Congress 1961 *Study Mission to Eastern (American) Samoa.* United States Government Printing Office, Washington, DC
Government of American Samoa 1990 *American Samoa Statistical Digest.* Government of American Samoa, Pago Pago
Schramm W, Nelson L M, Betham M T 1981 *Bold Experiment.* Stanford University Press, Stanford, California
Thomas R M 1980 The rise and decline of an educational technology: Television in American Samoa. *Educ. Commun. Technol.* 28(3): 155–67
Thomas R M 1981 Evaluation consequences of unreasonable goals—the plight of education in American Samoa. *Educ. Eval. Policy Analysis* 3(2): 41–50

Further Reading

Thomas R M 1986 *From Talking Chiefs to Videotapes: Education in American Samoa—1700s to 1980.* ERIC File—ED 273 544 (microfiche)

Antigua and Barbuda

J. Knowles

1. General Background

The State of Antigua and Barbuda consists of three islands of the lesser Antilles within the Caribbean Archipelago or West Indies. Antigua, the largest of the three and the main island, has a land mass of 280 square kilometers. Barbuda, the sister island, has an area of 167 square kilometers, and lies about 40 kilometers to the north of Antigua. The third island, Redonda, is a rocky uninhabited islet of about 1 square kilometer, lying about 8 kilometers west of Antigua.

Preliminary reports from the 1991 population census reveal a resident population of 63,880: about 2 percent of this number, 1,252, live on Barbuda. This shows a small decline when compared with the 1970 figure of 64,794. Over 7,500 people reside in the capital city of St John's. Descendants of African slaves, who were brought to Antigua in the eighteenth century to work on the plantations, constitute the majority of the population. English is the official language, but there are dialects, as well as other languages of immigrants from the region and beyond. Christianity is the dominant religion.

In 1967 full British colonial status was supplanted by Associated Statehood, in which the United Kingdom retained responsibility for defence and foreign affairs. Full Independence was granted in 1981, and the parliamentary system of an Upper House or Senate and a House of Representatives is modeled on that of the United Kingdom. There is an independent judiciary. In 1971, the Progressive Labour Movement formed the government for a single term, and since 1976 the Antigua Labour Party has held power.

Tourism and its related services account for about 60 percent of Antigua's Gross Domestic Product (GDP). It is therefore the principal industry and since the early 1970s has changed what was once a plantation economy to a service-oriented economy, accounting for the bulk of the nation's export earnings, domestic income, and employment. Growth rates in GDP in the 1980s ranged from over 5 to about 8 percent. The main tourism markets are North America, the United Kingdom, and the rest of Europe. Light manufacturing industry, agriculture, fishing, and livestock production are the other major contributors. However, because of several factors, such as weak linkages between agriculture and manufacturing and tourism, trade imbalances, and other structural problems, the economy experienced a serious downturn, especially during the global recession.

Efforts to diversify the economy met with little success. From the mid-1970s, cotton was planned as a replacement crop for sugar cane as the main agricultural produce, but the problems encountered with harvesting, parasites, unstable prices, and the absence of continued secure markets hampered its development. Though considerable incentives were provided by the government for the development of agriculture, fishing, and manufacturing, these industries were inhibited by the restricted local market, small labor force, and unfavorable natural conditions and protectionism in trade policies, even among the country's CARICOM partners. There is a serious problem of shortage of skilled workers. Attempts are being made by various government departments and other agencies to rectify this situation, however, there is much optimism for the future.

The standard of living compares very favorably with other advanced developing countries. In the mid-1980s the per capita GNP was US$2,030, and though no precise data are available, it is generally accepted that in 1993 this indicator was about 20 percent higher, and that unemployment was just under 10 percent.

Toward the end of the 1980s, Antigua and Barbuda experienced consistent social and economic growth. In the early 1980s, there was significant change in the emphasis on educational development. One special objective which motivated this change was the mounting of campaigns to improve literacy and to improve coordination of activities within programs for postliteracy and education for work.

2. Politics and the Goals of the Education System

The right to education is implicitly guaranteed in the 1981 Constitution. Further, the Education Act of 1973 set out the legal parameters which describe the principles of state education. It established the powers of the Minister responsible for Education with respect to the establishment of schools and the system of education. In the early 1990s efforts were being made to revise the Act.

In 1988, the government issued a White Paper on the development goals, objectives, and strategies for the period 1988–92 (Government of Antigua 1988). This stated that the main objective in the field of education will be to reorient and restructure the educational system in order to emphasize the built-in vocational training component designed to maximize its contribution to the economic and social progress of the country. A system of continuous assessment of the labor force will help to guide educational programs addressed to skills training in the areas critical to the development process. Specific training programs aimed at meeting the anticipated shortage of skills will receive high priority.

In the 1970s and 1980s, education and productive work was expected to play a key role in developmental strategies. In the early 1990s, learners, whatever their level, were expected to identify and integrate with their environment to assist in its change and the transformation of society. The whole process of education was to become a definitive practice, because the curricula had to become geared to, and be supportive of, real-life situations. Though the goals of education have been predominantly those of the Labour Party government, they are, in general, supported by rival political parties.

In October 1990, the ministers of education of the countries of the Organisation of Eastern Caribbean States (OECS) decided that it was prudent and necessary to establish a subregional strategy for the reform of education in the OECS. Such a strategy would provide the basis for development, the framework for subregional initiatives, and a focal point for regional cooperation in education within the Caribbean. An eight-man Education Reform Working Group was set up and mandated to develop a conceptual strategy for the reform of education in the OECS. In the working group's report, *Foundation for the Future: OECS Education Reform Strategy* (OECS 1991) it is stated that Education Reform can be approached from several different perspectives, and that the political perspective is one of three most frequently employed. It was pointed out that education policy and practice within the OECS are largely the product of compromises between policymakers and groups representing conflicting interests; with the result that there are no real solutions to education problems, only political trade-offs, so that reform is essentially the periodic renegotiation of the values, guiding policy, and practice that occur as there are changes of policymakers and shifts in the relative power of competing groups; and so that accordingly, reforms often consist merely of reinstating past policies with contemporary labels.

It is expected that the recommendations contained in the document will guide the reform and future development of education nationally and subregionally.

3. The Formal System of Education

The administration of education is chiefly the concern of the state. All state-controlled or public schools are free of charge. There are some privately operated schools which are fee-paying institutions, and a few of these receive annual grants from the government. Education is compulsory between the ages of 5 and 16, but the Education Act stipulates that a pupil can be retained at school beyond the 16-year limit until 20 years of age. Figure 1 presents the structure of the system.

3.1 Primary, Secondary, and Tertiary Education

Public primary education comprises three sections: infants, with two grades; juniors, with five grades; and seniors, with three grades. Of the 29 schools in this category, 18 have the senior section or postprimary grades. Most of the 14 private primary schools have adopted the same grading system.

There are 9 public and 3 private secondary schools in Antigua and Barbuda. Five grades or forms constitute the secondary stage of the system. A pupil gains a scholarship to one of the public secondary schools by successfully negotiating the annual common entrance examination which is written after completing the Grade 7 (Junior V) curriculum.

The Antigua State College (ASC) is the only public tertiary institution. It has six departments: teacher training, GCE Advanced level, engineering, commercial studies, business office training, and a first-year university studies department offering social sciences, natural sciences, arts, and general studies.

Students of both the teacher training and the advanced level departments do not pay tuition fees, but residential students in teacher training contribute to their board and accommodation, since they continue to receive their full salaries during the two-year period of training. All other students pay nominal tuition fees, as the College is highly subsidized by the government.

The quality of the output of the ASC, as in some other OECS tertiary institutions, is considered to be good. Analysis of the examination results, especially among teacher trainees and first year university students, reveals that results compare very favorably with the performance of students on the three campuses of the University of the West Indies (UWI).

3.2 Preschool Education

Preschool education is designed for children of 3–5 years of age. It is not mandatory, but is considered to be a very important stage in the development of the primary school child. It is privately operated but receives some government assistance through the Ministry of Education. The staff of the office of coordinator of Preschool Education are part of the Ministry's staff. The program of work receives some support from UNICEF.

3.3 Special Education

The following provisions have been made for special education in the public system:

(a) the Adele School for the Handicapped (chiefly mental retardation);

(b) the School for the Deaf (jointly administered by the local Red Cross Society and the Ministry of Education);

(c) an education program for the visually impaired which is partially integrated into one of the regular all-age primary schools, and partially conducted as an itinerant program which takes the specially trained resource teachers on home visits for orientation of parents and guardians of such pupils.

Provision of these services implements the government's policy of providing basic education for all children of school age.

There is also a Rehabilitation Centre for the Handicapped. This institution caters to the skills training and general development of those who pass through the above-mentioned special schools; it receives some support from the government, but is operated by the Antigua and Barbuda Council for the Handicapped.

3.4 Vocational, Technical, and Business Education

Technical and Vocational Education and Training (TVET) has high priority since it is the major strategy/mechanism by which the important objective of improving the quality of education and the efficiency of the school system is achieved. Technical and vocational education, of which business education is a part, is offered at three levels of the system; postprimary, secondary, and tertiary.

At the postprimary level, students follow a broad-based program consisting of courses in industrial arts,

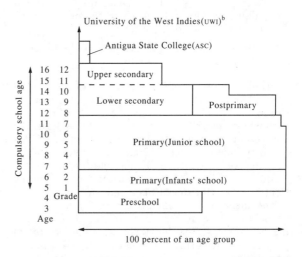

Figure 1

Antigua and Barbuda: Structure of the formal education system[a]

a Teacher training not included; about 25 candidates annually (all practicing teachers) take teacher training b 5 percent of pupils proceed to UWI the School of Continuing Studies, or private commercial schools

home economics, art and crafts. The industrial arts program is prevocational in scope, and includes a cluster of building trades, metalwork, automechanics and technical drawing. In home economics, students study food preparation, clothing and textiles, and home management. Three of the all-age primary schools have agricultural science as an optional subject.

Students at secondary school pursue the same courses as described above, but up to the craft level. In addition business education (typing, shorthand, accounting, related English, and mathematics) and agricultural science are electives.

At the tertiary level, the state college, the engineering department and the two business studies departments offer technical and vocational education up to an advanced craft level. Students graduating from the secondary level of the system generally enter these departments of the College. There are plans to expand the facilities to allow more students to enter these programs.

3.5 Adult and Nonformal Education

Since the mid-1980s, there has been a growing number of adult and nonformal education activities, characterized as opportunities for personal development and career improvement. The programs are of a wide range, and involve a number of governmental and nongovernmental agencies.

In 1982, an umbrella organization, the Antigua and Barbuda Adult Education Association, was established. Its stated objectives are to:

(a) act as a coordinating body, focal point, and promoter of adult education activities;

(b) keep educators and the community abreast of adult education activities, and to encourage the furtherance of adult education;

(c) help develop the professional skills of adult educators.

Prominent among other agencies involved in adult and nonformal education activities are the School of Continuing Studies (formerly the Extra Mural Department of the University of the West Indies), the Directorate of Women's Affairs (a division of this Ministry), the Agricultural Extension Division of the Ministry of Agriculture, Lands and Fisheries, the Youth Skills Training Unit, and the Hotel Training Centre of the Ministry of Economic Development.

The majority of programs carried by the various agencies address issues which fall primarily within the economic sector, but there are some important programs related to the development of the community, and to the social and national consciousness. The program activities may be categorized, in the main, as follows: development and improvement of basic literacy skills; skills training related to particular industrial and commercial business; craft training related

to self-employment and entreprenuership; and personal development, leadership roles, career guidance, and health and human sexuality.

There are several activities that are worthy of note. The University of the West Indies School of Continuing Studies has had particular success with its first-year university degree courses in social sciences; certificate courses in public administration, business administration and education; professional secretaries' courses, office procedures and practices; computer classes; and its distance education teaching courses.

The Agricultural Extension Division runs special pedagogical sessions for supervisors and extension officers to update their skills and expertise and also training sessions for farmers in crop production, agronomy, animal husbandry, forestry, and the economics of agriculture.

4. Administrative and Supervisory Structure and Operation

The administration of education is largely centralized, though in the case of the Antigua State College some measure of autonomy is allowed; to a lesser extent, the head and staff of each school are permitted to make certain decisions related to the day-to-day running of their institutions. The Ministry allocates resources, appoints staff, and formulates policies.

The Education Act confers upon the Minister responsible for Education the authority to devise, maintain and administer the system of education in the State. He is responsible to the cabinet, of which he is a member. Though he has the power to establish a National Education Advisory Council, such a council has never been put in place.

The Chief Education Officer heads the Education Division of the Ministry, and is considered the chief technocrat in education matters. All other professional/technical staff are directly responsible to this officer in the exercise of their duties. The Deputy Chief Education Officer is the direct link between the Ministry and the State College for routine matters, while the Senior Education Officer is administratively responsible for the secondary level of the system. Each education officer is responsible for one of the three zones into which all primary and postprimary schools fall.

Private schools are largely free from governmental control. Their registration and standards of accommodation and program delivery are channeled to the Ministry through the Education Planning Officer.

5. Educational Finance

The 1992 estimates of recurrent expenditure shows that some 13.5 percent of the total budget was allocated to the Ministry of Education, Culture, and Youth Affairs. Eighty-five percent of this allocation went to education, with primary education receiving 38 percent, secondary education 37 percent, and tertiary education 10 percent. However, personal emoluments account for about 76 percent of the Education Division's allocation. With just under 25 percent of the allocation going to all the other services, it is evident that educational financing is low. Yet out of this 25 percent allocation for goods and services, nearly half is directed to wages for part-time and other nonteaching staff. This poses serious problems, for it means that there is always a chronic shortage of teaching materials, including text and reference books, and badly needed equipment.

Funds allocated to education are grossly inadequate, despite what is considered a slight increase in the period 1987–93. When the developments of the 1980s are examined closely, it can be seen that much support funding has come from sources other than the government treasury. Funds for capital development, particularly for infrastructure and equipment, have mainly come from such agencies as the United Kingdom Development Division, CIDA and CDB/USAID.

As the reform processes continue, it becomes increasingly evident that the delivery of educational services demands greater financial and other resources. Since 1988, most of the educational institutions, public and private, have mounted programs for the express purpose of raising supplementary funds.

6. Supplying Personnel for the Education System

There were 719 public school teachers in the system, at the primary and secondary levels, at the end of the 1991–92 school year. In private primary and secondary schools there were 180 teachers. At the tertiary level, the Antigua State College, there was a total of 57 tutors and lecturers. 512 of the 719 teachers were trained; 95 of these were university graduates. It may be noted that about 75 percent of the teaching force is female. However, there is always some shortage of teaching staff during the course of the school year. This shortage is caused mainly by resignations (there is a high attrition rate of between 5 and 7 percent), and scholarships to overseas institutions of higher learning.

The minimum entry qualification for the teaching service is 4 GCE O-level subjects or Caribbean Examination Council (CXC) equivalents at general, or a combination of general and basic levels. Normally, new teachers spend about two years in the classroom as probationers before proceeding on scholarships to the teacher-training department of the Antigua State College for two years. At the conclusion of training, which is geared chiefly to the primary education level, graduates are awarded a diploma which is endorsed by the Faculty of Education of the University of the West Indies. Teacher-training institutions of the OECS are affiliated to this faculty.

Public-school teachers are civil servants and their appointments to the establishment are issued and regulated by the Public Service Commission through the Establishment Division of the Ministry of Home Affairs. Private school teachers are employed by the respective schools as the need arises and as funds permit. They sometimes apply for and receive scholarships to the State College at a subsidized fee structure.

In addition to the regular teacher training, teachers of vocational subjects such as industrial arts, home economics, and business studies receive one to three years' additional specialized training at overseas institutions and are awarded certificates, diplomas, or degrees.

The Antigua and Barbuda Union of Teachers has been negotiating with the government on behalf of the teachers for improved terms and conditions of service, which will assist in determining a structure for promotion policies. In 1993, promotion to headship of schools, and posts within the Ministry are determined by several factors, including qualification, seniority, and merit.

7. Curriculum Development and Teaching Methodology

There is a common curriculum for the primary and postprimary schools, and the lower three forms of secondary schools, the upper two forms, 4 and 5, follow the curriculum as set out in the CXC subject syllabuses. The core curriculum of the primary schools covers all aspects of language arts, mathematics, social studies, general science, and creative subjects like art, music and singing; the lower secondary forms add a foreign language—French and/or Spanish, the vocational subjects and one of the physical sciences. Physical education, sports and inter-school games such as cricket and football, are organised by the Sports Division of the Ministry.

Much emphasis is placed on technical and vocational education and training, and many inservice teacher education programs are mounted in order to equip teachers with the necessary skills.

A few schools, on their own initiative, have introduced some aspect of computer training, but it is government's intention to make this a regular part of the general school curriculum. There is a Resource Centre and together with an Infant Pedagogic Centre, teaching materials and equipment are made available to all schools. Notwithstanding what is prepared for them by these two facilities, teachers use their own initiative to prepare independently material and equipment to enhance the delivery of their programs.

8. The System of Examinations, Promotions, and Certifications

For the first seven years of formal schooling, pupils move automatically, chiefly by age, through the primary school, that is, from Infant I through to Junior V (Grades 1 to 7). A combination of age and performance is used for promotion in the postprimary grades, while performance is the criterion in the secondary schools.

Apart from the local internal examinations of each school, the first formal examination is taken by students when they reach the end of primary school. This is known as the common entrance or Junior School examination. All successful students receive a formal certificate and scholarship to one of the secondary schools. Unsuccessful students remain on the same campus and attend the postprimary division. After three years, these students take the postprimary examination, and if successful, are awarded a postprimary certificate and a scholarship to one of the secondary schools. Such students are normally between 14 and 15 years old, and enter the secondary subsystem at Form 3 (Grade 10). Unsuccessful students either remain and take examinations in specific subject areas, or they terminate their formal schooling. Individual certificates gained in subjects such as home economics and industrial arts serve as points of reference for other programs like that of the Hotel Training Centre.

Secondary school students work towards the CXC Certificate, either at Basic or General level. The CXC examinations are taken either at Form 4 or at Form 5 (Grades 11 or 12). Top students with 3 or more CXC subjects at general level compete for entry into the A-level department of the State College. Other secondary school graduates may go into either the engineering or business education department of the State College, or into the labor force.

All programs at the Antigua State College last two years. On completion of the second year, engineering and business education students take the Royal Society of Arts (RSA) examinations, while students of the advanced level department take the Cambridge board A-level examinations from the United Kingdom. It is this latter set of students, and those of the first-year university department who seek scholarships to pursue advanced studies overseas at universities and other institutions of higher learning. The College also issues its own diploma to all students.

9. Educational Assessment, Evaluation and Research

Since 1988, much consideration has been given, and is still being given, to ways of evaluating the education system, other than by means of the usual examination results. More emphasis is being placed on student performance over a period of years with a view to identifying strengths and weaknesses, and other useful indicators which point to the "successful products" or quality outputs of the system. Occasional reference has been made to the possible introduction of some formal instrument of evaluation, but this has not

been given any in-depth consideration. Rather, as a means of assessing the system's output, more serious attention is being given to the establishment of tracer studies.

One mechanism which has proved to be of some value in assessing the work in education is the publication of a biennial report. This report deals with staff at all levels, strengths and weaknesses in the quality of staff and pupils, favorable and unfavorable comments and observations about programs, and suggestions and ideas for improvement and reform.

No formal research capability exists. Each second-year student teacher in the College normally has to select an area, which in his or her view, constitutes a problem area, conduct some research locally to determine its cause, structure and administer an experimental program to address the problem, and then describe their findings. Other local research efforts are directed toward the preparation of theses for graduate or postgraduate studies at universities.

10. Major Reforms in the 1980s and 1990s

A major thrust in the development of education initiated in the 1980s and being intensified in the 1990s has as its general objective the improvement of the efficiency of the system, and the quality of programs offered to senior pupils of the all-age primary subsystem. Specifically, it aims to improve the efficiency of personnel who operate at this level of the system, and to make the educational offerings more relevant to the occupational needs of Antiguan society. Some of the important strategies being applied are:

(a) centralization of facilities for postprimary education;

(b) assistance, through inservice and advanced-level training for teachers to develop skills in curriculum development activities and teaching strategies;

(c) development of instructional materials and curriculum modules, especially in the areas of technical and vocational education;

(d) provision of the type and level of courses which are best suited to employment opportunities;

(e) introduction and expansion of the use of appropriate technology in the delivery of programs.

A significant development in this effort is the establishment of a comprehensive technical and vocational training center which will cater to postprimary students from five feeder schools on a day-release basis. The center will offer some sixteen courses in industrial arts, home economics, business studies, and arts and crafts.

The expected outcomes of this major reform strategy are:

(a) better qualified staff equipped with pedagogic skills, knowledge, and the expertise to deliver an improved curriculum;

(b) an improved curriculum which will strengthen the links between education and work;

(c) more adequate infrastructural facilities;

(d) students who are better equipped with the skills appropriate to the next educational stage to which they proceed.

Two other reform strategies worthy of note, and which were being planned in 1993 are: (a) the introduction of an Evening Institute program; and (b) the establishment of a National Training Board. The Evening Institute program will be delivered at two levels. The first will be for young adults who dropped out of the formal school system and who wish to upgrade or develop marketable skills for the labor market, especially in technical and vocational education. The other will cater to the needs of employees who wish to improve and/or develop academic, professional, and technical competencies. The latter will be based at the State College. The National Training Board will have public and private sector representation, and will seek, among other things, to coordinate all training efforts, especially in vocational education; establish an effective link between the formal and nonformal education sectors and the industrial and commerical sector, and to assist in establishing standards of certification and accreditation.

11. Major Problems for the Year 2000

Like many other developing countries, Antigua and Barbuda felt the effects of the global economic recession in the early 1990s. It is clear to education officials,

and other professionals in the field, that education for the twenty-first century will face serious problems in finding the resources to finance and support the reform and expansion of educational opportunities, especially at the upper levels of the system. Facilities at the State College are inadequate, and also for the projected developments in the areas of technical and vocational education and training.

The rapid social and economic changes of the 1980s placed great pressure on the education system. There are those who consider that educational institutions should provide all the answers to the challenges and demands of society, but the constant complaint is also voiced that the curriculum is already overburdened. The demands are growing. Another problem is the status of teachers vis-à-vis other civil servants. The teachers' representatives were agitating for new and revised terms and conditions of service, a career path for progress and promotion, and sundry other amenities. Primary school heads have acquired degrees and demand to be regarded. Shifts in population centres have begun to pose an accommodation problem.

These are grave issues that face the administrative personnel, who themselves have begun to realise that the present structure of the administration cannot deal effectively with the key issues that need to be addressed urgently. Inequalities and imbalances will therefore still exist for some time, even to the dawn of the twenty-first century.

References

Government of Antigua 1988 White Paper on development goals, objectives, and strategies 1988–92. Ministry of Economic Development, Department of Planning (Government Printing Office), St John's

Organisation of Eastern Carribbean States (OECS) 1991 *Foundation for the Future: OECS Education Reform Strategy.* OECS

Argentina

M. A. Petty

1. General Background

The Republic of Argentina is the second largest country in Latin America and is located in the southern cone of South America. It stretches over more than 2,800,000 square kilometers (727,201 square miles) from the highest Andean peak (Aconcagua: 6,959 meters), across the rich pampas, to the great eastern rivers north of the capital Buenos Aires and to the South Atlantic Ocean. Approximately half this vast area is a sparsely populated, semi-arid desert, yet 65 percent of the entire land is cultivable. Throughout these immense

areas, distance is among the main factors affecting the quality of rural education.

The land covered by Argentina today was part of the Spanish colony governed for two centuries (from 1617 to 1810) by a viceroy in Buenos Aires. In 1810 a revolution against the puppet Spanish king Fernando VII paved the way to the Declaration of Independence in 1816. The size and shape of the nation has not changed significantly since then.

The population of Argentina, according to the 1991 census, numbers 32,423,000, having increased by 14 percent since 1980. The population growth in the twentieth century is largely due to vast immigratory movements, particularly from southern Europe, around the turn of the century. In 1900, there were approximately 4 million inhabitants and this figure reached nearly 16 million by 1947. By 1980 the growth rate had slowed down to about half this pace, as immigration halted and urbanization rapidly increased. In 1900, urban and rural populations were equal in size, whereas in 1991, 86 percent was urban and only 14 percent rural. Nearly one-fourth (23%) of the entire population is centered in the greater Buenos Aires area.

Argentina is the most European of the Spanish-speaking Latin American countries, with over 90 percent of the population being of Spanish or Italian origin. A significant change that has taken place since 1960 is that most Argentine children have Argentine Spanish-speaking grandparents.

The remnants of nomadic tribes were reduced to insignificant numbers in the vast peripheral areas during the second half of the nineteenth century, due to unending wars and lack of immunity to European diseases. There was no important indigenous culture comparable to that of the Aztecs or the Incas, though the northwest was subject to Inca rule, and in the northeast the famous Guarani Indian missions flourished, reaching high cultural levels under the Jesuits for nearly two centuries until they were expelled in 1767.

According to the UNDP 1991 report, the Human Development Index (HDI) for Argentina is 0.854, which ranks the country as 43rd among those considered "high." The economically active population, including females, is highly concentrated in the service sector (53.1%), followed by industry (33.8%), and agriculture (13%). Agriculture, however, produced 55.5 percent of the 1984 national income.

Argentina's economic woes have been the main source of social and political problems during the past 50 years.

From being Europe's breadbasket up until the Second World War and one of the largest prime beef exporters in the world, from producing one-third of the world's wheat in 1913 and having one of the five most extensive railway systems in the world, the country reached an all-time low from the mid-1970s to the mid-1980s. It suffered grueling and repetitive combinations of hyperinflation and recession, as a result of clumsy industrialization projects together with inept political leadership and military rule. Under both forms of government, corruption prospered.

But it always rains in Argentina. Between 1940 and 1980 the total agricultural production doubled, and industry has evolved from being almost entirely oriented toward the production of consumer goods in order to satisfy the local market, to increased production of intermediary goods such as paper, chemical products, and industrial machinery.

The railways extend over 34,100 kilometers (21,189 miles), and have been run at a considerable loss for many years. The government is going ahead with dynamic privatization plans that will include most services. There are 1 million kilometers of road, 46,000 of which are paved. Now roads are maintained with a toll system.

In 1988 the average per capita income reached US$2,520. The foreign debt reached US$67.5 billion in 1991. By 1993 the Minister of Economics had totally deregulated the economy and permitted free convertibility of the dollar. His success is reflected in the reduction of inflation to practically zero per month, and economic growth had attracted at least US$5 billion in 1991. It would appear that the capital funds that fled the country in previous decades (estimated at US$60 billion) had begun to return in the 1990s.

The decade 1980–90 can be typified by two socially important developments: the transition towards democracy and the socioeconomic crises due to successive bouts of hyperinflation. However, during President Menem's government, a breath of fresh air, with new prospects of future prosperity, had been created by the Minister of Economics' stability, decentralization, privatization, and market deregulation plans.

President Menem took office in 1989, as the candidate of the Peronist Party. Perón and his party have dominated the political scene in the second half of the twentieth century. To understand this, a brief historical outline is necessary.

From 1915 to 1955, Argentina was ruled in turn by Conservatives (largely upper class), Radicals (middle class), and Peronists (working class). Each in turn encountered crises and was ousted by the military. Since 1930, with only brief interruptions, the country has been governed by a wide variety of military leaders, responding to the interests of different social strata or sectors. Since 1955 the basic political issue has been between Peronism and anti-Peronism, the military being found on both sides.

Perón ruled the country for three presidential periods, two from 1946 to 1955, and one from 1974 until his death in 1976. In the 1958 elections, President Frondizi (Radical) won, ruling until 1962 when he was ousted by the military and succeeded by Illia (also a Radical) until 1966. From 1966 to 1974 the military ruled the country, but ceded power to the Peronists for Perón's last term of office. After Perón's death, his widow governed until her regime collapsed through incompetence and the paralyzing effect of the insurgency movement, which unleashed the most extensive guerrilla war to date in Latin America. The military easily ousted Isabel Perón in 1976 and undertook the task of eliminating the guerrillas in a bloody civil war. The military acknowledged that many people "disappeared" during the war, but were unable to account for them.

In 1983, after defeat in the Falklands War with the United Kingdom, elections were held again, and Raúl Alfonsín (a Radical) was the clear winner. His major accomplishments during his first two years in office were a peace treaty with Chile, the trial of previous military presidents responsible for the "dirty war," and the "austral economic stability plan." Yet even this plan crumbled toward the end of his period, and hyperinflation was once again a problem until successive attempts by Menem's government finally brought inflation down to a reasonable 1 or 2 percent per month. Menem, who won the elections on a *peronista* ticket, moved decisively toward a more liberal free-market economy that finally showed signs of health in the early 1990s.

Throughout the periods of post-Peronist military rule, not only was popular participation absent from governmental decisions, but educational autonomy, particularly at the university level. was denied to state institutions. Probably the most important change that took place was the recognition of freedom of educational choice granted in 1956. This permitted private universities to exist, though without state support, and subsidies implying only very limited autonomy were granted to private primary and secondary schools.

A serious effort was made in 1969 to reform the entire system of primary and secondary education. However, its only lasting effect was the transfer of teacher education to the postsecondary level. Ten years later an important move was made to decentralize the administration of primary state schools, whereby these were handed over to provincial governments.

In 1984 a nationwide Pedagogical Congress was convened, in which supposedly the entire population could participate. Unfortunately, due to incompetent leadership, this initiative led only to the reappearance of obsolete ideological questions between liberals and Catholics.

2. Politics and the Goals of the Education System

The aims of the education system are officially stated in terms of the ideal of "integral" education. Thus, it is said that the aims of the system are to cover "the psychological, intellectual, aesthetic, social, civic, professional, and ethical aspects of the individual, taking both personal vocations and the common good into account." In other words, educational objectives are stated in such terms as to allow for the broadest possible interpretation, given the fact that at least equal access to primary schooling has already been achieved from a quantitative point of view.

There are differences between the two political parties (Radicals and Peronists). These differences are basically historical and philosophical: the Radicals are more liberal and the Peronists more Catholic.

However, the government is responsible for the financing of nearly all education except private universities and private high-tuition secondary schools. The advantage of this is that it can cover the expenses that no private groups would be able to, and the disadvantages resulting are low quality and poor standards. In other words, state schools are generally liberal (no

mention of God in the school), of poor quality, and spread thin. People seeking better education must go to private institutions, which are often run by Catholic organizations. In sum, the government in fact supports a low-quality, high spread of education. With very few exceptions, high quality must be paid for at private institutions.

These differences do not stem from differing goals of different segments of society, except those which are specific to different social classes. Upper- and middle-class groups generally seek better education for their children, whereas the working class tends to be satisfied with minimum standards.

3. The Formal System of Education

3.1 Primary, Secondary, and Tertiary Education

Figure 1 presents the structure of education and the percentage of an age-group enrolled all each grade level. Table 1 shows statistics of enrollments and resources in Argentine formal education.

Primary schooling is obligatory for all in the 6 to 12 year age-group. Dropout levels are moderate. Approximately 60 percent graduate within a seven-year period, but nine out of ten students stay in school for at least seven years. Repetition, particularly in the first grade, is high, reaching nearly 25 percent, and is between 10 and 20 percent in the remaining grades. Repetition is twice as high among the poor as among

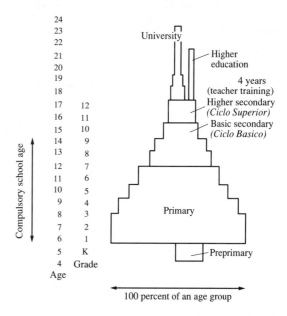

Figure 1

Argentina: Structure of the formal education system 1987[a]

a Adult education and nonformal education not included

the middle and upper classes, particularly in backward rural areas. Private schools cover only 18 percent of the enrollment.

Most pupils attend either morning or afternoon sessions only. The primary system was decentralized in 1978, and is now entirely in the hands of provincial governments. Nearly one-third of the students are located in the greater Buenos Aires area (30%). Another similar quantity is spread over the three largest provinces—Buenos Aires, Córdoba, and Santa Fe—and 40 percent are located in the remaining 20 provinces.

In 1993 the Ministry of Education planned to decentralize secondary education. The law approving this was being discussed in Congress at this time of writing this entry. Secondary schooling is for those aged 13 to 17, and it covers 44 percent of the age group. The main streams are *Bachillerato*, *Comercial* and *Técnico*. A small percentage attends agricultural or other types of schools. The first three years of schooling are basically the same for all streams, though each has specific additional subjects. Dropout rates are high, as on average only 50 percent of those entering the first year graduate. These high dropout levels are largely due to the immense growth of this level in recent years. Total secondary enrollments practically doubled from 1940 to 1950, and doubled twice again by 1974. The pace then slowed down but increased continuously reaching 1,859,325 in 1987. The largest stream is still *Bachillerato* (though many forms of it have developed) with 770,615 students.

All secondary streams are university-oriented. There are still only 51 agricultural schools in the country. The structure of the secondary curriculum is obsolete and encyclopedic.

Higher education is divided between university and non-university education. The latter is usually obtained at four-year teacher-training institutions, where over 90 percent of the students are women. University education comprises five- to seven-year study plans, few of which offer subject matter options.

There are 25 large state universities and 20 much smaller private institutions. These are organized in traditional faculties, following the Napoleonic model. Initiatives during the early 1990s included the establishment of business and agricultural faculties and the Technical University, which dates from Peronist times and trains technical engineers. This institution provides access to higher education for graduates from technical secondary schools. More recently, the proliferation of private universities with government approval is changing the scene at the higher level.

In 1987 there were nearly one million students (958,542) three-fourths of whom were attending universities. The number of students in higher education increased 54 percent since 1980. This immense quantitative increase has seriously affected quality in the entire system.

3.2 Preschool Education

The structure of the formal system proposes obligatory preprimary education for the 5-year old age-group in all provinces. Some provinces have obligatory schooling from the age of 4 years. In most large cities children are taken to daycare centers from the age of 3 or less. Kindergartens are usually attached to primary schools and financed in the same way. Private kindergartens are flourishing and provide for 31 percent of the total age-group. Social background is changing rapidly due

Table 1
Enrollment and resources in formal education 1987

| | Schools | | | Tertiary | |
	Primary	Secondary	Teacher training		University
No. of students	4,906,907	1,859,325	203,336		755,206
Percentage of age group enrolled:					
6–12	100	—	—		—
13–15	—	74	—		—
16–24	—	—	—	36[a]	—
No. of institutions	21,025	5,870	1,057		483[b]
Average no. of students per institution	233	316	192		1,563
Student–teacher ratio	19:1	7:1	6:1		18:1

a For all higher education 1985   b Includes all university faculties

to the growth of the attendance at this level. In 1987 there were 766,138 students in 8,677 schools.

3.3 Special Education

The overall policy in special education is that problem students should try to remain integrated in the normal school class. However, when this is not possible, children must be sent to special schools. There are primary schools for the blind, the deaf, and the mentally handicapped. These students continue studies in normal secondary schools. There are also schools for children with light and moderate mental disorders. In order to facilitate entrance to the labor force, there are "protected workshops" for children from 14–21 years of age.

3.4 Vocational, Technical, and Business Education

It is government policy that specific subjects in vocational, technical, and business education should be taught by teachers with the appropriate qualifications. For example, accountancy should be taught by public accountants or by professors in economic sciences.

The only major change in curriculum content is the introduction in some places of computer studies.

There are established percentages of income from cooperatives that should support business schools, and from industries to support technical schools, but these are not implemented in practice.

3.5 Adult and Nonformal Education

The National organization in charge of Adult education is the DIEA (*Dirección de Educación de Adultos*), which has provincial supervisory units. The state provides subsidies to private institutions, at national and provincial levels, and supervises them.

The main target groups are primary-level illiterates or functional illiterates over 14 years of age who wish to obtain a primary-school certificate, or adults with a primary certificate who seek a secondary-school certificate, the former being the larger group.

There are various types of nonformal programs including, for example, those given in labor unions and in prisons, those given to senior citizens and to soldiers, and special courses for women, which include cooking, sewing, health, and so on.

There are private institutions such as INCUPO in the northern provinces and the *Cruzada Patagónica* in the south, that cover a broad spectrum of education, community services, and economic development. INCUPO used to be one of the largest radio schools in Latin America, covering a radio audience of 1,200,000 inhabitants. It is now more centered on community development.

According to the 1987 statistics, there were 99,455 students in 1,594 schools for adults, and another 95,695 in 7,587 literacy training centers. The stated purpose of adult education is not the eradication of illiteracy, as the country is 95 percent literate. Rather, the purpose is to integrate those who need minimal training for their inclusion into the labor force.

4. Administrative and Supervisory Structure and Operation

The central state governing body is the Ministry of Education and Culture. Each province also has an equivalent organization. Between them they cover all educational programs, both formal and nonformal. The administrative structure of the system was highly centralized from the turn of the century until 1978, when administration, supervision, and the financing of preprimary and primary education was handed over to provincial governments. Secondary and higher education is still partially in the hands of the National Ministry of Education, though plans are being discussed for total decentralization by January 1993.

The financing of state universities is totally centralized, though rectors of these universities are elected by representatives of students, faculty, and graduates. Private universities are academically supervised by the state, but receive no support.

Educational laws are established by the National Congress or Provincial legislatures, according to constitutional principles.

Local supervisory systems are in the hands of supervisors, who hold the highest ranking nonpolitical jobs in the teaching service. Supervisors at preprimary, primary, and secondary levels cover all administrative and pedagogical aspects. At the secondary level they are organized by streams.

5. Educational Finance

A factual appraisal of investment in education is particularly difficult in Argentina, not only because data are not readily available, but also largely due to periods of hyperinflation and currency devaluations.

The traditional 14 percent of government costs dedicated to education was maintained for the period 1984–86. This was covered by 20.1 percent from the provincial budgets and 8.3 percent from the national budget. However, the total varied between 17.4 percent in 1975 and 9.2 percent in 1982.

As preprimary and primary education are, as of 1978, entirely in the hands of provincial governments, these have dedicated a very stable 81 percent of their educational budget to the primary level, another 17 percent to the secondary level, and barely 1.8 percent to higher (non-university) education. Over the same period, and in general, 52 percent of total costs have been awarded to primary schooling,

32.5 percent to secondary schooling, and 15.4 percent to higher education.

Given the economic crises, there has been a steady drop of investment in education since 1976, affecting all educational levels. Between 1979 and 1985 investment at the primary level dropped 61 percent and, for the same period, there was a reduction of 39 percent at the secondary level, and 51 percent for all higher education. Thus, it follows that teachers' salaries are, in general, relatively much lower than at the beginning of the 1980s.

Finally, it could be said that the private sector has absorbed a scant 13 percent of government educational resources; costs per student have been estimated at US$150 per annum; at the secondary level, costs per student have also diminished since the outset of the 1980s due to ever-increasing enrollments.

The major sources of income for private schools are parent-paid tuition fees.

6. Supplying Personnel for the Education System

Teachers are trained for primary and secondary levels. All university graduates may teach at the university level. There were 609,009 teaching positions in 1987, but from this statistical fact it is not possible to determine the exact number of teachers. However, from general appraisals, it would seem that there is no teacher shortage.

No specific training is provided for nonteaching personnel. All teacher training takes place at the postsecondary level, usually in four-year courses, though some are three and others five years long.

Many efforts are being made to improve the quality of initial education. Specific courses (either systematic or nonsystematic) are offered by state and private institutions, yet these are always isolated initiatives. Some courses are required in order to apply for managerial positions, whereas others are the usual inservice training courses. Some institutions are particularly well-known for the training they provide, such as the *Instituto Biedma* in Buenos Aires or the *Consejo Superior de Educación Católica* which provides distance training in leadership.

The government monitors, awards points, and evaluates all teacher inservice training courses. Certification examinations are not necessarily required, but some form of evaluation is.

7. Curriculum Development and Teaching Methodology

The subject syllabuses are prepared by the *Consejo Federal de Ministros de Educación*, which is a governing board for all provinces. Regional differences at the primary level are accepted in theory, though in practice they are insignificant, if any. There is no core curriculum since it is understood that the curriculum includes the basic syllabus of studies plus whatever local modifications should be made, either at provincial or local levels.

There is no central body that controls or approves commercially disseminated instructional materials except when contents are detected that could be considered to offend national identity. All texts follow established syllabuses, and are prepared by private groups.

There are no elective subjects throughout the system from primary level through to university. Students wanting specific courses in languages or music must attend private institutions.

English is the most popular foreign language and frequently taught. French and Italian are also taught.

The only way officials can ensure curriculum implementation is through supervision, which is carried out by the directors of the institutions or the supervisors.

The chief problem faced is the resistance to change among teachers. They would seem to be unable to be self-critical regarding their activity. This results in disconnected actions which follow no logical sequence.

8. The System of Examinations, Promotions, and Certifications

The state establishes minimum standards for promotion, and teachers must verify that the children have attained them. The selection system is not formal, as children tend to group by social classes. The quality of schooling is closely related to the social structure although few high-quality low social class schools can be found.

The system of evaluation in use in the 1990s at secondary schools was implemented in 1989 in an effort to distinguish evaluation from certification. The overall results have been that standards have fallen even more. Students are evaluated from 1 to 3 on a nominal scale (*superó, alcanzó, no alcanzó*), as opposed to the former system of a quantitative scale from 1 to 10.

The current system is not considered reliable, and many think it should be reconsidered. The problem is that necessary distinctions must be accepted between certification and evaluation, between evaluation of academic achievement and that of overall conduct, appraisals of dedication, capacity, hard work, and so forth. These obviously cannot be reflected by one single form of grading, but a consensus must be achieved as to the proper mechanisms.

9. Educational Assessment, Evaluation, and Research

There is no form of established assessment, and very little research is conducted on a nationwide basis. The official budget does not allocate funds for research, so what little exists is carried out by universities and private groups. There are groups of researchers, and a doctoral program in education has been initiated at the Catholic University of Córdoba, where there is also a REDUC (*Red Latinoamericana de Información y Documentación Educativa*) center that supplies educational research and information coming from all over Latin America. In the early 1990s an effort was being made to form a national REDUC network. The dissemination of previous studies is the basis of scientific research. Educational statistics are available only up to 1987.

10. Major Problems for the Year 2000

The Argentine school system has completed an important task in terms of "nation building," contributing positively to the consolidation of a minimal basis of national identity: one language, one flag, one government, practically no illiteracy, and no discrimination against women.

The centralization–decentralization problem has occupied the center of the scene since 1970, and it is closely related to problems of geographic and regional dominance of sectors. In the early 1990s this problem is close to finally being resolved.

Educational opportunity at the primary level has also ceased to be a pressing problem as practically all children now go to school, albeit with varying levels of achievement.

The arena would then be open for broad discussions on the quality of education, both at the primary and at the secondary levels. It is quite clear that students do not normally finish secondary school sufficiently well-trained for university courses. Yet all secondary graduates are theoretically capable of entering a university. Secondary graduation must be reconsidered as many students would do better with adequate job training, rather than going to university, whereas others would greatly profit from a university-preparatory education.

The entire problem is one of educational quality. This is also the case in teacher training which should include the introduction of a solid philosophical grounding for the entire teaching effort. Teachers are only trained in didactics and are often unaware of the theoretical implications of their work. Teachers need to be trained in problem-solving techniques. This would enable them to adopt more flexible attitudes toward modern science and the structure of modern knowledge, and to overcome the idea that there is a defined and unchangeable set of ideas that students must learn in order to graduate at the secondary level.

Education at the primary level in distant rural areas is in serious need of qualitative improvements. Schooling must be integrated with productive activities, as well as with community and economic development.

Teachers must be specially trained to work in those places and salaries should compensate adequately for the hardships they experience.

University education is in very serious need of change, since the famous 1918 Córdoba reform, by which rectors and deans are named by students, faculty, and graduates, has led to a situation in which political parties practically control university activity, and the decision-making process cannot function in order to solve real academic problems. The main problems at the university level are those of planning and administration. There is a fair reserve of good academics, but they have great difficulties in working adequately given the overwhelming administrative problems.

Bibliography

Amadeo J *La Universidad condicionada: La Universidad de Buenos Aires y su Lugar en el Proyecto político del Siglo XIX*. Centro de Investigaciones Educativas, Buenos Aires

Argentina 1968 *Educación Recursos Humanos y Desarrollo Económico-Social*, Vols. 1, 2. Secretaria del Consejo Nacional de Desarrollo, Buenos Aires

Argentina 1979 *Perfil Educativo de la República Argentina*. Dirección de Políticas y Programación Presupuestaria del Ministerio de Cultura y Educación de la Nación, Buenos Aires

Argentina 1981a *Estadísticas de la Educación, Sintesis 1971–1975*. Departamento de Estadística, Buenos Aires

Argentina 1981b *Anuario Estadístico de la República Argentina, 1979–1980*. Instituto Nacional de Estadística y Censos, Buenos Aires

Centro de Investigaciones Educativas 1979 *Educación y Justicia en la República Argentina*. Centro de Investigaciones Educativas, Buenos Aires

Llach J J 1977 *Estructura y Dinámica del Empleo en Argentina desde 1947*, CEIL Documento de Trabajo No. 2. Centro de Investigaciones Laborales, Buenos Aires

Martinez Paz F 1979 *La Educación Argentina*. Universidad Nacional de Córdoba, Córdoba

Martinez Paz F 1980 *El Sistema Educativo nacional, Formación Desarrollo, Crisis*. Universidad Nacional de Córdoba, Córdoba

Mulhall M G, Muthull E T 1985 *Handbook of the River Plate*, 5th edn. Buenos Aires

Petrei A H 1989 *Ensayos en Economía de la Educación*. Talleres Gráficos de BALADO, Buenos Aires

Petty M 1979 Prioridades de investigación educativa. In: *Perspectivas de la educación en América Latina*. Centro de Estudios Educativos, Mexico City

PNUD 1991 *Desarrollo Humano, Informe 1991*. Tercer Mundo Editores, Bogotá

REDUC–UCC 1988 *Segundo Encuentro sobre el Estado Actual de la Investigación Educativa*. Córdoba

UNESCO–OREALC 1990 *Situación Educativa de América Latina y el Caribe, 1980–1987*. (Argentina: pp. 65–74). UNESCO–OREALC, Santiago

United Nations Development Programme (UNDP) 1991 *Report*. Tercer Mundo Editores, Bogotá

Australia

P. A. McKenzie

1. General Background

Australia is a large island continent located close to Southeast Asia and the South Pacific. The land mass totals 7.7 million square kilometers and much of the interior is extremely arid. It is populated mainly by people of European background and the basic institutional framework is essentially British in origin. Large-scale immigration has slowly changed the ethnic mix and produced a more culturally diverse society. Although Australia is a relatively wealthy country, the 1980s and early 1990s were a period of considerable economic difficulty. Changing social and economic circumstances have prompted major educational debate and reform since the early 1980s.

British colonization commenced in 1788 with a penal settlement at Sydney, and by 1850 six major colonies had been established across the country. Each colony was administered directly from the United Kingdom until 1901 when they federated as the Commonwealth of Australia, the six former colonies became states, and the country gained substantial independence. In 1993 widespread public debate commenced on whether the remaining constitutional ties to Britain should be cut and an Australian republic formed. Under the 1901 federal constitution the states retained responsibility for education, although the federal government's financing and policy roles have increased since the early 1960s. There are also two territories with education powers similar to the states. There is no single Australian education system as such. However, there are few major educational differences between the states and it is likely that these differences will be reduced even further in the future.

In 1993 the population was 18 million. It is a highly urbanized society, especially in the southeast: two-thirds live in cities of more than 100,000 people, and the two largest cities, Sydney and Melbourne, between them account for about 40 percent of the population. Most of the country, though, is sparsely populated with small communities separated by vast distances. The techniques of distance education have thus long been important. Much of the character of Australian schooling results from nineteenth-century legislation designed to ensure uniformity of provision throughout each state. The highly centralized administrative structures which resulted were remarkably successful in this respect. However, by about 1970 it was clear that they were less well-suited to serve a more diverse, and demanding, society. Since the early 1970s, the states have moved with varying speed, and with varying success, to provide government schools with more autonomy for curriculum, assessment, and resource management. However, much uncertainty remains about the appropriate balance of state and local responsibility for schooling.

The population has more than doubled since 1950, largely due to immigration. One in three Australians is either a first- or second-generation immigrant. Fewer than half of the postwar immigrants have come from Great Britain or Ireland. Substantial numbers arrived from southern and northern Europe, especially during the 1950s and 1960s. More recently, the Middle East and Southeast Asia have been prominent sources of immigrants, including many refugees. These changes have generated a student population that is more diverse in its educational expectations and cultural backgrounds.

At the onset of British colonization there were an estimated 300,000 Aboriginal people in Australia. These numbers were severely depleted as the White population grew; by 1950 it was widely believed that the Aboriginal population would soon be virtually extinct. However, an increased birthrate and an enhanced appreciation of Aboriginal culture have meant that Aborigines now constitute a more significant part of society. About 2.5 percent of Australian children are of Aboriginal descent, many of them living in isolated communities, and there has been increasing recognition of the need for education to be more responsive to their needs. In general, though, Aboriginal people remain economically and educationally disadvantaged.

English is the language of virtually all activities. Education and labor market authorities provide language programs for immigrants from non-English speaking countries. Languages other than English continue to play an important role among some immigrant groups and Aboriginal people. In 1993 the state and federal governments agreed on a long-term plan for all school students from Years 1 to 10 to study a language other than English.

In its early years the Australian economy was dominated by agriculture and mining. These industries are still important, especially for export income, but they now employ less than 10 percent of the labor force. About 20 percent are employed in manufacturing utilities and construction, while the remaining 70 percent work in service industries such as construction, transportation, communications, sales, finance, education, and health. A general upward movement in the occupational structure of the labor force has been observed since 1950. Around 25 percent now work as either managers or professionals, 15 percent in skilled trades, and 15 percent in clerical occupations. In response to these labor market changes curriculum policies are placing an increasing emphasis on communication and research skills, computer literacy, and the ability to work in groups.

In 1993 just over half of the labor force held a postschool educational qualification (degree, diploma, certificate, or trade qualification). In the early 1980s the equivalent proportion was 40 percent. The growth in employment has been particularly rapid for degree holders. Since about 1970 the proportion of full-time workers with university degrees has tripled to about 15 percent. There has been some decline in the relative earnings of university graduates. However, demand for tertiary education continues to grow. Unemployment tends to be highest among those with the least education.

The fact that Australia is a relatively wealthy country is a further factor underpinning the demand for education. In the 1992–93 financial year per capita gross domestic product (GDP) was just under A\$23,000. The 1980s and early 1990s, though, were difficult economic times. Unemployment has remained high and overseas debt has grown. These difficulties prompted considerable national soul-searching, and much critical attention has been focused on education. The general political consensus has been that participation in education and training needs to be increased, curricula needs to be more relevant to national priorities, and that individuals and employers should finance an increasing share of the costs of educational expansion.

2. Politics and the Goals of the Education System

The dominant role of governments in financing and administering education means that the education policies of the major political parties are of considerable importance. These policies do differ in some respects. The social democratic party (the Labor Party) is more likely to emphasize equitable access, the need for compensatory programs, and the importance of teacher and parent involvement in decision-making. The Liberal and National parties tend to place more weight on the need to maintain academic standards, parental choice of school, and vocationally relevant curricula. The Labor Party has held office at the federal level since 1983, and also formed the government in most states for much of the decade to the early 1990s. In the early 1990s, Liberal–National party coalitions won office in most states and cut school funding to help reduce government debt. The funding cuts and accompanying policy changes—particularly greater monitoring of student performance and devolution of more management responsibilities to schools—have been controversial.

Since the mid-1980s the two major political parties have both advocated the deregulation of many economic activities and greater competition for public enterprises. These policies have also been evident in the education system, particularly higher education.

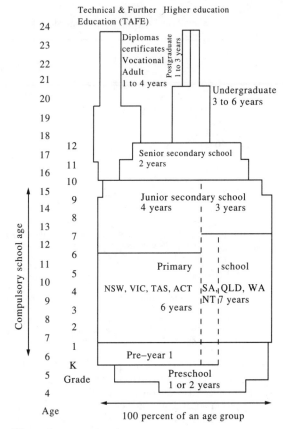

Figure 1

Australia: Structure of the formal education system 1990[a]

a Preschool, TAFE, and higher education data include part-time students

For example, universities now compete openly for fee-paying overseas students, a substantial proportion of research funds are allocated on a competitive basis, and in some areas of high employment demand—such as accountancy and computer science—academics are being offered more attractive employment packages than colleagues in other disciplines.

The broad purposes of the educational sectors and institutions are generally outlined in legislation and are supplemented by detailed statements of aims. These indicate a changing balance between individual and community needs as one moves through the education system. In the compulsory years of schooling the major emphasis tends to be on fostering individual development and general socialization. At the upper-secondary and tertiary levels, broader economic and social goals tend to become significant.

3. The Formal System of Education

3.1 Primary, Secondary, and Tertiary Education

Figure 1 outlines the structure of the formal education system. Key statistics on enrollments and resources in

Table 1
Enrollments and resources in formal education[a]

	Schools		Tertiary	
	Primary	Secondary	TAFE	University
Number of students[b]	1,816,000	1,282,000	1,043,000	575,000
Percentage of age group enrolled[c]				
Age 15–16	—	87	10	—
17–19	—	25	24	16
20–24	—	1	14	14
Number of institutions[d]	7,030	1,580	290	45
Average no. students per institution	220	530	3,700	12,800
Student–teacher ratio[e]	18.4	12.4	—	15.3
Expenditure per student[f] (A$)	3,800	5,400	—	10,000

a Caution is needed in making intersectoral comparisons due to differences in definitions, data collection methods, and reference periods. Unless otherwise indicated, the school and university data refer to 1993 and TAFE to 1992   b The school data include students enrolled in special schools. The TAFE data exclude enrollments in recreation, leisure, and personal enrichment courses; 90 percent of TAFE enrollments are part-time. About 30 percent of university enrollments are part-time   c School and university data refer to 1992, and TAFE to 1991   d The school data exclude 850 combined primary–secondary schools and 410 special schools   e The school data include special schools; teacher numbers include principles and other senior teachers with largely administrative functions. The university ratio refers to 1992 and is estimated from data on student numbers weighted for the level and type of enrollment, and academic staff numbers excluding those engaged solely in research   f The school data refer to the 1991–92 financial year and comprise estimates of government expenditure on government schools. The university data refer to 1992 and are derived from estimates of general recurrent institutional expenditure (excluding research programs) and weighted student numbers.

the major education sectors are provided in Table 1.

Education is compulsory from ages 6 to 15 (16 in Tasmania) and between these ages there is virtually 100 percent attendance at school. Most children, though, start primary school at the age of 5. The majority of 4-year olds attend kindergarten, normally part-time, before commencing primary school. Kindergarten programs, which are partly subsidized, are operated by local government and community groups. These programs generally focus on structured play. A large number of 3-year olds also attend a kindergarten or other preschool center. Programs for 3-year olds are usually not subsidized and parents pay full fees.

Primary education lasts for either six or seven years, depending on the state concerned. In 1993 there were 1.8 million primary students, of whom 25 percent were enrolled in private schools. The scattered rural population has necessitated a large number of very small primary schools, although this number is declining. All government primary schools and most private primary schools are coeducational. The primary school day normally contains about 5 hours of tuition and the school year comprises around 200 days.

Secondary education is available for either five or six years depending upon the length of primary education in the state. Students normally commence secondary school at about age 12. One of the most marked changes during the 1980s was the increase in the proportion of students who remain beyond the minimum school-leaving age of 15. The proportion of commencing secondary students retained to the

final year of school rose from 35 percent in 1980 to 77 percent in 1993. The secondary school completion rate is higher for girls than boys, largely because more boys than girls leave school to enter an apprenticeship. Almost all government secondary schools are coeducational, but the majority of private secondary schools are single sex. About 30 percent of secondary students enroll in private schools, a proportion that has gradually risen since 1970. The secondary school year operates for approximately 200 days, with about 5.5 hours of tuition per day.

The tertiary sector comprises colleges of technical and further education (TAFE) and universities. The TAFE colleges provide a wide variety of courses including pre-employment programs, apprenticeships, retraining and updating programs, and liberal adult education. TAFE is the most accessible part of the tertiary sector. In 1992 just over 1 million students were enrolled in award courses in TAFE. Just over 90 percent of these enrollments were part-time and half of the students were aged 25 or over. A further 0.7 million students enrolled part-time in recreation, leisure, and personal enrichment courses.

In principle, entry to many TAFE courses is possible after Year 10. However, the combination of a tight labor market and rising school retention rates during the 1980s meant that many TAFE entrants have now completed Year 12 at secondary school. The nature of TAFE makes it difficult to calculate student–teacher ratios, but they would probably be comparable to those in secondary schools.

Prior to 1990 higher education comprised universities and colleges of advanced education (CAEs). Relative to universities the CAEs placed more emphasis on teaching than research. In 1988 there were about 20 universities and 50 CAEs in Australia. In 1990 the formal distinctions between universities and CAEs were removed and amalgamations stimulated by the federal government reduced the number of separate institutions to about 45. Since the late 1980s several privately funded universities have been established, but high tuition fees have limited enrollments.

In 1993 total higher education enrollments were just under 0.6 million, a rise of 70 percent since 1980. Much of this increase was a progression from the substantial rise in secondary school completion rates noted earlier. About 50 percent of Year 12 graduates enter higher education within a year or two of completing secondary school. Entry to higher education is normally based on academic results in either school or external examinations. Competition is fierce for entry to the more prestigious faculties and institutions. Provisions also exist for entry by people who lack a Year 12 qualification. In 1993 about one in seven commencing undergraduate students was admitted on the basis of prior informal study or work experience. About two-thirds of higher education enrollments are full-time and around 20 percent of students are engaged in graduate study. Despite the rapid expansion in the system since the early 1980s, students are still drawn disproportionately from managerial and professional backgrounds. There has been substantial growth in the numbers of overseas students enrolling in secondary and tertiary educational institutions. Some of them are brought to Australia under overseas aid programs, but the total number of international students has grown rapidly since 1986, when public institutions were first permitted to enroll them and to charge fees. In 1992 there were 40,000 overseas students (mostly from Southeast Asia) enrolled in Australian universities, which represented about 7 percent of total enrollments. Around three-fourths of these overseas students paid full tuition fees (about A$10,000 per year, on average).

3.2 Special Education

Due to differences in the definition of disability and the criteria for access to special services, it is difficult to estimate the numbers of students with disabilities. A major study estimated that in 1992 about 2 percent of students in Australian schools had some form of disability. At that time, about 30 percent of students with disabilities were enrolled in one of 410 special schools, 25 percent were enrolled in special classes or units attached to primary and secondary schools, and the remaining 45 percent were enrolled in regular school classes. The latter proportion is likely to have risen over time as there has been an increasing emphasis on integrating students with disabilities into regular school classes. There is great variety in the forms of special education provision and staffing

levels. In general, special schools would be staffed on an average of about 5 students to each teacher. In integrated classroom settings it is common for students with disabilities to be accompanied by an aide for at least part of the week. It is widely recognized that to achieve the goal of inclusive schooling, classroom teachers will require enhanced professional training and access to adequate support services.

3.3 Vocational, Technical, and Business Education

Difficult economic conditions have focused attention on the provision of vocational, technical, and business education. All governments have expressed a commitment to the development of more diverse and flexible vocational pathways for young people. These pathways are intended to allow the achievement of industry-recognized vocational qualifications through varying mixes of classroom instruction in schools, TAFE colleges and other providers, paid employment, and unpaid structured vocational placements. These new approaches to initial vocational education are intended to overcome limitations in the long-established apprenticeship system. The organizational framework for these initiatives is provided by the Australian Vocational Certificate Training System, which is intended to be fully implemented by 1996. It draws together a number of relatively new concepts in Australian education and training: generalizable employment-related competencies; recognition of prior learning; credit transfer; a national framework for the accreditation of training providers; and the development of flexible pathways between education, training, and employment that people can use over the course of their working lives. During the early 1990s there was considerable developmental work on identifying empolyment-related key competencies for postcompulsory education and training; broad competencies were identified and these are having considerable impact on curriculum design, course delivery, and student assessment. There is no explicit policy as to which students should receive vocational training although government programs tend to be oriented to those considered to be at long-term risk in the labor market. Traditionally, many Australian industries have played relatively little attention to employee training. However, the imposition of minimum expenditure requirements on training for several years in the early 1990s redressed this situation somewhat. A further important contextual change has been the gradual reform of employees' industrial awards to encourage more flexible career paths, raise productivity, and provide greater incentive for retraining. Although these changes are not yet fully in place, they have substantial implications for the future of education–industry relations. General government policy is to re-emphasize the importance of vocational education and to recognize its increasing convergence with general education. As part of this, state and federal governments have agreed that by the year 2001, 95 percent of 19-year olds should have completed Year 12 or an initial postschool qualification or be participating in education and training.

3.4 Adult and Nonformal Education

Adult participation in formal education is increasing. During the 1980s the number of mature-age students commencing undergraduate courses in higher education rose by 25 percent, and about one-third of commencing undergraduate students were aged 21 or over. As noted earlier, adult participation in TAFE courses is even more extensive.

Enrollments in the nonformal (i.e., nonaward) sector are, by their nature, more difficult to estimate. Nonformal education is provided through a variety of agencies and institutions. Higher education institutions have long provided some nonformal courses, but TAFE colleges are probably the major providers of nonformal education. As noted earlier, in 1993 about 0.7 million students enrolled in recreation, leisure, and personal enrichment courses in TAFE. Nonformal education is also provided by a large number of neighborhood learning centers, ethnic groups, and those involved in adult literacy programs.

Programs provided in the nonprofit adult and community education include vocationally oriented courses, secondary school completion, personal development programs, and hobby and leisure activities. Educational authorities are encouraging a more market-driven approach to education that includes a role for the adult and community education sector in meeting vocational needs.

4. Administrative and Supervisory Structure and Operation

Education is the responsibility of the individual states and territories. State education departments recruit and appoint the teachers in government schools; supply buildings, equipment, and materials; and provide some limited discretionary funding for use by schools. In most states some responsibility for administration, staffing, and curriculum has been devolved to regional education offices and schools. Devolution of responsibilities to schools is likely to become more extensive as most states are now moving towards self-managing schools in the government school sector. Until about 1975 all states used inspectors to monitor government school and teacher quality. The inspectorate exercised considerable power and provided a direct link between head office and the schools. This situation has now changed substantially and inspectors play a prominent role in only one or two states. The demise of the inspectorate is one of the factors behind state efforts to develop alternative mechanisms for monitoring schools and assessing teachers.

Private schools are an important feature of the education system and in 1993 enrolled 28 percent of students. Almost all private schools have some religious affiliation, most commonly with the Catholic Church (70 percent of private students are enrolled in Catholic schools). Each state has a substantial system of Catholic schools. About 850 private schools are independent, that is, they do not belong to a system. These particular schools vary widely in type from long-established, prestigious schools to relatively new, religious and alternative education schools. Aside from having to meet prescribed minimum educational standards for registration and funding purposes, private schools are largely free from government direction. In practice, though, most provide a curriculum similar to government schools.

In the tertiary sector, TAFE colleges are operated by state governments, often through the mechanism of a training board which has substantial employer membership. TAFE colleges have considerable operational autonomy. In 1993 the Australian National Training Authority was established by the federal government in collaboration with state governments and industry to coordinate the joint funding and planning of Australia's training system. Higher education institutions are autonomous bodies established under state legislation. However, since 1974 almost all of the funding for higher education has been provided by the federal government and federal authorities have had a substantial influence on the shape of the sector.

Since the 1970s the role of the federal government in education has grown noticeably, in part due to the increased dependence of the states on federal funds. More than 50 percent of the funds available to the states for spending on all purposes, including education, are provided by the federal government. Political responsibility for the federal role is exercised by a minister who is accountable to the federal (Commonwealth) Parliament. The federal and state ministers of education and training meet regularly to discuss major policy issues.

Since the late 1980s the federal government has encouraged state governments to adopt common approaches on issues such as the school starting age, teachers' salaries, and curriculum reform. Traditionally, federal initiatives in schooling have been resisted by the states. However, the financial power of the federal government and the continuing pressures for reform suggest that the 1990s will see progress toward a more national approach to education.

5. Educational Finance

For the financial year 1990–91 total public and private expenditure on education was A$21 billion, which represented 5.5 percent of GDP. The proportion of GDP allocated to education has declined slowly from a peak of 6.3 percent in the mid-1970s. The decline can be largely attributed to relatively static school enrollments and a fall in education cost levels (principally teachers' and academics' salaries) relative to general price movements.

State and federal governments supply more than 90 percent of the funds for education. In 1990–91 about 55 percent of government outlays on education were directed to schools, 20 percent to higher education, 10 percent to TAFE, and 5 percent to preschool education. The broad division of governmental responsibility is that the states fund government schools and TAFE, and the federal government finances private schools, higher education, and student financial support. The federal government also provides supplementary resources to the states for government schools and TAFE. The states provide about 60 percent of all public expenditure on education, and the federal government 40 percent.

Private funding of education is mostly in the form of tuition fees paid to private schools. Parents do not pay fees to attend government schools. The fees levied by private schools range from about A$400 a year in some parish primary schools to about A$8,000 in some secondary schools. All private schools also receive some direct government funding. Federal government support is based on a measure of the capacity of schools to raise funds from private sources. In 1992 the federal grants ranged from A$400 per student in well-resourced primary schools to A$2,100 per student in the poorest secondary schools. State governments also contribute funds to private schools. For the more poorly resourced private schools (mainly in the Catholic sector) total government grants are about 80 percent of school income. Although not as divisive as in the past, government funding of private schools remains a contentious issue.

Full-time secondary and higher education students are eligible for financial assistance through means-tested allowances provided on a noncompetitive basis. In 1993 the maximum allowance ranged from about A$4,000 per annum for students who were financially dependent on their parents to A$6,000 for those who were independent. About 45 percent of eligible full-time university students received some financial support under the scheme.

Since 1989 higher education students have been required to meet part of the costs of their tuition. The figure in 1993 was about A$2,300 per year for full-time students which was equivalent to around 20 percent of average government expenditure per student. Students can elect to pay the annual sum on enrollment (and receive a small discount) or else pay through the income tax system after leaving higher education. The latter only starts to operate once a former student's income reaches about A$27,000 per year, a level that approximates average earnings in the community. This scheme, which is intended to help finance expansion of the higher education system, has increased the share of private contributions to education funding.

6. Supplying Personnel for the Education System

About 200,000 (full-time equivalent) teachers were employed in schools in 1990. A further 50,000 people worked in nonteaching positions. About 99,000 teachers were employed in primary schools and 103,000 in secondary schools. Some 60 percent of school teachers are female. However, men are more likely than women to occupy senior administrative positions in schools.

Until the late 1970s, teacher shortages were common and students were offered generous scholarships to enter teacher training. More recently, static enrollments, budget cuts, and reduced teacher recruitment rates have resulted in an oversupply of teachers in some subject areas and regions. Because of limited openings many teachers when they begin have to spend their first year or two in relief teaching. However, there seem to be perennial shortages of teachers in areas such as mathematics, languages, and the physical sciences. In addition, schools in isolated regions and unattractive suburbs are often difficult to staff. In some states government school teachers have to spend time teaching in rural schools before becoming eligible for a city position.

Teacher training occurs in higher education institutions. The states are responsible for determining acceptable teacher qualifications. The normal length of initial training for secondary teachers is now four years of higher education. This generally comprises a three-year degree in a major discipline followed by a one-year diploma of education. Primary teachers normally complete a three-year diploma of education. Many primary teachers later upgrade their qualifications by undertaking specialist one-year diplomas in areas such as librarianship, special education, and language teaching.

Government school teachers usually serve a one-or two-year probationary period before becoming eligible for permanent employment. The states vary in the extent to which teachers are required to undergo formal appraisal after this time. In some states, this only occurs when the teacher applies for promotion; in others appraisal occurs periodically. The states also vary in the balance of inspectorial, principal, and peer inputs to the appraisal process and decisions about teacher promotions. Private school teachers are normally employed directly by the school concerned although, like government school teachers, their salaries and conditions are determined by industrial tribunals.

In 1993 the average age of teachers was about 40. Evidence of the aging of the profession, limited promotion opportunities, relatively low salaries, and the declining attractiveness of teaching as a career have focused attention on teachers' career structures. Most school systems have moved to give more emphasis to merit, as opposed to seniority, in promotion decisions. In several states, though, reduced government expenditure on schooling has resulted in few promotion positions being available. The general

45

oversupply of teachers has had a substantial impact on teacher education programs in universities. Since the late 1980s most universities have reduced programs and staffing for initial teacher education students and have attempted to focus more on postgraduate studies and upgrading programs for practicing teachers. The importance of teachers' continuing professional development is also widely acknowledged, but there have been few systematic programs in this area.

7. Curriculum Development and Teaching Methodology

There is no common school curriculum across the country. Within states the general pattern is that central authorities specify broad curricular guidelines and schools have considerable autonomy in deciding curriculum detail and teaching methodology. This situation applies particularly at primary and junior-secondary level. Even at these levels, the curriculum differences between schools in any one system would be relatively minor. Practically all students would be exposed to a curriculum that provided some coverage of reading, writing, mathematics, science, social studies, humanities, the expressive and performing arts, physical education, and less frequently, a foreign language. In primary schools most of these subjects would be taught by a general classroom teacher, whereas in secondary schools various subject specialists would be employed. Until the end of compulsory schooling (about Year 10) most students would have few elective subjects and classes within a school would follow basically the same curriculum.

At the senior-secondary level the curriculum is more likely to be specified in detail by an authority responsible for examining and certifying students. At these levels students generally have more scope to specialize and a range of elective studies is usually provided. In 1993 around 25 percent of Year 12 students specialized in a humanities and arts course, 25 percent in mathematics and science, and 10 percent in commerce, while the remainder studied subjects from several discipline areas.

Foreign languages are taught in secondary schools and, less commonly, primary schools. The study of languages is generally not mandatory, however, and in 1993 only about 10 percent of senior-secondary students studied a foreign language. French, German, Italian, Greek, Indonesian, and Japanese are the most commonly taught languages. The federal government is keen to encourage more foreign-language teaching in schools, especially the languages of Australia's major trading partners in Asia.

A major development during 1989 was the adoption by the state and federal education ministers of a set of ten broad goals for schooling in Australia. The goals include development of students' knowledge and skills in literacy, numeracy, computing, languages other than English, the creative arts, and environmental understanding. The agreed goals are intended to provide a framework for cooperation in curriculum development and assessment. Extensive collaboration by the states on curriculum development has occurred since 1990, although the implementation of detailed curriculum profiles has met some resistance at state level. Nevertheless, the 1989 agreement on goals for schooling, and subsequent curriculum development, indicate the gradual adoption of a more national approach to schooling.

Learning materials and tests are prepared by a variety of agents including the curriculum sections of education departments, academics, commercial publishers, and teachers' subject associations. In a significant development in 1990, the state and federal education ministers established the Curriculum Corporation, a semiautonomous body with a charter to develop curriculum materials on a commercial basis. In general, schools and individual teachers have a great deal of independence in the selection of learning materials.

Key issues in curriculum include the more effective coordination of curriculum development between schools and central agencies, the development of new materials to reflect the increasingly multicultural nature of Australian society, the preparation of students for a more dynamic economic environment, and the pressures for greater national uniformity in curriculum provision.

8. The System of Examinations, Promotions, and Certifications

In most schools students are automatically promoted between year levels according to age. The first formal certificate is generally received at Year 10 based on internal school assessment. All states award a certificate based on successful completion of Year 12. In most states external examinations play a major role in Year 12 certification. In two systems, Queensland and the Australian Capital Territory, there are no external examinations at all: internal school assessments are adjusted against students' scores on an academic aptitude test to achieve comparability across schools.

There is considerable interest in developing statements that provide detailed accounts of student achievement in a wide range of academic, personal, and social areas. Similarly, there is increasing use of criterion-based rather than norm-referenced assessment. In part, these developments are a response to the perceived need for Year 12 programs to be broadened beyond a concentration on preparation for higher education.

9. Educational Assessment, Evaluation, and Research

Since the late 1980s there has been considerable activity in student assessment and the development of education indicators. There has been a change in focus by governments and others from monitoring resource inputs to monitoring student outcomes. Several states have commissioned the Australian Council for Educational Research (ACER) to assess student achievement in the basic areas of literacy and numeracy, and other states have initiated their own testing programs. The agreement on national goals for schooling has stimulated some development of national approaches to student assessment. A landmark in this respect was the 1990 publication of the first national report on schooling. This joint venture of federal and state education authorities involved the documentation of resource levels and student outcomes.

The only national tests of literacy and numeracy were undertaken by ACER in 1975 and 1980 on samples of 10- and 14-year olds. This testing program, which indicated a slight improvement in achievement between the two years, aroused considerable opposition from some groups and has not been repeated. ACER has also conducted national tests of student achievement in mathematics and science as part of the series of international studies undertaken by the International Association for the Evaluation of Educational Achievement (IEA). These tests suggested that Australian students generally performed at a similar level to those in other industrialized nations, but that Australia's relative standing has slipped slightly over time.

The 1980s saw an increasing emphasis on evaluation for accountability purposes. Independent evaluations are generally a requirement of federally funded programs. In most states government schools are required to undergo review and evaluation every few years. Federal and state education agencies are active in conducting their own research and in commissioning research projects. Federal agencies, in particular, have become major commissioners of research.

The activities of ACER give some indication of educational research priorities. For the 1993–96 period its program is structured around four broad themes: pathways between education, training, and work; making schools more effective; improving educational testing; and investigating assessment alternatives.

At the higher education level a major change in research policy was evident in the establishment of the Australian Research Council (ARC) in 1989. This federal initiative has sought to alter the "research culture" of higher education by placing more emphasis on applied research, shifting toward competitive allocation of research funds based on peer review, and identifying national priorities in research. A notable development in 1991–92 was a strategic review of educational research in Australia. The review was a cooperative exercise between major funding agencies, government authorities, and researchers' professional associations. The review documented the state of educational research, identified a medium- to long-term agenda, and proposed strategies for restructuring the funding and organization of research, and the training of educational researchers. The review estimated that about 0.35 percent of total education expenditure was directed to educational Research and Development (R&D). To help increase the national research effort, the review proposed that government funding authorities redirect a small proportion of the recurrent funding for schools, TAFE, and universities to an educational R&D fund that would be administered by a broadly based board to support research in priority areas. This recommendation was not endorsed by the relevant authorities. However, a number of the other recommendations are being implemented in various ways.

10. Major Reforms in the 1980s and 1990s

The 1980s were a period of considerable reform in many aspects of Australian education. One of the more notable changes was the dramatic rise in the proportion of young people who completed secondary education. This has stimulated far-reaching changes in curricula, assessment, and school structures. The need for the teaching career to be restructured to attract and retain able people has also been high on the reform agenda. In higher education the distinctions between universities and CAEs have been removed, fewer and larger institutions created through amalgamation, research funding revamped, and a form of student tuition fees introduced. In the nonformal sector a major scheme to expand employee training has been introduced.

Many of these changes share a common rationale: the need for education to assist the Australian economy to become more internationally competitive. The reforms have attracted considerable opposition from those who dispute the goal of more closely aligning education and the economy, and those who question the particular means proposed. The resolution of these tensions is likely to occupy Australian education for much of the 1990s.

11. Major Problems for the Year 2000

Finding the resources to support the continued expansion of senior-secondary and tertiary education will be a problem. Already, at the start of the 1990s, there are reports of overcrowding in higher education and indications of looming shortages of academics in key discipline areas. The educational demands of rapid social and economic change are unlikely to abate. It will be a major challenge to accommodate these demands without further burdening the curriculum. Teachers will need to acquire new skills and knowledge to assist their students anticipate and control the pace of change. The development of rewarding career structures for teachers and academics is likely to be a major problem.

In addition, some of the perennial problems of Australian education will almost certainly still exist. The difficulties of providing effective programs to scattered populations will remain. Finding an appropriate balance between central political responsibility for education and the encouragement of local school initiatives is still likely to be problematic. Program development to help redress social, gender, and economic inequalities will continue to be a challenge.

Bibliography

Australian Bureau of Statistics 1993 *Year Book, Australia 1993*. ABS, Canberra
Australian Bureau of Statistics 1993 *Schools, Australia 1993*. ABS, Canberra
Australian Education Council 1991 *Young People's Participation in Postcompulsory Education and Training*. Australian Government Publishing Service, Canberra
Australian Education Council 1993 *National Report on Schooling in Australia 1992*. Curriculum Corporation, Melbourne
D'Cruz J, Langford P (eds.) 1990 *Issues in Australian Education*. Longman Cheshire, Melbourne
Department of Employment, Education and Training 1993 *Education Participation Rates 1992*. Australian Government Publishing Service, Canberra
Department of Employment, Education and Training 1993 *National Report on Australia's Higher Education Sector*. Australian Government Publishing Service, Canberra
Department of Employment, Education and Training 1993 *Selected TAFE Statistics 1992*. Australian Government Publishing Service, Canberra
Department of Employment, Education and Training 1994 *Selected Higher Education Statistics 1993*. Australian Government Publishing Services, Canberra
Ingvarson L, Chadbourne R (eds.) 1994 *Valuing Teachers' Work: New Directions in Teacher Appraisal*. ACER, Melbourne
Logan L, 1990 *Teachers in Australian Schools. A 1989 Profile*. Australian College of Education, Canberra
McGaw B, Boud D, Poole M, Warry R, McKenzie P 1992 *Educational Research in Australia*. National Board of Employment, Education and Training, Canberra

Austria

H. Altrichter and P. Posch

1. General Background

Austria is a small landlocked country in the center of Europe. Its land mass totals 83,858 square kilometers; nearly two-thirds of the country is geographically part of the Alpine region. German is the first language for about 99 percent of its population of 7.884 million. There are small ethnic minorities of Slovenians, Croatians, Hungarians, and Czechs. About 81 percent of the population is Roman Catholic and 5 percent Protestant. Only minor population growth is expected in the 1990s and the first decade of the twenty-first century; this will be due mainly to increasing international migration and the aging of the population. It is expected that the size of the school population will further decline, the size of the work force will stagnate, and the size of the elderly population will greatly increase.

In 1992, about 7 percent of the labor force was employed in agriculture/forestry, 36 percent in industry, and 57 percent in the service sector.

In terms of Gross National Product (GNP), Austria has a good standing among the Western European industrial nations. In 1992, the unemployment rate was about 6 percent. The social security and national health systems are considered to be of a high standard. Austria's economic system has been called a "social market economy." Moderate privatization was the policy of the Austrian government at the end of the 1980s. The country is a member of the European Economic Area (EEA) and has applied for membership of the European Community. A characteristic feature of the Austrian economy is the system of social partnership. Its purpose is to solve wage, prices, and many other economic and labor-market decisions in "preparliamentary lobbies" comprising representatives of the employer organizations and the trade unions. This has resulted in a low incidence of industrial unrest, and great influence on the part of the organizations involved, and yet, according to some, also in a lack of open and public discussion of problems.

2. Politics and the Goals of the Education System

As a consequence of World War I the former Austro-Hungarian monarchy, a huge country of more than 600,000 square kilometers with a multiethnic population of over 50 million people, broke up. In 1918, the German-speaking parts of the former state were re-established as a republic. In the beginning of the newborn democracy new social groups, like the workers and their Social Democratic Party, were able to influence policy considerably for the first time and put forward some progressive programs for developing the social system and education. For example, a comprehensive secondary school for all 10–14-year olds was proposed, instead of the existing bipartite system. However, many of these programs soon got stuck in the increasing animosity between the two big political camps (Conservatives and Social Democrats) and were only partly realized in Vienna. Even these developments were stopped when a home-grown fascist regime took power in 1934. This soon ended in the occupation of the country by the German Third Reich.

After World War II, democracy was re-established and the school system was restored in its pre-War shape. In 1955, the "State Treaty" between Austria and the four allied nations was signed, making Austria an independent state which declared "Permanent Neutrality." Consultations to renew the Austrian educational system soon began; however, pre-War clashes over educational matters broke out again. Social Democrats were advocating a comprehensive school for all 10–14-year olds while the Conservative Party was insisting on the retention of the *Gymnasium* (grammer school) and, hence, of the bipartite system at the lower-secondary level.

In 1962, a law was passed which forms the basis of the educational system in the 1990s. It won the endorsement of the two big political parties by omitting controversial questions such as the structure of the lower-secondary level of education (Thonhauser 1992). The main aim of all Austrian schools was defined in the School Organization Act of 1962, as follows:

> It is the task of the Austrian School to foster the development of the talents and potential abilities of young persons in accordance with ethical, religious, and social values and the appreciation of that which is true, good, and beautiful, by giving them an education corresponding to their respective stages of development and to their respective courses of study. It should give young people the knowledge and skills required for their future lives and occupations and train them to acquire knowledge on their own initiative. Young people should be trained to become healthy, capable, conscientious, and responsible members of society and citizens of the democratic and federal Republic of Austria. They should be encouraged to develop an independent judgement and social understanding, to be open-minded to philosphy and political thinking of others, they should be enabled to participate in the economical and cultural life of Austria, of Europe, and the world and to make their contribution, in love of freedom and peace, to the common tasks of mankind.

(FPS 1990 p. 11)

Since the end of the 1960s it has been the explicit aim of the Austrian government to raise the general level of educational attainment. Policies have included: the provision of higher secondary schools in every district of the country; the rapid expansion of an upper and intermediate sector of vocational schooling; and making funds available to increase educational participation.

3. The Formal System of Education

Figure 1 presents a diagrammatic representation of the Austrian system of education. School attendance

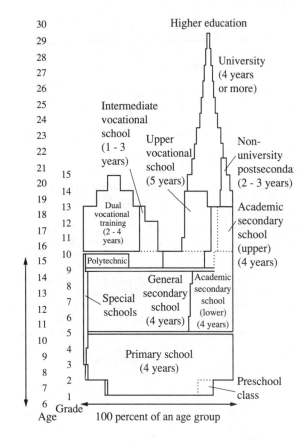

Figure 1

Austria: Structure of the formal education system 1989[a]

a   Diagram prepared by Lorenz Lassnigg and Adelheid Fraiji at the *Institut für Höhere Studien* (IHS), Vienna

is compulsory for all children between the ages of 6 and 15 who are permanently resident in Austria; actual attendance is virtually 100 percent within this age-range. In Fig. 1, the fact that some children aged 6 are not enrolled is due to the deadline for enrollment not being identified with the end of the year.

All state schools are coeducational. Class size is limited by law to 30; actual figures are usually lower. In 1992–93, about 8 percent of all Austrian students attended private schools, most of which were run by the Roman Catholic Church or affiliated institutions. Most private schools conform to state laws and can issue certificates equivalent to state schools.

The school year lasts from the beginning of September to the end of June. The school day starts about 8 a.m. There is no afternoon instruction in primary schools at all.

3.1 Primary, Secondary, and Tertiary Education

Parents must register their children for school. Children who have reached school age, but are considered by the school authorities to be too immature to attend the regular first grade (about 10% of the respective age group), attend a preschool class (*Vorschulstufe*) for a year which prepares them for attending primary school. A child's regular school career starts upon entering the *Volksschule* (primary school) which comprises 4 grades and aims at providing all children with a common elementary education.

Lower-secondary education lasts from 10 to 14 years of age. At the end of primary school, students have two options for further schooling: general secondary school (*Hauptschule*), which has no admission requirements (other than a fourth grade primary school pass) and is the historical successor to schools traditionally considered to be for the common people; or the lower cycle of the academic secondary school (*Allgemeinbildende Höhere Schule* {AHS} commonly referred to as the *Gymnasium*), which is the successor to schools traditionally considered as educating the learned sector of the populace. Admission to the latter type of school depends on children having obtained grades 1 or 2 (on a 5-point scale) in German, reading, and mathematics in their final primary school report.

Both school types have the same educational aims. Where the same subjects are offered, the syllabuses are identical. The general secondary school introduced a three-level setting system in German, foreign languages, and mathematics. This does not exist in academic secondary schools.

Only 5 percent of students from general secondary schools continue in an upper cycle of an academic secondary school, but about 24 percent continue in an upper vocational school. However, 65 percent of students from the lower cycle of the academic secondary school continue their studies at the upper cycle of this school type, while 30 percent enter an upper vocational school. Although efforts have been made to have students move from one type of school to another during the period of compulsory education, this has not occurred and the old segregation of the school types has persisted.

The *Mittelstufenproblem* (lower-secondary stage problem) is considered the major challenge for the future development of the lower-secondary school system. The academic secondary school—in the tradition of the old German *Gymnasium*—was originally conceived as a school for the top 5 percent of the student population, whereas general secondary schools were the "people's schools" catering for the other 95 percent. However, in 1992, the ratio was about 30:70 instead of 5:95. How this cycle of education should be reformed was still the subject of discussion in 1992 (Gruber 1990 p. 319).

While the main task of the primary and lower-secondary levels is to contribute to general education, a further task is added at the upper-secondary level—namely to provide vocational qualifications. The problem at the upper-secondary level is how to structurally separate, integrate, or mix general–academic-oriented education and vocational/professional education. The academic and vocational schools all form part of upper-secondary schooling.

The one-year polytechnical course (*Polytechnischer Lehrgang*) provides the completion of the basic general education within the range of compulsory education. About 24 percent of an age-group attends these courses. The students are typically those with the lowest aspirations and/or ability.

The four-year upper cycle of the academic secondary school (AHS-*Oberstufe*) consists of pre-academic general education. Although students specialize in certain subjects, they continue to study the whole range of pre-academic subjects. At the end of the course, students take a matriculation examination (*Matura*). Passing this exam gives them the right to enter university. In 1992, about 23 percent of the 14-year olds continued in these type of schools.

The five-year upper-vocational schools (*Berufsbildende Höhere Schule* or BHS) combine advanced general and advanced vocational education. Students train for careers in industry, trade, business, agriculture, or socioeconomic occupations. The curriculum mirrors the respective curriculum of the academic secondary school, but also includes theoretical subjects relevant to future professions as well as design and workshop practice. The final examination is equivalent to the AHS-matriculation exam and also to various levels of vocational qualification. Depending on the type of school attended, this qualification could be that of the intermediate vocational schools (for a range of apprenticed trades) or of a postsecondary professional kind. After three years of qualified work, graduates of the engineering, agricultural, and some trade courses in the upper vocational schools are awarded the professional title of *Ingenieur*. This "double qualification" is so attractive to parents and students that enrollments in these schools have increased. Further details of vocational education are presented in Sect. 3.4 below.

There are three types of university course. The first degree in all disciplines (with the exception of medicine, where a doctoral course of a minimum of 6 years provides the first degree) is obtained in a master's course (*Magisterstudium*). There are master's courses in 107 different fields. The legal minimum duration is between 4 and 5 years, but the actual duration varies from 6 (business economics) to 8.5 years (psychology). Only 6 percent of students complete their courses within the minimum time.

The second type of university course is the doctoral

course (*Doktoratsstudium*) of two years' minimal duration for students with a master's degree. A doctoral thesis has to be submitted which is assessed by two—usually internal—examiners. If this thesis is accepted, the student has to sit an oral examination in several subjects (*Rigorosum*), including defending his or her thesis. The third type of course consists of a variety of mostly nondegree-oriented, further education provisions.

In 1992, about 205,000 students were enrolled at the 12 Austrian universities and 6 fine arts colleges. Of these, 45 percent were female. About 20 percent of females and 24 percent of males in an age group is enrolled in the universities. Those with a university degree constitute 5 percent of the total labor force. With few exceptions (e.g., admission tests to the fine arts colleges), admission to university is open to all students who have obtained the *Matura*. There is an alternative path to university for those who have not earned a traditional upper-secondary education credential. After some professional experience and, optionally, after attending a preparation course they may sit an admission test.

Teacher-training academies (*Pädagogische Akademien*) provide three-year courses for primary, secondary, special, and polytechnical school teachers. The prerequisite for admission is also the *Matura*. Registered social workers are trained in three-year courses at academies for social workers (*Sozialakademien*) and are awarded a diploma (i.e., a nonacademic degree). Admission is through an aptitude test, plus the *Matura* qualification. The *Matura* may be waived if applicants attend a one-year preparatory course. At medico-technical schools, courses last for two to three years. Graduates receive nonacademic diplomas. Quantitatively, this nonuniversity postsecondary sector still plays a marginal role. About 89 percent of all postsecondary students are enrolled at universities, 3 percent at fine arts colleges, 6 percent at teacher-training academies, about 1 percent at medico-technical schools, and less than 1 percent at academies for social workers.

Problems exist in tertiary education in Austria. Universities, academies, and adult education (see Sect. 3.5) are three separate, largely uncoordinated systems (e.g., transfer from academies to university is not possible). The average duration of university study is long and the dropout rate is high. Only 57 percent of male and 44 percent of female students eventually graduate. There are virtually no postsecondary alternatives to universities. However, in 1993, legal provisions have been established for nonuniversity postsecondary institutions (*Fachhochschulen*) for professions other than teachers and social workers.

3.2 Preschool Education

Preschool education is noncompulsory and consists of crèches (*Kinderkrippen*) for the very young and kindergartens for 3- to 6-year olds. Preschool education is based on provincial legislation and is run both by private and public institutions. In 1989–90, about 70 percent of Austrian 3- to 6-year olds attended preschools, but the situation varies from province to province. There is considerable unsatisfied demand for places in preschool institutions.

3.3 Special Education

There are separate special schools (*Sonderschulen*) for mentally or physically handicapped children for the whole range of compulsory schooling. The schools have special syllabuses. Between 1.4 and 3.3 percent of an age group is enrolled. The number of pupils in special schools has been decreasing in line with a decrease in student numbers in schools in general. The movement for "integration" or "mainstreaming" of handicapped children has gained momentum. The legal basis for "integrated education" was created in 1989 and pilot projects have been conducted. They involved providing an additional (full-time or part-time) teacher for "integration classes." These teachers provided remedial instruction especially tailored to the needs of handicapped children (Gruber 1989). In 1993, these developments finally resulted in the 15th Amendment of the School Organization Bill. Parents of children with special education needs (*sonderpädagogischer Förderungsbedarf*) may opt either for an "integrated education" in mainstream schools (with additional special provision during parts of instruction time) or for a special school.

3.4 Vocational, Technical, and Business Education

In the system of dual vocational education (*duale Berufsbildung*) apprentices in business and industry receive practical vocational training at their place of work and also attend part-time vocational schools (*Berufsschulen*), typically for one day a week. There is some element of "general education" included. The teaching of a foreign language has been introduced. Admission to the dual system after the completion of compulsory education (i.e., at 15 years of age) depends on the individual having an apprentice's contract. About 47 percent of the school population in this age group in 1992–93 received this type of qualification. The length of courses varies from two to four years, but is three years for the majority (in addition to the polytechnical year). The vocational qualification obtained licenses the recipient to work in a legally defined trade. There are 227 different apprenticable trades. About 50,000 firms (of a total of approximately 200,000) train apprentices. Given the economic structure of Austria this means that about 80 percent of all apprentice training takes place in small and medium-sized establishments in commerce, trade, and tourism (FPS 1990 p. 17).

Intermediate vocational schools (*Berufsbildende Mittlere Schulen* or BMS) are basically full-time schools

Table 1
Responsibilities in the Austrian educational system

	Federal State	Province	Others
General legislation	state		
External organization (construction, equipping)	implementation for academic secondary, intermediate, and upper vocational schools	implementation for general secondary, primary, and vocational schools	passed on to municipalities by provincial by-laws
Teacher employment	as above	as above	
Administrative authority, inspection	federal Ministry is second instance for academic secondary, intermediate, and upper vocational schools	provincial education committee is first instance for academic secondary, intermediate, and upper vocational schools; second instance for general secondary, primary, and vocational schools	district education committee is first instance for general secondary, primary and vocational schools

equivalent to the dual system of school and apprenticeship. The curriculum is of one to four years' duration (but typically lasts three or four years). It comprises training in apprenticed trades, but with a good proportion of "general education." Successful completion results in vocational licences which are sometimes more extensive than the ones given by the dual system (Brezovich 1990 p. 26). In 1992–93, about 25 percent of all 14-year olds opted to enter these schools.

The vocational side of the upper-secondary level (and the upper vocational schools) has been and is the pride of the Austrian school system as it provides both well-qualified tradespersons and access·to higher education for a certain proportion of people. Discussions about upper-secondary education involve the following issues. Employers' organizations feel that too many persons attend academic secondary schools, and hence do not acquire basic vocational qualifications. Trade unions and some educational researchers have criticized the fragmentation and overspecialization of the dual vocational education, given the many trades and enterprises (Lassnigg 1989). The dual system is considered a kind of "educational dead-end" because it does not offer well-established opportunities for contination to higher or professional education. Academic secondary schools do not provide any vocational or professional qualification. Thus, the very type of school which benefits most at the lower-secondary level, and from which 65 percent of students continue to the upper cycle, virtually forces its students into higher education.

3.5 Adult and Nonformal Education

Tertiary education options are complemented by institutions of further or adult education. There is a range of institutions offering a variety of courses: state institutions, such as *Pädagogische Institute* responsible for inservice training of teachers; further education institutions of the Chamber of Commerce and Chamber of Labor respectively; semiprivate institutions which rely on regular state subsidies, such as the *Volkshochschulen* (people's adult education colleges); and private enterprises which sell their courses, such as management training institutions. There are long courses and short events, nonformal general interest courses, vocationally qualifying courses, and even courses which aim to prepare those who do not have the *Matura* for university admission. Since 1981, a development plan has existed for a cooperative system of adult education aimed at coordinating these activities. However, it has not had the desired effect (Schratz 1991).

4. Administrative and Supervisory Structure and Operation

General legislation for all educational affairs rests with the federal parliament (see Table 1). Provincial parliaments can pass minor bylaws. Thus, the organization of schools, their curricula, and the arrangements of school life are similar all over Austria.

All educational laws are constitutional matters. Thus, educational laws and amendments need a two-thirds majority in the lower house of the Austrian parliament. In this way, the two major political parties have ensured that no changes can be made without the consent of both. This has made the educational system relatively static, since compromises in controversial matters tend to be achieved by leaving unchanged existing structures. Provincial and district authorities have only very limited (mostly implementation or delegated) responsibilities.

The salaries of teachers in academic secondary and upper-vocational schools are paid directly by the state; those in all other schools are paid by the provinces, but refunded by the federal state (except for vocational schools, where only 50% of salaries are reimbursed).

School administration and school inspection are carried out by the Ministry of Education and the Arts. It has created special authorities at the provincial level (*Landesschulrat*) and district level (*Bezirksschulrat*) for this function. These bodies maintain a certain degree of independence from the center, primarily because they are composed according to the relative power of the political parties in the respective province.

Additionally, various consultation mechanisms exist. Before laws are passed, provincial governments and different lobbies (e.g., employers, trade unions, teachers' organizations, and parents' and youth organizations) are given the opportunity to comment and to propose changes. Advisory boards, such as the School Reform Commission, were founded to provide consultation for the Ministry. Parents' and pupils' advisory boards have been established at federal and provincial level.

At the secondary school level there are "school community committees" in which parents, teachers, and pupils are represented. They decide on issues such as school events (e.g., sports weeks), parents' consultation days, school regulations, career counseling, and health care.

It is a constitutional principle that science and the teaching of science is free from state constraints. However, this "academic freedom" is interpreted as an individual right and does not entail fully autonomous universities. Rather, there is a complicated system of direct and delegated state administration, as well as self-government of universities in operation.

All Austrian universities and fine arts colleges are state universities, regulated by federal law and mainly financed by the public purse (only 3.1% of their budgets are derived from sources other than the state). Most university personnel are civil servants governed by the general regulations for civil servants. However, there are some specific privileges for teaching and research staff.

Federal responsibilities are as follows: university law, budget, and staff; university appointments (including professors); staff management; establishment, denomination, and dissolution of departments; establishment of degree courses at universities; the construction and maintenance of buildings. Part of this public administration and, in particular, those matters concerning staff members has been delegated to the universities. Universities are self-governing institutions in those matters relating to the election of university bodies; coordination and control of university authorities and facilities; assignment of new posts; funds; recruitment of junior staff; temporary teaching appointments; proposals for the appointment of professors (professors are, however, appointed by the Ministry); determination of curricula; planning and coordination of teaching; administration of examinations; awarding of degrees; and research.

The university's chief executive is the *Rektor* who is a full professor elected by the university assembly (consisting of equal numbers of professors, other teaching staff, and students) for two years. He or she is responsible for the execution of decisions by the academic senate and for the internal regulations of the university. In 1993, a new law on university organization was passed which will substantially increase the autonomy of universities. Its implementation, which began in 1994, will take several years.

5. Educational Finance

Attendance is free at all public schools, as are transport to school and all textbooks. In 1988–89, about Sch 935 million (Sch 11.7=US$1) were spent on school books.

All fees for Austrian university students were abolished in 1972. Additionally, the state provides family allowances and free transportation up to the age of 27, reduction on income tax for students' parents, direct study grants, talent scholarships, subsidies for studies abroad, and subsidized health insurance for students.

The major contribution to education comes from federal taxes with very little direct payment by families and other private sources. For the year 1993, Sch 57,670 million were allocated from the state budget for education in the school system, and Sch 28,875 million for universities and research. This represented 7.25 and 3.63 percent of the state budget, respectively, and 5.6 percent of GDP. The percentage of the education budget devoted to the different levels of education were 5.8 to preschool, 17.1 to primary, 47.1 to secondary, and 19.7 to tertiary education in 1988 (BMUKS 1990b p. 15, CERI 1991 p. 15–17). In 1993, the federal government spent Sch 39,367 per pupil in all compulsory schools (i. e., primary schools, general secondary schools, polytechnic courses), Sch 61,902 per pupil in academic secondary schools (both lower and upper cycle), Sch 82,593 per pupil in technical intermediate or upper-secondary schools, Sch 79,907 per pupil in commercial intermediate or upper-secondary schools, and Sch 7,892 per pupil in vocational schools (BMUK 1993b p. 30).

6. Supplying Personnel for the Education System

In the school year 1992–93, 116,011 teachers were employed in the school system (including nonuniversity postsecondary institutions). A total of 63 percent of all

Table 2
Enrollments in educational institutions in the school year 1988–89

	Kindergarten	Primary	Lower-secondary General secondary	Lower-secondary Academic secondary	Vocational schools	Upper-secondary Academic secondary	Upper-secondary Upper vocational	Intermediate vocational[a]	Postsecondary Universities	Postsecondary Nonuniversity postsecondary[b]
Number of students	184,027	368,204	239,111	91,500	157,789	67,082	99,594	57,937	196,702	6,931
% of age-group										
age 3–6	70	—	—	—	—	—	—	—	—	—
age 10–13	—	—	69.6	26.6	—	—	—	—	—	—
age 15–16[c]	—	—	—	—	50.6	16.6	18.8	12.3	—	—
tertiary	—	—	—	—	—	—	—	—	18.9	4.6
entrance rate[d]										
Number of schools	3,876	3,383	1,187	314	244	314	285	619	18	35
Student–teacher ratio[e]	11.4	12.6	7.3	10.4	34.8	7.7	8.8		23	(4.3)

Sources: ÖSTZ 1990; BMUKS 1990a; BMWF 1990 a Without social and agricultural intermediate schools b Teacher training academies, academies for social work c Experimental computation for the age-group best suited the relative weight of upper-secondary options d Because of different duration of studies, dropout rates, and age of commencing of studies CERI-INES (1991 p. 36), entrance rates, have been preferred to age-group comparisons e Student–teacher ratios have been calculated from total student and teacher numbers in BMUKS (1990a). Academic secondary school teacher numbers have been evenly distributed to lower and upper cycle which results in overestimation of lower-cycle ratios and underestimation of upper-cycle ratios. In reality, ratios will be higher because teachers in nonteaching positions are included. The figures of nonuniversity post-secondary institutions misrepresent supervision relationships because they include teachers at "training schools" which are part of teacher training academies

teachers were female and 8 percent worked in private schools. The pupil–teacher ratio and other details are given in Table 2.

There are two major types of teacher qualification. The first type is for primary school teachers, special school teachers, and those at general secondary schools and polytechnical courses. They are educated at teacher-training academies. Their training takes 3 years and includes educational theory, curriculum studies, and a considerable portion of school practice, mostly in training schools (*Übungsschulen*) attached to the academies. The second type is for teachers of the academic subjects of academic secondary schools, and intermediate and upper-vocational schools. They are trained at universities in two academic subjects. About 20 percent of the training time (legally 4.5 years) is devoted to education (general education, curriculum studies, and school practice). After completion, graduates are entitled to participate in a one-year school-based induction phase (*Unterrichtspraktikum*) organized by the school authorities.

The typical workload of a teacher at a general secondary school comprises 23 lessons (50 minutes each) a week, while the workload of a university-trained teacher of foreign languages at upper-secondary schools is around 17 periods a week. Austrian teachers in public schools are awarded the status of tenured civil servants after a limited period of employment on a nonpermanent contract. The gap in salary between university-trained teachers and academy-trained teachers has increased between 1983 and 1992 from 8.4 percent to 15.3 percent. However, both are paid according to a salary scale on the basis of seniority. There are very few career opportunities in the profession apart from that of becoming a school principal.

Attendance at teacher inservice education courses is on a voluntary basis except on the occasions when new curricula or structures are being introduced. The overwhelming majority of all inservice courses are provided by Inservice Institutions (*Pädagogische Institute*) which exist in every province.

In 1988–89, Austrian universities employed 1,732 university professors, 5,294 lecturers, and 802 other academic staff. This results in a professor–student ratio of 1:101 and a university teacher–student ratio of 1:23. About 18 percent of all university teachers are female. As in the school system, the percentage of women occupying senior positions is low. Additionally, there are 17,991 temporary teaching appointments for specialized university teaching duties.

7. Curriculum Development and Teaching Methodology

Syllabuses for all schools (including nonuniversity post-secondary institutions) are uniform throughout the country. They are prepared by expert commissions within the Ministry of Education and the Arts after having been shaped by a complex consultation process involving all influential social interest groups, such as employers' and employees' organizations, churches, teacher associations, and so forth. They are issued by ministerial decree; the provinces have the right to be consulted before they are issued. These syllabuses specify the general purpose of education, objectives, and the didactic principles of the particular programs and subjects; they also contain a table of subjects listing the number of lessons per grade and week.

Although these syllabuses are considered "frame curricula" in need of selection and specification, schools are not expected to formulate any school policy with respect to the curriculum or to prepare a more specific "in-school curriculum." The 14th Amendment to the School Organization Bill, however, has provided schools with a little room to maneuver in curricular matters. Selection and specification of the topics provided within this content frame and the methods by which they are taught are left to individual teachers. In practice, however, textbooks define the content and methods to a large extent. Textbooks are published by commercial publishers who usually employ groups of experienced teachers to write them. All textbooks and other relevant teaching materials must be approved by expert commissions at the Ministry. The implementation of new curricula is ensured by inspectors and school principals, through additional curriculum-related inservice training, and through initial teacher education. However, this process is not usually closely monitored or enforced.

The primary school curriculum is not oriented toward teaching separate subjects and rote learning, but rather toward stimulating active learning in more complex environments. The aspiration is not just to develop intellectual but also social, emotional, and physical aspects of the child's personality. Starting with the third grade, a foreign language (usually English, sometimes French) is taught in an informal way. For both types of lower-secondary schools, the syllabuses are largely the same except for a few additional subjects offered in the lower academic schools. Thus, there is a national common core curriculum virtually identical in aims and content for all pupils from 6 to 14 years of age. At least one foreign language (usually English) is taught to all pupils from 8 to 15 years of age. The concept of elective subjects is quite new. Only in 1989 were a few elective compulsory subjects introduced into the upper cycle of the academic secondary school.

Major curricular reforms conducted in the 1980s concerned the primary curriculum, upper-secondary academic education, and computer studies. In the school year 1985–86, information technology was made compulsory for all ninth graders in academic secondary schools. The basic philosophy is to integrate new information technologies into existing subjects rather than to provide specialist training in hardware and software. Other new areas of societal interest, such as environmental, health, and civic education, were not established as subjects in their own right. Rather they were introduced as "learning principles" (*Unterrichtsprinzipien*), the responsibility for which is shared by all subjects.

8. *The System of Examinations, Promotions, and Certifications*

The system of examinations is regulated by law and largely based on continuous assessment by the respective class teacher. Successful completion of every grade is certified in an annual "school report" which is the basis for promotion to the next grade. The strong sense of legalism in the Austrian School System is underlined by the fact that these "school reports" are considered "administrative decrees" against which there is a right of appeal.

Examinations at Austrian schools are usually not very selective. Some 4 percent of all pupils were not promoted to the next grade in 1991–92. The grade repetition percentage for general secondary schools was 2.3, for polytechnical courses 8.6, and for vocational schools 2.9. For academic secondary schools (Grades 5 to 12) it was 7.2, for upper technical schools 12.9, and for upper commercial schools 11.8 percent.

Additionally, there is little difference among schools and universities in terms of their prestige and the value of their certificates on the labor market. Rather, the selectivity of the system seems to work via students opting out before having finished a specific school and, in particular, via choice at the ages of 10 and 14. Having opted for a specific type of school, students are channeled into specific educational careers which largely predetermine the next step. Students cannot easily break out of these educational channels without high investments of time and effort.

9. *Educational Assessment, Evaluation, and Research*

There is no external evaluation of schools and no external assessment of student achievement. Furthermore, inspections are focused on persons rather than institutions. The idea of accountability is rather alien to the centralist–bureaucratic Austrian tradition (Altrichter 1991). However, educational statistics are well-developed. They concern student and teacher numbers in programs and information on input indicators rather than on outcome indicators and quality differences.

There is no comprehensive plan for the development of the educational system nor a vivid public discussion on educational affairs in the national and regional media. Educational planning occurs in the interplay of political authorities, societal interest groups, and respective ministerial departments. Since 1970, the Ministry of Education has preferred to have research and development undertaken by its own departments rather than by external research institutes and universities. As a consequence, educational research and development at the ministerial and at the university level has been, to a large extent, uncoordinated. However, a fairly good documentation on educational research in Austria is regularly published (BMUKS 1990c) and also networked with the European Documentation and Information System for Education (EUDISED).

There has been little evaluation of the university system. However, in 1990, two lists ranking universities, faculties, and courses according to student opinion and to a few research indicators were published by newspapers. At the same time, the legal basis was provided for "performance examination" of universities and their subdivisions for the purpose of planning, formulating priorities in research and teaching, and assessing the impact of major investments. Research in physics was evaluated via a peer review procedure (ÖPG 1991) and a whole university was examined by a commercial consulting firm. These events have resulted in an increasing debate on accountability, evaluation, and effectiveness of universities (Altrichter and Schratz 1992), particularly since evaluation seems to be one of the centerpieces of the Ministry's new policy of reorganizing the university system in order to make it more flexible and competitive.

10. *Major Reforms in the 1980s and 1990s*

Legal and societal framework conditions do not favor reform and innovation (Gruber 1990 pp. 315–16). Legalism and bureaucratization are strong forces. On the one hand, they help to protect clients but, on the other, they stifle initiative. Continuity and harmony are highly esteemed social and administrative values. Change, if considered necessary at all, is thought of as setting "legal milestones" followed by long periods of consolidation rather than as a process of permanent adjustment. As Gruber (1990 p. 315) has pointed out, the school systems in German-speaking countries seem to be "particularly resistent to organizational and curricular change.... All three adhere to early selection for 'academic' secondary education and to a strict separation between general and vocational education."

Austria is no exception, and the 1980s were characterized by stagnation. Many reform initiatives were terminated early or failed outright; many problems were postponed without solution and few convincing new ideas were initiated (Thonhauser 1992 p. 637). Changes at the lower-secondary level were postponed even after successful comprehensive experiments had been conducted. This produced the *Mittelstufenproblem*. Curricular development at the whole secondary level hardly occurred because of the unresolved questions at the lower-secondary level. The structural separation of general and vocational education continued at the upper-secondary level. Legal organization of schooling was pursued to the point where more and more people consider schools to be "over-regulated." When there were reforms, they were either forced by the pressure of worldwide developments (such as the "computing curriculum"), or conducted against the will of the persons concerned (such as the new organization of primary schools for ethnic minorities; Gstettner 1988). Alternatively, they took place on the "margins of the curriculum" (such as environmental education; Posch 1990b). In retrospect, the only major reform of the 1980s that stands out is the reorganization of the primary curriculum. In the early 1990s, however, the situation has changed. Major educational reforms have been initiated by the University Organization Act of 1993, by the *Fachhochschulstudiengesetz* which established a legal basis for nonuniversity postsecondary education, and by the 14th and 15th Amendments to the School Organization Bill which provided for the integration of the handicapped into mainstream schooling and for some curricular autonomy of schools.

11. Major Problems for the Year 2000

There is a growing grassroots movement among teachers undertaking local development in their classrooms. Their schools are increasingly networking themselves and voicing their experiences and aspirations (Altrichter et al. 1993). Some regional inservice institutions are supporting such local development initiatives through courses, consultancy, and cooperative projects (Rasch 1991). Groups of parents are more clearly formulating their demands and pushing the authorities to develop new policies, as in the case of integration of the handicapped (Meister-Steiner et al. 1989).

Both the Ministry for Education and the Arts and the Ministry for Science and Research have been taken over by new ministers who seem to be keen on initiating new developments in the area of university reform (BMWF 1991), in increasing financial support for environmental education (a field in which there are many local initiatives on the part of teachers), and in giving more autonomy to schools (Posch and Altrichter 1992a). Despite all of this, there are many challenges (Thonhauser 1992; Posch and Altrichter 1992b). Deregulation will only be successful if schools prepare themselves for tackling the new tasks, and if measures are taken to establish structures for in-school development and decision-making, to develop local support structures, and to strengthen teachers' professionality. The structural problems of the lower-secondary bracket can no longer be ignored. Reform in this field will have repercussions on teacher education. Increasing migration and possible membership in the European Union will require new efforts in intercultural education. To prepare for the growing complexity and speed of societal developments, it will be important both to encourage access to further and recurrent education by removing educational "dead-ends" and to establish more complex and dynamic cultures of learning which shift emphasis from knowledge reception to problem definition and solution and to the development of local knowledge (education for "dynamic qualities"; Posch 1990a).

See also: Germany

References

Altrichter H 1991 Schulevaluation als Anstoss zu autonomer Schulentwicklung? *Schulheft* 64:204–16
Altrichter H, Schratz M (eds.) 1992 *Qualität von Universitäten—Evaluation und Entwicklung.* Studien zur Bildungsforschung und Bildungspolitik, Vol. 5. Österreichischer StudienVerlag, Innsbruck
Altrichter H, Posch P, Somekh B 1993 *Teachers Investigating Their Work. An Introduction to the Methods of Action Research.* Routledge, London
BMUK 1993a *Österreichische Schulstatistik 92/93.* BMUK, Vienna
BMUK 1993b *Kenndaten des Österreichischen Schulwesens.* BMUK, Vienna
Bundesministerium für Unterricht, Kunst und Sport (BMUKS) 1990a *Österreichische Schulstatistik 89/90.* BMUKS, Vienna
BMUKS 1990b *Education in Austria.* BMUKS, Vienna
BMUKS 1990c *Bildungsforschung in Österreich 1987–88.* BMUKS, Vienna
Bundesministerium für Wissenschaft und Forschung (BMWF) 1990 *Hochschulbericht 1990* 2 Vols. BMWF, Vienna
BMWF 1991 *Die neue Universitätsstruktur—Reformkonzept.* BMWF, Vienna
Brezovich B 1990 *Schulrecht-kurz gefasst.* Trauner, Linz
CERI–INES 1991 *INES—General Assembly on International Educational Indicators—Education at a Glance.* OECD, Paris
Federal Press Service (FPS) 1990 *The Austrian Educational System.* Federal Chancellery, Vienna
Gruber H 1989 Gemeinsamer Unterricht behinderter und nichtbehinderter Kinder in Österreich—ein Situationsbericht. *Erziehung und Unterricht* 139 (5): 262–69
Gruber K H 1990 School reform and curriculum development: The Austrian experience. *The Curriculum Journal* 2 (3): 315–22
Gstettner P 1988 *Zwanghaft Deutsch?* Drava, Klagenfurt
Lassnigg L 1989 *Ausbildungen und Berufe in Österreich.* IHS, Vienna
Meister-Steiner B et al. (eds.) 1989 *Blinder Fleck und rosarote Brille.* Österreichischer Kulturverlag, Thaur
Österreichische Physikalische Gesellschaft (ÖPG) 1991 *Bericht der Kommission zur Evaluation der physikalischen Forschung in Österreich 1990/91.* ÖPG, Linz
Österreichische Statistisches Zentralamt (ÖSTZ) 1993 *Statistisches Handbuch für die Republik Österreich 1993.* ÖSTZ, Vienna

Posch P 1990a *Towards a New Culture of School Learning.* ARGE Umwelterziehung, Vienna
Posch P 1990b *Dynamic Qualities and Environmental Sensitivity in Education.* ARGE Umwelterziehung, Vienna
Posch P, Altrichter H 1992a *Schulautonomie in Österreich.* Bundesministerium für Unterricht und Kunst, Vienna
Posch P, Altrichter H 1992b *Entwicklungsperspektiven des österreichischen Bildungswesens.* Österreichischer StudienVerlag, Innsbruck
Rasch J 1991 Das Pilotprojekt "Offene Lernformen" in der Mittelstufe. *Erziehung und Unterricht* 145 (9): 721–25
Schratz M 1991 Von der Systemanalyse zur innovativen Bildungsarbeit. *Die Österreichische Volkshochschule* 42 (159): 1–6
Thonhauser J 1992 Erziehung und Bildung. In: Mantl W (ed.) 1992 *Politik in Österreich. Die Zweite Republik: Bestand und Wandel.* Böhlau, Vienna

Further Reading

BMUKS 1990d *Kenndaten des österreichischen Schulwesens 1989/90.* BMUKS, Vienna
BMUKS 1990e *Austria: Development of Education: 1988–90.* BMUKS, Vienna
Dermutz S 1983 *Der österreichische Weg. Schulreform und Bildungspolitik in der Zweiten Republik.* Verlag für Gesellschaftskritik, Vienna
Österreichische Raumordungskonferenz (ÖROK) 1990 *Bevölkerungsprognose II.* ÖROK, Vienna

Bahamas

M. McLean

1. General Background

The Bahamas is the wealthiest of the independent states of the Caribbean, yet its economy has precarious foundations. Its population is small but its land area is widely dispersed. Cultural, political, and economic life has been strongly influenced first by Britain and more recently by the United States. The education system has been shaped by these conditions. Its future development is constrained by their continuing impact. The provision of schooling is relatively well-developed outside the remoter islands though postcompulsory and higher education suffers from problems of smallness. The achievement of the aims of education is weakened by the growth of forms of wealth creation in which the majority of the population do not participate and by a failure to develop a powerful sense of Bahamian cultural identity.

The Commonwealth of the Bahamas comprises an archipelago of about 700 islands and more than 2,000 cays and rocks stretching over 750 kilometers, yet having a land area of a little under 14,000 square kilometers. The proximity of its extremes to the Florida coast of the United States in the north, to Cuba in the southwest, and to Haiti in the southeast has had an impact on economic and foreign affairs. Of the 29 islands/island groups which are inhabited, Andros occupies over 40 percent of the total land area but the smaller territories of New Providence, Grand Bahama, Great Abaco, and Eleuthra are of equal or greater importance. The subtropical climate and island geography have helped the Bahamas to be a center of agriculture, fishing, and trade for much of its modern history.

The population in 1990 was about 255,000, of whom 172,000 inhabited the capital city of Nassau—which comprises most of the population of New Providence Island. Of the other islands, only Grand Bahama (41,000), Great Abaco (10,000), Andros and Eleuthra (each 8,000) have populations over 3,000. A population density of 18.7 per square kilometer indicates a sparseness which is most marked outside New Providence. The urban–rural distribution (59:41) reinforces this distinction. Educational provision for the people outside New Providence faces problems of size and dispersal.

The average annual population growth rate was 3.4 percent between 1970–80 and 1.9 percent between 1980–89. This relatively high growth by Caribbean standards was accounted for in part by immigration into a prosperous country. Birthrates at 20 per 1000 in 1989 were below those of other countries of the region. The equation of low economic expansion and high population growth which has restricted proper educational provision in other nonindustrial countries has not seriously affected the Bahamas.

Ethnic, linguistic, and religious structures are similar to those of other anglophone Caribbean countries. The ethnic composition has been described as 72 percent Black, 14 percent mixed, and 13 percent White. English is the official language and that of prevalent use, though creole versions are well-established. Most people profess Christianity apart from small Jewish and Muslim communities. The main religious affiliations are Baptist (31 %), Anglican (20 %), Roman Catholic (19 %), Methodist (6 %), and Church of God (6 %). The country benefits from the lack of acute cultural cleavages.

The occupational structure is oriented toward service industries. Over 40 percent of the working population has been employed in activities related to tourism compared with 14 percent in industry and 4 percent in agriculture and fisheries. There is still a division between a working population concentrated on service occupations in the main population centers and a traditional agricultural way of life in remoter areas. The unemployment rate of 12 percent is high, but not untypical of Caribbean countries. Government policy has emphasized the development of the agricultural sector to counter reliance on food imports and the expansion of light industries to supplement the growth of the construction industry which was stimulated by the demand for a tourist infrastructure of hotels and harbors. These policy imperatives are reflected in educational planning.

The economy of the Bahamas has been one of the most successful in the Caribbean in the second half of the twentieth century. The per capita Gross Domestic Product (GDP) in 1989 of US $11,370 was by far the highest among independent states of the region and compared with US $6,370 in Barbados, US $3,230 in Trinidad and Tobago, and US $1,260 in Jamaica. Economic growth was high in the 1970s and early 1980s but declined at the end of the 1980s to less than 1 percent per capita per annum.

The Bahamian economy has combined commerce and primary production throughout its history. Tourism dominates the economy and contributed over 50 percent of GDP in the mid-1980s. It is a major employer and stimulates capital projects. The government has invested heavily in this sector and educational provision takes account of this growth. While tourist arrivals, mainly from the United States, are expected to increase in the 1990s, the industry is vulnerable to rapid changes in demand affected particularly by economic changes in the sender countries. Other commercial and service industries have less impact on employment. The banking sector grew substantially in the 1980s as the Bahamas became a tax haven and offshore financial center. The Bahamas has a large open registry merchant shipping fleet which brings financial rewards. The unofficial economy of illegal drug-trafficking, in which the many islands provide staging posts for imports into the United States, and of facilitation of tax evasion has blighted Bahamian political, financial, and social life.

Traditional primary sector production of sugar and bananas has been replaced by a concentration on exports of tomatoes and subtropical fruits, crustaceans, and timber. Agricultural production has changed in the 1980s, through government initiative, to reduce dependence on imported foodstuffs. Plans to diversify agricultural production for both export and home consumption have relevance for educational development.

The pattern of industry changed in the 1980s. Petroleum refining, which was a mainstay of the industry, almost ceased in 1985 while mineral extraction (chalk, salt, argonite) also declined. Petroleum transhipment remains important while processing industries, notably rum, have grown. The major growth in the late 1980s was construction related to the tourist industry. The government has also tried to encourage the development of light industries.

Overall, the economy of the Bahamas is successful but fragile. Foreign debt has been low (16% of total debt). The trade surplus is produced by services rather than goods. Inflation averaged around 6 percent between 1980 and 1990. Yet there is overdependence upon tourism, while the illegal activities of the drug trade and some financial dealings threaten the stability of the whole society.

Education may play a major part in developing new economic activities but it still responds mainly to occupational opportunities in the established service industries. A shift to manufacturing and commercial agriculture will require the development of effective education and training. These priorities are accepted in official policy. There is less financial constraint on their achievement than in similar countries. Whether broader social and educational values can adapt is more questionable.

Political structures and goals reflect the history of a country which gained Independence from the United Kingdom in 1973. Though Spanish occupation followed Christopher Columbus's landing on the islands in 1492, which led to the transportation of indigenous inhabitants to other islands, the Bahamas were settled by British colonists and their slaves from Carolina and Jamaica in the mid-seventeenth century. British loyalists and their slaves swelled the population after the American War of Independence. A plantation slave economy survived until the 1830s and British landowners retained social and political dominance well into the twentieth century.

Representative parliamentary institutions were established by the British settlers, but political authority was in the hands of United Kingdom colonial officials until 1964, when the local assembly gained legislative power. The governor, appointed by the government of the United Kingdom, retained executive power until 1973.

A United Kingdom-style parliamentary government was established at Independence and remains in force. The Prime Minister and Cabinet are appointed by the Governor General, who is chosen by the United Kingdom government, but require the support of the House of Assembly, which is elected by popular franchise. The Constitution also provides for a nominated Senate and independent judiciary.

The Progressive Liberal Party (PLP) has held the largest number of seats in the House of Assembly since the 1960s. In the 1987 election, the PLP won 31 of the 49 seats. Its leader—Sir Lyndon O Pindling—became prime minister in 1962, an office he continued to occupy into the 1990s. There has been a high degree of political stability since the 1960s, marred only by a number of scandals in the late 1980s over political and official corruption as well as involvement in the drugs trade. In the 1990s, drug-trafficking has been less pronounced and there has been greater cooperation in attacks upon it with the United States authorities.

Political stability and authority has allowed the government to take an active role in economic and social affairs. There is intervention to encourage investment in tourism, and in agriculture and industry. Education is largely public and is seen by the government to have a significant role in overall development.

2. Politics and the Goals of the Education System

Education has not been high on the agenda of political debate since the mid-1970s. The major reconsideration of educational aims occurred in the mid-1970s when political independence and new social and economic goals had an impact on the declared objectives of education. The 1962 Education Act had declared the aims of education to be:

> to enable the children of the Bahamas to understand their privileges and responsibilities as members of the community, to contribute to the progress and well-being of the country by the full development of their natural abilities, and to earn an adequate livelihood as adults.

This statement reflected older and relatively unambitious colonial views of education.

The achievement of political independence was associated with the statement of expanded and more dynamic educational aims. The 1973 White Paper on Education emphasized individual-centered aims of equality of educational opportunity; extension of provision for citizens with physical, emotional, or intellectual handicaps; and the expansion of community-wide education for young people and adults for personal and social development. Society-centered aims stressed the contribution of education to the development of the labor force of the country; "the encouragement of a knowledgeable appreciation of the physical environment and the social and cultural heritage of the Bahamas"; and "the encouragement of the choice and acceptance of those ideals of conduct and endeavour that are valued by a Christian and democratic society." The educational objectives were to take account of appropriate developments in the methods and resources for teaching and learning.

Broadly these aims have been retained in the 1980s and 1990s. Schooling is the means by which individuals can gain opportunities for social advancement. Education should encourage an awareness of the cultural tradition of the independent state. Education is seen to be integral to the development of the economy so that plans for the development of technical and vocational education have been linked to economic policy on the expansion of the tourist industry as well as improved agriculture and new kinds of manufacture.

Debate about the purposes of education has not been pronounced since the 1970s partly because the Progressive Liberal Party has held political power since the first full elections in 1967. The opposition Free National Movement has focused upon charges of corruption of ministers and officials and their links with drug-related financial activities in the 1980s. As a consequence, education has not been the center of much debate.

The official aims of education may be challenged informally by two forces. First is the continued influence of churches through their schools and, second, the growth of private education. Church schools provide an alternative view to the materialism which has overtaken Bahamian life. Both church and private schools take their standards from those of the United Kingdom and, particularly, North America. The goal for parents and their children, where resources permit, is to gain entry to institutions of higher education in the United States. Individual aims of education are conditioned by these demands.

3. The Formal System of Education

3.1 Primary, Secondary, and Tertiary Education

The basic structure of education in the Bahamas is shown in Fig. 1. Education consists of six years primary education for children aged 5–11; three years of lower-secondary schooling for the 11–14 age group; and three years of upper-secondary education for those aged 14–17. A variety of postsecondary courses are offered at the College of the Bahamas and in the University of West Indies extramural department, but conventional full higher education is not available in the country.

Schooling has been compulsory in the Bahamas for children aged 5–14 since the Education Act of 1877. Participation rates have been high for many years. Almost all children are in school between the ages of 5–15. Over 70 percent of the age group completes

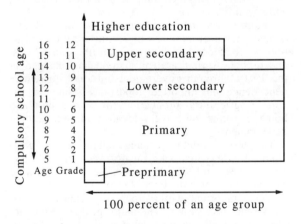

Figure 1

Bahamas: Structure of the formal education system

the full secondary school course. A majority of those succeeding in secondary schooling enter the College of the Bahamas or other forms of higher education.

In 1990 there were 101 primary schools with 25,452 students and 37 junior and senior high schools with 23,502 students. However, there were still 86 all-age schools with 10,739 pupils found mainly in the islands outside New Providence. In these remoter communities, participation in education is much more limited.

Obstacles to student progress within the school structure have been reduced since the early 1970s with the introduction of common secondary schools. Previously there had been academic secondary education, provided largely by voluntary religious organizations and modeled on the grammar schools of England. When a comprehensive system was introduced, the barriers to opportunity were lowered. While a system of selection from junior to senior high schools has been introduced, student dropout before the completion of full secondary schooling has been associated with social factors and, in the Family Islands outside New Providence, with the lack of accessible senior high schools which are often boarding institutions. There is very little difference between male and female rates of participation at any level of education in the Bahamas. Private as well as government-aided voluntary religious schools still provide over 20 per cent of school places. Private schools often give enhanced opportunities for educational and social advancement.

The main barrier to student advancement through the education system is at the end of the senior secondary course. Less than one-fourth of the students who complete this stage will gain the qualifications needed for more advanced general education. The retention of the University of London General Certificate of Education Ordinary-level (GCE O-level) examination as the terminal and selective qualification contributes to this high level of attrition.

The College of the Bahamas, with 2,051 students in 1990, provides a diversity of courses. It has parallels with community colleges in the United States except that students enter at the age of 17 with six rather than seven years of secondary schooling. The College was created in 1974 by amalgamating two teacher-training colleges, a technical college, and an upper-secondary school. It provides both general and vocational courses. The two-year associate degree in arts, science, and social science comprises the general element and is followed by around a quarter of all students. Teacher and nursing training are important though the industrial programs have been more limited. The largest number of students follow business studies programs including secretarial courses and those related to the tourist industry.

The Nassau branch of the University of the West Indies provides part-time courses to degree level in hotel management, tourism, and teacher education. The universities of Miami and St John's, New York

also validate studies in the College of the Bahamas. On completion of studies at the College, students may go on to higher level courses at the University of the West Indies in other Caribbean countries. A large number of Bahamian students pursue higher education in other countries, notably the United States. In 1989, there were 1,746 Bahamian students in higher education institutions in a number of foreign countries. Of this total, 1,480 studied in the United States, 219 in Canada, and 44 in the United Kingdom. The lack of capacity to provide higher education beyond the first level remains one of the weaknesses of the education system of the Bahamas. As a consequence, higher education at the more advanced levels, and the research associated with it, is not related specifically to Bahamian needs. Though there is little apparent discrimination against women, who form over half the students at the College of the Bahamas, some social groups will be able to gain particular advantage in gaining access to fee-paying higher education in other countries.

3.2 Preschool Education

Preschool education is not widely available and is the responsibility of private agencies.

3.3 Special Education

Education for children with special educational needs has been very limited. In 1990 there were five schools, largely private, with 268 students.

3.4 Vocational, Technical, and Business Education

Vocational education is concentrated on the College of the Bahamas. The emphasis in government policy since the 1980s on developing the infrastructure of the tourist industry is connected with the expansion of courses and students at the College related to tourism. A training college for the tourist and hotel industry was planned to open in 1992. However, the weight given in government policy to the development of light industry and commercial agriculture has not been matched by a growth of related technical courses which have had small numbers of students. In 1987 there were 103 graduates (at associate degree level or below) in commercial and business courses, 66 in education, and 108 in general education, but only 66 in engineering, craft, agricultural, and health-related courses.

3.5 Adult and Nonformal Education

Adult education has had a social and cultural rather than a basic or literacy education function since participation rates in formal schooling have been high for many years. There have been established traditions of inquiry into the history, social patterns, and language of the Bahamas which can inform such cultural courses though such research is often published outside the country.

4. Administrative and Supervisory Structure and Operation

Control of state education is concentrated on the Ministry of Education and Culture in Nassau which implements legislation passed by the House of Assembly. The Ministry provides resources for government schools and grants to independent schools. It appoints teachers, determines the curriculum and controls the junior secondary examinations. Senior secondary examinations still are linked to the University of London in the United Kingdom while American universities, as well as the University of the West Indies, have influence over the content and examination of higher education courses.

The system is highly centralized. There are no representative regional or local bodies. There is some concern about the control of schooling by commissioners of the central government in the outer islands and some demand for devolution of power to these remoter communities.

5. Educational Finance

Recurrent expenditure on education by the state was around 22 percent of total government spending in 1987. This proportion has been fairly constant since the late 1970s. Before Independence, in 1970, the percentage was 19. The proportion of gross domestic product spent by government on education rose from 4.9 percent in 1970 to 8.2 percent in 1978. It declined to 4.1 percent in 1987. Government spending per student at all levels of education was around US$1,500 in 1987. There were also substantial private contributions through fees to private schools. While the expansion of spending in the 1970s on education has not been maintained, government per capita expenditure is high by Caribbean standards.

6. Supplying Personnel for the Education System

There were 1,409 teachers in primary schools and 1,555 in secondary schools in 1986. The number of primary school teachers declined in the 1980s but there was an increase in secondary school teachers over the same period. The pupil–teacher ratio in primary schools improved from almost 25:1 in 1975 to around 18:1 in the mid-1980s. Since then the figure has risen to about 20:1. The increase in numbers of teachers

allowed the pupil–teacher ratio in secondary schools to fall from 27:1 in 1980 to 19:1 in 1986.

Though these figures indicate a reasonable provision of teachers in relation to the wealth of the society they also hide a number of disparities. There are considerable numbers of unqualified or underqualified teachers, notably in the areas outside New Providence Island where pupil–teacher ratios may vary markedly. The level of education and training of both primary and secondary school teachers is not high for reasons connected with the availability of higher level education. Well-educated and qualified teachers will have received their training outside the country or may be expatriates which poses difficulties in linking teacher training to local conditions.

There are two forms of teacher education available in the Bahamas. The Certificate of Teaching course lasts three years and is provided by the College of the Bahamas. The level of the course is not high since the entry qualification of the Bahamas Junior Certificate is mainly acquired at the end of the junior high school course and the academic standard of teacher education is not seen as much beyond upper-secondary level. A total of 37 students graduated from this course in 1989, which was hardly sufficient to replace natural wastage in the teaching force.

The more advanced three-year Bachelor of Education course for serving teachers has been run jointly by the College of the Bahamas and the University of the West Indies Faculty of Education. However the emphasis in the BEd is to enhance the general education or subject knowledge of teachers rather than their wider understanding of educational processes.

The problems of raising teacher quality are likely to remain perennial in view of the limited provision of higher education in a country with a small and scattered population.

7. Curriculum Development and Teaching Methodology

The school curriculum is decided centrally by the Ministry of Education. A curriculum division in the Ministry is charged with curriculum reform. The compulsory subjects in primary and lower-secondary schools are religious education, English, mathematics, science, social studies, physical education, and a practical subject (woodwork, technical drawing, home economics, or agriculture). Denominational grant-aided schools have their own religious education courses. There is also some provision for modern languages, especially Spanish, and for art and music.

The curriculum for upper-secondary schools permits more student choice in preparation for subject-centered Ordinary- and, sometimes, Advanced-level examinations of the General Certificate of Education of the

University of London. Traditional academic subjects prevail, though the government has urged more attention to technical and vocational subjects. Furthermore, there is an emphasis upon arts subjects and biology and a neglect of other sciences. In 1991, there were 2,594 candidates for GCE O-level English Language, 1,181 for Religious Studies, 995 for English Literature, 865 for History, and 865 for Human Biology, but only 288 for Chemistry and 263 for Physics.

Though the official curriculum is uniform for the country, many schools and pupils do not have access to all subjects especially in the physical sciences, foreign languages, and practical areas because of the lack of necessary equipment or qualified teachers. Students in many senior secondary schools prepare for examinations in a small number of subjects in which their schools can offer adequate teaching.

Textbooks and other learning materials have to be imported to a considerable degree especially from North America and the United Kingdom. This is an outcome of the small size of the system of education and is difficult to overcome. There are shortages of appropriate books and materials in a number of subjects.

8. *The System of Examinations, Promotions, and Certifications*

Students pass automatically through the grades of schooling. There are two types of school examination. The Bahamas Junior Certificate examination is entirely local in control and management. It is taken at the end of junior high schools (Grade 9) or in the first grade of senior high schools (Grade 10). A number of students leave school after this stage or enter other courses. Students may enter for differing numbers of subjects and are awarded certificates indicating the subjects which they have passed. English, mathematics, and religious education remain the most popular subjects.

The senior high school course leads to the General Certificate of Education (Ordinary level) of London University. This is also an academic examination with possibilities for students to enter and be awarded passes in individual subjects which may discourage study of vocational areas and also the peripheral general education subjects. The GCE is a barrier to higher education since passes with grades A–C in five subjects are needed for entry to higher education. In 1991, the proportions of candidates gaining these grades were 33 percent in English language, 20 percent in mathematics, 29 percent in English literature, 24 percent in biology, and 16 percent in religious studies. A high proportion of students are debarred from general higher education by this examination. However, the traditions of the GCE in England and Wales support high failure rates and, in 1991, less that 50 percent of

students in the United Kingdom achieved five passes at grades A–C in the equivalent General Certificate of Secondary Education (GCSE) examination. A small number of students (51 in 1991) sit for the Advanced-level GCE which is the normal requirement for entry to higher education in the United Kingdom.

9. *Major Problems for the Year 2000*

By the standards of many parts of the Caribbean, the system of education in the Bahamas is highly developed. Universal primary and lower-secondary education has been almost achieved. Expenditure on education is relatively high. However, since the early 1980s, neither participation rates nor expenditure have increased significantly. One danger in the system is that of stagnation because of a fairly high plateau of achievement.

The major problems are experienced at the apex of the education pyramid rather than at its base, but it should not be forgotten that there is a lack of even provision of educational opportunities at all levels in the peripheral islands. The proportions of the relevant age groups proceeding to postsecondary education are low and all full higher education has to take place outside the country. These deficiencies percolate down to the school system. There are no sufficiently qualified teachers in a wide range of specialisms including sciences and vocational subjects. There is an insufficient base of qualified people located in institutions within the country to give a distinctive Bahamian character to the curriculum, to textbooks and other learning materials, and to examinations. As a result, the Bahamas remains dependent upon foreign educational influences.

These problems have geographical and demographic roots. The population is too small to create a fully autonomous education system. Issues remain of how to control and channel the inevitable influences of foreign countries so that they are consistent with a national vision of educational development. The Bahamas has a further problem, not experienced by more compact Caribbean countries of similar population size, of providing educational opportunities for the minority of the people who live on remote and lightly populated islands. These problems have been chronic and their solutions are not easily devised.

Bibliography

Evans H 1989 Teachers and their preparation in the Western Caribbean and the Bahamas. Paper presented to the Caribbean Consultation on Education for All, Kingston, Jamaica

Lewis G K 1968 *The Growth of the Modern West Indies*. Monthly Review Press, New York

Ministry of Education and Culture 1973 *Focus on the Future: White Paper on Education*. Ministry of Education and Culture, Nassau

University of London Examinations and Assessment Council 1992 *General Certificate of Education Statistics 1991–1992.* University of London, London

Williams C 1982 *The Methodist Contribution to Education in the Bahamas.* Alan Sutton, Gloucester

Bahrain

N. Wahbe, L. Almannai and A. Almotawa

1. General Background

Bahrain is located 24 kilometers off the east coast of the kingdom of Saudi Arabia and a little further from Qatar. It consists of 33 islands. The capital, Manama, is situated on the main and largest island, Bahrain. The total land area is only 700 square kilometers. Bahrain is populated mainly by Arabs, originally from the Arabian peninsula.

After Bahrain gained its independence from Britain in 1971, state policy concentrated on establishing its infrastructure. Neither the size of the population nor its structure facilitated the achievement of this goal. Therefore, a qualified labor force was recruited from Arab and non-Arab countries. Hence, the growth of the total population is mainly a result of the large immigration of expatriates to Bahrain since 1971. The population was 350,798 in 1981 and, of these, 68 percent were Bahrainis. In 1991 the population was 508,037, with 63.6 percent Bahrainis. The majority of expatriates are males between the ages of 20 and 50 years and represented nearly 51 percent of the total expatriate population in 1991. Foreign nationals enjoy the freedom to practice their religion and to establish their own schools.

Nearly 41 percent of Bahrainis are under the age of 15, a fact which strongly influences the development of education. It also has a significant implication for the allocation of resources to education, as it is state policy to provide free education for Bahraini children.

All Bahrainis are Muslim and their language is Arabic. The English language is widely used and plays an important role in daily activities, especially in business. Therefore, starting from the 4th grade of primary school, English as a foreign language is taught at all levels of formal education.

Bahrain has a monarchical political system. It is an emirate. The Emir is from the Al-Khalifa family, which has governed Bahrain since 1770.

Pearls were the main source of income for the country before 1930. However, it lost a great deal of the market as a result of the advent of Japanese artificial pearls. The discovery of oil in 1932 contributed greatly to the economy and created many job opportunities, both in quarrying and oil refining and in other services. Government policy aims at establishing a broad commercial and industrial market. The strategic location of Bahrain in the middle of routes between Europe, the Far East, and Australia has contributed to reviving the economy, particularly in the two sectors of communications and services. The effect of this policy has been reflected in the share of oil, industries, and services in the gross national product (GNP) since 1975. The first has declined from 31 to 27 percent in the period 1975 to 1990, while industries have risen from 15 to 19 percent and services from 33 to 36 percent in the same period. Nearly 24 percent of the total labor force in 1991 was employed in the community, social, and personal services. Manufacturing industries employed nearly 16 percent, while the other 55 percent worked in service industries such as transport, construction, wholesale and retail trade, communications, and finance. The latest figures show that nearly 5 percent of the labor force worked in the educational sector.

2. Politics and the Goals of the Education System

Educational policy and goals are influenced and dictated mainly by Islam, the Constitution, and the requirements of development. In the state schools, the Ministry of Education ensures that all plans are drawn within the framework of the above criteria. In addition, the Ministry of Education ensures that the policy, objectives, and plans of the private schools do not conflict with national policy. At the higher education level, the University of Bahrain and the Arabian Gulf University design their policies independently. However, the Ministry of Education supervises their policies indirectly by having the Minister of Education as chairman of the board of trustees of both universities, and by having the president of the university nominated by the government.

Educational policy concentrates on three factors:

(a) Education for all: Although education is not compulsory, the Ministry of Education always emphasizes that every child has an equal opportunity to obtain education and to have access to all educational levels. This is confirmed by the fact that free education is offered to all children as well as free transportation to and from school and free textbooks.

(b) Quality of education : Since 1980 special emphasis has been placed on teacher education and training with a view to improving the standard of teaching. Major reforms in the content of education and teaching methods have also been introduced. In addition, several measures have been taken to link informal and formal education, especially in terms of content, evaluation, and equivalence.

(c) Linking education with the requirements of the job market: The expatriate labor force is, in many occupations, a real competitor to the national labor force. Therefore, official manpower planning concentrates on the Bahrainization of the relevant professions. The Ministry of Education plays an important role in this respect, particularly when awarding scholarships to higher education. Furthermore, educational planning has increased the capacity of technical education and links the curricula with the requirements of the labor market where possible.

3. The Formal System of Education

3.1 Primary, Secondary, and Tertiary Education

There are three types of schools in Bahrain:

(a) State Schools. These schools are totally financed by the state and provide free education for all children. Boys and girls have separate schools at each level. Subjects are taught in Arabic except for foreign languages such as English and French. In 1993–94 there were 167 public schools with approximately 106,599 students and 6,002 teachers.

(b) National Private Schools. These are coeducational and provide the national curriculum either comprehensively or as a major component of their curriculum. The Arabic language is taught to every student. Full fees are payable which range between US$1,300 and US$4,400 per annum. In 1993–94, there were six national private schools, which had 3,848 students and 304 teachers.

(c) Foreign Private Schools. These are owned by foreign societies in Bahrain and provide their own national programs. The Arabic language is compulsory for Arab students. Fees range between US$260 and US$10,000 per annum. In 1993–94 there were 25 schools, with 18,806 students of different nationalities, and 1,178 teachers.

Formal education in Bahrain was initiated in 1919. The first primary school for boys was established by a number of Bahrainis who contributed financially to the school. The school also received some assistance from the government. It was run by a public education committee and adopted the curriculum of other Arab

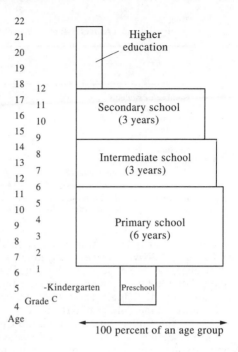

Figure 1

Bahrain: Structure of the formal education system 1993–94

countries. In 1928, the first formal primary school for girls was opened. However, it was not until 1930 that the government took over the administration of these schools. The first secondary school for boys was established in 1939 and for girls in 1952.

In the 1990s, formal schooling in Bahrain extends over 12 years and is divided into three main levels—primary (6 years), intermediate (3 years), and secondary (3 years). Figure 1 shows the structure of the formal educational system in Bahrain, and Table 1 presents student enrollments at school. The school year runs from mid-September to the end of June. Students at all levels attend school for 172 days per year. The school day for the first three grades lasts five hours, whereas it lasts six hours for the next three primary grades, and the intermediate and secondary levels. In 1993–94 there were 53,446 Bahraini children attending primary schools, 4.5 percent of whom were enrolled in private schools.

Almost all students who complete the primary level of education continue studying at the intermediate level. In 1993–94 the enrollment of Bahraini students at this level was 27,011 students, of whom 2.2 percent were enrolled in private schools. The secondary school system in Bahrain comprises three main sections: general, commercial, and technical. General education comprises arts, sciences, and applied science sections.

Higher education in Bahrain is available in several separate institutes:

Table 1
Enrollments and resources in formal education Bahrain 1993–94

	Primary	Intermediate	Secondary	Higher education[a]
Number of students	61,359	27,114	21,679	7,787[b]
Percentage of age-group enrolled				—
6–11	97			
12–14		80		
15–17			75	
Number of institutions	97	44[c]	25[d]	4
Student–teacher ratio	20:1	17:1	12:1	8:1
Cost per student per annum (BD)[e]	400	470	600–1400	—

a 1992–93   b Includes 638 postgraduate students   c Includes 19 schools primary–intermediate   d Includes 3 schools intermediate–secondary   e Bahraini Dinar equal to US$2.6 in 1994

(a) The University of Bahrain, which was formally established in 1986 when two existing colleges—the University College of Sciences, Arts, and Education and the Gulf Polytechnic—joined together. The University of Bahrain comprises five colleges as follows: the College of Arts, the College of Sciences, the College of Education, the College of Engineering, and the College of Business Administration. The total numbers of students enrolled in these colleges in 1993–94 were 2,861 males and 3,898 females, with a faculty of about 448 members.

(b) The College of Health Sciences was established in 1976 under the supervision of the Ministry of Health. It awards an associate degree in Health Sciences and a BSc in Nursing. In 1993–94, the total number of students enrolled in the college was 606, with a staff of 97 teachers.

(c) The Gulf University was formally established by the Gulf States in 1980. It is regarded as a distinctive university which emphasizes quality rather than quantity of education and concentrates on educational research and graduate education. It comprises three main colleges: the College of Medicine and Medical Sciences, the College of Applied Sciences, and the College of Education.

3.2 Preschool Education

Children under 6 years of age can attend privately owned kindergartens. Kindergarten institutions are classified as either: those owned by individuals or by philanthropic societies (e.g., women's societies, the Red Crescent Society, and religious bodies), or those attached to private schools.

In 1993–94 there were 80 kindergartens in the country serving nearly 7,765 children of different nationalities, 95 percent of whom were Bahrainis. There were 552 kindergarten teachers. The Ministry of Education is responsibile for supervising the kindergartens. This includes the location and design of kindergarten buildings, the objectives of the educational programs, and the professional level of the administrators and the teachers. Fees do not exceed US$520 per annum in the kindergartens owned by individuals or by philanthropic societies, though it reaches more than US$3,100 per annum at the kindergartens attached to private schools.

3.3 Special Education

There are three main institutes that offer special education for the handicapped in Bahrain:

(a) The Rehabilitation Center is financed and operated by the Ministry of Labor and Social Affairs. It serves mentally handicapped children as well as those who have impaired hearing. In 1993–94, there were 137 children enrolled at the Center.

(b) The Hope Institute for Handicapped Children was founded and is operated by a private society to serve the mentally handicapped between the ages of 6 and 15. The Institute receives financial assistance from the Ministry of Labor and Social Affairs, and from some private agencies. The program consists of both academic and professional training. Total enrollment in 1993–94 was 132 children.

(c) The Blind Institute was established in 1974 as a regional institute by the Middle East Committee for Welfare of the Blind. Children attending the Institute benefit from all residential facilities including accommodation, catering, clothing, medical treatment, and social care. The educational program includes an academic and a professional training component extending over 9 years. Students enrolled in 1993–94 numbered 96.

3.4 Vocational, Technical, and Business Education

Vocational education in Bahrain can be traced back to 1936 when the first industrial school for boys was opened. Vocational education comprises two sectors: technical (for boys only) and commercial (for girls and boys). The number of students has grown significantly since 1980. There were 6,078 students enrolled in 1993–94, whereas enrollment was only 2,749 in 1980–81. The Ministry of Labor has a training center which offers courses in several vocational subjects. It accepts all persons from the age of 12 up to 25 who have either graduated from intermediate level, or abandoned formal education. The expenditure at this center was nearly US$4,466,880 in 1993, while the number of students was 2,782. The Ministry of Information supervises the Hotel and Catering Training Center. It was established in 1974 with the object of the Bahrainization of the hotel sector. In 1993–94 there were 253 students enrolled in the Center with a staff of 23 teachers. In addition to this, the Institute of Banking and Finance provides inservice education in the banking sector and Batelco Training College provides inservice education in the telecommunications sector.

3.5 Adult and Nonformal Education

The Ministry of Education is responsible for literacy programs. In 1991, the illiteracy rate was 15.9 percent of the total Bahraini population (age 10 and above). The policy of literacy was reconsidered during the 1980s. It changed in terms of approach, curricula, financing, and attracting partnership in illiteracy actions. The Ministry of Education also provides adult programs in the English language, office practice, and the learning of Arabic as a foreign language. In 1993–94, there were 71 enrolled in such programs.

In 1994 there were more than 32 private educational agencies and institutes in Bahrain which provide various types of training such as: computing, management, secretarial studies, music, painting, photography, and languages. The University of Bahrain provides continuing education programs, which include higher education in business administration and engineering. There were nearly 300 students enrolled in 1993–94 from both public and private sectors.

4. Administrative and Supervisory Structure and Operation

The Ministry of Education recruits, appoints, and upgrades teachers in public schools. It is also responsible for supplying equipment, textbooks, transportation, and any other requirements to all schools. The Ministry uses curriculum specialists to supervise and direct the learning process within the schools. These specialists play an important role in linking schools and their concerns with the relevant official offices. Different committees within the Ministry have also a considerable power over organizing and directing schools' performance. These committees represent a form of

democracy and cooperation between the official departments in the Ministry. The University of Bahrain faculty is represented on some of these committees. Teachers are also invited to participate as regular members at some committees. There are nearly 15 committees with different professional and organizational functions. A new organizational approach has introduced a scheme whereby the school is considered as an independent educational unit. It aims particularly at promoting democratic practice within the schools. Though an administrative board or council represents the administrators and teachers, the board is mainly responsible for planning, supervision, and control of the educational and organizational policy of the school.

The University of Bahrain and the Gulf University enjoy relative autonomy and independence from the Ministry of Education. The policy of the universities is monitored by the University Council.

5. Educational Finance

Expenditure on education has risen significantly in the last 30 years. Only 1.2 million Bahrain Dinars (BD) was devoted to education in 1960. This had increased to BD70.4 million in 1994. In the 1960s and 1970s the educational budget was 20 percent of the state budget and 6.7 percent of the gross national product (GNP). This proportion has declined to 11 percent of the state budget and to 4 percent of GNP. This has been nearly constant since 1980. The primary level receives nearly 50 percent of the total educational budget, whereas the other 50 percent is distributed among the intermediate (24%) and secondary levels: general 13 percent, commercial 6 percent, and technical 7 percent. The higher education budget was nearly BD9 million for the University of Bahrain and BD1.2 million for the College of Health Sciences. Some private industries contribute continuously to financing higher education, and in 1990 a grant of BD53,000 was offered to the University of Bahrain by 5 such institutions.

6. Supplying Personnel for the Education System

In 1994, there were 6,623 full-time teachers working in public schools at all formal levels. Approximately 16.2 percent of male teachers and 7.1 percent of female teachers were non-Bahrainis. There is a shortage of Bahraini teachers in specific subjects, mainly English, science, mathematics, and technical subjects. Such positions are mostly filled by Egyptians. About 31 percent of Bahraini teachers hold associate diplomas in education, 50 percent BEd (Arts or Sciences) degrees, and the others (19%) had BA or BSc degrees. Teachers have to teach 22 periods per week at the primary level and 20 periods per week at the intermediate and secondary levels. All teachers and educators enjoy a special salaries' cadre, which awards an allowance of about 15 percent more than the normal occupations' cadre. Annual promotion is given to teachers over three categories of grades. Higher grade categories are restricted to senior teachers and administrators. Teachers can be promoted to the grade of senior teachers or administrators according to merit and seniority. At the beginning of the 1990s, the Ministry of Education was considering providing a wider scale of promotion within the teaching profession.

Teacher training is mainly undertaken at the University of Bahrain. The University of Bahrain, in cooperation with the Ministry of Education, organizes a special preservice program for the class–teacher system (one main teacher for each class). The length of the program is four academic years and it is financed by the Ministry of Education. Students attending this program are granted a scholarship and are obliged to teach, upon graduation, in the first three grades of the primary level. A diploma of education is awarded by the University of Bahrain mainly to two kinds of students: those holding BA or BSc degrees and intending to be employed as teachers, and those appointed in public schools but without any educational qualification. The latter enjoy a full scholarship from the Ministry of Education and a full salary.

Inservice training programs, workshops, and regular seminars are carried on continuously within the Ministry of Education. Private schools are responsible for the appointment of teachers, but the Ministry of Education is responsible for determining and supervising teachers' qualifications.

7. Curriculum Development and Teaching Methodology

Until the 1960s, the adopted curriculum in public schools was associated with the curricula in other Arab countries, mainly Egypt. Since the 1970s, the Ministry of Education has been involved in establishing a national curriculum. This has been done through the Department of Curriculum which achieved directorate status in 1975. The process of curriculum development for all grade levels begins and ends in the Department of Curriculum. In accordance to the general aims of education, the general objectives as well as the more specific learning skills are determined by specialized subcommittees within the Department of Curriculum. All concerned parties, inside or outside the Ministry of Education, are systematically consulted about the subject. The objectives of a project as well as the proposing of skills, syllabus, and contents which might embody them should, however, gain approval from a higher curriculum committee. Total legitimacy is gained with final approval from the Higher Committee of Education.

Once the approval has been gained, the specialists in the Department of Curriculum commence, on the one

hand, to try the new curriculum in the field and, on the other hand, to train all the teachers who are involved. The Educational Research and Development Center is sometimes called upon to ensure that the national examinations assess what was intended to have been learned by the students. Curricula are common to all public schools. The curriculum covers the Arabic language, mathematics, science, social studies, English language, fine arts, physical education, and music. Except for English language, all subjects are taught in the Arabic language. During the first three primary grades, the curriculum concentrates on the Arabic language (reading and writing) and mathematics. Students at the secondary level are presented with a choice of elective subjects such as French language, fine arts, electronics, and music. Students must attend 25 periods per week in the first three primary classes, 30 periods in the second three primary classes, and 35 periods in the intermediate and secondary levels.

At the secondary level the credit system is based on the following four groups of subjects: common, obligatory, optional specialized, and optional general courses. The academic requirements are 156 credit hours in general and commercial education and 216 credit hours in technical education. The curriculum concentrates on the self-instructional approach and adopts the formative evaluation process. There is also more emphasis on remedial teaching, particularly at the primary level. Considerable effort is being made to enhance the role of learning materials and visual aids in the educational process. The focus of such efforts is concentrated in a training program for all librarians. This program aims at establishing a learning resources center in each school.

8. The System of Examinations, Promotions, and Certifications

The evaluation process is conducted during the two semesters of the school year. In each semester the teacher assesses a student's performance continuously through a variety of methods. In the first three grades of primary level, the evaluation is carried out through observation of daily activities. The child's subsequent successful completion of the year and promotion is determined by teachers. Remedial classes are organized for slow learners at the primary level to enhance and promote a student's performance. The result of a student's performance in each semester (from the fourth primary to the third secondary class) is divided between daily coursework, the mid-semester test, and the final examination. A student cannot be promoted unless he or she attains a satisfactory level in the Arabic language in each class. At the intermediate and secondary levels, students who only fail in one subject can be promoted. However, the examination in such subjects should be resat by those students in the next class after they have attended at least 75 percent of the remedial lessons.

The first formal certificate is awarded at the end of the intermediate level according to the results of a public examination corrected by schools. The second certificate is awarded at the end of the secondary level according to the results of the public examination corrected by a central committee. In the credit-hours system in secondary schools the certificate is awarded by the school itself.

9. Educational Assessment, Evaluation, and Research

In 1983 the Ministry of Education established the Educational Research and Development Center. It became operational in 1988. Nearly US$78,000 from the education budget were allocated to research in 1990. This rose to nearly US$182,000 in the budget for 1992. Educational research is expected to play an important role in formulating educational policy. There are 47 research studies in the educational plan 1989–95. The research effort focuses on primary, intermediate, secondary, and adult education. It is concerned with the assessment of curriculum, teaching methods, teacher training, and the evaluation process.

10. Major Reforms in the 1980s and 1990s

At the primary level a class–teacher system (i.e one main teacher per class) has been introduced in primary schools. This started in 1983–84 in the first three grades. The system is expected to be gradually generalized to all primary schools before the end of the 1990s. It also involves changing and improving teaching methods, contents, and school buildings. It fixes the class size at 30 students. This means a reduction of about 10–15 students per class. In 1986–87, the Ministry of Education also introduced the associated class–teacher system into the next three grades, as a variant of the class–teacher system. This system distinguishes between two kinds of integrated subjects: languages and social sciences on the one hand, and mathematics and sciences on the other. Accordingly, it specifies a particular teacher for each integrated subject.

At the secondary level the most significant change occurred at the beginning of the 1990s with the introduction of the credit system to the secondary education system. The system is expected to have been extended to all secondary schools by 1995. It offers as much flexibility as possible for students, recognizes individual differences, and encourages self-instruction. Prior to this, technical education witnessed the introduction of the system's modules in 1988–89, which completely conformed to the credit system.

In 1983, the Ministry of Education made many changes in the organizational chart to meet the recent improvement of the educational system at the three levels. The new chart emphasized giving special prominence to the areas of educational information, technology, and research. It introduced an independent center for educational research and development. Special attention was given to computerization by setting up a new computer department within the Information and Documentation Center.

The school as a basic educational unit is a reform which has affected both the administrative procedures and the educational process within each school. The plan concentrates on transferring more autonomy to schools in order to empower the headteacher and the teaching staff to take various decisions. It commenced in 10 schools in 1990–91 as an experimental project and will be extended systematically in the future.

11. Major Problems for the Year 2000

The revenues of the state are affected deeply by the rise and fall of oil prices. In 1991 the Gulf Crisis affected all economic activity, and consequently the state budget, leading to financial restrictions. The Ministry of Education normally receives priority when resources are allocated. However, the education allocation is expected to be below the costs of the requirements of the aspirations and targets.

The significant changes in the 1980s, which adopted new approaches, either differed from or conflicted with the traditional ones. Although the teachers and administrative staff in the schools have high credentials, some serious resistance emerged while introducing such changes. The Ministry of Education made precautionary arrangements to ensure a minimum acceptance or a flexible reaction toward the reforms. An annual educational conference is organized, the objective of which is to discuss the new trends and the recent approaches introduced with a view to improving the educational process. These conferences are attended by teachers and administrators at the different educational levels.

Social values in Bahrain have restricted opportunities for girls in vocational education to commercial subjects. In 1994 commercial education enrolled 5.7 percent of all females at secondary level. The main problem arose when most females who graduated from commercial secondary education remained unemployed. The Ministry of Education initiated some special courses within general secondary education in 1979–80 in order to create opportunities for girls in the labor market. These courses were restricted to those that were acceptable to Bahraini society: health sciences, textiles, and hotel catering. There are still difficulties in attracting girls to these courses. Enrollment in these courses did not exceed 2 percent of the total number of girls enrolled in secondary education in 1990–91. However, attempts are being undertaken to introduce other kinds of vocational courses for girls, such as advertising and design.

Bibliography

Directorate of Plans and Programming 1990 *Educational Plan of Ministry of Education 1989/90–1994/95.* Ministry of Education, Bahrain

Directorate of Statistics, Cabinet Affairs 1982 *Bahrain Census of Population and Housing 1981.* Cabinet Affairs, Bahrain

Hammod R 1987 *Education in Bahrain.* Arab Bureau of Education for the Gulf States, Riyadh

Information and Documentation Center 1990 *Development of Education in Bahrain between 1987/88–1989/90. Report presented to the 42nd Session of the International Conference on Education, Geneva, 3–8 September 1990.* Ministry of Education, Bahrain

Information and Documentation Center 1992 *Educational Statistics 88/89, 90/91.* Ministry of Education, Bahrain

Saydawi A 1991 *Educational Change in Bahrain during the 1980s.* Ministry of Education, Bahrain

Bangladesh

M. M. Ali

1. General Background

Bangladesh is a land composed almost entirely of broad rivers, small waterways, and the low-lying land in between. Over 100 million people inhabit its 143,998 square kilometers of territory and 13 percent of the population lives in urban areas. The per capita GNP of Bangladesh was US$170 in 1988. The average annual growth rate for the urban population was about 5.5 percent in the period 1980–87. Although the poverty situation improved, the proportion of people below the poverty line in 1980 was still significantly high. About one-third of the population is unemployed. The agricultural sector provides employment for 61.3 percent of the labor force and generates 46 percent of Gross Domestic Product (GDP). According to the 1991 census, the overall adult literacy rate was 34.6 percent, with the male and female adult literacy rates at 45.0 percent and 23.44 percent respectively.

The fundamental principle of state policy on education, as laid down in article 17 of the Constitution, is "establishing a uniform mass-oriented and universal system of education and extending free and compulsory education to all children of stage as may be determined by law." The intention is to relate education to the needs of the society by producing properly trained and motivated citizens to serve these needs, and to remove illiteracy within a period stipulated by legislation.

2. Politics and the Goals of the Education System

Education is one of the basic requirements for developing human capabilities. Educational development in Bangladesh has expanded marginally and has continued to remain elitist in character. In order to remedy the imbalance in the education system, efforts were made after Independence to change the system, with a view to making it effective and making it more relevant to the people.

Bangladesh instituted a Commission Report in 1974, followed by another Interim Education Commission Report in 1977, which suggested a needs-based and work-oriented education system for the country. A new education policy was formulated in 1989 which implemented some recommendations of these commissions. This underlined the salient features of development strategy of the Bangladeshi education system. The main aims of this new policy can be summarized as follows:

(a) To create a significant base of literacy through effective implementation of primary education as basic education and to make a minimum of 5 years' education for all universal.

(b) To equip future generations with the knowledge, aptitudes, and the necessary skills to enable them to meet the challenges ahead.

(c) To make education open-ended throughout life by providing multiple entry points throughout the system.

(d) To create in students a sense of solidarity with the hopes and aspirations of the people of all countries of the world and to transform the students into practical, scientifically minded and socially well-integrated human beings.

(e) To inspire students to express their original ideas and develop free thinking in the society.

3. The Formal System of Education

3.1 Primary, Secondary, and Tertiary Education

The structure of the formal education system of Bangladesh is given in Fig. 1. In primary stage education, schools offer a uniform course of study from class I to

V, of five years' duration. The academic year begins in January and ends in December. Primary schools are run in two shifts. Children between 6 and 10 years of age are enrolled in primary education. In classes I and II, pupils study Bangla, arithmetic, and environmental science (general science and social studies); from class III onward, pupils take physical education, arts and crafts, music, and religion as additional subjects. English is taught as a second language beginning in class III. Primary education is free and compulsory for all children from 6 to 10 years of age.

Secondary education caters for adolescents between the ages of the 11 and 17 and is divided into three stages: junior secondary, secondary, and higher secondary. The duration of schooling is 3 years for junior secondary, and 2 years each for secondary and higher secondary (i.e., a total of 7 years). Junior secondary school comprises three grades, namely Grades 6 to 8. The curriculum is uniform and consists of Bangla, mathematics, English, general science, and social and religious studies.

Education is free for all girls studying up to Grade 8 in institutions located outside the municipal areas. The government provides 70 percent of teachers' and other employees' salaries. Each institution has a School Managing Committee (SMC) for the management and supervision of the school.

Secondary education comprises Grades 9 and 10. Most of the high schools in the country are privately managed. Although secondary schools provide mostly co-education, there are many single-sex institutions. A diversification of courses and curriculum is introduced at Grade 9, where students are separated into two main streams: sciences and humanities. Secondary education is administered by the Directorate of Secondary and Higher Education headed by the Director-general. The directorate has 5 divisional offices and 8 zonal offices and district offices headed by a District Education Officer.

Higher secondary education comprises Grades 11 and 12. Intermediate colleges in Bangladesh offer courses of higher secondary level. There are many degree colleges which combine Grades 11 and 12. The curriculum is divided into sciences, humanities, commerce, home economics, agriculture, and music. Intermediate colleges and intermediate sections of the degree colleges offering general education are also required to be affiliated to the regional Boards of Intermediate and Secondary Education (BISE) for academic and examination purposes.

Both the government-managed colleges and all nongovernment colleges receive 70 percent salary subsidy for all teachers and other employees. The management of the college consists of a governing body.

Higher education is open to students who have passed the Higher Secondary Certificate (HSC) examination. They are enrolled on either Pass or Honors courses for a bachelor's degree (2 years for Pass

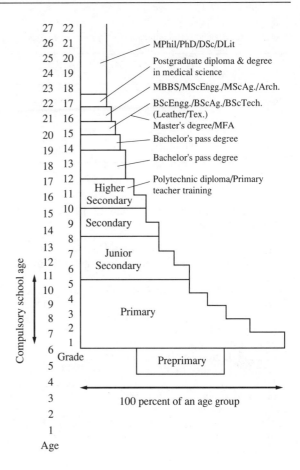

Figure 1
Bangladesh: Structure of the formal education system

and 3 years for Honors) in the degree colleges or in the universities. This may be followed by master's degree courses of one year's duration for holders of a bachelor's degree (Honors) and 2 years' duration for holders of a bachelor's degree (Pass). There are government and nongovernment degree colleges where degree courses including Honors and master's are offered. The degree colleges are affiliated to three affiliating universities—Dhaka, Rajshahi, and Chittagong—for academic and examination purposes. A national university has also been created to give accreditation to the degree colleges and hold examinations. This development has thus freed the three affiliating universities of responsibility for the degree colleges and thereby allowed them to concentrate more on academic activities. M Phil and PhD courses in selected subjects are also offered in the universities. The duration of studies for an M Phil degree is 2 years and for a PhD a minimum of 3 years after master's degree. Most universities follow either a course or semester system of examinations. In general, degrees

Table 1
Bangladesh: Stages of the *madrasah* system of education

Stage	Equivalent level	Duration
Ibtedayee	Primary	5 years
Dhakil	Secondary	5 years
Alim	Higher secondary	2 years
Fazil	Bachelor's degree	2 years
Kamil	Master's degree	2 years

are awarded in the First, Second or Third class on the basis of securing 60, 45, and 33 percent marks respectively in the final examinations.

An important aspect of education is the *madrasah* system of education. It parallels the secular state system in terms of general education, but also imparts religious instruction. Along with the Islamic religious subjects of the Koran and Hadith, Arabic, Bangla, English, mathematics, social studies, and science are included in its curricula. The stages of the *madrasah* system are outlined in Table 1.

Madrasahs are administered by the government's Madrasah Education Board as regards all forms of curricula and other functional matters. Public examinations are held at the stages of Dhakil, Alim, Fazil, Kamil and are conducted by the Madrasah Education Board. The system of examinations is the same as that in the general system of education. There are 16,000 *madrasahs* containing 5 grades of the primary level (*Ibtedayee madrasah*). These have been recognized as equivalent to primary education and have been developed in order to help implement compulsory primary education. *Qaumi* or *Nizamia madrasahs* arrange their academic programs according to grades of one year each, from Grade 1 to Grade 14. The grades are named in Arabic, the final grade being called *daurah*. Certificates are awarded to the students after successful completion of the *daurah* class. Furthermore, specialized higher courses of 2 to 3 years' duration are also conducted in some of the *Qaumi madrasahs*. There are about 3,000 *madrashas* of this type in Bangladesh. Some of them function as the most important seats of religious learning, attracting foreign students to pursue Islamic studies and research. These *madrasahs* are organized under the umbrella of a private board known as *befaqul madaris*, or the Qaumi Madrasah Education Board, situated at the Faridabad *madrasah* complex in Dhaka. This Board develops the curriculum and syllabuses, prescribes and publishes books, conducts examinations of various stages of all the *madrasahs* affiliated to the Board, and awards certificates and degrees. Most of these *madrasahs* are residential, and in many cases offer free board and lodging for teachers and students.

Sanskrit and Pali education should also be mentioned. It is normally imparted in the general schools, colleges, and universities where Sanskrit and Pali are elective subjects at all stages. The universities of Dhaka and Chittagong offer Honors as well as master's courses in these subjects. In the traditional system of education, Sanskrit and Pali are taught at the privately managed institutions in Bangladesh known as *Tolor Chatushpathi* colleges. These institutions are affiliated to the Bangladesh Sanskrit and Pali Education Board in Dhaka. It is mostly Hindus and Buddhists who receive this type of education. The minimum prequalification of entry to these institutions is the Secondary School Certificate (SSC) with specialization either in Sanskrit or Pali. The courses are offered in three grades of studies, each of one year's duration, known as *Adya* (Basic), *Madhya* (Middle), and *Upadhi* (Title). Higher accreditation is made according to the year of studies and attachment in these three grades.

3.2 Preschool Education

There is no official government recognition of preschool or preprimary education even though many primary schools offer such facilities. Nursery, kindergarten, tutorial, and pre-cadet schools are located in urban areas which have preprimary classes.

Mosque-based institutions such as the *Maktab*, *Forkania* and *Qurania madrasah* also offer preprimary education along with religious teaching. These institutions impart literacy as well as religious teaching and serve as feeder schools to primary schools and *madrasahs*. There are other institutions mainly for religious education such as the *Hafizia madrasah*, where pupils learn to read and to memorize the Holy Koran.

3.3 Special Education

Government and nongovernment organizations alike provide special education for the blind, deaf, and dumb. There are six blind schools and eleven deaf and dumb schools in Bangladesh.

3.4 Vocational, Technical and Business Education

Technical education in Bangladesh is organized in three phases, namely, certificate, diploma, and degree. The certificate course prepares skilled workers in different vocations for 1–2 years, after 8 years of schooling (class VIII), and the diploma courses, offered at the polytechnic institutes, are for the training of Diploma engineers. The Diploma course is of 3 years' duration, and its admission prerequisite is a minimum SSC. The two sets of courses may be briefly outlined as follows:

(a) *Certificate courses.* Vocational training institutes offer trade courses of 2 years' duration in the following trades: Farm machine maintenance, auto repair, electrical, radio and TV, machinist, welding, refrigeration and air-conditioning, woodworking and masonry, and plumbing. These institutes also offer various types of nonformal trade courses of shorter duration.

(b) *Diploma courses*. Diploma courses of 3 years' duration in the 18 polytechnic and 3 monotechnic institutes are offered in the following fields of technology: civil engineering, mechanical engineering, electrical engineering, electronics, architecture, chemistry and food technology, printing, ceramics, and surveying.

In addition, the Institute of Marine Technology and 11 Technical Training Centres (TTC) run by the Ministry of Manpower are affiliated to the Technical Education Board for academic purposes. Public examinations are held for various types of courses under the auspices of the Bangladesh Technical Education Board, and diplomas and certificates are awarded by them. The Board has full academic control over the technical and vocational institutions.

The Bangladesh University of Engineering and Technology (BUET) in Dhaka provides higher education in the field of engineering and technology. Four government engineering colleges have been restructured as autonomous degree-awarding institutes of technology under the Council of the Bangladesh Institute of Technology (BIT) and offer four-year BSc courses. In future, postgraduate degree and diploma courses will also be conducted in the BIT. The BIT situated in the Gazipur district offers a three-year engineering course for polytechnic graduates equivalent to the BSc engineering degree, thus creating an opening for the polytechnic diploma holders to pursue higher studies in engineering and technology. The College of Textiles Technology and the College of Leather Technology, both situated in Dhaka, are government-managed institutions under the Ministry of Education, which offer four-year degree courses.

An international organisation known as the Islamic Centre for Technical and Vocational Training and Research (ICTVTR) is situated at Tongi near Dhaka and is responsible for the preparation of skilled technical professionals for a number of Islamic countries. This institute offers certificates and diplomas in different technologies at the tertiary level of education.

There are other professional training institutes or schools throughout the country, managed publicly or privately, which offer certificate and diploma courses at the secondary level. The National Training and Research Academy for Multilingual Shorthand (NTRAMS), located at Bogra and run by the Ministry of Education, offers two-year courses leading to the diploma in commerce, equivalent to the HSC. There are many professional institutes which offer professional certificates, diplomas, and degrees.

Agricultural education encompasses education on the production, preservation, processing and marketing systems of all agricultural produce, animal husbandry, poultry farming, livestock, pisciculture, and so on. Diversified courses on agriculture are offered at the Agriculture University and three other agricultural colleges. The minimum entrance requirement for admission to the University and the colleges is an HSC (Science).

The government has established an Institute of Postgraduate Studies in Agriculture (IPSA). There is a Forest Research Institute at Chittagong, where Honors and master's courses on forestry are offered. In addition there is an institute within the University of Chittagong which offers courses in marine science of equivalent level.

The Ministry of Agriculture operates 11 Agricultural Training Institutes (ATIs) where a three-year diploma course in agriculture is offered after SSC. They are affiliated to the Technical Education Board.

There are eight government medical colleges providing courses in medical and health education. The Institute of Postgraduate Medicine and Research (IPGMR) is an apex institute for higher medical education and research. This institute, together with other specialized medical institutes in the country, offers various postgraduate courses.

A Dental College situated in Dhaka runs a four-year BDS (Bachelor of Dental Surgery) course, and a Nursing College in Dhaka offers a four-year BNSc (Bachelor of Nursing Science) course. Under the Directorate of Nursing Services, there are 42 schools of nursing which provide four-year senior certificate courses (3 years' nursing and 1 year midwifery). Of these, 38 are publicly managed. There are also 8 Medical Assistant Training Schools (MATS) run by the government under the Directorate of Health which offer three-year training courses. Two paramedical institutes exist in Bangladesh, providing three-year diploma courses in health technology, laboratory technicianship, radiography, sanitary inspection, pharmacy, and dentistry. The government hospital technicians can also participate in these courses.

There are 38 homeopathic medical colleges affiliated to the Homeopathic Board. Dhaka University has given academic recognition to some of the colleges to permit them to award degrees under its Faculty of Medicine.

The traditional Unani and Ayurvedic systems of medicine are very popular. Two types of courses are given in these systems of medical education: a four-year diploma course after SSC Alim, and a five-year degree course after HSC/Alim/Fazil. There is a Board of Unani and Ayurvedic Systems of Medicine recognised by the government. This Board prescribes syllabuses and curricula, conducts examinations, and awards diploma certificates.

3.5 Adult and Nonformal Education

Along with the introduction of universal primary education, more emphasis has been given to adult and nonformal education to realize the avowed objectives of eradicating illiteracy from Bangladeshi society. For this reason the mass education program was put under the direct supervision of the Primary and Mass Education Division of the Ministry of Education. The main objective of the project is to teach a functional level of literacy to the illiterate population between the ages of 11 and 45.

The aims and objectives of this project are the following:

(a) to enhance the existing adult literacy rate from 30 to 60 percent by the year 2000;

(b) to establish an organizational structure for ensuring that the mass education program remains effective and fruitful.

4. *Administrative and Supervisory Structure and Operation*

The Ministry of Education (MOE), headed by a minister who is assisted by a state minister, is concerned with policy formulation, planning, monitoring, and evaluation. The line directorates (Directorates of Primary Education, Secondary and Higher Education, and Technical Education) are responsible for the execution of policies laid down by the ministry and for the academic supervision of the institutions under their respective control.

The Bangladesh National Commission for UNESCO (BNCU) functions as a corporate body within the MOE. This is headed by the Minister of Education as chairman and the Education Secretary as the secretary-general. In pursuance of the government's policy of decentralization, there are separate units for accounts, compulsory primary education, and primary and mass education. The latter is headed by the Prime Minister.

The line Directorate of Primary Education is responsible for the entire primary education system, including implementation of universal primary education. The National Academy for Primary Education (NAPE) is an institution under the primary directorate and is responsible for bringing about qualitative improvements in primary education. It conducts inservice training and refresher courses for primary school teachers (including research and evaluation). It also conducts examinations for the Certificate in Education (C-in-Ed).

The Directorate of Secondary and Higher Education, which is headed by a director-general, is responsible for all secondary and higher education including *madrasah* and other special education.

The Directorate of Technical Education is headed by a director-general and is responsible for the management and administration of technical and vocational institutions.

In addition, the following staff departments of the MOE perform specialized functions assigned to them:

(a) The National Academy for Educational Management (NAEM) is responsible for inservice training of senior educational administration and teachers at the secondary and higher secondary levels. This academy also conducts foundation training for the Bangladesh Civil Service (BCS) Education Cadre Officers. It is headed by a director-general.

(b) The Bangladesh Bureau of Educational Information and Statistics (BANBEIS) is responsible for the collection, collation, compilation, publication and dissemination of information and education statistics from primary to university levels. It also functions as an apex institution for the country's Educational Management Information System (EMIS).

(c) The Directorate of Inspection and Audit is responsible for the planned improvement of the standard of education of institutions at the secondary and higher secondary level.

(d) The Directorate of Facilities is responsible for the construction of new buildings and repair work at all educational institutions from primary to higher levels and other government offices under the MOE.

(e) The National Curriculum and Textbook Board (NCTB) is responsible for the curriculum development, printing, and supply of all textbooks for the primary, secondary, and higher secondary levels.

(f) The Open University offers Bachelor of Education (BEd) degrees through distance teaching courses including programs on radio and TV and short-term practical courses held in all the teacher training colleges.

There are 64 districts and 494 subdistricts known as *Thana*. In each district there are district officers responsible for the implementation of education. At the primary level, 494 Thana Education Officers are responsible for the supervision, control, and management of primary education in cooperation with local government, which is referred to as *Union Parishad*.

5. *Educational Finance*

Public expenditure on education as a percentage of GNP increased from 1.1 percent in 1975 to 1.5 in 1980, 1.6

Table 2
Public expenditure on education, selected years 1974–92 (in millions takas)

Year	Revenue	Development	Total
1974	822.1	206.2	1,028.3
1979	1,728.2	446.6	2,174.8
1984–85	452.9	1,272.9	5,785.7
1989–90	10,938.5	3,186.6	14,125.1
1990–91	11,820.18	3,122.2	14,942.35
1991–92	13,815.77	4,368.4	18,184.17

in 1985, 1.7 in 1986, and around 1.9 percent in 1989. In absolute terms, expenditure on education more than doubled every five years, as shown in Table 2.

In 1990–91, primary education received 41.2 percent of the education budget. As a result of launching the CPE program in January 1991, the government decided to devote a larger share of budget to education and to ensure that the allocation to primary education was retained at a level commensurate with the increased requirement.

The Fourth Five-year Plan (1990–95) allocated about Tk23,727 million (US$600 million) which represented 4.8 percent of the total state budget. By comparison, the Third Plan allocation was 1.85 percent of the state budget. The government has accorded top priority to primary education, with nearly 50 percent of the sectoral allocation in the Fourth Plan.

6. Supplying Personnel for the Education System

There are five types of teacher training in Bangladesh: (a) primary, (b) vocational, (c) physical education at the second and third level, (d) technical teacher training at the second and third level, and (e) teacher training at the third level.

Primary teacher training lasts one year and is undertaken at Primary Training Institutes (PTI). The Vocational Teachers' Training Institute (VTTI) is responsible for the vocational teacher training institutions of Bangladesh. It offers two-year courses for teachers in the country's 51 vocational training institutes. The Technical Teachers' Training College (TTC) in Dhaka also offers short training courses (of about 4 weeks' duration) for the teachers of VTIs. Two physical education colleges situated at Dhaka and Rajshahi offer a one-year certificate (called the Junior Diploma in Physical Education Certificate) after HSC and a one-year Bachelor of Physical Education (BPEd) after a first university degree.

The Technical Teachers' Training College offers a one-year diploma in technical education and a two-year BEd (Technology) course for teachers (technical diploma holders) employed in the Polytechnic institutes. The College also runs inservice short courses for teachers in the polytechnic institutes and VTIs.

For the training of secondary school and *madrasah* teachers, there are ten teacher training colleges in the country offering a one-year BEd. Prequalification for this course is a first university degree or equivalent. In general, it is inservice teachers who are trained on this course. In some of the teacher training colleges, an MEd course is also available for BEd degree or diploma holders.

The National Academy for Educational Management (NAEM) is entrusted with the responsibility of conducting inservice short-term training courses in different subjects or disciplines for secondary and college teachers and educational administrators. The NAEM conducts training for all officers of the Bangladesh Civil Service (Education) Cadre.

7. Curriculum Development and Teaching Methodology

The subjects studied at all the various levels of education were given above in Section 3.1. The government attempts to convey the country's philosophy, ideology, and heritage through education. A national curriculum and textbook committee was called on to formulate syllabuses and curricula for primary and secondary levels. Furthermore, the National Curriculum and Textbook Board (NCTB) was created to review the progress of the implementation of the recommendations of the committee, update new concepts, and prepare textbooks for all grades.

8. The System of Examinations, Promotions, and Certifications

An examination is held at the end of each year of primary school beginning at the end of Grade 2. Promotion from one class to the next depends on pupils' results in their examination. At the end of Grade 5 there is a Merit Scholarship Examination for scholarships to secondary school. In Grades 6 and 7, during junior secondary school, no examinations are held. However, at the end of Grade 8 there is a nationwide scholarship examination known as the "Junior Scholarship" exam. Merit scholarships are awarded to successful candidates. In Grade 9 there are class examinations each year and promotion depends on the student obtaining the minimum prescribed marks. At the end of Grade 10 there is a national Secondary School Certificate (SSC) which is run by four Boards of Intermediate and Secondary Education (BISE) at Dhaka, Rajshahi, Couvilla, and Jesore. The minimum marks for the first, second, and third divisions are 60, 45, and 35 percent respectively. The minimum pass mark for an individual paper is 33 percent. Students who attain 75 percent receive a "star" award and those gaining 80 percent in each paper receive a "better" award.

9. Educational Assessment, Evaluation, and Research

There is an Examination Development Committee whose task it is not only to improve the examination system but also to create new assessment and evaluation procedures which can be used throughout the country.

School census statistics are collected annually. A special survey of all nongovernment schools was conducted in 1983 to help in determining government support for such schools. Various government institutes and universities conduct small-scale studies on various aspects of education. It is expected that the whole area of assessment, evaluation, and educational research will expand.

10. *Major Reforms in the 1980s and 1990s*

Major reforms or innovations carried out during the 1980s and 1990s were as follows:

(a) Outdoor primary education was instituted to make education attractive to young children through learning from their own environment.

(b) Introduction of population education programs at the school level to develop national attitudes among children about population matters.

(c) Organization of double shifts at schools to increase the intake capacity in the existing institutions and ensure full utilization of physical and other available facilities.

(d) Introduction of science and craft courses in the *madrasahs* in order to make the students of these institutions productive.

(e) Expansion of facilities for games, sports, and cultural activities in the educational institutions to keep the students fruitfully engaged during their leisure time.

(f) Nationalization of nongovernment schools and colleges to ensure better management and quality education.

(g) Organization of mobile libraries to increase library facilities in the rural areas.

(h) Establishment of community schools attached to some existing secondary schools in order to impart nonformal education in agriculture and technical subjects.

(i) Strengthening secondary education through the organization of curriculum-based broadcasting programs.

(j) Encouragement of women's education by developing at least one girl's high school in every *thana* headquarters which runs science and craft courses, by establishing polytechnic institutes for women, and through the extension of job opportunities for women (especially in teaching) with a view to ensuring quality education at the primary level.

(k) Establishing more vocational institutes in rural areas to make education production-oriented and to ease the pressure for admission to general education courses.

(l) Establishment of a Bureau of Educational Information and Statistics (BANBEIS) for the purpose of collecting, compiling, preserving, and disseminating educational information and statistics.

(m) Establishment of an Academy for Fundamental Education to improve standards, curricula, syllabuses, instructional materials, and inservice teacher training programs for primary education.

(n) Organization of voluntary social work by the student community in order to promote work-oriented education;

(o) Setting up of local education committees, to strengthen educational institutions through the participation of local people.

(p) Decentralization of administration of primary school education to the *thana* (subdistricts.)

(q) More than 150 nongovernment high schools were nationalized.

The Secondary Science Education Project (SSEP) was launched with financial assistance from the Asian Development Bank (ADB) in April 1985 and completed in June 1991. The main objective of the project was to improve the quality of secondary education, with particular emphasis on science education, through upgrading and expanding physical facilities for secondary schools and *madrasahs*, and improving the professional competence of teachers, teacher-trainers and educational administrators.

More than 1,000 laboratories have been built and equipped. Repair and renovation of another 4,000 has been completed. At the same time 8,000 science teachers have been retrained to ensure the proper use of science laboratories and apparatus.

One major development has been the creation of the education cadre of Bangladesh Civil Service. This provides teachers with a more secure and systematic service ladder. It is expected that this will contribute toward qualitative improvements in education.

To open up higher education to a growing number of students, 10 colleges were declared to be university-colleges where Honors and postgraduate courses in selected subjects are offered. At the same time, the physical plant of all universities has been repaired and improved. Three universities (Khulna, Sahjalal University of Science and Technology, and the Islamic University at Kushtia) were established.

Teacher training and educational facilities of teachers were greatly expanded. There were 47 Primary Training Institutes (PTI) in 1982 which increased to 53 by 1987. The National Academy of Primary Education (NAPE) has held inservice training courses for primary teachers, members of Primary Training Institute staff and primary school inspectors.

A Central Text Book Library and Book Bank was established in 1987. This has resulted in easy access to the central reading library for all educators and educational researchers. The Inspection and Audit Department was created to ensure the effective inspection of schools, colleges, and *madrasahs*.

11. Major Problems for the Year 2000

Priority in education in Bangladesh is given to the eradication of illiteracy, which still continues to be a problem. Institutional facilities exist, but there is still a need for a coherent management system. Community participation has diminished. It must be remembered that educational institutions have been nationalized. To develop a better educational management system the government created a national committee on Education For All (EFA) to suggest and recommend development strategies under a decentralized management system of primary and basic education and to involve community participation.

Bibliography

Bangladesh Bureau of Educational Information and Statistics (BANBEIS) 1988 *Educational and Reform Development of Bangladesh during the Years 1982–83 to 1987–88.* Ministry of Education, Dhaka

Bangladesh Bureau of Educational Information and Statistics (BANBEIS) 1989 *University Education in Bangladesh.* Ministry of Education, Dhaka

Bangladesh Bureau of Educational Information and Statistics (BANBEIS) 1990 *Primary Education in Bangladesh.* Ministry of Education, Dhaka

Bangladesh Bureau of Educational Information and Statistics (BANBEIS) 1992a *Financing Education in Bangladesh.* Ministry of Education, Dhaka

Bangladesh Bureau of Educational Information and Statistics (BANBEIS) 1992b *Education System of Bangladesh.* Ministry of Education, Dhaka

Bangladesh Bureau of Educational Information and Statistics (BANBEIS) 1992c *Bangladesh Education Statistics.* Ministry of Education, Dhaka

Education Directorate 1974 *Education in Bangladesh.* Education Directorate, Dhaka

International Conference on Education 1979a *Country Report Bangladesh.* Brief report on the development of Bangladesh during 1976–77 and 1977–78, 37th session of the International Conference on Education, Geneva, 5–14 July. Ministry of Education, Dhaka

International Conference on Education 1979b Speech of Prime Minister Mr. Azizur Rahman. 37th session of the International Conference on Education, Geneva, 5–14 July. Ministry of Education, Dhaka

International Conference on Education 1984 *Country Report Bangladesh.* 39th session of the International Conference on Education, Geneva, 16–25 October. Ministry of Education, Dhaka

International Conference on Education 1986 *National Report of Bangladesh: Development of Education 1984–86.* 40th session of the International Conference on Education, Geneva. Ministry of Education, Dhaka

Ministry of Education 1984 *New Life in Education.* Ministry of Education, Dhaka

Ministry of Education 1985 *Third Five-year Plan 1985–90.* Education sector document, Ministry of Education, Dhaka

Ministry of Education 1991 *Education in Bangladesh.* Planning cell, Ministry of Education, Dhaka

Ministry of Education 1992 *Education For All. Draft National Programmes of Action for Bangladesh.* Ministry of Education, Dhaka

Ministry of Finance and Planning 1989a *The First Five-year Plan 1973–78.* Planning Commission, Ministry of Finance and Planning, Dhaka

Ministry of Finance and Planning 1989b *The Second Five-year Plan 1980–85.* Planning Commission, Ministry of Finance and Planning, Dhaka

Ministry of Finance and Planning 1989c *The Third Five-Year Plan 1985–90.* Planning Commission, Ministry of Finance and Planning, Dhaka

Ministry of Finance and Planning 1990 *The Fourth Five-Year Plan 1990–95.* Planning Commission, Ministry of Finance and Planning, Dhaka

National Council for Science and Technology 1979 Summary of national paper on Bangladesh for submission to the United Nations Conference on Science and Technology for Development, Vienna. Ministry of Education, Dhaka

UNESCO 1979 *Country Report Bangladesh.* Sixth Regional Consultation Meeting on the Asian Programme of Educational Innovation for Development, Bangalore, India, 22–30 April 1979. Ministry of Education, Dhaka

Barbados

A. Layne and L. Atherley

1. General Background

Barbados, the most easterly of the Caribbean Islands, is 34 kilometers long and 23 kilometers wide, with a total land area of 432 square kilometers (166 square miles). It is comparatively flat; its highest point, Mount Hillaby, is only 340 meters (1,115 feet) above sea level.

Barbados is very small in terms of land area, but it is densely populated with a total of approximately 259,000 persons. In the period 1946–60, the population of Barbados grew at an average annual rate of 1.3 percent. However, since 1960, the average annual rate of population growth was only 0.3 percent (UNDP 1992). The low rate of population growth since

Table 1
Gross domestic product at factor cost by sector of origin, 1992[a]

Sector of origin	Bds(millions)	Percentage
Agriculture	168.3	6.1
Sugar	51.1	1.9
Other agriculture and fishing	112.7	4.2
Industry	422.2	15.7
Mining and quarrying	17.0	0.6
Manufacturing	203.2	7.6
Electricity, gas and water	100.6	3.7
Construction	101.4	3.8
Services	2,106.0	78.2
Wholesale and retail trade	489.9	18.5
Tourism	317.3	11.8
Transport, storage and communications	248.6	9.2
Financial and related services[b]	453.1	16.8
Government services	480.4	17.8
General services	107.7	4.0
Total GDP at factor cost	2,692.0	100.0

Source: Central Bank of Barbados, Annual Statistical Digest 1993
a Provisional   b Includes financial, insurance, real estate and business services

1960 was due mainly to two factors: large-scale emigration during the 1960s and 1970s, and a vigorous government-sponsored family planning program which came into existence in 1955.

According to the 1990 population census data, Blacks account for 92.5 percent of the population of Barbados. The remainder of the population is distributed racially and in percentage terms as follows: Whites 3.2, Mixed (Caucasian and Negro) 2.4, East Indian 0.8, Others 0.1, and Not Stated 1.0. The population is overwhelmingly Christian, and Anglicans are the single largest religious group. English is the official language and is the language of instruction in the schools.

Barbados has come a long way from the period of the slave regime (c.1640–1838) when a small master class of White sugar planters and merchants dominated every aspect of life in the then British sugar colony. The racial–class structure remained essentially intact for more than a century after the slaves were given their legal freedom in 1838. However, with the development planning which began at the end of the Second World War, and which was intensified with the attainment of (a) universal adult suffrage in 1950, and (b) political independence in 1966, the Black majority is now fully represented in the professions. However, the positions that carry the greatest renumeration and prestige—namely administrative, executive, and managerial ones—are still reserved for a very small section of the employed labor force, about 3.6 percent

in 1990 (computed from data provided by the Barbados Statistical Service). It is worth noting that throughout the post-colonial period, development planners and policymakers in Barbados relied heavily on education to function as a vehicle of upward social mobility.

Gross domestic product, in 1988 US currency stood at $1,488 million in 1990, having grown at average annual rates of 6.6 percent in 1961–70, 0.1 in 1971–80, and 0.3 percent in 1981–90 (Inter-American Development Bank 1991). It should be noted, though, that real gross domestic product (GDP) actually fell by 3.3 percent in 1990 from its level in 1989, further declined by 4 percent in 1991 (Central Bank of Barbados 1993), and stood at Bds$810 million in 1992, which was 4 percent lower than the level in 1991 (Barbados Economic Report 1992). The economy made a notable transformation after the Second World War from one based on sugar monoculture to one which is service-based. For example, as can be seen in Table 1, in 1992, sugar accounted for only 2 percent of GDP and the entire agricultural sector for approximately 6 percent. Industry has been making an important contribution to output, particularly manufacturing industry with its contribution of 8.0 percent, but it is the service sector which accounts for more than three-fourths of GDP. The sectors which make the largest contributions to GDP are: wholesale and retail trade (over 18%), government services (almost 18%), and financial and related services (almost 17%).

The employed labor force is to be found predominantly in the tertiary sector. In 1992, some 96,200 persons were employed, with the unemployment rate standing at 23 percent (1993–2000 Development Plan 1994 p.22). Of the 96,200 employed persons, agriculture and fishing accounted for 6.2 percent, industry (i.e., mining and quarrying, manufacturing, electricity, gas and water, and construction) for 19.9 percent and Services for 73.9 percent (1993–2000 Development Plan 1994 p.22). Government services accounted for the single largest share of the employed labor force: 21.7 percent.

In the light of Barbados' history of colonialism and slavery, the traditional domination of the economy by the white minority, the post-1990 economic decline, the rise of the service economy, and the rise in the level of open unemployment, educational planners in Barbados will need to pay very close attention to the political and economic aspects of what they do in a country whose population in the postcolonial period has continued to be made up predominantly of the descendants of the former slaves.

2. Politics and the Goals of the Education System

Barbados has a parliamentary form of democracy which is based on the Westminster model. Legislative power is vested in the Parliament, which comprises a 27-member elected House of Assembly, a 21-member appointed Upper House or Senate, and the Governor-General. Executive power is vested in the Cabinet, which comprises the Prime Minister and other Ministers of Government. The general direction and control of the Government rests with the Cabinet which is collectively responsible to Parliament. There are three political parties. All place great emphasis on educational development and there is little difference in the major thrusts of their policies.

As stated in the 1993–2000 Development Plan (Government of Barbados 1994a), the government has four broad goals which it expects to achieve through the planning process. These broad goals are: the maintenance and enhancement of the practice of parliamentary democracy as an inherent aspect of the Barbadian way of life, and as the framework within which major decisions affecting the people of Barbados will be taken by them and on their behalf; the resumption and acceleration of economic growth and development; attainment of a standard of living where all citizens, particularly the disadvantaged and the vulnerable, are able to satisfy their basic needs for food, clothing, and shelter; and the development and maintenance of a climate conducive to intellectual and artistic creativity and the promotion of a positive national identity.

The government is of the view that the development of Barbados is dependent on the excellence of its educational system, and has stated its commitment to "the development of an educational system which

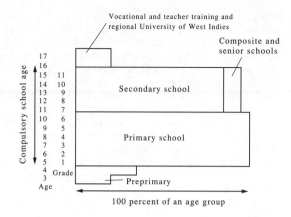

Figure 1
Barbados: Structure of the formal education system

enables all persons to realize their talents to the fullest possible extent" (Government of Barbados 1988 p. 63). It expects the educational system to help prepare the people of Barbados to meet the economic and social challenges of the modern world and of the twenty-first century, and to that end it has included in its development plans for education a number of strategies and programs.

There are a few key organizations which also contribute to the development of educational policy. The teaching force is well-organized with separate associations for each level of education. Local and regional nongovernmental organizations, especially in the areas of adult education and educational administration, are very significant. Finally, regional organizations, like the Caribbean Community Secretariat (CARICOM) are influential in the preparation of shared strategies for development.

3. The Formal System of Education

3.1 Primary, Secondary, and Tertiary Education

The structure of the school system is 6 years of primary and 5 years of secondary (see Figure 1). Barbados has a sizeable number of public and private formal education institutions. There are 3 government nursery schools and 117 primary schools (93 public and 24 private). There are 33 secondary schools (22 public and 11 assisted private). There are differences in prestige both between and within subsectors. In the first category are the 9 former "grammar" or "older secondary" schools. As a group, these 9 schools are the most prestigious of all the secondary schools, and 4 of them have sixth forms. The second category of secondary schools comprises the 5 former older secondary schools which do not have sixth forms. The third category comprises the 13 former newer secondary or comprehensive schools. The schools in this category are less prestigious than those in the preceding two. The former grammar and comprehensive schools are all government-owned and are now officially known simply as "secondary schools" even though the differences in prestige continue to exist. The final category of secondary school is the assisted private (there are no totally private secondary schools). As a group, the 11 assisted private schools are the least prestigious of the secondary schools, although the more expensive ones occupy a higher position in the prestige hierarchy than some of the "newer secondary." Occupying an intermediate position between the primary and the secondary schools are the "composite" and "senior" schools.

Admission to the government secondary schools is based on the score which the child receives in the Barbados Secondary Schools Entrance Examination, familiarly known as the Common Entrance Examination (CEE), and on parental choice of school. Those with the lowest "passing" marks are provided with bursaries to attend assisted private schools, while the few who "fail" are either kept in the senior departments of the composite schools or sent to senior schools.

There are four institutions which have been officially designated as providing tertiary education. Erdiston Teacher Training College provides a basic two-year education program for nongraduate teachers in primary and secondary schools. The Samuel Jackman Prescod Polytechnic (SJPP) was established to: (a) develop trade skills and occupational competencies up to the level of skilled craftsmen, (b) prepare the student for direct entry into paid employment, and (c) prepare students for entry into the Division of Technology of the Barbados Community College (BCC). The BCC itself was established to improve the facilities available to the community in a wide range of skills at the technician, paraprofessional, middle-management, and preuniversity levels. The fourth institution is the Cave Hill Campus of the regional University of the West Indies, which has Faculties of Arts and General Studies, Natural Sciences, Social Sciences, Medical Sciences, Law, and Education.

With regard to the flow of students throughout the system, the following facts should be borne in mind: (a) the net enrollment ratio for primary education is 98 percent, (b) the completion rate for primary education is 100 percent, and (c) about 96 percent of the children aged 11 years enter secondary school with the remaining 4 percent entering postprimary institutions (composite and senior schools). About 95 percent of the population aged 12-16 years is in school. A virtual policy of automatic promotion is in place in the primary schools, and the flow of students through the secondary school system is regular up to age 16 (fifth form). Approximately 7 percent of pupils at the primary level, and 18 percent at the secondary, are enrolled in private institutions. The enrollment ratio for tertiary education

is 19 percent, and is the same for males as for females (UNDP 1992).

The school day begins at 8.30 a.m. and ends at 3.00 p.m. The school year comprises three terms of 13-14 weeks and runs from September to July. The student–teacher ratio is about 18:1, both in the primary and the secondary schools.

3.2 Preschool Education

Preschool or nursery education is provided in the three government nursery schools, as well as in: (a) the nursery classes in some primary schools; and (b) any composite schools in which there is adequate space, facilities, and teachers; and (c) by the private sector. The three nursery schools have a total enrollment of 360 pupils (120 per school). Since primary school enrollment has been falling because of previous declines in the birthrate, the government has been promoting the use of available space at primary and composite schools to provide nursery education. In 1987, the latest year for which pertinent data on the enrollment ratio for children in the 3-5 age group are available, there were 8,325 children in the population aged 3-5 years, of whom 3,602 (43%) were receiving nursery education in government institutions.

3.3 Special Education

Special education is an area on which successive governments are placing increasing emphasis. It is provided at the School for the Deaf and Blind, the Challenor School for Mentally Retarded Children, and the Government Industrial School. The Government Industrial School is a residential school for children who have been referred by juvenile courts for detention. It offers both general and vocational education. The students range in age from 11 to 18 years and are divided into two age groups for the purpose of receiving education and training. The children in the 11-14 age group pursue full-time classes in general education, while those in the 14+ age group pursue vocational programs.

3.4 Vocational, Technical, and Business Education

Technical, vocational, and business education is provided mainly at the tertiary level, as far as the formal educational system is concerned; but it is also provided within the nonformal sector. Training is provided within the formal sector at the SJPP and the BCC, and both formally and nonformally by the National Training Board (NTB).

The courses of training offered at the SJPP are in the following areas: construction trades, electrical trades, engineering trades, commercial studies, human ecology, printing, and shoe repairs. They are offered on a full-time, part-time, or evening basis. They may lead to local certification, or to certification by the regional Caribbean Examinations Council, or to certification by the City and Guilds of London Institute. The SJPP has a total enrollment of about 1,311 students, 38 percent of whom are full-time and 62 percent part-time. The entry requirement for the SJPP is successful completion of an entrance examination which is set by the SJPP.

The BCC offers courses in its divisions of liberal arts, fine arts, health sciences, sciences, commerce, hospitality studies, technology, general and continuing education, the Language Centre, and the departments of computer studies and physical education. The courses of study are of two years' duration and lead to the Associate Degree in Arts or Applied Arts, Sciences, or Applied Sciences. The BCC has a total of about 2,200 students, the vast majority of whom are (a) day students and (b) enrolled in the division of commerce, followed by the division of science. The general entry requirement for the BCC is four Caribbean Examination Council (CEC) certificates at Grade 1 or 2 or four GCE O levels at grades A to C. These must include English Language.

The National Training Board is the main institution responsible for training in the public sector. It has on-going programs in the following four main areas: skills training, apprenticeship training, in-plant training, and special programs. The skills training programs are short intensive programs in manual skills, usually about three months in duration and are for unemployed persons between the ages of 16 and 35. The apprenticeship program provides on-the-job training for young people in several manual skill areas. The training is normally of three years' duration and is monitored by the NTB in conjunction with the employer, with the institutional training being provided at the SJPP or BCC. The in-plant program includes instructor training and refresher training for all levels of workers to increase efficiency and productivity at the plant. The NTB also has a pre-vocational training program for secondary school pupils aged 15–16 years. Altogether, the NTB trains about 1,200 persons per year.

3.5 Adult and Nonformal Education

Adult education is provided by the Ministry of Education and by several nongovernmental organizations (NGOs). The NGOs involved in adult education include the School of Continuing Studies of the University of the West Indies, the Barbados Institute of Management and Productivity, the Young Men's Christian Association, the Young Women's Christian Association, the Family Planning Association, the Barbados Workers' Union Labour College, the National Union of Public Workers Academy, and the Caribbean Regional Council for Adult Education. The educational programs offered by the organizations just listed span many areas and are tailor-made to meet the demands of the community. They include skills training for both hobby and potential employment generation, leadership training and development, public/community education programs on television, parent education, and the

performing and visual arts. In these programs, the traditional classroom teaching method is curtailed as much as possible.

In the estimates for 1992–93, the Ministry of Education earmarked Bds$3.9 million for adult education. This amounts to 1.8 percent of the estimated Bds$215 million to be spent by that Ministry during 1992–93. However, it should be noted that not all of the money which is spent by the government on adult education comes from the Ministry of Education. During 1990–91, the Ministry of Labour spent Bds$4 million on occupational training and specifically on the National Training Board (NTB). The NTB is in the nonformal sector and is the organization which has been charged by the government with the responsibility for (a) ensuring an adequate supply of trained labor in occupations in all branches of economic activity in Barbados, (b) supervision of apprenticeship and trainee programs, and (c) testing and certification.

4. Adminstrative and Supervisory Structure and Operation

Given the small physical size of Barbados, administrative control of the formal educational system is fairly highly centralized. The Ministry of Education was first established in 1954 under the portfolio of the Premier, at a time when Barbados was still a British colony. In 1958, a separate Ministry was created, with its own staff of administrative and technical officers, to assist the minister in the execution of the government's policy.

The Ministry is divided into two main sections, technical and administrative. The Chief Education Officer heads the technical staff and is the chief professional advisor, while the Permanent Secretary is the chief administrative officer with responsibility for finance. For administrative purposes, the two main sections have four subdivisions: the School Division, the Planning and Development Division, the Personnel Management and Services Division, and the Finance Division.

The primary schools are administered directly by the Ministry of Education, but the secondary schools have Boards of Management which are appointed by and answerable to the Minister of Education. All of the tertiary-level institutions also have Boards of Management, except for the University of the West Indies which is a regional institution with its own special administrative arrangements.

The Ministry of Education thus administers the formal education system and some adult education, but is not responsible for the entire education and training system.

5. Educational Finance

The education sector enjoys a sizable share of Barbados' financial resources and of the government

Table 2

Estimated expenditure by the Ministry of Education by program, 1992–93

Program	Bds	Percentage
Direction and policy formulation	7,808,307	3.6
Pre-primary	896,515	0.4
Primary and composite	66,045,995	30.7
Special schools	140,000	0.1
Secondary	76,015,297	35.3
Tertiary	39,545,663	18.4
Adult education	3,918,219	1.8
Special services	20,686,357	9.6
Total	215,056,353	100.0

Source: Government of Barbados, *Barbados Estimates 1992/93*

budget. In 1989, for instance, public expenditure on education amounted to 6.9 percent of gross national product (GNP), the highest proportion among the nonindustrialized countries in that year (UNDP 1992). Since Independence in 1966, there has been a substantial increase in education's share of total public expenditure. During the period from 1980–81 to 1990–91, education's share of total public expenditure fluctuated between 17.0 and 22.3 percent. However, with the economic downturn which Barbados has experienced since 1990 the education sector's share of the national budget was reduced significantly to an estimated 16.9 percent for 1992–93.

During the 1992–93 financial year, the Ministry of Education will have spent an estimated Bds$215 million on its various programs, as shown in Table 2. As far as the allocation of the state budget between the three main levels of education is concerned, it should be noted that 30.7 percent of the budget is earmarked for the primary (and composite) schools, 35.3 percent for secondary education, and 18.4 percent for tertiary education.

The unit costs of the three educational levels are, in approximate terms, as follows: US$672 for primary education, US$913 for secondary education, and US $1,200 for tertiary education. This gives approximate unit cost ratios of 1 for primary education, 1.4 for secondary, and 1.8 for tertiary. During the five years ending in 1990–91, the unit cost of education in Barbados grew on average by 12.2 percent per annum (Ministry of Education 1994b). It is useful to note that over that period the unit cost of secondary education rose by 11.4 percent and that of tertiary education by 10.3 percent, while the unit cost of primary education increased by 12.7 percent.

Data on private resources as a percentage of the total resources devoted to education are difficult to come by. It is worth mentioning, however, that within the public system of education no tuition fees are charged for citizens of Barbados, that some students at the secondary and tertiary levels do have to pay examination fees and incur transportation costs, and finally that students in tertiary education have to buy books. In indicative terms, private costs amount to 15 to 20 percent of the total costs of academic education as well as for technical education. Adult education classes tend to be geared to the maximization of cost recovery.

A brief word on tertiary education awards is appropriate. Each year, a number of Barbados Scholarships and Exhibitions are awarded by the government on the basis of the results of the Cambridge Local Examination Syndicate. A Barbadian scholar may pursue studies in the country of his or her choice as long as the course of study has been approved by the Minister of Education. An exhibitioner, on the other hand, must normally attend the University of the West Indies. There is no distinction between the level of allowances paid to scholars and exhibitioners. The government pays the full cost of tuition, related course costs, and a proportionate part of the maintenance costs.

Two other sources of financing tertiary education are the National Development Scholarships and the Student Revolving Loan Fund (SRLF). The National Development Scholarships are bursaries which are awarded to candidates pursuing studies at the University of the West Indies in areas regarded as necessary for national development. The SRLF makes repayable credits available to qualified beneficiaries to finance studies in specific professional and technical careers identified as being of primary importance to the economic and social development of the country (Government of Barbados 1990).

6. Supplying Personnel for the Education System

Data on the number of teachers in public schools are provided in Table 3 for the year 1989–90. In that year, there were 2,810 teachers in the public schools: 1,531 (54.5%) in the primary and composite schools, 49 (1.7%) in the senior, and 1,230 (43.8%) in the secondary. Over 71 percent of the teachers in the public schools were trained, and teachers with university degrees numbered 1,084 or 38.6 percent of the total number of teachers.

In the early 1990s, Barbados does not appear to have a shortage of teachers. Indeed, over the year 1991–92 a few hundred teachers were laid off as the government moved to implement its IMF-assisted "stabilization" program and to bring the student–teacher ratios in the primary and secondary schools up to levels agreed upon with the World Bank as a condition for financing of the Second Education and Training Project.

Teachers without degrees are trained at Erdiston College, while those with degrees are trained at the Cave Hill Campus of the University of the West Indies.

Table 3
Teachers in public schools by type of qualification, 1989–90

	Primary % Total	Primary % Trained	Senior % Total	Senior % Trained	Secondary % Total	Secondary % Trained	All public schools Total	All public schools Trained
Graduate	236	98.1	1	100.0	847	69.8	1,084	76.1
Special grade	6	100.0	—	—	31	80.6	37	67.6
Teacher	1,289	70.5	48	75.0	352	62.5	1,689	69.0
Total	1,531	75.0	49	75.5	1,230	83.6	2,810	71.9

Source: Government of Barbados 1990

Efforts are made to improve the quality of the initial training through workshops and seminars organized by the Ministry of Education, and through inservice programs such as that in Educational Management and Administration at the Cave Hill Campus.

7. Curriculum Development and Teaching Methodology

The curricula of the primary and secondary schools are wide-ranging and are prescribed by the Ministry of Education. The subjects which are taught in the primary schools are: English language, English literature, religious knowledge and moral education, science, mathematics, art and handicraft, agriculture, history, music, geography, social studies, health and physical education. The subjects which are taught in the secondary schools include: agriculture, art and handicraft, English language, English literature, religious and moral education, foreign languages, history, music, geography, social studies, mathematics, the sciences, health and physical education, and technical and vocational education (including industrial arts, home economics, clothing and textiles, and business education). At both the primary and the secondary levels, the curriculum is uniform, nationwide. The National Curriculum Development Council (NCDC) is the body which advises the Ministry of Education on policy and other matters related to the curriculum. It was set up by the Minister of Education, and comprises persons with a cross-section of interests. The NCDC collaborates with the Curriculum Section of the Ministry of Education with regard to the evaluation, revision, and implementation of school curricula.

Indigenous book publishing is limited, although several teachers and educators are contracted by publishing houses (mainly British in origin) to author (often jointly) textbooks for primary and secondary schools. The Audio-Visual Aids Department of the Ministry of Education produces posters, pamphlets, booklets and many items of stationery, videotapes, slides, filmstrips, prints, films, audiotapes, and so forth, for use in the schools and education system. However, the reality is that many of the resources used in the schools (especially textbooks) have to be purchased from outside because of the very limited local output.

Students who reach the fifth form and take the secondary school leaving examinations (normally of the Caribbean Examinations Council, CEC) are allowed to sit those examinations in up to seven or eight subjects. With an eye on those examinations, students choose their different options at the end of Form 3. There are two compulsory subjects, mathematics and English. Perhaps the most popular of the elective subjects is principles of business. Two foreign languages are taught, Spanish and French, and Spanish is the more popular. The Ministry of Education ensures that the curriculum is implemented through regular visits to the schools by its education officers and through meetings between principals of secondary schools and Boards of Management.

8. The System of Examinations, Promotions, and Certifications

The transition rate from primary to secondary education in Barbados is almost 100 percent and at the age of 11 children are awarded places in the different types of secondary school on the basis of their performance in the CEE. In the secondary schools, pupils are promoted on the basis of their performance at the end of the (three-term) school year. An average mark is used at the end of each year up to and including Form IV. Most schools have qualifying examinations for those students who wish to sit the external school leaving examinations at the end of Form V. Students are allowed to write the external examinations (e.g., CEC) in those subjects in which they do well in the qualifying examinations.

The main problems faced in the early 1990s in improving the examination, promotion, and certification systems center around the Common Entrance Examination (CEE) and the selection of pupils for the preferred secondary schools. There is clearly a need for a comprehensive system of assessment of the performance of pupils in the primary schools in particular. There is need for diagnostic testing of pupils at, say, ages 7 and 9. However, the problem of the CEE as a selection device needs to be solved otherwise there is a danger of any "diagnostic" tests which may be instituted becoming CEE-like in their function. It is only after the issue of transfer from primary to secondary schools has been resolved that attention can meaningfully be given to the question of assessment at age 11 and indeed at age 16.

9. *Educational Assessment, Evaluation, and Research*

Relatively little educational assessment, evaluation, and research is undertaken in Barbados. It would normally be expected that this would be undertaken by the Planning and Development Division of the Ministry of Education, teachers organizations, and mainly by the School of Education of the University of the West Indies. The little that is done deals mainly with the performance of pupils in the CEE, and the data derived from such analyses are sometimes fed back into the primary school system. Even here, there has been something of a lapse. The bulk of the research that is done by the Ministry is geared toward the preparation of statistics for possible projects with the various lending agencies, and is usually connected with the consultancies carried out (almost always by foreign experts) for those projects.

It is not known exactly what proportion of the primary and secondary school budget is allocated to assessment, evaluation, and research. These areas do not appear as a line item in the budget. The main emphases at the beginning of the 1990s were on cost-effectiveness in education and on vocationalizing the curricula. The most important educational indicators on which information is regularly collected are: enrollment by grade and sex, number and types of teachers, and expenditure on education as a percentage of the national budget.

Significant school-based research is carried out by graduate students in the University of the West Indies School of Education as part of the requirements for diploma programs and other advanced degrees. These studies are an important contributor to the development of educational policy. In addition, the University staff, as part of their own program, undertake research on educational issues.

The Caribbean is a region with well-developed regional institutions and all countries benefit from research undertaken on specific Caribbean problems. In this respect, relevant contributions are made by CEC in its research and analysis on assessment and by the Carribean Community Secretariat (CARICOM) in its educational policy and program development.

10. *Major Reforms in the 1980s and 1990s*

Several major educational reforms were completed in this period or are ongoing in Barbados and mention should be made of at least three of them. A new Education Act (the Education Act 1981) was proclaimed in 1983. The Education Act 1981 repealed the Education Act of 1890 which was, with amendments, the law of the land for almost a century. The main objective of the new Act was the democratization of education and the regularizing of the management and operation of all secondary schools. Under this Act, all teachers in government schools became members of the civil service. The Act is comprehensive and covers all aspects of education from school attendance, registration of private institutions, and duties of teachers to management of primary and composite schools and provision of special education. It was amended in 1984 and again in 1990, with the following principal aims: (a) to cement the process of bringing the former government grammar schools under the control of the Ministry of Education; (b) to clarify the legal rights of teachers who were on the staffs of the former government grammar schools prior to the proclamation of the Act but who chose to become public servants after the proclamation; (c) to provide clear definitions of education at the various levels; and (d) to spell out procedures for the handling of disciplinary problems, emergencies, and so forth.

A second major reform was the "restructuring" of the University of the West Indies (UWI). The UWI is a regional institution with three campuses: one at Mona in Jamaica, another at St Augustine in the Republic of Trinidad and Tobago, and a third at Cave Hill in Barbados. In October 1984, the University's original Charter, Statutes, and Ordinances were amended. The original Charter made it clear that the University was a regional institution, which, though funded by the regional governments was not answerable to any particular government. The restructuring which took effect in October 1984 involved: (a) the transfer of considerable functions and powers from the central organs of the University to newer organs at each Campus, (b) the erosion of the unitary concept which earlier prevailed, and (c) the effective placing of control of the campuses in the hands of the governments of the three campus countries (Layne 1989).

The third area of reform was that of coeducation. With the assistance of the World Bank and the Inter-American Development Bank, the government has been involved in a school building program to improve the quality and cost-effectiveness of primary and secondary education. In the process of amalgamating some of the primary schools and expanding some at the secondary level, the government took the opportunity to move away from the old system of single-sex schools and toward the promotion of coeducation as a matter of policy.

11. Major Problems for the Year 2000

Perhaps the most important problem faced by the education system is that of rising costs. Mainly because of its high per capita income and general level of development, Barbados does not qualify for as much aid as some other developing countries. Thus, in an effort to deal with this problem, the government has been cutting back on its expenditure at all levels of the educational system. This tendency has in some ways been promoted by some of the aid agencies in exchange for their granting loans. Two examples of these cuts are the government's reduction in its expenditure on the admittedly inefficient Textbook Loan Scheme for the secondary schools and the planned reduction during 1992–93 in the expenditure on the UWI from about Bds\$36 million to Bds\$22 million.

As the turn of the century approaches, the government will need to take steps to implement measures to unify the secondary school system. Staff and pupils in all secondary schools will have to be seen to have the same status and facilities. Indeed the crucial problem of transfer from primary to secondary school will have to be regularized to make the unified secondary school system possible. The cleavages within the public secondary school system are reinforced by status distinctions between the public and private sectors and within the private sector, all of which makes for a divided secondary school system which is acting as a brake on national development.

There is also the continuing problem of education and employment. Barbados has a large population, few natural resources, and high unemployment, and the opportunity for emigration has been reduced. Educational policy will therefore have to deal with the question of the type of education and training which is necessary to meet this situation.

Finally, Barbados has several problems frequently associated with small countries which are only now being confronted and tackled. These relate to dependence in the development of curricula, textbooks, examinations, and planning. The growing attention being given to small states by some organizations and researchers is the hope that some solutions may be proposed.

References

Central Bank of Barbados 1991 *Annual Statistical Digest 1991*. Central Bank of Barbados, Bridgetown
Central Bank of Barbados 1993 *Annual Statistical Digest 1993*. Central Bank of Barbados, Bridgetown
Government of Barbados 1988 *Barbados Development Plan 1988–93*. Ministry of Finance and Economic Affairs, Bridgetown
Government of Barbados 1990 *Education in Barbados*. Ministry of Education and Culture, Bridgetown
Government of Barbados 1992 *Barbados Estimates 1992/93*. Ministry of Finance and Economic Affairs, Bridgetown
Government of Barbados 1993 *Barbados Economic Report 1992*. Ministry of Finance and Economic Affairs, Bridgetown
Government of Barbados 1994a *1993-2000 Development Plan*. Ministry of Economic Affairs, Bridgetown
Government of Barbados 1994b *Country Paper: Barbados. International Seminar on Financing Education in the Caribbean Countries*. Organized by the International Institute for Educational Planning and the University of the West Indies, Pegasus Hotel, Kingston, Jamaica, 27–28 January
Inter-American Development Bank 1991 *Economic and Social Progress in Latin America 1991 Report*. Inter-American Development Bank, Washington, DC
Layne A 1989 *Higher Education in Barbados*. UNESCO/CRESALC, Caracas
United Nations Development Programme (UNDP) 1992 *Human Development Report 1992*. Oxford University Press, New York

Further Reading

Government of Barbados 1986 *Recent Developments in Education in Barbados*. Ministry of Education and Culture, Bridgetown
Layne A 1985 Government revenue and expenditure on education in Barbados. *Int. J. Educ. Dev.* 5(2) 95–104
Layne A 1987 Key issues in the allocation of pupils to secondary schools in Barbados as viewed from a democratic perspective. *Bulletin of Eastern Caribbean Affairs* 12(6): 1–15

Belgium

A. Philippart

1. General Background

Belgium, a member state of the European Community, is one of the smallest countries in Europe, with a total area of 30,521 square kilometers (11,779 square miles). It is bordered to the north by the North Sea and the Netherlands, to the east by Germany, and to the south and west by France. The capital, Brussels, is also the administrative center of the European Community Commission (ECC) and of the North Atlantic Treaty Organization (NATO). An independent country since 1830, Belgium has always been at the crossroads of several waves of immigration and was in the midst of the turmoil of the two world wars. At the beginning of the 1990s, its population formed an ethnically, linguistically, religiously, and philosophically diverse society. Nevertheless, Belgium is a wealthy country with nearly 10 million inhabitants. About 869,000 people of foreign nationality (9% of the total) are first-, second-, and third-generation immigrants. The result of this is a significant "segmented pluralism" which has an influence on education.

Belgium became a federal state in the early 1970s, as a result of revisions to the Constitution in 1970. These revisions created cultural communities and regions and, in 1980, some educational matters not subject to the *Pacte Scolaire* (school treaty) of 1958 were transferred to them. These included issues relating to personal problems, such as healthcare, and assistance to underprivileged citizens, and from August 8, 1988 educational matters were allocated exclusively to the communities. The Special Law of January 18, 1989, relating to finance of the communities and regions, lays down the financial and budgetary resources for a period of 10 years, in particular for teaching, education, and scientific research. It should be noted that education is free. From this date onward the three communities—Flemish (in the north; the inhabitants of Flanders and the Dutch-speaking inhabitants of Brussels), French (Walloons in the south and the French-speaking inhabitants of Brussels), and the small German-speaking community in the Ardennes (on the border with Germany)—have been given autonomy in these matters.

Several educational systems coexist in each of the communities, namely: (a) the official subsidized education in the 9 provinces and 589 districts; (b) the free subsidized education for about 92 percent Catholic, 6 percent nondenominational, and 2 percent for the Protestant, Jewish, and Islamic religions; and (c) the education of the communities formerly organized and financed by the State.

The increase in the number of school systems, organizing authorities, and educational establishments is the result of many factors associated with the political, economic, and social history of Belgium over a period of 150 years. The liberal bourgeoisie of the nineteenth century desired a general education for its children and skilled labor for its businesses. The Roman Catholic Church wanted an education that promoted the values that it espoused, allied with a spirit of social justice. Supporters of socialist doctrines advocated the principles of equity, egalitarianism, and education for all in State schools. Thus, colleges, *athenea*, secondary schools, local schools, vocational schools, and technical institutes were created throughout rural and urban areas to cover for education in all the new scientific and technical skills engendered by industrialization. Either separately or in coalition, the three social/political forces mentioned above have constituted the basis of all compromises concerning structure, financing, syllabus planning, and certification. Their influence dominates Belgian society (trade unions, insurance companies, hospital networks, cultural or charitable associations, the press, federations of all kinds, and so on). As power depends on universal suffrage with proportional representation at each level, and therefore on coalition, the political majorities in the communities and regions and in the provinces and districts may be different from those of the central government.

The linguistic division between Flemish and French speakers led to the splitting of the political parties and highlighted the need for party coalitions in order to enact the various executive powers. The *Pacte Scolaire* established academic equivalence and stability between the systems for nursery, primary, secondary, special, artistic, and higher nonuniversity education. The achievement of such a balance was made possible by Belgium's economic growth; all of the required compromises could be reached by increasing the budgetary resources for each school system.

As a result of population density (330 inhabitants per square kilometer), rapid urbanization (50% in cities, and 95% in all urban areas), the imbalance between Flemish speakers (60%) and French speakers (40%), and as a consequence of legal provisions, the number of schools increased massively (11,853 in 1983–84, decreasing by 5.3% to 11,222 in 1987–88).

In principle, parents have the right to a primary school within 4 kilometers of their home, a lower-secondary school within 12 kilometers, and an upper-secondary school within 20 kilometers. If there is no school within these distances, the communities must pay for transport. For higher education, there are 8 full universities, 9 university-level institutions, and 407 long- and short-term higher education establishments.

The Belgian population has a negligible growth rate and has experienced accelerated aging since the Second World War. Despite a higher birthrate among immigrants, this hardly compensates for emigration and general mortality. It is also estimated that the total population might decrease from 1992 onward. This phenomenon would have several implications for education, in particular a sharp rise in the age of the teachers themselves which would hamper recruitment of young secondary and primary school teachers, and an imbalance in the composition of classes between Belgians and foreigners. Some schools in areas with a high concentration of foreigners are subject to an erratic supply of teachers and to a reduction in educational standards.

The school population is also continually declining, resulting in a reduction in the number of teachers (according to the existing training standards). The educational boom of 1955–56 brought about massive teacher recruitment; these teachers will all retire before the end of the century. An acute shortage of teachers will then arise if their professional training, working conditions, salary, and social position are not significantly improved. Indeed, strikes centering precisely on these issues have been taking place since May 1990.

2. *Politics and the Goals of the Education System*

Despite its complex sociopolitical system—Belgium's major objective is to maintain its high educational standards. In fact, to remain among the world's top 15 trading powers but with a population of only 10 million, the political and economic decision-makers must invest in education, research, and training. It is insufficient to decree that education is compulsory up to the age of 18 in order to guarantee the balance between the supply of and demand for jobs. It is also necessary to implement adequate training, allowing flexibility in both its timing and its extent, according to prevailing economic needs and individual aspirations.

One of the principal goals of any system of education is to create a system that affords everyone the best opportunity for personal development as an individual, as a citizen, and as a participant in an economic system. Equal opportunities for women and for all social classes, special attention for the disadvantaged, and better preparation in general are the prime movers of the educational reforms of the 1970s.

The democratization of education has made great progress since 1950, but much work is still needed to create the appropriate structures, resources, and techniques to achieve all these objectives. Academic backwardness, even at the primary-school level, and academic dropouts (about 30% in secondary school; over 50% in higher education) raise fears of a lengthening of the period needed to reach these goals.

3. *The Formal System of Education*

Compulsory education of all children from 6 to 12 years of age was introduced in 1914 but only implemented in 1919 after the First World War. It was also stipulated that compulsory schooling would be extended progressively to 13, and then to 14 years of age. In 1970, the average school leaving age was 15

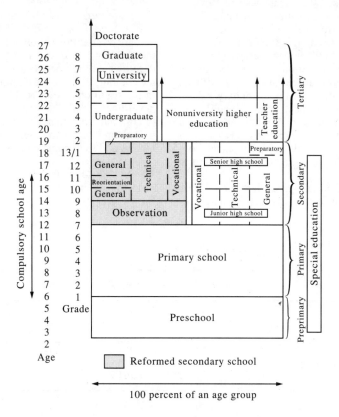

Figure 1
Belgium: Structure of the formal education system

years 8 months. The law of 1983 made it compulsory for all young people, regardless of whether they are Belgians or foreigners, to attend school for a period of 12 years beginining with the school year during which the child has reached the age of 6 and ending with the school year during which the young person reaches the age of 18.

However, compulsory full-time schooling cannot be imposed above the age of 16. Primary education and at least the first two years of full-time secondary education are compulsory and free of change. If a young person passes the examinations, then he or she can leave full-time education at 15 and attend part-time education. Otherwise, the student must wait until the age of 16 in order to enter into part-time education at a duly approved center with recognized training.

3.1 Primary, Secondary, and Tertiary Education

The educational system comprises four levels: preschool education (2–6 years), primary education (6–12 years), secondary education (12–18 years) and higher education (lasting 3, 4, 5, and even 7 years beyond secondary education).

As shown in Table 1, the number of pupils in the first three levels has decreased significantly since 1975. In contrast, higher education continues to expand.

Attendance in preschool education is about 30 percent up to 2½ years of age. It increases steadily from 3 years of age up to 99 percent between the ages of 5 and 6. For primary education there is pronounced unauthorized absenteeism in certain places with an underprivileged population. In the secondary school years (compulsory), attendance decreases steadily, according to certain studies, from 100 percent to over 40 percent between the ages of 15 and 18. Because of the lack of an appropriate regulatory mechanism, control is almost impossible and the means of constraint are illusory.

Some 60 percent of an age-group left school with at least a certificate in either general, technical or vocational lower-secondary education. In the 1980s, almost one child in three left compulsory education without a diploma at 18 years of age and from 40 to 50 percent of those who began university either abandoned their studies or reoriented themselves toward higher, nonuniversity education. Around 25 percent of young people who completed their secondary studies with a certificate actually obtained a higher education diploma.

Two types of secondary education exist in the French community (type I—law of July 19, 1971 on reformed education; type II—coordinated laws of April 1957) and one type in the Flemish community (since the decree of July 31, 1990 relating to the new general framework for secondary education).

The three structures reflect the complexity of a system which was designed to combine general, technical, artistic, and vocational education, by arranging transfers from one to another to enable young people to reorient themselves during studies according to the development of their abilities and to obtain the diploma which allows them entry to higher education or to complete the compulsory period of education with the best possible technical or vocational training.

3.2 Preschool Education

There are three groups of children in preschool education: (a) 2½ to 4 years; (b) 4 to 5 years; and (c) 5 to 6 years of age. Preschools are situated close to where the children live in order to teach the children within their own environments. The responsible agencies are the communities and the church. Teachers do not teach in the traditional way; rather, their main aims are to develop the children both mentally and physically, to stimulate their perception of their environment, to help them express themselves and communicate with others, and to become creative and self-sufficient.

3.3 Special Education

A 1970 law, modified in 1986, defines the policy of the Belgian state regarding physically and mentally

Table 1
Belgium: School population in 1974 and 1988 (in thousands)

	1974–75	1988–89	Difference	Percentage
Preschool	439	363	−76	−17.3
Primary	932	743	−189	−20.3
Subtotal	1,371	1,106	−265	−19.3
Secondary[a]	775	923	+148	+19.0
Higher nonuniversity	73	118	+45	+61.6
University	81	104	+23	+28.4
Total	2,300	2,251	−49	−2.1

a Increase linked to the extension of school attendance until 18 years of age

88

handicapped children from age 3 to 21 who are able to be educated, but outside the normal system of education. At the preschool, elementary, and secondary levels, the conditions for entry, the organization of the curriculum, the selection of students, and the personnel categories are required by law to parallel, as far as possible, the ordinary school system.

Special education takes place in specially designed institutions by either public or private bodies. The Ministry of Education is responsible for its administration and management, but the pedagogical and logistic aspects are decentralized to the eight institutional levels: mentally retarded, moderate or severely handicapped, personality problems, blind, deaf, motor coordination deficiencies, and those who are hospitalized for long periods of time. Entry to these establishments is as a result of a multifaceted assessment undertaken under the auspices of the ministry; the costs are covered by the Ministry of Education, but these are supplemented by donations from private persons and/or businesses and charitable organizations.

Approximately 60,000 pupils are enrolled in special education institutions. They either attend day schools or study at home or through correspondence courses. Those who are not able to be socially readapted or who receive vocational training in special environments receive an education according to their particular kind of handicap. The diplomas and certificates they receive are the same as in the normal educational system. The special education personnel are assisted by doctors, speech therapists, nurses, and social workers, all of whom work as a team.

3.4 Vocational, Technical, and Business Education

For the relevant level, these aspects of education are discussed in Sections 3.1 and 3.5 of this entry.

3.5 Adult and Nonformal Education

Several programs are available to adults and young people who have encountered problems during their formal education. The origins of education for social promotion can be found in the "adults' colleges" and "industrial colleges" which existed in the nineteenth century. Adult education enables around 255,000 people (120,000 in the French community—135,000 in the Flemish community) either to make up for basic education (vertical promotion), or to benefit from reorientation, proficiency, and updating in relation to their work or with a view to retraining or training (horizontal promotion). This form of education is extremely heterogeneous.

Distance learning has developed differently in the two communities. After 1984, the French Community reorganized this kind of education into four paths: (a) preparing adults for recruitment examinations or examining board tests; (b) participating in the continuous training of teachers; (c) catching up with primary education; and (d) developing the personality of those following the courses. Distance learning offers over 180 courses to just over 50,000 students in the French community.

The Flemish community linked its distance learning to two initiatives: (a) Heeflen Open University (in The Netherlands), and (b) Open Higher Education (with the support of universities and certain Flemish nonuniversity establishments).

The private business sector has also become involved in distance learning, above all in the fields of langues and computer science.

Other areas of nonformal training include the following: training army officers; alternate education–job training; professional training in branches such as construction, metal industries, electronics, chemistry, robotics, transport, the wood industry, clothing, languages, restaurants, secretarial, office administration, and so on; training programs called "apprenticeships," "on-the-job training", and "craftsmen and retailers' proficiency" of the French- and Flemish-speaking institutes for continuing education of the middle classes; and vocational training for agricultural personnel. This last sector is undergoing a complete transformation. Since 1960, the number of persons working in farming has decreased by 65 percent (from 264,000 to 91,600); the average farm size has increased from 6.2 to 15 hectares, and domestic production fulfills over 80 percent of national needs. The introduction of sophisticated, modern farming techniques has entailed great changes in training programs. All of these various professional training programs involve between 40,000 and 50,000 people annually.

4. Adminstrative and Supervisory Structure and Operation

Each community is empowered to take all decisions relating to education in its region except for the following: (a) the duration of compulsory schooling, (b) the minimum conditions for awarding diplomas, (c) pensions, unemployment and sickness/disability insurance for teachers. The respective ministries responsible for education are the *Ministerie van Onderwijs* (Flemish community) and the *Ministère de l'Education, de la Recherche et de la Formation* (French community). These administrative bodies exercise authority and supervision over the schools and establishments belonging to the three broad systems mentioned in the introduction, namely: education organized and financed by the communities; official, subsidized education (provinces and districts); and free, subsidized education.

The decrees on basic regulations and budgets are voted on by the community council (local parliament) in each community. The relevant decrees are passed in each community by the executive (local government).

Depending on the particular school system and establishment in each community, complex calculations are used to determine the training standards

Table 2
Number of teachers 1988–89

| | Flemish community | | | French community | | |
	M	F	Total	M	F	Total
Permanent	43,431	55,872	99,303	25,316	40,200	65,516
Temporary	7,784	11,845	19,629	4,677	11,109	15,786
Total	51,215	67,717	118,932	29,993	51,309	81,302

and numbers (either basic training, or overall number of teachers being trained), the number of teachers who can be employed (with a breakdown of figures for head teachers, secondary and primary teachers, auxiliary teachers, supervisory personnel, and secretariat), and the amounts of operational allocations. All salaries and wages of the personnel are paid directly by the administrative departments of each of the two ministries. Each establishment is run independently. Each network has its funds for school buildings, with financial intervention by the public authorities of each community.

Education that is organized and financed by the community is placed under the direct authority of the education minister in the French community, but in the Flemish community it comes under the aegis of the *Autonome Raad voor het Gemeenschapsonderwijs* (ARGO, or Autonomous Council for Community Education).

In education organized and financed directly by the communities, there is widespread decentralization in the day-to-day administration of educational establishments, in four main areas:

(a) Management and operational structures.

(b) Teaching (syllabus planning; conditions of admission and transition of pupils; teaching organization; distribution of teaching expenses).

(c) Selection and nomination of teachers.

(d) Accounting and financial management and purchase of materials.

However, the government is still responsible for ensuring standards. Management and teaching inspectors ensure that schools are well-run. Financial credits and subsidies and the recognition of certificates can be temporarily withheld from any school found guilty of disregarding the rules.

5. Educational Finance

Government expenditure on teaching has been decreasing as a proportion of the general state budget and of Gross National Product (GNP) since 1980. The large increase in demands on the general state budget is due to the heavy financial burden imposed by the public debt, and by unemployment. In 35 years, spending on education saw a 36-fold increase from 9 billion francs (BF) in 1955 to BF 323 billion in 1990; this amounts to a real growth of some 200 percent in constant francs over the same period (1990 figures).

The percentage of GNP allocated to education was 3.2 percent in 1960, 4.5 percent in 1970, 6.1 percent in 1975, 6.6 percent in 1980, 6.2 percent in 1985, and 5.1 percent in 1990. The overall amount of the education budget is likely to decrease further in the 1990s as a result both of a reduced birthrate and of measures instituted by the state to shift the burden of expenditure to other sources of funding (parental contributions, sponsorship and donations by private companies, etc.). These interventions outside the budget cannot be quantified, since educational establishments, by virtue of autonomy of management, are precluded from calculating them in their budgets.

6. Supplying Personnel for the Education System

The total number of people employed in all systems and on all levels of education in Belgium, from nursery through university, and including both teachers and administrative and ancillary staff, exceeds 7.5 percent of the working population. Teachers alone—from nursery to higher education—represent almost 200,000 full-time or part-time staff, the female proportion of which increased during the 1980s. Over half are employed in secondary education and almost one-third in primary education. The remainder are divided among nursery, special, and higher education.

The number of teachers in each community in 1988–89 is given in Table 2.

Women represented 57 percent of teachers in Flanders and 63 percent in the French community, with a higher proportion among temporary staff (particularly part-time positions). Nursery and primary education have almost 100 percent female staff.

The following factors have all contributed to the downgrading of the profession of teacher to the status of a second-income job in households: low salaries, the loss of social prestige, increased mobility of the population, the lack of job security, the absence of systematic ongoing training, and the expansion of the employment market.

The average age of permanent teachers is very high (about 43-years old in primary education and between 44- and 50-years old in secondary education); in the mid-term, this will create a problem of how they are to be replaced when the profession is no longer attractive to prospective young teachers.

The length of training (4 years for a university graduate and 3 years for a higher, nonuniversity graduate after secondary education) and the value of the diploma gives teachers the right to demand a higher social status, as they constitute a major asset in the dissemination of knowledge and expertise for economic development.

7. Curriculum Development and Teaching Methodology

In each of the three communities, setting of the curriculum and development of the study syllabuses for the basic (primary) and secondary levels are the responsibility of the respective education systems and establishments under conditions defined by the *Pacte Scolaire*; in particular, to follow a syllabus and a legally stipulated minimum timetable and to have them approved by the competent minister, in order to benefit from subsidies. Nonuniversity higher education is controlled by inspection, yet each organizing authority is free to determine teaching methods.

Materials for study (books, syllabuses, exercises, etc.) are produced by inspectors and/or teachers in a private capacity and marketed by private companies. Their concern is to ensure a complementarity between the levels of teaching and continuity in education. To coordinate the whole system, study syllabus committees exist in each system, presided over by the inspectors in the relevant subject. There is no central curriculum development institute.

Secondary education certificates and diplomas awarded by schools must be approved by an assessment committee (*commission d'homologation*) consisting of teachers from official and private schools. This committee checks if the standard provided for by the syllabus has been achieved. Teaching varies from one school to another within the same system, and even within a district or area; a necessary upshot of democracy and diversity. Thus, the parents are obliged to keep themselves constantly informed of the quality of one school in relation to another, sometimes over short periods of time. Such assessment is of necessity subjective, and conveyed by word of mouth, because there is no centrally accredited organization and no universally valid criteria by which to compare schools. Nevertheless, comparative academic results from Belgium and other countries indicate that educational standards remain at a high level and are comparable with the best foreign curricula.

8. The System of Examinations, Promotions, and Certifications

Primary education begins in September of the year in which the child reaches the age of 6; in order to be admitted into secondary education, the child must be 12 years of age, and have obtained the basic certificate of studies proving that he or she has successfully completed primary education.

However, in the absence of this certificate a child can still be admitted into the first year of the secondary school with the agreement of the parents, and subject to the advice of the psycho–medico–social center and the favorable opinion of the admissions council. There are many subsequent reorientation paths within the various secondary education sectors, subject to preestablished conditions being fulfilled. For entry into higher education the candidate needs a higher secondary education certificate (CESS) and, for entry to university, an aptitude diploma for entry into higher education (DAES).

In primary education, the teacher decides whether a pupil may progress from one grade to the next. In secondary school, decisions concerning orientation and upgrading to the next level are taken by a class committee which consists of all teachers teaching that grade.

Awarding certificates is the responsibility of each school. Criteria that are typically used are results in all subjects, discussions with the pupil and his or her parents, past academic history, and behavior. For vocational studies, success in a qualification test (*preuve de qualification*) is necessary and granted by a qualification board comprising teachers and professionals.

9. Educational Assessment, Evaluation, and Research

Evaluation and research in education are the responsibility of universities, a small number of centers and a few teacher-training colleges. There is no overall plan; rather, each researcher draws up a research or evaluation project on his or her own initiative or at the request of the ministry concerned. Financing is mainly of academic origin, according to the preeminence of the researcher. Since 1965 government funds have been made available to researchers to carry out studies relating to urgent and strictly delimited issues. Examples of issues covered are: teaching methods, educational technology (computer science), learning mechanisms, educational failures, financial flows and costs of education, health education, equal opportunities, academic paths, the education–employment relationship, and so on. It might reasonably be argued that financial and personnel resources should be much greater in this sector, given the problems which remain to be solved during the 1990s.

10. Major Problems for the Year 2000

The financing of education in Belgium is already a fundamental political and economic problem for all the reasons outlined above. The aging of the population, decline in the birthrate, high average age of teachers, problems of replacement, ongoing training, and adaptation of the curricula and teaching methods to scientific and technical changes and to economic objectives within an enlarged European context all constitute formidable challenges. Belgium's history indicates that similar challenges at the end of the nineteenth century and after the First and Second World Wars were met and resolved favorably. The democratization of studies, compulsory schooling, the integration of women and underprivileged social groups, and resolution of ideological confrontations, for example, were all successfully achieved. The essential thing is to become aware of them.

Bibliography

Alaluf M, Vanheerwynghels A 1988 *Adéquation enseignement–marché de l'emploi*. Fondation Roi Baudoin, Brussels

Brassinne J 1989 *Les nouvelles institutions politiques de la Belgique*. CRISP, Brussels

De Groof J 1989 *De grondwetsherziening van 1988 en het onderwijs—De schoolvrede en zijn toepassing*. Story Scientia, Brussels

De Landsheere G 1986 *La recherche en éducation dans le monde*. PUF, Paris

Devos G, Vandenberghe P, Verhoeven J C (eds.) 1989 *Schoolbeleid: Mogelijkheden en grenzen. Een empirisch onderzoek*. ACCO, Leuven

Leirman W 1990 Adult education and the state in Belgium and the Netherlands. In: Pöggeler F (ed.) 1990 *Adult Education and the State*. Peter Lang, Frankfurt

Ministère de l'Education Nationale 1988 *Le mouvement ducatif en Belgique: Développement de l'éducation 1986–1988*. Ministère de l'Education Nationale, Brussels

Ministère de l'Education, de la Recherche et de la Formation 1991 *Effectifs scolaires: Régime linguistique français 1990–91*. Coll. Etudes et Documents, Brussels

Ministerie van Onderwijs 1990 *Statistisch jaarboek van het onderwijs 1988–89*. Dienst onderwijsstatistieken, Brussels

Monard G 1990 Meer ruimte voor lokaal onderwijsbeleid? *Brandpunt* 17(8): 224–30

Organisation for Economic Co-operation and Development (OECD) 1991 *Les systèmes ducatifs en Belgique: Similitudes et divergences*. OECD, Paris

Van Haecht A 1985 *L'enseignment rénové de l'origine à l'éclipse*. Editions ULB, Brussels

Wielemans W 1987 *Structuur en organisatie van het educatiefbestel*. ACCO, Leuven

Ylieff Y 1990 *L'enseignement de l'an 2, ou 50 questions sur l'enseignement communautarisé*. Brussels

Belize

J. A. Bennett

1. General Background

Belize is located in Central America. It is bounded on the north by Mexico and on the west and south by Guatemala. Its total land area is 22,963 square kilometers. Formerly a British colony, Belize became an independent country within the Commonwealth of Nations in 1981. Its population consists of a diversity of ethnic groups, the major ones being Creoles of African descent, Mestizos, Mayas (Ketchi, Mopan, and Yucatec), and Garifuna (once called Black Caribs). There are also smaller populations of East Indians, Chinese, and persons of Middle-Eastern origin. The Spanish-speaking population has increased significantly during the last 20 years because of an influx of Central Americans fleeing the turmoil of war and the harsh economic conditions in their home countries. There has also been an increase of Asian immigrants, particularly Indians and Chinese.

The estimated population in 1991 was 191,000, of which slightly over 50 percent lives in rural areas. Nearly 60 percent is under 20 years of age. Some 45,000 persons reside in Belize City, the former capital of the country (replaced by the newly built capital, Belmopan, in 1970).

Although the economy of Belize was once dependent on its forestry industries, agriculture has become mainstay of the Belizean economy. The inhabitants are mainly engaged in farming, many of them being "slash and burn" cultivators.

The most important agricultural enterprises are the cultivation of sugar cane, citrus, bananas, and cattle. At the offshore cays—particularly San Pedro, Ambergris Cay and Cay Corker—scale fish, lobster, and shrimp fishing is a thriving industry managed by fishing cooperatives. Tourism is also a growing industry. The government is actively pursuing a policy of eco-tourism focusing on the natural environment and its conservation. In 1989 the labor force was 47,325, of which 40,700 were employed.

The Gross Domestic Product (GDP) in 1991 was Bze$645,136,000 and the per capita GDP was Bze$3,381. Total government expenditure for the same period was Bze$234,281,741 or 36.3 percent of the GDP. The expenditure of the Ministry of Education was Bze$45,384,363 or 7 percent of the GDP.

The Belizean economy experienced a downturn in the early 1980s because of the energy crisis of the previous decade followed by a serious fall in the price of sugar on the world market.

By 1990, however, it showed a marked improvement. The production of sugar, bananas, and citrus had increased and so had construction activity. However, inflation and unemployment remained high. The government's strategy for the 1990s is to achieve continued economic growth through a diversification of the economy. The implication for education is seen as that of enabling greater access to schooling for a growing population of young people and adapting the curricula of the schools to the priority needs of the country.

2. Politics and the Goals of the Education System

The stated mission of the Ministry of Education is that of being responsible for ensuring that all Belizeans have the opportunity of acquiring a well-rounded education for their own personal development, which enables them to participate fully and actively in the development of Belize. Nevertheless, the Ministry of Education acknowledges the partnership of the state with churches and other voluntary agencies.

The financing and administration of formal education in Belize has traditionally been based on a partnership between the churches and the state, and both the People's United Party and the United Democratic Party have supported the Church–State system of education. This acceptance has been of much significance in the formulation and implementation of national education policies which must take fully into account the views, perceptions, and preferences of religious denominational school managers regarding what is desirable and feasible in the educational programs of the schools. To this end, the present Education Act has made ample provisions for the authority and responsibilities of church managers of schools. These include such matters as the proprietorship of schools, and the hiring and firing of teachers and their posting. Both political parties support the policies of compulsory schooling for primary-school age children, improving access to secondary education, and providing for technical and vocational education throughout the educational system starting in primary school.

With regard to postsecondary education, both political parties support a policy aimed at the development of university-level education. However, the People's United Party has leaned towards the principle of amalgamating all postsecondary educational institutions under the aegis of a central university. This was the thrust of the effort to institute and develop the Belize College of Arts, Science, and Technology BELCAST (1978–86). The United Democratic Party, which ruled during the period 1984–89 disestablished BELCAST,

preferring an expansion of autonomous sixth-form level and other similar institutions serving as feeder schools to the two-year transfer-degree-granting University College of Belize (UCB). The administration of UCB would like to expand the institution into a three-year or possibly a four-year full-fledged university.

3. The Formal System of Education

3.1 Primary, Secondary, and Tertiary Education

Schooling is compulsory for all children between the ages of 5 and 14 years and the great majority of them enroll at the age of 5. Since the 1970s an increasing number of children between the ages of 3 and 5 have been enrolled in preschool centers. In 1990 there were 74 such centers in the country catering for some 2,680 children. The majority of these centers are run privately by individuals or by community groups with some assistance from the government. The primary schools are, with a few exceptions, all-age schools. The majority of them are rural schools, some of which are small. The primary-school course covers eight grades—Infants I and II and Standards I through VI. Tuition is free in all government and government-aided schools, but parents are expected to provide the required books for their children and contribute to fundraising activities. In 1991 there were some 46,023 pupils enrolled in primary schools. This represented about 90 percent of the primary-school age population.

Figure 1 presents a diagram of the system of education of Belize. Statistical data are difficult to obtain. The figure is based on the best estimates available.

Pupils transfer from primary to secondary school between the ages of 11 and 14 or 15. About 50 percent of the pupils who complete the primary-school course transfer to secondary schools; the rest leave school when they reach 14 or continue in all-age schools until they are 15 or 16 years of age.

At the secondary level, there are three categories of schools: (a) church-managed schools, (b) community schools which are managed by lay boards of governors, and (c) government schools. The government, of course, undertakes all responsibility for the operation of government secondary schools. The others are grant-aided. The government pays 70 percent of the salaries of teachers and of the recurrent expenditures of the schools. Grants are also made available on a 50 percent basis for all approved building projects.

Secondary education has grown significantly since 1980, both in the number of schools and in their enrollment. At least seven new schools were established during this period, some in rural locations. In 1990, there were 27 secondary schools enrolling 7,372 students, with a more or less even distribution in terms of gender.

93

The Belize Technical College, which conducted a two-year senior-secondary program as well as a sixth-form program was reorganized in the 1970s, thereby eliminating the secondary-school level program. This institution is now considered a tertiary-level college offering a diversified curriculum oriented towards the natural sciences and technical/vocational training. St John's College Sixth Form may be regarded as the counterpart to the Belize Technical College, which is a government institution. St John's College Sixth Form which developed out of SJC (St John's College), a Jesuit secondary school, offers a liberal arts program oriented to the Unites States Junior college system, but also prepares its students for the British A–level examinations.

Two other secondary schools offer courses at sixth-form level and there is also a teachers' college. The University College of Belize offers two-year first-degree programs for students who have acquired the necessary number of credits at the sixth-form or junior-college level of postsecondary education. Belize is also a contributing member of the University of the West Indies and is represented on the university's council. Those who wish to advance their education beyond the sixth-form level can now enter the University College of Belize (which offers baccalaureate programs in business administration and education) or must go abroad, mainly to the University of the West Indies or to colleges and universities in the United States, the United Kingdom, Canada, Mexico, or Central America.

In 1990 the total number of full-time postsecondary students was 1,649. The enrollment at the University College of Belize was 238.

English is the official language of the country but there are areas where the mother tongue is either Spanish, Garifuna, or Maya (Yucatec, Mopan, Ketchi).

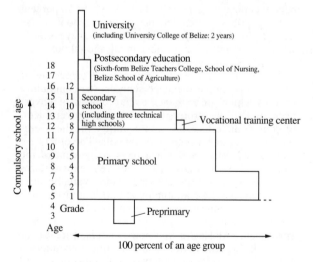

Figure 1
Belize: Structure of the formal education system

Creole is the *lingua franca* among Belizeans. English, however, is the universal medium of instruction in schools, and from the outset the aim is to enable school children to develop skill and facility in communicating in English, both oral and written. The teaching of English poses a challenge since, for the majority of children, it has to be taught as a second language and requires appropriate teaching methods.

3.2 Special Education

Stella Maris School is categorized as a primary school, though strictly speaking it is a special education institution. It serves some 100 physically and/or mentally handicapped students and has been very active in supporting a number of smaller units. There is need for better coverage of children with disabilities than is possible under existing circumstances. In Belize, special education is narrowly defined as the education of persons with disabilities and so far does not include the education of the gifted or of slow learners.

3.3 Vocational, Technical, and Business Education

There is an increasing awareness among the policymakers (and the Belizean people in general) of the need for a greater emphasis on technical and vocational education in the schools. There is also a growing demand among employers for a variety of skilled workers. In response to the demands of the labor market, and to the problems of unemployment, attempts have been made over the last 20 years to provide some practical training for the older primary-school students, through gardening in some rural schools and through a few rather small institutions such as manual craft and home economics centers. There is also a Vocational Training Center, which caters for a small number of primary-school leavers. At the secondary level, the schools have been called upon to diversify their curricula so as to provide for technical/vocational education in order to equip students with job-entry skills in some areas. At the post-secondary level, the Belize Technical College has been in operation since 1952 and has increased the range of courses it offers. Outside of the ambit of the Ministry of Education are the Belize College of Agriculture and the Belize School of Nursing.

In order to respond to the employment needs of young people, the Vocational Technical Training Unit (VTTU) was established in 1986. This agency provides support to the schools in their curriculum and teacher-training efforts. The national endeavors relating to technical/vocational education have not been without problems. Facilities, equipment, learning materials, and the trained labor force are generally inadequate. The personnel of the VTTU need to be upgraded, and linkages with industry need to be forged and strengthened to ensure relevance in the program being implemented in the schools. There is also a need to institute alternative programs which are more adaptable to the changing needs of industry. One such alternative is being attempted in the form of a Center for Employment Training.

3.4 Adult and Nonformal Education

Services in this aspect of education are available in a limited number of programs. Some cater for the academic needs of their clientele; others offer skills training. Programs exist mainly in urban communities. Nongovernmental organizations, as well as certain government ministries (e.g., Health, Social Services, and Agriculture) deliver services in the area of nonformal education.

The involvement of the Ministry of Education in nonformal and adult education has not been extensive. Other agencies which have been involved have not had the coordination necessary to ensure that programes are optimally effective. However, a recently designed literacy and adult education plan is expected to be receiving more support from the Ministry of Education during the coming years.

4. Administrative and Supervisory Structure and Operation

All matters relating to the national policy on education are ultimately the responsibility of the Minister of Education under the general authority of the new Education Act which was passed in the National Assembly in 1990. Under this act there is a National Council for Education which serves as an advisory body to the Minister and is expected to play an important role in giving direction to Belizean education.

Except for a few government schools, all grant-aided primary schools are managed by the churches. Grant-in-aid includes, in respect to recurrent costs, the total cost of teachers' salaries and a grant towards the maintenance of buildings, furniture, and equipment. The Government also makes grants available on a 50 percent basis for all *approved* building projects and provides some writing and other materials to the schools. Primary-school teachers enjoy a noncontributory pension scheme.

There is a very small number of private primary schools which operate as independent schools as a matter of policy. The remainder are private because they are not presently receiving grant-in-aid from the Government. However, they may become grant-aided whenever they are able to satisfy the conditions laid down for this and the required funds are available.

The Government makes grants available to approved secondary schools based on a formula which provides for the payment of 70 percent of the salaries of teachers and of the recurrent cost of operating the schools. The government also provides a number of scholarships annually to pupils completing the primary-school

course to enable them to continue their education at the secondary level. These scholarships meet the cost of tuition and include a book allowance. Scholarship students who must live away from home to take up their awards, and who are genuinely in need of assistance, receive a bursary to help meet the cost of their board and lodging. A scholarship is thus the equivalent of free education for those who receive the awards.

Responsibility for the administration of the Ministry of Education lies with the Permanent Secretary. The Chief Education Officer functions as the Chief Professional Officer and as advisor to the Permanent Secretary and the Minister. Other senior officers attached to the Education Section of the Ministry are one Deputy Chief Education Officer and two Principal Education Officers (Primary and Secondary). In addition, there are education officers whose main functions are to supervise the work in the schools and to assist teachers in improving the effectiveness of their teaching and in upgrading the standard of education.

Under the Education Act, all schools, private and grant-aided as well as government funded, are open to supervision and inspection by education officers.

Supervision and inspection are undertaken by education officers stationed at Belmopan (the capital), in Belize City and in the remaining districts. The orientation of supervision is toward improving the teaching–learning process, and it is recognized that this can only be achieved when teachers and education officers work together in partnership for the improvement of education. However, relatively few of the schools are supervised each year and it is realized that if the quality of learning in the schools is to be improved, the issue of adequate supervision will have to be addressed.

5. Educational Finance

Total educational expenditure has risen over the years, with a particularly sharp increase between 1986 and 1990, when education's share of total government expenditure increased from 16 percent to 23 percent. The sharp rise was caused mainly by increases in teachers' salaries in 1988. However, by the early 1990s it seemed that education's share of total government expenditure had reached a ceiling beyond which the government would find it difficult to sustain increased expenditure over a long period. For example, estimates of public expenditure for the 1992–93 budget year show a reduction of about 5 percent and a target share for education of 20 percent.

The budget for capital expenditure includes counterpart funds for projects which are financed externally. In 1990–91 the Ministry of Education budgeted Bze$1.8 million for locally funded expenditure, of which 48 percent, or Bze$865,000, was for the primary sector. The largest portion of the budgeted capital expenditure for primary education is the reimbursement to church managements of 50 percent of the capital expenditure undertaken by the churches. The totals do not represent the contribution of the churches. Education receives a relatively low amount of external assistance for capital expenditure from external sources compared with other key sectors such as agriculture. However, the primary-education project—partially funded by the World Bank—will significantly increase the proportion of externally funded capital expenditure in education.

An estimate of unit costs in 1991 indicates that for the primary level it was Bze$481, for secondary Bze$844, and for tertiary Bze$1,862. These estimates were based on the government's statement of recurrent expenditure. If private contributions were to be added, the amounts for the secondary and tertiary levels would be somewhat higher.

6. Supplying Personnel for the Education System

There were 1,749 primary-school teachers employed in government and government-aided schools in 1990. Of these, approximately 40 percent were trained—that is, had graduated from the Belize Teachers College. The remaining 60 percent were either certificated teachers who had qualified themselves through sitting between one and three of the annual teachers' examinations set by the Ministry of Education, or they were unqualified teachers. So far, the minimum educational attainment required for employment as a primary-school teacher is a primary-school leaving certificate. However, the majority of teacher recruits are now high-school graduates.

Formal teacher education is conducted by the Belize Teachers College whose program has comprised a two-year intramural course followed by a year of supervised teaching. In 1990, a three-semester program was introduced in an effort to increase the number of trained teachers at a faster pace. Under the Belize Primary Education Project which was officially inaugurated in early 1992, the Belize Teachers College is being considerably restructured to accommodate two levels of teacher training: (a) the newly introduced three-semester course, titled Level I Certificate in Teaching; and (b) the Level II Certificate in Teaching to which Level I teachers be admitted after an interval of classroom teaching. The Belize Teachers College's role is also being expanded to include a range of inservice teacher training.

There were 576 teachers employed in secondary schools in 1990. Of these, 201 were university graduates, some with professional training in teaching. Of the remainder, 96 were nondegree trained teachers; the others were unqualified, largely recruits from among sixth-form graduates. This last situation is changing as the University College of Belize produces teachers with education degrees from its baccalaureate program.

7. Curriculum Development

The Ministry of Education through its Curriculum Development Unit is responsible for providing curriculum guidelines for all government and government-aided primary schools. Principals and their teaching staff are expected to use these guidelines to prepare annual schemes of work which are relevant to their specific situations. Classroom teachers draw on the broad curriculum guides and the more specific annual schemes to prepare their weekly and daily teaching plans. There are curriculum guides in all the basic content areas including mathematics, language, arts, social studies, and science. There are also curriculum guides for health and physical education, and art and craft.

There is no common national system at the secondary-school level. Each individual school authority establishes its own curriculum policy and program. Even so, there is not a great deal of curriculum difference between schools. In all of them, for instance, English and mathematics are compulsory subjects during all four years of secondary schooling. Students are also expected to study Spanish, one or more of the natural sciences, and social studies or history. There is not a great deal of focus on the arts or physical education. For over 30 years secondary schools have been encouraged to diversify their curricula to provide for technical and vocational training, so that all attempt to offer commercial and elementary business courses, and home economics, mainly to female students. Some schools also attempt to provide opportunities for boys to engage in woodwork and metalwork and, where appropriate, agriculture.

In 1989, the Belize Association of Principals of Secondary Schools, in collaboration with the Curriculum Development Unit, prepared a curriculum policy for secondary schools which had the approval of the Ministry of Education. The policy document provides for a core curriculum to be adhered to by all secondary schools and a secondary school curriculum project has instigated work on curriculum development to provide guidelines and support materials for the content areas of English, mathematics, social studies, and science. The next facet to be worked on is that of preparing and instituting a national secondary-school leaving certificate examination which caters to the certificating needs of the "average" secondary student as well as to those of the higher achievers.

8. The System of Examinations, Promotions, and Certifications

At the primary-school level promotion varies, but as a rule it is based on the age and average grade achieved in the termly and final yearly school-based examinations. Upon completion of the eighth grade (Standard VI) primary-school pupils sit the Belize National Selection

Examination (BNSE) which serves for the award of a primary-school certificate and some 350 scholarships to secondary schools. The same examination serves as a device for screening the admission of children to secondary schools.

The BNSE is a norm-referenced examination and it has been suggested that it could be improved by being converted to a criterion-referenced test and by the reinstitution of a separate primary-school leaving certificate examination. With the establishment of a proposed Test and Assessment Unit it is expected that there will be some improvement in the present BNSE.

At the secondary-school level students are also promoted on the basis of success in the termly and final annual school-based examination. Upon completion of the four-year program, students sit the Caribbean Examination Council Examinations which have largely replaced the overseas GCE O-level examinations set by British examinations syndicates. At the end of the sixth-form program, students prepare for the GCE A-level examinations. Those who pursue technical studies may sit the British City and Guilds examinations.

9. Educational Assessment, Evaluation, and Research

There is no testing service in Belize at present nor is there any research agency. The proposed Test and Assessment Unit is expected to establish a system of diagnostic tests at different points in the primary-school program. It is also expected to undertake the institution of a national secondary-school leaving certificate examination. With the establishment of the planning unit within the Ministry of Education and the test and assessment unit increasing attention will be given to educational research. Classroom teachers are not very well trained in the preparation and administration of tests. Hence, there is an urgent need for such training. The Belize Teachers College and the University College of Belize should be playing a more prominent role in the preparation of practicing and prospective teachers for these areas of concern.

The Curriculum Development Unit of the Ministry of Education has been the principal agency for curriculum development and low-cost materials production. Established in 1975, the CDU has produced curriculum guides for the primary schools as well as some learning materials, largely for the primary schools. However, since 1989 when a Curriculum Officer for Secondary Education was appointed to understudy a consultant engaged with the assistance of the Overseas Development Administration of Great Britain. Some work has been done with regard to the secondary-school curriculum mentioned above. This work is expected to continue as human and material resources become more available. Since 1975, the responsibilities of the Curriculum Development Unit have been expanded to include schools broadcasts and tests and assessment.

In the near future there will have to be some revision of its structure and administration to accommodate the various subcomponents which are being added to the unit. This restructuring is expected to take place during the life of the Belize Primary Education Project which came fully on stream in 1992.

10. Major Reforms in the 1980s and 1990s

During the 1980s there were a number of significant developments in Belizean education. At the primary-school level REAP (initially the Rural Education and Agriculture Project, but subsequently re-named Relevant Education for Agriculture and Productivity in an attempt to expand the program of curricular activities into town schools) gained ground as the number of participating schools grew from some nine project schools in the mid-1970s to over 60 primary schools in 1991. REAP is an innovative project which is aimed at making the curriculum of the rural schools relevant and enriched. Its philosophy is child-centered, and its methodology integrative and activity-oriented. Instead of the compartmentalizing of the instructional program, "areas of study" are utilized so as to engage the children in learning from both the social and natural environment of their community. The use of the school garden as an outdoor education center is of special importance. Unfortunately, because of the perceived conflict of REAP with the traditional, compartmentalized curriculum the thrust of this innovation has decreased in strength.

Another reform of the 1980s was the introduction of the Belize National Selection Examination which primary-school leavers sit at the completion of the eight grade levels of the primary-school. Previously, primary-school leavers sat the primary-school leaving certificate examination. Those who were successful were awarded a primary-school certificate. The pass rate was very low. A selected number of "high flyers" sat a scholarship examination through which they competed for places in the secondary schools. The BNSE is a norm-referenced examination which is utilized to provide all primary-school leavers with a primary-school certificate as well as to admit children into the secondary schools, some of them as holders of scholarships funded by the Belize government.

At the tertiary level, the Belize College of Arts, Science, and Technology (BELCAST) was inaugurated in the late 1970s as the nucleus of a university-level institution. It commenced by offering a small range of technology-oriented courses, but in the early 1980s it widened its scope, absorbing the Belize Teachers College and worked toward amalgamating the Belize School of Nursing, the Belize Technical College, the Belize College of Agriculture, and other sixth-form level institutions. The University College of Belize (UCB), which replaced BELCAST, commenced (in affiliation with Ferris State University in the United States) to offer a two-year degree program to students who had successfully completed sixth-form or equivalent studies. At the beginning of the 1990s the University College was a viable university-level institution which had shed its dependency on a foreign institution and whose faculty was seriously engaged in forward planning.

In 1989, the Ministry of Education commenced negotiation with the World Bank for a loan to fund an educational project in Belize. The project was aimed at improving the quality of education, particularly at the primary level. The project was prepared during 1990 and the first half of 1991, during which time three components were identified for focus: the restructuring of the Belize Teachers College, principally a training institution for primary-school teachers; the institution and development of an educational planning unit within the Ministry of Education; and the mounting of an education development program with emphasis on curriculum, materials production, and student assessment.

11. Major Problems for the Year 2000

Some of the problems of the education system identified in 1981 are still present, although strenuous efforts are being made to solve them. At the primary-school level, for instance, overcrowding is severe and many classrooms need major repairs. Assuming a continuation of present demographic trends, the problem of meeting the social demand for school places will continue despite the continuing efforts to construct schools and to expand and repair school facilities.

There is a need to improve student achievement. Many factors contribute to unsatisfactory student performance in school. They include the high proportion of inadequately prepared teachers; unsuitable curricula or poor use of existing curricula; the scarcity of suitable textbooks, teaching materials, and equipment; and

the unsuitable physical conditions of schools. Serious efforts will be made to improve such conditions, but they are not expected to have disappeared by the year 2000.

The problem of the responsiveness of the educational system to the training needs of the country is very evident. The secondary and tertiary levels of the education system will need to be adapted to the problems of technical and vocational training as the twenty-first century approaches.

Bibliography

Belize Today 1991 (August) Issue devoted to Belizean economy 1981–91
Bethell G 1990 *Proposals for Examination Reform in Belize*. Ministry of Education, Belize City
Bridges D, Thompson C 1991 *Proposal for Teacher Training Component of the World Bank Education Project*. Ministry of Education, Belize City
Central Statistical Office 1990 *Abstract of Statistics 1990*. Ministry of Economic Development, Belize City
Curriculum Development Unit, Task Force III 1990 Curriculum, development, learning resources and assessment (draft), *Proposals for Education Development Component of the World Bank Education Project*. Ministry of Education, Belize City
Ministry of Education 1990 Prioritization with regard to proposals of Task Forces. *Proposed World Bank project to be initiated January 1991*. Ministry of Education, Belize City
Ministry of Education 1991a *Development plan 1990–1995* (draft). Ministry of Education, Sports, Culture, Broadcasting, and Information, Belize City
Ministry of Education 1991b *National Paper on Education Policy*. Ministry of Education, Sports, Culture, Broadcasting, and Information, Belize City
Penrose P 1990 *Educational Finance*. Ministry of Education, Belize City
SPEAR/CUBOLA 1991 *Education in Belize: Toward the Year 2000*. SPEAR/CUBOLA Productions, Belize City

Benin

R. Sack

1. General Background

Benin—known as Dahomey prior to 1975—is a small West African country that extends in a narrow strip for about 600 kilometers from the relatively pluvial Atlantic coast in the south to the more arid Sahel region in the north. The total land area of the country is about 113,000 square kilometers, and it shares long, north–south borders with Togo and Nigeria. Its estimated population of close to 5 million is growing at about 3.2 percent annually. About 36 percent of the

population live in urban areas. Benin is a multicultural society with five major ethnic groups and as many major languages, and two major nonindigenous religions (Roman Catholicism and Islam). Fon is spoken by a plurality of about 26 percent of the population. French is the official language of both government and schools, but is spoken only by a minority of the population.

The former Kingdom of Abomey, which had expanded in the seventeeth century, was assigned to the French by the Berlin conference of 1884. Full-scale colonial occupation began in 1892, and in 1904 Dahomey was incorporated into French West Africa. Self-government was granted in 1958 and full independence acquired in 1960. Western-style schooling first appeared in several coastal towns as a result of the activities of Portuguese missionaries starting in the sixteenth century. One result of such long-standing contact with Europeans was the concentration of Roman Catholic mission schools that produced relatively large numbers of African professionals and intellectuals. For this reason, Dahomey became known as the "Latin Quarter of Africa."

For the first 12 years after Independence, Dahomey was renowned in Africa for coups d'état, the last of which occurred in 1972 when the military seized power, and two years later proclaimed a Marxist–Leninist state. In order to further erase any vestiges of its colonial past, Dahomey changed its name to Benin in 1975. Because it does not have authority over the central bank that controls its currency (the CFA franc, a transnational African currency), the state became literally bankrupt in 1989 with accumulated salary arrears to its civil servants of up to 9 months. This precipitated a breakdown of the state and the end of the regime. The result was the first of the new wave of African democracies. The transition, which lasted approximately 18 months, was peaceful, and has yielded an open political system. This created pressure for a broad debate on educational issues that took the form of a national forum in 1990 (*Etats Généraux de l'Education*), attended by about 350 representatives from all sectors of society.

Benin's per capita income was US$360 in 1990, placing it near the bottom of the list of low-income countries. The mainstay of the economy is the primary sector which accounts for about 40 percent of GDP. The country is self-sufficient in food; cotton is its major export product. However, much of its economic activity depends on informal cross-border trade with Nigeria, making it vulnerable to developments in that country. A large part of the economy, commerce in particular, is within the so-called informal, or unstructured, sector. Well over half of the working population is within this sector.

2. Politics and the Goals of the Education System

As is the case in other former French dependencies, the formal arrangements governing Benin's education system call for a high level of financial, administrative, and pedagogical centralization. Informal reality, however, has created a situation in which there is a large degree of *de facto* decentralization. Nonetheless, general expectations hold that education is the responsibility of the state, expectations that were reinforced by the nationalization of almost all private schools by the military regime after 1974. As a first step toward consensus on the vital issues facing education and society in Benin, the newly created democratic

state quickly moved to convene the *Etats Généraux de l'Education*. This forum, which was partially empowered to make education policy recommendations, decried the qualitative degradation of the system. It made recommendations and established priorities, many of which are being incorporated into government policy. In addition to being founded on the consensus that emerged from this forum, government policy is based on an extensive set of policy research studies and planning tools that were realized over the period of 1989–92 with the assistance of UNESCO and the United Nations Development Program (UNDP).

The major thrust of government policy includes: (a) improving both the quality and the equity of the system, with an emphasis on primary education and pedagogy that stresses self-employment; (b) implementing rigorous learning norms for passage from one level to the next, with a clear preference for a system that would control student flows and become increasingly elitist as students progress up the ladder toward higher education (to offset the decimation of the country's intellectual elite under the military Marxist–Leninist regime, during which particularistic, political norms were given priority over more universalistic, achievement-oriented norms); (c) reforming technical/vocational education; and (d) diversification of sources of financing. These themes have been integrated into a government policy statement that also includes a call for rehabilitation of the institutional and managerial infrastructure of the education system based on a thorough organizational audit of the Ministry of Education.

3. The Formal System of Education

Figure 1 outlines the structure of the system; enrollments and resources are summarized in Table 1.

3.1 Primary, Secondary, and Tertiary Education

Children enroll in the 6-grade primary school at the age of 5–6 years. Gross enrollment rates declined slightly in the 1980s and were at about 60 percent in 1990, with about 55 percent of the eligible cohort enrolled in the first grade. Enrollment rates are about 74 percent for boys and 42 percent for girls. Regional disparities are strong, with enrollment rates close to 100 percent in the coastal provinces and much lower in the Sahelian north. Total enrollments in 1990 were 418,000, of which about 34 percent are female. Dropout and repetition rates are high, with only approximately 32 percent of an entering cohort reaching Grade 6, and about 16 percent graduating from primary school. The national average of 35 students per teacher hides the wide regional disparities, with vastly overcrowded classrooms in the main towns, and schools with as few as 15 students per teacher in rural areas. Private schools

Table 1
Enrollments and resources in public formal education 1991

		Secondary		
	Primary	General	Voc./Tech.	Higher
Number of students	486,000	74,000	3,700	10,900
Number of institutions	2,905	150	11	1
Student–teacher ratio	35:1	30:1	16:1	20:1
Expenditure per student (units of GNP per capita)	0.14	0.40	1.15	3.23

(mainly with religious affiliations) were eliminated under the Marxist–Leninist regime, but are beginning to reappear.

General secondary education consists of two cycles of four and three years respectively, with about 11 percent of the relevant age group enrolled. Girls constitute about 28 percent of enrollments. According to the new educational policy, access to each cycle will be dependent on an examination. Enrollments have declined by about 25 percent since 1985, reflecting: (a) the increasing rates of graduate unemployment (external efficiency); (b) declining quality, related to the very low rates of internal efficiency; and (c) decreasing family capacities to assume the costs (both direct and opportunity).

Benin has one university (UNB: Université Nationale du Bénin) with about 10,900 students enrolled. Access is automatic for holders of the secondary-school diploma (the *baccalauréat*). Whereas the primary and secondary levels have experienced declines in both their enrollment rate and number of students enrolled, university enrollments have increased. This can be explained by the lack of jobs for secondary school graduates, combined with negative opportunity costs, since about 30 percent of the students receive fellowships and all students benefit from subsidized room

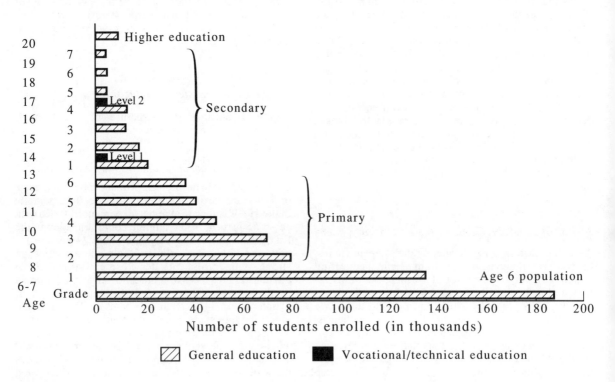

Figure 1
Benin: Structure of the formal education system 1990

and/or board. The University has two types of faculties: "open" faculties where there is no selection and admission depends only on the *baccalauréat*, and "closed" faculties where there is selection based on examinations and other procedures. Not unexpectedly, the latter have much higher unit costs and, more importantly, dramatically improved rates of internal efficiency.

3.2 Preschool Education

Preprimary education exists on a small scale and primarily in the major cities. Enrollments total about 13,000 in about 310 centers.

3.3 Vocational and Technical Education

Although identified as a priority by the government, only about 3,700 students are enrolled in the country's 11 public vocational/technical schools, a decline of about 10 percent since 1985. Enrollment in private institutions is about 1,500. There is also an extensive, informal apprenticeship training system, whereby youths pay fees to work directly (and in very difficult conditions) in small shops with no guarantee of future employment. In 1987 there were an estimated 40,000 apprentices in this "system."

3.4 Adult and Nonformal Education

There are little-to-no education activities organized by the Ministry of Education. Such activities have tended to be organized by ministries such as Agriculture and/or firms. An example would be training for adult women involved in agricultural activities in the context of Ministry of Agriculture extension services, where training includes functional literacy and numeracy as well as specific agricultural techniques and health-related subjects. An evaluation indicated that the numeracy learning was most highly valued by the participants.

4. Administrative and Supervisory Structure and Operation

Education is the responsibility of the Ministry of National Education, which was created in 1990 by consolidating two ministries (one for basic education, the other for secondary and higher). There is some delegation of authority to the six departmental (regional) offices of the Ministry. In the past, operations appeared highly centralized with all decisions being taken at the first level of command in the Ministry. In reality, however, many decisions are made locally, with or without prior ministerial authorization. This is particularly the case for relatively minor personnel decisions and pedagogical practices, where the need to act swiftly and with the available means takes precedence over lengthy formal procedures, exacerbated by a poor communication and information infrastructure.

A functional analysis (or audit) of the Ministry's organization and management was undertaken, which considered the Ministry as the largest firm in the country (in terms of budget, personnel, real estate, etc.). This management audit focused on the three major functional areas of strategic management, pedagogy, and logistics/administration, and came to the conclusion that the education system is deeply disoriented, disarticulated, and unstructured. This has resulted in a major effort at managerial reform and institutional rehabilitation of the Ministry of Education.

5. Educational Finance

Education has consistently consumed between 30 and 40 percent of the government budget since 1970. Total budgeted expenditures for 1992 are CFA Fr19,072 million, which represents about 33 percent of the national budget and about 4 percent of GNP. Primary education accounts for 63 percent of expenditures, secondary (general and technical/vocational) 19 percent, and higher education 18 percent. Government resources are used mainly to pay teachers' salaries, presently about 78 percent of the budget. Parents are expected to pay limited school fees for primary and secondary schools. These fees are used for expenses related to construction, maintenance, and supplies, and are controlled by the schools and the regional district offices. It is estimated that fees are paid by half of all parents. Only in higher education are there no fees. In addition to fees, parents and students are responsible for school uniforms, books, and school supplies.

6. Supplying Personnel for the Education System

The system employs about 17,000 full-time teachers plus about 2,200 administrators. Primary schools employ about 13,900 teachers, secondary (general and vocational/technical) about 2,700, and higher education about 550. Although the 35:1 student–teacher ratio is low (39:1 is the average for sub-Saharan Africa), the majority were hired during the previous regime with little secondary education and no teacher training.

Formal teacher training occurs in primary school training institutions and at the higher normal school (*Ecole Normale Supérieure*) for secondary school teachers. The primary normal schools have two course programs: (a) entering students with the first cycle of secondary school, who receive two years of training followed by a year of teaching practice; and (b) those who enter with the *baccalauréat* and follow a one-year course of study. The higher normal school admits *baccalauréat* holders on a very selective basis for a three-year course program.

The prevailing situation, characterized by an

oversupply of underqualified primary school teachers, is the product of a combination of factors: a lack of teachers in the late 1970s and early 1980s when enrollments were increasing, the massive recruitment of poorly schooled and untrained "young revolutionary teachers" in the early 1980s, and the decline in the enrollment rate.

7. Curriculum Development and Teaching Methodology

There is a common curriculum for all primary and secondary schools that is determined by the Education Ministry. The primary school concentrates on French (which is the language of instruction) and arithmetic, with social and natural sciences taught in the higher grades. Secondary school is divided into two cycles of four and three grades, respectively. The major components of first-cycle course work are: French (20%), mathematics and science (40%), English (13%), and history/geography (10%). Like the French system, the second cycle has streams for art, social sciences, natural sciences, and mathematics and the physical sciences, with coursework varying accordingly. The curricula in secondary technical/vocational streams include about 30 percent general education, 50 percent technical/vocational subjects, and the remainder for civics and related topics.

The few learning materials that exist are prepared by specialized commissions within the national pedagogical institute (INFRE—*Institut National pour la Formation et la Recherche en Education*). However, for a number of years, materials have amounted to little more than those supplied commercially by French publishers.

8. The System of Examinations, Promotions, and Certifications

The first formal certificate is awarded at the end of primary school. This is an examination that determines both certification and passage to secondary school. Success rates in this examination over the period 1980–90 have averaged 38 percent (with a standard deviation of 8). Promotion within primary schools is not automatic and depends on teacher evaluations. In 1990, about 25 percent of the enrolled pupils were grade repeaters. There is an examination at the end of the first cycle of secondary school that provides a certificate (BEPC) that is not related to promotion decisions. The end of secondary schooling is marked by the *baccalauréat* exam which provides both a secondary school diploma and automatic entrance into university. Pass rates on this examination have averaged 14 percent (with a standard deviation of 5) in 1980–90. In addition

to these examinations, there are several competitive entrance examinations (*concours*) that are used for selection into the "closed" university faculties, and examinations for the award of technical school certificates.

9. Educational Assessment, Evaluation, and Research

Basically, there is no institutionalized capacity in these areas. In spite of its name, INFRE produces no research, and systematic assessment and evaluation activities are nowhere to be found in the system. As is so often the case in other countries, most research is produced on an ad hoc basis by internationally funded and executed projects. A large-scale project of policy research was undertaken by UNESCO with UNDP financing. This project consists of an integrated set of studies covering the different levels and dominant themes of the education system. These studies are designed to provide the knowledge base required for sustainable policies for programs likely to depend on external financing.

10. Major Reforms in the 1980s and 1990s

Benin embarked on major reforms of its education system in the 1970s that were somewhat modified in the early 1980s. This reform, which was designed to make education consistent with the objectives of the newly installed Marxist–Leninist regime, was aimed at: (a) equalizing access according to geographic area; (b) making education free, secular, public and compulsory by bringing it under total state control and eliminating private schools; (c) controlling expenditures; and (d) making education better adapted to work environments by the introduction of practical skills into the curricula. Adjustments in the early 1980s represented partial recognition of the failure of this reform. By the late 1980s, and the demise of the military regime, it was generally accepted that these reforms had failed and that it was necessary to concentrate on quality of education and the reconstitution of the country's intellectual elite. In the 1990s, in addition to focusing on primary education, the government plans to overhaul the management and organization of the Ministry in order to improve its capability to deliver educational services.

11. Major Problems for the Year 2000

The major challenges in the final decade of the twentieth century will include: (a) developing new resources for all levels of education, (b) improvements in quality, (c) responsiveness and adaptability to social demand and to the demands and needs of the labor market, (d) improved management, and (e) controlling demand for higher education that is costly and of dubious economical value.

Bhutan

C. T. Crellin

1. General Background

The Kingdom of Bhutan is a small independent land-locked country in south-central Asia. It lies almost entirely in the Himalayan mountain range with the Tibetan Autonomous Region of China to the north and India to the east, west, and south. The land area of Bhutan is 46,500 square kilometers and it is 320 kilometers from east to west and 177 kilometers from north to south at the widest points. The northern border with Tibet is along a range of very high mountains, the highest point being at 7,554 meters. The southern, and part of the western, border with India is just inside the Indo-Gangetic Plain of northern India. The eastern border with India is mountainous. Most rivers flow from north to south, some rising in Tibet. The climate ranges from tropical along the southern border to a cold, high-altitude, tundra-like region in the north. The majority of the population lives along the southern border and in or near the fertile river valleys.

There are few roads and travel, especially from east to west, is difficult and occasionally impossible. Bhutanese citizens can use the roads in India, but most foreigners need a special permit to do so. There is an international airport at Paro about 60 kilometers from Thimphu, the capital.

The government has been carrying out a population census since 1989. Although the population was reported to be about 1,500,000 in 1991, by 1992 it became clear that the population was in fact considerably smaller. Indications are that the figure that will emerge from the census will be about 800,000. The population growth rate in 1992 was about 2 percent. There is a large immigrant population, not all of whom have official status. The government is attempting to regularize the situation and future immigration will be carefully controlled. Many illegal immigrants have left the country since 1989.

A considerable proportion of teachers, especially above the primary level, are immigrants, mostly from India. There are also many government officials of Indian nationality. It will be difficult to reduce this kind of immigration as the country is still short of qualified personnel and salaries are much higher than in neighboring countries.

There are a number of migratory tribes in the north and west of the country, some of whom regularly move across national borders.

About 87 percent of the population lives in rural areas. There are only two towns with more than 10,000 inhabitants. These are Thimphu, and Puntsholing on the border with India. The mountainous areas between the river valleys are sparsely populated.

Over 60 percent of the population are of Tibetan origin and speak one of a number of languages closely related to Tibetan. Nepali, an Indo-Aryan language, is spoken by about 25 percent of the population. The official language is Dzongkha which is based on the language spoken in the seven districts of Western Bhutan. As many traders are of Indo-Aryan origin, Nepali is spoken widely and is to some extent the language of commerce. English is used increasingly as the education system expands and improves.

The Nyingmapa or "Red Hat" sect of Buddhism is followed by 70 percent of the population including almost all Bhutanese of Tibetan and some of Nepali origin. About 25 percent of the population are Hindu and most of the remainder are Moslem.

The government of the country has been in the hands of people of Tibetan origin since the eighth century. From the earliest days civil and religious affairs were closely linked. Many men studied in the numerous monasteries and spent much of their lives as monks. The religious hierarchy remains important and has a status comparable to the ruling class which comprises a well-defined number of prominent families who support the king and the Royal Advisory Council.

While there is no social stigma attached to manual tasks on the family farm or in the home, many Bhutanese are reluctant to do manual work for payment. This kind of work was done at one time by slaves, often prisoners of war, and more recently by immigrants from India and Nepal. The government's decision to reduce the number of immigrants has resulted in difficulties in finding workers for many manual tasks.

The Gross Domestic Product (GDP) in 1988 was US$266,000,000. If a population of 800,000 is accepted as correct, the per capita income would have been about US$330. During the 1980s, the GDP grew at a rate of 7.5 percent per annum. In 1992 the United Nations listed Bhutan as a "Least Developed Country." In 1989, agriculture and forestry made up 45 percent of GDP and involved 87 percent of the working population. Electricity production accounts for 11 percent of GDP and 6 percent comes from industry, construction, trade, and transportation. Government service represents 10 percent of GDP.

Trade is mostly with India. Imports include road vehicles, machinery, textiles, and petroleum products. Most exports (93%) are to India, and include electricity, timber and wood products, and food of which some is processed. Total exports in 1987 were valued at about US$38 million and total imports at about US$48.5 million. Grants by the Government of India represented over half of the government income before the financial year 1987–88.

The government of Bhutan is a hereditary monarchy, and the king works with a Royal Advisory Council of 150 representatives. Of these, 120 are elected by village headmen (who themselves have been elected by villagers), 20 are appointed from the civil service, and 10 by the Monk Body.

The government continues to control the arrival and internal travel of overseas visitors. The reason for this caution is that it wishes to preserve the life and culture of the indigenous people. The government knows that influences from other countries will impinge on society and it wishes to guide the people to adjust to change in a well-planned way. The decision to provide a universal primary education system is a part of the government program of preparation for a modern society.

One of the more important goals of official policy is to reduce the current dependence on overseas personnel in the government service including education. This problem is being addressed but there are still a large number of expatriate government officials. In 1987, 54 of the 164 staff employed in the Department of Education in Thimphu and in other education offices were foreign nationals. Of 2,221 teachers in schools and colleges, 970 were from outside of the country.

2. Politics and the Goals of the Education System

Monastic education has been available, mainly for boys, for many centuries. This included the achievement of literacy in an ancient form of the present Dzongkha language. The ancient language form is still used in the many monasteries and the associated monastic schools.

Early in the twentieth century, prominent families began to send their children to Christian schools in northern India. When the first primary schools were established in the 1950s, their main purpose was to prepare children for secondary education abroad. The influence of these schools continues to be important.

The goals of education were examined with very great care in the 1980s. This was undertaken in cooperation between the Buddhist hierarchy and the government. It became apparent that an improved educational system was necessary if Bhutanese society was to benefit fully from economic and social development. On the other hand, the problem of the educated unemployed in neighboring countries was well-known. Until the 1980s, the education system typically provided a relatively safe path to government employment for the comparatively few young people who completed a rather rigorous course.

A decision was made to develop an improved education system with almost universal provision at the primary level and with less dependence on external education systems for teachers and teaching systems. In 1985 the Curriculum and Textbook Devel-

opment Division was established as a unit within the Department of Education.

Although the entry of foreigners from outside the immediate region has been tightly controlled, the government has made arrangements with some countries, such as the United Kingdom and Canada, to send teachers and a few specialists on curriculum and teacher education. A large number of teachers are engaged on a contractual basis from nearby countries, mainly India.

The decision to use English as the medium of instruction was made at a time when primary education was considered, in the main, to be a preparation for secondary schooling. To have chosen Dzongkha or any other Tibetan-based language would have created problems, since almost all teachers had to be recruited from abroad. The standard of English teaching in the primary schools is already high and improving, and there is little pressure to change the medium of instruction.

The fact that many of the people living in the country, including many citizens, speak Nepali, poses a more difficult political problem. From 1961 to 1989, Nepali was taught at the primary level in schools along the southern border.

The government followed a policy of relative isolation for many years. For this reason, those responsible for education in Bhutan had not kept in touch with educational development in Asia. Even developments in India were largely unknown as most teachers recruited from India did not bring either knowledge or experience of recent educational developments there. In 1991, Bhutan joined the Asian Program of Educational Innovation for Development (APEID) based at the UNESCO regional office in Bangkok. This will enable educators in Bhutan to exchange experiences with colleagues from all over Asia and the Pacific region.

3. The Formal System of Education

3.1 Primary, Secondary, and Tertiary Education

There are a few privately run kindergartens for preschool children and the government is considering the advisability of allowing other private primary and secondary schools to operate. However, most children in Bhutan attend government-run schools.

There is a seven-year primary school phase with children normally entering school for the first time at the age of 6. The first class is described as the "Preprimary" (PP) class. In 1989, there were 202 primary schools with 49,094 children and 1,668 teachers. Some 46 of them were small schools and are known as "Community Schools." They have classes from PP to Class 3. About 38 percent of the children in 1989 were girls. In 1989, the 31 secondary schools (junior-high schools) also had primary classes where there were 12,481 primary-school pupils enrolled. The average small school has 61 students. The normal primary school has, on average, about 300 children. The pupil–teacher ratio is about 30:1.

With a relatively high dropout rate at all class levels, class sizes are much larger in the PP year than they are in higher classes. There are often 50 or more children in the lower primary-school level classes.

Many children are overage and repetition rates can be as high as 20 percent each year. For this reason it is difficult to determine the true enrollment rate. It is estimated that it approaches 100 percent in areas of fairly high population density and is as low as 30 percent in some remote areas.

Most schools, including primary schools, provide boarding facilities. Apart from the relatively few children living in towns, most families live in large houses, usually accommodating an extended family, well-separated from each other. A typical rural village can cover 50 or more square kilometers. Parents are reluctant to send very young children, especially girls, to stay away from home. This probably explains why fewer girls than boys attend school. In urban areas there is no difference in enrollment nor is there any difference in the dropout rates for boys and girls at the primary level. In 1992, the government decided to provide Community Schools in any community where 30 or more children can be enrolled.

The National Education Policy published in 1984 states that secondary and higher education will continue to be selective and must be "appropriate to national needs and to those capable of benefiting from pursuing their studies."

Junior-high schools provide a two-year course and high schools a further two years. In 1989 there were 2,793 students at the junior-high school level in 31 schools and 1,452 at the high-school level in 10 schools. Pupil–teacher ratios are about 25:1 and 20:1 at the two levels respectively. The percentage of girls is lower at these levels; in 1989 it was 31 percent at the junior-high and 23 percent at the high-school levels.

A two-year precollege course is offered at the one academic college, but there are plans to offer similar courses at a number of high schools.

Until recently, an examination was set at the end of each school year, and the children that failed either repeated the class level or dropped out. There was a particularly high dropout and rate of repetition at the end of the PP year. Since the introduction of a new primary-school curriculum in 1990, the dropout rate has fallen from about 20 percent per year to about 10 percent at the end of the PP class, and 5 percent at other levels. Repetition remains high at about 20 percent annually.

The Planning and International Coordination Division of the Department of Education determined that over 12,000 of the 16,045 children in the PP Class in April 1989 were new enrollees. In 1990 it was estimated that about 67 percent of all children enrolled in primary schools. The government is planning to achieve universal primary education by the year 2000,

with at least 80 percent completing the primary-school phase of their education.

Figure 1 presents the enrollment pattern in schools. The numbers enrolled in technical, vocational, and higher education are too small to be shown on the same scale.

In 1959, the total school enrollment was 1,500 pupils in 59 schools and other institutions. In 1990, there were over 67,000 pupils in over 200 schools. This represents an annual growth rate of 13 percent. The annual growth rate at the end of the 1980s was about 7 percent. Plans are being made for a total enrollment of 138,000 by the year 2005.

The school year begins in March with a long break during the winter. Travel in the country is difficult during this season and a long school vacation is necessary to give children and teachers time to return to their homes. In the high altitude, sparsely populated northern region and in the densely forested south central region, it can take five or six days to walk to the nearest road. The school day is about five hours long, but since many children are boarders, there is a great deal of organized sport and other activities after school.

The traditional monastic schools continue to function as they have for many centuries, using Dzongkha as the medium of instruction. Monks receive education and training for work in the community. This form of education must be regarded as a parallel formal system. The Buddhist hierarchy does not form part of the executive of the government but no action regarding life in Bhutan, including the school system, is taken without consulting them. In 1989, the Department of Education supported five Sanskrit schools in the southern Hindu area.

There are two degree-awarding institutions. One is

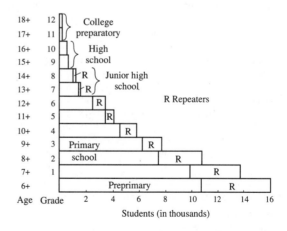

Figure 1

Bhutan: Structure of the formal education system[a]

a It was estimated that 67 percent of an age group actually enters school (1989 figures)

Sherubtse College in the eastern part of the country. In 1989 there were 186 degree-course students and 327 on precollege courses. Of the 29 lecturers, only seven were Bhutanese nationals. The other higher education institution is the National Institute of Education in Samchi in the southwest. There were 62 degree-course and 11 graduate students in 1990.

3.2 Preschool Education

The state education system does not provide for preschool education. A few privately run kindergartens operate in urban areas.

3.3 Special Education

In 1989 the only provision for handicapped children was a school for blind children with 19 boys and 8 girls. Of the 11 teachers, 9 were nationals.

3.4 Vocational, Technical, and Business Education

There are two vocational and technical institutions. The Royal Technical Institute (RTI) provides a four-year course for students who have completed the primary-school course. The Royal Polytechnic provides a two-year course for students from junior-high schools. These students and those from the RTI and high schools can then take a three-year course leading to a technical diploma. The Sixth Five-Year Plan (1987–92) provides for the establishment of a trade school with courses in carpentry, masonry, and plumbing for students who have completed primary education. A high percentage of skilled workers in the modern sector of the economy are foreign nationals. The Seventh Five-Year Plan (1992–97) includes an expansion of technical and vocational education and training.

3.5 Adult and Nonformal Education

The state education system has done little to provide educational opportunities for illiterates whether they be adults or young school dropouts; however, this problem is being addressed in the Seventh Five-Year Plan. The Buddhist monasteries have always provided educational services for the communities they serve. This now includes advice on such matters as health and agriculture. The government is considering the provision of nonformal educational services. There are plans to improve the national sound broadcasting system to assist in this work, but the mountainous terrain will make it difficult and expensive to provide a radio signal in all areas.

4. Administrative and Supervisory Structure and Operation

Education in Bhutan is administered by the Department of Education which is a department in the Ministry of Social Services. One deputy minister devotes most of his time to education. The Department of Education has a staff of 164 people including the staff in the 18

Dzongkhag (district) Education Offices. The country is divided into four zones each with a Zone Education Officer (ZEO).

The administration of schools is the responsibility of the *Dzongkhag* Education Officer (DEO). All DEOs and ZEOs are experienced teachers, many with training and experience in primary schools. The department has a small inspectorate. The inspectors are subject specialists and spend most of their time monitoring the effectiveness of the secondary schools. The DEOs and ZEOs visit schools far more often than do their counterparts in neighboring countries. They give advice to teachers and headteachers. They also collect information about schools and report regularly to the Department of Education in Thimphu. The ZEOs have a considerable responsibility in the selection of teachers for inservice training and for promotion.

The following divisions of the Department of Education are all in Thimphu: Planning and International Coordination; School Planning and Building Cell; Curriculum and Textbook Development; School Health and Agriculture; Personnel; Inspectorate of Schools, and Board of Examination.

School building will be an important activity in the 1990s. Although the government has provided all secondary-school buildings and primary schools in towns, the communities in rural areas have provided sites and buildings for very many primary schools. These are often large houses with rooms too small for the class size usually found in rural primary schools. The small schools established in 1980s are now called "Community Schools" and are linked administratively to an established primary or secondary school that may be more than one day's walk away.

The Department is cooperating with the International Bank for Reconstruction and Development (IBRD) in a program to provide several new primary schools. The architects working with this project are preparing standard school designs, many of them suitable for construction by parents.

A greater number of schools have boarders. The World Food Program (WFP) provides food for almost all schools. To supplement WFP food supplies most rural schools have gardens which the children tend. The Health and Agriculture Division provides buildings and kitchens for the schools.

The Board of Examinations prepares the examinations which take place at the end of primary school and of junior-high school. Until the late 1980s the Indian Certificate for Secondary Education Examination system was used to test the children at the end of their high-school course. The 1987–92 Five-Year Development Plan makes provision for the introduction of a national examination system.

5. Educational Finance

The government has increased its expenditure on education a great deal since the First Five-Year Development Plan in 1961 when 9.4 million ngultrum representing 8.77 percent of Plan allocation was provided. The 1987–92 Five-Year Development Plan allocates 778.8 million ngultrum or 8.2 percent of total expenditure. Spending on education has averaged about 7 percent of GDP. These figures do not include quite substantial payments for education abroad made by the Royal Civil Service Commission.

Parents are expected to provide very little in funds or in kind to enable their children to attend school. In addition to the provision of teaching services, the government provides school equipment and supplies, including textbooks and writing materials. Few schools in central Asia are so well provided for with sports and games facilities as well as recreational materials.

In the 1980s children were expected to make a small contribution for boarding but this was no more than a nominal sum and only just exceeded the equivalent of US$1 per year, or, in the case of high-school students, barely US$2 annually. The whole question of finance for education is being considered carefully. A commitment has been made to continue full financial provision for Bhutanese children in primary schools. However, some contribution may be required from the parents of foreign nationality and all parents of secondary-school students.

In 1989, the estimated annual expenditure per student was about US$70 for primary schools, US$120 for junior-high schools, and US$270 for high schools. The Seventh Five-Year Plan, which began in 1992, raised the government expenditure on education from 8.1 percent of total government expenditure to 11.2 percent.

6. Supplying Personnel for the Education System

Before the mid 1980s, the supply of educational personnel was largely a matter of recruitment from abroad. The establishment of the National Institute of Education in Samchi and the Teacher Training Center in Paro during the 1980s is beginning to address the problem. By 1990, 40 percent of primary, 51 percent of junior-high, and 56 percent of high school teachers were non-nationals. There are plans to increase the capacity and output of the two national teacher education institutions but there remains a need to recruit from abroad. In spite of a considerable increase in enrollment, currently about 7 percent per annum, the proportion of national primary-school teachers is increasing steadily, but the absolute number of non-nationals is not diminishing greatly.

There were two teacher education institutions in 1991. The National Institute of Education (NIE) at Samchi in the southwest and the Teacher Training Center at Paro, near Thimphu. In 1991, 183 primary-level teacher candidates were on two-year courses at the two institutions. At the NIE there were 71 students

on three-year courses leading to a BEd degree. In addition, there were 15 students on one-year Post-Graduate Certificate of Education courses.

There is a third institution that has its origins in Bhutan's culture. Originally the Simtokha Rigney School taught Bhutanese literature and painting, but since 1976 it has been training primary-school teachers mainly to teach Dzongkha. The school now provides a wider training, including the teaching of other primary-school subjects. In 1990 there were 442 students and 32 lecturers, 25 of whom were nationals.

A significant number of national teachers are only partially trained but almost all have at least a junior-high school certificate. A considerable proportion of the relatively large inservice teacher education program is committed to the training of these teachers. About 10 percent of all teachers receive at least two weeks' training each year.

Teachers recruited from abroad, mostly from India, are engaged largely on the basis of their ability to teach in English. Few are trained teachers at either the primary or secondary level.

With a relatively young team of national teachers, the wastage rate is low. Even if national policy did not require the replacement of non-national teachers, many would need to be replaced each year as few stay for long. Thus about 1,000 non-national teachers need replacement and about 150 new nationals are needed each year to cover losses through promotion and expansion of the system.

The status of teachers is high at all levels. In the late 1980s teachers salary scales were linked to those of the rest of the civil service. A factor that makes teaching an attractive career for nationals is that promotion to important administrative and higher education posts is largely from among teachers. All zone and district education officers are former teachers and many are from the primary schools.

One of the more important programs of educational development includes the training of educational administrators. A number of bilateral donors, including Switzerland and the International Bank for Reconstruction and Development (IBRD), have been involved in this.

7. Curriculum Development and Teaching Methodology

The modern school system created in 1961 was largely designed to prepare children for examinations set by the Indian Council of Secondary Education. The curriculum necessarily served the needs of the examinations and was associated with high repetition and dropout rates.

The subjects taught at the primary and secondary levels were similar and included: language (Dzongkha and English), mathematics, science, geography, and history. A wide nonacademic curriculum, including games and sport, art, and music is provided.

107

Following the introduction of the New Education Policy efforts have been made to develop a curriculum that would be relevant to the children of Bhutan and which would serve the needs of children and the nation. A Curriculum and Textbook Development Division was established in 1985 and has been developing a new curriculum known as the "New Approach to Primary Education" (NAPE) ever since. The new curriculum was tried out as it was being developed. This involved 13 schools in 1986 and 36 in 1989. An evaluation of the effectiveness of the NAPE was made in 1989 and a decision was taken to adopt the new curriculum beginning in the PP class in 1991.

The new curriculum is based on the specification of a number of educational objectives for each subject and at each class level. Teachers are expected to monitor the progress of each child by reference to the objectives. The new curriculum is intended to serve the needs of all children including those who will leave school at the end of the primary phase of education. One of the overall objectives was to decrease the drop-out and repetition rates. The evaluation carried out in 1989 indicated that this objective was being achieved.

The new curriculum integrates science, history, and geography into a new subject, designated "environmental studies." New textbooks have been prepared, since the ones in use before 1990 were prepared in India for Indian children. Much of the information in the older textbooks had little or no relevance for Bhutanese children. Exceptionally detailed teacher's guides have been prepared. These include detailed lesson plans and lists of educational objectives.

The secondary-school curriculum will continue to be a preparation for academic studies. A decision has been made to prepare a new curriculum at the junior-high and high-school levels. Parallel to the improvement of academic secondary education, efforts are being made to improve the vocational and technical education schools and institutes. To widen the scope of secondary education, employment-related topics will be introduced into the junior-high and high-school curriculum.

Higher education at Sherubtse College continues on a pattern similar to the practice in India. Courses are quite broadly based with four options: arts, commerce, bioscience, and pure science. The college is affiliated to Delhi University and this link is likely to continue. Consideration is being given to the creation of a national university.

8. The System of Examinations, Promotions, and Certifications

Examinations devised by teachers are set at the end of each school year to determine if children can proceed to the next class. The examinations at the end of the seven-year primary school and two-year junior-high school are prepared and administered by the Board of Examination in Thimphu which also assesses the papers. The examinations at the end of high school and college preparatory two-year courses are conducted by the Council for the Indian School Certificate Examination (ICSE) in New Delhi.

The introduction of a new primary-school curriculum in 1991 requires a new system of student evaluation. At the primary-school level, each child's progress will be monitored using a checklist of child capabilities. The examinations used at all levels up to 1991 required simple recall of information in Indian textbooks, much of which was innaccurate or irrelevant to Bhutan's students.

The degree-level examinations at Sherubtse College are carried out in cooperation with the University of Delhi, while those at the National Institute of Education are conducted in close association with the University of London.

9. Educational Assessment, Evaluation, and Research

Educational assessment systems are being developed in association with the development and implementation of the "New Approach to Primary Education." The curriculum includes a continuous assessment of student progress with a carefully prepared set of educational objectives for each subject and class level. Teachers are expected to record the progress of each child on a chart designed by the Curriculum and Textbook Development Division of the Department of Education.

In the process of evaluating the effectiveness of the new curriculum, achievement in mathematics and literacy of children in 20 urban and rural schools was assessed in 1989. This small-scale study was influential in determining whether or not to implement the new curriculum in all schools.

In 1992 the Royal Government of Bhutan prepared a National Plan of Action for Children. This plan included a number of educational and other goals for achievement in 1997 and the year 2000. The criteria, such as net enrollment associated with each goal will be monitored by the Planning commission with the technical assistance of the Central Statistical Office.

10. Major Reforms in the 1980s and 1990s

In the 1980s, the national education system underwent a detailed review. A decision was made to provide universal primary education in order to prepare children for life and work in the community and to prepare them for secondary and higher education. The government support of education at all levels which included the provision of tuition, all teaching and learning materials, and almost all of the cost of boarding, was questioned, and a decision was taken to impose some charges on the children of foreign nationals and on the children of Bhutanese nationals at the secondary and higher levels.

In 1989 it was decided to implement a new primary-school curriculum and to revise the examination system. Work also began on the revision of the secondary-school curriculum.

In the early 1990s a decision was taken to provide two-year college preparatory courses at a number of high schools. Until 1991 only Sherubtse College had made such a provision. A considerable number of junior-high schools will be established. In most cases, this will be done by expanding existing primary schools. There is a long-term plan to provide universal education for 9 years, that is, to the end of the junior-high school. A commitment has been made to provide universal primary education by the year 2000. It is hoped that this will be achieved in all but the remotest areas by 1995.

The feasibility of establishing a national university is being studied carefully, as is an expansion of the somewhat limited technical and vocational education programs.

11. Major Problems for the Year 2000

The main problem for Bhutan will be to maintain the rate of progress, both in quality and coverage, achieved in the 1980s. Bhutan has a relatively low per capita income and one of the most generously funded educational systems in Asia. It will be difficult to maintain this feature as enrollment increases and dropout decreases. As the educational system expands, a problem might arise when young people leave secondary education. In the 1980s there were jobs for all nationals with a successful secondary-school course behind them. In the absence of extensive industry and commerce, and following a government decision to control the expansion of the civil service, the danger exists of a growing number of educated unemployed young people, as in the case in neighboring countries.

The replacement of non-national labor might create a field for employment but this will require a new attitude towards employment, especially as regards manual labor. The greatest challenge will be to shape the education system to serve the needs of the dominant agricultural industry. This will require the development of new attitudes and techniques.

Bibliography

Hasrat B J 1980 *History of Bhutan*. Education Department, Thimphu

International Bureau of Education 1989 *Bhutan Country Report*. (41st International Conference on Education, Geneva) IBE, Geneva

Royal Government of Bhutan 1987 *Sixth Five Year Plan 1987–92*. Planning Commission, Thimphu

Royal Government of Bhutan 1992 *Bhutan National Plan of Action for Children for the 1990s*. Planning Commission, Thimphu

UNESCO 1991 *Statistical Yearbook*. UNESCO, Paris

UNICEF 1991 *Children and Women in Bhutan 1991: A Situation Analysis*. UNICEF, Thimphu

Bolivia

I. Classen-Bauer

1. General Background

Bolivia is situated in the heart of South America, surrounded by Peru, Brazil, Paraguay, Argentina, and Chile. The acting capital is La Paz, with about one million inhabitants; constitutionally, however, the capital is Sucre, a city of only 80,000 people. From an administrative point of view Bolivia is divided into nine *departamentos*: Chuquisaca, La Paz, Cochabamba, Oruro, Potosí, Tarija, Santa Cruz, Beni, and Pando. Bolivia is a large country with a diversity of geographical zones and a multicultural population. Its size is comparable to that of Spain and France, covering 1,098,581 square kilometers. The population is relatively small comprising about 6.9 million inhabitants. The average annual population growth rate is 2.8 percent and hence there is a large proportion of young people: 48.4 percent of the population is younger than 17 years of age. It has been estimated that between 1985 and the year 2000 the school-age population will increase by 1.2 million and these people will all need access to education. Until the 1970s the majority of the population inhabited the rural areas, particularly the mountainous part in the Andes with the high plateau of the Altiplano. Since that time, however, there has been a shift, so that in 1994 about 58 percent live in urban areas, mainly La Paz and Santa Cruz. This trend will certainly continue. The vast flat part of the country in the east is scarcely inhabited, with the exception of Santa Cruz.

Differences in altitude and climate have created contrasting landscapes that range from perpetual snow in the high peaks of the Andes through the barren plateau of the Altiplano and the dense rain forests of the Yungas valleys to the hot and thorny desert in the southeast. Equally diverse are the people and their cultures: more than half of the population speak indigenous languages, mainly Aymará and Quechua in the highlands but also Guaraní in the east. The official language is Spanish. The largest group belongs to the Quechua culture, still living in the territory ruled by the Incas up to the early sixteenth century. The second largest group is the Aymaras, whose language and way of life differ markedly from those of the

Quechuas. Both groups have kept their culture alive and live, dress, and worship much as their ancestors did in pre-Columbian times. In the cities, the Spanish culture predominates. There is a relatively small group of *criollos*, South Americans of Spanish descent, who dominate the political, commercial and cultural life of the country. About 35 percent of the population are Spanish-speaking *mestizos* who belong to both cultures but whose way of life is adapted to the mainstream of hispanic culture. They tend more and more to live in the cities.

The highland area of what is now Bolivia was conquered by the Spaniards in the middle of the sixteenth century and called Upper Peru (*Alto Perú*). Originally, it belonged to the Tahuantinsuyo, the Inca imperium which dominated a great part of the Andean region. Spanish colonization lasted until 1825 when Bolivia achieved independence through Simón Bolivar and his marshall, Sucre. Most of the people, however, did not gain significant independence or democracy until the middle of the twentieth century. Although there have been nearly 30 successive constitutions following the different revolutions or coups, the administrative realities have remained extremely centralized and dominated by only a small group of an urban elite. The vast majority of the people have remained unaffected by the political events, having no rights which allowed them to share in power. The only revolution which brought changes in the economic, political, and social structures was that of 1952, carried out by the National Revolutionary Movement (MNR), and which irreversibly changed the traditional distribution of wealth and power through the nationalization of the mines, an agrarian reform which gave the peasants land and an educational reform which offered better chances of educational and social participation.

However, in 1994 most of the people live under extreme and difficult circumstances. Bolivia passed through a heavy financial crisis in the 1980s. Mining, until 1983 the most important production sector, lost its importance as the main source of foreign currency due to the sinking prices in the international market and severe problems in the mining sector. In 1984 the inflation rate grew to 2,177 percent and in 1985 to 8,170 percent. The economic crisis hit the poor population in particular and affected mainly women and children. About half of children under five years old suffer from malnutrition; 12 percent are born underweight. Breastfeeding is common, but preparation of additional food is often not done under the necessary hygienic conditions so that diarrhoea is very common. As a consequence many children die from dehydration; the mortality rate is extremely high, with 282 deaths per 1,000 children under five years of age. Safe water and sanitary facilities are accessible only to about one-third of both the rural and urban population. Women usually have the task of getting water for the household, a very heavy and time-consuming task which is particularly difficult if a mother is pregnant or has small children. Health services are accessible to the majority of the urban population but not to the rural one, where only 36 percent have such services. Consequently the children living in the rural areas are not immunized and often die from measles, whooping cough, diptheria, tuberculosis, or other illnesses. Only 52 percent of mothers receive medical care to assist them during pregnancy. Indirectly, this situation affects educational achievement, since undernourished children who are often ill cannot concentrate or follow the courses at school properly. The general situation in the cities might be better as far as accessibility to education, health services, and sanitation are concerned, but the recession and the economic crisis has led to a feminization of poverty. Mothers cannot afford to maintain several children and abandoned and street children have become a serious social concern. There are about 280,000 working children who do unqualified work and have no access to the social welfare system and no real access to education. This is particularly hard for girls in rural areas: they start to work at 10 years of age, sometimes earlier, and often for 10 to 15 hours, so that they have no chance to attend school. This is reflected in the enrolment statistics: while in primary education 48 percent of the enrolled children are girls, the percentage in the intermediate level goes down to 38 percent and to 33 percent in the secondary level (see Fig. 1).

Street children mostly live in cities. The migration of thousands of families from rural to urban areas due

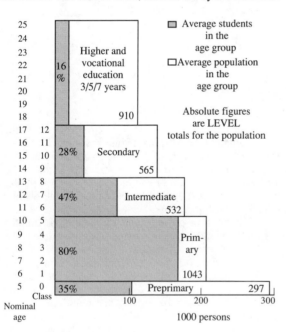

Figure 1
Structure of the formal education system since 1973
Source: Calculations based on statistics of the Ministerio de Educación y Cultura and estimated data published by the Instituta Nacional de Estadística, La Paz, Bolivia, 1988–92

to the economic crisis of the country in the decade 1980–90, with an inflation rate of 318 percent per year, has increased the number of street children in the cities. Working children still have their family connections and some of them also attend school, even if irregularly, but the street children have to seek shelter and food with their street companions. Sometimes they have remote ties to their mothers but this is not the case with abandoned children who are entirely on their own for their material and psychological survival. The principal causes of child abandonment are related to the rapid growth of both rural and urban poverty. The disintegration cycle for the family starts with migration to the city—not only does the rural population tend to leave the countryside, but miners' families have also lost their jobs since the decline of the mining industry. Since 1986 mining has contributed only 5.2 percent of the gross national product (GNP). In the cities, families are confronted by extreme urban slum poverty which soon leads to family disintegration, beginning with the abandonment of the family by the father. Progressively the disintegration of the family continues and there is a frequently high degree of violence, child neglect, and child abuse involved in the process. Often the children turn to drugs in the end. This enormous problem should be borne in mind when examining the system of education.

2. Politics and the Goals of the Education System

The first legal basis for the national educational system dates from December 1825, when Simón Bolivar, the first president of the nation, laid down the principles which were to rule education. This document stated that the first obligation of the state was to provide uniform and general education for all and to guarantee equality of opportunities—a goal which has not been yet achieved after about 170 years.

Several other laws gradually defined the aims and the structure of the educational system. The most important ones were those organizing the system of secondary education in 1845, the law of 1872 creating a private and a state system, the latter being free and compulsory; the law of 1909 regulating teacher education, the law of 1930 giving autonomy to the universities, and the law of 1956 which has to be seen in connection with the revolution of 1952, and implied a reform of the whole education system in the rural areas. As a result of this last reform enrollments increased enormously in the school system and in adult and vocational education. For several years this reform was considered one of the most progressive in Latin America. The organization of rural education based on the model of a nuclear system introduced by Elizardo Pérez as early as 1931 at the Warizata school has also been adopted in other countries, such as Peru. The system is closely related to the traditional organization of the Indian communities in *ayllus*, and Warizata was called the "*escuela ayllu*," where community participation was a basic principle.

The general structure of the education system was changed in 1973, accompanied by a revision of curricula. The new government installed in 1993, again by the National Revolutionary Movement (MNR), responsible for the big educational reform of 1956, started with a critical assessment of the present state of schooling. According to this assessment one of the greatest shortcomings was the inheritance of colonial goals and structures, which did not consider the different ethnic groups. Their traditional values and cultures should be respected.

Another aspect of the 1993 policy was to take account of the problem of marginalization. Only 52 percent of the school-age population attends school—in rural areas the percentage is 68.3 percent. This is due to a high dropout rate. Only 35 percent of children who start school continue through to the end of elementary education (5 years of schooling) and only 12 percent complete the intermediate level. One consequence is a high rate of recurrent illiteracy. This particularly affects girls: 80 percent of the illiterate population are women.

The new (1993) goals for the educational system are to change the structure, the curriculum, and teaching methods in order to make school more attractive for young people. The notion is that teaching should not be seen as a linear process from the teacher to the pupil but an interactive educational process, which should not necessarily take place in school buildings. Great emphasis will be given to a more practical approach to teaching and to the training of children for work. Furthermore, education will be bilingual (at least in the rural areas), so that children whose mother tongue is not Spanish have a greater chance of being educated. The one-sided academic approach of the traditional school will be abandoned in order to attempt to decrease the high dropout rate, particularly in the countryside. In the primary level of rural education only 36.8 percent of the pupils who started school are still enrolled in the fifth grade—the situation of girls is even worse, since only 28.6 percent complete this level.

The following concrete measures will have to be taken for the attainment of the newly designed educational policy:

(a) *Rural education first*. The goal is to bridge the enormous qualitative and quantitative gap between urban and rural education.

(b) *Municipal autonomy and decentralization*. There are about twenty cities that operate under different conditions and have to face different problems. Decentralization will give more flexibility to respond to the regional necessities. In the rural areas there should be more participation of the people in defining their goals of education.

(c) *Primary education for all children*. This recurring aim has never been achieved. Decentralization,

Table 1
Bolivia: Participation in the educational system, by age-group and sex, in urban and rural areas 1991

Corresponding structure of the education system[a] Level	Grade	Age-group Years	Urban population[b] male total	students	female total	students	Rural population[b] male total	students	female total	students	Total population total	students	Total schooling ratio (%)
Higher (3/5/7 Years)		18–25									910,400	146,809	16.1
	12	17	34,700	13,406	34,800	12,206	35,900	1,293	31,500	603	136,900	27,508	20.1
Secondary	11	16	34,200	16,189	36,700	15,016	32,100	1,758	30,000	828	133,000	33,791	25.4
(4 grades)	10	15	31,900	20,771	27,800	19,138	40,100	2,432	35,500	1,332	135,300	43,673	32.3
	9	14	44,100	26,299	43,900	23,496	37,600	3,469	33,900	1,907	159,500	55,171	34.6
Intermediate	8	13	43,000	29,273	41,700	26,496	47,600	7,092	43,200	4,136	175,500	66,997	38.2
(3 grades)	7	12	41,600	34,359	38,600	31,240	40,500	10,272	37,500	6,280	158,200	82,151	51.9
	6	11	47,500	41,108	46,900	35,952	54,300	14,921	49,300	9,571	198,000	101,552	51.3
	5	10	41,900	39,328	40,100	37,729	44,700	26,397	39,200	20,130	165,900	123,584	74.5
Primary	4	9	43,800	41,750	43,000	40,075	45,800	33,384	43,900	27,001	176,500	142,210	80.6
(5 grades)	3	8	45,500	43,562	44,000	42,245	42,900	41,402	41,800	36,142	174,200	163,351	93.8
	2	7	53,600	44,219	51,300	45,100	57,200	50,604	50,100	46,213	212,200	186,136	87.7
	1	6	74,200	49,182	72,800	48,063	85,300	64,610	81,700	60,716	314,000	222,5671	70.9
Pre-primary	0	5	70,700	34,831	68,500	33,983	79,800	18,865	77,800	17,701	296,800	105,380	35.5
Total Population[b]											6,616,000	1,500,884	22.7

Source: Calculations based on statistics of the Ministerio de Educación y Cultura and estimated data published by the Instituto Nacional de Estadística, La Paz, Bolivia
a The correspondence between age and grade is biased, because of the age-distribution in the single grades
b Data covers local resident population aged 5 years and more

higher financial support to rural communities, and the participation of the community in deciding on the aims of education in their area are expected to improve the standard of education. There should be more opportunities for sports, recreation, extracurricular activities, handicrafts, and arts and less emphasis on academic achievement.

(d) *Reduction and abolition of the illiteracy rate*. This should be achieved by attaining the enrollment of all primary school-aged children and the eradication of school dropout. In addition, there will be literacy campaigns for the adult population.

(e) *Improvement of teacher education*. The quality of teaching will have to be improved and the new educational approach introduced. It will, therefore, be necessary to have inservice teacher training courses; better salaries should be the incentive to participate in these courses. At the same time preservice teacher training will have to be improved.

3. The Formal System of Education

The present educational system operates along the lines defined by the 1955 Educational Code, the Su-

preme Decree 08601 of 1968 and the 1973 Law on Bolivian Education. Figure 2 depicts the educational system in a general way. Table 1 presents the enrollment breakdown for each grade by sex and urban/rural divide.

3.1 Primary, Secondary, and Tertiary Education

Elementary or basic education is subdivided into three cycles: preschool education, elementary education, and primary education as an intermediate level of vocational guidance. Preschool education is optional and involves children up to 5 years of age. Elementary education consists of 5 years of basic schooling which are compulsory for children aged 6 to 11 years. The intermediate cycle has a vocational orientation and is designed for children from 11 to 13 years of age.

Secondary education has four grades and two branches: arts and sciences (humanities) and technical–vocational for adolescents from 14 to 18 years. The arts and science branch has two cycles: introductory and general. After completion of these four years pupils finish their school education with a bachelor's diploma in humanities. The technical branch has the same length and is also divided into two cycles of two years each: general orientation and then differentiated

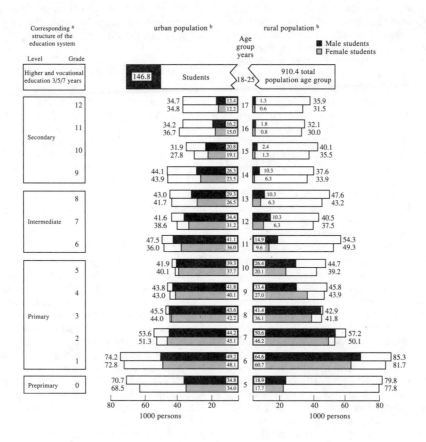

Figure 2
Participation in the educational system, by age-group and sex in urban and rural areas 1991

Source: Calculations based on statistics of the Ministerio de Educación y Cultura and estimated data published by the Instituto Nacional de Estadística, La Paz, Bolivia

a The correspondence between age and grade is biased, because of the age-distribution in the single grades b Data covers local resident population aged 5 years and more

courses in industry, commerce, arts, and agriculture. Pupils completing these courses acquire a bachelor's diploma in technology.

Higher education is provided in either universities or other institutions of higher education such as teacher training colleges or technical schools, in different areas covering four years of study. University studies cover the fields of social sciences and humanities in a five-year course, natural sciences and technology, also a five-year degree course, and medicine, which is a seven-year course. Universities are autonomous entities, but financially they depend on the Ministry of Education. There are three types of higher education: higher technical education (three years of study) either at a university or in a specialized technical college; studies to the level of a bachelor's degree (*licenciatura*), obtainable only at universities (five years of study), and master's courses which can be obtained after two further years of study, again only at

a university. From a total enrollment of about 900,000 students, 700,000 go to colleges and 100,000 go to university—about 20,000 have a vocational training and the others attend technical colleges or the Military Academy. While private education is relatively strong in the school area, it is not so pronounced in the tertiary level.

Figure 2 outlines the structure of the formal education system. In 1989 the population of school-age (6 to 15 years old) children was 2.5 million, of whom 49 percent were from rural areas and 51 percent from urban areas. Of these children, however, only 1.5 million attended school, an enrollment ratio of 77 percent. Of this figure, 52 percent are boys. School attendance is better in the urban areas, with a ratio of 83.5 percent as compared with 63.9 percent in rural areas. Absenteeism is also high. About 70 percent of the children who started school did not reach the fifth year of schooling.

Between 1970 and 1989 enrollment at the intermediate level increased by 5 percent in the cities; the rural population is heavily disadvantaged, since only 16 percent enter this level. From 10 years of age onward the poor situation of girls is much more noticeable, particularly in the rural areas. Here 37 percent of women have no formal education at all, 27 percent have attended the first three years of education, and only 19 percent could complete basic education with five years of schooling. For every 30 girls going to secondary school in the cities, only one has a similar chance in the countryside. It is not surprising that Bolivia has a very high rate of illiteracy, especially among women. In 1970 about 32 percent of men and 54 percent of women were illiterate. However, by 1990 only 15 percent of men and 30 percent of women were absolutely illiterate. Functional literacy, however, is lower. In rural areas children often do not attend school for more than three years of schooling; this gets them to the point where they can write their names and be officially registered as literate, but in reality they cannot cope with difficult texts. Hence the real illiteracy rate is about 55 percent; this means that every second person above 15 years of age cannot read properly. Two out of three illiterate people live in rural areas. Out of every ten illiterate people seven are women. It should, however, be acknowledged that in general illiteracy decreased enormousy in the 1980s (18.5 percent) owing to the great educational efforts, particularly in the rural aras. On the other hand, urban illiteracy decreased by only 7.6 percent—here one can see the effect of the increasing number of abandoned or street children.

Just over 60 percent of an age group attend the first level of basic education. Nearly 18 percent progress to the intermediate grades and only 14 percent continue their education at the secondary level. Secondary level—like the preschool level—is for a privileged group. One third of the secondary level school population attends private schools. In comparison, 12.7 percent of children in basic education attend the expensive private schools. These are in urban centers only. Secondary education in the countryside is practically nonexistent: there are only about 4,000 girls in rural areas who successfully finish the intermediate level (14 percent) and 600 go through the secondary level. In relation to the 60,000 girls who start school in the first grade this is a retention of 1 percent!

As can be seen from this analysis, the rural population, and particularly the girls in these areas are confronted with a very unfavourable situation. One reason for this is the attitude that formal education is only important for boys, and girls have to start work very early. Another reason is certainly the bad quality of education which does not encourage children to stay on at school. It can only be hoped that a new policy of introducing bilingual education and better trained teachers with a reformed and more relevant curriculum might improve the situation. A serious limitation is always the budget: Bolivia already spends 18 percent of its GNP on education (compared to 14 percent for defense and 2 percent for health) so that there is hardly room for an increment.

3.2 Preschool Education

Preschool education is available for a considerably higher proportion of children in the urban areas than in the rural ones. In the period 1980–91 enrollments in preschool education increased from 48,000 to 72,819. In comparison, in rural areas enrollment rose from 25,000 in 1980 to 39,673 in 1993. However, only 7.3 percent of the relevant age group were enrolled, making preschool education a very privileged form of education. Furthermore, about a fourth of these children attend private institutions.

3.3 Special Education

Special education is provided for students with physical, intellectual, or emotional disabilities in special establishments called *Establecimientos Educativos Especiales* (EEEs). They offer not only special education but also medical treatment and help for parents. Special education was expanded in 1985 with special financial aid from international agencies, although the first school for blind children was founded in 1927. Special education was provided only for blind children until 1946, when the first school for deaf children was founded. In 1953 there were courses provided for mentally retarded children. Through the help of external organizations such as *"Terre des Hommes"* special education gained importance and in the late 1960s and 1970s several institutions were founded in different cities. The International Year of the Handicapped (1981) was another milestone in the development of special education: a new National Department for Special Education was created in the Ministry of Education. This department worked very efficiently; in 1985 there were 33 institutions working in the field, and by 1993 they numbered about 50, covering different deficiencies. Parallel to this development there have been several courses for preparing the staff. However, not all children can regularly attend special education, since the relevant establishments are mostly concentrated in a few cities such as La Paz (13), Santa Cruz (15), and Cochabamba (10). Children with learning difficulties can only be taken care of in La Paz and children with emotional disturbances only in Santa Cruz.

3.4 Vocational, Technical, and Business Education

Vocational education in the formal system is provided in the first cycle of secondary education for children of 11 to 13 years of age. It has a differentiated curriculum and offers the opportunity to explore different fields of activity in addition to continuing the general education process. There are also secondary schools which differentiate their curricula to make them vocationally relevant and add a technical branch. The out-of-school vocational training is described in Sect. 3.5 below.

3.5 Adult and Nonformal Education

There are two branches of nonformal adult education: one for vocational, technical, and business education under the "Servicio Nacional de Educación Técnica" (SENET) which provides for industrial, commercial, and agronomic education and the "Servicio Nacional de Alfabetización y Educación Popular" (SENALEP). Both are decentralized organizations. Vocational education is provided for those having successfully completed primary education. The curriculum is designed for two years of study. There is no explicit policy as to how vocational training should be handled more effectively in the future.

The policy for SENALEP is more clearly defined. The target group is all those who did not enter or complete regular education. The main emphasis is on literacy programs. Following Freire's concept, literacy courses aim at increasing the consciousness of participants, enabling them to take fundamental decisions and increasing their social participation and autonomy in their organizations. Another feature—which is new for the country—is the multicultural and multilingual approach. Indian languages, especially Aymará and Quechua, are now considered as equally important in the educational process, so as not to discriminate against or exlude the rural population. In the multicultural approach, the participants' own values and cultural patterns are considered by including Indian representatives in the decision-making processes.

4. Administrative and Supervisory Structure and Operation

The basic document for the educational policy of the new government in Bolivia is the "Pink Book" (*Libro Rosado*), which includes the pedagogical, administrative and financial concepts of the government. Basically, the strategies are decentralization, curricular reform, and more social participation. These strategies resulted from a critical assessment of the present state of education. The assessment indicated rigid centralized planning and administration, anarchy in the teachers' unions due to very low salaries, and a static educational budget which did not consider the consequences of the population increase on the education system.

The centralized administration structure implied a static hierarchy which did not allow for social participation in the educational process and did not take the regional differences into account. This will be changed. National coordination will remain with the Ministry of Education and Culture, but more responsibility will be given to the regional and local authorities. The nine individual states (*departamentos*) will gain greater flexibility to deal with their own regional and local characteristics. Rural education will be strengthened according to the nuclear system developed by Elizardo Pérez, having a central school which covers at least the whole of primary education and which cooperates with smaller sectional schools in the remote villages. These, usually isolated, schools have only one teacher and do not cover the whole primary curriculum. Local participation of the community in all school matters will be insured, and nonformal adult education will be included in this. The teachers will thus be in direct contact with the community and be more autonomous in curricular and methodological decisions. The responsibility for all decisions at the local level will be with the directors of the nuclei; responsibility in the cities will be largely with the directors of the individual schools. Each state or *departamento* will have a coordinating and supervising function. They are responsible for the maintenance of the school buildings, payment of salaries, planning and management of the budget, and the appointment of personnel. The community will also be represented in these supervising agencies. Budgetary decisions, statistics, research, and general coordination will remain with the national Ministry of Education and Culture. The national Ministry is also responsible for the appointment of the directors of schools and supervising inspectors.

There are many private schools in the urban areas, particularly in La Paz, Santa Cruz, Cochabamba and Sucre. Nearly 19 percent of the students are enrolled in this sector at the primary and intermediate levels and 30 percent at the secondary level. Many private schools have a religious affiliation, most commonly with the Catholic Church. These schools are relatively free from government directions. They are, however, required to meet minimum standards for registration and funding purposes.

Higher education institutions are also mostly autonomous bodies, even if they get substantial support from the state. Administratively they are ruled by the Ministry of Education, which has three subsections: planning and coordination, education, and administration. The subsection of education has a department for each level of education, including higher education and adult education.

Supervision is not conducted in a uniform manner: generally supervisors in the cities specialize in a certain level of education, while in the rural areas this is not possible. Two main problems are that supervisors have not necessarily received adequate training for their job and they have difficulties in reaching the schools, which are widely dispersed throughout the country.

5. Educational Finance

The educational budget covers six different areas: administration at the central, regional (states or *departamentos*), and local (provinces) levels, and education at the different levels; that is, primary, intermediate, secondary, and higher education as well as the nonformal sector of adult education. For several years there has been no real budget, since inflation made any calculation very insecure. The first established budget dates from 1986. Bolivia used to spend a large amount of money on education: in 1982–83 it was 30 percent of the gross domestic product (GDP). This decreased to 19 percent in 1986. In the same period personnel costs increased by 90–98 percent, so that there was no money left for any new initiatives. In 1988, the budget amounted to 6,842,713,755 bolivianos (US$2.7 million). Two years before, petrol and some luxury goods such as cars, televisions, china, and tobacco were additionally taxed in order to increase the budget for education. The increase in the budget became absolutely necessary in order to cover the high personnel costs. The aim was also to increase the expenditure for rural education, with the aim of bridging the enormous gap between urban and rural areas.

6. Supplying Personnel for the Education System

There are about 80,000 teachers in Bolivia. Not all are well-trained and many lack motivation because of the low salaries. Many teachers have two jobs. In 1986 a school director earned the equivalent of US$100 per month and about 60 percent of the teachers earned the equivalent of US$25 per month. In comparison, teachers in private Catholic schools earned about US$60 per month. It was unsurprising that teachers started a lengthy strike and state schools did not work. It was very difficult for the government to decide on an increase in salaries given the general financial crisis. Supplying good personnel for the educational system is one of the major problems the system has to face. Qualified people will tend to leave the system and take other work which is better paid. Teachers receive no money for books, paper, or other didactic material.

Teacher-training is undertaken in four-year courses at specialized colleges. The courses include general orientation, teaching methodology, and teaching practice. In reality, however, they often study only the curriculum they will have to cover for the level where they will teach. Only a limited range of teaching skills is offered. Here again the scarcity of funds hampers having well-prepared lecturers. Some of the teacher-training institutions had to be closed down because they could not be financed. Funds are obtained either from external aid or from participants' fees, but the latter do not cover the cost. The new government intends to create a pedagogical institute at the University in Sucre.

7. Curriculum Development and Teaching Methodology

The curriculum used in the schools in 1993 was developed in 1973. There is one school curriculum for urban areas and another for rural areas, but there are no clear criteria for this differentiation. Very often the content is not sufficiently adapted to the requirements of the regions and thus not relevant to the students. The content is often far too theoretical and abstract. Teaching methodology concentrates only on the transmission of knowledge and is not sufficiently action oriented. It does not take into account the affective or psychomotor needs of the children. This is why they often lose interest in school and drop out prematurely. In addition, students in rural areas often have problems with the language since Spanish is not their mother tongue.

These problems have led to the conviction that a curriculum reform is necessary. The "Pink Book" of the government envisions accomplishing this through decentralization, thus giving schools more autonomy in deciding about curricular elements and teaching methods on the basis of broad curriculum guidelines. A reform is not only necessary in order to have greater flexibility according to the different requirements of the various geographical regions but also because, as mentioned above, the whole structure of education will be changed, resulting in a lowering of the school leaving age. In future there will be a 5–5 system, rather than a 5–3–4 system. Having only five years of primary and five of secondary education will be one of the steps aimed at decreasing the high dropout rate. The intention is also to have greater community participation in the decisions about what is taught in school, thus making the curriculum more relevant for the participants. A certain core curriculum will still remain valid for the whole country, but this will be accompanied by the introduction of certain regional options.

8. The System of Examinations, Promotions, and Certifications

In 1986 a UNESCO delegation evaluated the efficiency of the educational system. It pointed out that in order to diminish the high rate of school dropout and grade repetition there should be automatic promotion to the next grade in the first four years of schooling. Prior to this there had been final examinations at the end of the year and only pupils with an average of 3.6 in a scale ranging from a low of 1 to a high of 10 could be promoted to the next form. This will now only be the case for promotion from the basic to the intermediate level. However, pupils who do not reach this average in their marks will be able to take a four-week revision course at the beginning of the next school year. They can then take a second examination in the core subjects, namely language, mathematics, science, and social studies. If they pass all of them they will be promoted; otherwise they have to repeat Grade 5. Another innovation is to have the class teacher stay with his or her class from the first to the fifth grade, taking responsibility for the whole group over a longer period of time. In theory, the teacher will then see relatively early where a child is weak and what to do about it. If 90 percent of children can be promoted to the secondary level, the teacher will be rewarded with 15 points on the salary scale. If more than 30 percent of the children fail, the teacher will lose 10 points on the salary scale.

9. Educational Assessment, Evaluation, and Research

There is no state-run educational research. There are, however, some institutions which carry out research on certain problems which are also relevant to the educational system, such as the "Centro Estudios de la Realidad Boliviana" (Research Center of the Bolivian Reality), which deals for instance with the problems faced by women, and the "Centro de Investigación y Promoción del Campesinado" (CIPCA), which deals with all questions related to people in the rural areas.

10. Major Reforms in the 1980s and 1990s

In 1987 the "White Book" presented a document stating it was necessary to reform the education system. A national congress on education was held in January 1987 in order to discuss the issue. This reform was never carried out.

In August 1993 the *Moviento Nacionalista Revolucionario* was restored to power and will carry out the reform which is now documented in the "Pink Book." One of the main reforms is to shorten primary and secondary education in order to decrease the high dropout rate. The new system will have only five years of primary education and five years of secondary education. An optional preschool year and an optional year of postsecondary education preparing for university will provide educational opportunities for those who want more education. The curriculum will be more work oriented, bilingual, and multicultural, in order to attract more of the Indian population in the rural areas. Rural education is a special feature of this reform, as the majority of the marginalized people are in rural areas. Absenteeism is extremely high and from a thousand children who enter school, under 35 percent complete the fifth grade of schooling. A further important measure to improve the quality of education is decentralization. This will allow the community to have more social participation in all educational matters. More funds will be allocated to rural education and supervision. Inspection will become much more of a counseling and assistance service for the schools. The intention is to integrate urban and rural education gradually, rather than having them as two separate systems of education.

11. Major Problems for the Year 2000

The envisioned reform is one allowing a higher degree of democratization. The greatest problems in any change, however, will be financial factors, because teachers' salaries will have to be improved. Teachers have no time for inservice training or for a creative approach to the curriculum in the class. There are no teaching materials and no incentives for improving the quality of the teaching. Teacher training has been very traditional and although the reform would have to start here it will take a considerable time until a new generation of motivated teachers is in the classrooms. Previous attempts to foster a greater participation of the community in the decision-making process have shown that people have been very reluctant to accept it. Bilingual education will also be difficult to introduce—not all teachers are bilingual and communities often do not want to be taught in their language, but in Spanish, since this is the official language of the country and the language of the whole administration. School buildings are in bad repair.

Finding the resources to support the reform and the envisioned expansion in education for rural areas will also be a major problem. The reform itself will cost US$1.5 million and the existing educational budget will have to be increased through additional taxes. At the same time the demand for education is likely to increase. Bolivia has a very young population and even in 1994 there were not enough places for everybody in the system. Furthermore, there is no real approach to finding a practicable solution for the working and street children—an alternative way for their reintegration into society will have to be found and financed. These factors together create a heavy load for a poor country.

Bibliography

Cárdenas V H 1992 Un currículo intercultural y bilingüe. *Presencia* February 2
Gonzales S I M, Ipiña M 1993 *El desafío para el cuatrienio 1993–97.* Fundación Milenio, La Paz
Instituto Nacional de Estadística 1990a *Bolivia en Cifras, 1989.* INE, La Paz
Instituto Nacional de Estadística 1990b *Bolivia. Encuesta Nacional de Población y Vivienda. La Paz, 1988.* INE, La Paz
Instituto Nacional de Estadística 1991 *Resumen del Balance Estadística. Gestión 1991.* INE, La Paz
Ministerio de Educación y Cultura 1988 *Libro Rosado. Reforma de la educación,* 2nd edn. MEC, La Paz
Ministerio de Educación y Cultura 1991 *Bolivia. Estadística Global del Sistema con Indicadores.* MEC, La Paz
Ministerio de Educación y Cultura 1992a *Educación Especial.* MEC, La Paz
Ministerio de Educación y Cultura 1992b *Seminario Taller para Elaboración de un Plan de Trabajo de Educación de Adultos y Educación No Formal para la Gestión de 1992.* MEC, La Paz
Ministerio de Educación y Cultura 1993 *Estadística de alumnos a nivel nacional. Gestión 1992.* MEC, La Paz
UNESCO 1987 *Bolivia. Opciones y Estrategias para el Desarrollo de la Educación Regular.* Gisbert, La Paz
UNICEF 1990 *La situación de la Niñez y la Mujer.* Espacios/CIDEM, La Paz
UNICEF 1991 *Mujer y Pobreza.* Espacios/CIDEM, La Paz

Botswana

G. Kgomanyane

1. General Background

Botswana lies on the Southern African Plateau at a mean altitude of approximately 1,000 meters above sea level. The Tropic of Capricorn passes through the southern part of the country. Botswana shares borders with South Africa, Namibia, Zimbabwe, and Zambia. Most of the country is semiarid and is covered by a thick layer of the Kgalagadi sand, averaging 120 meters in depth. In 1885 the country became a British Protectorate, known then as "Bechuanaland." In 1966 it gained Independence and became the Republic of Botswana. The colonial administration showed no real interest in providing education in the territory. It was through the efforts of Christian missions and tribal chiefs that some form of education was provided to Botswana during the early years of British rule. When the country gained Independence in 1966 there were 251 primary schools, nine secondary schools, two primary teacher-training colleges, one trade school, and no university. The country was suffering from a critical shortage of well-trained workers required to staff the new public service in which expatriates predominated in the middle and senior grades. Education was thus to be given the highest priority in the government allocation of resources.

In 1966 the population was estimated to be almost 600,000, and it has since been growing at an average of 3.4 percent per year to reach 1.3 million by 1991. Most of the population lives in the eastern part of the country where soils and water resources are best. The people are predominantly of the Setswana-speaking stock, though there are other significant minority groups who speak a local language in addition to Setswana. There are also people of European and Asian origin. Setswana and English are the official languages.

The majority of the people live in rural areas, though there are fast growing urban settlements. The urban population is estimated to have grown from 17.7 percent in 1981 to 33 percent in 1991 due mainly to rural–urban migration resulting from growth in modern sector employment in towns. The more arid western parts of the country are characterized by small scattered settlements which are great distances apart, very limited water resources, and undeveloped road networks. The provision of social services such as health and education becomes a very costly undertaking in such a setting.

Schools are typically small, and boarding facilities in most locations, especially for the secondary school pupils, are an absolute necessity. Before the recruitment and deployment of teachers was centrally controlled, the staffing of these schools by district councils posed a serious problem and the performance of pupils in primary education was generally below the national average. So much so that entry requirements for postprimary schools were slightly lowered for pupils from remote schools.

There are indications that the Botswana rate of population growth may be slowing down which would mean that the number of children requiring schooling in future will grow less rapidly. In that event, some resources could be diverted away from physical expansion and be directed toward the qualitative improvement of the system.

In 1966 Botswana was said to be among the 25 poorest countries in the world or one of the poorest countries in Africa. The people depended for a livelihood on arable and livestock farming. Beef production was the mainstay of the economy in terms of output and export earnings, and it accounted for about 40 percent of the gross domestic product. The severe drought of the 1980s caused a considerable decline in the contribution that the agricultural sector made to the gross domestic product to the extent that by 1989 it contributed only 3 percent. It is, however, still regarded as a very important sector for providing the majority of the people with food, income, employment, and even capital. For this reason, agricultural education and training will continue to be given increasing attention.

The post-Independence period has been one of rapid economic growth fueled by revenues derived from minerals, especially diamonds. The average economic growth rate was 12.9 percent per annum. For the education system, this remarkable growth in the economy has meant a massive expansion of educational facilities at all levels in order to meet the growing demand for a trained workforce. It has also meant that the curriculum of the system must be reformed to make it more responsive to the needs of pupils and to the changing pattern of the labor market.

The post-Independence period also saw the expansion of the public service (central and local government, including teaching) and the growth of the private sector. Between 1972 and 1986 the compound rate of growth of formal employment averaged 8.8 percent per annum according to a study carried out by Colclough et al. (1988). The percentage of people in paid employment increased from 4 to 11 percent, and the number of expatriates in employment increased by more than 50 percent.

Some 90 percent of the workforce had no secondary education in 1972, but by 1986 one-third had some secondary schooling. Significant progress was made in the localization of the public sector; but in the private sector there continues to be a high concentration of expatriates in technical/professional occupations. In teaching, 41 percent of the secondary teaching force are expatriates. Given these facts, labor force considerations will continue to influence decisions on educational planning. The need to relate education and training to the labor needs of the economy has been echoed in all national development plans since Independence.

Botswana is a multiparty democracy. The Constitution provides for a unicameral elected legislature, the National Assembly, and a House of Chiefs with no legislative powers. The role of the latter is to advise on matters affecting custom and tradition. There are nine district councils, four town councils, and one city council, the members of which are popularly elected. These councils have responsibility, among other things, for primary education. They provide classrooms, teacher housing, school books, and equipment while the central government, through the Ministry of Education, is responsible for supplying teachers, developing the curriculum, and providing overall professional supervision of schools.

2. Politics and the Goals of the Education System

The goals of the education system were set forth in the government White Paper of 1977 entitled *National Policy On Education*. This followed wide-ranging consultations among major sectors of society or key stake-holders in education and politics, and the policy is based on the recommendations of the National Commission on Education appointed by the government in 1976 to review the entire education system.

The policy demands that education must foster and promote the four national principles of democracy—development, self-reliance, and unity which together lead to social harmony (*Kagisano*). In pursuit of this goal, the education system must move as rapidly as possible toward universal access to nine years of basic education of sound quality, preparing children for a useful and productive life after school, eliminating inequalities of educational opportunities, and meeting the labor force needs of the economy.

Debates about education tend to center around such issues as access and equity, quality and relevance, and the proper balance between academic and vocational education. School fees were abolished for primary schools in 1980 and for secondary schools in 1988 in order to reduce barriers to access. The government has assumed greater responsibility for the development and recurrent expenditure of community-managed junior-secondary schools to ensure that they are provided with adequate facilities to discharge their function.

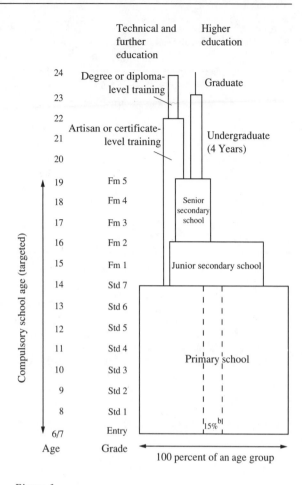

Figure 1

Botswana: Structure of the formal education system 1990[a]

a Preschool is not yet part of the formal system   b 15 percent of the eligible primary school age group cannot be accounted for

3. The Formal System of Educaiton

3.1 Primary, Secondary, and Tertiary Education

The structure of the formal education system is illustrated in Fig. 1. Table 1 presents the percentage of females of those in school at selected levels. The structure consists of 7 years of primary, 2 years of junior-secondary, and 3 years of senior-secondary education (7–2–3). It is envisaged that this structure will change to a 6–3–3 structure once open access to junior-secondary education is achieved or about to be achieved. In 1988, the minimum age for enrollment in the first year of the primary cycle was reduced from 7 to 6 years. In 1992, the primary school age population was aged 7–13 years. This will change as more and more children aged 6 enter primary school.

At the end of each of the three levels of formal education there is a terminal examination which de-

Table 1
Percentage female enrollment at various levels 1979, 1984, 1989

	1979	1984	1989
Primary			
Standard 1	52.4	50.6	50.2
Standard 7	60.4	56.4	55.9
Total	55.0	52.8	51.5
Secondary			
Form I	59.0	56.9	55.5
Year 1 senior[a]	44.0	43.7	50.3
Teacher training	79.9	84.1	82.3
Vocational			
training center	33.1	33.6	31.9
University	37.4	41.5	43.8

Source: Education Statistics (Botswana)   a   Form 4 in 1979 and 1984, and Form 3 in 1989

termines progression to the next level. Primary school children sit an attainment test in Standard 4 and if their progress is not satisfactory they repeat Standard 4; otherwise there is automatic progression from one standard to the next throughout the course of primary education. The medium of instruction is Setswana from standards 1 to 4, and thereafter English.

There are 654 primary schools, of these, 582 are council, 11 mission, and 61 private schools. A small number of private schools are referred to as "English-medium schools" and cater mainly, but not exclusively, for children of expatriates. Private schools are self-financing and are now steadily increasing in number because of the growing demand for expatriate personnel as the economy grows and diversifies.

The total enrollment at the primary level is 308,840 pupils. In Botswana, education is free but not compulsory. At the primary segment of the nine-year cycle of basic education (primary plus junior-secondary), Botswana has exceeded the target of 80 percent enrollment set by the 1990 World Conference on Education for All, and is making concerted efforts to move as quickly as resources permit toward universal access to nine years of basic education. The phenomenal growth in primary education may be illustrated by the fact that in the 20 years between 1962 and 1982 primary enrollment shot from 46,536 to 186,110 and is projected to reach 322,082 by 1992.

The average class size is 45 pupils per class, though it could be as low as 20 to 25 pupils per class in English-medium schools. The pupil–teacher ratio is 32:1. On each school day a pupil receives formal lessons for 5 hours. The number of school days in a year may not be less than 180 and not more than 200. Schools operate a three-term system commencing in January.

Pupils enter year one (Form 1) of the junior-secondary course on completion of primary education, subject to their satisfying certain admission criteria which include the grade of pass and the upper age limit. In 1992, the transition rate from primary to junior-secondary was 65 percent of all primary school leavers, and it is projected to rise to 77 percent by 1997. Junior-secondary schools increased in number from 42 in 1985 to 146 in 1991. Form 1 enrollments shot from 10,577 to 26,400 during the same period as a result of the accelerated expansion program launched to meet the demand for education beyond the primary level and to fulfill government commitment to universalize nine-year basic education.

Girls have always outnumbered boys in Botswana primary schools which is reflected in higher female enrollments in the first year of the junior-secondary school. The proportion is then gradually reversed as they progress through secondary school (see Table 1). The lower male enrollments at the primary level may be explained by the fact that traditionally boys spend time at the cattle posts, away from their villages where the schools are located. The higher dropout rate of girls, mainly because of pregnancy, accounts in part for their falling numbers further up the education ladder.

At the junior-secondary level, the class size is 40 pupils per class and the pupil–teacher ratio is estimated to be 26:1. The length of the school year is to be not less than 185 and not more than 200 days. Schools follow a three-term system. The first term begins in January. On average, instruction extends over 5.5 hours each day.

Although expansion of the senior-secondary school level has not been on the scale of the junior level it has nonetheless been quite impressive. In 1965, when the country gained self-government, only 129 pupils were enrolled in the senior-secondary level course. By 20 years later, in 1985, the number had reached 4,380. The figure for 1991 was 19,978, and is projected to rise to 23,576 by 1995. The proportion of junior certificate leavers proceeding to senior school is at present 31 percent of all junior certificate completers. The proportion is expected to decline to 25 percent by 1997 as the junior level continues to expand much faster than the senior-secondary education level, and other alternatives to proceeding on to senior school are identified and explored. The class size is 30 pupils per class and the pupil–teacher ratio is 18:1. The daily hours of tuition and the length of the school year are the same as for the junior-secondary school.

The senior-secondary level lasts for 3 years. About 33 percent of junior-secondary school leavers are not able to find places in senior-secondary school. They have traditionally had other options such as employment in the public service or training in nursing, agriculture, primary teaching, the police force, and private commercial schools. These options have become fewer as the number of senior-secondary school leavers unable to gain access to postsecondary school training and employment opportunities have risen. This situation has resulted from the very rapid expansion of the secondary school sector since about 1987. There were 35,966 pupils in both junior- and senior-secondary schools in 1984. This number reached 69,250 in 1991.

At the end of senior-secondary school, pupils sit the University of Cambridge Overseas School Certificate which is an entrance qualification to the University of Botswana for candidates with a first or second division pass. Other options for senior-secondary school graduates include diploma programs at the Botswana College of Agriculture, the Junior Secondary School Teacher's Diploma at the two colleges of education, the Diploma in Nursing, and technical courses at the Polytechnic which also offers degree programs validated by the University of Botswana.

The University of Botswana had its origins in the 1960s when a regional university for the High Commission Territories of Bechuanaland (Botswana), Basutoland (Lesotho), and Swaziland was established in 1964. This joint university continued to exist until 1975 when Lesotho unilaterally decided to national-ize it and to rename it the National University of Lesotho. In 1975, Botswana and Swaziland formed the University of Botswana and Swaziland with colleges in each country. In 1982 the two countries decided to establish separate universities. The University of Botswana is the only institution of higher learning in the country that awards degrees. Because Botswana emerged from the British colonial era with a critical shortage of skilled labor, the University has been given the mandate of training high-level labor of all types. In its initial development, the University con-centrated its efforts and resources on undergraduate studies in the basic faculties of education, humanities, science, and social sciences. At the end of the 1980s, it began to make a modest move toward offering master's degree programs. These initiatives are to be vigorously pursued. Its undergraduate programs have been expanded and strengthened; in collaboration with the Botswana Agricultural College and the Poly-technic, it has launched degree courses in agriculture and engineering. Enrollments at the University have increased from 1,400 in 1985–86 to just over 3,000 students in 1990.

3.2 Preschool Education

Preschool education covers a wide range of day care programs of varying quality operated by churches, women's groups, district councils, and the Red Cross.

The responsibility for overseeing day care programs rests with the Ministry of Local Government, Lands, and Housing. The Ministry is required to operate within the framework of guidelines drawn up in 1980. Summarized briefly, the guidelines require the Min-istry to monitor, supervise, coordinate and evaluate preschool activities in the country.

There are over 200 registered day care centers with a total enrollment of about 7,240 children. Over 200 teachers have been trained in Botswana and other countries. A preschool education teacher-training cen-ter has been established in the town of Lobatse, and it is supported by the United Nations Children's Fund (UNICEF). There has been little government support for the day care center program.

In the financial year 1991–92, the Ministry responsi-ble for the program was allocated P75,000 (US\$3,532). However, the 1991–97 National Develop-ment Plan acknowledges the government's commit-ment to the development of a comprehensive policy on preschool education which will link preschool education to the formal system in the long run.

3.3 Special Education

Special education is relatively new in Botswana. Pro-vision of special services for the handicapped came through the initiatives of nongovernmental agencies in the 1970s. Government intervention began only in 1984 when a Special Education Unit was established within the Ministry of Education following reports by the Swedish International Development Authority and UNESCO. The main function of the Unit is to plan, establish, develop, and coordinate special education services in the country. Special education services are provided through a variety of institutions. At the primary level there are purpose-built schools, two for the deaf with an enrollment of 126 children and one for the mentally handicapped with an enrollment of 42 children.

One junior-secondary and one senior-secondary school have provisions for visually handicapped stu-dents who follow a course of secondary education. A secondary school adjacent to a center for the deaf caters for the hearing impaired. The University of Botswana has a resource center for blind students who entered the Bachelor of Education program in 1982. Four vocational rehabilitation centers train dis-abled youth and adults in such activities as basketry, knitting, sewing, and carpentry.

A central resource center has been built adjacent to a teacher-training college near Gaborone. The function of the center is to provide assessment and counseling services, support teachers, gather informa-tion about the disabled population, and collaborate with all agencies involved in special education services. Teachers for special education have been trained outside the country, mainly in Zambia where primary teacher training colleges include special education in their curriculum.

3.4 Vocational, Technical, and Business Education

Vocational and technical education and training is open to school-leavers and persons in employment. The main objective of vocational/technical education is to promote industrial and rural development by providing training to meet skilled labor requirements and to increase the participation of women in vocational/technical training.

The providers of vocational/technical education and training include the Ministry of Education; some government departments such as roads, central transport organizations, and the Ministry of Agriculture; parastatals such as the water utilities, power, and telecommunication corporations; and private companies, especially in the mining sector. The Education Ministry provides education and training through the Botswana Polytechnic which offers artisan, technician, and degree-level courses in civil, electrical, and mechanical engineering and teacher education in craft, design, and technology. The Automative Trades Training School specializes in automechanics, while vocational training centers offer full-time training in all trades and part-time training for apprentices from industry.

The Brigade model of training was launched in the 1960s through the initiative of a private individual. The fundamental principle behind this model is to combine training and some academic studies with production, to generate income for the Brigade's operational activities, to create employment in the local area, to provide services and through these efforts to contribute to rural development. The target group was the primary school-leavers who could not be absorbed into the formal system of further education, which was seen as offering a narrow and elitist type of educaiton unrelated to the needs and lives of the majority of Botswani living in rural areas. Brigades are autonomous bodies, run by their own boards of trustees, involved in various forms of artisan training and a variety of small-scale commercial enterprises. They have become popular and receive an ever-increasing level of government subsidy.

In 1991 the enrollments at the various levels were Brigades 1,497, artisan 1,540, and technician 620 trainees. No fees are charged in Ministry of Education institutions for government-sponsored students. Privately sponsored students are required to pay a certain proportion of the training costs.

The Botswana Institute of Administration and Commerce offers accounting, commercial, and secretarial courses. It serves mainly as a government inservice center. The Institute of Development Management also offers courses in accounting and business management. Given the large numbers of expatriates in technical/professional posts in the public, parastatal, and private sectors, it is accepted that vocational/technical education and training will need to be accorded high priority.

3.5 Adult and Nonformal Education

At the time of Independence most adults had little or no formal education. As the majority of people lived and still live in rural areas, rural development was to be one of the government's top priorities. Without a literate population, rural development programs were bound to suffer serious setbacks.

A primary school teacher upgrading program was run between 1968 and 1973. The method of instruction was mainly through the use of printed materials supported by radio and residential courses, and 88 percent of the teachers on the program became qualified teachers. Following upon this success, a correspondence college was established in 1973 to offer an alternative route to attaining a secondary education qualification outside the formal school system. It also aimed at offering nonformal courses such as childcare, vegetable growing, cookery, and nutrition. The college worked closely with other government agencies involved in extension services of all types. It was incorporated into the Department of Nonformal Education within the Ministry of Education. The activities of the department have largely been directed toward correspondence courses at secondary school level, the national literacy programme, and home economics.

Of particular importance, is the National Literacy Programme launched in 1980–81 whose target was the men and women who had never been to school and who were estimated to number about 250,000. Although it had been designed to have a lifespan of six years, at the end of which it had been thought it would have helped to eradicate illiteracy, it has now been accepted as a long-term program. It will address the learning needs of poor urban and rural dwellers and nonsedentary remote area dwellers who are not served by formal education; facilitate cross transfer of learners between the formal and nonformal systems; and expand its activities beyond reading, writing, and numeracy into training for work and self-employment.

4. Administrative and Supervisory Structure and Operation

Primary education is the shared responsibility of two ministries. The Ministry of Local Government, Lands, and Housing has to provide primary school infrastructure, school books, and equipment. The Ministry of Education is responsible for all professional aspects, including the recruitment and salaries of teachers. District and town councils have no share in the control and administration of other levels or forms of education, except that they may be represented in boards of governors that may be set up at the local or district level to assist in the management of community-based junior-secondary schools. Apart form the role played by councils in the provision of primary school infrastructure, the education service is directed from the headquarters of the Ministry of Education. The system has expanded enormously during the post-Independence period and has now begun to experience the problems of long-distance management. The decentralization of some of the Ministry's operations is high on the agenda for future reform of the administrative structure.

At the apex of the administrative structure is the Permanent (Principal) Secretary who is supported by heads of departments with designations such as "Chief Education Officers" or "Directors" depending on whether the main function of the department is professional or managerial. Primary education has for a long time had a field-based team of professionals who perform the multiple role of supervising, advising, inspecting, and liaising with councils and education secretaries. Secondary education is beginning to decentralize some professional services. A skeleton of field-based senior officers has been deployed in the districts to provide professional support and supervision. A great measure of decentralization has been achieved in nonformal education which has a network of adult educators and literacy officers spread around the country. Other departments have no field staff and reach their institutions or clients through periodic visits.

The trend over the years has been toward increasing centralization of decision-making with all major decisions on the planning, development, and administration of schools being at headquarters. The development and recurrent costs of mission- and community-based secondary schools are met by the government. The staffing of schools is the responsibility of the Ministry. When secondary school fees were abolished in 1988 and the government became responsible for the running costs of community schools, they were required to comply with specific guidelines in the use of funds allocated to them.

The selection of primary school completers for junior-secondary school places has become a centralized operation for all schools financed from public funds. The process of decentralizing the Ministry of Education operations will require careful planning if its various district-level activities are to be properly coordinated and the duplication of resources avoided. The problem is that each department has worked on its own devolution plans without reference to its sister departments.

5. Educational Finance

In 1967–68, capital expenditure on education accounted for 19 percent of the total capital budget. In 1982–83, it was 16.9 percent and in 1990–91 it was about 18.3 percent. Expenditure here includes spending at the Botswana Agricultural College (Ministry of Agriculture) and the National Health Institute (Ministry of Health). Recurrent expenditure on education, expressed as a proportion of the total government budget, has increased from 18.4 percent in 1983–84 to 19.8 percent in 1989–90. Unit costs at various levels of the education system have increased, except in

Table 2

Unit costs of education 1984–85 and 1989–90 (in pula[a])

Level	1984–85	1989–90	% Increase
Primary	249	274	10%
Secondary:	1,142	1,363	19%
Junior	—	—	—
Senior	—	1,630	—
Teacher education	2,260	3,203	41%
Nonformal	40	63	58%
Technical education	4,925	4,575	–8%
Brigades	559	1,800	15%
University	12,591	12,394	–2%

Source: *National Development Plan VII*, Chap. 14. Government of Botswana   a One Pula = US$0.4710

primary education and the University. Unit costs for secondary education have increased as a result of the government taking over responsibility for the running costs of private secondary schools, which in 1984 only received a grant of P40 (US$19) per student. Table 2 gives the unit costs at the various levels.

The bulk of all funds going into education is provided by the central government. Councils receive a subsidy from the government to meet their financial commitments in respect of primary schools. Secondary schools, teacher-training colleges, and institutions offering vocational/technical education are fully government-financed, except that Brigades receive a grant per trainee. The University receives a government subvention calculated on the basis of the difference between estimated total expenditure and total revenue from fees and other sources. The government awards bursaries to students they sponsor. The costs of training outside the country are borne by the government, except that donor agencies do offer scholarships in certain areas of training.

Support is also provided by a number of outside agencies in various forms, such as the supply of equipment, teachers, educational materials, inservice workshops, and the like. Development funds come in the form of loans from institutions like the World Bank, the African Development Bank, the United Nations Capital Development Fund, or in the form of outright donations from the Swedish International Development Authority, the United States Agency for International Development, and several others.

The National Development Plan period covering the years 1991 to 1997 envisages the recurrent budget of the Ministry of Education growing at an average rate of 13.8 percent per annum, and the development expenditure allocated as follows: primary education (24%), secondary education (35%), vocational/university (17%), teacher training (5%), and others (2%). Economic forecasts indicate that the Botswana economy will slow down in the years ahead. In view of this prospect, consideration will have to be given to cost recovery measures.

6. Supply Personnel for the Education System

The Unified Teaching Service—a department of the Ministry of Education established in 1976—is the recruiting and employing agency for teachers serving in schools/colleges maintained out of public funds. It currently employs over 13,000 teachers, of which about 9,700 are in primary schools, 3,400 in secondary schools, 120 in primary teacher-training colleges, and over 70 in colleges of education.

Both primary and secondary schools have untrained teachers on their staffs. With the expansion of teacher education, their numbers are declining. The proportion of untrained primary school teachers has been reduced from about 26 percent in 1985 to about 16 percent in 1991; and that of secondary school teachers has dropped from 28 percent to 21 percent over the same period. The rapid expansion of secondary education and the shortfall in the supply of native teachers has necessitated the recruitment of large numbers of expatriate teachers. Approximately 40 percent of the secondary teaching force are expatriates.

The preservice training of teachers takes place at four levels:

(a) certificate-level for primary school teachers (2 years);

(b) diploma-level for junior-secondary school teachers (3 years);

(c) degree-level for teachers of senior-secondary schools (5 years);

(d) degree and graduate level for tutors and lecturers for teacher-training institutions (duration varies according to the type of program offered).

In order to improve the quality of primary school teachers, the two-year certificate is to be upgraded to a three-year diploma with a minimum entry of a senior-secondary school qualification. In addition, a network of inservice centers (commonly referred to as "education centers") has been established to facilitate the delivery of inservice education. The University has diploma and degree programs in primary education for serving teachers. Graduates of the diploma program are to return to the school system to occupy posts of responsibility in schools, while the graduates of the degree program are appointed to lecturer positions in teacher-training colleges or they may become education officers.

Teacher-training colleges follow a common curriculum and students are assessed on a common examination validated by the University of Botswana. Each college is required to organize blocks of teaching practice for its students.

7. Curriculum Development and Teaching Methodology

For the majority of school-leavers, formal education will terminate at the end of the nine-year cycle of basic education. With this fact in mind, curriculum designers have sought to expose all children to a broad-based curriculum and to incorporate into the various subject syllabuses as much practical skills as possible. This is different from the notion of vocationalizing secondary education. The rationale is that such an approach should better prepare students for alternative forms of training after they have completed their basic education.

The primary school curriculum consists of a core of English, Setswana, mathematics, integrated science, social studies, and religious education. Agriculture and home economics are also included to provide an orientation in practical subjects. Other subjects with a practical bias are arts and crafts, physical education, and music. For the junior-secondary level, there are also six core subjects, but agriculture takes the place of religious education in the core curriculum.

Curriculum in the senior-secondary schools is determined by the Cambridge Overseas School Certificate Examination, but there is room for electives. Because of the cosmopolitan composition of the teaching staff and considerable variation in their teaching competences and classroom experience, subject advisers play a very significant role in influencing the way in which teaching is organized and assessments made. Support instructional materials and teachers' guides are continually sent out to schools. Regular workshops are held to reinforce teachers' subject knowledge and to upgrade their professional skills.

In 1978, the Ministry of Education established the Department of Curriculum Development and Evaluation. Its mandate was to provide leadership and coordination in the development, implementation, and evaluation of the total instructional program of the school system. Its components are: curriculum development; research and testing; educational publications; guidance and counseling; and examinations. Its first task was to reform the primary-level curriculum and then move on to the junior-secondary level to complete the nine-year cycle of basic education.

The Department has been involved in activities such as syllabus revision, development and evaluation of teaching/ learning materials, trial testing, development of teacher handbooks, textbooks, and teacher inservice courses. There is interaction among curriculum developers, subject advisers in secondary and primary schools, inspectors, teachers, and lecturers in the colleges of education. The Department also drew on the wealth of expertise and experience brought in through projects funded by the United States Agency for International Development (USAID). The Primary Education Improvement Project (PEIP) focused on teacher education, the Junior-Secondary Education Improvement Project (JSEIP) on junior-secondary curriculum development, and Improving the Efficiency of Educational Systems (IEES) on management information systems. The department has grown from one professional officer in 1978, to six in 1985, and in 1992 it had 20 curriculum developers, including four advisers provided through donor funding.

Any efforts to reform the curriculum of the senior-secondary school will remain inhibited by the fact that the curriculum at this level is tied to a foreign examination. It will require a major political decision to detach senior-secondary education from this external examination.

8. The System of Examinations, Promotions, and Certifications

Two examinations are taken in the basic education program—the Primary School Leaving Examination and the Junior Certificate Examination—which are used for selecting students for higher levels of education. No account is taken of the school continuous assessment records in determining the students' examination results. Although schools set end-of-year internal examinations, these are not used to determine progression from one stage to the next. Their purpose is to assess progress made during the year and to pass this information on to parents through school reports. Promotion is automatic.

The two terminal examinations taken at the primary and junior-secondary levels are considered inappropriate or inadequate as they do not address the assessment of skill attainment or attitudes. Steps are now being taken by the Curriculum Development Department to move toward criterion-referenced testing and reporting. This exercise is being undertaken by examination subcommittees composed of curriculum developers, research testing officers, teachers, representatives of national subject panels, lecturers of teacher-training colleges, and education officers. To familiarize participants with criterion-referenced assessment procedures, inservice training workshops are to be mounted.

9. Educational Assessment, Evaluation, and Research

Education research and evaluation findings have been used as a basis for formulating policy in education and for the development of programs to improve the learning process. In 1976, the government set up a commission to undertake a comprehensive review of the education system which had been inherited from the colonial era. This resulted in the National Policy on Education of 1977. Another commission is to be set up in the early 1990s.

Other sets of assessments of the education system have targeted specific areas such as junior-secondary education. In 1984, for instance, IEES (Improving the Efficiency of the Educational System) produced a report on their evaluation of secondary education. The report, *Botswana Education and Human Resource Sector Assessment*, was updated in 1986. On the basis of this evaluation a program (Junior-Secondary Education Improvement Program) was developed to address the issue of curriculum development and teacher-training for the junior-secondary cycle.

The Ministry of Education does not have its own research unit, but it does commission other bodies or teams of experts to conduct reseach on its behalf. For instance, in 1988, three related studies on education funded by the World Bank were carried out to address questions such as the efficient use of resources, the country's labor force needs, school-leavers and the labor market, and so forth, which are continually being raised. These studies are: *The Cost Effectiveness of Technical and Vocational Education and Training* (Hinchliffe et al. 1988), *Investment Options in Post-Secondary Education* (Colclough et al. 1988), and *Education and Employment in Botswana* (Kann et al. 1990).

A considerable amount of research is done by the University through its various faculties, and through the University National Institute for Development Research and Documentation.

10. Major Reforms in the 1980s and 1990s

In the 1980s, the education system underwent significant change in size, structure, and complexity. The physical infrastructure has been greatly expanded, resulting in increased access to various levels of schooling and training. A total of four vocational training centers, a national resource center for handicapped children, two colleges of education, and an expanded and well-resourced network of inservice centers were some of the new additions to the stock of educational facilities. The scope of educational provisions was widened.

The restructuring of the system from 7–3–2 to 7–2–3 and the physical separation of the junior-secondary cycle from the the combined junior- and senior secondary course has given junior-secondary education its own identity. A program of junior-secondary education based on the needs of pupils of the appropriate age group has now been developed. It is being or to be executed by teachers trained specifically to handle this age group. A new partnership between the Ministry of Education and local communities in the management of junior-secondary schools has been forged.

The Department of Teacher Education was established and coordinates all inservice training activities for both primary and secondary teachers. Although the management of education remains centralized at the Ministry headquarters, the provision of support professional services has begun to move to the local level.

There were improvements in pass rates as measured by examination results. The effects of curriculum innovations on students' learning and their preparation for employment or for higher levels of education and training take long to manifest themselves in full. Innovations are often blamed by students, parents, and employers, even in the early stages of their implementation, should anything appear to go wrong in education. The curtailment of the junior-secondary course by one year in 1988 and the introduction of a new curriculum are viewed in some quarters as the cause of the unemployment of large numbers of school-leavers. The argument is that the course is short, which is true; and the curriculum is not relevant to the world of work, which is questionable. The fact that intake capacity at higher levels of education and the employment market do not expand at the same rate as junior-secondary enrollments is overlooked.

The curriculum for the nine-year basic education was initiated and is taking shape, though a great deal remains to be done to refine the contents of syllabuses, produce suitable instructional materials, train teachers, develop assessment and examination procedures appropriate to the new curriculum, and strengthen all the support systems necessary for the orderly and effective implementation of the reformed curriculum. These tasks will occupy a central place in any further transformation of the education system whether it be in relation to junior- and senior-secondary education, teacher education, or vocational/technical education for the next decade or longer.

11. Major Problems for the Year 2000

The number of Junior Certificate-leavers who cannot find places in senior-secondary schools or in training intitutions is rising each year. They cannot find employment because employers would prefer students who have passed the Cambridge School Certificate, and those who have are abundant. The result is a high unemployment rate among Junior Certificate-leavers. Parents and students do not understand that this is not only an educational, but also a labor market problem as well. Education could expand the senior-secondary school level to absorb more Junior Certificate-leavers, but then the unemployed school-leaver problem would be transfered from that level to the next.

The Ministry of Education will continue to be blamed for providing an education that leads nowhere; and it will have to explore other options for Junior Certificate-leavers or re-examine the curriculum with a view to determining what labor market skills can be incorporated into the curriculum. The government has already committed itself to the universalization of nine-year schooling and there is no likelihood of expansion at this level being scaled down to minimize the unemployed Junior Certificate-leaver problem.

The other challenge that faces the Ministry of Education both now and in the future is to move as fast as possible to produce personnel with technical, professional, and managerial skills to meet the ever-growing demand for such labor. Expatriates predominate in these occupations. Localization is one of the government's top priorities. While the private sector might help in making a contribution toward addressing some of the serious shortages in the technical, professional, and managerial labor force, education is looked upon as the main provider.

References

Colchlough C et al. 1988 *Investment Options in Post-Secondary Education.* University of Botswana, Gaborone

Government of Botswana 1991 *National Development Plan VII 1991–1997: Education and Manpower Development*, Chap. 14. Government Printer, Gaborone

Hinchliffe K et al. 1988 *The Cost Effectiveness of Technical and Vocational Education Training.* University of Botswana, Gaborone

Kann U et al. 1990 *Education and Employment in Botswana.* University of Botswana, Gaborone

Further Reading

Evans M, Yodder J H (eds.) 1991 *Patterns of Reform in Primary Education.* Macmillan, Gaborone

Government of Botswana 1989 *Botwana National Manpower Planning.* Government Printer, Gaborone

Kann U 1981 *Career Development in a Changing Society: The Case of Botswana.* Institute of International Education, University of Stockholm, Stockholm

Ministry of Education 1965 *Report of the Education Department 1965–66.* Government Printer, Gaborone

Ministry of Education 1977 *Education for Kagisano.* Report of the National Commission on Education. Government Printer, Gaborone

Ministry of Education 1985 *Annual Report 1985–86: Twenty Years of Education for Kagisano.* Government Printer, Gaborone

Ministry of Education 1990 *Improving the Quality of Basic Education.* (Country paper for Commonwealth Ministries conference:) Government Printer, Gaborone

Otaala B et al. 1989 *An Evaluation of the Day Care Programme.* Consultancy report for the Government of Botswana and UNICEF. Government Printer, Gaborone

Townsend Coles E K 1985 *The Story of Education in Botswana.* Macmillan, Gaborone

Brazil

C A C Gomes

1. General Background

Brazil is the fifth largest country in the world. Its territory covers an area of 8,511,965 square kilometers, almost half of all South America. This former Portugeuse colony was not divided into separate countries as was the case in Spanish territorial conquest. Its basic territorial configuration was defined during the second half of the eighteenth century through treaties between Portugal and Spain. This large nation has a great diversity of plant life, soil, agriculture, and climate. Such a large territory also implies remarkable economic, social, and educational disparities among its regions with industrialization still being concentrated in the south and southeast.

According to the 1991 census, Brazil had a population of 146,917,459 inhabitants, rating it as the sixth most populous nation in the world. This represents an increase of 26 million (23.5 percent) since 1980. The population growth rate declined from 2.99 percent in the 1950s to 2.48 percent in the 1970s. The gross mortality rate has remained relatively stable since the 1960s. Between 1955 and 1965 there was a small reduction in the fertility rate. This reduction increased through the 1970s and 1980s. Urbanization, modernization of social life in general, and, in the early 1980s and 1990s, the economic recession are factors associated with the declining growth rate. The urban population percentage rose from 36.2 in 1950 to 75.5 in 1991. Given Brazil's poor economic performance, the decline in the population growth rate prevented a greater deterioration in educational and other social indicators. However, population concentration in cities increased the social demand for schooling. Access to education in cities increased, at a lower cost than that in rural areas, although equality and quality of education became more serious problems.

As in most developing countries, Brazil's population is young. However, the participation of people under 20 in education diminished to less than half the total population in the 1970s and 1980s, whereas the participation of older age groups increased. According to a sampling research study conducted in 1990 (which excluded the Amazon Valley rural area), 44.5 percent of the total population was under 20. This implies that the global demand for school places should progressively reduce in the future.

The territorial distribution of the population is extremely asymmetrical. Beside the rural–urban population migration, new frontiers, particularly in the central western region, have attracted a large number of inhabitants. This results in a shortage of school places for the millions of people who migrate from one area to another. Thus, there is an excess of school buildings in rural areas and small towns, but a scarcity of schools in overcrowded cities and agricultural frontiers.

The Brazilian population of the 1990s is the result of a long process of interbreeding between Whites, Indians, and Blacks. Descendants from mixed races are increasing, while those from unmixed races are declining. In 1990, the percentage population distribution was as follows: Whites 55.3; Blacks, 4.9; mulattoes 39.3; orientals 0.5 (research study excluding the Amazon Valley rural area). In spite of the relative historical tolerance and the existence of an antiracial mentality, Blacks and Indians are disadvantaged in economic and educational terms. Blacks and mulattoes are systematically below other racial groups in terms of average years of schooling, achievement, and promotion, and above other groups regarding dropout rates (Barcelos 1993).

Notwithstanding the land's vastness and the numerous ethnic groups, Portuguese is spoken throughout the country. Indian communities in general speak their own languages and are given bilingual education.

Brazil's economy, after expansion in the 1970s, declined with the oil crisis and the increasing burden of interest rates of the international financial market. Between 1980 and 1991, the gross domestic product (GDP) expanded at an average annual rate of 1.5 percent. During the same period, however, the GDP per capita declined by approximately 6 percent. Inflation and recession aggravated income distribution. Salaries declined from 45 percent to 33 percent of the GDP in the 1970s and 1980s. Just over 50 percent of the total income is in the hands of the elite (10 percent of the population). As a reflection of income concentration and other factors, 7.6 percent of the labor force had higher level nonmanual occupations; 13.7 percent were in nonmanual occupations at the managerial level; and 66.5 percent were in predominantly manual occupations (22.7, 20.0, and 23.8 percent in the primary, secondary, and tertiary sectors respectively). Finally, 12.2 percent represented other occupations and missing data (Gomes 1988).

As a result of the industrial and urban expansion in general, the economically active population of the primary sector decreased from 32.5 to 23.4 percent during the period 1979–90. Meanwhile, the percentage of active individuals in the secondary sector varied from 23.9 in 1979 to 23.3 in 1990. The percentage corresponding to the tertiary sector increased from 43.6 to 53.3 between 1979 and 1990. In 1990, the economically active population was 50.1 percent. Their academic education was, on average, 5.9 years of schooling, whereas the average for the total population was 4.8 years (statistics exclude the rural population of the Amazon Valley). The export–import ratio was 1:527 in 1992.

Brazil has a federative state structure with 26 states and one federal district. Each state is subdivided into municipalities which are autonomous political–administrative units created by the states. The federal and state constitutions define the functions of the executive, legislative, and judiciary powers. The federal government provides higher education and technical education. The states predominantly offer primary and secondary education, while municipalities concentrate their efforts on preschool and primary education. Bilateral agreements have established collaboration between different government levels in order to reduce overlapping.

2. Politics and the Goals of the Education System

During the colonial era, the structuring of an education system was not considered a task of government authorities. The colony employed a large labor force of African and Indian slaves in the production of agricultural products and in the extraction of gold and diamonds. For the most part, education was delegated to the Jesuits and other Catholic orders. In the seventeenth century the civil government entered into conflict with the Jesuit order and expelled it from Portugal and its colonies. Educational matters were then transferred to the colonial authorities. During the following period—the Kingdom of Brazil and Empire (1808–89)—little educational expansion was registered, with the exception of the foundation of tertiary education at the time when the Crown temporarily moved from Portugal to Brazil (in the early nineteenth century). The Republican regime did not significantly change education. The first university was only founded in 1920. Brazil had an agrarian, oligarchical social structure, based on coffee production for export. However, the Great Depression affected this sector, resulting in industrialization, which was directed toward import substitution. In 1930 a revolution substituted the rural oligarchies with urban elites. Consequently, through a renewal movement largely based on progressivism, the state started to adopt a more objective and broad approach to education, resulting in the creation of the Ministry of Education and Health Affairs in 1931. During the following decades, educational policies began to acknowledge the relevance of the accelerating process of urbanization and industrialization. The government vigorously concentrated its efforts on extending primary education to the population in general.

In 1945, after some years under an authoritarian regime, Brazil started a new experimental period with democracy. Economic expansion and modernization led to a rapid increase in primary and secondary education enrollment. The military intervention of 1964 substantially changed the political system for a long period of time. Under military leadership the enrollments in tertiary education received a boost, especially in the private sector, as a means of meeting the middle classes' demands. Postgraduate education and research received substantial public investment. A reform of primary and secondary education in 1971 greatly limited its impact in terms of extending compulsory education to a broader spectrum of the population. The attempt to modernize secondary schools and higher education with the adoption of comprehensive school models was not successful.

The return to civil government took place in 1985, and it inherited economic recession and high inflation, a situation that has since been aggravated. The pace and trends of educational development have been affected by political changes. Nevertheless, progress has been made in the fields of decentralization and cooperation between different government levels. The Decennial Plan of Education for All is the result of discussion and collaboration among federal, state, and municipal governments, as well as nongovernmental organizations. There has been an increasing recognition of the fact that, once primary education has been made open to all, efficiency, quality, and equity are key priorities for the expansion and improvement of further educational levels.

3. The Formal System of Education

According to the 1971 reform, primary education consists of eight grades, and secondary education of three or four grades, depending on the complexity of vocational courses. Until then the country had a dual structure of academic and vocational secondary schools. With the aim of equalizing opportunity, the reform prescribed the generalization of comprehensive schools, a model which was rejected by society. In 1982, the country returned to the dual educational structure (see Fig. 1).

The academic year has a minimum of 180 days. Primary education comprises at least 5,760 hours, and secondary education 2,200 or 2,900 hours (depending on whether it lasts 3 or 4 years). Higher education is subject to a yearly equal number of days, as well as to the number of hours prescribed by the curriculum of each subject. Different courses have minimum, average, or maximum duration, according to more flexible rules.

3.1 Primary, Secondary, and Tertiary Education

The enrollment increase in primary education is one of the most remarkable factors of recent history in Brazil. The net enrollment rate jumped from 36.2 percent in 1950 to 84.2 percent in 1980. However, it decreased to 82.1 percent in 1989, which means that, despite universalization of primary schooling being nearly accomplished, the system has not progressed toward the integration of scattered rural populations and children living in pockets of extreme poverty in the outskirts of medium-sized and large cities. The total number of enrollments amounted to 27,557,542 pupils in 1989, while out-of-school children were estimated to be 4,922,010. Rates vary significantly from region but not by children's sex. The index of pupils in rural areas corresponded to 20.5 percent of the total (1989), although 65.4 percent of schools had a total of up to 50 pupils in 1987. The student–teacher ratio was 22.9:1 whereas the average number of pupils per class was 28.9 (1989). A total of 87.5 percent of pupils attended public schools in 1989. In overcrowded metropolitan areas a school day may last only two hours, while in some state educational centers, located in areas of lower income, there may be up to eight hours per day.

According to official data, based on the UNESCO model (1988), the fifth grade had the highest repetition rate (41.0%) while the fourth and eighth grades had the lowest (23.0%). The highest dropout rate was 13.0 percent for the first grade, whereas the lowest was 4.0 percent for the eighth grade. As a result, only

6 out of 100 pupils reached the last grade of primary school in 1986. In comparison, another model, using the National Household Sampling Surveys' data (Fletcher and Castro 1985) found that not only was the failure rate higher, but also that dropout rates result from several years of failure at school. In this case, the highest repetition rate was 51.1 percent for the first grade and the lowest one was 18.0 percent for the eighth grade. The dropout rates reached 20.8 and 4.1 percent for the eighth and second grades respectively. Consequently only 3 out of 100 pupils reached the last grade in 1986. On average, therefore, children spent 8.4 years at primary school and most of them did not proceed beyond the fifth grade (Oliveira and Castro 1992). Such a high proportion of failures led to about two–thirds of pupils being overage.

Expansion in secondary schools has also been outstanding. Yearly growth rate accelerated from 13.8 percent during the period 1960–70 to 19.2 percent during 1970–80, but declined to 18.0 in 1980–89, thus reflecting the fiscal crisis and general economic difficulties. In fact, net enrollment rates increased slightly from 14.5 percent in 1980 to 16.2 percent in 1989. The total number of enrollments was 3,477,859 in 1989. The most economically advantaged regions have greater access to secondary school. Girls tend to stay longer at school than boys, since the latter, in general, start work at an earlier age. The student–teacher ratio was 14.7:1 in 1989, while the average number of students per class was 23.5, according to the last available data (1987). The number of public school places was lower than in primary education (69.9 percent of total enrollment in 1989); however, state schools have offered the highest numbers of places (62.4 percent). Attrition increased during the 1970s and 1980s. The initial relation between enrollment and number of graduates decreased from 74 percent during the period 1970–73 to 49.9 percent in 1986–88. In turn, dropout rates rose from 6.4 to 21 percent in 1980 and 1986 respectively. School failures are, at least, partially due to the high proportion of night schools (78.6 percent of the total number of students studied at these in 1987). Despite serving as a filter between primary and tertiary education, secondary school has gradually opened its doors to students from the lower classes. Comparable surveys show that the percentage of students whose parents have a lower-class occupational status rose from 17 percent in 1963 to 51.4 percent in 1985. Meanwhile, the proportion of students whose parents maintain a middle-class occupational status dropped from 55 to 37.7 percent in the same period (Mafra and Cavalcanti 1992).

Tertiary education also experienced high expansion, although a steady reduction was observed in the 1980s. Undergraduate program enrollment was remarkably high during the period 1968–78 (increasing by 440.4 percent) and during 1980–91 (increasing by 113.6 percent), which challenged governmental control. Nevertheless, in 1991, enrollments comprised

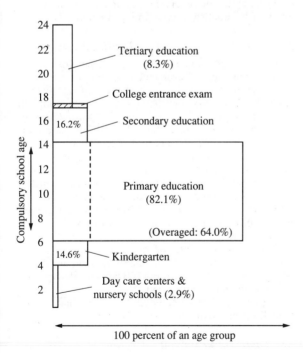

Figure 1

Brazil: Structure of the formal education system
a Gross enrollment ratio for higher education. Net enrollment ratio for the other levels. In all cases, 1989 data

1,565,056 undergraduate students and 52,053 graduate students. These numbers, when compared with total population figures indicate a slight decrease: 1,100 students per 100,000 inhabitants in 1991 against 1,162 in 1980. Enrollments are concentrated in the southeast. Women in general have a higher participation rate in a number of courses. Gross student–teacher ratio was 11.8:1 in 1991, an apparently low figure, given that the proportion of part-time professors was 56.6%. Most of the students (54.7%) attended universities, while the remaining studied at integrated colleges (14.4%) and colleges (30.9%). Public institutions accounted for 38.7 percent of total enrollments and federal institutions 20.5 percent. Thus, the majority of students were enrolled in private establishments (1991). Nevertheless, most of the graduate and research programs are implemented by federal and selected state and community universities. The dropout rate, estimated at 39 percent in undergraduate programs (1986–90), is an indication of modest productivity. Equity of access for lower-middle and middle-class students has improved in most courses as a result of the remarkable number of night classes. In 1967 the proportion of students whose parents maintained lower and middle occupational status was 10 and 61 percent respectively. A survey of graduates in 1983 revealed that these proportions had risen to 18.8 and 56.4 percent (Gomes 1988). These numbers, however, still conceal internal stratification by course and institution.

3.2 Preschool Education

Preschool education is offered at day-care centers (0–4-year olds), nursery schools (2–3-years olds), and kindergarten (4–6-year olds). It has expanded more than any other kind of education as a consequence of urbanization and the increasing participation of women in the economically active population. The net enrollment rate rose from 5.9 percent in 1980 to 17.4 percent in 1989. The total number of enrollments amounted to 4,043,570 children, concentrated in public institutions (69.4%), particularly those maintained by municipalities (43.3%). Significantly, in 1989 about 87 percent of the children were at urban institutions. Such an expansion has been partially due to voluntary work and improvization of facilities. In comparison, a significant proportion of personnel is underqualified, and day-care centers are often directed to satisfy nutritional rather than educational needs of children in underprivileged areas.

3.3 Special Education

Special educational programs are offered at regular schools and specialized institutions from preschool to secondary level. Programs in regular schools include support to students in regular classes, special classes, resource rooms, workshops, and itinerant assistance. Specialized institutions include special schools, rehabilitation centers, support centers, hospitals, clinics,

day-care centers, and so on. These institutions also provide resource rooms, itinerant assistance, workshops, and other relevant services. The number of special student enrollments in regular schools was 78,822 in 1989. Nearly 63 percent of this total were mentally retarded, 14.4 percent had hearing difficulties, 9.3 percent were physically handicapped, 4.4 percent had visual problems, 0.4 percent were exceptionally talented, and the remainder were classified in other categories. The enrollment total at specialized institutions, excluding those mentioned above, was 95,804 during the same year (multiple difficulties, 58.4%; mentally retarded, 19.7%; hearing difficulties, 11.9%; physically handicapped, 4.2%; visual problems, 3.4%). The total number of students enrolled in regular schools and specialized institutions was not determined.

State secretariats of education, as well as some municipal secretariats, have departments or divisions for special educational affairs, which maintain central services for curriculum planning, supervision, diagnosis, and assistance to students in several areas. There is a department in the Ministry of Education and Sports that assures technical and financial assistance to states and municipalities. Nongovernmental organizations also provide support, most of them with official resources. Support to students in the transition from school to work is provided by some specialized institutions (governmental or otherwise) by means of simulated enterprises, counselling, and placement centers.

3.4 Vocational, Technical, and Business Education

The federal government maintains a network of industrial and agricultural technical schools over the whole country. Parallel with the education system, several bodies such as SENAI (Serviço Nacional de Aprendizagem Industrial) and SENAC (Serviço Nacional de Aprendizagem Comercial), which are operated by business associations, provide training that corresponds to primary and secondary education. Each year, approximately 1.6 million individuals complete training programs, as compared with half a million students from secondary schools. These business institutions are largely financed by the tax of 1 percent on payrolls. Students at these institutions do not pay tuition fees.

Nonformal training for managers and other employees of micro, small, and medium-sized businesses is provided by SEBRAE (Serviço Brasileiro de Apoio às Micro e Pequenas Empresas). Private schools, offering on the spot and distance education, have had a traditionally prominent role.

3.5 Adult and Nonformal Education

Adult education includes programs of remedial schooling (second opportunity programs of primary and secondary education), and courses for qualifications, inservice training, and so on. The minimum legal age for completing a remedial program is 18 years for primary schooling and 21 years for secondary schooling.

The Ministry of Education and Sports, as well as the state secretariats of education, maintains a department or division which deals with adult education. In general, this manages programs and conducts special studies. Schools are supervised by state boards of education and inspection services. Nonformal education is subject to minimum control.

During the second semester of 1987, the total number of enrollments was 931,555 students. Literacy training courses corresponded to 5.4 percent; primary education, 78.9 percent; secondary general education, 11.0 percent; and secondary vocational education, 4.7 percent. In 1987, public institutions were responsible for 86 percent of total enrollment (state institutions 67.4 percent).

State secretariats of education also provide examinations for those who have reached the minimum legal age, regardless of whether they hold any previous certificates or have undergone any other type of studies. In 1989, 452,407 candidates sat for primary education examinations—an average of 64,630 per subject. The average success rate was 33 percent. During the same year, 860,399 candidates sat for general secondary education examinations—78,218 students per subject. Their average success rate was slightly lower, at 30.4 percent.

The declared expenditure on adult education is clearly underestimated, since it often does not include facilities, equipment, and personnel shared with regular education. The amount spent on adult education in 1989 was US$7.516 million, 99.3 percent of which came from federal government. Resources for adult education represented 0.1, 0.4, and 0.5 percent of the government's total federal, state, and municipal educational expenditures, respectively.

4. Administrative and Supervisory Structure and Operation

Since the early 1980s decentralization has characterized the distribution of fiscal resources, as well as educational administration. The Ministry of Education and Sports is not only responsible for a network of higher education institutions and technical schools, but also for technical and financial assistance to the states, Federal District, and municipalities. The Federal Board of Education establishes the general guidelines for curricula, particularly of higher education. Throughout the country, the inspection of private higher education is a task of the Ministry's offices.

The states have their secretariats of education, with planning and executive roles in connection with preschool, primary, and secondary education, and their own universities. They also inspect private preschools and primary and secondary schools. The state boards of education define the regional segments of curricula, among other things.

The municipalities in general are responsible for a variety of preschools and primary schools, especially in rural areas (state primary schools are largely predominant in urban areas). There are potentially overlapping activities at different government levels. Bilateral agreements have been one of the means to improve resources use. National associations of state and municipal secretariats of education have played an important role in collaborating with different government levels and in the decentralized definition of educational policies.

The schools have achieved some degree of autonomy. In several states, elected boards comprised of the principal, teachers, parents, and other members, assist the management of public schools. In some states, principals or boards receive financial resources for maintenance and small expenses. Principals are often elected by teachers, parents, students over 14, and other school staff, according to different criteria.

5. Educational Finance

The main sources of public funding, at the federal level, are:

(a) at least 18 percent of the budgetary resources from taxes;

(b) resources from mandatory business contributions, which are basically set aside for school lunch and health programs;

(c) resources from the "education wage", which represents 2.5 percent of payroll-based contributions from commercial and manufacturing enterprises and 0.8 percent of the rural products' commercial value in the case of agricultural companies, producers, and rural workers. The latter is destined exclusively for primary education. The federal government is responsible for administrating one third of the total, mainly to reduce regional disparities.

The states' sources of funding are as follows:

(a) at least 25 percent of the ordinary budgetary resources originating from state and federal tax revenues;

(b) the states' share of the "education wage";

(c) other funding from various sources, such as the federal share of the "education wage."

The municipalities' sources of funding are:

(a) at least 25 percent of the ordinary budgetary resources originating not only from tax revenues, but also federal and state tax revenues;

(b) other funding from various sources, for example, the Ministry of Education and the state secretariat of education.

The total public educational expenditure in 1989 was approximately 4.4 percent of the GDP. Upon the promulgation of the Calmon Constitutional Amendment, which established minimum earmarked resources for education in the mid 1980s, this index increased significantly, at least at the federal and state levels. As the economic crisis worsened during the 1990s, these resources decreased, according to partial data.

The proportions of total public expenditure spent on education were 4.6, 17.6, and 16.3 percent of federal, state, and municipal budgets respectively. The federal government allocated 40.6, 7.3, and 43.4 percent of its resources in primary, secondary, and tertiary education respectively. The corresponding percentages for the states were 48.3, 7.4, and 15.6 percent, whereas those for the municipalities were 76.6, 3.8, and 0.4 percent (1989). In spite of difficulties caused by accounting criteria, these statistics reflect the above-mentioned labor division, whereby the federal government is responsible for most of public higher education, the states for primary and secondary education, and the municipalities for primary education.

Expenditure per student shows a strong bias against primary education where the average was US$80.4 in 1986. The minimum cost was US$52.2 for municipal schools and the maximum US$146.3 for state schools. From the regional standpoint, the highest and lowest average costs were US$196.2 in the southeast and US$33.7 in the northeast (Xavier and Marques 1987). Average expenditure per student in secondary education was equivalent to US$1,759, 257, and 136 at federal technical schools, state, and municipal schools respectively (IPEA and Ministry of Education and Sports 1985). Average expenditure per student in federal higher education was US$4,301.80 and corresponded to US$435.70 for a selected number of confessional/community universities (IPEA and Ministry of Education and Sports 1986). The figure for federal higher education rose to US6,417.00 in 1991 (IPEA).

Equity is a serious issue. Unit costs reflect quality differences. Lower income students tend to enroll at free public primary and secondary schools, and often fail in public higher education selection examinations. It is noteworthy that students do not pay tuition fees at any level of public education. A reimbursable scholarship program for private higher education students is maintained by an official bank with resources provided by the Ministry of Education and Sports. The number of beneficiaries in 1991 (a critical year in terms of financial restrictions) was 89,468, or 9.3 percent of total enrollment in similar institutions. Total expenditure was US$54 million.

6. Supplying Personnel for the Education System

Teachers from the first to the fourth grades of primary education are trained in three-year courses at second-ary schools, although in medium-sized and large cities an undergraduate degree in education is regarded as desirable or even compulsory. Teachers for the remaining grades of primary and secondary education are trained for an average of four years at colleges and universities, often at private institutions' night programs. Higher education professors are trained through graduate programs.

Despite the large number of institutions and graduates, many teachers are underqualified. In 1989, preschool education employed 64,269 teachers (50.2% of whom were underqualified); primary education employed 1,201,034 teachers (at least 16.5% of whom were underqualified, and 84.2% of whom were in rural areas); and secondary education employed 236,081 teachers (27.3% of whom were underqualified). In 1991, tertiary education had 133,135 professors on undergraduate programs (31.9% of whom were underqualified). Paradoxically, the country has at the same time a surplus of graduates and shortage of teachers. According to an official estimate, during the period 1976–88 about one million college-graduated teachers had not yet been absorbed by the school market. However, the education system cannot replace most of the legally underqualified personnel. Mathematics, physics, chemistry, and biology teachers are often in shortage. Working conditions, particularly in rural areas, and underpayment in relation to similar occupations, tend to explain why graduates prefer not to work in education. In fact, the average monthly salary for a primary school teacher in 1982 was US$182.58 (US$149.07 up to the fourth grade and US$297.67 from the fifth grade on). In the northeastern rural area, the salary was as low as US$20.17 (Barreto, 1990).

In response to these challenges, numerous secretariats of education have invested in workshops and inservice training. Some intend implementing innovative programs in state higher education institutions.

7. Curriculum Development and Teaching Methodology

Curricula have historically been increasingly subject to decentralization. Primary and secondary education curricula are constituted both by a common core and diversified areas. The former, as defined by the Federal Board of Education, is mandatory for the whole country. The latter are determined by the state boards and schools and are based on regional and local needs and student differences. At least one foreign language, often English, is obligatory from the fifth grade on. The Federal Board of Education establishes the minimum curricula for higher and technical education. Syllabuses are not prescribed in any of these cases.

Despite relative freedom to organize curricula and programs, most institutions have not been able to put this into full practice. The inadequate training of principals and teachers, as well as geographically centralized production of textbooks, are but a few of the obstacles. Contrary to legal guidelines, curricula tend to be segmented and are often not relevant to communities and students.

The Ministry of Education and Sports is responsible for the National School Textbook Program which was expected to reach 28 million students in 1993. These textbooks are produced by private companies and schools select them according to preference.

8. The System of Examinations, Promotions, and Certifications

Students' promotion is decided by teachers in compliance with legally defined minimum levels of attendance and achievement. At primary and secondary schools decisions are frequently taken at staff meetings.

College entrance examinations are administered by each institution or group of associated institutions. They consist of a set of achievement tests on secondary school subjects, generally weighted according to the field of studies chosen by the candidates. In the 1980s, open-ended questions were increasingly adopted, with the intention of stimulating writing skills. As every secondary school graduate is eligible for higher education, the entrance examination has a classificatory nature according to the number of vacancies. The average number of candidates per vacancy was 3.8 percent in 1991. This average hides great variations, since higher education is stratified by course and institution.

9. Educational Assessment, Evaluation, and Research

The Ministry of Education and Sports, as well as some state secretariats of education, have designated private foundations to evaluate school outcomes through standardized tests applied to school samples, usually on a nonsystematic basis. However, the Basic Schooling Evaluation System (SAEB), created in 1987, and now administered by the National Institute for Educational Research (Ministry of Education and Sports), has become an important databank on achievement, costs, school management, and other features. Data have periodically been collected in a sample of municipalities throughout the country.

Educational research was begun by pioneer college professors and teachers early in the twentieth century. The first institution in this field was the National Institute of Pedagogical Studies (now the National Institute for Educational Research), an agency for the Ministry of Education and Health Affairs, founded in 1938. Directed toward psychopedagogical issues, it widened its

focus to social sciences and significantly expanded its activities in the 1950s. The most informative works in this area were directly sponsored and published by this Institute until the 1960s. During the 1970s, graduate programs in education opened horizons for a greater number of works written by faculty and students at universities. Scientific conferences, associations, and journals and other publications increased between then and the 1980s. The National Institute for Educational Research has become predominantly a sponsor and publisher, while universities and some colleges are responsible for almost the whole production in the area.

Research undertaken during the 1980s predominantly focused on relations between education, state, and society. During the 1990s, increasing focus is on curriculum development, the history of education, and instructional methods and strategies.

10. Major Reforms in the 1980s and 1990s

No major reforms were carried out during the 1980s and early 1990s. Despite political changes, the legal framework is similar to that stipulated by the 1968 University Reform and the 1971 Reform of Primary and Secondary Education, with little modification. A new law on directives and the basis for national education has been being discussed by the National Congress since 1988.

According to the previous Calmon Amendment, approved in 1983, the 1988 Constitution established earmarked resources for education. It also declared that primary education is a duty of both the family and the state (subject to legal enforcement), and defined several programmatic rights of citizens in this sector.

11. Major Problems for the Year 2000

According to estimates of the size of the labor force in the year 2000, if it maintains the same levels of technological modernization, productivity, and income distribution of the most developed regions, Brazil will have to increase the number of primary school graduates by between 134 and 200 percent, secondary school graduates by between 122 and 211 percent, and tertiary education graduates by between 169 and 259 percent (Costa 1987). Despite the declining fertility rate, the greatest struggle will be to acquire equity and quality in primary education; this will require the reversion of the traditional strategy of underinvestment in this level of education. Elitism has prevented schools from dealing effectively with low-income population and cultural diversity. Indicators of quality, equity, and efficiency reflect such an incapacity. The increase of efficiency and equity at primary school level will lead to the expansion of secondary and tertiary education. This implies substantial changes in management, curricula, and methodology.

A political agreement is necessary to establish a new

hierarchy of priorities, in opposition to the traditional model of economic modernization at high social costs.

References

Barcelos L C 1993 Educação e desigualdades raciais no Brasil. *Cadernos de Pesquisa* 86: 15–24
Barreto A M R F 1990 *Professores do Primeiro Grau: quem são, onde estão e quanto ganham.* IPEA, Brasília
Costa M A 1987 *Perspectivas e necessidades educacionais de mão-de-obra.* IPEA, Brasília
Fletcher P, Castro C M 1985 *Os mitos, as estratégias e as prioridades para o ensino de primeiro grau.* IPEA, Brasília
Gomes C A 1988 Curso superior e mobilidade social: vale a pena? *Educação Brasileira* 10(20): 63–84
Mafra L A, Calvacanti E C (eds.) 1992 *O ensino médio no Brasil.* INEP, Brasília
Oliveira J B A, Castro C M (eds.) 1992 *Ensino fundamental e competitividade empresarial: uma proposta para a ação de governo.* Instituto Herbert Levy, São Paulo
Xavier A C R, Marques A E S 1987 *Quanto custa um aluno nas escolas que os brasileiros frequentam.* IPEA, Brasília

Further Reading

Brazil, Ministry of Education and Sports 1993 *Education in Brazil: Situation and Prospects.* Ministry of Education and Sport, Brasília
Gomes C A 1991 Bildung und Erziehung in Brasilien in den neunziger Jahren. *Bildung und Erziehung* 44(2): 177–86
Harbison R W, Hanushek E A 1992 *Educational Performance of the Poor: Lessons from Rural Northeast Brazil.* The World Bank/Oxford University Press, Oxford
Plank D N 1990 The politics of basic education reform in Brazil. *Comp. Educ. Rev.* 34(4): 538–60

Brunei Darussalam

D. H. A. Abdullah

1. General Background

Brunei Darussalam (meaning "Abode of Peace") is situated on the northwest coast of the island of Borneo and occupies an area of 5,765 square kilometers. It has a coastline of about 161 kilometers along the South China Sea and is 442 kilometers north of the equator. It is bounded on the north by the South China Sea, and on all the other sides by the Malaysian state of Sarawak which divides Brunei Darussalam into two parts—the eastern part is the Temburong District, while the western part consists of the Brunei-Muara, Tutong, and Belait districts.

Brunei Darussalam is the oldest kingdom in the region. Documented evidence indicates that in the year 1414, Brunei Darussalam existed as a Hindu–Buddhist state which later converted to Islam in the middle of the fourteenth century. During the fifteenth century and the first half of the sixteenth century, Brunei rose to become a dominant power and one of the greatest empires of the archipelago with sovereignity over the whole island of Borneo and the present Philippines. The year 1571 saw the beginning of Spanish, Portuguese, Dutch, and British intervention, which reached a climax during the third quarter of the nineteenth century when Brunei's territories began to be eroded. In 1888, Brunei became a British Protectorate state. In 1906, Brunei dwindled to its present size of 5,765 square kilometers when Limbang (now part of Malaysia) was ceded to the British.

As a British Protectorate State, a Residential System was established where the British Resident, a representative of the British Government advised the Sultan on all matters except Malay customs, traditions, and Islam. In 1959 an agreement with the British Government established a written constitution which gave Brunei internal self-government. In 1971, this was amended to assert full internal independence except in defense and external affairs. In 1979 a second treaty was signed, giving full independence to Brunei Darussalam, which became the world's 159th sovereign state on January 1, 1984. This was followed by Brunei Darussalam's membership of the Commonwealth, the Association of South East Asian Nations (ASEAN), the United Nations, and the Organisation of Islamic Conference (OIC).

The country consists mainly of jungle with tropical forests covering 70 percent of the area, and is comprised of four districts—Brunei-Muara, Tutong, Belait, and Temburong. Of these, Brunei-Muara is the largest and most densely inhabited, with 61.5 percent of the population. The country's estimated population in 1989 was around 249,000. The indigenous people are mostly Malay and they make up nearly 70 percent of the population. This is followed by the Chinese (17.8%), other indigenous (5.3%), and others (8.1%). Males comprise 51 percent of the population.

Nearly 46 percent of the population is below the age of 20 and only 6 percent is above the age of 55. The median age is 21.9 years, and the annual rate of growth is 3.1 percent.

The national language of the country is Malay, although English is widely spoken and is also used in the education system.

Brunei Darussalam's small population is insufficient to provide all the labor force requirements of the country. As a result, it is heavily dependent on imported skilled and unskilled labor, the bulk of which comes from neighboring Malaysia, Thailand, and the Philippines. According to the 1986 population survey, the total working population was 86,000. The government was the biggest employer with 46,000 workers and most of the remainder of the population were employed by Brunei Shell Petroleum, Royal Brunei Airlines, and construction companies.

Brunei Darussalam's economy is heavily dependent on oil and gas. These two industries account for 93 percent of the country's revenue and 80 percent of its gross domestic product (GDP). Realizing that the country's economy should no longer be too dependent on oil and gas alone, the Fifth Five-Year National Development Plan (NDP) 1986–90 aimed at diversifying the economy, which had previously concentrated more on developing the infrastructure of the country.

His Majesty the Sultan and Yang Di Pertuan occupying the position of Prime Minister are the supreme executive authority in Brunei Darussalam. The administrative system is centered on the Prime Minister's Office, and the Sultan has followed a combination of traditional and reforming policies, moving away from a structure of a Chief Minister and officials to a full ministerial system with specified portfolios. As the supreme executive authority, the Sultan is assisted by the following councils: Religious, Privy, Cabinet Ministers, Succession, and Legislative.

2. Politics and the Goals of the Education System

The ministerial system, established after the resumption of independence in January 1984, brought the education system under the purview of the Ministry of Education and Health. A major reform in education policy took place which was based on the premise that the Brunei education system should no longer be diversified into different language streams. Consequently, the bilingual system of education was born in 1985. Prior to this new national education system, children aged 9 were subjected to a public examination which channeled the successful ones to English-medium schools, and those who failed to Malay-medium schools.

In 1984, selection examinations for 9-year olds were abolished and all children then had the opportunity of progressing according to their own potential without being subjected to unnecessary disadvantages through the bilingual system of education. "Bilingualism" in this context means that children study certain subjects in the national language (Malay) and certain subjects in English. The emphasis on either language as the medium of instruction is dependent on the level of education. There is strong emphasis on the Malay language as the medium of instruction at the preschool and lower-primary level. The use of English as the medium of instruction increases substantially as the level of education progresses. Subjects such as sciences, mathematics, and social sciences (except history) are taught in English. This recognition of the importance of the English language is based on the importance of academic achievement for facilitating the entry of Brunei students to institutions of higher learning outside the country where the medium of instruction is English.

The new national education system also emphasized the implementation of objectives which are based on recent developments in the nation as a consequence of the proclamation of independence in January 1984, with particular reference to the national philosophy that Brunei Darussalam is a Malay, Islamic monarchy. Inclusion of the Malay, Islamic monarchy philosophy in the national educational curriculum is intended to inculcate in children a state of mind, an attitude to life, and positive character traits that will all help create a society which embodies traditional Brunei virtues: strength in the Islamic faith, loyalty to the monarch, and a desire for progress and development.

Thus, the aims of the national education policy may be summarized as follows:

(a) to promote and sustain an educational system for Brunei Darussalam in which the Malay language will continue to play a leading role, without thereby neglecting the English language;

(b) to provide education in the Islamic religion, while ensuring that Islamic values and an Islamic way of life are integrated into the education system by means of an appropriate curriculum;

(c) to provide at least 12 years of education for every Bruneian child, namely 7 years in primary (including preschool), 3 years in lower-secondary, and 2 years in upper-secondary or vocational school;

(d) to provide a common curriculum and common public examinations for all schools in the country;

(e) to provide full opportunities for all children in Brunei Darussalam to play a useful role in the development of the country, in order that the needs of the country may be fulfilled through the active involvement of the people;

(f) to offer higher education to those who are capable and qualified, according to the changing needs of the country;

(g) to foster by all these means a national identity as a basis for inculcating loyalty to the monarch and Brunei Darussalam, while at the same time introducing efficiency and flexibility into the education system in order to further the development of the country.

Education in Brunei Darussalam is not compulsory

but it is universal, with almost every child entering school at the age of 5 and remaining there until the age of 14–15, at Lower-Secondary III.

3. The Formal System of Education

3.1 Primary, Secondary, and Tertiary Education

The structure of the formal education system is given in Figure 1. Education is not compulsory in Brunei Darussalam but virtually all children of 5 go to school for the one year of preschool education which is available in every school in the country. Primary education lasts six years and culminates in a public examination called the Primary Certificate Examination (PCE). Successful pupils are promoted to the three-year lower-secondary school, which culminates in another public examination—the Brunei Junior Certificate of Education (BJCE). The upper-secondary school lasts two years, or three years for those who need the extra year, and this also culminates in a public examination called the Ordinary-level Brunei Cambridge General Certificate of Education (BCGCE). After this, the students enroll in two year pre-university education at the end of which the students sit for the Advanced-level Brunei Cambridge General Certificate of Education. Successful and eligible students then enter universities either locally or abroad.

In theory, a child is provided with free education for 9–10 years as stated in the 1972 Education Policy. Yet in practice, because of the automatic promotion system of education up to Lower-Secondary III which allows children to repeat once in every level after which they have to be promoted irrespective of their performance, children are actually provided with a longer period of free education than 9 or 10 years. A child, however, becomes a dropout after a second unsuccessful attempt at Lower-Secondary III. In actual fact, a child is provided with free education up to tertiary level if he or she has succeeded at all the public examinations, except at Lower-Secondary III, and is eligible.

The dropout situation, arising as a consequence of unsuccessful repetition at Lower-Secondary III, entails unemployment, since those affected are below the minimum employment age of 18. The social problems associated with this resulted in the Ministry of Education introducing a new policy, to be implemented in 1993, which extends the provision of free education to 12 years, thus matching school-leaving age and employment age. The examination at Lower-Secondary III is expected to remain as a feature, but only as an instrument of final assessment, to channel the students into either an academic or vocational stream.

There are an average of 202 school days in the year, which begins in January and is divided into three terms, with the longest break during the period of Ramadan. Since the month of Ramadan is moving toward the early part of the year (it was in March in 1992, for example), this has resulted in the first term being short and the second term long. Efforts are being made, however, to organize the three-term system so as to have an almost equal number of days in each term and this may mean that schools will have to be open during Ramadan, as is already the practice in the country's higher education institutions.

Statistics on the enrollment of students and on resources are presented in Table 1. Statistics on enrollment are given for both government and nongovernment schools. The nongovernment schools receive no state subsidy, and many are nurseries and kindergartens, though some provide education up to upper-secondary level. These schools charge tuition fees which have to be approved by the Ministry of Education before implementation. The nurseries and kindergartens take children from the age of three and parents may transfer them into the free government primary schools, or continue to keep them in the private schools once they reach primary-school age.

The total implementation of the bilingual education policy of January 1992, requiring emphasis on Malay as the medium of instruction in primary school, is expected to result in more pressure in terms of enrollment on government rather than on nongovernment schools which formerly used English as the medium of instruction.

Brunei Darussalam has a second formal education system which comes under the aegis of the Religious Affairs Ministry. Children may take 6 years of religious education, normally when they are at the primary

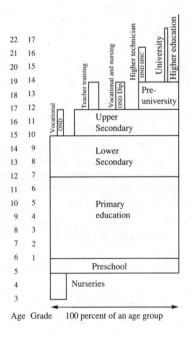

Figure 1
Brunei Darussalam: Structure of the formal education system

and lower-secondary level. This education is taken voluntarily in the morning by children who attend the mainstream schools in the afternoon and vice versa. At the end of 6 years the students sit for a public examination, the certificate of which qualifies them for entry into the Religious Teacher Training College which is also the responsibility of the Religious Affairs Ministry. The other educational institutions are the Institute of Islamic Studies which offers a Diploma and Advanced Diploma in Islamic Religious Studies; and two Arab Schools which offer a mainstream school curriculum except that they emphasize the use of the Arabic Language as a medium of instruction for certain subjects.

Before 1985 students from Brunei Darussalam obtained their higher education abroad, mainly in the United Kingdom, because of the absence of tertiary education institutions in the country. The upgrading of the Institute of Education from a teacher-training college in January 1985 marked the start of the degree program in Brunei Darussalam and ceased the total reliance on overseas higher education. This was followed by the establishment of the University of Brunei Darussalam in October 1985 which, in 1987, integrated the Institute of Education into the Faculty of Education. Due to the very small population of the country and concern for the cost-effectiveness of its functions, this is likely to remain the one and only

university. It offers programs geared towards fulfilling the labor force requirements of the country—hence the predominance of the teacher education program at the University. Brunei Darussalam is short of skilled labor and the paucity of teachers is symptomatic of this. Some 40 percent of the student population of the University is enrolled in teacher education programs. The other faculties of the University are the faculties of arts and social science, management and public policy, and science (which offers limited engineering programs).

In 1985 the Institute of Technology was also opened. It offers Higher National Diploma and Higher National Certificate courses in electrical and electronics engineering, business and finance, and computer studies.

The only other tertiary institution in the country is the Nursing College, established in 1987, which offers a 3½-year Diploma in Nursing and a one-year bridging course which enables Brunei-trained nurses (certificated) to earn a Diploma in Nursing.

With the availability of tertiary education in the country, government policy is not to provide government scholarships for overseas studies if the programs to be pursued are available locally. The University of Brunei Darussalam offers subdegree, undergraduate, and graduate programs limited to a master's degree in public administration and a postgraduate diploma and master's degree in educational management. This is due to constraints in various aspects of the facilities and

Table 1
Statistics on enrollments of students and number of teachers in formal education in Brunei Darussalam 1991

Type of institution	No. of institutions	No. of students	No. of teachers	Student–teacher ratio
Government schools				
Primary	117	32,136	2,198	15:1
Secondary	17	20,149	1,557	13:1
Nongovernment school				
Primary (+ preschool)	22	6,838	377	18:1
Secondary (+ primary and preschool)	16	11,979	517	23:1
Technical and vocational school		1,114	277	4:1
Tertiary				
Univeristy	1	891	17	5:1
Institute of technology	1	156	36	5:1
Nursing college	1	94	16	5:1
Islamic religious institutions				
Religious schools	110	25,941[a]	966	26:1
Teacher-training college	1	378	33	11:1
Islamic studies institute	1	64	12	5:1
Arab schools	2	1,575	134	11:1
Total	289	101,315[b]	6,140	16:1

a These pupils are accounted for in the figure for nongovernment and government student enrollments since they go to the mainstream schools either in the morning or afternoon (see sect. 3.1 above)   b The actual total of students enrolled in school because of the situation outlined in note a is 75,374 (i.e., 101,315–25,941)

other resources since the University is still operating on a temporary campus.

3.2 Preschool Education

Before entering formal primary education at the age of 6, nearly all children aged 5 attend a preschool for one year that is available in every primary school in the country. Apart from this year of preschool education, there are many private schools having kindergarten and nurseries for children aged 3 to 5.

The Ministry of Education's bilingual education policy states that in preschool education, the medium of instruction is the national language (Malay) and the English language is taught as a subject. The curriculum in preschool education comprises basic language, numbers, courteous behavior, basic Islamic religion, movement, self-discipline, singing, and the development of talents. These basics are taught through an integrated approach using informal teaching methods.

3.3 Special Education

There are three government agencies (namely the Ministry of Education, the Ministry of Health, and the Ministry of Welfare, Youth, and Sports) which are directly involved in caring for children with special needs. The Ministry of Education has yet to embark on providing special education programs for children with physical, intellectual, and emotional disabilities, apart from providing what is called "remedial education" to those children who have intellectual disabilities in the primary level of education. Such remedial education began in 1979 and is available in very few schools in each school district.

Since 1970, the Ministry of Welfare, Youth, and Sports has organized special classes for handicapped children and had its own center built in 1983. This center provides mainstream education at the primary level only. Upon reaching secondary-school age, children are provided with very basic vocational programs like basket weaving.

The Ministry of Health has a handicapped children's playgroup and once the children reach the age of 5, the representatives from the three ministries above decide whether these children should go to the mainstream schools or the special school.

Given the extremely limited opportunities for special education children, the Ministry of Education is examining ways of providing special education programs. There are 1,977 children classified as needing special education. Many more are unaccounted for since many parents are still reluctant to register their handicapped children. It is estimated that on average 18 handicapped babies are born every year and these are mostly categorized as mentally retarded.

3.4 Vocational, Technical, and Business Education

Since 1976, seven government-financed and controlled technical and vocational institutions have been established offering full-time and part-time courses and programs in a wide range of subjects to students, including adults. These courses cover craft and technical training in engineering, business and management, computing, agriculture, and arts and handicrafts. There are two more vocational schools planned which will cater for appropriately trained tradesmen and technicians for national development. Most vocational and technical institutions are governed by the Ministry of Education. However, the Ministry of Industry and Primary Resources is responsible for the Agricultural Training Center while the Ministry of Welfare, Youth, and Sports is responsible for the Arts and Handicraft Training Center.

Students tend to enter various vocational and technical schools after Grades 10 or 12. There was, unfortunately, a tendency to associate the entry into these education programs with low achievers. Consequently, the Ministry of Education is considering a policy which will no longer subject students to a public examination at Lower-Secondary III (or at the age of 15–16), but will have alternative assessment to channel them into academic or vocational/technical streams. This will also help eradicate the problem of dropouts at the age of 15–16 when they are too young for any form of employment.

In order to attract high achievers to vocational and technical education the government has set up the National Technical and Vocational Education Council which oversees the smooth running and implementation of vocational, technical, and business programs. There is an almost total reliance on the City and Guilds of London Institute, the Business and Technician Education Council, and the Royal Society of Arts for the awards of certificates and diplomas. In order to ensure that the Ministry of Education has independence in the design and development of relevant programs and their content, it is considered timely that Brunei Darussalam should have a locally controlled system of awards through a nationally recognized body. However, it is recognized that it is still essential to maintain links with overseas validating bodies over a phase-in period in order to maintain credibility and equivalence of current awards.

3.5 Adult and Nonformal Education

Continuing education is known as "further education" (which is also the name of the relevant section in the Department of Schools responsible for organizing courses for working adults and training for out-of-school youths). This type of education was initially introduced to eradicate illiteracy but has shifted its emphasis to improving the general education of individuals, their acquisition of technical skills, and the provision of programs for the enrichment of leisure activities, especially for housewives and working or nonworking women.

Increase in literacy has been quite dramatic. The rate increased from 26 percent in 1947 to above 90 percent in 1991. This figure is still improving and the government hopes that, with the steady expansion of formal education, the literacy rate will eventually fall to near zero.

Some government schools are used as centers for continuing education and classes are mainly conducted in the evenings or at weekends with teaching staff taken mostly from among government full-time teachers employed part-time.

Other programs include secondary education courses leading to Advanced-level examinations, commercial studies, education for the handicapped, City and Guilds technical subjects, home economics, and even education for prison inmates. Religious education is actively organized to promote a better understanding of the teachings of Islam and to improve the ability to read the Koran. These classes are not only conducted in centers in government schools, but also in mosques, offices, and public facilities. Nominal fees are levied on adults, but classes for basic literacy are free of charge.

4. Administrative and Supervisory Structure and Operation

The Ministry of Education is responsible for the mainstream school system up to higher education. The Ministry of Religious Affairs is responsible for Islamic religious education, including the supply of religious teachers for Islamic religious knowledge classes taught in the mainstream school system as part of the school curriculum. Both ministries have their own school inspectorate and, in the case of the Ministry of Education, the Inspectorate Department (which has a supervisory and advisory role) is one of the six main departments in the Ministry with the head having directorial status.

5. Educational Finance

Education offered by the public schools is almost entirely financed by the government. Although there is no compulsory education system, education is free to all citizens. If children live 8 kilometers away from the nearest school, they are either taken to and from school by school transport or are provided with free school accommodation including meals. There is also the school meals scheme which provides light refreshments to almost all children or a full meal at lunch for children in rural schools. Textbooks are loaned free to the children.

However, government policy is gradually shifting toward asking parents to meet part of the costs of their children's education; for example, the school meals scheme is gradually being withdrawn, and the provision of free exercise books has been totally withdrawn,

and so on. This does not imply that Brunei Darussalam is facing an unfavorable economic situation, but rather the government wishes to involve parents in sharing the responsiblity for their children's education and to initiate both parents and children into the fact that they should no longer take free education for granted.

The almost total state subsidy of education for citizens made the Ministry of Education one of the main claimants on the public purse. There was a substantial increase over the years in budget allocation until 1989 when it became government budgetary policy to reduce expenditure by all sectors of the government. By 1992 government policy was to budget on a 5 percent increase annually. Brunei Darussalam practices a five-year national development plan and budgets for education programs are quite favorably considered. Because of the peculiarity of budgetary allocation, expenditure, and accounting, it is rather difficult to determine what percentage of national budget is allocated annually to any particular government department or ministry. However, based on expenditure (which is accounted finally by the Department of Treasury at the end of the fiscal year), the expenditure by departments/ministries can be calculated, and here, once again, education appears to be one of the departments/ministries that has high expenditure. The figure for 1991 indicated that education was allocated 14 percent of the national budget.

Private schools do not receive any aid from the government except that they are provided with government-employed Malay-language and Islamic religious knowledge teachers. Children are charged tuition fees. Until 1971, the Chinese schools in the country were aided on a 1:1 basis by the government.

6. Supplying Personnel for the Education System

As indicated in Table 1, the total number of teachers is 5,103 for a student population of 71,153 (roughly a student–teacher ratio of 14:1). Some 83 percent of these teachers (4,259) are in government schools. Of these teachers 8.1 percent in primary schools and 32.6 percent in secondary schools are expatriates on three-year contracts with the government. In the vocational and technical schools, as well as in the tertiary institutions, the reliance on expatriates is even greater; in the first four years of operation of the University of Brunei Darussalam, there were fewer than 10 percent locals on the academic staff. By 1992, the University still had more than 80 percent foreign academics. Nongovernment schools also rely heavily on expatriates.

As mentioned above, Brunei Darussalam is extremely short of skilled labor, including teachers in all categories. Local teachers who are Certificate of Education holders are mostly trained locally, while graduates with the Postgraduate Diploma are mostly trained overseas, at least until the University was established and produced graduate teachers.

Teacher training for the certificate level lasts three years, while at the undergraduate level there is a concurrent four-year program. Until the University was established in 1985, graduates who had specialized in subject areas from overseas institutions had to take the Postgraduate Certificate or Diploma of Education, also overseas. If this was not done immediately after completion of the first degree, it had to be achieved within three years of service. Only after obtaining this professional qualification, and after having been assessed by the relevant authorities, can the teacher be confirmed in his or her position.

Expatriates are recruited mostly from the Commonwealth countries, particularly from the United Kingdom and Australia since this is a requirement of the Public Service Commission. Many are from Malaysia and Singapore. The improvement of the standard of education in Brunei Darussalam is receiving a great deal of attention from the Ministry of Education, and various programs are conducted not only to improve the quality of teaching but also the quality of school leadership. Different types of inservice courses, seminars, and workshops are expected to boost the effectiveness of school teaching and administration.

7. Curriculum Development and Teaching Methodology

As of January 1992, every school in the country, except for those schools which cater for nonlocal children, follow the National Education System. Hence, there is a common curriculum, a common syllabus, and a common examination system for all schools. However, particularly at the upper-secondary and pre-university levels, the curricula are greatly influenced by the Cambridge Examination Syndicate in the United Kingdom, which controls the public examination of these levels of education.

Examinations at the primary level (PCE) and lower-secondary level (BJCE) are controlled by the Brunei Darussalam Examinations Board. At the primary and lower-secondary levels, the curriculum and syllabus are developed by the Department of Curriculum Development.

The curriculum provides a coverage of reading, writing, mathematics, science, social studies, humanities, arts, and physical education, but very little foreign language which is only available at the secondary level. In primary schools, all the subjects (except for religious knowledge) are mostly taught by one general classroom teacher, whereas in secondary schools various subject specialists are used. There are very few elective subjects.

As a consequence of the Bilingual System of Education and the inclusion of the national philosophy of Brunei Darussalam as a Malay, Islamic monarchy, educational reform was accompanied by the implementation of the concept of the Islamization of knowledge.

This is a way of harmonizing the content of a number of subjects studied in schools and in other educational institutions with the teachings of Islam. The implementation of the curriculum is the responsibility of the School Inspectorate, the Curriculum Development Department, and the Monitoring Unit of the Ministry.

8. Educational Assessment, Evaluation, and Research

In Brunei Darussalam, there has not yet been any formal national assessment or evaluation studies, except those conducted by academics from the University of Brunei Darussalam as personal research projects.

9. Major Reforms in the 1980s and 1990s

From 1984, there was a period of considerable reform in the Brunei Darussalam education system. The most notable change was the Bilingual System of Education described above. Reforms of the school curriculum were undertaken and methods of teaching implemented which emphasized learning by discovery or student-centered approaches. There was also the extension of the national education system to nongovernment schools thus introducing the concept of a common school curriculum and syllabus and an examination system applicable to all schools in the country as promulgated in the new Education Policy.

Even though education is not legally compulsory, every school-age child is now in school. It is the improvement of the quality of education being provided to these children that is the challenge. The quality of the teaching staff is improved through inservice and preservice training and the intake of better-qualified candidates into the teaching profession. There was an increase in active parental and community involvement in the process of education. School administration and management efficiency was improved through leadership training, courses, and seminars.

10. Major Problems for the Year 2000

Financial resources do not present a major constraint to educational development. However, the problem of teacher shortage, caused by over-reliance on foreign teachers, will continue. The slow process of training qualified teachers is obvious since the duration of the training takes 3–4 years; but coupled with the shortage of interested and qualified candidates is the persistently small annual production of teachers locally.

Shortages of classrooms for secondary education

may still be a feature in the year 2000. Many more secondary schools need to be built not only to accommodate the increasing population, but also to abolish the double-session school system that still exists. Efforts are being made to increase the number of school buildings immediately. There is no doubt, therefore, that the objectives of improving the standard of education and providing an education which is in line with the aspirations of the nation as a Malay, Islamic monarchy without hindrance to national development are the major challenges now and in the future.

Bibliography

Curriculum Development Department 1985 *Education System of Brunei Darussalam*. Ministry of Education, Brunei Darussalam

Department of Examination 1991 *Analisa Keputusan Peperiksaan PCE, BJCE, BCGCE O Level (1980–1990)*. Ministry of Education, Brunei Darussalam

Department of Information 1990 *Brunei in Brief, 1990*. Office of the Prime Minister, Brunei Darussalam

Department of Planning, Research and Guidance 1989 *Educational Planning of Ministry of Education, 1989* Ministry of Education, Brunei Darussalam

Economic Planning Unit 1986 *The Fifth Five-Year Development Plan, 1986–1990, of Brunei Darussalam*. Ministry of Finance, Brunei Darussalam

Economic Planning Unit 1989 *Brunei Darussalam Statistical Yearbook 1989*. Ministry of Finance, Brunei Darussalam

Ministry of Education 1989 *Education in Brunei Darussalam, 1989*. Ministry of Education, Brunei Darussalam

Ministry of Education 1991 *Educational Statistics*. Ministry of Education, Brunei Darussalam

Office of the Prime Minister 1984 *Brunei Darussalam: Facts & Figures*. Office of the Prime Minister, Brunei Darussalam

State Secretariat 1972 *Report of the Education Commission Brunei*. State Secretariat Brunei, Brunei Darussalam

Bulgaria

M. D. Mateev

1. General Background

The Republic of Bulgaria is situated in the central eastern part of the Balkan peninsula in southeastern Europe. To the north Bulgaria shares borders with Romania, to the east with the Black Sea, to the south with Turkey and Greece, and to the west with the former Yugoslavia (the republics of Macedonia and Serbia). The total area is 110,994 square kilometers, and the population is 8,487,000 (unless otherwise stated, all statistics relate to 1992). Sofia (1,130,894 inhabitants) is the capital and main administrative and cultural center. Other large cities include Plovdiv (341,058), Varna (308,432), Bourgas (193,752), and Rousse (170,038). The general demographic trends are: a decrease in the birthrate (14.5 per thousand in 1980 to 10.5 in 1992; for the first time in 1990 the deathrate was higher than the birthrate); and a migration from rural to urban areas (in 1948 26.4%, in 1965 46.5%, in 1980 62.5%, and in 1992 67.2% lived in urban areas). The first trend influences enrollments and the second affects school construction in densely populated regions. The official language is Bulgarian (Slavic language group), which explains why the only Slavic international language, Russian, has traditionally been a part of the national curriculum. The mother tongue of 9.4 percent (800,052) of the Bulgarian population is Turkish and a specific educational problem arises connected with teaching this mother tongue. The second largest ethnic group is Bulgarian gipsies (313,396). There are difficulties in keeping children from ethnic groups like these at school up to the age of 16.

The traditional religion is Christian Orthodox, but 13 percent of the population is Muslim. Although there are no data available, a large proportion of the population is not religious. The Christian and Muslim religious institutions are separate from the state.

Some 40.5 percent of the labor force works in industry and construction (45.7% in 1985), 18.0 percent in agriculture and forestry (20.8% in 1985) and 41.5 percent in services and other (33.5% in 1985). From a total of 2,477,563 persons employed in the national economy, 490,326 have university or semihigher education, 441,312 have secondary vocational education, 703,661 general secondary education, and 842,264 lower education. The mean years of schooling of the labor force are: 9.0 in 1980, 9.6 in 1985, 9.8 in 1989, and 10.2 in 1990.

Since 1991 a major economic reform in the shape of a transition from a command to a free market economy has been carried out. The reform resulted in dramatic structural changes in the economy mainly caused by the reorientation of exports away from Council for Mutual Economic Aid (COMECON) countries toward the West and by the necessity of opening new markets to Bulgarian production. Liberalization of prices, severe monetary measures and state budget cuts, interest rates up to 70 percent, privatization, demonopolization of state industries, and agricultural reform oriented to private farming, resulted in rapid changes of the

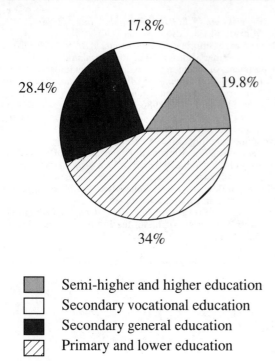

Semi-higher and higher education
Secondary vocational education
Secondary general education
Primary and lower education

Figure 1
Bulgaria: Educational stucture of the labor force 1992

economic and employment structure. Production decreased in 1992 by 51.5 percent and unemployment rose to 576,893 in 1992.

From September 1944 to November 1989 Bulgaria was governed by a Soviet-style communist totalitarian regime and was a member of the Soviet bloc military and political pact (Warsaw Treaty Organization). After November 1989 rapid political changes took place: free elections were held twice (in June 1990 and October 1991); the President was elected (1990 and 1992); and governments were formed democratically (in September 1990, December 1990, November 1991, and December 1992). A new Constitution was adopted (July 1991) and a new Education Law (October 1991) was passed by the Grand National Assembly.

The historical background of the Bulgarian educational system is connected with the development of what is one of the oldest state structures in Europe (Bulgaria has existed as a separate state since 681AD). The first schools were established by the students of Cyril and Methodius who invented the cyrillics—the alphabet which first became established in Bulgaria and then, together with Christianity, spread to other Slavic countries, including Russia. The biggest school was that of Kliment in Ohrid (c. 888AD) where more than 3,500 students were educated. After the Turkish

invasion of the country and during Ottoman domination (1396–1878) education only developed with great difficulty, but still more than 1,000 schools operated in Bulgarian lands in 1878.

Education developed quickly in the new, independent Bulgaria and by 1922 the compulsory length of education was seven years and tuition was free of charge. A national curriculum has always existed in the country. The first Bulgarian university was the University of Sofia, founded in 1888.

2. *Politics and the Goals of the Education System*

Policy relating to the development of the Bulgarian educational system is clearly determined by the total change of the political and economic system—from a totalitarian to a democratic society and from a command to a free market economy.

The critical analysis of the communist educational system showed that the so-called "class-party" approach which was applied through pedagogical pressure led to a strong and artificial enhancement of the ideology of one party over the general human values, to disregarding the rights of the individual, to intolerance of other people's opinion, to lack of initiative and creativity, and even to aggressiveness. Teachers were put in restrictive curriculum conditions, without any right to choose the ways and means to reach given educational goals, and under multilayer educational control which was far from being coherent and very often incompetent. There was a tendency for a uniformity of all schools including the absurd complete fusion of general and vocational education. The universities and the higher educational institutions were less damaged by the totalitarian regime, but major changes toward more flexibility, more choice, and more possibilities still needed to be given to students on their way to university degrees and further professional careers. No private schools or universities were allowed to exist.

Nevertheless, the infrastructure of the educational system, which includes kindergartens, schools, higher institutes, universities, and a large set of auxiliary establishments, was well developed throughout the country.

The Constitution and the Laws on School Education and Academic Autonomy are the present legislative basis of the educational system. The Constitution states that everybody has the right to education, that school education until the age of 16 is compulsory, and that secondary education is free of charge in state and communal schools. Under certain conditions education in the state universities is also free of charge. Private (independent) schools are allowed but the education there should be in compliance with the state educational requirements (standards), which are listed in the Law on School Education. Control over all kinds of schools is granted to the Ministry of Education.

The Law on School Education states that the education is secular; that schools and kindergartens are state-maintained, communal, and independent; and that they are legal entities. All heads of schools are appointed by the Ministry of Education. The school head exercises pedagogical leadership, manages the school budget, and appoints the teachers. There are two collective bodies in the schools—the Teachers Council which discusses and deals with major teaching matters, and the School Board which is an elective and consultative body advising the school head on a range of school problems. It consists of pupils, teachers, parents, and representatives of the community.

School education should promote knowledge of the Bulgarian language. Pupils whose mother tongue is other than Bulgarian have the right to study their mother tongue outside the state-maintained schools under the protection and control of the state. It is possible for these pupils to study their mother tongue for up to four hours a week from Grades 3–8.

Higher education is regulated by the Law on Academic Autonomy which states that all universities and higher education institutions independently decide all questions connected with their teaching and research, their structure and activity, the number and qualifications of their staff, the curricula and syllabuses, as well as the certification procedures for the students, their budget, and own economic activities. The universities and higher education institutions are governed by the general assembly, the academic council, and the rector. The rector and members of the academic council are elected by the general assembly, consisting of all professors and associated professors, as well as representatives of the non-teaching staff, the students, and distinguished representatives of industry, business, and society. All activities of higher education institutions, including business carried out by companies belonging to them, are free from taxes and duties. The state may reduce taxes to companies which invest in education.

3. The Formal System of Education

3.1 Primary, Secondary, and Tertiary Education

The structure of the educational system and graphical details of enrollments in different kinds of schools are outlined in Fig. 2.

School education begins at 6 or 7 years of age according to the wishes of parents. School education is general and vocational. General education is divided into the following stages: junior school education of 4 years' duration, presecondary school education of 4 years' duration, and secondary school education of up to 5 years' duration. There are 623 junior schools, 2,267 primary schools (from Grades 1–8), 39 presecondary schools, 83 secondary schools (from Grade 9 to the last grade), and 394 all-in

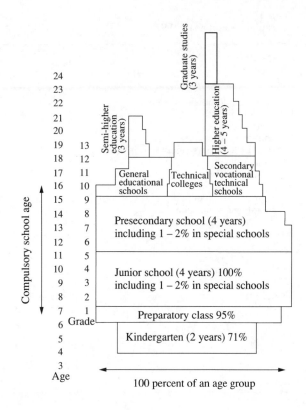

Figure 2
Bulgaria: Structure of the formal education system 1990

secondary schools (from Grade 1 to last grade). The total number of pupils in general education schools is 1,027,500 and there are 72,400 teachers. In 1992, 110,900 pupils completed presecondary education and 41,800 completed general secondary education. Schools are coeducational. The school week consists of 5 days while the school day covers 4–5 hours' teaching time in junior school and 5–6 hours' tuition in secondary school. The number of school days is 160–80 depending on the grade. In secondary general education there are many schools with a special profile: secondary schools with intensive study of foreign lanuages (French, English, Russian, German, Spanish, etc.) in which the first year is mainly used for the study of that particular language (22 hours per week). Some subjects are taught in the foreign language; for example, mathematics and science, sports (from Grade 6 to the final grade), and art and music. In the final grade all secondary general education schools have two options: (a) an indepth study of subjects connected with future university studies, or a broad profile vocational training mainly in services (e.g., tourism, commerce, communication, administration, and computers).

Table 1
Educational enrollments 1992

	Kindergarten	Schools	Semihigher education	Higher education
Number of children and students	263,000	1,265,498	30,261	162,009
Number of institutions	4,429	4,047	47	33
Number of teachers	27,400	93,440	3,081	18,895
Student–teacher ratio	10:1		10:1	9:1
general education schools		14:1		
special schools		6:1		
technical colleges		10:1		
secondary vocational schools		16:1		
Expenditure per student per year (US$)(1990)	—		666	666
general education schools		486		
technical colleges, special and vocational schools		563		
Age group enrolled	3 (47.1%)	6 (12.7%)	19–24 (22%)	
	4 (57.4%)	7 (96.7%)		
	5 (62.2%)	8 (99.1%)		
	6 (63.5%)	9 (97.6%)		
		10 (98.6%)		
		11 (96.5%)		
		12 (95.3%)		
		13 (93.9%)		
		14 (90.0%)		
		15 (84.0%)		
		16 (80.4%)		
		17 (65.9%)		
		18 (28.2%)		

In the 1992–93 school year, 9 private schools with 51 teachers and 539 pupils started to operate in Bulgaria.

There are three levels of higher education—semihigher education (2.5–3.5 years), higher education (an average of 5 years), and graduate education (3–4 years).

There are 30 state and 3 private institutions of higher education in Bulgaria. They provide education in different fields: 7 provide university education in natural sciences and humanities; 10 in the field of engineering and technology; 4 in economics and business; 2 in stockbreeding and agriculture; 5 in medicine, dentistry, and pharmacy; 4 in music, drama, and fine arts; and 1 in sports. The oldest and biggest is the University of Sofia with 14 different faculties.

Semihigher education exists within 47 faculties of different higher institutes or universities: 12 of them are in teacher training (mainly for kindergartens and junior schools), 17 in engineering and technology, and the rest in health and social services. The total number of students is 30,261 with a teaching staff of 3,081.

University students amount to 162,009 (almost twice as many as in 1980), 35,000 of them being correspondent students with a teaching staff of 18,895.

There are 2,965 postgraduate students; 331 of them were awarded with a PhD degree in 1992.

3.2 Preschool Education

The majority of children between 3 and 6 years of age attend kindergartens, which form an important part of their education. They are partially subsidized by the local authorities. The fee which lower income families pay is reduced. There are 4,429 kindergartens with 263,000 children (62% of the children of preschool age). A general trend for this number to decrease has been observed due to lower birthrate and the rise of unemployment. In both urban and rural areas there are more places than children (104 per 100 children and 140 per 100 children respectively). Nearly 90 percent of children attend full-time kindergartens. Some 27,400 teachers work in preschool education. Education in kindergartens is organized and carried out through a program devised by the Ministry of Education. This aims at the full intellectual and physical development of children through different activities, games, and occupations. For children suffering from chronic illnesses or with special educational needs there are special kindergartens.

Children are prepared for school in preparatory

groups attached to kindergartens or schools one year before school education begins. Special preparatory classes are organized for children who do not know the Bulgarian language well.

3.3 Special Education

The education, training, and rehabilitation of children with physical, intellectual, and emotional disabilities are provided mainly in 132 special schools with a total enrollment of 13,795 children. The student–teacher ratio is 7:1. The group of special schools (the greatest number of them being of the boarding school type) is sufficient for the country but the idea of moving some of the children with special educational needs into general education schools is strongly promoted by the Ministry of Education. This would help to create a more realistic environment for disabled children by integrating them socially with other children.

3.4 Vocational, Technical, and Business Education

Vocational, technical, and business education is provided in 269 technical colleges and secondary arts schools and 237 secondary vocational–technical schools. Education in technical colleges begins after completion of Grade 8 and is of 4 years' duration providing vocational education for technicians, technologists, economists, and accountants, as well as general secondary education. In many technical colleges (81 in 1991) education begins after Grade 7 with a year's intensive foreign-language study (English, German, or French) and then follows the ordinary technical college curriculum. Secondary vocational–technical schools prepare workers in 82 different vocations (as well as secondary general education) in 3 years. In 1990, 27,000 students were admitted to technical colleges and 47,000 to secondary vocational–technical schools (i.e., 23% and 37% from the total number of children who complete primary education). The total number of tuition hours in technical colleges is 4,290, of which 1,770 are allocated to general education and 2,520 to vocational training; in the secondary vocational–technical school the figures are 3,180, 1,467, and 1,713 respectively. The school year is 36 weeks. The changes which have to be made with the rapid transition from a command to a free market economy and the appearance of a labor force market are the most serious challenges to vocational education. These changes relate to the curriculum, the organization of training, and the need to broaden the profile of vocational qualifications in order to make them more adaptive to the labor market.

3.5 Adult and Nonformal Education

The state sector of adult and nonformal education has a variety of forms. There are 260 child centers for out-of-school activities in the fields of art, music, folk dancing, singing, and drama. About 111,220 persons participated in these activities in 1991.

Another group are the centers for pupils' technical and scientific activities (around 70 throughout the country with 28,383 participants) which work with talented and highly motivated children in the fields of mathematics, information science, sciences, applied engineering and construction, agriculture, and ecology. Children, as well as adults, can work and study at 10 public astronomical observatories. There are 38 regional sports centers housing 39,000 participants, each of them specially designed for training children in different sports and games.

The private sector consists of numerous small companies and individuals that provide a wide variety of lessons to both children and adults in foreign languages, mathematics, sciences, literature, management, business, etc.

Vocational schools also provide adult courses for qualification in different vocations. A set of evening schools are organized for adults who wish to continue their interrupted education. In 1991 a private open university was inaugurated in Sofia.

4. Administrative and Supervisory Structure and Operation

Management of the school education system (kindergartens, schools, and auxiliary establishments) is carried out by the Ministry of Education, which controls their activities in compliance with state educational requirements. For the school educational sector, the latter are determined by the Supreme Council of Experts to the Ministry of Education. One-third of its members are distinguished teachers. Pedagogical control over the results of teachers' work is undertaken by 600 inspectors of the Ministry of Education working in 28 regional offices. About 60 of them control and periodically assess the work of school heads and the school administration.

Local authorities have no pedagogical function but are responsible by law for the compulsory school education of children up to 16 years of age; the health and security of schools and kindergartens; children and pupils; the construction, maintenance, furnishing, and repair of communal schools and kindergartens; canteens, boarding houses, leisure and sports facilities; transport for chlidren, pupils and teachers; and for some of the scholarships and financial support for socially disadvantaged pupils.

The higher education institutes and universities are autonomous bodies, whose relations with the state are regulated by the Law of Academic Autonomy.

5. Educational Finance

The proportion of gross domestic product (GDP) allocated for education was 4.24 percent in 1980,

4.5 percent in 1988, and 4.05 percent in 1992. The budget is the main source of finance for the whole system. For instance, in 1988 the total expenditure for education was 4.5 percent of GDP and 95 percent of this money came from the state budget.

The budget in 1990 was distributed as follows: 31.5 percent for preschool education; 48.8 percent for primary and secondary education, including vocational schools; 10.8 percent for semihigher and higher education; 3.5 percent for nonformal education; and 5.4 percent for supporting activities, social help for teachers, and educational research. It should be noted that in reality the preschool budget is much less because the fees which parents pay are not subtracted and at a rough estimate they cover around half of the expenses. The proportion of the state budget allocated to education was 12.5 percent in the period 1980–84, 11.7 percent in 1985–89, 12.8 percent in 1990, and 11.3 percent in 1993. In 1990, the average cost of a student in a general education school was 8,750 leva (US$486) per year; in a technical college, secondary vocational school, or special school it was 10,150 leva (US$563) per year, and in a semihigher or higher institution it was 12,000 leva (US$666) per year.

Tuition in primary and secondary schools, as well as in vocational education, is free of charge. Textbooks for students up to the age of 16 are also free of charge. A high proportion of university students receive free tuition (up to 90%). Both secondary and university students can obtain fellowships depending on their performance at school and on family income. The fellowship for a secondary school student is 35 percent of the minimum salary in the country; for university students it is 60 percent.

Schools and universities in Bulgaria are still poor and serious efforts are being made to diversify the funding sources, including tax reductions for educational purposes, and some nonprofit economic activity of pupils, teachers and parents, and so on.

One of the greatest problems to be solved in the next 15 to 20 years is construction of school buildings in urban areas where there is a shortage of about 8,500 classrooms.

6. Supplying Personnel for the Education System

The total number of personnel in the school education system is 235,000. Of these 11,500 are school heads, head teachers, head teachers of kindergartens, their aides, or main accountants of schools; 140,000 are teachers (65,000 with semihigher and 74,000 with university education). Around 63,000 work in primary schools. About 5,700 different specialists, with a university or lower educational degree, work in the schools alongside 65,500 workers (a great number of them in vocational schools). Around 19,000 teachers and professors work in the higher education system.

Personnel in the kindergartens is exclusively female.

Almost 77 percent of all the teachers in the country are women. The number of women in the teaching profession has outstripped the number of men since 1960. The effect of this comparatively new phenomenon has not yet been analyzed.

English is the only subject in which there is a shortage of teachers. A special program for training teachers of English is to be started in 1992–93. Sometimes in rural areas it is difficult to find enough highly qualified personnel, although there is some teacher unemployment in urban areas.

Pretraining and inservice training for teachers is performed in higher institutes and universities. A greater number of kindergarten and primary school teachers complete 3 to $3\frac{1}{2}$ years of semihigher education, and the secondary school teachers 4 to 5 years of university study. Several months of practice in schools is obligatory before graduation. The inservice training of teachers is performed in four teacher-training centers attached to different universities. There are two graduate teachers' degrees. A first-class teacher qualification is given professional experience of a general, analytical, and experimental nature, documented in scientific publications, textbooks, study materials, computer software, and so on. A certain number of graduate examinations are also required. A second-class teacher qualification is awarded after success in examinations for a special program and a successful thesis connected with the professional career of the candidate. Inservice teacher training is financed both by the local authorities or by the state budget after a proposal presented by the school head.

The Ministry of Education and the scientific and professional societies sponsor the organization of annual national seminars and conferences for teachers, which summarize teaching and pedagogical innovations in different subject or topics of common interest, with the active participation of university academic staff.

7. Curriculum Development and Teaching Methodology

Until the 1989–90 school year there was a unified national curriculum in general education and for every type of vocational school. Moreover, the syllabus for each subject was approved by special commissions to the Ministry of Education and the teaching timetable, which was obligatory, was applied to each individual teacher and class. Such a system was too restrictive for both children and teachers. The latter could not choose the methods and teaching aids they needed to reach certain educational goals, and the education of the students was not in accordance with their personal qualities, abilities, and wishes. A liberalization of this restrictive regime was necessary.

In the 1990–91 school year and later, major changes were made to the curriculum and syllabus policies of the Ministry of Education. New educational standards for knowledge and skills had to be worked out and accepted by the Supreme Council of Experts to the Minister of Education. They stipulated only the goals to be achieved, whereas the methods and aids could be chosen either by the authors of different textbooks or by the teachers. Meanwhile three different curricula were proposed for the teachers' councils of general education schools to choose from. The curricula contain the list of the subjects to be taught, the number of school weeks, and the number of tuition hours for each subject and grade. They determine the obligatory and the optimal parts. The obligatory subjects form several groups (languages and literature, natural sciences and mathematics, society and philosophy, music and arts, physical culture and sports, techniques and technology). Two foreign languages are obligatory in Bulgarian schools (the students choose from Russian, French, English, German, Spanish, and Italian). Foreign language teaching usually begins after Grade 4, but an earlier start is not excluded. Pupils can choose up to four or five subjects according to their individual interests within the framework of the obligatory school time. In addition to that time, pupils from the first to the final grade may choose many different subjects. Among them is the teaching of the mother tongue to children whose first language is not Bulgarian.

New syllabuses were introduced, starting in the school year 1991–92. These contain a minimum compulsory element, with the remainder of the syllabus being chosen by teachers, in accordance with their pupils' interests and taking the teachers' own views into account.

The main change which is expected after the new educational standards for knowledge, skills, and assessment have been accepted and introduced is the appearance of a variety of textbooks and teaching materials, thus giving the pupils and teachers more freedom of choice and more motivation for excellence, so that national curriculum goals are achieved.

8. The System of Examinations, Promotions, and Certifications

The students in junior schools are automatically promoted according to age. In presecondary, secondary, and higher institutes there is a system of 5 marks: 2 is poor and indicates that the student must take the exam again, 3 is satisfactory, 4 is good, 5 is very good, and 6 is excellent. Students with poor marks must repeat the grade. The new law on school education states that primary and secondary stages of education are considered to have been completed after passing certified examinations. Their number and the corresponding procedure has not yet been determined. University students should take and pass between 30 and 40 different examinations, and at the end of their studies have to present a thesis or pass a state examination which encompasses the major parts of the speciality.

Each stage and grade of education is certified by a document which gives the student the right to continue onto the next stage or grade. Vocational qualifications are certified by a document after special examinations have been taken and passed.

9. Educational Assessment, Evaluation, and Research

Assessment is usually undertaken by teachers. However, there is a system of national examinations at the end of secondary school conducted by the Ministry of Education. In general, Bulgarian education needs a contemporary system of objective assessment both for knowledge and skills, together with a system for assessing the quality of teachers' work and of teaching materials. The system should have two levels—national and individual (for each school and teacher). In order to serve the two levels, a great deal of research and development needs to be undertaken and foreign experience should be used.

Research in the field of education is undertaken in many higher eduaction institutions, universities, and the Bulgarian Academy of Sciences. The Ministry of Education has its own research institute in eduaction. The main topics of current research are: alternative projects for the structure and content of the different stages of the educational system; principles and technologies for creating state educational standards; standards for knowledge and skills and two levels of assessment for difficult subjects; methods and systems for evaluating the results of teachers' work; new infrastructures in teaching materials and means; humanism, human and civil rights; functional illiteracy, and systems for adult education; teaching the Bulgarian language and the mother tongue in bilingual conditions; systems to reveal and develop talented children; interaction between the school and the cultural background and its use for the education of pupils; and cultural stereotypes and foreign language teaching.

For more than ten years, research has been conducted and the results tried out and implemented in many schools for an integrated teaching of different subjects from languages to science, mathematics, arts, computers, and social sciences, combined with bilingual and trilingual textbooks. The project is run by educators and scientists from the Bulgarian Academy of Sciences and the University of Sofia, and has achieved remarkable results especially in the first eight grades. Some of the features of the new system are already in common use.

There is a national system of collecting data on educational indicators connected with the enrollment of different ages, educational stages, and types of schools and higher institutions. A group of sociologists and an expert council reporting to the Minister of Education studies the public opinion about different educational problems and issues which are relevant to decision-making connected with the national educational policies.

10. Major Reforms in the 1980s and 1990s

The present educational reform is associated with the political and economical changes in Bulgaria. The framework of the reform and its principle features are the basis of the new Law on School Education: highly autonomous school, school heads and teachers' rights; the concentration of state control in a single competent pedagogical body—the inspectorate of the Ministry of Education; new educational standards and their role in the system with a great diversity of schools including independent ones; new financial rules; functions of the local authorities; and so forth.

The most important task in enacting the reform is research and development and the implementation of the new educational standards for knowledge and skills and their assessment both in general and vocational education. Some of the most difficult and basic problems are connected with the education of human moral values, the philosophy underlying life in a democratic society, human rights, civics, European awareness, the free market economy, and ecological knowledge. The common understanding is that these topics should be taught throughout the whole course of education, from the first grade through to the last, and using the programs of all the different subjects. The content of the syllabuses should be revised and updated with the help of the best existing educational standards in the world. Free competition in the area of textbooks and teaching materials is to be encouraged.

A major effort should be made in assessment both on the national and the individual school level. New assessment instruments and methods must be implemented in schools and universities.

A real challenge to the educators and the whole Bulgarian society is the reform in the vocational education and its orientation to the free market econo-my. With the help of many European countries and the United States, the reorganization of 15–20 pilot technical colleges has been planned in order to create examples of contemporary and proper education in such fields as individual farming, tourism, hotel catering and management, business schools, and so on. The rich experience which exists in vocational training together with the numerous highly qualified teachers, gives real cause for hope that a rapid change will occur throughout the country.

The improvement of the economical situation in the country will lead to a major improvement in equipment and technical resources for education. The most pressing task is the construction of almost twice as many schools in urban areas where nowadays teaching is performed in two shifts in almost every school. Modernization of school and university library systems into computerized, linked, and free access systems is of major significance. The reorganization and smooth transition of the publishing industry, especially where textbook production and distribution are concerned, under the free market economic system will be of paramount importance.

Bibliography

The Constitution of the Republic of Bulgaria 1991 *Darjaven vestnik*, No. 56 (July 13, 1991)

Education and Age Structure of the Personnel and Labor Conditions 1993. National Institute of Statistics, Sofia

General and Vocational Education 1993. National Institute of Statistics, Sofia

Kindergartens and Houses for Orphanages 1993. National Institute of Statistics, Sofia

Law on Academic Autonomy of the Higher Education Institutions 1990 *Darjaven vestnik*, Nos. 10 and 12 (February 2, 1990)

Law on School Education 1991 *Darjaven vestnik*, No. 86 (October 18, 1991)

Statistical Data Handbook 1993 (ISSN 0204-4889). National Institue of Statistics, Sofia

Burkina Faso

N. M. Ouedraogo and J. D. Nombre

1. General Background

Burkina Faso is situated in the Saheli region of West Africa. It is bordered by Mali on the north and west, by Niger on the east, and by the Ivory Coast, Togo, and Benin on the south. The total area covers 274,000 square kilometers.

In 1890 the first colonizers arrived (the Voulet and Charúne mission) via Mali and signed a treaty whereby the "country" became a French protectorate.

The territory was first occupied in 1896, when it was attached to the colony of Upper Senegal and Niger. In 1902 the colony became the colony of Upper Volta. The colony was declared to be the Republic of Upper Volta in 1958 and became politically independent in 1960.

In 1992 the population numbered 9.5 million inhabitants. About 80 percent of the population lives in rural areas. Just over 50 percent of the population is under 15 years of age and the average annual population growth rate is 3.05 percent. The population density is about 30 persons per square kilometer. The rapid increase in population—found in many developing countries— is due to several factors. The main factor is the introduction of modern medicine resulting in a higher life expectancy at birth.

The potential active population (those over age 15) is 51.7 percent of the total population. The workforce is made up of 92 percent in agriculture (including subsistence farming), 3 percent in industry, and 5 percent in commerce.

There is a high rate of illiteracy. In 1985 only 15 percent of the population was literate. This rose to 16.2 percent in 1990 and 18 percent in 1992. In 1985 just over 93 percent of women and 81 percent of men were illiterate. Literacy education is conducted in national languages; however, only 14 out of 60 national languages have a script. The official medium of instruction is French.

The economy is one of the weakest in the world. It is dominated by the primary sector, but has low productivity (rudimentary technology, slow modernization, and mostly illiterate workforce). The Gross Domestic Product (GDP) increases at a slow rate, mainly due to the fact that Burkina Faso is land-locked; it is also due to the persisting aridity, the decreasing quality of the soil, and to unfavorable international economic conditions. Furthermore, it is to be noted that the slow increase in the GDP is accompanied by a high increase in the population growth. The GDP per capita is less than US$200 per year.

The state budget has a deficit which has become enormous since 1988. The budgetary constraints affect the social services and, in particular, education.

2. Politics and the Goals of the Education System

Education is defined in the constitution as the right of every citizen. "Primary education aims at providing all young people in Burkina Faso with an education which will develop them physically, morally, and intellectually as well as to develop their personality in a harmonious way; education should also prepare them for their future tasks as adults, workers, and citizens." Such education must "within the availability of school places, be compulsory for all persons (males and females) from 6 to 14 years of age" according to the law. However, this is dependent on certain costs being met, including transportation, school meals for the underprivileged, and school equipment and supplies. Within the budgetary constraints it is difficult for the state to meet these costs.

Secondary school education is intended to reinforce that which has been learned in primary school and to prepare young people for working life. National policy has been to extend access to learning, and government has undertaken a massive school building program on the one hand to have enough primary

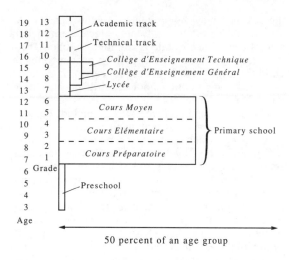

Figure 1

Burkina Faso: Structure of the formal education system

schools to attain the target of having all primary-age schoolchildren in school; on the other hand, the aim is to have one lower-secondary school (*collège d'enseignement général*) in each *département* (there are about 300 *départements*), one *lycée* in each province (30 provinces), and several permanent centers for literacy and training for those 15 years of age or older.

3. The Formal System of Education

Figure 1 presents an overview of the structure of the system of education. The scale at the bottom of the figure is 50 percent of an age group. It will be noted that there is still a lot of progress to be made before universal primary education is achieved.

3.1 Primary, Secondary, and Tertiary Education

Primary school lasts for six years and is subdivided into three parts: preparatory (2 years), elementary (2 years), and middle (2 years). Instruction is usually is French and occasionally in other authorized languages. There are 30 hours of instruction per week. The school year begins in September for the long course, but in January for the shorter course and there are 20 hours of instruction per week. There are separate schools for boys and girls except where there are not sufficient pupils for separate schools, in which case the schools are mixed.

Recruitment to primary schools is organized by a recruitment committee in each area. It consists of the recruitment chief or the mayor or their representative—the school principal—one or more teachers from the school, and a representative of the Parents' Association. The recruitment committee determines the school zone. Once a child is admitted to school, he or she receives a *fiche scolaire*, which accompanies the child throughout his or her school career. If a child is excluded from a public school, the child may not attend any other public school.

Those teaching in primary schools include teachers, assistant teachers, assistant pupil teachers, monitors (decreasingly), and special teachers for practical work.

There are two cycles of education in secondary school. Upon entering Grade 7 (Classe 6e.) pupils have three options, depending on their age. Entry depends on a competitive examination. If entry is at 13 years of age, the pupil may enter the *lycée* track; at 14 years or older, there is the option of the *collège d'enseignement général* or, if the age is 15 or more, there is the option of the technical school (*collège d'enseignement technique*). To enter the second cycle of secondary education (lasting for four years), the candidate must be younger than 19 years of age and have been selected. Within the second cycle there are two tracks: the academic and the technical. Within each track there are several "sections." Within the academic track there four "sections," each with a four year program: arts and science, economics and social studies, mathematics and physics, and mathematics and natural science.

Within the technical track there are six tracks. The first three have a four-year program and the second three a two-year program: technical administration, management skills; mathematics and technical subjects; mechanical production; electrotechnics, and accountancy, typing, shorthand, and topography.

Progress through school depends to a great extent on the work of the pupil. A pupil may only repeat a grade once within any one cycle of education. Grade repetition occurs if the pupil receives between 7 and 9.5 out of 20 in the first cycle of secondary school or between 7 and 9 out of 20 in the second cycle. If the child receives less than 7 out of 20 he or she fails and must leave school.

In 1991–92 the net enrollment ratios were 1 percent for preschool, 31 percent for primary school, and 6 percent for secondary school. There are large disparities among regions (82% in Kendiogo to 8.5% in Gnagua). There is also a disparity in terms of the number of classes in each school. There are fewer than 3 classes in 27 percent of all schools, exactly 3 classes in 37 percent of schools, and between 6 and 8 classes in 11 percent of schools. In 1990–91 10 percent of classrooms were being rebuilt.

Of all those in school, 91 percent are in state schools and 9 percent in private schools. In all cases, a higher proportion of boys than girls attends school.

Of the teaching force, 73 percent is male; only 20 percent have passed the *baccalauréat*; 70 percent are assistant teachers having graduated from the National Primary Teacher Training College, and 9 percent are monitors. The pupil–teacher ratio is 57:1.

There are two types of higher education. There is teacher training which takes place either at the National Primary Teacher Training College for primary school teachers or at the education faculty of the university for secondary school teachers. There is also higher education at the University of Ouagadougou. The university comprises faculties and institutes. Length of study ranges from two to seven years depending on the type of course and subject matter being followed. Some students study at universities in other countries.

3.2 Preschool Education

Preschool education is for children aged 3 to 6 years. It takes place in 42 kindergartens and 34 nursery schools (*garderies populaires publiques*). All come under the Secretariat for Social Action. In 1992 there was less than 1 percent of an age group enrolled in preschool education.

3.3 Special Education

There are no provisions for special education.

3.4 Vocational, Technical, and Business Education

The vocational, technical, and business education that takes place is undertaken within the formal education secondary school system (see Sect. 3.1) and within adult and nonformal education (see Sect. 3.5).

3.5 Adult and Nonformal Education

All adult and nonformal education programs are run by the Institute of National Literacy under the aegis of the Ministry of Basic Education and of Mass Literacy. This institute coordinates all activities and is responsible for the production of all materials. This education is aimed at the rural population. Its aims are the removal of ignorance in the population and helping the target group resolve its daily problems, and this involves their acquisition of knowledge and practical skills.

There are training programs for young people in agriculture and in artisan's crafts. Every effort is made to promote the participation of women in all spheres of socioeconomic development.

4. Administration and Supervisory Structure and Operation

The formal and nonformal systems of basic education are the responsibility of the Ministry of Basic Education and Literacy. Secondary and higher education are the responsibility of the Ministry of Secondary and Higher Education and Research. However, there is a certain decentralization in terms of administration.

The Directorate of Basic Education has several commissions through which it works. These include commissions on basic education, standards, examinations, competitions. It also organizes an annual conference of school inspectors and heads of training institutions, and an annual conference of peripatetic school advisers.

Burkina Faso is divided into 73 basic education areas in 30 provinces. These are headed by inspectors and are assisted by the peripatetic advisers and principal educators. The school principal is either a teacher or assistant teacher.

Secondary education is run by the Directorate of Secondary Education. Where there are sufficient secondary school inspectors there are no advisers.

It is to be noted that there have not been any major changes in the administrative system with the exception of decentralization to the provincial and basic education areas. Provincial directorates for basic education and literacy and provincial coordinators for secondary and higher education have been taken over by 10 regional directorates.

5 Educational Finance

The financing of education is jointly covered by the state and a number of other internal and external sources. This is because there is an insufficiency of state funding and because other sectors in the society must also be developed. Although there is a growing demand for schooling, the state is withdrawing its support from school building programs and the provision of equipment and supplies. Thus, the partners of the state for financing education are primarily parents and parents' associations who help fund buildings, equipment, and supplies. International agencies help with the development of the whole system. Now governmental and religious associations help not only with buildings, equipment, and supplies, but also with school canteens.

It was with the advent of the National Council of the Revolution that the notion of citizen participation in the financing of social infrastructure began. This included the building and maintenance of schools. However, the state pays all state school teacher salaries and this amounts to, on average, 70 percent of the education budget. Parental contributions vary between 35 and 44 percent for basic education, 40 and 50 percent in rural areas, and 47 to 57 percent in urban areas for secondary education.

6. Supplying Personnel for the Education System

Since 1985 primary school teachers have been trained in the Natural Primary School Teacher Training Institution (ENEP). In 1993 a second institution of this kind was being built. Entrants must have the *Brevat d'Etudes en Premier Cycle* (BEPC) and be between 17 and 24 years old. The course lasts for two years and comprises both theoretical and practical training.

Secondary school teachers attend a two-year training course at the National Institute of Education at the University of Ouagadougou. Those teaching in regular schools must obtain a *maître* or *license*; in *collèges d'enseignement géneral* (CEG) they must have a CAP-CEG, and for technical schools, a diploma.

7. Curriculum Development and Teaching Methodology

The curriculum, inherited from the French colonizers —as is the case in most former French colonies—has not been much change since Independence. Several proposed reforms have never really materialized. However, the existing curriculum has been enriched by the introduction of new areas such as vocational and computer training. In primary school the main subjects are: moral and civil education, French language, arithmetic, history, geography, scientific observation, drawing and manual work, sport, and environmental studies.

8. The System of Examinations, Promotions, and Certifications

Promotion from one grade to the next within a cycle of education is decided by the teachers in conjunction with the educational advisers.

At the end of the first cycle of secondary school, children sit for the *Brevet d'Etudes du Premier Cycle* (BEPC), the first examination in their school careers. At the end of the second cycle of secondary school students take the *baccalauréat* exam appropriate to the "section" in which they study. Certification is the receipt of a BEPC or *baccalauréat*.

9. Educational Assessment, Evaluation, and Research

There is no educational assessment, evaluation, or research undertaken, other than basic gathering of statistical data relating to enrollment and so forth.

10. Major Reforms in the 1980s

As already mentioned, there have been very few changes in the system of education since colonial times. However, in 1962 the curriculum for primary school was changed somewhat to adapt it more to the Burkina Faso context. In 1979 a large reform program began which affected all levels of education. However, after five years of experimentation, the program was abruptly stopped. In 1985 the nursery school system was begun. Nursery schools were to have been created throughout the country, but the parents of this age group of children has shown little interest. In 1992–93 an analysis of the problems and suggestions for possible reorientation was to be undertaken.

11. Major Problems for the Year 2000

It is clear to all involved in education that the content of education is inappropriate for the reality of life in the country. Plans for revision of the curriculum and for the expansion of the system are under way. Basic schooling will be the main focus of the effort to make education appropriate for the needs of the society. Universal primary education is expected to be achieved by the year 2010. However, by 1996, enrollment should be 40 percent of the relevant age group.

There has been no reform in secondary and higher education. One major problem is the high proportion of graduates from these levels of education that are unemployed. The authorities are concerned about this and the need to reform these levels.

Bibliography

Direction des Etudes et de la Planification 1989 *Rapport final du Séminaire d'Evaluation de Base du 9 au 10 Janvier 1989 à Koudougou*. Direction des Etudes et de la Planification du Ministère de l'Enseignement de Base et de l'Alphabétisation de Masse, Ouagadougou

Direction des Etudes et de la Planification 1992 *Annuaires Statistiques années 1990 et 1991*. Direction des Etudes et de la Plannification, Ministère des Enseignements Secondaire, Supérieur et de la Recherche Scientifique, Ouagadougou

Direction des Etudes et de la Planification 1993 *Annuaires Statistiques années 1990 à 1992*. Direction des Etudes et de la Planification, Ministère de l'Enseignement de Base et de l'Alphabétisation de Masse, Ouagadougou

Direction de la Planification de l'Education 1976 *Dossier Initial de la Réforme*. Direction de la Planification de l'Education, Minstère de l'Education Nationale, Ouagadougou

Institut National de la Statistique et de la Démographie *Recencement général de la population*. Institut National de la Statistique et de la Démographie, Ministère du Plan et de la Coopération, Ouagadougou

Mingat A, Jarousse J P 1987 *Coûts, Financement et Politique de l'Education au Burkina Faso*. Ouagadougou

République de Haute Volta 1965 *Décret no 289 bis 1965*. République de Haute Volta, Ouagadougou

Sous-Commission Education-Formation 1990 *Rapport, 2ème plan quinquennal*. Sous-commission Education-Formation, Ouagadougou

Burundi

M. Rwehera

1. General Background

Burundi is a small landlocked country in Africa, located very close to the Equator from which it is separated by less than 300 kilometers to the north. It has a surface area of 27,834 square kilometers and is far away from both oceans surrounding the African continent: 1,200 kilometers from the Indian ocean and 2,000 kilometers from the Atlantic. Located at the point of juncture between the River Zaire's basin and that of the Nile, Burundi belongs to the East African subregion. It is bordered by Rwanda to the north, Zaire to the west, and Tanzania to the east and south, with Lake Tanganyika alongside 60 percent of the western border.

Four different features can be observed in the country: the western part is a vast plain along the Lake Tanganyika and further to the north; then to the east a range of mountains runs from north to south reaching an average altitude of 2000 meters. This range is the dividing line in Burundi hydrography: all rivers and springs to the east of the range feed the Nile whereas those to the west feed into the Zaire River through Lake Tanganyika. The central area is made up of an elevated platform, crossed by numerous valleys and enjoying very favorable conditions for agriculture. Last, the eastern part of the country comprises a wide lowland with a hotter climate.

The Burundi population is highly homogeneous in its culture. It is one of the exceptional countries in Africa where a single language—Kirundi—is spoken and understood by all. However, the population is not ethnically homogeneous; three ethnic groups have existed in the country, not without some violent conflicts in recent history: these are the Hutu, the Tutsi, and the Twa in this order of numerical importance.

Burundi is proud to be the country where the southermost source of the Nile River is located. It was during one of the exploratory missions seeking to map the source of the Nile that Burundi was discovered by the Western world in the early 1870s. Soon after, the first group of Christian missionaries entered in 1893. A year later the Germans invaded the country and founded what is now the capital city, Bujumbura.

Prior to being "discovered," Burundi had existed as a highly centralized monarchy for several centuries. The political power as well as military leadership was held by the *Mwami* (king) on a hereditary basis. The regional power was assumed by lords appointed by the king. He was also the supreme head of the judiciary system. It was only in 1903 that the king recognized the German power and signed a treaty submitting to their "protectorate." They established their political capital in Gitega, a town built by them in the center of the country, keeping Bujumbura as a major port on Lake Tanganyika and an important economic center.

The missionaries played a key role in the development of the education system. It was common practice for them, particularly the Catholic, to have a school built at the site of every new mission. And of course the early school system was aimed at teaching children how to read the Bible.

The German protectorate over Burundi was terminated at the end of the First World War, with the defeat of the German army. The administrative authority over the country was taken over by the League of Nations. The League then transformed the country into a trust territory under Belgian tutelage. So Burundi became part of the Congo province (Zaire) together with neighboring Rwanda under Belgian administration. The colonial administration was headquartered in Léopoldville (now Kinshasa) where the Governor General had his offices; a lower level Résident with regional authority over Rwanda and Burundi had his office in Bujumbura. This rule continued until 1962 when Independence was gained.

After Independence, the monarchy carried on its political rule until it was itself overthrown in 1966 by Captain Micombero who went on to become the first president of the First Republic. The First Republic lasted 10 years, during which the most violent ethnic confrontation happened in 1972 and several tens of thousand people died. A second coup d'état under the leadership of Colonel Bagaza put an end to the First Republic on November 1, 1976 and declared the Second Republic. In his turn, Bagaza was overthrown on September 3, 1987 in a military coup led by Major Pierre Buyoya. It is under this president that a new political regime, based on multiparty system, has been put in place.

The total Burundi population was estimated to be 5.4 million in 1990, averaging a demographic density of 190 per square kilometer. Burundi is thus the second most densely populated country in Africa. The population is predominantly young, with as many as 42 percent being less than 15 years old, and 54 percent less than 20 years old. This particular population structure is bound to put a very strong pressure on the education system and its capacity to expand, because of the resulting high dependency ratio. Another consequence of the youthfulness of the population is the resulting acceleration of population growth. During the 1970s the demographic growth rate was 2 percent; it increased to 2.9 percent in the period 1983–87, and it is in the early 1990s estimated at 3 percent.

Burundi is a rural country: more than 90 percent of its population live and work in rural areas. The biggest city, Bujumbura, which is also the capital city of the country, has a population of less than 300,000 people; and the second largest town has less than 50,000. The total labor force was 58.1 percent of the population in 1987 and the overwhelming majority of them live off small subsistence agriculture. Sometimes agriculture is combined with informal rural activity like small scale trades, woodwork, or construction.

Only 13.2 percent of the labor force are active in the modern sector of the economy, both in the public and the private sectors.

The primary sector is by far the most predominant in the economy. It utilized 91 percent of the labor force in 1988, contributed 55.1 percent to the GNP, and 94 percent to the merchandise exports. Most of the activity in agriculture is producing food crops. Moreover, this food production is for the most part intended for family consumption only 9.7 percent being marketed. Cash crops production uses about 8 percent of the productive land to produce coffee, cotton, and tea.

The secondary sector represents 16.2 percent of GNP and the food and tobacco industry plays a major role within this sector, including beer, sodas, and cigarette production. In the area of energy consumption, according to a World Bank (1992) estimate, 70 percent of final energy demand is covered by wood, a state of affairs that represents a serious threat to the environment. Only 15,000 tons of peat are produced each year, a small proportion of the estimated reserve of 200 million tons. There is a role here for the education system, in helping to modify people's attitude toward the environment and to instill openness toward new technologies.

Burundi's economy suffers a lot from being landlocked: because of the higher costs of land transportation and of added transit fees paid to neighboring countries, its imports and exports are much more expensive and its competitivity much reduced. Furthermore, this total dependency over other countries adds a high degree of uncertainty: there is always a risk of transportation routes being disrupted.

The balance of payments shows a rising trade deficit and an increasing dependency over foreign aid. The percentage of imports paid for by exports revenue is only about 50 percent; the main export is coffee beans that are produced in increasing volumes but sold at fluctuating world prices, making government revenue very uncertain. As a consequence of increasing trade deficit the amount of public debt is on the increase: it rose from 2.36 billion Burundi francs in 1984 (the exchange rate was then about 180 francs to one US dollar) to 6.53 billion in 1988. As a proportion of current revenue, the debt service ratio doubled from 18.1 percent in 1986 to 36 percent in 1988. The government financial situation has also been deteriorating: the public deficit rose from 6.6 percent of GNP in 1986 to 12 percent in 1988. In reaction to the deteriorating economic condition, the Burundi government entered into negotiations with the International Monetary Fund and the World Bank about a Structural Adjustment Program that was started in 1986.

The declared major goal of the political authority of Burundi is to improve the living conditions of the population by increasing economic production and improving income distribution. In terms of economic growth, the stated objective was to reach an average annual growth rate of 5 percent and an average per

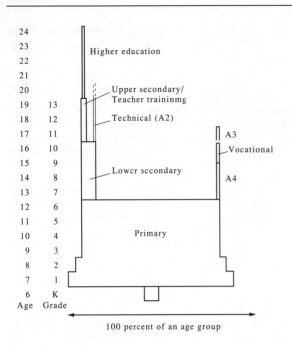

100 percent of an age group

Figure 1
Burundi: Structure of the formal education system 1992

capita GNP of US$245 in 1992. The leading role in economic development is to be played by the rural sector; the diversification of exports and the promotion of the private sector are also important strategic goals.

In terms of employment, the main goal is to increase employment both in the traditional and modern sectors. Reforming the investment codes, adjusting interest rates, and supporting small enterprises and rural cooperatives are seen as the major elements of the employment policy.

2. Politics and the Goals of the Education System

For most of post-Independence history, the Burundi system of government was based on a single party system. Therefore the aims of the education system as well as the major strategies for education development were outlined in official documents adopted by party congresses. Since the vote of the new constitution in 1990, UPRONA (union for national progress) is no longer the only party and has been joined by several opposing parties in the political arena.

A new Charter for Economic and Social Development was adopted in 1990 (see Conseil Economique et Social 1990). The Charter stresses the prime importance of human development. It emphasizes the strategic objective of a broad participative intervention by parents, central and local governments, nongovernmental organizations, and religious groups in order to develop a genuine school for community development. Universal primary education is to be pursued, illiteracy is to be eradicated, and school quality at all levels is to be improved. The Charter advocates enhancement of the scientific and technological dimensions in the content of education.

Given the predominantly rural distribution of the population, an ongoing debate arose in the 1970s on how to ruralize the content of primary education. The fact that the overwhelming majority of primary school completers cannot access to secondary education and have therefore to integrate agricultural activity in their rural community, led many to propose radical changes in the curriculum with a view to biasing it toward rural needs. Thus such strategies as putting more emphasis

Table 1
Basic data on formal education in Burundi in 1991–92

	Primary education	Lower secondary education	Upper secondary education	Vocational and technical education	Higher education
Number of schools	1,373	41	71[a]	33	1
Number of students	631,039	34,281	8,789	6,174	4,533[b]
% Female	45	39	35	35	24
% Repeaters	23	14	15	13	—
Number of teachers	9,582	—	1,701	—	510
% Female	47		22		21
% of education budget	44		29		24
Expenditure by student (1985, US$)	31	—	331	—	1,896

Sources: Bureau de la Planification de l'éducation 1992; UNESCO 1992; Rwehera 1991
a Institutions at this level combine both lower and upper secondary   b Including students abroad

on practical activies in school, more interaction with the economic actors around the school, the creation and exploitation of school fields, the organization of cooperatives in every school, and the reduction of the time devoted to study French language have been proposed.

However, there is some indication that parents' and children's real aim when they enroll in school is to gain access to the modern sector of the economy. Because of the poor conditions prevailing in the rural areas, wage employment is considered the best possible option. Thus a conflict between education objectives as viewed by the families on the one hand and by the policymakers on the other, may well be a disturbing but real fact.

3. The Formal System of Education

Table 1 presents some basic data about the number of institutions, students, teachers and expenditures for the school year 1991–1992.

3.1 Primary, Secondary, and Tertiary Education

The general structure of education in Burundi is of a 6–4–3 type. Figure 1 presents the structure of the system. The official school entry age is 7 years although a significant proportion of children enter at age 8. Primary education has a duration of 6 years. In 1991–92 there were 626,454 pupils attending public primary education (private education is very marginal in Burundi). This figure is below that for the previous school year when the enrollment was 633,203. The gross enrollment ratio is also on the decrease: it was 71.6 percent in 1989–90, 72.5 percent in 1990–91 and only 68.7 percent in 1991–92.

While a decrease in the gross enrollment ratio can take place when the growth in school enrollment is slower than that of the school-age population, in the case of Burundi it is alarming to note that the enrollment is decreasing even in absolute terms. Several factors can be invoked to explain this retrenchment which is obviously due not to a reduction in supply, but in the reduction of demand for education. Less confidence in the relevance of primary education in view of reduced opportunity for further education is one, financial constraints on families which reduce their ability to pay increasing school fees is another.

This negative trend takes place after a period of impressive educational progress. Burundi is one of the African countries where the gross enrollment ratio increased most in the 1980s: it was only 29 percent in 1982. Thanks to the introduction of double shifting methods and the creation of many new schools, the ratio rapidly and steadily increased to 72.5 percent in 1990–91. This was a remarkably impressive achievement which seems to be in great danger of being reversed.

At the end of primary education, pupils have to take a fiercely competitive examination for admission to high school. The reason why this examination takes on such a dramatic character is that the number of seats available at secondary level is disproportionately small in view of the number of primary school completers. The transition rate to lower secondary is less than 10 percent. Building new secondary schools is a very heavy investment for small economies such as that of Burundi; that is why it has not been possible to follow up expansion in primary enrollments with parallel developments at the secondary level, and why the transition rate has been decreasing.

Lower secondary education is available to those who pass the national entrance exam and has a duration of four years. The vast majority of these schools are public although some private schools are in operation with an enrollment of 10 percent as compared with the public sector. In order to partially compensate for limited financial resources from the central government, a new type of school, called *Collèges communaux*, built and equipped entirely by local government funds have been started. There were 18 such schools in 1991–92 enrolling 1,910 students. The teaching staff are paid by the Ministry of Education. In contrast with the public schools, whose catchment area is in principle the whole national territory, the *collèges communaux* have a local scope and it is the local authorities who determine the conditions for admission.

Beside general education, which enrolled 34,000 students in 1991–92, a few primary school leavers enter into vocational training in such skills as masonry, wood work, electricity, auto-mechanics, sewing, and various other fields. The duration of these vocational schools, commonly known as "A3" is five years. Many of these schools are privately managed and many government ministries, other than that of education, intervene in this type of training.

The transition rate to upper secondary level was about 30 percent in 1991–92. Here again a national test is imposed on all lower secondary completers, but as the probability of passing is higher than after primary, this exam is not as dramatic. Schooling at this level takes three years and four years in parallel technical education, known as "A2" schools. It is also at this level that the teachers for primary schools are trained in four-year courses. Within general education, three different tracks are offered presenting differences in the relative emphasis on science and arts. In 1991–92, there were 6,900 students in general education (upper), 1,900 in teacher training institutions and 1,900 in technical education ("A2").

Because of their limited number and thus the wide distances that separate them from students' homes, most public secondary schools operate under a boarding system. In 1991–92, 80 percent of the students were boarders. Under this arrangement, the students stay and live in the school area and can only stay with their families during vacation time. The additional expenses needed to pay for the boarding of students contribute heavily to raising the unit cost at this level in comparison with primary education.

Higher education is very limited in scope: total enrollment at this level was 4,533 in 1991–92, including students being trained abroad. There is only one university in Burundi, that is, the University of Burundi in Bujumbura, comprised of eight faculties and five institutes. Its present structure is the result of several changes that have been brought to the University since its birth in 1964. The faculties are: law, sciences, economic and administrative sciences, medicine, psychology and education sciences, agriculture, applied sciences, arts and human sciences. The institutes are higher institutions organized within the University but with well-marked professional orientation: ISA for agriculture, ITS for industrial higher technicians, ESCO for middle-level business technicians, IEPS for sports and physical education, and IP for teacher training for lower secondary schools.

Although four years is the most common length of studies, there are great variations between types of studies. In spite of quite rapid expansion in the programs offered by the University of Burundi, there are still a number of areas of study not available to students; consequently a number of students are each year given fellowships to study abroad with the assistance of bilateral and multilateral aid agencies: they were 729 in 1991–92. This number also includes students going abroad for graduate studies which are only being started in the University's medicine and sciences faculties.

3.2 Preschool Education

Preschool education exists in some urban areas with a very small enrollment in private establishments.

3.3 Special Education

There are only two schools dealing with special education in Burundi: one in Bujumbura and the other in Gitega, the two largest cities in the country. Both schools are devoted to the education of deaf children and are privately run.

3.4 Vocational, Technical, and Business Education

As stated earlier, a range of vocational and technical schools provide training at all levels. The aim is to train skilled workers and middle-level technicians in various fields. Some projections seem to show a relatively short supply of intermediate technicians in the longer run. All "A4" schools (three years duration) have been upgraded to "A3" (five years). New areas of skill training have been organized and the private sector has been encouraged to open such schools. There seems to be a division of labor between the private and public sectors, the former being more involved in

business-type of training and the latter in industrial-type training. Higher-level technicians are trained in five specialized institutes within the University of Burundi.

3.5 Adult and Nonformal Education

The directorate for out-of-school education is entrusted with the coordination of nonformal education. The directorate has been transferred from the Ministry of Education to the Ministry for Handicrafts, Vocational Training, and Youth. The directorate for out-of-school education takes care of youngsters who drop out of primary education, by developing special centers and workshops for practical activities where these youths can quickly acquire useful skills. It has also the objective of promoting self-employment among school leavers. Therefore, in 1981 so-called "multipurpose learning centers" (MLC) were created with a view to helping primary school leavers with training in agriculture, construction, animal husbandry, and so on. These MLCs increased in number (100 in 1988) but failed to achieve their real objectives: as they lacked technical equipment and had no credit system, the participants soon lost interest in them and were more interested in seeking wage employment in the modern sector, away from their rural milieu.

A national office for literacy has been set up with the aim of progressively eradicating illiteracy among adults. It designs literacy methods and primers for literacy activities which for the most part are implemented by private groups and nongovernment organizations (NGOs). There is one particular nongovernment organization, INADES (*Institut national pour le développement économique et social*) that manages a correspondence course aimed at adult rural population with information about fertilizers and other matters related to agriculture. Nearly 10,000 people have so far taken part in this correspondence course.

4. Administrative and Supervisory Structure and Operation

Two ministries are in charge of the formal education programs: the Ministry for Primary and Secondary Education and the Ministry for Higher Education and Scientific Research. Nonformal education is the responsibility of the Ministry for Handicrafts, Vocational Training, and Youth. However, most of the substantive programs in this area are run by NGOs, particularly religious institutions. Each institution has its own approach and coordination is almost nonexistent.

Primary and secondary education is administratively very centralized. Not only are all matters related to curriculum development and teaching materials design decided upon by the national education services, but they are also concerned with recruitment, posting, and remuneration of staff. Even the selection of primary school completers selected for admission to lower secondary education is done by the Ministry, which also determines very precisely which school they will go to.

However, as far as primary education is concerned, a number of administrative tasks are devolved to regional and local institutions. In each of the 15 provinces there is a provincial inspector who coordinates the work of two or three district inspectors. In 1991–92 there were 44 school districts (*cantons scolaires*) with an average 19 schools per district. The district inspector is in charge of administrative supervision, pedagogical support, and monitors and reports on classroom teaching in all the schools in his or her district.

Administratively speaking, primary schools are of two types: there are those dubbed "central" that offer a full six-year curriculum, are located in the more concentrated areas, and are closer to the mainstream communication networks. They are led by a dedicated headteacher with no teaching obligation. A "central" school is often coupled with one or more satellite schools called *succursale*, that may offer only a partial curriculum and are often located in the more remote areas. In case the school is incomplete, pupils are required to finish the curriculum in another school. The *succursales* fall under the administrative responsibility of the closest central school. There were in 1991–92 497 central schools and 857 *succursales* schools.

There is no regional administration for secondary education, but school principals enjoy limited autonomy in financial management. The University of Burundi enjoys extensive administrative and management autonomy. It is administered by a rector appointed by the President of the Republic for four years. Policy-making is the responsibility of a governing board, also appointed by the president and representing the major spheres of activity with connections with higher education development.

5. Educational Finance

Data on educational finance is very difficult to find in the published materials for several reasons: first, the voted budgets, always published at the beginning of the year are only theoretical and do not correspond to actual expenditures. The budgets are revised several times a year to adjust them to actual government revenue. Second, sources of education system finances are very diversified and there is no centralized accounting system for the nongovernment contributions such as those from local communities, families, enterprises, NGOs, and foreign assistance. Third, part of the contributions from local communities and families are in kind in the form of working days donated to the building or the maintenance of schools.

However, from what data is published, one can notice that public expenditure on education increased

slightly from 1985 to 1988. Thus government expenditure was 2.5 percent of GNP in 1985 and 3.1 percent in 1988. As a proportion of total budget, government expenditure on education is following the opposite direction: from its level of 17.1 percent in 1985, it decreased to 16 percent in 1992. Under hard economic circumstances and given the priority given to adjustment measures, education seems to be losing in the order of priority. This decrease may also be explained by the recent move to shift some of government expenses to local governments and to the families who have to pay increasing school fees. This increasing financial constraints over the families may partly explain the fall in demand for education and the resulting decrease in enrollments.

The internal allocation of financial resources between levels of education seems to show a steady movement not favorable to primary education. That level received 47 percent of the education budget in 1990, 45 percent in 1991 and 44 percent in 1992; the share of higher education in contrast is increasing from 22 percent in 1990 to 24 percent in 1992, whereas that of secondary education has stagnated at 29 percent. The reduction in the budget share of primary education is seen as a threat to the commitment to the objective of Basic Education For All.

Analysis of unit cost by level of schooling shows that in 1985 one primary pupil cost on average US$31, US$331 for a secondary school student, and US$1,896 for a student in higher education. Both the appallingly small amount spent on a primary school pupil and the extreme disparity among students in different levels are striking. The low level of unit spending in primary is not uncommon in the group of least developed countries (LDCs) of which Burundi is a member; this low spending, however, represents an absolute handicap to the provision of good quality education which requires motivating teachers' salaries and adequate learning materials.

The huge disparities between unit costs at different levels can be accounted for by the provision of students' assistance through boarding facilities in secondary and free fellowships in higher education. Wage levels for teachers are also much higher at those higher levels, contributing to raising unit costs.

6. Supplying Personnel for the Education System

During 1991–92, 17,000 full-time equivalent staff were employed in public and private schools. A quarter of this total were nonteaching staff. Of total staff, 60 percent were employed in primary schools, 28.6 percent in secondary and technical schools, and 11.4 percent in higher education. Central and regional administrative staff are not included in this figure, of which they represent a very marginal proportion.

For many years in the past, teacher shortages compelled the government to employ underqualified teachers as well as nonnationals in relatively large proportions. Thanks to the generalization of double shifting systems in primary schools, the problem of shortage has been significantly alleviated: in 1991–92 about 20 percent of the primary teachers were underqualified, down from 40 percent in the early 1980s. In the double shift system, each teacher teaches two different groups of pupils who spend half a day in school alternating mornings and afternoons every week.

The system of primary teachers' training has undergone many successive reforms in the recent past. In the 1960s the standard training system was in pedagogical schools offering one year of practical and theoretical training after lower secondary completion. Then in the late 1960s, a parallel system was introduced, whereby after completing lower secondary, prospective teachers entered the *école normale* where they received four years of general education in parallel with teacher training, so that after certification they could choose between entering the teaching profession or going ahead to higher education. Most of the graduates preferred further education. In the early 1980s both systems were abolished in favor of a new system where the prospective teachers, after completing lower secondary, entered the *école de formation d'instituteurs* for two years of teacher training without the option of further education. Finally, in the late 1980s, the *écoles de formation d'instituteurs* were replaced with *lycées pédagogiques* where the teacher training is organized in two cycles of two years each.

Secondary school teachers are trained in the University of Burundi from which they graduate after four years in the various specialities. Some teachers, specifically trained for lower secondary, are also trained in the IP (pedagogical institute) for two years.

Inservice training of primary teachers is a regular and important activity of the BER (office for rural education), a curriculum development agency. As new curricula and/or new teaching materials are developed, locally based courses are organized with the objective of acquainting the teachers with the new materials and updating their professional knowledge. Because of the large numbers of teachers involved, these courses are expensive to maintain and foreign assistance contribution is sought.

The BER also makes use of distance training by means of a weekly radio program for teachers. Every school is equipped with a radio set and collective listening is organized in the schools. Through the radio program, new methods are presented, views are exchanged, and practical problems solved by means of interviews, class observations, and reporting. A further opportunity is offered with the tradition of a monthly pedagogical day. The programs for such days follow a general plan set by BER but at the same time adjusted to the local needs. Similarly, a quarterly pedagogical day is organized in all school districts under the leadership of the inspector, with the help of BER. For underqualified teachers, upgrading sessions are usually organized during school vacations for longer periods of time (two months).

For secondary education, similar curriculum development agencies akin to the BER have been in operation, albeit with different methods: they are BEPES for general education and BEET for technical and vocational education.

In all three levels of education the teaching staff is predominantly male and more so in higher levels. The proportion of female teachers was 47 percent in primary, 21.6 percent in secondary, and 21.2 percent in higher education, during 1991/92.

7. Curriculum Development and Teaching Methodology

Curriculum development is centralized and is the responsibility of specific agencies already mentioned in the previous section: BER, BEPES, and BEET. All schools in the country, public as well as private, follow the same curriculum. For this reason the curriculum is usually very stable in time and changes are rare.

The BER is organized into as many units as there are subject areas taught in primary schools, plus some supporting units such as the evaluation unit. The areas covered are: Kirundi (national language), mathematics, environment studies, French, practical activities, physical education, sciences, history, and geography. Not all of the subjects are taught in all grades, the earlier grades concentrating on reading, writing, and simple arithmetic. French is introduced in Grade 3 as a subject and in Grade 5 as the medium of instruction. Religion is elective: parents can enroll their children in one of the main religions represented in the country (Catholic, Protestant, Islam, Kimbangism) or choose moral education instead.

The organization of time in school is fairly uniform all over the country. The school year is about 220 days long, organized in three terms separated by vacations totalling three months. As stated earlier, each nominal day is in effect a half-day because of the double shifting system.

The process for curriculum adoption is long and goes through several successive steps. When the final proposals are made by the responsible unit within BER, they are submitted to the minister who then authorizes their trial in a few selected schools and in a given grade. These experimental programs are followed up with frequent classroom observations and discussions between teachers and researchers from BER. They are then evaluated after one or two years. Depending on the results of the evaluation the programs are then improved and generalized to all schools. Along the way the relevant materials for the teachers and the students are designed and printed by RPP (*Régie des productions pédagogiques*), the printing unit of the ministry. This process is conducted in a grade-after-grade progressive manner. Nevertheless the progression is not uniform in all subjects because there are great differences in the time allocation and in the size and number of accompanying learning and teaching materials. The present cycle of curriculum development started with a major education reform in 1973.

In secondary education, the process is conducted by BEPES and BEET. There is a single curriculum for all lower secondary schools. The teaching time amounts to 38 teaching periods, each period being 50 minutes long. The teaching of French is intensified during the first few years in order to accelerate the transition from primary education where the language of instruction is Kirundi, to secondary and further education where instruction is given in French. English is the only other foreign language taught. It starts in Grade 9 till the end of secondary education. There are no elective subjects at this level.

At the end of lower secondary, students take a national test and their records are submitted to a national orientation commission in charge of guiding them into one of the several options opened to them for further education. They can enroll in general education (three tracks), in teacher training, or in various technical schools. Each of the schools is of limited capacity and many options are present only in a single institution in the country. Therefore the role of the orientation commission is, on the one hand, to make sure that the institutions can enroll those students whose aptitude best corresponds to their requirements, and on the other hand, that the students can find room in the institutions selected by them. Nevertheless, a fraction of the students are obliged to enter schools that they did not choose. It has been noticed that as educated unemployment increases, students' and parents' attitudes have been changing: whereas general education used to be considered the most prestigious option, opening the possibility to further education, more and more students have shifted their preference toward those institutions offering the safest job prospects, that is, technical and vocational schools.

Once the curriculum is adopted, it is passed as a compulsory regulation whichever level is concerned. In primary and secondary schools, on-site monitoring of curriculum implementation is done by headteachers and principals.

One issue in the area of curriculum is about the importance to be given to French at primary level. French is the *lingua franca* in administration, business, and external relations. Moreover, it is the medium of instruction after primary. It is therefore considered crucial for students to master it as early as possible. At the same time, however, many consider French to be of little use to the rural population where it is never used. Since 90 percent of primary school leavers may not go beyond primary, French should, in their view, be kept at a minimum. A satisfactory balance has not been possible to strike so far. It is an illustration of the well-known conflict between the terminal versus preparatory character of primary education.

8. The System of Examinations, Promotions, and Certifications

Repetition rates used to be very high and promotion rates very low in Burundi primary education, as is common in many Francophone African countries. The repetition rates in the early 1980s was on average as high as 30 percent in Grade 1 and 45 percent in Grade 6. Then in 1982–83 a system of near automatic promotion was introduced under which the repetition rate was to be kept below 10 percent in all grades. The objective was to reduce large internal inefficiency. But the measure has not been fully successfully implemented as can be seen from the following figures: in 1991–92, the repetition rates were 20 percent in Grade 1, 19 percent in Grade 2, 17 percent in Grade 3, 20 percent in Grade 4, 30 percent in Grade 5, and 35 percent in Grade 6. In lower secondary the rates were: 11 percent in Grade 7, 14 percent in Grade 8, 17 percent in Grade 9, and 20 percent in Grade 10.

Except for the terminal year of each level or cycle, promotions are decided based on internal assessment. Students take an examination in all subjects three times a year at the end of each term. While the difficult learning conditions (large classes and limited teaching materials among others) can explain such high repetition rates in the early grades, those in later grades have a different origin: many students pass the internal examination but fail at the external examination controlling admission to secondary education; they then choose to repeat and give themselves a second chance.

As noted earlier, this examination is nationally organized and quite dramatic. In 1991–92, for example, 53.4 percent of pupils passed the internal examination with success but only 8.5 percent passed the external exam. The success rate, however, is not a measure of students' mastery of primary education programs, but has everything to do with available capacity in secondary schools.

In secondary education, students are required to achieve 50 percent of maximum marks in all subjects in order to pass a class. In higher education, only one end-of-year examination is organized in which a 50 percent mark is generally required; two sessions are organized each year in such a way that students may retake in September the subjects they failed in June. Success rates are usually very low especially in the earlier years. By putting conditions before awarding fellowships to repeating students, the system means to pressure students against too much repetition.

9. Educational Assessment, Evaluation, and Research

With the technical and financial assistance of the French government, an assessment of primary education performance was conducted in 1989–90. Besides, the three pedagogical offices within the Ministry for Education monitor students' progress in the framework of their curriculum development activities. They also follow up with teachers' work in the course of the inservice training and classroom observations.

As far as quantitative data about the education system is concerned, the educational planning unit has been publishing such data annually since 1964. A school census is conducted every year in November in all schools, public as well as private, primary as well as secondary and tertiary. Then the forms are processed and indicators are calculated: enrollment ratios, age distribution, internal efficiency, teachers' qualification, and many other basic data. Some educational research is also done by the University of Burundi, particularly from the faculty of psychology and educational sciences. Many of the theses by graduating students in that faculty deal with various aspects of the education system and help understand it better.

10. Major Reforms in the 1980s and 1990s

One of the most important innovations that were implemented in the 1980s is the introduction and generalization of the double shifting system in primary education. By allowing every available classroom and classroom teacher to serve two classes of pupils instead of one, the innovation took the system one major step forward toward universal primary education. Primary school enrollment was raised from 260,253 in 1983 to 633,203 in 1991. True, the problem of declining demand remains to be addressed, as is that of deteriorating school quality.

Another noted innovation is the introduction of national testing at the end of each of the three major cycles: primary, lower secondary, and upper secondary. While the national examination at the end of primary has been in place for close to 30 years, the other two are recent measures. By allowing for an objective assessment of all students on an identical scale, these tests can be effectively used for quality enhancement.

Lastly, at the beginning of the 1990s, a move was started toward increasing access to secondary education by strongly encouraging communes to set up their own schools, the *collèges communaux*. That is a step down from an elitist view of secondary education to a simpler, more popular, and less selective type of school.

11. Major Problems for the Year 2000

In spite of all the efforts that have been made and of the impressive increase in school participation in the 1980s, the most important problem remains that of the exclusion of many children and adults from any educational opportunity. It is alarming that under conditions of economic hardship, even the advances made in the 1980s have started to be undone in the 1990s. Understanding this phenomenon better and indentifying its root causes remains a major challenge. This leads to enquiring into the factors influencing relevance of and demand for education in the rural areas.

The second major problem is the deteriorating school quality at all levels. The root cause of this situation is the extremely low level of educational spending (US$31 in 1985); unfortunately, there is little that can be done to solve the problem without finding ways to increase resources. The shifting of part of the burden to local governments and to the families has already been tried and can be unfavorable to the prospect of Education For All.

Another major difficulty lies in attracting and keeping a highly motivated and qualified teaching staff. The source of this problem is in the deterioration of teachers' salaries and the loss of purchasing power, this being the consequence of the more general economic problems. While it alleviated significantly the problems about participation in the educational system, the double shifting system has had a negative impact over the already unsatisfactory teachers' working conditions.

References

Bureau de la planification de l'éducation 1992 *Statistiques scolaires Annuaire 1991–1992*. Bureau de la planification de l'éducation, Bujumbura

Conseil Economique et Social 1990 *Synthèse du rapport— Etude et analyse des problèmes de développement*. Conseil Economique et Social, Bujumbura

Ministère du Plan 1992 *Vme Plan de développement économique et social, 1988–92*. Ministère du Plan, Bujumbura

Rwehera M 1991 L'état de l'éducation dans les pays les Moins Avancés. In UNESCO *Documents et Rapports sur Politiques Educatives*, No. 2. UNESCO, Paris

UNESCO 1992 *Statistical Yearbook 1992*. UNESCO, Paris

World Bank 1992 *World Development Report 1992*. World Bank, Washington, DC

Further Reading

Chrétien J P 1979 La société du Burundi: des mythes aux réalités. *Revue Française d'études politiques africaines* 14: 163–64

Greenland T 1984 The reform of education in Burundi: Enlightened theory faced with political reality. *Comp. Educ.* 10(1)

Ministère de l'Education 1992 *Rapport à la Conférence Internationale de l'éducation Genève 1992*. Ministère de l'Education, Bujumbura

Mworoha E (ed.) 1987 *Histoire du Burundi—Des origines à la fin du 19me siècle*. Hatier, Paris

Ndimurukundo N 1983–84 Une expérience originale d'éducation non formelle au Burundi: Les écoles Yagamukama. *Cahiers de Pédagogie africaine* 4–5

Cambodia

R. Lambin

1. General Background

Cambodia is situated between Thailand to the west and northwest, Laos to the north, and Vietnam to the south and east. The Gulf of Siam is to the southwest. It is divided into 18 regions and covers an area of 181,035 square kilometers. The central plain is the most densely populated area. Most of the population is of Khmer origin, and constitutes an important part of the Mon-Khmer linguistic group of people. There are a number of minority peoples, with Lao and Thai in the north and west and Vietnamese in the west. There are a few tribal people of Malayo-Polynesian origin in mountainous regions. The population was estimated to be 8.5 million in 1991 and the growth rate is believed to be about 3 percent per year. There has been no census since 1962. About 40 percent of the total population is aged under 14 years. Most of the population is Buddhist.

Between the ninth and the fourteenth centuries, the Angkhor civilization flourished. The kings organized a system of irrigation, cultivated the plains of the south, and developed a rich literacy culture. The Khmer kingdom based in Angkhor Wat was conquered by the Thais in 1431, but an independent Khmer kingdom based in Phnom Penh survived until the country became a French protectorate in 1863. In 1949, Cambodia regained its independence but remained associated with France. It obtained complete freedom in 1953 and left the French Union in 1955. In 1970, the monarchy was abolished and the Khmer Republic was proclaimed. The King, Norodom Sihanouk, formed a government in exile in Beijing. In 1975, a group known as the Khmer Rouge, supported by China, took control of the country. Initially with the support of Norodom Sihanouk, the Khmer Rouge formed a government which abandoned many aspects of modern life. All kinds of institutions such as schools and hospitals were destroyed and urban populations were forced to move to rural areas. From 1975 to early 1979, much of the population left the country, many to live in refugees camps, especially in Thailand. During the same period, many people died through direct Khmer Rouge action or through starvation. When a new government was established in Phnom Penh in early 1979 with military and political support from Vietnam, the population of Cambodia had fallen by at least 2 million. A high percentage of the educated people of the country were no longer available to assist in the recovery of society and the economy.

Since 1991, the United Nations has attempted to negotiate a resolution of the political difficulties. At one stage, the Khmer Rouge, the Vietnam-supported government group, Norodom Sihanouk's supporters, and the political groups that held power from 1970 to 1975 seemed to have reached an agreement. In 1993 an election was held, supervised by international monitors. The Khmer Rouge did not take part and attempted to prevent the election from taking place. From 1991 onward, a great deal of international support has been made available to help the Cambodian people recover from their difficult past.

The country is relatively dry in the north and very humid in the southeast. Drainage is necessary in the south and water reservoirs essential. The central plain is watered by the Mekong River and its tributary, the Thonle Sap. The capital, Phnom Penh, is at the confluence of the Mekong and the Thonle Sap. Before the devastation of the countryside, agriculture was the major economic provider, with products including rice, corn, cotton, tobacco, and rubber. The large forests were exploited for wood and spices. Fishery and cattle breeding were developed intensively. However, the uncontrolled exploitation of the soil and forests led to an impoverishment of the soil, a drastic diminution of water reserves, and a decrease in wildlife. The infrastructure, too, was largely destroyed. In 1993, it was estimate that agriculture provided 52 percent, industry 17 percent, and other sectors 31 percent, of the gross domestic product (GDP).

The economic state of the country has had a direct impact on the planning of education, mostly because parents tend to employ children in the fields or for home tasks rather than sending them to school. This is especially true for girls. Even though efforts have been made toward the compulsory education of adults, many of them drop out of their courses. Furthermore, many teachers were killed in the war and new teachers had to undertake their jobs with almost no training. In 1991, even though teacher quality had been improved, there were many teachers who remained poorly educated. The educational personnel responsible for curriculum development and educational planning were in the same position.

2. Politics and the Goals of the Education System

After having followed a path influenced by the French colonial system and comparable to that of its neighboring countries in the 1960s, the Cambodian educational system was entirely dismantled between 1974 and 1979. All educational institutions were closed or used for other purposes and the educational personnel were eliminated. Between 1975 and 1979 about two million people were killed and over half a million fled or were deported, among them many

Table 1
Enrollments at different levels of education 1979–91[a]

	1979–80	1985–86	1989–90	1990–91
Preschool education	8,229	56,165	56,017	49,277
Primary education	947,317	1,315,531	1,342,942	1,329,573
Lower-secondary education	4,803	297,775	244,842	201,496
Upper-secondary education	281	14,020	—	47,472
Higher education	702	2,213	—	6,640
Adult education	70,459	246,341	—	79,787
Secondary vocational, technical, and training education	378	2,859	—	11,234
Total	969,169	1,934,804	1,643,801	1,725,498

a Ministry of Education 1979–80 to 1990

skilled and educated workers. Although reliable statistics are not available, it is officially estimated that 75 percent of teachers, about 67 percent of primary and secondary level students, and almost 80 percent of students in higher education were killed or fled. Human resources were therefore badly lacking when the new government decided to rebuild the country and its system of education. Despite the situation of complete desolation, the new government of 1979 put a great deal of effort into the reconstruction of the education system to meet immediate priorities. It placed emphasis on a quantitative rather than qualitative expansion of the system. The government dramatically increased school enrollments, introduced systematic Khmerization at all levels, and significantly raised the literacy level of the total population. When the schools reopened, enrollment reached 900,000 students, ranging from those who had interrupted their education during the war to first-year primary students. Because the war had frozen instruction for a period of time, many children were older than normal when they restarted study. Population growth created a demand for an even more rapid expansion of the system.

In the 1990s, the main priority is to ensure that all persons have access to education and that full enrollment at the primary level be attained by 1995. The inefficiency of primary education and the urgent need for its improvement are of high concern to the Ministry of Education. The major aims are to provide basic skills in reading, writing, and mathematics from first to fifth grades.

The Khmer language has been adopted as the language of instruction in the whole country but there are difficulties because of a lack of material written in Khmer and problems in standardizing special terminology at the tertiary level. Priority is being given to the improvement of the quality of education through adapted and relevant curricula; provision of new school buildings, educational material, and textbooks; better teacher training; and an orientation toward making a clear connection between education and

work. Solutions to high dropout rates and uncontrolled repetition are well-known to be linked to the potential improvement of the quality of education.

To improve the quality of teaching, the government is attempting to develop higher education to provide training for educational personnel. The Inter-Ministerial Commission plans a restructuring of the system by decentralizing more power to the regions for the control of higher education facilities. The plan emphasizes the qualitative improvement of the staff rather than its growth. However, the withdrawal of many experts from the communist eastern countries after the fall of communism in Eastern Europe left Cambodia with a great shortage of personnel. Urgent replacement, especially in the technological sectors, is required.

The 1980s were spent rebuilding the system of education to its 1969–70 level. In the 1990s, new goals concerning education and work are emerging, with the government attempting to overcome the consequences of the country's former political and economic isolation and to open its system of education to the world by adapting education to the new country's technological needs and international exchanges. Policymakers are directing their efforts to establishing a strong link between education and the new economic demands by placing more emphasis on the teaching of business and language studies. They are also trying to restore a national identity through education, promoting the ancient culture. The government restored the status of Buddhism as a state religion and authorized the traditional religious institutions, such as the monasteries, to regain their place in society.

3. The Formal System of Education

The formal education system is of the 5+3+3 pattern. In 1991, "basic education," though not compulsory, was considered to cover primary school and was expected to be extended to Grade 8 by 1995. Schooling is

162

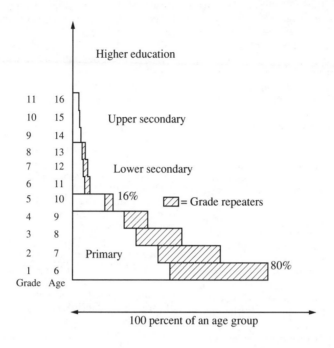

Figure 1
Structure of the Cambodian System

coeducational. About one-fifth of the population (1.7 million) is enrolled in educational programs. Table 1 shows the increases in enrollment between 1979 and 1991. It can be seen that the enrollment rate decreased somewhat at the end of the 1980s, especially at the preprimary, primary, and lower-secondary levels. This drop in enrollments may have several causes:

(a) the reopening of the closed schools which attracted many over-aged children and hence increased the numbers artificially has been followed by a return to a more normal situation;

(b) economic reasons, with a growing need to use children's labor as a result of the agrarian reform;

(c) growing distrust of education owing to the lack of qualitative improvement in teaching and school supplies, and to the irrelevance of the programs to their sociocultural and economic environment.

3.1 Primary, Secondary, and Tertiary Education

Figure 1 shows the distribution of students in primary, secondary, and tertiary education. The official age of enrollment in primary education is 6 years, but exceptions are made to ensure maximum access to schools. In 1991, the Ministry of Education estimated that 80 percent of children aged between 6 and 10 were enrolled in primary school. Of these, about 85 percent were enrolled in cities and only about 15 percent in the poorer rural areas.

Primary education represents five years of schooling (from 1979 to 1986, it consisted of four grades only). One-third of the total primary school age population are enrolled in Grade 1, but Grade 5 only contains about 10 percent of the children. Only about 20 percent of Grade 1 students reach Grade 5. This phenomenon is due mainly to grade repetition and dropout. Grade repetition can amount to more than 50 percent of first-grade students and this decreases gradually to about 20 percent of the fifth-grade students. There are classes with many over-age repeaters and, in some cases, this does not allow normal age students to enter school. Dropouts range from 10 to 25 percent in Grade 1 and are below 10 percent in the other grades. Thus, it can take an average of ten years for a student to complete primary school instead of the normal five years.

The geographical distribution of primary schools is uneven; there is a shortage of primary facilities in the mountainous regions and among the minority ethnic groups. Primary schools in rural areas are often small, with only two or three classes. Schools in cities are

overcrowded and often function in double shifts, while
normal schooling typically offers 50-minute lessons
between 7 and 11 a.m. The student–teacher ratio was
about 35:1 in 1987–88 and 40:1 in 1990–91 in primary
schools. However, in all grades, there is considerable
variation from province to province with a range of
about 100:1 to 40:1. Despite these difficulties, a minimum basic capacity has been created and can be used
as a starting point to expand the system and achieve
primary education for all children.

Primary education is followed by three years
(Grades 6 to 8) of a lower first cycle of secondary
education (*collège*), followed by another three years
(Grades 9 to 11) of a higher cycle of secondary education (*lycée*). In 1986–87, lower-secondary education
had an enrollment of 327,049 students in 304 schools.
By 1990–91, the number of schools had grown to 397
but enrollment had dropped by more than one-third to
201,496. This fall in enrollment was due to the dropout
in Grade 5 at the primary level. Enrollment in upper-
secondary education increased considerably between
1986 and 1990 from 18,799 students in 36 schools to
47,472 students in 66 schools. The transition between
lower- and upper-secondary education was 10 percent
in 1986 and 23 percent in 1990. In 1991, the distribution of upper-secondary schools was quite even
across the country: all of the 21 provinces except two
had at least one upper-secondary school. However, the
eastern provinces and the minority ethnic groups had
fewer schools and lower enrollment.

The secondary school curriculum has not been revised since 1979 because of a lack of supervision and
material. The time spent on instruction varies, ranging
from 27 to 33 hours per week, with most time being
spent on the teaching of mathematics, sciences, and
mother tongue. There is no teaching of subjects such
as music and art.

Higher education is the area which suffered the most
from the wars. Of 1,000 university academics and
faculty members, only 87 survived. In 1991, Cambodia
had seven establishments of higher education, run by
different ministries and offering a variety of programs.

The Ministry of Education is responsible for:

(a) the University of Phnom Penh, reopened in 1988
and offering training in social and natural sciences
(in 1991, it enrolled 2,327 students);

(b) the Institute of Advanced Technology, reopened
in 1981, and in 1991 enrolling 766 students;

(c) the Economic Science Institute, opened in 1984
and offering training in agriculture, business, and
economy (in 1991, it enrolled 987 students);

(d) l'Ecole Supérieure des Cadres de Gestion de
l'Education, opened in 1982 and offering short-
term inservice courses and long-term training
for school managers (in 1991, it enrolled 37
students).

The Ministry of Health is responsible for the Institute of Medical Science, enrolling 1,518 students
in 1991. The Ministry of Agriculture is responsible
for the Institute of Agricultural Sciences, enrolling
588 students. Finally, the Ministry of Information and
Culture is responsible for the University of Fine Arts,
enrolling 417 students.

In 1991, 6,640 students were enrolled in higher
education, of whom 15 percent were women.

3.2 Preschool Education

Preschool education, despite its growing recognition by the educational authorities, has traditionally
enrolled less than 9 percent of children between 3 to 6
years of age. Its growth, however, has been spectacular: between 1979 and 1988 enrollment increased more
than sevenfold from 8,229 to 61,349; the number of
kindergartens rose from 96 to 679, and the preschool
personnel from 267 to 3,209. In the period 1988–90, the
number of preschools decreased to 477 and enrollment
fell to 49,277. The reasons for this sudden decrease
have not yet been clarified but it is assumed that it
was due to rising costs and the uneven distribution
of preschool facilities, which are mostly found in
city areas.

Three types of preschool exist: state-run institutions,
former solidarity groups' institutions supported by
local authorities and factories, and private institutions
(two in Phnom Penh). They usually provide a light
breakfast with rice and other food donated by parents.
Their role is to prepare children for primary education
and to contribute to their development. The authorities
encourage mainly 5-year olds to enter preprimary education. They also encourage private initiative in order
to limit the government's expenses in maintaining the
system.

3.3 Special Education

The educational system in Cambodia is not yet strong
enough to provide adequate special education for
handicapped children.

3.4 Vocational, Technical, and Business Education

In 1979, the new government of Cambodia restored the
tertiary-level and the technical training institutions to
operational status with help of other socialist countries.
In 1991, in addition to the Ministry of Education, the
ministries of health, agriculture, and postal services
and telecommunications shared the responsibility for
and the supervision of vocational education. They
offered training in vocational primary-level training
schools, in specialized secondary schools, and in
transition schools between the primary and secondary
levels. Other institutions offering short-term training
for technical workers were also operating to meet
immediate needs. These were often situated in the
workplace.

Although the complete withdrawal of help from the ex-communist countries of the Eastern Bloc in the 1980s left Cambodian vocational education in a state of desolation, nonetheless there were around 30 vocational schools with various training objectives still operating. The main institutions are:

(a)   the school for training hospital personnel, opened in 1980, which offers training for hospital attendants, nurses, midwives, and laboratory technicians at primary and secondary levels with an enrollment of over 1,000 students in 1991;

(b)   the Soviet Frienship Higher Technical Institute, which opened in 1981, consisting of six faculties (construction, electronics, agriculture, hydraulics, mines and geology, and industrial chemistry), and with an enrollment of over 1,000 students in 1991;

(c)   the Chamcar Daung Agronomic Institute, which opened in 1985 with four faculties (agricultural sciences, veterinary sciences, agriculture mechanization, and fishery) and with an enrollment of over 5,000 students in 1991.

One institution in Cambodia offers business education and is run by the Ministry of Education. The Economic Science Institute, opened in 1984, offers training in agriculture, business, and economy, and enrolled 987 students in 1991. The Ministry of Planning's socioeconomic plan up to the year 2005 has among its objectives that of improving greatly the training of scientific, technical, and business personnel to meet the new economic situation.

One of the features of Phnom Penh in the 1990s is the proliferation of privately run commercial schools, usually associated with English language schools. In this they are following the trend seen in such places as Bangkok and Jakarta. These are often an unrecognized attempt to supply clerical workers for the many offices established in Asian capitals that use English as a working language.

3.5 Adult and Nonformal Education

In 1979, the new government of Cambodia developed adult education and organized literacy courses in the country to raise the literacy level at least to the level existing before 1975. The government therefore ran widespread campaigns for literacy and complementary instruction for adults (after their working day) in special complementary schools, semiregular schools, and normal classrooms used for adults after regular school. Literacy campaigns have been run by the government on a regular basis since 1981.

In the early 1980s, complementary education involved adults and young people attending classes on a regular basis in full-time primary education. In

1984, part-time and evening programs were set up and expanded. Complementary education has three levels: (a) three grades roughly equivalent to formal primary education Grades 2 to 4; (b) the equivalent of Grades 5 to 7; (c) the equivalent of Grades 8 to 11. Complementary education has 19 schools at the Province level, 140 nonformal institutions which are open after working hours, and 46 part-time schools functioning for four hours per day.

The government's goals for adult and nonformal education are to educate all state employees up to the secondary level, provide all adults (from 13 to 45 years of age) with a minimum of literacy skills, and provide minimal training to untrained adults. Each village or community chief must send 15–45-year olds identified as illiterate for complementary education. However, the general dropout rate for both literacy and training courses is very high.

Table 2 presents the enrollment figures for complementary education. It can be noted that the reform of 1984 which expanded the programs managed to stop the drop in enrollments observed in 1983.

4. Administrative and Supervisory Structure and Operation

The central administrative body of the educational system is the Ministry of Education, which acts on the policy decisions taken by the Council of Ministers. It sets pedagogical and management guidelines; ensures regular inspection of schools; develops and revises the curriculum; produces textbooks and distributes them to all educational institutions; provides supplies and equipment to all schools; and ensures the running of its higher education, technical, experimental, and professional institutions. The Minister of Education is assisted by three vice-ministers. The Ministry has 11 departments or administrative units employing 537 staff members. The 12 Ministry institutions employed 1,028 staff members in 1991.

A relatively large part of the responsibility for the financing and administration of education is given to the nineteen provincial and two municipal education offices as well as to district education offices. These institutions fall into three categories according to the size of the population for which they are responsible. They operate on a model similar to that of the Ministry: they are in charge of making the Ministry policy guidelines available to their schools; organizing complementary education and literacy classes; supervising schools and collecting school data; planning the educational system, including its facilities; supervising the distribution and use of school materials; providing preservice and inservice training for primary school teachers; and recruiting personnel. However, because of their large degree of autonomy, the provinces also lack coordination among each other and the help of an efficient network for planning. This lack of a

Table 2
Enrollments in complementary education (1980–91)

	1980	1982	1983	1985	1988	1991
Enrollments	70,459	241,678	2,642	246,341	214,118	79,787

common management of the system has resulted in a weakening of the administrative relations between the Ministry and the provinces. Inevitably, there have been administrative delays.

There are 146 district level offices, 17 provincial center level offices and six arrondissement-level offices. These offices are responsible for implementing educational policies and encouraging the local community to participate fully in the process of education and school maintenance and the provision of facilities. They work on integrating schools in their societal context, supervising the implementation of the syllabus for both formal and nonformal education, constructing new schools, and providing school maintenance and furniture. There are usually two or three staff members in the offices per 100 teachers.

The administrative staff members are, in general, not well-qualified in the field of education. This situation leads to serious problems in the management of the system. Because of the immediate needs created by the reconstruction of the country, most educational staff members have taken only short-term training courses for teachers. The increasingly complex development of the educational system in Cambodia in the 1990s requires better qualified personnel. Existing staff cannot, despite their good will and strong discipline, entirely fulfil the difficult tasks of consolidating the qualitative improvement of the whole educational system and of monitoring international assistance. The system also requires a better organized and larger unit of inspectors that should be provided with clear goals.

5. Educational Finance

In 1991, almost 8 percent of the national budget was spent on education. However, this percentage does not take into account the participation of the local communities in the financing of education. In 1991, the Ministry of Education spent 19.4 percent of its budget on personnel, 24.9 percent on administration and material, 37.8 percent on construction and equipment, 14.5 percent on student aid, and 3.4 percent on other expenses. The amount spent on personnel is small given the poorly trained nature of educational workers. Before 1982, teachers were paid with rice because

currency did not then exist. Since the re-establishment of the Riel (the unit of currency), teachers are paid in both currency and rice. Teachers often have other occupations with which to supplement their incomes. About three fourths of the public education budget is allocated to primary education. The Ministry is reimbursed by the provinces for the cost of textbooks but the amount of money given back to the Ministry is difficult to estimate.

The provinces and local authorities enjoy great financial autonomy: they control resource allocation and use, and cover a large part of recurrent expenditure and most school building expenses, except for the cost of imported material such as iron or concrete that is covered by the Ministry of Finance. Many schools have been built since 1979 with parents providing the labor. This ministry also finances the construction of school buildings in areas classified as "in difficulty." This decentralized structure leads to dynamic initiatives but, at the same time, to inequality between the provinces. The upper-secondary schools (except for one that is administered directly by the Ministry of Education) are controlled and financed by the provinces. It is still difficult to know exactly the real amount of education expenditure because of the existence of separate budgets allocated to the Ministry of Education, and the provincial and district education offices.

As mentioned above, there is a great need for a well-organized network of structures linking the Ministry and the provinces. The goal would be both to maintain national unity and keep the local initiative active in sharing the educational expenditure intelligently. The financial system is complex because of the lack of coordination between cooperation, assistance, and foreign aid institutions as well as the large number of other resources. The Department of Planning and Finance at the Ministry of Education also lacks trained personnel to undertake the tasks of reorganizing the educational financial system and setting up an effective monitoring plan.

6. Supplying Personnel for the Education System

Starting from virtually no teachers, the new government in 1979 hired more or less anybody who could

Table 3
Number of trained teachers at different levels of education in 1991

	Preprimary	Primary	Lower-secondary	Upper-secondary
Number of teachers	3,399	44,140	15,689	1,877
Number of trained teachers	423 (8+1 years)	12,404 (8+1 years) 499 (short period of training)	8,821 (8+3 years)	1,439 (11+3 years)

read and write. Only a few received short training courses, varying from three to six weeks in duration, given the urgency for reopening schools that had been closed during the war period. The most qualified teachers had been trained in schools for boys run before 1975 by Buddhist temples known as *Wats* and had followed a short inservice training at one of the teacher-training colleges created in 1979. By 1983, there were 33,000 teachers in Cambodia ranging from those with very little training to those with university training. The process of training was accelerated through 29 pedagogical schools in the provinces and its duration was extended over the years. By 1983, it was possible to demand eight years of general education training plus one year of pedagogical training to become a qualified teacher. In 1991, however, when 65,000 teachers were employed, there was still a severe shortage of trained teachers especially in foreign languages. This was due to Cambodia's isolation in the 1970s and 1980s.

Preprimary teachers are recruited through competition, usually after having completed their lower-secondary education in secondary school courses for preschool personnel. Their training is provided by pedagogical centers in Phnom Penh, Kampong-Cham, Battambang, and Kandal. Primary school teachers must follow the 8+1 years pattern and attend pedagogical schools and retraining establishments. Lower-secondary teachers are trained in regional training centers for pedagogy on a 8+3 years basis and higher-secondary teachers in teacher-training colleges and higher management schools on an 11+3 years basis. The University of Phnom Penh supervises the higher-secondary education teacher training and undertakes the training of teacher educators. In 1991, emphasis was put on the quality of teaching rather than the quantity for the first time. Table 3 presents the number of trained and, by implication, untrained teachers in the system in 1991.

Higher education faces a severe problem concerning the qualification of its personnel: the total teaching staff amounts to 180 professors of whom only 7 hold a PhD and about 20 more who are studying abroad. Foreign faculty members are badly needed, mostly in the fields of foreign languages and studies of other countries. The government tries to attract students by providing free scholarships and financial assistance.

7. Curriculum Development and Teaching Methodology

The Ministry of Education is responsible for the development and revisions of the curriculum. It is responsible for the writing, printing, and distribution of textbooks. A special committee is in charge of revising the curriculum and is composed of staff members of the Publication Department of the Ministry and school teachers. They meet irregularly. The teachers identify topics which are then covered in the textbooks written by the Publication Department staff members. The almost complete absence of critical steps which should always be undertaken in curriculum development leads to the omission of the definition of expected learning outcomes and their evaluation, the sequencing of learning, and the inclusion of new activities which could contribute to the improvement of learning.

The curriculum in 1991 had only been slightly revised since 1979 because of the lack of qualified people able to write and produce textbooks. The first curriculum for all levels was developed in 1970–80 by a few surviving teachers and university students who used both their own memory and old French textbooks as a basis for their work. A revision of the curriculum was initiated in 1985 with the help of more foreign examples and this revision had reached Grade 3 in science and mathematics by 1991. The revision process is very slow.

Instructional time varies from school to school but amounts to about 20 hours per week at the lower level and ranges from 27 to 33 hours at the upper-secondary level. The curriculum emphasizes, at all levels, the teaching of mathematics, sciences, and the mother tongue. The subjects covered at the primary and secondary levels are Khmer language, mathematics and sciences, history, geography, and moral education. The sciences are taught as general science at the primary level and are separated into physics, chemistry, and biology at the secondary level. At the secondary level, even more time is spent on the teaching of mathematics, sciences, and the mother tongue.

The implementation of the curriculum in schools is far from systematic: the lack of supervision and pedagogical material such as textbooks leads to a large variation between schools in terms of both the content of instruction and the time spent on each discipline. In upper-secondary schools, for instance, the teaching of the national language varies from four to six hours per week, the teaching of sciences from 12 hours to 17 hours, and that of history and geography from three to five hours per week.

There are still problems with instruction. In the 1990s, primary school students, with no textbooks provided, usually repeat together or individually what the teacher says and copy what the teacher writes on small pads of paper. Rote learning was the only method of instruction usually in the former *Wat* schools, and hence teachers were trained in that way. Even the scientific disciplines are learned by ear without the use of practical exercises related to experience. Results of scientific research are presented as facts to be memorized. Teachers often hesitate to use outside school materials to improve their lessons because they themselves have had no other training than the passive method of copying and memorizing what the teachers write. Extremely few active learning activities are provided at school with the exception of answering questions about what was learned. Methodologies for inducing thinking, the framing of inductive questions, the questioning of assumptions, problem-solving, the understanding of principles, making generalizations, or recognizing patterns are not used. Textbooks are produced without being linked to concrete learning situations and are isolated from what students learn in the classroom. In these circumstances, it is difficult for teachers to improve their teaching.

8. The System of Examinations, Promotions, and Certifications

Teachers make regular assessments of their students' achievement and grade repetition is high in general, although it is decreasing somewhat in secondary schools. At the end of each level of education, students must take examinations: at the end of primary school, they take the Certificate of Primary Education; at the end of the lower first cycle of secondary education, they take the Diploma of Lower Secondary Education; and, at the end of upper-secondary education, they take the Diploma of Upper Secondary Education (*Baccalauréat*) which can lead to university entrance.

9. Educational Assessment, Evaluation, and Research

Partly because of the decentralization of the Cambodian system of education and partly because of the lack of essential resources, it has been difficult to develop an efficient national assessment system (UNESCO 1991). No adequate measures and no valid data on the quality of the educational system are available and decision-making is rarely based on research. This negatively affects both the quality and the cost-effectiveness of the whole system of education. The Ministry of Education has a poorly run and inefficient research unit which has not yet provided valid and reliable data for planning and decision-making. The Department of Planning and Finance of the Ministry is in charge of the provision of the necessary information for educational planning but does not have the means to do this efficiently. The Department of Primary Education undertakes some educational research. The provincial education offices are asked to collect education statistics for the Ministry of Education but the staff is not yet adequately trained and suffers from the lack of resources for collecting reliable data.

Some universities undertake educational research. However, the improvement of the educational system as a whole also implies an assessment of the existing structures. Activities such as educational research could be centered in one institution, thus avoiding duplication of work. In 1991, a UNESCO mission's study (UNESCO 1991) encouraged the government to conduct its own research and to link it closely to planning.

10. Major Reforms in the 1980s and 1990s

In 1979, the whole system of education had to be re-established from scratch and literacy campaigns launched. The complete rebuilding of the system cannot be called a reform, because everything had to be done *ex nihilo*. The major intensive effort made by the government from 1979 onward was to build up an extended primary education system.

The first literacy campaign started in June 1980, for more than one million illiterate people and, in the first three years, more than 500,000 people were trained. The second campaign was conducted in the period 1984–86 and trained more than 400,000 people. Despite this admirable achievement, each year produced new illiterates because of the poor educational system, the lack of materials, and school dropouts after Grades 1 and 2. In 1990, about 98,000 new illiterates were registered by the government. If the staff of the Central Department for Adult Literacy from the Ministry of Education is not increased in number (it comprises 22 people), if new textbooks are not provided, and if primary education does not become compulsory, the level of literacy is likely to stagnate or to decrease (UNESCO 1991).

In the early 1980s, complementary education involved adults and young people attending classes on a regular basis in full-time primary education, but a drastic drop in enrollments was observed in 1983. In 1984, a major reform of the system was undertaken by the government: it had positive effects and managed to stop the drop in enrollments. The reform consisted of setting up part-time and evening programs and expanding them all over the country. In 1985, the government initiated a complete revision of the curriculum including ideas from abroad, such as an increase in the number of exercises, games, and diagrams in the textbooks, and the shortening of chapters and their contents to make the requirements easier for children to complete in a school year. The reform has continued and the revision reached Grade 3 in science and mathematics in 1991. In 1985, another major reform took place: the first cycle was extended from 4 to 5 years and the age of enrollment in Grade 1 was stabilized at 6 years.

11. Major Problems for the Year 2000

Those children entering school at age 6 numbered about 250,000 in 1990. It is hoped to increase this number to 270,000 in 1995 and to 300,000 in the year 2000. However, the fall in enrollments mentioned in Sect. 3 is alarming because the population growth rate is increasing rapidly. This raises the question of whether the goals of the government toward a full enrollment of 6–14-year olds can be met. The lack of reliable data is also an impediment to this problem being solved. To face this problem, the education system will first have to find the causes of the drop in enrollments and to adapt itself to the new economic and social situation of the country. The government will have to develop new policies and plans, revise the curriculum accordingly, provide better trained teachers, and improve access to school facilities and textbooks.

The decreasing number of girls enrolled at all levels is also very problematic: if enrollment in first grade of primary school is more or less even between boys and girls, then the percentage of girls later decreases drastically to only 10 percent enrollment in Grade 5. In 1985–86 girls represented 45.7 percent of all students in primary schools, but by 1989 this percentage had fallen to 43.4 percent. In 1986–87 girls accounted for 37.5 percent in lower-secondary schools, 35 percent in 1987–88, and 31.8 percent in 1988–89. In 1985–86 girls represented 25.3 percent in upper-secondary schools and this percentage dropped to 22 percent in 1988–89. This problem is due to the tradition of keeping girls out of school and to socioeconomic conditions which require girls, often as young as 8 years old, to stay at home and look after younger children. Urgent measures will need to be taken to reverse this trend.

Despite the several literacy campaigns organized between 1981 and 1988, in 1991 it was estimated that the total adult illiterate population had increased by more than 500,000 since 1979 and this was due to the high number of school dropouts. The Ministry of Education estimated, in 1991, that only 80 percent of 6–10-year olds were enrolled in primary school: a priority will be to make primary education accessible to all children. Measures will need to be taken urgently to prevent a further increase in illiteracy. Access, retention, and quality will need to be improved at the primary school level and adult and complementary education should deal with the dropout children and youth. To be able to enroll all children of primary school age, it would require a minimum of 1.6 million primary school places: the school network must be reorganized and new places must be provided. Classes must also be filled with children of the appropriate age group.

The government needs the requirements for basic schooling to be fulfilled—provision of schools, teachers, and textbooks—to enhance compulsory education. Compulsory education is expected to last eight years by the year 2000, thus forming what the government considers "basic education." Compulsory education would then cover primary and lower-secondary education. To achieve this goal, the problem of repetition and dropout at the primary level must be solved by better means of retention. The high number of grade repeaters and dropouts is both a cause and a consequence of the low quality of education.

Another major problem is the training of qualified personnel (teachers, school principals, and administrative personnel) at all levels of education which is contributing to lowering the level of achievement. In 1991, higher education enrolled only 6,640 students and the capacity of higher education to produce enough qualified personnel to meet demand is inadequate. Quality improvement of teacher training will help to resolve some of the problems being experienced at the beginning of the 1990s.

The last, but nonetheless important, problem is the lack of materials and facilities like toilets and clean water, and school materials such as textbooks. The production and distribution of appropriate textbooks and other materials for each level of education, including preprimary education, is a great problem because without such materials even the acquisition of reading skills becomes difficult. Students need books both to learn what they are taught in class and to exercise their newly acquired skills. In 1991, not all teachers had a textbook and most students had no textbooks. The persistent absence of books for students has the immediate effect of discouraging them from studying. A higher production of books and other reading materials like newspapers and the creation of local and school libraries would accelerate the process of learning and reduce drop-out rates. These are the challenges for the end of the twentieth century.

Bibliography

Kampuchea Needs Assessment Study (for UNDP) 1989 (August)
Ministry of Education 1979–80 to 1990 *Bulletin de statistiques de l'éducation de l'Etat du Cambodge.* Ministry of Education, Phnom Penh

Ministry of Education 1989–90 *Bulletin of Education Statistics.* Ministry of Education, Phnom Penh
Provincial Statistical Reports 1990–91
UNESCO 1991 *United Nations Educational, Scientific, and*
Cultural Organization, Inter-Sectoral Basic Needs Assessment Mission to Cambodia. 15 January–8 February 1991. UNESCO, Bangkok

Cameroon

O. W. Yembe

1. General Background

The Republic of Cameroon lies in a triangular wedge between West and Central Africa. Its rugged terrain rises steeply from the Atlantic Ocean and flattens out towards Lake Chad, covering about 475,000 square kilometers. There are tropical rain forests in the south and Saharan desert in the north.

Cameroon is surrounded by English-speaking Nigeria to the west and French-speaking African countries to the north, east, and south. Cameroon's bilingual education policy, although imposed by history, enhances this geopolitical position.

Cameroon was formally created by European colonization which ended in 1960 and 1961 when the country achieved Independence. Since 1571, when Cameroon appeared in recorded world history, Portuguese, Spanish, Dutch, English, and French explorers and traders came to trade along the River Wouri where the waters abound in prawns (or *cameroes*—the Portuguese word from which Cameroon derives its name). By the late eighteenth century when the Slave Trade reached its peak, the English held supremacy. Pidgin English became the language of business and of communication among the multiethnic groups of the region. Pidgin English is not officially used for instruction in the schools, but remains the third language of mass communication after French and English.

From 1884 to 1914, Germany controlled the region and determined the general boundaries that define the present republic. After the First World War, the German State of Kamerun was divided between France and Britain through a League of Nations mandate. France was assigned three-fourths of the eastern and northern portion of the country and Britain the remaining western fourth. The British administered their portion as part of their neighboring Nigerian colony and set up schools in which pupils were taught in English. English became the language of literacy, creating a local elite which eventually took over political leadership from the largely illiterate traditional rulers. The French established schools which became the instrument for assimilating "natives" into the French culture. By 1946, when the United Nations designated these mandated territories as "trusteeships," the former German State of Kamerun had indeed become French Cameroon and British Cameroon, thanks to the schools!

Following Independence, the southern part of British Cameroon opted to reunite with the new Republic of Cameroon, while the northern part remained within the Federation of Nigeria. In 1961, the new constitution of the Federal Republic of Cameroon declared English and French to be the official languages. Since then, the development of French–English bilingualism has become the greatest hope for national unity, yet also one of the greatest problems in education.

In 1972, the governance structure was changed to that of a united republic, and, in 1984, to the Republic of Cameroon. However, the coexistence of two educational systems ensures that Cameroonians still see themselves as either Anglophones or Francophones.

The population of nearly 12 million in 1991 was 60 percent rural, 55 percent under 20 years of age, and 50 percent female. The annual birthrate is nearly 3 percent. The population increase is about 5.5 percent in urban areas and about 1.8 in rural areas. It reaches 20 percent in the larger towns where the concentration of schools makes them the greatest pools for rural exodus.

Cameroon has over 230 ethnolinguistic communities. Language is therefore a crucial problem in both sociopolitical life and schooling. Although pioneer religious missionaries established schools in local languages, they are no longer used as the medium of instruction in the schools. Most youngsters in Cameroon begin schooling in either English or French, although the school is not their first contact with these languages. While there are some experiments in mother-tongue teaching in schools, fear of ethnic conflict makes official policy shy away from encouraging the development of one local language into a national language.

Since the establishment of the German protectorate, the structure of the economy has undergone enormous transformation. Originally it was a subsistence agricultural economy but at the beginning of the 1990s there were also modern agropastoral enterprises, industries, and petroleum exploration. Plantation agriculture had a very great early influence on the sociocultural life of the people, especially in terms of introducing salaried jobs, integrating multiethnic groups and, in spreading the importance of literacy and schooling into the hinterlands. However, few private individuals engage in plantation farming; nor have plantations had an impact on modernizing farming methods. Agriculture remains dominated by small household farms on which over 70 percent of the population depends for subsistence. Small one-family farms are the major producers of coffee, cocoa, and cotton, which until the advent of the oil industry in 1975 were the mainstay of the country's export earnings. Cattle rearing by nomadic herdsmen is the mainstay of the economy of the northern grasslands. Here, too, traditional methods prevail although increasing conflict between farmers and graziers is forcing government agencies to intensify the education of farmers in modern methods.

Family farm incomes, especially in rural areas, have had an enormous influence on financing schooling, enabling children in rural areas to stay longer in school, obtain higher diplomas, earn salaries, and climb the social ladder. This background applies to every elite or political leader. Agriculture accounts for about 30 percent of the Gross Domestic Product (GDP). The secondary and tertiary sectors cover 27 and 42 percent respectively. Since 1975, when Cameroon's first refinery went into production, oil revenues have accounted for about 30 percent of the national budget, although their contribution to educational expenditure is hard to determine.

The active population aged 15 to 55 constitutes about 50 percent of the total population. Of these, over 70 percent are engaged in subsistence agriculture where most of the work is still done by women. In 1987, the number of salaried workers in the public and parapublic sectors was estimated at about 500,000. The literacy rate is about 60 percent which is one reason for the high number of unskilled workers. However, many school leavers still shy away from manual jobs, despite increasing unemployment.

Government social and economic development planning started in 1960, making 1986–91 the sixth quinquennial. Three major goals of these plans are: to modernize, diversify, and expand the economy by creating new industries and services; to increase the productive capacity of the people; and to double the per capita income at the end of each plan (it was US $40 in 1960).

Education is intended as the main instrument to achieve these goals. It aims to instill a modern outlook in place of retrogressive traditional beliefs, attitudes, and practices. More importantly, technical education seeks to impart the new skills needed by industries and services. Thus, investment in human resources gave great impetus to the expansion of secondary and university education in the 1960s and 1970s.

Since the late 1970s, however, school graduates at all levels have outnumbered the capacity of the socioeconomic system to provide jobs. In the early 1990s massive unemployment is placing in doubt the goals of development plans of the past 30 years.

The federal government structure adopted in 1961 brought together the French and English parts of Cameroon under a presidential system which was dissolved in 1972. This was a logical corollary to the creation of a one-party political system in 1966. The system of administration is, therefore, highly centralized with little initiative for local school authorities, especially in matters regarding the school curriculum. However, 1990 began a new era in which, as elsewhere in Africa, there appeared to be a total rejection of the centralized totalitarian one-party system of government. It is difficult to predict the course of the turbulence affecting the country at the beginning of the 1990s and disrupting the school system. Nevertheless, the demand is for decentralization and popular democracy. Hopefully, the present political leadership will yield to the winds of change so that future developments will see greater harmony between the socioeconomic, political, and educational systems.

The above contextual factors have resulted in great regional diversity in educational development. Since 1960 the major effort has been to attain regional equilibrium in primary school enrollment rates between the northern and southern parts of the country because the introduction and expansion of the Western system of education was from the coastal south northwards. The goal of achieving universal primary education by the year 2000 has already been attained in many of the southern parts of the country. The largely Muslim-influenced northern provinces attained only about 60 percent enrollment in the 1990s despite the enormous school building program. This was about 14 percent in 1961.

The population growth rate has defied all efforts to provide schooling at all levels for those seeking it. Since the 1960s there has been a continuous lack of harmony between the education and socioeconomic subsystems. While these ideas are well perceived by educational planners, the old model of schooling has proven, at all levels, quite resilient to reform. The search for a new model of schooling is the major task for future planning.

One of the effects of the present economic crisis has been the drastic reduction in actual state expenditure on education. Parents, private individuals, and organizations are getting more involved in financing both running and capital development costs of education at all levels. The consequences of this change are already perceptible. The Ministry of Education is loosening its monolithic grip on some policy areas such as the school curriculum. Local school authorities are now forcing the schools to teach new and useful knowledge, "beekeeping," for example. Hopefully the exigencies of Cameroon society in the twenty-first century will force the emergence of relevant forms of education.

2. Politics and the Goals of the Education System

From its inception about 150 years ago, the school in Cameroon has been conceived as an instrument for achieving political and social goals. Religious mission-

Table 1
Expansion of enrollment from 1965–66 to 1990–91

	1965–66	1970–71	1975–76	1980–81	1985–86	1990–91
Nursery education	—	—	—	41,000	—	91,000
Primary education	742,000	923,000	112,300	1,380,000	1,705,000	2,100,000
Secondary grammar	29,000	310,000	105,000	169,000	259,000	397,000
Secondary technical	—	17,400	31,000	56,000	83,000	128,000
Teacher training	—	—	—	2,100	4,000	—
University education	—	2,600	7,200	10,400	24,650	30,000

aries who were pioneers of the present school system directed schooling toward evangelization. Colonial powers were anxious to train auxiliaries for the administration and to educate the "native" in the ways of the Europeans. Nationalists who fought for independence saw education as the means to produce the labor force needed to replace foreigners and to develop the citizens of the new nation. Thus, schooling was geared to salaried jobs and the diploma was highly prized. In addition to these goals, the reunification of the former French and British Cameroons brought national unity and integration as major goals to be pursued, especially through English–French bilingualism.

The advent of a multiparty system is producing much rhetoric about educational reforms. There is, however, no major divergence from earlier conceptions of the role of the school in society. Popular expectation is still for school graduates to get jobs commensurate with their level of schooling. The school remains the instrument for upward social mobility. However, the general direction of future policy seems to be toward greater individual opportunities in a less centralized school system which will fit into a diversified economic system in which the private sector will employ more than the public sector. What is needed is a new concept of education which will fit into the current demand for "sustainable development."

3. The Formal System of Education

Figure 1 shows the structure of the formal English and French education systems. Key statistical information on enrollments and resources in the major educational sectors are provided in Table 1.

Education is not yet compulsory in Cameroon, although a government white paper of 1980 advocated free and compulsory primary school education by the year 2000. This may not be possible but with careful planning Cameroon should be able to afford free education for over 80 percent of children of primary school age.

In 1990 there were over 90,000 children receiving nursery school education. Tuition is free in all public nursery schools which, in 1990, constituted over 60 percent of this level of education for children aged 4 and 5. Nursery education is available either in a separate institution, or, more generally, in a section of a primary school. Only a very small proportion of the age group attends nursery schools although enrollments have been increasing. The demand is greatest especially in the urban areas and is stimulated by the ever-growing number of working mothers.

All nursery schools follow the same programs directed by a special section of the inspectorate division of the Ministry of National Education. This division is also responsible for the training and certification of kindergarten teachers, many of whom have been instructed in the Montessori Method. Nursery schools function for only part of the school day, usually in the

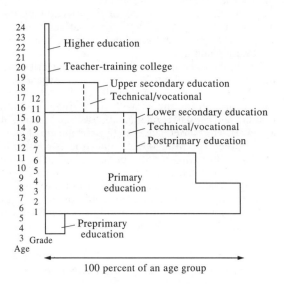

Figure 1
Cameroon: Structure of the formal education system

morning hours, between 8 a.m. and midday. The cost of education is much higher than in primary schools. Parents pay a subsidy in public nursery schools and must pay full fees in private schools.

3.1 Primary, Secondary, and Tertiary Education

Primary schooling begins officially at age 6, although many children begin at age 5. It lasts six years in Francophone schools and seven in Anglophone schools. In 1990 there were over 2.22 million primary school pupils of whom over 60 percent were enrolled in public schools. All primary schools are coeducational.

The primary school program in Cameroon is still organized by subjects distributed over 5 hours for each school day, 5 days a week, and about 35 weeks a year. The economic crisis which has hit Cameroon since 1985 has greatly affected the quality of primary school education, as can be judged from the diminishing number of trained teachers. Many classrooms are poorly equipped. Failure, grade-repeating, and dropout rates are high, often reaching over 40 percent for each cohort between the first and final years of primary school.

Language poses a major problem as the majority of school children begin learning to read and write in a foreign language. Schooling in the mother tongue is still in its experimental phase and even then concerns only about 5 of the 230 languages.

Primary schooling ends with the primary school leaving certificate examination and a competitive examination to enter secondary school. The national percentage passing the examination was over 40 percent in 1990, an improvement from the previous five years.

Two-year training courses after primary school are available in rural artisan training centers and home economics centers for primary school children who are too old for admission to secondary schools.

The development of secondary school education since 1960 has been phenomenal (see Table 1). However, less than 30 percent of primary school leavers can continue into this level of schooling, which begins at age 11 or 12 and lasts for 7 years. The number of girls is rapidly increasing and was over 40 percent in 1990.

The duration of the secondary school day is about 5.5 hours and schooling is divided into 3 terms totaling about 35 weeks per year.

Secondary school education still bears the imprint of the British and French systems. Attempts at harmonizing the two systems in order to create a national system have not succeeded largely for political reasons. However, both systems are dominated by the grammar type of general education school where the goals of instruction are the General Certificate of Education and the *baccalauréat*.

Stimulated by the lack of employment opportunities for secondary grammar school leavers the demand for secondary technical and vocational education was increasing at the end of the 1980s.

Expansion of public schools continues at a very rapid pace, while religious organizations have been reluctant to open new schools because of the difficulty of paying teachers' salaries. The number of private secondary schools established by private individuals increases every year as only about 30 percent of each primary school graduating cohort can be absorbed into existing secondary schools.

The introduction of bilingual schooling in which students receive instruction in both French and English is the most noteworthy curricular innovation since Independence. Modifications in subject matter content have kept abreast of changes introduced in the United Kingdom and France, especially through school textbooks supplied by publishers in those countries.

There was no university in the country in 1960. In 1979, four university centers were added to Cameroon's first university which were created in 1962. The number of universities was increased to six in 1993 when Cameroon's oldest university was split into two universities and the former four university centers were raised to the status of full universities. A free public higher education policy allows all successful candidates from secondary grammar schools to enter one of the three faculties of the University. Admission into the university centers and higher educational institutions is through competitive examinations. About 40,000 students were enrolled at this level in 1990. Over 35,000 were in the three faculties of Yaounde University. Higher education lasts from three to about seven years and prepares students for university degrees in the faculties and professional diplomas in professional higher educational institutions (French-type *grandes écoles*).

Language is one of the major problems in higher education, especially due to differences in the secondary school background of students who must follow lecturers in either French or English depending on the lecturer. Along with inadequate facilities, these problems produce failure rates reaching over 80 percent in some faculties.

In 1990, a Catholic University Institute was established, inaugurating private higher education and ending the state monopoly of higher education.

3.2 Preschool Eduation

Preschool education constitutes a very small part of the education effort. Preschool is available in the form of daycare centers run by private individuals and organizations who charge high fees. As with nursery schools, the number of these centers is on the increase in urban areas. Organized games and the basics of picture reading and drawing constitute the main program of these centers.

3.3 Special Education

Like preschool education, special education forms a very small part of education in Cameroon. There was no information on handicapped persons reported in the population census of 1987. Their welfare and education are handled by special services in a government ministry responsible for social and women's affairs. Four main types of special education programs date back to the colonial period. Rehabilitation centers for lepers are run at hospitals by religious missionaries. Centers for the blind are surprisingly few, especially as blindness is a very common phenomenon in the northern part of the country. Students are introduced to the basic elements of braille and are taught handicrafts and gardening. (It is worth noting that the first blind Cameroonian graduated with a PhD from Howard University in the United States in 1984.)

Psychiatric patients were once interned in penitentiary centers, but Cameroon now runs a major psychiatric hospital in the capital city, where one of the biggest centers specializes in treating the disabled. This center also runs a primary school program for both physically and mentally handicapped children of school age. Finally, a number of institutes admit young delinquents sent from the law courts. In addition to rehabilitation programs, inmates prepare for the primary school leaving certificate.

The majority of handicapped persons are generally taken care of by their families. However, physically handicapped persons who are able to attend school are generally admitted into regular school programs where no special provisions are made for them.

A small number of physically handicapped teachers are found in schools at all levels. They obtain employment on the basis of similar qualifications like any other person. Blind workers are less evident. However, in the Muslim north of the country, blind persons are teachers or *modibos* in the Koranic schools.

3.4 Vocational, Technical, and Business Education

Formal vocational, technical, and business education begins after primary school education from about age 13. Government policy, announced in the five-year development plans, has been directed to encourage this sector which enrolled about 237,000 students in 1990. Business education, in which students receive training in secretarial skills and bookkeeping, dominates this sector where the teaching of computer skills is being introduced even in some remote rural institutions. Vocational training in areas such as motor mechanics, carpentry, masonry, electronics, and similar trade skills enrolls mainly boys. Domestic arts centers remain reserved for girls, although such traditional biases are breaking down with the demand for trained personnel by the expanding hotel, tourist, and catering business.

The building industry in urban centers is the greatest stimulus for the growth of apprenticeship workshops which enroll more primary school leavers than secondary technical and vocational schools.

The structure of technical and vocational education at this level has been greatly influenced by curricular models of the French education and certificate system. This tradition also persists in professional training at the higher educational level.

The economic boom of 1975–85 gave this sector a great boost. It has since been declining because of the economic crisis, although many parents still advise their children to opt for this sector rather than secondary general education because of the possibilities it offers for self-employment. This sector is still a major priority in government planning.

3.5 Adult and Nonformal Education

Since 1960, great effort has been put into developing adult and nonformal education in three major directions. Extending agriculture through village agricultural officers has greatly contributed to modernizing agricultural techniques, resulting in significant increases in the production of some cash crops (coffee, cocoa, cotton, etc.). Community development has been directed to improving life in rural areas, especially for women. Adult literacy campaigns have not been very successful despite the enormous effort put in by the government and UNESCO in the 1970s.

The Ministry of Women's Affairs, which was created in 1985, has directed much of its energy to programs in which the major goal is to enhance the place of women in society.

The rapid expansion of evening classes in which adults prepare for primary and secondary school certificate examinations is one of the major developments in education since the 1970s. Female students are in the majority in these institutions which are generally run by private individuals outside school hours. They are regulated by the Law on Private Education and are fee-paying.

4. Administrative and Supervisory Structure and Operation

Constitutional responsibility for the education of the citizen devolves on the state which exercises this duty through free tuition in all public schools at all levels and also by granting subsidies to private schools. Major national education policies are published through laws and presidential decrees. For example, university institutions are established by these decrees. Thus, a highly centralized control of education is established in which two ministers execute presidential directives on elementary and secondary education on the one hand, and higher education on the other.

Public primary and secondary schools are the responsibility of the Ministry of National Education which establishes and equips schools, recruits teachers, and determines school programs and textbooks.

Teachers in public schools are civil servants and enjoy the same salary conditions as other government workers.

In 1990, public primary and secondary schools, absorbed over 13 percent of the national budget.

The administration of the public school system is structured like a giant pyramid with the Ministry at the apex and a provincial delegate or school superintendent in each of the ten provinces at the base.

The inspectorate system is also bureaucratic in structure with an Inspector General of Pedagogy (IGP) for each sector: primary, secondary grammar, and secondary technical and vocational. Each IGP is assisted by national subject inspectors who in turn have assistants in each province. National inspectors are responsible for school syllabuses, textbooks, school examinations, and the supervision of teachers.

The minister in charge of higher education takes final policy decisions regarding universities, although each university has a governing council. Councils have direct responsibility for personnel recruitment, promotion, and dismissal. However, the creation of new departments, degrees, courses, and changes in general regulations, such as admissions, must receive ministerial consent. Until January 1993 the university was considered a public institution and did not charge tuition fees. Each university received a budget from the state for its recurrent and capital development costs. The majority of students received a grant from the government in addition to free tuition. These student grants not only consumed over 50 percent of the total budget of each university but were the greatest source of unrest at Cameroon's first and biggest university.

Since 1993 student scholarships have not only been abolished, but students now pay fees, US$150 per student per year. This initial token figure will certainly increase in the near future. The private Catholic University charges over 10 times the above figure and Cameroon students pay fifty times the above rate in foreign universities. It is expected that this change in policy will be salutary, especially if the introduction of private financing stimulates a more dynamic role for universities in the private sector of the economy.

Several higher educational institutions do not fall directly under the Minister of Higher Education, but the Minister must ascertain that they meet academic standards. Some of these are directly run by other ministers and offer specialized training in areas such as agriculture, health, post and telecommunications, forestry, youth and sports, planning, public works, and so on. They award diplomas generally recognized as equivalent to a first degree, although these institutions do not have university status.

Private primary and secondary schools enrolled about 35 percent of the 2.5 million students receiving education at this level in 1990. Private schools are established by private individuals and organizations with the approval of the Minister of National Education. Proprietors must provide the initial funds for buildings and equipment. Personnel are recruited and paid by them although the government gives subsidies which cover about 60 percent of private school teacher salaries.

The Catholic Church is the largest private education organization. In 1990 it owned over 60 percent of private primary schools and, together with Protestant churches, owned 90 percent of private primary schools. Lay proprietors own 55 percent of the private secondary schools, although most of the old and more prestigious schools are owned by religious organizations.

Private schools are administered under conditions laid down in the Private Education Laws of 1976 and 1987. These provide for national representatives for each of the Catholic, Protestant, Islamic and lay private school authorities. Each national representative is assisted in each province by denominational supervisors, known as education secretaries.

All private schools must follow the same syllabuses and textbooks as public schools. They must be open to inspection by Ministry inspectors, and must prepare their students for official examinations.

Since the abolition of the federal structure in 1972, the administration and supervision of schools have become more centralized. However, the double dualism of Anglophone and Francophone schools on the one hand, and of public and private schools, on the other creates great imbalances in the implementation of national policies, especially curricular innovations.

The constitution of Cameroon (1961 and 1972) gives responsibility for policy decisions about the structure of the education system to the lawmaker. The present Francophone primary and secondary school system was instituted by laws passed in 1963 and 1964 while, in the Anglophone part of the country, the duration of primary and secondary schooling was determined by the education ordinance of 1952 and government policy decisions of 1955 and 1963. In 1964, 1976, and 1987, laws were passed allowing private schools run by individuals and organizations. However, since 1961 the organization of the university system, and especially the reforms of 1993, has been carried out by presidential decrees after consultation with advisory councils. Decisions on curriculum changes, the duration of schooling, instructional time for different grade levels, school holidays, etc., are all taken by the central Ministry of Education.

5. Educational Finance

The state, in the final analysis, bears the major financial burden for running both public and private schools. Parents are the next major source of educational financing as they bear the social cost of education. In addition, through Parent–Teacher Associations, they fund buildings and equipment, and, in some cases, pay teachers' salaries.

Before Independence and until the early 1970s, expenditure for school buildings, equipment, and teachers was a very significant part of foreign aid. In the early 1990s, this source has considerably diminished due to the establishment of indigenous churches.

In the 1990–91 fiscal year, US$300 million were allocated to education at all levels from the national budget of about US$1,500 million. Despite cuts in government expenditures because of the economic crisis, popular demand for education has put pressure on the government to expand schools and increase the education budget. Investment in education will remain a major priority for the next decade.

Table 2 presents the government budgetary allocations for each level of education in the fiscal year 1990–91.

Financial support for private education derives mainly from state subsidies and school fees paid by parents. The bulk of state subsidies (6 billion francs CFA in 1990) is paid to schools run by religious bodies and especially to the older and more prestigious secondary grammar schools. In 1990, over 80 percent of the expenditure on private primary and secondary schools was derived from school fees which were fixed by the Minister of National Education on the advice of a National Commission for Private Education, where all private school proprietors are represented.

At the levels of schooling, in both the public and private sectors, teacher salaries absorb over 70 percent of the school budget. In 1990, over 90 percent of the budgetary allocation for public primary and secondary schools was spent on salaries. Private school proprietors try to tackle this problem by employing part-time or temporary teachers, who made up over 70 percent of the staff of the majority of the schools in 1990.

The costs per pupil in 1990 were US$160 for primary, US$600 for secondary academic, US$10,000 for secondary technical and vocational schools, and US $13,000 for universities (US $ before 1992).

6. Supplying Personnel for the Education System

In 1990 there were over 67,000 teachers in primary and secondary schools. Men are in the majority, although the proportion of female teachers has begun to increase, reaching 35 percent of the 41,000 primary school teachers in 1988. Most institutions are headed by men although one of the six universities has a woman at its head.

Shortage of teachers is a chronic problem. Since 1987, there have been drastic cuts in the annual recruitment of teachers for public schools. Admissions to government primary school teacher-training colleges have also been stopped. The number of qualified experienced teachers is rapidly diminishing. About 50 percent of primary school teachers in 1990 has only a primary school leaving certificate.

At the secondary school level the situation is improving, especially for private secondary schools where unemployed university graduates are willing to accept low salaries. In general, schools in remote rural areas attract fewer female teachers, although they were in the majority in public primary school teacher-training colleges in the late 1980s.

Preservice training for primary school teachers prepares for three grades of certificates—Grade III, II, and I—awarded respectively after three years of training after primary school, two years after GCE

Table 2
Provisions for education in the national budget 1987–90 (in billions of francs CFA)

	1987–88	1988–89	1989–90
Total			
Education	123 (19%)	91 (16%)	112 (18%)
National	650 (100%)	600 (100%)	600 (100%)
Running			
Schools	66.9 (16.7%)	59.8 (10.8%)	67.3 (16%)
Universities	34 (9.6%)	27 (7.1%)	34 (8%)
Subsidies			
Private	6 (1.5%)	6 (1.6%)	6.5 (1.5%)
National	400 (100%)	375 (100%)	425 (100%)
Investment			
Schools	12 (4.8%)	5.3 (2.4%)	6 (3.4%)
Universities	12 (4.8%)	5.3 (2.4%)	6 (3.4%)
National	250 (100%)	225 (100%)	175 (100%)

Ordinary level, and one year after GCE Advanced level. Secondary school teachers are trained at the Higher Teachers School of Education at Yaounde University (*Ecole Normale Supérieure*) which offers three years of training after secondary high school and two years after the first degree. The majority of the teacher-training colleges are owned by the government and train teachers mainly for public schools. Only two private primary teacher-training centers exist for Presbyterian and Catholic training schools.

All teacher-training colleges follow official syllabuses from the Minister of National Education. Special training programs are offered for teachers destined for nursery schools, home economics, and technical vocational schools. Inservice training for all categories of teachers takes the form of correspondence courses, seminars, workshops, refresher courses, and travel abroad. Distance education existed up until the 1980s in the form of correspondence courses for obtaining the primary school teachers diploma. Enthusiasm for this type of training greatly diminished because of the abolition of the automatic salary increase for teachers on obtaining a higher teachers diploma. Furthermore, inservice training, in whatever form, is not compulsory.

Probationary periods are provided for in the salary conditions of untrained primary and secondary teachers. All teachers must be inspected every year by either national or provincial inspectors and headmasters, as a condition for earning a bi-annual salary increase.

One of the greatest problems in the schools is the rapid decline in the number of qualified experienced teachers because of aging. By 1970, Anglophone primary schools had over 70 percent trained teachers. In the mid 1990s, these schools have been depleted of the bulk of the experienced teachers produced in the 1960s and 1970s when this part of the country had over 12 primary school teacher-training colleges. The requirement of the International Monetary Fund in its Structural Adjustment Plan that Cameroon reduce teacher training and recruitment will certainly worsen the standard of education which, in countries like Cameroon, depends greatly on the quality of teachers.

7. Curriculum Development and Teaching Methodology

Although the curricula of primary and secondary schools is given for all schools by the Ministry of National Education, a formal statement of a core curriculum is nowhere stated as such. Statements of national goals can only be deduced from official educational statements and reports such as the Five-Year Socioeconomic Development Plans. Hence there is a disparity between some national goals and curricular practices.

The primary school curriculum comprises language (English or French), mathematics, natural sciences, history, geography, physical education, and manual work. The curricula of secondary schools is subject-oriented and similar to that of high schools in many Anglophone and Francophone countries. Technical and vocational schools provide training in a wide range of trade areas: motor mechanics, electronics, carpentry, masonry, painting, and so on. Religious instruction is permitted in public schools, but it is compulsory in institutions run by churches. Anglo-Arab and Franco-Arab primary schools exist for Muslim children.

Most instructional materials, especially textbooks, are imported from either France or the United Kingdom. Some foreign publishers use local authors to write or adapt materials to suit local syllabuses. However, new textbooks are generally approved by national inspectors who may seek the opinion of classroom teachers. Dissemination of textbooks is undertaken by local bookshops. In 1991 Cameroon negotiated financial subsidies with France in order to reduce prices for some primary school textbooks. This move could lead to a new textbook policy involving funding agencies which have so far been concerned only with building and equipping schools. Foreign organizations occasionally donate books to school libraries to help alleviate the pathetic dearth of reading materials in Cameroon schools. However, many of these books are not appropriate for Cameroonian children.

The *baccalauréat* usually provides for literary or science subject options. Some options contain electives such as Spanish and German. The GCE allows a choice from among 15 subjects. The best students take 10 subjects; English, French, and mathematics are compulsory for all candidates.

Beyond chalk and blackboard, improvements in learning facilities depend on the financial possibilities of each school. A few schools use videotapes for specific programs.

Since 1960, efforts made to harmonize the Anglophone and Francophone school curricula have not been very successful. Attempts to produce nationwide uniformity in school syllabuses have often provoked mutual antagonism between Francophones and Anglophones, erupting in strikes in 1983 and 1987.

Literary subject options attract more candidates, although this trend is changing in favor of science subjects in response to the general impression that students following science options easily find training opportunities in technical and professional training.

As official languages, French and English are compulsory subjects at all levels of the school system. However, from the third year of secondary school, students can choose to study an additional language: Spanish, German, Latin, or Greek.

All schools must follow the official curriculum under the supervision of the inspectorate division of the Ministry of National Education. Private school proprietors must pledge to follow official regulations and syllabuses. Otherwise, they face prosecution under the Private Education Law.

The overall inadaptability of the school curriculum to the socioeconomic realities of Cameroon is a general problem. This has further been aggravated by the use of imported textbooks and of foreign languages for instruction. Poor command of English or French is the major cause of failure at all levels of the school system.

The major duties of the inspectorate division of the Ministry of National Education include the selection of appropriate textbooks for each subject at various levels of schooling. Inspectors are involved in preservice and inservice teacher training where new teaching materials and textbooks are introduced. They supervise teaching and approve examination questions for primary and secondary school official examinations. Thus, they are responsible for ensuring that national examinations assess curricular objectives and content as determined in policy by ministerial fiat.

8. The System of Examinations, Promotions, and Certifications

Promotion from one year to the next throughout the school system is based on the results gained on tests devised by teachers, while promotion to a higher level of schooling is based on success at the national certificate competitive or selection examinations.

Francophone secondary schools still follow the *baccalauréat* while Anglophone secondary schools prepare students for the General Certificate of Education of the University of London. Both examinations were "Cameroonized" in 1969 and 1976 respectively. However, they still maintain the broad organizational features inherited from the 1960s. There is a dire need to introduce modern techniques of evaluation, as well as culturally appropriate subjects and tests into the examination system.

The job value of the diploma makes preparation for national examinations the major goal of instruction. The centralized examination system could facilitate the introduction of a Standardized Achievement Test which could provide a useful basis for curriculum evaluation throughout the school system and especially for nonexamination classes. However, such a development could take a decade to introduce! Examination questions are generally directed to testing knowledge rather than skills and competencies.

9. Educational Assessment, Evaluation, and Research

The planning divisions of the Ministries of National and Higher Education are responsible for assessment, evaluation, and research. A nationwide assessment (Labrousse 1970) of the school system was carried out in the 1970s focusing on factors including dropout, repetition, and per capita costs, in order to compare inputs and outputs. Some startling findings were made which continue to be valid in the early 1990s. For example, it was found that repeating classes was the greatest source of financial loss as many children took double the amount of time to complete their schooling. Fewer than 44 of every cohort of 10,000 first-year primary school pupils obtained the high-school diploma. These findings led to a policy of automatic promotion in Anglophone primary schools in 1970, and the plan to staff the schools with only trained teachers in the following decade. These innovations were abandoned in the early 1980s.

However, annual statistical surveys by the Ministry of National Education on indicators such as age, sex, enrollments, teacher qualifications, and so forth provide an overall picture of trends in the school system. Studies of achievement levels in writing, numeracy, and literacy skills at various stages of schooling would be very useful in providing an overall picture of the quality of education in schools.

Some form of annual evaluation is carried out in private schools by the National Commission for Private Education. This is based on indicators such as qualifications of teachers, organization, facilities, investment, and performance in official examinations. Such evaluation reports enable the Ministry to categorize schools for the purpose of distributing government subsidies. There have been suggestions that similar appraisals be extended to public schools which are not subjected to any systematic assessment or accountability.

Two research institutes were established in 1969 and 1974 to direct an ambitious effort to introduce massive changes in the primary school curriculum. Their impact has not been impressive. In 1973, the National Institute for Education was established and given a broad mandate for educational research on all aspects of education. An initial effort to review secondary school syllabuses and textbooks was abandoned in 1976. Since then this institute has not found a clear direction and focus for its activities. Therefore, in the absence of substantial research studies on crucial national policies such as bilingualism, it is difficult to assess the attitudes of policymakers toward research findings.

Expenditure on educational research and evaluation is difficult to estimate but it must be quite small if not negligible. However, occasional assessments of the functioning of the system are carried out through studies commissioned by international organizations such as the World Bank and UNESCO. In 1988, a World Bank study advised a drastic restructuring of the university system to reduce student numbers and cutting expenditure on scholarships. Both the pressure for more places at the university and the economic crisis have forced the government to revise its higher education policy completely. Six full-fledged universities were created in 1993. The thirty-year policy of free higher education and scholarships was changed and fees were introduced.

10. Major Reforms in the 1980s and 1990s

Several reform projects were attempted in the 1970s and 1980s. The ruralization of primary education with its key goal of getting school leavers back to the land and thereby checking rural exodus was introduced in 1969, but in 1990 this received little attention in policy statements. This reform has virtually been forgotten in its original ambitious form. However, one result is that manual work has been established as an important activity in the primary schools.

Bilingual education programs in which Anglophone and Francophone children attend the same schools have expanded since 1963. The teaching of a second foreign language has extended to most primary schools, although it is difficult to evaluate its effectiveness.

At the secondary school level, bilingual experiments which started in the late 1960s have crystallized into two models. Several cohabitational schools offer both the Francophone and Anglophone secondary schooling programs. Some schools use both English and French as the media of instruction in teaching content subjects.

Great interest has been generated among Francophone parents to send their children to Anglophone schools. An increasing number of Francophone students also undertake university studies in Anglophone countries. Although the 1983 reform of the GCE did not take place in the form that was planned, it has established French, along with mathematics and English, as compulsory subjects for this examination.

Latin and Greek were reintroduced into the secondary school curriculum in 1987 as electives, but it is not easy to ascertain the number of students taking these subjects at the *baccalauréat* level.

In 1993, as already mentioned above, a major reform of the university system was undertaken with the transformation of existing university institutions into six universities. The intention is that two of these universities should follow the Anglo-Saxon and French traditions of university education, while the oldest university will continue to operate bilingually. Many technical and professional institutions of higher education have been established in an effort to provide advanced training in various aspects of the socioeconomic system such as agriculture, post and telecommunications, hotel management, forestry, food technology, and so on.

But by far the most important reform is the introduction of tuition fees at the university level. This is a major change in the policy of free tuition practiced

since Independence. The state budget still bears over 80 percent of the cost of education in the public sector at all levels of education, but it is expected that this proportion will diminish if the current economic crisis continues.

11. Major Problems for the Year 2000

Overcrowding in classrooms at all levels in consequence of the phenomenal demographic explosion the country has experienced since 1960 is one problem the school system will continue to face in the 1990s. Ongoing efforts to cope with this include involving local associations in funding school projects.

Greater decentralization in which more responsibility for school and curriculum improvement is given to local authorities is a much needed direction for future change.

The quality of education has fallen because of teacher shortage, and poorer and overcrowded facilities. Poor handwriting at the upper levels of schooling is a strong pointer to falling standards. A sustained system of teacher training must be put in place, along with greater attention to factors that ensure greater retention of trained and experienced teachers who should be given security in a professional association.

A strategy for school curriculum renovation has still to be worked out so that reforms can be based on rationales that are clearly stated. Such reforms must be linked to the socioeconomic goals of the 1990s in ways that are realistic. The education system should impart marketable skills without making this the only goal of schooling. Greater diversity in the curriculum should replace the present rigid system. National goals of education should be more clearly stated. These goals must include a language policy that incorporates the teaching of Cameroon languages as a fundamental core of the curriculum at all levels of the school system. Finally, Cameroon must devote greater financial resources to education.

Bibliography

Blakemore K, Cooksey B 1981 *A Sociology of Education for Africa*. Allen and Unwin, London
Fanso G 1989 *History of Cameroon*. Longman, London
Gwei S N 1975 Education in Cameroon: Western pre-colonial and colonial antecedents and the development of higher education. Doctoral dissertation, University of Michigan, Ann Arbor, Michigan
Kale, J, Yembe O W 1980 Reforms in the educational system: A case study of IPAR Buea. In: Kofele-Kale N (ed.) 1980 *An African Case Study in Nation Building: The Bilingual Republic of Cameroon since Reunification*. Westview Press, Boulder, Colorado
Labrousse A 1970 *Le Financement de l'Education au Cameroun*. UNESCO, Paris

Lallez R 1975 *La Réforme de l'education au Cameroun.* International Bureau of Education, Geneva

Le Vine V T 1964 *The Cameroons: From Mandate to Independence.* University of California Press, Berkeley, California

Mveng E 1963 *Histoire du Cameroun.* Presence Africaine, Paris

Rudin H 1938 *The Germans in Cameroon.* Yale University Press, Princeton, New Jersey

Société Internationale de Linguistique (SIL) 1981 *Rapport Annuel 1980–81.* SIL, Yaounde

UNESCO 1962 *Report of the Advisory Commission for the Development of Higher Education in the Federal Republic of Cameroon.* UNESCO, Paris

UNESCO 1965 *Report of the Second Planning Mission to Cameroon, September–December 1963.* UNESCO, Paris

Vernon-Jackson H O 1967 *Language, Schools, and Government in Cameroon.* Teachers College Press, New York

Yembe O W 1979 Bilingualism and academic achievement in Cameroon secondary schools. Doctoral dissertation, Teachers College, Columbia University, New York

Canada

D. L. Berg

1. General Background

Canada is the second largest country in the world in area, but ranks only thirty-first in population. Its 27 million people represent cultural backgrounds as diverse as the land they inhabit. Geographically, the country encompasses large metropolitan areas, fertile plains, and farmlands, and great stretches of mountains, lakes, northern wilderness, and Arctic tundra.

Almost two-thirds of the population occupy urban areas concentrated in a more or less unbroken band along the border between Canada and the United States, and over 60 percent of Canadians live in two provinces—Ontario, with its largely English-speaking population, and Quebec where the primary language is French. In keeping with its history, Canada is a bilingual country. Its two official languages are French and English.

Politically, Canada is a federal state, divided into ten provinces and two territories. The Confederation Act of 1867 which brought together the four original provinces, was designed to build a strong central government, while ensuring autonomy and self-government for the participants in matters relating to their specific socioeconomic interests, language, religion, law (in the case of Quebec) and, significantly, education. These rights were extended to other communities as they joined the federation. Thus, Canada does not have a national system of education, nor a central office of education. Subject to the observance of certain guaranteed minority religious and language rights, education is exclusively under the control of each province and territory. A few exceptions exist for which the federal government has assumed direct responsibility. These include the education of Canada's aboriginal people (North American Indian, Inuits, and Métis), who represent about 3 percent of the population, armed forces personnel, and inmates of federal prisons. In order to ensure the provision of education in the official language of minorities (e.g., French

in Ontario), the federal government also provides financial assistance to support the additional costs of developing and maintaining these programs.

Natural increase accounts for about 65 percent of Canada's population growth. The 1990 annual rate of approximately 7.0 per 1,000 population was one of the highest in the industrial world, but the lowest in Canada's history. In the decade of the 1980s, the birthrate declined, resulting in a much smaller preschool and primary age group in 1986 than in the "baby boom" years of the 1960s. However, indications are that the rate (14 per thousand in 1992) will stabilize, or increase slightly, through the 1990s. Although the number of people under age 14 did not change much in the 1980s, the secondary school age group (14–18) decreased by 15 percent between 1981 and 1986. As a consequence of the declining birthrate and a gain in life expectancy, Canada has an aging population. The median age in 1992 was 33.8, the highest in the country's history.

Immigration is also a major factor in Canada's growth. Traditionally, most immigrants came from Britain, but in the 1991 census, 31 percent of all Canadians reported ethnic origins other than British or French. This included, in addition to European immigrants, an influx of West Indians and Africans in the 1970s, together with refugees from Latin America, the Middle East, and Asia in the 1980s. In 1991, Canada received approximately 231,000 immigrants, 53 percent of whom came from Asia. Although children under 18 normally represent only about 1 percent of the annual immigration, 70 percent of this number settle in the six major cities. The fact that as many as two-thirds of such children understand neither of the two official languages has created special problems for some urban school systems.

Canada has grown from a largely agricultural and resource-based economy to a prosperous industrialized country, although, like other such economies, it experienced recessionary periods in the 1980s and 1990s. According to the 1991 census, 2 out of every 3 Canadian workers were employed in service producing industries with the balance in the goods producing sector. Of the latter, under 4 percent of workers were employed in agriculture, fishing, and mining, in contrast to half the population in 1891.

Canada has a major financial commitment to education, which is second only to social welfare as a consumer of government funding. In 1992–93, educational expenditure represented about 8.1 percent of Gross Domestic Product (GDP). This commitment is reflected in the labor force; in 1989, 15 percent of workers had university degrees, and 42 percent had some postsecondary education compared with 29 percent a decade earlier. However, at the other end of the spectrum, 9 percent of the labor force had less than a Grade 9 education, and it has been estimated that as many as one-fourth of Canadians suffer from basic or functional illiteracy.

2. Politics and the Goals of the Education System

In addition to the Prime Minister of Canada and the Cabinet, each province has its own elected legislature, headed by a premier, to administer and delegate the responsibilities, including education, which fall under provincial control.

While the political parties in power in the various jurisdictions may differ and espouse philosophies either slightly to the left or right of center, Canada is not a country of political extremes. Moderation and pragmatism are Canadian characteristics. In a nation founded on democratic principles, the majority of its citizens share an ethic of equal opportunity, and the provision of universal, free schooling to the college or university level. Education is viewed as a process of imparting the necessary knowledge and skills to achieve a productive, rewarding, and fulfilling life. Differences, therefore, tend to focus on the interpretation of concepts such as "knowledge" and "skills" and the methods for acquiring them, rather than on the underlying principles.

It is also notable that with the growth in size and importance of education in the second half of the twentieth century, the federal government has inevitably played a more important role, even though direct participation is prohibited by the Constitution. Since 1963, when the Department of the Secretary of State was designated as the advisor to the Cabinet on postsecondary education, its responsibilities have grown to encompass the development, formulation, and implementation of all federal policies and programs on education. Most significant is its important role in the provision of financial support, especially at the postsecondary level. As a result, the economic and social priorities of the federal government inevitably have consequences for education which may conflict with provincial or regional objectives.

In the closing years of the twentieth century, Canada

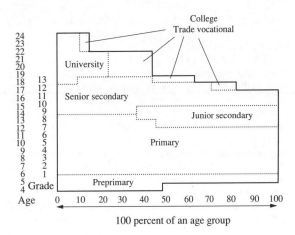

Figure 1
Canada: Structure of the formal education system
Source: *Statistics Canada*

is faced with serious economic and political decisions. The federal government's commitment to cut budget deficits implies less government spending on services. Federal policies on bilingualism and multiculturalism have been questioned. Most importantly, the resolution of Quebec's status as a "distinct society," either within the federation or as a sovereign state, as well as the question of self-government for native peoples, cannot help but affect all levels of education.

3. The Formal System of Education

3.1 Primary, Secondary, and Tertiary Education

Figure 1 illustrates the range of educational structures and years of study within provincial systems. There are three levels of education offered in Canada: elementary, secondary, and postsecondary. Attendance is compulsory for about ten years in every province. The starting age is 6 or 7, and the minimum leaving age, 15 or 16. The combined elementary–secondary program, however, usually extends over 12 years, although there are provincial differences. The definition of "elementary" and "secondary" also varies from province to province. In most jurisdictions, "elementary" refers to the first six grades; in others, Grade 7 and/or Grade 8 are included. The secondary level, therefore, may consist of five or six grades and may be further subdivided into junior and senior high schools. Quebec has a unique program of five years at the secondary level (Grades 7 to 11), followed by two or three years at a *collège d'enseignment général et professionel* (CEGEP).

At one time, secondary schools were primarily academic and prepared students for university. Vocational and technical schools were often separate institutions.

181

Although some of these still exist, most secondary schools are composite and offer both academic and vocational courses.

The majority of Canada's 15,600 elementary–secondary schools are public, meaning that they offer free, tax-supported education. In several provinces, provision is made for tax-supported "separate schools" on a denominational basis (usually Roman Catholic). Private schools, which represent only 4.6 percent of the total, are independent of the public system and charge fees, although provision is made for financial assistance in some provinces. Most public schools, with the exception of a few separate schools, are coeducational. In contrast, many private schools were established exclusively for either boys or girls, although some subsequently became coeducational.

Secondary school education to at least the Grade 12 level is often specified by business and industry as a minimum for employment. Despite Canada's commitment to education, retention rates at the secondary level are a concern. This situation has serious implications both for the country and for the young people themselves because of the increasing need for highly skilled workers and fewer opportunities for the unskilled or functionally illiterate.

Postsecondary education in Canada is essentially government-financed and has undergone a remarkable expansion since the Second World War. In 1993–94, Canada had 272 postsecondary institutions which included 69 degree-granting universities (compared to 28 in 1939) and 203 non-degree-granting "community colleges." The latter designation is used in the general sense because of provincial variations in terminology. These institutions offer a broad range of vocational, technical, and semi-professional programs and, in some cases, university transfer programs. Others specialize in specific areas such as art, fisheries, marine technology, or agriculture.

The structure of universities is relatively standard and degrees are offered almost universally at three levels: bachelor's (BA or BSc) and first professional, master's (MA or MSc), and doctoral (PhD) or professional degrees, such as Doctor of Medicine (MD). Each university sets its own admission standards, but the basic requirement is normally secondary school (or in the case of Quebec, CEGEP) graduation. Most institutions make allowance for the admission of "mature students," typically defined as people over 21 years of age who have been out of school for several years.

The school year at the elementary–secondary level averages 180 to 200 teaching days over the period from September to late June. At the postsecondary level, the academic year normally begins in September and continues until late April or early May. Most universities offer both full (two semesters) and half (one semester) courses, and some institutions operate year-round on a three-semester basis. Several universities have work-study programs in which students alternate between classroom study and supervised regular employment.

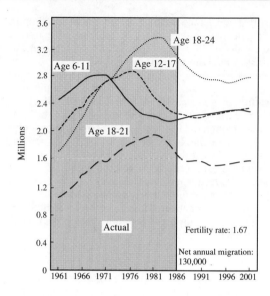

Figure 2
Selected age-group populations of relevance to school enrollment 1961–2001
Source: *Statistics Canada*

The majority of universities accept either full-time or part-time students, especially at the undergraduate level, and many offer off-campus courses, correspondence courses, or make use of communications technology. In a country as vast as Canada with many sparsely populated areas and severe climate, there are well-developed and innovative programs of distance education at all levels.

In 1991–92, just over six million Canadians, more than one-fourth of the population, were enrolled full-time in educational institutions. Since education is compulsory until age 15 or 16, virtually all of this age group attend school. Of the total full-time enrollment, elementary and secondary schools accounted for just over five million; nonuniversity postsecondary institutions for approximately 341,600, and universities for about 554,000. When part-time students attending universities are taken into account, the total enrollment was approximately 757,500 undergraduates and 110,000 graduate students. Figure 2 shows the actual and projected age-group population relevant to the three levels of education from 1961 through the year 2001.

In 1992, almost 120,700 bachelor's and first professional degrees were granted, an increase of 33,600 over 1982. In fact, between 1981 and 1986, the number of university graduates rose 432 percent, nearly seven times the growth rate of 65 percent for the population as a whole. Since 1982, the number of bachelor's degrees granted to women has exceeded those granted men, reaching about 57 percent in 1992. The number of master's and doctoral degrees awarded also increased over the decade, as did the percentage granted to women. Nevertheless, women are still underrepresented in senior administrative positions and full-time, tenured academic appointments.

Student enrollment includes an increasingly significant number of international students. In the fall of 1991, there were about 87,000 foreign students enrolled at all levels, the majority at the postsecondary level. Over half of these students were from Asian countries with Hong Kong sending about 16 percent of all international students.

Canadian university fees are heavily subsidized and vary by province, by university, and by faculty. Fees for international students are about five times higher than for Canadian residents, but are still considered competitive with the United States and many European countries. From 1981–82 to 1990–91 fees increased at an average annual rate of 10.8 percent. Nevertheless, with increases in public funding, student fees account for only about one-tenth of university income compared to one-fourth in 1960.

3.2 Preschool Education

Although the starting age for Grade 1 is usually 6 or 7, preschool programs, commonly called "kindergarten classes," are provided in most provinces in public elementary schools for 5-year olds. Some school boards in Manitoba, Ontario, and Quebec include 4- and 5-year old children in two years of noncompulsory schooling. Alberta operates a unique publicly supported program called "Early Childhood Services," which integrates educational, health, social, and recreational services, and enrolls children as young as $3\frac{1}{2}$ years old. In other provinces, or as an alternative to public school programs, pre-Grade 1 classes are offered in privately operated schools under varying degrees of provincial supervision. For 1992–93, it was estimated that 462,300 children would be in preschool programs. Pre-elementary enrollment has shown an upward trend since 1978–79, partly because of increases in the 4- and 5-year old population and partly because of a greater participation rate. The latter may be due to the considerable increase in the number of families in which both parents work and the growing number of single-parent families. In 1988, for example, both parents were employed, either full- or part-time, in 64 percent of homes with children; in the case of single parents, the figure was 69 percent. In general, day-care facilities are considered to be inadequate to cope with this trend. In some provinces, child care spaces are being incorporated in both elementary and secondary schools to provide facilities for older as well as younger children before and after the formal school day.

3.3 Special Education

Canada emphasizes the concept of equal educational opportunity for all children and attempts to provide for individual differences. Since the 1970s, there has been a trend to integrate "special needs students" (roughly 5 to 10 percent of all students) into regular classrooms. This often requires considerable adjustments in both curriculum and teacher training because of the diverse groups that fall into this category. Included are physically handicapped children and the learning disabled, as well as academically gifted children who are usually directed into enriched or accelerated programs. Special language and cultural needs of children who have recently emigrated to Canada, or of aboriginal children who enter the public school system, are also recognized. In addition, programs have been incorporated in some schools to encourage girls to participate in science and mathematics, subjects which have traditionally been male-dominated. Some critics have argued that the policy of equality of opportunity affects the quality of education and that gifted students, for example, receive less attention than those who lack ability.

There are also separate schools, both public and private, for various categories of disability, such as the severely mentally handicapped, or the visually or hearing impaired.

The education of registered Indian and Inuit children falls within the responsibility of the federal government through its Department of Indian and Northern Affairs. The Department is authorized to maintain schools for these children directly or to provide access to education in public or private schools. About half of Canada's aboriginal children attend provincial public schools. In 1986–87, the federal government owned and operated 141 schools on Indian reserves and, in addition, native band councils managed 244 schools under ministerial regulations. Since the 1980s, native peoples have become increasingly vocal in their demands for self-government. The dropout rate among native youth and problems relating to drug and alcohol use, together with a high suicide rate, have caught the attention of all Canadians and efforts are being made to remedy the mistakes of the past. One potential model for the future is a provincially funded secondary school opened in 1991 in Winnipeg, Manitoba. This school replaced a reserve school and has a program which, in addition to university and general courses, emphasizes instruction in native languages, history, and culture.

3.4 Vocational, Technical, and Business Education

Vocational preparation played an increasingly important role in secondary schools in the 1980s, although the earlier system of "streaming" students into vocational programs at age 14 was not reinstated. As a result of studies of the relationship between school and work, emphasis is given to a positive work attitude and ability to learn, rather than to specific job-related skills. The objective is to provide broader, transferable skills to enable young people to function in a society and a job market requiring flexibility to adapt to rapid technological change.

183

The prevalent Canadian view of education as preparation for work and the emphasis given to the relationship between income and formal qualifications was undoubtedly a factor in the widespread "community college" movement in the 1960s. These institutions originated a number of semiprofessional and technical diploma programs as adjuncts to, or replacements for, inservice training. Focus on the labor market is also reflected at the university level. Professional degrees have proliferated and are considered as prerequisites to employment not only in traditional areas such as law and medicine, but also in social work, teaching, librarianship, business administration, etc.

In addition to formal programs in composite secondary schools and postsecondary institutions, vocational and trade training is offered variously in community colleges, public trade schools, and vocational centers. In 1989–90, over 249,000 trainees were enrolled in such programs. On a small scale, training may also take place within industry in on-the-job apprenticeship programs. Most courses offered can be completed in less than a year and some for less complex occupations may last only a few weeks. Only people who have left the regular school system and who are older than the compulsory age are eligible to attend, and admission standards may range from Grade 8 to Grade 12. Historically, this kind of training was one of the first educational fields in which the federal government was involved since public schools and universities only rarely offered such programs. Initial participation was mainly financial and began with support of provincial programs after the First World War. After 1967, the federal government became more concerned with the types of training and the geographic distribution of programs. One of its priorities in the 1990s is to encourage business and industry to play a more active role in training.

3.5 Adult and Nonformal Education

Continuing education is an important element in Canada and more than three million Canadians register in adult education programs each year. Courses are offered by a variety of institutions, including school boards, provincial departments of education, universities, and community colleges. Programs are also sponsored or conducted by nonprofit organizations, professional associations, government departments, and business and industry. Instruction is offered by a variety of methods in addition to the conventional classroom. Communications technology has popularized "open learning" and enables learners in remote areas to gain access to educational opportunities.

University extension programs developed rapidly after the Second World War. At the postsecondary level, some courses are offered for academic credit, others are noncredit cultural or recreational programs for personal development. Professional development and refresher courses are also popular.

Programs to counteract illiteracy have been strengthened in all educational jurisdictions. Some embody an institutional approach and are offered through community colleges and evening courses in community-based schools. There are also a number of voluntary organizations that have developed informal and individualized assistance. These methods have received broad recognition and appear to be a more amenable approach to illiteracy at the adult level than formal programs.

4. Administrative and Supervisory Structure and Operation

Each province has a department of education headed by a minister who is an elected member of the provincial cabinet, or in the case of the Yukon and Northwest territories, a councillor. In some provinces, postsecondary education is a separate ministry.

While a provincial minister has responsibility for the overall policy and management of the system, the day-to-day operation and supervision of the department is carried out by the deputy minister and his staff who are permanent civil servants. Functions of ministries include the supervision and inspection of elementary and secondary schools; provision of curriculum and school organization guidelines; production of curriculum materials; finance; teacher certification; prescription of regulations for school trustees and teachers; and support services such as libraries, health, and transportation.

In all provinces, schools are operated by local authorities (boards of education), which are made up of elected or appointed trustees or commissioners. School board areas are delineated by the province. In recent years, many small boards have been consolidated into central, regional, or county units. The powers of the board are delegated by the province and pertain principally to the business and management aspects of education, including the establishment, maintenance, and purchase of facilities and equipment; the appointment of teachers; and budget preparation. The extent to which provincial school systems are decentralized varies. However, in most cases, there is an ideological commitment to local control in response to community needs.

The institutional structure of universities is established by provincial legislative acts. Traditionally, universities are governed by a two-tier system: a board of governors who are responsible for final policy decisions, and a senate which is the university's senior academic body. Although subject to the authority of the board, the senate is responsible for academic policy relating to matters such as admission requirements, approval of courses and programs, qualifications for degrees, and academic planning.

The majority of community colleges also have a board of governors whose members may be appointed by the provincial government, chosen by the municipality, or elected, although a few institutions, mainly institutes of technology, are under direct government control. Boards usually include lay people, as well as faculty and students. Other management models include a partnership between government, colleges, and school district boards (British Columbia), and, in Quebec, a partnership between the department of education and college boards, supplemented by a nongovernmental college association.

Provincial and territorial governments make every effort to accommodate individual transfers and movements between schools and from province to province. To assist this process, the Council of Ministers of Education, Canada (CMEC) regularly publishes *A Student Transfer Guide* describing secondary school structures and programs. The Council was established in 1967 to provide a forum and a voice for provincial ministers on matters of common interest, and to facilitate cooperation among its members. As concern with education as a pan-Canadian priority has increased, the CMEC has undertaken a number of significant national activities. One example is the establishment, along with Statistics Canada, of the Canadian Education Statistics Council, whose primary objective is to collect and disseminate comparable, agreed upon interprovincial data.

5. Educational Finance

In the period of expansion in the 1960s, expenditures on education grew by 15 to 20 percent annually, absorbing more than 22 percent of government spending and reaching a high of around 8.6 percent of GDP. From 1983–84 to 1993–94 spending (in current Canadian dollars) increased by 84.0 percent from $30.2 billion to $55.5 billion, an average annual increase of 6.3 percent. Elementary and secondary education accounted for nearly 65 percent of this total. Like other industrialized nations, Canada experienced downturns in the economy in the 1980s and 1990s. Increasing concern about high government deficits and the range of services to be supported, contributed to the lowering of the GDP ratio in 1992–93 to about 8.1 percent. The per-student cost for primary and secondary education was estimated to be CDN$6,134 in 1990.

More than 90 percent of educational revenue comes from government with the balance generated from private sources such as tuition fees, donations, and investment income. Traditionally, financing of elementary–secondary education was a municipal responsibility with local property taxes paying most of the cost of basic education. While local taxes are still important, the municipal share in 1993–94 dropped to an estimated 20.3 percent from 49 percent in 1960. In half of the provinces, the bulk, or all, of school board revenues come directly from the province. In the remainder of the jurisdictions, revenues from local

taxation range from approximately 35 to 50 percent. The relative contributions of local and provincial levels are adjusted to ensure minimum standards and to moderate local differences in income and wealth. The federal government's direct financing of programs under its jurisdiction amounted to an estimated 11.4 percent in 1993–94. In addition, part of provincial support actually consists of federal funds channelled through the provinces.

Postsecondary education is also essentially government financed, with the federal and provincial governments contributing over 80 percent of the total funding. Direct operating grants to eligible universities and colleges, in effect from 1951 to 1966, were replaced in 1967, except for sponsored research, by a system of transfer payments to provinces. A new method of financing was instituted in 1977, whereby federal contributions to postsecondary education, hospital insurance, and medicare were consolidated. Although about one-third of the allocation is expected to go to support education, provinces may allocate funds to the three programs as they see fit.

The federal government also operates the Canada Student Loans Program for students who do not have sufficient resources to cover the cost of full- or part-time studies at the postsecondary level. Interest on loans is paid by the government during a student's enrollment and repayment arrangements are made 6 to 18 months after the student graduates.

There is growing pressure from the universities for additional funding, with both faculty and students complaining of out-of-date facilities and equipment, crowded classrooms, and insufficient funds for research. Various proposals have been made from increasing fees to instituting a system whereby graduates would pay additional income taxes based on their salary levels once they are employed.

6. Supplying Personnel for the Education System

With the doubling of enrollment between 1951 and 1971, the number of elementary–secondary school teachers reached a new high of 284,900 in 1976–77, declined slightly until the mid-1980s, but has shown a steady increase since that time. Based on a student–teacher ratio of 17.9:1 (number of students per full-time teacher) in 1991–92, the estimated number of teachers for the school year 1993–94 was 301,400. It is probable that the increase is the result of educational reforms and new programs such as ESL (English as a Second Language) to accommodate a growing immigrant population, as well as the increased focus on computer technology. At the postsecondary level, it was estimated that there would be 37,900 full-time university teachers and 27,260 community college teachers in 1993–94.

About 94 percent of elementary–secondary teachers

are employed in public schools, 5 percent in private schools, and the remaining 1 percent in federal schools. In 1991–92, 60 percent of teachers were female, although three out of four public school administrators were men. As is the case with the labor force in general, the average age of teachers has increased owing to low recruitment and a high retention rate; in 1992, only 12 percent were under 30 years of age, compared to 40 percent 15 years earlier.

Teachers' working conditions depend on rules and regulations established by ministries or departments of education, as well as stipulations and policies of school boards who do the actual hiring. All provinces and territories require teachers to hold valid teaching certificates, or to be eligible for certification status. The eligibility requirement is normally a four-year Bachelor of Education (BEd) degree, or equivalent, from a recognized university. Alternatively, a one-year BEd degree may follow a first bachelor's degree in any field of study. Candidates for certification are assessed by the provincial department which also classifies the certificate level (general or specialist), subject area of specialization, and grade level. New teachers are usually required to complete a two-year probationary period. Salary levels are determined by certificate classification level and the number of years of successful teaching experience.

Canadian schools have faced many demands for new programs, ranging from second language instruction and computer technology to AIDS awareness, multicultural orientation, and integration of exceptional children in the regular classroom. The majority of provinces and territories offer inservice programs to help teachers adapt to innovations and learn new skills. Summer programs are also regularly offered by universities and departments of education.

At the postsecondary level, universities, with the exception of certain professional sectors of training, require a doctoral degree as part of the qualifications for entry to faculty tenure-stream positions. Some community college teachers also hold doctoral degrees, although work experience is the principal criterion for certain vocational and technical instructors. Universities and colleges employ a number of part-time or contractually limited lecturers and instructors as well. Virtually no provision is made for formal pedagogical training of postsecondary educators. This lack, and the importance many universities accord to academic research rather than teaching, was the subject of a 1991 report on Canadian university education (Smith 1991). While the relative importance of research and publications versus teaching is not a new issue, it is likely to receive more attention in the 1990s.

7. Curriculum Development and Teaching Methodology

Educational systems in Canada underwent sweeping reforms in the 1960s and early 1970s. Concepts such as child-centered learning, continuous progress, team teaching, discovery method, open-plan schools, and audiovisual aids were adopted, sometimes with little attention to the consequences for educational outcomes or teacher training. School programs that had been made up largely of compulsory subjects and texts specified by provincial departments of education also underwent considerable modification and many new programs were introduced.

Structurally, educational systems became more decentralized. Provinces continued to issue general guidelines, but local boards and individual schools had more control over implementation, materials, and methods. Teaching became less formal and more participatory as a counter-trend to the traditional lecture method and learning by rote. Less emphasis was placed on the learning of "facts," and more on the acquisition of skills to facilitate learning.

While these educational reforms had positive outcomes, especially in terms of providing for individual differences and community needs, and for implementing equal access policies, since the mid-1980s schools have become the target of considerable criticism from employers, from universities, and from parents. Complaints focus on a perceived decline in academic standards, and in literacy and mathematical ability. Public pressure has been exerted in two somewhat conflicting directions: the expectation that schools will incorporate programs pertaining to social and ethical issues, and, at the same time, provide a solid foundation in "the basics." The result has been a trend to redefining an essential "core" curriculum incorporating more compulsory academic courses, mainly in mathematics, sciences, language arts, and social studies (usually history and geography). Elective courses which proliferated in the 1970s have undergone scrutiny. There is, however, a recognition of essential new knowledge and skills beyond the traditional "3 R's." Curricula therefore incorporate computer technology and components such as critical and creative thinking, independent learning, and environmental studies.

In response to national social and cultural policies, considerable effort is made to eliminate racial and sexual stereotypes from learning materials. Second-language learning is emphasized, and in some provinces students have the opportunity to study the less commonly taught languages. Alberta, for example, offers Cree (a native Indian language) and Ukranian, two groups that have contributed to the provincial culture. Sex equity is also fostered by depicting role models for girls and encouraging them to consider nontraditional careers, especially in disciplines and professions involving science or mathematics.

Curriculum materials produced by departments or ministries of education are normally pilot-tested in the schools and revised before receiving official ministry sanction. Curriculum materials produced by the private sector are usually subject to an approval process involving ministry and school board officials before being sanctioned officially. Other materials are considered to be curriculum-support materials.

8. The System of Examinations, Promotions, and Certifications

Continuous progress is the norm in elementary schools. At the secondary level, credit systems are the rule and promotion by subject rather than grade is prevalent. Some jurisdictions have partially or entirely eliminated age-grouped classes. In general, the policy in Canada of open access to secondary education may be summarized as follows: although there is no automatic promotion, the school curriculum provides courses of studies at various levels so that differing abilities can be accommodated.

Graduation from secondary school is based on completion of the number of course credits specified by provincial guidelines. In most systems, examinations are prepared and students are assessed at the local level. However, in several provinces, notably British Columbia, Alberta, and Quebec (as well as the Northwest and Yukon territories which generally follow the programs of Alberta and British Columbia, respectively), graduation diploma examinations in certain subjects are centrally set by the department of education. The type and level of diplomas awarded differ within jurisdictions, but most provinces provide for general and advanced high-school diplomas in recognition of modified programs followed by students who do not intend to enter university. An average of over 60 percent of high-school graduates go on to some form of postsecondary education.

9. Educational Assessment, Evaluation, and Research

The trend to redefining a "core curriculum" and including more compulsory subjects has been accompanied by an emphasis on the measurement of educational outcomes. These focus not only on the assessment of student achievement, but also on the evaluation of programs, teachers, schools, and school systems.

At the elementary level, more attention is being given to the development of evaluation techniques to monitor student progress on a day-to-day basis, rather than summatively at the end of a term. Some provinces have instituted large-scale student testing in specific subjects at selected grade levels, a process which allows individual school systems and schools to be evaluated as well as students.

In 1989, the members of the CMEC combined their expertise in educational evaluation in order to develop the School Achievement Indicators Program. The program provides data to assist each province and territory in making policy decisions and planning program improvement. Indicators of student participation in the systems, as well as graduation rates, will form part of a profile that also includes indicators of the achievement of 13- and 16-year old students in reading, writing, and mathematics. The CMEC was to report to the Canadian public on all indicators in the fall of 1993.

Research in education is carried out in all provinces and territories, although the level of activity varies because of differences in population density. A significant number of studies are undertaken by members of university faculties of education, as well as by educational organizations and teachers' federations. The federal government, through the Social Sciences and Humanities Research Council, is a major source of funding, especially for university researchers. Provincial departments and some larger school boards also direct research efforts to matters of regional or local concern, such as program evaluation. Although there is a recognition of the need for national studies, such as the proposed CMEC assessment, because of the political structure of Canadian education, such undertakings are often difficult to implement and fund.

There are a number of channels for the distribution of research results, including scholarly journals, and manual and computer access to references to published papers by services such as the *Canadian Education Index*, published by the Canadian Education Association, ONTERIS (Ontario Educational Research Information System), and EDUQ (Education Quebec). At the national level, Statistics Canada, the official governmental body responsible for the census and the collection of data on all aspects of Canadian life, produces regular statistical reports, analyses, and projections relating to all levels of education.

10. Major Reforms in the 1980s and 1990s

Canada has undergone profound social and economic changes since the early 1970s that created a widespread awareness of the need to rethink educational objectives and the way in which they are implemented. The increasing racial and cultural diversity of Canadian society, native needs, issues of greater equality for women, provision within the systems for exceptional students, and other social issues have generated one set of educational priorities. At the same time, faced with an increasingly competitive world economy, education authorities have been pressured by the general public, the business community, the media, and students themselves, to provide more appropriate preparation and skills for the workforce. Moreover, especially since the early 1980s, this demand for better results has existed within a recessionary period of increasing budgetary cutbacks.

Given such diverse demands on twelve systems of education, it is perhaps not surprising that response to date has been somewhat piecemeal. As discussed in the previous sections, schools boards across Canada actively promote multiculturalism, equality of rights, and crosscultural understanding. Programs for English and French as a second language were expanded, as well as public and private-sector literacy programs. New information technologies led to the development of innovative programs and policies on the use of computers. In recognition of the role of education in preparing students for employment, a variety of school-to-work transition programs and cooperative work–study arrangements were implemented at both the secondary and postsecondary levels. The issue of what subjects should be considered compulsory and how educational outcomes can be best assessed, either at the classroom level or by large-scale provincial, or even national, testing became, and remains, a priority. Although considerable progress was made in identifying core curricula, emphasizing accountability, and instituting means of assessment, it is generally recognized that these changes can only be considered as part of an ongoing effort to reform systems to respond to complex social, economic, and political issues.

11. Major Problems for the Year 2000

It is probable that agreement on appropriate curricula, the measurement of educational outcomes, and remedies for functional illiteracy will still be major issues in the year 2000.

It is also likely that there will be an increasing recognition of the need to define the role of the school in a complex society and to identify priorities. In the last several decades, Canadian educational systems have given an almost "kneejerk" response to the multiple demands placed on them. It seems questionable whether schools can continue to pursue academic excellence and, at the same time, be expected to ameliorate social problems by providing the young with life skills, counseling, and moral and social values that were traditionally acquired within the family setting.

It has also been suggested that Canadians, despite their apparent commitment to education, do not value learning to the extent of some other cultures. Although Canada has one of the highest participation rates in the world in postsecondary education, it still lacks the highly skilled workers, particularly in scientific and technological areas, that are necessary if the country is to compete and prosper in a global economy. It has been estimated that nearly two-thirds of the jobs created between 1989 and 2000 will require a minimum of 12 years of schooling and 40 percent will require more than 16 years of training. The existing dropout rate in secondary schools will potentially create a large pool of unemployable, unskilled workers at the turn of the century. Opportunities for returning to school and for retraining are therefore likely to become priorities, as well as the development of new learning environments to promote continuing education.

Financial constraints will be the major concern for universities and other institutions offering postsecondary education. Alternative methods of financing and more efficient delivery systems may be debated. For example, there may be a trend to more specialization within institutions which presently offer programs across a range of academic disciplines and professions.

Finally, one cannot overlook the constitutional crisis of the 1990s which is likely to extend well into the twenty-first century. Educational systems cannot be considered in isolation from the politics, priorities, and culture of the society they serve, and any realignment among provinces, or between provinces and the federal government, will inevitably have a profound effect on education, as it will on all social institutions in Canada.

References

Council of Ministers of Education, Canada 1991a *Secondary Education in Canada: A Student Transfer Guide*, 6th edn. CMEC, Toronto

Smith S L 1991 *Report of the Commission of Inquiry on Canadian University Education*. The Commission, Ottawa

Further Reading

Canadian Education Statistics Council 1990 *A Statistical Portrait of Elementary and Secondary Education in Canada*. Statistics Canada and Council of Ministers of Education, Canada, Ottawa and Toronto

Corpus Almanac and Canadian Sourcebook 1991, 26th edn. Southam, Don Mills

Council of Ministers of Education, Canada 1988 *Recent Trends in Curriculum Reform at the Elementary and Secondary Levels in Canada*. Report presented to the OECD's Centre for Educational Research and Innovation (CERI). CMEC, Toronto

Council of Ministers of Education, Canada 1989 *Education in Canada, 1986–88*. Report to the 41st Session, International Conference on Education, Geneva, Jan. 9–17, 1989. CMEC, Toronto

Council of Ministers of Education, Canada 1990a *Adult Literacy, Canada*. Report to the 42nd Session, International Conference on Education, Geneva, Sept. 3–8, 1990. CMEC, Toronto

Council of Ministers of Education, Canada 1990b *Improving the Quality of Basic Education in Canada*. Prepared for the Eleventh Conference of Commonwealth Education Ministers. CMEC, Toronto

Council of Ministers of Education, Canada 1991b *Teachers' Working Conditions in Canada*. Report prepared in response to the International Labour Office questionnaire on The Conditions of Work of Teachers. CMEC, Toronto

Learning Well ... Living Well. Draft discussion paper for pre-consultation meetings 1990. Government of Canada, Ottawa

Statistics Canada 1986 *Canadian Social Trends*. (Quarterly) Statistics Canada, Ottawa

Statistics Canada 1990 *Education in Canada. A Statistical*

Review for 1989–90. Statistics Canada, Ottawa (Cat. No. 81–229)

Statistics Canada 1991 *Advance Statistics of Education, 1993–94*. Statistics Canada, Ottawa (Cat. No. 81–220)

Statistics Canada 1993a *Canada Year Book, 1994*. Statistics Canada, Ottawa

Statistics Canada 1993b *Canada, a Portrait*. Official handbook of present conditions and recent progress. Statistics Canada, Ottawa (Cat. No. 11–403)

Central African Republic

D. Limbassa

1. General Background

The Central African Republic is a nation of approximately 623,000 square kilometers located in the central region of Africa. Landlocked, it is surrounded by Chad, the Sudan, Congo, Zaire, and Cameroon. Topographically, the country lies on a high plateau, which serves as the watershed between Lake Chad and the Congo River basins. This area includes a system of inland waterways, which is important for transportation, commerce, and communications. Important river ports include the one at the nation's capital, Bangui, and those at Salo and Nola. The central plains rise to mountainous areas, including the Massif du Tondou and the Chaine des Mongos in the east and northeast and the Monts Karre in the west.

In 1988 the population was estimated to be about 2.7 million persons. Nearly 43 percent was under the age of 14 years. Some 63 percent of the population lives in rural areas and the density is 4 inhabitants per square kilometer. The population growth rate is 2.5 percent per year. The population includes a variety of ethnic groups. The largest are the Banda and the Baya, followed in number by the Mandjia, the Ubangi, the Sara, the Mboum, the Fertit, the nomadic Bororo-Fulani, and the Pygmies. A number of Europeans, mainly of French nationality, are concentrated around Bangui. French and Sango serve as the official languages. Some 60 percent of the population have traditional (mainly animist) beliefs, 20 percent are Roman Catholic, 15 percent are Protestant, and 5 percent are Moslem.

In 1989, the per capita Gross National Product (GNP) was estimated at US\$390 (or US\$290 per capita GDP). The majority of persons work in the agricultural sector and much of the agricultural production is at subsistence level. About 6 percent were employed in manufacturing, industry, and construction; 4 percent in commerce; and 1 percent in administration. Nearly 45 percent were unemployed. The main exports are cotton, coffee, and groundnuts. Minerals include diamonds, and there is the possibility of substantial uranium production. There is a deficit in the balance of payments.

Transportation is one of the main problems confronting economic development. There is a fairly extensive road network, but it has not been well maintained. Due to seasonal factors, the roads are only dependable at certain times during the year. The major source of transportation is the river system, especially the stretch of the Ubangi River which flows between Bangui and Brazzaville, Congo. There is a proposal for a Bangui–Yaoundé railway, and air transportation is facilitated by the major airport at Bangui and several smaller ones. The most widespread means of internal communication is radio.

The Central African Republic gained official independence from France in 1960. In 1976, the Constitution was amended and a new Constitution was adopted. In 1987, a democratic election was held and members of parliament were elected. In 1991, there was an amendment to the Constitution to create the post of a prime minister and to install a multiparty system.

In 1988, the illiteracy rate was 63 percent among all those aged 10 years or more. The primary school gross enrollment ratio was 67 percent (6- to 11-year olds) giving a net enrollment ratio of 49 percent. Average class sizes are 83 at primary level and 72 at secondary school in 1990. Of those in primary school, 17 percent succeeded in the end-of-primary-school exams and 19 percent of those in secondary school in the end-of-secondary-school exams.

2. Politics and the Goals of the Education System

The system of education was inherited from the colonial period at Independence and remained unchanged for 20 years. This academic system was geared towards the production of a small elite of administrators. The system was not appropriate for the socioeconomic needs of the country and it became increasingly apparent that there was a major crisis. For those in school, the majority were in academic tracks and few were educated in vocational and technical education because of only skeletal provision. At the end of secondary school, there was high enrollment in the arts subjects and little enrollment in the science subjects. This resulted in many graduates of secondary schools being unemployed. With the population increase and the democratization of education, the insufficiency of human and material resources for the school system exacerbated the crisis. Not only was there a decrease

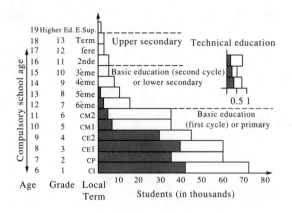

Figure 1
Central African Republic: Structure of the formal education system[a]
a The nonshaded part of each grade level indicates the number of children over age. The shaded part indicates the number of pupils of the equivalent age

in the quality of education, but also in the internal and external efficiency of the system.

In 1982, a national effort was focused on the problems of education and training. This has resulted in the establishment of a new school system responding to the realistic needs of the Republic. The goals of the new school system are to ensure the child's full intellectual, physical, moral, civic, and vocational development. The child must learn to read, write, calculate, and, at the same time, develop a sense of productive work and a sense of the responsibilities involved in being a citizen. The overall aim is for the system to provide a basic education for all, an education that is both general and practical, and relevant to the environment. Instruction will be conducted in French and Sango, the two official languages. The teacher has three roles: to teach, to be a leader in the community, and to involve parents and other members of the community in school affairs. The reform envisaged more emphasis on mathematics, science, and technology in the higher levels of secondary school.

3. The Formal Structure Of Education

3.1 Primary, Secondary, and Tertiary Education

Education is compulsory from the age of 6 to 17 (primary and secondary education). Figure 1 presents a diagram of the new educational system. Primary education (*Enseignement Fondamental, Niveau* 1) lasts for five years. Students enter at age 6 after having completed two years of preprimary school. After five years, the students enter either lower-secondary school or vocational centers. Lower-secondary education (*Enseignement Fondamental, Niveau* 2) lasts for

four years and has three tracks: general, vocational and technical, and agricultural and artisan. Upper-secondary school lasts three years and has general and vocational tracks. Higher education trains persons to a high level of proficiency either for the higher echelons of administration, the teaching service, or research. The University of Bangui has faculties of law, law and economics, the humanities, science, and medicine. There are also four *grandes écoles* for administration, business, and rural development, and a polytechnic. The University had an enrollment of 2,472 students and the *grandes écoles* an enrollment of 346 in the academic year 1989–90.

Grade-repeating rates in primary and lower-secondary school are high and in the order of 30 percent per year. There are 279 days (including Sundays) in the school year. This was computed by deducting all official holidays from 365 days. Officially, there are 4.5 hours of instruction per day in primary school.

3.2 Preschool Education

Preprimary education lasts two years. Children enter at the age of 4 years. The aim is to facilitate the transition from the family to school and to instill work habits in the children.

3.3 Vocational, Technical, and Business Education

Following primary school, students can either enter lower-secondary school or go to local vocational centers where they learn practical skills for the type of employment that exists in the local communities. For those entering lower-secondary school, students opt to enter either the academic track or vocational and technical tracks. The same is true at the upper-secondary school. The curriculum training centers cover such areas as masonry, carpentry, and metal work. The technical college attached to the *Lycée Technical* in Bangui runs courses for automechanics, electricians, and administrators. The Technical College for Women in Bangui has courses in domestic science. Finally, the National Center for the Training of Artisans runs courses in jewelry, basket-weaving and furniture-making, leatherwork, and metalwork.

Efforts are being made to increase the percentage of an age-group entering school and to encourage more students to take vocational courses.

3.4 Adult and Nonformal Education

Nonformal education is regarded as an integrated and indispensable part of the formal educational system. Literacy programs are run by the Division for Nonformal Education of the Ministry of Basic Secondary and Technical Education. This division is responsible for the production of literacy and post-literacy materials, the collection of data to do with literacy and recurrent education, follow-up and evaluation of the various literacy programs, and sensitizing the population to participate in mass literacy programs.

It should be noted, however, that there are difficulties in supplementing literacy activities because of a lack of funding. In 1992 there were only eight zones where these programs were in operation: three of these zones were in Bangui and five in the countryside.

Other bodies are involved in functional literacy programs, sometimes working on their own and sometimes in cooperation with the Division for Nonformal Education. Examples of such bodies are the Regional Centers of Education and Training (CREF), the Central African Agency for the Development of Ouham-Pende (ACADOP), the Evangelical Associations' Project for Agricultural Development (PREDAS), organizations for community and social development, and the National Civic Service for the Promotion of Youth (SCNPJ). The government has also created an ad hoc committee in the campaign against illiteracy in order to strengthen all literacy activities.

Another form of education that exists is that of Koranic education. This consists of teaching the Koran to children in Moslem communities. However, it is beginning to take on a more modern form in that new subjects are being introduced. These include grammar, Arabic, mathematics, and literature. It is said that the Arab–Islamic school comprises a pure Koran study part and an Arabic study part which is identical to the lay school.

4. Administrative and Supervisory Structure and Operation

Before 1986 all administration was centralized and in the hands of the Ministry of Education. After 1986 there was a reorganization of the administration in order to make it more effective. Decentralization took place and six *"inspections académiques"* were created. Modern methods of management and a permanent system of "control" (*Inspection Générale de l'Education*) were introduced. In addition, two institutions were established to help in the improvement of the administrative system. These were the National Center for Recurrent Training (*Centre National de Formation Continue*) and the National Institute for Educational Research and Development (*Institut National de Recherche et d'Animation Pédagogiques*).

The Ministry of Education has several tasks, among which are: the general administration of the educational system; the conceptualization, development, implementation, and monitoring of education as formulated in governmental decrees; the planning of all educational activities; the monitoring of the private school system; the conduct of all examinations and national competitions; research on the sources of financing; and the coordination of aid organizations in the field of education. One of its main tasks is funding of school buildings, school furniture and supplies, and teacher training, as well as the general administration of the system. A large amount of funding comes from France, and other funds in the form of loans or gifts come from the World Bank, the African Development Bank, and the United Nations Development Program.

5. Educational Finance

The percentage of the state budget allocated to education was 29 in 1980, 21 in 1989, and 19 in 1990. Two programs of structural adjustment took place in this period of time. These included the curtailment of the funds allocated to the social services and, in particular, to education. It should also be noted that the gross enrollment ratios in education decreased from 72 to 67 percent from 1980 to 1990.

In 1990, the education budget (19% of the state budget) was allocated as follows: Primary education (53.8%), lower-secondary education (14.4%), higher-secondary education (21.0%), administration (4.6%), and miscellaneous (6.2%).

The per student expenditures were US\$47 for primary, US\$86 for secondary, and US\$1,710 for higher education in 1990 (US\$1 = 282.5 CFA).

6. Supplying Personnel for the Education System

Primary school teachers are trained at the *Ecole National d'instituteurs* (ENI). The course lasts two years. To enter the ENI, a candidate must have passed the *baccalauréat*.

Up to 1986, those having a *baccalauréat* could compete for places at the *Ecole Normale Supérieure* (ENS) where there was a two-year training course to become a teacher in the second cycle of basic education (lower-secondary). In 1992, the training of second-cycle basic education teachers had been suspended.

Teachers for the upper-secondary school were recruited from university graduates possessing a degree (*licence*) for a one-year teacher training course at the ENS. By 1992, these teachers received a two-year teacher-training course at the ENS and qualified for a Certificate of Educational Aptitude in Secondary Education (*CAPES*). They are recruited from among those having a licence, as well as from practicing teachers in the second cycle of basic education.

Because of a deficit of primary school teachers, a crash program has been mounted. Candidates are recruited from university students who have not only the *baccalauréat* qualification, but also one or two university certificates obtained in the first or second year at the University. Thus far, this nine-month crash program has produced 234 teachers.

In some provincial schools, there are community teachers who have been recruited from pupils having graduated from the second cycle of basic education. They are employed by the local communities. In 1990, about 60 percent of all primary school teachers were of this category.

In 1990, there were 3,582 primary school teachers, 953 lower- and higher-secondary school teachers, and 410 faculty members in all institutions of higher education. In higher education there were 79 national, 57 foreign, and 274 part-time faculty members.

7. The System of Examinations, Promotions, and Certifications

In primary school, there are monthly assessments by teachers and an end-of-the-year examination. A certain standard must be reached in the end-of-year examination in order to be promoted to the next grade. However, for those pupils who have been working at the time of the monthly assessments or end-of-year examinations the teacher can decide on promotion. At the end of primary school there are two types of examinations: the first results in a Certificate of Primary Education (CEPE) and the second is a competitive examination in order to enter the second cycle of basic education.

In the second cycle of basic education (lower-secondary) there are term assessments. The average of the three term results determines promotion to the next grade. At the end of lower-secondary school there is a national examination for the *Brevet d'Etudes du Premier Cycle* (BEPC). Depending on a pupil's results in the different subjects, he or she is oriented to the general or technical streams in upper-secondary school.

The same form of assessment is undertaken in the upper-secondary school as in the lower-secondary school. At the end of upper-secondary, the pupils sit for the *baccalauréat* (*Second Degré*). The passing of the *baccalauréat* gives the right for admission to higher education.

8. Major Reforms in the 1980s and 1990s

In 1986, the reform of education was legislated and was to begin in the period of the five-year plan from 1986–90. Priority was awarded to the reform of primary education and the aims were to increase enrollment and improve the quality of education. At the secondary-school level, priority was awarded to the training of science and vocational teachers, and at the university level to the initiation of more science courses.

In 1990–91 there was a teachers' strike with the result that nothing happened in the schools, and this obviously affected any improvement in the system. There is a severe deficit in the number of teachers. Above all, there is a lack of funding to deal with the many problems of buildings, supplies, and teachers. Until this situation is improved little can be accomplished.

9. Major Problems for the Year 2000

As already mentioned, the lack of funding is likely to be a major problem for several years to come. Many noble words have been written about the rights of children to education, and the Central African Republic has endorsed the aims for education emanating from the World Conference on Education for All held in Jomtiem in 1990. However, there is much to be achieved in practice. The main aims in this country will be to decrease illiteracy (especially for girls), promote productive work at school, help students to enter the labor market, introduce health and environment education, improve teachers' conditions, and develop a private school system.

Given that education is the responsibility of each and every citizen, efforts will need to be made to involve local communities and parents in the educational school system in the communities. This is a necessary, but long and arduous task. The challenge is great.

Chad

T. D. Moadjidibaye

1. General Background

The Republic of Chad is situated in the heart of Africa. In 1979, it was dubbed the "soft lower chest of Africa" by journalists. It covers 1,284,000 square kilometers, stretches 1,440 kilometers from north to south and 720 kilometers from east to west and is land-locked. To the north is Libya; to the east, Sudan; to the south, the Central African Republic; and to the west; Niger, Nigeria, and Cameroon. The capital city is N'Djamena. The population was estimated at just over 5 million in 1984. In the period 1980 to 1985, the population growth rate was estimated to be 2.36 percent and could have been near 3 percent at the beginning of the 1990s. Over 30 percent of the population is under 20 years of age and there are over 1 million children in the age range

6 to 15 years. Of these 1 million, less than 50 percent (i.e., 300,000) of the children are in school.

There are two climatic zones separated by a wide transitional Sudano–Sahelian area. The northern zone tends to be barren and cattle-raising is the main activity. The southern zone is wooded savanna with humid river valleys and agriculture is the main activity. The inhabitants in the north tend to be nomadic or seminomadic Moslem herders, and in the south they are farming people who live in fixed abodes and tend to be animists or Christians.

The mainstays of the economy are cotton and livestock. The agricultural sector accounts for 90 percent of export earnings and 57 percent of Gross National Product (GNP). The most productive area is in the south (the *préfectures* of middle Chari, Mayo-Kekki, Tandjile, and the eastern and western Logones). Cotton alone accounts for 70 percent of export earnings. Animal husbandry, the traditional activity of the northern nomads, is the second largest earner (mostly to neighboring countries).

Through a process of partnership with France, a certain number of companies have been created in the south, including the Chadian textile company (STT) and a brewery (*Brasseries du Logone*). Pending the exploitation of oil discovered in the Lake Chad area and in the Valley of Logone, three oil companies (Mobil, Total, and Shell) operating a joint facility for the storage, sale, and distribution of refined oil, were established in the capital city, N'Djamena. Esso and its subcontractors operate in the south of Chad for a consortium of Esso, Shell, and Chevron.

French and Arabic are the two official languages. Chadian Arabic, the language of the north is also the *lingua franca* of the capital city. The most common languages spoken in the south are those of Sara-Bongo-Baguirmian or Sara Group—the Sara Madjingay, the Ngambay, and the Mbay Moissala to name but a few. Many other more or less structurally related languages are the Toubou, Kanembou, Kotoko, Massa, and so forth.

Chad became an independent republic in 1960. A succession of kingdoms characterize the early history of Chad. The cultural and political strife and tension between the Arabized northeast and animist south date back to those times. During the last half of the nineteenth century, the United Kingdom and France disputed the territory, and only in 1899 was agreement reached that France would assume control of the area. The colony of Chad was formally established by the French in 1920 and the territory of Chad was founded in 1946. After Independence, there was fighting between the north and the south. This was severe at the end of the 1970s. Despite numerous peace agreements and ceasefires, the civil war continued. The war had international ramifications, with France and the United States supporting one group and Libya the other. The relentless civil war, compounded by the protracted Sahelian droughts, resulted in all efforts and much

of the resources going into the war and fighting the drought. Resource priority for education was limited until 1982.

Economic and social well-being deteriorated during the period of droughts and war. School enrollment is one of the lowest in Africa. The literacy rate is only 25 percent. The pattern of schooling is still the same as that of the colonial power. Chad has few paved roads, no rail network, and only a few airfields capable of handling commercial aircraft at prohibitive costs. The Chari River, the largest in Chad, and one that runs through the capital, had no bridge until the end of the 1980s when the *Pont de la Chanson* was built. The name comes from the fact that the money to build the bridge was raised at a concert. Before the bridge was built, only means of transport across the Chari was by ferry.

2. Politics and the Goals of the Education System

At Independence, the aim was to provide basic education opportunities to all children and, when possible, to adults. Several efforts were made, over a 10-year period, to improve the formal system of education. However, because of the enormous financial constraints and the perceived nonrelevance of such education on the part of the parents, they have basically failed.

In 1962, within the framework of a large project named "Operation Mandoul" attempts were made to introduce farming into a number of pilot schools in the Koumra region of the country. This also included reforming the curriculum and revising teaching approaches. This costly venture had no substantial effects because the needs of the local population had not been taken into account. In 1968, attempts were made to extend some of the ideas of the 1962 experiment to more rural schools. This was primarily concerned with the integration of agricultural and handicraft subjects into the normal school curriculum in order to make it practically oriented.

In 1973, another project was begun. This was to change the colonial school structure. It was an ambitious scheme to create a school structure of four cycles, each cycle having its own specific goal:

(a) The first cycle was to last 5 years—children were to acquire basic knowledge and the ability to change according to the changing social environment and to think on their own.

(b) The second cycle was to last 3 years—this was aimed toward reinforcing and consolidating the previously acquired skills and knowledge.

(c) The third cycle was to last 4 years and included the main components of vocational training.

(d) The last cycle could be likened to an advanced training for the elite, with the focus being on the training of highly qualified persons needed for the socioeconomic development of the country.

This highly selective project planned ways and means for the school leavers to enter socioeconomic life from each stage of schooling. The most important outcome of the project was the creation of the Institute for Educational Sciences (*Institut National des Sciences de l'Education*—INSE) and, above all, legislation instituting the reform of the Chadian school system. The main idea behind this reform was to adapt the school system to socioeconomic development needs, promote Chadian cultural identity, reinforce national unity, and rationalize the utilization of human resources in order to foster economic development. In the wake of this reform process, the creation of "pilot schools" constituted the only concrete outcome.

By 1978, this philosophy resulted in the primary school providing basic conventional teaching coupled with about two hours of practical work each week for boys in intermediate classes and workshops where they were initiated into crop husbandry, ironwork, and carpentry by practical work instructors. The objective was to integrate the pupils into the productive system of the area where they lived. This objective was consistent with the new teaching philosophy and was to be extended later to secondary school in order to establish the structural link "elementary–secondary–vocational teaching complexes" combining regional production activities and formal education. The new school would be open to parent associations and village communities in collaboration with the regional development authorities.

In 1979 the civil war brought the whole process to a halt. None of the good intentions and schemes were translated into programs of action and no operational strategy was defined to implement the educational policy. Nevertheless, a few rewarding elements of these projects were kept, notably the "parent association" and "village community" which ushered in a sort of "local school system" era in Chad, providing a new educational partner for the future Chadian school system. It was this "partner" that operated the school system during the period of the war (1979–82), even without discontinuity in certain areas where the structures had been completely destroyed. In 1992, legislation was underway to institute and legalize the "Parent Association."

In 1982, schools all over the country opened again. The main objective of the Ministry of National Education was focused on restoring the school system to its prewar structure. Emergency schemes were implemented from 1985 to late 1988 to refurbish school buildings and train and retrain teaching staff. It was a challenging period, by the end of which most of the school system had been put on track again. The main education issues had been reassessed and rationally addressed, paving the way for the new Chadian School in the year 2000.

3. The Formal System of Education

The Chadian formal educational system is structured approximately according to the French educational structure. It includes preschool institutions, the basic or elementary institutions, and secondary and higher education institutions. Figure 1 depicts the overall structure of the educational system.

3.1 Primary, Secondary, and Tertiary Education

Basic or primary school lasts for six years. Pupils can enter at the ages of 6 or 7. At the end of primary school an examination is taken. On the basis of the results, students enter either secondary school or centers of vocational training.

Secondary school is composed of two cycles. The first cycle lasts for four years at the end of which students obtain the *Brevet d'Etudes du Premier Cycle* (BEPC) which is nothing more than the first secondary cycle leaving certificate. The second cycle leading to the *baccalauréat* is a prerequisite for admission to the higher education institutions such as the University of Chad.

The University of Chad, one of the most outstanding higher training institutions, constitutes the third level of the educational system. The University has four faculties: arts and social sciences, law and economics, exact and applied sciences, and medical studies. Each of these faculties is divided into two cycles: the first cycle terminating with the DEUG (*Diplome d'Etudes Universitaires Général*) which is the first cycle diploma. The second cycle ends with the *licence*

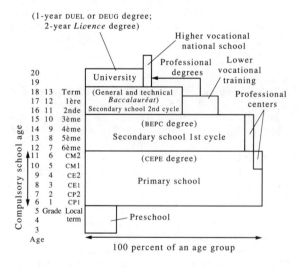

Figure 1
Chad: Structure of the formal education system

usually equated with a BA degree. The University of Chad has discontinued conducting the master degree program which was started in the late 1970s.

3.2 Preschool Education

Preschool education (*enseignement préscolaire*) institutions are more or less a combination of *écoles maternelles* and kindergartens. Children can enter these institutions at any time between the ages of three and five years. A very small proportion of an age group attends the *écoles maternelles*. They tend to exist in urban areas only. Attendance is free. The content of work is play-centered and basically socializes children for entering the primary school.

3.3 Special Education

Although there are mentally and physically handicapped children, there are no special provisions for them. They do not go to school but remain with their families.

3.4 Vocational, Technical, and Business Education

Following primary school, students can enter either vocational training centers or industrial–technical schools. The vocational centers are multipurpose school complexes that integrate technical and professional training along with manual and practical work in the forms of production in the areas where the centers are created.

There are two kinds of technical school. The first is a technical training school (*collège*) where the course lasts three years. To enter, a student must have completed one year of lower-secondary education. At the end of the course, the student receives a professional aptitude certificate (CAP). The second type of technical school is parallel to the upper-secondary school and is known as a *Lycée Technique Industriel*. To enter, a student must have successfully completed the BEPC at the end of the lower-secondary school and passed a special entrance examination. Courses last three years, at the end of which, upon successful completion of examinations, the student will receive a *Brevet de Technique* or a *baccalauréat* for technicans. There is also a parallel *Lycée Technique Commercial* which is similar to the *Lycée Technique Industriel* but focuses on commercial subjects.

At the higher education level, there are a number of professional training institutions. Students must have the academic, technical, or commercial *baccalauréat* to enter. Many of the professional institutions also have their own selective entrance examinations. The major institutions are:

(a) *Ecole Normale Supérieure* (ENS) where secondary school teachers and elementary school inspectors are trained. Those eligible for admission must be holders of the *baccalauréat* and pass a very selective test. There is just one ENS in the country and it is in N'Djamena.

(b) *Ecoles Normales* (of which, there are five) are in N'Djamena, Sarh, Moundou, Bongor, and there is also the Bilingual Normal school of Abeché (French and Arabic). They train elementary school teachers.

(c) *The Ecole Nationale d'Administration et de Magistrature* (ENAM) is located in N'Djamena and trains administrators and magistrates and other administrative agents. The holders of the *baccalauréat* are eligible for entrance and must also pass a competitive examination.

(d) Students can enter the public work school from the first and second cycles and are trained as public works engineers. It is located in N'Djamena.

(e) The National Public Health and Social School is located in N'Djamena and trains social workers, nurses, and midwives.

(f) The National School of Telecommunications is located in Sarh and trains post and telecommunication technicians.

(g) There are two agricultural schools located in Bahili and Sarh which train agricultural and forestry technicians.

4. Administrative and Supervisory Structure and Operation

The Ministry of Education is responsible for the administration of education and for carrying out the government's educational policies. The Ministry has five major departments: (a) cabinet; (b) *diréction générale*; (c) *diréction de services* (for the separate divisions for primary education, secondary education, and technical and professional education)–literacy and the protection of national languages; planning, examinations, and competitions; educational projects; sport, youth, and civic education; higher education and scholarships; scientific and technical research; and administrative, financial, and equipment; (d) *des services exterieurs* (meaning *préfectures* outside of the capital); and (e) *des établissements sous tutelle* (the higher education institutions). The Ministry of Education is headed by the Minister of Education who is backed up by the Secretary of State for Higher Education and a Secretary of State for Youth and Sport.

There are, however, other ministries which are responsible for certain aspects of education. These are the Ministries of Agriculture and Rural Development, Public Health, Public Works, and Post and Telecommunications.

There are 14 *préfectures* and in each *préfecture* there

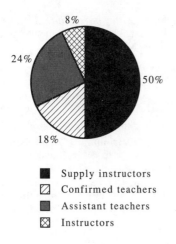

- ■ Supply instructors
- ▨ Confirmed teachers
- ■ Assistant teachers
- ⊠ Instructors

Figure 2
Distribution of teachers in elementary schools

is a *délégué à l'éducation*. There is a certain amount of decentralization, and since the end of the civil war there has been an increasing effort to involve village communities and parent associations in education through the *préfectures*. Inspectors are based at each large sub-*préfecture* and *préfecture*.

5. Educational Finance

In the past, the state financed all education. In 1992, the position was that there were three partners involved in the financing of education: the state (33%), external aid (61%), and parent associations (6%). The education budget in 1992 was 13.8 percent of the state budget. The state has pledged to raise this to 20 percent by the year 2000.

6. Supplying Personnel for the Education System

In the period up to Independence and up to 1987 there were two types of teacher-training institution: normal schools (*Ecoles Normale des Instituteurs*), for the training of elementary school teachers, the main intake of which came directly from the primary and the first cycle of secondary schools; and the normal higher training school (*Ecole Normale Superieure*) and the University of Chad.

In order to upgrade and improve the quality of teachers, it was decreed in 1987 that elementary or primary teachers should be holders of the *baccalauréat* (an *Ecole Normale des Instituteurs bacheliers* was therefore created) and those destined to teach in secondary schools should have at least the first university degree (DUEL or DEUG) or *licence*.

Two of the main characteristics of the Chadian elementary schools are the lack of required educational standards and understaffing. Yet the number of elementary school teachers has been estimated to be 6,215–90 percent of whom are actually teaching in classes and the remaining 10 percent being administrative personnel and supervisory staff. The distribution in terms of the level of education is the following: 1,098 are qualified primary school teachers (*instituteurs et institrices pleins*), 1,513 assistant primary teachers, 469 institutors (*moniteurs*), and 3,135 supply teachers with no pedagogical qualification at all (*maîtres suppléants*). In other words, at least 50 percent of elementary school teachers in Chad have no professional teaching qualification. The distribution of school personnel by category can be seen in Fig. 2. According to the 1989 census, there were 25,653 civil servants in the public sector so that the figure of 6,215 elementary teachers or about 24 percent is low. The total number of the elementary school pupils in 1988–89 was 425,000 pupils, and hence the pupil–teacher ratio was 68:1. This is very high compared to the median ratio for countries in the region where the ratio is 39:1. Even the ratio of 68:1 blurs disparities in the country because in urban areas such as N'Djamena, Sarh, Moundou, and Bongor, the size of classes reaches about 150 pupils.

There were about 1,210 secondary teachers in 1989, 45 percent of whom were not qualified to teach in secondary school. Moreover, there is a total lack of teachers in scientific subjects. The distribution of teachers according to their level of qualification is presented in Fig. 3.

In order to tackle the serious problem of understaffing in secondary schools, the structure of the unique Higher Normal Training School (*Ecole*

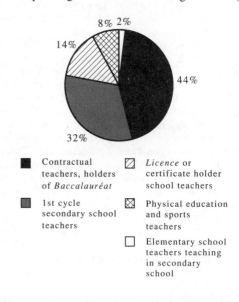

- ■ Contractual teachers, holders of *Baccalauréat*
- ▨ *Licence* or certificate holder school teachers
- ■ 1st cycle secondary school teachers
- ⊠ Physical education and sports teachers
- □ Elementary school teachers teaching in secondary school

Figure 3
Distribution of secondary school teachers by level of qualification

Normale Superieure—ENS) has been streamlined in such a way that first and second cycle secondary schools teachers are trained and recycled to acquire the required qualification.

In higher education in the academic year 1988–89, the total number of lecturers at the University of Chad was 57. There were 30 *maitre assistant* holders of doctorates and 27 assistant lecture holders of MA or MSc, and 10 laboratory assistants. Owing to the lack of full-time lecturers, the University has resorted to using the service of 67 part-time lecturers. Nevertheless, the lecturers and their assistants are still burdened by an enormous amount of teaching, leaving them with extremely little time for their research work.

7. Curriculum Development and Teaching Methodology

The whole process of curriculum development and design is the responsibility of the ISSED (*Institut Superieur de Science de l'Education*). In this process, the educational goals and objectives set by the government are taken into account. In terms of content, the curriculum is designed in such a way as to provide fundamental "know-how." Yet the curriculum had to be updated in 1983 in order to take account of social reality and adapt schools to the needs of the Chadian pupil. One of the main features of this adaptation was the attempt to introduce a national language into the school system. Through the international Francophone organization called CONFEMEN (*Conference des Ministres de l'Education Nationale*), the Chadian government realized that a child could easily learn the "3Rs" in its mother tongue. So the introduction of national language into the school system was considered to be a must. But there are two main obstacles to this:

(a) With a mosaic of Chadian languages, it has not been possible to choose one or two languages as a national language from among about 270 languages.

(b) Parents refused to accept that their children should be taught in a Chadian language—they prefer French.

8. Educational Assessment, Evaluation, and Research

Docimology or the science of evaluation and assessment is one of the educational areas in which there is no systematic work in Chad. Evaluation is administered at random according to the vagary of the educational background of the person involved. The prevailing evaluation system is that inherited from the French system, and there is no systematic evaluation at all.

The only examples of evaluation are those related to examination enabling students to move from one class to another. In this respect the traditional examination taken by candidates is not related to any set of specific objectives, but rather to subject matter and topics. This is, in part, because the Chadian curriculum is designed in terms of topics rather than specific objectives. The traditional examinations ranging from the "CEPE" of the elementary school to the *Maitrise* of the university are meant to evaluate the content of what is taught. In the early 1990s, such matters were improved. A *service d'evaluation et programme* was created within the Department of National Education. New goals and new objectives are being determined and tried out. The education system is expected to come to terms with the problems of assessment and evaluation in the near future.

9. Major Reforms in the 1980s

Since the civil war virtually wiped out the education system there was ample opportunity to create a new and modern system of education. However, little has been achieved except for the introduction of the new partnerships of "parent associations" and "village communities." Since the government was unable to rebuild and re-equip school buildings, the new partnership was essential if an educational system was to be re-established.

At the same time, it was important to identify the key aspects which had been responsible for the previous system's failing. The diagnosis of the weak points and proposals for the introduction of reforms has begun.

10. Major Problems for the Year 2000

The period of the two decades following Independence was marked by an education system evolving through false starts, and trial and error. Following the civil war, there was a great opportunity to capitalize on previous experience and to inaugurate a new era of a more reliable and stable system of education. This new system would:

(a) avoid wasting money on "white elephant" educational projects (as in the 1960s and 1970s);

(b) provide more incentives to parents associations to be involved in school affairs;

(c) set well-defined priorities along the lines of the Jomtien "Education for All" Conference in 1990

(d) place more emphasis on preparation for the working life in the Chad population.

It is also important to increase school enrollment.

At the primary school level, plans are in hand to increase the enrollment rates from 48 percent (1989) to 60 percent (2000) and ensure, at the same time, that dropout decreases and that the number of children receiving a primary school-leaving certificate triples. At the secondary school level, the increase in the number of students enrolled should move from 45,000 in 1989 to 76,000 in the year 2000. The increase would be more at the lower than at the higher secondary levels. In the industrial and commercial schools there would be a 20 percent increase. At the higher education level, the plans are to decrease by 10 percent the number of students at the University of Chad but, at the same time, increase enrollment in the Science Faculty and decrease enrollment in the faculties of arts and social sciences and law and economics.

Bibliography

Doromon M 1991 Problematique du système Educatif au Tchad. Unpublished paper
N'Djaména 1990 *Réunion se Suivi de la Table Ronde Genève III*. Conference held in Geneva
Pamdegue A 1991 Système éducatif Tchadien. Unpublished paper
Bourdon J, Orivel F 1991 *Cadrage macro-Economique de la Stratégie Education et Formation du Tchad*. Dijon

Chile

C. Rodríguez

1. General Background

Chile has been an independent republic since the beginning of the nineteenth century. It extends along the southwestern coast of South America, stretching on average 4,300 kilometers north to south and only 180 kilometers east to west. It is very mountainous, with plains occupying only about 20 percent of the country, and it has extreme geographic contrasts: a desert covers about one-third of the territory in the north, and broken coasts with deep channels and fjords occupy another third of the country in the south. These features give rise to a very uneven distribution of population, with a concentration in the central zone, that has traditionally absorbed about 90 percent of the total number of inhabitants and also contains the most important agricultural, industrial, and cultural centers. The metropolitan region (where the capital Santiago is located) alone has 40 percent of the total number of the country's inhabitants.

The population is highly homogeneous in terms of its ethnic background and language. This is due to a successful process of integration of the native inhabitants with their Spanish conquerors beginning in the sixteenth century and, later on, with groups of immigrants of European origin.

The implications of these geographical characteristics for the educational system are felt in both administrative and curricular matters. The difficulties in communication and the isolation of the regions in both extremes of the country, as well as of those zones located in the mountains, make the administration of the system particularly complicated. As far as curricular aspects are concerned, the difficulty lies in the fact that the system has to reconcile the cultural unity of the nation with the diversity existing in the different regions.

The population of Chile has increased at a fast rate: it doubled in the 55 years between 1865 and 1920, and it doubled again in the following 40 years (1920–60). The growth was less marked between 1960 and 1990. During this period it increased from 8,900,000 to 13,200,000 and between 1982 and 1991 the average annual growth of the population was 1.8 percent. These 13 million people had a per capita Gross National Product, (GNP) of US$1,770 in 1989. The annual growth rate of the GNP per capita was 0.3 percent in the period 1965 to 1989, and in 1989 the growth of the GNP was 10 percent. The export–import ratio of US$8,579 million:US$7,023 million was an additional indicator of the economic situation prevailing in the country in 1990. Due to migration from rural areas, the percentage of persons living in towns increased from 46.2 percent in 1920 to 82.2 percent in 1982.

Given that 30 percent of the population is aged under 15, economically active persons have represented between 30 and 35 percent of the total population in the 50 years to 1990, but their distribution in the different sectors of the Chilean economy varied substantially over this period. Whereas the percentage of individuals engaged in the secondary sector (industry) has remained fairly stable at around 20 percent, the tertiary sector (services) increased its share at the expense of agriculture and mining (the primary sector): it represented 35 percent in 1940, 65 percent in 1980, and 56 percent in 1990. The primary sector fluctuated between 43 and 22 percent in the same periods, with a 4 percent increase between 1980 and 1990 due to the substantial development that agriculture experienced in that decade.

The occupational structure of the population varied concomitantly, and while the percentage of professionals and technicians (9% in 1990), as well as manual workers, remained fairly stable, the proportion of salespersons and office employees grew from 14 percent in 1960 to 27 percent in 1980 and decreased to 24 percent in 1990. The percentage of fishermen, miners, and agricultural workers decreased from 29 percent in 1960 to 17 and 18 percent in 1980 and 1990 respectively.

From the point of view of the geographical distribution of economic activities, there were no important changes between the 1960s and 1990s. The metropolitan region continues to be the development center of the country; it has more than 40 percent of the workforce in the tertiary sector, which is the sector with the highest productivity. This excessive centralism has traditionally posed serious problems, since it has brought about not only a concentration of economic activities, but also disparities in per capita social investment, thus limiting the economic growth of many regions. A key element of the development strategy started in the 1970s was the regionalization of the country. A total of 12 regions plus the metropolitan area were designated in 1974, each with its own administrative system and also with autonomy in decision-making. These changes in the administration of the nation have been defined in accordance with the subsidiary role that the state adopted since the mid-1970s. In contrast to the period 1930–70 (which showed an increasing intervention of the state in the economy), in the early 1990s the role of the state was to carry out only those functions which cannot be performed by the private sector, either because of their nature or because of their interdependence with other functions. In 1991, the results of this strategy were just starting to become evident in terms of a better distribution of economic activities.

The stated objectives of this development strategy are to reach a steady economic growth and actively to seek equity through redistribution policies and mainly through increases in public social expenditure. Several factors have been identified as being important for the achievement of these goals and, among them, the improvement of human capital is considered essential. The new educational policies include changes in the regular system and also in adult education for the provision of vocational qualifications. Educational administration has become more decentralized.

2. Politics and the Goals of the Education System

In the twentieth century the political history of Chile has seen many changes, especially from 1970 to 1990. The long tradition of democratically elected governments acting in a presidential system was interrupted by brief periods of *de facto* governments in 1924–25 and 1931–32, and by an autocratic military regime in 1973 that lasted until 1990. Until the late 1930s, Chilean governments can be broadly defined as oligarchic. Between 1938 and 1952 the central–leftist tendencies dominated the political scene; after that time there were some independent and demo–Christian governments until the socialist and communist parties came to power in 1970. The socialist government lasted until 1973 and, following a 17-year military regime, a democratically elected president, supported by forces from the center–left, became the head of the Chilean government in 1990.

The concept of the state educating people (*estado docente*) has been important throughout the history of Chilean education, and is summarized by the motto of President Pedro Aguirre Cerda in the late 1930s: "To govern is to educate" ("*gobernar es educar*"). On the other hand, the educational bureaucracy constitutes a relevant part of the strong Chilean middle class.

Despite the political changes described, the main goals of the educational system have remained fairly stable since the 1920s. Traditionally, the state has emphasized equal opportunity of access to education for all citizens, mainly in order to lower the percentage of illiteracy (28.8% in 1940, 11.7% in 1970, and 5.4% in 1990) and to ensure that everyone completes at least primary education. At the beginning of the 1990s there were no important challenges as far as access to education was concerned, nor were there major dilemmas about the institutional organization of the sector. The core of the new educational policy is the quality of its internal processes and results, and the equity of the social distribution of them. The government is engaged in a midterm strategy aiming at the improvement of the quality and equity of Chilean education through a six-year program, financed with the cooperation of the World Bank, which started in 1991 (*Programa de Mejoramiento de la Calidad y Equidad de la Educación*—MECE). Additional objectives of this program are to broaden access to and improve the quality of pre-school education and to evaluate institutional and curricular alternatives in order to reform secondary education through increasing its pertinence, quality, and equity.

3. The Formal System of Education

3.1 Primary, Secondary, and Tertiary Education

The structure of the regular educational system in 1990 was 6 years of voluntary preprimary schooling (ages 0 to 6), divided into three levels: nursery, middle level, and transition; 8 years of compulsory primary school, in which the first 4 years use a global methodology; 4 years of secondary school, with two branches—academic and vocational (which in 1990 included commercial, technical, industrial, agricultural, and maritime education) both branches having equal right of access to the university; and 3 to 7 years of higher education, which were (until 1980) the responsibility of Chile's eight universities. As well as these levels, which absorb the majority of the Chilean school population, there is special education and adult education.

A new structure was implemented during the 1980s. The main differences from the one previously described are found in the postsecondary alternatives offered, which are more varied and more appropriate to the needs of the labor market. Modifications in higher education have been put into practice since 1981. Universities are no longer the sole bodies offering professional training. Professional institutes and centers for technical training also do so, except for 16 courses (leading to traditional professions such as law, medicine, architecture, and engineering) which can only be taught by universities.

The number of students enrolled in the system increased steadily from 1940 to 1990, but more accelerated rates have occurred in different periods in the four levels defined. The largest increase in primary enrollment took place between 1960 and 1965; in secondary enrollment between 1965 and 1970; and at the university level between 1970 and 1975. The slight decrease in primary enrollment observed in the period 1975–90 is due mainly to a decreasing birth rate. Preprimary schooling (even if the number of children enrolled has increased from about 5,000 in 1940 to 220,396 in 1990) still absorbs only a limited proportion of the children aged 0 to 6 (12.7%)

The net and gross rates of schooling for the population aged between 7 and 14 are 91 percent and 101 percent respectively, and the difference between these two percentages shows that average grade repeating is about 10 percent. Despite the fact that the criterion for promotion is attendance and not grades, 10 percent of first-grade students repeat, and this percentage is estimated to be higher in children belonging to families of low socioeconomic status. Grade repeating is also high in Grades 4 through 7. Although it is still a problem, grade repeating has decreased in the last 15 years, and in 1990 it was 7.8 and 12.4 percent in primary and secondary schools respectively. Permanent (vs. temporary) dropout in Grades 1 to 7 fluctuates between 1.0 percent and 5.8 percent (in 1990, the figures were 2.29% for primary and 7.37% for secondary education). Despite the problems of grade repeating and dropout, an estimated 80 percent of the students entering school finish primary education, even if 20 percent of them graduate from this level after having repeated one or more grades. On average, for each student who finishes primary education (which is formally 8 years), 10.1 years of schooling are necessary. The following data about the average number of school years of the economically active population provide additional information regarding the increasing retentivity of the system: 1970–4.33; 1980–7.60; 1990–8.58. Figure 1 presents the structure of the system. The grade repetition is reflected in the diagram, especially in the increased enrollment in Grades 6, 7, and 8.

Educational opportunities for males and females have traditionally been equal in Chile. The proportion of boys was slightly higher in primary school (51% in 1990) and that of girls higher at the secondary

level (51% in 1990), mainly in the academic track. At university, the situation (which was definitely more favorable for males in 1940, who then represented 75% of the total enrollment) has changed, and in 1990 only 56 percent of students were male.

In 1990, the total number of children enrolled in the lower levels of the system was 2,963,139, of which 7.4 percent were in preschool, 67 percent in primary, 15.7 percent in academic secondary, 8.6 percent in vocational secondary, and 1.3 percent in special education. Postsecondary education represents an additional enrollment of 249,482 students, of which 52.8 percent were at universities, 16 percent at professional institutes, and 31.2 percent at centers for technical training. The enrollment in adult education for the same year was 72,795, distributed among primary, technical, and academic and vocational secondary, the highest percentage being enrolled at the secondary level (54%).

·Rural enrollment represented a total of 12.4 percent in 1990, with an unequal distribution among the different regions of the country: the extreme north (I, II, and III), the extreme south (XI and XII), the center (V) and the metropolitan region having 8 percent or less, whereas in the more agricultural zones (Regions VI, VII, IX, and X) rural enrollment fluctuated between 25 and 28 percent.

Normally there are 30–33 weekly class periods of 45 minutes (40 minutes in Grades 1 to 4) in primary and 34–36 class periods a week in secondary school, the most common class size being 30–45 students.

3.2 Preschool Education

In 1994, the main aim of preschool education was to

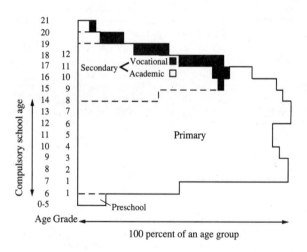

Figure 1
Chile: Structure of the formal education system

increase its coverage, its quality, and its equity within the context of decentralization and participation, as defined by the general principles that guide the Chilean educational system. Its further aims are to decrease deficit in the psychosocial development of children under 6 and to improve the entry conditions of children to the educational system in both the cognitive and socioeconomical areas.

The main institutions responsible for preschool education are:

(a) The Ministry of Education, supervising and assisting schools administered by municipalities and state institutions. It provides norms for private and public education as well as the official curricula for nursery schools (ages 0–2), middle-level schools (ages 2–4), and transition schools (ages 4–6).

(b) The *Junta Nacional de Jardines Infantiles* which carries out, directly and through agreements, programs of both a conventional and nonconventional kind for children aged preferably 0–5 years.

(c) The *Fundación Nacional para el Desarrollo Integral del Menor*, undertaking directly nonconventional programs favoring an integral development of children aged 0–6 who attend open centers together with their families and communities in order to ameliorate the children's entry in the school and society.

These institutions also develop different types of specific projects such as Centers for Expression and Creativity, the "Know your Child" program (urban and rural versions) from the Ministry of Education; the "Family Garden" program (nonconventional) and the "Distance Garden: Showing the Future" program (nonconventional) from the *Junta Nacional de Jardines Infantiles*. The National Center for Pedagogical Improvement, Experimentation, and Research, under the Ministry of Education, also carries out training programs for teachers and parents of preschool children.

The main objectives of preschool education are to create meaningful experiences, both within and outside educational institutions, that contribute to the development of children's thinking, autonomy, creativity, communication, expression and relationships, and identity and culture; and to teach them to value and care about their environment. Important factors to achieve these objectives are integrated work with parents, family, and community, as well as convergent actions with different sectors who are involved with children and with professionals of other disciplines.

3.3 Special Education

The main objective of special education is to rehabilitate children with learning difficulties in order to integrate them into the normal educational process, either permanently or transitorily, and thus to incorporate them into social life. It takes care of handicaps in learning, language, vision, mental retardation, motor deficits, and specific learning disabilities. The detection of these cases is undertaken by specialists in special centers for diagnosis which belong to the Ministry of Education. In 1990, a total of 31,746 children were enrolled in 336 special education units, 130 of which were located in the metropolitan region. About 84 percent of the children suffered from mental retardation, 10 percent from language problems, and 3.6 percent from hearing difficulties. The remainder had visual and motor problems. About 52.6 percent of these handicapped children go to municipal schools, 46.8 percent to private schools with fiscal subsidies, and less than 1 percent go to private schools. The Ministry of Education assigns a special subsidy for these children that is about 50 percent higher than for normal students. Handicapped children have special programs, mostly full-time, and most of them study in special education units since there are very few regular institutions that would accept them. Their transition to work is difficult in a country in which employment is still a problem.

3.4 Vocational, Technical, and Business Education

Vocational, technical, and business education is offered at both the secondary and tertiary levels. At the secondary level a total of 255,396 students were enrolled in 1990. This represents 35.5 percent of Chilean secondary education students (47.7% women and 52.3% men). Vocational education can be municipal or private, with or without fiscal subsidy, the highest percentage of students (42%) attending private schools which are subsidized. Of the 255,396 students enrolled in this type of secondary education, 41.6 percent are in the commercial branch, 17.3 percent in the technical, 3.3 percent in the agricultural, and 1.3 percent in the maritime branch. Only students attending private vocational schools that have no subsidy from the state pay tuition; the rest is free. At the beginning of the 1990s, significant efforts were being made to bring vocational education close to the requirements of future employment, since traditionally both curricula and the available material resources in the schools did not correspond well to the needs of the labor market.

At the tertiary level, there are 82 professional institutes and 156 centers for technical training that offer different programs, lasting from 2 to 4 years; the former leading to a technical degree in different specialties, and the latter to several technical and professional degrees. Only two of the professional institutes receive a subsidy from the state; the rest are private, and financed by students or their families. In professional institutes, the highest percentages of students are enrolled in the areas of administration and commerce (24.6%) and education (20.7%). In centers for technical training, 47 percent are in administration and commerce, whereas 29.9 percent are in the area of technology. Both options described in tertiary education are less popular than universities for those students who finish secondary education, because job opportunities and social prestige are much higher—and have traditionally been so in Chile—for the latter type of education.

3.5 Adult and Nonformal Education

Adult education is habitually offered in evening or night courses which aim at providing primary or secondary education to people who are older than 16, who for diverse reasons (e.g., temporary dropout or early age of starting work) have not been able to study when they were of school age. Two different types of programs are offered for adults. One is at the primary level with a maximum of 300 hours (fundamental education) and offers an elementary training in some technical specialty. The second lasts between 600 and 800 hours, at the primary or secondary level, and aims at providing training that will enable the person to enter the labor market with a technical specialty (elementary technical education for adults). Of the total of 72,795 persons enrolled in adult education in 1990, 21.7 percent was in primary, 1.5 percent in technical, 38.7 percent in academic secondary, 15.1 percent in vocational secondary, and 23.0 percent in a special two-year academic program. The majority of adults go to municipal schools which are free.

In nonformal education, action has been rather limited in scope and also tends to be irregular. Universities have contributed through their special community extension programs, among which orchestras, ballet corps, choirs, theater groups, television channels, and radio stations deserve special mention in addition to the many courses on subjects of general cultural interest which the universities habitually offer.

The Ministry of Education provides nonformal education both for school children and for adults. For children, provision is mainly through the Department for Out-of-School Education (*Departamento de Educación Extraescolar*).

Nonformal education is perceived as a basic element in the development of children, adolescents, and adults. It complements the function of the school. It attempts to integrate the family and the community through an adequate utilization of their free time by means of group activities (clubs, brigades, academies). The Department for Out-of-School Education has defined five areas of action: culture–arts, science–technology, sports–recreation, environmental education, and social participation and integration (e.g., discussions on topics such as peace, human rights, etc.). Specific events organized by this department include literary, scientific, and artistic contests; fairs; sports events; and drama and folklore festivals.

These are run both at the national and the international levels. The Department also trains specialists in out-of-school education, offering seminars and distance courses to teachers. Some examples of activities organized by this department in 1990 were the national contest of Chilean folk dance, with 120,000 students from primary and secondary education participating; a national contest on "*Pacifico Mare Nostrum 2000*" for primary school students with 2,500 works presented; a national contest of needlework, with 2,520 pieces exhibited; a scientific–technological fair in which 18,450 students took part; and a national sports event, which had 400,000 primary and secondary school students participating. Most of the events are organized by the Ministry of Education in cooperation with either private or public institutions. Teachers coordinate activities at the school level; at the central level there are supervisors for these activities in communes and in provincial departments. Programs for adults have been implemented only to a very limited extent.

4. Administrative and Supervisory Structure and Operation

Since the beginning of the 1980s, the administration and supervision of the Chilean education system has undergone drastic changes. The consolidation of the new administrative structure of the country had strengthened the functions of the mayor and municipalities. The administration of public schools, which had traditionally been in the hands of the Ministry of Education, was given to the municipalities and into private hands. In 1990, of the total number of schools (15,325), 64 percent were municipal, 28 percent were private with a fiscal subsidy, and 8 percent were private without any public subsidy, the percentage of primary municipal units being the highest (68 percent).

The Ministry of Education is responsible for the technical and pedagogical aspects of the educational process, that is, for establishing educational policies; for producing technical norms; and for supervising, orienting, and evaluating public and private education through its specialized departments. These are the subsecretaryship of education, and several technical divisions, such as the divisions for general education, for planning and budgeting, for personnel, and for higher education. Within each region, the Ministry has delegated its functions of planning and supervision to the regional secretaries of the Ministry of Education. Regional secretaries coordinate their action with the Ministry and the provincial departments (40 in total) which work with schools through teams of supervisors. Thus, certain powers are delegated from the regional level to the provincial level and in turn to the community and school levels.

Responsibility for the administration of primary and secondary public schools lies with the municipal authority. Schools are responsible for carrying out the teaching–learning process. School principals have certain responsibilities for the administration of personnel and the curriculum. They may, for example, adapt the curriculum according to the characteristics and needs of the students.

5. Educational Finance

The resources invested in public education come mainly from the central government (the state budget), from regional and community organs, from grants from the private sector, and from income originating in the schools themselves. Private schools are supported by student fees and by government Humanits subsidies when the schools are free. Contributions from municipalities and private bodies have increased with the transfer of responsibility for schools to these bodies. Self-financing has become particularly important in higher education, and several legal acts decreed in the 1980s gradually diminished the contribution of the state to higher education. The proportion of the state budget devoted to education was 15.95 percent in 1990, (17% in 1940, 12% in 1955, 21% in 1970 and 15% in 1985). As a percentage of GNP, the allocation has been between 2.0 and 4.1 percent over the 10 years up to 1991. The allocation of the budget among the various levels in the system was as follows in 1990: 7.5 percent for preprimary, 51.7 percent for primary, 10.7 percent for academic secondary, 8.1 percent for vocational secondary, and 20.7 percent for higher education. The high priority given to education is demonstrated by an increase of approximately 13 percent in the budget of 1991 as compared with 1990, which has been devoted mainly to increasing the salaries of the teachers and to supporting the poorest schools in the country.

It is important to stress that besides fiscal subsidies to municipal and some private schools, amounting (in 1990) to US$12 and US$14 a month per student in primary and secondary education respectively, there are several additional forms of financial assistance that the state gives to students, mainly in preschool and primary education. This consists of food (approximately 1,200,000 meals a day in 1990), textbooks (4,523,938 distributed in 1990), and special summer programs (918 schools participated in 1990). Information about private resources devoted to education (which mainly refers to private schools financed entirely by families) is difficult to obtain and no available statistics exist.

6. Supplying Personnel for the Education System

Teacher training has always been given great emphasis in Chile. The first public institution created for preparing teachers for secondary education (the *Instituto Pedagógico*) was founded in 1889 and was part of the Faculty of Philosophy and Humanities of the University of Chile. From then until 1980, the training of secondary school teachers was entirely in the hands of the universities and was regarded as postsecondary education. This training lasted five years, during which time prospective teachers studied general subjects, but specialized in one or two specific disciplines which they would later teach and in which they received special pedagogical training.

Primary teachers, on the other hand, were trained in normal schools until 1966, and afterwards (1967–80) in the existing universities. They are now trained in universities and also in some professional institutes. Normal schools belonged to the vocational branch of secondary education, and primary teachers received their professional training in parallel with secondary schooling. Preschool teachers and teachers for handicapped children were trained at the universities until 1980. From 1981, other institutions of postsecondary education as well as universities, prepare teachers for all levels of the system. Gradually, following a legal change introduced in 1990, universities will again be the only institutions which carry out teacher training.

In 1990, there were 134,389 persons working in the different levels of the system. About 89 percent were teachers and the rest were in administrative or technical positions. Of these 134,389 persons, 6 percent were in preprimary education, 2 percent in special education, 57 percent in primary, and 35 percent in secondary education. There is, in general, no shortage of teachers, and the teaching functions are performed to a large extent by qualified people. In 1990, for example, 98 percent of primary teachers and 92 percent of teachers in secondary schools had a degree in education. The distribution of qualified personnel is still uneven and some provinces, mainly in rural areas, are at a disadvantage in this respect. In general, there are more women than men teachers. In primary and secondary education, 75 and 55 percent respectively of teachers were women.

Inservice training for educational personnel is provided through staff-development programs, workshops, and seminars by many institutions. These are mainly universities, and coordinated by the Center for Inservice Training, Experimentation, and Educational Research of the Ministry of Education. Inservice training is considered to be so important that each teacher in municipal and subsidized schools receives a bonus in order to pay for the training he or she considers necessary. There is a wide selection of such courses for teachers. Increases in salaries are an additional stimulus for teacher training in Chile, both in public and private schools.

7. Curriculum Development and Teaching Methodology

The main curriculum reform took place between 1966 and 1970. The old curriculum was strongly content-oriented. In the new curriculum, the number of subjects was reduced and emphasis was placed upon student behavior and skills. The new programs included alternative content, types of activity, and evaluation procedures. These alternatives give teachers more freedom to carry out the teaching–learning process in accordance with the characteristics of their students.

In primary education, there is one uniform, nationwide curriculum developed by the Ministry of Education, starting with global activities in Grades 1 to 4, and gradually becoming more subject-centered. The curriculum for secondary education is nationwide as are the syllabuses of studies for the different subjects which contain general and specific learning objectives, the content being organized into units which contain a recommended bibliography. Vocational tracks have different curricula which initially are largely the same, as in the academic branch (70% of subjects), and later become more differentiated.

In academic secondary education, the curriculum included common subjects for Grades 9 and 10 (Spanish, world history and general geography, mathematics, natural sciences, foreign language, arts, physical education, religion [optional]) and a homeroom period. In Grades 11 and 12, there were also 8 common subjects, plus a set of electives which represented about 30 percent of the total number of weekly periods. The teaching of foreign languages starts with one (usually English) in the first cycle of primary, continues with two (English and French in most of the schools) in the second cycle, and then with one (mostly English again) in secondary education. Primary schools that do not have the necessary resources may be exempted from teaching foreign languages.

Since 1967, the Center for Inservice Training, Experimentation, and Educational Research of the Ministry of Education has had major responsibility for the planning and implementation of school curricula. In accordance with the *Ley Orgánica Constitucional de Enseñanza,* there is a council constituted of outstanding representatives of the academic community (*Consejo Superior de Educación*) which has to analyze and give its approval to the fundamental objectives for each grade-level of both primary and secondary education, and also to the minimum obligatory content that will facilitate the achievement of those objectives. Once the Ministry of Education has formally established them, the schools are free to define the curricula and syllabuses they consider adequate to comply with the objectives and content determined by the Ministry. The Ministry of Education has then to accept these curricula, proposing changes if necessary, and has to prepare a common nationwide curriculum for those schools that do not have their own. This has to be approved by the Higher Council for Education (*Consejo Superior de Educación*).

Textbooks are produced by private companies and schools select those they prefer. Every year the Ministry of Education buys several million textbooks and distributes them to public schools. The Ministry also prepares audio-visual materials which schools can buy at very competitive prices. This is also the case for methodological guides for teachers.

The Ministry of Education carries out its functions of orientation and supervision of the implementation of the curriculum through specially trained supervisors who belong to the provincial departments of education.

The main problem in the areas of curriculum and teaching methods is the emphasis placed on lower mental processes and traditional teaching methods in schools. This has produced an important gap between what goes on in schools and the demands and stimuluses of life outside the schools. Students thus perceive the curriculum as not being relevant, particularly at the secondary level.

8. The System of Examinations, Promotions, and Certifications

The decision as to whether a student is to be promoted lies with teachers and is based normally upon the performance of students in different types of tasks which test learning objectives in specific subject fields. No special examinations exist in order to pass from one level of the system to another, except for a nationwide examination that is held to select candidates for subsidized universities. The admission rate in 1990 was approximately 1:1.6 for these universities, which is very favorable compared with the situation prevailing in the 1970s and mid-1980s. It is due to the expansion of the private sector of higher education. The examination consists of a battery of tests, including an aptitude test (verbal and mathematical reasoning) and several achievement tests which the student takes according to the subjects to be studied. The tests are administered throughout the country on common dates, and more than 90 percent of the students finishing secondary education take them. Universities then select their students from among those candidates who obtained the highest scores in the tests and had the best average marks in secondary education. This system for selecting university students has been in existence since 1967.

9. Educational Assessment, Evaluation, and Research

Since 1988, and having as an antecedent a program for evaluating school outcomes (*Programa de Evaluación de Rendimiento*—PER, 1982–84), the Ministry of Education administers a nationwide examination alternatively to all students in Grades 4 and 8 (*Sistema de Medición de Calidad de la Educación*—SIMCE) in order to have a yearly diagnosis of the results of the educational process in terms of objectives attained. The system is based on the administration of multiple-choice tests in Spanish and mathematics to all children, and in history and geography and natural science to a sample of them. It also measures certain features of the personal development of students and some indicators of acceptance of the work of the school by students, parents, and teachers; and provides information on some indicators of school efficiency, such as pass / fail rates, the number of years studied, and the number of dropouts. The percentage of achievement in each one of the objectives measured is reported to every school in the country, by class, and schools can also evaluate their relative position by comparing their results to national outcomes, and to results obtained by similar schools which are also given to them. Recommendations are provided to schools to help them improve their education on the basis of the results attained, and schools use the information and the recommendations for the improvement of the teaching–learning process. The results obtained by schools have served as a basis for selecting the 900 lowest achieving schools located in poverty areas in order to provide them with material and human support to improve the quality of the education they offer.

Educational research may be traced back to the beginning of the twentieth century in Chile and has had continuous development. However, its importance in decision-making has been limited and only a few educational policies have been based upon the results of research. These have included coordinated efforts to reduce grade repeating, the provision of textbooks to primary schools, and the implementation of the entrance examination to Chilean universities.

From 1950 onwards, several public and private research institutions were created. Their work was to have an impact upon the reforms introduced in education after 1960. Among them, two at the University of Chile stood out: the Institute for Education and the Institute for Statistical Research. At the Ministry of Education, the main research organism was the Center for Inservice Training, Experimentation, and Educational Research founded in 1967. Among private institutions the main one was the Center for Educational Research and Development (CIDE), created in 1965 and initially connected with the Catholic University. Educational research was given high priority in the 1960s since its importance in deciding and evaluating the changes that were taking place in education was widely recognized. During this period, the tendency was mainly to study educational achievement and the variables associated with it, the flow of students through the different levels of the system, and descriptive statistics of the psychological and sociological characteristics of students.

During the 1970s, educational research became a more common activity in those universities having faculties of education, and since the late 1970s many nongovernmental organizations have also had an important role in educational research. The interest in determinants of achievement continued, but, in addition, emphasis was placed on dropout, language development, and the relationship between education and different elements in the social context.

At the beginning of the 1980s the main research issues were achievement, preschool education, nonformal educational programs, teacher training, and higher education. Starting in the late 1980s school processes have received great attention, with emphasis on qualitative–ethnographic methods. The topics that were most popular with researchers (according to the number of papers presented at the educational researchers' meeting held in 1991) were teaching–learning strategies (28); curricular experiences (25); family, community, and school (25); higher education (23); teacher training and development; and early primary education (20). Within the framework of the program for improving the quality and equity of education at the secondary level, the Ministry of Education has defined a number of research projects aimed at providing an information basis for restructuring secondary education according to the needs of Chilean society in the areas of curriculum, socialization and pedagogical practices, measurement of quality, internal and external efficiency, and teacher training. These projects will be financed with the cooperation of the World Bank.

At the national level, there is a National Commission for Scientific and Technological Research which finances research projects in all disciplines and which is the main institution for financing research in Chile.

The Ministry of Education collects and regularly publishes information on several important educational indicators such as school retentivity for children and adults, coverage, attendance, pedagogical retardation, quality of education (achievement of academic objectives), enrollments, human and financial resources, nonformal education, and illiteracy.

10. Major Reforms in the 1980s and 1990s

The decentralization of educational administration and changes in the role that the state had traditionally played in education had important consequences, and the consolidation of the new administration is still in progress. The major reforms expected for the 1990s will be oriented towards improving the quality and equity of Chilean education, mainly through participation, decentralization, efficiency, and open design to allow schools to develop their own educational initiatives. The first steps toward a reform of secondary education were taken in 1991 in order to make this level of the system more meaningful and more adjusted to the needs of society. The reforms of secondary education will be based on research data which will provide the basis for specific actions to be taken in the near future.

11. Major Problems for the Year 2000

Since the 1960s major efforts have been devoted to the quantitative expansion of the system, and increases in enrollment rates have been substantial. Efforts will have to be made in the 1990s to increase enrollments, not only in primary education but also in preschool and secondary education.

The major concern, both at the time of writing and in the near future, is the quality and equity of education. Many studies show serious discrepancies between the intended curriculum and the levels of student achievement and, particularly, in the equity of the social distribution of the quality of the educational process. The changes in the structure of the system and in the administration of the schools have begun implementation since the beginning of the 1980s. The curricular changes that are being studied and the efforts that are being made to enhance teacher participation in those curricular changes have as their ultimate goal the improvement of both the quantitative and qualitative problems. Yet education cannot be isolated from the whole social context, and its growth will therefore depend to a large extent on the development that takes place in the other subsystems of Chilean society.

Bibliography

Comisión Nacional de Educación Párvularia 1993 *La Atención Integral del Párvulo en Chile*. Comisión Nacional de Educación Párvularia, Santiago

Diario Oficial de la República de Chile, Santiago, 10 de Marzo de 1990, Ministerio de Educación Pública, Ley No 18,962, *Ley Orgánica Constitucional de Enseñanza*. Empresa Periodística "La Nación." Santiago

Fondo Monetario Internacional 1991 *Estadíisticas Financieras Internacionales. Anuario 1991*. Publication Services IMS, Washington, DC

Lemaitre M J (ed.) 1990 *La Educación Superior en Chile: Un sistema en Transición*. Corporación de Promoción Universitaria, Santiago

Ministerio de Economía, Fomento y Reconstrucción, Instituto Nacional de Estadísticas 1991 *Compendio estadístico 1991*. Imprenta INE, Santiago

Ministerio de Economía, Fomento y Reconstrucción, Instituto Nacional de Estadísticas 1991 *Encuesta Nacional del Empleo 1991 (Octubre -Diciembre, total del país)*. Imprenta INE, Santiago

Ministerio de Educación Pública 1981 *La Educación en Chile 1979–1980*. Informe de Chile a la 38ª reunión de la Conferencia Internacional de Educación. Ginebra 10–19 de noviembre, 1981. Oficina de Relaciones Internacionales, Santiago

Ministerio de Educación Pública 1991, 1989 *Revista de Educación* No. 79, (2nd edn. 1989), No. 94 (1982). Centro de Perfeccionamiento, Experimentación e Investigaciones Pedagógicas, Santiago

Ministerio de Educación Pública 1990 Compendio de Información Estadística 1990. Departamento de Estadística, División de Planificación y Presupuesto, Ministerio de Educación, Santiago

Ministerio de Educación Pública, División de Educación General, Departamento de Educación Extraescolar, 1991 *Documento de Trabajo: La Educación Extraescolar*. Ministerio de Educación, Santiago

Ministerio de Educación Pública 1991 *Resúmenes de los trabajos presentados al XI Encuentro Nacional de Investigadores en Educación*. Perfeccionamiento, Experimentación e Investigaciones Pedagógicas Serie de Estudios No. 226. Santiago

Ministerio de Educación Pública 1991 *Revista de Educación: Orientaciones Básicas, Objetivos y Componentes del Programa MECE*. Documento de difusión, Agosto 1991. Centro de Perfeccionamiento, Experimentación e Investigaciones Pedagógicas, Santiago

Schiefelbein E 1976 *Diagnóstico del sistema educacional chileno en 1970*. Universidad de Chile, Departamento de Economía, Santiago

Schiefelbein E, Grossi M C 1981 Antecedentes para un análisis de la eficiencia de la educación media en Chile. Corporación de Promoción Universitaria, Documento de Trabajo No. 229, Santiago

Schiefelbein E, Heikkinen S 1991 Chile—*Acceso, Permanencia, Repetición y Eficiencia en la Educación Básica*. Documento de Trabajo UNESCO-OREALC, 18 de abril de 1991.

World Bank 1991 *World Development Report 1991: The Challenge of Development*. Oxford University Press, Oxford

China, People's Republic of

Teng Teng

1. General Background

China is one of the largest countries in the world, with a total land area of approximately 9.6 million square kilometers accounting for 6.5 percent of the global land area.

In 1990, the total population of China (including Taiwan) reached 1.16 billion. With 540 million in 1949, the present figure represents a net increase of 620 million and an average annual growth rate of 1.87 percent. Since the 1970s, the birthrate has dropped from 35 per thousand to 20 per thousand in the early 1990s, and the natural growth rate has also declined from 25 per thousand to about 15 per thousand due to the family planning policy. The urban population in mainland China constitutes 26 percent of the total, while the rural population makes up the remaining 74 percent.

As a multinational country, China is comprised of 56 nationalities. The Han nationality accounts for 92 percent of the total population, and the other 55 national minorities together represent the remaining

8 percent. The Han people have their own spoken and written language, which is the most common and widely used language in China. Most of the other 55 national minorities have their own languages, but 34 of them did not have written forms prior to 1949. Since 1949 the relevant government departments have assisted ten national minorities in creating and standardizing the written forms of their languages. The Chinese government has stipulated that in the national minority region, classes should be conducted in the national language so long as the written form of the language exists, and that national pupils should master their own languages while also learning the Chinese language.

China is traditionally an agricultural nation. In 1952, agricultural workers constituted 83.5 percent of the total social labor force in the country, industrial workers accounted for 7.4 percent, and workers in the service sector for 9.1 percent. With the development that has occurred since the early 1950s, the value of fixed industrial capital assets has increased 50-fold, and an independent comprehensive industrial system has been established. Great progress has also been made in agricultural production. By 1989, the proportion of the agricultural labor force had fallen to 60.2 percent, while the industrial and service sectors had risen to 21.9 and 17.9 percent respectively.

The economic system of China is a socialist market economy based on public ownership. The state organizations of the People's Republic of China include: organs of state power—the National People's Congress and local people's congresses at various levels; state administrative organs—the State Council and various levels of people's governments; the state judicial organs—the people's courts; and the state law supervision organs—the people's procuratorates. In the early 1980s, the Chinese government formulated a three-phased economic development strategy for China's socialist modernization: the first phase aims to double the 1980 Gross National Product (GNP) and to solve the problem of providing food and clothing for the people; the second phase aims to quadruple the 1980 GNP by the end of the century and to raise the standard of living of the Chinese people to a comfortable level; and the third phase aims basically to realize modernization by the middle of the next century, with per capita GNP reaching the level of a medium-developed country.

2. Politics and the Goals of the Education System

Since the 1980s, the Chinese government has established, on the basis of sound analysis of China's national condition, the fundamental principle of undertaking economic construction as the central task, while upholding the four cardinal principles (i.e., socialism through the proletariat dictatorship, the leadership of the Communist Party, and adherence to Marxism–Leninism, and the ideology of Mao Tse-Tung) and maintaining the policy of reform and

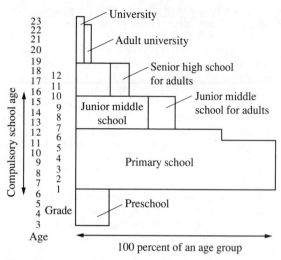

Figure 1
People's Republic of China: Structure of the formal education system

opening China to the outside world. The 1985 Communist Party of China (CPC) Central Committee Decision on the Reform of Educational Structure explicitly stated that "education must serve the purpose of socialist construction and socialist construction must rely on education." This document set out the correct relationship between education and economic development, and called for economic development to rely on the advancement of science and technology and the improvement of the quality of the labor force.

The guiding principle of Chinese education is that education must serve the cause of socialist modernization and be integrated with practical work in order to ensure the all-round moral, intellectual, and physical development of the builders of socialism and their successors.

The general objective for the development of Chinese education is to establish, by the end of the century, the basic framework of an educational system which is well-adapted to the needs of the socialist modernization drive, geared to the requirements of the twenty-first century, and which bears distinct Chinese characteristics.

3. The Formal System of Education

3.1 Primary, Secondary, and Tertiary Education

Figure 1 presents the structure of the education system. Education in China comprises four sectors: basic education (BE), technical and vocational education (TAVE), higher education (HE), and adult education (AE). BE covers preschool, formal primary, and secondary education; TAVE is carried out mainly in specialized secondary schools, skilled worker schools, secondary vocational schools, and the advanced technical and vocational colleges; HE essentially refers to the education of regular higher education institutions; and

AE offers literacy programs, various types of school instruction, and other forms of education which are targeted at adults.

The lengths of education at different levels and types of institutions are set as follows: kindergarten admits preschool children (age 3 or older); primary schools, lasting 5 or 6 years, enroll children at the age of 6; and secondary education consists of lower-middle school and upper-middle school, the former is for 3 or 4 years and the latter 3 years. In 1986, the National People's Congress adopted the Compulsory Education Act, which stipulates that a total of nine years of education should be made compulsory, covering primary and lower-secondary levels. Specialized secondary schools admit lower-middle school leavers normally for a four-year study program. The undergraduate courses of higher education institutions are mostly of four years' duration, medical and some engineering courses last five years, and a few medical universities even offer six-year courses. College diploma courses normally last 2 or 3 years. Graduate studies may be divided into master's degree courses and doctoral studies, with the former lasting 2.5 to 3 years and the latter usually 3 years.

In 1990, the enrollment of primary school-aged children reached 97.8 percent and the proportion of primary school leavers who proceed to lower-middle schools stood at 77.8 percent. In China, there are 766,000 primary schools with a total enrollment of 122.41 million pupils; 72,000 lower-middle schools with 38.69 million pupils; 16,000 upper-middle schools with 7.17 million students; and 1,075 regular higher education institutions with 2.15 million students.

3.2 Preschool Education

The development of preschool education in China has always been guided by the principle of reliance on the efforts of the public and local community. Apart from the endeavors of local governments, preschool education is mainly provided by various departments, work units, and social organizations within the framework of relevant laws and regulations of the state. Preschool education is mostly full-time. The training of children in the kindergartens is conducted through games, sports, classroom activities, observation, physical work projects, and daily activities. In 1990, there were over 170,000 kindergartens nationwide with an enrollment of 19.72 million children.

3.3 Special Education

The provision of special education has expanded substantially since the founding of the People's Republic. The number of special schools for the blind, deaf and mute, and the mentally retarded has grown from 42 before 1949 to 746, with the pupil population increasing from 2,000 to 72,000. Since the 1980s, a total of over 5,000 handicapped youths have entered higher education institutions.

3.4 Vocational, Technical, and Business Education

The rapid development of Technical and Vocational Education (TAVE) since the 1980s is an important indication that Chinese education is being further geared to serving the modernization process. In 1990, the total student population in the various types of technical and vocational schools all over the country reached 6.048 million, representing a fourfold increase in the 1979 figure. TAVE enrollment now accounts for 45.7 percent of the total enrollment at the upper-secondary level. Specialized secondary schools are run by the relevant ministries of the State Council and professional organizations. The purpose of these schools is to train middle-level technicians and line managers for the economic sectors. Skilled worker schools are run by local professional organizations and enterprises to train elementary- and middle-level skilled workers. The state guarantees employment for graduates from these two types of schools. Vocational schools include vocational middle schools and agricultural schools, which are run by local education authorities to supply elementary- and middle-level technicians and managerial personnel as well as the future labor force. Students in these schools are not guaranteed employment when they complete their studies. They may seek employment by their own efforts through a competitive selection process, and they may also try to undertake further study in their own discipline.

Funding for TAVE comes mainly from the state budget allocations (including the central budget and the local budgets) for the operation of various types of public schools and assistance to community-run institutions. At the same time, industrial enterprises, public establishments, organizations, individuals, and various social sectors are encouraged to raise funds to run such educational establishments.

3.5 Adult and Nonformal Education

Adult education is an important component of the Chinese education system. Its main purpose is to raise the quality of inservice personnel and contribute directly to socioeconomic development. As far as its forms are concerned, the provision of adult higher education in China includes radio and television universities, advanced staff development colleges, farmers' colleges, and the higher education self-study examination system. Elementary and secondary adult education provision includes specialized secondary schools or classes for adults and adult technical training schools. In 1990, there were 1,321 adult institutions of higher education in China with an enrollment of 1.56 million students, in addition to 58,501 secondary adult schools with 15.29 million students and 258,134 elementary adult schools with 22.82 million students. These adult education establishments have designed different modes of study to meet the needs of adult learners—for instance, classroom instruction, the provision of audio-visual materials and textbooks to assist distance learning, full-time and part-time studies, or sparetime studies. Although funding for an adult education program is primarily the responsibility of the organization that runs the program, the school may also charge students a small fee.

The Chinese government attaches great importance to literacy education. Since the founding of the People's Republic, a total of 169 million people have learned to read and write through literacy programs. From 1978 to 1990, 42.5 million illiterate people have benefited from the programs, with another 5.6 million people currently undertaking literacy study in China. It is estimated that over 50 percent of the counties all over the country have all but eliminated illiteracy.

4. Administrative and Supervisory Structure and Operation

The basic pattern of educational management system in China is that education authorities are established at the central, provincial (including autonomous regions and metropolitan municipalities), municipal (or prefectural), and the county levels to take the responsibility of national and local education administration. The departments of planning, finance, labor, and personnel of governments at all levels assist the education authorities in formulating educational development plans, budgets, and the basic personnel and salary systems. The State Education Commission (SEDC) is a professional organization of the State Council with overall responsibility for the administration of education throughout the country. In 1985, the Chinese government decided to delegate responsibility for basic education to local authorities and implement a system of management by various departments for education. The rural township governments are thus charged with part of the responsibility for local education provision.

Educational inspection in China is a system under which the higher government authorities undertake to monitor, inspect, evaluate, and provide guidance for the educational work of the lower-level people's governments, the education authorities, and schools (lower-secondary, upper-secondary, teacher-training schools, and vocational middle schools, in particular). Its purpose is to supervise the implementation of the laws and decrees, guiding principles, and policies governing education provision, and to ensure the realization of educational goals and the improvement of educational quality. An inspection network has been established.

5. Educational Finance

State financial allocation is the main source of educational funding in China. State financial allocation includes both central government allocation and fundings by local governments. Generally speaking, local financial allocations are spent on the educational provisions run and managed by local governments, whereas the central government finance is mainly used to support the institutions under various central government ministries and as special grants for specific national education development projects. In addition, considerable efforts are made by the people's governments at all levels to raise education funds through all possible channels. These include the education surcharge levied by government authorities, expenditures incurred by industrial enterprises for educational purposes, funds raised and donated by local communities, revenues generated through social services and work–study programs which are spent on improving the conditions for education, and incomes from tuition and other miscellaneous fees. In 1990, state finance provided a total expenditure of 43.3 billion Renminbi yuan (RMB yuan) on education, which accounts for 13.1 percent of the state revenue for that year; other educational funds and revenues amounted to about 11.6 billion RMB yuan. The state budget for education in 1991 was 115 RMB yuan per student at primary level and 255 RMB yuan per student at secondary level. Since 1981, China has been actively utilizing the World Bank loans for educational development.

6. Supplying Personnel for the Education System

In 1990, China had a total of 13.45 million teaching, administrative, and support staff in educational institutions of various kinds and at all levels—10.37 million of which were full-time teachers. This includes 5.58 million full-time primary school teachers, 3.63 million mainstream secondary school teachers, and 394,500 faculty members in regular higher education institutions. In comparison with 1980, the total number of employees in the school system has increased by 1.91 million; full-time teachers increased by 1.04 million. Thus, the size of the teaching force in China is sufficiently large and the primary task for the future is to raise its ideological and professional quality and optimize its structure.

To ensure the quality and standards of education and teaching, the state has laid down relevant academic qualification requirements and criteria for professional certificate assessment for primary and secondary school teachers. The state encourages teachers to upgrade their educational and professional levels through further training. There are two types of training provisions: full-time training and inservice training which are mainly provided by education colleges, teacher-training colleges, undergraduate or diploma teacher education courses run by higher education institutions, televized universities and teacher-training colleges, and correspondence schools. Such training may also be conducted through workshops and seminars on teaching materials and methodology. Teachers may also participate in the National Higher Education Self-Study Examination. Inservice training of teachers of higher education institutions is conducted through either the Senior Visiting Scholars Program or the

Advanced Teacher Training Course. In addition, there are interuniversity exchanges of teachers for training purposes. The government and institutions provide the necessary conditions for the training of teachers. Those who participate in training programs are paid in full during the training period and the costs for training are met by the state. The state recognizes the qualifications of the teachers after they have satisfactorily completed their training. Appropriate status will also be given to these teachers.

The Chinese government has adopted a series of positive and effective measures to stabilize the teaching force and to improve its quality. These measures include the following:

(a) Raising the economic status of teachers and improving their working conditions. The salary of teachers has been raised on several occasions in recent years. Primary and secondary school teachers are paid an additional allowance for their years of service. The salary scale for teachers is 10 percent higher than that of other public services. Teachers with 30 years of service are entitled to full pay after retirement in some provinces and municipalities.

(b) Setting up honors and reward systems for teachers. September 10 has been designated Teacher's Day. A National Fund for Kindergarten, Primary, and Secondary School Teachers has been established to reward those teachers who have made outstanding contributions.

(c) Establishing a tenure system in primary and secondary schools. Primary and secondary school teachers are included in the professional post system. They are thus entitled to the same salary scale as other professionals.

(d) Encouraging talented secondary school leavers to enter teacher education institutions so as to ensure the quality of the student intake of these institutions. Teaching practice is to be enhanced in order to raise the quality of teacher education.

(e) Introducing the professional certificate system for primary and secondary school teachers. It is estimated that a total of 1.62 million primary and secondary school teachers took part in the qualification examination between 1986 and 1990.

The overall quality of the teaching force is constantly improving as the state attaches greater importance to, and has effectively strengthened, teacher education and teacher-training programs.

7. Curriculum Development and Teaching Methodology

In order to improve the quality of the whole national effort and ensure the effectiveness of basic education,

the State Education Commission (SEDC) has formed expert groups and formulated curricula guidelines for the country's primary and secondary schools. In view of the huge regional socioeconomic disparity, SEDC permits the flexible implementation of the guidelines by the provinces, autonomous regions, and the metropolitan municipalities. Necessary adaptation can be made as appropriate to local conditions, provided that the basic requirements of the curricula are met. There are two versions of the six-year primary school curriculum: one for the urban schools and the other for rural schools. It offers ten subjects including moral studies, Chinese, and mathematics. The urban schools should, in addition, provide sports activities for Grade 1 and Grade 2 pupils, while rural schools should add provisions of agricultural studies for Grade 6 pupils. The five-year primary schools do not offer sports. The middle school provides 13 compulsory subjects, including moral education and politics, Chinese, mathematics, and a foreign language. The upper-middle school is required to offer optional subjects, the contents of which are determined in accordance with the wishes of the pupils, social needs, and the conditions of specific schools. English is the most common foreign language, although some schools also offer Japanese, Russian, French, German, and Spanish. The syllabus teaching materials for each subject are all developed by subject experts according to the requirements of the curriculum and are approved by the Primary and Secondary School Teaching Materials Board of SEDC.

As far as higher education institutions are concerned, SEDC laid down the basic requirements and principles for course designs. The institutions are responsible for the formulation of their curricula and syllabuses in line with SEDC requirements and in accordance with social demand, as well as their own conditions. As a general pattern, higher education institutions offer optional courses in addition to compulsory subjects. The development of standard textbooks for higher education institutions must be approved by specific subject committees organized by SEDC.

8. The System of Examinations, Promotions, and Certifications

Primary and secondary schools administer four types of examinations: term examinations (TE), school year examinations (STE), completion examinations (CE), and entrance examinations (EE). In primary schools, TEs, STEs, and CEs are all confined to the subjects of Chinese and mathematics. The entrance examination to the lower-middle school is being phased out. The upper-middle school EE is of a selective nature and is usually combined with the middle school CE. The upper-middle school CE is independent of the higher education EE. The former is a qualifying examination and the latter a selective one. The higher education EE is a common national examination with separate provisions for liberal arts candidates and science candidates. Successful CE examinees of primary and secondary schools are awarded completion certificates, whereas university students will be awarded the completion certificate and a degree after passing various examinations and assessments.

9. Educational Assessment, Evaluation, and Research

Educational evaluation is an important form of supervision of the performance of schools and institutions. Since the 1980s, educational evaluation has been given due emphasis and has experienced rapid development. In higher education institutions and specialized secondary schools, assessment mainly consists of qualification evaluation, standard evaluation, and excellence evaluation. At the primary and secondary levels, the evaluation normally covers the aspects of purpose, school management, educational quality, and school conditions. Educational evaluations are normally conducted by local governments and the educational authorities.

With regard to educational research, a multilevel research network has been established with over 10,000 full-time research personnel in the country. Research funding is provided by the state and the local authorities through special funds and projects. Apart from basic educational theories, the topics of educational research are mostly concerned with the changes and development of Chinese education as well as educational and teaching practices. Research results can thus directly serve both educational policy-making and the educational reform process.

In the early 1990s, the key research topics were as follows: the relationship between rural educational development and the advancement of rural society; the main issues concerning the theory and practice of ethnic minority education in China; the theory and practice of the integration of education with productive labor; the theory and practice of Chinese educational legislation; the reform of teacher education and the building of the teaching force; the reform of primary and secondary school curriculum and teaching materials; the reform of teaching methods and the examination system; literacy education in China, and so on.

10. Major Reforms in the 1980s and 1990s

Since the early 1980s, the Chinese government has undertaken a series of effective educational reforms. These include:

(a) The adjustment of the educational structure. In 1980, secondary education in China consisted pri-

marily of mainstream secondary schools, and the proportion of pupils in secondary technical and vocational schools accounted for only 19 percent of the total enrollment at the upper-secondary level. Following the adjustment, this proportion had increased to 46 percent by 1990. Progress was also made in the reform of the structure of higher education. In terms of the structure of subject areas, the disciplines with the greatest social demand were rapidly expanded. Between 1978 and 1990, the number of full-time students in finance and economics, politics and law, and liberal arts disciplines increased by 12, 32, and 2.2 times respectively. A large number of new and interdisciplinary subject areas were developed. With regard to the structure of program levels, the development of diploma education was accelerated. By 1990, the number of higher diploma institutions had grown to 455, accounting for 42.6 percent of the total number of higher education institutions, with an enrollment of 743,000 students representing 36 percent of the total student population in higher education. The ratio of graduate, undergraduate, and diploma students had been adjusted from 0.7:100:24 in 1949 to 7:100:56 in 1990, illustrating a rationalization of the structure of higher education.

(b) Change of the management system. A new decentralized management system was established, with local authorities being given the responsibility for basic education. With regard to the provision of education, the traditional mode—according to which the government assumed full responsibility—decreased and provisions by enterprises and social communities expanded substantially. In addition, the degree of institutional autonomy was extended. This change was marked by great success, particularly in the rural areas. In the early 1990s, efforts are being made to improve the macrocontrol and internal management systems of institutions.

(c) Comprehensive reform of education. Since 1987, SEDC has launched pilot projects in the comprehensive reform of education in 15 municipalities and 116 counties. The main contents of the urban comprehensive reform were: to enhance the overall coordination of economy, science and technology, and education (including all levels and types) by the government; to change the admission and job assignment system of the specialized secondary schools and the skilled worker schools, with corresponding reforms of the labor personnel system; to improve the overall structure of urban education; and to promote the diversification of upper-secondary education. The main contents of the rural comprehensive reform of education included: the overall coordination and integration

211

of agriculture, science and technology, and education: and the overall management of BE, TAVE, and AE, so as to facilitate coordinated socioeconomic and educational development.

11. Major Problems for the Year 2000

The main problems of Chinese education are as follows: a degree of irrationality in the educational structure (e.g., TAVE is not adequately developed); insufficient investment in education and poor school conditions; educational principles, contents, and methodology are out of touch with social reality to varying degrees; and the efficiency of the system is less than ideal. Thus, in general terms, the Chinese education system is not yet well-adapted to the needs of the national socialist development program.

The Chinese government has formulated a Ten-Year Program and the Eighth Five-Year Plan for educational development. It may be anticipated that, by the end of the century, the educational structure in China will become more rational, the education quality will be substantially improved, the force of specialized personnel will be expanded, and the quality and standard of the labor force and professionals will be further improved. The educational system will largely meet the needs of state economic and social development.

Bibliography

Liu Huozi (ed.) 1990 *Chinese Encyclopaedia.* Chinese Encyclopaedia Press, Beijing
Li Jian (ed.) 1989 *Chinese Education Yearbook.* People's Education Press, Beijing
People's Republic of China 1985 *The Central Government's Decision on Educational Reform.* Government Office, Beijing
People's Republic of China 1986 *The Compulsory Education Act.* Government Office, Beijing
Xue Muqiao (ed.) 1990 *Chinese Economic Yearbook.* Chinese Statistics Press, Beijing

Colombia

J. Mora

1. General Background

Colombia, located on the northwestern corner of South America, is the only country of the continent which borders on both the Atlantic and the Pacific Ocean. With a land area of 703,248 square kilometers, it is the fourth largest country in South America.

Colombia is made up of seven macroregions with different geographic, socioeconomic, and cultural characteristics which constitute peculiar environments for education. Variations in geographic conditions and in specific patterns of settlement of the population result in different degrees of educational opportunities as well as diverse kinds of available educational services.

According to the 1991 Constitution: "Colombia is a national state based on law, organized as a unitarian, decentralized republic, autonomous in its territory, democratic and pluralistic, founded on respect for human dignity and labor, on the solidarity of its population, and on the predominance of common interests" (Article 1). Since Independence in 1810, Colombia has been a republic with a centralized political organization that is now becoming decentralized in accordance with the new Constitution. In the past, education was the responsibility of the central government which defined policies and financed programs and projects. At the beginning of the 1990s responsibility shifted to regional and local governments for the implementation and financing of some programs and projects designed for their particular needs.

Colombia's population is made up of Whites of European origin, Blacks of African origin, Native Americans, *mestizos* (White and Native American), *mulatos* (White and Black), and *zambos* (Native American and Black). Populations of those with solely White, Black, or Native American roots are smaller than mixed groups.

Spanish is Colombia's predominant language; Native American groups tend to maintain their own language but use Spanish as a second language. Minor efforts have been made to develop educational materials in vernacular languages for the more isolated Native American groups.

According to the last national population census of 1985, Colombia had just over 30 million inhabitants, with a projected population of 33.6 million for 1991, 36.2 million for 1995, and 39.4 million for the year 2000. Since 1960, Colombia has undergone two significant demographic changes: urbanization and a decrease in population growth rates. The exponential rate of growth fell from 3.2 percent for the period 1964–73 to 2 percent for the period 1973–85. The rural population has fallen from 48 percent of the total population to 35 percent in 1985. This was due to such factors as expansion of educational opportunities, birth control campaigns, urbanization, and migration from rural to urban areas. These factors have been accelerated by political turmoil and by people's aspirations to improved living standards, particularly in large cities. For this reason, migration has led to higher growth rates for the four largest cities in the country—Bogotá, Medellín, Cali, and Barranquilla—than for other cities.

Urbanization and decreased rates of population growth have had a great influence on the distribution of educational opportunities and on improvements in the quality of education. Traditionally, considerations of educational opportunities involved two sectors of the population, rural and urban groups. Inadequate education for marginal groups in the so-called "poverty belts" in large cities has brought about the need to consider this new population sector. New educational content, materials, and strategies must be designed to meet their specific needs.

From an economic point of view, between 1958 and 1970 policies were aimed at promoting industrial development which would lead to the replacement of imports by home produced goods. Toward 1967, a period of growth began. It was fueled by increased foreign trade and new exchange and commercial policies. This growth declined by 1980 when an economic recession started. Between 1970 and 1974 the average growth of the Gross Domestic Product (GDP) was 6.1 percent, due to the increase of minor exports, world trade, and the dynamics of public and private investments. From 1974 to 1975, the GDP growth rate was only 2.3 percent; between 1981 and 1985 deterioration of the external sector led to recession, and the GDP increased only by 1.8 percent. Agricultural production in this period only increased by 1.3 percent compared to 4.3 percent for 1970–74 and 5.8 percent for 1975.

Before the 1950s the economy was based mainly on agricultural production and Colombia had one of the most underdeveloped educational structures in the world. By the 1960s, however, educational expectations had increased from 2 to 6 school years for Colombian children. This led to significant changes in the urban labor market and consequently in the distribution of income. Expectations of up to 9 years of basic education should be reached by the year 2000.

The National Socioeconomic Development Plan for 1990–94 calls for reinforcement of dynamic foreign trade; investment on physical infrastructure and on transportation and communications; a stimulus to private investments on agriculture, housing, and industry; and investments on human capital through formal and nonformal education for children, youths, and adults, and on scientific and technological research. By the end of the 1990s economic growth in Colombia is expected to reach an annual average rate of 5.35 percent.

The program for economic openness is designed to reorient the Colombian economy toward continuous and efficient growth, expanding production in order to increase employment, improving the quality and lowering the prices of goods and services. Since a strengthened society is a necessary complement to this process, educational needs become a significant factor in improving productive capacity. In addition, women's education is seen as a means to healthier children, and general education is considered a factor in greater social mobility, according to the National Development Plan for Education 1990–94.

2. *Politics and the Goals of the Education System*

Colombia once had only two major political parties, Liberal and Conservative. Since 1970, however, factions have emerged from the traditional parties, affecting their internal stability, and new political parties have appeared, notably the Patriotic Union (UP) and the National Alliance M–19. The former has been associated with, and the latter is a direct descendent of, guerrilla movements that achieved integration into the system of constitutional democracy through negotiations with the government.

On the other hand, the political dynamics of the country have become increasingly more complex as guerrilla movements, organized within a national coordinating body, advance peace negotiations with the government. As negotiations continue, it is likely that other new parties will appear in the political arena.

Each party and guerrilla movement has different philosophical and ideological positions concerning the policies that will lead to national, regional, and local development. However, there appears to be a consensus regarding education as a human right and as an important ingredient for the improvement of personal and social conditions. Consequently, policies that tend toward the implementation of universal basic education are widely supported. Nevertheless, conceptions of the strategies, means, and instruments needed to achieve this goal are not shared. For example, according to some political groups responsibility for basic education should lie with the public sector; for other groups, it should be shared by public and private sectors and by the communities.

In the past, differences between the two traditional parties regarding their position on education concerned who should be educated, the content of education, and whether official or unofficial education should be emphasized. On these issues, however, the two traditional parties seem to have come together. Healthy rivalry between official and unofficial institutions, particularly in higher education, is expressly emphasized in the National Development Plan for Education for 1990–94.

Since 1970, politics have also influenced education directly as parties, guerrillas, and other nongovernmental organizations (NGOs) have imparted political education, particularly to the more deprived sectors of the population in rural areas and to marginal sectors in the large cities. This political education is related to strategies for community organization, consciousness-raising in relation to rights and duties, the assimilation of participatory strategies and means for participative planning, and the development and monitoring of programs and projects for community development.

The stress laid by the 1991 Constitution on the participation of the people strengthens an existing and growing practice and formalizes it through political, normative, and institutional channels. State governors and city mayors were formerly appointed by the President; the first elected mayors will conclude their first term at the beginning of 1992, while the first elected governors will begin their first term in January 1992.

In sum, politics has played, and will continue to play, a significant role in determining educational conceptions, values, expectations, and actions, beyond the role played by political parties. Some questions, however, remain; among them, to what extent political parties, guerrilla movements, and NGOs have contributed to social consciousness-raising and to self- and community-improvement, and what role will they continue to play in such processes, including education.

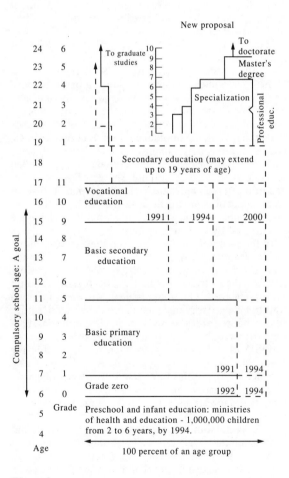

Figure 1

Colombia: Structure of the formal education system 1991

3. The Formal System of Education

3.1 Primary, Secondary, and Tertiary Education

Figure 1 outlines the structure of Colombia's formal education system; key data will be presented for each level of education in text.

Education in Colombia is compulsory for children from 5 to 15 years of age; it comprises a minimum of one year of preschool education and nine of basic education, as stipulated in Article 67 of the 1991 Constitution.

Previous constitutions, as well as the present one, state that education, especially at the elementary level, is a public responsibility. The present Constitution, however, adds that some academic costs might be met by those who are able to pay them. In actual practice, education does involve a financial cost to the family, in tuition or a proportion of fees, books and other learning materials, uniforms, or contributions.

Educational services are offered in official and unofficial institutions; both types of institution implement the curriculum approved by the Ministry of Education.

The present structure of the educational system encompasses four levels: one to two years of preschool education, five years of elementary basic education, four of basic secondary education and two of vocational secondary education, and two to ten years of higher education. As will be shown later, some reforms are being introduced which particularly affect preschool, vocational secondary, and higher education. Figure 1 presents not only the system in 1991, but expected enrollments in 1994 and the year 2000.

Public institutions have always had a large coverage of elementary education in Colombia. Public education at the elementary level has experienced significant growth in the past; enrollment rose from only 0.5 million students in 1933 to 3.5 million in 1976. Unfortunately, in the last 15 years the annual rate of growth for enrollment has decreased to the point where, between 1980 and 1984, it dropped to zero, with a rise to 1 percent between 1984–89. At present, 4.2 million students are enrolled in elementary grades, but 16 percent of school-age children do not attend school.

One of the major problems in elementary education in the past was enrollment; at present the main problem is keeping the students in school. In the 1980s, more than 90 percent of school-age children enrolled in first grade, but 40 percent of them did not complete elementary education. One-third of overall enrollment is made up of overaged children repeating grades, especially first grade. Strategies devised to control this phenomenon have not been effective. In addition, school days are short and school years even shorter: effective time for learning at elementary schools is approximately 5 hours per day and 180 days per year.

The goals of expansion of enrollment and improvement in the quality of education in rural areas have been sought through the *Escuela Nueva* methodology, in which elements of nongraded schools are combined with personalized strategies and active student participation techniques. These methods have brought about a positive change in the role teachers play in the learning process. Schools have also become focal points for communities, which in turn become involved in school activities.

Average class size has ranged from 45.3 in 1968 to 39.1 in 1984; for 1991, it has been estimated at 30. The student–teacher ratio was 52:1 in 1933 for urban and rural schools, 34.8:1 and 37:1 respectively for 1964, and 30.4:1 and 28.4:1 for 1984. For 1991 this ratio has also been estimated at 30:1. In elementary graded schools it is frequently the case that there is one teacher per grade; consequently, class size and the ratio of students per teacher tend to be identical. However, some schools work two shifts, particularly in deprived urban areas. In rural areas, where the *Escuela Nueva* methodology is applied, several grades are taught in the same classroom and by the same teacher. Up to now, no information about the ratios for *Escuela Nueva* have been made available.

Secondary education includes grades 6 to 11. In 1990, more than 2.6 million students enrolled in secondary schools, 60 percent of them in public and 40 percent in private institutions. The annual growth rate for enrollment was 5 percent in 1983–84, but since 1985 it has been close to 2.2 percent.

Major problems found in secondary education include the low coverage of educational opportunity (only 46% of the target population, aged 12 to 17, is enrolled in schools, of which 58% correspond to large cities and 36% to rural areas) There is also the fact that the structures of basic elementary, basic secondary, and vocational secondary education in the public sector do not lead to an integrated educational process from first to eleventh grade, as is common in private institutions. This disparity leads to decreases in enrollment in the higher grades, particularly in the transition from fifth to sixth grade; during the latter there are also high levels of dropout. The lack of integration has an additional negative effect upon the quality of education due to changes in norms, teachers, methodologies, and environment. A further problem, low levels in the quality of education, is evidenced in the data collected through state examinations for entrance to institutions of higher education. These low levels are due, among other reasons, to the low quality of teacher training, an obsolete curriculum, lack of adequate materials, and insufficient time dedicated to actual academic work since public institutions work in up to three shifts (morning, afternoon, and evening) per school day.

The low coverage of secondary education (46%) and its poor quality have led the present government to consider secondary education a priority for 1991–94. Policies included in the National Development Plan for 1990–94 aim at the integration of public and private efforts, to achieve 100 percent coverage of the population aged 12–17 by the year 2000. It is expected that by 1995 coverage will reach 70 percent. A project to integrate elementary and secondary public institutions is underway; emphasis on general education will be reinforced with vocational options for Grades 10 and 11, and transfer of technical and technological education as part of higher educational levels.

Available data indicate that in 1989 there were 236 institutions of higher education, 30 percent of which were public and 70 percent private. Over two-thirds of the institutions are universities and the rest are for technical and technological education. Enrollments for the same year totaled 475,000; of these 42 percent attended public and 58 percent private institutions. At the same time, 78 percent of total enrollment was in the universities, 13 percent in technological institutions, and 8 percent in technical professional institutions.

Enrollment in graduate schools for 1989 was 9,904 students, of which 87 percent studied education, health sciences, economics, and social sciences; 7 percent were in engineering; 5 percent in mathematics and basic sciences; and 1 percent in agricultural sciences. Some 56 percent of enrolled students were in specialization programs (one year of study after a professional degree) and 44 percent in programs leading to a master's degree. Only 15 students were enrolled in doctoral programs; half of them were in theology and the rest in basic sciences.

The main problems found in Colombian higher education are, in order of importance: low quality levels, institutional dispersion in the system, and unequal distribution of financial support by the government. Some major causes of these problems are lack of planning, low levels of credibility due to fast expansion without the requisite infrastructure, and loss of national leadership on the part of the universities.

Policies for higher education for 1991–94 are oriented to strengthening undergraduate general education and de-emphasizing specialization at this stage, to reinforcing curriculum flexibility and restructuring teaching strategies in order to place more value on the work of students and to facilitate participation of teachers and students in research. Additionally, there are plans to promote the development of new master's and doctoral programs associated with research programs and projects.

3.2 Preschool Education

In the 1980s great emphasis was placed on educating children under 6 years of age. Between 1982–86 enrollment in preschool education increased by 26 percent, although official institutions covered only 7 percent of the target population. In the past, preschool education has been entirely the family's responsibility. At present, 80 percent of the target population of 4–5-year olds remains unassisted. However, the ministries of Health and Education have developed a joint care program, aimed at the most disadvantaged sectors of the populace, for integral attention to children under

5 in welfare homes established under the care of a community mother.

The Educational Development Plan for 1991–94 includes a program for the establishment of a "Grade Zero" in all public elementary schools for children under 6 in order to prepare them for first grade. Repetition of the first grade has been high, particularly in deprived sectors of the populace. In 1987, for instance, first-grade repetition reached 21.9 percent for rural areas and 14.1 percent for urban areas. Grade Zero is expected to increase the level of internal efficiency of the educational process.

3.3 Vocational, Technical, and Business Education

The last two years of secondary education, Grades 10 and 11, include vocational education; at the same time, some options in technical and business education are offered.

Vocational, technical, and business education in Colombia have three purposes: first, to respond to the aptitudes and preferences of secondary-school students; second, to allow them to apply their knowledge to practical problems related to life and production; and third, to train dropouts from the educational system and students interested in learning a trade and in joining the labor market. The first purpose is being met through Grades 10 and 11 of vocational secondary education; the second is considered a pedagogical element at all levels of education, and the third is a responsibility of public and private institutions established for this purpose.

The most important institution of this kind is the National Apprenticeship Service (SENA), under the Ministry of Labor. It runs several schools which offer vocational training in options related to the specific circumstances and perspectives of each geographical region. Private institutions for vocational training are supported mainly by religious communities.

Vocational secondary education offers a variety of options including programs in industrial, agricultural, and business education. The Colombian system also includes the options of academic preparation for higher education (particularly for careers related to humanities and natural and social sciences) and teacher training, which prepares teachers for basic elementary education. In 1958, 70 percent of students enrolled in the preparatory option were men and 30 percent were women. In 1980, distribution was 59 and 41 percent respectively. For the teacher-training option 43 percent of the enrollment was made up of men and 57 percent of women in 1958; by 1980, women made up 60 percent of enrollment and men 40 percent. By 1990 the percentage of men had decreased even further.

Business vocational education is, after the academic preparation option, the second most popular in terms of enrollment. In 1983, over 77 percent of enrollment corresponded to the preparatory option and 12 percent to business education, while the percentages for industrial, agricultural, teacher training, and social work were 3.98, 1.71, 3.77, and 1.46 respectively.

3.4 Adult and Nonformal Education

The rate of illiteracy in Colombia for the population over 10 years of age was over 38.5 percent in 1951. By 1985, it had decreased to 12.2 percent, but there are still 2.3 million illiterate adults. In 1991, the percentages were 23.4 for rural and 7.3 for urban areas. The more deprived areas with regard to basic elementary education are the Atlantic and Pacific coasts. Literacy campaigns have been significant in the past; it has been difficult, however, to implement basic primary education as postliteracy programs for adults.

Major problems include lack of educational opportunities, inadequate curriculum, lack of special training for teachers to deal with adult learners, and lack of adequate materials. Unfortunately, provisions for 1991–94 do not include additional programs to improve educational conditions in adult and nonformal education. It is important to mention the contributions nongovernmental organizations have made to the development of programs of popular education through community development projects which include educational activities.

4. Administrative and Supervisory Structure and Operation

Traditionally, Colombia has had a centralized organizational structure for education; the reorganization of the educational system in 1968 and 1976 was aimed at decentralizing educational administration. National development plans formulated in the 1980s were oriented toward the growth of enrollment and the improvement of quality of educational opportunity through the implementation of projects that respond to regional characteristics and educational needs.

One strategy devised in 1982 in order to decentralize administration was educational mapping, which created local administrative units called "Nuclei for Educational Development." A nucleus is made up of communities that interrelate in social, economic, and cultural affairs. Several nuclei with similar characteristics make up an Educational District, the second-level administrative unit. A Secretariat of Education is the regional administrative entity in each of the politico-territorial units into which the country is divided. It constitutes a link between the region and the central units for educational administration. Until 1990 educational mapping had not been as successful as expected because it has failed to integrate with city governments.

Supervision has traditionally been an important element in the development of Colombian education. The first legal act to establish objectives and responsibilities for the work of national inspectors dates from 1936. Inspectors were to oversee the organization and operation of all public institutions of preschool, elementary, and complementary education, as well as public and private secondary schools. In 1949 inspection was organized by specialized subject areas and considered a link between the government and the people through the schools. In 1958 inspection was regarded as more of an academic than an administrative function, while in 1963 criteria for recognition and approval of curricula were established, and in 1970 a supervision manual, introducing the term and concept of "supervision," was published.

Lack of funds resulted in a decline in the importance of supervision for education development. It is likely that supervision as it now exists in Colombia will be abolished in the near future. Supervision as a function is becoming a responsibility of local and regional curriculum administrators such as academic vice-principals, pedagogical coordinators, and nuclei directors.

5. Educational Finance

In the 1970s and 1980s there has been a gradual increase in the percentage of the total national budget dedicated to education. In 1970, 13.6 percent of the budget was allocated to education; in 1975, it was 16.5 percent; and in 1980, it was 19 percent. In 1980, 37.69 percent of the educational budget was dedicated to elementary education, 21.1 percent to secondary education, and 22.1 percent to higher education.

Since 1971, Colombia has aimed at concentrating the financing of public education in the central government while decentralizing responsibility for the administration of the school system at the regional level. This policy was meant to empower the government to redress severe regional inequities in the distribution of educational expenditures and opportunities. As a result, by 1980 the central government financed 84 percent of expenditure in public education, as compared with 65 percent in 1970.

The government's financial effort to increase educational opportunities and to improve quality is based on Law 46 of 1971 (called "*Situado Fiscal*," or tax allowance) and Law 43 of 1975 (Law of Nationalization). The *Situado Fiscal* requires that at least 11.1 percent of the government's ordinary income be allocated to support elementary education. Nationalization requires that one-half of the sales tax returnable to departmental (state) capitals and the Special District of Bogotá be transferred to the Ministry of Education as financial assistance to secondary education.

At present, expenditure in education comprises public and private efforts; in the 1980s, they represented 5 percent of the GDP. The public sector contributed approximately 60 percent of total expenditure in education, as compared with 84 percent in 1980.

Programs and projects planned for 1991–94 will be financed as follows: 42 percent through the national budget, with the remaining 58 percent to be shared by municipalities, the private sector, and regional governments. National funds for investment in basic elementary education include part of a loan for projects tending to universalize elementary education.

Private institutions are financed by student tuition fees and contributions from private enterprise; in some cases, however, these schools receive some support from the government.

Public institutions of higher education charge tuition fees according to family or student income statements. Starting in 1992, tuition at public universities will be as expensive as at comparable private institutions. However, students will receive scholarships on the basis of scholastic achievement and financial needs. It is projected that in 10 years tuition will supply 33 percent of the money needed to run public universities. At present tuition represents 5 percent of the total income of these institutions.

In the 1950s, the Colombian Institute for Technical Studies Overseas (ICETEX) was created to help Colombians attend graduate school abroad. The Institute has served as a clearing house for scholarships and as a financial corporation for loans. From the 1960s, loans were also made available for professional studies, both in Colombia and overseas. ICETEX has retained both functions but its loan capacity does not meet increasing demands. Loans usually cover tuition, room and board, and books. Repayment starts after graduation, when the graduate enters the labor market, with a low rate of monthly interest. Policies for 1991–94 aim at creating new sources for loans; governmental banks will establish lines of credit for education for the benefit of students from low-income families.

6. Supplying Personnel for the Education System

Elementary and secondary education (basic and vocational) is imparted by 280,000 teachers. The public sector includes 200,000 of them, of which 120,000 teach in basic elementary schools and the rest in secondary. Private education employs 80,000 teachers, 62 percent of whom are in secondary schools.

Elementary-school teachers are trained in normal schools, a type of secondary school whose curriculum includes four years of general education and two years of specialized teacher training in all subjects taught in elementary school. In the 1980s special programs were established at universities to train elementary-school teachers. Some of these programs apply education-at-a-distance strategies, becoming inservice education programs. Data indicate that the educational level of teachers has increased. While in 1950 two-thirds of elementary-school teachers had little schooling beyond elementary level and the rest were graduates from normal schools, at present around 68 percent are graduates from normal schools, 17 percent from other types of secondary schools, and 15 percent from universities.

Secondary-school teachers usually receive university training at schools of education offering majors that correspond to the main subjects taught in high school. University-level teacher-training programs, like all higher education programs, are evaluated and supervised by the Colombian Institute for the Promotion of Higher Education (ICFES).

Data indicate that 21.51 percent of graduate programs are in education. However, a small fraction of teachers and educational administrators hold graduate degrees.

University faculties are made up of professionals from different fields of knowledge. Most universities grant some members of their staff paid study leaves to pursue graduate studies. Staff members are also encouraged to apply for scholarships to carry out graduate work. Some universities offer training programs on university teaching methods, especially for professors in the areas of engineering, health, and architecture.

Teachers at normal schools often supplement their income by teaching in adult education programs. In the 1980s, few undergraduate and graduate programs offered training for adult and nonformal education.

Foreseeable reforms for teacher training in basic education include abolishing normal schools, granting schools of education full responsibility for training elementary and secondary school teachers (Grades 6 to 9), and leaving the training of tenth- and eleventh-grade teachers in the hands of university schools of humanities, and natural and social sciences. Teachers for technical and technological education will be trained mainly by schools of engineering, architecture, and others as needed.

7. Curriculum Development and Teaching Methodology

Curriculum design and development have traditionally been the responsibility of the central government. There is a General Directorate for Curriculum Development within the Ministry of Education, with sections for curriculum design and development for basic elementary and secondary education (Grades 1 to 9) and vocational secondary education (Grades 10 and 11).

During the 1950s, the curriculum for elementary schools was different in urban and rural areas. By 1963, a new curriculum was designed, to give rural children access to knowledge formerly available only to children in urban areas. Consequently, a national curriculum was approved but implemented through traditional methodologies in which teacher and content were the center of the learning process. Later

the *Escuela Nueva* methodology described above was developed.

In 1978, the Curriculum Renovation Program was launched. This new curriculum includes four basic areas: mathematics, natural sciences, social studies, and Spanish and literature. Other subjects such as art, physical education, vocational training, and religious education complement the curriculum.

Different teaching materials have been designed for rural and urban areas. At present, materials for urban schools are published according to specific standards defined by the Ministry of Education. These materials are distributed free of charge to all urban schools along with small libraries as programmed by the project for universalization of basic elementary education. Learning materials for *Escuela Nueva* are designed by a technical team at the Ministry of Education and their publication contracted with a private firm.

The curriculum for vocational secondary education is also designed at the Ministry of Education according to the different options offered at schools. In the 1980s a more flexible approach was implemented for the creation of new options: localities and regions are invited to present proposals for vocational secondary education programs to respond to their specific needs. This has resulted in the creation of such vocational training programs as theater, ballet, music, tourism, and recreation.

In the case of higher education, each program designs its own curriculum. Teams of specialized teachers with the assistance of a curriculum expert design study plans for each career. The resulting curriculum is evaluated at different administrative levels of the institution, which must approve it before it is sent to ICFES. Only after ICFES approval is the creation of a new program or the curriculum reform authorized.

Specialization in a professional field begins early in most undergraduate curricula. Students are allowed to register in some elective subjects, but usually few electives will count as credits for graduation.

As far as methodology is concerned, the present teaching methods for elementary education are geared toward individualized learning, promotion of team work, and encouragement for children to play the central role in the teaching–learning process. These developments have been made possible by the adoption of new learning materials in the case of *Escuela Nueva* and of the new curriculum at urban schools. Teaching methods at vocational secondary schools tend to be more traditional but they also assume different characteristics depending on the type of program involved. At the level of higher education, teaching methods are adapted to each specific field: methodologies that allow students to come in contact with real situations are being emphasized in fields like engineering, architecture, and education. Methodologies stressing research as a means for learning are also being implemented.

According to the National Development Plan for Education for 1991–94, work will continue on the design of a new curriculum for basic elementary eighth and ninth grades. The secondary-school curriculum will be reformed to meet the requirements of basic education with optional subjects for vocational education. Higher education will have a new structure: three years of general education, two or three years of professional education plus the option of an additional year for specialization, and from two to five years of graduate education in master's and doctoral programs.

8. *The System of Examinations, Promotions, and Certifications*

Evaluation of learning at the elementary level is somewhat flexible and is focused on the quality of learning processes and on the achievement of objectives. Tests, written work, and direct observation by the teacher are the tools used by teachers to collect information for evaluation. Reports to parents are issued four times a year.

In urban schools where new teaching methods and evaluation strategies are used, all children enrolled in a grade are expected to be promoted to the next with remedial learning activities when necessary. Despite the fact that teachers have been trained to apply automatic promotion, traditional examinations measuring rote learning are still administered in some schools.

The *Escuela Nueva* methodology is flexible with regard to student promotion from one grade to the next. Because students learn at their own pace, promotion is possible in one or more subjects or in the whole curriculum. Parents are periodically informed of their children's progress and learning problems. This is made possible by parents' permanent involvement in school activities, even in those related to the learning process.

In secondary schools, both basic and vocational, the evaluation process is more rigid. Students must take frequent quizzes and partial examinations. Parents receive grade reports four times during the school year. Grades for all periods are averaged to arrive at the final grade, which determines whether the student is promoted to the next grade. Norms regulating secondary-school evaluation are being revised.

Secondary-school graduates who wish to enter higher education institutions are required to take a state examination. Some public and private universities also require applicants who have scored sufficiently high marks in the state examination to take an additional entrance examination. Each university determines the score an applicant should achieve to enter a particular program. Each university has its own norms in relation to the evaluation of student learning, and for graduation and certification.

One of the most significant problems in the areas of evaluation, promotion, and certification is the disparity at the elementary level between schools and between urban and rural schools, as well as the insufficient training of teachers to conduct these tasks. In secondary schools, norms tend to be too rigid. For universities and other institutions of higher education, the fact that quality differs from one institution to the next may constitute an obstacle when students need to transfer between schools.

9. *Educational Assessment, Evaluation, and Research*

A national evaluation system is in the process of being developed. It is geared to continuous evaluation of growth and improvement through basic and elementary education. Instruments for the evaluation of scholastic achievement in mathematics, sciences, and Spanish and literature are being prepared.

Traditionally there has been a lack of approved strategies for educational assessment. Specific programs (such as *Escuela Nueva*, the National Institutes for Diversified Secondary Education, or the normal schools) have incorporated their own evaluation processes. Only in the case of *Escuela Nueva* are the results used to refine and improve the methodology in order to expand its application.

At the end of the 1980s, the Ministry of Education invited schools of education to evaluate, on a regional basis, the effect of automatic promotion on student achievement. Results have not yet been published.

The National Planning Department and the Educational Planning Office of the Ministry of Education habitually carry out research as input for policy-making. In addition, some research centers and universities have contracts to conduct studies. Basic statistics are issued by the National Statistics Department (DANE), but in education statistics are insufficient and not always reliable. Colombia is expected to have developed a reliable information system by 1995.

Research is mainly the responsibility of universities and nongovernmental research institutions. COLCIENCIAS, an institute associated with the National Planning Department, is responsible for promoting research at universities and research centers. A National Plan for Scientific and Technological Research is being implemented. Under it, research and graduate training are expected to become a significant input for socioeconomic development.

10. *Major Reforms in the 1980s and 1990s*

The major reforms implemented in elementary education have sought to effect improvements in the quality of education. Through the project for universalization of elementary education, for instance, all schools in the country were endowed with a small library, textbooks for children, inservice training for teachers, teaching aids, and certain elements of infrastructure for schools and classrooms.

The introduction of automatic promotion at urban elementary schools brought about changes in teaching methods and evaluation strategies which represent a significant advance. Expansion of educational opportunity and changes in methodology through *Escuela Nueva* have resulted in improvements in the quality of the educational process.

Teacher training and some technical and technological programs have increased coverage through education-at-a-distance strategies.

Goals for the 1990s include achieving 100 percent elementary school coverage for school-age children, increasing coverage for secondary education from 46 to 70 percent by 1995, promoting graduate studies as well as scientific and technological research at universities, reorienting research toward projects that have a bearing on socioeconomic development, creating a Grade Zero for children under 6 years of age, and reinforcing decentralization not only in the administration but also in the financing of education.

11. Major Problems for the Year 2000

Major challenges for the educational system in Colombia in the 1990s and into the next century include:

(a) to find sufficient resources to support the continuous expansion of elementary education as population grows, to increase expansion of secondary and higher education, to cope with rapidly growing financial deficits at public universities, to expand scientific and technological research due to costs of infrastructure, and to meet foreign debt commitments (several programs are financed with foreign loans.);

(b) to respond to the great cultural differences that arise from social, economic, and cultural inequalities among the population;

(c) to improve the training of educators and their working conditions;

(d) to strengthen coordination between literacy programs and nonformal educational activities;

(e) to implement a general system of evaluation in the whole country;

(f) to establish a reliable system of information.

Bibliography

Constitución Política de Colombia 1991 *Vigésima Edición.* Editorial Tamis, Bogotá

ICFES 1990 *Calidad, Eficiencia, Equidad de la Educación Superiore Colombia, 1990. Seminario Permanente: Memorias,* Vols. I and II. Editorial Delfin Ltda., Bogotá

Presidencia de la República, Departamento Nacional de Planeación 1991 *La Revolución Pacífica: Plan de Desarrollo Económico y Social 1990–1994.* Impreandes, Bogotá

República de Colombia, Departamento Nacional de Planeación 1991a Plan de apertura educativa 1991–1994. Working paper (Documentos MEN-DNP-UDS-DEC-2518)

República de Colombia, Departamento Nacional de Planeación 1991b Plan de apertura educativa 1991–1994. Anexo Estadistico. Working paper (Documentos MEN-DNP-UDS-DEC-2518)

República de Colombia, Ministerio de Educación Nacional 1987 *La Planeación Educativa en Colombia 1950–1986,* Vols. I and II. Editorial MEN, Bogotá

República de Colombia, Ministerio de Educación Nacional 1988a *Análisis del Sector Educativo con Enfasis en sus Aspectos Administrativos y Financieros.* OSPE, Bogotá

República de Colombia, Ministerio de Educación Nacional 1988b *Un Siglo de Educación en Colombia 1886–1896.* Editorial MEN, Bogotá

Tirado Mejia A 1989 *Nueva Historia de Colombia. Vol. V: Economía, Café e Industria.* Editorial Planeta, Bogotá

Congo

M. A. Husain

1. General Background

The People's Republic of the Congo is in the central west part of the African continent and, astride the equator, it has an area of 342,000 square kilometers. There is a narrow coastal plain stretching from Gabon in the north to the Angolan enclave of Cabinda in the south. Inland there is the chain of mountains known as the Mayombe and between the coast and the Mayombe is a mountainous area known as the Chaillu. Between the Mayombe and the Chaillu there is the Niari valley and a vast region of sandy hills dominating the four Batéké plateaus to the north of Brazzaville, the capital city. The climate is warm and humid throughout most of the country, but there are two types of vegetation: forest and savanna.

The Congo became independent in 1960 and a People's Republic in 1969. The constitution is that of

1979. There was an interim government in 1992 and new elections were to be held shortly after that time. The Congolese Workers' Party—the only political party—was to allow a multiparty system consisting of the Presidential Movement, the Opposition, the Third Force, and the Independents. However, the President named a new government where the opposition was represented and to which party the new minister of education belonged. The official result of the elections held in May and June 1993 was announced late and was contested. This resulted in the dissension which only subsided at the beginning of 1994.

Although national unity became stronger after independence, ethnic groups are still very important, especially in rural areas and within family units in towns. There are about 50 different ethnic groups which can be categorized into 13 major groups. The most important of these are the Sangha, the Makao, the Mbosi, the Téké, and the Kongo. Apart from the pygmies, the population is part of the larger Bantu group. There are two national languages, Lingala and Munukutuba, but the language used by the administration and also used as the medium of instruction in school is French.

The 1990 census showed that there were 2.2 million inhabitants with a density of 6.4 inhabitants per square kilometer. The average density hides regional disparities because 57 percent of the population lives in towns and in particular, in the two towns of Brazzaville and Pointe-Noire which account for 91 percent of all people living in urban areas. This is due to a massive exodus of young people from the rural areas which in turn led to the rural population becoming older.

Only 17 percent of the age group able to work is active and more than half of them work in the public sector. Pupils and students account for 24 percent of those of an active work age. This factor accounts for the reported low unemployment rate with education soaking up most of the employable out of all proportion to the norms in neighbouring countries.

The situation in 1994, however, was characterized by increasing unemployment, due on the one hand to a decrease in economic activity and, therefore, fewer jobs and, on the other hand, by an increase in the demand for employment by those leaving the educational system. The economy is heavily dependent on the petroleum sector (39% of GDP), whereas agriculture contributes relatively little to overall productivity, and services are restricted to the public service.

In the early 1980s the high price per barrel of petroleum was able to support the whole economy but after then, the fall in the price of petroleum and the devaluation of the dollar resulted in an economic recession and the onset of the first structural adjustment plan. In one year, 1985–86, the value of petroleum production fell from 398 billion to less than 100 billion Congolese francs. The second structural adjustment plan (1986–87) did not achieve the expected results. The third plan had to be delayed in 1990 because the civil servants' claims resulted in recruitment and salary increases that were incompatible with the planned budget restrictions.

In 1992, the state income was 192 billion Congolese francs but state expenditure was 214 billion francs. The gross domestic product (GDP) was 725 billion francs making a per capita income of 329,000 Fr CFA (i.e., US$603) per inhabitant. The devaluation of the franc at the beginning of 1994 further aggravated the economic difficulties.

In mid-1944, the economic and financial recuperation relied heavily on the relations between the state and the funders, and on a renegotiation of the debt (which absorbed all income from the sales of petroleum). Economic improvement would require new and rigorous adjustment efforts based on a major reduction of the number of persons working in the public sector, a change in the fiscal arrangements in the petroleum sector, a privatization of the means of distribution of oil products, and a restructuring of the banking sector. The reduction of salaries in the public sector remains a major problem in public finances.

2. Politics and the Goals of the Education System

Since independence the main goals of education have been: (a) the generalization of education (i.e., 10 years of compulsory education, later reduced to 6 years); and (b) human resources opportunities for the development of the country.

More than 30 years of legislation has not succeeded in decoupling the Congolese system of education from the influence of the French model. For example:

(a) A law of 1961 enacted compulsory and free education for a cycle of 10 years in a common school from primary to college level (this structure will never be implemented).

(b) A law of 1963 nationalized private education in order to have one public school type where ideological values could be inculcated.

(c) A law of 1980 tied education to development at the "Peoples' School" making literacy education compulsory, and introducing national languages (which will never be taught) and the notion of "productive work."

In 1990, compulsory education was reduced to 6 years; ideological education in the schools was suppressed; literacy education was no longer compulsory; and private schools were reinstated.

3. The Formal System of Education

For the structure of the education system see Fig. 1. Table 1 presents some selected information about the education system.

Table 1
Enrollment, number of teachers, and pupil–teacher ratios, by level 1990–91

	Pupils total	Number of girls	Teachers	Pupil–Teacher ratios
Preprimary	5,810	2,897	645	9.0:1
Primary	503,918	234,479	7,578	66.5:1
Secondary general	144,623	64,453	3,286	4.4:1
Secondary technical	3,306	1,452	601	5.5:1
Trade centers	2,003	1,079	256	7.8:1
Agricultural centers	53	12	7	7.5:1
General *lycée*	25,786	6,746	1,638	15.7:1
Technical *lycée*	5,583	2,177	481	11.6:1
Vocational schools	1,611	660	582	2.7:1
University	10,671	1,885	1,112	9.6:1

3.1 Primary, Secondary, and Tertiary Education

The structure comprises:

(a) three years of fee-paying preprimary education, only accessible to the children of well-off parents in urban areas;

(b) six years of primary education culminating in a certificate of primary studies and also a competi-

tive examination for entry to the first cycle of secondary school;

(c) four years of the first cycle of secondary education divided into an observation cycle of two years and an orientation cycle of two years;

(d) three years of general secondary school following on from the four years of the two cycles of secondary education. The general secondary school ends with the *baccalauréat*.

Since 1988, the gross enrollment ratio in primary schools which had been the best in the region (120% in 1980) was only 88.9 percent. This can be traced to a reduction in the demand for education (given lower family incomes), a decrease in the quality of education provided, and too little hope of employment in the public sector.

Parallel to secondary education there exists vocational / technical education (see Sect. 3.4).

After finishing secondary school, the chance exists for higher education, which has two cycles, the third one being undertaken abroad. Higher education is provided by a national university, *écoles normales supérieures*, and institutes. The university, Marien Ngouabai, has a monopoly on higher education in the Congo. It has twelve establishments, all in Brazzaville, that can be categorized into three groups:

(a) four faculties: in sciences, humanities, law, and economics;

(b) five institutes: for administration (ISG), rural development (IDR), health sciences (soon to become the Faculty of Medicine) (INSSA), physical education and sport (ISEPS), and education (ENS);

(c) three vocational institutes: the *École Normale Supérieure* (ENS) and the *École Normale Supérieure* for technical education (ENSET) (both

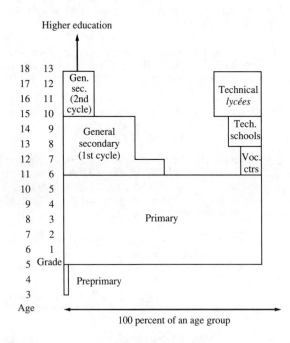

Figure 1
Congo: Structure of the formal education system

of which train teachers mostly for general secondary school and technical school), and the *École Normale d'Administration et de la Magistrature* (ENAM).

The four faculties have the highest enrollments (9,440 in 1992) with the rest of the establishments enrolling 2,600 (in 1992). Due to the decrease in scholarships, the number of students abroad considerably decreased after the academic year 1983–84.

3.2 Preschool Education

Lasting for three years, preschool education is only accessible to the wealthy (see Sect. 3.1). In 1990–91 there were 5,810 pupils enrolled with a pupil–teacher ratio of 9:1.

3.3 Special Education

No information on special education was available.

3.4 Vocational, Technical, and Business Education

Parallel to the general secondary education system there is a vocational and technical education system as follows:

(a) two years at a vocational center (*Centres de Métiers*) after primary school;

(b) two years of technical education that can be entered by those from the two-year vocational course or from the observation cycle in secondary education;

(c) three years at a technical and vocational *lycée* that can be entered by those from the two-year technical education course. In 1991–92 about 84 percent of pupils in these *lycées* were enrolled in Brazzaville and Kouillon.

While nearly 145,000 students were enrolled in general secondary education in 1990–91, about 36,000 students were enrolled in the various vocational and technical schools.

3.5 Adult and Nonformal Education

Nearly 47 percent of adults are deemed to be illiterate (57% women and 43% men). Literacy courses are held in firms, women's groups, and pre-cooperative groups, but the number of these "activities" decreased from 491 in 1984–85 to 209 in 1989–90 when there were only 4,632 participants.

Only a very small proportion of the population is involved in nonformal education which is mostly carried out by nongovernmental organizations in the form of evening courses. Craft courses and various courses for young people not having received a full primary education are part of "popular education" which, in 1988–89, had 17 establishments enrolling 2,246 persons (about half of them women) in 113 classrooms. Again, the number of these courses has decreased.

Unfortunately, pygmies most often do not receive any form of education.

4. Administrative and Supervisory Structure and Operation

The Ministry of Public Services (MFP) is responsible for the recruitment of personnel, the Ministry of Finance pays all salaries, and the Ministry of National Education (MEN) deploys the personnel and is responsible for their conditions of work.

The administration of primary and secondary education comes under four agencies and groups of services:

(a) *Direction général de l'administration et des services généraux* (DGASG) covers the following areas:

— the condition (appointments, holidays) and classification of personnel (promotion, re-classification, training, retraining, leaves of absence, retirement);
— equipment of the administrative and school infrastructures;
— Ministry budget for running and investment costs;
— purchase of supplies and equipment.

(b) The *Direction des études et de la planification scolaire et universitaire* (DEPSU) is responsible for the production of information on the following:
— pupil enrollment;
— administrative and school infrastructure and furniture in schools (teachers' desks, pupils' desks and benches, etc.);
— teaching and nonteaching personnel in schools;
— examination and competetive examination results.
   This agency also undertakes different studies on school mapping, human resources, the financing of education, and educational projects.

(c) Educational services (inspectorate, regional offices) collect data from all schools on such matters as school entry; the schools, pupils, infrastructure, and staff members; the organization of examinations; and budgetary requests.

(d) The *Direction de l'orientation et des bourses* (DOB) processes all information about student fields of study, grants, and scholarships,

Except for the data generated by DEPSU, many of the data produced are basically a subproduct of the administration and not conceptualized in terms of the needs of the users and of a modern administration system. Each agency thinks of itself as the owner of the data that it receives or produces and the dissemination of such information is more or less nonexistent. Thus, either identical or analogous information is produced by the different agencies and there is no attempt to have a common effort for data collection or for integrating the different data that have been collected by different agencies. Since the early 1980s there has been a serious and rapid deterioration in the collection and processing of data for the annual statistical census. A relevant and reliable system of data collection and processing needs to be created.

The administration of the system is characterized by a number of serious problems:

(a) The information system does not respond to the most rudimentary needs of the users because of insufficient coverage, lack of reliability, and delay of the availability of the results.

(b) There are uncertainties about the actual number of people working for the Ministry of Education and the allocation of personnel to schools and local, regional, and central authorities.

(c) There is a lack of personnel administration or, stated in another way, an administration characterized by delay in the processing of thousands of files.

(d) The needs of the schools are not taken into account when personnel are appointed and this hinders any kind of local organization and the implementation of school mapping.

5. Educational Finance

The financing of education is exclusively governmental with two exceptions: registration fees, and learning

Table 2
Public expenditure on education, percent of GNP, and percent of state budget for selected years in the period 1980–92

	Billions of CFA	% GNP	% State budget
1980	24.5	2.5	28.3
1985	40.1	6.3	13.2
1986	41.0	5.9	20.4
1988	37.4	4.7	23.6
1990	37.2	5.0	19.4
1992	61.9	—	28.9

tax (enacted by a law in February, 1983). In 1992, the percentage of the state budget allocated to education was 28.9. Table 2 presents the state expenditure on education for selected years in the period 1980 to 1992.

State expenditure on education, as a percentage of GNP, increased from 2.5 to 5.0 in the period 1980 to 1990. In 1992 salaries accounted for 85 percent of all expenditures, and scholarships for 12.5 percent which left 2.5 percent for all other expenditures. The central administration and nondesignated teachers accounted for 31 percent (8.9 billion Congolese francs) of all expenditures. An analysis of expenditure by level of education in 1992 (see Table 3) suggests that: (a) primary education receives a relatively small part (19.4% and this includes preschool); and (b) higher education receives most. This allocation bears witness to the fact that priority was given to postprimary education, particularly higher education, and that primary education was allocated a low priority. At the same time it should be noted that the expenditures on higher education reflect the large amount of money spent on scholarships.

In 1992 preschool education had an expenditure of about 1 billion Congolese francs but only for a small number of pupils; the unit cost is estimated to be 330,000 Fr CFA (US$605) per year. Primary education received 10.9 billion Fr CFA and the unit cost was 21,600 Fr CFA (US$40). General secondary school re-

Table 3
Expenditure on education by level of education in 1992 (in percentage of total)

	Primary and preschool	Secondary general	Secondary technical	Higher education	Administration
Including administrative expenditures	19.4	18.8	5.9	25.8	31.0
Excluding administrative expenditures	28.1	27.2	8.6	37.2	—

ceived 18.8 percent (11.5 billion Fr CFA) and the unit cost was 67,500 Fr CFA (US$124). Secondary vocational and technical received 3.6 billion (5.9%) and the unit cost was 342,900 Fr CFA (US$628). Finally, higher education received 16 billion (25.8% of the total) and this represented a unit cost of 1,499,400 Fr CFA (US$2,747).

The principal characteristic of the educational budget is its inertia: salaries and scholarships constitute 97.5 percent of all expenditure and it is considered that this cannot be decreased; the authorities have always, and exclusively given priority to the employment of their staff. Salaries, which account for most of the budget, remained stable from 1985 to 1990 when, as a result of salary increases and new recruitment, the salary component of the budget increased by slightly more than 50 percent. As a result of this, successive structural adjustment plans have not resulted in lowering educational expenditure. Indeed, in 1992, educational expenditure—61.9 billion Fr CFA—represented 28.9 percent of total government expenditure.

Family contributions are used for nonsalary expenditures in the schools. For example, parents pay 1,800 Fr CFA per year per child. Further to this, there are other parental expenditures: textbook purchase—500 Fr CFA, supplies and furniture—5,000 Fr CFA, uniform 3,000 Fr CFA or more, and examination fees (1,000 Fr CFA for the end of primary school examination).

Parents can also agree to a number of other special expenditures, such as maintenance of buildings and construction of new classrooms.

If one assumes that the annual cost of a pupil in primary school is 1, a pupil in general secondary school costs 3.1, a preschool pupil 15.4, a secondary technical pupil 15.9, and a higher education student 69.4. In Europe the difference between a primary pupil and higher education student is 1 to 5. Again it must be reiterated that the scholarship costs are 50 percent of the total cost.

6. Supplying Personnel for the Education System

In 1991–92 there were 32,030 persons involved in teaching: 26,601 certificated teachers (of whom 7,345 were female); 4,017 contracted teachers (of whom 1,035 were female); 299 expatriates (of whom 121 were female); and 1,113 volunteers (of whom 359 were female) who were recruited as *boursiers* or *appelés* in 1990 and 1991 and who are now demanding to be certificated.

The following number of persons were working at different levels of education: 20,710 in primary (of whom 6,271 were female); 5,981 in general secondary (of whom 655 were female); 1,471 in secondary technical (of whom 661 were female); 1,699 in administration (of whom 806 were female); and 757 in personnel service (of whom 87 were female).

Further to the 299 expatriates mentioned above it should be mentioned that there were also 1,112 working at the University.

There is a problem of over- and undersupply of some of the above categories in various parts of the country. For example, there are 97 primary school inspectors (of whom 27 are in Brazzaville covering 107 schools), assisted by 239 educational advisors (of whom 122 are in Brazzaville); preprimary education has 645 teachers and 3 to 4 social helpers per class covering 5,810 pupils—a clear case of oversupply.

There would appear to be an excess of positions: besides those teachers who are actually teaching, there are also those who have purely administrative functions and those who have been sent to work in other ministries. This situation creates an excess of 8,000 persons, originally teachers, who are now attached to other organizations receiving a salary, without actually working for the Ministry of Education.

The median age of teachers is about 40 years which explains the low rate of wastage: this was calculated to be 2.6 percent in 1991. The median age of administrative personnel was 44 years. The age groups 26 to 30 years and 50 to 55 years accounted for only 3.5 percent of all personnel. The number of new teachers who were hired is also low. The recruitment of pupil teachers was stopped and in 1993 the Ministry of Education recruited only 155 *bacheliers* as future teachers at the general secondary school and 60 *licentiates* as future teachers at the *lycées*. This represented a renewal rate of 4.3 percent for the general secondary school.

In general there are good conditions for preservice training, which includes

(a) three teacher-training colleges for the training of primary school teachers;

(b) the ENS which has a three-year course following the *baccalauréat* for general secondary school teachers, and a two-year course after the first university degree for teachers in *lycées*;

(c) the ENSET which trains technical teachers;

(d) some *lycées pédagogiques* which train primary school teachers; the higher institute of education (ISP) at Dolisie which trains teachers for the CEGP (polytechnic centers), and the CETF (technical centers for girls) which train female teachers and social auxiliaries for preprimary education.

In reality the above scheme is not always followed and there are certain gaps. In 1986 about 20 percent of primary school teachers were unqualified and 62 percent of teachers in general secondary schools were not fully qualified. However, just over 60 percent of *lycée* teachers were qualified. Furthermore, it might be added that among the qualified teachers there are those who reached this status by a special administrative decree and others who acquired the status through "exceptional procedures." The number of teachers allocated to administrative tasks exceeds the number required.

The preservice teacher training is traditional: courses in educational science, in practical work on the use of textbooks, in large group work, or in multigrade classes could all be considered as being given too little emphasis.

The inservice training of teachers is not very developed. A center for teacher training (CFM) under the division of inservice training in the Ministry has proposed preservice training during the summer vacation, but this has never taken off. The ENI in Brazzaville enrolls graduates of the pedagogical *lycées* but no longer enrolls pupil teachers. On the basis of a competetive examination the ENS and ENSET enroll practising teachers who wish to be promoted or who wish to prepare to enter the inspectorate.

There is an unbalance in training between subjects such as French, English, history, geography, and the natural sciences where inservice training may amount to six hours in one week, and other subject areas such as the physical sciences and mathematics with far fewer hours.

7. Curriculum Development and Teaching Methodology

Major modifications were made to the curricula imported from France. These involved changes to take the realities of the Congolese environment into account, the introduction of certain state ideologies, and innovations coming from world educational trends. For example:

(a) from 1967 onward, the Africanization of geography and history;

(b) in 1968, the introduction of the "whole word method" of reading;

(c) in 1969, modern mathematics;

(d) in 1970, ideological youth training with the National Pioneer Movement;

(e) in 1971, the introduction of African literature in the *lycée* and university;

(f) the teaching of Marxism–Leninism in the university in 1972 and in the *lycée* in 1974.

A national colloquium in 1970 marked the most important turning point when it proposed a completely new type of education. It took nearly 10 years of various attempts and of research to have the "People's School" which was to introduce the national languages of Munukutuba and Lingala, productive work, and criterion-referenced education. In reality, by the mid-1990s the national languages were not taught and productive work was not well perceived by either teachers or parents.

The last versions of the syllabi were produced in 1986 for the first cycle of secondary school and in 1988 for primary school. In both cases the curricula were developed by committed work groups of INRAP and were published by the INRAP.

Primary education. The timetable consists of 30 hours of instruction per week. The time allocated to each subject matter by day and by week is strictly defined. The subject matters which were to be the pivot of the reform have little time accorded to them. The syllabus gives priority to French—the language of instruction and communication—and to mathematics; the other traditional subject matters are grouped, as in France, into disciplines with either an intellectual or artistic bias. The study of reproduction, and even population education, is not in the curriculum. On the other hand, civic education has been reintroduced.

Secondary education. The timetable varies from 28 to 30 hours per week. The syllabi emphasize traditional subject matters, as in the French model, except for African geography and literature. Population problems are dealt with in geography and history.

In vocational and technical education the syllabi include an adequate theoretical basis and seems to be satisfactory. However, at the same time, there appears to be an obvious lack of realism in textbooks and, in particular, the educational and instructional means to implement the programs.

Higher education curricula favor the humanities and there is, as yet, no thought of introducing short technological courses for higher level technicians.

8. The System of Examinations, Promotions, and Certifications

There is poor internal efficiency at the primary level with average grade repeating rates of 30 percent, and even 40 percent in Grade 3. Dropout is low, except at the end of primary school. In this sense, primary education may be regarded as a failure except for the fact that it enrolls a very large number of pupils but in appalling conditions and with very poor results. The quality of education has been a major concern for a long time.

Internal efficiency is also very low in secondary school with grade repetition rates of nearly 40 percent in Grades 7 to 10. There is a particular problem with Grade 7 where the grade repeating rate is 43 percent and the dropout rate is 19 percent. This indicates the difficulties encountered at the beginning of secondary school by pupils with a poor level of education coming from primary schools. The dropout rate increased at the beginning of the 1990s. The success rate in the BETC is low but varies a great deal from one year to the other without any apparent reason. In 1992, the last year for which results were available, the pass rate was 14 percent.

Disaffection for practical forms of education such as those offered in agriculture and trades (CFA and CN) and the low number of pupils entering Grade 7 from primary school results in the fact that about 50 percent of primary school pupils leave the education system without any qualification and with no prospects.

In higher education the percentage of students in any one year acquiring a degree is 15 to 17 percent. This is not negligible given that the theoretical length of study is about 3 years (considering that three-fourths of students are enrolled in one of the faculties), even if one takes into account the increase in enrollment at the beginning of the 1990s. These figures do not include those students that have dropped out. However, they do confirm that a significant proportion of students complete their studies only after some of them have had to repeat a year.

9. Educational Assessment, Evaluation, and Research

The National Institute of Educational Research and Development (INRAP) is responsible to the Ministry of Education. Its work includes: curriculum development, the development of textbooks and learning materials, subject-matter research, and the conduct of educational research projects financed from abroad. However, without a budget for running costs, the institute is only ticking over.

Even in the central administration, for example, in the planning division, there are insufficient human and financial resources to conduct studies either on needs and social demand for education or on evaluation studies on the system of education and training.

This has resulted in a situation where all important studies are undertaken as a result of external initiatives and often under the direction of external agencies. At the same time, there is a lack of national research work that would be useful to the government for policy-making in terms of the real needs of national development and the available human and financial resources.

10. Major Reforms in the 1980s and 1990s

As can be seen from what has been stated above there were no reforms in the 1980s and at the beginning of the 1990s. Rather, there were a series of actions undertaken which involved proposals for reforms. It is these that will be reported here.

Proposals for reform must be seen within the global context of structural adjustment and the economic and financial situation of the country. Within this context, measures which are likely to have an effect on education are the reduction of public expenditure and improved methods for macro-economic management. The reduction in public expenditure should result in fewer personnel at the Ministry of Education and possibly also in further consideration of increased salary levels.

The beginning of the restructuring of the educational system should first of all focus on improving the capacity for educational policy-making based on sound technical studies and the creation of a system of gathering reliable information. This implies the creation of an operational educational policy and planning unit, the strengthening of the unit responsible for personnel management, and the availability of the necessary material and financial resources.

The restructuring of the system of education should also improve its internal efficiency and quality to meet the requirements expected by the end of the century. There is a proposal to have eight years of compulsory education consisting of five years of primary school followed by three years of secondary school. The conditions of teaching and learning could be improved by a series of measures including: reduction in class size, redeployment of teachers, revision of the curriculum, increase in the number of textbooks and learning materials, and more practical training of teachers. Appropriate measures should also be taken at the upper secondary and higher education levels to make the curriculum more relevant the the socioeconomic needs of the country but, at the same time, taking into account the budgetary constraints.

11. Major Problems for the Year 2000

The initiatives taken in the past to improve the system of education and adapt it to the development needs of the country have not lived up to expectation. Despite the demographic and financial constraints, the Congolese school system does not lack the resources. Rather, it is a matter of managing them better in order to support the Ministry of Education's policies and strategies in terms of: admission procedures, flow of pupils through the system, transition from one cycle of education to the next, teaching conditions, and the management of personnel and scholarships.

The failures of the past must be avoided and, as soon as possible, a global policy for education and training should be defined. Any approach which is fragmented, nonsystematic, and outside the national context will be doomed to failure. Above all, a realistic enrollment rate of about 95 percent should be achieved and, at the same time, equality of education should be improved so as to develop and not block public employment. For this to be possible and efficient, all changes within the system of education must be within the context of a structural adjustment program which takes into account the economic situation of the country.

Bibliography

République du Congo 1993 *Education et Formation. Etat, Perspectives et Proposition.* UNESCO / UNDP, Paris

Costa Rica

F. Reimers

1. General Background

Costa Rica is a country of 50,900 square kilometers located in Central America, bordering on Nicaragua in the north, Panama in the southeast, the Caribbean Sea in the east, and the Pacific Ocean in the west. Costa Rica gained independence from Spain in 1821 and emerged as a state after the break-up of the Federal Republic of Central America in 1829. Education has been a cornerstone of the political and economic system of Costa Rica and an important foundation for one of the oldest democracies in the region.

For many years, Costa Rica has had higher literacy and school enrollment rates than its neighbours in Central America and other Latin American countries. In 1990, only 7 percent of the population was illiterate and the average number of years of schooling of the population aged 25 years or over was 5.7. In 1990, Costa Rica had a population of 3,015,000, of which 47 percent lived in urban areas. Population growth between 1980 and 1988 was 2.8 percent. Some 36 percent of the population was aged 14 years or less. Most of the population is of European descent from the colonial period, with the exception of some regions in the Atlantic coast populated by Blacks who came from the Carribbean at the end of last century. Spanish is the prevalent language.

The Gross National Product (GNP) per capita in 1989 was US$1,780. In terms of the Gross Domestic Product (GDP), 17 percent came from agriculture, 27 percent from industry, and 56 percent from services. In 1983, 10 percent of the population in urban areas lived on only 1.1 percent of the income, while 10 percent received 40 percent of the income. The poorest 50 percent of the population lived on 19 percent of the income. The distribution of income is not significantly different in rural areas. The predominantly agricultural economy of Costa Rica is structured in a variety of patterns of land ownership, with many small and medium-sized farms. In 1973, about 55 percent of the owners had plots of 200 hectares or more, 4 percent had plots smaller than 9 hectares, 4 percent had plots from 10–19 hectares, 25 percent had plots between 20–99 hectares, and 13 percent from 100–199 hectares.

During the 1980s, Costa Rica experienced a severe economic crisis which saw a deterioration in living conditions which also affected the education sector. This crisis originated in the major slump in coffee prices in 1978 (coffee is the main commodity export of the country), the deterioration of demand of the Central American Common Market, oil crises, recession in the United States, and the debt crisis. The public debt increased from US$134 million in 1970 to US$3,480 million in 1989. In 1989, the total external debt was equal to 236 percent of the exports of goods and services and 91 percent of GNP, and debt servicing was 19 percent of exports of goods and services. Since 1980, the country has had seven stabilization/adjustment loans with the IMF and three with the World Bank. The exchange rate went from 8.6 colones per US$1 in the 1970s to 120.6 colones per US$1 in 1991; inflation reached 51 percent in the early 1980s. GNP growth which had averaged 2.5 percent in the 1970s became negative in the 1980s.

2. Politics and the Goals of the Education System

In the mid-nineteenth century, Costa Rica embarked on a liberal democratization project, of which education was a mainstay. The Constitution devised in 1869 established that primary education should be free and compulsory, under the direction of the municipalities. Between 1870 and 1882, the country was ruled by a dictatorship. From 1882 to 1888, education received a new stimulus from the Minister of Education Mauro Fernandez, a lawyer who had written extensively on the role of education in society. He proposed an education reform that would proceed in stages, addressing first primary education, then sceondary education, and lastly university. In 1885, a general Law of Education was passed, influenced by the ideas of Fernandez. The Law aimed to centralize educational administration which until then was in the hands of the municipalities.

Between 1908 and 1948, several reforms, influenced by the ideas of the "active school" were carried out to make schools instruments for national development. The curriculum was simplified to make it more relevant to everyday life, and education began to be perceived as an instrument for national development.

José Figueres, who won the Civil War of 1948, laid the foundations of modern Costa Rica. The Constitution approved in 1949 gave education a preeminent role. In the same year, the national armed services were abolished—in a symbolic act, the keys to the main military barracks were given to the Minister of Education. A new Law of Education was passed in 1957 to promote the reform and development of the education system.

Since 1953, Costa Rica has had democratic governments with a strong social democratic agenda. The Costa Rican social democracy, represented by the *Partido de Liberación Nacional* (PLN) (established by José Figueres) has virtually controlled the legislature and alternated in the presidency with a coalition of smaller parties espousing neoliberal views. The platform of the PLN assigns the state the role of main agent

Table 1
Enrollments in Costa Rica 1990

Level	Students	Teachers	Schools
Preprimary	50,377	2,373	755
Primary (cycles I-II)	422,021	15,671	3,236
Secondary	—	8,160	247
cycle III	104,807	—	—
cycle IV	42,214	—	—
Higher			
university	65,531	3,954	13
other	9,483	—	4
Expenditure per student (colones)[a]			
Preschool		20,545.21	
Primary		23,143.91	
Lower secondary		38,861.64	
Higher secondary		41,721.92	
University		123,985.83	

Source: World Bank 1991a Staff Appraisal Report: Costa Rica

a Unit costs were computed dividing total public education expenditures per level in 1990 over public enrollment in that level (in 1990, 91.58 colones = US$1).

in the promotion of development and general welfare. The Party espouses heavy state intervention in the economy and an aggressive social welfare policy.

The Costa Rican Constitution establishes that basic education is mandatory and free. Preschool and secondary education are also free. University students pay nominal tuition fees. The Constitution also establishes that the state will help students without means to pursue higher education and will provide food and clothing to poor students at the basic levels.

Though there has been much continuity in the goals assigned to the education system under democracy, personalism and the lack of institutional development account for substantial policy discontinuities with every change of minister. In 1970–71, a plan for education development was prepared as a result of a broad-based national consultation. This plan was the result of analytic work of 18 committees which involved ministry staff, the planning ministry, the teacher union, retired teachers, and the university. A total of 16 working sessions were organized in the 14 regions of the country to promote participation of community representatives in the diagnosis and programming of the plan. The plan had three main objectives: (a) to raise average levels of education of the population, (b) to modernize the education system to meet the needs of economic development, and (c) to maintain the present share of education in the budget. A new system of basic education was created which included the old primary education of 6 years and the first cycle of secondary of 3 years. These 9 years were proposed as the minimum level of education for all the population and the National Constitution was amended in 1973 to include

this extension of mandatory education from 6 to 9 years.

The teachers' unions, however, opposed the plan for the proposed education reform and embarked on a strike which lasted until the election of 1973. Although the *Partido de Liberación Nacional* won the election, the new Minister of Education was from a different faction of the Party and hence shelved the numerous reforms proposed in the document, which never reached schools and classrooms. The new Education Law proposed in this plan was never passed by Congress:

> Thus, three years after exceptional national efforts supported by considerable international assistance had been deployed in a movement which the Minister hoped would make history, changes in the classrooms were few and far between. Mention of the Plan now evoked no more than cynical smiles or regretful sighs. (Lourie 1989 p.108)

3. The Formal System of Education

The education system is structured in the formal system and in the parallel system. The formal system includes four levels: preschool education of two years' duration, nine years basic education divided into three cycles of three years each, diversified secondary education which may last two years (academic branch) or three years (technical branch), and higher education (see Fig. 1). Special education is also offered in the three cycles of general basic education. In practice, the first two cycles of basic education are typically offered in the same institutions while the last cycle is offered in the

229

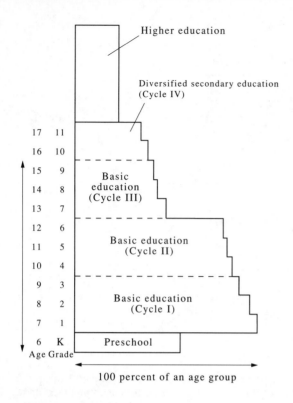

Figure 1
Costa Rica: Structure of the formal education system 1991

same secondary schools offering secondary diversified education; this reflects the institutional arrangements of the pre-reform model of 5–6 years.

The parallel system includes adult education administered by the Ministry of Education and vocational education administered by the National Institute for Learning (*Instituto Nacional de Aprendizaje*).

3.1 Primary, Secondary, and Tertiary Education

There have been sustained improvements in the expansion of education since the early 1960s. The number of primary school teachers and schools doubled between 1960 and 1990, while the number of secondary school teachers increased fourfold and the number of secondary schools doubled. The percentage of the population with incomplete primary education decreased from 75 percent in 1960 to 25 percent in 1990. The percentage of illiterate population aged 15 and over declined from 11.6 in 1973 to 7.4 in 1984. Figure 1 and Table 1 summarize basic statistics of the formal education system.

In 1990, 90 percent of the relevant age group was enrolled in basic education. Most of the enrollments in the first six years (94%) and in the last cycle of

basic education (84%) are in public schools. While all children enter school in Grade 1, only 80 percent complete six years; 99 percent of 8-year olds are enrolled in school. There are wide regional disparities in educational opportunity. While half of those children who enter Grade 1 complete the nine years of basic education in San José, only one student in four will complete the cycle in regions which are predominantly rural (e.g., Coto and Perez Zeledón). This is related to the fact that there are proportionately more untrained teachers and multigrade schools in rural areas. While only 5 percent of the schools have only one teacher in San José, in areas like Coto this figure is 49 percent. While 31 percent of the schools in the country have only one teacher, in rural areas this figure is 45 percent.

Grade repetition is a serious constraint on internal efficiency. Over 20 percent of the students in Grade 1 repeat. In basic education, the estimated cost of grade repetition is US$11 million. However, 90 percent of the students stay in school for at least five years. Among the students who complete the basic cycle, 10 percent do it after repeating three or more times. On average, students need 1.2 years to pass one year in school (Schiefelbein and Heikkinen 1992).

Students are learning too little, as indicated by the results of achievement tests administered in 1987 to students in Grades 4 and 12; less than 30 percent of the students passed those tests of basic subjects. The scores of rural students were 37 percent below those of urban students.

In theory the school year lasts 171 days, though in practice there is wide variation between regions. The school day lasts 4.5 hours in double-shift schools, which represent the majority (98.4%). The curriculum assumes 925 lesson hours a year of 40 minutes each. Urban schools provide 29 lesson hours per week of 48 minutes each, for a total of 600 lesson hours per year. In schools taught by a single teacher, teaching time is divided among the different grades, hence students receive 22 lesson hours of 40 minutes each, while per year they receive an average of 450 lesson hours.

While enrollment in private institutions amounts to a very small share of total enrollments (5%), the number of students in private schools increased 73 percent between 1980 and 1987 as a response to the widespread perception of declining quality in public schools.

The economic crisis of the 1980s affected secondary education the most dramatically. Salaries of secondary school teachers declined 42 percent between 1980 and 1987. Only 61 percent of the students who complete basic education go on to secondary, and 41 percent of the relevant age group is enrolled in this level. In 1990, there were 42,214 students in secondary schools, of whom 8 percent are in private institutions.

Enrollments at this level declined by 20 percent between 1980 and 1988. The subsector was influenced by disproportionate cuts in public expenditures, by the number of students who dropped out in order to contribute to the household economy, and by the increase in the price of school supplies.

There are four public and nine private universities, and four public institutes of higher education. In 1990, there were 2,478 university students for every 100,000 persons in the country, or 25 percent of the relevant age group. Enrollments in universities are disproportionately from higher-income groups; 43 percent of those enrolled belong to families in the top quintile of the income distribution, while only 10 percent come from the bottom quintile of the income distribution.

In the early 1970s, a university reform attempted to increase the equality of educational opportunity in higher education to all income groups. A study of that reform, however, found that even though more students from lower-income groups were admitted, the system became more stratified, with a higher proportion of well-to-do students gaining access to better universities. The reform did not change the distribution of students from different social groups (Mendiola 1989).

Enrollment trebled in the 1970s. The University of Costa Rica was converted into a multi-campus university. Most of the expansion in enrollments took place in satellite campuses, and the University of Costa Rica became more socially homogeneous. While 22 percent of entering students in 1972 came from private schools, in 1979, 33 percent of the new entrants came from private schools.

3.2 Preschool Education

Preschool education lasts one or two years and takes place in special centers or in classrooms attached to a primary school. There are 50,377 students enrolled in this level, of which 11 percent attend private institutions. Some 58 percent of the 5-year olds are enrolled in preschool institutions. The government has given priority to expansion at this level, and between 1980 and 1987 enrollments grew at an annual rate of 10 percent per year. The decline in birth rates has allowed services to expand at this level and for the relocation of primary school teachers.

3.3 Special Education

There is public special education at each of the three cycles of the basic education level. All special education takes place in special classrooms in regular schools; there is no mainstreaming in Costa Rica. In 1987, there were 10,478 special education students of which 86 percent lived in urban areas, and 531 teachers worked in these special education classrooms.

3.4 Technical, Adult, and Nonformal Education

Technical education is provided by the Ministry of Education and by the National Institute of Learning (INA). A technical stream exists for lower secondary (the last cycle of basic education) and higher secondary, in which students learn technical job-related skills in addition to the academic curriculum. Technical education receives 7 percent of all expenditures of the Ministry of Education. In addition, INA is financed by a 2 percent payroll tax

Enrollments in the Ministry's adult education classes decreased sharply during the 1980s, from 43,329 in 1980 to 28,343 in 1987. The number of teachers declined from 1,270 to 1,178 in the same period, and the number of schools from 92 to 59.

INA provides two types of training: apprenticeship and on-the-job training. Apprenticeship is a three-year program including education for students 15–20 years of age (e.g., carpentry). After completing the program, students are placed as apprentices in industry. This program includes instruction of basic and secondary education and provides funding to the students. On-the-job training is provided in the form of short courses lasting less than 6 months. There have been a number of changes in INA in the last few years to make it more responsive to an increasingly open economy. For example, public workshops in poor communities teach skills such as masonry, metal mechanics, welding, carpentry, and so forth, in which by using equipment from the INA, community members build products which are then sold in the local market. INA is also promoting micro-enterprise development, helping small entrepreneurs establish their own firms.

4. Administrative and Supervisory Structure and Operation

The state manages education through the Ministry of Education, the universities, and the *Instituto Nacional de Aprendizaje* (INA). The National Education Council is the highest education authority in the country. It includes the Ministers of Education and Planning and Economy, representatives from the universities, the national council of rectors, and the INA. The Ministry of Education is responsible for the implementation of policies designed by the National Education Council and it administers public education at the preschool, basic, and secondary levels. The Ministry is also responsible for the supervision of education in private institutions.

Universities are administered autonomously. There is a National Council of University Presidents which, together with the National Planning Office, coordinate education policy at that level. The National Institute of Learning (INA) is an autonomous institution, financed from a 2 percent tax on the payroll.

The Ministry of Education is organized into 5 divisions, 23 directorates, and 39 departments. It has a staff of 31,572, of which 87 percent are teachers. There are 17 regional directorates. Each regional directorate is nominally in charge of all basic and secondary schools in the area. Each region is divided into 5 to 12 districts each containing some 20 schools. Each district is administered by a school supervisor and each school has an association, made up of parents and the principal, that is responsible for oversight of school expenditures and the mobilization of resources.

In practice, administration is highly centralized as suggested by the fact that 90 percent of the administrative staff work out of the capital city, San José. All personnel management, school supervision, and resource allocation decisions are all made in the Ministry offices in San José.

Operating procedures in the Ministry are outmoded and inefficient. Many systems of information and control rely on old manual-based procedures, and computer equipment is rarely used. Budgeting is a process lacking all rationality, since the input of regional directorates is minimal. Budget requests are prepared by the Ministry in San José based on a 10 percent increment formula every year.

5. Educational Finance

Between 1980 and 1985, education expenditures in real terms declined 33 percent, and decreased from 26 percent of the government budget in 1980 to 22 percent in 1989. As a percentage of the GNP, they fell from 5.6 percent in 1980 to 4 percent in 1989.

The decline in education expenditures have affected the primary level disproportionately. Expenditures for this level declined from 66 percent in 1980 to 60 percent in 1989. Transfers to the universities increased from 22 percent of the education budget in 1980 to 36 percent in 1989, partly as a result of a constitutional provision that establishes a special fund for higher education which cannot be abolished nor reduced. Increases in primary school enrollment, together with decreases in resources for this level, reduced per pupil spending at this level by 32 percent between 1980 and 1988. Capital expenditures were slashed, declining from 23 percent of total education expenditures in 1980 to 1 percent in 1989. About 3 percent of education expenditures goes to administration, 35 percent to higher education, 58 percent to basic education, and the rest to other programs.

The economic crisis which affected the sector severely constrained all nonsalary expenditures, with consequent declines in quality. For instance, no new textbooks have been printed since 1984. Parents are asked to contribute 1,000 colones per year in primary school toward school supplies. In addition, the cost of notebooks, supplies, and uniforms add up to 7000 colones per year, which, added to the per pupil expenditure reported in Table 1, suggests that families bear over 20 percent of direct primary education costs in public schools. This share is higher in secondary education.

6. Supplying Personnel for the Education System

In 1990, there were 21,535 teachers working in 3,551 schools. Of these teachers, 13,651 taught in primary education and the rest in secondary schools.

In response to fiscal austerity affecting the sector, teacher salaries for primary level declined 33 percent between 1980 and 1987. As a result, the quality of education has continued to decline. For instance, enrollment growth between 1981 and 1989 was served with an increased number of untrained teachers. Of the 6,200 teachers hired during this period 44 percent were untrained ("*aspirantes*"). An achievement test administered to some of these *aspirantes* showed that only 10 percent of them attained pass marks in the four basic subjects at a Grade 6 level.

In 1989, 23 percent of the primary school teachers were untrained, with most of them teaching in rural and urban-marginal areas.

Since 1986, the Ministry of Education has developed a program where untrained teachers sign a contract committing themselves to enroll in a one-year certification program while they teach. Classes take place at weekends and during the summer. There is a shortfall in the output of the training programs which currently train 588 new teachers every year, while 1,377 new teachers will be required annually between 1991 and 1996.

7. Curriculum Development and Teaching Methodology

Curriculum development is the responsibility of the Ministry of Education. This curriculum is followed in all schools in the country. The Ministry inspects and approves all textbooks, to assess that they conform to the national curriculum.

In 1990, the Ministry carried out a curriculum reform in basic education which emphasizes core subjects while adding a strong social curriculum focusing on ecology, health, and values education.

The document which outlines the new curriculum policy emphasizes the role of learning from real life activities, as well as having a regional emphasis and a student-centered learning approach. The new curriculum highlights the importance of teaching using democratic approaches, active and participatory learning, and assessment focused in products as well as processes (Ministerio de Educación 1991a). To implement the curriculum reform, the Ministry printed new programs for each subject and various teacher guides, such as the book entitled *The Teaching and Learning Processes in a Democratic Society* which was distributed to all teachers. An additional mechanism to implement the new curriculum are the new textbooks which will be produced under the new education reform.

8. The System of Examination, Promotions, and Certifications

Promotion from one grade to the next, at all levels of education, depends on the grades given by the teacher based on performance throughout the year and in a final examination in each subject.

Costa Rica was one of the first Latin American countries to experiment with automatic promotion in basic education in the 1960s. Within each of the cycles, students were automatically promoted from one grade to the next. In addition, the entrance examination to secondary education was eliminated. Many educators in Costa Rica attribute to this the decline of the quality of education—more students were promoted but with less effective knowledge.

Concern with the decline in the quality of education stimulated the research carried by the University of Costa Rica at the request of the Ministry of Education, which developed criterion tests in all basic subjects (Spanish, mathematics, science, and social studies) to be administered to all students at the end of each cycle of basic education and at the end of secondary education. These tests were used for certification and university entrance. All students were tested in 1986 and 1987, and a random sample was tested in 1989. One of the consequences of the widespread concern generated by the poor performance of students in the basic achievement tests administered in 1987 was a revision of the system of promotion. At the end of each of the cycles of basic education, students will be tested in all basic subjects and a minimum passing score will be required for promotion to the next grade. Similarly, at the end of secondary education, students will be required to pass the test. While the original idea was to implement a national test to determine promotion, there has been a shift toward tests developed by each district on the basis of national criteria. These tests establish a minimum level required to graduate from primary and secondary school. The final grade received by each student is a combination of 50 percent of the test score and 50 percent continuous evaluation from the teacher.

9. Educational Assessment, Evaluation, and Research

Although there is a research unit ascribed to the planning division in the Ministry of Education, there is very limited research and policy analysis capacity within the Ministry. Research was one of the activities which was devalued during the economic crisis of the 1980s.

The Ministry collects standard educational data (enrollments, teachers) and computes a number of indicators (e.g., completion and repetition rates) of internal efficiency. In addition, there has been experience administering national achievement tests, and the education reform in operation in the early 1990s proposes establishing a regular system to monitor student performance.

The University has an Institute of Educational Research (*Instituto de Investigaciones para el Mejoramiento de la Educación en Costa Rica*) which has produced a number of influential reports, focusing especially on the low levels of achievement of students and teachers.

By and large, decision-making is informed by political and other considerations and technical analysis plays a relatively unimportant role in this process.

10. Major Reforms in the 1980s and 1990s

In spite of the financial strain on the education sector, there has been innovation and experimentation in Costa Rica to try to address the fundamental problems of inefficiency and inequity facing the education system.

In 1986, the Ministry of Education started an experiment in community participation in the formulation of the curriculum in the rural region of Los Santos. This coffee-producing area, 70 kilometers south of San José, was characterized by low completion rates in basic education, and the Ministry assumed that this was due to the fact that the curriculum was irrelevant to this community. This action-research project was launched to identify appropriate planning methodologies to design a curriculum responsible to local needs. The core of the experiment were a series of consultations and community mobilization activities which helped to design a profile of basic learning needs.

During the 1980s, the government financed the creation of a foundation (the Omar Dengo Foundation) chartered to develop a five-year experiment to introduce computers in some schools. This project was continued with subsequent funding from the World Bank and the Inter-American Development Bank in the 1990s. It was initially implemented in about 1,000 primary schools which were provided with Logo software, microcomputers, and teacher training. Pupils receive 80 minutes of Logo instruction per week. In addition, the Ministry established the Costa Rican Scientific Colleges, which are schools for gifted children.

As mentioned earlier, the Ministry supported several exercises to assess student performance which were carried by the University of Costa Rica. The ultimate aim is to establish a national testing system.

In 1990, Costa Rica requested and received loans from the Inter-American Development Bank (US$28 million) and the World Bank (US$23 million) to finance a program to improve the quality of basic education and to strengthen management in the Ministry of Education. An additional US$10.5 million of local financing went toward the project. This project will involve school repair and maintenance, curriculum development, textbook and teaching materials development including school libraries, teacher training, assessment systems, computers in schools, and management development in the Ministry of Education.

In 1991, the Ministry of Education initiated a reform which would devolve some of the administrative functions to the regions. The current system of administration based on 17 regions would be replaced by one of 6 regions, 12 subregions, and 150 zones. In 1992, the Ministry developed a new curriculum for basic education as a result of studies and a consultation to students, teachers, parents, university faculty, and private firms. There are four new areas that have been added to the curriculum: ecology, cultural revitalization, personal and collective security, and health and nutrition. Values education is included in the last three areas.

11. Major Problems for the Year 2000

Costa Rica faces the challenge of repositioning education at the core of its strategy of economic and political development. While the education sector has enjoyed this position since the consolidation of the modern Costa Rican state, the economic crisis of the 1980s took a severe toll in the education sector. The morale of teachers fell, partly as a result of lower teacher salaries, but especially as a result of continued confrontations between the Ministry of Education and the Teachers' Union. As part of the increasing confrontation, the Ministry blamed the teachers for the low achievement scores in the tests administered at the end of the 1980s.

The education sector's response to the adjustment programs made the distribution of benefits of public spending in education among income groups more inequitable. While 30 percent of the poorest households captured 31 percent of the education resources in 1977, by 1986 their share had declined to 27 percent. In contrast, 40 percent of the richest households increased their share from 38.6 percent in 1977 to 45.4 percent in 1986 (World Bank 1990).

A major challenge for the year 2000 will be the financing of necessary improvements in efficiency and equity in basic education. This will involve issues of overall allocations to education within the public budget, but especially the need to redistribute the education budget to make it more equitable. This requires exploring options to generate additional resources for higher education.

The decline in the working conditions of teachers, and the sustained confrontations between the Ministry of Education and the teachers' unions are likely to have a negative effect on the quality of education. This has resulted in the most highly trained teachers looking for alternative jobs. Furthermore, the signaling value of salaries is likely to further lower the quality of the supply of teachers in the future. The implicit policy in operation in the early 1990s of replacing teachers with candidates with lower levels of formal education, and providing them with short periods of inservice training, has yet to show its merits.

The education reforms initiated in 1991, and the attempts to enhance a social curriculum that place a premium on educating for democracy, are positive signs in the direction of helping the sector recuperate from the devastating damage of the 1980s.

As the political and economic situation improves in the Central American region, it might be easier for Costa Rica to return to human development as a central pillar of its democratic project. Solving the challenges of low efficiency and equity of the education sector will be a true test of the commitment to that project.

References

Lourie S 1989 *Education and Development: Strategy and Decisions in Central America*. UNESCO, Paris

Mendiola H 1989 Reform of higher education in Costa Rica: Effects on social stratification and labor markets. *Comp. Educ. Rev.* 33(3): 334–56

Ministerio de Educación Pública 1991a *Sintesis de la Política Curricular*. Ministerio de Educación, San José

Schiefelbein E, Heikkinen S 1992 Costa Rica: Acceso, permanencia y eficiencia en la educación básica. UNESCO–OREALC, Santiago (Unpublished manuscript)

World Bank 1990 *Costa Rica. Public Sector Social Spending*. World Bank, Washington, DC

World Bank 1991a *Staff Appraisal Report. Costa Rica: Basic Education Rehabilitation Project*. World Bank, Washington, DC

Further Reading

Carnoy M, Torres C 1991 Educational change and structural adjustment: A case study of Costa Rica. (Unpublished manuscript)

Horn R, Wolff L, Velez E 1991 *Developing Educational Assessment Systems in Latin America*. LATHR Regional Studies Program No. 9. World Bank, Washington, DC

Ministerio de Educación Pública 1990a *Serie de Documentos del Proyecto de Planificación Educativa*. Ministerio de Educación, San José

Ministerio de Educación Pública 1990b *Plan General de Educación. 1990–1994*. Ministerio de Educación, San José

Ministerio de Educación Pública 1991b *Memoria Anual de Labores 1990*. Ministerio de Educación, San José

Ministerio de Educación Pública 1991c *Programas de Estudios*. Ministerio de Educación, San José

Pérez Cordoba R et al. 1991 *Los Procesos de Enseñanza y Aprendizaje en una Sociedad Democrática*. Ministerio de Educación, San José

Reimers F 1991 The impact of economic stabilization and adjustment on education in Latin America. *Comp. Educ. Rev.* 35(2): 319–53

Rojas Y 1984 The politics of an educational reform process in Costa Rica: A case study. Unpublished doctoral dissertation, University of Wisconsin, Madison, Wisconsin

Sanguinetty J 1988 *La educación general en Costa Rica: La Crisis y sus posibles soluciones*. Development Technologies, San José

UNESCO–OREALC (annual) *Situación Educativa de América Latina y el Caribe. 1980–1987*. UNESCO–OREALC, Santiago

World Bank 1991b *World Development Report 1991*. Oxford University Press, New York

Côte d'Ivoire

P. D. Kokora

1. General Background

Côte d'Ivoire is a West African country, roughly square in shape, which is bordered by the Atlantic Ocean to the south, the Republics of Liberia and Guinea to the west, the Republics of Mali and Burkina Faso to the north, and the Republic of Ghana to the east. Its land mass covers 322,462 square kilometers, which represents only 1 percent of the African continent's surface. The country is divided into two quite distinct bioclimatic zones: a two-season regime (dry and rainy seasons) in the north and a four-season one in the south (short and long rainy seasons and two dry periods).

Large-scale immigration to Côte d'Ivoire by other West African groups began in the sixteenth century. Hence, when the country was declared a full-fledged colony by France on March 10, 1893, cultural zones had already been established by six major sociolinguistic communities: (a) Krou or Mangwé; (b) Southern Mandé or Peripheral Mandé; (c) Mandingo or Nuclear Mandé; (d) the Voltaic family of the Senoufo, Koulango, and Lobi subfamily; (e) the Angi-Baoulé subgroup of the Akan group; and (f) the "lagoon people" (i.e., the few small Akan groups who live by the lagoons that stretch along the coastal areas).

These cultural and linguistic zones still exist. In 1989, 46 percent of the population aged 15 years and above in Côte d'Ivoire were regarded as illiterate (World Bank 1989 p. 326). Different local languages are used for intercommunication purposes. Ivoirian leadership, however, has chosen French as the only acceptable and official language. Since the 1960s, it has been used for all official transactions—from church to educational activities, from politics to cultural contests, from small business to economic deals, and from administration to judicial practices. In 1986, the Ivoirian government announced that the official name of the country would thenceforth be "Côte d'Ivoire" rather than the "Ivory Coast."

In 1990, Côte d'Ivoire had a total population of 11,730,000, growing at an average annual rate of 4.3 percent (World Bank 1992 p. 11). The country's urban dwellers represented 46.6 percent of the total population with an average annual growth rate of 5.6 percent. In 1980, Abidjan was the only city with over 500,000 people, and it comprised 34 percent of the urban population of Côte d'Ivoire at that time. Indeed, Abidjan's population grew from 1.3 million inhabitants in 1978 to 2 million in 1988, including 500,000 African immigrants vying for jobs with Ivoirians (Lamb 1988 p. 120).

In the 1980s, Côte d'Ivoire's labor force totaled 3,547,000 (World Bank 1992 p. 282), with an average annual growth rate of 2.7 percent. Some 65 percent of this labor force was in agriculture, 8 percent in industry, and 27 percent in services. Their earnings at minimum wage decreased from US$1,581 per annum in 1980 to US$1,061 per annum in 1986 (World Bank 1992 p. 287). The education level attained by Ivoirian workers, in the 1980s, was estimated at an average of only 2.1 years.

In 1985, 11.2 percent of Côte d'Ivoire's school-age population was enrolled in the private primary institutions and 29.3 percent in private secondary institutions (World Bank 1992 p. 330). Thus far, the private sector has not invested in tertiary education. Its main investment has been in preschool education, whether of the "traditional" or modern type. In 1985, the gross enrollment ratio in primary schools was 70 percent, but for females it was some 18 percent less (World Bank 1992 p. 327). The dropout rate of the primary school population was 32 percent, while the number of repeaters per 100 pupils enrolled was estimated at 28. In that same year, the secondary school gross enrollment ratio was 19 percent, with the female rate trailing 8 points behind (World Bank 1992 p. 333). The number of repeaters per 100 students enrolled was 19, but for females it was 22 (World Bank 1992 p. 334).

These statistics are a sad reflection on the efforts and reforms in education introduced by the Ivoirian government since the 1960s. This high rate of dropout and school leaving may be due to the following reasons: (a) the insistence of the government on following the French system, hence abrogating the deep cultural forms of education already extant in Ivoirian society; and (b) the lack of political will to make the necessary changes.

2. Politics and the Goals of the Education System

Three decades after regaining its independence from France on August 7, 1960, Côte d'Ivoire's educational system is still modeled on the French school system. Like the French system, education in Côte d'Ivoire is regarded as the sole concern of the state and, therefore, is mainly secular. Historically, however, education in Côte d'Ivoire was initially a matter of family units, village communities thereafter, and eventually ethnic groups. This responsibility was taken away from those groups by the French colonial power and given over to denominational groups, mostly Christian and a few Muslims. In the early twentieth century, education became the charge of the French colonial power itself, and finally the sole responsibility of the Ivoirian government after Independence.

The educational system in the early 1990s appears to be well-structured, but a closer look reveals conflicting elements which are the result of a lack of cohesion between traditional and modern education systems. These conflicting elements did not surface during the years of prosperity in the 1960s and 1970s. The hardships of the 1980s have revived some of the unresolved problems. The Ivoirian government faces new (and old) challenges of educational reform.

3. The Formal System of Education

Côte d'Ivoire had an educational system in existence before the nineteenth century and the arrival of the French colonists. This "traditional education system" began during early childhood, as early as the "mother's back" stage (a reference to children always being carried on the mother's back) and extended to "age-group" settings. This traditional education system has continued up to the early 1990s. Based entirely upon the two basic concepts of "orality" and "apprenticeship," it still flourishes at the individual family level in urban areas. It is practiced more extensively by rural dwellers where the majority of Ivoirians continue to entrust the charge of dispensing education to a respected family unit elder, generally an aunt or uncle, or another knowledgeable adult. The lack of such an education is believed to detract from the active participation needed for the preservation of family values and economic survival.

In contrast, the modern educational system is so totally different that it relies exclusively on "writing" and "analysis procedure." Ong (1990 p. 9) portrayed the ways in which mental and social structures operate in "primary oral cultures." Ong argued that people from these oral cultures, who have been untouched by any writing system, learn by "apprenticeship." In other words, they acquire knowledge through the practice of listening and repetition and by assimilating a repertoire of common folk wisdom. Battestini points out, however, that it would be misleading to rule out any book-oriented knowledge in the traditional education system, given the existence of writings in African languages (Vaɪ[um], Bété, Mandé, Fulani). Traditional education has produced literates whose duties in their social group included diffusing knowledge for legal matters, medical purposes, geomantic predictions, ethical questions, and so on. Books were still scarce, and owned only by a few literates. The knowledge contained in these books was available to everyone through the "master of speech," or "alkitabi" (the man of the book). By contrast, the book-oriented knowledge which illustrates the trend of the modern educational structure focuses mainly on analytical and analogical skills (Bendor-Samuel 1984).

3.1 Primary, Secondary, and Tertiary Education

The Ivoirian school system is organized into a three-tiered system, each of which has a general goal (see Fig.

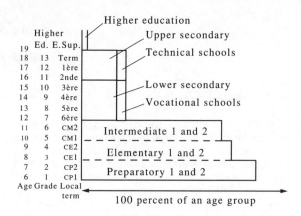

Figure 1
Côte d'Ivoire: Structure of the formal education system

1). The primary tier ensures an elementary education, the secondary tier secures a general and technical education, and the tertiary tier is intended to provide higher education for people to develop elite skills and be trained as professionals.

Primary education aims to reach all children aged 6 through 11 and is subdivided into three steps with a double entry per step: Preparatory classes I and II, Elementary classes I and II, and Intermediate classes I and II—identified here by their French acronyms CP1 (*Cours Préparatoire 1ère année*), CP2 (*2ème année*), CE1 (*Cours Elémentaire 1ère année*), CE2, CM1 (*Cours Moyen 1ère année*), CM2.

Figure 2 presents primary school enrollment statistics. In 1948, school attendance of all school-age

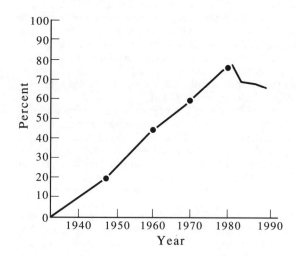

Figure 2
Primary school enrollment 1940–90

children was estimated to be 20 percent. There was a steady increase up to 1983 (77%). Enrollment then started to decline and, by 1992, it was estimated to be 66.5 percent.

General secondary education is available to pupils who have passed their secondary school entrance examination and whose full names have been registered on a nationwide list. The candidates are from 11 to 15 years of age, depending on how many times they repeated the final grade of primary school. The secondary tier is divided into first and second cycles: (a) lower general secondary, which extends over a four-year curriculum and leads to the middle course final examination called the *Brevet d' enseignement du premier cycle*, BEPC; and (b) upper general secondary, which lasts three years and prepares students to take the *Baccalauréat* examination. Upper general secondary students enter major areas of study, casually referred to as series "A, B, C, D, E, F, and G." These letters correspond respectively to the following domains of studies: (a) letters, arts, and human sciences—A; (b) economy and social sciences—B; (c) pure sciences and physics—C; (d) sciences of experimentation—D; (e) sciences and technology—E; (f) applied sciences, office techniques, trade and management—F and G. Success in the *Baccalauréat* examination in any of these disciplines ensures the candidate automatic access to higher education and to student allowances. However, the economic disarray of the 1980s forced the Ivoirian education authorities to modify this practice in higher education, in terms of both accessibility and financial support strategies.

In 1960, the general secondary school enrollment was 12,000. A decade later, it stood at 70,000, an almost sixfold increase, and by 1980, it had reached 238,000. Although the enrollment of 1983 totaled 269,000 students, the average annual growth rate of the 1960s and 1970s (16%) drastically decreased to 4.1 percent in the early 1980s (World Bank 1989 p. 126).

Higher education has a two-track curriculum: the university schools called *facultés* and specialized professional schools known as *grandes écoles*. The first track is composed of schools, such as law, medicine, and pharmacy. However, there are no specific job prospects as students progress toward their degree or diploma. Few jobs are available even for university graduates. The *facultés*-track also includes higher educational institutes devoted to fundamental and applied research (see Sect. 9). The National University of Abidjan (with only one campus until the academic year 1992–93) was founded in 1959 as the Center for Higher Education, under the leadership of the University of Paris. Starting in 1964, its internal schools were granted full autonomous status as required, but only when they satisfied the French university criteria of administrative and pedagogical autonomy.

University enrollment at Abidjan campus was 300 in 1960. It climbed to 4,400 in 1970 and reached a peak of 19,600 in 1980. In 1982, however, enrollment decreased slightly to a total of 17,900, but rose again in the late 1980s. In 1992, the student body totaled 20,000 regular full-time students and 3,000 evening students, enrolled in FIP (*Formation individuelle permanente*) training. All University facilities are used to their maximum capacities. The 23,000 student population makes for overcrowding in the institution, especially since the University was built to accommodate only 7,000 students. For this reason, policymakers decided to open, for the academic year 1992–93, a second campus in the city of Bouaké, which will accommodate about 3,000 new *baccalauréat* graduates.

3.2 Preschool Education

In the traditional educational setting, preschooling was quite different from the system implemented in Côte d'Ivoire in the 1970s. In the former case, the child received an informal preschool education while on the "mother's back." The parents' home, the field, or the village market were the natural milieu where this informal education was dispensed. This form of education was the beginning of the training of young Ivoirians into active membership in their communities—their first "contact with the adult world" (Roberts et al. 1973 p. 114). This was a serious undertaking, as it constituted the very foundation of any subsequent education.

In Côte d'Ivoire in the early 1990s, preschool education does not appear to be as serious a matter of concern for policymakers as primary, secondary, and higher education. Indeed, there are no specialized administrative or supervisory structures to run preschools. This is understandable—in fact, the issue is not really discussed in the public arena—insofar as the vast majority of rural women are self-employed workers who are not constrained to wage-earners' time as in the urban areas. Thus, these women satisfactorily meet the educational needs of their preschool-age children.

Nonetheless, Côte d'Ivoire policymakers have had to address the problem of the high mortality rate of children under 5 years of age (163 per thousand in the 1980s), who constitute a large percentage of the 1–14 age-group. This 1–14 age-group has shown a serious decline, from 48.3 percent in 1980 to 46.7 percent in 1990. The preschool population and its education has been considered more a matter for the Ministry of Social Affairs (with 91 maternal or kindergarten schools under its tutelage in 1987) rather than the responsibility of the Ministry of National Education.

3.3 Special Education

Special education endeavors to find a viable solution to the ever more pressing scholastic problems faced by policymakers as a result of the failure of the formal educational system to adapt to Ivoirian sociocultural settings. For instance, with 80 percent of students enrolled in the first grade of primary school, both private and public, Côte d'Ivoire may justifiably be proud of its record in making considerable progress toward universal primary education. However, the disadvantage of this progress is the high dropout and grade repetition rate (see Sect. 1). Special education is therefore an ad hoc response to limit the negative effects of the dropout and repetition phenomena affecting the overall school population.

The alternative education system does not usually fall under the supervision of the ministries in charge of formal education. Curricula and classes are organized by concerned ministries. For instance, the *Lycée agricole* of Bingerville is under the tutelage of the Ministry of Agriculture. The *Ecole de police* is supervised by the Ministry of the Interior. The *Ecole des infirmiers/infirmières ou des sages femmes* is under the tutelage of the Ministry of Health. The *Ecole des assistantes sociales* as well as the *Institut des aveugles et des mal-voyants* and the *Village des enfants d'Aboboté* are all under the supervision of the Ministry of Social Affairs, Youth, and Sports. Other specific ministries which take on educational responsibilities are: the former Ministry of Scientific Research and Culture; the National Defense Ministry; the Civil Service (*la Fonction publique et emploi*); the Ministry of Industry and Planning; the Ministry of Public Labors, Transportation, Construction, and Urbanization; and the former Ministry of Agriculture, Water, and Forest (Gideppe 1990 p. 197).

3.4 Vocational, Technical, and Business Education

In keeping with its ideology toward the colonized, French educational policy concentrated on vocational training. In fact, as early as 1892, the first school of agriculture was opened on Verdier's farm, in the Aboisso area of southeastern Côte d'Ivoire. Nevertheless, the history of vocational, technical, and business education in Côte d'Ivoire demonstrates that it was first considered only as an adjunct to general education, before gaining recognition through the creation of a full-fledged ministry, called the Ministry of Technical Education and Vocational Training (the autonomy of which was interrupted by a short-lived superministry of national education between 1983 and 1986). Roberts et al. (1973 p. 123) give the following appraisal of Côte d'Ivoire's vocational school policy: "The 20-odd institutions which existed in 1962 offered a variety of programs leading to certificates, diplomas and degrees covering a range of proficiency from craftsman to engineer." Hence, from its earliest beginnings, education was regarded by decision-makers as an investment in an academic education leading to white-collar jobs, rather than being considered a practical vocational or technical training.

The Ministry of Technical Education and Vocational Training manages all the technical- and vocational-related institutions at the secondary and tertiary levels, except for those coming under specific ministries (see Sect. 3.3).

3.5 Adult and Nonformal Education

The longstanding debate about the link between education and the labor market can be traced to colonial administration policies in all African countries. In an effort to contribute to a better understanding of the role of education, some educationists (Speak 1982 p. 98) have proposed a three-way classification of education: (a) "formal" education, (b) "informal" education, and (c) "nonformal" education. Speak argues that "formal" education is concerned with "the highly structured, chronologically graded system running from primary school through university." This mode of education has already been addressed above. "Informal" education is viewed as a "truly lifelong process whereby every individual acquires attitudes, values, skills and knowledge from daily experience and the environment" (this approach will be examined in Sect. 7). "Nonformal" education, in Speak's terms, "refers to organized activities outside the formal system intended to serve identifiable clienteles and learning objectives." Any range of activities from "literacy classes to driving instruction" comes under this category, which is discussed below.

The illiteracy figures quoted in Sect. 1 indicated that 60 percent of females and 33 percent of males aged 15 years or more were illiterate. In other words, the illiterate female population outnumbered male illiterates by 2 to 1. In an attempt to reach this population, the Côte d'Ivoire government has participated in "nonformal" education mainly through two of its ministries—the Ministry for Social Affairs, Youth and Sports, and the Ministry of Technical Education and Vocational Training. The former has a "center for literacy" through which French reading and writing skills are taught. The latter has within it the National Bureau of Vocational Training, which is in charge of inservice training of workers. In both cases, the teaching objectives seem to be limited to the training of holders of blue-collar jobs. The teaching objectives claim to reach the self-employed, in rural areas as well as urban environments. In Speak's terms, "nonformal" education as monitored by the two ministries has been limited to include the improvement of reading and writing skills for urban wage-earners.

Indeed, the concept of "nonformal" education extends beyond literacy viewed as the acquisition of reading, writing, and arithmetic. At variance with "formal" education, it aims at the acquisition of job skills. A study has shown convincingly that "formal" and "nonformal" education are not substitutes for each other but "prepare people for different careers" (Grootaert 1990 pp. 309–19).

4. Administrative and Supervisory Structure and Operation

Education is the sole responsibility of the state, and hence is always referred to as "national education." For a short period, between 1983 and 1986, a superministry was created which was committed to managing the whole educational system directly with the intent of realizing the ideal of a unified system of national education.

These years were the worst in the history of the school system management in Côte d'Ivoire. The depth of the school crisis in the early 1990s can be directly attributed to those three years of demagoguery and mistaken enactment of so-called "Moral Rearmament" (Gideppe 1990 p. 192). Indeed, under this leadership, state responsibility towards the Ivoirian school system was actually on the decline, notwithstanding the uplifting rhetoric about the "new Ivoirian school."

In reality, in 1983–84, only three new public schools were built under the new centralized system, in contrast to 20 new private institutions (FPI 1987 p. 141). At the same time, and without allowing any transition period, the state left to new and inexperienced mayoral authorities the planning and development of primary schools (Gideppe 1990 p. 192). The ensuing chaos resulted in a return to the multi-approach management policy which was still in effect in the early 1990s.

The Ministry of National Education is in charge of secondary and tertiary education. This ministry directly oversees the institutions of general education (the *collèges et lycées du secondaire*). Moreover, it sets the standards for all the private secondary education institutions. It is divided into as many regional directorates as necessary to cover the country's territorial divisions. It is the only institution which decides the validity of all diplomas earned and recognized from any other training institution, inside and outside the country (Gideppe 1990 p. 197). In 1991, the national university (*Université nationale de Côte d'Ivoire*), the teacher college (*Ecole normale supérieure*), and student union affairs (*Centre national des oeuvres universitaires*) came under the auspices of a new ministry called *Enseignement supérieur et recherche scientifique*.

Primary education falls under the supervision of the Ministry of Primary Education. This ministry was created when Côte d'Ivoire decided to launch a large-scale television teaching program—*le programme d'éducation télévisuelle* (PETV)—from October 1971 to June 1983. The Ministry oversees all the public grade schools at the primary level and sets the standards for all private schools at that level. It functions through regional directorates composed of as many primary education inspection personnel (*les inspections d'enseignement primaire* (IEP) as necessary. The head of each inspection unit monitors the competence of the teachers as well as the quality of the content of the teaching.

After a lengthy period of neglect (see Sect. 3.4), technical education and vocational training was put under the supervision of an autonomous administrative and academic ministerial authority which directly manages all the institutions of technical education and vocational training at the secondary and tertiary levels. At the secondary level, education and training are offered through the *Institut national de formation technique et professionnelle* (INFTP). At the tertiary level, the schools are known as the *Grandes écoles*, *Institut supérieur de l'enseignement technique* (INSET), *Institut pédagogique de l'enseignement technique et professionnel* (IPNETP). There are two other vocation-related institutions which come under the control of this ministry: the *Office national de la formation professionnelle* (ONFP) and *Fonds national de régulation* (FNR).

5. Educational Finance

The Ivoirian authorities have repeatedly maintained that education must be the overriding priority ("*la priorité des priorités*") because "education and culture are seen by them as one of the best investments if we {the Ivoirian people} want our country to reach in a short period of time to its full development" (Gideppe 1990 p. 188). Therefore, they were willing to devote up to 43 percent of the country's budget to creating several structures and hiring a full complement of teachers, with a highly attractive salary scale to encourage more candidates to apply and to retain those already in service. Thus, a special teacher salary scale was established within the Ivoirian civil servants' (*les fonctionnaires ivoiriens*) salary scale. This was known as "*le décrochage*," referring to the uncoupling of the teachers' category from all other civil servants' categories (Gideppe 1990 p. 192; also Komenan and Grootaert 1990).

During the first half of the 1980s, Côte d'Ivoire's expenditure and lending (minus repayments) on education was estimated at an average of 18.2 percent of the state budget (World Bank 1992 p. 191). Nonetheless, one may wonder whether mere lip service is being paid to the sacred principle of "*la priorité des priorités*" in matters of education in Côte d'Ivoire. One yardstick of comparison is the educational statistics of Cameroon, a quite similar country in terms of population size; these might provide an indication of whether the huge Ivoirian educational budget has been managed efficiently.

In mid-1990, the population of Cameroon, a middle-income African country like Côte d'Ivoire, was 11.6 million, compared with 11.7 million in Côte d'Ivoire. In 1985, primary school enrollment in Cameroon was 94 percent, as against 60 percent in Côte d'Ivoire. In 1989, secondary enrollment in Cameroon reached 27 percent, compared with 19 percent in Côte d'Ivoire. For the first half of the 1980s, Cameroonian government expenditure on education was only 11.0 percent of total expenditure and lending (minus repayments), as against 18.2 percent in Côte d'Ivoire. During the same period, Cameroon registered only 23.1 percent in real per capita education spending, compared with 67.6 percent in Côte d'Ivoire, almost three times higher. In 1980, the number of Cameroonian primary school staff was 26,760 including 20 percent females compared with 26,460 with 15 percent females in Côte d'Ivoire.

The Côte d'Ivoire–Cameroon comparison reveals that greater per capita public expenditure is not a necessary prerequisite of better achievement. Cameroon budgeted less per capita public expenditure than Côte d'Ivoire, yet the former had a better return to investment in education than the latter (Ogbu and Gallagher 1991).

6. Supplying Personnel for the Education System

Historically, education training has taken a variety of forms in Ivoirian society. Within the context of one such traditional education system, the sacred forest during "Poro" initiation among the Senoufo people was the required institution for supplying the personnel needed for their education purposes. In the pre-Independence era, personnel for educational tasks were supplied through a three-year normal course aimed at training teachers at the *Ecole primaire supérieure*, founded in 1925 in Bingerville, on the Ebrié lagoon, 17 kilometers from Abidjan.

In the 1930s, the *Cours normaux* teacher-training institutions were established in Dabou at the other end of the Ebrié lagoon. This new training policy was implemented throughout the country as Côte d'Ivoire gained more autonomy from the educational policy of *l'Afrique occidentale française*, based in Dakar, capital city of the West African Federation of French colonies. Guiglo and Bouaké were established as all-male training institutions in 1946 as well as Korhogo in 1953 and Bouaké as the all-female teacher-training institution, in 1957. With Independence, these institutions were transformed into *collèges d'enseignement général* (CEG), and lost their teacher-training institutions' characteristics.

In the early 1990s, there were two types of institutions supplying teachers for the Ivoirian primary and secondary education system: the *Ecole normale supérieure*, founded in 1964 in Abidjan; and the *Centres d'animation et de formation pédagogiques* (CAFOP). The latter were founded as supporting institutions to the nationwide *Programme d'éducation télévisuelle* (PETV) in the 1970s.

Teachers at the tertiary level (this applies to the university rather than the *grandes écoles* level) are hired upon obtaining a doctoral degree (*troisième cycle*) with a high pass mark. In the early 1980s, the francophone African countries created the *Conseil africain et malgache pour l'enseignement supérieur* (CAMES) which functions as a tenure committee overseeing the promotion of university teachers from assistant, associate, and to full emeritus professorship.

7. Curriculum Development and Teaching Methodology

A study (Roberts et al. 1973 p. 114) has described the different steps of a curriculum development and teaching methodology in *informal* education of the traditional type. They affirm that the 0 through 5 age-group is a period of "constant contact with the adult world," conveyed to the child via every gesture of the mother. There then follows the 5 or 6 through 8 age-group, which corresponds to a period of individualization and personal relationship with the environment. The curriculum for the period from age 8 until puberty is organized according to two criteria: age-group activities and gender job specialization.

However, the traditional curriculum was not based solely on an informal environment. In some ethnic communities, such as the Senoufo people in northern Côte d'Ivoire, there was quite an impressive formal curriculum. The "Poro" as an institution of initiation can be regarded as the survivor of the kind of formal education system indigenous to Côte d'Ivoire before the European-oriented system was imported. Indeed, the "Poro" is said to be a comprehensive school curriculum as well as a lifelong education system. The first three stages last seven years each and are compulsory for males of ages 7, 14, and 21.

The Senoufo female goes through a different and simplified "Poro" test from her early childhood to puberty, at which point the initiation process is suspended. After reaching her menopause, she is considered asexual and, therefore, is again eligible to pursue this lifelong education system. As a rule, the "Poro" initiation spans the Senoufo's life from cradle to grave, gradually teaching him or her self-control techniques and also the bulk of knowledge necessary to assume his or her social and professional status.

The 1990s public school curriculum is designed and monitored by central authorities operating at the level of the different ministries in charge of the educational system. The main task of these authorities consists in producing syllabuses for nationwide use. They assume more a pedagogical role than an administrative one. At the level of the primary school system, there is the *Direction générale des études et des programmes* (DGEP). Its counterpart at the secondary school level is the *Sous-Direction de la coordination pédagogique*. Finally, there is the *Commission nationale de pédagogie* which is more administrative than didactic. It is composed of the *Conseillers pédagogiques* and *Inspecteurs de l'enseignement* (one inspector per subject matter). The Commission periodically gathers its commissioners to discuss curriculum matters and to establish the national list of the different textbooks used in the country's primary and secondary schools. There is very little in this curriculum that reflects the cultural environment of indigenous Côte d'Ivoire.

8. The System of Examinations, Promotions, and Certifications

At the end of the first cycle of study (i.e., CP1 through CM1), pupils sit for two tests, the results of which will have different impacts on the course of their futures. The first is a school leaving certificate which provides neither social nor economic returns to the holder. The second test is a nationwide examination which allows the successful candidates to apply for entrance to the first grade of secondary education (CEG). It used to be the case that any Ivoirian who passed the second examination successfully was automatically eligible for a scholarship covering textbooks and school supplies. This is no longer the case, as resources are scarce, and parents are encouraged to share the financial burden of their children's education.

During the 1980s, there was a steady decline in primary education enrollment. In 1992, an average of 34.5 percent of all school-age children in Côte d'Ivoire were still denied access to formal primary education, despite the goal set for universal primary education in accordance with the 1961 Addis Ababa Educational Proclamation.

In addition, the system contains a severe factor of selectivity that produces a 30 percent dropout rate following the first grade and a 20 percent rate of primary school repetition. These three negative factors (34.5% school nonattendance rate, 30% dropout rate, and 20% repetition rate) confirm the impression that the Ivoirian educational system is of low effectiveness at best and provides low equitable access to the school system.

As the secondary school level is reached, further unduly selective factors are encountered which further curtail Ivoirian access to education: the Secondary School Entrance Examination (*Examen d'entrée en sixième*), the Secondary School First Cycle Examination (*Brevet d'études du premier cycle* {BEPC}), and the University Entrance Examination (*Baccalauréat*). These three consecutive parameters of selection result in a pyramid-shaped Ivoirian educational system characterized by a large base (82% of school-age children in the first grade of the primary level) narrowing sharply toward tertiary education (17% at middle-course, in the first year of the secondary level and 1% at the top, in the first year of higher education).

In the school year 1991–92, there were 241,489 candidates who sat for the CEPE (the second sixth grade) examination. The total number who succeeded was 147,045 (61%). At the BEPC level, the total of the candidates was 81,272, and 19,414 students passed (24.5%). Finally, 45,075 students registered for the *Baccalauréat* examination. The total number of successful candidates was 10,685 (23.7%). Again, at

61 percent, the pyramidal structure has a large base. Four years later, the steepness of the pyramid slope produces a loss of 36.5 points and the percentage drops to 24.5 percent. There is only 0.8 point in loss between those sitting the BEPC and the *Baccalauréat*.

9. Educational Assessment, Evaluation, and Research

Since Independence in 1960, Côte d'Ivoire has made various adjustments to the inherited colonial educational system. Early endeavors were aimed at achieving universal primary schooling by the mid-1970s. The launch of a nationwide television educational program formed an essential part of this first educational assessment (Egly 1986). A subsequent decision based on a tenuous evaluation that correlated education to the labor market (Bertrand et al. 1981) produced a measure by which the leadership attempted to subordinate educational needs to development and economic potentials. The 1977 Reform Law (which was never enacted) aimed at improving the integration of Ivoirian youth into the economic system.

In 1975, the Ivoirian leadership added an evaluation tool known as *Service d'évaluation* to the primary education system. The rationale behind the creation of this tool of educational performance measurement was to enable the Ivoirian policymakers to monitor simultaneously the multiple components of national distance education through television. This evaluation tool drew a great deal of support from internationally renowned scientific institutions, such as the *Laboratoire de pédagogie expérimentale* at the University of Liège, Belgium, and the Stanford University Institute for Communication Research. However, twelve years after its creation, the television program and its supporting evaluation structure collapsed, not due to economic, technical, and pedagogical difficulties, but because of sociocultural factors that policymakers did not address beforehand (Egly 1986 p. 343).

Since 1990, Higher Education and Scientific Research, which were under two separate ministries, have been combined into one department. At first glance, it appears as if Higher Education, which is concerned with teaching, and Scientific Research, traditionally an individual activity, are now being considered as two sides of the same coin. This policy has positive ramifications, since the two areas can now inform each other rather than operate autonomously.

Fundamental and applied research are performed in order to establish or consolidate the credentials of the university or the higher education institution. Between 1966–74, several university research institutes were created: the *Institut d'ethnosociologie* (IES), the *Institut de géographie tropicale* (IGT), the *Institut d'écologie tropicale* (IET), the *Institut de linguistique appliquée* (ILA), the *Institut d'histoire, d'art et d'archéologie africains* (IHAAA), the *Centre d'études et de recherches*

Conte d'Ivoire

Côte d'Ivoire

en communication (CERMOM), the *Criminologie*, the *Institut de littérature et d'esthétique négro-africaine* (ILENA), the *Institut de recherches mathématiques* (IRMA), the *Centre ivoirien d'études et de recherches en psychologie appliquées* (CIERPA), the *Centre ivoirien de recherche économique et sociale* (CIRES), the *Centre universitaire d'études françaises* (CUEF), the *Centre de recherches en architecture urbaine* (CRAU), and the *Groupe de recherches en tradition orale* (GRTO).

10. Major Reforms in the 1980s and 1990s

Experts on education in sub-Saharan Africa have called for a "revitalization" of the 1960s and 1970s "existing educational infrastructure" that could lead to "a properly conceived educational strategy" in the 1980s and 1990s (World Bank 1989 p. 3). In Côte d'Ivoire, the period from 1983–90 was described as a taking-in-hand of the educational system in order to rejuvenate it at both the moral and managerial levels (Gideppe 1990 p. 192). However, the serious school crisis of the early 1990s has shown this period to have been more political rhetoric and wishful thinking rather than actual reform. The main reason appears to be the superficial analysis of the real educational needs of the country's primary and secondary school population. In other words, the condition of the educational picture in Côte d'Ivoire in the early 1990s is troubling because there never has been a properly conceived educational strategy, only a series of innovations with no real plan for following them through.

The 1977 *Etats généraux* on education under the authority of Usher Assouan (the name of the Commission's President) and their output were never properly enacted. The 1983–90 educational reform in Côte d'Ivoire was assessed as a three-phase action conducted by the supervising ministry at that period. The first phase, called the "Third Education Project of the World Bank," in fact ran from 1980 to 1985 and was dubbed the "Moral Rearmament" endeavor. Its supposed aim was to win the trust of all the educational system's partners. The second phase, from 1986 to 1988, was launched by the *Etats généraux* on education, and set as its goals the reconstruction of the existing educational system by targetting definite objectives, such as the introduction of civic and moral education, pledging allegiance to the national flag, and singing the national anthem every morning. The third phase, starting in 1989, emphasized the administrative as well as the pedagogical management of the human and financial resources available, by decentralizing the primary and secondary schools' planning and development. In other words, education is now in the hands of the local jurisdictions.

11. Major Problems for the Year 2000

The phenomenon of rapid urbanization, with its series of socioeconomic and politico-cultural challenges in modern Côte d'Ivoire, will have tremendous impact on all educational issues for the rest of this century. During the 1980s, the urban portion of the total Ivoirian population saw an additional 1 percent increase per year. If this trend continues at the same pace the urban population will reach 57 percent of the total population by the year 2000. One implication is that by the beginning of the twenty-first century, more than half the Ivoirian population will be city dwellers and will rely less on the traditional channels of education, such as the "Poro" initiation ceremony.

Based on the history of education reforms and the emerging demographies, some tentative conclusions can be drawn in identifying the major education problems of the next century. These may be enumerated as follows:

(a) The reforms of the 1980s and 1990s, such as pledging allegiance to the country's flag and singing of the national anthem, will no longer be a viable ingredient of educational reform.

(b) The advent of multiparty rule on April 30, 1990 has brought to the forefront the necessity of a real debate on the kind of education the country wishes to implement. The student body has changed since 1990: student demands are no longer limited to increases in their allowances or the social concerns of previous decades. The claims are of a political and academic nature, regarding, for example, the change of leadership at the head of the ministry in charge of the education system, or the university presidency, or the student union directorate. Irrespective of whether these claims are justified or not, they must in any event be taken into account as Côte d'Ivoire prepares for a national dialogue on the educational system.

(c) The debate on the "new Ivoirian school" includes a variety of aspects which can be summarized as follows: economic returns to investment in education, equitable access to educational opportunities, and the education–labor ratio.

These are among the important issues to be tackled. Both government and opposition leaders will need to cooperate in laying down principles for the foundation of a new Ivoirian school system.

References

Bendor-Samuel D 1984 On the study of literacy. In: Kaplan R B (ed.) 1984 *Annual Review of Applied Linguistics 1983*, Vol. 4. Newbury House, Rowley, Massachusetts

Bertrand O, Timar J, Achio F 1981 The planning of training in the Third World. *International Labor Review* 120(5): 531–44

Egly M 1986 L'utilisation de la télévision scolaire au Niger, en Côte d'Ivoire et au Sénégal. *Int. Rev. Educ.* 32: 338–45

Front Populaire Ivoirien (FPI) 1987 *L'Education: Propositions pour gouverner la Côte d'Ivoire*. L'Harmattan, Paris

Gideppe (ed.) 1990 Education: La priorité. *Jeune Afrique Economi*. JAE, Paris

Grootaert C 1990 Returns to formal and informal vocational education in Côte d'Ivoire. *Econ. Educ. Rev.* 9(4): 309–19

Komenan A G, Grootaert C 1990 Pay differences between teachers and other occupations: some empirical evidence from Côte d'Ivoire. *Econ. Educ. Rev.* 9(3): 209–17

Lamb D 1988 A different path. *Wilson Q.* 12(4): 114–31

Ogbu S M, Gallagher M 1991 On public expenditures and delivery of education in sub-Saharan Africa. *Comp. Educ. Rev.* 35(2): 295–318

Ong W J 1990 *Orality and Literacy: The Technologizing of the World*. T J Press (Padstow) Ltd, Padstow

Roberts T D et al. (eds.) 1973 *Area Handbook for Ivory Coast*. US Government Printing Office, Washington, DC

Speak G (ed.) 1982 Education and literacy. In: *Cultural Atlas of Africa*. Mayfield House, Oxford

World Bank 1989 *Education in Sub-Saharan Africa: Policies for Adjustment, Revitalization, and Expansion*. The International Bank for Reconstruction and Development/The World Bank, Washington, DC

World Bank 1992 *African Development Indicators*. The International Bank for Reconstruction and Development/The World Bank, Washington, DC

Further Reading

Appleton S, Collier P, Horsnell P 1990 *Gender, Education, and Employment in Côte d'Ivoire: Social Dimensions of Adjustment in Sub-Saharan Africa*. Working paper No. 8, Policy Analysis. World Bank, Washington, DC

Chaudenson R, De Robillard D (eds.) 1989 *Langues et Développement: Langues, Economie et Développement, Vol. 1*. Didier Erudition, Paris

Glaze A J 1981 *Art and Death in a Senufo Village*. Indiana University Press, Bloomington, Indiana

Grootaert C, Kanbur R 1990 *Policy-oriented Analysis of Poverty and the Social Dimensions of Structural Adjustment*. World Bank, Washington, DC

Kanbur R 1990 *Poverty and the Social Dimensions of Structural Adjustment in Côte d'Ivoire*. World Bank, Washington, DC

World Bank 1989 *Sub-Saharan Africa: From Crisis to Sustainable Growth*. World Bank, Washington, DC

World Bank 1990 *Primary Education*. World Bank, Washington, DC

Cuba

E. Martin and Y. F. Faxas

1. General Background

The Republic of Cuba comprises both the island of Cuba itself and a large number of adjacent islets and keys. Its overall territory covers 110,860 square kilometers. It is located in the Caribbean section of Latin America. Cuba's population is about 11 million inhabitants; population density is 94 persons per square kilometer; of these, 75 percent live in urban areas.

The basic means of production are state-owned. The economy is fundamentally agro-industrial. In 1989 the proportion of the various sectors of production in the Gross National Product (GNP) was as follows: industry (46%), construction (9.3%), agriculture (15.4%), transport (6.9%), commerce (20.1%), others (2.3%). The productive sphere made use of 70 percent of the economically active labor force; the rest was in services. The country's main exports are sugar, fish, cigars, and minerals (mainly nickel).

Attention is being given to the development of such industries as tourism, pharmaceuticals, the manufacture of medical equipment, and the biotechnological industry. Joint business ventures are beginning to take place. Scientific research has been recognized as a fundamental tool for the country's social and economic development. In 1989, there were three and a half million civilian workers. Labor was distributed as follows: managing personnel (7.1%), technicians (21.3%), workers in the services (13.5%), administrative personnel (7.1%), and laborers (51%). The percentages of the labor force working in the primary, secondary, and tertiary sectors in 1989 were 20.8, 29.1, and 50.1 respectively.

In 1990 life expectancy was 76 years; infant mortality was 11.1 for every thousand born alive. There was one medical doctor for every 303 inhabitants, and one dentist for every 1,623. Healthcare expenses were 78 pesos per inhabitant, and were supplemented by a welfare system from which 9 percent of all Cubans benefit.

Educational planning should always aim to know the actual and future need of the labor force or the national economy in order to ensure an adequate answer in schooling and professional training, taking into consideration the best possible relation between the individual's and society's interests.

2. Politics and the Goals of the Education System

In 1959, Cuba's education system was a reflection of the social order imposed upon the country for over four centuries of colonial domination and 50 years of neocolonialism. Under such political regimes, very little attention was paid to education and culture.

In 1959, there were over one million illiterates (23% of the adult population); half of the children did not attend school at all; 72 percent of 13- to 19-year olds were unable to reach intermediate education; and there were only three official higher education centers, as well as a handful of private institutions, which, save for a few exceptions, were only for the privileged bourgeois elite. Paradoxically, 10,000 teachers were unemployed at that time.

Within the framework of the changes undertaken in the country's economic, political, and social structures, education began to be viewed as a means toward achieving moral development and as a means to help achieve social transformation. Three fundamental goals were set, all closely related to one another: education for the entire school-age population, a national literacy campaign, and the establishment of continuing education for the new literate population, in order to avoid functional illiteracy. One of the first steps was to expand the number of elementary schools. Ten thousand new schools were opened, which increased the number of 6- to 12 year-olds attending school to 90 percent. This was possible due to the efforts of all the teachers, supported by a detachment of 3,000 voluntary teachers who took education to the remotest places in the country.

In December 1959, the first Education Law was passed. It established a new educational organization and stated that the overall aim of education was full development. In 1961—known as the Year of Education—the National Literacy Campaign was held. Representatives of the entire population participated in the Campaign: 167,000 voluntary teachers (students, workers, unwaged women, and teachers proper) identified over 979,200 illiterate persons, of whom 707,200 were taught to read and write. Illiteracy as a social phenomenon has now been eradicated in Cuba, thanks both to the initial effort made in that respect and to the attention paid later to residual illiteracy.

The Law of Nationalization of Education was also passed in 1961, making it possible for education to take on a truly democratic stance. Education was declared public and free, and an untransferable duty of the state. Among the first group of reforms was the University Reform Law, passed in 1962. Among other measures, the reform comprised the following: access to university for the sons and daughters of peasants and workers; full participation of students and teachers in the government of the universities; the development of scientific research; an increase in the number of higher level studies in keeping with the country's needs; the establishment of the study–work combination; and the creation of a system of scholarships to provide students from low–income families with access to the university.

Article 1 of the constitution in force established that "Cuba is a socialist state of workers ...". Article 39 states that "... teaching is a function of the state and it is gratuitous ... The state supports an extensive scholarship system for students and offers a variety of studying facilities for workers so that they can reach the highest possible levels of knowledge and skills."

The goal of education is to shape people so that they develop integral, multifaceted personalities, and are able to carry out fully their social role, by developing their intellectual, physical, and spiritual capacities, and encouraging a more elevated level of human feeling and aesthetic taste, thus turning ideological principles into personal convictions and habits of everyday behavior. The school is the core of the education system, an institution in which the entire society takes part, and where the family plays an essential role. The state is entrusted with the function of providing education through the national education system. One basic principle of the education system is the combination of study and work, achieved through the linkage of theory and practice, of the school to life, and of teaching to production. The novel ways in which this principle has been implemented in the various school levels constitute an important contribution on the part of Cuban pedagogy.

Education as a right and a duty of all citizens is a principle whose application implies having achieved universalization first at the elementary level and later at the intermediate level, as well as the establishment of a system comprising all types and levels of education for children, young people, and adults.

Another principle of the Cuban education system is the correspondence between planning within the National Education System and the country's overall economic and social development, as well as the interaction between education and society. On the other hand, the implementation of coeducation at all levels within the national education system ensures that both men and women have access to schools, irrespective of the specialties and professions offered. Educational policy is strengthening the application of nonformal models in different subsystems.

3. The Formal System of Education

Cuba's national education system is made up of a number of interrelated subsystems, which in turn correspond to preschool education; general polytechnic education and education for work; technical and professional education; teacher training and improvement; adult education; and higher education. Figure 1 presents the overall structure of the system.

The entire system is managed by the Ministry of Education and by the Ministry of Higher Education. The latter is responsible for all higher education institutions, while the former is responsible for the schools and institutions corresponding to the other sections within the education system.

Preschool education is the initial stage in the system. Its role is to create the necessary conditions for the education of children up to 5 years of age, as well as to prepare them to enter elementary education.

The role of general polytechnic education is to aid in the integral development of the personality of children and adolescents, on the basis of the close relationship existing between education and work training. It comprises the preschool year, elementary education, and general education at intermediate level.

The preschool year is a one-year preparatory period prior to the elementary level. Children may take it either in the nurseries or in the elementary schools themselves.

3.1 Primary, Secondary, and Tertiary Education

Primary or elementary school lasts for six years (6 to 12 years of age). The elementary school is divided into two cycles. The first cycle (Grades 1 to 4) is general. More specialized subject matter knowledge is introduced in the second cycle (Grades 5 to 6). In 1991, there were 887,800 students (constituting 99 percent of the equivalent age groups) enrolled in elementary schools. Only an average of 2.6 percent repeated a grade (but this was 7.8 percent at Grade 2 and 4.4 percent at Grade 4) in 1991. Out of every 100 children entering elementary school 94 graduate.

Basic secondary education lasts for three years (ages 13 to 15) and upper-secondary also lasts for three years (16 to 18). In the upper-secondary education, there are also polytechnical schools for technical and professional education, with two- to four-year courses, depending on the students' schooling and the complexity of the specialty chosen.

Within technical and professional education, the so-called trade schools may be found, where underschooled youngsters, as well as dropouts from educational institutions, have the opportunity to learn a trade. Study and work are combined in multivalent workshops.

Upon successful completion of the upper secondary school students can enter higher education.

There are three forms of schooling: day schools, half-boarding, and boarding. At the elementary school level, students typically attend day schools, but schools sometimes have two shifts. It should also be noted that in some rural areas there are multigrade classrooms. At the basic secondary level there are some boarding schools, especially in remote rural areas. In some cases there are vocational schools with a particular bias, often boarding schools in urban areas.

However, they frequently take day students who live in the area.

There are 40 school weeks per year at the elementary school level. At the higher levels, there are 34 school weeks per year, and students must undertake productive work in rural areas for a further seven weeks.

The average number of grades of education per citizen rose from 2.4 school grades in 1953 to 9 in 1993. Moreover, 23.5 percent of the country's labor force have completed elementary education, 49.3 percent higher-intermediate education, 18.3 percent technical and professional studies, and 8.9 percent are higher-level graduates.

Retention has gradually increased in all sections of the education system. During the 1990–91 school year, retention was as follows: 98.7 percent in elementary schools, 95.7 percent in lower-intermediate education, 92.5 percent in higher-intermediate education, 91.2 percent in technical and professional education, 91.6 percent in teacher-training schools, and 97.3 percent in special education.

The role of higher education is to train higher-level professionals, as well as to keep them updated and requalify them. It is also in charge of carrying out scientific research related to objectives in keeping with the country's main social and economic problems. Institutions include universities, university centers, higher agricultural institutes, polytechnics,

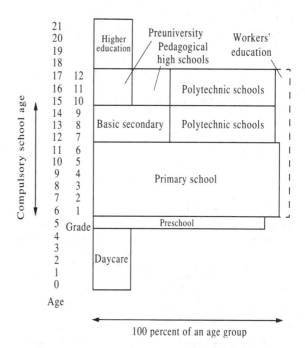

Figure 1
Cuba: Structure of the formal education system

teacher-training institutes, art schools, physical culture institutes, and medical science schools. Three kinds of courses are taught: regular courses, workers' courses (afternoon/evening and directed), and open directed or free courses. The main challenges for higher education are to improve the quality of training, improve achievement standards, and increase the amount of research conducted in universities.

In higher education, dropout figures are high, especially during the first two school years, though it has decreased by half since 1970. Among the main reasons why full-time students leave their studies are the fact that terms can only be repeated in exceptional cases, and that those students' academic proficiency does not reach the expected levels.

From 1959 to 1991 the number of schools doubled; most of the existing nurseries were opened; 1,871 new-type elementary and intermediate schools were built; almost all the special education schools were created, as well as many technical and professional schools, the teacher-training institutions, and provision for adult education. Furthermore, in 1959 there were only three universities. By 1991, this had risen to 46 higher education institutions. The number of teachers was 293,400 in 1991.

3.2 Preschool Education

Preschool education emerged as a response to the growing needs of women to become an active part of social production, which made taking specialized care of children up to 5 years of age essential.

In September 1991, there were 1,136 daycare centers, with more than 17,000 children enrolled (covering approximately 20 percent of the age group). These daycare centers include special education schools and 15 institutions for disadvantaged children. There are also kindergartens at age 5, and at that age about 90 percent of the age group is enrolled in preschool.

To provide preschool education for those not yet benefiting from it, experimental projects were developed to enroll more children up to 4 years old. These were successful, and in 1992 efforts were being made to extend them throughout the country.

3.3 Special Education

Special education ensures the proper development and training of children and youngsters with physical, mental, or behavioral impairments, both instructionally and for work. There are schools for the blind or visually impaired, deaf, mentally retarded, emotionally retarded, for children with behavior disorders, and for children who are physically impaired and with speech disorders.

3.4 Vocational, Technical, and Business Education

In the polytechnic schools (where students can go when they have finished at least the ninth grade or afterwards), the two- to four-year courses are aimed at training skilled workers and midlevel technicians. At the beginning of the 1990s, 43 new agricultural polytechnic schools were opened and 12,000 students enrolled. This is part of an attempt to increase enrollment in the polytechnic schools.

At the higher education level an increasing number of courses are being provided to produce high-level technical and managerial personnel.

3.5 Adult and Nonformal Education

The aim of adult education is to ensure the permanent general education of all citizens. It consists of workers' and peasants' education (elementary level comprising four one-semester terms), workers' and peasants' secondary education (intermediate level comprising four one-semester terms), and workers' and peasants' faculty (higher intermediate level comprising six one-semester terms).

Adult education takes place in classrooms at workplaces, in afternoon and evening schools, in classrooms in schools with a regular daytime schedule, and in other places. The system is very varied and flexible as to timetables and weekly schedules, and has contributed to a great extent to raising the population's level of education.

Medium-level polytechnical schools and higher education centers also provide adult education with formal and nonformal models.

Out-of-school education supplements, reinforces, and enriches the school's educational role through activities carried out both within and outside the school itself. These activities may be patriotic, recreational, sports, technical and scientific, related to vocational guidance or professional orientation, or cultural. They are organized by teachers as well as businesses, or by social, cultural, sports, patriotic, children's, or youth organizations.

4. Administrative and Supervisory Structure and Operation

All schools within the national education system are under the auspices of the Ministry of Education. It is responsible for general educational policy, designing and implementing syllabuses and curricula, suggesting teaching methods, and supervising and controlling education.

Higher education institutions are subordinated to specific national agencies, depending on the subject area. Thus, higher institutes of medical science are subordinated to the Ministry of Public Health, teacher-training institutes in charge of training elementary and intermediate level teachers are subordinated to the Ministry of Education, the Institute of Art is subordinated to the Ministry of Culture, and so on. Higher level institutions training professionals for agriculture, industry, the social sciences, and the humanities are the responsibility of the Ministry of Higher Education. The 1976 government reform gave more power to governmental education institutions. In the case of higher education centers, links with the community were strengthened. These links are being analyzed with a view to strengthening the role of the community.

Supervision and control is carried out at three levels (national, provincial, and municipal). Reforms of the system of management and organization have been aimed at greater decentralization and flexibility. This has provided the government at provincial and municipal levels with more power to take new initiatives and to form closer links with the community. Steps have also been taken to raise the status of teachers and school principals and to eliminate activities that overload school personnel unnecessarily. Efforts are being made to allow a more rational use of the teaching staff and avoid excesses that make education so costly.

School councils, comprising parents, neighbors, key citizens, and representatives of institutions have proved their effectiveness, though their potential has not yet been fully exploited. An example is both the support to the school by the community and the demands made on the former by the latter.

In higher education, there has been a trend toward raising the status of rectors, deans, and other executives, as well as toward decentralizing decisions on methodology. For example, in the curricula, which have been implemented nationwide, a number of teaching hours can now be determined by the higher education institution according to the characteristics and needs of the area where it is located. For graduate studies and scientific research, each institution reflects local interests, as well as the particular competencies of the institution's teaching and scientific personnel.

The systems of state control ensure the analysis and assessment of the teaching process at the various levels. These systems are under constant reform. Special attention is paid to the personnel performing such control functions. They are a small group of persons working on a full-time basis. Most are chosen on the basis of their experience and recognized professional prestige. Most of them are teachers, professionals from production, or researchers (the latter two in the case of higher education), who do their job on a temporary basis, in such a way that the role of supervisor combines with that of supervised.

An important role in the life of the school is played by the students' organizations. There is the Pioneers' Association in elementary and lower-intermediate schools; students in higher-intermediate and technical and professional schools are in the Federation of Intermediate-level Students (FEEM); higher education students are in the Federation of University Students

(FEU). Similarly, workers in the educational sector are in the Union of Workers of Education Science and Sports (SNTECD), which represents their interests and collaborates in the development of the school and its activities. There is also a Union of Science Workers.

5. Educational Finance

In Cuba all education is state-run and state-financed. In higher education some of the scientific and technical services and research undertaken for business are financed by the businesses themselves. The priority given to education may be seen in the constant growth experienced by the state budget for education from 11 pesos per inhabitant in 1959 to 175 in 1990. In 1958 the budget consisted of 79.4 million pesos (US$59.5 million); this rose to 648.5 million pesos (US$486.4 million) in 1970, 1334.5 million (US$1000.8 million) in 1980, and to 1823.4 million in 1990.

The percentage of the educational budget allocated to preschool, primary, secondary, and vocational and technical education was 81.7; for higher education it was 15.9; and for other educational activities it was 2.4. The per-pupil average unit expenditure per year was 513 pesos for preschool, primary, and medium level, and 1,023 pesos for higher education. All types of courses are included in each level of education.

6. Supplying Personnel for the Education System

The Cuban education system has experienced dramatic growth, both quantitatively and qualitatively. Teachers have been an important component of this growth. Systematic effort has always been devoted to the training and continuous improvement of the teaching personnel.

The training of teachers for the elementary and intermediate levels consists of constant follow-up and requalification to raise teachers' basic cultural background and their pedagogical/psychological level of instruction.

There are also schools for the training of librarians and of personnel for the nurseries, as well as higher education teacher-training institutes where teachers for the intermediate level, as well as those for special education and for technical and professional education, are trained. Higher-level teacher-training institutes also offer university-level education for elementary school and preschool teachers. Inservice training in general is compulsory. The higher pedagogical institutes and other higher education institutions have the overall responsibility of organizing postgraduate studies, courses, seminars, and scientific conferences for this purpose.

In addition to the emergent and regular courses designed for the training of teachers, great attention is paid to self-improvement. Ways of improving the selection system into teaching are being experimented with. An assessment of the studies offered by higher education institutions shows that students enrolling in education studies have not, in general, been of the highest quality when compared with those joining other studies. To overcome such a situation, emphasis is placed on the social recognition of the work done by applicants; forms of self-improvement are used. In 1992, a system of paid sabbatical years was introduced for elementary school teachers to improve their qualification. Both the implementation of the sabbatical year and the higher status for elementary school teachers will make it possible, by the end of the twentieth century, for most teachers to be university graduates which, in turn, should raise the quality of education. Among the most important steps taken to raise the quality of teaching in elementary and intermediate-level schools are the following: the participation of the students in the school's life; the growing independence granted to their professional activity; the adaptation of the school's curriculum to the needs of the local community; the participation of the school in the training of pedagogical cadres; and the use of the results of scientific research to solve teaching problems of various kinds.

7. Curriculum Development and Teaching Methodology

Curricula and syllabuses have a nationwide coverage at all educational levels. The objective is to ensure the homogeneity of the basic content taught at each level.

Curricula and syllabuses are subject to continuous reform to adjust the content to the changing demands of society. At the elementary and intermediate levels new curricula and syllabuses were implemented in the period from 1975–1981, first in the general polytechnic education subsystem, and then in the remainder of the subsystems.

Among the main aims behind the improvement of curricula and syllabuses (as well as of the teaching process) are the following: (a) to achieve a clearer description of the aims to be accomplished and of their specific relation to the actual conditions that will ensure their achievement; methodological stability, so that all teachers master the methods and procedures used and have a chance to put them into practice; (b) to grant more authority to the teacher and to the school in such a way that they can adapt the national curricula to their local reality; (c) to ensure the development of working skills responsibility, discipline, and awareness of the social value of work within the characteristic Cuban framework of the combination of study and work, so that citizens will be formed with a producer, not a consumer, mentality.

Curriculum, syllabuses and other teaching materials are written by collectives of selected teachers with a high professional performance and revised by the better specialists and scientists in the specific field of knowledge, regardless of their working place. In technical and professional education and in the universities, the participation of highly qualified technicians working in the different sectors of the economy is requested.

Changes in the curriculum are immediately taken into consideration in the teacher-training institutions in both the undergraduate and postgraduate courses.

The national examinations must be constantly improved to fulfill their tasks, and the systematic evaluation of the results of the educational process by teachers in their daily activities is greatly encouraged.

Efforts are also being made to ensure that there is greater interaction between the various levels of education in order to have intermediate exit points from the system and not just at the end of the 9th and 12th grades. Diversification will be introduced to respond more effectively to the students' individual characteristics and interests.

A general feature of the entire national education system is to broaden curriculum choice so that there is greater mobility in the process of work placement and so that skills specific to the workplace can be developed at a later stage.

The improvement of the quality of teaching is the main objective of the national education system. Besides curriculum improvement and decentralization, there are policies for linking school education to the economic, political, and social life of the community, the country, and the world.

8. The System of Examinations, Promotions, and Certifications

In the elementary school there is automatic promotion from the first to the second grade. Students experiencing difficulties are given special treatment without segregating them from their class.

In order to ensure that a specified minimum level of knowledge is attained in the 6th, 9th and 12th grades throughout the country, specific examinations are set at these stages. Furthermore, to enter higher education, a list of all the applicants is compiled on the basis of the grades obtained throughout the higher-intermediate school, together with the grades obtained in examinations designed at a national level.

Within the process of improving the evaluation system at the elementary and intermediate levels, more relevance is given to the teacher's assessment as a supplement to the results attained by students in the examinations. In the technical and professional schools more attention is given to the practical activities carried out by the students.

For each level of education the requirements to be met to obtain certification are defined. The national education system is designed in such a way that the different levels dovetail into one another. The two points in the system where the largest number of alternatives are to be found are the 9th and the 12th grades. However, to achieve greater flexibility, work is being undertaken to increase the number of exit points and to diversify training, thus satisfying students' interests and capabilities.

9. Major Reforms in the 1980s and 1990s

Due to a decrease in the country's population growth rate there are fewer students per grade in the elementary schools than in the lower-intermediate school. The expansion at the intermediate level resulted in an excessive growth at the higher-intermediate level enrollment during the 1980s. This is being adjusted in the 1990s by means of both diversification and enrollment growth in the technical and professional subsystem.

The period witnessed the greatest increase in undergraduate higher education enrollment, as well as an expansion of the network of institutions and studies. By the second half of the 1980s there was a slight decrease in the number of undergraduate students. All of this was associated with the needs of the country's economy and the individual interests of the population. Higher education institutions, especially through scientific research and graduate education, began to link themselves more effectively to socioeconomic reality, that is, to enterprises and local or national institutions.

A program was started to train elementary school teachers in higher education training institutes. The program includes the gradual elimination of intermediate-level teacher-training schools. By the end of the century, all teachers in the country will be university graduates.

10. Major Problems for the Year 2000

The austerity program will create a problem in terms of funding available to education. On the other hand, the "study and work" principle will alleviate this to some extent.

Illiteracy was a social phenomenon in 1961. The 1981 population census showed that there was 3.8 percent of illiteracy among those aged 10 years or

more and 2.2 percent among those aged between 15 and 49 years. Illiteracy among the population between 10 and 49 was 1.9 percent and between the ages of 10 and 34 was only 1 percent. In 1990 an exploratory survey was carried out to detect illiteracy, especially in the countryside and mountains. It was found that there were around 20,000 illiterates between the ages of 15 and 49. A special program was implemented to eradicate this residual illiteracy. Between 1962 and 1992 more than 1.5 million adults graduated from elementary school, and more than 900,000 from the lower intermediate school. In 1992 more than 90,000 adults were undergoing their high school studies, and around 25,000 were enrolled in language schools.

Adult education has made a large contribution to increase the average education level of the population. More efforts are being made to increase it further.

To improve the democratization process of education further, the following projects have been designed for implementation in the 1990s:

(a) expansion of preschool education and qualitative updating of the existing syllabuses in daycare centers;

(b) expansion of nonformal preschool educational projects and identifying new ways and means to achieve greater coverage of these options.

In the early 1990s Cuba's educational system is stronger than ever; it has recovered the creativity that characterized the first years of the Revolution. It pays close attention to the rich educational tradition of Cuban culture; it values highly the achievements of pedagogical sciences the world over, especially in Latin America, a region to which Cuba is linked in many ways. The people of Cuba are projecting themselves into the future, along a free and independent path and based on original and creative ideas.

Bibliography

Ministry of Education 1976 *The Plan for the Improvement of Cuba's National Education System*. Ministry of Education, Havana
Ministry of Education 1989 *Statistics Yearbook 1989*. Ministry of Education, Havana
Ministry of Education 1990 *Brief Information on Education in Cuba*. Ministry of Education, Havana
Ministry of Education *General Guidelines by the Minister of Education for the Development of Teaching and Administrative Work During the 1991–1992 School Year*. Ministry of Education, Havana
Ministry of Education 1991 *Summary of Work Done by the Ministry of Education in the 1990–91 School Year*. Ministry of Education, Havana
Ministry of Higher Education 1991 *Report on the 1990–91 School Year*. Ministry of Education, Havana

Cyprus

C. Papanastasiou

1. General Background

Cyprus is situated at the eastern end of the Mediterranean Sea. It is a small island, 226 kilometers long and 98 kilometers wide, occupying an area of 9,251 square kilometers. Two parallel ranges of mountains stretch from west to east covering roughly half of the island. Being a small island makes the introduction of innovations in the educational system easier and the interaction of influences from other educational systems faster. Turkey invaded Cyprus in 1974 and occupies about 37 percent of its area. One of the major problems that education in Cyprus still faces is the occupation, by Turkish troops, of a great number of schools, both elementary and secondary. The displacement of 200,000 Greek Cypriots, almost 40 percent of the population, as a result of the Turkish invasion led to an acute shortage of school buildings.

According to the first official census in 1881 the population of Cyprus was 186,173. The average annual population growth was 1.3 percent over the period 1881–1931 and 1.7 percent during the period 1931–60 (1960 was the year of Independence). In 1960, the population was 573,566 and by 1973 it was 631,778. In the period 1974–76 the population experienced negative growth (−0.9%) as a result of the Turkish invasion in 1974. In the following years, the population growth gradually increased by an average of 0.8 percent during the period 1976–82, and reached the maximum growth rate of 1.4 percent in 1984. Since then, the growth rate has declined steadily and the average growth rate during the period 1982–90 was 1.2 percent. The estimated population in 1990 was 706,900. The estimated population of the free area of Cyprus was 575,000 at the end of 1990, and the total urban population was nearly 70 percent. The main characteristics of population growth are declining fertility and emigration associated with political problems in Cyprus.

The estimated composition of the population for 1990 was 80.1 percent Greek Cypriots (including Armenians, Maronites, and Latins), 18.6 percent Turkish Cypriots, and 1.3 percent foreign residents mainly of British, Greek, and Lebanese origin. After Independence, each ethnic group maintained its own system of education, using either Greek or Turkish (the official languages) as the language of instruction. English is widely spoken and is mainly used in trade transactions between Cyprus and other countries. To some degree, the government has also retained the use of the English language.

According to the occupational classification system (International Labour Office 1990), craft and related workers (20.1%), service workers and shop and market sales workers (18.3%), elementary occupations (14.5%), technicians and associate professionals (13.2%), and plant and machine operators and assemblers (12.5%) form the major occupational groups. The rest were legislators, senior officials, and managers (3.2%); professionals (9.1%); and clerks (8.8%). This does not include agricultural establishments. At just 1.8 percent of the economically active population, unemployment in Cyprus is very low. Unemployment tends to be highest among graduates of secondary schools or persons who have not completed their studies at such schools (43.8%) followed by tertiary education graduates (30.7%).

The tertiary sector of the economy (trade, hotels, transport, and services) accounts for 57 percent of total employment. The secondary sector (manufacturing, electricity and construction), as well as the primary sector (agriculture and mining), declined to 29 and to 14 percent respectively in the period from 1980 to 1990. The government plays a significant role in the economic development of the island. In 1990, over half of the labor force held a secondary or postsecondary educational qualification (degree, diploma, certificate, or trade qualification). It has been estimated that in 1990 the average labor force member has 10.1 years of formal schooling compared with 8.9 years of schooling for the same group in 1980. Between 1980 and 1990 the proportion of the labor force with a secondary or postsecondary qualification rose from 46 to 58 percent.

Cyprus is an independent, sovereign republic of a presidential type. Under the 1960 Constitution, the executive power is entrusted to the President of the Republic who is elected by universal suffrage for a five-year term of office. The President ensures the executive power through a Council of Ministers appointed by him. Legislative power is exercised by the House of Representatives, consisting of 80 members elected by universal suffrage for a five-year term. The main political goal of the government is the survival of Cyprus as a unified independent and sovereign country. Part of the above general political goal is the educational principle of "I do not forget." This means that Cypriots do not forget the schools, churches, and houses in the occupied part of Cyprus. Since the quantitative expansion has reached very high levels, the government policy objectives on education are: the improved connection between school and the production processes, the satisfaction of the labor force requirements of the economy, the offer of equal opportunities to all, and the servicing of wider cultural objectives.

2. Politics and the Goals of the Education System

Education has been regarded as very important in Cyprus for the last two centuries. During the nineteenth century only a small percentage of people was educated. During the twentieth century, especially after the Second World War, the number of educated people increased rapidly. Before Independence in 1960, the main goals of education were the raising of the standard of living of the people, the inculcation of national ideas, and the strengthening of the national conscience. Church leaders supported education morally as well as financially, especially secondary education which was outside the control of the government.

After Independence, education has been seen by the people as a means toward better employment and improvement of their socioeconomic status. The government and political parties also considered education as the path to raising the standard of living of the people through better training, thus maximizing productivity and making the best use of natural resources. Furthermore, education has been regarded by the government as a human right, and as such it is the government's duty to provide equal educational opportunities for all citizens.

All of these determinants increased the demand for more education at all levels of education. The general aim of education in Cyprus is the development of a free and democratic citizenry with fully developed personalities who will contribute to the social, scientific, economic, and cultural progress of the island.

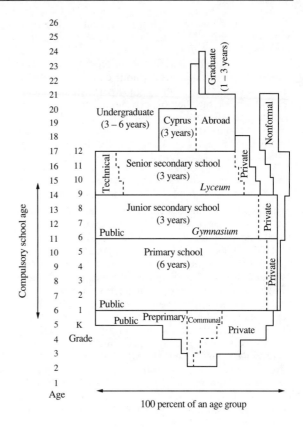

Figure 1
Cyprus: Structure of the formal education system

3. The Formal System of Education

Figure 1 presents the structure of the Cypriot formal education system, and Table 1 provides statistics on the number of schools, teachers, and students by level of education and per capita expenditure. The formal education system of Cyprus is centralized. Preprimary, primary, secondary general, secondary technical/vocational, special, nonformal, and some sections of tertiary education are under the authority of the Mini-

Table 1
Number of schools, teachers, and students by level of education in 1960–61 and 1989–90 and per capita expenditure per student in 1990–91[a]

Level of education	1960–61 Schools	1960–61 Teachers[b]	1960–61 Students	1989–90 Schools	1989–90 Teachers	1989–90 Students	Pupil–Teacher ratio	Expenditure per student 1990–91
Preprimary	14	27	603	540	917	22,008	24.0:1	C£349
Primary	548	1,940	68,773	378	2,824	60,841	21.5:1	C£536
Secondary	45	1,027	25,888	108	3,526	43,219	12.3:1	C£1,143
Tertiary	3	30	367	26	481	5,852	12.2:1	C£1,099
Special education	3	28	163	12	133	672	5.1:1	C£2,366
Nonformal	—	—	—	526	785	74,989	95.5:1	—
Public	570	2,623	85,279	928	6,750	145,032	21.5:1	—
Private	43	429	10,515	662	1,916	62,549	32.6:1	—

a Due to lack of adequate statistical information no data on the occupied part of Cyprus are included in the table   b Teachers = full-time equivalent

stry of Education which is the highest authority in educational policy. For the first time, in the academic year 1992–93, university education will be provided in Cyprus, in addition to the university education provided abroad. Apart from public education there are also a small number of private primary and secondary schools and a number of private tertiary education institutions. Education is compulsory from the age of five years and six months to the age of fifteen and between these age limits all students have to attend school.

3.1 Primary, Secondary, and Tertiary Education

Primary education covers six grades. All public schools use the same curriculum, but teachers are free to adapt it according to their local environment. In 1990, 60,841 pupils attended primary schools, of whom 4 percent attended private schools, 66 percent attended urban schools and 34 percent rural schools. There are primary schools in all towns and villages with 15 or more children of school age. Central schools serve small neighboring communities with 15 children or less of school age. Most of the large schools are divided into two cycles. Cycle A comprises the 3 lower level grades and Cycle B the upper 3. The school year extends over 205 days, and the primary-school day consists of approximately 5.5 hours of tuition. Primary education has been free and compulsory since 1962. Although not compulsory before 1962, education has been universal since 1945. The pupil–teacher ratio for public primary schools is 21.9:1 and 16.1:1 for private.

Public secondary education lasts for six years and is divided into two cycles, the *Gymnasium* (i.e., the junior-secondary school) and either the *Lyceum* or technical school (i.e., senior-secondary school). All primary-school leavers proceed to secondary school without any examination. The lower-secondary school provides a general core curriculum to all children. During the 1980s a marked change was introduced into the upper-secondary school. It was the introduction of LEM (Lyceum of Optional Subjects). Under this arrangement, students can choose one of five group of subjects (i.e., arts, science, economics, commercial/secretarial, foreign languages) according to their future plans and interests. Technical schools offer two types of courses, namely technical courses and vocational courses. The proportion of children of a certain age group who graduate from secondary school at the age of 18 is increasing steadily. The corresponding percentages were 62.7 in 1971, 71.9 in 1981, and more than 80 in 1991. The number of pupils of the *Lyceum* cycle is expected to increase from 14,000 in 1989–90 to 16,000 in 1993–94. This trend is expected to continue beyond 1993–94. The proportion of children of an age group who complete secondary education is almost the same for girls and boys. About 10 percent of secondary students attend private schools. In 1971 the percentage was 15.3 but it gradually decreased to 4 to 5 percent in

the period 1973–77 and has gradually risen since then. The decrease during 1973–77 can mainly be attributed to financial reasons in the wake of the Turkish invasion of Cyprus. The secondary-school year extents over approximately 180 school days, with 6 hours of tuition per day. The pupil–teacher ration is 12.2:1 for public secondary schools and 12.7:1 for private secondary schools.

The University of Cyprus began operating in 1992. Before 1992, students studied in universities abroad. Tertiary education in Cyprus is provided by public and private institutions which award diplomas equivalent to Higher National Diplomas. These colleges provide a wide variety of courses including forestry, engineering, computer studies, nursing, primary-school teaching, business, banking, accounting, hotels and catering, and so on. About 48 percent of the total secondary school leavers (38.5% of the age group) continue their studies either in Cyprus (50%) or abroad (50%). In Cyprus, there are 6 public and 18 private institutions, with 5 of these institutions offering only degrees of the Higher National Diploma level. There is one which offers a graduate diploma. Some of the private institutions are affiliated with polytechnics and universities in the United Kingdom and the United States and in many cases their examinations are associated with overseas examining bodies. In 1989 there were 9,410 students abroad attending tertiary institutions. Of these, 70 percent were full-time university students, 13 percent higher nonuniversity students, 8 percent graduate students, and about half of the graduate students were PhD students. The rest were students in vocational or preparatory studies. The level of higher education enrollments abroad decreased by almost 33 percent since 1980. At the same time there has been an increase of enrollments in tertiary institutions in Cyprus. This increase can mainly be attributed to financial reasons since it is more expensive to study abroad than at home. Also, when some of the local institution graduates resume their studies abroad, universities or polytechnics give them a number of credits for subjects they have already been taught. A further increase in the number of students attending private tertiary institutions in Cyprus is expected, in order to satisfy the local and foreign demand for this level of education. In 1990 there were 5,852 students in public and private institutions. Among them, 69 percent were students in private institutions. Since 1980 the number of students attending tertiary institutions in Cyprus has risen by 385 percent. Women accounted for 55 percent of the total number of students.

The student–teacher ratio for public tertiary institutions is 8.9:1 and for private institutions 14.5:1. The Cyprus Pedagogical Academy has ceased to function and the training of preprimary and primary school teachers is undertaken by the new University of Cyprus. The University will, in its first phase, have three schools which, when fully developed will have 4,000 Cypriot and foreign students: the School of

Humanities and Social Studies, the School of Pure and Applied Sciences, and the School of Economics and Administration.

3.2 Preschool Education

The great majority of children of preschool age (4½ to 5½ years' old) attend public, communal, or private kindergartens. In 1990, just over 22,000 children enrolled in preprimary schools. The attendance rate was 99 percent of the 4½–5½ age group, 56.4 percent of the 3½–4½ age group, 31.6 percent of the 2½–3½ age group, and 15.8 percent of the age group under 2½. Preprimary education is not compulsory and lasts from one to two and a half years. Kindergarten programs generally focus on structured play. Public kindergartens are established by the Department of Welfare Services and financed by the government. Community nursery schools are run on a nonprofit basis by Parents' Associations in the communities and are subsidized by the Ministry of Education. Private nursery schools are established by individuals on a profit basis who must be qualified in childcare. Community and private nursery schools are registered at the Ministry of Education and are supervised regularly. The pupil–teacher ratio for public preprimary schools is 22.3:1 and for private 25.0:1.

3.3 Special Education

By law, the government has undertaken the responsibility to educate any child, between the ages of 5 and 18, including those having learning and/or behavior problems. This Law also requires each district to form a committee for the handicapped children. Any child may be referred to the proper authorities for any possible special education program. During the school year 1989–90, 672 pupils attended special education schools. Special education programs are provided for students who are mentally retarded, physically handicapped, blind, deaf, or emotionally disturbed. In 1990 there were 12 schools providing programs for 672 students or about 0.6 percent of the student population. During the last few years the school for moderately retarded pupils provided training to children on speech therapy, occupational therapy, and self-care activities. The schools for the deaf and blind organize programs for the development of the abilities and the social adjustment of their pupils. The vocational rehabilitation centers for disabled people assist them in their efforts toward adjustment and integration into work and society. There are also homes for the severely retarded children. About 80 percent of the children who need special education attend certain programs. The policy of the government is not to segregate students with physical, intellectual, and emotional disabilities, but to give them the chance to grow and learn in a normal environment with normal students. They learn as much as they can in the normal schools which satisfies both their psychological and physical needs. The teacher of special education was adopted within the framework of primary schools. During the school year 1989–90, 508 children between 5½ and 13 years of age obtained help from specialized teachers in the primary schools, 37 in the first cycle of secondary education, and 127 in the second cycle of secondary education. The pupil–teacher ratio is 5.1:1 in public special schools.

3.4 Vocational Technical, and Business Education

Students enter technical schools after successful completion of the *Gymnasium* at the age of 15. Technical schools offer technical and vocational courses. Technical courses give particular emphasis to science and mathematics in addition to technical theory and skills. Graduates of the technical section, which lasts 3 years, may follow further studies in colleges or universities. Vocational courses also have a three-year duration. In the third year of the vocational courses, students follow a training program in industry for two days a week and attend school for the other three days. In the vocational section, more emphasis is given to practical skills.

The aim of public technical and vocational schools is to provide industry with technicians and craftsmen in various specializations such as mechanical and automobile engineering, computers, electronics, building, graphic arts, dressmaking, goldsmithery, shoe manufacturing, and many others. The government has planned to increase the number of students of technical schools up to 25 percent of the *Lyceum* pupils or 20 percent of the age group. Some of the plans are to provide improved information, to widen the spectrum of specialization, to build new technical schools, and to include certain provisions so that the technical school leaving certificate is recognized as a necessary qualification for posts in the various technical departments of the civil service. Public technical schools are free and the recurrent and capital expenditure is paid by the government. In 1990 the total number of public technical schools was 11. The students numbered 3,117, and 84 percent of them were boys.

3.5 Adult and Nonformal Education

Nonformal education includes evening and afternoon classes. Several public and private institutions provide courses at various levels. For some of these classes fees are charged, but for public nonformal institutions the government covers the rest of the expenditure. The goals of nonformal education are to help early school leavers to supplement their basic education, to help secondary-school graduates to enter the world of work, and to help working people acquire the necessary professional knowledge.

Enrollments in the nonformal sector are large. It is estimated that 9.5 percent of people above the age of 18 attend nonformal education which is provided through a variety of agencies and institutions. Evening *Gymnasia*, part-time institutes, adult education centers, the Industrial Training Authority, and the

Cyprus Productivity Center are some of them. They offer courses on languages, music, dance, physical training, school subjects at various levels, economics, computers, GCE, Teaching English as a Foreign Language (TEFL), and many others. Nonformal education attracted about 75,000 students in 1990; 20 percent of these were primary-school pupils, 30 percent were secondary-school pupils, and 50 percent were adults. There are 2,135 teachers in nonformal education institutes, and 26 percent of them are full-time.

4. Administrative and Supervisory Structure and Operation

According to the Constitution, following Independence in 1960 the Greek Cypriot and Turkish Cypriot Communal Chambers had competence to exercise legislative power on all educational, cultural, and religious matters. The two chambers were weakly linked to the central government in matters related to goals, planning, and implementation procedures. In 1965 the Greek Cypriot Communal Chamber asked the central government to take over its responsibilities. All the administrative functions were transferred to a new ministry, the Ministry of Education. Since then the government has been responsible for education in Cyprus. The whole structure of the public educational system is highly centralized. The government, through the Educational Service Commission, an independent five member body, recruits and appoints the teachers in public schools, as well as transfers and promotes teachers to headmasters and inspectors. The government also supplies buildings, equipment, and materials, and provides limited funding for use by schools. It is also responsible for administration, staffing, and curriculum. The Ministry of Education is responsible for the preparation of bills related to education and for the enforcement of educational laws. In Cyprus there are inspectors in preprimary, primary, and in secondary schools. It is their task to guide, supervise, and evaluate teachers. The inspectors have considerable power and provide a link between the directors of primary, secondary, and technical education and the schools.

Private schools are supported by fees paid by parents. The private foreign-language schools are run on a nonprofit basis by various religious groups and give more emphasis to languages and general education. The languages of instruction are English, French, or Italian. Private schools are owned and administered by individuals or bodies. The private schools are independent and do not belong to a specific system and are not accountable to the government.

The public tertiary institutions are administered by different ministries according to the institution. The Cyprus Forestry College is under the Ministry of Agriculture and Natural Resources; the Higher Technical Institute, the Hotel and Catering Institute, and the Mediterranean Institute of Management are under the Ministry of Labour and Social Insurance; and the School of Nursing is under the Ministry of Health. The private institutions are autonomous, but some of them have close relationships with foreign universities. Since 1987 a law has regulated the establishment, control, and operation of private tertiary institutions. All private institutions must register with the Ministry of Education. Registered private institutions are entitled to apply for accreditation of their programs.

5. Educational Finance

Public education is mainly financed by the government and local authorities of school committees. Parents do not pay fees for their children when the latter attend formal government schools. Private funding of education is in the form of tuition fees paid to private schools by individuals. In the case of private foreign schools, they are assisted by overseas authorities and organizations. Public education is not financed in the same way. Public kindergartens are financed by the Department of Welfare Services of the Ministry of Labour and Social Insurance. Community nursery schools are subsidized by the Ministry of Education. In public secondary schools, the government is responsible for the salaries of school personnel, scholarships, and grants-in-aid. The financing of public technical schools is undertaken in full by the government. Public schools of tertiary education are financed by different ministries.

Government expenditure on education has risen significantly since 1960 and in 1990 was 11.7 percent of the government budget and 3.6 percent of the Gross National Product (GNP). The expenditure for public and private education was 5.5 percent of GNP in 1989. For all levels of education, public expenditure increased from 163C£52.9 million (US$105.6 million) in 1984 to C£81.9 million (US$162.8 million) in 1989, an increase of 54.8 percent. Public and private expenditure was C£125.1 million (US$250 million) in 1989.

The amount of the total expenditure for education was distributed, in percentage terms, as follows: 4.9 for pre-primary education, 23.2 for primary education, 38.5 for secondary education, 4.8 for special and informal education, 4.4 for local postsecondary studies, 22.3 for studies abroad, and 1.9 for administrative purposes. For recurrent and capital expenditure in 1989, the cost per student was C£339 (US$678) for public and C£274 (US$548) for private pre-primary, C£493 (US$986) for public and C£260 (US$520) for private primary, C£1,031 (US$2,062) for public, C£1,751 (US$3,502) for technical, and C£1,251 (US$2,502) for private secondary. C£1,738 (US$3,476) for public local, C£725 (US$1,450) for private third level, C£1,987 (US$3,974) for public special education, and C£2,924 (US$5,848) for students abroad.

6. Supplying Personnel for the Education System

In 1990, there were 8,666 (full-time equivalent) teachers employed in schools in all levels of education.

A total of 10 percent were employed in preprimary education, 33 percent in primary schools, 41 percent in secondary education, 5 percent in tertiary education, 2 percent in special education, and 9 percent in nonformal education. About 55 percent of school teachers were female.

Between 1960 and 1970 there was a relative shortage of secondary-school teachers. By the end of the 1980s, however, due to relative static enrollments and reduced teacher retirements on the one hand, and the tremendous number of teachers graduating from universities on the other hand, there was a large surplus of secondary-school teachers in all subject areas. Some of them will never have the chance to be appointed. In primary education things are different. The students entering the Pedagogical Academy each year corresponded to the needs of the system at the time of their graduation and there has been no problem of redundancy.

Primary and preprimary teacher training has been offered by the Pedagogical Academy, an institution which offered three-year courses. As from 1991–92, the Pedagogical Academy did not accept new students and the Department of Education of the Cyprus University undertook this role by offering four-year initial teacher-training programs. All primary-school teachers attend a specific inservice program at the Pedagogical Institute for upgrading their professional qualifications and their salary scale. For secondary teachers, a university degree in a particular subject constitutes the only requirement for entering the profession. This degree generally comprises a major discipline. Considerable effort is being directed to improving the quality of teachers' academic qualifications. For this purpose, the Pedagogical Institute organizes optional as well as compulsory seminars free of charge. There are two compulsory seminars, one for secondary teachers on probation and another for secondary deputy heads. All secondary-school teachers on probation are obliged to attend a yearlong course specifically designed for them for two days a week at the Pedagogical Institute. Successful completion of this course is a prerequisite for permanent appointment. The second course also lasts for one year, but is conducted once per week.

The evaluation of teachers is carried out by inspectors. Normally teachers are assessed every two years. Inspectors and school principals cooperate in teacher evaluation, but the final decision rests with the inspector. For promotion purposes, the criteria are: teaching experience, teaching performance, and academic qualifications. Candidates for promotion must present themselves for an oral interview before the Education Committee.

7. Curriculum Development and Teaching Methodology

There is a core curriculum across the country. Curricula for all preprimary, primary, and secondary public schools are prescribed by the Ministry of Education. The development of the curricula is a common effort by teachers, inspectors, and school boards.

The Curriculum Development Unit contributes to the effort of linking the content of education with life by producing teaching materials. Pupils in all primary and lower secondary schools follow the same curriculum. All subjects are compulsory and there are no options. In primary schools most of the subjects are taught by the same teacher, but in secondary schools there is a specialist teacher for each subject. The students in the *Lyceum* (senior-secondary) are permitted to select some subjects apart from the common core of a certain domain, which is compulsory. In 1990 about 7 percent of the senior-secondary school students specialized in classics, 17 percent in mathematics and science, 44 percent in economics/commerce, 5 percent in languages, and 17 percent in technical and vocational courses, while the rest studied subjects from several discipline areas. One of the targets of secondary education is to prepare pupils for life. The development of the curricula and the introduction of new subjects, such as computers, are directed toward this objective.

Foreign languages are compulsory for all students in secondary education. English, which is by far the most popular foreign language in Cyprus, is compulsory and is taught for six years. French, as a third language, is also compulsory for four years. In elementary schools, the pupils are taught English in the two upper classes.

Teaching materials are prepared by the Curriculum Development Unit based on the modernized syllabuses on a noncommercial basis. In general, teachers have no freedom to select the textbooks they use. They have to use the books prepared by the Curriculum Development Service and some others used in Greece provided they fit the curricula of Cyprus. The curricula which the preprimary, primary, and special education sectors use have been developed by the inspectorate in cooperation with the teachers' union and the pedagogical institutions. Audiovisual aids like videorecorders, overhead projectors, tape recorders, television, visuals, and computers are widely used. The small number of students in each class makes it easier for the teacher to give more emphasis on the individualization of instruction and the introduction of remedial teaching.

8. The System of Examinations, Promotions, and Certifications

In Cyprus there are no entrance examinations for primary and secondary schools. In primary schools almost all pupils are automatically promoted to the next grade. Only in the first grade is there a failure rate of about 1.5 percent of students. The first certificate the students acquire after completion of the sixth grade of the primary school and is based on continuous assessment. This certificate is used for enrollment in secondary education. In secondary education every student receives a school report three times a year at the end of each school term. These reports include the scores on all subjects which are taught. The scores result both from oral and written examinations. At the end of Grades 9 and 12 all students take common final exams prepared by the Ministry of Education. In 1991 the Ministry of Education decided that the students in Grade 12 must take externally prepared final exams. The subjects for each specialization differ. As from 1992, Grade 9 students take compulsory common exams in 4 subjects.

Private schools are not considered as equivalent to public schools. Private school graduates cannot attend higher courses abroad whose entrance requirements include the possession of a public school leaving certificate. Those who wish to obtain a certificate which will be equivalent to a public school leaving certificate must take special examinations held by the Ministry of Education. Institutions of tertiary education award their own diplomas.

9. Educational Assessment, Evaluation, and Research

Since 1985 there has been considerable activity in student assessment for accountability purposes. Several projects have been undertaken by the Department of Research and Evaluation of the Pedagogical Institute. Student assessment focuses on mathematics, language, and science. All of these projects cover primary and secondary schools. The aim of the research projects is the creation of a bank of information to be used by the educational authorities in decision-making, as well as by teachers in organizing their teaching activities. The priorities of educational research are those relating to student achievement in the various subject areas, curricula, teacher education and evaluation, and general educational parameters.

National tests were commissioned by the Pedagogical Institute on Mathematics in 1990 for Grades 7, 8, and 9. New tests for language and science are in progress. Apart from the International Association for the Evaluation of Educational Achievement (IEA) international studies on reading literacy and mathematics and science, projects have been undertaken in cooperation with universities or research organizations in the United States, Germany, Greece, and the United Kingdom, mainly for comparison purposes. For the next five years, the main emphases in the field of research are: teachers and teaching; student achievement in the main subject areas; educational technology; the effects of problem-solving instruction; ancient Greek; evaluation of language, mathematics, and science; misconceptions in science; teachers' perceptions about mathematics learning; English as a foreign language; and computers.

10. Major Reforms in the 1980s and 1990s

In 1984, the "work-week" was introduced and all pupils in Grade 11 leave school for a week and work in factories, workshops, shops, and offices. In 1987–88, the post of department head was established and department heads were appointed to all upper-secondary schools and to a number of lower-secondary schools. Uniform final examinations for Grades 9 and 12 were introduced in 1991 and 1992. In 1991–92, the five-day working week was introduced on the basis of an agreement between the Ministry of Education and the professional organizations of teachers.

In 1990–91, a pilot curriculum for nine-year long compulsory education was implemented on an experimental basis in a sample of primary and lower-secondary schools. The most important point to underline is the re-allocation of the content of subject matter to the curricula of primary and lower-secondary education. This reallocation will provide satisfactory education both for those hoping to attend the upper-secondary school as well as for those who do not.

A significant development in 1990 was the introduction of design technology into the *Gymnasia* and courses on new technology into technical schools. The existing traditional craftwork in schools was brought into line with the needs of modern society. Computer science was introduced as a compulsory subject in Grade 10 of secondary general education.

A body consisting of representatives from various ministries, semigovernmental organizations, industry, trade unions, teachers' unions, and other bodies and associations concerned with technical and vocational education was established to act as a consultative body on matters of policy and development in technical education. An Advisory Committee on Tertiary Education was also established to examine problems related to the private tertiary educational sector.

A need has been identified for the introduction of a unified system of examinations. For this reason, the introduction of unified examinations is being studied for the award of a certificate of education which will be used to fulfill the entrance requirements to higher educational institutes and universities both in Cyprus and abroad, as well as for employment in private organizations. An intensive inservice training of all primary-school teachers will contribute to their academic upgrading and will bring their remuneration in line with that of secondary teachers.

11. Major Problems for the Year 2000

One major problem is the shortage of school buildings as a result of the Turkish occupation of about 40 percent of the schools, and the shortage of educational equipment. The expected increase in the school population will exacerbate the situation in secondary as well as primary schools. There is also an uneven distribution of pupils between urban and rural schools. The urban school population is increasing rapidly. The problem of the uneven distribution of pupils is dealt with by restructuring the existing educational areas and the establishment of new schools in rural areas. The provision of educational equipment, especially that of expensive advanced technology, has been left to the government but the problem has yet to be faced adequately.

A second main problem is the absence of compatibility to present social needs and to rapid technological developments which demand a versatile and adaptive labor force. Some aspects of this problem are the methods of instruction, the preservice training of personnel and continuous training thereafter, and the means that the system has at its disposal. The development of nonformal education indicates that there is insufficient satisfaction of the educational needs of the people. Problems also arise from the lack of homogeneity of the pupil population resulting from the universality of secondary education.

Further problems which strongly characterize all levels of education are the need for improved organization, the size of schools, and the quality of education offered in rural areas.

Bibliography

Demetriades E I 1985 Cyprus: System of education. In: Husén T, Postlethwaite T N 1985 *The International Encyclopedia of Education*, 1st edn. Pergamon Press, Oxford

Department of Statistics and Research 1990a *Statistics of Education 1989/90*. Series I, Report No 22. Printing Office of the Republic of Cyprus, Nicosia
Department of Statistics and Research 1990b *Registration of Establishments 1989*, Vol. II, Series I, Report No 16. Printing Office of the Republic of Cyprus, Nicosia
Department of Statistics and Research 1991a *Demographic Report 1990*, Series II, Report No 28. Printing Office of the Republic of Cyprus, Nicosia
Department of Statistics and Research 1991b *Labour Statistics 1990*, Series 14, Report No 9. Printing Office of the Republic of Cyprus, Nicosia
International Labour Office (ILO) 1990 *ISCO 1988 International Standard Classification of Occupations*. ILO, Geneva
Karageorgis A G 1986 *Education Development in Cyprus 1960–1977*. (Author publication, Nicosia)
Ministry of Education 1988 *Development of Education 1986–88. National Report of Cyprus*. Ministry of Education, Nicosia
Ministry of Education 1990 *Development of Education 1988–90. National Report of Cyprus*. Ministry of Education, Nicosia
Papastavrou A S 1988 Education system in Cyprus. In: Markou G et al. *Comparative Education. Education in Europe* (in Greek). Gutenberg, Athens
Persianis P 1981 *The Political and Economic Factors as the Main Determinants of Educational Policy in Independent Cyprus (1960–70)*. Pedagogical Institute, Nicosia
Planning Bureau Commission 1989 *Five-Year Development Plan 1989–1993*. Printing Office of the Republic of Cyprus, Nicosia
Press and Information Office 1990 *Cyprus*. PIO, Nicosia
Press and Information Office 1991 *Cyprus: The Way to Full EC Membership*. PIO, Nicosia

Czech Republic

J.Kotásek and J.Švecová

1. General Background

The Czech Republic (CR) is a state located in central Europe. It borders on Germany, Austria, Slovakia, and Poland. It covers an area of 78,864 square kilometers and has a population of 10.3 million. Population density is 131 inhabitants per square kilometer in 1994.

In 1918, after the First World War when the Austro-Hungarian Empire disintegrated, the Czechoslovak Republic was constituted, linking the Czech and Slovak nations in one unified state founded on the principles of parliamentary democracy. It was the only democratic state to the east of Germany. In 1939 the Czech part was incorporated into the Nazi German Reich as *Protektorat Böhmen und Mähren* (Bohemia and Moravia) while Slovakia became an independent but satellite state. Czechoslovakia was restored after the end of the Second World War in 1945. From 1948 to 1989 Czechoslovakia was part of the Soviet bloc where the Communist Party had exclusive political power. An attempt to liberalize the totalitarian system in 1968 (known as the Prague Spring) was marred by Soviet military intervention in August. About 450,000 Czechs and Slovaks emigrated in the period 1948–88. It was only in November 1989 that the "Velvet Revolution" launched the transformation of Czechoslovakia into a democratic and sovereign state striving for the observance of human and civil rights. The former totalitarian Czechoslovak Socialist Republic was transformed into the Czech and Slovak Federal Republic in 1990. The last troops of the Soviet occupation left Czechoslovakia in 1991.

257

After the 1992 Parliamentary elections the Slovak National Council decided to pass a new Constitution of Slovakia as an independent state. After negotiation, the Czech and Slovak political representatives accepted the proposal of the leading political parties to abolish the Federal Constitution and to set up two states: the Czech Republic and the Slovak Republic. The new Czech Constitution was passed by the Czech National Council later. Both republics started their independent existence with a Customs Union Treaty and other political, cultural, and economic agreements on January 1, 1993. The separation has been acknowledged as a peaceful solution of national aspirations for full sovereignty.

The CR is a state with a relatively high population density and a continuing process of urbanization. The relatively dense network of towns and suburbs, the small distances between them, and the large public transport network not only facilitates communication between the inhabitants of towns and suburbs but also makes commuting to school possible.

Ninety-five percent of the inhabitants are Czechs (formally those identifying themselves as Czech, Moravian, or Silesian) and 3.1 percent Slovaks. There are also small minorities of Poles (0.6%), Germans (0.5%), and Romanys (0.3%).

The transition from a central command economy to a market-regulated economy began in 1990. The program of economic reform comprised primarily price liberalization, which had a serious impact on the standard of living of the population, owing to inflation. Changes in ownership structures are represented by the process of restitution of property to original owners, denationalization, and privatization. Agriculture cooperatives were being transformed into cooperatives of share-holders. Small, middle-sized, and large private businesses were reappearing. These processes brought about the re-establishment of a private sector of the economy. As a consequence, the process of social stratification according to income began. The process of privatization was accompanied by a restrictive state monetary policy which created a highly critical situation for the education sector. The state budget was oriented to providing subsidies for agriculture, social allowances, administration, defense, public health care, and education. In 1991 the gross national product (GNP) began to decline as a result of the collapse of the former socialist economic system and its transformation into a market economy. After the economic recession, a 2 to 3 percent increase in GNP was predicted in 1994.

In 1992, 5.49 million persons were employed. Of these, 74 percent were in production sectors and 26 percent in nonproduction sectors. Of the former, 36 percent were employed in industry and 10 percent in agriculture. Unemployment in the CR reached approximately 3.5 percent of the workforce in 1994.

In 1993, women constituted 51.3 percent of the total population and made up 44.3 percent of the workforce.

The percentage of women employees began to drop as a result of a decrease in jobs. The CR has a high employment level of women. The living conditions of children are affected by a high divorce rate which, in the 1980s, exceeded 30 per 100 marriages.

The Bill of Fundamental Rights and Freedoms, passed by the Czechoslovak Federal Assembly on January 9, 1991 remains part of the constitutional order as one of the fundamental legislative acts confirming the change of the totalitarian political system into a pluralistic and democratic one. In harmony with accepted international agreements, the Bill defines personal rights, political rights, the rights of national and ethnic minorities, and economic, social, and cultural rights. These include the right to education. School attendance is compulsory by law. The citizens of the Czech Republic have the right to free elementary and secondary level education. Free higher education depends on the ability of the citizen and the resources of the state. Private schools may be established where instruction is implemented under conditions set by law.

The Constitution consistently separates legislative, executive, and judiciary power. Legislative power is exercised by parliament, which consists of two chambers, namely the Chamber of Deputies and the Senate. The president and the government represent executive power. The president is head of state and is elected to the post by parliament for a five-year term of office. The government, which is responsible to the Chamber of Deputies, is the supreme body of executive power. The president appoints the prime minister and, on the latter's suggestion, the other members of the government. The responsibility for education in the government rest with the Minister of Education, Youth, and Physical Culture. Judiciary power is implemented by independent courts. The supreme judiciary body is the Supreme Court. The Constitutional Court is a judiciary body which supervises the observance of the Constitution. The management of state property and the fulfillment of the state budget is controlled by the Supreme Control Office. The Constitution also provides territorial self-government at the level of localities and higher self-governing entities.

The main political goals are established by the government which, in 1994, was composed of representatives of conservative and Christian-democratic parties and supported by a significant majority of the citizenship. The goals comprise completion of the political and economic transformation of the country and the establishment of an open society of Western European standards. The constitution of forms of democratic legislation was all but completed but the implementation of economic reform will be a long-term process. The monetary and budget policy is fully subordinated to the effort to attain prosperity speedily. Consequently the budget for the education sector was very limited in 1994. The international goal of the

Czech Republic is full integration into the European Union and NATO.

2. Politics and the Goals of the Education System

Since 1989 fundamental changes have taken place in educational goals which have gradually been reflected in legislation: Education Act No. 171/1990 (Amendment of Act No. 29/1984), and Higher Education Act No. 172/1990, both passed by the Czechoslovak Federal Assembly; and the Act on State Administration and Self-government in Education, passed by the Czech National Council in 1990. The previous goals of "communist education" were formulated in the spirit of Marxism-Leninism as class ideology and complied with the interests of the ruling party and the state which it governed. The new postulates of education are the needs of the free human individual and of civic society, the principles of humanism and democracy.

The radical and relatively quick transformation of the society is a great challenge for the educational system, requiring global reform relating to all contexts and aspects of its activity. The difficulty of the reform is exacerbated not only by the rigidity of attitudes prevailing among the public and the teaching profession and the break-up of existing organizational structures affected by the economic reform, but also by the low esteem in which the educational system is held. In the political, economic, and social transformation, the necessity of introducing a long-term strategy of development of the educational system tends to be underestimated.

In the political program declared after the 1992 General Election the government set itself the goal of drawing up "a modern strategy of educational policy open to world development and aiming among the West European democracies." Cooperation with the public is to be intensified and the impact of the family, the community, and other parts of civic society on the school is to be strengthened. Within the process of decentralization substantial elements of authority and responsibility so far invested in central bodies of state power are to be transferred to schools and teachers. The state is to provide that all schools—state, private, and ecclesiastic—develop under comparable conditions. Another task is to define the basic core curriculum and educational standards allowing the provision of quality education which would correspond to the older home tradition and to the country's integration in Europe. In addition to these agreed standards space should remain for the plural diversification of schools. The government is convinced that the use of economic mechanisms and relations, namely in the field of funding, is one of the most effective means of transformation of the Czech education system. It therefore intends to apply these instruments consistently in its policy. State funding of basic and secondary schools will be related to the number of pupils and at higher levels funding will be supplemented by grants and loans to students. Conditions are to be created to allow schools to acquire further funds from sources other than the state budget. The introduction of school fees should abide by the principle of accessibility of all educational levels to all citizens.

3. The Formal System of Education

Education is carried out in the Czech language. Citizens of national minorities are provided with education in their native language on a scale adequate to the interests of their national development and right to education. In the Czech Republic the largest number of minority schools are schools with the Polish language as the medium of instruction (29).

Figure 1 depicts the structure of the education system in the CR.

3.1 Primary, Secondary, and Tertiary Education

The "basic school" provides a compulsory nine-year basic education. After the 1989 "Velvet Revolution" there were changes in the objectives and content of education as well as structural changes. The length of basic school was extended from eight to nine grades. At the same time, compulsory education was reduced from 10 to 9 years.

Basic school is divided into two study cycles. In the first cycle (Grades 1–4, in the future 1–5) pupils acquire basic knowledge in the mother tongue, mathematics, the natural sciences, and elementary civics. Art and physical education are part of this education, as is work education where pupils acquire basic work skills and habits. They are taught by only one teacher. Instruction at the first level of basic school lasts 4 hours a day on average.

The second level (Grades 5–8, in the future 6–9) is attended by 10- (11-) to 14- (15-) year olds. There is a different teacher (specialist) for every subject of basic school. Talented pupils attend basic school with extended language study courses, extended mathematics education, sports schools, and so on. Streaming is being increasingly introduced. There are 5 hours of instruction per day (in some cases 7 hours). The school year runs from September 1 to June 30. School vacations are as follows: Autumn (2 days); Christmas (approximately 10 days); Mid-term (1 day); Spring (5 days); and main vacations (2 months).

Most basic schools are state run. In 1993–94 there were 26 private and 13 church basic schools. Since the 1950s the number of basic schools decreased but the number of classes increased. This phenomenon was linked to the closure of small schools in isolated areas and to the establishment of large basic schools in new conurbations. In 1950–51 there were 15,144 schools with 50,697 classes; in 1993–94 there were 4,199 schools with 45,973 classes, with a maximum

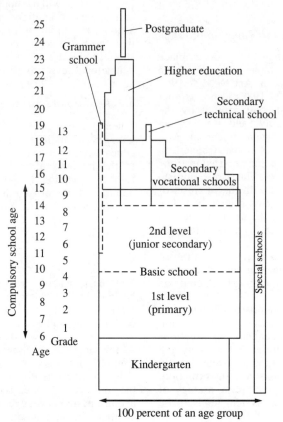

Figure 1
Structure of the formal education system

of 30 pupils to one class, an average of 23 pupils and a pupil–teacher ratio of 16.5:1. In 1992, many schools with a smaller number of classes in small settlements were being reopened.

Out-of-school education is an integral component of the educational system. It is implemented in after-school units and clubs (in 1993 there were 8,600 with 216,104 pupils, mainly in basic schools), houses of children and young people (in 1993 there were 318 with 311,088 members), basic art schools (formerly people's schools of art), language schools, boarding schools, and youth homes.

Secondary schools prepare pupils either for enrollment in higher education or for a vocation in industry, agriculture, trade, administration, culture, the services, or other sectors of the national economy. Applicants for secondary school enrollment come from eighth grade basic school leavers. If they are not admitted they attend the ninth grade of basic school and may re-apply for enrollment in secondary school.

Secondary schools comprise: grammar schools, secondary technical schools, and secondary vocational schools. In 1993–94, 14 percent of 15–16-year old students attended first grade of grammar schools, 32.5 percent technical schools, and 53.5 percent vocational schools. The number of students attending secondary technical school and grammar courses at secondary school increased slightly since previous years. By attending four- or five-year courses at secondary school and passing the final examination students acquire full secondary education, entitling them to apply for enrollment in higher education. By attending a two- or three-year course in a secondary technical or vocational school the student acquires secondary education. Part-time students may also take part in final examinations in secondary schools. Instruction in secondary school lasts 6 to 7 hours (8 hours maximum). In 1992–93 the highest number of pupils per class was set at 30. The pupil–teacher ratio is 17.9:1.

In 1993–94, there were 47 private grammar schools, 194 private and 20 ecclesiastic secondary technical schools, and 30 private vocational schools. The number of private secondary schools and their pupils is steadily growing.

Since 1948 grammar schools have undergone many changes. Attempts to preserve an academic-type school alternated with the enforcement of a general and polytechnic school of the Soviet type. The 1990 Act returned the grammar school to its initial purpose, namely a school offering demanding academic training for higher education. The Act also made room for establishing grammar schools offering more than four-year study courses. Now students can also study on eight-year courses at grammar school, starting at age 11, after the fifth basic school grade. There are also seven-, six-, or five-year grammar schools starting at corresponding ages and grades. Since 1991 there has been tracking in the first and second years of four-year study courses, namely the humanities, science, and general education streams. The senior grades are offered a modified curriculum. Over 60 percent of grammar school students are girls.

The Higher Education Act of 1990 restored the autonomy of institutions of higher education in all fields of activity. The Ministry of Education ceased to be in control of their work. A new body, the Academic Senate, elected by the academic community of each institution of higher education, makes basic decisions on the activities of its own institution. These decisions are on such matters as the statutes, internal organization, establishment of units, election of rectors and deans, approval of vice-rectors and vice-deans, nomination of professors, approval of members of the scientific council, supervision of budget and management, and study programs. The Council of Higher Education Institutions, composed of representatives from academic senates of all institutions, has become a consultative board to the Ministry in legislative and budgetary matters of higher education. A similar mission has been entrusted to the Rector's Conference. The Accreditation Commission was established as advisory body of the government to assess proposals for the establishment of new institutions of higher education and to evaluate the quality of teaching and research.

In 1993–94 there were 23 institutions of higher education with 105 faculties and 109,471 full-time day students. Forty-four percent of all university and college students were women. Nearly 15 percent of 18-year olds (after matriculation at secondary school and university entrance examination) were admitted to the university. This was approximately 40 percent of all applicants. The number of enrolled students had increased 2.8 times since 1948. In 1991 five new universities were established.

All higher education institutions have university status. A nonuniversity sector has not been developed. There are some moves to transform a number of secondary technical schools into postsecondary professional colleges.

Most institutions of higher education organize their study courses at two levels: basic and specialist. The first three years are usually general common core study courses which allow students to change their study courses within the framework of the faculty. Specialization takes place in the senior years of study. Higher education lasts 4 to 6 years. The 1990 Act also provided for three-year study courses for a bachelor's degree. Some short-cycle courses reflect the needs of the new labor market and are more vocational in orientation. In the early 1990s there was a great demand for admission to studies in law, the humanities, social sciences, management, teaching, and medicine. The major constraints on higher education development were and are limited capacity of premises, space for teaching and research, and an aging academic staff. There are problems about how to strengthen university research and how to cooperate with the Czech Academy of Sciences.

3.2 Preschool Education

Preschool education constitutes a compact system of educational work with children under the age of 6. Institutions of preschool education were first established in the 1830s, but it was not until 1948 that preschool education was incorporated into the education system. Nursery schools (nurseries and kindergartens) provide education for children from a young age up to the age of 6 years. Children up to the age of 3 years are educated in creches which are administered by the healthcare sector. Children between the ages of 3 and 6 are educated in nursery schools (kindergartens). In 1993–94 there were 6,600 nursery schools attended by 331,509 children; that is, nearly 87 percent of the respective age group.

Preschool education is free and includes regular medical care. Parents pay toward the cost of meals according to their income. In 1993 there were 16 classes in Christian and 44 in private nursery schools.

3.3 Special Education

Institutionally, the education of children and youth with special needs has been entrusted to two sectors; the education sector and the social care sector. The education sector runs special schools for children with special needs. The social care sector operates institutions of social care for heavily physically and mentally disabled children, youths, and adults. Special schools provide education to pupils with mental, sensory, and physical handicaps, and difficult and maladjusted pupils. Delicate children are placed in medical institutions. The curricula are adapted to the disability of the child. Special schools have smaller class sizes (in 1993–94 the average was 10.4 and the average pupil–teacher ratio was 7.5:1), a slower tempo of instruction, specially modified, and the possibility of extending school attendance (and a more demanding educational technology). Special education also includes speech therapy and educational and psychological counseling provided to families through schools of all types, and permanent medical care. In 1993–94 there were 1,250 schools attended by 70,099 pupils, that is 4.2 percent of the age group. The new trend is to integrate the pupils whose handicaps are not severe into ordinary schools.

3.4 Vocational, Technical, and Business Education

Secondary technical schools offer two-, three-, four-, and five-year courses, combining general and vocational education at different levels. A new and popular type of secondary education comprises two-year home economics schools attended mostly by girls.

Secondary vocational schools are practically oriented and provide vocational training as well as the foundation of general education. They provide secondary education within two-, three-, four-, and five-year courses. In 1993 there were 15 five-year courses. 116 four-year courses, 233 three-year courses, and 47 two-year courses.

Since 1992 the responsibility for secondary vocational education has been divided between the Ministry of Education and the Ministry of Economy. The Ministry of Economy is responsible for the secondary vocational training and its financial aspects. Vocational training is the subject of special discussions on the transformation of the Czech educational system. There is a trend to give preference to more universal fields of training or "despecialization." Emphasis should be placed on the variability and permeability of vocational training courses, and decision-making on the professional orientation of pupils should not be made too early. Another trend is to involve the social partners into vocational education.

Integrated technical and vocational schools are new types of secondary vocational education (there were 190 in 1994).

3.5 Adult and Nonformal Education

Until 1989 there was a unified system of adult education within the system of state schools, in state enterprises, and out-of-school institutions. The Socialist Academy was important, striving for ideological indoctrination of citizens. After 1989 the system of adult education disintegrated and by 1992 was redeveloping spontaneously. A number of agencies and institutions were established. The lack of coordination in this area led about 250 groups to set up the Association of Institutions of Adult Education. This is a nongovernmental and nonpolitical voluntary organization whose aim is to submit proposals for adult education and to cooperate with state bodies in the preparation and introduction of legislation and

other measures in the field of adult education, to cooperate with similar institutions, and to coordinate educational activities. Another endeavor for the improvement of adult education is the establishment of the University Distance Education Association.

In the system of state schools adult education is applied through part-time study courses such as evening courses, distance courses, correspondence courses, combined courses, postsecondary courses run by secondary schools, and part-time undergraduate and doctoral graduate study courses in institutions of higher education which are equivalent to day courses. The number of adults attending part-time courses considerably decreased except for in secondary vocational schools where skilled workers gain full secondary education. It is to be noted that a flourishing market of private language and management schools, and correspondence courses, exists.

4. Administrative and Supervisory Structure and Operation

Before 1989 all types of schools and the entire content of education were controlled by the apparatus of the Communist Party. Schools and the local authorities had only very limited powers. The 1990 Act on State Administration and Self-government in Education gave greater independence to individual schools, that is, to their principals, and to regional and local authorities. State administration in education is implemented by the school principal, the director (head) of the preschool institution, the community authority, the regional education authority, the school inspectorate, the Ministry of Education, and other central bodies of state administration. Self-government in the educational system is executed by the community respresentation and the regional council of education. The Act significantly strengthened the authority of the school principal, who can fundamentally affect the entire life of the school in terms of personnel and material. The principal is responsible for the implementation of curricula, for the standards of the educational work of the school, and for the efficient use of funds.

The activity of schools and other educational institutions is managed by regional educational authorities, which are organizations directly supervised by the Ministry of Education. They allocate funds for the salaries of teachers and other educational personnel, for textbooks, teaching materials, and other teaching costs which are covered by the state, and monitor the use of these funds. Maintenance costs of building and equipment are covered by the community budget.

In each territorial unit, there is a council of education which consists of representatives of the communities ($\frac{1}{3}$), representatives of teachers ($\frac{1}{3}$), and representatives of parents ($\frac{1}{3}$). The standards of education in state and other education institutions are supervised by the Czech School Inspectorate, a body of state administration directly controlled by the Ministry of Education. School inspectors control the educational standards, the staff and material conditions of educational activities, the efficient use of funds, and the observance of generally valid and educational legislation.

5. *Educational Finance*

Although education is free in all state schools and universities, fees are paid in ecclesiastic and private schools. These are approximately CK 6,000 to CK 14,000 per pupil per annum (CK 28=US 1). Within the scope set by the government all textbooks and learning materials are provided free. Students are entitled to reduced tram, bus, and train fares, and free medical care. Scholarships are awarded to those who come from poor social backgrounds.

It is very difficult to identify accurately how much of the state budget is allocated to education, because apart from funds allocated directly to the education sector, education also receives funds from the budgets of other sectors such as healthcare and industry. In view of the wide discrepancies in the methods of calculating such data, the sums quoted below are likely to suffer from significant error.

In 1975 it was alleged that 7.1 percent of the budget of the then Czechoslovak Socialist Republic went to education. In 1980 this was 7.9 percent, in 1985 8.1 percent, and in 1988 8.6 percent. The 1991 allocation to the Czech education sector was 4.34, in 1992 4.30, and in 1993 5.08 percent of the national revenue. Salaries account for approximately 55 percent of the budget allocation.

In 1994, the per student expenditure (based on recurrent expenditures) were CK9,902 for preprimary education and CK12,039 for basic education. The expenditure for secondary schooling varied from one type of secondary school to another: the lowest was CK17,094 and the highest was CK42,495. The same situation prevailed in vocational schools: the lowest expenditure was CK19,023 and the highest CK26,249. For grammar schools it was CK17,094, and for special education it was CK38,106.

6. *Supplying Personnel for the Education System*

In the school year 1993–94 there were 130,159 teachers, of whom 28,674 were in kindergarten, 64,030 in basic schools, 10,573 in secondary vocational schools, 8,100 in grammar schools, 13,529 in secondary technical schools, 8,372 in special schools, and 13,463 in higher education. Roughly 53 percent of all education personnel were women (in kindergarten 100 percent, in basic school 82 percent, in secondary vocational 56 percent, secondary technical 53 percent, grammar school 65 percent, and higher education 31 percent). In secondary and higher education there were also part-time teachers.

Teachers at basic and secondary schools must be university graduates. Only kindergarten teachers receive their training at the secondary school level. Primary, secondary, and special school teachers are trained either in university faculties of education (4 to 5 years' study) or in faculties of philosophy, science, mathematics and physics, physical education, or theology (5 years). The professional part of teacher training and initial training practice is more developed at faculties of education. Technical, economic, art, and agricultural colleges train teachers of vocational subjects for secondary schools. Teacher training courses end with a final examinations and thesis. Successful candidates are awarded the degree of Mgr (MA).

For inservice teacher education, teachers may choose from a wide choice of short-term courses or programs organized by pedagogical centers and various institutions and organizations, including universities. Teacher salaries are a function of the level of education attained and the number of years of teaching experience a teacher has. Salaries of teachers in private schools are determined exclusively by their principals.

7. *Curriculum Development and Teaching Methodology*

Curricula and syllabuses for the different levels of state school are approved by the Ministry of Education. Since 1989 they have developed in such a way as to allow the school principal (especially in secondary schools) to form the school profile through an essentially arbitrary modification of the syllabuses of the 10 percent designated for elective subjects. This 10 percent rises to 40 percent by the fourth year of grammar school. The content of the elective subjects is determined by the school principal in agreement with the heads of the respective subject areas in the school. Further to this modification, an individual teacher may change, complement, or modify 33 percent of the content of the subject taught. This depends on regional conditions, the development of the subject matter, the teacher's own experience, and so on. Private schools have their own syllabuses.

The curricula are developed by teams of educationalists and academics in cooperation with teachers and representatives of the professional groups. They must be approved by the Ministry of Education.

The writing and publishing of textbooks and other teaching materials is the reponsibility of individual publishers who also influence the choice of authors. The textbooks must be approved by the Ministry of

Education and, if approved, appear on the approved list of textbooks. The school principal is allowed (with state funding) to purchase for the students any approved textbook on the market. The distribution of textbooks is the responsibility of the publishers.

The main problem in curriculum development is the determination of the core subjects for schools of different types and levels, and the coordination of the content of the different subjects. There are also certain problems related to the insufficient representation of humanities and social sciences.

Teaching is mostly conducted using the direct instructional method. Most of the teaching profession is not willing or ready to introduce less traditional methods of teaching, even at the cost of partial failure.

8. The System of Examinations, Promotions, and Certification

Student achievement in basic and secondary schools is examined by continuous oral and written examinations, as a result of which students receive marks ranging from 1 to 5. Students receive reports on their achievement at the end of the first term and at the end of the school year (end of January and end of June). The primary grades are allowed to use verbal assessment.

Parents meet with the class and subject matter teachers about four times per year. Parents are informed about their child's achievement and behavior. Students are admitted to secondary school on the basis of their achievement in the basic school and on the basis of the results of entrance examinations. Since 1990, admission to secondary school has been decided by the secondary school principal. The content and process of the examination is the responsibility of the school principal.

Education at grammar and secondary technical schools ends with matriculation examinations of equal status. Passing this examination is a precondition for applying for admission to higher education. Basic school leavers are admitted to two- and three-year training courses on the basis of their achievement in basic school. However, those wishing to take a four- or five-year course sit an entrance examination, which is almost always in the mother language and one other subject as decided upon by the school principal. At secondary vocational schools the training course is terminated by an apprentice examination. Pupils attending four- or five-year courses take both a matriculation examination and an apprentice examination.

Admission procedures to higher education vary from one institution to another. General admission is based on the successful passing of the entrance examination and on the entrant's school achievement in secondary school, including the matriculation examination. All applicants may send their application to any number of institutions of higher education.

After the Final Examinations, graduates of 3-year courses are awarded an academic degree *Bachelor* (Bc.), of 4–6-year courses *Magister* (Mgr.), *Ingenieur* (Ing.), or Doctor of Medicine /Veterinary Medicine (MUDr./ MVDr.). Graduate studies for selected *Magisters* and *Ingenieurs* last 3 years. After successful defense of the doctoral thesis the graduate is awarded the research degree of Doctor (Dr.), equivalent to PhD.

9. Educational Assessment, Evaluation, and Research

Since the early 1990s educational research has been in a stage of transition. The standard and prestige of educational research was seriously damaged by its subordination to official Marxist ideology and by the one-sided orientation to Soviet pegagogy. Another weak point was its isolation from the international educational theory, practice, and educational policy. This led to a loss of prestige of educational research among teachers, parents, and scientists in other fields.

The organizational and institutional basis of educational research is weakening. In the early 1990s some of the previous research institutions and coordinating bodies were abolished and others underwent a process of reorganization. The budget of research institutions was cut. The main task was to increase their productivity by the new developed research grant systems. Grants for educational research and development are awarded by the Ministry of Education (School Research and School Development Fund, Higher Education Development Fund) and by the Government Research Grant Agency. A significant contribution was the analysis of the system of Czechoslovak higher education which was conducted for the OECD in 1992. Since 1993, the PHARE Program of the EU has stimulated two projects concerning renewal of the whole educational system, restructuring the labor force, and the improvement of vocational education and training in the CR.

School monitoring and evaluation services were not developed 1994 but it is expected that they will be established as part of the independent inspection service.

10. Major Reforms in the 1980s and 1990s

The political, economic, and educational reforms which took place after 1989 are considered to be the beginning of a long-term transformation process to bring the CR to a level corresponding to that of the European Union countries and one that is comparable with the other advanced countries of the world. Six teams of specialists were established and they have presented comprehensive programs for the development of the educational system. These programs were published in the press and were submitted for discussion to the teaching profession and to the public. The terms were in general agreement but differed in their emphasis on different aspects of the transformation. The most comprehensive of these programs recommended a quantitative development of the educational system so that 60 to 70 percent of the population would eventually have full secondary education. At the same time, the authors suggested that demanding examination standards should be set and observed. The program recommended a differentiated education of pupils in schools with a heterogeneous population. New public bodies for curriculum development should be established. Change should be brought about in the entire social and emotional climate of schools and activity methods should be used. Major decisions should be decentralized and schools should be given greater autonomy. Some of the major prerequisities for this were seen to be the improvement of the pre- and inservice training of teachers, and the enhancement of educational research and of innovation processes in the schools.

Other teams suggested giving priority to an internal reform of the educational system before quantitative growth and structural changes. A process of humanization of relations between students and teachers should be given priority. Still other teams gave preference to the development of private education—a radical liberalization of the structures, content, and methods of the school. These principles were opposed by those who advocate the view that a strong central control of the educational system should be maintained but quality should be improved through demanding examination procedures. These proponents strive for a return to a selective and vertically articulated system with academic elitist schools admitting children at the age of 11 on the basis of entrance examinations.

In the newly drafted education legislation there are proposals for more liberal curriculum policy. The Ministry should be responsible only for national curriculum and achievement standards at different levels of education. The main responsibility should rest on school-based curriculum development. Each school should become a fully responsible legal body and should establish a school council with a broader participation of parents and community representatives. The decentralization of educational administration will be according to a new scheme of general state, regional, and local administration. Emphasis should be put on a fundamental transformation and diversification of vocational and technical education for youth between the ages of 15 and 19 according to the needs of a changing labor market. There is expected to develop a new system of financing vocational training and modular curriculum systems. The discussion on the future of basic and secondary education has not yet been closed, nor have any final decisions been made on development strategies.

In higher education the following steps have been proposed:

(a) to define more accurately the relations between the state and the autonomy of higher education;

(b) to establish a state-wide "higher education strategy planning group," to stabiliize the internal control of higher education through an arrangement between academic senates and the institutional governing body;

(c) to increase the percentage of graduates of graduates in the population to 25–30 percent, together with the diversification of higher education and the creation of a nonuniversity sector;

(d) to reduce systematically the age of faculty staff, and improve their quality;

(e) to enhance staff development and modernize curricula;

(f) to integrate higher education and the existing academies of science, thereby enhancing the interaction of intstruction and research and obtaining another source of funding for higher education.

11. Major Problems for the Year 2000

As indicated above, there were many proposals for reform after 1989. Whichever policies are adopted, their attainment will depend on the stabilization of the political system, the success of the economic reform and the prosperity of industry, trade, and agriculture. After fulfilling the above-mentioned preconditions it will be possible to apply for membership of the European Union and to achieve the quantitative and qualitative criteria of education development. A further condition will be that educational reform and human resource development are given the highest priority. It will be of great importance to raise the social status, prestige, and initiative of teachers if reform is to be well-conducted.

12. Bibliography

Český statistický úřad 1993 *Statistická ročenka ČR.* SEVT, Praha
Federální statistický úřad 1992 *Statistická ročenka ČSFR.* SEVT, Praha
Gobyová, J 1994 Vývoj školství v České republice po roce 1989. Ústav pro informace ve vzdělávání, Praha
OECD 1992 *Education and the Economy in Central and Eastern Europe. Czech and Slovak Federal Republic.* OECD, Paris
Ústav pro informace ve vzdělávání MŠ/MT ČR 1993 *Statistika školství 1992/93 ČR.* Ústav pro informace ve vzdělávání, Praha

Denmark

M. Jansen and S. Kreiner

1. General Background

Denmark is a state distributed over an area covering 43,000 square kilometers. It is a low-lying country consisting of the Jutland peninsula and numerous islands. The Faroes and Greenland form part of a state union with Denmark, but enjoy extensive self-government. Since 1920 the frontiers of Denmark have remained unchanged.

The total population is slightly over 5.1 million with an average density of about 120 persons per square kilometer. Approximately 26 percent of the population live in metropolitan areas. In 1992, 11 percent of the population was 70 years old or more. This is expected to remain constant but after about the year 2010 it is expected to increase gradually so that by 2030 about 15 percent of the population will belong to the oldest age groups.

Immigration has been very modest (and mainly from North and West European countries). In 1992 immigrants formed 3 percent of the population. The immigration of persons from countries far from the Northern cultural areas has caused some educational problems.

Nearly 90 percent of the population belong to the state Lutheran Church. However, there is complete freedom of worship, and religion is considered a personal matter. Lutheranism—as well as other religions—is taught in school. (Parents may request that their children are exempted from this instruction, but this is seldom put into practice.)

Danish is the mother tongue of nearly everyone living in Denmark, apart from immigrants. Danish is also spoken in the Faroe Islands where the total population is about 47,500. The Faroese children are taught Danish from their third or fourth year of school. A part of their education is still conducted in Danish.

Greenland has a population of approximately 55,500. In certain aspects, it is still a separate administrative area of Denmark. Children are taught the Greenland language from their first years of school. The teaching of Danish starts in Grade 3. The objectives of the school are very similar to those of the Danish school, and quite a few teachers still come from Denmark.

In northern Germany, in the state of Schleswig-Holstein, there are about 5,000 children who attend Danish schools where they learn both Danish and German.

The family background has played an essentially larger part in relation to the tradition of seeking education than have geographical barriers or the degree of urbanization. This could create great imbalance were it not partly equalized by a well-developed further educational system and inservice training facilities which are provided in almost all parts of the country.

Agriculture used to be an important area of employment but in 1992 only about 1.7 percent of the total workforce was employed in this sector. The industrial sector employs about 22 percent of the population and about 34 percent is employed in education, health services, and social services as well as in public administration. Two other main areas of employment are the Danish mercantile marine operating abroad and tourism, which is rapidly increasing. Denmark is a relatively prosperous country. Nevertheless, for a number of years the country has experienced certain financial difficulties. There has also been increasing unemployment (just under 12% in 1994).

Denmark is a kingdom and the country is governed according to the principles of the parliamentary democracy. From the 1930s to 1980 Denmark was mainly ruled by the Social Democrats ("the Danish Labor Party"), usually supported by the Social-Liberal Party. However, since 1970 there has been considerably more political mobility than before and since the early 1980s, the country had been governed by a Center/Conservative government. In January 1993, this was succeeded by a majority government of four parties led by the Social Democrats.

2. Politics and the Goals of the Education System

In the Danish *folkeskole* (elementary and lower secondary school) it is a characteristic feature that there is both formal and, in particular, informal well-functioning cooperation with parents. There is a trend for the large parent influence on school to increase; thus far this has taken place in cooperation with the teachers. The legislative aims of the *folkeskole* are under constant debate. One main aim is that the individual must be able to develop optimally within the framework of the community.

The law about the *folkeskole* includes the following points:

1. The *folkeskole* is the municipal primary and lower secondary school offering education under the provisions of the present Act.
2. The task of the *folkeskole* is, in cooperation with parents, to offer opportunities for pupils to acquire knowledge, skills, working methods, and forms of expression which will contribute to the all-round development of each individual pupil.
3. The *folkeskole* shall, in all of its activities, endeavor to create opportunities for experience and self-expression

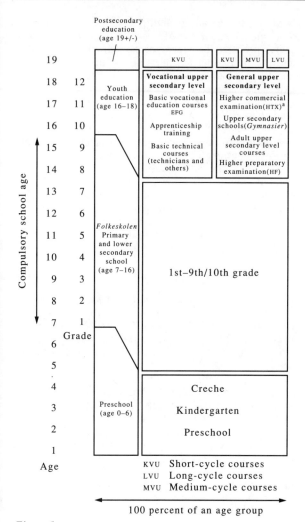

19   Postsecondary education (age 19+/-)

Age	Grade			
19		KVU	KVU MVU LVU	
18	12	Youth education (age 16–18)	**Vocational upper secondary level**	**General upper secondary level**
17	11		Basic vocational education courses EFG	Higher commercial examination(HTX)[a]
16	10		Apprenticeship training	Upper secondary schools(*Gymnasier*)
15	9		Basic technical courses (technicians and others)	Adult upper secondary level courses
14	8			Higher preparatory examination(HF)
13	7	*Folkeskolen* Primary and lower secondary school (age 7–16)	1st–9th/10th grade	
12	6			
11	5			
10	4			
9	3			
8	2			
7	1			
6	Grade			
5				
4		Preschool (age 0–6)	Creche	
3			Kindergarten	
2			Preschool	
1				

Compulsory school age

KVU   Short-cycle courses
LVU   Long-cycle courses
MVU   Medium-cycle courses

100 percent of an age group

Figure 1
Denmark: Structure of the formal education system[a]
Source: Ministry of Education and Research 1992 *Education in Denmark*
a The higher commercial examination is either taken after a 2-year supplementary course following the vocational upper secondary level or after a 1-year supplementary course following the general upper secondary level

that can promote the pupil's urge to learn, to expand the imagination, and to develop the capacity for independent judgment and opinion.
4. The *folkeskole* shall prepare the pupils for active participation in life and decision-making in a democratic society and for sharing responsibility for the solution of common problems. The educational activities of the school and its daily life as a whole must therefore be based on intellectual freedom and democracy.

3. The Formal System of Education

Education in Denmark is free, and is compulsory for nine years from 7 to 16 years of age (see Fig. 1).

About 90 percent of pupils attend the *folkeskole*. The remaining 10 percent attend private schools, supported by the state, which provides up to 80 percent of the expenses for teachers' salaries and other expenditures.

3.1 Primary, Secondary, and Tertiary Education

The Danish *folkeskole* has short school days (20–36 lessons per week, distributed over five days) and a relatively long school year (200 days). The average number of pupils per class is 19, and the pupil–teacher ratio is about 10:3.

The *folkeskole* is fully comprehensive in Grades 1–7. In Grades 8–10 the school is comprehensive except in mathematics, English, German, physics, and chemistry. In these subjects, the pupils can be differentiated into a basic course and an advanced course. Since 1975 more and more schools have applied a nonstreamed education. In 1992 there was, in practice, a nonstreamed comprehensive school for two-thirds of the pupils from Grades 1–9 (Skov 1992).

Grade 10 in the *folkeskole* is optional. This grade has been the subject of some discussion. It is regarded as being both a final school year preparing students for life outside education in general, and an entrance to other educational institutions. After Grade 9 the pupils may, in principle, leave school or enter further schooling. Over the years there has been much discussion about frequent restructuring of educational institutions.

There are many different youth and adult education programs. The municipal youth schools work in relatively close cooperation with the *folkeskole*. Some young people take subjects at a *folkeskole* while others take subjects at a youth school. Furthermore, there are quite a few continuation schools, in most cases boarding schools, for the same age groups. These schools offer formal education at the level of the *folkeskole*. In 1990, about 14,000 pupils attended these continuation schools which, to a considerable extent, receive pupils who want an education outside the *folkeskole* and private schools, but similar to Grades 8–10 of the basic school.

Approximately 57 percent choose vocational education, 34 percent upper secondary school or a higher preparatory course, while 9 percent leave school with no further education after compulsory basic education. The school enrollment rates in the late 1980s were 100 percent for basic education, 91 percent for the secondary level, and about 30 percent for the tertiary level.

Approximately one-third of a cohort takes a traditional three-year college preparatory course at a *gymnasium* leading to the Upper Secondary School Leaving Examination (*Studentereksamen*) or a two-year course leading to the Higher Preparatory Examination (*Højere Forberedelseseksamen* [HF]). Two vocationally oriented alternatives are the Higher Commercial Examination (*Højere Handelseksamen* [HH]) and the Higher Technical Examination (*Højere Teknisk Eksamen* [HTX]), both of which are comparable with the Upper Secondary School Leaving Examination, that is, giving entrance to higher education. Besides these four types of upper secondary education, it is possible to attend two-year day or evening courses leading to the Upper Secondary School Leaving Examination (*Studenterkurser*) or to take all or part of the HF examination on a single-subject basis, usually either at a *gymnasium* or at an adult education center (VUC).

Students who have completed Grade 9 or 10 of the *folkeskole* can be admitted to a *gymnasium* on the basis of a statement issued by their earlier school to the effect that they are qualified or partly qualified for studies at this level. Depending on their choice of course pupils must have passed the Leaving Examination of the *folkeskole* in certain subjects with a satisfactory result and have followed at least the basic course in certain other subjects.

The *gymnasium* is divided into two main tracks: one for languages and one for mathematics. However, about 50 percent of the time is taken up by compulsory subjects common to all students. The rest of the time is spent on optional subjects taught at two different levels: advanced and intermediate. In order to complete a course of study at a *gymnasium* successfully, students must sit a total of 10 written and oral tests for the *Studentereksamen*. The certificate gives access to universities and other types of higher education, although admission to some faculties is only granted to students with a pass in a particular branch of study. All other students may be required to pass supplementary examinations in subjects relevant to their chosen field of study. It is possible to supplement an Upper Secondary School Leaving Examination or a Higher Preparatory Examination in a number of key subjects.

The Higher Preparatory Examination (HF) was introduced in 1967 in a political climate of extending educational privilege to new groups in society. Originally the idea was to create a two-year course aimed specifically at prospective candidates for teacher-training. However, there was concern that this concept might result in an educational dead end, so the course design was changed into an alternative route to higher and further education, formally (though it has to be said not always in reality) equivalent to the existing three-year course leading to the *Studentereksamen*.

The students entering the new HF courses (sharing staff and buildings with teacher-training colleges and *gymnasiums*) were mainly adults. From the start, however, HF also appealed to young people who for social, personal, or gender reasons have not followed the straight route via the *gymnasium* to further education. Thus, HF is the "sweeper" of the general upper secondary education level. In the *gymnasium* there is (still) an overrepresentation of middle-class children, with male and female students equally represented, whereas HF recruits its predominantly female students from a broader base of society. The examination is

both written and oral and, as is the case with the *Studentereksamen*, the Ministry of Education and Research prepares the papers for the written examinations and the individual teacher sets the oral examination questions which must, however, be approved by the external examiners.

Higher education in Denmark is organized in such a way as to enable students to change from one institution or course of education to another without losing qualifications already acquired. Apart from the examinations mentioned above it is possible for applicants with other qualifications to be admitted after an assessment of their qualifications. However, limited capacity means that the *numerus clausus* is often applied for many educational courses.

In most cases, courses resemble those of most other countries on the European continent. The periods of study generally last for five or six years.

3.2 Preschool Education

Preschool education is voluntary. About 50 percent of children aged 3 to 6 attend kindergartens, which are not connected with the school. About 98 percent of any year group attends an optional kindergarten class (for children aged 5–6); this class is connected with the school.

Both in principle and in practice there is no formal education before Grade 1. Preschool education does not, or only to an extremely limited degree, include formal teaching in the subject areas of school (Danish, mathematics, etc.). The primary aim is a social education. Since the mid-1980s there has been cooperation between the preschool classes and their teachers on one hand and the teachers of Grades 1 and 2 on the other, called "coordinated school start." This coordination, which seldom aims at full integration, has no institutional connection with kindergartens.

3.3 Special Education

With strongly increasing social demands on Danish pupils in general there has been an interest in developing special education.

In 1991–92, 98 percent of all children were educated in the regular classroom setting, but 1.6 percent of all children were educated in special classes within the *folkeskole*, while 0.3 percent of all children were enrolled in special schools. In the 1970s, the development of special classes, and to a certain degree special schools, became the focus of developing special education within the framework of the ordinary school and preferably also within the ordinary class in such a way that "a principle of nearness" in relation to home and classmates was maintained.

Educationally, however, it was and is easier to try to meet the very different qualifications of the pupils (often very weak qualifications) within a system of special education than within the ordinary class.

Special preschool services are provided to children aged up to 6 years with disabilities. In 1992, approximately 2.3 percent of all children in this age group received such special support. Twice as many boys as girls receive special services.

The overall special education population attending Danish public schools is composed of children in each of the following categories:

(a) approximately 13 percent of children referred because of behavioral problems;

(b) approximately 14 percent of children referred because of intelligence problems;

(c) approximately 6 percent of children referred because of speech impairment;

(d) approximately 7 percent of children with identified sensory or physical impairments;

(e) approximately 60 percent of children referred because of "learning problems"; the vast majority of these children receive support in Danish, especially in reading.

About 12.5 percent of the overall school population enrolled in the Danish public school system receive special education services at any given time. Taking into account all forms of special education, approximately 25 percent of the overall school population will receive special education services for some period of time during their schooling. This covers both pupils who have received special education for only a very short period (perhaps a few lessons for a couple of months) and pupils receiving extensive special education during their entire schooling.

Separate classes within a *folkeskole* are usually offered to children within each of the following categories: (a) severe mental disorders; (b) brain damaged; (c) extreme reading difficulties; (d) severely hearing impaired; and (e) physically handicapped. Children with more severe disabilities are usually enrolled in special schools. There is no general formalized transition for severely handicapped children from special schools to a trade. However, in a few cases, a mentor may be responsible for the pupil for a period of time.

Young people of 14 to 18 years of age may attend youth schools offering education and training to increase their chances of employment and integration into society, or production schools receiving young unemployed people who have been unable to finish a qualifying training course and whose motivation for re-entering the educational system is limited or nonexistent. At the higher secondary school level special education may be provided for handicapped students.

The Act concerning special education for adults directs the counties to provide education and special educational support to adults with physical or mental handicaps for the purpose of redressing or limiting the effects of such handicaps. This education takes place at the county's speech clinics, institutes for the blind or hearing impaired, or at schools for persons with general learning difficulties (mentally handicapped), and persons with psychiatric handicaps. The counties may also enter into agreements with private organizations for the provision of special tuition. The number of pupils is approximately 75,000 per year, equal to approximately 1 million lessons. The expenditure of the counties for special education was about DKr 580 million for 1991.

3.4 Vocational, Technical, and Business Education

There is a limited connection between educational provision on the one hand (which formally endeavors to upgrade the most unqualified) and actual demand by both private enterprises and public institutions on the other. The whole system of vocational training was changed at the beginning of the 1990s. Adult vocational education comes under the 1990 Open Education Act; vocational education and training for young people was reformed in 1991 under the auspices of the Ministry of Education and Research. The overall purpose of this system is to ensure a high level of professional expertise together with a correspondingly high level of adaptation to the demands and requirements of production.

The basis of all vocational training in Denmark is a sandwich system; for young people, school and apprenticeship (the dual system); and, for adults the interaction between work and short courses (one-week or evening classes). A typical technical course lasts 4 years, of which 80 weeks will normally be spent at school. In the commercial field, the courses are of 3 years' (46 weeks in school) duration. The detailed structure of the courses is laid down by the trade committees. All courses are officially authorized, and targets are set by the government in coorperation with the social partners. For students who have a training agreement from the outset, the length of schooling is considerably shorter (60 weeks to 24 weeks in school).

Colleges are self-governing, which means that they have a high degree of freedom from local political influence. However, at the same time, local social partners relevant to the programs or courses are represented on the board of the self-governing institution. The Ministry of Labor offers short courses (week-long) for skilled and semi-skilled labor on a modular basis.

3.5 Adult and Nonformal Education

Apart from the above-mentioned vocational courses, adult education and, at least to a certain degree, youth education is noncompulsory. It is based on a very long tradition of freedom to study.

The Act concerning general education provides for support to the Danish adult education organizations with approximately DKr 1 billion per year. Moreover, about DKr 500 million is allotted to educational associations and approximately the same amount is given to the continuation schools (municipal, voluntary youth school). The many associations in Denmark—from house-owners' associations to trade unions, from housewives' leagues to environmental organizations—contribute considerably towards informal social education. Even though this does not form part of the formal education system, it is very important for informal (and essential) general education.

Evening schools for adults are very common. They cover a wide range of subjects, depending on the interests of the students attending classes once or twice a week for courses lasting a few weeks, six months, or more. A remarkably wide section of the population attends these evening schools, which cover extremely different spheres of interest. Previously, the evening schools were, in practice, free; they now charge fees of various sizes and this has caused considerable disturbance, both regarding application and contents. Ninety-four percent of adult education courses are arranged by private promotors (mostly large educational organizations or municipal organizations). The state awards a grant to approved open education courses in order to reduce the expense to users.

At the folk high schools, the pupils must be over 17 years of age. About 15,000 persons attend long courses of 5–8 months and about 44,000 persons attend courses, some being as short as one week. To a great extent, these schools (102 schools in 1992) were founded upon the principles represented by NFS Grundtvig (1783–1872), Danish pastor and poet, and inspirer of, among other things, a national involvement in all education. Public aid can be obtained for payment of residence at folk high schools.

The Act concerning education of adult immigrants directs the counties to offer education to immigrants, to make it possible for them to function in Danish society. Such education should consist mainly of courses in the Danish language, Danish culture and social conditions. The number of participants was about 36,450 in 1991; this is the equivalent of about 751,851 lessons. The counties' immigrant education budget for 1991 was about DKr 254 million.

The 1990 Open Education Act combines several fields of education under the Ministry of Education and Research in one law dealing mainly with government grants, whereas the responsibility for the content still lies with the respective advisory bodies, universities, Ministry of Education and Research, and so on. The aim of the Act is to provide further education opportunities to adults in the form of vocationally oriented qualifying part-time education courses and single-subject courses in order that the participants can upgrade their qualifications relevant for their present or future employment.

At the educational institutions under the Ministry of Education and Research, open education is offered in the field of vocational education and technical colleges, as well as in the field of higher education (universities, business schools, colleges of engineering, etc.). In order to be admitted, participants must usually meet the same requirements of previous education or qualifications that apply to ordinary students of the educational institutions. Courses must be organized in such a way that they can be attended outside working hours by persons in full-time employment and also so that persons maintain their unemployment benefits. Participation in open education activities does not entitle students to receive state educational support.

4. Administrative and Supervisory Structure and Operation

Denmark has a tradition of extensive local government; responsibility for the functioning of the educational system lies with the local authorities. The school system is decentralized, but the Minister of Education and Research has an overarching role. In principle, an attempt is made to limit the influence of the central administration on educational institutions in favour of some degree of local self-government for the individual institution. However, in practice, the budget is, to a large extent, centrally controlled.

Preschool education is administered by the Ministry of Social Affairs. Primary and lower secondary schools are run by the local authorities. The majority of upper secondary schools are run by the counties. The universities and higher educational institutions are mainly run by the state. All county, municipal, and private schools are subsidized by the state.

At the municipal level, responsibility for primary and lower secondary schools lies with the municipal council and its education committee. The general trend is markedly toward an increasing parental influence. Within the various sections of the education system attempts are made to secure a stronger position for the leadership, a fact which causes certain complications when viewed in connection with the traditionally strong staff influence.

Upper secondary education, the *gymnasier* (and HF) schools are, in general, the responsibility of the county councils. Each school has a school council. The school timetable must be approved by the school council which also has a say in how the school budget is spent. The daily administration of the individual *gymnasier* (including the institutions to which the HF courses are affiliated) is in the hands of school principals who are assisted by various governing bodies.

Further and higher education is provided at universities and at a number of specialist technical colleges (e.g., in engineering). The vast majority of these institutions are under the Ministry of Education and Research. The rector represents the institution externally and is responsible for the daily supervision of the administration. It is his or her responsibility to see to it that matters are put before the relevant collegiate board or committee when decisions are to be made. The management of the universities and the institutions of higher education has been the subject of violent debate. For a number of years the students have had a certain degree of influence and, in some cases, even a strong influence. However, in the early 1990s, negotiations were under way to change this so that the management of these institutions would have a stronger position.

5. Educational Finance

In 1991, Denmark spent DKr 38 billion on education, equal to 12 percent of total public expenditure, or 7.5 percent of the GNP. In comparison, social services accounted for approximately 40 percent and health for 9 percent respectively of the state budget.

The distribution of the expenses for the education system has changed considerably since the early 1980s. Primary and secondary education used to represent more than 50 percent of the total education budget. During the 1980s this share was reduced to 42 percent. The expenses for technical and vocational education and higher education have increased to approximately 20 percent each of the total education budget. However, the item to have increased the most is the one representing the expenses for adult education which was approximately 14 percent in 1991; this was double that of the early 1950s.

The state covers approximately 80 percent of the expenses of the public schools, while the parents pay the remaining 20 percent. Expenses for private schools have increased while, at the same time, the expenses for the *folkeskole* have been reduced.

In 1982, 6 percent of the total expenses for primary and secondary school were spent on private schools. By the early 1990s this share had increased to 7.25 percent.

The state educational support which includes both scholarships and study loans at all levels of the education system for students aged 18 and over was increased in the 1980s. In 1988 the educational support system was changed, and in the early 1990s was, to a large extent, conditional on the students' completing their studies within the stipulated time. There are also more scholarships and fewer loans.

6. Supplying Personnel for the Education System

In 1989–90, there were approximately 85,000 teachers. The number of part-time teachers in primary and secondary school declined during the 1980s. In 1992, there were 18 colleges for training primary and lower secondary school teachers. The vast majority of the teachers have had a four-year training. They have all passed the upper secondary school leaving examination or its equivalent. The curriculum covers psychology, educational theory, social studies, teaching practice, Danish, mathematics, religion, and different optional subjects.

After training, the teachers are qualified to teach all classes from Grades 1 to 10, and nearly all of them do so. To a large extent, the teachers apply for further training, especially at the Royal Danish School of Educational Studies, ranging from short courses to degree courses. There is also a variety of local inservice training courses; more importance has been attached to local inservice training than used to be the case. The inservice teacher training system is under considerable pressure due to a large number of applications for paid or partly paid further education.

Upper secondary school teachers are normally university graduates who have completed their university studies and a six-month course in educational theory and practice.

The state institute for the educational training of vocational teachers offers courses to permanent teachers at vocational schools. The teachers at the technical schools have very different qualifications. Many of them have completed higher education. Others have been educated within the various subject areas; the education is then supplemented in different ways.

University teachers and teachers at further and higher education institutions are graduates of these institutions. Emphasis is placed on their research qualifications.

Teachers in adult education have a diversified educational background. Most of them hold their positions for a season or in addition to their usual work.

7. Curriculum Development and Teaching Methodology

The Ministry of Education and Research sets the objectives for all subjects at each grade level. However, the local educational authorities and the individual school have a high degree of influence on the daily routine of the school. Teachers are free to choose whatever teaching method they consider best, and each individual school determines its own specific curriculum within the framework of the overall objectives mentioned above.

Teaching materials are written on a private basis and are mostly published by commercial publishing companies. There is no control of the scope and content of textbooks, and the competition is very keen. In some areas, technical development has resulted in a great reduction and readjustment of the production of textbooks. The introduction of new technology into the schools may well have an influence on the teaching materials. By the early 1990s, however, there has been more talk of such things as computers than actual procurement of such materials, especially in primary and lower secondary schools, where the replacement of materials has generally been modest for a number of years.

271

In a rapidly changing society such as the Danish one, and in a language area as small as the Danish one, it is neither technically nor financially possible to update the teaching material at the rate prescribed by the surrounding world. For instance, the school consumption of textbooks for geography, history, mathematics, literature, and so on, cannot possibly keep up with the frequent changes.

However, an effective utilization of the library system—public libraries, school libraries and local centers of educational materials—has, to a limited extent, remedied the gravest defects.

It is to be expected that foreign language education will be accorded more emphasis. At the same time there has been pronounced national backing of a strengthening of Danish mother tongue education, mainly in primary and lower secondary school, but also in other parts of the educational system. This strengthening of Danish reading, literature, and culture has taken place at the same time as Denmark has not only become more engaged in closer European cooperation but has also been experiencing more immigration.

Instructional differentiation, rather than pupil differentiation, is on the increase. Instructional differentiation is not only a question of the teacher's organization of the instruction. It is essential that both the individual pupil and the class gradually participate in the organization of their own learning. Hence, together with teacher and classmates, a pupil may participate in laying down individual and common objectives for a given period of learning. In the process, pupils learn to choose adequate working methods and materials and to share in the responsibility for instruction and for the subsequent evaluation of whether the objectives were achieved. This presupposes that the individual pupil has a realistic awareness of his or her own learning possibilities.

By 1993, there were no clear guidelines describing how instructional differentiation should form part of daily education. It is a principle and can only be put into practice if all parties involved in the education endeavor to share the responsibility for it.

8. *The System of Examinations, Promotions, and Certifications*

In all Danish schools, students are automatically promoted from one grade to the next according to age. In primary education there is no end-of-year examination and no marks are given for the first seven years of compulsory education.

In Grades 8–10, marks can be given on a 10-point scale. There is a leaving examination at the end of Grade 9, and an advanced leaving examination at the end of Grade 10. They may be taken on a single-subject basis and the pupils themselves decide if they will sit for the examination. There is no pass mark.

Under these circumstances, promotion is not a problem and only very few pupils are not promoted; however, there is an extensive system of special education within the class. A common marking scale is used throughout the educational system. In the *gymnasier* marks have a far greater importance; they are given regularly, and the students must pass an examination in each subject in order to obtain a leaving certificate. In the HF courses no marks are given except at the leaving examination for which there is a pass mark.

Examinations at universities and higher educational institutions are much the same as in other Northern and European countries. In the early 1990s, endeavors were under way to have the Danish educational system parallel educational systems both within the European Community and also in those countries to which Danish students often go to continue their studies.

In theory, a Danish pupil may pass through the educational system from kindergarten class up to the last month of Grade 9 without being faced with a single test or without being formally examined. However, in reading and spelling there is a tradition of using tests to some extent in order to decide whether a pupil should have some form of formal or informal special education. Should a recommendation for special education be the result, then a further test is administered by a specially trained test teacher, consultant, or school psychologist.

Commercially prepared tests in mathematics are used to a certain extent, but at the instigation of the individual teacher or school. In the 1980s, diagnostic reading and spelling tests were published by The Danish National Institute for Educational Research. These diagnostic tests are becoming popular in ordinary education. They cover mainly Grades 2 to 9.

9. *Educational Assessment, Evaluation, and Research*

From time to time there has been central interest in educational research and development.

Since the mid-1980s there has been an increasing interest on the part of the government in developing "quality programs." For example, folders, books, and booklets have been prepared with the purpose of inspiring schools and teachers to be more "quality oriented." An engagement in this respect can hardly be questioned, neither by government, nor by municipalities or pupils, parents, and teachers. However, there is no full agreement when it comes to methods of encouraging quality development or, for that matter, with respect to what constitutes quality.

Cooperation with the Organisation for Economic Co-operation and Development (OECD) and other Scandinavian and Western countries about evaluation is in progress. Researchers and government officials from these countries form "travelling teams," "panels," or groups in an effort to evaluate parts of the Danish education system.

Proposals for a systematic national evaluation program have been discussed—in particular with the Danish National Institute for Educational Research. So far no such proposals have met with approval. However, Denmark has participated in the International Association for the Evaluation of Educational Achievement (IEA) Reading Literacy Study and in the 1990s in the IEA mathematics and science study.

It is not possible to identify what parts of the budget for the school sector are spent on educational assessment, evaluation, and research; in comparison with what is seen in the other Scandinavian countries and in Western Europe—countries usually comparable to Denmark—it is probably a question of relatively limited amounts.

10. Major Reforms in the 1980s and 1990s

The Danish educational system has been under constant restructuring since the early 1970s, but the focus has shifted from level to level.

An administration of relatively flexible rules has further developed a long tradition in that adjustments may take place continuously within the framework of current laws and regulations. At the same time, there is a standing public debate about the education system. There is a tradition that legislation dealing with education—at least compulsory education—is practically always enacted with a very large majority.

11. Major Problems for the Year 2000

The period of nine years' compulsory education is likely to be continued. The education of young people is likely to receive greater vocational emphasis. "Recurrent education" (i.e., continuing further education as well as continuous inservice education) will probably emerge in various forms. In all likelihood, further education and inservice training will be financially demanding. Such training is likely to be run by public and private enterprises alike and take place within individual businesses and in public educational institutions.

An increasing percentage of an age cohort will receive more and more education but at a slightly reduced rate than before, and probably in such a way that further and inservice education will receive more emphasis. The trends indicate that individuals with intermediate and higher education will account for the majority of those attending further and inservice education, in spite of many public statements about offering more possibilities to less well-educated youth and adults.

The essential—and most difficult—task will be to establish a tradition of pupils using their specific educational competence in connection with their general knowledge and their specific and general prior knowledge and comprehension.

In the 1980s the term "functional illiteracy" was the subject of debate, which seemed unreasonable to most people, considering that an overwhelming majority of Danes read—and a very large proportion of them read a lot. The discussion seemed even more unreasonable given that the absolute number of functional illiterates will decrease as the older generations are replaced by younger and better educated generations. The Danish library system is one of the most developed in the world and the reading level of Danes represents a high figure internationally, especially where children are concerned.

However, there is still a problem of "functional illiteracy" linked to greatly increasing demands both of society and employers. Something similar may be expected to happen in other subject areas, resulting in a focus on "functional mathematics" and "functional competence in foreign languages."

There is a considerable and increasing dynamism in the demands made on the competence of the individual. It is anticipated that it will be difficult for the formal education system to live up to this dynamism which should result in the optimal education for all persons in any age cohort.

References

Ministry of Education and Research 1992 *Education in Denmark—The Education System*. Ministry of Education and Research, Copenhagen
Skov P 1992 *A Way to Improve Teaching — Differentiated Teaching through Formative Evaluation*. The Danish National Institute for Educational Research, Copenhagen

Further Reading

Blake M E 1984 Reading in Denmark: A relaxed atmosphere is the key. *Read. Teach* 38(1): 42–47
Danish School Libraries 1982 *Danish School Libraries*. The Danish Association of School Librarians, Copenhagen
Jansen M 1985 Language and concepts: Play or work? Seriousness or fun? Basics or creativity? In: Clark M M (ed.) 1985 *New Directions in the Study of Reading*. Falmer Press, London
Jansen M 1987 *The Fight Against Illiteracy—Described from a Danish Starting Point*. Report prepared for The International Office of the Ministry of Education and Research. The Danish National Institute for Educational Research, Copenhagen
Jansen M 1989 Literacy. In: Galton M, Blyth A (eds.) 1989 *Handbook of Primary Education in Europe*. David Fulton, London
Lundberg I, Frost J, Petersen O P 1988 Effects of an extensive program for stimulating phonological awareness in preschool children. *Read. Res. Q.* 23(3): 263–84
Mejding J 1992 Reading ability—More than basic skills. In: Belanger P, Winter C, Sutton A (eds.) 1992 *Literacy and Basic Education in Europe on the Eve of the 21st Century*. Swets and Zeitlinger, Lisse
Ministry of Education and Research 1973 *Special Education in Denmark*. Ministry of Education, Copenhagen

Ministry of Education and Research 1988 *The Folkeskole—Primary and Lower Secondary Education in Denmark.* Ministry of Education, Copenhagen

Ministry of Education and Research 1989 *Special Education in Denmark—with Particular Emphasis on Reading Disabilities.* The Danish National Institute for Educational Research and the Ministry of Education and Research, Copenhagen

Ministry of Education and Research 1991 *Act on the Folkeskole.* Ministry of Education and Research, Copenhagen

Ministry of Education and Research 1991 *Handicapped Students in the Danish Educational System.* Ministry of Education and Research, Copenhagen

Ministry of Education and Research 1991 *The Folkeskole.* Ministry of Education, Copenhagen

Ministry of Education and Research 1991 *The Danish Gymnasium.* Ministry of Education and Research, Copenhagen

Ministry of Education and Research 1991 *The Danish Higher Preparatory Examination.* Ministry of Education and Research, Copenhagen

Ministry of Education and Research 1993 *Facts and Figures. Education Indicators—Denmark.* Ministry of Education and Research, Copenhagen

Pagaard P E 1991 *Reading Development and Reading Comprehension.* The Danish National Institute for Educational Research, Copenhagen

Dominica

M. E. Peters

1. General Background

The Commonwealth of Dominica is the largest island in the Windward group and the English-speaking Eastern Caribbean. With an area of 750 kilometers, the island is located between the French islands of Guadeloupe and Martinique. Dominica has an extremely mountainous topography and is heavily dissected by valleys and rivers. It abounds in thick rain forests and has an average annual rainfall of 100 inches.

The geographical factor of climate influences the education system without one being aware of it. In Dominica's tropical climate, children start going to school at the age of 3. Although the climate should influence the selection of architectural design and construction materials, there are instances where the wide-open spaces in some institutions permit the uninterrupted entry of heavy rainfall. There is, however, an abundance of concrete, brick, and stone in the construction of educational institutions.

Preliminary reports of the 1991 census put the population at 71,794 a decrease of 3.8 percent over the 1981 figures. This drop in population has been attributed to migration. A substantial proportion of the total population—20,000 or 28 percent—live within the city limits of Roseau. This proportion is about the same as in the 1981 census. The percentage of the population that is either Black or of mixed race is over 97 percent, with most of the remainder being Amerindians.

Language presents a major problem in the planning and implementation of both formal and nonformal systems of education. The national language in Dominica is English, but there are also several dialects, each with its own uniqueness depending on the part of the island from which it emanates. These dialects constitute a serious interference with the writing and speaking of standard English. One method which has been devised to counteract this adversity is to teach English-as-a-Second-Language (ESL). In fact, ESL has been the focus of summer workshops for teachers for a number of years.

In the area of nonformal adult education, the Centre for Adult Education uses Creole for effective oral communication, but their written materials are in English.

The general development goals of Dominica are well-articulated in the Commonwealth of Dominica National Structure Plan, 1979–90. The overall objectives of the government's socioeconomic development policies is the elimination of poverty and the raising of the living standards of the population.

The government hopes to achieve this objective through the development of a mixed economy and the encouragement of private-sector development in the economic development process.

In addition, the decentralization of the development decision-making process appears to be a key policy element in facilitating the realization of overall objectives.

In order to create linkages between the overall development objective and the education system the following goals have been proposed in education:

(a) To increase the capacity of the people to participate in socioeconomic development and increase their level of welfare;

(b) to emphasize technical and vocational goals and provide educational delivery systems which will provide the needed labor for the present and future development of the nation;

(c) to increase the level of functional literacy among the population;

(d) to develop and encourage nonformal education in addition to formal education;

(e) to encourage accessibility to postsecondary education to qualified nationals of Dominica;

(f) to ensure local community participation and involvement in the education system.

Generally these goals are not primarily concerned with new buildings or plant at the primary level, particularly in the light of the stabilization of school enrollments. Efforts are being centered on adapting the education system to satisfy national needs and to improve various factors which influence educational outcomes. These include the following:

(a) The junior-secondary program and the establishment of centers of instruction;

(b) A national literacy program which was initiated with the goal of eradicating illiteracy from Dominica by the year 2000.

Community participation is encouraged and ensured in the areas of adult education and junior-secondary education.

Based on the 1989 labor force survey (Commonwealth of Dominica 1989), the labor force numbered 30,600. The overall unemployment rate then stood at 11.0 percent. According to the 1981 census, the employed were concentrated in three main occupational groups—skilled agriculture and fishery workers (19.7%), craft and related workers (17.6%), and unskilled manual and general occupations (20.8%). Among the first two categories, men were the most dominant. Women, on the other hand, dominated the secretarial and clerical personnel, and services and sales workers groups.

The four main industrial groups in which the men were employed were agriculture, forestry, and fishing; mining and quarrying; wholesale and retail; and construction. Women dominated wholesale and retail trade, manufacturing, agriculture, and other services.

The highest level of education and training received by most persons in the labor force was that of primary schooling. While 26 percent of women and 13 percent of men had received secondary training, approximately 85 percent of the labor force had no certificate or degree.

There is a higher proportion of females than males in the secondary school system. However, this is not the case in further education as there are less than half as many female as male graduates.

The economy of the country is heavily dependent on export-oriented agricultural products, especially bananas and citrus fruits. However, livestock farming and fishing are also important sources of income and employment. Agriculture remains by far the largest contributor to the Gross Domestic Product (GDP) (35%

in 1988), although there has been some increase in manufacturing's share as a result of efforts to diversify into textiles, agroprocessing, and component assembly.

Economic performance in the 1980s was mixed with annual GDP growth rates ranging from 1.75 percent in 1985 to 6.4 percent in 1986 and 5.6 percent in 1988.

During the third quarter of 1991, there were significant decreases in overall economic activity within Dominica's economy.

2. Politics and the Goals of the Education System

The chief political goal of the government is to educate its citizens so that they are equipped with the requisite knowledge, skills, and attitudes which would contribute to an improved quality of life.

The overall goal of the Ministry of Education is to establish and maintain appropriate procedures and systems of accountability in order to ensure cost-effective use of available resources in the provision of an education which will develop human resources to meet national goals and needs. In so doing, the Ministry will seek to enhance job satisfaction and stimulate the professional growth of individuals so that organizational needs can be met.

The specific tasks are to:

(a) encourage and develop a highly motivated staff so as to create effectiveness/productivity;

(b) guide/inform the policy-making process and to assist in policy implementation;

(c) develop or upgrade the existing information system so that gathering, storage, access, retrieval, analysis, and reporting of data can be more effective and accurate;

(d) develop management skills for staff so that organizational as well as professional needs can be met.

3. The Formal System of Education

3.1 Primary, Secondary, and Tertiary Education

Formal education begins at the primary level at the age of 5 and is compulsory for 10 years.

The structure of the primary school is similar to that found in other Organization of Eastern Caribbean States; a two-year infant stage followed by a five-year regular stage. The last three years of compulsory schooling is in the junior-secondary program. All of this is undertaken within a school building generally called an "all-age school."

There are 65 primary schools: 54 are government-owned, 5 are government-assisted (teachers' salaries are paid by the government) and owned by the Roman Catholic Church, and 6 are privately owned.

There are 14,314 primary-school students and 605 teachers. Except for four schools, primary schools are coeducational. The school day lasts for 5 hours and the school year comprises 195 days.

The Junior Secondary Programme (JSP) was introduced into Dominica's all-age schools in 1981. The main objective has been the development of community skills in Form I and the development of pre-vocational skills in Forms II and III. The program caters to the students who do not qualify for entry into the secondary school at the annual Common Entrance Examination.

The introduction of the secondary technical/vocational program affected the JSP in many schools. There was a reduction in enrollment figures and a decrease in the ability of entering students as a result of the technical/vocational program "creaming off" the more able students. The program was further hit by limited human and financial resources.

A plan for rationalizing the JSP was put into action in September 1991. Centralized schools were established as centers of instruction.

The majority of the graduates of the JSP prior to 1988 entered the job markets, while 25 top performers entered Form III of the academic secondary schools.

At the secondary level, there are 10 secondary schools: 3 of them are government-owned, 6 are government-assisted, and 1 is private. Some of these schools offer a predominantly academic program, while others offer a mix of academic and technical/vocational programs. In the last 3 years, the technical/vocational program has been introduced into at least four all-age schools. This program attempts, among other things, to provide continuity for students in the JSP.

In 1991, enrollment at the secondary level stood at 4,586 and the teaching staff numbered 251.

Figure 1 represents movement throughout the education system and the proportions of age groups at each level.

It is anticipated that with the expansion of the technical/vocational program there will be a higher percentage of students moving from the primary school into the secondary school. It is also expected that there will be an eventual phasing out of the JSP.

During the period from 1986–88 the largest number of dropouts were in the junior-secondary and secondary programs. From 1988, there has been a significant decline in the number of students dropping out of the junior-secondary program.

The tertiary education system centered in the Clifton Dupigny College of Arts, Science, and Technology, consists of a technical and academic division and a School of Nursing. It was established in 1988 with the merger of the Sixth Form College situated within the Roseau city limits and the Technical College, located 2 miles from Roseau.

Prior to the opening of the Dominica Teachers' Training College in 1973, school teachers in Dominica attended the Leeward Islands Training College in Antigua or Erdiston College in Barbados. In its first two years, the college ran two one-year emergency programs, after which two-year in-college programs were offered so that by 1982 the college had graduated 200 teachers. In 1982 the Teachers' College adopted another form of inservice training, in which the trainees initially remained at the College for two semesters, then returned to their schools and attended block workshops at the College.

In 1986 a decision was taken to revise the existing model to allow trainees to spend three terms in-college and three terms out-of-college.

3.2 Preschool Education

The main objectives of the preschool program are to:

(a) provide experiences within an enriched environment that would prepare preschoolers, in particular the disadvantaged, for school;

(b) increase the potential of children for initial success in school;

(c) provide children with opportunities to realize their individual potential.

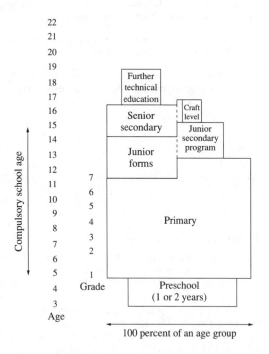

Figure 1
Dominica: Structure of the formal education system 1991

The preschool education program is conducted in 70 registered preschools. There are approximately 99 teachers in the program and approximately 3,000 children between the ages of 3 and 5. This represents some 75 percent of the children in this age group. An inability by parents to meet the termly or monthly fees accounts for a portion of the remaining 25 percent.

Some 49 of the 70 schools are private, while the other 20 are sponsored by the Social Centre and include 2 model schools in the Social Centre Compound. The Social Centre coordinates the training activities of the program and supplements these activities by visits to schools, demonstrations, and workshops.

The preschool program is administered by the Pre-School Advisory Committee on which the Ministry of Education is represented by the Education Officer for Pre-School and managed by the Director of the Social Centre.

3.3 Special Education

In Dominica, there is no legislation or policy specific to special education. However, the Ministry of Education and Sports plans to undertake a national survey to identify children with special needs. Following that survey, a policy paper will be formulated.

In the meantime, there are institutions and programs attempting to respond to the needs of exceptional children. The School for the Deaf caters for children with varying levels of hearing loss. In 1992, the School had 2 teachers, 1 designated Teacher-in-Charge, and a student roll of 16. The School operates through the assistance of local and overseas benefactors. The Alpha Centre, a school for mentally handicapped children, was established in 1974 by the Catholic Church and is managed voluntarily by a board of directors. On average, attendance is between 9 and 10 pupils, out of a possible enrollment of 12. Resource room settings exist in a few schools. They are manned by teachers with little training in special education.

3.4 Vocational, Technical, and Business Education

Entry into any of the divisions of the Clifton Dupigny College of Arts, Science, and Technology (CDCC) is based on well-stipulated requirements. Full-time students attending CDCC pay a fee of EC$20 a semester. Part-time students pay EC$200 annually. Funding is provided through the annual budgetry allocation, and materials are acquired through the occasional project.

The Organization of Eastern Caribbean States (OECS) technical/vocational project provides for the rehabilitation and/or extension of the training facilities of 9 educational training institutions (one of these was the CDCC); the acquisition and utilization of improved and updated equipment; and a program of fellowship training for 25 instructors/supervisors.

Educators in these divisions are constantly aware of modernization forces in the drafting of curricula.

In fact, on the OECS level, there has been a revision of the technical/vocational curriculum, now called the "New Curriculum." Additionally, computer literacy programs have been expanded. However, a limited supply of staff has prevented this innovation from coming on-stream.

3.5 Adult and Nonformal Education

The Ministry of Community Development and Welfare has established a Centre for Adult Education to carry out its programs. The Centre is staffed by the Adult Education Officer, the Assistant Adult Education Officer, the Supervisor of Field Operations, seven Zone Officers, and ancillary staff. Among the objectives of the Centre is the eradication of illiteracy by the year 2000.

The Centre offers a basic education program and skills programs—for instance, home economics (sewing, food and nutrition, and cookery) and the reading of building plans. They also run a postliteracy program on request, and inhouse classes at prisons, places of business, private homes, and so forth. Estimated enrollment at the beginning of the 1990s has been placed at 800 persons. The main target/participant groups are aged 15–99 years.

The Centre receives annual financial allocation from the Ministry but a large proportion of its materials resources are obtained through projects. The Organization of American States is one of its most prominent sponsors. The Caribbean Council for Adult Education and the International Council for Adult Education also play a supportive role.

Village adult education committees also exist, which are made up of civic-minded individuals with a commitment to the educational development of their community.

4. Administrative and Supervisory Structure and Operation

The organizational structure of the Ministry of Education (officially called the Ministry of Education and Sports) developed since Dominica's attainment of associated statehood with Britain in 1967 and then Independence in 1978.

The Ministry is headed by the Minister of Education who is responsible to the Cabinet of the Commonwealth of Dominica and accountable to the House of Assembly for the activities and programs of the Ministry.

The Permanent Secretary (PS) is administrative head of the Ministry and advises the Minister on policy. In addition, the PS supervises the implementation of policy, prepares budgets and keeps the accounts of the Ministry, and manages personnel matters.

The Education Division, which is the largest division of the Ministry of Education and Sports, is headed by the Chief Education Officer.

There are nine Education Officers (EOS) all answerable to the Chief Education Officer. There are four district EOs supervising the primary schools. The principals are responsible for the rest of the staff at their schools. There is an EO/Training, who is also the principal of the Teachers' College, who directly supervises the professional and ancillary staff at the College. The other EOs are for secondary education, curriculum, technical and vocational education, and preschool education, who supervises preschool education nationwide and chairs the Pre-School Education Committee.

The administrative system is centralized. Very limited autonomy prevails except for the submission of recommendations, reappointments, disbursement of funds, and so on, and the supervision that is undertaken at the schools in the districts. However, at the end of 1990, a proposal was made for the restructuring of the Ministry of Education and Sports so that authority could be decentralized.

5. Educational Finance

As a proportion of total government expenditure, Dominica allocated to education just over 17 percent annually during the period from 1984 to 1988. Personnel emoluments accounted for more than 90 percent of the allocation. In 1991–92, the percentage was 16.7.

Of the 1991–92 education allocation, 0.15 percent went to preschool, 57.9 percent to primary education, 25 percent to secondary education, 1.1 percent to junior-secondary, 2 percent to teacher training, and 4.8 percent to further education. The annual cost per student at the primary level is EC$1,006 and EC$1,275 at the secondary level. These funds are raised predominantly through local revenue.

6. Supplying Personnel for the Education System

There is no formal preservice training for teachers. Persons wishing to become teachers apply to the Chief Education Officer for primary schools and directly to the school for secondary education. Upon selection, these persons receive a one- or two-week orientation course. After 5 years of teaching they qualify for training at the Teachers' Training College. Entry into this program requires, apart from 5 years' teaching experience, four General Certificate of Education (GCE) or four Caribbean Examinations Council (CXC) subjects, or a combination of both.

There is no local training offered at the secondary level where the rate of teacher turnover is high and, since Independence, very few university graduates have pursued the Diploma in Education course offered by the University of the West Indies. Added to these circumstances, the diversification of the secondary curriculum has made the need for training at the secondary level even more urgent.

A teacher-training course for nongraduate secondary-school teachers in the OECS project was launched in 1991. The project is concerned with the training and certification of about 700 nongraduate secondary-school teachers within a four- to five-year period via distance education methodology.

Clerical and administrative staff also participate in orientation into the public service workshops which are conducted annually. In an effort to improve the quality of initial training, persons are encouraged to do the Certificate in Public Administration program which is taught by the School of Continuing Studies of the University of the West Indies. These public servants are given time off to study and paid increments on the successful completion of their programs. There are also ongoing staff development exercises and short-term local and overseas training workshops and seminars. The government is in the process of implementing an administrative reform program which would terminate the annual, automatic increments and replace the latter with a bonus-based system for the evaluation of all public servants.

7. Curriculum Development and Teaching Methodology

The Curriculum Development Unit is responsible for the preparation, distribution, and assessment of curriculum materials and the assessment of students in the school system. Limited human and material resources impose serious constraints on the effective functioning of the Unit generally and particularly in student assessment.

A new structure has been proposed for the Unit, which then would be called the Curriculum Development and Examinations Unit. A broad-based committee responsible for directing the process of curriculum development is already in place. Subject panels began work at the end of 1991. The preparation of curriculum material and support material for teachers and students will be the responsibility of these panels.

There is a national curriculum at the primary level and for the Junior Secondary Programme. There has been insufficient curriculum development at the secondary level. Curriculum development activities at the junior-secondary level have been uncoordinated, and no national curriculum exists for Forms I-III. However, at the senior level, the nature of the curriculum is determined by standards set by the Caribbean Examinations Council.

At the beginning of the 1990s a standardization exercise began. The primary goal of standardization was to ensure that students receive materials more in tune with the curriculum.

Implementation of the core curriculum is not problematic, but in areas such as health and family life education and music certain problems have arisen. It has been suggested that the lack of implementation stems not from unwillingness on the part of teachers, but from an inability to teach such subjects and, in the case of health and family life education, a misunderstanding of the nature of the subject.

At the junior-secondary level, students are required to take French and/or Spanish. However, at the senior levels, these become elective subjects.

8. The System of Examinations, Promotions, and Certifications

There are no national criteria and procedures for pupil evaluation in Grades 1–7. There is some level of automatic promotion. In some cases streaming goes on and children get promoted through streams. However, based on achievement, students are able to move across streams. In some extreme cases grade retention occurs.

The Common Entrance Examination is administered annually to Grade 7 students to select students for the secondary schools.

Form III students in the JSP take the National Assessment Examinations. Successful students receive a certificate at either Level I, II, or III.

At the secondary level, Form V students take the Caribbean Examination Council Secondary Education Certificate.

Promotion within the secondary school is dependent on achievement. Generally, repetition of the same form is allowed once.

Entry into tertiary-level institutions depends on well-stipulated criteria. For example, entry into the Secretarial Department is determined by four General Certificate Examination Ordinary-level subjects or four Caribbean Examination Council Proficiency-level subjects.

In addition to the possession of a certificate from external assessment bodies, persons seeking entry into the Technical Services Division of the CDCC must pass an entrance examination set by the College. At the end of two years, the students in the Technical Services Division sit the City and Guilds Examination, while the secretarial students sit the London Chamber of Commerce Examination. At the end of two years, the academic studies students sit the GCE at the Advanced level.

Trainees at the Teachers' College take an examination at the end of two years which is administered by the Joint Board of Teacher Education of the University of the West Indies.

Problems facing the examination, promotion, and certification systems revolve around the limited trained labor force and the shortage of financial and material resources.

9. Educational Assessment, Evaluation, and Research

Assessment data is used as the basis for promotion within a level, from one level to the other, for awards of scholarships, for entry into institutions, and for selection of persons for the labor market.

Provisions for assessment, evaluation, and research were made in the 1991–92 estimates under the educational administration allocation; 0.80 percent of that allocation is set aside for that purpose.

Some of the most important educational indicators on which information is regularly collected are enrollments at all levels, staffing at all levels, and assessment results.

10. Major Reforms in the 1980s and 1990s

The rationalization of the JSP is a major reform in education. The proposed restructuring of the Dominica Teachers' Training College (DTTC) plans to bring the Teachers' College under the umbrella of the Community College. There is a proposal to approach the Carribean Examinations Council to certify the craft-level courses taught at the DTTC.

Another OECS project involves the establishment of a College of Excellence in Agriculture in Dominica which would service the OECS. Colleges are already established in two other OECS states, one being the College of Business. The eventual establishment of a College of Excellence should have positive effects on the agricultural climate of Dominica.

The Prime Minister, in her 1991–92 budget speech, referred to the expansion in the service sector and agreed that "We must assist this expansion by developing the human resources necessary to service that sector." The government has commissioned a full study on the servicing of its development potential and the identification of the kind of policies that will be needed to further its expansion.

The author of the Education Sector Plan (1989–94) suggests a joint effort at revising the contents of the social studies curriculum for the school population (Ministry of Education 1990a).

In order to achieve excellence in education by 2002, a mission statement has been formulated:

Conscious of the need to maximize all resources available to Dominica, and dedicated to the overall development of every citizen, the Ministry of Education commits itself to:

(a) A participatory approach to planning, decision making, curriculum development, and evaluation;

(b) a systematic approach to the determining of priorities; and

(c) a continuous adaptation of innovation to the cultural reality of Dominica.

11. Major Problems for the Year 2000

The major problem predicted for the beginning of the next century is the unavailability of trained and competent teachers.

Bibliography

Broomes D 1991 *Teaching Training For Non-Graduate Secondary School Teachers In The OECS*. University of The West Indies, Cave Hill, Barbados

Central Statistical Office 1988 *Statistical Digest: Dominica Ten Years of Growth 1978–1988*. Central Statistical Office, Roseau, Dominica

Commonwealth of Dominica 1989 *Labour Force Survey*. Central Statistical Office, Roseau, Dominica

Commonwealth of Dominica 1990 *External Trade Bulletin Summary of Tables, 4th Quarter 1990*. Central Statistical Office, Roseau, Dominica

Commonwealth of Dominica 1991a *Labour Market Information Bulletin 1984–1990*. Central Statistical Office, Roseau, Dominica

Commonwealth of Dominica 1991b *Quarterly Economic Indicators Third Quarter*. Central Statistical Office, Roseau, Dominica

James-Reid O 1989 *Resources Management and Development in Some Caribbean Primary and All-Age Schools*. University of The West Indies, Cave Hill, Barbados

Matthew M 1990 *Report on the 1990 Junior Secondary Programme Assessment*. Ministry of Education, Roseau, Dominica

Ministry of Education 1990a *Education Sector Plan for Educational Development in the Commonwealth of Dominica 1989–1994*. Ministry of Education, Roseau, Dominica

Ministry of Education 1990b *Educational Statistical File 1988–1991*. Ministry of Education, Roseau, Dominica

Ministry of Education 1990c *Survey of Training Institutions in the Commonwealth of Dominica 1988–1989*. Ministry of Education, Roseau, Dominica

Ministry of Education 1990/91 *Staffing File 1989–90/ 1990–91*. Ministry of Education, Roseau, Dominica

Peters M E, Sabaroche H 1990 *The Organization and Management of the Ministry of Education: A Case Study*. Commonwealth Secretariat, Roseau, Dominica

Regehr W (ed.) 1990 *Developing a Common Vision in Education Through 2002*. Ministry of Education workshop paper, Roseau, Dominica

Sabaroche H 1989 *Report on the 1989 Junior Secondary Programme Assessment*. Ministry of Education, Roseau, Dominica

Shillingford D 1991a *Report on the 1991 Junior Secondary Programme Assessment*. Ministry of Education, Roseau, Dominica

Shillingford D (ed.) 1991b *Rationalization of the Junior-Secondary Programme: Retrospect And Prospect*. Ministry of Education, Roseau, Dominica

The New Chronicle 83(43): June 19 1991. Editorial "Parliament to seek approval for $209.7 million budget"

Turner T, Reid E H E 1979 *Dominica: An Evaluation of Its Education System*. University of The West Indies, Kingston, Jamaica

UNESCO 1982 *The Commonwealth of Dominica Education Sector Survey 1982*. UNESCO, Paris

Ecuador

Juan Samaniego F.

1. General Background

Ecuador is situated in South America and is bordered by Colombia and Peru, and to the west is the Pacific Ocean. Its area is 270,670 square kilometers, including the Galapagos Islands, which are located 1,000 kilometers from the Ecuadorian coast in the middle of the Pacific Ocean. The Andean Cordillera, which spans the countries of South America, divides Ecuador into three natural regions: coastal, mountain, and Amazonian. The topography of these regions has an influence on the physical characteristics, customs, and idiosyncrasies of their inhabitants.

The climatic differences of each region impinges on the school system. The school year in the coastal area is from May to January, and in the mountain and Amazonian areas, from October to July. The official language of the country is Spanish.

Ecuador registers one of the highest annual population growth rates in Latin America (2.19%), and its population density is the highest in South America:

almost 37 inhabitants per square kilometer. In 1990, the total population of the country was registered as 10,075,407 inhabitants. Some characteristics of the Ecuadorian population are as follows:

(a) equal numbers of men and women;

(b) predominantly young with the majority of the population between 5 and 14 years of age;

(c) a marked trend toward urbanization: in 1990, 55 percent of the population lived in urban and 45 percent in rural areas. Guayaquil and Quito, in that order, are the most populated cities;

(d) a considerable indigenous population (about one-third of the total population), the most numerous being Quechua. In the country there are 11 indigenous nationalities, each with their own language, and they occupy one third of the national territory.

Ecuador is rich in natural resources. Petroleum from

the Amazon region is the largest compenent of the gross domestic product (GDP). The export of fruit such as bananas and of beans (coffee and cacao) account for almost three million tons of annual production. Bananas are the largest single export. Ecuadorian industry began to develop in the 1970s. The most developed sectors of industry are food and textiles. Some 37 percent of the nation's industry is located in two towns: the capital, Quito, and the principal maritime port, Quayaquil. In the early 1990s unemployment was estimated to be 13 percent and underemployment 60 percent including both the informal urban and modern sectors of the economy.

Article 1 of the Constitution observes that Ecuador is "a sovereign, indepedent, democratic, and unitary State. Its government is republican, presidential, elective, and representative." Effectively, the structure of the government takes the form of three authorities: legislative (National Congress composed of 77 deputies), executive (President of the Republic and the cabinet of ministers), and jurisdictional (courts of justice).

The Law and the General Education Regulation lay down the rules for the administration, organization, and functioning of the education system. The Ministry of Education and Culture is the highest authority for everything concerning education, with the exception of the universities which have an autonomous administrative system.

2. Politics and the Goals of the Education System

The principle of the 1895 Liberal revolution sheds light on the philosophy of Ecuadorian education of the twentieth century. The Constitution of the Republic states that "education is the fundamental duty of the State. Special education is guaranteed. Parents must recognize the right to give their children the education which they had" (Art. 27). The Education Law in force provides, among others, the following principles:

"Education is a fundamental obligation of the State" (Art. 2,a).
"All Ecuadorians have the right to a full education and the obligation to actively participate in the national educational process" (Art. 2,b).
"The State guarantees freedom of education in accordance with the law" (Art. 2,d).
"Official education is secular and free at all levels. The State guarantees special education" (Art. 2,e).
"Education should have a moral, historical, and social meaning, inspiring the principles of nationality, democracy, social justice, peace, defence of human rights, and be open to current universal thought" (Art. 2,f).
"Education will have a democratic, humanistic, investigative, scientific, and technical orientation according to the needs of the country" (Art. 2,i).

Even though these postulates promote a close relationship between education and socioeconomic development with equality, the problems of the Ecuadorian system of education described below, determine that this relationship is still weak.

3. The Formal System of Education

The national system of education comprises two subsystems: one scholastic and the other nonscholastic. The scholastic subsystem comprises: (a) formal education (preprimary, primary, and middle levels); (b) compensatory education which has "a special system and is offered to those who are not admitted into or are not included in formal education"; and (c) special education, "aimed at physically, intellectually, psychologically, or socially exceptional students" (Law: Art. 5). The nonscholastic subsystem "promotes educational, cultural, and professional improvement through special teaching–learning and dissemination programmes, by mean of public and private efforts" (Law: Art. 6).

The presence of a considerable indigenous population has brought with it, in practice, the existence of two administratively autonomous systems of education (subject to stipulations in the law): one bilingual intercultural and the other Hispanic. In 1992 the National Congress reformed the Education Law institutionalizing Bilingual Intercultural Education and its administrative applications. The indigenous communities consider education as a means for reassessing, preserving, and developing national identity. The schools for indigenous peoples, principally in the central mountains and the Amazon, are bilingual (Spanish is taught as the intercultural relationship language). There are also bilingual teacher-training institutions.

3.1 Primary, Secondary, and Tertiary Education

Figure 1 presents the structure of the system of education by age and grade.

The school year lasts ten months. The enrollment at all levels is the same: equal numbers of males and females.

The primary level is divided into six grades of three terms. This complies with the education of the majority, that is, the age range between 6 and 12 years. In the early 1990s, accessibility to primary education reached high levels. At any one time, the entire population of school age was enrolled in Grade 1 of primary education. In the school year 1990–91, 96 percent of the population of school age was enrolled. The dropout rate was between 1.2 and 7.2 percent of pupils between the first and fifth grades. Fifty-four percent of pupils were from urban areas and 46 percent from rural areas (see Table 1). The deterioration in the quality of

Table 1
National enrollment at the various educational levels in rural and urban areas 1990–91[a]

Level	Urban	Rural	Total
Preprimary	90,425	24,599	115,024
Primary	994,305	852,033	1,846,338
Middle	692,520	93,324	785,844
Higher[b]	188,618	—	188,618
Total	1,965,868	969,956	2,935,824

a Ministerio de Educación y Cultura 1992 *Estadísticas de la Educación 1990–91*, Quito
b 1988 statistics. Source: CONUEP

primary education can be seen from the high level of grade repetition. Enrolled pupils require an average of 7.7 years to complete the 6 years of schooling. It is estimated that 7.8 percent of first grade pupils repeat the year. Just under half the rural schools have one teacher.

The middle level is organized in two courses: basic and diversified. The basic course lasts three years. A nine-grade school system (primary and basic courses combined) is being tried out but is still not official.

The marked growth in enrollment in the basic course in the 1970s and 1980s was a result of the expansion of the enrollments at the primary level. In 1990 percentage enrollment at the basic level was 63.9. The major problems at this level of education are those of coverage and quality.

The diversified course comprises three years of study and offers two types of baccalaureate: scientific and technical. The former is academically biased and is a preparation for university. The latter takes the form of intermediate courses in the areas of farming, industry, business, and administration and can lead to either employment or university education. Nearly 90 percent of schools with the diversified course are in urban areas. The majority of the teachers of this type of course are male, in contrast to the primary level, where most teachers are female. About 31 percent of pupils in the diversified course is enrolled in the technical baccalaureate; 75 percent of them are in the business and administration courses. In the diversified course there is a discrepency between the requirements of the university and productive sectors and the actual content of the courses. For example, more than half of the technical baccalaureate graduates work in areas unrelated to the subjects in which they specialized when taking the baccalaureate.

The cost of technical education is significant given that 50 percent of schools have fewer than 40 pupils. The lack of policy in the diversified course has led to some claims that the baccalaureate has a double profile: one with a solid scientific foundation and, at the same time, a second with necessary capabilities and skills to join the labor market. However, the characteristics of the education system and its incompatibility with the

productive sector has not allowed or resulted in the formation of baccalaureates with this double profile.

Some technical schools have postbaccalaureate specialization courses of 2 years' duration. These offer intermediate courses in branches of mechanics, farming, secretarial, and administration, among others. The total enrollment in these courses is not significant. There are 36 pedagogical institutes (IPED) responsible for the training of primary-level teachers. These offer two-year postbaccalaureate courses. Some 71.5 percent of the enrollment in these institutes is female.

With respect to higher education, in 1988 the

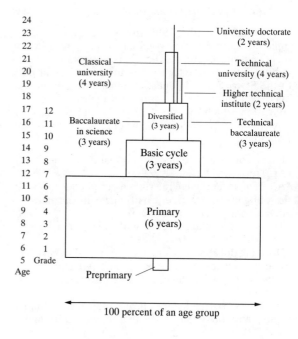

Figure 1
Ecuador: Structure of the formal education system 1990

national enrollment was 188,618 students (approximately 18% of the total population of the country). This enrollment was an enormous increase over that recorded in the 1970s. Of this total enrollment in higher education, 81.5 percent were enrolled in official universities. In Ecuador there are 21 main universities with 27 academic extensions. Only 26 percent of university students attend courses in technical colleges or polytechnics.

The Ecuadorian university system has fundamental problems of quality, similar to those of the middle level of education, in that it is unrelated to the productive and scientific requirements of society and to the employment opportunities available. With the exception of some polytechnic universities, the general academic level is low and resources for research are scarce.

3.2 Preschool Education

Preschool education lasts for one year and is aimed at 5-year old children. It is not a prerequisite for entry into the primary school. In 1990 enrollment was 44.2 percent of the 5-year old population. However, in rural areas only 21.4 percent of children of preschool age are enrolled in rural kindergartens.

3.3 Special Education

In 1990 there were 57 centers of special education, half of which were private and these cared for less than 2 percent of people with some kind of disability.

There is no policy for the training of teachers of special education. Furthermore this area lacks curriculum organization, infrastructure, materials, and appropriate resources. The efforts which are made are isolated and concentrated on certain areas of disability.

The lack of middle-term policies are apparent in the uncoordinated efforts carried out by public and private institutions and in the insignificant budget of US$5 per disabled child or youth, per annum.

3.4 Vocational, Technical, and Business Education

There is no official information or legislation regarding vocational education institutions in Ecuador. The majority of these are private and nearly all offer courses related to the service sector of the economy. The majority of students who enroll have their baccalaureate and wish to have an intermediate professional qualification before entering university. There is no set curriculum or form of administration for vocational education institutes.

The Ecuadorian Vocational Training Service (SECAP) is the only state body which, with economic contribution from the business sector, operates a network of institutions at national level which offer vocational training courses and have an annual intake of about 50,000 persons.

There are no regulations at an official level regarding business education. All efforts which are carried out are isolated and are almost exclusively dependent on the private productive sector.

3.5 Adult and Nonformal Education

Basic adult education (compensatory) is aimed at the young and adult population who, for various reasons, did not enter formal education. It is organized into three levels: (a) basic education: literacy, postliteracy (which is equivalent to the regular primary course), and the basic course; (b) diversified; and (c) craftwork level vocational education.

Literacy activities are ongoing. One example of a national literacy campaign was the *Monseñor Leonidas Proaña* National Literacy Campaign (1989). In 1990 (census), the illiteracy rate was 10.2 percent (731,093 people) of all persons over the age of 10 years. Some 73 percent of illiterates were in rural areas. Nearly 60 percent of illiterates are female. However, it is to be noted that the illiteracy rate has declined greatly since the 1970s. Between 1988 and 1992, 520,650 adults and young people attended various forms of compensatory education; the majority participated in the primary program.

Despite public and private efforts, problems with the quality of adult basic education services persist. The country does not have the economic resources to establish a competent network of teachers and materials for adult education.

The State maintains just over 1,500 centers for occupational training which cater mainly for females.

Nonformal education lacks adequate legislation. Public entities, municipalities, and others from the private productive sector undertake campaigns on issues such as health, human rights, the environment, vehicular traffic, and civic education.

4. Administrative and Supervisory Structure and Operation

The Ministry of Education and Culture includes two subsecretariats, various specialized boards of directors, and technical offices.

In each of the 21 provinces of Ecuador there is a Provincial Educational Board of Directors responsible for local organization of the system.

Two outstanding problems in the administration of education in Ecuador are (a) an excessive centralization in decision-making; and (b) a politicized, nontechnical, and bureaucratic management of the planning and operation of the system. The preprimary, primary, and middle levels of education institutions are supervised by Ministry of Education agents (supervisors) who, in the majority of cases, develop their role in an extremely legal manner. However, unless the supervisors have the appropriate training for assessing schools and colleges, their visits to such institutions are limited to ensuring that the institutions are run in accordance with the stated laws and regulations. In most cases, supervisors do not visit any one school more than once a year because of either geographic inaccessibility or the sheer number of institutions for which they are responsible.

5. Educational Finance

According to the Constitution, 30 percent of the state budget must be assigned to education. However, since the 1980s, the percentage has been only 20 percent. Since 1980 investment in education has been in inverse proportion to servicing the external debt; the greater the requirement of the debt, the less the allocation to education.

In 1993, the average investment per enrolled pupil (preprimary, primary, and middle) was US$11.14 per annum. Of the education budget, 24.49 percent was allocated to salaries and 53.59 percent to transferences (allocations to each school and kindergarten). There was a significant increase in the budgetary allocation to higher education programs between 1990 and 1991, in contrast with that for basic and middle education which fell significantly.

The budget is extremely low for teacher salaries and for materials and didactic resources. The starting salary for a teacher with a university degree is approximately US$70 per month. This situation has been further aggravated by the economic crisis which the country has been undergoing since the early 1980s.

6. Supplying Personnel for the Education System

In the school year 1990–91, there were 127,466 teachers in preprimary, primary, and middle levels in Ecuador (see Table 2). Seventy-seven percent of them worked in state institutions and 23 percent in private institutions. The majority of teachers work at the primary level which is where the largest proportion of pupils in the whole system are enrolled. In the same year, the pupil–teacher ratios were 18:1 at preprimary level, 30:1 at primary level, and 13:1 at middle level. Since the 1960s, the supply of teachers has increased by 280 percent; this is proportional to the increase in enrollments in the same period.

Some 86 percent of teachers at the preprimary level have no relevant qualification. At the primary level only 22.5 percent have a teaching diploma and at the middle level only 47 percent are qualified.

Teachers in Ecuador are trained in pedagogical institutes (for primary level) and in the faculties of Philosophy and Educational Sciences of public and private universities (for the middle level). This training does not include areas such as educational research and new trends in pedagogical thought. Moreover, much of the training is based on information which is out of date and unrelated to the psycho–pedagological requirements of children and young people.

There is no coordination between the Ministry of Education and the universities regarding the training of teachers. Furthermore, there is no request for the training of teachers in specific subjects in technical colleges.

7. Curriculum Development and Teaching Methodology

There are official study plans and programs which must be abided by all educational establishments. They are unique to the whole country with the exception of bilingual intercultural education. There tend to have a large amount of material for one year of study (the principal subjects of the primary level and the basic course are language, mathematics, social sciences, and natural sciences).

The content of the curricula of the preprimary, primary, and middle levels are largely disjointed. Much is repetitive. There is no curriculum policy which specifically requests the articulation of the regular education curriculum. However, a curriculum reform is being

Table 2
Enrollment, teachers, and schools[a]

	Preprimary	Primary	Middle	Total
Pupils	115,024	1,846,338	785,844	2,747,206
Schools	3,371	14,965	2,551	19,887
Pupil–school ratio	49:1	123:1	308:1	138:1
Teachers	6,301	61,039	60,126	127,466
Pupil–teacher ratio	18:1	30:1	13:1	22:1

a Ministerio de Educación y Cultura 1992 *Estadísticas de la Educación 1990–91*. Quito

discussed. It will focus its attention on the development of reading and writing and basic arithmetic skills in the first six years and on strengthening the nine grade school system.

Even though the new content will encompass less than before there is still the main problem of the work methodology in the classroom. This is characterized by the predominance of rote, cognitive development, and the passivity of the student. It has become apparent that the content of teacher-training programs and the needs of the pupils tend to be unrelated.

The school textbooks are of poor quality and there is no control over their production, distribution, and use. The textbooks are written by freelance authors or designed according to guidelines laid down by the state for any particular subject area.

The learning situation in the classroom is typically a rudimentary treatment of the curriculum content but somewhat unrelated to the pupils' age and ability. Apart from the relevance, or lack of it, of the study plans and programs, the poor quality of the Ecuadorian education system also stems from teaching processes and results in a weak academic education.

8. The System of Examinations, Promotions, and Certifications

At primary level, promotion within each grade is automatic from one grade to the next, according to achievement. In order to be promoted from one grade to the next an annual average score across all subjects of 10 / 20 is required. In the middle level cycle of education, pupils who obtain less than 23 / 60 in each of the study plan subjects are not promoted to the next level. There is also a system of supplementary tests for pupils who score between 24 and 43 points in a particular subject in any one year. There are similar regulations for promotion in adult basic education. Universities have their own system of promotion and certification; some have a "credit" system structure. On finishing the sixth year of the middle level cycle the pupil achieves the baccalaureate qualification.

At all levels in the system only the written examination is used as an evaluation strategy. These examinations are usually memory tests, based on single question, and often do not refer to the skill being tested. Even though an integral or continuous evaluation strategy has been officially stipulated, there is no funding for it to be implemented and, consequently, written examinations prevail.

9. Educational Assessment, Evaluation, and Research

Many studies have been carried out in Ecuador which report the state of the system of education. These are all of a quantative nature and have not explored the processes applied in the classroom. The methodological aspects of teaching and learning have hardly started to be researched.

The general tenor of the research has been to arrive at rhetorical and philosophical conclusions, announcing the poor quality of teachers, the rigidity of study plans, and teaching methodology as the principal reasons for the poor quality of the system.

Nongovernmental organizations have invested resources in socioeducational research in areas outside the teaching–learning process. However, there is still a great need for research to provide information on such matters as education and the community, satisfying the needs of the economy, the relationship between middle-level education and university, and intraclassroom pedagogical processes.

There are very few educational advisory institutions where diverse protagonists of society become involved. The production sectors and academics do not participate systematically in the search for solutions to the internal problems of the system of education.

10. Major Reforms in the 1980s and 1990s

There have been no significant reforms to the system of education carried out in the 1980s and early 1990s. The education law in force in the mid-1990s was approved in 1983 and the general regulation of the law was approved in 1985. The study plans and programs in force in primary and middle levels were approved in 1984. In the following years these legal documents were occasionally changed, as in the case of the creation of the National Bilingual Intercultural Education Office.

The trend since 1980 has been to execute large-scale educational programs with external funding (e.g., the World Bank) creating ad hoc bureaucracies. Some of these projects were as follows:

— Project for the Improvement and Enlargement of Technical Education (PROMEET): aimed at the improvement of middle-level technical training (technical colleges). It completed its activities at the beginning of the 1990s.

— Project to Prevent the Marginalization of Rural Schools (AMER): aimed at the improvement of the infrastructure of rural schools and the production of school textbooks. It ended its activities at the beginning of the 1990s.

— Project for the Improvement of the Quality of Basic Education (PROMECEB): aimed at the improvement of rural education, the creation of the nine-year school and major education centers (CEM). This program is envisaged to end in 1994.

— Project for the Development, Efficiency, and Quality of Basic Education (EB-PRODEC): having the same strategies as PROMECEB but for marginal urban sectors. This program is envisaged to finish in 1997.

There have been other projects carried out in the field of rural education (educational centralization) and bilingual intercultural education.

11. Major Problems for the Year 2000

A fundamental problem of the Ecuadorian system of education is the lack of continuity of policies that go beyond the interests of the government in power. However, the *Consulta Nacional Educación Siglo XXI*, which ended in 1992, was an important antecedent.

As the year 2000 approaches, the strategies being implemented for the improvement of the quality of the system of education must resolve the following problems:

(a) the lack of policies which relate education and the productive sector. There is an incompatibility of what the education system supplies with the demand of the labor market;

(b) universities having no systematic and sustained work in the field of scientific and technological research and which are isolated from other levels of the national system of education;

(c) reform of the specialization course to create a continuous nine-grade school;

(d) "legal" inflexibility and behavior of the supervisory and teaching staff. If this scheme changed, public schools and colleges would still not have the conditions for autonomous and creative management of the curriculum;

(e) training and remuneration of teachers. There is a need for revision of the funding of teacher-training institutes, particularly universities.

Mechanisms must be created to ensure better financial revenue.

Bibliography

Aspiazu P, Luna M 1993 *Aula: Geografía e Historia del Ecuador*. Cultural S.A. de Educación, Madrid

CONADE–GTZ 1991 *Ecuador Siglo XXI: Reorientación del Sistema Educativa Ecuadoriana*. CONADE-GTZ, Quito

Consejo Nacional de Educación 1992 *Consulta Nacional Educación Siglo XXI*. Final Report. Consejo Nacional de Educación, Quito

CONUEP 1992 *Universidad Ecuatoriana: Evaluación de la situación actual y perspectivas para el corto y mediano plazos de las Universidades y Escuelas Politécnicas*. CONUEP, Quito

CORDES 1988 *Educación: Entre la Utopía y la Realidad*. CORDES, Quito

Corpación de Estudios y Publicaciones 1993 *Leyes de Educación, Universidades y Escuelas Politécnicas, Cultura, Educación Física, Deportes y Recreación y Reglamentos*. Corporación de Estudios y Publicaciones, Quito

Ministerio de Educación y Cultura 1990–91, 1991–92 *Estadísticas de la Educación* Dirección de Planeamiento, Sección Estadística y Censo, Quito

Ministerio de Educación y Cultura 1992 *Documento Informativo para la Consulta Nacional Educación Siglo XXI*. Ministerio de Educación y Cultura, Quito

Montoya L et al. 1993 *1ra jornada Parlamentaria Educación y Desarrollo: Situación Actual de la Educación. Información Básica, Quito*

Pfister E 1991 *Costos y Financiamiento de la Educación Media*. PROMEET II, Quito

Rivera J 1992 Elementos para una estrategía de desarrollo educativo de largo plazo. *Ecuador Siglo XXI*. CONADE-GTZ, Quito

Salgado G, Acosta G 1991 *El Ecuador del mañana: Una ruta con problemas*. CORDES, Quito

Samaniego J et al. 1991 *La Educación Técnica en el Ecuador*. INSOTEC, Quito

Shiefelbein E, Heikkinen S 1991 *Ecuador: Acceso, Permanencia, Repitición y Eficiencia en la Educación Básica*. OREALC, Quito

Egypt

M. E. Mahrouse

1. General Background

The Arab Republic of Egypt is approximately one million square kilometers in size and occupies the northeastern corner of Africa and the Sinai Peninsula of southwestern Asia. Egypt is bordered on the north by the Mediterranean Sea and on the east by the Red Sea, the Gulf of Suez, and the Gulf of Aqaba. The Sinai Peninsula is separated from the rest of Egypt by the Suez Canal. Egypt borders on Libya, to the west and Sudan to the south.

The country is traversed from south to north by the Nile River and is divided into two regions: lower Egypt and upper Egypt. These two regions are subdivided into 26 governorates comprising 150 districts and 808 village councils of greatly varying sizes. Decentralization, which has occurred since 1979, has increased the powers of the governor as the local representative of the president and has stimulated greater community involvement in decisions concerning economic and social priorities at grassroots level.

The main topographical divisions are the western desert, the eastern desert and the Nile valley and its delta. The western desert, which comprises 68 percent of the land area, is an arid region covered by vast rolling plains of sand, shifting dunes, and large, deep valleys. Some of the valleys—such as Qattara, Siwa, and Faium—lie below sea level. In some valleys—such as Kharga, Farafra, Bahriya, Dakhla, and Faium—there is limited cultivation.

The eastern desert, also known as the Arabian Desert, is an elevated plateau broken up by deep valleys and covering 22 percent of the land area.

The basic human settlements are limited to the Nile valley and its delta. This comprises only 4 percent of the land area. In addition to the Nile valley and its delta, there are some inhabited points along the Suez Canal and the coasts on the Red Sea, the Mediterranean Sea, and the Gulf of Aqaba.

The population of the Arab Republic of Egypt was estimated at 55 million in 1990, and the population is expected to rise to 70 million around the year 2000. In the 1950s and 1960s the average annual population growth rate was 2.4 and 2.5 percent per year, respectively. In the 1970s it increased and almost reached 2.75 percent per year, one of the highest annual growth rates in the world. This is the equivalent of adding about 1.3 million people a year. The birthrate is estimated at 40.9 per thousand inhabitants and the deathrate is approximately 11.0 per thousand inhabitants.

Such a rapid population growth has had profound effects on the social structure. The pressure of population on land and living space in the inhabited zones of Egypt in the Nile valley and its delta has been intense and is still increasing from year to year despite efforts to extend the area of habitation. Within the populated areas (which amount to only 5.5% of the country's territory at present), the average population density at the time of the 1976 census was 695 persons per square kilometer, again one of the highest in the world; and it had increased to an estimated 835 persons per square kilometer by 1990, making it one of the most densely settled agrarian regions of the world.

The economically active population in Egypt constitutes a relatively small proportion of the total population. In 1987 only 14.5 million people, or 28.3 percent of the total population, were economically active. This is due to social and cultural factors in Egypt, the most important of which is the role of women in society. The participation rate of women, who constitute almost half of the total Egyptian population, is only about 5.6 percent. At the same time, this small percentage of the economically active population is also due to the age profile of the Egyptian population; almost 40 percent of the Egyptian population is under 15 years of age. This high proportion of children in the Egyptian population, as well as the small participation rate of women, implies marked unfavorable conditions in the country in consumption, expenditure, and investment.

Another important feature is the relatively high proportion of the population living in urban areas. The percentage living in urban areas increased steadily from 31.9 percent in 1950 to nearly 54.8 percent in 1985, and is expected to reach 64.3 percent by the year 2000. The population of the Cairo Governorate alone has increased from approximately 2 million in 1950 to an estimated 15 million in 1990.

Such rapid urban growth imposes a heavy burden on housing, transport, amenities, and other services, as well as on living space; the problem is aggravated by the encroachment of urbanization on farmland. It had been estimated that 15 percent of agricultural land would have been lost by the year 2000 if there had not been a proposal to build seven new cities on land unsuitable for agriculture during this period.

An examination of the distribution of the active population across the various economic sectors reveals that the proportion of agricultural workers diminished from 56.6 percent to below 38.5 percent in the period from the 1960s to 1990, while the proportion of the labor force in manufacturing increased from 12 to only 15.1 percent during the same period.

The total number of employed persons was 12.4 million in 1987. The percentage distribution among the government, public, and private sectors was 19.1, 10.3, and 70.6 percent respectively. Government employment increased by 137 percent from 1965 to 1988, while the population increased in the same period by 35 percent. Employment in agriculture decreased from 46.5 percent of the total number of employed persons in 1974 to 38.5 percent in 1988. Professional and technical workers increased from 6.0 to 10.5 percent during the same time.

In order to avoid massive unemployment among graduates, the government guaranteed, in principle, a job in government service or public enterprise to any person who could not find one in the private sector. This resulted in a vicious circle, as the guarantee of employment increased the demand for higher education and the resulting surplus of university-trained persons forced the government to increase the number of unnecessary jobs in the public sector, thus reducing the already low level of productivity in government and private enterprises.

Unemployed persons were estimated to comprise 11 percent of the total labor force in 1987. These unemployment figures are due to various factors, the most important of which is the limited capacity of Egyptian agriculture to absorb workers, because of the scarcity of land and the increasingly labor-intensive nature of agricultural work. Furthermore, the rapidly rising levels of education have made many young people dissatisfied with rural employment.

An examination of the educational level of the

Egyptian people reveals that in 1986 only 4.1 percent of them held a university degree (5.1% men and 2.85% women). The percentage of graduates at the secondary educational level at the same time reached 21.7 percent of the total (30.43% men and 17.45 % women). These figures are due to the expansion of secondary and higher education. Illiterates comprised 70.8 percent of all persons over 10 years of age in 1960, 56.3 percent in 1976, and 49.4 percent in 1986; the numbers of illiterate women being always 70 percent more than those of illiterate men. In spite of the marked improvement in percentages, the absolute number of illiterates is on the increase.

Islam is the state religion of Egypt, and Arabic is its official language. The democratic ideal has been pursued with a number of measures against feudalism, monopoly, and exploitation. Education is compulsory for five years at the primary level, and this can be extended to higher levels. Education is free at all state institutions. The state supervises all educational activities and guarantees the independence of universities and research centers on condition that they direct their efforts to societal needs and to productivity. Abolition of illiteracy is a national duty, and religion is a basic subject in the curriculum. There are a number of other articles relating to freedom, human dignity, equality of opportunity, security, and so forth.

The Arab Republic of Egypt has a People's Assembly consisting of 458 elected members of whom 10 are appointed by the president. Some 50 percent of the elected members are peasants and workers. Egypt also has a so-called "consultative council" and a body known as the "National Specialized Councils" whose function is to assist the president. The country is administratively divided into 26 governorates each headed by a governor appointed by the president. Under Law No. 43 of 1979, the governorates have important administrative functions in the fields of education, health, housing, agriculture, irrigation, transport, and so on. The central Ministry of Education is responsible for policies and overall plans, and for following them up, while the governorates are responsible for their implementation and administration.

2. Politics and the Goals of the Education System

In 1987, the Egyptian government declared that scientific development must take place in the Egyptian system of education. Therefore, it was decided that the concept, structure, function, and management of education should all be reviewed. Egyptian society was to be literate and educated, benefit from progress in science and technology, and be more productive. Education was also to be more flexible, diversified, and relevant to societal needs.

In 1989, the Ministry of Education stated the main goals of education to be the following:

(a) education is intended for the reinforcement of

democracy and equality of opportunity and for the formation of democratic individuals;

(b) it is also for the country's overall development, that is, to create a functional relationship between education productivity and labor markets;

(c) it should also be directed towards strengthening the individual's sense of belonging to the country and to the reinforcement of the Arab cultural identity;

(d) it should lead to further and lifelong learning through self-renewal and self-education;

(e) it should include development of students' knowledge and skills in literacy, numeracy, computing, languages other than Arabic, the creative arts, and environmental understanding;

(f) the goals are intended to provide a framework for cooperation in curriculum development and assessment.

These policies are general state objectives. Naturally, educational goals vary according to level of education, region, program, and the individual. Many Moslem villagers, for example, give as the main reason for wishing to become literate that they want to understand Islam better. Many parents send their children to school to help them avoid manual or physical labor in their future lives. With most people, education leads to a diploma, which brings a position with a regular income and security and ensures a respectable social status. However, this motive is losing importance because of the increase in the number of well-paid jobs in the private sector at the beginning of the 1990s.

The different sex roles have also given rise to differ-

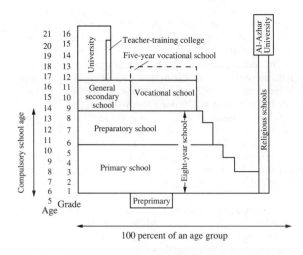

Figure 1
Egypt: Structure of the formal education system 1991

ences in educational objectives, but this gap is quickly disappearing. Finally, it should be mentioned that, in general, an academic emphasis of a verbal nature is gradually giving way to a more practical pattern of education.

3. The Formal System of Education

Egypt's educational system has two parallel structures: the secular structure and the religious Al Azhar structure. The secular structure is organized and administered by the Ministry of Education. The Al Azhar structure is run by the Ministry of Al Azhar Affairs: this is often called the Ministry of Religion in other countries. Apart from these two major structures there are other types of schools where a few pupils are enrolled. For example, handicapped children go to special schools, those wishing to enter the military go to military schools, and yet other young persons leave school and enroll in the nonformal programs run by different agencies.

According to 1988 statistics, only 92 percent of an age group entered school. Only 62 percent of an age group entered the second level of education (Grades 6–11). However, of the 92 percent in school, 3.6 percent of these were in the Al Azhar system. Figure 1 presents the two systems in diagramatic form. Table 1 presents some basic statistics.

3.1 The Secular School System

Compulsory education lasts for eight grades and is known as "basic education." There are some kindergartens and nurseries which precede basic education, but these are few in number and mostly situated in the cities. This basic education is split into two stages. The first stage (known as "primary school") goes from Grade 1 to Grade 5, and the second (known as preparatory school) from Grade 6 to Grade 8. The preparatory school was only made compulsory in 1984 and in this sense the label of "preparatory" is no longer appropriate.

Following the eight-year basic education, pupils have four choices: to leave school, to enter a general academic school, to enter a three-year technical secondary school, or to enter a five-year technical school.

Within the general academic school the first year (Grade 9) is common to all. In Grade 10 students must choose between arts and science for Grades 10 and 11.

Higher education in universities and specialized higher institutes follows general academic education. Study in some institutes lasts for two, four, or five years depending on the subject. Since 1991, some graduates from technical schools have been allowed to enter higher education.

The rapid population growth in the Arab Republic of Egypt resulted in an increased demand for education and, in turn, higher enrollments. This rapid growth of enrollment also resulted from the fact that, since the 1952 Revolution, Egypt has persistently striven to expand education as one of the necessary prerequisites for its social and economic development.

Between 1952 and 1988 total enrollment at all levels of education increased extremely rapidly from almost

Table 1
Key statistics on enrollments and resources in formal education 1991

	First level[a]	Second level	Third level
Number of students[b]	6,900,000	2,400,000	980,000
Percentage of age group enrolled:			
6–10	92	—[c]	—
11–16	—	57[d]	—
17–21	—	—	16[e]
Number of institutions	14,574	6,421	254
Number of teachers	214,500	175,500	16,600
Average no. students per institution	474	374	3,858
Student–teacher ratio	32	14	59
Expenditure per student (£E)	56.1	121.1	441.4

aBecause education was only compulsory at the primary level (6–11 years of age), and compulsory education has since been extended to Grade 8b(6–13 years of age), the levels of education are treated as follows: first level—basic education (primary level), second level—basic education (preparatory) and general and technical secondary stage, and third level—higher educationbthe education data refer to 1988c— = nil or rounded to zerodthe ratio is estimated from the 92percent of an age group who entered compulsory schoolethe ratio is estimated from the 27.7percent of third level to second level

1.9 to almost 10.3 million. The most substantial increase occurred at the first level of education where the number of pupils enrolled increased from 1.4 million (37.8% female) in 1952 to about 6.9 million (44.4% female) in 1988. The number of students enrolled in the second and third levels of education increased from 460,000 (19.4% female) and 54,000 to about 2.4 million (42.5% female) and 0.98 million (34.4% female) respectively during the same period.

The enrollment of females in schools is still below that of males at all levels of education. However, over the years, female participation as a proportion of the total number of pupils enrolled has increased considerably. The growth rate of female enrollment has been higher than that of male enrollment.

The number of pupils pursuing their studies beyond the first level increased both in relative and absolute terms. The ratio of second-level to first-level enrollment increased from 24.2 percent in 1960 to 62 percent in 1988. The ratio of third-level to second-level enrollment was 31.3 percent in 1960 and 27.7 percent in 1987. The first-level enrollment ratio (proportion of children in primary schools to total number of children between 6 and 10 years of age) rose from 66 percent in 1960 to 92 percent in 1988.

As far as higher education is concerned, the secular structure had 220 faculties and higher institutes with 16,000 teachers and 695,736 students (628,820 boys and 66,916 girls).

3.2 The Al Azhar School System

The Al Azhar school system is more or less identical with the secular system for basic education. The difference is that Islamic studies are given more emphasis. However, for ordinary school subjects, the curriculum is the same as for the secular schools. Grades 10 and 11 are common to all pupils. At the end of Grade 11 a pupil can choose to enter either two further years of general academic studies or a two-year religious course.

At the university level, the faculties are the same as for secular education but with a great deal more religious emphasis. Furthermore, those training specifically to be teachers in religious establishments at all levels can only be trained in the Al Azhar system.

Al Azhar schools have a small enrollment as compared with secular schools. In 1988, the percentage enrollment in Al Azhar schools was 3.6 percent of the total enrollment in the secular system.

In the realm of higher education the percentage enrollment in Al Azhar University in 1988 was 14.3 percent of the total enrollment in both secular and Al Azhar faculties and higher institutes. With the small enrollment at the Al Azhar school level, 14.3 percent at the university level seems high. However, there is an explanation for this phenomenon. It is that a higher proportion of the Al Azhar pupils proceed to higher education than those from the secular system.

There is no technical education in the Al Azhar system.

3.3 Vocational and Technical Education

Efforts to expand vocational and technical education started in the 1950s. The number of vocational and technical schools increased from 134 (with 31,800 students) in 1952 to 460 (with 115,600 students) in 1960. Between 1970 and 1988 total enrollment in the vocational and technical schools grew from 275,300 to 978,800. This represented 19.0 and 40.8 percent of the total number of students at the second level respectively.

In 1988, Egypt had 563 vocational and technical schools which represented 48.7 percent of the total number of secondary schools at the second level of education. Enrollment in these schools has been surpassed by that in the general secondary schools. While the number of students in the vocational and technical secondary schools in 1988 was 759,700 students, the total enrollment in the general secondary schools in the same year was 564,668.

Since 1970, the percentage of females enrolled in the vocational and technical secondary schools has increased considerably.

At the third level of education there were, in 1988, 34 higher technical institutes enrolling 59,400 students according to the National Center for Educational Research in Egypt. This represents 7.5 percent of total enrollment in higher education.

The number of teachers in the vocational and technical secondary schools (who usually graduate from higher colleges or institutes) increased from 13,700 (14% female) in 1970 to 42,800 (26% female) in 1987 which represented 23.6 and 28.7 percent of total second-level teachers respectively. Although enrollment in vocational and technical secondary schools has increased considerably over the years, the pupil–teacher ratio decreased from 20:1 to 8:1 during the 1970–88 period. At the third level, the number of teachers in technical institutes was 690 in 1988 which represented 4.3 percent of the total of third-level teachers.

3.4 Adult and Nonformal Education

Nonformal education has been defined as a set of planned educational activities outside the formal system that are intended to serve identifiable learning needs of particular subgroups in any given population, be they children, youth, or adults; males or females; farmers, merchants, or craftsmen; or from affluent or poor families. In Egypt, nonformal education is primarily connected with the eradication of illiteracy. Thus, the majority of the programs concentrate on this aspect of nonformal education. According to the 1960 Egyptian census 70 percent of the population over 10 years' old was illiterate. In 1976, Egypt registered a total of 13.3 million illiterate adults (over 15 years of age) or 61.8 percent of its entire adult population. By 1986 the total number of illiterates increased to 17.2 million, but the percentage of the corresponding adult population decreased to 49.4 percent.

Adult illiteracy is substantially higher among females than males. In 1976, 77.6 percent (or 8.2 million) of the adult female population was illiterate, while only 46.4 percent (or 5.1 million) of the male population fell into this category. By 1986, the rates were 61.8 percent (or 10.4 million) for females and 37.8 percent (or 6.8 million) for males. However, literacy programs include skills training for people aspiring to get a job, and if they already have one, further training to help them move up the occupational ladder.

Since 1967, the Ministry of Labor has offered vocational upgrading programs to train those who have completed primary-stage education and also those who have dropped out of formal education between 12 and 18 years of age. They are trained in some vocational skills appropriate to their environment and capability. Programs are typically nine months long: seven months are spent in vocational training centers and two months are allotted to on-the-job practical training on production sites. Trainees are then employed in both public- and private-sector factories.

In 1984, the Ministry of Labor initiated short-course vocational training programs to prepare groups of workers with limited skills to satisfy market needs in some jobs and to re-train workers whose jobs had disappeared or were about to disappear. These short courses are four months long. The trainees, between 18 and 45 years old, are provided with knowledge and skills that give them a reasonable start. Practical training is given in public- and private-sector factories, while theoretical lessons are given in the industrial schools.

Under the supervision of the Ministry of Industry, there are 33 centers in different governorates. These centers offer programs that aim at giving quick training to semiskilled workers, training skilled workers through industrial apprenticeship, and raising the skill level of technicians.

In the short-course vocational training schemes which aim at training semiskilled workers, trainees are about 17 years old. The training courses are four to six months long.

As for apprenticeship, a pupil who has finished basic education or decides to leave technical school can enter a nonformal three-year training course. This is divided into two parts: the first part is basic training for one year at the training center, and the second part lasts two years and is in one of the industrial companies.

To raise the skill level of employees, companies select a number of workers and foremen with a minimum of five years' job experience to attend three-month evening training courses which provide technical training.

4. *Administrative and Supervisory Structure and Operation*

Egypt's educational system is the responsibility of the state Ministry of Education. The central Ministry of Education is responsible for education up to and including the university level with regard to planning, policy formulation, quality control, coordination, and follow-up. The education offices in the governorates are responsible for all implementation. They choose the sites of the schools, construct and equip them, and ensure that they are well-run. They encourage local contributions and citizen participation. In short, they are responsible for everything that guarantees the efficient operation of schools.

The Ministry of Education is organized in the following sections:

(a) Office of Deputy Minister. This supervises the following: external cultural relations, educational planning and follow-up, public relations, statistics, directorate's affairs, and the coordination of supervisors' work.

(b) Minister's Office Sector. This includes a People's Assembly liaison office, a technical center, a security office, a general secretariat of higher councils, a complaints office, and a secretariat section.

(c) Primary Education Sector. This oversees primary education, teacher preparation, and adult education and literacy.

(d) Preparatory and Secondary Education Sector. This oversees preparatory education, secondary education, and general administration of coordination.

(e) Technical Education Sector. This oversees industrial education, cultural education, commercial education, technical equipment, and general administration of coordination.

(f) Sector of Educational Services. This oversees physical/military academies, social education, external relations, examinations, educational activities, and general administration of coordination.

(g) General Services Sector. This oversees educational methods, private education, nutrition, legal affairs, and office affairs.

(h) Sector of Administration Development. This oversees organization, training, and personnel.

(i) Administrative and Financial Affairs Sector.

The Minister meets at regular intervals with the council of undersecretaries and a number of other councils. The Minister also presides over the meetings of the

Supreme Council of Universities which is responsible for planning and policy making. The organizational structure of the governorates is similar in principle to that of the central ministry, but it is somewhat smaller and more simplified. The country is also divided into 140 separate education districts with a network of supervisors and administrators.

The Ministry of Al Azhar Affairs looks after the educational policy and plans of the Al Azhar University, and the Al Azhar colleges and schools.

Private schools are an important feature of the education system and in 1988 enrolled 8 percent of students. Private schools are largely supervised by the Ministry of Education. In practice, the private schools provide a similar curriculum to government schools.

5. Educational Finance

The rapid increase in the number of teachers and schools, improvements in equipment and rises in costs (including salaries) have caused an increase in educational expenditure. The 23 million Egyptian pounds (E) (US$77 million) budgeted in 1952 rose to about E126 million (US$420 million) in 1969. For the same period, public investment in education increased from E2.5 million (US$8.4 million) to about E33.3 million (US$111.2 million). After 1970, the allocation of funds to education began to increase at a higher rate than before. In 1984, public expenditure on education reached E1,186.5 million (US$1,163 million). This represented 8.9 percent of total government expenditure (4.1% of gross national product). Government expenditure on formal education in 1988 was 10.9 percent of the Gross National Product (GNP) and 18.5 percent of total public expenditure. Salaries absorbed more than 80 percent, while current expenses and investment accounted for the remaining 20 percent. Investment in school buildings increased at the beginning of the 1980s from 7 to 13 percent. There are still not enough school buildings and, if demand is to be met, more than E3 billion (US$2.94 billion) must be spent on construction in the next 10 years, according to estimates. From 1964 to 1978, expenditure on pre-university education increased fourfold, while expenditure on higher education increased more than fivefold. Higher education in 1970 used 20.4 percent of the country's total expenditure on education, and in 1978 it used 31.4 percent. Of the Ministry's total budget, primary education received 44 percent. Some maintain that this should be appreciably increased.

Egypt receives aid from the World Bank, UNICEF, UNESCO, and friendly countries such as the United States, Germany, the United Kingdom, and other Arab states. Although the aid received is substantial, there is a great deal yet to be achieved in education, particularly in the rationalization of management and of expenditure.

The present educational system considers the preparatory schools as the final stage in compulsory education. This has served to increase costs. Salaries for teachers at all levels of education increased at a higher rate in the 1981–88 period than before.

Despite the general increase in educational expenditure, the per-pupil expenditure, particularly at the first level, is still low (E56.1 in 1988) compared with a per-pupil expenditure of E121.1 and 441.4 at the second and third levels respectively. This indicates that the rapid growth of the school-age population did indeed affect the cost of education.

The appropriation for vocational and technical education rose from 6.2 percent of the total education budget in 1955 to 16.5 percent in 1986. In absolute figures the rise was from E5.2 million (US$17.4 million) to E92.8 million (US$54.6 million). The appropriation for 1986 was E105.8 million (US$62.2 million) or 14.6 percent of the total education budget. The figure of 14.6 percent for 1986 is a result of an increase of 29.2 percent in the total education budget since 1981.

For the financial year 1989–90 total outlays on education were E1.6 billion (US$0.7 billion), which represented 10.8 percent of gross domestic product. The Egyptian government supplies the most funds for education. Private funding of education is mostly in the form of tuition fees paid to private schools. Parents do not pay fees for their children to attend government schools. The fees levied by private schools range from about E200 a year in some primary schools to about E500 in some secondary schools. All private schools also receive some direct government funding.

6. Supplying Personnel for the Education System

The central Ministry of Education has slightly less than 2,000 professional and ancillary officials, usually very carefully selected. The planners, for example, are normally university graduates with an additional year of training at the Cairo Institute of Planning. As a rule preference is given to those who have demonstrated superior teaching skills. Suitable courses of training are given to those who will become inspectors, consultants, supervisors, technical assistants, senior masters, headmasters, directors, and so on. Elaborate evaluation methods are used for allocation and promotion. Between officials in the Ministry and those in the governorates there is a continuing exchange of information through regular meetings and other channels of communication.

The estimated total number of teachers in 1980—nearly 250,000—may be somewhat imprecise. The definition of a teacher in practice and as used for statistical purposes is not clear. If planning assumptions, school requirements, and the country's expectations are to be met, 13,000 new teachers are needed every year in order to reach a 95 percent enrollment ratio in Grade 1 by 1995. This means an intake to teachers' institutes and colleges of 13,500 in the first year. The universities are at present establishing primary education departments which will ultimately raise the level of the compulsory basic education of teachers.

Nearly 390,000 teachers were employed in Egyptian schools in 1990. About 55 percent of the total were employed in primary schools; about 22 percent in preparatory schools; and 16 percent in secondary schools. Only 7 percent of teachers were employed in Al Azhar and special schools.

Until the late 1980s, teacher shortages were common and students were offered generous scholarships to enter teacher-training institutes. More recently, enrollments have resulted in an over-supply of teachers in some subject areas and regions. However, there seem to be perennial shortages of teachers in areas such as languages and special education. Furthermore, schools in rural regions are often difficult to staff. Therefore, school teachers have to spend some of their time teaching in rural areas before becoming eligible for a city position. Teacher training occurs now within the universities, with four years of higher education being the normal length of initial training for primary and secondary teachers.

There are severe shortages in teachers of Arabic language and Islamic religion—a strange phenomenon. There are also shortages of teachers of art, agriculture, music, home economics, and the various branches of technical education. This may be because, in Egypt, teaching seems to be one of the least attractive professions. The status of teachers in general and teachers of Arabic in particular needs to be seriously reconsidered.

7. *Curriculum Development and Teaching Methodology*

In Egypt, curriculum construction is the result of teamwork. Committees are formed which include consultants, supervisors, experts, professors of education, and experienced teachers. There is usually one committee for each subject or group of subjects. The chairpersons of the various committees are invited to meet so that decisions may be coordinated. When a curriculum has been produced by a committee, it is referred to the Supreme Council of Preuniversity Education which formally issues it for implementation. By law, curricula may sometimes be adjusted to accommodate local conditions or specific events.

The National Center for Educational Research is responsible for collecting information about curricular teaching materials and implementation in the field. The results of such studies are channeled to the council of undersecretaries and if change is needed, a committee is formed and charged with the task. There are various ways to ensure relevance and to help in the dissemination of new programs. A large number of supervisors and consultants at all levels meet regularly with teachers for guidance and for collecting information. There are various training centers, experimental schools, and demonstration schools, all aiming at curriculum reform

and the improvement of methods. Once a curriculum outline is set, a small team similar to the ones described above is asked to write the textbooks. The curriculum text is not always identical to the curriculum implemented. The gap is due to a large number of factors such as classroom conditions, lack of aids and equipment, and teacher quality. Contrary to curriculum instructions, most teaching is verbally oriented.

In higher and university education, there is a great deal of freedom in curriculum construction and textbook usage. Factors such as progressively increasing class or course sizes, the scarcity of aids and resources, and so on, tend to lower the standards achieved by students. Dependence on one textbook and on the lecture method is prevalent.

Foreign languages are taught in secondary schools and, less commonly, private primary schools. The study of foreign languages is mandatory in schools. English, French, and German are the most commonly taught languages. The Egyptian government is keen to encourage more foreign-language teaching in schools, especially the English language.

Learning materials are prepared by a variety of agents including the curriculum committees of all the education departments, academics, and teachers' subject associations. In general, schools and individual teachers have some degree of independence in the selection of learning materials.

8. *The System of Examinations, Promotions, and Certifications*

The examination system in Egypt exercises a strong influence over the thinking of pupils, parents, and education authorities. The reasons for this lie in the importance attached to the results. Promotion examinations are set at the end of Grades 2, 4, and 5 and the first public examination is held at the end of Grade 8. The successful student obtains the Basic Education Certificate and can then proceed to further education. The aggregate score determines the type of school a student enters and is critical, as only the highest scoring students go on to the preferred option of the academic-secondary school leading to university. Otherwise, students register in technical schools or in training institutes. A youngster's future is thus determined by the aggregate score in the Basic Education Certificate examination, which makes it exceedingly important and creates a high degree of competition and anxiety throughout the country. Similarly, the secondary-school leaving examination determines, on the basis of the aggregate score, which faculty and even which university the student can enroll in. Highly competitive examinations held at the end of the year are responsible for the trade in "cram" or "crib" books and for the demand for private coaching.

There have been attempts at reform through, for instance, increasing the weight of the year's work in final assessments and using objective tests. The main solution would, of course, be to make examinations part of the process of effective learning.

9. *Educational Assessment, Evaluation, and Research*

Educational research began in Egypt with the establishment of the Institute for Teaching Education in 1929. It grew slowly but steadily until Ain Shams University incorporated the institute as one of its colleges in 1951. In 1955, a strong department of research was established in the Ministry and was replaced in 1972 by the National Center for Educational Research (NCER). Apart from the prolific work going on at the colleges and at the National Center, educational research is also carried out by the National Center for Social Research, the Center for Development of Science Teaching, and by a number of other organizations.

Several educational research studies are carried out in collaboration with the World Bank, UNESCO, UNICEF, and other United Nations organizations. Examples of these studies include: "Repetition and dropouts"; "Ill-effects of endemic diseases"; "Influence of nutrition on achievement"; and "The motivation to literacy among adult illiterates." Bilateral aid also supports educational research.

Since 1989 there has been considerable activity in student assessment and the development of education indicators. There has been a change in focus by the Egyptian government from monitoring resource inputs to monitoring student outcomes. Schools are required to undergo review and evaluation every few years. The focus of such evaluations tends to be on school improvement.

At the higher education level, a change in research policy was evident in the further development of the Egyptian Educational Research Center (NCER) in 1989. There is more emphasis placed on applied research, the shifting towards competitive allocation of research funds based on peer review, and on the identification of national priorities in research.

10. *Major Reforms in the 1990s*

At the beginning of the 1990s there was a period of considerable reform in many aspects of the Egyptian system of education. One of the more notable changes was the diminution in the length of primary school from 6 years to only 5 years. Thus, official compulsory education in Egypt lasts for the eight grades known as basic education. The other notable change was the rise in the proportion of young people who entered technical secondary education (65% of total graduates' basic education). This has stimulated far-reaching changes in curricula, assessment, and graduate unemployment in Egypt. In nonfomal education, a major scheme to expand employee training has been introduced.

Many of these changes share a common rationale: the need for education to help the Egyptian economy to become more competitive. The reforms have attracted considerable opposition from those who dispute the goal of more closely aligning education and the economy, and those who question the particular means proposed. The resolution of these tensions is likely to occupy Egyptian education for much of the 1990s.

11. *Major Problems for the Year 2000*

As a result of the rapid expansion of education, the Egyptian educational system suffers from a number of weaknesses, such as the shortage of qualified teachers, inadequate programs, the high rate of student dropout, inadequate school buildings, and a high pupil–teacher ratio.

The participation of people in education and training will need to be increased. Curricula need to be made more relevant to national priorities. Individuals and employers will have to finance an increasing share of the costs of educational expansion.

Unemployment and inflation have remained high and overseas debt has grown. Unemployment tends to be highest among all graduates of secondary and unversity education.

The most important educational task in Egypt is the qualitative and quantitative development of the basic compulsory school (the 6–13 age group) so as to create educated and productive citizens and to suppress the flow of illiterates into the adult community. The country's attempt to at least match the world's technological progress is at present jeopardized by the extent of illiteracy. This problem has many dimensions, including resources, buildings, aids for teachers, curriculum and so on. Related to this problem is the changing shape of the education pyramid—narrowing at the base and broadening at the top. The reconsideration of the education pyramid means taking demography, employment, culture, resources, and other factors into account.

Education suffers from the fact that the teacher has become little more than a mere transmitter of information and the student a passive recipient of it. The student should be developed into a positive, resourceful, self-reliant personality capable of effective and creative thinking. The student at any level should be educated in such a way that he or she is capable of independent thought and self-education.

The educational problems of Egypt, as in any country, are plainly evident, and one main defect is the consequent attempt to tackle them piecemeal, that is, dealing separately with examinations, teacher–pupil relationships, books, buildings, and so forth. Educational reform must be regarded as a system within a larger system and with its own subsystems. What is lacking is a total approach, with the immediate and long-range objectives and the individual and state objectives clearly thought out in advance.

Bibliography

Cochran J 1986 *Education in Egypt.* Croom Helm, London
El-Ghannam M A 1971 *Education in the Arab Region from the 1970 Marrakesh Conference.* UNESCO, Paris
El-Koussy A 1985 Egypt: System of education. In: Husén T, Postlethwaite T N 1985 *The International Encyclopedia of Education,* 1st edn. Pergamon Press, Oxford
El-Koussy A, Sanyal B 1982 *University Education and the Labour Market in the Arab Republic of Egypt.* Pergamon Press, Oxford
Hyde G D 1978 *Education in Modern Egypt: Ideals and Realities.* Routledge & Kegan Paul, London
International Labour Office 1987 *Yearbook of Labour Statistics.* International Labour Organisation, Geneva
Mahrouse M E 1990 *Effects of Education on Job Levels, Earnings, Vocational Aspirations, and Job Satisfaction of Industrial Workers: An Analytical–Empirical Study on Economic Benefits of Education.* Peter Lang, Frankfurt
Ministry of Education 1984 *The Development of Education in the Arab Republic of Egypt from 1981 to 1984.* National Center for Educational Research, Cairo (in Arabic)
UNESCO 1985 *Statistical Yearbook.* International Labour Organisation, Geneva
United Nations 1981 *Arab Republic of Egypt—Report of Mission on Needs Assessment for Population Assistance.* United Nations Fund for Population Activities, New York

El Salvador

R. Ruiz-Esparza

1. General Background

El Salvador is the smallest and most densely populated of the Central American countries. With an area of 21,041 square kilometers (8,124 square miles) it is bounded on the north and east by Honduras, on the south by the Pacific Ocean, and on the west by Guatemala. The country sits on top of 25 burnedout volcanoes and is subjected to occasional seismic activity (in 1986 the capital was heavily damaged by an earthquake). There are three distinct geographic regions: a tropical narrow Pacific coastal belt that produces cotton; a subtropical central region consisting of small valleys and plateaus where the dominant crop, coffee, is grown; and a mountainous northern region.

In 1991 the official estimate of the population was 5.3 million (World Bank 1993 p.238). An unofficial estimate for 1992 put the population at 5.4 million. Rapid population growth and population pressure on available cultivable land constitute two of the country's most fundamental problems. Besides creating social and political tensions over land ownership and the equitable distribution of wealth, these problems also place a strain on the provision of social services such as education, and complicate the task of planners and policymakers as they strive to meet the needs of the social sector.

The rate of population growth has been high during most of the twentieth century. From 1960 to 1978 the population grew at 3 percent per year, but that rate declined in the 1980s to 2.7 percent, still considered among the highest in Latin America. Official projections estimate that the population will be 6.7 million in the year 2000.

The ethnic composition of the population is about 93 percent Mestizo (a combination of Native American and White), 5 percent Native American, and 2 percent White. There are no reliable figures on the size of the Native American population because that minority group has been fairly well-integrated into Salvadoran society. El Salvador's Native Americans are descended from the Pipi tribes who inhabited the area when Spanish colonization began in 1525. As a result of cultural assimilation, and repressive policies in the past, there are now extremely few speakers of the native language which is known as Pipil. Spanish is the common language and the educational system does not have to deal with bilingualism when children begin school.

A prolonged period of instability and civil conflict began in 1979 and ended in 1992 when a peace agreement was ratified by the government and the opposition forces. Although considered tenuous, the peace agreement is expected to hold, thus giving the country an opportunity to rebuild and return to normalcy. The civil conflict resulted in the loss of an estimated 75,000 lives, the emigration of about 750,000 people, and severe damage to the economy.

Already plagued by financial problems during the 1980s, the government had to allocate a high proportion of its budget to national defense (23% in 1988). Defense spending coupled with debt interest payments consumed 41 percent of the national budget in 1988, and placed severe limitations on public social and economic spending. Funding for education and health declined the most as a percentage of the gross domestic product (GDP). From 1978 to 1982, GDP fell an alarming 22 percent, and even though the government was able to halt the downward trend in 1983, economic growth has only averaged 1.7 percent per year since then.

Agriculture, the mainstay of the economy, encountered serious problems during the 1980s, and continues to experience difficulties in the early 1990s. Output declined from 1982 to 1987 when the rest of the economy was showing signs of modest recovery. Coffee, the principal export product, has seen a drop in both production and exports. Since the rural areas were the main battleground during the period of conflict, large numbers of rural dwellers were displaced and agricultural activities were disrupted.

Manufacturing, which is centered in and around the capital city, grew at an average rate of over 7 percent in the 1960s and part of the 1970s, but from 1978 to 1982 output declined over 30 percent and employment fell by 19 percent. Since 1982 manufacturing has made a partial recovery, but output growth has only averaged about 2.3 percent, and in 1987 it was still below the level it had been in 1978.

The poor state of the economy and the civil conflict led to a decline in the labor force. Emigration, war casualties, and army recruitment contributed to a decline in the growth of the working-age population from almost 15 percent in the period from 1970–75, to only 5 percent in the period from 1979–85. The quality of labor supply fell significantly during most of the 1980s, mainly because those who left the country were better educated than the population at large, and also because school enrollments declined during that period. Toward the end of the 1980s, however, the labor supply began to improve and by 1987 the growth of the working-age population returned to 2.3 percent annually. In 1991 the Ministry of Economics reported that 24 percent of the labor force was engaged in agriculture, while 18 percent was in industry and manufacturing, and 35 percent was in services and commerce.

While reliable data on the educational attainment of the labor force are not available, that of the population as a whole was as follows in 1985: 31.7 percent had no schooling; 25.2 percent had 1–3 years; 21.4 percent had 3–6 years; 10.3 percent had 6–9 years; 8.7 percent had 9–12 years; and 2.5 percent had 12 or more years of schooling (Kast 1988). Assuming that this educational profile of the population has not improved significantly by the early 1990s, and that the economy as a whole is still striving to recover the ground it lost in the 1980s, it is not difficult to see that the educational system faces a monumental task. Educational planners and policymakers have to develop strategies and programs aimed at the gradual improvement of the educational profile, which would also have the desired effect of enhancing the quality of the labor force.

Although the country has had various constitutions since 1940, the structure of the government has been dominated by the military establishment. However, that pattern began to change in 1982 when a civilian interim president was appointed, and since then the presidents who have followed have been elected civilians. The basic role of the schools under the present structure of government is not unlike that of other countries, which is to promote education as the means by which the cultural, economic, and social development of the nation is enhanced.

2. Politics and the Goal of the Educational System

Given that education in El Salvador is centrally planned, financed, and managed, and that its goals are generally incorporated in the national Constitution, there are not many major ongoing conflicts among political parties or interest groups over fundamental educational issues. The time when educational issues are debated and resolved is when constitutional revisions pertaining to education are made, or when the Ministry of Planning prepares educational plans for a given period. In those cases, inputs from a wide range of interest groups are taken and given due consideration. The problem with most of the plans produced through this process is that they generally tend to proclaim lofty aspirations and prescribe idealistic remedies without any realistic consideration of cost and implementation factors.

3. The Formal System of Education

The formal structure of the educational system, which has not undergone any major modifications since the Reform of 1968, consists of five levels: initial programs, preschool, basic education, secondary education, and higher education (Escamilla 1981). Figure 1 outlines the structure of the system.

3.1 Primary, Secondary, and Tertiary Education

Basic education, designed to serve students between the ages of 7 and 15, is free and divided into 3 cycles of 3 years each. The first two cycles cover primary education (Grades 1 to 6) and the third cycle covers the lower-secondary level (Grades 7 to 9). Basic education schools are supposed to follow a school year extending from February 1 to October 31 with 175 days of instruction. However, during the period of civil conflict the school year was subjected to many disruptions, and countless days of schooling were lost each year. With the cessation of hostilities in 1992, authorities are encouraging students and teachers to adhere to the official school calendar. This and all other levels of the system are coeducational, and the proportion of males and females tends to be even in Grades 1 to 5, but tilts only slightly in favor of males in Grades 6 to 9. In 1989 about 59 percent of this enrollment was in urban schools, and the rest was in rural schools. It should be noted, however, that the majority of rural schools do not offer the full nine years of basic education.

There was a serious decline in the net coverage of primary education, which fell from 80 percent in 1979 to 61 percent in 1981 but climbed to 70 percent in 1990. The gross enrollment ratio in 1990 was 78 percent

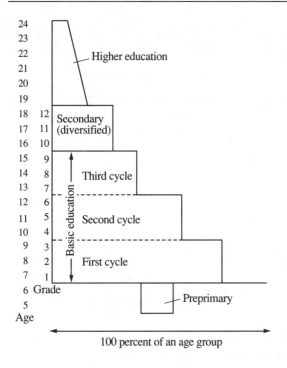

Figure 1
El Salvador: Structure of the formal education system 1988

(World Bank 1993 p.294). In addition to low coverage this subsector is burdened with low internal efficiency marked by low completion and high repetition and dropout rates. The completion rate for the urban cohort entering primary school in 1983 was estimated at 31 percent. In 1986 the primary level dropout rate was 15.1 percent, but the rate was considerably higher in rural schools where 23 percent of the students dropped out before completing the 6th grade. Repetition rates have been high since the 1970s when 11.5 percent of primary students repeated grades, and the rates diminished only slightly by 1986 to 9 percent (Kast 1988). Consequently, it is estimated that almost 11 years of schooling are required to produce one student who completes the 6th grade.

All of these basic education indicators are among the lowest in Latin America. Other related and unrelated factors contributed to the decline of basic education: (a) in 1987 about 66 percent of the basic education schools were incomplete schools, meaning that they offered less than 6 grades, and of these 29 percent offered only the first 3 grades; (b) as the civil conflict expanded in 1982 about 870 of the country's 3,000 schools were forced to close, and 575 schools remained closed in 1989 leaving about 100,000 children without a school to attend; (c) insufficient financial resources make it impossible to purchase textbooks, basic instructional materials, and supplies because almost all available

funds (96%) are used to pay employee salaries; and (d) school plant facilities are generally in need of repair or replacement.

Secondary education is designed to serve students between the ages of 16 and 18 in Grades 10 to 12 and enrolls a little over 100,000 students. In 1992 this level of the system enrolled 27 percent of the age group. The enrollment rate was 26 percent in 1979 but fell sharply to 20 percent in 1981 as a consequence of the civil conflict. By 1984, however, the rate was again on the increase, mainly because of an upsurge in the opening of private secondary schools. By 1988 about 50 percent of the total secondary-level enrollment was in private schools. The school calendar for secondary education covers the same nine-month period and 175 school days that is followed by basic education schools.

In rural areas most individuals cannot attend secondary schools because only 15 percent of such schools are located there. Reliable data on the flow of students through the secondary schools is lacking, but it is generally recognized that internal efficiency is low. Since the Reform of 1968, secondary schools have offered a diversified curriculum, which consists of a mix of general education subjects and vocational courses (Escamilla 1981). The latter were supposed to serve as vocational training, but in reality they provide pre-vocational training in most cases. From the start, the diversified program was designed to provide a mixture of general and vocational education in the following proportions: in the 10th grade, 80 percent general education and 20 percent vocational; in the 11th grade, 50 percent of each category; and in the 12th grade, 80 percent vocational and 20 percent of general education. The vocational areas included in this curriculum are: business administration, home economics, industrial arts, agriculture, hotel industry and tourism, navigation and fishery industry, health services, and teacher training.

Although there are some exceptions, the quality of most of these schools has declined gradually over time, as original equipment has worn out or become obsolete, and resources have not become available to maintain or replace that equipment. Consequently, diversified schools have tended to focus more on the academic phase of the curriculum than on the vocational phase. Private secondary schools generally offer the traditional academic curriculum and those that specialize in vocational programs tend to offer business administration.

Higher education served 17 percent of the corresponding age group in 1987 with a total enrollment of 92,510 students (Kast 1988). While the disruptive forces of the 1980s adversely affected all levels of the education sector, they were particularly harsh on the tertiary level. In 1979 there were two universities, the public University of El Salvador and the private Central American University. In addition, there were several specialized postsecondary institutions, such as the Polytechnic University of Engineering and

Architecture. As social and political unrest escalated in 1980, the government closed the public university. Dedicated members of the faculty, however, managed to keep the institution partially opened by renting space for classes in San Salvador and in other parts of the country. An estimated 10,000 students continued their university studies in this makeshift manner from 1980 to 1984 when the University was reopened. While it was closed the University was looted and vandalized, and it will be a long time before it recovers from those losses. The Central American University, on the other hand, managed to continue its operations during the troubled period, but only under precarious conditions, and despite the fact that it also suffered damage.

In order to fill the void left by the curtailment of operations at the two major universities, as many as 25 new private universities opened in response to the growing demand for higher education. Thus, by 1989 an estimated 48.6 percent of the total enrollment in higher education was in private institutions. Reliable statistical data on the state of higher education in the early 1990s are unavailable, but given its chaotic history of the past decade, it is not difficult to surmise that its educational indicators are low. In the 1990s universities face the daunting task of rebuilding and regaining some semblance of quality.

3.2 Preschool Education

Two separate programs comprise preschool education. The first is a relatively small program called "Initial Education" (early stimulation program), which basically provides child care to the 0 to 3 age group. This program is very undeveloped and served only 3 percent of the 380,000 children in the age group in 1987 (UNESCO 1990). Those children receiving service are generally urban orphans or urban children of working mothers. The program is administered by the Salvadoran Council of Minors of the Ministry of Justice.

The second preschool program is under the Ministry of Education and is intended to serve children between the ages of 4 to 6. In 1991 this age group consisted of about 600,000 children, of whom only 14 percent were enrolled, and the vast majority of these (89%) were urban children from middle- and upper-class families (UNESCO 1990).

Plans for the 1990s call for the expansion of preschool services for poor rural children as a means of improving the quality of the primary subsector. A UNICEF-sponsored "Program for the Integrated Attention of the Child of 0 to 6 Years of Age" was initiated in 1984 for impoverished rural children. The program showed considerable promise and by 1989 it was serving 13,500 children. Recognizing its potential, the government expects to replicate this model in a selected rural area in the 1990s with the aid of a project jointly financed by the World Bank and the United States Agency for International Development

(USAID). This project (World Bank 1991a) is expected to reach 25,000 rural children, and thereby increase the coverage of preschool from 14 percent to 18 percent by 1994.

In 1987 public-sponsored programs accounted for 62 percent of the enrolled preschool children, while the private sector attended to the remaining 38 percent. Participation of the private sector continued to increase so that by 1990 it was estimated that its share was from 40 to 42 percent. The student–teacher ratio in both public and private schools was 35:1 in 1989 (UNESCO 1990).

3.3 Special Education

In 1987 it was estimated that 216,900 young persons were in need of special education services and that 101,552 of these were under the age of 16. However, only 1.4 percent of the total (or 3,093) were actually enrolled in programs that year. The regular school system enrolled 1,754 special education students, and another 1,339 students attended special education facilities. In other words, the provision of special education is woefully inadequate.

Those limited programs being offered are directed at urban centers with attention given to those individuals with mental retardation and children with learning disabilities, and hearing and speech impairments. Financing for these programs comes from the government and from community contributions. Special education is administered by the Ministry of Education through its General Directorate of Basic Education.

3.4 Vocational, Technical, and Business Education

Reliable data on vocational, technical, and business education is very scant. It is apparent, however, that this component of the educational system is practically nonexistent below the secondary level. The vocational–technical track that was added to the secondary-level curriculum in the Reform of 1968 was intended to provide the labor force with workers trained with entry-level skills in a wide range of occupations, including mid-level technical areas. Although conceptually sound, the diversified secondary-school program is expensive to start and maintain, and the government has always had difficulty in providing sufficient resources for it. Thus, over a period of years the program has grown weaker. In addition to having obsolescent equipment, poorly trained teachers, and practically no operational funds, the program has only tenuous ties with the private sector.

Despite such limitations, graduates from these diversified secondary schools are able to enter the labor force, or pursue further training in any of the public or private postsecondary training institutions. Training in private vocational schools usually centers on selected areas in the field of business.

In the 1990s the government expects to improve the

vocational–technical programs in secondary schools with the aid of a US$14 million project from the Interamerican Development Bank. A separate project is being prepared with the assistance of the same institution to strengthen the program in the secondary agricultural school.

Private-sector training is generally done on an ad hoc basis and very little information is available about such efforts. With the assistance of USAID, the government initiated a project with the private sector in 1987 that will upgrade the skills of workers needed by private firms (Agency for International Development 1987). The main thrust of the project, which is scheduled for completion in 1992, is to establish training programs and create ties between private business and training institutions. Project management is being handled by a private foundation, the Foundation of Entrepreneurs for Educational Development (FEDAPE), which was formed by Salvadoran businessmen. In addition to identifying private-sector training needs, establishing training programs, financing scholarships and loans, and supporting industrial development training, the project will provide training to 2,800 persons, train an additional 2,300 workers on-the-job, improve management skills for 2,000 managers, and upgrade the skills of 100 vocational instructors. Perhaps more importantly, the project will provide a training model that the government can continue to use in the future.

3.5 Adult and Nonformal Education

The educational system makes little distinction between adult and nonformal education, both of which are managed by the Ministry of Education with funding from public and private sources. In 1987, 1.4 million persons who were aged 13 and over were considered in need of literacy training or adult education. That year the literacy training program enrolled 34,343 persons from urban centers, and 39,856 persons from rural areas. The coverage for literacy training was slightly over 5 percent (UNESCO 1990).

That same year (1987) programs designated as "adult education" enrolled a total of 67,807 persons, of whom 31,824 received literacy training, 32,733 persons enrolled in primary education classes, and 3,250 received basic occupational skills training. Again, those enrolled in these programs represented only 4.8 percent of the target group. The reasons for the poor coverage revolve mainly on the lack of adequate funding for the programs, and the disruptive environment created by the civil conflict.

4. Administrative and Supervisory Structure and Operation

With the exception of the universities, which in the Latin American tradition are autonomous, the Ministry of Education is responsible for administering all levels of the education system. Historically, the management of the system has been highly centralized in the Ministry, despite some attempts in the 1980s to decentralize some operations through a regionalization plan which met with very little success. However, during the unstable conditions of the 1980s the administrative links of the entire system were either broken, or severely frayed, resulting in a much weakened Ministry, whose financial resources have declined drastically, and whose administrative capacity has not been equal to the daunting problems it faces.

Overall management efficiency at all levels of the sector declined during the 1980s. The Ministry curtailed its school mapping operations, thus depriving itself of essential planning and diagnostic data for basic education. In fact, the Ministry's planning capacity has never been strong, since it lacks an integrated management information system capable of providing diverse sets of data on students, teachers, budgets, and facilities. Consequently, most educational planning is carried out by the Ministry of Planning.

Because of its centralized structure the educational system depends heavily on its program of school supervision to monitor the efficiency of school operations, teacher performance, and student outcomes, as well as to detect school needs and provide needed technical assistance. However, the supervisory program ceased to function in the early 1980s as a result of financial austerity and the civil conflict.

An educational project jointly financed by the World Bank and USAID will strive to strengthen some of the management functions of the Ministry of Education in the 1990s. Educational administration will be improved by initiating a decentralized process to deliver services to rural schools, an educational management information system will be established, the budget-making process will be reformed, and an improved school supervision program will be established.

5. Educational Finance

Education and the other social sectors have experienced severe financial constraints during the long period of political and economic instability. In 1980, education was allocated 3.9 percent of GDP, which compared favorably with other countries of the region. By 1993, however, education's share of GDP had fallen to 1.5 percent. Expenditures declined about 40 percent in real terms in the 1980s. This expenditure contraction meant that after payment of salaries (which consumed 96 percent of the budget in 1989) there was very little left for essential items such as instructional supplies and materials, equipment, plant maintenance, and school supervision.

Public education, which serves about 85 percent of those attending schools at all levels, is financed by the central government. In 1989 the distribution of total available funds for education was as follows: preschool 3.7 percent, basic education 70.5 percent, secondary education 4.5 percent, tertiary education 11.2 percent, literacy and adult education 2.8 percent, special education 1.5 percent, and culture 5.8 percent. The only difference in this distribution pattern from past patterns is that a little more was allocated to basic education at the expense of secondary and higher education. Private education, which serves about 15 percent of the enrolled school population, is financed by user fees. Reliable data on tuition levels and expenditures for private education are not available.

As financial resources for education dwindled during the 1980s and early 1990s, the government was forced to seek and accept foreign assistance and contributions from local communities. Foreign aid in 1989 represented about 20 percent of the education budget, and those resources were used mainly for school construction and repairs, textbooks, teacher training, and school food programs. For the 1990s the sector has already received commitments from external sources that amount to US$58.3 million, most of which will be forthcoming from USAID.

Voluntary community contributions to local schools were organized by parents who reacted to the deteriorating condition of their public schools. According to Ministry of Education estimates those contributions amounted to US$2 million in 1987 and increased to US$13 million in 1988, representing 10 percent of the education budget for the latter year.

6. Supplying Personnel for the Education System

Reliable figures are unavailable on the total number of the teaching force. In 1990 the Ministry of Education reported a total of 33,000 employees, of whom 24,629 were categorized as teachers, and the remaining 8,300 as administrators and support staff. A slightly more reliable picture was given in 1987 when the Ministry reported 1,939 teachers in preschools and 23,000 teachers in basic education. Although the number of secondary education teachers was not given in that report, one can estimate that there were about 2,800 teachers on the basis of the 99,300 students enrolled in secondary schools that year.

A number of variables account for the nebulous situation concerning teaching personnel, and most of them are related to the unstable political and economic climate in the country. For example, between 1978 and 1987 real wages for teachers fell by over 50 percent, while during the same period there was a surplus of about 6,000 teachers. Unfavorable salary conditions prompted many teachers to acquire second jobs, and this created conditions of low morale, low motivation, and high absenteeism among them. Teachers also became a very mobile group, as they joined the rest of the population in seeking safety from the dangers

of the civil conflict. Many rural teachers abandoned their jobs.

Preservice and inservice training for public school teachers, which used to be carried out by an institution called "*Ciudad Normal*," was transferred to a number of technological institutes and the two major universities. Given the surplus of teachers and the unstable conditions in the teaching profession, not much attention is being given to the preservice training programs. Inservice training, which had been greatly curtailed during the 1980s, is being reactivated in the early 1990s, mainly because various externally financed educational projects contain teacher-training components and will provide the funding to carry it out. It is expected that project-related personnel such as teachers, administrators, supervisors, and community groups will receive training to upgrade their respective skills. On a national level, inservice training for teachers is not compulsory.

Institutional infrastructure for providing teacher training of various types is inadequate, yet, there exists sufficient residual experience with regard to teacher training to ensure that this vital component of the education system can be strengthened in the future. Preservice teacher training, at least for the next few years, will not be a high priority given the existing surplus of available teachers.

7. Curriculum Development and Teaching Methodology

The general foundation for the primary and secondary education curriculum was established in 1970 after three years of preparation as part of the major Reform of 1968. Since then various curricular revisions and modifications have been carried out. Responsibility for curriculum development resides in the Department of Plans and Programs of the Directorate of Technical–Pedagogical Services in the Ministry of Education. However, initial direction for substantive curricular changes usually emanates in the Office of Planning and Organization of the Ministry (UNESCO 1990). When these entities undertake curriculum development work they seek out the participation of relevant groups representing a good cross-section of interest groups.

From their inception to the end of the 1970s the curricula for primary and secondary education were intended to be uniform throughout the country. However, during the 1980s the element of curricular flexibility was introduced to allow adaptations to local needs (Escamilla 1981). Nonetheless, the general framework of the curriculum is quite common nationally, with a core curriculum of academic subjects for the two levels of the system. The curriculum for the primary level was integrated into areas of study, but its application has not been successful in many cases.

There has been very little curriculum development

work since the late 1970s because of the lack of resources, except for that which has been stimulated by the projects financed with external assistance. Almost all such projects include some aspect of curricular revision or improvement. Those projects have also provided the stimulus and funding for the production and utilization of textbooks, teaching guides, and instructional materials. In the 1990s external assistance projects will continue to bring new infusions of textbooks and related materials to the preschool and primary levels. One such project will assist in creating a central textbook distribution unit in the Ministry of Education. Textbooks produced through these projects for basic education are generally made available to students on a loan basis so that other students can use them in subsequent years. Secondary school students generally have to purchase their textbooks in the commercial market from a list of books approved by the Ministry.

Classroom teaching methodology usually centers on the teacher–expository method, but most external assistance projects have emphasized the effective use of a variety of teaching methods. In general, teachers are aware that methods stressing student participation are more effective than teacher-centered instruction.

Although there are no restrictions on the teaching of foreign languages, the most common offering is English, which is usually taught at the lower and upper levels of secondary education. There are cases where selected private primary and secondary schools offer French or other languages.

8. The System of Examinations, Promotions, and Certifications

The high rate of students who repeat grades in primary and secondary schools attest to the fact that automatic promotion is not practiced in El Salvador. Promotion is determined by the classroom teacher and school principal on the basis of student classroom performance, which relies heavily on teacher-prepared tests. Certificates or diplomas are awarded to students at the completion of basic and secondary education. National examination systems are not used in El Salvador.

9. Educational Assessment, Evaluation, and Research

National, regional, and local assessment systems are nonexistent. The Ministry of Education produces annual reports which include school programs and a minimum of educational statistics. Objective assessments based on a set of predetermined evaluation strategies are processes that the Ministry will have to develop in the future. However, this will be difficult given the extremely low level of funding allocated to assessment, evaluation, and research.

Some rudimentary evaluation capacity is being institutionalized in the 1990s through at least one of the external assistance projects which will finance an annual formative evaluation of preschool and primary programs with the aim of determining their impact on child development and cost-effectiveness. In addition, educational planning will be strengthened, a management information system will be established, and the school mapping program will be reactivated.

10. Major Reforms in the 1980s and 1990s

The most significant reform in the 1980s was an organizational restructuring of rural schools through regionalization intended to decentralize rural school management. School mapping was used to organize rural schools into clusters known as "*nucleos*" with an administrative center for each *nucleo*. The end result was to be a "school nuclearization system" that would link each school to a support system that extended from the local school to the Ministry of Education. Three regional offices were created to decentralize management functions formerly handled by the Ministry. This reform basically failed because the funds to establish and maintain it were not provided. However, some of the basic structure of the system remains and is expected to be revitalized.

In the 1990s the most promising reform is a new approach to the decentralization and improvement of preschool and primary education which is being implemented with external assistance through a project that extends from 1992 to 1996. Through this effort the Ministry expects to delegate many of its school management functions to local community groups. This idea emerged from the remarkable support that parents and local communities gave to their schools during the 1980s. The project will reach 25,000 preschoolers and 45,000 primary students, and funding will be available to provide a package of quality enhancement inputs such as textbooks, supplies, teacher training, school lunches, supervision, physical facilities, and the strengthening of the regional offices. It is anticipated that the results of this effort will create a model that can be replicated in other parts of the country.

11. Major Problems for the Year 2000

El Salvador faces the formidable task of reviving its whole educational system, which is in crisis in the mid 1990s. That will require at least a decade of carefully planned and managed investment. Obviously, the first priority for the government is to resolve those social, political, and economic problems that stand in the way of establishing a peaceful national environment.

Although the national problems of the 1980s exacerbated the deficiencies of the education sector, the sector was already in crisis. Educational shortcomings have been mounting for a long time.

Educational planning has to be improved in the Ministries of Education and Planning to develop a phased approach for the recovery of the sector. Educational finance policies and procedures need reform, and the government must gradually increase funding for education. More privatization of education is being encouraged at all levels to reduce the public's share. External assistance should continue to play a significant role in financing educational development. However, the government has to be careful not to develop a dependency on this type of assistance.

Educational administration needs strengthening to ensure that investments are managed efficiently and maximized. Management models being tried out in projects might provide alternatives for addressing decentralization issues and the general complex mix of problems confronting the sector.

The rural poor population has to be provided with better educational opportunities, and the general coverage of the basic education age group has to be increased.

Internal efficiency at all levels needs to be improved, which means among other things, that the quality of teaching must be upgraded to reduce the wastage of scarce resources.

Finally, even though population growth issues are being addressed by the government, greater efforts are required to relieve the strain of an overcrowded country with limited land space.

References

Agency for International Development 1987 *Latin America and the Caribbean Overview: Education and Human Resources Development Portfolio*. USAID, Washington, DC

Escamilla M L 1981 *Reformas Educativas, Historia Contemporánea de la Educación Formal en El Salvador*. Ministry of Education, San Salvador

Kast M 1988 *Education Sector Report*. Salvadoran Foundation for Economic and Social Development (FUSADES), San Salvador

UNESCO 1990 *Situación Educativa de América Latina y el Caribe*. Oficina Regional de Educación para América Latina y el Caribe, Santiago

World Bank 1991a *Annual Report 1991*. World Bank, Washington, DC

World Bank 1991b *World Development Report 1991*. World Bank, Washington, DC

Further Reading

Disken M 1986 *The Impact of US Policy in El Salvador, 1979–85* (Policy Papers in International Affairs No. 27). Institute of International Studies, University of California, Berkeley, California

North L 1981 *Bitter Grounds: Roots of Revolt in El Salvador*. Between the Lines, Toronto

Russel P 1984 *El Salvador in Crisis*. Colorado River Press, Austin, Texas

Estonia

O. Must, J. Kõrgesaar and U. Kala

1. General Background

The Republic of Estonia, with a land area of 47,500 square kilometers, is the northernmost state in the Baltic region. Estonia borders on Latvia in the south and Russia in the east. The northern coast is formed by the Gulf of Finland and the western coast by the Baltic Sea. The capital of Estonia is Tallinn.

The ancestors of the inhabitants of Estonia settled the region over 5,000 years ago. Estonia was an independent state between 1918 and 1940. In 1940, Estonia was occupied by the Soviet Union. Since the end of the 1980s Estonia has been restoring its sovereignty. In 1992 a new constitution was passed, followed by the election of the parliament and president and the formation of the government. The strongly centralized totalitarian regime was substituted by a democratic and politically pluralistic parliamentary system. In 1991, there were 1.5 million inhabitants, of whom 61.5 percent were Estonians. The Soviet occupation changed the structure of population. Prior to 1940, 90 percent of the population was Estonian. The structure of population has been influenced by intensive migration from different areas of the Soviet Union. In 1993 Russians and other Russian-speaking people formed a considerable part of the population. There are Russian schools, newspapers, theaters, and cultural organizations, especially in the northeastern region where the Russian-speaking population dominates. In a number of areas, higher education professional training and corresponding activites were only or predominantly in Russian (military, diplomacy, navigation, police, government, etc.).

Most people live in towns (71.4% in 1991). Intensive urbanization began after the Second World War and lasted until the late 1980s. Urbanization is related to the economic structure of the country. At the end of the 1980s most people were employed in industry or services. Only 11 percent of the total labor force worked in agriculture. During the Soviet occupation there was no private sector economy. The structure of the economy has undergone fundamental changes since the early 1990s (privatization, new technology, reorientation to a market economy, introduction of a convertable currency, etc.). The reorganization of the economy has resulted in the closure, restructuring, and bankruptcies of several enterprises, huge loans to balance state and municipal budgets, increasingly unequal regional development and unemployment, all phenomena that were unknown under the Communist regime. Overall economic development demonstrates a low profile, but there was slight improvement in 1993 (GNP = US$3,100) after the 1992 crisis, when compared to 1991 (GNP = US$3,830).

Administrative reforms in 1993 aand 1994 introduced two levels of legislative power instead of three: between the state and municipality, at the county level, only the state's administrative representation remains. The main body of compulsory and vocational education institutions and all kindergartens are on the municipal budget and under the level's management. Teachers' salaries and the limited number of state special, upper-secondary, and the main body of higher education instituions are the responsibility of the state both managerially and budgetarily.

The Estonian education system started with cathedral and monastery schools established in the thirteenth and fourteenth centuries. The first *gymnasium* was established by Jesuits in 1583 and the university by King Gustavus II Adolphus of Sweden in 1632. The Lutheran Church had an impact on Estonian culture and education from the sixteenth century onwards. The first peasants' schools were established in the seventeenth century, and in the second half of that century, the two-year college for training native teachers for peasants' schools was established. By the end of the eighteenth century about two-thirds of all peasants could read. According to the 1881 Population Census, about 90 percent of Estonians were literate. The national educational system, including the university level, began to develop in Estonia as an independent state from 1918 with Estonian as the language of instruction. It was formerly German above the primary school level until the late nineteenth century and Russian at all levels between 1895 and 1917.

Estonia has to restore a comprehensive, independent, and integrated educational system, including the Estonian-oriented education of the Russian-language population. Vocational retraining has to be introduced and existing training restructured according to the needs and trends of the labor market.

2. Politics and the Goals of the Education System

Since 1940, the possibilities for developing independent educational policy in Estonia have been very limited. However, despite pressure to adopt the overpoliticized and unified Soviet educational structure and curricula, the Estonian educational system was able to maintain instruction in the Estonian language, and the differentiated school system.

The political renaissance at the end of the 1980s also stimulated Estonians' sense of national identity in educational matters. A depoliticized form of child-centered humanistic education was highly valued by politicians. By 1993, more precise guidelines on education were being drafted by social democrats and liberals.

The Estonian Educational Act, passed in 1992, states the following general goals of education: to promote the development of personality, family and the Estonian nation, as well as of national minorities, of Estonian economic, political, and cultural life and of nature preservation in the global economic and cultural context; to educate loyal citizens; and to set up the prerequisites of continuing education for everybody.

The Basic School and Gymnasium Act, adopted in 1993, sets out the obligatory nine-grade basic education between the ages of 7 and 17; differentiates between basic schools and *gymnasiums*, state, municipal, and private institutions; declares upper-secondary education to be open to all; and states that Estonian will become the only language of teaching in the state-financed upper-secondary institutions after the year 2000.

However, until May 1994 there was no political consensus reached in the egalitarian-elitarian dispute concerning upper-secondary education ("*gymnasium* for the chosen few" versus "comprehensive (upper) secondary schooling for all"). In addition, the issue of Russian-language upper-secondary education remains a "hot" one.

3. The Formal System of Education

At the end of the 1980s two essential innovations were introduced. First, the nine-year compulsory basic school replaced the compulsory secondary school. Second, four-year college-level institutions were introduced into tertiary education alongside universities. Private educational institutions started to function as alternatives to the existing public ones.

Estonia

The formal structure of education is shown in Fig. 1. The education system consists of preschool, primary, secondary, vocational, university / higher, and adult education. At all educational levels, except universities, there are Estonian or Russian institutions of education, according to the language of instruction. In universities there are also academic groups in which the instructional language is Russian. The percentage of students trained in Estonian is 61 in basic schools, 75 in secondary schools, 63 to 68 in vocational schools, and 84 percent in tertiary educational institutions.

3.1 Primary, Secondary, and Tertiary Education

Compulsory schooling begins at the age of 7, with the first four years as primary education. Secondary education is divided into two parts: basic education (Grades 5–9) and upper-secondary education (Grades 10–12). Primary and basic education (Grades 1–9) constitute compulsory schooling even if the student has not reached the age of 17 years. The basic school certificate provides students with the right to continue their education at the next level. There are two main options after the basic school: upper-secondary school (Grades 10–12) and vocational school. Some vocational schools provide secondary education parallel to vocational education. The certificate confirming secondary education gives students the right to continue their education either in universities or in other tertiary educational institutions.

In the 1991–92 academic year there were 666 comprehensive schools, 225 of which provided secondary education. The number of schools increased during the 1980s (in 1980–81 there were 537 schools). The number of pupils also increased but the growth was not so intensive. The average number of pupils per secondary school is 722. The average number of students per class is 24 (19 in rural schools) and this number is decreasing. The number of children starting Grade 1 is about 21,000 to 22,000 each year. In 1993, 1.7 percent of students dropped out from basic school and 0.27 percent were expelled.

Most graduates from the basic school continue their studies either in the secondary school (59% in 1991) or in different vocational schools (36%); about 5% do not continue their studies and, again, this number is increasing. Some 27 percent of secondary school graduates continue their studies in institutions of higher education and the same percentage in vocational schools.

Alongside secondary schools some three-year *gymnasia* have been established. Since these schools did not exist in the period from 1940–92, their role and function is not yet fully defined.

There were 10 public and two private tertiary educational institutions in 1991–92. The number of private institutions is rapidly increasing. From the academic year 1991–92 onward, tertiary education is divided

into two branches: universities and other institutions of higher education. There are six universities: Tartu University, founded in 1632 (8,000 students including part-time); Tallinn Technical University, founded in 1918 (9,000); Tallinn Art University, founded in 1938 (500); Tallinn Academy of Music, founded in 1919 (500); Estonian Agricultural University, founded in 1951 (4,000), and the Tallinn Pedagogical University, founded in 1952 (3,600). The total number of students in the academic year 1991–92 was 26,000 (including 5,300 first-year students) at universities, 760 in nonuniversity institutions, and 250 in private ones. The majority (88%) of students come from the general secondary schools. Undergraduate studies last

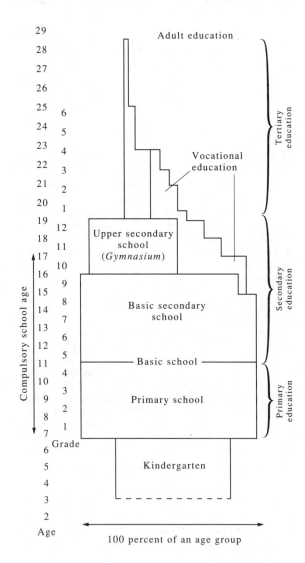

Figure 1
Estonia: Structure of the formal education system 1992

for four to six years. Nonuniversity higher educational institutions are new and based mainly on the former *technicums*.

3.2 Preschool Education

There were 794 preschool institutions, with an enrollment of 81,000 children in 1991. On average, there were 137 children per kindergarten in towns and 46 in rural areas. About 4 percent of 1-year old children, 38 percent of 2-year olds, 60 percent of 3-year olds, 68 percent of 4-year olds, 72 percent of 5-year olds, 69 percent of 6-year olds, and 25 percent of 7-years olds are enrolled. The media of instruction are Estonian (65% of children), Russian (28%), and both languages (6%). Regionally, neither municipal budgets nor parental charges can meet running costs.

3.3 Special Education

Children aged from 1–3 years with moderate and severe physical and/or mental disabilities are taken care of by some outpatient and related-area services that are available in larger cities. Children from three to seven years of age who need special speech, visual, auditory, orthopedic, or intellectual education and training, can attend special kindergarten groups in addition to the outpatient centers. This group of children (3–4% of the age group) has been decreasing slightly since the late 1980s.

In 1993 there were 50 special schools for children with physical, mental, or emotional disorders. About 13,700 pupils or 7.5 percent of the population in Grades 1 to 9 are provided with special education services. Among them 40 percent were enrolled in special schools and classes and 60 percent were provided with part-time remedial education and speech therapy. The average pupil–teacher ratios are: 2:1 in preschools / foundling hospitals, 4:1 in boarding schools, and 8–10:1 in special day schools. Since the late 1980s a process of mainstreaming has started. Enrollment in the primary grades of special schools has decreased, but there has also been an increase in the rate of functionally illiterate pupils with behavior problems from age 11 years onward. Since the early 1990s educational services for children with moderate mental retardation has expanded and a number of those children were able to study at special schools. Different and flexible solutions were introduced to educate children with learning disabilities in regular classes. The aim is to integrate persons with mental retardation, sensory, physical, and / or emotional disorders into independent life but the hope of accomplishing this has faded since the early 1990s. In order to combine early diagnostic identification and rehabilitation, outpatient sessions have been introduced to train both parents and their disabled children. Nongovernmental organizations of persons with handicaps, professionals, supporters, and parents have been active and cooperative. There is still a limited number of children with severe and / or multiple handicaps who are not integrated into the educational or social system.

3.4 Vocational, Technical, and Business Education

Until the beginning of the 1990s, vocational education was obliged to comply with Soviet policy, which placed artificial boundaries between tertiary and vocational educational systems. As a rule, compulsory secondary education was to be accompanied by a rigid form of vocational training. There are different curricula depending on the former educational level of the student. In 1981 there were 81 different vocational training institutions enrolling 28,000 students, training persons for more than a hundred different trades. Since the early 1990s there were six vocational educational institutions at the tertiary level. New programs to meet the national and market economy needs have been introduced (business management, navigation, aviation, tourism, police and military, etc.). The administration of nontertiary-level vocational education institutions is delegated to the local municipalities in order to ensure greater access. A number of secondary schools carry out some vocational training for the same purpose.

3.5 Adult and Nonformal Education

By the late 1980s, there were different forms of adult education in which general and / or professional pre- and / or inservice education could be continued. A wide range of cultural activities, taking place in different study groups, leisure-time activity clubs, recreation centers, and so on were organized for personal self-development. Since the early 1990s public and private educational institutions have been actively engaged into adult and nonformal education, especially in areas previously neglected such as the humanities, Estonian for the Russian-speaking population, modern languages, family therapy, business legislation and administration, computer application, and religion. Professional organizations and some state agencies are developing professional certification standards (medicine, engineering, jurisprudence, teaching, administration). There is a voluntary umbrella organization named "Andras," which is attempting to coordinate adult education activities.

The Adult Education Act, passed in 1993, differentiates between state- or employer-supported, professional qualification-oriented and general interest-oriented forms of continuing adult education.

4. Administrative and Supervisory Structure and Operation

Parliament determines the principles, budget, and general structure of the educational system. The government is responsible for the establishment and maintenance of state programs of education and regulates the governance of universities and other higher educational institutions. The Ministry of Culture and Education is responsible for the development and implementation of state educational programs and standards. It also grants licenses to private educational institutions.

Local municipalities are responsible for the development and functioning of the local educational system. They establish and finance local municipal educational institutions. Local self-governments form the structural units to administer preschool, primary, secondary, and vocational educational institutions.

Administrative and supervisory structures were still being developed in early 1993. The creation of educational standards has begun. The curricula of public educational institutions, except universities, are authorized by the Ministry of Culture and Education.

5. Educational Finance

Official figures of the percentage of the state budget allocated to education from 1989–90 to 1993 were: 11 percent in 1989–90, 12 percent in 1991, 16 percent in 1992, and 17 percent in 1993. These figures do not include expenditures made at the local level and from private and foreign sources. The ratio between per capita student costs at higher and secondary education is 2.5:1. Public primary and secondary education is still free of charge but at universities some categories of students must pay tuition costs. The stipend paid for students has been significantly reduced. A system of study loans has been introduced. Private finances and economic support from abroad cover a certain proportion of expenditures not only at the primary and secondary level but also in other forms of formal and nonformal education.

6. Supplying Personnel for the Education System

The number of comprehensive and secondary school teachers exceeds 19,000, forming 2 percent of the total labor-aged population. In 1992, the pupil–teacher ratios at different education levels were: 9.3:1 in preschool institutions, 17.9:1 in primary school, 11.9:1 in secondary school, and 8.8:1 in tertiary educational institutions. The educational level of teachers depends on the institutions in which they are employed. In preschool institutions teachers with two- or three-year tertiary education dominate and one-sixth have completed a full university education. Some 50 percent of primary and 81 percent of secondary school teachers have received a university

education. As a rule, the educational level of urban teachers is higher. Most teachers (85%) in primary and secondary schools are female, but in vocational schools 30 to 40 percent are male. Among the professional group 25 percent are under the age of 30 and 13 percent are at retirement age. The teaching profession has not been popular among young people since teacher salaries have been low for a long time. A perennial shortage of teachers, especially in some isolated rural areas, has made staffing schools difficult.

Educational personnel are trained at three universities and five educational colleges. At Tallinn Pedagogical University preschool teachers, primary school class teachers, and subject teachers for basic and secondary school levels are trained. There are also inservice training programs for teachers and school administrators. Since the beginning of the 1990s, social education tutors and school counsellors have also been trained. At Tartu University the qualification of the subject teacher for basic and secondary school levels can be obtained in a one-year course either following academic studies or simultaneously with undergraduate studies in the teacher's main subject. In 1968 the Department of Special Education where teachers for special and remedial education services are trained was established at Tartu University. Inservice teacher-training programs were also developed. Teachers for music education are trained at the Tallinn Academy of Music. Inservice training is not compulsory, but, for state and municipal employees, it may be an inevitable prerequisite to obtain higher professional certificates and salaries.

7. Curriculum Development and Teaching Methodology

Curricula, having been developed during the period from 1940–87 had to proceed from the general principles of the Soviet educational ideology. Despite the strict demand to unify the curricula, Estonia was able to maintain some of its educational traditions, for example, instruction in the native language, a number of textbooks written by Estonian authors, a year longer schooltime, and music education up to the end of secondary school.

The 1987 Congress of Estonian teachers started the process of restructuring, and changes in the curriculum began to take place in 1989–90. The curriculum was depoliticized, many syllabuses modernized, factual material diminished, the time allocated to optional subjects and to foreign languages increased, and new subjects introduced.

Students have to study at least two foreign languages, the choice of which is up to them. In Grade 3 a first foreign language is introduced and in Grade 6, a second foreign language. The most popular languages are English, German, Russian, Finnish, and French. It is also possible to study a third foreign language at the beginning of the upper-secondary level, but this is optional.

Russian schools in Estonia that had worked according to the Soviet curricula began to modernize their curricula in 1990–91. In the academic year 1992–93 the curricula of Estonian and Russian basic schools were identical.

The curriculum is nationwide for the core subjects but allows choices for the school and students in some subjects. According to the 1992–93 timetable the number of classroom hours per week were 20 hours in Grades 1 and 2, 25 hours in Grades 3 and 4, 29 hours in Grades 6 and 7 (plus two hours for options), and 32 hours in Grade 9 (plus three hours for options). At the secondary school level 24 hours per week form the core; there are a further eight hours for the type of differentiation subjects, and four hours for optional subjects. The total workload at the secondary school level is, therefore, 36 hours per week. At this level of schooling, the curricula of Estonian and Russian schools are not identical.

8. The System of Examinations, Promotions, and Certifications

The evaluation of students' achievement, the transfer of students from grade to grade and graduation from the school are regulated by the School Department of the Ministry of Culture and Education. The students' achievement is numerically evaluated on a five-point scale. The reports given at the end of each grade at basic and secondary school levels monitor the student's progress. Examinations, either oral or written, begin from Grade 6. Achievement tests are not used. The first formal certificate is awarded at the end of the basic school (Grade 9). The second certificate is awarded on completion of secondary education. Gold or silver medals are conferred on the very best students (in 1991, 50 students received gold medals and 312 silver medals).

Secondary education certificate does not confer an automatic right to enter tertiary educational institutions or universities. The applicants must pass the entrance examinations.

9. Educational Assessment, Evaluation, and Research

The Estonian educational system is being restructured. By 1993, several changes had already taken place in the structure of types of schools, as well as in the curriculum content, but it is too early for concrete feedback. It is expected that the results of contemporary changes will become evident in several years' time.

The evaluation of educational efficiency is based on the results of all-Estonian written papers in different subjects and on final examinations at various grade levels.

10. Major Reforms in the 1980s and 1990s

The only reform that took place in the 1980s was associated with the 1987 Estonian Teachers' Congress, at which the decision to restructure educational policy was approved. During the 1990s, the ideas of the 1980s will need to be corrected, improved, and developed. The Education Act was passed in 1992, the Basic School and Gymnasium Act, and Adult Education Act in 1993; as of May 1994 the Higher Education Act had reached parliamentary committees.

11. Major Problems for the Year 2000

The landscape of Estonian education in the 1990s reflects the breakdown of the totalitarian occupation regime and the regaining of independence and sovereignty. Nearly every aspect and sphere of education has been scrutinized and declared to be in need of revision and restructuring. Among the most acute aspects requiring attention were the following: the ideology and paradigms of education; the structure of education; the relationship between different levels of education; the quality of education; the relationship between education and the economy; the relationship between education and culture; the relationship between education, human rights, and freedom; territorial location and availability of educational institutions; legislation and administration of education; the relative proportions of public and private initiatives; and the supply of personnel and finances.

The chief problem as education in Estonia moves toward the year 2000 is how to develop an education system in a stable way and with an effective feedback system.

Bibliography

Eesti Õppeasutused 1991 / 92 Õppeaasta alguseks. Statistika aastaraamat. Eesti Vabariigi Riiklik Statistikaamet, Tallinn

Rajangu V 1992 *Educational Statistics Album of Estonia.* Eesti Vabariigi Haridusministeerium, Tallinn

Rajangu V 1993 *Das Bildungswesen in Estland. Grundlagen, Probleme, Perspektiven.* Böhlau, Cologne

Ruus V 1992 Eesti hariduse probleemistik ja eesmärgiseade. (Unpublished manuscript.)

Siimaste E 1992 Eesti haridus arvudes. *Haridus* 5, 6

Ethiopia

M. Belachew

1. General Background

Ethiopia covers an area of just over 1.2 million square kilometers and is located in the Horn of Africa. It is the tenth largest country in Africa. It has a coastline of about 1,000 kilometers and is bounded by Sudan in the north, Kenya in the south, and Somalia and Djibouti in the east.

Over the centuries, Ethiopia's civilization has been influenced by the Arabs (in particular, the Sabaeans who came from Saudi Arabia), the Romans, the Greeks, and the Egyptians. The capital was in the various parts of the country and it was only in 1899 that King Menelik II established the capital in the city of Addis Ababa. Haile Selassie I became emperor in 1930 and, compared with the regime that had previously ruled the country, did much for education. He was overthrown in 1974 and a military government, which was guided by Marxist–Leninist ideology (and headed from 1977 by Colonel Mariam Mengistu), ruled until 1991. It, in turn, was overthrown by the Ethiopian People's Revolutionary Democratic Front (PRDF).

At the beginning of 1992 Ethiopia was being ruled by a transitional government and it was expected that after a period of two to three years a new government would be elected. The administrative region of Eritrea created its own provisional government and, again, after a two-year period it was expected to decide its own future political destiny through a referendum.

In 1991, the total population was estimated to be nearly 50 million. Of these, 89 percent lived in rural areas. However, the population was unevenly distributed in the various rural areas, with some regions having five times more inhabitants than other areas. Some 73 percent of the population was under 18 years of age and the annual population growth rate was 3.22 percent. Only 49 percent of the population was economically active. Life expectancy was 46.9 years for both males and females.

Arable and livestock farming is the predominant economic activity, but productivity is low. Manufacturing activities are highly underdeveloped and accounted for only 11 percent of the Gross Domestic Product (GDP) in 1986. The per capita income in 1986 was US$121 per year, making Ethiopia one of the poorest countries in the world. The transitional government's Council of Representatives approved a new economic policy at the end of 1991. This was based on the principles of the market economy with large-scale privatization of the main sectors of the economy. This has had important implications for the knowledge and skills to be covered in the school curriculum (Central Statistical Authority {annual}).

Ethiopia is a multiethnic and multilingual society. The Amaras and Oromos form the two largest ethnic groups, but there are also Tigres and Eritreans. Amarigna, or "Amharic" as it is usually called, is the working language in the country. However, Oromigna is the predominant home language in several areas. Tigrigna and Wollaitgna are also other important languages.

In short, Ethiopia's education system is beset with difficulties. It is a very poor country, with 89 percent of its population in rural areas. Its labor force has a poor educational background and there are many health problems. There are different ethnic and language groups. The change of government which took place in 1991 has entailed great upheaval. Section 3 below indicates that less than 50 percent of an age group receives any formal education. Furthermore, money is in very short supply.

2. Politics and the Goals of the Education System

The goals of the education system emanate from the political orientation that the government has adopted in a particular period. For instance, between 1974 and 1991 curricula were based on the principles of Marxism–Leninism. However, in the last days of the Mengistu regime the ideological education component of the curriculum was eliminated by the government itself in response to the liberalization process resulting from the collapse of communism in the Soviet Union and Eastern Europe.

In February 1992, the transitional government had not yet issued detailed guidelines regarding the goals of the education system. But it was expected that when they eventually came out they would reflect the varied interests of the political organizations that are mushrooming in the country. In the meantime, the existing educational goals are by and large still in force.

The goals of general education aim at enhancing individual productivity which would in turn influence the overall level of production. Hence, the general education curriculum was restructured to include the following main disciplines: technical and vocational education, the arts, and physical education.

The specific goals of higher education are: to train the high-level and middle-level labor force, in both quantity and quality, that is required for accelerating national development; to conduct on-the-job training and continuing education programs, which focus on raising the technical and cultural levels of the people; to undertake research with particular emphasis on the

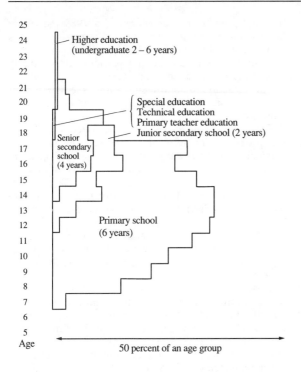

Figure 1
Ethiopia: Structure of the formal education system 1988

needs and problems of the people and to disseminate the research findings; and to establish a strong link between theory and practice.

3. The Formal System of Education

3.1 Primary, Secondary, and Tertiary Education

General formal education is free in Ethiopia and the system is coeducational. However, education is not compulsory. The Ministry of Education is responsible for kindergarten, primary, and secondary education, as well as for teacher-training and evening programs. Figure 1 indicates the structure of the formal education system.

There are eight types of institutions that are responsible for the provision of general education, namely: kindergartens or preschools, primary schools, junior-secondary schools, senior-secondary schools, technical and vocational education schools, primary teacher-training institutions, special education schools, and night schools.

The schools are divided into two categories: government and nongovernment. Government schools are usually regarded as offering low-quality education since they suffer from chronic shortages of qualified

teaching staff, finance, equipment, and materials; and have large class sizes. In consequence, the students of government schools largely originate from low-income families. In contrast, well-to-do families (which normally include members of the ruling class, high-ranking officials, successful businessmen, and highly educated professionals) prefer to send their children to the nongovernment or private schools.

As can be seen from Fig. 1, the scale is for 50 percent of an age group as compared with 100 percent in most other descriptions of school systems in this *Encyclopedia*. Children do not enter school at age 6. Even 16-years olds can enter first grade. Thus, grade levels are not given. Nevertheless, if it is assumed that primary school lasts six years, the age distribution can be seen.

In general, the number of educational institutions increased by 60 to 200 percent in the period 1974–89, with the exception of technical and vocational schools which decreased dramatically.

Primary school lasts six years, junior-secondary two years, and senior-secondary three years. After completing Grade 10, students may enter technical and vocational schools for three years. Teacher-training institutes for primary-school teachers accept students from Grade 12, and the course lasts one year.

Amharic is the medium of instruction in the preschools and in Grades 1 to 6. Thereafter it is replaced by English.

In 1989 the enrollments by level of education were as follows: 87,355 (preschool education); 2,855,846 (primary education); 447,587 (junior-secondary education); 426,413 (senior-secondary education); 1,537 (special education); 4,101 (technical and vocational education); 4,142 (primary teacher education); and 219,806 (adult education). Adult education is provided through evening programs. Although the students are fee-paying, these programs are highly popular. During the same year the percentages of girls in the primary, junior-secondary schools, senior-secondary schools, and night schools were 39, 41, 39, and 47 respectively (Ministry of Education 1989).

Higher education is free to the citizens of Ethiopia. The system is coeducational and is under the supervision of the Ministry of Education's main Department of Higher Education. There are three universities, three junior colleges, one polytechnic institute and one college. There are also other institutions of higher education that are supervised by other authorities. These consist of two colleges and two institutes.

The establishment of the University College of Addis Ababa (UCAA) in 1950 marked the beginning of higher education in Ethiopia. Between 1950 and 1961 four additional colleges were established. In 1961 the UCAA and these four colleges were upgraded and the Addis Ababa University (AAU) was established with a view to making it the major supplier of high-level workers (UNESCO 1984)

Initially the UCAA was mostly staffed by Canadian

Table 1
Total enrollments in higher education by programs 1989–90

Program	Total	Female
Regular diploma programs	6,713	1,004
Regular undergraduate-degree programs	10,327	845
Graduate-degree programs	573	37
Extension diploma programs	9,003	3,006
Extension undergraduate-degree programs	4,957	1,037
Summer teacher-training diploma programs	1,570	102
Summer teacher-training degree programs	639	30
Total	33,782	6,056

Source: Main Department of Higher Education, 1989–90

Jesuits and other expatriates. In 1961 the expatriates accounted for 75 percent of the academic staff and in 1973 this was 54 percent.

In 1953 a missionary congregation formed the Asmara University which was recognized by the government as a tertiary institution in 1963. Prior to the 1974 revolution, the Asmara University was the only nongovernmental tertiary institution in the country with mostly foreign staff and external financial support.

The total enrollments in higher education by program are provided in Table 1.

3.2 Preschool Education

Preschool is of two years' duration. Most preschools are private. Although there has been an increase in the number of preschools, the actual number of children attending them is so negligible that they have not been included in Fig. 1.

3.3 Vocational, Technical, and Business Education

The need for a middle-level workforce led to the establishment (by the Ministry of Education and the Ministry of Agriculture) of junior colleges offering two-year postsecondary diploma programs.

The former Alemaya College of Agriculture, which was under the administration of the AAU, was transformed into an independent university in 1984. It assumed the name Alemaya University of Agriculture, with the objective of serving as the center of excellence in agricultural education.

3.4 Adult and Nonformal Education

A literacy campaign, which aims at eradicating illiteracy, was launched in 1979. The ultimate objective of this campaign is to accelerate the socioeconomic development of the country. In 1974 only 7 percent of

the total population was literate. By 1989 the figure had risen to 76 percent. The literacy campaign focuses on reading and writing. In 1989 enrollment was about 13.1 million. Many postliteracy participants eventually enter the formal education system.

The structure of adult education is composed of the community skill training programs and distance education.

There are three types of community skill training programs, namely: skill training, development-oriented training, and transfer of knowledge. These are carried out through the Community Skill Training Centers (CSTCs). In 1989 there were 408 CSTCs. The number of participants was 151,671, and of these 21 percent were female. Participants are expected to return to their villages and teach their skills and knowledge to the other members of the community. In addition, the CSTCs serve as forums for expediting the activities of the various ministries such as Health, Agriculture, and Transport.

Distance education is carried out through the national radio network under the control of the Ministry of Education. It covers the regular school subjects in English, and numerous topics in agriculture, health, and civics in the Amharic, Oromigna, Tigrigna, and Wollaitigna languages for community development. The attendance was 5,985 in 1989, with 7.5 percent of these being female.

4. Administrative and Supervisory Structure and Operation

The government schools, colleges, and universities are administered by the government through the Ministry of Education. There are numerous regional educational offices dealing with current administrative affairs, but the curricula are centrally prescribed. The educational policy within the Ministry of Education is discussed by a Policy Advisory Committee comprising departmental heads under the chairmanship of the Minister. School-level administration is carried out in collaboration with school management committees elected by local organizations.

The nongovernment or private schools are operated by authorities other than the Ministry of Education. These are missionaries, the public, churches, and mosques. Nevertheless, even these private schools are obliged to follow the curricula developed by the Ministry of Education, since the national examinations taken at Grades 6 and 8 and the Ethiopian School Leaving Certificate examinations are set by or under the guidance of the Ministry of Education.

More specifically, higher education is administered by the Main Department of Higher Education, which is now under the Ministry of Education. It is a monitoring and coordinating agency for third-level education, which receives directives from the Council for Higher Education and collaborates directly with the Planning Committee especially in the area of manpower planning.

The universities receive policy guidelines and directives. The programs and budgets of the universities are processed through the Main Department of Higher Education which has granted internal autonomy to the universities.

The Main Department of Higher Education has a weak coordinating function with the AAU owing to the fact that the latter is the oldest and largest university in the country and as such has developed an autonomous status.

5. Educational Finance

The government has always been the major source of funds for the education sector, but there is also a heavy reliance on external financial sources. For instance, in order to implement the general education targets mentioned in the Ethiopian Ten-Year Plan, 39.2 percent of the investment is expected to be from internal sources and 60.8 percent from external sources.

In 1988 the recurrent and capital expenditure for the general education subsector was US$193,776. This was 3.6 percent of the GDP. The proportion of the GDP devoted to the general education subsector rose from 1.4 percent in 1971 to 3.6 percent in 1988. The recurrent and capital expenditure for the higher education subsector was US$37,558 in 1988. This was 0.7 percent of the GDP.

Between 82.5 and 85.5 percent of the recurrent budget is usually earmarked for primary, secondary, technical, and vocational education, as well as for teacher training and adult education. The rest goes to the higher education subsector. Capital expenditure represented between 3 and 24 percent of the total expenditure during the period extending from 1969 to 1988.

The unit costs in US dollars by level of education in 1981–82 were as follows: primary education (25), junior-secondary education (68), senior-secondary education (65), technical and vocational education (313), primary-school teacher training (549), and adult education (75). Higher education unit costs varied from US$1,429 for the AAU to US$381 for the Addis Ababa Junior College of Commerce. The AAU usually absorbs three-fourths of the total higher education budget.

6. Supplying Personnel for the Education System

The total number of teachers by level in 1989 were: 65,990 (primary), 10,500 (junior-secondary), and 10,720 (senior-secondary). The percentages of female teachers were 23.0, 10.6, and 9.1 respectively.

In 1991, the total number of nonteaching staff in the general education subsectors was estimated at about 18,000.

In the 1989–90 academic year, the total number of full-time Ethiopian academic staff in the higher education subsector was 13,978; of these, only 87 were female. During the same year the total number of full-time expatriate academic staff was 2,235 and, of these, 34 were female. Again during the same year there were 89 Ethiopian and 25 expatriate part-time academic staff. In 1989–90 the total number of the nonteaching or administrative staff in the higher education system was 5,467. Of these nearly 50 percent were female.

There are no shortages of administrative staff. Nevertheless there are grave shortages of qualified and experienced academic staff. The main causes are the uncompetitive salary scales, and lack of salary increments.

Teachers in the general education system may upgrade their knowledge and skills by joining either the regular undergraduate programs, the summer teacher-training diploma and degree programs, or the graduate programs if their employers are willing to sponsor them.

The academic staff of the institutions of higher learning may further their education by going abroad on scholarships or by joining the local school of graduate studies. In addition, the academic staff may develop their career through sabbatical and research leaves, short-term training, and seminars and workshops.

The main route for administrative staff to improve their knowledge and skills is by joining the evening programs. However, short-term training opportunities are usually available also. These are often purposely prepared within the workplace in order to upgrade the knowledge and skills of those employees that are not highly trained.

The work performance of the administrative staff in the entire school system is regularly evaluated on the basis of the guidelines issued by the Civil Service Commission.

7. Curriculum Development and Teaching Methodolgy

Prior to 1974, the education system at all levels was narrow and highly academic. The absence of adequate facilities for technical and vocational education resulted in a much larger number of students going on to academic education which in turn led to unemployment problems.

The old curriculum emphasized the teaching of academic subjects in a school system which envisaged entry to Grade 1 at the age of seven years. It consisted of offering largely general academic education in a school system comprising preschool education, junior-secondary education, and senior-secondary education.

Since 1974 many attempts have been made to

change the educational system. In 1974, a fully equipped and appropriately staffed National Curriculum Development Center was established. The Center, which forms the Curriculum Department of the Ministry of Education, now has over 70 professional staff. The structure of the Department includes offices for curricular and pedagogical research, polytechnic education research, and primary and secondary teacher education.

The new curriculum provides for a general education which is to be universalized to Grade 6 level in the first stage and then, as resources permit, to a unified system of general education to Grade 8 level. Above the level of Grade 8 there is a selective entry process to the four years of secondary education. In summary, the system which envisages entry to Grade 1 at the age of 7 has been defined as follows: general polytechnic education (Grades 1–8), higher polytechnic education (Grades 9–10), and extended polytechnic education (Grades 11–12).

The new curriculum has been issued to schools as a guide to program implementation, and a process of controlled implementation and evaluation was initiated in 70 pilot schools. The pilot school program includes a grade-by-grade intensive study of the viability of the new curriculum. The draft curriculum is then revised and finally published as the tested and approved program of studies for the grade.

The new curriculum includes the preparation and publication of student tests and workbooks, teachers' guides, and supplementary materials. Considerable efforts have been made in this area and Ethiopia is approaching a point where all teaching materials for the regular system will be prepared, printed, and published within the country by the Educational Materials Production and Distribution Agency established in 1975 as an autonomous unit under the Ministry of Education.

Foreign languages are usually elective subjects. French is perhaps the most popular elective subject. It is taught mainly in private schools. German is mostly taught in the AAU and a few other places.

8. The System of Examinations, Promotions, and Certifications

In the general school system, promotion from one grade to another is decided on the basis of the final examinations administered at the end of an academic year. Gifted students are usually entitled to what is locally referred to as "double promotion." In other words, they are allowed to skip their current year and be promoted to the next one. Nevertheless, this is not practiced uniformly in all schools.

Promotion to the seventh and ninth grades is determined by the Grades 6 and 8 national examinations prepared and administered by the Ministry of Education. Students are admitted to the institutions of higher education after passing the Ethiopian School Leaving Certificate examinations (ESLCE) which are prepared and administered by the AAU. As the available places are highly limited only very few students can enter institutions of higher education. These are often those candidates who earn the highest grade-point averages in the ESLCE.

Mid-semester and semester examinations are set, and frequent tests are also given during each semester in order to encourage the students to study regularly and ascertain the extent of their grasp of the subject matter. End-of-year examinations cover all the course materials discussed throughout the academic year. Certificates are awarded to those candidates who sit for Grades 6, 8, and 12 examinations.

In the colleges and universities, promotion is also determined on the basis of the final examinations administered at the end of an academic year.

In general, the examination system of the institutions of higher education is similar to that of the general school system. But there are certain differences. Students are entitled to resit examinations provided that they can produce satisfactory evidence for having failed to take the officially scheduled examinations. Supplementary examinations are also given to those students who have received low grades but have the potential for improving their grades if they are allowed to retake examinations in certain courses. Those students who are dissatisfied with their low grades, and who can submit justifiable reasons, may have their answer papers re-marked upon payment of about US$4.

Diplomas are awarded in the institutions of higher education usually at the end of two years of study, while first degrees are given after four years of study. Second degrees are awarded after a maximum period of four years, and terminal degrees after a maximum period of four years. Second degrees in engineering and MDs are awarded after five years of study. The award of diplomas and degrees to night-school students takes place after four and seven years of study respectively.

9. Educational Assessment, Evaluation, and Research

No systematic mechanism exists for educational assessment and evaluation. There have been, however, certain assessment studies of the functioning of the primary and secondary education levels. The Ministry of Education, concerned about the declining quality of education, undertook a number of intensive studies in the early 1980s. The studies covered the entire general school education system and proposed certain measures which would improve the quality of education. These proposals were not accepted by the former socialist government on two grounds: firstly, the proposals entailed solutions that were not politically acceptable; and secondly, the available resources were highly inadequate for implementing the proposals.

There is an annual educational evaluation seminar organized by the Ministry of Education and chaired by the Minister. The objective of the seminar is to evaluate the performance of the general education system during the preceding academic year. The main participants of this seminar are the high-ranking officials of the Ministry of Education and the regional educational officers. Every year the problems encountered are discussed and solutions are proposed. However, due to the grave financial constraints, the problems are merely transferred from one year to another.

Since 1974 the curricula of the higher education system have undergone numerous, and in some cases fundamental, changes and revisions. These changes and revisions focus on making the teaching and research activities more relevant to the development needs of the country. Moreover, the performance of the academic staff is continuously evaluated by the department chairmen, faculty deans, and the students. Some tracer studies have been conducted to evaluate the external efficiency of the institutions of higher education.

Research activities are mainly undertaken at the higher education level, particularly in the universities. In the AAU, research activities are coordinated by the Research and Publications Office. The AAU Press is responsible for the publication of books, monographs, and the like. Research activities are undertaken by the various colleges, faculties, and research institutes of the AAU: the Institute of Development Research and the Institute of Ethiopian Studies are notable examples. Currently there are 11 research journals whose reputation is recognized internationally.

The research projects completed by the University since 1974 number 670. Of these, 33 percent were concerned with teaching materials. The budget of the research institutes is normally 3 percent of the annual budget of the AAU, or about US$580,000. In addition, sizable external financial assistance is frequently obtained from regional, international, and UN donor agencies. This is usually in the region of 30 percent of the total research budget.

10. Major Reforms in the 1980s and 1990s

The 1980s were remarkable for the many curricular changes and revisions at all levels of education. Upon the eruption of Ethiopia's 1974 revolution, Marxism–Leninism became the philosophical foundation of education. In consequence, the schools and the institutions of higher education were required to change and revise their curricula on the basis of guidelines provided by the Ministry of Education and the then Commission for Higher Education. The former elitist education system was thus replaced by the broad-based education system which in theory was expected to cater for the educational needs of the masses.

Toward the end of the 1980s the Marxist–Leninist ideology was rejected and curricula started to reflect the pre-1974 capitalist mode of education.

11. Major Problems for the Year 2000

The Ethiopian school system is bound to suffer from the following deep-seated problems until the year 2000 and undoubtedly beyond: shortage of qualified staff; huge enrollment increases; inadequate orientation of curricula to Ethiopian circumstances; the absence of science and technology; and inadequate financial resources resulting from the previous dependence on external assistance in terms of staff, educational materials, and budgetary constraints.

The last problem is perhaps the most difficult one in the light of the new political orientation of the country. At the time of writing this entry, the transitional government had not yet prepared a new educational policy. However, it is likely that the major ethnic groups will be expected to use their own languages for instructional purposes, though perhaps only up to a certain level of schooling. This will certainly place a heavy burden on the limited resources available in the country.

References

Central Statistical Authority (annual) *Analytical Reports on Addis Ababa, Arssi, Bale, Gondar, Gojjam, Keffa, Shewa, Wellega and Wello Regions.* Central Statistical Authority, Addis Ababa
Ministry of Education 1989 *Basic Education Statistics 1989.* Ministry of Education, Addis Ababa
UNESCO 1984 *Ethiopia: Tertiary Education and National Development.* UNESCO, Paris

Further Reading

M. Belachew 1986a An analysis of tertiary education financing: The experiences of Addis Ababa University. In: USSR Academy of Sciences, *Proceedings of the Ninth International Conference of Ethiopian Studies*, USSR Academy of Sciences, Africa Institute, Moscow
M. Belachew 1986b Interregional variations and explanation of student achievement. *Ethiopian J. Development Research*, 8(2): 49–70
M. Belachew 1988 The need for regional educational planning within the context of integrated rural development: The case of Ethiopia. In: Treuner P et al. (eds.) *Regional Planning and Development in Ethiopia 2, A Seminar Report.* Institute of Development Research (Addis Ababa University) and the Institute of Development Planning, Stuttgart
Higher Education, Main Department 1991 *Statistics on Higher Education.* Ministry of Education, Addis Ababa
Pankhurst R 1990 *A Social History of Ethiopia.* Institute of Ethiopian Studies, Addis Ababa University, Addis Ababa
Provisional Military Government of Socialist Ethiopia 1984 *Ten-Year Perspective Plan 1984/85–1993/94.* Addis Ababa

Fiji

F. Mangubhai

1. General Background

Fiji is a south-central archipelago comprising over 300 islands, 100 of which are inhabited. It is 2,730 kilometers northeast of Australia and 1,830 kilometers north of New Zealand. The land mass totals 18,272 square kilometers spread across 1,127 kilometers of ocean north to south and 789 kilometers from east to west. Two main islands, Viti Levu and Vanua Levu, together make up 87 percent of the land mass. Its population of 771,104 (1993 estimate) is made up of 50 percent indigenous Fijians, 44.8 percent Indians, and 5.2 percent others. The growth rate is 1.7 percent, a small decline in rate compared to a rate of 2.1 in 1976, but substantially larger in comparison to the growth rate of 3.3 percent in 1966. More than 60 percent of the population lives in rural areas. The spread of islands has and continues to present a challenge to educational planners to make the provision of education in rural areas and on smaller islands equitable and economically feasible and possible.

The first European to sight and chart the islands was Abel Tasman in 1643. The first foreign residents at the beginning of the nineteenth century were "deserters, marooned sailors, derelict scourings of the ports of the Old World, among them some of the worst and lowest of their kind" (Derrick 1946 p. 37). They brought with them new diseases to the islands that were to take a heavy toll on the Fijian people.

Christianity in the form of Methodism arrived in 1835. The Methodist missionaries introduced the people to literacy in the Fijian language and taught them to read the Bible and other religious writings. The Methodists were followed by Catholics and together these two major Christian denominations were the primary providers of education for the next 80 years.

In 1874 the Fiji islands were ceded to the United Kingdom. Five years later the Colonial Government imported from India the first indentured laborers to work on the sugarcane plantations. By the end of the indentured system in 1920, some 60,000 Indians had arrived in Fiji. With natural increase and further migration from India, Indians in 1993 comprised over 44 percent of the population. The multiethnic composition of the islands has had many ramifications for education, not the least of which has been that from the 1920s onwards the Indian population has increasingly wanted more education and at higher levels, resulting in the Colonial Government having to provide some secondary education for both the Indians and the Fijians.

In addition to the ethnic diversity resulting from the indentured system and the subsequent migration, there also arose a diversity in religious affiliations (Christians of different sects, Hindus, and Moslems), as well as a diversity of languages (mainly Fijian, Hindi, Urdu, and English, but also Tamil, Telegu, Gujerati, Rotuman, and Chinese). These diversities have all put pressure upon the educational system to accommodate religious and language differences.

Historically, the language of education for the first 50 years after the arrival of missionaries was Fijian. All education was conducted by the Christian churches, even after Fiji was ceded to the United Kingdom. The Catholic Church was the first to teach English to students in its educational system. After 1916 when the Colonial Government formally set up an Education Department, English took on a greater importance in the education system, partly as a result of the needs of the Colonial Government for workers in the civil service and partly as a result of the pressure from the Indian population who wanted more education and more of it in English. After the 1930s, when the Methodist Church relinquished its primary schools to the Government, there was an increasing use of English in the school system so that by the time Fiji became independent in 1970, English was firmly entrenched as the language of instruction. The vernacular languages, Fijian and Hindi (and later Urdu and Rotuman, a Polynesian language) were used as medium of instruction for the first three years in the primary schools and thereafter became a subject of study until Form 4 (Grade 10). In the 1980s, the study of vernacular languages was extended to Form 6 (Grade 12).

In the 1980s particularly, Fijians began to show increasing concern about their language especially as it became evident that some urban Fijian children were neither proficient in their mother tongue or in the second language (English). By contrast, the Indian population, apart from some vocal educators, appeared to be less concerned about the cultural and linguistic impact of English. These linguistic concerns are likely to continue to surface whenever the focus of educational pronouncements shifts from an economic orientation to a more social and cultural orientation.

Much of the character of the educational system in Fiji has been determined by demographic factors. Until the 1960s much of the Fijian population lived in rural areas of the main islands or on smaller islands while the Indian population was massed in towns or areas near towns. This distribution of population resulted in largely monoracial classrooms. It was only with the advent of events leading to Independence in 1970 that a more concerted effort was made to make schooling in Fiji more multiethnic wherever it was possible. Despite these efforts, especially in the period immediately after

Independence, the historical patterns of enrollment have continued in most schools.

Like many other developing countries, Fiji is diversifying from agricultural production and exports to tourism and manufacturing. Tourism particularly has grown substantially. In 1976, of those over 15 years of age in employment, about 7 percent were involved in services. By 1986, this percentage had more than doubled to 15 percent. Historically, the Fijian population was involved in small-scale agriculture and also provided labor for the government administration, education, and medical services. The Indian population grew sugarcane, largely on leased land, and was involved in small-scale trade and commerce. Larger commercial ventures were run mainly by Australian-owned firms. After Independence, the Indian involvement in commerce and the professions increased substantially in size and scope. Since Independence, there has been a determined effort to involve the Fijian population more in the commercial life of the country.

In the late 1980s Fiji, like many other countries, did not escape the problem of unemployment. Concerns were expressed about school dropouts who did not wish to return to their villages but who also appeared to be equipped for no particular job. A nonformal education initiative was set up to provide such school leavers with a chance to acquire some skill that would make them either self-sufficient or to equip them to go back to the land. This concern continues to exercise Fijian educators rather more than the Indian since 82 percent of the land is owned by indigenous Fijians and cannot be sold. The Indians continue to see education as a means of "liberating" them from the land and as the chief means of social mobility. Aspirations of the two major ethnic groups have been different in the past and continue to be so. There have been, however, increasing pressures upon the Fijian people to participate more in the commercial life of the country.

The general educational level of the labor force has increased markedly in the second half of the twentieth century. Six to eight years of education was the norm in the first half of the century. Since Independence, with the development of junior-secondary schools in the rural areas, the norm shifted upward toward Grade 10. Among the population of 25 years or over, there are, nevertheless, approximately 11 percent with no schooling, and over 35 percent with incomplete primary schooling.

Most young people entering the civil service since the mid-1980s have completed at least 12 years of education. The development of a technical institute has provided skilled workers for the small manufacturing sector in the country.

The chief political goals of the country underwent a radical change after the military coups of 1987. In the mid 1990s, they are geared to ensure that the political power remains in the hands of the indigenous Fijians. To this end, the post-1987 Constitution has weighted

political representation in the parliament in favor of Fijians. This is in marked contrast to the constitution adopted at the time of Independence which allocated equal number of seats to the two major ethnic groups, and which did not stipulate that the prime minister must be an ethnic Fijian. The 1990s is likely to see further strengthening of the political power of the Fijians, with a likely curtailment of the educational opportunities of the Indian population. The goals of education for the Fijian people will continue to be ambiguous as efforts are made to encourage more Fijian students to undertake higher education and, at the same time, encourage them to retain their customs and culture.

2. Politics and the Goals of the Education System

The goals of education have changed dramatically since the beginning of the twentieth century. It was not until 1916 that the Colonial Government took some control of the education system in the country, which was geared to the development of basic literacy and numeracy. However, after the termination of the indentured system in 1920, there was a rising tide of demand for more education, especially at secondary level. The government had to respond to this demand, though it did it minimally. Religious groups, Christian and non-Christian, developed their own schools, leading to a situation where only 33 (3.6 percent) out of a total of 926 of all types of schools are government schools (1992 figures). The rest are controlled by religious, and special interest and subcultural groups.

Despite this large disparity between the number of government and nongovernment schools, the government has been able to influence the educational system through its control over the curriculum and the examinations, and through its system of grants-in-aid. In the 1970s, the Ministry of Education vigorously developed a Curriculum Development Unit which produced curricula and materials that were designed to be more relevant to the needs of an independent Pacific country. These materials have been used in all schools and the national examinations based on these materials have ensured uniformity of instructional goals in the country.

The broad aims of education enunciated by government five-year plans from the mid-1970s have been fourfold:

(a) to provide a program that would lead to the full development of individuals in a changing society, taking into account their abilities, interests, and aptitudes;

(b) to develop Fiji's human resources in such a way as to guide all citizens toward productive activity, in accordance with national needs, thereby accelerating economic development;

(c) to encourage a greater sense of national awareness, self-reliance, and pride in being a citizen of Fiji;

(d)   to promote the cultural identities of Fiji and its people amid increasing contact with the outside world (*Fiji Development Plan Eight,* 1981–1985 1981 p. 254).

The broad aims of education have not always been realized in practice as government goals have not necessarily coincided with personal individual goals or the goals of certain segments of the society. The lure of town or city life has resulted in an influx of young people from the rural areas with a slim chance of getting employment. White-collar jobs rather than blue-collar ones continue to hold greater attraction for young people so that the effectiveness of government policy on technical and vocational education is diminished.

3. The Formal System of Education

3.1 Primary, Secondary, and Tertiary Education

Education in Fiji is not compulsory and is not completely free. In 1972, the government introduced fee-free education in Grade 1 and extended it yearly until Grades 1 to 8 were fee-free. However, the grant of F$12 (US$10) per pupil is insufficient for running a school and has to be supplemented by monies raised through school fundraising activities.

The grade structure of schools is a mixture of patterns. Prior to 1969 the educational system consisted of an elementary / intermediate combination extending from Class 1 (Grade 1) to Class 8 (Grade 8), a secondary level from Forms 3 to 6 (Grades 9 to 12). The 1969 Education Commission recommended that the primary level consist of Classes 1 to 6, a junior-secondary level from Forms 1 to 4, and senior-secondary from Forms 5 to 6. However, the old and the new systems have continued side by side so that there are some primary schools where the highest grade is 6 and others where the highest grade is 8. Similarly in the secondary system, there are schools which begin at Form 1 and others that begin at Form 3. During the 1970s and 1980s, the concept of junior-secondary schools gradually became eroded as community pressures resulted in the Ministry of Education's approval to develop Form 5s and later Form 6s.

Beyond the primary and secondary levels of education there is the regional University of the South Pacific, established in 1968 to serve the needs of the countries of the South Pacific. In 1987 there were 879 full-time, 183 part-time, and 2,047 extension (distance education) students from Fiji enrolled at the University. In addition, there were a small number of students at the Fiji School of Medicine which offers Bachelor of Medicine and Bachelor of Surgery degrees, as well as

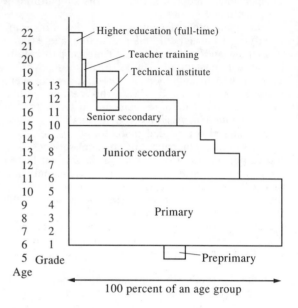

Figure 1

Fiji: Structure of the formal education system 1987

a number of paramedical courses. Other small tertiary institutions offer agriculture, theological studies (2 institutions), and nursing.

Figure 1 outlines the structure of the formal educational system. Key statistics on enrollments are given in Fig. 2. Both figures are based on the 1992 Ministry of Education Report. Some figures had to be estimated using the available data in the report.

With reference to Fig. 1, approximately 12.5 percent of children of preschool age were attending a preschool center. Of the 6–11 year age group, 99.5 percent were attending full-time school. There was a crude wastage rate of 20.9 percent for the first 8 years of education (this includes Forms 1–2). Between Class 8 / Form 2 and Form 4, there was a small dropout rate. Between Forms 4 and 5 there was a dropout rate of about 20 percent. Since 1987 there has been a two-year program leading to the Fiji School Leaving Certificate at the end of Form 6, and once students begin Form 5, the dropout rate is minimal between the first and second years. Since 1990, the Fiji government has not sent any students to do the foundation program at the University. Instead, Form 7 has been expanded so that in 1992 there were 2,328 students studying at the highest secondary level. The University numbers shown in the diagram represent just under 1,100 full-time students and did not take into account the 331 part-time students or the just over 3,400 students who were enrolled to study externally. About 10 percent of students were enrolled in formal technical and vocational courses in postsecondary technical institutions.

Approximately 8 percent of the students were enrolled in the University, and the primary training colleges.

3.2 Preschool Education

Preschool programs are offered to children aged 3 to 5.5 years. These are offered at preschool centers which are not normally attached to a primary school. In 1992, there were 334 preschool centers with an enrollment of 8,209, approximately 12.5 percent of the children at that age level. There were 422 preschool teachers.

Preschool education continues to grow but the arrangements are largely informal and the qualifications of teachers can be quite variable. While the Ministry of Education supports preschool education in policy, it has not devoted much resource to this sector. This is likely to change in the 1990s as more attention is focused on the lower end of the educational system.

3.3 Special Education

Special education is offered for the following types of disability: physical handicap, hearing impaired, intellectual handicap, and visually impaired. In 1992, there were 16 institutions centered mostly in urban areas which offered educational facilities to some of the above-mentioned categories. The visually impaired were catered for at only one institution.

These institutions are run by societies such as the Fiji Blind Society. In 1992, there were 61 teachers. More than half of these were untrained, and few of the trained teachers had specialist qualifications. Teachers' salaries are covered (wholly or partially) by the Ministry of Education but the institutions have to raise extra funds in order to meet other costs. There is no administrative structure for transition from these special schools to the workforce. Any student who does get employed does so through the effort of the institution and a good deal of luck.

The educational system does not have any administrative structure whereby students can be pulled out of classrooms for special tuition. Those that do not make it to the 16 special institutions remain in the classroom and perform as well as they can in the circumstances.

3.4 Vocational, Technical, and Business Education

Difficulties in employment opportunities for the school-leavers in the late 1970s and the 1980s resulted in calls for a broadening of the school curriculum. Subjects such as home economics for girls and industrial arts for boys were encouraged by the government. In 1992 there were 119 schools offering home economics at Form 4, but only 36 at Forms 5 and 6, and no schools offering the subject at Form 7. In the case of industrial arts, there were 98 schools at Form 4, 64 at Forms 5 and 6, and 15 at Form 7. Secretarial studies was offered at 25 schools at Form 4, 14 at Forms 5 and 6, and none at Form 7. Agricultural science is now emphasized, and in 1992 there were 68 schools offering it at Form 4, 40 at Forms 5 and 6, and 6 at Form 7. Efforts toward quality education are hampered by the large number of untrained teachers. The perception in Fijian society has remained that these subjects are alternatives for the less academically inclined students.

The school curricula relating to technical areas are determined by two issues: cost of modern technology and the notion of appropriate technology for a small island nation. Even if it were possible to address the first issue, it would seem that the second issue has a greater influence upon curricular decisions.

As a part of the strategy to develop technical skills in Fijian society, particularly in the rural areas, the government has developed a "multicraft program" for boys and girls who leave school at the end of Form 4. This program offers courses over two years in agriculture and fisheries, building crafts (including furniture-making and boat-building), light engineering, and homecraft and industries. The course is premised on the need to train students to an appropriate level for the environment in which they are expected to lead their lives. Such an environment is not likely to provide or support advanced technology. It is also an attempt to stem the flow of young people from rural to urban areas.

Vocational and technical education at the tertiary level is offered in the capital city and one of the smaller towns on the main island of Viti Levu. The Fiji Institute of Technology offers a variety of certificate- and diploma-level courses in engineering, business,

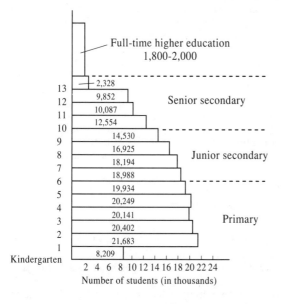

Figure 2
Enrollment figures 1987

hotel and catering, and printing. Some of the industries situated in the capital city are involved in this training through an apprenticeship scheme.

The government's intention to promote technical education is evident in its proposal to upgrade the Fiji Institute of Technology and make it autonomous, with a capacity to offer degree-level courses. This development may provide the link that has been missing between technical and vocational education within the school system and tertiary institutions.

3.5 Adult and Nonformal Education

The development of adult and community education accelerated in the 1980s as a result of dissatisfaction with the outcome of the formal school system, especially at the lower spectrum of achievement. A number of agencies are involved in this sector of education: the government runs some programs through the Ministry of Education, and others through the Ministry of Youth and Sport. In addition, there are organizations like the YMCA and YWCA, church organizations, and the University's Fiji Center that also provide adult and community education. A national committee comprising representatives from organizations involved in adult and nonformal education acts as an advisory body to the government.

There are a number of different schemes operated by the government. The government centers for adult and community education, small in number compared to the primary and secondary sector, are based in selected schools throughout the country. In 1987, there were 22 such centers, many of them in rural areas to target the rural population. Another scheme run by the government also within the school system is the multicraft program aimed at youth who have dropped out of school (referred to above). These latter centers have been developed since 1978 with the assistance of grants from the New Zealand government. The government also runs a National Youth Training Camp (78 in 1987) in agriculture, carpentry, and light engineering. While all these schemes are directed mainly at rural youth, urban students can undertake technically oriented courses at the Fiji Institute of Technology. In 1992, 5,163 students undertook a variety of courses at the Institute of Technology.

Nonformal education is carried out largely in the village environment, and since it is informal the numbers that participate in such schemes is difficult to estimate. The prime purpose of such courses is to provide information and skills that would enable rural people to lead more productive lives in their own environment.

The prime purpose of adult and nonformal education (excluding the Fiji Institute of Technology which is geared to producing skilled workers for industry) is to provide practical skills that can be used in a rural environment and thus reduce rural people's dependence upon urban servicing.

The total annual expenditure on adult and nonformal education is difficult to estimate since there is considerable amount of community input both in cash and kind. Nongovernment agencies raise funds through a variety of sources since government grants are small. In 1987, for example, NGOs received a total of F$20,250 (US$16,875). The overall government expenditure on adult and nonformal education in 1987 (excluding the Fiji Institute of Technology) was F$146,455 (US$122,046), 0.19 percent of the total expenditure on education.

4. Administrative and Supervisory Structure and Operation

Education is the responsibility of the Ministry of Education and many of the functions are centralized in the headquarters of the Ministry in the capital city. All policies, teacher appointments, curricular changes, examinations, and finance are centered in the capital city. Centralized policies are put into effect through four Educational Divisions which are in turn subdivided into 9 Education Districts. Each Educational Division is headed by a Divisional Educational Officer (at Principal Education Officer level). Each Education District is headed by a Senior Education Officer, who in theory should be the first point of contact for any school principal or headmaster.

Educational policies are formulated through the Minister of Education advised by a body called the Educational Forum and put into effect through a Permanent Secretary (Director of Education), three Deputy Secretaries (Professional, Technical and Vocational, and Administrative), and a hierarchy of education officers: Chief, Principal, Senior, and Education Officers. In theory and practice, policies and decisions move from the center to the periphery. The reverse process is true in theory but not always in practice: schools should first go through the District Office to the Divisional Office and thence to the Central Headquarters. Since most schools are nongovernmental they can put into effect policies particular to their school or system. In terms of the more fundamental issues of education, however, there is little difference between government and nongovernment schools.

5. Educational Finance

In 1992 a government budget of F$115,633,200 (US$96,361,000) was allocated to education, 16.84 percent of the total national budget, an expenditure of about F$60 (US$50) per head of school roll. In 1969, a year before Independence, it was just over F$38 (US$32). (No attempt has been made to adjust figures for inflation.) In 1987 and 1980, the percentage of national budget allocated to education was 17.4 percent and 17.6 percent respectively. Expenses for education incurred by churches and committees, a large portion of it coming from the community itself, is not included in these sums, nor is it possible to determine the extent of educational expenditure by nongovernment agencies.

The Government's recurrent grants-in-aid scheme for nongovernment secondary schools subsidizes 80 percent of the teaching and clerical staff salaries, amounting in 1992 to 5.1 percent of the total educational budget. (Since 1992, all government teachers sent to nongovernment schools have been fully subsidized by the Ministry of Education.) In addition, there is also a small per capita student grant given to nongovernment schools, as well as aid toward student fees based on parental income, amounting in 1992 to 0.5 percent and 1.3 percent of the total budget respectively. To this contribution of just under 7 percent of the budget must be added a very small percentage of funds provided to nongovernment schools as subsidies toward capital costs.

Since the middle of 1987, the formal education programs, academic and vocational, have been the responsibility of the Ministry of Education, while adult and nonformal education is the responsibility of the Ministry of Youth and Sport.

The government also contributes toward the running of the regional University of the South Pacific, calculated usually on the basis of the number of full-time, part-time, and distance education students from Fiji. In 1992, Fiji's contribution to the University budget was F$14,924,300 (US$12,436,920), which included a separate grant of F$5,399,208.

6. Supplying Personnel for the Education System

There were just over 8,321 teachers in the education system in 1992. Of these, 5,120 were employed in primary and kindergarten schools, 3,045 in secondary, 87 in special education, 586 in technical and vocational schools, and 69 in the teacher-training institutions. Since 1987, after the military coups in the country, a number of secondary teachers have migrated to other countries leaving a shortage that has been filled by untrained or volunteer teachers from abroad. In 1992, 47 percent of the secondary force was untrained, compared to just under 20 percent in 1987.

Overall the teaching force in 1992 was just under 53 percent female, with a larger percentage of women in the primary system. At the secondary level the percentages were reversed; there were about 53 percent male teachers. Senior administrative positions in schools were filled largely by men despite the number of women teachers in the system.

Primary teacher training is carried out in three teacher-training colleges, one run by the government and the other two by church organizations. The government training college and the Seventh Day Adventist College both run a two-year course, while the Catholic college runs a three-year course. The quality of the output from the teacher-training institutions has improved considerably since the 1970s largely as a result of a higher base education of the intake. While there are teachers in the system whose base education at the entry point into teacher training was completion of Form 4 (Grade 10) or lower (about 30 percent), applicants to the teacher-training courses tend to be overwhelmingly those who have completed either Forms 6 or 7 (Grades 12 or 13).

Until 1985, secondary teacher-training was conducted at the University of the South Pacific either through a concurrent program of first degree and teacher education or as an end-on teacher qualification. The junior-secondary teachers underwent a three-year diploma course. In 1984, the Minister of Education decided that future Fiji students going into the University and wishing to be teachers would do a three-year bachelor's degree. Thereafter, the Ministry of Education would run a secondary teacher-training program. Unfortunately this resulted in untrained graduates entering the secondary system as the Ministry was unable to start a teacher-training program. Since 1989, these teachers have been put through an intensive teacher education course spanning two summer vacations and conducted by Australian teacher trainers on an Australian aid scheme.

The Fiji government has sought aid from the Australian government in order to overcome the problem of training secondary teachers. As a result of it, a College of Advanced Education offering secondary teacher training became fully operational in February 1993. The primary purpose of this college is to prepare teachers for teaching Forms 1–4 (Grades 7–10) and to provide inservice teacher education for the untrained teachers in the secondary school system.

The Ministry of Education conducts inservice courses in the different educational districts for all teachers regardless of the system they are teaching in. These are aimed at familiarizing teachers with new curricula developed by the Curriculum Development Unit in the Ministry and at introducing them to newer teaching techniques. Financial constraints necessarily limit the length of these courses, normally from a couple of days to a week, and their frequency. In addition, the Ministry offers inservice awards to teachers to undertake a first degree at the regional university. In 1992, for example, there were 54 teachers on such awards. Inservice awards for specialist training overseas are also available to teachers. These are either through special Fiji government scholarships or awards provided by other countries as part of their bilateral aid to Fiji, or through agencies such as UNESCO or the Commonwealth Fund for Technical Co-operation. The Ministry personnel are also eligible to apply for these awards and this is one means of ensuring that the administrators of education are well qualified.

There are no special procedures for monitoring teacher education. The quality of courses offered in the training colleges depends both upon the quality of the lecturers and the quality of leadership provided by the Principal of the College. The University has its own system of external moderation and quality control.

Teacher appraisal forms completed by the principal are the chief means of monitoring teaching and providing information for promotion. Seniority used to be one of the chief criteria for promotion, but is now of lesser importance than formal qualifications. Ethnicity also has an influence on promotion, especially at the higher levels.

7. Curriculum Development and Teaching Methodology

There is a common curriculum throughout the country. Nongovernment schools, especially those run by religious authorities, may include some religious study in their curriculum, though it is not examined in any of the national examinations. Primary curriculum consists of social studies, elementary science, mathematics, English language, Hindi (for Hindu Indians), Fijian (for indigenous Fijians), Urdu (for Muslim Indians), Rotuman (for Rotumans on Rotuma), physical education, art and craft, and music. At the secondary level, all students must study mathematics, science, English, physical education and music or art and craft until Form 4. Thereafter, only English is compulsory until Form 7. In practice, however, most students do mathematics and sciences to higher levels, though there are options such as economics, geography, or technical subjects. Future developments include the writing of a syllabus and materials for vernacular languages. In 1992, a new Form 7 agricultural science curriculum was given a trial in six schools.

Syllabus prescription is the responsibility of the Curriculum Development Unit. Each subject specialist in the Unit has a Curriculum Committee made up of teachers, representatives from principals' association, teachers' unions, and private schools. This Committee finally approves a syllabus. While there is no formally constructed body that gives the final seal of approval, any dissatisfaction with a proposed syllabus may be discussed at a Ministerial Committee (the Educational Forum) comprising representatives from the various nongovernment agencies that provide education in the country.

The writing of the materials is either organized by the subject specialist in the Curriculum Development Unit or written by him or her. Such materials are vetted by the Syllabus Committee before being published by the Educational Resource Center of the Ministry of Education for trial. Feedback from trials in a number of representative schools is used to rewrite the material and then sent for publication to the government printery. Books are available through a central distributing system run by the government, independent of the Ministry of Education.

Inservice courses for the introduction of new curricula are held throughout the country and all teachers from state as well as private schools are invited to participate. Schools send at least one teacher to such courses as they like to get as much information about a new syllabus upon which national examinations are based.

Commercially available materials which reflect the syllabus are approved by the officers of the Curriculum Development Unit.

The chief problem faced by the Curriculum Development Unit is that, while its members may understand the philosophy underlying the content and the teaching methods to convey it, not all teachers are able to internalize this during the rather brief inservice courses. In conjunction with this, the prospect of national examinations (and peer as well as community judgment about teachers predicated on the pass-rate) results in few teachers wishing to experiment with the content or teaching styles. Teaching for examinations quite frequently goes against the delivery processes embodied in the new curricula. There is also a structural problem. The centralization of skilled labor in the Curriculum Development Unit necessarily requires curriculum officers to travel outside the capital city to conduct these inservice courses. This function is fulfilled to the extent there is provision for travel money, of which there is never sufficient.

8. The System of Examinations, Promotions, and Certifications

Students are automatically promoted at the end of each school year at the primary level. At the secondary level, examination results and availability of places may determine whether a student proceeds to the next grade level. Until fairly recently, at Class 6 level only the Fijian students sat for the Intermediate Entrance Examination. This enabled the more successful candidates the option of going to a number of well-established elite boarding schools, largely for Fijian students. Those that did not get selected to a school of their choice could move to a junior-secondary school in the vicinity or continue in Class 7 if the school was a Class 1–8 school. The trend is that more and more schools are offering students for this examination as a means of evaluating teaching and learning in the first six years. In 1992, there were over 15,000 candidates for this examination.

All students attending 1–8 primary school sit for the Eighth Year examination and attempt to get into a secondary school of their choice, depending upon their performance in this examination. Some students in junior-secondary schools in Form 2 (Grade 8) have also sat for this examination as a way of changing schools. In 1992, there were 13,536 candidates for this examination.

Secondary school national examinations have

undergone a dramatic change since 1987, which was the last year that the New Zealand Department of Education provided examinations for Form 5 (Grade 11) called the "New Zealand School Certificate" and the New Zealand University Entrance Board the Form 6 (Grade 12) examination called the "New Zealand University Entrance Examination." Fiji continues to set an examination at the end of Form 4 (about 11,700 candidates in 1992). Since 1987, there has been a two-year program after Form 4, with students required to sit for a national examination at the end of Form 6. Until 1989, the results in this examination determined, along with a policy of reserving 50 percent of the university places for ethnic Fijian students, who went into a university foundation program (pre-university) at the regional university. Since 1990, Fiji has greatly expanded its Form 7 (Grade 13) and now all successful students in the Sixth Form Examination can proceed to Form 7, subject only to the availability of places. The Form 7 examination and the policy of reserving 50 percent of places for Fijians, determine who will enter university. In short, examinations in the Fiji education system perform a gate-keeping function in terms of which schools become accessible to candidates, and at upper levels determine whether students proceed to the next grade level.

Certification of students after each of the examinations mentioned above takes the form of grades, with those below a certain grade designating a "failure" in the examination. No profiles of students' actual achievement in the classrooms is used in the selection process, that being determined solely by grades.

National examinations have a marked washback effect upon the school system. Much of the teaching is geared toward examinations. Reputations of schools are built or lost upon examination results. Another result of this feature of the education system has been that there is overall a uniformity of curriculum in the country.

9. Educational Assessment, Evaluation, and Research

While there has been a Research and Development Section in the Ministry of Education, it has limited itself to gathering quantitative data about the education system (number of students, number of teachers, number sitting examinations, etc.) to assist in planning and in the writing of annual reports. It has not undertaken research in terms of improving the quality of educational programs and their delivery. There is no specially earmarked money for the purposes of research in either the primary or secondary sector.

At the tertiary level, there is little research carried out in the teacher-training institutions or at the Fiji Institute of Technology. There is some research at the University of the South Pacific, but more widespread research in education is hampered by the limited amount of research money available to academics through the University budget itself and to some degree by the lack of a research culture in the societies which the University serves.

10. Major Reforms in the 1980s and 1990s

The 1980s were a period of considerable questioning about the emphases in the curriculum at both the primary and secondary levels. A greater effort was made to provide education in the vernacular up to the highest grade, rather than Form 4 (Grade 10) as previously. At the same time, there were rising pressures for more education so that a larger proportion of students entered the senior-secondary schools.

At the same time as formal education did not automatically lead to paid employment for many of the students, greater attention was devoted to alternative forms of education, including nonformal education.

Many of these reforms arose from a more deliberate attempt to achieve the goals of education enunciated in development plans, though the reforms may not necessarily be situated within the formal school system.

11. Major Problems for the Year 2000

The resourcing of a continued expansion in the secondary system and the development of a college of advanced education will continue to tax the government's finances. Developments in these two areas will necessarily reduce resources required to upgrade the delivery of education in the rural areas, thus continuing the perennial problem of marked differences between rural and urban education.

In addition, finding a balance between an education that leads to further higher education and an education that allows those who drop out of secondary schools before they reach the highest grades to lead full productive lives will continue to tax educational planners. This challenge will manifest itself as the rural drift to towns.

Issues of social equity, including equality of outcomes, the extent to which the country's educational system should pursue the development of technological expertise, and to what levels will also be a challenge to educational administrators and policymakers. The problem of making technical education more attractive and not be viewed as second best will also be a challenge as will be the improvement of educational administration throughout the system so that there is value for the large sums devoted to education.

The Indian aspirations regarding higher education will continue to be problematic in terms of availability of places. In the foreseeable future, the quota system of reserving 50 percent of the entries to the regional university for the indigenous Fijians will continue.

Problems in the educational system that have arisen from demographic, geographical, and social factors will continue to tax the educational administrators. Success in improving rural education will only lead to a migration to the town areas.

Finally, qualitative aspects of the educational system will continue to exercise the educational planners. Short-term inservice courses may have to be evaluated more thoroughly for their effectiveness, both short- and long-term, and other processes of inservice delivery will have to be explored in order to address issues of quality in education.

References

Derrick R A 1946 *A History of Fiji*. Fiji Government Printer, Suva

Further Reading

Education for Modern Fiji. *Council Papers 2/70*. Fiji Government Printer, Suva

Fiji Times, 6 August, 1987

Fiji Development Plan Eight 1981–1985. 1981 Fiji Government Printer, Suva

Gillion K L 1977 *The Fiji Indians*. Australian National University, Canberra

Mangubhai F 1984 Fiji. In: Thomas R M, Postlethwaite T N (eds.) 1984 *Schooling in the Pacific Islands*. Pergamon Press, Oxford

Mann C W 1935 *Education in Fiji*. Melbourne University Press, Melbourne

Ministry of Education 1987 *Annual Report for the Year 1987*. Parliamentary Paper No. 17 of 1990

Ministry of Education 1992 *Annual Report*

Rabukawaqa E 1992 Designing educational priorities for Fiji: Beyond the year 2000. Paper delivered to the 71st Principals' Conference held in Suva, April

Vakatale T 1992 Keynote address by the Honourable Minister of Education delivered to the 71st Principals' Conference held in Suva, April

Whitehead C W 1981 *Education in Fiji*. Australian National University, Canberra

Finland

M. Herranen

1. General Background

Finland is a republic in the Nordic community, located between Sweden and Russia. The country achieved independence in 1917 after having been an autonomous Grand Duchy within the Russian Empire from 1809. Prior to this period, also known as the "era of autonomy," Finland was an integral part of the Kingdom of Sweden for some six centuries. During the Swedish era, Scandinavian legal and social systems established themselves in the country, and the framework of the educational system was constructed. The first university was founded in 1640. Primary education and teacher training were modeled on Central European systems during the era of autonomy.

There are two official languages in Finland: although the majority speaks Finnish, about 6 percent speak Swedish. Official bilingualism has guaranteed the Swedish-speaking population equal opportunities with respect to education at all levels. The 1980s witnessed an increase in the cultural and linguistic rights of the Saami people, an ethnic minority of 1,700 people living in Northern Finland (e.g., more teaching in their native language, Saami, was made available).

Finland has a population of 5 million, of whom 65 percent live in towns and cities. The country is 338,000 square kilometers in area, of which 65 percent is forest and 10 percent interior waterways. On average, there are 16 inhabitants per square kilometer.

Nevertheless, more than half of the population lives in the south in an area covering about one-tenth of the country's area. Helsinki, the capital, has about half a million inhabitants. The population density for the northernmost part of the country is only two per square kilometer.

The Finnish population has increased by about one-fourth since the 1950s and will probably continue to increase at least up to the turn of the century. The 16–19 age group will increase, while that of comprehensive school age will undergo a gradual decrease. In the 1990s, the proportion of people of employable age will continue to be among the highest in the industrialized world thanks to the so-called "large age groups" born after the Second World War. The labor force is, however, aging. The employment of women has constantly increased, resulting in more than 70 percent of women belonging to the work-force.

The proportion of the population having some form of postcompulsory education has doubled since 1970. Finland is characterized by the high educational level of young people, especially young women. In 1989, 83 percent of 25- to 29-year olds had some kind of postcompulsory education. However, of the entire labor force, 38 percent had not completed education beyond the compulsory minimum. Adult education, especially vocational training, continues to be an important area for development.

Finland underwent a rapid change from a predominantly agricultural society in the 1950s to a modern service-oriented society in the 1980s. In 1950, 46 percent of the workforce derived its livelihood from agriculture and forestry, but 40 years later the figure had dropped to 8 percent. In 1990, 31 percent of the workforce was employed in industry and 61 percent in the services sector. Exports accounted for 23 percent of the Gross Domestic Product (GDP). The major branches of industry are wood processing, metal, food processing, and chemicals. During the period of economic growth in the 1980s Finland became one of the richest countries in the world with a per capita GDP of Mk105,000 (US$27,400) in 1990, and the trends in education budgets at that time were favorable. Since 1990, deterioration of the public economy has necessitated cuts in funding for education and research. The net reduction in spending on education and science between 1991 and 1994 will be about 12 percent. Another challenge to the entire system of education are the high unemployment figures, especially among young people.

Economic growth after the 1960s marked a time of expansion and reform at all educational levels: a nine-year compulsory comprehensive school was implemented in the 1970s, a reform of secondary education and training during the 1980s, and a reform of university administration and awards between 1977 and 1984. Education was also developed quantitatively, particularly vocational and higher education.

There is a comprehensive school in every Finnish municipality, and the network of upper-secondary schools and institutions of higher education is evenly spread over the entire country. Differences in education which were once consequences of regional and linguistic factors no longer play a significant role.

2. Politics and the Goals of the Education System

The Finnish parliament (38% of the representatives were women in 1992) decides on the overall lines of educational policy, passes educational legislation, and decides on funds for education from the state budget. The Council of State, the Ministry of Education, and the central educational authorities implement the decisions.

The system emphasizes the importance of political parties. Earlier major reforms in the educational system were carried through during a period when Finland was ruled by so-called "national front governments," which were coalitions of the political center and leftist parties. The reforms did, however, meet with the approval of the right-wing National Coalition Party. The Swedish People's Party has often participated in governments, thus defending the rights of the Swedish-speaking minority. The participation of the right-wing National Coalition Party in the government at the end of the 1980s and the nonsocialist government at the

beginning of the 1990s are demonstrations of changes in the values of the society.

In Finland, education has traditionally been held in high esteem, and its significance for the development of society and the economy is generally acknowledged. The traditional long-term objectives of Finnish education policy have been to raise the general standard of education and to promote educational equality. In June 1993, the government prescribed new lines of development for education and research. The long-term policy is to make Finland a country of knowledge and expertise, promoting education and research as part of a national strategy of survival. "Quality" and "internationalization" are keywords in this policy.

3. The Formal System of Education

The administration of education and research, as well as adult education, is largely centralized at the Ministry of Education. The Ministry stresses the development of the whole system according to the principle of lifelong education. The first overall five-year plan for developing the entire Finnish educational system was formulated at the end of 1991, and it was renewed in the summer of 1993.

3.1 Primary, Secondary, and Tertiary Education

The Finnish formal educational system comprises comprehensive schools, postcompulsory general and vocational education, and higher education (see Fig. 1). All educational opportunities are coeducational and mostly free of charge. In comprehensive schools and general upper-secondary schools, the length of the school year is 190 working days.

In Finland, compulsory school attendance is linked to the completion of comprehensive school. It begins at the age of 7 and continues for 10 years or until graduation. In special cases, a pupil may begin school one year earlier or later. Practically speaking, the entire age group completes compulsory education.

Comprehensive school lasts for 9 years. It is divided into a six-year lower stage and a three-year upper stage. At the lower stage the amount of weekly instruction varies between 19 and 26 hours, at the upper stage it amounts to 30 hours. Schools may also offer an extra (optional) tenth year.

In the year 1992, almost 595,000 pupils were attending comprehensive school. Some 6 percent of them were studying at Swedish schools, and a little over 1 percent at private schools. Until the early 1990s the lower-stage schools had to be located so that the pupils did not have to travel more than 5 kilometers to school. This is the reason for the relatively large number of schools, even though their individual size might be quite small. About 65 percent of these schools had in 1991 only one to three teachers. The number of upper-level schools is significantly fewer because of

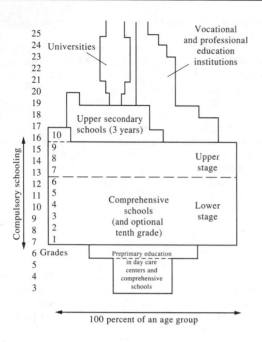

Figure 1
Finland: Structure of the formal education system 1990

the larger school districts. In the 1990s there has been a tendency to reduce the number of comprehensive schools, especially small lower-stage schools.

The upper-secondary school is a three-year general school ending with a matriculation examination. Instruction is given in the form of courses. Some of the schools function without a strict division into grades so that studies can be completed in 2 to 4 years. The number of weekly hours of instruction varies between 28 and 32. In the final grade, tests and the matriculation examination take up the lion's share of the spring term.

Vocational education is organized into 26 basic branches and these are further subdivided into more than 200 lines of specialization. Students are offered three levels of vocational qualifications: school-level certificates, as well as institute-level and higher-vocational-level diplomas. The length of time required for completing qualifications varies between one and six years, depending on field and level and on the student's basic education. The programs are designed differently for comprehensive and upper-secondary school leavers.

The system of postcompulsory education in Finalnd is very complex. Students can take parallel-level qualifications, for example, upper-secondary as well as a secondary vocational schooling. This feature of the system is one reason for the prolonged shape of the percentage in Figure 1 for both universities and vocational education. Students (especially matriculated students) often have to wait for several years to find

a place in a university. While waiting, they often take vocational diplomas. In the universities, students also often change their field of study and begin studying for another degree. Students start their university and higher vocational studies late and finish later in comparison to other countries. In 1991, 82 percent of the comprehensive school graduates continued their studies without interruption. About half of them continued to upper-secondary schools, girls (60% of female comprehensive graduates) more often, than boys (41%), and 32 percent went on to vocational education, boys (41%) more frequently than girls (23%). About 6 percent chose to attend the voluntary tenth grade. It is estimated that less than 10 percent of each age group of comprehensive school leavers do not proceed to these two forms of education.

Upper-secondary education has gained enormously in popularity since the 1950s. In 1990, approximately 45 percent of the 19-year old age group took the matriculation examination, while less than 10 percent did so in the 1950s. Since 1947, women have accounted for more than half of those taking the matriculation examination, Various efforts have been made to bridge the gap between general upper-secondary school and vocational education. Since 1970, these two forms of education have been developed in parallel, and since 1991, institute- and higher-vocational-level diplomas awarded by vocational institutions give the same eligibility for higher education as the matriculation examination. It has also been recommended that the proportion of unmatriculated students admitted to universities should be between 5 and 15 percent. The purpose of ongoing experimentation of education for young people (16 to 18 years) is to plan new unified forms of curricula for postcompulsory education.

Matriculated students can thus choose between vocational education and universities. More than half of them continue at a vocational institute, but only about one-fifth of them do so directly. Most of them begin to follow a curriculum designed specifically for matriculated students. In 1990, upper-secondary school graduates accounted for about 20 percent of those starting at school level, and about 60 percent of those starting at institute or vocational higher levels. University studies were begun by 16 percent of those who matriculated the same year.

Educational and labor authorities have made concerted efforts to guarantee a place in further education for school leavers. There are about 1.3 educational openings in vocational and higher education for each student leaving comprehensive and upper-secondary school. The total university intake corresponds to about one-fourth of the age group. Of the two groups of school leavers, 9 out of 10 go on to vocational education or universities. The problem is that finding a place to study can take several years. For example, only 19 percent of matriculated students can start university studies directly after matriculation. Multiple education, and transferring from one school to another without a diploma have all increased. A student may also apply to, and be admitted by, several places at the same time.

In 1994, there were 21 universities in Finland, each of which undertook research and provided postgraduate education. Since the degree reform in the 1970s and early 1980s abolished nearly all bachelor's degrees the basic Finnish university degree is a master's degree. Viewed internationally, the age of university students is comparatively high. The median age for first-year students is 21, and the master's degree is achieved, on average, at the age of 27.

Of more than 126,000 students attending university, roughly half are women. The number of students has gradually increased in the 1980s. It has partially been a consequence of a planned increase in the number of starting places, but it is also due to long study times in higher education. The number of new students increased by almost 4,700 from 1981 to 1993. The increase has been greatest in science and technology.

In 1991, an experiment with institutions of vocational higher education (*Fachhochschulen* or polytechnics) was begun. Its purpose was to raise the educational level of institute and higher level vocational education and to rationalize the structure of the system. These new institutions and higher education (nonuniversity) qualifications will be permanently introduced into the Finnish system in 1996.

3.2 Preschool Education

There are no actual preprimary schools in the Finnish education system. Voluntary preschool education is provided by the daycare system administered by the Ministry of Social Affairs and Health. In sparsely populated areas, where daycare services are difficult to arrange, education is given in conjunction with comprehensive schools. About 60 percent of 6-year olds and about one-third of the 3–6 age group participate in either form of education. The handicapped children who are not able to study at normal schools start school at the age of 6 with 2 years of preliminary instruction.

Since 1973, the municipalities have had a legal obligation to provide daycare to satisfy demand; the economic recession at the beginning of the 1990s has not made it easy for the municipalities to achieve this aim. The goal for the 1990s is to guarantee all 6-year olds the right to participate in preschool education of the existing type as a cooperative form of education and social welfare. It is also possible that the school-starting age will be lowered to 6.

3.3 Special Education

Compulsory education also applies to handicapped children. For children who are unable to study at a normal comprehensive school, compulsory education begins at the age of 6 (with 2 years of preliminary instruction) and lasts for 11 years.

Comprehensive schools give special education to disabled students who are unable to participate in normal school instruction. Education is given in special classes, or if the difficulties in learning or adjustment are of a minor nature, it is offered as part-time tutoring. Special schools, municipal or state-run or private, exist for the severely handicapped. In 1992, there were 349 such schools. They follow the objectives of the comprehensive school with some adaptations.

Special arrangements and facilities also exist to help disabled students who attend upper-secondary schools and institutions of higher education. In vocational education, depending on the need for special education, students can either participate in normal instruction, or follow special curricula, or they can attend special vocational institutions (there were 15 in 1992). The objective of this education is for these students to attain the same vocational qualifications as the other students.

Special education is given primarily for comprehensive school students, most often as a consequence of a speech, reading, or writing disability. In 1987, 17 percent of comprehensive school students participated in some form of special education. The majority of the students were boys. The proportion of emotionally disturbed and socially maladjusted students has increased slightly. Approximately 2 percent of the students attending vocational institutions were given special instruction, as were 0.2 percent of those attending upper-secondary school.

The labor force offices which function under the auspices of the Ministry of Labor provide special services for the handicapped when they enter the labor market. They receive assistance in choosing a profession and finding a suitable job, and experimental arrangements are made for them with respect to both work and education.

3.4 Vocational, Technical, and Business Education

Vocational education is developed as an integral part of the educational system. Efforts are made to respond to changes in working life by expanding educational opportunities, developing curricula, and delegating decision-making power to the local level and to the educational institutes. The curricula allow special regional demands to be taken into consideration. Vocational institutions may establish consulative councils to maintain and develop contacts with industry and to promote their activities.

Most vocational institutions have a unit for adult education. Separate vocational adult education centers have also been established. Since 1991, labor market officials have been able to purchase vocational education, according to the clients' needs, from these units as well as from universities, private organizers of education, or as inservice training.

Apprenticeship education is supervised by the Ministry of Education and administered by a local board.

Graduates of vocational institutions can also conclude contracts in order to obtain work experience. In Finland, apprenticeship training is a rather rare form of acquiring vocational qualifications; it accounts for only about 5 percent of basic vocational training. In 1993, however, the number of apprenticeship contracts was nearly doubled as a consequence of the legislative reform which made the system far more flexible.

3.5 Adult and Nonformal Education

Continuous changes in the world of work, the aging of the labor force, and trends in unemployment all underscore the importance of adult education. Efforts are made to integrate this education into the system according to the principle of continuing education. The government defined the present lines of development for adult education in 1978, priority being on the development of vocational education. Administration and organization were built up during the 1980s. Courses are offered in all parts of the country. Over 1,000 institutions and organizations provide education for more than 1.5 million adults annually. One-third of all adult participants are educated within the formal education system. Participation in education has increased rapidly since 1980, and the number of students in vocational adult education has grown tenfold. About 42 percent of employees attended inservice training in 1991.

General adult education is arranged by liberal education institutes such as adult education centers, folk high schools, evening schools, and study circle centers. Continuing education centers were established in all universities during the 1980s. Besides continuing education for university graduates, these centers arrange open university instruction in cooperation with other adult education institutions. The summer universities also provide higher-level adult education. A functioning network of public libraries serves as a good support for studies. Vocational adult education is provided mostly by vocational adult education centers, vocational institutes, special institutes run by business and industry, and as apprenticeship training. Labor market training is an important part of this education.

The institutions of adult education are financed by the state, municipalities, employers, the arranging organizations, and students. The tuition costs of students in vocational institutions are shared by the state and local authorities. The costs of liberal education institutions or organizations are covered from 50 to 80 percent by state subsidies (1991). Finland has a special financial aid scheme for mature students, who are entitled to obtain not only grants and loans but also compensation for the loss of income.

4. Administrative and Supervisory Structure and Operation

Legislation and the general lines of educational policy are decided by the parliament. The government and the Ministry of Education are responsible for actual implementation. The Ministry of Education is thus the highest educational and research authority. Almost all publicly funded education, including adult education, is subordinate to or supervised by the Ministry. Training relating to national security, order, and traffic is administered by the relevant ministries. The universities are directly subordinate to the Ministry of Education, and they have a considerable degree of autonomy with respect to their own internal matters.

The provincial offices and their school departments are responsible for regional administration, with the municipalities and educational institutions being responsible for local administration. Educational institutions may have either a governing board of their own or a joint board with other institutions.

The majority of comprehensive and upper-secondary schools are municipally run, with the remainder being state-run or private schools. These also receive most of their funding from the state or municipalities. Only about 1 percent of schools are private. In 1991, about 45 percent of vocational institutions were run by municipalities or federations of municipalities. More than one-third of the institutions were state-owned and the remaining 20 percent were private, but the latter are also supervised by local authorities. The policy of decentralization in existance in the early 1990s will gradually decrease the number of state-run institutions and they will be turned over to the municipalities.

Development measures have largely focused on administration. The principle has been that the government decides the framework for quantitative and qualitative development, but the decision-making power will increasingly be handed over from the central administration to local authorities, schools, and institutions of higher education. The National Board of Education, formed in 1991 through the combination of the National Boards of General and Vocational Education, is focusing more on educational development and providing expertise.

5. Educational Finance

Expenditure on the education system in 1989 was approximately Mk29 billion (US$7.25 billion) or 5.6 percent of GNP. Comprehensive schools accounted for 44 percent of the expenditure; upper-secondary schools for 8 percent; and vocational institutions, higher education, and adult education for 25, 15, and 8 percent, respectively. Public spending on education increased 2.7 percent on average during the period 1979 to 1989. The greatest increases were in higher, vocational, and adult education. In 1990 the costs per student amounted to Mk20,900 in comprehensive schools, Mk19,900 in upper-secondary schools, about Mk40,900 in vocational education (on average), and Mk26,800 in higher education.

As stated earlier, deterioration of the public economy has cut spending on education and research by about 12 percent between 1991 and 1994. Following a sharp downturn in the total GDP, education spending rose to over 7 percent. Savings in education and a new economic upswing will probably eventually bring spending to around 6 percent. Spending on public education accounts for some 15 percent of all public expenditure in Finalnd.

The state and the municipalities provide about 90 percent of the funds for educational institutions. A municipality receives state funds for schools according to its financial capacity. The ways of financing education were changed in 1993. A system of calculated state grants shared as block allocations was instituted, the decision upon the distribution of allocations being left to the municipalities. The institutions of higher education are financed directly through the national budget. By 1994 these institutions have gone over to budgeting by results, a change which will increase their power of economic decision-making and emphasize the importance of concrete results when allocating resources.

Instruction at school is free, as are the meals. At comprehensive school, even the teaching materials are free. The municipality arranges transportation (or accommodation) for comprehensive school pupils living far away from the school. Institutions of higher education do not charge for tuition. The state also subsidizes university students' meals, housing, healthcare services, and travel. However, the recession at the beginning of 1990s provoked thoughts of introducing some kind of fees to postcompulsory education.

Since 1969, the state has offered financial support for students in postcompulsory education. This comprises a nonrepayable grant and a government-guaranteed loan. Students' financial aid is granted on the basis of their achievement and financial standing. During the 1991–92 academic year, the maximum amount of this aid was Mk2,860 per month, of which Mk1,860 was a loan. For vocational and upper-secondary school students, the total amount was Mk300 less. The system of financial aid was revised in 1992, but only for university students at first. The proportion of the grant was raised, but also made taxable.

6. Supplying Personnel for the Education System

In 1991, the teaching staff at comprehensive and upper-secondary schools, vocational institutions, and institutions of higher education numbered 71,600, about 58 percent of whom were women. Comprehensive schools had 38,000 teachers (about 66% women), upper-secondary schools 5,700 (60% women), vocational institutions 20,100 (about 52% women), and universities 7,800 (about 34% women). According to employment figures, a total of 129,000 people were employed within the formal education system in 1990.

Since the 1970s, comprehensive and upper-secondary school teacher training has occured at universities. Studies lead to a master's degree. Training of class teachers, who teach most of the subjects at the lower stages, takes approximately five years. The education of comprehensive and upper-secondary school subject teachers consists of studies in their own subject, pedagogical studies, and teaching practice. Teachers at vocational institutions have either a university degree or a vocational diploma. They complete their pedagogical training and teaching practice at vocational teacher colleges. The main responsibility for teachers' further education lies with the organizations that run the schools, but with state support. Teachers' responsibilities include a short annual inservice training period.

Kindergarten teacher training, leading to a bachelor's degree, will be transferred to the universities by 1996. In the early 1990s, the training takes place in vocational institutions and only exceptionally in some universities, with the qualification being an institute-level vocational diploma. It takes three years to study for the diploma and this will also be the case for the new degree.

The qualifications required for teaching positions are laid down by law. The requirements are the same for a given type of post throughout the country. Teachers are appointed by the municipal school board or, in vocational and private schools, usually by their governing board.

Although the number of class teachers has almost doubled since 1970, there is still a lack of competent teachers in some subjects and in certain parts of the country. In 1991, 9.3 percent of the class teachers and 5.6 percent of the subject teachers at the comprehensive schools lacked formal competence, while less than 2 percent of the upper-secondary school teachers were in a similar position. Transfer of class teacher training to universities lengthened the studying times, and the numbers of subject teacher graduates have continually decreased. There has been a shortage of teachers in mathematics and art subjects, as well as of special education teachers. However, the shortage of subject teachers seems to gradually decline, for example, a little over 2 percent of the mathematics teachers lacked formal competence in 1991.

Measures which have been taken to expand teacher education to meet these demands include: increasing intakes, providing exceptional teacher training for diploma and degree holders, and supplementary training for formally incompetent teachers. Another effort is to unify education of different teachers to some extent to enable them to work in different sectors and levels of education. Particular efforts are made to develop the teacher training needed by vocational and adult education.

327

7. *Curriculum Development and Teaching Methodology*

The curricula and subjects taught at comprehensive and upper-secondary schools are defined in legislation. The Council of State decides on the distribution of lesson hours between subjects. The municipalities, or in the vocational institutions, their executive boards, compile the actual school curriculum (separately for Finnish and Swedish schools) according to the principles defined by the National Board of Education. Each school draws up an annual work plan. Schools and vocational institutions can form their teaching groups according to the lesson-hour quota system. Municipalities may include subjects of local relevance in their curricula, and schools may emphasize particular subjects (e.g., music). An upper-secondary school may function as a school specialized in languages, sports, arts, and so on. This range of choice will increase in the next few years and individual schools will begin to cultivate a more distinct image.

The lower stage follows a largely uniform curriculum. Children study their native language, either the other domestic language or a foreign language, environmental studies, biology, geography, civics (including student guidance), religion or ethics, history, mathematics, music, figurative art, handicrafts, and physical education. At the upper level, they still take an additional language, social studies, physics, chemistry, home economics, textiles, and technical work. Eighth grade students have to select six weekly hours from elective subjects. The most popular has been computer science; others include languages, and commercial and art subjects. A period of orientation into working life is also included in the curriculum. Religious instruction is given according to the faith of the majority of students, others can study ethics.

The Finnish school wants to provide children with a good all-around education. Both the rigidity of the curriculum and the obligation to study so many subjects have been the subject of criticism.

Finnish children study many languages. At comprehensive school and vocational institutions, students must study at least the second domestic language and one foreign language, which means English for the vast majority. The other possibilities are German, French, and Russian. In the upper-secondary school, students must study yet one more language or even two, depending on whether the student decides to take the general or enriched course in mathematics. Efforts are made to enable students to continue to study the language chosen in comprehensive school throughout the whole system. There has been some discussion concerning the necessity to study Swedish as a compulsory subject in the entire country.

Upper-secondary school is a general school providing education needed for further studies. Approximately 70 percent of the courses taught are compulsory, the rest are optional and elective. All instruction is given in the form of courses. For vocational education, effort has been taken to define a flexible curriculum, giving latitude for the institutions to take special local needs into consideration. About 30 percent of the hours dedicated to vocational subjects should be discretionary.

The national curricula for comprehensive and upper-secondary schools will be reformed in 1994. The reformed version will be more flexible; it emphasizes environmental and arts education, and stresses the importance of mathematics, the natural sciences, and information technology. Increasing internalization requires establishing foreign language medium blocks of studies, as well as classes and maybe also schools.

On a trial basis, in some upper-secondary schools and vocational institutions, students can include subjects from the other school form in their studies. It is also possible to study for a so-called "combination" diploma.

Textbooks are published primarily by private companies. The National Board of Education produces materials for limited distribution, such as Saami language material. There are plans to establish local teaching materials centers and to provide financial support for teachers producing instructional materials. Teachers will have more freedom to choose both the materials and the teaching methods. Students will be guided to independent, active study and mastery of wholes. Flexibility and individuality are, to an increasing degree, becoming bases for the planning of instruction.

8. *The System of Examinations, Promotions, and Certifications*

Evaluation of students at comprehensive and upper-secondary schools, as well as at vocational institutions, is an internal matter, with the relevant teachers functioning as evaluators. The National Board of Education provides the schools with directions for evaluation. Evaluation is numerical, except in the first four years of comprehensive school where it can also be verbal. Reports which are given every term and school-leaving certificates are valid throughout the country.

Low achievers may have to repeat a grade, or they may have to take a test during the summer in a subject which they failed. Decisions on promotion are made jointly by the rector and the teachers who have taught the students. The percentages of the students who have to repeat a grade are 0.5 in comprehensive schools and about 4 in class-form upper-secondary schools. In both categories, there are more boys than girls repeating. Grade repeating is most common in the first and final grades of comprehensive school and in the second grade of upper-secondary school. It must be noted that, most probably, all upper-secondary school instruction will be gradeless by the end of the 1990s.

Upper-secondary school may then be completed in 2–4 years.

Students are selected to upper-secondary schools and vocational institutions in a joint nationwide selection procedure. For upper-secondary schools, selection is on the basis of school achievement. For vocational education, interests and work experience are also taken into consideration and there may also be interviews and aptitude tests. Bonus points are given to applicants for a program where the preponderance of the opposite sex exceeds two-thirds. Admission to technical and arts and crafts institutions is by entrance examination. Additionally, there is a special procedure called "flexible" in which different individual factors such as previous studies, special aptitudes, study abroad, and questions of health are taken into consideration.

The nationwide matriculation examination is arranged and evaluated by the Matriculation Examination Board (appointed by the Ministry of Education). The examination consists of four compulsory tests: mother tongue, the second domestic language, a foreign language, and either mathematics or *realia*. (In *realia*, students choose tests from the following subjects: religion and ethics, psychology and philosophy, history and social science, physics, chemistry, biology, and geography.) Additionally, the candidate may take up to two additional tests in mathematics, *realia*, and foreign languages. The matriculation examination has been criticized for being too rigid exerting too great an influence on upper-secondary school teaching. Work is being done and experiments undertaken to reform the examination. The possibilities to choose among more subjects and to take the exams over a longer period of time have been discussed.

A student who has completed the matriculation examination is eligible for university education. Since there is usually a great number of qualified applicants, there is a *numerus clausus* in most fields of study. In addition to the matriculation examination, universities use entrance examinations and upper-secondary school certificates, aptitude tests, interviews, and so forth. Most of the first-year university students (about 95%) have matriculated. For applicants with an institute or higher-level vocational diploma, entrance examinations are usually the most important selection criteria. Academic degrees are valid throughout the country.

9. Educational Assessment, Evaluation, and Research

The new system of steering education and allocation of resources based on performance evaluation, which is being introduced into Finnish education will stress the imporatance of evaluation. The Ministry of Education and the Council of State have drawn up memoranda and reports in which education and educational policy were evaluated.

Statistics Finland and the National Board of Education provide information about schools. The key statistics on the operation of the institutions of higher education may be obtained from the Database on Higher Education Statistics (KOTA) maintained by the Ministry of Education. Finland also participates in the work undertaken by OECD concerning performance indicators in education (INES). Qualitative evaluation of education is the responsibility of the institutions. The national evaluation of disciplines and institutions is a joint responsibility of the Ministry of Education, the Council for Higher Education, the Academy of Finland, and the universities. Finland participates in international evaluation in different disciplines. The OECD evaluation work of Finalnd's higher education policy will be ready in 1994.

Research on education is financed by the Ministry of Education, the National Board of Education, and the Academy of Finland. The point of departure is that the research conducted by the first two provides follow-up studies and basic internationally comparative information on (and for) educational reforms in Finland. Besides its large-scale research on higher education, the Academy of Finland is presently funding a comprehensive study on adult education.

Research on education is conducted primarily within university faculties and research units specializing in education and social sciences. The largest research unit is the Institute for Educational Research at the University of Jyväskylä, which is divided into research divisions dealing with general education, vocational education, higher education, and the fundamentals of education. At the beginning of the 1990s the institute started a comprehensive project to clarify the manner in which new municipality-specific curricula are used to attain the educational aims of the comprehensive school. Since the 1960s, the Institute has participated in the IEA achievement studies. The results of these studies indicated that the differences in achievement between schools were small compared with other countries and, in general, the levels of achievement were deemed to be high.

To promote larger scale research on the relations between higher education and society, two new research units were established at the end of the 1980s: the Research Unit for the Sociology of Education at the University of Turku and the Work Research Center at the University of Tampere.

Since the end of the 1980s, research and development activity has been one of the most rapidly growing sectors in Finnish society. Particular attention has been focused on basic research and researcher training, in addition to rapidly increasing technical and other applied research.

10. Major Reforms in the 1980s and 1990s

Since the 1960s there has been a period of quantitative and regional expansion of education. Large-scale reforms were carried out on all educational levels. In the 1980s, the comprehensive school was functioning well and a network of institutions of higher education with a reformed system of degrees covered the entire country. Vocational education was reformed and legislation covering the comprehensive and upper-secondary schools was developed. The aging population shifted the emphasis to adult education, especially vocational education.

In the 1990s, the complexity of the education and degree system in post-comprehensive education was seen as the main reason for the inefficient utilization of student places and the main obstacle to a rational division of tasks between basic and adult education. The reforms which started in the early 1990s were aimed to streamline the education structure and make it internationally competitive. The experiment in secondary education provides a wider range of opportunities than before for completing a vocational diploma, upper-secondary school syllabus, or a combination of the two. A wide-ranging experiment in vocational higher education started in 1991, with 22 temporary polytechnics participating. After a careful assessment of this experiment, a permanent system of polytechnics will be introduced: the official division of higher education into a university sector and a nonuniversity sector will become reality in the late 1990s.

The core curricula of comprehensive school will be revised in 1994. A system of tuition for mixed age groups (gradeless school) will be introduced for upper-secondary schools, and experimented also on the upper stage of comprehensive school. The curriculum criteria and timetables will be revised in upper-secondary schools, with the emphasis on individuality and freedom of choice. Vocational education will be reorganized by establishing segmental and sectoral diploma programs broader than basic programs. The apprenticeship system will be expanded. In the university sector, the trend in most disciplines has been towards the adaptation of bachelor-level degrees and more broadly based curricula. The structure and the degree programs of the university and nonuniversity sectors will be coordinated. Adult education in the future will accord equal weight to competence acquired through education and through work experience. Teaching methods are being developed in all levels of education. The promotion of the use of information technology and telematics is a strong trend in the 1990s.

11. Major Problems for the Year 2000

In Finland, the last decade of the millenium began with an economic slump and an increase in unemployment. At the same time the rapid changes in the international environment, European integration and increasing mobility have caused quite new challenges to the education system.

According to the plan proposed by the Government in summer 1993, the Finnish education system should be developed in the direction of greater clarity and international compatability. The aim is a simple basic structure with flexibility in individual choice. The state and prospects of the national economy hold no promise of additional resources for carrying out the development program in the near future. That is why a greater efficiency is demanded of the schools, the institutions, and of the entire educational system. The policy must be implemented by rationalizing and reallocating existing resources. The size and number of education units will be reviewed and any excess trimmed. The measures involved will begin to save costs in the late 1990s.

The municipalities, institutions, and schools were granted more decision-making power in a situation of decreasing resources. They have been forced to shut down small comprehensive schools, to increase class sizes, decrease the number of employees and cut down their wages temporarily, and so forth. They are forced to make priorities also in the future. The idea of regional equality in education will also be challenged because of decreasing number of people in sparsely populated areas.

Changes in economy and occupational structure mean that the demand of education will change rapidly in several fields. There are also discrepancies between young people's aspirations and the needs of society. In general terms, developing the education system to meet the demands of a rapidly changing society and world will provide an ample amount of work long into the future.

Bibliography

Council of State 1990 *Suomen koulutusjärjestelmä, koulutuksen taso ja kehittämislinjat. Valtioneuvoston koulutuspoliittinen selonteko eduskunnalle 22.5.1990.* Government Printing Center, Helsinki

OECD/CERI 1993 *Education at a Glance: OECD Indicators.* OECD, Paris

Lappalainen A 1991 *Suomi kouluttajana.* WSOY, Porvoo

Lehtisalo L, Raivola R 1988 *Koulutuspolitiikka ja koulutussuunnittelu.* WSOY, Juva

LEIF—*Life and Education in Finland* 1991 (Special issue devoted to adult education) 26(2): entire issue

Ministry of Education 1990a *Higher Education and Employment: The Changing Relationship. The Case of the Humanities and Social Sciences.* Report prepared for OECD. Department for Higher Education and Research Publication Series No 73. Government Printing Center, Helsinki

Ministry of Education 1991, 1993 *Koulutuksen ja korkeakouluissa harjoitettavan tutkimuksen kehittämissuunnitelma vuosille 1991–1996.* Helsinki University Press, Helsinki

Ministry of Education 1992 *Developments in Education 1990–1992 Finland.* Reference Publications 16. Government Printing Center, Helsinki

Ministry of Education 1993a *Finnish Polytechnics: An Experimental Reform.* Printing Center, Helsinki

Ministry of Education 1993b *Adult Education in Finland.* Painorauma Oy, Rauma

Ministry of Education 1994 *Higher Education Policy in Finland.* Nykypaino Oy, Helsinki

National Board of Education 1991 *Vocational Education in Finland.* Government Printing Center, Helsinki

Statistics Finland 1991 *Education and Research 1991; Koulutus—Education in Finland 1991; Statistical Yearbook of Finland 1991.* Government Printing Center, Helsinki

Statistics Finland 1993 *Koulutus 1993.* Paino-Center Oy, Helsinki

France

A. Monchablon

1. General Background

France covers 551,000 square kilometers of territory and is the largest Western European state. Metropolitan France has an area of 543,965 square kilometers. Since 1918 when Alsace-Lorraine was returned to France, its frontiers have remained unchanged. However, the Alsace-Lorraine region retains certain German regulations from the 1871–1918 period, while laws voted on in France during the same period are only partially applied.

Climatic and geographical features have little effect on the educational system, at least in metropolitan France, apart from the existence of a boarding school system in mountainous regions (the Alps and the Pyrenees) which is gradually dying out elsewhere.

Regional differences play little part in the changing patterns of social and political life that have accompanied industrialization and mass communication, but there are significant regional variations in the status of private religious schools. In the west of France, 40 percent of pupils attend religious schools as compared to a national average of 17 percent.

According to the 1990 census, metropolitan France has a population of 56.6 million inhabitants, with a density of 102 inhabitants per square kilometer, making France the least densely populated major Western European country. Three-fourths of its population are city-dwellers, most of them massed in rapidly expanding urban areas of over 200,000 inhabitants (20.5 million people in all). The city and suburbs of Paris come foremost (9 million inhabitants) with Lyons and Marseilles (1.2 million and 1.1 million inhabitants respectively) trailing far behind. What by Western European standards is a high rate of natural population growth (+0.4%) promises to continue. Migratory movements in and out of the country have not changed appreciably and this results in a stable population of foreign residents (3.6 million in 1990 as compared to 3.7 million in 1982) most of whom have lived in France for over 10 years. Children from these families usually attend ordinary French schools. Special courses to learn the family's native language are optional. It is possible to study the local Basque, Occitan, and Corsican languages in secondary school.

Few pupils do (less than 1%) although this percentage is higher in Corsica (15%).

The working population stands at 55 percent of the total population, placing France among the more favored European Economic Community (EEC) countries. Salaried workers total 85 percent and can be divided into six categories: farmers and smallholders—5.1 percent; craftworkers, shopkeepers, heads of small businesses—7.2 percent; executive staff and the higher intellectual professions—9.6 percent; intermediate professions—19.3 percent; white-collar workers—28.6 percent; and blue-collar workers—30.2 percent (1989 figures). France's 2.1 million civil servants and 1.2 million municipal employees belong to the last four categories. The 1.05 million teachers represent half of the entire French civil service.

According to the 1992 International Labour Office (ILO) figures, there were 2.5 million unemployed in France, or 10.1 percent of the active population, with the categories most affected being manual workers and white-collar workers. This reinforces the belief that education and vocational training are key factors in the fight against unemployment. Women form 42 percent of the active population; their rate of activity (46%) is rising and a woman's career is less frequently interrupted by the arrival of a child than previously, due in part to the spread of day nurseries and nursery schools accepting children from the age of 2. Foreigners comprise 6.1 percent of the active population, 57 percent of whom are manual workers.

In economic terms, the primary sector represents a mere 6.3 percent of the labor market and 3.4 percent of the Gross National Product (GNP). The secondary sector (industry, excluding the building trades) represents 20.8 and 23.3 percent respectively. France has an open economy and exports amount to 22 percent of the GNP.

Some 51 percent of the population over 15 years of age and no longer in school are without a diploma or have only a certificate of primary education, whereas 11 percent of the population hold diplomas above *baccalauréat* level. Emphasis is on the need to train sufficient numbers of qualified workers and engineers to meet the country's economic requirements.

Government structure has remained unchanged for a century, but the 1958 Constitution increased the government's authority, and especially that of the French President elected by universal suffrage. For the various parties in office, education has always been an important issue, a theme of political debate, and of much public concern.

The educational system remains under the control of a centralized ministry but regions and *départements* have enjoyed greater administrative independence since the 1982–83 decentralization, which made them responsible for high schools (*lycées*) and colleges respectively. This in fact accorded them the same responsibilities that *communes* have had for over a century with regard to primary schools—limited to school buildings and maintenance. There is also joint planning of the school network by regions and state. In the early 1990s this concerned buildings only and exclude higher education, which remains a state responsibility, but local communities may well wish to play an increasingly important role in educational matters in the future.

2. Politics and the Goals of the Education System

As early as 1560 the Catholic Church's role in education came under Crown control. The Edict of Orléans made education a royal prerogative, even though effective responsibility remained in the hands of the religious orders. The idea of education as a national affair to be decided upon by those in power existed before 1789. The French Revolution adopted ideas which had been developed earlier in the eighteenth century, but in addition proclaimed that state education was the key to political freedom and to strong national identity, particularly through linguistic unification. Progress in this direction continued throughout the nineteenth century but the principal structures took shape in the early years of the Third Republic (1875). Efforts centered on primary education and, to a lesser degree, on universities. A series of laws were passed making primary education free (1881), compulsory between the ages of 6 and 12 (1882), and nondenominational (1882), thereby excluding the religious orders from state primary schools. Education became secularized 20 years before the separation of church and state in 1905. Universities enjoyed increased financial support and the monopoly of conferring academic diplomas.

Only slight reforms were introduced into the system of secondary education dispensed in high schools (*lycées*) which dated back to Napoleon's time, and in the even older Jesuit colleges founded during the old regime (the monarchy). These were fee-paying establishments frequented by a social elite and were to remain so for a long time. Unlike higher education, the secondary education system was composed of equal numbers of competing state-controlled and religious institutions.

Prior to 1945 there were two parallel networks rather than one educational system: first, the primary school (the *communale*), followed, for the best of its pupils, by "higher-primary school" (a secondary school), or even by one of the vocational schools created in 1919; these were met with indifference by teachers and parents alike. Second, the *lycées*, dispensing a classical secondary education and recruiting almost all their pupils from their own primary schools. Capping this classical education was the *baccalauréat* upon which university entrance depended (pupils from the higher-primary schools were not allowed to sit the *baccalauréat*). Each network had its own primary and secondary schools, its own teachers, and its own mode of recruiting pupils, and each was directed toward different goals.

Attempts by the *Front populaire* in 1936 to remove these differences failed. The term "democratization" came into use only after 1945 when efforts were made to create a truly unified educational system. In 1946 an article was inserted into the Constitution (where it still remains) stipulating that "it is the state's obligation to organize free, public, nondenominational education at all levels." Although no law or government statement followed the Langevin–Wallon Commission (1945–47), its findings were much debated and have influenced government policy, at least in part. For the first time educational goals were clearly defined: (a) to promote equal opportunities; (b) to provide the qualified personnel needed by the economy; and (c) to make it imperative to develop the personality of each child. France was now in a position to embark upon the unification of its educational system. Gradually the "prep schools" attached to *lycées* were closed down and the various branches of first-cycle secondary education assembled under the one roof of the college. Advancement of the school-leaving age to 16, a measure announced in 1959 but which became effective only in 1967, was another step towards democratization. In 1968, the students' rebellion succeeded in removing the limitations imposed on university entrance, considered contrary to the spirit of democratic schooling, and in transforming university administration.

Finally, the 1959 Debré Act introduced measures to bring private schools into line with state schools. In return for the financing of their personnel costs, private schools (Catholic for the most part) agreed to comply with Ministry of Education requirements concerning the syllabus, the organization of classes, and so on, and to accept pedagogical inspection. However, the funding of private education still remains a major political issue.

The Education Act of 1989 reaffirmed that the aim of school is to give all individuals the opportunity to develop their personality, to raise their educational level, to take part in social and professional life, and to enjoy full citizenship. It guarantees every person's right to education and training, this being the contribution of schools to the principle of equal opportunities for all. The chief objective is to enable every young person to reach a recognized level of qualification by a gradual process of orientation, for four out of five to reach *baccalauréat* level, and for those who pass to be able to continue on to higher education.

3. The Formal System of Education

3.1 Primary, Secondary, and Tertiary Education

Figure 1 presents the structure of the formal educational system in diagrammatic form.

There are no structural differences between state and private schools (17% of the school-going population). School attendance is compulsory between the ages of 6 and 16 (i.e., for 10 years). More and more young people continue their schooling, which comprised 82 percent of those between the ages of 2 and 22 in 1990 as compared to 66 percent in 1961. Schools are coeducational at all levels, classes are held morning and afternoon,

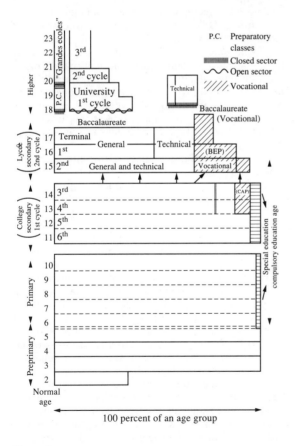

Figure 1
France: Structure of the formal education system 1990

and school hours vary from some 26 hours of teaching per week in primary schools to 30 hours or more in secondary schools. The 36-week academic year is divided into five equal periods.

Figures for primary school attendance have decreased (from 4.9 million to 4 million in 1992) due to a drop in the birthrate. Primary education lasts 5 years and caters for the 6–10 age group. In 1992 approximately 14 percent of pupils attended private schools.

School for this age group is compulsory, meaning that there are no dropouts. In addition, grade-repeating is decreasing. For instance, the percentage of pupils repeating the first year fell from 17.6 percent in 1971 to 8.1 percent in 1990. It is considered that a pupil's future may be jeopardized by having to repeat the first year of primary school. This explains why the last year of preprimary school and the first year in primary school are now associated. In 1991, 25 percent of pupils in their last year of primary school had lost one or more years as compared to 52 percent in 1961. It is recognized that grade-repeating occurs more often with pupils from underprivileged social backgrounds. However, the social gap is decreasing. In 1991 classes had an average of 22.5 pupils.

The most important quantitative and qualitative changes in recent years have been in secondary education. This is divided into two cycles. Pupils in the first cycle of secondary education spend four years in a college (the *6ème, 5ème, 4ème,* and *3ème* forms) which correspond to the final years of compulsory education. The grade-repeating rate remains stable overall (7–11%). Conversely, the percentage of pupils redirected into classes preparing them for a vocational education has fallen from 30 percent in 1984 to 14.5 percent in 1990. In 1975, 66 percent of pupils entering their first year of secondary school (*6ème*) reached the final *3ème* class, whereas in 1986 this figure rose to 75 percent. In 1991, the average number of pupils per class was 24.3.

The second cycle of secondary education has developed rapidly. Between 1960 and 1990, the number of pupils entering the second cycle has been multiplied by 2.5. In the 1990s, 70 per cent of an age group continue school beyond the age of 16, due to growing social aspirations rather than to demographic growth factors, and it seems unlikely that this tendency will be reversed.

The second cycle of secondary education is divided into two streams. General and technical high schools (*lycées*) prepare pupils in 3 years (the *2ème, 1ère,* and *terminale*) for the *baccalauréat*, which 7 out of 10 pupils sit. Enrollment in the second cycle comprises 40 percent of a cohort, meaning that since 1960 attendance has tripled, especially given the decreasing dropout rate at this level. Grade-repeating is high, however, with rates of 16 percent for the first year (*2ème*) and 12 percent for the second year (*1ère*). This explains an increase in the number of pupils per class—31 in 1991. Private schools enroll one-fifth of a cohort at this level. As a result of the higher rate of grade-repeating, the decrease in the average age of high school pupils came to a halt in about 1980. In 1991 only 36 percent of pupils in the final form were 17 years old (the theoretical age of pupils in that class) or younger.

Finally, 35.4 percent of pupils entering their first year of secondary school (*6ème*) in 1973 pursued their schooling up to the *terminale* compared to 45.6 percent for pupils enrolled in *6ème* in 1980.

Some 71 percent of the candidates sitting for the *baccalauréat* pass the examination. In a third of the cases this is a technical *baccalauréat*. Pupils from the less privileged social categories have been the ones to benefit most from this general rise. For instance, in 1973, 25.5 percent of children from families of qualified manual workers entered the terminal class as compared to 79.5 percent from families of senior executives, whereas in 1980 these figures rose to 35.4 and 83.7 percent respectively. Admittedly the major inequalities still exist, visible now in the choice of one or another type of *baccalauréat*, the scientific sections being those preferred by the wealthy and the technical sections by pupils from less favored backgrounds. Some people maintain therefore that high schools boast only surface equality, not true equality.

The other stream of the second cycle of secondary education takes place in vocational high schools (*lycées professionnels*). Attendance figures at these schools have doubled between 1960 and 1990, representing 30 percent of a given age group, but the dropout rate stands at 40 percent of the total number of school dropouts. Pupils in the vocational high schools follow a two-year program leading to a *Certificat d'Aptitude professionnelle* (CAP) or, more frequently now, the less specialized *Brevet d'Etudes professionnelles* (BEP). One-fourth of pupils attend private schools. In 1989 half the pupils with a BEP started work, a fourth returned to the general technical high school, and another fourth stayed on in the vocational high school to prepare for one of the vocational *baccalauréats* (*bacs pros*) created in 1987 and which, five years later, represented 10 percent of the total number of *baccalauréats* in that year. Their popularity is likely to grow.

Demand for education is such that the number of pupils leaving school each year without a diploma or with simply a *Brevet des collèges* has fallen from 39 percent of the total in 1983 to 31 percent in 1989. Of this 31 percent, school-leavers without any vocational qualification represented a near stable 14 percent of total exits. Some 44.4 percent of the relevant age group passed the *baccalauréat* in 1990 as compared to 11 percent in 1960 and 20 percent in 1970. The percentage of pupils reaching *baccalauréat* level rose from 30 percent in 1973 to 54.5 percent in 1990.

Female students are in the majority in the long second-cycle stream of secondary education (54%), but in the minority in the vocational high schools (46.8%), partly because girls get better results and partly because vocational education is traditionally oriented toward masculine careers.

Geographical inequalities are becoming reduced but more pupils reach *baccalauréat* level in the southwest and west of France than in the northeast. In 1990 the difference between extremes dropped to 13 points compared to 17 in 1975. This is not due to cultural reasons alone (i.e., the importance of industrial employment in the north), but also to reasons within the educational system itself; for instance, regions where fewer pupils reach *baccalauréat* level are often those which find it hard to recruit teachers.

Nine out of ten pupils with the *baccalauréat* continue their education and more and more students pass this examination, hence the growing demand for higher education. In 1992 there were 1,820,000 students and the student population will continue to increase. In France, universities (the open sector) dispensing general rather than professional education, and also involved in research, remain traditionally distinct from the *grandes écoles*, which select their students and dispense a professionally oriented higher education, though this difference is lessening.

Some 69 percent of the student population attend universities. Over half are women except in the sciences. One-third of students study the humanities and social sciences, a fifth study science, a fourth study law and economics, and one-tenth study medicine (the only discipline with selective enrollment). Half the university population are first- and second-year students, indicating the increased number of students and the high dropout rate at this level. It is estimated that one first-year student in five abandons university.

Professional training courses within the university system have been created since the 1970s, catering for all levels, ranging from technical engineer training in university institutes of technology to qualified engineer training. Entrance to these courses is usually selective. In addition, technical training courses are organized in the top classes of high schools: 12 percent of students are enrolled in these courses and numbers are growing rapidly.

Institutions known as the *grandes écoles* make up the second largest sector of higher education. These are principally engineering schools and schools of business and administration. They are often private institutions and are attended by a limited number of students (6%). Their policy is less to increase in size than to recruit the best pupils from the general scientific sections of high schools, through a competitive examination for which students prepare in the top forms of the *lycée* (the preparatory classes to the *grandes écoles* comprise 4% of students). Certain *grandes écoles* carry out research. These institutions are the direct route to leading posts in French society, and students from the upper social strata enroll in these institutions rather than in universities.

3.2 Preschool Education

France's preprimary school system is well developed. Teachers in these *écoles maternelles* hold the same qualifications as primary school teachers. The *école maternelle* is regarded as the place to identify possible difficulties at an early age and as a tool to reduce inequalities, mainly by developing the ability to talk. It accepts children from the age of 2. The proportion of 2-year olds is now stable (35.6% in 1990): 99 percent of 3-, 4-, and 5-year olds attend preprimary school as compared to 42 percent in 1964. In 1990 a total of 2.5 million children attended preprimary school (19% of the total school population), a figure which should not vary to any great extent in the future.

3.3 Special Education

Education for the handicapped mostly takes place in state schools. Primary education (concerning 1.1% of pupils) may be in special classes within ordinary schools or in special institutions. Since the mid-1970s the number of pupils concerned has been halved, essentially due to early diagnosis and the policy of integrating such pupils into the ordinary educational system.

Handicapped pupils continue their secondary education in special sections in ordinary schools or possibly in special schools where they receive vocational training. Their numbers have not varied in the 1980s. Finally, 0.8 percent are educated in institutions coming under the supervision of the Ministry of Health.

3.4 Vocational, Technical, and Business Education

Technical and vocational education have never been considered as important as general education in France. Despite official attempts to change this view, the latter is getting more and more attractive for students and parents.

Technical education, provided in general and technical high schools, leads to a *baccalauréat technique*, and then to technical higher education which lasts two years, provided either in the top forms of *lycées* (*Sections de technitien supérieur*) or in the universities (*Instituts Universitaires de Technologie*).

Vocational education is the responsibility of the *Lycées Professionnels*, where students follow a two-year program leading to a number of specialized diplomas—(250 different *Certificats d'Aptitude professionnelle*, and 34 different *Brevets d'Etudes professionnelles*). These are defined by employment organizations. About one-fourth of school time is spent in the workplace. Though *bacs pros* are developing, overall figures of vocational education are decreasing in favor of general education. Apprenticeship, which follows education, is also decreasing; fewer than 130,000 young people are following this path, mostly in the handicrafts sector. Since 1987, training programs may lead even to an engineer's diploma. The idea of increasing apprenticeships is now being discussed.

Business education is offered at selected higher education institutions, mainly private, for which students prepare in public institutions, the top forms of *lycées*.

3.5 Adult and Nonformal Education

Nonformal education consists principally of further adult education since France has no open universities. Under the 1971 Adult Education Act, employers are obliged to contribute to the major part of its monetary cost. All working people have the right to adult education, and each year one person in four benefits from it. The aim is professional improvement and better standards of general education. Surveys show that those who benefit most are quite well-qualified active males, for the most part between 25 and 40 years old. Training programs have, however, been created for young adults entering the labor market and for the unemployed. These programs are run by public and private bodies selected by employers. The Ministry of Education organizes about one-sixth of vocational training programs.

4. Administrative and Supervisory Structure and Operation

The French tradition of centralized administration applies also to the Ministry of Education, even given steps toward decentralization in 1982–83. Its control over educational matters is almost total, the one important exception being France's agricultural high schools (134,000 pupils in 1984) which are governed by the Ministry of Agriculture. Various institutions of higher professional education come under other ministries, such as the *Ecole Nationale de la Magistrature* (Ministry of Justice), the *Ecole Nationale d'Administration* (the Prime Minister's office), and the *Ecole Polytechnique* (the Ministry of Defense).

The Ministry of Education came into existence over a century and a half ago but was only named as such in 1932. Virtually all staff working in state schools are civil servants. Its payroll is the largest of all ministries and hence its budget occasionally tops all other state budgets. The Ministry of Education produces an abundance of regulations on questions of management (including curricula and timetables) and supervision with which the majority of private schools are also required to comply. In addition, a commission appointed by the Ministry of Education approves the diplomas delivered by many of the higher schools of business and engineering in the private sector.

France is divided into 28 academic zones. Each academy corresponds roughly to a region and is directed by a rector who represents the Minister of Education and to whom part of the latter's functions have been delegated. The rector is responsible for the management of primary and secondary schools and for the enforcement of national regulations within the academy. He or she is chancellor of the universities in the relevant academic zone and is required to enforce current decisions concerning higher education.

At the level of the *département*, the rector is represented by an academic inspector who directs the local education board and whose principal task is to supervise primary education. He or she is not entitled to intervene in higher education.

5. Educational Finance

In 1990, national expenditure on education amounted to FF414 billion (US$75.8 billion) or 6.4 percent of the GNP. Education is principally financed by the state. However, the financial contribution of local administrations (regions, *départements*, and *communes*) has increased (16.8% of national expenditure) with a proportionate decrease in state expenditure (66.5%), since the 1982–83 decentralization. The 6 percent contributed by employers to national expenditure on education is paid in the form of funds for adult training programs, without which employers are required to pay an apprenticeship tax. Finally the 9.9 percent borne by households represents their part in the financing of canteens (frequented by approximately half the school population), boarding schools (5% of the school population), and enrollment in higher education (in 1991 university entrance fees ranged from FF1000 to 2000—US$183 to 366). Teaching activities absorb 82 percent or four-fifths of national expenditure on education. Table 1 summarizes the evolution of the Ministry of Education budget.

The 1993 Ministry of Education budget amounted to FF281.8 billion (US$45.1 billion), 90.6 percent of which represented personnel costs, including pensions. Expenditure broken down by level of education, pensions excluded, is as follows: primary education: 26.1 percent (including state preprimary schools: 6.1%); secondary education: 53.5 percent (first-cycle state secondary schools: 18.2%, state high schools: 11.4%, state vocational schools: 6.9%); higher education: 14.4 percent; and general organizational expenses: 6 percent.

Table 2

Annual average per pupil unit cost at different educational levels (1991)

Preprimary	FF 15,600
Primary	FF 19,000
Secondary (1st cycle)	FF 31,600
Secondary (2nd cycle)	FF 41,200
IUT	FF 72,000
University	FF 36,500

The lower figures for primary school expenditure are due to a decrease in the number of pupils and the fact that until now the salaries of primary school teachers have been below those paid in secondary schools, where the number of pupils has risen rapidly.

Variations in average per student expenditure (see Table 2) according to educational level are principally due to fluctuations in the pupil–teacher ratio and in teacher salary scales. University institutes of technology, and engineering schools especially, incur high expenditures, given their heavy operating costs and large teaching staffs.

Family expenditure on school supplies and clothes, excluding canteen and boarding school costs and sociocultural expenses, increases as the educational level rises, from FF1000 (US$183)/year for a pupil in the first secondary year to FF1600 (US$293)/year for a *lycée* pupil. Half of this expenditure is incurred at the beginning of the school year. The average annual cost per student in higher education is estimated at FF30,000 (US$5,495).

Grants are provided principally by the Ministry of Education. There are none at the primary school level but one secondary student in every four receives a grant depending on family income. This proportion is higher for pupils attending the vocational secondary schools (one pupil in three). The size of the grant varies according to the level of studies with an average of FF1770 (US$324) allocated to a *lycée* student in 1991.

In France, pupils in primary school and the first cycle of secondary education receive their school textbooks

Table 1

Evolution of the Ministry of Education budget

	1952	1957	1960	1963	1965	1970	1975	1980	1985	1988	1989	1990	1991	1993
As percentage of state budget	7.4	10	12	13.6	16.3	16.9	18.1	19	16	18.3	17.9	18.5	19.3	20.5
As percentage of GNP	1.33	1.85	2.30	2.35	3.08	3.23	3.22	3.61	3.85	3.50	3.40	3.50	3.60	3.70

Table 3
Number of teachers by level of education 1990

Number of teachers	Preprimary	Primary (including schools for handicapped)	1st cycle	Secondary 2nd cycle (vocational)	2nd cycle (general & technical)	Higher[a] Full professors	Total
Public	300,409		181,837	61,119	122,461	15,204	57,429
Private	42,195 (1991)		42,070	85,163		—	—

a Private universities have no permanent full-time teaching staff

free of charge. Some 23 percent of students in higher education receive some form of aid. The majority of grants are allocated on the basis of family income (17% of the student population in 1990). In the early 1990s, the goal is to increase the size of grants (an average of FF13,000 (US$2,381 per year)) and for grants to be allocated to 25 percent of the student population. In 1991 a system of three-year bank loans guaranteed by the state was created for students who had completed their first year of higher education.

6. Supplying Personnel for the Education System

In 1992, 1,078,136 people were employed by the Ministry of Education, 778,217 being teachers. In France, school management, student guidance, and the supervision of pupils are tasks performed by people other than teaching personnel. Table 3 shows the numbers of teaching personnel at each educational level, including figures for the private sector.

Some 61 percent of state-employed teaching personnel are women. Percentages vary from 95 percent in preprimary schools and 74 percent in primary schools to 55 percent in secondary schools. In the private sector figures are still higher: 91 percent in primary schools and 65 percent in secondary schools.

In 1992 secondary school teachers outnumbered primary school teachers whereas until 1990 it had been the reverse. The number of teachers tripled in the period 1950 to 1990. While there used to be a great many auxiliary staff, owing to the shortage of teachers, in 1990 the percentage of state-paid auxiliary teachers was only 5 percent. Most are employed at the secondary level (12% of the teaching staff in state schools, 47% in private secondary schools).

Between 1991 and the turn of the century some 130,000 primary school teachers and 180,000 secondary school teachers will need to be recruited. This may be difficult, especially in the sciences.

Since 1991 the initial training of primary and secondary school teachers has been organized under one roof, in the university teacher-training institutes (IUFM) attached to universities. Candidates receive a mixture of university tuition and practical training besides developing the ability to transmit knowledge. Training lasts two years and a bachelor's degree is needed to enroll. Candidates sit for the different teacher recruitment examinations after the first year, becoming trainee civil servants if they pass. The second year emphasizes practical training experience. Civil servant status is acquired at the same time as the jury-conferred diploma.

The competitive *agrégation* examination to recruit *lycée* high-school teachers and open only to candidates with a master's degree (4 years of university studies) continues to exist. The IUFM also train candidates wishing to become high-school teachers. There are no training requirements for teaching personnel at the level of higher education.

The IUFM also provide inservice training. Primary school teachers are entitled to 36 weeks of further training in the course of their career and are replaced in the classroom during the one- or two-week training courses organized by the local board of education. Academic training programs for secondary school teachers exist, but at this level teachers have no contractual right to inservice training.

Teacher training ends with a series of qualifying examinations at the preprimary and primary school level or at the secondary level specializing in general education, technical education, or vocational education.

Inspectors visit classrooms regularly and teachers are marked on their classroom performance. This mark is important for career advancement.

7. Curriculum Development and Teaching Methodology

The French system makes no clear distinction between curriculum and syllabus. School programs are a mixture of both and are defined chiefly by their content of knowledge. There are strict stipulations concerning the number of hours to be devoted annually to programs at primary and secondary levels. Programs are drawn up by a National Program Committee composed of outside experts appointed by the Minister. There are no regional variations and programs are adopted at the national level by the Ministry of Education.

School textbooks and other teaching equipment are produced by private enterprises without ministerial control or approval, and play a *de facto* role in the interpretation of official programs.

More than 10 foreign languages are offered at the secondary level, and all secondary schools teach at least three languages. The study of one foreign language is obligatory and the study of a second foreign language may be made obligatory in the third secondary year (*4ème*). Students beginning the second cycle (*2ème*) may choose a third language as an option. In all, 85 percent of students choose English as their first language, and half choose Spanish as their second language.

On their classroom visits inspectors periodically verify that programs are being completed. In addition to this, practically all subjects studied in class are set as part of the *baccalauréat* examination.

The problem is different in the case of higher education. Universities are free to decide on their programs but before being able to confer state-recognized diplomas the content of their programs must be approved by the Minister. The National Program Committee has the task of ensuring that programs are coherent and progress in stages, with emphasis not only on knowledge but also on acquiring the necessary skills.

8. The System of Examinations, Promotions, and Certifications

Promotion is not automatic. At the end of each year teachers decide who is to move on to the next grade. At the primary school level this is a group decision taken by the teaching staff, but at the college and *lycée* levels the decision is taken by the class council. This decision must be accepted by the family in the case of college students whereas for high-school students families are able to appeal against a decision. Studies show that half of the students who appealed against a decision to repeat a class continued their schooling satisfactorily.

The class council (composed of teachers, representatives of parents and pupils, and the head of the school) also decides on how pupils are to be oriented, in the presence of guidance counselors. Families may also appeal against decisions orienting a pupil into one rather than another stream. Crucial decisions come at the end of the second year in secondary school and then again at the end of the first secondary cycle (*3ème*), when it is decided whether pupils should continue in the general education system or be directed toward

vocational training. Family influence counts but family expectations vary according to social status.

The first school diploma, called "*Brevet*," obtained at the end of the first cycle of secondary education, represents nine years of schooling and has no direct influence on a pupil's school career. The main school diploma is the *baccalauréat* which certifies completion of secondary education and allows a student to enter university (except where limitations are imposed on entrance, e.g., medical schools). In reality, not all *baccalauréats* enjoy the same prestige. To get into the closed sectors of higher education (*grandes écoles*, university institutes of technology, etc.) a general and preferably a scientific *baccalauréat* is needed.

University students obtain their first diploma at the end of their second academic year. The introduction of units to be earned may prevent students who abandon their studies at this stage from feeling they have gained nothing.

9. Educational Assessment, Evaluation, and Research

Assessment of education and the educational system is conducted at several levels. The Ministry of Education carries out statistical surveys to study school careers of various samples of students. The General Board of Inspectors conducts studies to assess teaching methods or even regional inequalities. There is also an evaluation in all schools of the skills acquired by pupils having completed their third year of primary education and also their first secondary year. The results obtained at the institutional level are not made public to avoid creating a hierarchy of schools.

These surveys include research on school learning processes, and the reorganization of preprimary and primary education in the early 1990s into cycles is in part a consequence of such research. Additional research themes concern factors other than the learning processes liable to induce scholastic failure or success; for example, the organization of educational institutions and their mode of functioning, the role of the various actors in the educational system, and regional disparities and differences between types of institution. Particular attention is paid to dropout rates at all educational levels, and to the numbers of pupils reaching the *baccalauréat* level.

10. Major Reforms in the 1980s and 1990s

The reforms being undertaken or already completed aim at improving the educational system by remodeling its structures rather than by setting out radically to transform it. The target is to educate 80 percent of an age group up to *baccalauréat* level by the year 2000 and for all pupils to reach at least the level of a vocational qualification. To this end preprimary and primary classes are being grouped into three cycles instead of divided into six compartmentalized classes, making it easier to follow each pupil over this six-year period and to avoid unnecessary repetition of a class. There are proposals to diversify the content of secondary education and teaching methodology but within the framework of a unified national program, with schools able to decide on how best to cover the program according to the needs of their pupils.

At the higher education level it should be possible to reduce the number of dropouts by reorganizing the first year and by providing training courses of a more professional nature.

Finally, future primary and secondary school teachers will receive a common core of training in the university teacher-training institutes (IUFM), with emphasis on the professional aspects of teaching.

11. Major Problems for the Year 2000

From the way in which the educational system is likely to develop, it can be inferred that the main problems will center on the need for more and better-trained teaching personnel as a result of the increased demand for secondary and higher education. It will also be necessary to deal with growing cultural differences within the school and student population. There is debate as to whether unstreaming at the college or even the *lycée* level will democratize education or whether it will be a cause of failure for pupils from low-income families. Generally speaking, the difficulty will be to strike a balance between educating a whole generation to a high and relatively homogenous level and the new concern

to focus training on the varied individual facets of a student's personality.

Finally, given the financial implications and the many ways of responding to the above problems, it can be expected that there will be a shift in the present balance between the role of the state and that of local communities.

Bibliography

Bienaymé A 1986 L'*Enseignement supérieur et l'idée d'université*. Economica, Paris
Cahiers français 1991 *Le système éducatif, 249*. La Documentation Française, Paris
Charlot B 1987 *L'Ecole en mutation, Crise de l'Ecole et mutations sociales*. Payot, Paris
Collège de France 1985 *Propositions pour l'enseignement de l'avenir*. La Documentation Française, Paris
Commissariat Général au Plan 1991 *Eduquer pour demain. Acteurs et partenaires*. La Documentation Française, Paris
Dubet F 1991 *Les lycéens*. Le Seuil, Paris
Durand-Prinborgne C P 1989 *L'administration scolaire*. Sirey, Paris
Legrand L 1982 *Pour un collège démocratique. Rapport au Ministre de l'Education Nationale*. La Documentation Française, Paris
Lesourne J 1988 *Education et société. Les défis de l'an 2000*. La Découverte, Paris
Ministère de l'Education Nationale (annual) *Repères et références statistiques*. Direction de l'Evaluation et de la Prospective, Paris
Prost A 1968 *Histoire de l'Education en France, 1800–1967*. Armand Colin, Paris
Prost A 1986 *L'Enseignement s'est-il démocratisé?* Presses Universitaires de France, Paris
Tenzer N 1989 *Un projet éducatif pour la France*. Presses Universitaires de France, Paris

Gambia

M. Ceesay

1. General Background

The Gambia is a small country on the West African Coast. It stretches 350 kilometers inland on either side of the river Gambia, varying in width from about 50 kilometers near the mouth of the river to about 24 kilometers upstream. The country is bounded by the Republic of Senegal and the Atlantic Ocean. The river Gambia runs the entire length of the country, starting from the Futa Jallon highlands in the Republic of Guinea to the Atlantic Ocean, dividing the country's inland areas of 10,689 square kilometers approximately in two equal halves—the South Bank and North Bank.

The population of the Gambia was estimated at 890,000 in 1992, growing at an annual rate of 3.4 percent overall and over 8 percent for the urban areas. The high rate of population growth is accounted for by the following factors: a net immigration rate of 0.6 percent coupled with a natural increase of 2.8 percent per annum. Fertility levels have been consistently high since 1970 with a crude birthrate of 49 per thousand while the total fertility rate remains at 6.4. The crude deathrate is 21 per thousand; mortality rates, particularly infant mortality, have fallen but still remain high. The infant mortality rate of children under one year is over 120 per thousand live births and of those under age 5 years is 240 per thousand live births. Life expectancy still remains 41 years for males and 44 years for females.

The youthful population structure is not unrelated to the high fertility levels. The under-15 age group forms approximately 45 percent of the population, while another 18 percent is between 15 and 24 years of age. The dependency ratio is 88 percent. Rapid growth in population, resulting in increased pressure on arable land, has led to a continuous outflow of population from rural to urban areas. Almost one-third of the Gambia's population lives in urban areas. In 1980, urban areas accounted for just over a fifth of the total population. Immigration from neighboring countries has also contributed to urban growth. This rapid population growth rate and growing concentration into one main urban area affects the distribution of school places.

The main ethnic groups include the Fula (19%), Wollof (15%), Mandinka (40%), and Jola (10%). Some 85 percent of the population is Moslem, which to some extent accounts for the mushrooming of *madrassas* (Koranic schools); 14 percent is Christian and 1 percent animist.

The official language is English with local languages, such as those of the above ethnic groups used in nonformal education and also in the first three grades of primary schooling as a medium of instruction. Arabic is taught in *madrassas*.

The illiteracy rate has been estimated at 83 percent, but the reliability of this figure is questionable.

The Gambia is a male-dominated society where women have little decision-making power. They are valued for their procreation roles and have generally accepted their socioeconomic status to be inferior to that of men. Generally, girls are given away early in marriage and this has been assumed to be one of the main causes of low female enrollment, especially in the rural areas. Numerous and closely spaced pregnancies, as well as childbearing early in life, have adverse effects on girls' and women's health. Early pregnancies for the unmarried young girls is also related to the dropout rate from the formal school system.

At Independence in 1965, the Gambia, like most African countries, inherited an economy that relied heavily on a single commodity—groundnut in this case. In 1990 almost 60 percent of cropland was under groundnut cultivation. The crop accounts for 75 percent of domestic exports. Structurally, agriculture is the mainstay of the economy, with more than 70 percent of the population engaged in subsistence farming, livestock-raising, and groundnut cultivation.

The labor-intensive nature of groundnut cultivation has required the participation of school-eligible and school-going candidates. This is even more evident at the start of the school year when boys do not enroll on time because they are busy helping their parents with farm work while the girls look after the younger ones at home in the rural areas. They can attend school full time only after harvest.

The industrial sector in the Gambia is very small and accounts for less than 8 percent of Gross Domestic Product (GDP). Manufacturing activities are limited to the processing (crushing) of groundnuts, baking, brewing, tanning, food processing, and the production of bricks, soap, and plasters. The sector provides employment for less than 3 percent of the country's labor force.

In addition to agriculture and industry, tourism and fisheries are important as sources of foreign exchange as well as of employment. The tourist industry provides employment to more than 2 percent of the labor force on a seasonal basis running from October through April. The industry also helps in the financing of education in the Gambia, though on a limited basis. Several schools in the rural areas had classroom blocks built by individual philanthropists who came out to the country as tourists. They also often give stationery and equipment, and sometimes sponsor students.

The Gambia is governed by a system of parliamentary democracy. The political party which wins a majority of seats in the House of Parliament in a General Election (held every five years) forms the government. The President, who is also elected by direct universal support, then appoints members of his party as Ministers with responsibility for various aspects of the business of the nation. Ministers are usually elected members of the House of Parliament but some of them may have been nominated members of parliament by the President. Each Minister is responsible for piloting through parliament all business relating to the Ministry for which they have responsibility. After legislation has been passed by the House of Parliament, the Minister is responsible for executing the approved policy through the Permanent Secretary as head of the agency of the Ministry.

Under this governmental structure, the Ministry of Education, Youth, Sports, and Culture is responsible for providing a basic education at the primary, secondary technical, and secondary high school levels. In addition, the Ministry is also responsible for the promotion and development of youth and sporting activities, and the safe custody of the country's cultural heritage. It is also committed to a program of functional adult literacy through a nonformal program of education.

2. Politics and the Goals of the Education System

The decade up to the mid-1980s was one of considerable expansion in enrollments. This unprecedented expansion was a reflection of Universal Primary Education (UPE) within the subregion after the Addis Ababa Resolution in 1961. Due to this expansion, the following problems resulted: qualified teachers, classrooms, furniture, and other software items all fell short of demand. Most glaring amongst these problems was the acute shortage of secondary school places due to the increasing number of primary school graduates. Even with the increased expansion, primary school enrollment was no more than 57 percent in 1988. Together, these problems form the basis of the New Education Policy 1988–2003. The policy document states three objectives: (a) to increase access to education; (b) to improve quality; and (c) to improve the relevance of education.

To achieve these objectives, strategies such as the restructuring of the education system to the 6–3–3–2 system of education (illustrated in Fig. 1) were taken. This new structure, particularly the middle school which forms the first tier of the basic education cycle, has generated considerable questions from the public; this is an indication of people's perception of change and innovations through the education system. However, population growth is on the increase, rural–urban, male–female disparities still exist, and at the same time, the cost of education is increasing.

The main objectives of education are to foster individual development and general socialization at the basic cycle, while at post-secondary levels the significance is focused on broader economic self-reliance through vocational education, skills and technical training, all through which also runs broader social goals.

3. The Formal System of Education

3.1 Primary, Secondary, and Tertiary Education

The Gambia's system of education in principle follows the structure inherited from the British Colonial

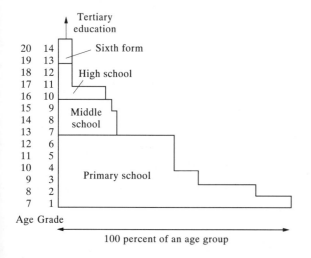

Figure 1
Gambia: Structure of the formal education system

period. Figure 1 outlines the new structure of the formal education system. It also presents expected enrollments (as a percentage of an age cohort) at each level of education. Primary education lasts for six years, at the completion of which students take the Common Entrance Examination (GCEE) to determine their eligibility for secondary school. Secondary education consists of a five-year academic stream (secondary high schools) and a four-year technical stream (secondary technical schools). Secondary high schools offer a five-year academic program (Forms 1–5) and prepare students for the Ordinary ("O") Level Examinations of the West African Examination Council (WAEC). Such qualifications provide access to some postsecondary educational institutions. Two of the secondary high schools offer Form 6 classes leading to Advanced ("A") Level Examinations of the West African Examination Council, which provide access to higher education either in-country at the Gambia College (two years' postsecondary) or abroad at universities and other postsecondary institutions. Technical secondary schools offer a combined program of academic education and skills in a terminal four-year program.

Education in the Gambia is not compulsory and is tuition-free at the primary level. Children can start nursery level at four years of age. The terms "nursery" and "kindergarten" are used synonymously in the Gambia. Such institutions are run by private individuals, community groups, and nongovernmental organizations.

In 1990–91, 86,101 students were enrolled at the primary level in 232 schools. Of these, 31 percent were in the most urban regions and only 18 percent in the most rural areas. The gross enrollment ratio in 1991 was 61 percent. However much fewer females than males were enrolled in the rural areas compared to urban areas. The low enrollment of girls in the rural areas is a reflection of a combination of factors, among which parental attitudes toward the education of girls has been very influential. Rural communities have lower modern sector employment expectations for their children following schooling, and preference is usually given to educating boys. Low enrollment ratios are in part also due to inadequate physical facilities. Religious and cultural factors also form other reasons for the low enrollment ratios at the primary level. All primary schools are coeducational. The primary school day normally contains about five hours of tuition, and the school year comprises 200 days. The student–teacher ratio is 30:1.

Secondary education was available for five years under the old system but under the new 6–3–3–2 system (See Fig. 1) O-level courses will last for three years. The secondary school completion rate is higher for boys than girls, largely because the attrition rate starting from the primary cycle is higher for girls. Most of the secondary schools are coeducational whereas some private schools, such as those under the Catholic Mission, are single sex. The secondary school year operates for approximately 200 days, with about 5.5 hours of tuition per day. The student–teacher ration is 28:1

3.2 Preschool Education

The purpose of preschool activities is to complement and supplement the informal education provided by the family and the home community, and to help to prepare children for entry to school.

The target group for preschooling comprises 3- to 7-year olds and, in 1992, the total number of preschools that existed was mapped by the Directorate of Schools Division of the Ministry of Education. The total number of children being served was not known. Despite this lack of data, it can be stated that preschooling has witnessed a rapid growth due to changes in parental and family circumstances, especially in urban areas were both parents may be working and where the extended family system may no longer be available to assist in looking after young children.

The preschool service offered will continue to function on a private basis and the role of the Ministry of Education, Youth, Sports, and Culture will be to act in a consultative and coordination capacity. The Ministry will coordinate preschool activities; organize training programs for preschool personnel; encourage research into preschool education; develop curricular materials; and assist in community, national, and international support for preschool education.

3.3 Special Education

Special education programs are provided for students with physical and mental disabilities. There are two special education institutions in the Gambia: a school for the blind which opened in 1971, and one for the deaf which opened in 1984. Both schools depend on philanthropic and religious organizations for support, while the government's contribution has been in support of staff salaries. The school for the blind has developed a program whereby students are integrated into primary schools and high schools after receiving basic academic and orientation courses. It should be noted that there is a need for educational provision to be made for different handicaps and for different levels of handicap but reliable statistics on these are not available and the probability exists that more children with disabilities are in the mainstream than in special schools.

3.4 Vocational, Technical, and Business Education

In spite of the government's efforts to offer a tuition-free but noncompulsory universal primary education, more and more children are leaving school at 14–15 years of age, and the majority are finding it difficult to gain employment in the formal sector. The fact that outputs from the education system serve as the major inputs to vocational and technical training programs in the Gambia, calls for the creation of more facilities to allow for a small and effective transition from one level to the other.

The objectives of vocational training institutions tend to serve varying purposes due to their diverse and complex nature, which to a large extent are not coordinated. Control of these institutions is lacking especially within the informal sector which is dominated by nongovernmental organizations. Another reason is the lack of an established framework to facilitate a smooth network of a system of operation.

The funds required for financing technical and vocational education will continue to increase and it will be difficult for the government to continue to shoulder this heavy responsibility alone. As a stopgap measure and to off-load this heavy financial responsibility, of which the major beneficiaries are employers in the commercial and private sector, a proposal has been made to introduce a levy system to assist the government towards the training and development of the country's human resources. The proposed system will have substantial implications for the future of education–industry relations.

3.5 Adult and Nonformal Education

Nonformal education activities in the Gambia are undertaken by government and nongovernmental agencies. The Nonformal Education Services Unit and the Department of Youth, Sports, and Culture run such activities, as well as the Ministry of Agriculture, the Department of Community Development, The Gambia Cooperative Union, the Women's Bureau, religious bodies, and nongovernmental organizations.

The principal target groups are 350,000 adults, (aged 15 years and over) requiring new skills to gain employability or develop self-employment opportunities, 48,000 out-of-school youths (aged 10–14 years), and 21,760 school dropouts (mainly girls and young women.)

The functions and purposes of adult and nonformal education are functional literacy and the need to sustain literacy. The latter applies to primary school-leavers. Nonformal education programs encourage the learning of new skills as a component of functional literacy activities. Given the varied character of nonformal education and the variety of agencies involved in its development, the key role of the Nonformal Education Services Unit (NFES) is to facilitate the coordination of these programs and activities. The NFES will supplement the programs and activities of NGOs where necessary.

The total annual expenditure on adult and nonformal education was one quarter of a million dalasis (US$28,090) which represented only 1 percent of the government's total expenditure on education. The main sources of finance are the government and agencies such as UNICEF, Danida, and the Women in Development (WID) Project.

4. Administrative and Supervisory Structure and Operation

Apart from private and religious organizations which administer schools at the preschool level, and the board of governors for the high schools, education in the Gambia is a government responsibility. At the primary level, which is directly funded by the government, the responsibility for administration, staffing, and curriculum has been devolved to the regional education offices through the Directorate of Schools headed by a Deputy Chief Education Officer (Schools). The Inspectorate Unit (under the Chief Education Officer) provides a direct link between the Ministry and particularly primary schools in the four education regions.

The active participation of religious missions, nongovernmental organizations, and private individuals underlines the need for some degree of decentralization in the administrative structure of schools. Most of the private schools are administered by the Catholic Mission which were long-established in the Gambia. Private schools are largely free from government direction, but have to follow the educational standards for registration and the annual subvention from the government.

Out of a total of 12 high schools in the Gambia, only one is run by the government. The remaining 11 are each administered by a Board of Governors. Postsecondary institutions are autonomous, although most of them receive a subvention from the government and the vocational education and technical training institutions are independently administered. A National Vocational Training Board (NVTB) is the body responsible for vocational and technical education programs and the major financial source for the board is the government.

The school starting age, the curriculum, and teachers' salaries remain standard for the schools whether government or privately sponsored.

While it is essential that the Ministry of Education retains central management control, the four regional offices are being strengthened to become strong arms of the system, both administratively and professionally. Each office is staffed by a Principal Education Officer and an Education Officer. The policy period, in effect in the 1990s, should see an increased measure of responsibility placed at the regional offices especially in the areas of financial management, personnel management, and the monitoring and administration of schools. High schools continue to be the responsibility of Boards of Governors appointed or approved by the Minister of Education, Youth, Sports, and Culture.

5. Educational Finance

The government's total spending from the national budget on education has witnessed an increase in real terms from D15–16 million (US$1.7–1.8 million) in 1979 to D35 million (US$3.9 million) in 1989. In 1991–92, the total Ministry of Education recurrent budget was estimated at D76.8 million (US$8.6 million). This refers to expenditure incurred through the Ministry of Education and does not include educational expenses arising through other ministries such as those incurred by the Ministry of Agriculture's education extension programs. In 1991–92, D32 million (US$3.6 million) were allocated to primary education, D7.9 million (US$888,000) to secondary technical schools, and D8.1 million (US$910,000) to high schools.

In the period 1979–89, the education share of the national budget increased. In 1991 it was 19 percent and it is expected to increase to 22 percent in the late 1990s. The government funds over 80 percent of the total recurrent allocation to primary education, pays all teachers' salaries at the secondary technical level, and gives an annual subvention (grant-in-aid) to all secondary high schools. Parents do not pay fees at the primary level. The fees levied by the secondary technical and high schools range from about D50–150 (US$6–17) per term which excludes books and maintenance; private schools such as the Senegalese school and Marina International receive no funds from the government.

The recurrent per capita cost is estimated at D500 (US$56) for primary, D800 (US$90) for secondary technical, and D1,500 (US$169) for secondary high schools.

Despite the increase in the government's allocation to education, the public, and parents in particular, have also borne their share of the increasing cost of education. However, the government will continue to bear the main burden of financing education. The share of the national budget devoted to education will need to be maintained at a high level if the targets specified in the Education Policy 1988–2003 are to be achieved.

6. Supplying Personnel for the Education System

In 1991 approximately 1,923 teachers were employed at the primary level, of whom 1,087 were qualified teachers and 836 were unqualified. These numbers exclude Koranic and home economics teachers. In secondary technical schools and high schools, about 470 and 290 teachers were employed respectively.

The unprecedented expansion of primary schools within the 1976–86 policy period led to numerous problems, such as shortages of qualified teachers which has been correlated with low internal efficiency within the school system and also the poor quality of education. The pupil–teacher ratio is 31:1 at the primary level, 23:1 at the high school level, and 28:1 at the secondary technical level. Teacher shortages occur in mathematics and sciences. Overall, approximately 65 percent of the total high school teaching force is non-Gambian. There is also a rural–urban disparity in the form of the qualified teacher–pupil ratio, which at the primary level is approximately 100:1 for the most rural region as opposed to 45:1 in the most urban region.

The Gambia College School of Education provides a two-year preservice teacher-training program for primary school teachers. Entry for this program requires four passes in the GCE O-level examinations. Those who successfully complete the course obtain the Primary Teacher Certificate, and are appointed at Grade 6 in the civil service salary scale. The production of primary teachers has averaged about 65 teachers per annum. There was a sharp increase in enrollment of student teachers in 1989–90. Out of 144 enrolled, 100 candidates were first year, and this has increased the number of qualified teachers geared toward the improvement of the quality of primary education. The Gambia College School of Education also trains secondary school teachers in a two-year Higher Teacher's Certificate (HTC) program. In 1989–90, 60 student teachers were enrolled in this program, of whom 47 were in the first year. Teachers for the upper levels of high school are trained at the degree-level in universities abroad.

There were mass promotions in 1991 and this has helped to boost teacher morale in a situation of declining attractiveness of teaching as a career. About 605 teachers will graduate from a series of inservice training programs in 1991. Considerable effort is also being directed to improving the quality of teachers. The Bristol University link with the Gambia College offers a two-year degree program to the College's graduate students, particularly those in mathematics and science. The new Education Policy 1988–2003 widely acknowledges the importance of teachers' continuing professional development, as a result of which programs have been delineated in this area.

7. Curriculum Development and Teaching Methodology

A distinction needs to be made between the curriculum for pre-1992 and that which was "prescribed" for 1992 onwards. In the pre-1992 curriculum, there was a partial common core curriculum at the primary level based on English language, mathematics, science, and social studies as core subjects. Physical education, arts and crafts, and economics are not examined; while in the realm of religious education, individual Arabic/Koranic teachers improve their own curriculum.

From 1992 onwards, a commonly prescribed core curriculum for Grades 1–9 became effective and the scope covers English language, mathematics, science, arts and craft for the first six grades, while for Grades 7–9 (i.e., the middle school level) there is a broad based curriculum. This includes English language, mathematics, science, social and environment studies, religious education, agricultural science, arts and craft, home economics, physical and health education, French, and Arabic. A new element has been introduced — national languages, however the problem of national language needs to go through a stage of experimentation and funding; the latter has yet to be obtained.

The Curriculum Research and Development Center (CRDC) translates policy into plans from a theoretical definition of pupils' learning needs and submits these proposals to the panel composed of curriculum specialists in a particular subject matter, other members from the Ministry, and others whose work is based on the subject matter.

The syllabus for each subject is also prepared by panels in the following steps. Step One reviews the curriculum, while Step Two expresses this curriculum in the form of a syllabus content, and makes recommendations about the materials required and the methods of teaching. The third step involves the drafting of teaching guides and pupils' books. Approval of these syllabuses takes the form of a syllabus validation exercise where one or two of the former panel members from CRDC sit in a larger panel chaired by an external member of CRDC. There is a uniform curriculum nationwide with no regional variations.

The Curriculum Development and Research Center is mandated with the preparation and making of recommendations for textbooks and modules. Most of the textbooks being used or about to be introduced have been adapted through the purchase of adaptation rights. The trial and dissemination is initially undertaken in a number of pilot schools identified by the Center. There is no institutionalized central body for approving commercially disseminated instructional materials, and in the absence of such a body, the CRDC should perform that role.

The Inspectorate Unit in collaboration with CRDC helps ensure that the curriculum is implemented by monitoring what is taught in the schools, while the Research and Evaluation Unit within the CRDC focuses on research for curriculum planning and renewal. A major problem is that developed curriculum is often not taught in schools due to the examination-oriented syllabus for selection purposes. The curriculum follows the examinations instead of vice versa.

8. The System of Examinations, Promotions, and Certifications

The norm in most schools is automatic promotion of pupils from one grade to the next without assessment. The first formal examination is the Gambia Common Entrance Examination (GCEE) given at the end of primary education (Grade 6) and is an external examination. Certificates are not awarded at this stage, but the results of the GCEE determines promotion into the secondary education cycle. The next major certificated examination is taken at the end of five years in secondary high school (the GCE O level), or at the end of four years in the secondary technical cycle. The former examination is externally administrated by the West African Examination Council (WAEC), while the Secondary Technical Leaving Certificate is administered by the same agency, but internally. Within both cycles, promotion is based on internal examinations offered by individual schools.

As stated earlier, the end-of-cycle examinations administered are more selective than curriculum-oriented. Because of their function as selection instruments, the Common Entrance Examinations, GCE O level, and the Secondary Technical School Leaving Certificate Examination all exert a strong influence on teaching methods and course content, and are no appropriate tool for assessing student accomplishment, particularly for those who do not continue their schooling. In the new 6–3–3–2 education structure which is in the process of implementation, the restructuring of the curriculum is intended to address the above problem. In essence, this will assist in the development of syllabus-based local examinations for primary and middle school leavers, replacing the GCE with a Primary School Leaving Certificate (PSLC) and introducing a new Middle School Leaving Certificate (MSLC).

9. Educational Assessment, Evaluation, and Research

The new Education Policy wishes to establish a continuous assessment scheme for Grades 1–9 and to develop an effective feedback system to monitor student performance over time and across schools.

There is no specific allocation from the education budget for assessment, evaluation, and research apart for D1,000,000 (US$112,000) under the Ministry's vote. This million dalasis which is just 1 percent of the total recurrent expenditure is allocated to examination charges. National research as such has not been conducted.

The main emphases of research at the beginning of the 1990s include: low enrollment rates (particularly female), parental attitude to formal education, and tracer studies on dropouts from Grade 6.

The most important education indicators on which data is collected annually by the Planning Unit of the Ministry of Education are on enrollment, teachers, textbooks, and furniture. The focus of such data is to improve the quality of education and budget preparation.

10. Major Reforms in the 1980s and 1990s

The new Education Policy resulted in considerable reform in many aspects of the Gambia's system of education. The lowering of the school entry age to 7

years, for example, was related to the drastic increase in primary school enrollments from 77,000 in 1988–89 to 86,101 students in 1990–91. The Ministry and the former Department of Education were integrated into a single Ministry. The new 6–3–3–2 education structure has far-reaching implications for changes in the curricula, assessment, and school structures for achieving the 1988–2003 Education Policy's objectives of increasing access and improving the quality and relevance of the education system. The need to improve the quality of education has required the training of more qualified teachers at Gambia College, and the building and refurbishment of more permanent classrooms at the primary level. Part of this program has also been the introduction of a Textbook Revolving Fund at the primary and middle school levels. National vocational education and technical training is in the process of review and strategies are being formulated to address the human resources and labor needs of the country.

These changes are all focused on the problems emanating from the unprecedented expansion at the primary level during the policy period 1976–86. They also share a common rationale: the need for the Gambian education system to assist in creating equality and efficiency. The reforms created considerable misgivings in the public mind, which needs to be enlightened about the new structure and, in particular, the middle school. The resolution of these doubts in the public mind is likely to loom over education in the 1990s.

11. Major Problems for the Year 2000

Attainment of the objectives described in the Education Policy 1988–2003 will require both major inputs of finance and the careful husbandry of all available resources devoted to education. The middle school spectre in terms of its location and the required labor force for the transitional period still looms. The cost of education is on the increase and is unlikely to abate in the face of external economic forces, and when most of the instructional and learning materials have to be imported, including textbooks. In essence, rewarding career structures for teachers are likely to remain a problem. Increasing access is likely to affect the quality of education, and parental attitudes toward the education of girls will be slow to change.

Bibliography

Ministry of Education 1991 *Education Statistics 1990–91.* Planning Unit, Banjul
Republic of The Gambia 1991 *Estimates of Recurrent Revenue and Expenditure 1991/92 with Estimates of Development Expenditure 1991/92.* Government Printer, Banjul
Republic of The Gambia 1988 *Sessional Paper No. 4 of Education Policy 1988–2003.* Ministry of Education, Youth Sports, and Culture, Banjul
World Bank 1990 *Staff Appraisal Report: The Gambia Education Sector Project.* World Bank, New York

Germany

R. H. Lehmann

1. General Background

In May 1945, a sovereign German government ceased to exist, as a result of the collapse of the National Socialist regime and Germany's unconditional surrender to the Allied powers. Only gradually were certain rights of self-determination restored, and in 1949 out of this situation two rival German states emerged: on the territory of the Soviet Occupation Zone, the German Democratic Republic (GDR), a Marxist–Leninist one-party state with a planned economy, and the pluralistic and economically liberal Federal Republic of Germany (FRG) within the limits of the American, British, and French Occupation Zones. Building on a long history of regional diversity, both states were originally organized with traditional historical territories (the *Länder*) constituting administrative subunits. Whereas these subunits were abolished in the GDR in 1952 in favor of a new centralized structure, federalism remained—as the state's official name indicates—an essential feature of self-government in the Federal Republic.

As a consequence of the dramatic changes in Europe at the end of the 1980s, the GDR was dissolved. Its original five *Länder* were reinstated and incorporated into the Federal Republic on October 3, 1990. Given the long period of divergent development in all segments of society, including education, the situation at the beginning of the 1990s was characterized by the need to equalize the living and working conditions in the two parts of the country.

Geographically, Germany is situated in the middle of the European continent and covers 356,957 square kilometers. The total population numbers about 80 million persons, of whom about 8 percent possess a nationality other than German. Many of the latter began to arrive in the late 1950s when the practice of recruiting manual labor from south European and Mediterranean countries was introduced. The largest single group (1.8 million) are Turkish by birth or descent. Other immigrants have entered the country in search of refuge from persecution, warfare, or economic hardship in their native countries. A third group of immigrants consists of ethnic Germans (even if German is not always their native language) from east and southeast European countries who—in contrast to the two previous groups—can claim citizenship immediately upon arrival. Given the enduring language handicaps even among long-term residents, let alone recent arrivals (approximately 500,000 in 1992), it remains a challenge for the educational system to integrate immigrant students and to offer them adequate opportunities for study and training. There are four language minority groups that have historical roots in the country: Danes, Frisians, Sinti (Gypsies), and Sorbs. None of these groups has more than 100,000 members. Special efforts are made to provide children from these minorities with mother-tongue instruction. German, however, is the dominant language, but with substantial variation in its regional dialects.

Germany is not rich in natural resources; nor does its agricultural production fully meet market demands. Thus, the country is heavily dependent on imported goods as well as on the export of finished products. As a rule, the West German balance of trade has been markedly positive, and German investments abroad by far exceed foreign investments in Germany. However, as a consequence of high wages and substantial labor costs within the mandatory social security system, Germany's favorable position as an export nation has been, and will continue to be challenged on the world trade markets. Obviously, this has implications for education. Research and development as well as the manufacture of high-value-added products require high standards of training. The same is true for the sectors of commercial and social services in Germany's rapidly changing society. In addition, the flow of capital since 1990 into the former GDR for financing reconstruction, improving the infrastructure, and implementing measures to combat unemployment places a heavy burden on government budgets, which, in turn, threatens to limit severely public expenditures on education.

The ratio of productivity levels between the two parts of the country was about 3.5:1 in 1990 in favor of the West; this was reflected by an estimated annual per capita Gross Domestic Product (GDP) of DM 20,059 (US\$34,100) for West Germany, and only DM 6,355 (US\$10,800) for East Germany. Unemployment rates also differed substantially. Whereas up to 1990 there was, officially, no unemployment in the GDR (however low the general productivity level), unemployment figures for the first quarter of 1992 stood at 6.3 percent for the West and 10.3 percent for the East. It is in the light of this contrast that the state of education in post-reunification Germany has to be evaluated.

2. Politics and Goals of the Education System

Historically, the provision of education in Germany has two distinct roots: the Church and the State. There is a tradition of church involvement going back to the early Middle Ages, and the *Länder* (or antecedent territorial powers) have long claimed responsibility for education. Proclamations of universal compulsory education in various territories since the end of the seventeenth century can be seen as landmarks. There are a few private schools, some of which have their origins in experiments in the reform movements during the early decades of the twentieth century. Quantitatively, however, their role is negligible. Church influence, in turn, has generally declined. Thus, it is very much left to the political forces—and the teachers, parents, and students as directly involved groups—to determine both the state of, and changes within, the educational system.

In the postwar Federal Republic, a period of reinstating the traditional tripartite school system as well as politically autonomous universities was followed by an era of unprecedented expansion and qualitative reform (1965–73). Since the Federal Constitution of 1949 had established state (rather than federal) jurisdiction over educational matters, variations in the distribution of power between the major political parties within and across the *Länder* soon came to dominate debates about the goals of educational reform. Whereas Social Democrat (and Liberal) state governments tended to stress education as a civil right, with an emphasis on individual self-fulfillment, equality, and compensatory action (and a comprehensive school system as a corollary), the more conservative Christian Democrat state governments insisted more on collective aims and actions for the public good such as the supply of highly qualified graduates. Several attempts were made to establish a new structure for the educational system as a whole to which both sides could subscribe (e.g. the *Strukturplan* of 1970 and the *Bildungsgesamtplan* of 1973). In most respects, however, these attempts failed. Nevertheless at least, mutual recognition of school-leaving certificates between the *Länder* was maintained.

Educational politics and the formulation of educational goals followed quite another course in the Democratic Republic. In 1946, even before any elections had taken place, the administrative authorities passed a law establishing a "democratic unified school" which was intended to "break the educational monopoly" of the privileged classes and to guarantee access to higher education for hitherto deprived groups ("children of workers and farmers"). By 1949 more than two-thirds of the teachers who had served under the National Socialists had been replaced by rapidly trained "new teachers", so that a high degree of compliance was quickly achieved with the established communist rule. A period of adopting Soviet models (such as the principle of "polytechnic instruction" (1958–59) followed, the official overall goal being that of a "universally developed socialist personality" (1952). Strict, centralized political control of the educational system, as well as the state doctrine of economic and social planning, led to a closer linkage between labor demands and educational planning than was the case in West Germany (Anweiler 1988). Consequently, education in the GDR also experienced a period of quantitative expansion and some qualitative reform (1963–71). But whereas

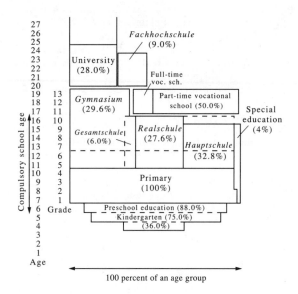

Figure 1
Germany: Structure of the formal education system

the general trend toward more prestigious educational certificates remained unbroken in the FRG, quantitative expansion in the GDR had leveled off by the 1970s, and since the early 1980s there was a noticeable trend toward fostering specially gifted and talented students in the interest of attaining a better position on international markets.

With the former ideological basis gone and the political system changed, reunification forced the East German *Länder* to adapt their educational system(s) to the established West German structure. Thus, provisions in the State Constitutions and/or preambles to special School and University Acts established broad educational goals emphasizing both development of individuality and participation in public life.

3. The Formal System of Education

Figure 1 depicts the formal structure of the West German education system, with graphic indications of the approximate percentage of the age cohort enrolled in a particular program. In 1992, with the East German *Länder* still undergoing fundamental reforms, no accurate picture can be given for the whole of Germany. Eventually, however, directly comparable school leaving certificates as implied by the diagram will also exist in East Germany, and since its population is only about 20 percent of the total, quantitative changes will be relatively minor.

3.1 Primary, Secondary, and Tertiary Education

Depending on the state, compulsory schooling lasts 9 or 10 years, with normal entry at age 6. Special regula-

347

tions cover the details as to when the requirements are fulfilled (e.g., in case of belated entry or grade repetition). If a student fails to obtain a leaving certificate, he or she is no longer legally entitled to the provision of formal education and will often face grave social and economic difficulties.

Primary education normally includes four years of formal schooling. The city-state of Berlin has a six-year scheme, however, and several other states organize instruction in fifth and sixth grade in special intermediary institutions which then feed their students into the various types of secondary programs. Still others have special provisions for easy transition between school types during the fifth and sixth grades. There are approximately 190 school days per year at the primary level and children attend school from about 8 a.m. to noon, depending on the grade.

At the end of Grade 4 (or 6, as the case may be) the students are allocated to the different programs of secondary education. These represent a clear three-level hierarchy in terms of the "academic esteem" of the leaving certificates conferred. In practice, if not in theory, the allocation process is markedly dependent on social background influence; the correlation between school-type attendance and parental education, for instance, is about 0.50 at Grade 8. Theoretically, the choice of a particular program rests in most cases with the parents. The role of the primary teacher in the decision is mostly restricted to that of giving a written recommendation based on attainment. Again, in practice, unwillingness to comply with this recommendation will often result in failure at a level which then proves to be too demanding. Thus, significant numbers of students drop back to a less ambitious program in or after Grade 7, at which level some secondary schools introduce a second foreign language.

In 1990, just over 34 percent of the West German students in Grades 7 through 9 attended the least academically demanding program, namely the *Hauptschule*. This school type provides instruction geared toward entering an apprenticeship after having received the leaving certificate. The curricular content provides special components intended to prepare the students for their later careers and also includes one foreign language (usually English). Quantitatively, the *Hauptschule* is in a state of decline as can be seen from the fact that in 1960 nearly 64 percent of the respective age cohort attended this program. Since the *Hauptschule* tends to attract many low-achieving students and a disproportionately high percentage of immigrant youth, this school type is sometimes cynically labeled as "the only choice left" (*Restschule*, cf. Tillmann 1988), and this situation has given rise to a mounting debate about its reform or abolition.

Of the corresponding cohort, 28.8 percent attend the next higher program, which is known as the *Realschule* or sometimes the *Mittelschule* (intermediate school). At least one foreign language is obligatory in this type of school and a second is usually offered. Traditionally, the *Realschule* has catered to students aspiring to enter subordinate white-collar professions. Since the 1970s its successful completion has become an entry requirement for some of the more attractive apprenticeship programs. The leaving certificate also appears to function increasingly as a key to alternative routes into higher education. There is some evidence that scholastic achievement among students attending the *Realschule* is, on average, higher in those *Länder* having a more selective/competitive educational system.

The third program at the secondary level is called the *Gymnasium*. It is attended by 30.8 percent of West German students in Grades 7 through 9. The overall aim is to prepare students for higher education programs, even though not all of its graduates will proceed to university studies. The number of female graduates is slightly higher than that of males although more male graduates continue with higher education. In Grades 5 through 10, the curricular content varies somewhat according to the type of school attended. It may range from a heavy emphasis on classical languages (Latin and Greek) to modern languages and special arts programs. Generally, at least two—and in some cases three—foreign languages are required, of which English is one. Beginning with Grade 11, students can choose specializations within a rather complicated framework that allocates approximately one-third to "language and arts," one-third to social studies (civic education, history or geography, religion or philosophy), and one-third to mathematics and science. Physical education is also compulsory.

Successful completion of the final examination at the end of Grade 13 entitles a student to attend university. A minimum grade point average may be required for some higher education programs (most notably in the medical field) but there is no strict and essential linkage between the student's specialization at the upper secondary level and his or her choice of higher education studies.

At the secondary school level, there are also about 190 days of school per year and children typically attend school from 8 a.m. to 1 p.m.

Since the early 1970s, plans to restructure the (West) German educational system focused on introducing comprehensive schools for all children in an area, with internal streaming by subject and differential leaving certificates. These plans aroused a great deal of controversy. Some of the early experimental programs of comprehensive schools (*Gesamtschulen*) were politicized and this made them unacceptable to a popular majority. Different *Länder* authorities also held very different views about the desirability of having truly comprehensive systems. Commissioned evaluation studies did not always help to take the ideological element out of the debate. As of the beginning of the 1990s the situation can be characterized by saying that the conservative *Länder* have decided to terminate the experimental programs, whereas the Social Democratic states have given the *Gesamtschule* the status of one among four types of regular secondary schooling. Thus, only 6.2 percent of the Grade cohorts 7 through 9 attend this type of school but because it often has to compete with *Realschulen* and *Gymnasien* for students, "creaming-off" occurs, so preventing the *Gesamtschule* from becoming comprehensive in the truest sense of the word.

At the tertiary level, there are two types of institution. First, there are colleges or polytechnics, the *Fachhochschulen* which basically train students in the practical applications of scientific knowledge (e.g., design, construction, and development in engineering or public administration in the fields of law, economics, social sciences). These institutions require only 12 years of successfully completed schooling. Their programs usually include a rather strictly prescribed curriculum with a strong emphasis on practical experience. Secondly, there are universities which are designed to integrate teaching with front-line research. Universities often allow students a great deal of individual choice, especially in humanities courses. No general studies are required before entering a particular program and there is no clear distinction between undergraduate and graduate programs. A first leaving certificate can be obtained after four to six years of study. However, the dropout rate is unacceptably high, and the average length of study exceeds the theoretical minimum by several years.

In West Germany there were attempts during the reform phase of the 1970s to combine *Fachhochschulen* and universities into a single institution (the *Gesamthochschule*). While some of these continue to exist, the model as such did not meet with enough enthusiasm to be implemented on a large scale. One exception, however, was the incorporation of teacher-training colleges into existing universities or their upgrading to become new universities. In East Germany, where no new universities were founded after 1945, many highly specialized tertiary institutions existed at the time of reunification. In the course of adapting the situation to West German standards, they are now being converted to both *Fachhochschulen* and universities. For a more detailed account of the system of higher education, see Kehm and Teichler (1992) and Möhle (1992).

3.2 Preschool Education

Preschool education has deep historical roots in Germany. In the eighteenth and nineteenth centuries, institutions existed for the welfare of needy children which originally provided basic biblical instruction and which sought to contain the adverse effects of early industrialization. As a result, even in the early 1990s only about one-third of kindergarten places in West Germany are provided by the government (usually the local community). The majority are supported by independent authorities, in most cases the

churches. Both public and independent institutions require parents to contribute to fees. Kindergarten education caters to children from age 3 to school entry, and its personnel are trained in special vocational schools. Preschool education does not normally contain literacy or numeracy instruction. For those children who have reached the age of compulsory school entry but who are judged not yet ready to follow regular instruction, some schools provide *Schulkindergarten* programs. Without actually covering first-grade content, these are intended to facilitate a smooth transition into regular schooling. On the basis of a similar pedagogical approach, there are also preschool "classes" for 5-year olds which operate on a voluntary basis.

Prior to the dissolution of the GDR, there were marked differences in the provision of preschool education between the two parts of the country. Only 1 percent of the age groups 0 to 2 years in West Germany was provided with some form of institutionalized daycare, as opposed to 56 percent in East Germany. About 80 and 94 percent of the age groups 3 to school entry attended kindergarten in West and East Germany respectively. There were substantial regional differences in the provision of places within West Germany, as well as great variation between the age groups ranging from 36 percent of 3-year olds to 90 percent of 6-year olds not yet enrolled in schools. These contrasts were related to differences in the rates of women's employment between East and West Germany as well as the East German party and state policy to exert maximum control over all educational processes under the jurisdiction of a single ministry (Ministry of Popular Education). With the exception of the *Schulkindergarten*, preschool education in West Germany was, and still is, mostly the indirect responsibility of the Ministry of Youth and Family Affairs which emphasizes pluralism and parental involvement.

The political and economic collapse of the GDR entailed—at least temporarily—a partial dismantling of the virtually universal provision of preschool facilities in East Germany which had, in fact, put a heavy strain on productivity levels and government expenses. At the same time, relatively low birthrates in West Germany led to the expectation that a sufficient number of places for 3- to 6-year olds will be available before the end of the 1990s. (For more detail see Tietze et al. 1989.)

3.3 Special Education

In 1989, in both East and West Germany, approximately 4 percent of students were in special institutions for handicapped children close to the end of lower secondary education. In addition, the GDR operated a system of special schools (*Spezialschulen*) for children with exceptional talent in academic subjects, the arts, or sports for about 1 percent of the respective age cohort. In West Germany special education for talented children was and continues to be almost completely neglected, with only very few experimental programs operating largely on the basis of private initiative. Therefore, only special education for the handicapped will be considered in this section.

Traditionally, handicapped children were classified according to the nature of their disabilities (e.g., blindness, physical problems, mental retardation). The establishment of special classes and sometimes schools closely follows this classification scheme. Accurate data on the distribution of students across the various categories are available only for the former West Germany. According to these, approximately 40 percent of all students in special education attended a program specifically geared toward problems deriving from medically defined impairments (including individual tuition in the case of long-term illness and special provisions for multiple handicaps). There are, however, two further categories which together constitute the major part of special education in Germany: 3 percent of those in special education are characterized as displaying "behavioral disorders" and 56 percent as having "learning difficulties." The latter category poses considerable difficulties in arriving at a satisfactory definition and clear diagnostic procedures.

Increasingly, efforts are being made to integrate handicapped children into mainstream classrooms, although—as of 1992—these were only beginning to lead to reductions in special school enrollment. The preferred model is to have a trained specialist and a regular teacher work as a team in the classroom, but there are obvious financial limits which, in conjunction with practical constraints, militate against its full implementation.

3.4 Vocational, Technical, and Business Education

Compulsory schooling in Germany is not limited to general education. Students who graduate with a general school-leaving certificate at the level of *Hauptschule* or *Realschule* and even those who leave without a certificate after nine years of schooling must attend, either part-time or full-time, some program leading to an officially recognized professional qualification.

The system delivering these qualifications has a rather complex structure with closely parallel provisions in the fields of vocational, technical, and business education. The most common type of program (the *Berufsschule*) caters to apprentices who, in addition to the practical training gained within their firms, receive both theoretical instruction in their trade and also some additional general education (e.g., in German and civic education). Instruction may take place regularly for one or two days per week or, alternatively, for blocks of several weeks. Since vocational education is provided by state-run schools, but the final certificate is awarded by the local Chamber of Trades, Industry, or Commerce, this scheme is often referred to as the "dual system." The certificates are official and recognized

by the state. However, there are nearly 400 registered professions and for each of these there are theoretical and practical training requirements which are issued by the relevant federal authorities.

Sometimes similar in content, but entirely under the jurisdiction of the educational authorities and operating on a full-time basis, the *Berufsfachschule* offers qualifications in areas in which apprenticeship schemes do not exist (e.g., for certain professions in early childcare) or where there are insufficient numbers of openings for apprentices (e.g., for some technical professions, such as chemical laboratory assistant). A general school-leaving certificate serves as an entry requirement and, as is the case in the dual system, the final diploma can often be used to enter more ambitious programs within the system.

Other programs are directed to relatively smaller groups with very special aspirations. The "year of basic vocational training" (*Berufsgrundbildungsjahr*) provides preparatory courses with a comparatively broad orientation. These are to help school leavers to improve their chances in securing an apprenticeship contract. The "supplementary vocational school" (*Berufsaufbauschule*) awards to its graduates who lack certain formal qualifications a certificate that allows them to enter more demanding programs. *Fachschulen* deliver this advanced instruction to trainees who have already completed a program of vocational, technical, or business education or who, alternatively, possess a higher school-leaving certificate. *Fachoberschulen* lead to certificates allowing students to enter the *Fachhochschule* within a given range of options.

A somewhat ambiguous function is performed by professionally oriented forms of the upper secondary stage (*Fachgymnasium*). Legally, they are part of the general academic system, and upon successful completion they also grant unrestricted admission to university-level studies. At the same time, their curricula are geared toward economic, social, and technical fields. They are also open to students who have already completed a vocational, technical, or business training program.

Thus, the system as a whole is governed by a host of regulations which cover the entry requirements, transition, and exit qualifications. It is, sometimes, characterized as being ruled by the "entitlement syndrome" (*Berechtigungswesen*). Nevertheless, it does provide multiple opportunities for students with a slow start in school, but high levels of later achievement and aspiration to move upward on the educational ladder.

In spite of modifications resulting from the almost complete abolition of private firm ownership in the former GDR, East Germany had retained some key features of the traditional "dual system." Similarly, its former practice of incorporating vocational/technical elements into the secondary school curriculum and its system of hierarchically structured qualifications offered functional equivalents to some parts of the complex West German array of opportunities for professional qualification. Thus, the implementation of the latter system in the East German *Länder* can build upon a set of common traditions in the provision of highly qualified workers which—in spite of all postwar divergence—had never been completely eradicated.

3.5 Adult and Nonformal Education

Adult education in Germany is usually classified into three broad categories: general, vocational (including technical and commercial), and political. Federal legislation dating back to 1972 encourages participation in adult education by entitling adults to financial support and additional holidays in order to attend vocational (and in some cases political or general) courses. These measures were taken in recognition of the fact that fast-changing economic, political, and social conditions require individuals to upgrade their qualifications in accordance with new demands. It is estimated that approximately 40 percent of the (West German) work force participates in some form of adult education each year.

General adult education is dominated by the *Volkshochschulen*, usually supported by the local community, although they may also be registered nonprofit organizations. The courses provided include (in decreasing order of hours offered): (a) languages; (b) economics, mathematics, and science; (c) health; (d) handicraft; (e) school equivalent; (f) politics and social science; (g) education, psychology, and theology; (h) literature and arts. Similar courses, but with a different order of relative importance, are offered by the churches.

Since some of the courses offered in the *Volkshochschulen* can be considered as vocational adult education, these institutions are also the most important providers of such programs. Other institutions are chambers of industry/commerce, or trade unions, certain vocational schools (*Fachschulen*), the tertiary sector, and institutes specialized in distance learning. No participation figures are available for in-firm and out-of-firm programs organized by employers, but it is safe to assume that all large modern enterprises operate such schemes and that many technologically advanced skills are transmitted through these mechanisms within the economy itself. Special attention must be given to qualification and retraining measures organized and/or funded by the unemployment agency (Federal Agency of Labor). Since 1990, this institution has promoted massive training programs for the East German work force. These programs have also bridged longer periods of unemployment for workers and employees whose firms were closed down.

Political adult education refers primarily to the activities of foundations that are closely linked to the political parties, as well as to courses provided by unions. The number of participants (about 500,000 per year) does not exceed 10 percent of those who acquire further professional qualifications through adult education.

Given the great diversity of programs and institutions involved in adult education, it is difficult, if not impossible, to distinguish between formal and nonformal activities. Relatively few of the activities are "formal" in the sense of being related to state-recognized certificates. However, many of the programs are implemented by specially trained staff with detailed curricula and teaching strategies. Thus, the practice of considering adult education as the "fourth sector" of the German educational system is not without some justification.

4. Administrative and Supervisory Structure and Operation

Since the Federal Constitution establishes *Länder* jurisdiction over formal education, several *Länder* have provisions in their own constitutions governing educational matters and all of them have passed special legislation establishing the goals, structures, instructional content, and procedures in their respective systems. Within the state, the responsibility for education rests with a ministry of cabinet rank often called the Ministry of Culture (*Kultusministerium*). In some of the larger states, schools are not directly controlled by the state ministry, but through regional administrative bodies which are part of the executive without any immediate parliamentary counterpart. The local community usually shares responsibility for providing the necessary infrastructure and may be involved in the appointment of staff.

The supervision, or inspection, of schools is either directly or indirectly subordinate to the state ministry. With very few exceptions, the state churches no longer exert any supervisory functions in schools. Formally, three different functions of school supervision are distinguished: pedagogical, legal, and civil service supervision. While the first of these functions is based on "advice and support," the other two refer to possibilities of direct intervention in cases of the violation of pertinent laws and to the implementation of civil service regulation (e.g., appointment, evaluation of service, and promotion). The latter applies because most teachers are tenured civil servants and as such are subject to special legislation. While, in theory, the supervision of schools is the most important instrument of control in the hands of the ministries, there is a clear secular trend away from the notion of control toward predominantly advisory functions.

Given the necessity of reconciling the pluralistic structure of education in Germany with the needs for some minimum homogeneity (expressed, for instance, by the mutual recognition of school-leaving certificates between the states), the Standing Conference of Ministers of Culture establishes—by unanimous decision—nationwide principles for education and also deals with international matters. The Joint Commission for Educational Planning and Research Support, in which federal and state governments share the voting power, formulates recommendations and commissions experimental programs. After a change in the Federal Constitution in 1969, some jurisdiction for the tertiary sector was transferred from the states to the federal government.

5. Educational Finance

With the exception of tertiary education, educational finance is entirely in the hands of the *Länder* and the local communities. As a rule, all personnel costs are borne by the state and the infrastructure is provided by the community. Federal government liabilities in the tertiary sector are primarily related to the physical installation and expansion of tertiary institutions, to the provision of research and teaching equipment, and in general to the support of research activities. Whereas nearly all educational programs including tertiary-level studies are free of tuition fees, the federal government grants supplementary payments to some secondary and tertiary students; some of these payments are granted on a loan basis. While the number of private (e.g., church-operated) schools is small, many of these institutions receive substantial support from the public budget (approximately 90% of the operating costs). Thus, such schools are often also free of tuition costs.

Public expenditure for education amounted to 3.7 percent of the (West German) Gross National Product (GNP) in 1990, to which 1.7 percent for research and individual support measures can be added. Private investments in research and development as well as adult education programs added another 3.9 percent so that the total expenditure in 1990 was just under 9.3 percent of GNP. It is to be noted, however, that the public share has steadily declined since 1975 which marked the end of the expansion of the system as a whole. It is somewhat alarming that the same trend has been followed by private educational expenditure since about 1985. In 1989, public unit costs were about DM6,200 (US$3,650) per student in schools and DM17,100 (US$10,060) per student in higher education.

6. Supplying Personnel for the Education System

Traditionally, only teachers in *Gymnasien* and some specialist teachers for commercial education were trained at the university level, with a heavy emphasis on subject matter at the expense of pedagogy. Teaching staff for all other school types, including the various forms of vocational and technical education obtained their training from other tertiary institutions, often with lower entry requirements. Much of this dualism survived in the GDR until 1990, whereas since the late 1960s in West Germany most of the former teacher-training colleges were incorporated into existing universities, or actually formed the nuclei of newly founded universities. There has been a general tendency to equalize the various forms of teacher education across target groups in the sense of providing qualifications of directly comparable status, although this aim has been fully achieved only in a minority of states.

As a general rule, subject-matter studies cover two disciplines to be taken at the respective university departments or faculties. For some specializations, general educational studies are supplemented by specific studies such as in the field of reading for future primary teachers or applied diagnostics for those who are intending to teach in special education institutions. Within the departments of education, the major emphasis is on historical, philosophical, and practice-oriented approaches.

For teaching personnel, certification is a state matter. University (or teacher-training college) studies are concluded by a state-supervised examination with university staff functioning as examiners. This is followed by an internship (*Referendariat*) which includes supervised teaching practice and additional coursework. This *Referendariat* training usually lasts for two years at the end of which there is a second examination run solely by the state. Since only a few students are able or willing to gain the first level of certification within the official limits of $3\frac{1}{2}$ to $4\frac{1}{2}$ years of university studies, fully certified teachers in West Germany are often almost 30 years old before they actually enter the classroom. This was markedly different from the situation in the former GDR, where primary teachers were normally 21 years old when they began their active teaching career.

7. Curriculum Development and Teaching Methodology

The state ministries of education (with a few exceptions in vocational and technical training) determine their curricula in accordance with existing legislation, and they do so by means of three different instruments: (a) tables prescribing the number of periods per week and subject by grade and school type, (b) curriculum guidelines, (c) the authorization of textbooks.

There is considerable variation from state to state. For instance, Bavarian students (Grades 1 through 10) receive approximately 20 percent more instruction in terms of teaching periods than the corresponding group in Hamburg (Mitter 1990). There is also some variation in the relative weight accorded to different subjects.

While the general aims are laid out in school legislation (often the preambles of the respective Acts of Parliament), specific objectives are published in the context of curriculum guidelines. These are decreed by the state ministry; they include syllabuses, recommendations on teaching methods, and sometimes model lesson plans. Only the syllabus itself is considered obligatory and decisions about methods are left to the teachers (subject only to advice from the supervising authorities). The guidelines are usually elaborated by appointed teams of experts, sometimes in collaboration with universities and/or research and development institutes. It is to be noted, however, that the guidelines are not primarily based on empirical research outcomes but rather they reflect purely normative considerations and have at times been subject to considerable political controversy.

No textbook may be used in a German school without prior approval from the state ministry. Schools and teachers are then free to choose from among the books on the approved list. While it has sometimes been argued that this mechanism provides the ministries with a powerful instrument of control, it should be noted that many teachers make extensive use of materials they have photocopied or prepared themselves. This adds substantially to the variation in learning opportunities between classrooms.

As stated above, the decisions about whether to use a particular teaching method are very much left to the teacher. With diminishing student–teacher ratios (down from more than 30:1 in 1960 to about 15:1 in 1980, primarily for demographic reasons), there has been a clear trend away from teacher-centered approaches toward work with small groups and a student-centered perspective. Since the late 1980s, the concept of "open instruction" which emphasizes self-directed student learning has become an increasingly popular model for primary schools and is also in the lower grades of some secondary schools.

8. The System of Examinations, Promotions, and Certifications

With very few exceptions, formal testing is not used for the evaluation of educational achievement. These exceptions refer primarily to diagnostic tests (e.g., for the purpose of identifying different types of dyslexia), although some commercially produced achievement tests are available (Trost et al. 1991). The normal approach which is used to assess student achievement relies entirely on teachers' evaluations of written tests and of the students "oral" cooperation. "The results are expressed either in a written progress report (mainly in primary grades), or as marks on a 6-point scale. Informal tests are given with a prescribed minimum frequency (in the higher grades of up to five hours duration), but greater weight is placed on successful participation in classroom interaction. Homework may also play a role.

Because of this variety of assessment procedures, students' marks or scores are not comparable across schools or even classrooms, since they depend on individual judgment and potentially quite different achievement tasks. Some states provide, on an annual basis, centrally defined tasks and standarized coding

schemes in order to facilitate feedback to teachers, but these are not part of the in-class evaluation of achievement.

Again, with some exceptions, there is no automatic promotion from one grade level to the next, although grade repetition is decreasingly exercised (1.5% per grade in primary schools and about 4% in secondary schools in 1990). A special case is the upper secondary stage of the *Gymnasium*, where credits for successful completion of courses (awarded on a 16-point scale) are weighted and accumulated over four semesters, and the marks for the written and oral final examinations are then added to form a total score.

All attainment documents (school-leaving certificates as well as university and state examination diplomas) have a legalistic and highly formalized character. They are mutually recognized by the states and entitle the student to enter higher-level programs, to receive higher levels of payment (e.g., in the extensive civil service), and to bear certain professional appellations (including academic titles). In the case of school-leaving certificates, it is for the state educational authority to ensure the attainment of minimum standards. Procedures vary: In most states, successful completion of the final grade of the *Hauptschule* and *Realschule* leads to a recognized certificate, while the tasks for the final examination in the *Gymnasium* are submitted to and approved by the ministry. In others, there are centrally set (and marked) tasks at all three levels. Still others have a mixture of these practices.

9. Educational Assessment, Evaluation, and Research

There is no national assessment of educational outcomes on a regular basis. The German component of the International Association for the Evaluation of Educational Achievement (IEA) Reading Literacy Study (Elley 1992) was the first achievement survey in two decades based on a national probability sample of students. This is despite the fact that there are several large, and in part federally funded, research institutes. Some of the *Länder* maintain their own state institutes, but these are politically controlled by the ministry and are, therefore, in a delicate position when controversial issues are investigated across state borders. Another typical form is that of a specialized central institute devoted to particular subject areas (e.g., science), a segment of the school system (in this case vocational, technical, and commercial education), or a particular field of research (e.g., internationally comparative studies).

Evaluation, defined in the sense of program evaluation, is almost entirely limited to commissioned research. At the federal level, the Joint Commission for Educational Planning and Research Support provides official recognition for experimental programs whose evaluation is then funded jointly by the federal and the state ministries. However, the appointment of evaluation teams (often, but not always, from universities) may be critical in such cases. Especially in the case of experiments in comprehensive schooling, some of the evaluation studies have been criticized for their rather obvious political bias.

As compared with other countries, Germany has not undertaken much empirical research in education (for an overview, see Ingenkamp et al. 1992). Similarly, relatively few methodological innovations have originated from German educational research groups. In the case of East Germany, there was a relatively broad tradition of small-scale empirical studies, often severely limited because of lack of access to computer facilities. The latter factor did not play a role in some centrally controlled research groups which were also able to conduct larger surveys, but many of these results were never published for political considerations. Neither of these limitations apply in West Germany where the strong historical and normative orientation resulted in many valuable monographs but which, at the same time, placed strong constraints on the influence of empirical studies.

10. Major Reforms in the 1980s and 1990s

The time of officially proclaimed major educational reforms ended in 1975 in West Germany with the abolition of the German Council of Education which had tried to implement a whole new education system. Since then, conservative state governments tended to maintain much of the traditional tripartite secondary education structure while, to some extent, the Social Democratic ministries tried to install the *Gesamtschule* as an alternative to, if not as a substitute for, the tripartite system. Nevertheless, there were major changes. There was a decrease in *Hauptschule* enrollment and a simultaneous increase at the *Gymnasium* level. Academic and vocational schooling at the upper secondary level have become more parallel, be it by the introduction of new professionally oriented courses in the *Gymnasium*, or by increased enrollment in such schools, or by the encouragement of the integration of several forms of upper secondary education. There were also changes in the university curricula for teacher training. At the level of classroom teaching, new methods began to gain acceptance. The same was true for new content areas; peace education, environmental education, and the study of women's issues serve as examples.

Very fundamental reforms, albeit applying to five states only, were initiated in 1990 with the reunification of the country. Because of their commitment to the communist system (often including the practice of infringing upon the civil rights of others, for example by cooperating with the Ministry of State Security), many teacher trainers lost their positions. The same applied to some groups of researchers, curriculum specialists, and school principals. Some institutions

were closed altogether. Others then began to appoint new staff, often "imported" from West Germany. All five East German *Länder* abolished the former unified system in 1992 and then installed schemes similar to one or the other of the West German ones. Inservice training which is intended to acquaint existing teachers with new curricula, new textbooks, and less teacher-centered methods was undertaken on a large scale. New administrative structures and new organizations for carrying out this massive program were set up and began to be implemented. At all levels, this process must be described not as one of internal reform, but rather as one of adapting conditions in East Germany to the firmly established West German system.

11. Major Problems for the Year 2000

Although not all problems refer to the immense difficulties in mastering the consequences of reunification, many major problems during the 1990s will undoubtedly be centered around the need to equalize opportunities in the two parts of the country. Apart from the institutional changes described earlier, it must be seen that the transition from a highly centralized and in many respects clearly collectivity-oriented (if not repressive) system to a liberal one is full of risks for all of the groups involved. Changing teaching styles and marking practices, completely new needs for decision-making (e.g., in the selection of a secondary school and even the relatively free choice of a profession), the internalization of unaccustomed values and the principle of individualization, all place a heavy burden on the entire population, and this all occurs against the backcloth of an extremely difficult economic situation. There can be no doubt that these problems will continue to loom large until the end of the century and beyond. In the meantime it is to be hoped, but by no means certain, that financial resources, political and administrative experience, and personal engagement will be sufficient to overcome the obvious difficulties. It should be noted, however, that the risks of transition also include the possibility that positive traits in the former East German educational system (such as its apparent relative success in dealing with weaker students or its ability to maintain generally high levels of achievement motivation) might diminish, if not disappear altogether.

The whole of Germany, meanwhile, will continue to face problems which (at the time of writing in early 1993) seem to be growing rather than being gradually solved. There is evidence of out-of-school problems having an increasingly negative effect in particular on the development of students from already problematic social backgrounds. The integration of growing numbers of immigrant children and their provision with adequate, if not fair, educational opportunities will continue to present a constant challenge to the system. Finding a balance between the need for the social integration of handicapped students and the delivery of optimal instruction will continue to be a focus of concern. To stop and, if possible, reverse the trend toward later entry into working life (particularly at the university level) will require major reforms. Finally, the protracted controversies over preserving or changing the structure of the German educational system as a whole may, at least in part, become redundant simply as a result of changing social demands for education as, for example, in the case of the beleaguered *Hauptschule*.

References

Anweiler O 1988 *Schulpolitik und Schulsystem in der DDR.* Verlag Leske and Budrich, Opladen

Elley W B 1992 *How in the World do Students Read? IEA Study of Reading Literacy.* International Association for the Evaluation of Educational Achievement, The Hague

Ingenkamp K, Jäger R S, Petillon H, Wolf B (eds.) 1992 *Empirische Pädagogik 1970–1990. Eine Bestandsaufnahme der Forschung in der Bundesrepublik Deutschland*, 2 vols. Deutscher Studien Verlag, Weinheim

Kehm B, Teichler U 1992 Germany, Federal Republic of: System of higher education. In: Clarke B R, Neave G (eds.) 1992 *The Encyclopedia of Higher Education*, Vol. 1. Pergamon Press, Oxford

Mitter W 1990 Grundfragen im Überblick. In: Bundesministerium für innerdeutsche Beziehungen (ed.) 1990 *Vergleich von Bildung und Erziehung in der Bundesrepublik Deutschland und in der Deutschen Demokratischen Republik.* Verlag Wissenschaft und Politik, Cologne

Möhle H 1992 German Democratic Republic: System of higher education. In: Clarke B R, Neave G (eds.) 1992 *The Encyclopedia of Higher Education*, Vol. 1. Pergamon Press, Oxford

Tietze W, Rossbach H G, Ufermann K 1989 Child care and early education in the Federal Republic of Germany. In: Olmsted P S, Weikart D P (eds.) 1989 *How Nations Serve Young Children. Profiles of Child Care and Education in 14 Countries.* High Scope, Ypsilanti, Michigan

Tillmann K-J 1988 Comprehensive schools and traditional education in the Federal Republic of Germany. *Int. J. Educ. Res.* 12: 474–79

Trost G, Ingenkamp K, Jäger R S (eds.) 1991 *Tests und Trends: 10. Jahrbuch der Pädagogischen Diagnostik.* Beltz, Weinheim

Further Reading

Arbeitsgruppe Bildungsbericht am Max-Planck-Institut für Bildungsforschung (ed.) 1990 *Das Bildungswesen in der Bundesrepublik Deutschland. Ein Überblick für Eltern, Lehrer, Schüler.* Rowohlt, Reinbek

Bundesministerium für Bildung und Wissenschaft (ed.) 1991 *Grund und Strukturdaten.* Verlag Karl Heinrich Bock, Bad Honnef

Bundesministerium für innerdeutsche Beziehungen (ed.) 1990 *Vergleich von Bildung und Erziehung in der Bundesrepublik Deutschland und in der Deutschen Demokratischen Republik.* Verlag Wissenschaft und Politik, Cologne

Führ C 1979 *Education and Teaching in the Federal Republic of Germany.* Inter Nationes, Bonn

Hüfner K, Naumann J 1971/86. *Konjunkturen der Bildungspolitik in der Bundesrepublik Deutschland*, 2 vols. Klett-Cotta, Stuttgart

Rolff H-G, Bauer K-O, Klemm K, Pfeiffer H (eds.) 1992 *Jahrbuch der Schulentwicklung. Daten, Beispiele und Perspektiven*, Vol. 7. Juventa Verlag, Weinheim

Statistisches Bundesamt (ed.) 1992 *Bildung im Zahlenspiegel.* Kohlhammer Verlag, Wiesbaden

Ghana

Y. Dwomoh

1. General Background

Ghana gained independence from British Colonial rule in March 1957 and was declared a Republic in July 1960. The country lies almost in the center of the countries along the Gulf of Guinea. To the east of Ghana lies the Republic of Togo, beyond which are Benin and Nigeria. To the west is Côte d'Ivoire (formerly the Ivory Coast) and to the north is Burkina Faso (formerly Upper Volta). Ghana has a total land area of 239,460 square kilometers and a coastline of 560 kilometers consisting mainly of sandy beaches.

The country has tropical vegetation of dense rain forest which tails off into savana and grassland toward the north and the coast.

The population of the country as of February 1991 was estimated to be approximately 15.2 million, growing at the annual average rate of 2.6 percent.

Ghana consists of small ethnic groups who speak some 50 languages or dialects. English is the official language and it is introduced early in schools.

Many of the major religions of the world are practiced in Ghana. About 62 percent of the population belong to the Christian faith. Moslems form about

15 percent of the population, with the remainder being minorities who adhere to other religions such as Hinduism, Buddhism, Judaism, and to indigenous traditional religions.

Agriculture is the mainstay of Ghana's economy, although efforts are being made since independence to expand other sectors of the economy. Agriculture accounts for about 55 percent of the Gross Domestic Product (GDP) and employs 55 percent of the labor force. The main source of the country's export earnings has been cocoa, which is exported in the primary form. Other sources of export earnings are minerals, timber, and surplus electricity from the country's two hydro-electric dams at Akosombo and Kpong. The two hydro-electric dams have combined installed capacity of 1,072 megawatts. The dependence on cocoa earnings, which fluctuate with changes in climatic situations and world market prices, has a large effect on the country's balance of payments, and on government budgets and gross levels of investment.

2. Politics and the Goals of the Education System

The foundation of formal education in Ghana was laid by the various churches and missionary bodies that operated in the country long before the introduction of formal colonial authority in 1844. Schools established at that time had a unique role to play in the plans and aspirations of the missionary bodies. Their basic aim was to produce a corps of literate youth groups, who would use their acquired knowledge to spread Christianity throughout the country. The educational system throughout the colonial period continued to have limited objectives. It was elitist and aimed at preparing middle-level administrators and other functionaries, such as clerks, interpreters, and tax collectors, needed to make the colonial system work effectively. Educational opportunity was basically limited to primary schools with very few post-primary facilities.

The launching of the Accelerated Development Plan for Education in 1951 by the first Ghanaian Minister of Education brought about the first upsurge in educational expansion in the country, particularly at the primary education level. By 1957, on the attainment of independence, there were 455,053 children in primary schools, about three times the figure for 1951 (Office of the Government Statistician 1959).

Educational development was given a further boost in the 1960s. The Education Act of 1961 made ten-year basic education (primary and middle education) free and compulsory for all children of school-going age which led to a significant rise in the enrollment in schools. There was a corresponding increased demand in secondary school places, and a special trust (Ghana Educational Trust) was set up in the early 1960s to promote the expansion of secondary education. The enrollment for basic education increased from 586,464 in 1960–61 to 1,404,939 in 1965–66, while the enrollment figures for secondary education during the same period increased from 12,922 to 31,241 (Ministry of Education 1973).

The quality of education was improved significantly by the provision of sufficient numbers of qualified teachers and textbooks and other educational materials. By September 1960, there were about 12,000 trained and 8,000 untrained teachers compared with 5,000 trained and 10,000 untrained teachers in 1952. In 1963, the government introduced a free textbooks scheme by which basic textbooks and other essential school materials were supplied to pupils in primary, middle, and secondary schools. The scheme operated until after 1966 when the government asked parents to make some contribution to the cost of supply of textbooks and educational materials.

Educational policies in the early years of Ghana's independence were aimed at preparing the young nation to take over the administration and governance of its resources and to bring modernization and improved living conditions to the population. By 1975, Ghana had the most developed educational system in Africa south of the Sahara. The country had produced personnel of admirable quality especially geared toward the administrative machinery and public services. Training facilities for technical and vocational education for the middle-level labor force and school leavers did not expand much during this period.

The decline of Ghana's economy from the mid-1970s as a result of the oil crisis reflected itself seriously in the deterioration of the quality of education, stagnation of school enrollments, reduced budgetary allocations for education, and the decline of proportion of the GDP devoted to education. The proportion of GDP for education declined from 6.4 percent to about 1.3 percent. The educational policies initiated by the government in 1987 were aimed at not only halting the downward trend, but also toward making major changes in the structure and content of education.

3. The Formal System of Education

Prior to 1987, the structure of education in Ghana consisted of 6 years primary education starting at age 6, followed by 4 years middle school, 7 years secondary (the first 5 years leading to O-level GCE certification and the last 2 years to A level) and 3 years for the first degree at the tertiary level. The system thus offered 17 years of preuniversity education.

The current system of education introduced in 1987 provides 9 years of compulsory basic formal education for every Ghanaian child from the age of 6 to 14. This comprises primary and junior-secondary schooling. The state provides approximately 93 percent of basic education, while the remaining 7 percent is provided by private institutions. The nine-year basic education is followed by three-year senior-secondary education and tertiary education of 4 years. A 6:3:3:4 structure has replaced the former 6:4:5:2:3.

3.1 Primary, Secondary, and Tertiary Education

Figure 1 presents the overall structure of the Ghanaian educational system. Primary education is of six years' duration for all children starting at age six. Enrollment in public primary schools has increased from 455,053 in 1957 to 1,803,148 in 1991, and is projected to increase to 3,088,418 or 98 percent flow rate by the year 2000 to achieve the target of near universal primary education.

The four-year middle school was completely phased out at the end of the 1989–90 school year and has been replaced by the three-year junior-secondary school. All children who complete primary Grade 6 move on to junior-secondary Form 1 (Grade 7). There is a transition rate of 95 percent for primary Grade 6 to junior-secondary Form 1, and a flow rate of 98 percent for the junior-secondary school classes. The junior-secondary school course provides opportunities for pupils to acquire basic pre-technical, pre-vocational, and life skills. Enrollment at this level of education has increased from 115,831 in 1957 to 569,343 in 1991, and is expected to reach 1,125,328 by the year 2000. Girls represent 41.3 percent of the junior-secondary school enrollment. At the end of the course, a basic education certificate examination is conducted and about 40 percent of the graduates are selected for admission to senior-secondary schools. The admission rate is projected to rise to 50 percent by the year 2000.

The new three-year senior-secondary school program launched in 1991 is operating alongside the old system which will be phased out by 1997. The new program caters for various aptitudes in the technical, vocational, agricultural, business, and general education fields, and has a common core to meet the minimum educational needs of the students. The total enrollment in the senior-secondary schools (old and new) in 1991 was 199,260, with an intake of 56,000 students for senior-secondary Form 1. Based on a flow rate of 95 percent, the total enrollment for senior-secondary schools has been projected at 332,213 by the year 2000.

Before 1987, higher education was available in the three universities in the country—the University of Ghana in Accra, the University of Science and Technology in Kumasi, and the University of Cape Coast in Cape Coast—and a few nonuniversity institutions. A number of Ghanaian students also receive higher education abroad, especially in Europe, the United States, Canada, Australia, and the former Soviet Union. Admission to any of the three universities in Ghana is based on performance at the GCE A-level examinations. This will be replaced by senior-secondary school examination after 1997. The total enrollment for the three universities was 10,689 in 1990. Facilities for higher or tertiary education are being expanded to consist of the existing three universities, the existing six polytechnics, the seven diploma-awarding colleges, the teacher-training colleges, and other post-senior-secondary school institutions.

The polytechnics and the teacher-training colleges are being regrouped to be known as "Regional Colleges of Applied Arts, Science and Technology" (RECAAST). It has been projected that 10 percent of the senior-secondary school graduates will be admitted to the universities from 1994–95 onwards, which will increase the present (1990–91) total enrollment of 10,689 at the universities to 26,979 by the year 2000. Enrollment in the diploma-awarding colleges, together with the RECAAST, will also increase from 20,923 in 1990–91 to 56,513 by the year 2000.

3.2 Preschool Education

Preschool education is not compulsory in Ghana. Preschool institutions are to be found in the urban centers with many of them being operated by private individuals, organizations, churches, and local communities.

In 1990, there were 4,527 preschools in the public system of education with an enrollment of 299,738, and 1,321 private schools with an enrollment of 121,484. To ensure proper operation of preschools, the government has established special training centers to train teachers and nursery attendants for both public and private preschools.

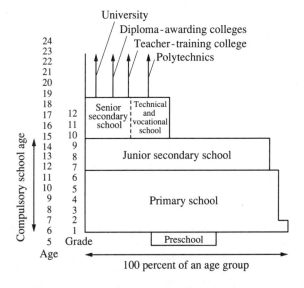

Figure 1
Ghana: Structure of the formal education system

3.3 Special Education

Education for the handicapped is available at all levels of education in Ghana. As of 1991, there were 17 special schools at basic education level with an enrollment of 1,935—11 schools for the deaf, 4 for the mentally handicapped, and 2 for the blind. There is 1 secondary technical school for deaf students with an enrollment of 51. The policy of integrating disabled students into mainstream schools is being pursued. Facilities have been provided for students in 3 senior-secondary schools, 2 teacher-training colleges, and the universities of Cape Coast and Ghana to enable blind students to pursue higher studies.

3.4 Vocational, Technical, and Business Education

Technical and vocational education are provided to support the national economy through the education and training of skilled personnel. Full-time courses which are run by the technical institutions for junior-secondary school leavers are of three to four years' duration. Courses offered by the institutions include basic building, block laying and concreting, carpentry and joinery, catering, and business studies. There are 20 technical institutes in the public system of education with a total enrollment of 14,759, and 371 private institutions. Information on enrollment for the private institutions is not available, but it is estimated that approximately 100,000 students are enrolled in these institutions.

The ministries of Education and Mobilization and Social Welfare set up a National Coordinating Committee for Technical and Vocational Education and Training (NACVET) in 1990 to formulate policies necessary for the administration of technical and vocational education and to coordinate facilities at the institutions.

There are six polytechnics in the country which provide two to four years training in mechanical engineering, electrical engineering, auto engineering, building and civil engineering, catering, accounting, secretarial services, and refrigeration. The total enrollment for the six polytechnics for 1990 was 9,135, out of which 4,551 were part-time students. Students enter polytechnics from senior-secondary schools. Links between technical and vocational institutes and industry are forged through industrial liaison units established in the institutions.

3.5 Adult and Nonformal Education

Adult literacy initiatives by voluntary organizations and churches in Ghana started as far back as 1948. In the 1950s, government, as well as religious and nongovernmental, organizations were heavily involved in adult education programs. Between 1952 and 1966, a total of 225,000 literates were produced by these governmental and nongovernmental organizations. The Institute of Adult Education of the University of Ghana has, since the 1960s, been engaged in adult education activities including distance education programs, evening classes for general certificate education (GCE) examinations and other professional qualifications, remedial classes, symposia, and lectures.

Adult and nonformal education suffered severely between the 1970s and mid-1980s as a result of the lack of coordination in the activities and the lack of government support and funding. The number of new literates produced annually fell from an average of over 22,000 during the 1950s to just over 2,000 in the mid-1970s.

In 1986, as part of an overall reform program for education, the government reactivated adult and nonformal education programs. The Non-Formal Education Division (NFED) was established within the Ministry of Education to coordinate the efforts of the various agencies involved in the literacy programs. The NFED has additional responsibility for the development, production, and distribution of instructional materials for adult education programs.

The NFED's strategy since 1990 has been to reduce the number of illiterates in Ghana by 10 percent annually to enable adult illiteracy in the country (affecting about 38% of the population) to be largely eliminated within a decade.

In 1990, the NFED and nongovernmental organizations opened classes for 290,000 learners in 15 different local languages. A total of 36,000 new literates are being produced annually.

In addition to the increased government budgetary allocation, significant amounts of foreign assistance have been given by foreign countries and agencies in recent years to support adult and nonformal education programs. Major donors have been the British Overseas Development Agency (ODA), Switzerland, UNFPA, UNICEF, WHO, and the World Bank.

4. Administrative and Supervisory Structure and Operation

The Ministry of Education is responsible for the provision and management of education in Ghana. The Ministry has various statutory bodies under it, including the Ghana Education Service, the Ghana Library Board, the Ghana Book Development Council, the Bureau of Ghana Languages, the National Commission for UNESCO, and the National Service Secretariat.

The Ghana Education Service is the largest statutory body as it performs about 80 percent of the Ministry's functions. It implements pre-university education policies formulated by the Ministry. The Service is headed by a Director-General who, assisted by high-level personnel, administers and manages education at the national, regional, district, and institutional levels. Each of the ten regions of the country is headed by a Director, while District Education Officers manage and administer pre-university education in the 110 administrative districts in the country.

The universities and other research institutions are administered by the Higher Education Division of the Ministry of Education. The Division is being expanded to cater for all tertiary institutions.

The Planning, Budgeting, Monitoring and Evaluation (PBME) Division, established in 1988 as part of the overall education reforms program, coordinates the planning, budgeting, and evaluation activities of bodies under the Ministry. The PBME Division undertakes policy analysis and prepares perspective and medium-term plans. Statistical data needed for planning and policy formulation are also collected and published by the Division.

5. Educational Finance

Financing of public education is the responsibility of the central government. The local communities (District Assemblies) provide buildings, furniture, and equipment for basic education institutions in their communities in accordance with the 1961 Education Act. With regard to deprived areas, especially the three northern regions of the country, the central government provides facilities for basic education. The government's assistance in the provision of physical facilities for basic education institutions has increased tremendously since the launching of the reforms in 1987.

The central government also pays the salaries of all teachers in the public system of education. Tuition fees remain free at all levels of education in Ghana. About 60 percent of students in the senior-secondary schools are boarders and parents generally pay the boarding fees. Between 35 and 40 percent of the boarding students in senior-secondary school receive government scholarships and bursaries based on merit and hardship. Since 1989, an interest-free loan scheme has been operating for students in all tertiary institutions.

Since independence in 1957, various governments of Ghana have made large budgetary allocations for the development of education in the country. By 1960, approximately 26 percent of the government's recurrent expenditure was devoted to education, while education's share of the GDP was 4.1 percent (Ministry of Education 1973). The country experienced protracted economic decline from the mid-1970s and early 1980s which seriously affected education services. Government budget allocations for education fell by about 60 percent in real terms between 1979 and 1985, while the proportion of GDP devoted to education declined from 6 percent in 1976 to about 1.3 percent in 1983.

The situation has improved considerably since 1987. Between 1987 and 1990, over 30 percent of the government's recurrent budget has been devoted to education, while education's share in terms of GDP has risen to 4 percent (Ministry of Education 1990). In addition to the increased government budget allocations, the country has received substantial assistance from the World Bank and other donor countries under Education Sector Adjustment Credit (EdSAC) to support the reforms program.

Approximately 80 percent of the education budget is devoted to pre-university education, while the remaining 20 percent goes to tertiary education and the other statutory bodies under the education sector. Higher education's share of the education budget is between 12 and 13 percent.

6. Supplying Personnel for the Education System

In the 1990–91 school year, a total of 62,859 teachers were employed in the primary schools, out of which 21,146 or 33.64 percent were untrained. Junior-secondary schools had 35,262 teachers, of whom 12,388 or 35.13 percent were untrained. The number of untrained teachers in primary and junior-secondary schools has been declining steadily since 1987. The proportion of untrained teachers in primary schools has declined from 49 percent in 1987 to 34 percent in 1991, and that of junior-secondary schools from 38 percent to 24 percent during the same period. There are 38 teacher-training colleges with a total annual output of 4,000 teachers for primary and junior-secondary schools. This output is expected to increase to about 8,000 annually from 1999 as the teacher-training colleges are being upgraded and expanded.

The three universities, the seven diploma-awarding colleges, and the other tertiary institutions provide teachers for the senior-secondary schools, the teacher-training colleges, the polytechnics, and the technical institutes. In 1990, these institutions had a total of 10,662 teachers, with the senior-secondary schools alone employing a total of 8,087 teachers. Almost all teachers at this level of education have the necessary qualifications.

The three universities also employed a total of 1,114 teaching staff in 1990, made up of lecturers, senior lecturers, and professors.

7. Curriculum Development and Teaching Methodology

There is a uniform curriculum approved by the government for all pre-university education in Ghana. The Curriculum Research and Development Division (CRDD) of the Ministry of Education is responsible for the development and preparation of curricula, as well as regular review and revision of syllabuses, textbooks, and instructional materials for pre-university education.

In the late 1960s, curriculum innovations such as elementary science, environmental studies, modern mathematics, and practically and vocationally oriented programs were introduced into basic education schools.

The reforms initiated in 1987 place emphasis on the teaching of Ghanaian languages, English, and practical agriculture at all levels of pre-university education. The environmental approach to the teaching of science is also being emphasized. Junior-secondary schools offer "pre-vocational" subjects designed to give students familiarity with, and practice in, using simple hand tools.

The curriculum for senior-secondary schools has a common core consisting of English, Ghanaian languages, science, mathematics, agriculture and environmental science, life skills, and physical education. There are also five broad programs of specialization which are offered, namely in the agriculture, technical, vocational, business and general arts, and science areas. Adequate qualified teachers to teach practical subjects, including vocational and technical subjects, is the major current problem for the implementation of the new curriculum.

The curriculum for teacher education has been reorganized to ensure the supply of adequately qualified teachers for the system.

8. The System of Examinations, Promotions, and Certifications

There is automatic promotion in all pre-university institutions between year levels. All pupils are promoted to junior-secondary school at the end of six years of primary schooling. A terminal basic education certificate examination based on continuous assessment and external examination conducted by the West African Examinations Council is taken by junior-secondary school pupils at the end of their course. This examination has replaced the former common entrance examination for selection to the senior-secondary schools and the middle school-leaving certificate examination.

The senior-secondary school examination, also to be conducted by the West African Examination Council, will be taken for the first time in 1993, and will replace the current GCE O and A levels which will also be conducted for the last time in 1996.

Technical and vocational training courses lead to professional certificates and diplomas in the special fields of study. The City and Guilds London Institute and the Royal Society of Arts (RSA) examinations for these courses have been localized to have Ghanaian orientation.

Higher education institutions offer both graduate

and graduate programs in a variety of fields, as well as specialist diplomas in areas of professional education. The diplomas and degrees awarded by the universities and colleges are internationally recognized.

9. Educational Assessment, Evaluation, and Research

Institutions and agencies responsible for assessment, evaluation, and research activities include the Curriculum Research and Development Division (CRDD); the Inspectorate Division of the Ghana Education Service; and the Planning, Budgeting, Monitoring and Evaluation (PBME) Division of the Ministry of Education. Other tertiary bodies, like the Faculty of Education, the Center for Development Studies, and the Institute of Education Planning and Administration (IEPA) at the University of Cape Coast, undertake assessment and research studies. While the CRDD, the Inspectorate Division, and the PBME Division undertake routine research studies, the University-based institutions are often commissioned by the government to undertake specific studies.

The CRDD has undertaken a number of student-based research studies, mostly on measurement and student outcomes or achievement. From the 1980s, studies needed for monitoring resource inputs and formulation of policies have assumed greater role because of the government's policy on accountability, effective management, and decentralization. The PBME Division has carried out studies on policy analysis, expenditure analysis and unit costs, teacher demand, and microplanning. Educational indicators developed by the PBME Division relate to class size, average school size, pupil–teacher ratio, norms for budgeting, gender and regional/district disparities, and trained and untrained teachers.

In the 1990s, research studies will continue to focus on resource inputs, the impact of the educational reforms program, cost-sharing and community participation in school management, and management at national, regional, and district levels.

It is difficult to identify the proportion of the educational budget earmarked for education assessment, evaluation, and research. It may be less than 1 percent, but it is likely to increase to about 2 to 3 percent toward the end of the 1990s in view of the increasing roles being played by the PBME Division and the CRDD in research studies.

10. Major Reforms in the 1980s and 1990s

In 1987, Ghana embarked on education reforms with the initial thrust on the nationwide implementation of the junior-secondary school program. The education reforms cover both structure and content and run through the whole system of education from primary to the university level. The broad objectives of the reforms program include increasing access to education throughout the system, improving the quality of education, and making education more relevant to socioeconomic conditions. There has been a marked increase in school enrollments since the reforms were launched in 1987. The gross enrollment at primary level for children in the 6–11 age group increased from 80.5 percent in 1988 to 82.5 percent in 1990. Primary Grade 1 intake has also grown by 11.8 percent between 1988 and 1990. At the junior-secondary school level, 1987–88 enrollments were 21.7 percent higher than comparable former middle school Form 1 enrollments. Under the new senior-secondary school system, 35 percent of the 1990 junior-secondary school enrollment cohort was admitted in 1991, as against about 25 percent under the old senior-secondary school system.

Reforms involving the tertiary subsector were launched in 1988. Between 1988 and 1993, a revamping, recapitalization, and expansion of facilities at the tertiary level of education are taking place to ensure sustainability. A system of cost-sharing between the government, local communities, parents, students, and institutions is being implemented. Course structures have been adjusted to accommodate working persons and viable linkages between different types of programs with the subsector have been provided. In response to the increased student population at pre-tertiary level, the tertiary system has been expanded to include all post-senior-secondary institutions.

Reforms have also been introduced into teacher-training institutions to prepare teachers for the new programs. An inservice training system with a cascading effect has been introduced to give intensive and extensive training to all serving teachers to reorientate them to the new reforms and also upgrade their level.

11. Major Problems for the Year 2000

In spite of the considerable achievements made since 1987, it will require additional financial inputs and constant monitoring to ensure that the goals of achieving universal basic education; the eradication of illiteracy; increased access to education; and coordinated, cost-effective management of the educational system are finally attained. The sustainability of the improved system will be a problem in future. There has been a considerable increase in the government's budgetary allocations (almost 40% of government recurrent expenditure is devoted to education) as well as increase in the external assistance for education. It

will be difficult to maintain this level of expenditure in the year 2000 to support the expansion already initiated.

The already over-crowded tertiary institutions, especially the universities, will find it difficult to cater for the increased demand from senior-secondary school graduates.

Some of the perennial problems of the education system, such as inadequate qualified teachers for technical and vocational education programs and inadequate textbooks and educational materials, will continue. Feeding and other maintenance problems in boarding institutions and unequal distribution of educational facilities within regions, districts, and localities are likely to continue in the year 2000. The functional literacy programs being implemented will also have heavy financial implications by the year 2000.

The problems for the year 2000 are likely to be intensified by external factors. Ghana, like all countries of the Third World, will continue to bear the burden imposed by the unfair world economic order which perpetuates the dependency relationship of poorer nations on richer ones.

Bibliography

Amonoo R F 1986 *Language and Nationhood: Reflections on Language Situations with Particular Reference to Ghana*. Ghana Academy of Arts and Sciences, Accra

Ghana Information Services Department 1991a *An Official Handbook of Ghana 1991*. Ghana Information Services Department, Accra

Ghana Information Services Department 1991b *Ghana, A Brief Guide*. Ghana Information Services Department, Accra

McWilliam H O A, Kwamena-Po M A 1978 *The Development of Education in Ghana*, new ed. Longman, London

Ministry of Education 1973 *Education Statistics 1970–71*. Ministry of Education, Accra

Ministry of Education 1990 Ghana's country paper for the World Conference on Education for All, Bangkok, March 1990

Office of the Government Statistician 1959 *Education Statistics*. Office of the Government Statistician, Accra

Pandit HN, Asiamah F 1988 *Forecasting Enrolment and Teaching Manpower Demand for Basic Education in Ghana*. PBME Division, Ministry of Education, Accra

PBME Division, Ministry of Education (annual) Basic statistics and planning parameters for school education in Ghana 1988–89, 1989–90, and 1991. Ministry of Education, Accra

PBME Division, Ministry of Education 1990 *Meeting Basic Education Needs by the Year 2000*. Ministry of Education, Accra

PBME Division, Ministry of Education 1991 *Costing of Education Reform Programmes of Ghana, 1991–2000*. Ministry of Education, Accra

Greece

G. Kontogiannopoulou-Polydorides, T. Mylonas, J. Solomon, and D. Vergidis

1. General Background

Greece lies in southeastern Europe and occupies the southernmost part of the Balkan peninsula. Its surface is nearly 132,000 square kilometers and in 1992 its population had reached about 10.3 million. It is a geographically fragmented country surrounded by sea on the east, west and south, with numerous large or small islands in the Aegean and the Ionian Seas and large mountain ranges. There are many scattered small communities and small rural schools. The number of such communities is decreasing. However, there is a large degree of urban concentration, with almost 60 percent of the population living in urban areas mostly located near or by the sea, while Athens, the capital city, contains about one-third of the population.

Demographic trends include a severe decline of the birth rate, creating new conditions for education; and the aging of the population. During the 1970s and 1980s there was an increase in the numbers of repatriating emigrants as well as massive repatriation of political refugees who had fled the country in order to settle in countries of Eastern Europe after the 1946–49 civil war. In addition, many thousands of Greek origin ex-Soviet or Albanian citizens moved permanently to Greece at the end of the 1980s. The problems of language and cultural integration faced by their children created a new challenge for Greek education which has not yet been successfully faced.

Greece's economy has traditionally been dominated by the agricultural sector. In the 1990s it is faced with the challenges of postindustrialism without, however, having gone through a stage of substantive industrialization. Economic developments have produced a redistribution of the labor force among the primary, secondary, and tertiary sectors. The 1961–81 period was characterized by large shifts of labor force between sectors. The primary sector lost 23 percent of the total labor force during that period and the secondary and tertiary sectors gained 10 and 13 percent respectively. The proportion of the labor force distributed among the three sectors in the early 1990s was 30:30:40.

A particular characteristic of the Greek economy is the large number of employers and self-employed amounting to about 40 percent of the total active labor force, as well as the relatively large number of auxiliary and nonpaid members of the family, related to the existence of a large number of small family-size units mainly in the areas of manufacturing and of agricultural production.

In contrast, an extended public sector constitutes an important source of employment. This is linked on the one hand to personal or political party relationships (which directly feed to the increase of the public sector) and, on the other, to the relative lack of entrepreneurship and industrial development which consequently results in a large deficit in the balance of payments and an enormous public debt. In close relation to these economic aspects is the extensive social demand for, and the predominant position of, general education.

The level of education among the population overall is still quite low but varies distinctly between the older age group and the younger. During the 1981 census nearly 55 percent of the total labor force had completed only primary education, while about 16 percent had not done so; and tertiary education degree holders represented only 11 percent. However these figures are rapidly changing.

The level of education by occupational groups reveals a clear relation between education and social position. Low education levels and illiteracy or semiliteracy affect primarily those employed in agriculture, followed by laborers and technicians. However, it is also clear that the education system is functioning, particularly since the 1950s, as the main channel of upward social mobility for the children of the lower strata, mainly toward the service sector.

The country's incorporation in the European Community in 1981 has had a certain influence on Greek education, to the extent that the member states of the EEC are fostering a converging educational policy aiming at the modernization and coordination of national education systems and thus at the unrestrained mobility of the labor force within an integrated Europe.

2. Politics and the Goals of the Education System

The Greek education system is highly centralized. General and particular goals and policy are conceived, formulated, and issued by the Ministry of National Education. Educational policy, mainly in the form of government laws and presidential decrees, is decided by the minister of education. Such a process holds the government directly accountable to the electorate, and thus subject to pressures from both the public and teachers' unions.

Consensus on educational issues among the major political parties alternating in power is hardly ever achieved and educational reform has been very slow and with endless oscillations. A few of the traditional conflicts between conservatives and liberals concern issues such as a formal language for education, the length of compulsory education, and the introduction of technical and vocational education as part of mainstream schooling. General agreement on these issues was reached only in the mid-1970s.

In the early 1990s it was possible to identify a certain lack of congruence in the relationship between the goals prescribed by the educational law for primary and secondary education, instituted by the Socialist Party in 1985, and the ideology underlying it, on the one hand, and the character of everyday educational practice and aims set and pursued by society at large, on the other. The 1985 Law has a liberal ideology, and its set goals are the promotion and development of the students' personality and creativity by means of child-centered, active and participatory teaching and learning. However, everyday educational practice focuses on transmitting and acquiring fixed knowledge and national cultural heritage and adopts traditional teaching methods. This character of educational practice clearly supports a mode of selection for higher education based on assessment of knowledge acquired from specific textbook items which in turn promotes the same educational practice.

Society at large is mainly concerned with ensuring wide and egalitarian access to higher education based on reliable and objective selection procedures. This tends to reinforce the demand for specific textbook-based entrance examination items, and indirectly tends to preserve the conservative character of schooling, and thus to undermine the implementation of the goals stated in the 1985 Law.

The argument for establishing private higher education, has created a major educational–political controversy. Opponents raise the unconstitutional nature of such decisions, since higher education is meant to be provided by the state and is free of charge for all. Proponents argue that the large number of students studying abroad is already indirectly violating the free higher education provision.

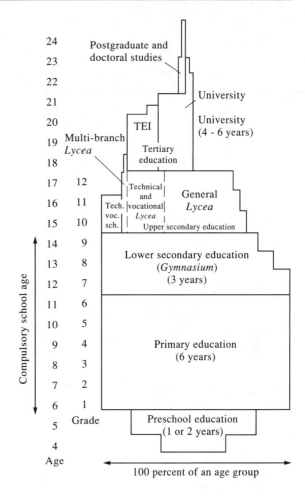

Figure 1
Greece: Structure of the formal education system[a]
a Rough estimates of enrollment figures in preschool and secondary education taken from Ministry of Education data

3. The Formal Education System

3.1 Primary, Secondary and Tertiary Education

The structure of the formal educational system is given in Fig. 1. Selected statistics for all the levels of formal education are presented in Table 1. Preschool education involves children at age 3½ onward and lasts for two years. Compulsory education starts at age 5½ and, since the 1978 reform, lasts for nine years. It is divided into primary school and lower secondary school (*gymnasium*). Upper secondary schooling is provided in various types of *lycea* and in technical and vocational schools. Students graduating from one level may freely enroll at the next, except for tertiary education, provided in technological educational institutes (TEI) and in universities, where entrance is based on achievement scores.

Primary schooling lasts for 6 years. The school year comprises 170 school days. There are five school days in a week, and each school day comprises five teaching hours. Following the decline in the birthrate,

the number of enrollments decreased in the 1980s by 11.2 percent. In 1991–92 there was a total of 791,000 pupils, representing nearly 100 percent of the relevant age cohort (approximately 7% of whom attended private schools). At the same time the pupil–teacher ratio reached an average of almost 20:1. All schools are coeducational.

After completing primary education, all children, normally at age 11½, are automatically enrolled into lower secondary education which consists of three years of schooling. There are 165 school days in a year and about six teaching hours in a school day. Schools at this level offer general education but there are a few schools specializing in sports or music. There are also a few ecclesiastic schools.

Implementation of the nine-year compulsory education policy brought more students into the *gymnasia*.

Table 1
Enrollments in formal education, Greece 1991–92

	Kindergarten[a]	Primary	Secondary		Tertiary	
			Lower	Upper	TEI	University
Students[b]	134,000	791,000	439,000	423,000[c]	73,000	119,000
Institutions	5,615	7,660	1,820	1,710	12	17
Teachers	8,200	39,000	28,000	30,000	5,000	5,900
Average number of students per institution	24.1	103	241	247	6,083	7,000
Student–teacher ratio	16.3:1	20.3:1	15.7:1	14.1:1	14.6:1	20.2:1

a Data for kindergartens concern only those institutions, public or private, under the authority of the Ministry of Education   b The data given refer to the 1991–2 school year except for enrollment data for TEI and universities which refer to 1990   c Including 2-year technical–vocational schools

In 1991–92 there were 439,245 students enrolled, of whom about 4 percent were in private schools. Ministry of Education data indicate that slightly over 80 percent of the students enrolled at the initial grade of *gymnasium* graduated in 1991. This was 70 percent in 1981. Repeating grades has been severely reduced but is still about 8 percent.

All secondary schools are coeducational. More girls than boys entering *gymnasium* reach graduation. This is attributed to girls' higher achievement level and to boys being forced to enter an apprenticeship earlier.

Upper secondary schools comprise three years of schooling in three types of *lycea*: general, "multibranch" (quasicomprehensive), and technical-vocational. At this level there are also a few ecclesiastic *lycea*. Finally several technical and vocational schools provide two years of schooling. The number of enrollments in upper secondary education increased in the 1980s by 38 percent. The vast majority of *gymnasium* graduates enroll in the various *lycea* and most of them choose to enroll at general *lycea*. Of the 378,000 students enrolled at *lycea* in 1992, approximately 68 percent were in general, 5.6 percent in multibranch, and 26 percent in technical–vocational *lycea*. There are many more boys than girls in technical and vocational education. Girls opt rather for general education where they are very much overrepresented.

Courses provided in the first two grades of general *lycea* are common for all students. Students in the third grade may follow one out of four option streams (cycles) in order to prepare for tertiary education entry examinations. A fifth option is available for those who will not pursue higher education. In technical-vocational and in multibranch *lycea* a wide range of option cycles of vocational and/or general education is provided. Government policy indicates that cycles in general *lycea* will be replaced by another system of options for students entering upper secondary education in 1993. A very widespread practice is for students preparing for tertiary education entry examinations to follow extra courses in nonformal, private cramming schools (*frondistiria*).

The Ministry of Education data indicate that the number of those abandoning upper secondary education exceeds 20 percent of initial enrollments. In 1991 77.5 percent of the students who graduated from upper secondary education, representing approximately 48.5 percent of the 17–18 age group, qualified for participation in tertiary education entry examinations.

Tertiary education comprises universities and technical educational institutes (TEI), which are colleges of higher education without a university status. Scores achieved on the annual national entry examinations combined in a complex way with the scores achieved at the end of upper secondary schooling provide the final score which may or may not allow a student's entry into one of the departments for which he or she has applied. A *numerus clausus* for entrants in each department is decided yearly by the ministry. Competition is fierce, particularly for some prestigious departments such as medicine and computer science, and especially in large urban universities.

In 1991 about one-third of the 128,000 candidates succeeded in entering tertiary education, 55 percent of whom were in universities. In 1980 and 1970 tertiary education entrants represented 28.5 and 25 percent respectively but the percentage of those entering universities was 58 percent in 1980 and as high as 80 percent in 1970 when nonuniversity higher education was very limited, and higher technical–vocational education practically nonexistent. In 1990 there were about 189,000 students in both types of tertiary education, a number significantly higher than in the 1970s and early 1980s.

Between 1975 and 1985 the participation of female students in tertiary education rose by more than 12 percent up to 48.9 percent of the total number of students (slightly above the ratio of girls in the relevant age group population). Girls are overrepresented in domains such as literature, education, fine arts, law, architecture, and medical sciences, but underrepresented in domains such as engineering, science, and mathematics.

University studies normally last four years except for medicine and architecture. There is no part-time study. Graduate studies have been practically nonexistent, except for limited doctoral studies. Several postgraduate courses are planned according to the 1985 and 1988 Education Laws but postgraduate certificates do not yet have a formal status.

As a result of the policy for the creation of new regional universities, together with the renaming and redefinition of the university status of several schools of higher education, there are 17 universities, all funded by the state and enjoying administrative and academic autonomy. The establishment of private or foreign universities in Greece is constitutionally prohibited, but this has not prevented discussions in the press as well as within and between political parties on this issue.

A problem that has faced Greek economy and society ever since the 1960s is the increase of university students abroad, mainly in Europe and the United States, both at first-degree and postgraduate levels. Despite the reduction of their numbers after 1985, due to the rise of enrollments in Greek tertiary education, their number remains sizable in the early 1990s. Another issue in the 1990s concerns the possibility of raising the level and status of studies and degrees provided by the TEI to those provided by universities. No decision has yet been reached.

3.2 Preschool Education

Before entering primary school, children at age $3\frac{1}{2}$ to $5\frac{1}{2}$ may attend a Ministry of Education kindergarten in the morning. Their daily programs are based on structured play and learning exercises aiming at the multisided development of the child, according to the guidelines provided by a 1989 presidential decree. In 1992 there were 5,600 kindergarten centers under the Ministry of Education. Of these about 2.6 percent were privately owned. The 133,600 children enrolled in 1992 represent about 50 percent of the relevant age group.

Additionally, daycare services are offered by infant schools run mainly by the Ministry of Health and Social Welfare and also by local authorities and state or private organizations. There are no exact data as to enrollments and attendance in these childcare centers outside the Ministry of Education's jurisdiction but it is estimated that about another 30 percent of the $3\frac{1}{2}$ to $5\frac{1}{2}$ age group may be attending such preschool services. Younger children from 40 days old up may be accepted at nursery homes for daycare.

Social demand for preschool education has grown immensely since the 1960s as a result of changes in the form of maternal employment, and its expansion has been impressive since the early 1970s.

3.3 Special Education

In the mid-1980s the state undertook the responsibility for the supply and control of special education which was until then supplied only by the private sector. The 1985 Education Law specified the provision of special education and special vocational training for students with physical, intellectual, and emotional disabilities, aiming at the overall development of their capacities and their full integration into society and production. The Law defined that this be pursued either by the creation of special classrooms and/or additional special courses in mainstream schools or special schools' programs. In addition, vocational schools for the disabled provide special training programs. In 1989 there were 164 special schools and 285 special classrooms in mainstream schools, with 850 teachers and 200 specialized staff providing programs for 8,200 students. These figures illustrate an unprecedented growth since 1980 when special education was virtually nonexistent.

3.4 Vocational, Technical, and Business Education

Throughout the twentieth century, efforts to establish and develop technical and vocational education have not succeeded in changing the general orientation of secondary education toward eventual university entrance. The 1976–77 educational reform promoted the establishment of technical and vocational upper level secondary schools, but the growth in the number of students has been less than expected due mainly to the low status of the technical professions compared with the higher status of the education provided by the general upper secondary schools. Nevertheless the number of students enrolled in all types of upper secondary technical and vocational education (*lycea* and two-year schools) including those in multibranch *lycea*, as a percentage of the total number of students in upper secondary education rose from 26.7 in 1981 to 37 in 1990.

The growth of the number of students in higher technical and vocational education (TEI) has been more impressive: in the 1980s their number more than doubled. The provision according to which 32 percent of the yearly entrants in the TEI must come from upper secondary technical and vocational schools has significantly promoted their expansion. Slowly but surely a two-track education system (general and technical–vocational education) is being created.

3.5 Adult and Nonformal Education

The development of adult and nonformal education in the 1980s aimed at bridging gaps left by the low level of development of mainstream technical and vocational education and at facing some of the problems of unemployment created by technological evolution and the needs for new technical knowledge and skills.

Adult nonformal education and training are provided by a variety of public and private agencies:

(a) public administration and private corporate bodies under the responsibility of various ministries;

(b) nonprofit foundations and public-minded agencies;

(c) trade unions and cooperative bodies;

(d) universities and TEIs;

(e) the private sector.

Since 1980 adult education programs aimed at the unemployed under the age of 25 and the long-term unemployed over 25 are partly (at a minimum of 55% of the budget) financed by the European Social Fund. This fact has promoted the development and improvement of adult education programs attended yearly by an estimated 200,000 trainees.

The Secretariat of Popular Education of the Ministry of Education provides programs of vocational pretraining and training, as well as those dealing with cultural and social interest, literacy, and basic skills for adults. The Ministry of Agriculture provides agricultural training courses. The Manpower Employment Organization of the Ministry of Labor provides training programs to unemployed workers or those at risk of unemployment, either in its own training schools or within private or public enterprises. Furthermore, management, marketing, public relations, and computer training courses are provided by a number of public and private organizations.

4. Administrative and Supervisory Structure and Operation

The Ministry of National Education constitutes the central authority from where virtually all decisions and guidelines stem. These concern administration, supervision, finance, curriculum development, textbooks, supply of personnel, and buildings and equipment at all education levels except, in many respects, higher education. The Pedagogic Institute is an advisory body attached to the ministry, geared to provide expertise for curriculum development and textbooks at the primary and secondary level.

The responsibility for the administration and supervision of all preprimary, primary, and special education schools and their personnel is carried out by the bureaus of primary education based in the capital of every administrative department or subdepartment of the country. Similarly, bureaus of secondary education carry the responsibility for all secondary schools.

These bureaus are agencies of the central education authority, with very little jurisdiction. They transmit the decisions made by the ministry to the schools and regulate issues of a technical character concerning the schools under their responsibility. The bureaus collaborate with school counselors who have an advisory role on issues of curriculum implementation and educational practice for the schools in their defined area. Every school unit is headed by a director, an experienced teacher undertaking mainly administrative tasks, who may collaborate with the school's teachers association and the pupils' or parents' representatives, particularly on issues of the school's orderly operation.

Higher education institutions regulate their own operations through self-governing bodies. The administration of the TEIs is conducted by an elected president and department directors. They collaborate with the council of the teaching staff and the students' representatives. Universities are to a large extent autonomous for both their teaching and research activities. Their administration is supervised by the elected rector and vice-rectors who work closely with the senate which comprises teaching staff representing the University's departments and representatives of the students' unions and of the administrative personnel. A University department's operation is regulated by the department's general assembly comprising members of the teaching staff and students' representatives and headed by an elected chair of the department. Decisions regarding programs of studies and hiring policies are taken at the department level. Decisions regarding resource and new teaching post allocation are taken at the senate and rector level. University-wide policies are subject to the deliberations of the rectorial council constituted by the rector and the vice-rectors, a representative of the students, and a representative of the administrative personnel.

5. Educational Finance

Public education is financed directly by the central state and is free of charge at all levels. The state budget devoted to education grew steadily in relation to the gross domestic product (GDP) from a mean of 2.65 percent in the 1970s to a mean of 3.47 percent in the 1980s, reaching a peak of 4.28 percent in 1991.

The proportion of the state budget allocated to education was about 8.3 percent in 1991, nearly the lowest percentage since 1970 (compared with 10.7% in 1984 and 12.2% in 1978). Preprimary and primary education's share of the total educational expenditure gradually decreased to 33 percent in 1991 (an average of 34.7% in the 1980s and 40.4% in the 1970s). Secondary education's share followed a reverse trend reaching 35.6 percent in 1991 (with an average of 34.5% in the 1980s and of 28.7% in the 1970s). These trends may be partly attributed to the decrease of enrollments in primary education due to the fall in the birthrate and the increase in secondary school enrollments particularly due to the extension of compulsory education.

During the same period university education's share increased from 13.6 percent to 20 percent in 1990, falling to 17.7 percent in 1991. Tertiary technological nonuniversity education's share also rose steadily reaching a peak of 6.7 percent in 1990 and falling to 5.3 percent in 1991.

Per pupil expenditures in preprimary and primary education (in 1980 constant prices) increased slowly but steadily and nearly doubled between 1970 and 1990, a trend primarily attributable to the decrease of enrollments. In secondary education per pupil expenditure rose significantly (nearly tripled) despite the increase of enrollments. University per student expenditure also increased significantly in the 1970–80 period but remained steady in the 1980s despite the growing enrollment figures.

State education is provided free of charge at all levels. In private schools parents have to pay tuition fees which constitute the main form of private funding. Total private educational expenditures are between 1.5 percent and 1.9 percent of GDP and thus represent about half of the state educational expenditure ratios. However, the ratio of private to public educational expenses for formal education has decreased steadily from 0.28 in 1970 to a mere 0.07 in 1988, due to a large increase of public and a reduction of private expenditure. The ratio of private to state expenditures for private preprimary and primary education decreased steadily from 26.8 percent in 1970 to 12.4 percent in 1988. For secondary education this ratio fell even more steeply from 41.8 percent in 1972 to 6.6 percent in 1988.

The relation of nonformal to total public educational expenditure is steady at about 7 percent. It is estimated that considerable private funds are directed to private preparatory cramming courses for national entrance examinations, foreign languages, and postsecondary courses outside of the educational system. Remarkably high private funds in the form of foreign currency for fees and living expenses are spent by parents for university studies abroad.

6. Supplying Personnel for the Education System

Public preprimary, primary, and secondary school teachers are hired by the Ministry of Education and are taken in serial order out of central priority lists of graduate applicants. In 1992 there were approximately 39,000 teachers in primary education and 58,000 in secondary education. Women represent about 52 percent of primary and secondary school teachers, but are underrepresented in upper administrative and counseling positions. In 1992 there were about 5,000 teaching staff members in TEIs and nearly 6,000 in universities. In 1985, 35 percent of university teaching staff were female but only 5 percent held professorial positions.

Preprimary and primary school teachers used to be trained for two years in colleges of education but these colleges ceased to function in 1989. Since the mid-1980s teacher education has been provided in university departments of education and these degree studies last for four years. General degrees in preprimary or primary education issued by the relevant university departments constitute the only qualifications necessary for entering the teaching profession.

Secondary school teachers are mainly holders of a university degree in a discipline matching or closely related to their subject or subjects of instruction at school. Some technical and vocational *lycea* teachers are higher technical education graduates, while a very small percentage have only a secondary school certificate. The educational qualifications in a specific discipline constitute the only necessary secondary school teacher professional qualification.

At the beginning of the 1990s there was a huge oversupply of teachers for all general education levels, except for a few rare specializations at the secondary level. Graduate applicants on the lists often have to wait more than 10 years in order to obtain a teacher post in a public school. Beginning teachers have to spend a few years in isolated regions, and also have family reasons before becoming eligible for being transferred into a city school near home. Promotion—no more than a small salary raise—is nonselective and is merely related to years of employment, unless it is connected with an administrative or counseling position.

University faculty members must have a doctoral degree. They are appointed by a committee consisting of relevant department members of the same or higher rank levels. TEI professors are appointed by a Ministry of Education committee.

Inservice training has always been very limited. The establishments responsible for it are being replaced by Regional Education Centers (RECs). Degree holders, before entering employment will receive four months, further training in educational sciences. In addition to the RECs there is one postdegree (nonuniversity) school in Athens and one more being created in Thessaloniki to provide two-year further studies for teachers wishing to become eligible for senior administrative and educational counseling positions and for staff positions at the RECs.

Teachers holding a two-year training degree can pursue additional courses in order to obtain a university degree in education. These have been provided since 1991 by some university departments of education.

7. Curriculum Development and Teaching Methodology

Centralization and uniformity are the main characteristics of curriculum practice. For all primary and secondary schools there is a nationwide uniform curriculum, the scope and detailed content of which are decided by the Ministry of National Education. A unique formal syllabus for each grade is prepared by the Pedagogic Institute and ratified by the Ministry. Textbooks are prepared by individuals or teams following specific guidelines, and are selected by the Pedagogic Institute and ratified by the Ministry. There is a unique textbook for every subject for each grade, matched with the syllabus. Along with the textbooks there are also centrally developed teachers' guides which suggest ways of conducting the lessons for specific contents for every grade. This is aimed at coping with the disparity or lack of teaching methodology training, particularly among secondary school teachers. Syllabuses, textbooks, teachers' guides, and other printed educational material are published by a central agency run by the Ministry. Textbooks are disseminated to students and teachers and the other publications to teachers in all public schools and are free of charge.

The subjects taught in general education are common and compulsory for all students in primary and in most of secondary education, and include a wide range of knowledge of language and humanities, mathematics, science, social science, and religion, as well as some art and physical education. Only in the final year of secondary schooling do students have to select among the four groups of subjects or "cycles" in addition to the core subjects, in order to prepare for relevant higher education specializations. In 1991 about 20 percent of the students followed stream A (leading to technology, architecture, engineering, mathematics, science, and education studies), 7 percent stream B (leading to health sciences, and education studies), 21 percent stream C (leading to humanities, law, social science, and education studies) and 52 percent stream D (leading to social science, political science, economics, and education studies).

The subjects and content taught in university departments are determined by the teaching staff and student representatives in each department's general assembly. Students normally have a number of core courses and in theory, but not so much in practice, a wide range of choice among elective courses offered. Course content is usually included in a single textbook for each course and given to students without charge.

In primary education all lessons are taught by a general classroom teacher while in secondary schools subjects are taught by specialists with no or very little pedagogical training. In practice, the traditional teacher-centered, subject and textbook-based teaching, with very few opportunities, if any, for classroom discussion, group work, or library or laboratory work still seems to constitute the main form of instructional practice at all levels. A gradual variation in teaching methods is likely to occur at primary level when graduates from the new education departments at the university level will enter service.

English or French are taught in secondary schools and only in some primary schools on a pilot basis. Proposals stemming from the Ministry include the introduction of English language courses in all primary schools and of a second foreign language (English, French or German) in secondary schools.

School directors and school counselors are expected to monitor the exact implementation and progress of the relevant syllabus in every classroom throughout the country by means of a register where teachers have to write down what they have taught in their classroom.

The focal issues in curriculum development and teaching methodology are how to find ways of keeping syllabuses and textbooks apace with developments in science and society, and how to train teachers at all levels in education sciences.

8. The System of Examinations, Promotions, and Certifications

Educational evaluation at both primary and secondary levels is the classroom or subject teacher's responsibility. It results from the teacher's assessment of individual student performance, based on the amount of information the student is able to reproduce as close to the content of the textbook as possible, either orally or in writing.

In 1981 written examinations for promotion were abolished at primary and lower secondary levels and grade repeating ceased to be practiced at the primary and was reduced at the secondary level. In 1991 written examinations were reinstated in the last two grades of primary and at the lower secondary schools, but contrary to official expectations the essence and practice of educational evaluation have not changed.

Normally, students are automatically promoted from grade to grade in primary and from primary to lower secondary level, at the end of which (year 9) students receive a lower secondary school-leaving certificate. This allows enrollment at any type of upper secondary school at the end of which (year 12), after passing internal school examinations students receive an upper secondary school-leaving certificate.

Examinations for entrance to higher education are national external examinations organized by the Ministry of Education. University students at the end of each academic semester, usually in February and in June, are examined and graded by the individual professors responsible for the instruction of the courses and for running the laboratory work followed during the semester. Examinations may take the form of a written and/or oral examination, and, rarely, may be based upon or followed by a written paper, according to the choice of the individual professor. Students failing in these examinations may have a single second chance in a special examination period in September. They are granted a university degree after having passed the courses and collected the necessary amount of relevant units, after being enrolled for at least four years.

9. Educational Assessment, Evaluation, and Research

The only form of educational assessment applied at a national level is achievement research conducted within the framework of the International Association for the Evaluation of Educational Achievement (IEA). Since 1987 IEA research has been undertaken by the IEA Greek National Center in the fields of reading literacy, computers in education, and mathematics and science. The projects have the support of the Ministry of Education and the General Secretariat for Research and Technology but it is at the discretion of the relevant agencies to take into consideration the respective data and findings.

Educational research has never been a major and organized activity and there is no particular research institution devoted to it. The Pedagogic Institute, the National Center of Social Research, the Center for Planning and Economic Research, and the Ministry of Education have rarely been engaged in educational research (a couple of projects have been conducted by each institution since 1960). More importantly, funding of educational research is very limited, while overall research policy as delineated by the General Secretariat of Research and Technology has given little priority to education. Available reports on Greek educational research and policy issues have been produced by university teaching and research staff and doctoral students in Greece or abroad, as well as international organizations focusing on related activities (e.g., OECD).

In the 1980s, three research traditions emerged in the field of education and their development can be attributed partly to the influx (following the restoration of civilian rule in Greece as of 1974) of researchers who had studied abroad and mainly to the establishment of university departments of education (as of 1985). These traditions have been fostered by education faculty members and researchers at universities. Some trends are identifiable: the first is mostly found at the University of Ioannina focusing on a radical (historical) perspective; the second is mostly found at the University of Thessaloniki, concentrating on a functionalist type of research from a liberal perspective; the third is a newly evolving experimental and achievement research tendency, from a structuralist-cum-radical perspective (with a historical dimension) including research conducted by the Greek National Center of IEA, at the University of Patras.

10. Major Reforms in the 1980s and 1990s

Major reforms in the 1980s concerned the organization and administration of universities and the opening of university departments for teachers' education. The 1982 Law for Higher Education introduced by the Socialist Party aimed at widening the participation and decision-making powers of members of lower professorial grades and of students in the administrative bodies at the level of the individual departments and of the university, and reduced the traditional powers of senior professors. Teacher education ceased to be undertaken in two-year colleges of education and was undertaken in four-year courses within universities.

11. Major Problems for the Year 2000

There is incompatibility between the supply of and the social demand for education and an educated labor force on the one hand and of pedagogic and technical deficiencies in educational provision and practice, on the other.

The social, economic, scientific, and technological developments in the 1970s and 1980s have resulted in an increasing demand for a specialized labor force and consequently for broadening the Greek educational system. More particularly the continuous change of the occupational structure, the changes in the patterns of production and consumption, the introduction of new technologies and Greece's potential role in the international division of labor, particularly after joining the EEC, have created new needs for social and vocational education and training.

As a result of existing deficiencies and the continuously increasing needs for change, it is anticipated that by the year 2000 Greece will be facing problems of:

(a) introducing innovation and diversifying educational content and practice, and improving teacher training and teacher hiring practices;

(b) providing modern school buildings (especially in urban areas where land costs are very high) equipped with laboratories, libraries, and modern educational materials;

(c) modernizing and continuously updating curricula and textbooks to keep up with the pace of social and technological evolution and change;

(d) creating and developing a high standard of graduate studies and thereby also helping to reduce the numbers of students abroad;

(e) modernizing the structure, content, and teaching methods of university studies and introducing new technologies across the disciplines;

(f) introducing new technologies in schools in an enriching and creative manner across the curriculum;

(g) developing and linking adult education and training with evolving social and economic needs;

(h) developing and linking educational research and assessment with national educational policy;

(i) broadening and developing compulsory education as well as providing all the necessary educational means for helping Greek society to reduce its social inequalities.

Bibliography

Dimaras A 1973–74 *The Reform Which Never Occurred*, 2 vols. Ermis, Athens

Ellou M 1988 *Educational and Social Dynamic.* Poria, Athens

Fragoudaki A 1987 *Language and Ideology, Sociological Approach to the Greek Language.* Odysseas, Athens

Gotovos A 1980 *The Logic of Existing School.* Contemporary Education, Athens

Kazamias A 1974 *Education and Modernization in Greece.* University of Wisconsin, Madison, Wisconsin (mimeo)

Kontogiannopoulou-Polydorides G 1989 The main characteristics of the entrance examinations. In: Varvaklon Alumni Association 1989 *The Transition from Secondary to Tertiary Education.* Varvakion Alumni Association, Athens

Kontogiannopoulou-Polydorides G 1991 Greece. In: Wilson M (ed.) 1991 *Girls and Young Women in Education. A European Perspective.* Pergamon Press, Oxford

Lambiri-Dimaki T 1967 Les chances d'accès à l'enseignement en Gréce. In: Castel R et al. (eds.) 1967 *Education, Développement et Démocratie.* Mouton, Paris

Makrinioti D 1992 *Childhood as a Social Phenomenon National Report, Greece.* European Center, No 36/12, Vienna

National Statistical Service of Greece 1990 *Results of Population Survey of 1981.* NSSG, Athens

National Statistical Service of Greece various years *Statistics of Education.* NSSG, Athens

Organization for Economic Co-operation and Development OECD (1980) *Educational Policy and Planning: Educational Reform Policies in Greece.* OECD, Paris

Papakonstantinou P 1990. *History of Education, I. Teachers' Training, II. Educational Reform and Social Distinction.* University of Athens, Athens

Pesmazoglou S 1987 *Education and Development 1948–1985.* Themelio, Athens

Psacharopoulos G 1980 *Returns to Education: An Updated International Comparison.* Staff working paper no 401, World Bank, Washington, DC

Tsoukalas K 1977 *Dependence and Reproduction: The Social Role of Educational Mechanisms in Greece.* Themelio, Athens

Guadeloupe and Martinique

C. Michel and G. Pigeon

1. General Background

Occupied by France as early as 1635, Guadeloupe and Martinique remain the last vestige of France's colonial incursion in the Western hemisphere. Their strategic position, their economy based on sugar production, and the resulting creation of an influential plantocracy made them prized possessions of the French government for a long time. A series of intermittent colonial wars finally gave France territorial domination over the islands and the peace treaty of 1763 confirmed its unchallenged mastery over the two budding colonies. It was only in 1946 that departmental status was granted to the colonies, *de facto* making them an integral part of the social infrastructure of France.

If the newly granted status of "Overseas Departments" brought to the islands a certain parity in civil rights matters, it nevertheless maintained their level of dependency on the metropole. Budget decisions and demands were argued and decided in metropolitan France according to needs perceived and defined in Paris until the creation of a Regional Council in 1974. The latter profited from President François Mitterand's liberal decentralization policy and, by 1983, had gained greater control over local taxation, police, and economic matters.

In regard to the social composition of these societies, the wavering interests of French colonial economy and politics brought to Martinique and Guadeloupe successive waves of imported labor. Black slaves were transported from Africa to toil in the sugar plantations and to replace the dwindling Amerindian population (Caribs) and the recalcitrant endentured servants (*engagés*). Although the French Revolution outlawed slavery, the slaves were not emancipated until 1848. By the end of the nineteenth and beginning of the twentieth century, colonial venturism and mercantilism brought waves of middle management personnel and workers. Thus, small numbers of Asians, East Asians, and Middle Easterners settled in the islands.

The rigidly stratified social structure which characterizes Martinique and Guadeloupe clearly originated from these colonial policies and from the miscegenation which resulted. If the Békés (descendants of the wealthy planters) still own most of the land, mulattoes usually control the upper and middle management in the private and civil sector. The great majority of the population is comprised of darker complexioned individuals, who constitute the lower echelon of society. Finally, French immigrants from the Hexagon, sent either after the debacle in Algeria (*Pieds-Noirs*) or as administrators of civil services (metro), have added to the kaleidoscopic nature of these societies as well as increased racial and class tensions among the various groups living in these islands.

Guadeloupe and Martinique are located in the western hemisphere and are part of the chain of

Lesser Antilles Islands in the Caribbean Sea southeast of Puerto Rico. Their territories are small, with Guadeloupe's two islands making up only 1,780 square kilometers (697 square miles) of land area and Martinique only 1,100 square kilometers (425 square miles). Both departments have small populations and low growth rates. In 1991, there were 344,897 people in Guadeloupe and 345,180 in Martinique, with an annual growth rate of less than 1 percent (0.8% in Guadeloupe and 0.9% in Martinique) (United States Central Intelligence Agency 1992 pp. 122, 199). The ethnic mix in each society is similar. In both territories, 90 percent of the populace are Black or mulatto, 5 percent Caucasian, and 5 percent East Indian, Lebanese, or Chinese. Roman Catholicism is practiced by 95 percent of the people, while the remaining 5 percent follow Hinduism or indigenous African religions (United States Central Intelligence Agency 1992 pp. 122, 199).

Although French is the official language, all native islanders speak a version of Creole consisting of French superstratum and African substratum. Due to a rise in cultural and nationalistic consciousness, Creole culture and language have attracted linguistic, political, and anthropological attention and have experienced a remarkable growth in political and trade union circles where they have become closely linked to the independence movement in both Martinique and Guadeloupe (Burton 1978 pp. 34–35). Although some attempts are made to incorporate the local language in the primary and secondary school system, Creole's most important impact has been at the university level where an Institute for Creole Studies has been created in Martinique.

The standard of living in the two departments is the highest in the Caribbean, with annual per capita incomes at the beginning of the 1990s of US$3,300 in Guadeloupe and US$6,000 in Martinique (United States Central Intelligence Agency 1992 pp. 122, 199). Their economy is based on agriculture, light industry, and tourism. Tourism has become the most important source of foreign exchange for Guadeloupe and Martinique and was, as of 1988, the major contributor to the overall economy of the region. The main agricultural crops are bananas, sugar cane, coconuts, plantain, and pineapples. Manufacturing has been slow to develop and the limited amount of industry is devoted to producing goods mostly for local consumption, including food processing such as sugar production, rum distillation, and flour milling. In the 1980s, economic instability resulted from loss of jobs due to mechanization in agriculture which was not being counterbalanced by the creation of new opportunities. High standard of living, weak agricultural and industrial production, and chronic trade deficit contributed to inflation and high unemployment rates in the two islands. In 1990, 30 percent (29,427) of the labor force was unemployed in Guadeloupe compared to almost 40 percent in Martinique with 52,094 unemployed

(Europa 1992 pp. 1121, 1125). The grim economic condition means that many of the islanders emigrate to metropolitan France. It is now estimated that as many Martinicans and Guadeloupeans live in the Hexagon as in the islands.

Although less obvious, the abject poverty typical in certain Caribbean islands is still present in the rural enclaves of the French West Indies. Starvation may be hardly existent, but malnutrition still remains an endemic problem, particularly in Martinique and Guadeloupe's poorer areas. Nevertheless, the economy of the islands enjoy some financial stability due to French government support, which seeks to provide its overseas departments with the same social and economic advantages available in the metropole.

2. Politics and the Goals of the Education System

Despite their status of overseas departments which make them an integral part of the French Republic, Martinique and Guadeloupe have over the years gained a certain level of internal autonomy. The budget allocated in France is now managed by a regional council which controls the distribution of funds according to the specific needs of each region. Although still headed by a Government Commissioner, each island is administered by elected general councils and has elected representatives in the French National Assembly and in the senate of the republic in Paris. However, assimilation of the overseas population into French culture is still the main ambition of the government and such a goal is to be achieved chiefly through the educational channel.

In this sense, the aim of education in overseas departments is the same as that in France, to raise the youth to be "perfect French citizens." It is for that reason that the structure and content of the educational system of Guadeloupe and Martinique remains identical to those in France, with nevertheless some attention paid to the islanders' geographical setting and African ancestry. Since the early 1970s, some efforts have been made to revitalize historical pride, and West Indian cultural specificities are slowly becoming part of the curriculum.

The concern of the French government to provide schooling opportunities equal to those in France has meant that public education in the islands is free and compulsory for 10 years, to children from the age of 6 to the age of 16 in public institutions. Some schools are coeducational, while others are single sex. Both public and private schools have an educational structure similar to that of France with primary, junior, secondary, and technical schools. Higher education is provided by the *Université Antilles-Guyane* with administrative offices located in Martinique and by the newly created IUFM (*Institut Universitaire de Formation des Maîtres*) which replaced the former teacher-training colleges.

Guadeloupe and Martinique

3. The Formal System of Education

Although an integral part of the metropolitan educational system, the three overseas departments of Martinique, Guiana, and Guadeloupe institutionally belong to a unique administrative structure called the *Académie des Antilles et de la Guyane* (the Antilles–Guiana Academy) administered by a *recteur*, but ultimately controlled by the French Ministry of Education.

Historically, the first Western-style education was offered by French missionaries. However, progress was slow due to the small populations in the islands and a limited economic base in these two societies. After the First World War, both state and mission schools forged ahead in enrollment. However, growth was slowed during and immediately after the Second World War, when France faced war conditions and subsequent problems of reconstruction. Not until 1946, when the two territories were accorded department status, did both primary and secondary schooling start to develop consistently. Most of the growth in schooling opportunities in Martinique and Guadeloupe has occurred in comparatively recent times, particularly in the public education segment. However, the success of the islands' basic educational system is reflected in the general literacy rate which is quite high compared to other Caribbean nations. In 1982, the average rate of adult literacy was 90 percent in Guadeloupe and 93 percent in Martinique (United States Central Intelligence Agency 1992 pp. 122, 199).

3.1 Primary, Secondary, and Tertiary Education

The structure of the system is depicted in Fig. 1.

Like its counterpart in continental France, compulsory education starts with primary education which pupils attend between the ages of 6 and 11. To reduce the number of students who are retained in the same grade for two or more years, to lower attrition rates, and in order better to adapt teaching practices to each individual's needs, a system of pedagogical "cycles" was designed at the national level. Originally, the Department of Martinique was selected for a pilot study on the implementation of these pedagogical cycles for primary education. However, the rectorate decided to extend the testing and as a result, as early as January 1992, the system was implemented in all the primary establishments of the *Academy*. These new pedagogical cycles are defined as follows: (a) a generalized cycle of instruction taking place in kindergarten schools followed by, (b) a more fundamental stage of learning which starts the last year of kindergarten and continues during the first two years of primary schooling, and finally, (c) a cycle of in-depth learning corresponding to the last three years of primary education, thus ending the cycle.

In 1964, primary enrollment in Martinique had reached 76,467. It increased by 16 percent in 1969 to

88,818, then diminished slightly to 88,024 in 1971. During the early 1970s, over 94 percent (264) of the primary schools were public, while the remaining 16 schools were private. By 1977, the number of primary schools had increased to 310 but enrollment had diminished to 50,142 by 1982 (Institut National de la Statistique et des Etudes Economiques 1982). By 1978, there were 53,798 pupils in the 312 primary schools in Guadeloupe. The enrollment figures had increased to 62,000 in 1982 (Institut National de la Statistique et des Etudes Economiques 1982).

In 1990, there were 222 schools in Guadeloupe, 39,290 pupils enrolled in public and private schools, and 2,064 teachers. As for Martinique, there were 210 schools and 32,649 pupils (public and private) in 1989, and 2,004 teachers in 1986 (Europa 1992 pp. 122, 199). At the start of the 1991 school year, 204 primary schools existed in Guadeloupe, and 189 primary schools operated in Martinique, servicing respectively 35,188 and 30,701 pupils in the public schools. During the same academic year, 3,343 students were enrolled in the private schools in Guadeloupe (Ministère de l'Education Nationale 1991 pp. 5–6).

Primary school is followed by seven years of sec-

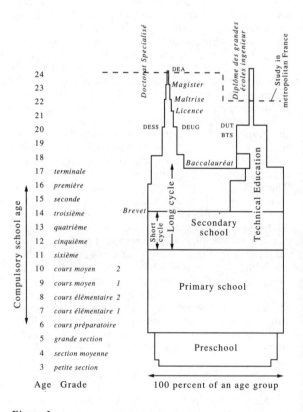

Figure 1
Guadeloupe and Martinique: Structure of the formal education system

372

ondary education that is divided into two segments: a four-year lower secondary cycle and a three-year upper secondary cycle. Therefore, the secondary cycle which begins immediately after the primary one is divided into two parallel and, at times, complementary tiers. The first tier can be either "long" or "short," depending upon students' ability and is essentially offered in establishments called *Collèges*. In these institutions, students are either placed on a "short track" of studies which ends after four years and gives them the opportunity to obtain what is called a *Brevet de Collège* which allows them to enter the workforce. Otherwise, they enroll in the "long track" which, after three additional years of studies, makes them eligible to take the *baccalauréat* examination sanctioning the end of the long cycle offered in high-schools. Those who pass receive their *baccalauréat* diploma and are entitled to apply to a university of their choice or to enter a newly developed two-year cycle of studies which prepares them for a BTS (*Brevet de Technicien Supérieur*). Those who fail the examination may, however, also qualify to enter the BTS program.

High school students enrolled in the long cycle usually attend an establishment called a "*lycée*" where they follow a three-year cycle of general study (*seconde, première*, and *terminale*) which leads to the *baccalauréat* in general studies. Students who choose to pursue the *baccalauréat d'enseignement général* (as opposed to those who decide to get a *baccalauréat technique* described below in Sect. 3.4), have the opportunity to elect one of the six "sections" available as part of the general studies curriculum.

Secondary schools in Martinique in the early 1970s totaled 52, with 43 of them public (83%) and 9 private (17%). By 1982, secondary enrollment had reached 44,000. In Guadeloupe, 52 secondary schools had been established, with enrollments of 46,692 in 1978 and 48,000 in 1982 (Institut National de la Statistique et des Etudes Economiques 1982).

In 1990, a figure of 49,846 pupils attending 75 schools (public and private) staffed by 3,237 teachers in Guadeloupe was reported (Europa 1992 p. 1122). In Martinique, in 1989, the number of students was 43,480; and the number of teachers working in Martinique's 75 secondary public and private schools was 2,745 (Europa 1992 p. 1126).

Due to the reforms which have taken place in the structure of the secondary cycle, the number of schools listed by the official publication of the Ministry of Education is as follows: in Guadeloupe, 63 public establishments divided into 9 high schools, 12 professional high schools, and 42 *collèges*; in Martinique the total is 62 establishments divided into 7 high schools, 13 professional high schools, and 42 *collèges*. To that total, Guiana adds 21 more schools giving the entire Academy 146 public establishments (Ministère de l'Education Nationale 1991 p. 14).

In the whole Antilles–Guiana Academy, the number of students enrolled in the first and second cycle of secondary study is steadily decreasing and went from 99,000 students enrolled in 1988 to 95,000 students in 1991. Only 6 percent of the students are enrolled in private institutions compared to 20 percent in continental France. Nevertheless, the Academy anticipates that by the year 2000, 48,500 students will be enrolled in Guadeloupe, 43,500 in Martinique, and 20,000 in Guiana (Ministère de l'Education Nationale 1991 p. 13).

Higher education is rather limited in the French West Indies, with most university studies aimed at preparing students for advanced professional certificates. In Guadeloupe, the *Centre Universitaire Antilles–Guyane* is composed of colleges of arts, law, and physical and natural sciences. In Martinique, there are colleges of economics and of law. Well-qualified candidates are encouraged to travel to France to obtain more advanced degrees, and the French government usually provides generous financial assistance to support West Indians in such overseas study.

The Antilles–Guiana Academy is directed by a president (*recteur*) who is appointed by France's President and is assisted in this task by academic inspectors named by the Minister of Education. The official residence of the Academy president, as well as one of the administrative officers, is located in Fort de France in Martinique.

Due to the geographical complexity of the *Académie des Antilles et de la Guyane*, scattered over three departments and bridging two continents, nagging problems of communication hamper the proper flow of administrative information as well as their coordination. As an example, scholarship or financial aid granted to some needy students is often delayed, causing great harm to deserving individuals. To remedy this situation, one of the goals of the administration is to reach by the end of 1992 a decentralization of its attribution, particularly in regard to the prerogative of each individual university as well as each IFUM (Institute for the Formation of Teachers). In this way, the attribution and/or distribution of scholarships will be carried out entirely by each university concerned.

Though extremely important, scholarship distribution and management is not the only problem raised by this geographical dispersion. The organization and articulation of courses and classes is also riddled with difficulty. Compounding these difficulties, the important migration of a poorly educated constituency coming from Haiti and Dominica (and even as far as Brazil and British Guyana) adds to the problems of insertion encountered by those who are essentially Creole speakers.

By 1977, higher education enrollment in Martinique totaled 1,656 and in Guadeloupe reached 1,645 by 1978 (Europa 1982 pp. 341–42). In 1988, there were 2,373 students in Guadeloupe and 2,743 in Martinique (Europa 1992 pp. 1126, 1222). The *Université Antilles–Guyane*, scattered in three campuses (Fort de France-Schoelcher, Martinique; Pointe-a-Pitre-

Fouillole, Guadeloupe; and Cayenne, Guiana) enrolled 5,840 students in 1989. In 1991, that number rose to 6,609 students.

3.2 Preschool Education

Between the ages of 3 and 6, children are first enrolled in a three-year cycle of pre-elementary schooling called "*Ecole Maternelle.*" The three years of preschool are assigned the important role of developing young children's linguistic competence in the French language and of teaching them social learnings that will enable them to succeed with the French curriculum when they enter primary school. In the mid-1980s, around 17,000 children in Guadeloupe and 19,000 in Martinique were in preschool education. In 1991, the number of preschoolers were 18,088 in Guadeloupe and 19,249 in Martinique. At the start of the 1992 school year, 84 and 117 kindergarten existed in Martinique and Guadeloupe respectively, numbers which are substantially higher than, for example, the 32 kindergartens operating in Guiana—also an overseas department of France (Ministère de l'Education Nationale 1991 pp. 5–6).

3.3 Special Education

On both islands, assistance is available for students who have learning disabilities and for those who are physically or mentally disabled. The Ministry of Education recognizes the rights of all handicapped children and youth to receive a quality education adapted to their special needs. Three type of program are available to foster the optimum development of these children and to encourage their mainstreaming into regular classrooms.

RASED (*le Réseaux d'aides spécialisées pour les élèves en difficulté*), a special network of assistance for the handicapped and disabled students, serves all public and private institutions of the Academy. Staffed by 198 special education teachers, 45 school psychologists, 90 psychotherapists, and 65 teachers, RASED offers in Martinique, for instance, various support programs to the learning disabled or handicapped students. The support of specialized teachers goes further than what is available in continental France (38% in Martinique vs. 30% in the Hexagon) (Bulletin d'informations 1991 p.4). These programs, newly restructured in the early 1990s, try to reintegrate special education students into the mainstream of the educational system.

3.4 Vocational, Technical, and Business Education

The term "high school" applies to two types of establishments. On one side are the so-called "professional high schools" (12 in Guadeloupe, 4 in Guiana, and 13 in Martinique for the 1992 academic year) (Ministère de l'Education Nationale 1991 p. 14) and on the other side

are the "secondary high schools" (9 in Guadeloupe, 7 in Martinique, and 2 in Guiana) which were discussed in Sect. 3.1.

In the professional high school, two cycles of education co-exist: (a) a short cycle of study which prepares for two degrees: a CAP (certificate of professional aptitude) and a BEP which is a more advanced certificate of professional competency; and (b) a longer cycle which leads to a more advanced technical and professional degree: the *baccalauréat technique* (technical high school diploma). (It should be underlined that in all Francophone educational systems, the term "professional" usually designates establishments where technics and technology form the basis of the curriculum. The CAP and the BEP are therefore diplomas leading mainly to technical and/or professional careers.)

In Martinique, by the early 1970s, there were eight public and private institutions offering technical courses. Vocational education opportunities have increased significantly, as both departments have established a variety of technical education colleges (*collèges d'enseignement technique*) to parallel the liberal arts curriculum of the secondary *lycées*. Courses in the technical colleges include home economics, agriculture, mechanics, commercial subjects, crafts, and others.

3.5 Adult and Nonformal Education

Clearly, one aim of public education in the French West Indies is to provide professional or vocational training to all youth and adults. The Ministry of Labor in each department, in collaboration with the Martinican and Guadeloupean Association for Professional Education, trains adults in bookkeeping, typewriting, electrical installation and repair, and hotel services for the islands' important tourism industry. In addition, courses are offered to medical professionals in public health practice, while the army provides training in various technical skills (Notes et Etudes Documentaires 1974 p. 28).

Correspondence courses offered through radio and television are becoming increasingly popular, and refresher courses (*cours de perfectionement*) are provided in vocational skills for employees who request inservice upgrading opportunities. The *Centre National d'Enseignement à Distance* (CNED), although primarily operating from various cities of metropolitan France, has a branch in Martinique. The catalog of this center for distance education is fairly exhaustive and offers courses in a wide range of subjects targeted toward people at all levels of education (Centre National d'Enseignement à Distance 1989). Tuition varying from US$90 to US$500 is usually paid by the enrollees depending on the degree pursued or the certificate or diploma sought. However, the young, the unemployed, teachers, and military draftees pay no fees.

4. Administrative and Supervisory Structure and Operation

Until 1973, the islands' systems of education were controlled by a French administrative body, the Academy of Bordeaux, and were directed locally by a vice rector. Subsequently, the West Indies assumed the status of an autonomous academy ruled by a rector residing in Fort-de-France, Martinique. The rector, as the regional director of education, is responsible for administering all teaching services in the region as well as serving also as chancellor of the University. As in the other French academies, inspectors assist the rector with youth activities and sports, medical and social services, and educational and vocational guidance.

Community participation is encouraged and public educational decrees, reports, and studies are often sent to representatives of teachers' unions and parents' associations for their reactions (Holmes 1980 p. 79). In 1990, the recently appointed *Recteur de l'Académie* put in place an organization which assures the articulation of dialogue and negotiation amongst the many interested parties (Heon 1990). Also, upper classmates at the various *lycées* of the Academy are invited to join the organization and offer their views on matters affecting their course of study.

5. Educational Finance

Local needs for educational finance cannot be adequately met by the state allocation raised through local taxes, so the French government continually adds to the funds for education in the two departments. In a September 1990 speech, the head of the Academy, the *recteur*, explained that the government increased its support for education by providing an additional 8.9 percent for that year. It was estimated that the increase would be 9.3 percent for the following year (Heon 1990).

In addition, in order to upgrade teachers' knowledge of child development and methods of instruction, the French government provides special funds to support both short-term and long-term inservice courses.

6. Supplying Personnel for the Education System

If in the past, most primary and secondary teachers studied in teacher-training college institutions in metropolitan France, more recently they have been recruited and trained in the islands and attended local Normal Schools. Since the start of the 1991 academic school year, the newly developed IUFM, *Institut Universitaire de Formation des Maîtres* (University Institute for Teacher Education), affiliated with the *Université Antilles-Guyane*, provides this training. It is for this reason that the University supports the strengthening of this Academic Institute (IUFM) and hopes that by the year 2000, it will provide about 150 better educated teachers, more competent to answer the specific needs of the Academy.

At the beginning of the 1991 school year, IUFM opened in Pointe-à-Pitre, Guadeloupe, offering four CAPES (Certificate of Professional Competency) for teaching in secondary high schools. Three other CAPES, one of which is more specifically geared toward teachers in physical education and sports (CAPEPS) will be implemented in the very near future.

Although part of the university system, the *Institut Universitaire de Formation des Maîtres* is a unit administered independently from the University. It contracts independently with the various universities of the academy for the use of some common educational resources, and with the rectorate and its inspectors for the formation and inspection of student teachers. It also makes agreements with the General Council for the utilization of buildings used by the former Normal Schools (teacher-training colleges). These IUFM satellites are usually located in university towns and have a two-year curriculum. Candidates for these institutes are recruited after the licence (bachelor's degree). The first year is reserved for discipline specialization and is sanctioned by a recruitment competition examination (concourse), and the second year is reserved for the specific development of teacher skills as education specialists in their particular fields and is sanctioned by the tenure of the candidate in institutions which belong to either the region (departments) or the nation.

The Academy of Antilles–Guiana, being acutely aware that its function is to first and foremost cater to the need of the Academy, pays special attention to both the instruction and placement of the student teachers enrolled in IUFM. In 1991, the number of positions available in the region were 50 for Guadeloupe, 25 for Martinique, and 100 for Guiana. Due to its sudden demographic increase, its newly developed technological emphasis, and its obvious greater instructional needs, the Department of Guiana was able to attract and facilitate the mid-cycle transfer of students from Martinique and Guadeloupe. Students who have attended the first year in an IUFM in Martinique or Guadeloupe successfully transfer to Guiana for the second year of studies and are able to obtain teaching positions in this fast-developing department.

7. Curriculum Development and Teaching Methodology

The Ministry of National Education in the French West Indies sets the curricula and issues instructions to teachers on how to implement the programs. However, teachers are allowed to select the textbooks they wish to use and have a certain level of flexibility in terms of pedagogical techniques. The subjects studied are the same as those in France. In primary school, children learn reading and writing in the French language, mathematics, moral and civic education, science, history, geography, crafts, and physical education. At the secondary level, several tracks of studies are available. Students learn literature, languages, economics, social sciences, natural sciences, mathematics, and technical and industrial subjects (Holmes 1980 p. 80). The *Institut National de la Statistique et des Etudes Economiques* reports that six areas of specialization are available for the general studies curriculum (*baccalauréat d'enseignement général*): A, Philosophy and Letters; B, Economy; C, Mathematics and Physical Sciences; D, Mathematics and Natural Sciences; and E, Technical Mathematics. The choices for the *baccalauréat technique* are: F, Industrial Emphasis; F8, Socio–medical Sciences; G, Social and Economic Studies; and H, Computer Science (Institut National de la Statistique et des Etudes Economiques 1982 p.38).

8. *The System of Examinations, Promotions, and Certifications*

The impact of social inequalities is clearly reflected in the high rate of failure reported in the three departments. If, in continental France in 1991, 8.1 percent of the students enrolled in preparatory courses were forced to repeat a grade, in the Antilles–Guiana Academy, this rate, during the same academic year, reached 11.4 percent. Also, according to the *Institut National de Statistique*, 66 percent of 15-year olds do not have diplomas in the Department of Martinique (Institut National de la Statistique et des Etudes Economiques 1982 p. 39) This number, which has remained consistently the same since 1982, is comparatively much higher than the number found at the national level. Furthermore, a 1986 survey of the elementary and intermediate secondary schools found that, in Martinique and Guadeloupe, students' achievement scores were 25 percent lower than their counterpart in continental France (Valo 1990 p. 57).

In urban areas, the age distribution by grade levels in schools is nearly the same as in metropolitan France. However, the proportion of repeaters at each grade level is somewhat higher than in France which explains why there are more overaged students in both primary and secondary schools in the West Indies.

In 1991, for the entire Academy, 74 percent of the students enrolled received their *baccalauréat* degree in general education and 52 percent received a *technical baccalauréat*. These numbers show a net increase since 1987 when the corresponding figures were 59 and 49.6 percent. For the *baccalauréat* of general education, the number of graduates in 1991 was 73 percent in Guadeloupe, 78 percent in Martinique, and 36 percent in Guiana. As for students enrolled in the professional baccalaureate, the numbers were 63 percent in Guadeloupe and 79.1 percent in Martinique (Ministère de l'Education Nationale 1991).

Of all the students enrolled in the CAP program, 53 percent in Guadeloupe, 51 percent in Martinique, and 63 percent in Guiana received their degree in 1991. For the BEP, the numbers were: 45 percent for Guadeloupe, 50 percent for Martinique, and 62 percent for Guiana (Ministère de l'Education Nationale 1991 p. 22). The rate of students' success is consistently improving.

9. *Educational Assessment, Evaluation, and Research*

At the national level, the Law of 1989 regarding the general direction of education mandated that careful attention be paid to the geographic and cultural specificities of the student body, and that every effort be made to integrate these concerns at all levels of the curriculum as well as at every stage of students' education. In 1991, the Rectorate of the Academy decided to select a committee charged to study the possible adaptation of the national dictate to local realities. It was the opinion of many members of the committee that the high level of failure (indicated by the low achievement scores) was due to the fact that the students, whose essential and functional language was Creole, were learning how to read in a language they did not speak. At the political level, the proponent of French Creole openly spoke of a "cultural decolonization" and recommended its daily use in school. However, in spite of a weak attempt at Creolizing the educational process and despite the official recognition of French Creole as a full-fledged regional language to be taught in the public schools, the malaise persisted. In 1986, a study conducted by the National Institute on Pedagogical Research found that 46 percent of low-income parents were opposed to the Creolization of schooling. They argued that for them the use of the French language was the most important tool for social improvement. On the opposite side, 25 percent of parents in favor of the Creolization of the educational system came from the middle- and upper-class stratum of society. They were accused of wanting to maintain the existing social inequalities by attempting to marginalize the French language, the only efficient tool for upward mobility. However in the 1990s, despite the controversy, research is still in progress to develop pedagogical models of integration of French in Creole-speaking environments.

The University is increasingly focusing on the need to engage in original research relevant to regional needs. Since for the most part, research conducted by the academy is of a regional nature, the Ministry of National Education signed a new research contract in January 1992 which will result in the creation of a comprehensive doctoral degree. Meanwhile, for the year 2000, one of the main goals of the Academy is to assert with efficiency and strength its place in both the Caribbean and American region. It is with that in mind that multiculturalism and plurilingual research are emphasized and that neighboring islands in the entire Caribbean basin are unblushingly considered natural partners in a cooperative and integrated educational system. Already, numerous faculty exchanges, as well as intensive language clinics for French teachers in Anglophone islands, are evidence of this form of inter-Caribbean cooperation. Furthermore, to show its commitment to research and development in the region, the French government has already helped set up many such programs. A regional cooperation committee, a commissary for cooperation, and funds for cooperative endeavor have been reserved for that purpose. Forecasting greater demand in the field of applied science, particularly in Guiana, home of France's space program, a special branch of the University exclusively dedicated to that field was to have been created by 1992.

10. Major Reforms in the 1980s and 1990s

During the 1980s, some modest efforts were made in Martinique and Guadeloupe to adapt both academic and vocational curricula to life in the West Indies rather than focusing so heavily on life in Europe. To that effect, more functional cycles of studies were implemented in primary and secondary schools. Also, more university degrees are offered, including a master's in economics, law, and sciences and the newly developed programs at IUFM.

After dominating the educational scene in the 1980s, the matter of maintaining French as the language of instruction in the islands continues to be an issue of debate in the 1990s. Nationalist-inclined local teachers who believe that West Indian children should be taught in Creole instead of French (which, according to them, may alienate students from their heritage) are among the strong proponents of the Creolization of the system. Political activists who wish the islands to become independent also believe that "the destiny of Creole is linked to the future development of the (West Indian) people" (Lucrece quoted in Burton 1978 p. 35). The various reforms which have taken place in Martinique and Guadeloupe seem to indicate support for the argument put forth by those in favor of the use of local culture and language in the educational system. It is interesting to note that a similar controversy in neighboring Haiti opposing French and Creole has been a major subject of debate since the early 1970s.

11. Major Problems for the Year 2000

As noted above, the structure of the educational systems of Guadeloupe and Martinique is essentially the same as that of France, with some attempts to adapt the system to the special needs and conditions of West Indians. A history of limited funds and a

shortage of qualified personnel consistently have stood as major obstacles which slowed the implementation of educational change in Martinique and Guadeloupe. Fortunately, the politics of decentralization and an acute sensitivity to cultural nationalism brought by the literary figures such as Césaire, Damas, Gratiant, and Glissant, as well as the independentist movement helped the authorities adjust allocations and encourage them to redress the endemic problems stated above. However, a barrier to change remains the attitude of the departmentalists, those residents of the islands who feel comfortable with curricula imported from the metropole and with the ties and prestige associated with the French language and culture.

Nevertheless, most islanders are struggling between these two poles. On one side those who consider themselves independentists are striving to liberate the islands politically and culturally from such a heavy dependency on France, whereas departmentalists are fiercely defending the status quo. Caught in the middle are those who are fearful of a hasty independence and wish for an intermediate stage of internal autonomy which they hope will ultimately lead to independence. The present structure, with its elected Regional Council, seems to give them some solace, but the future of the political status of Martinique and Guadeloupe hangs in the fragile balance which exists between these three forces: departmentalists, independentists, and autonomists. In the forthcoming decades, education will clearly play a decisive role in the battle to shape the destiny of these islands.

References

Bulletin d'informations de la cellule départementale d'action culturelle 1991 *Martinique Communication Culture 2000 MC2*, No.8 (September). Inspection Académique de la Martinique, Martinique
Burton R D E 1978 *Assimilation or Independence? Prospects for Martinique*. Center for Developing Areas Studies, McGill University, Montreal
Centre National d'Enseignement à Distance 1989 *Catalogue des Formations 1989/1990*. Ministère de l'Education Nationale, Paris
Europa 1982 *Europa Yearbook: A World Survey*, Vol. 2. Europa Publications, London
Europa 1992 *The Europa World Yearbook 1992*, Vol. 1. Europa Publications, London
Heon M 1990 Conference de Presse de Rentrée Scolaire 1990–1991 Introduction de M le Recteur Michel Heon. Martinique
Holmes B 1980 *International Yearbook of Education*. UNESCO, Paris
Institut National de la Statistique et des Etudes Economiques 1982 *Région Martinique: Tableaux économiques régionaux*. INSEE, Martinique
Ministère de l'Education Nationale 1991 *La Rentrée Scolaire 1990–1991 dans l'Académie des Antilles et de la Guyane*. Rectorat de l'Académie des Antilles et de la Guyane, Martinique
Notes et Etudes documentaires, No 4060 1974 *Les Départements d'Outre-Mer, La Martinique*. La Docu-

mentation Française, Secrétariat Général du Gouverne-ment, Paris

United States Central Intelligence Agency 1992 *World Factbook*. Central Intelligence Agency, Washington, DC

Valo M 1990 L'Inadaptation du système éducatif dans les DOM. Où créole ne rime pas avec école. *Le Monde de L'Education*

Further Reading

Claypole W, Robotton J 1990 *Caribbean Studies Book One: Foundations*. Longman Caribbean, Harlow

Claypole W, Robtton J 1990 *Caribbean Studies Book Two: The Inheritors*. Longman Caribbean, Harlow

Dossier d'Information 1990 *La Rentrée Scolaire 1990–1991 dans l'Académie des Antilles et de la Guyane*. Rectorat de l'Académie des Antilles et de la Guyane, Martinique

Heon M 1991 Conference de Presse de Rentrée Scolaire 1991–1992 Introduction de M le Recteur Michel Heon. Martinique

Knight F W 1990 *The Caribbean: The Genesis of a Fragmented Nationalism*. Oxford University Press, New York

Revue de l'Académie des Antilles et de la Guyane Juin 1991 *Education Avenir No. 0*. Rectorat de L'Académie des Antilles et de la Guyane, Martinique

Surhomme M, Biarnès J 1982 *L'enfant Antillais en France*. L'Harmatan, Paris

UNESCO 1982 *World Guide to Higher Education*. UNESCO, Paris

United States Central Intelligence Agency 1982 *World Factbook*. Central Intelligence Agency, Washington, DC

United States Department of State 1974 *Background Notes: Martinique*. United States Department of State, Washington, DC

Guatemala

M. Leyton Soto

1. General Background

Guatemala is a small country in Central America. To the north are the Republic of Mexico and the Caribbean Sea; to the south, the Pacific Ocean; to the east, the republics of Honduras and El Salvador; and to the west, the Republic of Mexico. Its area is 108,889 square kilometers. It is mountainous, being crossed from west to east by a large volcanic chain, from which two hydrological basins are formed with rivers flowing into the Gulf of Mexico, the Caribbean Sea, and the Pacific Ocean. The population consists mainly of two ethnic groups: the indigenous and the nonindigenous.

Administratively, the country is comprised of 330 municipalities within 22 departments, and these departments are within 8 regions. As with the other Central American countries, Guatemala has not been able to avoid the severe effects of the economic crisis that has affected almost all spheres of activity during the 1980s.

Before the European conquest begun by the Spaniards in 1524, the territory was settled by various peoples, descendants of the Mayan culture. Colonization as such began with the foundation of the city of Santiago de los Caballeros de Guatemala in 1524, the first city of the General Captaincy of the Kingdom of Goathemala (*Capitania General del Reyno de Goathemala*), which extended from the Isthmus of Tehuantepec in Mexico to Costa Rica. Juridically, it was responsible to the Viceroyalty of New Spain (*Virreinato de la Nueva Espana, Mexico*), and commercially it depended on the Spanish metropolis. During the colonial period, importance was given to education through the so-called "Schools of Elementary Education" (*Escuelas de Primeras Letras*) run by religious orders and destined, mainly, to catechize and to teach Castillian to the indigenous population. In 1676, the Royal and Pontifical University of San Carlos of Barromeo of Guatemala (*Real y Pontifica Universidad de San Carlos de Barromeo de Guatemala*) was founded—the fourth university on the American continent.

In 1821, the country gained independence from Spain, but remained annexed to Mexico until 1823, when total independence was declared. It remained united with the rest of Central America in a Federation of Central American States until 1847, the year in which the Federation was dissolved. From 1871, the Liberal Revolution reformed the country socially and economically, influencing education which became nonreligious, compulsory, and organized into a formal system.

In 1990, the population was estimated at about 9.2 million persons, the largest population in Central America. Some 38 percent of the population lives in the capital city and its metropolitan area, as well as in cities of more than 20,000 inhabitants, such as the main departmental towns. The rest of the population lives in rural areas and the majority of them are scattered communities of less than 2,000 inhabitants. The indigenous inhabitants (3.3 million) form about 38 percent of the population and comprise different ethnic groups, among which 25 languages are spoken with more than 100 different dialects. The majority are of Mayan descent, the most important groups being: Quiche, Cakchiquel, Kekchi, Mam, and Tzutujil. Due to this situation, and even though constitutionally the official language is Spanish, bilingual education (or Castillanization), in which children learn to read and write in their mother tongue and in Spanish as a second language, has been strongly promoted since the 1960s.

The country has always had a strong agricultural base, but industrial development has provoked a growing internal migration to the metropolitan areas. The selectivity of migration by age is shown by the fact that almost 50 percent of the urban migrants are between the ages of 15 and 44, which means a young population. This phenomenon has contributed to diminishing the levels of social welfare and the satisfaction of basic needs. It has also affected education, with a significant effect on literacy rates. The effects of armed violence have resulted in nearly 1 million displaced persons, about 50,000 refugees, and approximately 250,000 orphans. Government policy seeks a solution to this problem through the implementation of strategies such as regionalization and educational reform which promotes a wide variety of programs within the framework of "Education for All," and, in particular, the creation of the so-called "Schools of Peace" (*Escuelas de la Paz*).

The economically active population (EAP) of the country constitutes nearly 50 percent of the total population. Female participation is low (25.5%), and that of youngsters aged 10 to 24 years is high (36.1%). The educational levels of the EAP are extremely low, which implies that there will have to be sustained efforts both for the expansion of educational coverage and for qualitative improvement through extra-school programs and long-distance education.

2. *Politics and the Goals of the Education System*

For each governmental period, constitutionally lasting five years, policies for economic and social development are established for the country. This is the responsibility of the General Secretariat of Planning or SEGEPLAN (*Secretaria General de Planificacion*). Since 1985, a continuity process has been established between governments regarding the problems that must be faced.

The country, as signatory to international agreements, has formulated national educational development plans that strongly link it to the Central American subregion. In the long term, this allows the nation to tackle common educational problems that it shares with the Latin American and Caribbean countries. Thus, since 1985, the education system has assumed a very important role. It has been assigned specific policies that link it significantly to the needs of health, education, housing, employment, and the nutrition of the population with the planned support of private enterprises and other nongovernmental sectors.

The Ministry of Education is responsible for the conversion of these policies into guidelines and goals in such a way that its functions have been closely related to the need for increased public spending in education and its equal distribution to all educational levels. This

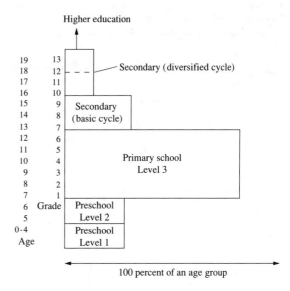

Figure 1
Guatemala: Structure of the formal education system

is especially the case at the preschool and primary levels so that their enrollment ratios and quality will improve. It is also responsible for curriculum revival and integrating into educational programs the basic ideals for the teaching of democracy, human rights, interculturalism, work, health, and environmental conservation. It must also provide compensatory measures (programs of integral assistance) for those students coming from disadvantaged social sectors.

Special attention is given to the training of personnel who work in the different subsectors of the system in order to achieve the required changes and qualitative improvement of education. There is a political commitment to the elimination of illiteracy, and programs are developed to stimulate participation of those needing the programs. Economic resources have been increased and there are joint efforts between government and private enterprise.

3. *The Formal System of Education*

Figure 1 outlines the structure of the system. Table 1 gives details of enrollment and resources in education in Guatemala.

The educational system is composed of school education and extra-school, or parallel, education. School education is organized by levels and divided into age groups; extra-school education is organized into modules and targeted toward the required qualifications for job performance. The government, as well as the private sector, intervenes in the development and financing of education in the country.

379

Table 1
Enrollment and resources in education 1991

| | Initial | Preprimary | Primary | Secondary | | Higher[a] |
				Basic Cycle	Diversified Cycle	
School-age population	1,607,886	591,016	1,583,602	685,419	812,881	—
Enrolled population	—	158,843	1,248,413	207,935	94,485	66,908
Percentage of enrollments per education levels						
0–4 years	—					
5–6 years[b]		28.5				
7–12 years			78.9			
13–15 years				30.3		
16–19 years					11.6	
Number of teachers	—	6,244	36,757	13,588	7,129	—
Number of students per teacher	—	27.0	33.9	15.3	13.3	—
Number of schools	—	3,496	9,362	1,277	526	5[c]
Average number of students per school	—	48	139	153	161	—
Cost per student (Q)	—	100	240	600		1,416

a Refers only to University of San Carlos for the year 1990 b From this level on there are students who are one or more years over-aged preprimary—younger than 5 years, primary—older than 12 years, basic cycle—older than 15 years, and diversified cycle—older than 18 years   c includes private universities

There are five levels: the first (or initial) level covers children of 0 to 4 years of age, and the second level is preschool, for children aged 4 to 6 years. (These two levels will be dealt with in Sect. 3.2 below.) The third, fourth, and fifth levels constitute primary, secondary, and higher education.

3.1 Primary, Secondary, and Tertiary Education

The third level, that of primary school education, is for children and youngsters between the ages of 7 and 14 (legally, the ages are 7 to 12) in 6 one-year grades. This level has historically received more support due to the fact that, for more than 100 years, it has constitutionally been free of charge and compulsory.

However, in 1991, 21 percent of the equivalent age group was not in school. This was due to socioeconomic phenomena such as displacements due to violence, internal migrations, high levels of poverty, and the dispersion of the rural population. Hence, 79 percent of school-aged children were enrolled in private and government schools. Although most schools are coeducational, there are some single-sex schools. The school day lasts an average of 5 hours and the school year is comprised of a maximum of 180 working days. Furthermore, there is also a specific accelerated formal education program for students of 14 years of age and older, in 4 one-year stages and equivalent in duration to that of the regular program.

The fourth level, or secondary education (*educación media*), is made up of two cycles. One is general or basic secondary education (*educación media básica*) with a duration of three years for young people who have completed primary school. The other, the cycle of diversified education (*educación media diversificada*), with a duration of two to four years of study, provides graduates of basic secondary schools with further education leading to high school diplomas or specialized training in teaching or accounting. In 1991, the cycle of basic education (*ciclo de educación básica*) served about 30 percent of the population aged 13 years and older, and the cycle of diversified education served almost 12 percent of the population aged 16 years and older. In both cases, students are enrolled in establishments, institutions, and private schools in morning, afternoon, and night sessions. The majority of the schools are open to both young men and women, but there are also single-sex schools in both the government and private sectors. Secondary education schools function for approximately 11 months a year in various shifts of about 5 hours per day.

Higher education (the fifth level) consists of universities and specialized institutions of nonuniversity higher education. The Constitution of the Republic declares that the San Carlos University of Guatemala is an autonomous body of the state. Together with four private universities—Rafael Landívar, Mariano Gálvez, Del Valle, and Francisco Marroquín—it is responsible for the direction, organization, and development of higher education. Each university has its particular set of courses (*cuadro de oferta*) for the formation of professionals in liberal, social, humanistic, and technological careers that the country requires both socially and economically. The San Carlos University, Rafael Landívar, and Mariano Gálvez have decentralized their services to the interior of the country, where they have created university centers, schools, and sections.

A secondary school diploma or degree is required for entering university. There are some courses that require six years of study. Each year is divided into semesters. There are also short programs of two to three years' duration that are of a more technical nature. These are organized into bimesters, trimesters, or semesters, depending on the subject area and the university.

The six-year programs generally culminate with the acquisition of the academic title of master or bachelor (*licenciatura*) and, in most cases, a professional degree is also awarded. In 1990, the state university was attended by a total of 66,909 students, 19 percent of whom were in their first year. In 1992, the state institution served more than 60 percent of the university population.

The institutions of higher nonuniversity education provide a variety of courses parallel to those of university and/or graduate degrees. Among them are the Feminine Institute of Superior Studies, or IFES (*Instituto Femenino de Estudios Superiores*), and the National Institute of Public Administration, or INAP (*Instituto Nacional de Administración Pública*).

3.2 Preschool Education

Childcare for children aged 0 to 4 years, whether by parents or within a school environment, is the first or initial level of education in Guatemala. The initial education program fundamentally develops activities targeted at health, nutrition, environmental education, and community and early childhood development. Early childhood development is under the direct care of private and governmental educational institutions such as nurseries, daycare centers, and kindergartens. In the early 1990s, its coverage was very low because it had just begun to be recognized as a right and duty of the population.

The second level—preschool—caters for children aged 4, 5, and 6 years. The general program is composed of psychosocial developmental activities so that the child will be prepared for formal learning of reading, writing, and mathematics in the primary school. For the major indigenous groups, there exists the National Program for Bilingual Education, or PRONEBI (*Programa Nacional de Educación Bilingue*), which provides children with education in their mother tongue and in Spanish as a second language. Preschool is the responsibility of the government as well as the private sector. However, coverage in 1991 did not surpass 30 percent of the targeted population.

3.3 Special Education

The problem of disability and its socioeconomic repercussions has still not been measured in Guatemala. Nevertheless, national estimates indicate that almost one million people are disabled. The institutions (mainly private) offer regular and nonregular programs to take care of cases of mental retardation and mental, audio, psychosocial, motor, and muscular-skeletal disabilities.

3.4 Vocational, Technical, and Business Education

Vocational education is part of the diversified cycle of secondary education and it is organized into four areas: general, technical, commercial, and teacher training. The student population enrolled in these schools comes from the basic secondary level where the students have received some vocational orientation to help them to decide their enrollment in one of the above-mentioned areas. Almost 14 percent of graduates from the basic secondary level enroll in technical education. Opportunities for technical preparation are very limited in the industrial and agricultural areas. There are only three technical government schools with various specialties, where applicants are admitted according to test scores; five further schools offer one technical specialty allowing students to acquire a secondary education diploma or certificate that is valid either to continue to higher education or to enter the workforce. Computer education has spread quickly but exclusively in the private sector, and mainly in the capital city with few establishments in the interior of the country.

Approximately 50 percent of the graduates from the basic cycle enroll in commercial education. There are various training opportunities in this area, since both private and government schools offer secretarial and accounting careers in various commercial specialties. Nevertheless, the demand for these services diminished at the beginning of the 1990s.

Private, industrial, agricultural, commercial, and other types of businesses pay little attention to the formal training in these technical specialties and, in many cases, their requirements are not fulfilled by the existing market of qualified persons.

The Technical Institute of Training, or INTECAP (*Instituto Técnico de Capacitación*), is an office of the Ministry of Work and Social Welfare (*Ministerio de Trabajo y Previsión Social*). It offers various programs for the training of qualified personnel for private businesses. The institute trains workers in short-term courses in a number of training centers situated both in the capital city and in other geographic areas.

3.5 Adult and Nonformal Education

The education system also has a parallel subsystem of out-of-school education. This system promotes formal and nonformal educational activities aimed at the marginalized population aged 15 or older. The branch offices of seven ministries (including those of education), the presidency of the Republic, the Popular University, state and private universities, municipalities, and 261 nongovernmental organizations are all involved.

Adult participation in formal extraschool education has been made possible by the implementation of a modular system. A series of learning modules have been developed and, between 1980 and 1981, Module No. 1 received special attention. This module introduces the adult to minimum basic knowledge related to health; economic, social, and cultural development; and acquiring basic literacy. The efforts in literacy training have been intensified because of the low level of instruction and the high illiteracy rate.

The participation of the adult population in nonformal out-of-school education is very difficult to quantify. Both private and government institutions participate in its development, and the emphasis is on education for jobs.

4. Administrative and Supervisory Structure and Operation

The Ministry of Education is the institution responsible for providing the population with a common basic education for the integral development of the human being, as well as providing the knowledge for the inculcation of a national and universal culture. In 1987, the Ministry of Education began a process of educational regionalization and decentralization. A total of eight educational regional authorities were established; each one to be in charge of the technical direction of the region, and integrated with technical–pedagogical and administrative units.

To make the Ministry of Education more effective, it has been restructured into four levels: (a) management, (b) coordination and execution, (c) evaluation and planning, and (d) support. The regional education directors are part of the second level. Management involves technical support services for the system as a whole, and the development of administrative procedures.

One of the major technical supports is the inservice training of personnel in different areas. A total of 1,500 people participated in events relating to school management, project formulation, curriculum development, and methodology at the beginning of the 1990s. The management level also awarded 104 officials with scholarships for study abroad. On the administrative side, laws and by-laws have been promulgated, such as the National Education Law of January 1991. It is also responsible for the elaboration of manuals, organization and implementation of census events, the creation of positions and improvement in salaries for teachers, and the provision of support for low-income students.

The Educational Coordination Units (*Unidades de Coordinacion Educativa*) are responsible for the monitoring of schools and the inspection and supervision of teachers in the educational system. This system is being decentralized from the regional directors of education to the departmental, municipal, and local levels.

In 1990, there was a total of 13,980 school establishments. Of these, 24 percent belonged to the private sector. Although private schools have some characteristics that differentiate them from government schools, the educational curriculum is similar. The characteristics that differ are that most private schools have better physical conditions, better technical resources, and their students come from homes with better economic and social conditions.

In general, the education service has developed more in the urban areas. Therefore, much of the ministerial efforts, especially in the 1980s, have been to spread the educational services to the rural areas.

5. Educational Finance

In the 1980s, the financing of education in the government sector has been from various sources— funds coming from the central government, donations of an internal or external nature, and loans given by international entities. The Ministry of Education is responsible for the execution of the annual budget. In the fiscal year 1990, the budget was Q494.7 million (US$99 million), equivalent to 16 percent of the general budget of the government and 1.8 percent of the Gross National Product (GNP). UNESCO has recommended to the Latin American and Caribbean countries that they allocate a minimum of 6 percent of their GNP to the education budget.

The government budget absorbs little more than 50 percent of the total annual financial availability. A total of 41 percent goes to the financing of salaries and, of this amount, 93 percent is for the financing of teacher salaries. Other programs are those of equivalent investment (a little more than 3% of the total) and currency transferences (equivalent to 46%). The investment program covered only primary education and the administrative improvement of the system. The transference program is composed of allocations mainly for the University of San Carlos and for the National Committee for Literacy (*Comite Nacional de Alfabetizacion*—CONALFA). In 1989, the general cost per student at the preschool level was calculated at Q100 (US$20), for the primary level Q240 (US$48), for the secondary level Q600 (US$120), and for the higher education Q1,416 (US$284).

The educational system also receives external financing in the form of loans and donations from international agencies and friendly governments. Between 1986 and 1989, this totalled Q71.7 million (approximately US$14.34 million).

The private sector receives its funding from state subsidies, donations, and school fees. These fees vary from US$40 to US$900 per child per year. Parents of children who study in government schools do not pay fees, except for an initial payment that is used to provide a daily snack for the children and school furniture. At the primary level, even when children receive some help with school supplies, parents must cope with all other costs. In the basic secondary cycle, there are establishments called "cooperative basic institutes" that function with financing from the government, municipalities, and parents.

6. *Supplying Personnel for the Education System*

In 1991, more than 60,000 teachers worked in private and public schools. Almost 7,000 teachers were employed in preschools, 37,000 in primary schools, and 21,000 in secondary schools. More than 60 percent of teachers are female. In preschool and primary levels, there are higher percentages of female teachers. However, most of the administrative positions are occupied by males.

Preparation for teaching in preschool and primary levels is given in teacher-training schools, of which there are 114 throughout the country. Most of them are private, and only 12 percent are government-owned. Teacher preparation for secondary schools is the responsibility of the universities. The program of teacher education in normal schools is of three year's duration in basic secondary education, and, in most cases, three years in the diversified cycle. In this cycle, the study plan is given according to specialization: preschool or kindergarten, urban primary, rural primary, bilingual primary, music education, physical education, and home economics education.

The teacher-training program for secondary school teachers is conducted in the universities and lasts for three years. Applicants must possess the equivalent of 12 years of schooling, which means having studied and completed the diversified cycle of secondary education. A large number of teachers graduate each year from normal schools and universities. This has resulted in a surplus of teachers at the primary level. However, there is a scarcity of teachers for bilingual education, and of subject matter specialists for secondary education. The biggest deficit is for teaching personnel for technical schools.

The procedure for teacher promotion is called "teacher scaling" (*escalafon*). It is administered by the Personnel Grading Board (*Junta Calificadora de Personal*) and works according to a scale based on years of service and scaling levels. All teachers enter the service with scaling level "A" and every five years they can be promoted until they reach the last level which is level "F." For each scaling level, there is a 20 percent salary increase that is begun at level "B" with 20 percent of the basic salary and ends at level "F" with a 100 percent increment. Teachers also receive extra pay known as "emergency allowance" (*bonificacion de emergencia*), which is given as an economic aid in times of catastrophe—for example, because of the 1976 earthquake.

Private school teachers can also benefit from this procedure, because the time they have taught in the private sector is recognized as experience when they enter government teaching. The professional careers of teachers can be terminated voluntarily or teachers can be fired. In both cases, teachers have a right to their retirement pension if they have accumulated a minimum of 20 years of service. They are entitled to indemnity payments if they are fired for an unjustified cause.

7. *Curriculum Development and Teaching Methodology*

The syllabus (or study plan) is common throughout the country. The Ministry authorities establish the curricular guidelines that must be followed in private and government educational institutions. However, each Regional Director of Education can incorporate some specific curricular elements according to the cultural, social, and economic characteristics of the region. Both private and governmental schools have considerable latitude in deciding on the development of study plans and more appropriate teaching methodologies. Practically all students are subjects of an educational process that provides them with: reading, writing, and grammar in Spanish; mathematics; science; social studies; and arts, music, and physical education.

In both preschools and primary schools, students are grouped by sections or rooms that are supervised by one teacher. The situation varies in rural areas because, in most of the primary schools, each teacher is responsible for various groups according to the grades in a particular school. As from the beginning of Grade 7 (the first year of secondary education), students are also grouped by sections; each section has various teachers specialized in one of the subjects that comprise the study plan. The same procedure is followed in the diversified cycle beginning in Grade 10. Thus, specialization of some teachers varies by the type of educational establishment—technical, commercial, or general.

The only foreign language included in the study plan is English in the secondary school. However, there is no rule that forbids the teaching of other foreign languages, especially in private establishments. The government encourages the teaching of native languages in groups of the indigenous population by providing a national program of bilingual education as referred to in the Law of Education.

In 1987, the Ministry of Education created the National Commission of Curricular Improvement (*Comision Nacional de Readecuacion Curricular*) whose brief is to start a project to establish an integral system of educational improvement. This system is the mechanism that will link the training of personnel, research, curriculum development, and generation of educational technology with community participation.

It is responsible for continuous curriculum innovation with its corresponding development. Curriculum improvement is a continuous process of adjustment to ensure the workability, pertinence, flexibility, and relevance of the curriculum. It also ensures that the pedagogical process responds to the demands of national, regional, and local development, as well as to the country's cultural and social environment. To this end, specific strategies of restructuring, reformulation, and decentralization were implemented. The National System of Improvement of Human Resources and Curricular Adaptation—SIMAC—was organized to facilitate the coordination and integration of processes and resources, including the fundamental variable of personnel training. To attain this, UNDP, UNESCO, and the government of the Netherlands provided technical and financial support.

The Ministry of Education's national textbook program produces reading materials, mainly textbooks, for government primary schools. There is great flexibility in the use of materials and textbooks, national or foreign, that are available.

8. The System of Examinations, Promotions, and Certifications

In order for a student to be promoted from preschool to primary, it is necessary for him or her to have reached the maturity level in reading and writing (*lecto-escritura*) and arithmetic. A certificate, or "proof" (*constancia*), is awarded. However, many children, mainly in rural areas, enroll in the first grade of primary education simply because they have become 7 years of age. Some enroll after the age of 7. For movement from the primary level to the secondary level, the student must have completed six school grades. A study certificate is given for grade-to-grade promotion and a diploma is awarded at the end of the cycle or level.

In secondary education, a diploma is also awarded between basic secondary education and diversified education; again, a study certification is given on a grade-to-grade basis. Finally, when students graduate from the diversified cycle, they receive a diploma in the case of high school graduates and secretaries, and a degree (*titulo*) in the case of teachers, accountants, and some secretaries. These credits allow students to enroll in higher education. The diplomas and degrees of secondary education are awarded by the regional education directors. In the system of equivalency of studies (*equiparación de estudios por nivelación*), different educational courses from both inside and outside the country are considered. It also provides for studies carried out in countries that are signatories to agreements ratified by Guatemala, mainly the Central American Covenant of Basic Unification of Education (*Convenion Centroamericano sobre Unificación Básica de la Educación*).

9. Educational Assessment, Evaluation, and Research

There is no system that combines the results of evaluation and research with the aim of helping students according to the results of academic achievement that the schools present annually.

The basis for a national system of pedagogical teacher training that allows a feedback for the teaching–learning processes that occur in school is being established by SIMAC. A national testing system, which will help to collect information on learning that leads to better school achievement, is also being formed.

Since 1980, the Ministry of Education's Student Welfare Office has handled the scholarship program and the study packages (*bolsas de estudio*) for students in secondary education. The study package consists of a monthly monetary allowance to help persons with little money, but good levels of academic achievement. A somewhat similar system exists in the private sector.

Materials, schools supplies, and textbooks, used in governmental and nongovernmental programs, can also be provided for poor students. In higher education, universities also develop scholarship programs for their students. The procedure is more precise than at the school level because students are formally evaluated. Each scholarship consists of monthly allowances and exemptions from paying school fees.

Contextual and institutional evaluation gained support at the end of the 1980s. The first resulted in positive approaches to the socioeconomic reality of the communities in order to make education more appropriate to their needs; the second revealed the successes and failures of the reforms in the administrative and teacher-training innovations that had taken place.

The lack of a clear policy on educational research will be rectified when legislation occurs to create the National Institute of Educational Investigations. Its task will be to integrate all research studies, investigations, and scientific research into the educational system in a systematic way.

10. Major Reforms in the 1980s and 1990s

The 1980s witnessed significant reforms in Guatemalan education. The political crisis of 1982 resulted in the imposition of austerity measures in order to achieve an economic and social re-ordering. In 1985, the Constituent National Assembly issued the new Constitution of the Republic which established the bases governing the educational system and brought about changes in its structure, organization, and functioning. Decentralization and regionalization of the educational system began in 1987 when the Ministry of Education issued a decree establishing eight regions under the supervision of regional education directors. Administrative decentralization helped considerably in improving the conditions in schools, and pedagogic decentralization helped in the qualitative improvement of the system. The participation of communities in curricular reform helped to make the content of what was taught fit more to the interests, culture, and social and economic needs of the areas served by the schools.

In 1989, the Ministry of Education created SIMAC and the new Law of Education came into effect in January 1991. The purpose of the Law is to achieve more consistency between the various reforms that had been implemented, and also to ensure that the development and consolidation of the regionalization and administrative and pedagogical decentralization processes of education will meet the nation's plans for socioeconomic development.

11. Major Problems for the Year 2000

During the 1990s, the generation of funds to meet the cumulative and emerging needs will continue to be a problem. Funding for education will require an annual increase of at least 1.5 percent if the twenty-first century is to begin with higher enrollments at all levels of the system. Precise strategies and procedures must be implemented in order to reach the dispersed populations in the rural and marginal urban areas.

At the same time, the training and professional development of teachers must be invested with vision in terms of the teaching abilities and skills which will be needed to develop the programs to face the demands of the future. The need to unite sectoral efforts will also persist so that nongovernmental institutions, and especially private enterprise, will lend, to a greater extent, their capacity (administrative as well as economic) to the solution of secular educational problems such as illiteracy and job training.

The challenge to the system will continue to be the development of educational processes that lead to a democratic and more just society with a clear national identity, given the wide variety of ethnic groups, languages, and cultures that exist in the country.

Bibliography

Instituto Nacional de Estadística (INE) 1990 *Encuesta Socíodemografica 1989*. INE, Guatemala City

Ministerio de Educación 1992 *Descentralización educativa en Guatemala*. Informe del Ministerio de Educación de Guatemala a la Primera Reunión de Nivel Ministerial con los países de Centro América, El Caribe y la Península Ibérica. Ministerio de Educación, Guatemala City

Ministerio de Educación, CENALTEX 1987 *Constitución Política de la República de Guatemala*. Ministerio de Educación, Guatemala City

Ministerio de Educación, CENALTEX 1991 *Ley de Educación Nacional. Decreto Legislativo 12–91*. Ministerio de Educación, Guatemala City

Ministerior de Educación/PNUD/UNESCO/UNICEF/ACDI 1990 *Propuesta del Plan Nacional de Acción de Educación par Todos, Guatemala*. Ministerio de Educación, Guatemala City

Ministerio de Educación SIMAC 1991 *Guatemala: Situación del Personal Docente en el País*. Ministerio de Educación, Guatemala City

Ministerio de Educación SIMAC 1992 Situación y perspectivas de la educación en Guatemala. XXIII Reunión del Consejo Interamericano de la Educación, Ciencia y Cultura de la Organización de Estados Americanos. Ministerio de Educación, Guatemala City

Ministerio de Educación/USIPE 1986 *Diagnóstico de la Educación Nacional 1981–1985*. Ministerio de Educación, Guatemala City

Ministerio de Educación/USIPE 1988 *Plan Quinquenal de Educación 1987–1991*, 2 vols. Ministerio de Educación, Guatemala City

Ministerio de Educación/USIPE 1989 *Plan Nacional de Acción 1989–1995*. Ministerio de Educación, Guatemala City

Ministerio de Educación/USIPE 1991 *Documento de Base para la Planifacación Educativa de Corto y Mediano Plazo 1992–1995*. Ministerio de Educación, Guatemala City

Ministerior de Educación/USIPE, Centro de Informática 1991 *Estadísticas de la Educación 1991*. Ministerio de Educación, Guatemala City

Ministerio de Educación-Asemblea Nacional del Magisterio 1991 *Reglamento de la Ley de Educación Nacional*. Ministerio de Educación, Guatemala City

SEGEPLAN 1991 *Proyecto "Lineamientos de Politica Económica y Social para Guatemala 1991–1995."* SEGEPLAN, Guatemala City

Guinea

H. A. B. Diallo

1. General Background

The Republic of Guinea is situated on the west coast of Africa, with Sierra Leone and Liberia to the south, Senegal to the north, and Mali and the Côte d'Ivoire to the east. A former French colony, Guinea was one of the first African territories to gain independence when it achieved self-rule in 1958. The capital is Conakry.

Its territory covers 246,050 square kilometers and the population is about 6 million. The annual population growth rate is estimated to be about 2.6 percent. The population comprises 3 major ethnic groups

(Fulani, Malinke, and Susu) and 15 minor tribes speaking 8 languages. French continues to be the official national tongue. About 75 percent of the population is Moslem, about 25 percent Animist, and less than 1 percent Christian. Agriculture and subsistence farming occupy about 80 percent of the labor force. Despite potential mineral wealth (particularly bauxite), the per capita annual income is very low at US$440 per year (1992).

With the advent of the Second Republic in 1984, Guinea was determined to create a strong united nation assuring each citizen the opportunity to develop his or her personality and creative faculties. It was within this framework that the government undertook a major reform of several state institutions, notably in the monetary, economic and financial, educational, and administrative spheres. At the same time a policy of decentralization was undertaken with the aim of giving initiative and responsibility back to local communities for their own socioeconomic development. This was to include such matters as school building, water points, and industrial and cultural development. In education, the reform was to include a redefinition of the principles and aims of education as well as the provision of the material conditions for improving the quality of education. The main principles and strategies were to be as follows:

(a) Education was to be democratic and non-denominational and was to be for all children of school age.

(b) Education was to be based on the values of African civilization.

(c) The curriculum was to be universal and enable a dialogue among cultures, people, and nations.

(d) National, African, and world languages should be taught.

(e) Education should involve a balance of theory and practice, a link between the school and the community, and ensure that the individual can live harmoniously in his or her environment.

(f) Education should be provided free of charge in all levels of state schools and parents should have the right to choose the school (state or private) to which they send their children.

(g) Education should be provided, in an appropriate form, at the following levels: preschool, elementary or primary, secondary, vocational, and higher.

The aims of the 1984 reform must be seen within the light of what happened during the First Republic. Upon Independence, the government wished to create a system of basic education for all children and to achieve the eradication, or at least decrease, of illiteracy. Despite enormous efforts in terms of finance,

building infrastructure, training of teachers, and so on, the slowing of the economy made it difficult for such aims to be met. Several of the planned reforms were not well-conducted. Although members of the public became more and more interested in having their children attend school, net enrollment ratios decreased from 33 to 27 percent between 1980 and 1984. At the same time the percentage of illiterate females was 86.

2. Politics and the Goals of the Educational System

The major goals of education are:

(a) to have young people acquire an adequate level of theoretical and practical knowledge as well as vocational skills and a love of manual work;

(b) to provide young persons and adults who are not in school with access to other modes of thought and expression;

(c) to provide special needs children with an appropriate education.

To overcome the deficits of education under the First Republic an overall strategy was developed, the main dimensions of which were:

(a) a transitional period (1984–90) for the progressive reform of education;

(b) renewal and/or adaptation of educational structures;

(c) more inservice training of teachers;

(d) the use of the French language as the medium of instruction from the beginning of the first grade in school;

(e) high priority given to the development of primary education;

(f) the provision of many more literacy courses to stem the increase in illiteracy;

(g) the diversification of vocational training to respond to the needs of the economy;

(h) the reorganization of learning strategies for those who leave school to enable them to enter the job market successfully;

(i) the strengthening of administration, planning, and inspection within the education system.

This overall strategy identified, in particular, the need for the acquisition of learning materials, the retraining of teachers, and the strengthening of the administrative services and the inspectorate. All of the above were embodied in the *Programme d'ajustement sectoriel de l'education* (PASE) which was launched by the government in 1990.

3. The Formal System of Education

Figure 1 presents the structure of the educational system in diagrammatic form.

3.1 Primary, Secondary, and Tertiary Education

Primary education begins at the age of 7 years and lasts for 6 years. In practice, however, urban children begin at 6 years of age and rural children at 9. In 1991–92 there were 359,405 pupils (less than a third of them girls) in 8,415 classes in 2,586 schools. In all, there were 7,374 teachers of whom only 21 percent were women. The discrepancy between the number of teachers and the number of classrooms means that some classes were taught by teachers teaching their second shift, or by unqualified teachers. Teaching consists mostly of imparting reading, writing, and arithmetic to prepare pupils to enter an active working life. At the end of primary school pupils may take the examination for the certificate of end of primary school studies (CEPE). If they are successful this gives them the right to enter secondary school.

General secondary school comprises two cycles; the first lasts four years and the second three years. At the end of the first cycle, pupils sit for the *brevet d'études*

du premier cycle (BEPC) which gives access to the first form of the second cycle, Grade 11. At the end of the second cycle, the first part of the *baccalauréat* is taken in Grade 12 and the second part in Grade 13. In 1991–92 there were 87,975 pupils (of whom nearly 24 percent were girls) enrolled in 177 *collèges*, 24 *lycées*, and 34 *lycées/collèges* in a total of 1,878 classes. There were 4,846 teachers, of whom 13 percent were female. Those possessing the BEPC may take a competitive examination for a place in vocational schools (*les écoles professionelles*). Similarly, those having passed the *baccalauréat* may compete for a place in higher education or in a national vocational institution.

Higher education comprises two universities (Conakry and Kankan), three institutes (Géo-Mines at Boké, Agro-Zootechnie at Faranan, and the Advanced Institute of Education at Coyah), eight institutes of research, and two documentation centers. All courses last for five years except for medicine, which lasts six years. In 1991–92, there were 5,366 students (of whom 6.5% were female); there were 527 full-time and 176 part-time faculty members. The research institutes employed 135 researchers, of whom 15 were female.

3.2 Preschool Education

Most nursery schools are to be found in Conakry. They come under the auspices of the Ministry of Public Health.

3.3 Special Education

There is only one special education school in the whole country and this is for deaf and dumb children; it is in Conakry.

3.4 Vocational, Technical, and Business Education

Secondary vocational and technical schools recruit their students, on a competitive basis, from Grade 10. There are *centres de formation professionelle* (CFP) providing courses for, for example, the technical, industrial, and construction trades. In the secondary schools there is vocational training providing training for jobs in offices, the health sector, and so on. The national institutes recruit their students, again on the basis of competitive examinations, either from Grade 12 (for primary school teacher training and sports) or Grade 13 (for secondary school teacher training, public health training, and agriculture). There were 10,268 students in these types of course in 1991–92, of whom 31 percent were female. In all there were 47 different institutions with 1,130 faculty members (9% female).

3.5 Adult and Nonformal Education

Nearly all efforts in this area come within the realm of literacy education. Within the basic "education for

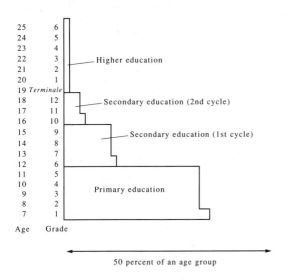

Figure 1
Guinea: Structure of the formal education system 1991–92

all" program (1991–95) it has been stated that there should be extensive and intensive implementation of all functional literacy programs in all rural, industrial, and artisanal areas, and with special emphasis on females and children who have never been to school or who have dropped out of school at an early age; 450 new literacy centers should be built; 450 literacy teachers should be trained and 36 percent of them should be female; and 1,350 basic literacy and postliteracy booklets should be developed and produced.

One subsector that has thus far received little attention is that of informal learning, or learning on the job. Some studies were conducted in the period 1983–89 but no efficient strategy about optimal modes of learning has yet been developed. However, because of the importance of this type of learning, an office for training and retraining in this area has been created (*Office de Formation et Perfectionnement Professionel*). A sector study was undertaken which has helped Guinea to formulate a national policy of vocational and technical training. This policy requires the improvement of the quality of trades and business, and increasing the participation of women in production.

4. Administrative and Supervisory Structure and Operation

The Ministry of Education and Training (*Ministère de l'Enseignement Pré Universitaire et de la Formation Professionelle*—MEPU-FP) consists of a secretary general, a cabinet, support services, national directorates, consultative committees, and several service units. The support services consist of an inspectorate general, a directorate of administrative and financial affairs, a central secretariat, an external relations and transport unit, a documental and archival information unit, an examinations and competitions unit, a statistics and planning unit, and a technical projects unit. The national directorates are those of elementary education, secondary education, and vocational and technical education. Connected with these directorates there are the National Literacy Service and the National Institute of Education. The consultative committees include the National Basic Education Committee from 1993 to 2000 (CONEBAT), the committee on the training of teachers and the teachers' teachers, and various national commissions. Finally, the service units comprise the regional school inspectorates (4 plus Conakry), 33 (plus 5 for Conakry) prefectural directorates, and 310 subprefectural school directorates.

The most important decisions taken by the Ministry of Education and Training concern orientations, priorities, and strategies for the implementation of orientations and priorities. The orientations, priorities, and strategies for each school year are set out in a letter of instructions written by the Minister to the heads of the levels, who write their centralized proposals. Other important decisions taken at ministerial level and concerning the whole system pertain to such factors as budget, distribution of material and personnel, and teacher training.

Regional or provincial problems are dealt with at the respective levels, and decisions concerning the everyday running of the schools are taken at the district level or by school heads.

5. Educational Finance

The percentage of the state budget allocated to education increased as follows from 1989 to 1993 (excluding interest on debt and investment): 1989 —12.9 percent, 1990 —14.2 percent, 1991—25.7 percent, 1992—25.2 percent, and 1993—26.0 percent. In 1992 the total educational budget was 18,263 million Guinean francs (US$15 million). Of this, half was spent on salaries in primary and secondary education and the primary education teacher-training college. Of the salary bill, 68 percent was spent on primary schools, 13 percent on secondary schools, 13 percent on vocational and technical schools and institutes, and 6 percent on the teacher-training college. About a quarter of the total bill went to higher education. The rest was spent on the other programs and on administration, including the inspectorate. Between 1991 and 1992 the overall increase in the educational operating budget was 1.16 percent.

6. Supplying Personnel for the Education System

The length of the teacher-training preservice education programs was given in Sect. 3. It is in inservice teacher-training that results have been encouraging. More than 60 percent of primary school teachers have been retrained in inservice teacher-training courses run at the prefectural level, and 60 percent of those teaching French and 65 percent of those teaching mathematics at the college of education have been retrained, while 71 teachers were trained how to teach multigrade classes. Over 100 of the college faculty members and educational advisers (*conseillers pédagogiques*) were trained at the Advanced Institute of Education at Manéah. At the same time 658 new primary school teachers were being trained in 1993. Further to this, seminars are held regularly to upgrade administrative personnel. Although inservice teacher training is not formally compulsory, all teachers attend such courses because it is important for them to obtain higher grades and professional development, and it is only through such inservice training that this is possible.

7. Curriculum Development and Teaching Methodology

Within the sectoral adjustment program in education

one major component is "revision of the curriculum and methods of teaching and adaptation and implementation of them." Ten activities are foreseen. These are:

(a) evaluation of the national textbook policy;

(b) readaptation and acquisition of textbooks for the learning of the French language for Grades 7 to 9;

(c) production and piloting of textbooks in mathematics and science for Grades 7 to 9;

(d) production of pedagogical support materials for collective use;

(e) trial and revision of all materials;

(f) distribution of all pedagogical materials;

(g) training of teachers to use the materials;

(h) printing of pedagogical support materials;

(i) educational research and innovation;

(j) sensitization of all involved in education to the use of media.

A council is regularly called to discuss issues on the curriculum, and comprises inspectors, directors, and teachers. The decisions they take at this level become official and are applied throughout the country. These activities will be the beginning of continuous reform of the curriculum. All of these efforts are aimed at the improvement of the quality of education in the primary and secondary schools.

8. The System of Examinations, Promotions, and Certifications

The national unit for examinations is responsible for organizing, in collaboration with the regional inspectorates and prefectural directorates of education, the examinations given at the end of each cycle of education. These are the CEPE (end of primary school studies certificate) which, if passed, admits a child to secondary school, the BEPC at the end of the first cycle of secondary school, and the first and second *baccalauréat* examinations, taken in the 12th and 13th grades of school respectively. There is a competitive examination for those who have passed the second part of the "bac" to gain entry to the university. The examination at the end of university studies results in a *diplôme d'études supérieures* (DES).

Within each cycle of education there are internal examinations set by the school at the end of each grade. Upon passing the examination the pupil is promoted to the next grade.

9. Educational Assessment, Evaluation, and Research

Efforts are being undertaken to assess the achievement of pupils in various subjects at selected grade levels.

At the same time, studies are planned to follow up pupils after they leave school in order to evaluate the external efficiency of the system. Certain studies are undertaken in order to have information on the requirements of the economy in terms of the knowledge, skills, and values to be produced by the schools. The results of such studies are used to modify the educational objectives embedded in the curriculum. An institution called the Institut Pedagogique National (PN) is responsible for carrying out research on curriculum.

10. Major Reforms in the 1980s and 1990s

By the mid-1980s it had been established (at two national educational conferences) that there was: (a) an underqualification of teachers, (b) teaching that did not take account of national languages, (c) insufficient equipment in the classrooms, (d) no pedagogical support materials and equipment in the schools, (e) insufficient and poor conditions of school buildings, (f) a lack of planning, and (g) poor administration. As a result of these meetings, efforts had to be made to rethink and make precise the principles and aims of education in the republic. All technical, financial, human, and institutional resources had to made available to achieve the above aims.

An intermediate plan of action was adopted for the period 1984–90. This plan included the following:

(a) all teaching would be in the French language, but at the same time recognizing the importance of local languages;

(b) a massive program for training educational advisers and the inservice training of teachers;

(c) the development of infrastructures, buildings, and equipment to make it possible for all children of school age to attend school;

(d) the replacement of mainly academic schooling with more practical training, to be of more direct use to the economy;

(e) a transformation of teacher promotion and structures at all levels of schooling;

(f) a redeployment of teachers to ensure that they would be teaching in a school appropriate to their level of qualification.

Work was conducted in the period 1984–89 by nationals, with some help from outsiders. This work resulted in 1989 in an educational policy declaration. This policy declaration has become the reference for all educational activities in Guinea. Activities were then planned and became the agenda for the 1990s or, in other words, what had to be attained by the year 2000.

The objectives for the year 2000 are:

(a) to increase admission rates to the first year of primary school to 50 percent;

(b) to reduce the amount of grade repeating and dropout;

(c) to improve the quality of education and to adapt education to the needs of the job market;

(d) to increase the percentage of the state budget allocated to education (after having allowed for debt) to 20;

(e) to have 10–12 percent of the investment program allocated to education;

(f) to accord higher priority to basic education and increase the percentage of the educational budget to basic education from 35 percent in 1993 (it was 30% in 1988) to 40 percent in 2000.

The structural adjustment in education has planned the details of how the many subobjectives implied in the above activities will be achieved. The World Bank, the French Coopération, and the United States Agency for International Development have together helped with a sum of US$58 million. In particular, these agencies will require several improvements which can be grouped into four major categories:

(a) restructuring educational administration and strengthening the skills of the current personnel;

(b) pooling human resources and rationalizing the preservice and inservice training of teachers;

(c) improving the conditions of work in classrooms and improving the inputs of equipment and supplies;

(d) revision of curriculum and methods of teaching.

11. Major Problems for the Year 2000

The government's desire to adapt education to the needs and economy of the country will be pursued. Efforts will be made to decrease the dropout rate, to improve the quality of education at all levels of education.

In primary education there should be a net enrollment ratio of 53 percent. This requires the building of a large number of schools/classrooms and the production of the required number of teachers. Quality should improved in order to improve the general level of education and also to decrease substantially the amount of grade repeating. Continuing efforts will be made to plan for education for all. In secondary education the enrollment rate of 12 percent should be maintained. To keep pace with increasing births this will mean more schools/classrooms and laboratories. There will need to be changes in the curriculum in order to have it conform with realities of life in the country. The same can be said about higher education.

Illiteracy rates should be decreased from 74 to 40 percent. This implies the production of more literacy helpers and more learning materials.

Bibliography

Agency of Cultural and Technical Cooperation (ACCT) 1991 *Report of the Regional Seminar on Upgrading of Diagnostic Methods and Educational Planning*. Agency of Cultural and Technical Cooperation (ACCT), Conakry

CIEP 1991 *Report of the Seminar on the Rationalization of Educational Policy by Systematic Analysis in Francophone African Countries*. CIEP, Sèvres

Diallo H A B 1989 *Déclaration de Politique Educative*. Paper presented at specialized seminar for francophone journalists, September

Ministry of Education 1984–85 *Texts from the National Conferences in Conakry 1984/85*. Ministry of Education, Conakry

Ministry of Education 1992a *Memorandum on the Aims and Activities of the MEPU-FP. Ministry of Education, Conakry*

Ministry of Education 1992b *Annual Statistics, 1991/92*. Ministry of Education, Conakry

Ministry of Finance 1993 *Année Financière 1993. Budget Analyses for Education in Respect of the Funds Available for PASE*. Ministry of Finance, Conakry

Guinea-Bissau

W. D. S. Leal Filho

1. General Background

The Republic of Guinea-Bissau is a country located on the western coast of Africa, having Senegal and Guinea as its northern and southern neighbors, respectively. It has a total area of 36.1 million square kilometers, which includes, besides its territory in continental Africa, the 40 islands (20 of which are inhabited) which constitute the archipelago of Bijagoz. Guinea-Bissau has an estimated population of around 1 million. Its capital, Bissau, is the country's largest and most densely populated city with 140,000 inhabitants.

GDP per capita was estimated at US$190 (1993) for the country as a whole, but less than US$100 in the interior of the country. The average rate of population growth is estimated at 4.1 percent per annum. In the city of Bissau the rate is estimated at 5 percent. The birth rate is fairly high (the average family size is 6.3 persons), but the infant mortality rate is also high (14.3 percent). Life expectancy is around 41 years for men and 44.6 years for women. The annual growth of the country is an estimated 3.3 percent. There is a 450,000 strong workforce distributed over agriculture (82.4%), industry (3.5%), and trade and services (14.1%). The female workforce totals 42 percent (Mazzolenis 1993).

One of the implications of the above distribution of the workforce in terms of educational planning is the fact that emphasis needs to be given to the education of those living in rural areas and who are thus likely to be involved with agriculture. In addition, educational planning also needs to take into account the training of those working in the trade and services industry.

As a former colony of Portugal, the country still has Portuguese as the official language, although Creole and other native dialects are widely spoken. Animists, Muslims, and Christians are among the main religious groups. The 10 September is "Independence Day," when celebrations are held to commemorate the formal establishment of the country, which separated itself from Portugal in 1974.

Guinea-Bissau is poor in minerals. Apart from oil, only bauxite and phosphorous are commercially produced, despite the existence of significant reserves (Mazzolenis 1993). It is essentially an agricultural country which produces rice, beans, manioc, and timber. Agriculture is the main economic activity of about 85 percent of the population and it accounts for approximately 79 percent of its Gross National Product (GNP) of US$147 million (1990). The GNP has been growing at a rate of 0.8 percent per year since 1987. Agriculture suffers from the effects of the climatic variations typical of the Sahelian region with extended droughts, but at the same it benefits from the high level of periodic rainfall in the country. However, the rainfall often inundates the southern regions during the rainy season. In fishing, forestry, and mineral resources, there would appear to be an underuse of the agricultural potential of the country. For example, in 1992 only 400,000 hectares of the available arable land of one million hectares were under cultivation; in addition, fishing catches represent only 25 percent of the potential annual catch of approximately 100,000 tons of fish. In the case of mineral resources, large reserves of phosphate (35 million tons), bauxite (250 million tons), and offshore oil remain unexploited while their potential is considered. Agriculture workers live in 3,600 villages that are the basic units of settlement. After 500 years of colonialism, the rural world of Guinea-Bissau has remained fundamentally traditional. The consumption of energy is unevenly distributed. Whereas in the interior the per capita consumption is less than 5 kilowatt hours, the city of Bissau consumes seven times as much energy as the rest of the country.

In political terms, Guinea-Bissau has a main political party, the African Party for the Independence of Guinea and Cap Verde (PAIGC), whose existence has been complemented by new political parties such as the Social Democratic Front and Guinea-Bissau Resistance/Bafata Movement. At Independence in 1974, PAIGC inherited glaringly underdeveloped economic and social infrastructures: harbors and asphalted roads were scarce, built only to connect Portuguese army camps, and the industrial base was extremely limited. Health and educational facilities were concentrated in urban centers and military posts: there was one doctor per 10,000 inhabitants, and the literacy rate was about 5 percent. The tasks of the first government of Guinea-Bissau were enormous: to develop a productive sector, to create the economic infrastructure that is the prerequisite for the development of the productive sector, and to develop the human potential of the country by creating health and education facilities for the entire population (SIDA 1982).

During the first years of Independence, when ambitious plans in all these fields were made, there was a series of dry years and agriculture suffered. The estimated food deficit was 60,000 tons in 1981. As a result, exports declined dramatically and there was an estimated balance of payments deficit of about US$100 million in 1981 and US$553 million in 1993. It is against this background that the country's education sector has to be viewed.

2. Politics and the Goals of the Education System

Education is the right and duty of every citizen. Over recent years, as part of the ongoing attempts to fight illiteracy, new schools have been opened in the remote parts of the country, especially in the south and in the islands, and the number of pupils has increased noticeably at all levels of education. Considerable efforts have been made to improve the country's educational system in spite of the lack of planning experience and capacity; of trained teachers; of adequate curricula, textbooks, and teaching materials; and of school buildings.

Soon after Independence, primary education was restructured to include Grades 5 and 6. New curricula and more relevant textbooks were progressively introduced.

During the first two years of Independence, teaching in Guinea-Bissau continued within the Portuguese structure. It was not possible to implement straightaway the wide-reaching reforms envisaged by the PAIGC given the complexity of the situation and the numerous difficulties encountered. A gradual and planned change took place, whose description is relevant to the explanation of the system in the early 1990s.

The colonial system was divided into two parts:

a primary education of four grades and a secondary education including a *lycée*, technical schools, and teacher-training colleges. The transition between primary and secondary was made through a preparatory cycle of two years.

Another important characteristic of the colonial educational system was the emphasis on preprimary education. The objective of that level was to help the child adapt to the culture of the school. For various reasons, including a lack of resources, the Ministry of Education decided to abolish this level as a separate stage, preferring to include it as the first grade of primary school. This, according to SIDA (1982), also explains the big increase in enrollments in the first grade in 1976–77 when this scheme was introduced. Taking into consideration that the language of instruction—Portuguese—is a foreign language for the majority of the people, it seemed obvious that, in order to enable children to adapt themselves, there was a need for some kind of preparatory stage for them, independent of its formal name. At each of the other levels, the colonial system was highly selective and discriminatory. The function of the preparatory cycle was to prepare students for the *lycée*. In principle, the education in technical schools provides a better preparation for an active productive life, but in reality students graduated from them without an adequate preparation and were unable to integrate themselves into the economic life of the country. Finally, there was a teacher-training course, but it was so designed that very few actually succeeded in completing the training.

The whole situation imposed on PAIGC the necessity to make urgent structural changes in order to affirm not only its political, but also its cultural and economic, hegemony. The principles of the educational reform which are given below are based on the assumption that the content and shape of the education system should be in accordance with the political choices and principles laid down by the PAIGC and should be oriented towards the achievement of its objectives.

(a) Education should promote the complete development of an individual, in order that he or she can assess the choices open to him or her in the light of the principles laid down by the party.

(b) The democratization of education, whether understood as equality of access or as equality of opportunity for success, requires a reform of the whole system in terms of structure, organization, and administration.

(c) Education should incorporate all the positive aspects of traditional African knowledge, both through its research activities and through integration into the community.

(d) An adaptation of the programs and of teaching methods should be undertaken to fit reality and national needs.

Based on these principles, the Ministry of National Education introduced a series of reforms. The first was in the content of teaching: the curricula and textbooks which had been used in the liberated zones were adapted to the new reality of national Independence and introduced into the first four grades. Only later was there an attempt to change the overall structure of the education system. The following system was introduced:

(a) a first level of basic education with six grades;

(b) a second level with three years of schooling corresponding to general polyvalent education, postprimary professional training, and the training of primary teachers;

(c) a pre-university level: the training of secondary teachers and polytechnic education provided by the institutes.

It is important to underline that the first significant reform was the introduction of a new system of basic education with the ultimate objective of providing six years of free schooling for each citizen. In this way the old preparatory cycle, which had been part of secondary education, was transformed into a second cycle of basic education. Even more important was the new orientation given to basic education which was no longer seen as a preparation for the *lycée*, but rather for life outside school.

One other important feature is that the curricula for Grades 5 and 6 were developed scientifically. The objective of the second level of teaching is to prepare skilled personnel (both administrative and technical) so that in their productive life they will be able to carry responsibility for projects and tasks within the development programs.

3. The Formal System of Education

The educational system is divided into two main levels: primary and secondary. There are no universities in the country. Two technical schools cater for the further education of 594 students. Guinea-Bissau's illiteracy rate was about 68 percent in 1991. The country's 807 primary and secondary schools cater for a student population of just over 90,000. Spending on education amounted to 5.2 percent of the country's GNP.

3.1 Primary, Secondary, and Tertiary Education

Figure 1 presents an overview of the structure of education.

Elementary basic education lasts for four years. Of the total of 95,267 students attending all kinds of educational institutions in the country (1980 figures), more than 72,000 or 75 percent were in elementary basic education, which is compulsory. In 1992, only 54 percent of an age group entered elementary basic education.

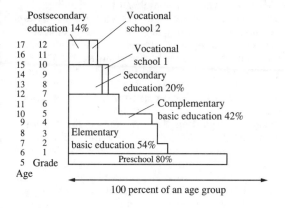

Figure 1
Guinea-Bissau: Structure of the formal education system

Complementary basic education lasts for two years. In 1977–78, there were 14 establishments at this level of education and in 1981 this number had increased to 21, of which four were in the Autonomous Sector of Bissau. A total of six more were created between 1982 and 1989. From 1977–78 to 1981–82, there was a total increase of 54 percent in the daytime (students) numbers. The number of female students increased by 84 percent. From 1977–78 to 1980–81, the number of teachers at this level of education increased by 89 percent leading to a decrease in the student–teacher ratio from 24:1 to 18:1. This relatively low ratio is due to the fact that each teacher teaches only 18 sessions a week and only in one subject. Despite the lack of reliable statistics, it is acknowledged that there is a perceived problem with regard to the number of teachers who are fully qualified. There are also no courses specifically designed for those teaching Grades 5 and 6.

Secondary education covers Grades 7 to 9 or 7 to 12 (in the case of postsecondary education). Since 1980 the number of teachers in secondary education has increased by 49 percent. The proportion of nationals in this number has increased from 51 to 76 percent. The National Lycée Kwame N'Krumah includes Grades 7 to 12, whilst the remaining *lycées* include only Grades 7 to 9. More than 50 percent of the pupils enrolled in secondary education go to the National Lycée Kwame N'Krumah.

Following Grade 9, there are only two "middle schools": the National School of Physical Education and Sport and the School of Law, both with approximately 80 entries per year. There is also a medical school (2 years) and a training college for secondary school teachers. University studies are undertaken outside the country.

While the number of students in Grades 5 and 6 and in secondary education has increased by about 46 percent since 1987–88, there has been a slight but steady decrease in enrollment in Grades 1 to 4 during the same period. This decrease can partly be explained by the fact that the rate of grade repetition has gone down. Furthermore, the decrease is concentrated among children above the age of 9. There is a slight increase in participation of children aged 6, 7, and 8, but even with these explanations the fact remains that the participation rate has decreased rather than increased. One reason for this could be the clash with the traditional culture with its age-stratified teaching–learning system and the modern school. Another reason might be the parents' skepticism toward the utility of the teaching given at the school. It is also the case that children are often needed to help in the family farming, a trend also seen elsewhere in the developing world (Leal Filho 1991).

The 1979 census showed that the average enrollment rate of children between the ages of 7 and 14 was 44 percent. There is large variation in access between the regions, between rural and urban areas, as well as between the sexes. The proportion of girls in primary school has been stable at about 33 percent since Independence.

The transition between Grades 4 and 5 is a critical stage since there is a dropout of 50 percent between the end of Grade 4 and the end of Grade 5. Those girls who do continue their studies usually remain in their home region, whilst most of the boys transfer to the city.

3.2 Preschool Education

With the objective of increasing the possibility for children to succeed in the first grade of basic education and, specifically, to facilitate their comprehension of Portuguese—the language of instruction—the Ministry of Education reinitiated preschool activities in 1979–80 for children aged 3 to 6. The number of children in preprimary education increased from 300 in 1979 to 419 in 1980, being more or less steady since then. Until the early 1980s, nearly all preprimary classes were concentrated in Bissau. Although the development of these activities was stressed in the program of the Provisional Government in 1981, there are still no resources for spreading the provision any wider. Plans are being developed in the Ministry for preschool education. These are expected to lay down the framework and correct orientations for those organizations which are meant to operate preschools in all areas of the country.

3.3 Special Education

There are registers of attempts to make provisions for those with special education needs. Education of the handicapped is nonetheless at an early stage in Guinea-Bissau, partially due to the lack of a systematic policy about such an issue and partially due to financial constraints. Some overseas development agencies are providing support to initiatives aimed at improving the educational provisions for the handicapped.

3.4 Vocational and Technical Education

Vocational training is divided into two levels: that offered to students who have completed Grade 6 and immediately seek a professional qualification (level 1), and that offered to those who complete Grade 9 and wish to study more specialized subjects (level 2) such as Law and Physical Education in the framework of postsecondary education which are also considered as "vocational" (Ramos 1992). In 1979, the Technical Institute for Professional Training (ITFP) was created. In this institute, courses of professional training lasting three years are provided for those graduating from Grade 6. Approximately 2,000 students took courses in civil construction and general mechanics at the Institute, which, since 1980, organizes intensive courses and upgrading courses in general mechanics (enrollment of 9–12 students per year), electricity (15–19 students), administration (26–31 students), civil construction (22–27 students), and rural mechanics (15–19 students). The Institute has also organized courses not only in Bissau, but in different regions of the country.

There is only one agricultural college in Guinea-Bissau: the residential school of the Comrades Institute in Boe. It offers a three-year course, taken after graduating from Grade 6, with an annual intake of approximately 100 students per year. Apart from this, there are provisions to train nurses in Bissau, Bolama, and Njala organized by the Ministry of Health. Applicants should at least have completed Grade 6 prior to being considered for admission.

Finally, there are also courses organized internally by the various factories and development projects. There does not appear to be any efficient coordination of these different types of technical education.

3.5 Adult and Nonformal Education

Since Independence, there has been a system of night courses for adults. These are run parallel to the normal daytime educational system. There has been a decrease in the number of adults in such courses for elementary basic education, but an increase in the numbers for secondary education courses. The numbers involved in literacy programs have not shown a similar development. In the first seven years of Independence, and until 1994, there have been many literacy projects. Due to a variety of difficulties, the results have not been very satisfactory. Of the approximately 4,000 students who enrolled initially in the culture circles, only a small percentage followed the programs and learned how to read and write successfully. As from 1982, literacy courses in Creole have started and learning materials are being prepared for literacy courses in other national languages.

4. Administrative and Supervisory Structure and Operation

The educational system of Guinea-Bissau is under the auspices of the National Ministry of Education and the Minister, who is a member of the Cabinet. The Ministry is divided into various sections which are responsible for planning and implementing education at various levels. A committee of inspectors appointed by the Ministry is responsible for ensuring that all work is properly conducted. In addition, individual schools have officials who are responsible for monitoring progress of students and for supervising the normal school routine.

Decisions regarding the structure of the teaching system at all levels are made by the Ministry of Education. The Commissariat of State for National Education and Culture, headed by the Minister of Education, provided for many years advice with regard to the structure of the teaching system and with regard to decisions related to the curriculum. In terms of time spent on various subjects at grade levels, there are the so-called "minimal provisions," nationally set; these provisions ensure that basic subjects such as maths, science, and Portuguese have a suitable proportion of school time and are in line with the existing policy of reducing illiteracy.

Both during the years of the liberation struggle and since Independence, PAIGC has viewed education as a basic human right, as a vehicle for integrating the individual with the surrounding society, and as a means for economic and social development. As such, the government is trying to ensure that the development of the education sector is in accordance with proper administrative and supervisory procedures, compatible with social and economic realities, and with the development goals.

5. Educational Finance

Official figures set the education budget at 300 million pesos (US$60,240) for the period 1990–91. This is the equivalent of just over 5 percent of the country's GNP. A considerable portion of the education budget comes from contributions from international donors and development agencies. Salaries and administration costs consume over 60 percent of the budget, leaving little money for investment in teacher training and improvements in school buildings.

In percentile terms, preprimary education and primary education consume over half of the educational budget. The rest, approximately 38 percent, is spent on secondary technical and vocational education. As over a quarter of the funds used in education originate from foreign agencies and over half the budget is spent on teachers' salaries, there are no reliable figures on the real cost per pupil at each level of education.

The planned investments in education decreased considerably over the 1980s, with an average of 3 to 4 million pesos decrease per year. This could be ascribed to a higher degree of realism on the part of government planning, given the known restrictions in the country's implementation capacity. The bulk of investments are financed through external assistance (grants and loans); domestic resources financed about 12 percent of the total. Of the foreign financial aid received, only a fraction was spent in Guinea-Bissau. Most of it was used to pay for the purchase of goods abroad and for training and technical assistance.

6. Supplying Personnel for the Education System

Guinea-Bissau suffers severe difficulties in the supply of personnel to occupy teaching positions, especially qualified teachers. Only 8 percent of teachers are qualified for the job (Rosengart 1981). Even though the prospect of a career in teaching means a lifetime job, not many people wish to enter the profession.

Recruitment of personnel is undertaken actively, but it is not an easy task. A small proportion of teachers working at the secondary level is composed of locals who went to study abroad, predominantly in Europe. The low wages and the difficulties faced in teaching combined with the shortage of teaching materials also represent obstacles for the regular supply of personnel for the education system. Santos (1988) indicated that only 9 percent of the teachers in elementary basic education in 1987 could be considered sufficiently qualified.

There are a variety of training and upgrading courses designed to improve the level of teachers. These have been implemented since the time of the National Liberation struggle. There are also the so-called "directed courses" providing on-the-job training for teachers without qualifications. The plan is to train more than 800 monitors or teachers by 1994.

There are also teacher-training colleges which have trained over 5,000 students over a ten-year period. In the first years (1977 to 1981), there were 630 teacher candidates. From 1982 onwards the Amilcar Cabral Teacher-training College has functioned as a residential institution with a capacity of about 200 teacher candidates.

In 1979–80, the pedagogical vanguard unit Chico Te was created with the aim of producing teachers for secondary education. This unit, which had designed a four-year training course, enrolled 67 students in 1979–80 and 109 in 1980–81, and has steadily enrolled new students since then. During the first few years there were many dropouts, but this has improved, especially since 1986. The Centers for Integrated Popular Education also train their own teachers and 38 graduated in 1979–80 and 58 in 1980–81. No other data are available.

There are also programs for upgrading teachers and, during the long vacation, the Ministry organizes 2–4 week courses in Bissau. At the end of the 1980s and early 1990s, more than 1,500 teachers took part in one or other of these courses. Finally, during the school year, there are study committees, which are groups of 12 to 25 teachers directed by an experienced teacher; these committees meet every two weeks and participation is obligatory.

7. Curriculum Development and Teaching Methodology

As mentioned earlier, curriculum development is overseen by a specialist group at the Ministry of Education. The National Institute for Educational Development also plays a key role in the execution of curricular policies. In terms of teaching materials, although a proportion of the materials used at schools is written locally by a working group, there are various teaching instruments which are adapted from foreign publications (especially from Guinea, Senegal, and Portugal). The teacher-training schools are regularly informed on educational developments and some staff provide assistance to the Ministry of Education. This is acknowledged as being a useful way to relate curriculum developments to the training of teachers and at the same time provide favorable conditions for realistic examinations.

Given that more than 80 percent of the population are peasant farmers, the curriculum is meant to cater for the rural reality of Guinea-Bissau, so that the students can be integrated into farming activities.

In 1992, national curricula still stressed topics and theoretical approaches which were rather too academic for students. The link between productive work and the improvement of the country's economic performance need to be improved. School-leavers do not seem motivated to remain in rural areas.

It has been suggested that the high dropout rate is a result of the content of the curriculum being heavy and detailed and not sufficiently related to the local environment. One other explanation is that the main language of instruction is Portuguese, which is spoken by only about 10 percent of the population.

There is a lack of interdisciplinary approaches in teaching. This may well be a consequence of the lack of qualifications of most teachers. However, efforts are being made to upgrade teachers. The few qualified teachers who do exist are being sent to the rural areas.

8. The System of Examinations, Promotions, and Certifications

The assessment system is based on a continuous monitoring of a student's progress throughout the years. This is done by the teachers themselves. Students are assessed monthly or quarterly and the cumulative results of these assessments are used to judge whether a student should proceed to the next class or not. Certificates are issued at the end of every school year and also after completion of a certain level (e.g., primary or secondary) of education. Successful students are awarded a diploma.

9. Educational Assessment, Evaluation, and Research

The availability of records on educational assessment and research is limited. The National Institute of Education started an evaluation research exercise in 1994. This is in line with the awareness at the Ministry of Education that these information needs should be met as soon as possible.

10. Major Reforms in the 1980s and 1990s

A school construction program is being carried out in rural areas. A considerable part of the investment budget is spent in the countryside, but a comparatively larger part of the current budget is spent in the urban centers where the complementary basic education class 5 to 6 schools and virtually all secondary education is located.

During the 1980s, adults were integrated into the education system in two ways: via evening classes parallel to the normal daytime courses and through literacy projects. Enrollment in evening courses increased for Grades 5 and 6, but decreased slightly for Grades 1 to 4.

Literacy remains the greatest challenge for the 1990s. Despite political declarations about the importance of literacy, the various projects have not been successful and very few participants have become literate.

In August 1981, a working group within the Ministry of Education presented a proposal for a new school system entitled "Bases for the Implementation of a National System of Education and Training" (SNEF). The text of this proposal starts with a critical analysis of the existing situation, encompassing both the problems of parents' motivation to send children to school and the difficulties of recruiting teachers. The proposal was approved at the 4th National Meeting of Professional Staff and the final decision concerning the reform of the educational system was made in late 1992. There are, in 1994, few signs that it has been fully implemented.

The proposal for reform implies a heavy investment in primary schools, adult education, and professional training, all of which are to be organized in a practical fashion. Each cycle of schooling should be considered as a complete and integral phase of education and not as a springboard to the next cycle. The official teaching program should be better adapted to the country's requirements and the whole educational system should be designed to reflect the intimate relation between theory and practice, education and work, and schooling and working life.

The *lycée*, in its existing form, is considered to be a colonial hangover and should be replaced by an education system which is professionally oriented toward specialities in various sectors. The SNEF report also discusses the possibility of distributing educational services among the population in a fairer way. This distribution should be accomplished by requiring work experience from students requesting entry to these higher levels of education, or through allocating fixed percentages of places to the different social groups. The SNEF also discussed a limit on the number of years which each student is allowed to repeat, suggesting a maximum of two, together with a maximum age of entry of 15 to the end of complementary basic education. Priority should also be given to literacy courses and occupational training for adults through intensive and frequent courses in the workplaces. These forms of literacy and postliteracy education should progressively substitute the parallel night schools to elementary basic education.

11. Major Problems for the Year 2000

In order to improve both its effectiveness and social role, the teaching system of Guinea-Bissau faces a number of challenges. First, it must overcome its primary difficulty, namely the lack of resources. More money should be invested in education as a whole in order to cater for long-lasting improvements. Second, there is a need for better materials and facilities, through which teachers may be able to reach their goals. Third, more effort is needed to provide systematic teachers-training programs, both preservice and inservice. It should be aimed at familiarizing teachers with the didactic resources and methods they may use in order to stimulate interest among students. Teachers' knowledge of their subjects should also be updated.

The fact that nationals need to go abroad to complement their education also needs to be addressed in the medium term. It is known that many bright and promising young people do not return. To address this problem, thought might be given to the foundation of a national university.

References

Leal Filho W D S 1991 *Environmental Problems and Structural Development in Africa: Cultural Challenge*. UNGLS, Geneva
Mazzolenis A 1991 *Almanaque Abril*. Abril, São Paulo
Ramos P 1992 Personal comment.
Rosengart G 1981 *Educacao na Guiné Bissau*. SIDA, Stockholm
Santos J dos 1988 *Indicativos educationais da Guiné Bissau*. (pamphlet.) Ministerio da Educacao, Bissau.
SIDA (Swedish Development Agency) 1982 *Education in Guinea-Bissau 1979–1981*. SIDA, Stockholm

Further Reading

de Sena L 1987 *Education et developpement rural: une experience d'integration de l'education en Guinee-Bissau*. IRDEF, Paris
SEPAEC 1987 Guiné-Bissau—sintese da situacao economica-financeira e perspectivas de médio prazo. SEPAEC, Bissau.

Haiti

C. Pierre-Jacques

1. General Background

Haiti is part of an island, the other part being the Dominican Republic, in the Caribbean. It is 90 kilometers from Cuba and 147 kilometers from Jamaica. It has an area of 27,000 square kilometers and its population density is 120 persons per square kilometer. In all, there are about 6.5 million inhabitants of whom 30 percent live in urban areas and 70 percent in rural areas. The average annual population growth rate in the period 1990–95 was 2 percent. However, 43.6 percent of the population is under the age of 15 and the demand for education is high. Having been a French colony, the language of instruction and administration in schools is French. The majority of the people speak Creole and the Creole-French issue is a major educational problem.

Forty years of dictatorship created a socioeconomic situation that resulted in waves of emigration. There were two types of emigrants: peasants who represented the so-called "boat people" who headed for Florida; and the professionals who went to Africa, the United States, and Canada thus depriving the Haitian education system of its higher cadres.

The social and economic conditions deteriorated rapidly from 1991 onward. The development projects initiated by the democratically elected government in February 1991 were all jeopardized by the coup d'état in September 1991.

The social system in Haiti is very heterogeneous. There are large social inequities particularly in the differences between the urban and rural populations. These differences (often unjust and harsh) also apply to the system of education. Economically, 5 percent of the population possesses 50 percent of the country's wealth. The ratio of the poorest to the richest incomes is 1:176 making this type of imbalance the highest in all of Latin America. Families of the privileged minority tend to send their children to European and North American schools for their education. Since the 1980s Haiti has become a typical example of a society unable to rise above a status of underdevelopment, a society in regression. At a United Nations meeting held in Paris in 1981, Haiti was the only Latin American country said to represent the "fourth world." Many things still indicate this status: agricultural production is insufficient for the needs of the population; there is famine in several regions of the country; and malnutrition is particularly serious among children of preschool age (75% suffer from it).

A 1992 report from the Inter-American Development Bank stated that "... only 31 percent of the population meets the recommended energy consumption and 50 percent the recommended protein consumption levels." The report also indicated that in general the incidence of malnutrition, at a rate of 27 percent, was much higher in Haiti than in other countries in the region (e.g., 12.8% in the Dominican Republic in 1986). The following facts give an impression of the economic situation and its social consequences: the trend of lower agricultural production has continued since 1991; the 1991 GDP had decreased by 0.7 percent since 1990 and by 1.4 percent since 1989; per capita production decreased from 199 in 1980 to 155.6 in 1991; an inflation rate of 20 percent in 1991 badly affected the purchasing power of the poorer sections of society; and finally, products that had previously been exported were consumed locally.

An economic and commercial embargo decreed by the international community in 1991 in order to force the military (responsible for the 1991 coup) to remit power to the constitutionally elected government, resulted in the following:

(a) a halt to exports resulting in unemployment;

(b) a partial halt to the import of primary materials;

(c) a budget deficit (a decrease in income and an increase in civil service expenditure);

(d) the suspension of international assistance.

In 1990, the last year for which official figures are available, per capita income was US$300 per year, primary school enrollment stood at 66 percent, life expectancy was 55 years, illiteracy was 66 percent, and 50 percent of the workforce was unemployed. Furthermore, the qualification level of the workforce was low.

In the same year, 63 percent of those in work were employed in agriculture, 11 percent in industry, and 26 percent in commerce and services. In the primary sector, 84 percent of those employed were illiterate, 14 percent had completed primary education, 0.1 percent college level, and 0.2 percent university. In the secondary sector, 38 percent were illiterate, 47 percent had completed primary education, 17.2 percent secondary education, 0.1 percent college level, and 1 percent university. In the tertiary sector, 55 percent were illiterate, 25 percent had completed primary education, 16.5 percent secondary education, 1.3 percent technical education, 0.9 percent college, and 0.9 percent university. In general, there was (and still is) a great dearth of technically qualified personnel, for example, engineers, medical doctors, and teachers.

Such a precarious socioeconomic situation has repercussions on the educational system which reflects the state of the country's structural underdevelopment.

2. Politics and Goals of the Education System

Since Independence in 1804 there has never really been a defined philosophy of education adapted to the social, economic, and cultural environment of the nation. Toward the end of the nineteenth century, and under the direction of the Catholic Church, it was conceived as a process of the internalization of norms and values and school was seen as everybody's main preoccupation in this process. Since the dominant social classes were, in effect, the state, a typical candidate for education would be a subject of the state and a future member of its serving personnel. France always "inspired" those responsible for the school system in their choice of policies and orientation. It was forty years later that Maurice Dartigue, a minister of education, who began to articulate an educational philosophy that was specifically Haitian but the political constraints at that time did not allow him to have much practical effect. Nevertheless, the basic ideas of Dartigue were taken up in the 1979 reform under the auspices of UNESCO and the World Bank. In the 1990 electoral campaign all political parties claimed to award education a prime role in the development of the country, insisting on the social role of education and the desirability of having an education system that responded to the needs of the community. The 1987 constitution obliged the State to guarantee the "right of education to all with emphasis on physical, intellectual, moral, vocational, social, and civic education."

3. The Formal System of Education

Figure 1 presents the structure of the Haitian school system. (The figure is approximate because of the shortage of statistical data. Further explanations are given in the text.)

3.1 Primary, Secondary, and Tertiary Education

Haiti has the lowest enrollment ratios in the Caribbean and Latin America. In 1990 it was 60 percent and there were large regional disparities (ranging from 41 to 77%). Urban–rural differences were large with some rural areas having an enrollment ratio of only 30 percent. The legal age of primary schooling is from 6 to 12 years. In 1991–92 enrollment in all primary schools (state and private) was 787,553. Of all schools, 75 percent were private and 25 percent state. Fifty-two percent of pupils were boys and 48 percent girls. Again, it must be noted that there are large regional and urban–rural differences.

In state primary schools the pupil–teacher ratio was 54:1 and the average class size was 55, but in rural areas these figures were 73:1 and 65. In private primary schools the figures were 36:1 and 39 in urban areas and 40:1 and 47 in rural areas.

The vast majority of private schools are run by religious organizations. Dropout and grade repetition rates are very high in primary education. In the school year 1987–88, the percentage dropout rates for Grades 1 to 6 were as follows: 24.2 at Grade 1, 23.1 at Grade 2, 26.8 at Grade 3, 29.2 at Grade 4, 29.2 at Grade 5, and 31.3 at Grade 6. Table 1 represents the percentage dropouts by grade for the period 1980–88. Of all children starting Grade 1 only 16 percent reach the end of primary school. The proportion of overage children in primary school is 72 percent in Grade 1 and 89 percent in the last grade.

Secondary education consists of seven grades. Of all secondary schools, 10 percent are state schools and 90 percent are private (33 *lycées* and 542 secondary schools). Nearly all of the schools are in urban areas, a fact that explains the difficulty experienced by rural children in accessing secondary schools. In 1991–92 there were 193,624 pupils enrolled in secondary education. In 1986–87 dropout and grade repetition rates were both high. Only about 7 percent of those entering secondary school reached the final grade without repeating at least one grade. At the beginning of secondary school 48 percent of pupils are girls but this falls to 36 percent in the last grade. An indication of dropout rates in both primary and secondary education runs as follows: out of 1,000 children about 900 enter

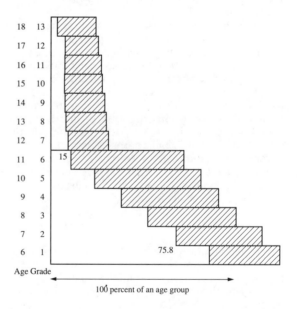

Figure 1
Haiti: Structure of the formal education system (approximate)

Table 1
Percentage primary school dropout rates, by grade—public and private sectors 1980–88

Year	1980–81	1981–82	1982–83	1983–84	1984–85	1985–86	1986–87	1987–88
CP1 (Grade 1)	7.5	12.1	20.1	1.7	4.6	2.9	28.6	24.2
CP2 (Grade 2)	3.7	14.3	9.3	3.2	10.5	9.7	29.7	23.1
CE1 (Grade 3)	4.0	12.9	6.3	6.0	17.2	15.7	25.8	26.8
CE2 (Grade 4)	3.3	16.2	8.4	10.2	17.4	15.7	18.5	29.2
CM1 (Grade 5)	-1.0	14.3	6.2	10.0	18.8	17.0	15.7	29.2
CM2 (Grade 6)	26.9	9.2	27.6	39.3	32.9	31.6	25.2	31.3

Grade 1; 245 reach the last grade of primary school; 128 enter the first grade of secondary school; 105 enter 11th grade; 26 Grade 12; and only 19 achieve the *baccalauréat* without repeating. Figures on enrollment in secondary education in the years 1980–89 are given in Table 2.

As far as higher education is concerned the State University of Haiti, operating under the Department of National Education, supervises both public and private tertiary education. Public institutions include the School of Law and Economics; the School of Medicine and Pharmacy; the School of Odontology; the School of Agronomy and Veterinary Medicine; the School of Human Sciences; the School of Ethnology; the School of Sciences; the Applied Linguistics Center; the Superior Normal School; and the National Institute of Administration, Management, and Advanced International Studies. All are located in Port-au-Prince. There are also three private centers for engineering and electronics. There are four private law schools operating under the supervision of the Faculty of Law and Economics at the State University. They are located in Cap Haïtien, Gonaives, Cayes, and Jérémie. Enrollment at the State University of Haiti in 1991–92 was about 6,300 students of whom 70 percent were boys (see Table 3).

From the mid-1980s there was a proliferation of private tertiary institutes primarily because the State University was not able to respond to the increased demand. The American University of Les Cayes, which teaches English has practically no Haitian students. In 1990 the University of Quisqueya was founded. This is a private university that had, in 1991, 400 students, 13 professors, and about 50 junior staff members. It has five faculties: sciences, agriculture and ecology, economics and administration, education, and a faculty of civil engineering. There is also the University of Roi Christophe in the north of the country with three faculties: medicine, engineering, and agriculture with a total enrollment of 100 students.

3.2 Preschool education

The preschool division within basic education at the Ministry of Education was created in 1982. Since 1989 this division has coordinated the program known as *Konesans se lespwa timoun* aimed at the education of parents of children up to 6 years of age. Of the 1.34 million children within that age range only a small minority (5%) attends preschool and this is due to the poor economic situations of most families. Since 1985 a large number of *jardins d'enfants* has appeared.

Table 2
Secondary education enrollment, by sex, and repeater rates—public and private sectors 1980–89

Year	1980–81	1981–82	1982–83	1983–84	1984–85	1985–86	1986–87	1987–88	1988–89
Girls	40,228	45,867	47,052	57,809	64,662	60,369	65,367	71,842	75,896
Boys	47,452	50,729	51,518	59,272	69,615	67,668	74,055	83,400	79,165
Total	87,680	96,596	98,570	117,081	134,277	128,037	139,422	155,242	155,061
Repeater rate (percentage)	—	12.5	7.7	3.4	3.7	16.9	16.2	6.7	8.9

In 1991–92, the private sector was responsible for 89 percent of children attending preschool.

3.3 Special Education

There is no formal structure of special education in he country. There are only four schools, sponsored by foreign religious missions that offer programs for handicapped children.

3.4 Vocational, Technical, and Business Education

Haiti has three nursing schools, one laboratory technicians' training school, and one medical helper school operating under the School of Medicine and Pharmacy. The College of Agronomy and Veterinary medicine supervises four agricultural vocational schools. The Department of National Education sponsors an intermediate school of geology and the Department of Social Affairs has a hotel training school. Following the 1979 educational reform, technical and vocational training was placed under the jurisdiction of the National Vocational Institute (*Institut National de Formation Professionelle*). In 1987–88, there were 3,600 students being trained in the areas of dressmaking, cabinet-making, shoemaking, electricity, mechanical fitting, metal construction, and the mechanics of sanitary installation. There were about 55 commercial and accounting schools. In 1991–92 there were six teacher-training colleges (four state and two private) with an enrollment of 1,091 students and with a staff of 113 members.

3.5 Adult and Nonformal Education

Because of the low rate of enrollment, nonformal education should play a major role in educational planning in Haiti. Both public and private bodies run nonformal education. Some provide general education with an emphasis on literacy; others stress community development; and yet others provide courses in technical subjects (agriculture, animal breeding, home economics, hygiene, etc.). The National Office of Literacy and Community Action is run by the Ministry of Education. Within Mission ALPHA (an offshoot of the Episcopal conference), 30,000 adults were taught to read in 125 centers from 1986–88. The Ministry of Social Affairs runs courses on syndicalism and related matters. The Ministry of Agriculture offers courses which deal with the technical aspects of such themes as the fight against erosion, reforestation, and animal breeding. Finally, the Ministry of Public Health and Population offers training programs in preventive medicine, public hygiene, birth control, and mother–child care.

4. Administrative and Supervisory Structure and Operation

The Ministry of Education, Youth and Sports (MENJS) is responsible for all government policies and public activities in education. The minister is aided by a cabinet of advisers and secretariat. In the Ministry there are the divisions of planning, inspection, educational support, personnel, and administration. There are nine regions each with ten districts and they are responsible for the day-to-day running of the educational system. In 1989–90 the private primary school organized themselves into the Haitian Education Foundation (*Fondation Haïtienne pour l'Etude Privée*). The Ministry of Education subsidises a certain number of private schools. The rectorate of the State University of Haiti reports to the Ministry of Education and is responsible for running all state tertiary institutions and, in theory, for supervising the private tertiary institutions.

5. Educational Finance

In the year 1989–90, 1.41 of the GNP was earmarked for education. This represented 20 percent of the state budget. The sum allocated for education was 192.3 million gourdes (US$38.5 million). The percentage allocation was: 9.5 for general administration, 60.6 for primary education, 12.6 for secondary education, 6.2 for technical education, 6 for tertiary education, 2 for literacy, and 2 for youth and sports.

Per capita expenditure on education was US$3.8. The state covers only 20 percent of the cost of education in the country. Parents cover 50 percent and a further 30 percent comes from external assistance. Many organizations such as UNDP, UNESCO, UNICEF, ILO, and the World Bank provide both financial and technical aid to the education system. The USA, France, and Canada have aid programs in Haiti.

Table 3
Enrollment at State University of Haiti, by sex 1981–90

Year	1981–82	1982–83	1983–84	1984–85	1985–86	1986–87	1987–88	1988–89	1989–90
Girls	1,273	1,247	—	1,399	1,446	—	—	—	1,933
Boys	2,672	2,724	—	3,494	3,255	—	—	—	4,345
Total	3,945	3,971	4,655	4,893	4,701	5,204	—	5,362	6,278

6. Supplying Personnel for the Education System

There are no studies that present a global view of the personnel in the system of education. Double employment makes it difficult to classify personnel in mutually exclusive categories. For example, secondary school inspectors often also work as teachers in *lycées* and colleges. Staff records are neither accurate nor updated; only 5,000 of the 13,700 employees are registered on the payroll. Thus, there are only fragmented data. In 1986–87 there were 23,900 teachers in primary education (8,200 in public schools and 13,800 in private schools). The figures for secondary schools were 1,093 in public schools and 6,827 in private schools—a total of 7,920. At the tertiary level there were 563 professors (478 men and 85 women) in eleven faculties; however, only 58 of the 563 work full-time. The number of women diminishes as one ascends the education hierarchy. At the primary level 49:8 percent of all teachers are women but this figure is only 15 percent at the tertiary level. Despite action that was taken in 1974 to improve conditions and standing of teachers in the society their situation in 1994 was very precarious. It is estimated that 300 teachers leave the profession each year.

7. Curriculum Development and Teaching Methodology

Apart from the teaching of Haitian literature and history the curriculum is entirely based on the French system of education. At the beginning of the 1980s an effort was made to introduce textbooks that better reflected the social reality of the Haitian pupil. However, textbooks produced and distributed by the private sector are mostly in French and this has been the case for many years. Given that private schools are attended mainly by urban children of wealthier parents this situation has exacerbated the disparity in communication skills. At the secondary school level all textbooks are imported from France. At the tertiary level there are both American and French books. Few schools use active teaching methods, so that memory plays a key role in instruction. The schools use frontal teaching with the teacher lecturing to passive pupils. There was resistance to the use of Creole as the medium of instruction because parents perceived it as an attempt to lower the standards of education. Only a few elite schools have science laboratories. In general, didactic material is either rudimentary or nonexistent.

8. The System of Examinations, Promotions, and Certifications

The evaluation of learning is based exclusively on what pupils can remember. This is even the case in science where it could be argued that it is practical and laboratory work that is important. The primary studies examination (CEP) was abolished under the reform so that there is no longer any uniform method of evaluating what pupils have learned. At the secondary school level the Ministry of Education organizes the *baccalauréat* exams (first and second parts) twice a year. If they are passed a pupil receives a diploma. At the university level most faculties organize examinations in July, the end of the academic year. It is possible to retake these examinations in September. Upon the successful completion of a cycle of studies the faculty issues a diploma that is sanctioned by the Ministry of Education.

9. Educational Assessment, Evaluation, and Research

There are both units of evaluation and research at the Ministry of Education. Given the competition of external agencies, especially UNESCO and the World Bank, a number of studies have been undertaken: for example, enrollment rates, urban rural disparities, the conditions of teachers, literacy, etc.

The evaluation of the effects of the 1980 reform was the responsibility of the National Institute of Education. Research at the university level is rudimentary in that only three of the eleven faculties have small research units and all of them are dependent on external funding.

10. Major Reforms in the 1980s and 1990s

The early 1980s witnessed an awakening of the national conscience toward Haitian educational problems. In the mid-1970s there were criticisms of the humanist approach to education and a movement toward the "developmental" approach which perceived education as an investment for the future development of the country. It was deemed that the Haitian system of education had failed in terms of its organization, management, productivity, and pedagogy. A 1974 UNESCO report based on two years of work financed by the Canadian International Development Agency (CIDA) pointed to the quantitative and qualitative deficiencies of the system. It was on the basis of such reports that the Minister of Education, Joseph Bernard, launched his reform. The reform was based on the following principles:

(a) Education should be a global process.

(b) Education should be aimed at economic development.

(c) Education should promote democracy and class equity.

The purposes of the reforms were:

(a) extending basic primary education to the whole of the teachable school-age population;

(b) reforming secondary school teaching in order to adapt it to national realities;

(c) developing teaching techniques;

(d) orienting university education toward research and the training of highly competent cadres in the technical and scientific fields;

(e) extending the extracurricular educational system;

(f) reinforcing the institutional structures and rationalizing the administration of the system;

(g) improving school achievement and teaching standards.

From 1982–86 school building was undertaken; pre- and inservice training of teachers was reformed, the number of places in teacher-training colleges was increased; and an evaluation of nonqualified teachers was initiated. The language policy was revised and both Creole and French were taught from Grade 1 onward. Despite these initiatives there were difficulties in the reform being implemented. The Haitian government faced formidable problems of a financial and managerial kind. At the same time, there was considerable opposition to the introduction of Creole as a language of instruction. The privileged social classes who supported the traditional form of education perceived the introduction of Creole as an attempt to diminish the influence of French and the privileges that went with it; the lower social classes perceived it as a way of never letting them learn French and hence depriving them of the means of being able to climb the social ladder.

All of this resulted in the "reform" being only partly implemented. Only 9.5 percent of children in private primary schools and 25 percent of those in public primary schools are enrolled in schools affected by the reform. Furthermore, the participation rates in the reform schools varies from region to region: in the south, southeast and the Grande Anse, it is 20 percent while in the west and in Port au Prince it is 11.2 percent. It is the destiny of this reform (which has already cost a lot in human and financial resources) that constitutes the fundamental problem faced by the system of education in the years to come.

11. Major Problems for the Year 2000

Before turning to the problems to be faced until the year 2000 it must first be stated that the coup d'état of 1991 has considerably aggravated the situation. The political repression and the international embargo caused irreparable damage to the system both in terms of the quality of education and access to education

particularly of the underprivileged groups. Not only did the different *de facto* governments since the coup have no educational policy but they took steps that will affect the system for years to come. For example, they re-employed incompetent civil servants that had already been dismissed by the legitimate government, increased without reason the number of civil servants, and closed the teacher-training colleges for secondary school teachers. Senior members of the universities left their posts and international aid, representing 30 percent of the expenditure on education was stopped.

From the above, it is clear that the educational system has nearly insurmountable financial and human resource problems to face as the year 2000 approaches. Five major problems can be identified.

Illiteracy. The illiteracy rate in Haiti is 75 percent. This is an anachronism in the Caribbean and Latin American region. It reflects a system where the interests of the privileged group work against the interests of the majority of the population and of the nation. Illiteracy is the major problem.

Insufficient resources allocated to education. The lack of resources for education is an obstacle for the efficient running of the educational system. It must be borne in mind that the army and defense receive twice as much money as education and the priority accorded by the state to education might well be queried.

Lack of productivity of the system. The third major problem to be resolved by the Haitian society is the lack of productivity of the educational system. Despite an increase in the educational budget and considerable external aid in the 1980s, instructional delivery did not improve because of a lack of inservice training and inadequate instructional materials such as books.

Inadequacy or lack of training of teachers and other educational personnel. Official requirements for teaching are ten years of formal education; however, about 80 percent of rural teachers and 33 percent of urban teachers did not possess this level in the early 1990s. In 1988 about 50 percent of secondary school teachers had inadequate training (university diploma or a qualification from the secondary teacher-training institute).

Urban–rural disparities. Whether it be the pupil–teacher ratio, enrollment ratio, illiteracy rate, or the quality of school buildings and resources, schools in urban areas always have a distinct advantage over schools in rural areas. This disparity is reflected in the financial allocation to the different regions. Nearly 80 percent of all educational expenditure goes to urban areas where only 30 percent of the population lives; by definition only 20 percent of the resources are allocated to rural areas where 70 percent of the population lives.

The educational problems of Haiti can only be solved in the long run in a just and human society which places education within a strategy of economic and social development.

Bibliography

Alexis J E, Larose S, Morin C, Pierre-Jacques C, Louis E 1989/90 *Université et Développement en Haiti*. Editions CIDIHCA et Henri Deschamps, Montreal and Port au Prince

Bourdon J, Perrot J 1990 *Analyse économique du secteur de l'éducation*. Projet Haiti/PNUD/UNESCO—Education pour le dévelopement. IREDU, Université de Bourgogne

Commission gouvernementale du gouvernement constitutionnel 1993 *Etat du système d'éducation et actions prioritaires pour relancer le secteur*. Port au Prince

Inter-American Development Bank 1992 *Socioeconomic Report—Haiti*. Inter-American Development Bank, Washington, DC

Ministère de l'éducation nationale de la jeunesse et des sports 1988 *Annuaire Statistique 1985–1986*. MENJS, Port au Prince

Ministère de l'éducation nationale de la jeunesse et des sports 1991 *Politique Educative*. Port au Prince

Pierre-Jacques C et al. 1987 *Rapport final de la mission d'évaluation de la réforme éducative en Haiti*. Geneva

Poster R C, Valdam A (eds.) 1984 *Haiti—Today and Tomorrow: An Interdisciplinary Study*. University Press of America

World Bank 1994 *Statistical Yearbook for America and the Caribbean*. Johns Hopkins University Press, Baltimore, Maryland

Honduras

A. L. de Valle

1. General Background

The Republic of Honduras is one of the smallest countries in Latin America. It has an area of 112,088 square kilometers and had a population of 4,443,721 in 1988. The average annual growth rate was 3.4 percent (but 4.5% in rural areas) in the period 1974 to 1989. The population density is 39 people per square kilometer. Just over 60 percent of the population lives in rural areas, primarily in the departments of Francisco Morazan (Tegucigalpa) and Comayagua and Cortes (San Pedro Sula), known as the "central corridor." About 2.5 million persons live in villages of less than 1,000 people. This hampers the integration of the population into the development process of the nation.

There is an equal number of females and males and 46.8 percent of the population is less than 15 years of age. In 1988 nearly 50 percent of the population aged 10 years or more was considered economically active while in 1974 it was 44 percent. In the same period female participation rose from 13 to 21 percent. This was, in part, due to the improved status of women in the society but was also due to the deterioration of the economic situation and the significant drop in real income for men.

At the beginning of the 1980s, the increase in the size of the available labor force was faster than the number of jobs available; in the period 1980–86 the labor force (15 to 65 years of age) increased by 20 percent, but employment increased only by 13 percent and many of the economically active population could not be absorbed by the economy.

In the early 1990s, Honduras was experiencing an economic crisis. In the 1980s production had a lower rate of growth than the population increase; in 1980, population growth was about 3.4 percent, while economic growth in the period 1980 to 1987 was about 1.4 percent and per capita income decreased. The per capita income is one of the lowest in Latin America and there are problems about the basic needs of the poor being met. In 1988 about 1.5 million people were deemed to be extremely poor and another million could not satisfy their basic needs.

This extreme poverty is accompanied by a high rate of illiteracy, deficient medical care in the rural and marginal urban areas, increasing lack of housing, and high rates of unemployment. At the same time, the possibility of integrating all the economically active population into the formal economic sector is not very promising. An indicator of poverty is that the average annual per capita income dropped from US$526 in 1986 to US$177 in 1990 when the Structural Adjustment Program was initiated. However, these indicators are relative considering that in 1988 the richest 20 percent of the population had 60 percent of the total family income.

In the period 1979 to 1990, the Gross Domestic Product (GDP) increased, on average, by 1.9 percent—clearly lower than the 8.8 percent in the period 1976 to 1979. The GDP declined throughout the period 1979 to 1990 with an accompanying deterioration in the average standard of living. The national economy is subject to the external fluctuations of demand for and prices of its main exports such as bananas and coffee, which represent 80 percent of all exports. Irrigation, fisheries, and agriculture account for 60 percent of the GDP. However, only 6 percent of students receive formal training for agriculture. There is great demand for training in the service sector, where the market is saturated. The migration from the rural areas to the cities has created a great demand for basic services in the social sector (health, housing, and education) and infrastructure (drinking water, electricity, drainage, access, and transport). Despite large government efforts much remains to be done. All of these factors have created a socio-economic situation which limits the development of a sound educational system.

2. Politics and the Goals of the Education System

Compulsory education (ages 7 to 13) provides a basic education aimed at engendering scientific and rational attitudes to natural and social phenomena; skills that will contribute to the economic and social development of the country; hygienic habits that will conserve and improve health; and social habits for the development of the family, good citizenship, and democratic values. Middle level education is a continuation of primary education and aims at preparing young people for careers and for further education.

The following statements are taken from the educational laws and are indicative of the goals of education:

(a) Education is an essential function of the government in order to conserve, promote, and diffuse culture and benefit the society without any discrimination. The national system of education will be of long duration and will be based on the essential principles of democracy. It will instill among the students strong feelings of affinity with Honduras, and should be directly linked to the social and economic development process of the country.

(b) Parents will have the right to choose the type of education that their children will have.

(c) The government is obliged to develop basic education for all people and to create the necessary administrative and technical organization under the direction of the Secretary of Public Education.

(d) All education officially provided by the government will be free, and basic education, besides being compulsory, will be totally paid for by government.

3. The Formal System of Education

The educational system of Honduras consists of the following: preprimary, primary, and lower and upper secondary education. All of these are directed and supervised by the Secretary of Public Education (SEP). Higher education is coordinated by the National Autonomous University of Honduras (UNAH). Fig. 1 presents the overall structure of the system.

3.1 Primary, Secondary, and Tertiary Education

According to the Honduran constitution, primary education is compulsory and free. It covers the ages of 7 to 13 years. A high priority is placed on this level of education. In 1980 just over 83 percent of children of the appropriate age group were in school and by 1990 this had risen to 85 percent. In 1980 there was a total of 5,517 schools (5,351 governmental and 166 private) while in 1990 there were 7,704 schools (7,388 governmental and 516 private). The majority of these schools are located in rural areas and consist mainly of only one classroom. In 1990 there was a shortage of 1604 classrooms and 137,653 desks. This problem is being solved with the aid of the Honduran Social Fund (FHIS).

A total of 16,385 teachers were employed during 1980 at this level and 25,118 in 1990. The student–teacher ratio was 37:1 in 1980 and 35:1 in 1990. In the past a good percentage of teachers were not qualified, but by 1990 this had fallen to only 5 percent. The attrition rate in primary school is about 4 percent which is considered appropriate. However, 13 percent of students have to repeat a grade.

Middle level education is a continuation of the primary level and lasts for three years (ages 14 to 16). This level of education is divided into two cycles: the common cycle and the diversity cycle. The first is directed and supervised by the General Directory of Middle Education and the second by the General Directory of Technical Education. The diversified cycle follows immediately after the completion of the common cycle.

The common cycle consists of four programs: (a) general, (b) industrial, (c) polyvalent, and (d) technical. The general program provides the student with a basic general culture, gives some vocational orientation, and develops the basic knowledge and skill to be able to function effectively in society and continue studying in any of the branches of the diversified cycle.

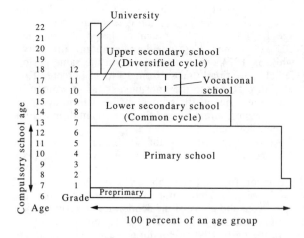

Figure 1

Honduras: Structure of the formal education system

The industrial program provides a general technical training based on a curriculum that involves practical skills in laboratories and workshops. Upon completion of three years of the industrial program a student may continue to the diversified technical cycle or undertake courses for qualified labor.

The polyvalent common cycle provides students with the general content of the curriculum of the general program and also with basic technical skills which will enable them to acquire employment in the labor market. Upon completion of this program students can subsequently choose a technical speciality in the diversified cycle should they decide to study for the technical baccalaureate.

The technical program provides students with the knowledge and basic abilities required for handling tools and should equip them to enter the job market.

The diversified cycle provides courses leading to certificates for practicing a profession or undertaking higher education studies. There are several different areas.

Normal education trains primary education teachers, and is coordinated by the Middle Education General Directory through the Department of Normal and Artistic Education. The curriculum has a three-year duration after completion of the common cycle. There are 12 normal schools throughout the country, 11 of them governmental and one semigovernmental. There is also the National School of Arts which trains teachers in the visual arts. In 1987 it had 119 students. Music education is provided in three institutions. Of these only the National School of Music trains teachers in music education and the other two accept students who have completed six grades of primary education. Normal education trains 4,000 teachers each year.

The diversified cycle also includes a program culminating in the baccalaureate. Courses can last from two to three years. Students are prepared either to continue their studies in higher education or to enter the labor market. Students may select their areas of interest such as arts and sciences, social work, administration management, industrial technical subjects, agriculture, or artistic education. This diversification allows young people to broaden their employment opportunities and also provides a better-trained workforce for both public and private organizations.

The diversified cycle also includes courses for careers such as: accountancy, secretarial work, practical agriculture, and work as a practical industrial technician. There are also institutes for dress design and dressmaking and beauty and cosmetology. These are private organizations but their programs are approved by the Secretary of Public Education.

The enrollment of 14- to 19-year olds in diversified courses was 27.6 percent of the age group. In the period 1980 to 1989 middle level enrollment increased by 8 percent and technical education by 29.2 percent. This increase was due to the fact that the number of free courses increased and also because there was an increase in interest in such courses in order to participate in the labor market. The enrollment of 14- to 19-year olds in both middle and diversified education was 47.8 percent in 1989. Most students are enrolled in state schools but the proportion in the private sector is increasing.

The student–teacher ratio was 29:1 in 1980 and 23:1 in 1990, but the main problem is that the majority of the teachers rely upon practical experience and have neither completed nor satisfied requirements as graduate teachers, and thus, the quality of teaching process is deficient.

Enrollment in higher education increased by 5 percent in the period 1980 to 1990. In 1990 41 percent of the students were female. There are five main institutions of higher education. The Central American Technology University was founded in 1986 and in 1990 had an enrollment of nearly 1,000 students. It offers technical courses. The Honduran National Autonomous University offers 35 different undergraduate courses and 14 graduate courses on its three campuses using distance education procedures. Its enrollment was nearly 33,000 students in 1990. It is criticized for having low academic quality and high costs, and for allowing students to take too long to graduate. The private University of Jose Cecilio del Valle, founded in 1977, is run by the Honduran Association for Promoting Higher Education (AHFES) which is a private, nonprofit, nonpolitical body. It offers academic and technical training. Its enrollment was 423 students in 1990. The University of San Pedro Sula has seven faculties in the service sector. The National Pedagogic University "Francisco Morazan" was founded in 1989. Before that, it was the Superior School for Teachers. It has a school of humanities and a school of sciences and technology. It has two campuses and trains teachers for all levels of the school system, but mainly for the upper secondary level.

In general, there is an overproduction of graduates in the humanities. Most faculty members are part-time (half-day, or hourly), a condition that is widely assumed to have negative effects on the teaching and learning process.

3.2 Preschool Education

Preprimary education comes under the direction and supervision of the General Directorate of Primary Education and covers children aged 4–6 years. Its purpose is to contribute to the child's psychological, physical, and social development with special emphasis on the learning of good attitudes and behaviors that will help the child in primary school. Preprimary education is organized into three cycles: prekindergarden (children of 4–5 years of age), kindergarden (5–6 years of age), and preparatory (6–7 years of age). The enrollment rate increased from 9 percent of the age group in 1980 to 12.4 percent in 1990. In order to increase enrollment, a total of 395 new nonformal preschool centers (CEPENF) were established. In 1990, over 442 community centers for scholar initiation (CCIES) were opened and enrollment rose to 16.2 percent of the age group. In 1990, there were just over 1,700 teachers. The student–teacher ratio was 40:1 in the first year and 33:1 in the last year of preschool education.

3.3 Vocational, Technical, and Business Education

Lower level vocational education takes place at the common cycle level, the more advanced and technical at the diversified level, and advanced technical and business education at the university level, as described above.

3.4 Adult and Nonformal Education

There are more than 150 nongovernmental organizations (NGOs) operating in the country. They provide training in agricultural development, marketing, community organization, health, and other programs. Some of these programs operate in coordination with governmental institutions which are mainly concerned with literacy and adult education.

For adult education for vocational and technical training and retraining there is the National Institute for Professional Training (INFOP). In 1990 its training programs were focused on commerce and services (49%), the industrial sector (26%), and the agricultural sector (25%). In the period 1980 to 1990 it trained a total of 332,102 people. At the same time there are 19 vocational education centers functioning throughout the country. There are also other institutions that have developed training courses in different areas of the country. Most of the ministries (Natural Resources, Health, Labor, Education, Social Welfare, etc.) operate their own programs. However, this is usually done in coordination with NGOs and other institutions.

4. Administrative and Supervisory Structure and Operations

The educational system of Honduras is regulated by administrative procedures established by the government. Education from preprimary to upper secondary education (diversified cycle) is controlled by the Ministry of Public Education. Higher Education is coordinated by the National Autonomous University of Honduras. All the educational levels are directed and supervised by the Secretary of Public Education, who is responsible for different decisions at different levels, through the Directors of Primary Education, Middle Education, and Technical Education.

The following legal points are of interest:

(a) Formal education is under one set of legislation.

(b) The University of Honduras is a governmental autonomous institution with its own legal capacity and has the exclusive right to organize, direct, and develop higher and professional education. The government contributes to support the National University with an annual allocation of not less than 6 percent of the net income of the Republic, excluding loans and donations.

(c) Teacher training is a function and exclusive responsibility of the government.

(d) Teachers working in primary schools are exempt from all kind of taxes on earned salaries.

5. Educational Finance

The government of Honduras is responsible for financing all public educational centers in the country. The financing is accomplished primarily through yearly budget allocations to the Ministry of Education. In 1992 the government allocated a total of approximately 683 million Lempiras (US$108 million) to the Ministry of Education and this was 14 percent of the state budget. Since 1980, the budget assigned to education averaged a 10 to 15 percent yearly increase. A total of 310 million Lempiras (US$49 million) (45 %) are devoted to the primary level, and 73 millions (11%) to the middle level.

Higher education is financed mainly by the Honduran National Autonomus University, which receives, from the government yearly, an allocation of 4 percent of the total operational budget.

6. Supplying Personnel for the Educational System

The teaching personnel engaged in the educational system (both public and private) are supplied mainly by the government through the Ministry of Education. Primary level teachers are prepared in four regional institutions located in Tegucigalpa, Danli, La Esperanza, Intibuca, and La Paz. Middle level teachers are prepared in the National Pedagogic University "Francisco Morazan." There is a shortage of teachers due mainly to lack of funding for buildings and salary payments.

The upgrading of the knowledge and skills of teachers is achieved through regional seminars, workshops, and intensive short courses developed every year by the Ministry of Education. Each participant is individually evaluated and, upon completion, a certificate is issued.

7. Curriculum Development and Teaching Methodology

The system of education has a commonly prescribed core curriculum for each level of education and is developed by the Ministry of Education. Curricula for higher education are developed by the Academic Council of the National University.

The Ministry of Education issues to each institution formally approved syllabuses of study containing the objectives (goals for student behavior), content allocation, intensity (theory and practice hours), and teaching methodology. The curriculum is uniform nationwide and is supervised by personnel from the Ministry of Education by periodic visits to the institutions.

Learning materials such as textbooks, manuals, and modules are usually prepared or written by experienced teachers and submitted to the Ministry of Education for approval. These materials are disseminated through public bookstores at reasonable prices. In some cases, Ministry of Education personnel recommend foreign books from neighboring countries. These are also made available through local bookstores but at higher prices.

English is the only foreign language officially included in the curriculum. Private institutions are allowed to teach other languages such as French and German, but English is the most popular. A commonly prescribed curriculum for urban and rural areas is actually hampering rural development since children generally only complete three grades of primary school and when they are 10 years old start to work with their parents in agricultural activities. The lack of simple audiovisual equipment and materials is a problem affecting the teaching and learning process.

8. The System of Evaluations, Promotions, and Certifications

The decision as to whether a pupil is to be promoted to the next grade or level of primary schooling is based on regular bimonthly examinations with approval given to students with grades from 60–100 percent. Grades from 40–59 percent are "not approved." This implies that the pupil must take an additional examination. During the year the pupil has four opportunities to be finally promoted. Pupils obtaining grades from 0–39 percent are considered totally deficient, and with two failures of this type, they must remain in the same grade next year.

At the secondary level the same scale of grading in bimonthly examinations is also used, but pupils have only two opportunities to be finally promoted at the end of the year, after the regular final examinations have been completed.

A certificate is issued to each primary pupil upon finishing each year of schooling stating whether he or she has been approved or disapproved. A certificate is issued to secondary level students who have satisfactorily completed the three years of the common cycle. This certificate makes them eligible in order to continue studies in the diversified cycle (e.g., teaching, computation, business education, vocational schools, baccalaureate). Another certificate is issued for students who have completed the diversified cycle. All of these certificates are terminal, except those issued for the Baccalaureate because these students generally continue studies at university level.

In order to improve the quality of the students it would be convenient to raise the minimum approval grade from 60 to 65 percent and eliminate additional examinations.

9. Educational Assessment, Evaluation and Research

The educational system has no provision for educational assessment, evaluation, or research. Only a few research projects mainly in physics, biology, basic sciences, and commercial education have been conducted in the schools at the primary and secondary level. This is due mainly to lack of adequate laboratories and materials. Available funds for such activities are very limited.

10. Major Reforms in the 1980s and 1990s

There were no major reforms in the educational system during the 1980s or at the beginning of the 1990s.

11. Major Problems for the Year 2000

The country has a small qualified labor force, but education has not provided sufficient qualified human resources for the economy. The technological area needs more people in intermediate positions in order to accelerate industrial development. Only a very small percentage of students complete studies at the university level. Attrition rates have increased and young people who leave the educational institutions are incorporated into the labor market but are underclassified as well as underpaid.

One major problem is the need to establish more teacher-training institutions in order to prepare a greater number of people at the primary level.

Yearly allocations from the government to the Ministry of Education will have to be increased if new schools are to be built and more teachers hired.

A complete revision of the curricula of the different levels (including higher education) should be undertaken in order to make them more adequate for the preparation of well-qualified personnel for the labor force.

Bibliography

Secretaria de Planificación Económica, Ministerio de Hacienda y Crédito Público. Tegucigalpa, M.D.C., Honduras

Secretaria de Education Publica, Tegucigalpa, M.D.C., Honduras

Universidad Autónoma de Honduras, Tegucigalpa, M.D.C., Honduras

Hong Kong

M. Bray

1. General Background

The territory of Hong Kong comprises the island of Hong Kong, a number of other islands, and part of the Chinese mainland. The island of Hong Kong became a British colony in 1842. The territory was subsequently enlarged by addition of sections of the mainland and neighboring islands. The greatest enlargement occurred in 1898, when colonial authorities took a 99-year lease of an area known as the "New Territories." The implications of this lease, which would require the reversion of Hong Kong to Chinese sovereignty in 1997, were perhaps underestimated at the time. Because in the twentieth century the boundaries between the New Territories and the rest of Hong Kong had become indistinct, it became clear to negotiators in the 1980s that sovereignty of the whole territory would revert (i.e., including parts that had been ceded "in perpetuity"). Hong Kong has a land area of just 1,071 square kilometers.

The population of Hong Kong is approximately six million. Almost 98 percent are Chinese, for the majority of whom Cantonese is the mother tongue. Among the remainder, the largest groups are from the Philippines, the United Kingdom, the United States, and the Indian subcontinent. Most primary schooling and much secondary schooling is conducted in Cantonese. The majority of other schools are English medium, though schools also operate in French, Japanese, and other languages for children of expatriates.

At the end of the Second World War, the population was a mere 600,000. However, the return of many people who had left the territory during the Japanese occupation raised the population to 1.8 million at the end of 1947. Hong Kong subsequently received many immigrants from China, especially following the takeover of its communist government in 1949. In the 1980s, however, the Hong Kong authorities began to impose stringent immigration controls. These reduced the average annual growth rate to 1.3 percent and, among other effects, reduced pressure on education facilities.

Census data reveal aspects of human capital as reflected in educational qualifications. In 1961, only 13 percent of the population aged 15 and over had attained upper secondary or higher qualifications. A mere 2.4 percent were graduates. By 1991, respective figures were 44 and 5.9 percent. Gender disparities were indicated by the fact that 7.2 percent of males and 18.2 percent of females over 15 years of age had received either no schooling at all or only kindergarten education.

The bulk of Hong Kong's population lives in urban areas. Pressures on space require schools to have constricted playgrounds, and 60 percent of primary schools are bisessional. However, the territory still has a rural periphery with some two-teacher schools and multigrade classes.

Economically, Hong Kong is well-known for its high rates of growth. In company with Taiwan, South Korea, and Singapore, Hong Kong is known as one of the four "Asian Dragons." In 1991, Hong Kong was estimated to have a per capita Gross Domestic Product (GDP) of US$16,400. The economic growth has greatly facilitated expansion of education.

Because of its limited natural resources, Hong Kong has depended on imports for virtually all food, fuels, and capital goods. In 1992, the total volume of visible trade (comprising domestic exports, reexports, and imports) amounted to 254 percent of the GDP. Agriculture and fishing contributed only 0.3 percent to the GDP. Manufacturing contributed 16.7 percent, while commerce, restaurants, and hotels contributed 24 percent. Finance, insurance, real estate, and business services contributed 20.6 percent.

It was decided in 1984 that Hong Kong would remain a British colony until 1997, and then become a Special Administrative Region (SAR) of the People's Republic of China. The Governor is advised by an Executive Council consisting of various ex officio and appointed members. Legislation, including that on finance and schools, is enacted by the Legislative Council.

2. Politics and the Goals of the Education System

The colonial education system in the immediate postwar period was highly selective and elitist. It served mainly to provide the small public and international sectors of the economy with necessary bilingual labor. Although many Chinese-medium schools operated at both primary and secondary levels, the fact that all tertiary education was in English obstructed advancement from Chinese-medium institutions. Many competent pupils from these schools went directly into family businesses instead of further education (Sweeting 1993, Morris and Sweeting 1991).

During the 1960s and 1970s, this situation changed markedly. The establishment of the Chinese University of Hong Kong in 1963 provided an apex to the Chinese-medium school system. Also, the population became increasingly aware of the financial benefits to be gained from tertiary education. Pressure to expand provision at all levels led the government in 1971 to make six years of primary education compulsory. Three years of junior secondary education were made free in 1978 and compulsory in 1979. The 1980s and early 1990s brought rapid expansion of tertiary education.

Nevertheless, the goals of education were shaped within a colonial context. Students were not encouraged to develop national pride, for example, though major changes were initiated when it became clear that sovereignty of Hong Kong would return to China in 1997.

The framework for the Special Administrative Region was set out in a Basic Law in 1990. Concerning education, the Law (Governments of Hong Kong/China 1990 p. 47) states that:

> On the basis of the previous educational system, the Government of the Hong Kong Special Administrative Region shall, on its own, formulate policies on the development and improvement of education, including policies regarding the educational system and its administration, the language of instruction, the allocation of funds, the examination system, the system of academic awards and the recognition of educational qualifications.

It remains to be seen how far the Hong Kong SAR will actually operate autonomously. Some tensions in the education sector during the transitional period are analyzed in Postiglione and Leung (1992).

3. The Formal System of Education

3.1 Primary, Secondary, and Tertiary Education

The structure of formal education is shown in Fig. 1,

and enrollment figures for 1993–94 in Table 1. Primary schooling begins at the age of six, and lasts for six years. Maximum class size is 45 pupils in ordinary classes, or 35 pupils in classes with activity methods. About 40 percent of classes use activity methods in primary grades 1–3. The typical primary school has 24 classes and a pupil–teacher ratio of 26:1. Each teacher specializes in three subjects, and any class on an average school day would be taught by two to four different teachers.

Secondary schools offer a five-year course in the broad range of academic subjects leading to the Hong Kong Certificate of Education Examination (HKCEE). The majority of institutions are grammar schools, though some are named technical or prevocational schools. Out of the 448 secondary schools existing in 1994, only 22 were technical schools and 23 were prevocational schools. Prevocational schools must devote at least 40 percent of the curriculum to technical subjects. However, no such requirement is placed on secondary technical schools, and in practice their curricula strongly resemble those of grammar schools. Secondary teachers usually specialize in one to two subjects, so each class is likely to be taught by six or more different teachers a week. The typical secondary school has 24 to 30 classes, with about 40 pupils per class. The overall pupil–teacher ratio is about 22:1 in government and aided schools, and 31:1 in private schools.

Candidates for the HKCEE may enter a two-year sixth form course leading to the Advanced-level examination to prepare for admission to the universities and polytechnics. Since 1992, this course has been available in prevocational schools as well as at grammar and secondary technical schools.

At the primary level, about 6 percent of pupils attend government schools, 84 percent attend government-aided institutions, and 10 percent attend private schools. Comparable figures for the secondary level are 9 percent, 79 percent, and 12 percent. While most of the private primary schools are prestigious institutions,

Table 1
Institutions and enrollment by level, Hong Kong 1993–94

	Institutions				Enrollment			
	Government	Aided	Private	Total	Government	Aided	Private	Total
Kindergarten	—	—	730	730	—	—	187,549	187,549
Primary	47	551	75	633	30,725	406,683	48,103	485,061
Secondary	39	323	86	448	39,246	358,429	58,260	455,935
Special education	—	61	—	76	148	8,131	—	8,279
Colleges of education	4	—	—	4	2,315	—	—	2,315
Approved postsecondary	—	—	1	1	—	—	2,787	2,787
Adult education	—	—	123	123	—	—	22,185	22,185

at the secondary level many have low status and cater for pupils unable to gain places in government or aided schools.

Hong Kong has six universities, all of which are owned publicly. The University of Hong Kong, founded in 1911, is the oldest. It operates a broad range of courses, and teaches in English. The Chinese University of Hong Kong, as noted above, was established in 1963. It also operates a broad range of courses. Although most teaching is in the medium of Chinese, many programs require students to read materials in English. The Hong Kong University of Science and Technology opened in 1991, and teaches most courses in English. In 1994, the two polytechnics, which had been founded in 1972 and 1984, were granted university status. The Baptist College, which had been founded in 1956, also achieved university status. Lingnan College, which was established in 1967, offers degree courses but does not have university status.

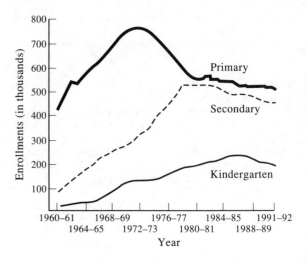

Figure 2
Enrollments in kindergarten, primary, and secondary schools, Hong Kong 1960–61 to 1991–92

Growth of formal schooling is shown in Fig. 2. The graph charts dramatic expansion in the 1960s and 1970s. The fall in enrollments during the 1980s chiefly reflected declining birthrates.

Higher education enrollments have also grown markedly, though more recently. In the early 1980s, fewer than 3 percent of the age group could study at local universities. This forced many people to go abroad, and at one point as many Hong Kong people were studying overseas as at home. In the mid-1980s, the government announced ambitious expansion targets, which were subsequently made even more ambitious. Because people had misgivings about reunification with China in 1997, Hong Kong had begun to suffer severely from brain drain. Partly to replace the talent lost, and partly as a public demonstration of self-confidence, in 1989 the governor announced that first-year first-degree places would expand from about 7,000 in 1990 to 15,000 in 1995. This projection indicated that 25 percent of the age group would have tertiary education places (Morris et al. 1994 p. 131). By international as well as local standards, this is a dramatic figure.

3.2 Preschool Education

Preschool education caters for nearly 90 percent of children aged 4 to 6. Some children receive preschool education from the age of 3.

Most preschool education is provided in kindergartens, which are registered with the government's Education Department but are operated privately. Some children attend nurseries which are registered with the social welfare department. The government operates one demonstration nursery, but the others are

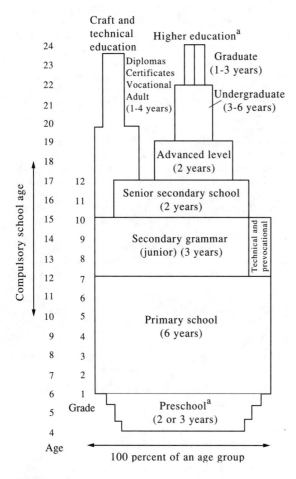

Figure 1
Hong Kong: Structure of the formal education system 1994
a Preschool and higher education data include part-time students

private. Some are commercial enterprises, but many are run on a nonprofit basis.

The enrollment figures indicate that most parents consider preschool education to be an essential part of the lives of their young children. However, the government holds that there is no firm basis to assert that kindergarten is essential, and provides minimal support (Opper 1991 p. 36). Government officers do inspect kindergartens and do advise managers, teachers, parents, and the public, but direct expenditure on kindergartens is below 1 percent of the total Education Department budget.

Partly because of this official policy, the sector suffers in quality. Basic professional training is available at one of the colleges of education, but only a quarter of preschool teachers are actually trained. This reflects salary structures, for few trained teachers gain higher salaries in recognition of their training. Kindergarten teachers generally receive low salaries, and many leave the profession after a short period for better-paid jobs elsewhere in the economy.

3.3 Special Education

In 1993–94, 15,000 special places were provided for handicapped children, of which 8,000 places were in 61 schools for the severely handicapped. These included the blind, deaf, physically handicapped, mentally handicapped, and maladjusted. A total of 17 special schools provided 950 residential places. All these schools were operated by voluntary agencies, but were in the aided sector. In addition, 416 special education classes in ordinary schools provided 6,200 places for the partially sighted, the partially hearing, and students with learning difficulties.

The classes in special schools have from 8 to 20 pupils each, depending on the types of children served. The staffing ratio ranges from 1 to 1.5 teachers per class.

Screening and assessment services help to identify special educational needs among school-aged children so that remedial action can be taken as early as possible. The government also provides training and advisory support. Emphasis is on early diagnosis and the prevention of a mild impairment from becoming a serious or permanent handicap.

The Centralized Braille Production Centre was established in 1986 and is operated by the Hong Kong Society for the Blind under government subvention. It produces braille reading material in both English and Chinese.

3.4 Vocational and Technical Education

The Apprenticeship Ordinance provides a legal framework for the training of craft workers and technicians. It requires an employer to enter a contract of apprenticeship when engaging a person aged between 14 and 18 in one of the 42 designated trades. The contract must be registered with the Director of Technical Education and Industrial Training. Contracts for apprentices in nondesignated trades, or for individuals over the age of 18, may be registered voluntarily. Most apprenticeship training lasts for three or four years.

The Vocational Training Council (VTC) operates eight technical institutes which provide courses at craft and technician levels. Full-time courses last for one or two years, while part-time courses last up to three years. Some part-time courses operate through daytime "block release," while others operate in the evenings. Many of the courses aim to update the knowledge and skills of people already in employment.

The VTC also provides industrial training. Individual centers train labor for 16 different industries. The centers provide off-the-job basic or updating training for over 21,000 trainees a year on a full-time or part-time basis. The skill levels range from operative to technologist.

At the apex of the system, the tertiary institutions run courses ranging from diploma to graduate levels. In 1992–93, the Hong Kong Polytechnic had 10,200 full-time and sandwich course students, and 15,000 part-time students. The City Polytechnic was smaller, with 7,800 full-time, 5,700 part-time, and 380 sandwich course students.

3.5 Adult and Nonformal Education

The Adult Education Section of the Education Department provides formal and nonformal education in the evening through a number of courses and activities, and assists voluntary organizations through a subvention scheme. Formal courses cover remedial education, second-chance education, and education for personal development at all levels. Some courses are jointly operated with other government departments. Nonformal courses cover cultural, social, recreational, and educational activities to stimulate social awareness, cultivate creativity, and develop individual talents and skills. There are 10 adult education and recreation centers operating in various administrative districts. In 1994, over 100,000 people participated in these courses and activities.

Subvented courses run by voluntary agencies supplement and complement those operated by the government. In 1992–93, government subsidies were granted to 363 projects operated by 67 organizations.

The Open Learning Institute was established in 1989. It provides a second chance for those who have been unable to go on to further education after leaving school, as well as opportunities for workers and managers to update their qualifications and extend their personal development. It offers degree programs through four schools: Science and Technology, Business and Administration, Arts and Social Science, and Education.

4. Administrative and Supervisory Structure and Operation

Hong Kong has a unitary system of administration, with a single government and no provincial or state

411

authorities. However, the Education Department does operate 19 offices located in various parts of the territory in addition to its main office. Also, at the end of the 1980s and beginning of the 1990s there were moves to decentralize at least some powers to the school level through a School Management Initiative (Government of Hong Kong 1991).

The director of education is responsible for general supervision of education at kindergarten, primary, and secondary levels. The director also supervises institutions registered under the Post Secondary Colleges Ordinance, and directly controls all government schools. All other schools, with minor exceptions, must be registered under the Education Ordinance. All schools are regularly inspected by the Education Department, and those receiving financial assistance from the government under codes of aid are subject to controls on such matters as staffing and conditions of service.

The Education Commission, established in 1984, is the government's highest advisory body on education. Its terms of reference are to define overall objectives, formulate policy, recommend priorities for implementation, coordinate the planning and development of education at all levels, and initiate education research.

The Board of Education is a statutory advisory body established in 1920. It helps plan and formulate policies for the school sector.

The University and Polytechnic Grants Committee (UPGC) advises the government on the development of higher education. It also administers grants for tertiary institutions. Its history dates back to 1965.

The Vocational Training Council, mentioned above, was set up in 1982. Its role is to advise the governor on measures to ensure a comprehensive system of technical education and industrial training, and to set up, develop, and operate training at various levels. Under the Council are 20 training boards and 7 general committees. The training boards cover all major economic sectors, while the general committees focus on training relevant to more than one sector of the economy.

5. Educational Finance

Education generally consumes between 15 and 20 percent of the total government budget, and around 3.0 percent of GDP. The mid-1980s brought an increase in expenditure, though proportions declined at the end of the decade. Expansion of higher education has required heavy financial commitments in the 1990s, but education has to compete with other sectors, most notably infrastructure, including a new, high-cost airport.

Within the education sector, expenditure on primary education has consumed about 30 percent of the total, with slightly more being devoted to secondary education and about 25 percent for "others." Because Hong Kong is compact, the government avoids the costs of

administering education in a large area. The government also devotes very little money to adult education.

In government and aided schools, education is free of charge up to Form 3. Thereafter, standard fees are charged. In 1991–92 they were HK$2,100 (US$270) per annum in forms 4 and 5, and HK$2,550 (US$331) per annum in forms 6 and 7.

Fees are also charged at the tertiary level. Until the 1990s, the highest fee level was charged in 1962 at the University of Hong Kong, when income covered about 16 percent of recurrent costs. In subsequent years fee levels slipped, so that by 1982 fees covered only 3.8 percent of recurrent costs at the University of Hong Kong and 5.8 percent at the Chinese University of Hong Kong. However, in 1987, the government drew up a schedule for progressive increase in fees, aiming to cover 12 percent of recurrent costs by 1994. This target was subsequently raised to 18 percent.

Since 1969 the government has also operated a system of student loans. The scheme aims to ensure that no student who has been offered a place in an institution of tertiary education should be unable to accept it for lack of means. To a large extent, the authorities seem to have been successful in this goal (Bray 1992). The scheme allows for grants as well as loans, with the former covering faculty expenses, tuition charges, and student union fees, and the latter covering living expenses. The loans used to be interest free, but a 2.5 percent annual charge was introduced in 1987. Loans normally have to be repaid within five years of graduation.

6. Supplying Personnel for the Education System

In 1994 Hong Kong had over 45,000 teachers. Wide variations exist in their academic qualifications, professional preparation, and terms of service. Although the government aims in the long run to achieve an all-graduate profession, very few primary school teachers were graduates in 1994. Even at the secondary level, one-third of teachers were nongraduates. Most of these teachers had been trained, but about one-fourth of the graduate teachers were untrained.

Four colleges of education train nongraduate teachers for primary and secondary schools. In 1994, they were directly financed and staffed by the government and administered by the Education Department, but plans had been prepared to merge the colleges into a single Institute of Education. Three of the colleges have a general focus, while the fourth focuses on training for technical subjects in secondary and prevocational schools. The colleges provide both full-time initial teacher education and part-time upgrading courses.

Training for graduate teachers is provided at the University of Hong Kong, the Chinese University of Hong Kong, and the Baptist University. The universities offer a one-year full-time teacher education course, and a two-year part-time one. The part-time course provides training for graduates who are already teaching in schools. Although government permits untrained graduates to teach, it limits their career prospects.

The University of Hong Kong and the Chinese University of Hong Kong also offer MEd programs on both a full-time and a part-time basis. These programs serve administrators and lecturers in colleges of education as well as ordinary teachers and other groups.

7. Curriculum Development and Teaching Methodology

The government's Education Department includes a Curriculum Development Institute (CDI), which was set up in 1992. It is responsible for developing curricula, and for helping schools to implement curriculum policies and innovations. It also provides a secretariat for the Curriculum Development Council (CDC), which is an advisory body composed of employers and parents as well as educators.

The primary curriculum is dominated by Chinese, English, mathematics, social studies, science, arts and crafts, music, and physical education. Schools run by religious bodies also offer studies appropriate to their faiths. Similar subject offerings are found in the secondary schools. The two languages and mathematics are allocated at least one period a day, while most other subjects have only two or three periods a week.

In the 1970s, the government introduced integrated science and social studies at junior secondary level to replace the academic disciplinary studies. Integrated science is firmly established, but social studies has been resisted by principals and specialist teachers strongly wedded to academic disciplines. Efforts to increase the place of practical subjects have also been resisted, with the result that junior secondary education, although universal and compulsory, remains highly academic. This tendency is even stronger in the postcompulsory stage, where studies are dominated by public examinations (McClelland 1991).

All textbooks are produced by commercial companies, and competition has encouraged high quality products. However, schools are only permitted to use books which are on an approved list. Books are only added to the list if they are educationally and politically acceptable.

Viewing of Educational Television (ETV) programs has become a normal part of school life for pupils of primary grades 3 to 6 and secondary forms 1 to 3. These programs are produced jointly by the Educational Television Section of the Education Department and Radio Television Hong Kong. They are a useful audiovisual supplement to classroom teaching.

8. The System of Examinations, Promotions, and Certifications

Children are admitted to primary schools by the Primary One Allocation Scheme, which takes pa-

rental choice into account but is mainly governed by geographic area. On completion of the primary course, pupils are allocated Form 1 places according to the Secondary School Places Allocation System. The system uses internal school assessment, scaled by a centrally administered academic aptitude test. It also takes account of parental choice and geographic area.

The most significant public examination is the Hong Kong Certificate of Education Examination, sat by most students at the end of five years of secondary schooling. It is administered by the Hong Kong Examinations Authority, an independent statutory body established in 1977. The authority also operates the Advanced-level examinations, and conducts some examinations on behalf of overseas examining bodies.

Within the school system, pupils are generally promoted automatically from one grade to the next. Schools may require pupils to repeat grades, but repetition is normally permitted only once during a student's primary school career. At the secondary level, official policy restricts repetition to 5 percent in any one year.

9. Educational Assessment, Evaluation, and Research

Most evaluation and research in education is undertaken by the government's Education Department and by the institutions of higher education. The research in the Education Department mostly focuses on the government's own programs and policies. Work in the higher education institutions is extensive and multi-faceted.

The territory has a thriving Educational Research Association which holds annual conferences and publishes the *Educational Research Journal*. The Faculty of Education at the Chinese University of Hong Kong publishes an education journal, and the Faculty at the University of Hong Kong publishes periodic *Education Papers* on specific topics.

Hong Kong has participated in several projects undertaken by the International Association for the Evaluation of Educational Achievement (IEA). Projects have included ones on mathematics, science, preprimary education, and literacy (Brimer and Griffin 1985, Holbrook 1990, Opper 1992). The projects have provided useful comparative indicators, though have not always fed as much into policy-making as might be desired.

It is difficult to identify the share of the total budget allocated to assessment, evaluation, and research, but it is unlikely to exceed 1 or 2 percent.

10. Major Reforms in the 1980s and 1990s

The rapid pace of change in the 1980s did not slow in the early 1990s. Many of the reforms were directly or indirectly linked to the resumption of Chinese sovereignty in 1997.

One far-reaching initiative, already mentioned, is dramatic expansion of higher education. The policy has had a major impact not only on the tertiary institutions themselves, but also on the schools which feed those institutions. The expansion was expected to have a marked effect on the labor market toward the end of the decade.

Another significant initiative is the Direct Subsidy Scheme (DSS). Under the scheme, aided secondary schools are able to become private institutions but still receive substantial government grants. Existing private schools can also apply to join the scheme and thereby obtain government grants. The DSS was proposed by the Education Commission in 1988, and launched in 1991. The system appears elitist, and is designed to dismantle some of the uniformity which administrators over the decades have devoted much effort to establishing. The scheme has provided an avenue for left-wing schools that were formerly excluded from government assistance to come within the fold; but it also diffuses the control of other key institutions. The latter may be considered especially important by those who fear centralized manipulation of the school system after 1997.

The 1980s and early 1990s also witnessed extensive discussion over the language of instruction. Although advocates of mother-tongue schooling push for Chinese-medium education, many parents prefer English-medium education because it enhances opportunities in the labor market. The fact that many so-called "English-medium schools" actually operate in Chinese or in mixed mode highlights the complexities and contradictions.

In 1989, the Education Department issued a consultation paper which suggested that all primary Grade 6 pupils would be subject to an English test to determine their ability to benefit from a secondary education in English. On the results of this test, 30 percent of Form 1 pupils would be taught most school subjects strictly in English, and the remaining 70 percent strictly in Chinese. Mixed mode teaching was to be abolished. The proposal earned the Department praise for a strong stand on a difficult issue, but met widespread opposition. In the end, schools were left to determine their own policies, rather as before.

11. Major Problems for the Year 2000

By the year 2000, Hong Kong will have been incorporated in the People's Republic of China. Despite the statement in Hong Kong's Basic Law that the territory will be permitted to maintain its own education system, there will be inevitable requirements for adjustment and harmonization.

Some tensions have already been foreshadowed. The discussion on language issues, above, referred chiefly to the respective roles of English and Cantonese. Reunification with China will also require added attention to Putonghua. A place for Putonghua will have to be found in the curriculum, and teachers will have to be trained. It is also likely that the system will increasingly use the simplified Chinese characters employed in the People's Republic of China rather than the complex characters that have been the standard in Hong Kong.

Another set of issues will concern control of the education system. Although Hong Kong has been promised a high degree of autonomy, questions of influence and control in the decision-making bodies will inevitably arise. These questions will concern the school level as well as the territory as a whole.

Further questions will concern recognition of qualifications from mainland China. In the decades following the Second World War, the colonial government in Hong Kong refused to recognize credentials from north of the border. However, it seems unlikely that this position can remain tenable after reunification.

Finally, and partly linked to the above issue, reunification with mainland China may bring pressures on Hong Kong salaries. Teachers and other educational personnel in Hong Kong have long been paid far higher salaries than their counterparts in China. Increased supply of professionals from China, and pressure to reduce differentials, is likely to alter this situation significantly.

References

Bray M 1992 Financing higher education through student loans: The Hong Kong system in comparative perspective. In: Chung Y P, Wong R (eds.) 1992 *The Economics and Financing of Hong Kong Education*. Chinese University Press, Hong Kong

Brimer M A, Griffin P 1985 *Mathematics Achievement in Hong Kong Secondary Schools*. Centre of Asian Studies, University of Hong Kong, Hong Kong

Holbrook J 1990 *Science Education in Hong Kong: Achievements and Determinants*. Education Paper 6, Faculty of Education, University of Hong Kong, Hong Kong

Hong Kong/China Governments of 1990 *The Basic Law of the Hong Kong Special Administrative Region of the People's Republic of China*. The Consultative Committee for the Basic Law of the Hong Kong Special Administrative Region of the People's Republic of China, Hong Kong

Hong Kong Government of 1991 *The School Management Initiative: Setting the Framework for Quality in Hong Kong Schools*. Education and Manpower Branch/Education Department, Hong Kong

McClelland J A G 1991 Curriculum development in Hong Kong. In: Marsh C, Morris P (eds.) 1991 *Curriculum Development in East Asia*. Falmer Press, London

Morris P, Sweeting A E 1991 Education and politics: The case of Hong Kong from an historical perspective. *Oxford Rev. Educ.* 17(3): 249–67

Morris P, McClelland J A G, Leung Y M 1994 Higher education in Hong Kong:The context of and rationale for rapid expansion. *High. Educ.* 27(2): 125–40
Opper S 1991 Trends in early childhood education in Hong Kong. *East West Education* 12: 26–47
Opper S 1992 *Hong Kong's Young Children: Their Preschools and Families.* Hong Kong University Press, Hong Kong
Postiglione G A, Leung J (eds.) 1992 *Education and Society in Hong Kong: Toward One Country and Two Systems.* M E Sharpe, Armonk, New York
Sweeting A E 1993 *A Phoenix Transformed: The Reconstruction of Education in Post-War Hong Kong.* Oxford University Press, Hong Kong

Further Reading

Bray M 1992 Colonialism, scale and politics: Divergence and convergence of educational development in Hong Kong and Macau. *Comp. Educ. Rev.* 36(3): 322–42
Lee W M 1993 Education. In: Choi P K, Ho L S (eds.) 1993 *The Other Hong Kong Report.* Chinese University Press, Hong Kong
Hong Kong, Government of (annual) *Hong Kong 19xx.* Government Printer, Hong Kong
Post D, 1993 Educational attainment and the role of the state in Hong Kong. *Comp. Educ. Rev.* 37(3): 240–62

Hungary

Z. Báthory

1. General Background

The Republic of Hungary is a small East Central European country in the Danube Valley surrounded by the Carpathian Mountains. Its territory covers 93,030 square kilometers (35,918 square miles)—about 1 percent of the surface area of Europe. The Danube River separates the eastern plains from the hilly region in the west.

The Carpathian basin was occupied by the Magyar tribes in the tenth century, and, after the adoption of Christianity, Hungary became an independent kingdom. The zenith of the country's economic, political, and cultural development was reached during the reign of Matthias Corvinus, in the fifteenth century. Soon after this, Hungary became a buffer state between the expanding Ottoman and Hapsburg empires. The Austro–Hungarian monarchy existed from 1867 to 1918. The Peace Treaty of Trianon (1920) reduced the territory of Hungary. The country lost 70 percent of its territory and 60 percent of its population. Between the two world wars, social and economic development advanced slowly. The Second World War devastated the country. The "socialist" period started in 1949 and lasted until 1989. For forty years, the country became a satellite of the Soviet Union. The short glory of the 1956 revolution was crushed by Soviet troops. From the 1960s, political reconciliation paved the way for limited economic growth and cultural development. The "change of regime"—as the change from autocracy to democracy is called—gained impetus in 1990 during the first free elections. Hungary in the early 1990s is a pluralist democracy striving for a free market economy and aspiring for full membership in the European Community. It is clear that all the political and social changes affected the whole system of education:

values, administration, curriculum and curriculum policy, and the structure of formal education.

The population grew steadily to over 10 million by 1980, then the trend changed and the average annual growth rate became negative (−0.1%). In 1992, the population totalled 10,337,200. The density of the population is 113 inhabitants per square kilometer. There was a steady flow from rural to urban areas in the period 1950 to 1990. Nevertheless, there are still many small villages in the countryside. Whether these villages should have their own (elementary) schools is a question under consideration. Budapest, the capital, is a large European-style city.

Urban–rural differences pose an educational problem. Even after accounting for parental socioeconomic status, a large part of the variation in students' achievement may be explained by the location (urban–rural) of the school.

Ethnically, the population is fairly homogeneous: 96.6 percent are Hungarians. Ethnic minorities include (in descending order of size): Germans, Slovaks, Serbs, Croats, Romanians, and Slovenes. An estimated 5 percent comprises the Gypsy ethnic group, consisting of several linguistic subgroups. For a long time, the Gypsy issue was ignored.

The revival of religions and religious life after forty years of "socialism" is one of the new aspects of life in Hungary in the 1990s. It strongly influences both educational thinking and practice. According to an opinion poll (INFO 1991), about half of the population considered themselves to be religious while 46 percent declared themselves as nonreligious. About two-thirds of religious people are Roman Catholic. Calvinism, Lutheranism, and Judaism are also common.

In 1992 the per capita Gross Domestic Product (GDP) was US$3,400 with a decrease of 4–6% as a consequence of the economic restructuring and the recession in the last few years. In economic terms, therefore, Hungary is a poor country as compared to, for example, Hungary's western neighbor, Austria, where the per capita GDP is nearly seven times higher. However, culture and education traditionally enjoy a relatively high prestige, and despite its low economic standard, Hungary has gained high esteem in the world for many of its cultural and educational achievements.

Industry has long been regarded as the most important sector of the Hungarian economy. The "socialist" industrialization of the country was rapid and enforced in the 1950s. However, the Hungarian economy—partly for historical, and partly for geographical reasons such as the shortage in mineral resources and the country's surface and climate—still has an agricultural character.

The active workforce constituted 46 percent of the total population in 1992. Just over 48 percent were in the service sector, 35 percent in industry, and 13 percent in agriculture. The number of workers in agriculture and industry decreased slowly from 1970 to 1990, while those in the services increased rapidly. Both the absolute number of the population and the ratio of the active workforce to the total population have decreased during the 1980s. Blue-collar workers, in general, and especially semi-skilled, unskilled workers, and female (49%) workers constitute a relatively high proportion within the labor force. Unemployment is a new phenomenon in Hungary's economic and social life. In 1993, about 13 percent of the workforce was unemployed and this is predicted to remain the case. This fact causes concern. The occupational distribution is strongly connected with the educational level of the population (see Table 1). Although development was significant, only 10 percent of the population holds a college or university degree. The so-called "planned" economy and "socialist" political system in Hungary were unsuccessful in establishing wealth and achieving a high level of production. At the beginning of the 1990s, the major task is to overcome that past and to catch up with Western societies.

In the 1990s, the Cold War is over. The world has

witnessed amazing political changes in East Central Europe. In Hungary, the economy, society, and culture has entered into a state of transition from socialism of the Soviet type to democracy of the Western type. By 1992, all the major institutional bases of a pluralist democracy had been laid down. However, the economy was stagnating and the standard of living was deteriorating. On the one hand, privatization of former state property and a shift from the planned to a market economy were in progress, but on the other, unemployment and disillusionment had appeared. Political disturbances occurred in the wake of economic constraints. The "transition" affected individual and social life, including education.

2. Politics and the Goals of the Education System

To place the trends in educational policy at the beginning of the 1990s into perspective, it is important to bear in mind that education has had a long tradition in Hungary and that the 1990 political changes induced far-reaching changes in the values, goals, content, and even in the system of education.

The cultural heritage goes back almost one thousand years. The first school was opened as early as 996 AD. The first royal decree on state curriculum was issued by Empress Maria Theresa in 1777 (*Ratio Educationis*). The first Educational Act dealing with public education was passed by the Parliament in 1868, along with similar acts adopted in the Western countries. The 1868 Act granted compulsory schooling for children between 6 and 12 years of age.

In contemporary Hungary, the basic aims of educational policy are to evolve democracy in all aspects of education, to secure free schooling for all strata of society, and to modernize education in order to catch up with the developed world. Both the government and the opposition consider public education as a strategic sector for social and economic reconstruction.

Democracy means first of all—after many years of indoctrination—a free choice of education and everyone's right to enhance their personal growth. The government should not impose a single-value system on education and schools. Education is essentially secular. Teachers—in contrast to what was requested of them during Soviet domination—are not supposed to state what is "good," what is "true." Schools and teachers should follow the values expressed in the constitution of the country, in the Declaration of Human Rights, and in the Charter for Children.

The state monopoly of school ownership was abolished at a stroke in 1990. The state became responsible for maintaining schools but ownership is shared with municipalities, churches, foundations, and private persons. All such legal entities may open schools if they meet the legally set criteria.

Efforts to modernize the Hungarian system of education started in the late 1970s. Decentralizing

Table 1
Development of educational level in four relevant age cohorts

Age cohort[a]	1970	1980	1990
10+	1.9	1.1	1.0
15+	51.4	66.1	78.1
18+	15.9	23.4	30.1
25+	4.3	6.5	9.4

a 10+: at least 10 years old and having no school instruction at all; 15+: at least 15 years old and having completed 8 grades; 18+: at least 18 years old and having passed final examination of secondary education; and 25+: 25 years old or more and having graduated from college or university

educational administration and giving more autonomy to schools and teachers constituted the major goals of that reform movement. In 1985, a still controversial education act was passed (Halász 1987). That act is considered by many people to be a milestone in reforming Hungarian education. With the "change of regime," old aims were reinforced and new aims also emerged. New Education Acts were passed in 1993 on public, vocational, and higher education.

All those interested in the modernization of public education seem to agree on the following three major tasks: (a) extending general education for all from eight grades to ten grades encompassing the compulsory years (6–16); (b) extending the scope and improving the quality of academic and vocational secondary education; and, (c) providing more places for students at institutions of higher education (colleges and universities). The second and third tasks express the common concern that Hungary—in these two respects—belongs to the group of least developed countries in Europe.

Education is still considered the main channel for social mobility. It is widely agreed that the existing social differences should be diminished by schooling.

3. The Formal System of Education

3.1 Primary, Secondary, and Tertiary Education

The structure of the Hungarian system of public education in transition is presented in Fig. 1. The basic types of schools are: general school, academic secondary school (grammar school), and various types of vocational secondary school and trade school. This structure hardly changed in the forty years of the Party state. This explains why it is generally considered a rigid system and no longer complying with the changing social and educational needs. Therefore, it was not surprising that at the first touch of political freedom, structural alterations were initiated before anything else. Elitist and democratic considerations as well as experiments emerged. Two structural changes in particular should be mentioned: the eight-grade grammar school and the six-grade secondary school. The eight-grade grammar school used to be a traditional and basic component of the school structure before the end of the Second World War. Innovators of this school frequently also refer to the German *Gymnasium*, whereas reformers of the six-grade secondary school refer to West European and American patterns. Naturally there are experts who argue strongly for the reform of the existing eight-grade general school in order to catch up with the Scandinavian model. At the beginning of 1992, there were only 57 schools in the secondary sector taking part in different structural experiments but since then there has been a constant increase in the number of applications submitted to the Ministry to get allowances for opening classes or schools of these new types. Table 2 presents data on the number of schools, students, and teachers in the system at the beginning of the 1993–94 school year.

It is likely that in the mid-1990s—as a result of the new Education Act—new types of school will take over. A rather strong differentiation of schooling (appearance of different types of school) is expected to take place at the lower- and upper-secondary grades. Consequently, it may happen that the early 1990s' pattern of public education (4+4+4 or 4+4+3) will gradually give way to the patterns like 8 + 2, 4 + 8, 6 + 8, 8 + 4, or 12.

In 1992, the general school consisted of eight grades for pupils in the 6–14 age group and was divided into an elementary and a lower-secondary part. There were class teachers at the four elementary grades and subject teachers for the four upper grades.

In rural areas, many small and mostly ungraded schools were closed in the period 1970 to 1990 for the sake of improving the standard of teaching. In 1970, there were 5,450 general schools in the country, including 3,103 entirely or partly ungraded schools. By 1993, that situation had completely changed: out of 3,771 general schools, only 586 had remained partly or entirely ungraded. Only 1,127 schools had only elementary grades. New regulations have allowed municipalities to open or reopen small schools. Many think that small schools are best tailored to the educational needs in rural areas. Schools also play a social role in their local communities.

The general schools and the special schools for

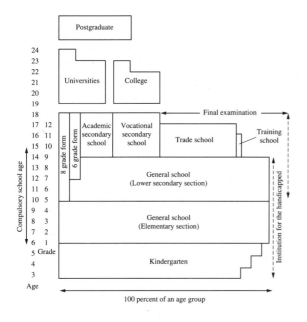

Figure 1
Hungary: Structure of the formal education system

Table 2
Number of schools, students, and teachers (1993–94)

Type of school	Number of schools	Number of students	Number of teachers
General school	3,771	1,009,416	89,655
small school[a]	1,686	—	—
church school	94	19,449	1,521
foundation/private school	21	2,212	283
Academic secondary school	270	131,373	11,305
church school	38	10,248	—
foundation/private school	12	—	—
six-grade form	86	5,674	—
eight-grade form	68	7,152	—
Vocational secondary school	446	80,351	13,992
Academic and vocational secondary school	150	—	—
Secondary school (total)	866	—	—
Trade school and trade school with vocational secondary classes	332	174,184	11,251
Training school[b]	329	25,016	1,258
Special general school for handicapped children[c]	191	} 34,454	} 6,538
General school with special classes for handicapped children	452		
Adults' general school	123	8,982	221

a General schools only with elementary grades (1,127), ungraded general schools (412), partly ungraded general schools (174)   d Shorthand-typist and nursing schools   c Mentally retarded (172), deaf (9), blind (4), motor disabled (4), speech defections (2)

Table 3
Enrollment in general schools

Academic year	Thousands of pupils in		Percentage of 1st graders coming from kindergarten
	General schools	1st grade	
1960–61	1,392.4	229.1	36.5
1970–71	1,115.4	138.9	54.7
1980–81	1,162.2	171.3	85.6
1984–85	1,286.6	171.9	90.0
1990–91	1,130.7	125.7	92.1
1991–92	1,080.3	125.7	92.3
1993–94	1,009.4	125.7	92.3

Table 4
Institutions and students in tertiary education

Year	Number of institutions	Number of students	Percentage of students in evening and correspondence courses	Number of teachers
1970	74	53,821	49	9,791
1980	57	64,057	58	13,890
1990	77	76,601	34	17,302
1993	91	103,713	29	18,670

period of work. Two-thirds and one-third of the students admitted to institutions of higher education come from grammar schools and vocational secondary schools, respectively.

Trade schools and training schools train skilled workers. The accent is put on specialized vocational education: on practical knowledge and skills. Vocational education is in a state of transformation.

Most secondary schools are concentrated in the urban areas although there has been a tendency to establish some grammar schools in the countryside. Some small cities ("school cities") have traditionally been famous for their grammar schools.

Institutions of higher education include colleges and universities. The number of students has increased slowly but steadily since 1970 and dramatically in the last few years (see Table 4). Nevertheless, this is still a very low enrollment and causes much concern. The number of students per 100,000 inhabitants was 970 in 1990 (World Education Report 1993), but 2,668 and 3,326 and 1,216 in Austria, Finland, and Czechoslovakia, respectively. (Only Albania and Romania are lower on this indicator in Europe.)

Another concern in tertiary education is the relatively high number of students attending evening and correspondence courses. The quality of teaching and learning is undoubtedly lower in these sections. Therefore the decrease (since 1980) in this indicator may be interpreted as a sign of improving quality.

The number of institutions of higher education fluctuated strongly since 1970. In the 1970s, several institutions such as small colleges were integrated into different universities. Since 1980—in accordance with the demand for a considerable expansion of higher education—many colleges and even some universities were founded and several former institutions reorganized. The political events of 1990 gave an impetus to that process. Some of the new institutions are privately owned and churches are also opening colleges and universities. The autonomy of higher education has been widely accepted and assured by legal means. University life is traditionally connected with large economic and urban centers, such as Budapest, Debrecen, Szeged, Pécs, Veszprém, and Miskolc.

handicapped children enroll virtually the whole of any school generation. Since 1960, the rate of enrollment has been practically 100 percent, fluctuating between 98.2 and 98.9 percent. Table 3 contains the most important data on enrollment in general schools. A brief glance at the first and second columns reveals the consequences of demographic waves.

Most students complete the eight grades in eight years but some repeat a grade and complete the eight grades one or two years later. Compulsory schooling lasts until age 16 and students who cannot complete eight grades by that time generally drop out. Some of them, however, take up schooling later at an institution for adult education.

After the successful completion of general school studies, students may choose from among three types of secondary school: academic secondary school, vocational secondary school, and trade school. Close to 90 percent of all general school pupils continue to study at secondary school. In 1990, 42 percent were in trade school, 27.5 percent in vocational school, and 21.1 percent in academic secondary school.

Academic secondary schools, or grammar schools (in Hungarian, *gimnázium*), offer general education. This type of school is popular among those who wish to continue learning at universities and also possess the required abilities. Students who are undecided often choose this type of school. In general, girls and boys constitute two-thirds and one-third of the students, respectively. The dropout rate is around 10 percent per year.

Vocational secondary schools offer general education and basic skills and practice in broadly defined vocational fields. These schools have particular vocational orientations, such as mechanical engineering, chemical engineering, animal husbandry, and economics. The dropout rate in vocational secondary schools is around 15 percent per year.

Vocational secondary school graduates either may be admitted to tertiary-level education—especially to the colleges and universities that fit their vocational orientation—or start to work. The latter can become skilled workers or technicians after a relatively short

3.2 Preschool Education

Preschool education is for children from 3 to 6 years of age. In 1992, 88.8 percent of the age cohort attended kindergartens of various kinds. In 1992, there were 4,730 kindergartens in operation. From 1950 onwards, preschool institutions were maintained either by the state or by big factories. The latter opened kindergartens in order to attract young women (the cheapest workforce available) to their workplaces. By the beginning of the 1990s, most municipalities had started to maintain kindergartens, but churches and private persons have also opened such institutions. There are whole-day and part-day kindergartens.

Kindergarten education is traditionally one of the most developed branches of education in Hungary and is considered by many people to be a basis for human development and socialization (first of all for school studies). Paradoxically, it also reflects a kind of intrusion into family affairs by the state. Kindergarten fitted well into the image of family life in "socialism": the mother goes to work while the child gets education, controlled by the state, from a very early age.

3.3 Special Education

As shown in Table 2, a large number and variety of kindergartens and general schools provide special care for children suffering from different disabilities (e.g., mental retardation, blindness, deafness, and motor disabilities). Some 2.5 percent of an age cohort need some kind of special care. It is a general view and practice that disabled children should be educated together with their nondisabled schoolmates. Mentally retarded children should be educated either in integrated or special classes (or even schools) depending on the measure of their handicap. Special teachers for the different tasks are trained in a Budapest college. The Petö Institute and College trains "conductors" specialized in the care of motor-disabled children and adults.

3.4 Vocational, Technical, and Business Education

The controversy between general and vocational education characterizes well the 1950 to 1990 period of secondary education in Hungary. There were periods when school policy stressed the importance of general education (providing a good base for several streams of learning) but more often the priorities went to vocational education. The main argument emphasized the practicality of vocational education. At the same time, workers' families tended to prefer vocational education whereas middle-class families preferred general academic education for their children. Vocational education, continuously influenced by labor force needs and considerations, suffered much from internal problems such as how to define the basic content of the major branches of vocational education and how to avoid extreme specialization at the secondary grades. Worse still, the most famous vocational secondary institutions (technical schools) were transformed into technical colleges in the mid-1970s. Thus higher education gained at the expense of secondary education.

Two levels of vocational training can be identified in the public education sector: (a) vocational secondary education in ten broadly defined areas (industrial, technical, commercial, agricultural, etc.); and (b) special training offered at trade schools and training schools in 24 areas and almost 100 trades.

3.5 Adult and Nonformal Education

The practice and institutions of nonformal education developed in Hungary after the end of the Second World War as a means to provide an opportunity for those who could not attend school—mostly for social reasons—in due time. Schools for adults also played an historical role in overcoming illiteracy. Beginning with the 1970s, however, this function gradually lost ground and gave way to another function: compensation. In the early 1990s, it was more or less an educational channel for those having dropped out of school or compelled to leave school before reaching the upper limit of the compulsory age of schooling (16) either for social or behavioral reasons. More than half of the students enrolled in adults' general schools are below the age of 16 and the dropout rate varies between 30 and 40 percent. Simultaneously, attendance at general schools for adults decreased tremendously indicating the outdated nature of this form of nonformal education. It can be reasonably expected that alongside new forms of nonformal education (e.g., the open university type of learning) old forms from the long forgotten past (e.g., the movement of People's High Schools) will emerge.

4. Administrative and Supervisory Structure and Operation

Allowing more autonomy to individual schools and reducing the hitherto heavy administrative and political control was already among the objectives of the educational reform launched in the late 1970s. In other words, the extremely centralized state administration gradually gave way to a decentralized system (Halász 1990). The 1990 change of regime facilitated all these changes.

By 1993, educational administration was a responsibility shared by three levels: the Ministry of Culture and Public Education, the municipalities (those maintaining schools), and the school boards (including representatives of the teaching staff). The Ministry provides for the financial funds from the state budget, conveys basic information to orient teaching (by means of a frame curriculum and examinations), and exercises legal supervision over the whole of the system. Local authorities (municipalities) own, maintain, run, and advise schools according to the needs of their clients. In normal circumstances, but to varying degrees depending on their resources, they are supposed to complement the financial funds granted by the state. It is also envisaged that the respective local curricula of schools will be approved by the local authorities. School boards consist of members elected from the teaching staff, the parents' organization, and the municipality. They carry out advisory tasks.

Only the Ministry is experienced in school administration and many municipalities are inexperienced. In this administrative vacuum, many schools are irresolute about ways of coming up to professional and political expectations.

The prevailing system of school supervision was strongly criticized even in the latter years of the past political regime. The controversies focused on the "inspectors or advisers" issue. In general, school principals and teachers favored a system of advisers while the authorities favored that of inspectors. In the administrative vacuum, which exists in the early 1990s, there is only a small chance for any reasonable compromise in the near future. It can be expected, however, that both advisers and inspectors will be needed for ensuring the highly professional goals of such a complex system.

5. *Educational Finance*

In 1992, the public education budget represented some 7–8 percent of the yearly national income. As a percentage of the GDP, it was 7.13. The annual expenditure spent on education is rather low in Hungary compared with highly developed countries in the European region. However, there is a marked development in this domain in recent years.

The percentage of the educational expenditure allocated to various sectors was the following in 1989 (in percent of GDP): preprimary 0.71, primary 2.16, secondary 1.26, and higher education 0.75. The percentage of total educational expenditure allocated to the various sectors was the following in 1992: preprimary 12, general schools 40, secondary sector 25, higher education 16, and other 7.

The 1992 per student expenditures by school type exhibit marked differences between the different sectors of public education (see Table 5). In 1991, the system changed: a normative way of state financing—per capita calculation—was introduced. The per student expenditure, as indicated in Table 5, will rise since municipalities may complement the per capita calculated sum given by the state—and most municipalities actually add such contributions.

The rather high expenditures in secondary and high-er education include different social benefits (student hostels, dormitories, meals, student grants, etc.). In the period 1970 to 1990, regular support was given to more than 80 percent of the students in higher education. This system will presumably change in the years to come: while many students will still be given support, several other students will have to pay fees according to their family's income.

6. *Supplying Personnel for the Education System*

Teachers for the various levels of public education are trained and specialized at colleges and universities. There are different colleges for kindergarten teachers (three-year training), for elementary grade teachers (three- or four-year training), and for lower-secondary grade teachers (four-year training). Secondary school teachers are trained at universities (five-year training). Kindergarten teachers are also trained at vocational secondary schools. In 1992, more than 40,000 undergraduate students were trained at 35 colleges and universities belonging to the above five types of institutions. Compared with 1980, there was a slight increase in the number of students. The structure of the training system has mostly remained intact. The content, however, has changed radically.

Several problems have emerged in teacher training since the 1980s. It is often argued that the selection procedure for future teachers is based on exaggerated intellectual criteria and that teaching abilities play only an insignificant role. The educational content of teacher-training courses is also severely criticized. Experiments are underway aimed at building up a new unified but graded system of teacher training.

Demographic irregularities and the relatively low ratio of participation in the tertiary sector seriously affect the educational personnel. After many years of a shortage of teachers in general schools, teacher unemployment has appeared. There is a serious shortage of teachers of English and German, whereas there is

Table 5
Expenditures per student in different educational sectors 1960–92 (in Forint)

| Year | Kindergarten | General school | Trade school | Secondary school | | Higher education |
				Academic	Vocational	
1960	2,596	1,414	4,314	4,175		19,267
1970	4,379	2,713	4,955	5,878		29,367
1980	9,941	8,822	16,646	15,840	19,973	59,667
1985	15,919	13,651	21,448	17,339	24,576	78,013
1990	39,583	37,169	47,728	48,877	58,974	200,133
1992	62,790	71,222	89,647	86,544	103,448	342,715

an abundance of teachers of Russian. Former Russian teachers must either begin to study English or German languages or they may well become unemployed.

Inservice teacher training of various types has long been strongly recommended but not made compulsory. Courses take place at higher institutions, county pedagogical institutions, or at school level. The restructuring of the Hungarian education system unfavorably hit inservice training which is now to be in the field of innovative approaches.

7. Curriculum Development and Teaching Methodology

The centrally designed, approved, and implemented curriculum played a significant role in Hungary during the forty years of the Party state and also between the two world wars but, in fact, the tradition of having a central curriculum goes back nearly two hundred years. However, especially in the 1980s, educational researchers strongly opposed the extreme centralization of curriculum policy and tried to find different intermediate solutions. Facilitated by the 1990 political changes, a well-balanced curriculum policy, containing central and local components as well, is under consideration. As part of this process, the specification of a national core curriculum and the adoption of a new public examination system were initiated. The core curriculum does not impose any single ideology or religion to follow in schools and offers many different ways for individual schools to adapt their curriculum (Nagy and Szebenyi 1990, Báthory 1993). Beyond the core curriculum, schools and teaching staff are free to decide upon all aspects of the content of teaching in their respective schools. They are encouraged to develop their own local or school-based curricula. This new and somewhat unusual curriculum policy for many teachers assumes that a fairly long transition period will be needed. This is also true for the provision of inservice training for teachers and the establishment of a market for different syllabuses, frame curricula, textbooks, and teaching aids.

In terms of content, significant changes have been made in such school subjects as history (social sciences) and literature. There seems to be a consensus that schools, in the future, should put more emphasis on the humanities (e.g., a basic knowledge of ethics and religion), even at the expense of science and mathematics. The most radical changes have occurred in foreign language teaching. Russian, formerly a compulsory subject for all Hungarian students, was the dominant foreign language. Now English and German are in demand, but there is a shortage of teachers. Although the number of those studying English and German is rapidly increasing, the actual number of students studying English represents not more than 30 percent of primary school students (aged 6 to 14) and 20 percent of secondary school students. German is the second most popular foreign language course at both levels.

Methods of teaching vary a great deal depending on the objectives and content being taught. Teachers are strongly encouraged to introduce new methodological elements and to be innovative. The way to identify the most effective teaching strategy is a constant subject of debate among teachers. Student motivation and active participation in the process of learning are considered essential.

8. The System of Examinations, Promotions, and Certifications

There are two decisive transition points in the system of public education. After graduating from general school, almost all students go on to further education without taking any examinations. However, the type of school they may choose is determined by their respective past achievement expressed in marks. This transition point is strongly criticized because it imposes choice at a rather young age (10–14). It appears that it is, in many cases, the parents who make the choice.

In all secondary schools, the graduating (Grade 12) students (17- to 18- year olds) may choose whether or not to take a final examination (called "maturity examination"). When taking this examination, most students are examined by a board of examiners headed by a high-ranking education official not employed in the same school. Students at trade schools also take a final examination in order to obtain a certificate.

Students intending to enter tertiary education have to pass an entrance examination set by a university board. The entrance examination includes oral and written parts. The total score is calculated from the points scored at the examination and the marks received in the last two secondary grades in a few key subjects such as literature and mathematics. The minimum total score necessary for admission is determined by the universities and colleges themselves. Numerous higher institutions have in the early 1990s introduced less strict admission requirements in the spirit of a desirable expansion of higher education.

The system of promotion is strongly criticized. In order to improve the effectiveness of teaching (especially at the secondary grades) and to comply with the new curriculum policy a new system of state examination is being considered. It is anticipated that this examination system will have two steps: the first after the completion of the last compulsory grade (10), and the second at the end of secondary education ("maturity examination"). It is widely argued that such a new examination system should counterbalance the fairly liberal curriculum policy. Consequently, the methodology of assessment and examination also will be modernized: objective and standardized methods will be introduced.

9. Educational Assessment, Evaluation, and Research

International educational evaluation has been accepted in Hungary since 1968. Nine surveys have so far been carried out in cooperation with the International Association for the Evaluation of Educational Achievement (IEA). Hungary has also joined an organization based in the United States: the International Assessment of Educational Progress (IAEP). Evaluation at the international level prompted several national and regional surveys. In 1986, a national monitoring system covering the field of basic knowledge (reading comprehension, mathematics, computer literacy) was developed, with follow-ups in 1991 and 1993 (Csapó 1992). Beyond making state-of-the-art reports, the Center for Evaluation Studies of the Institute of Public Education reports on achievement trends. Assessments with diagnostic aims have been worked out and they have become widely applied by schools. Evaluation is considered a vital source for school policy at both regional and national levels. The collection of descriptive statistics on schools has a long tradition in Hungary. The OECD indicator program is well known to Hungarian researchers.

For a long time, educational research was influenced by theoretical reasoning and a marked historical approach. Empirical research emerged only in the 1960s. The impetus came from urgent social needs and from experience in other social fields such as sociology and psychology. In the early 1990s, the following research priorities and emphases have been formulated:

(a) research on the content of teaching in the domains of the new national core curriculum and in the area of methods of developing school-based curricula;

(b) research on the structure of public education (as indicated above, the types of school and the whole structure are in a state of flux);

(c) research on alternative education (theories, approaches, applications)—in particular, the humanistic approach and the various religious interpretations of education attract attention (as a result of these activities, alternative—that is, "new", nonconventional, and "free" (Waldorf type)—kindergartens and schools have been established);

(d) research on the teaching–learning process—this is a complex field of investigation aimed at establishing a differential approach to teaching and the various sides of school life, as well as at increasing the effectiveness of education in general (aspects of curriculum development and evaluation, as well as national and international surveys belong to this sector of research).

Other research topics cover teacher training, educational administration and finance, educational media, and so forth. Needless to say, this list is far from being complete.

10. Major Reforms in the 1980s and 1990s

Since the early 1980s, there has been a strong and continuous social pressure aimed at updating all important aspects of education. In the wake of the democratic changes the focus of reform shifted radically and was given new impetus. Apart from the usual modernization aims (like content, structure, and administration), the philosophical and political aspects of education have also gained ground: school ownership, distribution of power, values and aims, and so on.

11. Major Problems for the Year 2000

Much has been mentioned about the social, political, economic, and educational problems, changes, reforms, and expectations. Hungarian education seems to have two major problems that should be solved not later than the year 2000. First, it is vital that schooling be organized and administered along democratic lines, independent of the rapidly changing scenes in the political theater and of the tactical priorities set by different political parties. Second, Hungarian education should be thoroughly modernized and updated to meet Western (probably Scandinavian) standards so that schools can offer proper humanistic education, effective teaching and learning, and social safety. Such schools will presumably have every chance of assuring equal opportunities to all of their respective clients.

References

Báthory Z 1993 A national core curriculum and the democratization of public education. *Curriculum Studies* 1(1)
Csapó B 1992 Educational testing in Hungary. *Educational Measurement: Issues and Practice* 11(2)
Halász G 1987 A new Educational Act. *The New Hungarian Quarterly* 28(106)
Halász G 1990 School autonomy and the reform of educational administration in Hungary. *Prospects* 20(3)
INFO 1991 Társadalomtudomány, 17. szám
Nagy J, Szebenyi P 1990 Hungarian reform: Towards a curriculum for the 1990s. *Curriculum Journal* 1(3)

Further Reading

Báthory Z (ed.) 1992 Achievement surveys in Hungary. *Stud. Educ. Eval.* 18(1)
Mihály O, Horváth A 1990 Globalization of education and Eastern Europe. *Prospects* 20(2)
Szebenyi P 1991 Teacher education in Hungary: Standardization versus autonomy. *Br. J. Educ. Stud.* 34(2)
UNESCO 1993 *World Education Report 1993* UNESCO, Paris

Iceland

H. Lárusson

1. General Background

Iceland is an island in the North Atlantic Ocean, lying south of the Arctic Circle and midway between Norway and Greenland. It covers 103,000 square kilometers (39,768 sq. miles), and 78,000 square kilometers (30,116 sq. miles) of its surface lie over 200 meters above sea level.

Originally, Iceland was almost entirely settled from Norway, with the first settler arriving in 874 AD. Iceland was for a long period under the rule of Denmark and only gained final Independence in 1944 after a protracted struggle.

Settlements in Iceland are only found along the coastline and in the valleys that stretch into the interior. Reykjavik, the capital, is in the southwest corner of the country. More than one-half of the country's population live in Reykjavik and the townships that surround it.

Table 1 shows population growth since the turn of the last century and the proportion divided between urban and rural settlements.

From the time of the first settlement in the ninth century, the population of Iceland did not increase for nearly a thousand years. In 1801 the number of inhabitants was only 47,200 people. However, the population of the country has more than doubled since 1940 to about 260,000 in 1991. During the twentieth century, there has also been a considerable migration from rural areas into towns as Table 1 shows.

The shift in population distribution from rural to urban areas was caused by changes in the traditional industries of the country and the introduction of technical innovations to agriculture and the fishing industry. At the same time, there has also been an increase in the production of other industrial goods, especially since the 1970s. As a result of these changes and the improved standard of living that accompanied them, there has also been a considerable increase in general services and commerce within the Icelandic economy.

In the past, few foreigners settled in Iceland. It has only been in relatively recent years that the number of people from other countries has begun to rise. The official language of Iceland is Icelandic, and this is the only language used in daily communication. However, many Icelanders speak one or more foreign languages, most commonly English and one Scandinavian language. Problems that relate to differences in language and race are virtually nonexistent.

Table 2 indicates the relative number of workers employed by the various industries in Iceland between 1982 and 1990. In the decades between 1960 and 1980 the main change in the make-up of the labor force was

a reduction in the numbers of workers employed in fishing and agriculture and an increase in the number of employees working for the state, for banks, and for insurance companies.

In the 1980s, the number of students at the upper-secondary and the university level began to increase gradually. Further education has been perceived to be the key to better jobs in the long run. Therefore, people now entering the labor market have more years of schooling behind them than used to be the case. Previously, it was fairly common for young people who were offered a reasonable job to choose not to continue their education or to drop out of school. Such options have been curtailed by the increased economic difficulties of the last few years and the growing demand for specially trained employees in various industries.

Since Iceland became an independent country in

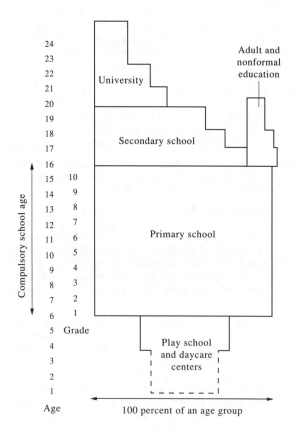

Figure 1

Iceland: Structure of the formal education system 1991

Table 1
Population increase and the relative distribution of inhabitants in urban and rural settlements 1901–91

Year	Population size (thousands)	Urban (in towns of more than 300 inhabitants) (%)	Rural (%)
1901	78.5	26.9	73.1
1920	94.7	45.7	54.3
1940	121.5	66.7	33.3
1960	175.7	82.3	17.7
1970	204.6	85.9	14.1
1980	229.2	88.6	11.4
1991	259.6	90.4	9.6

1944, all governments have involved a coalition of two or more parties. However, there has been a general consensus concerning the aims and the structure of the Icelandic school system, regardless of which political parties have been in power.

The increased autonomy of public institutions have been gradually implemented, and private enterprise has replaced government operated businesses insofar as that has been deemed feasible.

Education has also been affected by these trends. Schools are expected to be productive, and an effort is being made to ensure that the various industries can exert a greater influence on the structure and organization of the courses of study that prepare students for work in a particular field. Increased competition among schools is being discussed, and every effort is being made to guarantee the best possible use of funds for education. It has furthermore been suggested that students at Icelandic universities and upper-secondary schools should pay their share toward the operating

Table 2
Occupational distribution of the Icelandic workforce in 1982 and 1990

Major occupation (%)	1982	1990
Agriculture	7.2	4.9
Fishing	5.0	5.7
Fish processing	8.6	6.1
Industry (other than the fishing industry)	14.5	12.5
Construction and power plants	11.2	10.8
Commerce, hotels, and catering services	13.6	14.5
Transport, communications	7.0	6.7
Banking and insurance	5.6	8.1
The public sector	16.7	18.3
Various services and other operations	10.6	12.4
	100	100

costs of these institutions. Opinions are divided on these issues, and it is not clear what the final outcome will be.

2. Politics and the Goals of the Education System

In the laws concerning education in Iceland it is a fundamental principle that everyone should have an equal right to education and that complete equality of the sexes should be observed both among teachers and students. Furthermore, the law stipulates that pupils must be given equal opportunities of education regardless of where they live.

Although all Icelandic governments have been coalitions, they have usually been characterized as being left-wing or right-wing depending on which political party has led the coalition. Despite the broad consensus on aims in education, there are political differences as to how those aims should be accomplished. On the one hand, there is the view that society should make every effort to help students to get the best possible education, and on the other hand there are those who argue that it is the responsibility of the students themselves to seek the education or vocational training in which they are interested and to avail themselves of the opportunities that the educational system has to offer. Neither of these points of view is dominant in the Icelandic system of education, and as a result the best possible compromise is usually adopted as policy.

3. The Formal System of Education

3.1 Primary, Secondary, and Tertiary Education

Figure 1 shows the structure of the Icelandic school system, and Table 3 indicates the number of students and government funding towards education.

School is compulsory for children between the ages of 6 and 16. As a result, enrollment is virtually 100 percent among students in this age bracket. There are about 4,300 students enrolled in each year of school and in 1990 there were 220 compulsory schools in the country.

The aim of compulsory school is:

in cooperation with the home, to prepare the pupils for life and work in a continuously developing democratic society. The organization of the school as well as its work shall, therefore, be guided by tolerance. Christian values and democratic cooperation. The school shall foster broad viewpoints and develop the pupils' understanding of the worlds and its inhabitants, Icelandic society, history and characteristics and their sense of duty to society as individuals.

Compulsory school shall endeavor to organize its work so as to harmonize with the nature and the needs of the pupils

Table 3
Some basic statistics on the Icelandic education system

	Compulsory schools	Upper-secondary schools	Universities	Abroad
No. of students:	42,450	17,817	6,161	2,395
Percentage of age group enrolled				
16 years		83	—	—
17 years		72	—	—
18 years		62	—	—
19 years		60	1	—
20 years		34	9	2
21 years		22	16	2
22 years		17	17	4
23 years		12	17	4
24 years		10	15	5
25 years		8	11	5
26 years		7	7	5
27 years		6	5	5
28 years		4	4	4
29 years		4	3	3
No. of schools	213	62	7	—
Average no. of students per school	199	287	880	—
Student–teacher ratio	15:1	13:1	—	—
Expenditure per student in US$	1,945	3,247	5,252	—

as well as possible, and develop their general abilities conducive to the maturity, health and education of each individual.

Compulsory school shall give the pupils the opportunity to gain knowledge and develop skills and train them in such methods of work as will lead them to make constant effort to improve their education and reach further maturity. The school shall, therefore, lay the foundation to independent thinking and foster the spirit of cooperation.

Upper-secondary schools are four-year schools, but certain courses of study can take anywhere from one to four years depending on the kind of education that is being offered. Student enrollment of the upper-secondary level has been on the increase. In the autumn of 1991, 83 percent of all 16-year old students entered upper-secondary schools. In that group, more girls than boys were enrolled. More students in urban areas enter upper-secondary schools than in rural districts.

The aim of upper-secondary school is:

(a) to prepare students for living and working in a democratic society by providing conditions that make it possible for all to study and mature;

(b) to prepare students for work by providing vocational training that leads to formal qualifications;

(c) to prepare students for further education in special schools and at the university level by providing

them with the necessary education and practical training.

In Iceland, a few schools provide education at the university level. The education that is available at this level is both theoretical and practical; that is, aimed at providing training for a variety of professions. The largest of these schools is the University of Iceland, attended by the vast majority of students studying at the tertiary level in Iceland.

Courses offered at the university level are to some extent limited in Iceland, and as a result a number of students enter universities abroad (see Table 3).

3.2 Preschool Education

Iceland has play-schools and daycare centers for children between the ages of six months and 6-years old. Laws concerning these schools only date from 1991. Local municipalities are responsible for establishing and operating these schools. When a local municipality wishes to establish such a school, the Ministry of Education makes certain that proper facilities are provided and grants permission for the school to operate. The Ministry provides play-schools and daycare centers with an educational program that stipulates the role that such schools are to play in the upbringing and education of children. The aim of these schools is to provide a wholesome educational environment that allows children to work and play in a way that stimulates every aspect of their development and encourages their creativity and means of communicating with others. During the 1990–91 academic year, one-half of all children in the aforementioned age bracket attended play-schools and daycare centers.

3.3 Special Education

The general policy in respect to handicapped pupils who need special assistance is to encourage them to attend ordinary schools and avail themselves insofar as they can of the education that they have to offer. These pupils are provided with special assistance according to their handicap.

Special courses are also set up for pupils whose handicap prevents them from attending an ordinary school. These courses are aimed at providing the pupils with some knowledge of certain jobs or at showing them how they can help themselves when and if they have to fend for themselves.

Severely handicapped pupils attend special schools or institutions that are specifically designed to cater to the needs of pupils with a particular form of handicap.

3.4 Vocational, Technical, and Business Education

Vocational and technical training is offered at schools at the upper-secondary and university level, as well as in the workplace. At the upper-secondary level, this kind of education is provided by upper-secondary comprehensive schools and by special schools. The same rules apply to this form of training as to any other education that these schools have to offer. Anyone who wishes to enter into vocational training may do so, and the same demands are made of teachers of vocational subjects as teachers of academic subjects.

Students who are training to become skilled workers in certain fields may choose between two different ways of completing their studies. First, they can become apprenticed to a master craftsman who is responsible for the practical aspect of their training, and then go back to school for the theoretical part of their education. Second, both practical and theoretical training take place at school.

Curricula for vocational training are to a large extent written by people who represent a particular skilled trade. In many cases they also stipulate what skills the student needs to master in order to receive his or her vocational qualifications.

Business studies are no different from any other forms of education except in the sense that the students receive a practical training course by working briefly for a particular company, wherever that can be arranged.

Enrollment in vocational, technical, and business courses of study has decreased. A comparison between enrollment figures for 1984 and 1991 shows that vocational and technical training now attracts 5 percent fewer students, while 4 percent less opt for business studies. At the same time, enrollment for other courses of study has increased by a corresponding margin.

Those who complete their vocational, technical, or business training at the upper-secondary level can continue their education at a technical college or a university, and obtain further qualifications at that level.

3.5 Adult and Nonformal Education

Adult education is provided by various parties. Many upper-secondary schools offer adult education in the form of evening classes. In addition, they organize and run specialized courses in cooperation with industries or labor unions for employees in particular fields. Those who attend such courses pay a minimum of one-third of the cost of tuition.

Efforts have been made to establish distance learning in certain fields and for certain professions. This form of education is likely to increase over the next few years.

A correspondence school is jointly operated by a group of various associations. It receives some support from the state but its main income is through tuition fees.

Various institutions and societies also offer adult education which is not connected with the general system of education. Furthermore, there are a few private schools which offer courses in specific areas, such as computer studies and foreign languages.

4. Administrative and Supervisory Structure and Operation

The Icelandic parliament, the Althing, debates any proposed legislation concerning education, and bills are either passed or defeated. The Althing thus formulates, in the main, educational policy that is being followed at any particular period. The minister of education is responsible for putting into effect any measures that are stipulated by educational laws.

Upper-secondary schools come directly under the Ministry of Education and are entirely funded by the state. Compulsory schools, on the other hand, are operated by local municipalites. Iceland is divided into eight educational authorities with a director of education in each authority. The director of education is in charge of all compulsory school operations in the district and directly represents the Ministry.

The Ministry of Education appoints teachers at compulsory schools and upper-secondary schools. In upper-secondary schools teachers are hired by the headmaster, but they are hired by the local director of education in compulsory schools.

The Ministry of Education is responsible for supervising school work. This supervision mainly applies to school budgets and less so to the actual teaching that goes on in the school. Education is professionally supervised through nationally coordinated examinations, surveys that are sent to the schools by the Ministry, and by visits to the schools.

5. Education Finance

Play-schools and daycare centers are funded and operated entirely by local municipalities. Compulsory schools are operated by local municipalities which also pay for the construction of any school buildings at that level. Teachers' salaries and educational expenses, however, are paid for by the state. Upper-secondary schools are operated exclusively by the state, but local municipalities contribute 40 percent of the cost of new school buildings. Schools at the university level are operated exclusively by the state.

Sufficient information on the total expenses borne by local municipalities in the operation of schools is not available.

In 1990, 14.77 percent of the state budget went toward education. This represents 3.93 percent of the Gross Domestic Product (GDP). The 14.77 percent was divided as follows: 5.14 percent went to compulsory schools, 3.42 percent to upper-secondary schools, 2.19 percent to schools at the tertiary level, 2.33 percent on loans and grants, and 1.7 percent to other activities in the educational sector. State funding towards education rose proportionally from 12.74 percent in 1980 to 14.77 percent in 1990.

6. Supplying Personnel for the Education System

The training of teachers takes place in schools at the university level. The University College of Education trains teachers for work in compulsory schools. Teacher trainees at that school have traditionally completed their education in three years, but a fourth year was added to the program in 1992. The University of Akureyri has also been authorized to train teachers for the compulsory level through a three-year course of study. The Akureyri training course is expected to stress aspects that are different from the program of the University College of Education.

Teachers at upper-secondary schools receive their education at the University of Iceland where they complete a four-year course of study: two years (or three, if a one-year minor is not selected) of studying a particular subject in which they major and one year of education.

In the academic year of 1990–91 there were 2,741 teachers employed in full time positions at compulsory schools. Of that number, 2,266 had full qualifications as teachers and 475 had something lacking in their training according to the legal requirements that stipulate what their qualifications must be.

At the upper-secondary level, 1,360 teachers were employed in full-time positions in the 1992–93 academic year. Of that group, 980 were fully qualified to teach at that level.

As these figures show, there is a shortage of fully qualified teachers in Iceland. It is mainly in rural areas that this lack is most keenly felt. Rural locations provide less than towns in terms of social services, and have little to offer that might attract teachers to come and work there. There is also a general shortage of specially trained mathematics and science teachers; a major reason for this is that people with such qualifications find it easy to get work in other fields. Teachers' unions maintain that the poor pay they receive is largely to blame for qualified teachers not being attracted to work in the schools.

7. Curriculum Development and Teaching Methodology

The Ministry of Education issues a curriculum for the schools. The curriculum applies to the country as a whole, and the schools all have to follow the main points that it stipulates.

The law concerning compulsory schooling specifies which subjects should be taught there, and the curriculum for that level explains what should be the main aims in the teaching of particular subjects, the contents of the education, assessment procedures, and makes suggestions with regard to teaching methods. The schools have some freedom in deciding how many lessons they want to spend on the teaching of individual subjects. Compulsory schools, Grades 1–10, teach the following subjects: mother tongue (27%); modern foreign languages; that is, English and Danish (9%); mathematics (17%); natural science (6%); social studies (10%); arts and crafts (17%); physical education (10%); and other subjects (4%). Most schools write their own study programs based on the curricula issued by the Ministry. The school curricula take into consideration those local factors that are seen as useful elements in the education of the children.

In the eighth, the ninth, and more often in the tenth grade, students are free to choose between certain subjects. They can elect to receive more instruction in subjects that are on their regular timetable or select other optional subjects that are specifically being offered by their school. The most popular optional subjects are: bookkeeping, domestic science, biology, arts and crafts, computer studies, and typing. More than 25 percent of all tenth grade students select one or more of these subjects.

The National Center for Educational Materials supplies compulsory schools with textbooks and other educational materials. Students at this level receive their textbooks free of charge.

The curriculum for upper-secondary schooling applies to all nonspecialized schools at that level. It contains general rules concerning the rights and duties of the school and the students, which both teachers and students are to take note of. It furthermore defines the courses of study that individual schools can offer and lists the subjects that pertain to each course of study. The aim of courses of study at the upper-secondary level is to train students for work or to prepare them for further education at special schools or schools at the university level. The subjects that are required for each course of study are of course varied, but a few subjects, i.e., mother tongue, modern foreign languages, and mathematics, are common to all of them. All students are required to learn some modern foreign languages. Students in language streams study more modern foreign languages than the rest (i.e., four in all: Danish, English, German, and French). In some cases students opt to take Spanish instead of German or French.

In most of the courses of study the students can select from among optional subjects. This mainly applies to academic coursework that leads to matriculation. The courses of study include optional subjects which have been defined in the curriculum, so all students have to choose subjects within that particular framework.

No single institution has the role of providing the upper-secondary schools with textbooks. Students have to buy them themselves from whatever bookshop the school may recommend. There is some shortage of suitable textbooks, and to remedy this, the Ministry of Education annually gives a few grants to authors of textbooks for the upper-secondary level.

Curricula for compulsory and upper-secondary schools are written by experts that are specifically appointed for that task and supervised by Ministry of Education employees. The Minister of Education ratifies the curricula for both levels before they are put into effect.

Students arrive at the upper-secondary level with very different preparation from their various compulsory schools, and also vary in regard to their learning ability. The main problem of upper-secondary schools is to be able to meet all the different needs and requests of the students both in respect to the courses that are offered and the methods of teaching. Solving problems of this kind calls for increased funding for schools, different training of teachers, and more expert assistance.

8. The System of Examinations, Promotions, and Certifications

At compulsory school, students move automatically from one grade (or year) to the next regardless of their academic performance. Assessment at compulsory school is carried out by the teachers themselves, except in the case of the nationally coordinated examinations that are held in two subjects at the end of the 10th grade. Although marks are given, no official examination certificate is issued until the student completes his or her compulsory education.

Most upper-secondary schools are organized according to a so-called "unit-credit system." At the outset of their studies, the students work out a plan of

which courses they intend to take and when they are to be taken. In each course, certain minimum requirements have to be met in order to go on to the next course in the same subject. The writing of examinations and assessment is exclusively done by the teachers themselves.

It is generally recognized that more information is needed about the students and their academic status than is available. This need is primarily felt when the students apply for upper-secondary school or schools at the university level. To improve this situation, it has been suggested that more nationally coordinated examinations should be introduced, in addition to systematic evaluation of the work that goes on in individual schools.

9. Educational Assessment, Evaluation, and Research

The early 1990s economic recession that affected both the state and local municipalities, and consequent efforts to make the best possible use of funds for education, have raised questions about the efficiency of the Icelandic system of education. The lack of assessment of the work that goes on in the schools has been a weak link in the school system, and there is growing interest in resolving this problem. For this reason, the possibility of introducing more nationally coordinated examinations is being studied. Thus far, students only take a nationally coordinated examination in two subjects at the end of compulsory school. Practical methods of evaluating comprehensively the work that goes on in individual schools are also being examined. Such evaluation would make it possible to make improvements in the operation of a particular school in whatever areas that might be needed.

10. Major Reforms in the 1980s and 1990s

In the 1980s, new legislation concerning play-schools and daycare centers was prepared. According to the law, which was passed in 1991, these schools are for children between the ages of six months to six years. Local municipalities are responsible for establishing and operating play-schools and daycare centers, but professional administration of this school level rests in the hands of the Ministry of Education. Local municipalities are to plan a few years in advance what developments they intend to make in respect to preschool education. Putting this new law into effect will be one of the major tasks of the next few years.

Laws that were passed in 1991 made it compulsory for 6-year old children to attend school. Compulsory education was thus extended from nine to ten years.

Efforts are also being made to decentralize educational administration in Iceland. For this purpose, local educational authorities and individual schools are now being given tasks that used to be in the domain of the Ministry of Education. New laws have been passed that change the role of the state and local municipalities concerning the operation of compulsory schools. With this change, the local municipalities now carry a greater responsibility for the operation of the schools that they did before.

Plans are also being made to increase the independence of the schools. This will probably mean that the schools will be given more freedom to decide those matters that concern their operation and the number of lessons that go into the teaching of individual subjects.

A new curriculum for compulsory school was issued in 1989. The new curriculum reflects the changes that have affected policy-making in education since the writing of the old curriculum which it replaced.

11. Major Problems for the Year 2000

Although much was achieved in the 1980s in the field of education, many problems remain unsolved. The rapid development in the field of science and technology and the quick changes that Icelandic society has gone through have made it difficult for the schools to meet the demands that are being made on them. Legislation concerning compulsory and upper-secondary schools was being revised in the early 1990s, and other educational factors, such as the training of teachers, will also be examined.

The areas that need to be studied in this context include the structure of the school system, the education that the schools—mainly upper-secondary schools—can offer, and the increased participation of industry in policy-making in the field of vocational training and the organization of vocational courses of study to ensure that this form of training prepares the students for their work in the best possible way. It is also important to reassess the training of teachers in Iceland in the light of changed social conditions and the different role that schools now have to assume.

Bibliography

Gumundsson G 1992 *The Changing Role of Vocational and Technical Education and Training*. Menntamálaráuneyti, Reykjavik
Hagstofa Islands 1992 *Landshagir: Statistical Abstract of Iceland*. Hagstofa Islands
Háskóli Islands 1992a *Undirbúningur náms vi Háskóla Islands*. Kennslumálanefnd Háskóla Islands
Jónasson J T 1992 *Abyrg og stjórn í íslenskum skólum*. Samfélagstíindi
Jónasson J T, Jónsdóttir G A 1992 *Námsferill í framhaldsskóla*. Félagsvísindastofnun Háskóla Islands
Menntamálaráuneyti 1989 *Aalnámskrá grunnskóla*. Menntamálaráuneyti, Reykjavik
Menntamálaráuneyti 1990 *Námskrá handa framhaldsskólum*. Menntamálaráuneyti, Reykjavik
Menntamálaráuneyti 1992 *Nám a loknum grunnskóla*. Menntamálaráuneyti, Reykjavik
Nordisk Ministerråd 1990 Skola och Skolförvaltning i Norden. *Nord* (1990): 8. Nordisk Ministerråd, Copenhagen

India

A. Bordia

1. General Background

With a tradition of learning and education as old as the history of civilization, India presents a picture of impressive scientific and technological progress side by side with massive illiteracy and a weak educational system. In terms of numbers of institutions, students, and teachers, as well as in the variety of educational activity, the Indian educational system is highly diversified and one of the largest in the world. However, in spite of much effort, it remains divorced from the overall objectives of the country's socioeconomic development.

The 1991 census records an overall literacy rate of 52.1 percent for the population aged 7 years and above. For the first time in the history of independent India the number of literates has exceeded the number of illiterates. There are, however, wide disparities. While Kerala has achieved a literacy rate of 94 percent, the four states in the Hindi belt—namely Bihar, Uttar Pradesh, Madhya Pradesh, and Rajasthan—have very low literacy rates and account for 47 percent of the illiterates in the country. Two-thirds of the illiterates are female, and the level of illiteracy among the Scheduled Castes and Tribes, the economically and educationally disadvantaged groups, is even lower.

With an area of 3,287,263 square kilometers (1,269,000 square miles), India is the seventh largest country in the world. In the last census (1991) its population was approximately 844 million, second only to China. About 74 percent of the population lives in the rural areas. The main religious groups are Hindus (83%) and Moslems (11%), with Christians, Sikhs, and Jains forming small minorities. A large number of languages and dialects are spoken in India, most of which have their own scripts and a rich literature.

India's economy is essentially agricultural. Agriculture and allied activities (such as animal husbandry and fishing) account for 34 percent of the country's national income, and performance in this area has a direct impact on performance in the manufacturing sector, which accounts for 27 percent of the national income. There is roughly one worker to every two nonworkers. The nonworkers are mainly housewives, the aged, students, and the unemployed. The agricultural sector absorbs nearly 69 percent of the country's workforce, of which more than one-third are agricultural laborers who are generally illiterate and dependent on seasonal work.

India has a planned economy, the guiding consideration of which is growth with social justice. Between 1951 and 1991, the country has had seven five-year plans, with ad hoc annual plans in the other years. Planning in India encompasses the public as well as the private sector, including the social services and human resource development, of which health and education are a part. During the 40 years of planned development, the national income has increased, in real terms, at a rate of 3.8 percent per annum, agricultural production has risen by 2.95 percent per annum, industrial production by 6.3 percent, and installed generating capacity from 2.3 to 70.5 million kilowatts showing an average growth of 9.3 percent per annum.

In spite of these gains, with an estimated per capita income of Rs. 4,252 (US$200) in 1989–90, India is among the poorest countries in the world, with wide disparities of income and wealth distribution. According to official estimates (1987–88), about 30 percent of the population is below the poverty line (that is, with a nutritional intake below the minimum requirement).

For about 150 years India was a part of the British Empire, until it gained independence in 1947. The British systematically destroyed the indigenous system of education and introduced the teaching of European education through the medium of English. The British–Indian system educated a select few, leaving a wide chasm between the educated and the unlettered. At the time of independence, 14 percent of the population was literate and only one child out of three had been enrolled in a primary school.

During the British raj, too, a number of educational pioneers, who were also leaders in the struggle for freedom—for example, Sri Aurobindo, Rabindranath Tagore, and Mahatma Gandhi—explored ways of reviving the spirit of Indian culture and of building an educational system suited to Indian conditions. During the first few years after independence, there was serious debate between those attempting to retain the British–Indian educational system and those advocating an alternative model, particularly the one designed by Mahatma Gandhi.

2. Politics and the Goals of the Education System

The Indian Constitution, promulgated in January 1950, sets out the framework for a federal political system and lists the sectors for which the central and state governments are respectively or concurrently responsible. Education was in the state list, and although an amendment (1976) has placed it in the concurrent list, the responsibility for education rests essentially with the states. The central government's responsibility is mainly for the maintenance and coordination of standards of higher and technical education. Directive principles of state policy in the constitution direct the state to provide free and compulsory education for all children up to 14 years of age. The state also provides equal educational opportunity for all and special protection of religious and linguistic minorities.

Soon after independence, priority was given to the introduction of "basic education" (*nai taleem*, in the words of Mahatma Gandhi), the objective of which is to develop the total personality of the child by providing instruction related to manual and productive work. While Gandhian basic education provided guidelines for the planning of primary education, the search for a suitable system of secondary and higher education led the government of India to appoint two commissions, in 1948 and 1952 respectively. Although some reforms were introduced as a result of the recommendations made by these commissions, a nationally accepted structure of education (of 10+2+3 years) had to await the report of the Education Commission (Ministry of Education and Social Welfare 1966).

On the basis of the recommendations of the Education Commission, the central government, after consultations with state governments and with the approval of parliament, announced the National Policy on Education in 1968. It called for "a transformation of the system of education to relate it more closely to the life of the people; a continuous effort to expand educational opportunity; a sustained and intensive effort to raise the quality of education at all stages; an emphasis on the development of science and technology; and the cultivation of moral and social values."

Early in 1985 the central government reviewed the educational situation and decided to bring about a new education policy. The new education policy and a program of action for its implementation were prepared in consultation with the state governments and were adopted by the federal parliament in 1986 (Ministry of Human Resource Development 1986). The new educational policy envisages a national system of education which would take determined steps for the universalization of primary education and the spread of adult literacy, thereby becoming an instrument for the reduction of disparities. It is based on a national curricular framework which contains a common core along with other, flexible, region-specific components. The common core cuts across subject areas and is designed to promote values such as India's common cultural heritage, egalitarianism, democracy and secularism, equality of the sexes, protection of the environment, removal of social barriers, observance of the small family norm, and inculcation of the scientific way of thinking. While the 1986 policy lays stress on widening of opportunities for the masses it calls for consolidation of the existing system of higher and tech-

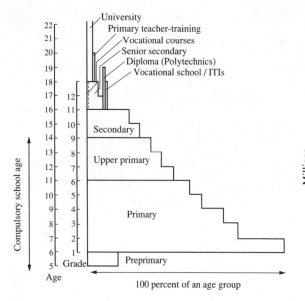

Figure 1
India: Structure of the formal education system

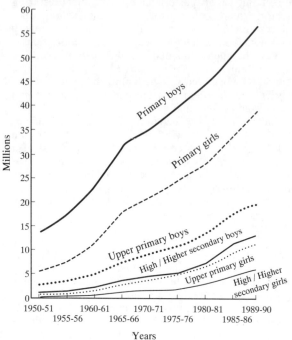

Figure 2
Trends in school enrollment in India 1950–51 to 1989–90

nical education. It also emphasizes the need for a much higher investment in education of at least 6 percent of the national income.

Pace-setting residential schools intended to provide quality education to children with special talent or aptitude irrespective of their capability to pay, have been established in various parts of the country. These schools, called *Navodaya Vidyalayas*, seek to promote excellence along with equity and social justice by enrolling children largely from the rural areas and the backward sections of society. One-third of the total places in these schools are reserved for girls. In all, 280 *Navodaya Vidyalayas* had been opened by 1990.

The 1986 policy envisaged its review as occurring every 5 years. The government of India set up a committee for review in 1990 and minor modifications were made in 1992. The Seventh Five-Year Plan (1985–90) postulated decentralized planning and organizational reforms, promotion of nonformal and open learning systems, the forging of links with industry and development agencies, and the mobilization of community resources and societal involvement. Primary education and adult literacy were included in minimum-needs programs, to which the plan attached a high priority. The Eighth Plan (1992–97) lays emphasis on the universalization of primary education in the threefold dimensions of enrollment, retention, and achievement, and on the eradication of illiteracy, particularly in the 15–35 age group.

While the earlier approach to educational planning assumed that the supply-side constraints were the major factor in educational underdevelopment, experi-

ence has shown that the mere provision of facilities does not ensure their utilization. The causes of low enrollment and high dropout are rooted in the socioeconomic structure and the cultural milieu. To overcome this malaise various alternatives and possibilities are being worked out. Some significant attempts include the foreign-assisted projects for achieving the goals of basic education for all. These projects include the Andhra Pradesh Primary Education Project with the assistance of the Overseas Development Administration of the United Kingdom, the UNICEF-assisted Bihar Education Project, the Lok Jumbish project in Rajasthan with Swedish International Development Agency (SIDA) assistance, and the Dutch-assisted Mahila Samakhya which views education as important in achieving the goal of women's equality. The main literacy campaigns started after the launching of the National Literacy Mission (1988) also lay stress on the generation of demand for literacy among illiterate adults.

3. The Formal System of Education

3.1 Primary, Secondary, and Tertiary Education

Since independence (1947) there has been an attempt to have a common structure of the educational

Table 1
Number of educational institutions from 1950–51 to 1989–90

	1950–51	1960–61	1970–71	1980–81	1989–90
Universities	27	45	82	110	146
Colleges of general education	498	1,043	2,598	3,425	4,755
Colleges of technology and professional education	102	470	641	727	891
Secondary schools	7,288	17,257	36,738	51,594	70,633
Upper-primary schools	13,596	49,663	90,621	116,447	143,747
Primary schools	209,671	330,399	408,378	485,538	550,700

system. The Education Commission (1964–66) had recommended a 10+2+3 pattern, which was adopted in the 1968 educational policy. The emphasis in this pattern is on a common school curriculum up to class X, with vocational and technical courses starting at the secondary stage. Professional courses for primary teacher training, medicine, and engineering commence after the two-year senior-secondary course (see Fig. 1.).

Wide disparities in facilities and standards of various types of institution have been observed. At one extreme are the "public schools," so called after their British models, and the newly established *Navodaya Vidyalayas*. At the other extreme are the ill-equipped, insufficiently staffed, and poorly supervised government rural or municipal schools. In between these extremes are a variety of private schools, the well-funded "central schools" mainly for the children of central government employees, and the basic and postbasic schools run by people inspired by Gandhi's ideas on education.

Primary schools are, by and large, coeducational. School sessions commence at the end of the summer, and there are autumn and summer vacations. Generally speaking, the number of working days is about 200 in an academic year. The four-year secondary stage is equally divided between the secondary and senior-secondary levels. While standards of education in practically all schools funded and managed by govern-

ment or quasigovernment agencies are unsatisfactory, the quality of buildings and school facilities, and numbers and qualifications of teachers at the secondary stage are comparatively much better.

General higher education is provided in universities and colleges. All central universities and a few others are primarily residential. About 83 percent of enrollment in higher education is in affiliated colleges. Technical and professional courses range from three to five years for a first-degree course and from two to three years for a postdegree course. Admission requirements in general education courses are not very demanding, but admission to engineering and medical courses is very competitive. Universities also provide facilities for research and many of them, particularly the agricultural universities, have developed strong extension programs. The number of educational institutions by different levels is given in Table 1.

Little attention has so far been attached to preprimary education, except through the Integrated Child Development Services Program, which has health, nutrition, and education as its components. Priority is given to provision of primary education. Gross enrollment in the 6–11 age group was 99.9 percent in 1989–90, representing a 115.5 percent increase for boys and 83.6 percent for girls since 1950–51 (see Fig. 2). The growth of enrollment since 1950–51 is shown in Table 2.

Table 2
Enrollment at different stages 1950–51 to 1990–91 (in thousands)

	1950–1		1960–61		1970–71		1980–81		1990–91	
	Male	Female	Male	Female	Male	Female	Male	Female	Male	Female
Pre-primary	15	13	97	82	190	168	501	417	732	621
Primary (I-VIII)	16,356	5,919	28,667	16,475	45,155	25,195	59,220	35,278	78,100	51,407
Secondary (IX-XII)	1,058	162	2,340	547	4,872	1,708	7,593	3,201	11,552	5,660
Higher	90	14	277	73	1,016	392	2,943	1,049	3,685	1,493

The position regarding enrollment varies widely from state to state. Most states have a system of incentives to encourage participation in school. These include attendance scholarships, midday meals, free uniforms, free textbooks, and so on. Dropout between classes I and V has been a bane of India's primary education system. In 1986 the dropout rate was about 46 percent (as against 60% in 1951). Enrollment is particularly low and the dropout rate high among girls and certain social groups that have traditionally been backward.

With a view to ensuring that all primary schools are brought to the minimum standard of facilities, the "Operation Blackboard" scheme was launched in 1987. It provides for (a) the minimum of a two-room building usable in all weather with toilets, (b) at least two teachers, and (c) essential furniture and teaching–learning equipment. By 1991 about 66 percent of the schools in the country were covered under Operation Blackboard.

3.2 Special Education

In consonance with the policy of providing a complete package of education and welfare services to physically and mentally handicapped children, a number of programs have been initiated by the central Department of Education and by the Ministry of Welfare. The Integrated Child Development Services and the Early Childhood Care and Education projects emphasize the preventive and developmental efforts. The coverage under these schemes constitutes less than 12 percent of the corresponding age groups requiring these services. Special schools for educational provision, integrated schools, special rehabilitation services and so on, have been in operation for many years. The coverage under the scheme of integrated education of the disabled is about 30,000 children in nearly 6,000 schools. Four national-level apex institutes are engaged in education, training, vocational guidance, counseling, research, rehabilitation, and development of service modules in each major area of disability. On the whole, educational facilities for the handicapped are extremely insufficient and they have not kept pace with the advances taking place in this sphere.

3.3 Vocational, Technical, and Business Education

Traditionally, the system of education in India is divorced from work and vocation. The system of Gandhian education, which evolved during the struggle for independence, laid emphasis on the interaction between learning and productive work. After India's independence, pressure also began to be felt on the educational system as a result of growing unemployment among educated persons. Efforts for the introduction of vocational courses were made from the beginning of the 1960s, but progress was slow. The education policy of 1986 made a strong plea for the introduction of vocational courses as a distinct stream at the senior-secondary level. The policy envisaged that by 1995 about 25 percent of the students at senior-secondary level would be in vocational courses. In 1992, about 6 percent of the students at this level were in vocational programs.

Technical education is comprised of two levels: technician education of approximately 3 years' duration after the secondary stage, and technical higher education of 4 to 5 years' duration after senior-secondary level. There are approximately 1,315 polytechnics in the country for technician education with an intake capacity of approximately 80,000 and 277 engineering colleges or university engineering faculties with an intake of approximately 40,000. About 140 institutions offer facilities for graduate courses and research in technical education. These include five Indian institutes of technology which are internationally recognized institutions of excellence, and four technican teacher-training institutes which provide training to polytechnic teachers. The All India Council of Technical Education, which was given statutory status in 1987, is the apex organization for the promotion of technical education and the maintenance of standards.

Large-scale industrialization started in India in the 1960s. Much of it was in the public sector. A total of four Indian institutes of management have been set up to meet the needs of a high-level management labor force. In addition, there are 54 universities with graduate courses in management. Management education in India mainly serves industry and trade with little attention to public systems and the management needs of the rural sector.

3.4 Adult and Nonformal Education

A noteworthy development is the creation of a nonformal education system—from the primary to the university levels. This system complements the formal education system and meets the educational needs of children and adults who cannot attend the full-time educational programs.

At the primary education level a start was made in part-time educational programs in the Sixth Plan (1980–85) and extended by the 1986 policy. The overall program envisages flexibility in regard to course content, duration, place, and hours of instruction, and decentralization in management. The actual running of the program will be done with the involvement of voluntary agencies, local government institutions, and specially funded government projects. The curricula and teaching–learning materials to be used will be relevant to the work, life, and environment of the learners. The new policy emphasises that the level and opportunities of learning in the nonformal stream should be comparable with the corresponding stage in the formal system. The program had acquired a momentum by the end of the Seventh Plan (1990). By 1990 there were nearly 260,000 nonformal education centers with an average enrollment of 22 learners per center.

The National Open School (NOS) for providing distance education programs at the secondary education level was established in 1985. The NOS offers courses for classes IX to XII and has also initiated some vocational courses for continuing education of middle-level workers. The 1991 enrollment of NOS was about 160,000.

Universities began to start correspondence courses in the 1960s. By 1990, 40 universities were organizing correspondence courses with an enrollment of about half a million, comprising about 10 percent of total enrollment at the tertiary level. The courses are, by and large, a duplication of regular bachelor's or master's programs, relying almost exclusively on correspondence. Radio and television are not used to supplement correspondence instruction. In the 1980s, the University Grants Commission developed an ambitious country-wide classroom program, through which supplementary instruction is provided via television.

The Indira Gandhi National Open University (IGNOU) was established in Delhi in 1985. It lays stress on continuing education with a view to improving knowledge and skills, and promoting the educational opportunities of the community in general and disadvantaged groups in particular. The states of Andhra Pradesh, Rajasthan, Maharashtra, and Bihar have established their own open universities. One of the functions of IGNOU is to oversee the standards of distance education in all institutions of higher education. It has established a Distance Education Council for discharge of this responsibility.

Although a variety of adult education programs had been organized since independence (1947), they were small scale. All of these programs merged into the National Adult Education Program (NAEP) which was launched in 1978. NAEP attempted to involve all official and nonofficial agencies in adult education programs, the content of which included literacy, functionality, and awareness. Approximately 250,000 adult education centers were being run under NAEP in 1980. A state resource center was established in every state for production of instrumental materials, training, and evaluation. Evaluation of NAEP revealed that while the spread of programs was wide, there were serious deficiencies in quality and overall performance.

Taking into consideration the strengths and weaknesses of NAEP, the central government launched the National Literacy Mission (NLM) in 1988. The NLM's aim is to provide functional literacy to 80 million illiterate persons by 1995. Shifting emphasis from the provision of a delivery system, it attempts to stimulate mass action and creation of an environment in which a genuine demand for literacy is engendered. There is an insistence in the NLM on attainment by all persons of a well-defined level in language and arithmetic. Special instructional materials have been developed to see that learners' motivation is sustained, and it is possible to

assess the level of literacy achieved at the time of evaluation. A program of total eradication of illiteracy was launched in the Ernakulam district of Kerala to coincide with International Literacy Year (1990). In that district 280,000 illiterate persons were made literate within one year. This impressive success has generated enthusiasm throughout the country. A campaign for the total eradication of illiteracy has been launched in 75 districts (1991), which accounts for 15 percent of all the districts in the country. It is estimated that nearly 20 million persons were made literate under the NLM between 1988 and 1990.

4. Administrative and Supervisory Structure and Operation

The Government in India is federal in character. Although under the Constitution, the central and the state governments have joint responsibility for education, it is essentially treated as a state matter except in some well-defined areas. The responsibility of the central government is for educational planning and policy, for coordination and maintenance of standards in higher and technical education, for promotion of research and training relating to school education, adult education, promotion of languages, and so on. The Ministry of Human Resource Development (which comprises the Department of Education, Culture, Youth Affairs, and Sports and the Department of Women and Child Development) has the principal responsibility in respect of education.

The central government set up the University Grants Commission (UGC) in 1956 to discharge its responsibility for higher education. The UGC (like its British counterpart, the UFC) is a statutory, autonomous body. Although its principal function is to coordinate the development of higher education and to ensure maintenance of standards, over the years the UGC has become the central government's arm for assessing the financial needs of universities and colleges and disbursing funds to them.

The central government has set up three national agencies which help it in its work. The National Council of Educational Research and Training (NCERT) has the role of improving the quality of school education. Its main contribution has been in the sphere of curriculum design, production of textbooks, and examination reform. The National Institute of Educational Planning and Administration (NIEPA) undertakes diverse programs of research, extension, training, and consultancy. It plays an important role in educational reform and much of the professional support for the implementation of the new education policy is being provided by NIEPA. The National Institute of Adult Education is responsible for providing research support to literacy and adult education programs.

In each state, there is a secretariat for education and separate directorates for higher education, school edu-

Table 3
Number of teachers in schools (in thousands)

| | 1947 | | 1988–90 | |
	Teachers	Percentage of trained teachers	Teachers	Percentage of trained teachers
Primary	344	67.1	1,602	89.8
Middle	50	58.3	1,048	91.7
High/Higher secondary	93	54.9	1,264	91.4

cation, technical education, and adult and nonformal education. The state-level administration lays down policy and regulates the educational system. At the head of the district education administration is a district education officer with several deputies and sub-deputies who together inspect and supervise the schools. Given the 1986 emphasis on decentralized micro-level planning and management of education, the infrastructural and institutional support is being strengthened at the district level. The heads of schools set school timetables, attend to discipline among pupils, and supervise the work of teachers.

5. Educational Finance

Education is financed by the central government, state governments, local authorities, and a variety of private sources. The education budgets of the central government as well as the state governments are divided into two categories: developmental expenditure (Plan) and maintenance (Non-Plan). Over the years, there has been a remarkable increase in expenditure on education, both as a percentage of the gross national product (about 3.8% in 1990) and as a percentage of government expenditure (about 20% in 1990).

Although the proportion of government expenditure on education has been increasing, the burden of private costs continues to be substantial. These costs comprise the increasing expenses on textbooks and stationery, school clothing, and attendant expenses. Private funding for education has not expanded appreciably, although it still comprises a significant segment of the total investment in education. Private sources of funding include individual and family charities, student fees, and community contributions in the form of buildings and equipment. Fees are very low in schools run by government and local authorities and in institutions of higher, professional, and technical education. A comprehensive program of scholarships exists to aid equalization of educational opportunity. Almost every student from an economically and socially backward group who pursues higher education is eligible for a scholarship. The estimated per student costs at the primary, secondary, and tertiary levels of education (1989–90) were approximately Rs. 610,

Rs. 2,655, and Rs. 5,570 (US $29, US $125, US $262) respectively.

6. Supplying Personnel for the Education System

With the support of the federal Department of Education, the salary scales of teachers at universities and colleges have been substantially improved. There is a wide difference in the salary scales of teachers, although this has narrowed. Differences from one state to another have also tended to narrow down. The average monthly pay of a primary school teacher is Rs. 2,000 (US $94) and that of a higher secondary school teacher Rs. 3,500 (US $165). The figure for a university/college lecturer is Rs. 4500 (US $212) and that for a professor Rs. 6500 (US $306). Table 3 provides information on the numbers of teachers in India's schools.

Practically all teacher appointments are made from among trained personnel. The requirement for admission to primary teachers' colleges is completion of higher secondary education and for secondary teachers' colleges it is a university degree. On the recommendation of the National Council of Teacher Education most states have introduced a two-year certificate course for primary school teachers. The duration of the degree-level teacher-training course is determined by the universities and they continue to have the Bachelor of Education degree course of one year's duration. Under its faculty improvement program, the University Grants Commission provides financial support for teachers wishing to pursue research. There are four training institutions for teachers in polytechnics. Since the 1986 Education Policy there is an increasing emphasis on inservice training of teachers. About 275 (out of 1500) primary teacher-training institutes have been upgraded to district institutes of education and training with the principal function of running inservice courses, and the UGC has funded 43 academic staff colleges for the continuing education of university-level teachers.

The NCERT and its state counterparts have endeavored to upgrade the quality of teacher education. NCERT has assisted the state authorities in the improvement of teacher-training curricula. In December 1991, the federal government took a decision to give statutory status to the National Council of Teacher Education to improve standards of teacher training and regulate private teacher-training colleges which commercialize the growing demand for teachers.

7. *Curriculum Development and Teaching Methodology*

Curricula at the higher education level are the responsibility of the universities, which also prescribe them for the colleges affiliated to them. There is a board of secondary education in each state with responsibility for devising curricula and prescribing textbooks for secondary and higher secondary classes. For the primary and middle stages, the responsibility rests mainly with the state education departments. The geographical coverage of curricula in universities extends only to affiliated colleges, and there is a common curriculum for secondary and primary education throughout each state.

The UGC, the boards of secondary education, and the NCERT make substantial efforts to improve curricula at all levels. The UGC has paid particular attention to the restructuring of first-degree courses and relating them to the needs of the rural and urban environments. The federal Department of Education funds the publication of university-level books in Hindi and regional languages. The NCERT has also been engaged in the task of evolving school curriculum which conforms to the national policy guidlines. State boards of secondary education continually undertake research and experimentation aimed at the improvement of curricula. In pursuance of the mandate given in the 1986 education policy, the NCERT, in consultation with the relevant state authorities, has developed the National Curricular Framework for classes I to X, suggesting national learning norms and the inculcation of values such as patriotism, national integration, faith in democratic institutions, women's equality, protection of the environment, and observance of the small-family norm. Textbooks at the secondary and primary levels are written mainly by teachers. Other measures to encourage the implementation of curricula reform include retraining teachers and the introduction of modifications in instructional methodology to emphasize the interaction of learners with the environment and laboratory experiments in science teaching.

Mahatma Gandhi pleaded for a needs-based, differential curriculum in which learning is organized around productive manual work. Reiterating this, the Education Commission (Ministry of Education and Social Welfare 1966) also called for increasing emphasis on work experience, national and social service, and ethical and moral values. While several efforts have been made to improve the curriculum and include socially useful productive work, in practice it continues to be devoid of manual work. The traditional method of rote memorization and the habit of regarding education as synonymous with book-learning still holds sway.

8. *The System of Examinations, Promotions, and Certifications*

Examinations occupy a dominant position in India's educational system. Traditionally, what has mattered is the score obtained in an examination rather than the quality of education—and the two are not necessarily related.

In practically all parts of the country, stages in the educational system are divided into grades or classes. Promotion from one grade to the next depends on continuous pupil assessment through terminal tests and, invariably, an examination at the end of the school session. At the initial stages, examinations are flexible and the internal concern of each school, but in the higher stages an external element in evaluation tends to increase, as do rigidities in the system. No retention policy is followed for first few years of schooling, which implies that practically all children progress from class to class till the 5th standard without having to repeat. Certificates provided by school authorities are accepted for purposes of admission to secondary schools.

While examination of pupils at the end of Grades IX and XI is the responsibility of schools, boards of secondary education conduct examinations at the end of the secondary (Grade X) and higher secondary (Grade XII) stages. In setting question papers and practical tests in science and certain other subjects, and in the checking of answer books, the boards employ the help of experienced school and university teachers. On the basis of the results of examination, they award certificates which are required for admission to further courses or for employment.

Examination at the higher education stage is the responsibility of universities. Generally speaking, each university has an examination branch which, in consultation with the academic faculty, appoints personnel to set question papers, as well as superintendents of examinations and examiners. In some universities, and other institutions of higher learning, the academic session is divided into semesters and evaluation is undertaken at the end of each semester by the faculty.

Reform of the school examination system has been a continuous endeavor since independence. The Central Examination Unit was established in 1958 (it merged with NCERT in 1961) and a program of systematic reform was started. The present reform program is, by and large, based on the recommendations of the Education Commission (Ministry of Education and Social Welfare 1966) and the experiences gained since then. These reforms cover external examinations as well as school evaluation and include a scheme for the intensive training of various personnel responsible for examinations. The reforms have been adopted by practically all boards of secondary education.

The 1986 education policy underscores the need for examination reforms as a means of bringing about qualitative improvement in education. It seeks to de-emphasize memorization and to eliminate the element of chance and subjectivity. With a view to lessening the overriding importance of examinations and certification, and with the explicit intention of restoring the essential teaching–learning process to its rightful position, the policy seeks selectively to detach degrees from jobs. Whereas the need for rendering education free from the subjugation of the job market had been felt for several decades prior to the formulation of the policy, it is only in the policy, that it has been possible to put the suggestion more firmly. The National Evaluation Organization has been set up to conduct tests, to be taken on a voluntary basis, to determine the suitability of candidates for specified jobs, and to pave the way for emergence of norms of competence across the nation. The NEO will also pay attention to the improvement of learner evaluation at the school stage.

9. Educational Research

Systematic educational research is of recent origin in India. Research in universities leading to a PhD degree began only after independence. With sociopolitical changes in the country, interest in educational research increased rapidly, and by 1972 about 50 universities provided facilities for doctoral level research in education. In the 1950s, a number of institutions were set up by the central government for research in various aspects of education. In 1961, these institutions were amalgamated into NCERT. The number of PhD degrees awarded has increased from 9 in 1961–62 to 295 in 1987–88. Although NCERT was also expected to undertake periodic assessment of educational research, it has not created any machinery to do so.

In the middle of the 1970s, the Indian Council of Social Science Research initiated a program for surveying research in the social sciences, including education. The Association of Indian Universities publishes, at regular intervals, subject lists of all dissertations approved in Indian Universities. In the early 1970s, at the instance of UGC, the Center of Advanced Study in Education of the University of Baroda undertook a project for abstracting all published and unpublished research studies, and published two monumental surveys. Subsequently, NCERT took over the responsibility and has brought out two surveys, the last one in two large volumes published in 1991. These surveys contain classified abstracts of several thousand research works.

The areas which have attracted the largest effort are educational measurement and evaluation, as well as correlates of achievement. Closely following this group of topics are those of personality, learning and motivation, curriculum, teaching methods, and textbooks. While the coverage of some subjects is impressive, the deficiencies are glaring. For example, language teaching, school duration, wastage and stagnation, and student unrest—all burning topics of Indian education—have received insufficient attention. Similarly, the long-term impact of educational programs, particularly of primary education and adult literacy, has received scant attention. Although there is no well laid out system for the use of research findings in decision making, persons engaged in research are associated in decision-making processes.

10. Major Problems for the Year 2000

An opportunity for the transformation of education in India was available soon after the attainment of independence in 1947. The whole nation was imbued by Jawaharlal Nehru's call of "tryst with destiny." The alternative of Gandhian basic education was universally accepted and persons with a profound understanding of the role of education in the building up of the new nation—Mahatma Gandhi, Jawaharlal Nehru, Abul Kalam Azad, Rajgopalachari, and Radhakrishnan—were at the center of affairs. However India's "brahmanical tradition" (the age-old system in which instruction is imparted in a language known to a small coterie and where formal education remains the preserve of a certain class of society) has prevented educational reconstruction. Notwithstanding the achievements, educational reform remains an unfinished task. While India has large numbers of highly trained technical, scientific, and management personnel, the vast majority of Indians continue either to remain deprived of education altogether or receive poor quality education.

The 1986 education policy is faced with tremendous odds, for, it does not seem to be in tune with the socioeconomic trends in India. While there are signs of rising religious fundamentalism, the policy stresses secularism; while the government favors a free market economy, the policy stresses egalitarianism and socialist society; while separatist and disintegrative forces are raising their heads in several parts of the country, the policy calls for the creation of a national system of education which would give a new sense of Indian identity and enable the country to move towards a new framework of national integration and social cohesion; with increasing centralization and authoritarianism in the central and state governments, the policy stresses the need for decentralization, institutional autonomy, and support for innovation. Perhaps, in the short run, something that is more disquieting is the prevailing atmosphere of dispiritedness and lack of accountability among the teachers and students in the university system. Yet, it is this situation which makes the implementation of the education policy a momentous and challenging task. There are already indications of the government's seriousness and of new initiatives which may have far-reaching influence.

The government has decided that 6 percent of the national income will be spent on education by the mid-1990s. Every effort will be made to consolidate the existing system and to create the necessary management apparatus for implementation of the new policy. Large projects for reform and renewal of basic education have been started in the states of Andhra Pradesh, Bihar, and Rajasthan. The programs of mass literacy have already taken the shape of a movement which may transform not only the literacy and primary education situation, but the entire development scene. The 1990s will show whether India is capable of taking concrete decisions to transform the educational system with a view to bringing about fundamental changes in the socioeconomic order, or whether it will remain a soft state.

References

India, Ministry of Education and Social Welfare 1966 *Education and National Development, Report of the Education Commission (1964–66)* Ministry of Education, New Delhi
India, Ministry of Education and Social Welfare 1978 *National Adult Education Programme: An Outline*. Ministry of Education, New Delhi
India, Ministry of Human Resource Development, Department of Education 1986a *National Policy on Education 1986*. Ministry of Education, New Delhi
India, Ministry of Human Resource Development, Department of Education 1986b *National Policy on Education 1986—Programme of Action*. Ministry of Human Resource Development, New Delhi

Further Reading

Buch M B (ed.) 1974–79 *A Survey of Research in Education*. Centre of Advanced Study in Education, Maharaja Sayajirao University of Baroda, Baroda

Buch M B (ed.) *Third Survey of Research in Education, 1979–83*. NCERT, New Delhi
Buch M B (ed.) 1991 *Fourth Survey of Research in Education*. NCERT, New Delhi
Gandhi M K 1953 *The Problems of Education*. Navjeevan Publishing House, Ahmedabad
India, Ministry of Education 1985 *Challenge of Education—A Policy Perspective*. New Delhi
India, Ministry of Education and Culture (annual) *Education in India: A Statistical Presentation*. New Delhi
India, Ministry of Education and Social Welfare 1951 *The Report of the University Education Commission*. New Delhi
India, Ministry of Education and Social Welfare 1953 *Report of the Secondary Education Commission*. New Delhi
India, Minsitry of Education, Social Welfare and Culture (annual) *Annual Report*. New Delhi
India, Ministry of Human Resource Development, Department of Education, 1991a *Report of the Review Committee on NPE, 1986: Towards an Enlightened and Humane Society*. New Delhi
India, Ministry of Human Resource Development, Department of Education 1991b *Selected Educational Statistics*. New Delhi
Naik J P 1982 *The Education Commission and After*. Allied Publishers, New Delhi
National Council of Educational Research and Training 1963–67 *Indian Year Book of Education* 4 vols. NCERT, New Delhi
National Council of Educational Research and Training 1989 *Fifth All-India Educational Survey*. NCERT, New Delhi
National Institute of Educational Planning and Administration 1990 *Education for All: The Indian Perspective*. New Delhi
Nurullah S, Naik J P 1974 *A History of Indian Education*. Macmillan, Delhi
Saiyidain K G, Naik J P, Hussain S A 1966 *Compulsory Education in India*. Universal Publication, Delhi
Singh A, Altabach P G (eds.) 1974 *The Higher Learning in India*. Vikas, New Delhi
Srivastava H S 1979 *Examination Reforms in India*. UNESCO, Paris

Indonesia

Moegiadi and Jiyono

1. General Background

The Republic of Indonesia covers most of the world's largest archipelago, a domain of over 3,000 equatorial islands stretching more than 5,000 kilometers east to west across seas that separate continental Southeast Asia from Australia. It is the world's fifth most populous nation, with over 180 million residents at the end of the 1980s. The average annual growth rate for the period 1985 to 1990 was 2.1 percent. It is estimated that the population size will be over 210 million by the year 2000. In 1990, about 41 percent of the population was under 18 years of age. Despite this, some

92 percent of the 6-year olds and 97 percent of 7-year olds were enrolled in school. Nearly all are in primary schools with separate classrooms for each grade level. However, in sparsely populated areas there are so-called "small schools" with mixed-grade classes and only three teachers per school.

The extent of Indonesia was originally determined between the early seventeenth and early twentieth centuries by a succession of Dutch colonial conquests. Over a 350-year period, sea traders and soldiers from the Netherlands won control over more and more islands, eventually forming the Netherlands East Indies colony as it existed prior to the Second World

War. Throughout this same period the Moslem religion, introduced earlier by traders from India, spread throughout the islands' peoples to become the dominant religion of the region (the Sunni faith following the Syafei school of Islamic law). There are, however, some pockets in North Sumatra and North Sulawesi that are Christian.

In 1942, the Japanese army and navy captured the East Indies, ousted the Dutch colonists, and ruled the territory until the Japanese themselves were defeated by Allied troops in late 1945. Following the Japanese surrender, the Dutch returned to reclaim the region. However, in August 1945, the indigenous peoples of the archipelago declared their independence and then fought the Dutch army over the next four years until they won uncontested self-rule at the close of 1949.

The nature of the present-day Indonesian educational system has been significantly influenced by both the geography of the nation and the people's experience under Dutch colonialism and under Islam. One outcome of the geography of widely dispersed islands was the emergence over the centuries of a multiplicity of distinctly different cultural groups, a diversity of societies caused by peoples being separated by barriers of seas, mountains, and dense jungles. This isolation fostered the development of over 400 languages and dialects.

Such ethnic and linguistic variety has posed problems for both political leaders and educators. The question of what language would best serve as a national tongue, unifying the many societies, was settled when Independence was declared in 1945. The Republic's leaders chose a version of Malay as the official language and labeled it "Bahasa Indonesia." Since that time, Indonesian has been learned willingly by virtually everyone. It has served as the language of government, of mass communication, and of instruction at all educational levels above the second grade of primary school. Local languages have been the media of instruction in the first two primary grades and have been taught as subjects in upper grades. Such a pattern of instruction is designed to promote the national motto of "unity in diversity" (*Bhinneka Tunggal Ika*). This language policy has faced educators with special problems in textbook production, teacher training, and teacher placement.

At Independence, only a minimal school system was in place, catering to a relatively small proportion of an age group. Textbooks were in Dutch. Education was awarded high priority by the government, but it is since 1970 that enrollments began to expand dramatically from 3 million students in primary and secondary school in 1970 to 38 million in 1990. In 1990 over 1 million children attended private kindergartens and there was universal access to primary school for the age group 7 to 12 years of age. There were 27 million children enrolled in primary school (with an equal representation of boys and girls) and 7 million children in lower-secondary school which represented slightly less than 50 percent of an age group for the 13- to 15-year olds. However, it is estimated that 25 percent of primary school children drop out during primary school and 40 percent of the primary school graduates do not enter lower-secondary school.

The country is divided into 28 provinces, 324 districts, 3,500 subdistricts, and over 66,000 villages. The number of persons per household was 4.6 in 1985. The illiteracy rate was 19.1 percent for all of the population aged 10 years or more. The Gross National Product (GNP) per capita was US$570.

The nation's geography, and the way the population is distributed across the islands, have affected the efficiency of administering the centralized system of schools from the capital city of Jakarta on the island of Java. Because of the great distances between islands and the shortage of transportation facilities, school supplies and directives sent to remote islands can take months to arrive. The task of collecting accurate statistics from all parts of the nation for purposes of national planning has been difficult.

Most of Indonesia's wealth comes from oil and mineral resources, followed by agricultural products such as coffee, rubber, and palm oil. Although most of the population lives in rural areas, the government is wholeheartedly committed to developing economic potential in the industrial sector through the introduction of modern technology and hence planned investment in education for producing the required knowledge, skills, and values began in the 1970s.

In 1990, some 60 percent of the labor force was engaged in agriculture, 10 percent in industry, and 12 percent in services. As more leave agriculture to enter the other sectors, the basic curriculum must be changed. As already mentioned the country is very large. There are also many cultures ranging from the very rural areas of Irian Jaya to the modern culture of Jakarta. On the one hand, a national curriculum is needed and, on the other hand, the different needs of different cultures must be taken into account. Communication from the Ministry of Education in Jakarta with the provinces and districts has been a problem but are now much easier than before. Bahasa Indonesia is now widespread and despite the differences in local languages and scripts there are no problems in using the national language as the medium of instruction from Grade 3 onward. Every effort is made through the National Curriculum Center to establish a balance of national and provincial curricula. At the same time examinations must take the different curricula into account. The examinations center has established a continuously updated item bank to allow for students with a common curriculum and partly different curricula to be assessed and brought onto one national scale.

It should be borne in mind that at the end of the Dutch occupation only about 8 percent of an age group had received basic formal schooling (in Dutch). Less than 50 years later nearly all children receive primary school education (in Indonesian) and a good proportion also receive secondary education (also in Indonesian).

2. Politics and the Goals of the Education System

The national goal as laid down in the Preamble of the 1945 Constitution is "to protect the whole of the Indonesian people and their entire homeland of Indonesia in order to advance the general welfare, to develop the intellectual life of the nation and to contribute to the implementation of an orderly world which is based upon independence, ability, peace, and social justice." In order to meet the goal, the development of the intellectual life of the nation is the main task and responsibility of the Indonesian national education system. The Constitution further states that "Every citizen shall have the right to obtain education, and . . . the government shall establish and conduct one national system of education which shall be regulated by statutes."

The Ministry of Education and Culture is assigned to implement part of the general task of the administration and development in the field of education and culture. The state ideology, *Pancasila*, the 1945 Constitution, and the Guidelines of the State Policy are the basic principles upon which the Ministry of Education and Culture carries out its task.

The 1989 Education Law stipulated that the aim of national education was to develop the intellectual life of the Indonesian people as a whole person, namely men and women who have faith in and full devotion to the one and only God and who possess knowledge and skills, who are physically and mentally healthy, and who have a strong and independent personality and a sense of responsibility for the society and the nation.

The national education system is based on the state ideology, *Pancasila*, the Five Principles of the state's philosophy; and the 1945 Constitution. These five principles are: (a) belief in one God; (b) just and civilized humanity, including tolerance to all people; (c) unity of Indonesia; (d) democracy led by wisdom of deliberation among representatives of the people; and (e) social justice for all.

3. The Formal System of Education

Figure 1 presents the structure of the formal system of education in Indonesia. However, it should be borne in mind that there is a very large out-of-school education program.

School education consists of general, vocational, professional, religious, and armed forces education. General education prepares students to obtain basic abilities to continue to further education or enter the world of work. Vocational education prepares students to master certain skills to enter the world of work and

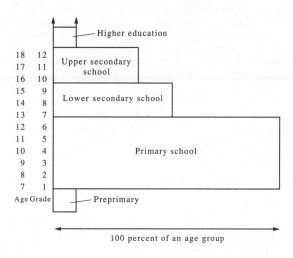

Figure 1
Indonesia: Structure of the formal education system

simultaneously to equip them to continue to higher vocational education. Professional education improves the competence of students in carrying out their tasks. Religious education prepares students for their tasks in religious fields. Armed forces education prepares and enhances the capabilities of students in carrying out their tasks as members of the Indonesian Armed Forces.

In terms of level of education, the existing structure of education consists of primary education, secondary education, and higher education. Formal schools are under the Ministry of Education and Culture and also the Ministry of Religion; namely, the Islamic School (*Madrasah*). *Madrasah* has *Ibtidaiyah* (primary level), *Raudatul Athfal* at the preschool level, and the Institute for Islamic Religion (IAIN) at the higher education level. The Ministry of Religion is also responsible for supervising a great number of Islamic educational establishments called "*Pesantren*."

3.1 Primary, Secondary, and Tertiary Education

The primary school is one unit and education lasts six years. In 1988–89, there were nearly 146,000 primary schools with an enrollment of nearly 27 million pupils. Nearly all of these schools were state schools. An age group consists of just over 4.5 million children. Of the 4.5 million entering school, 3.4 million graduate from primary school.

Secondary education consists of junior secondary followed by senior secondary school. The first consists of general, technical, and vocational schools, each lasting three years. Those eligible for the junior secondary school, be it general, technical, or vocational, are primary school graduates. In 1988–89, there were 20,334 junior secondary schools with an enrollment

441

of 6.5 million children. A grade group consists of 2.2 million children; of these, 1.9 million graduate.

The senior secondary school consists of a general, technical/vocational, and teachers' school. Each one of them is one unit and has a three-year program. However, some technical and vocational senior secondary schools have four-year programs. They are open to junior general secondary school graduates. Those finishing technical or vocational junior secondary school can only continue at relevant technical or vocational senior secondary schools. In 1988–89, there were 10,682 senior secondary schools with an enrollment of 3.9 million pupils.

Higher education has two types of courses: degree and nondegree. The degree program has various levels: Level 1 (*sarjana* or master); Level 2 (magistrate); and Level 3 (doctorate). The nondegree program offers the following courses: three-year Polytechnic, Diploma 1, Diploma 2, Diploma 3, Diploma 4, Specialist 1, and Specialist 2. Basically, nondegree courses are terminal. The degree programs emphasize academic or professional academic work, whereas the nondegree courses stress more professional and technical work.

To provide opportunities for society to pursue higher education without necessarily leaving their home or work, an Open University was established. It is organized in such a way that students can learn at home. The self-instructional materials are presented in printed form and supported through media such as radio broadcasts and television. The Open University has faculties of pedagogy and education sciences, economics, social sciences, mathematics, and applied statistics. It offers S-1 (Master) degree programs covering several fields of study. There are also nondegree D-2 (Diploma) programs in mathematics, English language, social sciences and *Pancasila* moral education. The Open University has also been given the task of developing and executing distance education to retrain primary school teachers. In 1988–89, there were 792 institutions of higher education with an enrollment of over 1 million students. Of these 792 institutions, only 48 were state institutions.

3.2 Preschool Education

Education before a child begins primary school is considered to be mainly the responsibility of the family. However, in 1988 there were 36,190 kindergartens (of which 57 were public) with an enrollment of over 1.5 million children. These programs last a maximum of three years (ages 4, 5, and 6). Given the great social diversity in the nation and the cost of financing preschool education, it will be some time before the state will be able to plan and afford preschool education.

3.3 Special Education

In 1988–89 there were 447 special schools, of which 22 were public. Nearly 20,000 children were enrolled in these schools. They were mostly children with severe physical and mental handicaps.

3.4 Vocational, Technical, and Business Education

As mentioned in Section 3.1 and as will be seen from Section 7, there is a certain amount of vocational, technical, and business education provided in secondary education and in higher education. There were about 300 junior secondary schools that were vocational/technical and nearly 1,000 such senior secondary schools. Most of these were private. Furthermore, as mentioned in Section 3.5 great efforts are made in the out-of-school programs to train those who have never been to school with skills to help them earn a living.

3.5 Adult and Nonformal Education

Out-of-school education comprises skills education; education aimed at broadening the outlook; family education; and educational programs aimed at the development of students in sociocultural and religious fields, skills, and/or expertise. Through this type of education, every citizen can widen his or her intellectual outlook and personal quality by applying the principle of lifelong learning. Skills education prepares students to obtain the abilities to carry out certain work. This kind of skills education may take the form of services such as typing or sewing. The "broadening of outlook" education makes it possible for students to widen their intellectual outlook. Family education provides basic knowledge and skills, religion and belief in God, moral values, social norms, and life views that students need in order to be able to live in the family as well as in society.

Activities concerning out-of-school education are geared towards providing the participants with learning experiences that can give them sources of income to improve their standard of living and make community members more able to conduct educational and cultural activities in community life. The general targets of out-of-school education programs are community members aged 7 to 44 years who have never had educational opportunities or who are school dropouts. They may also consist of people who had already acquired certain educational certificates but who did not go to higher formal schooling, or people who need additional knowledge and skills in order to be able to improve their living standards.

Out-of-school education in Indonesia which is implemented through community education offers a Package A learning group and an income-generating learning group. Package A learning is directed towards the eradication of illiteracy, the mastery of the national language, and the acquisition of basic education. The income generating learning group, on the other hand, is directed towards increasing the mastery of knowledge and skills, especially in the technical and vocational fields. In preparation for nine-year compulsory basic education, Package B is being developed as a continuation of Package A. Package A is supposed to be equivalent to primary school and Package B to junior secondary school.

4. Administrative and Supervisory Structure and Operation

The Ministry of Education and Culture (MOEC) is responsible to the government for the planning and execution of education. The minister reports directly to the president of the republic. The minister is assisted by a secretary general, who heads a secretariat general; four directors general (primary and secondary education, higher education, out-of-school education, and culture); an inspector general for supervisory work; and a director of research for research and development for policy formulation (the Office of Research and Development) within the Ministry. In addition, there are also other units within the organization serving as executors of various other activities.

For each province there is a provincial office of education. Within each province there are also district offices of education and even subdistrict offices of education. However, secondary schools come directly under the provincial office. The system is mainly centralized, with each unit carrying out the requests of the higher unit. However, in matters of curriculum development, provinces have begun to play a greater role. The provincial offices are not responsible for the management of higher educational institutions. The management of higher educational institutions is directly under the responsibility of the Directorate General of Higher Education, and in the province it is assisted by the coordinating office for private higher education.

5. Educational Finance

In Indonesia, education is the joint responsibility of the family, community, and government. Resources to support educational development come from different sources of funding. Government provides an annually recurrent budget, mainly for salary, travel, provision of office facilities and the maintenance and development budget to support development projects. Families contribute funding at different levels of education in cash or sometimes through the Parent–Teacher Association. Formal tuition fees are collected only at secondary and higher learning institutions. Primary education is free, and the community voluntarily provides support as a reflection of community participation in education.

The size of the budget for education in 1990 was about 2.95 percent of the total Gross National Product (GNP), and about 13.8 percent of the total state budget

is allocated to education, which is not limited only to programs under the Ministry of Education and Culture. In 1989–90, for example, the recurrent budget was Rp. 1.19 trillion (US\$595 million) or equivalent to about 5 percent of the total recurrent national budget.

6. Supplying Personnel for the Education System

The most important personnel in the educational institutions are the teachers or lecturers, school principals or headteachers, and school supervisors. For example, in 1989–90 there were 146,558 primary schools, 20,985 junior secondary schools, and 11,550 senior secondary schools. There are about as many school principals as the number of schools. In these schools there are 1,141,486 primary school teachers, 467,122 junior secondary teachers, and 347,425 senior secondary school teachers. According to the regulations, one school supervisor should be responsible for a maximum of 15 schools. There are also several kinds of nonschool supervisors. These include supervisors for community education, sports, and for youth and cultural programs.

Primary school teachers previously were graduates of SPG (school for primary school teachers), which was a three-year teacher education program following junior secondary education (at the same level as the senior secondary school). However, in order to improve the quality of primary school, the government decided to increase the education of primary school teachers from secondary education to higher education level with a two-year diploma course (DII program) following senior secondary education. The DII course for primary school teachers is conducted by the Institutes of Teacher Training and Educational Sciences (IKIPs). At the same time, the government has launched a national inservice training program for primary school teachers throughout the country using the Open University. Its objective is to train existing teachers to the equivalent level of the Diploma II.

Teachers in junior secondary schools are mostly supplied from the graduates of PGSMTP (equivalent to DI or DII teacher training), and DII teacher training run by the institutes and faculties of teacher education. There are some teachers with higher degrees such as DIII and Level 1 degree (IKIP graduates) who teach in junior secondary schools. Now, junior secondary school teachers should have at least DII education. The teachers of senior secondary schools are mostly recruited from the graduates of PGSLA (equivalent to DII teacher training), DIII, and Level 1 degrees. There are still a number of teachers whose level of education is below that required by the regulation, or who have no teaching background (e.g., subject matter specialists with no teacher training).

The school principals for schools at a particular level are recruited from the teachers at that level. Those who are appointed to be school principals are also expected to meet other criteria such as a stipulated minimum level of education, number of years of teaching experience, a certain civil service rank, or managerial ability. School supervisors are usually recruited from among school principals. They, too, must meet certain minimum criteria.

The criteria used to recruit the nonschool supervisors (supervisors for community education, youth affairs, sports, and for culture) are less clear than the criteria for school supervisors. For example, there are no specific criteria concerning a minimum level of education or number of years experience which should be met by the nonschool supervisors. The impression is that the criteria for recruitment are left in the hands of the head of the Provincial Office of Education and Culture.

New lecturers of higher education institutions are generally recruited from at least Level 1, the graduates of higher education.

7. Curriculum Development and Teaching Methodology

A curriculum is designed on the basis of the objectives of the national education system, taking into consideration the development stages of the students, the local environment, national development, scientific and technological development, and the arts.

The implementation of the teaching–learning activities in a given educational institution is based on a core curriculum for all students and elective programs which are adjusted to the needs of the environment in which the educational activity takes place. The core curriculum constitutes general guidelines for both in-school education and out-of-school education and is composed of a number of subject matters.

The content of the curriculum consists of sequenced materials. These materials are written on the basis of the curriculum outlines, and are tried out and revised before being implemented. The whole content of the curriculum is classified into: *Pancasila* (state ideology), religion, citizenship, culture sciences, skills, and sports and health.

The primary school curriculum in use at the beginning of the 1990s was an improved version of the 1975 curriculum, having 10 subject areas. The nine original subject areas were: religious education, *Pancasila* moral education, Indonesian language, social studies, mathematics, science, sport and health education, arts education, and skills education. A new subject area, introduced in 1984, was the history of the national struggle for independence, which covers Indonesian history and politics.

Each day children receive instruction in most subject areas. The total amount of instructional time per week varies from 26 hours for Grades 1 and 2 to 36 hours per week for Grades 4 to 6. There are 245 official school days per year but the actual number of days in

Table 1
Primary school curriculum

Subject	Grade Level					
	I	II	III	IV	V	VI
Religious education	2	2	2	3	3	3
Pancasila moral education	2	2	2	2	2	2
Indonesian language	—	8	8	8	8	8
Social studies	8	—	2	2	2	2
Mathematics	6	6	6	6	6	6
Science	2	2	3	4	4	4
Sport and health	2	2	3	3	3	3
Arts education	2	2	3	4	4	4
Skills education	2	2	4	4	4	4
Total lesson hrs/week	26	26	33	36	36	36

which instruction takes place is less. Table 1 shows how weekly hours are allocated for each subject area. A class period lasts 30 minutes for Grades 1 and 2 and 40 minutes for Grades 3 to 6.

The Junior Secondary School has a curriculum developed in 1984. It has three parts, namely general education, academic education, and skill education. In general education emphasis is given to *Pancasila* moral education and religious education, which reflect the nation's universal moral values. In addition to these, sports and health education and arts education are other subjects in the general education category.

Academic education consists of six subject areas, which are Indonesian language, local language, English, mathematics, science, and social studies. Skills education consists of required skills and elective skills, which are both practical skill subjects. The required skills subjects are taught in odd semesters, while the elective skills subjects are given in even semesters. The time allocation for general education subjects are two lesson hours per week for each subject except for sport and health education, which are three lesson hours. Academic education is taught in four lesson hours a week except for the Indonesian languages and mathematics, which are five lesson hours a week. Skills education is allotted six hours per week.

The senior secondary school (SMA) also has a curriculum developed in 1984. In the first year it is the same for all students and consists of 15 subject areas. In the first semester of the first year there are as many as 14 subjects taught, while in the second semester there are 13 subjects. All of the subjects taught in the first year are labeled as the "core program." Some of the subjects in this core program such as *Pancasila* moral education, religious education, Bahasa Indonesia, and world history are taught continuously through the third year. Beginning in the second year, students are assigned to one of four streams: Program A–1: physical science, Program A–2: biological sciences, Program A–3: social science, Program A–4: language and arts. There are 38 hours of instruction per week in Grade 10, and this reduces to 36 in Grade 12.

The curricula of the preprimary school, primary, lower-, and upper-secondary schools were being reviewed at the beginning of the 1990s in order to adjust them to developments in science and technology and also the requirements of the newly adopted Education Law (1989). The nine-year basic education curriculum has been placed as the first priority. The new curricula will be implemented in the 1994–95 school year. The main feature of the curriculum is that the Ministry is only responsible for developing the national core curriculum, which is about 80 percent of the total curriculum. The other 20 percent is related to local content and will be prepared by the provincial office in conjunction with the schools. In some cases, the national core is adjusted to local conditions and needs; this includes curricula to meet the most specific characteristics of certain educational institutions. This new policy has direct implications for the preparation of teachers, textbooks, and other types of instructional materials, as well as the management, supervision, monitoring, and periodical evaluation of the curriculum.

8. The System of Examinations, Promotions, and Certifications

School examinations are conducted at the end of the school year, from primary to senior secondary schools. The national leaving examination (EBTANAS) is taken by every student enrolled at the last grade of every school level (i.e., Grades 6, 9, and 12). It is planned nationally and administrated locally to determine the level of students' achievement in key subjects. The examination serves the purpose of providing scores on each key subject which are used as major components in each student's total scores in the school certificate. Furthermore, student scores on the national examinations are usually used for selection into the next higher cycle of schooling.

Not all subjects taught in school are included in the national examinations. For instance, for primary school the examinations include *Pancasila* moral education, Indonesian language, mathematics, science, and social studies. Other subjects such as religion, sports, vocational skills, and others are not included, although the students' scores on the subjects based on the teachers' assessment are included in the certificate awarded by the school.

The test blueprints for primary, junior secondary, and senior secondary schools are developed at the national level with input from the provincial office. The test items for the senior secondary schools are constructed in the provinces and selected for the examinations at the national level. The test items and the

tests for the primary and junior secondary schools are also developed at the provincial level but subsequently 5–7 "parallel" tests are developed for each subject included in the examinations, two of which are set aside for future use. The province can choose three out of five sets of the parallel test to be used for the examinations for junior and senior secondary schools, while the district in each province can choose three out of the five parallel tests for the examinations.

For the administration of the national school examinations, a regulation specifying every step is issued by the Directorate General of Basic and Secondary Education. This regulation includes, for instance, the time schedule of the examinations, scoring the results, and the rules for determining whether a student passes. In practice, a committee is set up at the provincial level to oversee these matters. It deals with all steps from the printing of the examination materials to the determination of who passes. A committee for this examination is also set up at the national level.

The promotion of students from one grade to another is based on their performance during the school year. Their performance is assessed by their teacher(s), a classroom teacher for primary school, and subject matter teachers for junior secondary and senior secondary schools. The performance levels of the students are shown in their school progress report. There is no automatic promotion in the Indonesian educational system. In fact, the grade repetition rate in primary school is still very high. In 1989–90, it was 9.8 percent. On the other hand, in junior and senior secondary schools the repetitions rates were 1.2 and 1 percent respectively.

As mentioned above, the national examinations scores are only one of the components of the final or total scores included in the school completion certificate. In the school certificate (STTB), the final score is derived from the scores on the national examinations, and the scores of the students in the school progress report. The decision on a student being awarded a certificate is determined by these final scores. Specific formulas are given in the regulations on how to determine this, but basically they deal with the scores derived from the national examination and from the students' school progress report. However, as mentioned earlier, school entrance to the next level of schooling is usually based on the students' scores in the national examinations, rather than on their final scores mentioned in the school completion certificate.

9. Educational Assessment, Evaluation, and Research

Basically there are two kinds of institutions engaged in major educational research (including assessment and evaluation). One is the Office of Educational and Cultural Research and Development (*Balitbang Dikbud*) and the other is the IKIP and the faculties of education (FKIP) in universities. The *Balitbang Dikbud* is a principal unit within the Ministry of Education and Culture (MOEC). Its main task is to plan, conduct and coordinate educational policy research and development within the MOEC. The IKIPs and FKIPs are institutions whose main task is to train teachers for secondary schools and to conduct primarily basic research in education and applied research in teaching and learning processes. A number of policy research studies are also sometimes conducted by these institutions, but the scope of these studies is usually small-scale. Policy research studies with a national scope conducted by these institutions are usually contracted from the directorates within the MOEC. *Balitbang Dikbud* also often works with these institutions in conducting its research studies. On the other hand, *Balitbang Dikbud* conducts a greater number of large-scale policy research studies on a regular basis.

Balitbang Dikbud has four centers and one secretariat. The four centers are the Center for Policy Research, the Center for Computing and Statistics (*Informatik*), the Center for Curriculum Development, and Center for Testing Service. There is another center outside *Balitbang Dikbud* which is technically under the supervision of the head of *Balitbang*, called the "Center for Educational Technology" (known as "*Pustekkom*"). This center formerly belonged to one of the centers within *Balitbang Dikbud*, and then became an independent center structurally under the Secretariat General of MOEC.

The Center for Policy Research has the major task of planning, conducting, and coordinating policy research in education and culture in general. The Center for Computing and Statistics plans, conducts, and coordinates data collection related to school statistics; it compiles annual school statistics and conducts quantitative planning studies in education and culture (e.g., conducting the preparation of a five-year development plan in the field of education and culture). The Center for Curriculum Development is in charge of research and development related to school curricula, especially for primary and secondary education. The Center for Testing Service is responsible for conducting research and development related to school testing and examination, such as the development of a test item bank, and methods of effective testing and examination. The Center for Educational Technology conducts research and development of innovative technology in the delivery systems at school and training (e.g., developing innovative educational media such as slides, audio cassettes, video programs, and films).

10. Major Reforms in the 1980s and 1990s

Educational development programs are part of the five-year national development plans (1992 was the fourth year of the fifth five-year plan). There have been many educational reforms conducted in education in terms of quantitative as well as qualitative aspects. The following are a few examples.

Student enrollment in primary school more than doubled from 1971 to 1988–89 (from 12.9 to 28.9 million students). In 1992, the net enrollment ratio was 99.6 percent. The rest who are still deprived primary education are pupils living in isolated areas, those from poor families, or those who are physically and mentally handicapped.

Enrollment at the junior secondary school also increased from 2.9 million in 1979–80 to 7.7 million pupils in 1988–89, with an enrollment ratio of 20 and 65 percent respectively. At senior secondary level the net enrollment ratio rose by 12 and 37 percent in the same period. Similarly, the net enrollment ratio rose from 2.2 to 8.5 percent at the tertiary level. To achieve these increases, many development activities had to be conducted such as the construction of thousands of new school buildings and the recruitment of a great number of new school teachers. To accommodate primary school-age children living in isolated areas the government provided primary schools with multiple grade teaching (known as "small schools"). Packet A, the out-of-school program was provided to young children and adults who could not attend school regularly everyday. The open junior secondary school (SMP *Terbuka*) is being implemented for 13- to 15-year old pupils who live in remote or isolated areas. Research is being undertaken to develop a model of the universalization of nine-year basic education.

The Open University was established in 1984 in order to provide education to secondary school leavers and teachers who have difficulty in attending lectures every day at higher education institutions. It provides written modules, radio programs, audiocassettes, and television programs. About 137,000 students were enrolled in its various programs in 1988–89.

Since 1977 the government has produced over 900 million copies of textbooks for students and teachers, has provided inservice training programs for most of the school teachers, and has provided teaching aids such as science kits to schools. All of these measures have been taken to improve the quality of primary and secondary schooling.

Based on evaluation studies, the 1975 curriculum was improved in 1984. Further research on curriculum is being undertaken to develop content suitable for local conditions to be taught in schools in addition to the national core curriculum which is the same for all schools. The core curriculum is also being revised to ensure its continuity between school grades and levels. In this endeavor, more emphasis is put on teaching arithmetic to respond to the fact that many primary school leavers were having problems with arithmetic calculations.

To improve primary school quality further, research and development was undertaken to develop a teacher support system and active learning. It started in 1979 in three subdistricts at the Cianjur district, in the West

Java province. The main objective of the system is to promote better and more active learning at school. The outstanding feature of the system is that it adopts an "active learning" approach involving more discussion in lessons and more pupil questions to their teachers instead of too much teacher talking and students listening. This system has been disseminated to more schools in the Cianjur district itself, and to selected districts in other provinces.

Research has shown that the quality of primary school teachers is, in general, still low. To improve the quality of teachers, the government has abolished the SPG teacher training and is replacing it gradually with a DII program (two years after senior secondary school). This DII program is now being run by IKIPs and FKIPs. The Open University is running programs for upgrading existing primary school teachers with SPG education to obtain DII diplomas within three years. Both government support and teacher self-financing programs have been conducted since 1990 and 1991. Under a 1989 government regulation, better teachers will be promoted faster than the others.

11. Major Problems for the Year 2000

In the Fifth Five-Year Development Plan (Repelita V), from 1989–90 to 1993–94, one of the most important goals of educational development is to improve the educational quality of all types of education at all levels. This endeavor is conducted through various programs including the improvement of teachers' quality through preservice and inservice training programs, the improvement of teachers' welfare through a better promotion system and better salaries, the improvement of the school curriculum, the provision of textbooks and other school facilities, allowing higher education institutions to be, among other things, more autonomous.

Despite all these efforts, it is predicted that low educational quality at all educational levels and types will still be a major problem in the 1990s. This is due to the fact that the educational resources and funding available for education will always be limited, and by its nature the improvement of educational quality can only be done gradually alongside the improvement of all aspects of the educational system and the economic development of the nation.

Just as an example, the inservice DII equivalency program for primary school teachers (totaling over 1 million people) will take more than 20 years, according to 1993 estimates. Besides that, most schools have textbooks and other facilities that are inadequate in terms of both quantity and quality. To improve this situation will take many years. It also takes a long time to improve such things as the learning and teaching habits or the school and social environments which could lead to more effective learning.

A second problem will be improving access to education. So far, Indonesia has been successful in accomplishing the universalization of primary education for 7- to 12-year old children. During Repelita VI, which starts 1994–95, the nation will embark on launching the universalization of a nine-year basic education for 7- to 15-year old children. Various activities have been undertaken in preparation for this program, including: the establishment of a range of types of junior secondary schools to serve children from various types of communities, the establishment of new school buildings and new classrooms, the recruitment of new teachers, and the provision of school facilities. Despite all these efforts, it is estimated that by the year 2000, the next enrollment ratio for the junior secondary school (13- to 15-year old children) will still be as low as 72 percent, and for the senior secondary school and higher education 45 and 12 percent respectively. This will certainly be a major problem for the human resource development of the country.

The relevancy of education will also still be a major problem in the future at all levels of education. At the level of basic education (primary and junior secondary education), the problem concerns how to provide a curriculum with local content (about 20% of the total curriculum). At the senior secondary level (including vocational education), the problem involves such things as the ideal proportion of general and vocational education, considering the various types of employment available in the society. At the higher education level, the problem is especially related to the imbalance between the science and social/humanities majors (faculties), because most students are enrolled in social/humanities programs.

Finally, it is predicted that educational efficiency will still be a major problem in the future. This is shown by such indicators as high dropout rates and repetition rates, especially in primary school. For example, the repetition rates in primary school in 1990 was as high as 10 percent. The average dropout rates from 1971–90 in primary school, junior secondary school, and senior secondary school is about 5.2 percent, 5.8 percent, and 5.0 percent respectively.

Educational inefficiency involves various components of the educational system such as teacher deployment (lack of teachers in certain schools/areas and an oversupply of teachers in other schools/areas), problems with the implementation of educational decentralization on the part of the school personnel, and inequality of resource allocation across schools and areas.

Bibliography

Boediono W, Mcmahon W, Adams D (eds.) 1992 *Education, Economic, and Social Development*. MOEC, Jakarta
Ministry of Education and Culture 1988 *Fifth Five-Year Development Plan*. MOEC, Jakarata
Ministry of Education and Culture 1989 *Education Law No. 2/1989*. MOEC Jakarta

Ministry of Education and Culture 1990a *Educational Indicators: Indonesia*. MOEC, Balitbang

Ministry of Education and Culture 1990b *Compilation of School Statistics 1989–90*. MOEC, Jakarta

Ministry of Education and Culture 1992a *Education in Indonesia in Brief*. MOEC, Jakarta

Ministry of Education and Culture 1992b *Education in Indonesia*. MOEC, Jakarta

Iran

H. Aziz-Zadeh

1. General Background

The Islamic Republic of Iran is a mountainous, high-plateau country with an area of 1,648,000 square kilometers. It stretches from the Caspian Sea and allied independent countries in the north to the Persian Gulf in the south and from Turkey and Iraq in the west to Afghanistan and Pakistan in the east. Iran thus forms strategically the land-bridge between the Middle East and Asia.

The country is rich in minerals (i.e., copper, oil, gas, and coal), and exportation of petroleum is the principal source of foreign currency.

According to the census taken in 1986, the population then numbered 49.8 million. Some 45.5 percent of the total population were under the age of 15, and 3 percent were aged 65 and over. The annual growth rate between 1976 and 1986 was 3.2 percent. According to that census, 38.3 percent of the population aged 6 and over were illiterate.

Nearly 66 percent of the Iranian people are of Persian origin while 25 percent have Turkish origins, 5 percent have Kurdish origins, and 4 percent Arab origins. Nearly 99 percent of the people of Iran are Muslims and 91 percent of them are followers of the shiite sects. The official language of Iran is Persian, and Persian and Arabic scripts prevail in the country.

Prior to the Arab conquest and the propagation of Islam in 642 AD, the Zoroastrian religion dominated the area emphasizing three duties which parents and society were supposed to teach the children: pious thoughts, good deeds, and kindly speech. Physical education was also taught to ensure a sound body. After 642 AD and the country's conversion to Islam, the mosques became centers of learning. The Koranic schools emerged with a curriculum of scripture, logic, Arabic, and grammar. These schools, the *Maktabs*, dominated for centuries until a state education system was introduced in 1894 based on the centralized French model. The system, however, still reached very few and illiteracy remained high. New attempts to improve and expand education were made in the 1950s and 1960s. Iran participated in the UNESCO/UNDP world literacy program and a World Conference of Minsters of Education was convened in Tehran in 1965. An international institute for adult literacy was established in the Iranian capital in 1968, and literacy rates increased to 55 percent for males and 30 percent for females. However, millions of persons could still not read and write and school enrollment rates were low, particularly in rural areas and among women.

Following the Islamic Revolution of 1979, the education system was changed so that all teaching would conform to Islamic principles. Much emphasis was placed on guaranteeing that children and teenagers were brought up as committed Muslims. Efforts were also made to use the Holy Koran, the traditions of Islam, and the Constitution of the Islamic Republic as a basis upon which the aims of education are set.

2. Politics and the Goals of the Education System

The Constitution of the Islamic Republic of Iran lays down the basic framework for educational development in Iran. According to Article 3 of the Constitution, the government is responsible for providing free educational opportunities up to secondary level for Iranian citizens. The same principle is stressed again in Article 30. The latter obliges the government to provide free education and further facilitate access to higher education.

The goals and objectives of education are derived from a number of sources including the Constitution and reports of the High Council for Fundamental Change in Education appointed by the Higher Council for Cultural Revolution. They underline national development as the primary aim of education. Education should be developed to increase productivity, achieve social and national integration, and cultivate social, moral, and spiritual values with great emphasis placed on strengthening and encouraging the faith of Islam. They emphasize the role of education in developing labor for different levels of economy and thus education is visualized as an investment in the future.

3. The Formal System of Education

The structure of the formal education system is presented in Fig. 1.

3.1 Primary, Secondary, and Tertiary Education

Primary school begins at the age of six and lasts five years. Then follows a guidance or orientation course

Table 1
Growth of enrollment during the period 1980–1990

| Level of education | Enrollment in thousands and % Female | | | |
	1980	% Female	1990	% Female
Preprimary	172	47	227	48
Primary	4,799	40	9,370	46
Lower-secondary	1,575	38	3,233	41
Upper-secondary	1,143	36	1,819	41

lasting three years. These eight years of education are assumed to be general education. Secondary education lasts four years and is divided into two main branches: technical–vocational and academic.

The education structure of Iran at the beginning of the 1990s gave all students a reasonable chance to study according to their attitudes and aptitudes. It also kept the door open for a majority of senior secondary school graduates to proceed to higher education. Institutions of higher education include universities, teacher-training centers, and colleges of technology. For student admission, these institutions require the completion of upper-secondary schooling. A university has one or more undergraduate faculties which offer courses usually lasting four years, but six years for medical, dental, and veterinary courses.

Table 1 presents enrollments in 1980 and 1990 in the different levels of education. During the period 1980–90 the number of pupils enrolled in regular education (primary, lower-secondary {guidance schools}, and upper-secondary education) increased from 7.5 to 14.5 million, a relative increase of 93 percent. Female enrollment increased more than male enrollment at all levels of education.

In 1990 gross enrollment ratios for primary, lower-secondary, and upper-secondary education were 119, 86, and 43 for boys, and 106, 63, and 32 for girls respectively. In the period 1980–90, enrollment in higher education expanded. There were 126 higher education institutes with 312,000 students in 1990. Close to 90 percent of the students were enrolled in 61 universities. An "open university" with several units throughout the country was established in 1984. It enrolls some 200,000 students; a "distance university" was also opened in 1987 in which teaching is mainly through correspondence courses and audio visual materials.

3.2 Preschool Education

The one-year preprimary education system enrolled 227,500 in 1990. Most of these children speak Farsi and thus belong to the ethnic majority of Iran. There are, however, major ethnic groups speaking Arabic, Turkish, Kurdish, and other languages.

The government has expressed its intention to expand preprimary education to economically deprived regions and to the ethnic minority groups. Preschool typically takes place in private institutions. The overall aim is to prepare children for school education. Activities include group games, narrating stories, singing, acting in plays, and handicrafts with simple tools.

3.3 Special Education

There are schools for the mentally and physically handicapped.

3.4 Vocational, Technical, and Business Education

The percentage of students in technical, vocational, and agricultural education was about 12 percent in 1990 at the upper-secondary level of education. There are also courses in technology and business administration in higher education.

3.5 Adult and Nonformal Education

In the 1980s, great interest and effort were devoted to nonformal education, particularly to literacy work. The

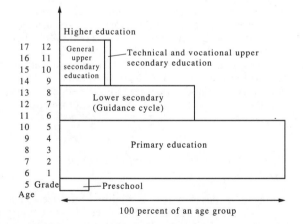

Figure 1
Iran: Structure of the formal education system

literacy program has two parts: an initial stage of 180 hours followed by a second stage of 288 hours. Some 10 million illiterates participated in literacy classes in the period 1980–90. About 65 percent of these classes were allocated to women and more than 60 percent of them were held in rural areas. The literacy rate has, as a result of these courses and the expansion of primary education, increased from 48 to 62 percent during the whole period.

4. Administrative and Supervisory Structure and Operation

The organization of the modern educational system in Iran was closely modeled on that of France, and is, therefore, highly centralized. The Ministry of Education through its central bureaucracy and regional representatives administers and finances the schools at primary and secondary levels of education. The Higher Council of Education, as an autonomous and legislative body, approves all policies and regulations related to education at preuniversity level.

Efforts are being made to establish regional education councils and to develop their authority in allocating funds and a considerable range of administrative duties. In the second five-year plan (1994–98), the government has indicated its intention to expand nonprofit schools which are financed by parents.

The administration and management of educational activities in higher education is vested in the Ministries of Science and Higher Education, and Health and Medical Education. There is also a Higher Council for Cultural Revolution which approves policies mainly related to higher education.

5. Educational Finance

For the financial year 1990–91, the total budget for primary, guidance, and general secondary levels of education was R1,711 billion (approximately US $1 billion), which represented 3.2 percent of GDP. The proportion of GDP allocated to these levels of education declined from 3.8 in 1982 to 3.2 in 1990.

Government supplies more than 90 percent of the funds for education. In 1991 less than 1 percent of the students were enrolled in private (or nonprofit) schools. Education is free in public schools although parents, in some cases, contribute funds for recurrent materials and maintenance. The fees levied by private schools are not considerable.

About 20 percent of the total government budget is spent on education, and 90 percent of the recurrent education budget goes on teacher salaries. Schools receive public allocations for materials and maintenance on a per student basis which is too small to allow for any acceptable provision of teaching materials or maintenance.

6. Supplying Personnel for the Education System

Nearly 450,000 teachers were employed in schools in 1990. A further 150,000 persons worked in nonteaching positions. About 260,000 teachers were employed in primary schools, 110,000 in guidance schools, 73,000 in secondary schools, and 4,000 in special schools. Nearly 50 percent of all teachers were female.

From 1973 until the Islamic Revolution of 1979, the major constraint on the growth of the education system was personnel and not money. The unsolved crisis of Iranian education was, and remains, the provision of qualified teachers for extending education in rural areas and the expansion of vocational schools at secondary education level.

The enrollment growth in Iran has been significant. In 1917–18, there were only 24,000 pupils in schools; by 1960–61 this had increased to 1.5 million, by 1980–81 to 7.5 million, and by 1990–91 to 14.5 million. It is obvious that supplying personnel for such an expansion deserves special attention. Iran has developed various strategies to solve the teacher supply problem. The teaching staff for primary education and guidance cycle, as well as teachers for handicapped students are trained in two-year teacher-training centers. Secondary school graduates are admitted, through a nationwide entrance examination, to these centers. The number of teacher-training centers has increased from 28 in 1979 to 175 in 1989, and 152,000 teachers were trained in these schools during the period 1979–89.

The required teaching staff for upper-secondary schools are trained at universities and higher education institutes. A four-year postsecondary program comprises courses in relevant subjects, as well as courses in educational sciences and psychology. In 1989 there were 35,000 students and 3,800 graduates.

The teacher-training centers and the universities have not been able to meet the teacher demand in rural areas. The government has therefore, been forced to use military conscripts as teachers in rural and less-developed areas. Soldiers teach for two years instead of doing their regular military service. Training teachers for technical, vocational, and agricultural schools is a major problem, since the teacher salaries are not attractive to those already in industry or similar activities. Similarly, the rapid expansion of higher education has created a demand for qualified faculty administrators.

7. Curriculum Development and Teaching Methodology

Curriculum development is highly centralized. The 5+3+4 pattern of education introduced in the country envisages a broad-based general education for all pupils during the first eight years of school education. The curriculum at primary and lower-secondary (guidance) levels of education is nationwide and all curricular areas are compulsory.

The focus of the curriculum in primary education is on development of basic skills of literacy and numeracy, study of environment in terms of physical and social phenomena, and religious training.

The content of education in guidance schools is directed to the consolidation of knowledge, skills, attitudes, and values acquired at primary education. At this stage, the pupil is required to continue with the curricular areas introduced in primary school but in greater depth. The study of foreign languages (Arabic and English) starts at this stage, and the government is keen to encourage more foreign languages. These schools are intended to help the students become familiar with sciences through numerous activities in order to help them identify their area of interest and choose their field of study at the next level of education.

The curriculum at the upper-secondary level of education is designed to equip the students either to take up higher level courses of study to prepare for entrance into higher education or to equip them for vocational courses at technical colleges or to enter the world of work. The curriculum in upper-secondary education consists of the study of foreign languages, mathematics, science, work experience, social sciences, physical education, and religious training. Science includes physics, chemistry, and biology; while social sciences include the study of history, geography, and civics.

The comprehensive review of school curricula resulted in a fundamental change in education objectives and content after the Islamic Revolution of 1979. The teaching of religion, emphasizing Muslim values; work experience; and computer education were allocated more time.

8. The System of Examinations, Promotions, and Certifications

Promotion from one grade to the next is mainly based on the results of an end-of-year internal examination. In each subject, children's work is scored on a 0 to 20 scale. An average score across subjects of at least 10 is required for promotion. Those falling below 10 must repeat the year. This system holds for primary and secondary education. At the end of primary education, a regional test is administered and a certificate is awarded to the successful candidate.

A provincial test is administered at the end of the lower-secondary level of education and again a certificate is awarded to successful students. Admission to upper-secondary education requires certain levels of performance in each specific subject area.

The test at the end of upper-secondary education is administered at the national level, and the admission to higher education is based on the results of an annual multiple-choice nationwide test.

9. Educational Assessment, Evaluation, and Research

Research in education is generally conducted by universities and research institutions. The Council for Educational Research identifies the research priorities, supervises research activities, and devises plans to involve university staff in conducting educational research.

Analysis of the research reports available indicates that a large number of projects are undertaken in the areas of educational administration, teacher training, tests and measurement, and guidance and counseling. The area of curriculum has also been researched. There has been criticism that the findings of these studies are not considered in policy-making processes.

10. Major Reforms in the 1980s and 1990s

Social, political, cultural, and economic changes came about as a result of the Islamic Revolution in 1979, and it became a matter of urgency for the Ministry of Education to examine the philosophy, goals, objectives, and policies of the educational system. In 1980, the Higher Council of Cultural Revolution was created. The Council formed several committees in order to revise different aspects of education at all levels. The Council for Fundamental Change in Education was responsible for the revision of the educational system at primary and secondary levels of education. This Council prepared a draft about principles, goals, structure, and policies of education based on the Islamic doctrine which was approved by the Higher Council of Cultural Revolution in 1992.

The new educational system will be in the form of 6+3+3 years of education. The structure in upper-secondary education would change from a grade system to a credit one, and automatic promotion would be introduced in general education. How the new educational system will turn out in practice remains to be seen.

However, apart from these efforts for the 1990s, the period 1980–90 has been a period of considerable reform in many aspects of education. Two of the more notable changes were the dramatic rise in enrollment ratios and the proportion of female enrollment at all levels of education. Children continued to turn up in schools in large numbers to learn their classrooms had been destroyed by bombs. The government responded by increasing the share of the education budget, providing double-shift schools, broadcasting educational programs on television, and similar measures. The establishment of nonprofit schools in 1990 was another attempt to deal with the rapid expansion of education.

In 1991–92, new forms of high schools were established for adults. Those who had not completed their secondary education could enter this flexible credit system of evening classes and receive their certificates. It is believed that a considerable percentage of regular high school pupils will also attend these new schools.

Many of the changes that took place in the 1980s share a common rationale: to find new resources or to manage the available resources better in order to support the continued expansion of the educational system.

11. Major Problems for the Year 2000

Iran will face some difficulties in the functioning of its educational system in the 1990s. Finding the resources to support the expansion of upper-secondary and tertiary education will be a major problem. There are already reports of overcrowding in higher education. In 1990 there were 126 higher education institutes with 312,000 students and about 23,000 full-time and part-time staff in facilities planned for half as many students. Schools are also overcrowded and are sometimes housed in buildings not designed as schools. Appropriate facilities and equipment are generally missing and maintenance is poor due to the shortage of existing resources for education. It will be a major challenge to accommodate the high demand for education without a deterioration of quality.

Teacher training for secondary and tertiary education will be another problem. Teachers will need to acquire new skills and knowledge to assist their students with the implementation of the new education system approved in 1992. In addition, some of the perennial problems of education will remain: the difficulty of providing qualified education in rural and scattered populations, and shifting from a centralized to a decentralized system.

Bibliography

Aziz-Zadeh H 1988 *Educational System and Development of Education in the Islamic Republic of Iran.* Paris
Aziz-Zadeh H 1989 *Educational Development in the Islamic Republic of Iran: Past Trends and Future Perspectives (1976–2001).* Paris
Ministry of Culture and Higher Education 1991 *Statistical Yearbook 1990.* Ministry of Culture and Higher Education, Tehran
Ministry of Education 1990 *Education in the Islamic Republic of Iran, Now and in the Future.* Ministry of Education, Tehran
Ministry of Education 1990 *The Development of Education.* Ministry of Education, Tehran
Ministry of Education 1991 *Statistical Yearbooks 1980–1991.* Ministry of Education, Tehran
Redjali S M 1985 Iran: System of education. In: Husén T, Postlethwaite T N (eds.) 1985 *International Encyclopedia of Education*, 1st edn. Pergamon Press, Oxford

Ireland, Republic of

J. Coolahan

1. General Background

The island of Ireland is situated on the northwestern periphery of Europe. Prior to 1922, the island formed part of the United Kingdom of Great Britain and Ireland. The island was then partitioned, with six counties (called "Northern Ireland") remaining within the United Kingdom. The rest of the country became independent as the Irish Free State. It adopted its present Constitution in 1937 and became a republic in 1949. The country has extended its international linkages in recent decades. It became a member of the EEC in 1973 and has adopted a strong pro-European stance since then. It was a founder member of the OECD and of the Council of Europe, and was admitted to the UN in 1955. Because of its high levels of emigration, Ireland retains many cultural and social links with countries such as the United States, Canada, and Australia.

The Republic of Ireland occupies 70,000 square kilometers, equivalent to 84 percent of the area of the whole island. The population of the Republic of Ireland was 3,523,401 in 1991. Unlike the pattern in other European countries, Ireland experienced a fast-growing young population from the early 1960s until the early 1980s. Since then, however, the annual birthrate has fallen from 74,000 in 1980 to 52,000 in 1990, with consequences for school provision and planning in the immediate future (Department of Education 1992 Statistical Appendix). The population is characterized by its youthfulness, with about half of the population under 25 years. Almost one-third of the population is engaged full-time in education and training. The Republic of Ireland has the lowest density of population, at an average of 50 inhabitants per square kilometer, of the European Community countries. There has been a significant drift of the population from rural to urban centers, with Dublin, the capital, accommodating one-third of the population. Emigration is a long-established tradition within the community; in 1987, those who emigrated amounted to 32,000, but, the recession in many countries has led to a significant decline in emigration in more recent years. The majority of the people is affiliated to Christian religious denominations, with over

90 percent of the population declared as Roman Catholic.

The Republic is a parliamentary democracy with a written Constitution. It has a bicameral House of Parliament; an elected president (*Uachtarán*), who is Head of State; and a prime minister (*Taoiseach*), who is Head of Government. The Constitution states that the Irish language, as the national language, is the first official language. It recognizes English as the second official language, and English is, in fact, the language of everyday usage for the vast majority of the population. The Irish language is now spoken as an everyday language only by about 55,000 people in what are known as " *Gaeltacht*" areas, along the western seaboard, and by some families in urban areas.

The Irish economy up to the 1960s was predominantly based on agriculture and operated within protected market structures, with a heavy reliance on exports to the British market. A more dynamic approach to economic development was adopted from the first Economic Programme of 1958, which contributed to a period of sustained economic growth and prosperity into the mid-1970s. Annual growth rates reached about 4 percent. Improved educational standards were seen as a vital ingredient in this development, and education was one of the social services which benefited from greatly increased investment. Industry, manufacturing, and the services sector ousted agriculture as the major source of employment. In 1961, 42 percent of the workforce was employed in agriculture; by 1987 this had fallen to 15.7 percent. A more liberal free trade policy and a greater range of markets boosted exports. Much foreign investment was attracted to the country which helped to fuel the economic drive. Per capita income rose from US$1,360 in 1970 to US$7,541 in 1987, which still leaves Ireland as one of the poorer of the OECD states (OECD 1991). The momentum of this drive was reduced with the oil crises of the mid- and late-1970s. Agriculture, however, experienced a boom period following accession to the EEC in 1973. The public and foreign debt reached dangerously high levels by 1980 culminating in a balance of payments crisis, high inflation, and high taxation. In line with many other countries, cutbacks in public expenditure became a feature of life in subsequent years. Since 1987, the economy has staged a significant recovery with a surplus balance of trade, annual growth rates of 2 to 4 percent, reduced interest rates, low inflation, and greatly increased export earnings. The black spot on this improved economic horizon is the continuing extremely high level of unemployment, which is about 20 percent of the workforce, one of the highest in OECD countries (OECD 1989).

2. Politics and the Goals of the Education System

There has been little ideological conflict between the political parties regarding education, and changes of government have not led to dramatic changes in educational policy. Commonly accepted goals of the system are set out below and they reflect economic, cultural, egalitarian, administrative, and partnership concerns.

There is a general commitment to the all-round, balanced education of the person for his or her individual and social purposes. The curricula of schools are conceived in broad, comprehensive, liberal education lines up to the end of secondary schooling. There is no early specialization or dual-track system. Within this comprehensive curricular policy, however, emphasis is being placed by the government on greater take-up of scientific and technical subjects, allied to a stated concern to foster an enterprise culture for greater economic development.

A major educational policy goal following Independence was the revival of the Irish language as part of the cultural nationalist agenda. While the educational system achieved a great deal in promoting a knowledge of the language, the schools on their own could not achieve such a fundamental social revolution. There is now a more realistic view of what can be expected of schools. Yet their role is still seen as of central importance in achieving the national goal of general bilingualism in Irish life.

Another widely shared goal of the educational system is to establish greater equity in education, particularly for those who are disadvantaged socially, economically, physically, or mentally. The impressive quantitative expansion and qualitative reforms which took place since the 1960s, led to great improvements in equality of educational opportunity. For instance, between 1965 and 1991 there was an increase of 130 percent in those enrolled in secondary education and an increase of over 230 percent in higher education (Department of Education 1992). However, a more sophisticated understanding of equality of participation and outcome, linked to the pressures arising from new social changes, have re-emphasized the need for more comprehensive and well-targeted action, which was being proposed by the government in its Green Paper on education (Department of Education 1992).

A new goal of the system is to alter the strong centralist tradition with its dependency culture and to foster greater autonomy at institutional level with improved local school management. This is to be allied to a reformed role for the Department of Education which will concentrate activities on strategic planning, quality assurance, and budgetary responsibilities. Allied to these policy changes is the promotion of much greater accountability and transparency at all levels of the education system.

In line with developments in many countries, Ireland is now laying much greater emphasis on liaison and partnership between educational institutions and the world of work and industry in the wider community. In the context of Ireland's closer integration within the European Communities, it is also a goal of policy to promote a greater European dimension within the

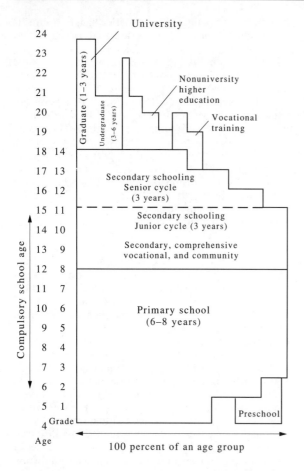

Figure 1
Republic of Ireland: Structure of the formal education system

the freedom to decide where that education should take place. The Constitution obliges the state, for its part, to ensure that children receive a certain minimum education. The Constitution's balancing of private and public responsibilities is reflected in the structures and operations of the educational system. The system is predominantly a state-aided one, whereby the state provides the vast proportion of finance for capital and current expenditure, although most of the institutions are not publicly owned or controlled. The great majority of the schools are denominational.

The roots of this "balance of power" lie deep within struggles between Church and State in the nineteenth century on the control of schooling, neither of which could exercise full control on its own (Coolahan 1981). A collaborative rapprochement evolved whereby the state controls curricula and assessment, sets out the regulations for management, staffing, organization and physical facilities, while local management is responsible for a portion of school costs, the appointment of teachers, and the implementation of policy at school level. Regular contact and access exist between the Department of Education and the interest groups such as school managements, teacher unions, and parent associations.

The state has not attempted to introduce an overarching comprehensive education act since Independence, contenting itself with ad hoc pieces of legislation and various unrelated statutory instruments. Much of the education system is controlled by Departmental or Ministerial regulation rather than by statute. The state has adopted a more comprehensive approach to policy formulation in recent years as indicated by the publication of the government's White Paper, *Educational Development* (Department of Education 1980), the *Programme for Action in Education* (Department of Education 1984) and, most recently, the Green Paper, *Education for a Changing World* (Department of Education 1992). The government has announced its intention of proceeding to a White Paper in late 1992 followed by a range of educational legislation which will provide the up-to-date legal framework for educational development into the new century.

education system in a variety of ways, including the promotion of modern European languages.

3. The Formal System of Education

Figure 1 shows the distribution of students in the formal system of education. Following Independence, the administrative and policy formulation roles of the education system became very centralized within the state Department of Education. Vocational Education Committees were instituted by legislation in 1930 with responsibilities for a small sector of the postprimary schools and some higher education colleges. Otherwise, the Department relates directly with individual schools. No intermediate tier of local education authority exists and no national representative advisory council exists for education. The Constitution recognizes the right and duty of parents to provide for their children's education, and guarantees to parents

3.1 Primary, Secondary, and Tertiary Education

Primary education for over 95 percent of Irish children takes place in the state-aided national schools (henceforth referred to as "primary"). There are 3,225 such schools catering for about 540,000 children (Department of Education 1990). Compulsory attendance is from age 6 to 15 (soon to be raised to 16). A long tradition exists for pupils to attend from ages 4 and 5. At present, about 85 percent of such children attend these primary schools. The pupils are divided by age into eight year-groups, or classes, from Junior Infants to Sixth Class. The normal age for completing school is 12. Over 80 percent of the schools are coeducational. The vast majority of the schools are denominational in their intake and management. Yet, no child may be refused enrollment on the grounds of religion and the child enjoys constitutional protection for his or her religious beliefs within the school. A small number of multidenominational schools have been established in response to local parental demand, and these receive state support on the same lines as denominational schools. There are a small number of private primary schools catering for about 2 percent of the pupils at this level, but these schools receive no state aid or state supervision.

The state provides a minimum of two-thirds of the building costs of primary schools, most of the current expenditure, and all of the teachers' salaries. The ultimate responsibility for each primary school lies with the "patron" who is usually the bishop of the relevant denomination. School boards of management—comprising representatives of the patron, teachers, and parents—are responsible for the day-to-day running of the school, repairs and maintenance, the appointment of teachers, and the application of the Departmental rules. Many of the primary schools are very small, with 43 percent having three teachers or less. The schools are required to be in operation for 184 days per annum.

Participation in secondary education has expanded enormously, by about 150 percent, since the mid-1960s, and retention rates are high. For instance, at the postcompulsory stage, over 90 percent of 16-year olds, 75 percent of 17-year olds, and about 50 percent of 18-year olds are in full-time schooling. Some 73 percent of the age group complete secondary schooling, which is now a six-year cycle of studies. A variety of school types has come into existence to cater for the demand—secondary schools, vocational schools, comprehensive schools, community schools, and community colleges. The secondary schools are the oldest type and evolved on traditional grammar school lines. Secondary schools are private institutions and almost all of them are denominational in character. They amount to 60 percent of all schools and enroll 62 percent of the student body. Vocational schools were established originally to provide a strictly job-oriented curriculum of vocational and technical subjects, but now offer the complete range of secondary studies for about 25 percent of the student body. They are controlled by locally elected Vocational Education Committees (VECs). Some of the schools under their aegis have been designated "community colleges." Comprehensive schools, which date from 1966, were set up by the state to act as exemplar schools with a more comprehensive curricular policy. The community schools, which date from 1973, were a development of the comprehensive school concept with a greater role in community education and the use of their resources by the local community. The comprehensive and community schools cater for about 13 percent of the pupils in this sector of education. While differences exist between these schools relating to their origins and traditions, there has been a growing convergence with regard to their pupil clientele, the training of their teachers, the curriculum offered, and the pedagogy employed in all schools. Overall, there are just over 800 schools which cater for 343,000 pupils (The sector will be referred to henceforth as "secondary education"). The pupil–teacher ratio in secondary education is 19.5:1, but it is planned to reduce this in the immediate future. Schools tend to be small with over one-fourth of them having less than 250 pupils, and only one-third of them have over 500 pupils.

The higher education sector has expanded and diversified greatly since the mid-1960s. Student numbers have grown from 20,000 in 1965 to 75,000 in 1992, and it is planned to raise this figure to 100,000 by the year 2000 (Department of Education 1992). There is a wide diversity in the type of institutions—universities, technological colleges, regional technical colleges, colleges of education, and a number of other institutions which provide courses in areas such as art, music, commerce, and theology. There are four universities, one of which (the National University of Ireland) is a federal university, with three constituent and four recognized colleges. Almost half the higher education students are enrolled in universities. About 40 percent of the age group go on to higher education and about half the intake proceeds to degree-level programs. About 50 percent of students benefit from state grants linked to means, ability, and area of domicile.

The Higher Education Authority (HEA) was established in 1968 as a planning and budgetary agency between the government and the many designated institutions. The National Council for Educational Awards (NCEA) was set up in 1972 to validate courses and confer awards for colleges in the nonuniversity sector. The Central Applications Office (CAO) was set up in 1976 and acts as a clearinghouse for almost all applications to higher education institutions.

Trends in higher education in the early 1990s include new funding mechanisms based on a unit cost analysis, modularization of courses, closer links with industry, the establishment of performance indicators in the interests of quality assurance, and the introduction of new legislation to meet the changing needs of the institutions and their relationship with modern society.

3.2 Preschool Education

In Ireland, the tradition of early entry into mainstream schooling is long-established. Almost all 5-year olds and two-thirds of 4-year olds attend the infant classes of the national (primary) schools. In a sense, much of what is considered preschooling in other countries is incorporated into the primary school system. Responsibilities in relation to preschools per se rest with the minister for health. Both the Department of Education and of Health make grants-in-aid available to voluntary bodies to provide preschooling for children with disabilities and for certain disadvantaged groups. A

455

small minority of parents pay fees for privately run preschools for their children.

3.3 Special Education

Although only about 2 percent of school children are involved in special education, this aspect of educational provision has become increasingly important in public policy over the last 30 years. A comprehensive system of special education is now provided for children suffering from various forms of handicap or disability including mental, physical, sensory handicap, and those who are emotionally disturbed. Such children are catered for in special schools, in special classes in ordinary schools, or in certain voluntary centers where appropriate educational services can be provided. The proportion of the total population of compulsory school attendance age (6–15 years) enrolled in special schools is approximately 1.29 percent, which is small by European standards. Nevertheless, government policy is to seek integration of those with special educational needs in mainstream schools, as far as possible.

Pupil–teacher ratios are very much smaller in special schools and special classes than in ordinary schools, and an extensive system of school transport has been developed to assist parents and pupils. Cooperation exists between teachers in special education, the Schools' Psychological Service, and the health authorities to ensure that the needs of pupils are responded to satisfactorily. Policies to facilitate disabled pupils to participate in secondary and higher education are also in operation. Visiting teacher schemes for children confined at home also exist. Specialized training courses exist for teachers in special education. In September 1991, the minister for education set up the Special Education Review Committee to submit recommendations for improvement of the services for special education.

3.4 Vocational, Technical, and Business Education

With the establishment of the Vocational Educational Committees (VECs) in 1930, vocational and technical education came predominantly under the aegis of these committees. In the 1960s, the vocational schools were allowed to offer the whole secondary school range of subjects and enter pupils for all the public examinations. National policy favored a comprehensive type of curricular provision. The policy, as it stands in the early 1990s, is to strengthen the vocational and technical dimension within secondary education. Among the means being employed to do this are the expanding of the Leaving Certificate Vocational Programme from its up-take in the early 1990s by about 5 percent of pupils to 30 percent at senior level. Pupils will also be required to take a science course and a new subject, Enterprise and Technology, as compulsory subjects. Work experience is being incorporated in more school courses and representatives of industry and commerce are being recruited to school managements. The approach to training is that it be broad-based rather than job-specific, and that higher level skills and competencies will be based on good standards of general education.

There has been a significant expansion of vocational education and training for those leaving the formal school courses before taking up employment. Some 19,000 young people avail of the Vocational Preparation and Training Programmes, VPT1 and VPT2. The Industrial Training Authority, FAS, regulates apprenticeship in designated trades and 10,000 participants take their off-the-job education in vocational schools. Arrangements for a new apprenticeship system, based on standards reached, rather than on time served, is being introduced in 1993. "Youthreach" programs exist for those who dropped out of school and involve Community Training Workshops. Training for the hotel and tourism industries is provided by CERT and the Vocational Education Committees. The VECs also provide the Vocational Training Opportunities Scheme (VTOs) for the long-term unemployed. The establishment, on an ad hoc basis, of the National Council for Vocational Awards is the forerunner of a planned new body, the Council for Educational and Vocational Awards, to operate a comprehensive system of national certification and validation of standards for all vocational education and training programs.

3.5 Adult and Nonformal Education

In line with developments internationally, adult education has been receiving greater public attention and support and the concept of "lifelong learning" is now generally accepted. The range of institutions and agencies providing adult education is very wide indeed. The VECs have played a central role in the provision of adult education with the help of their 50 Adult Education Organizers and of their Adult Education Boards. Community, comprehensive, and, increasingly, secondary schools are also taking on roles in adult education. The Regional Technical Colleges and most of the university institutions offer adult education and extramural courses. Increasingly, second chance provision is enabling adults who were early school leavers, to return to secondary schooling. Universities operate flexible schemes which facilitate the entrance of mature students to higher education. A National Distance Learning Centre has begun to make diploma and degree courses available to locations at a remove from university centers.

A host of other agencies, such as trade unions and voluntary groups, provide a very diverse range of adult education courses. Adult literacy courses are particularly target areas. AONTAS, the National Association of Adult Education, is the main advisory and consultative body in adult education and acts as a general reference agency for all those involved in adult education.

It receives a grant-in-aid from the Department of Education.

4. Administrative and Supervisory Structure and Operation

All schools, except for a minority of voluntary secondary schools, are administered by management boards representative of trustees, parents, and teachers. Some secondary schools also have representatives of local industry and commercial interests on the boards. In the case of vocational schools and community colleges, the boards refer back to the Vocational Education Committees. Other schools relate directly with the Department of Education. The Green Paper (Department of Education 1992)—*Education for a Changing World*—envisages a common structure for all school management boards, more extensive powers, and greater accountability.

A school inspectorate acts as the supervisory agency for primary schools, responsible for general maintenance of standards. There is also an inspectorate for secondary schools, but its powers are less intrusive. Success in the public examinations is also a public indication of standards of schools. Most schools operate formal parent–teacher meetings and provide feedback to parents on the continuing educational progress of their children. The control exercised by the minister for education is mainly based on the recognition of schools, specification of national curricula, monitoring by the inspectorate, teacher recognition, and administration of public examinations in secondary education. Most higher education institutions have statutory governing bodies and most of them liaise with the Higher Education Authority on budgetary and planning matters. The traditional academic autonomy of the universities is increasingly influenced by the national budgetary considerations, and the government is also planning the introduction of performance indicators in the interests of quality assurance.

5. Educational Finance

Almost all public authority spending on education comes from the central government. Total public expenditure on education in 1992 amounted to Ir£1.6 billion (US$2.3 billion), representing almost 20 percent of total government expenditure on public services and 6 percent of the Gross National Product (GNP) (Department of Education 1992). This represents a substantial increase in allocation of resources to education in comparison to 1965, when the corresponding figures were 15.8 percent and 3.6 percent respectively. The changing nature of pupil participation is reflected in changes in the proportionate expenditure between the sectors. In 1966, primary education accounted for 52 percent of the expenditure, second level for 30 percent, and third-level, or higher education, for 8 percent. In 1992, the respective proportions are about 35, 37, and 22 percent between the sectors. The cost of the central administration of the system in 1992 is 5 percent of the total expenditure (Department of Education 1992). Teacher salaries account for about 80 percent of the current expenditure on education.

Statistics are not precise on the matter, but it is estimated that about 85 percent of the cost of education in the country is met by government, and the remaining 15 percent by local contributions and student fees. Tuition is free in all state-aided primary schools and in 93 percent of secondary schools. The costs of school textbooks and uniforms are borne by parents, but the state makes grants to a minority of needy pupils for such items. School transport, beyond a 4 kilometer limit from the local school, is mainly free, but some parents do pay transport levies.

A grant scheme exists for students in higher education, linked to ability, means, and geographical location. Some of these are provided through the European Community Social Fund. Significant increases in the grants were introduced in 1992 and, under the new regulations, about 53 percent of students in state-aided higher education institutions benefit from some form of grant. It is planned to introduce a unit cost mechanism for all education institutions in the immediate future on the basis of which they will be allowed more discretion in the deployment of their budgets.

6. Supplying Personnel for the Education System

In 1990, there were 20,321 full-time teachers in primary schools, 11,630 in secondary schools, 4,825 in vocational schools, and 2,293 in comprehensive and community schools. There was also the equivalent of a further 1,345 teachers working part-time in secondary education. Pupil–teacher ratios in schools tend to be high, at 26.5:1 in primary schools and 19.5:1 in second-level schools in 1992. The demographic decline has led to reduced demand for teachers in primary schools and this is also affecting secondary teachers. Teaching as a career traditionally has been held in high social regard and it has continued to attract people of high intelligence and personal caliber.

Trainee teachers for primary schools undergo a three-year concurrent Bachelor in Education degree in colleges of education which is validated by the universities. Their probation year in the schools is monitored by the school inspectorate. Most teachers for second-level schools take a consecutive teacher-training program, whereby they follow their undergraduate university degree by a one-year professional diploma course in education within the university. Teachers of specialist subjects, such as physical education, art, home economics, woodwork, undergo four-year concurrent degree courses, most of which are validated by the universities, with a minority by the National Council for Educational Awards. The Secondary Teachers' Registration Council is the registering body for most second-level teachers.

A common salary scale exists for all teachers, with extra allowances for qualifications and responsibility. The inservice education of teachers is regarded as an issue of particular priority, if planned reforms are to be achieved. The vast majority of teachers are members of the three teacher unions which have proved strong in defense of teacher interests.

Support personnel for the school system, such as inspectors, are recruited from well-qualified, skilled teachers and are trained by the senior inspectorate. School psychologists are recruited usually from teachers who have also obtained university qualifications in psychology. Special graduate courses exist for school guidance personnel and remedial teachers. While not yet obligatory, school administrators increasingly take diploma courses in school management or graduate degrees in education.

7. Curriculum Development and Teaching Methodology

Curricula for primary and all secondary schools are approved by the Department of Education of the central government. With the establishment of the National Council for Curriculum and Assessment (NCCA) in 1987, as an advisory body, the Department is assisted by this body in planning and devising curricula. The curriculum for the primary school, introduced in 1971, replaced a rather narrow, rigid program with a more child-centered one, incorporating a wide range of subjects and encouraging an active style of pedagogy linked to local needs and environment. This curriculum has been endorsed by the report of a Review Body on the Primary Curriculum (1990) in basic principles, but it seeks more emphasis on the "3Rs" and seeks more targeted objectives. The Green Paper of 1992 took the same view, emphasizing the importance of literacy and numeracy, and a more focused program for science and physical education. It also sought the more universal use of standardized tests at the ages of 7 and 11 for diagnostic purposes.

Since the mid-1960s, the government has favored a comprehensive approach to curriculum in second-level schools, whereby all schools offer a wide program up to the end of senior cycle to suit students of varying aptitude and ability. The expansion of the clientele in secondary schooling has led to much curriculum development and experimentation, notably by the Dublin Vocational Education Committee's Curriculum Development Unit and the Shannon Curriculum Development Unit. The Irish Association for Curriculum Development, founded in 1971, reflected teacher interest in such developments. Ireland participated in a range of curriculum development projects on school-

to-work in association with other EC countries, in the late 1970s and early 1980s. It proved difficult to absorb much of the curricular experimentation into the mainstream courses.

However, with the establishment in 1989 of a new Junior Certificate for secondary schools, examined for the first time in 1992, there is a more clear articulation with primary school curriculum and a more innovative approach to the content, pedagogy, and assessment of the first three years of secondary schooling. The design of new syllabuses has involved many teachers with a keen interest in curriculum reform. Work is underway to design a new Senior Certificate course appropriate to the needs of the greatly increased student body in the 15 to 18 age group. The aim is to try to preserve a comprehensive, unified, senior cycle school framework within which a variety of options can be accommodated. There has been concern expressed by employers and the government that a more vocational and technical emphasis should be given to the school programs. The senior cycle is now of three years' duration. The methodology in secondary schooling has traditionally been of a teacher-centered, didactic style by subject teacher specialists. It is hoped that a methodology more focused on student engagement in problem-solving, divergent thinking, and promoting self-reliance can be developed to assist the creation of an enterprise culture.

Guidance and psychological services exist to assist students in educational and vocational planning. Supporting textbooks are usually written by skilled teachers for a range of educational publishers. The publishers liaise with the Departmental inspectorate on appropriate content: books have to be officially approved for use in the primary schools.

8. The System of Examinations, Promotions, and Certifications

Traditionally, public examinations have played a very prominent part in the Irish education system at the secondary level. There is no formal assessment at the end of primary school, but school principals may transfer a cumulative record card of pupils' profiles to the school to which the pupils transfer. Promotion within primary schools from grade to grade is automatic. The Green Paper of 1992 expressed concern at the lack of any standardized, objective criteria to measure pupils' progress from the age of 4 to 15. Accordingly, it is planned to introduce standardized testing at ages 7 and 11, primarily as a diagnostic aid. The results will be confidential to schools and to parents, but will be available in aggregated form to the Department of Education.

At the end of three years of secondary schooling, pupils take the Junior Certificate Examination, an external examination administered by the Department of Education. This has been largely based on terminal, written examination papers. It is planned that school-based assessment should form a much greater proportion of the examination, involving teachers assessing their pupils on much more varied criteria, and seen to be more integral to the content and pedagogy which is sought. However, there is strong reluctance by many teachers to be so directly involved in the public certification of their own pupils. The report of a special committee on pupil assessment is expected in the autumn of 1992.

The issue of school-based assessment becomes more acute at the end of senior cycle education when the final examination carries a heavy burden of selection for higher education and for employment. The Leaving Certificate has been taken by most pupils after two years study. It is a very competitive examination which relies heavily on performance in the written examination papers. Most students present 6 subjects from an approved list of about 35 subjects. There has been much criticism that the Leaving Certificate courses and examinations are not suitable for many of the enlarged pupil clientele of the schools. The NCCA, in association with the Department of Education, is seeking to devise a new Senior Certificate Program which will be more flexible, allow for more options, and be assessed in more varied ways. The Leaving Certificate has had high public acceptability among employers, higher education institutions, and parents. The challenge is to devise a replacement for a universalist student cohort of 90 percent of the age range.

The National Council for Vocational Awards was set up in 1991 to act as the validating and coordinating agency for a wide range of vocational courses, within and out-of-school, which are not included in the mainstream system.

9. Educational Assessment, Evaluation, and Research

In the context of a greater emphasis on accountability, transparency, and quality assurance reflected in the Green Paper (Department of Education 1992), tighter controls on the overall education system are being planned. The measures include more comprehensive reporting by the Department of Education, a restructuring of the role of the inspectorate, greater responsibility and public accountability on school boards of management, the introduction of standardized testing for all schools, the employment of performance indicators, and public reportage for higher education institutions. While the OECD *Review of Irish Education*, in 1991, returned a favorable overview of the system, it is considered that the role and costs of the education system are such that more regular formal monitoring and reportage on the system is in the public interest.

With regard to educational research, recent decades have witnessed a significant growth in this area with the participation of a wide variety of institutions and agencies. The OECD *Review of Irish Education* found that the study of education was well developed in Ireland, and that the volume and variety of research was impressive for a small country. It pointed out the need for more policy-related research to underpin educational development.

Among the key research agencies are the education departments of the universities, the Educational Research Centre, the Linguistics Institute, and the Economic and Social Research Institute. The Educational Studies Association of Ireland acts as an umbrella association for educational researchers. The research covers a wide range of issues including policy analysis, school effectiveness, curriculum reform, economic aspects of education, language teaching and bilingualism, evaluation techniques, social equity and gender issues, modes of school organization and subject availability, education and the labor market, and teacher education. Dissemination of research occurs through conferences, symposia, educational journals, and media reportage. To help coordination and establish priorities for educational research, a Research and Development Committee was established in 1992 within the Department of Education, which will include some external advisers.

10. Major Reforms in the 1980s and 1990s

Despite the difficulties encountered in the 1980s because of retrenchment on educational expenditure in line with public sector spending generally, the momentum for educational reform was sustained. Among the significant reforms was the continued quantitative expansion of participation in secondary and higher education. It is planned to extend the 73 percent of the population who complete secondary education in 1992 to 90 percent during the 1990s, and to increase the age group who enter higher education from 40 to 45 percent. Linked to the great improvements in participation are the curricular issues to ensure that the education young people receive is satisfactory and beneficial. The curricular experimentation of the 1980s is being harnessed into mainstream provision in the 1990s with the new Junior Certificate and the planned new Senior Certificate. These are being guided forward by the NCCA, set up in 1987. Links between school and the world of work, pioneered in the 1980s, are being continued in secondary schooling. Efforts are still in progress to reform the assessment procedures so that they become more varied and flexible in response to changed curricular policies.

Teacher education at preservice level has also been experiencing on-going reform, and a greater role for the universities in teacher education has been taking place. The acceptance of a coherent teacher education program involving initial, induction, and inservice education has been gaining greater acceptance. The further expansion of the inservice education of teachers is regarded as particularly important in the 1990s, but limited resources impede its more comprehensive provision.

Within the remarkable expansion of higher education from a level of 21,000 students in 1965 to a projected 100,000 by the year 2000, a great diversity of institutions and programs has been achieved. Furthermore, it is planned to develop the links which have been forged between higher education and industry in a variety of ways. Another area of on-going reform is the expansion of access to higher education for mature students and the extension of distance education facilities to the regions.

11. Major Problems for the Year 2000

One of the major problems is the rationalization of school provision. The declining pupil population will involve even smaller primary schools than exist at present, when 43 percent of the primary schools have three teachers or less. The aim is to try to establish the four-teacher school as the minimum size. However, this is a very controversial area as many rural localities have a very close attachment to their schools, seeing them as symbolic of their well-being for the future. The issue will also be acute at secondary level where it is calculated that the existing 800 schools will be reduced to between 500 and 600 by the year 2000. New curricular policies make it imperative, particularly at senior cycle, that rationalization of school provision takes place. Some 25 percent of the schools have less than 250 pupils enrolled and, with a declining population, there is a battle for survival between local schools. This is a matter of major concern for the good of education and for preserving the social fabric of local communities.

The policy shift toward greater school autonomy and accountability involves significant problems of a cultural, attitudinal, and skills character for local schools if the policy is to be met successfully by the year 2000. It involves significant challenges for the quality of management and leadership within the schools. Significant changes are being sought from teachers whereby an older tradition of teacher individualism yields to a more teamwork approach and a tradition of schools as discrete organizations yields to closer integration and collaboration with the local communities.

The achievement of greater equality in the education system related to social group, gender, ability level, and region is a major problem for the years ahead. A particular target will be those living in disadvantaged areas and the low achievers, or early leavers from the education system.

The senior-secondary school cycle presents significant problems relating to curricular balance, curricular diversity, teaching methodologies, assessment processes, and institutional climate. The challenge here is unprecedented as never before has society aimed to involve 90 percent of the relevant age cohort in full-

time schooling. One of the difficulties here, and also underlying many of the problems leading up to the year 2000, is the limited financial resources that can be made available to achieve the ambitious targets laid out for a quality education system at all levels, in the context of a small, open, island economy with a very high unemployment rate. Aspirations are high, but it will take great commitment by all concerned to achieve the planned targets by the year 2000.

References

Coolahan J 1981 *Irish Education: It's History and Structure.* Institute of Public Administration, Dublin
Department of Education 1980 White Paper: *Educational Development.* Stationery Office, Dublin
Department of Education 1984 *Programme for Action in Education, 1984–87.* Stationery Office, Dublin
Department of Education 1990 *Annual Statistical Report.* Stationery Office, Dublin
Department of Education 1992 Green Paper: *Education for a Changing World.* Stationery Office, Dublin
OECD 1989 *Employment Outlook.* OECD, Paris
OECD 1991 *Review of Irish Education.* OECD, Paris
Review Body of the Primary School Curriculum 1990 *Report.* Stationery Office, Dublin

Further Reading

Akenson D H 1975 *A Mirror to Kathleen's Face: Education in Independent Ireland, 1922–60.* McGill–Queens' University Press, Montreal
Barber N S J 1989 *Comprehensive Schooling in Ireland.* Broadsheet Series Paper No. 25 Economic and Social Research Institute, Dublin
Clancy P 1988 *Who Goes to College? A Second National Survey of Participation in Higher Education.* Higher Education Authority, Dublin
Department of Education 1991 *Rules and Programmes For Secondary Schools.* Stationery Office, Dublin
Hannan D F 1986 *Schooling and the Labour Market.* Shannon Curriculum Development Centre, Shannon
Hannan D F, Boyle M 1987 *Schooling Decisions: The Origins and Consequences of Selection and Streaming in Irish Post-primary Schools.* Economic and Social Research Institute, Dublin
Hannan D F, Shortall S 1991 *The Quality of Their Education: School Leavers' Views of Educational Objectives and Outcomes.* Economic and Social Research Institute, Dublin
Higher Education Authority 1991 *Accounts and Student Statistics 1989–90.* Higher Education Authority, Dublin
Mulcahy D G 1981 *Curriculum and Policy in Irish Post-primary Education.* Institute of Public Administration, Dublin
Mulcahy D G, O'Sullivan D 1988 *Irish Educational Policy: Process and Substance.* Institute of Public Administration, Dublin
National Council for Curriculum and Assessment 1991 *The Curriculum at Senior Cycle.* NCCA, Dublin.
O Buachalla S 1988 *Education Policy in Twentieth Century Ireland.* Wolfhound Press, Dublin
Primary Education Review Body 1990 *Report.* Stationery Office, Dublin

Israel

E. Shmueli

1. General Background

The State of Israel was established on May 15, 1948, upon the termination of the British Mandate and following the United Nations' resolution on the partition of Palestine between Jews and Arabs of November 29, 1947. Soon after this resolution, a war broke out (the War of Independence in 1948) between the new state and its Arab neighbors. The outcome of this war, and the armistice agreement that followed, determined Israel's borders, and its land mass now totals 28,000 square kilometers (the green line). There are also 1,176 square kilometers of the Golan Heights (which were officially annexed to the State of Israel after the Six Day War in 1967), 5,706 square kilometers of the West Bank, and 1,352 square kilometers of the Gaza Strip (which are still under Israeli military occupation).

Israel is situated on the Mediterranean coast, south of Lebanon, west of the Arabian Desert, and north of the Sinai Peninsula. Israel's climate is humid in the north and arid in the south. Its natural water balance is estimated at 1.7 billion cubic meters per annum. The continuous growth of its population and its special needs for industry and agriculture have resulted in a water shortage which could eventually lead to limitations in the water supply.

The Negev Desert in the south (which constitutes 60% of Israel's area) and Upper Galilee are sparsely populated. Despite their relatively short distance from the center of the country and the special and intensive efforts to develop these areas, they still remain comparatively underdeveloped. The most populated areas are the cities along the narrow coastal plain. Most of the economic and cultural activities are conducted in Jerusalem, Tel-Aviv, and Haifa.

The first census in Palestine was conducted in 1922 under the British Mandate. The population was then 757,182. In the second census in 1931, it had increased to 1,035,825. From 1948 to 1951 the population increase was 25 percent annually. Most Israelis are either first- or second-generation immigrants.

The Israeli population totaled 4,960,000 by June 1991, 82 percent of whom are Jews and 18 percent non-Jews (Moslems and Christians). During the first eight months of 1990, 100,000 newcomers immigrated to Israel, seven times more than in former years. This large number of immigrants arrived mainly from Russia and Ethiopia and had a great impact on the ethnic mix. It also resulted in a more culturally diversified society, which prompted major educational problems and plans for absorption and social integration. In 1991, special extra hours of teaching were allocated to introduce Hebrew and Israeli culture to these new immigrants.

Israel's economy is based on industry, agriculture, building construction, high technology, and tourism. Out of 1,603,000 persons in the labor force (1989), 91.1 percent (1,461,000) were employed, while 8.9 percent (142,000) were unemployed. Export of agricultural products amounted to 3.5 percent of the Gross Domestic Product (GDP) and totaled 527 billion INS (Israeli New Shekels) (3 INS=US$1). Building construction accounted for 8.5 percent of the GDP and the income from tourism amounted to 1.5 billion INS.

The annual state budget for social services in the fiscal year 1990–91 amounted to about 65 billion INS. Defense took the largest share (about 20%). The education budget comes out of the social services allocation and amounts to 7.4 percent of the state's budget.

Israel is a parliamentary democracy with elections every four years and has a multiparty system. Governments can be formed by coalition only. The 1991 government coalition was comprised of the right-wing conservative parties (Likud, Moledet, Tzomet, and Hatchiya), the religious national party (Mafdal), and the orthodox religious parties (Aguda and Shas). Labor and left-wing parties were in the opposition. On June 11, 1990, the Knesset (parliament) approved the new government's political goals: absorption of the newcomers (housing, labor, employment, and education), securing Israel's independence and welfare, and striving for peace with its neighbors.

The educational system is highly centralized. The Ministry of Education and Culture is responsible for the content of education (curriculum and approval of textbooks), educational policy, supervision of schools, teachers' recruitment and placement in primary schools, budgeting, and development.

The Ministry's representatives report to the Education Committee in the Knesset. A National Board of Education, comprising representatives of the different political parties and the Ministry's officials, convenes rarely and has little impact on the Ministry's everyday work.

2. Politics and the Goals of the Education System

The political goals of the Ministry of Education, ever since the establishment of the state, have been: to absorb newcomers and adjust the system to their needs, bridge social and cultural gaps, and strive for better relations between Jews and Arabs.

The state's Law of Education (1953) defined the goals of the education system as follows:

to base elementary education on the values of Jewish culture and the achievements of the sciences, on love of the homeland and loyalty to the state and the Jewish people, on practice in agriculture and manual work, on pioneer training, and on striving for a society built on freedom, equality, tolerance. mutual assistance, and love of humankind.

The state's school population is mainly secular (70%) and all students receive a general education without practicing religion inside the school premises. Differences between various social segments exist mainly between religious and secular communities. Over the years the religious policymakers have developed nuances in their religious and political behavior and these affect the daily schoolwork of the children of these groups.

In general, the religious Jewish community is divided into moderate religious and ultra-orthodox communities. Both groups have developed their own school networks. The ultra-orthodox schools are supervised and financed by the Ministry of Education, but as far as curriculum and teacher recruitment are concerned, they are independent. The network of the national religious party (Mafdal) is supervised by the Ministry of Education and is totally controlled by it. Religion is practiced in schools of both the ultra-orthodox and Mafdal networks.

3. The Formal System of Education

3.1 Primary, Secondary, and Tertiary Education

The school system is divided into the following levels:

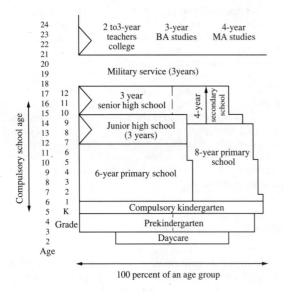

Figure 1
Israel: Structure of the formal education system

kindergartens for children ranging from 3 to 5 years of age; primary schools for 6–12 (or 6–14) year olds; secondary schools from 12–18 (or 14–18) year olds and teachers' colleges, community colleges, and universities. Those who are exempt from military service can continue their studies immediately after their matriculation examination at the age of 18; otherwise, all graduates first serve in the army for at least three years. Figure 1 presents a diagram of the school system and the proportion of an age group enrolled at each level.

Primary schools are district-oriented and cater for students from their neighborhood. Secondary schools have three different tracks: academic, technical (and vocational), and agricultural. In the early 1960s the technical schools were transferred from the Ministry of Labor's supervision to the Ministry of Education and Culture, in order to broaden the students' general education alongside their vocational training. Since 1970 there has been a significant increase in the number of students in the technical educational system. In 1987–88 approximately 42 percent of upper-secondary school students (Grades 10–12) studied in it. Most were from the disadvantaged population.

In the late 1970s, capable students of high academic standard began to attend the technological tracks to graduate as qualified technicians and practical engineers. Graduates of technical tracks are encouraged to serve in technical units of the Israeli defense forces to continue their studies in institutes of higher education.

Technical education offers a wide variety of courses from design and hairstyling to electronics and telecommunications. At the end of the 1980s and beginning of the 1990s, there was a rise in the numbers of students enrolled in computer studies, robotics, and industrial automation studies. There are no differences in enrollment between the sexes, in either urban or rural schools.

Hardly any private (profit-making) schools exist in the country. All primary schools, Jewish or Arab, are maintained either by the state or by nonprofit organizations.

Schools are open six days a week. The Ministry of Education is considering a five-day learning week to comply with the Teachers' Union demands to adjust the educational system to the national five-day work week in industry and other services. It has been decided to postpone this plan because of social and economic pressures. The school day in primary schools is relatively short (from 8.00 a.m. to 12 noon). Junior and senior high schools continue into the afternoon (8.00 a.m. to 2.00 p.m.). The school year is from September 1 to June 30 in primary schools, and from September 1 to June 20 in secondary schools. The average class size is 30 students.

3.2 Preschool Education

Investment in preschool education responds to a number of social and national needs. It enables mothers to join the labor force, and it offers an acceptable solution for children whose families do not provide an environment conducive to their optimal development.

Kindergarten education in Israel started as early as 1884. Later, formal kindergartens were established by women's voluntary organizations, welfare agencies, and eventually by the local authorities. The Compulsory Law of Education (1949) included one year of kindergarten education at the age of 5.

The early childhood education network includes the education of children from 0–6 years of age. Within this framework the Ministry of Education is responsible for children from age 3 to 6 years. The 5-year olds receive free education according to law. Precompulsory kindergartens (age 3 to 5) are organized by the local authorities, by women's organizations, and by private individuals or groups. They charge graded school fees according to the parents' income.

The Ministry supervises all of these settings. In the 0 to 3 age group the Ministry is involved mainly through programs intended to improve parenting skills, thereby advancing the development of infants and toddlers. For instance, 64 percent of the 2-year olds attend daycare centers.

The early childhood education network is responsible for approximately 420,000 children. The average percentage of the age group attending early childhood education amounts to 96 percent in the Jewish sector and 50 percent among Arabs.

3.3 Special Education

The percentage of special education students ranges from 8–10 percent of the total number of 1,463,945 students enrolled in primary and secondary education.

Special education programs are provided by law. Programs are provided for students with physical, intellectual, and emotional disabilities. During the early years of statehood, special education was totally separated from the main system. Since the end of the 1980s, there has been an attempt to integrate, as much as possible, "special students" in separate classes in a regular school. In order to be able to cope with different learning disabilities, different kinds of schools have been established: for example, schools for autistic, blind, and deaf children. These special schools and classes are supervised by the Ministry of Education and Culture.

"Special students" are tested, screened, and approved by professional local committees composed of Municipality and Ministry psychologists, educators, and social workers. Dissatisfied parents are entitled to appeal to a higher authority in the Ministry.

A few special education classes exist within hospitals, and are run by the Ministry of Education in cooperation with the Ministry of Health.

There is limited guidance for dealing with the issue of transition from school to the work market. The fact that all high-school graduates are recruited into the armed services immediately after graduation constitutes a time-gap between school and work or between school and higher education. Special guidance services, mostly nongovernmental, help young people find suitable work after they have completed their military service.

3.4 Vocational, Technical, and Business Education

Vocational and technical education is free up to Grade 12 of the secondary school. Students have a choice between academic, vocational, technical, nautical, or agricultural high school after graduating from primary school. Business education is a part of the regular vocational school studies.

Vocational and technical education is financed by the Ministry of Education. In some cases, nonprofit public organizations take responsibility for managing and financing these schools, dividing the expenses between themselves, the Ministry, and the local authorities. The nonprofit vocational school networks of ORT (Organization of Rehabilitation by Training), Amal Amit, and WIZO (Women's International Zionist Organization) also raise funds abroad to help maintain their schools and cover special financial needs which are not covered by the Ministry.

The only agencies to combine vocational and special education are the "Youth Centers" run by the Jewish Agency in cooperation with the Ministry and the local authorities. These centers attract dropouts from regular schools, and provide special vocational education for students who do not wish to pursue academic studies. Industry also plays a partial role and there are only a few vocational high schools (run by the Ministry of Labor), within the industrial enterprises. These schools are similar in their educational tasks to the "Youth Centers" mentioned above.

3.5 Adult and Nonformal Education

Adult and nonformal education are two separate entities in the Ministry. Adult education deals mainly with college education, the teaching of Hebrew to newcomers and tourists in *Ulpanim* (special institutes established to teach Hebrew to newcomers), and with the education of illiterates. In the early 1980s, regional colleges were established in the rural areas. They offer a variety of courses in general knowledge, arts, and crafts. At the beginning of the 1990s there were 12 colleges with 4,787 students in different parts of the country. The students pay tuition fees according to the number of courses they attend. These colleges are supervised by the Ministry.

Nonformal education consists of extracurricular activities, school trips, premilitary training and the teaching of educational values, and political and nonpolitical youth movements, such as the National Scouts. The National Council for youth movements, in cooperation with the Ministry, provides supervision and allocates budgets for these activities. Young people and adults are encouraged to join special activities initiated by the Society for the Preservation of Nature which deals mainly with ecology and environment preservation.

In high schools, all of these activities are compulsory and supplement the educational curriculum. Students receive credit in their final high-school diplomas for having participated in the different youth activities.

The total expenditure on adult education amounts to 56,500,000 NIS (US $20,635,500), which is approximately 1.5 percent of the Ministry's budget. Nonformal education's budget amounts to 48,253,000 NIS (US $17,623,447) and this represents 1.28 percent of the Ministry's budget.

4. Administrative and Supervisory Structure and Operation

The Israeli educational system is highly centralized. Its headquarters in Jerusalem deal with administrative and educational matters. The Ministry is in charge of the recruitment and placement of primary-school teachers. Primary-school supervisors review their work, and are in charge of the allocation of extra teaching hours according the the school's needs.

Educational policy is made in the Ministry's headquarters. Its execution is carried out by the Ministry's administrators and the local authority officials. Each year, the Minister of Education and the Minister of Interior meet and coordinate, by law, the registration and zoning policy for the local educational councils.

Secondary education is free up to the age of 18 years. It is under the jurisdiction of the local authorities and voluntary organizations and is administered by them.

Secondary-school teachers are recruited by the local authorities or by the public networks (Ort, Amal, etc.). They are hired and fired by the agencies that recruit them. Most of the teachers in the country are graduates of teachers' colleges, and are supervised by the Ministry's inspectors. A teacher cannot be fired unless the school's inspector gives a negative report on his or her accomplishments. A second opinion should be received from an additional inspector from a different inspectoral district.

Religious school supervisors are under the jurisdiction of the state's religious council.

5. Educational Finance

The national expenditure for education is comprised of all the education costs, educational services, and funds for new buildings and equipment. More than half of the national expenditure on education is allocated to primary and secondary schools. The balance is allocated to post-secondary schools, universities, the building of new schools, and equipment. The total expenditure on education (1991) was 3.7 billion NIS (US $1.35 billion), 88.1 percent of which went to formal education. This represents 8 to 9 percent of the Gross Domestic Product (GDP).

The total regular budget allocated to education is NIS7,315,509,000 (US$2,938,503,000). Of this budget, 6.2 percent goes to preprimary education, 29.7 percent to primary education, 39.1 percent to secondary education including vocational education, 3.2 percent to the private sector, 13.9 percent to administration, and 7.9 percent to other educational and cultural organizations.

The per unit costs are per preprimary pupil NIS3,500 per capita (US$1,667), per primary pupil NIS4,000 per capita (US$1,333), and per secondary pupil NIS7,500 per capita (US$2,500).

Since 1985–86 there has been a moderate increase in the national expenditure on education as a percentage of the GDP. However, it is still a lower percentage than that of 1984–85 (9.3%). Government and local authority participation in financing national education decreased from 84 percent in the years 1975–80 to 76 percent in the year 1988–89. There is, however, some indication of an increase in the share of the nonprofit institutes (e.g., the Jewish Agency, the United Jewish Appeal) in this financing.

6. Supplying Personnel for the Education System

There are just over 49,000 teachers in primary schools. There is no shortage of teachers. Most of the Russian immigrant teachers teach science, music, and physical training. Primary school teachers are trained for three years in teachers' colleges. Secondary school teachers are trained in the various departments of the universities, and undergo a further year of educational training in a university school of education. They are evaluated periodically by the Ministry's supervisors. Teachers are encouraged to attend inservice training courses in the universities during the summer vacations.

7. Curriculum Development and Teaching Methodology

The Ministry is responsible for curriculum development in both primary and secondary schools. Curriculum is prepared by subject matter committees composed of university experts within the Ministry. Secondary schools are encouraged to develop special subjects, media studies, interdisciplinary studies, and so on. These subjects must be approved by the school's supervisor before they are introduced into the school. Students who participate in them are entitled to take final diploma examinations in these subjects, which are recognized by the Ministry.

Textbooks are written by private authors and are approved by the Ministry. In most cases the authors cover the official curriculum in particular subject areas.

The Curriculum Center's role is to define the curricula for the different subjects statewide. The Center revises the curricula and introduces the necessary changes according to sciences development and the teaching methodology of the subject. The Center receives feedback from the school principals and supervisors, and rewrites the curricula accordingly.

The formal state language is Hebrew. English is a compulsory foreign language from the fifth grade onwards all over the country. Arabic, French, and Spanish are optional and are taught in high schools to interested students.

8. The System of Examinations, Promotions, and Certifications

The structure of Israeli matriculation examinations has undergone a number of changes over the years. In 1975 a reform was tried out in a small number of schools. It proved to be so successful that it was then implemented throughout the whole system. The reform enables students to choose most of their study courses and to take examinations at different levels according to their capabilities. Graduates are also encouraged to write a paper instead of taking a final written examination.

In 1989, 58 percent of the examinees studied in the academic track, 42 percent in the technological and agricultural tracks, and 78 percent took final examinations. During 1987–89, there was an increase in the percentage of graduates from the technological track taking final examinations

Nationwide tests are conducted periodically in primary school classes in order to examine the students' scholastic achievements. (These tests include the comprehension of texts and mathematics.) Special attention, extra teaching hours, and a lot of encouragement are given to "needy" schools.

9. Educational Assessment, Evaluation, and Research

Educational research is carried out by the academic staff of the schools of education in the universities. The Henrietta Szold Institute for Research in Behavioral Sciences serves the system by conducting research studies upon request. Topics for study include: the screening of the potentially gifted, community schools, long-day studies, and enrichment programs. The Center of Educational Technology concentrates on the development of new methods for improving educational achievement.

The Ministry of Education makes use of research results. In some cases the Ministry initiates research in order to decide on its educational policy. For example, following the results of research on grouping, the Ministry decided to stop this policy in the schools and encouraged new techniques in teaching heterogenous classes.

10. Major Reforms in the 1980s and 1990s

The 1980s found the educational system preoccupied with strengthening education for coexistence between Jews and Arabs. During the early 1980s the Ministry launched a special program for this purpose. Special guide books were prepared to aid educators in this important task. Schools conducted mutual visits to each other's premises. These encounters have resulted in constructive understanding and in open dialogues between Arab and Jewish students as well as acquainting them with each other's culture and language.

Educating the gifted has become a declared policy. Special classes for the gifted have been opened within regular schools. The Henrietta Szold Institute for Research in Behavioral Sciences has developed special techniques for identifying these gifted students as early as possible in primary schools.

In the early 1990s, the Academy for Sciences and Arts opened the doors of its boarding facilities to senior high school graduates from all over the country. The Minister of Education is planning special schools for students who are in search of knowledge in the arts, sciences, and theater in addition to the regular formal curriculum. These new schools are apt to face strong opposition from the teachers unions since they constitute a threat to the integrated high schools which were established as a result of the reforms in the 1970s.

11. Major Problems for the Year 2000

The main problem the educational system is facing in the mid 1990s and will still be facing in the year 2000 is the absorption of the expected new waves of immigrant students mainly from Russia and Ethiopia. The growing need for buildings, laboratories, equipment, teachers, and psychological and guidance personnel calls for additional funding, reconsideration of old teaching methods, and adaptation to the cultural and personal needs of the new immigrant students. The education system will have to confront the problems of "re-educating" teachers, and acquainting both parents and students from totally different climates of schooling with the existing democratic, liberal system.

The majority of the Russian immigrants are well-read and most of them have university diplomas. The main objectives of the educational system in absorbing these newcomers are: cultural and social integration, providing the skills needed to function and live in a democratic, pluralistic society (as opposed to their former regime and environment); acquainting them with their Jewish heritage, through their learning Hebrew; and helping them to become an integral part of their new nation and country.

The educational demands for such rapid social changes and concepts require new skills and efforts from the educational system. Special courses for immigrant teachers to help them master their "new" profession and Israeli teaching methods, special coaching of administrative and supervisory personnel, special programs for Hebrew-language teaching, and special aids such as video cassettes were all introduced into the educational system to facilitate this absorption.

Israeli teachers attend special courses to enable them to achieve these goals quickly, successfully, and efficiently. More than 140 schools use modern computer programs for teaching Arabic. In Grades 6 to 9, computer-programmed texts provide immediate feedback, pinpointing weaknesses to enforce corrective measures to improve students' mastering of Arabic. In 1991, more than 1,900 Grade 12 students will take their matriculation examinations in Arabic. This constitutes an increase of 30 percent over the number of students who studied Arabic in 1990.

Bibliography

Bentwich J 1965 *Education in Israel.* Routledge & Kegan Paul, London
Eisenstadt S N 1967 *Israel Society.* Basic Books, New York
Israel Government 1990 *Year Book.* Israeli Government, Jerusalem
Ministry of Education and Culture 1990 *Facts and Figures on Education and Culture Systems in Israel.* Ministry of Education and Culture, Jerusalem
Ormian C (ed.) 1973 *Education In Israel.* Ministry of Education and Culture, Jerusalem
Wallach J, Lissak M (eds.) 1980 *Carta's Atlas Of Israel.* Israeli Ministry of Defense Publishing House, Jerusalem
Yifhar Y (ed.) 1984 *Laws of Education and Culture.* Ministry of Education and Culture, Jerusalem

Italy

A. Visalberghi

1. General Background

Italy was the first ancient European country to reach a fair level of political, cultural, and linguistic unity. This was achieved through expansion of the Roman Republic (third to first centuries BC, whose Latin language became the universal *lingua franca* of the peninsula even if there were slight local differentiations based on previous ethnolinguistic variations. After some centuries, both political and linguistic unity disintegrated. Neo-Latin dialects (considered, in some cases, as genuinely different languages) developed, and only after several centuries, culminating in the Renaissance period, was a new standard Italian established. A new political unity and independence was gained only in the middle of the nineteenth century and completed after the First World War. The most crucial problems of the state were, therefore: (a) consolidating the new, precarious unity (and to achieve this, the choice has been a highly centralized administration, including that of education); (b) reducing underdevelopment, compared with most other European countries, in the economic and educational fields; and (c) reducing the large economic and educational gaps between the northern and southern regions of Italy itself.

In the middle of the nineteenth century, Italy was among the few largely illiterate nations of Europe. Figure 1 shows the relationship between the increase of elementary school enrollments, progressively achieved, and the decrease of the illiteracy rate from the beginning of Italian unity and independence. The dramatic reduction of enrollments after 1971 is a mere consequence of the fall in the birthrate, a phenomenon typical of almost all industrialized countries since the 1960s.

Figure 2 shows the radical transformation of the Italian economy from 1871 to 1991. During this period Italy changed from an agricultural to an industrial country, with even some postindustrial features (services plus public administration largely exceed industry). The Gross National Product (GNP) multiplied by a factor of about 12 and per capita GNP income by a factor of about 5.

Italy became one of the most industrialized countries of the world as a result of the high rate of economic growth in the 1950s and 1960s when considerable migration from agriculture to industry and from southern to northern regions took place, alongside both permanent and temporary emigration to other European countries. Thus, the birthrate (relatively high at that time, chiefly in the south) was partly compensated. The birthrate later declined steadily and by the early 1990s, the country, which had doubled its resident population since 1871 (from 28 to 57 million), had almost reached a zero population growth rate.

The educational system in Italy also changed greatly after 1860, both in quantitative and in structural terms, although it retained some of the characteristic features

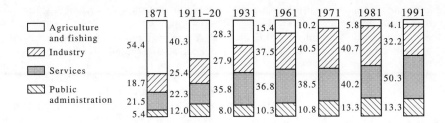

Figure 2
GNP by occupational sector (%), selected years

existing from its foundation. Many of its problems in the late twentieth century spring chiefly from the contrast between already implemented changes and old structures and habits of mind which resist further, greatly needed reforms to make the system capable of coping with the tremendous growth in enrollment rates (see Fig. 3).

The Italian school system was nationally established in 1859–61. However, schools—both popular schools and institutions for the ruling class—were already operating in the various states. Generally, schools were religious, but sometimes they were run by the municipalities. In a short period of time, Piedmont extended the educational legislation it had developed to other regions, in the form in which it had been restated and improved by the *Legge Casati* (1859), issued when Lombardy was annexed. This law emphasized centralization. Even though some educational tasks were assigned to the municipalities, all basic powers, including the formulation of syllabuses for all types of school, were concentrated in the hands of either parliament or the minister of education and exercised through central inspectors and provincial *provveditori*

(superintendents). Most open-minded scholars voiced bitter criticism of such a "Napoleonic" system. This system, strengthened during the Fascist era (1922–43), lasted without any major change until the 1980s.

Gentile, who became the Minister of Education in 1922, introduced the single most important educational reform (*Riforma Gentile*, 1923) since the *Legge Casati*. It halted or eliminated several trends toward more flexibility which had taken place (e.g., the possibility of being admitted to scientific studies at university without having studied Latin). Latin became again the decisive entrance ticket not only for academic studies and university, but even for the technical sector of upper-secondary schools. The educational system was centralized further and even the rectors of the universities had to be appointed by the minister of education. The *Riforma Gentile*, however, also had some positive aspects: elementary schools were given a richer and more creative curriculum and extended in duration from four to five years. New syllabuses also stressed a historical–critical approach, chiefly in

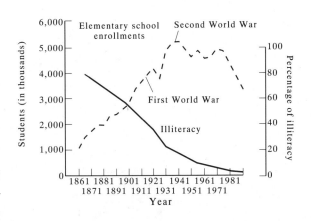

Figure 1
Elementary school enrollment and illiteracy rates 1861–1991

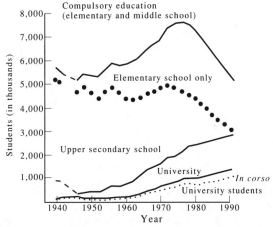

Figure 3
Enrollment in compulsory, upper-secondary, and higher education 1940–80

467

the classical *lyceum* and the new scientific *lyceum*. The fascist ministers of education who followed stressed centralism and rigidity, introduced political propaganda into schools on a massive scale, and emphasized the increased religious instruction that had been reintroduced by Gentile.

2. Politics and the Goals of the Education System

After the Second World War, there was no substantial change for a while. The centrist political tradition was taken over and emphasized by the Christian Democrat Party which acquired a relative and sometimes absolute majority in parliament and government. It administered public schools through the *provveditori* appointed in the 100 provinces by the minister of education, but attempts to support private (mostly Catholic) schools officially from public funds failed because of strong opposition by most of the other parties. In spite of the fairly democratic educational principles contained in the 1947 Constitution, the first important structural change was discussed and approved by parliament only in 1962—a single middle school lasting three years to be provided after primary education as a final cycle of the eight years of compulsory education prescribed as a minimum.

The Italian Constitution allows for more power to be given to local communities (cities, provinces) and chiefly to the 20 regions, some of which enjoy greater autonomy than others even in the educational field because of their ethnic, linguistic, or historical peculiarities. "The Republic dictates general norms about education and establishes state schools for all orders and grades," whereas the regions have both legislative and administrative power in matters of "artisan and vocational instruction and scholastic assistance." It was only in 1977 that a "law of principles" was approved about the practical procedures for implementing such a division of responsibility. It established that the state was responsible for preprimary schools, compulsory education, and upper-secondary and higher education for the provision of general culture, including science and technology. Vocational education, operated or supervised by the regions, was limited to short cycles (not more than two years) aimed at providing highly specific knowledge and training and acting as an interface between state education and the labor market. Regional instructional systems have developed at different speed (faster in the northern regions).

The prevailing centralized tradition for state schools was partially broken by a law in 1973 and by the ensuing "delegated decrees" issued by the government in 1974. New elective bodies involving the participation of parents, pupils, and citizens, and partial self-government were created at different levels: school level (and even class level), district level (a new dimension with total populations ranging from 50,000 to 200,000 and with councils endowed with formal

rather than effective powers), provincial level, and national level.

At the regional level, special regional institutes for educational research, experimentation, and inservice training of teachers (IRRSAE) were created, together with a national Library of Pedagogic Documentation in Florence and a European Center for Education in Frascati (Rome). The same decrees also allowed educational experimentation, even in new curricula and structures, to be initiated by single schools and approved by the ministry or planned by the ministry itself. Thus the rigidity of the system was somewhat reduced.

A centralized management of education, although criticized, was generally accepted as the least evil system considering the cultural heterogeneity, chiefly between the north and south of the country. This disparity was repeatedly shown in research studies. International comparisons also showed that elementary school average achievement was good, middle school a little worse, and in the final grade of the upper-secondary school achievement was unsatisfactory and geographically more heterogeneous. The "maturity examinations" did not prove to be a good instrument for ensuring more homogeneity of achievement.

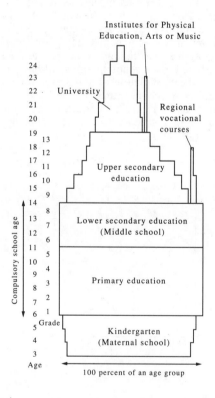

Figure 4
Italy: Structure of the formal education system 1990

3. The Formal System of Education

The most striking feature of the Italian educational system is the contrast between the completely unitary structure of its compulsory level (five years of elementary and three years of lower-secondary or middle school for all pupils) and the intricate jungle of upper-secondary schools. Figure 4 presents the approximate distribution of the various age groups at the different levels of schooling, but it cannot show the different types of upper-secondary schools because of the great number of school types in the technical and vocational sectors. The industrial technical institutes have 31 different tracks, and the vocational institutes (*instituti professionali*) of various lengths have 18 different prescribed curricula for different qualifications. Not even the private schools are separately represented: they are mostly Catholic and enroll about 8 percent of elementary pupils, 4.5 percent of lower-secondary pupils, and 9 percent of upper-secondary students.

The transition rate from middle schools to upper-secondary schools is high (more than 86% in 1990). The percentage of graduates going from high school to university is also relatively high (in 1990, about 76%). But a general feature both of postcompulsory secondary education and of higher education in Italy is the dropout rate. In 1990, less than 45 percent of the age-group completed secondary education and only about 10 percent obtained a university degree.

3.1 Primary, Secondary, and Tertiary Education

Both elementary and middle schools are uniformly organized, and a national curriculum is studied. A law of 1990 prescribes a normal weekly school length of 27 hours plus 3 hours if a foreign language is also taught. A few primary schools are recognized as institutionally "experimental," and a set number of other schools are authorized to experiment with new curriculum content and methods. Indeed, they are encouraged to do this mostly in connection with the teaching of a foreign language and the organization of the so-called " *moduli*" (modules), that is, the progressive and eventually universal introduction of a ratio of three teachers for two classes, or in some cases four for three classes. The result is that a certain number of elementary schools have a weekly number of lessons and activities up to 40 hours ("prolonged" and "full-time").

Elementary education has a fairly good tradition of intelligent search for innovation, founded on advanced psychological studies and carried on in the past by forerunners like Maria Montessori, Giuseppe Lombardo Radice, and Ernesto Codignola, to quote the most prominent. The French educator Céléstin Freinet has also exerted a wide influence through the Italian "Movement of Educational Cooperation" fostered by excellent teachers like Giuseppe Tamagnini, Bruno Ciari, and Aldo Pettini. In general, the main objective is to give the child an active role in his or her learning processes, often through the promotion of free and playful activities, group work, and communicative and artistic expression. Such features are actually more or less present in the common schools. Stimulating relations with the environment are also encouraged. Such a learning atmosphere may account for the good cognitive achievement of Italian primary children as seen in international comparative research.

Classes and schools are small (on the average having about 16 and 126 pupils respectively) and the pupil–teacher ratio is very low, about 10.5:1. This situation results from the fact that, in the period 1980–90, the fall in the birthrate reduced elementary school enrollment by 31.3 percent, but the number of teachers increased by 2.5 percent. Such a policy, favored by the teacher unions, was justified because of the demand for specialized teachers (for the care of handicapped children, experimentation of new modules, foreign language teaching, etc.).

Secondary education presents very different features at its two stages: the lower (middle school) and the upper (*lycea*, and a great variety of other institutes). The middle school is part of compulsory education and is practically nationwide. Such schools usually have a modest average size of slightly less than 230 pupils. Although there is a national curriculum for middle schools, there is room for some flexibility of implementation by teachers. Each class has several subject matter teachers: one for the "literary subjects" (Italian, history, geography, civics), one for the scientific subjects (mathematics, physics, biology, and earth sciences), one for foreign languages, one for music, one for graphic expression, one for technical education, one for physical education, and one for Catholic religion (for those pupils choosing it, and they are the overwhelming majority).

The situation of upper-secondary education is very different. Attempts at structural reform of the extremely sectorial framework has failed since the creation of the middle school. The main tracks of upper-secondary schools remain into the 1990s: classical *lyceum* (with Latin and Greek, and no foreign language in the last three years except on experimental grounds), scientific *lyceum* (without Greek, with one foreign language, and more mathematics and sciences), and technical institutes (integrating general culture with technologies of various kinds, up to 31 in the industrial sector). They all last five years. The artistic *lyceum* and the *instituto magistrale* (for elementary teachers) lasts four years. The *scuola magistrale* (for kindergarten teachers) lasts three years. There are also the *instituti professionali* (vocational institutes), created by successive ministerial decrees after the Second World War, lasting three years. They have expanded to include a variety of more than 160 qualifications for middle-low level jobs. A law of 1969 started additional postqualification courses so that, in general, a "professional maturity" can be achieved after a cycle of five years. However, in both the technical and the vocational sectors, national

Table 1
Enrollment in types of upper-secondary schools as percentages 1990

Type of schools	Total enrollments	Those entering university
Vocational institutes	18.9	7.8
All technical institutes	45.5	37.0
Industrial institutes	(11.5)	—
Commercial institutes	(23.3)	—
Surveyors institutes	(5.9)	—
Schools and institutes for teachers	6.5	7.6
Scientific lycea	17.7	26.0
Classical lycea	8.0	15.2
Art institutes and lycea	3.4	6.4
Total	100.0	100.0

experimental plans have progressively transformed this situation (see Sect. 10 below).

Table 1 shows the percentages enrolled in the main types of secondary schools and the percentages entering university.

Some of the upper-secondary schools maintain their traditional academic and preuniversity character, but the technical and even the vocational sector also have many more students entering higher education than in the past.

Higher education is attended by a growing proportion of the eligible age group: from less than one-fifth in 1980 to one-fourth (23.8%) of the 19–24 age group in 1990. There are 45 universities, two polytechnics, and a few "higher institutes" chiefly for foreign languages and education. Some of the universities are among the oldest in the world, with Bologna (founded around 1170) being regarded as the eldest. Some are among the youngest like the III University of Rome and the II of Naples. A detailed description of higher education in Italy was provided in English by Martinelli (1992) and readers are referred to that publication.

3.2 Preschool Education

From 0 to 3 years of age, Italian children can attend both private and public nursery schools (the latter are operated by local authorities). From 3 to 6 years of age, 9 out of 10 children attend kindergartens called *scuole materne* (maternal schools), one-half of which are directly managed by the state and the other half by municipalities or private associations, most of which are religious. Italian kindergartens have a long pedagogical tradition stretching back to the nineteenth century, but the huge expansion started in the 1970s. It was in 1968 that a law finally gave the kindergartens the full status of an "educational stage," so that, according to the Constitution, the state ought to create its own schools at this level. Since 1968, their number has risen rapidly, new syllabuses have been

created and updated, and special inspectors have been appointed.

3.3 Special Education

Since the late 1960s, Italy has developed a policy of the integration of retarded and handicapped children into the normal mainstream classes. The separate special schools have been reduced in number and size, limiting them to the particularly serious cases. Special classes have been abolished. Specialized teachers and assistants for the individual care of problem pupils are trained in two-year university courses. Classes hosting up to three special needs children have been reduced in size to not more than 20 students. The general principle is to emphasize social adjustment and to retain the problem pupils year after year with the same classmates, even if their achievement is below minimum standards. If necessary, however, they can repeat a class if this appears to be useful for better cognitive growth. Such decisions are taken by a team of teachers and hot discussions may follow among parents and the public. In general, this flexible solution seems to work satisfactorily in the compulsory education grades. However, at the upper-secondary level a lot of problems have arisen, mainly in connection with the transition of the handicapped and/or retarded young people to the workforce. "Protected laboratories" have been created in some places for them. Sometimes they are employed for assistance to younger pupils with similar problems. This is particularly true for those with Down's syndrome.

There are special institutions for minors lacking family care, or those coming from morally unreliable families. Most of these institutions are private, very often managed by religious organizations, and can be roughly divided into residences hosting some 40–200 young people and houses or communities having not more than 12 guests on the recommendation of a judge or the social services. Minors from 14 to 18 years of age, if found guilty of crimes by special courts, are sent to particular detention houses, where, according to the law, an "educational project" shall be worked out for each of them. In all cases, minors receive the forms of education appropriate to their age and attend boarding schools or more often ordinary schools outside the institutions hosting them.

3.4 Vocational, Technical, and Business Education

There are state-managed schools for technical education and also for vocational education, in spite of the fact that the latter, according to the Constitution, is the responsibility of the regions. Technical education enrolls about 42 percent of upper-secondary school students. There are five-year courses in institutes for industry, agriculture, sea and air transportation, and business and accounting (the latter two having the major enrollments). There are 31 different types of industrial institutes. They prepare *periti* (experts) for middle-high specialized jobs. State vocational education (*instituti professionali*) enroll more than 22 percent of upper-secondary school students and offer a very large range of courses leading to different qualifications in almost all fields of middle-low jobs. But students may also study further in the same institutes and obtain a "professional maturity" giving access to university. In 1992, a ministerial decree reduced the tracks in vocational institutes to 18. After a three-year qualification course, further specialization can be obtained in collaboration with the regions.

Regions operate short cycles of vocational instruction and training of two year's duration at three different levels: for students with only the middle school licence, for students having attended two or more grades of upper-secondary school, and for students having completed upper-secondary education. The students of the regional courses number about 270,000—only half of the total number of students in state vocational institutes in 1991. Regional vocational courses may be organized directly by the regions or delegated to recognized associations. Their number, as well as the number of students enrolled, is much higher in the north than in the south of the country.

In most sectors of low- or middle-level professions, the general tendency is to increase the requirements for certification: for instance, nurses have traditionally qualified through three years of study and training in hospitals after having attended at least the first two years of some upper-secondary school, but, since the early 1990s, new rules and practices are being progressively put into action requiring the "professional" nurses to have completed a postsecondary three-year course, managed or controlled by a university.

Regions must also organize "apprenticeship" courses that are compulsory for young artisans under 18 years of age. This is also the case for the new type of apprenticeship for industry and service enterprises called "formation-labor."

Private agencies play a large role in vocational education, mostly in business education, either by authorization given to them by the regions or autonomously, especially in informatics, design, and fashion. Such agencies are often organized by labor unions, professional associations, or groups of enterprises. The large enterprises usually have internal training activities for inservice training.

3.5 Adult and Nonformal Education

There are many initiatives in the field of adult education including those of the "university of the third age." Most of them are managed or financed by local authorities. Several technical and vocational state institutes offer evening courses. In the 1970s, the labor unions obtained special forms of paid leave of absence for workers during which they are able to avail themselves of special educational opportunities. In some cases, these are offered free by the state and are mostly at the lower-secondary level, including about 2,500 experimental courses attended by some 70,000 students with a majority of them male and one-third of them below the age of 18. There are more than 4,000 teachers engaged in such activities; the majority of them being female. There are also experimental courses for about the same number of illiterate people. This number is slowly declining because of decreased demand. The total costs of these state initiatives is about 2 percent of the cost of compulsory education. Adult education has no formal institutional status: proposed legislation to be implemented by the regions have never reached parliamentary discussion. It should be noted that state-managed radio and television stations (and to a lesser extent, private ones) broadcast various educational programs. These range from courses for illiterate people to refresher courses for medical doctors and teachers.

4. Administrative and Supervisory Structure and Operation

For preprimary, primary, and secondary education, the core administrative structure is represented by the different branches of the Ministry of Public Instruction responsible for these stages or even for different sectors of the upper-secondary level, such as the classical and scientific *lycea*, the technical institutes, and the vocational institutes. There are 100 provincial superintendents (*provveditori*) who are charged with enacting local laws and regulations. Several hundred administrative and "technical" inspectors work either centrally or at regional or provincial level. The technical inspectors, through class visits, control the teaching–learning activities in their fields of competence, however such activities are monitored more closely and continuously by the principals of the individual schools. They enjoy a limited degree of initiative, but are often overburdened by administrative duties. Teachers, parents, and students at the upper-secondary level participate in the organization of extracurricular school activities. The rigidity of this highly centralized system is partially offset by the traditional degree of freedom the individual teacher has over content and teaching methodology. The schools authorized by the ministry to implement experimentation have much more freedom. Many schools are engaged in national experimental plans, programs of health education, and the "study and work alternation" programs prompted and partially financed by the European Community.

Higher education is centrally coordinated by a Ministry of Universities and Scientific and Technological Research, but the main responsibilities are in the hands of the individual institutions, their elected bodies, and, chiefly, the deans for the faculties and the rector for the university as a whole. However, the secretary general of each university is a public officer appointed by the minister.

5. *Educational Finance*

Public education is financed either directly by the state (about 74%), or by the municipalities (about 18%), the provinces (about 4.5%), and the regions (about 3.5%). Some 98 percent of the state's expenses are for salaries. Technical and vocational schools enjoy administrative autonomy and can sometimes obtain additional money through contracts with private and public agencies. Compulsory education is free of charge and textbooks are completely or partially paid for by the municipalities of the state. For upper-secondary schooling, families pay modest fees. University fees are higher, but cover only a small fraction of the costs. In both cases, students with low family income can be exempted. Most university funding is provided by the relevant ministry. Several other ministries contribute very small fractions of their budget to the expenses for culture and education. Such allocations do not represent more than 0.5 percent of the expenses of the ministries of public education and universities.

Public expenses for education and culture rose a lot during the 1960s and 1970s, but later plateaued or even declined as percentages of both the GNP and the state budget: in 1990, these percentages were 5.9 and 8.3 respectively—slightly below the average for OECD countries. At the tertiary level, the negative difference was 23 percent.

6. *Supplying Personnel for the Education System*

The teaching staff for preprimary and primary schools was traditionally prepared by upper-secondary schools (*scuole magistrali* lasting 3 years, and *instituti magistrali* lasting 4 years) and by universities for all grades of secondary education. Almost all secondary teachers should possess a *laurea* requiring 4 or 5 years of university study in order to obtain full tenure (through nationwide or regional public selections) or even for temporary employment, in both public and

"legally recognized" private schools. But a recurrent shortage of graduates in the scientific and technological field results in university students being used. School principals and inspectors are usually recruited from among existing teachers. At the end of the 1980s, librarians, guidance counselors, educational technology specialists, and teachers responsible for retarded or handicapped pupils were also employed. Female teachers monopolize the preprimary level and are a great majority at the elementary and lower-secondary levels, but male teachers prevail in technical and vocational courses at the upper-secondary level.

Nonteaching staff (secretaries, janitors, porters) have no particular training to operate within schools. The central and the provincial administrative staff is composed of state employees who have graduated in law or economics. This can cause some problems when they interact with the teaching staff about educational issues.

7. *Curriculum Development and Teaching Methodology*

The curricula are primarily determined by the syllabuses that are issued by ministerial decree. However, they are adapted by the teachers to some extent to suit local needs. Experimental schools can be authorized to develop new curricula. Methods of teaching are developed by schools, teams of teachers, and individual teachers. The general tendency as implemented both by circular letters of the ministry and by local decisions is to develop cooperation and planning within the schools and the classes, stressing interdisciplinary and multidisciplinary approaches.

8. *The System of Examinations, Promotions, and Certifications*

There are examinations at the end of each main educational cycle (primary, lower-secondary, and upper-secondary). There are no entrance examinations for particular types of schools. Promotion from one grade to the next in the same cycle of education is decided by the teacher team for each class. In compulsory schools the "repeat" examinations during the September session were abolished in the 1960s and grade repetition is rare and only allowed in well-documented circumstances. The situation is very different at the upper-secondary level where negative "selection" occurs either at the end of the school year or by failure in the September examinations that can still be required for specific subject areas. Evaluation in both primary and lower-secondary schools is on the basis of cooperative compilation of special forms made by the teachers and regularly sent to the parents. After each cycle of education, certification documents are awarded to pupils. This allows them to enroll in any type of further study, but in several cases single schools can limit enrollment using the criteria of merit and territorial distribution of family homes. Primary and middle schools use a 5-point scale of proficiency in the different subjects. Upper-secondary schools employ a 10-point scale, where 6 is the minimum for promotion. The most important certificate is obtained at the end of secondary school. This is based on the results of the "maturity examination," which is organized by commissions appointed by the ministry and external to the schools. However, there is one school member involved. The examination includes two written essays on themes that students choose from among those sent by the ministry, and an oral examination in two out of four possible subject areas. The subject areas change each year and are set by the ministry.

9. *Educational Assessment, Evaluation, and Research*

Pupil assessment during the compulsory education years has become "positively" oriented, linked with counseling and individualization of teaching, and is decreasingly oriented toward negative selection. There are laws and regulations on how judgments should be made for cognitive, social, and emotional development. These are also oriented toward giving suggestions for further educational treatment. Grade repeating has been progressively reduced because of this approach and is now very rare at the primary level. At the upper-secondary level, the most common assessment procedures are radically different: the individual teacher gives marks based on the achievement in his or her own subject matter as assessed by written and oral examinations. The assessment for each student tends to be a mechanical aggregate of scattered and independent elements. Written essays are used (at least in the subjects where a mark in written proficiency is prescribed) but objective testing is rarely employed. Practical abilities are important in technical and vocational education. Social and emotional maturation is not assessed. Evaluation of programs and innovations is not common. In general, Italy has a good tradition of theoretical and historical educational studies, but empirical educational research has only developed modestly. A 1992 report of an ad hoc committee appointed by the Minister of Universities and Scientific and Technological Research points out that the volume, if not the quality, of empirical research places Italy in the last third of European countries.

10. *Major Reforms in the 1980s and 1990s*

Most innovations in Italian schools implemented or initiated in the period 1980–92 took the form of experimentation with new ministerial syllabuses and also of new structures autonomously proposed by individual schools or outlined by the ministry. For instance, linguistic *lycea*, for which a special maturity examination had been foreseen in the early 1970s, were only in private institutions or in experimental state schools. By

1992, they were more widely diffused in state schools as experimentation of new syllabuses that had been prepared by experts and proposed by the ministry. The most important innovations, apart from those already mentioned in compulsory education, were based on national plans for "assisted experimentation" in the technical and then in the vocational sector. Both plans were intended to rearrange and simplify structures and update curricula. In the vocational sector, the experimentation concluded in 1992 with generalized structural changes: not only were the huge number of different qualifications reduced to about 20, but the first two years were culturally enriched and made more homogeneous; the third year concentrates on a not-too-narrow type of qualification that leads either directly to the world of work, or to further specialization through regional courses assisted by the same state institutes, or to transfer to a technical institute, or to study for the professional maturity examination.

Minor experimental plans for secondary schools were developed either for integrating curricula (computer science, foreign languages) into the overall curriculum or as a first trial of restructure and/or enrichment programs (elementary schools, first "unitary" biennium of upper-secondary education).

On the whole, about 50 percent of Italian schools are engaged in some type of experimentation which will hopefully be followed by refinement and generalization to the system. However, for upper-secondary education the problem has been much more difficult because of contention in parliament about the ways of increasing the age of finishing compulsory education to 16.

11. *Major Problems for the Year 2000*

The most likely major problem to be solved by the end of the century is that of high dropout rates at both the upper-secondary and university levels. This issue will become increasingly important because of the already insufficient output of middle- and high-level qualified people as shown by OECD international comparisons. There is a risk that this will be aggravated by the forecasted decrease in enrollment at both secondary and higher education levels which has been calculated at about 28 percent for the year 2003 compared with the situation in 1990. Such absolute figures take into account both the decreasing birthrate and the natural increase of transition and retention rates. To increase the retention rate without lowering standards is a rather difficult task. The need for a better continuity between school levels is generally felt to be very important. However, the main efforts should be concentrated on the first years of upper-secondary and of postsecondary education. A few research and development programs on "dispersion" in the high schools are underway, but they should be replicated in the different geographic, cultural, and social settings.

At the postsecondary level, it will be necessary to develop "short cycle" courses not only within universities as planned and encouraged by the university ministry, but also in the regional system in cooperation with both upper-secondary schools higher education. Structural reform of upper-secondary education and of the final certificate (maturity examination) is urgently needed.

Other important issues concern didactic and administrative autonomy being increased for the universities and largely granted to schools at all other levels. Connected with school autonomy is the need, now largely stressed by both experts and teachers, to create a national educational evaluation service. However, in order to move seriously toward such targets, empirical and experimental educational research should be systematically developed to reach levels attained in several other countries.

Reference

Martinell A 1992 Italy. In: Clark B R, Neave G R (eds.) 1992 *The Encyclopedia of Higher Education*, Vol. 1. Pergamon Press, Oxford

Further Reading

Ambrosoli L 1988 *La scuola alla Costituente*. Paideia Editrice, Brescia

Battistoni L, Ruberto A 1989 *Percorsi giovanili di studio e di lavoro*. Franco Angeli, Milan

Borna E, Genovesi G (eds.) 1988 *L'istruzione secondaria in Italia da Casati ai giorni nostri*. Cacucci, Bari

CENSIS (Centro studi investimenti sociali) 1991 *Sulla situazione sociale del paese (25th report)*. Franco Angeli, Milan

CERI (Center for Educational Research and Innovation) 1992 *Education at a Glance*. OECD, Paris

Gattullo M, Visalberghi A (eds.) 1986 *La scuola italiana dal 1945 al 1983*. La Nuova Italia Editrice, Florence

ISFOL (Instituto per lo sviluppo della formazione professionale dei lavoratori) 1991 *Rapporto 1991*. ISFOL, Rome

ISTAT (Instituto italiano di statistica) 1991 *Le regioni in cifre*. ISTAT, Rome

ISTAT 1992 *Bollettino Istruzione 4*. ISTAT, Rome

Malizia G 1992 *La prolongación de la enseñanza obligatoria en Italia*: CESE (Comparative Education Society in Europe) *Reformas e innovaciones educativas en el umbral del siglo XXI: una perspectiva comparada*. UNED, Madrid

Ministero della pubblica istruzione 1990 *Nuovi modelli nella formazione post-secondaria*. Le Monnier, Florence

Ministero dell'università e della ricerca scientifica e tecnologica 1992 *Formazione e ricerca nell'area della pedagogia e delle scienze dell'educazione*. Istituto Poligrafico dello stato, Rome

Moscati R (ed.) 1989 *La sociologia dell'educazione in Italia*. Zanichelli, Bologna

Trivellato U, Zuliani A 1979 *The Determinants of Student Achievement in Italy*. Almqvist and Wiksell, Stockholm

Vertecchi B (ed.) 1991 *Una scuola per tutta la vita*. La Nuova Italia, Florence

Visalberghi A 1981 Aspetti generali del sistema scolastico italiano: sua storia e sua organizzazione. *Scuola e città* 10: 417–29

Jamaica

V. R. Been and R. R. Morris

1. General Background

Jamaica is the third largest of the Caribbean Islands. It is situated 144 kilometers south of Cuba and 600 kilometers south of Florida. The island is 235 kilometers in length and varies between 35 and 82 kilometers in width, producing a total area of 11,292 square kilometers. A sinuous central mountain ridge runs northwest to southeast separating the island into northern and southern coastal areas. The crest of this ridge attains its highest elevation at the Blue Mountain Peak, 2,256 meters above sea level. The mountainous terrain of the country renders some areas inaccessible, which in turn seriously impacts upon teacher quality, supervision, and access to secondary education.

Jamaica became a British colony in 1655 and flourished as a sugar plantation society employing a large labor force of African slaves and, to a lesser degree, East Indian and Chinese indentured labor. The advent of the plantation system has been the single most significant element in the evolution of the racial mix, social structure, and educational development of modern Jamaica. Jamaica, described as a melting pot of people, has a population in which the majority (95%) is of African origin, and the rest is comprised of East Indians, Chinese, Syrians, Lebanese, and Whites. Jamaica has a stratified social structure in which color and class bear a strong correlation. The White and fairer skinned people—a small, powerful elite group—occupy the apex of the social ladder and are often the descendants of the wealthy plantocracy. The majority, who are primarily descendants of African slaves, occupy the base of the social ladder and account for the semiskilled, the unskilled, and the unemployed. The middle of the social hierarchy has evolved out of the intermixture of the top and bottom strata producing an influential group of professionals, technicians, and bureaucrats.

The 1982 census recorded Jamaica's population as 2,190,357. The preliminary results of the 1991 census estimated the population to be 2,366,067—an increase of 7.4 percent over the 1982 figure and an average annual growth rate of 0.86 percent.

English is the official language, however the ethnic presence of a strong African heritage is reflected in a Jamaican creole which is spoken and understood by the majority of Jamaicans. This duality between the spoken and the official language has created a barrier in the delivery of the curriculum at all levels. In an attempt to reduce this disparity, reading materials are developed locally and place strong emphasis on the use of local settings and materials. In addition, the teaching of English as a second language is to be introduced at the primary level.

Some 38 percent of the employed labor force is in self-employed occupations, followed by 17.1 percent in the skilled trades, 15.3 percent in service occupations, 12 percent in clerical occupations, and 9.4 percent in the unskilled category. Professional and managerial occupations comprise another 8 percent of which 60 percent is female. In 1990, 15 percent of the labor force was unemployed and mainly comprised persons under 25 years, women, and the unskilled.

Jamaica gained full independence in 1962 and the Jamaican constitution, based on the Westminster model, was adopted. Jamaica enjoys a parliamentary democracy with a House of Representatives of 60 members chosen every 5 years.

The structure of the education system of post-independence Jamaica continues to resemble the traditional British system. In an attempt to provide an education which was relevant to local needs, the government adopted strategies to localize the curriculum and reading materials at the primary level. British external examinations were replaced by regional external examinations. Despite these developments, the secondary system of education is still elitist and needs major reform in order for equal educational opportunities to be provided for all. The unfavorable economic conditions since the 1970s have thwarted the political goal of both governments to reform secondary education system.

Historically, the Jamaican economy was largely dependent on agriculture. Since 1970 there has been a shift of economic activity from agriculture to services. In 1990, 27 percent of the labor force was employed in primary industries compared to 42 percent in 1960. In 1990, 15 percent worked in the manufacturing sector and 57 percent was employed in the service sector, compared with 15 percent and 43 percent respectively in 1960. The export–import ratio between 1985 and 1989 decreased from 1:96 to 1:78. This marginal decrease may be attributed to one of the government's objectives to improve the balance of payments.

In 1978, 77 percent of the labor force completed primary education, 21 percent completed secondary education, 26 percent had no formal education, and less than 1 percent had acquired tertiary education. The mean years of schooling of the labor force was 6.9 years. In 1982, approximately 65 percent of the population had completed 6 years of schooling, 17.5 percent secondary education, and 1.3 percent had acquired tertiary-level education.

In the 1989–90 financial year the per capita Gross Domestic Product (GDP) was approximately J$9,000 (US$400). Even though there was economic growth in the 1980s, there is still the problem of inflation and debt burden crisis. Debt servicing utilizes 40 percent of export earnings, thus reducing the resources available for the social services.

Despite these limitations, however, there was an expansion of educational expenditure in the 1980s and 1990s, especially at the tertiary level. In the information age both government and the private sector have found that it is in their best interest to invest in education and training in order to keep abreast of technological developments.

2. *Politics and the Goals of the Education System*

The two political parties—the Jamaica Labour Party (JLP) and the Peoples National Party (PNP)—have implemented similar educational policies over the last four decades which have resulted in the achievement of universal primary education and expanded access to secondary and tertiary education.

During the 1960s, the JLP expanded access to secondary education with the provision of 50 junior secondary schools with accommodation for 37,530 students. In the 1970s the PNP added grades 10 and 11 to these schools and announced a policy of "Free Education." This was made possible by resources obtained from a levy on bauxite exports.

In the 1980s, the debt crisis forced the JLP government to impose a so-called "cess" (tuition fee) on university students as a contribution to their education. Boarding grants were abolished, except for students attending the overseas campuses of the University of the West Indies (UWI) and teachers' colleges. Secondary schools, especially high schools (on their own initiative), introduced a variety of fees (except tuition). Emphasis was placed on the improvement of the quality of primary education with very little expansion of access to secondary education. Both governments, have pursued policies which resulted in a highly differentiated, stratified secondary education system. The JLP government introduced a reform at the secondary level to reduce the variety of institutional types. With the change of government in 1989, there

Jamaica

has been continuity in the implementation of these policies. Major emphasis continues to be placed on improving the quality of primary education. Steps continue to be taken to unify the secondary system. The cess has not been discontinued, despite promises made by the PNP while in opposition in the 1980s. The Five-Year Education and Training Plan (1990–95) stated that cost recovery schemes are to be implemented at the upper-secondary and tertiary levels of the education system.

3. The Formal System of Education

3.1 Primary, Secondary, and Tertiary Education

Formal education (comprised of early childhood, primary, secondary, and tertiary levels) is offered primarily by the public sector with a low level of private sector participation. Figure 1 is a diagrammatic representation of the age cohort structure of the formal education system. The distribution of enrollment, pupil–teacher ratio, and the unit cost per student by level is presented in Table 1.

Children in the age cohort 6–11 years receive 6 years of primary education in Grades 1–6 of public primary and all-age schools and privately owned preparatory schools. Universal primary education has been attained but irregular attendance is a major problem. The public sector accounts for 95 percent of total enrollment—an increase of 6 percent since 1970. All public primary schools operate within the legislated daily minimum of 5 hours of contact teaching time for whole-day schools and 4.5 hours in shift schools. The minimum length of the school year is 190 days. Some

62 percent of primary school enrollment is offered in the primary grades of all-age schools (Grades 1–9), located primarily in rural Jamaica where the population density is low. Secondary education is offered in six different types of publicly administered secondary institutions and a number of privately owned secondary schools, with the public sector accounting for 95 percent of total secondary enrollment.

Secondary education consists of two cycles. The first cycle is of three years' duration, comprised of Grades 7–9 and caters to the 12–14 age group. In 1990, the transition rate from the primary level to Grade 7 was 98 percent. In 1990, 80 percent of the population was enrolled at this cycle, with females accounting for 51 percent of the total enrollment. Second-cycle secondary education is for 2 years (Grades 10 and 11). Some secondary high schools continue to Grade 13 (sixth form). In 1990, the transition rate from Grade 9 of the first cycle to Grade 10 was 71 percent, with females accounting for 52 percent of the total enrollment.

The provision of tertiary education is almost the exclusive domain of the public sector. Institutions at this level offer degrees, diplomas, and professional certificates. The tertiary level of the educational system is expected to provide the professional, executive, and managerial skills needed to satisfy national labor force needs. Between 1970 and 1990 the enrollment at the tertiary level recorded a significant growth of 221 percent moving from approximately 7,800 to 22,500; this was a gross enrollment rate of 8.7 percent. It should be noted that females comprise 60 percent of Jamaican students enrolled at the University of the West Indies (UWI).

3.2 Preschool Education

Early childhood education is provided for children in the 3–5 age group in public, private, and community-operated institutions islandwide. In 1990, 85 percent of the total population of 3–5 year olds was enrolled at this level.

The educational provision at this level is designed to provide compensatory as well as holistic and integrated approaches to readiness for formal learning. Children in the 4–5 age group attend public infant schools, the infant departments of primary and all-age schools islandwide, or private nursery schools, kindergarten departments of preparatory schools, and community-operated basic schools. Basic schools which meet specified minimum requirements set by the Ministry of Education are eligible for operational subsidies. Such recognized basic schools provide the early childhood level for 70 percent of the enrolled 3–5 year olds.

3.3 Special Education

Special education is designed to meet the educational needs of children aged 4–18 years who are identified as

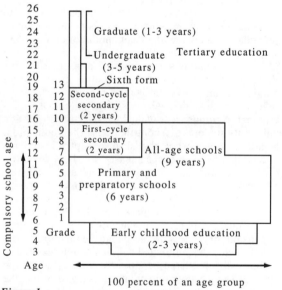

Figure 1
Jamaica: Structure of the formal education system

having mental, physical, and intellectual capabilities which deviate significantly from the norm expected of their age group. Educational provision for children with special needs is undertaken primarily by private voluntary organizations which receive annual budgetary allocations from the Ministry of Education.

Special education provision is offered in the following six specific areas of disabilities: the blind and visually impaired, the deaf and hearing impaired, the mentally retarded, the multiple handicapped, the physically handicapped, and those with learning disabilities. In addition to the school-based provision of special education, voluntary agencies provide limited services for severely disabled children either in their homes or in community centers. In 1990, initiatives were taken to establish an Institute for the Gifted with the objective of developing enrichment programs designed to facilitate advanced placement of intellectually gifted students in schools.

3.4 Vocational, Technical, and Business Education

Public provision of vocational, technical, and business education is designed for phased and smooth integration into general education from as early as the primary level, where art and craft is taught. During the first cycle of secondary education at least three vocational technical subjects are offered. At the second cycle, prevocational training is offered primarily in Grades 10 and 11 where students select a vocational option from five vocational subject areas. The major aim of the vocational and technical program at this level is to provide graduates with skills which can facilitate on-the-job training or which can form the basis for further education. Specialized training for vocational and technical education teachers is offered at various tertiary-level institutions at the diploma and degree level. Certificate courses for vocational instructors are also offered by one nonformal institution.

At the beginning of the 1990s the relationship between vocational, technical, and business education and special education was limited in scope. Skill-training at this level is confined to the hearing impaired and involves collaboration with voluntary organizations.

Under the formal education component of the Basic Skills Training Project (1984–90), several private-sector advisory committees were established under the Ministry of Education. The business sector also participates in the work experience program of new secondary and technical high schools. In addition, the Jamaica Computer Society has been instrumental in designing and developing the computer science syllabus for the regional Caribbean Examinations Council (CXC) at the general and technical proficiency levels.

One of the policy initiatives for the 1990s is the expansion of vocational, technical, and business education to satisfy employment needs at the middle and higher labor force levels. In response to high labor demand for technical personnel in such areas as accounting, computing, and commerce, the scope of the technical, vocational, and business education was broadened. Computer studies were introduced into the curriculum, and a management information system has been introduced in all technical schools. The facilities at the College of Art Science and Technology (CAST) have also been expanded for additional types of courses. The major thrust at the UWI is in the area of business education. The facilities and number of faculty members have increased and a new course has been added.

There is no formally established mechanism for linking job development and vocational, technical, and business education. In 1991, a National Training Agency (NTA) was established to facilitate the coordination and harmonization of vocational and technical training. The NTA will be responsible for policy formulation, research studies, establishment and monitoring of standards, program development, and evaluation. Under NTA, a national council for technical and vocational education and training with linkages to related professional associations will provide systemwide accreditation and promote private sector–public sector partnerships.

3.5 Adult and Nonformal Education

Traditionally, adult education has been provided by nongovernmental agencies attached to churches and

Table 1
Distribution of enrollment, pupil–teacher ratio, and unit costs by level, 1990

Institutions	Number	Enrollment	Pupil-teacher ratio	Unit cost (J$)[c]
Primary and all-age	787	387,023[a]	39:1[b]	951.04
Special	11	2,511	—	5,563.76
Secondary	149	165,947	19:1	2,164.10
Tertiary	16	22,500	—	14,030.27

a Data includes 59,761 Grade 7–9 students   b Computation of the ratio include teachers at Grades 7–9 of all-age schools   c Unit cost data represent public expenditure only

voluntary social groups. Since the 1970s, government involvement in the provision of adult education has increased significantly, with the establishment of the Jamaican Movement for the Advancement of Literacy (JAMAL). Since 1973 JAMAL has made over 248,000 persons functionally literate, thereby reducing the illiteracy rate from 45 percent in 1973 to 18 percent in 1987. In 1988–89, J$4.1 million (US$182,000) was allocated to JAMAL which is 0.5 percent of the recurrent budget, a decline from 1.8 percent in 1983–84.

The Human Employment and Resource Training (HEART) Trust was developed in response to the need for the provision of skilled workers to meet the developmental needs of the country and to equip the unemployed, especially the youth, with skills which are either in demand on the labor market, or necessary for self-employment. Established in 1982 as a statutory body, the HEART Trust was empowered to finance, coordinate, and monitor all nonformal skills training programs. In order to achieve its objectives, HEART coordinates four programs to train approximately 10,500 trainees islandwide. Employers with a wage bill above a prescribed minimum are obligated by law to contribute 3 percent of their wage bill to the Trust fund or provide assistance with on-the-job training of school leavers. In 1991, the HEART Trust levy yielded J$115 million (US$5.1 million) which became their operational budget for the year.

4. Administrative and Supervisory Structure and Operation

The Ministry of Education is responsible for administering the education system. Each educational institution is administered by a board of management appointed by the Minister of Education for a three-year period. The composition of the boards of management differs according to the level of education and ownership of the school facilities. Approximately 27 percent of public schools are housed in buildings owned by the Church. Boards of management recruit and temporarily appoint teachers and other staff. Their appointments are confirmed by the Ministry of Education. In the case of principals, boards of management interview potential candidates, submit the names of three candidates in order of priority to the Teachers Service Commission who makes recommendations to the minister of education for appointment. The Ministry of Education supplies buildings, furniture, equipment, and funding for the purchase of class materials and supplies. At the primary level, textbooks are supplied by the Ministry of Education. At the secondary level, schools operate a book-rental scheme with textbooks provided by the Ministry of Education. Rental fees provide a revolving fund for the periodical replacement of textbooks by the Ministry of Education.

A team of education officers supervise school administration and the quality of teaching. The supervisory system operates on a regional basis from six regions and is headed by the chief education officer. Other administrative functions are administered centrally from the Ministry of Education's headquarters in the capital city. Statutory bodies administer literacy, skill training, school feeding, and library services.

In 1989, independent (private) schools enrolled 5.6 percent of students at the early childhood, primary, and secondary levels. Some private schools are owned by the Church, but many are operated by individuals.

Independent schools which satisfy certain prescribed minimum requirements are registered by the Registrar of Independent Schools.

The University of the West Indies (UWI) is a regional institution which serves 14 independent Caribbean countries including Jamaica. The Mona campus (one of three campuses) is located in Kingston and is the site of the central administration of the university. The University Council of Jamaica (UCJ) is a statutory body established in 1987 by the University Council of Jamaica Act to increase availability of university-level training through the accreditation of courses and programs offered by other tertiary institutions. In 1991, a joint committee for tertiary education was formed to provide a mechanism for consultation and collaboration among tertiary institutions. Legislation is being drafted for the establishment of a national council on education which will have wide representation from various interest groups to advise the minister of education on educational policy. Educational policy-making is the responsibility of the minister of education in collaboration with the Cabinet of ministers.

5. Educational Finance

For the financial year 1989–90, expenditure on education was J$1,245 million (US$55.4 million) which represented 6.2 percent of GNP. The proportion of GNP allocated to education increased from 1.3 percent in 1962–63 (Independence) to a peak of 7.7 percent in 1977–78. By 1986, the allocation to education declined to 5.1 percent. This decline was due to the debt crisis and the implementation of a structural adjustment program designed to increase foreign exchange earnings and reduce the budget deficit.

Education is financed centrally and the government provides most of the funds for education. In the 1989–90 financial year, 68 percent of the budget was allocated to primary and secondary education, 20 percent to tertiary education, 2 percent to early childhood education, and 8 percent to nonformal education. Private sources of funding for education come from tuition fees paid in private schools. These fees in private schools may be as high as J$15,000 (US$668) per year. Public schools do not charge tuition fees, but parents are asked to pay fees for other charges such as book rental, upkeep of facilities, and other miscellaneous fees. These vary from one school to another, but may be as high as J$1,200 (US$53) per year.

Teachers and parent–teacher associations also raise funds for schools. Since 1983–84 employees are required to pay an education tax which is now 2 percent of their gross salary. Each employer with a payroll above a prescribed minimum is required to pay a levy to the HEART Trust. In the 1989–90 financial year the education tax yielded J$204 million (US$9.1 million), while the HEART Trust provided J$95 million (US$4.2 million). Since the 1987–88 financial year, university students pay a cess as a contribution to the cost of their education. The cess varies according to the faculty but ranges from J$1,400 (US$62) for arts and general studies to J$1,850 (US$82) per year for full-time students in the Faculty of Medicine. Part-time students pay a lower rate.

The Examination Assistance Program was introduced in the 1984–85 financial year to assist needy secondary-level students. In the 1991–92 financial year J$4.5 million (US$200,300) was allocated to this program. At the tertiary level, students may apply for loans from the Students' Loan Bureau which was established in 1970. In the 1990–91 financial year 2,593 students received loans amounting to J$13.5 million (US$601,000). Loans can be obtained for local or overseas courses (i.e., those not available locally). Students are required to undergo a "means test." Repayments form a revolving fund and begin one year after graduation at an interest rate of 12 percent. Some university students are eligible for boarding grants. This grant was introduced in 1973–74 for all students attending UWI and CAST, but since 1985–86 the grant is only available for UWI students at the Cave Hill (Barbados) and St Augustine (Trinidad and Tobago) campuses. In the 1988–90 financial year, 220 grants were given for J$654,000 (US$29,000). This represents a decline from a peak of J$3.4 million (US$151,000) in 1985 for 4,092 students.

6. Supplying Personnel for the Education System

In 1990, the stock of teachers employed by the public sector at the early childhood, primary, and secondary levels was 18,825—an increase of 25 percent over the number employed in 1980. The pupil–teacher ratio at the primary level is 35:1, and 19:1 at the secondary level. These statistics obscure the fact that in some small rural primary and all-age schools the ratio is as low as 17:1 and as high as 60:1 in the urban centers. The implication of this is an oversupply in some areas and an undersupply in others, producing an imbalance in teacher distribution. To alleviate this situation, the Ministry of Education has been working with the Jamaica Teachers' Association since 1987 on a program of voluntary relocation in order to achieve a 42:1

ratio in all primary and all-age schools as the Ministry of Education has no power to transfer teachers. At the secondary level there is a shortage of qualified teachers in English and mathematics, particularly in Grades 10 and 11. This has implications for student performance on terminal examinations and may, in part, account for the low levels of performance which characterize this stage of the the education system.

Training for preprimary, primary, and secondary school teachers at the diploma level is provided at the tertiary level. The UWI offers undergraduate and graduate programs in teacher education. A three-year program was reintroduced in the teachers' colleges in 1981–82 to replace the two-year certificate course. Total enrollment in the diploma programs declined from 3,589 in 1983–84 to 2,646 in 1987–88. In recognition of the need for ongoing systematic professional development of teachers, all major internationally funded projects include inservice teacher training. In the Five-Year Education and Training Plan it is proposed to establish a professional development unit in the Ministry of Education to coordinate the professional development of educational personnel.

The Joint Board of Teacher Education (JBTE) assesses students for the purpose of certification of teachers for the early childhood, primary, and secondary levels. The JBTE achieves this objective by recommending and/or approving the syllabuses of teachers' colleges and the examination and assessment of the work of students in training. Appraisal of practicing teachers is the responsibility of the Operations Division of the Ministry of Education. Education Officers submit evaluation reports to the School Services Division and the Teachers Services Division which are responsible for the appointment and promotion of teachers.

7. Curriculum Development and Teaching Methodology

At the primary grades (Grades 1–6) of public schools, curriculum guides for each grade have been provided since the late 1970s and the early 1980s. Each curriculum guide suggests topics, objectives, weekly learning activities, resources, and evaluation methods for the following subjects: language, arts, mathematics, social studies, science, religious education, music, physical education, and arts and crafts. The curriculum is usually taught by a classroom teacher and teachers are expected to modify and restructure the curriculum to suit the needs of the students. The curriculum guides were written by the staff of the Core Curriculum and Technical and Vocational Education units in the Ministry of Education with the participation of classroom teachers.

At the lower-secondary level (Grades 7–9) there is no common curriculum. The subjects offered are similar in the various school types with options usually confined to industrial arts and home economics. With the assistance of the World Bank, work has started on the development of a common curriculum for the lower-secondary level. At the upper-secondary level (Grades 10–11) the curriculum is determined by the syllabuses of external examinations such as the Caribbean Examinations Council (CXC). Most students pursue English language and mathematics with the other subjects being optional. The syllabuses and examinations are written and marked with the participation of teachers throughout the Caribbean region. In new secondary schools, students in Grades 10 and 11 spend 40 percent of the timetable pursuing a vocational option. At Grade 13 students sit the General Certificate of Education at the Advanced Level. At the secondary level, teachers are usually subject specialists. Spanish and, to a lesser extent, French are the foreign languages offered. The education officers (see Sect. 4 above) monitor the implementation of the curriculum.

Learning materials for the primary level are provided through a primary textbook program with financial assistance from external funding agencies as well as from the local private sector. Some textbooks are written and published by the Ministry of Education, while others are selected from the marketplace. The Ministry of Education annually contracts out the printing and distribution of textbooks for the primary grades. Publishing firms are paid royalties for each book printed. At the secondary level, a textbook rental scheme has been organized. A small number of books are selected for each subject, procured from British publishers and distributed to schools for rental to students. The rental scheme was established in 1987 with the assistance of the Overseas Development Agency (ODA) of the United Kingdom.

A key issue at both the primary and secondary levels is the quality of education. The past three governments have stated that the implementation of a common curriculum at the lower-secondary level is an objective. A major concern is that equal educational opportunities are not being provided at the secondary level. A major thrust is being implemented to unify and rationalize the secondary system of education.

8. The System of Examinations, Promotions, and Certifications

Student movement from one grade to the next within a given level is achieved primarily through age promotion. At the end of Grade 6, transition to the various types of secondary institutions is achieved through several mechanisms. The Common Entrance Examination Eleven Plus (CEE 11+) is used to select 95 percent of students entering secondary high schools. Awardees are also placed in comprehensive high schools which admit students by automatic promotion from designated feeder schools as well as through CEE selection from other neighboring schools. Placement through the CEE mechanism accounts for 21 percent of the Grade 7 population. The remaining students flow automatically into new secondary and all-age schools. After Grade 7, approximately 3,000 children from all-age schools gain entry to high schools through selection examinations. At Grade 11, most students in the high schools sit the Carribean Examinations Council (CXC) examination which is offered at basic, general, and technical proficiency levels. The Secondary School Certificate (SSC) examination, a local examination administered by the Ministry of Education, is taken by new secondary school students. At the end of the sixth form (Grade 13) students sit the GCE (Advanced Level) of Cambridge University.

The major problem in the system of promotion from the primary to the secondary level is a consequence of the existence of a variety of secondary institutions each different in admission criteria, curricula, social currency, and unit expenditure. The early screening of children by the CEE11+, a mechanism which is highly selective and elitist in nature, mainly benefits the middle and upper socioeconomic groups. The Ministry of Education in an attempt to resolve this issue has embarked on a program of rationalization of secondary education. Another problem is in the area of certification at the end of the secondary cycle. Performance levels continue to be relatively low in many subjects and in the CXC General Proficiency clusters at the 30–40 percent range. This has grave implications for enrollment at the tertiary level and severely threatens the thrust towards the provision of the trained and qualified labor force needed for national development.

9. Educational Assessment, Evaluation, and Research

In the late 1980s, a National Assessment Programme (NAP) was designed with technical assistance from the Inter-American Development Bank. Work has been initiated on a Grade 1 readiness inventory, achievement and diagnostic tests for Grades 3 to 5, and a Grade 6 achievement test. The Grade 6 achievement test has been administered for three years, but is still at the developmental stage.

In the long term, it is envisaged that a common curricular program will be implemented between Grades 1 and 9 eliminating the need for selective examinations below Grade 9. A school-based continuous assessment program will be implemented from Grades 1 to 9 after which selection will be made for entry to the upper-secondary level. Just under 1 percent of the recurrent budget was allocated in 1990 to educational assessment. This includes the contribution by the government to the regional Caribbean Examinations Council.

Educational research is mainly carried out at the Faculty of Education of the University of the West

Indies. It is difficult to estimate how much is spent annually on educational research. During the late 1980s several policy studies were conducted with assistance from the United States Agency for International Development (USAID) and the World Bank. The policy studies, funded by a grant from USAID, concentrated mainly on primary education. Many of the recommendations of these studies were being implemented at the beginning of the 1990s. A study on research capacity of the education system made recommendations which include: the allocation of 0.5 percent of the educational budget to research, the establishment of an endowment fund for the Educational Research Centre at the Faculty of Education at UWI, the establishment of a consultative group, and the upgrading of the research section in the Ministry of Education to a unit.

Educational indicators on which information is regularly collected include enrollment rates, attendance rates, pupil–teacher ratios, the percentage of girls participating at all levels of the education system, per capita costs, percentage budgetary allocations to each level, as well as educational expenditures as a percentage of the total budget, GDP and GNP.

10. Major Reforms in the 1980s and 1990s

The debt crisis and the implementation of policy measures designed to achieve structural adjustment of the economy reduced the financial resources available for all social sectors. Development aid was mobilized in the form of loans and grants. Major emphasis was placed on improving the quality of basic education. The development of a system of continuous assessment for the primary grades was initiated during this project with the design of the National Assessment Programme (NAP). At the secondary level, curriculum development at the lower-secondary level was initiated with a loan from the World Bank, to develop a common curriculum for Grades 7–9 of all secondary schools. A school-mapping project was implemented between 1984 and 1990 with the assistance of the International Institute for Educational Planning, UNESCO, and UNDP which resulted in the preparation of a school map for each parish. Proposals for the consolidation and amalgamation of Grades 7–9 of all-age schools were also included. A ten-year implementation plan for the first phase of the reform of secondary education is being prepared.

The administration of the education system is being decentralized. Many administrative functions presently being carried out from Kingston will be administered from six regions. A loan has already been obtained from the World Bank to establish six regional offices. The establishment of the National Council on Education to advise the minister of education on educational policy should go a long way

in improving community participation. In the area of skill-training, the Human Employment and Resource Training (HEART) Trust was introduced in 1982. This training program was financed by a levy on employers.

11. Major Problems for the Year 2000

Finding resources to improve the quality of primary education to acceptable levels and provide equal educational opportunities by unifying the highly differentiated secondary system will be a major challenge. In addition, providing the much-needed labor force to develop the economy to a stage which will reduce the debt burden, increase foreign exchange earnings, and improve our ability to compete on the international market will require substantial resources. Resources will also be needed to compensate skilled labor at levels which will reduce the brain drain as well as attract and retain highly qualified persons in the teaching profession. Girls have been out-performing boys at all levels of the education system. Ways and means will have to be found to redress this imbalance.

Bibliography

Figueroa P M E, Persaud G (eds.) 1976 *Sociology of Education: A Caribbean Reader*. Clarendon Press, Oxford
Jamaica Gazette 1981 *The Education Act, The Regulations 1980*. Jamaica Gazette, Kingston
Miller E L 1990 *Jamaica Society and High Schooling*. Institute of Social and Economic Research, University of the West Indies, Mona, Kingston
Ministry of Education 1977 *Five Year Education Plan Draft Two (1978–1983)*. Ministry of Education, Kingston
Ministry of Education 1977 *Jamaica Education Sector Survey*. Ministry of Education, Kingston
Ministry of Education 1991 *Education Statistics 1988–89*. Ministry of Education, Kingston
Planning Institute of Jamaica 1991a *Economic and Social Survey 1990*. Planning Institute of Jamaica, Kingston
Planning Institute of Jamaica 1991b *Jamaica Five Year Development Plan 1990–1995 Education and Training*. Planning Institute of Jamaica, Kingston
Psacharopoulos G, Arriagada A 1986 The Educational composition of the labour force: An International comparison. *Int. Lab. Rev.* 125(5): 561–74
Statistical Institute of Jamaica 1986 *Population Census 1982*, Vol. 3. Statistical Institute of Jamaica, Kingston
Statistical Institute of Jamaica 1989 *Statistical Yearbook 1989*. Statistical Institute of Jamaica, Kingston
Statistical Institute of Jamaica 1991 *The Labour Force*. Statistical Institute of Jamaica, Kingston
Students' Loan Bureau 1991 *Twenty-first Anniversary 1970–1991*. Bank of Jamaica, Kingston
UNESCO 1983 *Development of Secondary Education— Jamaica*. UNESCO, Paris

Japan

T. Kanaya

1. General Background

Japan consists of more than 3,000 large and small islands stretching along the northeastern rim of the Eurasian continent, the longest span from north to south being 3,000 kilometers. Its total land area is 378,000 square kilometers, of which only 15 percent is arable. Systematic provision of school education was inaugurated in 1872 with the introduction of *Gakusei* or Education System Order by the Meiji Government.

The population of Japan was 124 million in 1992, of which 26 percent lived in the Tokyo metropolitan area which occupies only 4 percent of the total land area. In 1992, those over 65 years of age formed 13.0 percent of the total population while those under 15 years of age formed 17.2 percent. The aging of the population is a marked trend and it is estimated that in the year 2010 those over 65 years of age will form more than one-fifth of the total population. The natural population growth rate was only 2.9 per thousand and the total fertility rate was 1.52 in 1992. The urban concentration of the population and the decrease in the proportion of young persons causes various problems and issues in education.

Ethnically, Japan is a homogeneous country and foreign residents number 1.2 million. The Japanese language is the sole official language and medium of instruction from preschool to higher education stages.

Japan is known as a highly industrialized country. The Gross Domestic Product (GDP) in 1991 was ¥450,795 billion, (US$3,665 billion). Of this, 28.9 percent came from manufacturing, 21.2 percent from the service industry, 12.9 percent from commerce, and agriculture, fishery, and the forestry industry formed only 2.3 percent of GDP. In terms of the labor force composition, 59.4 percent of total employees belong to the tertiary industry and 33.9 percent to the secondary industry.

Since the enactment of the 1947 Constitution, Japan has had a bicameral legislature whose members are elected by direct voting. The national government operates through a party cabinet system and since 1948 the Liberal Party and its successor, the Liberal Democratic Party, monopolized the national government until mid-1993 when a coalition government was formed excluding the Liberal Democratic and Communist parties. The Ministry of Education, Science, and Culture (*Monbusho* in Japanese, and hereinafter referred to as the Ministry of Education) assumes the responsibility of educational administration at the national level.

Administratively, Japan is divided into 47 *To-Do-Fu-Ken* (prefectures) and further subdivided into 3,238 *Shi-Cho-Son* (municipalities). Local autonomy is systematized to an extent. Each prefecture and municipality have their assemblies formed by elected representatives, and the heads of their executive organs are elected by direct voting. The responsibilities to establish and maintain prefectural and municipal schools, which are called "public schools," rest on the shoulders of these prefectural and municipal governments which establish boards of education for education administration.

2. Politics and the Goals of the Education System

Until 1993, there had been no shift of political power in terms of the government party in power since 1948, and the national education policies were developed jointly by the Liberal Democratic Party and bureaucrats at the Ministry of Education. The other political parties had expressed their education policies from time to time in the form of election manifestos and other means, but thus far they have had less influence on the actual education policies.

The goals of education in Japan are enunciated in the Fundamental Law of Education issued in 1947 which, as prescribed in the first article, is as follows:

> Education shall aim at full development of personality, at rearing a people, sound in mind and body, who love truth and justice, esteem individual values, respect labor, have a deep sense of responsibility, and are imbued with an independent spirit as the builders of a peaceful state and society.

This statement of educational goals has been cast in more specific terms as laws, notices, and recommendations of the Ministry of Education. The latest example of such a statement was the final report of the National Council on Educational Reform which had worked out educational reform proposals in 1987. The National Council kept the Fundamental Law of Education as the basis of their deliberations for educational reform measures, and in its final report the National Council stressed, as the aims of education, the full development of the individual personality and the rearing of healthy nationals as the builders of a peaceful state and society as expressed in the Fundamental Law of Education. The report further stated that the most important objectives of education for the twenty-first century are: (a) the development of broad mindedness, a healthy body, and creativity in individuals; (b) the rearing of the spirit of freedom, self-reliance, and public awareness; and (c) educating the Japanese individual to live in the global human society.

Table 1
Number of educational institutions and enrollment 1993[a]

Type of institution	Number of institutions				Enrollment			
	Total	National	Public	Private	Total	National	Public	Private
Kindergarten	14,958	49	6,205	8,704	1,907,110	6,740	379,857	1,520,513
Elementary school	24,676	73	24,432	171	8,768,881	47,226	8,654,680	66,975
Lower-secondary school	11,292	78	10,578	636	4,850,137	34,678	4,588,523	226,936
Upper-secondary school	5,501	17	4,164	1,320	5,010,472	10,363	3,518,187	1,481,922
	(91)		(69)	(22)	(157,003)		(97,681)	(59,322)
College of technology	62	54	5	3	55,453	48,053	4,364	3,036
Junior college	595	37	56	502	530,294	16,705	22,802	490,787
	(9)			(9)	(42,341)			(42,341)
University	534	98	46	390	2,389,648	561,822	74,182	1,753,644
	(13)	(1)		(12)	(184,425)	(46,537)		(137,888)
Special training school	3,431	161	198	3,072	859,173	18,232	32,230	808,620
Miscellaneous school	3,055	3	75	2,977	366,536	58	5,827	360,651

a Figures given in parentheses represent the number of institutions and enrollment for correspondence courses, except the figures for National University which represent the University of the Air and its number of students

3. The Formal System of Education

3.1 Primary, Secondary, and Tertiary Education

Figure 1 outlines the structure of the formal education system, and Table 1 presents statistics on the number of educational institutions and their enrollments in major education sectors. Throughout the country, the school year begins in April and ends the following March. This is the case from preschool to higher education. A growing number of institutions of higher learning adopt the semester system.

Schooling is compulsory for nine years and begins with the six-year elementary school at the age of 6 years. The elementary school activities consist of learning of specific subjects, moral education, and special activities. The actual number of subjects studied and the number of hours spent at school differ by grade. Sixth-grade children study eight subjects for a minimum of 1,015 periods a year. Each period is 45 minutes long. The school textbooks, which are authorized by the Ministry of Education for school use, are distributed without charge.

In 1993, there were approximately 24,700 elementary schools with an enrollment of slightly less than nine million children, of which 99 percent were in public elementary schools. The elementary school population was over ten million in 1987, and the decline in the school population causes problems such as difficulty in maintaining elementary schools in remote and rural areas, over-supply of elementary school teachers, useful transfer of school facilities, and so on.

Those who complete elementary school proceed to the lower-secondary school which is three years in duration and the second stage of compulsory education. In addition to the subject areas taught at elementary school, lower-secondary school pupils learn health and prevocational subjects. Foreign languages are elective subjects, but almost all lower-secondary schools teach English as a foreign language. The minimum number of periods a year in the lower-secondary school is

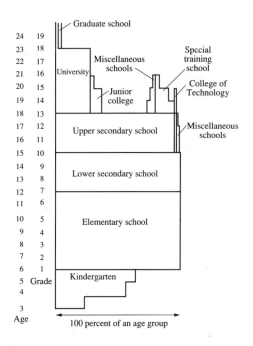

Figure 1
Japan: Structure of the formal education system

1,050, each period being 50 minutes long. Textbooks authorized by the Ministry of Education are also free of charge.

In 1993, there were 11,300 lower-secondary schools with an enrollment of nearly five million pupils. In all, 5 percent of the pupils were in private lower-secondary schools. The lower-secondary school enrollments have since in the late 1980s decreased by one million pupils.

The upper-secondary school is the second half of secondary education and is not compulsory. Entrance examinations are organized for applicants and 96 percent of graduates from lower-secondary schools go to upper-secondary schools. Tuition fees are required and textbooks, also authorized by the Ministry of Education for use, are no longer free.

There are two types of upper-secondary schools distinguished by length of study period: full-time school for three years, and part-time and correspondence school for three or four years. A new type, called the "credit-system upper-secondary school" was inaugurated in 1988. Its aim is to offer learning opportunities to meet learners' needs and conditions. Streaming starts at this stage and approximately 74 percent of students enroll in a general course. Specialized courses include technology, commerce, agriculture, mathematics/science, English language, informatics, and so on.

In 1993, there were 5,500 upper-secondary schools with 5 million students enrolled in them. The upper-secondary school population has also begun to decrease. Some 30 percent of the upper-secondary school population was in private institutions and it is expected that the decrease in the size of the population may affect these privately established institutions more severely than public schools.

Institutions of higher learning in Japan can be classified into three categories: *Daigaku*, or university; *Tanki-daigaku*, or junior college; and *Koto-senmongakko*, or college of technology.

Daigaku or the university is a traditional academic center of higher learning leading to the bachelor's degree, and the number of years of study vary from four to six according to discipline. The entrance requirement for *Daigaku* is the completion of upper-secondary education and passing an entrance examination. *Daigaku* may set up *Daigaku-in* or graduate schools leading to the master's degree in 2–3 years and to the doctoral degree in 4–5 years. There are a few independent graduate schools which have no undergraduate courses.

There were 534 *Daigaku* offering either full-time or part-time undergraduate courses with enrollments totaling 2.4 million in 1993. Almost three-fourths of them were private. A total of 40 percent of students were in social sciences, 20 percent in engineering, 16 percent in humanities, 7 percent in education, and 3 percent each in natural sciences, agriculture, medicine and dentistry, and others. In addition, there is one *Hoso-daigaku* or "University of the Air" and there

are 12 *Daigaku* offering correspondence courses. They had an enrollment of about 137,000 in 1993. There were 860 graduate courses for the master's degree and 614 graduate courses for the doctoral degree in 1993. Engineering comprises 45 percent of the master's degrees, and 38 percent of the doctoral courses were in medicine and dentistry. The total number of graduate students was more than 120,000.

Tanki-daigaku or junior colleges were created in 1950 to respond to the demand for the popularization of higher education. The length of study is 2–3 years, but there are no courses in junior college for the study of the natural and medical sciences. The majority of courses in junior colleges are in the humanities, home sciences, education, and social sciences. There were 595 junior colleges with an enrollment of 530,000 students in 1993. In terms of numbers, 84 percent of institutions and 93 percent of students were in private *Tanki-daigaku*. In 1993, 92 percent of junior college students were female.

Koto-senmongakko or colleges of technology (created in 1962) are a unique form of higher education institution providing mainly technology and engineering education for those having completed lower-secondary school. The courses last 5 years. There were 62 *Koto-senmongakko* with 55,000 students in 1993. Most of the *Koto-senmongakko* were national institutions.

The demand for higher education in Japan is high and 34 percent of graduates (42% in the case of female graduates) from upper-secondary school proceed to either *Daigaku* or *Tanki-daigaku*. There were 51,000 foreign students in higher education institutions in 1993. Of these, 12 percent were Japanese government scholarship students and 32 percent were in graduate courses.

The University Council, an advisory organ to the Minister of Education on higher education was created in 1987 on the recommendation of the National Council on Educational Reform. It proposed several drastic measures to improve higher education with a view to coping with the changing needs of society, rapid progress in science and technology, and the population trend. Some measures have been implemented, which include the improvement of the quality of higher education and the enhancement of graduate education.

3.2 Preschool Education

A majority of children attend kindergarten or nursery before their entrance to elementary schools. Kindergarten is an institution for preschool education catering for children of 3–5 years of age. Nursery is a social welfare institution for children up to 6-years old. Educational programs of nursery for children of 3-years old and above are organized according to the kindergarten education guidelines set by the Ministry of Education. In 1993, 64 percent of 5-year old children were enrolled in kindergarten, while 31 percent of the same age group attended nursery. In 1993, there were 15,000 kindergartens with an enrollment of nearly two million. Of these about 80 percent were private.

3.3 Special Education

Special education programs exist for individuals who cannot study in ordinary classes of elementary and secondary schools due to their physical or mental difficulties. Such special programs are provided in schools for the blind, the deaf, the mentally retarded, the physically handicapped, and the health-impaired. In 1993, there were 964 special schools from kindergarten to upper-secondary education levels with an enrollment of about 90,000 pupils. In addition, those who are less handicapped but still have difficulty in studying in ordinary classes are educated in special classes attached to ordinary elementary and lower-secondary schools. In 1993, there were 22,000 special classes with 70,000 pupils.

Curriculum guidelines for the special education programs for kindergarten through upper-secondary level are set by the Ministry of Education. From the viewpoint of integrated education for handicapped children, measures to encourage learning in normal classes with additional guidance in special classes are undertaken. The increase in demand for upper-secondary level education for handicapped youth is another issue to be tackled.

Nine years of attendance at the special schools has been compulsory for blind and deaf children since 1948, and for otherwise handicapped children since 1979.

3.4 Vocational and Technical Education

Vocational and technical education is provided both in formal and nonformal education settings. Due to the increase of higher education opportunities and changes in the industrial employment structure, the ratio of students in vocational and technical streams at the upper-secondary level has decreased since the 1970s. Approximately 24 percent of upper-secondary students were in vocational or technical courses in 1993. Measures to revitalize vocational and technical education at the upper-secondary level have been taken. These include the establishment of new courses such as electromechanics, biotechnology, and others in order to keep abreast progress in technology and changes in the industrial structure; the establishment of new comprehensive vocational upper-secondary schools where students can study subjects over and above the course they belong to; the improvement of the curriculum; and the renewal of facilities.

Special training schools are also institutions for vocational and technical education. The system of special training schools was inaugurated in 1976 by upgrading miscellaneous schools. There were 3,431 special training schools with 860,000 students in 1993.

Technological and engineering courses accounted for 42 percent of male students, whereas 32 percent and 20 percent of female students were in medical services and business courses respectively in 1993. Some of the miscellaneous schools also provide vocational and skill training courses. Vocational training institutions under the Ministry of Labor organize a number of training courses. In 1992, a capacity of 36,000 places were offered for basic and advanced vocational training courses for young people.

3.5 Adult and Nonformal Education

Increased free time, higher incomes, aging, the progress of science and technology, and other factors have created the demand for lifelong learning. Ample opportunities for nonformal learning are provided not only by the education sector, but also by institutions of social welfare, vocational training, and the like. There are two types of nonformal educational settings. One is in the form of schooling and the other in the form of seminars and workshops.

The more than 3,000 special training schools and 3,000 miscellaneous schools are strong vehicles for the nonformal education program under the jurisdiction of the Ministry of Education. In particular, advanced courses of special training schools have a reputation equivalent to the junior college. The Ministry of Labor provides vocational and technical training opportunities. The Ministry of Agriculture, Fishery, and Forestry also organizes various training programs for junior farmers, fishermen, and forestry workers.

Nonformal education in Japan is known as "social education" by the Ministry of Education. This ministry provides facilities for social education activities such as libraries, museums, citizenship halls, youth centers, women's education centers, and social education centers, where various types of seminars and workshops are organized. Some other government agencies also establish facilities to provide nonformal education programs, exemplar facilities being community centers, young workers homes, and children's homes.

Mass communication media provides nonformal education programs which are quite wide in content and high in quality. The private sector also provides good opportunities for nonformal education. Lecture series and workshops provided by cultural centers, and correspondence courses for skill training are typical examples. Extension services are provided by universities, junior colleges, and upper-secondary schools.

An increasing number of universities and junior colleges are opening up learning opportunities for adults by means of special arrangements for entrance examinations and special quotas for occasional students. In some cases, credits obtained in these nonformal education and training institutions are approved as the equivalent to the credits obtained in the formal secondary and tertiary educational institutions. Those who have completed some designated special training schools are entitled to qualification for university education.

4. Administrative and Supervisory Structure and Operation

At the national level, the Ministry of Education, Science, and Culture is the agency which shares responsibilities with the Cabinet and the Diet for preparing budget estimates, drafting educational legislation, formulating educational policies, and maintaining educational standards. The Ministry allocates financial aid to prefectural and municipal boards of education, and assists such boards with advice and technical guidance. The Ministry prescribes guidelines for the curriculum, the courses, and credit requirements for kindergarten through higher education. Curricular standards for elementary and secondary schools are described in the form of "courses of study" issued by the Ministry. The Ministry is also responsible for authorizing textbooks in elementary and secondary schools.

The Ministry is responsible for formal national education institutions from kindergarten through graduate school, national social education institutions, national sports and physical education facilities, and national research institutions. National cultural facilities, such as national museums and national theaters, come under the Ministry's jurisdiction. Approval of and supervision of higher education institutions are tasks assigned to the Ministry. Promotion of research and sciences; international exchange in education, science, and culture; sports and physical education activities in society; and cultural activities also come into the Ministry's sphere.

As mentioned elsewhere, each of the 47 prefectures has a board of education to administer local education affairs. The five-member boards administer prefectural institutions of education and organize educational and cultural programs in the prefecture. In addition, the prefectural boards issue teaching certificates, recruit and supervise personnel for public educational institutions within the prefecture, provide inservice training programs for teachers, purchase and manage instructional materials, promote social education activities, protect cultural assets, and offer advice and guidance to municipal boards of education.

Each municipality maintains, either independently or jointly in the case of smaller municipalities, a three- or five-member board of education whose major functions are to establish and manage municipal educational institutions, administer personnel matters in such institutions, adopt textbooks for municipal elementary and secondary schools, and provide advice and guidance to educational institutions under its jurisdiction. The municipal boards are also responsible for promoting social education, and cultural and sports programs, providing inservice training opportunities for school teachers, and protecting cultural assets.

5. Educational Finance

Public educational expenditure is shared by national, prefectural, and municipal governments with funds obtained from taxes and other revenue sources. In 1990, its total amount reached ¥20,258 billion (US$115 billion) which represents 4.64 percent of the GNP and 16.51 percent of the total public administration expenditure. In the same year, it was estimated that a parent spent ¥263,015 (US$1,963) for all educational activities of a child attending public lower-secondary school.

Total school education expenditure (education expenditures of national, public, and private schools) was ¥22,536 billion (US$168 billion) in 1990, of which 47.5 percent went on compulsory education, 18.6 percent on upper-secondary education, and 25.6 percent on higher education. In the same year, the per unit costs of public education expenditure (education expenditure by national and local governments) were ¥537,787 (US$4,013) for kindergarten education, ¥666,924 (US$4,977) for elementary education, ¥721,835 (US$5,389) for lower-secondary education, ¥737,398 (US$5,503) for upper-secondary education, and ¥3,523,046 (US$26,291) for higher education.

During the 1980s, the national government had a national budget policy to reduce the issuance of deficit-covering national bonds. This forced a tightening of national administrative expenditures including education. The rate of increase of the public education budget has always been lower than the growth rate of GNP. Once in 1980, the public education expenditures were 5.71 percent of the GNP. The scientific research expenses in the private sector (including enterprises) showed an increase of 162 percent during the 1980s, while research funds at universities had only a 59 percent increase.

In order to maintain national standards of education, the Ministry of Education can provide further subsidies to the local boards of education for educational personnel expenses, school buildings and facilities, instructional aids and materials, and other educational programs. More than half of the Ministry's budget is always for the national treasury's share of compulsory school expenditures. This means that half of the total teachers' salaries bill for compulsory schools is paid by the national government.

Since the private educational institutions play a great role in the formal education system, the national government takes various measures to maintain and improve the educational conditions of private institutions. In the case of private higher education institutions, 13 percent of its current expenditure was covered by national government's subvention in 1991. In 1980 it was nearly 30 percent.

6. Supplying Personnel for the Education System

Teachers for kindergarten, elementary, and lower-secondary schools are trained in teacher-training universities, education departments, and teaching certificate courses in universities and junior colleges sanctioned by the Ministry of Education. Teachers for upper-secondary schools are trained in universities and graduate schools. Teaching certificates, classified into two for kindergarten, elementary, and lower-secondary schools and one for upper-secondary schools, are granted for life by the prefectural boards of education and are valid in all prefectures. Teachers with a master's or doctoral degree are given special teaching certificates.

An elementary school teaching certificate qualifies the teacher to teach all subjects in an elementary school, whereas a secondary school teaching certificate authorizes the teacher to teach specified subjects only. To obtain a post in a public elementary or secondary school, a candidate should apply to take a recruitment examination. This is organized by individual prefectural boards of education.

Due to the shrinking school population, the demand for teachers is also declining. However, the shortage of teachers is constantly seen in specific subject areas such as science and technology at the secondary level.

Teachers in public schools are treated as local public officials. Promotion to administrative posts such as deputy principal or principal in public schools usually requires a selection procedure set by the individual prefectural boards of education.

In order to enhance teachers' qualifications, teaching certificate requirements were improved. A one-year initial on-the-job training was enforced for newly recruited teachers, and several education universities for inservice advanced study by teachers were established.

Inservice training programs are widely provided by educational administrative agencies, educational research and inservice training institutions, teachers' professional associations, and others. Participation in these inservice training programs are voluntary in nature, but participation can be enforced in some of the inservice training courses organized by educational administration agencies. In-school voluntary study programs are actively organized by teachers themselves.

7. Curriculum Development and Teaching Methodology

The school curriculum is based on the course of study prescribed by the Ministry of Education, in which the basic framework for the curriculum at each grade level including instructional objectives, content, standard time allotment, and others are stated. The prefectural and municipal boards of education prepare guidelines for curriculum development in the schools in their areas, and individual schools are required to organize their own detailed instructional programs on the basis of the courses of study and the guidelines.

The courses of study prepared by the Ministry are revised approximately every ten years with a view to overcoming educational defects and improving the educational content and activities responding to social changes. Revision work was undertaken in the latter half of 1980s and newly revised courses of study were implemented from 1992 for the elementary school, 1993 for the lower-secondary school, and 1994 for the upper-secondary school. The principles for the revision of courses of study were (a) to place emphasis on basic and essential knowledge and skills, (b) to enhance educational programs to give full play to a pupil's individuality, (c) to keep consistency in the curriculum for each subject area among different levels of schooling, (d) to nurture the capacity to cope positively with changes in society, and (e) to develop self-learning ability.

Revision of the school curriculum has the following steps. The Curriculum Council of the Ministry of Education, the Minister's advisory organ on matters of school curriculum, prepares the basic guidelines, on the Minister's request, for revising a course of study. The guidelines prepared by the Council are utilized by the Ministry's subject specialists and their collaborators as the basis for writing the course of study for each grade and subject. Teachers' guidebooks for each grade level and subject are also prepared by the subject specialists in the Ministry with the assistance of experienced teachers in accordance with the newly revised courses of study.

The pupil–teacher ratios for elementary, lower-secondary, and upper-secondary were 20:1, 17.4:1, and 17.7:1 respectively in 1993. Simultaneous collective instruction at a class was common practice in elementary and secondary schools, but individualized teaching, small group instruction for homogeneous achievement, and other teaching methods are encouraged in order to deal with the increasing curriculum burden and the diversified learning abilities and aptitudes of students.

School textbooks serve as the main instructional material in the classroom. The textbooks are developed, except for a few which are compiled by the Ministry, by commercial publishing companies on the basis of the courses of study. They then have to be authorized by the Ministry and adopted by the local boards of education for use in schools.

8. The System of Examinations, Promotions, and Certifications

There is no external examination scheme in Japan. Promotion and certification of completion are made on the basis of internal assessment. Grade-to-grade promotion in compulsory education is practically automatic. The minimum requirement for graduation from the upper-secondary school is to acquire 80 credits. One credit can be earned by the attendance of 35 class periods, and by the approval of satisfactory achievement by the teacher in charge. Certification of graduation is issued by the individual school principal.

Entrance examination for public upper-secondary school is organized by the relevant boards of education, whereas the private upper-secondary schools organize their own entrance examinations. The Ministry of Education set up a National Center for University Entrance Examination to organize a nationwide test every January to assess the level of applicants' academic achievement acquired at upper-secondary schools. The test results are used by individual national, public, or private universities together with the school reports from upper-secondary schools and the results of interviews, essay tests, achievement tests, and practical skill tests of their own for consideration for admission. Use of the National Center's test results is decided by individual universities, and a majority of private universities prefer to organize their own entrance examination rather than to use the Center's test results. Junior colleges select students by using their own examinations.

There is a University Entrance Qualification Test Scheme for those who have not completed an upper-secondary school course. Those who pass the test are granted qualification for university entrance.

9. Educational Assessment, Evaluation, and Research

The Ministry of Education conducts a nationwide scholastic achievement survey from time to time either on the basis of census or probability samples. Its results were utilized for the improvement of curriculum standards. The National Institute for Educational Research, a research agency under the jurisdiction of the Ministry of Education and affiliated to the International Association for the Evaluation of Educational Achievement (IEA), conducts nationwide scholastic achievement surveys in specific subject areas in collaboration with prefectural institutes of educational research with a view to compare scholastic achievement of Japanese students at an international level.

The National Institute for Educational Research also covers whole areas of education, except special education which is covered by the National Institute for Special Education Research. Both institutions carry out theoretical as well as action-oriented research. The National Institute of Multimedia Education is another government agency which conducts research work related to higher education using broadcasting media.

In the Ministry of Education, there is one division for educational research and statistics which carries out policy-oriented research. In all prefectural and major municipal boards of education there is an institution called either "education center," "education research institute," or "inservice education center." This institution aims at providing inservice training programs for teachers in the area. At the same time, it conducts various action-oriented research activities.

The Ministry of Education and the local boards of education encourage school-based research by classroom teachers for the improvement of teaching methods and materials. University faculties in education are also a strong wing for educational research. Several of them have their own educational research institutes or centers.

10. Major Reforms in the 1980s and 1990s

Rapid social changes have greatly affected education and a variety of problems and difficulties have emerged. These include, among others, the social climate which puts too much weight on the educational career of individuals, excessive competition in entrance examinations, antisocial behavior or nonchalant social attitudes of young persons, the increase of school absenteeism and violence, and dropout from learning activities. On the other hand, changes in the industrial and employment structure, progress in science and technology (particularly in informatics), and globalization in various sectors of society required that education be made more relevant to these changes and developments. A National Council on Educational Reform was set up in 1984 as an ad hoc advisory organ to the Prime Minister for the purpose of working out possible measures for educational reform.

The Council identified causes which need drastic reform in every sector of education, and presented three major principles for reform with suggested measures: (a) the principle of putting emphasis on individuality; (b) transition to a lifelong learning system; and (c) coping with changes in society, including internationalization and the spread of information media.

The Council disbanded in 1987 having produced four reports, and the Cabinet issued a policy paper for the implementation of educational reform which clarified strategies in six areas, namely the development of lifelong learning structures, reforms in elementary and secondary education, reforms in higher education, the promotion of scientific research, reforms for coping with the changing times, and reforms in educational administration and finance. The Ministry of Education is implementing reform measures derived from these strategies in order to make education relevant to the twenty-first century. Provision of lifelong learning systems, diversified upper-secondary education, and the re-vitalization of higher education are, among others, major reform measures that the Ministry undertakes.

11. Major Problems for the Year 2000

The decrease in the size of the school-going population will affect greatly every education sector and, in particular, higher education in the early years of the twenty-first century. With this population issue, it will be a vital problem of Japanese education to break down the long prevailing uniformity in school education and to make education relevant to the diversified individual needs of learners. How to cope with the increasing demand for new knowledge will continue to be a problem. Enhancing the scientific research capacities of higher learning institutions is another problem for the society at large, while the systematization of lifelong learning is another major problem to be tackled.

School education is also expected to cope with problems arising from family and social changes such as the increase of working mothers, the move to a five-day working-week system, and other changes. Increasing demand for the provision of public education for children of non-Japanese residents poses quite a new problem for Japanese education. Finally, the teaching of emerging global issues such as environmental problems, population issues, poverty and North–South issues will be another basic task that the Japanese education system will have to undertake for the twenty-first century.

Bibliography

Asian Cultural Center for UNESCO 1990 *Outline of Education in Japan 1991*. Asian Cultural Center for UNESCO, Tokyo

Cummings W 1980 *Education and Equality in Japan*. Princeton University Press, Princeton, New Jersey
Dorfman C H (ed.) 1987 *Japanese Education Today*. A report from the US Study of Education in Japan. US Government Printing Office, Washington DC
Duke B C 1986 *The Japanese School*. Kodansha, Tokyo
Leestma R, Walberg J (eds.) 1992 *Japanese Educational Productivity*. Center for Japanese Studies, University of Michigan, Ann Arbor, Michigan
Ministry of Education, Science, and Culture 1980 *Japan's Modern Educational System-A History of the First Hundred Years*. Government of Japan, Tokyo
Ministry of Education, Science, and Culture 1988 *The University Research System in Japan*. Monbusho, Tokyo
Ministry of Education, Science, and Culture 1989 *Japanese Government Policies in Education, Science and Culture 1989: Elementary and Secondary Education in a Changing Society*. Government of Japan, Tokyo
Ministry of Education, Science, and Culture 1992 *Education in Japan. A Graphic Presentation*. Government of Japan, Tokyo
Ministry of Education, Science, and Culture 1993a *Monbusho*. Government of Japan, Tokyo
Ministry of Education, Science, and Culture 1993b *Wagakunino Bunkyo-seisaku*. Government of Japan, Tokyo
Nakane C 1973 *Japanese Society*. Penguin, Harmondsworth
White M 1987 *The Japanese Educational Challenge: A Commitment to Children*. Free Press, New York

Jordan

M. Masri and T. Bermamet

1. General Background

Jordan is a small country with an area of 91,000 square kilometers. Desert and semidesert areas predominate in the eastern part of the country, and constitute more than four-fifths of the total area. The central spine of the country, the hilly region that runs from north to south, is the seat of the capital—Amman and other main cities. To the west, the Great Rift Valley runs the entire length of the country and includes the Jordan Valley, the Dead Sea, Wadi Araba, and the Aqaba Gulf at the northern part of the Red Sea.

Jordan is a developing country which emerged in 1921 under the leadership of Prince Abdullah who was later proclaimed King of the Hashemite Kingdom of Jordan after the country gained its independence from Britain in 1946. Following the Arab–Israeli War of 1948, part of Palestine (the West Bank of Jordan) united with Jordan in 1950. The West Bank fell under military occupation following the 1967 Arab–Israeli War.

Jordan is governed by a parliamentary system and a constitutional hereditary monarchy. Under the Constitution, the King is vested with wide powers which he exercises through the Council of Ministers. Legislative powers reside in the National Assembly (People's Council), consisting of the Senate (Upper House) and the House of Deputies.

Jordan is an Arab country, and the great majority of Jordanians are Muslim. Christians constitute about 4 percent of the population. Arabic is the official language although English is widely spoken, and is taught as a second language in all schools.

In 1979, the population of Jordan (not including the occupied West Bank) was 2.15 million. The estimate for 1990 was 3.45 million, of which two-thirds resided in urban areas. The annual rate of population growth is 2.7 percent.

The economy of Jordan suffers from a narrow productive base, and is highly susceptible to various internal and external influences such as external aid, the price of phosphate which has traditionally been the main export, and even the amount of rainfall. Under such circumstances, it is natural that human resource development in general, and education in particular, have acquired a prominent place among national development plans and policies. In this respect, it is worthwhile noting that new entrants to the labor

Table 1
Net enrollment ratios (as percentage of age group) according to cycle and sex 1974–75 to 1989–90

Educational cycle/age	1974–75		1979–80		1984–85		1989–90	
	Male	Female	Male	Female	Male	Female	Male	Female
Kindergarten/4–6	7.9	6.1	16.2	13.4	20.9	18.6	30.6	27.9
Basic/6–15(16)[a]	97.1	86.0	92.7	85.2	88.8	89.1	90.4	92.5
Secondary/15(16)[a]–18	53.8	37.8	76.1	61.0	68.6	69.7	58.6	63.9

a Starting from the academic year 1988–89, basic compulsory education covered the age range 6–16

market have, on average, more than 11 years of formal education.

Jordan is both an importer and exporter of labor. Unemployment rates fluctuated sharply in the period 1970–90. Rates of about 8 percent were usual until the early 1970s, dropping to less than 2 percent in the late 1970s, and rising to more than 20 percent in the early 1990s following the Gulf Crisis that caused many Jordanians working in the Gulf countries to return home. The Jordanian labor force constitutes only 21 percent of the total population. It is distributed as follows: 8 percent in the agricultural sector, 22 percent in the industrial sector (including construction and mining), and 70 percent in the services sector (including education, health, finance, commerce, transportation, etc.). The low percentage of the population in the labor force is due to the fact that about half the population is under the age of 16 which is also the last year of compulsory schooling. The demands on the education system are consequently high.

Despite high rates of unemployment, the labor market in Jordan is characterized by the presence of a high percentage of expatriates from neighboring Arab countries who occupy low-skill occupations. This casts doubt on the external efficiency of the education system which is increasingly under pressure to respond better to labor force needs and labor market requirements.

2. Politics and the Goals of the Education System

Despite the parliamentary system of government in Jordan, the Council of Ministers does not usually represent one political background or line of thinking. This contributed to the fact that many government agencies, especially those concerned with public services such as the Ministry of Education, have a great deal of freedom in conducting their affairs with minimum cabinet-generated policies and guidance. Nevertheless, many agencies and individuals outside the education system usually participate in developing education policies and legislation.

In general, Islamic heritage and Western cultural influences constitute the two main sources that lie at the background of educational policies in Jordan. The

principles from which the philosophy of education emanates are identified by the Education Law to include the belief in God, the unity and freedom of the Arab homeland, the parliamentary system of government, international cooperation, and participation in the development of human civilization. Such principles also include respect for the integrity and freedom of the individual, as well as the appreciation of the general interests of society.

In basic education, emphasis is placed on the development of the individual—physically, mentally, socially, and emotionally. This is continued in secondary and higher education and in addition emphasis is placed on societal needs and the requirements of socioeconomic and human resource development.

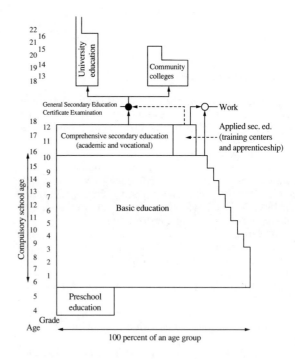

Figure 1
Jordan: Structure of the formal education system 1990

3. The Formal System of Education

3.1 Primary, Secondary, and Tertiary Education

Figure 1 represents the structure of the Jordanian education system. Key statistics on enrollments are provided in Table 1.

Basic education is compulsory and free in public schools. It consists of ten years of common non differentiated general education, divided into six years of primary education and four years of preparatory (junior or lower-secondary) education. To be admitted to the first grade of the primary school, a child should have reached at least the age of 5 years and 8 months by September of the relevant year.

In the academic year 1989–90, Ministry of Education schools accommodated 76.4 percent of the basic education population. The rest was catered for by the United Nation Relief and Works Agency (UNRWA) schools (15%), private schools (7.6%), and other government schools (1%).

Among the 6–16 age group, 90.4 percent of boys and 92.5 percent of girls were in school during the academic year 1989–90.

Since the abolition in 1988 of the National General Examination which used to mark the end of compulsory education, access to secondary education has become almost unhindered. The type of education a student enters is dependent on academic achievement, individual choice, and the availability of vacancies. The Ministry of Education has adopted a new procedure for streaming students in the various kinds of secondary education based on their school results in Grades 8, 9, and 10.

On completing compulsory basic education, most students continue their education for two years, either in comprehensive secondary education or in applied secondary education which aims at the preparation of skilled workers in training centers and formal apprenticeship schemes. The aims of secondary education are: preparation for citizenship, preparation for higher education, and preparation for work through vocational education and training.

In 1989–90, Ministry of Education schools accommodated 86.6 percent of the secondary education population. The rest was catered for by private schools (5.5%), UNRWA schools (0.5%), and other government schools (7.4%). Among the 16–18 age group, 58.6 percent of boys and 63.9 percent of girls were in school. The following is a brief description of each type of school in secondary education:

(a) The comprehensive secondary school replaced the separate general (academic) and vocational type school that dominated the education system until the early 1990s. The curriculum for comprehensive secondary education will be effective from the academic year 1993–94, and consists of a common general culture core as well as a specialized academic or vocational group of disciplines leading to the General Secondary Education Certificate Examination.

(b) Training centers have vocational education programs which are free and run mostly by the Ministry of Education. There are two years of specialized vocational preparation, almost exclusively in the industrial and women's crafts field. These centers prepare students for direct access to jobs as skilled workers.

(c) Formal apprenticeship is considered part of the "applied secondary education" stream. It consists of two years of vocational preparation implemented in cooperation with employers, and one year of supervised employment.

In tertiary education there are community colleges and universities. Community colleges are multidisciplinary formal educational institutions that offer 2–3 year courses in more than 100 specializations in engineering, business, paramedical, agricultural, catering, social, educational, and other fields. There are about 60 such colleges in Jordan, more than half of which are private. These colleges are mostly coeducational, and accept students who pass the General (Academic or Vocational) Secondary Education Certificate Examination. Annual enrollment figures amount to nearly 20,000 students.

To avoid a decline in the educational standards of community colleges, especially due to the growth of private sector involvement, a general comprehensive examination was introduced in 1983. Since then, certification of community college graduates has become a centralized responsibility of the Ministry of Higher Education which also applies an accreditation system to community colleges.

Jordanian universities admit students who pass the General Secondary Education Certificate Examination, mainly from the academic streams. In addition to first-degree courses that usually last four years, higher diploma and master's (second-degree) courses are available in most disciplines. Doctoral degrees, on the other hand, are available only in a limited number of disciplines. There are four public and five private universities, with an annual intake of about 13,000 students, more than three-fourths of whom are accommodated in public universities.

In 1988, enrollment in higher education institutions in Jordan totaled nearly 60,000 students, divided almost equally between universities and community colleges. In addition, about 20,000 Jordanian students study in Arab and foreign universities.

3.2 Preschool Education

Preschool education in Jordan is neither compulsory nor free. It lasts for two years, and is run almost exclusively by private agencies. To be accepted for preschool education in a kindergarten, a child should have reached the age of 3 years and 8 months by September of the relevant year.

During the academic year 1989–90, 30.6 percent of the boys and 27.9 percent of the girls in the 4–6 age groups were in preschool education. Table 1 shows the development of preschool education in the period 1974–90.

The Ministry of Education is responsible for the licensing of kindergartens as well as for maintaining standards and certifying teachers for preschool education. Although no formalized curricula exist, guided activities and play occupy most of the children's time, and a child is expected to have some skills in the "three Rs" by the time he or she enters primary school.

The Ministry of Education issues manuals and instructional guides to assist kindergarten teachers, almost all of whom are females. The child–teacher ratio in preschool education averages about 24:1.

3.3 Special Education

The Ministry of Social Development is the government agency responsible for supervising educational, clinical, and social services for the handicapped through special centers run by the Ministry itself or, more frequently, by voluntary organizations. The trend is to integrate disabled children into ordinary government or private schools supervised by the Ministry of Education, if their disabilities allow such integration. In general, special education services for the handicapped fall short of the needs.

3.4 Vocational, Technical, and Business Education

Vocational, technical, and business education for the preparation of craftsmen and skilled labor is provided through two-year courses in four types of educational and training institutions: comprehensive schools, specialized vocational schools, training centers, and formal apprenticeship centers. The types of vocational education and training programs available cover the industrial, agricultural, business, nursing, and catering fields. About 30 percent of all students (40% males and 20% females) who complete basic compulsory education at the age of 16 enter vocational education and training institutions. The Ministry of Education plans to raise this percentage to 50 percent by the year 2000.

Vocational education in comprehensive and specialized vocational schools is almost exclusively provided by the Ministry of Education. It is a balanced type of education with practical training, technical theory disciplines, and general education subjects occupying 40 percent, 20 percent, and 40 percent of the study plan respectively. Such education leads to a general examination and hence to higher technical education.

Training centers (which are run by the Ministry of Education, UNRWA, and some voluntary agencies) offer industrial and women's craft programs which are heavily biased to the needs of the profession, with practical training, technical theory disciplines, and general education subjects occupying 60, 20, and 20 percent of the study plan respectively.

Formal apprenticeship schemes are implemented by the Vocational Training Corporation in cooperation with employers. The content of the program is similar to that of the training center referred to earlier. Typically, a trainee would spend half the working week in a training center for general education, technical theory, and basic training and the other half at the employers' premises for supervised on-the-job training.

3.5 Adult and Nonformal Education

The main facilities in the field of adult and nonformal education in Jordan are listed below.

Literacy programs are provided mainly in schools and after working hours by the Ministry of Education and, to a lesser extent, by voluntary organizations. In 1991, the literacy rate for those over 15 years of age was 82 percent. The Ministry of Education plans to raise this rate to 92 percent by the year 2000. The number of adults of the various age groups, who joined literacy classes during the academic year 1989–90 amounted to about 9,000, of whom 88 percent were females.

The Vocational Training Corporation offers a variety of inservice and pre-service training programs for adult workers. Such programs, a good proportion of which are implemented in cooperation with employers, include retraining, upgrading training, and supervisory training. In 1990, about 5,000 participants joined such programs. Universities and community colleges, on the other hand, offer many nonformal training programs through their extension and continuous education departments. The Jordan Institute of Public Administration and the Jordan Institute of Management provide inservice administrative and managerial course to participants from the public and private sectors.

Private centers for adult education are profit-making centers that provide educational and training programs in such fields as business, finance, computers, languages, vocational training, women's crafts, fine arts. In 1990, about 18,000 adults joined such programs in 181 centers all over the country.

Voluntary nongovernment organization (NGO) centers play a role in the provision of special adult and nonformal education programs, especially for women.

Employers' inservice training programs are a wide range of on-the-job and off-the-job training programs, provided by employers in private and public sectors, and are directed to upgrading the skills of their employees.

4. Administrative and Supervisory Structure and Operation

The Ministry of Education has an overall responsibility over the whole system of pretertiary education, including basic (primary and junior-secondary) and secondary education. The responsibilities of the Ministry include the allocation of funds to the various educational activities and directorates within the provisions of the budget, the certification of teachers, the building of government schools, and the designation of curricula and textbooks. The minister of education is assisted by a secretary general who heads an administrative structure comprising a number of "General Directorates" that deal with education, planning and research, finance, administrative affairs, student affairs, examinations, inservice training, cultural and public relations, projects and school buildings, curricula and textbooks, and financial and administrative monitoring. Vocational education is dealt with by an administrative unit within the general directorate of education.

At the local level, a director of education heads each of the 23 directorates of education, which have an overall responsibility for the school system in their areas including inspection.

Private agencies, some of which are affiliated with various religious groups, have a significant role in Jordanian education, despite the relatively small percentage of students in private schools. A private school is normally governed by a board representing the owners. As no financial support is given by the government to such schools they enjoy an autonomous status administratively and financially. Nevertheless, they must have the same curricula and textbooks as in government schools. On the other hand, their educational activities are supervised by the relevant local directorates of education. However, in Amman, a separate directorate of education has been established to look after the affairs of the relatively great number of private schools there.

UNRWA provides free facilities for basic compulsory education, and some vocational and teacher education, to Palestinian refugees. UNRWA schools have the same status as private schools.

The Vocational Training Corporation (VTC) is a public agency that enjoys a degree of administrative and financial autonomy. The VTC board of directors, which is chaired by the minister of labor and appointed by the cabinet, consists of representatives from the Ministry of Labor, the Ministry of Education, the Ministry of Public Works, the Ministry of Planning, the Chamber of Industry, the Engineers Association, the VTC, the Workers Trade Unions, and some individuals in their personal capacity.

The VTC is mainly concerned with that type of vocational education and training undertaken in cooperation with employers. This includes formal apprenticeship, skill training, and upgrading training.

The Ministry of Higher Education, which was first established in Jordan in 1985, is generally responsible for the supervision and development of tertiary (postsecondary) education. Such responsibilities include the allocation of government funding to public universities, the accreditation of private universities, and the approval of specializations and size of enrollment in universities which otherwise enjoy a high degree of autonomy in administrative and academic matters. For community colleges, the responsibilities of the Ministry of Higher Education additionally cover the approval of curricula, general examinations and certification of graduates, and the direct administration of a number of such colleges. Other government agencies, such as the Ministry of Health, the Ministry of Social Development, and the Telecommunication Corporation, administer some specialized community colleges.

A policy of decentralization has given almost full responsibility to local directorates of education in the fields of school supervision, personnel affairs, and staff development and inservice training for teachers. The Ministry of Education still controls curricula and textbooks, school buildings, teacher certification, and fund allocation.

5. Educational Finance

For pretertiary education, the Ministry of Education bears about 74 percent of the educational cost while UNRWA, the private sector, and other government agencies bear about 11 percent, 14.5 percent and 0.5 percent of such costs respectively.

Jordan provides free education for the basic (primary and junior-secondary) and secondary cycles in public and UNRWA schools. Textbooks are distributed free of charge to students in basic education and at cost price to those in secondary education. Private schools, on the other hand, charge fees to cover their expenses.

The sources which finance the educational activities of the Ministry of Education are listed below.

(a) The national budget accounts for about 95 percent of the recurrent expenditure.

(b) Education tax amounts to 3 percent of the estimated rent value of buildings and for about 2 percent of the recurrent expenditure. In practice, the proceeds are spent on land acquisition for school buildings, maintenance and minor construction for schools, and payment of rents.

(c) Nominal contributions by students in Ministry of Education schools account for about 2 percent of the recurrent expenditure. Such contributions are spent mainly on the development of school facilities. In the early 1990s, they varied between US$5–10 per student annually.

(d) Community contributions vary in size and nature, and are usually made by individuals, enterprises, or parent–teacher associations. In practice, such contributions are spent on specific projects, or on the development of school facilities.

(e) Local or foreign loans are frequently utilized for the funding of capital expenditure, especially for funding the construction and equipment of new educational institutions. Foreign loans are usually secured through special agreements, either with international agencies like the World Bank, or with other countries on a bilateral basis.

(f) Local or foreign grants are frequently available in the form of technical assistance or funds for specific educational projects, especially from other countries that have friendly relations with Jordan.

In the 1980s the Ministry of Education budget averaged about 8 percent of the state budge and more than 3 percent of the Gross National Product. The proportion of the state budget allocated to education rose from 7 percent in 1960 to 8.75 percent in 1990. In 1989–90 the student unit costs were JD153 (US$221) for basic and general secondary education, JD298 (US$430) for commercial secondary education, JD419 (US$605) for industrial secondary education and over JD1,000 (over US$1,443) for agricultural and hotel secondary education.

Employers also make a direct contribution to the cost of vocational training. In addition to the payment of reduced wages to apprentices, employers' contributions including the provision of training facilities for on-the-job training and, in the case of big employers, paying the wages of full-time in-plant instructors, as well as providing other facilities.

Tertiary education is, in general, not free. A system of scholarships is available for students of good academic achievement. Student fees in government community colleges and public universities account usually for less than half the educational costs; in private community colleges and universities such fees are designed to cover all costs. Besides student fees, the sources of finance for government community colleges are similar to those referred to above for basic and secondary education. In addition, public universities have a regular income from the special tax of 1 percent on all goods imported into Jordan.

6. Supplying Personnel for the Education System

The 1988 Education Law specified a university degree qualification as a requirement for the teaching profession. For basic compulsory education (Grades 1–10), four-year degree courses that comprise pedagogical education, are available in public universities. Teachers for secondary education (Grades 11–12), on the other hand, are recruited from university graduates in the various relevant disciplines, and are required to obtain a postgraduate diploma or degree in education before or after joining the teaching profession.

To be allowed to take up employment as a teacher, an applicant should be certified as such by the Ministry of Education. Teachers in government schools are civil servants. Accordingly, matters related to their recruitment, classification, promotion, and retirement are subject to the Civil Service Law.

Despite the fact that teachers get a special allowance and other fringe benefits that are not obtained by other civil servants, it is felt that teachers' salaries are not adequate in view of the importance attached to education within the national priorities for development.

In 1990, the number of Jordanian teachers, excluding those in community colleges and universities, was nearly 45,000. The administrative, supervisory, and support staff, on the other hand, amounted to nearly 24,000. The Ministry of Education employed 77 percent of the total workforce in education. UNRWA, private schools, and other government agencies employed 6 percent, 15 percent, and 2 percent respectively. Females constituted about 62 percent of the teaching staff and 44 percent of the administrative staff.

In general, there is a surplus of female graduates who apply to join the teaching profession. The surplus is not as big in the case of males where there are even some minor shortages in English, mathematics, and the physical sciences. Some difficulties are encountered in recruiting teachers for remote and less attractive locations despite extra allowances.

To be in line with the provisions of the new Education Law (1988), a ten-year certification program has been initiated in public universities to upgrade the qualifications of more than 20,000 practicing teachers from a community college diploma to a university degree.

Inservice training for teachers, especially in instructional methodology, is a prominent feature of Ministry of Education activities. Universities provide inservice postgraduate diploma and degree courses for the various categories of teachers and administrators.

7. Curriculum Development and Teaching Methodology

Curriculum and textbook development is a national centralized activity of the Board of Education, which is chaired by the minister of education. It is composed of 18 members representing concerned ministries and agencies, as well as other individuals.

In basic education, which caters for the 6–16 age group, there is a national nondifferentiated curriculum for the whole country. A minor exception is found in the teaching of religion to non-Muslim students, and in prevocational education. In addition to the exact, natural, social, and human sciences, curriculum in basic education includes physical, art, music, prevocational, and computer education.

In (senior) secondary education, which caters for the 16–18 age group, two main educational streams exist. In comprehensive secondary education, there is a common core curriculum, in addition to a specialized academic or vocational parcel of disciplines chosen by the student according to his abilities and inclinations. Common core subjects take up 40 percent of the study plan, and comprise Islamic culture, Arabic language, English language, civics and social science, and general science.

In applied secondary education there is a common core curriculum that occupies 20 percent of the study plan and is derived from the comprehensive stream. In addition, there is a specialized vocational parcel of disciplines aimed at the preparation of skilled workers for industry and women's crafts, in training centers and formal apprenticeship schemes.

All curricula and textbooks are prepared by special committees, whose members are chosen mostly from among university professors, Ministry of Education supervisors (inspectors), and practicing teachers and professionals.

English-as-a-foreign-language is a mandatory subject in Grades 5–12. French is taught in many private schools and a limited number of government schools.

A major development is a complete review of curricula and textbooks, with the objective of enhancing the experimental approach to learning, critical thinking, and catering for individual differences. Such elements have been highlighted by the Education Development Plan, launched in 1987, as in need of development in terms of teaching methodology.

8. The System of Examinations, Promotions, and Certifications

The Jordanian education system is an open one where no national or general examinations exist except after the end of secondary education when a General Secondary Education Certificate Examination is held by the Ministry of Education to monitor the flow to higher education. A school certificate is also issued at the end of secondary education.

Although regulations are issued by the Ministry of Education, defining the general outlines for examinations and promotion, evaluation of students in basic and secondary education is the sole responsibility of the teachers. Repetition of school grades is allowed to a limited degree. A student may repeat twice between Grades 5 and 9 but only in consultation with parents.

One of the challenges faced by the Education Development Plan has been identified as the need for the development of the examination and evaluation system in order to be able to measure more than just the cognitive elements of learning.

9. Educational Assessment, Evaluation, and Research

There are two general directorates concerned with educational assessment, evaluation, and research in the Ministry of Education. The topics they cover include assessment of student achievement, development of evaluation techniques, applied educational research, studies on the economics of education, and publishing relevant statistical information. Research plans are drawn by an Educational Research Committee composed of members from the Ministry of Education and Jordan University.

To enhance educational research in Jordan, a National Center for Educational Research and Development (NCERD) was established in 1989 to conduct field-oriented research, establish a national education database, and provide support for the Educational Development Plan. Furthermore, the colleges of education in three of the Jordanian universities conduct research at master's degree level in the field of education. The main emphasis of research at the beginning of the 1990s included the economics of education, evaluation of educational inputs, and teacher performance.

10. Major Reforms in the 1980s and 1990s

In 1987, a ten-year Education Development Plan was launched after two years of critical review of the education system. The major reforms adopted by the plan included:

(a) extending basic compulsory education from nine to ten years, starting in 1988;

(b) the development of preschool education, both quantitatively and qualitatively;

(c) the radical review of curricula and textbooks for the various educational cycles, with emphasis on activity-oriented disciplines, experimental approach to instruction, critical thinking, and catering for individual differences;

(d) increasing the proportion of students in vocationally oriented streams of (senior) secondary education from 30 percent to 50 percent by the year 2000;

(e) reforming the examination systems, both at school and national levels;

(f) raising the minimum qualification needed for the teaching profession from a community college diploma to a university degree and the necessary pedagogical education.

(g) expanding university education when the ban on private universities was lifted. (The number of universities jumped from four in the late 1980s to ten in the early 1990s.)

11. Major Problems for the Year 2000

Three major problems can be identified that will most likely be faced by the education system by the year 2000. The first is the need to improve the match between the outputs of the education system to the needs of society and national development plans, especially in view of the great surplus and high unemployment of graduates of higher education, and the corresponding shortage of labor at the basic occupational levels. The second is related to teachers, and is mainly an attitudinal one, where the need is felt to improve their skills in modern instructional techniques. The third problem concerns the shortage of resources needed to support the continuous expansion of education, and the need to improve its quality, taking into consideration the relatively high annual rate of population growth.

Bibliography

Central Bank of Jordan *Monthly Statistical Bulletins*. Central Bank of Jordan, Amman

Masri M 1987 *Issues and Models in Vocational Education*. Amman

Masri M, Durra A, Aruri F 1991 *Population and Education (In Jordan)*. National Population Commission and UN Population Fund, Amman

Jordan Ministry of Education (annual) *The Educational Statistics Yearbook*. Ministry of Education, Amman

Jordan Ministry of Higher Education (annual) *The Annual Statistical Report on Higher Education in Jordan*. Ministry of Higher Education, Amman

Jordan Vocational Training Corporation *Annual Report, 1990* (and previous years). Vocational Training Corporation, Amman

Tall A Y 1979 *Education in Jordan (1921–1977)*. National Book Foundation, Islamabad

Kenya

M. Kariuki

1. General Background

Kenya is a country on the East African coast, with a land mass of 582,646 square kilometers. To the north it is bordered by Ethiopia, to the north-west by Sudan, to the west by Uganda, to the south by Tanzania, and to the east by Somalia. It has a coastline of about 400 kilometers along the Indian Ocean. Kenya is a land of contrasts: coastal lowlands to plateaus, highlands to the great Rift Valley to the largest fresh water lake in Africa, Lake Victoria. The Highlands are bisected into the Western and Eastern Highlands by the Rift Valley; the Eastern Highlands comprise Mt. Kenya (the second highest mountain in Africa) and the Aberdare Ranges which rise to 5,200 meters and 2,992 meters respectively and the Western Highlands rise to the highest peak at Mt. Elgon.

While the country enjoys a variety of climates, only 18 percent of the total land mass receives a mean rainfall of 750 millimeters per year. Four-fifths of the country's land comprises arid and semiarid zones with unreliable weather conditions including droughts of up to six months or more every two to four years. In fact 39 percent of the total land mass of the country is too dry for any agricultural activities and can only be used for nomadic pastoralism. The diversity in relief, climate, and availability of water has a direct effect on the economic activities of the people; it affects the people's ability to participate in educational activities and accounts for the existing regional disparities in access to education and retention rates.

According to the 1989 population census, Kenya had a population of 21.4 million people of whom 10.8 million were female. This population was projected to rise to 22.9 million in 1990 with a growth rate of 3.4 percent. The growth rate has declined from 3.8 percent in the 1970s and early 1980s owing to a successful population education program and family planning strategies by both governmental and nongovernmental organizations. However, 50 percent of the population is made up of youth under the age of 15 years. This explains to a large extent the insatiable demand for education and the continuing need to expand educational facilities.

The majority of the Kenyan population is rural, with only 18.6 percent (1990) living in urban areas. There has been, however, a remarkable growth of the urban population at a rate of 4.8 percent, rising from 2.3 million in 1979 to 3.8 million in 1989. Nairobi, the capital city and the seat of government, has a population of 1.3 million and Mombasa, the second largest town and the major port, has 0.46 million people. The rapid population growth in the towns can be attributed to the rural–urban migration brought about by the search for employment by school-leaving youth.

The population distribution by region is determined by geographical factors, with regions like the Central, Nyanza, Western, and parts of Eastern and Rift Valley provinces having high population density while the Coast, North Eastern and the northern parts of the Eastern and the Rift Valley provinces are sparsely populated.

There are about 42 local ethnic/language groups in Kenya and in addition to these there are a number of other languages spoken among the migrant communities, such as Hindu, Gujarati, and Urdu. The education system endeavors to preserve and promote the rich culture, values, and heritage transmitted through these different languages. The language policy states that the mother tongue, within the catchment area of a school, be used as the language of instruction in preschool, the first three years of the primary cycle, and in adult education programs.

English is the official language and the language of instruction from upper-primary school level to the secondary and higher levels of education. Kiswahili, the national language, which is widely used as the *lingua franca* all over the country and the whole of the East African region extending as far as the Eastern part of Zaire, is taught as a compulsory subject and second language at both the primary and secondary levels of the education system.

In the absence of significant mineral resources, agriculture is the largest sector and the mainstay of the economy, accounting for about 27.3 percent of the total GDP and employing about 80 percent of the total labor force. Sixteen percent is employed in the modern urban sector and 5.3 percent is employed in the informal sector. About 0.7 million of those employed in the modern sector work in the public service and government organizations.

At the end of the 1980s, Kenya experienced unfavorable economic conditions with the situation worsening during the 1990s. The deterioration of the economy resulted from both international and domestic factors. The major external factor is the economic recession being experienced the world over. Other factors include the heavy debt burden (about 30 percent of Kenya's foreign exchange earnings are absorbed by debt service payments), and falling prices of primary commodities in the world market which has had a negative effect because of the low prices now fetched by Kenya's traditional foreign exchange earners, coffee and tea. The domestic factors include unreliable weather conditions which have led to food deficits, high costs of imports, a rapidly growing population, a high inflation rate which stood at 19.6 percent in 1991, and high urban unemployment rates of about 16 percent (1988).

The above factors have had a great impact on the economy, especially the agricultural sector whose growth rate in its value added fell from 4.4 percent in 1988 to 1.1 percent in 1991, and the manufacturing sector whose real added value rose by 3.8 percent in 1991 as compared with 5.2 percent in 1990. This has resulted in a decline of the real per capita income to a rate of 0.3 percent in 1991 (US$360 in 1989).

The Republic of Kenya is a multiparty democracy headed by a president who is elected through universal suffrage. It has a legislature, the National Assembly, composed of 188 elected members and 11 national or nominated members. The legislature is the supreme authority in the land and has ultimate responsibility for government. From among the members of parliament, the president appoints ministers who advise the president on issues concerning their ministries and are responsible to the National Assembly for action taken under the authority of the president or vice-president or under their own authority. The Executive consists of the president, vice president, and ministers responsible for initiating and directing national policies. The ministers are responsible for guiding policy decisions and for political matters within their ministries.

Kenya has a single civil service appointed by the Public Service Commission. The civil service is the instrument of the executive authority vested in the president. The country is divided into eight administrative provinces: Central, Coast, Eastern, Nairobi, North Eastern, Nyanza, Rift Valley, and Western. Each province is headed by a provincial commissioner. The provinces are divided into districts and districts are divided into divisions which are further divided into locations which are further subdivided into the smallest administrative unit, the sublocation.

The government of Kenya is committed to ensuring that all the citizens participate meaningfully and effectively in the social, political, and economic development of the nation. Since Independence in 1963, the government has committed itself to developing national unity and ensuring the freedom and human dignity of every individual Kenyan. One of the key factors identified by the government as a vehicle through which it can achieve these objectives and goals is by having an educated population.

2. Politics and the Goals of the Education System

The educational policy and the objectives of national education have been clearly stipulated, since independence, in various national documents and policy papers. Policy guidelines on education are stated in the Constitution, the Kenya African National Union (KANU, the ruling party) manifesto, the Sessional Paper No.10 of 1965 on *African Socialism and its Application to Planning in Kenya*, and the Five Year Development Plans.

As the country evolves, new challenges arise which need to be addressed from time to time. The government of Kenya, owing to the importance it has placed on education has, over the years, set up commissions to examine and re-examine the national education system with a view to making it universal at the first level and making it relevant to the needs of the nation as a whole on the one hand and to those of individual Kenyans on the other. These commissions have produced reports which were consequently used as policy guidelines in the development of education. These important documents include *The Kenya Education Commission Report* (1964), *The Education Act* (1968 and revised 1970), the *Report of the National Committee on Educational Objectives and Policies* (1976), the *Report of the Presidential Working Party on Second University in Kenya* (1981), and *The Report of the Presidential Working Party on Education and Manpower Training for the Next Decade and Beyond* (1988).

The government of Kenya endeavors to provide

education that has a national outlook, is democratic, and which caters for the cultural aspirations and development of its people. The educational objectives are in consonance with the national philosophy, which encompasses the universal principles of political equality; national unity; human dignity; freedom of religion and conscience; social justice; freedom from want, ignorance, and disease; equal opportunity for all citizens regardless of race, religion, or color; equitable distribution of the national income; and the promotion and preservation of the cultural heritage.

The opposition parties' manifestos do not present a major departure from the objectives stipulated in the ruling party's manifesto. The differences that may arise are procedural in nature, touching on the structure of the educational system and curricular

content but not on the general objectives of education as such.

3. The Formal System of Education

3.1 Primary, Secondary, and Tertiary Education

Education in Kenya has undergone tremendous growth and expansion in terms of educational institutions and enrollment at all levels. The physical expansion has been as a result of the commitment of the government to education, thereby making a great investment in educating the youth and the effort of the people through the well-known Kenyan motto of *Harambee* (pulling together). It is through the partnership of government and communities that remarkable growth has been realized. In 1963 there were 6,058 primary schools, 151 secondary schools and one public university. In 1991 there were 17,650 primary schools, 2,647 secondary schools, four public, and 11 private universities. In 1991 there were about 7 million youths enrolled in various educational institutions as compared to about 1 million in 1963.

The 8–4–4 system of education consists of eight years of primary education, four years of secondary education, and four years of tertiary education, depending on the discipline and duration of the particular training. The overall structure of the formal system of education is presented in Fig. 1.

Primary education starts for most children at the age of 6 years. In 1991, there were about 5.5 million children enrolled, as compared with 892,000 in 1963. The national participation rate was 96 percent in 1991 of the total number of children within the age bracket of 6–14, although this rate varies in different provinces and districts. However, only about 69 percent of a given cohort reaches Standard 8, at the end of primary school. Girls make up 48.7 percent of the total enrollment but there are disparities in enrollment by gender between provinces. Most schools at this level are coeducational with the exception of a few private schools. The school day at this level lasts from about three and a half hours for the first two grades to about five hours for the other grades.

Secondary schools are categorized as public and private schools since former Harambee schools, which were financed and managed by local communities, have been taken over by the government in an effort to create equity within the public schools. The total enrollment in 1991 was 614,161—27 percent of the relevant 15–18 year age group—while enrollment in 1963 was 2,647. The growth rate, however, declined to 0.75 percent in 1991. Participation of girls at this level was 44 percent.

There are four public and 11 private universities in the country with an enrollment of 41,674 students in the public universities for the 1991–92 academic year. Only about 2 percent of those joining the formal

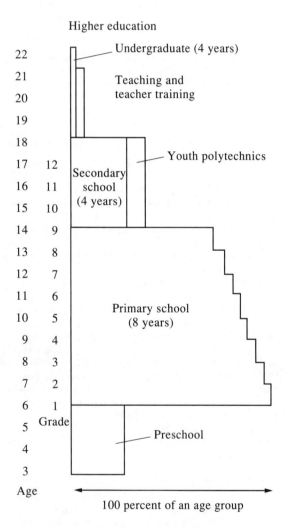

Figure 1
Kenya: Structure of the formal education system

school system make it to higher education because, while there may be more students who have the necessary entry requirements, the universities lack adequate facilities and staff to cope with the demand for education at this level. However this level of education registered the greatest rate of growth in enrollment of 4.9 percent in 1991.

3.2 Preschool Education

Preschool education forms a basic preparatory stage for formal education. It was in this light that the Ministry of Education took over preschool from the Ministry of Culture and Social Services in 1983, with the aim of full integration of this level within the mainstream of the formal system of education. The Ministry of Education is responsible for setting policy guidelines, registering schools, developing curricula, training teachers, and supervising and inspecting the quality and relevance of preschool education.

The Ministry of Education, apart from expanding professional and administrative services, has established, with assistance from donor agencies and international nongovernmental agencies, the National Center for Early Childhood Education (NACECE) at the Kenya Institute of Education. The Center coordinates the work of 18 district centers for early childhood education (DICECE) and 10 associate DICECEs as well as providing inservice training for DICECE staff and providing guidance on early childhood education.

In 1991 there were 17,650 preprimary schools in the country, enrolling about 25 percent of the 6 million children estimated to be within the 3–6 age group. The financing and management of the preprimary schools is a partnership between the central government, local authorities, local communities, religious organizations, and individuals. About 70 percent of preprimary schools are financed and managed by parents' associations while the government provides professional and administrative support.

3.3 Special Education

In 1968, the government produced the Sessional Paper No.5 on Special Education which formed the framework for government policy on the education of the disabled child. This was followed by the establishment of a rehabilitation center in Nairobi in 1971 and the creation of a Special Education Section within the Ministry of Education.

In 1980 the president launched a program for the disabled, and declared 1980 as the national year of the disabled in preparation for the UN Decade for the Disabled. This program aimed at not only raising funds for the disabled but also at focusing attention on the plight of handicapped people by sensitizing and creating awareness in the Kenyan public. It also had as an objective stepping up efforts to provide rehabilitation and training programs, and removing

prejudice and discrimination against disabled people.

In 1984 the Ministry of Education established 25 educational assessment and resource centers (EARs). This number rose in 1988 to cover 41 districts. The role of the EARs is: to provide educational assessment, peripatetic and resource services; to identify handicaps in children at an early age; and to provide professional advice to parents and guardians on their rehabilitation and integration.

The Kenya Institute of Special Education (KISE) was established to offer training of teachers, to carry out research and to act as an advisory center. It is also involved in the production of teaching aids, assessment of children with disabilities, and the development of programs for independent living.

In 1991 there were 95 special institutions/units in the country, with an enrollment of 8,808 handicapped children. The participation rate of the disabled in education is only about 6 percent. There is a need to carry out a national survey for updating data and information on the various types of disabilities and the proportion of school-age children among the handicapped for improving coverage in education for this category of children and for establishing appropriate intervention measures.

The policy of the government is, whenever possible, to integrate handicapped children within the normal schools. As a result 210 units have been established within ordinary primary schools. This has been possible especially for the visually impaired and the physically handicapped who have been able to go to normal schools, especially at the secondary and postsecondary level institutions.

Provision of vocational rehabilitation for the handicapped has taken place at the Industrial Rehabilitation Center and at the rural vocational rehabilitation centers. Artisan courses are offered and graduates of these institutes are provided with tool kits to assist them in self-employment. Similar programs are offered by local and international nongovernment, and religious organizations.

3.4 Vocational, Technical, and Business Education

The reform of educational curricula at the primary and secondary levels introduced a vocational/technical element in an effort to relate education to the world of work and also to provide prevocational skills in preparation for further training.

Postschool training is also offered in various institutions for different cadres. The youth polytechnics are attended by primary school leavers and some secondary school dropouts. The institutes of technology (formerly known as Harambee institutes of technology) and the technical training institutes provide a higher level of instruction for secondary school leavers. The training at the institutes of technology is predominantly at the skill/craft level but more and more courses are now being offered at the technician level. Higher level training which caters for secondary school leavers is offered at the national polytechnics, which also provide training for more specialized institutions and industries.

Government provides instructors as well as grants-in-aid to institutes of technology based on student numbers. Most of the capital equipment continues to be provided by foreign donors while recurrent costs are shared between the government and the communities. The trainees pay a certain fee annually. The national polytechnics recruit trainees from among apprentices who are sponsored by their employers. Students attending courses in business, management, and other nontechnical courses are self-sponsored. The government pays the tutors' salaries and funds recurrent expenditure.

Business and industry have a role to play in technical training since they are the main consumers of the products from the training institutions. The National Industrial and Vocational Training Act introduced a training levy which employers have to pay as a way of sharing training costs. The Directorate of Industrial Training (DIT) liaises between the government and industry. A number of industries and private companies have established training programs and institutions for their own employees.

In addition to the above-mentioned institutions, 583 youth polytechnics, 20 institutes of technology, 17 technical institutes, and 2 national polytechnics fall under the Ministry of Technical Training and Applied Technology. Different ministries have training institutions for their personnel in specialized fields. There are also 16 training centers under the National Youth Service which are financed and managed by the Office of the President.

3.5 Adult and Nonformal Education

One of the major goals of the government is to provide basic education to all Kenyans, and while efforts are being made to universalize primary education, there are also special courses for the adult illiterate population. According to a survey carried out in 30 rural districts in 1988, about 46 percent of the population aged 10 years and above were found to be illiterate, while 54 percent of the total population of women in Kenya is illiterate. While one of the main objectives of the government is to eradicate adult illiteracy it has also been conviction of the government that an educated people would be more productive and better informed and hence participate more effectively in national development.

Adult Education programs broadly include programs in adult literacy, occupational skill training, youth programs with educational purposes, and community programs. Nonformal education is coordinated by the Department of Adult Education which was established in 1979 in the Ministry of Culture and Social Services. Previously the Board of Adult Education had been established through an Act of Parliament in 1966, to act as the policy body on all matters relating to adult education. The Department of Adult Education works in close collaboration with nongovernmental organizations in the implementation of nonformal education.

Adult education is offered to people who are over the age of 16 years and not engaged in continuous full-time formal education and training. There is, however, an increasing number of younger children who have dropped out of the school system participating in the nonformal education program. In 1991 there was a total of 128,107 adults enrolled in the program, with a total number of 7,140 teachers.

The different programs include literacy, postliteracy, skills training for the youth employed within the informal sector (popularly known as *jua kali*), and functional literacy for adults and for street children. One of the most successful programs run by a nongovernmental organization is the Undugu (brotherhood) Society which has an educational and training program for the rehabilitation of street boys.

4. Administrative and Supervisory Structure and Operation

The Ministry of Education provides administrative and professional services in education at the national, provincial, and district levels. The minister of education is the political head, the permanent secretary, the overall administrative head, and the accounting officer of the Ministry, while the director is responsible for all professional matters in education. In the field, there are provincial education officers, district and municipal education officers, and divisional education officers at the divisional level.

The management of professional services within the Directorate of Education involves the administration, supervision, and inspection of educational programs; development and implementation of various curricula; and development and production of programmed materials, in collaboration with the relevant institutions and departments of the Ministry.

Within the Directorate of Education there are various sections which are responsible for the administration of the different levels of education; preschool education, primary education, secondary education, and university education. There is also the Inspectorate, headed by the Chief Inspector of Schools, which is responsible for curriculum supervision and inspection of schools.

The introduction of the District Focus Strategy for Rural Development (1983) by the government initiated a decentralization program for more efficiency in the provision of services and more participation in decision-making at the grass-roots level. The district education boards which had been established earlier, were to work in close collaboration with the district development committees (DDCs). The role of the district education board was to provide advice in the development and management of education in their respective districts.

The management of public secondary schools and training institutions is vested in boards of governors appointed by the minister of education. Their main functions include the development of the institutions and the day-to-day management of the institutions and the employment of nonteaching staff. At the primary school level, school committees are appointed to manage and develop primary schools and ensure the maintenance of high standards of education and discipline. These committees are made up of members from local communities and parents.

Parent–teacher associations (PTAs) are playing an increasingly important role in the development of both primary and secondary schools in collaboration with governing bodies and school administrators. Their contribution has been significant especially in the provision of physical facilities, equipment, textbooks and, in some cases, teachers' houses. Different sponsors of educational institutions, mainly from the various religious denominations, who contribute toward financing the development of education, have a role to play in the management of these institutions mainly through representation in the management committees and boards of governors.

Public universities, while financed by the Ministry of Education which is also responsible for general policy guidelines for the institutes of higher learning are, to a large extent semiautonomous bodies. Each one of them was established through an act of parliament and has got its own charter. The university councils are policy decision-making bodies while the senates are responsible for the day-to-day management and maintenance of academic excellence in the universities. The President of the Republic is the chancellor of all the public universities, and each university is headed by a vice-chancellor.

The Commission for Higher Education was established by the Universities Act of 1985, for the coordination and harmonization of university education and to advise on the establishment of universities and for accreditation. The role and functions of the Commission, however, sometimes overlap with those of the individual universities.

5. Educational Finance

The expansion of the education sector has been financed largely through public funds and, as a result, expenditure on education has more than doubled since 1963. The increase in government expenditure on education has hardly kept pace with the high rate of population growth and the subsequent demand for education. In 1963–64, the recurrent expenditure on education was Sh135,670,000 (US$2.1 million)

or 22.5 percent of the national recurrent budget, while Sh9,000,200 (US$137,000) or 3.2 percent of the development budget was spent on education. The annual national budget allocation rose from 10 percent at independence to 27 percent in 1990–91 for both recurrent and development expenditure (or 40% of the total recurrent vote). The public and private sectors combined spend about 9 percent of GDP on education and training. Owing to an unprecedented expansion at the university and tertiary level there has been a higher budgetary allocation to higher education especially in the development vote. In 1990–91 government spending on higher education was 23 percent as compared with 17 percent and 47 percent in secondary and primary education respectively.

Allocation to preprimary level accounted for only 0.12 percent of the total recurrent expenditure while the parents, communities, local authorities, and private organizations were responsible for development. The government per pupil expenditure for primary schools, in 1989, was 44 percent of a total of Sh2,100 (US$32) and 27 percent of Sh7,500 (US$115) for secondary school, while it accounted for more than 60 percent of the unit cost—Sh72,500 (US$1,108) per year at the university level. For the teacher training colleges and the polytechnics, government expenditure was more than 80 percent of Sh13,000 (US$199) and Sh14,000–38,000 (US$214–581) which was the cost per student.

For primary and secondary school education there is a large contribution by parents and local communities. At the university level there has been, since 1974, a students loan scheme for funding nontuition expenses. A form of cost-sharing was also introduced at the university in 1991–92 requiring students to pay a nominal fee of Sh6000 (US$92) per year.

Private contributions are in the form of fees paid in the private schools and in the form of scholarships for outstanding students in the national examinations especially at the end of primary school. There are also contributions from private firms and organizations for the development of schools through the Harambee Funds Drives.

6. Supplying Personnel for the Education System

In 1991 the total number of personnel employed within the education sector was 250,900. Out of these 208,467 were teachers for the primary and secondary sectors with primary schools having a total of 173,370 teachers and secondary schools 35,097. At primary and secondary level 37 percent of the teaching force is female while 90 percent of the teachers at the preprimary level is female. The pupil–teacher ratio at the primary and secondary levels were 31:1 and 17:1 respectively while the percentage of untrained teachers was 25.5 and 36.5. There has been a shortage of teachers in the technical subjects as well as mathematics and the sciences at all levels and in other specialized subjects like music and foreign languages.

The training of teachers is carried out at different institutions and uses different delivery methods for the different categories of teachers. A two-year inservice training program comprises two phases: the residential courses offered during school holidays and distance education (radio and correspondence) for both preprimary school teachers and adult education teachers. Primary school teachers have a two-year preservice programme which is run in 20 public and 4 private teacher colleges. An inservice training program is also offered for serving untrained teachers. Trainees for the primary teachers colleges are recruited from among secondary school graduates. The preprimary, adult, and primary school teacher training curricula is developed at the Kenya Institute of Education. Secondary school teacher training is offered at two different levels: a diploma program run in four colleges and bachelors degree program in education in the faculties of education of the universities. Those entering the diploma colleges and the universities were previously A-level certificate holders and the training program lasted two and four years for the diploma course and degree program respectively. With the intake from the 8–4–4 system the duration of the training has been increased by one year.

Teachers and teacher trainers for special education are trained at the Kenya Institute of Special Education. The Kenya Technical Teachers College trains teachers for technical and business education. Courses at this institute are becoming more diversified to cater for the growing demand for technical and business teachers by offering programs for artisans and technicians to train them to teach at different institutions. The college also offers part-time courses in different skills for professional and personal advancement in the evenings and on Saturdays. Teacher trainers (except for preprimary teachers who are trained through an inservice program run by the National Center For Early Childhood Education) are trained at Kenyatta University where they pursue a masters degree in education.

Teacher trainees are evaluated and assessed throughout their training through college-based examinations, microteaching and teaching practice and the end of the course examination. Posttraining assessment is conducted by school inspectors particularly for purposes of evaluation for promotion. Except for specialized subjects, inservice and training workshops, and seminars are not regularly organized for all categories of teachers.

7. Curriculum Development and Teaching Methodology

The Kenya Institute of Education is the national curriculum development center charged with the responsibility of preparing national curricula for preprimary, primary and secondary education, teacher education, technical institutes, and adult education. The universities, through their senates, develop their own curricula. Curriculum development for the educational and training institutions is a participatory process. Participants are drawn from relevant subject inspectors, teachers, representatives from the Kenya National Examinations Council, curriculum specialists from the Institute of Education and interested parties from government and nongovernment organizations. The Steering Committee, chaired by the director of education, formulates broad policy guidelines and objectives for each syllabus. The subject panels, chaired by their respective subject inspectors, then design the initial syllabuses. The course panels, whose chair is the chief inspector of schools, review curricula designed by subject panels and make recommendations to the Academic Board, again chaired by the Director of Education, which approves the curriculum for implementation.

The Kenya Institute of Education is also the institution in charge of preparation and development of textbooks. This is also done in collaboration with the Inspectorate and uses a participatory approach by using experts in the various subjects drawn from schools and other educational institutions. The teaching and learning materials are tried out in pilot schools and evaluation is carried out after which necessary modifications are made and manuscripts are approved for publication. The manuscripts are then published by the Ministry's two publishing houses: The Kenya Literature Bureau and the Jomo Kenyatta Foundation. Books published commercially are scrutinized and approved for use in schools by the Academic Board.

At the primary school level, all children cover a common curriculum nationally. This includes languages (English and Kiswahili), mathematics, science, agriculture, social studies, art and craft, music, and physical education. At the primary level these subjects are taught by a general classroom teacher except for the upper classes where there are specialist teachers.

The secondary school curriculum is more diversified. The main disciplines are: communication, mathematics, science, humanities, applied education, and physical education. The students are examined in eight subjects of which English, Kiswahili, mathematics, biological and physical sciences, geography, history, and government are compulsory. Students must also offer a subject in applied education and/or religious education. Foreign languages are mainly introduced in the secondary schools. The more popular languages are French and German. Arabic is taught in some schools and at the University of Nairobi. Other languages include Gujarati and Hindi which are taught in a few schools.

Curriculum supervision is the responsibility of

the Inspectorate of Schools but evaluation of the curriculum is also ensured through examinations.

8. The System of Examinations, Promotions, and Certifications

Promotion from one class to the next at both the primary and secondary levels is automatic but pupils may be advised to repeat a class if their performance is not satisfactory. The pupils' performance is evaluated through continuous assessment in class work and tests. There are end of term and end of year examinations which are normally school-based. In some cases these examinations are prepared at the zone, division, or district level for evaluation of the schools' performance and for comparison purposes. At the end of this cycle children sit for the Kenya Certificate of Primary Education (KCPE) which is also used for selecting students to move to the next cycle. Only about 50 percent of those completing the primary cycle enter into secondary schools which is only 27 percent of the relevant age group. At the end of the secondary cycle students sit for the Kenya Certificate of Secondary Education (KCSE) which is used for selecting students for university education and other postsecondary institutions.

The external examinations are very competitive, since their results determine a pupil's promotion to the next level and for the primary school graduates it determines what kind of secondary schools they enter. Some of the problems arising from this mode of examination include (a) repetition of grades in the hope that candidates will attain better results, (b) dropouts owing to failure to achieve, and (c) the tendency for teachers to teach and drill children specifically for the national examination. Although the 8–4–4 system was supposed to move away from an examination-oriented system toward the vocationalization of the curriculum, with more emphasis on continuous assessment, the examination system remains the same and teachers continue with their old methods of teaching.

9. Educational Assessment, Evaluation, and Research

The Kenya National Examination Council is the body responsible for management of examinations and certification for primary and secondary education and for postschool training institutions except for universities and diploma teachers colleges which administer their own examinations. The Kenya National Examinations Council operates through various committees comprising specialists and professionals from the Ministry of Education, Kenya Institute of Education, universities, and relevant bodies in the public and private sectors. The subject panels which

report to the relevant professional committees deal with the development of examinations, criteria and method of awarding certificates, as well as desirable changes in the syllabuses.

Research in education is mainly carried out at the Kenya Institute of Education (KIE), The Institute of Development Studies (IDS) of the Nairobi University, the Bureau of Educational Research (BER) at Kenyatta University, in addition to other research activities carried out in the faculties of education in the various universities. The Kenya National Examinations Council has a research unit which is concerned with issues of assessment and evaluation. Recent research activities have focused on nonformal and adult education, the implementation of the 8–4–4 education system, and women's education. There are still gaps in research on relevance and quality of education, education and the world of work, wastage and repetition, education for the pastoralists and nomadic groups, factors affecting the education of women, and higher education.

10. Major Reforms in the 1980s and 1990s

At independence Kenya inherited a racially segregated educational system that catered for three major racial groups at different levels. Education for Africans was initially left in the hands of missionaries but later, as Kenyans fought for their independence, formal education was viewed as an important tool toward liberation and Africans mobilized resources and built up their own schools. One of the major tasks of the Kenya government at independence was to abolish the segregated education systems and the racially designed educational programs and to assume central responsibility for education at all levels by removing responsibility from various communal and religious bodies who managed the segregated system. The government introduced measures to facilitate national unity in a pluralistic society, expand educational opportunities to ensure access and equity in the provision of basic education, and to expand education at the tertiary level to meet the labor needs of a newly independent nation. There was also the need to revise the curriculum to make it more relevant to the national education objectives.

With the phenomenal growth of primary and secondary schools within the first two decades after independence, issues of quality and relevance became a major concern for the government especially because of growing unemployment among the secondary school leavers. The education system was largely to blame since the curriculum and general orientation prepared youth for white-collar jobs in the urban and administrative centers which resulted in a growing rural–urban migration of youth. In an effort to remedy the situation, the Ministry of Education introduced a major structural reform in the education system in

1984, following recommendations of the *Report of The Presidential Working Party on the Second University* (1981). A new 8–4–4 system was introduced to replace the previous education structure which was based on the British education system with students sitting for the O- and A-level examinations at the end of the fourth and sixth forms respectively (11th and 13th school years).

The new education system introduced a restructuring of education and training with a view to improving curriculum content with greater orientation toward technical education and moving away from education being examination centered. The new system provides for vocationalization of the curriculum to enhance the development of vocational skills and to impart attitudes of self-reliance and national development. The main objective of the 8–4–4 system was to make education more relevant and responsive to the economic needs of the country and develop relevant skills for further training and/or self-employment.

11. Major Problems for the Year 2000

One of the major commitments of the government is to ensure universal primary education (UPE) and eradicate adult illiteracy by the year 2000 in an effort to provide basic education for all. This is a major challenge to the government, taking into consideration the high rate of population growth, budgetary constraints, and debt repayment pressures which have affected the country's ability to finance education adequately, a sector whose recurrent expenditure has risen to 40 percent of the total government recurrent expenditure. To attain UPE by the year 2000, the growth rate of enrollment would have to be increased from its present level of 2.25 percent a year to 3.8 percent and appropriate measures would have to be taken against factors that militate against the provision of basic education for all. Two major factors are the high wastage rate (especially at the primary school level) and high attrition rate in the adult education program.

The other major issue that the government is addressing is improvement of the quality of education especially at the primary school level. There is a lack of adequate facilities, equipment, teachers, and a low pupil–textbook ratio; these are a result of the tremendous growth of the education sector and could compromise the quality of education. The untrained teacher factor still plagues the education sector at all levels. The government has addressed itself seriously to this problem and hopes to have all untrained teachers in the primary schools trained by 1997 through the expansion of existing training facilities and no recruitment of new school leavers into the training colleges until all untrained teachers have received formal training. The fact that there is growing unemployment among school leavers (especially from the primary and secondary levels) creates pressure on the government to expand higher education and acts as a deterrent to parents sending their children to school. The issue of the mismatch between the educational curriculum and the demands of industry and also between the trained workforce and actual requirements in various professions and occupations still poses a big problem of the relevance of the present vocationalized curriculum and future orientation of the curriculum to reduce the imbalance between education and the world of work.

The government also faces the challenge of ensuring provision of education to disadvantaged groups, which include girls and women in some cultures, street children, children with disabilities, children in arid areas, and increasingly, children of refugees. The rapid expansion of higher education also poses a problem of quality and relevance of education to the labor market. There will be a need to increase and strengthen the existing research capacity and improve financing in this area, which is crucial for enhancing educational development.

References

Government of Kenya 1964 *Kenya Education Report*. Government Printing Office, Nairobi

Government of Kenya 1968 (revised 1970) *The Education Act*. Government Printing Office, Nairobi

Government of Kenya 1968 *Special Education*. Seasonal Paper No. 5. Government Printing Office, Nairobi

Kenyan African National Party (KANU) 1965 *African Socialism and its Application to Planning in Kenya* Paper No. 10. KANU, Nairobi

National Committee on Educational Objectives and Policies 1976 *Report*. National Committee on Educational Objectives and Policies, Nairobi

Presidential Working Party 1981 *Report on the Second University in Kenya*. Presidential Working Party, Nairobi

Presidential Working Party 1988 *Report on Education and Manpower Training for the Next Decade and Beyond*. Presidential Working Party, Nairobi

Further Reading

Government of Kenya 1991 *Development and Employment in Kenya. A Strategy for Transformation of the Economy*. Government Printing Office, Nairobi

Government of Kenya 1992 *Development of Education 1991 to 1992*. Government Printing Office, Nairobi

Government of Kenya 1992 *Economic Survey*. Government Printing Office, Nairobi

Government of Kenya 1990, 1991 *Statistical Abstracts* Government Printing Office, Nairobi

UNESCO 1992 *National Report for the UNESCO International Conference on Education, September 1992*. UNESCO, Paris

Kiribati

J. N. Johnstone

1. General Background

Kiribati was formerly joined with what is now Tuvalu as a British colony called the Gilbert and Ellice Islands Protectorate. Kiribati obtained its Independence in 1979. The delay for Kiribati resulted because of a protracted legal battle with people from the Island of Banaba (formerly Ocean Island) who claimed damages and unpaid royalties from the British Phosphate Commission.

Kiribati consists of three groups of islands. The main group is the Gilberts (17 islands), located about the equator and about 174° longitude. Moving in an easterly direction, one comes to the Phoenix group (8 islands) lying about 4° south of the equator and about 174° east, on the other side of the International Date Line from the Gilberts. Finally there are the Line Islands (8 islands) which are about 5° north of the equator and about 157° east. Hence Kiribati spans a large expanse of the Pacific Ocean from north of New Zealand to South of Hawaii.

The 33 coral atolls in the three groups are all fairly small although their total land area is 719 square kilometers. Christmas Island (in the Line Islands group) is the largest coral atoll in the world at 388 square kilometers. The dispersion of the Kiribati islands along the equator for about 4,000 kilometers gives the country a very large EEZ of over 3.5 million square kilometers. Most of the islands are less than 1.5 meters above sea level although one island—Banaba—has a point which is 84 meters above sea level. That island had very significant phosphate deposits. The capital of Kiribati is Tarawa which is located in the Gilberts group.

The country has a population of about 72,000 people. Most of these live in the Gilberts group, especially in Tarawa which accounts for over one-third of the total population. A significant number work overseas in Nauru, Tuvalu, or elsewhere in the Pacific or on ships. The population density is about 100 people per square kilometer as an average across the country. However it is about 1,600 persons per square kilometer in Tarawa itself. Urbanization is about 32 percent. The literacy rate is estimated at about 90 percent.

The I-Kiribati are generally described as Micronesian ethnically although it is believed the original inhabitants were Melanesian. There are also strong ancestral links to Samoa dating from about the thirteenth century. The local and official language (Gilbertese or I-Kiribati) is a Micronesian dialect which is common to all the islands. There are also a number of people who speak Tuvaluan because of the original links with Tuvalu. English is commonly spoken in Tarawa and understood in all government offices. It is not so commonly spoken on the outer islands. In schools, students begin to learn English by at least Grade 5 although some begin from Grade 1.

Development in Kiribati is constrained by a lack of natural resources and a narrow productive base. It also suffers from its isolation from potential markets, poor soil, lack of adequate human resources and a scattered population. The major industries are copra, handicrafts, clothing, and fish. About 80 percent of the economically active population are engaged in the traditional or subsistence sector. Seaweed is becoming an important product for export and is becoming a substitute for copra farming. There are about 1,200 sailors working overseas on ships (mainly German) and their remittances together with fees from fishing licences are the major sources of revenue. Prior to Independence, the Kiribati economy also depended heavily on the export of phosphate rocks from Banaba. Revenue from this single source accounted for 50 percent of government revenue and 80 percent of export earnings. Mining has, however, now ceased.

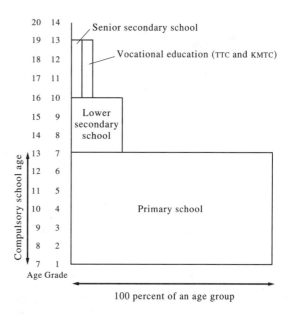

Figure 1

Kiribati: Structure of the formal education system

Table 1
Summary of basic education statistics, Kiribati 1990

	Primary	Secondary	Technical/ Vocational
No. of Students	13,860	3,005	395
No. of Teachers	486	192	—
No. of Institutions	110	6	3

The government of the Republic of Kiribati has been very stable since Independence. It has a 41-member unicameral legislature elected for a four-year term. The two main political parties are the Gilbertese National Party and the Christian Democratic Party. The president, Teatao Teannaki, was elected in 1991. He succeeded Ieremia Tabai who had been president since Independence and who is now secretary of the important regional organization—the Forum Secretariat—in Fiji. The vice president is Taomati Iuta. There are not more than eight ministers in the Cabinet.

2. Politics and the Goals of the Education System

There was no change to basic education policy when Independence was conferred. Hence the same policy as was evolved in 1975 continues to apply. In summary, this policy states that government must:

(a) provide free and compulsory education to all primary school children;

(b) have a single unified system of primary education;

(c) have a set of "community high schools" which provides a rural-oriented curriculum;

(d) provide sufficient places in secondary education to meet the needs of the economy.

3. The Formal System of Education

3.1 Primary, Secondary, and Tertiary Education

Figure 1 outlines the structure of the formal education in Kiribati while the key statistics on enrollments and resources in the major education sectors are provided in Table 1.

Primary education now provides seven years of schooling and is compulsory. There are 110 government-provided primary schools throughout the islands, enrolling 13,860 students and employing 486 teachers. There are also two private primary schools run by the Seventh Day Adventist Church and the

Church of God. The government has offered to absorb these schools into its system if the churches so wish but so far the offer has been declined.

The secondary system consists of seven years. There are three years at the junior secondary level with up to four more years required before achieving university entrance. There are six academic secondary schools throughout the country. All are coeducational and provide boarding facilities. They are intended to provide technical, professional, and administrative training. The schools are: the Catholic Senior College on North Tarawa, the Catholic Junior College on Abaiang, the Hiram Bingham High School on Beru, the Seventh Day Adventist School on Abemama, the South Tarawa-Moroni High School (Mormon), and the King George V (boys section) and Elaine Bernacchi (girls section) School on Tarawa. All community high schools have been closed and reclassified as either primary schools or academic high schools.

Prior to 1980 the system had a six-year lower primary course with a three-year upper primary stage. Students had to pass an examination at the end of Grade 6 to proceed to an academic secondary school. Very few children—approximately 8 percent—passed this examination and entered the secondary levels, while most of the rest stayed on to the upper primary levels which provided a village-oriented curriculum. The academic secondary schools were not considered to be offering education which was relevant to Kiribati development. Hence in 1975, a review recommended the primary cycle be limited to six years with a three-year community high school to follow it and to parallel the academic secondary stream. A pilot scheme involving four schools began in 1977. Later investigation showed that these schools were not viewed by parents or students in terms of their stated objectives but were considered to be comparable to academic schools. Indeed a statement to that effect was even made in Parliament, supporting a motion to provide more community high schools.

School fees were charged prior to 1983 however thereafter, fees were abolished except for students in South Tarawa and in the Line Islands.

Higher education is offered in Kiribati through the Extension Center of the University of the South Pacific. Links to the main campus in Fiji are through satellite while radio telephones allow people in the outer islands to communicate to the USP Center in Tarawa. Various courses can be studied in this way. Most students, however, travel overseas to obtain tertiary education. Most go to the University of the South Pacific, New Zealand, or Australia on aid-funded scholarships.

3.2 Preschool Education

There are no preschools operated by the Ministry of Education. There are, however, several preschools operated by private interests; one in Tarawa mainly for children of expatriates, and some small organizations provided by the churches.

3.3 Special Education

There was no provision for special education in Kiribati in 1993 although the issue is being debated in various ways. Lack of adequate finance is a critical problem.

3.4 Vocational, Technical, and Business Education

Vocational and technical training is provided by the Tarawa Teachers College in the form of full-time, part-time, and evening courses. A wide range of courses is on offer from the traditional trades courses through secretarial studies, accountancy, and clerical courses, to basic computing courses. For various reasons, there has been a significant decline in enrollments over past years from 659 in 1983 to 362 in 1985, and 226 in 1990.

There is also a Kiribati Marine Training Center which offers one-year courses in basic seamanship (e.g., OS-Deck, OS-Engine and OS-Catering) as well as various short courses (e.g., firefighting and life-boat). Students must have passed at least the Form 3 examination. Many students have graduated from the school with over 1,000 I-Kiribati employed at present on overseas ships.

3.5 Adult and Nonformal Education

There is little provision for adult and nonformal education. The main possibility is the University of the South Pacific Extension Center from which a variety of courses can be taken. As noted above, the Tarawa Technical Institute also offers evening courses. There are also courses offered from time to time by various agencies, including the churches. These courses cover a variety of areas from small business operation to family planning.

4. Administrative and Supervisory Structure and Operation

Education is administered by the Minister of Education who appoints a permanent secretary. There are the usual divisions of responsibility and supervision. Administration is centralized with little authority given to individual schools.

5. Educational Finance

Finance for education is provided by the government, by the churches, and by parents. Contributions have also been made by aid donors, especially for some of the capital works. In 1993, education accounted for about 25 percent of the national budget. Government also supplies most of the recurrent funds required for the church-operated schools.

A significant proportion of government revenue comes from the Revenue Equalization Reserve Fund which was established during the colonial administration out of phosphate revenue. The aim of this fund was to assist fund expenditures after income from phosphate ceased. The falling interest rates throughout the world, led to reduced income from the investments thus severe constraints have been placed on the Kiribati annual budget.

6. Supplying Personnel for the Education System

Basic primary level teacher training is the responsibility of the Tarawa Teachers College. Both preservice and inservice courses are offered. Enrollments satisfy the demand and have steadily increased since the early 1980s. Entrance to the College requires at least three years of secondary education to have been completed successfully.

Secondary teacher education is conducted overseas. Students receive aid scholarships especially to study at the University of the South Pacific, in Australia, or in New Zealand. A number of teachers, Teachers College staff and ministry personnel have been supplied by the United Kingdom, in particular through Overseas Development Aid (ODA). Other donors have also supplied some personnel from time to time. The supply will diminish substantially in the 1993–95 period as the United Kingdom in particular withdraws its funding for such appointees.

7. Curriculum Development and Teaching Methodology

Curriculum development is the responsibility of the Ministry of Education through its Curriculum Development Center. Subject organizers are appointed and convene subject panels who revise material, and produce and test new versions. This pattern is the same for both primary and secondary levels. Curricula in all subjects have been revised and improved incrementally for several years. On occasions, assistance has been received from aid donors who have assigned academics mainly from Australian institutions or the University of the South Pacific for short-term visits. By 1993, however, there had not been a comprehensive revision of the curriculum for a number of years.

While the community high schools operated, considerable confusion existed as to what purpose they served and therefore which curriculum should be followed. The minister of education stated that the schools were "to teach children or help them to know the Kiribati culture and domestic duties." The Ministry stressed the nonacademic character of the schools and their existence was to provide an alternative to academic schools. Parents, however, criticized the teaching of traditional skills, claiming this teaching was better done by parents than schools. With the government all but abandoning the community high school concept in 1980, the pilot scheme was closed and the academically oriented curriculum continued.

8. The System of Examinations, Promotions, and Certifications

There is a National Entrance Examination conducted at the end of the primary cycle to select students for the secondary schools. Competition is intense because of the limited number of places available. Pass rates are about 20 percent.

At the end of Form 3 there is an examination leading to the award of the National Junior Certificate. One achievement consequent upon obtaining this certificate is that a person is then eligible to join the Kiribati civil service. About one-third of Form 3 students are able to proceed to senior secondary school studies although they may have to change school.

At the end of Form 6, students can sit the School Certificate examinations set by Cambridge University or the Pacific Senior Secondary Certificate. The latter examination is prepared by Kiribati authorities in association with the South Pacific Board of Educational Assessment (SPBEA) in Fiji. The students who pass this examination then have one more year to complete—the University of the South Pacific Foundation Year—before entering university. The USP is phasing out the Foundation Year, so alternative arrangements for accreditation will have to be made possibly involving SPBEA.

9. Educational Assessment, Evaluation, and Research

Kiribati has not participated in any international research studies to assess the educational provision in the country. Nor has it attempted its own assessment directly, although some individuals—particularly those who are from or associated with the Teachers College—have attempted some assessment in particular subjects in an ad hoc way.

10. Major Reforms in the 1980s and 1990s

There has been little attempt to introduce major reforms into the education system in the 13 years since Independence. The fact that the pre-Independence aims for education are still quoted—despite the limited applicability of some aspects—reflects the prevailing attitude of maintaining the status quo.

The major experiment in Kiribati education has been with the community high school concept which was discussed in previous sections. That experiment was a practical demonstration of the frequently held educational planning debate about academic versus vocational schools. It is unlikely that any additional major reforms will be planned in the 1990s especially given the tight budget constraints.

11. Major Problems for the Year 2000

Kiribati education will face a continuation of its present problems in the year 2000. It is unlikely that all children hoping to receive even junior secondary education will be able to enter such a school. Places will be limited because of the limited funds required for capital works. Job prospects will continue to be few.

The major problem facing I-Kiribati educators will be the relevance of the education provided at the primary and secondary levels. As there are no real prospects for the development of major enterprises—except perhaps for a site in Christmas Island in the Line Islands group—I-Kiribati children will continue to be educated both for life in a subsistence economy and for the possibility of joining an elite who will work in a modern sector. The question of the purpose of education is vexatious and not addressed fully. The traditional need for full discussions to be held about most issues in Kiribati might mean that the answers to this question will remain unclarified in the year 2000.

Bibliography

Hindson C E 1985 Kiribati: The search for educational alternatives in a Pacific microstate. *Int. J. Educ. Dev.* 5(4): 289–94
Ministry of Finance 1987, 1992 *National Development Plans (6th Plan 1987–1991 and 7th Plan 1992–1996)*. Government Printing Division, Tarawa
Pacific Islands Year Book 1992 Pacific Publications, Sydney.
Pollard S J 1987 *The Viability and Vulnerability of a Small Island State, Islands/Australia*. Working paper 87/14. National Centre for Development Studies, Canberra.
University of the South Pacific 1979 *Kiribati: Aspects of History*. University of the South Pacific, Suva.

Korea, Democratic People's Republic of

Gwang-Chol Chang

1. General Background

The peninsular country of Korea is situated in central eastern Asia, and covers 222,209 square kilometers, 122,762 square kilometers of which comprise the Democratic People's Republic of Korea (North Korea). To the north, the borders with China and Russia are marked respectively by the Amnok and Tuman rivers, and the country is surrounded on all other sides by the sea. The Korean landscape is extremely varied: the mean altitude is 440 meters and mountains cover almost 80 percent of the country. The highest peak is Mt Paektu (2,750m), which forms the national symbol of Korea. The climate is typically températe, with distinct variation between the four seasons.

The total population of Korea is 70 million, of whom 20 million live in the North. Sixty percent of the population in this part of the country live in conurbations. Birthrate figures for the years 1944, 1970, and 1989 were respectively (per thousand of population): 31.4, 44.7, and 22.2; mortality rates 20.8, 7.0, and 5.4; and natural growth rates 10.0, 38.0, and 16.8.

After five thousand years as a sovereign country, Korea became a Japanese colony in 1905. As a result, the Korean populace found themselves deprived of the right to learn or speak in Korean, and suffered the all-too-familiar miseries of an occupied people. After an armed popular uprising, led by President Kim Il Sung, the country was liberated from Japanese colonialism. This liberation coincided with the end of the Second World War, and the partition of the country. Consequently, despite sharing a common language, culture and territory, the Korean people are divided and are compelled to follow two divergent paths in all walks of life, be they political, economic, cultural or educational.

Before liberation, 2.3 million Koreans (i.e., 76.1% of the adult population) were illiterate. Over 60 percent of school-age children did not attend school. However, in less than four years, the literacy campaign led by the Party and Government of North Korea had eradicated illiteracy.

Compulsory education, introduced in various stages to meet a constantly growing social need, has now been fully implemented: in 1956, compulsory primary education for all was introduced, and in 1958 this was extended to secondary education (first cycle). In 1967 compulsory 9-year technical education was implemented and finally, in 1972, compulsory education lasting 11 years. A ruling of the Council of Ministers in April 1959 established free education: the state is responsible for funding more than a third of the population, namely 8.5 million schoolchildren and students.

The Democratic People's Republic of Korea came into existence in 1948. A unique system of government was established in 1958 after the socialist revolution had been completed, and was based on the Juche Idea. This forms the guiding ideology of the country, the central philosophical tenet of which is that everyone has control over their own destiny and according to which the people are is responsible for, and are the prime mover in, the country's social and economic program. The people are also charged with upholding the principle of *Chajusong* (or national sovereignty) in the realm of politics, and the principles of economic independence, and self-determination in matters of national security. The Democratic People's Republic of Korea is concerned to represent the interests of the entire Korean population: its President is Head of State, elected by the Supreme People's Assembly. There are three political parties: The Korean Workers' Party, the Korean Social Democratic party, and the Chondokyo-Chongwoo party.

The country's economy has seen an unprecedented period of growth since the Second World War. Only some 45 years ago, it was a backward, feudal society whose sense of national purpose had been destroyed by decades of colonial rule and whose infrastructure had been completely devastated by the Korean war of 1950–53. As a result both of the wise strategy of economic reconstruction adopted by president Kim Il Sung and of the intensive rebuilding efforts of the Korean people, industrialization was achieved in 14 years, over the period 1957–70 and, by 1984, industrial output had increased by a factor of 431 in comparison to 1946. In the early 1990s it takes the country less than 13 hours to produce the same output as the entire annual industrial production of 1946. In this same period, industrial production has experienced an annual growth rate of 17.3 percent.

By 1974, per capita income had exceeded US$1,000, by 1979 had reached US$1,920, by 1985 US$2,200, and by 1988, US$2,530.

Medical care is free for all the population; workers receive annual paid leave of between 14 and 28 days. Women have the right to 150 days of paid maternity leave (60 days prior to birth, 90 days after). Average life expectancy is 74.3 years (70.9 for men, 77.3 for women). As of the end of 1989, all citizens are qualified at least to the level of secondary school leaver (second cycle).

In the 1990s, North Korea is seeking even closer economic and technical cooperation with foreign countries, and to diversify its export base. Ultimately, however, the highest goal of the Korean people is reunification, according to the principles of independence, peace, and unity within an overall national confederation.

2. Politics and the Goals of the Education System

Education in North Korea is regarded as an especially vital area of national concern, shaping the whole country's future. Since the foundation of the independent state, the Government of the Democratic People's Republic of Korea has endeavored to develop education in concert with political and economic advancement, and to accord it top priority.

Since 1975, all children have entered school at the age of 6 after a compulsory year of preschool education in a kindergarten. Compulsory education lasts thereafter for at least 10 years, at the primary and secondary levels.

Universal 11-year compulsory education enables all young people to receive, free of charge, a secondary education up to the age when they embark on paid employment. Even in the second cycle of secondary education, the various elements comprising education are always invariable throughout the country (with the exception of some special schools). There is no division of education into separate areas of general education, technical–vocational education, and so on, such as is the case in the majority of other countries. All pupils follow the same curriculum nationwide.

The objectives of the North Korean education system are as follows:

(a) To bring about a clear improvement in the quality of education and to strengthen the material and technical foundations of the education system, by applying the general principles outlined in the work *The Thesis on Socialist Education* (Kim Il Sung 1977).

(b) To extend education throughout the whole of society by improving the system of continuing higher education for those already working, alongside the traditional system of tertiary education.

3. The Formal System of Education

The structure of the formal education system is shown in Fig. 1, and Table 1 presents some statistical information on the system.

3.1 Primary, Secondary, and Tertiary Education

All children of school age (5–16 years) are included in the education system. This system of 11-year compulsory education is intended to ensure the continuity and coherence of all forms of education from preschool through to the second cycle of secondary education, and combines a high level of achievement with a broad general education and scientific training. Within this

system, pupils are required to gain a solid grounding in a scientific approach to the world, equip themselves with a knowledge of the fundamental principles of the natural world and of society, and to attain at least a basic grasp of technical skills.

Before Independence in 1945, there were no institutions of higher learning in North Korea. In the early 1990s, universities and colleges number 280, and there are 456 specialized institutions of higher learning. All young Koreans are able, if they so wish, to enter higher education. All higher education institutions, such as Kim Il Sung University, Kim Chaek Technical University, and the Kim Hyong Jik Advanced Teacher-training College are all split-site institutions, divided according to requirements between the capital Pyongyang and the provinces. Each district of a province contains at least one specialized higher education institution, and every region of the country has several institutions of higher learning: colleges of industry, agriculture, medicine, teacher-training institutes (both basic and advanced), and so on.

Within universities and other higher education establishments, there are research and doctorate-awarding institutes. Universities (*Jong-hap dae-hak*) and colleges (*Dae-hak*) make up the country's scientific and technical cadres, while other higher education institutions (*Dan-kwa dae-hak*) are responsible for training engineers who work in production units, and specialized institutes (*Kodung jon-mun hak-kyo*) train highly qualified technicians. All students receive a state grant. Much effort is devoted to the development of national cadres through a constant process of retraining, while at the same time ensuring growth in their numbers. The state, which has already trained 1.6 million higher education graduates, accords great importance to implementing a system of compulsory higher education for all, in the service of intellectualizing the whole of society. This goal is conceived as a principal task of the country's cultural revolution, whose aim is to raise the cultural and technical level of awareness of all citizens to that of higher education graduates. Once this aim has been achieved, the intelligentsia will no longer exist as a distinct social group separate from the rest of society.

3.2 Preschool Education

Preschool education takes the form of a 2-year kindergarten. The upper class of the kindergarten, the first stage of the 11-year system of compulsory education, prepares children for academic learning. Kindergarten pupils learn the basic vocabulary necessary for daily life and for academic learning, accepted linguistic modes of expression, simple arithmetic (addition and subtraction), singing, dance, and drawing.

3.3 Vocational, Technical, and Business Education

Two factors distinguish the North Korean system of education from the system of vocational and business education, open universities, and so on existing in other

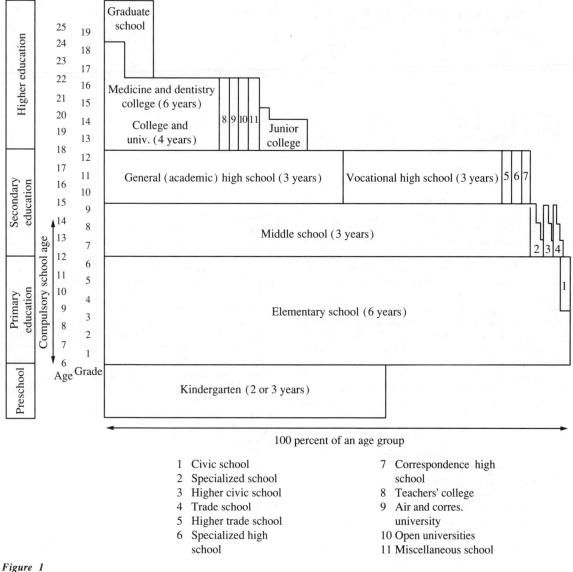

Figure 1
Democratic People's Republic of Korea: Structure of the formal education system

countries: (a) all workers are educated to secondary school standard (second cycle), and (b) the system of ongoing education throughout employment. This allows all workers, should they so wish, to pursue their studies under favorable conditions without having to give up work to do so.

Workers can participate in postsecondary education in a variety of ways: in colleges for industrial workers (*Gong-jang dae-hak*), for agricultural laborers (*Nong-jang dae-hak*), for fisherman (*O-jang dae-hak*), and through correspondence courses, evening classes, and the system of continuing study for cadres and workers.

The duration of the various types of continuing education is as follows: 2–3 years for specialized institutions of higher learning, 4–5 years for advanced teacher-training colleges, 4 years for university-level institutions, 5 years for universities and equivalent colleges and 6–6½ years for medical schools.

Workers educated through this system to the level of engineer or subengineer contribute enormously to the economic, scientific, and technical development of the country.

4. Administrative and Supervisory Structure and Operation

No private schools exist in the Democratic People's Republic of Korea: all institutions of learning are

Table 1
North Korea: Data on the education system 1991

| | General education | | Higher education | | | Kindergarten[a] |
	Primary	Secondary	Specialized colleges	Institutes and universities	Total	
No. of institutions	4,789	4,697	456	280	11,407	14,762
No. of students	1,601,000	2,169,000	188,000	401,000	5,000,000	728,000
No. of teachers	59,000	111,000	12,000	23,000	212,000	—

a 1989 figures, not included in the total

public and belong either to the state, or to political, social, or cooperative organizations.

The State Education Commission (*Kyo-yuk wiwon-hoe*), which comprises both the Ministry of Higher Education and the Ministry of Education, devises and implements in a coordinated way the country's educational development plans, and designs the curriculum for all establishments of learning. It is also the role of the Commission to resolve strategic questions of administration which arise in the system; for example, how to organize and direct the publication of teaching materials and research into educational studies, and to facilitate the centralized production and distribution of school equipment.

Local administrative bodies are empowered to undertake the following tasks: school construction projects, selection of pupils for higher education, recruitment and placement of teaching staff, and the smooth implementation of the unified curriculum by the educational establishments within their area.

Some establishments come under the jurisdiction of the Ministry of Culture and Arts, the Ministry of Health, and so on. Educational establishments are governed and administered according to the same management principle pertaining in all economic organizations in North Korea. This combines the following elements: political, economic, and technical management; overall governance by the state; promotion of individual initiatives by schools; democracy and coordinated policy making; and material, political, and moral considerations.

5. Educational Finance

The state provides the great majority of funding for education. All sources of revenue are public cooperatives, be they centralized or required. Kindergarten, primary, and secondary schools, medical and agricultural schools, and both basic and advanced teacher-training colleges are all locally financed, whereas degree-granting institutions, specialized higher education institutions, and colleges for industrial workers receive their funding from the respective government departments in whose domain they fall. All

other higher education establishments are in the State Education Commission's budget. The overall state education budget continually increases (see Table 2).

The state gives considerable benefits to all schoolchildren and students. During a course of education lasting from crèche to university level, an individual receives grants in the order of 15,800 won(US$7,524). In 1991, the additional average state support for a student was approximately 1,000 won (US$476), for a secondary school pupil 419 won (US$199), and for a primary school pupil 342 won (US$163). The state provides the following subsidies: over 60 percent of the real cost of learning materials in primary and secondary education, and over 40 percent of those of higher education; 20 percent on school uniforms and 50 percent of the cost of clothing for kindergarten children. Thus, the average education subsidy per capita of population is 90 won, and 396 won per family unit.

Table 2
Increase in government expenditure and the education budget 1981–91

| Year | Government expenditure | | |
	Total[a]	% increase over previous year	% increase in education budget
1981	20,333,000	7.9	7.6
1982	22,203,600	9.2	5.0
1983	24,018,600	8.2	4.7
1984	26,158,000	8.9	7.0
1985	27,328,830	4.5	4.2
1986	28,396,000	3.3	—
1987	30,085,100	5.9	5.8
1988	31,660,900	5.2	—
1989	33,382,940	5.4	5.6
1990	35,513,480	6.4	4.8
1991	36,909,240	3.9	3.9

a in thousands of wons

6. Supplying Personnel for the Education System

There is a comparatively well-structured system of teacher training. Three years of training in a basic teacher-training college (postsecondary level) are required to become a teacher in kindergarten or in primary schools, and 4–5 years in advanced teacher-training college to become a teacher in a secondary school. Teachers at the tertiary level undergo 4–6 years training in universities and equivalent higher education institutions (3–4 years training in technical institutes for teachers who are responsible for practical education), and teachers in technical institutes are educated for 4–6 years at university (or equivalent), followed by 2 years' research experience and 3–3½ years' work on a doctoral dissertation.

In 1988, teachers at all levels numbered some 212,000: the teaching labor force in primary education was 59,000, in secondary education 111,000, and in tertiary education 23,000. There was a relatively high percentage of women in the teaching profession: they accounted for 100 percent of teachers in kindergartens, 90 percent of primary school teachers, 70 percent of secondary school teachers, and 61 percent of teachers in higher education.

The state accords great importance to the inservice retraining of teachers in order to enhance their technical and professional skills. For example, the following kinds of retraining are offered to university lecturers:

(a) Retraining in basic and advanced science, organized by the State Education Commission. Teachers are retrained over a period of 1–2 months, or even 3–4 months, every 4 or 5 years, so that they may be kept abreast of recent advances in their field.

(b) Retraining through intensive courses. These take the form of one-, two-, or three-week courses organized by the cadre of the State Education Commission and the universities, and are designed to improve both the awareness of current scientific advances and the professional and practical aptitudes of teachers.

(c) Retraining in the workplace. Teachers join workshops, or they learn on the job as they teach. The period of training in this instance spans 3–6 months every 5 years, and 6 months to 1 year in the field of technical drawing.

(d) Retraining in research institutes, and through doctoral degrees.

7. Curriculum Development and Teaching Methodology

The State Education Commission draws up both long and short-term plans for the development of educational policy and of teaching materials.

Education programs are developed by the State Academy for Research in Education and teaching materials are drawn up and edited by the state's educational publishing houses, working from a program laid down centrally by the state. Once they have been worked out, developments in educational programs are subject to final approval by the State Education Commission: changes in textbooks are undertaken by the National Commission for the Revision of Textbooks, and then are ratified by the Commission prior to publication.

Education programs are comprised of two parts: the curriculum and the education plan. The curriculum determines the course of studies, the distribution of subjects and their timetabling—for instance, academic semesters, holiday periods, and periods of examination and inspection. The education plan, on the other hand, stipulates the limits and the levels of teaching to be given to any one year group in any particular subject, the forms of teaching, the subjects which are to be taught, and how they will fit within the total school year.

The Democratic People's Republic of Korea lays great emphasis on the teaching of foreign languages. Secondary school pupils must learn more than one foreign language (Russian and/or English), and students must take two or three languages from among the following: English, French, Russian, Chinese, Japanese, and German.

8. The System of Examinations, Promotions, and Certifications

The purpose of educational evaluation is to assess the results of study. In the Democratic People's Republic of Korea, evaluation consists of discovering whether the pupil's education by the teacher (i.e., as regards content, teaching procedures, and teaching methods) is properly conducted and whether the pupil has attained the objectives of the education process, as defined in the state's education programs.

Evaluation of the results of study basically consists of regular question-and-answer sessions, checks on homework assignments, and intermediate tests. Finally, there are examinations in selected subjects at the end of the semester and each academic year. If a poor result is achieved in an end-of-term examination even after resits, the pupil must repeat the year. The final secondary examination is based on questions set by municipal or district education committees. If pupils fail their final examination, they receive only a certificate of education, which means that they have to resit the exam the following year in the subjects in which they failed, if they are to obtain the secondary education diploma.

9. Educational Research

The State Academy for Research in Education (*Kyoyuk Gwahak-won*), which has a research staff of 400, undertakes research into teaching theory, the psychology of education, and the content and methodology of general education (primary and secondary). Research in teacher training is conducted by the Teacher Training Research Institute (*Sabom kyo-yuk yonku-so*) at the Kim Hyong Jik Advanced Teacher Training College. The Institute of Higher Education (*Godung kyo-yuk yonku-so*) is responsible for research in higher education.

The State Education Commission coordinates the efforts of all the educational research institutions.

10. Major Reforms in the 1980s and 1990s

Structural reforms in education and training have mainly taken place in higher education, with the aim of reorganizing and developing the scientific and technological system of education. The reforms may be outlined as follows:

(a) Increasing the number of technical institutes and specialized colleges of higher education, improving specialized technical education, and training technicians to a higher standard for work in industrial units, in accordance with the demands of the national economy and with contemporary trends in science and technology.

(b) Improving the education of highly qualified workers by enhancing training opportunities.

(c) Further development of the education system in the area of continuing education in employment, in parallel with improvement of the traditional system.

In order to implement these reforms successfully, more institutions of higher education for workers, peasants, and fisherman were created. Managing them efficiently according to established business and administrative practice is accorded priority. Special effort has been devoted to creating the new departments needed and to broadening their training scope, by encouraging the formation of technical cadres in industrial sectors such as mechanical and electronic engineering and cybernetics, and by developing important areas of scientific advancement such as electronics, biotechnology, and thermo research.

Reforms in the content of education and training have also been undertaken in the 1980s and 1990s in the domain of higher education:

(a) Primarily, urgent attention is being given to strengthening education in the areas of science and technology, as outlined above.

(b) The amount of practical training is being increased in order to raise the standard both of content and of methodology in the teaching of technical drawing and in work experience programs.

(c) Higher education has combined teaching and research by closely allying specialized practical training and technical drawing with endeavors in scientific research and technical innovation in the workplace.

11. Major Problems for the Year 2000

The major tasks facing primary schools is to improve the general standard of education. In order to achieve this, the Korean Workers' Party and the North Korean Government are endeavoring to enhance teachers' skills.

In secondary education, the following tasks are vital:

(a) To augment scientific and technical education. This area of education must be based on a thorough general grounding in core subjects such as mathematics, physics, chemistry, and biology.

(b) To ensure that secondary school pupils learn more than just a single technical subject, in line with the demands of the national economy and the fundamental principles of production and technology.

(c) To eradicate didactic teaching methods in favor of adopting heuristic modes of instruction, which concentrate on fostering independent thought and creativity in pupils. It is therefore regarded as important to raise the standard of teachers' skills and to introduce modern equipment and teaching methods.

The major problems confronting higher education are to maintain a balance between, on the one hand, the urgent need for graduates and thorough training and, on the other, between the development, goals and quality of education under the long-term perspective of the scientific and technical advancement of the nation. In addition, it is essential that the policy of compulsory higher education for all be realized as soon as possible.

References

Kim Sung Il 1977 *The Thesis on Socialist Education*. Pyongyang

Further Reading

Chang Gwang-Chol 1993 *Etudes comparatives des systèmes d'enseîgnement supérieur*. Paris
Charvin R 1984 *La République Populaire Démocratique de Corée*. Paris
KCNA 1980–91 *Korea Central Yearbooks*. Pyongyang
Kim Jong Il 1984 *Pour un dévelopment continu de l'enseîgnement*. Pyongyang
Pang Hwan Ju 1988 *Korea Review*. Pyongyang
Vishwanath 1992 *Encyclopedia Kim Il Sung*, Vol.2. New Delhi

Korea, Republic of

Se-ho. Shin

1. General Background

The Republic of Korea (South Korea) occupies the Korean Peninsula in the eastern corner of the Asian continent and faces the Japanese islands. Korea is ethnically a highly homogeneous country and has its own unique language. South Korea has 42 million people in a land area of 90,000 square kilometers. Its Gross National Product (GNP) per capita was US$5,569 and its share in world trade ranked twelfth in 1990. The literacy rate is over 97 percent.

Korea's national and cultural identity has been developed over its 4,000 year history, based on its sustaining sovereignty and on its own unique cultural tradition. The origin of Korea's history goes back to the "Ancient Chosun," which as a tribal state, ruled the northern part of China and the Korean Peninsula from about 100 BC to around 43 BC. After the "Ancient Chosun" period, several kingdoms emerged. The kingdoms were unified by the Sylla dynasty, which was replaced by the Koryo dynasty, which ruled the Korean Peninsula with Buddhism as the state religion. The name "Korea" originated from "Koryo."

In 1392, the Koryo was supplanted by a new dynasty, the Chosun. In the Chosun period, new inventions such as the Korean alphabet, known as the "hangul," were made. However, the heavy reliance of the ruling class on Confucianism as the new sovereign ideology increasingly dominated the intellectual climate and discouraged diversity of thought. This "hermit" dynasty was forced to open its door to foreign industrial powers in the late nineteenth century. Since then, Korea has undergone a series of hardships and turbulent changes. In 1910, Chosun was occupied by the Japanese colonial regime and Korea's cultural pride was much damaged by this colonization. Though Korea was liberated in 1945, its independence was not guaranteed with the division of the country into north and south by the world's superpowers. The Korean War followed, leaving the country riven and destitute, and ever since South and North Korea have remained hostile. In 1992, Korea still had the ultimate mission of reunification, and the two Koreas are engaged in a series of talks for a peaceful unification.

The teaching of Confucianism was dominant in traditional schools before the advent of modern style schools in the late nineteenth century. During the Koryo dynasty and the Chosun period, higher civil officials were selected through a state civil examination system which tested their proficiency in Chinese classics. The system made the learning of Confucian classics an educational tradition of the elite class. Learning for practical life was accorded a lesser status.

In this way, all public *and* private learning focused on the recitation of Confucian classics until the late nineteenth century.

Modern schools were introduced in the 1880s by Christian missionaries. A Royal Decree for Educational Reform was announced in 1885, through which modern state schools, including primary schools, normal schools, and vocational schools, were established in the capital and in the provinces. Many private schools were also founded around the country. In the period 1910–45, there was a Japanese colonial education system, and during this time Korean's own identity was lost.

The school system existing in the 1990s was established after 1945. The government adopted a 6–3–3–4 ladder system, known as the "American model," as the formal school system in 1949. Enrollment in primary school reached its universal level by 1960 and secondary schools by 1980. From 1991, the enrollment rate was 100 percent for primary school, 95 percent for middle school, 88 percent for high school, and 38.1 percent for higher education. The proportion of students to the total population is 26.7 percent. Just over 11,000 students attend about 20,000 schools and about 400,000 people are involved in the teaching profession.

There is fierce competition for college entrance and those who fail to gain admission take college entrance preparatory courses for another year or move into private tutoring halls. Education is one of the most powerful sources of mobility for individuals. It is also the primary instrument for training and supplying qualified labor for nation-building. However, there are many discrepancies between the intended goals and achieved outcomes in educational reality. Students' academic achievement at the upper levels of education does not meet the expected standards. Students at high school level are not very well-equipped to make their own career choices in a way that is conducive to their own abilities. This lies at the root of many problems in Korean education. In this vein, there have been several efforts by the government to reform the education system since the mid-1980s. Reflection and commitment are still needed to reform the Korean education system in order to meet the nation's needs in the twenty-first century.

2. Politics and the Goals of the Education System

Education in Korea has served as a means of political socialization. It has also created public awareness of political participation as well as supplying political and administrative personnel. Enlightenment of the people, the internalization of democratic values, and the development of leaders have been some of the basic aims of education.

Education has contributed to the internalization of new values in the Korean people by providing them with an orientation towards the future and instilling in them a sense of commitment to modernization and citizenship.

The basic aims of Korean education according to an official publication were:

(a) Education for the subjective consciousness through the production of people motivated to inherit, develop, and transmit the nation's cultural heritage to succeeding generations.

(b) Education for the whole person for a balanced assortment of knowledge, character, and sound development of mind and physical health.

(c) Education for creativity which is considered pivotal for the nation's survival in the rapidly advancing frontiers of the world technology race.

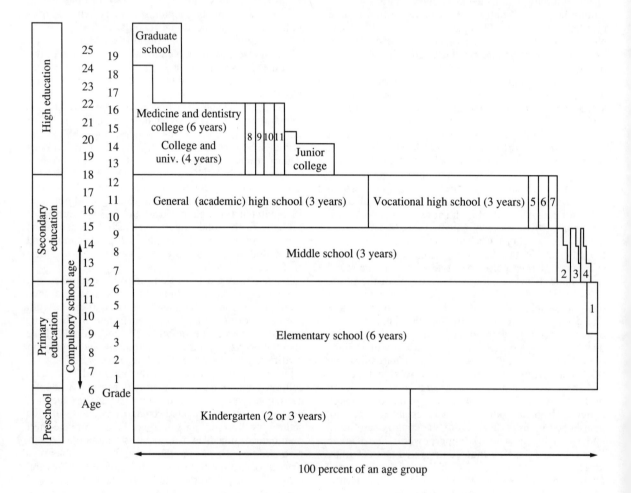

1 Civic school
2 Specialized school
3 Higher civic school
4 Trade school
5 Higher trade school
6 Specialized high school
7 Correspondence high school
8 Teachers' college
9 Air and corres. university
10 Open universities
11 Miscellaneous school

Figure 1
Republic of Korea: Structure of the formal education system

(d) Education for the future in the sense of developing skills appropriate for application and adaptation in the future world.

(e) Ensuring excellence in education which requires highly qualified teachers, diverse programs, and teaching methods that cater to individual needs.

(f) Diversity of operation involving stretching the student's potential to the fullest measure. Diversity and flexibility should be reflected in managing schools so that these attributes complement instruction catering to individual needs.

(g) Autonomous educational administration by granting a great deal of antomony to schools. A full degree of autonomy develops a sense of responsibility and accountability. In this regard, each school is encouraged to manage itself with its own creativity and resources.

(h) Humanization of the educational environment by creating clean neighborhoods and school environments that are humane in terms of classrooms and schools.

(i) Linking the school to social organizations. This can be done by intensifying the educational efforts of all people in such a way that the whole society is converted into a learning site. Efforts will be made to restore the educational function of the home, and greater efforts should be made to tap the educational function of the mass media.

3. The Formal System of Education

3.1 Primary, Secondary, and Tertiary Education

Figure 1 outlines the structure of the formal education system. Key statistics on enrollments and resources in the major education sectors are provided in Table 1. Education is compulsory from 6 to 14 and between these ages there is virtually 100 percent attendance at school. The majority of 4–5-year olds attend kindergarten before commencing elementary school. Elementary school lasts for 6 years. In 1991, there were 4.8 million primary students, of whom 1.4 percent were enrolled in private schools.

The scattered rural population has necessitated a large number of small primary schools. All primary schools are coeducational. The primary school day normally lasts for 4–6 hours of instruction and the school year for more than 220 days.

Secondary education lasts for 6 years; 3 years in middle school and 3 years in high school. Students normally commence middle school at age 12, and high school at age 15. The entrance examination to middle school was abolished in 1969 and now students are assigned at random to one of the middle schools in their residential district. In rural areas, free compulsory education has been extended to middle schools. This is being extended to the middle school level in other areas on an incremental basis. About 60 percent of middle schools are coeducational and about 30 percent of students are enrolled in private schools.

High schools are divided into general (academic) high schools and vocational high schools. Since 1974, a new entrance system has been used in areas where high school education has been "standardized." There is a preliminary nationwide examination to establish the hierarchy of eligibility for admission. In these areas, candidates for vocational high schools are given tests to compete for entrance earlier than the entrance tests for general high schools. Following this, the candidates who had opted for general high schools and those who failed to obtain entrance to vocational high schools take another examination. Those who pass

Table 1
Enrollments and resources in school education 1991

	Primary	Secondary Middle	High	Higher
Number of students	4,759,000	4,443,000 (2,232,000/2,211,000)		1,540,000
Percentage of age group enrolled				
Age 6–11	102.4	—	—	—
12–14	—	95.3	—	—
15–17	—	—	87.6	—
18–21	—	—	—	38.1
Number of institutions	6,245	2,289	1,702	580
Average number of students per institution	760	890	1,300	2,700
Student–teacher ratio	34.4:1	24.2:1	23.2:1	29.9:1[a]
Expenditure per student (in thousands of won)	655	855	1,000	2,247[a]

a College and university only

this examination are assigned to a high school in their respective residential district by computer lottery. In 1991, 97.4 percent of middle school graduates went on to high schools. Some 40 percent of high schools are coeducational and about 60 percent of students enroll in private schools. Secondary school operates for more than 220 school days a year, with about 4–7 hours of instruction per day.

The tertiary sector comprises colleges, universities, junior colleges, and other institutions, including teacher's colleges, the air and correspondence university, and the open universities. In 1991, one million students were enrolled in 115 colleges and universities, and 400,000 students in 118 junior colleges. In addition, there were 11 teacher's colleges, one air and correspondence university, and eight open universities.

In 1991, about 1.5 million students were enrolled in various types of higher learning institutions. The higher education enrollment rate was 38.1 percent. Competition is severe for entry into higher education institutions, especially for the more prestigious colleges and universities.

The junior vocational college is a two- to three-year postsecondary program leading up to Grade 14 level and is the direct outgrowth of the increasing demand for technical labor force required by rapid industrialization. The aim of junior vocational education is to produce middle-level technicians equipped with the combination of theoretical knowledge and practical skills. Their specialized courses are grouped into the following: technical, agricultural, nursing, fishery, sanitation, commercial and business, home economics, arts, and athletics.

College and university courses at the undergraduate level are 4–6 years in duration, and medical and dentistry colleges require 6 years of study. With 140 academic credits, a student is entitled to a bachelor's degree. Class attendance for over 16 hours per term earns one credit unit.

3.2 Preschool Education

Preschool education is provided by kindergartens for 3- to 5-year old children. The specific objectives of preschool education are:

(a) to form lifetime habits for good health, foster basic perceptual and motor skills, and develop the body and mind harmoniously;

(b) to develop basic communicative skills to express oneself effectively as well as to understand others;

(c) to cultivate interest in the various phenomena present in everyday life and develop an inquiring attitude toward them;

(d) to help children gain confidence in themselves, and assist them in expressing their feelings and thoughts about everyday happenings in their lives;

(e) to foster, in children, a sensitive and caring attitude toward family and friends.

The aforementioned objectives of kindergarten education narrow down into five areas, namely: physical, language, cognitive, emotional, and social development. The national curriculum for kindergarten was first established in 1969 and is revised periodically. The teaching materials are provided by the Ministry of Education. Most kindergartens are private; however the government is making an effort to increase the number of public kindergartens and the number of those enrolled, and to improve the quality of kindergarten education.

3.3 Special Education

Special education children are classified into seven different types: the visually impaired, the hearing impaired, the mentally retarded, the physically handicapped, the emotionally disturbed, the communicatively disordered, and "others." Children in public special schools are educated with full financial support and those in private special schools are partially supported.

Standard curricula for exclusive use in special schools was developed in 1989 and becomes effective in 1993. Efforts are being made to provide more time and better facilities for career education.

Special education programs are provided to special children from elementary to high school level. There is no formal special education at the preschool level. There are 104 special schools for the handicapped where 19,971 students and 2,757 teachers are involved as of 1990.

In 1991, there were 2,502 special classes in elementary schools and 668 special classes in high schools. The numbers of students served by special education in special classes in regular schools were 24,202 and 5,645 in elementary and high schools respectively.

An Act for the promotion of employment of the handicapped was legislated in 1991.

3.4 Vocational, Technical, and Business Education

Vocational education for employment is provided mainly at vocational high schools and two-year technical colleges. However, prevocational courses are provided even in elementary schools as a part of general education. Practical arts education is required for all students at the elementary school level for orientation toward the world of work, jobs, and technology. For prevocational education at middle school and general high school, students are required to take a technology education course and one of the elective courses such as agriculture, industrial technology, commerce, fishery and marine studies, and home economics.

Vocational high schools supply technicians for industrial development. Most vocational high schools are established and financed by the government, except for commercial high schools which are mostly private. Students pay for tuition in the same way as general high school students, but the vocational students have a greater chance of receiving scholarships than the general high school students.

Vocational high schools provide three-year programs for technician education. The course requirement for vocational high school ranges from 204 to 216 units. Within the course requirement, each school principal can decide how many units are required for graduation, depending upon school conditions. Vocational courses consist of 82–122 units and they correspond to 40–60 percent of the total requirement.

Middle school graduates can apply for admission to vocational high school. Applicants are selected by means of an entrance assessment consisting of an examination score, middle school records, a letter of recommendation from the middle school, and a screening test. Vocational high school students form about 30 percent of the total number of high school students. Upon completion of the three-year program, every vocational high school student receives a graduation diploma. Most of them also obtain the second-class technician's certificate by taking a national qualifying test. Certificate-holders have more chance of employment. However, most graduates are employed, except for a small number of graduates who continue their studies at a two-year technical college or four-year university.

Field work is required of all students and ranges from one to six months for technical high school, one to three months for agricultural high school, and one month to one year for fishery and marine high school.

There are five types of vocational high schools: agricultural, technical, commercial, fishery and marine, and home economics. With rapid industrialization, the number of agricultural high school students has been gradually declining and this trend is expected to continue. On the other hand, technical high schools have been gradually expanded by government policy in order to meet technical labor force demands for industrialization. The number of commercial high school students accounts for more than 50 percent of the total number of vocational high school students. The number of female students has gradually increased at commercial high schools.

National policy emphasizes the strengthening of vocational education. In 1989, the ratio of general high schools to vocational high schools was 2.5:1. The Ministry of Education (MOE) is making an effort to change the ratio to 1:1. The MOE is also conducting a long-term plan to reorganize the whole system of vocational high school education in terms of fields of study, student enrollment, field experience programs, teacher training, and school–industry cooperation.

3.5 Adult and Nonformal Education

Adult and nonformal education in Korea is defined as all forms of education, other than formal school education, and is based on the concept of life-long education. The Adult and Nonformal Education Promotion Law, which was enacted in 1982, establishes criteria for the recognition of nonformal education institutes and programs as the equivalents of formal education corresponding to each school level. The adult and nonformal education programs can be categorized into: (a) paraschool (semiformal) education, (b) occupational and technical education, and (c) general or liberal education.

Paraschools are excluded from the main ladder of schools in the sense that they do not require daylong and full-time attendance at school. Paraschools include civic schools, higher civic schools, trade schools, higher trade schools, industry-attached night schools (middle and high), school-attached night classes (middle and high), air and correspondence high schools, the air and correspondence university, and open universities.

Institutes provide occupational and technical education programs in job training centers under the Ministry of Labor Affairs and vocational schools for youths under the Ministry of Education. Privately run commercial institutes, monitored by the respective board of education, offer occupational training. The armed forces and penitentiaries also offer training programs on practical vocational skills.

Public and private organizations provide general and liberal education programs aimed at enhancing the cultural refinements of women, youth, and elderly people. These programs—dealing with the kinds of activities that meet diverse educational needs, such as the art of entertainment, and the like—are intended to help individuals make the best use of leisure. Universities also run extramural or extension programs, such as child care, home economics, business management, and health, as nondegree courses.

4. Administrative and Supervisory Structure and Operation

Educational administration consists of the Ministry of Education, the municipal and provincial offices of education, and the district offices of education.

The Ministry of Education is the central authority responsible for discharging the constitutional mandates for national education. Based on government education policies, the Ministry develops national education plans; implements the plans; publishes and approves textbooks for elementary and secondary education; enacts laws related to education; executes the educational budget of the country; directs and coordinates subordinate agencies for educational policy planning and implementation; and supervises the municipal and provincial boards of education, the institutions of higher education, and other national schools. The Ministry has many auxiliary organs under its supervision and control.

Within the Ministry of Education there are three offices—the Planning and Management Office, the Supervision and Textbook Compilation Office, and the University Education Office and five bureaus—the Elementary and Secondary Education Bureau, the Teacher Affairs Bureau, the Science and Technology Education Bureau, the Nonformal and International Education Bureau, and the Educational Facilities Bureau. The municipal and provincial offices of education are responsible for the administration of elementary and secondary education under their jurisdiction. There are 15 offices of education: 6 municipal and 9 provincial. Offices of education are under the authority of the Board of Education as well as the Ministry of Education.

The boards of education are responsible for ordinances, budget approval, and auditing the offices of education. The boards of education consist of members elected by the municipal and provincial assembly. The superintendent of education for each municipal and provincial office of education is elected by the relevant board of education.

The district office of education is the lowest unit of educational administration. The district office of education is an educational administrative organization of a city or a county under the direction of the municipal and provincial office of education. There are 179 such offices. The head of the district office of education is appointed by the municipal and provincial office of education of each municipality or province. The head of the district office of education (supervised by the municipal and provincial office of education) carries out all the administrative affairs concerning education; maintains educational facilities; enacts educational regulations; and supervises all kindergartens, elementary, and junior high schools in its jurisdiction.

5. Educational Finance

There are three major sources of educational funding: central government, local government, and private education finance. Grants from the central government and tuition fees are the major sources of financing education in Korea. Contributions from school foundations and the private sector are relatively marginal compared with those of foreign countries.

The major source of central government educational expenditure is tax revenues. Expenditures are for the Ministry of Education, national universities, research institutes, and elementary and secondary education incurred by local autonomous government. The Ministry general account includes current operational costs, grants for local education, and subsidies for national universities and public schools and its subsidiary organizations. The special account includes a special account for the improvement of educational conditions, a special educational tax account, a special private education fund account, and a special account for national university hospitals.

In 1991, general account revenue was W131.4 billion (US$400 million), composed of W73.8 billion (US$225 million) from entrance fees and tuition at national universities, W4.4 billion (US$13.4 million) from application fees for entrance examinations, W51.7 billion (US$13.4 million) from foreign loans, W1.5 billion (US$4.6 million) from shop/laboratory practice, and others. The general account expenditures include W5,161.9 billion (US$15.7 billion) for the Ministry of Education and national research institutes, W541.4 billion (US$1.7 million) for national universities, and W4,286.6 billion (US$13.1 billion) to subsidize local education.

The general account excluding subsidies for local education amounts to W1,245.3 billion (US$3.8 billion) which consists of remuneration (W480.7 billion {US$1.5 million}, 38.6%), operational cost (W117.1 billion {US$357 million}, 9.4%) and the cost of financing educational services (W647.6 billion {US$1.97 billion}, 52.0%).

The special account for the improvement of educational conditions invests W370 billion (US$1.13 billion) per year for three years beginning in 1990. This investment takes the form of transfer from the central government to finance the improvement of educational conditions for elementary and secondary schools in local areas.

The special educational tax account sets aside revenue from educational taxes for raising the quality of elementary and secondary school teachers. This account pertains to subsidy for local education.

The special private education account fund is intended to create a private education fund to help private schools with the expansion or renovation of shop and laboratory facilities. The targeted amount of the fund is W20 billion (US$61 million). Added to this are the scholarship fund amounting to W20 billion (US$61 million), which is to be made available to bright and needy students, and W6 billion (US$18 million) to attract bright students into the teaching profession.

The special account (W175 billion {US$533 million}) for national university hospitals is intended for use in their operation. Its expenditure consists of the remuneration of medical treatment, investment in facilities, and other costs.

The total education budget in 1991 was W6,597.9 billion (US$20 billion), and was 22.8 percent of the total government budget of W28,972.2 billion (US$88.3 billion). The local office of education prepares education budget bills based on estimated needs for providing elementary and secondary education and forwards them to its respective local autonomous body.

To stabilize the financing of local education, the central government is responsible for total remuneration of teachers in compulsory education, and 11.8 percent of internal tax revenue is earmarked as a grant to local education. Special accounts are institutionalized to set aside a fixed percent of the general account for transfer to local education and to perpetuate educational taxes to be used for improving educational conditions.

The major sources of financing private education are entrance fees and tuition. In terms of number of students, private schools account for 72.3 percent at kindergarten; whereas, due to compulsory education, the private school accounts for only 1.5 percent at the elementary school level, as compared to 27.8 percent, 61.9 percent, and 80.1 percent for middle schools, high schools, and colleges and universities, respectively. The private schools play a vital role in education and deserve government support. The government enacted a law exempting private schools from taxation in the acquisition and sales of properties and it provides subsidies and loans to help them with the expansion and renovation of facilities. The subsidies also include scholarships, research grants, and partial coverage of pensions for private school teachers.

In 1990, the total budget of private schools was W2,661.3 billion (US$8.1 billion).

6. Supplying Personnel for the Education System

In order to ensure the professionality and the public accountability of teachers, graduates of teacher-training institutes are required to be licensed according to criteria established by law. They are classified into teachers, assistant teachers, special education teachers, librarians, teachers responsible for practical work, and nursing teachers.

Institutes responsible for teacher education vary in type and level, and include teacher's colleges, colleges of education, teacher education courses or departments of education in colleges and universities, junior colleges, air and correspondence colleges, and graduate schools of education. These institutions turn out nearly 30,000 teachers annually.

Kindergarten teachers are trained at four-year colleges, junior colleges, and the air and correspondence colleges. Elementary school teachers are produced by the 11 teacher's colleges. During the period 1981–84, the two-year junior teacher's colleges were upgraded to four-year colleges granting bachelor's degrees. Students are exempt from entrance fees and tuition and are entitled to scholarships, but they are obliged to serve as a school teacher for a given number of years upon graduation.

Secondary school teachers must be graduates of colleges of education, departments of education, or teacher education courses in colleges and universities, or graduate schools of education. Students must pay some tuition. The entrance examination to colleges of education has become more strict with the addition of an aptitude test and an interview.

. Special education teachers are educated according to the level of schools where they are expected to teach. School librarians must be graduates of universities and colleges with a major in library science. Nurses are qualified to become teachers upon graduating from a junior college or a university and obtaining a registered nurse license.

7. Curriculum Development and Teaching Methodology

There is a very strongly prescribed common curriculum across the country. Under the present system of curriculum, which is called the "fifth revised curriculum," almost all of the specific details of curriculum are determined by the Ministry of Education (MOE), thus making the school curriculum content and time allocation very uniform with only few variations at the regional and local levels.

At elementary and middle school levels, most subjects are compulsory. At the high school level, however, the scope of studies varies depending on the course, even in the same general academic school. Students in the humanities–social sciences stream study different subjects from those in the science or vocational streams, but 12 subjects out of a total of 26 are compulsory for all students, regardless of their streams. School teachers, subject-matter specialists, curriculum specialists, professors, and educational administrators form committees which prepare a draft of the syllabus. A final version is formally promulgated by the MOE.

At the elementary level, all textbooks, and at the secondary level, the textbooks for three subjects (Korean language, moral and education, and Korean history), are developed by educational research institutes authorized by the MOE. The MOE reviews, revises, and finally approves these textbooks known as "Type I" textbooks. Textbooks for other subjects are developed by private publishers, and are then reviewed and approved by "textbook review committees" organized by the MOE. These sort of textbooks are classified as "Type II" books. In the case of Type I textbooks, only one kind of textbook is available for each subject, while Type II textbooks can be of several kinds: five for the middle school level and eight for the high school level. In the case of Type II textbooks, schools select one that seems most appropriate for them, for each subject from five or eight.

The sixth revised curriculum will be effective from 1994. In middle school, one subject from several in the "practical art and home economics" area can be selected. In high school, one foreign language out of many on offer and one subject in the field of "practical art and home economics" can be chosen. But these subjects are selected by the school, not by each student. Once selected by a school, students attending that school must study that subject; in this sense, these subjects are more appropriately called "compulsory electives."

English is taught from the beginning of secondary school. Chinese, which is somewhat different from that used in China, is also taught at the secondary level. English is also taught in some elementary schools as an elective subject in extracurricular time. At the high school level, students must study one more foreign language in addition to English. It is selected from among Japanese, Chinese (as used in China), French, German, and Spanish. Russian will also be available in the new curriculum from 1995.

How the curriculum is being implemented by classroom teachers is monitored mainly by school principals and by a supervisor from the provincial school board in some special cases. Supervisors from the MOE sometimes monitor the status of curriculum implementation in each provincial school board.

There are many problems related to curricula and teaching methods. First, the process of curriculum determination is very centralized with little allowance being made for special regional or district needs. Second, the structure of the curriculum is too uniform and rigid. Third, the implementation (or management) of the curriculum is too rigid and controlled. This problem is closely related to the first problem in that the curriculum is both developed and imposed by outsiders. The curriculum implementers (namely, the teachers) do not have a strong intrinsic motivation to implement it well. Finally, there is the problem of the effectiveness of the school curriculum. Schools are not generally successful in improving student achievement.

The problems of teaching methods are also numerous. The most serious being that teaching is undertaken without consideration of individual differences among students: teaching materials, classroom instruction methods, homework, and evaluation methods are the same for all students. In a word, teaching is conducted in total disregard for individual differences among students. A second problem is that teaching methods are relatively simple and rigid. Teachers are heavily dependent on lecturing, regardless of the characteristics of instructional objectives. Large class sizes, large school sizes, lack of school facilities and of teaching–learning materials are major problems which are responsible for poor teaching methods.

8. The System of Examinations, Promotions,.and Certifications

Within each level of school education, the promotion of students from grade to grade is generally automatic. The first, second, and third certificates are awarded upon successful completion of the six-year primary school, the three-year middle school, and the three-year high school. They are based on internal school assessment. Applicants for vocational high schools are given an entrance examination. Each vocational high school selects their students based on the score of the examination. Applicants for academic high school have to take a city or provincial examination.

Colleges and universities select their students on the basis of the composite score of the Scholastic Achievement Examination for College Entrance (SAECE) and on high school academic records. The entrance examination for colleges and universities underwent drastic changes in the 1980s. Until 1968, colleges and universities were authorized to select their students on the basis of the applicant's score on the entrance examinations conducted by individual institutes. From 1969 to 1979, the new entrance system stipulated that the applicants who passed the Preliminary Examination for the College Entrance (PECE) be allowed to take the main entrance examinations conducted by individual institutes. Subsequently, the college entrance examination system was modified in accordance with the educational reform launched in 1980. The PECE was replaced by the Scholastic Achievement Examination for the College Entrance (SAECE). The SAECE scores are not the only determinant of eligibility for entrance. Achievement in high school and scores in essays administered by individual institutes are also important determinants since 1985. What is unique about this system is that applicants are required to select universities or colleges before they sit for the examination.

From 1994, colleges and universities will have more autonomy in selecting their students. Each college or university will have to make a choice to select students with one score among the following four patterns: (a) the composite score of high school academic records, the National Learning Ability Test for College (NLATC), and an examination given by each college or university; (b) the composite score of high school academic records and NLATC; (c) the composite score of high school academic records and an examination given by each college or university; and (d) the sole score of high school academic records.

9. Educational Assessment, Evaluation, and Research

School-based assessment consists of objective paper-and-pencil tests to measure cognitive achievement and, since the early 1980s, essay tests and affective domain assessments have played a greater role. Teachers of elementary and secondary schools keep records of students' affective behaviors. These records are based mainly on observation. There is also the record used for the guidance of school life and careers in general, with assessment in particular of the twelfth grade students which will be used as one criterion or university entrance selection as of 1994.

Regional assessment is undertaken at elementary and middle schools. Participation of (primary) schools in the test is mandatory in many regions, except in some big cities. The regional board uses the test results as a guide for enhancing the quality of education of the schools under their supervision by informing each school of its own mean scores and standard deviations with corresponding regional means and standard deviations.

For national assessments, there are governments tests provided by the National Institute of Educational Evaluation (NIEE) and private institute tests. Nationwide achievement testing is undertaken annually to monitor national standards of achievement in eight subjects in Grade 3, 13 subjects in Grade 7, and 12 subjects in Grade 10.

Private institute tests are developed and administered by private test development institutes. The majority of schools voluntarily participate in this testing. Nearly all twelfth grade students in general high schools and the students registered at private institutes take these tests almost every month.

Educational research can be exemplified by the studies carried out at the Korean Educational Development Institute (KEDI), which is a government-supported research and development organization. The institute undertakes about 40 to 50 research or development projects every year. They cover educational foundations and policy studies, curriculum research and development, research on computer education and on educational data and information, and evaluation studies of air and correspondence education.

It also undertakes ambitious long-term research projects on topics such as how evaluation should be formulated to enhance quality education and accountability of school education, how university entrance examination systems can be improved, how democratic citizenship can be implemented, how creative and critical thinking can be taught, and how education should be reshaped to prepare for the future. These research studies started in 1990.

At the same time, there are ongoing research studies into each subject area: early and special education, environmental education, vocational education, computer education, and adult and nonformal education. The research results, depending on their characteristics, are used by schools as teaching and learning materials, as guides for policy changes, and/or other academic resources.

There are many other types of research studies. The Ministry of Education supports individual research projects from various schools, universities, and research institutes which must compete for research funds. In 1991, there was a total of US$25 million available for 3,744 research projects. The NIEE also undertakes research on the entrance examination, nationwide achievement tests, and affective domain assessments.

Accountability of schooling has been of great concern since the late 1980s. Consequently, school self-evaluation has become widespread in the 1990s at every level of schooling from the elementary to the university level. Universities are also evaluated and rated by the Korean Council for University Education.

The Ministry of Education and the NIEE produce an annual statistical yearbook of education every year. It provides an overview of the overall status of education. KEDI publishes *Educational Indicators in Korea* each year.

Korea participates in international assessments conducted in mathematics and science, in the International Mathematics Olympiad (since 1988), and also in the mathematics and science assessments sponsored by the National Science Foundation and the National Center for Educational Statistics of the United States which took place in 1990.

10. Major Reforms in the 1980s and 1990s

Innovative efforts to streamline the Korean educational system have been carried on in the 1980s. Provisions outlining the direction of promoting lifelong education were added to the Constitution. Production of the "whole person" was adopted as the aim of education. Education aimed to perfect character and the development of a humane perspective was given new emphasis. Moral education was given more weight. Science education should prepare youth for living with the advancing frontiers of science and technology. Lifelong education should prepare youth for the future by fostering self-directed learning.

The immediate effect of educational reforms was felt on the chronic problem of private tutoring (which had grown out of proportion to school education) as an added insurance of passing competitive examinations. To diminish this problem, the entrance examination system was reformed: the college-and university-based entrance examination was abolished, achievement in high school was given a heavier weight in screening, the curriculum was readjusted in terms of workload, enrollment quotas were expanded for all types of higher education institutions, teacher's colleges were upgraded to four-year colleges, an educational tax was created to finance educational reforms, the physical facilities of universities were expanded and updated, teachers were given incentives, and the government and its affiliated agencies changed the criteria for employment.

To assist the President in educational matters, the Presidential Consultative Commission on Educational Policy was established in 1989. The educational system is being reformed to stress local and institutional autonomy in the 1990s. In order to improve the local autonomy of educational administration, a local board of education was reinstitutionalized and new board members were elected with lay majority from 1991. Individual schools and universities also gained more power to decide on their own educational matters. A new college and university entrance examination system will be introduced in 1994.

11. Major Problems for the Year 2000

The problems listed below indicate the key educational problems to be dealt with by the year 2000:

(a) The problem of a "college fever" and examination-oriented education system. Examination-oriented education neglects the broader and more fundamental function of school education for the development of character and the whole person. The current system of education does not take account of the majority of students who are not in the college track in providing them with adequate provision for career preparation.

(b) The neglect of education for character-building, the formation of sound values and affective development. Excessive competition for college entrance has led to a widespread "diploma disease" and credentialism. Education fails to cultivate a personality that values cooperative spirit and fraternity.

(c) The problem of inappropriate educational content and methods. The school curriculum is unable to provide diverse educational programs based on the aptitudes, interests, and abilities of individual students. Knowledge-oriented school curriculum only aggravates the already heavy study burden of students. The schools neglect to emphasize practical work such as field observation and laboratory work. Various types of teaching–learning media and educational technology which stimulate learning are virtually nonexistent in schools.

(d) The problem of a dilapidated educational environment. Excessively large school sizes (e.g., 453 schools out of a total 999 elementary schools have more than 49 classes) in major cities lead to bureaucracy and formalism. Huge class sizes also hinder effective instruction which takes into account individual difference and character development. In-school laboratory and workshop facilities are below the legal requirement levels and existing facilities are of poor quality.

(e) The problem of low morale of teachers. There are excessively large numbers of students per classroom (50 for primary, 53 for middle and 55.1 for academic high schools in major cities).

There are heavy weekly teaching loads (over 30 hours, especially in the case of upper-grade teachers of elementary schools), and excessive administrative workloads.

(f) The problem of education which fails to prepare for the future. Primary- and secondary-level science and technology education is far from effective due to the lack of adequate laboratory and experiment facilities, and inflexible teaching and learning methods. Computer education in schools is inadequate for preparing students for the coming of information society. There is a lack of adequate school and classroom facilities for mentally and physically handicapped students. Gifted children are being deprived of opportunities to develop their potentials to the fullest. Schools are not providing relevant and effective programs in international education.

(g) The problem of higher education which lacks adequate standards for quality. There is a lack of autonomy of individual institutions: academic and student administration is still very much uniform and close-minded. The ability to attract internationally competitive faculty is extremely low, and creates heavy teaching loads for individual professors. There are also adverse research environments and a lack of sufficient funds for research.

Bibliography

Korea Education Newspaper 1991 *Korea Education Annual.* Korea Education Newspaper, Seoul
Korean Educational Development Institute (KEDI) 1991a *Educational Indicators in Korea.* KEDI, Seoul
Korean Educational Development Institute (KEDI) 1991b *The 7th Five-year Economic and Social Development Plan* (Sectoral Plan on Education). KEDI, Seoul
Ministry of Education (MOE) 1991 *Statistical Yearbook of Education.* MOE, Seoul
Ministry of Education (MOE) 1992 *Education in Korea.* MOE, Seoul

Kuwait

M. G. Hussein

1. General Background

Kuwait is situated on the northwestern shore of the Arabian Gulf, and has an area of 9,600 square kilometres. It is bounded on the west and north by Iraq, on the east by the Arabian Gulf, and on the south by Saudi Arabia.

Before the middle of the eighteenth century, Kuwait was inhabited by a few small Arab tribes and groups of fishermen. Then a number of families of the Anaiza tribes migrated from the interior of Najd in Saudi Arabia to settle on the shore of the Gulf where Kuwait is now. The Sabah family, the present rulers, are descended from these people. There then followed migrations of people from other neighboring countries including

Iraq and Iran, and slowly the number of people increased.

In 1899, a Protection Treaty was signed between the Shaikh of Kuwait and the United Kingdom. The main points of the treaty were that the Shaikh promised not to lease any part of Kuwait to any foreign country except the United Kingdom and its subjects, and not to accept foreign representatives except with the approval of the United Kingdom government. On its part the United Kingdom agreed to provide economic aid to Kuwait and to provide protection from any outside invasion.

The treaty remained in force until 1961, when the two governments reached a peaceful agreement and declared Kuwait an independent state. In November 1962 a new constitution proclaimed the Kuwaiti government as a democratic government, the people being the source of all executive powers. The constitution also recognized that the Al-Sabah family would retain rights in the succession to the throne.

Kuwait depends mainly on oil revenue for financing all aspects of life. Before the Iraqi invasion of Kuwait in August 1990, the country had established an industrial scheme that would have seen a gradual replacement of oil over a 10 to 20 year period, but this was completely destroyed and its replacement will take a long time. The educational services are completely financed by the government which spends about 10 percent of its revenue on education. The Ministry of Education's budget for 1992–1993 was 385 million Kuwaiti Dinars (1 K.D = US$3.4).

Education for foreigners (including foreign workers) is mainly confined to the private school system. The government helps but does not supply financial aid for private education.

2. *Politics and Goals of the Educational System*

Kuwait's constitution defines the framework and principles underlying the structure of the society and the state with its different institutions. Among these fundamental principles are those concerning education and its position in the society, and those which emphasize the philosophical elements adopted by the state; together they form one of the main sources for defining the educational objectives in Kuwait.

The public education system in Kuwait is guided by the following constitutional principles: (a) youth care is the responsibility of the state; (b) education is an essential factor for the progress of the society, secured and patronized by the state; and (c) education is a right for Kuwaiti citizens and is compulsory in its elementary stage.

The 1987 law concerning general education states that:

Education aims at providing opportunities for the students, which will help them integrally and comprehensively develop, spiritually, intellectually, and physically within the ultimate limits of their aptitudes and potentials as well

as within the context of Islamic principles, the Arabic legacy, modern culture, the nature of Kuwaiti society and its traditions. Such education should implant in the students the spirit of nationalism as well as loyalty to the homeland and the Emir. Also it should ensure balance for the students' self-realization and qualify them to contribute to the advancement of Kuwaiti society in particular and the Arab nation in general.

Education in Kuwait stems from the nature of Muslim, Arabian Gulf, and Kuwaiti society in terms of values, culture, conditions, potentials, needs, problems, and attitudes. Thus, it aims at: (a) implanting faith in the principles of Islam in the students; (b) introducing students to their Islamic/Arabic legacy as well as Kuwait's history and the development of its society and traditions; (c) establishing a feeling of belonging to Kuwait, the Arabian fatherland, and the Islamic world; (d) strengthening the nation's solidarity and family spirit; (e) preparing individuals for a democratic society; (f) acquainting individuals with their rights and duties; (g) promoting the ability to think according to scientific methods; (h) guiding students toward innovation and modernization; (i) raising the levels of their ambitions; (j) attending to both gifted students and handicapped students; and (k) educating a strong generation characterized by seriousness, fortitude, sacrifice, and the possession of such abilities, skills, and attitudes that qualify them to hold responsible roles in the future.

The more specific aims for primary education can be said to be:

(a) promoting the child's spiritual and mental growth and character in accordance with the principles and ideas of the Islamic religion;

(b) providing the basis of a knowledge of the three skills: reading, writing, and arithmetic;

(c) encouraging the child's participation in art and craft subjects;

(d) aiding the child to appreciate the ideas of society, particularly the qualities of co-operation and responsibility;

(e) construction of the national character and consciousness of the child through studies in national history.

For intermediate education the main aims are:

(a) enabling students to acquire an understanding and knowledge of their national character and of the following subjects: the Arabic language, social sciences, elementary sciences, mathematics, and English;

(b) guiding the pupil's abilities and aptitudes as a preparation for the secondary stage of education;

(c) providing an opportunity for the pupils to gain technical skills and experience of manual work.

3. Formal Structure of Education

The Kuwaiti educational ladder is of the 4–4–4 pattern: four years primary, four years intermediate, and four years secondary education. This general education is preceded by a two-year kindergarten stage.

Figure 1 presents, in diagrammatic form, the structure of the school system together with the percentage of the equivalent age groups enrolled in school.

3.1 Primary, Secondary, and Tertiary Education

The primary stage is concerned with children of ages 6 to 9 years, and is compulsory. The intermediate stage covers the schooling of children from ages 10 to 13 years. All children at this stage go to the same type of school, known as the general preparatory.

The secondary stage covers the education of pupils from the age of 14 to 18 years. The pupils enroll at the secondary schools after four successful years at the intermediate stage. At this stage the students are mainly prepared for the university and higher education. All the students in the first two years of this stage follow a common curriculum, then in the third year they are allowed to choose either the scientific or the liberal arts path of study. In 1992 almost 60 percent of the students chose the liberal arts path. This is causing some concern within the Ministry of Education, which has already started an investigation to determine the causes of this bias.

The Religious Institute accepts students after they have completed their primary stage education. In it the students are prepared to specialize in Islamic jurisprudence and the structure of Arabic literature and language before entering the Ancient Institute of Islamic Learning in Cairo, or Dar al-Uloom also in Cairo. Since 1966 students also enter Kuwait University, Al-Sharia College, or religious colleges in Saudi Arabia. The curriculum of the Religious Institute is designed to offer both a general education and a deep knowledge of the Koran, Islamic traditions, and Islamic jurisprudence.

Aside from the public schools which are financed and supervised by the Ministry of Education, there are various private schools which are either owned by individuals or by foreign missionaries. In order to ensure a satisfactory education for children who enroll in these schools, the Ministry of Education keeps a close watch on them. They are given all necessary advice and those schools which teach in Arabic are supplied with books and other financial support. These schools are attended by expatriate children who cannot find any place in the public schools. The regulation for expatriates to be allowed a place in the public school is that the parents should have been living in Kuwait for no less than 10

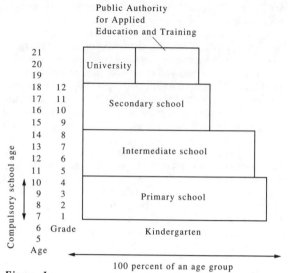

Figure 1

Kuwait: Structure of the formal education system

years. There is a very small number of Kuwaitis who attend either the American or the English schools.

There was a great increase in the number of students attending private schools between 1971 and 1989. In 1971, there were 7,162 students in private schools and 23,091 in Kuwaiti schools. By 1989, the numbers were 93,135 and 39,132 respectively.

Until 1966 all Kuwaiti students who wanted to pursue higher education had to attend universities in either other Arab countries or Western ones such as the United Kingdom and the United States. In the early 1960s the number of Kuwaiti students in such universities increased rapidly, as did the country's need for specialists in various fields. It was such developments, with all their far-reaching consequences, which finally led the state to establish a university in Kuwait.

The university opened in 1966, at which date there were only two faculties (science and arts). By the early 1980s there were faculties of arts, science, commerce, law, engineering and petroleum, medicine, allied health, education, and Shar'ai and Islamic studies. The enrollment rose from 418 students in 1966 to 14,106 in 1988.

3.2 Preschool Education

The kindergarten stage is concerned with children aged 4 and 5, and is not compulsory. The main aim is to introduce children to the school atmosphere, to provide them with companionship, and to develop social behavior in their life. It is the only stage which is co-educational. The children are usually introduced in a formal way to very basic ideas in the following subjects: Islamic religion, Arabic language, arithmetic, elementary science, arts, physical education, and music.

3.3 Special Education

In addition to the various kinds of educational institute already mentioned, the State of Kuwait has endeavored to provide special educational facilities for the handicapped. In particular the Ministry of Education has built a number of institutes for the physically and mentally handicapped. These institutes are provided with all the equipment and aid needed to facilitate the teaching of handicapped students so that they can adjust to their physical and social situation.

3.4 Technical, Vocational, and Business Education

This type of education is conducted in the Teacher Training Institute, the Commercial Institute, the Institute of Public Health, and the Kuwait Institute of Technology. Students can apply to enter these institutes after successfully completing secondary education.

Students are accepted at the Teacher Training Institute after they have successfully passed the Secondary School Certificate Examination. The Institute offers a four-year course with curricula geared to providing a knowledge of educational theory and practice to prepare teachers for the primary stage. Academic studies are specialized from the beginning in one of the following branches: (a) science (general science and mathematics), (b) liberal arts (Arabic language, Islamic religion, and humanities), (c) art, (d) physical education, and (e) music.

The Commercial Institute provides the different commercial and industrial establishments in the country with specialists in the following branches: banking, insurance, computer operating, and management. This institute has been successful in leading a number of establishments to employ young Kuwaiti graduates and stem the flow of expatriates into the country.

The Institute for Public Health aims to provide trained nurses who will serve either in the schools or in the hospitals. Usually the students who attend this institute are those who obtained a low grade in their Secondary Examination Certificate.

The Kuwait Institute of Technology provides the country with trained technicians in the following branches: mechanics, electricity, and electronics. In order to encourage young Kuwaitis to attend this institute they are given a monthly allowance of US$200. In addition to this all the top students sent after graduation to colleges outside the country for further training are provided with full scholarships. So far the country has not felt the impact of this institute's graduates, although the Institute has been established for more than 10 years.

3.5 Adult and Nonformal Education

Adult education is under the supervision of the department of Adult Education and Eradication of Illiteracy.

It includes two stages: the intermediate and secondary stage. The intermediate stage offers 20 or 21 hours of instruction per week in Islamic education, Arabic language, English language, mathematics, science, social studies, and national education. At the secondary level, there are 24, 26, or 27 classes per week. The third grade of secondary school is split into arts and science subjects.

Improved curricula in general education schools have been used in the centers of adult education, in the fields of Islamic education, national education, and mathematics.

The department of Adult Education and Eradication of Illiteracy is continuing its efforts to open morning classes for those who are unable to join the evening classes to encourage them to continue their studies. This experiment is being followed up and evaluated to assess its results. In general, morning classes have met with approval by both male and female students and has helped them in their regular attendance.

Programs of hygiene awareness have been supplemented in all centers and stages of adult education and centers of evening religious education for adults. These programs include hygiene, treating problems at the local level, and international problems like AIDS as participation in the program of the International Health Organization. A competition for preparing research studies in intermediate and secondary stages has been arranged. Recreational, sports, arts, and practical programs are conducted for the purposes of artistic expression and entertainment, in addition to training in practical programs for daily living skills.

Nonformal education is supervised by various bodies related to ministries and educational and scientific institutions. The Koran memorization centres offer study to all students over 18 who desire to learn by heart chapters from the Holy Koran and to learn the principles and history of Islam, and history. The duration of the study in these centres is four years for three days a week. Students are awarded an annual bonus according to reports on their regular attendance according to regulations. The literate are also awarded a certificate of success in each school year. Textbooks are distributed free of charge.

The Institute of Islamic Studies under the Ministry of *Awkaf* and Islamic Affairs is a center for religious education to upgrade the scientific levels of the graduates of these centers and specialize in legislative sciences such as the Holy Koran, the Prophet's teachings (*sunna*), and jurisprudence in Islam in order to prepare them to serve as prayer leaders (imams), preachers, and teachers.

Finally, the Ministry of Social Affairs and Labor is responsible for the Youth, Sports and Childhood sector. It runs youth centers, children's playgrounds, youth houses, camps, the Kuwait Club for the Handicapped, and a center for training sports leaders. The aim of these activities is to provide the opportunity for

Table 1
Distribution of the ministry budget (in percent) on education in the years 1985–1990

Programs	1985–86	1986–87	1987–88	1988–89	1989–90
Public divan	7.85	7.95	6.85	6.42	6.48
Kindergarten	7.77	8.40	8.65	9.09	9.07
Primary instruction	24.84	23.72	22.45	22.29	22.06
Intermediate instruction	25.61	25.40	24.90	24.57	24.70
Secondary instruction	17.50	17.64	19.52	19.73	21.43
Other instruction type	2.77	2.66	2.63	2.32	2.40
Public instruction services	6.45	6.60	7.10	7.85	8.58
Other services, missions, private schools support, etc	7.21	7.63	7.90	7.74	5.30
Total	100	100	100	100	100

young people to develop their personal abilities and their personality.

Other nonformal education activities are the public utility societies under the Ministry of Social Affairs and Labor; the Community Services and Continuing Education Office under the Public Authority for Applied Education and Training, and the Community Service Center of Kuwait University.

4. Administrative and Supervisory Structure

Education in Kuwait is administered by the central government which supports most of the schools. Nevertheless it should be noted that the central administration has experimented with some kind of decentralization by dividing the country into regions, each with its own board of education. It has already established five boards of education: the Al-Ahmadi, Al-Jahra, Al-Hawally, Al-Asema, and Al-Farwaneiah. There is also a central governing board at the Ministry of Education in the capital city. This board is formed by the minister, the undersecretary and all the assistant undersecretaries, with the participation of the directors of the five educational regions.

Both the minister of education and the undersecretary have a number of special boards or committees that advise and help them. The undersecretary has five assistant undersecretaries, each of whom is responsible for a department. These are: financial and administrative affairs, educational services, informative student affairs, public education, and planning and development. Each of these departments has between five and nine divisions.

The Ministry also has a number of advisory boards, one for each area of the country and one for private schools. The advisory boards are recognized as an important element in the Ministry of Education. The advisors represent the Ministry in overseeing the schools. They are also responsible for curriculum development, drawing up new syllabuses, preparing new textbooks and supervising their introduction to schools. Advisors are appointed by the Undersecretary of the Ministry of Education, and are all experienced teachers chosen from the best heads of departments in the secondary schools.

The advisory board is subdivided into departments, each department being concerned with a particular subject. Thus, there are boards for mathematics, Arabic, English, religion, science, French, social sciences, physical education, fine arts, musical education, home economics, library education, and handicrafts. Each advisory board consists of the general advisor and chief advisors for each educational board, and for private schools, with their advisors.

Table 2
Number of teachers

	Number of teachers						
	Kuwaitis	Male expatriates	Subtotal	Kuwaitis	Female expatriates	Subtotal	Total
1988–89	2,944	8,988	11,932	8,915	6,987	15,902	27,834
1989–90	3,100	8,848	11,948	9,125	6,914	16,039	27,897
1990–91	3,414	5,599	9,013	8,812	3,266	12,078	21,091

5. Educational Finance

It is the strong belief of the nation that expenditure on education is a great investment in future. Young Kuwaitis are guaranteed free education from the day they enter kindergarten (which is not compulsory) to the day they graduate from university. Free education in Kuwait means that not only are there no tuition fees, but also all necessary textbooks and equipment are provided. Therefore, not surprisingly, Kuwait's top budget priority is education. However, the Ministry of Education's budget rose from 181.3 million Kuwaiti dinars in 1980–81 to 385 million Kuwaiti dinars in 1992–93 (1 Kuwaiti dinar = US\$3.4 in 1992). The Iraqi invasion and occupation of Kuwait for seven months (August 1990 to February 1991) meant that the majority of educational establishments were looted and destroyed. This forced the government to spend millions of dinars on the re-establishment of schools and other educational institutions.

Table 1 presents the distribution of funds to the various sectors of the educational system.

6. Supplying Personnel for the Education System

When the educational system started, the government looked for educational personnel from outside its borders. The first group of teachers and administrators were Palestinians and Egyptians. With the growth of the number of students and schools, the demand for educational personnel increased. Table 2 shows the number of teachers (Kuwaitis and expatriates) in the period 1988 to 1991.

7. Curriculum Development and Teaching Methodology

The Gulf Arab States Educational Research Center (GASERC) has its headquarters in Kuwait. It began a project in mathematics and science in 1981, consisting of four main phases. The first concerned defining the 1981 status of the two subjects in all Gulf States and, with this as a basis, developing general and specific objectives for all grades. These were reviewed and amended. Suggestions were also made for the design of the textbooks and teacher handbooks. The second phase involved the trial and revision of the textbooks for grades two to four, the training of teachers, and implementation. Phase Three consisted of the trial and revision of the textbooks for Grades five to nine, teacher training, and revision. The fourth phase (1992) consisted of the same steps for Grades 10 to 12.

In the Kuwaiti primary schools there are 30 periods per week. The main emphasis is on the learning of Arabic (10 or 11 periods per week), arithmetic (4 or 5 periods), religion (3), general science (2 or 3), arts (2 or 3), physical education (2 or 3), and music (2). Social studies is introduced in Grade 4. There are also one or two free activities periods.

At the intermediate stage there are 37 to 39 periods per week: English and Arabic (8 periods each), mathematics (4), general science (3 or 4), social science (2 to 5), religion (2 to 3), physical education (1 or 2), and music (1). For arts and home economics a distinction is made between boys and girls, with boys having four periods of arts instruction in Grades five and six, and girls having only two periods. However, girls receive three periods of home economics instruction in Grades five, six, and eight, whereas boys receive none. In Grades seven and eight both boys and girls have two periods in arts.

Table 3 presents the prescribed study scheme for the secondary stage of general education.

Four specific eras of curriculum can be identified. In the "old era," before the 1950s, Kuwait depended completely on Egypt for textbooks in all subjects. Therefore, what was taught to Egyptian students was also taught to Kuwaiti students.

The "era of development" from the 1950s to the 1970s concerned the renewal of the content and methodology of teaching. Kuwait pioneered the change of curriculum in the Gulf Area. This not only caused a drastic change in mathematics teaching, but also awakened other specialists in other subjects. This was followed by the formation of special steering committees to develop curricula in various subjects to fulfill the needs of students in Kuwait.

The "era of adjustment" up to the mid-1980s saw the refinement or adjustment of the new curricula after implementation in the schools and after feedback from the schools about the new curricula had been obtained. The development committees started the adjustments of these curricula, including the rewriting of textbooks.

The "unification era" which is expected to last until the mid-1990s concerns the development of a unified curriculum for the Gulf States.

8. The System of Examinations, Promotions, and Certifications

One of the departments within the Ministry of Education is the Department of Examinations and Evaluation. This department is responsible for all certificates which are achieved by Kuwaiti students from all over the world. In addition it organizes through subboards the secondary examination which is held at the end of the secondary stage (Grade 12).

In primary schools, the students' promotion depends on monthly tests. The pass mark is 50 percent, which is achieved by the vast majority of students. Of the small number of students who do not achieve 50 percent, only those who fail to achieve the 50 percent level in more than two subjects are asked to repeat the same class. A small percentage repeat a grade.

At the intermediate and secondary levels, the promotion of students depends on two types of grade. One type is their results on the daily, weekly, or monthly tests. The other is on the general test which is held at the end of the school year. These types of tests are written by the head teacher of each subject at the school, after consultation with the advisors of the subject.

The 12th grade examination is solely the responsibility of the Department of Examination and Evaluation. The examinations are written by the advisors in the Ministry of Education in co-operation with specialists in Kuwait University. Each 12th grade student must achieve at least 50 percent in each subject in order to be awarded the Secondary Examination Certificate. If any student does not achieve the 50 percent in any subject, he or she can take another examination in the same subject two months later. The students are not allowed to retake more than three subjects. If this happens, the student is required to repeat the same grade next year, and this will be his or her final chance. Otherwise the student will not be allowed to continue schooling.

9. Educational Assessment, Evaluation, and Research

In 1985, His Highness the Emir of Kuwait issued a decree creating a high level committee for evaluating the Kuwaiti educational system, under the chairmanship of the minister of education. The committee formed a number of subcommittees, which evaluated the Kuwaiti education system from all aspects and submitted its report in 1987. The results and the findings of the report were conveyed to each body concerned with education. This has been the only evaluation of the system, but there are plans to undertake an assessment of student achievement in 1993–94.

The Education Research Center is an important part of the Ministry of Education. This center is concerned with (a) developing the educational aims for every educational stage and for each subject; (b) assessing different aspects of the curriculum; (c) undertaking research studies for curriculum planning; and (d) collecting all documents and references concerning curriculum development regionally, nationally, and internationally.

10. Major Reforms of the 1980s and 1990s

In early 1980, the Ministry of Education began experimenting with the credit hour system schools, aiming at a major change in the secondary system of schooling. The experiment started with two schools (one for boys and one for girls). Each ensuing year the number of experimental schools was increased, until it reached more than 20 schools in 1992. Another 12 schools will be converted into the new system in the school year 1992–93. The Ministry of Education hopes that by 1996–97 all the secondary schools will be functioning on the new system. The Ministry of Education will also experiment with the so-called "new directed schools" in 1992–93. It will start with two schools in each stage. This adds up to six schools in each educational region, and there will be 30 schools in total. The aim of this experiment is to give the schools more freedom to manage themselves, with the Ministry of Education acting as advisor.

Table 3
Prescribed scheme of study for the secondary stage

| | Number of periods per week | | | | | |
| | | | Arts | | Science | |
	1st Year	2nd Year	3rd Year	4th Year	3rd Year	4th Year
Islamic education	3	3	2	2	2	2
Arabic	7	6	7	8	5	5
English	6	5	7	7	6	5
French	—	—	5	5	—	—
Mathematics	5	5	1	—	6	6
Science	3	6	1	—	11	12
Sociology	3	3	7	8	—	—
Free activity, practical studies, and fine arts	2	2	—	—	—	—
Home economics (for girls)	2	2	2	2	2	2
Physical education	2	2	1	1	1	1
Total Boys	31	31	31	31	31	31
Total Girls	33	33	33	33	33	33

There was a major curriculum conference in November 1992, in order to develop a new curriculum to enable Kuwait to recover from the lack of schooling during the Iraqi invasion and occupation of the country for seven months in 1990–91.

11. Major Problems for the Year 2000

Since the beginning of the educational system, Kuwait has faced the challenge of a shortage of teachers. Before the Iraqi invasion of the country, Kuwait had almost established a stable channel for supplying well-qualified personnel for the education system from almost all Arab countries. When Kuwait was occupied by Iraqi soldiers, Kuwait lost most of its qualified teachers in many different ways. Some were not allowed back by Kuwait itself after the liberation of the country; others chose not to come back for personal reasons. So, the major problem for the 1990s will be to form a new group of well-qualified teachers. The Ministry of Education, in cooperation with Kuwait University's teachers college and the teachers college at PAAET (Public Authority for Applied Education and Training), has already established a plan by which, during the 1990s, the majority of all teachers will be from within Kuwait itself.

It should be noted that the Government gave priority to the rebuilding of schools following the liberation of Kuwait. About 300 million US dollars were spent to enable 80 per cent of the schools to open and start work again.

The other major problem is renovating the curricula to fulfill the needs of the future generation of Kuwaitis scientifically, and to solve the psychological effects of the Iraqi invasion and occupation of the country.

Bibliography

Gulf Arab State Educational Research Center 1992 *GASERC's Scientific Efforts in the Domain of Developing Education in Arab Gulf States*. Arab Bureau of Education for the Gulf States

Husein M G 1987 *The Mathematical Attainment of 13-year-old Students in Kuwait*. Ministry of Education, Kuwait

Kuwait University 1989 *Kuwait University in 22 years*. Kuwait University, Kuwait

Ministry of Education 1992 *Midyear Report*. Ministry of Education, Kuwait

Ministry of Education 1992 *Ministry of Education Annual Report*. Ministry of Education, Kuwait

Ministry of Planning 1990 *Statistical Abstract in 25 Years*. Ministry of Planning, Kuwait

Laos

R. Duberg

1. General Background

The Lao People's Democratic Republic (Lao PDR) is a small country with a land area of 236,800 square kilometers, stretching more than 1,700 kilometers from north to south and between 100 and 400 kilometers from east and west. It is a landlocked country bordering China in the north, Vietnam in the east, Cambodia in the south, and Myanmar and Thailand in the west. The western border follows mainly the north–south course of the Mekong River. Some 80 percent of the country is mountainous and almost half of it is covered with forest (47%). The mountains pose difficulties for transportation and communication. Together with an abundance of rivers, however, the mountains produce vast potential for the development of hydroelectric power. Forests consist of a wide variety of species, including hardwoods. Sizeable deposits of minerals such as iron ore and coal are scattered across the mountainous area.

Laos is the least densely populated country in Southeast Asia with 17 persons per square kilometer. The 1990 population was estimated at 4.17 million,

and is projected to grow at 2.9 percent per year. Most of the population live in rural areas in or near small villages. The capital, Vientiane, has a population of 442,000 inhabitants and a density of 140 persons per square kilometer. Luang Phrabang in the north has 44,000 inhabitants. Two other major cities are situated in the south—Pakse with 45,000 inhabitants and Savannakhet with 51,000. The physical characteristics and lack of development have led to wide disparities in economic conditions, health, education, and other aspects of life, particularly in the rural areas.

In addition to the Vientiane Prefecture, the country is divided into 16 provinces, each one divided into districts and villages.

There are a large number of diverse ethnic groups. The major categories are the Lao Loum (55%) occupying the lowland plains, the Lao Theung (27%) occupying the mountain slopes, and the Lao Soung (18%), who occupy the high mountain tops. Emphasis is being placed on finding ways to integrate more fully all ethnic groups into the economic and social life of the country.

Most of the labor force (85%) are employed in the agricultural sector, which includes livestock, fisheries, and forestry, mostly within the subsistence economy. Women make up 45 percent of the labor force. The primary agricultural activity is the cultivation of irrigated lowland and upland rice. Other crops include coffee, tea, cotton, tobacco, sweet potatoes, cassava, maize, and peanuts. The livestock holdings include buffalo, cattle, pigs, and sheep. The remaining 15 percent of the working population is employed within the service and public sectors. The industrial and service sectors of the economy currently account for about 40 percent of the Gross Domestic Product (GDP). The annual per capita income is estimated to be US$180 (1990), excluding the nonmonetized segment of the economy. Under the incentives of the New Economic Mechanism, adopted in 1986, the industrial, manufacturing, and wholesale and retail trade in the services sector are steadily growing. The real growth of GDP is 8.4 percent. The annual inflation rate (CPI) in the capital is 19.6 percent. The ratio of imports to exports is 3:1. The budget deficit is 81.51 billion kip (US$1=694 kip). Current Government Expenditure (1990) is 69.86 billion kip.

The commercial opening across the Mekong to Thailand is vastly enhanced by the New Bridge (1994) which connects Laos with Thailand at Thadeua–Nong Khai.

The crude birthrate is 44 per 1000. Infant and under-five mortality rates are 104 and 156 per 1000 live births, respectively. Life expectancy is 50 years. Improvements in health and sanitation are vital.

Literacy, as well as primary school enrollments, varies from province to province. Adult literacy ranges from 45 to 76 percent and gross enrollment ratios from 57 percent in Louang Namtha to 131 in the Vientiane Municipality. In some rural areas, only 25 percent of the children enroll in school.

Primary schools do not exist in every village. In many mountainous areas there are no schools at all; in others only one, two, or three grades are offered and the children are unable to complete the whole five-year primary cycle. In numerous rural primary schools, multigrade teaching is practiced by unqualified or untrained teachers who lack necessary school materials.

For centuries Laos suffered from the competing ambitions of two regional powers, Thailand and Vietnam. The French colonized Laos for strategic reasons. After they left in 1953, Laos endured two decades of civil war, aggravated by the wider conflict in the area. The communist Pathet Lao movement brought stability when it took power in 1975. Isolation and stagnation endured till late 1986 when the Laotien politburo introduced a Southeast Asian version of *perestroika*—the "New Economic Mechanism."

The President is the head of State, and the main organ of government is the Council of Ministers, headed by the Prime Minister. The main legislative body is the Supreme People's Assembly. The local government structure extends from the provincial level through the district level to the village level. The Lao People's Revolutionary Party (LPRP) is the only political party. It is governed by a Central Committee, headed by an Executive Committee. The Party organization extends downward to the district and village levels, in parallel with the government's administrative structure.

Many small and isolated provinces and districts have encountered problems in discharging their administrative functions effectively. Major shortcomings are connected to the lack of trained personnel, poor communications, and financial shortcomings. Steps are being taken to rationalize the division of responsibilities at the central, provincial, and district levels. In particular, moves toward centralization of most tax and customs collections and major government spending decisions are part of a broad program of fiscal administrative reform.

2. Politics and the Goals of the Education System

A national Conference on Education was arranged in June 1990 to establish national policy coordinating as a follow up to the Jomtien, Thailand Conference on Education for All in 1990.

In response to the goals for Education for All by the Year 2000, the Laos government's objectives for education are to achieve universalization of primary education (UPE) for all children in the 6–14 year age group by the year 2000, improvement of access to secondary education in all areas, and improvement of the quality and efficiency of both primary and secondary education. As from 1996, the government emphasis is to be on the development of nonformal education for disadvantaged populations and ethnic minorities as well as the development of technical, vocational, and higher education.

The following national goals for education have been recommended by the World Bank:

(a) to increase the availability of books and teaching materials;

(b) to improve teacher training;

(c) to allow automatic graduation from one level to the other for the first three years of primary education;

(d) to encourage schools to become nonformal "cultural centers;"

(e) to reduce the number of subjects taught at primary and lower-secondary levels;

(f) to reduce the number of textbooks, lower prices, and ensure better distribution;

(g) to simplify teacher training and reduce the number of teacher-training schools.

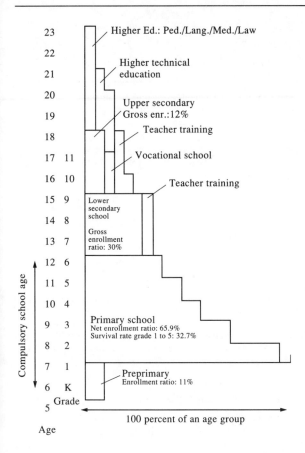

Figure 1
Laos: Structure of the formal education system 1990

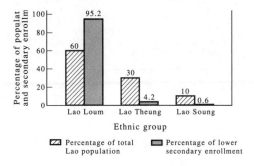

Figure 2
Ethnic representation in Laos
Source: ADB data 1989

3. The Formal System of Education

Figure 1 outlines the structure of the formal education system. Key statistics on enrollments and resources in the major education sectors are provided in Table 1.

3.1 Primary, Secondary, and Tertiary Education

The Laotien education system was reconstructed in 1975. It now consists of five years of primary, three years of lower-secondary and three years of upper-secondary school (5+3+3). Kindergarten, where available, is offered to children aged 3–6. The number of years of compulsory education is five. Normally children start school at the age of 7.

As primary school teachers normally are trained by their own provinces, primary teacher-training institutes are available in several provinces. Technical and vocational schools, however, as well as university-level institutions, are mainly located in Vientiane.

Traditionally, girls did not have access to the

Buddhist *wat* schools as their services were required in the household, looking after younger children, and so forth. In 1989–90, the number of boys enrolled in primary school exceeded that of girls by 13 percent. As the education level becomes higher, the gender gap enlarges. The proportion of female teachers decreases significantly from preschool level to higher education. Also, there are high disparities in school enrollments between urban and rural/mountainous areas, between regions (provinces), and between ethnic groups. This arises because of the problems the government encounters in trying to provide education in the face of difficulties in communication, a low population density in the hills, and the diversity of language and culture.

Student enrollments at the primary level vary from province to province. Gross primary enrollment ratios (nationally reported at 102) range from 57 percent in Luang Namtha, a province bordering China and Myanmar, to 131 percent in Vientiane Municipality. Net primary enrollment ratio in the country is reported at 65.9 percent. Even within a province, ratios differ between rural, mountainous, and other areas. In Luang Namtha, only 25 percent of the children in rural areas enroll in school. This relates not only to ignorance or negative attitudes toward schools, but is also a result of the quality of the education provided to them.

The grade repeating rates are very high. The national average for repeating rates for primary education in 1988–89 was 23.4 percent, with the average for the first grade being 39.8 percent. This means that four out of ten students failed by the end of the first grade.

The survival rate in the primary education system is quite low. The national average for first to fifth grade is 32.7 percent (i.e., 33 out of every 100 first graders complete the fifth grade—the other 67 are drop-outs). Naturally, regional differences are vast. While the national average is 32.7 percent, the survival rates are 15.6 in the mountainous regions, 33.4 in the rural areas, and 40 percent in the urban zones.

Net enrollment ratios for secondary schools are

Table 1
Enrollment and resources in formal education, Lao PDR 1990

	Kindergarten	Primary school	Lower-secondary	Upper-secondary	Teacher training[a]	Tertiary education[b]
Number of students						
Girls	14,008	245,005	37,758	12,251	3,512	2,737
Boys	14,159	318,729	55,987	19,640	4,187	6,556
Total	28,167	563,734	93,745	31,891	7,699	9,293
Net enrollment rate	—	65.9	13	—		5
Gross enrollment rate	—	102.1	23		—	
Number of institutions/schools	638	6,435	698	119	64	30
Number of teachers	1,519	19,970	7,441	2,607	1,105	1,265
Teacher–student ratio	1:18	1:28	1:12	1:7	1:7	

a Teacher training includes primary and lower-secondary teacher colleges   b Includes beside university, pedagogical and technical colleges, also vocational schools

calculated to be 13 percent (gross 23), and 5 percent for tertiary institutions. Preliminary calculations show a gross enrollment ratio of 30 percent for lower-secondary schools and 10 percent for upper-secondary schools. As the survival rates to Grade 5 are low, very few students have a chance to continue on to the secondary level. Figure 2 shows the ethnic representation in the general population and in lower-secondary schools. As can be seen in Figure 2 only 14 percent of the Lao Theung (uplands) and 6 percent of the Lao Soung (highlands) were able to attend secondary schools in 1988.

3.2 Vocational, Technical, and Business Education

The current educational system also includes three levels of vocational–technical education: two years of vocational training following lower-secondary education, three years of technical training following upper-secondary education, and three years of higher technical training following completion of upper-secondary school or the technical colleges.

Specialized higher education institutions belong to different ministries: the School of Medicine belongs to the Ministry of Health, the School of Law to the Ministry of Justice, the Institute of Foreign Languages to the Ministry of Education, the School of Communication and Transport to the Ministry of Communication, and so forth.

In spite of a relatively large number of vocational schools and specialized technical colleges, the needs for trained and skilled personnel are not being met. Vocational schools, in particular, fail to attract enough students to fill available spaces. One problem might be that the curricula used do not correspond to the current needs of the country. A constant problem in all

educational institutions, including higher education, is the lack of funds, competent personnel, and teaching materials.

3.3 Adult and Nonformal Education

In the early 1990s, only three main types of nonformal education programs were being offered: (a) literacy training for out-of-school adults, usually organized at the village level using regular teachers and volunteer students from secondary schools; (b) upgrading programs for the general adult population, the equivalent of full-time compressed programs; and (c) upgrading programs for government cadres organized at both provincial and district levels in order that these people will gain a lower- or upper-secondary education.

4. Administrative and Supervisory Structure and Operation

A number of educational reforms have been implemented since the liberation in 1975. Educational administration has been decentralized to provincial and district levels in order to achieve relevance to local needs. Many primary schools have been built and have become the responsibility of local governments and communities. However, the decentralization has not been accompanied by a legal framework which could harmonize the administrative procedures at central, provincial, and district levels. Nor have the changes been accompanied by an appropriate training program for local school administrators. These shortcomings have caused regional disparities in educational quality, curriculum, and financial and administrative systems.

The previous inspectorate system was suppressed without being replaced by any new structure, which implies difficulties in maintaining a sound personnel management.

Since 1991, a move toward centralization has been made with the intention to create an effective organizational structure at national, provincial, and district levels. The immediate goals are to create sufficient autonomy, flexibility, and local engagement to achieve universalization of primary education for all children in the 6 to 14 year age range by the year 2000.

5. Educational Finance

The government faces urgent problems in financing education. In the early 1980s, the education budget represented more than 15 percent of the national budget. In 1988, the proportion had fallen to 7 percent. The World Bank Report (1991) notes that education absorbs 3.8 to 4.0 percent of GDP in Laos, compared to an average of 3.5 percent in Asia as a whole.

The 1991 education budget (local funds) is 8,202 million kip or US$12 million which constitutes 1 percent of the Gross National Product (GNP). External contribution to education is approximately US$33 million (see Table 2).

Investment costs for school buildings and equipment for primary schools are carried by the local communities. The Ministry's endeavor to give free textbooks to students has not been very successful due to the lack of funds and an appropriate distribution network. Teachers are paid by the national government.

6. Supplying Personnel for the Education System

The government reports that, since 1975, around 18,500 new primary teachers were trained in the teacher-training colleges. Out of about 20,000 employed primary teachers in 1990, approximately 35 percent were unqualified, leaving only 13,000 trained teachers in the system. This indicates that even if a substantial number of primary school teachers are employed in the secondary school system, many trained teachers are abandoning the teaching profession. The rate of teacher time-on-task has also been

Table 2
Expenditure on education 1991

Local funds	US$12 million (1% of GNP)
External funds	US$33 million
Total	US$45 million

Source: Ministry of Education and Sports, Department of Planning and Finance

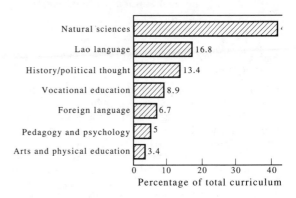

Figure 3
Primary teacher training curriculum 1986–87
Source: Ministry of Education and Sports

proved to be low, mostly because the teachers have to perform other duties in order to support themselves and their families. Teacher salaries in Laos are lower in relation to GDP per capita than in other Asian countries. According to a World Bank report (World Bank 1991), teacher salaries should be increased by 40 percent at the primary level and 75 percent at the secondary level.

Teacher training at primary level is the responsibility of the provinces. Teachers for lower-secondary schools are selected from students having completed lower-secondary education and trained for three years at teacher-training colleges. Teachers for upper-secondary schools are selected from students having completed upper-secondary education and trained for four years at the Pedagogy Institute at Dong Dok in Vientiane.

In general, three systems of primary teacher training are offered: (a) five years of primary and three years of teacher training; (b) five years of primary, three years of lower-secondary, and one year of teacher training; and (c) eight years of primary plus secondary education and three years of teacher training. The teacher-training curricula is reported in Fig. 3. As can be seen in Fig. 3, only 5 percent of the teaching time is allocated to psychology and pedagogy. Teachers at the primary school level need much more training in methods of instruction and evaluation and in curricula development. Inservice training programs for teachers and supervisors are being planned for five of the 17 provinces.

Among five subprojects proposed by the Asian Development Bank in 1991 are the following: (a) production and distribution of textbooks, (b) strengthening of pre-service teacher-training colleges, (c) establishment of a Teacher Development Center at the Pedagogy Institute at Dong Dok, and (d) conduct of a feasibility study for the conversion of the Pedagogy Institute at Dong Dok into a national university.

7. Curriculum Development and Teaching Methodology

During the colonial period, the French language was used at all levels of education. After Independence, some efforts were made for the "Laoization" of primary education, but secondary education continued to take place in French. After 1975, a new curriculum in the Lao language was introduced at all levels of education. However, the adaptation of this curriculum to the national context is in need of improvement. A curriculum reform project, including learning programs, teacher guides and materials, has therefore been drafted in collaboration with the Educational Sciences Research Institute and the teacher-training schools. It is expected that methods of teaching and evaluation of student learning will be developed along with the curriculum reform. Since primary school learners compose a diversity of minority groups, a project on specific training for ethnic minorities is also being proposed.

It has been commented that the teacher-training curricula in mathematics, physics, chemistry and biology (see Fig. 3), which comprise 41.3 percent of total time allocations, would seem to be better fitted to regular high school students than prospective teachers.

8. The System of Examinations, Promotions, and Certifications

The promotion of primary and lower-secondary students from one grade to the other is decided by the teacher or teachers, based on the students academic record and level of maturity. Because of deficient pedagogical standards, the students very often fail to reach the desired academic level, which implies that there are very high repetition rates. The repetition rates for 1988–89, for example, were, on average: 39.8 percent in Grade 1, 19.8 percent in Grade 3, and 13.6 percent in Grade 5. In certain areas, the repetition rates exceed 70 percent in Grade 1. This implies a high degree of educational wastage and makes the education unnecessarily costly. Discussions have therefore resulted in a suggestion to allow automatic graduation from one level of primary education to the next for the first three years.

Secondary education promotions are mainly based on internal assessments, day-to-day accomplishment of specific behavioral objectives, and subject-oriented achievement tests. Entrance to higher education is by selection, based on the completion of upper-secondary education and previous accomplishment.

9. Educational Assessment, Evaluation, and Research

Except for donor-based programs, virtually no systematic research in education is performed on a national basis in Laos. However, in order to identify the needs for "education for all," a national seminar was organized by the Ministry of Education and Sports in Vientiane in August 1990. Also, a study on wastage in the primary education system has been conducted. Enrollment ratios and repeater and drop-out rates in rural and mountainous areas were investigated. Important findings of this study confirmed disparities in educational practices at the primary level.

The recently drafted Curriculum Reform Project, performed in collaboration with the Educational Science Research Institute and the teacher-training schools, also deals with methods of teaching and evaluation of student learning.

The educational strategy to the year 2000 emphasizes the necessity to make every effort to combine education with production application and scientific research. Technical and vocational institutes therefore must be closely linked with production units. This strategy calls for a general revision of curriculum and training programs.

10. Major Reforms in the 1980s and 1990s

Since the founding of the Lao People's Democratic Republic in 1975, the role of the Ministry of Education has been to train new socialist men and women and to serve the work of the revolution through education. In the early 1980s, emphasis was put on adult literacy, preschooling, and general, technical, and higher education. Teaching material and manuals were revised to conform with the new policies of the government. Educational administration has, in the 1980s, been decentralized to local authorities at district and provincial levels.

Late in 1986, the Laotien Politburo announced a version of *perestroika*, followed by a number of activities enhancing democracy. Since 1989, market orientation and privatization of selected state enterprises has been encouraged by the government. All these political and social reforms naturally have a great impact on educational policies and practices.

During the IVth Party Congress, it was announced that the government's objectives for primary education were focused on the achievement of universalization of primary education (UPE) for all children in the 6 to 14 year age group by the year 2000.

Believing that development of education in the Lao PDR is best achieved through the establishment of new structures, systems, and administrative procedures accompanied by the upgrading of personnel, equipment, materials, and facilities, and that this process must commence at the national level and set single national standards, Laos is again experiencing tendencies to centralize educational leadership and administration.

In view of the economic constraints, but with a willingness to invest in the development of human resources, the Lao PDR government has invited international agencies, like the World Bank and the Asian Development Bank, to study the possibilities for educational development. These invitations have resulted in a set of new and progressive goals for education in Laos, which most likely in turn will result in a number of reform actions in the 1990s. However, a deeper analysis of the country's education and development requirements shows that the rapid and somewhat mechanical reforms of education initiated in 1992 suffer from a number of difficulties.

11. Major Problems for the Year 2000

The capital-intensive methods of education development, especially loans, place a heavy burden on the Lao economy. The various commitments, when it comes to locally financed parts of development projects, such as staff payments and local material, put high strains on the economy. Lack of funds is an increasing problem in the development work.

Trained labor, including well-trained teachers, supervisors, and administrators, is a common problem throughout the country. Because of the lack of infrastructure and development, and poor communication, it is difficult to encourage young professionals to engage in education development work in the remote rural and mountainous areas. Although necessary to form national standards, requirements, and procedures in education, centralized activities easily suppress local initiatives. It will require great efforts to encourage and maintain practical community-based

education approaches which meet locally determined needs that are well integrated into local lifestyles. This problem is greatly enhanced by the ethnic disparities in the country.

Bibliography

Far Eastern Economic Review 1991 *Asia Yearbook*. Review Publishing Co. Ltd., Hong Kong
Iinuma T 1992 *Country Gender Analysis for the Lao People's Democratic Republic*. Swedish International Development Authority (SIDA), Stockholm
Phonekeo K 1966 *History of Education in Laos*. Ministry of Education, Vientiane
Phonekeo K 1975 *The Lao Challenge: An "Education Non-polluting", Perspective 1*. Ministry of Education, Vientiane
State Statistical Center 1990 *Lao PDR: Basic Statistics*. Ministry of Economy, Planning, and Finance, Vientiane
Sudaprasert K, Kampe K 1991 *Educationally Disadvantaged in Laos and a Community-based Approach to Education-Development: An Assessment and Program Proposal*. UNDP/Lao PDR, Bangkok
The Economist 1990 *Vital World Statistics, The Economist Books*. Hutchinson, London
The Economist 1990 *Atlas, The Shape of the World Today*. Guild Publishing, London
UNDP Development Corporation 1990 *Report*. UNDP Development Corporation, Vientiane
UNESCO 1989 *Areas for External Assistance to Education in Lao People's Democratic Republic*. UNESCO Principal Regional Office for Asia and the Pacific, Bangkok
UNESCO 1992a *Statistical Yearbook*. UNESCO, Paris
UNESCO/International Bureau of Education 1992b *International Yearbook on Education*. UNESCO, Paris
Whitaker D P et al. 1971 *Laos, A Country Study, Foreign Area Studies*. The American University, Washington, DC
World Bank 1991 Aide-Memoire, Project de Développement du Secteur de L'education, Mission de Pre-evaluation. World Bank, Washington, DC

Latvia

A. Piebalgs

1. General Background

Latvia is a small and relatively new country. Its area is 64,000 square kilometers. Latvia borders on Estonia, Lithuania, and the Commonwealth of Independent States (the former USSR). It was founded in 1918. In 1940, Latvia was occupied by the Soviet Union and became incorporated into it. On May 4, 1990, as a result of drastic changes in the whole territory of the former Soviet Union, the Latvian parliament passed the Declaration of Independence of the Republic of Latvia.

On September 17, 1991, Latvia became a member of the United Nations.

According to the 1990 census, the population of Latvia was 2.7 million with 70 percent of the people living in cities and 30 percent in rural areas, mostly in villages and small towns. Some 34 percent of the inhabitants live in Riga, the capital of Latvia, while most of the countryside is scarcely populated. The government of Latvia has worked out a series of economic reforms, one of the most important of which is land reform. People are encouraged to become farmers and, consequently, the social infrastructure in rural areas must be renewed. An integral part of this process is the opening of small country schools (some with no more than 10 pupils). The greatest problem in city schools is the lack of space that results in them having to work in two shifts (20% of the pupils go to school in the afternoon). At the beginning of the 1990s there were also changes in kindergarten and nursery school attendance, as more and more parents chose to keep their children at home until they started school.

Before the First World War Latvia had a population of 2.55 million; this fell to 1.6 million after the war in 1920. The number of inhabitants increased to 2 million before the Second World War and decreased to 1.1 million in 1950. During the next 40 years, the population practically doubled due to immigration from Russia, Byelorussia, and the Ukraine; this changed the national balance of the republic to the disadvantage of Latvians. Before 1940 there were 70 percent Latvians and 30 percent other nationalities; in 1990 the population comprised: 52 percent Latvians, 34 percent Russians, 2.3 percent Poles, 4.5 percent Byelorussians, 3.4 percent Ukrainians, and 3.8 percent others.

Before the Second World War there were a number of schools for national minorities in Latvia, but in the Soviet period there were only two languages of instruction—Latvian and Russian. There was also a strong movement of "Russification." At the beginning of the 1990s, a number of schools for national minorities (Poles, Estonians, Lithuanians, Ukrainians) were reopened. Schools were also reopened for Jews in Latvia, and teachers for these schools were in part recruited from Israel. There is a plan to provide primary education in most of the languages spoken by the national minorities of Latvia. At the same time, much attention is paid to the teaching of Latvian, which has been proclaimed the state language. For a number of years there were certain fields of education (e.g., aircraft engineering, shipping) that did not provide instruction in Latvian. All state-financed higher educational establishments now have to introduce Latvian as the language of instruction. There are also special Latvian-language teaching programs for the Russian-speaking community of Latvia.

Before the Second World War Latvia was predominantly an agricultural country. At the beginning of the 1990s, 30 percent of the labor force was employed in agriculture, 40 percent in industry, and 30 percent in the service industries (education, health care, culture, etc.). However this situation is likely to change due to the transfer to a market economy. This may well bring unemployment and the educational system will have to provide opportunities for acquiring new knowledge in specialized subjects such as computer operating and management. Although, in 1990, the average employee had 12 years of formal education and 60 percent of employers had also some further education, these figures were satisfactory because the level of practical knowledge required was quite low.

However, with the new conditions, the level must be improved.

In the early 1990s Latvia faces an economic crisis: the level of production is decreasing, there is hyperinflation, and there is the likelihood of unemployment. The government of Latvia is introducing free market prices, transferring to private enterprise, and creating Latvia's own currency. Latvia is not rich in natural resources, but it has an advantageous geographical position that makes it "a bridge" between the East and the West. This specific position also determines the necessity for highly educated people able to work under the new economic conditions.

2. Politics and the Goals of the Education System

Latvia is still a centralized country and the federal government plays an important role. During the 50 years of Communist Party dictatorship there was an over-ideologization and Russification of education. In 1988, the Latvian Popular Front demanded the humanization and democratization of the school system and strongly opposed the ideologization of academic work.

By 1991, the Communist Party had lost its power and influence, the process of the formation of new political parties flourished and the political spectrum was quite vast. In the early 1990s, very few of the political parties had concerned themselves with education problems. Their programs for education were quite similar and vague, but emphasized high academic standards and up-to-date curricula. There was debate about whether or not tuition fees should be introduced at the universities and other higher educational establishments. The objectives of Latvian education system is for compulsory general education to foster the individual development of a person, and for upper-secondary and higher education to provide high academic standards and thorough professional training.

3. The Formal System of Education

Figure 1 shows the structure of the formal education system. Basic statistics on enrollment and resources in major sectors of education are provided in Table 1.

3.1 Primary, Secondary, and Tertiary Education

Education is compulsory for children aged 6–15 years. At the time of writing, children start school at 6 years of age, but the coming reform envisages the age of entry being raised to 7 years. Given this situation, it will be seen from Fig. 1 that the age of 6 years and 6 months has been selected for 100 percent of an age group as entering school. A number of children under 6 attend kindergarten, where they are also taught through a form of structured play. Kindergartens are subsidized

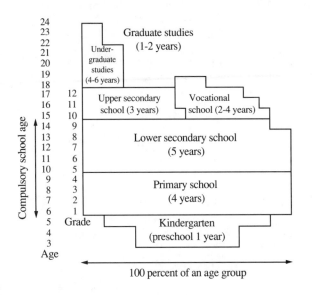

Figure 1

Latvia: Structure of the formal education system[a]

a Preschool, vocational education, and higher education data include part-time students

by local government and parents have to cover only a fourth of the costs.

Primary education comprises 4 years. The children study in public coeducational schools. These schools are government subsidized. The first private schools were opened in 1991. The pupils have four classes a day during the first two study years and five classes a day in the third and fourth grades. The total school year is about 180 days.

The next stage is lower-secondary education which comprises five years. At this stage, the number of subjects taught increases; there are more teachers to teach different subjects (in primary school nearly all classes are conducted by one teacher). There are different class masters or class mistresses at the lower-secondary education stage. There are usually six classes a day and, again, the school year lasts about 180 days. In 1992, there were no private schools. All existing schools are coeducational. There is practically no dropout at this stage of education.

About half of the children who have completed the course of compulsory education continue their studies in the upper-secondary school which prepares the students for further studies in higher education. The rest go to vocational school. Proportionally there are more girls who choose the academic route, while most of the boys choose vocational education. On average, there are seven classes a day and the school year consists of about 200 days. Yet the upper-secondary education system is closely connected with the compulsory

lower-secondary education system as it is provided by the same teaching staff.

If a person has completed a course of compulsory education, he or she can enter a vocational school (about 35% of the lower-secondary school graduates enter these schools). There are technical schools (2–4 years), medical schools (4 years), agricultural schools (4 years), teacher-training schools (4 years), and art schools (4 years). These schools emphasize professional training. Reforms are also expected in this sphere of education.

There are ten higher education establishments in Latvia: Latvia University, Riga Technical University, Latvia Medical Academy, Latvia Music Academy, the Academy of Agriculture, the Academy of Arts, the Culture Academy, the Sports Academy, and the teacher-training colleges in Daugavpils and Liepaja. In 1990 the total number of students was just under 10,000, an increase of 25 percent over 1989. About 49 percent of upper-secondary school graduates enter higher educational establishments within one or two years of finishing secondary school. Students are accepted on the basis of entrance examinations and their academic success at school. About half of the total number of students study in part-time or correspondence departments. Again, drastic changes in the system of higher education are expected.

3.2 Special Education

Special educational programs are provided for physically, intellectually, or emotionally handicapped pupils. In 1990 there were 54 schools for disabled children comprising 6,805 pupils or 2 percent of the total number of school children. There is a teacher for every four or five pupils in schools of this type. A major aim is to integrate handicapped children into regular schools as much as possible.

3.3 Vocational, Technical, and Business Education

Many schools of this type are changing their curricula in response to the changing economic situation in the country. In the higher educational establishments more attention is paid to those subjects connected with business, economics, and computers, thus making the graduates competitive in the new job market. Trainee courses are also very popular.

3.4 Adult and Nonformal Education

There is a sizeable number of adult students in formal education, but there is an age limit for full-time students (35 years of age). There is no limit for part-time or correspondence students. Approximately half of the part-time and correspondence students are older than 25 years.

Nonformal education is provided by a number of different organizations. The purpose of nonformal edu-

Table 1
Enrollment and resources in formal education, Latvia 1991

	Primary and lower-secondary	Upper-secondary	Vocational schools	Higher education
Number of students[a]	309,990	28,220	67,409	45,953
Percentage of age group enrolled[b]				
Age 15–16	10	41	45	—[c]
17–18	—[c]	20	51	9
20–24	—[c]	—[c]	8	19
Number of institutions	979	377	153	10
Average no. of students per institution	317	75	440	4,177
Student–teacher ratio[d]	10.2:1	8.1:1	7.1:1	8.0:1
Expenditure per student[e] (in roubles)	957	1,220	2,660	4,116

a The school data includes students enrolled in special schools. The vocational schools data refer to 1990; 10% of enrollment is part-time. About 50 percent of higher education enrollment is part-time   b All data refer to 1989   c —= Rounded to zero   d The school data exclude special schools. The higher education ratio is estimated from data on student numbers weighted from the level and type of enrollment, and academic staff number   e The data refer to the 1991 financial year

cation is to enrich the knowledge and experience of an individual. A number of these courses are financially supported by the government.

4. Administrative and Supervisory Structure and Operation

The system of education in Latvia is subject to the parliament's legislative power. The Ministry of Education is responsible for general education policy, research, and sports activities; the Ministry of Agriculture supervises professional agricultural education; and the Ministry of Culture deals with art and music schools. There are also some national councils for various types of education. These councils actively cooperate with the Ministry of Education.

Kindergartens, primary, and secondary schools are under the authority of local municipalities, while vocational and higher educational establishments acquire more and more freedom.

There is certainly a strong tendency toward decentralization, the responsibility of maintenance and supervision of kindergartens and schools being fully transferred to local governments (specifically, the school committees appointed by the municipal councils). The duties of the school committees include appointing headmasters and teachers, determining school budgets, and evaluating the teaching process.

The Ministry of Education provides general curricula for primary and secondary schools. The Ministry of Education also appoints school inspectors whose task it is to provide assistance and advice concerning innovations in the teaching–learning process as well as to supervise the general educational standards. Private schools are practically independent of any government control. Vocational education is quite centralized and most of the vocational schools are directly subject to the Ministry of Education.

The higher educational establishments are free to provide their own courses and set academic standards, while the ministries determine the type of degree a specific higher educational establishment can give as well as the general budget. The entire education system is legally based on the Education Act of 1991.

5. Educational Finance

Education has high priority compared with many other public activities. In 1990 about 567 million roubles (6.9% of Gross National Product—GNP) were spent on education. In the mid-1980s this figure amounted to 6.1 percent, but it is difficult to compare these data, as in 1990 Latvia had to make its first independent state budget since the Second World War. It should also be noted that the GNP of 1990 was 3 percent lower than in 1989, yet the expenditure for education ranked second after the expenditure for agricultural subsidy and constituted 19 percent of the state budget.

Practically all education is state financed and is divided as follows: 45 percent to schools, 25 percent to vocational education, 15 percent to higher education, and 15 percent to kindergartens. As a rule, schools and kindergartens are financed by local authorities, while higher and vocational education is financed by federal authorities. Vocational school and university students receive grants (state scholarships) which are the equivalent of approximately 50–60 percent of a minimal salary. There are no tuition fees in state schools. In private schools the situation is different, although they are very few and in the 1990s they were partly government subsidized.

All higher education is state financed and Parliament determines these expenditures as part of the annual budget. About 5 percent of higher education expenditures are covered from independent sources (contracts, research work, etc.). The current economic situation shows that there should also be private contributions to education funding, so the government encourages the enterprises to donate money to education.

6. Supplying Personnel for the Education System

In 1991, there were 31,561 teachers in Latvian schools and of these, 1,628 worked in special schools. Some teachers worked both in lower- and upper-secondary schools. In 1991, 85 percent of the teaching staff was female and 60 percent of the school administration personnel was male.

There is no shortage of teachers in Latvia in general, but there are shortages of good foreign language, music, and physics teachers. There are some problems in the staffing of isolated country schools. The qualifications of the teaching staff also need improving as only 80 percent of the teachers have had special training. In 1990 the average age of teachers was 35 years in cities and 40 years in rural areas. There were also many teachers working beyond retirement age (55 years for women, 60 years for men). The teaching profession is not considered to be prestigious and salaries are relatively low. In 1991 the Ministry of Education introduced a new teacher rating system thus providing the possibility for highly qualified and competent teachers to receive higher salaries. According to this system the teachers are classified as follows: teacher, senior teacher, teacher methodologist, and advanced skills teacher.

Teachers are trained at Latvia University, teacher-training colleges in Liepaja and Daugavpils, and three teacher-training schools in Riga. Teachers of physical education are prepared at the Latvia Sports Academy. Applicants are selected on the basis of their entrance examination results and their previous academic achievement at the upper-secondary school. The students study for four or five years and have both theoretical courses and teaching practice in schools. There is no probation period for newly appointed teachers.

The improvement of teacher training is a priority and a special Teacher Training Act determines the academic requirements for different categories of teachers (kindergarten, primary, lower- and upper-secondary school teachers). The education reform also envisages inservice training. A number of courses for inservice training are provided by Latvia University, the teacher-training colleges, and the Institute for Education Advancement. The length of the courses varies from a few days to three months.

7. Curriculum Development and Teaching Methodology

According to the Education Act of 1991, teaching in schools should be in accordance with the curriculum guidelines provided by the Ministry of Education. The curriculum guidelines include an outline of the basic principles and objectives of compulsory education, the framework of the content of various subjects, and the allocation of teaching periods. The guiding principle is to make the children aware of their future role in community life. Emphasis is laid on the interaction of the school and the community. On the basis of these guidelines schools are expected to provide their own study programs. Schools are responsible for curriculum planning and the detailed definition of syllabus content. It must be noted, however, that children of national minorities should be provided with the same opportunities as Latvian children. The upper-secondary school pupils can choose a number of subjects according to their interests, but there is a set number of compulsory courses: the native language, mathematics, a foreign language, history, and sports. The Latvian language is also compulsory in national minority schools.

In the early 1990s, foreign-language teaching gained unprecedented importance in Latvia. A number of foreign languages can be studied. The first is introduced in the third grade, the second in the fifth grade, and the third in upper-secondary school. Children can choose from English, French, German, and Russian. In some schools they can also study Finnish, Swedish, and other languages. In 1991, the most widely studied language was Russian due to the 50-year long attempts to Russianize the country; however, the most popular languages were English and German.

Teaching materials are prepared by the Curriculum Section of the Ministry of Education in cooperation with academicians, teachers, and teaching associations. To ensure the implementation of the curriculum, the Ministry of Education provides a set of tests.

Generally, the new system of education is oriented towards the preparation of young people for living in the new social and economic conditions. Much attention is also paid to environmental education.

8. The System of Examinations, Promotions, and Certifications

Compulsory education is completely comprehensive. A class is preserved as a heterogeneous unit till Grade 9. This is regarded as important training both socially and educationally. A class master (or mistress) is appointed for each class. The basic approach applied is individual differentiation within mixed ability groups and the school should provide teaching suited to the pupils' abilities. Very rarely are there cases when a child is kept in one grade for two successive years (only in cases where the child would definitely benefit from it). There are two exams at the end of compulsory education: an essay in the native language and an examination in mathematics. If a person wishes to continue his or her education in the upper-secondary school, these examinations must be passed satisfactorily.

On finishing the upper-secondary school, the pupil receives a certificate. In order to finish the upper-secondary school the pupil has to pass five examinations—an essay in the native language, and four exams of the pupil's own free choice. In national minority schools, the exam in the state language is obligatory. There will also be a compulsory examination in a foreign language.

9. Educational Assessment, Evaluation, and Research

The curriculum guidelines provide various forms of assessment at all levels. Emphasis is laid on the forms of assessment that would stimulate further progress of the pupil. Parents should be informed (in writing) about their children's achievement at least twice a year. There is no formal assessment during the first three years of school.

A national survey of achievement was conducted and the results were published in 1992. Latvia also participates in international studies undertaken by the International Association for the Evaluation of Educational Achievement (IEA). The aim of these activities is to provide a factual basis for decision-making to improve the general level of education.

10. Major Reforms in the 1980s and 1990s

The reforms introduced during the 1980s followed the changes in the former Soviet Union's education policy and were concerned mainly with administrative structures and primary schooling. Since the restoration of independence the situation has changed considerably but most of the changes are yet to come. The old financing system, curriculum development, and teacher training will all have to be changed. The aim of the changes is to make Latvian education (and consequently the economy) internationally competitive.

11. Major Problems for the Year 2000

Finances will still be the greatest problem Latvian education will have to face. The economic and social demands set for the education system will certainly increase. One of the main tasks of education will be the integration of national minorities (especially Russians) into the Latvian community.

Bibliography

Builis A 1975 *Vidējās izglītības problēmas*. Zvaigzne, Rīga
Builis A, Gailīte G 1984 *Tautas izglītības perspektīvas Latvijas PSR*. Latvijas PSR Zinību biedrība, Rīga
Builis A 1985 *Mūsdienu skola*. Zvaigzne, Rīga
Drīzule M 1967 *Latvijas skolu vēsture*. LVU, Rīga
Inkis R 1966 *Tautas izglītība Latvijā agrāk un tagad*, Dokumentu krājums (edited volume of documents). Liesma, Rīga
Latvian Bureau of Statistics 1990 *Year Book, Latvia 1990*. LBS, Riga
Latvian Ministry of Education 1991 *Brief Survey of School Statistics*. LME, Riga
Staris A (ed.) 1987 *Tautas izglītība un pedago giskā doma Latvijā līdz 1900*, Rakstu krājums (edited volume of articles). Zinātne, Rīga

Lebanon

G. Zouain

1. General Background

The Republic of Lebanon is situated on the eastern shore of the Mediterranean Sea. It has an area of 10,450 square kilometers (4,035 square miles). The predominantly mountainous nature of the Lebanese territory has helped the country maintain an almost uninterrupted autonomy or independence throughout its history and attracted persecuted religious and ethnic groups to seek shelter in its mountains. It is the site of some of the oldest human settlements in the world (Byblos, Sidon, Tyre).

After the fall of the Ottoman Empire, Lebanon was administered by France (1920 to 1945) through a mandate given by the League of Nations. In 1975, and after several flares of violence caused by its fragile equilibrium and its extreme sensitivity to the Palestinian issue (Lebanon houses nearly 500,000 Palestinian refugees on its territory), war erupted in the country which had several aspects (regional, religious, clanic, left vs. right, etc.); foreign involvement increased progressively in the conflicts and the country was occupied several times. It was only in 1990 that a process of reconstruction of a central authority began. At the time of writing, the country still remains occupied by Israeli and Syrian troops.

Lebanon is a member of the United Nations, a founding member of the Arab League, and has joined the Arab League Educational, Cultural, and Scientific Organization (ALECSO).

Modern Lebanon is a republic with a parliamentary system of government. The Constitution promulgated in 1926 provides that the National Assembly elects the President of the Republic for six years. The Government is responsible to the Parliament. By an unwritten convention (1943), the President must be a Maronite, the Premier a Sunni Muslim, and the Speaker of the Assembly a Shiite. In order to avoid friction among the 17 religious factions which reside in Lebanon, quotas are assigned to each of them at various levels of the government and civil service according to the numerical importance of each group. Traditionally, this has made the government weak, since major decisions must be unanimously accepted. The signed agreements made in the Saudi town of Taef (in 1990) under the auspices of an Arab committee brought amendments to the above, by distributing more evenly the power of decision between the President (Maronite), the Prime Minister (Sunni), and the Speaker of the Parliament (Shiite).

Lebanon has a liberal economy with a predominant tertiary sector due to the importance of trade, banking, tourism, and communication. This sector contributed 70 percent to the gross national product (GNP) in 1991. The contribution of the industrial sector was 21 percent of GNP in 1991, but the destruction of many industrial suburbs and basic infrastructure since 1975 has severely reduced its productive capacity. Giant investment efforts have to be made to enable the manufacturing sector to recover. Agriculture, for its part, though very promising, had a share of only 10 percent of GNP in 1991.

After 16 years of violence, the country is faced with a profoundly damaged infrastructure. The rehabilitation and modernization of the water supply, electricity, telecommunications, and roads is a priority for the reconstruction of the Lebanese economy.

The trade balance has always been negative. The value of exports has fluctuated since Independence in 1945 between 20 and 40 percent of that of imports. However, the balance of payments has shown surpluses of between 5 and 40 percent of the value of imports because of the flow of capital to Lebanese banks, triangular trade transactions operated by Lebanese business institutions, and the earnings of Lebanese emigrants in oil-rich countries. The increase in emigration of mainly technical and professional people since 1975 has increased the flow of capital into the country. It has also had a negative impact on the national economy

because of the impossibility of replacing this loss with a qualified labor force. This is also the case of the civil service which has been decimated and can no longer cope with the reconstruction requirements.

In the absence of an official census, individual studies and surveys must be used for population data. The total population was estimated at 2.75 million inhabitants in 1991; this represents a net loss of at least 250,000 since 1975. Most of the population lives in cities (80%), and mainly in Beirut and its suburbs. The violence which began in 1975 provoked, among other things, an internal and external emigration and a decrease in the population growth rate (2.3% in 1975 and 1.1% in 1990).

2. Politics and the Goals of the Education System

Both French and American influences are visible in the Lebanese education system. Educational activities by French missions started early in the nineteenth century and schools of a Western type were established during the *Mutasarrifiah* period of autonomy (1861–1914) through the efforts of missionaries. In 1866, an American Presbyterian mission founded the American University in Beirut (AUB), and in 1882 the French Jesuits founded Saint-Joseph University (USJ).

Initially limited to a political and intellectual elite, the number of schools and universities increased steadily, literacy became among the highest in the Middle East, and Lebanese technicians and university graduates continue to represent a major element of the economy of the Gulf oil-rich countries while Lebanese publishers have the largest share of the Arab publishing industry. Since 1975, however, education in Lebanon has suffered from its isolation and the lack of innovation and investment. Its quality has decreased as has the numbers enrolled. Illiterates, for example, have grown to an unprecedented 380,000 (UNESCO 1991a). There is still no legislation on compulsory schooling in Lebanon.

More than half of the Lebanese people are bilingual. At every level of schooling, students learn two languages: Arabic (the official language) and French (75% of all school students) or English (25%). Students frequently learn a third language, particularly in the private schools.

There is no stated national educational policy nor are there clearly stated educational goals in Lebanon. Education is, however, built on certain guiding principles to which all parties continue to adhere, the most important being that of the freedom of education: freedom to provide education and freedom to choose the type of education desired. Educational institutions must respect the Constitution, register with the Ministry of Education, and follow the Lebanese curriculum if the diplomas are to be recognized in Lebanon.

In a country with very limited natural resources, a population density of around 300 per square kilometer

Table 1
Development of enrollment 1974–75 and 1986–87

Level and type	1974–75	1986–87
Preuniversity general education	756,992	808,468
Preuniversity technical education	25,791	31,045
University education	33,427	83,891
Total	816,210	923,404

Table 3
Development of preuniversity enrollment by sector 1974–75 and 1988–89

	1974–75	1988–89
Public		
number	320,825	237,054
percentage	42.4	32.9
Private/fees		
number	195,924	352,515
percentage	25.9	48.9
Private/aided		
number	240,243	130,146
percentage	31.7	18.2
Total		
number	756,992	719,715
percentage	100	100

has always experienced strong inward and outward migration flows (refugees on the one hand, and Lebanese seeking better opportunities on the other), education ranks very high on the social scale of values and any debate on education becomes an important political issue in which passions and conflicts develop very rapidly. Hence, the difficulty of opening a national debate on education or of making decisions.

In 1991, the Ministry of Education organized a national seminar on the goals and objectives of education. Agreement was reached on the broad lines of education: education for all, compulsory primary education, primacy of the Arabic language, teaching of foreign languages, importance of technical and vocational education, and freedom of education.

3. The Formal System of Education

3.1 Primary, Secondary, and Tertiary Education

In Lebanon, there are private and state schools and universities. Private institutions are supported financially by student fees and enroll mainly from the high- and middle-income strata of the population. Public institutions are run and supported financially by the government, and their students come mainly from low- and middle-income groups.

At the primary level, there is also a third type of school: these schools are privately run, but subsidized by the government. Their students come from low-income families who cannot afford to pay the high fees of private schools but who do not live near a public school. Such schools, which were, at one time, supposed to support public education have become a hindrance to the Ministry of Education: their quality is low and their cost too high.

Statistical data on student enrollment have been irregularly published by different departments in the Ministry of Education and their availability and re-

Table 2
Student enrollment by level of education and by sex 1988–89

Age group	Level	Enrollments	Gross enrollment ratios[a]		
			Total	Male	Female
4–6	Kindergarten	131,217	—	—	—
6–11	Primary	346,534	125	116	106
11–15	Intermediate	172,424			
			66[b]	61	57
15–18	Secondary	695,554			
Over 18	University	83,891	24.8	31	18.9

a Male and female gross enrollment ratios are for 1988, totals are for 1988   b Intermediate and secondary gross enrollment ratios are combined

Table 4
Higher education enrollments 1986–87

Institution	Enrollment	Percent
Lebanese University	39,654	47.3
American University of Beirut	5,308	6.3
Saint-Joseph University	5,404	6.4
Beirut University College	4,300	5.2
Saint-Esprit University	3,055	3.6
Arab University of Beirut	24,039	28.7
Lebanese Academy	555	0.6
Others	1,576	1.9

liability have suffered much since 1975. Some data can be found in reports by the Center for Educational Research and Development since 1973, in the World Education Report (UNESCO 1991a), and those collected by the UNESCO mission to Lebanon in May 1991. Table 1 compares enrollments between 1974–75 and 1986–87 by types of education.

Between 1986–87 and 1988–89, enrollment at the preuniversity level fell from 808,468 to 719,515. Primary, intermediate, and secondary level enrollments fell by about 13 percent. Enrollments of each of the relevant school ages reveal that 20 or 30 percent of primary school-age children (6–10 years old) and 50 percent of young people aged 11–17 were out of school (UNESCO 1991b). Table 2 provides student enrollment in all types of education for the year 1988–89 (public and private). Data show that sex differences in enrollments at all levels are negligible.

These figures represent a fall of 5 percent compared with those of 1975, though total numbers reportedly reached 808,000 in 1986 but subsequently declined rapidly. The main reasons quoted for this decline are outward migration and the lack of nearby school facilities.

In 1989–90, the public sector enrollment was 237,054 pupils compared with 320,825 in 1974 (see Table 3). Despite the decline in enrollment, the number of teachers in public schools increased by over 25 percent and brought the pupil–teacher ratio down to nearly 8.8:1. However, this increase has been quite detrimental to the quality and geographical distribution of teachers (see Section 6 below).

After preprimary education (offered by a few private schools), the five-year primary school level is followed by a seven-year secondary level (4 years of intermediate education which is either general or vocational and 3 years of secondary education, general or technical). This leads to the official baccalaureate diploma which opens the door to university education.

Higher education in Lebanon has played a decisive role in shaping the intellectual and academic life, and also the political destiny, of most of the Middle East countries.

The system is made up of seven major universities. The enrollments are shown in Table 4.

Hostilities caused changes in the organization of the universities in Lebanon. While most campuses used to be concentrated in and around the Greater Beirut area, regional branches were created after 1975 to cover most parts of Lebanon in order to be able to reach its target populations. Although the private sector accounted for 52.7 percent of total university enrollment in 1987, the share of the public sector rose steadily from 29.3 percent in 1977 to 47.3 percent in 1987. This was because of the drop of the value of the national currency and the rise of education fees.

The relative composition of the student body between nationals and foreigners also changed: the percentage of foreigners was 26 percent in 1988 as compared with 57 percent in 1975.

A characteristic of higher education in Lebanon in 1991, as well as before, was the continued predominance of enrollments in arts, literature, and humanities (75%), and the small percentage of courses devoted to science and technology fields (except for Saint-Joseph University and the American University of Beirut).

3.2 Preschool Education

The private sector is playing a leading role in providing preschool education, mostly in urban areas. In this subsector, three-fourths of teachers are untrained, the curriculum has not been revised since 1971, and a severe shortage of appropriate teaching materials prevails. There is also a need to expand the system with a view to covering the needs of the economically disadvantaged and displaced population. The Kindergarten Unit in the Ministry of Education is responsible for developing the curriculum, preparing teaching material, and the training of teachers. However, the unit is poorly staffed and organized to handle the badly needed teacher training and revision of the curriculum, and address the confused status of preprimary education.

During the period 1981–82 and 1991–92 preprimary enrollment increased by 9 percent. The increase occurred largely in the private sector which, in 1991–92 enrolled 83,540 pupils (63.7%) in 83 kindergartens and 25,500 (19.5%) in private-aided preschools. Only 22,000 pupils (16.8%) were enrolled in 15 public kindergartens and in 842 primary schools offering preprimary classes.

3.3 Special Education

Special education is provided mainly for the physically handicapped, by charitable organizations with the help of a few foreign nongovernmental organizations. There are no statistics available, but the schools are few.

3.4 Vocational, Technical, and Business Education

There are 210 vocational and technical education institutions (22 public and 188 private): 68 percent are in the Greater Beirut area. For the academic year

1986–87, the total enrollment in all public and private institutions was 31,045 students (8,246 in public, 16,373 in private official, and 6,426 in private special programs), representing a mere 3 percent of all preuniversity education.

Since Independence and more particularly since the 1960s, Lebanon has attempted to develop its technical and vocational education streams. A Directorate General for Technical and Vocational Education was created together with a National Pedagogical Institute for Technical Education (which is in charge of curriculum development and teacher training), and an autonomous *Caisse nationale de l'enseignement technique et professionnel* to organize and develop working relations with the industrial sector.

This has led to a progressive shift from vocational education to higher levels: between 1954 and 1987 the share of vocational education in the total sector (technical plus vocational) declined from 85 to 7.7 percent. Participation of girls represented 40.2 percent of the total enrollment.

The basic problems of this type of education in Lebanon are, on the one hand, the nonexistence of textbooks written in conformity with the curriculum, which, moreover, dating from the early 1960s has become obsolete and, on the other hand, the lack of social recognition, though this is beginning to change. The quality of education in private vocational and technical institutions is, in general, quite low, contrary to the quality of general education.

3.5 Adult and Nonformal Education

The Ministry of Education does not deal with this type of education and has never embarked on literacy campaigns or nonformal education programs. This has been the responsibility of the Ministry of Social Affairs and of the semipublic Office for Social Development, which before the war conducted several programs of literacy for adults and nonformal job training activities in several sectors (handicrafts, agriculture, etc.).

Since 1975, the private sector has progressively replaced the public institutions active in this field through the emergence of a multitude of nongovernmental organizations and charitable associations. However, a structured and organized large-scale effort is urgently needed in these types of education and training (literacy and numeracy, organized apprenticeship, or accelerated vocational training programs) to help the social reintegration of the youth who have been active members of the various fighting militias.

4. Administrative and Supervisory Structure and Operation

The structure of the Ministry of Education is highly centralized. It consists of five divisions which come under the direct control of the Minister: the Mixed Administration Organ, the National Music Institute, the Directorate General of Youth and Sport, the Directorate General of Technical and Vocational Education, and the Directorate General of Education. There are also three autonomous bodies, the Sports City Authority, the Lebanese University, and the Center for Educational Research and Development (CERD), created in 1971. Since 1991, the Ministry has increased its authority over the Lebanese University.

Responsibilities for organizing, controlling, and managing the education sector in Lebanon are shared between the Ministry of Education and CERD. The Ministry is responsible for the overall management of schools, and for the recruitment, appointment, and transfer of teachers. The Directorate General of Education consists of two departments, one for primary education and the other for secondary education, in addition to a division of private education.

CERD is, in principle, responsible for all technical aspects of education: planning, curriculum development, educational technology, preparation of textbooks and teaching aids, research on new administrative structures to guide educational reforms, school buildings, research and development, and the administration of 24 public teacher-training institutions.

A few years after the creation of CERD, and as a result of hostilities, the country was divided into small entities and areas of political influence in which the central government lost all power. Thus, CERD has not had the chance to carry out all its functions and to prove its credibility and viability. Within the context of the reconstruction of education in Lebanon, the functions for which CERD is responsible should urgently be recreated within an overall reform of education and its management—which remains very traditional.

An important characteristic of the Lebanese system is that the inspection of schools, which is a part of the functions of the Ministry of Education in most other countries in the world, is the responsibility of the General Inspectorate, directly attached to the Office of the President of the Republic. However, schools have rarely been inspected since the early 1970s.

The curriculum taught in all schools of Lebanon is standard. Private schools must observe the main lines of the official curriculum and their pupils must sit the national examinations. At the university level, there is more flexibility.

5. Educational Finance

The Ministry of Education and Fine Arts' share of the overall state budget varied between 22 percent (1974) and 11.7 percent (1987) with an average of about 16.5 percent for the whole period. In 1988, the share was 16.8 percent. Since 1984, capital expenditures in education have been virtually nonexistent because of the loss of government revenues. Most of the expenditure on education—as for all other sectors—went to cover recurrent costs (mainly salaries). Hence, the Ministry's budget was expended on sustaining the system; no improvements or renewals were possible from national resources. Repairs of buildings, replacement of equipment, or erection of new facilities took place only through foreign assistance.

The share of the Ministry's budget fell from 22.1 percent of total state regular budget in 1974 to 15.6 percent in 1982, 9 percent in 1987 and 7.9 percent in 1991. In 1992 it increased to 12.5 percent. This decline can be explained by the growing proportion of public spending devoted to debt servicing.

The lack of statistical data is a serious obstacle to a study on the various aspects of the financing of education in Lebanon. It is necessary that the Ministry of National Education, Youth, and Sports presents disaggregated budgetary data by level of education, by type of expenditure, and by region. Private education institutions should also provide the Ministry with reliable data concerning schooling costs, financing, and resource utilization.

Meanwhile, the share of the private sector in enrollment continuously increased (57% in 1975; 67% in 1989). The decreasing share in total enrollment of public schools, including private-aided schools, is an indication that during hostilities, all components of education experienced more disruption in public and aided schools than in private schools. Private schools which were affected by hostilities could be repaired and rehabilitated rapidly and could continue to offer education services. Thus they were able to attract students from the public sector.

The results of a study conducted by CERD in 1980 show that in private schools, parents paid an average of L£1,240 (US$0.72) per child at the preprimary level, L£1,650 (US$0.96) at the primary level, L£2,150 (US$1.25) at the intermediate level, L£2,790 (US$1.62) at the secondary level, and L£4,350 (US$2.53) at the university level. In the public system, the total costs are, on average, 20 percent less.

6. Supplying Personnel for the Education System

An important change due to hostilities is that the number of teachers in Lebanon has continuously and greatly increased since 1975. More precisely, the number of teachers in the public sector increased at a greater rate than that of the private sector, while there was a decrease in the number of teachers of private-aided schools.

The overall pupil–teacher ratio decreased from 17.9:1 in 1975 to 13.8:1 in 1989 (8.8 in public schools; 17.3 in private schools [UNESCO 1991b]). The number of teachers in 1982 was 52,017, of whom 26,895 were in public schools, 20,305 in private schools, and 4,817 in private-aided schools (see Table 5).

Table 5
Development in the numbers of teachers 1974–75 and 1988–89

Sector	1974–75	1988–89
Public		
enrollment	320,825	237,054
no. of teachers	21,244	26,895
pupil–teacher ratio	15.1:1	8.8:1
Private/fee		
enrollment	240,243	352,515
no. of teachers	14,250	20,305
pupil–teacher ratio	16.9:1	17.3:1
Private/aided		
enrollment	195,924	130,146
no. of teachers	6,691	4,817
pupil–teacher ratio	29.3:1	27.0:1
Total		
enrollment	756,992	719,715
no. of teachers	42,185	52,017
pupil–teacher ratio	17.9:1	13.8:1

Even though the number of teachers has increased, this has not been the case for their qualifications. As can be seen in Table 6, the qualifications of public-sector teachers have deteriorated drastically.

In addition to attrition, another factor (due to the loss of authority by the government) caused this fall in the qualifications of teachers: militia leaders have forced the government to enroll, in large quantities, members of their "clientele" in the public sector. Education took its share by enrolling large numbers of totally unqualified teachers who appear on the payroll of the Ministry but seldom teach. Furthermore, the teacher-training colleges were shut down at the end of the 1980s.

The rapid increase in the number of teacher-training colleges from 9 in 1973 to 18 in 1982 and 21 in

Table 6
Percentage of qualified teachers 1974–75 and 1986–87

Category	1974–75	1986–87
Primary/intermediate teacher-training colleges	44.2%	42.0%
University degrees	9.8%	1.0%
Baccalaureat or equivalent	35.0%	23.1%
Primary education or below	11.0%	33.9%

1986 was justified because of the need to decentralize teacher-training facilities in order to attract candidates from rural areas. It may also have been caused by the changes initiated by hostilities, including the dislocation of the population and the drawing of demarcation lines between the various factional groups and areas, which necessitated the provision of separate teacher-training facilities to serve the needs of small geographical areas.

Some 9,460 teachers were trained between 1973 and 1987. This is not enough to meet the yearly need for trained teachers for the primary and intermediate levels, because there were and still are a lot of teachers in public schools who remain untrained. CERD has stopped providing extensive inservice teacher training, while 5,000 untrained teachers have been appointed by the government as an emergency measure to continue to provide essential basic education services during the last years of the war. It will be recalled that the teacher-training colleges were shut down.

The training of preprimary and primary public school teachers is undertaken by CERD through a ten-months training period after the completion of secondary education. In addition, intermediate-level teachers complete 2 years of university education in their specialization. Second-level teachers must have a university diploma in their field of teaching and undergo a two-year training program at the Faculty of Education of the Lebanese University.

In the private sector of education, teacher training at all levels is provided by universities such as the American University of Beirut, Beirut University College, or Saint-Joseph University.

The administrative staff of the Ministry of Education, already weak before 1975, has reached a skeleton stage both in terms of quantity and qualifications. Retirements, resignations, and the inability to control the effective presence and work of the Ministry's personnel prevent the Ministry from meeting the pressing needs of rehabilitation, training of staff, and adaptation of the system to the new realities.

7. Curriculum Development and Teaching Methodology

As stated earlier, the Lebanese curriculum has remained unchanged since the 1960s. Established in 1971 and entrusted with the responsibility of educational research and development, CERD had neither the time nor the political power to tackle the issue of curriculum change before 1975.

A major political issue in the 1970s was the "Arabization" of the curriculum (i.e., the teaching of all of the curriculum in Arabic); this was opposed by the private educational institutions due to the lack of qualification of public sector teachers to teach foreign languages. To improve the quality of language teaching and provide a more equal opportunity to learn foreign languages, the Ministry of Education has now embarked on a large-scale inservice training program of preuniversity teachers in the use of foreign languages.

Science education at preuniversity level is also being given great attention: the laboratories of all public schools are being re-equipped with standardized modern teaching equipment and the training of science teachers is being prepared.

In technical and vocational education—even though the national curriculum has not been revised since the 1960s—a serious attempt for its modernization has been under way since the mid-1970s. This attempt has been slowed down by the many years of violence, but it is now being relaunched and the Ministry is giving priority to the renewal of technical and vocational education in view of the reconstruction requirements of the country.

Once the curriculum content has been officially decided there is complete freedom in the writing and publishing of textbooks which are usually easily approved by the Ministry. In public primary and intermediate schools, the production of teaching materials is the responsibility of CERD. In principle, the CERD materials should cover all levels of preuniversity education. However, private schools are free to select from the range of books available on the market.

Despite the war, teaching methods in some private schools have evolved and in some cases compare easily with the most advanced methods available in industrialized countries.

8. The System of Examinations, Promotions, and Certifications

The promotion of a student to a higher grade is decided by the teacher and the school, except at the end of the intermediate and secondary levels, where official examinations are held. They are respectively: the *Brevet d'Etudes Moyennes*, which opens the door to the second level of secondary education or to technical schools; and the two *baccalauréats* (Levels 1 and 2) which are required for university entrance.

Despite the old methods used in these examinations and the strong political pressures exercised by leaders to satisfy their clientele, the government has managed to keep the *baccalauréat* examination highly selective (pass rates vary between 50% and 10%).

At university level, the situation is more complex and the various universities are entitled to provide their own diplomas and organize their own examinations. However, in the fields of medicine, dentistry, pharmacy, and law, there is great similiarity in the content, thanks to the professional bodies that have been able to press for a control of standards. Otherwise, any Lebanese graduating from a university in Lebanon or abroad in a field other than the above can practice freely in Lebanon.

9. *Educational Assessment, Evaluation, and Research*

In the public sector, educational assessment, evaluation, and research were conducted by two bodies: CERD and the Faculty of Education of the Lebanese University. If institutionally such programs have progressively come to a halt since 1975, individual efforts by Lebanese researchers in the public sector have continued, either through these bodies or in cooperation with private educational institutions.

In the private sector, and contrary to the public bodies, the war has provoked an increase in such activities: the American University of Beirut, the Saint-Joseph University, the Makassed Educational Institution, and religious educational congregations have all conducted several in-depth research and assessment studies in education.

10. *Major Reforms in the 1980s and 1990s*

No major change or reform took place in education since 1970 because of the war which started in 1975. It is only since the end of the violence in 1991 that reform of education in Lebanon has been given further consideration. The United Nations and bilateral agencies have been requested to help and to contribute in the reform of the system. A thorough sector survey of education and training in Lebanon was expected to begin in 1992.

11. *Major Problems for the Year 2000*

As a consequence of years of violence, Lebanon is confronted with rebuilding a nation—both physically and mentally. Its educational system has been profoundly damaged. The system which existed before the war has evolved in a random way, spontaneously adapting to the conditions of life during hostilities (decentralization of universities, increasing numbers of untrained teachers). The system has also adapted to the changing needs of a country at the end of the twentieth century. At the same time, its resources diminished drastically. The public revenues were reduced to a minimum, and the national currency lost more than 100 times its value. Teachers and civil servants have left without being replaced, and schools and universities have been damaged and looted.

The most important issue for the year 2000 is the improvement of the quality of education. This is particularly necessary in the public system, where:

(a) 45 percent of teachers at the primary level are unqualified;

(b) damage, theft, and lack of funding have reduced

the availability of teaching aids, materials, and furniture;

(c) 86 percent of the schools are not considered functional—some were originally designed as residential units while as many as 250 were destroyed or damaged after 1975;

(d) within the Ministry of Education and Fine Arts, there appears to be a lack of coordination, while the capacity to manage and plan an educational program has greatly diminished.

At the university level, there is a definite need to reassess the situation in terms of the role of the Lebanese University in the reconstruction of the country and in terms of immediate improvements.

Overall, the first steps towards a rethinking of the role of education and training in Lebanon needs to be intensified and coordinated. The future of education needs to be studied and conceived in terms of a national approach, avoiding partisan attitudes.

Three specific aspects which must be urgently addressed are:

(a) the improvement of the quality of education within the public sector schools with emphasis on upgrading teaching skills, provision of materials and aids, and the central management and planning capabilities of the sector;

(b) the restoring of the physical capacity of the sector through the rehabilitation of damaged public school buildings and the building of new schools with improved standards according to a school mapping exercise;

(c) the improvement of the curriculum of technical and vocational education, thus increasing its social value and its enrollments in a significant manner.

Another problem which is of utmost urgency is the need to reintegrate former members of fighting groups or militias into society through a properly devised scheme of vocational training and civic education.

How the Lebanese authorities will manage to finance and most importantly to plan, organize, and implement the above is still unclear. Lebanon's human and financial resources have been destroyed and what is left is barely sufficient to keep the system alive. Any rehabilitation or improvement will require a long time, but the need is urgent and the demand for educational services, adapted to the new reality, is increasing.

References

Center for Educational Research and Development (CERD) 1977–81 Educational Statistics. In: CERD 1977–81 *Yearbook for 1973–74 and Preliminary Statistics for 1977–78, 78–79, 79–80, 80–81*. CERD, Dekwané

UNESCO 1991a *World Education Report—1991*. UNESCO, Paris

UNESCO 1991b *Needs Assessment Mission in the Fields of Education and Cultural Heritage—Lebanon (8–18 May 1991)*. UNESCO, Paris

Further Reading

Abou-Rejeily K 1986 Displacement of population in Greater-Beirut, *Plus*, 4: 50–56

Al-Chehoumi A M 1988 *Integration of the Handicapped in Technical Education in Lebanon*, (arabic). UNEDBAS, Amman

Bryce J, Armenian H 1986 *In Wartime: The State of Children in Lebanon*. Kuwait Society for the Advancement of Arab Children, AGFUND, American University of Beirut, Beirut

Chidiac L-M, Kahi A, Messara A N (eds.) 1989 *La génération de la relève, pédagogie nouvelle pour la jeunesse Libanaise de notre temps*. Bureau Pédagogique de la Congrégation des Saints-Coeurs, Beirut

El-Amine A, Nizam J 1987 Les programmes scolaires au Liban: étude de l'équilibre des programmes scolaires dans l'enseignement général. In: UNEDBAS 1987 *L'éducation nouvelle*. UNEDBAS, Amman

Faculté des Lettres et des Sciences Humaines 1991 *Annales de la Faculté des Lettres et des Sciences Humaines, Université Saint-Joseph, Vol. I: Propositions pour une réforme des programmes scolaires, Vol. II: Vingt ans d'enseignement au Liban, bilan et perspectives*. Université Saint-Joseph, Beirut

Labaki B 1989 *Lebanese Emigration during the War (1975–1989)*. Centre for Lebanese Studies, Oxford

Lesotho

A. N. Seitlheko

1. General Background

Lesotho is situated in southern Africa, and is entirely surrounded by the Republic of South Africa. The terrain is very mountainous with elevations ranging from 120 to 3,300 meters above sea level. It is a small country with a total land area of 30,300 square kilometers, of which less than 15 percent is suitable for cultivation due to the steep terrain and soil erosion. Thus, two-thirds of the country consists of mountains where only limited livestock production is possible. The climate is cold and dry in winter and warm and wet in summer, with long dry spells which make agriculture unreliable.

By 1831 most of the Basotho recognized as their paramount chief the great Moshoeshoe who had fought against Zulu invasions and united his people. It was in the 1830s that the Basotho first encountered Boer trekkers and lost land and people to them. On the advice of the French missionaries who had settled among the Basotho in 1833, Moshoeshoe sought protection from Britain and this was granted in 1868. The country remained a British protectorate until October 1966 when it was granted independence and became a constitutional monarchy.

Lesotho has a population of some 1.7 million with an estimated annual growth rate of 2.7 percent. The bulk of the population lives in the lowlands. The mountain areas are sparsely populated with scattered villages. Unlike most African countries, Lesotho has no serious internal tribal or linguistic divisions. Sesotho, the national language, is spoken throughout the country and is used as the medium of instruction in the first four years of primary education. Sesotho and English are the official languages.

Communications are a major problem, though much development has taken place. Since Independence,

a large road construction program has succeeded in connecting all the major towns of the lowlands and foothills and is now reaching far into the mountain areas. The launching of the Lesotho Highlands Development Project has made a significant contribution to the improvement of roads in the project area. A domestic airline also reaches many of the mountain areas on a regular schedule. However, there are still a number of villages in the mountains which either have poor roads often blocked by rain and snow, or are accessible only by horse or on foot. This has an important bearing on the provision and administration of education in these remote areas.

Lesotho is basically a poor country with few natural resources. Most of the people are engaged in subsistence farming; agriculture thus accounts for only about 21 percent of the gross domestic product (GDP). Local employment opportunities are limited; 25 percent of the labor force is employed in the service sector which accounts for half the country's GDP. The industrial sector, though expanding, is limited, providing employment to only about 10 percent of the labor force. However, with the implementation of the Lesotho Highlands Development Water Scheme, the proportion may be expected to increase moderately. The scheme, which involves a lot of engineering and construction work to transfer water from the highlands of Lesotho to the Republic of South Africa, is expected to bring considerable revenue to the government and create employment opportunities for both skilled and semiskilled labor, with additional jobs being created in supporting industries.

Because of its geographic situation, Lesotho's economy and infrastructure is highly dependent on the Republic of South Africa. It has a customs union agreement with South Africa (as well as with Botswana,

Namibia, and Swaziland) which provides for some 65 percent of government revenue. Over 95 percent of Lesotho's imports, including a significant percentage of basic foodstuffs, come from South Africa. A significant proportion of the labor force (about 40% of the male labor force and 30% of the total labor force) is employed in South Africa. The migrant workers are of vital economic importance to Lesotho, making a major contribution to the country's employment, household income, and gross national product (GNP) (almost 46% of the country's GNP is generated by migrant workers). However, in the early 1990s increased competition from South African workers and the risk of the tightening of legal restrictions on Basotho labor migration to South Africa as a result of the ongoing political changes in that country, suggest that future employment prospects for Basotho in South Africa's mining sector may be relatively limited.

2. Politics and the Goals of the Education System

Long before the Basotho nation was exposed to influences from Europe, a pattern of culture and education was firmly established. The learning of children and youth was informal, oriented toward practical activities in the home and in the fields. Learning culminated in a formal initiation school, taught by local leaders, traditional doctors, and wise elders, where boys and girls separately learned cultural values and philosophy, personal and family responsibilities, and duties to one's clan and people. There were no dropouts from this system, and the "examinations" were a way for youth to demonstrate their mastery of the skills and knowledge essential to the physical and cultural needs of the community. Some of the more important elements of traditional education included forms of respect and communication; knowledge of clan members, elders, and ancestors; family and community expectations of one's role and work; the exercise of memory and reasoning skills through riddles, stories, and games; values of cleanliness, sharing, and charity toward strangers and the needy; and cultural expression through songs, musical instruments, and dances. Although the traditional system of education continues to a limited extent even in the 1990s, the formal schools have largely replaced the system of learning through precept and example that characterized traditional education.

Lesotho is often cited as having a relatively high literacy rate (estimated at 50%) for such a rural country. The work of the religious missions has been of great importance in this regard. The education system in Lesotho owes its beginnings and early development entirely to missionary enterprise. The greater part of its history is the history of the three missionary bodies, namely: the Paris Evangelical Missionary Society (PEMS), the Roman Catholic Mission, and the English Church Mission. Later the government supplemented the work of the missions by a system of grants-in-aid, but it was not until 1905 that the first steps were taken toward unifying the system under government control.

Formal education began with the arrival of the missionaries of the PEMS in the early nineteenth century, who established schools as a facility to proselytization. From then on any Christian mission that came to Lesotho introduced itself by opening a school for the instruction of its followers. This tradition of initiative by missionary bodies in the provision of education and the scarcity of direct government control encouraged an unhealthy competition between the missions, the result of which was an organic proliferation of schools all over the country rather than a school system. These schools were established without working to a plan; the result of this is the inefficient and uneconomic manner of running them in terms of finance, personnel, administration, and productivity.

In the period 1900 to 1946 several major reports were published. In 1905 there was the Sargant Report. In 1909, the Central Board of Advice was created and consisted of the Director of Education and representatives from the missions. In 1925 came the Smith Report, recommending, inter alia, that the government should assume complete control of educational policy in the country. In 1946 was the Clark Commission, which resulted in the Education Act that defined the roles of government and the churches in the management of the schools. It also established the Central Advisory Board which consisted of representatives from government, district advisory committees, the missions, and the teaching body.

Education continued to progress steadily and was marked by strong cooperation between the government and the missions which is still characteristic of the educational system in Lesotho in the 1990s. School ownership and control has remained largely in the hands of the missions, with the government giving direction and financial support mainly for payment of teachers. In this context education is widely regarded as a joint government/church responsibility with the latter owning and operating 97 percent of the primary schools and 86 percent of the secondary schools. However, major postsecondary institutions, including the Lesotho Agricultural College (LAC), the National Teacher Training College (NTTC), the National University of Lesotho (NUL), the Lerotholi Polytechnic (LP), and the National Health Training Center (NHTC) are government owned.

In all five-year development plans it has been a stated objective for government to exercise greater control over the policies and development of the education system. On the other hand, it has also been a stated policy that government will not "take over" the church schools. The improvement of the partnership between the government and the churches in the operation of the schools has thus remained the basis for all government policies on education.

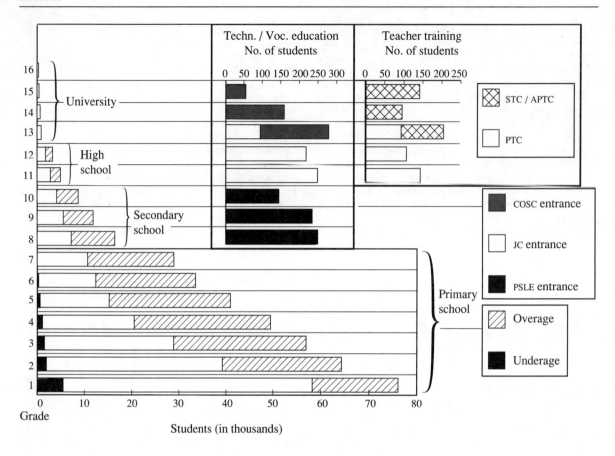

Figure 1
Lesotho: Structure of the formal education system 1990

3. The Formal System of Education

The structure of the formal education system in Lesotho is outlined in Figure 1, and Table 1 provides key statistics on enrollments and resources in the primary and secondary education sectors. The education system consists of seven years of primary education, five years of secondary education (three years of junior-secondary and two years of senior-secondary education), and four to six years of higher education.

3.1 Primary, Secondary, and Tertiary Education

There are 1,190 primary schools, most of which are located in the lowlands. Schools in the sparsely populated remote mountain areas are small and a majority of them do not offer the complete seven-year primary course.

Primary education provides the only formal education which the majority of children can hope to have. It is not compulsory and it is not free, yet the majority of parents make every effort to send children to school. The official entry age into primary schools

Table 1
Enrollments and resources in primary and secondary schools, Lesotho 1990

	Primary	Secondary
Number of institutions	1,190	175
Number of students	351,632	46,301
Number of teachers	6,448	2,217
Certificated	5,178	1,824
Uncertificated (%)	20	17
Expatriate (%)	—	21
Student–teacher ratio	55:1	21:1
Number of classrooms	3,552a	1,254
Number of classes	6,659	1,231

Source: Ministry of Education
a The number of classrooms does not include 840 church halls used for this purpose

is 6 years and the maximum is 9 years. However, many older children are enrolled and an increasing number of younger children, particularly in township and semi-urban areas, are also enrolled due to the influence of preschool and kindergarten programs. In 1990 there were 351,652 pupils enrolled in primary schools. About 2 percent of the pupils were below the age of 6 years and 33 percent were older than 12 years. A number of children whose families reside in South Africa go to school in Lesotho. With the underage and the overage children and those coming from the Republic of South Africa, the actual enrollments exceed the numbers of the 6- to 12-year old children in the country. Thus, the overall participation rate for primary schools is about 116 percent.

All primary schools are coeducational. The normal primary school day is 6 hours long and the school year comprises 190 working days. Instruction in the first four years of primary education is in Sesotho, the national language, and in English in the last three years. The policy of automatic promotion adopted in 1970 encountered strong resistance from both parents and teachers and was officially dropped in 1980. Ever since, primary education has been characterized by a very high wastage rate, particularly in the first three classes where at least 22 percent of the pupils repeat classes each year and about 13 percent drop out.

There is a critical shortage of classrooms and school facilities in primary schools, and classrooms in most of the existing schools are in poor condition. This shortage, coupled with the enrollment of underage and overage pupils and the high repetition rates, results in severe overcrowding. In addition, primary education suffers the problems of teacher shortage, unqualified teachers, and poor supervision by unqualified headteachers. About 20 percent of the primary teachers are unqualified.

Major reforms in the primary sector are aimed at reducing overcrowding through the construction of additional classrooms, particularly in the underserved mountain areas; improving the quality of learning by increasing the supply of instructional materials; recruiting additional teachers to reduce the pupil–teacher ratio; increasing inservice training opportunities; limiting the enrollment of underage and overage children; and reducing the amount of repetition.

Secondary education extends over three or five years (three years junior-secondary and two years senior-secondary education). Progression from junior-secondary to senior-secondary school is through the nationally administered Junior Certificate (JC) examination of the Examinations Council of Lesotho. The Junior Certificate is the minimum requirement for admission into primary teacher-training courses, and craft-level courses and other forms of prevocational training. Senior-secondary education culminates in the external examination of the Cambridge Overseas School Certificate (COSC) of the University of Cambridge Examinations Syndicate. This is the entry requirement for most tertiary programs, including higher education.

Largely because of the increasing public demand for more education opportunities, the number of secondary schools increased from 96 in 1979 to 175 in 1990. The total enrollment in secondary schools was 46,301 in 1990, 40 percent of which were boys. Girls outnumber boys in every grade. This rapid expansion of secondary schools puts a strain on the staff, facilities, and finances.

The secondary education sector is extremely inefficient in terms of quality and cost-effectiveness and it suffers from problems of teacher shortage; poor (sometimes even lacking) special facilities such as libraries, laboratories, and workshops; and a high percentage of unqualified teachers. There is also a high percentage of expatriate teachers, particularly in the areas of mathematics, science, and practical studies. The pupil–teacher ratio is very low, at 20:1. The total number of teachers is 2,213, 17 percent of whom are unqualified and 485 of which are expatriate teachers who make up 27 percent of all degree-holding teachers.

The school year comprises 180 days and the normal school day is 8 hours long. Instruction in secondary schools is entirely in English. Reform strategies in the secondary sector concentrate on the improvement of quality and efficiency; improvement of local-level school management, administration, and use of resources in schools; improvement of the quality of teaching–learning processes; strengthening of the teaching of English, mathematics, and science through the provision of additional instructional materials; the construction of science laboratories; and inservice workshops and professional support to teachers.

Higher education is provided by the National University of Lesotho (NUL), the only institution of higher learning in the country. The NUL is autonomous and is administered by a council. It offers degrees in education, the humanities, the natural sciences, agriculture, the social sciences, and law.

3.2 Preschool Education

Preschool education does not form part of the formal school system provided by the Ministry of Education. Preschools have been established by local communities in much of the country and, in urban areas, by private individuals.

There are approximately 800 preschools catering for about 10,000 children between the ages of two and six years. This figure represents only about 4 percent of all children between the ages of two and six years. The standard of care and education provided in these centers varies greatly across the country as does availability and access. Coverage is much lower in the rural and isolated mountain areas.

The Early Childhood Development Unit of the Ministry of Education supports the program with training, curriculum development, registration and supervision of centers, development of training materials, and the creation of greater public awareness of the needs of young children. The Unit has developed guidelines which will enable the Ministry of Education to control the expansion of preschools and to ensure that the programs are of uniform and acceptable standards.

3.3 Special Education

Existing special education centers only cater for children with physical and emotional disabilities. These centers, with the exception of the Resource Center for the Blind which receives an annual subvention from the government, are almost entirely funded by nongovernmental organizations. There are approximately 250 disabled children in the centers. Of these, 150 have physical disabilities, mostly as a result of polio, and attend schools adjacent to the centers. There are three specially trained teachers of the blind supporting a total of 40 blind children integrated in schools adjacent to the Resource Center for the Blind. There is one residential school for the deaf with one trained teacher catering for 40 children aged 7–16 years. Another center has successfully integrated children with emotional disabilities and children with a variety of learning problems with other children.

3.4 Vocational, Technical, and Business Education

Technical and vocational education and training are offered in some secondary-level and postsecondary-level institutions run by the churches and under government control. A number of the vocational schools are for girls only, offering home economics as a three-year postprimary course. Another five institutions offer craft-level training in leather work, bricklaying, carpentry and joinery, fitting and turning, plumbing, motor mechanics, electrical installation, basic electronics, masonry, and upholstery. The Lerotholi Polytechnic, a government-owned institution, offers diploma courses in architecture, civil engineering, electrical engineering, mechanical engineering, commercial studies, dressmaking, and tailoring.

In 1990 a total of 1,690 students were enrolled in technical and vocational institutions (see Fig. 2), of whom 672 were girls enrolled in the home economics courses. The remaining 1,018 students were enrolled in technical and vocational training, of whom 785 were boys. In addition to vocational training under the Ministry of Education, there is also the Lesotho Agricultural College (under the Ministry of Agriculture), the National Health Training Centre (under the Ministry of Health), and a variety of smaller training institutions. The participation rate for tertiary education (including teacher training and higher education) is only 2 percent of an age group.

Government policy attaches high priority to the improvement of technical and vocational education and training as a key element in the development of Basotho industry and in the creation of local employment opportunities, especially in view of declining employment availability for Basotho workers in the South African mines. In 1987 the Lesotho Technical and Vocational Training Act was passed. The Act makes provision for the establishment of the Department of Technical and Vocational Education and Training within the Ministry of Education and for the constitution of the Technical and Vocational Training Board comprising representatives of government ministries of industry, trade and commerce, and the donor community. The purpose of the Act is to make provision for the development of persons for skilled occupations in trade and industry. It is in the plan of the government to upgrade and expand existing tertiary vocational training institutions to improve the quality of craft-level training, integrating these diverse institutions into a coherent national system.

3.5 Adult and Nonformal Education

Although the literacy rate is estimated at 50 percent, there are still a number of people in need of basic education. The literacy programs cover only about 4 percent of those classified as illiterate. There is clearly a need for alternative programs not only for adults, but also for those children who for various reasons are unable to attend primary schools or drop out of school before attaining functional literacy.

Adult and nonformal education is offered by the Ministry of Education through the Lesotho Distance Teaching Center (LDTC) and the National University of Lesotho through the Institute of Extra-Mural Studies (IEMS). The Institute offers short-term courses throughout the country to varied groups of adults. As a part of the University, it also offers off-campus business studies and adult education programs at certificate and diploma levels.

The Lesotho Distance Teaching Center (LDTC) was established in 1974 to provide alternative educational opportunities for people who do not have access to formal education. To achieve this the Center has assumed a number of functions which include providing correspondence courses at the Junior Certificate and Cambridge Certificate levels; sponsoring formal and nonformal education radio programs; assuming responsibility for the adult nonformal education programs of the Ministry of Education; running literacy and numeracy programs for out-of-school youth and adults; providing support services and education materials for a variety of nonformal education programs run by private agencies and government departments; and providing support to the mass media in Lesotho. The Distance Teaching Center has undertaken research and surveys and produced reports and publications on various aspects of adult and nonformal education. It also plays a significant role in the Lesotho Inservice Education for Teachers (LIET) program run jointly with the NTTC. The program is intended to upgrade the academic and pedagogic skills of some primary school teachers and headteachers.

4. Administrative and Supervisory Structure and Operation

As indicated above, education is a joint responsibility shared by the government, the church, and the community. The government pays the salaries of more than 95 percent of the teachers in the schools. However, the immediate responsibility for hiring, transferring, and disciplining teachers rests with the school manager who communicates his decisions for approval by the government through the Educational Secretary. The community is represented through school management committees whose role is to advise the school proprietor in the administration and management of the school. The Ministry of Education is decentralized to the districts through the inspectorate. The role of the inspectorate in the schools is largely advisory; reports are sent to headteachers, school managers, and educational secretaries for action and to the Ministry of Education for information and, if necessary, follow-up action.

With the exception of three technical/vocational institutions which are church owned, all tertiary institutions are operated by the government either directly as government departments assisted by boards of control or through councils, as in the case of the University which is autonomous. Plans are under way to grant autonomy to the National Teacher Training College and the Lerotholi Polytechnic.

In addition to the payment of teachers, the government provides school facilities through its capital budget. The government is also responsible for the pronouncement of policy, determination of the curriculum and syllabuses, the setting of standards, and the monitoring and evaluation of the education system.

5. Educational Finance

Government recurrent expenditure on education increased from M26 million (US$7.6 million) in the financial year 1980–81 to M121 million (US$35.5 million) in 1989–90. (The Maloti (M) has a 1:1 relationship with the South African Rand). In addition, parents have continued to pay about 30 percent of the total costs of the schools. To this amount should be added fees and contributions made for nonformal and vocational education, as well as church contributions and community contributions in kind for school buildings. In 1990–91 the allocation for recurrent expenditure on education was approximately 27 percent of the total government recurrent expenditure. The per pupil expenditure for a primary school was M213 (US$63) and for a secondary school M327 (US$96). In the area of school buildings and maintenance there has been a significant shift toward all capital financing through government with the assistance of a variety of bilateral and international agencies. This financing also includes food aid to primary schools in the remote and mountain areas, technical-assistance financing for specific projects and scholarships for training in Lesotho, in the region, and abroad. Full-time students in higher education are eligible for financial assistance through the Loan Bursary Scheme administered by the National Manpower Development Secretariat. In 1990, about M4 million (US$1.2 million) was paid by government as sponsorship for 1,038 students studying at the National University of Lesotho. The loans are repayable by the students upon completion of their studies, at the rate of 100 percent of the loan for those who seek employment outside the country, 65 percent of the loan for those who seek employment in the private sector, and 50 percent for those who work in the public service. See Table 2 for a breakdown of per-pupil expenditure and percentage allocation of the state budget for each sector of education.

Table 2
Per-pupil expenditure and percentage of the budget allocated to primary, secondary, technical, and higher education

	Per pupil expenditure[a]	Percentage allocation of the state budget
Primary	213	52%[b]
Secondary	327	30%[c]
Technical	3,513	2.4%
Higher education	15,024	15%
Other (administration)		1%

a In Lesotho Maloti   b Primary includes all the activities of the Ministry of Education relating directly to primary education, including teacher training   c Secondary includes all Ministry of Education activities relating directly to secondary education, including secondary teacher training at the National Teacher Training College

6. Supplying Personnel for the Education System

Primary and junior-secondary teacher education is provided by the National Teacher Training College (NTTC). The College opened in 1975 following the phasing out by the government of the seven mission-owned teacher-training colleges and it met a long-felt need for a centralized teacher education institution for both preservice and inservice teachers. It offers a variety of three-year programs leading to the Primary Teacher Certificate, the Advanced Primary Teacher Certificate, and the Secondary Teacher Certificate. In 1980, the NTTC introduced a program of teacher training in technical subjects for secondary schools (the Secondary Technical Teachers Certificate—STTC), and in 1990 the Diploma in Technology (Education) was launched for STTC graduates. Many of the teachers graduating from the NTTC later upgrade their qualifications by undertaking the diploma courses in education leading to the Bachelor of Education degree of the National University of Lesotho (NUL). The NTTC, in collaboration with the LDTC, also trains primary school teachers through a part-time, inservice program known as the Lesotho Inservice Education for Teachers (LIET) program. The program has been in operation since 1976 and approximately 1,500 unqualified teachers have received professional certificates through it. In 1986 the NTTC launched an inservice program for primary school headteachers in educational leadership. The first intake of 85 received their certificates in 1989.

The Faculty of Education of the National University of Lesotho provides senior-secondary teacher education programs. These are comprised mainly of the four-year Bachelor of Science Education (BSc Ed) program; Bachelor of Arts Education (BA Ed) program, and/or a four-year degree in a major discipline followed by a one-year certificate in education—the Postgraduate Certificate in Education. In 1989–90, 487 students were enrolled in education programs at NUL.

Support for teachers is provided through a number of inservice training activities run by the inspectorate, the National Curriculum Development Centre (NCDC), the National University of Lesotho (NUL) and the teachers' associations. Attendance at all these activities is voluntary.

The NCDC provides inservice training about new curriculum materials. The inspectorate provides inservice training in school management and administration for headteachers and school administrators and for teachers in the various subject areas. School-based inservice training for teachers is provided through the Area and District Resource teacher network focusing on teaching methodology, classroom management, and general administration.

The NUL faculty of education runs induction courses for new entrants into the teaching service. Participation in such courses is voluntary and is confined to secondary school teachers graduating from the NUL, and the NTTC. The NUL also provides school-based support for teachers of mathematics and science in secondary schools.

Nearly 8,665 teachers were employed in schools in 1990. Of these, 6,448 were employed in primary schools and 2,217 in secondary schools. Some 85 percent of the teachers are female, and it is not unusual to find an entire school staff comprised of female teachers.

As has been noted above, both the primary and the secondary sectors suffer serious teacher shortages and are plagued by a high mobility of staff, resulting in high losses of trained teachers, especially to neighboring countries. In April 1991, teacher salaries and conditions of service were improved. To relieve the acute teacher shortage in schools, plans are under way to increase the output of the NTTC.

7. Curriculum Development and Teaching Methodology

In 1980, a National Curriculum Committee was established to advise government on all curriculum matters. Curriculum development is highly centralized and is based at the National Curriculum Development Center (NCDC). The NCDC works through national subject panels comprising representatives of teachers, teacher-training institutions, the inspectorate, and teachers' associations. All curriculum materials intended for use in the schools are approved by the government on the advice of the National Curriculum Committee. The Instructional Materials Resource Center (IMRC) is closely linked to NCDC to assist in the production of prototype instructional materials developed by the subject panels. Another important link, the Schools Supplies Unit, provides procurement services for the curriculum materials and is responsible for the timely distribution of such materials to the schools.

All primary schools follow a common curriculum and a common syllabus determined by the government. Instructional materials in the form of pupils' textbooks and teachers' guides and other supplementary materials are prescribed by the government and provided to the schools through the national book loan scheme.

The primary curriculum includes Sesotho, English, mathematics, science, social studies, and practical studies (gardening, agriculture, home economics). There are still shortages of supplementary materials and pupil workbooks despite the government's book loan scheme. The teaching of English in the first three years (i.e., Grades 1–3) is supported through the provision of radios and support materials to schools and the broadcast of daily radio lessons for each grade. This has had a significant impact on the teaching–learning of English in primary schools.

The curriculum in secondary schools is guided by the government policy of diversification. While core subjects such as Sesotho, English, mathematics, science, and social studies are offered, the introduction of practical subjects that will give secondary education a vocational bias is a requirement. This is being implemented with visible promise of success in an increasing number of secondary schools where the teaching of agriculture, home economics, basic handicrafts (woodwork, metalwork, and technical drawing), commercial studies, and development studies is taking place. The aim of this policy is to help to prepare students for the world of work and to provide a sound academic base for those with the potential and the resources to proceed into tertiary education.

8. The System of Examinations, Promotions, and Certifications

The education system in Lesotho is highly examination oriented. End-of-year examinations are a characteristic feature in all grades culminating with a public examination at the end of primary education (the Primary School Leaving Examination—PSLE—organized by the Curriculum Center), at the end of junior-secondary education (the Junior Certificate Examination—JC—organized by the Examinations Center of Lesotho), and at the end of senior-secondary education (the Cambridge Overseas School Certificate examination—COSC). The external examinations (public examinations) mainly serve as a selection instrument for the next educational level.

There is an urgent need for one institution for examinations at the various levels from primary through to O-level. This will help to remove unnecessary duplication of effort and contribute toward efficient use of available resources.

Furthermore, concern has been raised about the relevance and appropriateness of the Cambridge Overseas examinations to the needs of the country and individual students. It is becoming more and more expensive each year and, in 1990, at least M1.4 million was paid to the Cambridge Syndicate. In response to these problems, steps have been taken to prepare for the localization of the O-level examinations.

9. Educational Assessment, Evaluation, and Research

Educational evaluation is undertaken by the Testing and Evaluation section of the Curriculum Center on a very limited scale due to problems of staffing. This consists mainly of the preparation and pretesting of items for the primary school leaving examination to assess their psychometric properties. The section also produces analyses of both the JC and the COSC examinations to provide useful data for the NCDC, the inspectorate, the schools, and other interested bodies.

The Lesotho Distance Teaching Center also engages in research and evaluation for internal use by the Center and also on behalf of other organizations involved in nonformal education programs.

The Institute of Education of the National University of Lesotho undertakes research in various subjects of educational interest. There is also the Lesotho Educational Research Association which is an independent body whose main objective is to promote educational research. The association collaborates with similar associations in the sister countries of Botswana and Swaziland and organizes seminars and symposia to share results of studies and research undertaken.

10. Major Reforms in the 1980s and 1990s

The following objectives for education were identified at the beginning of the 1980s:

(a) to increase access to education so that all Basotho children are assured of at least primary education;

(b) to ensure that educational programs are relevant to the country's economic development; and

(c) to ensure that sufficient numbers of individuals are equipped with appropriate occupational, technical, and managerial skills to facilitate the country's socioeconomic development.

Significant progress was made toward the achievement of these objectives in the 1980s. Primary school enrollments increased by about 40 percent from under 250,000 to nearly 350,000, and the number of secondary schools increased from 100 in 1980 to about 180 in 1990. In addition, the number of unqualified teachers was reduced and several programs to improve the teaching of mathematics, science, and English were substantially strengthened. Enrollments in technical and vocational education also increased from about 1,200 in 1980 to about 1,700 in 1990.

11. Major Problems for the Year 2000

In spite of the achievements outlined above, education in Lesotho still suffers various problems, including deterioration in the quality of education, lack of relevance to occupational and social realities, high dropout and repetition rates, very poor facilities and staffing in both the primary and the secondary sectors, high costs to government and parents, weak management, poor professional supervision, and lack of effective quality control.

In response to these challenges, the government intends, during the Fifth Plan period (1991–92 to 1995–96), to focus explicitly on addressing these quality and efficiency issues while restricting further expansion of the education system to a minimum. Two general priorities have been adopted for the development of the education system. First is the policy of providing basic education for all. By basic education is meant those skills and competencies required for individual development and social interaction. This is to be achieved, in the first instance, by providing for complete primary education for all children and by providing the opportunity for continuing education for youth and adults, particularly those who have no access to formal education. The second general priority is to provide sufficient numbers of people with appropriate occupational, technical, and managerial skills to ensure the development of the modern sector of the economy. This will be achieved through both formal and nonformal education.

Bibliography

Basutoland, Ministry of Education 1950 *Annual Report by the Director of Education for the Year 1950*. The Government Printer, Maseru

Central Planning and Development Office 1988 *Kingdom of Lesotho Fourth Five-Year Development Plan 1986–87 to 1990–91*. Ministry of Planning, Economic and Manpower Development, Maseru

Hawes H R 1977 Primary school curriculum change in Lesotho (a consultancy report). Maseru

Ministry of Education 1978 Report on the views and recommendations of the Basotho nation regarding the future of education in Lesotho. Report of the National Dialogue and Seminar, Maseru

Ministry of Education 1984 Secondary and high schools in Lesotho—strategies for improvement. Report of a Study Team on Secondary and High Schools in Lesotho, Maseru

Ministry of Education 1988 *Clarification of Lesotho's Education Policies and Priorities*. Ministry of Education, Maseru

Stevens R P 1967 *Lesotho, Botswana and Swaziland: The Former High Commission Territories in Southern Africa*. Frederick A Praeger, New York

Liberia

R. Duberg

1. General Background

Liberia is situated between the fourth and ninth latitudes north of the Equator on the west coast of Africa. It is bounded by the Atlantic Ocean, Guinea, Sierra Leone, and Côte d'Ivoire. The area is 111,369 square kilometers. The flat costal plain, which is 15 to 55 kilometers wide and 570 kilometers long, includes swamps, forests, and savannah. The northern highlands contain Liberia's greatest elevations, including the Nimba and Wologisi ranges reaching up to 1,752 meters above sea level. Almost 60 percent of the surface is covered with rainforest. The climate is tropical with an average temperature of 21 to 28 degrees Celsius and a humidity of about 90 percent.

The 1989 population was 2,508,000 with a growth rate of 3.2 percent. The crude birthrate is 4.5 and the mortality rate 1.3 percent. Average life expectancy is 55 years. Due to the civil war, more than 700,000 people left Liberia during 1990–91, most of them settling in refugee camps in neighboring countries. Approximately 30,000 Lebanese, American, and European people also left the country during the war.

The economy has been in rapid decline since 1980, partly because of mismanagement but also because of massive capital flight and generally poor world prices for the main exports—rubber and iron ore. In 1989, per capita Gross National Product (GNP) was US$395, external debt US$1.68 billion, exports US$505 million, and imports US$394 million. External aid, mainly from the United States, the European Community, the International Bank for Reconstruction and Development (IBRD), Japan, and Germany, amounted to US$65 million.

In 1989, 70 percent of the working population were occupied within the agricultural sector, 9 percent within industry, and 21 percent within services.

The main groups composing the Liberian population are the 16 indigenous African tribes, nontribal Liberians descending from the settlers (freed American slaves), and non-Liberian Africans from neighboring African countries. The major ethnic groups include Kpelle, Bassa, Gio, Kru, Grebo, and Mano. Each of these tribes represents 100,000 to 300,000 people. Other tribes representing 100,000 people or less include the Krahn, Gola, Kissi, and Vai. Although each tribe has its own language, English is the official language of the country.

Liberia is officially considered to be a Christian state. Less than one-fourth of the population are Muslims. The traditional belief system constitutes an important part of village life in Liberia. Liberians of tribal descent have managed to preserve their social structure and norms. Their lives are still governed to a great degree by gender-oriented secret societies—Poro for men and Sande or Bundu for women. Through a traditional school system and other village activities, the secret societies transmit the tribal culture from one generation to the next.

The demographic pattern of Liberia is characterized by a number of features typical for developing nations: almost half of the population is below the age of 15; the growth rate in the capital and in coastal districts is comparatively high; and migration toward urban centers is vast, implying social problems such as a high rate of unemployment, slum formations, and increasing crime.

The Constitution provides for the division of the government into three independent branches: the executive, the legislature, and the judiciary. The executive power is vested in the president. An interim president was inaugurated in November 1990, and an interim government of national unity was appointed in January 1991 pending presidential and general elections.

For more than 130 years Liberia has been known as one of the most stable countries in Africa. Instances of political upheaval other than minor tribal conflicts have been few and far between. The True Whig Party governed Liberia from the time the Republic was established in 1848 (by freed American slaves) up to April 1980 when a military coup led by Master Sergeant Samuel K Doe took place in Monrovia. A failed coup attempt in November 1985 spurred accusations of tribal genocide. A formal installation of a civilian government in January 1986 did not lead to the internal stability and international acceptance President Doe had hoped for. In December 1989, Liberia was invaded in the northeast border region of Nimba County by a rebel military force led by Charles Taylor, a former government official. The fighting in Nimba developed into a conflict between President Doe's ethnic group, the Krahn, and their allies, the Mandingo, against the local Gio and Mano tribes.

During Doe's ten years in power, he failed to accomplish social change and to allow democracy to prevail in Africa's oldest republic. On the other hand, he executed several former associates, altered the results of the 1985 election, imprisoned opposition leaders, closed a number of newspapers, and reawakened tribal antipathies. In July 1990, about 600 people were massacred by Doe's forces while they were seeking refuge in a Monrovian church. In September of the same year, Doe was captured, tortured, and killed. On November 22, Amos Sawyer was installed as interim president under the auspices of the Economic Community of West African States (ECOWAS) in Monrovia.

Despite peace negotiations, the civil war was continuing in 1992. Several schools and hospitals were closed, and Liberia was convulsed by a civil war that took a severe toll on its citizenry, its economy, the political system, and the moral values of its society.

In 1992 Charles Taylor still refused to recognize the Sawyer government. He addressed himself as President and was moving his military and administrative operations to Gbarnga, northeast of Monrovia, where he created his capital center for a new bureaucracy. His troops were estimated by analysts at 10,000. Many of the soldiers were boys aged 9–10, who instead of carrying books and attending the village schools, were carrying machine guns at village checkpoints.

2. Politics and the Goals of the Education System

It has long been recognized that one of the most serious constraints adversely affecting development and modernization programs in Liberia is the lack of suitably qualified labor. While the 1980s witnessed an unprecedented expansion of education facilities in many developing countries, Liberia was adversely affected by the ongoing civil war. Not only were schools closed down because of unrest, but students were drafted as soldiers and many teachers left the country.

The response of an individual to education is to a great extent affected by the social structure within which he or she functions, the environment in which he or she lives, the economic circumstances of his or her existence, and his or her state of health, both physical and mental. The quality of the response will, in turn, affect the extent to which the individual is able to influence, control, and modify his or her environment to meet not only personal needs but also the social,

political, and economic needs of society. In short, education influences and is in turn influenced by society and the state of affairs in all sectors of the economy.

The present system of education in Liberia is inefficient and poorly managed. Liberia and its educational system is in great need of peace and stabilization. The educational goals as expressed in the 1980s are still valid and viable: to develop human capital; to eradicate illiteracy; to increase the number of schools; to expand community schools; to make education available for all; to raise the quality of teachers and teaching; to make education relevant to the needs of the country; to revise curricula; and to improve facilities.

The strategy of rural development as the route to national development is the main thrust of national policy in Liberia. The provision of relevant and suitable education and training is a prerequisite for rural development. There is a need for inservice training for government staff to be engaged in rural development and there is a need to offer training and education to people in the rural areas in a manner which is relevant to their major economic activities and which also opens new opportunities for wage employment as well as for self-employment and for diversification of the rural economy.

3. The Formal System of Education

3.1 Primary, Secondary, and Tertiary Education

Figure 1 shows the formal system of education in Liberia. As can be seen in Fig. 1, there are three main levels in the (6+3+3) education system. The preprimary and primary level including kindergarten, pregrade school, and an elementary school of six years (Grades 1–6); the secondary level comprising three years of junior high school (Grades 7–9) and three years of senior high school (Grades 10–12); and the tertiary or higher education level, including undergraduate and graduate university courses and various subdegree courses.

The number of students in the school system (primary and secondary) varied roughly between 250,000 and 300,000 during the 1980s. About 60 percent of the students are boys. Liberia has approximately 1,800 schools and 9,800 teachers, of which two-thirds are underqualified. Net enrollment ratio for primary education is 40 percent. At the University of Liberia, 3,300 students were enrolled in 1988.

Institutes of higher learning include the University of Monrovia, the Cuttington University College, the WVS Tubman College of Technology, and the Teacher Training Institutions at Kakata and Zorzor.

3.2 Preschool Education

The demand for preschool education has been increasing. In schools where kindergartens are available, the small classrooms are often overcrowded and pose health problems for the children. Efforts were made in the mid-1980s to improve preschool education through a number of workshops. However, inadequate appropriations for preschool education has remained a problem.

3.3 Vocational and Technical Education

The WVS Tubman College of Technology, which was opened in 1978, trains technicians expected to fill jobs between the professional engineers level and that of skilled workers. Successful students are awarded an associate of science degree in technology.

The Rural Development Institute at Cuttington University College offers a two-year agricultural technical degree program directed to subprofessional agricultural workers for extension service and agricultural development projects of the Ministry of Agriculture, as well as private institutions and business in the agricultural sector.

Once reconstructed, maintained, and with proper planning and systematic coordination, the vocational and technical education institutions that have been established in Liberia since the 1960s could very well meet the needs of the country for professional and skilled workers.

3.4 Adult and Nonformal Education

"Nonformal education" connotes any organized and systematic learning activity which takes place outside the formal education system. In Liberia, this takes the form of adult education or literacy classes, as well as various programs conducted under the aegis of the agricultural and health sectors to increase the productivity of subsistence farmers and to enable the rural population to acquire knowledge and skills to improve its living conditions.

The adult education program is an integral component of the Community School Project. In accordance with the strategy of integrated rural development, the community schools are to provide a relevant basic education for youth through the introduction of practical skill-oriented courses, as well as functional literacy classes for adults, as a preliminary step to the introduction of other nonformal education activities.

Problems in the operation of nonformal education include lack of coordination of the courses offered by the various ministries and other agencies and lack of a comprehensive development plan for each county which would ensure a fair distribution of available resources.

A community schools program operates rural schools as community centers where adult literacy is taught. Liberia continues to experience serious education problems, with an estimated illiteracy rate of 60.5 percent of the adult population in 1990

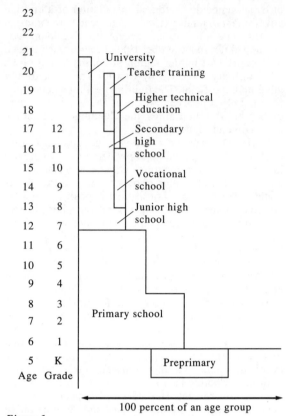

Figure 1
Liberia: Structure of the formal education system

(males 50.2%, females 71.2%). Literacy textbooks and postliteracy materials are inadequate, and this affects the efficiency of adult education programs.

4. Administrative and Supervisory Structure and Operation

Education is provided by the government, missions, and other agencies such as concessions, local communities, and private institutions. It is officially compulsory for nine years between the ages of 7 and 16 years.

Three departments constitute the Ministry of Education: the Department of Administration, the Department of Instruction, and the Department of Planning and Development. The Bureau of General Supervision, under the Department of Instruction, is headed by an Assistant Minister whose responsibility is to provide administrative as well as instructional supervisory services to schools at all levels across the country. The country is divided into three educational regions each headed by a Senior Regional Supervisor. Each county educational administration is headed by a Chief

Educational Officer assisted by District Educational Officers.

Problems encountered include the lack of: funds, qualified managers, teachers and public servants, adequate educational material, and sufficient transportation.

5. *Educational Finance*

Education is free in all government (public primary and secondary) schools, although pupils have to buy their own textbooks and uniforms. Apart from government-operated schools, there are many private and mission schools throughout the country. Some of the private schools do charge tuition fees. However, tuition fees are not standardized. The government provides a 50 percent subsidy for university education.

Government provision for education during the 1980s varied between US$35 and US$45 million per year. The 1988 education expenditures amounted to US$42 million, equivalent to 17.5 percent of the total government spending.

The Liberian economy was already in a crisis situation prior to the start of the civil war. During the 1980s, the GNP decreased by 2 to 3 percent per year. The export volume dropped from US$600 million in 1980 to US$430 million in 1985. The war created a still worse situation. Almost one-third of the population left the country, as did all foreign expertise. The collapse of the education system alone will mean large investments in school reconstruction and in the provision of learning materials. The future government of Liberia will have to exercise extreme caution and use government revenues wisely to provide basic social services for its people.

6. *Supplying Personnel for the Education System*

The entire teaching staff for primary and secondary education in Liberia has, since the early 1980s, numbered between 7,200 and 9,800, of which only approximately one-third have met the formal requirements for teacher qualification.

There are two institutions mainly responsible for the training of teachers for the primary level. They are the Kakata Teacher Training Institute (KTTI) and the Zorzor Teacher Training Institute (ZTTI). The KTTI is mainly an institution for training of preservice teachers, while ZTTI concentrates on inservice training. Tuition, boarding, and textbooks are provided free of charge to trainees at both institutions. The two institutions have a capacity to accommodate about 630 students, but total enrollment is normally much below this figure, mainly because of too few qualified applicants. The number of graduates from the two institutions seldom exceeds 250 per year.

The University of Liberia and the Cuttington University College also train teachers for the primary school at degree level but their total contribution, in terms of number of teacher graduates, is less than 10 per year.

The extension centers that were set up during the 1980s to upgrade the professional competence of under-qualified primary school teachers failed to meet their objectives. As a result Liberian schools continue to run their programs with the majority of the staff underqualified.

Teachers for the secondary school level are trained at the University of Liberia and Cuttington University College. The number of graduates amounts to 30–50 per year from the two institutions.

The activities at the teacher-training institutions were constantly interrupted during the civil war (1990–92). Thus, the supply of personnel to the education system, which has been a continuous problem in Liberia in the past, will certainly remain as an obstacle for development for a number of years to come.

There is no institution in Liberia which provides training for technical and vocational education teachers. However, inservice training programs for vocational education teachers have been arranged from time to time at the Booker Washington Institute (BWI) in Kakata.

7. *Curriculum Development and Teaching Methodology*

Curriculum development is the responsibility of the Division of Curriculum Development of the Department of Instruction at the Ministry of Education, a division also responsible for the evaluation of learning materials at all levels of instruction. Regionally, there are a number of county curriculum centers serving as extensions of the Ministry's instructional program. These centers also conduct workshops and seminars for teachers.

During the 1980s, the curricula for elementary and secondary education were revised. The elementary social studies program was completed in 1985 and new textbooks were produced. Revision of mathematics textbooks for Grades 4 to 6 was also completed during the mid-1980s. An adequate school atlas for the secondary schools has been edited and printed. Several units of the general science curriculum for junior high school have been completed. In the regional county curriculum centers, story-books, word lists, and simplified reading material have been produced. However, many schools still operate without a syllabus. Textbooks as well as instructional materials are generally in short supply in most schools.

8. *The System of Examinations, Promotions, and Certifications*

The promotion of primary education students from one grade to the next is decided by the class teacher. The most serious problem at the preprimary stage is the persistence of the pregrade school classes for children of school-going age. It is estimated that more than 90 percent of all beginners start at this level, and the duration is between one and three years. Because of the relatively high level of maturity of most of these children and the relative irrelevance of the instruction to their needs, it is assumed that more than 40 percent of them drop out before reaching Grade 1. About 40 percent of the cohort entering elementary school (Grade 1) reach Grade 3, and only 25 percent reach Grade 6.

The promotion from junior high school to senior high school is decided by the teachers based on the results of the National Examination for Grade 9. Graduation from senior high school is based on the National Examination for Grade 12. Given that less than one-third of the teachers in the national system are qualified, there is an acute shortage of teachers qualified to teach mathematics, languages, the sciences, and technical subjects—a fact that is evident from the results of the National Examination. It was estimated in 1985 that 52 percent of the Grade 7 cohort reach Grade 12, and that about 45 percent graduate.

Entrance to higher education is mainly based on the completion of senior high school and the results of the National Examination for Grade 12.

9. Educational Assessment, Evaluation, and Research

The indigenous school system in Liberia was examined in some studies during the 1970s (Zetterström 1976, Duberg 1978). An anthropological study of the cultural context of learning and thinking is reported by Cole et al. (1971). The Harvard Institute of International Development made a preliminary survey of the educational system in Liberia (1976). The effect of education on earnings was reported in Duberg (1982). The University of Liberia, through its various colleges, has undertaken research in several areas including education during the mid-1980s. A lack of finance and transportation, however, meant that the Division of Research at the Ministry of Education was very cautious not to embark on new research projects during the 1980s. Its activities during this period were mainly limited to monitoring and continuing ongoing projects, including the 1984 National School Survey and the 1988–89 Liberian Country Analysis by UNESCO.

10. Major Reforms in the 1980s and 1990s

During the 1980s, a new Liberian Constitution was promulgated (January 6 1986); the Ministry of Education was reorganized in order to improve quality of administration in the various areas of educational planning, personnel management, educational administration, and fiscal management; revised objectives and strategies for primary and secondary education were set; and curriculum reforms were carried through. However, shortage of funds and political instability, and the civil war, brought the entire education system to collapse early in the 1990s.

11. Major Problems for the Year 2000

The reconstruction of a society brought to an almost total collapse by the civil war will call for support and funds which are well beyond the means of Liberia. Support from international donors like the World Bank, USAID, and the African Development Bank is a prerequisite for dealing with the problems facing the educational system and institutions.

Those problems embrace low enrollment ratios; an imbalance in access to primary, secondary, tertiary, and adult education; a high proportion of unqualified teachers; high wastage rates (failure, repetition, dropout) at all levels; inadequate financing; and the lack of all kinds of educational facilities, including school buildings and material.

References

Cole H et al. 1971 *The Cultural Context of Learning and Thinking: An Exploration in Experimental Anthropology*. Basic Books, New York
Duberg B R 1978 *Forces Influencing Education Policy Making in Liberia: Socio-economic Changes and Educational Relevance*. University Microfilms International, Ann Arbor, Michigan
Duberg B R 1982 *Schooling, Work Experience, and Earnings: Determinants of Earnings in a Third World Corporate Setting*. Studies in Comparative and International Education, No. 6. Institute of International Education, University of Stockholm, Stockholm
Zetterström K 1976 *The Yamein Mano of Northern Liberia*. Institute of General and Comparative Ethnology, Uppsala
Harvard Institute for International Development 1976 *New Directions for Education and Training in Liberia: A Preliminary Survey*. HIID, Monrovia

Further Reading

Clapham C 1991 *Liberia in Africa: South of the Sahara 1992*, 21st edn. Europe Publications, London
Falk M (ed.) 1992 *Liberia and Sierra Leone*. The Swedish Institute of International Affairs (306), Stockholm
Dunn D E et al. 1988 *Liberia: A National Polity in Transition*. Scarecrow Press Inc., Metuchen, New Jersey
Guluma E L 1991 *The Trouble with Liberia*, UFSI Field Staff Reports, Vol. 1990–91 No. 4. University Field Staff

International, Indianapolis, Indiana

Holman M 1990 Liberia's agony unlikely to end with Doe's departure. *Financial Times* 1st August 1990

Liberia 1985 *Second National Socioeconomic Development Plan*. Government of Liberia, Monrovia

Ministry of Education 1984 *Annual Report to the Ministry of Education to the Interim National Assembly*. Ministry of Education, Monrovia

Nelson H D (ed.) 1984 *Liberia. A Country Study*. Foreign

Area Studies. American University, Washington, DC

New African 1992 *Liberia: Slow Peace Process*. IC Publications Ltd, London

Noble K B 1992 In Liberian ashes, a guerrilla's flawed empire. *New York Times* 15th April 1992

The Economist 1990a *Vital World Statistics, The Economic Books*. Hutchinson, London

The Economist 1990b *Atlas, The Shape of the World Today*. Guild Publishing, London

Libya

K. Gezi

1. General Background

The Socialist People's Libyan Arab Jamahiriya is located in North Africa, bordering on Egypt and Sudan to the east, Tunisia and Algeria to the west, the Mediterranean Sea to the north, and Niger and Chad to the south. Libya occupies 1,775,500 square kilometers of land, most of which is desert, 6 percent is agricultural, and 1 percent is forested. Its population in 1991 was 4,350,742, of whom 76 percent live in urban areas and 24 percent in rural areas. While its average population density in 1989 was 2.3 persons per square kilometer, Tripoli, the capital, had 360 persons per square kilometer. About 80 percent of the population live close to the Mediterranean Sea. The population growth rate in Libya is approximately 3.9 percent annually, and 51 percent of the population is under 15 years of age. The mortality rate in 1989 was 0.7 percent.

Ethnically, 97 percent of the population are Sunni Muslims of mixed Arab and Berber ancestry, and the remainder are composed of Berbers, Tuareg, and Black Africans. The official language is Arabic, but English, and to a lesser degree Italian and French, are spoken in major cities even though it is government policy to use Arabic in written and oral communication.

Libya is the largest producer of petroleum in Africa and one of the largest producers in the world. Oil revenues have contributed to the increase in its Gross National Product (GNP) and per capita income and have transformed it from a poor country to a rapidly developing nation with the highest per capita GNP in Africa.

While Libya has depended throughout its history on foreign skilled and nonskilled labor, the Qadhafi policies have consistently called for the "Libyanization" of the country's workforce and the shrinkage of the private sector. The number of foreign workers fell from 560,000 in 1983 to 154,700 in 1989, with 840,700 Libyan workers constituting the remainder of the labor force who run much of agriculture, business, and industry as "partners not wage workers."

Libya's GNP has increased from LD1,288,100 million in 1970 to about LD7,223,500 million in 1989. Per capita income has also increased from LD642 in 1970 to LD1,575 in 1989. In addition to petroleum, Libya's main industries include food processing, textiles, home products, and handicrafts. Its major agricultural products are wheat, hay, vegetables, fruits, meats, milk, eggs, and honey. However, 75 percent of Libya's food is imported. In 1987, Libya's exports totaled LD2,432 million and its imports amounted to LD1,278 million.

Libya's history is replete with foreign domination from the ancient Greeks and Romans to the Arabs, Ottomans, Italians, British, and French until its Independence in 1951 when a constitution was approved for a kingdom ruled by King Idris I. But in 1969, the Free Officers Movement led by Muammar Al Qadhafi ousted the king and gained power, proclaiming the new Libyan Arab Republic and a system of direct democracy. According to this system, the authority of the people is based in theory on the General People's Congress (GPC) which acts as the legislative and executive body. It is led by the General Secretariat with the General People's Committee serving as a national cabinet. People's committees of different sectors such as agriculture, education, health, and housing are formed each with its own secretariat. Syndicates, associations, or unions are run by the people's committees which are responsible to their own popular congresses. In reality, the military exerts a very strong influence on all major policies.

Colonel Qadhafi became the leader of the government, and in 1973 advocated the cultural revolution and Arab nationalism. A new constitution was formulated in 1977, renaming the nation as the "Socialist People's Libyan Arab Jamahiriya" (Jamahiriya is translated as the "state of the masses"). Political participation is conducted through the Arab Socialist Union, the only political party in the nation.

2. Politics and the Goals of the Education System

The 1969 constitution decreed compulsory free education through the ninth grade, increased efforts in adult literacy and teacher education, and focused on providing more educational opportunities to women, Bedouins, and rural inhabitants. When Qadhafi's cultural revolution began in 1973, public education was identified as an important means of contributing to the achievement of the goals of the revolution. School curricula were to emphasize Arab Libyan culture, and Arabic became the language of educational texts and educational programs. The objective of the cultural revolution to implement Islamic socialism, which is a mixture of elements from capitalism and communism, became the major goal of education. This type of socialism was aimed at social and economic equity and workers' management of agricultural and industrial companies as partners not as employees. Qadhafi, in his *Green Book* (Part 3, pp. 48–49), advocated that "society should provide all types of education, giving people the chance to choose freely any subjects they wish to learn. This requires a sufficient number of schools for all types of education … knowledge is a natural right of every human being which nobody has the right to deprive him." He also emphasized the need to teach religion in the schools.

Education is seen as a key to achieving the country's future development. Students in public schools are instructed in Qadhafi's *Green Books* and are encouraged to participate in political activities in support of government policies. However, on occasions, university students have protested against certain government policies such as compulsory military training and attempts to disband the faculties of French and English at Al-Fatah University.

Table 1
Enrollments in formal education, Libya 1989

Educational levels	Number of classrooms	Number of students	Class size
Primary	31,296	852,593	27.2
Intermediate	11,467	341,044	29.7
High school	2,922	95,576	32.7
Technical education	912	27,301	29.9
Teacher-training institutes	1,374	37,050	26.9

Source: Department of Statistics and Census 1989

3. The Formal System of Education

3.1 Primary, Secondary, and Tertiary Education

Figure 1 depicts the structure of the formal educational system in Libya and Tables 1 and 2 indicate enrollment statistics and resources. Libyan public education is free and compulsory between the ages of 6 and 15. Primary education lasts 6 years. In 1989, there were 852,593 students in 31,296 classrooms with an average class size of 27.2. The school year commences in September and it spans 280 days per year with students attending school six days per week.

After the primary school there are three parallel tracks of secondary education. The first is the general preparatory, the second is the general teacher training which runs for 4 years and prepares teachers for preschools and primary schools, and the third is vocational training. In 1991, 138,860 pupils enrolled in general intermediate schools (50% female), 39,491 students in teacher training (73% female), and 37,157 students in vocational education (64% female). During the same year, there were 11,429 teachers in general intermediate schools (36% female), 4,113 instructors in teacher training (34% female), and 2,959 faculty in

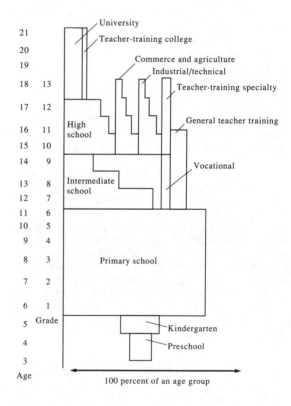

Figure 1
Libya: Structure of the formal education system

vocational programs (27% female). Academic secondary education consists of two stages. The intermediate school or the general preparatory is 3 years in duration, and the high school or the general secondary school also lasts for 3 years. The first year of high school consists of general courses for all students after which students can opt to enroll either in the sciences stream or the humanities stream for the remaining 2 years of high school. In 1989, there were 341,044 students attending intermediate schools in 11,467 classrooms with an average class size of 29.7. In the same year, there were 95,576 students attending high schools in 2,922 classrooms with an average class size of 32.7. Grade repetition rates are about 12 percent in primary schools and about 10 percent in secondary schools. The dropout rate at the end of the tenth year is about 6 percent, and is greater for boys than for girls. More students attend primary school and the rate of school attendance declines as one moves up the educational ladder. It was estimated that if the failure rates for 1980–81, as reported by the Arab League Educational, Cultural and Scientific Organization (ALECSO), were to persist in 1992, intermediate schools would incur about 20 percent student failure in the seventh grade, and 15 percent in the eighth and ninth grades. In high school and technical schools, failure rates are about 5 percent in the tenth grade, 3 percent in the eleventh grade, 8 percent in the twelfth grade, and 7 percent in the thirteenth grade of technical schools. In general, there are more males in schools than females, even though the enrollment of girls has steadily increased in primary schools.

Coeducation in public schools presents a mixed picture. In East Libya, the schools are coeducational, but in the West and South, males and females attend separate schools. Even in Tripoli, this separation is maintained at all levels except kindergarten. In the rural areas, where schools have a small number of students, boys and girls attend the same school out of sheer economic necessity, with the boys sitting at the front of the class and the girls at the back.

Parallel to the general secondary stage, there are the following three other tracks: commerce and agriculture, industrial secondary, and teacher education specialty which prepares teachers for upper-primary grades and intermediate schools.

In addition to the public schools, there are the Islamic or Koranic schools which instruct students in religion and the Koran. Private schools constituted about 3 percent of all schools in the 1970s, but the government's policy has been to discourage the existence of private schools throughout the country and consequently they now play an insignificant role in the educational system.

Higher education is the domain of ten higher institutes and universities. The public universities are Al-Fatah at Tripoli, Gar Yunis at Benghazi, and the Technical University at Marsa Brega. Higher technical institutes in different cities provide more student access to higher studies. The total enrollment in the higher institutes and in the universities in 1989 was 47,300 students. In addition, the Islamic University of Sayid Muhammad Ali Sanusi offers specialties in religious higher education for graduates of the Koranic secondary schools and others interested in further studies of Islam. In general, students have a relatively high rate of repetition in higher education.

3.2 Preschool Education

Children aged 3 are admitted to preschools which are available not only in cities but also in rural areas. In 1985, there were 78 kindergarten schools offering 390 classes with a total student population of 15,028 of whom 7,785 were boys and 7,243 were girls. The class–teacher ratio was 2.70:1. The teaching staff in these schools consisted of 1,051 female teachers. Most preschools are publicly supported but a number of them are private (UNESCO 1993, Faraj 1988). In 1976, there were 37 private preschools which had 235 students taught by 117 teachers (Massialas 1988). As for the curriculum of preschools, it includes teaching the alphabet, the Koran, supervised play, and general childcare.

3.3 Special Education

Learning handicapped and physically handicapped students are taught in special education schools. These schools, which exist in large cities, provide special curricula, individualized learning opportunities, and teachers who are trained specifically to work with children having mental or physical disabilities.

Table 2
Resources in formal education, Libya 1975–86

	1975	1986
Total educational expenditure [a]		
amount in millions	224,908	636,260
as % of GNP	5.9	10.1
as % of total government expenditure	14.5	20.8
Current educational expenditure [a]		
amount in millions	122,485	506,260
as % of the total	54.5	79.6
as % of GNP	3.2	—
as % of current government expenditure	—	—
capital expenditure	102,423	—

Source: UNESCO, *Statistical Yearbook 1991*. UNESCO, Paris
a In Libyan dinar equivalent to US$3.13 in 1986 and US$2.66 in 1991

Furthermore, special efforts are made to meet the needs of gifted students in public schools. Outside of large cities, special education students are instructed along with other students in regular classrooms. No specific enrollment data on special education are available.

3.4 Vocational, Technical, and Business Education

With the trend toward "Libyanization" of the workforce and less dependence on foreign labor, there has been a concerted effort to recruit and encourage women and men to enroll in technical, vocational, and business programs. As Table 2 indicates, in 1989 there were 27,301 students enrolled in 912 technical and vocational classes with a density of 29.9 students.

In addition, there were 89 general training centers accommodating 16,293 trainees, which are funded by the various secretariats in order to recruit new workers or to provide inservice education for current employees. Furthermore, there are postsecondary-level institutes in agriculture, business, commerce, health, industry, and social work which offer further specialized training.

Vocational, technical, and business education is viewed as a means for achieving the goals of Islamic socialism of increased productivity and economic self-sufficiency.

3.5 Adult and Nonformal Education

In 1990, it was estimated that the rate of illiteracy of the over 15 years age group was 34.2 percent, which totals 890,300 persons. About 49.6 percent of the women in this age group were illiterates compared with 24.6 percent of the men in this group. When a comparison is made between the illiteracy rates of 1991 and 1973 (51%), it is evident that literacy efforts have made progress.

Literacy campaigns, literacy and cultural centers, public libraries, and television programs have been augmented by special training programs provided by each secretariat to its own employees with salary and release time incentives. The length of these nonformal programs ranges from several months to over 4 years depending on the goals of the program. While the basic literacy programs aim at developing language and mathematics competence at the fourth-grade level, secretariat and industry programs may focus on the development of a given set of skills relevant to the worker's specific job. Despite these efforts, illiteracy is still a major problem facing Libyan society.

4. Administrative and Supervisory Structure and Operation

Education in Libya is highly centralized. The Secretariat of Education and Scientific Research is in charge of all regular schools, Islamic schools, special education schools, and teacher-training institutes. As regards vocational and technical institutes, the Secretariat of Education is responsible for its own institutes and colleges such as the commercial and applied engineering colleges. While other secretariats such as agriculture and industry are responsible for budgetary and administrative functions of their own institutes, the Secretariat of Education remains in charge of the educational supervision and final examination for these institutes.

The Secretariat of Education and Scientific Research establishes national policies for education while the directors of education and their technical staff in each of the 46 zones are charged with supervising the implementation of these policies in public and private schools. People's committees administer universities and the Secretariat of Higher Education is in charge of their supervision.

5. Educational Finance

Since public education in Libya from preschool through the university level is free, the financing of education has been a national responsibility. Allocations from the national budget to public education are made annually.

As indicated in Table 2, total and current expenditures on education have increased, making Libya one of the top Arab countries in expenditures on education. While total expenditures in millions on education in 1975 were LD224,908 constituting 5.9 percent of the GNP and 14.5 percent of total government expenditures, educational expenditures in 1986 grew to LD636,260 making up 10.1 percent of the GNP and 20.8 percent of that year's total government expenditures. Similarly, current educational expenditures in 1975 were LD122,485 constituting 54.5 percent of the total and 3.2 percent of GNP. In 1986, these expenditures increased to LD506,260 making up 79.6 percent of the total and 8.1 percent of the GNP. Capital expenditures also grew from LD102,423 in 1975 to LD130,000 in 1986.

Fees charged by private schools are regulated by law.

6. Supplying Personnel for the Educational System

Primary school teachers are prepared at four-year institutes after the primary stage. Graduates undergo a curriculum consisting of subject matter preparation for the first two years and pedagogy and student teaching in the remaining two years. Intermediate school graduates can opt to enter four-year teacher institutes with specialization in certain studies to enable them to teach in the upper-primary grades or in intermediate schools. Secondary school teachers are prepared at the university teacher-training colleges and institutes. As Table 1 shows, in 1989, there were 37,050 students in attendance at 1,374 classrooms in teacher-training institutes. The average class size was 26.9.

Libya has been facing the problem of teacher shortage for a number of years. Two major solutions were utilized. The first was to recruit more women and university graduates into teaching their subject matter without having had any pedagogical training. The second was to import foreign teachers to fill the manpower shortage. Several years ago, Libya proclaimed an open door policy for other Arabs. Every Arab was entitled to come and live in Libya. This encouraged many Arab educators, the majority of whom were Egyptians, to work in Libya mainly in secondary schools and in specialized institutes such as those for teachers. In addition, non-Arab foreign experts have been imported to teach in technical institutes and universities where there are positions that could not be filled by Libyan citizens or other Arab teachers.

The number of foreign workers in general has fluctuated over the years. In 1975, 33 percent of the labor force were foreigners, but Libya expelled many of its foreign workers for political reasons in 1985 and 1986. In the 1980s, about 10 percent of the personnel in education were foreign. The total number of teachers for primary, secondary, university, and equivalent institutions in 1985–86 was 79,043. The number of teachers in kindergarten, primary, secondary, technical, and teacher-training institutions in 1986 was 78,840. More females taught in kindergarten and primary schools, but more males taught at secondary, technical, and teacher-training institutions. The overwhelming majority of teachers taught at primary schools. The inadequate quality of teacher preparation and the shortage of teachers, especially in technical subjects, represent two of the major challenges facing Libyan education.

7. Curriculum Development and Teaching Methodology

There is a common curriculum throughout the country as set by the Secretariat of Education and Scientific Research. Weekly, there are 26–35 periods in primary schools, 36–39 periods at intermediate schools, and 42 periods at high schools. Each period is 45 minutes long.

The primary school curriculum consists of Arabic, religion, arithmetic, science, social studies, fine arts, music, physical education, agriculture for boys, and home economics for girls. The intermediate school curriculum includes mathematics and English in addition to the primary school subjects. The curriculum of the first year of secondary school focuses on general education which includes advanced studies in the subjects mentioned above plus the French language. The

curriculum of the second and third years of secondary school vary depending on the student's choice of the sciences or the humanities stream. The common subjects to both are religion, Arabic, English, and French. More males *and* females tended to enroll in the humanities stream. The *Green Book* by Qadhafi is studied by students each week. The curriculum of the Koranic schools is similar to that of the regular public schools, but with greater focus on Islamic studies and Arabic culture. Technical and vocational schools offer engineering, agriculture, medicine, commercial subjects, social sciences, and arts. Work training is also provided.

The dominant method of instruction is lecturing, and all textbooks are published by the Secretariat of Education. Rote learning is the general tendency. The availability and the use of educational technology in the classroom are limited, even though new approaches using public television in literacy training have been attempted.

Overall, the regular school curriculum is limited and is not relevant to student and community needs or the world of work. It needs to include critical thinking and application. It needs to be based on modern materials that challenge students and invite their creativity. As the country reaches out for modern technology, foreign languages should have a permanent place in the school curriculum.

8. The System of Examinations, Promotions, and Certifications

In addition to classroom examinations, there are two major statewide examinations that determine student promotions from one level of schooling to another higher level. At the end of the intermediate school, students need to pass the state-mandated examination in order to be admitted to a secondary-level school or institute. At the end of the last year of secondary school, students must take and pass another state-mandated examination to be admitted into a postsecondary institution. These examinations are developed by teachers and professors commissioned by the Secretariat of Education and Scientific Research and are offered at specific dates and locations to all students throughout the country. The completed examination papers are read and evaluated by another group of teachers and professors assigned by the Secretariat to accomplish this task. Examination results are then communicated to each student and are usually published in the major newspapers.

The exams are rigid and are information-based, emphasizing memorization, and are related marginally to classroom instruction. A number of students fail these exams and are then forced to repeat their classes and prepare to take these examinations the following year. Failure to pass these examinations causes some students to drop out of school. Promotion from one grade to another within a certain stage depends on the passing of teacher-created examinations which rely mainly on memorizing information.

Examinations represent a problem in the educational system. They need to be aligned with what students are taught in the classroom and with the skills they need to succeed in society. Examinations should test, in addition to knowledge, higher mental processes such as analysis, synthesis, and evaluation. Problem solving, reasoning, and creativity should be important ingredients in classroom instruction and curriculum materials, and hence in all examinations.

9. Educational Assessment, Evaluation, and Research

Data are scarce on these topics. From time to time, the government issues plans for educational development, the implementation of which is not known. Examinations, which are rigid and rote-learning-oriented, constitute the basis for assessing student abilities and serve as a means for channeling students into vocational, technical, and scientific studies.

Efforts of the Secretariat of Education and Scientific Research seem to be focused more on information gathering than on systematic research and evaluation of the system of education. A number of research centers have been established leading to optimism that research may play a role in the reform of public education in the future.

10. Major Reforms in the 1980s and 1990s

Spurred by oil revenues and the determination to make education an instrument of national development, several advances were made in these decades. Efforts were made to encourage more females to attend primary schools, secondary schools, and postsecondary education. Such efforts resulted in the fact that females constituted 46 percent of all students in 1986. Escalation in the construction of new primary, secondary, and vocational schools and the provision of more teachers further expanded educational opportunities to all students. The war on illiteracy was waged with a national effort expanding literacy and cultural centers, as well as public and mobile libraries, bringing the rates of illiteracy down from about 80 percent in 1951 to 34.2 percent in 1990.

Education became free and university students were assisted with government grants in 1987. Compulsory school attendance between the ages of 6 and 15 years was reinforced. More universities and technical and agricultural institutes were established. A number of new university departments, such as nuclear and electronic engineering and pharmacy, were developed. As shown in Table 2, total expenditures on education represented 10.1 percent of GNP and 20.8 percent of the total government expenditure in 1986.

The emphasis on the history and cultures of Libya, Islamic and Arabic studies, and efforts to recruit more students into science and technology studies were also major trends. The expansion of technological education has emerged increasingly as a primary goal of government.

The preparation of more teachers has also become a focal point of effort in order to provide the personnel needed for a variety of subjects in an expanding system of public education.

11. Major Problems for the Year 2000

Despite the strides made in educational development in Libya, there are several vexing problems which will still face the nation in the year 2000. Education in Libya is highly centralized and controlled. A balance needs to be established between the role of the central government and the role of local education authorities. Local authorities, teachers, administrators, students, and community groups should participate in educational planning and the development of flexible programs to meet their own needs.

Libyan education is also highly politicized. It is viewed by the government as an instrument of its policy. The government, for instance, dictated compulsory military training for male and female students resulting in the 1976 student riots in Tripoli and Benghazi. As part of military mobilization, the government began weapons training in secondary schools and universities in 1981. The government's intention of halting the impact of the West led to attempts at phasing foreign languages out of university offerings.

Despite some progress, there is an insufficient supply of qualified Libyan teachers. This will hamper the national effort to provide quality and equity in education to all of its citizens. Teacher education programs need to be reformed to train teachers who are proficient both in subject matter and pedagogy. Teacher salaries should be improved to attract better candidates to the profession. Continued reliance on foreign teachers is influenced by fluctuating political and economic considerations which caused the influx of foreign teachers and workers into Libya and also their expulsion from the country. Another example is the government's policy in the 1980s to end the granting of student fellowships for study abroad and to recall Libyan students from the West, terminating their grants. To encourage the development of highly skilled and specialized Libyan teachers in science, engineering, medicine, and technology, scholarships for study abroad should have been increased and foreign languages should have been emphasized in the curriculum.

While school construction has expanded, school attendance is still a problem. Rural youth and ethnic minorities do not have equal access to schooling similar to their colleagues in metropolitan areas. More females need to be encouraged to attend schools, especially secondary schools, technical institutes, and universities.

Enrollment in the scientific and technical streams is lower than in the humanities and literary programs. The country's needs for the twenty-first century cannot be fully addressed unless there is a balance between supply and demand in personnel in the technology and vocational fields.

The school curriculum is highly theoretical and based on rote learning and outdated books. The process and quality of education need to be enhanced by emphasizing modern strategies of teaching and pursuing the development of higher order mental skills in the classroom.

The system of examinations is very rigid and is not very well-coordinated with student needs or classroom learning. Examinations tend to emphasize more the recalling of information than reasoning and application. These examinations have resulted in 32,256 repeaters, constituting 12 percent of all students in 1982, and a number of dropouts each year.

In spite of the progress in literacy training, there is much still to be done in this field especially among women, minorities, and rural inhabitants.

Finally, educational planning for the year 2000 requires systematic data gathering, realistic assessment, and strategic evaluation. The process of planning should follow a collaborative model where all involved in the educational enterprise are partners in the change effort. The goals of reform should be realistic and the process of implementation should be supported by national and local authorities as a means of achieving a viable education for all youth.

References

ALECSO 1983 *Educational Statistics Bulletin for the Arab World, 1980–1981*. Department of Documentation and Information, Tunis

Department of Statistics and Census, Socialist People's Libyan Arab Jamahiriya 1989 *Facts and Figures*. Department of Statistics and Census, Tripoli

Faraj A 1988 *Education in the World*, International Yearbook of Education, Vol. XL. UNESCO, Paris

Massialas B 1988 Libya. In: Kurian G (ed.) 1988 *World Education Encyclopedia*. Facts on File Publications, New York

Qadhafi M n.d. *The Green Book, Parts 1–3*. The Public Establishment for Publishing, Advertising, and Distribution, Tripoli

UNESCO 1993 *Statistical Yearbook*. UNESCO, Paris

Further Reading

Massialas B, Samir A 1983 *Education in the Arab World*. Preager, New York

Metz H (ed.) 1989 *Libya—A Case Study*. US Government Printing Office, Washington, DC

UNESCO 1991 *Statistical Yearbook*. UNESCO, Paris

US Department of State 1985 *Background Notes: Libya*. US Government Printing Office, Washington, DC

Lithuania

M. Lukšiené and Z. Jackūnas

1. General Background

On March 11, 1990, Lithuania declared its Independence. It had been annexed by the Soviet Union in 1940. Governmental structures are being restored and a new educational system developed which will be based on Lithuanian educational traditions. It aims at being reintegrated into the European educational system.

The Republic of Lithuania is situated on the eastern shore of the Baltic Sea. Its territory covers 65,200 square kilometers and the population density is 58 inhabitants per square kilometer (1989). There were 3,723,000 inhabitants in 1990, with 57 percent of them being of working age. Of these, 30.2 percent were occupied in industry; 17.8 in agriculture; 11.9 in construction; and 9.8 percent in education, culture, and the arts. Some 69 percent (1990) live in towns. The natural annual increase is 4.8 percent. The most populated city is the capital Vilnius (592,000), followed by Kaunas (430,000), and Klaipéda (206,000).

The ethnic composition of Lithuania in percentages is: Lithuanians 79.6, Russians 9.4, Polish 7.0, Byelorussians 1.7, Ukrainians 1.2, Latvians 0.1, Germans 0.1, and others 0.9. Followers of the Jewish religion constitute 0.3 percent.

The Second World War decimated Lithuania's population and radically altered its national structure. From 1940 to 1953, Lithuania lost about one million of its inhabitants: 300,000 were deported and 210,000 were murdered by Nazis, among them 135,000 Jews. Prior to the war, the Jews had formed about 7 percent of Lithuania's population.

Lithuanian belongs to the Baltic language group, which is a branch of the Indo-European group.

The development of the formal education system began in the fourteenth century and was completed by the sixteenth century. It was connected with the founding of Vilnius University in 1579. Before then, young people studied at home schools set up in manor houses. Others went to universities in the West. Both the structure and the subjects taught were those of the European system. The language used for instruction in the upper grades of schools was Latin.

Toward the end of the Lithuanian–Polish union at the end of the eighteenth century, an educational reform required the change from Latin to a living language as the medium of instruction. However, it was Polish that was used in the upper grades. In general, Lithuanian was considered the language of the people.

During the Russian occupation of Lithuania in the nineteenth century, there were several uprisings against the Tsarist regime. After the 1830–31 uprising, Russian was introduced as the medium of instruction. After the uprising of 1863, there was no place left in the schools for either the Lithuanian language or culture. The teachers and pupils were punished for using the Lithuanian language. That was why many secret Lithuanian primary schools were created in the country. The situation became easier only after the revolution in Russia in 1905.

In 1918 Lithuania regained its Independence as a democratic republic. However, it was too agrarian and had been ruined by the First World War.

One result of the rule of the Russian occupation was that over 30 percent of the population was illiterate. The main concern of the new, independent government was to organize education. By 1938, some 15 percent of the state budget was designated for education. Adult education was extended by organizing classes (450 courses for adults in 1928). As a result, only 2 percent of the people remained illiterate by 1940.

During the Soviet period (1940–90), schools were used only as a means of enslavement by the occupying power. The educational system in Lithuania became ideological, political, and centralized. With total control in the hands of the Soviet regime, it did not differ from that of the Soviet Union.

In conducting educational reform in the 1990s a great deal of attention must be paid to the ethnic and demographic structures of Lithuania, to the demands of economic development, and to the political aims of strengthening the nation and the state.

In 1991, there were 995,000 workers, of whom 228,000 were in agriculture and 453,000 in services. A total of 73 percent of the workforce was employed in industry and 27 percent in nonindustrial jobs. Out of 1,000 workers, 145 had some college education and 734 were high school graduates.

The two main branches of the Lithuanian economy are industry and agriculture. The main industrial fields include electrical engineering and fuel industry, machine building and metalwork, chemical and petrochemical industries, forestry, paper and pulp manufacturing, light industry, and food production. The number of private owners is increasing in agriculture. The sphere of service jobs is expanding. While reforming the field of professional education, one aim is to have more specialists for developing these areas.

Lithuania is a parliamentary republic. The highest institutions of government are the Seimas (which enacts the laws) and the Government of the Republic of Lithuania (which fulfills the functions of the executive branch). The main goal of these institutions is to create a rich democratic state based on the tenets of private ownership of property and universally recognized individual citizen's rights and freedoms. These are the main foundations for the forthcoming reforms.

2. Politics and the Goals of the Education System

The main goals of Lithuania's educational reform were formulated in the Law of Education of the Republic of Lithuania of 1991. It states that: "Education is a priority of State—a supported sphere in the development of the Republic of Lithuania." Education must contribute to the nation's cultural, social, and economic progress; and strengthen people's solidarity, tolerance, and cooperation. It is stressed that the main task of the educational system of Lithuania is to enhance the spiritual and physical powers of the individual, to lay a firm foundation for morality and a healthy lifestyle, and to stimulate the intellect by creating conditions for the development of individuality. Other tasks are to afford the young generation the opportunity to acquire both general and professional education, corresponding to the contemporary level of science and culture; to develop a sense of civic duty, an understanding of personal rights and obligations to the family, nation, society, and the state of Lithuania, as well as the need to participate in the cultural, public, economic, and political life of the Republic. In the course of the reform, it is recognized that there will be a need

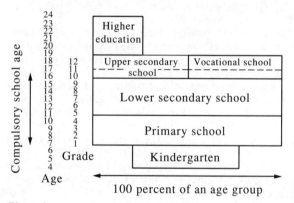

Figure 1
Lithuania: Structure of the formal education system

to develop a variety of educational structures and to stimulate private initiatives in the sphere of education.

3. The Formal System of Education

3.1 Primary, Secondary, and Tertiary Education

Figure 1 presents the structure of the school system. Education is divided into primary grades (1 to 4), lower-secondary grades (5 to 9), and upper-secondary and vocational grades (10 to 12).

However, there are three types of school: primary (Grades 1 to 4), elementary or nine-year schools (Grades 1 to 9), and secondary schools (Grades 1 to 12). There were 2,042 schools in 1990: 778 of them were primary, 590 were nine-year, and 674 were secondary; 461 (22.5%) were in towns and 1,581 (77.5%) in the country. Since 1980 the rural population declined due to increased migration to towns and a lower birthrate. The number of nonurban schools and, at the same time, the general number of schools in the Republic as a whole, had been decreasing. In 1970 there were 3,778 schools (86%) in rural areas, in 1980 there were 2,205 (81.8%), and in 1985 there were 2,103 (79%). Before the Second World War (1939), there were 2,319 primary schools and 116 *gymnasiums*. There were four types of *gymnasium*: humanitarian with intensive teaching of Latin, those with intensive teaching of foreign languages, "real" *gymnasiums* with intensive teaching of mathematics and natural sciences, and commercial *gymnasiums*. A total of 37 of them (32%) were private.

In 1990, some 525,000 students were studying in public schools: 14,800 of them in primary, 48,800 in nine-year, and 438,100 in secondary schools. In addition, 11,400 students were studying in special schools for the physically and mentally handicapped, and 12,100 students in evening schools of general education.

Children begin attending primary school between the ages of 6 and 7 years. Education is compulsory till the age of 16. According to law, 14-year old children may leave secondary school and begin attending professional (or vocational) school. Because education is compulsory until the age of 16, there is no dropout problem.

In terms of ethnicity, Lithuanian schools reflect the composition of the Republic. In 1990, 82.6 percent of Lithuanian school children were in Lithuanian schools, 15.1 percent in Russian schools, and 2.3 percent in Polish schools. The number of Russian schools has been declining since 1989, but the number of Polish schools has been increasing. These changes are mostly connected with two circumstances: Russians have begun to leave Lithuania and some of the Polish children have left Russian schools and now attend Polish schools.

There is an insufficient number of secondary schools. In 1990, 293 schools (14.3%) were working

in two shifts; the vast majority of these were in towns. The number of such schools increased from 222 in 1985 to 281 in 1989. The number of school children continuing their secondary education after completing compulsory schooling (soon to be increased from 9 to 10 years) is changing. In 1990, about one-half entered upper-secondary school and the other half entered vocational school (see Fig. 1).

The secondary school system is comparatively well-provided with personnel. Of the 40,300 teachers working in daytime secondary schools in 1990, 85 percent had completed higher education and over 80 percent were women. The pupil-teacher ratio was 13:1. A serious problem is that a considerable number of qualified teachers do not work according to their university major (or specialization). Approximately 38 percent teach subjects for which they were not professionally prepared.

The school year in Lithuanian secondary schools begins on September 1. The number of school days are: 175 for Grades 1 to 4, 195 days for Grades 5 to 8, 180 days for Grade 9, 195 days for Grades 10 to 11, and 175 days for Grade 12. It is at the end of Grades 9 and 12 that final examinations are taken. The weekly number of lessons for students in 1990–91 was: 87 for Grades 1 to 4, 149 for Grades 5 to 9, and 93 for Grades 10 to 12.

Educational reform of the secondary system is anticipated. There will be a basic and an advanced program. A choice of subjects will be available. The goal is to encourage students to continue at secondary school for as long as possible and to postpone the time when they choose a professional education. Trade and manufacturing schools will be established where students will be able to continue their studies according to their abilities and, at the same time, prepare for a career.

Curriculum changes will also be undertaken. More attention will be paid to moral education, aesthetic and ecological awareness, ethnic culture, the basis of healthy lifestyles, and modern languages. Instruction in religion will also be introduced as an option. Those not selecting religion will be instructed in other subjects related to moral and civic education.

There are 15 colleges or universities in Lithuania with 67,300 students and 5,000 to 6,000 faculty members. The most prominent of them are: Vilnius University (15,200 students), Kaunas Technological University (13,700), and Vilnius Technical University (6,300). In 1989, the Great Vytautas University was re-established and, in 1991, Klaipéda University was opened. The others are: Vilnius Pedagogical University and Shiauliai Pedagogical Institutes, Lithuanian Academy of Music, Vilnius Academy of Art, Lithuanian Agricultural Academy, Lithuanian Veterinary Academy, Lithuanian Physical Culture Institute, Lithuanian Police Academy, Kaunas Theological Seminary, and the Kaunas Medical Academy.

In 1991, there was an approximately even number

of male and female students. There are departments where the language of instruction is Russian or Polish. After completing two stages of studies, a bachelor's and a master's degree are awarded. Following graduate studies and the successful defense of a scientific thesis, a doctoral degree or *habilitation* are conferred.

3.2 Preschool Education

In 1940, there were 197 kindergartens. During the Soviet period (1940–90) the preschool system was highly centralized and unified. The children were trained according to traditional scholastic methods.

In 1992 the preschool system consisted of creches (for children aged 1.5 to 3 years), kindergartens (for 3- to 6-year olds), a combination of creches/kindergartens and preschool groups (for 5- to 6-year olds), and a combination of kindergartens and schools (for 3- to 10-year olds). Almost all preschools are run by the state. Private kindergartens are very rare. In 1991 there were: 5 creches, 351 kindergartens, 4 kindergartens/schools, and 1,314 creches/kindergartens.

By the end of 1990, 24.5 percent of an age group attended preschool until the age of 3, and 58.6 percent from the age of 3 to 6 years. The percentage was higher in towns than in rural areas. Since 1985 there has been a decrease in the percentage of an age group attending kindergartens, especially in rural areas.

In 1991 there was a desire to create the best learning conditions for children from various ethnic groups. One method of developing this field is to stimulate the establishment of monolingual (one-language) kindergartens. During the years of Soviet domination such conditions had been created only for Russian children, while children of Polish or Jewish descent or from other nationalities had hardly any opportunity to learn their native language or culture. In 1991, there were 115 Russian language preschools (15,000 children), 19 Polish (450 children), and 1 Jewish (23 children) preschool.

By the end of 1991, 18,400 teachers were working in preschools. Only 9,860 of them (53.6%) had a background in preschool education. New kindergarten programs have begun, based on the humanitarian psychological precepts of Erikson and Piaget. Kindergarten programs are being prepared for those who follow the Montessori and Steiner models.

3.3 Special Education

During the Soviet period, children with severe mental impairment were considered uneducable and, in most cases, were directed to homes for invalids. More attention was given to those with only slight mental impairments or those with visual, hearing, speech, or orthopedic handicaps. After the restoration of Lithuania's independence, the education of children with special needs and their adaptation and integration into society were given more consideration.

In 1990, there were 101 preschools for handicapped children: 5 for those with hearing deficiences; 64 for those with speech deficiencies; 16 for those with visual deficiencies; and 7 for the mildly mentally handicapped. There were also 3 residential schools for children with medium and severe mental and physical impairments. In 1990, about 4,500 children were educated in special preschools.

There were 56 schools of general education (10 of them in rural areas) for physically and mentally handicapped in 1990, and 11,400 children were educated in them. In addition, there were 33 special classes for such pupils. All in all, 8,933 mentally retarded children (1,424 of them orphaned or abandoned) are taught and educated in the Republic.

A logopedic school for the communications handicapped (with 279 pupils), a school for children experiencing the consequences of poliomyelitis and cerebral palsy (with 153 pupils), schools and classes for the blind and visually impaired (347 pupils), and special institutions for deaf children (473 pupils) are included among special education institutions.

The primary task of these schools is the training of such children for an independent life and for integration into Lithuanian society.

The Ministry of Culture and Education supervises 5 special schools for juvenile delinquents, 10 preschool children's homes, 11 students' homes and boarding schools for orphans, 15 secondary boarding schools, and 3 sanatorium schools. Some 5,786 pupils study and live in these special facilities.

In 1991, the first preschools were organized for children having mental impairments and groups of invalid children were established in kindergartens. Special institutions have been organized to meet the needs of these children: the Center for Psychotherapy, the University Center for Children's Mental Health, the Diagnostic Service for Developmental Disorders, and the School Psychological Service Center. These service centers will help to improve the diagnosis of children's developmental disorders and the selection of children for special groups. Classes or schools will give qualified help to parents and pedagogues.

3.4 Vocational, Technical, and Business Education

The first lower- and higher-level vocational and apprenticeship schools in Lithuania were established in 1919. Lower-level training lasted 2 to 3 years and higher-level training lasted 4 years. These schools were particularly for agricultural workers, but there were also apprenticeship housekeeping schools for girls. In 1939, there were 78 apprenticeship schools and courses, and 38 agricultural schools and courses in Lithuania.

After the annexation of Lithuania in 1940, vocational schools were rendered state property and attached to the Republican Board of Labor Reserves (in 1945). They were two-year apprenticeship and six-month factory and workshop training schools. In 1956, technical schools were established where graduates from general education secondary schools could study. In 1959, the labor reserves schools were reorganized into town and rural vocational–technical schools (VTS), and the Republican Board of Labor Reserves became the State Vocational Technical Training Committee.

In the 1960s and 1970s, there were vocational schools (the term of study being 2 to 2.5 years), technical schools (1 to 1.5 years), and a few secondary vocational–technical schools. At the end of the 1970s and the beginning of the 1980s, it was decided that vocational training would be oriented toward preparing highly qualified workers. Vocational–technical schools were reorganized into secondary vocational–technical schools in which a student could acquire both a profession and a general secondary education within 3 years. In 1984, vocational schools of various types were reorganized into secondary vocational schools. In 1990, 23,200 qualified workers graduated from these schools.

There were also 64 *Technikums* (with 46,500 students) which were halfway between vocational schools and universities and which prepare qualified specialists for the national economy. In 1991, they were reorganized into college-level vocational or technical schools.

Administratively, vocational–technical schools are supervised by the Ministry of Culture and Education, agricultural schools by the Ministry of Agriculture, and high schools by the Ministry of Culture and Education.

Vocational–technical schools, high schools, and industry cooperate with each other. Businesses and farms often provide vocational schools with equipment and materials, and employ students for industrial practice. Representatives from the private sector are present at the state examinations and at the defense of students' graduation theses. Since 1990, graduates look for jobs themselves and make labor agreements with employers. In this way, the labor market is actively being formed. The register of trades will be revised and the curricula will be more aligned with those of other European countries. The principles of a dual vocational training system will be adapted.

3.5 Adult and Nonformal Education

Before 1990, there were evening adult and youth schools of general education, vocational training schools, advanced training facilities, and a variety of extracurricular establishments for children. After independence, a modern adult education system has been organized, and nonformal educational opportunities for children are being reorganized. In 1992, the Lithuanian Adult Education Association was established. New, nonstate private informal adult education establishments have arisen, in which people are mostly taught foreign languages or trained in various practical skills (sewing, knitting, driving, etc.). As unemployment rises, the problems associated with changing professions is becoming more urgent.

In 1990, within the realm of adult education, there were: 4 college-level schools (41,300 students), 7 high schools (19,200), 15 vocational schools (12,700), and 59 schools of general education (12,100). In all, 85,300 adults studied at these schools (attending evening schools, advanced training courses, or studying by correspondence). Adults also studied at 175 state-run schools. The activities of these establishments are partially regulated by the state by means of registration and licencing.

At the end of 1990, there were more than 400 extracurricular establishments with 220,000 students; 55 student palaces and centers, 16 young technicians' clubs, 11 young naturalist clubs, 152 students' summer camps, 94 music and arts schools for children, 137 sports schools for children and youth, and 26 children's libraries, among others. At these establishments, children can develop their talents and satisfy their needs for self-expression and self-education. Most of the adult and nonformal education facilities are either fully or partially maintained by the state. The new system of adult education will be an integral part of a lifelong educational system. The Scandinavian model is expected to be a guide. The network of workers' advanced training and trade-changing centers will be rapidly developed.

4. Administrative and Supervisory Structure and Operation

The administrative system can be defined as a centralized system with considerable elements of self-government. Preschools and schools of general education are subordinate to local administration; vocational schools (with the exception of agricultural schools, which are under the jurisdiction of the Ministry of Agriculture, and some other vocational schools which belong to other departments) are administered by the Ministry of Culture and Education. The activities of the high schools (having wide rights of autonomy) are supervised by the Information, Science, and Studies Department of the government. The Ministry of Culture and Education supervises the pedagogical activities and the teaching of general education subjects in all state and private schools through central and local inspection offices. The reorganization or liquidation of educational establishments is subject to the Ministry of Education. All educational institutions use syllabuses, curricula, and textbooks which must be approved by or agreed with the Ministry. Local educational supervision is undertaken by the Offices of Culture and Education of the institutions of local government, which are under the jurisdiction of the Ministry.

The beginning of decentralization and autonomy is represented by school self-government institutions such as school councils, teacher councils, and student councils, whose activities and rights are defined in the Law on Education. An important role in building national educational policy is played by the Lithuanian Educational Board. The Board is a public institution and functions as a scientific expert and consultant group on the strategic problems of education.

5 Educational Finance

The main source of the financing of state educational establishments was and still remains the state budget. Most expenses are covered by municipal bodies. They finance preschools, general secondary schools, and extracurricular establishments.

There are governmental norms for legal subsidies to privately owned educational institutions in order to ensure an education which meets the level of state standards.

Table 1 presents data on educational financing in Lithuania from 1965 to 1990. Annual expenses were not usually more than 12 to 13 percent of the state budget, but per capita expenditures continually increased. In 1990, they were 555 roubles in preschools, 446 roubles in general secondary school, 1,977 roubles in auxiliary school and childcare facilities, 1,471 roubles in vocational schools, 915 roubles in high school, and 1,084 roubles in universities. Advanced students of colleges and universities are provided with state scholarships.

In future, a multichannel network will be developed for both regional and national funding. Charitable donations will be stimulated and the revenue system will be arranged in such a way that it will also support education.

6. Supplying Personnel for the Education System

Teachers are trained at the Vilnius Pedagogical University for teaching students in Grades 1 to 4 and 5 to 12 in general public schools, at the Siauliai Pedagogical Institute for teaching students in Grades 1 to 4, and at 4 college-level pedagogical schools for teaching preschool children. In addition, teachers are also prepared in other institutions of higher learning, such as the University of Vilnius, the Lithuanian Academy of Music, the Vilnius Academy of Arts, the Lithuanian Agricultural Academy, the Lithuanian Institute of Physical Education, the University of Klaipéda, and Vytautas Didysis University of Kaunas.

There is no teacher shortage in Lithuania, but there is the problem that 38 percent of the teachers are teaching subjects in which they have not specialized. Teachers of vocational education, fine arts, and music are badly needed in schools. Teachers of the Lithuanian language and literature are also badly needed in the eastern regions of Lithuania where there are large numbers of Poles, Russians, and Byelorussians residing in compact areas.

Teachers are trained in the pedagogical institutes for 4 or 5 years and in the college-level pedagogical schools for 3 years. There is a feeling that the quality of teacher training is not "modern" enough in terms of educational psychology, comparative education, and in the philosophy of childrearing; furthermore, the syllabuses and curricula do not accord well with the new educational reform. The essence of the higher education reforms is to introduce scientific degrees of bachelor and master of science in order to improve this situation. A few establishments in universities provide inservice teacher training. Most of the teachers (about 15,000 teachers per year) improve their qualifications at the Inservice Teacher Training Institute. Raising teachers' qualifications is closely associated with their certification. Teaching certification will be divided into four categories: teacher, superior teacher, teacher–methodologist, and teacher–expert. Each teacher's salary will depend on his or her qualifications and prior work experience.

Table 1
Educational financing 1965–90

	1965	1970	1975	1980	1985	1990
Expenses for education[a]	149.7	198.0	281.8	362.0	442.4	581.8
Percentage of the annual state budget	6.09	12.08	12.98	14.15	11.63	12.95
Percentage allocated to:						
preschools	8.4	11.9	13.5	15.3	16.5	15.6
general secondary schools	55.2	47.3	42.9	38.3	36.9	39.4
vocational schools	6.7	7.9	10.1	11.5	12.2	12.6
college-level schools	9.3	9.5	9.9	9.3	7.9	7.2
universities	11.7	13.1	12.6	13.2	11.8	12.5

a in millions of roubles

7. Curriculum Development and Teaching Methodology

Under the Soviet regime, syllabuses and curricula were largely unified and centrally prepared. The development of new national curricula for all subjects was begun after the restoration of independence. These curricula are approved by the Ministry of Culture and Education. This Ministry also approves the syllabuses for all schools. The curricula are developed by experts at the Institute of Pedagogics. The experts are assisted by experienced, practicing teachers and university lecturers. The drafts of curricula are discussed, revised, and approved by the Experts' Commissions at the Ministry. These commissions also approve the drafts of textbooks and other teaching aids and literature.

The national curriculum is obligatory in all schools. In educational establishments for national minorities, syllabuses and curricula can be supplemented by courses about ethnic culture (especially in the areas of ethnic language, literature, and art). However, the schools function five days a week and there is little free time for optional subjects.

Until independence, Russian language and literature was compulsory in all schools. In addition, one other foreign language (English, French, or German) was taught. The new Law on Education made all foreign languages equal, and their teaching is coordinated with parents' wishes and with the options available to the school.

The new curriculum will have eight cross-curricular courses which will be common to all school types and levels of schooling. These are Lithuanian language, ethnic culture, moral education, ecological culture, aesthetic education, health, civic education, and work education. In addition, interdisciplinarity will be introduced in terms of general laws and concepts, as reflected in such disciplines as philosophy, the general theory of science, social philosophy, cultural theory, aesthetics, natural philosophy, general linguistics, and so on. In the preparation of the new curricula, an overemphasis on the memorization of facts is being avoided, while contemporary scientific thinking and apprehension of reality are being stressed. A greater variety of optional subjects will be introduced. The two-level curricula (i.e., basic and intensified) of some subjects, and both basic and secondary school graduation examinations will be legalized.

8. The System of Examinations, Promotions, and Certifications

Up to Grade 9, promotion to a higher class depends on the pupil's grades as assessed by the teacher. At the end of Grade 9, all students must take an examination in three subjects: native language (written), mathematics (written), and native language (oral). Those who pass receive the Basic School Certificate. At the end of upper-secondary school, students must take an examination in five subjects, four of which are compulsory: Lithuanian language and literature (written and oral), mathematics (written), history (oral); with the fifth subject being selected by the student. In the schools for national minorities, students take three compulsory examinations: native language (written), mathematics (written), and state language (oral), and two optional subjects. Students who pass the examination receive the (Graduation) Diploma Certificate, which gives them the right to enter a college or university.

In future, the reform will require three subjects in which all must take an examination: native language (written), mathematics (written), and foreign language (oral). Examinations will also include two optional subjects. Every attempt will be made to make the Lithuanian education system more like that of other European education systems, but at the same time retaining elements of the ethnic features of Lithuanian schooling.

A national system of end-of-cycle (level-of-schooling) examinations will be developed. This will allow universities to form judgments about students' future studies because student results will be on a national scale.

9. Educational Assessment, Evaluation, and Research

Academic research is mostly conducted by the Institute of Pedagogics and by specialists of the pedagogical departments of universities. The main thrusts of these research studies are: teaching typing to students in Grades 9 to 12 of the general secondary school, integration of social–cultural and intersubject content, continuous instructional development, and vocational training. A computerized data bank on teachers and schools is being established. Much of the data on education in the Republic is being collected by the State Statistical Service.

10. Major Reforms in the 1980s and 1990s

The reform of the Lithuanian educational system was begun in 1988 when the concept of reorganization of general secondary schools was declared. In accordance with the fight to restore Lithuania's independence, it stressed the role to be played by ethnic culture in the nation's schools. Democratic and humane aspirations for schools were declared. In 1989–90, the theoretical foundations for the reform of other areas of the

Republic's educational system were prepared and the draft of the new Law on Education was written. During the 1992–93 academic year, preschools and the first general secondary schools will start to work according to the new curricula.

Given the new economic conditions, vocational schools will be reformed. Training and, in particular, retraining will be of utmost importance. Preference should also be given to adult education, the continuous development of instructional systems, and the task of integrating the educational system into those of Europe. Realization of all these goals will decide the evolution of education in Lithuania until the year 2000.

Bibliography

Baltic States. A Reference Book 1991 Estonian Encyclopedia Publishers/Latvian Encyclopedia Publishers/Lithuanian Encyclopedia Publishers/Tallinn, Riga, and Vilnius

Bendrojo lavinimo mokyklos ir ikimokyklines istaigos 1990 metais. 1991 Šviesa, Vilnius

Lietuvos statistikos metraštis: 1990 metai. 1991 Lietuvos Statistikos Departamentas, Vilnius

Ministry of Culture and Education of the Republic of Lithuania 1991a *Education in Lithuania*. The Publishing Center, Vilnius

Ministry of Culture and Education of the Republic of Lithuania 1991b *The Educational System of Lithuania: Aims—Structure—Reforms*. The Publishing Center, Vilnius

Ministry of Culture and Education of the Republic of Lithuania 1991c *The Law on Education of the Republic of Lithuania. The Law on Science and Studies of the Republic of Lithuania*. Šviesa, Kaunas

Tautinerp mokykla 1989 T. I. Mokyklu tipu koncepci-ju projektai. Šviesa, Kaunus

Tautinerp mokykla 1990 II. Ugdymo turinio koncepci-ju projektai. Šviesa, Kaunas

Universaliosios ugdymo programos (Eksperimentines) 1991 Lietuvos Respublikos Kultūros ir švietimo ministerijos Leidybos centras, Vilnius

Luxembourg

M. Ant

1. General Background

The Grand Duchy of Luxembourg, established as an independent country at the Congress of Vienna in 1815, is situated in the very heart of Western Europe. Bordered by Belgium in the north and the west, Germany in the east, and France in the south, the country has an area of 2,586 square kilometers and approximately 389,900 residents. Some 14 percent of the population lives in the northern, hilly, and relatively infertile region called the *Oesling* (32% of the territory). The central and southern part of the country, or the *Bon Pays*, includes the capital, the City of Luxembourg, with 20 percent of the population concentrated on less than 2 percent of the country's surface, as well as the southern industrial areas with more than 30 percent of all inhabitants.

In 1993, the number of foreign residents exceeded 30 percent of the population, representing the highest proportion of foreigners in any country of the European Community. Ninety percent of the foreign population originate from countries of the European Community, including large and still growing Portuguese (40.4%) and Italian (19.8%) communities. While the number of children born to Luxembourg families was decreasing, the opposite was true for foreign families. In 1991 the birthrate per 1,000 inhabitants was 11.4 for Luxembourg families and 15.8 for foreign families. The demographic distribution of the Luxembourg population is no longer pyramidal, that is, there is uncommonly high growth in the proportion of elderly people, as can be seen from Table 1. These circumstances have led to a number of problems for the Luxembourg education system, as it has not yet adapted to instruct foreign children, who often cannot speak the languages used in schools.

The linguistic situation in Luxembourg is based on a superposed trilingual structure with, at its base, the mother tongue, Luxembourgish. Promoted in 1984 as the national language, it functions as a vernacular to the native population in everyday communications and increasingly as a literary language. French and German are the official languages of the country, used in administrative and legal matters. Most Luxembourgers speak all three languages and many are fluent in English as well. No ethnic language groups exist.

Luxembourg is an independent constitutional monarchy, headed by a Grand Duke. The constitution states that the sovereign power resides with the nation, and political responsibilities are divided between the government, the parliament (60 members, eligible for 5 years) and the jurisdiction. The country is governed by a large social consensus with at least two of the three major political parties (Social Christian Party, Socialist Workers Party, Democratic Party) typically being represented in the government since 1945.

Luxembourg has undergone major economic changes since the second half of the nineteenth century. The discovery of iron ore in the southern regions transformed the purely agrarian country into a modern industrialized nation within the last 100 years. Table

Table 1
Breakdown of population by age and nationality from 1971 to 1991 (percent)

Age	1971			1981			1991		
	Luxembourg	Foreign	Total	Luxembourg	Foreign	Total	Luxembourg	Foreign	Total
0–14	17.0	5.1	22.1	11.6	6.9	18.5	11.3	6.0	17.3
15–64	53.0	12.3	65.3	49.6	18.3	67.9	46.4	22.0	68.4
>65	11.6	1.0	12.6	12.5	1.1	13.6	12.3	2.0	13.4
Total	81.6	18.4	100.0	73.7	26.3	100.0	70.0	30.0	100.0

2 shows the distribution of workers over the principal sectors of the Luxembourg economy from 1970 to 1992.

Whereas the number of persons active in the agrarian sector (animal, crop, and wine production) has remained more or less stable since the early 1970s, heavy industry, consisting of mainly steel production, has been in decline. The production of steel dropped from 6.4 million tons in 1974 to 3.4 million tons in 1991, with a corresponding reduction of workers from 25,000 to about 9,900, respectively. In response to this decline, the Grand Duchy promoted investment in other industries (mainly chemical and glass production, tourism, banking, and small and medium-sized enterprises). These diversification efforts allowed the Grand Duchy to achieve from the 1970s onwards one of the best records of economic performance in Europe. For example, Luxembourg has become an international banking and finance center, with the number of banks growing from 19 in 1960 to 213 in 1992 and the number of employees from 1,321 to 17,250 over the same period. The total number of active persons equals 201,300 (1992), of which 43,910 are frontier workers from France, Belgium, and Germany. The unemployment rate at 1.4 percent was by far the lowest in western Europe in 1993.

Exports and imports represent about 75 percent of the country's gross national product, which is estimated at LF947,000 per capita (US$31,600). Of the country's exports, steel accounts for 38 percent, chemical, plastic, and rubber products for 18 percent, and textile production for 6 percent. Imports are more diversified and include mainly coke, iron ore, and fuels (13%), in addition to a wide range of general consumption goods.

Since the 1960s, successive governments deployed considerable efforts in the development of the national infrastructure. New waterways and motorways were built, while the railway system and the telecommunications network were expanded and improved. The international airport of Luxembourg became a major platform for international air transportation, including a large part of air-freight business. In addition, the audiovisual sector became a growth industry, as new internationally broadcasted radio and television programs were produced increasingly in the country. Efforts were and are being made to develop Luxembourg as a film production center and, in 1985, a satellite launching company was founded which will operate four satellites by 1994.

The City of Luxembourg is the site of the Secretariat General of the European Parliament, the European Court of Justice, several departments of the European Council and Commission, the European Investment Bank, and the European Monetary Fund, among others. Although the Luxembourg economy pays a large tribute to international economic circumstances, the country has remained fairly prosperous with one of the highest per capita incomes in Europe. The diversification, expansion, and the high tech revolution as well as the constant need for a small country to adapt quickly to changing economic circumstances challenges the Luxembourg education system, forcing the Ministry of Education constantly to review the existing school curricula and to develop new courses and new diplomas.

Table 2
Persons employed in the principal sectors of economic activity 1970–92

Sector	1970	1980	1990	1992
Agriculture	1,600	1,200	1,500	1,500
Industry	46,100	42,300	37,900	34,900
Construction	12,400	15,100	17,900	20,600
Services	39,400	61,300	93,400	105,200
Public administration	13,100	17,100	20,700	21,400
Independent	27,600	21,200	17,700	17,700
Total	140,200	158,200	189,100	201,300

2. Politics and the Goals of the Education System

The general political approach towards the Luxembourg education system, which was mainly oriented

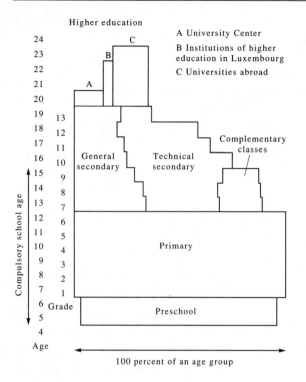

Higher education

24
23
22
21
20

A University Center

B Institutions of higher education in Luxembourg

C Universities abroad

Figure 1

Luxembourg: Structure of the formal education system 1990–91

towards knowledge acquisition processes, was redefined in *Demain l'école* (Ministry of Education 1992). It focuses on the development of global skills, competences, and autonomous learning capacities, as well as at a redefinition of the system of promotion and a larger cooperation with the economic environment. Finally, large efforts will be made to integrate the children of immigrant workers better into the Luxembourg school system and to develop teaching and learning methods to increase the number of graduates.

3. The Formal System of Education

3.1 Primary, Secondary, and Tertiary Education

The education system of Luxembourg is divided into four stages: preschool, primary, secondary, and higher education. Education is compulsory for a period of two years at the preschool level and for a period of nine years in the formal school system. Figure 1 presents the structure of the system.

Primary education, which starts at the age of 6, lasts for six years and is run by the local community authorities. These public schools do not charge fees. The Ministry of Education is responsible for the primary curricula, which apply throughout the country. Primary

education in Luxembourg focuses mainly on the disciplines of reading, writing, arithmetic, art, physical education, environmental studies, and development of social behavior. There are 30 teaching lessons per week, from Monday to Saturday, with four lessons in the morning and three times two lessons in the afternoon (Monday, Wednesday, Friday). However, the teaching environment in Luxembourg remains unique due to the specific language situation: teaching in primary schools begins with Luxembourgish as well as with German, the latter becoming the teaching language for practically all subjects in primary school. French is taught as a foreign language from the middle of the second school year.

Pupils must attend some form of full-time postprimary education for at least three years after completion of primary school. To be admitted to either general secondary or technical secondary education, they must pass an entry examination. Students who do not want or mainly cannot pass on to either of the secondary systems, must complete their compulsory curricula in the complementary classes. In a three-year course, those pupils are taught general subjects and have lessons in practically oriented subjects which prepare them for the transition to adult and working life.

General secondary education following the reform of 1989 is divided into the lower stage (the first three years) and the upper stage (the following four years). The first year is called orientation class and allows pupils to adjust to secondary education. In the second year, it is possible to choose between a classical section, which offers Latin as the third and English as the fourth language (starting in the third year), or the modern section, which requires English as the third language. The language of instruction is German throughout the lower stage, but changes to French in the upper stage. The upper stage comprises the polyvalent cycle (fourth and fifth year) and the specialization cycle (sixth and seventh year). The 1989 reform was designed to delay the choice of specialization, which previously occurred after the third year, and offers a more diversified range of optional courses. The polyvalent cycle offers a choice between literary and scientific subjects, the main difference consisting in the degree of difficulty in mathematics, and a more specific subject choice through one or two optional courses. In the specialization cycle, pupils opt for one of seven specific sections within either of the two disciplines. At the end of the seventh year, pupils must pass a written secondary education completion diploma allowing them to continue their studies at universities and institutions of higher education in Luxembourg and abroad.

The lower stage of technical secondary education, also called the observation and orientation cycle, covers a period of three years and completes the compulsory education. Its objective is to deepen the pupil's general training and to prepare for vocational training.

Table 3
Recent evolution of the total primary and secondary school population 1988–91

School system	Number of students 1988–89			Number of students 1989–90			Number of students 1990–91		
	Public	Private	Foreign	Public	Private	Foreign	Public	Private	Foreign
Preschool	7,977	—a	—	7,965	—	—	8,354	—	—
Primary	24,996	534	—	26,538	575	—	26,612	633	—
General secondary	7,258	475	—	7,518	486	692	7,589	509	745
Technical secondary	11,976	1,562	—	11,740	1,564	462	11,341	1,599	469
Total	52,207	2,571	—	53,761	2,625	1,154	53,896	2,741	1,241

a = not available

These three years offer a wide range of subjects, with a twofold diversification in the second year and a threefold in the third, maintaining a general basic program, but differing in the importance attributed to different subjects and by the teaching methods. They are called pedagogical orientations and are meant to address the differing abilities of each pupil. The intermediate and upper stages are divided into three sections: vocational, technician's and technical. The vocational section, or apprenticeship, consists of a three-year course combined with part-time practical work in a firm during the third year. The final diploma is the certificate of vocational and technical proficiency. Pupils having difficulties with the theoretical training may attend two-year technical and professional initiation courses. They correspond to a basic vocational training allowing candidates to learn the theoretical part at their own pace parallel to an apprenticeship agreement with a firm. Pupils are encouraged to acquire the certificate of vocational and technical proficiency. The technician's section, situated between the vocational and the technical section, trains students for skilled jobs mainly in industry. The curriculum lasts for a period of four years and closes with the technician's diploma. It allows students to enter immediately into professional life, but enables them also to attend schools of higher education in their respective field. The technical section emphasizes theoretical and general subjects, including some specialized vocational courses. The final diploma enables students to pursue university studies and is equivalent to the general secondary completion diploma.

Private schools in Luxembourg are nearly all Roman Catholic institutions, yet are subject to very strict authorization by the government. To be recognized by the Ministry of Education, a private school must teach the same topics, use the same textbooks, and follow the same programs as any public school. In 1991–92, 680 pupils (or 2% of the total primary school population) and 2,108 secondary school students (509 general secondary and 1,599 technical secondary school) attended private schools. Between 1988 and 1993, the number of children enrolled in private primary and technical

secondary schools increased by 46.5 percent, whereas the number of private general secondary school children decreased by 34 percent. Furthermore, a study by the Ministry of Education showed that in 1990–91, 1,241 Luxembourg resident secondary school children (or 5.5% of the total secondary school population) attended schools outside of Luxembourg, mainly in Belgium (85%), France, or Germany. This circumstance is certainly due to the demanding Luxembourg school system, which overstresses to a large extent the teaching of languages and the number of subjects instructed.

Other private schools are: the European School of Luxembourg, which provides teaching in nine different languages for children of employees of the European Community; the American School of Luxembourg and the Luxembourg branch of Miami University, Oxford, Ohio (USA), both for American students only; the French primary and secondary school; and the Waldorf school.

Although a developed university system does not exist in Luxembourg, the country has several institutions of higher education. The University Center Luxembourg runs first-year university courses in three different departments (law and economics, arts and humanities, and sciences) which are in line with syllabuses of universities in neighboring countries. The principal entry requirement is either a Luxembourg or a foreign secondary school diploma. The language of instruction is French. Students who have successfully completed the year at the University Center are given certification and may register as regular students for second-year studies at most universities in Austria, Belgium, France, Germany, or the United Kingdom. The department of law and economics also offers a two-year course of practical and applied economics and information science for students interested in entering their chosen profession more quickly. The Superior Institute of Technology delivers a three-year technical training course to students holding a general secondary or technical secondary school diploma. The curriculum, divided into mechanics, electrical engineering, civil engineering, and computer science, leads to the diploma of a technical engineer. The languages of instruction are French and German. The Superior Institute of Pedagogical Studies and Research, a three-year course, was founded in 1983, replacing a former two-year course, and is a specialized institute for preschool and primary school teacher training. The Institute of Educational and Social Studies offers one section for graduated educators for holders of a secondary school diploma and one for educators with at least five years of secondary school education. The normal curriculum lasts three years, but may be extended to six years for students who already work part-time in the field of special education. In 1990, a new postsecondary two-year technician's course was created, which offers the following practical disciplines: secretarial studies, accounting and business management, and animated motion pictures production. These studies are essentially practical.

During the school year 1990–91, 4,407 students (2,000 in 1975 and 2,500 in 1980) continued their higher education either in Luxembourg (totalling 1,156 students, of which 611 were at the University Center, 214 at the Superior Institute of Pedagogical Studies and Research, 254 at the Superior Institute of Technology, and 77 at the Institute of Educational and Social Studies), or at a university abroad (3,033 students). Most students go to Belgian universities (43.4%), followed by France (27%), Germany (20.8%), and Austria (4.3%). The total student population represents 2.2 percent of the total working population.

3.2 Preschool Education

Preschool institutions are free of charge and under the authority of the Ministry of Education which contributes to the financing of about two-thirds of the schools. One-third of the costs, the administrative and maintenance functions fall under the responsibility of the local communities. Less than 1 percent of the preschool children attend private institutions. In 1990–91, 8,354 children were enrolled in preschool education, of which approximately 30 percent speak a mother language other than Luxembourgish. Although no formal teaching is given, preschool education is expected to foster the physical, intellectual, and social development of the children and to prepare them for entry into primary school.

3.3 Special Education

The Special Education Administration of the Ministry of Education includes the Department of Child Guidance which is a diagnosis and counseling service for handicapped children and their parents. The department is organized regionally with 12 psychologists undertaking more than 5,000 consultations per year. Serious cases of deficiency and inadaptability are reported to the National Medico-psycho-pedagogical Commission, a group of experts which decides, in conjunction with the parents, on the institution best suited

to the child's needs. The Psycho-pedagogical and Educational Treatment Department includes a school for children with auditory and speech disabilities, an institute for children with visual defects, one for children with cerebral conditioned motor deficiencies, and one for severely handicapped children. Furthermore, there are several institutions run by the local communities and assisted financially by the Ministry of Education for children with various deficiencies, several centers that undertake the elementary manual training of young handicapped children enabling them to work in protected workshops or even industry, an institute for physically disabled children, some institutions devoted to children with social behavior problems, and a school for autistic children. Overall, 240 psychologists, specialized teachers, educators and education aids care for 1,000 handicapped and young children, amounting to 0.5 percent of the ordinary expenses of the state budget.

3.4 Vocational, Technical, and Business Education

The vocational and technical education in secondary school was described in Sect. 3.1. The Department of Professional Training of the Ministry of Education aims to develop continuous professional training initiatives in the context of technological and economic change. Through professional training centers, the Ministry of Education organizes orientation courses for young people and re-education courses for people with insufficient or inappropriate professional qualifications, as a means to prevent unemployment. In 1990, 800 persons benefited from this initiative. The professional training of potentially unemployed people is under the authority of the Ministry of Education, while the professional training of employed people is organized by the National Institute for the Development of Professional Training, a private institution of public utility. Its objective is to analyze the training needs of companies, to develop appropriate training strategies and to create specialized training units.

3.5 Adult and Nonformal Education

The Department of Adult Education of the Ministry of Education, created in 1991, primarily organizes evening classes in languages (Language Center Luxembourg, 3,962 participants in 1991–92), secondary school courses for adults (296 participants), and courses of general interest (1,120 participants).

Professional associations, particularly the Luxembourg Association of Banks and Bankers through the Institute for Training in Banking, also organize professional training courses but on a private basis. Founded in 1989, the *Emploi-Formation* functions as a two year curriculum to train young bank employees on the basis of 65 percent practical work in a bank, combined with a 35 percent part of theoretical banking courses. The Institute for Training in Banking also organizes general and specialized courses and seminars for bank employees, and created in 1992 the European Bank Academy, a two-year MBA level professional training course.

4. Administrative and Supervisory Structure and Operation

The Ministry of Education is responsible for the organization and general control of the Luxembourg education system. At preschool and at the primary level, a college of inspectors is in charge of administration and staffing. The principals of general and technical secondary schools are responsible for administration of their respective schools as well as the execution of teaching and learning.

5. Educational Finance

Since 1970, the part of the state budget devoted to education increased in absolute terms by a factor of 14, the major part being teacher salaries. In 1993, 43.68 percent of the total education budget (11.40% of the state budget) went to preschool and primary education, as shown in Table 4, and 19.84 percent, respectively 28.31 percent of the state budget to secondary education. General and running costs are covered either by the communities or other parts of the state budget.

6. Supplying Personnel for the Education System

Preschool and primary teacher training is organized in a three-year curriculum led by the Superior Institute of Pedagogical Studies and Research. Candidates are selected based on their ranking in the national general secondary school diploma, and since 1992 on their results in an oral examination in Luxembourgish, French, and German, as well as in a practical test in either

music, arts, or sports. The number of candidates admitted is generally very limited (50–60 per school year), and thus an important shortage of qualified teaching personnel has arisen. This represents a severe problem for the Luxembourg education system, as many classes are directed by unqualified instructors. Until the beginning of the 1990s, admission to a teaching position was strictly limited to candidates who successfully completed the Superior Institute of Pedagogical Studies and Research course. Due to European regulations, however, candidates from foreign teacher training schools have also become eligible and from 1994, all candidates must pass a function admission exam. In 1992–93, 1,614 teachers taught primary school classes, 250 preschool, 181 complementary, and 93 special classes (totalling 2,138 teachers).

Both general and technical secondary school teachers must complete four years of studies at a university abroad in a subject matter which is taught in Luxembourg secondary schools. In order to be admitted to the training courses for secondary school teachers, candidates must pass an entrance examination, as there are normally more candidates than actual teaching positions available. The courses comprise a three-year period of practical teaching in a secondary school, combined with teacher training courses held at the Pedagogical Department of the University Center Luxembourg and the writing of a thesis in a specialized subject. In 1992–93, the Ministry of Education employed 840 secondary school teachers, including 81 who attended the teacher training courses.

7. Curriculum Development and Teaching Methodology

At the primary school level, new curricula are determined by the inspectorate and developed in collaboration with specialists and teachers. At the secondary education level, the curricula are proposed for each subject area by national commissions composed of specialized teachers. These commissions also propose the textbooks to be used. For both school levels, the

Table 4
Evolution of the state budget dedicated to education by school system (percent)

	Preschool and primary education	General secondary school	Technical secondary school	Higher education	Special education	Total percentage of state budget
1970	47.22	29.52	19.51	1.59	2.13	8.92
1980	50.09	21.06	21.60	1.73	5.51	9.20
1990	44.08	20.01	28.00	2.41	5.49	10.69
1993	43.68	19.84	28.31	2.81	5.36	11.40

individual teacher has no influence upon these but does decide on the method of teaching.

8. The System of Examinations, Promotions, and Certifications

The primary school year is divided into three terms. A system of continuous control is applied and promotion to the next class is determined by averaging the results of the three terms in French, German, and arithmetic. In order to continue to a general secondary school, an entrance examination must be passed in French and German dictation and language exercises, and in arithmetic. Children who are not admitted to either of the secondary school systems must enter complementary classes which require no examination. The same three-term system applies for secondary education. With the exception of the last year of secondary education, where a final national examination has to be taken, advancement from one grade to the next is based on the weighted average of marks across the terms with weights of one-sixth for the first term, one-third for the second, and one-half for the third. The decision on promotion resides with the class council at each school and is based on the final results within each subject. Since 1989, a system of compensation is applied in order to avoid unnecessary penalization. The final secondary school examinations last over a period of eight half-days and attempts are made to include the results of the school year as well as oral abilities in the final results. The Ministry of Education delivers the following diplomas: the general secondary school diploma, the technical secondary diploma, the technician's diploma, the certificate of vocational and technical aptitude, and the certificate of manual ability.

9. Educational Assessment, Evaluation, and Research

The Department of Pedagogical Innovation and Research of the Ministry of Education, to be replaced by the Department of Coordination of Pedagogical Research and Innovation (SCRIPT), and the Department of Psycho-pedagogical Research of the Superior Institute of Pedagogical Studies and Research are responsible for educational research and for evaluating existing and proposed curricula. The different departments comprise Luxembourgish teachers and research specialists, and an increasing number of research projects are organized with the aid of foreign universities and specialists.

Research projects have focused on the introduction of information and communication technologies at all school levels; the development and evaluation of new curricula in primary, vocational, and professional education; the development of a national school television

system; and the integration of children of immigrant workers in order to reduce general school problems and the number of children that leave school without qualifications.

10. Major Reforms in the 1980s and 1990s

While there were very few reforms in the 1980s, a large number of projects and reforms are planned for the 1990s. As a consequence of the new definition of the general primary curriculum, textbooks and teaching materials are being redeveloped. At the postprimary level, the complementary classes are being restructured and integrated into technical secondary education, and profiles of professional needs and adapted training measures are being established for vocational training. At the lower levels of technical secondary school, classes and programs are being introduced with French as the medium of instruction and at the upper levels, oral competencies are taken into account for evaluation. Finally, a general framework for continuous teacher training is being defined.

11. Major Problems for the Year 2000

Due to the multilingual situation in the country which is primarily attributable to the large proportion of foreigners in Luxembourg, fundamental reforms of the Luxembourg school system must be implemented. The organization of special classes for children of immigrant workers does not suffice in order to integrate this population into Luxembourg society and to give foreign children an appropriate education. It is essential to reduce the number of school failures and to increase the number of graduates, without decreasing the general level of instruction and achievement, as it is certainly not enough, in a country where natural resources are virtually nonexistent, that of all the children born in 1960, only 40 percent proceeded to secondary school, with only 13.2 percent passing their final examination and 7 percent obtaining a university degree. Hence, the major challenge is to develop a less selective school system with more adequate structures and teaching methods (including computer-based training and multimedia learning) that no longer overemphasize the acquisition of knowledge, but put individual skills and aptitudes as the main focus of interest.

The absence of a university becomes increasingly noticeable and discussions result in more and more adherents supporting the creation of a full curriculum university in Luxembourg, based in a European context. Despite the advantages arising from the fact that Luxembourg students study in various countries, the creation of a university should enable the country more readily to encounter the social and economic implications of rapid industrial and technological development.

References

Ministère de l'Education Nationale 1992 *Demain l'école. Le sytème éducatif luxembourgeois face au changement.* Ministère de l'Education Nationale, Luxembourg

Further Reading

Ant M, De Cillia S 1991 Logique d'une formation professionnelle moderne. *Letzebuerger Land* 24: 53
Gengler C 1991 *Le Luxembourg dans tous ses Etats.* Editions de l'Espace Européen, La Garenne-Colombes
Kaiser L, Levy J 1990 *Population étrangère, langues et enseignement vus par les Luxembourgeois.* Service d'Innovation et de Recherches Pédagogiques, Ministère de l'Education Nationale, Luxembourg
Press and Information Service of the Luxembourg Government 1993 *The Grand Duchy of Luxembourg.* Press and Information Service, Luxembourg
Statec 7/1992 *Luxembourg en Chiffres.* Luxembourg
Unité Nationale d'Eurydice 1991 *Education in the Grand Duchy of Luxembourg.* Ministère de l'Education Nationale, Luxembourg

Macau

C. Almeida and M. Bray

1. General Background

The territory of Macau, on the south coast of China, is just 18 square kilometers in area. It consists of a peninsula of the mainland plus two islands. The southern island is joined to the northern one by a causeway, and the latter is joined to the peninsula by two bridges. A population of approximately 400,000 gives Macau a density of 23,500 persons per square kilometer. This far exceeds the density even of Hong Kong, which has about 5,600 persons per square kilometer (see *Hong Kong: System of Educaton*).

Because Portugal remained neutral during the Second World War, Macau, as one of its colonies, became home to many Chinese and European refugees. The population grew from 142,000 in 1938 to 400,000 in 1940, but fell again to 150,000 in 1945. It then commenced more steady growth to 267,000 in 1980. A burst of legal and illegal immigration from China brought about 100,000 more people in the 1980s. The scale of population growth put great pressure on education facilities.

Over 90 percent of the population is Chinese by race. However, two significant minority groups are a small cadre of Portuguese, and a mixed-race group known as the "Macanese." Many of the Portuguese have been recruited on short-term contracts to assist with administration, education, and other services.

As a distinct political entity, Macau's history dates back to 1557, when Portuguese traders secured rights of settlement from the Chinese authorities. The Europeans were allowed considerable autonomy, and an 1887 treaty brought explicit recognition of Portuguese sovereignty (Pires 1991).

Although the Portuguese were primarily interested in Macau for economic reasons, the territory also played a major religious and cultural role. The Catholic Church established many schools, one of which became a university in 1594 and taught theology, humanities, Greek, Latin, rhetoric, and philosophy. The university operated until 1762, but was closed when the religious conflict in Europe led to a ban on Jesuits in all Portuguese territories. Nevertheless, the Jesuits subsequently returned, and Macau was a major conduit through which Western education and science entered China, Japan, and Korea.

After the mid-seventeenth century, Macau's fortunes declined. Portugal was unable to hold her empire together, and competition for East Asian trade became increasingly intense. The foundation of Hong Kong in 1842 was a scrious blow, for its far superior port eclipsed Macau's strategic significance. Macau became little more than an inward-looking backwater.

Although after the end of the Second World War the Chinese government wished to repossess the territory, it was unable to force the issue. For a time, policies were left at the level of official pronouncements. However, China's 1966 Cultural Revolution led to violent riots in Macau and to vigorous anti-Portuguese propaganda. Unexpectedly, as soon as the Portuguese announced that they intended to leave, the Communists altered their stance. The Chinese authorities recognized Macau's role as an outlet for international trade, and found it more useful to retain Macau as a foreign port than to repossess it.

Portugal itself experienced a revolution in 1974. Its new government had a very different view of world affairs, and immediately set about decolonizing its African territories. In Asia, East Timor was unilaterally seized by Indonesia. However, the Chinese maintained their refusal to reassert sovereignty over Macau.

Finally, in 1987, the Portuguese and Chinese governments agreed that Macau would revert to China in 1999. Macau is expected to remain a Special Administrative Region for at least 50 years after the transition.

Meanwhile, it is considered a "Chinese territory under Portuguese administration."

Official figures placed the 1992 Gross Domestic Product (GDP) per head at US$13,200. Manufacturing contributes about a third of GDP, with textiles, toys, and artificial flowers holding the greatest share of exports. There has also been a major growth in tourism, part of it linked to gambling. Being a highly urbanized society in which land commands high prices, Macau has a negligible agricultural sector.

Economic growth has greatly facilitated expansion of the education system. However, the general level of education in the population is quite low. The 1991 census indicated that 4.9 percent of the working population had no schooling, that another 13.9 percent had incomplete primary education, and that a further 31.5 percent had only primary qualifications. At the other end of the scale only 6.6 percent of the working population had tertiary education, and 43.1 percent had secondary education.

2. Politics and the Goals of the Education System

Until the 1980s, government involvement in education was minimal. The authorities provided a small number of Portuguese-language schools for the children of officials and others desiring this type of education, but most schools operated privately without official control or even monitoring. Even in 1979, only 2.1 percent of the budget was devoted to education. This was one of the lowest proportions in the world. The lack of official interest in education for the bulk of the population may be attributed partly to colonial policies (Bray 1992).

However, the 1980s and 1990s brought dramatic changes. Many were stimulated by awareness of the precise date on which sovereignty would be returned to the People's Republic of China (PRC). The government of Portugal realized that it was about to lose its last foothold in Asia, and embarked on strategies to strengthen influence which could last beyond 1999. Interest was also stirred locally, for the people of Macau were keen to ensure that structures were in place prior to the change of sovereignty.

Certain provisions on education were enshrined in the Basic Law (Macau 1993), Chapter VI of which indicated that:

> The Government of the Macau Special Administrative Region shall, on its own, formulate policies on education, including policies regarding the educational system and its administration, the language of instruction, the allocation of funds, the examination system, the recognition of educational qualifications and the system of academic awards...
> The existing educational institutions of all kinds in Macau may continue to operate. All educational institutions in the Macau Special Administrative Region shall enjoy their autonomy and teaching and academic freedom in accordance with law... Students shall enjoy

freedom of choice of educational institutions and freedom to pursue their education outside the Macau Special Administrative Region.

This is very similar to the provision for Hong Kong (see *Hong Kong*).

The legal framework is derived from a pair of laws (Macau 1991a, 1991b). One covers higher education, and the other covers kindergarten to secondary education.

3. The Formal System of Education

3.1 Primary, Secondary, and Tertiary Education

Until the early 1990s, Macau could not be said to have a single, distinctive education system. Instead it had an uncoordinated collection of institutions based on models in Portugal, the PRC, Taiwan, and Hong Kong (Alves Pinto 1987). The number of years in the primary, junior secondary, and senior secondary cycles varied according to the model. The Portuguese model followed a 4+2+3+2+1 pattern, the model imported from the PRC was 6+5, and the Taiwan one was 6+3+3. The principal model borrowed from Hong Kong had a 6+5+1 structure (see Fig.1).

Within this categorization was a wide collection of combinations (see Table 1). This diversity reflected the haphazard way in which education in Macau had been allowed to develop. However, some overarching features could be identified (see Fig. 2), and the 1991 Education Law brought much greater coherence.

The Education Law also set out a long-term goal of nine years of compulsory and free schooling. However, even in the absence of compulsion, enrollment rates were high. In the early 1990s they exceeded 95 percent.

Although most schooling is in Chinese, some schools operate in Portuguese or English (see Table 2). Government schools form about 10 percent of the total. The others, the vast majority, are private institutions run by religious bodies, social service or-

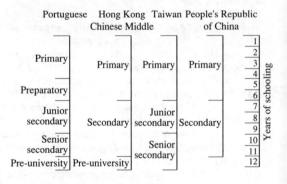

Figure 1

Macau: Structure of school systems

ganizations, commercial enterprises, and individuals. About 50 percent of the schools are operated by the Catholic Church. Private schools have been free to recruit their own teachers, determine conditions of service, and decide on the size of classes. All government schools are coeducational, but some Church schools are single-sex.

The Portuguese-medium official schools have one teacher per class in the first cycle of four years and one teacher per subject in the second cycle of two years. Average class size is about 20 pupils. Private Chinese-medium schools use a combination of the class system and specialist teachers throughout the six-year primary cycle, and most schools have about 50 pupils per class.

Macau's principal postsecondary institution is the University of Macau. It was founded in 1981 as a private, commercial enterprise, and until 1991 was known as the University of East Asia (UEA). Because its owners perceived the English-medium market to be larger than that of Chinese or Portuguese, they made English the principal language of operation. In 1988 the main part of the university was purchased by the government. More courses are now taught in Chinese and Portuguese than was originally the case, but English has remained the institution's principal language.

3.2 Preschool Education

In 1991–92, 21,000 children aged 3–5 attended preschools (see Table 2). Although most institutions were private, some were operated by the government. Programs are free of charge in government institutions, and subsidized in private ones.

In the past, private kindergartens have strongly emphasized instructional teaching as a preparation for primary school. The 1991 Education Law discouraged this approach and emphasized the need for broader attention to play and exploration. Some progress is being made toward this goal.

3.3 Special Education

Until the 1980s, the only provision for children with special education needs was through the churches. This provision met some needs, but was inadequate. Schooling was provided for some deaf and some mentally handicapped children.

In 1982 the government opened a special school for mentally handicapped children, and offered some support for children with various learning difficulties who were integrated into the official regular schools. Over the following decade provision gradually expanded, though a 1990 survey indicated ongoing inadequacies.

In 1990 the budget for special education was raised to 1 percent of the total education budget. Services were made free of charge, and efforts were made to improve training and professional support. The principal focus of activity was children with mental handicaps, though the authorities tried also to cater more effectively for other children with special needs.

By 1991 special education programs catered for 412

Table 1

Number of schools by type and level, Macau 1989–90[a]

	Language of curriculum					
	Port-uguese	Chinese	Chinese & Portuguese	English	Others[b]	Total
Preschool	1	8		1		10
Preschool and basic	1	34	4	2		41
Preschool, basic, and secondary	1	12		1		14
Basic	2	2				4
Basic and secondary	1	4	1	4		10
Basic and secondary-technical-professional		1		1		2
Secondary	1	5		1		7
Secondary and teacher-training		1				1
Secondary and higher			1	1	2	
Teacher-training		1				1
Nursing school		1	1			2
Higher				3		3
Total	7	69	6	14	1	97

Source: Governo de Macau, Inquerito ao Ensino 1989/1990 (Macau: Direcçaõ dos Serviços de Estatística e Censos, 1991) p. 72

a The sizes of these institutions vary widely. A table showing enrollments would indicate rather different proportions in each system

b The column "others" refers to the use of different languages at the University of East Asia

students aged 3–21, who represented about 0.5 percent of the student population. The special school and special classes have an average student–teacher ratio of about 7:1, but few teachers have received specialist training. The main strategy for development of special education emphasizes mainstream integration of disabled pupils into regular government schools. Teaching conditions in private schools do not yet encourage an optimistic forecast for comparable strategies in the nongovernment sector.

3.4 Vocational, Technical, and Business Education

In 1990 the polytechnic and junior colleges were separated from the rest of the university. They formed an independent polytechnic which focuses on such skills as computing, hotel management, travel management, and social work. The institution runs two-year diploma/certificate and three-year bachelor's courses in the media of Cantonese and English.

The Industrial Training and Development Center was established in 1985 under the umbrella of the government's Department of Industry, with an annual budget of US$250,000 for full- and part-time training. By 1988 it had enrolled over 2,000 students on various short courses at technician, craft worker, and operative levels. The long courses at the technician level include the Diploma in Fashion, which trains people who are not in the trade but wish to join it. Shorter craft worker and operative courses serve sewing machine mechanics, cutting operators, pattern graders, and similar personnel.

Other training is offered by the Association of Industry, which operates regular industrial training courses with government subsidies. Also, the Macau Management Association's Vocational Training Center offers courses on tax returns, languages, computers, banking, and advertising.

3.5 Adult and Nonformal Education

In the 1940s, the Chinese Chamber of Commerce began vocational courses for adults in such areas as bookkeeping and Mandarin. The school of Commerce is an evening school which began in these early days and still exists. Institutions such as the Kang Wu Evening Primary School and courses organized by trade unions help adult workers to acquire basic literacy and numeracy skills. Some programs receive government subsidies. However, the number of adults studying the equivalent of primary education at evening schools has been small, despite the large proportion of the population that has never completed primary education.

Establishment of the university and the polytechnic created new opportunities for mature students who lacked earlier opportunities to extend their studies. Students who have not completed secondary school can sit examinations for entry to some faculties.

Table 2
Number of schools in Macau 1992–93[a]

	Preprimary	Primary	Secondary
Official			
Chinese	6	6	1
Portuguese	1	2	1
Private			
Chinese	54	55	24
Portuguese	2	4	2
English	2	6	7
Total	65	73	35

a The total number of institutions differs from that shown in Table 1. This is partly because the figures refer to a different year, but also because multilevel schools are here counted as if their component parts were separate institutions

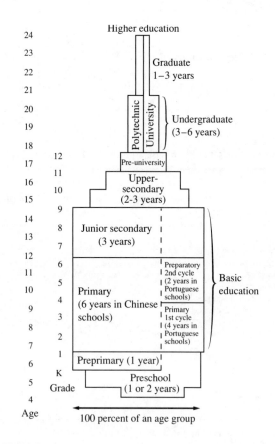

Figure 2
Macau: structure of formal education system

Also, in 1990 about 2,000 adult students enrolled in Portuguese-language courses run by government institutions.

4. Administrative and Supervisory Structure and Operation

Education is a shared responsibility between the government and private sectors. Private schools have considerable autonomy. Government coordination and control have increased, but the Education Law recognizes the autonomy of educational institutions.

The government's Department of Education plans, manages, and evaluates the official schools. The central authorities recruit and appoint teachers, and supply equipment, materials, and meals for preprimary and primary schools. At the secondary level, official schools have some autonomy in the management of school resources and appraisal of teachers.

Two collective bodies coordinate most of the private schools: the Association of Catholic Schools and the Chinese Education Association. The latter plays a particularly strong role with the left-wing schools.

The Education Council has representatives of different social sectors and is consulted on all major matters of government policy. A permanent Executive Committee composed of education professionals appraises and monitors education policy implementation.

5. Educational Finance

Although government expenditure on education until the late 1970s usually represented less than 3 percent of the budget, the activities of the 1980s required substantial budgetary growth. By 1989 education was consuming 7.6 percent of the budget, and by 1991 the figure was 11.6 percent. These figures reflected not only increased activity in the school sector, but also the government's purchase and operation of the university. However, commitment to other infrastructure projects required subsequent reduction of the proportional allocation to education.

As part of the efforts to forge a coherent education system and to reduce inequalities in access, the government has made extensive grants to parents and private schools. In 1991–92, these subsidies comprised 5 percent of the total education budget and supported 14 percent of the school population.

While for the first seven years of its existence the owners of the University of East Asia (UEA) were anxious to avoid the image of rapacious capitalists, they nevertheless charged the highest fees that were consistent with their aspired image and the ability of the market to pay. After the government's purchase of the institution, local students were given 40 percent subsidies.

Since the early 1980s, the government has operated a scholarship scheme for overseas study. The scheme was mainly intended for study in Portugal, though it also permitted study elsewhere. In 1986 the scheme was enlarged to encompass local study at the UEA, and it now includes a loan as well as a grant element (Bray 1991).

6. Supplying Personnel for the Education System

Many of Macau's teachers are imported. This is especially true of the official Portuguese-medium schools, where almost all staff are from Portugal. Church and other private schools employ more Macau teachers, but they also recruit large numbers from the PRC and elsewhere. Figures for 1991–92 showed that only 38.7 percent of teachers had been born in Macau. As many as 29.6 percent had been born in China, though not all were recent immigrants. Teachers from Hong Kong formed only 7.9 percent of the total, chiefly because Macau salaries and job opportunities compared poorly with those in Hong Kong. The local staff were concentrated in the lower levels of the system, while Portuguese and PRC staff were concentrated in the secondary schools. The majority of Hong Kong citizens were in the postsecondary sector.

Macau has long had a problem of teacher training, especially for primary schools. In 1987–88, for example, 50 percent of primary teachers had only secondary education. At the secondary level, 16 percent of teachers had only secondary education.

The high proportion of untrained teachers was partly attributable to the small size of the territory, for the authorities found it difficult to establish institutions of sufficient size to gain economies of scale. However, teacher-training institutions have not been completely lacking. Since 1952 the Roman Catholic Church has operated a one-year full-time course for preprimary and primary teachers, and in 1984 the government established a small Portuguese-medium institution to train teachers of adults and of preprimary and primary age children. Also, some primary teachers have received training on a three-year part-time correspondence course run by the South China Normal University.

In order to improve the situation, the Macau government has trained teachers through the University of Macau since the late 1980s. In 1987, an inservice program was launched for 24 preprimary and 40 primary teachers, and two years later, full-time preprimary and primary teacher-training courses were launched for Form 5 leavers. For secondary teachers the university set up a full-time BEd program for Form 6 leavers; and in 1990 it launched a postgraduate certificate in education program. However, inservice training is not compulsory.

In 1991, the Education Department employed about 1,000 people. Of these, 58 percent were teachers, while

8 percent were senior officers and technical staff, 7 percent were administrative staff, and 24 percent were auxiliaries.

7. Curriculum Development and Teaching Methodology

Major questions have surrounded the relevance of school curricula in the second half of the twentieth century. They arise particularly from the colonial origins of the official system, the multiplicity of other imported models, and the lack of local textbooks (Bray and Hui 1991). Like other aspects of the education system, curriculum development has been *laissez faire*. Schools have adopted syllabuses and curricula from other countries on a largely ad hoc basis. Portuguese-medium schools have used syllabuses and textbooks imported from Portugal, while private schools have used materials from such places as Hong Kong, Taiwan, and China. The combination of official neglect of nongovernment schools and the small size of the market meant that until the 1990s no textbooks were published directly for Macau's private schools.

The Basic Law gives a continued place to the Portuguese language in education for 50 years following 1999. It also upholds the autonomy of private schools in their own selection of curricula. However, the role of Portuguese is likely to decline over time; and all schools need assistance with curriculum development.

8. The System of Examinations, Promotions, and Certifications

Until the 1990s, Macau had no territory-wide examination system. Pupils in the Portuguese-medium schools followed the assessment system from Portugal, while students in private schools either sat foreign examinations or no examinations at all.

The chief factor permitting Macau to exist without a territory-wide examination system was its small size. Whereas larger societies need national examinations to allow employers to compare different job applicants, employers in Macau could learn most of what they needed to know from personal contacts. Applicants to the civil service sat a written Portuguese-language test, but were otherwise selected on the basis of reference letters and interviews.

To some observers, the lack of examinations might seem a blessing, for in other contexts critics have decried the distorting effect of examinations on educational processes. However, in Macau, younger schools had no yardstick against which to prove their ability and compete with the prestige of older institutions. Also, while some students who wished to study abroad could do so because their schools had agreements with specific tertiary institutions in Hong Kong, Canada, and the United States, other students were disadvantaged by their inability to present standardized credentials. Some school-leavers met the same problem in the labor market.

Since 1990, the university has held an entrance examination open to all schools in the territory. The arrangement is not without problems, for the examination has considerable influence on secondary school curricula and it is set by a tertiary institution rather than by an independent examinations authority. However, the examination does help to unify the education system.

9. Educational Assessment, Evaluation, and Research

The government now takes a much more active role in assessment and evaluation. Its detailed work is assisted by the small size of the system and the personalized nature of the society. Among the important instruments for planning are a detailed annual survey of schools.

Nongovernment research is limited, but has nevertheless expanded significantly. The research output of the Faculty of Education in the university remains restricted by the small number of staff and by other pressures on their time, but the institution has helped build up a corpus of published information about education matters.

10. Major Reforms in the 1980s and 1990s

During the 1980s and 1990s, the situation has been transformed from one of official neglect for all but the government schools to one of extensive government activity. While much remains to be done, there is now considerably greater shape to the education system. It serves more people, and does so in a more effective way.

Since the mid-1980s the government has also taken a much more active role in higher education. In 1986 the government appointed a delegate to the University of East Asia and in 1988 the government bought the main campus of the university from its private owners. According to the government delegate (quoted in Hui 1994):

> The greatest heirloom that Portugal can leave in Macau should be a university built according to the modern mode. This university will be the focus point of knowledge transmission and the bridge for eastern and western communication.

This quotation summarizes official aspirations for the university.

The early 1990s also brought discussion about privatization of the Portuguese-medium official schools. This move would permit the government to devote its main energies to Chinese-medium institutions.

With the gradual change of administration before 1999, the number of expatriate officers and teachers from Portugal will diminish. A major effort to train local personnel will be made, especially in the area of management and in the inspectorate.

11. Major Problems for the Year 2000

By 2000, Macau will again be part of the People's Republic of China as a Special Administrative Region. The major challenge will be to preserve its identity while operating within the larger framework. Considerable tension may be anticipated between competing social, political, and economic forces.

On a more specific note, it seems inevitable that Putonghua will occupy a stronger place in the school curriculum. The challenge then is to find space in timetables which are already crowded, and to secure sufficient qualified teachers in the subject. Other issues will concern the place of the Portuguese and English languages, the nature of links with Portugal, and ways to strengthen the quality of schooling.

References

Alves Pinto M C 1987 *Ensino em Macau: Umas Abordagem Sistémica da Realidade Educativa.* Gabinete do Secretário-Adjunto para a Educacao e Cultura, Macau

Bray M 1991 Strategies for financing higher education: Perspectives from Hong Kong and Macau. *High. Educ.* 21(1): 11–25

Bray M 1992 Colonialism, scale and politics: Divergence and convergence of educational development in Hong Kong and Macau. *Comp. Educ. Rev.* 36(3): 322–42

Bray M, Hui P 1991 Curriculum development in Macau. In: Marsh C, Morris P (eds.) 1991 *Curriculum Development in East Asia.* Falmer Press, London

Hui P K F 1994 Decolonization and higher education development: The transfer of state power in Macau. In: Mauch J, Sabloff P (eds.) 1994 *International Perspectives on Reformulation and Change in Higher Education.* State University of New York Press, Albany, New York

Macau 1991a Ensino superior em Macau, Decreto-Lei no.11/91/M. *Boletim Oficial de Macau* 5: 435–46

Macau 1991b Sistema educativo de Macau, Lei no.11/91M. *Boletim Oficial de Macau,* Supplement to No.34, pp. 3693–703

Macau 1993 *Lei Básica de Regiaõ Administrativa Especial de Macau da República Popular da China.* Conselho Consultivo da Lei Básica da Regiaõ Administrativa Especial de Macau da Republica Popular da China, Macau

Pires B V 1991 Origins and early history of Macau. In: Cremer R D (ed.) 1991 *Macau: City of Commerce and Culture,* 2nd edn. API Press, Hong Kong

Further Reading

Bray M, Hui P 1991 Structure and content of education: Evolution and reform in the transitional period. In: Cremer R D (ed.) 1991 *Macau: City of Commerce and Culture,* 2nd edn. API Press, Hong Kong

Edmonds R L 1989 *Macau.* World Bibliographical Series, vol. 105. Clio Press, Oxford

Ngai, M C 1993 Ensino em Macau no período de transição. *Administração* (Macau) 22: 831–37

Rangel J 1991 Prospects and directions for education. In: Cremer R D (ed.) 1991 *Macau: City of Commerce and Culture,* 2nd edn. API Press, Hong Kong

Teixeira M 1982 *A Educaçaõ em Macau.* Direcçaõ dos Serviços de Educaçaõ e Cultura, Macau

Vong C S 1990 Sobre o problema das vagas escolares no ensino primário e secundário em Macau. *Administraçaõ* (Macau) 10: 815–29

Yee A H 1988 Universities in Hong Kong and Macau: A tale of two colonies. *Journal of Higher Education Policy* 1(4): 16–22

Yee A 1990 A comparative study of Macau's education system: Changing colonial patronage and native self-reliance. *Comp. Educ.* 26(1): 61–71

Madagascar

R. Rakotondrazaka

1. General Background

Situated in the Indian Ocean, Madagascar is a large island with an area of 587,041 square kilometers. Separated from the African continent by the Mozambique channel, which is 400 kilometers wide, it is predominantly a tropical country. The country is divided into four major geographical regions. The main rice growing region (rice being the Malagasy staple food) is situated in the highlands in the center of the island, and includes the capital city of Antananarivo and many urban centers. The luxuriant eastern plain is bounded by the Indian Ocean and the steep slopes of the highlands, and certain regions become inaccessible during rainy seasons. The south is characterized by a semidesert climate and the north, one of the wealthiest regions of the island (growing coffee, vanilla, cocoa), is inaccessible during the rainy seasons. Geographical isolation, climate, social organization, and poor communications all have strong effects on education development in the different regions of the island.

Madagascar gained its independence in 1960, after 65 years of annexation by France. Apart from the fact that the missionaries had left an educational heritage in the highlands in the precolonial era, the majority of the educational infrastructure was set up in Antananarivo during the French colonial period. The differences between the highlands and the coastal regions in both economic and cultural fields will affect educational policy in the years to come.

Madagascar's population was 11,197,000 in 1990, with a national average density of 19.1 inhabitants per square kilometer. Half of the population is concentrated in the central highlands, where the average density is twice as high as the national average. Just over 23 percent of the population lives in two large provinces in the western part. These two provinces occupy half the land area of the country. This unequal distribution of the population has a direct effect on the location of schools for the population. The supervision and the administration of the educational system is not easy because of the wide distances and poor communications. The population more than doubled from 1950 to 1990. The population growth rate was 2.76 percent in 1990. This high rate is due to a decrease in mortality, better medical care, and a birthrate which has remained high. Children are considered by the Malagasy people as a source of wealth and as labor for agriculture and stock farming. This phenomenon appears among the causes of the rather high dropout rate and the low school attendance rate at the primary school level in rural areas, where 78 percent of the population lives. The population is young: half of the people are less than 20 years old.

The island has been populated by successive groups of people from Asia, the eastern coast of Africa and the Persian Gulf; there are 18 ethnic groups in the country. Despite this diversity, the Malagasy people have a common language, Malagasy, of Malayo–Polynesian origin, but there are dialectal variants.

Madagascar is a predominantly agricultural country. The labor force represents 55.5 percent of the population, of which 90 percent lives in rural areas. Traditional agriculture monopolized 87 percent of the national labor force over the age of 12 years in 1985; the informal sector represented 6 percent; the remainder was 7 percent of the modern sector, divided into 2 percent for the modern public sector, 3 percent for the private sector, and 2 percent for modern private sector service. Based on self-subsistence agriculture, the money income of the rural population remains very low. Employment is a major concern. The crisis in the public sector and parapublic sector, together with low economic growth, have decreased the number of remunerated jobs. Various measures of structural adjustment were introduced after 1980, and in 1992 there was a liberal restructuring of the economic sector. The government favors the creation of small and average firms. Instructional programs will be made more appropriate to the needs of the national economy.

In 1990 the per capita gross national product (GNP) was US$198. The distribution of the GNP between sectors was 40.5 percent agriculture, 16.1 percent in the sec-ondary sector, and 31.6 percent in the tertiary sector. In 1984, half of the women living in rural areas and over 15 years of age had never been to school. The percentage of illiterate women in rural environments is three times more than that of illiterate women in urban environments. Literacy rates have improved because of the expansion of the education system and efforts made in the training of adults, especially adult women, in the 1980s.

The First Republic ended in 1972. By 1972 the educational system had not changed much as compared to the structures inherited from the colonial system. In 1975 Madagascar chose socialism. Power was shared between central bodies on the one hand and decentralized communities on the other. Central bodies comprised the executive level composed of the president of the Republic, the Supreme Revolutionary Council, and the government. The legislative level constituted the National Assembly. The country is divided into six *Faritany* (Provinces), 110 *Fivondronampokontany* (communes), 1250 *Firaisampokontany* (districts), and 11,300 *Fokontany* (villages). Political and administrative reorganization has led to the establishment of territorial structures which coincide with the decentralized communities. Three fundamental principles are embodied in the Constitution as far as educational policy is concerned. These are: democratization, Malagasization, and decentralization, and they resulted in establishing schools throughout the different communities and providing equal opportunity to all. This structure ended in 1991. There is a transitional period of 18 months, at the end of which the Third Republic will be proclaimed. However, the strategy applied since 1990 in the educational sector remains and will have six emphases, namely: (a) teaching quality improvement; (b) management improvement; (c) control of costs and financing; (d) reorganization of vocational training; (e) the establishment of an efficacious postsecondary training; and (f) the management of student flow.

2. Politics and the Goals of the Education System

Given that one of the roles of the state is to educate its people, a large part of the state budget will be allocated to education. Efforts have been made to make primary education accessible to a larger number of people. The major task of primary education is to educate the greatest number possible so as to give them the knowledge and skills to enable them to join the working population. The system should also provide the nation with technicians in accordance with its future and present needs. For part of the population, the education system and especially general education is the privileged way to climb the social ladder, and is perceived to be the way to higher levels of certification, which means a better paid and stable job in government service. In government service, the salary scale depends on the level of certification.

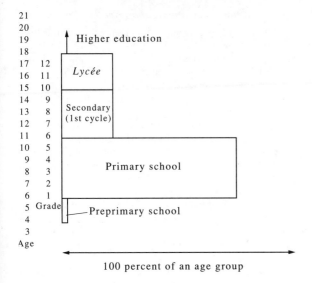

21
20
19   Higher education
18
17 12
16 11   *Lycée*
15 10
14   9
13   8   Secondary
12   7   (1st cycle)
11   6
10   5
 9   4
 8   3   Primary school
 7   2
 6   1
 5 Grade   Preprimary school
 4
 3
Age

100 percent of an age group

Figure 1
Madagascar: Structure of the formal education system

The rapid growth of school enrollment at the primary level has led to social pressure in favor of general secondary education which, in turn, saw its enrollment increase rapidly to the detriment of enrollment in vocational training. In higher education, university studies are organized around a hierarchy of degrees. Enrollment in faculties which lead to the highest degrees have increased, to the detriment of enrollment in training which prepares students directly for a job. About 80 percent of *baccalauréat* holders enroll in higher education. Many of these students fail to find employment and have no other alternative than to enroll at the university, which provides a generous policy of grants. Those who are already inside the system remain there, even if they repeatedly fail courses for the same reasons. Some parents think that after the *baccalauréat* the state should assume responsibility for studies. Others think that scholarships are disguised unemployment benefits which secure social peace.

3. The Formal System of Education

Figure 1 is a diagrammatic representation of the Madagascar system of education.

3.1 Primary, Secondary, and Tertiary Education

The educational system is divided into four levels. Level I, also called "primary education" or "basic education," begins at six years of age and lasts for five years, at the end of which students obtain the *Certificat*

d'Etudes Primaires et Elémentaires (CEPE). There are 13,555 primary schools. Decentralized communities are in charge of the construction and equipment of the public schools at this level, while the state provides subsidies. From 1975 to 1985 school enrollment at all levels increased rapidly, due to the policy of democratization and decentralization. The growth was 62 percent at the primary level. Since 1986, there has been a slight decrease, partly explained by the fact that many schools (1,700) closed down in rural areas. The Direction for Planning of the Ministry of Public Instruction recorded 19 reasons for schools closing down. These reasons varied from the bad state of buildings caused by bad weather or lack of maintenance to a state of insecurity in the countryside. The net enrollment ratio is 73.5 percent for children between six and ten years of age, but there are disparities between regions. There were 1,522,312 students in primary school in 1990, 17 percent of whom were in private schools and more than half in the two provinces in the highlands. Female participation is high (48%). Internal school achievement is quite low, with an average annual grade repetition of 34.7 percent. The average size of a class is about 40 pupils and the pupil–teacher ratio is 40:1. The school year lasts 204 days with 25 to 30 instructional hours per week.

The medium term objective is to increase the number of newly enrolled pupils in the first year of primary school by 4 percent per year. Within this framework, all children should be in primary school by the year 2000.

Level II, secondary school first cycle, lasts four years in a *collège d'enseignement général* (lower-secondary school) established in each *Firaisampokontany*. The average gross enrollment ratio in 1989–90 was 21.5 percent, but this varied between 16.4 in the south and 27.8 in the central highlands. In 1990, there were 260,958 pupils, with 49 percent of girls and 99.3 percent in general education. Enrollment in private schools decreased from 50 percent in 1975 to 32 percent in 1990. Freezing the growth rate of those enrolling in the first year of the first cycle at 2 percent is under consideration.

Level III *lycées* (upper-secondary schools), established in each *Fivondronampokotany*, provide three years of upper-secondary education. In theory, this level should lead to effective employment as a medium executive with multiple abilities. The average gross enrollment ratio in 1989–90 was 21.5 percent and varied between 16.4 in the south and 27.8 percent in the central highlands. Enrollment doubled between 1975 and 1990. In 1990, 43 percent of students were in private schools, 63 percent were in the central highlands, and 49 percent were girls. The percentage in technical education (17%), though low, is improving. Internal achievement is low and so is success at the *Baccalauréat* examination (20%). Setting the growth rate in the first year of studies at this level (Form 10) at 1 percent is under consideration.

Level IV, higher education, is dispensed either in

universities or in technological institutes of higher education which train senior technicians in two years. In universities, education is in the hands of establishments of higher education. Access is automatic for all *Baccalauréat* holders. In vocational schools of higher education, selection is on the basis of a competitive examination. The length of studies varies according to the school/establishment chosen and ranges from four to seven years. There are six universities, one in each major city in the *Faritany*. In 1990 there were 37,046 students amounting to 330 students per 100,000 inhabitants. Nearly 77 percent of students were in establishments of the faculty type, and 23.2 percent were in the 10 vocational schools/establishments. In vocational establishments 64 percent of students were in the first two years of study, and 74.7 percent in the University of Antananarivo. More than half of these students were grant-holders and 43 percent were women.

From 1975 to 1985 there was a large increase in school enrollment, with an average annual growth rate of 19.5 percent. This period corresponded to the phase of intensive implementation of the decentralization and democratization policy. From 1985 to 1990, higher education enrollment remained stable at about 37,000 students. In 1991 there were two technological institutes of higher education with seven training tracks, mainly in civil engineering, the industrial area (especially maintenance), and the tertiary area. Further institutes of this kind will be established in other provinces.

3.2 Preschool Education

Preschool education is still at an embryo stage. The percentage of 3- to 5-year olds enrolled in 1987 was 2.6 percent. There are 480 centers and most of them are in the capital city (54%). More than half are in the hands of Catholic and Protestant missions, 38.5 percent are owned by private individuals, and 3.3 percent have been founded by the state under the auspices of the Ministry of Population. Private institutions charge fees and only parents with a certain income can benefit from them.

3.3 Special Education

Special education is dispensed to physically and mentally handicapped children and adults. Most of these schools are organized by private and denominational agencies with financial support from nongovernmental organizations and small subsidies from the state. In institutions reserved for deaf-mutes, apart from specialized education, a training similar to primary school training is dispensed. Training is mostly vocational, that is, formula training production. After their training, the students start their own businesses or obtain employment at the production workshops of the institution.

3.4 Vocational, Technical, and Business Education

Technical and vocational education is accorded high priority by the government. It will be reorganized and redefined in order to arrive at a practical training linked with the problem of employment. A coordination structure will be established. This reorganization will be financed within the framework of multilateral and bilateral cooperation.

Dispensed in public and private institutions that depend on the Ministry of Public Instruction, technical and vocational education covers Levels I, II, and III. Level I provides two-year practical courses after the end of primary school. Level II provides similar courses after the first cycle of secondary school (1,780 pupils for 31 institutions). Colleges and technical *lycées* provide, for students holding the certificate for achievement of the first cycle of secondary school, three-year courses for technical A-level type examinations and the *Brevet technique* (technical certificate) and *Brevet d'agent d'exécution*. In the public institutions, the students do not pay school fees. At the level of higher education, technical training is dispensed within schools of higher education.

One of the major problems in the field of vocational and technical training is the fact that the training is inadequate for the type of labor needed. Added to this are the decrepit facilities, obsolete equipment, and poorly qualified teachers. Those who emerge from this system enroll, for the most part, in higher education, where their failure rate is high.

In 1992, businesses were becoming aware of the need to invest in education and of the need for a tight relationship between businesses and vocational schools for the training of future labor. The outcome of this is expected to be a new form of cooperation: business training organization.

3.5 Adult and Nonformal Education

There is a host of organized nonformal education activities, which are in general haphazard and poorly coordinated. There is no coherent policy of lifelong education. Continuing education of the vocational type is run by many ministries as well as private and public organizations. Continuing education courses are of two types: (a) the long-term formal type (one year or more) for basic training, with access often being via competitive examination; and (b) the nonformal type, lasting not more than six months and mostly centered on further training and retraining. The majority of these centers also provide training in the tertiary sector. At the end of the 1980s and beginning of the 1990s, centers began to provide courses in computer studies. Very few courses were oriented towards the agricultural and industrial sectors.

Literacy and postliteracy activities are carried out for young dropouts and rural adults who request it. The Head Office for Literacy and Adult Education, via its decentralized branches, trains teachers and provides equipment and a rural press. The number of adults taught to read and write is estimated to be 20,000 a year. Literacy makes up an initial phase insofar as these adults have never been to school, the objective being the eradication of illiteracy. Agencies such as UNESCO and UNICEF bring their support to these programs.

Another aspect of nonformal and adult education is youth training within the framework of youth sociocultural activities. The purpose of these different activities is to help reduce unemployment and create jobs.

4. Administrative and Supervisory Structure and Operation

The Ministry of Public Instruction (MIP; formerly the Ministry of Primary and Secondary Education) is in charge of primary and secondary education, and the Ministry of Universities (formerly the Ministry of Higher Education) is in charge of higher education. Other educational activities come under the responsibility of other ministries (Health, Population, Employment and Training, Agriculture, etc.).

There are regional and local structures at the level of Ministry of Public Instruction. The Ministry is responsible for the implementation of the government's education development policy. The MIP has five departments, one of which is that of education planning. Its tasks are to implement educational policy, develop educational plans and strategies, and program and follow up the implementation of the plan. The Department of Educational Planning works out the plan in collaboration with primary, secondary, and technical departments at the Ministry of Public Instruction. The central level recruits and places teaching staff. The central level is responsible for school premises and equipment for Levels II and III. Provincial departments established in the major town of each *Faritany* are the decentralized structures of central services. Primary education administration and supervision, secondary education, financial and administrative control, and primary teacher self-training are the responsibility of school districts (CISCO) at the level of the *Fivondronampokontany* and for educational "animation" areas in the *Firaisampokontany*. However, these regional structures sometimes have neither the means nor the qualified staff necessary to carry out these tasks. This results in inconsistency between services and educational realities. Inspectors and consultants often do not visit schools for several years. Despite this so-called "decentralization," decision-making is still centralized at ministry level. It is to be noted that these structures and attributions are those which exist at the beginning of 1992, but they are likely to be changed in the course of the Third Republic.

The universities and institutes of higher education are the responsibility of the Ministry of Universities. Although the universities are autonomous, many decisions are made at the central level. The state provides the money for almost the total budget, including the salaries of teaching staff. Within the proposed reform, the role of the Ministry will be limited to the support, follow-up, and control of university activities. The development policy as carried out by universities must be consistent with the sectorial strategy. At the national level, a Conference of Rectors (vice-chancellors) will be established to discuss problems common to the universities.

Denominational and nondenominational private education have their own central and regional administrations. Contact with the MIP is ensured by the National Bureau for Private Education. In theory, these institutions must submit to ministry control. But there are some institutions which are not affiliated with the Bureau and which have teaching programs that differ from those of the state schools.

In 1987, a National Advisory Committee for Cultural Affairs (CONACOAC) was created. This is a very high-level committee that creates dialogue between the government and representatives of social groups directly concerned with cultural issues in general and with education in particular. Proposals made by this committee serve as a basic document to those responsible for the general improvement of the education and training system.

5. Educational Finance

The budget allocated to the two ministries in charge of education represents 3 percent of the gross national product in 1989. Education ranked first in the state's budget with 30.3 percent in 1989. On average, 73 percent of the education budget is allocated to primary and secondary education and 27 percent to higher education. Some 95 percent of the MIP's budget is used to finance salaries and the remainder is used for administrative expenses. This leaves nothing for pedagogical purposes in schools. Primary education, secondary first cycle, and secondary second cycle spent 49.6 percent, 19.9 percent, and 9.4 percent respectively of the MIP's budget in 1989; 4.8 percent was allocated to vocational and technical education. Unit costs are low at all levels.

In higher education, the money for training and research is limited because almost 60 percent of expenditure is absorbed by social expenses (grants, food) and 8 percent by the administration, leaving only 32 percent for training and research. The average cost per student was estimated to be US$600 in 1988.

The state's budget alone is insufficient to cover educational expenses. In private schools (primary, secondary), school fees vary between US$30 and US$250 per student per year. This represents a considerable sum for a family's budget. Added to this there are registration fees and examination fees in public schools (primary, secondary, higher education) and expenses for school equipment.

Table 1
Allocation of the budget by level of schooling and unit costs by level, 1990[a]

Level	% of education budget to different levels	Unit costs by level (FMG)	Unit costs by level (US$)[b]
Primary	43.3	35,435	22.9
Secondary	21.3	101,157	65.3
Technical	4.0	399,916	258.0
Higher education	31.4	877,072	565.8
	100		

a This includes teachers' salaries and salaries of nonteaching personnel working in the Ministry of Education and the Ministry of Higher Education. The central and local administration expenditures and transfer costs are taken into account. They are categorized by level of education proportional to the number of students at a given level. b The exchange rate used was that of February 1990: US$1=FMG1,550

6. Supplying Personnel for the Education System

In 1990, there were 54,893 teachers at all levels. There were 37,932 in primary education, 10,807 in the first cycle of secondary, 5,093 in the second cycle of secondary education, and 1,061 in higher education. The number of nonteaching staff amounted to 4,111 in higher education.

The rapid growth of enrollment at the primary level required a massive recruitment of teachers. The academic and pedagogical weaknesses of these teachers are one of the causes of poor student achievement. It is estimated that 85 percent of the teachers need to be retrained. In the first cycle of secondary education, there is a lack of teachers who have received initial training. Students who are called to national service are paid by the Ministry of Defense and placed at the school's disposal for a year. They represent almost half of the staff. At the beginning of the 1992 academic year, there was a big shortage of teachers because the government abolished national service for those having the *Baccalauréat*. There is a plethora of teachers for arts subjects and a shortage of teacher for subjects such as mathematics, physics, and chemistry. There are also more qualified teachers in urban than in rural areas. This lack is, in part, due to the lack of money for teaching posts at the MIP.

In the second cycle of secondary education the qualification level of teachers is higher. At this level, 90 percent of teachers hold a bachelor's degree. There are also several foreign (mostly French) technical assistants. There is a shortage of faculty members in higher education. Teachers work overtime to the detriment of their research. To mitigate this shortage, the universities take on part-time teachers. There is a need not only for more teachers but for more qualified teachers. There is a low percentage of professors of the highest rank (only 13.3%), especially in the new uni-versities. The highly qualified professors, especially in medicine, are nearing retirement.

In primary education, the pedagogical training of the national service volunteers lasted three months for holders of the CFEPCES (end of the first cycle of secondary education certificate) and five weeks for those who hold both CFEPCES and CAE/EB (certificate of aptitude for teaching in primary education). After serving two years as a teacher, volunteers were entitled to be teachers. Since 1990, training has taken place at Level I teacher-training colleges, to which trainees have access via a competitive examination. The training lasts two years. Level II training takes place in Level II teacher-training colleges. Recruitment is via a competitive examination. The course lasts three years, at the end of which teacher trainees sit for *Baccalauréat*-level examinations in education. Now this type of training has been replaced by a two-year training course of *Baccalauréat* holders at Level II National Teacher Training College (ENNII). Again, entry is via a competitive examination. For the second cycle of secondary school, teacher training takes place at Level III teacher-training colleges (EN3) within the universities. Access is via a competitive examination and training lasts five years. Examinations are organized at the end of each academic year; at the end of the fifth year students have to defend a thesis.

The retraining of teachers will be undertaken by means of a combination of pretrained consultant visits, periodical seminars in the region, and through the school pedagogical committees. The MIP will provide materials, equipment, and a teacher's guide as well as means of transportation for inspectors and consultants. At the level of higher education, studies and research scholarships in foreign universities will be granted, with a view to improving the qualifications of the teachers.

7. Curriculum Development and Teaching Methodology

There is a common curriculum for all state schools, and the books and materials are the same. At Level I there is only one teacher per class; at Levels II and III each subject is taught by a different teacher. At each level of higher education, specific courses and degrees are the same all over the country; however, new texts are being worked out. In the first three levels, the learning objectives, the school timetable, and directions on how to conduct the lesson appear in the curriculum guides.

Before 1990 the National Council for Curriculum Development (CNEP) was in charge of designing the school syllabus at the primary and secondary levels. In 1990, a Pedagogical Study and Research Unit (UERP) was created to arrange and fine-tune the curricula. The materials were tried out in pilot schools, evaluated and then discussed at the level of CNEP before the final version was issued. UERP evaluates and selects from among existing textbooks those that meet the demands of the curriculum. It also produces or coordinates the production and distribution of textbooks, teacher guides, and pedagogical aids. In the production and textbook writing stages, UERP uses teachers. As of 1992, the distribution of the books is organized by the School Book Bureau. The books are sent to the school districts and from there are sent to the educational "animation" areas and finally distributed to the schools. The books are either sold or rented to the pupils at a fixed price all over the country. A study of textbook distribution conducted in 1992 by the Direction for Education Planning showed that there are problems with distribution, due to communications and transportation difficulties. For other levels of education, the books can be obtained from bookshops in big towns.

Since 1976, Malagasy has been the language of instruction in primary schools and state secondary schools. In higher education, the teaching language has always been French. French is a compulsory subject in primary and secondary schools; English is a compulsory foreign language in Levels II and III; German, Spanish or Russian are optional foreign languages at Level III. French remains the foreign language used for communication and is therefore the most popular.

One of the biggest problems is the adaptation of syllabuses and course content to the profiles of pupils who are in their last term of studies while taking into account their everyday environment. A need is felt, especially in Levels I and II, to modify the curriculum with a view to adapting it to the needs of the majority who will not continue their studies, rather than for those wishing to go to university. Such an adaptation is made even more difficult by the low qualifications of the teachers and the severe lack of equipment, materials, and textbooks.

8. The System of Examinations, Promotions, and Certifications

Within each level of schooling, an examination system based on reference norms is used. The average marks obtained in these examinations is the criterion which determines promotion, grade repetition, or dropout. National examinations are organized at the end of each level of schooling in order to award national certificates (CEPE after primary studies; CFEPCES after the first cycle of secondary education; *Baccalauréat* after the second cycle of secondary education). On the other hand, competitive examinations for gaining access to higher education (Levels II and III) in some public institutions are coupled with these national examinations.

The examination system emphasizes essentially academic knowledge and encourages competition for certificates. Teaching and what teachers teach are largely oriented to the examination syllabus. There is also the problem of fairness. The Level I examinations militate against rural pupils. Once these pupils leave school, they often become illiterate again.

9. Educational Assessment, Evaluation, and Research

Evaluation of achievement acquired by a given group of students has never been carried out. Information about student achievement and aptitude is mostly on the basis of teacher judgment. Indicators collected at the national level are mostly centered on access to the different levels of the system and on the academic course of study.

Within the framework of these activities, the UERP could be called on to conduct studies of educational achievement together with the relevant educational directions.

10. Major Reforms in the 1980s and 1990s

In the 1980s, reforms which had taken place in 1978 took effect in the schools. The socialist trend in 1975 led to the adoption of a law in 1978 which set a general framework for education: the use of Malagasy as the medium of instruction and the reduction of the number of years of primary schooling entailed changes in the curriculum. The University of Madagascar was transformed into six autonomous universities. The 1980s saw the creation of private institutions of higher education. At the beginning of 1990, the technological institutes of higher education were founded.

In the early 1990s, studies were being undertaken with a view to restructuring Malagasy universities. Reforms coming from these studies will undoubtedly be implemented in the years to come.

11. Major Problems for the Year 2000

The Malagasy educational system is confronted with the following problems: loss of quality in teaching at all levels with a low internal and external efficiency; inadequacy of technical and vocational training for the employment market; enrollment explosion, especially in higher education, aggravated by low achievement; a double imbalance of costs and financing between the various levels of teaching; and in higher education an imbalance between educational expenditure and student grants. All this is further aggravated by weakness in the administration and management of the system.

Efforts to remedy these problems will involve: modification of the curriculum content and teaching methods; retraining and initial training of teachers at all levels; supervision of teachers; and the production of teaching materials. Special support was given to the Planning Department to reinforce its personnel's skills with priority on the improvement of the data collection system, data processing and data analysis, as well as to the dissemination of the results. Measures concerning the management of student flow, ways of making resources profitable, and of improving of the administration will all be studied.

Bibliography

Ministère de l'Enseignement Secondaire et de l'Education de Base 1990 *Annuaire statistiques 1989–1990*. Direction de la Planification et de l'Orientation de l'Enseignement, Antananarivo
Ministère de l'Enseignement Supérieur 1990 *Donneés statistiques 1989/1990*. Direction de la Planification et de l'Orientation de l'Enseignement, Antananarivo
Ministère de l'Enseignement Supérieur 1990 *Rapport d'activités 1989 et 1990*. Ministère de l'Enseignement Supérieur, Antananarivo
Ministère des Universités 1991 *Repères et Références Statistiques de 1975 à 1990*. Direction de la Programmation et des Investissements, Service de la Statistique et Etude, Antananarivo
Office Statistiques et Informatique pour la Programmation du Développement 1990 *La structure de l'Emploi dans le Secteur Moderne à Madagascar 1990*. Antananarivo
Rajaoson 1985 *L'Enseignement Supérieur et le Devenir de la Societé Malgache*. Antananarivo
Rasera J 1988 *Financement, coût, efficacité*. Université de Madagascar, Antananarivo
UNESCO 1986 *Priorités, contraintes et Perspectives du Développement de l'Education: Republique Démocratique de Madagascar*. UNESCO, Paris

Malawi

S. Nyirenda

1. General Background

Malawi is situated in southern East Africa. It has an area of 119,140 square kilometers, of which 20 percent is covered by water. Malawi is landlocked; it shares borders with Tanzania to the north, Mozambique to the east and south; and Zambia to the west.

The total population was estimated at 9 million in 1990; of which 1 million were Mozambican refugees. The population is estimated to be growing at 3.7 percent per annum. Malawi has a very high population density by African standards, estimated at 94 people per square kilometer in 1990. Slightly over 10 percent of the total population live in urban areas. It is estimated that Malawi's population will grow to 12 million with a population density of 229 per square kilometer of arable land by the year 2000.

The labor force was estimated to be 3,142,000 in 1990, of which 498,000 or 16 percent were in the paid employment sector. There were 2,338,000 small-holder farmers (74%) and 136,000 or 4.3 percent were unemployed.

Between 1964 and 1986, Malawi's development strategy emphasized the development and support of directly productive sectors rather than social sectors. Government expenditure was therefore concentrated in such sectors as agriculture, transport, and communica-

tions. The expansion of the educational system has in turn been constrained by the availability of resources and the competing needs of other social sectors as well as productive sectors.

During the 1990s, the intention is to increase expenditure on education. This initiative is being tempered by resource constraints because of the economic difficulties the country is undergoing and the growth of the school-age population.

2. Politics and the Goals of the Education System

The goals of the education system in Malawi have remained basically the same for many years. At primary level, the ultimate aim is to achieve universal education gradually, with special attention to geographic areas of low enrollment. Secondary and tertiary education have always been geared toward meeting skilled and educated labor force needs for the modern sector. The stock of skilled and educated workers was estimated to be 80,000 in 1987. Since the formal school system alone can not reduce the illiteracy level to any extent (estimated at 61% in 1990), the adult literacy program supplements formal education.

Primary education and the adult literacy program attempt to cover universally relevant target groups,

Table 1

Enrollments and resources in formal education, Malawi 1990

	Primary	Secondary	University	Primary teacher-training	Vocational technical training
Number of students[a]	1,325,453	29,326	2,685	2,909	7,702
Percentage age group enrolled	52	4	—	—	—
Number of institutions[b]	2,693	86	1	7	5
Average number of students per institution	492	341	2,685	416	154
Student–teacher ratio	64:1	27:1	11:1	15:1	13:1
Expenditure per student (MK)	39	425	6,690	1,886	2,181

Source: MOEC, Education Statistics, 1990
a Excludes the Malawi College of Distance Education centers students   b Covers only the 5 colleges under MOEC

while secondary and tertiary education are targeted at meeting the wage economy labor force needs. Since the supply of educated and skilled labor for the paid employment sector is more or less stable "the emphasis is increasingly toward equipping the nation's youth with the skills and desire for self-employment and entrepreneurship rather than conventional employment."

3. The Formal System of Education

3.1 Primary, Secondary, and Tertiary Education

Malawi has a basic 8-4-4 system of education with some deviations when it comes to secondary and tertiary education. Figure 1 shows the structure of the education system while Table 1 shows enrollments and resources for 1989/90.

The duration of primary education is eight years. Official entry is at age 6 while the exit age is 13 years. Although access to primary education is open, it is not compulsory. Total enrollment in 1989/90 was 1,325,000, of which about 45 percent were girls. The net enrollment ratio was about 52 percent and the average pupil-teacher ratio was 64:1. Government expenditure per pupil was MK40 (US$9.3). For 1989–90, only 8 percent of those who passed the Primary School Leaving Certificate Examination (PSLCE) gained admittance to conventional secondary schools, Form 1. The overall pass rate at PSLCE was 68 percent in 1990. The pass rate for boys was 70 percent compared to about 60 percent for girls. The primary school year is 210 days long.

Secondary school education lasts 4 years in the majority of schools (with the exception of a few externally oriented schools which offer six-year courses). Secondary education is conducted in two stages. The first part prepares students for the Junior Certificate Examination (JCE) which is taken after 2 years of study. The majority of successful students at JCE proceed to the two-year Malawi School Certificate of Examination

(MSCE) course. The MSCE is the normal entry qualification to university. In 1990, about 4,400 candidates passed the MSCE and about 750 or 17 percent gained admission to university. Students who do not gain entry into university proceed to other forms of postsecondary courses or join the labor market.

In 1990, there were 86 secondary schools in Malawi, of these 66 were government-assisted while 20 were

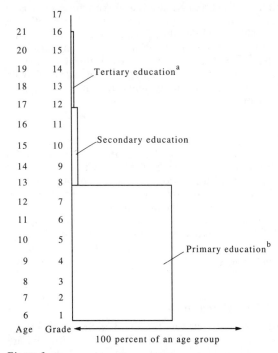

Figure 1

Malawi: Structure of the formal education system 1990
a Less than 1 percent of the age group (estimated figure)
b Preprimary education virtually nonexistent

597

private. Total enrollment was over 29,000 and the net enrollment ratio of the relevant 14–17 age group was about 4 percent. The average enrollment of each school was 340 pupils and the student–teacher ratio was 27:1. Government expenditure per pupil was about MK425 (US$98.8).

Malawi has one university with five constituent colleges. Bunda College offers diplomas and degrees in agriculture while Chancellor College offers degrees in arts, education, law, science, and social sciences. The Polytechnic offers diplomas in business studies, engineering, laboratory technology, management studies, and public health. In addition, it offers degrees in commerce, technical education, and engineering. Kamuzu College of Nursing offers diplomas and degrees in nursing. The newly opened College of Medicine will be offering degrees in medicine. In addition, the Malawi College of Accountancy offers technician and professional courses in accountancy.

In 1990, the University had a total enrollment of 2,685 students of which 574 or 21 percent were females. Teaching staff totalled 235 giving a student-staff ratio of 11:1. It is estimated that less than 1 percent of the relevant 18–21 age group attends the University in Malawi. Government expenditure per student was MK6,690 (US$1,556) in 1990.

The University's strategy during the 1990s is to increase efficiency in the utilization of facilities and staff, reduce staff turnover, and raise the quality of diploma and degree courses. It is also intended to expand facilities to permit an increase in full-time enrollment to 3,000 (including 200 medical students) and external diploma students to 500. Where appropriate, graduate programs will be introduced. By 1996, it is planned to transfer all courses below technician level from the Polytechnic to the planned Institute of Technical Education.

3.2 Preschool Education

Malawi had an estimated 1.2 million children in 1990 who were below the age of 6, which was about 20 percent of the total population. A pilot project on "Early Childhood Care and Education" began in 1992. The project covers six to eight thousand children. It combines the education and health needs of young children. The Government provides technical support while each community provides the needed resources. It is intended that the project will cover over 1 million children by 1995.

3.3 Special Education

A survey conducted by the National Statistical Office in 1983 estimated that 190,000 people in Malawi are disabled. It was also estimated that 93 percent of these people live in rural areas. In addition, the survey found that 45 percent are in the 15–49 age group and more than half of the disabled aged 10 years

or more had never received any education. A sample survey conducted in February 1991 showed that 431 or 19 percent of the disabled children were in school. Montfort School for the Blind caters for the visually impaired. The coverage of these schools is limited. An estimated 4 percent of Malawi's population is mentally disabled. Limited resources have resulted in little attention being devoted to children in this category. There are no special government programs for mentally retarded children—nevertheless, the government gives assistance to nongovernmental organizations (NGOs) to provide for severely disabled children.

3.4 Vocational, Technical, and Business Education

Vocational, technical, and business education institutions are run by a number of government ministries and departments, parastatals, and some nongovernmental organizations (NGOs).

The Ministry of Education and Culture (MOEC) trains primary school teachers. In 1990 there were nearly 3,000 full-time students in its seven teacher-training colleges and the throughput was 1,472. It also had about 4,500 trainees on its special distance teacher-training program. In addition, MOEC had nearly 800 full-time students and 60 teaching staff in its five technical colleges. These colleges and the Polytechnic offer technician courses in brickwork, carpentry, electrical work, plumbing, motor mechanics, painting and decorating, diesel fitting, secretarial work, and accounting. The Polytechnic Board of Governors had about 400 students and 50 teaching staff in 1990, giving a student-teacher ratio of 8:1. From time to time the Malawi College of Accountancy mounts professional or non-technician courses in computing, management, and accounting. The Ministry of Works offers a number of engineering-related courses at its training center in Lilongwe.

The Natural Resources College (NRC) under the Ministry of Agriculture trains field assistants, veterinary assistants, surveying assistants, homecraft workers, fisheries assistants, surveying assistants, and parks and wildlife assistants. The Malawi College of Forestry under the Department of Forestry offers certificate and diploma courses in forestry.

The Lilongwe School of Health Sciences under the Ministry of Health offers courses in several paramedical fields. The Zomba School of Hygiene, also under the Ministry of Health, and a number of church institutions offer courses in nursing and midwifery and other health sciences. All the other ministries, departments, and some parastatals mount courses specific to their needs if it is cost-effective to do so; otherwise training has to be done centrally in Malawi or abroad.

3.5 Adult and Nonformal Education

The National Adult Literacy Program (NALP) had 2,185 literacy centers and 44,150 learners in 1990, of which about 85 percent of those enrolled were women. Its goal over the next 5 years will be to reach at least 65 percent of the adult illiterate population with a target of reducing adult illiteracy from 59 percent to 30 percent by the year 2000.

In addition to adult literacy programs, other nonformal education programs are administered by various sectors to meet their particular needs. Examples include the Ministry of Agriculture which provides agricultural training, while the Ministry of Health provides training in health education. The Malawi Young Pioneers organization trains about 2,000 boys and girls per annum in life skills.

4. Administrative and Supervisory Structure and Operation

Historically, the formal education system has been highly centralized. The administration filters from the Ministry of Education and Culture Headquarters at Capital Hill in Lilongwe to the Regional Education Offices in Mzuzu in the North, one in Lilongwe itself in the center, and the other one in Blantyre in the South. The Regional Education Offices are broken down into 28 district education offices as follows: Northern—6, Central—10, and Southern—12.

The MOEC is the largest employing ministry in government. Well over 33 percent of civil servants are teachers. In 1990, MOEC's share of the national budget was 15 percent. The highly centralized system of its administration makes MOEC ineffective in utilizing its human, physical, and financial resources.

The Education Service Review Report of 1988 and Department of Personnel Management and Training (DPMT) Inspection Report of 1990 recommended the following broad reforms to improve the situation:

(a) geographic decentralization and rationalization of decision-making so that top levels of administration can concentrate on policy issues;

(b) clear definitions of work objectives and base performance reviews on achievement;

(c) restructuring of the MOEC;

(d) implementation of a series of actions to enhance career development given that MOEC career paths are the most static in government.

Although the recommendations in the two reports can improve the organization and management of MOEC, much depends on whether in practice the recommendations will be implemented. Otherwise, there will not be much deviation from the status quo of the early 1990s in the future.

5. Educational Finance

According to the *Statement of Development Policies 1987–1996*, the share of education in the national budget is planned to be raised from about 10 percent in 1987 to about 15 percent by 1996. This target allocation is unlikely to satisfy educational requirements given the rapid school-age population growth estimated at 4.8 percent per annum, the existing low levels of enrollment or unmet demand, and the declining quality of education. The unstable economic environment and heavy debt servicing obligations make it uncertain that targets will be met in real terms.

The planned target expenditures are also low by sub-Saharan African standards. According to the World Bank's *Education in Sub-Saharan Africa* (1988), the medium African country allocated 18.5 percent of its budget to education in 1980 and 15.3 percent in 1983. Government expenditure on education is around 3 percent of GDP in Malawi. This compares with over 5 percent in Kenya and Zambia, nearly 7 percent in Zimbabwe, and more than 8 percent in Botswana.

Planned government expenditures alone are unlikely to increase access and improve quality significantly during the rest of the 1990s. More resources than those obtained hitherto will be mobilized from individuals, communities, private organizations, foundations, NGOs, the donor community, and so forth to raise access to and improve quality of education.

6. Supplying Personnel for the Education System

At the primary school level, there is an acute shortage of teachers. In 1990 the pupil-teacher ratio was 65:1 and the target is to reduce this ratio to 55:1 by 1996. It is planned to raise the number of teacher-training college places from 1,640 in 1987 to 3,840 by 1996. Output of teachers is to be raised from the 1992 level of 1,700 per annum to 1,920 a year. Because of the acute shortage of teachers, the MOEC launched a massive special three-year distance teacher-training program in 1990 to alleviate the problem. There are about 4,500 trainees on the program. The teacher supply and quality situation is not encouraging in Malawi College of Distance Education (MCDE) centers. The centers are manned mostly by primary school teachers instead of trained secondary school teachers.

The situation in normal secondary schools and tertiary education is much better. In 1990, the student–teacher ratio was 27:1 in secondary schools. However, there is a shortage of teachers in science subjects and mathematics. The student–teacher ratio in primary teacher-training colleges was 15:1 and in technical colleges the ratio was 13:1. At the university level, the student–teacher ratio is 11:1. In short, the staffing situation is by and large satisfactory in conventional secondary schools and the tertiary sector, while in primary schools and MCDE centers there is an acute shortage of teaching staff.

7. Curriculum Development and Teaching Methodology

Several shortcomings have been observed in the primary school curriculum. The curriculum is too theoretical and it emphasizes rote learning. There is heavy dependence on textbooks, and teaching and learning aids are not used much. The textbooks are also in short supply. The number of subjects taught is excessive and the subjects are compartmentalized. Subjects are also overloaded. The treatment of subjects is perfunctory and each one is given only 1 hour per week. Pupils receive less than 15 hours of instruction each week. Textbooks on which teachers' guides are based do not reflect the realities of Malawi. The curriculum review aims at redressing these shortfalls.

The primary school curriculum review started in 1988. The review started with Standards 1–4 and the final phase will cover Standards 5–8. All basic subjects will be covered. Supervisors, administrators, and teachers will be trained. The whole process is envisioned to be completed by 1995, at the earliest.

There are also too many subjects at the secondary level. Students are required to take eight prescribed core subjects and up to three out of seven optional subjects. In practice, the number of subjects offered is determined by the availability of staff and physical resources. The number of subjects needs reducing and the curriculum needs updating especially in mathematics, science, and agriculture.

8. The System of Examinations, Promotions, and Certifications

At the primary school level, pupils write internal examinations from Standard 1 up to Standard 7. These examinations are the basis for promotion for the Primary School Leaving Certificate Examination (PSLCE), a prerequisite for entering into secondary school education. About 10–12 percent of those who pass the PSLCE find places in conventional secondary schools. The rest go to MCDE centers, repeat Standard 8, or simply drop out. After two years of secondary school education students sit for the Junior Secondary Certificate Examination (JSCE) to qualify for Form 3. In Form 4, students sit for the Malawi School Certificate Examination (MSCE). The MSCE is a basic entry qualification into most tertiary institutions. All tertiary institutions have got their own internal and sometimes external examinations and certification arrangements.

9. Educational Assessment, Evaluation, and Research

Each major institution or agency has its own research and evaluation unit to cater for its own policy and practice requirements. These institutions include MOEC, MCDE, Malawi Institute of Education (MIE), Malawi National Examinations Board (MANEB), and the newly formed Centre for Educational Research and Training (CERT) at Chancellor College of the University of Malawi in Zomba. The center is expected to be policy-oriented. All these institutions are represented on the Co-ordinating Committee for Education Research (CCER) which acts as a clearinghouse for educational research work to reduce duplication. In general, research is constrained by inadequate funding and a shortage of staff.

10. Major Reforms in the 1980s and 1990s

Major reforms in the educational system revolve around tackling issues related to improving access and equity, quality, internal efficiency, and management. Access and equity has to be improved, particularly at primary and secondary levels, because of the low enrollment levels and geographic variations. With regard to quality, there is a need for relevant curricula, more effective examination systems, and better learning and teaching materials in primary and secondary schools. There is also a need to improve on the frequency and quality of school supervision. Internal efficiency has to be improved through reducing repetition and dropout rates, thus lowering the high cost of producing each graduate. Finally, management has to be improved; in particular, this means strengthening planning, research, budgeting, and administrative capabilities.

11. Major Problems for the Year 2000

If the reforms cited above are to bear fruit at all, the share of education in the national budget will have to be raised beyond the target of 15 percent. In addition, more resources will have to be mobilized from other supporting sources such as NGOs, churches, foundations, communities, the private sector, the donor community, and so on. Given the 1990s economic difficulties, it is evident that mobilizing adequate resources to implement envisaged reforms may not be realistic.

An effective decentralized system of operation is inevitable, otherwise the sector will continue to be unresponsive to society's educational requirements. Finally, the supply and quality of teachers will have to be improved, particularly at the primary school level.

The system is in need of several far-reaching changes. However, introduction of reforms is coming at a time when the school-age population is growing rapidly and the economic conditions are not favorable to meet the challenges.

Bibliography

Economic Planning Division and Development 1988 *Statement of Development Policies 1987–1996*. Government

Printer, Zomba
Economic Planning and Development 1991 *Economic Report 1991*. Government Printer, Zomba
International Labour Organisation (ILO) 1988 *Comprehensive Human Resources Study*. Montfort Press, Blantyre
Malawi Government 1990 *Malawi: Towards Education for All*. Government Printer, Zomba
Ministry of Education and Culture 1984 *Education Plan 1985–95*. Government Printer, Zomba
Ministry of Education and Culture 1990 *Education Statistics (1990)*. Montfort Press, Blantyre

Ministry of Education and Culture 1991 *Education Indicators for Malawi: 1985–1989*. Government Printer, Lilongwe
Mmanga W R 1990 *Projections of Primary and Secondary School-going Age Population (1977–2012) and Status of Primary Education*. Government Printer, Zomba
National Statistical Office 1987 *Population and Housing Census Preliminary Results*. Government Printer, Zomba
Price Waterhouse 1988 *Education Service Review—Final Report*. Price Waterhouse, London
World Bank 1988 *Education in Sub-Saharan Africa*. World Bank, Washington, DC

Malaysia

A. A. Aziz and S. Maimunah

1. General Background

Malaysia covers an area of 330,307 square kilometers, occupying the Malay Peninsula and the states of Sabah and Sarawak in the northwestern coastal area of Borneo Island. These areas are separated by about 531 kilometers of the South China Sea. Peninsular Malaysia consists of eleven states (Perlis, Kedah, Pulau Pinang, Perak, Selangor, Negeri Sembilan, Melaka, Johor, Pahang, Trengganu, and Kelantan) and the federal territories of Kuala Lumpur and Labuan, with an area of 131,537 square kilometers bordering on Thailand in the north; while Sabah and Sarawak cover an area of about 198,847 square kilometers, bordering the territory of Indonesia's Kalimantan.

Malaysia's history began with the period of the Melaka Sultanate founded just before 1400 AD. Melaka's growth was due largely to its position as a trade center at the meeting point between East and West Asia. It was conquered by the Portuguese in 1511, and later by the Dutch in 1642, and finally by the British who established the Straits Settlements (Melaka, Pulau Pinang, and Singapore) in the early nineteenth century. The establishment of British administration through the later part of the nineteenth century led to an increase in commercial enterprise and development, especially in the rubber and tin industries. This period also saw an influx of Chinese and Indian immigrants in response to the labor shortage, thus transforming the demography and the homogeneous nature of the indigenous society.

The population of Malaysia is multiracial, multicultural, multireligious, and multilingual. The national cultural policy, implemented to strengthen national unity, is a prerequisite to establishing a national identity and national unity. The school system makes provision for the diverse first languages of the population by providing primary education in three different media of instruction—the National Language

(Bahasa Melayu), Chinese, and Tamil. The estimated population of Malaysia in 1990 was 17.769 million, with about 13 million in Peninsular Malaysia, 1.5 million in Sarawak, and 1.2 million in Sabah. The three major races in Malaysia are Malays and other *bumiputeras* (indigenous peoples), Chinese, and Indians. In Peninsular Malaysia, the Malays and other *bumiputeras* make up 56.5 percent of the population, while the Chinese comprise 32.8 percent, and Indians 10.1 percent. In Sarawak, 70.1 percent of the population are *bumiputeras* and 28.7 percent are Chinese. In Sabah, *bumiputeras* form 84.1 percent of the total population and Chinese 14.9 percent.

The rate of population growth is 2.6 percent, with 2.5 percent in Peninsular Malaysia, 2.7 percent in Sarawak, and 3.9 percent in Sabah. A high fertility rate and an increase in migration are the main factors leading to the high population growth rate in Sabah as compared to the other parts of the country.

The population is essentially rural. During the 1981–85 period, the urbanization rate increased rapidly due to migration from rural to urban areas, the natural population growth rate in urban areas, the growth of new towns, and expansion in township administration. The urban population thus increased from 34.2 percent in 1980 to 37.4 percent in 1985.

Bahasa Melayu (Bahasa Malaysia) is the national language of the country. It was declared the official language in Malaysia in 1967 following the passing of the National Language Act by Parliament. In the effort to develop the national language, it has been made the main medium of instruction in schools and institutions of higher learning in the country, as well as being the official language in government administration. While the national language is promoted by the government to foster national unity, the people are free to use their mother tongue and other languages. English as the second language is widely used in business.

Table 1
Population, enrollment, and enrollment ratios by level of education for the year 1990

	Age group	Population	Enrollment	Enrollment ratio
Primary (Years 1–6)	6+–11+	2,415,800	2,447,206	99.8%
Lower-secondary (Forms 1–3)	12+–15+	1,135,300	942,801	83.0%
Upper-secondary (Forms 4–5)	16+–17+	735,500	361,411	49.1%

Source: Educational Planning and Research Division, Ministry of Education, Kuala Lumpur

In the past, the country's economy was largely agriculture based, with the focus being on the production of rice. Other primary products include tin and rubber. Since the 1960s, however, the nation's economy diversified into industries. In 1990, active sectors of the economy were manufacturing, construction, and services. The rate of unemployment in 1990 was 6 percent. Under the country's Sixth Malaysia Plan (1991–95), the employment situation is expected to remain favorable, with employment projected to grow at 3.2 percent per annum to reach 7.8 million in 1995, an increase of 1.1 million new jobs. While overall the supply of young and trainable labor in the country will increase, the rapid expansion of industries at particular locations will place pressure on local labor markets. As a measure to ease the tightening of the labor market, the government will undertake programs to equip female workers with more marketable skills.

The increasing adoption of modern manufacturing technologies and production processes to increase productivity will place greater demand on the availability of skilled labor to complement capital-intensive operations. Toward this end, training programs to make the skill delivery system more responsive to market and technological demands, as well as encourage greater public–private sector collaboration and a greater role by the private sector are being formulated.

2. Politics and the Goals of the Education System

The diversity of schooling offered in Malaysia at the time of Independence in 1957 challenged the educational system to develop so as to be a unifying force, to bring the citizens of the country to be one populace united to work for the economic, social, and political development of the country. Hence, all five-year development plans have emphasized the importance of education as a means for unity and integration as well as labor force planning and development. Educational programs up to the 1970s emphasized academic development. In the 1980s, education moved toward the holistic development of the individual as manifested in the National Education Philosophy:

Education in Malaysia is an on-going effort towards further developing the potential of individuals in a wholistic and integrated manner, so as to produce individuals who are intellectually, spiritually, emotionally and physically balanced and harmonious, based on a firm belief in the devotion to God. Such an effort is designed to produce Malaysian citizens who are knowledgeable and competent, who possess high moral standards, and who are responsible and capable of achieving a high level of personal well-being as well as being able to contribute to the harmony and betterment of the society and the nation at large.

Education as an instrument for national development, national unity, and personal development has been given priority over defense in terms of financial allocation. In the spirit of private sector participation in the progress of the country, education is also being privatized especially at the higher education level, both as a means to increase educational opportunities as well as to share the financial burden of providing quality education for the labor requirements of the country.

3. The Formal System of Education

The structure of the formal school system is found in Fig. 1 while statistics for enrollment in government-aided schools at all levels are in Table 1.

3.1 Primary, Secondary, and Tertiary Education

Education is provided free to all children. Although it is not compulsory, enrollment figures at the primary school level denote a near universal participation and this figure has remained at 99 percent since 1988. The duration of primary education is six years with children starting schooling at the age of six.

Education at the primary level is provided in three language media—the National Language (Bahasa Melayu), Chinese (Mandarin), and Tamil. Parents are free to choose the type of schools (national, national-type Chinese, or national-type Tamil) for their children. In 1990, enrollment figures in the respective schools were 1,770,004 for national schools, 581,082 for national-type Chinese, and 96,120 for national-type Tamil. The number of primary schools was 6,828.

The dropout rate at the primary school level is small—0.6 percent. The transition rate between primary and secondary levels was 86 percent in 1990 and this figure had remained constant for the last three years. The 14 percent who do not continue their education in secondary school in the main system include those who choose to study in private Chinese schools, Islamic religious schools, and other private schools.

Secondary education is available over five or six years and is divided into lower- and upper-secondary levels. The former is of three years' duration, while the latter is of two years' duration. Pupils from the national-type Chinese and Tamil primary schools spend a year in the Remove class before the transition to secondary schools. This is to enable them to get sufficient exposure to and opportunities to enhance their proficiency levels in Bahasa Melayu, which is the medium of instruction in secondary schools, before joining Form I the following year. In 1990, there were 1,327 secondary schools including fully residential schools. The latter are special schools established to provide better educational opportunities for high ability students, especially those from rural areas. Apart from these schools, the MARA Junior Science Colleges under the Ministry of Rural and National Development also provide similar opportunities.

Upper-secondary education consists of arts, science, technical, and vocational streams. Selection of students into the various streams is based on their performance in the Lower Certificate of Education

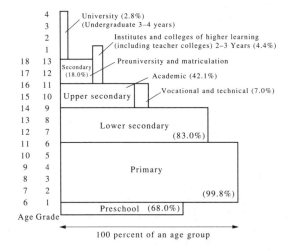

Figure 1
Malaysia: Structure of the formal education system

Examination held at the end of Form III (Grade 9). For some, this examination is terminal as those who fail leave the system to join the labor market. In 1990, the transition rate between lower-secondary and the upper level was 67.18 percent. While students previously were selected for streams based on academic performance, as from 1992, under the Integrated Secondary School Curriculum, students studying at Form IV (Grade 10) in general academic schools will be allowed to select electives from various groups apart from the core subjects.

In 1992, there were two programs offered at the postsecondary level—the sixth form and matriculation classes. Sixth form education prepares students for the Higher School Certificate Examination (conducted by the Malaysian Examination Council) which is the requirement for several courses conducted at local universities. Matriculation classes prepare students to meet specific entry requirements of certain universities. In 1990, the number studying in postsecondary education was 138,302, which accounted for 18 percent of the total 17+–18+ age group.

Apart from the two programs mentioned above, postsecondary education is also offered at the MARA Institute of Technology and colleges. Fields offered include: technology, commerce, management, and administration. Polytechnics offer education and training in commerce and engineering at the technician and junior executive levels. The number of students in these colleges was 45,144 in 1990.

Schools operate on a semester system and the school calender begins in the first week of December. There are 41 weeks in a school year. Schools normally start at 7.45 am. Many schools in Malaysia, especially in the urban areas, are on double (i.e., morning and afternoon) shifts.

Boarding facilities are provided to pupils in the lower income group from rural areas and those whose homes are far from schools. Pupils pay a nominal fee for food and lodging. Needy and deserving pupils at both primary and secondary levels are given scholarships based on merit. This financial assistance is provided by the Ministry, state governments, and the private sector. Needy pupils are also given textbooks on a free loan basis.

Higher education is provided in the seven universities, one of which is international in status. These universities offer courses both in the pure and applied arts and sciences. In 1990, enrollment at the seven universities was 58,286 which is 2.8 percent of the 19+–20+ age group. Scholarships are awarded by the government and by quasi-government agencies to selected students in order for them to pursue their education abroad.

Private education is available at all levels, from primary right up to preuniversity. There are three main types of private education, namely: the Chinese private secondary schools, Islamic religious schools, and the elite private schools. The elite private schools, though small in number, are growing. Private secondary schools have to abide by regulations set by the Ministry of Education, that is, the common curriculum and the common examination. Other courses taught also must meet the approval of the Ministry of Education. In 1990, a total of 98,553 students enrolled in these schools from primary to secondary levels. At the postsecondary level, private education offers both academic and professional courses leading to diplomas and certificates. A growing number of private colleges have arranged twinning programs with universities abroad, whereby students spend the first year of university education in Malaysia and the next two years in the foreign country.

3.2 Preschool Education

Preprimary education is widespread, and about 70 percent of the pupils enrolled in Year One in 1990 had preschool experience. Efforts are being taken to widen access to preschool education. In 1990, there were 6,046 preschool centers catering to 328,813 children. About 77 percent were operated by government agencies and statutory bodies, while the rest were managed by private bodies and voluntary organizations. All preschool centers charge fees, but the amounts charged vary among centers.

3.3 Special Education

"Special education" refers to education of students with physical, intellectual, and emotional disabilities. There are two programs for this group of pupils. The first is conducted in special schools, while the second is provided in normal schools where these pupils are integrated into the mainstream. In 1991, there were 4,717 students in this category and the Ministry of Education was managing three of the special schools catering for the visually disabled and those with hearing disabilities. However, the Ministry is giving more emphasis to the integration of these students into mainstream schools and classes.

3.4 Vocational, Technical, and Business Education

Vocational and technical education offers students basic courses to equip them with relevant knowledge and skills. In vocational secondary schools, students are also offered practical training in individual trade skills.

In 1990, there were 57 vocational and 9 technical schools. Under the sixth Malaysia Plan, 8 more will be built. In addition, vocational subjects are incorporated into the secondary school curriculum in line with the policy of allowing students in general academic schools the opportunity to study vocational subjects under the new curriculum. In an effort to cope with the increased demand for skilled and semi-skilled labor in line with the Prime Minister' vision of Malaysia by the year 2020, the intake into vocational education is ex-

pected to be increased substantially from the 7 percent level of the early 1990s. Students in vocational schools either follow the academic or skills training program. Those with interest in and aptitude for skills training are streamed after Form 4 into the skills training course which lasts for two years. Those academically inclined proceed to Form 5 when they sit for the *Sijil Pelajaran Malaysia Vokasional* (Malaysia Certificate of Examination {Vocational}). Technical schools offer technical-based subjects.

Efforts are also being made to specialize vocational schools according to industry location. The close proximity to industries will provide the advantage of industrial exposure to students as well as facilitate hands-on experience.

Technical and vocational education at higher levels are offered at the polytechnics, teacher education colleges, the MARA Institute of Technology, and the Tunku Abdul Rahman College where professional courses leading to certificate and diplomas are available.

3.5 Adult and Nonformal Education

Nonformal education is available as a form of training for youths and adults in specific skills and vocational trades. The objectives, among other things, are to prepare candidates for productive activity to participate actively in commerce, industries, and other economic enterprises and to promote an awareness of the working environment, hence bringing about changes in society. Among the government agencies providing education and training programs are the Ministry of Human Resources, the Ministry of Youth and Sports, the Ministry of Agriculture, the Ministry of Land and Regional Development, the Ministry of Rural and National Development, and several statutory bodies. Programs include courses in apprenticeship, skill upgrading, instructional and technical skills, leadership, business, agriculture, preschool education, electrical and mechanical engineering-related fields, and commerce.

4. Administrative and Supervisory Structure and Operation

The administrative structure of the Ministry of Education consists of four levels, namely: federal, state, district, and school. In Sabah and Sarawak, the districts are known as "divisions."

The federal level, which is the Ministry of Education, translates the national educational policy into education plans, programs, and projects in accordance with national objectives and aspirations. Guidelines for the implementation and management of education programs are also formulated at the federal level.

The Ministry consists of a professional and an administrative section. The professional section gets its leadership from the Director-General of Education while the administrative section is headed by the Secretary-General.

The Ministry uses the committee system in its decision-making procedures. Highest of these committees is the Educational Planning Committee chaired by the Minister of Education. This committee is concerned with the formulation, coordination, and implementation of policy guidelines. There are six other committees that deal with specific issues such as those concerning curriculum, development, finance, higher education, scholarships, training, and textbooks.

The Ministry is organized into 12 professional and 8 administrative divisions. The Educational Planning and Research Division is responsible for overall educational planning, policy analysis, educational research and evaluation, educational statistics, and staff development. Implementation of educational programs, projects, and activities come under the purview of the Schools' Division. Planning and implementation of teacher-training programs at the preservice and inservice levels are the responsibilities of the Teacher Education Division.

Curriculum development is undertaken by the Curriculum Development Center. This center also produces support materials, and disseminates effective teaching methods and strategies as well as new curricula programs. The Examination Syndicate has the responsibility of conducting all national examinations and of administering other approved examinations. Examinations at the Higher School Certificate level are the responsibility of the Malaysian Examination Council.

Inspection and supervision of effective instruction and management are conducted by the Federal Schools Inspectorate. Technical and vocational education, including the curriculum for secondary schools and polytechnics, comes under the ambit of the Technical and Vocational Division. Educational support in the form of educational media and educational technology services are provided by the Educational Technology Division. All matters pertaining to Islamic religious education come under the Islamic Religious Division.

All government and private educational institutions must comply with the rules and regulations governing the registration of schools. This responsibility is undertaken by the Schools and Teachers Registration Division. The Textbook Division handles evaluation of textbooks, use of approved textbooks, and the management of the Textbook Loan Scheme. The Aminuddin Baki Institute is responsible for upgrading professional and managerial skills and the competence of education administrators.

Matters concerning the establishment and service of both professional and nonprofessional staff are handled by the Establishment and Service Division. The management of education funds for the Ministry of Education is dealt with by the Finance and Accounts Division. The Development and Supply Division deals with the planning of physical school

requirements, the design of school plans, the supply and maintenance of equipments and materials, and foreign loans for educational programs. Higher education is managed by the Higher Education Division. The External Affairs Division manages regional and international cooperation in education. Financial assistance to students for specific courses in education, as well as for the teaching force, is dealt with by the Scholarship Division. This division is also responsible for the management of Malaysian students departments abroad. Computer facilities, technical expertise in management information services, and computer consultancy services are provided by the Computer Service Division.

At the state level, the State Education Departments are headed by directors. These departments are responsible for the implementation of all educational programs, projects, and activities in the state. They also conduct monitoring of curricular programs in schools as well as give professional advice to teachers. Inservice courses, particularly those pertaining to the training and dissemination of new curricula, have become a major activity at state level. Regular feedback on the implementation of educational programs is relayed to the Ministry through regular meetings and discussions between these departments and the Ministry.

District/Division education offices have been set up in all but three states with the purpose of forming linkages between schools and State Education Departments. These education offices assist the state departments in the supervision of educational programs in the schools within the district.

The State Resource Centers and the district Teachers Centers have been established to improve teachers' accessibility to media services and reference materials with the aim of enhancing teaching–learning processes. These centers also provide an environment where teachers can work and interact with one another and receive assistance and guidance. Activities

Table 2
Educational expenditure by sector 1990

Sector	Expenditure[a]
Administration	179,017,534.58
Primary and secondary	3,290,994,040.45
Technical and vocational	111,254,306.07
Student welfare	256,219,947.02
Planning and research	38,507,957.75
Higher education	778,189,179.57
Teacher education	190,756,987.60
Total recurrent expenditure	4,844,939,953.04
Total development expenditure	1,487,025,274.13
Total educational expenditure	6,331,965,227.17

Source: Educational Planning and Research Division, Ministry of Education, Kuala Lumpur   a Figures in Malaysian singgit

conducted at these centers include workshops and inservice courses for teachers.

5. Educational Finance

The extent of the emphasis on education can be seen from the proportion of financial allocation given to it. In 1990, the total expenditure for education against total government expenditure was 18.3 percent. This represented about 5.91 percent of the Gross National Product (GNP) at market price. Under the Sixth Malaysia Plan (1991–95) the average allocation for education accounts for 15.5 percent of the total public development allocation of the Gross Domestic Product (GDP) and of the national budget. Funding for government schools other than MARA Junior Science Colleges comes under the Ministry of Education. The latter is funded by the Ministry of Rural and National Development. Educational expenditure by sector for 1990 is presented in Table 2.

Unit recurrent costs by level of education in 1990 were: M\$770 (US\$308) (primary), M\$1,296 (US\$518) (secondary general) M\$2,916 (US\$1,166) (secondary vocational) M\$2,083 (US\$833) (polytechnic), M\$7,829 (US\$3,132) (teacher training), and M\$10,360 (US\$4,144) (universities).

6. Supplying Personnel for the Educational System

In 1989, the total number of teachers employed in government and government-aided schools was 178,666, with 111,729 teaching at the primary level and 66,937 teaching at the secondary level. Of these teachers, 13.9 percent were university graduates, 79.0 percent were college trained, and 7.1 percent had other forms of academic training.

A shortage of trained teachers has been a problem for the system. With the emphasis on science and technology subjects, teachers specializing in these subjects, including mathematics, are constantly in demand. In 1992, the system was also facing a shortage in the supply of teachers for languages, including Bahasa Melayu and English, and for history and geography. The shortage is more critical in rural areas and in the states of Sabah and Sarawak. In order to alleviate the situation, newly trained teachers are often posted to rural schools, as well as to Sabah and Sarawak, for a period of time, before giving them the opportunity to serve in urban schools.

Teacher training, both at preservice and inservice levels, is mainly conducted by the Teacher Education Division and the universities. There are 28 teacher-training colleges under the supervision of the Teacher Education Division, and these prepare teachers to serve in primary and lower-secondary schools. In the early 1990s, the shortage of graduate teachers for several

subjects in secondary schools led to selected teacher-training colleges undertaking the training of graduate teachers as well. Universities prepare teachers for the upper- and postsecondary levels of education. Other divisions in the Ministry of Education, State Education Departments, and District/Division Education Offices also conduct inservice courses.

Teachers trained at the teacher-training colleges go through a five-semester training program and receive a certificate in teaching. Graduates who are trained in the universities, as well as selected teacher-training colleges, are awarded a diploma in teaching.

All teacher trainees undergo a cocurricular component to prepare them to organize and run extracurricular activities in such areas as uniformed units (Scouts, Girl Guides, Red Cross, and St John's Ambulance), clubs and societies, and sports and games.

The appointment and posting of trained teachers is done centrally by the Ministry of Education.

In 1990, the government implemented a new service scheme for all teachers, categorizing them into two groups—graduate and nongraduate teachers. Nongraduate teachers, particularly those who do not have the prerequisite qualities, need to undergo short-term professional courses to enable them to be placed into the group. This serves as an encouragement for teachers to attend short inservice programs offered at teacher-training colleges, as well as those conducted by state and district education offices.

The emphasis on the quality of trained teachers has also encouraged several teacher-training colleges to mount additional one-year inservice courses in various specialized areas such as pedagogy in Bahasa Melayu, English as a second language, mathematics, the use of computers in the teaching of Bahasa Melayu, remedial education, and the place of drama in language teaching. In addition, short fourteen-week courses have been introduced in such special areas as man and environment, remedial mathematics, the use of media in language teaching, enrichment and remedial programs, and evaluation and assessment in language teaching.

The Teacher Education Division constantly monitors the five-semester teacher-training program to ensure its relevance to the curriculum reforms under implementation. In 1992, it undertook to review the five-semester program, and a new program is expected to be implemented in 1994.

7. Curriculum Development and Teaching Methodology

All schools in Malaysia follow a common content curriculum formulated by the Curriculum Development Center using national objectives, the Rukunegara and the National Educational Philosophy, as important sources of reference. A holistic and balanced development of the child in the cognitive, affective, and psychomotor domains, and the nurturing of desired moral values and attitudes are the main thrust of the school curriculum. Other areas of emphasis include the cultivation of citizenship values and national consciousness as well as the production of trained and skilled labor for the nation. The school curricula is developed centrally with representative participation from practicing teachers and teacher educators and officers from the state and district education offices. Bahasa Melayu is taught to all pupils. English is taught as a second language.

The primary school curriculum, revised in 1981 and implemented in 1983, places emphasis on the overall and balanced development of the child in the physical, intellectual, spiritual, social, emotional, and moral domains. It is divided into two phases.

Table 2 provides the subjects and time allocation for the primary school curriculum. The curriculum is designed to provide basic education. Thus its main thrust is the acquisition of the basic skills of literacy and numeracy. However, the development of physical, affective, and personality characteristics are also given importance.

Such aims are to be achieved through a child-centered instructional approach. Teaching–learning strategies used include a variety of approaches such as the flexible groupings of students appropriate to the skills being taught; greater attention to individual needs of the child through remedial and enrichment activities; integration of skills and knowledge in lessons taught; and the utilization of a variety of materials. Orientation to science and technology is achieved through the subjects "Man and the Environment" and "Manipulative Skills," both new subjects introduced in Year 4 of primary schooling.

The integrated secondary school curriculum is an extension of the primary school curriculum and is currently implemented in all classes up to Form IV (Grade 10) throughout the country. This curriculum is designed to provide general education. It is modeled on an integrated approach which fuses knowledge, skills, and values; theory and practice; the curriculum and cocurriculum; and school culture.

Special emphasis is given to the acquisition of knowledge and skills which promote the development of thinking abilities to enable students to analyze, synthesize, explain, draw conclusions, and produce ideas that are both constructive and useful. The teaching of moral values and the correct usage of Bahasa Melayu to acquire knowledge and promote thinking skills are other areas of emphasis.

At the lower-secondary level, the core subjects are formulated with the aim of providing general education for all. At upper-secondary level, beside the core and additional subjects, several electives are offered to cater for students' interests and talents.

In line with the increased demand for a workforce with a technical–vocational bias, efforts have been taken to introduce elective subjects in the vocational and technical group at upper-secondary level in normal academic schools. At the lower-secondary level, "living skills," a new subject which comprises elements of manipulative skills, entrepreneurship, and family life education, has been introduced.

At the lower-secondary level, the total teaching time per week is 1,800 minutes divided into 45 teaching periods of 40 minutes each.

Cocurricular activities are undertaken to complement teaching and learning activities in the classroom. Pupils are encouraged to participate in at least one activity in each of category of programs—sports and games, uniformed units, and clubs and societies activities.

8. The System of Examinations, Promotions, and Certifications

In all government and government-aided schools, pupils are automatically promoted up to Grade 9. However at the end of Year Six all pupils sit for the *Ujian Pencapaian Sekolah Rendah* (Primary School Assessment Test) in language and mathematics. At the end of Form 3 (Grade 9), students take another national examination leading to the *Sijil Rendah Pelajaran* (Lower Certificate of Education). Based on performance in this examination, students are placed either in the academic stream or technical and vocational schools. From 1993, this examination will be replaced by the *Penilaian Menengah Rendah* (Lower-Secondary Assessment). This examination has both the components of central and school-based assessment. At the end of Form 5 (Grade 11), students take the *Sijil Pelajaran Malaysia* (Malaysian Certificate of Education) or the Technical and Vocational Certificate Examinations. Based on their results, the students either follow a two-year preuniversity course to enable them to sit for the Higher School Certificate for placement in universities, or join institutions such as the teacher-training colleges or the polytechnics in preparation for employment. Some students leave to join the labor market after the Malaysian Certificate of Education.

With the emphasis on preparing students for gainful employment in the private sectors, there is less emphasis on academic qualifications and more effort is given to prepare students for employment or further training before employment. Participation in extracurricular activities also are given more emphasis than previously.

9. Educational Assessment, Evaluation, and Research

The reforms at both the primary and secondary levels in the 1980s were aimed at the development of the individual child to his or her full potential in all areas—

intellectual, emotional, physical, and spiritual. Holistic development calls for a continuous evaluation of the child. This evaluation should be criterion based rather than norm-referenced. The emphasis on the acquisition of the "3 Rs" at the lower primary level requires that pupils be assessed individually. Tests are thus more school-based and classroom-based. Toward this end, teachers have been trained to develop suitable items based on the needs of the schools and pupils. Ultimately, national examinations will only be conducted at the end of Grade 11. The system also encourages teachers to conduct self-assessment as a means toward self-improvement.

Educational research is coordinated by the Educational Planning and Research Division of the Ministry of Education. All research to be conducted in schools and classrooms needs to get approval from this division, to ensure that the design and questions would not have any negative effects on the system or students. Other coordination aspects include determining priority areas in which research is required and the dissemination of research findings, thus improving the quality of education. Funding for research is also disbursed by the Educational Planning and Research Division.

There is growing interest in the Teacher Education Division's efforts to encourage teacher-training colleges to conduct small research projects which would feed into efforts to improve classroom teaching.

10. Major Reforms in the 1980s and 1990s

The 1980s was a period of consolidating qualitative educational improvements within the system. Major curricular reforms at the primary and secondary levels were followed by major reviews of the teacher-training courses and the introduction of several one-year and fourteen-week inservice programs. The administrative structure of the system was decentralized with the establishment of some District/Division Education Offices.

In terms of assessment and evaluation, the system has attempted to give more attention to the overall development of the individual. Continuous evaluation of the child within the classroom has increased in emphasis to assist teachers in tailoring programs to the needs of the individual child.

In the 1990s, further projects were implemented to assist teachers in terms of support and efforts. The idea of teacher centers was explored and 350 such centers were established throughout the country to provide teachers with a venue and a system to help them think through classroom problems and find solutions together. Resource centers were established to help alleviate the scarcity of audiovisual materials required by classroom teachers.

In 1991, the Prime Minister announced "Vision 2020," which is the government's blueprint for the nation's development and progress to the year 2020.

"Vision 2020" envisions a fully developed nation, able to take its place within the international economic and social framework, by the year 2020.

11. Major Problems for the Year 2000

While strides have been made in terms of qualitative improvements, there remain issues which confront the education system. Disparity in achievement between rural and urban areas, especially in secondary mathematics, science, and English, continue to be a problem and if not addressed will pose constraints in fulfilling aspirations related to national manpower requirements and the development of human resources in related fields. This is especially so in an environment of rapid industrialization where scientific and technological skills and access to current information are of extreme importance. Thus special efforts need to be mounted to address the problems confronting learning in rural schools.

Another area of concern is that of technical and vocational education. Related concerns include the need to produce a workforce qualified in this field and a better articulation between school and the world of work. This necessitates more students being given exposure to this field. (About 8 percent of upper-secondary school enrollment is in technical and vocational education.) The Integrated Secondary School Curriculum which provides opportunities for students to study subjects under the technical and vocational group of electives is a positive step toward addressing the problem. However, the vocationalization of normal academic schools and the expected increase in the number of vocational schools would increase the demand for more trained staff and facilities. This would incur considerable expense on the part of the government. Thus, efforts need to be taken to find the most cost-effective and feasible solution.

Bibliography

Curriculum Development Center 1990 *The Integrated 1 Curriculum for Secondary School (ICSS).* Ministry of Education, Kuala Lumpur

Educational Planning and Research Division 1990 *Education in Malaysia 1989.* Ministry of Education, Kuala Lumpur

Educational Planning and Research Division 1992 *Educational Statistics of Malaysia 1990.* Ministry of Education, Kuala Lumpur

Government of Malaysia 1991a *Sixth Malaysia Plan 1991–1995.* National Printing Department, Kuala Lumpur

Government of Malaysia 1991b *The Second Outline Perspective Plan 1991–2000.* Government Printers, Kuala Lumpur

Maldives

A. H. A. Hakeem

1. General Background

The Republic of Maldives is an archipelago of approximately 1,200 coral islands located southwest of the Indian subcontinent. Only 200 of these islands are inhabited. The islands form 26 natural atolls which for administrative purposes are grouped into 19 units, also called atolls. Most of the islands are small, with few having a land area in excess of one square kilometer. The average elevation of the islands is 1.6 meters above mean sea level. For this reason, concern with the rising sea level has become a major national issue.

The total land area of the islands is 298 square kilometers, only 10 percent of which is suitable for agriculture. A major beneficiary of the new Law of the Sea, the Maldives has an Exclusive Economic Zone of some 90,000 square kilometers—more than 3,000 times its land area.

The Maldives are believed to have been settled by Aryan immigrants from India and Sri Lanka in the fourth and fifth century BC. The Buddhist culture of the early settlers prevailed in the islands until the people embraced Islam in the twelfth century. Since then Islamic culture has been established and has shaped traditional schooling. The Maldives have enjoyed self-rule for most of the country's known history. In the period from 1887 to 1965, when the Maldives gained full independence, the country was a British protectorate.

The population was estimated in 1990 to be 213,215 and growing at the rate of 3.4 percent per annum. The population is dispersed among the 200 inhabited islands. Some 90 percent of these islands have a population of less than 1000, and only 4 islands have more than 4000 each. More than 25 percent of the population is concentrated on Male', the capital island. The country's population is an increasingly young one and this has major implications for the educational system. By 1990, the proportion of the population under age 5 was 18.5 percent (compared with 16.8% in 1977). Those under 15 years of age represent 48 percent of the population.

The principal economic bases for the Maldives are fishing, tourism, and trade. The country has few natural resources, no known minerals, a relatively small domestic market, and an extremely small area of cultivable land. The Maldives is confronted by a formidable array of development constraints. The extreme dispersal of population and the small sizes of the island population give rise to severe diseconomies of scale in the provision of essential infrastructure.

Added to this are the high costs of intra-country transport and telecommunications. Other impediments to development include the paucity of land-based resources, the severe shortage of a qualified labor force, a rapid rate of population growth, and constraints imposed by the natural environment and the fragility of small-island ecology.

The Maldives is also endowed with numerous assets which translate directly into tangible development potentials. These include the country's unique physical attributes; an abundance of marine resources; a common history, religion, language, and culture; and a positive attitude to change and development on the part of the people.

2. Politics and the Goals of the Education System

The current National Development Plan (1991–93) outlines the country's main development objectives as follows:

(a) securing improvement in living standards and the quality of life;

(b) ensuring the equitable sharing of the benefits of development;

(c) achieving greater self-reliance.

In the area of education and training, the priority development goals have been stated as follows:

(a) providing universal basic education (Grades 1–5 level) by 1995;

(b) providing universal extended basic education (Grades 6–7 level) by the year 2000;

(c) increasing the trained and trainable labor force for national development;

(d) improving quality in education while sustaining quantitative growth.

3. The Formal System of Education

Before describing the actual structure of the formal school system, it is important to comment on the overall educational scene.

3.1 Primary, Secondary, and Tertiary Education

A major transformation took place in the development of education in the Maldives in the period

609

1978 to 1990. From a small system of schools in the capital Male', and a largely informal network of traditional educational structures that extended over the whole country, the framework for a modern system of education has consciously been developed. The transformation was brought about through four main programs: construction of new school buildings and the upgrading of selected existing ones; the development of a national curriculum and the production of new educational materials; the training of teachers and headteachers; and the development and expansion of nonformal education programs, including the production of educational radio programs.

The educational scene in the Maldives presents a unique mix of traditional and modern education. The country has a high literacy rate of just over 95 percent (in 1989) with a marginally higher rate for females than for males and presenting no rural/urban disparities. There is a system of traditional indigenous educational institutions which are owned and operated by the island communities. These have developed and thrived on the wisdom, creativity, and indigenous knowledge of the population and provided them with basic learning. This system has survived through the centuries and served the island communities well. Traditional schools provide basic religious education, basic literacy, and numeracy for preschool and school-age children. The traditional system operates through different levels and categories of institutions which include *edhuruge* or *kiyavaage* (neighborhood Quranic Schools), *makthabs*, and *madhrasa*.

The *kiyavaage* or *edhuruge* is a gathering of children in a private home with the objective of making the pupils learn to read the Koran, to read and write Dhivehi (Maldivian language), and to provide some rudiments of arithmetic. The *makthab* is more formal, offers almost the same curriculum, but is in a separate building. In the *madhrasa*, the curriculum is wider.

Parallel to this, a modern formal English-medium school system has been established in Male' operated both by the public and private sectors. This system provides primary, secondary, and higher-secondary education culminating in GCE O and A levels set by London University. There are separate government schools for boys and girls leading to O level and a Science Education Center—a coeducational institution—which teaches to A level. The Government is progressively creating similar educational facilities in the islands by establishing atoll education centers and atoll primary schools in each atoll. Both the atoll education centers and the atoll primary schools offer a modern curriculum which includes seven subjects. Many island community schools are now being modeled after the atoll primary schools and atoll education centers as they receive more trained teachers and have access to textbooks and curriculum materials. Hence the traditional, indigenous system of education in the country is in the process of blending with the more modern and formal structure that, in

the past, existed primarily in Male'. This trend has been encouraged by the regulation of the Ministry of Education requiring the adherence to a unified, national curriculum for Grades 1–7.

As with most educational systems, the Maldivian educational structure involves academic, occupational, formal, and nonformal delivery systems. Figure 1 presents the basic structure of the national education system of the Maldives. The primary level of education is a 5-year cycle which students are expected to begin at age 6. In Male' the primary cycle is preceded by a two-year cycle of a modern preprimary education. In the other islands, this preprimary system does not yet exist, but many students attend informal neighborhood preprimary activities. The sixth and seventh year of education are labeled "middle school." Traditionally considered part of the secondary cycle, they have now been redefined as part of the seven-year "extended basic education" for all children. Thus, the five primary and two middle school years will become the expected (but not yet compulsory—no compulsory education exists in the Maldives) level of minimum educational attainment for all children by the year 2000.

The secondary level of education (Grades 8 to 12) is a 5-year cycle divided into lower-secondary (Grades 8 to 10) and upper-secondary (Grades 11 to 12) levels. There is no university education available in the country. Students crossing the threshold of higher-secondary education and intending to go up to tertiary-level education have to go abroad, either on various scholarships or through their own resources.

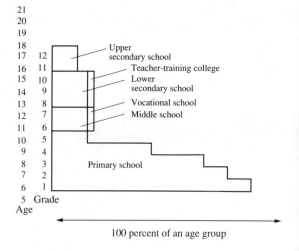

Figure 1

Maldives: Structure of the formal education system

Students are ready to sit the University of London GCE O level and A level examinations after completing the lower- and higher-secondary levels respectively. There are also two national examinations called SSC (Secondary School Certificate) and HSC (Higher Secondary School Certificate) for two subjects: Islamic Studies and *Dhivehi* language.

At the primary level enrollment is over 85 percent, but the enrollment ratio progressively declines thereafter with overall enrollment in secondary education averaging 20 percent of the relevant age group in 1989. However, the equivalent figure in 1977 was 2 percent.

Women in the Maldives have traditionally had access to educational opportunities in their community. As a consequence, female literacy rates are relatively high and gender disparities do not exist in educational participation rates at the primary level. Girls, therefore, account for an equal enrollment in primary schools. However, disparities creep in at the higher-secondary level.

3.2 Special Education

A special program to cater for a limited number of primary-age deaf and dumb children began in 1985. The program is conducted in a regular primary school in Male' with a specialist teacher in charge.

Another program for the disadvantaged is provided in the reformatory for delinquent children in a school with hostel facilities. This school offers primary education which involves a significant vocational component. The Maldives has a long way to go in the provision of education for disabled children.

3.3 Vocational, Technical, and Business Education

There is a vocational training center in Male' which produces semi-skilled and skilled workers in seven trades. The center currently has four branches (rural youth vocational training centers) in the atolls. These branches provide training in five different trades.

Specific technical/occupational training is carried out by the respective ministries and departments. These include: the Institute for Health Science of the Ministry of Health, the School of Hotel and Catering Services of the Ministry of Tourism, the Institute for Teacher Education of the Ministry of Education, and the Maldives Center for Management and Administration.

Other ministries and departments—including the Ministry of Planning and Environment, the Ministry of Transport and Shipping, the Ministry of Fisheries and Agriculture, the Department of Women's Affairs, the Department of Civil Aviation, and the Youth Center—also provide short-term training in various trades and vocations in response to specific sectoral needs.

3.4 Adult and Nonformal Education

In 1978, when the government expanded and accelerated the educational development programs, nonformal educational programs encompassing all age groups in the community were introduced.

In most cases, the atoll education Centers are the venues for adult education classes in health and nutrition, history, culture, social living, and vocational skills. Short courses are conducted in a range of different kinds of trades, vocations, and skills. These courses are both target group and situation-oriented and purely nonformal in their organization and conduct. Among the teaching responsibilities of the Nonformal Education Unit the following areas are covered: commercial classes, *Thaana* (local script) calligraphy, English for atoll teachers and government officials, and special courses for over-age primary-level students. The Unit also performs an important information dissemination role. A monthly newsletter and a quarterly magazine are published.

Since 1984 the focus of nonformal education has shifted to some extent from community-oriented education to the educational needs of the large over-age school population and out-of-school boys and girls. In response to this situation the Nonformal Education Unit has developed an innovative program of instruction in which the Grades 1–7 primary syllabus is condensed and accelerated into three years. It is envisaged that this Condensed Education Program (CEP), when it operates fully, will accelerate the achievement of universal basic education and will further provide a source of supply for various training courses, particularly teacher training.

Another new initiative in the area of nonformal education was the introduction of a Population Education Program in 1984 to increase awareness of the implications of the size of the family, the growth of population, and the roles and rights of the members of the family and their relationships. The program is also aimed at increasing awareness of the relationship between the size of the population and the quality of life.

The Nonformal Education Unit has begun a distance education program as one of its educational activities. The major objectives of this program are as follows:-

(a) Establishing a technical administrative infrastructure for distance education in the Maldives;

(b) training tutors in the 19 atolls enabling them to conduct, monitor, and evaluate distance education courses;

(c) training staff for central service in scriptwriting, course programs, feedback, and evaluation;

(d) adopting the condensed curriculum of Grades 6 and 7 and related materials for distance education.

4. Administrative and Supervisory Structure and Operation

Monitoring improvement in school quality and the degree to which educational policies are implemented in schools require the regular supervision and evaluation of teachers. In addition, such supervision ensures that the national curriculum is followed and provides required assistance for teachers.

The management of the educational system in the Maldives, until the late 1970s, had been limited to a few government schools in the capital, Male'. With the expansion of educational facilities throughout the country, effective administration and management of the system is becoming increasingly difficult. Major constraints include the lack of an effective supervisory and monitoring mechanism especially for the atolls, and a shortage of qualified personnel to direct and implement programs. The quality of administration is highly variable among the major educational institutions and this is a serious problem given the critical changes occurring in the country.

Most island schools are managed by local island communities with the island chief as the head. Owing to the fact that the chief has duties and responsibilities other than those of education, the island chief often has little time to look into the affairs of the school which are generally entrusted to the senior teacher in the school. Lack of formal education and training prevents the island chief from providing professional and administrative support to the school. Plans are underway to extend managerial support to atoll schools through the atoll education centers which have trained headteachers.

A major change in the educational decision-making process was introduced in 1989 when the government formed the National Education Council to formulate major educational policies. The Council is chaired by the Maldivian President and includes six members of the cabinet and representatives from the atolls, private schools, and the Ministry of Education.

5. Educational Finance

There are a number of sources that finance formal and nonformal education in the country. These can be broadly classified as follows: Government, island communities, fees, and international cooperation.

The government budget, largely via the Ministry of Education, covers all expenses of government schools in the country, including the administrative overhead costs of the Ministry. At the end of the 1980s, the government started a scheme providing financial assistance to island community schools that have been in continuous operation for ten or more years. In addition, many island community schools

have been physically upgraded on a cooperative basis with the community meeting the requirement for labour and local construction materials, while other requirements are met by the government. Many schools have also been provided with trained teachers or temporary untrained teachers paid by the government. These forms of assistance have proved to be positive and encouraging with far-reaching implications for both the expansion and the improvement of the quality of education in the country. Almost 80 percent of government financing goes to government schools in Male' which are responsible for less than 40 percent of total enrollment. The second source of finance, the island community, contributes to education through ad hoc arrangements such as fundraising or through payments in kind.

Government schools, both in Male' and in the atolls, do not levy fees while most private and island community schools charge pupils with a school fee. All nonformal education courses conducted by the government are free of charge.

Education's share of the government budget has an encouraging and regular growth. The percentage of the total government budget for education increased from 9.3 percent in 1982 to 16 percent in 1989. This increase paved the way to taking limited but effective measures to enhance the quality of education. Individual and community contributions have also been significant, reflecting the strong social demand and respect for education.

The Maldives has a history of active community participation in education. The majority of primary schools in the Maldives are financed and operated by island communities. It is important to grasp the historical, socioecological reality in which these schools came into existence. The islands are isolated communities with little contact with the outside world. Even in the 1990s access to these islands is very difficult owing to the poor transportation facilities. It is in this context that the indigeneous institutions were created by the island communities on a self-help basis to fulfill their educational requirements. Since they have been owned and operated by the island communities themselves, they have survived, and more recently, have been activated by the encouragement and support given by the government. Most island schools are funded through individuals' accounts or through ad hoc fundraising. Community contributions also come in the form of labor for construction, part- or full-time teachers, and various donations in cash or kind.

6. Supplying Personnel for the Education System

A major achievement in the period 1977 to 1990 was the institution of systematic teacher education in the country. In 1977 the island community schools in the atolls were staffed predominantly by untrained and part-time teachers.

The majority of teachers in the English-medium schools in Male' were expatriates who presented the problems of short tenure, difficulties with the local language, and a lack of familiarity with local conditions. An adequate supply of trained teachers with sufficient educational attainment was imperative for the development of the education system and for the effective use of syllabuses and educational materials. Hence the institution of a systematic course of training was given high priority. Consequently the teaching force of the 1990s comprises a significantly large proportion of trained teachers as well as a greater number of locals. These trained teachers are making modest progress in providing their pupils with an education that goes beyond rote learning and routine skills to genuine understanding.

Regular and systematic preservice primary teacher training in the Maldives began in 1977. Three main courses are currently conducted at the Institute for Teacher Education:

(a) a two-year Dhivehi-medium course to train teachers for the atoll schools,

(b) a one-year English-medium course designed primarily to meet the needs of primary schools in Male',

(c) a one-year course to train Dhivehi-language subject teachers for schools in Male'.

In the period between 1977 and 1990 more than 850 primary teachers were trained. Over 130 teachers were trained through these courses in 1990. The current situation of the teaching force reveals that a large number of teachers in the atolls are poorly educated and untrained. Many have not studied beyond the primary level. However, the recent increase in salary of government teachers has served to attract a large number of candidates with better qualifications for teacher-training courses.

Inservice training is not as systematic and effective as pre-service training. It has been hampered by the constraints of a shortage of teacher educators, trained headteachers, and supervisors with the professional ability and skill to help teachers in their teaching.

Since 1984 an innovative program of training untrained teachers in the atolls has been underway. Under this program two-week intensive training courses for untrained teachers are conducted in their respective atolls as part of a four-week practice-teaching program for trainees who undergo preservice teacher training. The untrained teachers are provided with the opportunity to observe the trainee teachers using modern methods of instruction. They also attend theoretical classes in the evening. Ra-

dio has been used for inservice education through a regular weekly program called *Teacher's World*. It has provided some form of inservice training particularly to the untrained teachers in the outer islands.

Significant developments at the end of the 1980s contributed towards improvement of the quality of teachers and included the following:

(a) conducting of the practice-teaching program of the two-year Dhivehi-medium course in the atoll schools, which trains teachers primarily to serve in atoll schools;

(b) using closed circuit television in micro-teaching clinics;

(c) holding workshops in teacher-training courses to develop low-cost teaching aids;

(d) applying multigrade teaching techniques and techniques for teaching in difficult situations in the training system;

(e) conducting inservice training for untrained teachers in the atolls;

(f) providing inservice training to atoll teachers through a program of on-site teacher education;

(g) making changes in the teacher-training curriculum and reorganizing the teacher-education program;

(h) training additional teacher educators and upgrading those in service.

7. Curriculum Development and Teaching Methodology

The first attempt at a unified primary curriculum was made in 1980 with the development of the Five-Year Unified Curriculum. Prior to this there were vast differences in what was taught in the different schools of the country. In the atolls, it could occur that two schools in the same island used completely different curricula. A few traditional texts intended for adults were often used in schools.

The Five-Year Unified Curriculum was revised and in 1984 the Primary and Middle School National Curriculum came into effect. All schools in the country adopted this new curriculum which comprises seven subjects. Most of the texts, workbooks, and teacher's guides for this curriculum have been developed. A major challenge in the 1990s is to begin a revision cycle of the existing texts.

The new curriculum encourages a variety of group and individual activities as well as active participation of pupils to achieve real learning and to help them develop responsibility and creativity. It also emphasizes the importance of evaluation by the teacher on a continuous and systematic basis. Teachers are being oriented to the new curriculum and teaching–learning materials.

The curriculum for the secondary level is derived directly from the University of London preparatory requirements for the O and A level examinations. The only exceptions to this are the national courses in Dhivehi language and Islamic studies and the locally developed fisheries science.

At the secondary level, the most remarkable achievement is the introduction of the locally developed fisheries science as a University of London GCE level subject. The syllabus was designed with a view to providing students with a basic knowledge of ecology and fisheries in the Maldives and creating a greater interest in the fisheries industry which is vital to the economy of the Maldives.

Curriculum development in the Maldives is still in its infancy, and the government is encouraging the training of additional curriculum developers for the improvement of textbooks.

The major transition from a limited curriculum to the expanded modern curriculum expects a higher level of knowledge and competency among the teachers. The shortage of adequately trained teachers with the required level of education is a major constraint in the effective implementation of the new curriculum. In reality, the content covered and the level of instruction is mainly determined by the knowledge and ability of teachers. Hence the curriculum, in terms of implementation, varies among schools depending upon the ability of teachers and resources available.

8. Educational Assessment, Evaluation, and Research

The systematic collection of educational statistics is a recent activity in the Maldives. The period 1983 to 1990 witnessed considerable improvement in the collection, processing, and publication of educational statistics. The Ministry of Education established a statistical cell in which all of the tabulation and calculation of statistical data are done. In order to modernize the management of education, a computer-based Educational Management Information System (EMIS) was developed and installed at the Ministry of Education in 1987. In-depth analysis of data spanning the period 1978 to 1989 has now been made possible in order to give a comprehensive description of past progress and current status of enrollment, schools, teachers, finance, facilities, and attendance. Educational research in the Maldives is in its infancy. Limited action research in curriculum and teacher-training effectiveness has been undertaken in recent years.

9. Major Problems for the Year 2000

An analysis of the development of education in the period 1980 to 1990 revealed certain shortcomings. The most significant is an imbalance between the quality and quantity of schooling. The rapid expansion in enrollment has not been accompanied by a parallel improvement in the quality of teaching in most schools. In addition, the development of the new curriculum and the production of new educational materials have not kept pace with the increase in enrollment and the construction of new schools, mainly due to a lack of qualified personnel and the technical difficulties of book production in the country. An acute shortage of professional staff has also prevented the organization of sufficient inservice teacher training particularly in the use of the new curriculum. Many of the traditional island schools still do not have trained teachers. Quality suffers in two dimensions: first, the full span of the national curriculum is not covered; and second, the treatment of the subjects that are actually taught is superficial.

The Maldives also faces the following problems:

(a) a rapidly rising share of enrollment in government schools (from 18% in 1978 to 40% in 1990);

(b) issues of internal efficiencies due to wastage arising from repetition and dropout rates—a need exists to identify the patterns of wastage by location (atolls/islands) and to study the factors that contribute to this wastage;

(c) the limitations, both in content and coverage, of nonformal education programs;

(d) the relative scarcity of secondary education opportunities in the outer islands.

Bibliography

Institute for Teacher Education 1990 *Yearbook 1990*. ITE, Male'
Ministry of Education 1985 *Education and Human Resource Development Plan 1985–1995*. MOE, Male'
Ministry of Education 1990a *Development of Education: 1988–1990: Maldives Country Report to the International Conference on Education*. MOE, Male'
Ministry of Education 1990b *Framework for Action to Meet Basic Learning Needs: Republic of Maldives*. MOE, Male'
Ministry of Education 1990c *The Edhuruge*. MOE, Male'
Ministry of Education 1990d *Development of Island Community Schools*. MOE, Male'
Ministry of Planning and Environment 1991 *Republic of Maldives: Development Constraints, Plans and Strategies, Vol. I.* MPE, Male'
Windham D M 1991 *Education Sector Review: Republic of Maldives*. MOE, Male'

Mali

A. Ouane

1. General Background

The Republic of Mali, with an area of 1,204,000 square kilometers, is one of the largest countries in West Africa. Mali is a former French colony that attained its independence in September 1960. It is a landlocked Sahelian country which has been drastically affected by a persistent drought since the early 1970s.

Politically, the country has been marked by the colonial period; the first post-independence government which opted for socialist-oriented development; and the so-called "Second Republic" which resulted from the 1968 coup d'etat that established a very authoritarian military regime which lasted for 23 years and was dominated by corruption and repression. The Third Republic was shaped by the popular upsurge which took place in March 1991, in which the leading role was played by unemployed graduate students and out-of-school children and young people. These events are reflected in educational development landmarks ranging from the 1962 Reform to the National Debate on Education held in September 1991.

The 1987 census put the total population at 7,696,348 inhabitants, of which 43 percent were actively employed. The population growth was then 2.5 percent but was expected to reach 3.2 percent in the 1990s. If this trend prevails, the population will be 12.7 million in the year 2000, and 63 million in 2050. In the early 1990s, about 82 percent of the population lived in rural areas. The population density is low and its distribution between regions unequal.

Such geographic and demographic features have implications for the location of schools and the provision of educational services. In the cities (particularly in the capital, Bamako), the annual growth of the 7 to 12-year old population was 4.2 percent and higher than the educational provision for the same target which had been based on 2.3 percent, thus creating a large unmet demand for education. In rural areas, only 14.1 percent of an age group was enrolled in school. It was estimated that about 2,000 villages of about 500 inhabitants each did not have elementary schools and that the average distance between 2 primary schools was more than 18 kilometers in more than 80 percent of the districts (Bureau Central de Recensement 1991, Ministère de l'Education Nationale 1991, UNDP 1991).

Another factor playing an important role in the planning of education is the ethnic and language situation of the country. There are 15 major ethnic groups and about 12 languages. Several of these languages cross the boundaries of neighboring countries. These regional languages are: Bamanan (Bambara, Maninka, Mandingo, Jula), Fulfulde (Fula, Fulani, Peul), Hassanya (Arabic), Songhoy (Sonrhay, Jarma), Syenara-Mamara (Senoufo, Minyanka), and Tamasheq. This heterogeneity was further complicated by the colonial language policy which resulted in an exoglossic situation whereby a hitherto foreign language—French—is used as an official and national language. Except Tifinagh (an almost secret alphabet) for Tamasheq, and the individual use of Arabic characters for Fulfulde and Songhoy in certain areas and families, the Malian languages acquired alphabets only in the 1970s (Ouane 1991).

Agriculture, animal husbandry, fishing, and forestry account for 45 percent of the Gross National Product (GNP) and provide income for 85 percent of men and 78 percent of women. Only 0.8 percent of the active population is unemployed, owing to the fact that the rural population is marginally concerned with this phenomenon.

The rate of unemployment of the 55 percent deemed to be illiterate amounts to 0.5 percent, while the average unemployment rate of those with secondary, vocational, or higher education reaches 8 percent. Scientific, technical, and liberal workers account for 40 percent of the unemployed, with a rate of unemployment as high as 20 percent. The distribution of the active population according to the level of instruction shows that 87 percent of men and 93 percent of women have not received any formal instruction. Among those with instruction, 0.4 percent have completed literacy courses, 7 percent have acquired basic education, and 0.7 percent have a level of education equal to or higher than secondary education (Bureau Central de Recencement 1991).

According to the United Nations Development Program (UNDP) *Human Development Report 1991*, Mali is ranked 156 out of 160 countries with a Human Development Index (HDI) value of 0.0072 as compared to 0.993 for Japan, which heads the list. From this report, it is worth mentioning the following observations regarding Mali:

(a) A total of 44 percent of the population lives below the poverty line.

(b) The amounts of the GNP spent on public education and public health are 2.8 and 0.7 percent respectively.

(c) In 1987, 19 percent of the total Official Development Assistance (ODA) received by the country was spent on education.

(d) Military expenditures rose from 1.7 percent of

GNP in 1960 to 2.5 percent in 1986. This constituted 71 percent of the combined education and health expenditures. In the same year, the country had one member of the armed forces for every 2,000 inhabitants. This represented 38 percent of the teacher ratio for the same population. Furthermore, imports of arms represented 40 percent of the total imports in 1987.

(e) Debt servicing represented 14.2 percent of exports of goods and services in 1988, compared to 1.4 percent in 1970

2. Politics and the Goals of the Education System

Prior to the colonization of the country by France, education was organized according to the rules of the traditional society where the dominant form of provision was the initiation—a type of generational transmission of knowledge, skills, and attitudes. Through learning and cultural rites, this form of education aimed mainly at achieving social integration, imparting manual skills, and providing intellectual training in order to help the "youngsters enter the world of men (adults)."

The modern schools stem from the colonization process and follow the itinerary of French penetration in the country. In 1886, Gallieni opened the first school for "hostages" (this referred to the children of traditional chiefs of countries who were taken by force to be enrolled against the will of their parents). In 1910, this school was renamed "School of Sons of Chiefs and Interpreters." Modern education then spread into the interior of the country. It was only in 1916 that the first vocational school, *L'Ecole Primaire Supérieure* (First High School), was opened.

It is impossible to speak of education in Mali without referring to the 1962 Reform which aimed at accelerating the political and economic emancipation of the people of Mali and the emergence of a modern nation. The reform was based on democratic and socialist principles: social justice, equal educational opportunity, and the cultural de-alienation of the citizen. This reform had five main goals:

(a) to promote mass education of high quality;

(b) to decolonize people's mentality;

(c) to provide education able to maintain equivalency with education provided in other modern countries;

(d) to promote not only African and Malian values, but also universal values;

(e) to promote an education system able to provide, in a very short time, all the cadres needed in the production process (Diakité 1985).

Shaped from the services inherited from the colonial period and structured by the educational reform of 1962, Mali's educational system constitutes both a correction of the colonial heritage and a principal instrument of social and economic development. The implementation of this policy necessitated developing the education system along two axes: firstly, the provision of a basic education to all citizens, which would enable them to become active agents of development (horizontal development), and secondly, the promotion of a rational policy for the development of human resources (vertical development).

Conferences held in 1964, seminars in 1968 and 1978, and a sector study carried out in 1979 showed that, on the whole, the goals set for the school system had not been achieved despite a change of political regime. The *Etats Généraux* of Education held in 1989 and the National Debate on Education in 1991 paved the way for a more democratic and efficient education for all, heavily drawing on the Declaration of the World Conference on Education for All (WCEFA), held in Jomtien, Thailand in March 1990.

In particular, the National Debate on Education, organized within the framework of the transition to a Third Republic, reviewed the structures and organization of education and made recommendations for reform. The proposed changes aimed at providing basic education to a large majority of the population by facilitating access to learning and democratizing the functioning of the schools. Among the measures suggested were the expansion of public and private schools, the setting up of cooperative or basic schools, the reform of the *medersas*, the creation and strengthening of the school cantines in deprived areas, and the use of double divisions and double shifts in order to increase the opportunities for access.

3. The Formal System of Education

3.1 Primary, Secondary, and Tertiary Education

Figure 1 outlines the structure of the formal education system.

Since the 1962 Reform, basic education is said to be compulsory, coeducational, free, and secular. However, in 1981, an executive order stated that education was only compulsory within state budget limits. Basic education is composed of two cycles. The first cycle lasts six years (6–7 to 12–13 years of age) and consists chronologically of two years of initiation, two years of aptitude, and two years of guidance. At the end of the first cycle, pupils sit for the CFEPCF (*Certificat de Fin d'Etudes du Premier Cycle Fondamental*—Certificate of First Level Completion) which gives access to Grade 7. The second cycle (7th, 8th, and 9th grades) lasts three years (12–13 to 15–16 years of age), at the end of which pupils sit for the DEF

(*Diplôme d'Etudes Fondamentales*—Basic Education Diploma).

Basic education is provided in 1,619 schools for a population of 577,000 pupils. About 12,000 teachers serve these schools. There is a big gap between demand and supply due to the development of the educational infrastructures that did not follow the growth of the school-age population. The 1987 census showed that out of a total population of 6-to 9-year olds of 923,381, only 162,815 were able to read and write in French, Arabic, or one of the national languages. The district of Bamako, the capital, exemplifies the situation: more than 40,000 children of enrollment age did not have access to school in October 1990. In reality, the enrollment rate, which increased from 9 percent in 1960 to 27 percent in 1981, barely reached 30 percent in 1991. This low rate might be explained by two factors: the high birthrate (45% of the population is below 15 years) and the lowering of the enrollment age from 8–10 to 6–8 years in 1972 (Ministère de l'Education Nationale 1991).

Special mention should be made of the Koranic schools and the *medersas*. The former provide a bilingual Arabic–French religious education. While 80 percent of the population are Muslim, it is estimated that only 6 percent are able to read the Koran. In order to struggle against the high illiteracy rate and to provide more educational places, the government started implementing a reform aimed at creating "improved" Koranic schools and more secular *medersas*. The new Koranic schools, while keeping their religious character, will introduce a curriculum based on teaching reading, writing, and computation in national languages or French in ad-

dition to elements of moral and civic education and ruralization.

General secondary education is composed of two strands. General secondary education lasts three years and leads to the *baccalauréat*, the first part of which is taken in Grade 11 and the second in Grade 12. Technical grammar schools running parallel to general secondary education, also last for three years and lead to the technical *baccalauréat*.

General secondary education is provided in 20 *lycées* of general education, and 2 technical *lycées* (1 of which is oriented toward agriculture). However, 40 percent of the general secondary schools and 70 percent of technical schools are in the district of Bamako. Bamako has 46 secondary education schools and teacher-training colleges, while the region of Timbuktu in the north has only one. At secondary education level, the enrollment of boys is five times higher than that of girls (11.1% as against 2.8% of an age group respectively).

Higher education has a particular configuration. There is no university, only separate higher education and training centers. Higher education is provided in seven higher education centers. The duration of the courses varies from two years as in the EHEP (*Ecole des Hautes Etudes Pratiques*—School for Higher Practical Studies) and the ENPT (*Ecole Nationale des Postes et Télécommunications*—National School for Postal Services and Telecommunications) to four years in engineering, management, and teachers' training schools, and to six years for the ENMP (*Ecole Nationale de Medecine et de Pharmacie*). A three-year postuniversity degree can be obtained in the ISFRA (*Institut Supérieur de Formation et de Recherche Appliquées*—Higher Institute of Applied Training and Research).

Access to tertiary education is obtained through direct selection from among those who passed the *baccalauréat*, or through a competition for working people who have completed secondary education level. Apart from the IPR (*Institut Polytechnique Rural*—Rural Polytechnic Institute) located in Katibougou, all other higher education centers are concentrated in the capital. The enrollment rate at this tertiary level is 3.3 percent, representing 5.8 percent for males and only 1.8 percent for females.

The present structure of higher education has been the center of debate since the 1962 Reform. Studies on the creation of a university in Mali have been carried out in 1983 and 1985 with the assistance of international agencies. Based on these studies, a law was promulgated in 1986 stipulating the creation of a decentralized and vocationalized university, with a capacity to enroll up to 6,000 students. Follow-up studies were undertaken in the early 1990s. All of the studies concluded that the proposed option for a decentralized university was not only expensive, but would also create a problem of coherence with the other levels of education without solving the burning

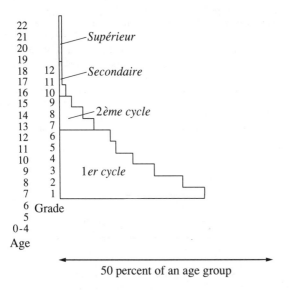

Figure 1
Mali: Structure of the formal education system

problem of unemployment of graduates from higher education institutions.

Formal school is confronted with high dropout and repetition rates. Table 1 gives an overview of the situation at the different levels of education. This table shows that the internal efficiency of the system is improving from one level to the next. The rate of efficiency increases from 19 percent in the first cycle of basic education to 23 percent in the second cycle, reaching 50 percent in secondary and 54.8 percent in higher education, while the dropout rate decreases from 81 percent in the first cycle of basic education to 45.2 percent in higher education.

3.2 Preschool Education

A very limited number of kindergarten and day nurseries provide preschool education for the urban elite. This system is privately run and monitored. In the early 1990s, the state attempted to create its own network and to regulate the system in order to integrate it into the basic education structure. The Koranic schools also provide some preschool education in Arabic.

3.3 Special Education

Special education is a very underdeveloped sector of education in Mali. The consequence of such a situation is the quasi-integration of physically handicapped students into the already narrow mainstream. The mentally and emotionally disabled are hardly catered for at all in the education system. A special effort is being made for the rehabilitation of young delinquents. Among the handful of institutions of special and remedial education are: the education centers for the handicapped, the National Institute for the Blind, and the Bolle and Mabile centers for rehabilitation (for young delinquents). Enrollment in this system is unstable and fluctuating, making it difficult to collect and maintain statistics.

3.4 Vocational, Technical, and Business Education

Vocational, technical, and business education is provided by a myriad of institutions at various levels

from the first cycle of basic education onward. There is, however, a concentration of these schools at the secondary education level. At this level there are four-year intermediate technical and vocational education courses leading to the various specialist diplomas called BT (*Brévets de Technicien*), and two-year technical and vocational education courses leading to the CAP (*Certificats d'Aptitude Professionnelle*—Certificates of Vocational Proficiency).

There are 53 institutions of technical and vocational education, all affiliated to the Directorate of Secondary Education. These centers also provide business education. The institutions provide trade courses ranging from typing and sewing to skills training in banking, custom clearance, business administration, and so on.

3.5 Adult and Nonformal Education

Adult education includes multidimensional literacy activities, extension training in rural areas (rural animation), vocational and income-generating training activities in urban areas—both in the formal and informal sectors of the economy, community development programs, and labor force training (Ouane 1991).

Adult literacy was one of the components of the 1962 Reform. After the failure of an initial attempt to provide a remedial elementary education in French to the adult population which had missed primary education, the country turned to functional literacy in local languages and, in 1967, joined the World Experimental Literacy Programme, launched after the well-known World Conference of Ministers of Education on Functional Literacy, held in Teheran in September 1965.

Two types of functional literacy program were developed: the programs integrated into rural development agencies and nonintegrated programs. In 1972, literacy was integrated into rural development operations to serve extension purposes. It started with the OACV (*Opération Arachides et Cultures Vivrières*—Operation Groundnuts and Food Cultivation) and the CMDT (*Compagnie Malienne de Développement des Textiles*—Textile Development Company of Mali). By the early 1990s, about ten

Table 1
Indicators of efficiency by level of education (in percent)

Indicators	Basic 1st Cycle	2nd Cycle	Secondary	Higher
Rate of efficiency	19.0	23.0	50.0	54.8
Relapse	81.0	77.0	50.0	45.2
Dropout	70.4	64.2	48.2	65.4
Repetition	29.6	35.8	51.8	34.6
Average duration of courses (in years)	7.2	3.9	3.8	4.6

rural development authorities had built-in literacy components. The nonintegrated programs are mainly run by nongovernmental organizations and the DNAFLA (*Direction Nationale de l'Alphabétisation Fonctionnelle et de la Linguistique Appliquée*—The National Directorate for Functional Literacy and Applied Linguistics).

According to statistics collected in 1990 by the DNAFLA, out of 12,000 villages in Mali, 4,197 had access to literacy programs. Some 5,073 functional literacy centers were operating, involving 9,654 facilitators, 574 of whom were female. These centers were attended by some 100,000 learners, 3,777 of whom were female. The same campaign found that there were 18,732 neoliterates, the majority of them (11,593) being female (MEN/DNAFLA 1991).

Despite rather slow quantitative progress, functional literacy programs became firmly established in the period from the 1970s to 1990 in all rural areas of Mali. Evaluation studies have shown that literacy has made an impact on the life and progress of the rural areas; the extension of agricultural techniques; improvement in livestock husbandry; the organization in the villages of primary health care and environment protection; and management by the villagers of credit, provisions, marketing, and local social organization.

Many workers develop their trades through self-learning sometimes with, and sometimes without, the guidance of a master. Among the trades covered are: sewing, batiks, metal work, leather work, auto mechanics, electronics, and so forth.

4. Administrative and Supervisory Structure and Operation

Education is organized, administered, and controlled by the Ministry of Education. The administration of the education system is centered at three levels: the cabinet, those departments called "vertical," and those called "horizontal."

The cabinet is the central decision-making body. Special services such as the Bureau of Education Projects, the Secretariat of the Malian National Commission for UNESCO, and the Higher Institute for Applied Training and Research are attached to the cabinet. The vertical departments manage and administer one given level or type of education. They include: the National Directorate of Basic Education, to which are attached some 32 "inspectorates"; the National Directorate of General, Technical and Vocational Secondary Education; the National Directorate of Higher Education; and the National Directorate for Functional Literacy and Applied Linguistics.

The horizontal departments intervene in the form of research, training, administration, and financial management for all levels and types of education.

These functions are performed by the National Pedagogical Institute and the Administrative and Financial Division.

There are also eight Regional Education Offices in charge of administering all educational matters at the intermediate level, which should also be included in the category of horizontal units.

In addition to these structures, consultative bodies (such as the Higher Council of Education and Culture and the National Union for Education and Culture), partners in development (such as the parents association), and certain development agencies play a key role in the organization of education programs.

As part of the proposed reforms, it has been suggested that a new Ministry for Basic Education (comprising four directorates in charge of basic education, literacy, preschool education, and special education) should be created. The parents association will be consolidated and two new consultative bodies set up at the school level—namely the School Cooperative, with present and former pupils, and the School Council, for monitoring the development of the school.

5. Educational Finance

Since independence, education in Mali has been largely supported by public funding. The average public annual spending on education, which reached 33 percent of the state budget in the early 1970s, decreased steadily to 28 percent in 1988 and stabilized at 26 percent after 1990. This decline led to a growing participation of families and local communities in financing education, particularly at the basic level. In 1975, the contribution of families represented 10 percent of the budget of the Ministry of Education, and 20 percent of that of basic education.

For the fiscal year 1991–92, the government earmarked Francs CFA 18.5 billion (about US$74 million) for education, which was about 5.3 percent of the GDP. An additional amount estimated at 4.9 percent of the education budget and 0.53 percent of the national budget was spent on education and training under other government ministries. Almost 90 percent of government outlay on education was devoted to the payment of salaries and scholarships. Investments in materials and infrastructures were left to parents, local communities, and the partners in development. This explains why education in Mali is so underequipped.

On average, 59 percent of education funding is for basic education. However, the bulk of this amount is spent on personnel. The resources devoted to the first cycle of basic education (34%) are still below the target of 37 percent. As far as unit costs are concerned, a secondary level pupil costs 7.6 times more than a basic education pupil (Ministère de l'Education Nationale 1991).

Parents pay a per capita contribution in addition to payment for textbooks, uniforms, transportation, health costs, and fees in private schools. The special contributions of parents associations were used to build, maintain, and equip schools. Since 1988, these contributions have been merged with others to form the so-called "Local and Regional Tax for Development." The authorities are confronted with serious difficulties in levying this tax. Furthermore, the proportion for education foreseen in this tax is less than the former contribution of the parents associations.

Mali depends on foreign aid for its development. From 1985 to 1989, it is estimated that 3–5 percent of the total aid given to the country went to the education sector. This amounted to an additional yearly income of Francs CFA 6–7 billion (US$ 25–26 million). Bilateral sources contributed largely to this amount in the form of grants. It should, however, be noted that its share has gradually declined from 79 percent in 1985 to 51 percent in 1989. Among the multilateral donors and funding agencies, the World Bank since the early 1970s and the African Development Bank (BAD) in the mid-1980s have been engaged in lending for learning through various education projects. The Fourth Project, which started in January 1990, was supported by a grant of US$20.7 million for the structural adjustment policy and a World Bank loan of US$32 million.

6. Supplying Personnel for the Education System

According to the 1987 census, 18,640 persons listed teaching as their principal activity. Among them, 19.7 percent were female. Basic education accounted for 80 percent of the teaching personnel, secondary education for 12.8 percent, and higher education for 1.5 percent.

The pupil–teacher ratio at the first and second levels of basic education was 24:1, but there are disparities among regions. Some 44 percent of all female teachers work in the capital. They accounted for 34.8 percent of all teaching personnel in the city. There are also disparities in class size. The national average estimate of 47 masks variations which range from 83 in Bamako, the capital, to 54 in Ségou and 28 in Gao (Bureau Central de Recensement 1991).

Teachers are trained in so-called "normal schools." Basic education teachers undergo preservice training in two kinds of teacher-training colleges: the *Instituts Pédagogiques d'Enseignement Général* (IPEG—Pedagogical Institutes for General Education); and the *Ecoles Normales Secondaires* (ENSEC—Secondary Teacher Training Colleges).

Until 1984, there was direct access to these institutions to graduates with the DEF either for a two-year course in the first category of college, or a four-year course in the second category. Since 1984, however,

there is competition for access among the graduates who have completed the *baccalauréat*.

Teachers for secondary general education are trained in the *Ecole Normale Supérieure* (ENSUP—Higher Teacher Training School), for four years.

Teachers' performance and motivation have gradually decreased due to harsh working conditions, poor and irregularly paid salaries, and limited promotion opportunities. As a result, there is a mass exodus to neighboring countries such as Côte d'Ivoire, Mauritania, and Niger, or to more affluent countries such as Gabon and Libya.

7. Curriculum Development and Teaching Methodology

Curriculum is centrally determined, developed, and controlled. The national educational goals are transformed into syllabuses and textbooks by central institutions such as the National Pedagogical Institute (IPN).

For basic education, central teams of specialists and educationists carry out, for each subject matter, the whole curriculum development exercise from needs assessments to the determination of learning objectives and sequences which are reflected in the primers and textbooks. These technical teams undertake all the operations linked to the conception and production of learning/teaching materials. Camera-ready copies are prepared and the printing is subcontracted to textbook publishers or printers. About 2,000 copies of each of the accompanying teacher guides are produced by the IPN.

This central approach was inherited from the colonial period. The nationally defined and implemented core curriculum was thought to preserve the quality of the curriculum and the whole school system, and, at the same time, to cement national unity. This is also why the various national languages did not enter the school curriculum until the mid-1980s. The cultural diversity, reflected in these languages, was wrongly perceived as a threat to national unity. A study of the content of basic education and the modalities of its provision to a large majority of the population conducted in the late 1970s recommended a regionalization of education and decentralization of the curriculum development process. This only resulted in an administrative decentralization with the setting up of regional directorates for education.

Central control is kept on the so-called " *disciplines d'éveil*" such as history, geography, and social and environment studies. As far as language and science are concerned, the curricular materials tend to be an adaptation of textbooks designed and produced in France for francophone Africa. A further innovation introduced in the late 1970s aimed at achieving more curricular relevance for pupils in rural schools by adjusting the school calendar and the curriculum content to the specificity of rural areas.

English as a first foreign language is introduced in Grade 7, and a second foreign language can be studied from Grade 10 onward.

The curriculum policy is translated into a school book policy with two aims: (a) producing textbooks based on the prescribed curriculum content, thus creating learning situations based on cultural settings familiar to the learners; and (b) selling the textbooks at a reasonable price, enabling the parents to purchase all the books required for basic education. (It should be noted that at secondary and higher education levels, the books are provided by the state through a scholarship scheme.)

In addition to fixing book prices, this policy also includes working out efficient distribution procedures and setting up a textbook revolving fund. The number of textbooks to be produced is determined every year according to enrollment figures. The government also subsidizes school textbooks through grants and loans received from bilateral and multilateral donors and funding agencies. The Fourth Education Project launched in the early 1990s kept the basic education textbooks within the purchasing power of the parents by fixing their average prices between Francs CFA 500 and 1000 (approximately US$2 and $4).

8. *The System of Examinations, Promotions, and Certifications*

Within one cycle of education, school-based continuous assessment procedures are widely used within schools for deciding on the promotion of pupils from one grade to the next. However, the promotion from one cycle of education to the next is based on national examinations.

The Certificate of First Level Completion (CFEPCF) is the first nationally organized examination. Admission to lower-secondary level was slightly above 50 percent throughout the 1970s and 1980s. At the end of lower-secondary level, students sit for the Basic Education Diploma (DEF). During the 1980s, between 40 and 45 percent of the pupils passed the DEF which provides direct access to general secondary education and to selected institutions of vocational and technical secondary education.

The *baccalauréat* is in two parts and is taken in Grades 11 and 12. There is also a series of vocational proficiency diploma examinations. Passing the *baccalauréat* gives direct access to a few higher education institutions and gives students the right to take competitive examinations to enter other tertiary education institutions.

Apart from the obvious issue of access, the education system is confronted with a huge problem of quality and efficiency. A system of continuous assessment of achievement and the monitoring of progress is needed, but in view of the limited places available within the system, selection is unavoidable.

9. *Educational Assessment, Evaluation, and Research*

There is no system of built-in evaluation and no significant activity related to student assessment and the development of education indicators. The only indicators produced are those on promotion, repetition, and dropout. The few instances of large-scale assessments were those undertaken within the framework of on-going experiments related to reading, writing, arithmetic, or science. Studies were undertaken by the Center of Applied Linguistics of Dakar (CLAD) on specific methods for reading and writing in basic education. The subsequent reforms and innovations developed in the 1980s by the *Centres d'Entrainement aux Méthodes Actives d'Education* in France and the National Pedagogical Institute (IPN) were based on these studies.

There is no specific allocation in the education budget for assessment or research. Applied educational research is mainly carried out by the National Pedagogical Institute and the National Directorate for Functional Literacy and Applied Linguistics. Two areas have benefited greatly from these research efforts, namely the ruralization of the curriculum and the experiment on the use of local tongues in the school curriculum. These topics, combined with an urgent need to find answers or alternatives to persisting and alarming population and environment issues while trying to enter the new communication age, resulted in research studies on the integration, balance, and multidisciplinary approach to curriculum development and implementation.

The Division of Scientific Research within the Department of Higher Education is in charge of research activities, many of which are carried out by specialized units of selected higher education institutions focusing more on overall development problems than on educational issues.

10. *Major Reforms in the 1980s and 1990s*

Democratizing functioning of the school system, increasing access to education, improving curriculum relevance, improving the internal efficiency of the education system, and achieving the fit between education and employment are the aims of the major reform attempts carried out in the 1980s and 1990s.

The 1980s were marked by the "ruralization" of the education system (i.e., adapting the curriculum to improve the relevance of education to the learner's immediate surroundings). Its main objective was to link the schools with concerns directly affecting life in the rural communities. As a result, learning and production should be harmoniously integrated, and schools should achieve self-financing as much as possible. The National Pedagogical Institute launched an experiment on "ruralization" in nine schools in the Sikasso region in the second cycle of basic education. These schools were equipped with workshops for technology and home economics, laboratories for science, and tools for practical work in agriculture, market gardening, and animal husbandry (Ministère de l'Education Nationale 1991). "Ruralization" as practiced in the 1990s is more production-oriented than pedagogical and this creates resistance from the parents.

An issue permanently raised in all forums held on education is the introduction of the various local languages into the school curriculum. In 1979, the National Directorate for Functional Literacy and Applied Linguistics (DNAFLA) was authorized to carry out a small-scale experiment in four rural schools. Opting for a gradual bilingualism built on the children's mother tongues, the experience was positively evaluated. A large-scale approach started in the mid-1980s and was coupled with the use of a "converging methodology" to facilitate and improve the transition to French language.

Double shifts (use of the same classroom by two different groups at a different time) and double division (use of a classroom at the same time by two groups of different level under the same teacher) were introduced in many areas to face the pressing demand for enrollment. These limited practices were extended within the framework of the Fourth Education Project. During the school year 1990–91, double shifts prevailed in 117 classes, of which 82 were located in Bamako. The statistics for the same period indicated that double division operated in 18 percent of all classes in the country.

11. Major Problems for the Year 2000

Most of the perennial problems of the Malian education system will remain in the year 2000. The most acute are the lack of resources, the issue of access, the need to improve the internal efficiency of the system, and the growing unemployment of graduates from higher education institutions.

The share of the parents and the local communities in education funding and the capacity of the state to contract more loans for schooling have already reached unbearable limits. However, at the same time, there is a need to raise the enrollment rate to about 70 percent by the year 2000. In addition to a search for alternative and dynamic strategies, efforts will have

also to be deployed to correct gender disparity, and to improve access for the deprived sectors, in particular for the nomadic populations bordering the Sahara.

The education system is also confronted with a very low internal efficiency. High dropout and grade repetition rates are the two major factors affecting the schooling system.

References

Bureau Central de Recensement 1991 *Fréquentation Scolaire, Scolarisation et Alphabétisation. Recensement General de la Population et de l'Habitat au Mali: Analyse, Vol. 4*. Ministère du Plan et de la Coopération Internationale, Direction Nationale de la Statistique et de l'Informatique, Bamako
Diakité S 1985 Mali: System of education. In: Húsen T, Postlethwaite T N (eds.) 1985 *The International Encyclopedia of Education*, 1st edn. Pergamon Press, Oxford
Ministère de l'Education Nationale 1991 *Débat National sur l'Education*. Ministère de l'Education Nationale, Bamako
Ouane A 1991 L'Harmonization des langues maliennes: Entre l'intégration nationale et régionale. *Int. Rev. Educ.* 37(1): 99–114
United Nations Development Programme (UNDP) 1991 *Human Development Report 1991*. Oxford University Press, Oxford

Further Reading

Belloncle G 1984 *La Question Educative en Afrique Noire*. Karthala, Paris
Dave R H, Perera D A, Ouane A (eds.) 1984 *Learning Strategies for Post-Literacy and Continuing Education in Mali, Niger, Senegal and Upper Volta*. UNESCO Institute for Education, Hamburg
Easton P 1984 *Education des Adultes en Afrique Noire: Manuel d'Auto-Evaluation Assistée*. ACCT/ Karthala, Paris
Ministère de l'Education Nationale 1973 *Contact Spécial: 10 Ans après la Réforme*. Ministère de l'Education Nationale, Bamako
Ministère de l'Education Nationale 1978 *Quelle Education pour Quel Développement: Rapport Final de l'Etude sur l'Education de Base*. Ministère de l'Education Nationale, Bamako
Ministère de l'Education Nationale 1979 *Deuxième Séminaire Nationale sur l'Education 1 and 2*. Ministère de l'Education Nationale, Bamako
Ministère de l'Education Nationale 1979 *Deuxième Séminaire National sur l'Education: Documents peparatoires*. Ministère de l'Education Nationale, Bamako
Ouane A 1984 Alphabétisation et formation des formateurs: L'expérience de l'Afrique Francophone. *Int. Rev. Educ.* 30(3): 329–50
Ouane A, Amon-Tanoh Y 1990 Literacy in French-speaking Africa: A situational analysis. *African Studies Review* 33(3): 21–39

Malta

C. J. Farrugia

1. General Background

The Republic of Malta comprises the three small islands of Malta, Gozo, and Comino which lie 90 kilometers south of Italy and 290 kilometers north of the African mainland. In 1991, about 345,000 Maltese lived within a total land area of 316 square kilometers, to render Malta one of the most densely populated nations. The population was on the increase following a substantial decrease in the 1950s when many young adults emigrated to Australia, North America, and the United Kingdom. Improved economic conditions had practically eliminated emigration, while social and medical services had extended life expectancy and eradicated infantile mortality. The annual birth and death rates were 17 and 10 per thousand respectively.

Malta's earliest known inhabitants were Stone Age farmers whose temples date back to 5000 BC and are the oldest known free-standing stone monuments in the world. The islands' strategic position at the center of the Mediterranean, together with their excellent natural harbors, rendered Malta a much sought after commercial and military base for the dominant powers of the Mediterranean from the time of the Phoenicians. The population speaks Maltese, which is derived from Maghreb Arabic. In addition, most Maltese speak English (the second official language), which is the second language of tuition at the university and in secondary schools. Many Maltese speak Italian as a third language. The majority of Maltese are practicing Roman Catholics. Historical events have intermixed with geographical circumstances to influence the highly independent nature of the Mediterranean islanders. For example, the Maltese educational system evolved into its present indigenous blend from educational ideas and practices that emanate both from European and Anglo-Saxon influences.

In 1787, Napoleon expelled the Knights of St John who had been Malta's rulers for 268 years. The Maltese in turn expelled the French three years later with the help of the British who stayed on as the last colonial power until Independence in 1964. Malta declared itself a republic in 1974 to enhance its political self-reliance as a genuine parliamentary democracy with general elections being held every five years. Gozo, the smaller island, is fully integrated into the political and social life of the country. The islands' international political status is that of a nonaligned nation with strong political and economic ties to Western Europe. It is a member of the United Nations, the British Commonwealth, and the Council of Europe. Following 27 years of close economic links with the European Economic Community, Malta applied for full membership in 1991.

For centuries Malta's economy has been conditioned by the demands of its colonial rulers so that in times of political instability or warfare in the Mediterranean the islands served the military exigencies of its occupying power, while in peacetime Malta's natural harbors functioned as a central point for the mercantile trade in the region. As a result, the Maltese could not develop a local industrial base to compensate for the islands' gradual loss of importance as a military fortress. Under colonialism, the inhabitants were unable to reduce their dependence on the income derived from military occupation and substitute it with nonmilitary foreign exchange.

After Independence, successive Maltese governments embarked on extensive economic programs to diversify from military-derived income to an export-oriented industrial base. This now includes the production of high-quality textiles, precision engineering and electronics, specialization in shipbuilding and repairing, and offshore banking. The islands' natural and historical attractions, together with the traditional hospitality of the Maltese, contribute to the expanding tourist industry which, with 800,000 tourists in 1991, had become the major foreign currency earner. The real per capita gross national income increased from US$924 in 1980 to US$1,347 in 1991. The 1991 per capita Gross National Product (GNP) was US$3,787.

Throughout the 1970s and 1980s, a socialist administration aimed for a mixed economic structure where the government laid down central economic policies to regulate growth and, at the same time, to enforce a higher level of direct state participation in the economic sector. The change of government in 1987 encouraged reliance on a free market economy, deregulation, decentralization, and a stronger emphasis on private enterprise. The changed orientations were also reflected in the government's policy on education. The previous administration had enforced the adoption of utilitarian courses at all levels, especially at tertiary level, and attempted to bring the private education sector under state control. The new government lays greater emphasis on liberal and general education, and has introduced legislation which aims for decentralized educational policy-making, and which safeguards the existence of private schools.

2. Politics and the Goals of the Education System

A variety of schools have existed in Malta since the fourteenth century; the origins of the University of

Malta date to 1592. However, concentrated attempts to introduce universal education began in the late nineteenth century. Legislation for compulsory school attendance was enacted in 1924, but full enforcement had to wait until the end of the Second World War. The Education Act of 1946 made primary schooling compulsory for all children between the ages of 6 and 14. Universal secondary education came into effect in 1971. By 1988 compulsory schooling was from 5 to 16 years of age. Tuition-free university education became available in 1970. In 1978, the state introduced wage-sponsored university education in selected utilitarian courses, a system that was eventually extended to students in state postsecondary schools. Since 1987, all students in postsecondary and tertiary education receive stipends which enable them to pursue their studies regardless of their parents' income.

3. The Formal System of Education

3.1 Primary, Secondary, and Tertiary Education

Compulsory education begins at age 5, but 83 percent of the children aged 3 and 4 attend nursery or kindergarten centers run by both the state and private schools.

The primary phase of compulsory education lasts 6 years from age 5 through to age 10. All Maltese chil-

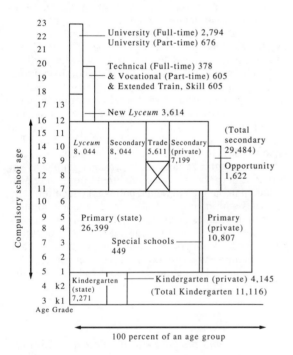

Figure 1
Malta: Structure of the formal education system 1990

dren receive primary education: 26,399 in state schools where tuition is completely free, and 10,807 in private schools which charge nominal fees but will become fully state-supported and tuition-free in 1992. All state and most private primary schools are coeducational with an average class of 30 pupils. The objectives of primary education in Malta are stressed in the National Minimum Curriculum which came into effect as part of the new education legislation in September 1989 (Government of Malta 1988).

The National Minimum Curriculum (NMC) encourages primary teachers to adopt an integrated pedagogical approach through methods that "stimulate reactions from the child, which rely on problem-solving and which make use of the satisfaction to be derived from the achievement of success in learning to endear young people to the learning process" (Government of Malta 1989 p.v). Such methods, stress the authors of the NMC, aim to provide pupils with "self-control, self-confidence and self-reliance."

As the competition for more and better schooling intensifies, scholastic stress has become a major feature of Maltese primary schools. Educators and legislators are anxious to render primary schooling as stress-free as possible for pupils, their parents, and the teachers. Competition and stress have always featured in the Maltese education system, but these have become even more pronounced since the 1970s when the state secondary education sector changed radically from a highly selective grammar-type to fully comprehensive schooling. Fearing a lowering of academic standards the majority of parents attempted to transfer their children to the more traditional grammar-type schooling in private schools which could not accommodate all those who sought entry. Eventually the state itself re-established a small number of selective secondary schools with the result that entry to the more academically rigorous private and public secondary schools became more competitive and highly selective than ever.

These events had, and still have, a strong impact on the teaching methods adopted at the primary level where children are trained, coached, tested, and examined in readiness for the entrance examinations into state and private secondary schools. A more liberal secondary-school entrance policy, supported by mass-media educational programs aimed at parents and teachers, are making some headway in reducing the competition and anxiety. Yet, many parents, while agreeing with the educational arguments, are reluctant to risk their children's chances of entering a popular secondary school. Consequently, the competition and the stress, albeit at a reduced level, remain high.

At 11 years of age all Maltese pupils transfer to secondary single-sex schools where they are required to remain for 5 years until the end of compulsory schooling at the age of 16. Pupils who are successful in the Secondary Schools Entrance Examination proceed to the grammar-type state junior lyceums or private colleges; the remainder attend state area secondary schools.

In 1991, the numbers of students in state and private secondary schools were 14,879 and 7,199 respectively. At the end of the second year of secondary education, students can opt to go to the state's trade schools, which were attended by 5,611 students in 1991 seeking to obtain training and basic qualifications in a craft or trade.

The average class size in the first two years of secondary education is 30 students, which is reduced to 25 in the remaining three years. Trade schools have a high level of student absenteeism due mainly to the students' lack of motivation and the perception that their studies are irrelevant for postschool life. All secondary education, whether in state or private schools, is tuition-free since private schools are maintained through state subsidies and voluntary contributions by parents.

Secondary education in Malta is also guided by a National Minimum Curriculum, which attempts to ensure a *minimum* level of educational competence to widen the students' intellectual, moral, physical, and social development, as well as to prepare them for the world of work (Government of Malta 1990).

The tripartite system of education creates serious problems. The rigid pedagogical approach at the primary level is repeated even more strongly at the secondary level. Furthermore, the rigid examination-based selection process for entry to the limited places in the grammar-type schools arbitrarily discriminates against potentially good students who end up being labeled as academically weak. The label is even more indiscriminately applied to those students who transfer to trade schools. Unofficially qualified as academic failures, most of these students linger on for three years in an unstimulating scholastic environment until the age of 16 and the end of compulsory education. The educational authorities are seeking to eliminate the academic and social differences between these schools. For example, the availability of places in junior lyceums are being increased so that all the students can enter them, thus phasing out the area secondary schools. Furthermore, the trade schools' curriculum is being altered gradually to render it less exclusively craft-oriented and to provide the students with a more balanced education.

In spite of these shortcomings, Malta's system of secondary education provides a good foundation for those students who seek formal academic qualifications, such as Ordinary-level certification in the University of Malta Matriculation or the General Certificate of Education offered by British universities, which open the door to postsecondary education.

Postsecondary education in Malta takes several forms with the sixth form or upper lyceums being the most popular, since they lead to Advanced-level qualifications in the Matriculation and the General Certificate of Education and to university entrance.

State upper-secondary schools cater for 3,209 students, while 405 students attend their private counterparts. These schools generally have three streams: the liberal arts and language stream, the mathematics and science stream, and the commercial stream which is becoming increasingly popular.

The University of Malta is the highest tertiary-level institution in the islands. It has ten faculties which include architecture and civil engineering; arts; dental surgery; economics, management and accountancy; education; law; mechanical and electrical engineering; medicine and surgery; science; and theology.

An important development in the structure of the university has been the establishment of institutes or centers to cater for interdisciplinary studies or specialized areas of excellence. The institutes and centers include: Anglo–Italian studies, distance learning, energy technology, healthcare, linguistics, and Mediterranean studies. Furthermore, the Foundation for International Studies at the University of Malta acts as a catalyst and organizer of research and training programs of an international nature. The Foundation houses a number of institutes including the International Environment Institute, the Euro-Mediterranean Marine Contamination Hazards Center, and the Mediterranean Social Sciences Network. The International Marine Institute at the university reflects Malta's keen interest and international initiatives in global environmental matters, especially those related to the common heritage of mankind, marine studies, and human rights.

The university faculties and institutes offer undergraduate, graduate, and higher studies in their specific teaching and research areas. In October 1991, 3,470 students were attending the University of Malta on a full-time or part-time basis. This number represents 13 percent of the 18–22 age cohort, an increase of 9 percent in the age cohort over the 1981 figures.

The dramatic increase results from three major factors. The most important results from the universal social phenomenon which leads people, whose needs are satisfied at one educational level, to seek more, better, and higher educational facilities. Thus, following the implementation of universal primary and secondary education, many Maltese now seek postsecondary and higher education. The second factor is undoubtedly an economic one. Many Maltese families are in a financial position to forego the income from their children's employment until they complete their university studies. Students' economic security is further enhanced by generous stipends and guaranteed vacation employment offered to postsecondary and university students. The third major contributing factor to account for the increase in the number of tertiary education students results from political and administrative changes. The policy of the previous administration was to restrict university studies and entry to strictly vocational and utilitarian courses which guaranteed employment on the conclusion of one's studies. A strict *numerus clausus*, or limited university entry to vocational courses, was enforced according to estimated requirements while general arts and science courses were suppressed. The present administration has adopted an open entry policy in all faculties and aims to increase university enrollment for the 18–22 age cohort to 25 percent by the year 2000.

3.2 Preschool Education

The stated aims of preschool education are to introduce children to an educational environment outside the home and help them to socialize through organized play. The availability of kindergarten centers also makes it possible for young mothers to join the workforce, an option which an increasing number of Maltese women are taking. The average class size in state kindergartens is 35–40 children with two kindergarten assistants; the ratio in private nurseries tends to be higher.

3.3 Special Education

The education of handicapped students is catered for by schools for the blind, the deaf, the severely physically handicapped, the mentally handicapped, and the maladjusted. Although the special services offered by these schools will be maintained, education policy in Malta is to integrate handicapped students in mainstream schools whenever possible.

3.4 Vocational, Technical, and Business Education

The trade schools at the secondary level have already been mentioned.

Postsecondary technical education is catered for at the technical institutes with 378 full-time and 605 part-time students. Students who wish to continue with their education when they have completed trade school can proceed to the Extended Skills Training Scheme which consists of study-cum-apprenticeship courses and which directs the more promising students to the technical institutes. Prevocational schools, such as the School of Nurses, the School for Agriculture, the Builders School, and the Nautical School, prepare students who have decided to pursue a specific line of employment.

3.5 Adult and Nonformal Education

Nonformal education is catered for by both government and nongovernment organizations such as the university, professional bodies, trade unions, church organizations, the political parties, sports and cultural clubs, and philanthropic associations. Nonformal education courses vary in nature, duration, and level of academic attainment; they are extremely popular, and attendance, especially to those that are vocationally oriented, is on the increase.

4. Administration and Supervisory Structure and Operation

The Ministry of Education sets policies and is ultimately responsible for the national educational service whether provided for by the state or by the private sector. The Director of Education heads the state's Department of Education with its primary, secondary, and postsecondary educational sections, each under the responsibility of an assistant director of education. The Department employs teaching and support staff, sets curricula, owns and maintains school buildings, provides teaching materials, and centrally administers all formal and nonformal public education. Although headteachers in state schools are nominally responsible for all academic and school administration matters, the Department exerts considerable influence on all local school matters. The small size of the islands and the efficient communication network make it easy for officials from head office in Valletta to keep in touch with the remotest schools. Communications between head office and schools are maintained through direct contact between the head of school and the assistant director of education responsible for the particular section. Area education officers reinforce the links, and generally ensure that official policies are followed.

Until the mid-1970s, education officers were known as "school inspectors" whose function was to evaluate and to report on teachers' competence as well as to pronounce on the academic, administrative, and leadership qualities of heads of schools. Having the seniority and the power, inspectors were deferred to by school personnel. However, the Reorganization Agreement of 1975 between the government and the Malta Union of Teachers altered their role radically, and their title was changed to education officer in order to emphasize an advisory rather than a supervisory function. They also lost their senior standing in the Civil Service scale in relation to headteachers and, as a result, their administrative clout was greatly reduced. In the 1980s, the changed administrative style, which coincided with rapid growth in the secondary and trade school sector, created a management and power vacuum especially in schools with weak or inexperienced heads. Teaching personnel now accept that the inspectorial function of education officers should remain, albeit in a greatly reduced form, and that their main role should be to provide pedagogical guidance and specialized advice in specific areas of the curriculum.

The Education Act of 1988 introduced a new development in local school administration by establishing school councils. These replace the previously informal role of parent–teacher associations and take a greater measure of responsibility for the nonpedagogical administration of individual schools. The membership of each school council is made up of: a chairperson nominated by the Minister of Education, the head of school who acts as secretary and treasurer, three elected representatives of the teaching staff, and three elected representatives of the parents whose children attend that school (the latter three can be elected from among the students who are over the age of 16). School councils are encouraged to deal with nonacademic administration matters for the school, such as maintenance, purchase of equipment, and administration of school funds and services. They have no power to change curricula, or to interfere in the teaching duties of staff. The government looks upon school councils as a vehicle to reduce the traditional high degree of centralization, and to change the culture of central control which dominate all sectors of public administration in Malta. It is still too early to conclude that school councils will provide state schools with the degree of autonomy they seek, and which their counterparts in the private education sector enjoy.

The private education sector in Malta has always been strong. It expanded considerably in the 1970s when the state sector went through a series of academic and administrative upheavals which prompted parents to seek the more stable environment of private schools. In 1991, one-third of the parents still preferred to send their children to private schools. These schools are mainly affiliated to the Catholic Church, although the demand for private schooling has led to the expansion of non-Church schools, and has encouraged private organizations or foundations to establish independent ones.

According to the law, the state's Department of Education is empowered to supervise the academic and administrative work of private schools. For example, in order to operate, private schools must obtain a state license and teachers (as in state schools) must possess a Teachers' Warrant. In practice, apart from the requirements to meet the academic provisions of the National Minimum Curriculum and to abide by nationally set standards for accommodation, school premises, and teaching personnel, private schools, even those which are heavily subsidized by the state, are administratively autonomous.

5. Educational Finance

The Maltese authorities regard education as a major contributor to the islands' human resource base, and in the 1980s successive governments devoted an average of 8 percent of the national budget to education. In 1990, US$75 million were spent on education compared with US$77.5 million on health, US$2.6 million on social security, US$117 million on energy and utilities, US$144 million on the infrastructure, and US$21.6 million on the military. In addition to the money spent by the state, another estimated US$4 million are spent by the private education sector.

Recurrent expenditure and salaries consume the bulk of the educational budget since the islands are fairly well provided with school buildings in every sector. The University of Malta is the exception since it has had to double its space in order to cater for the much larger influx of students. Educators in Malta are aware of the islands' limited finances and appreciate that the nation's income has to be shared among the other social services and national needs. However, there is serious concern about insufficient funding for educational research, the development of new curricula, and the continuous professional development of teaching personnel. The shortcomings are particularly acute in the technical education sector which needs substantial investments for the recruitment of new staff, the upgrading of equipment and laboratories, and the development of new methodologies.

6. Supplying Personnel for the Education System

The number of teachers currently employed in the Maltese education system is 3,322, of which 2,249 teach in state schools, and 1,073 in private schools. In addition, almost 250 personnel were employed by the Ministry of Education as nonteaching staff; comparable figures for nonteaching personnel in private schools are not available. Almost two-thirds of the teachers (63.2%) are female.

Nearly 29 percent of teachers in state schools hold a teacher's degree or diploma-level or higher teaching qualification, 43 percent hold a teacher's certificate, 2 percent hold technical qualifications, while 26 percent have postsecondary qualifications but do not have formal teacher training. Complete figures are not available for private schools, but the indicators are that teachers' qualifications there are similar to those in state schools.

The percentage of teaching personnel who lack formal teaching qualifications reflects Malta's endemic teacher shortage. This declines when the economy is depressed and young people seek secure employment in the public service. When the economy recovers, the teacher shortage becomes more acute, and the education service has to rely on the temporary employment of untrained postsecondary educated young people. In 1991, the economy was booming and the high level of untrained personnel employed in Maltese schools was alarming. Unfortunately, all the major factors militate against the declared objective of an all-trained graduate teaching profession. First, the Maltese education system has been expanding rapidly with ever-increasing demands for a more numerous and better qualified teaching force. Second, in spite of the recent increases, teachers' salaries still compare badly with those in industry, business, and the service sectors. Third, in spite of their enhanced standing through the 1988 Education Act's recognition of teachers' professional status, many teachers still complain of occupational stress, work fatigue, and an acute lack of promotion opportunities.

The formal route to teaching is through one of two initial teacher education courses offered by the Faculty of Education at the University of Malta, namely the four-year Bachelor of Education (Honours) degree course, or the one-year Postgraduate Certificate in Education. These programs prepare an average of 170 candidates annually to teach either in primary or secondary schools. The Department of Education at the Ministry of Education organizes induction courses in basic pedagogy for untrained temporary teachers, as well as inservice courses for its regular teaching personnel. The University of Malta, the state's Department of Education, the Malta Union of Teachers, and private schools collaborate to offer courses in the Continuous Professional Development of Teachers Program organized by the Faculty of Education. They also sponsor experienced teachers who enroll in evening diploma courses which the Faculty offers in educational administration and management, guidance and counseling, librarianship, and the education of children with special needs. Since 1977, the Faculty has been offering a Master's in Education course and intends to launch a doctoral degree program in the 1990s. The Faculty of Education also leads and coordinates research in various educational spheres, more notably in the professional development of teachers, educational development in small states, curriculum innovation, teachers' occupational stress, environmental studies, and the evolving social context of Maltese education. Other faculties at the University, more notably the faculties of Arts and Science, contribute to enhance teachers' "subject content" in their specialized field of interest.

7. *Curriculum Development and Teaching Methodology*

Universal primary and secondary education in Malta evolved soon after the Second World War when the Maltese felt a special affinity with the British, and at a time when many locals sought to emulate the British way of life. The education path followed the British system of that time. Since most students sat for examinations run by British examining boards, the syllabuses and curricula reflected British rather than Maltese concerns. The sections of the Education Act of 1988 dealing with the National Minimum Curriculum aimed at rectifying these shortcomings.

Until 1988, schools were technically free to devise and develop their own curricula, but in reality the central authoritarian culture of the state system meant that schools had to follow the syllabuses dictated by head office, while private schools followed the demands of public examinations. However, it was still possible for individual schools to neglect one or more important subjects. For example, when in the late 1970s, physics and Arabic became compulsory subjects for entry into sixth form, most schools simply dropped history and geography; some private schools ignored the teaching of Maltese and Maltese history. The National Minimum Curriculum legislation identifies the basic

subjects that are to be taught at the primary, secondary, and postsecondary levels.

Primary-school pupils are taught by one teacher. The curriculum is differentiated into several subjects, but teachers are encouraged to adopt an integrated approach round themes selected by the teacher and the pupils. In the early years, most instruction is in Maltese with a gradual introduction of English so that children are able to speak and read both languages at the end of primary school. Most students become bilingual by the time they complete their secondary education. Subjects are clearly differentiated and taught by specialist subject teachers in secondary schools. In the first two years, students follow a common core course, and are able to opt for some subjects in the last three years. Students who proceed beyond fifth form take options in the Advanced-level subjects in the Matriculation and the Secondary Education Certificate examinations.

The emergence of a more assertive national identity is being reflected in the re-examination of school curricula to reflect local culture and needs more strongly, and to reinforce the islands' close links with Europe. This revaluation extends beyond the revision of syllabuses; it includes the extension of the local Matriculation and Secondary Education Certificate examinations to cover, by June 1992, all the subjects previously offered by foreign examination boards.

8. *Major Problems for the Year 2000*

The shortage of financial resources is a constant source of concern to educators in small countries such as Malta. Demands by equally deserving projects, each competing for a limited number of personnel and for restricted funds, cause perennial problems.

The shortage of human resources constitutes another constant source of frustration. In very small states like Malta, the shortage reaches endemic proportions especially in the labor intensive nature of educational services. Regardless of its size, Malta requires a basic educational administration including a Ministry of Education, an education head office, education officers, personnel and finance sections, a special education unit, an examination branch, a physical plant maintenance service, etc. In effect, it requires the basic services and facilities needed in a country a thousand times larger. The actual number of people employed in the educational sector is much fewer in Malta than in Italy, for example, but the difference is not proportional to the total number of inhabitants. As a result, the per capita financial costs and the demands on human resources for the provision of an adequate educational service become proportionally much higher in Malta than in larger countries.

As the economy expands and the standard of living improves, the demands for a wider variety and better educational services become more exacting. Increases in the tourist industry, export drives to Continental

Europe, industrial diversification from garment manufacture to electronics and sophisticated technology, and the islands' objective to become an offshore banking and commercial center all have their implications for changes in the curriculum for further languages to be taught and the introduction of new vocational and business courses.

Consequently, first the secondary schools and later the University have had to introduce courses which cater for the new developmental needs. These in turn entail resource investment in new courses, extended buildings, and the training of additional staff. The actual sums of money and the number of people involved are small by international standards, but in relation to the islands' financial and human resources, they are exorbitant.

The small educational system will soon be facing a major demographic problem caused by an aging teacher population. In the late 1990s, the recruits of the 1960s will be due for retirement and, unless replacements are found, the teacher shortage at the beginning of the 1990s will become even more acute. The number of retiring teachers amounts to 21 percent of the teacher complement in the state sector. Several propositions are being considered to overcome the problem, including extending the retirement age beyond 61, encouraging trained married women teachers to rejoin the service, and offering better salaries and conditions of work. Each has to be evaluated carefully in order not to upset the finely tuned social and economic ecology. For example, the extension of the retirement age will have the negative effect of blocking the promotion opportunities of younger employees: a dilemma that on the one hand plays on the requirements of the educational systems, and on the other hand affects the personal aspirations of younger staff.

Restricted promotion opportunities are the highest cause of frustration in the small educational system since many capable and ambitious young teachers feel that their professional and economic growth are seriously stunted. They are attracted by better opportunities in larger, more prosperous countries and it is a constant effort to contain the brain drain and the loss of valuable, often highly skilled expertise. The problem is exacerbated by the employment pattern in the state sector with its particular phenomenon of a skewed organizational pattern made up of a large number of personnel at the lower end of the salary scale, but tapering off sharply at the top. This structure renders promotions rare and highly competitive. At the beginning of the 1990s, a reorganization of teachers' salary scales was undertaken. Teachers can move to a higher grade and a better salary without having to abandon classroom teaching. Thus, a larger number of experienced and deserving teachers are promoted, and at the same time continue to provide the service for which they are best qualified rather than having to move to an administrative post for which they may be unsuited.

Since Independence the Maltese have had to generate their own income, establish their own national and international policies, and nurture an almost dormant national identity. Self-confidence and self-reliance are becoming more apparent in most national enterprises, from local industry to education. This will continue in the 1990s. The University of Malta is planning new faculties and institutes. Some of this has begun and the investment is paying off. In spite of the limited number of people in education working with very restricted resources, the Maltese educational system is experiencing an upsurge of local initiatives. Professional educational literature, curriculum development, experimental pedagogy, instructional projects aimed at specific local needs, and a small but flourishing textbook production industry reflect the many attempts to shed dependence on foreign ideas and products. Within the Maltese education system, the University serves as the principal generator for new ventures including those in local industry, indigenous technology, local theater, the arts, folklore, the Maltese language, and cultural tourism: all contributing to the renaissance of the Maltese identity.

Small states have an ecology of their own, and the Maltese educational system has to cope with academic, social, administrative, economic, and political forces that in many respects are unique. In global terms, Malta's educational problems may seem insignificant, but to the Maltese the issues are real and important and the islanders are striving for an efficient and forward-looking educational system to deal with them.

References

Government of Malta 1988 *An Act to Consolidate and Reform the Law Relating to Education in Malta*, Act No. XXIV. DOI, Valletta

Government of Malta 1989 *Education Act 1988, National Minimum Curriculum Regulations 1989 (Primary Level)*. DOI, Valletta

Government of Malta 1990 *Education Act 1988, National Minimum Curriculum Regulations 1990 (Secondary Level)*. DOI, Valletta

Further Reading

Borg M, Riding R, Falzon J 1991 Stress in teaching: A study of occupational stress and its determinants, job satisfaction and career commitment among primary schoolteachers (in Malta). *Educ. Psychol.* 11(1): 59–75

Director of Education 1991 *Department of Education: Annual Report 1990*. DOI, Valletta

Farrugia C (ed.) 1988 *Education in Malta: A Look to the Future*. UNESCO, Paris

Farrugia C 1990 Malta: primary education. In: Pusci L (ed.) 1990 *Primary Education in Europe*. CEDE, Frascati

Farrugia C (ed.) 1991 *A National Minimum Curriculum for Malta*. University of Malta, FIS, Ministry of Education, Valletta

Farrugia C 1992 Authority and control in the Maltese education system. *Int. Rev. Educ.* 38(2): 57–73

Farrugia C 1992 Malta: Educational development in a small island state. *Prospects* 21(3)

Farrugia C, Attard P 1991 The Malta case-study. In: Bray M (ed.) 1991 *Ministries of Education in Small States.* Commonwealth Secretariat, London

Fenech J 1991 Laying the foundations for cultures of teaching. *Education* (University of Malta) 4(2): 2–8

Sultana R (ed.) 1991 *Themes in Education: A Maltese Reader.* Mireva Publications, Msida

Wain K 1991 *The Maltese National Curriculum: A Critical Evaluation.* Mireva Publications, Msida

Xerri C 1990 *The Development of Education: 1988–1990—National Report For Malta.* Planning Section, Department of Education, Valletta

Mauritania

D. A. Ousmane

1. General Background

The Islamic Republic of Mauritania covers an area of 1,030,691 square kilometers. It is a link between North Africa and South Saharan Africa. It is bordered to the south by Senegal, to the southeast by Mali, to the northeast by Algeria, and to the west by the Atlantic Ocean. It has a straight 600 kilometer coastline edged by a cordon of dunes. Inland there are a few mountains with a minimum altitude of 915 meters and isolated rocks (guelbs) which are often rich in minerals (iron and copper). There are four climatic areas:

(a)   The Sahelo–Sudanese area on the south tip of the country. This area has yearly rainfalls of between 500 and 600 millimeters.

(b)   The river valley (Chemama) with rainfalls from 300 to 500 millimeters in the period June to October.

(c)   The Sahelian area, a cordon of 80 to 250 square kilometers stretching from the north of the Senegal River to the Mali border.

(d)   The Saharan area in the north with little rain.

In 1988, the population was estimated at just under 1.9 million inhabitants. There are two major ethnic groups: the Arab–Berbers who live mostly in the north, and the Mauritanian Negroes, who live mostly in the south. The latter group contains the Halpularen, the Soninkés, the Ouolofs, and a few Bambaras. Each of these ethnic groups has its "traditional" forms of living, including a hierarchy of castes. The highest caste level is known as "free people" (the nobles), the second as the "caste people" (craftspeople), and the third as the "slave people" (slaves who are emancipated and those who are still not yet emancipated). The slaves of the Arab–Berber ethnic groups are composed of persons originating from the Mauritanian Negro ethnic groups.

There have been many changes in the composition of the population since 1965. At that time, 70 percent of the population were nomads. By 1988, only 30 percent were nomads. This was brought about by a policy of providing permanent homes for the nomads, a process known as "settling." This process was accompanied by an exodus from the north to the south. However, most nomads still live in the center of the country. Since the 1970s there has been a high rate of urbanization— almost 22 percent per year. The population density is low at 1.07 persons per square kilometer. There is a rising population growth rate and a limited life expectancy (only 6% of the population is over 60 years of age). About 44 percent of the population is younger than 15 years of age.

Agriculture (with a large cattle breeding subsector) predominates as an occupation. The iron ore and fishing industries have increased rapidly since the 1970s. The per capita Gross National Product (GNP) increased at a rate of 3.6 percent per year between 1985 and 1989. In 1992, the per capita GNP was US$440. In the 1980s, there were economic and financial imbalances and structural adjustment programs had to be adopted to restore the macro-economic balances in order to boost the economy.

Mauritania became independent in 1960. It was formerly a French colony and known in Arabic as *"Trab El Chinguit"* (Land of the Chinguit). Mauritania's administrative organization was inherited from the French and is very centralized. The country is divided into twelve regions plus the district of Nouakchott, the capital. Each region is headed by a Governor and is divided into *départements*. Each *département* is headed by a *préfet* and is subdivided into districts. Each district is headed by a chief who reports to the *préfet* of the *département*. The village and the encampments are the smallest administrative units for the settled population and for the nomads.

French is no longer an official language according to the constitution. Arabic, and its dialects (Hassaniya), is the official language. National languages include Pulaar, Soninke, and Ouolof.

The educational system is based on the French model. It began with three *medersas* (schools) in the Arab–Berber area. Instruction was in both French and Arabic. This form of bilingualism was a tradition for many years but since Independence there has been a policy of Arabization and by 1992 this had been nearly totally achieved. The state system of education developed alongside the traditional Koranic schools. The Koranic schools are financed by the students' families and still enroll many children. As mentioned above, under 50 percent of children enroll in state schools. Only 0.7 percent of all pupils attend private schools. These schools are based on modern models of education and all are located in Nouakchott.

The illiteracy rate is very high: 61 percent of the population over ten years of age is illiterate. About 70 percent of women are illiterate. Less than 10 percent of the population possess any form of education certificate. Half of this 10 percent do not even have the BEPC—the certificate awarded at the end of the first cycle of secondary school. Those with higher education qualifications represent 0.22 percent of the active population. Only 0.69 percent have a baccalaureate, 0.38 percent have a DEUG (two years of university education), and 0.03 percent possess a doctorate.

The financial constraints must be borne in mind when considering the educational system. The national debt is very high. The interest needed to service the debt in the period 1989 to 1991 was the equivalent of 37 percent of all benefits and services. State expenditures had to be reduced by this amount. Education expenditures come from the state budget.

2. Politics and the Goals of the Education System

The creation of democratic institutions was achieved with the first pluralistic elections in the country (President of the Republic, National Assembly, and Senate) in 1992. The aims of the state system of education are laid down by the government. The educational system has both a cultural and economic aim: cultural in the sense of the Arabization of the system and economic in the sense of training workers of different levels to create the human capital required for economic development.

As already stated, the Arabization of the system has been in progress since Independence and has nearly been achieved. However, with the institution of a multiparty system, the issue of using the French language as a medium of instruction was raised again and represents one of the major points of difference between those political parties in government and those in opposition. The opposition parties propose keeping French as a working language. The government parties advocate, in accordance with the constitution, the exclusive use of Arabic.

Mauritania has subscribed to the aims of the World Conference on Education for All (WCEFA) and particularly to education for all by the year 2000. However, because of the increase in the size of the educational system since Independence and because of the constraint of structural adjustment the most immediate priorities are:

(a) speeding up the expansion of primary education and the improvement of its quality and relevance;

(b) improving the internal and external effectiveness of the educational system by investigating ways and means of fitting the educational system to the needs and demands of national development;

(c) improving the organizational capacity, planning, management, and supervision of all educational activities.

3. The Formal System of Education

3.1 Primary, Secondary, and Tertiary Education

Figure 1 presents the structure of the formal education system and Table 1 presents key statistics on enrollment and resources. Schooling consists of three levels: primary school and two cycles of secondary school stretching, in theory, from the ages of 7 to 18 years.

Children enter a six-year primary school at 7 or 8

Table 1
Enrollments and resources in formal education, Mauritania 1991

	Primary	Secondary	Schools Technical	Normal	Higher
Number of students	166,036	35,221	800	676	5,339
Percentage of age group enrolled					
7–12 years	45%	—	—	—	—
7–14 years	25%	—	—	—	—
Number of institutions	1,253	51	2	2	6
Average number of students/institution	133	690	400	338	890
Student–teacher ratio	45:1	17:1	7:1	15:1	26:1
Expenditure per student	UM8,467	UM3,503	—	—	UM150,000

years of age. At the end of primary school pupils can obtain a CEP (Certificate of Primary Studies) and/or take a competitive examination to enter the first year of secondary school. In 1990–91, there were about 166,000 pupils enrolled in primary education. The medium of instruction for 92 percent of those enrolled in school was Arabic. The gross enrollment ratio was between 45 and 46 percent. There are large regional differences in enrollment. Nearly 40 percent of these pupils are enrolled in only two regions of which one is the capital city. Classrooms in the cities are crowded and have double sessions, while in the encampments most schools have only one classroom. The National Languages Institute is undertaking trial studies on the use of three national languages as media of instruction. This pilot work is limited to very few schools.

The secondary school is divided into two cycles. The first cycle lasts 3 years at the end of which students can take the BEPC (*Brevet d'Etude du Premier Cycle*). If they gain at least 10 out of 20 points, they may enter the second cycle—also of 3 years' duration—and at the end of which they may take the baccalaureate examination. If successful, they may apply to enter higher education. In 1990–91, the total number of students in the baccalaureate course was 35,221, of which 20,168 were in the first cycle. Girls represent 32 percent of all secondary school pupils. Some 78 percent of students were taught in Arabic and 22 percent were taught bilingually (i.e., Arabic and French). Most secondary schools are located in the regional capitals. The *collèges* have only the first cycle of education whereas the *lycées* have both the first and second cycles of secondary education. There are 25 *lycées* and 26

collèges throughout the country. Of these, 6 *lycées* and 4 *collèges* are in the capital city.

Higher education consists of training colleges and a university. To enter such institutions students must have passed the baccalaureate. After 2 or 4 years of study, students receive a diploma to become a second-cycle secondary school teacher (studying at the teacher-training college—*E[ac]cole Normale Supérieure*) or they obtain a bachelor's degree either at the *Institut Supérieur Scientifique* (ISS) or in one of the two faculties at the university (law and economics or arts and humanities).

In 1990–91, there were 5,339 students in higher education. Of these, 4,495 were enrolled in the university and 97 in the Advanced Center for Technical Studies (CSET). The rest were in training colleges. In the 1970s, most students went abroad for their higher education. By the beginning of the 1990s, this number had fallen to only about 2,000.

3.2 Preschool Education

Preschool education is relatively new and only to be found in the capital city. The cost of a child attending kindergarten is paid for by the parents. The cost varies from UM1,500 (US$13.3) to UM3,000 (ouguiyas) (US$26.5). In the state-run institutions the cost is UM1,500 (US$13.3) per month per child and instruction is in Arabic. These are for Mauritanians only. The kindergartens for the children of expatriates and a few Mauritanian families cost UM3,000 (US$26.5) per child per month and the instruction is in French.

3.3 Special Education

The National Union for Mentally and Physically Handicapped Persons (UNHPM) is the only institution providing training in special education. It has a braille school for blind people and a technical training institute for craft and administrative skills.

3.4 Vocational, Technical, and Business Education

Many people in Mauritania learn their skills on the job. Vocational and technical education runs parallel to secondary education. It is provided only in Nouakchott and Nouadhibou (the economic capital of the country). It is divided into two cycles. The first cycle lasts three years. At the end of the first cycle, a student may obtain a CAP (*Certificat d'Aptitudes Professionelles*) which is a type of vocational/technical diploma. This certificate also allows a student to enter the second cycle which also lasts 3 years. The examination at the end of this cycle is a technical baccalaureate. Again, if successful, the student may proceed to technical higher education.

In 1990–91, about 800 students were enrolled in technical education. Over 630 of these students were enrolled in Nouakchott where emphasis is on electrical engineering and the building trades. There are few girls

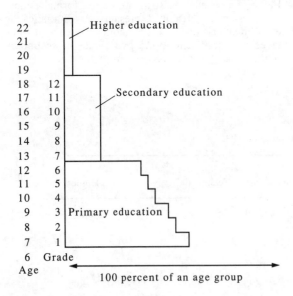

Figure 1
Mauritania: Structure of the formal education system

in this kind of education. Nearly 60 percent of the students are taught in both French and Arabic.

Vocational, technical, and business education is the weak part of the educational system despite the fact that skilled personnel are sorely needed in the economy. Training for jobs in the service sector has basically been taken over by the private sector. In 1991, the private sector was training over 1,500 students of whom just over 1,100 came from the state school system. However, there is no coordination between the different businesses, no supervision of the quality of the training, and no technical or educational assistance rendered by the state.

3.5 Adult and Nonformal Education

Adult education has received priority since 1988 when an office of a Secretary of State for the elimination of illiteracy was created. There are 700 permanent adult education centers. In 1990–91, over 18,000 persons were enrolled. About 70 percent of the learners were women. The language used for creating literate citizens is Arabic.

4. Administrative and Supervisory Structure and Operation

The Ministry of National Education is responsible for the development and implementation of the government's educational policy. A Higher Council for Education develops the educational objectives taking into account priorities established for economic development and the advice of various bodies, including technical counselors; two boards of inspectors (one for primary schools and one for secondary and technical schools); and the various directorates of the Ministry such as those for finance, curriculum, supervision, and primary, secondary, technical, and teacher education.

Primary education is managed and supervised at the regional level by the regional directorates of primary education (DREF) which are responsible to the directorate of primary education (DEF). The DREFs are responsible for ensuring that the schools function well, for the supervision of primary teachers, and for the posting of teachers to schools within the region.

The Ministry of Culture and Islamic Orientation provides training and supervision of the Mosque *Imans* and is also responsible for the AWGHAF foundation, a higher institute for Islamic studies. The Ministry of Public Works, Labor, Youth, and Sports has a directorate that is responsible for vocational and technical education institutes (CFPP) and the National School for Administration (ENA). This directorate was not fully operational in 1992.

5. Educational Finance

The proportion of the state budget allocated to national education rose from 18 percent in 1975 to approximately 23 percent in 1989. It was 21 percent in 1990. Nearly half of the education budget goes to primary education. Secondary education receives somewhat less and the remainder goes to other forms of education. The per-student expenditure is one of the highest in Africa. For primary education it is UM8,467 (US$75) (ouguiyas), for secondary UM35,034 (US$310), and for higher education students it is UM150,000 (US$1,327). At the primary and secondary levels 95 percent and 93 percent of their respective budgets are used for teacher salaries. The investment budget for 1990–91 was UM1,496 billion (US$13.25 billion). Just over 16.4 percent was devoted to the sector of human resources.

The self-financing of Koranic education cannot be quantified. In the encampments, students contribute to the cost of their education by doing fieldwork. In urban areas, students bring back to the master an agreed amount (typically UM40 or UM50) each day. This has led to the practice of begging behind trading centers, banks, and religious places. Some Koranic schools (*mahadras*) receive a state grant.

There is a lack of funding for the state education system and, although there has been some development of a private sector of education, the need for education far outstrips the funding available. This is and will continue to be a difficult problem to overcome.

6. Supplying Personnel for the Education System

Primary school teachers are trained in two teacher-training colleges (*Ecoles Nationales des Instituteurs*—ENI) in Nouakchott and Aioun. Entrants to the teacher-training colleges possess a BEPC or are from any level of the second cycle of secondary schools. The training course lasts 3 years in general, but only lasts 1 year for those possessing a baccalaureate. In 1990–91, 671 students were enrolled in the ENI. Just over 200 possessed a baccalaureate, 175 were girls, and 515 were instructed in Arabic.

Secondary school teachers are trained at the *Ecole Normale Supérieure* (ENS) and the course lasts 2 or 4 years. Entrants must possess a baccalaureate or a DEUG. Those already possessing a bachelor's degree only do a one-year course at the ENS.

In 1990–91, there were 3,741 teachers in primary schools, 2091 in secondary schools, 115 in technical education, 47 on the faculty of teacher-training institutes, and 206 faculty members in higher education. Of the total number of teachers in secondary and primary education, 16 were women. Those using Arabic as the medium of instruction constituted 66 percent of all teachers in primary and secondary school. The minimum age of teachers in secondary education is 28 years.

Teacher boards have been created for providing further training in the field at the primary and secondary school levels of education. To become a member of a board, teachers must already be qualified and have had two years of practical experience followed by a supervisory period. Teachers with diplomas from foreign universities can gain access to a teacher board after recognition by the Diploma Equivalence Commission. Teaching boards are relatively new and the members have relatively little experience.

Despite the fact that a bonus has been awarded to teachers and that an attempt has been made to give more social prestige to the job, many teachers end their careers early in order to earn more money in other sectors of the economy.

7. Curriculum Development

Syllabuses are developed by the National Education Service. They are the same for all schools. Textbooks are prepared and supplied by the National Education Institute. Their availability in the schools is, however, very variable depending on subject area, the distribution mechanism, and the extent to which care is taken of them in the schools. Only one in ten pupils owns a book. About 80 percent of teachers have no teacher guide book. The syllabuses and content of the textbooks are often too theoretical and too general. Teachers often use teacher handbooks from wherever they can get them and this results, in practice, in great heterogeneity of what is actually taught in the classrooms.

At the secondary school level 39 percent of all secondary school pupils are enrolled in the humanities track, 44 percent in the natural sciences track, and 17 percent in the mathematics track. At the higher education level only 10 percent of students are enrolled in mathematics: of these, 1.7 percent are girls.

As mentioned above, French is still used as a medium of instruction in some schools despite the policy of Arabization. French is studied as a foreign language in secondary school. English is introduced in the first grade of the second cycle of secondary education.

8. The System of Examinations, Promotions, and Certifications

Before commenting on the system of promotion, it must be mentioned that less than half of the 7- to 12-year old population goes to school. If one takes the 7- to 14-year old population, only 25 percent go to school. The dropout rate in primary school is high. Of 100 pupils entering Grade 1, only 81 proceed to the second year, 71 to the third year, 69 to the fourth year, 73 to the fifth year, 72 to the sixth year, and only 27 graduate from the primary school.

Promotion from one grade level to the next is dependent on success in a school-set examination. To move from one cycle of education to another, students must succeed in an externally set competitive examination. The BEPC is not a sufficient condition for access to the second cycle of secondary education because a

student must have at least 10 out of 20 points. The baccalaureate is a sufficient condition for entry to university. External national examinations are organized by the relevant department of the National Ministry of Education.

9. Educational Assessment, Evaluation, and Research

There is relatively little educational research. The National Languages Institute conducts pilot studies on the use of national languages as media of instruction. The National Education Institute conducts research on teaching methods in the basic subjects of arithmetic, Arabic, natural sciences, and French. There is no testing for national assessment. Educational evaluation is conducted only by teachers using very traditional methods.

10. Major Reforms from 1960 to 1990

There have been four reforms since 1960. The first, in 1960, began the movement to have Arabic as the language of instruction. The second, in 1967, continued the emphasis on Arabic and defined the duration and content of the various cycles of the educational system. The third, in 1979, continued its efforts to have the country's official language as the language of instruction. It reduced the length of primary schooling from 7 to 6 years and that of the first cycle of secondary education from 4 to 3 years. The 1978 reform made Arabic compulsory as the medium of instruction but with French being allowed at certain levels.

11. Major Problems for the Year 2000

The Mauritanian education system is confronted by a vast number of problems. There is a low percentage of the population going to school and there is a high level of dropout. There is still the problem of there being two languages of instruction which increases costs. In addition, most of the population is illiterate.

There are too many students enrolled in the humanities tracks and an insufficient number in the scientific and mathematics tracks. The content of the curriculum is not appropriate for the needs of a developing country. There is too little vocational and technical education. Girls are underrepresented at school. There are serious quarrels and debates which continue about the reforms in the educational system. Social prestige is still given to those with academic titles even though their knowledge and skills are of little, if any, use to the practical development of the economy.

This is a bleak picture and given the lack of funding

it is clear that it is unrealistic to believe that Mauritania can achieve universal primary education by the year 2000. These problems are worrying. The development of education and the improvement of its quality will necessarily have to rely on the capacity of the state to define a policy of reallocation of resources, a more efficient use of such resources, and an increase in the private financing of education.

References

Ministry of Education 1989 *Statistical Yearbook of National Education*. Ministry of National Education, Nouakchott

Ministry of Education 1990a *Statistical Yearbook of National Education*. Ministry of National Education, Nouakchott

Ministry of Education 1990b *Expert Planner 1990*, activity report term no. 5. Directorate of Planning and Cooperation, Ministry of National Education, Nouakchott

National Office of Statistics 1989 *Statistical Yearbook of Mauritania 1989*. National Office of Statistics, Nouakchott

UNDP 1991 *Fifth-cycle program per country 1992–1996: Sector-based program for Mauritania*. UNDP, Nouakchott

Further Reading

Baduel P R 1990 *Mauritanie, entre Arabité et Africanité, Revue de Monde Musulman et de la Mediterranée*. Edition EDISUD, Aix en Provence

Ousmane D A 1982 Système productif et système éducatif en Afrique (Doctoral thesis, University of Dijon)

Mauritius

S. Munbodh

1. General Background

Mauritius, an island in the Indian Ocean, has a democratic system of government based on the British pattern and a system of education which has also developed from the British pattern. The island is of volcanic origin, and has an area of 1,864 square kilometers. The first school was opened around 1767 and, by 1992, more than 97 percent of the primary school age-group was in school. The 1980s was a period of rapid development when the mass of unemployed was absorbed by the economy. The changing social and economic structure put a lot of pressure on the education system and prompted a review of the whole system. A master plan for the development of education to the end of the century was published in 1991.

Although Mauritius was visited by the Arabs and Portuguese during the sixteenth century, it was first settled by the Dutch (1598–1710), who remained for about a century. In the early eighteenth century, French colonists and forced labor from Madagascar and Africa settled on the island. In the early nineteenth century, the French used the country as a base to fight the British in the Indian Ocean and even in India. In 1810, the British conquered the island and made it a British colony. With the abolition of slavery in 1834, the emancipated labor left their former masters, and labor (mainly from India) was brought in to cultivate the fields. The country became independent in 1968 and a republic in 1992. It is a member of the British Commonwealth.

By 1990, the country had a network of 1,865 kilometers of tarred road, and communication between schools and the Ministry of Education and other organizations is easy. School supplies are easily transported and the relatively good transport system allows teachers to travel to and from school daily. Tap water and electricity are available all over the island. Most of the schools have telephones. National radio and television broadcasts cover the entire country.

In 1993, the estimated population of Mauritius was 1,098,000 and the population density was 638 per square kilometer. After the eradication of malaria in the 1950s, the annual population growth rate rose to 3.1 percent. This declined over the years and by 1993 it was 1.20 percent. This reduction in growth rate—due mainly to better education, better health care, and aspiration for a better quality of life—made the provision of education to all citizens less difficult.

Mauritius is a multiracial, multilingual, and pluricultural country with people whose ancestors came as settlers from Europe, Africa, and Asia. It is a country where the official language is English, the officially spoken one is very often French, the common *lingua franca* is Creole, and in the home it can be Bhojpuri, Hindi, Urdu, Tamil, Telegu, or Mandarin, among others. The teaching of the different languages and the level at which they should be introduced in the school curriculum has always been controversial. Children start studying English, French, and an Asian language in their primary schools.

The country has very few natural resources. Its main economic activity was the production of sugar for export, mostly to the European Economic Community until the late 1970s. Its situation in the cyclonic belt renders such an economy very fragile. In the 1970s, the government established an export processing zone in an effort to create more employment. In the 1980s, manufacturing and tourism were also promoted. In 1958, sugar accounted for 34.2 percent of the gross national product (GNP) and represented 99 percent of Mauritian export. In 1993, the share of agriculture in the gross domestic product (GDP) was 9.97 percent and represented 21 percent of gross export earnings, while manufacturing accounted for 23 percent of GDP and represented 70 percent of gross export earnings. Gross earnings from tourism stood at Rs5,200 million in 1993. The country, which has a relatively educated population, is diversifying its industrial base and is making special efforts to develop the service sector. In 1993, the estimated GDP at factor cost was Rs44,900 million and the workforce in large establishments numbered 288,600 or about two-thirds of the total workforce.

There was a dramatic increase in employment in the 1980s. It was largely attributed to the buoyancy of the manufacturing sector. Employment in that sector grew at an average annual rate of 14 percent in the period 1983 to 1993. The female share in total employment increased from 22.7 percent in 1983 to 38 percent in 1993. In 1994, the percentage of labor working in the primary, secondary, and tertiary sectors was 14.2, 45, and 40.8 respectively.

Historically, Mauritius has placed a great premium on education, which has resulted in high social mobility in the population. In July 1983, unemployment stood at 71,681 with 62 percent having only between one and six years of education and 13.3 percent having at least the Cambridge School Certificate. In 1993, unemployment was reduced to 1,184 with 61 percent having one to six years of education and 13 percent with the Cambridge School Certificate. An educational profile of those employed is not available. However, it is noted that the level of education of the unemployed has increased.

Mauritius has reached a stage in its development where the quality and relevance of the education it provides to its people will determine its competitiveness in the world market. An Education Sector Master Plan was prepared in 1991 to improve the quality of education at the the primary and secondary levels and to increase institutional capacity at the tertiary level. It is in the process of being implemented.

Mauritius has a democratic system of government with the President as head of state and the Prime Minister as head of the government. The parliament is made up of 70 members with 24 ministers with responsibilities for the different sectors. The Ministry of Education and Science has responsibility for the education sector and is accountable to Parliament which approves its budget. The Education Act of 1957, which has subsequently been amended, provides legislation for uniformity of provision of education facilities all over the island. The centralized administrative structure for education has been quite successful in managing the system. However, since the end of the 1970s, attempts have been made to decentralize the administration and supervision of education.

2. Politics and the Goals of the Education System

More than two centuries ago, education was available to the French settlers, but not to the slaves and the labor class. Gradually, the government took over the responsibility for education and nonfee-paying primary education was introduced for a small group of the population as far back as 1815. The emancipated slaves and the laboring class quickly discovered that one of the basic preconditions for their complete liberation was education. Thus, political parties which were formed to defend the rights of the laboring class gave high priority to the education of the classes they represented. The Labour Party, formed in 1936, included the following provisions among its objectives for education:

(a) free primary education for all;

(b) free medical service for everyone attending school;

(c) mid-day meals and shoes for the pupils;

(d) better physical and recreational facilities.

Prior to 1948, the right to vote at general elections was limited to those who were owners of property. In 1947, the British government gave the right to vote to all those who could sign their name in any language. Sociocultural organizations launched campaigns to teach the working class to read and write and to sign their names. This measure increased the thirst for education among all workers. By 1949, the primary school population had increased to 5,315. The *Parti Mauricien* was formed in 1955 to safeguard the interests of the ruling class. With the advent of universal suffrage in 1959, the electorate returned the Labour Party with an overwhelming majority to the Legislative Council.

With the introduction of universal suffrage, a change in the social policies of the right-wing parties occurred. They also pledged to provide access to education to a larger proportion of the population. The difference between the goals of the political parties was reduced and they all vowed to provide better education, better health care, and better living conditions for the population.

The goals of education, as stated in all the development plans since independence in 1968, lay stress on:

(a) equality of opportunity;

(b) a diversified curriculum;

(c) promotion of science, technical, and vocational education;

(d) improvement of the quality of education.

Prior to 1977, secondary education was fee-paying

for all except for the few students who benefited from state scholarships. From 1977, education was made nonfee-paying at all levels, including the tertiary level. In 1978, a major policy decision was taken by the government which restricted access to secondary schools to those who had passed the end-of-primary cycle examination. Thus, about one-third of the population, who did not succeed in the Certificate of Primary Education examination, was provided with facilities for an alternative type of education under the Community School Project. The alternative was a three-year school, run in the afternoon in junior-secondary school buildings, which laid stress on the learning of practical subjects like woodwork, metalwork, cookery, sewing, and agriculture. The project did not meet with great success and was abandoned in 1982.

A 1984 White Paper gave a new orientation to the education system. Greater emphasis was placed on the review of the curriculum, examinations, and teaching methodology to adapt them to the changing needs of the country. Subsequently, international seminars were organized to obtain inputs on the different sectors of education to help redefine the goals of the education system. Inputs were obtained from UNDP, UNESCO, the World Bank, and the ILO, and a master plan for the development of education was published in 1991. The main aim of the plan is to improve the quality and relevance of education at all levels.

At the tertiary level, a university was set up in 1965, an institute of education in 1973, and the School for Oriental and African Studies, based at the Mahatma Gandhi Institute, in 1976. In 1988, the Tertiary Education Commission was set up to plan, coordinate, and monitor education at the tertiary level. The goals of the education system are published in the development plan, and relevant legislation is passed to enable the goals to be translated into operational terms. In 1991, education was made compulsory to the age of 12 years. It is to be noted that individual needs differ from the needs of the community. While all the plans stressed the need for science education, the number studying science has been declining, especially since 1982. At the lower levels, more stress is laid on the overall development of the child, while at the higher levels the goals are much nearer to the socioeconomic needs of the country.

3. The Formal System of Education

Responsibility for education is vested in the Ministry of Education and Science. Education is free at the primary level, the secondary level up to the age of 20 years, and since 1993–94 a fee is charged for part-time courses at the University. The country has a 6-5-2 education system as represented in Figure 1.

As from 1991, education has been compulsory from the ages of 5 to 12 years. The enrollment ratio

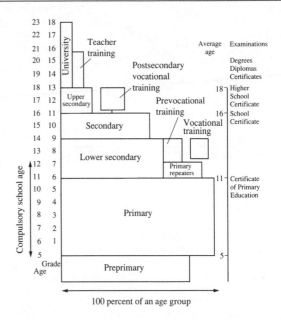

Figure 1
Mauritius: Structure of the formal education system

between these ages is estimated to be more than 95 percent.

3.1 Primary, Secondary, and Tertiary Education

Primary education lasts six years for most pupils and a seventh year for those who are unsuccessful at the Certificate of Primary Education (CPE) examinations. A large proportion of those pupils who are not successful after a second attempt at the CPE examinations, but who have acquired some reading, writing, and counting skills, can move to the pre-vocational training centers run by the Industrial and Vocational Training Board. These centers provide courses in English, French, and mathematics, and in practical subjects like agriculture, electricity, home economics, metalwork, and woodwork. Those leaving the PVT Centers join the apprenticeship system or Vocational Training Centers. Those who pass the CPE examinations are admitted to secondary schools where, after five years, they take the Cambridge School Certificate examinations.

Enrollment at the primary level, which amounted to 117,591 in 1961, reached 125,543 in the 281 schools in 1993 after peaking at 151,614 in 1972. More than 90 percent of the children attend the 223 government and 53 government-aided primary schools with the remainder attending the 5 non-aided private schools.

Some 97 percent of the primary school age population are at school. Dropout is negligible at the primary level. All primary schools are coeducational. The pri-

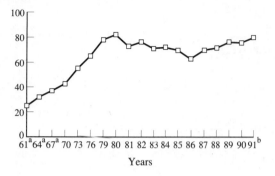

Figure 2
Mauritius: Secondary school enrollment 1961–91

mary school day normally lasts for six hours, including recreation time, and the school year is around 185 days in length.

Secondary education lasts five years, at the end of which students take the Cambridge School Certificate. Students obtaining a minimum of four credits in these examinations and who are below 19 years of age on December 31 of the previous year qualify for the two-year Higher School Certificate course. Students normally start secondary school at about age 12. Enrollment at the secondary level has improved and about 50 percent of a particular cohort reach the School Certificate level and 12 percent, the Higher School Certificate level.

Enrollment at the secondary level, which was 24,851 in 1961 increased to 87,661 in the 123 schools in 1993. A total of 23 of the 123 schools are state-owned, catering for 20 percent of the school population, while 97 are aided with 79 percent of the enrollment. There are also 3 private non-aided schools with about 1 percent of the enrollment. Only 20 percent of the facilities obtained in the private schools compare favorably with the facilities in state schools. Figure 2 presents the enrollment data from 1961.

The secondary school completion rate is higher for girls than for boys because the examinations are still testing the lower cognitive abilities where girls do better. There are 50 coeducational schools and 73 single-sex schools, of which 34 are for girls. The secondary school year has 185 days, with an average of 5.5 hours of tuition per day.

The tertiary sector comprises the Mauritius College of the Air (MCA), the Mahatma Ghandhi Institute (MGI), and the University. There are a number of training centers offering postsecondary training to about 11,500 persons in electronics, the hospitality industry, textiles, electrical and mechanical engineering and building construction, and management and business education. The Mauritius Institute of Education is the only teacher-training institution and its enrollment for 1993 was 1,512. Of these, 1,318 followed award courses while 992 followed nonaward courses. Over 80 percent of the enrollment was part-time, with 134 students following postgraduate certificate courses in

1992. The minimum requirement for entry to the certificate courses is a good Cambridge School Certificate, while for the diploma and degree courses, it is the Cambridge Higher School Certificate.

Prior to 1990, the University of Mauritius provided certificate, diploma, and degree courses only in agriculture, administration, and technology. With the growing demand for a better qualified labor force, the University has diversified its courses and, as from 1992, it offers certificate, diploma, degree, and higher degree courses in its five faculties—Agriculture, Engineering, Science, Law and Management, and Social Studies and Humanities. The enrollment, which was 470 in 1980, increased to 1,799 in 1991.

Another institution, the Mahatma Gandhi Institute, also runs certificate and diploma courses in fields such as music and dance, oriental and African cultures, and fine arts.

In 1991, the total enrollment in higher education was 3,626 representing more than five times the 1981 figures. A large proportion of the students follow part-time courses. Much of this increase is due to the higher number completing the Higher School Certificate and the development of the economy requiring a better educated and trained workforce. Competition for entry to the higher education institutions is fierce and many secondary school leavers go overseas (mostly to India, France, Canada, Australia, and South Africa) for further studies.

3.2 Preschool Education

The majority of 4-year olds attend the 1,400 privately run preprimary schools offering a variety of curricula and run very often in substandard buildings. The school day lasts from a few hours to more than six hours. A small proportion (about 20%) of 3-year olds attend playgroups or half-day preprimary centers.

The aim of the government, which runs some 71 preprimary centers, is to have all children of preschool age in good quality centers by the year 2000. The government provides counseling services, a toy and reference library, and training opportunities to those running the preprimary centers.

3.3 Special Education

Special education programs are provided for children with physical or intellectual disabilities. At the end of the 1980s and beginning of the 1990s the number of children aged 3 to 18 years with one or more disabilities was estimated at around 6,000. Children with minor handicaps tend to be in the normal primary and secondary schools. Some of the children with moderate to severe handicaps are educated in special schools such as the school for the blind, the school for the deaf, schools for subnormal children, and schools for the handicapped. These centers are mostly operated by nongovernmental organizations, aided by the government, and are located in the urban area. Pupils from rural areas have difficulty attending them because of transport problems. A shortage of devoted and trained staff, proper equipment, and physical infrastructure further slows down the growth of special schools.

The Trust Fund for the Disabled, set up by the government in 1988, sponsors trainees for institutional and on-the-job training. The idea is to integrate the disabled into the normal work environment.

3.4 Vocational, Technical, and Business Education

Mauritius has a long history of vocational education. As far back as the nineteenth century, vocational training was provided through apprenticeship in horticulture, mechanical engineering, and needlework. However, technical education which was meant for the working class never flourished.

Several attempts were made in the 1960s and 1970s to provide vocational education to primary and secondary school leavers through the setting up of central schools, senior-primary schools, junior-technical schools, and junior-secondary schools, but never with much success. These types of schools came to be perceived as for those who either dropped out of the academic stream or who could not pay to attend secondary schools prior to 1977 when secondary education was fee paying. Such an approach to technical education, compounded by the lack of proper physical facilities, equipment, and materials, further handicapped its development.

The high rate of unemployment among school leavers and the rapid industrialization of the country in the early 1980s led to a change in parental, community, and student attitudes toward vocational education. The creation of the first proper technical education school in 1982 also helped to change attitudes, and by 1990 abler students were opting for the study of technical subjects. Many secondary schools offer accountancy, commerce, and economics, which are in high demand in the labor market. Some schools offer technical subjects like craft, design, and technology; fashion and fabrics; food and nutrition; and so on. As from 1988, students can sit for the Business School Certificate or the Technical School Certificate in addition to the academic School Certificate.

The setting up of the Industrial and Vocational Training Board (IVTB) in 1989, a parastatal organization, further boosted the learning of technical and commercial subjects. The IVTB has four main objectives:

(a) to advise the Minister on matters relating to training;

(b) to monitor the needs for training in consultation with relevant authorities;

(c) to administer, control, and operate training schemes;

(d) to provide for, promote, assist in, and regulate the training or apprenticeship of persons who are or will be employed in the commercial, technical, or vocational fields.

The IVTB promotes training in all sectors of the economy and at all levels. Traditionally, training for the only major industry—the sugar industry—was on-the-job. The first industrial trade training institution was set up in 1968. In 1992, the IVTB—managed by a council made up of an equal number of members from the private and public sectors—set up a system to encourage more industry-based training with a greater involvement of the private sector. Many industries, in addition to sending their workers to training institutions, have set up their own training centers. The levy-grant system operated by the IVTB has enhanced training geared toward the acquisition of new skills and increasing productivity. From a relatively low level, the number of persons following a training course jumped to around 14,000 in one year. This figure is expected to increase further.

3.5 Adult and Nonformal Education

With the country diversifying its economic activity and moving rapidly toward industrialization, adult participation in education is increasing. In 1991, it was estimated that 5,000 mature students attended education and training courses. Nonformal education plays an important role in the development of the country and many different courses are organized outside normal school hours. Some 3,000 to 4,000 attend nonformal education courses.

Adult education classes are run by the government, the municipalities, and by charitable and private organizations. Courses include science and technical subjects, cookery, dressmaking, homecraft, shorthand, typing, secretarial courses, and numeracy and literacy. These classes aim at providing an opportunity to those who could not benefit from the formal education system and to those who wish to carry on self-learning.

The thirst for more education among the people and the efforts made by the different communities to preserve their cultural identities led to the further development of the nonformal education sector. Classes in oriental languages subsidized by the government are held in representative cultural institution halls and clubs and are attended outside school hours by children of the different ethnic groups.

4. Administrative and Supervisory Structure and Operation

Education is the responsibility of the government, which enacts laws pertaining to all levels of education. Within these laws, the Ministry of Education and

Science determines the policy and requirements for the different levels of education.

The permanent secretary, the responsible officer of the Ministry, is the adviser to the minister. The Ministry of Education and Science administers the government schools, and the Roman Catholic Education Authority and the Hindu Education Authority the government-aided schools.

At the preprimary level nearly all schools are private. At the primary level less than 1 percent of the enrollment attends private fee-paying schools; the rest are in government and government-aided schools. At the secondary level, as from 1977, education was made nonfee-paying even in private schools. The Private Secondary Schools Authority, a parastatal body set up in 1977, is responsible for the administration of the government grant for these schools, as well as the supervision of education. There are four private non-aided secondary schools managed by a trust which cater for 1 percent of the enrollment.

At the tertiary level, different institutions are managed by councils or boards set up by the government for that purpose. They are all funded by the government.

Since the early 1980s, education has been nonfee-paying at all levels to provide access for a much larger proportion of the population. University education is free, except for part-time courses which are fee-paying since 1993–94.

5. Educational Finance

Education in Mauritius is financed principally by the government. In 1968, at independence, the share of the budget devoted to education was Rs30.9 million which represented 10.9 percent of government spending and 3.7 percent of GDP. The percentage of the total budget devoted to education varied little until 1976, when about 92 percent of secondary school pupils attended private fee-paying aided schools.

In 1977, education was made nonfee-paying and the education budget increased to 17 percent of government expenditure. In 1990–91, it stood at 14 percent. Rs1,440.2 million or 13.4 percent for 1992–93 of recurrent government expenditure was devoted to education in the same year. The sectoral allocation is presented in Table 1.

The existence of different types of school, mostly at the secondary level, combined with the desire of parents to see their children in a good school, encourages competition throughout the system. Nearly all parents have recourse to private tuition for their children and this considerably inflates the private expenditure devoted to education. A study carried out in 1988 revealed that an average of Rs500 million is spent on private tuition each year. One of the private non-aided secondary schools levies a fee of Rs21,000 per student per annum.

Since 1989 the government provides free textbooks to all primary school children, in addition to free meals. At the secondary level, the needy students—about 1 percent of the population—benefit from a similar scheme. At the tertiary level, the students buy their own requisites.

An extremely ambitious plan has been worked out for the development of education at all levels, and an estimated investment of Rs600 million will be made in the next few years to improve the infrastructure and equipment to give a boost to science and technical education.

6. Supplying Personnel for the Education System

Some 10,240 teachers work in the primary and secondary schools with an additional nonteaching staff of 4,150. Of the 6,500 teachers at the primary level, 80 percent are in government schools and most of the rest are in aided schools. Of the 3,740 teachers at the secondary level, 74 percent are in the aided schools. Some 1,500 teachers work at the preprimary level with 90 percent being either self-employed or working for

Table 1
Government recurrent expenditure by sector of education 1992–93

Sector	Amount[a] (Rs m)	Percentage	Annual per unit cost in Rs
Primary	541.2	37.6	4,367
Secondary	574.1	39.9	7,000
Tertiary	133.5	9.3	40,320
Technical/Vocational	33.5	2.3	12,602
Unallocated	157.9	10.9	—
Total	1,440.2[b]	100.0	

a in millions of Rs   b estimate

an individual. Teachers for the government primary and secondary schools are recruited by the Public Service Commission. Those working at the primary level follow a compulsory two-year preservice training course at the Mauritius Institute of Education (MIE), which took over the function of the Teacher's Training College founded in 1902. Compulsory inservice courses are also organized for teachers. Teachers for science and technical subjects are more difficult to recruit.

Prior to the setting up of the Mauritius Institute of Education in 1973, teachers for the secondary level had to go abroad for their training, and only a small percentage of the teachers were qualified and trained. Teachers employed at the secondary level are increasingly following certificate, diploma, and graduate courses run by the institute. About 3,000 of the secondary school teachers were trained between 1980 to 1990. The University runs a three-year degree course for diploma holders to increase their educational competence.

In 1993, the pupil–teacher ratio at the primary and secondary levels were 29:1 and 22:1 respectively. The job market for teachers has declined as the school population has not been increasing. Teaching jobs at school are scarce.

There is a system of confidential assessment of the teachers carried out by the head of the school and inspectorate to diagnose the weaknesses of the teachers. Considerable effort is being made by the government to improve and update the quality of the teaching force. The possibilities offered by distance education will be better utilized in addition to workshops and seminars which are organized to help teachers and the managers of education.

7. Curriculum Development and Teaching Methodology

The Ministry of Education and Science has overall responsibility for curriculum implementation in all the schools. The Curriculum Development Center, operating under the aegis of the Mauritius Institute of Education, collaborates with the Ministry to plan and develop new curricula for the primary and secondary schools. The Secondary Curriculum Reform Project (1975–80) and the Primary Curriculum Development Project (1981–88) have been completed. A Continuous Assessment and Remedial Education Project (CARE) is in progress, and a Lower-secondary Curriculum Renewal Project was nearing completion in 1992.

The primary schools have a uniform curriculum. In addition to English, French, mathematics, environmental studies, needlework, and handicrafts, the children have an opportunity to study one of the following languages: Hindi, Tamil, Telegu, Marathi, Urdu, Arabic, or Mandarin. The teaching of languages occupies a large share of the timetable. The amount of time given

for each language and the level at which it should be introduced is much debated. Learning of different languages starts as from Standard 1.

At the lower-secondary level, students follow a core curriculum including English, French, mathematics, environmental studies, physical education, and integrated science, and choose from the following optional subjects: agriculture, arts and crafts, home economics, commerce, music and dance, and one additional language. At the middle-secondary level, the curriculum varies with the facilities available at the schools and is biased toward the teaching of nonpractical subjects. It is also conditioned by the University of Cambridge Local Examination Syndicate (UCLES), which has increased the subject options available to students to about 70. New subjects, like fashion and fabrics, food and nutrition, education for life, family life education, design technology, and design communications, have been introduced. In primary schools, a class teacher is responsible for the teaching of all subjects except for the Asian languages, which are taught by specialist teachers. At the secondary level, subject specialists are used.

Teaching materials for the implementation of the curriculum at the primary level and the lower-secondary level are prepared by the Mauritius Institute of Education and are prescribed by the Ministry of Education and Science. In addition to the prescribed materials, teachers also have recourse to books and question papers produced by individual local authors to help them in their teaching. At the upper-secondary level, books prescribed by the UCLES and imported from abroad are mostly used.

A major criticism about the curriculum is that it is overloaded, and teachers and pupils, mainly at the primary level, are not able to cope with it. A National Center for Curriculum Research and Development has been set up to review the curriculum constantly and to adapt it to the needs of the pupils and the country and for use by the teachers.

8. The System of Examinations, Promotions, and Certifications

Pupils sit for national and international examinations at the end of each cycle. At the primary level, promotion from one grade to the next is automatic until Grade 6 when the pupils sit for the Certificate of Primary Education (CPE) examination. Promotion throughout the system has been described in Section 3 above.

The present system of examination does not promote the learning of nonexaminable subjects and the overall development of the child. It lays stress on the acquisition of cognitive skills. The system of recruitment and promotion from one level to the other is based on certification, with much importance attached to the national and international certificate—the latter awarded by the University of Cambridge Local Examination Syndicate and the University of London. As a result, international examinations dominate the curriculum. Learning is geared toward the acquisition of skills and abilities to move to the higher grade.

9. Educational Assessment, Evaluation, and Research

Internal assessment of the performance of pupils by means of oral and written tests and homework is a regular feature of the system for remediation. Such an activity is left to the school. However, performance of the pupils at the end-of-cycle examinations shows that not all schools are carrying out such remediation properly. In an attempt to improve the internal efficiency of the system and the performance of the pupils, the government has planned a national assessment at Grade 3 to diagnose the slow learners who will be directed to a four-year course instead of the three years normally required to complete the CPE. Continuous assessment will also be introduced and will carry a weight of 20 percent of the total mark for the award of the CPE certificate.

By 1992, the only national means of assessment of literacy and numeracy levels remains the CPE examination which is used both for certification and for selection to secondary schools. There is a plan to introduce a new assessment scheme (Essential Learning Competency) to test the numeracy and literacy skills of the pupils for promotion to secondary schools.

There is no system of evaluation for accountability purposes in the schools. Since the setting of the Mauritius Examinations Syndicate (MES), a few research projects have been attempted. Issues such as the causes of failure at the primary level, the validity of the CPE examination, and the mechanics and methodology of evaluation studies have been covered and the findings are used to redefine educational policy. The MIE and the University of Mauritius have also carried out a few research projects on issues connected with curriculum development and private tuition to help reorient the education system. The research priorities for the 1990s are being defined by the Tertiary Education Commission.

Thus far, educational research has been undertaken on an ad hoc basis with no clear objectives. The budget has also been allocated on the same basis and, on the whole, less than 1 percent of the recurrent expenditure is estimated to be spent on research.

10. Major Reforms in the 1980s and 1990s

Attempts to vocationalize the education system started in the mid-1970s on the recommendation of the World

Bank, but were dropped. The capacity for teacher education, especially for the secondary level, was increased.

The primary school curriculum was reviewed and the lower-secondary school curriculum was "Mauritianized." Curriculum materials were produced locally and a uniform curriculum was implemented in all primary and lower-secondary schools.

The use of the shift system at the primary level was eliminated as a result of the construction of additional school buildings. Textbooks were made available free to all primary school children and to the needy at the secondary level. Enrollment in higher education increased between six and seven times in the 1980s and courses have been made available in a larger number of subjects.

The examination system is being reviewed to promote the learning of nonexaminable subjects, to test essential learning competencies, and to incorporate school-based assessment in the award of the CPE Certificate.

The Industrial and Vocational Training Board was set up to promote training and to improve the link between education and the world of work.

There are school places for primary and secondary level students. The major thrusts of the reforms in the 1990s will be directed to the improvement of the quality and relevance of education to the needs of the country at all levels, the provision of nine years of basic education to all, and the expansion of capacity at the tertiary level.

11. Major Problems for the Year 2000

Mauritius has reached a crucial stage in its socioeconomic development. The economy is warming up with almost frictional unemployment. It will thus be difficult for it to remain competitive with low-level education and skills. The changing socioeconomic conditions will put further pressure on the education system and the school curriculum. The major task to be tackled will be, at the primary level, the improvement of the efficiency of the system; at the secondary level, the promotion of science and technical education; and at the tertiary level, capacity building. The level of education and training of the whole population will have to be raised further.

Bibliography

Chinepeh V 1983 *Participation and Performance in Primary Schooling: A Study of Equality of Educational Opportunity in Mauritius*. Institute of International Education, University of Stockholm, Stockholm

Mauritius, Central Statistical Office 1990a *Annual Digest of Statistics 1990*. Central Statistical Office, Port Louis

Mauritius, Central Statistical Office 1990b *Digest of Educational Statistics 1990*. Central Statistical Office, Port Louis

Mauritius Institute of Education 1990 *Annual Report*. University of Mauritius, Reduit

Mauritius, Ministry for Civil Service Affairs and Employment, Employment Service Division 1991 *Statistical Review on Unemployment Jan–April 1991*. Government Printer, Port Louis

Mauritius, Ministry of Economic Planning and Development *National Development Plan 1988–90 Education*. Government Printer, Port Louis

Mauritius, Ministry of Economic Planning and Development 1991 *Economic Indicators No. 137, Survey of Employment and Earnings in Large Establishments*, 20 December. Government Printer, Port Louis

Mauritius, Ministry of Economic Planning and Development 1992 *Economic Indicators No. 138 Educational Statistics 1991*, 17 January. Government Printer, Port Louis

Mauritius, Minstry of Economic Planning and Development *National Development Plan 1992–94*. Government Printer, Port Louis

Mauritius, Ministry of Education *Annual Reports 1982/84, 1985/86, 1987/88*. Government Printer, Port Louis

Mauritius, Ministry of Education 1984 *White Paper on Education*. Government Printer, Port Louis

Mauritius, Ministry of Education 1991 *Masterplan for the Year 2000*. Government Printer, Port Louis

Ramdoyal R D 1977 *The Development of Education in Mauritius 1710–1976*. Mauritius Institute of Education, University of Mauritius, Reduit

University of Mauritius 1987 *Visitor to the University of Mauritius June 1987*. University of Mauritius, Reduit

University of Mauritius 1988 *The Private Costs of Education in Mauritius 1988*. Government Printer, Port Louis

University of Mauritius *Calendar 1991–1992*. University of Mauritius, Reduit

Mexico

M. E. Reyes

1. General Background

The United States of Mexico is a federal country located in the North American continent. It has a total area of nearly 2 million square kilometers. To the north it has a border of over 3,000 kilometers with the United States of America, and to the southeast it is bordered by Guatemala and British Honduras. To the east is the Gulf of Mexico and the Carribean Sea, and to the south and west there is the Pacific Ocean. Mexico has 31 states and one federal district. Each state is organized into municipalities of which there are 2,402 in the whole country.

Mexico has a population of 81.4 million inhabitants (1990 census). With one of the highest population growth rates in the world, Mexico has had more than a fivefold increase in its population since the beginning of the twentieth century, when the population was 15.1 million. Although in the period from 1970 to 1990, the annual population growth rate decreased, 60 percent of the population is under 24 years of age. An enormous effort was required to offer educational services to such an expanding population, and this explains why enrollment in the formal school system is only 31 percent of the total population.

The population is unevenly distributed. Population density in the states ranges from 43 to 5,500 inhabitants per square kilometer. The Federal District and one neighboring state include 22.2 percent of the total population. The percentage of the population living in urban areas increased from 42.2 in 1950 to 58.7 in 1970 to 71.3 in 1990. From 1970 to 1990 the percentage of the population living in cities of greater than 100,000 inhabitants increased from 23 to 44.4 percent.

Spanish is the official language, although more than 93 languages and dialects are still used by 5 million inhabitants, of whom nearly 1 million do not speak Spanish. Among the most important languages are the Mayan and the Nahuatl. Nearly 90 percent of the population is Roman Catholic.

The labor force comprised 24 million persons in 1990; of these, 19.6 percent were female. Nearly 23 percent of the active population was engaged in agriculture but contributed only 8 percent of the Gross Domestic Product (GDP). Some 28 percent of the labor force was in the secondary sector and 46 percent in the tertiary sector; these sectors contributed 23 and 52 percent to the GDP respectively.

Since the early 1980s, Mexico has gone through a series of transformations after the severe crisis triggered by the decline of oil prices at the beginning of the 1980s, and with and external debt burden of more than US$150 billion.

After joining GATT in 1986, Mexico moved away from protectionist policies to raise industry competitiveness. In 1993, it signed a commercial agreement (NAFTA) with the United States and Canada, which will start to operate in 1994.

The public sector deficit representing 16 percent of the GDP in 1987 was transformed into a financial surplus in 1993. Strong adjustments were made in terms of size and activities in the public sector. A large number of state-owned enterprisies were privatized, and changes in public expenditure resulted in increased resources towards social development.

Exports have changed since the early 1980s. In the early 1980's, oil exports accounted for a considerable proportion of total exports, but in 1992, although oil exports 18 percent of total exports, the manufacturing sector accounted for 77 percent.

Mexico has been able to negotiate its external debt successfully through the use of different mechanisms, and significant payments of the internal debt were made. The public net debt moved from a proportion of 62.4 percent of its GDP in 1988 to 28.4 percent in 1992.

After several years of high inflation and low or negative rates of growth, the economy achieved an annual economic growth rate higher than 3 percent from 1989, and single figure inflation is expected by 1993. However, there is still a strong unequal distribution of income. Furthermore, there was, in 1993, still the challenge to create more than 800,000 new jobs per year for a young and increasing population. The informal sector had increased considerably and the need to train workers was still on the agenda.

According to the results of the 1990 census, schooling levels for the total population were still low but 83 percent of the 15- to 19-year old age group had completed primary school. More than 10 percent of the population was still illiterate, with slightly more females than males being in this condition. However, only 4.3 percent of the 15- to 19-year olds were illiterate.

2. Politics and the Goals of the Education System

Goals for education were stated in Article 3 of the Constitution of 1917. They expressed a series of principles which embodied Mexican attitudes toward education and its role in society. Education should be integral, nationalist, humanist, objective, and democratic. It should be secular and free when provided by the state. The Constitution has passed through a series of reforms since 1917. In particular, in 1991–92, two modifications were passed. Strong objections had been made by some groups in Mexican society about the explicit prohibition of religious corporations to offer education. The Constitution was amended to eliminate this restriction. Secularity was maintained as a principle but not applied to private schools. The conflict was not completely solved. There are still some groups in favor of eliminating completely the declaration about the secular character of education.

Education in Mexico is provided mainly through public schools at all levels. The federal government is responsible for establishing and supervising the implementation of curricula in primary and secondary education, teacher-training institutions, and all education provided to workers and peasants. Provision of educational services and the recognition of studies offered by private educational institutions and schools are shared among the federal government, the state, and municipal governments.

In 1992, the length of compulsory education was lengthened from 6 to 9 years in recognition of the need to raise the level of schooling of the Mexican population. As from 1993, the federal government ceded to state governments the running of all preschools, primary and secondary schools, and teacher-training institutes, except in the Federal District.

From the 1950s onwards there was a tremendous expansion of educational opportunities. Nevertheless there are still strong disparities among regions. To reduce educational inequalities, specific programs were launched to increase coverage (i.e., the percentage of an age-group in school) and retention in basic education of the less privileged states and in primary schools in all states with high rates of retention and dropout.

Raising the quality of education, a long-time declared objective, created efforts to revise the curricula in basic education and to improve substantially the working conditions of teachers and the frequency and quality of inservice teacher-training programs. An explicit policy of greater participation of communities and parents in the school itself will result in new forms of organization and cooperation.

Public higher education institutions are facing serious problems in quality and a downturn in prestige which can be explained by several factors. These include the enormous increase in student enrollment without a sufficient number of well-prepared faculty members, the outflow of teachers and researchers because of the low salaries and poor conditions both for teachers and researchers, and the low academic level of students entering the system. In addition, higher education has not been able to attract candidates for careers which are considered basic for future economic growth. Different schemes have been explored for the evaluation and self-evaluation of institutions that could lead to an increase in quality. The establishment of a

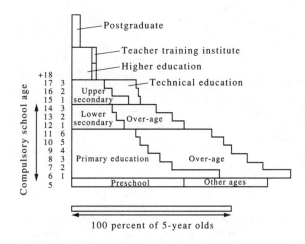

Figure 1
Mexico: Structure of the formal education system 1993

National System of Researchers has allowed researchers to benefit from complementary income through an evaluation process of their research programs.

3. The Formal System of Education

Figure 1 presents the structure of the formal educational system and proportions of age-groups attending different cycles.

Children can attend preschool from the age of 4 years, but it is expected that 5-year olds will have already completed one preschool year before entering primary education. As the figure shows, 72.5 percent of 5-year olds and 46.7 percent of 4-year olds are in preschool.

The official entrance to primary education is at 6 years of age but, in effect, children can start to attend the formal system between 6 and 14 years of age. Although late-comers to primary education have been reduced almost to zero, repetition rates and re-entrance have brought about a considerable proportion of over-age pupils in each grade (more than 30%) as can be seen in Fig. 1. This phenomenon also occurs in subsequent cycles in the educational system.

The differences between nominal and real age of pupils makes it difficult to determine real survival rates. As a point of reference, Table 1 presents the survival rate for the 20 to 24 years age-group drawn from data from the 1990 census. To compare changes in time, the same data are presented for the 40- to 44-year old age-group.

The total population in the formal education system rose from 3.3 million students in 1950 to 24.6 million in 1990. In spite of the fact that this growth required the creation, on average, of more than 500,000 places per year, the total enrollment of all children in the basic

Table 1
Survival rates for two age groups

Years of schooling	Percent of age-group achieving	
	20–24	40–44
1	93.4	80.9
2	92.6	77.8
3	90.2	69.7
4	86.1	58.5
5	82.6	52.7
6	79.5	49.3
7	60.8	28.8
8	58.5	27.4
9	54.6	25.1
>9	35.1	17.1

Source: XI Censo General de Población y Vivienda, 1990. Estados Unidos Mexicanos. Resumen General. Primera Reimpresión, 1992, INEGI, Mexico

Table 2
Percentages of enrollment in public and private schools

Cycle	1970			1991		
	Public	Private	Total	Public	Private	Total
Preschool	83.4	16.6	100	91.4	8.6	100
Primary	92.2	7.8	100	93.7	6.3	100
Lower Sec.	71.9	28.1	100	91.9	8.1	100
Technical	61.1	38.9	100	71.2	28.8	100
Upper Sec.	72.5	27.5	100	77.8	22.2	100
Teachers	65.2	34.8	100	73.4	26.6	100
Higher Ed.	86.1	13.9	100	81.4	18.6	100

Source: Anexo Estadístico, 4o. Informe de Gobierno. Mexico, 1992

education age-group is still far from being achieved. Furthermore, growth of educational opportunities has not been on an equal footing in all regions of the country, neither in urban nor rural areas, nor for different ethnic groups. Regions in the northern part of the country and around the Metropolitan Area of Mexico City have attained high enrollment ratios but states in the southeast regions have lower rates.

Education is provided by public schools managed by the different government levels (i.e., federal, state, and municipality) and by private institutions. Basic education is mainly through public schools. Its share of the enrollment grew considerably since 1970 especially for preschool and lower-secondary education. Private participation in the middle-level cycle of education is stronger, even though it decreased in the 1970–91 period. Private participation for teacher-training institutions decreased, mainly because the form of teacher training was changed from a four-year cycle after secondary education to the higher education level. Lastly, participation of the private sector in higher education has also increased since 1970.

Table 2 shows the distribution of enrollment in private and public institutions for basic, middle-level, and higher education.

3.1 Primary, Secondary, and Tertiary Education

The structure of the school system is organized into basic, middle-level and higher education. Basic education comprises preschool, primary school, and the lower cycles of secondary school. Up to 1992, six grades of primary education, was compulsory by constitutional mandate. Since then compulsory schooling covers 9 years: 6 years of primary and 3 years in lower-secondary education.

After basic education there is middle-level education which has two streams: students can follow technical studies with a duration of between 3 and 4 years, or the upper-secondary cycle, called *bachillerato*, with a average period of 3 years of study that enables them to pursue higher education studies.

Table 3
Estimated percentages of selected age groups having completed primary education

Age-group	Percentage having completed primary education
15–19	83.1
25–29	72.7
35–39	57.2
45–49	40.5

Most of the higher education institutions offer courses lasting from 4 to 7 years, including teacher training for basic education. Graduate courses comprise specialization, master, and doctoral degrees.

Total enrollment in primary education grew from 3.0 million pupils in 1950 to 14.7 million in 1980, with an average annual growth rate of nearly 5 percent. There are no reliable data to estimate enrollment rates or admission rates for the years previous to 1976. An approximate measure is given by the percentage of different age-groups having completed primary education, as shown in Table 3. The number of new entrants to primary education decreased after 1981 and the same was true for total enrollment after 1984. This was mainly due to the diminishing population growth rate and to the reduction in the number of latecomers. This trend is expected to continue.

Total enrollment in lower-secondary education grew from 70,000 students in 1950 to 4.2 million in 1991. From 1971 to 1982 gross transition rates rose from 60.0 to 84.3 percent. After 1982 transition rates remained almost constant at about 81 percent. Since 1989, with a decreasing number of pupils enrolled in sixth grade, enrollment in first grade and total enrollment in secondary education diminished. For the mid-1990s an increase of 25 percent in the total student enrollment given the policy of 9 years of compulsory education.

Enrollment in middle-level education rose from 313,000 students to 2.1 million during the period 1970–91. Before 1981, 90 percent of new entrants enrolled in the *bachillerato* stream and in teacher training institutions. However, after that year, technical schools grew considerably and, by 1991, 19.2 percent of total enrollment was in technical education. However, in both types of education, retention rates are low at about 50 percent.

After a large increase in enrollment in higher education (12.4 percent annually from 1970–1980), and the creation of many up-to-date institutions during that period, there was a slower growth in the period 1980–90 with total enrollment showing an annual growth rate of 3.1 percent. The retention rate in higher education is very low, with less than 60 percent of students completing their studies, and an even smaller proportion obtaining their degree.

In primary education, the average capacity of one-shift schools is 200 pupils, although in large and middle-size urban areas, they cater for approximately 400. Around 23 percent of primary schools are one-teacher schools and 15 percent do not offer all six grades. The school day lasts for 4 hours, and the school year has 200 days. Since 1993, efforts have been made to increase the number of days in the school year and to reduce teacher absenteeism. The ratio and the class size vary greatly, but, on average, the student–teacher ratio is 30:1 and the average class size is 23.

Secondary schools are larger and, on average, have 400 students. Class sizes vary from 21 to 36 students. The average student–teacher ratio is 18:1. In upper-secondary education, class size varies from 42 students in public schools to 31 in private ones. On average, class size for technical schools is lower, with 28 students per class. The student–teacher ratio is 52:1 in upper-secondary education and 11:1 in technical education. School size in upper-secondary education is much larger with 1,500 students per school, while for technical schools the average size is 220 students.

Higher education institutions have, on average, 9,000 students, but campuses vary considerably in the number of enrolled students: from more than 100,000 in the National University to less than 3,000 in some state universities. The average student–teacher ratio is 10:1.

Special modalities in primary public schools exist for ethnic groups and children living in small and remote areas. Approximately 4.3 percent of pupils attend bilingual schools where, apart from Spanish, they are taught their own language. In small and isolated communities, many located in mountainous areas, graduate secondary students teach around 100,000 children in schools with fewer than 30 pupils each.

Lower-secondary schools have two tracks: general and vocational education. Additionally, in remote areas, public schools provide education by transmitting previously recorded lessons to students by means of a television network and the assistance of a tutor. Vocational schools represent 27.3 percent of total enrollment, and technical secondary schools 10.9 percent.

In the past, most of upper-secondary education was part of higher education. In the 1990s, all federal schools were separated from higher education. Many universities, however, continue to offer this cycle. Upper-secondary education represents 80.8 percent of the middle-level cycle, with 33.6 percent of the students enrolled in federal schools, 44.2 percent in state schools, and the rest in private schools. Technical education has 53.9 percent of its total enrollment in federal schools and 28.8 percent in private schools.

Public institutions enroll 81.4 percent of higher education students. They can be grouped into three categories: a system of federal technology institutes including the National Polytechnic Institute, state and autonomous universities together with the

National Autonomous University of Mexico, and teacher-training institutes. Technology institutes are smaller in size than universities, and offer courses in the engineering and management fields, whilst universities have a wider range of courses. There are over 94 technology institutes all over the country, enrolling 16.8 percent of all higher education students. There is at least one public university in each state (38 in total) and the larger universities have campuses in different cities. This is also true for the most important private institutions.

In all of higher education, the faculties of management and the social sciences have the larger proportion of enrolled students (50.6 %), followed by engineering and technology (35.5 %), and medical studies (6 %). No more than 2 percent of students are enrolled in natural sciences and mathematics.

Higher education institutions offer graduate courses and conduct research programs. In 14 states, including the Federal District, doctoral studies enroll 1,250 students, 28,500 were enrolled as master's degree students, and 16,300 as specialization students. In the 1990 census, 350,000 persons were registered as having graduate education. Of these, 55 percent were concentrated in four states and 24 percent in the Federal District. Most avenues for pursuing graduate studies are still to be found outside Mexico.

Most universities are organized by schools but a few that were created after 1970 have a departmental structure. There are also public research centers which offer graduate programs in the social sciences, industrial sciences, and engineering.

3.2 Preschool Education

Enrollment in preschool education rose from 400,000 children in 1970 to 2.8 million in 1991. In 1970, 23.5 percent of the children aged between 4 and 5 years attended preschool; in 1980 the enrollment rate was 47 percent, and in 1990 it reached 58.5 percent.

It is strongly advocated that children should attend at least one school year before entering primary education. As in the case of primary education, specific programs are provided for ethnic minority groups and for children in scattered areas. The latter have secondary graduate students as teachers, who, at the same time, study for a technical career in the open system. Preschool for ethnic groups represents 5 percent of the total enrollment, whilst for isolated communities it represents 6 percent.

The average student–teacher ratio is 25:1, the average class size is 21, and the average school size is 56 children. Schools work from 9 a.m. to noon. Many of them have one or two groups with 20 children in each. Children from poor families are provided with breakfast.

3.3 Special Education

There are several public agencies as well as private institutions that offer services to children with different degrees of handicaps. However, enrollment is low; it is 239,000 children from an estimate of 2 million or more when the UNESCO criteria are used.

The largest type of handicap covered is that of learning problems, with nearly 140,000 children. Programs to train teachers to be able to identify children with problems have been created; the development of teaching materials for children with visual or hearing deficiencies has been undertaken, and there are some trials to establish whether the use of computers can help deaf and mute children or those suffering from dyslexia. But material is limited; there are few Braille textbooks and only few libraries with Braille catalogs. Very few children are identified as gifted and no more than 2,000 receive special treatment.

A great effort will be required in the future to train enough skilled personnel to give skills to inservice teachers and to persuade families to accept help from outside.

3.4 Vocational, Technical, and Business Education

Technical training is offered as part of the middle-level cycle after nine years of basic education. Although for many years this type of education was considered important, and technical schools for training had been part of the educational system for a long time, it is only since 1980 that a huge effort has been made to expand this type of school. In that year, a target was set to have 40 percent of students in the middle-level cycle in technical schools. The argument was to invert the ratio of five professionals to one middle-level technician in the labor market. In 1993 the actual percentage of students entering the middle-level cycle was 21.3. Many youngsters, when choosing to pursue their studies, still prefer a more general academic option. Just as for upper-secondary education, the dropout rate is very high.

Technical education covers a broad range of options, but most are in industry and commerce. In each school, between three and six options are offered. The average weekly teaching time is 35 hours.

Public technical education is still managed by the federal government. Since 1978, equipping the schools has, to a large extent, been financed through international loans. At the national level, as well as at the institutional level, there are many mechanisms which endeavor to link the productive sector with schools, including the participation of enterprises in school boards and the organization of sandwich training courses. At the national and regional levels, there are agreements between chambers of commerce and industry and educational authorities. In some regions, and for some schools, this joint coordination has been successful. Some schools are able to sell their products.

Graduates have difficulty in entering the jobmarket. Their youth and lack of experience do not always guarantee them a job according to their training. Sometimes lack of employment opportunities pushes them to underemployment or informal activities.

3.5 Adult and Nonformal Education

Adult and nonformal education consists of special programs for illiterates and for adults who have not completed their basic education; particular attention is given to initial education activities and to ethnic groups. There are also open and semiformal systems for technical education and post-lower-secondary schooling.

In 1981 the different agencies involved in adult education were combined into the National Institute for Adult Education, and their principal aim was to reduce illiteracy among the population and to offer alternatives for the completion of primary and secondary education among the adult population. Part of the effort was oriented to vocational training for these adults.

The Institute's activities are based on the 1975 National Law for Adult Education. Mexico still has 13 percent of adult illiterates with a higher rate for women (15%) in contrast to 10 percent for the male population. This implies that, in 1990, over 6 million adults were still to be made literate. Even if there are slightly more than 800,000 illiterates between 15 and 24 years of age, the main target group is older, which makes the task much more difficult. The Institute develops its activities by soliciting cooperation within the community and from business enterprises. Young people are engaged to teach illiterates how to read and write in exchange for remuneration which can only be termed symbolic. Agreements with business enterprises and trade union organizations constitute the framework for the Institute's activity. On average, the Institute enrolls a population of 700,000 illiterates annually.

According to data from the 1990 Census, there were 11.3 million persons aged 15 years or more who did not complete their primary education. More than 1 million adults are registered for primary and secondary education, but many adults drop out of the program before completing the curriculum.

Apart from this type of adult education, there is also training for parents and communities, and for ethnic groups. Initial education is provided through health and social security institutions, and specific activities designed for the different ethnic groups are catered for by the Instituto Nacional Indigenista.

Training for work is offered to individuals older than 15 years having only primary education. Short courses with an average duration of three months are offered through 3,500 centers, mainly private, to around 400,000 persons. Different institutions, public and private universities, and the Ministry of Education itself offer open or semiformal programs for technical and upper-secondary education as well as for higher and graduate education. Most of the population is attracted to open upper-secondary education, and

graduate programs for inservice teachers. In addition to activities implemented by the educational sector, a new Ministry of Social Development was created in 1992. It offers training activities in accordance with its overall mandate. Within the educational sector, around 3 percent of the total budget is allocated to adult education.

4. Administrative and Supervisory Structure and Operation

Although the 1917 Constitution had assigned the provision of educational services to municipalities, a main change was introduced in 1921 granting to the federal government functions for providing educational services all over the country shared with the state and municipalities' governing bodies.

In 1921 the creation of the Ministry of Education laid the basis for organizing the federal educational services which, for the next 72 years, not only fulfilled a normative function in relation to curriculum definition and design, authorizing and supervising educational services, but also ran more than 70 percent of existing schools in the country. For seven decades the Ministry and the federal agencies in the states had various organizational structures, and attained a size, both in the number of personnel and in the number of functions, that was not efficient.

Until 1992 there were parallel systems of administration, supervision, and certification for basic education by both the federal and states' governments. An exception was the Federal District where education was, and continues to be, fully under the Ministry of Education.

A major administrative change occurred in 1992 when basic education services and teacher-training institutes were brought under the jurisdiction of the states after adjustments had been made to both the Constitution and the Federal Law of Education. Since 1993, state governments are responsible for all public schools; in other words, all federal schools became state schools. A period of transition from centralized to decentralized administration will take place up to the end of the 1990s. Funds are allocated annually from the federal to the states' budget.

The Ministry of Education, with a reduced size, remains the body in charge of all normative and policy-making functions in education. Specifically, it is responsible for formulating national plans and curricula; authorizing teaching material for basic education and teacher training, implementing the free textbook program for primary education; establishing evaluation procedures for the educational national system; and maintaining programs such as inservice training, improvement of efficiency in primary schools, literacy programs, as well as all programs aimed at reducing inequalities among regions.

The existing supervisory system is more administra-

Table 4
Federal budget. Millions of constant nuevos pesos (1980 = 100)

Sector	1983 Amount	%	1988 Amount	%	1992 Amount	%
Social development	308.1	28.02	295.1	31.97	492.7	50.90
Education	127.4	11.59	127.9	13.86	202.2	20.89
Others	180.7	16.43	167.2	18.11	290.5	30.01
Other sectors	791.4	71.98	628.0	68.03	475.3	49.10
Total	1,099.5	100.00	923.1	100.00	968.0	100.00

Source: La Política Social en México. Instituto Nacional de Solidaridad. Secretaría de Desarrollo Social. Agosto 1992

tive than academic. There is an inspectorate for schools with each inspector having 25 schools under his or her auspices. The quality of inspection is varied.

Parallel to the administration, there is a network of technical councils, at the national, state, and school levels which provides an environment for consultation, communication, and feedback processes of academic programs. There are other federal agencies which are involved in educational activities. Agricultural education institutions are associated with the Ministry of Agriculture. Initial school and some preschools are in the health sector.

There is no unique agency devoted to middle-level education which comprises technical and upper-secondary education. All systems coexist with different curricula, academic structures, training programs for the teachers, and growth policies. At most, in places like the Metropolitan Area of Mexico City, there has been an effort to coordinate entrance quotas.

Universities have self-governing bodies with differences in the level of autonomy. Federal institutions are regulated by the central government. In the case of federal schools, together with federal higher education institutions, the mid-1990s will witness a shift to a more decentralized management. Since 1979, a planning scheme for higher education institutions was implemented to establish coordination among institutions. There are planning committees at the national, regional, and state level. In 1991, a national evaluation committee was created to encourage institutions to establish systematic self-evaluating procedures which could allow for funds allocation criteria addressed to improve quality and efficiency in higher education. There is a National Association of Higher Education Institutes (ANUIES) by means of which policies and programs can be jointly agreed.

There is a national law which regulates and recognizes different types of professions. Any individual completing his or her undergraduate studies, and having fulfilled the academic requirements for holding a degree, should be registered as a professional.

This law also regulates the existence of professional associations.

Teachers and administrative personnel who belong to the federal system are organized in a national trade union. State teachers have their own trade union organizations. When federal schools were transferred to the states, state authorities recognized this national organization. Universities and other public education institutions have their own trade union organizations.

5. Educational Finance

In 1992 total expenditure on education was US$15.6 billion representing 5 percent of GDP. Government expenditure as a percentage of total expenditure on education was 91 percent, of which 77 percent came from federal funds.

Restructuring of the federal public sector allowed a redistribution of the budget by sectors, benefitting the social development sector, and in particular education. The percentage of the federal budget allocated to education increased from 11.6 to 20.9 percent between 1983 and 1992. Table 4 shows the distribution of the federal expenditure for the years 1983, 1988, and 1992. From 1988 to 1992, the education budget increased by 67 percent. This resulted in a large increase of teacher salaries which had been seriously affected by the period of greater inflation.

Since 1978, 42 classrooms for basic education were built every day. The Administrative Committee for the Promotion of School Construction (CAPFCE) is in charge of establishing norms for the construction of educational areas. Norms include standardization of physical areas and equipment. The budget allocated for maintenance increased in the period 1988–92 with voluntary work from the communities and funds from the Solidarity Program.

Administration expenditure represented 10 percent of the budget in 1991. However, higher education received more than its proportional (based on enrollment) share. Public funds for autonomous and state universities come from the federal and the state government. On average, 70 percent of their revenues are from federal funds. Revenues other than from subsidies are generally very low. Student fees are very heterogeneous, varying from less than US$1 per year up to US$50 and contrast strongly with some private universities, where fees can reach US$1,200 per semester per student.

Special programs are addressed to give financial aid to more than half a million children for completion of primary education. Private institutions at all educational levels must assign 5 percent of their enrollment to free-tuition students. Apart from a few special programs, there is no system of loans or scholarships to students enrolled in upper-secondary and undergraduate studies. The National Council for Science and Technology provides around 10,000 scholarships for graduate students enrolled in national institutions. This has led to an evaluation of graduate courses through ad-hoc committees formed by prestigious teachers and researchers from different fields. Around 2000 scholarships were awarded for graduate studies abroad.

6. Supplying Personnel for the Education System

Teacher training became part of higher education in 1984. At that time there were 437,000 teachers in primary schools, and 110,000 teachers in preschool education. Alternative ways for inservice teachers to obtain an undergraduate-level education and certification were organized through semiformal and open systems; different economic incentives were given to attract teachers to complete their studies. From 1987–92, 175,000 graduates of this new generation of teachers were produced, and around 60,000 teachers enrolled to complete their studies in inservice courses.

Until 1984, graduate students were guaranteed a position as teachers in federal education. From that date onwards, graduates were required to pass an examination in order to be assigned a post.

A shortage of preschool teachers and a surplus of primary teachers led to the establishment of programs for training primary school teachers to become preschool teachers. Despite this, total enrollment in teacher-training institutions is less for the preschool level than for primary education. A career in teaching has become less attractive given the real salaries, and many teachers have left education for more remunerative jobs.

Teacher-training curricula are being revised. First, a common core will be designed for the three levels of basic education, with an accent on learning to learn and on skills of observation and practice in the classroom. At a second stage, a major reorganization of the curricula will be undertaken.

An emergent plan for inservice training has also been established, combining distance education with formal courses, collective study sessions, and information exchange.

In 1993, a new promotion system was established which alleviates low salaries through a mechanism of horizontal movement. The model is interesting as it allows for the evaluation of teachers through their pupils' performance as well as their sitting for examinations. Procedures for both sets of evaluation have been approved jointly by the authorities and the trade union organization. In this way, teachers will attain higher salaries and, at the same time, the proposed mechanism tends to promote efficiency. In addition, teachers have benefited from salary increases, which in the period from 1990–93 meant that the minimum salary paid to a teacher doubled its value.

In postsecondary schools, most systems have well-defined profiles and recruitment systems. Most teachers had been trained in a higher education institution. However, there are many (more than 40%) who did not complete their studies.

In some higher education institutions, a professor must have at least a master's degree. The large majority of professors are part-time and few have a full-time status. There are some programs to improve teaching and professional skills.

7. Curriculum Development and Teaching Methodology

The federal government, through the Ministry of Education, is responsible for designing the curricula for basic education and teacher training. Curricula modifications and revisions are by means of a participatory process through the National Technical Council of Education, and involve the existing network of state councils and technical councils in each school. The resulting syllabus is authorized by the Ministry of Education and it is compulsory for all basic education. There are regional variations in the curriculum.

In the case of primary education, there is a main core curriculum, although special modalities in public schools exist for ethnic groups and children living in small and scattered areas. A great effort has been made to provide children speaking other languages and dialects than Spanish with material written in their own language. Despite the fact that the dropout rate in primary education is decreasing, children leaving school before completing third grade will become functionally or totally illiterate. In order to give attention to this group of children, there are some specific programs for children between 10 and 14 years of age who have dropped out of regular school in urban and rural areas.

In primary education, seven subjects form the core curriculum: mathematics, language, history, geography, civic education, health, and environmental education. There is what is called the single textbook for primary education which the government has produced and has distributed free to all pupils since 1958. For new textbooks, the federal government calls for proposals. Proposals are evaluated by a jury composed of different groups of specialists, academic experts, and representatives of social groups. When the book is finalized, it is printed and distributed by the government. In 1992, 9 million copies were printed and distributed.

General lower-secondary education has a 35 hours per week load. The curriculum is organized by subjects and includes mathematics, mother tongue, world and Mexican history, geography, civic education, and natural sciences. Vocational secondary schools add extra technical activities making 42 weekly hours. Secondary education textbooks are developed by private publishing companies but, for the book to become officially accepted, it requires the authorization of the Ministry.

In secondary education, English is the main foreign language taught in schools. In federal upper-secondary schools, 70 percent of the subjects prepare the students to continue their studies in higher education, and 30 percent of the curriculum gives them a technical training with a wide range of options, some oriented to specific industrial or primary sector activities, and others with more horizontal mobility. The school weekly load is 35 hours. The Minister authorizes curriculum changes. Until 1982 there were many syllabuses, curricula, and courses. From 1993 all different types of schools will have a common core.

Autonomous or state schools are organized in two or three different administrative subsystems, and there is a wide range of curriculum models as each system autonomously establishes its own academic program. Several efforts have been made to establish a common core, but models differ among them, not only in the sequence of subjects but also in number of hours taught in each subject and the overall teaching approach.

There is a body called the University Council which authorizes proposed changes or modifications to curricula from different institutions and faculties. Within each institution or faculty there is a technical council which deals with all academic aspects, including proposals for curriculum revision to be presented at the University Council. This Council is generally composed of members of the faculty; student representatives; and the directors of schools, departments, or institutes.

8. The System of Examinations, Promotions, and Certifications

In primary and secondary education, promotion from one grade to the next is the responsibility of the teachers in the school, but they must comply with the Ministry norms. It was formerly the case that tests were rarely administered. However, in 1993 a national standard examination was introduced for primary and secondary education.

Certificates are awarded to pupils and students by state authorities. Up to 1992, certificates were awarded only after pupils completed primary education; so-called "grade certificates" and "cycle certificates" were awarded for lower secondary education.

To obtain a place in a lower- or upper-secondary school or a university, each system sets its entry examination which students must pass to be admitted to the institution. Where upper-secondary schools are attached to universities, promotion is in many cases automatic for those obtaining the minimum final grade.

Private institutions, with a few exceptions, must have their academic program approved by a federal or state authority, or through a public institution.

9. Educational Assessment, Evaluation, and Research

Systematic evaluation studies have been conducted on students graduating from teacher-training institutions. The results were used to allocate teachers to schools and the information was also fed back to the institutions for their own use.

Adhoc studies are conducted at different levels of education. An example is the survey of teachers, parents, and students in relation to the teaching and learning of Spanish in basic education. The results of the survey coordinated by the National Technical Council of Education formed the basis for proposing changes in the curriculum.

Many surveys are undertaken by different institutions, but there are no systematic, well-established mechanisms to communicate or interchange results.

As already mentioned, examinations have to be passed by candidates to be admitted to upper-secondary education and higher education insititutions. Registers of examinations presented by candidates for entrance to different levels of education can become a source for evaluation procedures of the educational system. Unfortunately, information obtained over the years was not necessarily used for evaluation purposes nor were the data accessible to researchers. One exception to this was a critical analysis undertaken by the National University to assess the level of preparation of secondary graduates entering the university upper-secondary schools.

There are well-established systems for data collection, analysis, and dissemination. Mexico has an educational statistics system which was created at the beginning of the 1970s and that has been sustained and improved over the years. Twice during the school year, schools complete information on enrollment and human resources. Summary data are published and they form part of a national information system including the population and economic censuses, the national and public accounting system, and geographical data. In particular, the education sector maintains historical time series data on enrollment and resources. The main indicators include rates of admission, enrollment ratios, survival rates, promotion, repetition, and drop-out rates. Education expenditure data of various kinds are also generated.

Research on education is carried out by private and public institutions. Proposals and critical analysis have served to launch programs and correct policies. However, the number of total research projects is low and the budget allocated for this kind of activity is also very low.

10. Major Reforms in the 1980s and the 1990s

The transfer of the administration of schools from the federal to the state level dismantled an operational structure that was no longer efficient. Schools will benefit from the change if they have more access to information and resources and better mechanisms for communicating with other schools and with authorities. The participation of the community and parents in school matters should increase if the communities now work for their own shcools.

Changes in federal expenditure have resulted in more resources being allocated to social development programs and, especially, to education.

Transforming teacher-training institutions into higher education institutions in 1984 laid the basis for having better teachers. But the transformation was not easy. Time was required, some institutions resisted changes, and not enough human and financial resources were allocated for the transformation.

At other times, curricula changes had been proposed and implemented. Changes proposed in the early 1990s dealt with a general feeling in the society that education has to bc improved, not only for the sake of modernization but because Mexican children have to be prepared for a complex and highly competitive life and, at the same time, they have to preserve their individuality and their social and national identity. Recognition of the need to change the various curricula is important for the authorities and for society, but the crucial role is in the hands of the teachers and their organizations. The decade of the 1990s will witness progress in the proposed changes.

11. Major Problems for the Year 2000

A central problem, possibly the most important of all, will be to raise the quality of education. The first task is to raise the quality of primary education. The first steps have been taken. To find a functional but lasting way to implement changes that can offer visible results in opening new roads to children every day and every year will be the most important challenge up to the beginning of the twenty-first century. Very strong and effective actions must be pursued if teachers are to be individuals with self-respect, social standing, and effective preparation.

Factors influencing repetition rates will have to be minimized to ensure that the maximum number of children can complete primary education in six years. Expansion of secondary education should be envisaged. This requires planning for training the required number of teachers and to mobilize enough resources to avoid having quantity without quality.

Training for work of the young population will require the rcvision of existing programs and the participation of the employer of the school graduates. Mexico needs more highly skilled personnel for professional work and for research. It has groups of researchers and experienced individuals but institutions must have an adequate environment and conditions where new generations can be trained.

References

Anexo Education 1992 IV Informe Presidencial 1992. Government Printer, Mexico City

Instituto Nacional de Estadística Geografía e Informática 1992 *XI Censo General de Población y Vivendia 1990. Perfil Sociodemográfica, Estados Unidos Mexicanos.* INEGI, Mexico City

Instituto Nacional de Estadística Geografía e Informática 1992 *Resumen General del XI Censo General de Población y Vivienda, 1990.* INEGI, Mexico City

Instituto Nacional de Solidaridad 1992 *La Política Social en México, Síntesis gráfica y estadística.* INEGI, Mexico City

Further Reading

Acuerdo Nacional para la modernización de la educación basica. Government Printer, Mexico City

Comentarios del Centro de Estudios Educativos al Acuerdo Nacional para la Modernización de la Educación Básica 1992 *Revista Latinoamericana de Estudios Educativos (México)* 22(2)

Diez J C, Lizaur M P, 1975 *Historia de las Universidades.* SEP, Mexico City

Economic Commission for Latin America and the Carribean 1991 *Educación y Conocimiento: Eje de la transformación productiva con equidad.* Comisión Económica para América Latina y el Caribe, Santiago

Economic Commission for Latin America and the Caribbean 1992 *Economic Survey of Latin America and the Caribbean, 1990*, Vol. 1. Economic Commission for Latin America and the Caribbean, Santiago

Instituto Nacional de Estadística Geografía e Informática 1991 *Anuario Estadístico de los Estados Unidos Mexicanos.* INEGI, Mexico City

Instituto Nacional de Estadística Geografía e Informática 1992 *Sistema de Cuentas Nacionales de México. Cuentas de Producción del Sector Público 1987–1990.* INEGI, Mexico City.

Interamerican Development Bank 1991 *Economic and Social Progress in Latin America 1991 Report* Interamerican Development Bank, Mexico City

Larroyo F 1970 *Historia comparada de la educación de México*. Porrua Mexico, Mexico City

Latapi P 1992 Libertad religiosa y legislación escolar. Las recientes reformas constitucionales de México ante el derecho internacional. *Revista Latinoamericana de Estudios Educativos (México)* 22(1)

Modernizar la escuela primaria. Siete propuestas de acción del Sindicato Nacional de Trabajadores de la Educación. 1991 *Revista Lantinoamericana de Estudios Educativos (México)* 21(3)

Padua J 1984 *Educación, industrialización y progreso técnico en México*. El Colegio de México y UNESCO, Mexico City

Secretaria de Educación Pública 1990 *Compendio del gasto educativo*. Secretaria de Educación Publica, Mexico City

Sierra F B 1992 *Estudio prospectivo de las ingenierias*. Mexico City

Sierra J B 1976 *Conversaciones con Gastón García Cantú*, 4th edn. Siglo XXI, Mexico City

Solana F, Raul C R, Raul B M 1981 *Historia de la educación pública en México*. Secretaria de Educación Pública, Mexico City

Textos de la historia mexicana, Independencia y Revolución. 1985. SEP, Mexico City

Urquidi V I 1992 El convenio trilateral de libre comercio entre México, los Estados Unidos y el Canadá. *El Trimestre Económico* 59(2): 234

Vázquez J Z et al. 1981 *Ensayos sobre historia de la educación en México*. El Colegio de México, Mexico City

Mongolia

S. Spaulding

1. General Background

Mongolia, home of the Mongols, covers an area of 1,565,000 square kilometers, more than twice the size of Turkey and four times that of Japan. Mongolia is landlocked, bordered on the north by Russia and the south by China. The distance from west to east is as far as from Paris to Moscow. It has an average altitude of about 1,600 meters, and can be divided into roughly three regions: upland steppes, semi-deserts, and deserts. Nearly four-fifths of the country consists of pasture lands that support immense herds of grazing livestock. The remaining area is divided between forests and barren deserts. An important part of the country is covered by the Gobi Desert and three major mountain ranges that thrust into the country from the north and west. The country is divided into 18 *aimaks*, or regions, and three large cities: Ulan Bator (the capital), Darkhan, and Erdenet. The *aimaks* are subdivided into *somons*, or districts, of which there are over 350. These units are governed by *aimak* and *somon Hurals* (councils of deputies). A new constitution came into effect on January 12, 1992, stipulating that the structure of the *aimaks* and the *somon Hurals* would change during 1993 and onward.

An early thirteenth century Mongol leader was Genghis Khan who is credited with establishing a strong central government and codes of honesty, incorruptibility, and fairness. In the mid-seventeenth century, a Manchurian state in northeastern China took advantage of tribal warfare among the Mongols and established a colonial rule in 1691 that lasted until 1911 when the Mongols overthrew the Manchu Qing dynasty. The then *Bogdo-gegen*, or Living Buddha (head of the Lamaist church), became the ruler, though the Kyakhta Agreement in 1915 with Russia and China denied Mongolia the right to establish relations with other countries. After the October Revolution in Russia, the *Bogdo-gegen* government invited Chinese troops to return to defend the country against possible Russian intrusion. In 1921, however, Sukhbaatar organized, with the help of the Soviet government, a revolutionary movement that overthrew the government in 1924 and established a People's Republic, closely allied with the Soviet Union and following the socialist policies of that country. The Mongolian Constitution, adopted in 1960, stated that the country is a socialist state of workers ("*arats*"), organized in cooperatives, and working intellectuals, in the form of a people's democracy (Dash et al. 1990, Spaulding 1990).

Since the earliest days of the People's Republic, the Lamaist religion has been separated from both government and educational activity, although formal freedom of worship has existed and there have been elements of a variety of religious practices (Lamaistic, Buddhism, Shamanism, Islam, and others) in the country. The Mongolian People's Revolutionary Party was the sole party until the late 1980s when a process of peaceful change led to the establishment of a multiparty system and a market economy. The name of the country was changed in late 1991 by the legislature from the Mongolian People's Republic to simply Mongolia. Elections in mid-1992 further altered the power relationships between the various factions in the new multiparty system and there are signs of a resurgence of interest in religious thought that is also felt in the political arena. The President, Prime Minister, and legislature have powers similar to those of the former Party and its Chairman and most Party assets have been passed to the legislature.

The population numbers 2,294,100 (1993), with well over half of the population under 20 years of age, and three-fourths under 40. The average population density (late 1980s) is only 1.37 people per square kilometer. During the last 15 years, the average annual rate of population increase has been 2.6 to 2.7 percent, resulting in a doubling of the population. In 1985, 44.8 percent of the population was in the 1–15 age group. For every 100 people of working age, there were 112 below that age, including 95 children. About one-third of the population is economically active. Life expectancy for men is 64.6 years and for women, 66.5 years.

Although it is estimated that two-thirds of the economically active population is engaged in rural activity—primarily as herdsmen, farmers, and livestock breeders (UNESCO 1990, 1991), there is a tendency to abandon the nomadic life and it is estimated that 53 percent of the population are now settled in cities and towns, 26 percent in the capital, Ulan Bator, alone. Urban dwellers, especially in the larger towns, are increasingly alienated from traditional agricultural occupations, particularly pasturable cattle breeding, while at the same time there is unemployment in the urban areas.

The main agricultural resource consists largely of great herds of livestock (about 70% of all agricultural production) that have increased throughout this century and that provide a valuable export commodity. Most livestock is produced by giant cooperatives, mostly organized in the late 1950s, averaging 1,700 square miles in area. Less than 1 percent of the total land mass is arable and, because of short summers, only one annual crop is possible. About four-fifths of the cropland is in grain, and the rest in fodder crops (hay). Potatoes and vegetables occupy only a tiny fraction of the crop area. About four-fifths of the cropland is formed by state farms (averaging 700 square miles in size), and the rest by cooperatives. The government, however, has embarked on a process of privatization and many of these state cooperatives and farms will be divested in the 1990s.

Mongolia is rich in mineral resources (coal, iron, tin, copper, gold, and silver), some of which is exploited. The northern rivers of Mongolia have great potential for hydroelectric development and timber is logged from mountain forests that cover about 10 percent of the land area. Much of Mongolia's industry is engaged in processing raw materials or meeting basic domestic consumer needs. Processing industries for livestock raw materials, together with food and other light industries, contribute about 40 percent of the aggregate industrial and agricultural output. There is a mining operation at Erdenet that concentrates copper and molybdenum ores and that accounts for about 40 percent of the country's exports. Ulan Bator is the center for light industry and heavy industry is concentrated in Darhan, where there are a number of projects that have been developed in cooperation with the former Soviet Union and Eastern European countries. Forest products are processed in Sukhbaatar. There is a small, but well-established, tourist industry, attracting visitors worldwide, that concentrates on organizing hunting expeditions into the rugged mountains where a number of exotic wild animals exist in abundance.

Until 1990, the Gross National Product (GNP) was estimated at US\$1,600 per capita. In 1990 the country joined the World Bank and the International Monetary Fund. These organizations did a reassessment of Mongolia's GNP and concluded that the per capita GNP for 1990 was actually US\$463, placing Mongolia among the least economically developed countries. Its educational system, however, is far better developed than the country's economic ranking might suggest.

The 1990s have ushered in a plan for "structural adjustment" under the tutelage of the World Bank and the International Monetary Fund. Before 1991, the government had been running a deficit of about 15 percent of the country's Gross Domestic Product (GDP), according to World Bank figures. During 1991, 1992, and 1993, budgets in the social sectors have been slashed; the Ministry of Education in mid-1994 had less than 50 professional officers, down from twice that in earlier years. Budget cuts were affecting enrollments, with some kindergartens cutting back on spaces, and boarding schools for nomadic children beginning to close because of lack of funds for food. Some of these trends will be noted further below.

2. Politics and the Goals of the Education System

At its 19th Congress in May 1986, the Mongolian People's Revolutionary Party (the ruling party of the then one-party state) decided on a national strategy of restructuring the economy and society in general. Subsequently, reformer Jambyn Batmonh, then Secretary General of the Mongolian People's Revolutionary Party, suggested at the country's trade union congress in May 1988, that there was a "lack of dynamism" in carrying out Party resolutions and that trade unions should rid themselves of bureaucracy and practice openness, frankness, and democracy. Later, in December 1988, the Party's Central Committee at its 5th Plenary Meeting, decided that renewal (*shinechiel*) and restructuring of all sectors of the socioeconomic structure should be intensified.

From 1989 through early 1992, reform had accelerated dramatically. In March 1990, after several demonstrations and hunger strikes, moderates took control of the legislature and replaced Jambyn Batmonh as head of the Party with Punsalmaagiin Ochirbat, until then the Minister of Foreign Economic Relations and Supply. The People's Great *Hural* (the upper house) then abolished the constitutional clauses that had validated the Party's leading role in Mongolian society and a new Constitution was debated and passed during 1991 and it took effect on January 12, 1992. In late 1991, the parliament renamed the country simply "Mongolia," dropping the socialist nomenclature, "People's Republic." The monetary system was liberalized so that private groups can offer whatever exchange rate necessary to raise the foreign capital they need for their businesses.

More significantly, perhaps, on May 20, 1991, the *Baga Hural* (the upper house of the legislature) adopted a plan to privatize as much as 70 percent of the Mongolian economy. Under the plan, every man, woman and child alive on May 20, 1991, received one voucher with three pink coupons attached, each package worth an estimated 10,000 tugreks or about US$1,600 at the government bank's rate of exchange when they were issued, or about one-tenth that amount if exchanged at the Cooperative Bank. The pink coupons are for the purchase of more or less mobile assets of the state, including livestock, cars, equipment, and even small shops. The main vouchers (imprinted with a picture of Genghis Khan) are being exchanged for shares in some 500 corporations being formed from large state enterprises. These shares are traded on the Mongolian stock exchange located on the main square in Ulan Bator (The Economist 1991, Shapiro 1992).

These changes are dramatically altering the educational system. The entire system is being reformed with an eye toward preparing young people for a new political and economic reality. A new sense of nationalism is emerging, with renewed interest in the traditional Mongolian script (*Ourgen*), which was dropped in the early 1950s in favor of a Cyrillic alphabet and that is now being re-introduced in the schools. The education system in general is moving toward a more Western model and away from the Russian model that has dominated the country since the 1920s. An open door policy is encouraging scholars and academics from Western nations to visit Mongolia and there is much encouragement for Mongolian educators and policymakers to undertake further training in Western nations. A serious lack of funds, however, may limit the government's ability to effect the dramatic reforms it wishes to undertake, though there was some indication by 1994 that some funding agencies were concerned that the education sector was being neglected in the then current external aid programs. The Asian Development Bank, for instance, had funded an education sector study and had indicated its intention of providing US$5 million credit to assist the government in its educational reform efforts. Also, the Danish assistance authorities were assisting in the improvement of administrator and teacher training and, in cooperation with UNESCO, in the education of nomadic women.

3. The Formal System of Education

3.1 Primary, Secondary, and Tertiary Education

Figure 1 outlines the structure of the formal education system following a new education law passed in 1991. Key statistics on enrollments at the various levels appear in Tables 1 (primary and secondary), 2 (higher education), 3 (preschool education), 4

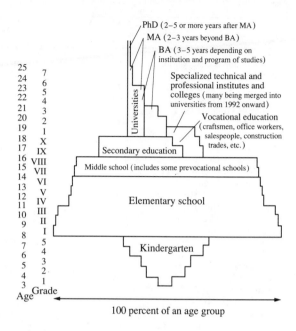

Figure 1

Mongolia: Structure of the formal education system 1992[a]
Source: Working session between Seth Spaulding, rectors of the colleges and universities and officers of the Ministry of Education, R. Bat-erdene, Ts. Undracht and others, Ulaanbaatar, June 1, 1992.

a The postsecondary degree structure on this chart was agreed upon in early 1992. Degrees offered earlier were as follows: *Diploma*, after five years of postsecondary study; *Candidate*, after 3 more years of *Aspirant* or postgraduate study; and *Doctor* after 2.5–3 years of additional study. Under the new system, there is some talk of offering a *Doctor* after the PhD because of the feeling of some academics that the old Russian *Doctor* was of higher level than the PhD

(technical/vocational education), and 5 (technical/professional education). A total of about one-third of the kindergarten-age children go to kindergarten. Nearly all the children go to primary and secondary school, though an increasing number (around 10%) drops out along the way. About 26 percent of the country's population of about 2,100,000 are enrolled in some level of education. Even though nearly half the population is rural and nomadic, there is less than 10 percent illiteracy. Official statistics suggest that in 1989 only 2.8 percent of the population in the age group 35–44 had not completed secondary school; in 1979 the figure was 10.3 percent, thus showing considerable growth within the ensuing decade. Since 1987, ten years of schooling have been compulsory, although some students who wish to work may leave after eight years and continue their studies through adult education or evening classes or return to school later.

The Ministry of Science and Education estimates that, as of 1990, the population in the modern sector

Table 1
Mongolian primary and secondary education 1986–92

Year	1986	1988	1990	1992
Total primary and secondary schools	591	607	634	679
number of 10-year schools	155	195	267	398
number of 8-year schools	339	317	271	185
number of primary schools	97	95	96	96
Number of students (in thousands)	423.1	438.2	440.9	369.1
in grades 1–3	155	162.9	166.2	138.4
in grades 4–8	230.4	236.9	233	198
in grades 9–10	37.7	38.4	41.7	32.7
Enrollment in Grade 1 (in thousands)	54.2	55.8	57.1	51.9
Enrollment of 7-year old children	9.6	11.5	17.7	8.8
Enrollment in Grade 9	19.4	20.1	21.6	17.2
Graduation, Grade 8 (in thousands)	41.3	43.6	45.2	38.1
Graduation, Grade 10	16.7	18.2	19.1	18.7
Number of children who go to a special school or class	3,154	3,588	3,540	2,856 (1991)
Number of workers schools	304	342	210	—
number of students (in thousands)	17.6	20.1	10.4	2.8
graduation (in thousands)	7.8	6.7	5.3	—
Staff members of schools	33,886	36,785	39,707	34,199
principals	527	517	546	617
vice Principals	1,088	1,163	1,137	1,019
teachers	17,461	19,183	20,629	19,441
a) primary schools (only three grades)	5,072	5,409	5,917	6,165
b) comprehensive schools (first grade through eighth or tenth)[a]	12,389	13,774	14,712	13,276
Number of seats in school buildings used for secondary schools	256,800	270,909	289,800	—
Number of children in inadequate school buildings	36,800	38,420	42,110	—
Average number of shifts in schools	1.65	1.62	1.52	
Number of children who live in school dormitories	75,466	73,331	64,362	35,368
their percentage of all students	17	16.7	14.6	—
Number of beds being used in dormitories	52,000	52,900	55,234	—
Number of children in inadequate buildings	4,450	4,560	4,730	—
Number of children per 100 beds	145	139	117	—
Total expenditure on comprehensive schools (not including dormitory expense) in tugreks	282,921.2	315,513.2	363,656.9	839,926.6[b]
Total expenditure on dormitories	110,868.2	117,861.1	92,030.5	—
Repeaters in comprehensive schools	—	—	3,016	—
percentage of all comprehensive school students	—	—	.68	—
Leavers of comprehensive schools (drop-outs)	—	—	3,292	48,411
percentage of all comprehensive school students	—	—	.75	11.7[c]

Source: Compiled from data supplied by the Ministry of Science and Education, November 1993
a Schools with Grades 1 through 8 or 10 are called "comprehensive schools," though schools with only Grades 1 through 8 are labeled "incomplete" b By 1992, the value of the tugrek had declined from about 7 = US$1 to about 100 = US$1. By 1994, the tugrak appeared to have stabilized at about 400 = US$1. c 417,503 students were enrolled in January 1992 and 369,092 were enrolled in December 1992.

averaged 8.5 years of schooling. There were 260 "complete" secondary schools of ten years' duration (including the primary school cycle) and 271 "incomplete" secondary schools of eight years' duration (including the primary cycle) (see Table 1). There were 96 four-year primary schools independent of secondary schools. About 440,000 pupils were enrolled in the entire elementary and secondary system in 1990.

Children enter basic education at the age of 8 or 9 and complete six years before entering two years of basic secondary education followed by two years of specialized secondary education. A second option after the first six years is a third year of professional secondary school. In addition, there is a twelve-year track for a small number of talented young people. Thus, elementary and secondary education may be either eight, nine, ten, or twelve years, depending on the track pursued (see Fig. 1). In practice, however, the eight-year certificate is considered an incomplete secondary certificate; only the nine-year professional certificate, the ten-year specialized secondary program, and the twelve-year gifted student program are considered complete. The nine-year track terminating in a professional secondary school diploma is either terminal or it can lead to higher vocational technical schools. Students in all other tracks can gain entrance to any postsecondary institution, including universities, depending on how they place on entrance examinations (see Fig. 1).

Most young people graduate from at least an eight-year elementary/secondary program (often called the "comprehensive school") with less than a 1 percent dropout rate during the first eight grades. Children in urban areas tend to complete Grades 9 and 10, although many in rural areas (despite boarding facilities at many rural comprehensive schools) do not. There appears to be some repetition at the various grade levels, though this diminished from a cumulative total of 14,136 repeaters in Grades 1 through 9 in 1975 to only 3,016 in total in 1990 (see Table 1).

A major problem in the mid-1990s is the dropout rate. With the closing of residential schools for nomadic children and with deteriorating conditions in many schools, many parents are withdrawing children from schools. The dropout rate jumped to 11.7 percent of total enrollment from January 1992 to December 1992. As of the latter date, a cumulative total of 20 percent of children once in school had dropped out since 1988.

Until 1990, there was only one university in Mongolia—the Mongolian State University (since 1993, the Mongolian National University). There were eight additional higher education institutions considered to be university-level: the Polytechnic Institute, the Russian Language Institute, the State Pedagogical Institute (Ulan Bator), the Pedagogical Institute (Khovd), the Agricultural Institute, the Medical Institute, the Management Institute, and the Military Institute. All of these institutions, with the exception of the Management Institute, offered postsecondary preparation of roughly the same number of years and issued certificates considered to be the equivalent of a university degree.

During 1990–91, the Russian Language Institute became the Institute of Foreign Languages and was merged with the State Pedagogical Institute to become the Pedagogical University. The Polytechnic, the Agricultural Institute, and the Medical Institute all became universities. The Management Institute became the Institute of Administration and Management Development and it now enrolls graduates of other

institutions who wish one-year or short-term inservice management training. In addition, there is an Economic College, offering a three-year program (leading to a bachelor's degree) in banking and finance, accountancy, and business management; and a Higher Political College of the Great People's *Khural* that is being transformed into a school of public administration. The latter offers a one-year postuniversity or higher institute program to train graduates in public administration techniques. The College of Commerce and Industry, established in 1991, was once a specialized training center attached to the Ministry of Trade and Industry. It now prepares specialists to the bachelor's level (three years postsecondary) in business administration and management, business accounting, and marketing. In addition to the several government colleges, as of June 1992, 15 private postsecondary institutions had been authorized (most small, dealing with specialized areas such as Mongolian knowledge, languages, and other special areas) and, in early June 1992, an association of private postsecondary schools was established, probably with the idea of becoming a kind of accrediting agency and self-study group.

The eight universities and higher institutes enrolled 13,397 students in 1990. Some 3,513 students were enrolled in foreign universities and higher institutes in 1990, down sharply from the norm of around 6,000 in the mid-1980s (see Table 2). Most of those going abroad went to the former Soviet Union and a few (perhaps 10%) to the Eastern European countries then affiliated with the Soviet bloc (primarily the German Democratic Republic and Czechoslovakia). Trends in the future will be for students going to these countries to diminish and those going to Western European countries, the United States, Japan, and other countries, to increase, both because of the reduction in numbers of scholarships available from the former socialist countries and because of the increased interest of the Mongolians in the educational systems of countries with mature market economies.

Until the early 1990s, the Mongolian higher education system was very similar in structure and content to the Soviet educational system. The main stage of higher education led to the acquisition of a specialist diploma, which usually entitled the holder to exercise a profession, and was awarded after a five-year course that usually included a thesis (four to five years at the Pedagogical University and five to six years at the Medical University). A further stage could be undertaken, during which time the student was a *candidat*, usually by those already teaching in the university. The graduate course lasted at least three years, included individual research, and concluded with a *doctorat*. Final examinations were taken in relevant fields.

Beginning in September 1992, the universities changed over to a degree structure of bachelor's (three to five years of study, according to the institution), master's (two to three years of graduate study), and PhD (several years beyond master's study plus a dissertation). There is some talk of maintaining the former *doctorat* beyond the PhD because of the concern of some who feel that the *doctorat* is a more advanced degree than the PhD.

All in all, the many higher education institutions prepare specialists in over 100 different professions, from physicians to veterinarians, from secondary school teachers to engineers and research workers. The average age of learners in higher education institutions is 25 years and the term of study averages between 5 and 6 years. In 1988, the country had 185 students per 10,000 population studying in higher education, and there were 265 higher education graduates per 10,000 population (State Committee 1988). In addition, there were, in 1988, over 100 foreign students from more than 10 different countries studying in Mongolian higher education institutions with all tuition and expenses covered by the government.

The quality and relevance of higher education are coming under new scrutiny. Profound reforms are called for in higher education in order to "radically improve the quality of training and better define the structure of professional disciplines" (Dash et al. 1990). Reforms are envisaged that will: put a greater emphasis on polytechnic education; create new specialties that will be needed in such new areas as environmental science; and expand international cooperation in developing and applying the new information and communication technologies in teaching.

Research in Mongolia generally has taken place in research institutes sometimes, but not necessarily, connected with the higher education institutions. It is estimated that there are about 60 scientific institutes attached to the Mongolian Academy of Sciences which is the country's main scientific organization.

Higher education policy in the 1990s suggests moving research back into universities and the elimination of many of the former research institutes. As of November 1991, for instance, the former Law Research Institute of the Academy of Sciences was absorbed by the Faculty of Law of the Mongolian National University. In early 1992, the agricultural institutes under the Academy of Sciences were negotiating to join the Agricultural University. It is expected that others will do the same. Current thinking is also affecting research in the social sciences. It is being candidly admitted "that sociological research ... has been dominated by a dogmatic vision, which has led to blind copying and simplification, instead of opening up new vistas as regards development" (Dash et al. 1990).

The Academy of Sciences did not report through the Ministry of Education until early 1993 when the Ministry of Education became the Ministry of Science and Education. This will ensure that the research institutes of the Academy will be pulled closer to the universities. At the same time, there are several institutes within the Academy which have established a Technology University, with the idea of becoming a small high technology research and training center. How this will develop, considering the limited resources available for new institutions and with a Technical University already in existence, remains to be seen.

Until the early 1990s, the number of students admitted to the various institutions of higher education was controlled by the State Planning Commission which no longer exists. The Ministry of Education, through the Institute of Education, sets entrance examinations to universities. Graduates of secondary school, with a ten-year *gerchilgee* certificate, can select examinations in humanities, engineering, agriculture, or language as options, in addition to the general examinations.

Table 2
Mongolian higher education 1986–92

Year	1986	1988	1990	1992
Higher education institutions	7	7	8	8
Total students, university/higher institutes[a]	23,516	20,732	16,910	16,364
in local institutions	17,358	15,074	13,397	13,464
in foreign institutions	6,158	5,649	3,513	2,900
New entrants	4,884	4,184	3,768	2,100
in local institutions	3,774	3,322	3,061	2,058
in foreign institutions	1,110	862	707	41
Graduation	4,758	4,435	3,510	2,433 (1993)
from local institutions	3,857	3,522	2,849	2,433 (1993)
from foreign institutions	901	913	661	—[c]
Staff members	3,002	3,014	3,023	2,952
teachers	1,488	1,462	1,429	1,499
Total expenditure (in thousands of tugreks)	75,374.7	77,931.6	77,143.1	215,513.6[b]

Source: Compiled from data supplied by the Ministry of Education, October 1991 and Ministry of Science and Education 1993
a The distinction between universities and institutes of university level appears to be disappearing, with most institutes either becoming universities or being merged into universities. b The value of the Tugrek fell from about 7 = US$1 in 1990 to about 400 = US$1 in late 1992. c By 1992, foreign study financed by the government had all but evaporated. Only 42 students embarked on study around programs in that year, largely sponsored by technical cooperation programs of other countries.

Universities then choose the top candidates who opt for their institutions. Secondary education may take place in general schools of polytechnic education that combine general subjects with those relating to production in a specified sector of agriculture or industry. Another method of entry to higher education (though generally not university) is that which follows upon a two- or three-year vocational course given at the end of eight years of general schooling. Institutions of higher education also have many students who have attended evening classes or secondary schools for adults.

Although investment in higher education has remained fairly stable over the past several years, enrollment has dropped by about 30 percent from 1985 to 1990 (see Table 2). In addition, students studying abroad (mainly in the former Soviet Union, the former German Democratic Republic, and Czechoslovakia) declined by about 43 percent. The latter decline is due, in part, to lack of scholarships and the fact that study abroad will increase dramatically in the direction of the developed market economy nations in the 1990s. The decline in domestic enrollment may be due in part to the perceived lack of opportunity for higher education graduates in the weak economy of the late

1980s and in part due to restrictions in admissions by some institutions.

The Ministry of Science and Education has prepared several strategy papers for the reform of higher education and is seeking bilateral and multilateral aid for reform efforts.

3.2 Preschool Education

The number of kindergartens in the country increased from 542 in 1975 to 909 in 1990 and is now declining. In 1992, there were 806 and estimates for 1994 suggest a dramatic decline, in part because enterprises are no longer financing kindergartens and government budgets are similarly being cut. In 1975, there were 1,367 kindergarten teachers (all female) and 36,900 children enrolled (49.3% female). In 1992, there were 85,671 children enrolled (52.3% female) representing about 30 percent of all children aged 3 to 7.

Most of these kindergartens are directly financed by the state, but 35 of the 806 kindergartens (enrolling about 10% of the total enrollment) were financed by businesses in 1992, in part to provide daycare facilities for their employees. There were, in 1992, about 14,408 staff members in the kindergartens, of which most had

Table 3
Mongolian preschool education 1986–92

Year	1986	1988	1990	1992
Number of children of kindergarten age (less than school entrance age of 8)	317,000	314,000	276,700	—
Children enrolled in kindergarten	69,746	81,029	97,212	85,671
state financed	65,566	75,047	88,395	81,817
enterprises financed	4,180	5,982	8,817	3,874
Number of kindergartens	696	770	909	806
state financed	654	695	779	771
enterprises financed	42	75	130	35
Number of beds being used in kindergartens	59,890	65,900	72,739	—
Number of children in inadequate kindergarten facilities	12,685	12,400	12,512	—
Number of children per 100 beds	116.5	123.0	133.6	—
Staff members of kindergarten	9,141	11,288	15,358	14,408
principal	609	676	801	708
teachers	2,349	2,767	3,747	3,732
with higher education training	28	32	62	60
with specialized (10 to 12 years) secondary education	2,087	2,329	2,959	3,074
with complete middle (8 years) education	226	392	688	58
with incomplete middle education (less than 8 years)	8	14	38	0
Total expenditure (in thousands of tugreks)	11,047.9	132,042.1	166,390.1	333,001.9[a]

Source: Compiled from data supplied by the Ministry of Science and Education, November 1993
a 1991 The increase in funding is due to a gradual decline in the value of the tugrek during 1990–91

full secondary education preparation. The government estimates that about 15 percent of the children in kindergarten are in substandard facilities (see Table 3 for complete figures, including expenditures on kindergartens). The austerity budgets of the early 1990s are affecting kindergarten enrollments. Many kindergartens in rural areas have been closed and, in the urban centers, many parents are withdrawing their children from kindergartens in part because of increases in the fees charged. Kindergarten fees rose from 35 tugreks per child per month in 1990 to 166 tugreks in 1992.

3.3 Special Education

There are six schools for mentally and physically handicapped children in Ulan Bator and there are classes in several schools for handicapped children in each *aimak*, or region. In addition, there are two schools in Ulan Bator for exceptionally talented children: one specializing in languages and one in technology. Government figures for 1990 suggest that 3,540 children of the total enrollment of 440,900 at the primary or secondary levels attended special education schools or classes (see Table 1 for enrollment figures from 1985 onward).

3.4 Vocational, Technical, and Business Education

Vocational, technical, and business education is offered at various levels, from the upper level (years 9

through 10 or 11) of basic education to specialized institutes at the postsecondary level and universities (see Tables 4 and 5). There were, in 1990, 26 technical vocational schools at the postsecondary level, enrolling 26,431 students in programs ranging from one to two years. In addition, there were 2,636 students studying abroad in postsecondary vocational schools (mostly in Russia and Eastern European countries that were formerly affiliated with the then Soviet bloc). The numbers enrolled abroad are dropping, having declined from a high of 1,882 in 1985 to 820 in 1990 and to 194 in 1992 (see Table 4).

In addition, there are specialized professional/technical schools that offer programs which extend two to three years beyond secondary school. There are 31 such schools enrolling 8,116 students (1992 figures). There were 587 students studying at comparable institutions abroad (down from 1,311 in 1989 and from comparable figures in earlier years) (see Table 5). Changes are anticipated in these postsecondary schools. Many will become a part of universities; others may become colleges. Others may be closed because of lack of funds in the austerity period of the mid-1990s.

3.5 Adult and Nonformal Education

The Ministry of Science and Education maintains a section which deals with education of employers and workers and which encourages inservice training. Most universities and colleges offer inservice training and

Table 4
Mongolian postsecondary technical/vocational education 1986–92

Year	1986	1988	1990	1992
Total Technical/Vocational (T/V) schools	41	43	44	44
specialized T/V schools	22	26	26	26
Total enrollment (in thousands)	29,276	33,797	29,067	11,685
in specialized T/V schools	16,372	21,858	20,825	—
Enrollment in local T/V schools	25,036	30,574	26,431	11,491
Enrollment in foreign T/V schools	4,240	3,223	2,636	194
New admissions (in thousands)	14,207	14,820	10,517	4,812
in local T/V schools	12,857	13,622	9,697	4,812
in foreign T/V schools	1,350	1,198	820	0
Graduation (in thousands)	11,842	11,884	13,872	9,820
from local T/V schools	10,371	10,491	12,778	—
from foreign T/V schools	1,471	1,393	1,094	—
Staff members (total)	4,117	4,683	4,168	—
teachers	1,916	2,278	1,817	746
Number of seats in buildings being used as T/V schools	16,810	22,151	23,471	13,180 (1993)
Average number of shifts in schools	1.49	1.38	1.13	—
Total expenditure (in thousands of tugreks)	102,516.8	118,498.2	108,170	—

Source: Compiled from data supplied by the Ministry of Science and Education, November 1993
a These schools are one or two years of postsecondary study and accept entrants from professional secondary schools (9 years of study) or the comprehensive school (10 years of study). See Fig. 1

most ministries offer inservice training in their fields of competence. In addition, the Mongolian National Center for Children provides a range of creative experiences for children throughout the teenage years. These institutions provide instruction in art, music, drama, and other areas, and are patterned after similar institutions in other former socialist countries.

Higher technical and professional institutes provide short courses for those already working. The Institute of Administration and Management Development, for instance, offers such courses (in addition to a one-year university-level program leading to a certificate). These courses cost (in 1991) 600 tugreks (about US$10 at the then free market rate) for a nine-month course and 140 tugreks (approximately US$2) for a one-week course. Some institutes and universities offer correspondence courses. By 1993, the exchange rate was about 400 tugreks to US$1, and fees had increased accordingly.

Although there is little illiteracy in the country, there is a possible problem of lack of use of literacy skills especially among women in nomadic families. A Danish-funded project for nomadic women in the Gobi Desert was begun in early 1992. It was designed to reach the women through radio education, reading materials geared to the needs of nomadic women, and other forms of training and education.

4. Administrative and Supervisory Structure and Operation

At the national level, the education system is administered by the Ministry of Science and Education. In the past, higher education policy was developed by the State Committee for Higher and Specialized Education and by the Mongolian People's Revolutionary Party (MPRP). Since the installation of a multiparty system and the disengagement of the MPRP as a decision-making body, the Ministry of Education and the legislature have developed new policy and administrative structures.

In 1991, for instance, a Higher Education Reform Commission was established by the legislature, jointly chaired by a representative of the legislature and the first vice-minister of the Ministry of Science and Education. In addition, a private "foundation for higher education" was established to encourage private industry and individuals to contribute to the development of higher education. There is some talk of combining these two groups in the future to form a National Higher Education Council which would both work with universities on policy and planning issues and interface with the private sector in the development of universities and colleges.

5. Educational Finance

Tables 1 through 5 include expenditures from 1985 through 1990 by educational level. It will be noted that expenditures have generally risen except for vocational/technical education. These figures are in tugreks, which, throughout 1990, were officially pegged at about 6 to US$1, though by 1991, the unofficial rate offered by the Cooperative Bank in Ulan Bator was 60 to US$1, and by June 1993, the free market rate was in excess of 400 tugrek to US$1. For comparison purposes, however, the rate of about US$1 to 8 tugreks would probably be fair for the period prior to 1991.

About 13 percent of GNP was spent on education in the 1980s and the average cost per student from

Table 5
Mongolian postsecondary specialized technical/professional education 1986–92

Year	1986	1988	1990	1992
Total specialized technical/professional schools[a]	28	29	31	31
Number of students	23,212	22,556	18,476	8,703
in local institutions	21,714	21,248	17,609	8,116
in foreign institutions	1,498	1,308	867	587
Number of new entrants	7,376	6,023	5,617	1,786
in local institutions	7,011	5,690	5,408	1,780
in foreign institutions	365	333	209	6
Staff members	2,451	2,581	2,679	—
teachers	1,224	1,201	1,260	460
Total expenditure (in thousands of tugreks)	71,217.1	72,967.8	75,306.9	—

Source: Compiled from data supplied by the Ministry of Science and Education, November 1993
a These schools are two to three years beyond the ten-year comprehensive school program and do not admit students from professional secondary schools as do the postsecondary technical/vocational schools listed in Table 4. See Fig. 1

1985 to 1989 was 1,862 tugreks. The educational budget was allocated as follows: those schools in the basic education program of 10 years, about 40 percent; kindergartens, about 12 percent; vocational schools, about 11 percent; technical colleges, about 7 percent; and higher education, about 8 percent. About 22 percent went for administration, new facilities, teaching materials, and other infrastructural expense. About 30 percent of the budget is allocated to teacher and staff salaries.

In the past, all education was free (with the exception of fees for kindergarten), though children have always had to purchase their own books. Many primary and secondary schools in rural areas have dormitories so as to provide living quarters for children of nomads. Austerity budgets are affecting these boarding schools, however, as the government often cannot supply the necessary meals. There was a serious drop in enrollment in these schools in 1991 and 1992. There is also some indication that with the economic problems of the early 1990s and unemployment among the educated that the nomads are losing interest in advanced education for their children.

A new higher education fees policy was introduced in 1993. From September of that year students have to pay tuition fees to the university they are attending; these fees are to be used to defray instructional costs of the university. Students may borrow the necessary fees (and living expenses) from the government, but this loan must later be repaid when they begin working. If they work for the government or teach for a specified time, the loan will be waived.

In the past, students accepted into the university not only had tuition paid, but received a living expense stipend. At the time of writing this entry, the effect of this new policy is not known, but it is likely that enrollment in some university programs will decline and others rise as students choose those programs which they feel will give them better chances at jobs when they complete their training.

Austerity budgets have affected the quality of educational facilities. The government feels that many of the facilities are substandard at all levels. Tables 1 and 3 list the number of kindergartens and schools that the government feels must be upgraded if the educational system is to meet its obligations to the public within the context of the new social and economic imperatives. A typewritten memo prepared by the Ministry of Education in 1991, the Draft Project on Getting Assistance in the Field of Education, suggests the need for external assistance of some US\$28.4 million to strengthen and improve the universities (US\$20.8 million); rural education and distance teaching (US\$2.5 million); teachers' qualifications (US\$2.5 million); teaching of the Mongol script (US\$1.7 million); computer education (US\$0.425 million); and educational printing facilities (US\$0.425 million). These figures will undoubtedly change as funding agencies carry out sector studies and other analyses, but it is clear that

Mongolia will need sizable foreign assistance if it is to improve its educational system consistent with its goals of joining the world's market economy and of establishing a thriving multiparty democracy.

6. Supplying Personnel for the Education System

Most teachers and administrators for the preschool through the secondary levels are prepared by the Pedagogical University in Ulan Bator and the Pedagogical Institute in Khovd (for the western region of the country). In addition to preservice training, the Pedagogical University has a Professionalization Institute to offer inservice training for teachers. Both institutions also have inservice training in educational administration. Traditionally, teachers must complete at least a one-month refresher course each five years. Some school teachers, especially in fields such as mathematics, chemistry, physics, and other scientific areas, are trained at the Mongolian State University.

There are very few teachers at any level without the necessary teaching credentials. The teacher–student ratio in comprehensive schools (i.e., the first ten years of schooling) is 1:28; in vocational schools and technical colleges, 1:15; and in higher education institutions, 1:12. About 66.9 percent of the education budget was spent on teacher and staff salaries in 1990. There is an oversupply of available teachers in Ulan Bator, and a shortage of teachers in rural areas.

7. Curriculum Development and Teaching Methodology

Most curriculum materials and textbooks in the past were translations from Soviet editions. There is now much urgency to prepare new textbooks and to begin using traditional Mongol script (*Ourgen*) which was replaced by Cyrillic in the early 1950s. Most curriculum and teaching materials development is done by the Institute of Education under the Ministry of Science and Education and by the Institute for Curriculum Development, Research, and Training under the Pedagogical University. The latter chooses authors of textbooks once a curriculum is approved. The Institute of Education engages in the preparation of nationwide examinations which are given at the eighth and tenth grade. Apart from these levels, promotion is more or less automatic, with local schools giving their own examinations.

Many secondary-level schools have sizable audiovisual facilities and projection materials provided by the Ministry of Education. Many of the audiovisual materials seem to be of the static variety (exhibits, models, etc.), with few programmed teaching materials. In the past, these were developed by special "methodological centers," set up with the help of the Soviets. With the lessening of Russian collaboration, it is not clear who will continue such work.

The Pedagogical University has several desktop computers and is attempting to develop computer-assisted instruction and instructional materials dealing with computers. All secondary-level schools are supposed to offer a computer course, though many do not, in fact, have computer facilities. All higher education institutions have some computer facilities, but most are very limited in scope.

8. The System of Examinations, Promotions, and Certifications

National examinations at the pre-higher education level are prepared by the Institute of Education under the Ministry of Science and Education and administered by the Ministry. The Ministry of Science and Education, through its higher education section, sets university entrance examinations. University faculty are engaged by the Ministry to do the actual writing of the examinations. Otherwise, the individual schools and universities examine their own students and set the grades. At the elementary and secondary level, Grade 3 is a pass, while Grades 4 and 5 are good and excellent respectively.

9. Educational Assessment, Evaluation, and Research

Apart from work in developing examinations for the various levels, there has been little educational research or assessment and evaluation of students, teachers, or faculty. With the new goal of integrating research with universities, it is expected that more research will be initiated in the future.

10. Major Reforms in the 1980s and 1990s

Major reforms are embodied in the new education law passed in July 1991 and in continuing policy decisions through 1994. The 1991 law speaks of "open education" whereby students may, after a basic education of at least eight years, leave the system and return at a later date. As seen from Fig. 1, there are various routes a student can take and all routes lead to some kind of continuing, inservice education if the student wishes to take advantage of it.

Curriculum changes at the elementary and secondary levels mandated for the 1990s include more natural science (a new subject); much less physics and astronomy; and new subjects such as history and social studies (combined course), practical arts and home economics, physical education and health, and moral education. At the ninth and tenth years, there will be 15 hours a week of diversified vocational studies. Essentially, the ninth and tenth grades (the last two years of basic education) will become a prevocational course for most students.

For the undiversified school (those without the heavy offering of prevocational work at the ninth and

tenth grades) there will be two options open to students. Those students who wish can pursue optional studies in lieu of the traditional academic program in physics, chemistry, biology, and geology.

Vocational–technical schools will be available beginning Grade 7 for those students who wish them. These will be of four years' duration with options to allow students to express individual interests. The tenth grade curriculum of the vocational schools is left up to the geographic regions to decide with the idea that there will be programs differentiated to meet the employment needs of each region.

The planning of higher education spaces, based on the number of specialized jobs anticipated, has been dropped and enrollment planning is now considerably decentralized. There is still, however, a highly complex system of classifying jobs in the labor market (a sizable manual exists with hundreds of jobs listed, each with a number), and the universities, institutes, and specialized secondary schools prepare individuals who are certified for one or more of these posts. With the universities changing over to Western-style bachelor's, master's, and doctoral programs not specifically geared to highly specialized job descriptions, there will be major adjustments to make in both the curriculum and in job market specifications.

Austerity budgets were already beginning to have major effects on the system at all levels by mid-1993. The tuition fees which students at the higher education level are charged will have a major effect on enrollments. The movement toward combining research with teaching at the universities and parallel diminishing of the importance of the Academy of Sciences will be interesting to track.

Essentially, there is some danger that the Mongolian education system, one of the most advanced of any developing nation, may retrogress over the next several years, with less nomads attending school, less children attending kindergarten, less young people finishing secondary school, less vocational and technical training available, and less secondary school graduates attending university. Already by mid-1994 the trend in this direction was significant.

Those managing the structural adjustment program, including the World Bank and other international agency advisors, must think carefully about the long-term effects of de-emphasizing the education system during the period of adjustment. It may take years to recover from the relative financial neglect of the 1990s if the neglect is allowed to continue.

11. Major Problems for the Year 2000

As Mongolia moves toward the year 2000, it will become more and more integrated into the world economy. It is attempting to restructure its educational system so that it is comparable to systems in the major industrial nations of the West. As it does this, it will encounter major issues in terms of content, methodology, staffing, structure, finance, and management. The challenge will be to build on the strong educational traditions that already exist and to modify, add, and otherwise develop programs that improve and make more efficient what already exists.

With the abandonment of the centralized manpower planning system, and with the universities now competing with each other for students, tuition fees, research funds, and other income, an entire new educational environment is developing. Also, as the market economy increases in vigor, jobs in the public sector such as teaching will become less attractive. As Mongolia's economy develops (as it will), the education system will have to compete with much higher paying opportunities in business and industry, much as in the richer countries.

The country has made a remarkably rapid start in its major reform effort. It will now need a major infusion of technical and financial cooperation in order to achieve its goals. At the same time, the Mongolians are moving ahead with major reforms designed to make the education system more efficient and relevant to their needs. With the high motivation and dedication of the Mongolians, one can expect to see continuing change, improvement, and revitalization of the education sector.

References

Dash M, Nyamaa D, Damdin D 1990 *Mongolia by the Year 2005*. UNESCO, Paris (BEP/GPI/60; BEP-90/WS/3)
The Economist 1991 The free market comes to Mongolia. 321(7729):92
Shapiro F 1992 A reporter at large: Starting from scratch. *The New Yorker*, January 20, pp. 39–58
Spaulding S 1990 Educational development and reform on the Soviet periphery: Mongolian People's Republic and Lao People's Democratic Republic. *J. Asian and African Affairs* 2(1): 109–24
State Committee for Higher and Specialized Secondary Education (Mongolia) 1988 *Post-secondary Education and Its Diversification in Relation to Employment*. International Bureau of Education, Geneva (microfiche SIRE/02239)
UNESCO 1990 Mongolia: Re-introduction of the Traditional Ourgen Alphabet. Draft project proposal, UNESCO, Paris
UNESCO 1991 *Statistical Yearbook 1991*. UNESCO, Paris

Further Reading

Academy of Sciences MPR 1990 *Information Mongolia: The Comprehensive Reference Service of the People's Republic of Mongolia: (MPR)*. Pergamon Press, Oxford
Akiner S (ed.) 1991 *Mongolia Today*. Routledge Chapter and Hall, London
Bawden C R 1989 *The Modern History of Mongolia*, 2nd edn. Kegan Paul International, London
Middleton N 1993 *The Last Disco in Outer Mongolia*. Orion Books Ltd., London
Morgan D I *The Mongols*. Basil Blackwell, London
Severin T 1991 *In Search of Genghis Khan*. Hutchinson, London
Storey R 1993 *Mongolia: A Travel Survival Kit*. Lonely Planet, Hawthorne, Australia
Worden R L 1991 *Mongolia: A Country Study*, 2nd edn. US Government Printing Office, Washington, DC
Yusuf S 1992 *Developing Mongolia*. World Bank, Washington, DC

Morocco

M. Radi

1. General Background

Morocco has a form of government known as a constitutional monarchy. There are 14 political parties and 8 large trade union organizations. Its land area is 710,850 square kilometers. In 1991, its population was estimated to be about 25 million persons. Slightly over 50 percent lived in rural areas. The average density of the population is 35 persons per square kilometer. The average annual population growth rate was 2.26 percent between 1982 and 1991. At the beginning of the 1990s just over 50 percent of the population was under 20 years of age.

Administratively, the country is divided into a series of units: 7 economic regions, 5 *wilayas*, 59 urban communities, 9 municipalities, 40 autonomous centers, and 760 rural communities.

In 1983, a series of measures were taken within a structural adjustment framework with the result that the Gross Domestic Product (GDP) rose from 99,140 million Dhs in 1983 to 207,000 million Dhs in 1990. In the 1980s, there had been a slight decrease in the amount of expenditure on education but by the onset of the 1990s it began to rise again and the proportion of the state budget allocated to education ranges between 18 and 26 percent.

The structure of the urban workforce is such that 4.6 percent work in the agricultural sector, 33.6 in industry (which mostly consists of manufacturing, mining, and handwork), and 15.2 percent in commerce. The comparable figures for rural areas are 78.3, 11.8, and 4.0. Arabic is the official language, but French is often used. Nearly all inhabitants are Moslems. The infrastructure has been much improved and it is only in remote areas that there are problems of communications.

Given the need to have a literate workforce, the government has made great efforts to eradicate illiteracy through schooling and through adult literacy programs, especially in rural areas.

2. Politics and the Goals of the Education System

Morocco achieved Independence in 1956. Since that time, the principles of equality of access to education and free educational provision have had the highest priority at all levels of education. Basic education now lasts for nine years and consists of a first cycle of six years and a second cycle of three years. Equality of access across all socioeconomic groups has not been achieved for secondary education and tertiary education, as is the case in many countries. Furthermore, given the high, and ever-increasing, costs of education it is difficult for the Ministry of Education to compete with other sectors of the society requiring government support.

The 1988 to 1992 development plan, based on the educational reform of 1985, stressed the need to expand the number of students enrolled at the different levels of the system but in a regulated way depending on the resources available. Particular emphasis is placed on the improvement of the quality of education offered at the first cycle of basic education in rural areas and on the diversification of secondary education with special attention to the expansion and upgrading of vocational training. As already stated above, more literacy programs have been instituted. At the university level, the policy is to continue the decentralization already begun, to make the content more relevant to the needs

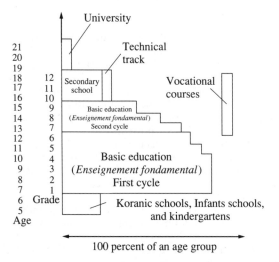

Figure 1
Morocco: Structure of the formal education system

of the labor market, to improve the quality of teaching, and to foster more applied research to help in the economic development of the country.

3. The Formal System of Education

3.1 Primary, Secondary, and Tertiary Education

Figure 1 presents a diagram of the structure of the education system. Children enter school at 7 years of age. The first cycle of basic education lasts for six grades (ages 7 to 12). In 1992, there were 2,485,000 pupils enrolled in this stage of education. Those enrolled represent 75 percent of the relevant age group. The second stage of basic education lasts for three years (ages 13 to 15); about 60 percent of the relevant age group enrolled. Those not entering this second cycle of basic education may attend vocational courses in special centers. Indeed, as pupils drop out of the second cycle of basic education at each of the grade levels 7, 8, and 9, they may enter these vocational courses. At the end of Grade 9, students are oriented to either general and technical or vocational tracks in secondary school. Secondary school lasts for three years (ages 16 to 18). At the end of secondary school, students sit for the *baccalauréat* which in turn leads to either academic or vocational higher education. Because of financial constraints, the percentage of students transferring from the second cycle of basic education to secondary school is fixed at 40 (i.e., 40% of the 60% of the age group enrolled in the second cycle of basic education). In other words, about 24 percent of an age group is enrolled in secondary school: 5 percent of these students are enrolled in vocational schools. There are also private schools. For comparison purposes, there are 2,485,000 students in the first cycle of basic education in state schools, 790,200 in the second cycle, and 333,500 in secondary schools. The comparable figures for the private school system are 93,500, 16,800, and 8,600.

There are two types of institutions in higher education. The first is the universities run by the Ministry of Education and the other is the training establishments run by other ministerial departments. In 1992, there were 220,000 students enrolled in higher education. Of these, about 4,000 were foreigners. About 90 percent of all students were to be found in the academic faculties (in the faculties of arts, sciences, law, social sciences) in 11 universities throughout the country. About 6 percent were in the faculties of medicine and engineering. The remaining students were in technical institutions. Efforts are being made to increase the number of faculties. There is also a form of higher, but nonuniversity, education. This comprises specialized schools and institutions run by different ministries to train their own technical personnel in such matters as engineering, administration, agriculture, telecommunications, public works, mining, and so on. It also comprises pedagogical training centers and special centers run by the Ministry of Education for training teaching personnel, supervisors, and administrators.

3.2 Preschool Education

Preschool education belongs to the private sector, but is under the supervision of the Ministry of Education. There are two types of establishment, one being the Koranic schools. In 1992, 788,400 children were enrolled in preschool institutions. About 83 percent of these children are enrolled in these schools which dispense a renovated, but traditional type of teaching (i.e., Koranic schools). Other children are enrolled in infants schools and kindergartens which are based on more modern methods of education.

3.3 Special Education

There are few institutions concerned with special education. In 1990, there were 15 institutions: 10 institutions belonging to the Alaouite Organization for the Blind, with 238 pupils enrolled; and 5 institutions for the handicapped (deaf and dumb, mentally retarded, etc.) with an enrollment of 319 pupils.

These institutions, which belong to nongovernmental organizations, are subsidized by the state. There are also other institutions of special education which belong to the private sector.

3.4 Vocational, Technical, and Business Education

Vocational training and education is being restructured in order to make the content more relevant to the socioeconomic needs of the country. There are three levels of vocational training. The first, known as the "specialization" level, receives pupils from Grades 6, 7, and 8. The second, known as the "qualification" level receives pupils from Grades 9, 10, and 11. The third, known as the "technician" level receives pupils from Grade 12 and also those from the first degree level of the university. The specialized level has a two-year course, after which the graduate becomes a specialized (craft) worker. The qualified level also has a two-year course, after which the graduate becomes a qualified worker. The technician level has courses of varying duration at the end of which the graduate receives a technical diploma. In 1991, about 105,000 persons were enrolled in vocational institutions.

3.5 Adult and Nonformal Education

Nonformal education in Morocco comprises literacy programs for adults. In 1991, about 255,000 persons were enrolled in such courses. The literacy programs have a basic phase, a complementary phase, and a follow-up phase. The basic phase lasts six months with six hours of instruction per week. The objective is for the participants to acquire the fundamental principles of reading, writing, and arithmetic. The complementary phase also lasts six months and provides basic knowledge and skills in the use of literacy for daily life and work. Finally, the follow-up phase is of unlimited duration and aims at maintaining communication with participants by means of an information bulletin and continues to convince them of the utility of education and of the dangers of falling back into illiteracy.

4. Administrative and Supervisory Structure and Organization

The Ministry of Education is divided into two parts: one for basic and secondary education, and a second for higher education. Both parts are headed by the Minister who is assisted by the Cabinet and General Secretary. Beneath the General Secretary are a number of directorates, and within directorates there are several divisions. The task of the Ministry is to develop and implement all institutional and pedagogical measures reflecting government policy. In particular, it is responsible for the construction and equipping of all educational institutions.

For basic and secondary education, there are regional, provincial, and local offices which are responsible for the implementation of Ministry policy in their areas. For higher education, all institutions come directly under the Ministry.

There are also other ministries that are responsible for various aspects of education. The Ministry of Public Works is responsible for coordinating all activities of vocational training. The Ministry of Social Affairs is responsible for all literacy programs. The Ministry of Youth and Sports supervises educational activities for pupils having dropped out of school.

5. Educational Finance

Most of the financing of educational and training activities is provided from the state budget. The budget for basic secondary and higher education in 1991 was 26.3 percent of the state budget. This represented 5.76 percent of the Gross Domestic Product (GDP). However, since 1990, local communities have taken over the construction of schools for the first cycle of basic education. This represents about one-third of the investment budget of basic and secondary education. It should also be mentioned that the departments of the other ministries responsible for different aspects of education also have their own budgets for financing their activities.

Loans have been received from the World Bank and the African Development Bank. Contributions, generally in the form of gifts, have also been provided by other international and regional organizations such as the EEC, UNFPA, UNICEF, and so forth.

In 1991, the amount spent on education by the state and local communities was 13,278 million Dhs of which 12,430 million Dhs (94%) came from the Ministry of Education and 848 million Dhs from other ministries. The per pupil expenditure was 1,490 Dhs per year for the first cycle of basic education, 3,600 Dhs for the second cycle, 6,630 Dhs for secondary education, and 7,940 Dhs for higher education. (The exchange rate in June 1992 was about US$1=8.35 Dh.)

6. Supplying Personnel for the Education System

The preservice training of teachers is different for the different levels of education. For the first cycle of basic education, the training is of two years' duration in teacher-training centers. The entry requirements are the possession of a *baccalauréat*. However, for those students who have obtained a certificate at the end of the first cycle (two years) of university studies, only one year of study at the teacher-training center is required.

For the second cycle of basic education, teachers are trained in regional pedagogical centers. The training lasts two years for those having the *baccalauréat*, and one year for those having successfully completed the first cycle of university studies. Although the academic requirements for entering the teacher-training centers and the regional pedagogical centers are the same, there is a difference in the level of marks required for entry and in the specialization in the content studied.

The training of secondary school teachers takes place in *Ecoles Normales Superieures*. For those having the *baccalauréat*, the course lasts four years; and for those having a university degree (licence), it lasts one year.

The National Center of Inspectors is responsible for training supervisory personnel. All teachers having had at least four years of teaching experience may apply. The course lasts three years for the inspectors of the first cycle of basic education and two years for the second cycle of basic education and secondary school.

The Educational Planning and Orientation Center runs a two-year course leading to a diploma in planning or guidance counseling (orientation) for teachers from the second cycle of basic education. Entry is on a competitive basis. If successful in the course the planners or guidance counselors may continue on to take a further course to become an inspector.

Teachers and administrative personnel also attend inservice training. This training may last from a few days to a few weeks. It consists of seminars, workshops, conferences, information days, and refresher courses. The main aim of inservice training is to upgrade skills in teaching, inspection, planning, and administration. When systemwide innovations are introduced, regional and national seminars are organized.

7. Curriculum Development

Syllabuses and textbooks for basic and secondary education are the responsibility of specially appointed commissions composed of inspectors and teachers. Their activities are supervised by pedagogic directorates within the Ministry of Education. The textbooks are written on the basis of the syllabuses. They are piloted in judgment samples of relevant schools and revised before being implemented in the school system.

In general, syllabuses and textbooks are revised every four years. The use of these syllabuses and textbooks by private schools is compulsory. Mostly, they are produced in Arabic, including scientific materials; and in French, English, and Spanish for foreign language teaching. Textbooks are either bought or rented by pupils. Each pupil may rent the set of grade textbooks at a very low rate for the whole year. Every year there is an official list of textbooks. In 1991, this list contained 42 for the first cycle of basic education, 30 for the second cycle, and 57 for secondary education.

8. The System of Promotions, Examinations, and Certifications

Teachers are trained to conduct both formative and summative evaluation in their classes. Teachers are issued with formative evaluation materials in order that both teachers and pupils can see the results of the pupils' learning. At each grade, there are standard school term and year examinations. In the first cycle of basic education, promotion from one grade to the next is based on the teachers' assessments of pupils' homework and classwork. For promotion from the first to the second cycle of basic education, the teachers' assessments and the results on an examination at the end of the cycle are taken into account.

The same procedures are used for promotion from one grade to another within the second cycle of basic education. Again, each school sets standard term examinations. The transition from the upper cycle of basic education to secondary school is based on the results of the term examinations. A committee within the school, composed of teachers and guidance counsellors, recommends to each pupil whether he or she is better suited for entry to academic or vocational secondary schools. Entry to secondary schools depends on the number of places available.

In secondary schools, there are two regional examinations per year. These examinations are meant to help teachers and pupils to maintain their efforts in order to finish their courses on time. Obtaining the *baccalauréat* depends in part on the average performance on each of the two examinations per year over the three years. The new form of examination uses different techniques of evaluation including written and oral questions, practical exercises, and homework. The results on this *baccalauréat* diploma determine whether a pupil enters higher education in a university, higher education in an nonuniversity institution, or a vocational training establishment.

All studies in higher education for a licence last four years. A further two to three years are required for a *Doctorat de Troisieme Cycle* or three to five years for a *Doctorat d'Etat*. Promotion from year to year is based on the results of two mid-term examinations per year. However, courses in medicine last seven years and five years in pharmacy and dentistry.

In engineering institutions, students must have completed two years of study in *classes preparatoires* and the courses then last three years for a State Engineering Diploma, five years for a Research Preparatory Certificate, and eight years for a doctorate in science.

9. Educational Assessment, Evaluation, and Research

The Ministry of Education is responsible for research and evaluation activities. These increased in number at the end of the 1980s after the educational and vocational training reforms had become effective.

The major areas of research which have received most attention cover curriculum, teaching methods, evaluation of achievement, administration, school management, personnel training, access of rural children to education, educational finance, educational planning, and school and vocational guidance.

10. Reforms in the 1980s and 1990s

Changes in the 1970s in the economic and social structure of the society as well as the rapid expansion of the educational services led to certain dysfunctions between the educational system and its environment. There was a decline in the efficiency of the educational system and there were disparities between urban and rural areas in terms of demand for education. To overcome this situation, the government reformed the structure and content of the school system. It created a basic school divided into two cycles of six and three years of education. Secondary school consisted of three years of education with academic and technical tracks. Priority was given to basic education and vocational training. The various aims of this reform were:

(a) that 78 percent of seven-year olds should be enrolled in school by 1992;

(b) that the transition rate from the first cycle to second cycle of basic education should reach 80 percent by the school year 1992–93;

(c) in terms of vocational training, 20 percent of

Grade 6 pupils should enter the specialization level, 40 percent of Grade 9 pupils should enter the qualification level, and 40 percent of Grade 12 pupils should enter the technician level;

(d) that the promotion rates from one grade to the next should be 80 to 85 percent. (Grade repeating should be about 10 to 15% and should not exceed 20% at the end of a cycle.)

In terms of the quality of education, the reform envisaged updating the content of textbooks, the local adaptation of curriculum for rural areas, experimenting with new methods of teaching, special educational activities for slow learners, and a review of all courses for personnel upgrading.

Further accompanying measures were implemented. These included the upgrading of teachers in rural areas, the upgrading of social services in terms of food and health, the improvement of planning procedures, and the decentralization of educational services.

11. Major Problems for the Year 2000

On the eve of the twenty-first century, Morocco, because of its geographic position and economic condition, can play an important role in the region on condition that it enhances the level of its population's education and vocational training. The challenge of the 1990s is related to democratic access to education and to the improvement of the relevance of education to the socioeconomic development needs of the country. It is envisioned that all children of school age, regardless of their sex or place of residence, will have access to school. Furthermore, all efforts will be made to keep all of those entering Grade 1 in school up to the end of Grade 9. To this end, priority will be given to enrollment and the quality of education in the basic school. More second cycle basic education schools will be built in rural areas and more effort will be made to enroll girls. The aim is to have 80 percent of pupils completing the first cycle entering the second cycle. The enrollment of those entering secondary school will be kept at 40 percent of those finishing the second cycle of basic education. Vocational training at this level will be enhanced. More vocational and technical courses will be provided at the higher education level. Private institutions in private education will be encouraged by the state. Finally, bridges or pathways between higher education institutions and vocational institutions will be formed to allow movements of students between the two.

Bibliography

Banque Mondiale 1989 Projet d'appui au premier cycle de l'enseignement fondamental en milieu rural (unpublished research report)

Banque Mondiale 1991 Projet d'appui au deuxième cycle de l'enseignement fondamental en milieu rural (unpublished research report)
Ministère de l'Education Nationale 1990a *Bilan et perspectives de réforme et de développement de système éducatif.* Ministère de l'Education Nationale, Rabat
Ministère de l'Education Nationale 1990b *Le mouvement éducatif au Maroc.* Ministère de l'Education Nationale, Rabat
Ministère de l'Education Nationale 1990c *Recensement annuel de l'enseignement primaire.* Ministère de l'Education Nationale, Rabat
Ministère de l'Education Nationale 1990d *Recensement annuel de l'enseignement secondaire.* Ministère de l'Education Nationale, Rabat
Ministère de l'Education Nationale 1991 *Note d'orientation sectorielle pour la préparation du plan 1993–97.* Ministère de l'Education Nationale, Rabat
Ministère de Plan 1987a *Population active rurale, résultats détaillés.* Ministère de Plan, Rabat
Ministère de Plan 1987b *Population active urbaine, résultats détaillés.* Ministère de Plan, Rabat
Ministère de Plan 1990 *Annuaire statistique de Maroc.* Ministère de Plan, Rabat
Ministère de Plan 1992 *Projections de la population du Maroc a long terme.* Ministère de Plan, Rabat

Mozambique

A. Nhavotto

1. General Background

Mozambique's 783,000 square kilometers of territory is cut by five major river basins in a west to east direction that effectively divide the country into a northern section of highlands and a southern section of fertile lowlands.

The 1980 census established Mozambique's population at 12.1 million, and projected 15.7 million for 1990 and 18.1 million for 1995. Fertility has been consistently high and fairly stable. From 1950 to 1980 the crude birthrate varied only from 50 to 47 births per 1,000 persons. There is a decline in mortality: the crude deathrate declined from 35.2 per 1,000 in the period 1950–55 to 20.7 per 1,000 in the period 1975–80. As a result of the continuous reduction of the mortality level and the prevailing high fertility, the Mozambican population is experiencing rapid growth. The annual population growth rate is estimated at 2.7 percent per year. A corollary of this is the youthful population which increases the demand not only for educational services, but also for such amenities as health care, transport, communication, housing, and employment.

Only 1 percent or less of the population has Portuguese as mother tongue, and the majority of the population speaks one or more of the 20 different Bantu languages. It should be noted that there is no single national mother tongue in the country and that Portuguese has therefore been adopted from Grade 1 onward as the language of instruction. This seems to be one of the most important causes of the high repetition and dropout rates.

The potentially active workforce (aged 15 to 59) is estimated to be 6.1 million persons, of which about 50 percent are thought to be economically active. The formal private sector employs approximately 200,000 workers, while public administration accounts for 100,000. These totals suggest a wage-earning sector of about 10 percent of the economically active population. It can be assumed that the remaining 90 percent are employed in agriculture, in the informal urban and rural sectors, or are unemployed.

Within the formal private sector, manufacturing is the biggest employer, accounting for about 10 percent of total employment, followed by commerce (22%), agriculture (14%), and construction (11.5%). The formal private workforce is unevenly distributed by province and gender. Maputo City (44%) and Maputo Province (15%) account for the biggest shares of the workforce. Sofala has 14 percent, while Zambezia and Nampula (the two most populous provinces in Mozambique) have 8 and 7 percent respectively. Men dominate the workforce in all provinces and in all economic areas. Women represent less than 13 percent of those employed.

Mozambique is by a considerable margin the poorest country in the world according to the United Nations. The per capita Gross Domestic Product (GDP) in 1990 was estimated at approximately US$80. Two-thirds of the population are believed to live in absolute poverty as a result of the continuing effects of war and the devastating drought affecting the country. Foreign aid comprises fully two-thirds of measured GDP and the export–import ratio was estimated at 0.35:1 in 1992.

Mozambique has eleven provinces including Maputo, the capital. Second to the Mozambican Parliament, which is legislative in power, there is the Council of Ministers. There are about 20 ministries and some secretariats of state. At the local level, there is a provincial government which, among other things, includes a Provincial Directorate of Education. In the first years of Independence (1975), a one-party system with a highly centralized government was established. In the early 1990s there was a move toward decentralization, following a shift in 1987 from a centrally planned to a market-oriented economy. There were also major political changes in 1990, shifting from a single to a multiparty system. This decentralization policy, however, will take some time to take effect, and in 1993 it was still common for decisions to be made at the central level.

Mozambique in 1993 was in a transition phase from a single to a multiparty system. It had just come out of one of the bloodiest wars in Southern Africa which had lasted 20 years. The chief political goal the country aspires to is the establishment of a long-lasting peace which, it is believed, will lay the basis for democracy and socioeconomic development.

2. Politics and the Goals of the Educational System

The politics and goals of education can be found in the 1983 and 1992 laws. It is stated that the educational system must eradicate illiteracy in the adult population, establish a free, universal, and compulsory seven-year primary education and train the cadres judged necessary for the country's socioeconomic development. At the same time, equal access to education is to be given to all Mozambicans.

Although these goals were established under single party rule, their value is so universal that they are endorsed by other political parties and, in practice, differences tend to be more of degree than of substance.

Following criticisms from different sectors of society that the educational system involved a lot of Marxist–Leninist ideology, there was a revision of the law in 1992 that removed this ideology, but did not change either the content or the structure of the system.

3. The Formal System of Education

Figure 1 presents the structure of the National System of Education (SNE).

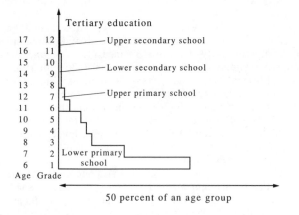

Figure 1
Mozambique: Structure of the formal education system

At Independence in 1975, there was an illiteracy rate of 93 percent, one of the highest worldwide, and the educational system at the time was organized in a discriminatory way. There were official schools, mainly in the urban areas, attended by the children of the Portuguese settlers and a minority of Mozambicans, children of "*assimilados*"—faithful servants of the colonial regime. The vast majority of Mozambican children either had no access to education, because of the discriminatory nature and insufficiency of the system, or attended the few missionary schools that existed, mainly in the rural areas. Apart from the missionary schools, there were a few private schools in the urban centers and these were generally attended by pupils who could not get access to the official schools.

In order to guarantee nondiscriminatory and equal access opportunities to education for all Mozambicans, the government decided to nationalize education and abolish the private and missionary schools. Curricula and educational programs with typical colonial content, such as the teaching of the history and geography of Portugal, were replaced by content relevant to Mozambique. Despite these curricular changes, the government later started an education review program which resulted in the introduction of a new system of education in 1983. One grade is added every year and the system will be completed in 1994 with the introduction of Grade 12. Education is, in practice, not yet compulsory and the school population pyramid is wide at the bottom, with about 500,000 children in Grade 1, and narrow at the top, with only 1,000 students in the 10th Grade and about 300 entering university each year. Less than 1 in 500 students entering the system has the chance of finishing secondary education.

The distribution of students in the different levels of the system is as follows: 86 percent in lower-primary; 9.5 percent in upper-primary; 3.7 percent in lower-secondary; and 0.3 percent in higher education.

3.1 Primary, Secondary, and Tertiary Education

Lower-primary education (EP1) begins at the age of seven and consists of five grades. Pupils are in the 7–11 age group. In 1991 over 1.2 million pupils attended the lower-primary school. This was 14 percent less than in 1979 when a maximum of 1.4 million pupils attended this level of education. Girls represented 41 percent in 1991 compared with the maximum of 44 percent in 1986, but there is a drop in this percentage in the higher levels of education. From 1975 to the 1980s, the average annual growth rate of the school population was around 16 percent compared with the 2.7 percent for the whole population. This rapid school population growth should have allowed a significant reduction in the illiteracy rate in the country. However, throughout the 1980s, the gross and net schooling rate dropped from 75.5 to 54 percent and from 50.6 to 37.5 percent from 1981 to 1989 respectively. This decline was mainly due to the destabilizing war in the country which caused the destruction or closure of 3,400 schools. This corresponded to 58 percent of the school network at this level and affected about 1.3 million pupils in the period between 1983 and 1991.

Because of the large flux of people from rural to big urban centers, the demand for education dramatically increased in these areas and the government has been unable to meet it satisfactorily. In an attempt to minimize the problem, the government decided to run three shifts in all of the lower-primary schools in the major urban centers instead of the two originally planned. As a consequence, the number of teaching hours per pupil/year has decreased by about 30 percent (from 850 to 595 hours). A 9 percent increase was planned for 1993. Some schools also have an evening shift devoted to the teaching of adults and teenagers who could not obtain places in the other shifts.

Private education is minimal, owing to the fact that it was abolished in 1975 and was only reintroduced in 1990.

In general terms, lower-primary education is highly inefficient, having high repetition and dropout rates; the promotion rate is invariably below 60 percent.

Upper-primary education (EP2) consists of only two grades (6 and 7) and is attended by pupils who have successfully completed the lower-primary grades and are in the 12–13 age range. Unlike lower-primary education, upper-primary has witnessed a steady growth. In 1991 there were 119,000 pupils in upper-primary schools. In spite of the efforts made at this level of education, the enrollment rate remained low, and, in 1991, barely 10 percent of those in lower-primary went into upper-primary. In 1975, girls represented 44 percent of the total upper-primary school population, but in 1991 only 39 percent. In absolute terms, however, the figure rose from about 9,000 to over 46,000 in the same period. Between 1982 and 1987 the transition rate from lower- to upper-primary was 70 percent on average. However, because of the increase of the number of lower-primary graduates and the lack of places in upper-primary schools, the transition rate was approximately 64 percent in 1991. Internal efficiency in the upper-primary is also very low. Grade 7 graduates represent just over one-third of the pupils that entered Grade 6.

Lower-secondary education (ESG1) consists of Grades 8, 9, and 10, and officially it is attended by the 14 to 16-year old age group. Pupils are mainly graduates from the upper-primary school, but also from elementary technical and vocational schools. These pupils, if they so wish, can also enroll in the basic technical and vocational education or in primary teacher-training courses. Lower-secondary education is relatively important as it meets the country's demand for a professionally trained and qualified workforce as well as preparing persons for higher education. However, there is only a limited number of these schools in almost all the eleven provinces. There has been an increase in enrollment in lower-secondary education and 26,000 pupils were enrolled in 42 schools in 1991,

representing a mere 2 percent of the upper-primary population, although the transition rate was 55 percent from Grade 7 to 8. Over 40 percent of the lower-secondary enrollments are in Maputo. The female population in lower-secondary education is very low despite the relative upward trend. It rose from less than 20 percent in 1975 to 34 percent in 1991. Again, the efficiency of the lower-secondary school is very low. For example, in 1990, 52 percent of the lower-secondary students failed at the end of Grade 8 and the system was able to produce only 3,000 new lower-secondary school graduates.

Upper-secondary education (ESG2) comprises Grades 11 and 12. In official terms, this level of schooling is also known as preuniversity education, and it is attended by students between 17 and 18 years of age. All students may attend who have either finished lower-secondary education or basic technical and vocational education. These graduates can pursue their studies either in technical and vocational education or in upper-primary teacher-training courses. The importance of upper-secondary education lies both in providing a middle-level, trainable labor force for the labor market and in preparing students for higher education, and thus for eventual positions of leadership in political and economic spheres.

Despite their crucial role, however, in 1991, upper-secondary schools were only in 6 out of the 11 provinces and were attended by 3,400 students (32% of whom were female) and about 50 percent of the students were in Maputo. The total number of students enrolled represented only 0.3 percent of the total lower-primary school population. In 1991, the transition rate from lower- to upper-secondary school was 44 percent. However, as a result of the increase in the number of Grade 10 graduates and the stagnation of the upper-secondary network, the transition rate may decrease, even though the Ministry of Education intends to maintain the 1991 levels by extending the network to all the provinces by 1995–96. Internal efficiency is low. In 1990, when the population exceeded 15 million, the system produced only 500 new upper academic secondary graduates.

The higher education sector comprises one university (Eduardo Mondlane University), one teacher-training institute for secondary school teachers (Higher Pedagogical Institute), and one institute for diplomacy and political sciences (Higher Institute for International Relations). There are no graduate courses. Enrollment in 1991 was about 5,000 students. There are gender and regional disparities. The majority of the students are from the southern part of the country (mainly from Maputo) and the proportion of women, for example in 1991, did not exceed 25 percent in any of the tertiary education institutions.

3.2 Preschool Education

Preschool education is not compulsory and takes place in the kindergartens, which are few in number and mainly concentrated in the urban areas. There are some kindergarten programs which are operated by community groups in suburban areas. The Ministries of Education and Health and the Secretariat of State for Social Welfare determine the opening, functioning, and closure of preschool centers.

3.3 Special Education

Special education is designed for children and young people with physical and sensory disturbances. It provides general and vocational training to enable pupils to reintegrate in regular schools and normal life. Both the number of schools and enrollments are minimal, although it is recognized that the war greatly increased both the number of children with disturbances and the gravity of their traumas.

3.4 Vocational, Technical, and Business Education

The main objectives of technical and vocational education are to prepare young people to carry out their jobs in a given field; to develop the right attitude toward work; and to develop the ability to investigate, innovate, organize, and conduct work scientifically. There are three levels: namely, elementary, basic, and middle, each of which is divided into three areas: agricultural, industrial, and commercial. In relation to general education, the elementary level lasts for two years and is equivalent to upper-primary; the basic and middle levels last for three years each and are equivalent to lower- and upper-secondary, respectively.

The agricultural courses include agriculture, animal husbandry, and forestry. The industrial courses include civil construction, mechanics, electricity, mining, and the like. The commercial field includes courses such as accountancy, secretarial, management, and information and technology.

There are two types of elementary schools: arts and crafts, and agriculture. The number of these schools decreased from 12 in 1975 to 1 in 1991 as a result of the war. After that date, however, some schools reopened and the building of new ones began. In 1991, the basic level of technical and vocational education had an enrollment of 7,600 students in schools spread throughout the provinces (enrolling 12.8% in agriculture, 27.2% in commerce, and 60% in industry). Girls represented 20.7 percent of the total number of students enrolled in the basic level (15.2%, 44%, and 11.2% of students enrolled in agriculture, commerce, and industry, respectively).

Middle-level schools run courses in more than 20 different subjects, but in 1991 they functioned in only 8 educational institutions in 6 of the 11 provinces of the country. In that year 2,100 students attended this level (20.8% in teacher-training courses for technical education, 26.1% in commercial courses, 17.5% in agricultural courses, and 35.6% in industrial

courses). Female participation in middle-level schools was only 13.6 percent (2.5% in teacher training, 8.3% in agriculture, 8.8% in industry, and 32.2% in commerce).

3.5 Adult and Nonformal Education

Measures taken by the government soon after Independence to democratize access to education created favorable conditions for adults to participate in literacy campaigns or in technical and general education by attending evening classes. Literacy campaigns and adult education are formalized. Nonformal education for adults is almost nonexistent.

The illiteracy rate decreased from 93 percent in 1975 to about 72 percent in 1980 in accordance with the general population census carried out in that period. The number of adults participating in literacy campaigns rose from about 275,000 in 1978 to 415,000 in 1980. The number of participants then decreased to 46,600 in 1989. This decrease was due mainly to the devastating effects of war, excessive formalization of literacy programs, the use of the Portuguese language (when many adults cannot understand or communicate in this language) as the medium of instruction, and the poor quality of literacy teachers and adult educators.

4. Administrative and Supervisory Structure and Operation

Up to 1975, Mozambique was regarded as one of the provinces of Portugal. The educational system was, therefore, run by the Provincial Education and Inspection Services. Most of the staff of these two services were Portuguese nationals and soon after Independence they fled the country. In 1975 the Ministry of Education and Culture, which included physical education and sports, was created. Because of the shortage of specialized and qualified personnel, several civil servants, teachers included, with no prior training in educational management and planning, were recruited to Ministry posts.

By 1993 the Ministry of Education (MINED) was no longer responsible for culture, physical education, and sports, and was primarily in charge of the planning, management, and supervision of the National System of Education (SNE). The curricula and educational programs, with the exception of those for higher education, were of national scope and approved by the Ministry of Education. That is, the management of the educational system was centralized in principle, but decentralized at the implementation level with the delegation of some central functions to the province, district, and school levels.

At the central level the Ministry comprises three national directorates and eight executive directorates and departments. The former are the directorates of primary education, general secondary education, and that of vocational and technical education. The latter are directorates such as planning, human resources, administration and finance, and school social welfare. There are also the *Instituto National de Desenvolvimento da Educação* (INDE) and the *Instituto para o Aperfeiçoamento de Professores* (IAP) which are central bodies that enjoy a certain degree of autonomy in relation to the central Ministry. The Eduardo Mondlane University (UEM) and the *Instituto Superior Pedagogico* (ISP) are higher education institutions with administrative autonomy. At the provincial and district levels there is a Provincial Directorate of Education (DPE) and a District Directorate of Education (DDE), respectively, and in both cases the directors are appointed by the Minister of Education despite the fact that they are subordinate to both the provincial governor and the district administrator. In general, schools are run by a director, a deputy director, and an administrator.

5. Educational Finance

In 1980 expenditure in education accounted for about 12 percent of the public budget and 4 percent of GDP. After 1980 expenditure experienced a sharp decline before stabilizing at about 8 percent of the 1988 budget. As a percentage of GDP, government expenditure fell from 4.5 percent in 1983 to 2.5 percent in 1987, increasing to 4.8 percent in 1989. In constant 1980 prices (US$1 used to be approximately MT40), per capita government expenditure on education, which had reached MT255 in 1981, dropped to MT128 in 1987 before rising to an estimated MT199 in 1989. In 1987 total education outlays were, in constant prices, about two-thirds of what they had been in 1980. By 1989 they had nearly recovered to the peak 1981 level. However, in 1993, levels were still not commensurate with the expectations placed upon the sector.

Education suffered a larger reduction of resources than other public sectors in the adjustment process at the beginning of the 1990s. However, users of the system did not bear the entire burden of the decline in education expenditure in the 1980s as actual cuts affected mainly teachers' real salaries which fell steeply during the period (a drop of about 50% between 1986 and 1987). Nevertheless, this trend, as well as expenditure cuts on items such as maintenance and school supplies, most probably had a tangible impact on the quality of education being provided.

The share of education in the recurrent budget which was about 18 percent between 1980 and 1982 dropped sharply to 10 percent in 1987 as result of the economic crisis and ensuing economic rehabilitation program. In real terms, recurrent expenditures fell 17 percent per year on average between 1980 and 1987, the year when they reached their lowest level. Real unit expenditures were reduced by half between 1982 and 1987.

Beginning in 1988, resources allocated to education began to increase again. The rise in sector recurrent expenditures can be explained by a relatively faster increase in the number of enrollments in the upper levels of education which have higher unit costs.

In 1993 nonsalary outlays funded by external assistance were higher than internal budget allocations and represented half of the total recurrent aid. This shows the fundamental role aid can play. However, these contributions are concerned with only a few items such as textbook production, food, assistance for import duties and shipment, and some inputs for the central and provincial administration. Many other important school inputs such as educational materials for teachers and basic supplies for the classrooms are considerably underfunded.

The relative share of nonsalary expenses varies largely according to the level and type of education. In lower-primary schools, the per pupil expenditure on nonsalary items out of the provincial budgets were US15¢ in 1990 (1% of the recurrent unit costs). In upper-primary, the same expenditure was 10 percent of the recurrent unit costs. Nonsalary unit expenses were much higher in secondary, teacher-training, and technical schools, but this was related, to a large extent, to a high number of boarding students, and a large share of these nonsalary expenses was devoted to housing and feeding students. At the Eduardo Mondlane University, more than 60 percent of the recurrent expenditures (exclusive of technical assistance) were nonsalary expenditures. Student aid (28%), international cooperation (16%), and room and board (14%) are the major items. Per pupil expenditures are more than 200 times larger at the University than they are in lower-primary schools.

As a proportion of government investment, education declined from an average of 3 percent in 1980–81 to 1.5 percent in 1986–87. In 1988, the sector recovered and surpassed its 1980 real investment level. However, the average share of education investment expenditures in public investment for the period 1980 to 1989 was only 2.6 percent and insufficient even to replace schools destroyed by war. The lack of investment affected particularly primary education facilities.

6. Supplying Personnel for the Education System

Data on personnel is not reliable because the war caused the closure of approximately 60 percent of the schools and displaced about 1 million pupils and a substantial number of teachers. In fact, there are variations in the data from different sources such as the finance, human resources, or planning department and the Provincial Directorates of Education. According to the planning directorate of the Ministry of Education, Mozambican schools employed 27,000 teachers and 9,700 people in non-teaching positions in 1992. About 91 percent of all teachers were working in primary schools, 6 percent in secondary and vocational schools, and the remaining 3 percent in tertiary and teacher education. There is a shortage of teachers in general, but this is particularly true in primary education.

Teachers for lower-primary schools are trained in three-year courses in the primary teacher-training centers. In 1993 courses began in Grade 7. It is anticipated that the entrance level will be increased to Grade 10 and the course length will be reduced to 2 years only. The entrance requirement to teach in upper-primary schools is Grade 10 and qualified candidates are trained in the medium pedagogical institutes for 3 years. The higher pedagogical institutes train teachers for lower- and upper-secondary schools. The entrance level is Grade 12 and the course lasts for 4.5 years. There are specific teacher-training institutes for vocational schools.

Inservice training is either scanty and unsystematic, or virtually nonexistent. However, plans have been made to start a crash program based on auto-instructional materials and focusing on the use of textbooks, the management of groups in multigrade classrooms, and other problems related to the management of classrooms in deprived conditions. The Ministry of Education will also revitalize the integrated pedagogical zones (ZIP) and an inservice training program using radio lessons, printed material, and tutoring.

Both written national examinations and practical teaching are used to evaluate teacher candidates, and certificates are issued at the end of each type of training.

7. Curriculum Development and Teaching Methodology

A common curriculum for all schools is approved by the Ministry of Education. All students are exposed to a curriculum that provides some coverage of reading, writing, mathematics, science, social studies, aesthetics, and physical education. English is introduced in Grade 8 and French in Grade 11. Environmental, population, and family life education will be added to the curriculum. In primary schools, all subjects are taught by a general teacher, whereas in secondary schools teachers combine two subjects such as mathematics and physics, chemistry and biology, and so on. In upper-secondary schools, students may specialize in either the natural or social sciences according to their abilities and in terms of what they expect to study later at the University.

The National Institute for Educational Development (INDE), under the Ministry of Education, used to prepare syllabuses for all subjects and grades, specifying both content and teaching methodology. It also developed pupil textbooks and teacher guides and provided inservice training for teachers. Since 1991, this institute has prepared the syllabuses which are then approved by the Ministry of Education but the writing of the textbooks is put out to tender. The Ministry of Education evaluates and approves one single textbook per subject per grade which is then used nationwide.

One problem with the textbooks is that, due to lack of time, they were not tried out and, for primary schools, they were developed without taking sufficiently into consideration the cultural and linguistic competence of the pupils. Teachers complained (and evaluation reports confirmed their complaints) that the syllabuses were too demanding and lengthy. Furthermore, the use of Portuguese as the medium of instruction in primary schools (especially in rural areas) and the emphasis on teaching methods that inhibit verbal interactions and foster passivity and rote learning have become a common characteristic in the teaching–learning process.

In the mid-1990s there will be a thorough revision of the curriculum in line with the sociopolitical changes which have taken place in the country. Particular attention will be given to multicultural education, regionalization of curricula, and education for peace and common understanding. The use of Mozambican languages in the first years of education in the primary school—particularly in rural areas—is foreseen.

8. The System of Examinations, Promotions, and Certifications

There are national examinations in Grades 5, 7, 10, and 12, which correspond to the end of the lower-primary, upper-primary, lower-secondary, and upper-secondary schools. Upon successful completion, certificates are awarded. The government adopted a system of automatic promotion from one grade to the next within a cycle of education in 1991. However, although it is too early to evaluate this policy, there is a certain resistance to adopting it since the teachers were not involved in making the decision.

9. Educational Assessment, Evaluation, and Research

Educational assessment is practically nonexistent, but evaluation studies are gaining momentum. The beginning of the 1990s witnessed three important studies: the pedagogical evaluation of primary school textbooks; the evaluation of the management and administration of the educational system; and the evaluation of the purchasing capacity of parents vis-à-vis textbook prices. In the period 1991 to 1993, Mozambique participated in an International Study of the Assessment of Mathematics.

Research is underfunded and the few funds available are provided by foreign and international agencies. Educational researchers work in isolation and research findings are rarely used for policy formulation. There are plans that research will focus on school effectiveness, by identifying factors which may have impact on the quality of education, particularly in primary schools and in the context of a poor country; sociology and culture of education through the study of the interrelationships between the school and the communities and the pupils and the teachers; on linguistics and education, in view of the multilingual situation of the country; on psychology, with particular focus on conceptual studies; on didactics for improving the quality of the teaching of mathematics and sciences; on environmental and population education; and on policy analysis research that will enhance policy formulation in education.

10. Major Reforms in the 1980s and 1990s

Given that the reform of the Mozambican educational system that was introduced in 1983 will come to its final stage only in 1994, no major changes to the structure of the educational system are foreseen before the year 2000. However, some research on the effectiveness of the system suggests that some changes in curriculum should be made in order to make it more learner centered, including the use of Mozambican languages in primary schools. Appropriate changes in the teacher-training programs should also be made.

There are plans to have only one teacher, or a maximum of two teachers, for the whole primary cycle (from Grades 1–7) in order to make it possible to expand upper-primary schools into rural areas with sparse populations in a cost-effective way. Plans are also underway to create a regular inservice teacher-training scheme, particularly for primary education using tutorials, printed materials, and radio lessons. The preservice teacher-training programs will be restructured.

There is likely to be a reform in vocational and technical education given that a study of the policies and the strategies for the development of this kind of education, as well as the drawing up of the master plan for the period from 1994 to the year 2000, is underway. This reform will entail the need for more involvement on the part of the potential employers, trade unions, and other associations in defining the courses, and also having areas of specialization according to the skilled workforce's needs in particular areas of the country; and, the evaluation of graduates from technical schools. Finally, the system of funding will be reformed.

11. Major Problems for the Year 2000

Given serious governmental financial constraints, the absolute poverty of the majority of the population, low enrollment ratios, an increase in the size of the school population, and a high dropout rate, Mozambique faces a dilemma between improvement in the quality of education and the expansion of school places. Access to basic education is increasingly limited, particularly for rural, poor children, and, in some areas, for girls. The quality of education is seriously jeopardized: by the poor quality and quantity of instructional materials and textbooks; by poorly educated and trained teachers; by inadequate teaching facilities (many without running water or toilets); by a very short school year calendar with less than 3.5 hours of instruction per day; and by overcrowded classrooms with children from different ages, abilities, and talents. In addition, more than a decade of civil war has left emotional and psychological scars on the country's children and youth.

The internal efficiency of schools is another important problem in the whole system of education. For example, in a cohort of 1,000 pupils who enroll in Grade 1, only 77 graduate after five years of lower-primary education.

There is a crucial need to improve the institutional capacity of the educational sector at all levels in terms of technical skills, administration, management, and educational planning. Special attention should be paid to schools, the seat of the teaching–learning process, and where the need for professional training and inservice training and specialization of staff at central, provincial, and district levels is urgently required in order to guarantee and enable the formulation and definition of educational policies that are realistic and compatible with the context in which they are set. This will also allow gradual and progressive decentralization of some tasks to the provincial and district educational authorities.

For an efficient management of the educational system, the administrative services of education need to improve their horizontal and vertical coordination, and their communication system.

Bibliography

Assembleia da República 1983 *Lei e linhas gerais do Sistema Nacional de Educação. Boletim da República*. Imprensa Nacional, Maputo

Assembleia da República 1992 Lei no 6/92 do Sistema Nacional de Educação. Boletim da República, Serie 1, 19: 8–14. Imprensa Nacional, Maputo

Dzvimbo P, Plank D, Torres C, Verhine R 1992 *Mozambique: Education Sector Assessment*. IEES/USAID Project. Florida State University, Tallahassee, Florida

INDE 1992 Primary school textbook evaluation project. Reports no. 1 to 23. INDE, Maputo

Martins Z 1990 *Population Growth and Universal Primary Education in Mozambique*. University of Ghana, Faculty of Social Sciences, Legon

Martins Z 1992 Aproveitamento escolar no SNE: contribuições para um estudo das disparidades regionais e de sexo com referência ao ensino primário do 1o grau. *Cadernos de pesquisa do* INDE 1. INDE, Maputo

Ministry of Education 1981 Linhas gerais do Sistema Nacional de educação. Imprensa Nacional, Maputo

Ministry of Education 1988 Relatório do Minist-ério de Educação ao Conselho de Ministros. Mimeo

Ministry of Education 1990 *Balanço da introdução do SNE. A Educação em Moçambique*. Colecção documentos Nº1. Editora escolar, INDE, Maputo

Ministry of Education/World Bank 1992 *Education Sector Expenditure, Management and Financing Review*. World Bank, Washington, DC

Nhavoto A 1982 *Le système educative au Mozambique:*

Essay de diagnostic. UNESCO/IIEP, Paris

Nhavoto A 1991 Custos e despesas do ensino em Mocambique: a busca duma racionalidade. *Cadernos de pesquisa do INDE*

Nhavoto A, Rego M, Sitoi A 1985 Balanço dos primeiros dez anos de educação em Moçambique. Mimeo. Ministry of Education, Maputo

Palme M 1992 *O significado da escola: repetência e desistência na escola moçambicana*. Cadernos de pesquisa nº2. INDE, Maputo

Myanmar

C. T. Crellin

1. General Background

The official name of the country is the Union of Myanmar. From 1962 to 1988, the official name was the Socialist Republic of the Union of Burma. The word "Union" acknowledges that the country unites a number of different ethnic and linguistic groups. The dropping of the older name "Burma" is to further national integration by removing reference to one ethnic group even though the Burmese constitute almost 70 percent of the population.

Myanmar is in tropical Southeast Asia and has an area of 676,577 square kilometers. There is a long coastline on the Bay of Bengal and the other borders are largely along mountain ridges. Bangladesh and India are to the west, China to the north and northeast, and Laos and Thailand to the east.

Two river systems, the Irrawaddy and the Sittang, irrigate large, highly fertile basins; there are also large fertile coastal plains. Most of the rest of the country is densely forested and has begun to be affected by excessive logging.

The population in 1990 was 41,675,000 and the population growth rate has been about 2.1 percent for many years. Most of the population lives in the coastal areas and the basins of the Irrawaddy and the Sittang. The population consists mostly of descendants of people who moved into the country during the last 2,500 years. Migration into Myanmar from Yunnan continued in recent centuries and has not yet entirely ceased. Prior to independence in 1947, there was a considerable inward migration from India and China, most of the newcomers settling in the few large cities. Many, especially those from India, left Myanmar after Independence.

There is only one city with a population of over one million. This is Yangon (known formerly as Rangoon), the national capital. Two others have over 200,000:

Mandalay at the northern end of the Irrawaddy plain, and Mawlamyine (Moulmein) in the south. Internal movement of the population has been controlled by the government since 1962. Perhaps for this reason, migration to large and overcrowded cities is less of a social problem in Myanmar than in most neighboring countries.

The Burmese people came from the north and were well established in the Irrawaddy basin over 1,000 years ago. At about the same time the Mon came from what is now Cambodia and occupied the Sittang valley. By the middle of the eighteenth century, the Burmese controlled all lowland areas. The British ruled the country as a province of India from 1855 to 1937. For a short time the country was ruled from London. The Japanese occupied Myanmar from 1942 to 1945. Independence was achieved in 1948.

The imposition by the British of the use of English as the language of commerce and administration added to a complex linguistic situation. The Mon and Burmese languages are unrelated, while the many hill tribes mostly originated in central China and have languages related only remotely to Burmese. The Burmese constitute about 70 percent of the population. The Mon constitute only 2.4 percent. Of the remainder, the Shan, ethnically and linguistically related to the Laotians and Thais, form 8.5 percent of the population. The national language, now officially called "Myanmar" is the language of the major ethnic group. This article refers to this language by its long established name, "Burmese."

Almost 90 percent of the population is Buddhist. About 3.9 percent are Christians who live mainly in the few large cities and among some of the hill tribes, such as the Chin and the Karen. Some 3.8 percent of the population are Muslim, living largely in the cities and near the border with Bangladesh.

Although the people have mainly come from the north and the east, the cultural influence of India is considerable. Buddhism came from India, probably via Cambodia with the Mon people. The Burmese script is a derivative of an ancient Indian script. Nevertheless, culturally and socially, the people of Myanmar have much more in common with the people of East and Southeast Asia than they have with India. An important social factor is that for many centuries women have had the same legal and social status as men. Women own, in their own right, half of all family property and keep their own name after marriage.

About 76 percent of the population lives in rural areas. During the period of British colonial rule, much of the administration was carried out by people of Indian origin. At the same time, ethnic Chinese became heavily involved in all kinds of commercial and industrial activities. One of the problems which faced the newly independent country in 1948 was to develop an educational, social, and administrative system to enable Burmese and other long-established national groups to take important positions in government and administration.

There is little in the culture or religion to hinder social mobility as it can in the Indian subcontinent. The lack of secondary schools in rural areas before 1947 did inhibit social mobility. On the other hand, Myanmar's society and British rule did little to give status to manual activities.

Although Myanmar shares with its neighbors in Southeast Asia rich natural and human resources, in 1988 the per capita income was US$250, one of the lowest in the world. In December 1987, Myanmar was recognized as a "less developed country" (LDC). Agriculture, which includes forestry, represents almost half of the Gross Domestic Product (GDP) and employs about 64 percent of the working population. Manufacturing, mining, and construction represent 10.6 percent of GDP and employ 10.1 percent of the workforce. The service sector, including transport, trade, and administration, constitutes 37 percent of GDP and involves 19 percent of employment.

Exports in 1988 were about US$276 million and imports US$668 million. These figures must be treated with some caution as there is a great deal of informal and unregulated import and export of goods. Agricultural and forestry products together with gems, often leave the country illegally. Consumer goods, including clothing and pharmaceuticals, enter through unregulated borders. Remittance by nationals working abroad, especially seamen, is a significant element in the national balance of payments.

From 1948 until 1962, Myanmar had a constitution based on a multiparty political system with national elections at regular intervals. In 1962 a military government took power and the Constitution was suspended. A new constitution was established in 1974 with the Burma Socialist Program Party (BSPP) as the only political party allowed. A very high proportion of government ministers and senior civil servants were serving or retired army officers.

In 1988 there were widespread political protest meetings. The government and administration based on the BSPP was overthrown, a military government took over, and the State Law and Order Restoration Council (SLORC) was established. The military government permitted the formation of a number of political parties and increased foreign involvement in commerce and industry. Elections were held in May 1990 and the party supported by SLORC was defeated. The government did not allow a transfer of power and most foreign providers of aid reduced or curtailed their support.

Since Independence, governments have insisted on neutrality in the dealings of the people of Myanmar with the rest of the world. This policy has been applied with considerable intensity since 1962 and has resulted in near isolation of its people and institutions from contact with developments elsewhere.

In 1991 Myanmar did join the Asian Program of Educational Innovation for Development (APEID), a UNESCO program based in Bangkok. Most countries in Asia and the Pacific have been exchanging experiences through this program since 1975. Consideration was also being given to joining the Association of Southeast Asian Nations (ASEAN).

2. Politics and the Goals of the Education System

Once the early Burman kingdoms were established in the Irrawaddy valley, monastic schools provided religious and basic elementary education for most boys and many girls. A high level of literacy was achieved and to this day, most parents are prepared to support schooling for their children.

The British introduced schools based on their own experience, beginning in 1825. English was used as the medium of instruction for many primary schools, and for all secondary and tertiary institutions. These English-medium schools were fee-paying and mostly in towns and the few large cities. Christian missionaries provided many schools, including some in the rural, often mountainous areas. Burmese-medium primary-level schools supported by the local population were established alongside the traditional monastery schools. Partly because of the English language requirement for education above the primary level, few children proceeded from the Burmese-medium schools to the secondary level.

During the period of Japanese occupation from 1942 to 1945, a single school system was established with Burmese as the medium of instruction.

Independent Myanmar made a commitment to the provision of universal primary education. Burmese continued as the medium of instruction in an educational program to foster national unity and the establishment of Burmese as the language of commerce and administration in all areas of the country. English was taught as a subject at all educational levels and was used for many years as the medium of instruction at the tertiary level.

After 1962, English was removed from the primary-school curriculum and was retained at the secondary level almost entirely to foster reading and writing with little or no emphasis on English as a spoken language. It was believed that such instruction would be sufficient as a preparation for the use of textbooks written in English that are used at the tertiary level of education. English as a written and spoken language was reintroduced at the primary level in 1981. In the late 1980s, English became the medium of instruction at the tertiary level, and in 1991 English became the medium of instruction for science, mathematics, and economics at the high-school level.

Government financial support for primary education was minimal prior to Independence and provided little more than the teacher's salaries after Independence. Primary-school buildings are usually provided by communities, and parents pay for textbooks and writing materials. Primary education for a period of 5 years from age 5 to 10 was decreed to be compulsory from 1985 onwards.

In the early days of Independence, insufficient provision was made for primary education where the mother tongue of the children was not Burmese. The problem was first addressed in 1964 when the University for the Development of National Groups was established. The University provides a longer period of training for primary-school teachers than in the other 13 teacher-training schools.

Myanmar has retained the highly selective educational system inherited from the British. The goal of education has been seen by parents and the government as a preparation for higher education. Only in the 1980s was serious consideration given to establishing other goals. Although most children enter primary school, only about 10 percent complete the primary phase in the scheduled 5 years. Another 19 percent complete the course but take up to 9 years to do so. No more than 4 percent qualify for higher education after 11 years of primary and secondary schooling.

The education system has been disturbed many times during periods of civil unrest in recent years. As many of those involved in urban disturbance were higher education students, the government attempted to disperse them by establishing 17 regional colleges in 1978 where students studied for two years before proceeding to the two universities in Yangon and Mandalay to complete their studies. This system lasted only a few years. Schools, universities, and colleges have been closed many times. In August 1988, all educational establishments were closed. Schools reopened a year later but higher education institutions did not reopen until mid-1991.

3 The Formal System of Education

3.1 Primary, Secondary, and Tertiary education

The national system is based on 5-year primary, 4-year middle, and 2-year secondary schools. This statement is an over simplification as there is a great deal of class-level repetition. The average number of years taken by the relatively few children who complete the nominal 5-year primary-school course is 7 years. Private schools are not recognized by the government but a few privately-run kindergartens and a few English-language schools operate in large cities. Several unofficial private schools operated during the period 1988–89 when all schools were closed but some were still open in the early 1990s. Private tuition of children enrolled in government schools is widespread and involves nearly half of all children.

A feature of the educational system is that many children are over age at each class level while very few

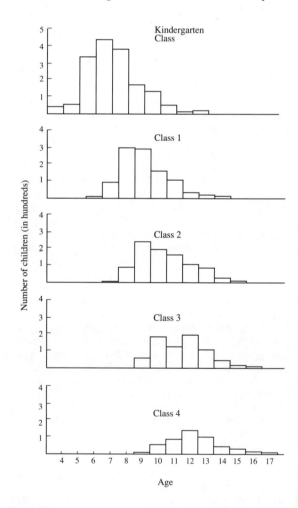

Figure 1

Age distribution, 16 urban and rural primary schools, Myanmar

are under age. This is partly due to late enrollment, but mainly because of very high repetition rates. Figure 1 shows the age distribution in 8 urban and 8 rural schools in 1989. The data are taken from a study by the Myanmar Education Research Bureau (MERB), a unit within the Ministry of Education in Yangon.

In 1987, 5,046,470 children were enrolled in primary schools. The gross enrollment ratio is about 100 percent. Studies by MERB and the Department of Planning and Statistics in the Ministry indicate that about 80 percent of all children enroll in a primary school at some time. Studies indicate that enrollment in 1989 was 25 percent less after a year's closure of all schools.

In 1987, the pupil–teacher ratio was about 43:1 at the primary level and 23:1 in secondary schools. The standard school week is of 35, 40 minute lessons at all school levels. Teachers are expected to teach 30 lessons a week at the primary level and 28 at the secondary level. A shorter day is worked in urban schools operating on a shift basis. Class sizes are usually quite large at the lower primary-school level. Many primary schools, especially in rural areas, have several classes of 60 or more pupils in one large room. With the chanting of passages from the textbook as a standard "learning" technique, noise is a considerable problem.

Enrollment in middle and secondary schools was reported in 1987 to be 1,336,199 for the six class levels. Dropout rates average 17 percent annually over the nominal 6-year course. Repetition rates are also very high. Only about 20 percent of final-year students pass the high-school leaving examination. Enrollment in secondary-level technical and vocational schools was 15,631 and there were 6,958 inservice teacher trainees in primary-level teacher-training schools. There were 202,381 students enrolled in tertiary-level institutions in 1987. Of these 87,881 were studying by correspondence.

There are two long established arts and science universities at Yangon and Mandalay. A third was opened in 1991 at Mawlamyine (Moulmein). These offer 3- and 4-year courses. The Yangon Institute of Technology and the Mandalay Institute of Technology (opened in 1991), offer 4- and 5- year courses. There is one Agriculture Institute. Figure 2 shows the sequence of educational courses in Myanmar.

Figure 3 depicts the structure and enrollments of the Myanmar system of education. As has already been explained, there is high grade repetition and also the problem of over-age students because they begin school late. Thus Fig. 3 has divided each grade level into a normal progression and over-age or grade repeating students.

3.2 Preschool Education

Preschool education does not form a part of the official school system supported by the Ministry of Education.

The first class in the primary schools is described as the "kindergarten class," but is organized in a similar way to the first-year classes in other national primary-school systems. The official age of entry to primary school is 5 years, a year younger than in most other countries in Asia. There is some education of mothers in nonformal education programs that includes some early childhood education. There are some small privately run kindergartens in urban areas.

3.3 Special Education

Very little is done to provide an education for children with physical and mental handicaps. The requirement that children pass an annual examination quickly eliminates children that have any difficulty in keeping up with the fairly rigorous school curriculum.

3.4 Vocational, Technical, and Business Education

Although the objective for education in these fields is preparation for employment, there is a lack of practical training facilities. Moreover the examination and testing system used in technical, commercial, and vocational education institutions gives little emphasis to practical matters.

3.5 Adult and Nonformal Education

It became apparent in the 1960s that many children were dropping out of school before they had reached a sustainable level of literacy. A large-scale effort was made with guidance from the Institute of Education of the University of Yangon and using university students to visit towns and villages. Special books were prepared and claims were made for a considerable reduction in adult illiteracy. The program gradually faded away, but in any case, most small communities have little in the way of reading material available to sustain and use any literacy skills that may have been acquired.

The Department of Social Welfare has developed voluntary primary night schools mainly serving school dropouts in urban areas. In 1990 there were 187 such schools with 13,281 students and 508 voluntary teachers.

The Department of Technical, Agricultural, and Vocational Education of the Ministry of Education has established a number of voluntary schools for young literates aged over 16. In 1990 there were 7 handicraft schools, 2 machinery and maintenance schools, and 6 schools for home science. These schools rely on voluntary teachers, mostly from technical and vocational institutions.

Government encouragement of traditional monastic schools has fluctuated since 1948. There has been increasing interest in these schools in recent years and one report indicates that about 10 percent of rural children attend monastic schools.

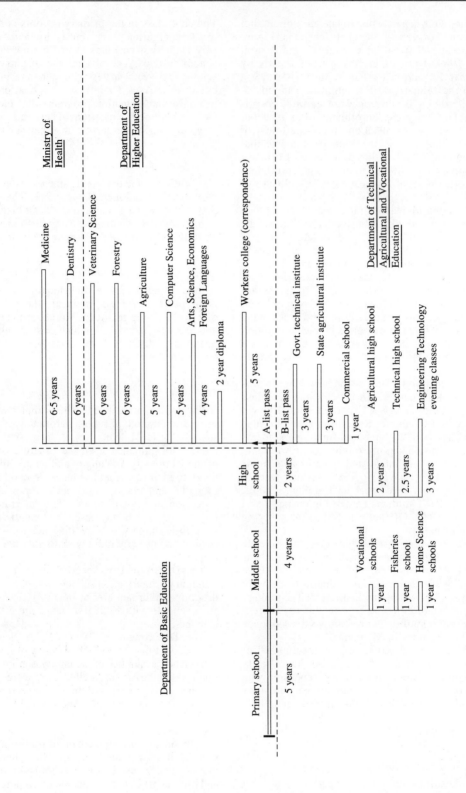

Figure 2
Myanmar: Educational sequence

4. *Administrative and Supervisory Structure and Operation*

The administration of education is highly centralized with almost all policy decisions made at the Ministry of Education in Yangon. Educational institutions and schools are administered by three departments: Basic Education; Higher Education; and Technical, Agricultural, and Vocational Education.

The Department of Basic Education is responsible for all primary, middle, and high schools, and also for teacher education at the primary- and middle-school levels. This department controls 90 percent of the staff and funds of the Ministry. A very high proportion of the officials have had successful experience as middle and high-school teachers.

The Department of Higher Education administers the three arts and science universities, the two institutes of technology, and the institute of agriculture. This department also administers a number of smaller units such as the Universities Central Library, the Burmese Language Institute, and the Foreign Language Institute. Teacher education for high-school teachers is undertaken by institutes of education within the universities.

The Department of Technical, Agricultural, and Vocational Education administers 66 institutions: 14 technical, 9 agricultural, and 3 commercial high schools which offer courses for students from middle schools. Students from these schools can go on to 3-year courses at 11 technical or 7 agricultural institutes.

There are also 24 vocational schools which recruit from primary and middle schools. This department administers the Technical Teacher Training Institute.

Other units of the Ministry of Education include: The Examination Board, which is responsible for the examinations set at the end of the primary, middle, and high-school levels; The Myanmar Educational Research Bureau; and The Department of Planning and Statistics.

There are seven Divisions and seven States in the Union of Myanmar. Each has an education office under the Department of Basic Education. The office has a small administrative staff and a team of inspectors. These offices deal largely with the middle and high schools. There are 318 Township Education Offices each with a Township Education Officer. Some of these officers are also principals of high schools. The administration and supervision of the primary schools is almost entirely in the hands of these offices. State, Division, and Township offices are staffed almost entirely by officials who have had successful teaching experience. A serious deficiency is that very few will have qualifications or experience in primary-school education.

5. *Educational Finance*

In 1987, 1,290,519,000 kyat (about US$210 million) was allocated by the government to the Ministry

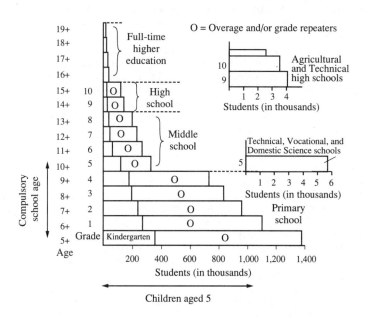

Figure 3
Myanmar: Structure of the formal education system

of Education. This represented 15.3 percent of total government expenditure. Of this, 13 percent was spent at the tertiary level, and almost all the rest was spent at the primary- and secondary-school levels. All but 1.4 percent of the budget allocation was spent in 1987. It has been estimated that about 2 percent of GDP is spent on education.

Government expenditure was about US$33 per primary- and secondary-school student, and US$140 per tertiary-level student. The parental contribution for school facilities is quite high at the primary level, and for books and writing material it is high at all levels.

Success in school examinations is extremely important for the future educational progress and ultimate employment of students. For this reason private coaching is a very important activity in all communities, but especially in towns and cities. School teachers rely to very large extent on the income from private tuition. Private tuition fees impose a burden on parents that only the moderately prosperous can afford.

Almost all of the input for nonformal education is from the community in the form of voluntary administrative and teaching services.

6. Supplying Personnel for the Education System

Preservice teacher education no longer exists in Myanmar apart from the few hundred students at the University for the Development of National Races. This university is administered by the Public Service Selection and Training Board.

Up to about 4000 serving, but untrained, teachers are selected each year for inservice training for one year in teacher-training schools and institutes. This is a costly process as teachers are paid their salaries while under training at residential institutions. Little can be offered in primary-school pedagogy as the instructors seldom have experience or training at the primary-school level. Over 40 percent of primary-school teachers have not received training.

A feature of the teaching situation is that teachers at the primary- and middle-school levels seek "promotion" to the next level. Some inservice teacher training supports these aspirations. A primary-school teacher can become a headteacher, but educational administrators, inspectors, and teacher educators are usually recruited from high-school teachers.

Since 1988, the government budget for the appointment of teachers has been increased appreciably and recruitment has been at a rate greater than that at which training is provided. Assuming a 4 percent "wastage" rate and 2.1 percent population growth rate, it would seem that about 7,000 new primary and 3,600 middle and secondary-school teachers are needed each year. This will require a substantial increase in the teacher-

training program as well as an improvement in the content of the curriculum of that program.

On the positive side, it is reported that about 40 percent of primary-school teachers are university graduates and a further 20 percent have qualified for university admission. This favorable situation will be offset by the fact that all tertiary educational institutions were closed from 1988 to 1991. On the other hand, some primary-school teachers have no more than a middle-school certificate.

There is little formal training of educational administrators. Relatively few of the personnel working in the various fields of education have had education and training abroad.

The whole question of the training of educational personnel is being examined carefully and external assistance is being sought. There is some support from multilateral and bilateral organizations, especially for vocational and technical education, teacher education, and for English-language teaching.

7. Curriculum Development and Teaching Methodology

There is a Curriculum Development Unit in the Department of Basic Education. It could be more accurately described as a textbook-writing unit. One of the consequences of the isolation of Myanmar educational personnel from developments abroad is that little is known of current curriculum development practices and techniques.

In principle books should be revised or rewritten every three years. Textbook writers refer to overseas textbooks but as they are all subject specialists rather than education specialists and little is added to the national textbooks to improve student learning experiences. Overseas textbooks that include such provision, usually assume that teachers are quite well trained. Very little new information finds its way into textbooks; the atlases in use include out-of-date maps, and science and economics data are often either incorrect or out of date.

A noteworthy feature of textbook provision, quite common in low-income countries in Asia, is that it is assumed that books will be replaced each year. Whenever a new set of textbooks is specified, there are long delays, well into the academic year, before they become available.

The curriculum is specified by the Department of Basic Education and is in practice determined by the external examinations. There is no variation for different parts of the country and virtually no elective subjects. Very few changes have been made in the list of subjects to be taught since Independence. Myanmar has not introduced the teaching of science and environmental studies into the primary-school curriculum as in most other Asian countries. When a policy decision is made to make a substantial change in the curriculum, such as the introduction of the teaching and use of English, little is done in the form of curriculum development and teacher education to support the policy decision.

8. The System of Examinations, Promotions, and Certifications

The examination system controls almost every aspect of the education system in Myanmar. The national system of education sees all levels of education as a preparation for the next stage on an academic ladder leading to employment in a government office. The examinations needed before a primary, middle, or high-school leaving certificate is awarded are controlled by the Examination Board which is a unit in the Ministry of Education. The only attribute tested is simple recall of textbook information.

The examination at the end of the middle school has six papers: Burmese, English, mathematics, history, geography, and general science. Most students in the last class take the examination and about 60 percent pass. Selection for admission into three streams in the high school depends to a large extent on performance in mathematics and science.

In 1988, 217,193 students took the Basic Education High School Examination, 42,001 (19.34%) were given an A-list pass and 9,951 (4.58%) a B-list pass. The failure rate was 76 percent. Only A-list students can proceed to higher education. In theory B-list students should proceed to technical and vocational institutions but many prefer to resit the examination a year later. It is not possible to resit individual subject examinations, nor is there a chance to resit the whole examination until the next year.

End-of-year examinations at each grade level are extremely important at all school levels and are modeled on the end-of-course external examinations. Dropout rates average about 14 percent per annum at the primary level and about 17 percent per annum at the middle-and high-school levels, with above average peaks at the end of the first, ninth, and eleventh years. Repetition rates are about 20 percent per annum at the primary level and 25 percent at the middle-and high-school levels.

9. Educational Assessment, Evaluation, and Research

The Myanmar Education Research Bureau is a small but efficient unit that has studied the education system in Myanmar for many years. It has limited funds and much work carried out by the Bureau has been funded by external agencies such as UNICEF, UNESCO, and UNDP. Unfortunately, little publicity has been given to the reports of the Bureau, even within the country.

The Department of Planning and Statistics has carried out a number of important studies in recent years, but little has been widely disseminated.

Officials of the Department of Basic Education and the Department of Technical, Agricultural, and Vocational Education include many with a great interest in the work of the schools and other institutions that they administer. They also visit schools more than is common in other low-income countries. The Township Education Officers also visit schools a great deal. Officials in the Ministry of Education in Yangon have a very good knowledge of the current status of education in Myanmar. Lack of contact with educators and others from abroad and an attitude of tight control of government information has combined to shelter knowledge of the educational system from anyone not in the Ministry.

10. Major Reforms in the 1980s and 1990s

An Education Sector Study was carried out in 1990 and 1991, by UNESCO and UNDP. One of the reasons for the commissioning of this study was that the government became aware of the current status of education in Myanmar. Little had been changed in the administration and implementation of the educational system for over 30 years. One major change was made in 1981. This was the introduction of English as a subject in all primary schools from the first year.

11. Major Problems for the Year 2000

The entire educational system is in need of reform. It is difficult to determine where work should begin. Perhaps the Educational Sector Study completed in 1991 is the first step on the road to reform.

The following fields need urgent attention: curriculum development at all levels; teacher education; educational assessment, including the monitoring of the effectiveness of the education system and the monitoring of the progress of individuals; education as a preparation for employment; adult and nonformal education; and educational administration.

Bibliography

Myanmar, Ministry of Education 1987–88 *Education Statistics*. Ministry of Education, Yangon
Myanmar, Education Research Bureau (MERB) 1990 *Report on the In-School and Out-of-School Activities of Primary School Children*. MERB, Yangon
UNDP Burma 1986 *Annual Report*. UNDP, New York
UNESCO 1991 *Statistical Yearbook 1991*. UNESCO, Paris
United Nations 1990 Myanmar (Country Presentation), Second United Nations Conference on the Least-Developed Countries. September 1990. United Nations, Geneva

Namibia

M. H. Craelius, U. Kann and M. J. Mukendwa

1. General Background

Namibia is located in the southwestern part of Africa and covers an area of 824,000 square kilometers—more than three times the area of the United Kingdom. The Tropic of Capricorn crosses the center of the country, which means it lies half in the tropics and half in the southern subtropics. The overall climate is dry and mostly hot. The average temperature in Windhoek, the capital, is 24°C during January and 13°C during July. Windhoek has 81 millimeters of rain in March and none in August.

The country has four major regions: a desert in the west, a semiarid high plateau in the middle, a second desert in the east, and a tropical region with rain in the far north. The deserts dominate. The Namib Desert along the Atlantic coast is 65 to 165 kilometers wide and 1,600 kilometers long from the north to south. Only two major roads and two railroads cross it. In the middle of the country is the central high plateau, often 2,000 meters above sea level. The plateau is somewhat more hospitable, lending itself to animal husbandry, and has a scattered small population and a few towns. The east, like the west, is dominated by a major desert, the Kalahari, with few inhabitants. The only part of the country which houses a fairly large population and lends itself to traditional African subsistence farming is the north, near the Angolan and Zambian borders. Consequently the majority of the population lives there.

The last population census was made in 1991 and it is estimated that the 1994 population is approximately 1.5 million. Namibia has a population density of only two persons per square kilometer. About one third of the population live in urban areas and the urbanization rate has been rapid since independence. The annual population growth is 3.1 percent. Life expectancy is 60 years and is among the highest in Africa; public health is thus good by African standards. The population in Namibia is, as in most African countries, ethnically very diversified. The San (Bushmen) constitute the aboriginal population, but are a minority of a few thousand. They have so far been almost totally outside mainstream society and its education system.

Over half of the population lives in the northern part of Namibia, where water is more abundant and the soil more arable. The language situation is complicated and requires, to be fully understood, a few words about Namibian history since its occupation over a hundred years ago. This will also explain the existence of a small White population (7%) in Namibia.

What is now Namibia was occupied by Germany in the early 1880s and at the Berlin Congress of 1885 it was recognized by the European powers as a German colony. The group of German farmers, military people, and civil servants who settled in the country referred to it as "German South West Africa". The Germans settled primarily in the high tableland and in the coastal towns of Swakopmund and Lüderitz. A German school system was introduced which involved, almost exclusively, the children of German immigrants. Finnish missionary groups had, some decades earlier, established missionary stations with schools in the north, but they involved only small groups of the indigenous people. The Germans and the Finnish were more successful in their religious conversions and in 1990 about 75 percent of the population was listed as Christian—mostly Lutheran.

At the outbreak of the First World War in 1914, a British/South African army occupied the country. The Treaty of Versailles gave the United Kingdom, through South Africa, the right to administer Namibia as a mandate of the League of Nations. A condition for this administration was that the Black population should be assured of social development, including education. This did not happen. On the contrary, South Africa gradually introduced apartheid and even restricted Black population groups to the north of the country to make room for additional White immigrants. In the beginning, very little attention was given to any education or training of the Black population. The language situation became more complicated. Many Germans remained in the former colony and the German language survived. The official language became Afrikaans (the old Dutch dialect spoken by a large number of South African Whites). This had the result that the language of instruction in the country's secondary schools and in most "White" schools, apart from in the German schools, at all levels became Afrikaans.

Upon Independence in 1990, it was decided that the official language of Namibia should be English. This decision while politically well-justified, has not been easy to implement. In primary lower schools, the local language is the language of instruction and English is taught as a subject. In upper primary and in secondary schools, the local language is a subject and English is both a subject and the language of instruction. At the tertiary level, English is the only acceptable language in the lecture hall. It is, however, not unusual to have English used in the classroom, but Afrikaans or a local language being used by both students and teachers everywhere outside the classroom.

As will be discussed later, the majority of Namibian teachers are under- or unqualified and this is particularly so as regards their teaching and use of English. The non-White teachers have their indigenous language and are also, with few exceptions, fluent in Afrikaans. However, they have so far had only limited reason to speak, read, or write in English. They are now having to teach in their third language.

Thus, in 1992, the situation in Namibia was that there were 10 major African and three European languages which were all in use. Oshindongwa and Oshikwanyama, both Bantu languages, were the most common. There is every reason for those involved in education to examine carefully learning achievement in Namibian schools and relate it to the ethnic and language situation of the students. It is very important to have a system which does not discriminate against certain ethnics groups. It has been claimed that in the past the language policy in education was a deliberate part of apartheid and a means by which to deprive the Black population of a fair social, cultural, and economic development.

Namibia is by African standards well-off. The gross national product (GNP) per capita is estimated at US$1,610 (1993) and only some minor African countries do better. The main reasons for this fortunate situation are the rich mines of diamonds, copper, gold, and, at least before independence, uranium. Cattle and sheep ranching with approximately 5,000, mainly White, ranchers have also produced important income although insufficient precipitation renders traditional agriculture difficult in most parts of Namibia. The climatological situation is somewhat more favorable in the north and some 120,000 Black families farm there. It is, however, subsistence farming at a fairly underdeveloped level. The standard of living of the Black farmers is therefore low compared with that of White ranchers. Fishery and tourism have indicated promising developments since independence. Thus, while GNP per capita is relatively high in Namibia, there are substantial differences between high- and low-income earners and a fairer distribution of assets and incomes among various population groups is given a high priority.

In 1991 commerce and services accounted for 50 to 60 percent of the Namibian GNP, mining 25 to 30 percent, agriculture and fishery 10 percent, and other industries 5 to 10 percent. The White minority has so far dominated commerce, mining, and the most profitable part of agriculture, while the Black majority has been involved in subsistence farming and low-paid jobs in commerce, industry and as laborers on commercial farms. Tourism is, as mentioned above, becoming an important source of income, but this sector, too, has so far been dominated by the White labor force.

Of the 1.4 million persons in Namibia (1991), 200,000 are in the formal labor force, 440,000 are not in the labor force and 350,000 are in the nonformal labor sector (all of whom are Black and most of whom live in the north). A high proportion, perhaps 50 percent of the latter, are illiterate. It must be asked: what kind of education and training should they and their children be offered in independent Namibia? The apartheid system and the past segregation into separate ethnic nationalities gave them few chances for development. Following independence policies have stressed fair and equal opportunities. Practice has shown that implementation of these policies will take some time.

2. Politics and the Goals of the Education System

In 1990 the new Ministry of Education outlined the broad education goals in a document entitled *Education in Transition: Nurturing our Future.*

During 1990–91 the efforts, energies, and initiatives of the Ministry of Education and Culture were directed toward the creation of strong foundations from which programs could be initiated and activities launched. Central to the creation of such strong foundations was the establishment of a unified, nonracial, nonethnic, and nonsexist national education system.

It should be emphasized prior to the presentation of the educational system that the education goals by the government in power after independence clearly indicates that the previously existing education system did not correspond to the needs of Namibia—economically, socially, or culturally. It was unequal and its enrollment, content, staffing, and so on were biased in favor of the White minority. The goals expressed, programs produced, and subsequent actions should be viewed in that light.

In 1993, the Ministry of Education and Culture presented its policy document *Toward Education for All—A Development Brief for Education, Culture, and Training.* This document consolidated a number of policies developed during the first years of independence. Consistent with the government's national development objectives, the Ministry of Education and Culture has five broad long-term goals. These are:

(a) the expansion of *access* to education;

(b) the improvement of the *quality* of the education delivery service;

(c) the *equitable* distribution of resources both between the regions and within each region;

(d) the promotion of *culture* and the arts;

(e) increased *efficiency* in the management and use of resources at the disposal of the Ministry.

Underpinning these goals are the principles of *lifelong learning* and an active *partnership* between the Ministry and both the national and the international community.

3. The Formal System of Education

Figure 1 presents the structure of the school system. It will be seen that the number of averaged pupils is

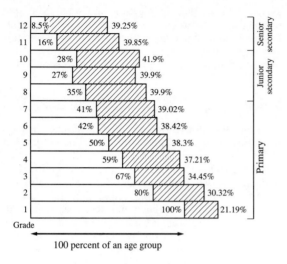

12	8.5% ///// 39.25%	Senior secondary
11	16% ///// 39.85%	Senior secondary
10	28% ///// 41.9%	Junior secondary
9	27% ///// 39.9%	Junior secondary
8	35% ///// 39.9%	
7	41% ///// 39.02%	
6	42% ///// 38.42%	
5	50% ///// 38.3%	Primary
4	59% ///// 37.21%	
3	67% ///// 34.45%	
2	80% ///// 30.32%	
1	100% ///// 21.19%	

Grade

← 100 percent of an age group →

///// Overaged pupils, that is, pupils that are four or more years older than the minimum age for a grade

Figure 1
Namibia: System of Education 1992

high at each grade level. The number of pupils of 6 and 7 years of age in Grade 1 was taken to represent 100 percent of the equivalent age group.

3.1 Primary, Secondary, and Tertiary Education

Pre-independence Namibian education was basically South African. There were external examinations after primary as well as junior and senior secondary schools. Parallel to the general senior secondary education system was a small vocational/technical/agricultural education system stretching into the tertiary level.

Students who passed their secondary education examination could proceed to tertiary education, which comprised an institution referred to as the "Academy" and consisted of several colleges at various levels. Some students, especially Whites, continued their tertiary education in the Republic of South Africa. In addition, some students who had fled the country during the liberation struggle, received secondary and tertiary education in other parts of the world, while in exile.

The new post-independence education system in Namibia consists of a seven-year primary system followed by a three-year junior secondary phase, and thereafter a two-year senior secondary phase, which concludes with the International General Certificate of Secondary Education (IGCSE) examination. This examination has replaced the old Cape Education Department Matriculation Examination. A small group of learners opt to take the Higher International General Certificate of Secondary Education (HIGCSE). In the long run the intention is to establish a Namibian Certificate of Secondary Education. There is a Namibian Junior Secondary Certificate at Grade 10, but no national examination at the end of primary school level. A few schools offer technical education at senior secondary level. Vocational training is the responsibility of the Ministry of Labor and Human Resource Development and agricultural training mainly takes place at colleges under the auspices of the Ministry of Agriculture.

In early 1994, there were 482,500 students in some 1,350 schools with 14,900 teachers. Since independence, in 1990, the system has increased by approximately 25 percent. At primary level the student–teacher ratio ranges from 43:1 in Ondangwa to 22:1 in Keetmanshoop and 25:1 in Windhoek, with a national average of 32:1. The schools averaged an enrollment of 360 students, and only 20 schools have more than 1,000 students.

Of the total number of learners in the education system, 375,000 (77%) are in primary schools and 103,000 in general secondary schools. Some 15 percent of the students in general secondary school take prevocational or vocational subjects such as agriculture, industry, domestic sciences, and commerce. Since 1994 overall vocational training is the responsibility of the Ministry of Labor and Human Resource Development, and the system is under review.

Rough estimates indicate that gross enrollment ratios in primary education are 131 and net enrollment ratios 83. This indicates a large number of overage and some underage students. It is particularly so in the northern regions, and less so among the White population. A similar estimate would give a gross enrollment ratio of 41 percent in secondary education, indicating a high rate of dropout after primary education.

There are serious regional differences in education. A grade-by-grade comparison by region shows that there were as many as 49,000 students in primary Grade 1 in Ondangwa in 1994, but only 6,000 in Grade 12. However, there has been a substantial improvement since 1990, when Ondangwa had only 600 students in Grade 12. By comparison, Windhoek region had 9,800 Grade 1 and 2,500 Grade 12 students in 1994.

There are, however, rather small gender differences. Of the total enrollment at primary and secondary level in 1994, 51 percent were girls (246,000 of 483,000). This is true for almost all regions, Rundu being the exception where girls constitute only 40 percent at secondary level. There are, as in most countries, differences between urban and rural enrollment, but the difference is somewhat compensated for by a large number of boarders from rural areas. There are no less than 60,000 boarders in Namibia's schools. The percentage of repeaters is also very high. In 1991, the repetition rate in Grade 1 was 37 percent. Many students repeat a grade several times. This, of course, is rather inefficient and costly.

There is a considerable age difference within the

school classes, most markedly in the two Ondangwa regions. The large age differences within the school classes is a pedagogical problem for the teacher as well as for the pupils.

The supply of physical facilities varies much among the regions. Windhoek has many schools in very good buildings with excellent classrooms, laboratories, workshops, and, as mentioned, good materials. In rural areas the situation might be very different and in the north even "under the tree" schools exist. The situation has, however, improved somewhat since independence. School mapping surveys are being conducted and major donor-funded school construction programs have started. However, these programs cannot keep pace with the expansion of the system.

Given the small population of Namibia it is understandable that the tertiary education system is limited in size, with an estimated gross enrollment of 3.2. It comprises the University, the Technicon, the College of Out-of-School Training (COST), three agricultural colleges, and four teacher-training colleges. An institution referred to as the Academy was established around 1980 in order to provide basic tertiary education to Namibians. It consisted of a university, the Technicon and the COST. However, it ceased to exist in 1992 when the University of Namibia (UNAM) was established by an Act of the National Assembly. There are plans to convert the Technicon into a Polytechnic.

The University, which has approximately 2,700 students (1993), offers some 30 degree, diploma, and graduate courses in the arts, economics, management, education, health, and science. It also offers distance teaching in order to upgrade teachers. The Technicon has some 1,200 students and offers courses in agriculture, nature conservation, management, public administration, accounting, secretarial training, languages, commerce, legal training, and the like. In 1993 COST had 2,100 students.

Namibia also has three agricultural colleges with good facilities. However, they have not been operating to full capacity. There is a great need for agricultural development in the north and it would be desirable to have all colleges in full operation, and with curricula specifically related to the development of small-scale farming. There are plans to convert one of the colleges into a Faculty of Agriculture within the University.

3.2 Preschool Education

Preschool education plays a minor role in Namibian formal education. In 1994, it enrolled only 4,700 children in 12 institutions—perhaps 10 percent of the relevant age group. White, urban children were, as would be expected well-represented. While considering early childhood education and development an important aspect of basic education the Namibian government recognizes that it does not have the resources to provide this service to every child. Thus, the Ministry of Education and Culture has accepted responsibility for the training of trainers and for curriculum development, but is leaving it to communities and nongovernmental organizations to establish and run centers for this level of education.

3.3 Special Education

The Ministry of Education and Culture has established a directorate of special education to manage and coordinate programs in special education for the physically, emotionally, and mentally handicapped; the blind, and the hard of hearing. Few schools exist. The government runs six schools and nongovernmental organizations run four. The demand for special education has not been met. It has been decided to expand it, by building an Institute for Special Education in Windhoek. Construction work started in 1993 and will be completed at the end of 1995. Use of these facilities will be phased in gradually.

3.4 Vocational, Technical, and Business Education

The vocational/technical educational system is small in Namibia. It comprises—if some diversified secondary schools, polytechnics, agricultural colleges, and private schools are included—22 institutions. Only about 15 percent of the senior secondary school students are in prevocational or vocational programs, while it could be claimed that the figure should be 40 to 60 percent at this stage of Namibia's development. The fact that vocational subjects are being offered also in junior secondary schools does not change the situation to any large extent. According to the 1991 Population Census there are less than 10,000 people in the country with some kind of vocational/technical education or training.

The link between public vocational/technical schools and the employers and labor market has been weak in Namibia. No formal links existed in the past. A National Council on Vocational and Technical Education was created in 1991. It deals with curricula, examinations, and testing in vocational/technical schools, apprenticeship schemes, staff recruitment and development, best use of facilities in existing schools, and so on. A very important issue is to establish a close cooperation between the Ministries of Education and Culture, Labor and Human Resources Development, Trade and Industries, Mines and Energy, Fisheries and Agriculture, and Water and Rural Development in the area of vocational/technical education. The fact that vocational/technical schools have to compete in the open market for staff and that they are also very expensive are two important issues in this sector of education which must be faced.

3.5 Adult and Nonformal Education

Before independence the government's involvement in nonformal education and training was minimal.

Instead, this system was run by mining companies, transport and power enterprises, and many construction firms. Church and other nongovernmental organizations were also involved. These entities also offered literacy courses in connection with the vocational training activities to reduce the high percentage of illiteracy among Blacks.

At independence a new Directorate of Adult and Nonformal education was established within the Ministry of Education and Culture. A National Literacy Program was started to cater for those who had never attended school or had dropped out before they had become literate. The adult literacy rate is estimated at between 40 and 60 percent. In 1992 the National Literacy Program had 15,000 students in Stage 1. In 1993, after the introduction of Stages 2 and 3 the number of students in the program was 34,000. There are also continuing education programs for those who have dropped out of the formal education system, distance education opportunities, mainly directed at teachers for upgrading of formal education qualifications, and an adult skills development program.

4. Administrative and Supervisory Structure and Operation

In order that the offices for the administration of educational policies, programs, and services achieve the goals listed earlier an effort was made to create an organizational structure for the Ministry which was flexible, interactive, unified, and decentralized. Its main functional features were, and still are: (a) policy planning and formulation, (b) management and administration, (c) supervision and control, and (d) unification and decentralization of education services.

The policy planning and formulation function of the Ministry is led and conducted by the offices of the Minister, Deputy Minister, and senior administrative personnel. This function encompasses curriculum and teaching, personnel and logistic services, program development, research, policy analysis, information management systems, institutional development and resources control, and the overall supervision and control of all aspects of the Ministry's portfolios.

The management and administration of the Ministry's functions are coordinated by the office of the Permanent Secretary and the Education Management Team (EMT). The functions are distributed in several portfolios, namely: formal education programs, adult and continuing education, libraries, arts and culture, and regional education offices. These are supported by the Directorate of Planning and Development and the Directorate of General Services, both of which fall directly under the Permanent Secretary's office.

The supervisory and control functions of the departments are vested in departmental divisions and units. At this level, policies and programs are translated into activities and actions for implementation, monitoring, and control.

Whereas the portfolios and functions of the Ministry are unified into the National Ministry of Education and Culture Headquarters, their implementation is decentralizaed to seven regional offices. In mid-1994, a rationalized structure was implemented in an attempt to streamline the fairly large administrative system.

5. Education Finance

Namibia is, by African standards, an affluent country (GNP/capita US$1,610). It spends about 10 percent of its GNP on education, which is about twice the world average. The percentage of national budget going to education is also fairly high—28 percent. However, just as the per capita income is very unevenly distributed, as a legacy of the apartheid system, so is the educational expenditure, both between and within regions. Thus, equitable distribution of resources is one of the main objectives of the Ministry of Education and Culture. The distribution of the budget by level in 1993 was as follows: preprimary and primary education, 58 percent; secondary education, 31 percent; tertiary education, 8 percent; and adult/nonformal education, 2 percent. This includes administrative costs, which are high. Salaries account for 75 percent.

The allocation of funds for adult/nonformal education is low considering the great need for literacy training, particularly in the north. However, the above estimate does not include donor funding, which is substantial to the literary program. About 12 percent of all pupils are boarders and the Ministry spends 13 percent of its total current budget on feeding and housing. While boarding facilities are necessary in this very sparsely populated country the Ministry is investigating ways and means of sharing the cost of this service with the pupils and their parents.

Student–teacher ratios vary, as already stated, from 43:1 in the north to 21:1 in Keetmanshoop which implies large differences in per student–teacher salary costs; from 600 N$ per student per year to over 4,000 N$. The average per pupil cost (1993–94) was 1,370 N$ in primary education and 2,830 N$ in secondary education, after the reduction of the large boarding cost. The costs include salaries, equipment, furniture, books, maintenance, and so on.

The annual allocation of capital funds amounts to 6 percent of the recurrent costs. This does not include donor contribution to classroom building projects. The pre-independence unequal distribution of physical facilities leaves the situation in the northern part of the country still lagging substantially behind with respect to classrooms, laboratories, libraries, and teacher accommodation.

School costs are mainly financed by the central government. The role of regional and local authorities as regards education is under development. After independence a large number of international and bilateral agencies started helping Namibia to improve its education system and particularly to help reduce the

Table 1
Professionally qualified teachers by region 1993

Region	Number of qualified teachers	Percentage of qualified teachers
Katima Mulilo	738	70
Keetmanshoop	766	67
Khorixas	724	61
Ondangwa	4,064	64
Rundu	664	44
Windhoek	3,331	84
National Total[a]	10,287	67

a Total number of qualified and unqualified teachers was 15,280

inequity in educational opportunities between ethnic groups and geographical regions. Investments in the north have had preference. Undoing apartheid has, however, turned out to be more difficult than could be expected.

6. Supplying Personnel for the Education System

The supply of qualified teachers in Namibia is unsatisfactory. There were some 15,300 primary and secondary school teachers in 1993. On these approximately two-thirds had professional teacher training. However, many of the teachers are qualified to teach at primary level, but are in fact teaching at secondary level and many of those teaching mathematics, science, and English are not qualified to teach those subjects. The teachers are divided into 12 categories depending on their education and training which varies from full secondary education and 7 years of training for the most qualified category to Grade 9 or lower with no teacher training at all.

Black teachers were traditionally underpaid in Namibia. After independence a substantial salary increase was provided in order to equalize salaries between various population groups and minimize differences between the lowest and highest paid teachers. In 1993, professionally qualified teachers were distributed among educational regions as shown in Table 1.

The table shows substantial differences throughout the regions. Among teachers in vocational/technical schools, the lack of industrial/practical experience is a serious deficiency. At the University of Namibia many Namibian lecturers do not have the required background, that is, a master's degree.

What renders the situation of the unqualified teachers even more difficult is the uneven workload among the groups. In Ondangwa schools the high student–teacher ratio means very large classes of some

40 students or more. In former White schools classes are often half this size. The most unqualified teachers have thus so far had the largest classes and thus the heaviest workload. The result has been large differences in examination results, dropout rates, and grade repitition.

In order to improve the situation a number of inservice teacher-training programs have been started in areas such as mathematics, science, and English. Upgrading of management skills of principals at all levels of the educational system is an additional focus of inservice training. Most of these inservice training programs are supported by various foreign donor agencies. However, it has to be recognized that it will take many years to arrive at a situation of fair regional distribution of teachers in Namibia.

Teacher training is provided for secondary school teachers in the Faculty of Education in the University of Namibia and for primary and partly for junior secondary school teachers in educational colleges in Windhoek, Ongwediva, Rundu, and Katima Mulilo. The total number of students in preservice teacher training at the colleges was 1,545 in 1994.

Pre-independence teacher education gave excessive emphasis to subject content with insufficient time allowed for teaching practice. A new preservice teacher education curriculum has been developed and implementation of this 3-year Basic Education Teaching Diploma (BETD) started in 1993. This program, which draws upon experiences of a teacher education program for Namibians in exile, is applying a pupil-centered approach and includes substantial teaching practice referred to as school-based learning. Work has also started on the provision of the BETD by distance education, for un- and underqualified practising teachers, who for one reason or another are not in a position to spend three years away from home. In addition, a network of teacher resource centers have been established in various parts of the country and the colleges in Rundu and Katima Mulilo, previously operating from secondary schools are soon going to be accommodated in purpose-built buildings.

In conclusion, while the teacher situation was disastrous before independence, it can now be said that much has been done, but much remains to be done, not least in the fields of science, mathematics, and English.

7. Curriculum Development and Teaching Methodology

Curricula and syllabi in the general primary and secondary school have been considered somewhat irrelevant to the needs of independent Namibia, and in many ways outdated. The teaching methods and the examination system demanded much rote learning. In the late 1980s Namibia and South Africa were probably among the most examination-dominated countries anywhere. Failure rates were also high.

Textbooks have also constituted a problem as they were mostly produced in South Africa and reflected apartheid South African situations and values. Lately a number of Namibian textbooks have been published, but shortage of funds is a serious problem in this area.

There are 40 to 45 periods per school week with each period lasting 30 to 40 minutes. The school year comprises 198 days, almost a quarter of this time used to be devoted to revision and examinations. The examination system is under revision to include more continuous assessment and fewer formal examinations. The South African Matric examination after Grade 12 is being phased out and replaced by the International General Certificate of Secondary Education (IGCSE) and the Higher International General Certificate of Education (HIGCSE). There is a national junior secondary examination after Grade 10, but no national examination at the end of the primary cycle (Grade 7).

In 1991, a commonly prescribed curriculum and approved syllabi common for all students in primary and secondary education regardless of ethnic background was introduced. The major responsibility for this sector of education rests with the National Institute for Education Development (NIED) and the National Examination and Assessment Authority. These institutions are systematically reviewing and updating curricula and syllabi to make them relevant to the needs of Namibia. An important aspect of the new curriculum is the introduction of English as the medium of instruction from Grade 4.

The subject content at the preschool level of education in Namibia includes language development (home language), social skills (toilet training, living together, etc.), arts and crafts, discovering the environment, and fun with numbers.

In primary schools the main general areas concerned are language skills (speaking, reading, and writing in English and Namibian languages), social skills (social studies, religious, and moral education), arts and crafts (drawing, music and dance, physical edcuation and hygiene, gardening, and handwork), and mathematics and environmental science.

In junior secondary schools the main general areas covered are language arts (English and home language); social sciences (history, geography, religious, and moral education); science and mathematics (mathematics, physical science, life sciences); art and sports; and prevocational skills from which two of the following are chosen: domestic science, woodwork, metalwork, commerce, needlework or dressmaking, and agriculture production. Senior secondary school has language studies; sciences; humanities and social sciences; mathematics; physical education; and creative, technical and vocational studies as its core subjects. Options are wide, but are dependent on the field of study chosen and the availability of physical, instructional, and human resources in the school.

The technical secondary schools have the following core subjects: English language, technical theory and practice, technical drawing, and mathematics. The following are available as options: bricklaying and plastering, electricity, motor mechanics, metalwork and welding, and woodwork.

The curriculum at the vocational institutes is under revision.

It should be noted that agriculture is offered as early as the junior secondary level, although many junior secondary schools have no land for agricultural practice.

The complicated language situation in Namibia implies that a large part of teaching time must be given to language teaching at the sacrifice of other subjects. This has been built into the syllabi at all levels.

8. Prospects for the Year 2000

Namibia became independent in 1990. In many aspects it began its independence with a better base for educational development than other African countries. However, the available resources in the form of classrooms, teachers, and equipment are extremely unequitably distributed following the policy of the previous apartheid regime. In fact, Namibian education can appear as being from developed nations and underdeveloped nations at the same time. Thus, the main objective is to distribute the educational resources among the people of Namibia more equitably than in the past. However, it is clear that undoing the impact of apartheid on the Namibian education system will take time, effort, and additional resources. The assistance from abroad is important in this context. There is every reason to believe that the country will succeed in achieving the official goals as listed in Section 2 above.

Bibliography

Angula N 1990a *The National Integrated System for Emergent Namibia. Draft Proposal for Education Reform and Renewal*. Ministry of Education, Culture, Youth and Sport, Windhoek

Angula N 1990b *Change with Continuity: Education reform directive, 1990. A policy statement of the Ministry of Education, Culture, Youth and Sport*. Ministry of Education, Culture, Youth and Sport, Windhoek

Angula N 1991a *Educational policies in post-colonial Namibia: Challenges and prospects*. Ministry of Education, Culture, Youth and Sport, Windhoek

Angula N 1991b *Education and Culture in Namibia: The Way Forward to 1996. Broad policy directives for Education Reform and Renewal in Namibia*. Ministry of Education and Culture, Windhoek

Angula N 1992 *Pedagogy in progress: challenges and opportunities—Phase 1*. Ministry of Education and Culture, Windhoek

Craelius M H 1990 *Vocational Education and Training in Namibia*. SIDA, Stockholm

International Labor Organization 1989 *Namibia Training*. ILO, Geneva

Ministry of Education 1990 *Namibia: Statistics of Schools 1986–1989*. Ministry of Education, Windhoek

Ministry of Education and Culture 1990 *Education in Transition: Nurturing our Future*. Ministry of Education and Culture, Windhoek

Ministry of Education and Culture 1991 *Explanatory Note and Remarks*. National Assembly, Windhoek

Ministry of Education and Culture 1991 *Pedagogy in Transition, the Imperatives of Education Development in the Republic of Namibia*. Ministry of Education and Culture, Windhoek

Ministry of Education and Culture 1992 *Curriculum Guide for Formal Basic Education, Version 7*. Ministry of Education and Culture, Windhoek

Ministry of Education and Culture 1992 *National Language Policy for Schools 1992 to 1996*. Ministry of Education and Culture, Windhoek

Ministry of Education and Culture 1993 *Toward Education for All—A Development Brief for Education Culture and Training*. Gamsberg Macmillan, Windhoek

Ministry of Labor and Manpower Development 1991 *Draft Document on Vocational Training*. Ministry of Education and Culture, Windhoek

Turner J 1990 *Education in Namibia*. Overseas Development Agency, London

United Nations 1989 UN *Institute for Namibia Report: International Conference on Teacher Education for Namibia*. UN, Lusaka

UNDP 1989 *Education in Namibia*. UNDP, New York

Nepal

T. R. Khaniya and M. A. Kiernan

1. General Background

The Kingdom of Nepal covers an area of 145,504 square kilometers and has a population of 18.46 million (1992 census estimate). Demographic density is highly related to topological structure: the high mountain areas bordering on China contain 7.2 percent of the population and have a density ratio of 25.1 per square kilometer; the central hills share 46 percent of the population and have a density ratio of 116.8 per square kilometer; while the low-lying Terai belt, bordering on India, has 46.8 percent of the population and a density ratio of 192.7 per square kilometer. Children under 15 years of age constitute 41.2 percent of the total population. Over 90 percent of the population live in rural areas though urban growth is increasing at a rate of 7.4 percent per annum.

A population growth rate of 2.1 (1992) is surprisingly lower than that estimated in 1982 (2.62) yet remains the greatest threat to the development strategies of Nepal. The low educational status of the majority of adults and the paucity of medical and social services, compounded by prevalent poverty (71% described as living in absolute poverty, World Bank 1990), are the greatest obstacles to population growth control. Estimated per capita income is US$180 and Nepal is placed in the 131st position (out of 160 countries) according to the Human Development Index of 1991. While mountain areas have least access to social services, western and far-western regions of the country also suffer both from their comparative remoteness and government neglect.

Though a strongly unified nation-state, Nepal is geopolitically open to the influence of its major world-power neighbors, China and India. Internally, Nepal is characterized by a highly complex ethnic and language composition which, together with the ruggedness of the physical landscape and inaccessibility of remote areas, presents considerable obstacles to national development. The national language, Nepali, is the mother-tongue of 51 percent, and spoken as a *lingua franca* by 75 percent. There are approximately 12 major different language groups in Nepal. Nepali is the medium of instruction at all levels of the educational system, with English taught as a second language from Grade 4. Use of ethnic languages was prohibited by the one-party state system but the new democratic constitution of 1991 has guaranteed the cultural rights of all ethnic minorities. As yet the implications for education of this constitutional provision have not been worked out.

Agriculture is the occupation of 80 percent of the working population; agricultural products account for 56 percent of GDP (1988, a fall from 60% in 1980); and a growth rate of only 2.5 is not encouraging. Industrial development, influenced by the power of neighboring India's industrial infrastructure, has a higher growth rate (8.6%) but accounts for only 17 percent of GDP. What is particularly striking in this situation is the fact that while unemployment is estimated at 3.10 percent, underemployment is estimated at 41 percent in the rural, and 46 percent in urban areas. A sizable proportion of the labor force in Nepal is engaged in government and commercial sectors (5.4%) and it is these sectors which absorb the outputs of the educational system. The apparent contradiction between dramatic increases in the output of schools with rising underemployment is a major issue for the newly elected democratic government of Nepal. The government's planning strategy is carried out by the National Planning Commission, an appointed body charged with the development of the nation's five year development plans. The FYDP 1992–97 has poverty alleviation as its primary theme, and increased investment in human resource development is its major thrust.

Agriculture accounts for 52 percent (65% in 1965) of GDP, with the service sector accounting for 25 percent and industry only 6 percent. The balance of payments situation is structurally weak with a heavy reliance on foreign assistance to finance essential components. The Indian economy dominates that of Nepal, especially with regard to employment-creating growth. The greatest challenge to the economy is the massive increase in urbanization with only limited potential for industrial growth. With the labor force expected to double by the year 2010, and with the saturation of arable land, off-farm employment presents the only hope but also the biggest challenge to the future of the economy. Education policies are not as yet addressing the implications of this situation.

Nepal felt the world-wide impact in recent years of the democratization process: in 1990–91 a popular movement led to the overthrow of the Panchayat (the nonparty, but *de facto* single party system, under the absolute authority of the monarchy). A new constitution based on democratic principles, the multiparty system, and constitutional monarchy was promulgated in November 1990. The first free general elections since 1960 were held in 1991 and national and local elections were conducted in 1992. Political stability seems to be emerging after the turbulence of the popular movement and the first year of the new government. The most important decision of the government is its decentralization policy, giving considerable powers to local authorities. It is expected that this will greatly affect the shape of development in the future, empowering as it does the local communities themselves through the elective process. In the previous system local officials were elected only after nomination by the single party apparatus. Demand for educational facilities is expected to increase, which will greatly strain the central authority's ability and capacity to provide the technical and administrative backup support required.

2. Politics and the Goals of the Education System

The policies and goals of education are developed by the National Education Committee and ratified in parliament by education acts. Education development began very tentatively in the 1950s in Nepal and was both initiated and largely funded by foreign donors. In 1971 the first national plan for education was developed, the National Education Systems Plan, which specified the government's role in education and was the first clear statement of educational policy: "The Plan is primarily aimed at counteracting the elitist bias of the inherited system of education by linking it more effectively to productive enterprises and egalitarian principles ... The plan calls for unifying education into one productive system that serves the country's needs and aspirations ... and regards education as an investment in human resources for the development of the country." The immediate outcome was an almost exponential increase in school enrollment, particularly at primary level. However, the administrative and managerial capacity, and the policy-monitoring structures needed to sustain this effort, were lacking and by the 1980s serious problems emerged, especially with regard to quality, access, and equity. By the late 1980s, the government, worried by popular dissatisfaction with the pace of development, issued its Basic Needs Policies for the year 2000 AD, which included the provision of free primary education for all, and increased access to secondary and higher education.

The political changes in the early 1990s, while not leading to an abandonment of the Basic Needs approach, did result in greater emphasis on policy and planning issues and on providing a greater role for the private sector. Thus major studies were initiated into primary, secondary, and tertiary levels of education, culminating in the establishment of a National Education Commission charged with developing those educational policies consonant with a rational assessment of the current situation within the new political context. The Commission presented its report in mid-1992 and following its adoption by parliament this will provide the framework for educational planning in the 1990s. The fact that political parties have not operated freely in Nepal for many years, with the accompanying absence of public debate on education, can account for the Commission's report being somewhat generalist in tone, without clearly specifying the options and policy alternatives available to government.

Government's role in education is dominated by two issues: (a) its responsibility to improve access, equity, and quality of education, and (b) the increasing level of public expenditure needed even to maintain the present level of services. With the poverty level as it is the chances of increasing revenue from the community is limited, and in any case increased privatization would favor urban and relatively well-developed regions of the country. Considerable savings could be made by reducing the degree of internal inefficiencies in the system: it reportedly takes between 9 to 12 years to complete the five-year primary cycle; only 15 percent of the secondary entry cohort complete secondary education and only 30 percent of that group pass; university course pass rates vary from 5 to 10 percent. The long-term solution will depend very much upon political responsiveness to this situation, coupled with significant improvement in the professional development of educational services.

3. The Formal System of Education

Analysts of school enrollment data produced by the Ministry of Education have often to face the problem of lack of systematized, consistent, and reliable data. This is due to the absence of a professional information management system but further complicated by such factors as, for example, highly inflated Grade 1 enrollment figures as a result of tying grants-in-aid with teacher number which is determined by student number. Therefore the structure of the formal education system (Fig. 1) can only be regarded as an approximation, showing trends rather than indicating absolute quantitative levels. While the Ministry of Education reports (for primary education) a net enrollment ratio of 79.8 percent (1991), another survey (the Demographic Sample Survey of 1987) reported an NER of only 36 percent. It is hoped that the census of 1992, which has enumerated the population by education level and also by caste and ethnic origin, will provide a clearer picture of the situation.

3.1 Primary, Secondary, and Tertiary Education

The progress of primary education in Nepal can be indicated by the dramatic increase in the number of schools: from less than 300 schools in 1950 to 14,500 in 1992. However, increasing population combined with public pressure for education and government's commitment to equitable social services, will involve not only additional schools but also the high cost of providing education for the estimated 20 percent of the primary age-group not receiving education. This group lives in the more inaccessible areas and can be characterized as disadvantaged. Very few studies are available on access and participation issues; one (CERID 1984), examined the determinants of educational participation in rural Nepal. These were chiefly three: (a) child-related variables such as the gender of the child and the extent to which the child contributes to household activities and earnings; (b) the child's immediate cultural environment as represented by father's level of education, household occupational and economic status; and (c) school-related variables such as the

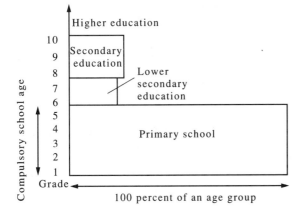

Figure 1
Nepal: Structure of the formal education system 1990

teacher and school characteristics. Anecdotal evidence in recent years indicates the perceived irrelevance of primary education among rural parents as a reason for the slow-down in enrollment growth rates which began to appear in the mid-1980s.

The primary cycle is five years, though until 1981 only three years of primary schooling was mandated. Some 55 percent of all the schools in the country are independent Grade 1–5 units, a further 20 percent operate in combination with lower secondary classes (Grades 6–7), and 10 percent have all grades (1–10). Private primary schools are allowed but as they do not qualify for government grants-in-aid (teacher salaries and free textbooks) their numbers are few (less than 4% of students are enrolled in private primary schools). However, increasing dissatisfaction with the quality of primary education has led to an increase in private primary schooling, mostly in urban areas.

The greatest problem of the primary sector is its internal inefficiency. According to the 1986 Ministry of Education study, 70 percent of all dropouts occur at Grade 1 level, as do 53 percent of all repetitions. The whole cycle has an estimated efficiency rate of 35 percent. Reasons are multiple: poor teaching, lack of supervision, no student assessment, poor or nonexistent school–home relationships, and irrelevant and poorly produced teaching/learning materials; however, there is little research evidence to support any of these explanations.

External efficiency is equally poor. The goals of primary education are basic literacy, numeracy, and acquisition of basic life skills. Again recent data is not available but a study in 1984 on achievement of primary graduates indicates very low scores in mathematics, social studies, and science. There is no standardized primary school terminal examination.

The structure of secondary education has shifted three times since 1970. Initially there was a 5+3+2 system (primary, lower secondary, upper secondary). In 1971 this was changed to 3+4+3 and in 1981 changed again to 5+2+3. There are plans to combine lower and upper secondary and to add a higher secondary course to accommodate the 60 percent of the university population who take nondegree courses, thus giving a 5+5+2 system. These frequent changes in structure were accompanied by changes in goals and curriculum, factors which have greatly weakened the sector, despite quantitative gains.

From 1951–1985 the number of secondary schools increased from 11 to 4,899 and students increased from 4,899 to 496,821. Approximately 25 percent are girls. In 1990 there were 3,964 lower-secondary schools with an enrollment of 344,138 students and 1,953 secondary schools with an enrollment of 364,525 students. The gross enrollment rates were 41 and 29 percent of the age-group respectively.

The government's support for the goals of "Education For All By 2000" presents the most serious matter of policy, as it will lead to the inevitable expansion of secondary education and consequent pressure on limited financial resources. In 1991, the new government announced that first-year secondary (Grade 6) would be "free" (that is, government would provide the same grants-in-aids assistance as to primary grades), indicating already the dual impact of increased output from the primary level and the political pressures of the new multiparty system.

The critical issues in secondary education relate to internal and external efficiency, access, participation and equity, administration, supervision and financing. The dropout rate of students at lower-secondary level is 45 percent; 50 percent dropout at the upper level; less than 30 percent pass the final (SLC) examination. While the participation rate of 24.9 percent is relatively high for developing countries, the rate for girls is only 13 percent. Secondary schools are unevenly distributed with regards to population, a situation partly to be ascribed to topography but also to political motivation. Kathmandu Valley, the seat of political power, has the highest percentage of the age-groups in secondary schools. The Ministry of Education attempts to monitor the quality of secondary education by stopping its grant-in-aid to schools who fail to have at least a 15 percent pass rate for three consecutive years. However, penalties can be avoided by schools controlling the number of students presented for examination. A high proportion of teachers are temporary. There is no mandatory professional training, materials are scant and only marginally adequate, and the rote-memorization style of learning is reinforced by a final examination which has a very high percentage of recall-type items.

Higher education enrollment in Nepal doubled in five years from 1985 to 1990, tripled in the decade from 1980 to 1990 and quadrupled in 15 years from 1975 (22,765 students) to 1990. The enrollment ratio of 5 percent (1991) is remarkable for one of the lowest income countries in the world. The 1992 enrollment of 115,772 will reach 300,000 by the year 2000 on current projections. The problems this will cause can be dramatically illustrated by the fact that at present the physical capacity of the university is only 30–40,000 students on a single shift basis; many campuses run three to four shifts, resulting in serious deterioration of quality.

The principal body of the higher education system is Tribhuvan University, which consists of 65 constituent campuses and 130 associated campuses. The constituent campuses are publicly funded and account for 80 percent of enrollment, while the associated campuses, privately funded, account for the remaining 20 percent.

The major issues are (a) rapid expansion of enrollment, (b) underfinancing of the system, (c) poor management and administration, (d) structural problems, and (e) outdated curricula. The rapid expansion of enrollment without improvement of quality inputs will further deteriorate a weak system. The system is also producing unemployable graduates, a situation likely to increase in view of the sluggish state of the economy. A recent survey showed that more than 25 percent of graduates have been working in jobs requiring less education than they obtained.

From 1985 to 1991 enrollment doubled without provision for any additional classrooms, laboratories, or other facilities. Curricula have not been updated since the mid-1960s. Centralized control of finance stifles initiatives and innovations for mobilization of necessary resources by local governments, communities, and the campuses themselves. A recent survey revealed that 90 percent of the professors are obliged to take a second job after a second shift in an affiliated campus in order to support their families. Student fees are nominal, less than US$1 per month set against an average cost of US$300 per student per annum. The university has a staff of 5,065 teachers, but an administrative staff of 5,511.

Most of these problems stem from the fact that almost 60 percent of campus students are studying at nondegree level (mostly a two-year certificate course). Some 30 percent of the students study at bachelor level and 8 percent study at master's level. More than 80 percent of the students are enrolled in the humanities, social sciences, management, and law, while less than 10 percent are enrolled in engineering, agriculture, forestry, and medicine. Women account for less than 25 percent of students, with only 15 percent in the latter-named faculties. The new government is addressing these problems in a realistic manner but its options are limited.

3.2 Preschool Education

Preschool education is a rarity available only to an extremely small minority of Nepalese in urban areas and based almost exclusively on economic factors. All preprimary schools are private with average monthly fees of 200 rupees (US$4.36) (cf. 40 rupees (US$0.87) per month for tertiary study). However, the fact that an estimated 5 percent of the total primary enrollment is under age (3-, 4-, and 5-year olds, generally brought by their elder siblings) demonstrates that there is an acute need for preschool education, not only for the children's necessary psychosocial development but also to allow Grade 1 teaching to start correctly.

3.3 Special Education

Disability rates are comparatively high in Nepal, particularly deafness, caused more by preventable diseases than by birth defects or by accidents. Education facilities are very limited, provided mostly by international and national nongovernmental organizations. However, the government has now recognized the educational rights of the disabled. A National Council for Special Education has been established and the Ministry of Education has allocated a specific budget for special education activities. Disabled children are catered for either through integrated (14) or segregated (26) schools, with the majority in the central development region.

3.4 Vocational, Technical, and Business Education

Despite public awareness of the need for skilled and motivated labor in order to sustain development, provision of opportunities for technical and vocational training have been very limited. In the 1950s and 1960s higher level technical labor was procured externally or through training programs for Nepalese abroad. The National Education System Plan (1971) emphasized the need for training of large numbers of basic level skilled workers. Lower-secondary schools were asked to provide prevocational courses and 22 percent of the curriculum of upper-secondary schools was devoted to technical subjects. These efforts failed mostly because of inadequate resources and lack of skilled teachers. Parental interest in education focused more on preparation for higher education than in the acquisition of terminal usable skills. These early efforts were replaced by a Trades School Plan, managed by a Technical and Vocational Education Committee (TVEC) with the Directorate of Technical and Vocational Education, a division of the Ministry of Education, as its secretariat. In 1979 the Committee decided to separate vocational schools entirely from general schools and to establish a skills-intensive vocational training program instead.

The system of technical–vocational education and training in the early 1990s covers a broad range of activities from informal on-the-job training, through apprenticeship, to fully fledged and certificated technical schools. Technical schools are of the following three types lower-secondary level, secondary level, and higher-secondary level. Other ministries, particularly the ministries responsible for labor and industry, run training programs to produce workers for their own activities only. Expansion of the limited number of technical schools, while strongly advocated by planners and policymakers, is constrained by high unit costs and by the slow development of the economy, particularly the industrial sector.

3.5 Adult and Nonformal Education

Literacy rates are difficult to define in Nepal as a result of changing and/or ill-defined concepts of literacy, and the absence of any assessment systems. Even the 1992 census figures will only reflect each adult's own estimation of his or her literacy level. The accepted figures in the early 1990s are a literacy rate of 52 percent for males and 18 percent for women (from 9.5% and 0.7% respectively in 1952). Illiteracy is most pronounced in rural areas, in particular among disadvantaged groups and lower castes. The Education For All (Jomtien Declaration) impetus has led to a much more pronounced emphasis on adult education, both for its own sake and as a tool for national development.

A national campaign has been under way in a phased manner, since 1990, aiming at providing literacy to an estimated 5 million adults by the year 2000 AD. The goals are to (a) enable individuals between 15–45 years of age to read, write, and do simple mathematical calculations; (b) increase adults' awareness of their own environment and develop positive attitudes and self-confidence; (c) provide information essential to daily life; and (d) inform participants about democratic principles and the political and developmental systems of Nepal. The Ministry of Education has been successful in developing an integrated program which is used by over 50 nongovernment agencies operating in most areas of the country. Despite this, however, only 100,000 adults are being reached yearly against a target of at least 600,000 if the 2000 AD goals are to be met.

A number of problems threaten the future of adult education in Nepal: (a) less than 2 percent of the annual education budget has traditionally been allocated to adult literacy; (b) implementation suffers from poor monitoring and supervision; (c) there is very little provision for postliteracy programs; and (d) the absence of any measurement of literacy will continue to weaken the whole planning process. Government attention to adult education, particularly in welcoming the involvement of the private sector and the empowerment of local communities to develop their own strategies, provides some cause for optimism.

Nonformal programs other than adult literacy are few. Of particular interest, however, is a nonformal approach to basic education for children, especially girls, of school age. It is estimated that 1.2 million children do not attend formal school and this is the target group of the "Out-Of-School" program which at this stage operates on a small, through promising, scale. While the scale of the problems at postsecondary level has led to calls for nonformal approaches such as distance teaching and open university systems, nothing concrete has been established.

4. Administrative and Supervisory Structure and Operation

Nepal's administrative system has developed from two traditions: that of the early monarchy and the oligarchic Rana system which was concerned with security and internal control, and the influence of the Indian Civil Service administration, which itself was largely influenced by the British colonial system. The chief legacies are therefore a strongly centralized system and an emphasis on loyalty more than on technical or professional competence. Attempts at administrative reform started with the first post-Rana government in 1956, further developed by the Nepali Congress government of 1959–60, but little progress was made. The Panchayat system politicized the administrative system, thus incapacitating its declared policies of decentralization and meritocracy. The newly elected government of 1991 has given high priority to administrative reform, prompted by the urgent need to dismantle a large civil service which resulted from the patronage system implemented by previous governments.

The Ministry of Education is highly centralized; staff at the highest level are burdened by a decision-making chain which allows for little delegation of authority. A National Education Committee is the policy formulation body but only has advisory status. Education plans are approved under the five year development plan system. The education secretary is responsible for day-to-day operations and reports directly to the minister, who is a member of the Cabinet. There are three major divisions at central level (planning, educational administration, and general administration) and a number of directorates for the developmental activities. There is a system of regional educational directorates and district education offices, the former having a technical support role and the latter a purely administrative function. In practice, and on account of budgets going directly from central to district level, the regional offices have little authority and less funding for developmental work.

Until the advent of the new democratic system the district educational authorities were more subject to the local political system than to the Ministry of Education. People's participation has been limited to school management committees, but here too, until recently, members were political nominees more concerned with political control than educational advancement.

A peculiar aspect of education management is the semi-autonomous powers of donor-assisted projects, which, while providing a more task-oriented, quality-conscious, and accountable environment, run the risk of establishing parallel structures within the ministry itself. Supervision at all levels is weak. The ministry has a nominal program evaluation section, regional offices seldom carry out district inspection tours, and district supervisors, through qualified, cannot carry out any meaningful supervision of schools because of the absence of a supervision system for education. Major reforms of the system are being planned but the scarcity of qualified and trained workers will hinder the implementation of desired reforms.

The King is the chancellor of the university, an honorary and symbolic position. The minister of education is the prochancellor and a university council of 85 is the governing body, functioning as a board of trustees. The daily operation of the university system is managed by the vicechancellor, assisted by the rector, the chief academic officer, and the registrar, who is the chief administrative officer. The Tribhuvan University Service Commission is an independent body responsible for recruiting and promotion of university staff.

5. Educational Finance

It is only since 1971 that the government assumed substantial responsibilities for financing all levels of education, largely in the form of teacher salary support and a free primary textbook scheme. However, expenditure in the education sector has not expanded as fast as total government expenditure. Education accounts for 2.2 percent of gross domestic product (GDP) (regional average is 4%), and government spending on education as a percentage of total government expenditure has been deteriorating from an average of 10 percent in the late 1980s to 8.6 percent in 1990–91. Figures from 1991 show that 50 percent of education expenditure goes to primary level, 17 percent to secondary, and 24 percent to tertiary (the corresponding figures in 1978 were 44, 22, and 27%).

Secondary schools are partially financed by government. In lower- and upper-secondary schools, 75 percent and 50 percent of salaries respectively, are paid by government. The cycle costs for a graduate of the secondary education cycle, including a school-leaving certificate, are estimated to be 13,000 rupees (US$283.32), with government contributing approximately half of that amount. If the system was fully internally efficient the total cycle costs are estimated at 4,000 rupees (US$89.12)

The major sources of educational financing are grant-in-aid provided by the government, local communities support, and foreign resources. Local communities contribute with cash, land, and voluntary labor for school construction. Foreign assistance, mostly "soft" credit-loans from the World Bank's International Development Association (IDA) and the Asian Development Bank (ADB), with additional grant funding from the United Nations Development Program (UNDP), UNESCO, UNICEF, JICA (Japan), Danida (Denmark), GTZ (Germany) and the Overseas Development Administration (ODA) (UK). There are a number of nongovernment agencies assisting, as well as international voluntary agencies such as the Peace Corps and Voluntary Service Overseas. However, government has been reluctant to borrow substantially for the social sector and it is difficult to foresee how the "Education For All by the year 2000" goals can be met if current trends prevail. It is estimated that the government would have to spend 16 percent of its total national expenditures on education and raise the allocation to the primary sector to 60 percent if it intends to enroll an estimated 3.4 million children of primary school age by the year 2000.

Over 90 percent of higher education expenditure is salary payment, with little for nonsalary recurrent expenditure items such as instructional improvement, materials, laboratory and library supplies, etc.

Improving internal and external efficiency rates, increased and more judicious use of donor assistance, the introduction of cost–recovery systems, especially at tertiary level, and much greater private investment in education, are strategies that the government will have to implement even to maintain the early 1990s level of access and participation.

6. Supplying Personnel for the Education System

The public sector is the largest employer of educated workers with educational institutions accounting for 80,000 of the estimated 200,000. Tribhuvan university is the main producer of middle and higher level workers. Primary teachers, who number 67,000 (less than 10% of whom are female), have only a school-leaving certificate, and this qualification was introduced only as late as 1989. The majority of teachers are untrained, a consequence of a policy decision taken in the mid-1980s not to make professional training mandatory. The National Staff Development College provides some management training and the bulk of teacher training (mostly secondary) is provided by the Faculty of Education of the national university. In 1989 the government decided on a mandatory 150 hours basic training for teachers, but this has been poorly implemented and is under review. The major problem is the absence of a comprehensive teacher-training policy, supported by quality programs within the context of a clearly defined career path for teachers. The recruitment and training of district personnel is especially weak, and this, compounded by frequent transfers and a high attrition rate, accounts for the general weak level of educational administration.

While all gazetted level appointments are made by the Public Service Commission, this has not proved to be an effective intervention in enhancing the technocratic and meritocratic aspects of the education service. The National Administrative Reform Commission of 1991–92 is expected to recommend drastic staff reductions and to place increased emphasis on initiative, responsibility, qualifications, and training at all levels of the public service.

7. Curriculum Development and Teaching Methodology

The strong traditions of centralized powers in Nepal are reflected in the history of curriculum development. All curricula are centrally set and are embodied for the most part in the official textbooks, one per core subject. A student entering university is unlikely to have read anything beyond set textbooks from Grade 1 to 10. Curricula at all levels are largely irrelevant to the needs of the students, are mostly outdated, and have not undergone any of the accepted processes of curriculum development. For primary and secondary levels curriculum development is the responsibility of the Ministry of Education's CTSDC, (Curriculum, Textbook, and Supervision Development Center). Other levels and institutions set their own curricula, and all must be approved by the National Education Committee, though in the case of tertiary studies this function is carried out by the University Council.

The inadequacies of the official curricula and the poor standard of the textbooks are but two of the major reasons for the qualitative decline of education in Nepal. The CTSDC is more an administrative than a developmental institution, especially as curriculum development until very recently has been based on the contractual authorial method. All publishing and printing of textbooks has been carried out by the Janak Educational Materials Center, a government corporation, and distribution is carried out by Sahja Publishers, a public enterprise.

The major problems stem from the absence of the process approach to curriculum development: no needs assessments are carried out, materials are not pretested, curriculum planners and designers are exceedingly few and where available are mostly self-taught. There is an almost total absence of editorial, design, and publishing skills. There is little, if any, evaluation. Textbooks are poorly produced and have a life expectancy of less than one year. There is considerable paper wastage, largely due to old machinery and lack of quality control at all levels of operation. Textbooks do, however, get to most parts of the country and transport costs are built into the book price, thus not unduly penalizing students in the remote areas. Project-initiated exercises in curriculum reform are beginning to make an impact on primary curriculum development. In 1993 a New Primary Curriculum was introduced throughout the country and by 1997 will cover the whole primary cycle. While not all aspects of the process approach have been addressed in the preparation of the new curriculum, there has been at least a three-year test and trial phase. There are plans under way to reform secondary and tertiary curricula; the actual implementation of these plans will require considerable technical inputs not available in the country in the early 1990s.

The structure of the primary curriculum is dual: lower primary focuses on the acquisition of basic literacy, numeracy, and some social studies skills, the latter including some health education. English and science are added to the upper primary curriculum together with moral education, work education, physical education, and arts and crafts. However only the examined subjects (languages, mathematics, science, and social studies) tend to be taught. The curriculum for lower secondary includes 10 subjects, the relative weight given to each, in terms of instructional time and the examinations which follow, is assigned by a system of "marks": Nepali language gets the most, 120 (17%), mathematics 100 (14%), and health 20 (3%). At upper-secondary level optional subjects are available, though most are not offered because of the absence of teachers. Nepali, English, mathematics and "vocational" are the core subjects. Science is an option.

Teaching methodologies are controlled by the textbooks and since these are content overloaded and written by academics rather than by curriculum developers, the most common methods are rote memorization, note-copying, and lecturing. The lack of teacher training, especially in pedagogics, further exacerbates this situation.

8. The System of Examinations, Promotions, and Certifications

Primary terminal examinations are set by individual districts and do not constitute any serious barrier to advancement to secondary (fee-paying) school. After Grade 5 there is no further exit point until Grade 10 when students sit for the School-Leaving Certificate Examination (SLC). Increasingly, many faculties are setting their own entrance examinations, a reflection of the inadequacy of the SLC as a means of determining attainment and aptitude. As there is no continuous assessment, final examination scores are the critical factors. Raw scores only are tabulated and a cut-off score of 32 percent indicates a "pass." Examinations are poorly constructed; marking and scoring are apt to be erratic; and there is no feedback mechanism to allow schools, teachers, or students to analyze their achievement. Pass rates are very low, estimated at 30 percent for secondary and between 5–20 percent at tertiary level institutions.

9. Educational Assessment, Evaluation, and Research

Examination results are the only type of assessment in operation. Only SLC and higher level examination scores are recorded. There are some moves to introduce student assessment as a component of the new primary curriculum but this will at best be done on a sample basis. Research in education is sporadic, dictated more by advanced degree theses than by the needs of the system itself. Whatever significant research that has been carried out was pioneered by the University's Center for Educational Research, Innovation, and Development (CERID). However, lack of government funding and reliance on donor, project-specific assistance has prevented the development of systematic research. A particularly weak area is that of policy research. The Ministry of Education is developing its own educational management information system and a school mapping exercise is under way which will provide very valuable baseline data for use in future evaluations. Gross and net enrollment rate, dropout, promotion, retention ratios, and gender ratios, are some of the most important indicators used by the Ministry of Education to monitor educational development.

10. Major Reforms of the 1980s and 1990s

The 1980s in Nepal can best be characterized by project-based experimentation. In 1981 the primary cycle was increased to five years and during that decade a number of projects focused specifically on the issues of access, equity, quality, and management. A Basic and Primary Education Master Plan was developed in the early 1990s and this has led to the formulation of a basic and primary education program which is being jointly and cooperatively financed by the government, the donor agencies (credit-loan banks, multilateral and bilateral), and the community. Serious attention is being given to the problems of secondary and tertiary levels, and the decision to create a new level of senior secondary to accommodate the high percentage of hitherto nondegree university students is an indication of the will to change. Increases in tertiary level fees, though small, are significant in times of increased student activity following the recent reintroduction of democracy. The new primary curriculum, which can be faulted on a number of grounds, is a major improvement on its predecessor and has, by virtue of the process approach, the capacity to change and adapt according to the feedback mechanism.

11. Major Problems for the Year 2000

All the problems in education are closely linked to the problem of finance. If quality is the major issue then there will have to be increased investment in nonsalary categories if any significant qualitative gains are to be achieved. There is also a great need for a fundamental change in the approach to education, to focus more on the acquisition of thinking and application of knowledge skills and to bring the education system more into line with the needs of the rural, agricultural sectors of Nepal. "Education For All by the Year 2000" should not be the goal as it is logistically impossible at this stage; instead, Nepal should seek to have a functioning, cost-effective and cost-beneficent educational system in place by the year 2000, capable of serving Nepal in the twenty-first century.

References

CERID 1984 *Determinants of Educational Participation in Rural Nepal*. Center for Educational Research, Innovation, and Development, Kathmandu

Ministry of Education and Culture (MOEC) 1991 *The Basic and Primary Education Master Plan*. MOEC, Kathmandu

Ministry of Education and Culture (MOEC) 1991 *Education Statistic Report of Nepal*. MOEC, Kathmandu

Ministry of Education and Culture (MOEC)/USAID 1988 *Educational and Human Resources Sector Assessment*. MOEC, Kathmandu

World Bank 1990 *Nepal: Relieving Poverty in a Resource-Scarce Economy*, Vols. 1 and 2. World Bank, Washington, DC

Further Reading

Aryal C N, Pant Y R, Kafle B D 1990 *Promotion of Primary Education for Girls and Disadvantaged Groups*. Ministry of Education and Culture, Kathmandu

CANEDCOM International Limited 1988 *Nepal Teacher Education Project: Final Report*. CANEDCOM Int. Ltd., Toronto

UNICEF 1992 *Children and Women in Nepal: A Situation Analysis*. UNICEF, Kathmandu

World Bank 1989 *Nepal Social Sector Strategy Review*, Vols. 1 and 2. World Bank, Washington, DC

Netherlands

E. J. Vuyk

1. General Background

The Netherlands is one of the smaller member states of the European Community (EC). The land mass totals approximately 40,000 square kilometers. The surface is flat: only in the south and east are there some hills. About 27 percent of the land surface is below sea level and some 60 percent of the population lives in this part. The territory of the Netherlands is divided into 12 provinces. Each province is subdivided into a number of municipalities, varying from 6 (Flevoland) to 125 (Noord Brabant). Normally, primary schools are within very short distance of pupils' homes.

With a population of 15.1 million and 442 people per square kilometer, the Netherlands is one of the most densely populated countries in the world. Between 1964 and 1985, there was a decrease in the birthrate; in 1990 the number was 200,000. The composition of the population is still changing significantly. The ageing of the population is a significant demographic phenomenon.

In the Netherlands there is separation of church and state. There is no state religion. In 1989 Roman Catholics formed the largest religious group (36%), Dutch Reformists (Protestants) accounted for one-fifth, and one-third of the Dutch population was without registered religion. The spoken language is Dutch, a Teutonic language. Both Frisian and Dutch are official languages in provincial and municipal settings in the province of Friesland. In Frisian schools both Frisian and Dutch are taught, and Frisian can be chosen as the official language in schools in Friesland.

Dutch society is becoming increasingly multiethnic. Migrant workers from Mediterranean countries and immigrants from former overseas territories have settled in the Netherlands since the 1960s, chiefly in the older districts of cities in the west of the country and in a number of industrial cities elsewhere. In 1992, about

Table 1

Enrollments and resources in formal education, The Netherlands 1990

	Primary	Secondary	Tertiary
Number of students (×1,000)	1,545[a]	1,613[b]	385[c]
Percentage of age group enrolled			
4–11	99.4[d]	—	—
12	44.0	55.5	—
13–16	3.7[e]	95.0	—
17–18	—	75.0	5.5
19–23	—	19.3[f]	8.4
24–28	—	5.4	5.7
Number of institutions	9,426	1,835	141[g]
Average number of students per institution	164	880	2,730[h]
Student–teacher ratio[i]	17.5	15.8	11[j]
Expenditure per student (×1000 DFl.)[k]	5.2	5.7[l]	8.4[m]

Source: CBS-vademecum educational statistics 1991
a Including special education (106) b See Fig 1: Preuniversity education (VWO) and general secondary education (AVO). First 3 years (480) and next 3 years (209), secondary vocational education (VBO) numbers (176), IBO (49), MBO (248), vt-KMBO (27). Including part-time students in secondary education and adult education (DAO 119), dt MBO (15), LLW (138), Vormingswerk (8) and other secondary education (149)) c Higher Vocational Education (HBO) full-time (183), HBO part-time (50) and University Education (161) d The number of pupils in (primary and secondary) special education increases until the age of 11 and then decreases (age 5: 1%, age 10–11: 7%, age 15: 3%) e Secondary *special* education f Including part-time education, excluding education by correspondence, out of school oral education, and business courses g HBO (73 institutions for full-time education; 56 institutions for part-time education), WO (12 Universities) h HBO full-time (2,507) students), HBO part-time (967 students), Universities (13,879 students) i All numbers concerning personnel are given in full-time equivalents (fte's) j Excluding administrative and support staff, excluding personnel research institutes (OI). Including all this personnel, ratio would be 5,7 students k Personnel, material, housing, rest l Financial report Min. O&W 1990 m Including student contributions (*collegegelden*)

7 percent of the population consisted of immigrants of non-Dutch nationality, and a further 2 percent came from outside the Netherlands but possessed Dutch nationality. Children from ethnic minorities can be given five lessons maximum per week in their own language and culture.

Unemployment among people from ethnic minorities was over 30 percent in 1992 and many had a low level of education.

Basic industries are transport, commercial services, and a highly developed agricultural and horticultural sector. Export of goods (including natural gas) and services accounts for just over 50 percent of GNP. The rate of unemployment has been a major problem since the 1970s. In 1992 the rate was 8 percent. This problem is expected to stay during the 1990s, especially among ethnic minorities and people with low levels of education. Women's participation in paid jobs is considerably below average European levels. Women's economic independence has long been discouraged, partly by social security schemes and tax regulations.

About 5 percent of the labor force is in agriculture; 27 percent in construction and manufacturing; and 68 percent in transport, services, and the public sector. The Netherlands has been a constitutional monarchy since 1848 with a parliamentary system since 1815. The Constitution provides that the members of the Second Chamber, the 12 provincial councils, and the approximately 700 municipal councils be elected directly. The 75 members of the First Chamber are elected by the members of the provincial councils. There is a multiparty system. In 1917, the Netherlands adopted universal suffrage for adult men, and in 1922 for women. Educational policy is generally made at the national level, but the municipality plays a specific role as the authority in charge of public schools.

2. Politics and the Goals of the Educational System

The end of the nineteenth century and the early twentieth century saw the pooling of influences and interests along political and religious lines in virtually every field of social life. This "pillarization" has been typical of administrative and social structures in the Netherlands. The role of pillarization as the dominant principle of social organization declined in importance after the 1960s, but it is still clearly discernible in some fields. Education offers one of the most striking examples of this. Freedom of education is laid down in the Constitution. This characteristic finds expression in virtually all facets of the Dutch educational system. The threefold freedom—to found schools, to organize them, and to determine the religious or other convictions on which they are based—is the reason for the wide variety of schools in the Netherlands. Two out of three primary schools are private, mostly Catholic or Protestant. Their funds are provided by the state

(since 1917). The essential characteristic of their being designated as private is that they have their own independent board of governors. This independence is a very influential characteristic in the Dutch school system.

Equal educational opportunities, the improvement of educational quality, and the development of personal and civic responsibility are the main political goals of education. At the same time improving efficiency will be the only way to achieve those goals, as funds for the educational system are, and are expected to remain, relatively stable.

3. The Formal System of Education

Figure 1 shows the enrollment statistics in the various levels of education. Figure 2 outlines the structure of the formal educational system. Key statistics on enrollments and resources in the major education sectors are provided in Table 1.

3.1 Primary, Secondary, and Tertiary Education

Education is compulsory from ages 5 to 17 and between these ages there is virtually 100 percent attendance at school.

Until the passage of the 1955 Nursery Education Act, central government bore no responsibility for nurseries, as distinct from primary education. The 1985 Primary Education Act integrated nursery and pri-

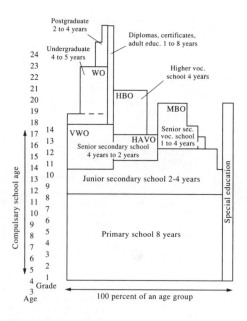

Figure 1

The Netherlands: Structure of the formal education system

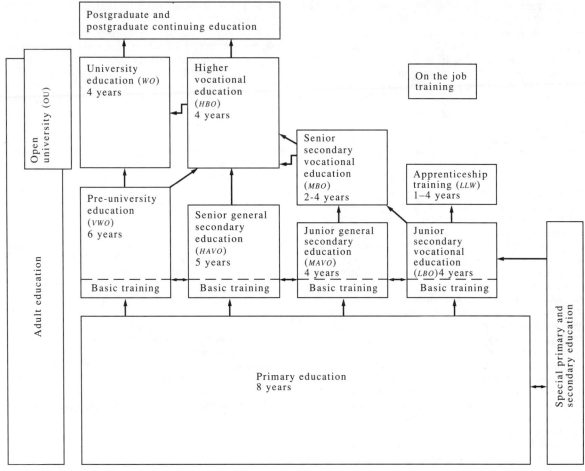

Figure 2
The Netherlands: Organizational diagram of the education system   Source: Netherlands Ministry of Education and Science

mary schools, creating the new-style primary school. Primary education lasts for 8 years. In 1980, there were 1.74 million pupils enrolled in 8,727 primary schools. In 1988, these figures dropped to 1.43 million and 8,426. Since then the number of pupils has been increasing and is expected to rise to 1.62 million in the year 2000. Schools in the Netherlands fall into a number of categories: public authority schools (attended by 31% of the pupil population); private nondenominational (5%), Roman Catholic (33%) and Protestant (33%) schools.

In 1990, the number of "competent authorities" (local schoolboards) was approximately 3,585, of which 2,197 incorporated only one primary school, 996 more than one but less than six, and 392 ran six or more schools.

Over the first three years, children must be taught for a total of 2,240 hours, with a minimum of 480 hours in any one school year. For the rest of their primary careers, they must receive at least 1,000 hours of schooling per year. The maximum amount of teaching

time in one day is 5.5 hours. In determining how this time is to be spent, the need for a balance of activities is taken into consideration.

Secondary education is available for four to six years and follows on from ordinary and special primary education. It caters for pupils from 12 to about 18 years of age. The secondary school system distinguishes between general and vocational education. During the 1980s, the number of students decreased due to demographic trends. Especially in junior secondary vocational education participation rates tumbled.

The transition class, the first year of secondary education, bridges the gap between primary and secondary education and links together the various types of secondary schools. Throughout that part of secondary education covered by compulsory schooling, schools are open five days a week. The total number of lessons given varies between 960 and 1,280 per year, corresponding to 24 to 32 lessons (of 50 minutes) per week.

Preuniversity education (VWO) lasts six years and prepares pupils to enter universities or colleges of higher professional education (HBO). Senior (HAVO) and junior (MAVO) general secondary education courses last for five and four years respectively. Senior general education is primarily designed to prepare pupils for higher professional education. After junior general secondary education, pupils may go on to the fourth year of senior general education, take a senior secondary vocational education course (MBO), join the apprenticeship scheme, or attend part-time nonformal education.

Junior secondary vocational education (VBO) provides a four-year course of prevocational education.

The apprenticeship system (LLW) is a vocational training scheme which involves spending one or two days a week at school and receiving practical training for the rest of the week. The theoretical component is taught on a day-release basis at an apprenticeship training institute, a VBO school or, more rarely, at a nongovernment-funded company training school. Practical work is done in industry or a trainee workshop. There are two parts to the apprenticeship system: elementary training (2–3 years) at the end of which the apprentice takes an examination and is awarded a diploma, and an optional advanced course lasting 1–2 years. Apprenticeship does not require an VBO or MAVO certificate.

Short MBO programs (2–3 years) are designed for VBO and MAVO graduates (with certificate) who cannot find a suitable course in MBO or the apprenticeship system. These courses offer young people, aged 16 and over, the opportunity to be trained for junior positions. Practical work, both in and outside the school, is an important element.

Since 1975, it has been compulsory for those 16-year-olds who do not wish to continue to attend school full-time to attend a course of part-time education for one or two days per week for one year. Part-time nonformal education embraces a complex of related social and educational activities for young people who come under the compulsory part-time education ruling. The activities are led by experts. The aim of the courses is to further personal and social development in a way which is relevant to the individual's present and future situation. The educational institutes active in this field must be affiliated either to the National Organization for Part-time Education for Young Working People or the National Protestant Organization for Part-time Education for Young People in order to receive funding. Both organizations monitor standards.

Tertiary education comprises higher professional education, the universities, and the Open University. Higher professional education (HBO) provides theoretical and practical training for occupations which require a higher professional qualification. It follows on from the higher types of secondary education (HAVO, VWO, and MBO). In the 1960s and 1970s, higher professional education, which was regulated by the Secondary Education Act, increasingly came to be regarded as a form of higher education. Its status

as such was acknowledged in 1986 and in 1992 by education acts.

University education comprises training in the independent pursuit of scholarship and preparation for positions in the community for which a university degree is required. The universities offer a highly diversified and extensive range of nearly 100 degree courses within which students can, to some extent, compile their own individual programs by their choice of optional and main subjects.

Because of the limited number of places available a decision is taken every year as to whether admission to certain courses should be restricted. Students are admitted to these *numerus fixus* courses by means of a weighted draw. In 1991/92 there were 23 courses subject to a *numerus fixus*.

Since 1982, tertiary education has had a two-tier system; the first phase, or undergraduate level, may last up to four years. There are 14 universities, ten state, one municipal and three private. There are eight teaching hospitals, each of which is attached to a university. The universities (including the Open University and those specializing in technology and agriculture) have operated a two-tier system, comprising the first phase (4 years to graduate) and the second phase (1–4 years) for a small number of graduate students. Admission to university is possible with a VWO or HBO-certificate.

Successful students are awarded the title of drs. (meaning "doctorandus"), mr. (law graduates) or ir. (engineering graduates); internationally they may use the title of Master. Students in the second phase courses are trained as researchers, teachers, or specialists (medical sector). Doctorates in most cases take four years extra study.

3.2 Preschool Education

Since August 1985, separate preschool education has not existed formally in the Netherlands, due to compulsory education starting at age 5. Almost all children attended school at age 4 (see Table 1.) A large number of 2- and 3-year olds attend kindergarten, normally part-time before commencing primary school. Programs for 2-year olds are usually not subsidized and parents pay full fees. Kindergarten programs are run privately or by local authorities, but the Ministry of Welfare, Health, and Cultural Affairs has helped to stimulate their growth. Some schools have organized kindergartens inside their buildings. Some types of special school accept children at the age of three.

3.3 Special Education

Special schools cater for children from the age of 3 who, owing to a handicap or to learning or behavioral difficulties, require more help than ordinary primary and secondary schools can offer. In principle, special primary schools are attended by pupils of the same age group as ordinary primary schools. The age at which a child can be admitted to special education varies from one type of school to the other, and ranges from 3 to 6. Special secondary education is for pupils aged 12 and over. The maximum age is 20. Exemption from this rule can only be obtained in exceptional cases.

The competent authority of a special school decides whether to admit a child to the school on the basis of advice and selection by a board of experts. The pupils are re-examined every two years.

The number of different kinds of special schools has increased. There are various types of special primary and secondary school, each suited to the particular learning difficulties which children may encounter. There are schools for children who are deaf, partially hearing, have severe speech disorders, are blind, partially sighted, physically handicapped, hospitalized, chronically ill, mentally handicapped, severely mentally handicapped, severely maladjusted, have learning and behavioral difficulties, are attached to paedological institutes, or have multiple handicaps; and for preschool-age children with developmental difficulties. Although the absolute increase in the overall number of pupils is fairly small, there has been a considerable relative increase, especially considering the decline in the number of pupils in this age category. It is striking that in special education as a whole boys outnumber girls by more than two to one. In 1991 there were 1,004 special schools providing programs for about 109,000 pupils at preprimary (3,000 pupils), primary (74,000 pupils, 4.7%) and secondary (32,000 pupils, 2.7%) level. The average student–teacher ratio is about 6:1. Attendance is growing and expected to grow in the 1990s. The participation of children from ethnic groups is rising considerably, both absolutely and relatively (1991: 12% of the special school population).

About 60 percent of the pupils leaving special education enter secondary education, 6 percent enter primary education, and the rest leave the educational system. Support for transition from special school to work is organized at local level.

There is an increasing emphasis on integrating disabled students into mainstream schools and classes. Children with physical handicaps have been integrated into ordinary schools to an increasing extent. In 1985 the Special Education Interim Act (ISOVSO) was introduced. It contains many provisions similar to those contained in the Primary Education Act as it aims to encourage transfers from special to ordinary schools, for both educational and financial reasons. Cooperation between special and ordinary schools are encouraged.

Teaching is based on a school work plan, which affords an overall view of the organization and content of teaching. The curriculum must include the same subjects as those taught in primary schools, although it may be modified for children with multiple handicaps. Children under the age of 7 must be taught for at least 880 hours and older children for at least 1,000 hours in each school year. Lessons last for between 2.5 and 5.5 hours per day.

3.4 Vocational, Technical, and Business Education

Traditionally there were separate junior secondary schools for technical, business, and administrative training as well as for domestic science. Many of these separate schools have merged into institutions for secondary education during the 1980s and early 1990s. Differentiation and specialization increasingly takes place in senior secondary vocational education (MBO) and higher vocational education (HBO), as well as in universities.

In junior secondary vocational training (VBO) pupils choose from technical courses (including nautical education), domestic economics, business education, retail trade education, and agricultural education. However, the first two years are mainly devoted to general subjects, including Dutch, arithmetic, one modern language, and general studies. The third and fourth years are more vocationally oriented, but the general subjects continue to feature in the timetable.

Senior secondary vocational education (MBO) courses last for two to four years and train pupils to occupy middle-ranking posts in industry, the service sector, and the public sector. The MBO schools provide education in the different VBO courses (technical, domestic economics, business, retail trade, agricultural), and develop their own programs (e. g., social work, health care). At the end of the courses students must pass examinations, the pass levels for which are set by the minister of education based on proposals from a committee of representatives from both business and industry and also the education sector.

In higher vocational education (HBO) differentiation is made between seven sectors: agriculture, teacher training, technical education, commercial education, social work and community education, health care, and the arts.

In university education (WO) there are three institutions specializing in "applied" technology (Delft, Eindhoven, Twente) and there is one university specializing in agricultural sciences (Wageningen). Most general universities also offer technical and medical sciences allied to eight academical hospitals. All universities are subdivided into several study areas, normally specializing in scientific disciplines from the first year.

There are also private institutions in tertiary education which offer certificates and diplomas in business, religion, and other disciplines. Some of them are connected with foreign universities and offer international standard diplomas such as BSc, MSc, MA, and MBA.

3.5 Adult and Nonformal Education

The organization of adult and nonformal education both public and private, is the responsibility of the state. Adult education is available for persons aged

18 years and over, and comprises adult basic education, adult secondary education, vocational courses, and nonformal adult education. Adult basic education refers to activities that enable adults to require the minimum in knowledge, aptitudes, and skills necessary to function on a personal level and in the community. Special provision is made for ethnic minorities to be taught within their own cultural context, for example using their own language as the language of instruction. The primary objective, however, is that participants learn to make their way in Dutch society. Evening and daytime classes are available in MAVO, HAVO, VWO, and senior secondary commercial education (MEAO). These courses lead to a diploma, though it is also possible to study one subject at a time. The minimum requirement for admission is that students have completed compulsory schooling. For HAVO, VWO, and MEAO there are specific admission requirements.

Adult vocational education encompasses educational provision for adults designed to lead to an occupational qualification. Adults may apply for training on their own initiative or at the suggestion of third parties, for example regional employment offices.

Limited information is available on adult education which is not publicly funded; however, it appears to be a large sector. About 226,000 persons took courses in 1989/90, and 130,000 attended postschool face-to-face education. The registered number of people following television courses was 162,000 in the same year.

The Open University, which started in 1984, offers distance learning courses in higher education. There are no admission requirements other than a minimum age of 18 years. There are 18 study centers throughout the Netherlands. Open University students are largely free to compile their own programs of study and may study at home at their own pace. Teaching is done mainly by correspondence. University or HBO qualifications may be obtained in a number of disciplines. In 1990, 53,000 persons were enlisted in one or more of the 150 available programs. More men (over 60%) than women study within the Open University. The number of students who already have a higher education qualification is strikingly high; the majority of students are in paid employment. During 1988–90 there was a yearly growth of more than 25 percent.

Total annual expenditure on adult and nonformal education is about 650 million DFl. (US$325 million) (1992) and accounts for about 2 percent of the state expenditure on education. The main sources of finance are private, considering the large number of people involved in this sector. Regional and local programs are sometimes subsidized by international (mainly European) funds.

4. Administrative and Supervisory Structure and Operation

The Dutch educational system rests on a strong statutory foundation, which serves as the basis for more detailed regulation in particular fields. Such regulation usually takes the form of an order in council. Parliament may enact that such an order in council must be submitted to Parliament before it enters into force. Legislation is directed in particular at the funding and organization of education.

A distinctive feature of the Dutch educational system is that it has a centralized education policy. Central government's chief responsibilities lie in the spheres of organization, funding (including legal status of personnel), inspection, examinations, and promoting innovation. The provincial authorities are charged mainly with supervisory duties, but also have a role in adult education and are lately more included in planning and advisory tasks. The management and administration of schools is organized on a local basis. The municipal executives are the competent authorities for publicly run schools and foundations or associations perform the same function for private schools. The municipal authorities also perform a wide variety of executive duties for all schools, such as ensuring that compulsory education legislation is observed. They also pay expenses for public and private schools facilities.

The Ministry of Education and Science is headed by the minister of education and science, who is responsible for coordinating science policy as well as for education. The minister is assisted by a state secretary with special responsibility for primary and secondary education. The inspection of education is the responsibility of the minister of education and science and is carried out by the Education Inspectorate. This is a decentralized body. In 1990 it had 14 regional offices with a staff establishment of 500 full-time equivalent posts, 237 of which are occupied by inspectors. The duties of the Inspectorate are to keep up with developments, ensure compliance with statutory regulations, promote the development of education and report to the minister, either upon request or on its own initiative. The Inspectorate for Higher Education is in addition responsible for organizing and providing support for review committees in universities and colleges of higher professional education in connection with self-evaluation. The inspectorate submits on its own responsibility an annual independent report on the state of education to Parliament.

Decisions about the structure of the system of education are taken by the national parliament based on proposals of the central government (Ministry of Education and Science). Decisions about the curriculum are made by heads of schools and teachers, but the final goals for education programs and almost all final exams in secondary education are nationwide standards. Provincial authorities spend most time on the geographical planning of educational institutions. Local authorities spend most time making decisions relating to social problems and to the Educational Priority policy for disadvantaged pupils.

External advisory bodies advise the minister of education and science on the policies he or she should adopt. The Education Council and the Advisory Council for Education make recommendations on education policy in general. The minister discusses policy plans with various consultative bodies comprising representatives of educational establishments, parents, staff, and students. The HBO colleges and the universities each have an organization of their own for joint consultation. Organizations of interested parties exert influence on education policy through various consultative bodies. There are four umbrella organizations, one for Catholic, one for Protestant, one for private nondenominational, and one for public authority schools, which represent parents' organizations, teachers' unions, school board organizations, organizations working in the field of part-time nonformal education for young adults, and the educational advisory centers in consultations with the minister of education and science and the state secretary. Every school must set up a participation council on which parents and staff participate.

5. Educational Finance

Formal education is funded by the Ministry of Education and Science, except for agricultural education which is funded by the Ministry of Agriculture and Fisheries. These funds are derived from tax revenues and, to a limited extent, from school, course, and tuition fees. Higher education establishments can earn income from teaching or research carried out on a contract basis. Nongovernment-funded education also constitutes a sizeable sector, being paid for entirely by the participants, or their parents or employers. Government funds are allocated to regular education in accordance with certain conditions. Separate rules govern the funding of staffing costs, capital costs, and running costs. Relevant factors include the number of pupils at the school, the average length of time for which pupils attend that type of education, class size, and the teachers' salary scales. The "overspend" regulation, which stems from the financial equality of public authority and private schools under the Constitution, means that if, in the course of a particular school year, a municipality overspends on public authority education, it must pay an equivalent amount to the local private schools. In 1987, local community authorities spent about 680 million DFl. (US$340 million) in educational facilities.

The Netherlands is among those Organisation for Economic Co-operation and Development (OECD) countries which devote the highest percentage of their gross national products to education. Between 1976 and 1987 government expenditure on education in the Netherlands continually increased. As a percentage of the national income it remained about the same (7%), but as a percentage of the national budget there was a clear fall (1975–83), after which it settled down at about 15 percent. In 1990, out of the funds available to the Dutch government, 15.5 percent was allocated to the Ministry of Education (13.2% if the budget for the student allowance system is omitted).

Of the funds available to the Ministry of Education and Science for 1992, 21 percent was earmarked for primary education; 5 percent for special education; 20 percent for general secondary education, preuniversity education, and junior secondary vocational education; 9 percent for the rest of vocational education and adult education; 24 percent for higher education, science, and research policy; 18 percent for scholarships; and 3.4 percent for teacher training, the educational support structure, the inspectorate and general expenditure.

The costs per pupil in full-time education (1982–88) have risen in primary and secondary education. In higher professional education the costs per student decreased by 15 percent while the costs per pupil in special education increased by 18 percent. In 1988 a pupil in primary education cost 3,612 guilders (US$1806), in special education 12,641 (US$6321), in general secondary education 5,583 (US$2,792), in junior vocational education 6,493 (US$3,247), in senior vocational education 5,461 (US$2,731), in higher professional education 7,867 (US$3,934), and in university education 10,120 guilders (US$5,060).

6. Supplying Personnel for the Education System

Teacher training is part of higher education. Primary school teachers are trained at colleges of higher professional education or colleges of education specifically for primary schoolteachers (PABO's). The courses, lasting four years, ensure that every primary school teacher must be able to teach every subject taught in primary schools. The number of students enrolling in these courses is increasing rapidly (1987: 3,000–4,000 students, 1990: 6,000 students) after a serious fall of numbers in the years before 1987. The number of graduates is also increasing (1987: 1,700 graduates, 1989: 2,600 graduates).

Secondary school teachers have either a grade one or a grade two qualification. Grade two teachers may teach the first three years of VWO and HAVO and in MAVO, VBO, and MBO schools. Grade one teachers are qualified to teach every age group in all types of secondary school. The full-time course for grade two teachers in general subjects, run by colleges of higher professional education, lasts four years. Students specialize in one subject and may only teach their subsidiary subject at certain levels. Since 1979 there has been an experimental full-time course in technical subjects which lasts five years. The number of students at these courses is increasing (1987: 3,148 students, 1990: 4,427 students), though the number of graduates is still decreasing (1987: 2,254 graduates, 1989: 1,755 graduates).

In order to obtain a grade one teaching qualification, it has become necessary to take a one-year graduate teacher-training course at a university after completing a university degree. The second-tier university teacher training courses are fully paid by the government. For teaching in special schools it is necessary to take a two-year course over and above the HBO teacher training qualification. The number of students attending these courses is decreasing (1987: 2,192 students, 1990: 1,484 students). Part-time teacher-training courses for grade one and grade two teachers are also available at higher professional education level. The number of people attending these courses is decreasing. Negative reporting in the media, low salaries in comparison with other professions, few promotion opportunities and a lack of mobility seem to have made the profession less attractive. The recruitment and training of new teachers consequently gives causes for concern.

Primary school teachers normally work 40 hours per week. The standard weekly workload for secondary school teachers is 29 teaching periods. A teacher's work involves both teaching and nonteaching duties. Teachers who have been given extra duties, for example, as careers officers or tutors, are partially released from teaching.

University staff are governed by a separate set of regulations based on those which apply to public servants but modified to take account of the specific circumstances in universities.

7. Curriculum Development and Teaching Methodology

The freedom of education enshrined in the constitution is subject to the standards imposed by the Ministry of Education and Science. Such standards include the subjects which are compulsory under the law in a particular type of school and other binding regulations governing the content of school-leaving examinations. Attainment targets have not yet been laid down for all types of school. The minister of education and science takes the view that, in keeping with the ideological and curricular freedom of schools, the production and assessment of teaching materials should not be subject to central regulation. The school board is responsible for the chosen curriculum.

In primary education the school workplan is the principal instrument of the school board. Organization and content of the educational program is prescribed at least every two years on proposals from the teaching staff. It contains choice of study materials, teaching methods, and the way in which progress of pupils is examined and reported. Each year an activity program is designed for teachers' and pupils' activities for specific lessons. The school workplan is sanctioned by the inspectorate; the activity plan is made available to the inspectorate.

In secondary education the teaching staff develops the syllabuses and lesson plans. These are sanctioned by the inspectorate. Detailed information must be given about subjects, times, organization of groups, and the way in which the school deals with the fact that students are living in a multicultural society. There is a minimum and a maximum time set for each given subject by the minister of education. From 1993 on, students in all types of secondary education will receive instruction in 15 "core-curriculum" subjects (3,000 lessons each year). About 20 percent of the school curriculum can be chosen by the school board.

Curriculum development began to be systematically organized in the 1960s. The National Institute for Curriculum Development (SLO) was founded in 1975. The SLO's main task consists of developing proposals for curricula, or having these developed. Associations of schools determine which proposal(s) to adopt and individual schoolboards then decide on implementation. In addition to the SLO, some university research and development centers develop curricula in experimental form.

The production, distribution, and sale of teaching materials is a commercial private sector activity, though in many cases based on SLO contracts. The Educational Publishers' Group (GEU) represents 30 publishing houses whose combined turnover (1990: 300 million guilders, US$150 million) accounts for 90 percent of the total market in educational publications in the Netherlands.

8. The System of Examinations, Promotions, and Certifications

In most primary schools pupils are automatically promoted from grade to grade. Generally the first formal certificate is received at age 12 based on a test, which is designed at the central institute for development of tests (CITO). In 1990, 58 percent of the primary schools used these tests. External examinations have become rare.

In general secondary education the final examinations embody two parts: a school part and a nationwide examination. Both examinations are held in the last year. The school examination precedes the central examination. The central examinations are held for each type of school at the same time. In junior secondary vocational education, examinations are held at four different levels. The two most difficult examinations are determined by the minister of education. In senior secondary vocational education, examination programs are determined by the minister of education when a central examination is held. In most cases schools set their own examinations which are related to the "attainment goals."

In tertiary education there are examinations at the end of the first year (propaedeutic examination) to decide if students are allowed to take courses in the next three years. At the end of the four-year educational program, students must take a final examination. The school board (in HBO) or faculty council (university) is responsible for the organization and quality of the examinations. Normally each faculty or department has its own examination committee.

9. Educational Assessment, Evaluation, and Research

Assessment studies—investigations into the education provided and the level of achievement—can assist in quality control. In primary education each subject is assessed once every eight years. The results may prompt the government to intervene. Schools can also compare their own results with the national figures and make their own adjustments.

Research on the causes of the increase in the number of pupils in special schools revealed a number of reasons: inflexible curricula in primary education, lack of motivation among teachers, the fact that special schools are losing their stigma, and the fact that the balance between the children's potential and abilities, the expectations and demands which they face and the support they receive at home and at school has been disturbed. The increase was not due to increased learning difficulties among children but rather a socially determined process.

At the same time as increasing the autonomy of higher education institutions the government also placed more emphasis on the quality of teaching and research. Procedures for quality control, for which the universities and higher professional education institutions are themselves primarily responsible, have been developed. The inspectorate now plays a less conspicuous role, its main function being to stimulate and organize quality control and quality assessment.

10. Major Reforms in the 1980s and 1990s

The new-style primary school was introduced in 1985. This should allow pupils to follow an uninterrupted process of development. In special education many provisions were made to encourage transfers from special to ordinary schools. The number of different types of special schools rose.

In 1975 after a period of extensive debate between the advocates and opponents of the idea of education as an instrument of social reform, the minister proposed the introduction of comprehensive education (*middenscholen*), one type of school for all pupils between the ages of 12 and 16. Differences between pupils were to be catered for through differentiation within the classroom. After quite a strong debate 15 experimental *middenscholen* were set up. A period of deadlock followed until 1986 when the Advisory Council on government policy published a report on "basic" education (*basisvorming*). The Council's report shifted the emphasis in the discussion from the structure of education to its content. Because pupils' choice of subjects at secondary school gave rise to problems in further and higher education all pupils, but

particularly girls, were encouraged to take mathematics and science subjects. It will be compulsory to take two foreign languages and, in senior general secondary schools and preuniversity schools, mathematics. Basic education was implemented in secondary schools in 1993.

All secondary school pupils must take one more examination subject than in the past. Philosophy and social studies have been introduced as examination subjects in an attempt to achieve a more balanced combination of examination subjects. Computer and information literacy has been introduced voluntarily in almost all schools while special projects are being conducted to determine whether information technology should be taught as a separate subject for one or two hours a week in the intermediate years of senior secondary education and preuniversity education.

The structure of higher education changed significantly in the 1980s. The length of undergraduate courses, which provide a general university education, was reduced to four years. More autonomy was given to institutes of higher education. The two-tier system was introduced and higher professional education has achieved considerable economies of scale. A merger process aimed at achieving economies of scale was concluded. The 350 establishments which used to exist were amalgamated to form 51 large, multisectoral institutions, while 34 remained independent. Most of these were primary teacher training colleges. The mergers were considered to be necessary for increased autonomy and for curricular innovation and improvement. Institutions must now have at least 600 students on their roll.

In 1982 and 1986 two major reforms took place in university education. The first was designed to achieve cuts in expenditure of 317 million guilders (US$158 million) while at the same time permitting a review of teaching and research responsibilities and how these were distributed among the universities. As a result 53 courses were closed, the number of faculties of dentistry was reduced from three to one, two pharmacy faculties and four philosophy departments were closed, and there were cutbacks in social sciences and humanities and in medicine. Sixty million guilders (US$30 million) was to be made available for innovation. The second reform began in 1986. The Minister of Education and Science had to take measures himself because the universities did not submit proposals again. The amount to be saved was 129 million guilders (US$64 million) of which 70 million (US$35 million) was to be channelled back into universities for innovation.

11. Major Problems for the Year 2000

Although the Primary Education Act (1985) aims to give pupils an uninterrupted process of all-round individual development, the progress made in achieving the objective is still far from satisfactory. Only 35 percent of schools work with forms of differentiated and individualized teaching, both of which are deemed to be necessary tools for achieving this goal. Furthermore, nursery education, in practice, still constitutes a separate kind of education. Many schools have still not effectively integrated nursery and primary teaching. The implementation of intercultural education is difficult although there is broad agreement about its importance. The increase in the number of pupils from ethnic minorities makes it even more necessary.

Educational priority policy (OVB) aims to combat the educational disadvantage which has been found to exist in practice, the focus being on pupils' socioeconomic background and ethnic origin. Extra money is channelled into areas where there are a lot of educationally disadvantaged pupils for use in joint projects involving schools and welfare organizations. Assessments show modest success in combating educational disadvantage. However, an increasing number of schools in certain parts of the major cities are turning into "Black schools," because most of their pupils come from ethnic minorities. White parents tend to withdraw their children from these schools. For ethnic minorities (in 1990 about 10% of the pupils at primary level) extra funds are given to schools.

Junior secondary vocational education is increasingly regarded as a last resort. Basic education should provide individuals with a core on which they can build for the rest of their lives by acquiring new knowledge and skills.

There has been an increase in the number of pupils leaving full-time secondary education without any qualifications. Some of these pupils go on to part-time education and still obtain qualifications. It is difficult for unqualified school leavers to find employment.

Many of those qualifying from preuniversity education and senior general secondary education experience difficulties in higher education because of an inappropriate choice of subject. The interface between senior general secondary education and higher professional education is problematic and the percentage of senior general secondary school leavers among the higher professional education intake has therefore fallen. The number of students in senior general secondary education will drop in the years ahead. This is a matter of concern.

In teacher training the problem is a shortage of teachers for secondary education and university education in certain subjects (mathematics, economics, exact sciences, and technology). Retraining, more places on training courses, and measures to boost intake may remove the shortages.

Bibliography

Central Bureau for Statistics 1992 *Statistical Yearbook*. CBS, The Hague

Inspectorate of Education 1992 *Onderwijsverslag over het jaar 1991*. Inspectorate of Education, The Hague

International Association for the Evaluation of Educational Achievement (IEA) 1988 *Science Achievement in Seventeen Countries; A Preliminary Report*. IEA, Oxford

Ministry of Education and Science 1989 *Richness of the Uncompleted Challenges Facing Dutch Education. Reviews of National Policies for Education. The Netherlands' Report to OECD*. Ministry of Education and Science The Hague

Ministry of Education and Science 1989 *School op weg naar 2000, Een besturingsfilosofie voor de negentiger jaren*. Ministry of Education and Science, Zoetermeer

Ministry of Education and Science 1990 *Basic Education in the Netherlands. Newsletter No. 45E*. Ministry of Education and Science, Zoetermeer

Ministry of Education and Science 1990 *Education Funding in the Netherlands. Newsletter No. 38E*. Ministry of Education and Science, Zoetermeer

Ministry of Education and Science 1990 *Primary Education in the Netherlands. Newsletter No. 40E*. Ministry of Education and Science, Zoetermeer

Ministry of Education and Science 1990 *Weer samen naar school: perspectief om leerlingen ook in reguliere scholen onderwijs op maat te bieden: hoofdlijnennotitie*. J Wallage, Zoetermeer

Ministry of Education and Science 1991 *Referentieraming 1991*. Ministry of Education and Science, Zoetermeer

OECD/OCDE 1990, *Education in OECD countries 1987–88, A compendium of Statistical Information*. OECD, Paris

Science Council for Government Policy (WRR) 1986 *Basisvorming in het onderwijs*. WRR, The Hague

New Zealand

J. M. Barrington

1. General Background

New Zealand lies in the southwest Pacific Ocean and consists of two main islands and a number of smaller islands, whose combined area of 268,000 square kilometers is similar to the size of Japan or the British Isles. From the time New Zealand became a British colony in 1840, British institutions and forms of life have strongly influenced the development of the country's government, legal system, religious and social life, and its education system. Since about 1960 however, as the Maori population has become larger

(14.4% of the total in the early 1990s), more urbanized, and more effective politically, there has been a growing acknowledgment of Maori institutions and ways of life and of the importance as a founding document of the Treaty of Waitangi signed between the British Crown and Maori chiefs in 1840. During the same period, New Zealand experienced a new wave of Polynesian migration: Pacific Islanders who have either migrated to New Zealand or been born there, and make up nearly 4 percent of the total population. There are also small groups whose forebears came to New Zealand from various countries in Europe or Asia—German, Swiss, Scandinavian, Dutch, Polish, Italian, Greek, Yugoslav, Indian, and Chinese are the most numerous.

In 1990 the population was 3.3 million. Dramatic changes have taken place in the New Zealand population as a whole since the late nineteenth century in a pattern similar to those experienced by other Western countries. The population has become highly urbanized despite continued reliance on agricultural exports, and the historical trend for the greater proportion of people to live in the north of the country has persisted with a steady movement from south to north.

The growth in the size of the Maori population, its youthfulness (39% of Maori were under 15 years of age, compared with 24.4% of the total population in 1986), and increased visibility as the result of urban migration has focused attention on the need for greater acknowledgment of the notion of partnership as embodied in the Treaty of Waitangi. Implications for schooling have included demands for recognition of the Maori language as well as English in instruction, and means of improving the academic performance of Maori students in relation to Europeans.

New Zealand has experienced, like other Western developed countries, a continuation of the long-term growth in the proportion of the employed population in the "white collar" category and a corresponding decline in the proportion working in manual occupations. Historically, agriculture has dominated the New Zealand economy but, while agricultural and related occupations remain important, the numbers of workers in them have steadily declined as a proportion of the employed. The fastest growing group has been that of "administrative management." Unemployment has grown steadily and in 1991 affected 10 percent of the labor force. The proportion is much bigger amongst the young and Maori: in 1990 Maori made up 8 percent of the labor force, but 20.5 percent of the unemployed; 30.8 percent of Maori unemployed are in the 15–19 age group, compared to 23 percent of non-Maori. These various developments have given a new urgency to questions such as what should be the purpose of schooling and what are the most suitable subjects of instruction, and have also contributed to more students staying on longer at the top of the secondary school.

Historically, the central government has always had a major influence on the economy, using monetary and regulatory instruments to moderate or alter the workings of the free market in most areas. However, the entry of the United Kingdom into the European Common Market ended New Zealand's traditional reliance on it as the major assured export market. Subsequently, the speed and scope of financial and economic changes with a strong deregulation or "more market" emphasis begun by the Labour Government in 1984 were probably not equaled in either other Western countries or the Pacific region over the previous two decades. Important parallel changes also occurred in public administration with the State Sector Act (1988) which redefined the relationship between ministers and permanent heads of departments. These significant economic and political changes were matched by major changes in the education system.

2. Politics and the Goals of the Education System

New Zealand's provincial form of government was abolished in 1876, and central government soon became dominant. A national system of education, centrally funded with all public money appropriated for education authorized by Parliament, and with an increasingly strong central Department of Education developed. The legal authority for all public educational institutions derives from the Education Act and other acts of the New Zealand Parliament.

The first Labour government elected in 1936 created the welfare state. A statement made by the Minister of Education in 1939 was handed down as the overriding philosophy regarding what New Zealanders expected the education system to achieve for themselves and their children: "all people, whether {they} be rich or poor whether {they} live in town or country, have a right as citizens, to a free education of the kind for which {they are} best fitted and to the fullest extent of {their} powers." Welfare Labourism portrayed education as a public good that the central state had a responsibility to provide, expand, improve in quality, and make freely available, and these general principles were adopted by both main political parties.

The policies of deregulation and a more free-market approach initiated by Labour after 1984 have been continued by the current national government. In December 1990 the Prime Minister announced an economic and social initiative which he said was made necessary by the prevailing economic situation. This was subsequently described by the Minister of Education as very apposite to the government's education policy. The principles were:

(a) Fairness—adequate access should be available to those in genuine need, but those who can make greater provision for their own needs should be encouraged to do so.

(b) Self-reliance—government programs should not foster dependency on state provision but increase the ability and incentives to enable individuals to take care of themselves.

(c) Efficiency—social services should be provided so that quality and quantity represents the highest possible value for each dollar invested.

(d) Greater personal choice—alternative providers in health, welfare services, housing, and education would provide people with a wider choice to meet their needs.

A more market approach to the supply of educational services has become evident in some areas, and the government has increased financial support to private schools. It is also shifting more of the costs of education onto those in the community it feels can afford to pay, while maintaining the principle of free public schooling for those in the years of compulsory schooling (ages 6–16).

The charters introduced as part of recent reforms incorporate both national and local goals of schooling for each individual institution. Each institution and its community, acting in a spirit of partnership, are asked to reflect on their particular aims and character and then develop a mission statement outlining the educational purpose of the institution and the outcomes intended. The board of each institution is required to annually detail the manner in which it will consult with its community. This includes making decisions about and developing local curriculum goals and objectives, taking into account the particular aspirations and resources of the community, any special skills and qualifications of the staff, and the individual needs and interests of students. The mission statement then provides a reference point for all major planning decisions.

National goals and guiding principles which are nondiscretionary are also incorporated in the charter. New Zealand has had a national curriculum since 1877 and each school is required to meet New Zealand curriculum objectives prescribed by the Minister of Education. The board of trustees of each school is expected to approve a policy statement and incorporate it in the charter detailing how the school will deliver the curriculum. The board is also expected to ensure that the curriculum is implemented through the learning and teaching programs developed by the staff. These will include specific learning objectives and realistically stated outcomes in terms of a range of achievements. Equity goals and objectives are also incorporated in the charter.

3. The Formal System of Education

3.1 Primary, Secondary and Tertiary Education

Figure 1 outlines the structure of the formal education system. Education is compulsory from six years of age, but children usually start primary schooling at the age of five. Most children attend an early childhood center before the age of five. The primary and secondary school day usually lasts for 5 hours of tuition, the primary year for 200 days, and the secondary for 190 days.

Attendance is compulsory until the age of 16 years. The final two years of the primary course (Forms 1 and 2) may be taken at a full primary school, an intermediate school, an area school, or a Form 1–7 composite school depending on where a child lives. On completing Form 2, usually after 8 years, students normally enter Form 3 of a secondary school. In 1990 there were 420,426 primary students of whom 12,890 were enrolled in private schools.

Most state secondary schools are coeducational and, in 1990, 242 schools enrolled 191,000 pupils. A total of 11 private schools, the majority of which are single sex, enrolled 3,560 pupils. These schools comply with defined standards of accommodation and teaching as a prerequisite for compulsory registration. The Private Schools Conditional Integration Act of 1975 allowed for the voluntary integration of private schools into the state system and this has happened progressively.

At the secondary level, a noticeable trend has been for students to stay on beyond the school leaving age of 16. The proportion of commencing secondary students retained in the final year of school rose from 16 percent in 1981 to 36 percent in 1990. Further

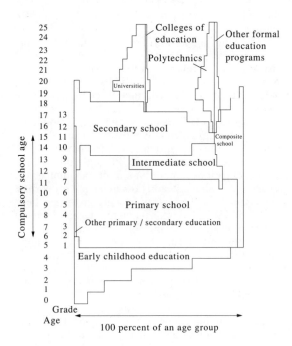

Figure 1
New Zealand: Structure of the formal education system

improvements need to take place for New Zealand to match the proportion of students in some form of post-16 education in comparison with most developed OECD countries. There is also continuing concern that Maori students are much more likely than others to leave secondary school before the end of the third year.

The consolidation of smaller rural schools has been a feature of the last 30 years, in order to give children in rural districts the advantage of special equipment and more specialized teaching in larger schools. Composite schools have also been developed to bring together larger concentrations of children. They provide education at primary and secondary level and are known as "Form 1 to 7 schools" and "area schools."

In an effort to cater more effectively for the population in remote areas the government established the National Correspondence School in 1922. It is located in Wellington and is administered by an elected board of trustees composed of parents, community and school representatives and a student. It provides courses for four major categories of students: early childhood and full-time students obtaining their education through the school, students enrolled in New Zealand primary or secondary schools but doing one or more subjects with the Correspondence School, and adult part-time students who wish to continue their basic education.

The school roll on July, 1 1989 was 21,213, made up of 519 early childhood, 900 primary, 17 special needs section (pupils with significant educational handicap), 1,205 individual program section (pupils needing remedial tuition), 1,203 secondary full-time students at secondary schools, and 10,260 part-time adult students. Personal contact between students and the school is strengthened by resident teachers based in major centers who visit families regularly.

In 1990 the majority of university students (49,546) were internal full-time students—an increase from 30,989 students in 1980. There were also 15,748 part-time internal students and 13,625 external students in 1990. Polytechnics, which total 24, provide a diverse range of vocational education courses and cover an increasing number of subjects at various levels of sophistication.

3.2 Preschool Education

Approximately 90 percent of four-year olds are enrolled in some form of preschool education. The main organizations involved in providing part-day sessional programs are the New Zealand Free Kindergarten Union and the New Zealand Playcenter Federation. Such programs are also provided through mobile early childhood units, early childhood classes in primary schools, and hospital early childhood groups. A wide range of child care centers provide both part-day and full-day programs and are administered by a variety of community and church groups, voluntary agencies, and private and commercial operators. All early childhood centers wishing to receive

government funding must have a charter, and those not having a charter must be licensed.

Kohanga Reo (language nests) have been established usually by Maori initiative, with government funding, to increase the proportion of Maori children in preschool as well as providing an environment in which Maori language and cultural values can be taught. In 1989, 73 percent of Maori children under 5 years of age attended some form of preschool, and of these approximately 45 percent attended *Kohanga Reo*.

3.3 Special Education

Special education was affected, like other education services, by the major restructuring of education in New Zealand carried out in 1989–90. In 1989 the Special Education Service (SES) was established as an independent Crown agency. Its prime function, as specified in the Education Act (1989), is to "provide advice, guidance and support for the benefit of people under 21 with difficulties in learning or development." It carries out this function in accordance with a "stewardship agreement" with the Ministry of Education and annual contracts of service negotiated with the Minister of Education. A seven-person board oversees the performance of the services provided under these agreements.

The SES brought together in a coordinated manner hitherto disparate groups of professionals—school psychologists, speech and language therapists, advisers on deaf children, and visiting teachers (the latter being responsible for liaison between schools and homes in cases of children with learning difficulties or behavioral problems). It also took on a new range of functions to do with providing a comprehensive early intervention service for infants and preschool children with special needs and their families. The SES has approximately 700 staff located in its 12 districts and a national office.

3.4 Vocational, Technical, and Business Education

Much of the vocational education and training in New Zealand is provided by 24 polytechnics. The Open Polytechnic provides instruction in many vocational courses not available elsewhere, and the Central Institute of Technology is another provider in this area. Polytechnics have developed transition courses including the Link program by which secondary school students can undertake specialized vocational education and training.

The 1990 Education Amendment Act established the Education and Training Support Agency to administer and develop programs relating to noninstitutional labor market education and training. The Career Development and Transition Education Service provides information and resources on education, training, and occupations, and assists educators and trainees to run transition and career education programs on a diverse range of sites.

In the early 1990s, government initiatives have also included an announced intention to include a new subject—technology—in a forthcoming revised national curriculum. For those adults returning to study, who wish to further their education and training in the workplace or at places of learning, a National Certificate is being developed to offer the opportunity to achieve a national qualification. It will also be possible for secondary students to attend both school and follow National Certificate courses which suit their preference.

These steps are increasingly viewed as part of an urgent need to improve the overall educational qualifications of the labor force, by better equipping students for successful transition not only to higher education but to further vocational education and training, and to improve opportunities for the kind of retraining and upskilling the modern economy requires.

3.5 Adult and Nonformal Education

Prior to 1987 the National Council of Adult Education provided the Minister with advice on the development of adult education. However, the needs and funding of nonformal education groups is now administered by a trust as a national resource center funded from the Ministry of Education by contract through Community Learning Aotearoa New Zealand. This latter group will advise the Ministry of Education on nonformal community education and disburse grants to nonformal community education groups.

All seven of New Zealand's universities have centers for continuing education. Diverse approaches and courses characterize the programs and a large number of university teaching staff are co-opted in order to supplement the activity of the full-time continuing education staff.

However, most organized adult education is provided by day schools and community education classes based at secondary schools. An amendment to the Education Act in 1975 allowed adults to return full-time or part-time to secondary schools in day classes. This led to increases in adult classes leading to the school certificate examination and a wide range of other examinable and nonexaminable courses.

Community centers which opened experimentally some 40 years ago were the forerunners of today's school-based community learning centers. A total of 13 such centers have been established in association with primary and secondary schools.

Many voluntary organizations make some provision for continuing education. For most of them, such as the Playcentres Federation and the Country Women's Co-ordinating Committee, continuing education is only one aspect of their overall activities. However, several organizations, such as the New Zealand Workers' Educational Association, have community education as their primary purpose.

4. Administrative and Supervisory Structure and Operation

From 1989, the administrative structure of every sector of the education system from early childhood to tertiary level has undergone major reform. Features of the reform include decentralization of greater responsibility to each individual institution in such areas as setting of goals and aims, financial management, and staff appointments; measures to increase accountability of individual institutions both with regard to the local community and the Minister of Education; and new procedures for reviewing the performance of institutions against their agreed goals. A new Ministry of Education replaced the former Department of Education, with a mandate to focus more on policy analysis and advice, and less on direct oversight of all details of the system and direct supply of educational services. Until October 1989 there were 57 secondary and 102 primary school inspectors throughout the country, all of whom were officers of the Department of Education recruited from the teaching service. In addition to their evaluative role, they provided support in professional, curriculum, management, and general decision making. The disestablishment of the Department created the need for a new organization to measure the effectiveness of the performance of teachers and schools, and the Education Review Office, an agency independent of the Ministry, was established to provide this.

The tertiary sector has also been affected by the reforms. Previously the University Grants Committee (UGC) advised the government on needs for university funding, education, and research. However, tertiary reforms in 1990 abolished the UGC and introduced a greater degree of decentralization. The Ministry of Education now has the responsibility for making recommendations to the Minister on funding of tertiary institutions, and to this extent inherits, for universities, the role previously performed by the UGC. An increasing trend is for the government to deal with the tertiary sector (universities, polytechnics, and colleges of education) as a whole and in ways which are as identical as possible. For example, all are now covered by a single Act of Parliament, funding is conducted as one exercise and on one basis and the structure of governing councils is identical (with some freedom for variations), as are the accountability requirements.

Polytechnics and colleges of education have greatly increased powers of responsibility for decision making, equivalent to those traditionally held by universities. A major change is that all tertiary institutions now have the authority to set their own fees.

5. Educational Finance

Funding for public primary and secondary schools comes from the central government. The reforms of the early 1990s gave elected boards of trustees limited financial autonomy through a bulk grant, but the costs of teachers' salaries, school transport, capital works, and long-term maintenance are provided directly by the Ministry of Education. In 1991 the Government was wishing to include salaries in the bulk grant to boards, but was meeting strong opposition from the teachers' unions. Parents of pupils in state schools do not pay fees but are asked to make an annual voluntary donation to assist with school activities. Changes to tertiary student allowances introduced targeting by parental income and a student loans scheme.

For the financial year ended June 1990, total outlays on education were over NZ\$4 billion, which represented 5.8 percent of Gross Domestic Product (GDP). The proportion of GDP allocated to education has increased annually slowly but steadily from a figure of 4.5 percent in 1986. Education as a proportion of net government expenditure rose from 11.3 percent in 1985 to 15.7 percent in 1990. Almost 60 percent of government outlays on education are directed to schools, 28 percent to higher education, and 3.5 percent to preschool education.

6. Supplying Personnel for the Education System

Out of a total of 33,855 full-time and relief teachers in 1990, 1,363 were in the early childhood sector, 18,396 in primary, 13,145 in secondary, and 951 in area schools (Forms 1 to 7) and the Correspondence School. An additional 516 teachers taught in special schools and there were also 5,623 part-time teachers in all categories of schools.

More recently, falling enrollments have resulted in an over-supply of teachers in some schools, regions, and subject areas. However, shortages remain in some areas such as mathematics, making the offering of the full range of secondary subjects in some smaller schools outside the main centers sometimes difficult to achieve.

The training of teachers is carried out at seven colleges of education which provide a two-year early childhood course, a three-year primary course, and an end-on one-year course for secondary trainees. Primary trainees are encouraged to undertake university study, and conjoint Bachelor of Education degrees have been established at several institutions.

The reforms introduced important changes for teacher selection and education. Previously annual recruitment numbers were centrally determined and selection was carried out by regional officers of the Department for secondary teacher education and regional education boards for primary. Much greater autonomy, including responsibility for selection, has now been given to reconstituted college councils, although the Ministry retains the authority to set minimum levels to ensure equitable staffing levels in schools are maintained. Entry to teacher education is

no longer restricted by zoning, which means applicants can apply to any college in the country.

A wide range of professional education examinations is offered for the continuing education of teachers, the majority intended to provide credits towards diploma qualifications and service increments. The Advanced Studies for Teachers unit at Palmerston North College of Education caters for the continuing education of teachers and other adult learners through distance education.

7. Curriculum Development and Teaching Methodology

New Zealand has a long-established tradition of a national curriculum which has established the framework and much of the detail of what is learnt in schools. The curriculum of primary and intermediate schools, as set out in the syllabuses, covers English (including oral and written language, reading, spelling, and handwriting), mathematics, social studies, arts and crafts, science, physical education, health education, and music. The number of schools teaching Maori language has increased, and there are official bilingual state primary schools. A total of 75 primary schools and 20 secondary schools have official bilingual units. At intermediate level (Forms 1 and 2), the curriculum includes workshop craft and home economics.

The secondary curriculum is based, for the first two years, on a common core consisting of English, social studies, general science, mathematics, music, arts and crafts, and physical education. Secondary schools are required to give all pupils a minimum number of units of instruction in the common core subjects. At the fifth to seventh form levels, students may choose from a wide range of subjects.

Foreign languages are taught in secondary schools and some primary schools. In 1990, French remained the most frequently offered language (296 schools), a decline from 321 schools in 1986. Other languages to experience a decline over the same period were German (155 to 135 schools) and Latin (74 to 50 schools). The number of schools offering Maori increased from 217 to 233, as did those offering Japanese (73 to 145 schools).

In a 1990 brief to the government, the Ministry of Education stated that: "with the administrative reforms largely completed we can now turn more of our attention to learning and assessment, which are at the heart of education. It is time to focus again on curriculum development, for instance, and on appropriate assessment methods." In December 1990 the Minister stated the government wanted educational reform to "once again largely be driven by matters of curriculum, learning and assessment."

National curriculum objectives were being reviewed in 1992. The government announced a new "achievement initiative" linked to its aim of further improvements in achievement levels in schools. This included the need to establish clear achievement standards for all levels of compulsory schooling and explore the development of new subjects such as technology. Organizational changes have also affected curriculum development. The Learning and Assessment group within the Ministry's Policy Division retains responsibility for setting national curriculum objectives and provides policy advice on a range of curriculum matters, including, the National Languages Policy. Unlike the former Department, the Ministry is not a direct provider of curriculum development, which is now undertaken by contractual arrangements with it. A new learning media group within the Ministry now provides services that were formerly carried out by the Department of Education, including the planning, development, production, dissemination, and promotion of resources for learning. The emphasis is on materials that document and support the curriculum for schools—for example, syllabuses, teachers' handbooks, pupils' books, and classroom materials in all media. All curriculum materials are tried out and revised before being used in schools. Support of early childhood education has been an important new focus.

8. The System of Examinations, Promotions, and Certifications

Primary and lower-secondary school students are generally automatically promoted between year levels according to age. The school certificate examination is taken by most pupils at the end of three years of secondary education. With the exception of part-time students, each candidate's course of study must include English, although the student is not required to sit the examination in that subject. A candidate may enter the examination in any number of subjects up to six and is accredited with a grade for each subject.

A sixth form certificate is awarded, on a single-subject basis, to pupils who have satisfactorily completed a one-year course beyond school certificate level. No more than six subjects can be taken.

Previously students sat a university entrance examination in the sixth form, but this has now been abolished. A higher school certificate is now awarded after a five-year course of study to pupils who have been accepted for entry to Form 6 and have satisfactorily completed an advanced course of two years. It is also awarded to pupils who have obtained a B bursary qualification from the University Bursaries Examination. The University Bursaries Examination and the University Entrance Scholarship Examination, usually taken by secondary school pupils in Form 7, are competitive examinations for supplementary awards for study at a university.

The government is reforming senior-secondary school qualifications through the introduction of a national certificate in 1993, linked to and part of a totally new national qualifications framework.

9. Educational Assessment, Evaluation, and Research

The establishment of a ministerial working party on assessment for better learning in 1989 reflected growing interest in the development of more appropriate methods of assessing student learning. Its report (*Tomorrow's Standards*) emphasized that just as school achievement needed to be systematically monitored and reported on to satisfy a variety of purposes, so the methods of monitoring and reporting also needed to be diverse. A wide range of school quality indicators needed to be developed.

The Ministry of Education has established an Education Assessment Secretariat to oversee and coordinate policy development and projects relating to more effective monitoring of the assessment of student achievement and the reporting of this information to parents and the wider community. Among a number of activities undertaken in 1991 was a national *hui* (meeting) for Maori educators on assessment issues and priorities for Maori students, and a national workshop in educational assessment for teachers college and university staff teaching preservice and inservice courses and others involved in educational assessment work.

An Education Review Office was established as part of the reforms to monitor the effectiveness and efficiency of schools and other learning centers in meeting their agreed objectives as set out in school charters. The Office, which is independent of the Ministry of Education, replaced the former system of school inspectors. In addition to external review, it will also assist schools to improve their own monitoring and reporting systems.

National standards are monitored by the Progressive Achievement Tests (PATs) which are nationally standardized achievement tests developed by the New Zealand Council for Educational Research for use with pupils from Standard 2 to Form 4. Results on most questions show there has been remarkably little difference in student competence from 1968 to 1990.

New Zealand has participated in the International Association for the Evaluation of Educational Achievement (IEA) studies which provide evidence of how New Zealand students compare with their overseas counterparts. Since joining IEA in 1968, New Zealand has participated in five major studies, and generally New Zealand pupils have performed well. For example, in the 1981 second international mathematics study they performed at a similar general level to those in England and Wales, the United States, Finland, and Israel.

The New Zealand Council for Educational Research founded in 1933 has been supported by state funds, contributions by education bodies, its own trading activities, and, increasingly, contract research. The Council's research priorities also reflect national concerns. These are educational achievement (assessment, monitoring, and reporting), educational institutions in change (policies and practices), and Maori language and policy issues.

The Ministry of Education funds a vigorous and diverse staff and contract research program through its Research and Statistics Division. This includes funding a major three-year longitudinal study to monitor the impact on schools of the administrative reforms in areas such as characteristics of board members, the operation of boards, school charters, equity issues, evaluation, school–community relations, and management practices. Some other typical reports from the Ministry's program include: parent support and education, a summary report from the Curriculum Review Research in Schools Project (CRRISP) on collaborative decision making in education, bilingual mathematics education, teacher training in assessment developments, a moderation trial for Sixth Form Certificate French, nontraditional polytechnic training for women, and the need for resources in Pacific Island language. Reports in progress include: funding of out-of-school care, school-based work exploration schemes, infants and toddlers in New Zealand child care centers, and pupils' attitudes to technology.

Tertiary sector reform, combined with the creation of a government-funded Foundation for Research, Science and Technology, have had implications for research funding and direction. The Foundation funds public good research from a contestable pool. Its funds are available to social scientists working in universities or other tertiary institutions, in research institutes, or in the private sector. Graduate students undertaking social science research as part of their course requirements are also eligible to apply under certain conditions. For 1992–93, funds were allocated to research projects which fit the following areas: New Zealand history, culture, and *Te Ao Maori*; social and personal development, relationships, and well-being; political, economic, and international relationships; and knowledge, education, and training.

10. Major Reforms in the 1980s and 1990s

Various aspects of the major reform of virtually the entire education system since 1988 have been briefly described in sections above. For fuller accounts, see the bibliography at the end of this entry.

11. Major Problems for the Year 2000

In the early 1990s, the effect of economic recession is creating strains in various parts of the education sector which will need to be ameliorated when the economic situation improves. The provision of equal education for all remains a key goal. Maori remain a critical target group, since Maori students' achievement remains markedly less than that of other groups in the population. Despite steady improvements, the country still lags behind a number of other OECD countries in the percentage of students entering senior-secondary and tertiary institutions, and in the education qualifications level of its workforce. These are seen as other areas where further improvements are needed.

Bibliography

Barrington J M 1990 Historical factors for change in education. In: McKinlay P (ed.) 1990 *Redistribution of Power? Devolution in New Zealand.* Victoria University Press for the Institute of Policy Studies, Wellington

Committee to Review the Advisory Services 1990 *School Development.* Committee to Review the Advisory Services, Wellington

Lauder H, Hughes D 1990 Social inequalities and differences in schools outcomes. *New Zealand J. Educational Studies* 25(1)

McLaren I A 1974 *Education in a Small Democracy: New Zealand.* Routledge and Kegan Paul, London

Minister of State Services 1991 Address to Education Sector, March 6

Ministry of Education, 1989–90 *Annual Report.* Ministry of Education, Wellington

Ministry of Education 1991 *New Zealand Education at a Glance.* Research and Statistics Division, Wellington

Monitoring Today's Schools Research Project 1990 *Report No 1: Getting Started, Report No 2 Who Governs Our Schools?* University of Waikato, Hamilton

New Zealand Council for Educational Research 1990 *The Impact of Tomorrow's Schools in Primary Schools and Intermediates.* Highlights from the NZCER 1990 Survey, Wellington

New Zealand 1988 *New Zealand Yearbook.* Government Print, Wellington

OECD 1990 OECD *Economic Surveys: New Zealand.* OECD, Paris

Office of the Minister of Education 1989 *Tomorrow's Schools: The Reform of Education Administration in New Zealand.* Government Print, Wellington

Report of the Taskforce to Review Education Administration 1988 *Administering for Excellence.* Government Print, Wellington

Report of the Early Childhood Care and Education Working Group 1988 *Education To Be More.* Early Childhood Care and Education Working Group, Wellington

Scott G, Bushnell P, Sallee 1990 Reform of the core public sector: New Zealand experience. *Governance: An International J. Policy and Administration* 3(2)

Treasury 1987 *Government Management: Brief to the Incoming Government, Vol 2: Education Issues.* Government Print, Wellington

Working Party on Assessment of Better Learning 1990 *Tomorrow's Standards. Learning Media.* Minister of Education, Wellington

Nicaragua

H. Belli

1. General Background

Until 1979, the Nicaraguan education system consisted of two clearly defined and autonomous subsystems: that of nonhigher education which was directed by the state by means of the Ministry of Education, and that of higher education, established by the National Autonomous University and the Central American University.

Between 1980 and 1990 the Sandinista regime stripped the higher education system of its autonomy and converted the education system into a single system which depended totally on central government. The creation of this centralized structure was a result of the government of this era's intention to use education as a means to ideologize and dehumanize.

Nevertheless, as a result of the election of 1990 which was won by the United National Opposition, the Sandinista regime, as a political strategy, split the Nicaraguan education system into four subsystems. In the early 1990s, four institutions exist with separate organic laws, coordinated and linked by a newly created National Council for Education. These subsystems are as follows:

(a) The Ministry of Education (MED), whose principal role consists of attending to the population registered in programs of primary, preschool, special, adult and secondary education, and teacher training.

(b) The National Technological Institute (INATEC), whose social function is to educate and train the members of the labor force, such as technicians at intermediate and basic levels and qualified workers, which the country needs for the development of production, particularly in agriculture and industry.

(c) Higher education, which has the responsibility of training professionals and advanced-level technicians (*técnico*) to guarantee the fulfilment of the economic plans of the country.

(d) The Institute of Culture, related to museums, music, dance, and the intepretation and promotion of national customs and traditions.

2. Politics and the Goals of the Education System

The Nicaraguan government's Plan of Social Development has the following broad aims:

(a) The ultimate objective of the social policy of Nicaragua is to promote the development of the social, economic, political, and citizenship qualities of individuals so that they are capable of satisfying their essential needs.

(b) In all these efforts, the satisfaction of the basic necessities of children and of young people will receive high priority.

(c) The country proposes to establish, as one of its principal plans of social action and national reconciliation, the support and strengthening of the family as the driving force of society, and the natural medium for the growth and well-being of all of its members.

(d) Special attention will be given to the objective of facilitating the participation of women in different forms of life in Nicaraguan society, guaranteeing their receipt of the various services of health, education, work, housing, food and nutrition, training, and career training.

(e) The country will try to give protection to children who are in especially difficult circumstances, and to achieve the elimination of the root cause of these difficulties.

(f) Greater national concern will be generated concerning the importance and viability of the peace process and the great benefit it will bring to the national population if it is supported by all Nicaraguans.

(g) Incentives will be restored to the private sector in its widest sense, within the context of a competitive market economy, for a far-sighted social policy.

The social responsibility of the government is to create conditions which allow the preservation of the mental and physical health of the individual, and also the participation of young people in the development of the country as agents of modernization and social change. In this area, the government proposes to give particular attention to the primary subsector, especially to the first grades. Adult education will focus preferentially on young women and the municipal divisions where there is the most acute poverty. The program of bilingual intercultural education for the Atlantic zone will continue to be offered, with the objective of incorporating the indigenous population of this zone into the community, without destroying their own cultural identity. (In fact this program has been seriously jeopardized by government cuts and lack of support.)

The government proposes to strengthen cultural education from infancy, making the students conscious of their tasks and responsibilities as actors in the new reality. In the area of sports, government efforts will concentrate fundamentally on promoting and developing sports programs in the school, university, and military sectors, and also in the population at large. In technical education, the emphasis will be on various types of agricultural education and attention will be given to young people and adults demobilized from the army and the Resistance (in other words, the contra and indigenous armed groups who fought to try to overthrow the Sandinista revolution).

In higher education the focus will be on the decentralization of the education service and the revision of the system of admissions, at the same time as the revision of the courses in accordance with the development plan of the government.

The goals for the school year 1992 included:

(a) the registering of 1,147,043 students into the three subsystems;

(b) the raising of the rates of completion (*retención*) and advancement (*promoción*) of the programs of the different subsystems;

(c) the improvement and adaptation of the curriculum of the primary, preschool, secondary evening school, teacher-training, agricultural technical education, training, and prioritized courses in higher education;

(d) the training of teachers of primary, adult, bilingual, intercultural, preschool, special, industrial, technical, and graduate programs;

(e) the development in administration and institutional management of the basic information of educational statistics, manuals of organization, and new models of planning and design of strategic educational projects;

(f) the provision of infrastructure and furniture, especially in primary and technical education.

3. The Formal System of Education

3.1 Primary, Secondary, and Tertiary Education

The objective of education at these levels is to make available to the population the opportunity to develop in the first six grades the basic aspects of reading and writing, mathematics, sciences, and, at the same time, Christian moral values. This program takes first priority in the country in the area of education. Children leave school after completing six grades trained to continue secondary studies or intermediate technical courses, basic courses, and courses in teaching primary education. Figure 1 is a diagrammatic representation of the education system.

The objective of secondary education is to prepare young people fully for entry into universities, and particularly to centers which teach courses at intermediate and higher technical levels. High-school students graduate after five years of study and students in the basic cycle after three years study.

The objective of higher education is to train professionals and technically skilled people at the advanced level to accelerate the technical, economic, and social development of the country. The programs are: agricultural sciences, medical sciences, educational sciences, technological sciences, national sciences and mathematics, economic sciences, humanities, and legal and social sciences. There are private and state universities which make up the council of higher education.

3.2 Preschool Education

Children attend preschool from 4 to 6 years of age in order to create the requisite psycho-pedagogical conditions for their entrance to the first grade of primary school. There are two types of preschool: formal and nonformal.

3.3 Special Education

The special education system caters for the disabled population who have visual or hearing problems, or

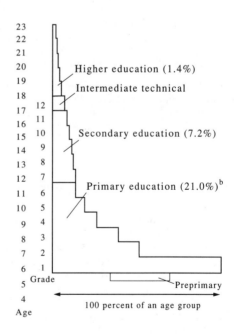

Figure 1

Nicaragua: Structure of the formal education system[a]

a There is a high percentage of over-age students in primary education and the basic cycle of secondary education   b Percentage of students who pass their grades at the end of each year in the various subsystems

are mentally or physically handicapped. At the same time, the objective is to integrate the handicapped population into the world of work. In formal education, the population up to age 18 attends special centers of education; the study plan lasts for six years and at the end of the period they leave having undergone the equivalent of primary education.

3.4 Vocational, Technical, and Business Education

In terms of formal education, technical courses are offered at basic and intermediate levels in nearly all the departmental capitals of the country. There are three programs which are offered in various forms: agricultural technician, industrial technician, and administration and economics. The nonformal part of training is becoming increasingly important for the young people who pass the basic cycle, for daytime and evening secondary school students, and for demobilized combatants.

3.5 Adult and Nonformal Education

The educational demands of the adult population, both in the rural and urban areas, are addressed by adult education programs. The programs are on several levels:

(a) literacy training work with voluntary teachers, trained and supported by the Ministry of Education;

(b) evening classes lasting five years, where adult high school graduates can choose to study an intermediate level technical course or continue onto higher education in the universities;

(c) for adults who have not completed primary education, an intensive form lasting three years. They can opt to continue their technical studies (intermediate or basic) or secondary education at night school.

4. Administrative and Supervisory Structure and Operation

The central activity of the Ministry of Education is to direct the education of the country by means of policies, norms, and regulations to improve institutional efficiency. The education system under the supervision of the Ministry consists of various levels of responsibility including:

(a) the Executive Committee (*Dirección Superior*), which is responsible for policies, organization, systems, and decrees;

(b) the General Secretariat, which functions in a supporting capacity and is a member of the Executive Committee, with its primary role being the management of external resources and aspects of protocol;

(c) the General Planning Board, which since 1991 has been the permanent advisory body to the Executive Committee and assumes responsibility for development of plans and projects;

(d) the General Supervisory Board, which was created after 1992 with the aim of supervising and advising the introduction of the educational policies, plans, and programs directed by the Ministry. It is also responsible for supervising the fulfilment of the proper use of resources, norms, laws, and regulations directed by the Ministry of Education;

(e) the General Board of Education, which takes care of everything related to the substantive work of the institution and is formed by the boards of preschool, special, primary, secondary, and adult education and teacher training, whose objectives have already been outlined. Also part of the General Board of Education is the Curriculum Board, which has the task of implementing educational policies issued by the Higher Executive, as well as coordinating all aspects of the plan of study, programs of study, and the evaluation of the educational system;

(f) the General Board of Administration, which has responsibility for guaranteeing the administration and control of human, material, and financial resources of institutions to contribute to the achievement of the objectives and targets.

In the realms of higher education INATEC has a similar structure to the Ministry of Education, but with the interpretation of university autonomy, each faculty and university has its own structure for administration and supervision. The Institute of Culture also enjoys budgetary autonomy and it is structured according to the type of functions which it assumes.

5. Educational Finance

The relation between the budget of the educational sector with the 1992 global budget (US$494,060,000), ordinary budget (US$337,400,000), and GDP (Gross Domestic Product) (US$1,707,640,000) is as shown in Table 1.

6. Supplying Personnel for the Education System

Administrative and teaching personnel of the subsystem of the Ministry of Education are given in Table 2.

In terms of the subsystem of higher education, the rectors of the universities have indicated that they have

Table 1
Education sector budget 1992

	Budget 1992[a]	% General Budget	% Ordinary Budget	% Education budget	% GDP
Education sector	93,209,528.22	18.86	24.69	100.00	5.45
Ministry of Education	56,147,100.11	11.36	14.87	60.23	3.28
INATEC	9,246,005.65	1.87	2.44	9.91	0.54
Institute of Culture	1,610,422.46	0.32	0.42	1.72	0.09
Universities	26,206,000.00	5.31	6.96	28.14	1.54

a Figures calculated in US dollars

4,154 employees, including teachers and administrative staff to cater for 32,550 students. With respect to INATEC, it has, in the early 1990s, 19,450 students located in the following sectors: agriculture, industry, and economic administration.

7. Curriculum Development and Teaching Methodology

The process of teaching and learning in the Nicaraguan education system is developed essentially on the basis of a national curriculum of a centralized nature which is in the process of being decentralized through the promotion of planning at the micro level and curricular improvement at the municipal and local levels.

The 1991–1992 curriculum was regarded as a transitional curriculum and included the following features: it responds to the policies of the New Government of National Salvation in terms of the depoliticization of school programs and texts, and it strengthens objectives and content with regard to fundamental values: peace, democracy, reconciliation, freedom, human rights, family unity, and respect and love of the country and all its values. The use of diverse methods of teaching, texts, and educational materials is promoted.

The curricular development plan has two programmed stages: improvement and transformation. Improvements to the curriculum were still in the process of being planned and programmed with a view to implementation during 1992 in all grades of general education, and training of primary school teachers. The stage of transformation, responding to the newly approved curricular policy, will emphasize the search for more broadly based forms of curricular organization, the revision of the systems of evaluation and advancement, and development of a more creative and participative learning process. Pilot studies are being carried out with respect above all to reading, writing, and arithmetic in the first grades of primary education. Higher education reforms are centered on the revision of its administrative structure and the creation of regional centers with courses in accordance with regional

Table 2
Administrative and Teaching Personnel[a]

Program	Total general	Administrative	Teachers in classrooms	Urban	Women
Preschool education	2,291	248	2,043	1,775	2,525
Primary education	20,817	1,578	19,239	11,240	17,552
Adult primary education	425	22	403	218	294
Secondary education	6,388	1,665	4,723	5,794	3,769
Adult education (CEDA)[b]	562	65	497	508	413
Special education	226	29	197	226	217
Workers education (CECO)[c]	38	—	38	38	35
Total	30,747	3,607	27,140	19,799	24,532

a In the head office the subsystem has 363 employees comprising of directors, advisors, technical staff, and support staff   b Educational center for adult development   c Educational center for workers culture and national socioeconomic development. Technical education will revolve around agricultural technical education and the training of young people and de-mobilized fighters, with the objective of increasing educational provision and production.

8. The System of Examinations, Promotions, and Certifications

In the early 1990s, there is no system of evaluation, although this is being worked on. The period of evaluation is used to select the activities developed in the different periods of the school year with a view to advancement. There are systematic, partial, and final evaluations.

The grading scale is from 0 to 100 points, with the following categories: 90–100 (Excellent); 80–89 (Very Good); 70–79 (Good); 60–69 (Average); and 0–59 (Fail). Conduct is evaluated qualitatively in the programs of the Ministry of Education, but not in technical and higher education. In order to be eligible for final evaluation in a course run on an annual or semesterly basis, it is absolutely necessary to have attended 80 percent of classes, or, in the case of illness, 60 percent.

In primary and secondary education, grade certifi-cates are given out at the end of the school year, showing the grades for each subject. When a student is failed or referred in more than three subjects, no certificate is given and he or she must repeat the school year. In the last months of the school year there is a preregistration which is officialized at the beginning of the following school year, in the respective period. Only in higher education is there an entrance examina-tion for the new intake, given the shortages of places on the different courses.

The rewards at the end of the programs are as follows: the Certificate of Primary Education (on fin-ishing 6th grade): the Certificate of the Basic Cycle (on concluding the third year of secondary education); the Certificate of the Diversified Cycle of the High School Leaving Certificate (on concluding the fifth year of secondary education); and qualifications (*título*) in professional and higher technical courses on conclud-ing a plan of study (which can be of three, four, five, or six years).

The programs of the Ministry of Education, of the National Technological Institute, and the higher edu-cation institutions have their own respective norms for examinations, promotion, and certification.

9. Educational Assessment, Evaluation, and Research

At the beginning of the 1990s, with the new govern-ment, different international organizations undertook social studies and reports, looking particularly at primary education. This has enabled the fundamental improvement and relevant adjustment of the overall and institutional policies of the Ministry of Education and the National Technological Institute.

Within the institutions research and/or reports are carried out by means of the educational projects which are supported economically by UNESCO, FINNIDA (Finnish Aid Organization), UNICEF, FISE, OPS-INCAP (The Panamerican Health Organization); OAS (Organization of American States); Italian Cooperation; Red-Barnam (a Swedish Children's charity); IPADE-Spain; EDESAR; DANCHARCHAID (Danish Church Aid); the European Economic Community; and REDUC. These activities are carried out as part of the programs of the Ministry of Education and the National Technological Institute.

The personnel usually engaged in this work are tech-nical staff from the respective institutions, and, in some cases, consultants and/or foreign or national specialists are contracted. Pilot projects and experiments play an important role in the majority of the curricular research or experiments.

The higher education system has specialized depart-ments for carrying out research at macro and specific levels. In general, they are concerned with formal research which also has the financial support of for-eign countries, universities, and organizations. This research is being carried out by research departments in the different private and state universities.

Research makes up a large part of the work of universities and has an important role, as much for their growth as for their influence on national development.

10. Major Reforms in the 1980s and 1990s

The educational reforms of the 1980s were based on the premise that education, both formal and nonformal, was a suitable resource to achieve the consolidation of Marxism throughout the population. From this perspective, Sandinism opted for two well-defined strategies regarding the roles of nonformal and formal education. Nonformal education was given the task of creating popular organizations as a means to bring its philosophy to the population. In formal education, the following relevant activities were carried out:

(a) The National Literacy Crusade, considered as a politico-educational project, which succeeded in reducing illiteracy to 12.5 percent in 1981. The lack of follow-up did not allow the consolidation of the project and by 1985 illiteracy had risen to 22 percent according to the PNUD in its 1990 statement.

(b) The curricular transformation, which had as its objective the institutionalization of a materialist education with the advice of socialist countries, principally Cuba and the former East Germany.

It is important to recognize that in this period educational coverage was extended to sectors of the population traditionally marginalized from the education system and an attempt was made to adjust teaching to the agricultural and occupational reality of the country.

Two facts are worth noting as a consequence of this educational policy. First, the deterioration in the quality of education throughout the system, and, second, the total abandonment on the part of the government of this era of the infrastructure to such an extent that despite the efforts of the new government, there were still schoolchildren without chairs and school buildings in a state of lamentable deterioration in the early 1990s.

11. Major Problems for the Year 2000

Thorough evaluations and reports on the educational system have been made, with an emphasis on primary education, by means of international and national organizations, which have discovered the following problems that significantly affect the functioning of education:

(a) lack of a sectoral education policy which impedes the development of an adequate strategy;

(b) high grade repetition and dropout rates, particularly in the first grades of primary education;

(c) a high percentage of schools in the rural areas which do not teach all grades or which teach several grades at the same time (which in the majority of cases only provide education up to third grade);

(d) a high percentage of untrained teachers and the low quality of teaching technique;

(e) lack of staff and inadequate teaching materials;

(f) lack of suitable, reliable, and relevant educational information;

(g) lack of a coherent decentralization policy;

(h) lack of necessary resources in order for primary education to offer an efficient service;

(i) weakness in administration capability and the lack of a planning model for taking decisions;

(j) the adult education program as a whole does not respond to the need of the adult students to work and the quality of the teaching is very low;

(k) the percentage of illiteracy is approximately 40 at the national level and 40 in rural areas;

(l) the existing curriculum and its development process do not guide basic education toward the formation of individuals for the world of work and family;

(m) research needs to be linked to business and production;

(n) the handicapped, demobilized fighters, and children at risk are not adequately incorporated into the system;

(o) efforts are lacking to rationalize resources and appraise technical agricultural programs of all types.

Niger

H. Bergmann

1. General Background

Niger has been an independent state, *La République du Niger*, since 1960, but before that it was one of the territories of French West Africa (*Afrique Occidentale Française*). Its capital is Niamey. It is divided into the seven divisions (*départements*) of Agadez, Diffa, Dosso, Maradi, Tahoua, Tillabery, and Zinder.

Niger covers an area of about 1,267,000 square kilometers. It is one of the Sahel countries with a large proportion of its northern area belonging to the Sahara desert. Its longest international boundary through inhabited territory is with northern Nigeria, extending practically from 4° to 12° eastern longitude. As far as cultural and historical factors and their effect on educational policy are concerned, this is a major source of influence.

In 1991, the total population was estimated at 7,960,900 inhabitants (49.5% male, 50.5% female). Based on the 1988 census, the annual population growth rate was estimated at 3.41 percent which is high even in the context of sub-Saharan Africa. Life expectancy is still relatively low (47.7 years on average) with only a small difference between the sexes. Infant mortality remains high at 134 per thousand.

Overall urbanization is low: 15.3 percent in 1988, 19.5 percent in 1990, and an estimated 27 percent for the year 2000. Due to the ecological characteristics of the country, the population is heavily concentrated in the southern regions, suitable for rain-fed agriculture and extensive animal husbandry. Thus while the overall population density is only 6 inhabitants per square kilometer, it is 163 inhabitants per square kilometer of agriculturally usable area.

Niger is inhabited by nine ethnic groups, each of which speaks its own language (see Table 1). The Hausa population has strong links to the Hausa states of northern Nigeria where Hausa is a language of culture and instruction in both traditional and modern settings. Most other ethnic groups and languages are shared with a number of other countries in the region, for example, Fulfulde, the language of the Fulbe cattle grazers in the whole of West Africa, the Zarma-Sonraï and the Touareg with Mali, the Gourmantché and the Mossi with Burkina Faso, and the Kanuri with Nigeria. Most minority language speakers master at least one of the major languages, with Hausa being understood by a majority of those whose mother tongue is different.

Relations between the ethnic groups are far from easy. Tensions build up between the Hausa and the other groups, with certain Hausa groups claiming Niger to be a Hausa state. The region-wide unrest among the Touareg population has not spared Niger. The conflict over the Touareg claim for a far-reaching internal autonomy is not yet settled.

The country is far more homogeneous in terms of religion. Of all Nigériens 98.6 percent are Muslim and less than 1 percent practice traditional beliefs. The strong fundamentalist undercurrent in the Muslim world has also reached Niger. Thus, the national conference and the following interim government were faced with demands for a nonsecular, Islamic state.

The modern sector of the economy employs only a very small proportion of the country's labor force. Of the less than 51,000 employees, 48.7 percent are civil servants or employees in the administration. Only 29.6 percent are employed by the private sector. The majority of the population is self-employed in agriculture and animal husbandry. Trading and crafts have a long standing, autochtonous tradition with certain crafts (e.g., blacksmithing, leather work, weaving) restricted to castes. This feature of traditional society makes practical subjects in primary school difficult.

Table 1
Ethnic group composition of the population (in percentages)

Hausa	52.89
Zarma-Sonraï	21.08
Touareg	10.57
Fulbe	9.81
Kanuri-Manga	4.55
Toubou	0.45
Arabs	0.32
Gourmantché	0.28
Mossi	0.05
Total	100.00

Table 2
Education level of the population 1988 (in percentages)

Level of education	Male	Female	Total
None	69.9	87.6	78.9
Koranic school	15.7	4.6	10.1
Primary school	11.2	6.6	8.8
Secondary school	3.0	1.2	2.1
Higher education	0.2	0.05	0.14

Due to the late development of the formal school system, the educational level of the general population is low, as can be seen in Table 2.

The incidence of illiteracy is very high, with 89.8 percent of the adult population (15 years and above) being deemed to be completely illiterate (males: 85.3%, females: 94.2%). Between 2 and 3 percent are literate in local languages but not in French (males: 4.8%, females: 0.5%), and 7.6 percent are literate in French.

As in most other Sahelian countries, the economy is predominantly agricultural. In 1988, agriculture and animal husbandry accounted for 39 percent of Gross National Product (GNP). Government's share was 15 percent of GNP (administration), 14 percent was trade and tourism, 9 percent services other than administration (banking, insurance), 12 pezrcent manufacturing and construction, and 6 percent mining. In the early 1980s, uranium mining was the dominant sector of the country's economy. Its decline contributed heavily to the economic breakdown in the early 1990s. This breakdown has led to a shrinking of the formal (revenue-generating) sector of the economy and to a growth of the informal sector. The poor economic performance since the mid-80s did not create the job opportunities needed to absorb all secondary school graduates, let alone primary school leavers. Niger, like Burkina Faso, is a net exporter of labor to the coastal countries.

Until 1989, Niger was governed by a one-party structure. The military took over the country on several occasions. In 1991, after prolonged political unrest, the military government and its political movement, the single party MNSD—*Mouvement National pour la Société de Développement*—were replaced by a sovereign national conference which, in turn, put in place an interim government which had to prepare free elections. The name of the former single party stood for the overall political goal—creating a development-oriented society.

2. Politics and the Goals of the Education System

The interim government has not defined an educational policy of its own. However, the goals as stated in the action plan Education For All, approved in 1990, are still valid. Its main elements are the democratization of basic education and quality improvement. This includes mother-tongue teaching in the first three years and practical subjects in primary school in order to make education more relevant. It would seem, however, that the way in which people perceive the purpose of education is much more important in shaping participation in the system and political pressures on the state.

People's perception of education is that of a machine for upward social mobility, giving access to administrative jobs and public office. Based on past experience, this perception is correct but is being more and more frustrated. This perception will be decisive for the acceptance of the reform goals and the policies to implement it, for example, introducing African languages as medium of instruction, or introducing practical subjects.

3. The Formal System of Education

The traditional, precolonial system of Koranic schools will be included in the description of the formal structure of education. Although it is not controlled by the state, it is certainly formal in that it has a definite curriculum, specialized teachers, and examinations. It did, on the other hand, prompt the colonial administration to introduce, as part of its formal education system, the *medersas* (*écoles franco-arabes*—French-Arabic schools) where alongside the official curriculum religious subjects were taught, and where Arabic was both a subject and a language of instruction.

Koranic schools cater for the religious instruction of boys; girls may enroll but do so only to an insignificant degree. They are organized by religious teachers (*mallams*) who offer their services to local communities. Boys may enroll as early as 3 to 4 years of age. Parents pay a small fee to the teacher. The first stage of teaching/learning consists of memorizing the Koran in Arabic, and learning to write in Arabic script. Performance is examined, and pupils who distinguish themselves in Koranic recitation may continue for further studies, learning Arabic as a second language, and learning to understand and interpret the Koran and other sources of learning.

According to the 1988 census, Koranic instruction was far from universal. In the group aged between 16 and 30 years, 9.8 percent had been taught at Koranic schools without any further formal instruction. Among those older than 30 years of age, this proportion was 11.6 percent.

3.1 Primary, Secondary, and Tertiary Education

There are six years of primary education (*études du premier degré*), divided in three phases of two years' duration each. The first phase consists of the beginners' class (*cours d'initiation*) and the preparatory

class (*cours préparatoire*); the second of the elementary course (*cours élémentaire 1ère année, cours élémentaire 2ème année);* and the third of the middle course *(cours moyen 1ère année, cours moyen 2ème année)*. Final examinations at the end of Grade 6 lead to the first school leaving certificate (*certificat de fin d'études du premier degré*). Primary education is provided in regular schools called *écoles traditionnelles* (94.2% of all schools) with French as the language of instruction throughout; in *medersas* or *écoles franco-arabes* (4.1% of all schools); or, very rarely, in experimental schools where the language of instruction is the children's mother tongue. In 1990, the number of primary schools was 2,305.

Secondary education consists of three types: general secondary education, teacher training, and technical –vocational education. General secondary has two levels: the first and the second cycle. The first cycle lasts for four years and is common for all those who have been admitted to secondary education. Successful completion is certificated with the *"Brevet d'Etudes du Premier Cycle"* (BEPC), a certificate which is the precondition for further secondary education. The second cycle consists of three years of study at the end of which, if successful in the examination, a student receives the *baccalauréat*. This examination provides access to higher education at university level. While the first cycle is taught in general colleges (*Collèges d'Enseignement Général*), the second cycle is taught in high schools (*lycées*).

Higher Education is provided in the National University Abdou Moumouni Dioffo in Niamey, and in an Islamic institution of higher learning which applied for official recognition in 1992. The National University consists of six faculties: humanities and social sciences, natural sciences, medicine, agriculture and related sciences, economics and law, and pedagogy. The Faculty of Pedagogy trains all secondary school teachers, the pedagogical advisers (*conseillers pédagogiques*), and the inspectors.

In addition, there are three research institutes, the IRSH (*Institut de Recherche en Sciences Humaines*), the IREM (*Institut de Recherche en Mathématique*), and the IRI (*Institut de Radio-Isotopes*). In 1990, just over 4,000 students were enrolled at the university, representing 74.2 percent of the nation's university student population, while the rest studied abroad. The total university enrollment represents about 0.5 percent of the corresponding age group.

Figure 1 presents the structure of the educational system. As can be seen, there is quite an amount of grade repeating in primary school. However, although the figures are presented in terms of thousands of children enrolled, it must be recognized that Niger is one of the five countries with the lowest enrollment rates in the world. In 1990, the gross enrollment in primary school was 28.8 percent and the net enrollment was 16.6 percent. From very low enrollment rates in 1960, gross enrollment rates grew rather steadily, moving

Table 3
Gross and net enrollment rates for boys and girls in urban and rural areas

Zone	Boys		Girls		Total	
	gross	net	gross	net	gross	net
urban	64.1	47.7	53.5	41.3	58.8	44.5
rural	19.5	15.0	9.8	7.6	14.9	11.5

Girls represented about 36 percent of primary school pupils in 1990. Their participation was slightly higher in the *medersas* (38%) and the experimental schools (39.7%). Female participation has been rather stable over time, rising from 31 percent in 1963 to 35 percent in 1973, and reaching 36 percent in 1987. Regional differences in female participation are quite pronounced. Girls make up 49 percent of primary school pupils in the capital, but only 26.7 percent in the *département* of Maradi. One of the main factors explaining these differences seems to be the proportion of female teachers. Just as the proportion of girls in primary school rises over time as the proportion of female teachers increases, so there is a parallel between these two proportions in urban and rural areas. In urban areas, the proportion of female teachers is much higher than that of male teachers; in rural areas, it is just the reverse. There is no evidence that religious or cultural factors play a role in this respect.

from 11 percent in 1970, 16 percent in 1975, 26 percent in 1980, with an all-time high of 30 percent in 1986 and 1988 before dropping to 28 percent in 1992. This drop was probably related to the economic difficulties of the late 1980s when the building of schools slowed down considerably.

The gross enrollment in secondary education was 5 percent and net enrollment 4.1 percent in 1990. These rates have been remarkably stable over the years.

Enrollment in adult literacy courses represented 1.6 percent of the group between 15 and 30 years of age from which the majority of participants are drawn, and 0.8 percent of all adults above the age of 15 years.

The 1988 census made it possible to estimate regional and gender differences in primary school enrollment as can be seen in Table 3.

The urban/rural enrollment differences (see Table 3) are enormous. Rural enrollment rates also vary according to the division. Reasons for these differences have not been established. It is plausible, however, to assume that the concentration of job opportunities and opportunities for self-employment, where education is of some help, in urban areas explain most of the difference. The demonstration effect of the economic utility of education is located in the towns.

Private schools enroll 3.3 percent of all primary school pupils. This is probably due to the fact that

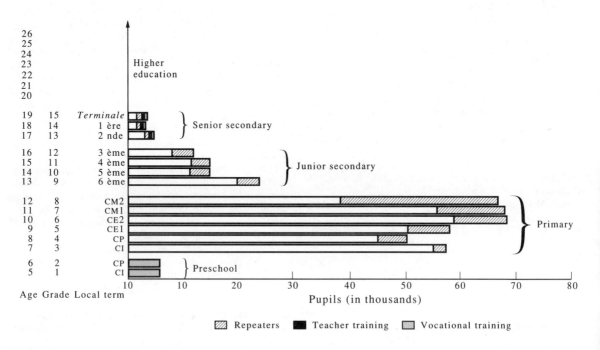

Figure 1
Niger: Structure of the formal education system 1991

mission schools were not allowed to operate in Niger. As far as secondary education is concerned, the French high school in the country's capital is privately run and receives a large number of Nigérien students.

The length of the school day in primary school is 6 hours. The school week has 5 days and the school year consists of 34 weeks. Thus, the number of hours taught is 1,020. The official school calendar of the year 1990–91 has a total of 1,014 hours. After deduction of the breaks (30 minutes per day), the net amount of time devoted to teaching is about 930 hours. However, this does not take teacher absence into account, and the estimate of 780 hours which forms the base of the mathematics syllabus might be a more realistic estimate. The school year is the same for secondary education. The weekly teaching time is not known but one may safely assume that it does not exceed 30 hours either.

Average class size varies from 27 in the Diffa region to 55 in Niamey (the capital). Two things have to be kept in mind, however:

(a) Class sizes vary a lot; in Niamey, final years with 60 to 70 pupils are not exceptional.

(b) In many rural areas, the average classroom consists of pupils in different school years, sometimes covering the whole six years, so that multigrade teaching is necessary. In fact, multigrade classrooms with at least two grades per classroom are the rule in rural areas.

The pupil–teacher ratio at the primary level was 38.8:1 in 1990–91. The same considerations as for the average classroom size apply. The student–teacher ratio at the second level is 26:1, but it is 29:1 in general secondary school, 15:1 in teacher training, and 7:1 in vocational school.

3.2 Preschool Education

Preschool education was introduced in 1977 and is still in its infancy. At the beginning of the school year 1989–90, about 11,500 children were enrolled, corresponding roughly to 2 percent of the 4–5-year olds. All of the 71 preschool facilities are located in urban areas with 40 percent of them being in the country's capital. Preschool work has suffered a drawback which is hopefully only temporary. In the school year 1990–91, there were only 65 preschools with 262 teachers and 9,434 pupils (48% of whom were girls).

3.3 Special Education

There are no data on special education programs.

3.4 Technical, Vocational, and Business Education

Preparation for employment in the formal sector of the country's economy and in the administration has been governed by a manpower planning approach which originated with independence. Given the extreme scarcity of trained manpower (primary school enrollment was still at only 11% in 1969!) all secondary school leavers were assured jobs but had to follow a tightly controlled career orientation. This career orientation started to operate during the second cycle of secondary school and, of course, at the university level. All the costs of secondary and higher education including subsistence and lodging were borne by the state. The resulting comprehensive scholarship schemes are extremely onerous and have introduced an element of rigidity in the sector budget, due to the enormous political pressure of the students.

Vocational, technical, and business education is just beginning. There is one technical college, the *Lycée technique Dan Kassawa* at Maradi, and a professional training institute, the *Lycée d'enseignement professionnel Issa Beri* at Niamey. The technical college at Maradi confers the *baccalauréat de technicien*, a certificate equivalent to the one issued at the end of general secondary education, and leading toward further studies. The professional training institute provides the *brevet d'aptitude professionnelle* after two years of training, and the *diplôme d'aptitude professionnelle* (a certificate for a fully qualified, technically skilled worker) after three years.

In 1990, the number of students undergoing formal vocational training was 843. It is provided in a number of specialized institutions, apart from the above mentioned training institutes. These are the Center for the Training of Adult Literacy Specialists, the Center for Trades Related to Water and Electricity, the National Training Center for Post and Telecommunications, the Animal Husbandry Training Center, the Mining School of the Air, the National School of Administration, the National School of Public Health, the National Institute of Youth and Sports, and the Practical Institute for Rural Development.

There has been an attempt to introduce elements of the dual system in the apprenticeship system of the informal sector, organized and cofinanced by the German Volunteer Service. It had to be abandoned, however, for lack of trainees—which, in turn, was due to the fact that employers were not willing to pay for the training of their apprentices in the difficult economic situation at the beginning of the 1990s.

3.5 Adult and Nonformal Education

Adult and nonformal education is mainly limited to the national program of adult literacy. Its goal is to eradicate illiteracy by the year 2000. It is the responsibility of a department in the Ministry of Education and Research, the DAFA (*Direction de l'Alphabétisation et de la Formation des Adultes*) with 8 divisional inspectorates and 18 district inspectorates.

The main target groups are illiterate adults, both male and female. It is seen as complementary to primary education, catering to the learning needs of those who could not go to school or who failed to terminate primary education successfully.

The literacy program takes the form of an annual campaign. For an adult to become permanently literate, two years of participation are thought to be necessary. Each annual campaign starts in November with a drive to sensitize public opinion and, in particular, the target population. Communities are encouraged to open literacy centers, which means little more than constituting learner groups which would meet in classrooms or other suitable places. Literacy instructors are recruited and briefly trained so that in February, course work can start. The course work of 2½ months is rather intense; 6 days a week, 3 hours of intensive courses are taught, providing a minimum of 180 hours of instruction. Teaching is done in 5 African languages. This period is followed by a month of consolidating what had been learned. The evaluation of each annual campaign ends in August.

The 1990 campaign had about 1,400 learner groups with about 25,400 participants. However, attendance was low (an average of 17 to 18 learners per group at registration) and irregular, and dropouts were high (one third of the initially registered participants). Women constituted 8.5 percent of the participants. This was due to a number of reasons, among others that it is very difficult to recruit female literacy instructors.

Success is rather limited, and progress slow. Initial evaluation of the literacy level of course participants has shown that a number of people enroll several times in the literacy programs. Irregular attendance and dropout are additional factors of inefficiency. Thus, although the monthly allowances for the literacy instructors are modest and costs for reading materials low, the unit cost per literacy graduate has been estimated at nearly four times that of a first school leaving certificate.

4. Administrative and Supervisory Structure and Operation

Education is administered by the Ministry of National Education and Scientific Research, the MEN/R (*Ministère de l'Education Nationale et de la Recherche*). In each region (*département*) and the capital, there is a regional inspectorate of primary education, a regional inspectorate of secondary education, and a regional inspectorate of adult education. In addition, there are two inspectorates for Arabic education who supervise the *medersas*. The inspectorates organize the educational service in their districts, work out proposals for the posting of teachers, administer and distribute school supplies, run workshops where school furniture is made, and organize teacher inservice training in the form of education days (*journées pédagogiques*).

At the subregional level, there are inspectorates of primary and adult education, while inspectorates of secondary education cover several subregions at a time. There are three senior posts at each regional and subregional inspectorate for primary education, two for the inspector and his deputy, and one for an education adviser (*conseiller pédagogique*). The latter is supposed to provide professional guidance to teachers in a situation that is free of the tension which often occurs with a formal school inspection. Budgetary limitations, however, make separate visits impossible. Thus, at least part of the purpose for which the post of education adviser had been created cannot be attained. Education advisers and inspectors are trained at the Faculty of Pedagogy. Inspectors are recruited from the ranks of the education advisers.

While administrative control is decentralized in theory, it is highly centralized in practice. Even most disciplinary matters are dealt with at the central level. Teachers are paid at the regional and subregional headquarters.

The responsibility for programs such as the curriculum lies with the central level and no local adaptations are foreseen.

5. Educational Finance

In 1989, the total education expenditure amounted to 19,873 million FCFA (US$67.5 million). This figure represented 3.1 percent of GNP. While the share of education in GNP was stable between 1980 and 1989, its share in total government expenditure dropped sharply from 22.9 to 9.0 percent. During the same period, the proportion of current expenditure rose from 47 percent in 1980 to 78.2 percent in 1989.

The allocation of the education budget was: primary 48.6 percent, secondary 25.8 percent, and "other types of education" 25.6 percent. Students in secondary and higher education are entitled to scholarships not only to cover the cost of tuition but also the living costs. Scholarships accounted for 11.1 percent of the current expenditure for secondary education. There are no data on the percent allocation for preprimary and nonformal education.

In 1990, budgetary allocations in the Ministry of National Education were as laid out in Table 4 (figures refer to the *budget de fonctionnement*).

For 1990, salary expenditures could not be broken down according to levels of education. The expenditure under the item materials amounts to 1,200 FCFA (US$4.08) per primary school pupil. The sum of 600 million FCFA (US$2.04 million) had been set aside for classroom building and maintenance.

Unit costs per primary school pupil amounted to 33,200 FCFA (US$112.83) in 1987 and 31,000 FCFA (US$105.35) in 1990, and are among the highest in the whole region. Only Mauritania had higher unit costs (36,300 FCFA in 1985).

Table 4
Budgetary allocations in the Ministry of Education 1990

Item of expenditure	FCFA (in thousands)	percentage
Teaching and supervisory personnel	17,040,000	79.6
Central administration	1,200,000	5.6
Subtotal salary	18,240,000	85.2
Nonsalary items primary education	813,980	3.8
Materials	443,000	
Transport, vehicle maintenance, fuel	98,340	
School feeding programs	206,000	
Telephone	36,270	
Water and electricity	30,370	
Nonsalary items secondary school	2,346,594	11.0
Subtotal nonsalary expenditure	3,160,574	14.8
Grand total	21,400,574	100.0

6. Supplying Personnel for the Education System

In 1990, there were 262 preschool teachers, all of them female. This implies a stagnation in the development of this sector since figures have gone down slightly, compared with the previous year.

In 1991, there were 9,473 primary school teachers (35.6% of them women). There were three grades of teachers, according to qualification: 21.3 percent fully trained teachers (*instituteurs*), 69.1 percent partly trained teachers (*instituteurs adjoints*), and 9.6 percent untrained teachers (*moniteurs*).

In 1989, teaching staff in secondary education were distributed among the three branches of secondary education as laid out in Table 5.

Student teachers are recruited after four years of secondary education, at the BEPC level. Recruitment is

Table 5
Distribution of teaching staff in secondary education 1989

	Male	Female	Total
General education	2,019	430	2,449
Teacher training	65	12	77
Vocational training	58	5	63
Total	2,142	447	2,589

undertaken by the manpower division (*Direction des études et de la programmation*) of the Ministry, based on the BEPC results after the first four years of secondary education. Fully trained teachers are trained in long cycle teacher training colleges (*écoles normales/cycle long*) and undergo four years of training. Three of the four years are identical to secondary education at the *lycées*. One year is devoted specifically to teacher training. Partly trained teachers study for two years in short-cycle teacher-training colleges (*écoles normales/cycle court*).

There are two short cycle teacher-training colleges, one for girls at Tahoua, and one for boys at Dosso. There are also two long cycle teacher-training colleges, the one at Tillabéri for girls, and the one at Zinder for boys. Those who successfully pass the *baccalauréat* examination in the long-cycle teacher-training colleges can opt for one year of further studies in order to become primary school teachers, or to continue their studies at the Faculty of Education of the university where they are prepared for work as secondary school teachers.

Efforts to upgrade knowledge and skills are of two kinds: courses of variable duration in the inservice teacher-training college at Maradi, and one-day workshops organized by the inspectorate. The long courses at the inservice college lead to an upgrading of trainees; most unqualified teachers have been promoted to the grade of partly trained teacher through such courses.

The four-year teacher training is felt to be too costly and, at the same time, not efficient enough. There are plans to change the training of fully qualified primary school teachers completely—recruiting student teachers at the *baccalauréat* level and giving them two years of professional training, geared almost exclusively to pedagogy and teaching methods, and very little to content.

7. Curriculum Development and Teaching Methodology

Curricula in Niger are nationwide, with no scope for local or cultural adaptation. For primary education, there are three variants: one for the mainstream "traditional" schools, one for the Arabic-medium *medersas*, and one for the experimental schools using African languages as the medium of instruction. Apart from the classical disciplines (language, mathematics, natural science, geography, history, physical education), the general syllabus features practical subjects and domestic science, and civics. Since language lessons mean French, they take up a large proportion of the weekly teaching time (55% in the first two years of primary education, 41% in the elementary course, and still 36% in the middle course).

The curriculum of the *medersas* contains, as additional subjects, Islam, Koranic studies, Arabic grammar, religious singing, and history of the Arab world.

727

The curriculum of the experimental schools covers the same subjects as those in mainstream schools, but African languages are also taught, and the number of French lessons is reduced accordingly.

Curriculum development is part of the responsibilities of the INDRAP (*Institut National de Documentation, de Recherche et d'Animation Pédagogique*). There are three divisions in the institute:

(a) the humanities (*lettres et sciences humaines*), responsible for French, history and geography, English, African languages, and philosophy;

(b) natural sciences (*sciences exactes*), responsible for mathematics, the sciences, and practical subjects (*activités pratiques et productives*);

(c) guidance, documentation, and inservice training (*animation-documentation et formation permanente*), responsible for all training activities, audiovisual apparatus, the library, and curriculum evaluation.

Curriculum development and the writing of instructional materials is done by groups of authors (*cellules rédactrices*). New materials and teachers' guides are trialed in ten trial schools for about four months, with at least three follow-up missions by INDRAP. Trialling results are fed back to the authors for revision and final editing.

The inspectorate ensures, through on-the-spot checks and the analysis of class registers, that the curriculum is implemented.

8. The System of Examinations, Promotions and Certifications

All examinations are centrally set, and organized by the inspectorate in schools selected as examination centers.

Primary education ends with the final school leaving certificate CFEPD (*certificat de fin d'études du premier degré*). It covers eight domains, three of which are in French and two in mathematics. In addition, pupils are examined in writing, environmental studies, and drawing or needlework. The pass mark is 70 out of 140 points. The *medersa* education is certified by the *Certificat d'Etudes Primaires Elementaires Francoarabe*, with a pass mark of 50 out of 100 points. Papers are marked by a jury installed by the divisional inspector.

Results are discouragingly poor. In 1990, 30.9 percent of all candidates were admitted but admission rates were slightly higher in earlier years (43.3% in 1975–76; 43.0% in 1978–79; and on several occasions, they fell to 25% or below). Mean results per subject were very low; most of the time they were rather below 10 out of 20 than above. The lowest

results were registered in dictation. Problem-solving in mathematics yielded poor results but it must be noted that they involve more language skills than the four operations.

Promotion in primary school is automatic from Grade 1 to Grade 2. In the other grades, grade repeating is limited to 15 percent and only in Grade 6 is an unlimited number of repeaters allowed. The following percentage repetition rates bear this regulation out:

(a) Grade 1–Grade 2: 2.5%

(b) Grade 2–Grade 3: 9.9%

(c) Grade 3–Grade 4: 12.3%

(d) Grade 4–Grade 5: 13.3%

(e) Grade 5–Grade 6: 17.5%

(f) Grade 6: 41.7%

Needless to say, the restriction placed on repetition has not solved the problem of poor learning results in primary school.

Promotion in secondary school is not automatic; total repetition in 1990 was 19 percent with very high repetition rates in the final classes of junior secondary school (30%) and senior secondary school (43%).

9. Educational Assessment, Evaluation, and Research

There is no educational assessment. Evaluation and research are among the responsibilities of the INDRAP.

10. Major Reforms in the 1980s and 1990s

While an experiment to use television extensively in primary education was abandoned in 1975–76, other reform efforts have been more continuous although not as successful as initially planned. In the years 1974 and 1975, a thorough reform of the whole system had been envisaged. It was supposed to introduce African languages as languages of instruction in the first three years of primary education, and practical subjects (*activités pratiques et productives*) in order to make education more relevant, particularly in rural areas. These topics received further attention in the 1980s, with national seminars on education held in 1982 and 1987.

The language of instruction issue has been trialed in a number of experimental schools, starting with one Hausa-medium school in 1973. By 1993, there were 38 experimental schools teaching in the 5 major languages of Niger. No systematic evaluation of the experience is yet available, but there are indications that the approach is successful, and the average examination results seem to be slightly superior to those of the mainstream schools. Pupils are said to participate much more freely, being less inhibited and restrained by the language barrier.

Practical subjects were introduced at the national level in 1985. There is little systematic evidence about how successful this innovation has been. However, the record does not seem to be more favorable than in most other countries where this idea has been tried out, although a few schools do show outstanding performances.

In 1987, curriculum reforms were discussed, and the content of certain subjects was updated.

11. Major Problems for the Year 2000

Enrollment will remain low. Its growth will depend on how the economy grows, and how much external support can be mobilized. However, expansion of primary education will hardly keep pace with population growth.

Bibliography

Barnes V 1984 *Niger Education Sector Assessment: Florida State University/Howard University.* Institute for International Research, Albany, New York

Bergmann H, Yahouza I 1992 *Niger—étude sectorielle sur l'éducation de base.* Rapport pédagogique, No.55. GTZ, Eschborn

Comité National de suivi et d'évaluation des recommandations de la Conférence Mondiale sur l'Education pour tous 1991 *Rapport sur l'évolution du système éducatif nigérien.* Comité National, Niamey

Ligappa S/UNESCO 1977 *L'éducation et l'environnement socio-économique—développements récents au Niger.* UNESCO, Paris

UNICEF 1989 *Société en crise et éducation au Niger.* UNICEF, Niamey

Nigeria

E. A. Yoloye

1. General Background

Nigeria is a fairly large geographic unit on the west coast of Africa. It lies completely within the equatorial zone. It has a roughly rectangular shape, the widest distance from north to south being about 406 kilometers and from east to west about 438 kilometers. Its area is estimated at about 222,919 square kilometers. It is bordered on the west, north, and east by the Francophone countries of Benin, Niger, and Chad, and by Cameroon respectively, while in the south, the Atlantic Ocean washes its coastline for about 313 kilometers. Until independence from British colonial rule in 1960, southern Cameroon (which is Anglophone) was administered as part of Nigeria. It was then joined with Francophone Cameroon, making Nigeria narrower on the coastline by cutting off the southeastern corner. The introduction of French into the Nigerian school curriculum shortly after Independence was largely inspired by the fact that the country is completely surrounded by Francophone countries.

Since independence, population census has become a sensitive political issue. The 1963 census, under UN supervision, put Nigeria's population at 55.6 million. The 1973 census figures were rejected by the government because of obvious inflations in many areas. For nearly 30 years, therefore, Nigeria's population was based on projections from the 1963 census using a growth rate of 2.5 percent, the same as the estimated average growth rate for Africa. Independent studies suggest that the actual growth rate is slightly higher than 3 percent. The 1991 census, the first results of which were released in March 1992, put the population at 88.5 million which was much lower than expected from projections. Details of urban–rural distribution, age distribution, occupational distribution, and the like, have (as of May 1994) not yet been released. The long period of uncertainty about the size and details of the population clearly make educational planning a hazardous affair. Educational indicators such as enrollment ratios were likely to have been inaccurate and the delay in the release of the details of the 1991 census has compounded the problems of planning.

Nigeria is a multiethnic and multilingual country. Hansford et al. (1976) report that there are 394 different languages and as many ethnic groups. Brann (1977) points out that three of these languages—Hausa, Yoruba, and Igbo—are spoken by over 54 percent of the population, being spoken by 21.7, 18 and 17.6 percent of the people respectively according to the 1963 census. Further, 9 other languages (Fulfulde, Efik/Ibibio, Kanuri, Tiv, Ijo, Edo, Igala, Nupe, and Idoma) account for another 31 percent. Thus, these 12 languages account for over 85 percent of the population.

One legacy of Nigeria's colonial history is that English is the official language of business, administration, and, to a large extent, education. The government has designated Hausa, Yoruba, and Igbo as the major national languages, and the national policy

Nigeria

on education requires that each child in secondary school should learn at least one of these three major languages other than his or her own. The policy further states that the medium of instruction in the first three years of primary school shall be the mother tongue or the language of the immediate community and thereafter English. Considerable controversy surrounds the policy of using the mother tongue as a medium of instruction. Opponents claim that certain mathematical and scientific concepts cannot be taught in the mother tongue because they do not exist in the Nigerian languages. A longitudinal research project conducted at the University of Ife between 1969 and 1985 in which the experimental group was taught in Yoruba throughout the six years of primary school has largely debunked such arguments (Fafunwa et al. 1989).

The real problem for education is that most of the smaller languages are not written and so production of instructional materials in them is difficult. The 12 larger languages, however, all have well-developed orthographies.

At independence in 1960 about 80 percent of the total working population was engaged in the agricultural sector. With increasing industrialization, the occupational structure has changed considerably. Accurate statistics are not available, but it is estimated that those in agriculture amounted to about 60 percent at the beginning of the 1990s. Educationally, the government has a deliberate policy of encouraging production of more workers in science and technology for industrialization and modernization. At the tertiary education level, the government has adopted the 1982 Tannanarive Conference on Higher Education recommendation that the ratio of science to humanities in student enrollment in African universities should be 60:40. The industrial and manufacturing sector has, however, not developed as much as anticipated. Consequently, there is considerable unemployment even among graduates in science and technology. At the beginning of the 1990s, the banking, finance, and business sectors seemed to thrive better than the industrial and manufacturing sector. This is beginning to affect student choice of careers at tertiary level. Overall, an increasing professional elite has emerged in the country.

The economy of the country has undergone fundamental changes since independence. At independence, agriculture contributed over 85 percent of the country's foreign exchange earnings and the industrial sector's contribution was only 3.6 percent.

The discovery and exploitation of oil during the early 1970s boosted the Nigerian economy. Oil became the major foreign exchange earner, accounting for over 80 percent. The agricultural sector became neglected and its contribution to the economy dwindled rapidly. With the oil boom, there followed a period of uncontrolled spending, especially on imported goods including food. When the price of oil began to fall in the early 1980s, the nation's foreign exchange earnings plunged steadily downward while foreign debt continued to rise. In spite of a structural adjustment program with stringent fiscal measures embarked upon by the government in 1986, the national economy has remained in a poor state.

The repercussions on education have been quite severe. Infrastructural facilities have deteriorated and become quite inadequate; there is a gross shortage of instructional materials in institutions; and educational personnel have become scarce in many institutions partly because of nonavailability, a shortage of funds to employ those who are available, and the massive brain drain to wealthier countries mostly in the developed world. Textbooks, journals, and scientific equipment have become scarce, especially in tertiary institutions because of foreign exchange problems. On the positive side, the government is making strenuous efforts to stimulate local production of textbooks and scientific equipment, and these efforts began to yield results in the early 1990s; for example, two science equipment manufacturing centers were established and one more is under construction.

Nigeria has moved progressively from a federation of 3 large regions in 1960 to a federation of 30 states and a federal capital territory in 1991. It operates 3 clearly defined tiers of government, namely the federal, state, and local levels. In 1992, there were 589 local governments. The administration's emphasis is on decentralization and development from the grass roots. Government business is run through ministries at federal and state levels and through supervisory councillors at local government level.

Responsibility for education is shared out between the three tiers of government. Primary education is completely under the control of local governments. Secondary schools are predominantly under the control of state governments, although there are federal government secondary schools called "Unity Schools" controlled by the federal government in practically every state. Tertiary education is also shared between federal government and state governments.

2. Politics and the Goals of the Education System

Nigeria had five years of democratic rule immediately after attaining independence. A military coup in January 1966 ushered in a military regime which lasted for 14 years. Power was handed back to a democratically elected government in 1979, but another coup brought in the military again in 1983. Since then, Nigeria has been under a military regime. A program of transition back to civil rule began in 1989. There are two political parties which have been created by government fiat and with prepared constitutions. One of them—the National Republican Convention (NRC)— is supposed to lean a little to the right ideologically, while the other—the Social Democratic Party (SDP)— is supposed to lean a little to the left. Registration for membership began at local government level working up to federal level. As

730

of 1992, local government councils and state executive and houses of assembly have been democratically elected on the platform of the two parties. The federal house of representatives and the senate were elected in 1992.

A presidential election—the last phase of the transition program—was held in early June 1993. It was adjudged nationally and internationally to be free and fair. However, after over half of the results had been announced and a clear winner seemed to be emerging, the then president of the country annuled the election. An Interim National Government was installed but this was overthrown a few months later in a bloodless military coup. The two political parties and all previously elected democratic organs of government were dissolved. Since then the country has reverted to full military rule.

The clearest articulation of the political objectives of Nigeria is to be found in the Second National Development Plan (1970–74) which was prepared under a military regime. The objectives were the building of:

(a)   a free and democratic society;

(b)   a just and egalitarian society;

(c)   a united, strong, and self-reliant nation;

(d)   a great and dynamic economy;

(e)   a land of bright and full opportunities for all citizens.

These five objectives form the bedrock of the national policy on education first promulgated in 1977 and

revised in 1981. They are reflected in the content of the curricula, as well as the planning and administration of education at all levels. Between 1967 and 1970, there was a civil war occasioned by the attempt of the then Eastern Region to secede and form a separate nation called "Biafra." The attempt failed. The event has, however, made Nigeria particularly sensitive to the issue of national unity with the related issues of universalization of access to and equity in education. These concerns receive prominent attention in the policy and practice of education.

One of the most difficult problems is that of "educational imbalance," especially between northern and southern states, created by the religious and educational histories of the country. Islamic education and religion were first brought into northern Nigeria by itinerant Moslem scholars as far back as the eleventh century. Western education on the other hand was brought by Christian missionaries via the coast to the southern parts of the country in the first half of the nineteenth century. There was stiff resistance to Western education in the northern states. The colonial government, in order to retain the goodwill of the northern emirates, found it expedient to maintain the dichotomy in education systems between north and south, with the result that the north lagged behind the south in Western education.

Efforts to correct the imbalance have led the government to establish such educational policies as quota systems of admission into federal secondary and tertiary institutions and differential cut-off points for different states in entrance examinations to these institutions. Such policies have naturally generated much controversy and have led to pressure for more state-owned educational institutions at the tertiary and secondary levels.

3. The Formal System of Education

The formal education system is referred to as a "6-3-3-4 system," implying 6 years of primary school, 3 years of junior-secondary school, 3 years of senior-secondary school, and 4 years of university education for a normal bachelor's degree. In reality, secondary education also goes on in technical and vocational schools and Grade 2 teacher-training colleges for training primary school teachers. Tertiary education also covers polytechnics and colleges of technology, as well as colleges of education for training middle-level teachers for primary and junior-secondary schools.

3.1 Primary, Secondary, and Tertiary Education

Primary education is free and supposed to be universal, but it is not compulsory. Indeed, there is no compulsory age for attending school in Nigeria, although the official age of admission to primary schools is 6 years. Over 95 percent of primary schools are government-owned, but there is increasing private enterprise in

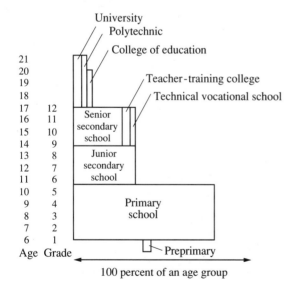

Figure 1
Nigeria: Structure of the formal education system

the establishment of primary schools. These private schools are usually fee-paying and therefore tend to be elitist. They receive no government subsidy.

The age of entry to junior-secondary school is normally 12 years. Tuition fees are charged in all secondary institutions. After junior-secondary school, the students may proceed to senior-secondary schools, technical and vocational schools, or Grade 2 teacher-training colleges.

At the tertiary level, colleges of education run three-year programs leading to the Nigerian Certificate in Education (NCE). Polytechnics and colleges of technology run two- and four-year programs leading to National Diploma (ND) and Higher National Diploma (HND) respectively. Usually an ND holder must do a year of industrial attachment before proceeding to HND. Universities run a wide range of programs lasting 4 to 7 years. Tertiary education is tuition free.

Primary and secondary schools usually operate a three-term system of 13 weeks each (i.e., 39 weeks a year). Daily schedules last about 6 hours. Tertiary institutions run two-semester systems with about 15 weeks of instruction per semester while 2 to 3 weeks are additionally allowed for administrative activities such as registration and examinations.

Figure 1 outlines the structure of the formal education system, while Table 1 shows enrollment-related statistics for primary schools, secondary/commercial schools, and universities. Statistics for other institutions are not readily available.

In 1992 there were 31 universities, 2 of which have been established since 1990. Roughly two-thirds of the universities, one-third of the polytechnics and colleges of technology, and one-third of the colleges of education are federal government-owned, while the rest are state-owned with the exception of a couple of colleges of education owned by religious bodies. There are no private universities or polytechnics. However, private universities did make a brief appearance in 1983 and 1984 when a supreme court ruling declared that there was nothing in the Constitution and laws of the country preventing the establishment of private universities.

Within 6 months of the ruling, 26 private universities were established or proposed in the country. The immediate response to this was that the federal military government, which had again come in via a military coup in December 1983, promulgated a decree in 1984 abolishing the existing private universities and prohibiting the further establishment of private universities.

Within the last year (1993–94), the government has reconsidered the issue of private universities. The prohibition has been lifted and new guidelines for the establishment of private universities have been issued. Already a couple are under serious consideration for approval.

3.2 Preschool Education

In the cities and urban areas, many children attend nursery schools between the ages of 3 and 5+. These

Table 1
Trends in enrollment in formal education 1975–90

Level and Variable	1975–76	1978–79	1981–82	1984–85	1987–88	1989–90
Primary						
No. of institutions	21,223	35,328	37,614	35,281	34,266	34,904
Enrollment	6,165,547	10,798,550	14,311,608	13,025,287	11,540,178	12,721,087
Percentage female enrollment	42.5	43.5	43.0	44.3	43.5	45.5
Gross enrollment ratio	—	—	—	80.1	70.8	68.7
Pupil—teacher ratio	35:1	36:1	37:1	42:1	37:1	—
Transition rate to secondary	—	—	—	38.9	46.2	43.2
Secondary						
No. of Institutions	1,513	2,249	5,594	5,406	5,547	5,868
Enrollment	601,652	1,194,479	2,880,280	2,689,586	2,662,085	2,723,791
Percentage female enrollment	34.5	33.3	28.9	41.4	43	42
Gross enrollment ratio	—	—	22.52	24.9	22.2	19.9
Student—teacher ratio	84:1	60:1	35:1	28:1	21:1	—
University						
No. of Institutions	13	13	24	25	29	29
Enrollment	32,286	46,423	70,365	97,546	160,767	180,871
Percentage female enrollment	16.0[a]	—	22.5	22.8	25.8	27.0
Student—teacher ratio	11:1	9:1	—	—	14:1	15:1

Source: Statistics Branch, Federal Ministry of Education, Victoria Island, Lagos
a new entrants only

nursery schools are entirely run by private individuals and groups (religious and secular). They are fee-paying and only fairly well-to-do families can afford to enroll children in them. The government provides guidelines for the operation of nursery schools and each is required to register with the state Ministry of Education.

3.3 Special Education

Special education is given considerable attention in the national policy on education. Government intervention began in the late 1960s. Before then, a number of voluntary philanthropic organizations and religious bodies had set up special schools in a few cities, particularly for the blind, the deaf and dumb, and the physically handicapped. In 1992, departments of special education existed in federal and state ministries of education. Special education teachers are trained in a number of universities and a special college of education established by the federal government.

Government policy is largely in favor of integrating the handicapped into the normal school system at the secondary and tertiary levels. Such integration is restricted to a few selected schools at secondary school level. Mentally retarded children are catered for only in special schools.

To facilitate transition from school to work, many state governments have established rehabilitation centers where the handicapped are taught special skills for gainful employment. Such centers are usually run by the Ministry of Social Development, Youth, and Sports.

In the late 1980s, a program of education for gifted children was launched by the federal Ministry of Education. The program was still largely experimental in the early 1990s, but a secondary school for gifted children has been established in the federal capital territory. As of 1989, it was estimated that only about 0.4 percent of school-aged handicapped children were actually in school.

3.4 Vocational, Technical, and Business Education

Vocational education takes place in post junior-secondary school institutions. There are as many as 39 trades taught, with the duration of training ranging from 4 months (welding) to 3 years (automechanics, carpentry/joinery). In 1986, there were 300 such schools with an enrollment of 73,741. The National Directorate of Employment (NDE) organizes a National Open Apprenticeship scheme. In this scheme, young secondary school leavers are attached to master craftsmen and craftswomen as apprentices for periods ranging from 6 months to 3 years. During this period, each apprentice is paid a small monthly allowance. As of 1989, the 25 most subscribed trades had enrollments ranging from a low of 1,420 (leather) to a

high of 15,817 (typing and shorthand) throughout the country.

3.5 Adult and Nonformal Education

Organized nationwide, adult education programs began in 1949 with the help of the Oxford Delegacy. A Department of Extramural Studies was established at the newly created University College Ibadan. The program started with a philosophy of nonaward liberal education for self-improvement. By the end of the first decade, it had become increasingly geared toward examinations such as the GCE O level and A level for youths and adults who had either dropped out of secondary schools or never had the opportunity of secondary education.

By 1992, a variety of certificate-oriented, job skills-oriented, and general enlightenment-oriented programs existed in universities, polytechnics, colleges of education, government ministries, and in private businesses. There is no open university, but a number of universities run part-time programs leading to a first degree.

At the end of the 1980s, the federal government set up the National Commission for Mass Literacy, Adult and Nonformal Education to coordinate adult and nonformal education throughout the country. Available Ministry of Education records show that, in 1989, there were 338,855 people enrolled in adult education programs. Of these, 189.554 (i.e., 55.9%) were female. In 1991, there were 72,010 literacy centers with a total enrollment of 910,110, of which about 47 percent were female.

4. Administrative and Supervisory Structure and Operation

Until the late 1960s, most primary and secondary schools were owned and controlled by voluntary agencies (religious and secular). Most, however, were grant-aided by the government which also paid the salaries of all teachers. The government then completely took over all the schools and paid compensation to the original owners. Private primary schools were allowed and, in special cases, a few private secondary schools were allowed.

As stated earlier, the position in 1992 was that all primary schools were under the control of local government education authorities, secondary schools (except the unity schools) were under the control of state governments, and tertiary institutions were owned and controlled partly by the federal government and partly by state governments.

Each state ministry of education and local government education authority has an inspectorate for supervision and quality control of its institutions. There is, however, also a federal inspectorate with branches in all states of the federation. They are free to inspect any secondary or primary school. Their reports usually go to the respective authorities and the heads of the institutions.

In spite of the decentralized administration of educational institutions, there are a number of federal organs of coordination.

At the tertiary level, there are three national commissions/boards as follows:

(a) the National Universities Commission (NUC) for universities;

(b) the National Board for Technical Education (NBTE) for polytechnics and colleges of technology;

(c) the National Commission for Colleges of Education (NCCE) for colleges of education.

Each commission or board sets minimum standards for curricula and management of the institutions under their control and organizes accreditation of academic programs. They have no state counterparts and are responsible to the federal Minister of Education.

The National Commission for Mass Literacy, Adult and Nonformal Education, on the other hand, works through state agencies and NGOs via literacy centers in the states. Some aspects of adult education are controlled by other ministries such as Health, Agriculture, and Social Welfare.

At the policy level, there are two powerful federal government organs which ensure broad-based consultation. These are: (a) the Joint Consultative Committee on Education (JCC), and (b) the National Council on Education (NCE).

The Joint Consultative Committee has the more broadbased membership, including the directors-general of the federal and state ministries of education and representatives of university faculties and institutes of education, the West African Examinations Council, the Nigerian Union of Teachers, and the National Manpower Board. It has several reference committees dealing with different sectors of education. Proposals from various educational agencies go first to the appropriate reference committees from where they are processed to the main JCC.

The National Council on Education comprises the federal Minister of Education (who is the chairman) and all the state commissioners of education. It considers recommendations from the JCC and the various commissions. Its decisions become education policies after approval by the federal executive council.

5. Educational Finance

Statistics on the percentage of gross domestic product (GDP) spent on education are not readily available.

However, it is known that the education budget as a percentage of total national budget has declined steadily since 1977. In 1976, when universal primary education (UPE) was introduced, education alone consumed about 25 percent of the national budget and, of this, about 60 percent went to primary education.

With the subsequent economic recession, allocation to education declined to a little over 5 percent of total budget by 1984 and has remained at about that level. Proportional distribution to different levels of education has also altered with secondary and tertiary education now having larger shares. Indeed, primary education deteriorated so much that, in 1989, the federal government had to intervene to inject federal funds into primary education through the National Primary Education Commission (NPEC) which it set up. Among other things, the federal government undertook to contribute the equivalent of 65 percent of the calculated teaching and nonteaching staff salaries to the primary schools. However, the NPEC was dissolved in January 1991. The rapid deterioration of primary education that followed the dissolution of the NPEC compelled the Government to reinstate it in late 1993. The impact of this new arrangement is yet to be felt.

In general, more and more of the financial burden of education has devolved onto parents as government subsidies for accommodation, meals, and textbooks have been withdrawn. Tuition fees are not charged at primary and tertiary level, but they are charged at secondary level. Bursaries and scholarships are being gradually reintroduced and plans are also afoot to introduce a student loan scheme.

Unit costs of education at the different levels of education are difficult to determine partly because of inadequate statistics, partly because of the instability of the national currency, and partly because of the considerable decentralization in the control and financing of education. The last detailed information on financing was for 1983 which gave unit costs in different states for secondary schools, Grade 2 teacher-training colleges, colleges of education, and polytechnics. Unit costs varied widely with the relative affluence of the states and the student population for which they catered. States with high student enrollment tended to spend less per student and vice versa. Thus, for secondary schools, unit costs ranged from a low of US$176 in Oyo State to a high of US$808 in Sokoto state. For Grade 2 teacher-training colleges unit costs ranged from a low of US$355 in Anambra State to a high of US$1,433 in Bauchi State. For colleges of education, it ranged from a low of US$972 in Ogun State to US$3,843 in Plateau State. For polytechnics it ranged from a low of US$991 in Plateau State to a high of US$3,975 in Oyo State. The National Annual Statistics of Education present no such details in subsequent years, but in 1989 information was provided that put the unit cost of secondary education for Nigeria as a whole at US$852. It should be understood that in each of the cases given, it is the unit expenditure by government that is reported and not the unit cost of education. There is, for example, no information on parental input into the cost of education.

6. Supplying Personnel for the Education System

Teachers are trained for the school system in three kinds of institutions: Grade 2 teacher-training colleges, colleges of education, and university faculties of education.

Grade 2 teacher-training colleges train teachers for the primary schools. They run three-year courses after junior-secondary school which lead to the Grade 2 Teachers Certificate.

Colleges of education mainly run three-year courses after senior-secondary school which lead to the Nigerian Certificate in Education (NCE) qualifying graduates to teach in junior-secondary schools. Some of these colleges have been authorised to run bachelor's degree programs in education in affiliation with some universities.

University faculties of education offer bachelor's degrees, as well as Postgraduate Diploma in Education courses to produce teachers for senior-secondary schools. They also run higher degree programs for those who will teach in colleges of education. Associateship certificate in education programs lasting one year for experienced Grade 2 teachers are also run to prepare graduates for administrative posts, such as head of primary school or inspector of primary education.

The national policy on education requires that by 1998 the NCE will be the minimum teacher's certificate in the education system. Consequently, Grade 2 teacher-training colleges are being phased out and all teachers with Grades 1 or 2 certificates are undergoing upgrading courses, sometimes through distance learning, to attain the NCE.

Universities usually recruit their teachers from the crop of master's and doctoral students produced in the various faculties. Most of the teachers at tertiary level are now Nigerians. The overall percentage of expatriates is less than 5.

Although there is a shortage of qualified teachers at all levels, there is still unemployment among qualified teachers because the government often does not have enough funds to pay additional staff.

Refresher courses, workshops, and seminars for updating the knowledge of teachers and other categories of educational personnel are organized by federal and state ministries of education and local government education authorities. Other agencies that organize such programs are universities, professional educational associations, and teachers' unions.

Many universities run degree courses for other categories of educational personnel such as planners, administrators, and managers; guidance counselors; librarians; adult educators and extention workers; educational evaluators; and sports coaches. These programs are run at both undergraduate and graduate levels.

7. Curriculum Development

At the primary and secondary levels, subjects to be taught in school are prescribed in the national policy on education. Curriculum development, in the sense of producing instructional materials in these subjects, is entrusted to the Nigerian Educational Research and Development Council (NERDC). This agency produces national curriculum guidelines, textbooks, teachers' guides, and other instructional materials. It has a special education unit which produces specialized materials (e.g., brailled books) for handicapped children.

Some professional associations (e.g., the Science Teachers Association of Nigeria), often in collaboration with commercial publishers, do produce textbooks based on the NERDC curriculum guidelines. Sometimes, too, commercial publishers, on their own, assemble scholars to produce textbooks based on the NERDC guidelines.

For many years, the West African Examinations Council (WAEC) determined the secondary school curriculum, which was the same for all the five Anglophone member countries. Before the WAEC took over, the Cambridge Examinations Syndicate played the same role for most British colonies. By the end of the 1980s, there was a trend for each country to develop its own curriculum. In Nigeria, the WAEC prepares examination syllabuses for the senior-secondary school based on NERDC guidelines.

At the tertiary level, each institution usually develops its own curriculum guidelines and range of subjects taught. There is a measure of central control through the National University Commission, the National Board for Technical Education, and the National Commission for Colleges of Education through the accreditation process for which the commissions set minimum standards in the curriculum. In terms of instructional materials, each institution selects from materials available in the market from various sources.

The contemporary concern in curriculum development at all levels is relevance to local realities as well as to national aspirations for social and economic development.

8. The System of Examinations, Promotions, and Certifications

The National Policy on Education (Federal Republic of Nigeria 1981), interalia, stated

(a) Ultimately, there will be no formal examination at the end of the first six years of primary education. Certificates will be based on continuous assessment, and will be issued by the headmaster of the school.

(b) Junior-secondary school-leaving certificates will also be based on continuous assessment and will be issued by the headmasters or principals of the junior-secondary schools.

(c) The senior-secondary school-leaving certificate will be based on a combination of continuous assessment and a final formal examination.

In practice there are still formal examinations organized by the state ministries of education at the end of primary and junior-secondary schooling. The certificates are, however, based on a combination of continuous assessment and the final examination just like the practice at the senior-secondary school level. At the senior-secondary school level, the final examination is administered by the West African Examinations Council. As a national policy, continuous assessment at each level carries a weight of 30 percent and the examination a weight of 70 percent.

At the tertiary level, each institution administers its own examinations. The principle of combining continuous assessment with final examination scores is practiced to varying extents by the various institutions and there is no fixed proportion for combining the two scores. Traditionally, colleges of education are affiliated to universities which moderate their certification examinations and issue the certificates. There is a move to make the colleges of education independent of the universities while the NCCE exercises the function of monitoring of standards.

The universities and polytechnics adopt the system of external examiners for moderating internally set certification examinations. Colleges of education are likely to adopt the same procedure in future.

Promotion from one grade to another is usually based on performance during the school year in primary and secondary schools. In primary schools, however, because of the pressure of fresh intakes, only a very small proportion of pupils may be detained in any class.

Selection examinations to educational institutions have become increasingly centralized. The Joint Admissions and Matriculation Board (JAMB) conducts Joint Matriculation Examinations (JME) to the three categories of tertiary institutions. However, final selection is done by the institutions in consultation with JAMB. Admission is based on both the JME and the senior-secondary certificate.

The West African Examinations Council (WAEC) conducts common entrance examinations to federal government junior-secondary schools (unity schools) as well as to state-owned junior-secondary schools where the state governments so request. In many states, however, the ministries of education conduct entrance examinations to state-owned junior-secondary schools. Selection from junior- to senior-secondary schools is generally based on performance in the junior-secondary school certificate.

There are two new national examination bodies which have been established in order to reduce the examination load of the West African Examinations Council. One will deal with vocational and technical examinations, while the other will deal with selection examinations at secondary school level. The WAEC will thereafter concentrate mainly on senior-secondary school examinations.

9. Educational Assessment, Evaluation, and Research

The structure of the public service requires that every ministry should have a department of planning, research, and statistics. Such departments exist in the federal Ministry of Education and in all state ministries of education. They also exist in all the commissions (NUC, NBTE, NCCE, and the Mass Literacy Commission). These departments are supposed to organize assessments, evaluation, and research related to their respective portfolios.

Statistics of education are collected routinely on an annual basis. They cover such things as student enrollment, the number of teachers, graduate output, educational expenditure, transition rates, and enrollment ratios. Attention is paid to state and gender distributions.

Periodically, special research studies are commissioned by the federal Ministry or state ministries of education on specific problems such as educational inbalance; survey of resources for teaching science, mathematics, and technical subjects; tracer studies of products of the educational system; labor market surveys; standards of examinations; situation and policy analysis surveys; and so forth.

By 1992, there was no regular and systematic assessment of the performance of the system on a national scale, although such assessments are being planned.

Much education-related research goes on in tertiary institutions, and such institutions occasionally get involved in international surveys. For example, the University of Ibadan Institute of Education has participated in six of the IEA international surveys of educational achievement.

University budgets usually have specific allocations for research which vary in amount from one university to the other. The role of research in educational planning and management is becoming increasingly recognized.

10. Major Reforms in the 1980s and 1990s

The major educational reform has been the implementation of the new national policy on education first promulgated in 1977 and revised in 1981. The main structural change was in the secondary school.

Hitherto, secondary schooling consisted of five years up to GCE O level, followed by two years up to GCE A level. This structure was replaced by three years of junior-secondary and three years of senior-secondary schooling. The GCE O level and A level have consequently been phased out, and replaced by the Junior School Certificate and Senior School Certificate. The content of the secondary school curriculum has also changed. Junior-secondary schools have become both academic and prevocational. Graduates of junior-secondary schools may proceed into one of three categories of institutions: (a) senior-secondary schools, (b) technical/vocational colleges, and (c) teacher-training colleges.

Another area of reform was in curriculum. Curricula had to be modified at all three levels of education to conform with the national philosophy of education and national development goals spelt out in the new policy. There is an increased leaning toward science and technology. There is also a new emphasis on general studies in the universities intended to give a broad-based knowledge in addition to specializations. New areas, such as environmental education and population education, have also been introduced into the curricula at primary and secondary schools.

There has been increased centralized control of tertiary education through the three national commissions and the introduction of accreditation to enforce certain minimum standards in tertiary education.

Finally, there is a policy of decentralizing public examination bodies such that, in addition to the monolithic West African Examinations Council, there are two other national examination bodies. Associated with examinations is also the insistence on continuous assessment.

11. Major Problems for the Year 2000

Like most developing countries in the world, a major problem for the education system is the attainment of "education for all by the year 2000" as presented in the *World Declaration on Education for All* at Jomtien, Thailand in 1990. Universalization of access and promotion of equity in basic education pose formidable problems in Nigeria.

In 1992 a Commission on the review of higher education in Nigeria was created. Its recommendations (already submitted) are likely to have far-reaching effects on the control, funding, and management of tertiary institutions, especially universities. Some of the current problems are: (a) an arbitrary increase in the number of universities; (b) inadequate funding of existing ones; (c) pronounced deterioration of existing facilities; (d) massive brain drain of tertiary education teachers; (e) persistent erosion of university autonomy by government; and (f) a serious lowering of the standard of education.

One of the most intractable problems in 1994 was the question of appropriate renumeration for university academic staff. This problem led to closure of universities and other tertiary institutions for long periods of time with the result that students, in some cases, lost a complete year of studies. Another difficult problem was the emergence of "secret cults" in the tertiary institutions. These cults constituted themselves into an independent force for manipulating life in general in tertiary institutions, largely in a negative direction involving brutal initiation ceremonies and considerable violence in the imposition of their norms.

The implementation of the Commission's recommendations for tackling these problems is likely to extend to the year 2000 and beyond.

The general political, social, and economic instability in the country arising largely from the scuttling of the transition to democracy by the former military government has had serious repercussions on the educational system as a whole. With the dissolution of the state houses of assembly and local government councils, a state of uncertainty prevails at the secondary and primary education levels. It is true that even before the scuttling of the democratic process, problems of inadequate funding and management existed at these levels but they have now been compounded many times over.

In general, the major problem for education in Nigeria in the coming years will be the establishment of a new basis for confidence in the education system. In the early 1990s, such confidence is at its lowest ebb.

References

Brann C M B 1977 Language planning for education in Nigeria: Some demographic, linguistic and real factors. In: FME National Language Centre 1977 *Language in Education in Nigeria. Vol. 1: Proceedings of the Language Symposium of November 1977*. National Language Centre, Lagos

Fafunwa A B, Macauley J T, Sokoya J A F (eds.) 1989 *Education in Mother Tongue*. University Press, Ibadan

Hansford K, Bendor-Samuel J, Stanford R 1976 *Studies in Nigerian Languages*. Ghana Summer Institute for Linguistics, Accra

Federal Republic of Nigeria 1981 *National Policy on Education (Revised)*. NERDC Press, Lagos

Further Reading

Chizea C A (ed.) 1983 *Twenty Years of University Education in Nigeria*. National Universities Commission, Lagos

Fafunwa A B 1971 *A History of Nigerian Higher Education*. Macmillan, Lagos

Federal Republic of Nigeria 1977 *Implementation Committee for the National Policy on Education: Blueprint 1978–79*. Federal Government Printers, Lagos

Ozigi A O L 1981 *Education in Northern Nigeria*. Allen and Unwin, London

Taiwo C O 1980 *The Nigerian Education System*. Nelson, Lagos

Yoloye E A 1989 Cross currents in the evolution of educational planning strategies: The Nigerian experience. In: IIEP 1989 25th Anniversary Workshop Booklet No. 5 *Educational Planning in Practice*.

Norway

I. R. Bjørndal

1. General Background

Norway, with an area of 200,000 square kilometers, is comparable in size to Britain, Poland, or Italy. Its coastline is 2,656 kilometers long, and many of the numerous fjords reach far into the country. Its population of 4 million inhabitants, twice as many as in the late nineteenth century, give it a population density of 21 persons per square kilometer, the lowest in Europe after Iceland. Industrial growth since the middle of the nineteenth century brought more people into towns, particularly in the southeast. However, much of the population is still widely dispersed, and most of the towns are small; it is the many small, local communities that give Norwegian society its distinctive character.

There is broad political agreement on maintaining this population pattern which contributes so much to the quality of life in Norway. Educational institutions are an important factor in ensuring its survival.

Modern Norway has a substantial degree of social and economic equality, a high standard of living, and a largely homogeneous population. A measure of immigration has nevertheless given the larger towns a more varied cultural and ethnic population. In the far north there are the Sami people, an ethnic minority whose livelihood has been based largely on reindeer herding, hunting, and fishing. They speak a language totally different from Norwegian, and have preserved much of their traditional culture.

The year 1814, when the 400-year union with Denmark was brought to an end, marks the start of Norway's modern history. A democratic constitution was drawn up and a constitutional monarchy established. The new union with Sweden lasted from 1814 to 1905.

The Labor Party (social democratic) held power, with two short breaks, from 1935 to 1981; minority governments have since then been formed alternately by the Labor Party and the center/right-wing parties.

The structure of industry has changed considerably since the Second World War. Employment in primary industries has declined dramatically. Heavy industry saw a fall in employment, while the service industries expanded considerably, with a 55 percent increase in numbers employed between 1972 and 1989. The percentage of the labor force working in primary, secondary, and tertiary sectors are 5.8, 38.2, and 56.0 respectively.

The decline of the traditional industries and the growth of the tertiary sector seem to have important implications for educational planning. It leads to a need to raise the level of education nationwide and get away from too much early specialization. The need for a better system of recurrent education and opportunities for life-long education seems to be another implication.

A levelling of incomes has occurred since 1890, and class distinctions are few in Norway. Economic growth and full employment have been important political goals. Until 1987–88 unemployment was very low, but in 1990 it was up to 5.2 percent. Unemployment has hit young people hardest, and the authorities have used the educational system as a tool in the fight against unemployment.

Norway has large offshore oil and gas resources. Production has expanded rapidly, providing a substantial contribution to national income. Norway is now regarded as one of the world's richest countries.

Equal opportunity for all, regardless of social and cultural background, gender, or place of residence, has been an important goal of educational policy. As early as 1920, Parliament established the unitary school, ensuring that all further education should build on the foundation of a complete, seven-year period of compulsory schooling.

It is important that as many children as possible should receive an education up to the completion of upper-secondary school without having to move away from home. This means that very small schools are commonplace in Norway.

Everyone has an equal right to education. Education at all levels in public schools and universities is free of charge; practically all children at the primary and lower-secondary level attend public schools, as do 96 percent of pupils at the upper-secondary level. All schools accept pupils of both sexes, and all classes are mixed. The curriculum is the same for both sexes.

2. Politics and the Goals of the Education System

There has been full agreement on providing the same basic primary and lower-secondary schooling for all. It is unthinkable, in Norway, to separate children at the age of 11 or 12 and send them to different kinds of schools. But the right-wing parties do support a certain amount of organizational differentiation in the final stage of lower-secondary education and somewhat stricter curriculum guidelines. Nevertheless, the differences of opinion are small.

Greater disagreement emerged over the structure of upper-secondary education. When the 1974 Act on Upper Secondary Education was debated in Parliament, the Labor Party wanted all schools for 16–19-year olds to be organized as combined schools (i.e., schools offering a broad range of courses, academic and vocational, on one campus with one administration). Parliament would not accept this. The majority felt that the regional authority, as owner, ought to decide how the individual school should be organized. It is, therefore, interesting to note that all schools built since 1974 have been planned as combined schools, regardless of the political color of the region. One reason for this is that organizing schools in this way has made it possible to establish separate upper-secondary schools in sparsely populated areas. But even in urban areas combined schools have been preferred. Pupils in combined schools receive the same standard of teaching and take the same examinations in their chosen subjects as they would in separate schools.

There is agreement in Norway that education at all levels is primarily a public responsibility, but that the state ought to support financially schools that have a religious foundation or offer an interesting pedagogical alternative. The right-wing parties would like to see more private schools receiving state support at all levels, to give state schools stronger competition. They wish to give pupils freedom of choice among schools, while the other parties wish to avoid a system in which schools differ widely in quality.

One might say that the Labor Party and the parties of the center place more emphasis on equality of opportunity, while the parties to the right emphasize academic standards and the needs of commerce and industry. However, the differences are more of degree than of kind. When Parliament debates proposals relating to education, there is seldom disagreement about aims and principles.

There was, however, always a certain amount of disagreement about the National Council for Innovation in Education, which had responsibility for innovation and development work in Norwegian schools for 30 years. The Council played a major part in the introduction of the nine-year compulsory school (1969) and the Act on Upper Secondary Education (1974). The center/right parties abolished the Council after they came to power in 1981, and proposed instead that innovative work should on the whole be based on the individual school, and should derive from local initiatives and needs.

3. The Formal System of Education

3.1 Primary, Secondary, and Tertiary Education

Figure 1 presents the structure and enrollments of the educational system. Table 1 provides figures on enrollments and costs.

The 1887 Education Act established a compulsory seven-year period of schooling for all. The Basic Education Act of 1969 extended compulsory education to nine years and abolished the differences between urban and rural schools.

Primary education covers Grades 1 to 6, while lower-secondary education covers Grades 7 to 9. Where numbers are high enough there is a preference for separate schools for Grades 7 to 9; this makes it possible to provide more specialized equipment and also gives the pupils a change of environment.

The Ministry of Education determines the subjects taught, the minimum teaching hours, and teachers' qualifications. The curriculum guidelines for primary and lower-secondary education establish the national framework of learning and teaching. They state the principles; define the goals and central, compulsory

Table 1
Enrollments and resources in formal education, Norway 1990

	Schools		Higher education	
	Primary and lower secondary	Upper secondary	Regional sector	University sector
Number of students	473,000	224,000	70,000	60,000
Percentage of age group enrolled				
age 16–17		95		
17–18		80		
18–19		70		
19–26			—[a]	—[a]
Number of institutions	3,406	678	131[b]	14[c]
Average number of students per institution	139	330	535	4,286
Student–teacher ratio	14:1	12:1	14:1	14:1
Expenditure per student (NKr)	35,000	33,000	27,000	61,000

a Figures not available   b Includes 22 private colleges with government grants   c Four universities and ten research colleges, including four private with government grants

contents of all the subjects; and give advice on methods, aids, and pupil assessment. More detailed syllabus planning is left to the individual school.

The maximum number of pupils per class is 28 in primary and 30 in lower-secondary school. The average number is 18 in primary school and 22.5 in lower-secondary school. Large schools are viewed as inimical to a good learning environment, and the maximum size of new schools is set at 450 pupils.

The total number of lessons in Grades 1 to 3 has been increased. A reduction of the starting age to 6 will take place from 1997. The starting age of 7 was justified by hard winters and the distance from home to school.

With more one-parent families and working mothers, the need for more organized activities beyond the normal school day has been recognized by the government, which is strongly encouraging developments in this area.

The upper-secondary school is responsible for all education between compulsory and higher education. It covers Grades 10 to 12, and the pupils are generally aged 16 to 19. The proportion of older pupils is rising, because increasingly more return to school to complete or supplement their education. Upper-secondary education is open to all who have completed compulsory education.

The Upper Secondary Education Act was passed in 1974 after 10 years of development work. The Act had its origin in a wish to build a more comprehensive and flexible system which would correspond better to the different interests and abilities of the pupils, and the needs of industry and society. The aim was to strengthen practical areas of education, make possible a combination of academic and practical studies, and encourage the large majority of young people to gain an upper-secondary education.

Regional authorities were given responsibility for planning and running upper-secondary education. They were charged with providing places for all applicants and with meeting, as far as possible, the individual educational wishes of the pupils. While attention was paid to the needs of industry, the wishes of the pupils themselves were emphasized. A further goal was the expansion of upper-secondary education in all parts of the country, thus satisfying the ideal of equal opportunities for all.

Pupils could choose either general studies or one of the nine vocational areas of study, or a combination of the two. When there are more applicants than places, previous school marks are the main selection criterion.

The educational debate in Norway has occasionally been lively. Critics have asserted that the standard of upper-secondary education has fallen. Most of the debate centers on general studies. Those who defend the new upper-secondary system draw attention to the fact that the proportion of young people taking general studies has risen from 15 to 40–45 percent of the age cohort since the early 1960s, and that it has been necessary to offer a greater degree of freedom in the choice of subjects in order to provide an education that meets the needs of a more differentiated body of pupils. While this necessarily results in a wider range of achievement, the mean level of education in the population as a whole has risen.

Apprenticeship is a tradition in technical and industrial fields. A number of incentives have been provided by the authorities to encourage businesses to offer more apprenticeships. Many trades can now be learnt either by receiving all the training in a company, or almost all of it in school, or by a combination of the two.

The traditional European ideal of an elite school has been abandoned, and upper-secondary education for all who have completed compulsory education is fully accepted by all political parties. All education at this level—general studies as well as vocational training—has been gathered into one system under one Act.

The Organisation for Economic Co-operation and Development (OECD), in its 1987 report, found the expansion of upper-secondary education in Norway remarkable; but they saw the need for more thorough work on course content and questioned the extent to which the national goals and values so strongly emphasized by Parliament could be ensured (OECD 1987). OECD also recommended exploring methods of evaluating the work done in schools and establishing a body of statistics that would provide a solid basis for educational planning and management. These recommendations are now being effected.

In 1980, 80 percent of the age cohort entered the first year of upper-secondary education, 70 percent

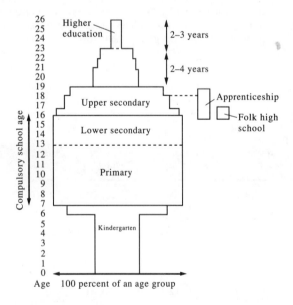

Figure 1
Norway: Structure of the formal education system 1990

entered the second year, and 50 percent the third. By 1990 the figures had risen to 95, 80, and 70 percent respectively. The course in general studies is developed fully enough for almost all pupils to be able to complete all three years. In several vocational areas, however, there are insufficient second- and third-year courses, even when apprenticeships are included. The deficiency became marked as the number of applicants increased during the 1980s, and many pupils enrolled on successive foundation courses because they were unable to advance to the next level. The government therefore set up extra classes and met all the costs in order to avoid rejecting large numbers of young people and aggravating the unemployment situation.

The aim is to provide three years of upper-secondary education for all who wish it, either in school or in a training scheme; from 1994, this is a legal right for the individual.

Higher education includes all education beyond the upper-secondary level. Originally all higher education was provided by traditional academic institutions. The oldest and largest of these is the University of Oslo, founded in 1811. After the Second World War, further universities were established in Bergen, Trondheim, and Tromsø.

What characterizes these institutions is their double function—research and teaching—and their high degree of autonomy. The four universities offer three levels of degrees: lower (after four years), higher (after five to seven years), and doctorates. In addition, the universities and other higher-level teaching and research institutions provide five- to seven-year courses in such professional areas as law, medicine, agriculture, and engineering.

The other group of post-secondary institutions is the regional colleges, of which the oldest are the colleges of education. At the end of the 1960s a new type of regional college (*distriktshøgskoler*) was established to offer shorter courses which prepare students for specific areas of work, as an alternative to the longer university courses. They attract large numbers of students.

Regional colleges also relieve pressure on universities by offering basic courses in such areas as modern languages and traditional arts subjects. In many cases students can combine courses at regional colleges and universities.

Regional colleges have played an important part in the decentralization of higher education in Norway. The goal has been to offer educational opportunities to as many people as possible at this level, and to provide a higher level of professional competence in the regions.

During the 1970s and 1980s several kinds of institutions have been upgraded to higher education level. These include colleges of education, nursing, and engineering. Entry requirements are the same as for other types of higher education, and teaching qualifications have been raised. Regional colleges also conduct a certain amount of research, often directly related to the needs of the region.

The upgrading of existing colleges and the growth of new regional colleges provide a widespread network of state-funded regional colleges. A number of the colleges are very small, however, and work is in progress to merge institutions which lie close to each other, partly with a view to achieving a more rational use of resources, and partly to give the institutions more academic muscle.

Numbers in higher education rose from approximately 75,000 to 115,000 in the course of the 1980s. Since 1988 many additional places have been provided, and in the autumn of 1994 student numbers in public institutions reached 160,000. About half of them are in regional colleges. Some 35–40 percent of the age cohort now receives some form of higher education.

Costs in higher education are met entirely by the state. There are a limited number of approved private higher institutions which offer studies in economics, technical subjects, and theology; they are regarded as a supplement to the state institutions and receive a high level of government support, but students pay a fee for the teaching.

Norway has a long and solid tradition of studying abroad. Despite the considerable expansion of higher education, between 8,000 and 9,000 young people still study in other countries. Additional government scholarships and loans are available for studies regarded as especially relevant for the country.

3.2 Preschool Education

Kindergartens are run both by public and private organizations in accordance with the 1975 Act. Private kindergartens receive a large measure of financial support, provided they meet requirements concerning buildings and equipment and employ qualified staff. Activities in kindergartens focus principally on structured play. The local authority is responsible for the expansion of kindergartens, but central authorities give financial help. During the 1980s the number of kindergartens doubled, but the proportion of Norwegian children under school age who attend kindergartens is still only 40 percent. The training of preschool teachers, and building of more kindergartens are therefore priority issues.

3.3 Special Education

The Education Act of 1975 gave handicapped children the same right to education as other children. They are to be provided with schooling in their home environment and at their local school. This is a basic principle. In classes containing handicapped pupils, additional resources are provided. If pupils cannot be fully integrated, they are taught in small groups. A few special schools remain for those whose needs cannot otherwise be met (2%).

The 1985 changes in the Upper-Secondary Education Act gave handicapped pupils with attested needs priority of admission, and by 1990 6 percent of the age cohort were admitted under this rule. The Act also requires local and regional authorities to establish a pedagogical/psychological advisory service to provide support in this work.

3.4 Vocational, Technical, and Business Education

Training in vocational, technical, and business courses takes place partly in school and partly at the place of work. After the 1974 Upper Secondary Education Act the area of study for commercial and clerical subjects expanded greatly; it now offers a full three-year course satisfying matriculation requirements. In the area of study for technical and industrial subjects, substantial efforts have been made to establish more apprenticeships, and the number has now doubled to approximately 20,000. The authorities encourage pupils to take the first two years of basic training in school and the final, specialized stage in industry.

Training councils, nominated by the different trades, develop training programs for the individual courses which are coordinated with the subject syllabuses used in the schools. Local examining boards are responsible for the award of subject and craft certificates. The syllabuses used in schools are based on training programs in industry. The representatives of industry therefore have substantial influence on the content of vocational courses in schools.

3.5 Adult Education

Adult education is seen as an important part of the educational system; there is a long tradition of adult education in Norway, partly under the auspices of independent organizations, partly in the form of folk high schools.

Adult education not aiming at specific qualifications and examinations is traditionally the responsibility of independent organizations. Responsibility for courses preparing for public examinations is primarily in the hands of the schools. Another section of adult education is the labor market courses, in line with the government's employment policy. With growing unemployment, these courses have expanded considerably. Distance learning, which began as correspondence courses, also has strong roots in thinly populated Norway. Some 16 correspondence schools were receiving support under the Correspondence School Act in the early 1990s. In 1988–89, 745,000 people (of whom 57% were women) took part in courses run by the independent adult education organizations.

Folk high schools provide young people and adults with a liberal education, building on basic schooling. There are around 100 folk high schools in Norway in the early 1990s, largely boarding schools run by a variety of organizations. Most of their costs are met by state grants.

4. Administrative and Supervisory Structure and Operation

Education in Norway is a national responsibility. The local authority is responsible for compulsory education (Grades 1 to 9); the regional authority is responsible for upper-secondary education (Grades 10 to 12); and central government is responsible for higher education (universities and university-level institutions).

Parliament passes laws, approves the Ministry's annual budget, and debates the long-term aims of educational policy on the basis of government white papers.

The government provides financial assistance to the running of primary, lower-secondary, and upper-secondary schools. The costs of universities and other institutions of higher learning are wholly met by central government.

In the 1970s and 1980s there was a clear tendency toward a decentralization of administrative responsibility within all parts of the educational system. Responsibility for primary and lower-secondary schools in individual local authority areas rests with the education committees, bodies appointed by the local authorities. Responsibility for upper-secondary education rests with the regional education committees appointed by the regional authorities.

Higher education is organized in two sectors. The first includes the universities and traditional scientific research institutions. These have always had a large measure of autonomy, underlined in the University Act of 1 January 1990. Each institution is headed by an elected principal and a board on which representatives of faculty, students, and other employees sit. The other sector consists of the regional colleges. They too have a large measure of autonomy, coordinated by a regional board of higher education appointed by the Ministry.

The Ministry of Education, Research, and Church Affairs has final responsibility for education at all levels. Comprhensive changes have been carried through in the organization and administration of the educational system. The national school councils, who arranged the national examinations, worked out the framework for subject syllabuses, and advised the Ministry on all sorts of educational matters, were terminated from 1991 after 100 years of existence. The regional offices for primary education, with a similarly long tradition were abolished in 1992. The tasks formerly performed by these organs were transferred to the Ministry, to a new National Center for Educational Resources, and to the new national education offices representing the Ministry in the 18 regions of the country.

5. Educational Finance

Funds for higher education and research are apportioned by the Ministry to the different institutions. The financing of upper-secondary education is calculated according to specific criteria, and the funds are transferred to regional authorities as part of the general grant. Similarly, funds for primary and lower-secondary education are transferred to local authorities.

Businesses which accept apprentices and offer them contracts receive state support. Apprentices receive wages at 50 to 90 percent of the average full rate.

In the 1990 financial year the total education and research budget (public funding) was in the region of NKr46,000 million. Expenditure on education measured as a percentage of Gross National Product (GNP) rose from 2 percent in 1945 to 6.4 percent in 1980 and 7 percent in 1990. In the mid-1990s education accounts for approximately 15 percent of public expenditure. These figures place Norway among the countries with the highest per pupil expenditure. The government intends to spend more, in relative terms, on higher education and research throughout the 1990s.

In 1993, 46 percent of the budget went to primary education, 30 percent to upper-secondary education (including vocational education), and 27 percent to higher education.

6. Supplying Personnel for the Education System

A total of 54,000 full-time teachers worked in the public school system in 1990: 34,000 were employed in primary and lower-secondary schools, 1,000 in special schools for handicapped children, and 19,000 in upper-secondary schools. Some 43 percent were female.

All teacher training for schools is controlled by the 1973 Teacher Education Act. This Act states the level of subject competence needed to qualify as a teacher at different levels from preschool to upper-secondary school. The Act also defines the three levels: teachers with basic qualifications, teachers with first-degree qualifications, and teachers with higher degrees. To qualify as a teacher in technical and industrial subjects in the upper-secondary school, a trade certificate and work experience are required in the appropriate trade, as well as a period of pedagogical training.

Teachers with first-degree qualifications have studied for at least four years; teachers with higher degrees have at least six years of study behind them. They must have studied at least two teaching subjects and attended a one-semester practical/pedagogical course. Most teachers in the general area of study have this academic background. The academic level attained determines the teacher's salary scale, while the type of school and subjects taught determine the number of class contact periods the teacher will have.

There generally has been strong recruitment to teacher-training colleges since the Second World War. Graduate courses, on the other hand, have had more varied recruitment, and there has at times been a shortage of higher-degree candidates to the teaching profession. The authorities have introduced measures to encourage more students to take higher degrees, both in school-related subjects and in other subjects.

The status of teachers is still, on the whole, quite high as the level of applications to teacher-training colleges indicates. Training institutions and education authorities run many inservice courses at which attendance is, in the main, voluntary. There is a shift toward more school-based inservice training.

7. Curriculum Development and Teaching Methodology

The first curriculum for primary and lower-secondary schools that presented guidelines rather than detailed syllabuses was introduced in 1971 (revised 1987). It emphasizes attention to the needs of the individual pupil.

During the first seven grades at school all pupils have largely the same set of subjects. In Grades 8 and 9 some optional subjects can be taken in addition to the compulsory subjects, but the same class units continue to the end of compulsory schooling, except in optional subjects where pupils are recruited from different classes.

The first foreign language is English and is a compulsory subject from the age of 10 years. Importance is given to encouraging an active use of the language and most younger Norwegians speak English fairly well. Pupils can take a second foreign language at the age of 14 years; German is the first choice and French the second. The proportion of pupils taking a second foreign language in addition to English is an unsatisfactory 40 percent.

The curriculum now has more solid roots in the local situation of each school; but it must be emphasized that it is still the Education Act and the curriculum guidelines that are the basis of work in all schools.

The overriding aims of upper-secondary education are concretized in the general section of the curriculum; when a subject syllabus is drawn up, content selected, and methods proposed, these elements are seen in the light of the overriding aims. Subject syllabuses in the upper-secondary school are also in the form of guidelines, but the demands of examinations and certificates are a powerful controlling factor in the schools. This is a dilemma.

All pupils take three categories of subjects: general subjects, area of study subjects, and optional subjects. A large number of vocational courses give very limited time to general subjects and optional subjects. There is greatest flexibility in the general area of study.

The most important learning tool is still the textbook. Course books are subject to approval by the Ministry, but are published by commercial publishers. The Ministry did, however, take the initiative in the middle of the 1980s in producing an action plan for information technology in schools, partly with the aim of developing pedagogical software.

8. The System of Examinations, Promotions, and Certifications

There is no formal assessment of pupils in primary schools. In lower-secondary schools, pupils are awarded grades in compulsory subjects twice a year. A final written examination administered over the whole country is held in Norwegian, English, and mathematics. Although upper-secondary education is open to all who have completed compulsory education, pupils must satisfy minimum requirements to proceed from one level to the next.

In the general area of study and the area of study for commercial and clerical subjects in the upper-secondary school, national examinations are held in Norwegian and one or two selected advanced subjects. The pupil's certificate includes both the grade awarded by the school and that obtained in the examination. In other areas of study, local examinations are the rule. Successful completion of the general area of study or the area of study for commercial and clerical subjects, or certain other combinations, satisfies general matriculation requirements. For many higher studies, specific subject combinations are demanded.

9. Educational Assessment, Evaluation, and Research

The 1987 OECD report pointed to the need for new evaluation procedures to ensure that national educational aims are put into practice (OECD 1987). Norway, like other countries, is attempting to arrive at some means of achieving a reasonable degree of supervision of what schools do, while at the same time stimulating a process of renewal and development in the individual school. From 1992, the Government Director of Education in each region has the task of collecting and processing information about the entire educational scene in the region and contributing to the central authority's overview of developments.

Research in education has traditionally concentrated on the area of pedagogy, and there is some criticism that this research has been too theoretical and of little help to practitioners. More recently, it has become common to make arrangements for the external evaluation of all larger projects, and evaluation research has come into the foreground. A five-year program by the Ministry aims at stimulating educational research.

10. Major Reforms in the 1980s and 1990s

In primary and lower-secondary education, the 1987 curriculum guidelines will be revised to comply with a greater emphasis on management by objectives as applied to the individual unit. The position of the second foreign language will be strengthened. Further, the development of a first year of primary education for 6-year olds from 1997 and the so-called "all-day school" will be given priority.

In upper-secondary schools there has been a continuing expansion of places, particularly in vocational areas of study and in apprenticeship training. There are too few places in the advanced technical and industrial courses. The disappearance of work opportunities for young people and the need for higher qualifications make it necessary to create more places both in schools and in industry.

In addition, the structure of vocational education in the upper-secondary school will be simplified and much broader foundation courses provided, with later specialization and more emphasis on theoretical subjects; this is in keeping with a new White Paper (1992). A stronger foundation for lifelong learning and new ways into higher education should result. Further objectives are that languages should be strengthened, not only in general studies, but also in vocational areas; that all branches of education should offer courses of three years' duration; and that all courses should lead to matriculation or a trade certificate. At the same time, admission to higher education should be less rigid, and also open to people with vocational backgrounds.

Within higher education, higher degrees, doctoral programs, and research will be strengthened. In the regional sector, smaller colleges will be amalgamated from 1994 to form 26 larger study centers. Together with the universities and university-level institutions they will form a national network with shared responsibilities, offering students the opportunity to switch between institutions.

11. Major Problems for the Year 2000

Changes in the employment situation mean that continued schooling is the only available activity for most young people when they complete their lower-secondary education. At the age of 18 apprenticeship is a possibility, but too few contracts are available. Many who enter upper-secondary schools have little motivation, and to offer courses which pupils in this category find useful and relevant is a huge problem. If these problems are not solved successfully, a deterioration of the learning milieu may result. This, in turn, will place an additional burden on the teachers. Teachers are not sufficiently well-trained to cope with the considerable differentiation problems that will arise. The massive influx of students to higher education will place greater pedagogical demands on this sector than before. Teacher training will therefore have to be strengthened at all levels.

Another problem is to find the balance between national control and local freedom and initiative. The

Ministry is seeking to establish a national system of school evaluation which will give national authorities a reasonable degree of certainty that national goals are being pursued, while at the same time stimulating renewal locally and encouraging improvement in the individual school.

References

OECD 1987 *Reviews of National Policies for Education, Norway*. OECD, Oslo

Further Reading

Bjørndal I R 1992 *The Norwegian Educational System*. Royal Ministry of Foreign Affairs, Oslo

Central Office of Statistics 1991 *Statistical Yearbook of Norway*. Central Office of Statistics, Oslo
Ministry of Education 1991a *Education in Norway*. Royal Ministry of Education, Research, and Church Affairs, Oslo
Ministry of Education 1991b *Government White Paper on Organization and Management in the Educational Sector*. Royal Ministry of Education, Research, and Church Affairs, Akademika, Oslo
Ministry of Education 1991c *From Vision to Work*. Government White Paper on Higher Education. Royal Ministry of Education, Research, and Church Affairs, Akademika, Oslo
National Council for Compulsory Education 1990 *Curriculum Guidelines for Compulsory Education in Norway*. National Council for Compulsory Education, Oslo
Rust V D 1989 *The Democratic Tradition and the Evolution of Schooling in Norway*. Greenwood Press, New York
Ness E (ed.) 1990–91 *Skolens Årbok*. Aschehoug, Oslo
Telhaug A O 1986 *Norsk skoleutvikling etter 1945*. Didakta, Oslo

Oman

A. M. Al-Shanfari

1. General Background

Oman is situated in the eastern corner of the Arabian peninsula and has a coastline which extends for 1,700 kilometers. To the west the country borders Saudi Arabia and the Emirates, to the south Yemen, to the north the Strait of Hormuz, and to the east the Arabian Sea. The total land area is 322,000 square kilometers. Most of the country is either desert or barren land, with sand and gravel covering at least 80 percent of the country. There are several islands near the coast in the Gulf of Oman and in the Strait of Hormuz, as well as the Islands of Masirah and Al Halaniat Islands (Kuria Muria) in the Arabian Sea. The climate varies from north to south. In the coastal areas, it is hot and humid in summer, while in the interior it is hot and dry. In the southern region the climate is more benign.

The majority of the population in Oman is Arab. There are other ethnic minorities in the country, mainly Balushies, Khojas Lawatiyas, or Hyderbadiyin who originated from India and Pakistan. There are also smaller numbers of Persians and Hindus. The other groups are Zanzibaris, Arabs of Oman who once lived in Zanzibar and returned to Oman. It has been estimated that the Arabs in Oman constitute 85 percent of the population. The official language is Arabic but English is widely spoken and used for commercial purposes.

There had never been a population census in the Sultanate of Oman until 1993. According to the December 1993 census Oman is inhabited by 2.018 million people.

Agriculture and fishing were the backbone of the economy in Oman up to 1970. Even in the 1990s, in a period where petroleum production is high, over half the population is engaged in agriculture and fishing. Out of 100,000 hectares of cultivable land, 60,000 are under cultivation in 1994, and the government is aiming to achieve self-sufficiency in food by the year 2000, thus achieving an annual growth rate of 6.6 percent. Oil was discovered in Oman in 1954, but the export of crude oil only began in 1967. The whole aspect of the economy was changed when HM Sultan Qaboos took power in 1970. This was related to two main factors: first the new pattern of government, and second the export of crude oil. The crude oil exports and the subsequent rise in government income brought great change in the economy of the country. Besides oil, copper has also been found. The production of copper was 20,000 tons in 1985 and in 1992 it was estimated at 38,000 tons.

The fundamental problem that faced the country after 1970 was the shortage of labor. The Five Year Development Plans emphasized the importance of human resource development. Government policy towards developing human resources has been emphasized in its training policy. A number of technical schools and institutes have been established in order to prepare qualified indigenous labor. Investment in education and training has been a priority target for the government since 1970.

2. Politics and the Goals of the Education System

Modern education was not known in Oman before 1940. The most common form of education at that time was the *kuttab*, where a group of boys or girls were taught to recite the Koran, and sometimes learned basic writing and arithmetical skills. This kind of education took place in mosques, houses, or even under trees. There were no organized classrooms, no chairs, and no well-defined textbooks, apart from the Koran. The teachers were responsible for everything from organizing the teaching method to the type of books from which they were teaching.

The first official supervisory body for education in Oman was established in 1940. When Sultan Said bin Taimur was in power from 1932 to 1970, he established three schools in the country. During the period 1940–1970, there were only 909 male students in those schools and 30 teachers in the whole country. Although the *kuttabs* remained the main form of education the three "modern" schools taught other subjects as well as Islamic teachings. However, in 1970 a period of great educational development and devolution began. The aim was to have every child enrolled in school even if it meant receiving instruction in the shade of a tree or in a tent. At the same time, it was recognized that there should be an improvement in the quality of education.

The education system is based on Islamic and Sharia (Law of Islam) principles. At the same time it aims to be modernized to be in line with the technological developments of the modern world. Education should aim at freeing individuals and groups from ignorance and backwardness and should prepare citizens to acquire the necessary technical and professional knowledge and skills for the development of the country.

Education is a right for all individuals in Omani society. The Sultanate responds to the social demand for education without limits. Education aims at developing the mental faculties of individuals to enable them to understand scientific facts and acquire practical skills. It also aims at strengthening the individual's belief in God by teaching the basic fundamentals of the Islamic religion and the ideals that are derived from it, so that students' religious life may guide their deeds and conduct. Education seeks to develop positive sentiments and attitudes in individuals in order that they respect nature and appreciate its beauty; it also helps the individual to value intellectual and scientific innovations, particularly the contribution of Islamic thought in these fields.

It is intended that education should pay sufficient attention to the physical growth of students to allow them to acquire good habits to promote health. The growth of the individual's body should be in accordance with the growth of his or her character and mind. Education also aims at developing the idea of patriotism and citizenship as well as respect for the heritage, national achievements, and pride in the Arab people.

Finally, education aims to work for the best interests of individuals and their society.

3. The Formal System of Education

3.1 Primary, Secondary, and Tertiary Education

The education system is based on a 6–3–3 pattern. This consists of six years primary, three years preparatory, and three years secondary education. These three levels are similar to most Arab countries which have adopted the recommendation of the Arab League conference of 1965, held in Cairo. The educational structure of the Sultanate of Oman is divided into a number of stages (see Fig. 1).

There is no compulsory education for children of school age. Enrollment at the primary level is open to all children in the country within the school age limit (6–8). Those who are over 8-years old can join the adult education schools. There is no coeducation in Oman.

Children who have reached the age of six years can enroll for primary education which provides basic education and prepares them for preparatory and then secondary education. The curriculum covers the teaching of Arabic and English languages, Islamic education, general science, arithmetic, social studies, fine arts, and physical education.

The preparatory level is a three-year program after primary level. Although introduced during the academic year 1972–73, there was considerable demand that resulted in rapid growth.

Secondary education comprises the final three years of school after preparatory education. Students at this level are generally prepared either for university education or other specialized education necessary for the employment market. This level of education commenced in the academic year 1973–74. The first year provides general education and during the second

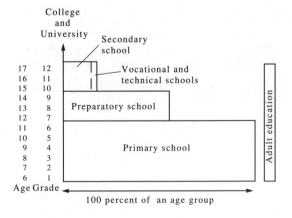

Figure 1

Oman: Structure of the formal education system

year students choose either science or arts sections. The science section includes mathematics, biology, physics, and chemistry while the arts section includes geography, history, sociology, and psychology, apart from Arabic and English languages and Islamic studies, which are taught in both sections.

Another type of secondary education is Islamic education. This type of education emphasizes Islamic teachings. There are seven institutes of this type in the whole country.

Agricultural, commercial, and technical secondary schools offer vocational education in their respective sections. Students at these schools are normally prepared for the employment market, although some acquire training in their respective field in order to assume medium supervisory level in employment.

There are three types of higher education programs existing in the country. The first is teacher training. The Primary Teacher Training Institute was officially founded in 1979, but teacher training had already begun in 1977 as a full-time class which was accommodated in one of the boys' secondary schools. This class, together with two new classes in 1978, provided the nucleus for the new institute. In 1984 the Ministry of Education introduced a new policy which upgraded teacher training for two years after secondary education. The name of the institute was changed to Intermediate College. The new policies are aimed at Omanizing teachers at the primary stage for both sexes. There are nine colleges, five for boys and four for girls.

The Oman Industrial College was opened in the academic year 1985–86. It was under the supervision of the Ministry of Social Affairs and Labor and later the Ministry of Labor and Vocational Training. There are two main courses, the technical section and the commercial section. In 1992 the Organization for Vocational Training took charge of the supervision of the college.

The Sultan Qaboos University was opened in the academic year 1986–87 with five colleges: science, medicine, agriculture, engineering, and education and Islamic studies.

It should be noted that there are two types of private school in the country. Some of these schools are run by Omanis, and others are established by communities living in the country. Schools such as the British school, Indian schools, Pakistani schools and others follow their countries' system of education, while the private schools follow the Omani curriculum. The Ministry of Education grants licenses to citizens who wish to operate general education private schools. The Ministry supervises these schools in order to ensure that their students enjoy appropriate educational facilities, and that instructional standards equivalent to those in state schools are maintained. This sector of general education caters for a good number of both native and expatriate students. The private schools use the same curricula and textbooks as the state schools. Examinations and certificates awarded are also the same.

3.2 Preschool Education

Preprimary nurseries are privately owned and few in number. The government has banned child minding, in the interests of the parents and children, and only licensed nurseries are allowed to operate under the supervision of the ministry concerned. The Ministry of Education issues licenses for running private kindergartens. Standardized curricula, teacher guides, and books are prepared by the Ministry of Education. Supervision of these schools is the responsibility of the Ministry of Education, which facilitates regular inspection visits to the private kindergartens. Teacher training and refresher courses are regularly organized by the Ministry of Education for those who work in kindergartens.

3.3 Special Education

There is one special educational school known as the Hope for Mutes school. It is located in the capital, Muscat, and offers mixed class programs for both males and females for two years. The educational policy in respect of the handicapped who are able to pursue their education is that they can join the handicapped schools in other Gulf States, especially in Bahrain and Kuwait.

3.4 Vocational, Technical, and Business Education

Vocational training is relatively new and can be dated back to the year 1967, when the Petroleum Development of Oman (PDO) attempted to train its lower level technical and clerical staff. A center was opened in Darsait, mainly to improve the skills of specific members of the technical and clerical labor force. By 1973 the vocational center in Darsait was under the supervision of the Ministry of Social Affairs and Labor. This was the first vocational center run by the Government of Oman officially. Since 1973 remarkable changes have taken place with regard to the development of vocational training in the whole country to fulfill the demands for labor force training. A Directorate for Vocational Training was established within the Ministry of Social Affairs and Labor. The Council for Vocational Training was introduced in the Ministry of Social Affairs in 1975. The main purposes of the Council were:

(a) specifying the needs of the country for a trained labor force in all specialties;

(b) planning vocational training programs to meet the demand for a trained labor force;

(c) recommending ways and resources for financing vocational training programs;

(d) setting the standards needed by the training programs.

An important target for the government was to expand vocational training by establishing vocational centers in different regions in order to offer facilities in all regions to enroll for training in different job skills.

By 1979 two types of technical secondary school were established. Commercial and agricultural schools were established in order to meet the needs for skilled labor in the Sultanate. Technical secondary education is now the responsibility of the Ministry of Education under the supervision of the Department of Technical Education. The Ministry of Education and the Ministry of Social Affairs and Labor have both taken responsibility for technical education and vocational training in the Sultanate.

The Second Five-Year Development Plan was a maturing period for technical education and vocational training. There were nine vocational training centers in the country. In 1984 these centers were upgraded from the preparatory to the secondary level in order to make vocational training more attractive.

Until 1983 technical education and vocational training had been a male domain, but in that year the first Commercial Secondary School for Women was opened. In 1985 a ministerial decree was issued to establish an industrial school in order to provide highly skilled labor to help in the development of the country.

Three main factors have affected the development of technical education and vocational training in the country: (a) the substantial development which took place in Oman from 1970 up to the 1990s; (b) the export of oil which brought with it substantial financial revenue; and (c) the shortage of skilled and semiskilled labor in the newly developed country.

The Third Five-Year Plan (1986–90) stressed the further development of technical education and vocational training centers, the necessity to raise the standard of vocational training, and the desire to improve productivity in all sectors of the economy. A further challenge is to decrease the number of expatriate workers in Oman.

Technical education is the responsibility of the Ministry of Education, while vocational training is that of the Ministry of Labor and Vocational Training. Technical and commercial secondary schools are well-organized by the Ministry of Education to provide students with knowledge and skills needed for semiskilled labor. The Ministry of Labor and Vocational Training also used to run vocational institutes to help graduating semi-skilled laborors. However, as from the school year 1993–94 these institutes have been converted by the Council for Vocational Training into technical colleges. Postsecondary school students graduate from these colleges after three years as members of the technical labor force.

3.5 Adult and Nonformal Education

The introduction of nonformal education took place in the absence of any formal education in Oman for many years except for three primary schools. In the early 1970s the government committed itself to providing education for those who had not had the chance of attending school.

Literacy and adult education centers are run by the government in a joint effort by the Ministry of Education and the Ministry of Labor and Vocational Training. Contributions from individuals in the form of help with setting up study premises and transporting teachers and students from houses to classes are also accelerating the rate of progress in this field. Literacy courses last two years. After successful completion, students who wish to continue their education can join adult education centers, where they receive the same instruction as is available in formal education schools and colleges.

The Ministry of Education is responsible for developing adult education. The Ministry offers four years of primary, three years of preparatory, and three years of secondary education. In addition, students can register as home students and attend the final examinations only. There are four subjects at the primary level: Islamic education, Arabic language, mathematics, and general culture. At the preparatory and secondary stage students are taught the same subjects as at the general preparatory and secondary levels.

4. Administrative and Supervisory Structure and Operation

The education system in Oman is controlled by the government, which provides free education to all. However, preprimary schools (kindergarten) are privately owned, together with a few private and community schools. The Ministry of Education is responsible for general education as well as for some specialized vocational education such as agriculture, commerce, and technical education at the secondary level.

The Ministry has established nine regional education departments which are responsible for ensuring that school systems in the respective regions are run efficiently and education is made available to all.

A Committee for Educational Planning composed of the Undersecretary for Education and the director generals in the Ministry headquarters has been set up, chaired by the Minister of Education. Its goal is to establish educational planning, making decisions on issues such as curriculum, teacher training, and staffing. A Supreme Committee for Educational Policies lays out and balances the educational policies according to the needs of the country and directives of the government.

5. Educational Finance

The finance for all government and quasigovernment education and technical and vocational training in the

Sultanate of Oman is provided by the government, and hence education at all levels is free for all. Budget allocations for education increased tremendously over the years, from 5 percent of the total civil expenditure in 1971 to 16 percent in 1984, and this has been increasing annually.

The per student cost at the primary level was the equivalent of US$176; at the preparatory level US$277; at the secondary level, US$320; and at the higher education level US$1,336 in 1992.

6. Supplying Personnel for the Education System

Table 1 shows numbers of teaching and nonteaching personnel at the different levels in 1991–92.

Most of the teachers in Oman other than at primary level are expatriates. This is due to the delay in the introduction of modern education and teacher training in the country. In 1989–90 the number of Omani teachers at primary level was 3,057 while the non-Omanis numbered 5,639. At the preparatory level there were 211 Omani teachers while the number of non-Omanis was 3,437. At the secondary level there were 83 Omanis compared to 1,268 expatriate teachers. Importance is put on teacher training in order subsequently to replace teachers at all levels with suitably qualified Omanis.

There are three establishments in charge of teacher training, namely, the Primary Teacher Training Intermediate College, the faculty of Education in the Sultan Qaboos University, and the Institute of Education.

7. Curriculum Development and Teaching Methodology

Up to 1970 Oman used Qatari textbooks. This practice imposed Qatari education in Oman, which had different aims and objectives that had been specified by its own particular values and needs. By adapting and modifying the Qatari textbooks some of the goals pertaining to the social and economic plans of the reform movement were achieved. However, it became evident that it was necessary to design an Omani

curriculum which could cope with Omani objectives and the philosophy and development of Oman. In 1974 the need to develop an Omani curriculum was realized whereby specialized committees were set up to design the school curriculum.

Within the Department of Curriculum all school subjects are dealt with by experts and technicians employed to develop the curriculum. General educational objectives are dealt with at the higher administrative levels in the Ministry, while specific teaching aims and assessment objectives are decided by curriculum experts and chief inspectors for subjects. All new textbooks are subject to trial and development by the experts in the Department of Curriculum, together with the teacher-training colleges' and institutes' staff.

8. The System of Examinations, Promotions, and Certifications

All students who successfully complete the sixth grade become automatically eligible to enter the preparatory level. After three years in the preparatory cycle, students sit for a national examination and, if successful, receive the General Preparatory Certificate. The students may then be eligible to enroll at the secondary level. After spending three years in the secondary school, students sit for a national examination. If they pass the examination successfully they are awarded the General Secondary Certificate.

Within each level of education the promotion from grade to grade is at the discretion of the teacher.

In order to secure a high degree of reliability, comprehensiveness, and consistency in examinations, the Ministry of Education has set up a technical committee whose responsibility is to set out the behavioral and assessment objectives for each school subject. This will help in setting national examinations that assess exactly what should have been learnt.

9. Educational Assessment, Evaluation, and Research

The Department of Educational Research in the Ministry of Education supervises the educational studies pertaining to the evaluation of curriculum. In addition, some relevant studies are undertaken by educational faculty members at the University.

10. Major Reforms in the 1980s and 1990s

Enrollments in primary school rose from 91,652 in 1980–81 to 272,068 in 1991–92. For the same period enrollments in preparatory school rose from 13,729

Table 1
Personnel, schools and students in 1991–92

Stage	Schools	Teachers	Administrators	Students
Primary	381	9,816	417	209,003
Preparatory	359	4,686	628	48,129
Secondary	83	1,973	361	31,092

to 84,129 and for secondary school from 1,551 to 31,092. From these figures it can be seen that the total enrollment of all those of preparatory school age has still to be attained.

Great efforts were made in the areas of vocational training and technical education. Furthermore, Omani teachers increased as a proportion of the total teaching force.

11. Major Problems for the Year 2000

Following on from what was stated above, it is clear that efforts must be made to increase the proportion of an age group enrolled in preparatory school. Much remains to be done to increase the number of Omani teachers. The quality of education and in particular of educational achievement must be improved. Vocational and technical education must be expanded to prepare a highly qualified cadre of efficient national workers. The Organization for Vocational Training, formed in 1992, will help in this regard. Existing programs will be reviewed and reformulated. New curricula and modern workshops will be developed. The private sector will become involved in training. In this way Omanis will be trained to replace the expatriate workforce.

Bibliography

Ahuja Y L, Birks J S 1982 Manpower and development in the Sultanate of Oman. Unpublished report presented to the Ministry of Social Affairs and Labor

Al Khabori B K 1985 Manpower planning and training development in the Sultanate of Oman. Master's thesis, University of Leeds

Al Ougaly A 1990 Omanization Policy. Unpublished paper submitted to the Training Week, May 23–27 Seminar, Oman Chamber of Commerce and Industry, Muscat

Al Raesi I et al. 1989 An evaluation of technical education schools and institutes in the Sultanate of Oman. Ministry of Education, Muscat

Al Shanfari A M1990 Technical and vocational education in Oman. Conference Paper presented at a Conference on Planning and Management of Education and Human Resource Development in Small System, Institute of Education, University of London

Al Shanfari A M 1991 The development of government policy in technical education and vocational training in the Sultanate of Oman. (Doctoral thesis, University of Wales)

Al Shanfari S M1989 Impact of oil revenue on the economic development of the Sultanate of Oman. (Master's thesis, Colorado School of Mines)

Ali H A1988 Vocational training: Its aims and its reflection upon Omanization in the government and private sectors. Unpublished report presented to the Seminar, Direction of Omanization in Both Sectors, Government and Private, Muscat

Arab Bureau of Education for the Gulf States 1980 *Industrial Education in the Gulf States: Comparative Study*. Arab Bureau of Education in the Gulf States, Riyadh

Arab Bureau of Education for the Gulf States 1988 *Higher and Intermediate Education: Technical and Vocational. Special Study*. Arab Bureau of Education in the Gulf States, Riyadh

Birks J S, Issa M A, Ahuja Y L 1983 Education training and manpower needs in Oman. Overview and leading issues. Manpower Report No. 4 presented to Ministry of Social Affairs and Labor, Muscat

Development Council 1976 *The First Five-Year Development Plan, 1976–1980*. Development Council, Muscat

Development Council 1978, 1987, 1989 *Statistical Year Book*. Development Council, Muscat

Development Council 1987 *The Third Five-Year Development Plan, 1986–1990*. Development Council, Muscat

Development Council 1988 *Oman Facts and Figures*. Development Council, Muscat

Ibraham M 1990 A plan of manpower strategy. Unpublished memorandum presented in Development Council, Muscat

Ministry of Education 1978 *The Philosophy of Education in the Sultanate of Oman*. Ministry of Education, Muscat

Ministry of Education 1979 *The Educational Development in the Sultanate of Oman between 1976–1978*. The Omani National Commission of Education, Culture, and Science, Muscat

Ministry of Education and Youth 1982a *Focus on the Development of Education in Oman*. Ministry of Education and Youth, Muscat

Ministry of Education and Youth 1982b Low enrollment in technical and vocational education and its impact upon the development plans in Oman, with special solutions. Seminar, Baghdad

Ministry of Education and Youth 1985a *The History of Education in Oman: Overview*. Ministry of Education and Youth, Muscat

Ministry of Education and Youth 1985b *Development of Illiterate Education in Oman*. Ministry of Education and Youth, Muscat

Ministry of Education and Youth 1987, 1988, 1990, 1991 *Annual Report*. Ministry of Education and Youth, Muscat

Ministry of Education and Youth 1988 Educational Planning Committee recommendation: Formal letter on 15.12.88 regarding the evaluation of technical education. Ministry of Education and Youth, Muscat

Ministry of Education and Youth 1989 Agricultural education and its role in meeting the demands of agricultural development in Oman. Unpublished working paper presented to the Arab Regional Experts for drawing new strategy for developing agricultural education, Alexandria

Ministry of Education and Youth 1990 Local seminars recommendations for technical education. Unpublished

Ministry of Information 1988 *Oman*. Ministry of Information, Muscat

Peterson J E 1978 *Oman in the Twentieth Century*. Croom Helm, London

Rakhyoot A M 1991 Freedom of passage for Arabian gulf oil is of vital importance to the world economy. Oman's role and contribution.

Razik T 1987 Evaluation of curriculum. The case of Oman: Primary Level. Part 1. Unpublished paper, Ministry of Education, Muscat

Razik T, Kight H R 1985 Student occupational preferences and the implications for education. Vocational training, planning and manpower development in Oman. A Preliminary Study. Unpublished paper, Ministry of Education, Muscat

The State Consultative Council 1988 The recommendations of the State Consultative Council for developing the policies of education and TVT and traditional handcraft. Unpublished notes, Seminar, October 2–6, 1988, 4th session

Townsend J 1984 Philosophy of state development planning.

In El Azhary S (ed.) 1984 *The Impact of Oil Revenue on Arab Gulf Development*. Croom Helm, London

Turky A, Gahfar S 1985 Suggestions for the fundamental trends for education and instruction in the Second Five-Year Development Plan: 1981–1985. Unpublished note, Ministry of Education, Muscat

Pakistan

A. Ghafoor and R. A. Farooq

1. General Background

Pakistan came into existence on August 14, 1947, when the Indian subcontinent was divided, with the Hindu and Muslim majority areas becoming separate sovereign states of Bharat or India and Pakistan. Initially, Pakistan had two constituent parts. These were East Pakistan and West Pakistan, which were separated from each other by 1,600 kilometers of Indian territory. In December 1971 East Pakistan seceded, giving birth to the new state of Bangladesh, and West Pakistan became Pakistan. Pakistan comprises four provinces: the Punjab, Sind, the North-West Frontier Province (NWFP), and Baluchistan, besides the federal capital Islamabad and the federally administered areas. It is bordered by Afghanistan and the People's Republic of China in the north, India in the east and southeast, and Iran in the west.

According to the 1981 census, the population of the country was 83.8 million, as compared with 65.3 million in 1972 and 32.5 million at the time of Independence in 1947. In January 1991 the population was estimated as 103 million and was projected to be 153 million by the year 2000. The population growth rate was 3.1 percent per annum. According to the 1981 census the density of the population was 106 persons per square kilometer which was estimated to rise to 142 persons in 1990. The population was unevenly distributed among the provinces. Punjab was the most populous province comprising 56.1 percent of the total population, followed by Sind (22.6%), NWFP (13.1%), and Baluchistan (5.1%). The proportion of urban population, which was 22.5 percent of the total population during the 1961 census, rose to 25.4 percent in 1972 and 28.3 percent in 1981. Over 3.7 million Afghan refugees arrived in Pakistan during the period 1979–90. They had to be provided with social services on humanitarian grounds. The existing educational facilities which were already inadequate to cope with the requirements of the indigenous population came under severe pressure to accommodate the additional school-age children of the Afghan refugees.

Pakistan is predominantly an agricultural country with wheat, rice, cotton, sugar cane, and tobacco as its principal crops. It is one of the leading exporters of rice and cotton. The estimated labor force in 1990–91 was 32.8 million, of which about 24 million were rural and 8.8 million urban. An estimated 1 million of the labor force were unemployed in 1991. About 51 percent were estimated to be employed in agriculture. The second major sector—manufacturing—accounts for nearly 13 percent of the employed labor force. Trade, construction, and transport are other major sectors which provide employment. The output from the education system is usually employed in the modern sector of the economy which is comparatively very small in Pakistan. The agricultural sector has not been capable of providing employment opportunities. Educated youth have become alienated from work in the agricultural sector, especially in the rural areas. In 1974, agrotechnical education was introduced at the secondary level of education but that too was restricted in scope and coverage. About 46 percent of students opted for premedical and engineering groups and were exempted from agrotechnical education. Other exemptions were also allowed. Thus a small percentage of students (about 20–25%) had to study agrotechnical subjects which were not examinable. Teachers were ill-equipped, there were inadequate laboratory and workshop facilities, and there was a lack of financial resources. The government liberalized its policy and now encourages private entrepreneurs to invest in the modern sector so as to increase employment opportunities for the educated youth.

About 97 percent of the people are Muslim. Urdu is the national language and is understood throughout the country. There are regional languages such as Punjabi, Sindi, Pushtu, and Baluchi. English is widely used in commercial, legal, and other official transactions. It is also the medium of instruction in colleges and universities. The high population growth rate, the cultural barriers (especially in the education of females), the predominant agrarian structure of society in rural areas, and the low level of socioeconomic development have kept the literacy level depressingly low. According to the 1981 census, the literacy rate was estimated as 26 percent, with 47 percent in urban areas and 17 percent in rural areas. Among males the literacy rate was 35 percent and among females 16 percent. This is the lowest literacy rate among developing countries in the early 1990s, and yet it shows a significant increase from 13 percent in 1951, 18 percent in 1961, and 21 percent in 1972. Literacy rates tend to vary widely from province to province. In order to promote literacy, attempts are being made to universalize primary education through the provision of basic education facilities and the launching of adult education programs through formal and nonformal educational institutions. A Literacy and Mass Education Commission (LAMEC) established in 1981 was renamed as the National Education and Training Commission (NETCOM) in 1990 and made responsible for launching adult education programs. Simultaneously, the Allama Iqbal Open University in Islamabad also initiated functional literacy programs. Pakistan has not yet been able to overcome the problem of illiteracy which is considered a stigma of backwardness.

2. Politics and the Goals of the Education System

Ever since Independence, attempts have been made to relate the educational system to the requirements of an independent sovereign state. An All Pakistan Education Conference was held in 1947. This was followed by the appointment of various commissions which submitted their reports periodically. These reports, at later stages, constituted the basis of various education policies. The 1959 Report of the Commission on National Education enjoys a peculiar position in the history of educational reforms. It is considered to be the most comprehensive and elaborate document on the educational problems of Pakistan. It dealt with various levels and aspects of education. Its recommendations were incorporated into the Second Five-Year Plan (1960–65) which is also considered to be an important landmark in the planning history of the country. There were several other commissions and policy statements over the subsequent 15 years. Invariably each

policy emphasized: (a) the orientation of education toward Islamic ideology and character building, (b) the universalization of primary education and promotion of literacy, (c) the orientation toward science and technology, (d) the qualitative improvement of education, and (e) the reduction in inequalities of educational opportunities.

The 1973 Constitution provided that the state shall: (a) promote with special care the educational and economic interests of backward areas; (b) remove illiteracy and provide free and compulsory secondary education within a minimum possible period; (c) make technical and professional education generally available and higher education equally accessible to all on the basis of merit; and (d) enable the people of different areas, through education, training, agricultural and industrial development, and other methods to participate fully in all forms of national activities including employment in the service of Pakistan.

A series of educational conferences was held in 1988 and 1989. A draft education policy was presented in 1991. A Commission on Islamization of Education was also appointed by the government in 1991 to ensure that the educational system of Pakistan is based on Islamic values of learning, teaching, and character building. The policy formulation process has, therefore, been postponed until the submission of the report by the Commission on Islamization of Education.

3. The Formal System of Education

3.1 Primary, Secondary, and Tertiary Education

Figure 1 outlines the structure of the formal education system. Key statistics of educational institutions, their enrollment, and the number of teachers by various levels of education are provided in Table 1. The formal educational system has a multistage structure. The first

Table 1

Number of educational institutions, their enrollment, and the number of teachers during 1947–48 and 1990–91

Levels of	No. of institutions		Enrollment		Teachers	
	1947–48	1990–91 Estimated	1947–48	1990–91 Estimated	1947–48	1990–91 Estimated
Primary I–V	8413	127,575	770[a]	8,856[a]	17.8[a]	218.3[a]
Middle VI–VIII	2190	7,389	221[a]	2,531[a]	12.0[a]	70.2[a]
High or Secondary IX–X	408	6,215	58[a]	866[a]	6.8[a]	114.0[a]
Secondary/Vocational	46	930	4[a]	108[a]	—	8,722
Arts and Science Colleges	40	426	14[a]	496[a]	—	17,593
Professional Colleges	—	99	4,368	85,500	—	4,032
Universities	2	22	644	77,400	—	4,425

Source: Pakistan Economic Survey 1990–91
a thousands

is the primary stage which lasts 5 years and enrolls children aged 5–9 years. Universalization of primary education remained a cherished goal of successive governments in Pakistan. Unfortunately, this goal does not seem to be attainable during the 1990s. The participation rate at primary level is estimated to be 58 percent. There are numerous constraints on the attainment of universal primary education. Some of them are: (a) a low level of female participation, (b) a rapid increase in the population of children aged 5–9 years, (c) a dropout rate of about 50 percent, (d) a lack of access to primary schools, (e) inadequate financial resources, (f) unattractive school hours, (g) poor school buildings in rural areas, and (h) teacher absenteeism. The female participation rate varies from province to province. It was 8 percent in Baluchistan and 26 percent in Punjab. Some of the factors responsible for a higher dropout rate are poverty, parental attitude, illness, unattractive schools, the poor quality of teachers, and the perceived irrelevance of curricula.

The primary stage is followed by a three-year middle stage, a two-year secondary stage, and a further two-year higher secondary stage. The participation rate at the three-year middle stage is estimated to be 36 percent and at the two-year secondary stage as 22.5 percent. The higher secondary stage is also called the "intermediate stage" and is considered a part of college education. The participation rate at this level is estimated to be 7.3 percent. To obtain a degree, 4 years of higher education after 10 years of primary and secondary schooling is required. Students who pass their first-degree stage are awarded a baccalaureate degree in arts or science, typically at the age of 19 years. In order to complete an honors course, an additional year's study is required.

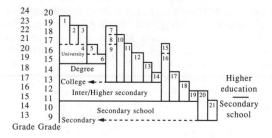

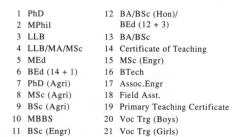

1 PhD	12 BA/BSc (Hon)/
2 MPhil	BEd (12 + 3)
3 LLB	13 BA/BSc
4 LLB/MA/MSc	14 Certificate of Teaching
5 MEd	15 MSc (Engr)
6 BEd (14 + 1)	16 BTech
7 PhD (Agri)	17 Assoc.Engr
8 MSc (Agri)	18 Field Asst.
9 BSc (Agri)	19 Primary Teaching Certificate
10 MBBS	20 Voc Trg (Boys)
11 BSc (Engr)	21 Voc Trg (Girls)

Figure 2
Detailed diagram of educational system in Pakistan from Grade 9 onward

The duration of postsecondary education varies in technical and professional fields. The polytechnic diploma is a three-year course. A bachelor's degree in medicine (MBBS) requires 5 years of study after the intermediate stage (12 years of schooling). Similarly, a bachelor's degree course both in engineering and veterinary medicine is of 4 years' duration after the intermediate examination. An additional 2 years after the bachelor's degree are required to complete a master's degree. A doctoral degree may require 2 to 3 years of study after the completion of a master's degree course. The participation rate in higher education is estimated as 2.8 percent. Figure 2 presents the different types of course at the higher levels of education.

Pakistan has severe climatic conditions for which the educational institutions are not properly equipped. Several educational institutions are, therefore, closed during winter and summer. These vacations vary from region to region. Taking into account all of the official vacations and other holidays, the academic year lasts only 6 to 7 months. Schools remain open for about 6 hours per day with a recess of about 30 minutes. Friday is a public holiday.

Side by side with the modern system of education introduced during the British period, is the traditional religious education system which provides education in the Islamic religion based on the Quran, the Hadith, Islamic jurisprudence, logic, and so forth. At the elementary level, there are *maktab* schools (attached to mosques) for the learning and memorization of the Quran and imparting elementary religious instruction. *Madrassah* (or *darul-uloom*) impart advanced instruc-

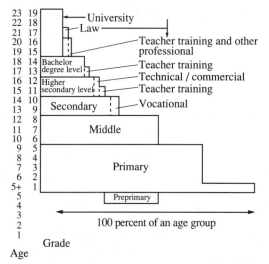

Figure 1
Pakistan: Structure of the formal education system

tion on various aspects of Islamic education. Together they constitute the organizational structure of religious education. In order to provide an effective integration of the religious education system with the formal school system, attempts are being made to introduce modern subjects into the *madrassah* system. These institutions have their own management system without interference from either the provincial or federal governments. However, grants-in-aid are provided to these institutions by the government. According to a survey carried out by the Ministry of Education in 1987, there were 2,862 such institutions with an enrollment of 207,448. Graduates of the *madrassahs* are called " *fazils*" and are qualified to be appointed as religious teachers in secondary schools.

3.2 Preschool Education

With the encouragement of the private sector, a number of nurseries and kindergarten schools have sprung up which provide preschool education to children who are not yet 5 years old, the normal age of entry to the regular school system. There are public schools both in rural and urban areas which provide preschool education as a part of the socialization process. The children in these preschool programs are not taken on the school register but, after 6 months, they are promoted and registered as regular students in Grade 1.

3.3 Special Education

Special education is a new and developing field in Pakistan. The nonavailability of trained staff was the main hurdle in the speedy expansion of educational services. The Allama Iqbal Open University (AIOU) Islamabad, and the universities of Karachi and Islamabad started courses leading to a master's degree in special education. A National Mobility and Independence Training Center has been established at Islamabad for providing training to teachers and visually handicapped persons. Collaborative links with international agencies such as ODA, WHO, UNICEF, UNESCO, and UNDP/ILO were established to plan and develop projects in the fields of labor force training, equipment support, consultancy services, development of national programs, and orientation visits and training fellowships to foreign countries. The National Institute for the Handicapped at Islamabad was strengthened during 1989 and 45 special education centers enrolling 3,500 children were established. A National Training Center for the Disabled was established at Islamabad. In order to spearhead pioneering work in the area of special education and rehabilitation of disabled persons, the office of Director General Special Education was established under the Ministry of Health, Social Welfare, and Special Education in 1985.

3.4 Vocational and Technical Education

Engineering universities, colleges of technology, and polytechnics operate under the provincial education departments and the federal Ministry of Education. There are 7 universities of engineering/colleges of engineering, 9 colleges of technology, 26 polytechnics (19 male and 7 female), 13 colleges of commerce, and 70 institutions of commerce. However, there are also vocational training institutions which are administered by the provincial labor departments and the Ministry of Labor, Manpower, and Overseas Pakistanis under the National Vocational Training Project. There were 235 vocational institutions with an enrollment of 12,113 in 1988–89. These institutions produce skilled workers at the operator level like carpenters, masons, machinists, welders, electricians, and such like. There are other organizations such as the Directorate of Social Welfare, the Department of Local Government and Rural Development, the Small Industries Corporation, the Agency for Barani Areas Development, the Directorate of Agriculture (Punjab), the Directorate of Industries and Commerce, the Directorate of Mineral Development, the Overseas Pakistanis Foundation, and the Agriculture Cooperative Department, and so on which also impart vocational training in 2,924 institutions with an enrollment of 92,737 in 1988–89. Government vocational institutes for girls conduct training programs in handicrafts and household skills such as sewing and cutting, embroidery, knitting, leatherwork, woodwork, food preservation, cooking, hairdressing, shorthand, typing, and so on.

3.5 Adult and Nonformal Education

The Allama Iqbal Open University (AIOU) was established as an institution of nonformal education and distance learning under the Open University Act of 1974. The main objectives of the University are to: (a) provide facilities for those who cannot leave their homes and jobs; (b) provide facilities for educational improvement for the masses; (c) provide facilities for the training of teachers; and (d) hold examinations and award and confer degrees, diplomas, certificates, and other academic distinctions to persons who have been admitted to the University and have passed its examination under the prescribed conditions. The AIOU provides a wide range of courses at different levels allowing students a fairly wide choice of subjects which can be clustered together to form major areas of study. The main clusters are humanities, teacher education, technical education, business management, commercial education, social sciences, Arabic, Pakistan studies, Islamic studies, home economics, and women's education. The University offered as many as 204 different courses through its media-based and tutorially supported nonformal/distance education system during the academic year 1989–90. These courses have an extremely wide range, from literacy to M Phil levels. The University had a total enrollment of 235,259 during the academic year 1989–90.

In pursuance of the National Education Policy of 1979, the Literacy and Mass Education Commission

(LAMEC) was established in 1981 to develop plans for the promotion of literacy and to suggest ways and means to use nonformal education as a mass approach for adult literacy programs. In 1989, the name of this organization was changed to the National Education and Training Commission (NETCOM). A variety of literacy programs were launched, but so far it has not had the desired impact owing to the lack of political commitment and financial support.

4. Administrative and Supervisory Structure and Operation

Education has been and is primarily a provincial matter, though under the federal Ministry of Education. The federal government continues to be the overall policy-making, coordinating, and advisory authority on education. The educational institutions located in the federal capital territory, the centers of excellence, and the area study centers and other nationalized institutions in various parts of the country are administered by the federal Ministry of Education. Universities located in various provinces are administered by the provincial governments, but are exclusively funded by the federal government through the University Grants Commission.

The federal Ministry of Education is headed by the Minister of Education. The most senior civil servant in the Ministry is the Education Secretary. The provincial education departments are headed by the education ministers of the respective provinces. The senior civil servants in these departments are called "education secretaries."

Each province is divided into regions for the management of education. Each regional office is headed by a director. The regions are further divided into districts and the officer in charge of a district is the district education officer. The supervision of primary schools falls under the jurisdiction of the district education officers; secondary schools are under the administrative control of the regional director of education. For colleges, there are separate directorates of education. Universities are autonomous bodies supervised and controlled by their own syndicates which are appointed by the governors of the respective provinces. Each syndicate is headed by a vice-chancellor who is the academic and administrative head of the university, and who also heads the syndicate and the various academic and administrative bodies of the university. The governors of the respective provinces are ex officio chancellors of the universities in their domains. Universities located in the federal area have the President of Pakistan as ex officio chancellor.

5. Educational Finance

For all development activities, the federal government provides funds for capital expenditure, whereas the provincial governments have to provides matching funds for recurring expenditure. According to the economic survey of 1989–90, the total estimated expenditure on education was Rs 32,089 million (25 rupees=US$1). A sum of Rs 8,397 million was spent on primary education; Rs 7,262 million on secondary education; Rs 2,607 million on colleges; Rs 4,874 million on universities; Rs 2,119 million on technical education; Rs 386 million on teacher education; and Rs 6,443.5 million on other items. These figures represent percentages of the overall expenditure of 26, 23, 8, 15, 7, and 1 respectively. The same trend is expected to persist in the years following 1990. In order to generate additional revenues for education, the government levied a 5 percent Iqra surcharge on imports under the Finance Act of 1985. A total of 4 billion rupees was collected through this surcharge during 1985–86 and these revenues gradually rose to 6 billion rupees in 1990–91.

The additional revenues collected through the Iqra surcharge were not totally provided for the education sector. Had the additional revenues been used solely for education, the percentage expenditure would have risen to 3 percent of the Gross National Product (GNP). Total expenditure on education, which was 2.44 percent of the GNP in 1988–89, declined to 2.33 percent in 1989–90 and 2.25 percent in 1990–91. In view of the scarcity of funds, the government has adopted a liberal policy to encourage the private sector, through a package of incentives, to establish educational/research institutions. Educational foundations are being established at both the national and provincial levels to encourage the private sector to establish educational and research institutions. Per student public expenditure at primary level is estimated at US$27, US$50 at secondary level, and US$1,335 at tertiary level.

6. Supplying Personnel for the Education System

Teaching is an unattractive profession in Pakistan. The majority of the graduates joining the teaching profession have a poor academic background. This places a burden on preservice and inservice training institutions which have to be properly equipped and staffed. While the preservice training institutions cope with the demand, the inservice training institutions have problems, especially when the curricula are revised and teacher competencies must be upgraded. In some isolated areas it is difficult to find qualified teachers. In order to promote education in such areas, a relaxation of the minimum qualification is under consideration.

The size of enrollment and the number of teachers at various levels of education can be seen in Table 1. The student–teacher ratio at primary and secondary levels is estimated as 40:1 and 36:1 respectively. At subsequent levels the ratio falls, except in the secondary and vocational levels where it is 80:1.

At the beginning of the 1990s elementary-teacher training programs were offered in 87 training institutions. There are two kinds of program: the Primary Teaching Certificate (PTC) and the Certificate of Teaching (CT). Both of these programs last one academic year. The PTC program is meant for teachers in Grades 1 to 5. Admission to the PTC program requires that the applicant should have matriculated (10 years of schooling). The CT program prepares the teachers to teach all the subjects up to Grade 8 including English. For admission, candidates are required to have an FA/FSc certificate representing 12 years of schooling. The Allama Iqbal Open University also offers PTC and CT courses on a distance education basis. The curriculum used for teacher education at the beginning of the 1990s was issued in 1983 by the Ministry of Education.

The institutions preparing secondary-school teachers are known as "colleges of education," and those offering advanced training leading to MAEdu/MEd degrees are called "institutes of education and research" or "departments of education" in the universities. In the early 1990s there were four institutes of education and research, two departments of education, and 11 colleges of education preparing secondary school teachers. Two types of program are offered for the training of secondary-school teachers: (a) a one-year BEd program (14+1 model), and (b) a three-year BEd program (12+3 model). The basic requirement for admission to the degree of BEd is a bachelor's or master's degree from any recognized university.

The postqualification professional development of teachers is the responsibility of the curriculum bureaus and extension centers. The courses offered to teachers vary in their frequency according to local conditions. There are four types of inservice training program: (a) inservice training of untrained staff on a full-time basis (and with salary) at an elementary college, (b) crash programs of three months' duration run by curriculum bureaus and extension centers, (c) short-term refresher courses run by curriculum bureaus and extension centers, and (d) limited private ventures such as the Teachers Resource Center at Karachi supported by the Agha Khan Foundation (AKF) which offers workshop courses on a systematic basis to teachers in both the private and public sector. Throughout the country there are 13 inservice teacher education centers / institutions which conduct inservice refresher courses for teachers.

An Institute for the Promotion of Science Education and Training (IPSET) has been established at Islamabad to train science teachers and to develop research-based curricula and teaching kits for the improvement of science education. There is a National Technical Teachers Training College (NTTTC) at Islamabad which trains junior and senior instructors at polytechnics and colleges of technology. There are no separate programs for preservice or inservice training of college teachers. There is a National Academy of Higher Education (NAHE) at the University Grants Commission which provides inservice training facilities to university teachers. The Academy of Educational Planning and

Management (AEPAM) at Islamabad trains supervisory personnel such as principals of colleges, subdivisional and district education officers, divisional and regional directors, and planning directors in the field of educational planning and management. The Asian Development Bank has initiated a survey of teacher-training institutions on the basis of which a project is likely to be developed for financial assistance from the Bank.

7. Curriculum Development and Teaching Methodology

At the federal level, the National Bureau of Curriculum and Textbooks is a constituent part of the Ministry of Education. There are also curriculum bureaus and centers, and textbook boards in the provinces. The National Bureau coordinates the activities of the provincial bureaus. The development of curricula is initiated by the provincial bureaus, but is finalized jointly by the national and provincial bureaus.

The medium of instruction at the primary level is the national language (Urdu) or an approved provincial language. Urdu is used as the medium of instruction at the secondary and higher secondary levels. Higher education is usually conducted in English.

The courses offered are generally the same throughout the country. Diversification of courses takes place after Grade 8. Three streams of courses (arts, science, and technical/vocational) are available, from which students can choose according to their interest and aptitude. Medicine and engineering are the most prestigious courses and competition for these is greatest.

Textbooks are produced by the provincial textbook boards. Writers are appointed in consultation with the curriculum bureau. At the higher education level, particularly in scientific and technical fields, foreign textbooks are usually prescribed. Since the cost of foreign books is prohibitive, most students can never own a book for intensive study. A National Book Foundation (NBF) has been established by the government to reproduce such books locally and make them available for students. Book banks have also been established on the campuses of the universities. Side by side with the National Book Foundation, a National Book Council has been established as an autonomous body. This council encourages local scholars to write books in various disciplines and ensure their nationwide distribution.

8. The System of Examinations, Promotions, and Certifications

There is automatic progression of students from Grades 1 to 9. Students wishing to apply for a scholarship take the Grade 8 examination conducted by the respective provincial education departments. Public examinations are held at the end of Grades 10 and 12. These examinations are conducted by the Boards of

Intermediate and Secondary Education. The students who pass the Grade 10 examination are awarded a secondary school certificate, and those passing Grade 12 are awarded a higher secondary school certificate. There are separate boards of technical education which conduct examinations and award certificates in various technology subjects. Universities conduct their own examinations and also those of the colleges affiliated to them. The system of public examination has been under criticism for a long time. It is considered as invalid, inefficient, and to some extent also corrupt. After the failure of the semester system, annual examinations have been reintroduced. In order to improve the evaluation system, a national testing service is being contemplated by the Ministry of Education.

The institutions imparting religious education and funded by public donations have their own system of examinations and certification. Those who complete elementary education are awarded certificates such as *Nazira* (Reading of Holy Quran), *Hifz* (Memorization of Holy Quran), *Tajweed-o-Qiraat* (Techniques for the Recitation of Holy Quran). The *Tahtani* examination covers Arabic language and literature, Islamic law and jurisprudence, and the translation of selected chapters of the Holy Quran. The *Tahtani* examination is equivalent to the completion of secondary education in the formal education system. *Mauqoof Alaih* is an advanced level which covers Arabic language and literature, history, logic, translation of Holy Quran, and certain sections of the sayings of the prophet Mohammad. It is equivalent to a bachelor's degree. *Daurai Hadeeth* (specialization in the meaning and interpretation of the sayings of the prophet Mohammad) is equivalent to a master's degree. Equivalence has been established with the formal education system enabling the graduates of religious education to seek employment in the formal education system as teachers of religious education.

9. Educational Assessment, Evaluation, and Research

There are very few institutes of educational research. The principal institutes are located at Islamabad, Lahore, Peshawar, and Hydrabad. Individual studies are undertaken by the students in these institutes as a requirement for their master's degree. A National Institute of Education and Research at the federal level is expected to coordinate all research efforts. A Bureau of Educational Planning and Management used to exist in the Ministry of Education to undertake specific studies for planning and policy formulation. This bureau was converted into an Academy of Educational Planning and Management (AEPAM) in 1982 to provide training and conduct research in the fields of educational planning and management. The Academy has produced a substantial number of reports based on its training seminars and workshops. It has also carried out a number of studies on various aspects of education. Under

collaborative arrangements with the Harvard Institute for International Development (HIID), the Academy conducted extensive surveys on various aspects of primary education under the BRIDGES Project. In addition, there is a planning wing in the Ministry of Education to carry out routine activities such as the formulation, appraisal, implementation, and evaluation of educational projects and the securing of funds from the Ministry of Finance. The Pakistan National Commission for UNESCO (PNCU) prepares comprehensive reports on the education sector for presentation in the annual meetings of UNESCO and the International Bureau of Education (IBE). A National Education Council (NEC), established in 1972, has undertaken monitoring and evaluation of the national education policies in the country. The Council met only once in 1981 and could not discharge its evaluative functions properly due to lack of encouragement and support from the Ministry of Education which had established a parallel forum in the form of an Inter-Provincial Education Ministers Conference. The National Education Council produced a number of reports on primary, secondary, technical, and female education. Research into curriculum issues is conducted by the provincial bureaus of curriculum development.

10. Major Reforms in the 1980s and 1990s

In order to provide universal access to primary education, independent institutions have been set up by mosques for boys' primary education, whereas for girls *Mohalla* ("cluster of houses") school was introduced. Under the Fifth Five-Year Plan (1978–83) the number of mosque schools opened was 8,200. During the Sixth Five-Year Plan (1983–88) this figure rose to 17,193, and during the Seventh Five-Year Plan (1988–93) to 20,000. To increase the effectiveness of supervision, a new tier of learning coordinators was introduced which reduced teacher absenteeism and dropout. It improved the quality of teaching and increased the professional status and motivation of the primary school teachers. Separate directorates of primary education were established by the provincial governments. At the secondary level, the number of boards of intermediate and secondary education was increased by the provincial governments. A National Technical Teachers Training College and an Institute for the Promotion of Science Education and Training were established in Islamabad for the inservice training of teachers.

As a result of the governemnt's liberal policy, the Agha Khan University of Medical Sciences and Lahore University of Management Sciences were established by the private sector. The burdon on the public sector was reduced by the establishment of English-medium primary and secondary schools in the urban areas of the country. Educational foundations have been established by the federal as well as provincial governments to help the private sector in the establishment of educational institutions. The National Education Management Information System (NEMIS) has been established to carry out the planning and development of human resources.

11. Major Problems for the Year 2000

The major problems encountered in the 1990s are the universalization of primary education and the promotion of widespread literacy; the relevance of secondary and technical education to the world of work; the promotion of scientific and technical education at higher levels; the improvement of the internal efficiency and external effectiveness of the education system; the achievement of equality of educational opportunity by sex, social class, and geographic regions (especially rural areas); and the development of a sound research base for scientific analyses of educational problems and the development of educational policies. The problems related to the unemployment of educated youth will continue to exercise the minds of policy decision makers, planners, and administrators in the country.

Bibliography

Akhtar R 1988 *Pakistan Year Book 1988–89*, 16th edn. East and West Publishing Company, Karachi

Farooq R A 1990 *A Survey of Pedagogy, Research, and Curriculum Development in Pakistan*. Academy of Educational Planning and Management, Islamabad

Ghafoor A 1980 Financial management of education in Pakistan. *Educ. Rev.* 1(5): 112–29

Ghafoor A 1988 *Technical and Vocational Education in Pakistan*. Academy of Educational Planning and Management, Islamabad

Haq S 1965 *Education and Development Strategy in South and Southeast Asia*. East-West Center Press, Honolulu, Hawaii

Mufti A G 1980 Human resource development through education in Pakistan (occasional paper). Pakistan Manpower Institute, Islamabad

Pakistan Government 1972 *Education Policy 1972–80*. Ministry of Education, Islamabad

Pakistan Government 1974 *Pakistan Education—A Sector Assessment*. Ministry of Education, Islamabad

Pakistan Government 1979 *National Education Policy*. Ministry of Education, Islamabad

Pakistan Government 1988 *Deeni Madaris Pakistan Ki Jame Report*. Ministry of Education, Islamabad

Pakistan Government 1989a *Special Education and Social Welfare Division—Performance 1989*. Ministry of Health, Special Education, and Social Welfare, Islamabad

Pakistan Government 1989b *National Education Conference Working Papers*. Ministry of Education, Islamabad

Pakistan Government 1990–91 *Pakistan Economic Survey*. Economic Advisor's Wing, Ministry of Finance, Islamabad

Panama

M. A. Gandásegui

1. General Background

Panama is a relatively small country with a total area of 77,000 square kilometers. It stretches from east to west at the base of the Caribbean Sea and joins together North and South America. Panama became a springboard in the conquest of the Western Hemisphere after Balboa claimed the Pacific basin for the Spanish Crown in 1513. Panama City was founded in 1519 and since then the Isthmus has played a key role in world commerce. Panama was a Spanish colony for over three centuries until it decided to break its political ties in 1821. At the center of the Isthmus, the Panama Canal was built at the turn of the twentieth century.

In 1903 Panama became an independent state. In 1993, Panama's population was 2.4 million with a declining annual population growth rate of approximately 1.9 percent. The people are Spanish speaking and can be considered a blend of European, African, and Native American stocks. There are seven indigenous nations with their own languages and customs with a population close to 120,000. Approximately 44 percent of the Panamanian families live below the poverty line. The districts with most problems are those populated by the indigenous groups.

Almost 35 percent of the population in 1990 was under 14 years of age. Children with an urban background have a higher probability of success than do rural children. The infant mortality rates are 25 percent higher in rural areas. In the urban areas, 99 percent of the children are born with professional assistance but this occurs for only 76 percent of children in rural areas. Other studies reveal that 30 percent of rural school children suffer some kind of nutritional problem but this is true for only 10 percent of urban children.

Panama's economy was based on a strong service sector fully integrated into the world market. With import substitution industry taking off in the midst of the Second World War and the growth of an internal market, the country's social fabric was rapidly transformed. A dynamic middle class of entrepreneurs and professionals, along with a growing working class demanded a place in Panama's day-to-day decision-making process. Education became a major issue for producing the skilled labor to help fulfill economic goals and also for assuring social mobility for the younger generations.

Liberalism as an ideology has played a dominant role in Panama. It has challenged the Catholic Church's traditional leadership so entrenched in most of Latin America. During the second half of the twentieth century, liberal ideologists justified the use of the state in order to guarantee economic growth. During this period a massive system of education was set up across the country reaching into the most remote villages.

Illiteracy rates at the beginning of the twentieth century were over 90 percent. The first Ministry of Education (1904) successfully created a network of primary schools throughout the country and a National Institute at Panama City. In the 1950s illiteracy rates had dropped to 50 percent. But progress was considered insufficient and a massive effort was set in motion to eradicate illiteracy. Primary, senior, and junior high schools were started throughout the countryside and in the cities. The illiteracy rate in 1990 stood at 11 percent.

Economic depression and productive stagnation, however, characterized Panama in the late 1970s and in the 1980s. The education system's growth has leveled off and other structural problems are attracting more attention. This addresses the fact that close to 33 percent of children aged 4–9 did not attend school full-time in 1991. Over 16 percent of the 10- to 14-year olds did not attend school at all.

2. Politics and the Goals of the Education System

The constitution mandates that all children between the ages of 6 and 15 attend school. It also guarantees free education. The state promotes university studies by maintaining extremely low enrollment fees (US$26 per semester). After having overcome ideological barriers in the 1970s, preprimary education grew rapidly. Education facilities for special training were also expanded. Vocational training stagnated as a result of economic depression.

Panamanian law states that the education system is divided between "official" and "private" education. Official education is financed mainly by the state. "All education is public because schools, official and private, are open to students without distinctions of race, social position or religion" (UNESCO/Ministerio de Educación 1992).

Constitutional mandate gives the state a strategic role in all matters concerning education. Through the Ministry of Education it has the responsibility of the coordination, supervision, and control of the system. Besides the Catholic Church, the state is the sole institution involved in supporting education.

3. The Formal System of Education

Figure 1 presents the structure of the educational system together with the approximate enrollment of each age group in school.

3.1 Primary, Secondary, and Tertiary Education

Primary school lasts, in theory, for six years and secondary school for a further six years. Between 1960 and 1980 the primary school enrollments doubled from 161,000 to 338,000. This was accompanied by an increase in the number of teachers from 5,397 to 12,107. In 1990, there were 351,000 pupils with 13,505 teachers.

Secondary school has two cycles. Lower-secondary education lasts for three years and builds on what pupils learned in primary school. Upper-secondary education lasts for three years and offers a more diversified and specialized curriculum. In 1960, most of the 108 secondary schools were private. By 1980, there were 310 schools and nearly two-thirds of them were public schools. Student enrollments increased more than five times between 1960 and 1980 (from 36,000 to 172,000 students). By 1990, there were 9,754 teachers and 196,000 students. However, as can be seen

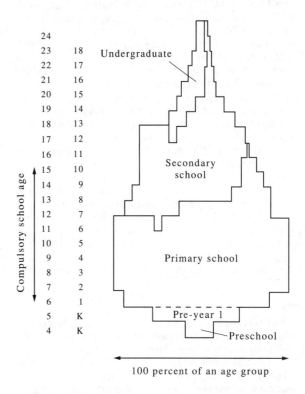

Figure 1

Panama: Structure of the formal education system 1990

from Fig. 1, grade repeating is rife and there are many overage pupils in the classes.

In higher or tertiary education, the University of Panama (*Universidad de Panamá*), founded in 1935, is responsible for setting down all guidelines relating to the universities in the country. In 1993, there were two public universities and four private establishments of higher learning. In 1990 the two public universities had a registration of 46,990 students. The private universities totaled 5,520 students.

The public universities, *Universidad de Panamá* (UP) and *Universidad Tecnológica de Panamá* (UTP), share a campus in Panama City and have regional centers in most of Panama's 9 provincial capitals. The UP has 14 faculties where most arts and science areas are covered and students are offered close to 50 degrees (from lawyer to medical doctor to nurse and interior designer). The UTP has 7 faculties where engineering degrees are awarded. The UP and the UTP have not developed a strong research base and, with a few exceptions, do not offer graduate degrees. Traditionally the UP has been an effective means for upward social mobility. This held true especially in the period of economic expansion of the 1960s and 1970s. The UP's yearly budget was close to US$55 million in 1992. Over 90 percent was state sponsored.

The private universities include a Catholic University (Universidad Santa María la Antigua) founded in the mid-1960s. This university struggled financially in the 1970s and 1980s, but in the early 1990s it started to receive private grants and foreign aid. The other private establishments, *Universidad del Istmo, Universidad Interamericana de Educación a Distancia*, and *Universidad Latinoamericana de Costa Rica* are spearheading a movement to diversify higher education, as well as to introduce graduate studies. Upper-middle class people and wealthy families generally send their offspring to foreign universities.

However, in 1993 most of the top enterprises hired their managers, lawyers, and engineers with degrees from United States universities. There is a strong correlation between a degree from a university in the United States, upper-class membership, and the ownership of the top enterprises. Stronger competition is felt in top government posts where upper-class university graduates were displaced in the 1960s by up-and-coming and aggressive middle-class professionals. This situation was countered after the 1989 United States invasion.

3.2 Preschool Education

The first formal kindergarten was created in Panama by the *Instituto Panamericano* (IPA), a Methodist Church-run school. A few years later two prestigious Catholic schools followed suit, *La Salle* (1947) and *Javier* (1948). The Education Ministry considers preprimary education "as nonobligatory with the objective of promoting the integral growth of each of the participants, stimulating and developing their sentiments

Table 1
COIF registration (matriculation)

Type	Area and type of school 1980		
	Urban	Rural	Total
Public	8,598	3,336	11,934
Private	6,108	94	6,202
Total	14,706	3,430	18,136

Source: Comisión Coordinadora de Educación Nacional (1985) Vol. 5, Table 38, p. 42

and good habits . . . This education includes kindergartens as well as daycare centers" (Ministerio de Educación 1992).

The daycare centers (*Centros de Orientación Infantil Familiar*—COIF) represent one form of preprimary education geared to satisfy the needs of 2- to 5-year olds with the intention of promoting the adequate development of their emotional, physical, and intellectual faculties.

A study funded by UNICEF that focused on the COIFs concluded that "the system was accepted by the community, that it was economic, efficient, flexible, and multi-institutional. It also discovered several problems. Its financial structure was weak; its training of personnel was limited; its supervision mechanisms needed much improvement; and, the health component for the children was not sufficiently organized" (Comisión Coordinadora de Educación Nacional 1985).

Over 80 percent of the children who were participating in the COIF programs were from urban areas. This indicator gives an idea of the problems that education programs have in the rural areas where over 40 percent of the population lives. Figures for 1980 are presented in Table 1.

The growth of COIFs was extremely rapid in the 20-year span between 1960 and 1980. This was due mainly to two factors. On the one hand, bureaucracy in the public sector grew fivefold during that period, from 25,000 employees to a total of 125,000. On the other

Table 2
COIF and preprimary teachers according to level of education 1980

	Total	University degree	Other degree	No degree
1960	104	0	73	31
1980	645	99	545	1

Source: Comisión Coordinadora de Educación Nacional (1985) Vol 5, Table 3A, p. 41

hand, employment in business and industrial activities multiplied several times. The demands for education and daycare establishments were concentrated mainly in the urban areas.

The number of COIF and preprimary teachers according to their qualifications is given for 1960 and 1980 in Table 2.

3.3 Special Education

Special Education serves children who have physical or intellectual difficulties. Children who are blind or deaf-mute are considered to have physical problems. Children with behavior problems are considered to have mental deficiencies. The programs provided are designed to permit such children to recover or develop basic abilities that will integrate them into society. The Panamanian Institute for Special Recovery (*Instituto Panameño de Habilitación Especial*—IPHE) had an enrollment of 6,015 students in 1991.

IPHE was created in the early 1960s and is financially autonomous. It receives grants from the government and other private sectors. The Institution has specialized workshops for sewing, cabinet-making, metalwork, toys, and binding. There are secretarial courses and there is also a training farm. At a cattle ranch set up with Dutch aid (IPHE-Holland) the Institutio runs a dairy farm and offers horticulture courses.

3.4 Vocational, Technical, and Business Education

There are two- and three-year vocational courses in secondary school followed by periods of practical training. Business education courses are provided at the tertiary level.

Although it is not clearly set out in the Ministry's organigram and it has not had high priority, vocational education is an integral part of Panama's education system. At present the Education Ministry is stressing in its reports the need to develop the level of professional and technical education that includes commercial, industrial, and agricultural high school degrees.

The Education Ministry is also preparing plans to enhance a National Policy on Computer Education. There are no specific dates but the plan wants to incorporate 70,000 students in 84 school establishments.

3.5 Adult and Nonformal Education

The Ministry of Education has two definitions for adult education. On the one hand, it serves a large fraction of the population that is considered technically illiterate (i.e., has not attended school). On the other hand, it has special courses for men and women who were not able to finish their primary or secondary education.

According to the 1990 census, approximately 145,000 persons were officially considered illiterate. In 1991, over 16,000 persons received literacy courses in 458 centers where 784 teaches worked.

Adult education is oriented toward the needs of the illiterate population and to those who have not culminated their formal studies. It also offers vocational courses and seminars of popular culture. Total registration for these activities reached 30,277 students in 1991. The distribution was as follows: literacy courses —4,935 students; primary courses—6,012; popular culture—5,147; and secondary courses—14,133.

There are also three schools that offer courses for workers (*Educación Laboral*). It is an open and flexible system that promotes the self-esteem and sense of security of the adult. The adult is stimulated to study on her/his own and reach new stages of knowledge based on their psychological maturity.

The Ministry of Education also has programs for the inmates of the different penitentiary establishments around the country. There are no statistics available concerning the number of students. However, the courses include both primary and secondary education as well as literacy courses and popular culture seminars.

4. Administrative and Supervisory Structure and Operation

The Ministry is organized into national bureaus (*direcciones*) responsible for revising curricula, recruiting personnel, and coordinating training programs. The Ministry also has provincial offices that supervise programs on a permanent basis. The state also oversees the private schools that must use the Ministry's curricula. There is only one curriculum valid for the entire system.

On the one side, there is a technical structure that deals with all problems related to teaching. On the other, there is an administrative structure. Both structures function on a hierarchical basis stretching from the minister's office all the way to the smallest rural school.

Panama's legislation identifies three different levels of responsibility in the educational system. The highest level is responsible for political leadership and institutional development. A second level is responsible for the support system. It generates the necessary resources and other requirements that guarantee the process of education. A third level—the schools—is where the programs and plans are executed.

In 1957, 12 hierarchical levels of command were established. At the head was the General Directorate of Education (*Dirección General de Educación*), followed by the National Directorates of Primary, Secondary, and Private Education; the inspection, auxiliary, and supervisory services; down to principals, assistant principals, and finally teachers. In 1968 the National Directorate of Vocational and Technical Education was created along with Directorates of Auditing, Student Affairs, Administration, and Budget.

The education system is well backed by the constitution and an array of laws. However, there are some operational levels whose origins are difficult to trace. According to some critics this is partially due to the reforms that were introduced in the 1970s. For instance, the General Directorate of Education not only has the divisions created by law but also has divisions that are responsible for literacy and for adult education.

Another Technical Directorate is responsible for curriculum and education technology, professional educational orientation, a teacher's center (cooperative), the art and culture center, educational television, and the national library.

5. Educational Finance

Public education in Panama represents an investment of over US$250 million which is approximately 22 percent of the central government's budget. Table 3 presents the education budget for 1992.

6. Supplying Personnel for the Education System

Primary school teachers (*maestros*) are trained at Normal Institutes (teachers colleges) and can also receive further training at the University of Panama. Secondary school or high school teachers (*profesores*) are trained exclusively at the university level. The University has an Education Faculty where primary school teachers receive special courses, a Liberal Arts (*Humanidades*) Faculty where high school teachers are trained, and an Institute of Higher Education (ICASE) where graduate studies for teachers are conducted.

The official school system stimulates teachers to take courses in order to develop their abilities. A personnel board (composed of teachers and ministry personnel) makes decisions about their promotion. The system was originally set up in 1947 with seven categories for teachers. Secondary school teachers were divided into three categories according to their university degrees. A 1979 law established 22 grades with a total of 136 categories taking account of all the positions in the system. The categories reflect the years of education, degrees, responsibilities, and effort.

Table 3
Education Budget 1992

	Total (millions US$)	Percent
Central government	1,248	100
Education sector	257	22
Ministry of Education	187	15
Other sectors	70	7

Source: Ministerio de Educación (1992) Table 17, p. 216

The Ministry emphasizes that the efficient use of human and material resources should guarantee the fulfillment of the education system's objectives. Following on this, the Ministry maintains a permanent inventory of personnel. In this way the higher echelons can plan according to the country's needs and in step with the progress of science and technology.

In 1993, there was no difference in purchasing power between the average teacher and average blue-collar worker.

7. Curriculum Development and Teaching Methodology

All syllabuses are determined by Ministry of Education personnel. The curriculum unit is responsible for the writing of the school textbooks which in turn must be approved by the Ministry.

A 1992 UNESCO report stated that the updating of Panama's curriculum would be preceded by research involving teachers along with administrative personnel, parents, and students (UNESCO/Ministerio de Educación 1992). This collective effort would enable teachers to incorporate cultural and social features of their communities into the curricula. The report also pointed out that teachers were still using traditional methods and outdated curricula.

8. The System of Examinations, Promotions, and Certifications

Students who have completed all six grades of primary school are promoted automatically to the middle-school level. Students must present their Grade 6 Report Card and a Primary School Certificate before registering in secondary school. In order to enter the Second Cycle (4th year of secondary school) the student must present his or her credits to the school authorities. There are no examination requirements. The school's principal may give advice to the student on several of the special degree courses the establishment offers during the Second Cycle. In order to enhance this distribution process the student may be asked to take a test.

Grades are scored from one to five. A student must reach a minimum of three to pass a course. Panamanian Law states that promotion in secondary schools is according to each course passed. Any course that a student fails to pass must be given priority at the start of the following academic year. Students who have courses pending cannot move on to the next stage. A student counselor studies the aptitudes of each candidate before approving his promotion, which must also be approved by the school's principal.

When a student fails in four or more courses in the same year or when a student fails in the same course two consecutive years, the school authorities will usually recommend to his or her parents that transfer to another section or school would be preferable.

The school year is divided into four "bimesters," each being of two months' duration. Teachers test students at the end of each bimester. However, students should be given prior warning of the tests which must also be approved by the principal. The final grades are the result of the average of the four bimestral tests. The decimal points are preserved in the final grade. Teachers must always be able to justify the final grade given to a student.

9. Educational Assessment, Evaluation, and Research

The Ministry of Education considers the teacher's evaluation process as part of its general system of supervision. "The evaluation process should stimulate professional progress and serve as a showcase of the teacher's efforts."

The Ministry evaluates two main areas. On the one hand personality, and on the other efficiency. The area of personality is divided in five distinct aspects: health and vitality, personal appearance, tone of voice, leadership, and human relations. The area of efficiency is divided in four aspects: teaching qualities, administrative efficiency, interest, and ability to progress.

The reports are evaluated by the Ministry on an annual basis. They are a combination of a self-evaluation on the part of the teachers, the principal's evaluation, the supervisor's review, and a final approval by the provincial director.

10. Major Reforms in the 1980s and 1990s

There were some minor bureaucratic and organizational changes but no major reforms.

However, in the early 1970s an aggressive reform was pushed through a highly sensitive education system. The nucleus of the changes proposed were based on the concept of the "productive school." The child was supposed to be familiarized with notions set in the framework of modern industrialized societies. The curricula and the school teacher would be made more attractive by relating the student with means of production. In rural areas students would come in contact at a very early age with modern agricultural technology as well as with notions of productivity and market competitiveness.

Strong political opposition was mustered to defeat the reforms. After a decade of struggle to implement the new ideas the government was forced to abandon the program. Conservatives, the Catholic Church, and the political parties opposing the government were able to check the reforms. The victory of conservatism in part has to be explained by the fact that the teachers themselves were not part of the process. A once proud teachers' guild that occupied an important place in society had lost much of its influence. Finally, partly because they were not listened to, the teachers sided with the conservative forces.

11. Major Problems for the year 2000

Given the economic crisis, the government has identified two priorities for the 1990s. The first priority links Panama's role in the world to its ability to integrate science and technology in all phases of life. Education must "cooperate with economic development through technology adapted to the requirements of modernization of all productive sectors. Knowledge of science and technology must be promoted throughout the country," (UNESCO/Ministerio de Educación 1992).

The second priority aims at those sectors of the population who live in extreme poverty. "Education and social action must give priority to those groups who are most affected by poverty." The Ministry of Education hopes to find support among nongovernmental organizations in its support of those programs that deal with the poverty question.

Education has still to come to terms with the times and the demands for more complicated training in the fields of science and technology. The 1990s do not seem to be overly concerned with these questions. Panama still has three tasks left over from its effort to modernize the educational system. It has to complete the process of widening the base through which children have access to education. Modern technology has to be introduced on a massive scale into the education system. Finally, the quality of training has to be enhanced at the higher education level.

References

Comisión Coordinadora de Educación Nacional 1985 *Estructura administrativa y régimen legal del sistema educativo panameño*. Ministerio de Educación, Panamá
Ministerio de Educación 1992 *La educación en Panamá. Informe anual 1991*. Ministerio de Educación, Panamá
UNESCO/Ministerio de Educación 1992 *Plan nacional de acción de educación para todos*. UNESCO, San José.

Further Reading

Arosemena D 1988 Discurso inaugural (Escuela Normal de Santiago, 1938). *Revista Lotería* 372
Bernal J B 1991 *Desarrollo y equidad en la educación de base para adultos*. ICASE, Panamá
Candanedo A 1989 Educación y democracia. *Revista Panameña de Sociología* 5
Céspedes F 1979 *Informe sobre la Reforma Educativa*. Ministerio de Educación, Panamá
Comisión Coordinadora de Educación Nacional 1983 *Filosofía de la educación panameña*. Ministerio de Educación, Panamá
Duncan J 1921 La educación pública en Panamá. *Memoria*
Fernández B, Garrido C 1990 Proyecto nacional y política científico–técnica. *Tareas* 75
Ministerio de Educación 1984 *Propuesta para estructuración del sistema educativo*. Ministerio de Educación, Panamá
Mejía B 1993 Situación actual del sistema educativo panameño. In: Picón C (ed.) 1993
Picón C (ed.) 1993 *Educación para todos en Panamá*. Ministerio de Educación, Panamá

Papua New Guinea

N. Hoi and P. Wari

1. General Background

Papua New Guinea, with its over 800 languages and difficult geography, has always made it a challenge to its leaders in bringing unity to the country. Since it gained Independence in 1975, education has always been given top priority by various governments. With the country going through the mineral boom in the early 1990s, the demand for more national participation has highlighted the need to expand access to education at the primary and secondary education level. Major changes have taken place in education over the years and more recently the system has been reviewed to make it more responsive to the needs of the public. The central issue at the primary level is retention, while the central issue at the secondary is access, or opportunity for enrollment.

Papua New Guinea lies just south of the Equator and approximately 150 kilometers north of Australia. The country is made up of the eastern part of the mainland of New Guinea and some 100 smaller islands that lie in the Bismark and Solomon seas to the north and east of the main island. The total land area is just 463,840 square kilometers. The mainland accounts for about 85 percent of the total area. The country shares a land border with Indonesia.

The mainland is divided by a massive mountain range and includes the highest peak in the Pacific (12,500 feet). Covered by tropical rain forest the climate is generally hot all year round, averaging up to 34°C in the coastal regions.

The 1990 census estimated the population to be approximately 4 million, over one-third of which live in the Highlands region. Physical characteristics of the people are broadly that of the Melanesian group. However, within the country, there is a diversity of physical characteristics, language, and culture depending on the province of origin. The heterogeneity of group is best highlighted by the fact that there are more than 800 languages.

Formal schooling in Papua New Guinea only began after the first European settlement in 1873. Schooling at that time was the responsibility of missions and focused on teaching basic literacy so that the Bible could be read. Real growth in education began when the Department of Education was formed in 1946 as part of the Combined Territory of Papua New Guinea administration. In 1952, the first Education Ordinance came into being which defined in law the right of the administration to exercise control over schools (registration and exemption), the certification of teachers, and payments of grants-in-aid. This however, was not exercised until 1955 when the Territory's first syllabus appeared on a trial basis. Control over registration and certification of teachers followed.

In reality, there were two independent education systems operating in the 1950s: one system under the administration and the other under the churches and missions. The systems that were active and effectively managed normally contributed finance or materials to the schools in their areas. In the late 1960s it was recognized that a system was needed to coordinate all the activities relating to education and the administration appointed a three-man advisory committee (Weeden Committee) to investigate education in the Territory.

The Weeden Report (Weeden 1969) resulted in the establishment of two important laws: the Papua New Guinea Education Ordinance (1970) and the Papua New Guinea Teaching Service Commission (1971). These two ordinances brought about many changes to the education system and together they outlined the objectives of the national education system.

After the country gained Independence in 1975, the Organic Law on Provincial Government established the provincial government system and certain responsibilities for education were decentralized to the provincial level. This meant that provinces theoretically had almost full responsibilities for planning, financing, staffing, and maintaining community schools, vocational centers, and provincial high schools. However, the National Department of Education kept some control over the distribution of national funds. Curriculum in community, provincial, and national high schools, including time allocation, syllabus content, assessment, and inspections is a national responsibility. Control over national high schools, technical colleges, and primary teachers' colleges are also national functions.

Decentralization has benefited some provinces in that provincial public servants are in a better position than national staff to identify local needs and coordinate required services. However, decentralization also has its disadvantages. The divided nature of responsibilities has made the management of education a most complex task. The creation of 19 provincial divisions of education, together with the drive for localization, make it difficult to determine, agree upon, implement, and enforce nationwide policies or strategies concerning the many areas of education where responsibility is shared or unclear.

2. The Goals of the Education System

The main aim of the education system is to provide a quality education. "Quality education" is defined as an education which strengthens citizens' identification with rather than alienation from their own communities. In this context, the system emphasizes education of the appropriate attitudes, knowledge, and skills relevant to community development. The system also aims at providing individuals with a degree of competence in English, mathematics, and science to ensure the development of citizens who are committed to their own personal development and who view education as a continuing life-long process. It also encourages the development of education fitted to the needs of the country and to establish, preserve, and improve the standards of education throughout the country and make the benefit of such education available to as many people as possible.

3. The Formal System of Education

Education is the largest consumer of national resources and the largest single employer in the country. Education provides a complex system ranging from preschool to university study. Formal education is provided at three levels—primary, secondary, and tertiary. Figure 1 presents the structure of the education system.

3.1 Primary, Secondary, and Tertiary Education

Primary school education is aimed at providing basic skills in reading, writing, and mathematics. Primary schools are called "community schools" because of their close link and association with the community and cover the first six years of education. Although the official age of entry to school is 7 years, children older than 7 years of age also enroll. It is a national government policy to provide basic education for all children from the age of 7 by the year 2000. In 1992, only about 73 percent of the age group enrolled in schools.

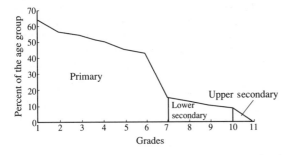

Figure 1

Papua New Guinea: Structure of the formal education system 1979–89

There is no formal preprimary education, although, some provinces have a one-year preparatory class to provide initial literacy in a language which the children speak before they commence formal schooling.

In 1992, there were approximately 2,510 community schools and 26 International Education Agency schools providing education to approximately 413,089 students and the national gross enrollment rate was 73.2 percent with an average annual increase of 1 percent. Some 44 percent of community school pupils were girls. The national male–female distribution was 52:48. The pupil–teacher ratio was 32:1 in 1989. In 1990, there were approximately 12,514 teachers. The percentage of teachers who were female was 31.6.

Secondary education is comprised of two levels—lower-secondary education for Grades 7 to 10 and upper-secondary for grades 11 to 12. Lower-secondary education for the 12 to 16 age group aims at educating students to become useful and productive members of society with special emphasis on the application of acquired skills and knowledge and the development of positive attitudes, as well as providing opportunities for students to achieve personal fulfillment.

Secondary schools are known as "provincial high schools." There were approximately 130 provincial high schools in 1991 with some 53,494 students, 37 percent of whom were girls. The gross enrollment rate shows a very low average for female students, which in 1989 was 12.1 compared with the average male enrollment rate of around 18 percent. The pupil–teacher ratio was 27:1, but this varies somewhat from province to province.

Upper-secondary education covers Grades 11 and 12 in national high schools and is viewed as the continuation of general education leading to university entrance. Some 2,000 Grade 11 and 12 students enroll in the four national high schools. In 1992, 29 percent were females. The pupil–teacher ratio stood at 19:1.

Apart from the mainstream structure, an alternative distance route for students who are not able to enter the mainstream schools exists at the lower-secondary education level through the College of Distance Education and in vocational centers at provincial centers. Alternatives to upper-secondary education are provided by the adult matriculation courses offered by the Extension Studies Department of the University of Papua New Guinea.

Tertiary education offers a variety of options from technical and teacher training, to university degrees, diplomas, and certificates. The higher education sector comprises sixty colleges and two universities. There are eight community teachers' colleges and four technical colleges. Most of these institutions have not been founded, but rather have grown up in response to the initiatives of missions of government departments. To a large extent, the institutions have met the country's needs for technical personnel, but they have been found to have high unit costs, insufficient response to labor force needs, and sometimes the quality of their graduates is low.

Attrition rates are as high as 46 percent, and facilities, equipment, and staff time are underused. The Commission for Higher Education is responsible for coordinating higher education in Papua New Guinea. Its objectives include fostering a rational development of higher education in the light of Papua New Guinea's needs in terms of resources and delivering higher education efficiently and cost-effectively and maintaining quality. The National Higher Education Plan prepared by the Commission for Higher Education has outlined strategies to meet these objectives.

3.2 Preschool Education

While the formal education system starts at Grade 1, an increasing number of preparatory schools or classes have developed around the country. This development resulted from the concern by communities that children needed to acquire initial literacy in a language which they speak, and be more closely bonded to their culture. Known as *Tok Ples* schools, these schools originally offered mainly initial literacy in the vernacular, but the curriculum of most of them was broadened to include numeracy and health.

There was a wide range of financial support systems and coordination strategies for preparatory classes. Some preparatory classes were run in separate institutions while others were established in association with a community school. The length of preparatory courses varies from one to two years. In 1991, many training courses for preparatory class teachers were run by different groups. These courses were run over a period of six weeks and included materials and costs of approximately K800 (US$821) per graduate.

3.3 Special Education

It was estimated that in Papua New Guinea there were about 24.7 percent of disabled persons per 1,000 of population in 1980. Most of the disabled persons have been found to be suffering from deafness and blindness which means that a great number of the disabled children in the country have not benefited from normal schooling and require education in a special school.

There are very few schools in Papua New Guinea for disabled or handicapped children and most of these schools are located in main urban centers. These schools are permitted schools outside the national education system and are coordinated by the National Board for the Disabled.

3.4 Vocational, Technical, and Business Education

Under the Organic Law on decentralization, vocational centers were categorized as nonformal education and therefore were seen as provincial government responsibilities. In 1991, there were 105 vocational centers, with 6,000 trainees and 400 instructors, costing over K5 million (US$5.13 million) per year.

Vocational training is aimed at producing either the ability to be self-employed or run a small business, or enhancement of subsistence has become highly relevant. However, compared to high school or technical education, it has not been given commensurate support in terms of support of teacher education or funding.

Technical education in the country is concerned with giving people the skills to fit into established niches in the formal sector. Technical education is carried out in six technical colleges and two business colleges. The colleges come under the direction of the Technical Division of the National Department of Education.

The main programs offered are the one-year pre-employment technical training courses, designed to fit students for later apprenticeships or in the case of the business college, direct employment. The second type of courses are known as extension courses of eight weeks' duration, which are provided within the framework of apprenticeship training. Then there are courses which lead to certificates and are geared to a higher technical level. The fourth type of courses are specific responses to demands of the economy, for instance, welding or hydraulics.

3.5 Nonformal and Adult Education

Nonformal education in Papua New Guinea includes village-based literacy for children, youth, and adults; agriculture and health programs; provincial and community libraries; and distance education for school leavers. Despite its importance in the development of individuals, communities, provinces, and the nation as whole, government support for nonformal education has often been sporadic and disorganized. Fortunately nongovernmental organizations have given the most support to nonformal activities and the efforts of these organizations are generally supported.

At the provincial level, 20 Adult Education Officer positions were created in 1973. These positions were later changed into Provincial Nonformal Education Officers and given the responsibility of vocational centers. Only a very few provinces had nonformal education embracing a variety of aspects of adult education.

4. Administrative and Supervisory Structure and Operation

The Ministry of Education is responsible for the universities, the Commission for Higher Education, the National Department of Education, and the Teaching Service Commission. The administration of education in Papua New Guinea is a complex task. The efficient delivery of education is complicated by factors such as the existence of a large number of agencies and the lack of line authority for the entire system.

The universities are self-administered, but responsible to the national government through the Minister for Education. The functions of the Teaching Service Commission hinge on overseeing all matters relating to the terms and conditions of service of the teaching service. The Commission for Higher Education deals with all matters concerning higher education.

The National Department of Education was established to manage education for all of Papua New Guinea under the direction of the National Education Board and is the executive arm of the Ministry of Education. It has some responsibility for community (primary) and secondary education and full responsibility for higher education. Under a 1991 restructuring, the Department was divided into four wings according to the type of education services they provide, namely, Special Education, Standards, General Administration, and General Education.

Education management and planning takes place at three levels: nationally through the National Education Board, provincially through the Provincial Education Board, and at the school or local level through the local governing board, the headteachers and teachers.

Provincial Divisions of Education operate under the direction of Provincial Education Boards. Each Provincial Division of Education has officers to oversee specific areas of education management. The headteachers, teachers, and the boards of management in community schools and boards of governors in high schools manage and plan for education at the school level. Table 1 presents an overview of the responsibilities of the national, provincial, and local levels.

5. Educational Finance

The educational system in the country has been greatly affected by the lack of funds over the years. Between 1978 and 1988 there was a 39 percent fall in real public expenditure on education. Between 1983 and 1991 there was no increase in real terms in the amount of money allocated to education, even though the total number of students enrolled in the system increased from 374,524 to 488,524 in the same time period. With the government requiring greater increased retention and expansion of the primary and secondary systems in the future, it will be necessary to increase the level of funding of the system. In 1989, the unit cost was estimated to be around K200 (US$205) for primary education, K350 (US$359)

Table 1
Distribution of primary and lower-secondary education functions by government level

Function	National	Provincial	Local
Planning	x	x	
School siting, expansion, or consolidation		x	x
School and teacher housing construction, equipment, and maintenance		x	x
Determination of number of teaching posts	x	x	
Teacher training	x		
Teacher inservice training	x	x	
Teacher certification	x		
Teacher grading, inspection, promotion, and tenure	x		
Teacher appointment, transfer, and payment			x
Teacher discipline	x	x	x
Maximum pupil–teacher ratio	x	x	
Teacher hours	x	x	
Extracurricular teacher duties		x	x
Student selection	x	x	
Student discipline		x	x
Curriculum content and language	x	x	
Length of schooling (years/days per year)	x	x	
End-of-cycle examinations	x		
Student promotion and repetition	x	x	
Learning materials	x	x	
School fees—setting and collection		x	x
School/teacher-training college grants-in-aid	x	x	
Establishment of school boards		x	x
School closure	x	x	

767

for secondary, and κ2,000 (US$2,053) for Grades 11 and 12.

6. Supplying Personnel for the Education System

The purpose of education is not just to contribute to individual development, but also to provide suitably educated, qualified, and well-motivated members of the workforce. Overall, Papua New Guineans make up approximately 96 percent of the country's workforce. Localization has progressed at a steady rate over the years. The growth in localization was also reflected in the vast progress made in training Papua New Guineans to take over jobs in the education system. In 1990, secondary education employed some 2,021 teachers, of which 207 were non-Papua New Guineans.

The Department of Education's localization policy is considered very important because it is felt that: (a) Papua New Guineans should be running their own country and making their own decisions; (b) due to scarcity of employment opportunities preference should be given to employing citizens; and (c) because the recruitment of contract officers is expensive, the fewer contract officers employed will mean more money can be used to fund other educational developments.

The Staff Development Unit of the National Department of Education was set up in 1984 with its function to monitor localization programs and to provide inservice training for Papua New Guinea staff employed by the Department of Education and Teaching Service Commission. The Staff Development Unit is organized into two committees, both of which supervise and coordinate the selection, assessment, and training of officers and select officers within the education system for courses and conferences.

For the training of community school (primary) teachers there are eight community teachers' colleges, of which seven are run by churches and one by the government. In 1991 there were 1,419 students mostly coming from Grade 10 of which 25 percent were female. The colleges had a total of 144 academic and 127 nonacademic staff. Lower-secondary teacher education takes place on two campuses of the University of Papua New Guinea: Goroka and Waigani. Of these, Goroka is the principal source of lower-secondary teachers.

Vocational center instructors formerly were trained through two programs at the Port Moresby Inservice College (a one-year course for male and two years for female instructors). The preservice training programs lacked facilities, support, materials, equipment, and status. Recommendations were made under the 1991 Education Sector Review to strengthen the training programs through training vocational and technical instructors over a two-year period in one institution.

7. Curriculum Development

There is a growing concern that education in Papua New Guinea is failing to help the majority of people to participate usefully in the activities of the community and the development of the nation. Attempts are being made to develop a curriculum that will be more relevant to the vast majority of the population. The adopting of a philosophy of education in 1986 led to the beginning of a restructuring of the curriculum.

All curriculum and materials development is carried out by the Curriculum Development Division of the National Department of Education. The work of the curriculum unit is guided by Boards of Studies which review and approve syllabuses and supervise curriculum and material development through Curriculum Advisory Committees.

The curriculum at the primary level in the proposed reformed primary system will provide for initial literacy in a language that the child speaks, and the transfer of these skills to English; integrated activity-based elementary and lower-primary education, with the introduction of discrete subjects at upper-primary level; and a renewed emphasis on social, cultural, spiritual, ethical, moral, and vocational education.

The latter emphases will also apply to all secondary level as well as more integrated teaching. At the upper-secondary level, changes in curriculum and examination structures will allow for different student abilities, including advanced courses to enable the most able students to gain international recognition.

8. The System of Examinations, Promotions, and Certifications

The award of school certificates to students within the national education system is the responsibility of the National Department of Education. The Measurement Services Unit of the Department of Education is responsible for the production and administration of national examinations at Grades 6, 10, and 12. The final results for each level are presented in slightly different ways although they are all used for the same basic purposes—selection to the next level of education.

At Grade 6 students take two 25-mark basic skills, criterion-reference tests which assess competency in English and mathematics basic skills. A certain level of achievement is recommended on each of the two papers for a student to be considered for selection into secondary school. Final selections are made on the basis of a 50-mark combined subjects paper. The provinces, however, use a variety of criteria to make final selections. Each student receives a certificate to state that he or she has completed six years of primary education and the examination results are not reported on the certificate.

At Grade 10, students are assessed on the basis of both internal and external marks. National examinations are worth 50 marks each for English, mathematics, science, and social science. National examination marks are moderated with internal marks to compare students on a national basis. Each student receives a certificate to state that he or she had completed four years of secondary education. Moderated results are recorded on the certificate as grades, whereas other subjects, which are internally assessed, are reported in terms of the student's position in the school. Students are required to score at particular levels in the four examined subjects in order to be selected for further education.

Grade 12 students are nationally examined in a number of subjects. Results on the national examination are used to moderate internal assessment marks to compare on a national basis. Each student receives a certificate to state that he or she has completed two years of national high-school education. Moderated results are recorded on the certificates as grades. Students are required to score C or better in their chosen subjects to be considered for matriculation into universities. About 65 to 70 percent of Grade 12 leavers matriculate, and most of the rest find their way into other tertiary institutions.

9. Educational Assessment, Evaluation, and Research

The are three main institutions which undertake educational research. They are: the Research and Evaluation Unit of the National Department of Education, the University of Papua New Guinea, and the National Research Institute. The Research and Evaluation Unit was originally set up in 1981, primarily to evaluate World Bank projects. In 1984, the Evaluation Unit was further expanded to include the already existing research branch of the department. The responsibilities of the unit now include coordinating a range of research and evaluation studies, both within and outside the National Department of Education.

The Research and Evaluation Unit carries out research and evaluation activities requested by the National Department of Education and the Provincial Divisions of Education. The Unit fulfills its role by identifying evaluation and research needs and priorities, conducting studies, reporting results, and monitoring external studies approved by the Department. A Research and Evaluation Committee is responsible for monitoring and overseeing the Unit's activities.

Although research has been undertaken on many aspects of education over the years, most of this can be categorized into the following: educational administration and technical planning, staff training and development, curriculum development, literacy, higher education, and vocational and technical education.

10. Major Reforms in the 1980s and 1990s

The main educational issues which affect national development are: universal primary education, retention, female enrollment, expansion of access to upper- and lower-secondary, curriculum relevance, decentralization, equal opportunities, localization, quality, funding, human resources, and employment.

In the 1980s, most of the developments in education that addressed these issues were in the form of major projects. These projects were designed to meet the needs of particular levels of education and a large share of the cost of the projects were met through loans from outside agencies such as the World Bank. The national and provincial governments also funded some projects with several provinces giving special attention to nonformal and nutrition education through their integrated rural development plans. However, until 1992, the education system has continued to place its emphasis on formal education, despite the realization that not all of the educational needs of the population could be met through the formal system.

The Department of Education in conjunction with UNESCO completed an education sector review of the status of education in the country (Department of Education 1991). The review aimed at identifying the deficiencies in the current education system and built on successful provincial initiatives in a proposal for major educational reform.

The proposed reforms are wide-ranging and encompass a restructuring of the education system (see Fig. 2). More specifically, the proposed reforms call for: (a) increased access to school for 6-year olds and initial literacy and early education in a language which the child speaks; (b) greater cultural bonding as a result of the above, and 11 years of education located in or near the home and no more Grade 6 leavers; (c) increased retention and improved standards as a result of a change in language policy and the provision of a more integrated activity-based curriculum; (d) increased access (by almost 50%) to both the lower- and upper-secondary levels; (e) a major improvement in the place of vocational education within the secondary stream; (f) the development of biases at matriculation level—technical, agricultural, commercial, including a "School of Excellence"; and (g) an increased number of Grade 12 leavers but at a much lower cost. Due to the comprehensive nature of the reforms recommended, strategies are being developed to ensure that very careful and thorough planning is undertaken.

11. Major Problems for the Year 2000

For the year 2000, the major problems will be access, retention, and relevance. There is a great disparity in the ages of children enrolling in Grade 1. Initial

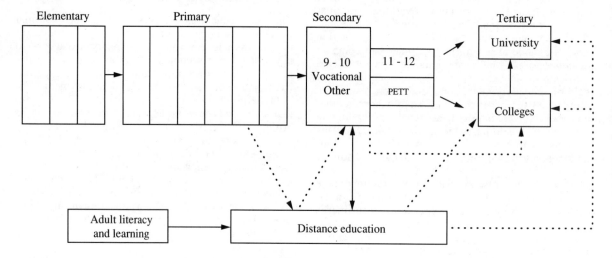

Figure 2
Papua New Guinea: The proposed restructure of the education system

literacy and education is largely provided in a foreign language resulting in many children leaving school as functionally illiterate. Only about 73 percent of an age cohort enroll in a community school. Of those who enroll, only 55 percent complete Grade 6. This means that the goal of universal primary education is still a long way away from becoming a reality. Furthermore, as only 32 percent of the children are able to continue their education beyond Grade 6, there is a great public demand to have opportunities for continued education.

At the lower-secondary level, only 15.5 percent of the school age group (13–16 year-olds attend school. A further 20,000 students do secondary-level courses by correspondence studies through the College of Distance Education. Of those who enter Grade 7, only about 66 percent complete Grade 10, and of those who complete Grade 10, only about one-third are selected for further education or training. About 3.8 percent of the upper-secondary age cohort (17–18 year-olds) have access to Grade 12 education or training at technical or teachers' colleges. In addition, there is a serious shortage of teachers. Most of these problems are now being addressed by the National Education Reform Task Force and hopefully strategies will be developed to address the problems.

References

Department of Education 1991 *Education Sector Review, Deliberations and Findings*, Vol. 2. Department of Education, Port Moresby

Weeden W J 1969 *Report of the Advisory Committee on Education in Papua New Guinea*. Department of Education, Port Moresby

Further Reading

Commission for Higher Education 1985a *Towards a Strategy for Higher Education in Papua New Guinea*. Commission for Higher Education, Port Moresby

Commission for Higher Education 1985b *Annual Report*. Education Printshop, Port Moresby

Department of Education 1981 *Education II Project Documents, 1981–1987: A World Bank Project on Primary Education in Papua New Guinea*. Department of Education, Port Moresby

Department of Education 1985 *Five Year Education Plan: Community School Sector 1986–1990 1976–1980*. Department of Education, Port Moresby

Department of Education 1985 *Growth of Education Since Independence 1975–1985*. Department of Education, Port Moresby

Department of Education, Planning Branch 1991 *Facts and Figures 1991*. Education Printshop, Port Moresby

Hees R, Allison C, Bahr K, Russell P, Johnson C M 1987 *The Costs and Financing of Education in Papua New Guinea*, Report No. 6767-PNG. World Bank, Washington, DC

Papua New Guinea, National Planning Office 1984 *Medium Term Development Strategy: Education Strategy 1984*. Discussion paper. Government Printing Office, Port Moresby

Papua New Guinea, Department of Finance and Planning 1986 *National Manpower Assessment 1982–1992*. Government Printers, Port Moresby

Pearson M R 1988 *A Report on the State of Localization in Various Areas of the Papua New Guinea Education System for the Year 1988*. Department of Education, Port Moresby

Weeks S 1988 *A Proposed Plan for Educational Development in Papua New Guinea 1989–1993*. National Research Institute, Port Moresby

Paraguay

D. M. Rivarola

1. General Background

Paraguay was constituted as a republic in 1811. There have been changes to its boundaries, principally because of two long wars (1865–70 and 1932–35). The country covers 406,752 square kilometers and is bordered by Argentina, Brazil, and Bolivia. It has two very different regions: the Chaco Paraguay or the western region, covering an area of 246,925 square kilometers and inhabited by 5 percent or so of the total population, and the eastern region, covering 159,827 square kilometers. Since 1960, the population of the latter region has changed in terms of its spatial distribution due to internal migration. At the same time the country has also received important influxes of migrants, principally from Brazil but also from some Asian countries such as Japan and Korea.

According to the 1982 census, the population was four million, and in 1992 it was estimated to be about 5.5 million. There has been much racial mixing since the colonial period. In 1992 the indigenous population did not exceed 2 percent of the total population, and was still declining. One result of this mixing has been bilingualism, that is to say, the retention of the native language alongside Spanish. According to the 1982 census, 40.1 percent of the population spoke Guaraní only, 7 percent Spanish only, and the remainder spoke Japanese, German, and Portuguese, the last of which is rapidly expanding, mostly in the frontier area. The varied cultural composition of the population is recognized as being of utmost importance in the process of education and cultural development as well as an essential element of national identity and the recently approved constitution has recognized both Spanish and the indigenous language as the official languages of the republic.

The economy is predominantly agricultural. Around 80 percent of exports are from the agricultural sector, which accounts for approximately 45 percent of the economically active population. In the early 1990s the rate of growth of the Paraguayan economy declined significantly. In 1992, it grew by only 3.1 percent. The minimum salary was equivalent to US$168 and inflation in 1991 was approximately 34 percent. The value of exports, largely made up of primary products, was approximately US$1 billion in 1991. At the same time the external debt of Paraguay was US$2 billion.

2. Politics and the Goals of the Education System

In contrast to the influential countries of the River Plate region, to which it has historically been culturally integrated, the political development of Paraguay has been characterized by a succession of authoritarian regimes. Since the collapse of the liberal regime following the War of the Chaco (1932–35), there was a dictatorial regime until February 1989 when free elections were held and fundamentally democratic institutions were reestablished. This radical change in political orientation had very important effects on educational development at a time when education was undergoing a serious crisis largely brought about by political parties' interests in the management of education, with the abuse of power within the education system. One of the first measures of the new democratic government was to recognize education as one of the priority areas of its social policy. This measure led to the creation of a special commission composed of well-known specialists in the field of education to support and advise the government in the process of educational reform. Since then this commission has continued to function, with responsibility for setting out the fundamental guidelines for educational reform, designing its strategy, and participating in the process of implementation. Both chambers of the National Congress firmly supported the reform, and have announced important laws such as that which governs the functioning of the universities. The new 1992 Constitution paid particular attention to education and included the implementation of bilingual education and the statutory allocation of 20 percent of the national budget to education.

With the inauguration of democracy, important steps have been taken to confront the evident decline in the quality of Paraguayan education: the educational

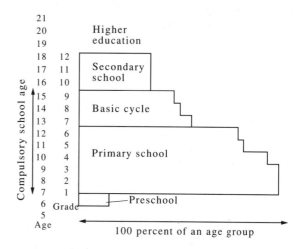

Figure 1

Paraguay: Structure of the formal education system

budget was significantly raised, the salary of teachers was improved, infant education was decreed to begin at six years of age and the regional centers of education were reorganized to allow the participation of the community in the management of learning activities. This latter point was a first step in the administrative decentralization considered to be one of the priorities of educational reform. Flexibility in terms of the requirements for the creation of new universities also permitted the organization of an appreciable number of private universities.

3. The Formal System of Education

The National Constitution establishes that basic school education lasting nine years is compulsory and free. It is the responsibility of the state to promote secondary, technical, agricultural, industrial, and higher or university teaching. The Ministry of Education and Culture is the governmental office responsible for this function. Figure 1 presents the structure of the system.

3.1 Primary, Secondary, and Tertiary Education

Primary education lasts six years. Since 1993 the age of entry to school is 6 years. This stage is followed by the basic cycle of 3 years, and is followed by diversified secondary school teaching (where students choose to specialize in a particular subject), which also lasts 3 years.

After a period of very slow growth between the second half of the 1940s and the first half of the 1950s, rates of school attendance underwent a sustained increase. In 1980 the net level of school attendance was 90 percent, 93 percent in 1989, and 94.5 percent in 1990. In 1991, of the total school age population (7–12 years), 720,983 pupils attended school, and an estimated 40,000 did not. Of the total school population in 1992, 85.9 percent attended public schools and 14 percent attended private institutions and the distribution was: 44.5 percent urban and 55.5 percent rural. Table 1 presents 1991 data on primary schools.

Table 1
Registration, teaching posts, and schools. Primary education 1991[a]

	Total	Urban	Rural
Students	720,983	319,948	401,035
Teaching posts	29,172	11,402	17,770
Schools	4,649	1,002	3,647
Student–Teacher Ratio	25:1	28:1	23:1
Student–School Ratio	155:1	319:1	110:1

a Source: Ministry of Education and Culture 1992

Although the attendance rate at primary school reaches significant levels, serious problems still persist. In general terms, differences between rural and urban areas continue to be important. For example, according to 1989 data, the completion rate for primary education at the national level was 47 percent, but only 32 percent in rural areas. The national average success rate was 43 percent, but only 29 percent in rural areas. The drastic decline in the quality of education—and consequently success rates—according to the urban or rural location or the public or private status of the school has been corroborated in various studies (Rivarola 1977, Rivarola 1991, Rivarola et al. 1977, Corvalán 1981, Corvalán et al. 1981).

One of the most serious problems is the failure of students to pass their grades and consequently having to repeat a year. According to Schiefelbein and Heikkinen (1991), this is a particular problem among students who come from poor families which lie below the 50th percentile line of income distribution, where nearly 40 percent have to repeat grades.

There are serious limitations in educational resources. At the national level, students fail to complete their schooling in 33 percent of schools. Of these, 81 percent are located in rural areas where a significant number only reach third grade (29%) or second grade (14%). Furthermore, some 28 percent of teaching posts are held by unqualified teachers. In general, 42 percent of teachers in rural areas are unqualified, and in some areas this is 75 percent.

Since the 1960s illiteracy has declined, although there are signs that this situation has deteriorated since the mid-1980s. Even so, the illiteracy levels are relatively low compared with other Latin American countries. According to the last national census, 14.2 percent of the population aged 15 years old and older were illiterate. Some 30 percent were in rural areas, and of these 19.1 percent were men and 22.9 percent women.

Secondary education began to undergo expansion toward the middle of the 1950s. This was related to the high level of coverage which had been achieved by primary education. Levels of school attendance at the secondary level experienced a sustained increase (20.3% in 1972, 27% in 1980, 30.9% in 1985, and 32.5% in 1990).

In 1991 a total of 166,894 students were enrolled in secondary education, 151,391 (90.7%) of which were in educational institutions located in urban areas, and the rest (9.3%) in rural areas. At the same time, 78.4 percent were enrolled in public schools that reflected the central role which the state had come to assume in the expansion of secondary teaching since 1965.

Secondary education consists of two cycles: basic education and the diversified cycle, both lasting three years. The latter cycle is divided into three branches: diploma in human sciences, diploma in business studies, and a technical diploma. The first two can lead to entrance to the university or to the Institute of

Table 2
Coverage of the formal education system by level 1989[a]

Registration	Quality	Percentage of all students
Preschool education	30,019	3.4
Primary education	656,877	74.6
Special education	1,286	0.1
Literacy and adult education	31,393	3.6
Secondary education	157,458	17.9
Teacher training	3,384	0.4

a Source: Ministry of Education and Culture 1990

Teacher Training. The technical diploma can lead to entry into postsecondary level institutions in the fields of industry or agriculture. In 1991 the distribution was as follows: 65 percent in the basic cycle, 28 percent in the diploma in human studies, 6 percent in the diploma in business studies, and 1 percent in the technical diploma.

According to 1989 estimates, only 37 percent of young people between the ages of 13 and 18 enter the formal education system. At the same time, secondary school attendance accounts for only 17.9 percent of all students, as can be seen from Table 2. The expansion of secondary education is greater in urban areas. In 1989, 81 percent of secondary education institutions were located in urban centers; in 1991 this increased to 90.7 percent.

Compared with the national average completion rate, which was 45 percent in 1989, in rural zones it was only 17 percent. One of the reasons was the considerably reduced number of educational institutions which teach up to the level of the diploma. Around 40 percent of the institutions do not have full school attendance. Just over 80 percent of the institutions which handle the six courses in secondary teaching are located in urban areas. Of the total number of secondary educational institutions only 2.1 percent provide technical education.

One of the serious problems in secondary schools is the low level of achievement, particularly in the rural areas in the central section of the country. One of the principal reasons is the lack of qualified teachers and equipment.

Until 1990, higher education was offered in two universities: the National University of Asunción (UNA) which was founded in 1886, and the Catholic University which was established in 1960. With the installation of the democratic regime in the country in 1989, a series of restrictions governing the organization of new universities, which had been imposed by the authoritarian regime, were eliminated. This resulted in the emergence of five new centers of higher education. The new Constitution authorized the running of a center of university education which was established by the National Congress. In 1991–92, four new universities were created.

Since 1950, there has been a rapid increase in university enrollment, albeit with certain fluctuations. Since the 1970s this has intensified due to two main factors: first, the expansion of secondary teaching and the opening of university centers in the interior of the country and second, the economic boom of the 1970s, which opened up the possibilities for social sectors with fewer resources to gain access to university education.

In 1990, the National University of Asunción had 19,742 students, while the Catholic University had approximately 11,000. The rate of annual increase in university enrollment was 8.8 percent in the period from 1975 to 1980; 5.1 percent from 1980 to 1984 and 6 percent from 1985 to 1990. The decrease observed in the 1980s reflected the grave economic crisis which has affected the Paraguayan economy since then.

For entrance into the two traditional universities there are somewhat different entrance exams. In the period from 1970 to 1990, the average rejection rate was approximately 45 percent, although this has begun to decline (50.4% in 1981, 48.6% in 1985, and 43.5% in 1990). The new universities have dispensed with the entrance exam, which has resulted in an increase in registration.

University education is passing through a profound crisis, primarily because of its low completion rates and the grave deterioration in its levels of quality. One of the determining factors is the limited resources available to finance basic equipment, organization, and salaries. Indeed, there is no research activity and almost all the lecturers are part-time and receive a meager wage. The average salary of a qualified lecturer fluctuates between US$210 and US$180 per month.

3.2 Preschool Education

In 1989 there were 814 educational kindergartens with a combined enrollment of 30,019 children, 45 percent of whom are enrolled in state kindergartens and 55 percent in private ones. Of these children, 86 percent were in urban areas and 14 percent in rural areas. The expansion of preschool education is primarily hampered by economic factors. This explains the slow progress of the public sector and also the fact that around 70 percent of registration at this level is concentrated in the capital city, Asunción, and the central zone (surrounding Asunción), which constitutes the region of greatest population increase.

3.3 Special Education

The development of special education has been very slow, although it had a strong impetus in the late 1980s. There are 75 institutions for disabled students, 71 of which are located in urban areas. Of these establishments 75 percent are public and depend on state subsidies. The total number of students enrolled in these schools in 1991 was 2,753, of which 1,629 were males and 1,124 were females. In the same year, public establishments had a total of 234 teachers and the private sector had 104 teachers.

3.4 Vocational, Technical, and Business Education

The technical and vocational education system of the early 1990s is based on the educational reform which was drawn up in 1956. That year a special commission was formed to study reform at the high school level. Based on the commission's work, the Plan of Study (curriculum) was passed in 1960 for business education, and was revised over the next few years as it began to be implemented.

An important landmark in technical education was the creation of the Pte. Carlos A. López Vocational Technical School. The school's main objective was to update the curriculum at this level, adding new programs. The private sector also participated. In 1959, the Salesian Technical School was created by the Catholic Salesian order. In 1972, the Department of Technical Education was established to develop programs in such areas as electricity, electronics, mechanics, and refrigeration. Throughout the 1970s, the Ministry of Education and Culture implemented a series of initiatives to expand vocational education.

In the early 1970s high school education was divided into three separate programs: business, technical–agrofishery, and humanities. Despite the emphasis that the public and private sectors placed on technical, vocational and commercial education, there has only been slow progress since the early 1970s. The majority of students are still enrolled in the humanities. In 1991, 80.7 percent were concentrated in humanities, 15.8 percent in the commercial program, and only 3.5 percent in the technical program. As a result, a major restructuring of the high school curriculum in general, and a new look at technical and vocational education, is receiving high priority.

Finally, business education programs have grown in the late 1980s with the expansion of educational institutions—principally through the creation of new universities—that concentrate on accounting, business administration, management, and computer science.

3.5 Adult and Nonformal Education

Although it is recognized that needs are increasing, the institutional capacity of the Ministry of Education for adult and nonformal educational programs continues to be extremely limited, in terms of both human and material resources. However, it should be noted that the armed forces are responsible for literacy courses: conscripts doing their military service participate in these activities.

In 1991, there were 540 centers for literacy and adult education in operation. Of these, 61 percent were

Table 3
Literacy and adult education registration by zones 1990[a]

	Total	Adult literacy	Basic edcuation	Vocational training
Total	29,707	1,171	18,323	10,213
Urban	22,680	896	13,062	8,722
Rural	7,027	275	5,261	1,491

a Source: Ministry of Education and Culture 1990

located in urban areas and the rest in rural areas; 13 of the centers were responsible for literacy, 509 for basic adult education, and 8 for training.

The provision of this type of program appears to be insufficient when it is considered that the number of illiterate people in the country in 1989 was 259,000 but the total registration for literacy courses was 1,171. Table 3 presents information on adult and nonformal education enrollment for 1990.

4. Administrative and Supervisory Structure and Operation

The most noticeable characteristic of the Paraguayan educational system is its high degree of centralization. A high concentration of the decision-making power lies with the minister of education and other high officials within the Ministry, as well as with the departmental directors and supervisors. There is agreement that this extreme centralization is one of the determining factors in the inefficiency and failure of operation in projects organized by intermediary and regional groups. According to a study conducted by the Advisory Commission for Educational Reform (1992), the most critical factors affecting educational administration are the following: (a) institutional inadequacy which prevents the initiation and orientation of actions at the regional and national levels; (b) excessive centralization at the technical curricular level, both in supervision and financial administration; (c) little coordination among the technical and administrative educational units, as well as between the different regions and educational communities; (d) lack of norms for selecting personnel and assigning them to specific positions, and an absence of any kind of mechanism for evaluating the work and skills of the permanent staff; (e) disorder and inadequacy of the present set of legal practices, norms, regulations, and bureaucratic proceedings.

It is also widely agreed that there are serious deficiencies in the supervisory structure. These involve: poor functioning, a prevailing authoritative work style among the supervisors, and a strong political party influence which has determined the choices of supervi-

Table 4
Recurrent and capital budget allocation to education levels 1982–91[a]

Expenses	1982	1985	1989	1990	1991
Recurrent	82.6	85.7	96.6	98.7	94.3
Primary school	33.7	34.5	37.7	40.4	42.0
Secondary school	15.5	17.9	19.7	20.3	24.9
University	19.3	19.2	23.8	24.3	16.9
Teacher training	1.4	1.4	1.4	1.4	1.1
National University	17.9	17.7	22.4	22.9	15.7
Catholic University	0.0	0.0	0.0	0.0	0.0
Other programs	14.0	14.2	15.4	13.6	10.6
Capital	17.4	14.3	3.4	1.3	5.7
Total	100.0	100.0	100.0	100.0	100.0

a Sources: Treasury Department. National Budgets

sory personnel and the duties they have been assigned. It has been suggested that the supervisory structure suffers limitations such as: (a) the predominance of political party criteria in selecting personnel and supporting their work; (b) lack of systematic training received by the majority of the supervisors in order to equip them to better the quality of education; (c) a shortage of supervisors which overloads them and makes it impossible for them to attend to everything under their jurisdiction; (d) an authoritative style and a large concentration of power, which make the supervisory structure one of the most serious obstacles for educational change.

This perception of the structures for educational administration and supervision has led the Advisory Commission of Educational Reform and the National Education Congress to set them as top priorities in the reform of the Paraguayan educational system.

5. Educational Finance

In 1990, governmental support of the educational sector represented 1.2 percent of the gross domestic product, and around 12.4 percent of the total budget of the central government. This did not vary significantly from the budget profile during the 1970s. As already stated, democratic government installed in May 1989 established that education would constitute a priority in government policy. Table 4 presents the recurrent and capital budget allocations for selected years.

The Ministry of Education obtains the major part of its ordinary finances from the central government. A minimal percentage comes from other sources, such as income from sale of stamps, fees for examination and qualifications, and income obtained from donations and special fees. Another important source is that of international organizations which provide funds in the form of loans or donations.

According to available estimates, in the public sector the annual per student expenditure is US$32. This is considered to be one of the lowest in Latin America and, to a large extent, explains the low quality of primary education, particularly the provision for the poorest sectors of society. In terms of secondary education, the annual per student expenditure is US$124, a figure which is closer to the prevailing average in Latin America than that for primary education. A significant aspect of educational finance is the advantage which both secondary and university education obtain in terms of subsidy, in comparison with the primary sector.

Expenditure in the private sector is much greater than in the public sector. Some estimates suggest that this expenditure is three times as great. This, in turn, explains the differences in quality between the two sectors. Under such conditions, it is understandable that students coming from public schools—especially those from the interior of the country—have less opportunity to compete for entry into the better quality secondary educational establishments or universities.

6. Supplying Personnel for the Educational System

In general, there is an insufficient number of teachers for both the primary and secondary levels. There are also inadequacies and disparities in terms of their training. In 1991 there were 20,534 primary education teachers: 13,691 (66.7%) of these had teacher training, 5,000 (24.3%) were without teacher training, and 1,643 (8.0%) had special subject training.

The requirement for entry to teacher training is two years' study after the completion of the high school diploma. After completion of this cycle, it is possible to embark upon the training necessary for teaching at secondary level which is given in the Higher Institute for Education (Instituto Superior de Educación—ISE) and the regional centers of education established in various cities in the interior of the country.

Teacher training represents a minimal component of higher or tertiary education in terms of registration. It accounts for only 0.4 percent of enrollment. In 1989, just over 300 secondary level teachers graduated in different areas. This represented a very small quantity given the increase in enrollment, particularly in the interior of the country. The principal reason for this was the economic decline, which affected the already precarious teaching salary. This trend was reversed in 1990 by successive increases in salary granted by the government. The deficit in teacher training is a serious problem. There are not more than 500 trained teachers, while an estimated 1,500 teachers per year are needed to meet the levels of demand existing in the early 1990s.

Teaching is a two-year course of study in all institutions of the country. A curriculum of three years of an experimental character is being developed at the Higher Education Institute of the Ministry of Education. There is also a one-year course of professionalization. It is designed to train teachers at the primary level in areas with a shortage of teachers.

The Ministry of Education attributes the low rates of success observed in the training of teachers to two principal factors: (a) academic failure owing to socioeconomic difficulties; and (b) low educational training of the incoming graduates, especially those coming from the interior of the country.

With respect to university lecturing, the requirement of fulfilling special courses for a semester in the ISE has been established as the prerequisite for university teaching, so that a considerable proportion of university lecturers are qualified to teach purely on the basis of a professional qualification and other academic merits.

7. Curriculum Development

The curricula for both basic and secondary education are developed and implemented by the Ministry of Education's Curriculum Development department. At the university level, the National University has autonomy for the development of the content and structure of its courses. However, private universities must present their curricula for ministerial approval. Control of the implementation and evaluation of programs in public and private schools is the responsibility of the Ministry's Department of Supervision. This department has a network of supervisors who have been strongly criticized as much for their professional conduct as for their political involvement in the past authoritarian regime.

The standard practice of the last regime was that official approval had to be sought for the publication of books, both for private publications and for texts developed by the ministry itself. This mechanism, which became an element of political maneuver, was a determining factor in the low quality of the set texts. This system has been abolished. Poor quality materials have begun to disappear, and new and better texts have slowly begun to appear.

8. The System of Examinations, Promotions, and Certifications

One major concern in primary education is students repeating grades, particularly in the first two grades where the repetition rate continues to be high. In response to this situation, the oriented automatic promotion system, which is based on attendance, was introduced. This requires that students attend 80 percent of the classes conducted over the academic year. In addition, in the second cycle of primary education (third through sixth grade), the criteria used are: (a) maintenance of a continued evaluation system similar to that used in the first two grades; (b) evaluation of conduct; and (c) promotion from one grade to the next is based on: a minimum of 75 percent attendance and overall satisfactory performance, expressed in terms of a general grade average. In summary, promotion in this cycle is based on two criteria: attendance and performance.

In 1982, due to operational difficulties, the Ministry of Education established a guideline that first grade students should be promoted to the next grade as long as they satisfied the requirements of 80 percent attendance: a grade of Satisfactory in the area of responsibility; and a grade of Satisfactory in the three most important subjects (reading, writing, comprehension, ability to perform arithmetic operations and problem-solving). After the third grade, students are promoted to the next grade if they satisfy the requirements of 75 percent attendance; a grade of Satisfactory in the area of responsibility; and an acceptable average in each field or area.

There have been serious objections to the system of promotion in primary education, and it is in the process of being revised. The main criticism is that students are promoted to the next grade without having acquired the skills necessary to allow them to function at that level. This might explain the high dropout level and the general impression that students lack a strong educational base when they reach the middle or junior high school level.

With regard to high school and university education, the examinations and promotions are determined by course, allowing students three opportunities to pass each course during the academic year. The certificates awarded at the high school level are: (a) humanities, awarded after having successfully completed the three years of middle or junior high school and three years of the humanities program, which then allows students to proceed to any university program: (b) business, which requires three years of middle or junior high school and three additional year-long courses, and then allows students to proceed to the university to study economics; and (c) technical, which is a terminal degree with the exception of agronomy which allows students to proceed to the university to study agronomy.

9. Educational Assessment, Evaluation, and Research

Compared with other countries in the region, educational research work has been very limited. This can be explained by four main factors: (a) the meager development of scientific research in general and of social science research in particular; (b) the strongly restrictive stance taken by the authoritarian regime towards this type of activity; (c) lack of resources for research, both in the university and in governmental organizations; and (d) the limited support of external assistance. In the period from 1945 to 1989, of a total of 311 research studies, 25 percent came from private institutions, 60 percent from state, 1 percent from universities, 9 percent from international organizations, and 5 percent from various independent organizations.

Research topics have varied over time. In the 1960s and part of the 1970s, the principal focus of interest revolved around problems of the education system's performance, that is to say, specific aspects such as grade repetition, dropout, and low school completion rates. Since the beginning of the 1980s, a crucial aspect both for researchers and planners has been bilingualism, in terms of its direct relationships with educational performance and its bearing on the process of teacher training. Other topics have covered administrative centralization and regionalization. At the end of the 1980s, the ministry developed a program of centralization of the educational system. This received favorable external support and stimulated research into the theme of regionalization.

A notable fact about educational research in Paraguay is the minimal attention that has been given to secondary and higher education. An exceptional case is that of technical education, which (partly because of having been strongly promoted by external cooperation) has been the subject of an appreciable number of studies. Little attention has been paid to education because of the restrictive political context which prevailed for many decades.

Finally, it is important to point to the exceptional progress that has been made in the field of educational documentation by means of the REDUC network. In addition to the specific task of documentation, REDUC has made a huge effort in the preparation and publication of analytical summaries. This program constitutes one of the central elements for future educative research in Paraguay.

10. Educational Reform in the 1980s and 1990s

Upon its installation in May 1989, the new government took three important measures: (a) to decree that education should be a priority of the social policy of the government; (b) to increase the budget for the educational sector, and (c) to create the Advisory Commission for Educational Reform. The functions allotted to this commission were: to prepare a report on the education system, to formulate a project of reform, and to participate in its execution. The Commission is presided over by the Minister of Education and has 12 members: three of them belong to the ministry itself and the remaining nine members are researchers, educationalists, academics, and intellectuals involved with the topic of education. The principal achievement of the Commission has been a first document for the guidance of the process of reform. It defines seven central lines of work: (a) a reformulation of the objectives of Paraguayan education; (b) the reform of the system of teacher training; (c) educational decentralization, which has made room for the organization of regional educational councils with broad participation of the community; (d) the administrative reorganization of the Ministry of Education with a view to its decentralization; (e) the democratization of the educational system, which includes as one of its central points the implementation of a program of bilingual education at the national level; (f) the depoliticization of the educational system; and finally (g) a reformulation of the financing of Paraguayan education.

11. Major Problems for the Year 2000

Paraguay is not one of the countries with a marked deficiency in its education development. Its progress in certain areas—such as the extension of basic education—has been very significant. Nevertheless, since the mid-1980s, the educational system has experienced serious difficulties in confronting the problems created by the crisis of external debt and chronic inadequacy of resources. An appreciation of the difficulties can be gleaned from the objectives which the Ministry of Education has formulated: (a) to raise the average level of school attendance with special emphasis on basic and professional technical education; (b) to respond to the increasing aspirations and demands of society by means of diversified subsystems; (c) to orient education toward the working world; (d) to confront the problem of illiteracy; (e) to offer alternatives that benefit exceptional people (people with educational difficulties or especially talented people); and (f) to democratize and modernize the educational system.

This vision has been significantly broadened by attempts at educational reform. In this sense, what is most striking is the global character of the education crisis which demands a broad response both from the state and from society in general. One of the major problems is the sustained decline in the quality of education at all levels, a phenomenon which will involve reform of the system of teacher training, the structuring and implementation of a vast program of bilingual education, curricular reform, improvement of salary levels of teachers, improvement of educational equipment, and so on.

Another critical aspect concerns the issue of equality. While trying to reverse the process of educational fragmentation experienced at all levels of the educational system, it must avoid becoming another instrument of social differentiation. This lack of relevance of the current curriculum to the world of work is marked and is considered as a problem of great urgency. The great effort made since the 1960s to promote technical education has not been consolidated, nor have viable alternatives been created. Finally, there is a broad consensus about the essential factors inhibiting educational development: insufficient public sector investment in the educational system, and the persistence of a centralized and deficient administrative structure.

References

Corvalán G 1981 *Paraguay: Nación Bilingüe.* Centro Paraguayo de Estudios Sociológicos, Asunción
Corvalán G, Marecki S, Schiefelbein E 1981 *Estimación del efecto de escolarización en el analfabetismo en el Paraguay.* CPES/REDUC, Asunción
Paraguay Comisión Asesora de la Reforma Educativa 1992 *Informe de Avance del Consejo Asesor de la Reforma Educativa.* Comisión Asesora de la Reforma Educativa, Asunción
Paraguay Ministerio de Educación y Culto 1990 *Diagnóstico del Sistema Educativo. Año 1989.* Ministerio de Educación y Culto, Asunción
Paraguay Ministerio de Educación y Culto 1992 *Anuario 1991. Desarrollo Educativo en Cifras.* Ministerio de Educación y Culto, Asunción
Rivarola D M 1977 *Educación y Desarrollo en el Paraguay.* CEPAL/PNUD/UNESCO, Asunción
Rivarola D M, Corvalán G, Zuñiga L 1977 *Los Determinantes del Rendimiento Educativo en el Paraguay.* Centro Paraguayo de Estudios Sociológicos (CPES), Asunción
Rivarola D M 1991 *Educación y Desarrollo Rural.* Universidad Católica/Centro Paraguayo de Estudios Sociológicos, Asunción
Schiefelbein E, Heikkinen S 1991 *Paraguay: Acceso, Permanencia, Repetición y Eficiencia en la Educación Básica.* UNESCO/OREAL, Santiago

Further Reading

Banco Interamericano de Desarrollo (BID) 1980 *Paraguay, Informe Socioeconómico.* BID, Washington, DC
Centro Paraguayo de Estudios Sociológicos 1991 *Paraguay: Situación Económica, Política y Social.* CPES, Asunción
Centro Paraguayo de Estudios Sociológicos 1992 *Paraguay: Perfil Socioeconómico.* CPES, Asunción
Paraguay Ministerio de Educación y Culto 1991 *Informe. Cuarta Reunión Intergubernamental del Proyecto Principal en el Esfera de la Educación en América Latina y el Caribe (PROMEDLACIV), Quito-Ecuador.* Ministerio de Educación y Culto, Asunción
Paraguay Ministerio de Educación y Culto 1991a *Paraguay. La Experiencia de la Descentralización Educativa.* Ministerio de Educación y Culto, Asunción
Paraguay Ministerio de Educación y Culto 1991b *Plan de Desarrollo Educacional. Periodo 1991–1993.* Ministerio de Educación y Culto, Asunción
Rivera Pizarro J 1991 *Investigación sobre Educación en algunos Países de América Latina.* IDRC, Ottawa

Peru

V. H. Díaz Díaz

1. General Background

Peru is situated on the west central coast of South America. Its 1,285,216 square kilometers cover vast geographical differences, with climates ranging from tropical to glacial, extremely arid ground to highly productive soil, and flatlands to rugged mountainous regions. The Andes mountain range runs along the Sierra, or highlands; the tropical rain forest occupies 57.6 percent of the country. In terms of population, there was a fusion of the Andean societies with the Western colonizing culture (the Spaniards) in the sixteenth century; this group is known as *mestizaje* (mixture of races). In Peru's early republican life there was immigration from Asia and Europe.

Traditionally, the coast has been the economically privileged region, and the highlands, marginal. From the time of the Spanish conquest, social relations have been loaded with a heavy ethnic component; the Native Americans are the most exploited people and have the least access to education. However, the economy created a series of links that joined the various regions of the country and integrated the indigenous with the Hispanic world, organized on the basis of external demand, especially through mining, which is a principal source of export.

Since 1940, the population has increased dramatically. In the 1980s, the population growth rate was 2.2 percent. It was estimated that, in 1990, there was 21.5 million Peruvians, of whom 70 percent lived in urban areas (47% in cities with over 100,000 inhabitants and 30% in Lima, the capital city). The process of urbanization is attributed to natural growth and rural migration. The latter came about because of a birthrate explosion, destruction of the rural society, rigidity in the land tenure system, and the effect of the broadening of mass media communications (especially the radio) which reaches those areas where there are many illiterates.

According to the 1981 population census, 27 percent of the inhabitants over 5 years of age were vernacular speakers (80% of whom speak Quechua). The state promotes the study and knowledge of aboriginal tongues and should guarantee the rights of the Quechua, Aymara, and other native communities to receive primary education in their own language. Various experiences in bilingual education (Spanish and mother tongue) in the highlands and in the tropical rain forest have permitted advances in the development of a series of linguistic and sociocultural traditions as well as the production of texts and other didactic materials in those languages.

Spanish is the official language. Quechua and Aymara are also official languages in certain areas within the limits that the law establishes. Aboriginal tongues constitute the cultural inheritance of the nation.

In 1990, the economically active population (EAP) was 7.3 million; 34 percent in agriculture, 15.6 percent in commerce, 10.5 percent in manufacturing, and 26.7 percent in services. In the 1980s, the levels of employment deteriorated markedly: in the city of Lima, which constitutes 65 percent of the industrial gross national product (GNP), the EAP under-employment rate increased from 33 to 94 percent. Meanwhile, the per capita GNP fell from US$938 in 1980 to US$674 in 1990, the level of 1960. The increase in poverty that affects more than two-thirds of the population explains the higher number of women and children seeking jobs, the anguish of many educational system leavers who do not find employment, and the growth of an informal economy which, in recent studies, reaches almost one million productive units and occupies 50 percent of the EAP.

The educational levels of the working-age population improved substantially between 1961 and 1981; the noneducated level descended from 32.8 to 13.5 percent, while those with secondary and postsecondary levels rose from 14 to 42.4 percent. These changes took place primarily in urban areas. In rural areas, where there is low agricultural productivity, there is a low educational level amongst the peasants.

The fall in the per capita GNP has been accompanied by a reduction in social expenditure. The 1991 *Human Development Report* by the UNDP stated that Peru, next to Angola, Chad, Pakistan, Syria, Uganda, and Zaire, spent twice as much on military affairs as on education and health. In the 1980s, social expenditure was half of the amount spent in Latin America (10%). State expenditure on education, which was 3.82 percent of the GNP in the 1970s, was reduced to 2.93 percent in 1980 and 2.21 percent in 1989.

2. Politics and the Goals of the Education System

Both the state and the society have the formal obligation to guarantee educational services to the whole population of the country, recognizing the principle of the freedom to learn. The state directly administers public educational centers, such as schools under the jurisdiction of the Ministry of Education, institutions belonging to other ministries, state universities, and municipal teaching establishments. However, its actual functions are essentially twofold: to formulate educational policies and to administer education.

Educational policy is in force throughout the whole country, in all public and private educational establishments. The 12 regions into which the country is divided are economically and administratively autonomous. They are responsible within their territory for primary, secondary, and technical education. However, they are always subordinate to national legislation.

In the 1960s, there was a policy for the expansion of educational opportunities. The enrichment rate rose to above the average in Latin America. The enrollment growth rate was higher than the population growth rate. The level of illiteracy decreased from 38.2 percent in 1963 to 11.4 percent in 1990. The ratio of enrollment in higher education per 100,000 inhabitants increased from 514 to 3,164. University enrollment exceeded the country's ability to finance it and of the labor market to absorb it.

All political groups are concerned with improvement of the quality of the system and especially the training of teachers. There is also a consensus that priority should be given to primary education and literacy programs, and that failure rates should be decreased. To support progress, the state promotes and stimulates intellectual and artistic creativity, scientific and technological investigation, and professional and cultural development. The Ministry of Education is responsible for these activities.

3. The Formal System of Education

Figure 1 presents the structure of the educational system. Statistical data on enrollment and resources per educational level are given in Table 1.

3.1 Primary, Secondary, and Tertiary Education

Education provided by the state is free for all. For economically poor students, health services, food, social assistance, and school materials are provided. Economic aid is also dependent on the student's achievement.

779

Primary education consists of six grades and is compulsory. Pupils begin school at the age of 6 years, but primary education is also offered to those who did not continue school or did not receive schooling in time. According to UNESCO data, Peru, as well as Colombia and Mexico, registered the highest gross enrollment rates in Latin America and the Caribbean. In 1990, 3.9 million children went to school. Of these, 12 percent were in private schools. Due to the low density of the rural population, there are about 15,000 one-teacher primary schools. Nearly all primary schools are coeducational. Officially, there are 30 class periods a week and 38 school weeks per year.

Secondary education is compulsory and should be organized in two cycles: the first, for all students, lasts two years; the second, three years long, is where the scientific–humanistic and technical options are diversified. In practice, however, since 1990 there are two well-differentiated branches: the first is oriented towards the study of sciences and humanities, and the second towards the technical areas; both operate from

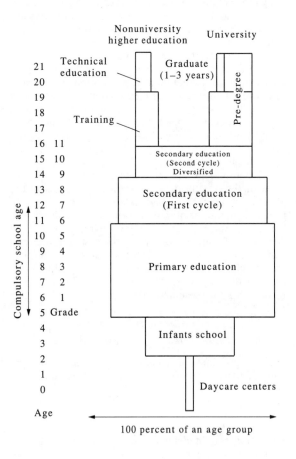

Figure 1
Peru: Structure of the formal education system

Grade 7. Secondary education is normally offered to adolescents between the ages of 12 and 16; however, adults may also attend. In 1990, 55 percent of those who began their secondary education five years earlier were able to complete the course; in 1984 the estimate had been the same. Of the 1.9 million secondary students, there were slightly more boys than girls. However, the enrollment rate of girls rose rapidly in the 1980s. Most secondary schools are coeducational. Some 14 percent of students attend private schools; this proportion was 34 percent in 1950. At this level of education, there are 36 class periods a week and 38 school weeks a year.

Higher education is provided in higher education centers, schools, and institutes, and in higher centers of graduate education and universities. The higher institutes offer training programs for teachers and a variety of technical options for careers of between four and ten academic semesters long. In 1990 there were 242,000 students enrolled, the majority being between the ages of 17 and 25. The majority of them study and work at the same time.

The percentage of the population over 25 years of age that has attained a level of higher education is comparable to that in the United Kingdom, and higher than other countries with more development of scientific and technological capacities. In absolute numbers, though, the 650,000 students that once took higher education studies do not reach the standards required to initiate national development.

In 1990, there were 51 universities, 28 of which were private. In 1960, there were only 9 universities. The major growth was between the 1960s and 1980s. This fact is evidenced by the accelerated rhythm of growth in secondary education and the strong and assertive demand for university studies. Entrance to the universities operates on the basis of an entrance examination. Applicants who failed these examinations rose from 181,000 in 1980 to 251,000 in 1990. Of those passing the entrance examination in 1988, 49 percent were female (a rise of between 10 and 15% over the period 1980–87).

In the 1980s, there were changes in the choice of subjects studied. The proportion of students studying for degrees in engineering and medicine remained at 18 and 10 percent respectively; enrollment in the economic and social sciences, agriculture, and the natural and exact sciences decreased by between 3 and 1 percent; enrollment in education and law courses increased. The rate of completion of university studies is low.

3.2 Preschool Education

Preschool education is offered in two forms: scholarly, in daycare centers for children under 3 years old; in kindergartens for children between 3 and 5 years old; and nonscholarly, destined for poor children of the rural and marginal urban areas. The private sector comprises 12 percent of the scholarly enrollment, while the Ministry of Education is in charge of almost all nonscholarly programs. The objective of preschool education in Peru is to develop the intellectual and physical abilities of the child for the successive steps of formal education and, in a broader sense, for life in society. Preschool education for 5-year olds is compulsory.

3.3 Special Education

Special education encompasses both those that suffer mental or organic deficiencies or maladjustments of social conduct, and those that show excellent progress in learning, although the provisions for this latter group have not yet been organized. In 1990, 324 centers of special education had an enrollment of 26,300 students, of whom 11 percent were in private schools.

3.4 Vocational, Technical, and Business Education

Since the beginning of the 1970s, special importance has been given to workshop education in the educational system and even to including it as a subject starting in primary education. Courses for technicians increased noticeably during the 1980s. A wide variety of private institutions of variable quality were established. There are also institutions that qualify their students for modern sectors of the economy and that are real alternatives to universities. Their former students are those who acquire jobs more readily, while the rest of the young people have difficulties in entering the occupational market. Facing these situations, various measures of accelerated qualification for youth in search of jobs are being studied.

Some sectors have organized their own mechanisms of training. The National Service of Industrial Technical Training (SENATI) trains qualified laborers for industry. Its programs include apprenticeship, inservice training, mobile units, and other activities. In the case of the construction and tourism industries, education courses are run by the National Service of Training for Construction (SENCICO) and the Center of Touristic Studies (CENFOTUR).

3.5 Adult and Nonformal Education

Adult education, in terms of formal courses, is almost totally offered by the state. In 1990, about 330,000 students were registered in primary and secondary programs of adult education. However, there are also centers of occupational education whose purpose is to train adults and adolescents (whether they are working or not) in occupations related to the various productive branches. The programs offered are short, generally of less than one year's duration, and have a flexible pedagogical design, adapted to the characteristics of those participating. In 1990, enrollment in this form of education was 330,000, 53 percent of whom attended private centers.

Nonformal education is still a somewhat unknown world as far as its coverage, working methods, and levels of qualification are concerned. There are many institutions under (and not under) the guardianship of the Ministry of Education that operate as adult literacy centers; train people for industry qualifications; and offer instruction in feminine arts, languages, secretarial work, health and hygiene, human relations, and

Table 1
Enrollments and resources in formal education, 1990

	Preschool	Primary	Secondary	Higher Nonuniversity	University
Number of students[a]	504,200	3,955,100	1,906,600	242,500	442,900
Percentage of age group enrolled[b]					
3–5	49	—	—	—	—
6–11	—	95	—	—	—
12–14	—	2	88	—	—
15–19	—	—	65	19	34
20–24	—	—	—	12	23
Number of institutions[c]	9,490	29,036	5,610	421	51
Number of students per institution	53	136	340	576	8,684
Student–teacher ratio	27:1	28:1	20:9	19:2	16:2
Expense per student (US$)[d]	61	53	122	133	269

a Enrollment in primary and secondary considers only the modality of minors, excluding that of adults; and in the case of nonuniversity higher education, the higher technological institutes, the higher pedagogical institutes, and the art education schools   b Gross scholarity rates   c Primary and secondary institutions for adults are excluded when they occupy the same areas in which the modalities for minors operate   d The average exchange rate for 1990: US$1=Sol 547.50. The data refer to the cost of public education. Investigation expenses are included in the information for universities

rural matters. There is an increasing awareness of the importance of nonformal education as an alternative to formal training.

4. Administrative and Supervisory Structure and Operation

Administration in education is a decentralized process that began in 1962. Administration is organized at three levels: central, regional, and local. The central level is the Ministry of Education and its basic function is technical, normative, and political. At the regional level, the departmental directorates of education are part of the Regional Development Organization, but they maintain an operational relationship with the Ministry. The departmental directorates of education implement the educational policies related to their jurisdictions and control and administer the educational services. Finally, at the local level, the functions are essentially operational and are the responsibility of Educational Services Units (USES) and education centers. The provincial municipalities have the obligation to cooperate with primary education and supervise its normal operation.

The control of the administrative, technical, and pedagogical supervision of education is the responsibility of the National Supervision and Evaluation Directorate and its equivalent bureaus on the regional and local levels. This is a permanent mechanism and ensures the operation of all educational institutions and courses as well as assessing the teaching–learning processes and guiding the qualitative development of the curriculum. Financial difficulties concerning nonsalary expenses have limited the exercise of this supervision.

The state recognizes, supervises, and guides private education. According to law, no private education center may offer educational knowledge at a lower level than that offered by its state counterpart. This type of education is offered by 10 percent of the local schools with 15.6 percent of national enrollment. Schools administered by religious bodies comprise about 25 percent of private education.

Universities are founded by law. They may be public or private. Every university is autonomous in its academic, economic, normative, and administrative aspects; universities are ruled by law and by their statutes.

5. Educational Finance

In 1989, the state subsidized education to the amount of Sol 2.5 million (US$580 million), which represented 2.2 percent of the GNP and 15.6 percent of the state budget. Since the beginning of the 1970s, there has been a progressive decrease in expenditure on education. This has been reflected in the per student cost

and especially in teachers' salaries. Nearly all public expenditure on education is financed by the government. Its own income represents less than 1 percent of the total expenditure. Foreign financial cooperation obtained since the 1970s has been directed particularly toward the building and equipping of schools.

The Constitution ensures that education should have priority on the government's ordinary budget in each year. Education received little more than 10 percent in 1983 and 1984. On the other hand, changes in the enrollment structure affect the pattern of the expenditure. Primary education, which in 1979 received 51.2 percent of the education budget, received 36.3 percent in 1989; secondary and higher education expenditure increased by 2.6 and 7.3 percent respectively, reaching 27.3 and 28.3 percent. The cost per student in 1990 was: primary US$57, secondary US$93, and higher education US$250.

In 1988, the university student per unit expenditures were, on average, less than a third of their level in 1970. Internationally, it was quite low: in 1988 it was US$255, whilst in Belgium, for example, the annual expense per student was over US$18,000. Universities and other educational centers are thus far exonerated from all tax. By law, there have been incentives to favor donations and contributions to these institutions; also, enterprises are encouraged to help finance centers of education. For example, textile factories employing more than 15 employees participate in financing SENATI with 1.5 percent of the total of their salaries, a minimum regulated by law. Similar procedures are established in the cases of training institutes in other sectors.

School fees in private schools are based on decisions taken by the Fees and Scholarships Committee (COPEBE) of each institution. The Committee consists of the director, the principal or the principal's representative, a teacher representative, and a representative from the Parents' Association. The level of school fees varies, ranging between US$15 and US$300 per month. Some educational centers administered by clergy and private centers of special education receive a subsidy from the state in the form of teacher salaries.

6. Supplying Personnel for the Education System

About 310,000 teachers worked in the educational system in 1990: 146,000 in primary education; 91,000 in secondary education; 40,000 in higher education; 22,000 in preschool education; and the rest in other forms of education. Almost half of the teaching population is female and 17 percent work in private education.

Teacher training takes place in 85 pedagogical institutes (ISP) and 58 university programs. The ISPs have a common program of studies, whereas the university programs vary.

Low wages for teachers has resulted in a huge exodus of qualified teachers from the system and an increase in nonqualified teachers (50% in 1990). Many teachers must take on extra jobs in order to survive. There is an increase in absenteeism and a reduction in the time dedicated to the preparation of subjects and evaluation of students. This explains the relatively low average of years of teacher experience (between 10 and 15). However, the demand for careers in education is still high. This is, in part, due to the prospect of employment at the end of studies; however, not all those trained are the most adequate in terms of vocational and professional abilities.

The training service is the responsibility of the National Directorate of Educational Research and Teacher Training, the ISPs, the departmental directorates of education, and the universities. The state made great efforts in the 1970s and 1980s in technical pedagogical areas, but there still remains much to be done. In rural areas, working conditions are very hard as there is not even a minimum of resources for learning to take place. No strategy has yet been identified to ensure that the teacher attends school each day. Inservice teacher training is not compulsory but is urgently required to enable teachers to work in multigrade centers, to organize the work in their class, to use and produce educational materials at low cost from local resources, and to overcome learning difficulties derived from existing teaching methodologies.

7. Curriculum Development and Teaching Methodology

Except for university education, the Ministry of Education establishes all syllabuses and course outlines for all schools. By law, study programs are in force for a minimum of 6 years, after which modifications are made to improve them. The detailed content and suggested teaching strategies are the responsibility of the local and regional educational authorities. This task has not been completely achieved because there is not always sufficient evidence about how to deal with factors such as the linguistic differences, the characteristics typical of each region, and the production of adequate educational materials.

The preschool curriculum aims at: (a) the promotion of the child's integral development, care of the child's feeding, health, and recreation; (b) the prevention and discovery of the biological, psychological, and sociological problems of the child; and (c) the contribution towards the improvement and perfection of the family. It emphasizes that educational activities must take into consideration the multilingual situation and the cultural values of the community. Since the 1970s, important steps have been developed that have permitted the development of a curriculum specifically for this kind of education.

In primary education, courses are established with a flexible number of hours per subject for Grades 5 and 6. In the other grades, it is the teacher who undertakes the planning. Before the beginning of the school year, teachers develop courses on the basis of study programs and analysis of the student's environment and community. The Ministry of Education may authorize the use of experimental curricula, organization systems, and grading methods. The teaching methods used in the classroom world are varied. The teacher determines the techniques and selects the ways and the materials necessary to aid the process of learning on the basis of criteria like the degree of maturity of the students, the use of playing and verbal activities of the child, stimulus of self-learning and learning in groups, the use of the resources that are offered in the environment and their relation to the nature of the subjects offered. The introduction of modern technologies, such as computers, began in the 1980s in private schools.

Since 1970, great efforts have been made to enable children from the poorer strata of society to have access to school texts. However, in rural areas, such materials do not exist in the majority of schools. This is also the case in urban peripheral zones. The establishment of school libraries, as a mechanism to help with this deficiency, has still not been developed.

8. The System of Examinations, Promotions, and Certifications

Three types of student evaluation are used: progressive, general complementary, and recuperation and supplementary. Progressive evaluation is undertaken every two months. General complementary evaluation is used on the basis of the contents, aspects, or essential activities developed in the four bimesters of the school year. The grading scale ranges from 0 to 20. In primary education, an average of 11 and a passing grade in either language or mathematics is necessary to be promoted. In secondary education, evaluation is by subject. Recuperation and supplementary evaluation is done in March, one month before the beginning of the school year, for those who have failed up to three subjects the previous school year. Students who have been absent for 30 percent of the school days in a year also fail.

Certificates are issued on the successful completion of primary and secondary education. Universities award the degrees of bachelor, master, and doctor, as well as certificates and professional titles of licentiate, including certificates for further specialization. Institutes and higher education centers award degrees of professional, technical, and expert, as well as for further forms of specialization.

The state recognizes and certifies primary studies that have been done independently and validates studies undertaken in foreign countries. Educational centers are authorized to evaluate and certify only one grade of studies per year. There are also placement tests for those entering the system late.

9. *Educational Assessment, Evaluation, and Research*

The Ministry of Education, through INIDE, directs, promotes, supervises, and evaluates research programs. The law states that conducting research is free in the sciences of education and the development of didactical methods and materials. The Ministry of Education promotes experimenting with technical–pedagogical innovations and new materials.

Since the beginning of the 1970s, there has been a noticeable increase of nongovernmental organizations dedicated to education. Many of them have undertaken research studies to create indicators of the quality of the educational system. However, there are no common evaluation tests for the students which might result in the adoption of new policies and objectives.

Some studies reveal worrisome data about student achievement. A 1981 study by the Ministry of Education of 1,600 students in Grade 6 revealed that 75 percent of students fail in mathematics, 38 percent fail in the social sciences, and 23.1 percent fail in general sciences. Another study in 1991 by the National Interministerial Commission for the Plan of Action in Favor of Childhood confirmed that between 1980 and 1990 the annual primary school failure rate per year increased from 15 percent to 16.7 percent. The dropout rate also rose from 7.9 percent to 11.2 percent. Schiefelbein (1989), in his report for UNESCO, considered that the number of failures in primary school is, in reality, twice the number officially declared, and that in Grade 1 it reaches 46.8 percent.

An important study of school efficiency was, at the time of writing this entry, being carried out in private education by the institution responsible for Catholic schools. It consisted of a battery of tests in different schools in the country to evaluate the areas of language and mathematics in primary and secondary education. It is the beginning of the application of standardized tests to all students. Facing the need to strengthen the policies of improvement in the quality of education, studies of school progress and the factors that influence it have become vitally important.

There are few universities where there is any noticeable research effort and where national, binational, or multinational resources support them.

10. *Major Reforms in the 1980s and 1990s*

The major progress in the 1980s was that enrollment increased despite the notable fall in government expenditure on education. UNESCO statistics show that many Third World countries with less severe economic problems have seen their enrollment levels affected in the 1980s. On the other hand, the quality of education has been sacrificed, especially in state schools. Even so, the country did bring about the nonscholarly experiences of preschool education within the concept of integral attention, with multisectorial and communal participation. Some higher education institutes are providing practical and positive alternatives for the country. These include the Higher Technological Institute (TECSUP) and the Peruvian Institute of Business Administration (IPAE). These and other institutions encourage other training centers to adopt the same types of improvement and modernization of their teaching services.

Another element of renovation is that of nonformal education, particularly popular education. Since the middle of the 1980s, it has advanced and changed orientation. Active methods and techniques, participation or group dynamics are the main points of interest in meetings, seminars, and so forth. The systematization of previous experiences is encouraged, and it passes from the level of concept to the level of practice.

11. *Major Problems for the Year 2000*

The effects of the economic crisis will still be felt at the beginning of the twenty-first century, and there is little hope that there will be major changes in the level of public resources for education. The greatest impact will be on those members who need more, not less, governmental aid in order to gain access to education. A prime objective in the 1990s is to improve the quality of education. The greatest challenge in terms of quality is in primary education in order to ensure a minimum of basic learning needs. The key role in this process of the improvement of learning will be that of the teacher. Conditions of teacher employment will need to be changed, and more professional teacher training is needed.

Insufficient information is known about the relationships between education and employment. Studies are needed to guide policy-making. All effort from the state and private sectors is needed to ensure effective planning in order to articulate efforts and successfully adapt them to the needs of development. In the perspective of employment, the challenge will be of organizing imaginative formulas so that young persons may develop their own occupational alternatives.

References

Ministry of Education 1981 *Diagnóstico del Rendimiento Académico de los Educandos del Sexto Grado de Educación Básica Regular*. Ministry of Education, Lima
National Interministerial Committee for the Plan of Action in Favor of Childhood 1991 *Prioridades Sociales del Desarrollo Humano, la Reconstrucción Nacional y la Paz*. Lima
Schiefelbein E 1989 *Repetición: última barrera para universalizar la educación primaria de América Latina*. Bulletin N° 18. Principal Project of Education in Latin America and the Caribbean. UNESCO-OREALC, Santiago de Chile

SONRA (Consortium of Catholic Schools in Peru) in press *Evaluation of Scholarly Achievement in the Areas of Language and Mathematics Service*. SONRA, Lima

UNDP 1991 *Human Development Report 1991*. Oxford University Press, Oxford

UNESCO 1987 *Statistical Yearbook 1986*. UNESCO, Paris

Further Reading

Cardó A, Díaz H, Vargas R, Malpica C 1989 *Planificación y Desarrollo de la Educación en el Perú*. Report of Research Nº 77. UNESCO, Paris

Lizarzaburu A 1984 L'Expérience de l'alphabétisation intégrale des adultes au Peou: de l'utopie. *La Planification de la Education dans le Contexte des Problémes Actuels du Development*. Vol. 2. UNESCO, Paris

Ruiz D G 1983 Experience of educational microplanning in Perú through nuclearisation. *Educational Administration and Multilevel Plan Implementation: Experience from Developing Countries*. UNESCO, Paris

UNESCO–OREALC 1988 *Educational Situation of Latin America and the Caribbean. Principal Education Project 1980–1985*. UNESCO, Santiago de Chile

UNICEF 1991 *The State of the World's Children 1991*. UNICEF, New York

Philippines

M. C. Sutaria

1. General Background

The Republic of the Philippines is a chain of some 7,107 islands stretching over a length of 1,150 miles on the western side of the Pacific Ocean. The total coastline comprises 11,500 miles. The total land area is 118,850 square miles and is diffused over some 500 square miles of oceanic waters. Its largest islands, Luzon in the north and Mindanao in the south, together represent about two-thirds of the total land area of the country. Its middle portion consists of a diffusion of islands which form the Visayas, the third major region of the country. The archipelagic characteristic of the Republic makes monitoring and supervision of its schools difficult and expensive.

There are some 111 linguistic, cultural, and racial groups speaking a total of about 87 languages, 11 of which are spoken by a large portion of the total population. While the Philippines has a national language, Filipino, largely based on Tagalog which is predominantly spoken in Metro Manila, English is used as a medium of instruction in school and for communication in government.

The country's population of about 62 million (1992) is unevenly distributed. The population growth rate of 2.4 percent reported in 1980 has not dramatically changed. About 70 percent of the population resides in rural areas. The urban population is heavily concentrated in Manila and its suburban cities and towns. Some 46 percent of the population is under 15 years of age. Persons aged 16 and above are classified with the "older half" of the population. Those above 65 years of age constitute less than 3 percent of the population. A young age structure is the result of a sustained high birthrate and a steadily declining death rate due to improved medical services and living standards, and to better health and nutrition.

The Philippines is a democratic and republican state. Legislative power is vested in the Congress which consists of a senate and a house of representatives. Executive power is vested in the president, and judicial power in one supreme court and several lower courts.

The National Economic and Development Authority (NEDA) is the overall planning agency responsible for the formulation of national policies and economic and social development plans. The development plan aims to alleviate poverty and address unemployment which unfavorably affects the attainment of the nation's educational goals and objectives. The industrial sector is being rationalized toward greater export competitiveness and stronger linkages with the countryside. To stem the rapid migration to more developed areas, industries are being dispersed to outlying regions.

Agriculture represents about one-third of the Gross Domestic Product (GDP) of the Philippines and supplies a large share of its exports. Over 10 million acres are under cultivation and about two million acres grow two or more crops a year. The country has a variety of natural resources, with copper being the major mining product. Its several thousand islands and extensive coastline provides a natural fishing ground whose waters cover 5.5 times its land area.

Developments in the second half of the 1980s created new challenges for education. The economy revived during this period. The economic growth rate was 1.9 percent in 1986, but it was 5.9 percent in 1987, 6.7 percent in 1988, and 5.8 percent in 1989. This growth was translated into higher expenditures for education and other social services. Education continued to constitute the bulk of the social service expenditures representing a share of 69 percent in 1988 compared with 62 percent in the previous year.

Natural and man-made calamities impeded the development of the country in the early 1990s. The

785

destructive eruption of Mount Pinatubo; the strong typhoons that devastated Cebu, a rapidly developing island, and Ormoc City in the Visayas; and a few pockets of insurgency in the three major regions of the country set back its economic and social development.

A huge debt burden has exacerbated the country's problem of adequately providing for development programs and has constrained the allocation of more resources to education. Debt servicing accounted for a substantial 46.1 percent share of total expenditures in 1988. This was, however, reduced to 41.3 percent in 1989. As a result of this reduction, the share of education in government expenditures in 1989 rose to 13.8 percent, while its share in the total amount of social services expenditures rose to 11.1 percent. The situation, however, remains untenable when viewed from the perspective of a rapidly increasing school population competing for scarce facilities and resources.

2. Politics and the Goals of the Education System

A new constitution was adopted in 1987. The goals and objectives of the Philippine education system are articulated in the new Constitution, the Education Act of 1982, and the 1987–92 Philippine Development Plan.

The Education Act of 1982 provided for the establishment and maintenance of an integrated system of education, aimed at unifying and centrally coordinating the education system. Such integration covers formal education, nonformal education, and specialized educational services.

The 1987 Constitution provided that "the State shall protect and promote the right of all citizens to quality education at all levels and shall take appropriate steps to make such education accessible to all." It further mandated the state to:

(a) establish, maintain, and support a complete, adequate, and integrated system of education relevant to the needs of the people and society;

(b) establish and maintain a system of free public education in the elementary and high school levels without limiting the natural right of parents to rear their children (elementary education is compulsory for all children of school age);

(c) establish and maintain a system of scholarship grants, student loan programs, subsidies, and other incentives which shall be available to deserving students in both public and private schools, especially to the underprivileged;

(d) encourage nonformal, informal, and indigenous learning systems as well as self-learning, independent, and out-of-school study programs,

particularly those that respond to community needs;

(e) provide adult citizens, the disabled, and school leavers with training in civics, vocational efficiency, and other skills.

The abovementioned provisions of the Constitution were translated into specific objectives and strategies in the medium-term Philippine Development Plan prepared by the National Economic and Development Authority in consultation with all sectors of government. According to this plan, the major tasks of the Department of Education, Culture, and Sports for the period 1987 to 1992 were:

(a) to improve the quality and increase the relevance of education and training;

(b) to increase access of disadvantaged groups in all educational areas;

(c) to accelerate the development of the middle- and high-level labor force toward economic recovery and sustainable growth, as well as to enhance their employability, productivity, and self-reliance;

(d) to maintain an educational system that is truly Filipino in orientation and open to constructive ideas from everywhere, but alert to influences inimical to national dignity.

In 1992, the following philosophy of education, grounded in the 1987 Philippine Constitution, was articulated:

Education for the Filipinos shall be rooted in their culture and traditions which are anchored on positive values and beliefs of the people. It shall develop an enlightened and nationalistic citizenry, imbued with democratic ideals, unselfish in their commitment to serve the national community, and proud of being Filipinos, yet receptive of international developments. It shall further develop God-loving, creative, disciplined, productive and self reliant citizens leading meaningful lives.

3. The Formal System of Education

The Philippine educational system has features similar to those of other countries. The system may be divided into the formal and nonformal, both of which may be further subdivided into public and private.

"Formal education" refers to the hierarchically structured and chronologically graded system of traditional schooling, for which certification is required for the learner to move to the higher levels. It corresponds to the three levels of education, namely, elementary, secondary, and higher education. "Nonformal education" refers to any organized educational activity outside the established formal system that is intended to serve specific clientele.

The private sector plays a very important role in the delivery of education in the Philippines. In 1991, 6 percent of the primary school enrollment and 37 percent of the total secondary school population was in the private sector. This secondary school ratio is drastically changing because of the government's implementation of the free secondary education program which was launched in 1988. Private institutions of higher learning provide education to about 85 percent of all tertiary-level students.

3.1 Primary, Secondary, and Tertiary Education

The structure of the formal education system is outlined in Fig. 1.

Formal education in the Philippines starts at the age of 7. It consists of six years of primary education (except in a few private schools which offer a seven-year primary education course), four years of secondary education, and from four to nine years of higher education.

Primary education, which is free and compulsory, is for children aged 7 to 12 years. In 1991–92, about 10.6 million (or 99.5%) of the school-age population

were enrolled in the nation's 34,081 primary schools. Of these, about 7 percent were in private schools.

Secondary education is free but not compulsory. In 1991–92, 4.2 million were enrolled in the Philippines' 5,500 secondary schools. About 45 percent of the students were in private schools.

Public secondary schools are classified according to the government office that gives them financial support; for example, municipal, provincial, and city schools. Among the several types of secondary school, the academic variety offers a four-year college preparatory curriculum. Most of the private schools offer a general curriculum which is designed to meet the needs of students who plan to go to college as well as those who will seek employment or become homemakers immediately after graduation. The general curriculum is now the standard type of public secondary school in the Philippines except for the trade, agriculture, and normal schools. Trade schools offer two-year and four-year secondary studies. The main aim of the two-year curriculum is to provide intensive training to train students for immediate employment. Agricultural and rural high schools offer a secondary agricultural curriculum which is designed to train students in the farming regions for agricultural occupations and for rural homemaking (female students take courses in home economics). A secondary fisheries curriculum is designed to give technical training in fishing.

Graduates of any of the four-year secondary schools are eligible for admission to the collegiate or university level provided that they qualify in the National College Entrance Examination (NCEE).

Tertiary education in the Philippines is largely delivered by the private sector. Of the 2,071 tertiary education institutions, 1,261 are postsecondary technical vocational schools and 809 are degree-granting institutions. Only 80 belong to the state. In 1991–1992, 2.06 million were enrolled in tertiary education institutions.

Tertiary education courses range from one to nine years, but a formal baccalaureate degree takes four years to complete. The larger tertiary education institutions offer graduate and postgraduate courses.

A Board of Higher Education serves as an advisory body to the Secretary of Education in the formulation of policy. Technical panels in the various disciplines provide advice to the Board in formulating policies and standards. These panels are composed of representatives from academe, both public and private; professional organizations; and business and industry.

The government has been addressing the problem of quality at the higher education level by strengthening the system of voluntary accreditation in all colleges and universities.

3.2 Preschool Education

Preschool education in the Philippines is largely in the hands of the private sector. However, the public el-

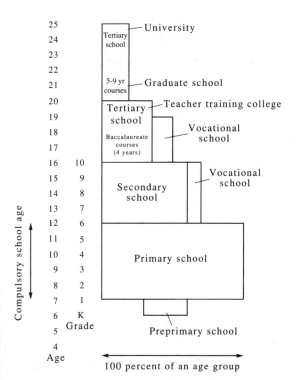

Figure 1
Philippines: Structure of the formal education system

ementary schools have increasingly offered preschool education supported by parents. To broaden opportunities for preschool education, these public schools allow the free use of their facilities for preschool classes while the salaries of the teachers are borne by the parents or the local government or volunteer groups. The more traditional kindergarten and nursery schools have sprung up everywhere, although these are relatively expensive and cater mostly to the upper and middle classes.

In 1990–91, nearly 400,000 children attended preschool. This figure is expected to increase dramatically as the 1990s progress as a consequence of the inclusion of early childhood care and development as an important component of the country's National Plan of Action for Education for All.

3.3 Special Education

Since its inception in the early part of the twentieth century, special education has grown to include special services for eight major categories of individual with exceptional needs. These are the physically handicapped, mentally retarded, mentally gifted, visually impaired, hearing impaired, speech defective, children with behavior problems, and children with special health problems. Enrollment figures reveal that there are more programs for the intellectual deviates—the mentally gifted and mentally retarded—than for other areas of exceptionality.

The programs that were identified as the most feasible in the regions are: (a) the self-contained classes in special education centers for the gifted, the mentally retarded, the deaf, the physically handicapped, and children with behavior problems; (b) integration and itinerant teaching for the blind; and (c) resource room services in regular schools. In the National Capital Region, there is a concentration of special schools, both public and private, and a variety of service delivery systems: programs on mainstreaming including reverse mainstreaming. By 1992, nearly 1,000 school teachers had trained in special education under the teacher-training program in special education of the Department of Education, Culture, and Sports. Of these, 64 percent were actively involved in special education programs. With an average of 15 exceptional children per class, this number of teachers is hardly sufficient to respond to the needs of all the exceptional children identified.

Special education has become a significant component of general education in the country. The extent of special services is, however, still inadequate. As of the school year 1990–91, there were 8 special education centers, 25 special schools, and 97 elementary schools with integrated classes. Only 22,096 children with special needs were enrolled in the government schools. The number served is less than 2 percent of the estimated exceptional population in need of special services.

3.4 Vocational and Technical Education

Vocational and technical education is provided by both the public and private sectors. It is the level of education which equips the skilled workers and operatives, craftsworkers, and technicians with the appropriate attitudes, aptitudes, and skills for specific levels of technology.

It covers five main fields, namely, trade (technology, communication, electronics, computers, transportation, etc.), agriculture, fisheries, home industries, and nontraditional courses. These comprise more than 250 different courses of six months' to three years' duration. These courses include formal school work in the field of specialization and related academic subjects. In the one-, two- and three-year courses, these are combined with supervised industrial training in a cooperating firm.

As of 1990–91, there were 335 government and 926 private vocational and technical schools; a total of 1,261 schools.

Quality improvements have been implemented by increasing the number of training institutions that simulated the nature of work in the industrial setting. Some 20 technician education institutions were upgraded by improving their facilities and equipment, curriculum design, and instructional systems and staff.

3.5 Adult and Nonformal Education

Both public and private schools offer adult and nonformal education programs in the areas of functional literacy, vocational and technical skills, or livelihood skills training and civic and citizenship education.

To give substance and meaning to the government program of education for all, nonformal/continuing education caters to a broad spectrum of people. These include those not enrolled in formal schooling but who are of school age, dropouts, and a great number of unemployed/underemployed adults who are skilled or semiskilled and who may be literate, semiliterate, or illiterate. In 1990–91, 4,627 public elementary school teachers handled functional literacy classes for 116,493 school leavers and adults, 4,046 taught livelihood skills to 107,473, while 2,235 offered both functional literacy and livelihood skills classes.

4. Administrative and Supervisory Structure and Operation

The Department of Education, Culture, and Sports is at the helm of the Philippine educational system. Charged with the task of administering and supervising the educational system and with regulating its institutions, it is vested with the powers to formulate general objectives and policies, to adopt long-range educational plans, and to promulgate rules and regulations for the school system.

The Department of Education, Culture, and Sports has undergone a series of reorganizations to enhance its effectiveness and efficiency in delivering service to its clientele. It has been decentralized, and the task of responding to the unique needs and concerns of the different regions is the responsibility of its regional directors who report directly to the Secretary of Education.

The staff bureaus (namely, the Bureaus of Elementary; Secondary; Higher; Nonformal, Technical, and Vocational Education; and Physical Education and Sports Development) of the Department, each headed by a director, exercise functional supervision over the regional and field offices. The Bureau of Higher Education administers various study grants and scholarship programs.

The 14 regional offices (not including the autonomous region of Muslim Mindanao), which report directly to the Secretary of Education, are responsible for the supervision and evaluation of activities of the Department within the region. This setup is intended to make education more responsible to local needs.

Under the regional offices are provincial and city school divisions, each headed by a superintendent, assisted by one or two assistant superintendents who are responsible for the overall coordination and supervision of the school division. Each school division has subject supervisors who supervise instruction in the schools in the whole province or city.

In each school division, there are district offices headed by district supervisors responsible for the supervision of school principals, who are in charge of managing and supervising the instructional program. There is, however, a plan to phase out the position of district supervisor by not filling the positions of those who retire.

The supervision of instruction is a function of the school principal, the district supervisor, and the various subject supervisors in the division and regional offices, and the academic staff of the central office who exercise functional supervision over schools throughout the country.

5. *Educational Finance*

In 1970, the outlay for the Department of Education, Culture, and Sports was P829,945,302 (US$29,640,900) which was nearly 25 percent of the national budget. It plunged to 9 percent in 1980 and fell further to 7.6 percent in 1981. This decline can be partly attributed to the shifting of government priorities to national defense and infrastructure.

In 1989, the budget for the Department was P27 billion (US$ 1 billion) and represented 20.15 percent of the total state budget, but this decreased to 17.26 percent

in 1990. If the appropriation for state colleges and universities were added to the Department's budget, then the total outlay for education in 1990 would be 20.20 percent of the total state budget.

In 1993, 0.30 percent of the education budget was spent on preschool education and this decreased to 0.28 percent in 1994. As regards elementary education, 58.87 percent of the budget was spent on this sector in 1993 and 65.39 percent in 1994. The allocation for secondary education was 15.95 percent in 1993 and 18.78 percent in 1994. Technical and vocational education was allocated 2.32 percent in 1993 and 2.49 percent in 1994. Higher education was given 4.65 percent in 1993 and 4.35 percent in 1994, while nonformal education had 0.12 percent and 0.23 percent for 1993 and 1994 respectively.

In 1993, the per capita cost for preschool education was P1,694 (P27.40 = US$1), for elementary education it was P2,003, for secondary education it was P1,831, for technical and vocational education it was P7,396, and for higher education it was P24,272.

The investment in education as a percentage of the Gross National Product (GNP) is 1.3 percent. This is expected to increase in the 1990s as the economy grows, as well as because it would be in keeping with the constitutional provision to accord education the highest budgetary priority and the emphasis President-elect Fidel V Ramos places on education.

Private funding for education is mostly in the form of tuition fees paid to private schools and to state colleges and universities which levy lower tuition fees than the private educational institutions.

Parents contribute substantial amounts to Parents-Teachers Associations (PTAs) which initiate improvements in the schools. In some towns and cities, parents and other members of the community finance school projects, such as the installation of electric lighting systems, the construction of classrooms and school furniture, the purchase of learning resources, and the building of toilets. Whenever government appropriation for urgent school projects is inadequate, the parents and community are generally willing to contribute in order to provide better schooling conditions for their children.

The government subsidizes scholarship and student assistance programs which seek to democratize access to higher education and equalize educational opportunities for poor but intellectually endowed students. The same attention is given to students from the countryside, including members of national cultural communities, hill tribes, and qualified returnees or former dissidents who have returned to school to take up professional and occupational courses geared to regional personnel needs.

The State Scholarship Grant Program, which was established in 1965 and is known as the State Scholarship Law, gives scholarships to poor but gifted students in the fields of science, arts, and letters. The beneficiaries of this program are selected throughout the country through a scholarship examination. The National Integration Study Grant Program and the Selected Ethnic Group Educational Assistance Program are designed primarily for cultural communities. The Work Study Grant Program also benefits rebel returnees.

The "study now pay later" plan is basically a loan agreement between a grantee and a lending institution with the latter providing the grantee with funds to cover tuition fees, book allowance, and living and personal expenses for the duration of his or her studies. The program is administered by five lending institutions which appropriate P50 million (US$1.8 million) each for this purpose.

The average amount of scholarship grant a year per student ranges from P7,000 (US$250) to P8,000 (US$286). The average student loan granted for degree programs is P5,000 (US$179) and, for nondegree programs, P3,500 (US$125).

To concretize the government policy of assistance to private education, a law was passed in 1989 providing for, among other things, tuition fee supplements for students enrolled in private high schools, colleges, and universities charging tuition fees below certain defined limits. Tuition fee supplements serve as a means of absorbing the annual tuition fee increases usually charged by private schools. Additionally, student overflows from public secondary schools are enrolled in nearby private high schools and the government pays the tuition fees. Scholarships are also provided to tertiary students enrolling in priority courses in private schools. Altogether, about 1.4 million students benefit from this government assistance program every year.

6. Supplying Personnel for the Education System

In 1992, the Department of Education, Culture, and Sports had more than 440,000 personnel who accounted for about one-third of the total workforce of the national government. About 380,000 were classroom teachers while about 41,000 were school administrators (e.g., head teachers, principals, district supervisors, and school superintendents) and their staffs which included subject supervisors.

The teaching force in government elementary schools during the school year 1990–91 numbered 306,181. This number included 8,551 school principals, 7,283 head teachers, 23,148 master teachers, 266,210 teachers, 280 guidance coordinators, 101 guidance counselors, and 6 school librarians. It can be inferred from these figures that not all schools have librarians, guidance coordinators, and counselors. However, the common practice in schools is to designate part-time librarians, guidance coordinators, and counselors from among teachers who are qualified for these ad hoc assignments.

Master teachers, who are classroom teachers promoted to the position for excellence on the job, assist the principal in conducting teacher inservice education. In general, it is master teachers who are promoted to the position of principal. Master teachers who opt to remain as teachers can receive a salary rate equivalent to that of a principal. This system insures the retention of competent teachers by providing incentives for remaining in the teaching branch.

The basic preservice education of teachers includes a four-year course leading to a Bachelor of Science in Elementary Education or Bachelor of Science in Secondary Education degree. The course for secondary school teachers provides that they major in a specific subject area. A graduate of either of these courses needs to pass the Philippine Board Examination for Teachers (TBET) in order to qualify for a permanent or regular civil service appointment as classroom teacher.

For college or university teaching, at least an appropriate master's degree is required. For higher ranks in the tertiary-level institutions, such as professor and dean, an appropriate doctoral degree is required.

In the regional and national education systems, administrative and supervisory positions require at least a master's degree, but many of those who hold such positions also possess a doctoral degree. To qualify for the position of schools superintendent or assistant superintendent, one must have passed the schools superintendent examination which is given once every five to ten years, depending upon the number of positions to be filled. Only personnel who have had sufficient supervisory experience and who meet the educational and performance qualifications required are allowed to take this examination. Those who pass the examination are not certified for appointment unless they obtain a passing mark in the superintendent's training program.

Those who are appointed to the positions of bureau director, assistant bureau director, regional director, assistant regional director, assistant secretary, and undersecretary are usually required to go through a career executive service training program conducted by the Development Academy of the Philippines. If successful, they are assigned a Career Executive Service Officer (CESO) rank and their salaries are adjusted accordingly.

Efforts are being made to upgrade the competencies of teachers, administrators, and supervisors. A system of Learning Action Cells (LACs) has been set in place for the purpose of maintaining a continuing inservice education program for all education personnel. A National Education Academy was established for the purpose of providing a venue for the retraining of key personnel.

Besides the inservice education programs, there are opportunities for key personnel to upgrade their competencies further through training courses offered by institutions both within the country and abroad.

One such institution is SEAMEO/INNOTECH (Southeast Asian Ministers of Education Organization Regional Center for Educational Innovation and Technology) located in Quezon City, which by 1992 had trained about 820 Filipino key education personnel in the areas of planning, management, innovation, technology, supervision, research and evaluation, computers applied to education, and nonformal education. They now provide leadership in initiating changes and reforms to improve the efficiency and effectiveness of education in their own systems.

7. Curriculum Development and Teaching Methodology

Learning materials are prepared by curriculum specialists from the central and regional offices or from the teaching and supervisory staffs. The materials are validated and refined on the basis of evaluation feedback obtained and Department guidelines, and with the help of master teachers and subject matter experts from teacher-training institutions.

Textbooks for elementary and secondary schools are prepared by both the public and private sectors and are chosen on a competitive basis. Those judged to be the best are developed, printed, and distributed by the Instructional Materials Corporation. While textbooks are distributed free of charge, the ideal ratio of one textbook per student has yet to be met because of severe budgetary constraints.

Books and other instructional materials that are used as textbooks or required learning material for tertiary education are prepared by subject experts. Trial copies are reviewed by instructors/professors with regard to validity, relevance, and correctness of the materials. Colleges and universities are given the freedom to determine and adopt the textbooks to be used by their students. In many instances, most of the textbooks they adopt are foreign-authored volumes which have been reprinted by book dealers under special arrangements with their publishers.

At the tertiary education level, the technical panels and the Board of Higher Education play an important role in the determination of the various curricula. They ensure that the curricula for the different courses are relevant and of acceptable quality.

The approved curriculum is disseminated to the field for effective implementation by the different regions. Seminars and workshops are organized for disseminating it, and the subject supervisors of the regional and division offices oversee implementation. Inservice education programs are geared to the changes in the curriculum to prepare the teachers, administrators, and supervisors for its implementation. Central and regional office personnel monitor and evaluate the implementation of the curriculum, and initiate and implement inservice education programs for the purpose of further upgrading the teachers' capability to implement the curriculum.

Since the early 1980s, the Department of Education, Culture, and Sports has pursued its goal of raising the quality of outcomes of education. It has provided teacher inservice education programs addressed to improving teaching methodology.

These programs emphasize greater understanding of the learner, development of desirable attitudes toward the job, and the development of learning-oriented teaching methodology.

An important development in the elementary school system is the establishment of learning resource centers which have contributed greatly to the improvement of teaching methodology through the use of a multimedia approach. Almost all elementary schools have learning resource centers. However, these vary according to the leadership in school.

8. The System of Examinations, Promotions, and Certifications

Students at the elementary level are annually promoted from one grade to the next provided that they meet the achievement standards set for the grade. Exceptionally bright students may be accelerated to the next higher grade (though in Grades 1 to 5 only) within the year on the basis of their performance in a nationwide test conducted for the purpose of identifying high-achieving boys and girls and their maturity level.

In Grades 1 to 6, students are rated in every subject four times during the year. A cumulative rating system is used as the basis for promotion. The pass grade is 75 percent. The periodic ratings are reported to the students and their parents through an individual report card which provides for a brief narrative evaluation of the student's behavior. After satisfactorily completing the six-year elementary curriculum, the students receive a certificate of graduation from the elementary school.

No examination is required for admission to public secondary schools. Some private schools administer an entrance examination to prospective high school students. As in the elementary school, secondary school students are rated four times a year. If a student fails in a particular subject, he or she repeats the subject the next year, but is, nevertheless, promoted to the next higher year. A certificate is issued to secondary school graduates.

All high school graduates seeking admission to postsecondary programs requiring a minimum of four years' study are required to qualify in the National College Entrance Examination (NCEE) administered by the National Educational Testing and Research Center. This Center administers a Philippine Educational Placement Test (PEPT) to dropouts desiring to go back to the formal system and, on the basis of their test scores, assigns them a grade level at which they may be readmitted to school. This system of accrediting nonformal and informal education has broadened access to formal education, especially at the higher levels. Studies on the performance of dropouts whose learning has been accredited confirm that nonformal and informal education can be just as effective as formal education in promoting learning. Among the more mature dropouts who took the PEPT, several were readmitted to school at a level two or three grades higher than the last grade they attended in school.

9. Educational Assessment, Evaluation, and Research

Since the mid-1970s, evaluation, research, and educational assessment have been receiving greater emphasis and support and have been contributing to the attainment of better quality education. A number of research projects have been addressed to the problems spawned by unprecedented expansion of the education system as a consequence of a rapid school population growth rate.

The most significant research conducted in the 1970s was the Survey of Outcomes of Elementary Education (SOUTELE). It was an attempt to ascertain empirically the extent to which the elementary education system had succeeded or failed in its efforts to provide good elementary education. One of the important findings of SOUTELE was the need to reform elementary education. Its recommendations included decongesting and revising the curriculum, greater flexibility in scheduling, narrowing the gap between urban and rural schools, improving teacher competence, improving physical facilities, developing more effective and relevant learning materials, redressing differences between regions, and adopting more innovative approaches to the solution of serious problems in the sector. The survey provided the basis for a major reform program in elementary education—the Program for Decentralized Educational Development (PRODED)—which introduced a revised curriculum, provided new textbooks, expanded and improved classroom equipment and facilities, initiated a continuing teacher development program, and provided for research on significant educational problems.

In 1979, a research study on literacy retention in Philippine elementary schools was undertaken. One major finding was that Grade 3 appears to be the threshold grade level at which permanency of literacy and numeracy is at its optimum.

In the 1980s and early 1990s, a longitudinal survey was conducted to determine the effects of school, household, and community factors on school outcomes and school participation. The results provided direction for developing intervention programs calculated to further improve the quality of outcomes of elementary education.

An evaluation of bilingual education in the Philippines was conducted in 1987, and its findings and recommendations provided the basis for reviewing and

reformulating the language policy of the Department of Education, Culture, and Sports. The evaluation consisted of a quantitative study which analyzed the results of nationwide testing of students and teachers and provided institutional profiles of schools where these students and teachers were located. Companion studies of a less quantitative character were also undertaken.

Several interventions were introduced at all three levels of formal education as well as in nonformal education to improve the efficiency and effectiveness of their programs. For each intervention (e.g., a training program), there was a built-in evaluation component to determine if its objectives had been met. Evaluation feedback is used as a feed forward for improving future performance and to insure the cost-effectiveness of similar efforts. To evaluate the effectiveness of educational programs at the elementary and secondary levels, criterion-reference tests are administered at national, regional, division, and school levels during and shortly before the end of the school year. This is imperative for all schools in order to determine whether they are meeting their target of raising achievement levels by at least 2 percent each year.

10. Major Reforms in the 1980s and 1990s

The reforms initiated in the 1980s and early 1990s have their antecedents in studies conducted on the educational system (such as SOUTELE) which clearly indicated the direction that reforms should take. The most important reforms were the revision of the elementary and secondary education curricula.

At the elementary level, the revision and implementation of the curriculum was the pivotal point of other related reforms in the sector. All of these reforms made up a massive program undertaken by the Department of Education, Culture, and Sports to improve the overall efficiency and quality of elementary education. This Program for Decentralized Educational Development, more popularly known by its acronym PRODED, was implemented from 1982 to 1988.

Among the significant outcomes of PRODED are an increase in student achievement level from 37.8 to 47.3 percent, a reduction of dropout rate from 3.8 to 1.8 percent, and an increase of the participation rate of 7-year olds from 74 to 93 percent. In terms of policy, there has been a more rational allocation of resources based on regional needs so that disadvantaged regions are given more, there is maximum utilization of teacher services through the use of nontraditional schemes, the teacher–class ratio in the intermediate grades has reduced from 5.3:1 to 4.3:1, student intake has improved, and progression schemes have resulted in better holding power on the part of the school system thereby minimizing educational wastage.

The secondary curriculum was restructured in preparation for the first graduates of the elementary school under PRODED. Like PRODED, the Secondary Education Development Program (SEDP) provides for a revised and revitalized curriculum whose main features are emphasis on values education, a strong science and technology orientation, stress on skills which promote further learning, and development of vocational technical skills. It is intended to prepare the student adequately for college and for the world of work, and to develop him or her into an effective citizen in a just and humane society.

Free public secondary education was implemented starting in 1988. Access to secondary education increased dramatically. The national government took over the operation of high schools previously funded by local governmental units, including the payment of teachers' salaries.

In line with the global movement for Education for All (EFA), the period 1990–99 was declared to be the "Decade for Education for All." A ten-year National Plan of Action for Education for All was prepared. It introduced reforms and improvements in the EFA-related programs: institutionalization of early childhood care and development, universalization of quality primary education, and the strengthening of alternative systems for the eradication of illiteracy and continuing education and development.

The deregulation of operations of private educational institutions by giving recognition to excellent programs and/or excellent schools, providing incentives for quality education, and streamlining the Department of Education, Culture, and Sports bureaucracy promoted an environment conducive to private sector initiative.

An agenda for reform was submitted by the Congressional Commission on Education in 1991. The significant recommendations included emphasis on basic public education; the development of alternative learning modes for the illiterate; the use of the vernacular and Filipino as medium of instruction; enrichment of technical vocational education; restructuring of the Department of Education, Culture, and Sports; ensuring greater access of the poor to education; and making state college and university education more relevant. Legislative action will be necessary to actualize these proposed reforms.

11. Major Problems for the Year 2000

Rapid social and economic development, which the Ramos government envisions for the country toward the end of the millennium, and the high population growth rate, which is taking time to curb, are expected to pose great challenges to the education system in the future.

The education budget cannot grow fast enough to finance all of the requirements of basic education which it has been suggested, should include both elementary and secondary education. To make basic education available to all Filipinos through both the formal and nonformal systems, billions of pesos will be needed to eliminate teacher and classroom shortage, increase the salaries of the teaching personnel, train teachers, develop more relevant curricula, and produce adequate textbooks and other learning materials.

As more and more Filipinos have access to secondary education, tertiary education will need to expand to accommodate more students. The high cost of education (especially private education) and the limited capacity of the government, private schools, and parents to cope with such cost will require fresh and viable approaches to this perennial problem which has defied solution for some time. Private schools will have to absorb increases in their operating and capital costs, which have to be financed from tuition fee increases in many cases. The economy must improve dramatically if the government and parents are to be able to afford the escalating cost of higher education. It will be a great challenge for the government to meet the demands on education of a country that is determined to put its development on a fast track.

Bibliography

Cariño I D 1992 *Is Education Manageable?* Department of Education, Culture, and Sports, Manila

Congressional Commission on Education 1991 *Making Education Work: An Agenda for Reform.* Congress of the Philippines, Manila

Department of Education, Culture, and Sports 1991a *Inventory of DECS On-going Projects, Calendar Year 1991.* DECS, Manila

Department of Education, Culture, and Sports 1991b *DECS Statistical Bulletin, School Year 1990–91.* DECS, Manila

Department of Education, Culture, and Sports *Handbook on Special Education.* DECS, Manila

Fund for Assistance to Private Education 1991 *Philippine Educational Indicators.* Fund for Assistance to Private Education, Manila

Fund for Assistance to Private Education 1992 *Policy Issues in Philippine Education.* Fund for Assistance to Private Education, Manila

Gonzales A, Sibayan B (eds.) 1987 *Evaluating Bilingual Education in the Philippines.* Manila

National Committee on Education for All 1991 *Education for All: A Philippine Plan of Action 1991–2000,* Vol. 1. NCEA, Manila

National Economic and Development Authority 1990a *Philippine Development Report.* NEDA, Manila

National Economic and Development Authority 1990b *Updates on the Philippine Development Plan 1990–92.* NEDA, Manila

Sutaria M C, Elequin E The educational research environment in the Philippines. In: Gopinathan S, Nielson H D (eds.) *Educational Research Environments in Southeast Asia.* SEARRAG/IDRC, Singapore

Sutaria M C, Guerrero J S, Castaño P M 1989 *Philippine Education: Visions and Perspectives.* National Book Store, Manila

Poland

H. Komorowska and A. Janowski

1. General Background

Poland is situated in central Eastern Europe. It's territory totals 312.683 square kilometers and it is inhabited by 38.3 million persons. In the west, Poland borders Germany in the south, the Czech and Slovak Republics in the north, the Baltic Sea and part of Russia, and in the east, the states created after the disintegration of the Soviet Union (i.e., Lithuania, Byelorussia, and the Ukraine).

Most of the country is low lying. In the south there are the country's only two mountain chains: the Sudeten and the Carpathians. In the north of the country there are numerous lakes. The climate is moderate. Poland's capital is Warsaw.

Education in Poland in the late twentieth century is the outcome of a number of events which have taken place over a period of 200 years. The former Polish state was established over 1,000 years ago, but it disintegrated at the end of the eighteenth century. The people who then tried to save the country were aware of the importance of education. Thus, in 1773, 20 years before the partitioning of the Republic, the Commission for National Education was created. It was the first Ministry of Education in the world. In 1795 the Polish state ceased to exist and its territory was partitioned by three neighboring states: Russia, Austria, and Prussia. During the following 120 years these states implemented their own educational policies, mostly contradictory to the needs and aspirations of the Polish nation. Prussia developed elementary schooling and attempted a linguistic and cultural "Germanization" of the students. Education in the Russian partition was poorly developed and its main purpose was the "Russification" of Polish society. Only in the decade immediately preceding the outbreak of the First World War did the teaching of the Polish language in schools become possible again. The educational situation was relatively most favorable in the Austrian sector where there were two universities that could educate the Polish intellectual elite in the Polish language. In the remaining two sectors, this possibility was nonexistent.

The independent Polish state emerged as the result of the First World War, following 120 years of slavery. The shape of the borders of this state did not much resemble Poland in the early 1990s. Furthermore, 33 percent of the population was not of Polish nationality—these were mainly Ukrainians, Germans, Jews, and Byelorussians. Postwar Poland inherited relatively good education conditions from the former Austrian and Prussian partitions and bad conditions in those territories which formerly belonged to Russia. In some regions, particularly in the countryside, illiterates comprised 65 percent of the population. Immediately after the First World War, elementary school enrollment was less than 50 percent. In the interwar period, the development of education was one of the state's priorities. At the end of this period, 90 percent of children of 7 to 14 years of age attended school. Secondary education was also well-developed, although the trend was more humanistic than technical. At the end of the 20 interwar years, only about one-third of primary school leavers continued their education in secondary schools, including vocational schools. The number of students in higher education was almost 50,000.

All these efforts, which brought slow but steady improvement to the state of education, were rapidly halted by the outbreak of the Second World War. On September 1, 1939, Poland was invaded by Hitler's Germany, and on September 17 by Stalin's Soviet Union. The Germans only allowed elementary education for Polish children. Both Germans and Russians implemented a detailed program of destroying the intellectual elite— Germans through deportation to concentration camps, and Russians through deportation to Siberia. Despite the invaders' prohibition of education, an underground education developed: nonformal groups arranged secret meetings and studied elements of secondary and higher education curricula. Nevertheless, the postwar period in Poland commenced with the intellectual elite having been mostly destroyed and the situation where there had been no continuous secondary and higher education for five years.

As the result of the Yalta and Potsdam treaties, Poland became a satellite state of the Soviet Union, with about one-third of Polish territory being annexed. Many minorities then had to live in the Soviet Union, as well as historical centers of Polish culture becoming part of the Soviet Empire. What remained of Poland was given a large territory on the west and north which had formerly belonged to Germany. The interchange of territories triggered a population migration. This resulted in an educational network in some territories having to be developed almost from the beginning.

Despite political differences dividing the nation, the postwar years witnessed extensive rebuilding of the educational system. The number of peasant children attending school increased from 55 percent in 1948 to 83 percent in 1955. Educational aspirations and the willingness to study in secondary and higher schools rose. Unfortunately, the increase in quantity was not matched by an increase in the quality of education. The educational model was almost entirely based on the Stalinist pattern—even translated Soviet textbooks were introduced. Although, after 1956, the ideological pressure on syllabuses became less, it was a fact that during the whole period of communist rule the point of view of the ruling party was compulsory in the curricula of social and humanistic subjects. A reform of curricula was implemented in the 1960s.

The birthrate at the beginning of the 1980s oscillated between 7 and 9 percent. From 1985 onwards it declined rapidly and, in 1991, it was 3.7 percent. It is estimated that, by the year 2000, the population will be about 39.5 million people, 20 percent of whom will be children and youth. Up to the year 2000, the number of children in primary schools will decrease, though it is expected to increase in secondary schools.

About 35 percent of the population live in agricultural areas, and the rest in cities. There are three highly urbanized and industrialized regions (Katowice, Warsaw, and Lodz agglomerations) which are inhabited by over 20 percent of the population. In the less densely populated north and east regions of the country, the question of choice arises between larger, better equipped but poorly located schools to which students have to be transported, and badly equipped small schools with easy access. Financial reasons mean that student transportation is poorly developed.

Poland is exceptionally uniform from a nationality point of view. The small minority groups (German, Ukrainian, Byelorussian, Lithuanian, and Slovakian) do not account for more than about 2.5 to 4.0 percent of the whole population. To understand the situation in the early 1990s it is particularly important to realize that over a million people, mainly young and well-educated, left the country in the 1980s. Economic reasons for emigration still exist. The provision of aid to satisfy the educational needs of over 1 million Poles who live in Lithuania, Latvia, Byelorussia, Ukraine, and Kazakhstan is considered a task of the Polish educational authorities.

At the end of the 1970s, the workforce accounted for 45 percent of the population (working women formed a large part of it). About 70 percent of the workforce was employed in state institutions and about 30 percent in the nonstate sector. These were mainly agricultural workers and minor craftworkers. Relatively few persons worked in the service sector. Far-reaching transformations, which started at the end of the 1980s, resulted in the formation of a group of small entrepreneurs. At the same time, however, a group of 2 million persons became unemployed (11% of the workforce). This group has increased to 3 million.

Prior to 1989, the socialist economy functioned in five-year plan cycles. In the postcommunist economy, which is developing toward a market economy, no system of long-term planning has yet been introduced.

In 1990, in the population group aged over 15 years, 7 percent were high school graduates, 25 percent had vocational nonfull-time secondary education, 39 percent had completed primary school, and 6 percent had not completed primary education.

In the period 1945–89, the government was the Party's executive organ, and the parliament functioned as a facade institution. In 1989, partially normal parliamentary elections took place; in the autumn of 1990, presidential elections were held; and in the autumn of 1991 free democratic parliamentary elections were held. The results of the elections testify to considerable fragmentation of political preferences with the result that it is difficult to form a strong government. The main task of the government is to continue the restructuring of the economy, advancing from the so-called "socialist economy" to the effective market economy in such a way as to minimize social problems.

2. Politics and the Goals of the Education System

In 1991, far-reaching goals for changes in the educational system were drawn up. Although they will influence the form that education will take in the 1990s, at the time of writing it is not clear how far they will be developed. The goals were formulated in the autumn of 1991 when the financial situation of the state was very difficult. This situation will no doubt continue in the coming years. In 1991, teachers' salaries declined considerably compared with 1990. The share of Gross National Product (GNP) apportioned to education was cut. Thus, even if the goals are commonly accepted, those requiring high implementation costs may be delayed.

Within primary and secondary education, more weight will be placed on the applied aspects of acquired knowledge, and not on the rote learning of facts. Foreign languages will be given high priority. At the end of the twentieth century, the whole population of students completing secondary education should have a command of English, French, German, or Russian with 70 percent of them also being proficient in another foreign language.

Common computer education introduced at the early stages of primary schools is of particular relevance. On completion of secondary education, every student should possess basic skills in the operation of computers. An important task is the transfer of weight placed on general and on vocational education. The existing system is characterized by the fact that only about 50 percent of primary school graduates complete full secondary education, and above 40 percent of them enroll in three-year long basic vocational courses offering training for narrowly specialized jobs. The experience of developed countries shows that the ability to respond flexibly to changes in the labor market is acquired through general education, and not through overspecialized vocational training. The acceptance of this assumption requires a restructuring of the educational system so that a larger proportion of an age cohort can proceed to general secondary schools. The proposed reform of education strives to increase teachers' influence on curricula (although the Ministry of Education retains the right to create core curricula), to expand their autonomy in selecting teaching methods, and to create an open market for curricula and textbooks.

Changes in the system of tertiary training are also indispensable. The 1992 proportion of only 10 percent of secondary school graduates proceeding to higher education must be increased to 20 percent by the 2010. If this is to be achieved, then the old five-year courses will have to be replaced by shorter two- or three-year courses similar to those in other countries.

Another important task will be to restructure adult education which, in the new political and social situation, should better prepare adults for labor market changes.

3. The Formal System of Education

3.1 Primary, Secondary, and Tertiary Education

The Polish system of education consists of the following levels: kindergartens, primary schools, secondary schools, and higher schools. Figure 1 presents the system in more detail. All schools are coeducational.

The primary school lasts eight years and is common and compulsory for everybody. A child starts school in the year of his or her seventh birthday and continues to completion of primary education, but not past the age of 17. Primary school attendance is almost 100 percent.

The goal of primary education is to provide for the comprehensive social, intellectual, moral, and physical development of students and to prepare them for secondary general or vocational education.

Primary curricula are uniform for the whole country, but schools may create their own individual curricula if they receive permission from the regional educational authorities (*kuratoria*). Grade O is a special phenomenon in the Polish system. It is compulsory for 6-year olds and exists either as the highest class in kindergarten or as the lowest one in primary school. There are two levels in primary school: elementary education (Grades 1 through 3) and systematic education (Grades 4 through 8).

In 1990–91, there were 19,446 primary schools attended by 5,146,982 students and taught by 313,401 teachers. It is anticipated that by 1995 the number of primary-school children will increase slightly, but after that date it will decline to 4,600,000.

There are 20 periods per week in Grade 1, 21 in Grades 2 and 3, 25 in Grade 4, 27 to 28 in Grade 5, 28 to 29 in Grade 6, 27 to 29 in Grade 7, and 28 to 30 in Grade 8. However, it should be pointed out that in 1990–91 cuts made it necessary to reduce the numbers given above temporarily by 4 per week. These reductions also affected secondary and vocational schools. The decisions on which subjects had to be cut were made by head teachers. These reductions are likely to be in force until 1994 or 1996.

The average grade size is 25 to 35 students and depends mainly on the location of the school. In the large cities, grades tend to be more numerous, while in the countryside their sizes are smaller.

Nearly 98 percent of the 7- to 14-year old age group is enrolled in primary school. Again, the quality of the education tends to be better in urban schools than in rural schools.

Postprimary schools in Poland comprise general secondary schools (4 years), vocational *lycées* and technical schools (4 or 5 years), and basic vocational schools (3 years).

About 95 percent of students who complete primary education proceed to postprimary schools. In 1992–93, 26 percent of primary school graduates entered general secondary education, 27 percent vocational *lycées* and technical schools, and 42 percent the basic vocational schools. However, some of the students either drop out of their courses or transfer to shorter courses. Only 83.5 percent of the 15 through 18 age cohort complete postprimary school. About 1,500 general secondary schools were attended by about 20 percent of the 15 through 18 age cohort. Only 1.7 percent of general

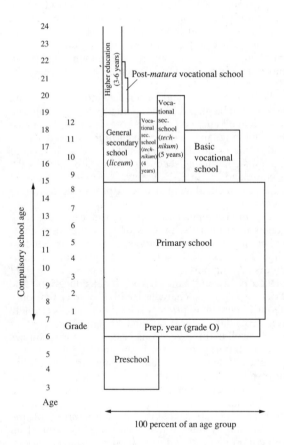

Figure 1
Poland: Structure of the formal education system

school students came from rural areas (where about 35% of the population lives), and only 1.2 percent from families of unskilled workers. This type of school is selected mainly by better educated parents in cities. The majority of students in general schools are girls (60–70%). Boys tend to think that general secondary schools do not offer any vocational skills, so only the most able or those who are not sure what to do with themselves enroll in them.

From the first year of the general secondary school students may choose from the following streams: humanities, classical, mathematics/physics, biology/chemistry, pedagogical, and general. This type of school provides the basis for entering higher education or further vocational training. There are 28 to 30 class periods per week. Students must study two foreign languages (3 hours per week each). English is studied by about 50 percent of the students, French by about 16 percent, German by about 44 percent, and Russian by some 85 percent.

In 1989, it became legal for private schools to be created, and in 1992–93, there were 500 such schools with the total number of students being 38,000. Half of these schools are primary and half are general secondary schools. Most private schools are nonprofit organizations and are attended mainly by children of highly educated parents.

The school year lasts from September 1 to about June 20, during which time there are three breaks. Summer holidays last from about June 20 to August 31. The school year consists of about 190 working days.

Higher education is free. Higher education institutions are supervised by the Ministry of Education (MOE) and several other ministries. In 1991, there were 234,691 students enrolled in institutions supervised by the Ministry of Education. The attendance was 96,902 students in the 10 universities, 64,045 in 18 higher technical schools, 27,682 in 9 agricultural schools, 17,967 in 5 economic institutes, and 28,095 in 10 teacher-training institutes.

Other ministries supervise 11 medical academies (35,883 students), 2 sea navigation schools (1,979 students), 17 art schools (6,853 students), and 6 physical education schools (9,449 students). Apart from the above, there is one private university (the Catholic Lublin University with 4,731 students) and two theological academies (1,339 students).

The total number of students in higher education is about 280,000. Furthermore, evening and extramural courses are attended by about 85,000 students. The normal length of higher education studies is 4.5 to 5 years.

It should be added that there are also two- or three-year postsecondary schools not categorized under higher education. These are referred to as "postsecondary vocational schools." There are about 900 of them and they are attended by about 111,000 students.

3.2 Preschool Education

Preschool education in Poland is conducted in kindergartens for children from the age of 3 through to 6 years, and in classes which are organized for 6-year old children in primary schools which offer an introductory preschool course (so-called "Grade 0"). Kindergartens are established and supervised by regional authorities (*gminy*). There are also private kindergartens. Children are divided into groups consisting of 7 to 30 persons. Children attend from 5 to 9 hours per day.

The total number of children attending kindergartens in 1990 was about 35 percent of the 3 through 7 age cohort. Just over 92 percent of 6-year olds were enrolled in preschool education. Since 1991, the number of children in preschool education has declined. There are three factors which account for this decline. First, the supervision of kindergartens has been delegated to regional authorities for whom they are not a priority. Second, the costs of maintaining the child in kindergarten are paid by parents, and these have risen substantially. Third, the increasing unemployment of women has resulted in their staying at home and looking after their children themselves.

3.3 Special Education

Children with various forms of handicap are enrolled in special education posts. These are: special kindergartens, separate classes in regular kindergartens, and so-called "integrative classes" in regular kindergartens. Special kindergartens are organized for children with sight and hearing defects, and for mildly and severely mentally retarded children.

At the primary and secondary levels, there are special primary schools, educational centers, and special forms in public primary schools. Individual tutoring is also possible. These schools have special Ministry of Education curricula, but also make use of the curricula for normal children, although adjusted to the potential of their students.

About 3 percent of children and young people are enrolled in special education schools. Those who complete education in special vocational schools take up work either in regular enterprises or in cooperatives for the disabled. The Ministry of Labor and Social Policy is responsible for their employment.

The majority of special education posts function as separate schools, although there are forms for special-care children in regular schools.

3.4 Vocational, Technical, and Business Education

Most students who complete primary education proceed to vocational schools whose task is to train technicians and skilled workers.

Basic skill qualifications can be acquired on completion of three-year (on rare occasions, two-year) basic vocational school. These schools train the bulk of the workforce and offer minimal general education which theoretically makes a basis for further education in secondary schools for adults. In practice, however, the vast majority of vocational school graduates do not undertake any further education, and thus these schools are not regarded as full secondary schools. In 1992–93, the enrollment in these schools was almost 800,000 students (about 43% of the 15–18 age cohort) with boys outnumbering girls. This type of education dominates in this age cohort.

A technician's diploma is awarded on completion of secondary technical school or a vocational school offering four- or five-year courses.

Secondary vocational–technical schools offer secondary general and vocational education. The courses are 4 or 5 years long and upon successful completion of the course the student receives a *matura* certificate. Secondary art, medical, and music schools are organized in a similar way. The enrollment in this type of secondary vocational–technical school was over 700,000 in 1992–93 (about 33% of the 15–18 age cohort). The number of periods per week is 30 to 40.

In 1992–93, the enrollment in all types of vocational schools was about 1,500,000 students. Most vocational schools are supervised by regional educational authorities (*kuratoria*) which report directly to the Ministry of Education, but some schools are supervised by other sectoral ministries. These are schools specializing in forestry and the lumber industry, mining, power, sea and river navigation, sea fishing, railway transport, agriculture, medical care, and art. There are also vocational schools attached to enterprises or associations. Vocational schools are financed by the state budget and tuition is free.

Preparatory work on changing the model and the curricula of vocational training is under way. There is participation from the various economic sectors in establishing vocations, qualification requirements, and vocational subjects curricula. The task of these curricular bodies is to update the curricula of vocational subjects and to adjust them to economic and technological changes.

3.5 Adult and Nonformal Education

School adult education is administered by *kuratoria*. The enrollment in the 170 primary schools for adults is about 14,000, and about 50,000 in the 234 secondary general schools for adults. There are 1,900 vocational schools for adults with an enrollment of about 200,000 students. These schools offer extramural or evening courses.

A particular feature of the educational system is postsecondary vocational schools for both nonworking and working students. This is not part of higher education. There are about 900 such schools and the enrollment (mostly adults) is about 110,000 students.

There is no state organization which organizes and administers extramural adult education. It is organized by social bodies, associations, foundations, companies, trade unions, private people, and inservice and preservice training centers in enterprises and in economic sectors, as well as by several research institutes. This area of education is undergoing spontaneous development, but data on the size of these activities are lacking.

Adult education is provided in day, evening, and extramural courses. It is mainly for adults, who, though either employed or unemployed, are nevertheless able to perform a job. It is fully paid for by the participants and, as the fees are often high, it is only undertaken by those who can afford it. Normally, it is enterprises that pay the costs of training for their employees.

Curricula vary considerably. The most popular courses are those which update and complement knowledge; provide training which makes it possible to undertake a new job; improve qualifications; and those which allow students to acquire skills for personal use and personality development.

Since the end of the 1980s there has been a considerable increase in the demand of the general public for foreign language (mainly English) courses as well as courses in bookkeeping, banking, management, marketing, and computer operating. The main providers of these types of courses are private individuals, companies, foundations, and associations.

A number of vocational courses are offered by the Skill Development Center (ZDZ), the Polish Economic Society (PTE), the Head Technical Association (NOT), and the Academic Association of Organization and Management (TNOiK).

In the face of political and economic transformations, the role of adult education is steadily increasing but the state has no overall policy in this field. Some research and development work has started. Out-of-school adult education is financed mainly from private and business resources. The state budget's contribution is extremely small (about 1% of all educational expenditure).

4. Administrative and Supervisory Structure and Operation

The whole system of education is administered and supervised by the Minister of Education. Certain vocational secondary and higher schools courses supervised by other sectoral ministries are monitored jointly by these two ministries.

Administratively, the country is divided into 49 *voivodships*. Within a *voivodship*, education is supervised by the *kurator* who is the head of the *kuratorium*. The *kurator* represents the Ministry of Education and supervises all educational matters in the *voivodship*. Schools are financed by the *kuratorium*, but kindergartens are financed from resources of smaller administrative units (*gminy*). From 1996, the *gminy* will probably be responsible for financing primary schools as well.

Most teaching syllabuses are developed by the Ministry of Education, or under its supervision. Teachers are helped in the implementation of these syllabuses by regional methodological centers within every *kuratorium*.

Higher educational institutions are also supervised by the Minister of Education. The body advising the Minister in this respect is the Senior Council of Higher Education. Universities and other tertiary institutions are highly autonomous in terms of their teaching curricula and daily activities. Their autonomy is limited only by the fact that their resources are allocated by the Ministry of Education from the state budget.

5. Educational Finance

The percentage of the GNP allocated to education has varied from 1958 to 1990. In 1958, it was 6.5 percent, in 1977—3.3 percent, in 1985—4.8 percent. On average it was 4 percent. In the period 1985 to 1990 expenditure for education rose, but in 1991 there was a sharp decline to 3.8 percent of the GNP.

Table 1 indicates how the expenditure for particular types of schools was allocated in 1991. The characteristic feature of these expenses is that only 8.8 percent is to be spent on investment and the remainder on running costs. Some 75 percent are personnel costs.

The very low student–teacher ratio is not a result of small classes, but of low teaching contact hours guaranteed by teachers' contracts and officially named *pensum*. In secondary and primary education the *pensum* amounts to 18 hours per week, and in higher education 4 to 7 hours per week. Thus, the student–teacher ratio in primary education is 15.5:1, in secondary 17.9:1, and in higher education it is 5.8:1.

Tuition, as already stated, is free. However, since the end of the 1980s, students in higher education have had to pay if they repeat a year. The burden of paying for books and other materials rests on parents.

Table 1
Budget expenditure for education in 1991

	%
Kindergarten and day care	3.9
Primary	54.1
Secondary	
General	3.5
Vocational	15.4
Higher	18.2
Others[a]	4.9
Total	100.0

a Includes allocations to foster homes, school camps, vocation houses, sports, other activities, tourism, transportation, and donations

Private nonprofit-oriented schools charge fees, but the state subsidizes 50 percent of student unit costs in these schools. In 1991, about 9 percent of secondary school students and 54 percent of higher education students received grants.

6. Supplying Personnel for the Education System

In 1991, the total number of employees in education was about 1,100,000. Of these, the number of primary and secondary school teachers was 620,000 and the number of academic teachers 65,000. There is a shortage of qualified teachers; about 15 to 17 percent lack proper qualifications. This is because there are few university graduates qualified in teaching foreign languages, mathematics, and Polish as well as the fact that the very low salaries cannot compete with other sectors of the economy. The annual demand for new teachers is about 30,000.

Teacher training is conducted at 10 universities, 10 pedagogical universities, 92 three-year teacher *studia*, and 29 pedagogical technical *studia*. All of these institutions select students who have a *matura* and who have passed an entrance examination usually consisting of one foreign language and two other subjects. In 1990, 55 three-year foreign language teacher-training colleges were established and 14 *collegia* which offer three-year courses for kindergarten teachers, teachers of elementary school subjects, and mathematics and physics. These courses emphasize subject-matter knowledge and teaching methodology, whereas the university studies offer more academic and theoretical courses.

Inservice teacher training is coordinated by the Center for Inservice Teacher Training and the 49 regional methodological centers. Their task is to organize, in cooperation with research centers and universities, methodology conferences, workshops, seminars, and courses. On-the-job help is offered by so-called "teacher consultants in methodology." Participation in inservice training is not compulsory. It is estimated that the average teacher participates in training activities for 3 to 5 days a year.

As teachers improve their qualifications through acquiring three specialization degrees, their salaries increase.

7. Curriculum Development and Teaching Methodology

There is a set of curriculum guidelines for every grade and for every subject; each of them presents the selection and the structure of the content to be taught. They have been fiercely criticized as being overloaded with factual, nonintegrated information and, since 1990, changes have begun to be made. Work has also started on the development of core curricula by curricula teams comprising academics, teachers, and other professionals chosen by the Minister of Education. Furthermore, independent experimental curricula are being developed which, after approval by educational authorities, may be implemented in individual schools.

Up to 1990, the company responsible for the selection of authors, the development of teaching materials, and the publishing of textbooks was the Publishing House for School and Pedagogical Books which cooperated closely with specific departments in the Ministry of Education. This monopoly has been phased out and it is now possible for every author and every publishing company to develop textbooks and apply for the Ministry of Education's approval.

In Grades 5 to 8 (ages 11–15), the first foreign language is introduced. This may be English, Russian, French, or German. In Grades 9 to 12 (ages 15–19) of secondary school, a second foreign language becomes compulsory and the students may select from those mentioned above, plus Spanish. Sporadically schools offer courses in other languages such as Swedish, Hungarian, Japanese, and Italian. The most popular language is English, followed by German, and then French. Although Russian is not very popular, it is taught in many schools because there are many qualified Russian teachers but a shortage of teachers of Western languages.

The implementation of the curriculum in the schools is supervised by inspectors employed in the *kuratoria*.

Religion is optional in all schools as are a second foreign language in primary school and informatics in secondary school.

8. The System of Examinations, Promotions, and Certifications

Students are promoted from grade to grade on the basis of marks ranging from 6 (excellent) to 1 (not satisfactory). Only those receiving a "1" at the end of the year are not promoted. When the mark in one subject is not satisfactory, conditional promotion is possible. The nonpromoted student repeats the whole school year, that is, two semesters. Gifted children can be promoted more quickly for either all or specific subjects.

Students take entrance examinations to enter secondary schools and also to enter higher education. The examination taken at the end of secondary education is the *matura* which consists of examinations in the Polish language, another subject according to the type of school which the student attends, and, in general secondary schools, a foreign language.

The main problem of the education system in this area is connecting the *matura* to the higher education entrance examinations and modernizing the forms of selection to higher education.

9. Educational Assessment, Evaluation, and Research

In the 1970s, research on school achievement was undertaken either for comparative purposes on an international scale or for comparing the levels of schools in a region. However, this has since been abandoned.

Educational research is conducted in education departments in universities and research centers such as the Institute for Educational Research or the Institute of the History of Education, the second of which is affiliated with the Polish Academy of Sciences. Research is also undertaken by those preparing a doctoral or *habilitation* dissertation. Most research concerns specific problems of teaching particular subjects or educational aspirations of children and parents and attitudes toward school. Other focuses of interest are able students, individual differences, and social pathology in certain groups of young people.

Qualitative methods are gaining in popularity and diagnostic projects and action research are replacing quantitative experiments and surveys.

However, the role of small-scale research in educational change is often irrelevant. Small-scale research does not allow generalizations. The researchers have not yet followed world trends in educational research because for many years pedagogy was kept inside an ideologically controlled system.

10. Major Reforms in the 1980s and 1990s

Changes in the late 1980s and early 1990s consisted of rejecting communist content in curricula and starting the teaching of foreign languages other than Russian.

The major reform in the educational system was the reform in preservice and inservice teacher training. The new system of three-year *collegia* gives priority to training in the methodology of teaching the subject closely linked with practice.

The reform of primary and secondary curricula is under way. Its main purpose is the development of core curricula and the defining of blocks of subjects from which the student can choose. Disparate subjects will also be integrated into larger subject blocks.

11. Major Problems for the Year 2000

The main factor which will influence either the development or the stagnation of education is the financial situation of the state. All predictions concerning the tempo and the effectiveness of the transfer to a market economy show that the 1990s will be financially difficult. Schools lack basic teaching materials and equipment. Teachers are badly paid, which is one reason for the low quality of didactic work. To increase the effectiveness of education, it is necessary to increase the student–teacher ratio and to introduce more accountability.

The basic problems to be solved are the same as those given in Sect. 2 above. It will be necessary to develop foreign language teaching, to overcome computer illiteracy, to restructure secondary education further so that a larger number of young people can receive general secondary training. Higher education will have to develop new, shorter forms and enroll more students. A clear policy of the state towards adult education and permanent education will also have to be developed.

Bibliography

Edukacja narodowym priorytetem 1989 *Raport o stanie i kierunkach rozwoju edukacji narodowej w P. R. L.* Panstwowe Wydawnictwo Naukowe, Warsaw

Glowny Urzad Statystyczny 1993 *Szkolnictwo 1992–93.* Glowny Urzad Statystyczny, Warsaw
Institute for Educational Research 1991 *Changes in Poland: The Implications for Education.* Institute for Educational Research, Warsaw
Janowski A 1992 Polish education: Changes and prospects. *Oxford Studies in Comparative Education* 2:
Komorowska H 1991 Second language pedagogy and language planning in Poland. In: *Proceedings* 1991 Georgetown University Round Table on Languages and Linguistics, Washington, DC
Ministerstwo Edukacji Narodowej 1991 *Szkolnictwo Wyzsze—informator.* Ministerstwo Edukacji Narodowej, Warsaw

Portugal

J. M. Rau

1. General Background

Portugal was formed as a result of various interacting political, economic, cultural, and geographical factors. The country's roots lie in the Christian reconquest of the Iberian Peninsula over eight centuries ago. Within a few years, Portugal had established virtually all the main borders it still has at the end of the twentieth century.

Almost rectangular in form, mainland Portugal occupies around 15 percent of the area of the Iberian Peninsula, with a surface area of 88,944 square kilometers, in addition to 3,041 square kilometers in the autonomous regions of the Azores and Madeira. There is a large area of mountains and an Atlantic climate in the north and plains, and a Mediterranean climate in the south. The climate of the two island regions is determined by their location in the Atlantic Ocean and by variations in altitude arising from their volcanic origin.

Portuguese is the official language in all state schools for compulsory education. All children (native and immigrant) are deemed to be equal. Extra classes for immigrant children are available in order to speed up the process of learning the language.

Until 1970, there was a slow decrease in the size of the population, particularly due to emigration. There then followed a population explosion, especially in 1974 and 1975, when high rates of growth were recorded, due particularly to the return of many Portuguese from former colonies. This was followed by a stable demographic growth of around 1 percent per year. The population was about 10.3 million in 1992.

The distribution of population in Portugal in the mid 1990s is to some extent a legacy of the past. The population is mainly concentrated in the north and near the coast because of more fertile soils, a milder climate, and greater concentration of industry, greater employment opportunities, and better amenities. The urban areas continue to attract people and have a greater population density. Meanwhile media/means of communication, literacy, and ease of access to higher education have contributed toward the fact that the rural population is changing its life-style. There is a strong concentration of schools in metropolitan areas and coastal districts.

Economic growth began during the 1950s. This was followed by a marked decline in the agricultural sector in sharp contrast to manufacturing industry. At the time of the political revolution in 1974, however, agriculture was still the dominant sector. In subsequent years, the level of unemployment increased, partly as a result of great political and economic instability.

In the 1980s, there was a considerable increase in employment in the tertiary sector. In 1992, 47.9 percent of the workforce was employed in the tertiary sector, 34.1 percent in the secondary sector, and 18 percent in the primary sector. Unemployment was only 4.7 percent.

Agriculture accounts for 6.7 percent of the Gross Domestic Product (GDP), the secondary sector for 38.3 percent, and services for 55 percent.

Since the Portuguese economy is open to the exterior, it is firmly integrated into the European Common Market, which is responsible for 71 percent of exports and 63 percent of imports. The leading exports are from traditional sectors such as cork, wine, textiles, clothing, and footwear.

Some 58 percent of the working population has four or fewer years of schooling, 38 percent have between five and eleven years, and only 3.2 percent have a higher education qualification.

The Portuguese Republic was established in 1910 after some eight centuries of monarchy. The republican ideals of equality and democracy were never realized, however, because of the subsequent period of political instability. Salazar's *Estado Novo* (1933), while intending to bring political and financial stability to the country, was also a highly centralized and totalitarian system. The democratization and development of education almost came to a stop. In its later years, the *Estado Novo* introduced some reforms into the education system (extension of compulsory education to six years, creation of new institutions of higher education, etc.), but only after the April 1974 movement did the general political democratization and decentralization affect democratization and decentralization in education: the two streams of secondary education were replaced by comprehensive secondary education, and decentralization of the system began with the transfer of responsibility to the local authorities and the schools themselves.

The government elected in 1991 has stated that it will have a policy of development, modernization, and decentralization based on the following principal objectives and goals:

(a) external cooperation,

(b) promotion of Portuguese language and culture,

(c) modernization of public administration,

(d) local power and decentralization,

(e) dialogue and social consensus,

(f) promotion of culture and education,

(g) social welfare and equal opportunities.

2. Politics and the Goals of the Education System

Following democratization of the country, the various political parties and civic organizations have largely tended to agree on the general objectives of the education system. In 1986, a Comprehensive Law on the Education System was passed with the following general principles:

(a) All Portuguese citizens have the right to education and culture.

(b) The state is responsible for promoting the democratization of education and guaranteeing the right to fair and effective equality of educational opportunities.

(c) All Portuguese citizens are ensured respect for the principle of freedom of learning and teaching and of choosing what to learn, bearing the following principles in mind:

   (i) the state may not assume the right to program education and culture according to philosophical, aesthetic, political, ideological, or religious doctrine;

   (ii) state education shall not be religious;

   (iii) the right to create private and cooperative schools is guaranteed.

(d) The educational system will address the needs of society and contribute to the personal development of the individual to produce responsible independent citizens and productive members of the workforce.

(e) Education promotes the development of a democratic and pluralist spirit with respect for other people and their ideas.

In 1989, the Educational Development Program defined three principal objectives and proposed measures for achieving them:

(a) General access to education involving: the development of nursery education; construction and equipping of new classrooms; construction and equipping of halls of residence; development of special education; development of vocational education; expansion of adult education; and development of higher education.

(b) The modernization of school infrastructures, involving: rescaling the First-Cycle school network; maintaining and renovating the school network; constructing sports areas; general access to information technologies; and the development of school *mediatheques*.

(c) Improvement in the quality of education, including: the promotion of educational success; vocational information and guidance; and inservice training of basic and secondary education teachers.

3. The Formal System of Education

3.1 Primary, Secondary, and Tertiary Education

The 1986 Education Law established the general organization of the Portuguese education system, involving nursery education, school education, and out-of-school education. School education includes basic, secondary, and higher education. Figure 1 presents the structure of the system.

Basic education is compulsory, universal, and free; lasts for 9 years; and is subdivided into three stages or cycles. The First Cycle is provided in public, private, and cooperative schools and teaching is global and administered by a single teacher; it covers the first four grades of schooling. The Second Cycle comprises two types: direct education in preparatory schools and indirect education making use of television for peripheral and remote zones. This latter type is declining since measures have been taken to cover the whole of national territory by direct education; it is organized by interdisciplinary areas, with one teacher per area. The Second Cycle involves Grades 5 and 6. The Third Cycle involves Grades 7, 8, and 9 and is run in preparatory/secondary and secondary schools; a unified curriculum involves diversified vocational areas with one teacher per subject or group of subjects. A certificate is awarded upon completion of basic education.

Secondary education is optional and lasts for three years (Grades 10 to 12) after compulsory education. It involves courses geared mainly toward working life as well as those toward further studies. Transfer between these two courses is provided for. Each teacher is theoretically responsible for a single subject. A certificate is awarded on completion of secondary education. The courses geared toward working life constitute the necessary qualification for entering active life. The courses geared toward further studies, followed by an entrance test, allow students to enter higher education.

Higher education involves universities and polytechnic institutes. Universities award the *licenciatura* (4 to 6 years of study) and master's and doctoral degrees. Polytechnic institutes offer specialized courses in particular areas that can be associated in wider units under various names according to regional interests and/or the nature of the schools. The degree of *bacharel* (3 years of study) is awarded by these schools. After two or more years of study, a student may be awarded a specialized studies degree, equivalent to a *licenciatura*. People over 25 years of age with no secondary education certificate can be admitted to higher education after passing a special test.

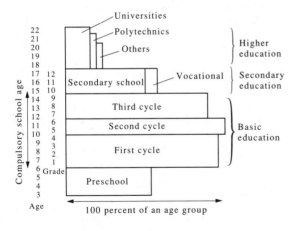

Figure 1
Portugal: Structure of the formal education system 1991–92

The school year lasts 197 days in schools open on Saturdays and 167 days in the remainder of schools. Schools in the First Cycle of basic education function 25 hours per week from Monday to Friday (5 hours per day). In the Second and Third cycles of basic education, classes are run from Monday to Friday (or Saturday), with an average of 31 hours per week. In secondary education, the number of hours per week varies between 28 and 33.

The average number of pupils per class is 25 in the First Cycle of basic education, and 26 to 34 pupils (according to the area of the classroom) in the Second and Third cycles of basic education and secondary education.

The calendar for higher education is fixed by the executive bodies of each institution. In most higher education institutions, the academic year is divided into two semesters (generally of 15 to 16 weeks), although some subjects can be organized in an annual structure.

3.2 Preschool Education

Nursery education complements family education and is optional for children between 3 years of age and the age of entering basic education; it is run on the initiative of central, regional, or local authorities or other private entities.

3.3 Special Education

Special education involves a series of measures for pupils with special educational needs in public education establishments at basic and secondary level. These measures include: remedial education facilities; material and curriculum adaptations; special conditions of enrollment, attendance, and assessment; adapted organization of classes; additional pedagogical support; and special education.

The state is responsible for promoting and supporting special education and for defining the general standards of implementing this sector, particularly in pedagogical and technological terms. Special education initiatives may be taken by central, regional, or local authorities or private institutions. According to available statistics, about 10 percent of the school population is provided with services, either in special schools or on the basis of a mainstreaming system.

3.4 Vocational, Technical, and Business Education

In addition to complementing the preparation for working life begun in basic education, vocational education is geared toward entry into active life and constitutes an alternative to academic secondary education. The aim of this vocational education is to train skilled professionals in intermediate technologies.

Vocational courses last for three years and involve three components: sociocultural, scientific, and technical–technological. Each of the first two correspond to 25 percent of the course and the last to 50 percent. Successful completion of the course confers the right to a vocational certificate and a secondary education diploma with the possibility of further studies, including access to higher education.

3.5 Adult and Nonformal Education

Portugal had an estimated average illiteracy rate of 13 percent in 1990. Those affected are mainly older people, those in rural areas, and women. Adult education can be classified into two subsystems. Recurrent education is a special type of academic education, with its own methods and organization conferring certificates at the same level as in formal education. Further education consists of the range of state or privately organized activities geared to the integral development of individuals in the community. These activities can be complementary to or substitutions for school education. The different courses in recurrent education for people of over 15 years of age involve three cycles equivalent to the three cycles of basic education and conferring the same diplomas and certificates as those in regular education. Distance learning also exists both at school and at higher education levels. It is provided by the Open University. Special courses for inservice teacher training are also included.

4. Administrative and Supervisory Structure and Operation

Education is run by the Ministry of Education, which defines the formal and nonformal education and sports policy. In specific cases, such as vocational education, it is run jointly by the Ministry of Education and the Ministry of Labor and Welfare. There is also close cooperation with other ministries and public or private bodies in order to capitalize on the structures and resources available.

The organizational framework of the Ministry of Education involves central and regional bodies. The central departments, which ensure the application of laws at national level, are also responsible for issuing guidelines for consultancy, techno-administrative and planning support, coordination of research and development, orientation and coordination of the education system, supervision, guidance, and coordination of social policy. The Ministry of Education constitutes a number of advisory, technical and planning, and coordination bodies for the running of the system.

The advisory bodies are the National Education Committee, the Private and Cooperative Education Coordinating Committee, the Committee of Higher Education–Enterprise Cooperation, and the National School Sports Committee. Their roles are as follows:

(a) The National Education Committee is a senior body of the Ministry and is independent, has administrative and financial autonomy, and is made up of representatives of the different bodies directly involved in education, whether producers or users, and the political and social sectors. The chairperson is elected by parliament and is responsible for issuing opinions, reports, and recommendations on all global matters concerning education policy.

(b) The Private and Cooperative Education Coordinating Committee is responsible for proposing measures to the Minister of Education for making the participation of private and cooperative education in the education system viable. It is made up of the director-generals of education, the inspector-general of education, regional education directors, representatives of private and cooperative teaching establishment associations, the national association of parents' and students' associations, and trade unions.

(c) The Committee of Higher Education–Enterprise Cooperation is responsible for proposing national cooperation policy between higher education establishments and firms, organizations, and financial institutions and for promoting measures likely to achieve this policy.

(d) The National School Sports Committee is an advisory body that participates in defining guidelines for developing school sports.

The roles of the technical and planning bodies are as follows:

(a) The General Secretariat provides technical and administrative coordination and support in the areas of organization, information technology, personnel and equipment management of ministerial offices, central services, and regional education departments.

(b) The Planning and Research Bureau is responsible for consistently and systematically studying problems related to education and proposing solutions to help draft general policy. It is also responsible for developing proposed activities emerging from international cooperation and financing agreements.

(c) The Financial Management Bureau drafts proposals for the Ministry's budget; distributes funds among the various departments, services, and units; and supervises the economic and financial management of all funds.

There are two research and development coordinating bodies, whose roles are:

(a) The Institute for Portuguese Language and Culture is responsible for the propagation of Portuguese language and culture abroad and for sponsoring and subsidizing meetings on this theme.

(b) The Institute for Educational Innovation is geared toward developing research in the different areas of educational development.

The units responsible for coordinating the education system are: the Directorate-General for Higher Education; the Directorate-General for Basic and Secondary Education; the Directorate-General for Adult Education; the Directorate-General for School Administration; the Technological, Artistic, and Vocational Education Bureau; and the Regional Education Departments (the regional departments are responsible for operating and managing education in each of the five regions).

Until 1974, basic and secondary schools were run by directors and rectors appointed by the Minister of Education. The situation was very unstable immediately after 1974, and various establishments formed "management committees." This spontaneous movement was institutionalized by subsequent legislation which transferred the management of preparatory and secondary education establishments (Grades 5 to 12) to three bodies—the Executive Committee, the Pedagogical Committee, and the Administrative Committee. The administration of primary education (Grades 1 to 4) was more simple. It consisted of an elected head teacher and the school committee was made up of all teachers.

In 1991, legislation was drafted establishing a new school management model to be run by four bodies: the School Committee, the Pedagogical Committee, the Administrative Committee, and the Executive Director. This new system is considered to be more appropriate to the decentralization and regionalization processes under way in the early 1990s and to school autonomy. It also includes a stronger participation of parents.

At the university level, each university is granted the right to draft its own statutes, ratified within 60 days by a ruling of the Minister of Education and published in the official gazette. The organizational units of each university also have scientific, pedagogical, administrative, and financial autonomy. The governing bodies of the universities are: the University Assembly, responsible for approving the university's statutes and electing the Rector who represents and runs the university; the University Senate which, in addition to exercising disciplinary power, is responsible for approving the general guidelines of the university, its development plans and annual activity reports, draft budgets, and the annual report and accounts and all academic programming and management; and the Administrative Committee, which performs the administrative, asset, and financial functions of the university.

Polytechnics draw up their own statutes, ratified by a ruling of the Minister of Education. Polytechnics are managed by the following bodies: (a) the president, elected by an administrative body made up

proportionally of teaching staff, students, administrative staff, and representatives of the community; (b) the General Committee, composed of representatives of students' associations, teaching staff and students of each school, nonteaching staff, and the community; and (c) the Administrative Committee, made up of the president, vice-presidents, and the administrator, which performs the administrative, financial, and asset functions of the institute.

5. Educational Finance

Educational expenditure in 1970 was only 1.9 percent of GDP and 11.1 percent of the state budget. In 1975, following political changes, this rose to 4.3 percent and 18.5 percent respectively. In 1989, the figures were 4.9 percent and 17.5 percent. In 1989, the allocation of the education budget was 2 percent to nursery education, 47 percent to basic schooling, 30 percent to secondary, and 18 percent to higher education. Special and adult education and teaching of Portuguese abroad received 3 percent.

Private universities emerged for the first time in the second half of the 1980s and rapidly absorbed 20 percent of students. In 1989, private financing of education (considering only the fees paid in private education establishments) was estimated to be 6 percent of total expenditure.

Socioeducational support in basic and secondary and, separately, higher education in 1989 was 1.6 percent and 1.7 percent of total expenditure respectively. In basic and secondary education, 26 percent corresponded to socioeconomic support and 64 percent to school refectories and the provision of a food supplement in the First Cycle (first 4 years of schooling). In higher education, support went to halls of residence (11%), subsidized refectories (59%), and grants (30%). In addition to this, the local authorities provide school buildings, for which they have been responsible since the 1984–85 academic year.

Per unit costs for the different levels of education (1991) are as follows: per preprimary pupil Esc118,500; per basic and secondary pupil Esc189,124; and per higher education pupil Esc588,845. No separate data are available for primary (1st Cycle) education, or the Second and Third Cycles of basic and secondary education. Estimates, however, for the First and Second Cycles of basic education are: First Cycle (primary) Esc260, 302; Second Cycle Esc256,279 (Esc170.35=US$1)

6. Supplying Personnel for the Education System

The total number of teachers in state education in 1989 was 133,077. Of these, 2.6 percent were in preschool education, 29.3 percent in the First Cycle of basic school, 20.3 percent in the Second Cycle, 38.3 percent in the Third Cycle and secondary education, 9.9 percent in higher education, and 1.0 percent in other schools. The number of teachers in the First and Second Cycles decreased somewhat in the 1980s because of decreases in pupil enrollment due to the fall in the birthrate. At the same time, there was an increase in the number of teachers in the Third Cycle of basic, secondary, and higher education as enrollments increased.

The training of nursery and First Cycle basic education teachers takes place in special initial training courses run by schools of higher education in polytechnic institutes. The training lasts three years, at the end of which the graduates receive a professional qualification. For schools at other levels of education, the percentage of teaching staff with an educational qualification as well as an academic degree is about 60 percent.

For teachers of the Second and Third Cycles of basic education and for secondary teachers, there are two ways of being trained. If they already have an academic degree (*bacharelato* or *licenciatura*) and have already been selected for teaching in schools, they can enter an inservice course that lasts for two years and involves theoretical and practical training. The courses are organized by faculties of education at universities or by schools of education, in close cooperation with teachers of basic and secondary education schools. If they do not already have an academic qualification, they take an integrated course of 4 to 5 years' duration in a university providing subject matter and educational training.

The inservice training of teachers takes place in the schools themselves, universities and polytechnic institutes (education faculties, departments, and schools), and in various public and private organizations, such as foreign language institutes and teacher associations.

In 1990, there were nearly 62,000 nonteaching personnel. The Directorate-General of School Administration and the regional education departments are responsible for the training of nonteaching staff through a cooperative system. The objective of the Directorate-General is to train monitors and produce training programs and supporting material. The regional education departments are responsible for promoting courses in the field geared towards the various nonteaching bodies; technical and technical–vocational personnel; and administrative, operative, and auxiliary staff.

7. Curriculum Development and Teaching Methodology

There is a national curriculum for basic education, although some optional subjects are possible (namely, personal and social development or religious education in the First Cycle, the same plus foreign language options in the Second); in the optional area of the Third Cycle, pupils can choose one of three possible subjects: a second foreign language, musical education, and technological education.

Secondary education is organized in a double track system: one track geared to continuation of studies in higher education, the other geared to entry into active life. Both tracks are organized into three components, each including several subject matters: general common core, specific components per track and per area and course, and technological component per track and per area and course.

In the Second Cycle, there are 12 hours per week devoted to language and social studies (including 4 hours for foreign language learning); 7 hours for mathematics and science; 8 hours for art, technology, and music; 3 hours for physical education; and 1 hour for personal/social/moral education.

In the Third Cycle, the same subjects are studied, but history, geography, and a second foreign language (optional) are added. However, more time is devoted to science, especially in Grade 8.

Table 1 gives a breakdown of secondary education teaching hours.

Textbooks and occasionally materials produced by the teacher are the main form of learning aids used. Textbooks are typically written by teachers and published commercially. The Ministry of Education, through the General Directorate for Basic and Secondary Education, establishes criteria by which schools abide when selecting textbooks.

Table 1
Number of hours per curriculum component in secondary education

	Track geared to continuation of studies			Track geared to entry into active life		
	Grade 10	Grade 11	Grade 12	Grade 10	Grade 11	Grade 12
General core of subjects common to all students	12/13	12/13	7/6	12/13	12/13	7/6
Specific component	12/13	12/13	15/18	12/13	8	6
Technical component	6	6	6	10	10	10

A major investment has been made since the beginning of the 1990s better to equip schools with science laboratories and computers.

8. The System of Promotions, Examinations, and Certifications

In the First Cycle of basic education, teachers assess their students on a continuous basis. Promotion is decided upon by the school committee. In the Second and Third Cycles of basic education, as well as in secondary school, teachers award marks for each subject on a scale of 1 to 5 (or 0 to 20 for secondary school). At the end of each cycle, if students receive a 3 in two or more subjects they may have to repeat a year (this is also decided by the school committee). However, grade repeating is rare. In secondary education, the passing mark per subject is 10.

National achievement tests are administered across all schools at the end of basic education and at the end of secondary education. These are used for deciding upon the award of a certificate.

Academic achievement is assessed by means of mandatory examinations for pupils attending private and cooperative education schools. Individuals taught at home may also apply to take these examinations.

In order to move from secondary to higher education, three different sources are used: marks on the general examinations at the end of secondary schools, marks on specific tests, and marks on a national entrance test for university.

9. Educational Assessment, Evaluation, and Research

Until the 1980s, assessment was mainly based on statistical surveys (which provided information on school attendance, and repetition and dropout rates) as well as on some other indicators which made it possible to monitor the system and, eventually, to estimate effectiveness rates.

In the first years of the 1980s, studies were being undertaken on the entry of young school leavers into the labor force. However, by the end of the 1980s, educational assessment studies began on a regular basis in the form of Portugal's participation in international projects such as those run by IEA, ETS, and OECD (CERI's International Education Indicators Project). At the same time, a national system of education statistics developed. By analyzing the nationally collected data, it became possible to monitor and assess the system at any given time, and to develop further studies on the supply and/or demand of education. Of the indicators available in 1990, those which had most impact on decision makers and public opinion were:

(a)   school attendance, retention, dropout, and success rates by students' geographical, social, and economic background;

(b)   distribution of secondary education students (academic or vocational schools);

(c)   higher education entrance rates and distribution of students by level and area;

(d)   performance level of students in Portuguese, mathematics, and natural science;

(e)   employment chances after leaving school;

(f)   rates of return to education.

10. Major Reforms in the 1980s and 1990s

The major reforms in the 1980s and beginning of the 1990s were:

(a)   expansion of compulsory education from 6 to 9 years;

(b)   development of polytechnic higher education as a real alternative to university higher education, the former being more geared toward vocational qualification;

(c)   change of the school management system allowing for a more active participation at local level (parents, local authorities, economic, and cultural interests);

(d)   reform of the school education curricula to assure greater integration of subjects in disciplinary areas, sequence of subject contents in the different cycles, and lesser diversity in secondary education areas (Grades 10, 11, and 12);

(e)   decentralization of education through the setting up of regional education authorities which enforce the laws and decisions made at central level;

(f)   state support to vocational schools for the private sector (this constituted an alternative to postbasic formal education after Grade 9 and trained youths at intermediate level).

11. Major Problems for the Year 2000

The heterogeneous nature of the school population, due to the expansion of the system together with the raising of compulsory schooling to nine years, led to problems in the quality of teaching. At the level of secondary education, the economic growth of the country has led to increased demand for education which has created bottlenecks and emphasized the shortage of resources. Meanwhile, the lack of a systematic program for updating and training teaching staff generally makes it difficult to solve problems rapidly and adequately.

In the years leading up to 2000, the Portuguese education system will have to cope with major problems which are in themselves a great challenge to its effectiveness:

(a) the quantitative as well as qualitative development of school conditions in terms of school equipment and facilities to meet the increasing demand for education, mainly at secondary and higher education levels, and for greater access to teaching/learning materials;

(b) the systematic and generalized teacher inservice training activities which, by fostering new attitudes in teachers, may lead to new teaching practices, motivating students (more and more attracted by the world outside the school), thus avoiding school failure and dropouts; and

(c) the provision of vocational education courses geared toward entry to the labor force which may constitute an attractive alternative to more traditional courses and, at the same time, improve the quality of the labor force.

Bibliography

Assembleia da República 1986 *Lei de bases do sistema educativo, Lei no. 46/86, de 14 de Outubro*. Assembleia da República, Lisbon

Direcção-Geral do Ensino Básico e Secundário (annual) *Ensino especial: dados estatísticos 1989/90*. Ministério da Educação, Lisbon

Direcção-Geral de Extensão Educativa 1990 Execução financeira de 1990. Ministério da Educação, Lisbon

Gaspar J 1981 *Portugal em mapas e números*. Livros Horizonte, Lisbon

Gaspar J 1989 *Ocupação e organização do espaco: uma prospectiva*. Fundação Calouste Gulbenkian, Lisbon

Inspecção-Geral de Ensino (annual) *Análises de conjuntura*. Inspecção-Geral de Ensino, Ensino

Instituto Nacional de Estatística 1982 *Inquérito ao emprego: 1982*. INE, Lisbon

Instituto Nacional de Estatística 1984 *Estatísticas da educação: 1984*. INE, Lisbon

Instituto Nacional de Estatística 1986 *Estatísticas da educação: 1986*. INE, Lisbon

Instituto Nacional de Estatística 1989a *Estatísticas da educação: 1989* INE, Lisbon

Instituto Nacional de Estatística 1989b *Estudos demográficos: 1989*. INE, Lisbon

Instituto Nacional de Estatística 1991a *Inquérito ao emprego: 1991, 20. trim. INE, Lisbon*

Instituto Nacional de Estatística 1991b Portugal em números: 1990. INE, Lisbon

Marques A H O 1985 *História de Portugal, vol. 1*. Palas Editores, Lisbon

Ministério da Educação 1989 *Decreto-Lei n.344/89, de 11 de Outubro*. Diário da República: I série, Lisbon

Ministério da Educação 1991 *Folha informativa para os pais e encarregados de educação dos alunos dos ensinos básico e secundário: ano 1990/91*. Ministério da Educação, Lisbon

Ministério da Educação, Gabinete de Estudos e Planeamento 1992 *Sistema educativo português 1990: situação actual e tendências*. GEP, ME, Lisbon

Presidência do Conselho de Ministros 1991 *Programa do XII Governo Constitucional, cap. III*. Conselho de Ministros, Lisbon

Unidade Portuguesa de EURYDICE 1992 Dossier nacional sobre o sistema educativo português. Gabinete de Estudos e Planeamento do Ministerio da Educação, Lisbon

Universidade de Lisboa 1991 Portugal económico: do vintismo ao século XX. In *Análise social: revista do Instituto de Ciências Sociais da Universidade de Lisboa, vol. 26*. Universidade de Lisboa, Lisbon

Qatar

A. A. T. Al-Subaie

1. General Background

Qatar is a peninsula situated halfway along the western coast of the Arabian Gulf. This location has made Qatar of strategic importance. It has an area of about 11,427 square kilometers. The landscape is generally flat and low lying except for some modest hills to the northwest. In the north there are areas of vegetation. The south is arid, with stretches of salt flats.

In 1992, the population of Qatar was about 400,000. More than three-fourths of the population lived in Doha, the capital. The rest were scattered in the oil areas, in small villages, and in the desert.

The majority of the inhabitants came to Qatar in three main immigration movements. In the 1870s, families from tribes living in Kuwait and the eastern coast of the Arabian Peninsula came by land to reside in Qatar. About the end of the nineteenth century, during the expansion movement of the Wahabbis, groups of families originally living along the eastern coast of the Arabian Peninsula emigrated by land to Qatar. The third immigration movement, over the first half of the twentieth century, was when inhabitants of the neighboring coasts of the Arabian Gulf came by sea, mostly from the western coasts of Persia.

All Qataris are Moslems; the majority are followers of the Sunna sect, and the minority (of Persian origin) are Shiites. Qatari society is conservative and its customs and traditions have their origins in the Islamic values and the traditions of nomadic tribes.

The State of Qatar became fully independent in September 1971. Since then it has been a full member of the Arab League and the United Nations Organization.

Independence marked the start of a real and essential change in the political, economic, and social life in Qatar; its effects have been more obvious in the cultural field in general and in the educational field in particular. The surge of education in Qatar did not start with Independence. There has been a continuous effort since the beginning of the twentieth century. This culminated in the declaration of the generalization of education in 1956–57.

2. Politics and Goals of the Education System

There have been several statements about the educational objectives of the Qatar education system. The constitution of the state of Qatar specified the aim of education as:

> Building a nation whose members are physically strong, mentally sound, believers in God, well-behaved, proud of Islamic traditions, aware of their duties and rights, and equipped with knowledge.

The Qatari educational curricula have adopted the general objective approved by the Arab cultural Unity Agreement which stipulates:

> Building a generation of believers in God, proud of and adhering to Islam, loyal & dedicated to their nation, filled with the sense of justice and benevolence, integrated in their development of soul, mind, body and conscience and filled with an urge to work and struggle for themselves, their nation, religion and humanity at large.

In 1982 a statement of educational policy was adopted. In 1989–90, a group of UNESCO experts evaluated the education system and proposed that the objectives should be recast. A specialized joint committee from the Ministry of Education and Qatar University developed general educational objectives. These objectives, still under consideration at the time of writing this entry, are as follows:

(a) To develop educated generations of believers in God, who adhere to their Islamic doctrine, well-aware of their perspective to humanity, universe, and life, committed to their principles: doctrine, worship, morals, and behavior.

(b) To develop generations proud of their association with the Arab Nation, convinced of its genuineness and role in the world civilization, and aware of its unity and integrity, and of the problems and challenges it is facing, equipped with all means to confront them.

(c) To foster Qatari, Arabic, Islamic, and humanitarian adherence of educated persons, and to strengthen their will to fulfill their rights and obligations thereto.

(d) To develop citizens with educated and physically, mentally, psychologically, and socially integrated personalities.

(e) To encourage the continuous acquisition of developed and useful scientific and technological knowledge in conformity with an individual's growth stages and capabilities to develop abilities to relate scientific knowledge with relevant applications, and to comprehend scientific and technological achievements utilizing their advantages and avoiding the disadvantages.

(f) To encourage individuals to acquire knowledge and develop self-education tendencies and skills for the purpose of achieving an educated society.

(g) To develop the artistic and literary interests of educated persons and enable them to express such interests; and to develop health attitudes which care for the principles and balance of public and psychological health, safety and treatment, and security and safety requirements.

(h) To develop social interaction skills that may be freely practiced and to respect the opinions of others. All persons should be trained in critical thinking, cooperative work, and in interaction with their environment and society.

(i) To develop citizens who, through their behavior, observe the constructive traditions of their society as well as its cultural and civilization heritage.

(j) To ensure the continuous vital interconnection among the generations of Qatari society and the positive interaction between those generations and their society.

(k) To develop the talents of all citizens and to link these talents with the vital interests of the society; citizens should be trained to utilize developed technology to meet the development requirements.

(l) To develop the awareness of students and their ability to cope efficiently with relevant facts; and prepare students for playing a major role in the advancement of human civilization, and in international understanding based on rights, justice, freedom, and equality, and to establish just peace among all nations.

(m) To develop an awareness of other nations' cultural civilization and experiences: while adhering to their own identity, Arabic and Islamic culture, values, and traditions.

3. The Formal System of Education

There was no official education in Qatar before 1956. It was in that year that the first government school was established. This was followed by a rapid increase in the number of schools and students. Initially, Qatar depended on other Arab countries for curriculum development, teachers, and books. Gradually the system developed and Qatar produced its own textbooks within the framework of Arab cultural agreements. In the 1970s, there was rapid quantitative and qualitative development. The University of Qatar was established in 1973 with a faculty of education in two parts, one for male students and the other for female students. In all, the University has five faculties.

3.1 Primary, Secondary, and Tertiary Education

There is no compulsory education in Qatar, yet the state spares no effort in providing the facilities needed to make education available to all. A draft law for compulsory education has been prepared which was still under consideration in 1992.

Figure 1 shows the Qatari system of education in diagrammatic form. The educational system comprises six years of primary school, three years of preparatory school (lower-secondary school), and three years of secondary school (higher-secondary school). The primary school is for all students, while there are two types of preparatory school, namely: general and religious. The secondary school comprises four types,

namely: general, religious, technical, and commercial. There are no community colleges in Qatar. There are also two specialized institutes: one for nursing, affiliated to the Ministry of Public Health, and the other for music, affiliated to the Ministry of Information and Culture.

There is a special institute for language teaching, mainly established for government officials. In this institute, English and French are taught to Arabs while Arabic is taught to non-Arabs. The institute runs a four-year course. The Ministry of Education also runs the Institute of Administration, which accepts Qatari government administrative staff who have completed their secondary education. The institute runs a two-year course.

Education is free for all residents regardless of race, origin, language, or creed. Ages of enrollment are 6–16 years in primary school, 11–19 years in preparatory school, and 14 years and above in secondary school.

In 1990–91, there were 63,596 students in the Ministry's day schools. This was an increase of 2.7 percent over the previous year. There was approximately an equal number of boys and girls enrolled.

There is some nongovernmental private schools for Arabs and foreigners. The number of students in private Arab and foreign schools in the school year 1990–91 was 23,187 students in 126 schools, distributed as shown in Table 1.

3.2 Preschool Education

There is a number of private kindergartens with an enrollment of just over 6,000 pupils. These are attended mostly by children aged 5 years.

In the early 1990s, the Ministry was considering the possibility of establishing a government preschool to act as a model for other private preschools and as a center for training preschool teachers.

3.3 Special Education

Two institutes for the handicapped were established in 1982 (one for boys and one for girls).

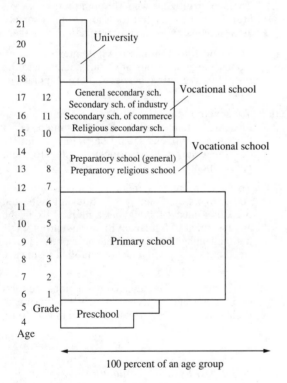

Figure 1
Qatar: Structure of the formal education system

Table 1
Number of students in private Arab and foreign schools 1990–91

	Boys	Girls	Total
Preschool	3,262	3,136	6,398
Primary	7,132	5,455	12,587
Preparatory	1,454	1,404	2,858
Secondary	670	674	1,344
Total	12,518	10,669	23,187

In the year 1991–92, the number of students was as follows: 247 at the mental education institute (153 boys and 94 girls) and 93 at the acoustic education institute (49 boys and 44 girls), making a total enrollment of 340.

3.4 Vocational, Technical, and Business Education

As a result of technological development, the Ministry has worked on the constant development of the secondary school of industry in terms of administration, organization, content, and training. To this end, experts at regional, Arab, and international levels were invited to the country on several occasions. In support, the Cabinet approved the construction of modern premises in the Abu Hamur area at a cost of QRs4,050,000 for equipment, in addition to construction costs. The number of students at the school was 409 in 1990–91 and 412 in 1991–92.

Since its establishment in the mid 1960s, the secondary school of commerce has not witnessed any significant development. Hence, the UNESCO team of experts gave special attention to the modernization of the school. The Ministry is providing the school with an advanced business workshop comprising computers, note-counting machines, communication facilities, and so on, to acquaint students with the latest developments in this field. The number of students at the school was 110 in 1990–91 and 129 in 1991–92.

3.5 Adult and Nonformal Education

Qatar's system of adult education includes literacy programs. The number of students attending evening literacy classes or classes to improve their standards of education reached 6,759 in the year 1990–91; of those 3,956 were men, and 2,803 were women. The classes are held in 65 centers covering all towns and large villages.

4. Administrative and Supervisory Structure and Operation

The level of efficiency of any activity mainly depends upon the level of qualification, awareness, expertise, and competence of its leadership. It also depends upon the administration methods adopted by the leadership in a way that objectively secures a better investment of all available resources, aiming for the largest returns against the lowest costs. Decisions related to educational policy, its strategic framework, and long-term plans are adopted by the Cabinet after consultation with the Advisory Council. The execution of educational policy is the responsibility of the Ministry of Education after consulting all relevant departments. There is a group of advisory committees which participate in preparing and executing the decisions. These are curriculum committees (for science, mathematics, English, and social studies) and committees for educational evaluation, educational research and studies, personnel, tenders, and scholarships.

Before a final decision is taken, the opinions of educational administrative experts, students, teachers inspectors, and school administrative staff are explored through questionnaires, opinionnaires, or general discussions. In this way, there is a counterbalance between centralization and decentralization.

In 1974, the Ministry of Education decided to conduct comprehensive research on productive efficiency in the schools using the procedure of following up a particular cohort of pupils. The Ministry first conducted a number of courses and seminars for school principals and their deputies, based on lectures and dialogues concerning concepts, modes, and factors related to promoting educational efficiency. Following this, a comprehensive research study entitled "Educational Efficiency in Qatari Schools" was launched. It is expected that the results of this study will help improve efficiency in schools.

The central educational administration was developed during the first year of Independence in 1971–72. Further developments were introduced in the school year 1990–91. The Ministry is restructuring the organization of the administration in accordance with the latest methods. The central administration has been provided with a highly qualified and specialized staff ever since the beginning of the generalization of education. In the year of Independence (1971–72), the Ministry's administrative staff totalled 213 (182 males and 31 females). In 1992, the total was 992 (758 males and 234 females).

Since Independence, the "Qatarization" of leading posts has been sought to ensure that national responsibilities are shouldered—whenever possible—by competent nationals, and to present them with the opportunity to acquire and refine experience and develop competence.

In 1990–91, the status of educational leadership was as shown in Table 2.

In 1990–91, the total number of Ministry employees, including teachers, was 7,778 (3,212 males and 4,566 females), of whom 4,258 were Qatari employees (614 males and 3,644 females).

5. Educational Finance

In 1985–86, the Ministry's budget totaled QRs 1,012,358,900 (US$1 = QRs3,65) and was allocated as follows: salaries and wages: QRs542,322,200 (53.5%); recurrent expenses: QRs224,311,700 (22.1%); expansion and maintenance: QRs17,500,000 (1.7%); and construction: QRs228,225,000 (22.5%).

In the school year 1990–91, the budget rose to QRs928,795,115, an increase of QRs11,439,675 (1.2%) over the previous year. The budget for 1990–91 was

Table 2
Educational leadership 1990–91

| | Qataris | | Non-Qataris | | | Total | |
	Male	Female	Male	Female	Qataris	Non-Qataris	Percentage
Undersecretary	1	—	—	—	1	—	100
Assistant undersecretary	4	—	—	—	4	—	100
Director	24	4	3	—	28	3	90
Assistant director	12	5	1	—	17	1	94
Head of section	31	10	13	—	41	13	76
Total	72	19	17	—	91	17	84

as follows: salaries and wages: QRs731,000,000; recurrent expenses: QRs173,027,000; secondary capital expenses: QRs5,790,000; and general capital expenses: QRs18,978,115.

The Ministry of Education has sought the adoption of a provision orientation program to work out a more realistic budget with the aim of reaching the optimum use of available resources and providing the necessary financial support to educational development schemes.

The State of Qatar still maintains a general budget for the education sector in terms of expenditure, costs, and funding. Accordingly, a uniform unit cost is given to each student in each stage. In the school year 1991–92, this unit cost was QRs15,000.

6. Supplying Personnel for the Education System

Between the years 1956 and 1965, Qatar depended on expatriates in the field of teaching, particularly those from Egypt, Jordan, Syria, Lebanon, and the Sudan. In 1965, the first batch of teachers graduated from the Qatari Teachers Training Institute, all of whom were males. The first batch of female teachers graduated in 1971. All graduates, however, were employed as primary school teachers, while both the preparatory and secondary school teachers were still expatriates employed either through direct agreements or within the framework of bilateral agreements.

In the early 1980s, the shortage in preparatory and secondary school teachers, which existed after Qatar University graduates (Faculty of Education) had been appointed, was covered by hiring teachers from other Arab countries.

The standard of primary school teachers (Teachers Training Institute graduates) was unsatisfactory and resulted in the gradual abolition of this institute by the Ministry. As from 1975, primary school teachers have been trained at the Faculty of Education.

In 1992, the procedure was to select a number of female graduates from secondary schools and enroll them at the Faculty of Education to obtain a general or special diploma to raise their educational standard, after which they immediately became teachers. The first group of such teachers under this procedure assumed their responsibilities as teachers in 1978. Afternoon studies for secondary school graduates qualifying them for a BA degree in primary school education began in 1979–80. By 1990, no teacher was employed who did not hold such a diploma. Qatari University graduates take part only in educational and school administration.

To overcome the national school teacher problem, the Ministry of Education and Qatar University decided to introduce inservice teacher training as follows:

(a) A General Diploma of Education was initiated to raise the standard of teachers in the first four years of the primary stage. The diploma is obtained after two years (72 credit hours) of evening study sessions. Holders of this diploma may proceed with their studies to obtain a bachelor of arts degree in primary education (144 credit hours), provided that they have worked as primary school teachers for two consecutive years.

(b) A Special Diploma of Education was initiated to raise the special educational standard of teachers in the fifth and sixth grades of the primary school, through a two-year evening course (72 credit hours). This course places emphasis on two main areas: religious and Arabic language studies or mathematics and science. Holders of this diploma may pursue their studies to obtain a bachelor of arts degree in primary education, provided that they have worked as primary school teachers for two consecutive years.

(c) A general diploma degree in education was instituted for preparatory and secondary school teachers who are university graduates but not qualified teachers. This degree is obtained after a one-year course (36 credit hours).

(d) A specialized diploma degree in education was instituted for holders of the general diploma degree, after they had completed a one-year course (36 credit hours).

7. *Curriculum Development and Teaching Methodology*

Before Independence, the state of Qatar had already shifted from school curricula taken from a number of Arab countries to curricula reflecting the context of Arab cultural unity. It then moved on to the stage of having specific Qatari curricula based on such unity. Qatari books were written, printed, and in the hands of students from Grades 1 to 12 by 1971, the year of Independence.

The Curricula and School Books Department was established in 1966. Its task was to develop curricula and supervise the writing and publication of textbooks. However, due to the limited resources of the Department at that time, the curriculum committee helped the Department a great deal. In addition, education inspectors participated in developing the curriculum and in writing books. Ever since, the Department has been in constant development.

A series of efforts have been made since the 1970s in curriculum development in various subject areas. For example, Qatar had its own curriculum developers in mathematics who worked on their own but also in collaboration with the Arab Bureau of Education and the Arab Education Research Center. As a result of these efforts, the first nine grades of school have uniform textbooks in mathematics. The same is true for science for the first six grades of school.

In 1970, Qatar introduced English as a foreign language from Grade 5 onward using British tutors. In 1974, a local team was established to develop a curriculum with the aid of a British expert. A curriculum and a set of textbooks were developed. The Arab Bureau of Education has also begun to develop a curriculum and textbooks for all schools in the Gulf States.

Curricula and textooks were also developed for Arabic, history, geography, civics, and the social sciences. In all cases, the general procedure was to determine the general aims and specific objectives, write the materials, try them out, revise the materials, train the teachers through pre- or inservice training, and launch the new materials in the schools.

In 1987 the government decided to introduce computers into schools. A first study was undertaken in 1990–91 in seven secondary schools. The ultimate aim is to introduce computers into all secondary school grades, where they are to be used as educational aids and an informatics system.

Grades 1, 2, and 3 in primary school receive 30 hours of teaching per week; Grade 4 receives 33 hours; and grades 5 and 6 receive 36 hours. The following subjects are taught: religion, Arabic, English (5th and 6th grades only), mathematics, integrated science, civics (3rd–6th grades), fine arts, and physical education.

At the secondary stage, students also receive 36 hours of teaching per week with an extra 6 hours for students in their subject(s) of specialization.

Subjects taught in Grade 10 (i.e., the first class of the general secondary school) are: religion, Arabic, English, modern mathematics, science (physics, chemistry, biology), fine arts, and physical education. In Grades 11 and 12, there are two streams: the science stream and the literary stream. Specialization in either stream starts in Grade 11.

8. *The System of Examinations, Promotions, and Certifications*

Examinations play a major role in the education system. Up to Grade 11, teacher-made examinations are given at the end of each semester. To proceed from one grade to another, a student must obtain a minimum passing mark. Until 1989, a national examination used to be set and conducted at the end of Grade 9 by the Department of Examinations of the Ministry of Education. In 1991, the supervision of such examinations came under the auspices of each school. As from 1991, national examinations are held at the end of Grade 12 only (general and specialized secondary school certificates).

9. *Educational Assessment, Evaluation, and Research*

The Ministry of Education, through its department of technical research, has established a special committee for studies and surveys. Research projects include case studies and surveys covering all inputs and outputs of the educational process, that is, students, teachers, textbooks, curricula, school buildings, extra curricular activities, and teaching aids.

Another general committee comprising educationalists and specialists in the Ministry and the University of Qatar was formed to make practical suggestions emanating from the results of research projects. In 1980, an Educational Research Center was established at the University of Qatar.

Since 1990 educational research has focused on the links between education and development plans and on matching educational outputs to employment. Research projects have included linking University outputs (graduates) with the existing labor market through: single-subject specialization versus specialization in two subjects at the university; retraining of female teachers in other subject areas where applicable; reorganization of the English Language department at the University to match its outputs with the needs of developed English Language curricula at different educational stages; evaluation of the efficiency of the faculty of arts; and a tendency toward the introduction of community colleges to meet certain requirements. In addition, a group of research studies on the diversification of secondary education was prepared, among which were: the introduction of productive work in the educational process; streaming in secondary education; curriculum at the secondary education level; the introduction of "computers in education" as a subject; and shifting between the secondary education streams. Finally, other topics for research have included: performance evaluation of teachers and students at each of the education stages; upgrading of private schools; evaluation of the model schools experiments; and introduction of practical studies in different stages of education.

10. Major Problems for the Year 2000

Independence and the financial boom of the early 1970s led to development in various fields, among which was the construction industry. The population chose to live in certain areas and avoided others. This, in turn, resulted in problems in the location of schools. The population increased greatly as a result of the arrival of large numbers of expatriates from Arab countries for work and also the return of many Qataris. This produced a turbulent population growth rate which made the establishment of medium-term plans difficult.

There are difficulties in providing the necessary class capacity in school buildings, which are sometimes not ready on time. Several ministries are involved and this problem must be solved. A comprehensive development plan at the state level will need to be developed if effective educational planning is to be undertaken. The centralization of the state financial system does not allow the Ministry to act freely within its budget since it has to have permission from the Ministry of Finance and Petroleum for every financial dealing. Steps will need to be taken to devolve some of the decision-making on educational expenditure.

There are no government kindergartens. Consideration should be given to introducing them because of their importance as a transitional stage between home and school.

New forms of education must be introduced to meet the needs of Qatari development. Innovations abroad should be carefully examined and, where appropriate, trialed in Qatar.

There were no objective national plans in any ministry until after the establishment of the Supreme Planning Council in 1989 which started demanding objective plans from the ministries. The Ministry of Education then prepared a three-year development plan (1992–95). Despite the official censuses in the year of Independence and again in 1986, detailed statistical data were not published. Planning without a reliable statistical data base is difficult. An efficient system of collecting and disseminating educational data must be instituted to enable authorities to make decisions on the basis of studies and their findings.

Continuous modernization of the content of education, its methods, aids, and system of evaluation (i.e., systematic, continuous curriculum development) is needed. More stress must be placed on technical education to keep pace with modern developments and to meet the real needs of society. Teacher pre- and inservice training must be improved.

Bibliography

Ministry of Education 1983 *Education Policy in Qatar*. Ministry of Education, Doha
Ministry of Education 1990 *Education System in Qatar— Assessment and Evaluation—A Report by the* UNESCO *Team of Experts*. Ministry of Education, Doha
Ministry of Education 1991a *Education in Qatar in the 20th Century*. Ministry of Education, Doha
Ministry of Education 1991b *A Three-year Educational Development Plan, 1992–95*. Ministry of Education, Doha
Ministry of Education (annual) Reports on the development of education in Qatar from 1970 to 1990. Ministry of Education, Doha
Ministry of Education (annual) Statistical reports from 1970 to 1990. Ministry of Education, Doha
Ministry of Education 1992 *Achievements of the Ministry of Education during the School Year 1990–91—Report*. Ministry of Education, Doha

Romania

G. Vaideanu

1. General Background

Romania, in the southeast of Europe, is bordered by the Black Sea, the Ukraine, Hungary, the former Yugoslavia, and Bulgaria. The landscape, dominated by the Carpathians, is varied: 33 percent plain, 36 percent hills and plateaus, and 31 percent mountains. Romania had a surface area of 237,500 square kilometers and a population of 22.3 million in 1980 and about 23.0 million in 1991. In 1930, the population was only 14,280,729. At the beginning of the 1980s, 54 percent of Romania's people lived in towns, as opposed to 23 percent in 1948. The population is 88 percent Romanians, 8 percent Hungarians, 4 percent Gypsies, 1 percent Germans, and some Serbs, Turks, Ukrainians, and others. The structure and vocabulary of the Romanian language originate from Latin, and it belongs to the Indo-European family of languages.

The land of the Romanian people has been inhabited since earliest times. The Dacians and Geti lived there well before the Christian era, organizing their territories and entering into relations with the Greek cities on the Black Sea coast and with other neighboring peoples. The first written mention of the Dacians and Geti occurs in the work of Herodotus (sixth century BC), who calls them "the bravest and the most righteous among the Thracians," adding that the Thracian population was "the second most numerous after the Indians."

In August 1944, after the national uprising, the Romanian army turned against the German army and played an active part, in conjunction with the Soviet army, in freeing north Transylvania, Hungary, and Czechoslovakia. After the Second World War, the Soviet army imposed communism in Romania. This difficult period lasted from 1944 to 1989. Following the advent of the new social and political situation in Eastern Europe after 1985, the Romanian people succeeded in abolishing the communist dictatorship in December 1989. Without the pressure brought to bear by the over 2 million people determined to fight for their rights from December 16 to 22, 1989, in Timisoara, Bucharest, Cluj, and Sibiu, as well as in other towns of Romania, the abolition of the totalitarian communist regime would not have been possible. The most recent Constitution was proclaimed in December 1991. The president of the republic is elected for four years.

In 1979, the gross national product (GNP) was US$3,426 million, an average of US$1,580 per inhabitant. In 1979, 35 percent of the active population worked in industry, which contributed 60 percent of the national revenue. Between 1948 and 1979, industrial production increased 53 times. Chemical and petroleum industries, the building of machines, and the textile and foodstuff industries are the most important. The educational system was developed in order to train the qualified personnel required by a swiftly growing industrial sector, and the other subjects tended to be neglected in the 1980s both at the preuniversity level and in the universities. In 1979, 30 percent of the working population was involved in agriculture, which accounted for 15 percent of the national revenue. In the early 1990s, it still remains a sizeable part of the economy and its modernization is a priority. Stock breeding is particularly important.

As in several Eastern European countries, Romania underwent large-scale political change at the beginning of the 1990s. A new system of education was under discussion. It is this system that is described in this entry and not the pre-1990 system of education.

2. Politics and the Goals of the Education System

A series of inconveniences and gaps in the old system were done away with as early as the beginning of 1990, following decisions of the government or of the Ministry of Education and Science, as well as a number of initiatives put forward by educators or students. The latter were aimed both at the structures and the content of education and at the quality of the teacher–student relationship, including evaluation. A shift in the content of education has been achieved through the promotion of the humanities, philosophy, and the arts, which had been discarded previously. Until December 1989, so-called "production training" and the technologies related to various occupations had a large share of the timetable and often led to frequent interruptions in the teaching–learning process. At the same time, about 90 percent of the upper-secondary schools were industrially and economically oriented; the remainder of the upper-secondary schools, focusing on the teaching of the humanities and the arts, were rare and thus had a low profile. In the new context, the beginning of 1990 witnessed the teaching of human rights, civic education, and democracy education for all pupils. All the ideological aspects which served for the promotion of an inaccurate picture of modern society and culture were removed from curricula and textbooks. This had raised many obstacles to the Romanian school system establishing communication with other schools and cultures.

The main goals of the Romanian educational system in the 1990s could be briefly summarized as follows: (a) the provision of a relevant, open, and thorough training for all students enrolled in the 9- or 10-year compulsory school (the length of studies was still under discussion in 1992; compulsory 12-year schooling, or 9+2 years of vocational training); (b) the achievement of a more balanced scientific–technical education, on the one hand, and humanistic–artistic education, on the other; (c) the training of all students in the spirit of love toward the national culture and respect for the universal culture and for the cultures of the minorities—the attainment of this goal will be fostered by nonformal education as well as by informal education (with television playing a significant role); (d) the educational and vocational guidance of pupils according to their interests and aptitudes, which is the task of teachers and counselors with a psychopedagogical training—the latter carrying out their activity in upper-secondary schools and in departmental school inspectorates; (e) orientation of learning from the perspective of lifelong education and the development in pupils of self-evaluation aptitudes; (f) the continuous democratization of the teacher–student relationship and an increase of the participation of teachers and students in the management of schools and universities; (g) the improvement of the evaluation subsystem of students, as well as of the entrance examinations to upper-secondary schools and universities; (h) the implementation of a relevant policy in the identification and promotion of talented students; and (i) the implementation of a set of measures aimed at supporting students experiencing learning difficulties, orphans, students from broken families, as well as handicapped children. The existing school network will be expanded and served by highly qualified staff.

3. The Formal System of Education

In 1980, the school-age population numbered approximately 5,585,000 people. The beginning of the 1990s marked a decrease in the school population, so that, in the 1990–91 school year, only some 5 million pupils and students were registered, representing 21.6 percent of the total population. There are approximately 200,000 higher education students, but it is expected that their number will increase as more places become available for first-year students. It is to be noted that six new state universities were founded at the beginning of the 1990s. There are approximately 40,000 teachers in nursery schools, 60,000 primary school teachers, 144,000 secondary school teachers (Grades 5 to 12), and over 14,000 tenured academics. Large numbers of Romanian pupils and students from Moldavia were given grants to study in Romania. All minorities have their own schools where they use their own mother tongues: Hungarian, German, Serbian, Ukrainian, and so forth.

3.1 Primary, Secondary, and Tertiary Education

Figure 1 presents the proposed structure of the new educational system. The proposed structure of pre-university education is 4+5+3, and compulsory schooling will last 9 years. The original 10 years of compulsory education was abandoned to avoid breaking the secondary education into two levels (2+2) and to ensure, at the same time, that the quality of compulsory education (9 years) is equally good in both urban and rural areas. Thus the complete structure will be as follows.

Preprimary education is for children 3, 4, and 5 years of age. There are kindergartens in which the young children can remain 5 days a week and enjoy good conditions; a second category is represented by kindergartens in which the children stay for some 8–9 hours a day, with a meal included; finally, there is a third category of kindergartens, where children learn 4–5 hours a day. Some kindergartens have introduced the teaching of foreign languages.

Primary education is for children from 6 to 10 years of age. The artistic disciplines and physical education will be taught by specialized teachers. A distinction will be made between the introductory year, the intermediary grades (2nd and 3rd), and the 4th grade, which is devoted to assessing and revising the knowledge acquired and preparing the pupils for the next level. The

teachers will be assisted by counselors—specialists in psychopedagogy.

The *Gymnasium* or upper-primary school will be for students from 10 to 15 years of age. Both the pedagogical dossier and teachers' and inspectors' assessments will be used. It is planned that standardized tests will be used in all schools in Romania. The pupil's dossier will include both the results of the summative tests and the proposals of the Commission for Educational and Professional Guidance made in collaboration with the counselors (one for each important secondary school, or one for two to three smaller secondary schools). These dossiers will help orient the students either toward different types of vocational school (2 to 3 years in duration) or to upper-secondary schools.

Upper-secondary school (*Lyceum*) will last three years and school-leavers will obtain the baccalaureate diploma. The presidents of the baccalaureate commissions will be university teachers. There will be core curricula for the different types of upper-secondary schools, according to their profiles: sciences, humanities, technology, teacher training, arts, and physical education.

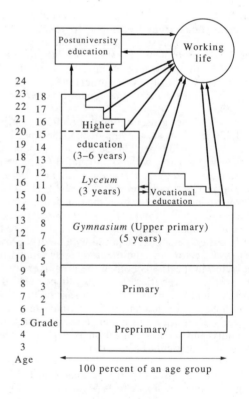

Figure 1
Romania: Proposed structure of the formal education system

A post-upper-secondary education (nonuniversity) system will be created. Courses will last one to two years and they will train specialists in subjects including cosmetics, cooking, typing, and tourism.

Either the Ministry of Education or the schools have, as a major concern, to better articulate formal and nonformal education. At the same time, national and local authorities and different cultural or religious institutions are preoccupied to reorient and intensify adult education.

Higher education will include three-year colleges which will train preprimary and primary school teachers, subengineers, and other categories of specialist. The universities will undertake the training of specialists (in mathematics, economics, or geography), with courses which will take four years, and students will be awarded a diploma upon satisfactory completion. Gifted students will have the opportunity of taking another year of specialization (4+1) and, after graduation, work either in research or in higher education institutions. For some faculties, the courses will last five years, while for others (medicine, architecture) they will last six years. Graduate education will comprise the doctorate (either full-time, with a duration of four years, and with financial aid in the form of scholarships, or by correspondence), as well as further specialization through training courses. Special attention will be given to the identification, development, and assertion of gifted people by means of adequate methods and with the help of teachers trained for teaching gifted children.

3.2 Preschool Education

As stated earlier, preprimary education is for children aged 3, 4, and 5 years. The method and learning materials are relevant for this age, but the syllabus for the final year is difficult for some of the children. Children start to learn a foreign language at age 4 or 5, especially in the cities: English, French, or German are taught. There are kindergartens in which young children can remain 5 days a week in good conditions. A second category is represented by kindergartens in which children stay for some 8 to 9 hours per day and a meal is included. Either the Ministry of Education or businesses help these categories of kindergarten. In a third category of kindergarten, children learn for 4 to 5 hours every day. The parents can choose which of the three categories they wish their children to attend. In future, the educators (always women) will be trained in three-year colleges after having passed the baccalaureate, or will be trained as social assistants in universities (4 years).

3.3 Special Education

Special education was neglected during the 10 to 12 years before December 1989. In all the university faculties, the training of teachers for different types or categories of handicapped children was suppressed. In 1992, the situation is completely different in that the budget for this subsystem of education, including services at the central and regional levels, has been much increased. The National Institute for Educational Research has a sector for special education and the old universities—Bucharest, Cluj, and Iasi—have created sections for the training of such teachers. The main preoccupations are how to integrate the handicapped children progressively into schools for normal children or, alternatively, how to integrate them into vocational schools.

3.4 Vocational, Technical, and Business Education

Enrollment in vocational schools is high, probably because the majority of students want to obtain a profession and a salary as soon as possible after completing compulsory school. The popular types of vocational schools are services (hotels, restaurants, etc.) and some branches of industry. The percentage of academic secondary schools was higher in 1992 than in the past. The schools include special secondary schools for talented children in music, painting, and choreography.

After December 1989, either the central or the regional authorities maintained a large number of technical secondary schools: industrial, economical, medical, and so on. At the same time, the Ministry of Education renewed the curriculum content introducing elements of informatics, marketing, management, statistics, and so forth. In the early 1990s, some postsecondary schools for business, private market, and management were organized in collaboration with ministries of education or foundations from other countries.

3.5 Adult and Nonformal Education

Adult and nonformal education is as important as it was before December 1989. Although students want to organize excursions and competitions, and want to meet and travel, they do not want to utilize the former structures of youth organizations or the former personnel. In 1991 and 1992, some initiatives of the churches, the Scouts, and foundations for culture, sport, or the protection of the environment were launched in some cities. In 1992, the Ministry of Culture, in cooperation with the Council of Europe, organized a meeting in order to relaunch and reinforce this subsystem of adult education.

4. Administrative and Supervisory Structure and Operation

The Ministry of Education and Science will continue to play an important role, but the new Education

Bill foresees a large amount of decentralization. Both the schools and the county school inspectorates will have important responsibilities. School heads will be elected by the teachers' councils. The recruitment of inspectors will be based on competitive examinations. Both school heads and inspectors will attend training courses. University autonomy is now real. This is clear from such activities as the nomination of heads of departments, deans, and rectors; the selection of teaching content and research themes; and contacts with other universities in Romania or abroad. The National Rectors' Conference and the National Certification Committee (for doctoral degrees and professorships) are active at the national level. An academic board is being organized, the functions of which will be the evaluation of higher education institutions, the certification of private education, and the confirmation of decisions made by the discipline committees in universities.

Upper-secondary and higher education will have full-time, correspondence, and evening courses. The intention is to make the structures more flexible in order to meet the pupils' and students' learning needs. Private education institutions may enroll pupils at all levels of education provided that they comply with the provisions of the law.

5. Educational Finance

As a consequence of the reduction of the maximum number of students per class (from 40–44 to 30), the reduction of the weekly workload of the teachers, and the payment for various activities which were not remunerated before 1990, the 1991 budget allotted 10 percent of the national budget to education. It will probably be maintained at this level, or even increased, since a massive school building program will have to be undertaken. Textbooks are still free of charge. The number of scholarships will be increased, especially in the area of vocational training.

6. Supplying Personnel for the Education System

Preschool and lower-primary school teachers will undergo a three-year training program following the baccalaureate. Upper-primary and secondary school teachers will be trained in a four-year course at the universities. The leaving certificate granted by the teacher-training colleges (pedagogical-seminar) is compulsory. Technical teachers will be trained at polytechnic or agricultural institutes. Preservice training is conducted within the framework of lifelong education. Inservice training is a well-structured subsystem which includes compulsory courses every five years, an examination after three years of teaching in order to obtain a full qualification, and the possibility of becoming a Category 2 and later a Category 1 teacher upon proof of a good mastery of teaching and the ability to be innovative in teaching. Much attention is focused on the training of the teacher trainers and on the link between educational research and teacher training.

Teachers in higher education include teaching assistants, and the various ranks of teacher up to that of professor. Teaching assistants are selected from the best students at the university. All other positions are obtained on a competitive basis according to graduate degrees, publications, and teaching experience.

7. Curriculum Development and Teaching Methodology

Specialist committees—composed of subject matter specialists, researchers, university personnel, and teachers—prepare the syllabuses for all subjects based on the time allocated to those subjects. These committees (e.g., for mathematics, biology, or foreign languages) are coordinated by a central committee. The syllabuses, approved by the Ministry of Education, act as a basic guide for teachers and the authors of school textbooks. This curriculum (syllabuses and textbooks) is identical for the same school types throughout the country; this unity of content eases the problem of examinations and evaluation both within the same district and throughout the whole country. At each level, there are compulsory and optional subjects. In 1992, the government was considering establishing a National Council for the Reform of Curriculum. The Institute for Educational Research is increasingly being requested to develop and implement curricula. The content of teacher-training programs is worked out on the basis of the school curriculum.

Within higher education, each faculty and department develops its own curriculum. An effort is being made to devise more interdisciplinary curricula. At every level of education, every possible educational and epistemological effort is being made when devising curriculum content.

8. The System of Examinations, Promotions, and Certifications

The different methods of evaluation (oral, written, and practical, continuous, and periodic) require that the pupils should not merely recapitulate and reproduce the information they have acquired but also make syntheses, selections, and new combinations. A special effort is being made to use more initial and formative evaluation. In practice, systematic pupil evaluation is carried out by each teacher in the classroom. Periodic evaluation occurs at the discretion of the local inspector (in order to evaluate and compare the performances of the pupils in one particular subject matter). A re-examination of the evaluation methods used at the preuniversity and university levels is under way in order to devise improved evaluation, one more suited to the educational objectives and to the expectations of the young. Competitive entrance examinations are still used for the upper-secondary school and for higher education; this involves written examinations and tests in subjects designated by the Ministry of Education.

9. Educational Assessment, Evaluation, and Research

The Institute for Educational Research in Bucharest is the major educational research institute; research is also conducted in the departments of education and psychology in universities and in teacher-training establishments; in the universities of Bucharest, Iasi, and Cluj-Napoca, professors are assisted by a number of specialized researchers. Other units of educational research include the Center for Youth Problems and the Section for Education of the National Commission for UNESCO. This last Section is, in 1992, undertaking research on the "Curriculum for a New Europe" in cooperation with 11 secondary schools.

The Ministry of Education is the principal beneficiary of these research studies. Attention is paid to the transfer of research results into practice and, in this context, to the organization of experimental schools; at the same time, attempts are made to strengthen the connections between systematic research and spontaneous educational innovation as practiced by teachers in their own schools. Publications of research fundings aim, on the one hand, at making the public and the school authorities aware of new ideas (e.g., permanent education, the systematic approach to the process of education, assisted teaching) and, on the other hand, at keeping educators informed and their interest stimulated in their professional work. The research effort focuses on the problems of the quality of education, pupil achievement, and, more particularly, ways of improving curriculum organization, active methods, formative evaluation, and the fit of the teaching–learning process.

10. Major Problems for the Year 2000

Developments in education in the 1990s are perceived as being related to those taking place in other countries of Europe and in other fields (such as economics, urban life, cultural life), and the aspirations of the young. Research of this type is part of the socioeconomic program for the 1990s and concerns the likely evolution of the world of work, science, and culture, and so forth, and the impact of this evolution on education. An increase in the quality of compulsory schooling is envisioned, as is the promotion of new methodologies for the selection and sequencing of curriculum content, and a better adaptation of structures, objectives, and methods to the demands of lifelong education and education for democracy.

Bibliography

Academy of Social Sciences 1980a *A Concise Geography of Romania*. Editura Stiintifica si Enciclopedica, Bucharest
Academy of Social Sciences 1980b *A Concise History of Romania*. Editura Stiintifica si Enciclopedica, Bucharest
Giurescu D 1981 *Istoria ilustrata a Românilor*. Editura Sport Turism, Bucharest
Malita M (ed.) 1981 *Enciclopedia statelor lumii*. Editura Stiintifica si Enciclopedica, Bucharest
Niculescu A 1981 *Outline History of the Romanian Language*. Editura Stiintifica si Enciclopedica, Bucharest
Romania, Ministère de l'Education et de l'Enseignement (Direction Scientifique G. Vaideanu) 1973 *L'Enseignement dans la République Socialiste de Roumanie*. Ministère de l'Education et de l'Enseignement, Bucharest
Romania, Ministère de l'Education et de l'Enseignement 1978 *Loi sur l'éducation et sur l'enseignement*. Editura Didactica si Pedagogica, Bucharest
Vaideanu G 1982 Les structures de l'apprentissage en Roumanie: Unité et diversité. *Int. Rev. Educ.* 28: 210–26
Vaideanu G 1991 *Vers un curriculum de l'éducation européenne*. UNESCO, Paris

Russia

N. D. Nikandrov

1. General Background

The developments of 1991 in the so-called "socialist camp," especially the dramatic changes in the Soviet Union after the failure of the August coup d'etat, have placed many things in the balance. At first it seemed that what had once been the USSR (Union of the Soviet Socialist Republics) was heading toward a loose union of sovereign states with the second "S" being taken for "sovereign" rather than "socialist." It was also not quite clear how many republics there would be in the Union, though Latvia, Lithuania, and Estonia had already become independent states.

The formation of the Commonwealth of Independent States makes it impossible to speak about a single "system" of education for the now extinct Union since all decisions on education now rest with the states themselves. However, since educational systems have a lot of inertia (for good or bad) it is unlikely that drastic changes will appear soon. So this entry reflects the status quo in October 1992; while "Russia" means, in this particular context, the Russian Federation as one of the former 15 republics of the Soviet Union.

The former Russian Empire that existed before the "Great October Socialist Revolution" of 1917 had been amassed partly by military force and partly by negotiation. From December 1922 it was a union of 15 republics until 1991 when the three Baltic republics left the union. The vast territory and the great ethnic variety (more than 100 nations and a large number of ethnic groups with as many languages) make it nearly impossible to generalize on the density of the population and its rate of growth. There was a "baby boom" after the 1941–45 war when the population grew almost 2 percent a year (1.3% in 1946, 1.7% in 1950, 1.78% in 1960). Since about 1965, however, there has been a steady decline in the growth rate all over Russia (8.4% in 1989), although it is higher in the countryside and much lower in the large cities. Over two-thirds of the population now live in cities. The density of population is 10.6 people per square kilometer (the Russian average) while it is 327.6 in the Moscow region and 0.3 in the Siberian region of Yakutia.

Russian is the natural language of communication among all nations and ethnic groups, though some republics inside the Russian Federation are reluctant to retain it as a second state language which it formerly was because they are increasingly conscious of their national identity. Most non-Russians speak Russian which makes it easier to communicate and learn in postschool educational institutions.

Before 1917 over 75 percent of the population lived in rural areas and were mostly engaged in agriculture. With the predominance of the urban population the former Russia still has a greater proportion of so-called "farmers" or "peasants" as compared to other industrialized countries (37.1% in 1989). Some 17.8 percent of the workforce living in the cities have higher education as opposed to 8.7 percent in the country.

The economy was very highly centralized from the middle of the 1920s within the overall control of the Communist Party. Even production quotas for particular goods (including consumer goods) were decided upon in the higher echelons of the Party and transferred down the line to factories and collective farms (*kolkhozes*). This centralization (termed the "command and administrative system" under Gorbachev's *perestroika*) brought the economy to stagnation. This, combined with the timid steps made toward a market economy in 1990–91, added fast decline and chaos in almost all fields of the economy. Some very unpopular decisions to overcome the situation were being taken or were in the offing in the early 1990s. Forecasting the results is certainly very difficult; what is true, however, is that in November 1992 more than 40 percent of the population was below the poverty line.

2. Politics and the Goals of the Education System

The difficulties mentioned in the previous section are increased by an uncertain political future. The union structure has crumbled and the new sovereign states have taken practically all power into their own hands. However, Russia is itself a conglomerate of ethnic territories and groups many of which claim their independence in their turn and this havoc does not help to stabilize (let alone improve) the economy of the country. Political uniformity of the past (with the overall goal of building the communist society, the primary principle of which was to be "from everyone according to his abilities, to everyone according to his needs") is now gone with no adequate substitution. Some speak about returning to capitalism, some stop short of it but emphasize market relations as the primary goal (not as a means to reach prosperity). No clear-cut policy accepted at national level is in existence and this also adversely affects educational planning. Formerly, the overall political goal of building communism was combined with the "all-round development of the personality" to form the ultimate educational goal. The state was considered the adequate interpreter of what society needs; as to the individual, his or her interests and needs were hardly taken into account. It followed then that severe disproportions appeared between what many people wanted and what the state offered (in the choice of schools at all levels, in salaries hardly dependent on the quality and quantity of education received, etc.). The most important consequence, however, was that the prestige of education fell very low and though many fine words are spoken in the early 1990s about education as a budgetary priority, people are for the most part wary about all this. It is all the more expected since in many cases salaries vary inversely with the years of schooling.

Although education was proclaimed to be a priority in the Law on Education adopted by the Russian Parliament in 1992, it is as yet very poorly financed. In the same law, six "principles of the state policy on education" are declared, that is: the humanistic character of education and the priority of general human values; the unity of the cultural and educational space of the Federation; the accessibility of education to all people; the existence of lay (church-free) education in the state institutions of learning; freedom and pluralism in education; and the democratic administration of education and the autonomy of institutions of learning. The task of elaborating the federal standard of general education is to be undertaken in the near future. Until this is done, the goal of general education is also set in very general terms as creating the favorable conditions and prerequisites for the mental, moral, emotional, and physical development of the personality; acquiring a scientific world outlook; and acquiring a system of knowledge on nature, society, people, and their work as well as on ways to work independently.

It is considered very important that any particular institution of learning should have its own package of educational values and goals which is in sharp contrast with the overcentralization of the former times. This is not to say that what is allowed and encouraged is current practice; sometimes schools and other state-run institutions of learning are just not prepared for the autonomy that private nonstate-run schools are so eager to have.

3. The Formal System of Education

3.1 Primary, Secondary, and Tertiary Education

Figure 1 is a diagrammatic representation of the Russian system of education.

Until the middle of the 1980s, schooling began at the age of 7 with very few exceptions (6, in many schools of the Caucasus) and 10 years of schooling were obligatory (11 in the Baltic republics—Latvia, Lithuania, and Estonia). The school reform of 1984 proclaimed the school starting ·age to be 6 which caused an outcry on the part of many scholars and

many more parents. The reason was a belief (and this was certainly true to a great deal) that schools are not prepared to take in such young students who were thus "deprived of their childhood." Comparisons with other countries did not convince the opponents. As a result of the furore, it is up to parents to decide at what age children go to school and they are helped in the decision by the schools' medical and psychological commissions that test if a particular child is ready for school.

Primary education is technically part of the secondary school system and takes 4 years to complete. Primary schools as such exist only in isolated villages. The goal of primary education is to give children basic study skills and basic facts about everyday life. For the most part, each class is taught by one teacher with very loose subdivision into school subjects. Sports and arts are mostly taught by specially trained teachers unless the school is very small. In extreme cases, there can be as many teachers as students in a school. Before about 1970, such schools gradually were being closed but it then appeared that such closures led to the virtual dying-out of villages as young parents left them seeking schools for their children.

The fifth form is the beginning of secondary education with the subdivision of school subjects which are taught by specialist teachers.

According to the 1992 Law on Education, the requirement for the complete secondary education of 11 years has been dropped. Although it is recommended for those children who are prepared to take it, the required minimal number of years of schooling is 9 (the so-called "basic secondary education").

The 11 years of complete secondary education can be realized in a number of ways. A student can spend all these years in a secondary school of general education; or 9 years in the school followed by some time at a vocational school gaining additional general education; or the choice of going on to a secondary special school (*technicum*—a type of junior college) where again some additional general education plus vocational

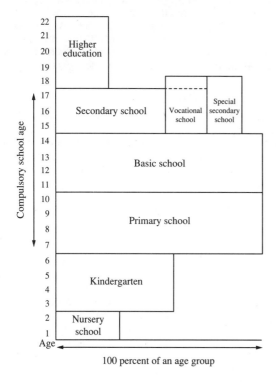

Figure 1
Russia: Structure of the formal education system

Table 1
Statistics on the formal education system, Russia 1993

	Number of institutions	Number of students	Number of teachers
Preschools	87,800	9,634,700	968,300
Schools of general education	67,098	20,169,600	1,596,800
Vocational schools	4,273	1,741,600	(no data)
Schools of secondary special education	2,607	1,993,900	154,958
Schools of higher education	548	2,542,900	228,800

education for blue-collar occupations are given. More and more alternative (nonstate-run) schools are being organized. At the beginning of the 1991–92 academic year, there were 600 *liceums* and *gymnasiums*. Though it is very few compared with the total number of schools (see Table 1), this is only the beginning and the growth rate is hampered more by lack of school buildings than by any administrative constraints.

Higher education includes universities, institutes, and academies. Though it is still true that universities are in general more prestigious and give a wider education, the term of study in most cases is the same (5 years) with the exception of 7 years for medical education.

Admission to higher education is on the basis of competitive entrance examinations with the number of applicants varying greatly from one institution to another. The general pattern for many years has been that the number being admitted to study humanities is higher than the number admitted to study engineering. With the gradual transition to a market economy, there are more and more applications to study economics, marketing, and so forth. Competition is the highest in the performing arts, painting, sculpturing, and so on. Though there has been a steady decline in competition for higher education over the years, the decline has been surprisingly small in view of the fact that there is very little material benefit through higher education to be gained in almost all workplaces.

It is usually the task of higher education institutions (abbreviated to *"vuz"* both in everyday and professional language) to provide continuing education for those who already have higher education. Typically a specialist with a higher education diploma is supposed to go through extension courses once in 5 years and, in most cases, the programs are run by the *vuz*'s.

3.2 Preschool Education

Children from birth till the age of 3 can attend maternity schools (crèches) followed by kindergartens before they go to school. In 1992, 9,634,700 children attended preschool institutions. They can also spend only part of their time in preschool institutions, the proportion being determined by their parents and depending for the most part on the family income. In most families, the total income is too small to allow mothers to stay at home; it is also true that many mothers do not like the idea of being housewives only.

For the most part, preschool education includes just daycare and the overall physical, mental, and moral development of children. However, some subjects are also taught in the kindergartens (a bit of the "3Rs," some art education, and, occasionally, the beginnings of a foreign language). All of this cost very little until quite recently. In the early 1990s, fees increased and there are some private kindergartens for those parents who are prepared to pay quite a high amount; the figures, however, differ greatly and the only steady tendency is toward increase.

3.3 Special Education

In the 1991–92 school year, 1.5 percent of children in the 6 to 17 age group went to schools for the mentally or physically handicapped. Although more children need special treatment, they do not receive it because of insufficient resources. There are also cases when parents are reluctant to send their children to special schools, sometimes hoping against hope that it will somehow be all right in an ordinary school. Since the number of available schools is far below the number required, such cases are not infrequent.

There are schools for the blind (or weak-sighted), for the deaf (or weak-hearing), and for mentally handicapped children. There are also centers for children who practically cannot be educated for they are too severely handicapped (mentally and physically) from birth. There are also schools for children with weak health (sometimes called "schools in the wood," though they may be situated anywhere in fine natural surroundings) and with more serious physical disabilities. In 1993, there were 1,861 schools for handicapped children with 400,000 students.

The programs that are offered naturally depend on how severely handicapped a particular child is. There are about a dozen typical programs that are supplemented or otherwise changed by schools themselves. It is unusual for mentally normal but physically severely handicapped children to go to ordinary schools (which is often the case in some other countries). Again, cases vary very much as to part-time or full-time attendance. Sometimes children go to classes only; sometimes they also get board and lodging in special schools (*internat*).

3.4 Vocational Education

Vocational schools train skilled workers and offer programs of two types. Those who enter them after 9 years of schooling take a program of 3 years in which general secondary education is completed in tandem with vocational education. If a student has completed his or her 11-year secondary education, then only one year of study in a vocational school is required, although the program is limited to professional training. Enrollments in vocational schools differ substantially from one region to another.

Special secondary schools (*uchilishche* or *technicum*) also offer two types of program. After a complete secondary education of 11 years, the term of study is 2 years; whereas it is 4 years if a student has completed only 9 years of schooling. In both cases, graduates get diplomas of special secondary education and become "technicians" (junior engineers), librarians, primary school or preschool teachers, and so forth.

3.5 Adult and Nonformal Education

Up to about 1970 there was always a high proportion of people who studied in evening classes while working in the daytime. With the objective of complete secondary education for everyone, the numbers are quickly falling in schools and falling more slowly in higher education. In 1992, 10 percent of those attending school studied in evening classes and about 40 percent of the higher education students studied in evening and distant classes.

The All-Union Society *"Znanye"* (literally "knowledge"), comprising sections in all union republics, has existed since the 1940s. Through numerous programs, "folk universities," study circles (both free-of-charge and paid-for), working groups, and lectures, the *Znanye* Society has run adult education services on a very wide scale. The teachers (lecturers) are usually university professors, but also include people from workplaces and factories, art institutions, and so on.

Along with the disintegration of practically all of the Soviet Union's institutions and severe financial restraints in existence in the early 1990s, the *Znanye* Society as a monolithic uniform organization has been transformed into a number of independent associations working on a self-finance basis. In addition, many educational institutions (universities, institutes, *technicums*, etc, but also schools of general education) run different education services for adults. Some are paid for by the adult students, some by their employees. Since the arrangement is quite new, no statistics exist as yet.

There has always been and continues to be a problem of student motivation in adult education. With a shortage of time for leisure (all the more acute because of shortages of all consumer goods and day-to-day services), there should be a strong intrinsic motivation for a student to go to any adult education service. As yet, very few people feel that education has any market value or that it adds anything to their material well-being. This is why adult education has even more problems than the formal education system. Its financial basis is also unclear. Formerly, most expenses were shouldered by the state which supported the *Znanye* Society. With the advent of self-support, most organizations are left to their own affairs and it is even impossible to say (statistically) how much is actually spent on adult education. Nevertheless, the principle of continuing education is adopted by all authorities responsible for education at all levels and the hope is that if (and when) conditions in the country change for the better interest for education on the part of adults will rise again. What is true, though, is that there are practically no illiterate people in Russia. However, the problem of functional illiteracy has not been addressed.

For many years, more than half of Russia's higher education students studied by correspondence or through evening courses. The quality of those programs always left much to be desired. However, the worst was that these courses were close replicas of full-time studies and no heed had been taken of the particular interests of grown-ups (e.g., there was no choice of courses). It was not until quite recently that the Russian open university was instituted which takes into account Western ideas of distance education as well as the particular interests of (mostly young) people with differing motivations for study.

4. Administrative and Supervisory Structure and Operation

Here, once again, everything is in an uncertain balance. Since the 1984 education reform there have been many changes. The Union Ministry of Education was abolished, and the State Committee for Education created. The idea was to have a single body responsible for the overall planning of education on the territory of the whole united Union. That is now in the past. In 1990s Russia, there are two highest governing bodies for education: the Ministry of Education responsible for all but higher education, and the State Committee for Higher Education in the Ministry for Science, Higher Education, and Policy in Technology which is responsible for higher education only. The former Soviet Union President Gorbachev issued a decree (*ukaz*) proclaiming all universities and similar higher education institutions to be autonomous, stipulating, however, that charters of autonomy should be given after a check-up process called "attestation" (similar to accreditation in the US) whereby the quality of education given in any one institution is officially approved by a competent body. This is being gradually implemented in the early 1990s.

In most former republics, many institutions of education are administered by ministries of education. At the regional and city level, there are also committees of education but their concern is only for the schools of general education and (sometimes) vocational schools. School principals ("directors") were always appointed by the regional or city authorities. At the peak of *perestroika*, which brought more democracy into all spheres of life, school principals began to be elected by school councils which were composed of the teaching body, elected representatives of senior pupils, and parents. The school councils were to possess considerable power in choosing the personnel and electing the principal, and in determining a large part of the curriculum (the so-called "school component"). However, experience showed that the school councils were often powerless or, on the contrary, abused the power they had in the interests of particular groups and persons. There is a strong movement to return to the nomination of principals. As to the content of education and pedagogy, more and more power is given to the schools themselves. This is especially pronounced in the alternative schools which as yet take less than 1 percent of the whole number of children. They are called "schools," "*gymnasiums*," "*lyceums*," or "colleges," with the difference sometimes not clear to the people who work in them. Usually *gymnasiums* are schools with a more pronounced humanities part of the curriculum. *Lyceums* are schools for senior students only with a strong orientation toward the sciences or the humanities and the specific purpose of preparing pupils for higher education. Colleges usually function under the patronage of a university or other higher school with most pupils going to this higher education institution after leaving school. Often these alternative schools charge fees, whereas all other state education is free of charge including higher education.

Though alternative schools are by definition less dependent on the curriculum and pedagogy imposed by the Ministry of Education, administratively and financially they are still subordinate to it. And the relationship of a particular school and the Ministry (or other administrative body) depends very much on who is in charge of them. In some cases, the role of those in charge is still that of close control and in others that of help and support.

Nonformal education has always been a service outside the ministries of education. The *Znanye* society was in theory independent and in fact rather closely controlled by the Communist Party officials at all levels. With the Party control gone and the *Znanye* society disaggregating into separate societies and associations working on a self-support basis, it is not clear how the system will develop, how it will be financed, and how (if at all) it will be supervised.

Supervision belongs to all levels of administration, though it is the closest at the regional and city levels. Under the former system, a city or region may have been picked out for inspection by the republican Ministry of Education (as far as schools of general education were concerned) or the State Committee for Education (for postschool education). This had some importance in the absence of a national testing service. In the early 1990s, with the decentralization process on the increase, inspections are mostly limited to the region or city levels.

Inspectors were always supposed to be the best teachers who chose to be inspectors. In reality, low wages made poor teachers who failed at school teaching choose the job which resulted in the attitude of schools and teachers to the inspectorate being that of resignation and sometimes resistance. Since the late 1980s, the role of a school inspector has been presented as being that of a helping hand rather than that of a severe judge. However, it will take longer to change the psychology of both teachers and inspectors for the role to be accepted that way.

5. Educational Finance

Up to about 1988, educational financing was strictly centralized. The all-Union authorities allocated overall budgets for each republic, also indicating the share of it to be spent on particular services such as education. Since that time, control of the money has gradually transferred to the republican level and by the end of 1991 practically no money was allocated for education

programs by the all-Union authorities. The formation of the Commonwealth of Independent States changed the whole pattern. Attempts are being made in Russia in the early 1990s to establish a reasonable distribution of educational financing between the state, the city, and the district levels. However, the situation here is not clear either. In some cities, administrators and policymakers find inspiration in the idea of large sums of money being allocated for education (at least to schools in their own territory) through taxation channels; in other places, more traditional approaches like central allocation of the money is preferred, except that there is no all-Union "center" any more.

There is a general understanding that education needs much more money than it is getting. This is, by the way, one of the stimuluses for decentralizing the educational finance system to make local authorities also spend some money on education in addition to what it already gets from the center. But the situation in the early 1990s promises little chance for change in this respect. From the end of the Second World War educational finance has been slowly rising in real terms but there have been no dramatic changes as in some other countries (see Table 2). At no time was it easy to calculate realistically the percentage spent on nonformal education, and, for reasons explained above, it is practically impossible in the early 1990s.

Attempts are being made to attract some private money for education. Formerly, no big private money legally existed in the country. With the transfer to a market economy there are numerous stock exchanges, private enterprises, and businesses and some of them are prepared to spend money on education either altruistically or for (as yet only promised) lower taxation. No statistics exist and one can only say that the practice will increase and that the sums themselves vary substantially. They vary from small donations to alternative schools by parents of the pupils who

Table 2
Educational finance in Russia

	1970	1980	1985	1990	1992
National income (in billions of roubles)	119.4	182.3	217.2	224.3	—
Total outlay for education (in billions of roubles)	8.1	12.2	14.4	15.7	211.7[a]
Percentage of national income	6.8	6.7	6.6	7.0	—

a Because of rocketing inflation in 1992, the seemingly large figure of 211.7 should not conceal the fact that in real terms education is still worse financed than in the past

study there to scholarships for university students and direct financial support to schools and universities by private firms.

All education (except for some informal programs like circles for knitting, photography, and the like, and some alternative schools) has always been free at all levels. However, more and more educational establishments, (especially alternative and university-level schools) are charging fees for tuition, which are sometimes very considerable. All higher education students and pupils in vocational schools get scholarships ("stipends"). They are low and barely sufficient for subsistence so many students also work in the evening and sometimes during classes. High achievers can get stipends 25 to 50 percent higher than those of others; there are also higher stipends bearing the names of outstanding people from politics or science.

Discussion was underway in the early 1990s as to whether some sort of loans could be given to postschool students by the state or private enterprises, but no documents to this effect are available. However, the 1992 Law on Education does provide for choice of schools. In practice it means that if a student prefers a private school charging fees, the student (or his or her parents) receive a cheque for the sum that would have been spent on the student in a state-run free-of-charge institution; this cheque should in law be accepted by any private school, with the rest of the money being supplied by the student. This is only a general idea; the corresponding paragraph of the Law will be made binding later.

6. Supplying Personnel for the Education System

Table 1 gives an idea of how many teachers at different levels of education there are in Russia. Teachers are trained in 42 universities, 4 pedagogical universities, 93 pedagogical institutes, and 353 pedagogical secondary schools with the latter training teachers for preschool and primary school levels only. Competition to enter the teaching profession has always been low and the road was (and is) very often taken by those who would prefer entering another type of institution but are afraid of failing the entrance examinations. Another exception is the foreign language and history departments but here many students do not in fact plan to become teachers after graduation.

Teacher-training programs at all levels include the component of general education (formerly largely taken up by ideological subjects such as history of the Communist Party), the special component (the subject or subjects to be taught later), and the professional component (psychology and education). The proportion of the components is different depending on the level of education for which teachers are trained. The professional component is the greatest for the teachers trained for preschool and primary-school level and smaller for secondary school teachers. There are no

special programs to train university (or other kinds of higher education) teachers. They are employed from the ranks of better students from higher education establishments and pass through a system of inservice training every five years. There are also candidate and doctoral programs in the institutions of higher education. Candidate of sciences is the first scientific degree requiring at least three years of preparing a thesis and its defense. It typically includes a program for teaching at the university level in order to prepare for the teaching profession, though too little time is allocated for this to change markedly the teaching potential of the candidate (e.g., a few lectures on the theory of education and some practice teaching).

The supply of teachers has always been irregular in the sense of there being oversupply of some subject teachers and an undersupply of others. But in later years, with the salaries of teachers growing much slower than those of other workers, there is a tendency for teacher shortage almost everywhere, in big cities as well as in far-off villages. In the latter case, poor housing conditions and an acute shortage of consumer goods exacerbate the problem. In addition classes are of very different sizes, and overcrowded classes (sometimes containing over 40 students) are a severe strain on teachers, many of whom cannot tolerate the situation any longer and seek another job.

A fairly good system of inservice training for teachers exists. In each large city there is a so-called "institute of inservice training for teachers" which serves the city and the region. Programs include lecture and workshop periods of several weeks, intermittent workshops for teachers of all subjects, and so forth. School principals and their deputies also have an inservice training period of two to four months every five years, with the training being organized at special departments attached to universities and pedagogical institutes. This also applies to university teachers themselves. The frequent opportunity of going to larger universities (in bigger cities) is usually very attractive to teachers who work in smaller far-off cities, the distances sometimes being measured in many hundreds of kilometers.

Inservice training for all teachers typically includes courses in their subjects as well as psychology and education, and, very often, computer training. These programs are all the more important for teachers since high teaching loads during the school year (24 45-minute periods or more each week for many university teachers) leaves them little time and energy for independent study.

7. Curriculum Development and Teaching Methodology

As mentioned above, the Soviet Union has always been a country with a highly centralized system of government in all spheres of life, including education. The noticeable movement toward decentralization began in about the middle of the 1980s, but got a strong impetus at the end of the decade. Now some provision is made for the all-Russia part of the curriculum (as far as general education is concerned) and higher education institutions are getting more and more independent in their curriculum decisions.

Though part of the content of education is still recommended from the (republican) center, 60 percent or more of it is now determined at the city and individual school level, and "the school component" is to grow further. Educationists in Russia do not use the word "curriculum" in the wider sense of the word that includes the enumeration of the subjects and the methods and media used. There are the "study plans" (the subjects taught with the number of hours for each of them) and the syllabuses for particular subjects which give a concise coverage of what is taught in this or that subject. Formerly, there was the all-union "core curriculum" including the Russian language and literature, mathematics, physics, chemistry, history of the Soviet Union and world history, geography of the Soviet Union and world geography, and biology. Now the Russian Federation decides on the native language and literature, history of Russia, physical culture, and some other things specific for the Federation as a whole—the general idea being that, in this respect (as in all others), individual institutions of education should get increased independence.

Though technically approved by the ministries of education and then by the State Committee for Education, all "study plans" and syllabuses and most textbooks for schools of general education are prepared by researchers from the Academy of Pedagogical Sciences. Some textbooks are written by school teachers or scientists working elsewhere. As far as textbooks for postschool education are concerned, these have always been written by teachers from universities and institutes. This is partly the case in the early 1990s with the difference being that the USSR Academy of Pedagogical Sciences has been reorganized into the Russian Academy of Education and many institutions of learning prefer to use alternative textbooks prepared anywhere, which is now encouraged.

Up to the middle of the 1980s there were no electives in school curricula, though schools had the right to offer courses in addition to those in the prescribed curriculum. The school reform of 1984 gave an impetus to the idea of differentiated learning and up to 10 percent of the curriculum time was taken up by electives. There have also been schools with an emphasis on a particular school subject or subjects (like foreign languages, physics, mathematics, etc.). Beginning in 1990, alternative schools came into being where "the emphasis" is still more pronounced and about 30 percent of the time can be taken up by electives.

Foreign languages are taught from the third form and in all schools. There are exceptional cases where there are no foreign language teachers; though this is not often, it does occur in some rural schools. In almost 60 percent of cases, English is the main language being taught, with French and German taking second place, and other languages being only very rarely taught. With international contacts becoming easier and with the spirit of entrepreneurship gaining strength, popularity of foreign language learning is also growing. Since schools as a rule do not give a working knowledge of languages, out-of-school groups and private teaching (sometimes for very high fees) have also grown in numbers.

Teaching methods are considered a matter for any teacher to decide upon in the early 1990s. This has not always been so as educational researchers formerly prepared plenty of literature not only on general methods but also very detailed "methods recommendations" on particular points in the syllabus, particular lessons on a given topic, and so forth. Some teachers do prefer to have these detailed guides. But in most cases the guiding principle is that of activating learning, making monologue lecturing less frequent than group talks, question-and-answer periods, and so on.

8. The System of Examinations, Promotions, and Certifications

Since the early 1940s, there have been frequent changes as regards examinations, promotions, and certification. Just after the Second World War, all children took yearly examinations in many subjects from the fourth form onward. Then examinations were taken only after the eighth form and at the end of the tenth (or eleventh) form when a certificate of finishing school (*attestat*) was given. This is also the case in the early 1990s except that schools themselves have the right to decide on whether to have any examination above a prescribed minimum. In other forms, progress during the school year is taken into account by teachers when deciding whether a pupil should be promoted to the next form. This progress is measured in a cumulative way while pupils are given grades for answering the teachers' questions, the highest grade being 5 and the lowest 1. The pass mark is 3; if a pupil gets a 2 in two or three subjects he or she can still be promoted to the next form. If a 2 is received when finishing school, the corresponding subject is not listed in the pupil's certificate and this can bar the student from entering a higher education institution where the subject is important.

Throughout almost the entire history of Soviet schooling, the guiding principle has been that of equal opportunities and no differentiation. It meant, too, that all pupils should somehow be brought to at least a 3 in all subjects irrespective of their interests and abilities. This is no longer the case, though many teachers still disagree and make life really too difficult for some of their less able pupils.

9. Educational Assessment, Evaluation, and Research

The tendency in the early 1990s for decentralization leaves little possibility for assessment or evaluation at the level of Russia as a whole, as the whole does not exist in the shape it existed in just a few years ago. Formerly, the examination system was centrally planned and administered (see Sect. 8) though anything like a central educational testing service never existed. The most important reason was that testing itself was for a long time considered "reactionary" and "bourgeois." However, since about 1970 or even earlier this has no longer been the case; tests are not produced in large numbers and teachers use their own homemade tests. Sometimes the Soviet Ministry of Education and the republican ministries did administer "control works" (test papers) at selected schools, but there has never been any policy on the way the results should be used. In most cases, the control works were followed by a ministerial decree reprimanding directors of poorly performing schools and ordering them to correct the situation.

The 1992 Law on Education provides for regular assessment of the state of education in Russia which makes it imperative to work out different testing procedures and also the so-called "all-Russia standard of (secondary) education." However, all this is only in the planning stage.

Since 1967, the USSR Academy of Pedagogical Sciences has existed as the most important institution for educational research (it has been re-christened the "Russian Academy of Education"). There are over 20 research institutes in the Academy with about 1,700 researchers. Some of them do mostly theoretical research; others prepare curricula, syllabuses, and textbooks. Previously the Academy was interested only in the schools of general education; in the early 1990s it is oriented to research in the whole system of continuing education.

Educational research is also done at chairs of education which function at all universities and pedagogical institutes (teacher-training institutions).

10. Major Reforms in the 1980s and 1990s

The most recent reform of general and vocational education was proclaimed in 1984. It extended the length of obligatory schooling (to 11 instead of 10 years), made vocational education obligatory in some form or another, decreed the school starting age to be 6, made some provisions for better equipment of schools and better pay for teachers, and called for more effective teaching by means of activating student learning. However, very little money was allocated for the implementation of the reform and what is more, with the advent of *perestroika*, the reform itself appeared

insufficient. In the following years, further documents appeared which made provisions for democratizing the government of education (e.g., creating school councils with considerable powers), decentralizing it, and allowing alternative schools to function.

The same ideas of democratization and variability were introduced into postschool education and the idea of continuity was adopted for the whole educational structure.

The new element in the strategic planning of education is the provision for a federal program of educational development (contained in the Law on Education) which is to be worked out on a competitive basis by policymakers, administrators, and scholars. It should be a basis for future educational innovations instead of spontaneous reforms. In 1991, a Program for Stabilization and Development of Education was adopted by the Ministry of Education. The lines along which education is to be reformed are determined by the principles described in Sect. 2 above.

11. Major Problems for the Year 2000

The all-important problem in the years leading up to the year 2000 will certainly be for all the former Union republics (including Russia) to find their identity in education (as in all other areas). Sovereignty of the republics was proclaimed on a wave of criticism of the former Union but destruction is much easier than construction. It means in fact that the new states should better provide for national specificity in education, and for Russia it is no less important than it was for the Soviet Union because of ethnic differences in the Federation itself.

It will be still more difficult to find ways to finance education better than was done under the rule of the Union. A provision for education as a priority exists in law; but to put it into practice will certainly not be easy.

Additionally, of course, the quality of education will be an important issue. Too much experimentation in education with too little money combined with insecure social conditions made motivation for learning very low and many brighter people think with good reason that they will get better pay in areas other than education (which makes it a formidable task for training good teachers), whereas brighter students think that they will earn good money sooner without education than later with it.

The very important transition from authoritarian to democratic schooling (and management of it), and from strictly imposed unity to diversity will certainly be slow in most educational institutions, and less slow in the alternative ones. School textbooks are published in many languages; it is easy to imagine the formidable costs if—as the ideology of diversity requires—they are published in several alternative variants. It will be no less difficult to implement fully the idea of choice of schools by parents and older children. Overcrowded schools, with two (sometimes, three) shifts in them, and the costs of bringing many children to a distant school of their choice are very real difficulties to overcome.

It is very probable that these and similar problems will find their solution only when a new generation of teachers (and even parents) comes along.

Bibliography

Dneprov E D et al. (eds.) 1991 *Rossiyskoye obrazovaniye v perekhodniy period: Programma stabilizatsii i razbitiya.* RSFSR Ministry of Education, Moscow

Goskomobrazovaniye 1990 *Norodnoye obrazovaniye v SSSR v 1989/1990 uchebnom godu.* State Committee for Public Education, Moscow

Goskomobrazovaniye 1991a *Pedagogicheskiye kadri obshcheobrazovatel'nikh shkol 1986–1989.* State Committee for Public Education, Moscow

Goskomobrazovaniye 1991b *Statisticheskiye materiali po obshcheobrazovatel'nim shkolam 1986–1990.* State Committee for Public Education, Moscow

Ministerstvo Finansi i statistica 1989 *Narodnoye obrazovaniye i kul'tura v SSSR.* Ministry of Finance and Statistics, Moscow

Ministerstvo Finansi i statistica 1990 *Narodnoye khozyaystvo SSSR v 1988 i 1989 godu.* Ministry of Finance and Statistics, Moscow

Ministerstvo nauki, vysshey shkoly i tekhnicheskoy politiki Rossii 1992 *O gosudarstvennoy politike v oblasti vysshego obrazovaniya.* Ministry of Science, Higher Education, and Policy on Technology in Russia, Moscow

Ministerstvo obrazovaniya 1992 *Sistema obrazovaniya Rossiyskoy Federatsii.* Ministry of Education of the Russian Federation, Moscow

Nauchno-issledovatel'skiy institut problem vysshey shkoli 1990 *Vissheye obrazovaniye segodnya: tsifri i fakti.* Research Institute for Higher Education, Moscow

Zakon Rossiyskoy Federatsii ob obrazovanii. *Uchitel'skaya gazeta*, 4 Avgusta 1992 goda, N. 28

Rwanda

P. B. Ndengejeho

1. General Background

Rwanda, a country of 26,338 square kilometers with a per capita income of about US$310 (figures as at 1989), is one of the least developed countries in Africa. A number of constraints impede its economic development, among which are: (a) its landlocked position, which adds considerably to transportation costs; (b) its lack of resources; (c) its narrow export base, comprised mainly of coffee, which renders the economy vulnerable to external factors; (d) its lack of a trained labor force; and (e) the growing scarcity of arable land, which has come about as a result of the continued rapid growth of its population.

With a population estimated in 1989 at 7.3 million, Rwanda is the most densely populated country in Africa, with an average density of 280 people per square kilometer. This puts heavy pressure on the availability of land. About 95 percent of the population is rural, engaged mainly in subsistence agriculture on family farms with an average size of one hectare. In the early 1990s the annual population growth rate was estimated at 3.7 percent, one of the highest in the world. Among the consequences of this high rate of population increase is a sharply rising demand for education, training, and productive employment.

From 1887 until the First World War, Rwanda was a German colony. From 1917 until 1962, the date of Independence, Belgium administered the country.

According to the national census of 1978, the social structure of Rwanda is made up of the following three ethnic groups: the Hutu (89.7%), the Tutsi (9.77%), and the Twa (0.46%). In addition, foreigners comprised 0.8 percent of the population, and naturalized citizens 0.67 percent. The great imbalance between the three ethnic groups has significantly influenced education and its implementation, depending upon which ethnic group was in power. The languages used in Rwanda are Kinyarwanda and French; the former, the mother tongue, is shared by the three ethnic groups; French, which is taught as a school subject, is used in administration together with Kinyarwanda. Swahili and English are taught at the secondary level.

Agriculture plays a predominant role in the economy, contributing 46 percent of Gross Domestic Product (GDP). Agriculture is comprised of 80 percent subsistence crops and generates about 85 percent of total export earnings (64 percent of this figure is accounted for by coffee). However, the contributions of the manufacturing and services industries have increased since 1964 to almost 20 percent and 33 percent respectively. Nevertheless, the precarious balance between domestic food supply and the rapidly growing population has become more problematic, not only because of limitations on land, but also due to deforestation caused by the use of firewood, amounting to 90 percent of total energy consumed. This problem is compounded by serious unemployment and underemployment, a high illiteracy rate, malnutrition, lack of primary healthcare, and lack of natural resources. A final important contributory factor is the high rate of population growth which largely outstrips the government's capabilities in terms of investment and job creation. These developments have had an extremely adverse impact on the country's budget. For example, the overall budget deficit in 1987 was about 11.5 percent of GDP, and in 1988 about 8.7 percent. This deficit has prompted the government to introduce a number of measures consisting mainly of budgetary restraints, import restrictions, and the adoption (in 1990) of the structural adjustment program.

Administratively, Rwanda is divided into 11 provinces of prefectures and 147 communes.

2. Politics and the Goals of the Educational System

School is a social entity; in other words, it is a social structure reflecting the society it comes from and which, in turn, it shapes. Thus, a cogent and exhaustive understanding of the needs of individual citizens, ethnic groups, and the nation as a whole is required in order to understand the problems faced by education. Rwandan education is a multiethnic system. Social structures and the Rwandan educational system are, and always have been, closely linked. Education in Rwanda is organized by the state, although the NGOs (nongovernmental organizations) play a significant and vital role. The government is responsible for financing and administering education through policies which encompass both public and private schools.

During the monarchical regime led by the minority Tutsi (up to 1959), the main goal of education was to provide local administration with assistants and a lower grade workforce. Since the administrative system was Tutsi-directed, it needed other Tutsi to help it lead the remaining ethnic groups. Consequently, only Tutsi children were educated, except for a very few members of other ethnic groups who were preparing for the priesthood or teaching at the elementary level.

In order to break the Tutsi monopoly and correct the previous imbalance, the First Republic (1962–73), made education available to all. The founding of the National University of Rwanda was the most significant event during this period.

From 1962 to 1977 the main aims of the education system were as follows:

(a) democratization of education;

(b) preparation for vocational life and entry into the labor force;

(c) preparation for higher education.

From 1977 to 1991 the educational reform embraced:

(a) democratization of access at all levels of education;

(b) qualitative and quantitative improvement of the skilled labor force required by the economy;

(c) promotion of the national language and culture through the education system while maintaining openness to the outside world through the teaching of foreign languages.

These goals were to be achieved in three ways:

(a) curriculum reform emphasizing rural/agricultural needs;

(b) diversification away from academic secondary education;

(c) orientation of higher education toward developmental priorities, including agriculture.

In 1991, there was a shift away from a system of 8 years schooling at the primary level back to the traditional 6 years of the period from 1962 to 1977. School entry age was changed from 7–years old (as in the 1977–91 period) to 6–years old.

3. The Formal System of Education

In 1977, the government decided to reform the formal education system. It initiated implementation of the reform for primary education in 1979 and for secondary education in 1981. Its general objectives have been described above. Both the primary and the secondary schools in Rwanda are mainly of missionary origin

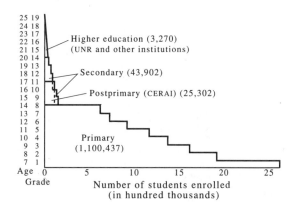

Figure 1
Rwanda: Structure of the formal education system

and are still largely supported by the Roman Catholic Church. Figure 1 presents the structure of the system.

3.1 Primary, Secondary, and Tertiary Education

At Independence in 1962, the Rwandese education and training system (ETS) was embryonic and ill-adapted to the needs of the majority of the populace. In the period from 1960 to 1979, primary education lasted 6 years. A 2-year postprimary cycle (*classes complémentaires*) emphasized practical courses in agriculture and basic crafts for boys, and household skills for girls. Primary education was declared free and compulsory for all children of school age. A double-shift system from Grade 1 to Grade 3 was created to meet the growing demand for education. There was a significant increase in school centers and classrooms, thus increasing the enrollment capacity from 197,656 pupils in 1960 to 463,422 pupils in 1977–78. The proposed reform in 1972 was not implemented for lack of sufficient public consultation. A major reform in 1977 which was actually instituted in 1979 included a major structural change with the following implications: (a) prolongation of primary education from 6 to 8 years for the 7–14 years age group with introduction of practical subjects in Grades 7 and 8 in workshop extensions to schools and with the target of UPE (Universal Primary Education) by 1986; (b) the entry of 90 percent of primary school leavers to CERAI (*centres d'enseignement rural et artisanal intégré*) for elementary vocational training in Grades 9–11; and (c) the entry of 10 percent of primary school leavers to the reformed secondary school system. Other planned actions included the discontinuance of the secondary 3-year common school (orientation cycle) retraining primary teachers in practical subjects, increasing the proportion of day-students, increasing coeducation, increasing secondary school size to a minimum enrollment of 240,

and the termination of the double-shift and automatic promotion systems. Up to 1991 primary education was of eight years' duration, and was divided into three cycles. The first three years focused on literacy and numeracy and the second three on general education with the introduction of French as a curriculum subject, while the last two years of training emphasized practical agriculture and basic crafts. While the basic objectives were sound, the proposals to achieve them were controversial and the overambitious targets for enrollments, teachers, buildings, and equipment were not achieved because of financial constraints, lack of teachers, and undercapacity of the construction industry. Automatic promotion in primary schools was dropped in 1981 and the double-shift system retained. Of the 1,290 CERAIS planned for construction only 195 were achieved. Participation rates improved steadily in primary education but varied among the 11 prefectures. Table 1 shows that 49 percent of total enrollments and 42 percent of teachers are female. The student–teacher ratio improved to 57:1. However, with the rapid increase in enrollment, the percentage of unqualified teachers rose to 66 percent for Grades 1–6 with deleterious effect on quality of training. The teaching of workshop subjects in Grades 7–8 is generally weak as the required retraining of teachers was substandard. Expenditure on textbooks and educational materials is miniscule. Standards of school buildings seem to be improving with 78.8 (estimates 1998–89) having stone or brick walls and hard roofs, though furniture, basic equipment, and lighting in many schools are either lacking or very poor.

At the postprimary level, because the former CERARS (*centres d'éducation rurale et artisanale du Rwanda*) and the so-called *sections familiales* were combined to form 328 CERAIS only in 1988, they have yet to be fully recognized by the public. They evolved

Table 1
Basic data on the education system 1987–88

Educational establishments		Enrollment	% Girls	Student–teacher ratio
Primary	1,633	969,908	49	57:1
Postprimary (ERAI grades 9–11)	328	27,220[a]	46	14:1
Secondary (grades 9–14)				
Public	74	20,743	35	14:1
Subsidized	10	2,688	—	15:1
Private (not recognized)	58	7,471	52	19:1
Higher education (1986)				
Public	9	1,675	15	7:1
Private	5	400	—	—
Abroad	—	700	—	—

a Less than in 1984–85, when the figure was 31, 245

from a nonformal system of education. Girls comprise 46 percent of enrollments. The teaching program aims at providing skills relevant to improved rural living but curricula remain improvised and teaching is frequently faulty. The aims are the same as those in primary Grades 7–8 and the small enrollments in Grades 9 to 11 make it difficult to use resources efficiently. The student–teacher ratio is very low at this stage. However, with the development of a two-stream enrollment size of about 200 students, this may improve. Teaching is conducted in Kinyarwanda with French taught as a curriculum subject.

Secondary education is organized into a 6-year cycle (Grades 9–14). As part of the reform's objectives to create a skilled labor force, this level has a strong vocational orientation that combines general and technical courses through 12 tracks subdivided into 28 streams. In 1990–91 the 142 schools (comprising 74 public, 10 subsidized, and 58 private and not recognized) were still small, with an average enrollment of around 210. The schools are not evenly distributed but selection of entrants aims to redress the imbalance. Percentages of girls are 40.4 percent in public schools, 43.4 percent in private schools and 48 percent in subsidized schools. The student–teacher ratio is 14:1, 15:1, 19:1 in public, subsidized, and private schools respectively (1988–89). Reformed curricula were introduced in 1980–81 without sufficient consultation of school staff and with a lack of teachers trained to teach the diversified curricula. Sixty-nine percent of the teaching workforce were qualified in 1984 and 75 percent of all teachers were Rwandese. Education quality is mixed due to the low standard of entrants and insufficient textbooks and learning materials, Entrants' weaknesses are particularly marked in the French language, which is so vitally important for success, especially after the 1977 education reform.

The chief institution of tertiary education is the National University of Rwanda (UNR), which has three campuses comprising 10 faculties. There are also four private religious institutions of higher learning, a 4-year Military College, a 2-year High Institute of Agriculture, a 2-year Applied Economics Institute, a Pan-African Institute of Applied Economics, and a 2-year Public Finance Institute. The enrollment at the UNR is 1,630 students and 300 at the other institutions. Seven hundred students study abroad. Females account for only 17 percent of total enrollments. The average student attrition rate which, at 43 percent, is very high is even higher in the science and commerce faculties. The main causes of this are: (a) secondary school curricula insufficiently related to UNR studies; (b) weaknesses in selection in that it is largely based on regional ethnic criteria; (c) shortcomings in UNR teaching, together with a lack of reference books; and (d) the low percentage of qualified faculty members in 1983, only 23 percent of faculty members had PhD degrees. In addition, the management information system is not adequately organized to allow for the comprehensive collection and processing of information relevant to policy analysis and related measures.

3.2 Preschool Education

Only in 1991, was a division for preschool education created in the Ministry of Education. Until that time, creation of preschool institutions was at the initiative of either local communities and organizations, or parents. Since 1992, however, preschool education has become one of the prime targets for action by the Ministry of Primary and Secondary Education, through the *Programme National d'Action* and the *Plan Cadre d'Opérations* UNICEF-RWANDA. The preschool period ranges from 2½ years to 6–years old, when the child is supposed to enter primary school. In 1992, there were 188 trained teachers in preschools scattered all over the country but especially in urban areas. The major objective of preschool education is the promotion of the overall development of the child, preparing him or her for further formal and nonformal education.

3.3 Special Education

There are two institutions for the handicapped. The first provides primary and secondary education for the physically handicapped and, at the secondary level, they are trained in laboratory assistance. The second institution is for the deaf and dumb and provides them with primary education using the Braille method. However, there is practically no secondary education for them due to a lack of trained teachers and appropriate material.

3.4 Vocational, Technical, and Business Education

In Grades 7 and 8 there are courses to develop the creative and manipulative skills of students. At the secondary school level, there are agricultural, commercial and paramedical courses but these are prevocational in nature. There are a few vocational schools that provide middle-level skills. At the upper secondary level, there are six schools offering two commercial courses. Technical training in agriculture, veterinary science, and forestry is provided in four schools. Following school, there are a few apprenticeship schemes comprising learning on the job and complementary practical/academic training leading to certification. The main form of practical training is through the traditional indentureship system in which trainees work with experienced craftsmen over extended periods and the skills are learned informally.

Paramedical training takes place in two schools and for senior nurses there are two schools with an output of ten per year.

Much development is required in the area of vocational and technical education including a better dovetailing of supply and demand and better learning materials.

3.5 Adult and Nonformal Education

The main thrust of adult and nonformal education is provided by six ministries. The Ministry of Civil Service and Professional Training (MINIFOP) serves as a national employment agency and provides preservice and vocational upgrading courses. The Ministry of Youth and Cooperatives (MIJEUMA) provides training for young people not in school. The Ministry of the Interior (MININTER) oversees a system of continuing education centers and also courses for training rural leaders and continuing education courses for adults. Within this system the commune provides the equivalent of primary school education as well as postprimary nonformal education. The Ministry of Public Works and Energy (MINITRAPE) provides a 4-year engineering course for graduates from CERAI. The Ministry of Defense (MINADEF) runs a 4-year technical and social science training course in a military college. Entrants are secondary school graduates. Finally, the Ministry of Posts and Communications (MINITRANSCO) has three training schools for postal services, telecommunications, and civil aviation and meteorology.

In addition to these planned courses by various ministries, there are many initiatives undertaken by a number of public and private organizations.

4. Administrative and Supervisory Structure and Operation

Two ministries are responsible for the administration of the education sector: the Ministry of Primary and Secondary Education (MINEPRISEC), and the Ministry of Higher Education and Scientific Research (MINESUPRES). At the regional level, MINEPRISEC is represented in the prefectures by the prefectural inspectors (*inspecteurs d'arrondissement*), and in the communes by the sector inspectors (*inspecteurs de secteur*). However, not all the communes have an inspector.

The major departments within the ministry responsible for primary and secondary schools are listed below.

The Department of Planning is directly attached to the office of the Secretary General and includes the school mapping and school statistics divisions. Among its main responsibilities is the planning of the development of primary, secondary, and long-term plans. It has three education planners attached directly to the director's office. The main output of the planning department is an annual statistical bulletin, the school map, and some ad hoc reports.

The Department of Studies and Evaluation is also attached to the Office of the Secretary General, and is basically a public relations office in charge of receiving, informing, and orienting visitors to the Ministry. It also has the responsibility of gathering necessary information and making it available to the Minister and

Secretary General. Despite its name the department undertakes very few studies and evaluations, due to a lack of human and material resources.

The Department of Financial Services is attached to the General Directorate of Administration and is responsible for the preparation of budgetary forecasts for schools as well as the implementation of the budget allocated to schools, payment of subsidies to schools, relations with agencies providing funds to educational establishments, and the payment of salaries to teachers.

The Division of Financial Control is also attached to the General Directorate of Administration, and is responsible for the verification and control of management of credit, settling financial claims, analyzing financial reports, calculating the operating costs of schools, and controlling the receipt and use of parents' financial contributions. However, it lacks the resources to undertake any effective financial control.

Attached to the office of the Secretary General, the Division of Credit Management and Supplies is mainly in charge of the elaboration of annual and multiannual budgetary forecasts for the central services of MINEPRISEC, the execution of the budget of these central services, and the distribution and the management of equipment and offices to each department.

The Department of Examinations and Orientations has three major divisions: (a) the Division of Studies and Statistical Analysis of Examination Results, (b) the Division of School and Professional Orientation, and (c) the Division of Examinations. Lack of the required infrastructure (administration facilities, qualified personnel, transport, finance, etc.) has hampered the government's aim of decentralizing administration to the 11 prefectures. The inspection system is also handicapped for similar reasons. Under the direction of the central inspectorate (6 inspectors for primary schools, 11 for CERAI, and 6 for secondary schools) the 11 *inspecteurs d'arrondissement* control 97 sector inspectors and principals responsible for 340 zones who follow up educational and administrative matters in schools. Because of the emphasis since the early 1990s on quantitative expansion of the ETS and reform, inspection has been rather neglected with detrimental effects on educational quality. The standard of school management varies depending upon the principal. Increased attention must be paid to selection and training of inspectors together with the preparation of administration and inspection guidelines. Church-related schools are generally better run.

Since March 1981, the administration and supervision of the education sector has been the domain of two ministries: MINESUPRES (tertiary education) and MINEPRISEC (primary and secondary education). The primary inspection level (both regionally and locally), suffers from certain serious shortcomings from a pedagogical and an administrative point of view. Educationally, the support and advice given to teachers is inadequate, and administratively, regional and local inspectors lack the resources necessary to manage the system adequately.

5. Educational Finance

The distribution of all educational finances in terms of the type of education and the source of the financing are shown in Table 2. The share of the government's estimated recurrent budget devoted to education in 1987 was 24.4 percent and of the total recurrent budget of 1987, 70% was allocated to primary education, 16% to secondary education, and 14% to higher education. However, real recurrent expenditures as a percentage of the government's total were 25.7 percent in 1987, and this figure is not expected to increase. Consequently, the prospects for improving access to and the quality of education depend largely on the growth rate of the recurrent budget and the extent to which the duration, structure, and content of education are modified and physical resources used more effectively.

Communal revenue amounts to about 8 percent of central government revenues. The share of education in the total communal budget is very low (about 2% in most of the communes) and much of this funding is used for literacy programs. Thus, the formal school system basically depends on support from the central government and the primary school fee (*minerval*) of 300 Rwandan francs (about US$2.4).

There is no effective policy framework for promoting private financing of education. The government almost entirely subsidizes the religious schools at both the primary and secondary levels. Most of the private schools created by parents' associations have not

Table 2
Distribution of educational finance

Unit cost (1986)	Rwandan francs (FRW)	Ratio to primary
Primary	4,004	1:1
Postprimary	15,467	4:1
Secondary	49,352	12:1
University	43,978	85:1

Educational expenditures 1987 (in millions FRW)[a]				
	Recurrent	%	Capital	%
Primary	3,861	70	—	—
CERAI	—	—	68	18
Secondary	848	16	204	53
Higher education	735	14	110	29

a Percentage of the total recurrent budget of Rwanda: 23; total expenditure (recurrent and capital) on education as percentage of GNP

been recognized by the government, a situation that sends a negative signal to potential benefactors. Users' fees at the primary level represent about 6 percent of the unit recurrent costs, while at the secondary and higher education levels where such fees were introduced in the early 1990s (FRW 9,000 and 20,000 respectively), they represent about 80 percent and 6 percent respectively. The registration and boarding fees for private secondary and higher institutions are substantially higher.

While the allocation of sectoral resources among the levels of education is efficient (64.5% for primary education and CERAI, 14.6% for secondary education, 15.4% for higher education, and 5.5% for administration) quality-related inputs such as classroom materials are underfinanced, a situation that is worsening. For example, in 1987, the salaries MINEPRISEC paid to teachers amounted to 86.2 percent of the recurrent education budget, whereas the share allocated to improving quality was only 2.4 percent. The trend is discouraging: between 1982 and 1988 the share of teachers' salaries in the budget increased from 78.7 percent to 86.2 percent, whereas the share allocated to quality-related inputs declined from 3.89 percent to 2.39 percent. The same applies to MINESUPRES: between 1982 and 1986, the share of fellowships and administration rose from 26.5 percent to 31.3 percent of the MINESUPRES recurrent budget.

Compared with other African countries, recurrent unit costs are relatively low at the primary level and high at the university level. In 1986–87 they were only FRW 4,004 (about US$50) at the primary level, FRW 49,352 (about US$640) at the secondary level and FRW 343,978 (about US$500) at the higher education level (the figure for the CERAI was FRW 15,467, about US$200). These high unit costs reflect the poor and inefficient use of resources, as well as the lack of economies of scale in higher education.

6. Supplying Personnel for the Education System

In 1989 there were 17,000 teachers in primary schools. Only 52 percent were qualified teachers. Underqualified teachers accounted for 78 percent of the staff in the first cycle of primary school (and this can be considered the most important cycle for the acquisition of basic skills and attitudes), 40 percent in the second cycle, and 48 percent in the third. The average student–teacher ratio was about 57:1. Teachers in the CERAIs numbered about 2,100 and the student–teacher ratio was 10:1. About 500 civil servants in the MINEPRISEC offices in the capital, Kigali, administer the staff in the schools. This yields a management–staff ratio of about 1:42. In secondary schools, only 69 percent of teachers are qualified. The university has 212 teachers, most of whom are not qualified. In 1989, it employed about 1,100 auxiliary staff, or about 1 for every 1.5 students. While senior management personnel generally have higher education qualifications, their effectiveness is compromised by their lack of training in administration and frequent changes of post. There are no facilities for training in administration in Rwanda and only a limited number have been trained abroad in this discipline. The standard of personnel and office management suffers accordingly.

7. Curriculum Development and Teaching Methodology

One major qualitative innovation of the 1977 education reform was the development of curricula based on the objectives approach. The aim of this approach was to ensure that by the end of each level most students would have mastered the achievement objectives established for that level. However, the internal efficiency of the education system has remained weak. In fact, the pedagogical directorate for primary and rural education, which is responsible for the development and try-out of curricula, textbooks, and teaching guides as well as for methodological inputs into the inservice training of primary teachers has not been able to achieve its qualitative objectives. Its main weaknesses are an inadequate mix of skills and poor operating conditions, including a limited recurrent budget, all of which leave it removed from the reality of the classroom. The curriculum implementation is for all schools, whether public or private. To ensure that the curriculum content is implemented, regular inspections of national, prefectural, and sectoral levels are carried out by the relevant inspectors responsible for each level. However, inspection is hampered by a lack of means of transport for inspectors. Also, not all the communes have an inspector.

8. The System of Examinations, Promotions, and Certifications

At the primary and secondary levels, there are examinations at the end of each quarter to assess the student's achievement. Promotion from grade to grade depends on the results of these exams. Grade repetition is high. At the end of primary school a national competitive examination for access to secondary education is held (*cours national d'accès à l'enseignement secondaire*), designed to rank students and compare schools but not to provide any information on student achievement or information that would help assess the strengths and weaknesses of students and guide improvement. Its purpose is to select students competitively for the limited number of places in secondary education (in 1988–89, out of 58,105 candidates only 7,057 were admitted). Thus the indirect feedback received by the schools does not encourage raising the level of achievement of all students

but instead encourages "cramming" for achievement to a higher level of education that will benefit only a few students. The national competitive examination is prepared by the pedagogical directorate for primary and rural education and is the same for all schools. A similar examination, also prepared by the pedagogical directorate, is taken by secondary graduates. The pass rate in the secondary school examination is higher than in the national competitive examination. At the university level, examinations are prepared by the teacher and taken regularly throughout the academic year (*évaluation continué*) regardless of the quarters. At the end of university studies, bachelor's degrees (BA, BSc) are granted to undergraduates and master's degrees (MA, MSc) to graduates.

9. Educational Assessment, Evaluation, and Research

In order to improve the capacity for policy analysis and development and to monitor and evaluate MINEPRISEC's programs, a Directorate of Studies and Evaluation has been created. With the help of inspectors at the national, regional, and zonal levels this analyzes data about the quality of education and identifies measures necessary to carry out compulsory changes in the educational system. This directorate needs to be strengthened so that it can better discharge its actual and potential responsibilities. At the beginning of the 1990s, there was no special emphasis on research for its own sake, but rather on development-oriented research in progress. Apart from the awards foundation, which supports special promotion of research, other incentives are given to school and education researchers, such as training abroad, specialist services and equipment, and incremental operating costs. The most important educational indicators on which information is collected regularly are the school map, educational expenditures, the development and implementation of curricula, pedagogical methods of teaching, and the growth of the rate of students admitted to primary, secondary, and higher education.

10. Major Reforms in the 1980s and 1990s

The length of primary schooling was reduced from 8 to 6 years. The age of entry to school was moved from 7 years of age to 6. The CERAIS (*centres d'enseignement rural et artisanal intégré*) were formed for postprimary education. Universal Primary Education was to be achieved by 1986 and, hence, there was a dramatic increase in primary school enrollment. The provision of qualified primary school teachers—especially in the lower grades—proved to be a problem.

At the university level, the length of a course has been reduced from 3 to 2 years for the undergraduate level while the graduate level has remained unchanged (2 years). None of the existing faculties lead to a PhD degree. To meet the needs of the reform program launched in secondary education in 1979 it was necessary, at the university level, to design new curricula and train teachers to implement their content in secondary schools. Concretely, the main objectives of this reform of higher education were to: (a) train the skilled labor force required by the economy, (b) diversify the financing of higher education and improve the efficiency of allocation and use of resources, and (c) review the length of undergraduate programs and improve the quality of teaching.

11. Major Problems for the Year 2000

Given the two overriding factors of continuing severe financial constraints and rapid population growth, the major issues to be faced in developing the Rwandese Educational and Training System may be summarized as follows: (a) clear definition of rational educational objectives, striking a reasonable balance among political goals which frequently conflict; (b) application of rigorous cost control; (c) improvement of efficiency; (d) amelioration of quality as the system expands; (e) preparation and implementation of an appropriate scheme for technical teacher training; (f) preparation and implementation of an appropriate scheme for institution building, especially with regard to central and regional administration; (g) continuous evaluation of the ETS with a view to gearing it to meet job opportunities for school leavers; and (h) planning and coordination of programs to improve the literacy rate of the population.

In primary education the increase in enrollments does not, and is not expected to, correspond to the percentage of qualified teachers; books are relatively scarce and not sufficiently used when they are available; the strategy employed thus far to introduce the reform's pedagogical innovations at the school and classroom levels is not well-articulated and targeted. The average repetition rate of 7.8 percent and the drop-out rate of about 12.8 percent are not expected to decrease. In rural education, although two-thirds of the staff are qualified primary school teachers, they are not prepared to teach preprofessional courses. Moreover, while the buildings and furniture are adequate, the lack of workshop equipment, consumables, and textbooks have adversely affected quality.

While the objective of the CERAIs is training for employment in the rural environment, the lack of employment opportunities and resulting student defection raise questions about the relevance of this type of education. In secondary education, the effectiveness of the vocational component is questionable and the need for the large number of streams debatable, given the limited range of employment opportunities in a poorly diversified economy. Some 30 percent of teachers are not qualified, and the resultant quality of the teaching of science and technical courses is poor.

In higher education there are serious efficiency problems, at the University of Rwanda the repetition rate in the first year is about 20 percent and the drop-out rate about 25 percent. This is due to several factors, namely, the inadequate selection and guidance of students, the lack of relevance of the secondary school curriculum to the UNR program and the encyclopedic design of the latter, and finally the low percentage of qualified teachers.

Bibliography

International Bank for Reconstruction and Development (IBRD) 1981 *Republic of Rwanda: Education Sector Memorandum.* Report No. 3559-RW, The World Bank, Washington, DC
International Bank for Reconstruction and Development (IBRD) 1984 *Controlling the Costs of Primary and Secondary Education.* The World Bank, Washington, DC
National University of Rwanda 1983 *Etude des causes d'échecs à l'université.* UNR, Butare
National University of Rwanda 1988a *Evaluation de l'enseignement primaire réformé.* UNR, Butare
National University of Rwanda 1988b *Evaluation de l'enseignement primaire, secondaire et ERAI: Rapport de synthèse.* UNR, Butare
Rwanda Ministry of Education 1978 *Réforme de l'enseignement au Rwanda, Historique, orientation et identification des besoins.* MINEDUC, Kigali
Rwanda Ministry of Education 1979 *Education et culture.* Report No. 4 (May/August). MINEDUC, Kigali
Rwanda Ministry of Education 1983 *Etude et programmation des besoins en enseignants au Rwanda 1983–2000.* MINEDUC, Kigali
Rwanda Ministry of Education 1984 *Statistiques de l'enseignement: Année scolaire 1982/83, 1984.* MINEDUC, Kigali
Rwanda Ministry of Education 1989 *Analyse des rapports des commissions d'évaluation de la réforme de l'enseignement rwandais.* MINEDUC, Kigali
Rwanda Ministry of Planning 1982 *IIIème Plan de développement économique, social et culturel 1982–1986.* MINIPLAN, Kigali
Rwanda Ministry of Planning 1989 *Analyse de la situation économique et propositions de mesures de redressement.* MINIPLAN, Kigali
Rwanda Ministry of Primary and Secondary Education 1978 *Recueil des principaux textes lé et réglementaires régissant l'enseignement rwandais.* MINEPRISEC, Kigali
United States Agency for International Development 1981 *Rwanda: Short Assessment of the Education Sector.* USAID, Washington, DC
World Bank 1988 *Report on the Costs and Financing of Primary, Secondary, and Higher Education* (Annexe 3: Rwanda). The World Bank, Washington, DC

Saudi Arabia

H. M. Al-Baadi

1. General Background

Saudi Arabia occupies most of the Arabian Peninsula. Of the latter's total land area of about three million square kilometers, the Kingdom of Saudi Arabia comprises nearly 2,200,000 square kilometers. The country is bounded by the Arabian (Persian) Gulf, Qatar, and the United Arab Emirates to the east; Oman and Yemen to the south; the Red Sea and the Gulf of Aqaba to the west; and Jordan, Iraq, and Kuwait to the north.

The official name of the country, the Kingdom of Saudi Arabia, came into existence in 1932 when Abdul-Azeez Ibn Abdur-Rahman āl-Saud, who was simultaneously King of Hijaz and Sultan of Najd and Dependencies, united the two parts of his state under one administration and one name. The word Saudi itself is derived from the name of the ruling house of Saud. The house of Saud has ruled most of what is now Saudi Arabia on and off since 1744 when its founder, Mohammad Ibn Saud, emir (ruler) of Diri'yah, a small semi-independent village state in Najd (the central region of Arabia), entered into a political-religious alliance with Muhammad Ibn Abdul-Wahhab, a fundamentalist Muslim reformer. The alliance provided the Saudi emirate with legitimacy and the fundamentalist reformer with military and political support in his crusade to "purify" the popular faith and rid it of unorthodox beliefs and practices. In the 1990s this alliance was still active between the descendants of Muhammad Ibn Saud, on the one hand, and the descendents of Muhammad Ibn Abdul-Wahhab and the network of Wahhabi ulama (religious savants), on the other and constitutes an essential part of the Saudi state's legitimacy.

Geographically, the country is divided into three major slices or chunks of land extending from its far north to its far south. The eastern slice comprises the Eastern Province; the central slice the Central Province (or Najd); and the western slice contains two provinces: the Western Province (or Hijaz) and the Southern Province (or Asseer). Except for the mountainous southwestern province of Asseer, Saudi Arabia is a predominantly arid desert that receives an average annual rainfall of about 100 millimeters.

Historically, the country's harsh environment, coupled with malnutrition and the lack of healthcare facilities, resulted in a low population density. During the 1930s the population was estimated at 1.5 to 2 million people (Stacey International 1977). The increases in oil income, especially during the 1960s and 1970s, and the subsequent improvements in education, nutrition, and health care, resulted in a reduction in infant mortality, a rise in life expectancy, and the elimination of emigration.

In 1991, the last year for which there are documented, though unofficial statistics, the total population of the country was about 16 million, of whom 11.5 million (72%) were citizens and 4.5 million (28%) were expatriates who were overwhelming guest workers and their dependants. The population growth rate for the native population was about 3.65 percent, mainly through births. For expatriates, the growth rate was 4.3 percent, mainly through immigration.

The oil industry and development-related works and projects resulted in the rapid urbanization of the peasant and nomadic population. In 1970, some 20 percent of the population was estimated to be living in metropolitan areas (towns of more than 100,000 people); 20 percent in small towns; and 60 percent in rural areas. Corresponding percentages for 1980 were 42, 12, and 46 percent respectively (Ministry of Planning, Third Development Plan 1980). The fully nomadic (bedouin) people was almost completely settled. However, between 2 and 4 percent of the population was still seminomadic in the sense that it lived simultaneously in the desert (usually in the spring time) as well as in settled (rural or urban) areas. In seminomadic households, men often work and live in the settled areas while womenfolk and other dependents remain in the desert. Men commute to their households during weekends and monthly leaves.

Prior to the beginning of commercial production of oil in 1938, government income was very meager and came mainly from foreign aid, revenues from foreign Muslim pilgrims, and an annual tax (tithe), levied on the land's animals and agricultural produce. Prior to 1938, the government's total income may never have exceeded US$5 million in any single year (Cheney 1958). In 1945, the government received its first sizable royalty from oil, US$20 million. The oil income has since rocketed. In 1980, it peaked at more than US$120 billion. Ten years later, in 1990, it leveled at nearly US$32 billion, still 1,600 times what it was in 1945. These income increases resulted in fundamental demographic, social, and economic changes such as rapid urbanization of most of the population, an almost total dependence on oil-based income, the diminution of the value of most forms of traditional production (e.g., agriculture, herding, and fishing) and an unprecedented rise in the importance of the government's role as receiver of national income, provider of social services, and planner and administrator of "national development" (a first five-year development plan was initiated in 1970, followed since by four others). The major goals of the 1990–95 development plan are:

(a) the stabilization of the national economy;

(b) organizational development of public and private sectors;

(c) expansion of the private sector;

(d) development of the economic structure;

(e) improvement of economic performance and competitiveness;

(f) development of Saudi workforce and improving its efficiency;

(g) preserving the quality of life in Saudi society;

(h) achievement of balanced regional development;

(i) speeding the acquisition of science and technology;

(j) expanding Saudi Arabia's international relationships (Ministry of Planning 1990).

2. Politics and the Goals of the Education system

Education has been a major concern in Saudi Arabia since the unification of the country in 1932, and especially since 1954 when the Ministry of Education was first established. The Development Plans have institutionalized this concern, formalized its objectives, and sought to bring it close to the mainstream of national development. Within the national development effort, the educational system is charged with three objectives: (a) to provide at least basic education for all citizens; (b) to provide students with the skills that are required by the changing needs of the economy; and (c) to educate students in the beliefs, practices, and values of the Islamic culture.

A Supreme Committee of Education has the official role of coordinating the educational effort in Saudi Arabia. This committee comprises the top officials of the major educational bodies in the country, plus other notables. These bodies are administratively independent of each other although their goals and functions are interdependent and often parallel each other. Each of these bodies is briefly described below.

The Ministry of Education was established in 1954 to replace the Directorate General of Education which had been in charge of the educational effort since 1926. Prior to 1926, the educational effort was mostly limited to Koranic schools (kuttabs) that taught the fundamentals of religion, literacy, and arithmetic. Trades and crafts were learnt through apprenticeship. Scholarship had an almost exclusively religious nature and talented Kuttab students obtained further training in Arabic and the Sharia (Islamic) law by attending more specialized lectures from established authorities in these subjects.

Attempts to introduce more secular topics were started in the late 1800s by Moslem philanthropists from other lands. A few partly secular schools were established in Al-Hijaz, the western province of Arabia. In 1926, when the Directorate General of Education was established, the country had about 12 such schools with a total enrollment of about 700 pupils (Jamal 1945). Nearly 25 years later, in 1950–51, the country had 325 government schools and 40 private schools, with a total enrollment of about 42,000 students (Twitchell 1953).

3. The Formal System of Education

3.1 Primary, Secondary, and Tertiary Education

While the organizations that administer formal education in Saudi Arabia are various and independent of each other, the basic plan of their programs is almost identical. There are six years of elementary school that begin after the child has reached the age of 6. The next stage is the intermediate or middle stage which lasts three years. A third stage is the secondary stage which also lasts three years. Students who go on to college spend an average of four years obtaining a bachelor's degree in the social sciences or arts or an

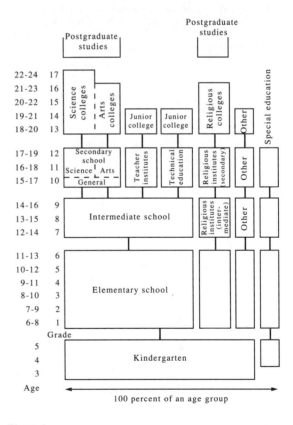

Figure 1

Saudi Arabia: Structure of the formal education system

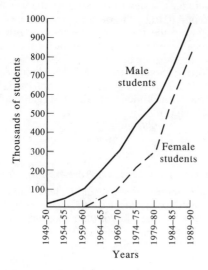

Figure 2
Elementary school enrollment 1950–90

average of five years obtaining a bachelor's degree in science. Figure 1 represents the general flow of the educational system in Saudi Arabia. Figures 2, 3, and 4 represent developments in elementary, intermediate, and secondary enrollment since the 1950s.

The rise in school enrollment reflected the changes in the socioeconomic conditions of the country. These changes have continued to take place and in 1990–91, nearly 37 years after its establishment, the Ministry of Education operated 8,782 schools with a total enrollment of 1,446,226 male students at predominantly the elementary, intermediate, and secondary stages. This number accounted for nearly 47 percent of the total student body in the country, a drop from 57 percent in 1978–79. This drop represents the rising numbers of students belonging to other educational authorities, especially female students.

The General Administration of Girls' Education (GAGE) was established in 1960. Objections from concerned parents and *ulama* (religious savants) to girls' schools, based on the fear that such modern schools might have undesirable effects on girls, delayed the establishment of these schools by the government until 1960. Girls' schools were put under the ulama's own administration and were thus independent of the Ministry of Education. In its first year, GAGE opened 16 schools. About 30 years later, in 1990–91, GAGE operated 6,644 schools, mostly elementary, intermediate and secondary, with a total enrollment of 1,247,498 (female) students, making up nearly 40 percent of the total student body in the country (GAGE 1992 pp. 34, 38).

In 1989–90 almost 8.7 percent of all students in Saudi Arabia were enrolled in educational institutions that did not come under either the Ministry of Education or GAGE. These institutions were operated by the Ministry of Higher Education or the ministries

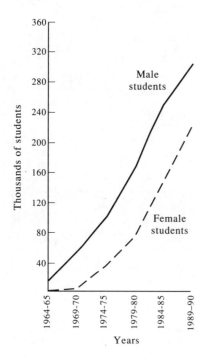

Figure 3
Intermediate-school enrollment 1965–90

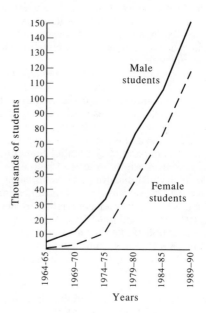

Figure 4
Secondary school enrollment 1965–90

of Defense, Health, Social Affairs, Communications or one of the other government agencies which offer specialized kinds of instruction.

Chief among these agencies are the General Organization of Technical Education and Vocational Training (GOTEVT) and the General Administration of Religious Institutes.

Private schools are the oldest type of school in modern Saudi Arabia. Prior to the availability of government schools, well-off families used to send their children to private schools in neighboring countries or to the few private schools that existed inside Saudi Arabia. In 1950–51, private schools constituted about 11 percent of all schools in the country (40 out of 365). In 1979–80 they made up about 4.3 percent of all schools (437 out of 10,018). The decline in the share of private schools in the overall total number of Saudi schools reflects the government's fast and expanding takeover of the educational effort in the country, especially after the establishment of the Ministry of Education. However, there has been an actual increase of 393 private schools between 1950–51 and 1979–80. That number has been growing steadily since then, reaching 829 schools (out of 16,767) in 1989–90. This growth in private education in the country reflects several demographic and socioeconomic factors. First, the high birthrate among Saudis has meant an increasing pressure for admission into government schools. As Saudis are given preference in admission, expatriates often relocate their children into private schools. Second, the increase in the number of working Saudi mothers has often meant sending their small children into day care centers and kindergartens, which make up nearly one-third of all private educational institutions. Third, the upper and middle classes have expanded in Saudi society, with the side effect that a growing number of their members often choose to send their children to better quality private schools. In 1989–90, there were 130,084 private-school students in the country (78,188 boys and 51,896 girls) accounting for nearly 4.3 percent of the total student body.

3.2 Preschool Education

All preschool education in Saudi Arabia, whether public or private, is under the supervision of GAGE. The reason is that all personnel (both administrative and teaching) in preschool institutions are female. These institutions are almost all coeducational, grouping boys and girls together until the age of seven when they go separate ways with boys going to Ministry of Education Schools and girls going to GAGE schools.

In 1985–86 there were 492 preschool establishments (176 public, 316 private) serving 51,604 children (27,950 boys, 23,654 girls). Five years later, in 1989–90, the number of kindergartens was 551 (238 public, 263 private) and the number of children 79,940 (37,852 boys, 42,088 girls). In a country of 16 million people, that figure (i.e., the number of children enrolled

in preschool education) is very unimpressive. It is, however, expected to take off in the next few years reflecting the following factors: (a) the headstart effect—enrollment of children in preschool can help them later in school, (b) the growing number of working mothers, (c) the growing number of unemployed female college graduates is likely to propel authorities to open more preschool centers (especially kindergartens) to employ them.

Preschool education in Saudi Arabia is not only underdeveloped in numbers; it is also by and large underdeveloped in quality. There are a few good preschool centers in the country; the majority, however, are poorly staffed, poorly equipped, poorly financed, and unprofessionally managed and supervised. Curricula and activities are shallow and haphazard at some centers, and rigid and formal at others. Despite all of the drawbacks, studies show that even after socioeconomic factors are controlled, preschool education of one year or more improves children's academic performance in elementary school, especially in the first three grades. The positive impact of preschool starts to fade out in Grade 2 and almost disappears altogether in Grade 4 (Badawood 1986, Al-Uqaili 1986, Al-Jeraisi 1986).

3.3 Special Education

In 1985–86 there were 27 special education institutions serving 2,820 students (1,840 males, 980 females). Five years later, in 1989–90, the number of institutions was only 35 serving 4,551 students (2,953 males, 1,598 females). These students were distributed as follows: 833 in nursery schools, 2,918 in elementary schools, 480 in intermediate schools, 108 in secondary schools, and 212 in vocational programs.

The overall number of students served in special education programs is far below what the country needs. This is obviously a very backward part of Saudi Arabia's educational system. Regular schools are not equipped or staffed to take children with mild handicaps and, without enough special education institutions to serve them, the overwehelming majority of Saudi handicapped children go uneducated, untrained, and institutionally uncared for.

3.4 Vocational, Technical, and Business Education

Vocational and technical education is completely separated from general education in Saudi Arabia in both curricula and administration. While the two systems are parallel to some extent, they are independent of each other to the point where they are often mutually exclusive. Prior to 1980, both the Ministry of Labor and Social Affairs and the Ministry of Education ran different aspects of the technical and vocational education subsystem. In 1980, the General Organization for Technical Education and Vocational Training (GOTEVT) was set up to be in charge of this subsystem and independent of both ministries. Different forms of technical education, however, are offered by other government agencies with special needs.

In 1985–86, there were 86 secondary level technical institutions in Saudi Arabia serving 17,885 students. Five years later, in 1989–90, there were 67 such institutions serving 22,183 students. Postsecondary institutions increased from six (with 576 students) in 1985–86, to 11 institutions (serving 2,680 students) in 1989–90. The distribution of secondary and postsecondary students by specialty was: 6,815 (industrial), 7,564 (business), 399 (agricultural), 6,782 (health), 2,314 (technical), and 989 (others). The total (24,863) does not account for students in military institutes or university colleges. But, still with only a little over 7 percent of all students in secondary and postsecondary education, technical and vocational education in Saudi Arabia has a very long way to go in order to satisfy not only the country's development-related labor needs but also students' demand for technical education. As the labor force gradually becomes more professionalized and the government's ability to employ general education graduates (for civil service jobs) declines in proportion to population growth, demand for technical and vocational education has greatly increased, specially at the postsecondary level.

In 1993 the country's subsystem for technical, vocational, and business education was unable to satisfy the demand. While the causes of this inability are many, and some are beyond GOTEVT's influence, the results are disturbing. One result is Saudi citizens' relative absence from technical and vocational jobs in the labor force at all levels, especially in the private sector. Another result has been the mushrooming of privately owned, privately managed technical centers and institutes. With little or no supervision from GOTEVT, and with no functioning accreditation system, these private organizations often offer training programs of doubtful quality and with questionable standards.

3.5 Adult and Nonformal Education

Of the country's 1989–90 student enrollment of 3,020,442, about 4.5 percent (135,209) were enrolled in adult education programs that were administered mostly by the four major educational institutions that administer formal education programs. The shares of nonformal students between these institutions are shown in Table 1.

The general purpose of adult education in Saudi Arabia is the eradication of illiteracy. Between 70 and 80 percent of all Saudi adults of 15 years of age and older were estimated to be illiterate in 1982. This was a reduction from a UNESCO 1962 estimate of 97.5 percent. While illiteracy eradication is a goal in itself for some, the majority of adult students probably enroll in order to obtain the basic literacy requirements of private and government employers or to improve their chances for promotion with such employers. Skill training is not an objective of adult education in Saudi Arabia except in a small number of private and government women's schools where programs to teach typing, and other skills are becoming increasingly popular among women who want to join an increasingly specialty-oriented job market.

It is interesting, however, to notice that the share of nonformal education in the country's overall educational effort in fact declined from 142,370 students (or 9.8% of 1,451,754) in 1979–80 to its 1989–90 numbers. There are institutional and socioeconomic factors that explain this phenomenon. First, nonformal education in Saudi Arabia is an adult version of precollege general education, lacking any vocational or job-related training. Second, while the country remains officially committed to the eradication of illiteracy, little is actually done to achieve this goal. In fact the opposite sometimes happens as financial resources are moved from nonformal education into formal programs. Third, as income, generated from oil and related enterprises, rises across the different classes through government and nongovernment handouts, subsidies, and welfare programs, many would-be recipients of nonformal education are finding that it is either irrelevant to their immediate welfare or, at best, remotely so and, thus, not worth the effort (Hamidi 1992).

4. Administrative and Supervisory Structure and Operation

During the school year 1989–90, Saudi schools had a total enrollment of 3,020,442 students. Of these students, nearly 47 percent (1,405,862 males and 1,598 females) were at schools operated by the Ministry of Education; nearly 39.4 percent were at GAGE schools (6,463 males and 1,181,170 females); nearly 9.3 percent (175,157 males and 106,145 females) were at schools run by other government organizations; and nearly 4.3 percent (78,188 males and 51,896 females) were at private schools.

The Ministry of Education specializes in general elementary, intermediate, and secondary education of males, although it also operates a number of special-

Table 1
Distribution of students in adult education.

Institution	Total number of students	Male	Female
Ministry of Education	62,930	62,930	—
GAGE	61,167	—	61,167
Other government agencies	8,854	7,402	1,452
Private schools	2,258	2,258	—
Total	135,209	72,590	62,619

Table 2
Government expenditures on education in selected years

Years	Expenditure on Education (thousands of riyals)	Share of Total Budget (%)
1945	130	6.3
1949–50	9,433	7.5
1954–55	48,000	6.3
1959–60	122,068	16.5
1964–65	408,000	13.0
1969–70	596,000	10.0
1974–75	3,760,000	8.2
1979–80	16,269,082	10.2
1984–85	23,031,700	11.5
1989–90	22,504,900	16.0

ized institutes. The General Administration of Girls' Education has an almost identical function with respect to females except that it also operates its own women's colleges. The Ministry of Higher Education supervises the country's universities. These universities serve different provinces. The King Saud University in Riyadh, King Abdul-Azeez University in Jeddah, King Faisal University in Dammam, offer programs in arts and sciences. The University of Petroleum and Minerals predominantly offers programs in engineering. The Imam Muhammad Ibn Saud Islamic University in Riyadh and the Islamic University at Madinah are religiously oriented and offer mainly training in religious studies, Islamic law, and Arabic.

The overwhelming majority of schools in Saudi Arabia are administered at three levels: a building level, a district level, and a national level. At the building level, the school principal handles the day-to-day operation of the school (discipline, scheduling, attendance, registration, supervision of teachers, etc.). All schools in a particular district belong to a district directorate which constitutes the link between the individual school and the ministry or central government organization it belongs to. The district directorate handles the placement of teachers, disputes between teachers and principals, parent petitions, school logistics, and the like. The ministry or other national-level agency is located in the country's capital Riyadh. Its general functions are the hiring of personnel, setting of educational policies and curricula, allocation of financial resources, planning, textbook selection and printing, and the overall supervision and administration of the educational effort.

5. Educational Finance

Except for private schools, which depend largely on tuition fees paid by the students' families, all schools in Saudi Arabia are free of charge to all students. Some educational institutions (e.g., colleges, religious institutes, and technical and special education institutes) even offer their students a monthly allowance. As shown in Table 2, government expenditure on education greatly increased after the 1960s, reflecting two interdependent factors: the increase in the government's revenue from oil and the expansion of the educational effort both horizontally and vertically.

Although there has been a steady increase in government expenditure on education over this period, the sudden jump in the 1979–80 allotment reflects to some extent the government's determination to establish and multiply the physical facilities for education at all levels. However, a majority of elementary and intermediate schools still function in rented buildings, many of which are considered unfit. A 1979 government publication stated that "a very rough calculation indicates that the government is spending a little over 500 riyals per head in the total population on education and incurring an average of about 4,000 riyals per student enrolled in various levels and types of education" (Ministry of Education, Center for Statistical Data 1979 p. 109). That figure has nearly doubled in 1989–90 to 7451 riyals (about US$2000) per student per year.

6. Supplying Personnel for The Education System

The speed with which the educational effort has expanded in Saudi Arabia has resulted in shortages in numbers of personnel and in qualified personnel. Three main policies have been adopted to deal with these shortages: (a) the recruitment of foreign personnel, most of whom were teachers from neighboring Arab countries; (b) the employment of Saudi teaching and administrative staff whose training in education was often deficient; and (c) the building of training facilities for Saudi personnel. The qualifications of Saudi personnel have improved over the years. In their early years, the Ministry of Education and GAGE often hired teachers who possessed no higher qualification than literacy.

To provide the expanding elementary school system with the teachers they needed, elementary teacher-preparation institutes were built. These institutes offered a two-year program after elementary school. They were later upgraded to provide three years of teacher training after the intermediate school and now provide most of the Saudi teachers at the elementary level. Intermediate and secondary school teachers are predominantly four-year college graduates although some Saudi teachers at the intermediate level come from two-year teacher-training programs. In 1989–90 there were 127 teacher-training institutes at the secondary level (13 for males and 114 for females). These offer a three-year program below the college level. In the same year there were 40 postsecondary training institutes, mostly two-year junior colleges of education that are being upgraded into four-year autonomous

Table 3
Subject matter areas and weekly hours of classroom study assigned to them

Subject	Grade 1	Grade 6	Grade 9	Grade 12 (science)	(arts)
Religious subjects	12	9	8	4	4
Arabic subjects	9	9	6	3	11
Social science	—	3	4	—	8
Mathematics	4	6	5	9	—
Science (and health)	2	4	4	12	—
Drawing	3	2	2	—	—
Physical education	2	2	2	1	1
English	—	—	6	6	6
Total	32	35	36	35	30

colleges of education. Of these, 22 serve males and 18 serve females. Aside from these, there are six university colleges of education that serve both sexes, albeit separately. There are also seven full-fledged colleges of education that are exclusively for women and operate under GAGE's Agency for Colleges. Besides preparing first-time teachers, these colleges often offer in-service training programs for school principals, supervisors, and teachers.

Of the 162,620 teachers who worked for the Ministry of Education and GAGE in 1989–90, about 71 percent were Saudi nationals, a jump from 1979–80 when Saudis were 60 percent of all teachers, and an obvious reflection of two factors. First, salaries paid to Saudi teachers are very competitive in comparison with salaries paid in most other branches of civil service or the private sector, making teaching an attractive profession for an ever increasing number of Saudis. Second, there are, as indicated before, various facilities for training teachers. It is an irony that a country that suffered a severe shortage of teachers only a few years ago will in a few more years be graduating more teachers than it can absorb. This is already happening in the major cities and at the elementary level throughout the country. One possible solution of this problem, occasionally discussed, is to convert some teacher-training junior colleges into multispecialty polytechnic or community colleges.

7. Curriculum Development and Teaching Methodology

With little prior expertise in modern education, the educational system in Saudi Arabia basically adopted the curricula of other Arab countries, especially those of Egypt, adding a heavier emphasis on religious subjects. The curricula of both boys' and girls' schools

of the same stages are practically identical except that girls' schools offer home management as an additional subject, and boys' schools offer physical education, which girls' schools do not offer. Private schools are required by law to offer the same curricula as those of their public counterparts. However, many private schools can and do extend their daily schedules to offer popular subjects such as more English language or computer classes.

Both the Ministry of Education and GAGE have a curriculum department, although little has changed in their educational programs since their inception. Both organizations hire the authors of the required textbooks, print the books, and distribute them among their schools. Thus, there is a uniform curriculum in the country. The general composition of this curriculum is shown in Table 3.

Implementaion of the curriculum is ensured through a variety of means such as the school principal and visits by inspectors from the district office, as well as by a system of final examinations which cover all the material that is supposed to be taught in a particular semester.

Teaching methods differ from subject to subject. Teachers of religious subjects emphasize memorization of religious texts and rarely use any teaching aids other than the blackboard. Teachers of Arabic use the blackboard and also require a fair amount of text memorization. Teachers of science subjects use laboratories when they are available in their schools. Most school laboratories, however, are deficient either in equipment or in qualified personnel, or in both. Language laboratories exist in some elite schools for teaching English.

Arabic is the language of instruction throughout the elementary, intermediate, and secondary levels. At college, Arabic is the medium in the arts, humanities, and social sciences. English is the medium of instruction in engineering, medicine, and the natural sciences. There is a scarcity of college-level textbooks in Arabic, and college instructors who have to use Arabic often type up their own notes and use them as basic required texts. The result is a shallowness in educational standards in some college departments.

The teacher–pupil relationship is characterized by formality. Class management depends on a mixture of moral and chronological authority, persuasion, admonition, and punishment. Corporal punishment is officially prohibited but is commonly practiced at the elementary and intermediate levels. Officially, there are parent–teacher associations but they have little or no authority and meet only once or twice a year.

8. The System of Examinations, Promotions, and Certifications

In Grades 1 through 12, the school year is divided into two semesters. The required instructional material for a year is divided into two halves. At the end of each semester, there is an examination that covers one half. The student's marks in two semesters are added up to make up his or her mark for the whole year. If the final mark is below a certain percentage, usually 50 percent, the student fails in that subject and sits another examination in the subject at the end of the summer recess. If the student fails again to attain the required minimum mark, he or she has then to repeat the whole year, retaking all subjects of that year, including those already passed. Success in passing examinations thus constitutes the only criterion for promotion from one year or grade to a higher one.

Colleges also operate on a semester basis but in a number of universities the credit-unit system was adopted and, thus, students who failed a particular subject did not have to repeat the whole year or semester but, rather, only the subject they failed, if it were a required one.

In 1991, however, the credit-unit system came under heavy criticism and was dropped from all Saudi universities except the King Fahad University of Petroleum and Minerals. And so the other universities have gone back to the uniform-track annual system where electives have been minimized, flexible schedules disappeared, and departments decide what college students must take and when to take it as part of their study program for a particular degree.

9. Educational Assessment, Evaluation, and Research

There was a noted improvement in the quality of educational research in Saudi Arabia in the 1980s. Most of the improvement, however, was confined to research

work undertaken by professors and graduate students in colleges of education. Research centers at the Ministry of Education and GAGE are understaffed and underfinanced and the research they produce remains deficient in quality, quantity, and scope.

However, while the scientific quality of academic degree-related research is, in general, acceptable by common standards, it is characterized by a lack of focus. There are no research maps and no research priorities. The major educational establishments in the country rarely finance any research or even suggest topics for research. As a result, the overwhelming majority of educational research is mostly irrelevant to the country's educational practice or immediate problems. Professors and their graduate students choose research topics rather haphazardly, and so the country's ability systematically to accumulate related research is flawed. Educational research in Saudi Arabia remains fragmented.

10. Major Problems for the Year 2000

Saudi Arabia has made some impressive progress in the expansion of its educational system. Some serious problems have grown alongside that expansion. The most important of these are the following:

(a) While lip service is paid to coordinating the educational effort with the goals of development, there, in fact, is a large gap between the two. In a country dependent on expatriate technical knowhow, for example, only 8.6 percent of Saudi secondary school students are in vocational schools, and only 2.6 percent of postsecondary students are in technical colleges, and only 20.6 percent of university students are in science and applied fields as opposed to 79.4 percent in humanities and theoretical fields (al-Rasheed and al-Baadi 1992).

(b) By the mid-1990s, Saudi Arabia will be self-sufficient in teachers, but the quality of recruits, and their training programs remains inadequate. Inservice programs for teachers and school personnel are also inadequate. Most important, accountability must be assured; lax civil service evaluation forms do not distinguish or encourage quality performance, and tenure is automatically obtained with assignment.

(c) School buildings, facilities, and equipment remain a big problem. Most are unfit for education and this is inexcusable in a very rich country like Saudi Arabia.

(d) Illiteracy, at 48.9 percent remains a very serious problem (Hamidi 1992). The whole adult education effort will have to be redefined, focused, and energized.

(e) Special education is an area where much remains to be done. At 4,551 students (in 1989–90), the number is far too small for the country's needs. Most children with severe and moderate handicaps either remain in their family homes or are sent abroad for care and training.

(f) A great deal needs to be done in technical education: it needs to be expanded, it needs to include more female students, it needs to be better aligned with the needs of the job market, and it needs to improve access from and into general and higher education.

(g) The country remains without a system of compulsory education. As a result, an estimated 10–15 percent of all school-age children go uneducated in the deserts and remote parts of the country as well as among lower socioeconomic classes in the sedentary areas.

(h) The educational system loses an estimated 20–30 percent of its charges to attrition. Its internal efficiency is further hampered by the phenomenon of "grade-repetitive", or "failures" as they are commonly known, where a student repeats a whole academic year if he or she fails to pass the final exams and then fails again at the end of the summer recess. Through this phenomenon, the average number of years male students spend to finish the 12-year course of precollege education (Grades 1 through 12) is 18 years; the corresponding length for girls is 15 years (Ministry of Planning 1990). The system is obviously inefficient and ineffective. With its limited native labor force, Saudi Arabia cannot afford to lose so many of its young to attrition and failure.

(i) Another problem faced by Saudi education at the postsecondary level is the provision of seats for the ever-increasing numbers of male and female graduates of high schools. The government has been reluctant to allow the opening of private colleges, but the pressure (from parents who want college education for their children and from businesses unsatisfied with graduates of public colleges) is growing and at some point private colleges will have to be allowed. The challenge is to regulate these institutions by setting up an accreditation system that ensures their quality.

In sum, Saudi education has grown remarkably fast, satisfying most of the immediate needs of a burgeoning population. As it approaches the twenty-first century, it shows normal signs of fatigue and maladjustment. Its challenge now is to tune itself so that it becomes more sophisticated, more efficient, more effective, better coordinated, and more sensitive and responsive to the needs of a different era and a different socio-economic landscape.

References

Al-Jeraisi A 1986 The economic social, and familial background correlated with school failures among female students of the first elementary grade in the city of Riyadh. (Unpublished M A thesis, College of Education, King Saud University, Riyadh)

al-Rasheed M, al-Baadi H 1992 External efficiency of university education in the GCC countries and its relationship to their development plans. Paper presented to the Fifth Symposium of GCC University Rectors, University of Kuwait, Kuwait

Al-Uqaili R 1986 The influence of kindergarten on school achievement of female students throughout the elementary school years in the city of Riyadh. (Unpublished MA thesis, College of Education, King Saud University, Riyadh)

Badawood A S 1986 The impact of kindergarten on the increase of vocabulary of female students in the first elementary grade in Riyadh City. (Unpublished M A thesis, College of Education, King Saud University, Riyadh)

Cheney M S 1958 *Big Oil Man from Arabia*. Ballantine Books, New York

General Administration of Girls Education 1992 *Girls' Education in Thirty-two Years 1960–1991*. GAGE, Riyadh

Hamidi A S 1992 *An Introduction to Andragogy*. al-Farazdaq Press, Riyadh

Jamal A M 1945 Matha fi al-Hijaz? Dar Ihyaa al-Kutub al-Arabiyyah, Cairo

Ministry of Education, Center for Statistical Data 1979 *Progress of Education in Saudi Arabia*. Ministry of Education, Riyadh

Ministry of Planning 1980 *Third Development Plan*. Ministry of Planning, Riyadh

Ministry of Planning 1990 *Fifth Development Plan*. Ministry of Planning, Riyadh

Stacey International 1977 *The Kingdom of Saudi Arabia*. Stacey International, London

Twitchell K S 1953 *Saudi Arabia*. Princeton University Press, Princeton, New Jersey

Further Reading

al-Hammad M A 1974 Notes on the educational systems in Saudi Arabia and the Arab countries. (Unpublished Notes in Arabic, Mu'assassat al'Talib, Riyadh)

al-Zaid A M 1977 *Education in Saudi Arabia: A Different Model*. Dar Ukaz lit-Tiba'ah, Jeddah

Arab Information Center 1966 *Education in the Arab States*, Information Paper No.25, Arab Information Center, New York

Ministry of Education, Center for Statistical Data 1978 *Educational Statistics*. Ministry of Education, Riyadh

Ministry of Education, Center for Statistical Data 1980 *Preliminary Summary of Statistics on Education*. Ministry of Education, Riyadh

Thomas A Jr 1968 *A Study of the Educational System in the Kingdom of Saudi Arabia*. American Association of Collegiate Registrars and Admission Officers, Washington, DC

UNESCO 1955 *World Survery of Education: Handbook of Educational Organizations and Statistics*. Les Petits-Fils de Leonard Danel, Paris

Senegal

M. Sow

1. General Background

Located in Sub-Saharan African, Senegal covers an area of 196,200 square kilometers (74,730 square miles). Bounded on the west by the Atlantic Ocean, on the east by Mali, on the north along the Senegal River by Mauritania, and on the south by Guinea and Guinea Bissau, this former colony of France is divided into two parts by the enclave of the Republic of the Gambia.

As in most other African countries, Senegal's population (estimated to be 7 million in the census of 1988) is growing fast (estimated at 2.8 percent per year in 1988). Although the government has adopted a population policy, demographic factors will continue to absorb most of the growth in real income for some time to come. The population is mainly concentrated in the coastal western border. The density in general is estimated at 35 inhabitants per square kilometer, but in almost two-thirds of the country the average density is around 5 inhabitants per square kilometer. The main ethnic groups are the Wolof (more than 40%) the Fulani, the Diola, the Serer, and the Mandika. Immigrants from other bordering countries (Guinea, Mauritania) or from Arabic countries (Lebanon, Syria) constitute an important segment of the population. Moslems make up 85 percent of the population and the remaining 15 percent are mostly Christian, although there are a few followers of traditional African religions.

An important feature of the country is the high concentration of people in Dakar, the capital city (inherited from the colonial period), and the coastal belt. This area constitutes a modern sector in employment with commercial facilities and social services resulting in large urban–rural and interregional disparities in employment in the country as a whole. Widespread government participation or regulatory controls—although this was changing in the early 1990s—have been, since Independence in 1960, another feature influencing occupational and social class structure. A new program aimed at considerably reducing the size of the public sector in favor of private entrepreneurs and organized communities (decentralization) has been implemented since 1989.

Despite considerable efforts at modernization, the Senegalese economy has not escaped dependence on the traditional mainstays: millet cultivation and cattle raising for domestic consumption, and groundnut production for export. Moreover, this traditional economy is in stagnation, as is also the case in much of the modern sector. Nearly half of Senegal's resource-poor and relatively open economy is highly vulnerable to climatic vagaries and adverse movements in the terms of international trade. Lacking the rich agricultural potential or mineral resources of other countries on the West African coast, Senegal's growth prospects are mainly based on the quality of its human resources. Table 1 shows the size of the different sectors in the economy.

Since 1976, Senegal has shifted from a one-party political system to a multiparty system. In 1992, there were 17 parties. At the summit of the government structure, the President of the Republic, elected by universal direct suffrage for a five-year mandate, conducts national policy with the assistance of ministers. In 1991, the appointment of a Prime Minister to coordinate and implement the national policy was accompanied by governing the country together with the majority of representatives from the opposition political parties. A monocameral parliament elected along with the President of the Republic and for the same period assumes the legislative power (there are 100 members of the parliament). Through four- or five-year socioeconomic development plans, governments have tried to promote Senegalese society. Thus far, because of excessive centralization, the different sectors of the socioeconomic system, including the education sector, have achieved only limited success. In fact the inadequate resources of the government can neither satisfy all the needs nor correct the large imbalances both in the economic and social sectors.

2. Politics and the Goals of the Education System

The formal type of education in Senegal was introduced by French colonizers in the early nineteenth century (1817 at Saint Louis), even before the conquest of the whole country had been completed. Its mission was to train selected persons from all French West Africa in order to meet the labor needs (mainly clerks) required to help conduct an ever-growing

Table 1
Labor force distribution 1990

Sector	Percentage of labor force
Agriculture	77
Industry	10
Services	13
Total	100

business. Assimilationism was the basic strategy, and it aimed at promoting the French language, French values, French history, and French ways of life. It was only in the period 1930 to 1940 that a few persons were allowed to go beyond the boundaries of clerical skills and be exposed to education aimed at developing leadership. Nevertheless, the perspective was the same: those highly educated people were a form of hostage or simply ambassadors of France to their own people. Large postprimary educational institutions were built in Senegal for training students from all of the French West African states: the William Ponty Teacher Training College; the Medical School; technical schools providing training in railways, postal, and telecommunication services; and two *lycees Faidherbe*, at Saint Louis and Van Vollenhoven in Dakar. The University of Dakar was created from the Institute of Higher Studies established in 1950. The elitist emphasis dominated, and after one century of schooling, the gross enrollment rate in primary school was still very low, at only 12 percent in 1960.

Senegal gained Independence on April 4, 1960 and with it came a tremendous number of changes in the political, economic, and social fields. The word "development," a leitmotiv in every policy paper, was more or less synonymous with catching up with the Western world. In many areas, the replication of models and strategies of development from the former colonial power was undertaken without taking into account the historical context which was so necessary to the understanding of many social phenomena. Education, because of its importance, did not escape the general drive of remodeling. Education was assumed to fulfill new functions different from those previously assigned to it by the colonizers. It was also the strategical unit that was to carry changes to the other subsystems in particular, and to the whole system in general.

The following goals were set for the first educational reform in Senegal in 1971:

(a) developing and consolidating national identity;

(b) promoting self-sufficiency and self-reliance;

(c) reducing cultural and psychological dependency;

(d) strengthening local institutions;

(e) localizing the expatriate labor force;

(f) developing individual potential fully;

(g) extending schooling to every part of the country (universal primary education was the major recommendation of the Addis Ababa Conference in 1961).

The impact of the reform was minor. The structure of the system, its organization, and its dynamism were left almost the same as during the colonial period and thus could not provoke the longed-for turnaround.

Neither the human nor the material environment were conducive to great changes. Teachers and administrators received no training to provide them with new mentalities, new approaches in the execution of their tasks, or even new skills to adjust to a changing reality. The power of the comfortable routine continued.

Apart from the environmental constraints, the lack of a well-rounded and well-designed program of educational reform was the major problem. There was bad coordination between different components of the reform, inadequate timing of action, and an absence of any evaluation process in order to measure the levels of attainment and to regulate action. All of these factors combined were characteristic of a sort of improvization which considerably limited the impact of the 1971 reform.

Between 1977 and 1980, the government of Senegal faced another pressure—that from the teachers' unions demanding more radical change in the educational system. The demand for a more adequate school system was recurrent and led to the reform of 1981. A change in political leadership again provided a favorable opportunity to question the educational system. A national gathering (including politicians, professionals from various fields, representatives from religious organizations, business people, administrators, teachers, and students) was organized to develop the system that would take into account the respective needs and preoccupations of all groups, and in so doing, achieve a national consensus. The meeting was called historically *Les Etats Généraux de l'Education* (after the French Revolution gathering of 1789, when all the social components of the nation met to define a new political charter). Key ideas were collected and committees were set up to design the project. They completed their work five years later in 1985, and the government took one year to study it for approval. Finally, the implementation was planned to begin in 1988.

The time that elapsed from the first step of the reform (1981) to its implementation seven years later did not impose a review or an updating of objectives and strategies. However, the main problem faced by the reform was and is the implementation cost. In fact, they are estimated at more than the entire 1981 national budget and, even if spent over a long period of time (15 years), they remain extremely high for a country which is undergoing a very serious financial crisis. A participative strategy involving all of the population is expected to take care of a considerable part of the operating costs. Again this is not a given fact, but still only a wish. This option has not yet yielded the expected fruit.

3. The Formal System of Education

3.1 Primary, Secondary, and Tertiary Education

Figure 1 outlines the structure of the formal education system. Key statistics on enrollment in the major education sectors are provided in Table 2.

846

Education is compulsory from the ages of 7 to 12 (although the reform aims at mandatory education from 3 to 16), and between these ages approximately 48 percent of an age group attends school. Many children start primary school at the age of 6 years, provided that they have already attended kindergarten. Very few 3- to 6-year olds (1.5%) attend kindergarten before commencing primary school. Kindergarten programs are mainly operated by private individuals. The few which are under government control are financed through public funds, but parents pay most of the operating costs (except for teachers' and administrative salaries).

Primary education lasts for six years. In 1991, there were 708,448 primary school students, of whom 9.8 percent were enrolled in private schools. The scattered population has necessitated a large number of very small primary schools, mainly in rural areas. The primary school week normally contains about 28 hours of tuition and the school year comprises 1,116 hours. Because of the demand for primary education, multigrade classes in rural areas and double shifts in urban areas were introduced in 1986–87 in order to respond more adequately to this demand within the framework of persistent scarcity of resources.

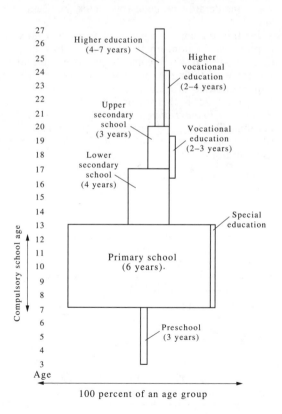

Figure 1
Senegal: Structure of the formal education system 1990

Secondary education is divided into two cycles: lower-secondary and upper-secondary. Lower-secondary is available for four years. However, transition from primary education to lower-secondary is not automatic, but mediated by a national test which promotes about 20 percent of primary school leavers. In 1991, there were 134,148 lower-secondary students, of whom 25 percent were enrolled in private schools. Access to upper-secondary is achieved through an orientation mechanism which promotes almost 50 percent of lower-secondary leavers (government policy aims to reduce it to 40%). It is available for three years and it provides for many options: art, science, technical subjects, economics, and so forth. In 1991, there were 47,022 upper-secondary students, of whom 22.2 percent were enrolled in private schools. Female students represent 30.4 percent of the total enrollment at this level of education. Since the early 1980s, the government has promoted scientific and technical education, but the lack of equipment, facilities, didactic materials, teachers, and laboratory assistants, has prevented the attainment of this objective. All these constraints mean that enrollment in technical education is very low (12.4%). The secondary school year operates for approximately 1,176 hours, with about 7 hours of tuition per day.

The tertiary sector comprises two universities (the second one was opened in 1991 in Saint Louis), six institutes, and four colleges. The institutes and colleges provide a wide variety of courses, including mainly pre-employment programs, but thus far, apprenticeships, retraining, and updating programs and liberal adult education are not well-developed. In 1991, some 18,410 students were enrolled in the tertiary sector. In principle, entry to the tertiary sector is possible after graduation from upper-secondary education. However, adults already working in the public or private sectors can gain entry through competition.

The major problem faced at this level is the dizzying pace at which tertiary education has grown: enrollment doubled in the period 1982 to 1990 and the main campus of the University of Dakar now houses 16,000 students in facilities designed for only half that number. Dropout and failure rates are abnormally high (fewer than 40% of economics students and 25% of science students in any entering class graduate within 4 years).

3.2 Preschool Education

The small amount of preschool education that exist in Senegal was mentioned in Sect. 3.1.

3.3 Special Education

In the early 1990s, special education for students with physical, intellectual, and emotional disabilities was still not well-developed. There were only 5 special schools in 1992 providing programs for about 400 students. Because of the lack of reliable statistics in this field, the total needs of the country in special education are not well-known. It is interesting to note that most of the centers for special education have been functioning since 1981, which was the international year for the disabled. The integration of disabled students (mainly those with physical disabilities) into mainstream schools and classes is undertaken.

3.4 Vocational, Technical, and Business Education

After having completed three years of education in lower-secondary schools, students can be offered vocational training in technical secondary schools, vocational schools, or some specialized job centers. The programs provided are in agriculture, animal husbandry, water and forestry, fishing, gardening, mechanics, electricity, metal construction, boiler-making, carpentry, secretaryship, accountancy, computing, trade, and handicrafts.

The major problem facing vocational training is that of decreasing enrollment. Most of the schools are state schools and their aim is to provide qualified personnel for government offices. However, since 1985, Senegal has embarked on an adjustment program which has among its many objectives the reduction of the number of civil servants. An innovation introduced in 1990 aims at having enrollment in public vocational schools from private institutions and from private individuals. This enrollment is adjusted to the capacity of the training structures which is insufficient for the country's needs. Because of the lack of state provision, there has been a proliferation of private vocational schools (particularly in Dakar) offering courses in business training (secretaryship, accountancy, and computing).

An aim of the 1990 innovation was to make vocational training more appropriate to labor market demand both in terms of quantity and quality. This intention has remained a mere slogan, since adequate mechanisms for linking working and training places had not yet been established in the early 1990s.

3.5 Adult and Nonformal Education

There is no age limit to access to higher education. Therefore, adult participation in formal education, which was low in the period 1960–1970, increased considerably during the 1980s. It is estimated that adults comprise 15 percent of the total enrollment of formal schooling. About two-thirds of these adults are aged 25 years or more.

Enrollments in the nonformal sector are, by their nature, more difficult to estimate. Nonformal education, which is provided by the literacy ministry and some nongovernmental organizations, aims at reducing the high illiteracy rate (62%). Vigorous action has been taken in this area since 1984, with the help of many donors. The government is responsible for the definition of strategies and methods, for the conception and production of didactic material, and for the training of trainers. Achievements have included the production of textbooks in six local languages and the training of more than 15,000 teachers. The number of illiterates was considerably reduced (by 25.9% between 1970 and 1990).

Job training has emerged as an area of considerable importance in nonformal education. However, the taxation system which compels employers to allocate 1 percent of their payroll to the government for the implementation of training programs has not yet had a major impact in this sector. The *Office National de Formation Professionnelle* (National Office for Professional Training), which was set up for this purpose, was still in the process of organizing nonformal job training in the early 1990s.

Table 2
Enrollment at the different levels of education 1983–84 and 1989–90

Level of education	1983–84 Number of Schools	Number of classes	Enrollment	1989–90 Number of schools	Number of classes	Enrollment
Preschool	95	121[a]	9,414	145	485	15,964
Primary	2,150	9,822	533,394	2,422	11,171	682,925
Middle						
lower	197	1,947	88,890	253	2,512	127,375
secondary	—	—	—	—	—	—
General and technical						
secondary	43	641	24,127	59	1,033	39,288
Tertiary	—	—	11,293	—	—	15,231

Source: DPRE (1990)
a figure is for public schools only

4. Administrative and Supervisory Structure and Operation

Education is the responsibility of the government in Senegal. The Ministry of Education recruits and appoints the teachers in government schools; supplies buildings, equipment, and materials; and provides some limited funding for use by schools. However, responsibility for administration and staffing has been devolved to the regional inspectorates for education. The inspectorates provide the direct link between Head Office and the schools. A 1993 reform aims at giving more power to inspectorates (deconcentration policy).

Private schools must meet prescribed minimum educational standards for registration and funding purposes and must teach the national curriculum. There is one office in the Ministry of Education that is in charge of controlling the quality of teaching that is provided in these schools and of determining government subsidies to them.

5. Educational Finance

Funds for education come mainly from the government's national budgets and, at a lower level, from local funds (rural and urban communities, parent–teacher associations); and finally from foreign aid (especially in capital investment). Table 3 presents information on recurrent expenditures for the period 1986 to 1989.

Recurrent education expenditure increased by about 22 percent in nominal terms and by 26 percent in real terms between 1986–87 and 1989–90, increasing its share in the overall recurrent budget from 22.3 to about 26.0 percent. This increase was attributable to a 14 percent increase in salaries and a 55 percent increase in expenditures on transfers (mainly to higher education). However, nominal expenditures on supplies and maintenance stagnated, thus falling in real

Table 3
Education recurrent expenditures, 1986–90[a]

	1986–87	1987–88	1988–89	1989–90
Wages	38.8	40.3	40.9	44.5
Supplies and maintenance	2.7	1.9	2.8	3.0
Transfers	9.7	11.4	11.4	15.0
Total education expenditure	51.3	53.6	55.2	62.5
Total government expenditure	230.0	236.4	241.6	242.0

a in billions of CFA francs (US$1 = CFA 270 (1990))

Table 4
Estimated unit costs per student in US dollars, 1990[a]

Level	Unit cost
Preschool	348.7
Primary	140.7
Lower-secondary	607.4
Upper-secondary	788.8
Tertiary	3,003.7

a US$1=CFA 270 (1990)

terms. This pattern of expenditure has contributed to the deterioration of the school infrastructure to such an extent that expansion is jeopardized by the magnitude of resources that must be set aside for rehabilitation. Budget allocations for operating expenditures are generally committed as a whole. However, payments are usually very slow owing to the cash flow difficulties that the state experienced for several years.

As for capital expenditure, it should be noted that local communities have built more than 50 percent of the total primary school infrastructure. Donors, through various projects, have played an important role in this field (mainly at postprimary levels).

Education is free according to the law. Nevertheless, in higher education, students are required to meet part of the costs of their tuition. The figure is set at about US$18 per year, except for those students eligible for financial assistance (10 to 15% of the total enrollment). At lower levels (primary and secondary), Pupils' Parent Associations raise funds in many schools to help in the implementation of educational initiatives. There are no reliable statistics about the exact amount of such fundraising. The estimated unit costs per student in 1990 are given in Table 4.

6. Supplying Personnel for the Education System

In 1990, the number of full-time teachers employed in schools was 16,130. Nearly 1,790 people worked in nonteaching positions. About 11,395 teachers were employed in primary schools and 4,735 in secondary schools. Nearly 22 percent of school teachers were female. However, men were more likely than women to occupy senior administrative positions in schools.

Since 1970, vigorous measures have been taken to cope with teacher shortages and to localize teaching staff. There seem to be perennial shortages of teachers in areas such as mathematics, physical sciences, and classical languages (Latin and Greek). Schools in rural areas and unattractive suburbs are often difficult to staff. Government policy consists of posting new teachers to these areas for at least two years before examining their application for a position in urban schools. There is an annual average of 2 percent resignation rate among teachers. Structural adjustment programs implemented since 1979–80, which include reducing the size of public offices, have limited drastically the supply of teachers since at least the early 1980s. This situation has led to the intensification of teacher utilization, especially in primary schools.

Teacher training occurs in teacher-training institutions. The government is responsible for determining acceptable teacher qualifications. There are two types of primary teacher-training institutions, according to whether trainees have completed lower- or upper-secondary education. Both courses last one year. A total of four years of higher education is required to enter secondary teacher-training institutions for a one-year training course in education. The training of private school teachers is provided by the schools themselves. Catholic schools have set up their own training institutions to cope with their own needs.

Teacher promotion in the public sector is automatic and depends on the provisions of teachers' career structures that are defined by law. Every year, only 60 percent of those eligible for promotion are promoted due to budget constraints. Seniority rather than merit determines promotion.

Considerable effort is directed at the improvement of the quality of teachers' initial training. The Human Resources Development Project to be implemented in the mid-1990s is expected to modernize facilities and equipment and enhance the competence of trainers. Teachers' continuing professional development is not well-organized. Nevertheless, at the primary level, it is interesting to note that a compulsory two hours per week peer coaching has been organized in every school since 1972.

7. Curriculum Development and Teaching Methodology

All students, at every level of the system, are exposed to a standardized curriculum provided by the government. At the primary level, the curriculum covers many subjects: reading, writing, arithmetic, science, history and geography, expressive and performing arts, and physical education. They are taught by one classroom teacher. In secondary schools, foreign languages are introduced as mandatory subjects: one in lower-secondary, and two in upper-secondary. Students choose between English, German, and Arabic as their first foreign language, and one of these languages or Spanish, Portuguese, Italian, or Russian as their second foreign language.

Learning materials are mainly imported from France. However, considerable effort is being directed to set up a national capacity in this field with the help of the World Bank and Japanese cooperation. At the primary level, some books are produced by the Ministry. A project aimed at restructuring this endeavor into a more commercial unit is being implemented.

8. The System of Examinations, Promotions, and Certifications

In every Senegalese school, students are promoted from grade to grade according to their performance and the decision of the board of teachers. The first formal certificate is awarded to students at the end of primary school after they have successfully passed the external national examination (CEPE). A national external examination is organized every year for those who have completed primary, lower-secondary, or upper-secondary school. Students' academic achievement during their career within any cycle of education is only considered at the end of the secondary school examination and especially when the performance of a student at the external examination is slightly below average.

Educational assessment and evaluation are not very well developed. There is an increasing emphasis on research, basically encouraged and funded by donors. In the early 1990s, no national priorities had yet been defined in this field. Higher education, which is supposed to be the catalyst for research, has not yet developed an educational research tradition.

9. Educational Assessment, Evaluation, and Research

The pressure for more quality in education has caused the Ministry of Education to show additional concern geared toward improving pupil achievement. This is all the more necessary because the system is operating in a diversity of situations (double shift classes, multigrade classes, conventional classes) resulting from the need to adjust to the economic crisis the country is undergoing. For that purpose, the government designed in 1993 a system which seeks to cost-effectively collect and disseminate valid and reliable information about student achievement throughout the country. The Ministry is also interested in monitoring progress, measured by outcomes, over time into the future.

At national level, many institutions (both governmental and nongovernmental) have been chosen in order to guarantee objectivity, accountability, and efficiency. A foreign institution which specializes in this field has been selected to help the country set up a reliable system of assessing achievement. The assessment, which is sample-based, is designed on the criterion-referenced model in French, mathematics, and science. The target population is Grades 2, 4, and 6 of elementary education, over a period of 5 years. Particular emphasis is made on the development of software that can facilitate sampling procedures collection and analyses of data. Special attention is given to training and report writing for different target populations. The implementation cost is estimated to be around US$186,000 and is comprised of various activities (training, technical assistance, software development, computer equipment, testing operations).

The management of the assessment system is the responsibility of the National Institute for Research and Actions for the Development of Education (INEADE). The National Examination Service, along with the Teachers Training School (ENS), the Board of Regional Inspectors, and the Directorate of Educational Planning and Reform, are the key institutions that are cooperating in the National Assessment System.

It is expected that such assessment and evaluation activities will promote research in education which has thus far been very poorly developed. In fact, even though the government has always declared its intention to give more emphasis to research, educational institutions have not been organized to absorb the findings. Sectorial researches done by educational services are not edited and disseminated because of a lack of policy in this area. That is why, despite the presence of INEADE (created in the late 1970s), the culture for research has not yet spread across the institutions.

10. Major Reforms in the 1980s and 1990s

After the important meeting called *Les Etats Généraux de l'Education* in 1981 and the report that followed in 1985, the government of Senegal decided in 1987 to undertake a serious reform of its educational system. The main objectives of this reform were:

(a) implementation of a national, democratic, and popular education program,

(b) compulsory free education for children aged from 3 to 16 years,

(c) progressive introduction of national languages into the curriculum,

(d) introduction of productive activities into schools in order to give some practical skills along with the traditional theoretical ones,

(e) the reshaping of educational time and space,

(f) improvement of the mechanisms of grade promotion and the changing of the examination-oriented pedagogical practices.

The authorities have been cautious thus far in the strategies adopted to implement the reform. This can be explained by at least four factors:

(a) the complexity and variety of sectors to cope with at the same time (training, equipment, facilities, curricula, extramural activities, partners, etc.),

(b) human resources capacities,

(c) institutional capacity,

(d) huge financial needs.

Therefore, the option of proceeding step by step had led the Ministry of Educaiton to start the reform by changing teaching methods (pedagogy by objectives, modular system). Some experimentation classes called "pilot classes" have been opened in both government and private schools in every region in Senegal. By 1991–92, a further big step forward was taken with the experimentation of "pilot schools." This phase of the reform aims at changing the organization of the schools through the following:

(a) design and implementation of school projects based on the opportunities provided by the environment where schools are located and which foster skills like agriculture, husbandry, commerce, etc.;

(b) involvement of local communities in different activities undertaken by schools (e.g., policy designing, financial and professional support, etc.);

(c) partnership with all economic or cultural agents operating within the environment of the schools.

A total of 100 pilot schools have been chosen for the experimentation. Nevertheless, some nongovernmental organizations working in education have been authorized to experiment with the reform on samples selected by themselves. They are expected to report their findings to the Directorate of Educational Planning and Reform. Generalization may take place after the evaluation which is scheduled for 1996.

Apart from this structural reform, minor changes in the educational system include the introduction of different courses aimed at meeting new learning needs (health, family and population, environmental protection, etc.) promoted by donors.

Reforms in Senegal have suffered greatly from the high turnover of ministers in the Department of Education (4 different ministers held the position from 1988 to 1992). Therefore, instability in the political management of the system can be considered to be a major element in the delay experienced in the progress of the 1981 reform. In addition, economic crises have made the shifting of national priorities from education to other sectors more rewarding. In such an environment, the model of schooling contained in the 1981 reform is extremely hard to implement.

11. Major Problems for the Year 2000

The major problems faced by the Senegalese educational system for the year 2000 will be:

(a) the construction of a system which can promote social, cultural, scientific, and economic progress;

(b) the availability of resources to support the expansion of basic education for all and the development of the quality of education at postprimary levels;

(c) the correction of major gender, regional, and economic disparities and inequalities;

(d) the modernization of the educational system so that it is compatible with world progress in the areas of science and technology;

(e) the decentralization of school management,

planning and financing to local communities;

(f) the development of private education at the tertiary level to cope with growing demand.

Bibliography

Direction of Educational Planning and Reform (DPRE) 1990 *Statistical Yearbook of Education.* Ministry of Education, Dakar

Direction of Planning *Senegal's 8th Social and Economic Development Plan (1990–1996).* Ministry of Planning and Cooperation, Dakar

Director of Reform and Basic Education 1987 *Senegal: The New School.* Ministry of Education, Dakar

Seychelles

B. Shamlaye

1. General Background

The Republic of Seychelles, in the southwest Indian Ocean, is one of the smallest sovereign states. It consists of some 115 islands with a total land area of 455 square kilometers, spread over a sea area of 1 million square kilometers. Originally uninhabited, the Seychelles experienced first French and then British colonial rule before achieving Independence in 1976. The population of 67,378 people (1990 estimate) is of mixed African, Asian (Indian and Chinese), and European descent. It is concentrated on the four main islands of Mahe, Praslin, La Digue, and Silhouette. The average annual growth rate between 1980 and 1990 was 0.6 percent.

Seychellois Kreol is the mother tongue of virtually the whole population and is the first national language, the others being English and French. English remains, however, the main language of business and government and is the main medium of instruction after the first four years of schooling.

In 1990, the number of persons in formal employment was 23,500, some 35 percent of the total population. The trend since about 1970 shows a decline in primary-sector employment with an increase in the secondary and especially the tertiary sectors. The increase in the latter sector reflects the growth of tourism as well as of the social services, notably education and health. Not surprisingly for a small country, the Seychelles is heavily dependent on imports. The 1990 import–export ratio was estimated at 11:1. Tourism is the main foreign exchange earner,

with fisheries steadily increasing its contribution. The gross domestic product at 1989 market prices was Seychelles Rupees (SR) 1,703 million (US$328 million). The Gross National Product (GNP) per capita was SR24,145 (approximately US$4,643).

The development of the Seychelles at the end of the 1980s and beginning of the 1990s was shaped predominantly by the policies of the government in office since 1977. The aims of this government (formed by the Seychelles Peoples Progressive Front [SPPF]) were stated as being to maintain the independence of the country; to improve the standards of living of its citizens; to respect human rights and guarantee the equality and dignity of all; to utilize the natural resources of land and sea for the development of the country; and to follow a policy of positive nonalignment in foreign relations. The government has brought significant changes in the social, economic, and cultural life of the country. Education, seen as a key factor in the transformation of society, has itself undergone major changes.

While upholding the fundamental principles upon which its program has been based, the government decided to change the political system from a single-party popular democracy to a multiparty democracy and a new constitution will be promulgated and elections held at the end of 1992.

2. Politics and the Goals of the Education System

Education policy in the Seychelles is guided by three main principles: education for all; education for life;

and education for personal and national development.

Education is considered to be a crucial factor in the creation of national unity as well as of a more egalitarian society. In the late 1970s and early 1980s, the school system was changed from one with better provision for the more economically and socially advantaged to a unitary system offering equality of opportunity to all. This was in line with the government's commitment to providing all Seychellois with the opportunity to achieve their full potential consistent with their abilities and interests and with the needs of society. Educational programs aim to develop knowledge, skills, and attitudes for personal development as well as for participation in society. At the higher levels, the system aims at meeting the labor force requirements of the country.

3. The Formal System of Education

3.1 Primary, Secondary, and Tertiary Education

Figure 1 outlines the structure of the formal education system.

A structural reform of the education system was begun in 1978. Primary schooling was extended from six to nine years, all children went to their district school, and schooling was made free and compulsory. In 1981 the two-year residential National Youth Service (NYS) was established for students wishing to continue at secondary level. In 1983 the Seychelles Polytechnic, regrouping the former upper-secondary and vocational schools and expanding the range of courses, was opened.

In 1991 another restructuring of the system was undertaken. Primary schooling of six years is to be provided in 25 district schools, followed by four years of secondary schooling in ten regional schools. The NYS is to last only one year. The program of school conversion and construction in line with the restructuring will be completed by 1995. New administrative structures are also being set up.

Education is compulsory from age 6 until the completion of the fourth grade of secondary school or the age of 17. There is virtually 100 percent attendance.

Primary education lasts for six years. A total of 10,078 children were enrolled in 25 schools in 1991. The average annual increase since 1970 was 0.4 percent. All schools are state schools and coeducational. The school day contains a little more than five hours of tuition. The school year comprises 200 days. The student–teacher ratio since 1989 has been 19:1.

As of 1991 compulsory secondary education lasts for four years. In that year there were 6,003 pupils at that level, compared with 1,980 in 1970, 3,614 in 1977, and 5,944 in 1985. Since 1970 the average annual increase has been 9.7 percent. The school day and school year at secondary level are similar to those of the primary school. In 1991 the student–teacher ratio was 18:1.

The NYS constitutes a fifth year of secondary schooling and also provides a global education that seeks to develop in students a spirit of solidarity and comradeship and qualities of self-discipline, initiative, and responsibility. Over 90 percent of secondary-school leavers join the NYS. In 1992 it had 1,378 students, almost equally divided between the two sexes. Students live in one of two residential villages for the one-year program, going home monthly and during the school holidays in April and August. The NYS also has a 200-day school calendar with around 6 hours of tuition per day. Its residential nature permits a large number of cocurricular social and cultural activities as well as organized study time. Students completing the NYS either go on to further studies or vocational training at the Seychelles Polytechnic (some 55%) or enter the world of work, some through apprenticeship schemes or work experience programs.

The Seychelles Polytechnic consists of 12 schools providing training courses in various vocational fields as well as preuniversity academic studies.

Table 1 indicates the number of students enrolled in 1991 in the schools of the Polytechnic (following courses ranging from one to four years) and also the number of successful graduates in that year.

Apart from courses in management run by the Seychelles Institute of Management, tertiary education is not available in Seychelles. Scholarships, a

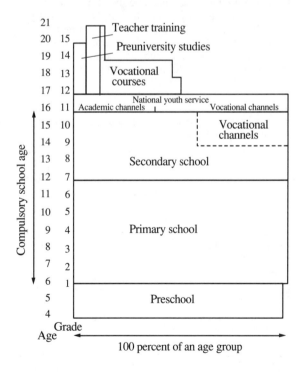

Figure 1
Seychelles: Structure of the formal education system 1992

number of which are funded through cooperation agreements with foreign states and organizations, are provided by the government for further education overseas. In 1991 there were 300 students in full-time education in some 25 countries.

Education and training is provided at no direct cost to the student throughout the formal education system.

3.2 Preschool Education

The state provides two years of free preschool education. The age of entry is 3½ to 4 years and virtually all eligible children attend. In 1991, 3,228 were enrolled in 33 preschools, administered as part of primary schools.

3.3 Special Education

The School for the Exceptional Child receives children with physical, mental, and emotional disabilities from the age of 4 to 16 or 17 years. In 1991 there were 75 pupils. Encouragement is given to integrating children with less severe disabilities into mainstream schools. Support structures in schools need to be developed.

3.4 Vocational, Technical, and Business Education

Vocational, technical, and business education is provided in the relevant schools of the Seychelles Polytechnic. The Seychelles Institute of Management provides courses in management, accountancy, and computing for persons already in employment.

In the Polytechnic schools, new courses are introduced or existing ones modified in response to

Table 1
Total enrollment in school of the Seychelles Polytechnic and number completing in 1991

	Enrollment	1991 Graduates
Agriculture	54	45
Art and design	150	27
Business studies	255	98
Construction studies	138	40
Education and community studies	302	51
(Education)	(241)	(44)
Engineering	158	70
Health studies	101	17
Hotel and tourism	132	69
Humanities and science	226	60
Maritime studies	80	27
Media studies	8	8
Total	1,604	512

emerging needs in the country's economy and changes in industry. Liaison with industry and employers generally as well as with the Ministry of Manpower is done through consultative committees. As part of their training, students undertake work experience attachments in industry.

The curriculum in secondary schools is being broadened to include prevocational studies in line with that of the NYS.

3.5 Adult and Nonformal Education

The School of Continuing Education of the Seychelles Polytechnic provides fee-paying evening classes in a range of subjects for adults. Participants attend in order to improve their secondary education, or trade skills, or to enhance employment prospects.

The school is also responsible for the organization of literacy and numeracy classes in the various districts of the country. These aim at the eradication of illiteracy, and the self-realization and increased participation in the affairs of society of individuals who did not have adequate schooling opportunities.

4. Administrative and Supervisory Structure and Operation

Not surprisingly given the size of the country, the education system is highly centralized with all functions executed by the different sections of the Ministry.

A principal secretary responsible to the Minister for Education is the head of the Ministry, which is divided into three main divisions each headed by a director-general. The Planning and Administration Division is responsible for physical planning and administration; the Education Management Division is responsible for the management of primary and secondary schools, the NYS, and the Seychelles Polytechnic; and, the Education Development Division is responsible for curriculum development, evaluation and research, and student assessment. Each division is made up of several sections, each headed by a director. An International Cooperation Section coordinates relations with foreign countries and international organizations and also administers scholarships for overseas courses.

Working groups are constituted as necessary to consider specific matters and make recommendations to an Education Planning and Development Committee which advises the Minister. There is also a permanent Management Committee consisting of the Minister, principal secretary, and directors-general which deals with both policy and administrative matters. Decisions on major policy issues are taken by the Council of Ministers.

5. Educational Finance

The state finances virtually the total cost of education. In 1991 educational expenditure accounted for 18.7 percent of the national budget and an estimated 7 percent of the gross domestic product. The proportion of the education budget allocated to general education (i.e., primary, secondary including the residential NYS, and preschool) was 57.5 percent and 16.5 percent to the Seychelles Polytechnic. A total of 11 percent was spent as the government's contribution, alongside that of donor countries and organizations, to overseas tertiary education costs. The annual unit cost for a primary/secondary pupil was SR3,967 (US$763), for an NYS student SR22,550, (US$4,337), and for a Polytechnic student SR14,606 (US$2,809).

6. Supplying Personnel for the Education System

In 1991 there was a total of 1,321 teachers in all educational establishments with 170 in preschools, 501 in primary schools, 335 in secondary schools, 102 in the NYS, and 194 in the various schools of the Seychelles Polytechnic. The Education Development Division had a staff of 50 persons, mainly curriculum developers. The Ministry of Education employed another 1,200 persons consisting mainly of administration personnel, youth workers in the NYS, and support staff. The teachers in preschools and primary schools are predominantly female, while at secondary and in the NYS and Polytechnic there are about equal numbers of women and men. The majority of headteachers of primary–secondary schools are female. Women are also well-represented in senior administrative positions in the Ministry of Education.

The significant expansion of education provision after 1978 necessitated the recruitment of teachers from abroad. In 1991, 40 percent of the teaching force at secondary, NYS, and Polytechnic level was expatriate. Efforts to attract young persons to the teaching profession are meeting with only a fair degree of success considering that the expanding economy provides many other job opportunities. A Teacher Scheme of Service with improved salary scales and gratuities to reward length of service was introduced in 1990. Links exist with overseas universities for the training of secondary teachers. In 1988 a program under which teachers train for two years at the School of Education before completing another two years at the University of Sussex in the United Kingdom to obtain a Bachelor of Education degree was started.

The School of Education only used to train teachers for preschools and primary schools. It now offers diploma (equivalent to the first year of university) courses for secondary-level teachers and has introduced teacher training in vocational subjects. Courses contain substantial teaching practice sessions in schools and trainees are assessed on practical teaching and, through examinations, on the theoretical compo-

nents. Teachers serve a one-year probation period before becoming eligible for permanent employment. Annual appraisals of teacher performance are made by headteachers and submitted to the Schools Section at the Ministry head office. Appraisal may be used to facilitate teacher counseling and the identification of professional development needs.

Inservice training sessions are held, mostly during part of the school holidays, to familiarize teachers with new materials or methodologies. Diploma courses, run on a part-time basis, provide opportunities for knowledge and skills upgrading as do short courses and degree courses overseas. Attention is also being paid to improving the administration of schools and a course has been set up in collaboration with the University of Quebec at Trois-Rivieres, Canada for the training of headteachers and school administrators in that domain.

7. Curriculum Development and Teaching Methodology

The Curriculum Development Section (CDS) of the Education Development Division of the Ministry is responsible for curriculum development for schools and the NYS. The CDS (staffed by curriculum development officers) prescribes the syllabuses for the various subjects, determines in great part the learning materials, and recommends the methodology to be used. Teachers are involved in varying degrees in the work of the CDS. Textbooks for primary schooling are in the main produced locally by CDS personnel, while a large proportion of textbooks for secondary classes are imported.

Since 1981 the medium of instruction in the first four years of schooling is Seychellois Kreol. English is introduced in the second term of the first grade (P1) of primary and becomes the medium for most subjects from P5. French is introduced in P4.

Pupils follow a common curriculum from P1 to the second year (S2) of secondary schooling, after which they enter into one of two channels of studies. One channel contains more vocational-oriented work (agriculture, art and design, social economics, and technology), whereas the other is more academic. In the S4 vocational channel students choose one of the vocational subjects as an option which they continue in the NYS. The core subjects of mathematics, English, French, science, history, and geography as well as physical education, art, and social education are taken by all pupils throughout the years of schooling. Music is limited to primary schools owing to a shortage of teachers. Computer studies were, in 1992, restricted to the NYS, but there are plans to extend this subject to secondary schools.

Work is in progress to modify the curriculum so that it will address the varying abilities and needs of pupils. At each level, learning objectives will be

855

defined in terms of core objectives attainable by the majority of pupils and extension objectives for the more advanced. Attention is also being given to slower learners.

Headteachers and studies coordinators are responsible for monitoring the implementation of the curriculum. Personnel from the CDS are in close contact with schools and teachers. However, more support could be given to teachers to help them in adapting the prescribed curriculum to the needs of their own pupils.

8. The System of Examinations, Promotions, and Certifications

Pupils are automatically promoted between year levels according to age with repetition occuring only in exceptional cases. Selection of students for the various courses at the Seychelles Polytechnic occurs at the end of the NYS.

The smallness of the system facilitates the testing of whole cohorts of pupils through national examinations. These are administered by the Education Development Division of the Ministry and occur at the end of Year 6 (P6), Year 8 (S2), and Year 11 (NYS). A number of students at the NYS and Polytechnic also take O-level examinations from English examining boards. A-level examinations, important for access to tertiary education overseas, are taken by students in certain schools of the Polytechnic.

Certificates are issued at the end of primary schooling (P6), compulsory schooling (S4), and the NYS. The Polytechnic issues certificates to students successfully completing its courses.

New methods of pupil assessment such as profiling and assessment through coursework are being introduced to give recognition to a wide range of academic, practical, and social achievements and to decrease dependence on end-of-cycle examinations. Emphasis is increasingly being placed on assessment serving curriculum aims and not subverting them. Counseling of students for study and career decision-making is also growing.

9. Educational Assessment, Evaluation, and Research

With increasing emphasis being placed on the qualitative improvement of education, the development of an evaluation and research capacity to inform decision-making has become a recognized necessity. In 1992 the Evaluation and Research Section was established.

Priorities for research include the use of the three national languages in schooling; teachers and teaching; the cognitive development of the Seychellois child; vocational education; and ability grouping of pupils.

10. Major Reforms in the 1980s and 1990s

The education system experienced considerable reform in the late 1970s and 1980s as a result of the government's program for social and economic transformation. Increased provision and equitable resourcing of schools resulted in education at all levels being accessible to young people regardless of socioeconomic background. These changes, together with changes in society generally, resulted in new challenges. The need to diversify and broaden the curriculum to suit the comprehensive nature of the school population and to respond to the demands of a developing economy continue to retain the attention of administrators, curriculum developers, and teachers in the 1990s. The restructuring of the system, begun in 1991, also indicates a concern with making it more efficient and cost-effective. The introduction of private schooling as an alternative to the state school is a likely development.

11. Major Problems for the Year 2000

Finding the resources for the further improvement of the system as well as for training the greater number of students at tertiary level needed for the country's development will be a major challenge. Dependence on overseas institutions will continue and it is unlikely that the idea of a regional university of the Indian Ocean with faculties in member countries will be realized in the 1990s.

The reduction of the high proportion of expatriate teachers by attracting young persons to the teaching profession will remain a key objective, as will the professional development of teachers and education personnel generally. Curriculum development, student assessment and counseling, greater parental participation in education, and school administration are other priority areas for attention. Generally, the challenge will continue to be that of strengthening the national capability to maintain and develop an educational system responsive to the needs of a small but dynamic developing nation.

Bibliography

Management & Information Systems Division 1991 *Republic of Seychelles Statistical Abstract*. Government of Seychelles, Victoria
Ministry of Education 1985 *Education for the New Society*. Government of Seychelles, Victoria
Seychelles Government 1991 *National Development Plan 1990–1994*. Government of Seychelles, Victoria

Sierra Leone

W. A. Taylor and A. B. Sesay

1. General Background

Sierra Leone lies on the west coast of Africa. It has an area of approximately 73,326 square kilometers. It extends approximately 328 kilometers from west to east, and is bounded on the west and southwest by the Atlantic Ocean; on the northwest, north, and northeast by the Republic of Guinea; and on the east and southeast by the Republic of Liberia.

For administrative purposes, the country is divided into the Western Area (in which is located Freetown, the capital city) and the Provinces which, prior to Independence in April 1961, were known as the Protectorate. There are in all three provinces—the Northern, Eastern, and Southern. These are in turn divided into districts with the North having 5, the East 3, and the South 4.

The founding of the colony of Freetown in 1787 was prompted by, among other factors, the desire to establish a land for Africans liberated from slavery. Owing to this humanitarian background, schools were established almost from the arrival of the first settlers in the colony. The arrival of the missionary societies from 1804 onward, led by the Church Missionary Society and the Wesleyan Society, saw an expansion in the number of schools, and these two societies had between them 28 schools in the colony by 1840. It was not until the hinterland of the colony became a British protectorate in 1896 that missionary bodies like the United Brethren Church in America and African Methodist Episcopal Church began to open schools in Sierra Leone. This early contact with Western civilization by the Western Area gave it an edge over the rest of the country in terms of educational provision and development. Following closely are the Southern and Eastern provinces, with the Northern trailing. Although much has been achieved by way of closing the gap, the historical pattern in the establishment of schools is still evident in the education scene in the 1990s.

According to the provisional figures of the 1985 census, the population stood at 3.7 million, which represents a 28.5 percent increase over the 1974 census figures. It has an annual average growth of 2.9 percent. The settlement pattern shows that the majority of the population lives in settlements of less than 1,000 people, and 17.2 percent of these settlements contain less than 100 persons. Such communities tend to be too small to support a full school. This situation has resulted in the establishment of "feeder schools" in the small villages. Such schools may usually have students up to class II level, after which they may transfer to bigger schools in larger neighboring villages.

There is a considerable ethnic variety in the population. Over 13 tribal languages are spoken, with Mende and Temne being spoken by a majority of the people. An important medium of communication is Krio, the *lingua franca*, which is widely understood. English continues to be the official and commercial language of the country. In addition to traditional African religions and customs, Christianity and Islam are widely practiced and educational institutions sponsored by both religions abound.

Sierra Leone has substantial economic potential as it possesses minerals and other natural resources as well as a favorable climate for the cultivation of tropical crops. Agricultural activities account for about 65 percent of the labor force and constitute about 30 to 35 percent of the Gross National Product (GNP). The mining industry and services sectors constitute the rest.

The early 1980s witnessed the continued decline of the economy as a result of both internal and external factors. The reduction in exports and the gradual depletion of the country's mineral resources resulted in low domestic income and a sharp increase in the price of imported oil. In addition, an over-valued domestic currency (the Leone) depressed producer prices for exports such as coffee and cocoa. The scarcity of foreign exchange limited the import of agricultural inputs which resulted in low production and the establishment of parallel market activities.

Economic performance has tended to fluctuate from year to year but the overall trend has been a deceleration in growth. The average Gross Domestic Product (GDP) growth rate decreased from 37 percent in 1965–73 to 1.9 percent in 1973–83. Per capita GDP was estimated at US$260, $128, and $102 in 1984, 1985, and 1986 respectively.

Financing of the current account deficit was mainly through external borrowing resulting in an external outstanding debt of US$512 million in 1982, rising to US$659 million in 1987. Consequently the country has outstanding arrears to financial creditors and other donors.

Despite the Government efforts at economic reforms in 1988 and 1989, external fiscal and financial imbalances have persisted. The government has therefore decided to carry out a comprehensive economic reform program with the International Monetary Fund (IMF) and the World Bank.

2. Politics and the Goals of the Education System

The All People's Congress (APC) has virtually ruled Sierra Leone since it came into power in 1968. Its position was reinforced when, after a referendum in 1978, Sierra Leone became a one-party state under the APC. With effect from October 1, 1991, a multi-party system was once again restored by an Act of Parliament.

The Government's overall policy regarding education has been guided by several comprehensive policies and programs. Among the most important have been: The Addis Ababa Conference of African Ministers of Education (1961); the Report of Education Planning Groups (1961); the Ten Year Economic and Social Development Plan (1962–63 to 1971–72); the White Paper on Educational Policy (1970); the Sierra Leone Education Review (1974); the Education Sector Review (1979); and the Second National Development Plan (1981–82 to 1985–86).

The general aim of educational policy has been to provide every child with an education which takes fully into account character development; interest, intelligence, and aptitude; the country's labor force needs; and the economic resources of the state, so that the child's education may become useful to the country and at the same time provide him or her with opportunities to succeed in life.

Against the foregoing background, the policies have resulted in the rapid expansion of educational institutions at all levels throughout the country. Greater emphasis has been put on primary, secondary, technical/vocational training, and the ruralization of education.

3. The Formal System of Education

3.1 Primary, Secondary, and Tertiary Education

Table 1 presents enrollments in the major education sectors. Figure 1 presents the structure.

The present formal system of education consists of six years of primary schooling (6–11 age group), five years of secondary (12–16 age group) and a two-year higher-secondary (17–18 age group) followed by tertiary education, particularly teacher training and

university education. Entry from the primary to the secondary level is through the Selective Entrance Examination (SEE) conducted by the West African Examination Council (WAEC). The examination consists of tests in English, mathematics, and verbal and quantitative aptitude. Successful candidates are admitted into a limited number of Form One places at the secondary level.

Despite the 30 percent increase in enrollment between 1980 and 1987, the enrollment ratio at the primary level remains very low. In addition, there are large disparities between urban and rural areas and these can be as high as 73 percent for urban and

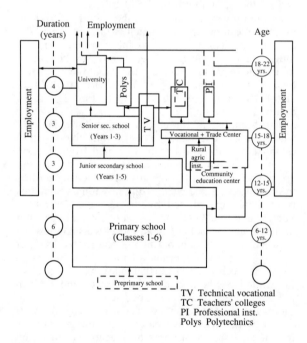

TV Technical vocational
TC Teachers' colleges
PI Professional inst.
Polys Polytechnics

Figure 1
Sierra Leone: Outline of the new structure of the education system 1992

Table 1
Enrollments in formal education, Sierra Leone

	Primary 1988–89	Secondary 1988–89	Teachers College 1989–90	University 1989–90
Number of students	393,593	101,695	3,120	2,125
Number of institutions	2,312[a]	205	6[b]	1[c]
Number of teachers	12,272	5,418	—	—
Student–teacher ratio	32:1	25:1[d]	—	—

a Includes 942 feeder schools   b Five out of six train primary-school teachers   c Comprises three constituent colleges   d Used to determine number of teachers to which a school is entitled

20 percent for sparsely populated areas. Limited access to primary school could be attributed to geographical factors (e.g., difficult rugged terrain, population settlement patterns {about 63% of the population live in settlements of less than 1,000 people which could not support a primary school}). Thus, children have to walk long distances to reach a school. Other factors are poverty and poor quality of education. Parents have had to bear about 85 percent of the cost of schooling their children by providing them with textbooks, exercise books, and school uniforms, which not many parents can afford. The poor state of many school buildings, overcrowded classrooms, inadequate furniture and equipment, and a high percentage of unqualified teachers contribute to the poor quality of education.

The normal secondary cycle is five years in length and leads to the General Certificate of Education Ordinary-level (GCE O-level) examination of the WAEC. A very limited number of students go on to do the GCE Advanced Examination also conducted by the WAEC. The system is very academic and is heavily oriented toward passing the Advanced level in order to go on to university. The situation at the secondary level is slightly different from that at the primary. An enrollment increase of 57 percent was recorded between 1980 and 1987, and the estimated growth enrollment ratio of 17 percent in 1983 is just below the average of 18 percent for sub-Saharan Africa. At the secondary level, the state of school buildings is comparatively better although lack of equipment and the shortage of teachers to teach special subjects such as metalwork, technical drawing, and mathematics also constitutes a major problem. The pupil–teacher ratio is 32:1 for primary and 25:1 for secondary schools. However, this in no way limits the size of classes which may exceed 50 at both levels.

Tertiary education is offered at five primary and one secondary teacher-training colleges, two technical institutes, and the University of Sierra Leone with its three constituent colleges—Fourah Bay College, Njala University College, and the College of Medicine and Allied Health Sciences.

Although higher education in Sierra Leone has the longest history of all West African countries—Fourah Bay College having been founded as early as 1827—tertiary institutions today suffer from a variety of problems which are mainly linked to the country's economic difficulties and insufficient budgeting allocations made by the government, the payment of which is often delayed.

The majority of the primary, secondary, and postsecondary institutions in the country are mixed. There is no legal restriction on access to all levels of education regardless of ethnic, sectional, political, or religious affiliation.

The school day lasts for approximately 5 to 6 hours, and the school week runs from Monday to Friday, with a few Moslem schools operating from Sunday to Thursday. The academic year consists of three terms running from September to July at the primary and secondary levels, making a total of 39 weeks. The duration of the academic year at the tertiary level is approximately 37 weeks.

The move taken by Nigeria and Ghana to withdraw from the O- and A-level examinations conducted by the WAEC, in order to have their own national school-leaving certificates by 1991, had far-reaching implications for the education system in Sierra Leone and the other member countries. With both Nigeria and Ghana withdrawing from the WAEC, the unit cost for developing these examinations becomes prohibitive. In addition, the computer personnel and other resources in Sierra Leone and the Gambia are not adequate to service the examinations for the smaller countries. Against this background, the government of Sierra Leone set up a task force to, among other things, study the possibility of Sierra Leone conducting its own national high-school leaving certificate examinations and, at the same time, seek international recognition for such certificates. The task force also recommended a new structure of 6 years in primary school, 3 years in junior-secondary, 3 years in senior-secondary, and 4 years in tertiary education scheduled to come into effect in the 1992–93 academic year.

3.2 Preschool Education

Preschool education in Sierra Leone dates back to 1966 when the first nursery school, Dove Cot Nursery, was founded in Freetown. There are in all about 80 nursery schools in the country, most of which are located in Freetown and other urban areas. They cater for children aged 2 to 5 years. They are mainly established by the Nursery Schools Association. Preprimary education is voluntary and the government is not directly responsible for this level of education. The government does, however, contribute to the salaries of teachers in these schools.

3.3 Special Education

A National Association of the Societies of the Handicapped comprising the Sierra Leone Society for the Deaf, the Sierra Leone Blind Welfare Society, the Sierra Leone Society for the Mentally Retarded, and the Sierra Leone Cheshire Home Foundation (which deals with the physically handicapped) has been formed. Each of these societies runs a primary school, with the schools for the blind and the mentally retarded respectively being residential. All the schools are located in Freetown, with the exception of the Cheshire Home which has a branch at Bo, the provincial headquarters of the Southern Province.

All four societies share the conviction that educational efforts for the handicapped should be integrated with the normal school system and work toward that goal. To this end, some blind students have been able to go through university, and other physically handicapped children are enrolled in regular primary and secondary schools.

However, it is estimated that the number of students registered in schools run by the four societies account for only 1 percent of the total number of physically handicapped children of school age in the country.

3.4 Vocational, Technical, and Business Education

Since 1970, the Sierra Leone government has emphasized the importance of technical, vocational, agricultural, and commercial education and pledged to give them priority.

Equipment has been provided for the diversification of the curriculum of secondary schools. Two technical institutes and two trade centers have been extended and upgraded. The emphasis on technical and vocational education continued in a project with the provision of buildings and/or equipment for 19 secondary schools and trade schools. A technical and vocational training program for teachers for secondary schools was also established at the Milton Margai Teachers College to produce the much-needed teachers for secondary schools. In the Sierra Leone National Development Plan 1974–75 to 1978–79, one of the major policy objectives was that of an acceleration of the expansion of technical education.

Technical, vocational, and business education are provided for within the formal education system at secondary schools, technical and vocational institutions, and at trade centers. There is no policy regarding which students should receive vocational training. However, until the 1980s, low status was attached to technical and vocational education and there was a feeling that only low achievers entered vocational streams in schools.

There is little or no relationship between training and labor market requirements, and there is also inadequate liaison between training institutions and employers. Consequently, a number of certificate holders leaving a trade center could not find employment in the trade in which they had their training.

The demand for teachers in these areas also poses a great problem for the system. The conditions of service for teachers are still lower than for other comparative positions. As a result, teachers with professional qualifications and industrial experience are in short supply.

Mention should be made of the program at the Young Women's Christian Association (YWCA) Vocational Institute which leads to the Certificate in Vocational Studies. The emphasis here is on vocational training with a strong practical bias for occupational middle-level fields. Designed to train adolescent girls for employment, the three-year program leads to the award of the first indigenous vocational certificate in the country.

3.5 Adult and Nonformal Education

The government's involvement in adult literacy dates back to 1946 when the Provincial Literacy Bureau (subsequently renamed the Bunumbu Press) initiated a national literacy campaign. The overall policy was to make as many people as possible literate in their vernacular language. This was considered a precondition for literacy in English. Until 1967 the Ministry of Social Welfare was responsible for adult literacy education. In 1967 the Ministry of Education assumed overall responsibility for adult education in the country.

In 1976, the Adult Education Unit was established within the Ministry of Education with a limited operational capacity and meager financial resources. The activities of the Unit were restricted to urban centers.

The rapidly increasing social demand for formal education during the 1970s reduced the out-of-school programs. The present illiteracy rates, estimated at 85 percent nationally and 90 percent in the rural areas, might be a direct consequence of the neglect of nonformal education in the 1970s.

The general objectives of the literacy program include the elimination of illiteracy in Sierra Leone by coordinated efforts directed toward the provision of literacy, basic education, vocational and technical skills, and continuing education among youths and adults.

The number of adult education providers has increased over the years. The *National Directory of Adult Education Providers in Sierra Leone*, published by the Institute of Adult Education and Extra Mural Studies in 1986, listed 144 organizations/institutions, both governmental and nongovernmental, providing adult education. Their activities range from literacy education to community development, health education, agricultural extension, and labor education.

The Adult Education Unit of the Ministry of Education serves as the secretariat for the National Literacy Committee (NLC), which is chaired by the Chief Education Officer. The NLC is a forum for adult literacy educators and provides support services such as training and materials production. Actual disbursement by the government remains small and the bulk of support has come from external sources, in particular the German Adult Education program (DVV).

4. Administrative and Supervisory Structure and Operation

The entire system of education, including the university, comes under the Ministry of Education. The system is highly centralized, although regional principal education officers have been appointed to head the Ministry's offices in the three provinces. Private schools account for a very small percentage of all schools in the country. They are largely free from governmental direction as they receive no government

Table 2
Educational recurrent expenditure percentage of government budget (thousands of Leones)

	1980–81	1981–82	1982–83	1983–84	1984–85	1985–86	1986–87	1987–88	1988–89	1989–90
Total government budget	361,859	442,558	427,074	608,097	545,591	899,541	1,287,710	1,579,647	2,321,296	4,249,229
Total education budget	47,204	58,249	60,750	63,991	82,991	97,717	224,983	425,418	420,224	576,552
Percentage of education share	13.00	13.20	14.20	10.50	15.20	10.90	17.47	26.93	18.16	13.51

funding. Prior approval for them to operate, however, has to be obtained from the Ministry and they are obliged to meet prescribed minimum educational standards.

The administration of the primary system is largely carried out in cooperation with employing authorities, which for the most part consist of religious bodies, both christian and muslim; municipal and local authorities; and private groups. At the primary level, the day-to-day running of the school is delegated by the Ministry to the employing authority which for the most part leaves it in the hands of the headteacher. There is also close supervision by supervisors and inspectors of schools (primary) from the Ministry of Education.

At the secondary level, this task is carried out by boards of governors which are jointly appointed by the Minister of Education and the proprietors of the respective schools. Each board comprises five members representing the proprietors and seven representing the Ministry of Education. There are also inspectors of schools (secondary). It should be mentioned that the government owns and controls a few secondary schools (13) and a number of district education committee schools which were, until 1972, run by the district councils.

The heads of trade centers and technical institutes are responsible directly to the Principal Education Officer (Technical and Science) at the Ministry.

The Ministry of Education determines the fees to be paid in all of these institutions, as well as the dates of terms and holidays. The salaries of all approved teachers are paid by the Ministry which also pays running costs to all assisted schools and gives development grants on request.

At the tertiary level, the Principal Education Officer (Teacher Education) administers the five primary teacher colleges through boards. The Ministry is represented on the council of the Milton Margai Teachers College, an autonomous college, by an Act of Parliament. The university, comprising three constituent colleges, is financed by government mainly through subsidies paid to each of the colleges as statutory bodies.

5. Educational Finance

Recurrent expenditure for education as a percentage of total recurrent budget 1980–81 to 1989–90 is shown in Table 2.

The government's recurrent expenditure on the education sector for the period 1980–81 to 1989–90 accounts on average for 15.3 percent of the government's total recurrent budget.

By far the largest share of the educational budget comes from government. However, funds provided by nongovernmental organizations, parents, religious bodies, and the private sector, as well as external assistance from international and multilateral sources, constitute significant contributions. The latter are usually in the form of financial and technical assistance with experts and consultants, scholarships, fellowships, construction of physical facilities, and the supply of equipment and materials.

Table 2 also shows that although education's share of the recurrent budget appears to increase in absolute terms from Le47,204 (US$86) in 1980–81 to Le576,552 (US$1048) in 1989–90, in relative terms the figures are declining. The recurrent budgetary provision for the education sector in 1989–90 is higher by 0.5 percent than the provision made in 1980–81, notwithstanding the increasing demand for educational resources and the need to make increasing financial provisions to offset the depletion of funds through inflationary pressure.

Of the overall sectoral allocation, about 85 percent of education's total recurrent expenditure was allocated to meet salaries and other personal emoluments of teachers, leaving 15 percent for nonsalary items such as equipment and maintenance.

The early 1990s have witnessed a considerable increase in the number of fee-paying students at the tertiary level. Only a very limited number of students now enjoy grants-in-aid from the government. This is in complete contrast to the 1970s and early 1980s when most students were on full government scholarships.

The financing of education in Sierra Leone must be viewed against the background of the generally poor performance of the economy, severe shortage of foreign exchange, and an accelerating rate of inflation—

all of which have generated continuing crises for government expenditure and growing budget deficits. Like other ministries, the Education Ministry has been a victim of this trend, with its problems compounded by the rapid expansion of the school system.

6. Supplying Personnel for the Education System

There are approximately 18,000 teachers employed in schools all over the country. Out of this number, about 30 percent are female. Secondary-school teachers account for 30 percent of the total teaching force. Since Independence in 1961, teacher training has been accorded a high priority in order to cope with the phenomenal expansion of enrollments and, at the same time, to enhance the quality of education.

At the nongraduate level, there are five teachers colleges offering courses for primary-school teachers. These courses lead either to the Teachers' Certificate or the Higher Teachers' Certificate for primary-school teachers. Primary-teacher training consists of three years after Form 5 and leads to the Teachers' Certificate (TC). Entrance is by examination, except for those candidates who have passed the GCE O level in appropriate subjects.

Secondary-teacher training is concentrated in three institutions in the country. They are Milton Margai Teachers College (MMTC), Fourah Bay College, and Njala University College, the latter two being constituent colleges of the University of Sierra Leone. Milton Margai Teachers College offers a three-year course leading to the Higher Teachers' Certificate (HTC). In principle, MMTC prepares teachers for the lower forms (Forms 1–3) of secondary schools, but in practice there is an increasing tendency for HTC holders in areas such as mathematics and science to teach up to Form 5. In addition, in the early 1990s, MMTC was the only national venue for training teachers in specialist areas such as music, art and crafts, and technical and commercial subjects. The faculty of education at Njala University College offers a four-year course which integrates academic and professional disciplines leading to a BA in Education, a BSc in Education, a BSc in Agricultural Education, and a BSc in Home Economic Education. The Department of Education at Fourah Bay College offers a one-year graduate diploma in education to graduates who have studied at least two subjects taught in secondary schools in the country.

In spite of the efforts of these institutions to provide a teaching force of qualified Sierra Leoneans in quantitative terms, there is evidence that teacher supply falls far short of demand. In view of the high annual demand and the relatively low output from the teacher-training colleges, it is unrealistic to assume that the large number of unqualified teachers in the system (estimated at about 60%) could be phased out in the immediate future. Furthermore, the retention of trained teachers, especially at the secondary level, is a big problem in the face of more attractive conditions of service in other occupations relative to those of teaching and the low professional status teachers hold in the country.

The college supply of teachers in special subjects like science and mathematics is very low and the dropout rate of the qualified teachers in these subject areas is very high. Consequently, the system has to utilize the services of "part-time teachers" such as university lecturers, personnel from other professions, and non-Sierra Leoneans who are employed on contract or as volunteers from such organizations as the American Peace Corps or the British VSO (Voluntary Service Overseas).

The uneven distribution of teachers between urban and rural areas persists in spite of the Government's introduction of Remote Area Allowance as an inducement to teachers to teach in the rural areas.

Once appointed, teachers generally serve a probationary period of one year. Not many opportunities exist for further training after the initial training apart from ad hoc seminars and workshops.

7. Curriculum Development and Methodology

The Institute of Education has the major responsibility for curriculum development. The National Curriculum Development Centre (NCDC) within the Institute has emerged as the single unit in curriculum development at national level.

Mention should be made of the primary school syllabus with a rural orientation developed by the Bunumbu Teachers College. This has now been incorporated into the Harmonized Primary Syllabus developed by the NCDC. It comprises the four core subjects (English, mathematics, social studies, and science), creative practice, religious education, physical and health education, and prevocational studies. This syllabus is now in use in primary schools, and textbooks in the four core subject areas were produced by the task force for primary textbook production set up in 1985.

Other materials developed by the NCDC include the New General Teachers' Certificate Syllabus and the Revised Harmonized Higher Teachers' Certificate Primary Syllabus. Between 1986 and 1988, a National Teaching Syllabus for secondary schools was developed and put into operation in the 1988–89 school year. It comprises the four core subjects, as in the primary school syllabus, and home economics, agricultural science, French, and technical studies. This syllabus covers the first three years in the secondary school, and there are plans to develop one for the senior-secondary schools.

At the primary level, a class teacher generally teaches all the subjects in a particular class based on the primary school syllabus. Mention has already been made of "feeder schools" where there may be two or even three classes being taught by a single teacher.

At the secondary level, there is a common program in the first three years, followed by variations in the senior school where there is specialization and diversification based on an arts, science, commercial, or technical orientation. At the senior school, principals normally plan their school courses within the framework of the WAEC GCE O-level examination, or those of the English Royal Society of Arts or City and Guilds respectively. At this level, teachers may teach one or two subjects depending on their field of specialization and the staff situation in a given school.

English is compulsory, being the official and commercial language, and French is the only foreign language being taught in secondary schools for the most part. It is also offered by a few private primary schools.

A key issue in the area of curriculum development and learning materials preparation is funding. This restricts the number of inservice courses that can be run for teachers as well as the quantity of materials that are produced. The schools receive far less than they require.

8. The System of Examinations, Promotions, and Certifications

Examinations are generally taken each term. The final term's examination each year is the most important for promotion to the next class. Some secondary schools base promotion on cumulative grades. The pupils are tested throughout their course. Weekly assignments and monthly tests are used in assessing them. The pass mark generally ranges from 40 to 50 percent, and students who fail to reach the minimum pass mark are asked to repeat the class during the next school year.

Entry into secondary school from primary school is based on success in the Selective Entrance Examination (SEE) which is administered by the West African Examination Council. The examination consists of papers in verbal aptitude, quantitative aptitude, mathematics, and English. For most students, the next major external examination is the GCE O level which is taken in Form 5. It is also conducted by the WAEC. There are criticisms of the SEE on the grounds that it is not sufficiently broadly based to cover all the significant learning experiences of primary-school children.

With the introduction of the 6–3–3–4 system of education during the 1993–94 academic year, both the Selective Entrance Examination and the GCE O level will be replaced by the National Primary Education Examination and the National Certificate of General Education Examination.

9. Educational Assessment, Evaluation, and Research

All over Sierra Leone schools administer nonstandardized tests and examinations. These are mainly written and designed by teachers to assess student performance. The tests and examinations are conducted on a termly or yearly basis. Financial constraints mean that continuous assessment and assessment of practical skills are minimal. The Selective Entrance Examination, which is mainly an aptitude test, and the General Certificate of Education Ordinary and Advanced Level Examinations conducted by the WAEC are also terminal examinations.

School assessment data are mainly used for promotion to the next class and, at times, for remedial lessons. The SEE results are used for admission to secondary schools, whereas the GCE O- and A-level results are used for employment, certification, and admission into vocational institutions, teachers' colleges, and university. The GCE results are increasingly being used for research purposes, either to improve the examination system or by colleges and other research students for dissertation and thesis work. In the 1990s, the main emphasis on research will be in the development and evaluation of new examination syllabuses for both the junior and senior schools and into the psychometric properties of examinations.

Important educational indicators on which data are regularly collected include enrollment ratios, pupil–teacher ratios, and distribution of teachers by qualification, sex, and region.

10. Major Reforms in the 1980s and 1990s

Prior to 1985, the entry age at the primary level was 5 and the duration of the primary course was 7 years. During the 1985–86 school year, both the entry age and the duration were brought to 6 years. This was in line with one of the recommendations of the 1976 Education Review. The rationale behind these changes was geared toward reducing expenditure on primary education and ensuring greater internal efficiency. However, an evaluation of the impact of this reorganization on internal efficiency has yet to be undertaken.

At around the same time, tuition fees at both primary and secondary levels were abolished. This development only proved ephemeral as students at both levels have resumed the payment of other charges.

Perhaps the most far-reaching reform will be the introduction of the six-year primary, three-year junior-secondary, three-year senior-secondary, and four-year tertiary structure of education. The implementation of this system, which commences in the 1993–94 academic year, will have very far-reaching financial implications for the education system up to the year 2000 and beyond.

11. *Major Problems for the Year 2000*

With the continued growth in demand for educational resources, projections into the mid-1990s indicate that expenditure would have to be increased about four times above the 1990 level to maintain the current enrollment, pupil–teacher ratio, and grants. In addition, the rebel incursion and occupation, in April 1991, of parts of the Eastern and Southern provinces of Sierra Leone by armed bandits of the National Patriotic Front of Liberia has turned the educational clock backwards in those areas. Educational institutions were vandalized, equipment and furniture stolen, and, in some cases, even the buildings were razed to the ground. The rehabilitation of such institutions will extend beyond the year 2000. The most important problem will be finding the resources to take care of such pressing demands.

Furthermore, the problem of the low level of literacy will have to be tackled. Estimates put the level of illiteracy in the country at about 85 percent generally and up to 95 percent in some rural areas. Phasing out the large numbers of untrained and unqualified teachers from the education system and stemming the exodus of competent and experienced teachers from the teaching profession to the more attractive conditions of service of other occupations are also problems that will have to be addressed.

Bibliography

Alie J A D 1990 *A History of Sierra Leone*. Macmillan, London
Porter A T 1966 *Creoledom*. Oxford University Press, Oxford
Sierra Leone Government 1970 *White Paper on Education Policy 1970*. Government Printing Department, Freetown
Sierra Leone Government 1974 *National Development Plan 1974–75 to 1978–79*. Government Printing Department, Freetown
Sierra Leone Government 1981 *Education and Development Sector Study 1979*. Sierra Leone International Development Agency Project Unit, Freetown
Sierra Leone Government 1989 *Report of the Task Force on External Exams for Secondary Schools in Sierra Leone*. Ministry of Education, Youth, and Sport, Freetown
Sierra Leone Government 1990 *Annual Statistical Digest*. Central Statistics Office, Freetown
Sierra Leone Government 1991 *Report of the Advisory Committee on the Management of Schools*. Government Printing Department, Freetown
Sumner D L 1963 *Education in Sierra Leone*. Government Printing Department, Freetown
University of Sierra Leone 1976 *Sierra Leone Education Review: All Our Future*. University of Sierra Leone Press, Freetown

Singapore

O. C. Yeoh

1. *General Background*

Singapore is an island nation with a total land area of about 633 square kilometers. This includes the main island—approximately 42 kilometers long from east to west and 23 kilometers wide, together with some 58 islets within its territorial waters. On the global map, Singapore appears to be at the center of Southeast Asia and is linked by the kilometer-long causeway in the northern end of the island to its immediate neighbor, Peninsular Malaysia. To the south is a vast expanse of the Indonesian islands, and eastwards across the South China Sea is the independent nation of Brunei and the Eastern Malaysian States of Sabah and Sarawak. Within the Region, Singapore is a member the Association of Southeast Asian Nations (ASEAN) and the Southeast Asia Ministers of Education Organization (SEAMEO).

Singapore has a relatively high daily temperature and rainfall all year round; the lush vegetation is rich and diverse, evergreen, and grows rapidly. The government has taken great care to exploit these advantages and has created the image of Singapore as the "garden city." This is expected to be "a city with a clean and healthy environment, and an environmentally conscious and responsible people who are committed to the concept of sustainable development and who participate actively in international fora on the environment" (Ministry of Environment 1990).

With the exception of about three and a half years of Japanese occupation during the Second World War, Singapore was under the influence of British Colonial rule since it was founded by Sir Stamford Raffles in 1819. In 1959, with the proclamation of the Singapore Constitution Order in Council, Singapore achieved internal self-government, although the British still ruled in matters of foreign policy.

In 1965, Singapore became a fully independent and sovereign nation when it separated from Malaysia (Singapore was merged with Malaysia from 1963 to 1965). Since Independence, Singapore maintains a multiparty political system of parliamentary democracy. At the general election in 1991, the ruling Peoples Action Party (PAP) was returned for the eighth time to form the government.

By 1990, Singapore had "become a thriving modern economy with the second highest standard of living in

Asia" and with a per capita indigenous GNP of s$20,031 (US$12,381) (Ministry of Trade and Industry 1991); it has about 87 percent home ownership. In order to attain the vision of Singapore, the government is committed "to invest heavily in the people and to enable them to move up to higher value-added and hence better paid jobs" (Government of Singapore 1991).

In 1990, there were 3,002,800 residents *(Ministry of Communication and Information 1991)*. In the multiracial society, there were 77.7 percent Chinese (2.09 million), 14.1 percent Malays (380,600), 7.1 percent Indians (191,000), and 1.1 percent other ethnic groups. About 5.3 million visitors passed through Singapore in 1990. This is almost twice the local population. The median age of the resident population is 29.8 years. Just over 23 percent of the population was 15 years or younger in 1990 compared with nearly 28 percent in 1980. Those who are 60 years or older increased from 7.5 percent in 1980 to 9.1 percent in 1990. Malay, Chinese (Mandarin), Tamil, and English are official languages. While Malay is the official national language, English is the language of administration and commerce. In addition to these languages, among the older Chinese and Indian generation a variety of dialects are spoken at home. All these factors have a direct implication on the purpose of bilingual education for all children (starting in preschool). The bilingual policy of learning English and the mother tongue that was first introduced to the schools in 1979 continues to be sustained and improved upon in the 1990s.

2. Politics and the Goals of the Education System

Singapore's vision in *Next Lap: Singapore 1991* (Government of Singapore 1991) is to become a well-educated society. Toward this end, the goals for education in the 1990s are fourfold, namely:

(a) to educate each individual to his or her maximum potential;

(b) to develop more thinking individuals with creative and flexible skills;

(c) to nurture leadership qualities and good work ethics;

(d) to cultivate civic and moral values.

Toward these ends, the education system aims to provide at least ten years of general education for all children. The system also incorporates flexibility so that children of different abilities are offered the opportunity to develop themselves fully.

3. The Formal System of Education

3.1 Primary, Secondary, and Tertiary Education

Figure 1 sets out the formal education system as recommended in the Report of the Review Committee

in *Improving Primary School Education* (Yip/Review Committee 1991). With effect from 1994, the refinements to the primary school system and the consequent changes at the secondary and postsecondary levels will be phased in to replace the system already in place since 1979 (Goh/Review Committee 1978).

As of 1991, every child in Singapore receives at least ten years of general education. This comprises six years of primary and at least four years of secondary education. In order to cater to the various needs of the students, the system provides opportunities for a wider choice of technical–vocational or preuniversity and tertiary courses of study after secondary school.

The objectives of the primary system of schooling are to give all pupils good grounding in English language and mathematics as well as an adequate proficiency in the mother tongue and to prepare them for secondary education. Education at the primary level is structured in two stages, the foundation stage and the orientation stage.

The foundation stage (Grades 1 to 4) emphasizes basic literacy and numeracy. The school maintains a profile of each pupil's progress in the first three years of school and at the end of primary four, pupils are streamed according to their level of performance in English, mother tongue, and mathematics. Parents are informed of their children's aptitude for the various academic subjects and are further advised on possible educational paths for them. The final decision on the

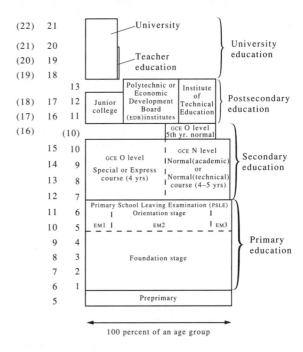

Figure 1

Singapore: Structure of the formal education system 1991

language stream best suited for the child rests with the parents.

The orientation stage (Grades 5 and 6) offers pupils one of the three language streams, depending on their standard of performance at the primary four national level of assessment.

Pupils are streamed into EM1 (English and mother tongue as first languages), EM2 (English as first and mother tongue as second language) or EM3 (English as first language and mother tongue for oral proficiency). A fourth stream, ME3 (mother tongue as first language and English oral) is available only if there is sufficient demand. The two-year orientation not only allows for further assessment of pupils' abilities, interests, and aptitudes but also allows for lateral transfer from one language stream to another.

At the secondary level, students have the choice of four alternative academic courses to match their learning abilities and interests. Hence, they undergo four to five years of secondary education, each having a different curricular emphasis.

The special course caters to the top 10 percent of the student cohort who are academically excellent and competent in language learning. These students therefore offer English and the mother tongue at the first language level. In contrast, students in the express course (about 50 %) study the mother tongue at the second language level.

The normal (academic) course students (about 20–25 %) enroll in the academic stream but are allowed an additional fifth year before they qualify to sit for the General Certificate of Education (GCE) O-level examination because they are less academically able than the express course students.

The normal (technical) course is the new four to five year technically biased course that is designed for the remaining 10–15 percent of students who are the least academically inclined. This will be phased in for the first time in January 1994 at secondary one normal. The aim of the technical course is to continue to enhance the students' proficiency in English and mathematics. These, together with computer applications, which focus on keyboard skills and use of software packages, make up the three compulsory subjects which students offer at the GCE Normal (N) level examination at the end of secondary four. Those who qualify can then proceed for the fifth year in the same course that leads to the GCE O level examination. With the introduction of this course, the academically weaker students have the opportunity to benefit from the ten years of general education that is so necessary if students choose to continue beyond secondary education.

For the 1985 cohort, it was reported that the dropout rate of primary school pupils is 1.7 percent. In 1993, the dropout rate for secondary school students was reported to be about 2.7 percent.

Students who choose to pursue further academic studies beyond the ten years of general education may either go on to the junior colleges (Grades 11 and 12) or seek alternative studies at either the polytechnics or the vocationally oriented Institute of Technical Education. Admission to these institutions is strictly on the basis of academic merit, a system of points that is based on the students' performance at the GCE O level examination.

About 25 percent of the students who qualify for admission to the junior college complete two years of the GCE Advanced (A) level studies that prepare them for tertiary education. Admission to the universities depends on their excellence in academic performance at the A level Singapore-Cambridge public examination.

The target for polytechnic education is for about 40 percent of the students who have the aptitude and prerequisite O-level and/or A-level qualifications to pursue technical, business, design, and nursing education at any one of Singapore's four polytechnics. As of 1993, the polytechnics offer a wide range of 59 full-time and 69 part-time courses, with a total enrollment of 30,736 full-time and 7,079 part-time students. With the academic staff strength of 3,488, this gives rise to a student–staff ratio of 10.8:1.

The full-time courses lead to the award of the three-year Diploma or two-year Certificate. The training is broad-based, with attachments to the industrial and commercial sectors. The courses that were most popular in the 1993 intake were architectural technology (8.8 times oversubscribed), followed by tourism management, biotechnology, building-related courses, shipbuilding, and offshore engineering.

Other forms of technical training are also offered by the Economic Development Board (EDB) institutions such as the French-Singapore Institute, the German-Singapore Institute, and the Japan-Singapore Technical Institute. These specialized institutes train the pool of technologists in computer software design, microprocessing, computer applications, industrial automation, and mechanical technology.

The Institute of Technical Education is targeted at about 25 percent of those who successfully completed the five-year normal (technical) course. The two to three year full-time courses are vocationally oriented and lead to the award of the National Trade Certificate–Grade 2 (NTC-2). More able students can advance to higher level courses whose training leads to the award of the certificate in fields such as business studies and office skills.

The aim of the education system is that by 1997 at least 90 percent of a cohort of students will have two to three more years of postsecondary education. The target is to have about 20 percent of students entering University. Admission to the National University of Singapore (NUS) and the Nanyang Technological University (NTU) is based on the students' academic performance at the GCE A level examination, and in the case of selection for teacher training, there are also interviews. As of January 1994, the alternative program to full-time studies by means of distance learning can be pursued at the proposed Singapore

Open University which is being set up jointly with the Singapore Institute of Management.

The NUS has eight faculties, 50 departments, four postgraduate schools (in medicine, dentistry, management, and engineering) and three advanced institutes (the Institute of Molecular and Cell Biology, the Institute of Systems Science, and the Institute of Microelectronics). The enrollment in 1990 was 15,193 students, plus 2,263 full-time and part-time graduate students together with about 1,400 academic staff. The faculties offer degrees and postgraduate studies in arts and social sciences, architecture, building and estate management, business administration, law, science, engineering, medicine, and dentistry. The institutes provide research and development in information technology (IT) applications, biotechnology, and microelectronics.

The NTU (originated from the former Nanyang Technological Institute) is a second comprehensive university, established in July 1991. The five schools in civil and structural engineering, electrical and electronic engineering, mechanical and production engineering, accountancy and business, and applied science are complemented by the other four schools under the National Institute of Education, namely, the schools of science, arts, education, and physical education. The NTU has joint collaborative research and teaching with top institutions such as the Sloan School of Management and the Massachusetts Institute of Technology, and joint research studies with the Mechanical Engineering Laboratory (MEL) of Japan. Close collaboration between the University and local industry and business ensures that the training courses are realistic and relevant.

In 1991, there were 262,876 pupils (or 58.83%) in primary school, 156,746 (31.6%) at the secondary and 42,553 (9.5%) in Junior Colleges (Ministry of Education 1991a). School is not compulsory but there is almost 100 percent enrollment of all eligible pupils. Table 1 summarizes the changes and trend in the

Table 1
A summary of the number of schools, teachers, and pupil enrollment 1976–91

Category	Characteristics	1976	1981	1986	1991
Number of schools	Primary	353	304	222	194
	Secondary and full schools	123	137	144	146
	Preuniversity, junior college and centralized institute	31	26	34	40
Number of teachers	Primary (government aided)	10,597 (67.0)	9,465 (66.5)	10,264 (69.7)	9,843 (72.8)[a]
	Secondary (and preuniversity)	6,855 (50.5)	7,690 (55.6)	7,596 (58.4)	7,532 (62.2)
	Junior college	—	580 (57.6)	1,099 (62.8)	1,601 (64.6)
	Total	17,434 (61.1)	17,735 (62.2)	18,959 (66.1)	18,976 (69.1)
Pupil enrollment	Primary and preparatory year	315,973 (47.3)	288,622 (47.7)	273,603 (47.2)	262,876 (47.3)
	Secondary (government aided)	161,779 (50.9)	157,307 (50.2)	173,538 (49.5)	156,746 (48.9)
	Junior college, Preuniversity centralized institute	14,391[b] (54.2)	18,153[c] (58.3)	27,598[c] (55.0)	27,224 (56.3)
	Arts stream[d]	60,631 (60.1)	34,433 (63.9)	42,434 (64.9)	35,522 (62.6)
	Science stream[d]	5,509 (42.1)	25,336 (48.6)	36,225 (42.9)	43,044 (45.9)
	Technical stream[d]	19,951 (27.2)	18,330 (23.0)	21,601 (20.2)	15,330 (15.1)
	Commerce stream[d]	5,328 (71.8)	10,066 (76.2)	17,768 (70.8)	19,198 (71.7)

Source: Ministry of Education 1991 *Education Statistics Digest*   a Values in brackets refer to percentage of female teachers b Junior College enrollment only c Junior College and Preuniversity enrollment d Enrollment from Secondary 3 to Preuniversity

number of schools, teachers, and enrollment from 1976 to 1991.

The vast majority of schools, especially the government schools, are coeducational. The single session schools operate from 7.30 am to 1.00 pm. Together with improved school facilities, schools provide a diverse range of extracurricular activities and enrichment programs in the afternoons. In double session schools, the second session is from 1.00 pm to 6.30 pm.

There is a series of special programs in schools which are worthy of mention. The Gifted Education Program (GEP), offered in selected primary and secondary schools, is designed to challenge those who are intellectually gifted. In the 1992 O-level examination, the GEP students scored a mean aggregate of 7.2 for their best six subjects. This meant that they achieved the distinction (A1) for almost every subject. The Science Research Program is intended to encourage a selection of the junior college students to experience scientific research while working directly under a university mentor.

The Music Elective Program is available in selected secondary schools to develop pupils who are talented in music as well as to enhance their appreciation of music. The Art Elective Program is introduced in selected secondary schools for students with an aptitude in art.

The Humanities Award is promoted to encourage students who are academically excellent in the sciences to study the humanities instead at the junior college level, and subsequently at the university. The purpose is to spread the most able students in the humanities and sciences.

The Language Elective Program in selected junior colleges is designed for linguistically talented students to master a third language, namely Chinese, French, German, or Japanese, at A level.

3.2 Preschool Education

Preschool education is not compulsory. Since parents place a premium on education in general, almost 99 percent of children experience one to three years of preschool education.

Although preschool education is private, strict guidelines and supervision are provided by the Ministry of Community Development (MCD) for the running of the childcare centers while the Ministry of Education (MOE) oversees the running of the kindergartens. In 1992, there were 345 centers and kindergartens with an enrollment of 94,318 children aged from 6 months to 6 years. Of these, 18,732 or 20 percent were enrolled in full-day or half-day childcare programs. It was reported that with the annual birthrate of about 50,000 babies, one of the childcare agencies expected to more than double their enrollment from 62,185 in 1992 to 147,556 by 1994 (*Straits Times* February 1992). Some of the childcare centers are in the workplace so as to facilitate mothers returning to full-time employment. For preschooling at the childcare centers, the MCD

provides a subsidy of s$130 (US$80) per child in the full-time center. This accounted for about s$6.5 million (US$4 million) a year (*Straits Times* March 1993). Unlike the childcare centers, the kindergartens offer daily programs that run for three to four hours only, either in one or two shifts.

The preschool centers provide graded instructional programs generally to enhance the overall development of the preschoolers and to lay a good foundation for formal education. To this end, most preschool centers offer a program of daily activities which include exposure to two languages, preprimary work, indoor free choice activities, outdoor play, story/rhyme time, music and movement, and social skills activities. Parents usually enroll their children in those centers that will meet the language needs of their children.

In 1993, there were over a thousand trained kindergarten teachers and three times that number of childcare assistant teachers, teachers, and supervisors. Corresponding to the rapid expansion of enrollment in the childcare centers, the teachers who are trained in NIE are awarded the Basic or Intermediate Certificates for teachers and the Advanced Certificate in Early Childhood education for the supervisors. In some centers, a core of senior experienced teachers are trained as childcare teacher trainers, also by the NIE. They in turn provide inhouse training to the untrained teacher aides. For a long period of time, the availability of qualified preschool teachers will determine the pace of expansion of the preschools.

3.3 Special Education

Special education is under the purview of the MOE but it is administered by the tripartite Coordinating Body for Special Education that is made up of representatives from parents, the voluntary welfare organizations (VWOs) and the ministry. Their role is to manage the educational needs of the disabled and to disburse the funds to the special schools.

The goals of special education are to develop the intellectual, physical, and social potential of disabled children for integration into society and to prepare them for further education and employment. The *Report of the Advisory Council on the Disabled* (Ministry of Community Development 1988) endorsed and recognized the eight different VWOs (e.g., the Movement of the Intellectually Disabled in Singapore or the Association for Educationally Subnormal) as agencies who are most competent to manage the 14 special education schools. They are known for their missionary zeal in the pursuit of their commitments. Also, their autonomy permits them to respond flexibly and quickly to the changing needs and demands of the disabled.

There are no exact numbers on the enrollment of the disabled but the agency promotional pamphlets reported a total of 8,403 people. Of these, 6,438 or 75.5 percent are in the 14 different special education schools. About 70 percent are classified as educationally subnormal, about 4.3 percent experienced profound multiple handicap, and the remainder are either cerebral palsy sufferers (7.2%), visually handicapped, or hard of hearing. Altogether, they account for approximately 3 percent of the school-going population. For the 2,100 disabled students who are in the special schools, the pupil–teacher ratio is about 8:1. Of the 271 teachers, about two-thirds are teacher aides who are untrained. The children–specialist staff (such as therapists and counselors) ratio is around 100:1.

Qualified teachers possess the three-year part-time Certificate or the two-year full-time Diploma in Special Education that is awarded by NIE. There is a great need to accelerate the training of paramedical professionals at the University, especially speech therapists.

The extent to which the children are integrated in their training with the regular schools depends on the degree to which they can benefit from regular school education. The majority enroll in the special schools, and only a small proportion (mainly visually handicapped) are totally integrated in selected schools and in the polytechnics.

The Bizlink Center is the agency that provides centralized vocational assessment and a job placement service for disabled persons who are suitable for open market employment and actively promotes the employment of disabled clients through public education. In 1993, there were about 1,300 individuals in the Center's care.

In 1992, the VWOs and related agencies received about s$13.5 million (US$8.3 million) to manage the programs. In addition to the per capita grant of s$3,000 (US$1854) per annum, which is twice the sum for primary school children, the Ministry seconds qualified teachers to supplement the shortage of teachers and expertise in the special education schools. In 1992, the cost per disabled pupil was about s$3,740 (US$2312). The government accepts the premise that the capitation grant for special education should be four times more (s$6,000 [US$3709] per annum) if the standards are to be comparable to those in the United States and United Kingdom.

4. Administrative and Supervisory Structure and Operation

Education in Singapore is managed centrally by the Ministry of Education. It exercises control of the development, administration, and implementation of the government's educational policy in the schools and in all institutions under the Statutory Board, namely the universities, polytechnics, the Singapore Science Center, and the Institute of Technical Education. The private schools, regular schools, special education schools, and the kindergartens come under the overall policy direction of the Ministry.

On matters pertaining to the professional concerns of the schools and schooling, at least four of the seven divisions of the Ministry (Schools, Curriculum Planning, Research and Testing, and the Curriculum Development Institute of Singapore) work closely with the schools under the director of education while the Administrative, Personnel, and Information and Services divisions answer directly to the Permanent Secretary (Education). The inspectorate of the Schools Division offers guidance through their supervision and appraisal of the schools. This includes the management of programs such as extracurricular activities, special language studies, pastoral care, and career guidance. In addition, the division is in charge of the registration and inspection of the private schools (a total of 340 with 4,714 teaching staff and an enrollment of 132,990 full-time and part-time students) and the kindergartens.

5. Educational Finance

Two major responsibilities of the government are to finance and to administer the education policies. In 1991, the Ministry of Education was the single biggest employer with a total number of 25,316 or 40.9 percent of all public employees. The development expenditure in 1990 was s$234.6 million (US$145 million) or 5.6 percent of total development expenditure. This was a 62.02 percent increase over the 1989 expenditure of s$144.8 million (US$89.5 million). In comparison, s$1,791 million (US$1,107 million) or 19.8 percent of the recurrent expenditure accounted for only a 9.9 increase over 1989. The budget of the MOE for 1993 was s$3.2 billion (US$2.0 billion), 20 percent higher than in 1992. This accounts for 20 percent of government expenditure.

The Ministry already subsidizes each child at about s$2,000 and s$3,000 at the primary and secondary levels respectively. This is reflected in the nominal school fees which pupils pay, ranging from free primary schooling to only five or six Singapore dollars per student at the secondary and junior college levels for Singaporeans. The independent secondary schools (thus far six in number) charge a fee that ranges from s$70 to s$200 per month. Students who cannot afford to pay the fees may apply to the Ministry for a full subsidy.

With effect from 1993 an additional educational subsidy is paid annually by the Ministry into each child's EduSave Account while the pupil is between 6 and 16 years of age. The purpose is for parents to use the account to pay school-related course fees, such as enrichment and remedial classes or the money is to be saved for future education. Parents ultimately make the choice on the use of the EduSave which is deemed to be an investment in the children and in the future of Singapore.

6. Supplying Personnel for the Education System

The Personnel Division of the Ministry is in charge of the recruitment and placement and the development of teachers for the schools. Together with the schools division, the division monitors the personnel needs of the schools and projections are made in accordance with the requirements of the educational policy. By 1994, for example, 800 more graduate teachers are required to staff the secondary schools when the new education policy is phased in to provide students with at least 10 years of general education (*Straits Times* March 1993). The Ministry has embarked on a systematic and extensive campaign to promote the teaching profession through the media and at career fairs. Each year, the number of applicants for training as teachers far exceeds the vacancies available. However, a shortfall persists due to the stringent criteria used at the selection interviews for candidates who must not only have the requisite entry qualifications but also show evidence of having an aptitude for and a commitment to teaching.

The National Institute of Education (NIE) of the Nanyang Technological University is the sole teacher training institute in Singapore. It provides all levels of teacher education, ranging from the preservice training of teachers (both graduate and nongraduate teachers) to inservice training for teachers, heads of departments, vice-principals, and principals.

The academic year consists of two semesters beginning in July and January, with 15 weeks each. The overall student enrollment for each academic year is about 2,000. The minimum matriculation requirement is the full GCE A-level Certificate obtained in one sitting. All candidates who are admitted to the preservice teacher training programs are awarded a Ministry of Education Teaching Bursary. The amount varies from s$3,200 (US$1,978) per annum for the undergraduate to s$1,300 (US$804) per month for the graduate teacher trainee in the first year of training, and s$700–750 (US$433–464) per month for the nongraduate trainees in the two years of training. In 1991, the average cost per teacher trainee was s$13,035 (US$8057). Of this amount, the Ministry subsidizes about 90 percent for those who are Singaporeans (Republic of Singapore 1991). On graduation, the trained teachers are obliged to serve the government for a period of three to five years, depending on the nature and duration of training.

The NIE offers four types of programs up to degree and postgraduate levels.The preservice full-time programs include (a) the four-year Bachelor of Arts/Science with Diploma in Education/Physical Education, (b) two-year Diploma in Education/Physical Education, (c) two-year Physical Education (primary/secondary), and (d) one-year Postgraduate Diploma in Education (primary/secondary).

The inservice programs include the Further Professional Diploma in Education for heads of departments, the Diploma in Educational Administration for prospective vice-principals and principals, the Advanced Diploma in Education for Chinese, Malay, or Tamil Language Teachers. A variety of short inservice teacher training courses are offered to update teachers in teaching the different subjects.

The postgraduate programs include the Master of Education program by course work and dissertation and a PhD in education by research. Masters and PhD programs are also offered in arts, science, and physical education by research only. The other programs include the consultancy programs in preschool teacher training as well as the full-time two-year diploma or part-time three-year Certificate in Special Education.

7. Curriculum Development and Teaching Methodology

The Division of Curriculum Planning in the Ministry of Education is responsible for the ongoing review and systematic revision of the National Curriculum which sets out the goals of the educational policy in terms of the range of core and elective subjects that are taught across the schools. For each subject, the subject syllabus outlines in detail the rationale and specific objectives for teaching the subject at the primary, secondary, or postsecondary levels. These are accompanied by the curriculum framework in which the lists of content topics are integrated across each grade level. In addition, guidelines and suggestions on the methods of teaching are highlighted, together with a clear statement of the intended standards of achievement. The syllabus then concludes with the suggested list of readings and available instructional resources.

The teaching and examination syllabus provides a clear framework and structure for the centralized administration, management, and implementation of the intended national curriculum. While the curriculum for Grades 1 to 8 (primary to the lower secondary school) are locally prescribed, the subject syllabuses at Grades 9 to 12 are jointly determined by the Singapore–Cambridge Board of Examinations that lays down the content and standards of assessment for the General Certificate in Education (GCE), Normal (N), Ordinary (O), and the Advanced (A) level examinations.

Given the approved subject syllabuses, both the curriculum developers or writers and the media specialists in the respective project teams collaborate with practicing teachers under the direction of the Curriculum Development Institute of Singapore (CDIS) to translate the syllabus into the multimedia package of teaching and learning materials. For each subject for a specific grade, the package generally consists of the student's textbook, the activities workbook, the teacher's guide and/or resource book and a range of audiovisual materials, such as wall charts, picture cards, audio and videotapes, and color transparencies. The design of such an instructional package for use in Grades 1 to 8 generally goes through the cyclic process of pilot-testing in schools, followed by the systematic feedback that is obtained during the trial period. These are then incorporated into the publication of the final edition for school use.

At this juncture, the subject specialist inspectors (officers of the Curriculum Planning Division) and staff in the Textbook Unit of the Schools Division review the textbooks and the relevant materials before they are approved for use by schools. Both the CDIS-developed materials and those published by the commercial publishers are subject to the same stringent measures of authorization. The aim is to ensure that the contents of the textbooks match the intended aims, content, and standards in the prescribed syllabuses.

Teachers are free to choose the instructional materials that will best satisfy the needs of the students in their respective schools. Generally, prior to the adoption of the CDIS-published materials, the teachers concerned are briefed on the appropriate use of the materials. At the same time, the NIE trains the teachers in pre- and inservice courses to comprehend the changes made and the innovative methods that are intended for the effective use of the materials to aid the teaching and learning of the subject.

Table 2 sets out the national curriculum in the primary, secondary, and postsecondary schools. The learning of two languages, namely English and the mother tongue, together with mathematics, is compulsory for at least 10 years. This stresses the importance of being bilingual in a multiracial society and also

Table 2
Summary of curriculum at the primary, secondary, and postsecondary levels

---

All Grades (compulsory subjects)
Examinable subjects (Grades 1–12): English language; mother tongue (Malay, Mandarin, Tamil)
Nonexaminable subjects: Moral education (Grades 1–6); civics and moral education (Grades 7–10)

Primary level (Grades 1–6)
Examinable subjects: English language; mother tongue; mathematics; science (from Grade 3)
Nonexaminable subjects: Moral education; social studies (from Grade 4); art and craft; music; physical education; health education (from Grade 5); school assembly
(Notes: At Grades 1–2 there are 47 perids per week of 30 minutes each. At the "foundation stage," i.e., Grades 1–4, the two languages and mathematics accounts for 80 percent of curriculum time. At the "orientation stage," i.e., Grades 5 and 6, there are 49 periods per week. The core subjects take up about 78 percent of curriculum time. In the 11+ examination in core subjects, pupils in the EM3 stream are not examined in science.)

Lower secondary level (Grades 7–8)
Examinable subjects (Special Course/Express Course/Normal [Academic] Course): Two languages; mathematics; science; literature; history; geography; art and craft; design and technology or home economics
Nonexaminable subjects (Special Course/Express Course/Normal [Academic] Course: Civics and moral education; physical education; music; school assembly
Examinable subjects (Normal [Technical] Course]: Two languages; mathematics; computer applications; science and technical studies; home economics
Nonexaminable subjects (Normal [Technical] Course): Social studies; civics and moral education; physical education; art and craft; school assembly

Upper secondary level (Grades 9–10/11)
Core examinable subjects:
Special Course/Express Course: English; mother tongue; mathematics; one subject in humanities; one subject in sciences; 2–4 electives (see below)
Normal (Academic) Course: English; mother tongue; mathematics; 2–4 electives (see below)
Normal (Technical) Course: English; mother tongue (oral); mathematics; computer applications (use of software); 1–3 electives (see below)
Elective examinable subjects:
Special Course/Express Course/Normal (Academic) Course: Further mathematics; literature; history; geography; home economics; general science; physics; chemistry; biology; human social biology; economics; computer science; music
Normal (Technical) course: technical studies; science; food and nutrition; fashion and fabric; elements of office administration; art and craft
Nonexaminable subjects: civics and moral education; physical education; music

Junior college level (Grades 11–12)
Core examinable subjects at A/O level: General studies; mother tongue
Elective examinable subjects at A/O level: maximum of four chosen from the following
    Science: physics; chemistry; biology; physical science; mathematics; further mathematics; computer science
    Humanities: English literature; geography; history; economics; mathematics; further mathematics; art; music
    Commerce: principles of accountancy; business management; economics; mathematics

---

guarantees that children are equipped with the basic skills of literacy and numeracy to function in a modern industrialized economy.

The teaching of moral education at the primary school for six years followed by civics and moral education for the next four years at the secondary school as a nonexaminable subject (taught in the mother tongue) demonstrates the strong commitment of the system of education "to keep pupils in touch with their cultural links" and thereby "to grow up to be a responsible adult, loyal to his country and concerned for his family and society."

The system of core subjects (both examinable and nonexaminable) plus the opportunity to select from a range of elective subjects guarantee that students who are tracked in the different language streams or academic courses (secondary level) are given sufficient flexibility "to develop himself to the limits of his ability and talent." To facilitate the effective implementation of curriculum innovation and change in schools, the teachers are trained or retrained to use the CDIS-designed package of multimedia instruction materials. While these may not always guarantee the faithful and effective implementation of the intended curriculum, nonetheless, over time the teachers' approach to curriculum change will approximate more closely to the intended goals and aims of the national curriculum.

8. The System of Examinations, Promotions, and Certifications

In the centralized system of education, the national examination, like the national curriculum, sets the standard for school attainment. Pupils sit a national placement examination called the Primary School Leaving Examination (PSLE) at the end of Grade 6. They are tested in four subjects: English at the first language level, the mother tongue at second language level (oral and written), mathematics, and science. Pupils who attain the necessary standards are then admitted to the special, express, or normal course in secondary schools.

The EM3 pupils generally need more time to learn. They offer only English, the mother tongue (at oral proficiency level), and mathematics at the PSLE. On attaining the required standards, they are admitted to the secondary normal (technical) course.

Students who complete four years of studies in the normal course (academic or technical) sit for the qualifying GCE N-level examination. Those who qualify then proceed for the fifth year in the normal course. At the conclusion of either five years of normal or four years of special or express course studies, these students sit for the common GCE O-level examination. On the merit of their O-level performance, students may either continue with two years of junior college or proceed to join the polytechnics. Attainment in the

junior college is assessed by the national GCE A-level examination. Strictly on the merit of their performance at the A level, students compete for admission to the universities or failing that, together with the O level graduates, seek admission for further training in the polytechnics or EDB institutes and Institute of Technical Education.

In addition to the use of the national public examinations to evaluate the standard of student and school performance, schools also maintain a system of continuous, formative assessment to monitor the students' progress in academic studies and extracurricular activities. These consist of the monthly tests or quizzes and the midyear examination whose scores are aggregated (suitably weighted) with the end-of-year final examination to offer a profile or index of the student's progress over the school year. This is one of the sources of feedback that are used to counsel students at the annual teacher–parent conferencing.

9. Educational Assessment, Evaluation, and Research

These functions are the main responsibilities of the Examinations and Assessment Branch, the Research Branch, and the Monitoring and Evaluation Branch of the Research and Testing Division, in the MOE. Together they administer the national examinations, set the standards of attainment and provide continuous and timely feedback on organizational, curricular and examination matters pertaining to the goals and specific aims of the educational system. There is a strong belief in and commitment to the use of systematic research to establish a knowledge base for an informed process in decision-making concerning the effectiveness of educational policies, programs, and practices.

Concurrently, both conclusion and decision-oriented research are pursued either individually and/or in teams under the coordination of the Center for Applied Research in Education (CARE) in the National Institute of Education. In addition to managing the studies of postgraduate students in the Master of Education and PhD programs, the Center has concluded studies such as: (a) the 10-year study of the cognitive and social development of preschool children (sponsored by the Bernard Van Leer Foundation 1983–93), (b) development and testing of the computerized career guidance system for students called JOBS or Jobs Orientation Backup System, (c) the primary school pupil profiling project, (d) the continuing monitoring and analysis of school and teacher effectiveness, and (e) the investigation of pupil learning strategies in the three different languages and in mathematics. Jointly with the Institute of Policy Studies, CARE is exploring the construction of the Quality of Life Indicator and an evaluative framework on the Management of Ethnic Relations in Singapore.

A comprehensive systematic framework of educational studies was created under CARE to coordinate research in teacher education (RITE) in four broad domains, namely: (a) the provision of an integrated knowledge base arising from the input-throughput-output (ITO) studies, (b) the theory-practice linkage (TPL) in teacher training (c) the school teacher effectiveness (STE) studies, and (d) studies that explore innovative teaching and learning (ITL) methods.

Much of the prevailing research and testing studies have emerged in response to changes made in the implementation of the New Education System, since 1980. Numerous evaluative studies have been reported by Kam and Soh (1990). These included the monitoring of academic streaming of students by ability; the intrinsic, formative, and summative evaluation of the innovative changes introduced in the revised curriculum programs; the impact and consequences of the bilingual education policy and the socio-psycholinguistic issues that arose therefrom; the efficacy of the moral education programs across the entire primary and secondary school grades; studies on the influence of preschool on readiness for entry to primary school, and the extensive evaluation and testing of reading and language skills in the four language media.

The Ministry has jointly engaged with the International Association for the Evaluation of Educational Achievement (IEA) in at least three large-scale international surveys of reading literacy (1989–1992), the Second International Science Study (1983–87), and the Third International Mathematics and Science Study (1991 on).

Among the many innovative measures introduced in the areas of testing and examinations, one of the most significant developments is the creation of the item banks for English language, Chinese, Malay, Tamil, mathematics, and science for schools to use in the end-of-year school based examinations. While the items are continually revised to keep up with changes in the syllabuses, key personnel in the primary and secondary schools are trained extensively on the skills of test construction. In view of the importance of examinations for purposes of selection and placement of students into the different language streams or academic courses, for the first time in 1983 item response theory (one-parameter model) was introduced to test the comparability of performance over time.

Funds for the conduct of all the research, development, and testing activities are generously supported by provisions within the annual budget of the Ministry and the universities.

10. Major Reforms in the 1980s and 1990s

The education system has undergone major changes following the Report on the Ministry of Education (Goh /Review Committee 1978) that led to the radical reform and implementation of the New Education System in 1979. A comprehensive account of the Evolution of Educational Excellence (Yip and Sim 1990) set out the 25 years of educational development and change in the Republic of Singapore.

Since then, different cohorts of students have flowed through the school system and have been fluent in at least English and their own mother tongue. The mother tongue helped to foster links with their culture that are rooted in the traditions of Asian values. The system of language and academic streaming at the primary and secondary levels, on the whole, enabled students to progress through the program of studies best suited to their abilities. These have resulted in improved standards of educational attainment.

The Curriculum Development Institute of Singapore has bridged the gap between curriculum planning and syllabus changes on the one hand and the means of meaningful curriculum development and implementation, on the other. Teachers have participated directly or indirectly in the process of change. For the innovative changes in the new curriculum to succeed as intended, teachers have begun to accept their role as the agents of change.

Computerization of the entire school system through the creation of School Link has given teachers and schools direct access to on-line information in the Ministry's pupil, teacher, school, and test-item data banks. Professional decisions concerning students and/or policies are now based on the immediate access to up-to-date information and timely availability of data for decision-making.

Increasingly, the use of information technology in schools has opened up new and innovative ways to supplement school learning. With the extension of interactive video technology to schools through the computer-based CAI/CML programs and, increasingly, students' access to Teleview in schools and at home, the teaching and learning systems are progressively customized to satisfy the individual differences and needs of students in schools.

11. Major Problems for the Year 2000

Educational objectives will need to be reviewed and modified continually. Emphasis must shift because of changing and rising expectations of students and parents, resulting from the globalization of Singapore's economy. The provision of quality education is a service to the people. But more important, it is an investment, because the future of Singapore depends on her youth, the most precious and only resource. This is the perennial problem for Singapore with only a very limited population.

The report *Improving Primary School Education* (Yip/Review Committee 1991) focused on the development of human resources to meet the need for an intelligent and skilled workforce and to facilitate the inculcation of sound Asian values that will serve as the cultural ballast in the face of rapid economic progress and social changes.

In the context of the drive for bilingual competence, the challenge is to ensure that the school and the curriculum are responsive to the differences in abilities and talents of the students. The goal is to make the learning experiences in school relevant and fulfilling for all.

In the decade of the 1990s and beyond, labor shortage and the quality and productivity of the workforce will loom as the most serious obstacles to further growth. Hence, "Singapore needs every one of its people and needs them all to be better—the best to be brilliant, the average to be good, and the weak to be stronger" (Editorial, *Straits Times*, March 7, 1991). Failure to achieve this would lead to wastage for both the individual and the nation.

References

Goh K S, Review Committee to the Ministry of Education 1978 *Report on the Ministry of Education*. Ministry of Education, Singapore

Government of Singapore 1991 *Next Lap: Singapore 1991*. Times Editions, Singapore

Kam K W, Soh K C 1990 25 years of research and testing. In: Yip J S K, Sim W K 1990

Ministry of Communications and Information 1991 *Singapore 1991*. Ministry of Communications and Information, Singapore

Ministry of Community Development 1988 *Report of the Advisory Council on the Disabled. Opportunities for the Disabled*. Ministry of Community Development, Singapore

Ministry of Education 1991a *Education Statistics Digest: 1991*. Ministry of Education, Singapore

Ministry of Education 1991b *Education System, 1991. Implementation Guidelines. Primary School*. The Schools Division, Ministry of Education, Singapore

Ministry of the Environment 1990 A Statement on the Concept of the Model Environment City. *Straits Times* Dec 27 1990

Ministry of Trade and Industry 1991 *Economic Survey of Singapore, 1991*. Ministry of Trade and Industry, Singapore

Republic of Singapore 1991 *Budget for the Financial Year 1991/92*. Presented to Parliament, February 1991, Singapore

Straits Times (daily). Singapore

Yip J, Review Committee to the Ministry of Education 1991 *Improving Primary School Education*. Ministry of Education, Singapore

Yip J S K, Sim W K 1990 *Evolution of Educational Excellence: 25 Years of Education in the Republic of Singapore*. Longman, London

Further Reading

Ang W H, Yeoh O C 1990 25 years of curriculum development. In: Yip J S K, Sim W K 1990

Yip Y S W, Eng S P, Yap J Y C 1990 25 years of educational reform. In: Yip J S K, Sim W K 1990

Slovak Republic

J. Vantuch

1. General Background

The Slovak Republic was established on January 1, 1993 by the division of Czechoslovakia. The area of Slovakia, situated in Central Europe between the Danube River and the Tatra Mountains, is 49,014 square kilometers. This predominantly hilly territory is inhabited by 5.27 million people in 2,846 municipalities. About 17 percent of the population is scattered among 1,952 villages which have less than 1,000 inhabitants. In the early 1990s, 12.3 percent of all 2,472 primary schools have 25 students or less, 40 percent of all primary schools have 100 students or less, and 2.6 percent have over 1,000 students. There are only 11 cities with populations of over 50,000, including the capital, Bratislava, which has a population of 440,000.

Eighty-five percent of Slovakia's population are Slovaks, 10.8 percent are Hungarians (Magyars), 1 percent are Czechs, and 0.6 percent are Ruthenians / Ukrainians. The estimated population of Romanies (Gypsies) is around 7–9 percent, but according to the 1991 census only 1.5 percent of the total population declared themselves Romanies.

In 1900, Slovakia's population was 2.78 million; in 1950, 3.44 million; afterwards there was a population boom which meant that by 1991 the population had risen to 5.27 million. In some localities of southern and eastern Slovakia Romanies account for 40 percent of the population under 15-years-old. For the educational sector this clearly signals the need to anticipate future specific needs of the Romany population.

Slovakia is a country with traditionally strong Catholic influence. According to the 1991 census, 60.3 percent of the population is Roman Catholic, 6.2 percent is Protestant, 3.4 percent is Greek Catholic, 9.7 percent is without denomination, and 17.5 percent failed to respond. According to recent sociological findings, the higher the level of education, the lower the confidence in the church and the higher the level of support for political change after 1989 was registered.

In 1990, at the very beginning of the transformation of the economy, 73 percent of the population was employed in the production sector, of which 33.1 percent worked in industry, 12 percent in agriculture (34% in 1960), and 10.2 percent in construction. The nonproduction sector employed 27 percent of the population, of which 7 percent worked in education and 4.8 percent in health services. Only 0.3 percent of the population was employed in the financial sector and 0.1 percent in insurance. It should be noted that 8.1 percent of university graduates and 16.9 percent of secondary school graduates were employed in jobs requiring lower levels of qualification.

The transition to a market economy was accompanied by a decrease of 14.5 percent in GDP in 1991.

Metallurgy, mechanical engineering, industry linked to military production, petrochemical industry, and the construction sector were all affected by economical recession. Consequently, in these employment sectors it is difficult for school leavers to find work. National levels of unemployment among school leavers rose to 32 percent in 1993. In 1994 the Slovak economy had overcome its major problems related to the economic reform. While GDP increased by 4.8 percent, inflation decreased to 13.4 percent (see Table 1).

2. Politics and the Goals of the Education System

Until 1918, the territory of Slovakia formed part of the multinational Hungarian kingdom. In the latter half of the nineteenth century Magyar politicians started a policy to create a linguistically homogeneous nation. Consequently, Slovak secondary schools were closed and Slovak as a language of instruction was gradually replaced by Magyar. In 1918, with the establishment of Czechoslovakia, 2 million Slovaks had at their disposal 300 Slovak-speaking primary school teachers and 20 secondary school teachers. The most important goal of the new educational policy was to establish a complete network of schools which taught in the Slovak language. Twenty years later, shortly before the first signs of the disintegration of Czechoslovakia, Slovakia already had 11,496 primary school teachers, 1,884 secondary school teachers, 1,535 secondary grammar

Table 1
Macroeconomical indicators 1993

GDP (in millions of US$)	10.92
GDP decrease (in percentage, constant prices)	4.1
State income saldo/GDP (in percentages)	6.86
Export/GDP (in percentages)	49.6
Inflation rate (in percentages)	25.1
Unemployment rate (in percentages)	14.4

school teachers, 1,437 vocational school teachers, and 109 special school teachers.

With the establishment of the Slovak State in 1939, the liberal Czechoslovak school was replaced by a rather conservative, religion-linked type of school. Co-education was abolished, compulsory prayers were introduced to schools, and teachers were obliged to take part in religious acts. Nevertheless, a school system continued to develop as far as the growth of higher education institutions was concerned.

The Slovak national uprising in August 1944 demonstrated the nation's rejection of its subjigation by Germany and single party rule. However, at the same time it contained the seeds of a future antiliberal development in education which was started by the taking of all schools into state control as a reaction to the excessive influence of the church. This development continued with the creation of the "unified school" with unified principles of organisation and curriculum, and was finished by the subordination of the whole educational system to the doctrines of the Communist Party after it took power in 1948.

After 1989, subordination of education to a single ideology was abolished and school autonomy was legally increased. According to the law, all education should be based upon scientific knowledge and adhere to principles of patriotism, humanism, and democracy.

In the early 1990s, Slovakia is a parliamentary democracy with a one-chamber parliament and a president elected by the parliament. There are not great differences between the political parties as far as the general goals of education are concerned. However, there are still indicative differences such as: liberal parties support private schools, parties to the left do not. Christian Democratic parties encourage a return to traditional Christian values in education, other parties stress the secular character of education. Slovak nationalist parties support partial instruction in Slovak in schools for minorities whilst Magyar parties stress the need for establishing independent schools for their minority.

3. The Formal System of Education

3.1 Primary, Secondary, and Tertiary Education

The structure of the formal educational system is depicted in Fig. 1. Some key statistics are provided in Tables 2 and 3.

Since a nursery is not recognized as a part of the Slovak educational system, the first link of the educational chain is a kindergarten. Up to the end of the 1980s practically every child came to school from kindergarten. The enrollment of 5- and 6-year old children declined from 92 percent in 1989 to 77 percent in 1993, and in 1995 is still declining. This decline is due to the growth in unemployment among married women

Table 2
Schools—Trend data 1960–93

Number of Schools	Year				
	1960	1970	1980	1990	1993
Kindergartens	1,901	2,645	3,723	4,025	3,642
Basic Schools	4,163	3,837	2,506	2,358	2,472
Grammar schools	141	126	128	132	165
Secondary specialized schools	206	197	179	182	315
Secondary vocational schools	304	248	273	311	348
Special schools	135	264	319	417	419
Higher education colleges	36	41	45	50	59

and extra fees required for kindergarten attendance. Although average enrollment per class is 22, in reality, daily absenteeism causes attendance to be substantially lower. Nationally, the children–teacher ratio is 10.9:1.

Children start going to primary school—*základná škola*—(i.e., basic school—BS), when they reach the age of 6. Enrollment in BS is practically 100 percent. The school director has the authority to delay compulsory attendance by one year. The decision is usually based on the results of a school maturity test which is administered by the psychological–educational guidance center.

Until 1990, BS lasted 8 years. However, the duration of compulsory education was fixed at 10 years and had to be completed at secondary school. Problems with student attendance at secondary school led to the decision to shorten compulsory education by one year, and extend BS from 8 years to 9 years. The ninth grade was drawn up as a bridging grade between a basic school and schools preparing pupils for working professions. In spite of the original intention and efforts to implement an up-to-date curriculum, attendance at ninth grade represents only 3 percent of the population. In practice, BS lasts for 8 years,

with a four-year first stage and a four-year second stage.

In the first and second grades pupils usually have only one teacher for all subjects. Then, in the third and fourth grades there also exists specialized instruction of some subjects. In the second stage all subjects are taught by specialists. The maximum number of pupils allowed in the first grade class is 30, and in higher grades, 34. Classes with fewer pupils are created for instruction in some subjects, such as foreign languages.

Forty-six percent of all first grade pupils attend extra classes outside school hours. Older pupils can attend school clubs, while 9- and 10-year olds usually leave school after lunch.

The average number of pupils per class is 24; the national pupil–teacher ratio is 17.7:1. Pupils have twenty-one 45 minute lessons per week in the first grade, increasing to 26 lessons in the fourth grade. In the second stage pupils have from 28 to 31 lessons per week. Repetition rate at primary and secondary school is about 2 percent.

There exist three main streams of secondary education: *gymnázium*—grammar school (G), *stredná odborná škola*—secondary specialized school (SSS),

Table 3
Students—Trend data 1960–93

Number of Students	Year				
	1960	1970	1980	1990	1993
Kindergartens	83,875	119,026	231,155	216,336	188,502
Basic Schools	711,494	758,748	669,960	721,687	704,119
Grammar schools	19,799	42,950	53,891	55,648	63,522
Secondary specialized schools	42,607	83,050	85,990	87,149	103,793
Secondary vocational schools[a]	60,185	109,471	137,712	149,981	139,408
Special schools	6,732	12,609	19,107	30,415	29,182
Higher education facilities[b]	20,455	40,111	56,640	52,669	55,564

a In 1960—apprentice training center only
b Citizens of the Czech and Slovak Republics only

and *stredné odborné učilište*—secondary vocational school–apprentice training center (SVS–ATC).

Grammar school prepares students for study at higher education institutions. Traditionally, about 15 percent of the population entered a four-year grammar school, gradually increasing to 18 percent. From this type of school a five-year bilingual grammar school developed. The first year is devoted mainly toward foreign language (e.g., English, German, French, Spanish, and Italian) acquisition. In the following grades the foreign language is used as a teaching medium in the chosen subjects, and the curriculum and textbooks of that country are used as well. The popularity of eight-year grammar schools has increased as children were saved the unpleasantness of entrance examinations to secondary schools and parents preferred the better learning environment and expected higher quality of foreign language instruction.

The learning load for students is 30 lessons per week. The average class size is 32 with a maximum of 38 students; the national pupil–teacher ratio is 13.7:1.

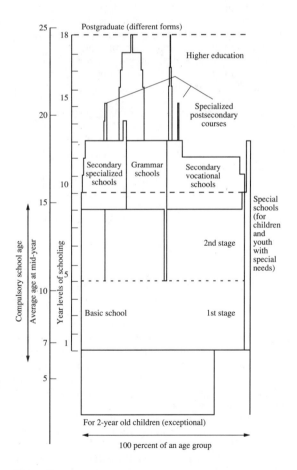

Figure 1
Slovak Republic: Structure of the formal education system 1993

Secondary specialized schools prepare students mainly for technical universities and for professions requiring a good quality, general and professional education with a firm grounding in theory. They are specialized in technology, economics, agriculture, forestry, library studies, and preschool teacher training, as well as health care (four-year courses) and conservatoires (six- to eight-year courses). Academies offering five-year courses in the hotel trade are very popular. Specialized schools for girls offering two to three-year courses have been established in the early 1990s.

The ratio of students entering SSS increased rapidly from 22 percent to 33 percent of the population which enrolled in 1993. The average weekly learning load is 32 lessons, average class size is 31 pupils, and the student–teacher ratio is 13.2:1.

On the basis of the 1976 school reform, SVS had to become the mainstream of secondary education. Indeed, at the end of the 1980s 60 percent of the population attended these schools. Since 1990, the number of students enrolled in these schools has fallen; in 1993 it was 48 percent of all students at this level. At SVS students can study in 41 four-year courses, 104 three-year courses and 49 two-year courses in various groupings of specializations. Together with a number of various specializations there are 351 different courses.

In four-year courses 80 percent of the time spent during the first two grades is devoted to general theoretical education, while 20 percent of the time is devoted to practical training. During the second half of the course, 40 percent of the time is devoted to practical training. In three-year courses this ratio is 1:1, theory and practical training alternating in weekly blocks. Practical training for jobs dominates two-year courses. The average class size is 24, and student–teacher ratio is 22.7:1. The problem of SVS is that the practical training in factories is difficult to guarantee due to the financial difficulties of many enterprises.

In 1993–94 the number of state schools with Magyar as the first language of instruction was as follows: 405 kindergartens with 617 classes and with an average class size of 21; 300 primary schools with 2,096 classes and an average class size of 22.1; 19 grammar schools with 154 classes and a class size of 29.4; 22 secondary specialized schools with 171 classes and with an average class size of 28.1; and 25 secondary vocational schools with 215 classes and an average class size of 25.3.

The number of state schools with Ukrainian as the language of instruction, serving the Ruthenian / Ukrainian minority is as follows: 47 kindergartens with 66 classes and an average class size of 18.1; 13 primary schools with 65 classes and an average class size of 11.6; 1 grammar school with 8 classes and a class size of 20.1; and 4 secondary technical schools with a class size of 31.5. Moreover, there exist 27 primary schools with the Ukrainian language as a subject with 125 classes and an average class size of 15.8.

After 1989 primary schools were established for the German minority with instruction partially offered in German, as well as an experimental school using Romany as the language of instruction. In 1992, the first Romany reader was published.

The school year begins in all state schools on September 2 (September 1 is a state holiday), and at the latest on September 5, and ends on June 30. The school year usually comprises 195 teaching days. Summer holidays are in July and August, weekly winter holidays vary regionally and occur in February or in March. Also there are longer school holidays during Christmas and Easter.

A special form of school, not illustrated in Fig. 1, is a basic school of art—*zácklad ná umelecká škola*—providing art education in one or more of four areas: music, dancing, visual arts, and drama. Students attend these schools to complement their primary or secondary school education. Schools can also be attended by adults. However, a tuition fee has to be paid for instruction. There are 169 schools and 103 affiliations with a total number of 77,201 students.

There are 14 institutions of higher education, two of them being classical universities with 59 faculties in 1993. In the 1990s nonuniversity higher education institutions started to emerge as colleges of professional studies and by the upgrading of six selected secondary schools. The Accreditation Commission has been established and the accreditation of all higher education institutions is in progress.

Higher education study for a bachelor's degree takes three years, and for a master's, five years. Some studies take four years, for example, teacher training for primary schools; and some six years, for example, theological and medical training. Approximately 17 percent of 18-year olds enter higher education. Since 1990 the number of new students has been rapidly increasing (e.g., by 25% between 1992–94). This rise in numbers is a reaction to OECD recommendations to increase the number of students to 20–25 percent of the relevant age group by the year 2000. However, unless there is faster development in the nonuniversity sector, the recommended expansion in numbers will not be reached.

3.2 Special Education

This stream of education is attended by approximately 3 percent of the population. In 1994 there were 417 state schools: 79 kindergartens, 296 primary and auxiliary, 2 grammar, 5 SSS, and 35 SVS—a total number of 29,033 children. This included mentally handicapped children, deaf children and children with hearing difficulties, children with speech problems, blind and poorly-sighted children, physically handicapped children, and multiply handicapped children. The average class size is 9.5 and student–teacher ratio is 7.5:1. There are 4,051 teachers and 1,259 educators serving in these schools. Fifty-one percent of teachers and 22 percent of educators are fully qualified; that is to say, they are graduates of special pedagogy at a Faculty of Education or they have finished a supplementary study of special pedagogy.

3.3 Vocational, Technical, and Business Education

In 1994, approximately 85,000 students finished various types of secondary schools. It was expected that 20 percent of them will go on to continue their further education, 45 percent will go on to work, and some 35 percent will remain unemployed. Besides economic recession there is a problem with the professional profile of school leavers. At present, the labor market is very atypical; schools are not yet prepared to meet increasing needs for economically educated, entrepreneurially oriented people with a good knowledge of foreign languages. Moreover, insufficiently formulated policies of economy change do not stimulate schools to change the profile structure of leavers.

Through entering predominantly SVS–ATC, but also SSS, 14- and 15-year old students are indirectly choosing their future profession. To prevent professional differentiation being realized too early, a model of gradual preparation is happening at SVS. In this model all students have the same study program for the first two years. Then, after a year of specialized preparation, they can obtain a certificate of apprenticeship and there is the possibility of obtaining a full secondary education certificate after another year of study.

Also, experimental two-year vocational schools are being founded at SSS and SVS. The leavers can be enrolled in the third grade of SSS or SVS. Nationally, there was a strong tendency to leave school with specializations that are too narrow. With respect to expected changes in the labor market, the profile of leavers will change toward more general skills.

Until 1990, SVS–ATC were operated by economy sectors. Schools were usually attached to enterprises which provided practical training for students, and later employed many of them. They also prepared workers for other enterprises. Students of SVS were contracted to the enterprise they were trained for which then financed their studies. So with the increase of enrollment in SVS, secondary education costs were almost completely carried by such enterprises. In the early 1990s 90 percent of SVS students were unable to find an enterprise that would subsidize their studies and provide future employment. Therefore these costs were financed from part of the state education budget. Legally, the Ministries of Education, Economy, Agriculture, Transport, etc., which represented the state became founders of relevant SVS, whereas only five enterprises maintained financial support for their SVS. However, this phase is likely to be a temporary one, since the involvement of the Chamber of Commerce and other such like professional associations in assessing and evaluating the design of vocational programs is increasing.

3.4 Adult and Nonformal Education

Interest in part-time secondary study decreased with the development of secondary schools. For instance, between 1960 and 1990, numbers fell from 2,676 to 305 in grammar schools and from 25,937 to 6,283 in SSS. Secondary education for adults was gradually concentrated in SVS–ATC. In part time courses, selected workers were able to complete the secondary education required for lower managerial positions in companies, as well as for possible entrance to institutions of higher education. After 1989, this form of study significantly decreased. A similar situation also developed in higher education.

Education financed by business enterprises has also declined with their financial difficulties. On the other hand, there is rapid development of new job-oriented education and training organized by Job Centers of the Ministry of Labor, Social Affairs and Family.

The University of the Third Age and *Academia Istropolitana*, the country's first Institute of Advanced Studies, were established in the early 1990s. The Socialist Academy was established by the former regime, originally for supporting socialist ideology, formed the organizational basis for the Open University which was founded in 1992. City universities were established where there was sufficient interest in regional development of human resources. Legally, they do not count as institutions of higher education, but rather collaborate with city universities abroad to provide specialist training courses. Moreover, the technology involved with distance education could compensate for the loss of quality teaching in higher education.

4. Administrative and Supervisory Structure and Operation

Due to legislative changes in 1990, the state monopoly of education was reduced, educational selfgoverning bodies were founded, and the process of decentralizing decision-making commenced.

Legislative proposals for the establishment of private and church preschool institutions were worked out in 1993, for primary and secondary schools in 1990,

Table 4
Nonstate schools 1993–94

	Private	Church
Kindergartens	1	0
Primary	1	81
Grammar	7	19
SSS	8	4
SVS	12	4

and for higher education in 1995 (see Table 4). It is not yet possible to establish schools which would be both nonprofit-making and radical.

The total number of students studying at private schools is 3,749 as opposed to 29,867 students studying at church schools. There is a marked increase in the number of church schools, whereas the number of private schools is stagnating and no new schools are being founded. It is worth noting that at private schools only 57 percent of students are of Slovak origin, while at church schools the figure is 97 percent.

There were three types of educational selfgoverning bodies created in the early 1990s: university and faculty senates to control rectors and deans, school boards to control school directors, and district school boards to control local (district) educational authorities. Selfgoverning bodies have the right to scrutinise the most important decisions of top management, allocation of finance, organizational changes, staff changes, and curriculum or program innovations.

Higher education institutions became fully autonomous by law. The Ministries of Education and Finance have retained their power to allocate funds.

Education at a lower level is administered by 46 school district offices. Slovakia is divided into 4 districts which administer regional institutions, predominantly secondary schools, and into 42 districts which administer mainly primary schools and other locally important educational institutions. In 1993 there was a total of 1,316 people working in administration in local educational authorities (LEA) and 250 working at the Ministry of Education. This is a one-third decrease on the 1989 figure.

Although primary and secondary state schools will not have full educational autonomy, they could legally have institutional autonomy. However, until it becomes transparent how the funds will be allocated, institutional autonomy will be questionable.

In accordance with the Act on State Administration and Self-government in Education, LEAs have to co-operate with municipalities. However, municipalities have no power regarding education, with the exception of founding kindergartens. They do have the right to delegate their representatives to selfgoverning bodies. This administrative structure is regarded as being of a temporary nature brought about by the need for internal change in education without the interference of local economical and political fluctuations.

The system of school inspection for primary and secondary education, with the Central Inspectorate and Inspection Centers in each school district, is headed by the chief school inspector who is subordinate only to the minister. Inspection centers are independent of school district offices. The inspectors monitor the schools and are responsible for the delivery of reliable information about quality control of education. There are teacher-training departments in school district offices which should improve the quality of education within the district by organizing local inservice training. Experienced teachers, employed part-time in these departments, provide assistance to colleagues from primary schools and kindergartens. There are four bigger independent teacher-training centers serving primarily secondary schools, but also managing larger inservice projects to the other schools and educational institutions.

This model of inspection and teacher training in methodology is based on the conviction that valid and reliable measurement of educational output is only possible when the evaluators themselves are not responsible for educational outcomes. This model of inspection does not go without criticism, but it is not yet clear if this criticism is founded on the model itself or by the lack of quality inspectors.

5. Educational Finance

During the period between 1965 and 1989, the expenditures on education fluctuated from 6.5 to 7.5 percent of the state budget and represented 5 percent of the national income. In 1993, the budget was US$0.58 billion which represented 5.5 percent of GDP. The educational budget for 1994 represented 12.6 percent of the state budget, that is 5.2 percent of the expected GDP. This increase of the share of educational expenditure from the state budget is a result of different legislative and financial methodology. The actual decrease of state budget from 1990–94 turned out to be 56 percent in constant prices of the originally allocated sum in 1990. Consequently, teachers' wages increased by a maximum of 30 percent while the cost of living increased by 260 percent.

Table 5 shows expenditures per capita in US$ spent in 1993, index comparison with proposed budget for 1994, and index comparison with 1991.

Church schools receive the same financial support from the state as state schools, and financial support from their founders. The amount of state contribution to private schools is not fixed. In 1993 it was approximately 85 percent of the expenditure of comparable state schools. Every year, the Ministry of Education makes a decision about the amount of this contribution

depending on the state budget. A legitimate claim would not cover more than 20 percent of expenditures. This situation makes budgeting for private schools complicated. Contemporary legislation does not stimulate enough private sector finance to sponsor schools.

In 1992–93 financial aid was allocated to 25,101 higher education students, in total an amount of US$1.337 million. A total amount of US$0.15 million was allocated to 1,730 students at state secondary schools, US$2,830 to 16 students at private schools, and US$5,635 to 61 students at church schools. A new system of grants and loans for payment of tuition fees is under consideration for secondary and higher education students.

6. Supplying Personnel for the Education System

As Table 6 shows, with the exception of higher education, there are generally too many women teachers.

As regards teachers' age in primary schools, 20.7 percent of teachers are younger than 30 years, 28.1 percent are between 30 and 40, 32.4 percent are between 40 and 50, and 18.8 percent are more than 50-years old. It is worth noting that in the first stage of BS 40 percent of teachers are more than 50-years old. Another point of concern is the small number of student teachers, representing only 3.3 percent of the number of all teachers teaching at primary schools.

In Slovakia, the higher education qualification required of primary and secondary school teachers was passed by law in 1946. In principle, the teaching qualification can be obtained in two ways: through studying for a master's degree in education or a two-year complementary teacher-training course.

Teacher training for the first stage of BS comprises a four-year program at a faculty of education. At these faculties, there is also the possibility to study a five-year program to become a second stage primary school teacher or a secondary school teacher. There are also other faculties at classical universities which provide five-year teacher-training programs. However, the graduates are predominantly trained for secondary schools. At these faculties, complementary

Table 5
Expenditures in US$ per capita in 1993, index comparison with proposed budget for 1994, and index comparison with 1991

	Operational costs			Wages and operational costs		
	1993	1993–94	1991–93	1993	1993–94	1991–93
Kindergarten	95.8	57.5	112.3	303.5	84.0	110.6[a]
Primary	63.9	75.9	130.4	230.1	95.1	114.9[a]
Grammar	67.2	68.0	200.2	243.0	90.2	114.2
SSS	93.8	72.4	179.3	296.7	91.1	113.2
HE	373.2	62.7	137.7	952.6	86.6	105.0

a comparison of 1992–93 only

teacher training study is available. Teachers of specialized subjects for SSS and SVS–ATC obtain their qualification after completing studies at the relevant HE institution (engineering, economy, etc.) and a two-year teacher training course at the relevant institution, or with a complementary teacher-training course after completing master's study. Student teachers usually undertake two subjects.

Since the second half of the 1970s, there has been a problem with postgraduate teacher training. Inservice training was and still is organized by a network of specialized methodological institutions. However, the lack of financial support means that further education is in danger mainly in rural areas, since teachers no longer have their travelling expenses paid. In the mid-1990s there are only 7 percent of primary teachers attending long-term further training.

The teaching load of teachers is 21 lessons per week at secondary school and 22 lessons per week at the second stage of primary school. At the first stage of primary school the teaching load corresponds to the weekly learning load of pupils; however, the maximum teaching load is 23 lessons.

7. Curriculum Development and Teaching Methodology

The Ministry of Education is responsible for curriculum development. Curricula and related documentation are developed by the State Pedagogical Institute in cooperation with advisory bodies.

It is generally accepted that liberalization of curricular policy is necessary, it is unfortunate that centralized curricular policy preserves existing mistakes and oppresses teachers' initiative. However, the situation is changing slowly. At some schools, teachers have the right to change 30 percent of the subject matter and adapt it to regional specificities, school objectives, or to their own professional point of view. However, this right is not sufficiently used by teachers because of the lack of experience in curriculum development and the lack of motivation. Directors of SVS–ATC now have the right to shift 10 percent of weekly load to the subject which is most important for the school profile.

If it is approved by the school directors, teaching staff, and the school board, there is a possibility to introduce arbitrary optional subjects at every school.

Textbooks prepared by different authors were evaluated by the State Padagogical Institute and submitted for approval by the ministry. Textbooks were usually written by teams. However, the authority of theoreticians usually prevailed, and so textbooks are usually very difficult and overburdened by facts and terminology. Thus, textbooks are addressed more to teachers than students. So far, publishers have been reluctant to take risks because schools have insufficient funds to buy teaching and learning aids, and the financial contribution from the state can only be used to buy a limited number of set textbooks and not alternative ones.

In the past the emphasis has been on teaching large amounts of subject matter rather than concentrating on teaching methodology. However, certain changes are taking place as follows:

(a) teachers taking responsibility for designing their own methodology rather than it being in the hands of the educational authorities;

(b) student-oriented rather than subject-oriented instruction being considered essential for achieving better educational results. This is reflected in teachers concentrating more on pupil performance and assessment.

In higher education there is absolute freedom in curriculum design, and also no supervisory body. However, curricular changes will occur as programs become more structured incorporating both modular units and a credit scheme.

8. The System of Examinations, Promotions, and Certifications

At the end of each school year, with the exception of the first two primary grades, a student's performance is evaluated in individual subjects by a five-degree scale from 1 (excellent) to 5 (unsatisfactory). Rules of assessment were set out by the Ministry of Education.

Table 6
Teacher distribution 1993

	Full-time	Part-time	Qualified (%)	Women (%)
Kindergarten	17,218	—	—	100
Primary	39,867	—	82	82
Grammar	4,659	719	95	67
SSS	7,812	3,037	91	60
SVS–ATC[a]	6,112	1,007	91	61
HE	8,103	1,248	100	34

a There are 19,201 other educators (foremen, instructors, etc.)

For example, students must be examined at least twice in each of two five-month school terms. They must not only be evaluated by written examinations but also by oral ones.

In each school grade a student receives an annual report card approved by either the state or a school founder. Nevertheless, only the following are of practical importance: the final report card from basic school confirming completion of primary education, the Maturity Certificate from grammar school, SSS and SVS confirming completion of full secondary education, and the Certificate of Apprenticeship from SVS–ATC confirming completion of vocational training. Higher education institutions award the academic degrees (such as batchelor, master's, and other doctorate degrees).

The organization of entrance examinations for secondary schools is regulated by the Ministry of Education. However, examination content is the responsibility of the individual school. The school must also make public the criteria of assessment before, and the applicants' marks and grade after, the examinations.

Higher education entrance examinations are not bound by special regulations. A dean, in cooperation with his advisory bodies, makes decisions regarding the content and organization of an examination. At present a *numerus clausus* for the acceptance of students is still operative.

Determination of the ratio between entrance examination results and prior school assessment presents a serious problem in student selection to any school. Difficulties arise because marks from basic and secondary school report cards are assessed by each individual school which means that it is very difficult to compare final results across the spectrum of schools. In the Slovak Republic a great deal of importance is put upon both examination results and average marks obtained from all subjects.

9. Educational Assessment, Evaluation, and Research

There is the lack of legitimate nationwide results, since research facilities are limited and no special allocation of finance is made for educational assessment and evaluation. Only after 1991 did Slovakia make an attempt to become more involved in IEA activities.

Financial means for research are allocated through the Ministry of Education's Grant Agency. Due to a reduction in financial support original research data is at a premium both quantitatively and qualitatively. Areas of research which are considered to be most important are

(a) investigation of standards of achievement, especially in relation to Grades 4, 8, and 12;

(b) methods of qualitative assessment and evaluation to investigate the increase in verbal assessment rather than written reports;

(c) curriculum development, especially in the social sciences (e.g., civics, ethics, health, sex education, and drug addiction prevention);

(d) computer-assisted learning and new technologies used especially in vocational education;

(e) teacher–student and teacher–parent relationships.

10. Major Reforms in the 1980s and 1990s

In the 1980s, primary and secondary schools underwent large curricular and structural reform. After extensive preparation at the beginning of the 1970s, the so-called "new conception of education" has been implemented since 1976.

It is indicative, that ideolization of good intentions together with an unrealistic approach to what was happening in schools led to opposite results. It was essential to overcome the necessity for encyclopedic learning. Instead, the highly theoretical explanation of the subject matter, advocated by the thesis about "acceleration of a child's development in a socialist society," led to the memorization of textbooks full of abstract concepts and overburdened with terminology. Stressing the relevance of school to real life led to the implementation of unpopular vocational subjects even in the preuniversity oriented grammar schools.

Those involved in future reforms should learn from the following mistakes:

(a) unrealistic demands through ideological and political pressure;

(b) student textbooks that were too abstract and not conducive to individual study;

(c) extensive, but ineffective inservice training, concentrating more on subject matter innovations than teaching methodology;

(d) no refresher teaching courses at higher education institutions.

Reform movements in 1990 started to look at different approaches to education because of the increased freedom throughout the country. However, curricular reform has suffered from a rejection of envisaged projects in favor of innovations, which taken together with the stagnation of teachers' wages has led to a decrease of activity in schools. Also, the conception of legislative changes suffers because of key obstacles— financial restrictions and the limits that they put on decision-making.

11. Major Problems for the Year 2000

The shortage of quality teachers is the biggest problem for future education. New reforms must involve resource management, wage differentiation and a proper promotion scheme. Working in an education authority, as an inspector or methodologist, is still considered to be an escape route for a teacher away from the teaching load rather than a place where a teacher can either advance in his or her profession or find a new challenging and more socially acceptable position.

Legal stipulations of a comprehensive system for both collection of the necessary data for decision-making and the delivery of information to the public have also to be considered. Every level of management will have to be clear about its role with clearly defined structures regarding its work and information duties so that it can be regulated by self-governing bodies and the public. Systematic quality control will also be essential. This can only be achieved through the introduction of appropriate nationwide assessment and evaluation, at least for Grades 4, 8, and 12.

Bibliography

Center for Social Analysis 1993 *Current Problems of Slovakia after the Split of the CSFR*. Report of the Socio-logical Survey. Center for Social Analysis, Bratislava

Harach L et al. 1992 *Higher Education in the Czech and Slovak Federal Republic*. Report to the OECD. Prague/Bratislava

Hobéon Management Consultancy 1994 *Feasibility Study on Upgrading of Pilot Schools in Vocational Education and Training in the Slovak Republic*. PHARE LMR Program. Hobéon Management Consultancy, The Hague

IIPEYS 1990 *Development of Education 1989–1990. The Czech and Slovak Federal Republic*. Institute of Information and Prognoses of Education, Youth and Sports (IIPEYS), Bratislava

IIPEYS 1992 *Development of Education 1990–1992. The Czech and Slovak Federal Republic*. IIPEYS, Bratislava

IIPEYS 1992 *The Effectiveness of Schooling and of Educational Resource Management, Country Report: Czechoslovakia*. IIPEYS, Bratislava

IIPEYS 1993 *Education in Figures. The Slovak Republic* IIPEYS, Bratislava

Ministry of Education and Science 1993 *Education in the Regions with Mixed Nationalities in Slovakia*. Ministry of Education and Science, Bratislava

Statistical Office of the Slovak Republic 1993 *Statistical Yearbook of the Slovak Republic 1992*. Statistical Office of the Slovak Republic, Bratislava

Slovenia

B. Marentič Požarnik

1. General Background

Slovenia, one of the youngest European states (having gained Independence on June 25, 1991, and international recognition in January 1992), lies at the crossroads of many influences, in both the geopolitical and the ethnic sense.

Geographically—covering an area of 20,200 square kilometers—it comprises Alpine, Pannonian, Karst, and Mediterannean subregions ("Europe in miniature"). The Slovenians are surrounded by national states of German, Roman, Finno–Ugric, and Slavic origin and have had to assert themselves throughout history against their mighty neighbors, especially the Bavarians (later Austrians) and Italians.

Historically, the Slovenian territory was part of the Austro-Hungarian Empire until the end of the First World War, when the largest part of it became incorporated into the newly created State of Serbs, Croats, and Slovenes, later named Yugoslavia. There, it was no more than an administrative unit inside a centrally governed state.

At the onset of the Second World War, Slovenia was occupied and divided between Germany, Italy, and Hungary, a partition which posed a major threat to its national existence. After the War, during which most Slovenians joined in the Resistance movement, Slovenia acquired the status of a federal republic within the Federative Democratic (later, Socialist) Republic of Yugoslavia. Refusing to join the Soviet Bloc of Eastern European countries in 1948, the Communist government gradually introduced certain forms of self-government and a degree of decentralization, but did not succeed in solving the national problems.

In Slovenia, the transition from the one-party system to a parliamentary democracy, with the first free elections being held in Spring 1990, proceeded fairly smoothly; the step to independence from the rest of Yugoslavia, decided by a referendum in December 1990 and implemented in June 1991, was followed by a violent but short-lived military intervention by the Serbian-controlled Yugoslav Army. Finally, the international recognition of the independent Republic of Slovenia in early 1992 gave impetus to the normalization and further development of its political, economic, social, and other structures.

The specific geohistorical situation of the Republic means that the Slovenian educational system has been influenced by the Austrian system, and there is a high regard for education in general.

In 1991, there were 1,960,000 inhabitants in Slovenia, of whom 87.5 percent were Slovenes by ethnic origin. Others include Croats, Serbs (together about 100,000), and other immigrants from other parts of Yugoslavia at different historical periods, in addition to a Hungarian and an Italian minority, and some other ethnic groups.

Many Slovenes live outside the present Slovenian borders. The borders, created in 1918, excluded large portions of the Slovenian population in Italy, Austria, and Hungary. The waves of economic and political emigration increased the number of Slovenians on all continents.

In the 1980s there was a stagnation of the population growth, and even a decrease as the result of a very low birthrate, in spite of low mortality. In 1981, there were 15.2 children born per 1,000 inhabitants, 13.5 in 1985, and 11.2 in 1990. There is therefore, a major concern that precious human resources (e.g., through high dropout rates, etc.) should not be wasted.

The prevailing religious denomination is Catholic. There are also small Protestant, Orthodox, Moslem, and other religious groups, and an increasing number of people with no religious affiliation.

The Slovene language belongs to the group of Slavic languages. It is spoken as the first language by about 1.7 million Slovenians within the Slovenian borders, and also by Slovenians living abroad (including about 50,000 in Austria, 10,000 in Hungary, and 100,000 in Italy).

Throughout its history, the Slovenian language and culture has had to assert itself in order to survive against the pressure from its mighty neighbors. Thus, education has been regarded primarily as a vehicle for promoting cultural and national identity, and not so much economic growth. The men who earned recognition for shaping Slovenian history were poets, and not scientists or military and political leaders.

There is a concern, even written into the Constitution, to promote education in the Slovene language and culture for Slovenian children living abroad, and an equal concern and respect for the educational needs of Italian and Hungarian minorities in Slovenia. Some models of bilingual education developed in Slovenia are regarded as model solutions by international standards.

Slovenia, which before the Second World War was still a predominantly rural society, has undergone changes due to rapid industrial growth. The proportion of those employed in the primary sector (mainly agriculture) decreased from 9 percent in 1960 to 2.6 percent in 1990; the corresponding percentages for manufacturing are 63 and 54; for service industries 28 and 43.5 (these values pertain to those employed in the public sector). The percentage of the population living in towns increased from 27 in 1948 to 51 in 1991. The per capita gross national product was US$6,186 in 1992.

After the Second World War, the number of schools, teachers, and pupils increased dramatically at all levels. The growth leveled out in the late 1970s. The proportion of unskilled and semiskilled workforce decreased from 38 percent in 1976 to 31 percent in 1991; at the same time, the proportion of those having secondary education or higher, increased from 24 to 35 percent. In 1986, the whole population over the age of 15 had, on average, 9.3 years of schooling. Those employed in the public sector had 9.9 years of schooling; the educational level of the unemployed was somewhat lower (9.1 years in 1989) (Bevc 1991).

Planning in the socialist era was rather rigid and more oriented toward the needs of the manufacturing sector than to the future. The transition to a free market economy has brought a reorientation in educational needs. It has also been accompanied, in the first phase, by an increase in unemployment (the unemployment rate increased from 4% in 1989 to over 12% in 1992) which represents a new challenge to education. The employment rate of women is among the highest in the world (in 1990, 45.5% of all employed persons were women). This has influenced the educational system, especially at the preschool level. Equal chances of access to different levels of schooling for both sexes are being attained. There are, however, discrepancies in some fields; women are underrepresented in the fields of natural science and technology, and in leading positions in the economy and in politics.

Major political changes in the post-Independence period involving a transition from a rigid monoparty system with a planned economy through a system of self-management socialism to that of a parliamentary democracy have all left their mark on the educational system.

Since 1990, attention has been directed toward establishing a pluralistic, democratic society with respect for human rights; on developing a market economy (with reprivatization of property); and on developing international relations on the new basis. The basic functioning of an independent state had first to be secured.

The vision of the future socioeconomic development of Slovenia has not yet been developed in detail. It is inclined toward a decentralized—"soft" and "medium"—ecologically safe and labor-intensive technology.

2. Politics and the Goals of the Education System

The change from a monoparty to a pluralistic governmental and political structure has involved a restructuring of the goals of the educational system. The government has not yet specified its respective visions in this area in great detail, owing to having other urgent tasks. There was a consensus that the one-sided ideological (Marxist) orientation had to be excluded from the curricula. There was also a trend toward a more diversified school system, with a shift away from a unified system which disregarded individual differences.

The need for more highly trained personnel, educated to secondary or tertiary level, is being stressed with a flexible, broad, but not too specialized and internationally comparable educational profile. More entrepreneurial spirit, which was stifled under the socialist economy, has to be developed.

The general aims of schooling are directed toward the improvement of the quality of life of the individual and of society as a whole, as well as toward securing basic human rights in education. Apart from providing minimum competencies, education should provide for other qualities such as: respect for others; tolerance and the reduction of conflicts arising from differences in ethnic, cultural, and historical backgrounds (interpersonal dimension, European dimension); individual development; personal autonomy and creative initiative at the workplace (individual development dimension); and the development of a healthy physical and cultural environment (ecological dimension). Specific demands upon educational systems in small countries should be added—compatability of systems, observance of the recognised criteria for proficiency, the study of foreign languages at all levels of education (Ministry of Education and Sport 1993).

The basic aims of compulsory schooling are to enable pupils' personal development in accordance with their abilities and developmental needs; to help them to acquire knowledge and competencies for critical, independent, efficient, creative action when dealing with the social and natural environment; and to provide the foundation for further education and training. Self-confidence should be encouraged and a positive self-concept fostered. Among the specific aims being stressed are the ability to participate in democratic, pluralistic society, tolerance, cooperation, responsibility, and respect for the rights of others (Piciga 1992b).

3. The Formal System of Education

3.1 Primary, Secondary, and Tertiary Education

Figure 1 presents the basic structure of the school system which is an 8+4+4 system, with some deviations from this general rule.

Slovenia has had a long tradition of compulsory elementary schooling; the compulsory six-year school was established in the rule of Maria Theresia in 1764 for the whole territory of the Austro-Hungarian Empire. It was extended to eight years in 1869. After Grade 4, pupils could stay in elementary school for another four years or go to an eight-year gymnasium.

To decrease the influence of the socioeconomic origin of school-going children, a comprehensive eight-year elementary school was introduced throughout Yugoslavia by a federal Act in 1958. This had the positive result that the proportion of children from different social strata who successfully completed eight years of schooling has in fact substantially increased. However, individual differences were neglected within a unified curriculum.

In Slovenia, in the years 1984–89, between 95 and 99 percent of children successfully completed Grades

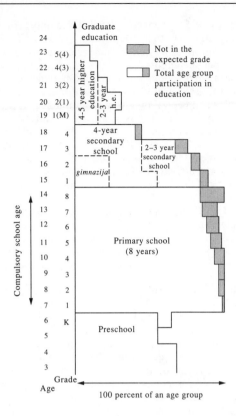

Figure 1

Slovenia: Structure of the formal education system
a Source for all data is Republican Bureau of Census. Data refer to end of school year 1990–91 for primary and secondary education; but for the winter semester 1990–91 for higher education. Data on preschool education are based on the population census in Spring 1991. Population data are estimated by the permanent residents register for the date December 31 1991 b The base of the diagram in the age of the student and percentages given are the participation rates of an age group in all kinds of education. Shaded areas (in primary and secondary education) are estimates of students who are in a lower grade than expected by age. No such estimates were possible for preschool and tertiary education c Data for secondary and tertiary education are overestimated, since students regardless of their permanent residence are compared to the population of permanent residents of Slovenia. It is estimated, that there are more students who come to study in Slovenia from other republics of former Yugoslavia, than there are students from Slovenia who study outside the country. This effect is highest in the age groups 14–15 and 19–20 years. Data for secondary education are underestimated for adult students, but their number is low d Unexpected high participation rate of 14-year old students in the educational system is due to immigration, their enrollment in primary as well in secondary education, and enrollment in a group of courses in secondary education (*skrajšani programi*, "shortened courses"). They make it possible for students who did not successfully finish all eight classes but were going to primary school up to the compulsory age 14 to enroll e *Gimnazija* does not last for only two years, as could be perceived from the graph, but was only recently re-introduced into the educational system, so that grades 3 and 4 were not yet operative in the critical year f Male students had to enter military service after secondary school for one year. This explains the lower participation rate of 19-year old students. This regulation was introduced in 1981 and discontinued after independence in 1991 g No official data on graduate enrollment is available for this year

1 to 8 and over 95 percent completed elementary school (including the 2–3% that took 9 years to do so). Table 1 presents information on the number of pupils in the various types of schools.

Children enter school when they are between 6 and 7 years old; at the end of the 1980s, the age of entry to school was lowered by a few months but it is still somewhat higher than in most European countries. The first four grades of primary school involve mainly general classroom teaching, while in the last four grades specific subject teaching is introduced; this transition presents some difficulties for certain pupils.

Pupils have 20 to 24 weekly lessons in the lower grades and 30 to 33 in the higher grades; the teachers' workload is 20 lessons per week. There are about 190 school days in the year (some of them reserved for sports, cultural events, etc.). Most schools are half-day schools and have a 5-day week. The teacher–pupil ratio is between 1:14 and 1:16, and the average classroom size is 25.

Small country schools are gradually disappearing. Large schools (over 1,000 pupils) in new urban settlements have not proven to be the best solution.

Many elementary (and also secondary) schools have a school counseling service where students and their teachers can obtain professional help in dealing with personal, educational, and other problems.

Traditionally, secondary education comprised at least three types of schools: two- to three-year vocational schools, four-year professional schools (technical, medical, etc.), and general secondary schools (*gymnasia*) leading to university studies.

Starting in 1974, a major reform of the secondary school system was launched at the federal level, to replace the "tripartite" system with a single type of multipurpose, comprehensive, vocationally oriented (directed) secondary school. Starting with a "common core" curriculum in the first two years, it offered a vast number of branches with general, vocational subjects and practical work in enterprises.

Every school had to perform a double purpose: to prepare pupils for work in a certain area and also for further studies. Other stated purposes of this comprehensive system were: to postpone early career decisions, to prevent "dead ends" in schooling (especially for young people from the lower socioeconomic strata), and to broaden general education for the whole population.

In Slovenia, this system—with some modifications—was introduced in 1980 and had, from the very beginning, to cope with serious difficulties, especially in teaching classes with students of such heterogeneous abilities, interests, and vocational plans. This gave rise to controversies. The most important of the gradual changes until 1990 was to re-establish a modernized version of the tripartite system of secondary education. A broader selection of schools for different trades and vocations is opening up.

In the year 1989–90, about 61 percent of those entering secondary education went to four-year schools (about 22% attended *gymnasia*), 31 percent entered three-year schools, while the remainder went into shorter forms of schooling (2 years and less). In 1983–84, the corresponding percentages were 50, 12, and 38.

The goal to extend secondary schooling to a whole generation has not yet been achieved. Between 5 and 10 percent of those who complete elementary school successfully do not enter secondary school. The dropout rate from secondary schools is about 20 percent (Piciga 1992a).

About one-half of those finishing the four-year secondary school proceed to the tertiary level.

The long-term wish of Slovenians to have their own national university was fulfilled only after the First World War, when in 1919 the University of Ljubljana

Table 1
Numbers of institutions, teachers, and students at different levels, Slovenia

	Institutions	Number of students	Teachers	Assistants
Preschool	942	76,279	3,957	—
Primary schools 1–8	831	229,932	14,840	—
Secondary schools 9–12	161	92,405	6,700	—
Higher education 12+	28	36,506	1,376	786
Special education 1–12	64	4,458	893	—
Musical education	96	18,750	1,068	—
Schools of national minorities				
preschool	11	798	47	—
elementary	19	1,931	207	—
secondary	5	475	68	—

Source: Nacionalni program 1992

was founded. The second Slovene university was founded in 1975 in Maribor.

The University of Ljubljana consists of 22 institutions and the University of Maribor of 6 institutions with two-year, four-year, and sometimes five- or six-year undergraduate studies. In 1991–92, there were 36,504 students in both universities (40,239 in 1993–94), but 15 percent of them were part-time. The number of part-time students declined during the 1980s. In 1980, 30 percent of students were part-time. Slightly more than half of the students and graduates are women.

All institutions of higher learning are part of either Ljubljana or Maribor university. Plans are being made to establish a parallel system of more vocationally oriented colleges. The number of teachers in higher education is given in Table 1. Some 17 percent of them are women but 39 percent of the assistants are women. The average teaching load is 6 to 9 hours per week for professors and 10 to 12 hours for assistants, with a tendency to the lower figures. There was an explosion in the numbers of students, teachers, and institutions, especially in the 1960s and 1970s; the numbers leveled off in the mid-1970s and went up again slightly in the early 1990s. In 1993, there were 202 students per 10,000 inhabitants. This is still lower than in most European states. Entry to higher education is regulated by a *numerus clausus* and there are entrance examinations to some institutions (medicine, architecture). Most of them will be replaced by *"matura"* in 1995.

University curricula are relatively fixed (no electives) and overburdened with a high number of subjects and contact hours. Most students have up to 30 lessons to attend per week (25 under the new regulations) which leaves them little time for individual study.

There is increasing public concern about the low efficiency of university studies. There is a high dropout rate (nearly half of all students are in their freshman year); only about 60 percent of those entering the system actually graduate. The average duration of studies is very long, for example, in 1986 it was 6.7 years. There are only between 25 and 30 graduates per 10,000 inhabitants each year. The ratio of graduate students is also very small. In 1991, 3,046 students completed two-year undergraduate studies and 2,393 students four-year studies. However, only 352 obtained their master's degree and 121 their doctorate. The corresponding figures for 1993 are: 2,991, 2,952, 725 (including specialist degrees), and 192. Among all employed persons, there are 6 percent who have completed four years of higher education.

International cooperation is being expanded, through interuniversity exchange programs and different schemes like PHARE/TEMPUS, ERASMUS, LINGUA, and others.

3.2 Preschool Education

Because of the very high employment rate of women, a well-developed system of preschool education is a necessity. After a one-year maternity leave, many women put their baby into a preschool institution. In 1981, 9 percent of children under 2 years, 53 percent of children between 2 and 4 years, and 51 percent of those aged 5 to 6 years were enrolled in preschool institutions. The corresponding percentages for 1991 were 12, 67, and 55. The costs are subsidized for families in lower income brackets. The first private kindergartens began to appear under the new political system and are increasing in number.

In the 1980s, an obligatory school preparatory program was developed for all children, including those who do not regularly attend kindergarten. The aim is to make the transition to elementary school easier.

There are special programs for children of national minorities and for children with special needs.

3.3 Special Education

Some institutions of special education (for children with impaired vision or hearing) have a longstanding tradition, stemming from the mid-nineteenth century.

In 1990 there were 64 institutions (mainly at elementary school level) for children with different kinds of disabilities. The average teacher–pupil ratio was 1:5.

There are trends toward integrating more children, especially borderline cases, into normal schooling. This requires a change in teachers' attitudes. It also requires specialized knowledge and methods of work which are not yet present to a sufficient degree.

There are very few specialized institutions (shorter vocational courses and schools) for youth with special needs at the secondary level. Pupils are encouraged and are given special support to get into "normal" schools, up to the university level. They do, however, face employment problems.

3.4 Vocational, Technical, and Business Education

The main features of this system have already been described in Section 3.1.

Apprenticeship training (with alternate periods of on-the-job training and formal schooling) nearly disappeared in the 1980s under the system of vocationally directed comprehensive schools. It began to reappear at the beginning of the 1990s in order to fulfill the needs for traditional crafts and also for new vocational areas such as car mechanics and electronics.

The reorientation from a planned to a market economy has given rise to the need for more efficient and diversified training in areas such as marketing, business management, banking, and accounting.

Educational and curricular planning in this area is becoming increasingly a matter of partnership between the Minstry of Education and Sport and corresponding chambers of commerce and professional associations.

3.5 Adult and Nonformal Education

In the first decades after the Second World War, adult education, mainly institutionalized in the form of "workers' universities," had primarily a compensatory function: to "fill-in" the gaps in elementary and secondary schooling of the existing workforce. Later, other functions emerged: training and retraining of semiskilled and skilled workers for new jobs and for new skills that were required, such as use of computers, foreign languages for special purposes, finance, and management. In 1992 the proportion of adults included in schools and in other types of formal education was 1 in 10.

The radical change of the political system in the 1990s has meant a decline in courses on self-management and similar courses of a sociopolitical nature. The range of courses in the areas of personal development, leisure, general education—also offered by private firms—has increased. The important contribution of the "Third Age University" for the retired, founded in 1984 and functioning mainly on a voluntary basis should also be mentioned here.

Many enterprises (banks, computer firms, railways, etc.) have their own systems of training and retraining their employees at various levels.

Every year, about two-thirds of adults are included in different forms of adult education, but the shorter forms prevail (in 1989, the average duration was 3.6 hours per person per year) and those not directly linked to upgrading vocational knowledge and skills. Only 10 percent of adult education has been linked to specific professional training for existing or new tasks.

Until 1992, very little public money was invested in this sector (about 0.09 of the GNP). It has been financed largely by firms and the candidates themselves.

The Andragogical Center founded in 1992 intends to serve as an organizational, training, research, and development center in this area. It is developing extensive new programs involving functional literacy and study circles.

4. Administrative and Supervisory Structure and Operation

Since there was no federal Ministry of Education in Yugoslavia, there was a certain level of independence in school administration and management in Slovenia even before Independence. All attempts to unify curricula were strongly resented.

The Slovenian Ministry of Education and Sport is responsible for school policy and for the management and financing of all schools, including preschool education (where the responsibility was previously shared with the Ministry of Health and Social Affairs) and higher education (where the Ministry of Science and Technology manages and finances research activity).

School inspection which used to be a part of the counselling function at the Board of Education and Sport was legally (1994) separated from it and placed under the responsibility of the Ministry of Education

and Sport. The Board of Education and Sport remained responsible for school counselling and development—fostering innovative projects—as well as for organizing inservice training (especially for school heads and teachers during the induction period).

There is a trend toward centralizing the whole system of education. New laws have been prepared (on higher education in 1994; on school financing in 1993) or are in preparation.

5. Educational Finance

In the era of self-management socialism (1976–90), the so-called "self-management communities of interest" were the place where the representatives of "associated labor" as "users" and schools as "producers" met and negotiated questions of finance, curricula, and management of schools in different sectors (health, building, economy, etc.). Since 1991, the system has been changed to one of public expenditure (budget) with the new law on organization and financing.

Previously, the financing of secondary and higher education had been coordinated at the national level and the financing of primary education was at the level of the local communities; this resulted in inequities among richer and poorer communities. Since 1992, the salaries of primary teachers have also become part of the national responsibility and teachers have become public servants. However, the other expenditures of elementary schools have remained at the local level.

Teachers' salaries are fixed by law. Schools have some freedom to decide about expenditures for material costs. They also submit proposals on maintenance and investment costs to the Ministry of Education and Sport.

The percentage of Gross National Product (GNP) allocated to education is subject to some variations: 4.0 in 1984, 3.5 in 1990, 4.3 in 1992, and (as estimated) 4.9 in 1993. In 1993, the percentage of the state budget spent on tasks which were the responsibility of the Ministry of Education and Sport was 18.3 The analysis of expenditures by level shows that in 1993, about 12 percent went to preschool level, 23 percent to the primary (Grades 1–4), 44 percent to the secondary (including Grades 5–8), and 19 percent to the tertiary level. Expenditures "per pupil unit" amounted in 1992 to 1,040 ECU for primary (Grades 1–4), 1,140 ECU for secondary (including Grades 5–8) and 3,410 ECU for higher education. Across levels, in 1990 about 60 percent of expenditure was for teacher salaries (50% in 1992), 28 percent for school administration and teaching materials, and 4.4 percent (7.3% in 1992) for study grants (Tratnik 1991).

Primary and secondary education is free of charge. Parents pay for textbooks and extracurricular activities. In tertiary education, regular undergraduate study is free. Part-time and graduate students pay fees.

6. Supplying Personnel for the Education System

The numbers of teachers at different levels are presented in Table 1. There is a lack of qualified teachers in mathematics, natural science, and technology, and a slight surplus in the humanities and social science.

There has always been a marked dualism between the training of primary and secondary teachers: the first had a thorough professional and practical, but less academic, preparation; the reverse was true for secondary teachers (Marentič Pözarnik and Kotnik 1988, Marentič Pözarnik 1991). The traces of this dualism are still visible. Since teacher training rose to the university level, its professional components have been reduced.

Teacher-training colleges have evolved from secondary-level teachers' schools (*učiteljišča*, which existed from the mid-nineteenth century) which became two-year institutions in the 1960s and four-year institutions in the 1980s. Since 1987, all teachers (including classroom teachers) have been educated through four-year courses. Only courses for preschool teachers are still of two-years' duration.

Teachers of vocational subjects (engineering, etc.) receive their professional training through inservice courses in education, psychology, teaching methods, and so on, after having completed their basic studies.

Increasing attention is being paid to the induction period (courses and professional support for teachers in their first year) and to inservice training. The central catalog of courses and workshops is published regularly. A three-tiered system of teacher promotion, linked to increases in salaries, has begun to be implemented since 1992. It is based on outstanding teaching, inservice training, mentoring functions, publishing, and innovative and developmental work. For this purpose, teacher quality is assessed by head teachers; this assessment system will be refined. This far, it has given a new impetus to inservice training which is not compulsory; every teacher can claim up to 5 days per year for inservice training. This is a trend toward active experimental methods rather than mere lecturing.

7. Curriculum Development and Teaching Methodology

There is a nationally prescribed core curriculum for all subjects and grades in primary and secondary schools. It is approved by the Professional Council (committee of experts) appointed by the Parliament. Curricula prescribe the scope of individual subjects, their goals, and content. The level of provision is monitored by school supervision. Teachers and schools are autonomous in the choice of methods and textbooks. Minor adjustments for local differences (as in teaching geography and history) are possible and even encouraged, especially in the lower grades.

In general there are very few electives, though they are increasing in number. There are movements toward greater flexibility. The "ideological" subjects such as Marxism, self-management socialism, and premilitary education have disappeared from syllabuses. After some discussions in 1990, religion was not reintroduced as a school subject, but a new subject—"civic" education—has been developed.

Thinking about curricula, teaching materials, and methods has been affected, to a certain extent, by the processes of adaptation of international curricula like "new maths," BSCS (Biology Science Curriculum), the CHEM Study Project and by taking part in international projects (IEA, TEMPUS). Some textbooks written by groups of experts are tried out systematically; others are just presented by individual authors. Though all have to be officially approved there exists freedom of choice from among approved textbooks.

All children (except for some in special education) learn a foreign language from the fifth grade onward. In most cases (about 85%), they learn English and the rest learn German. There is an official agreement to start learning foreign languages two years earlier. The second foreign language, taught in many four-year and some three-year secondary schools, may be German, French, or—in some cases—Italian, Spanish, Latin, or Russian.

There is a general problem of overburdening curricula with numerous disconnected subjects and a large quantity of data. At the same time, it is difficult to introduce new cross-curricular topics such as health, environmental education, civics, and intercultural education. Many feel that curricula should become less content- and product-oriented and more goal- and process-oriented. This also means a reorientation from expository teaching to more problem-solving, project work, and other active methods. There is a need for more highly trained experts in teaching methods and curricular theory.

8. The System of Examinations, Promotions, and Certifications

Grades 1–5 (1 being unsatisfactory) are given at the primary and secondary level on the basis of internal assessment. Promotion at the primary level is based on satisfactory achievement in all subjects, moderated by an overall assessment of the pupil's achievement.

There are two trends which should be noted: first, the replacement of numerical grades in the first three years of primary school by verbal accounts of pupils' progress in different areas, and, second, the introduction of external examinations at certain points, especially at the end of primary and secondary schooling. Some teachers fear that this will be an attempt to control the quality of their work.

Extensive preparations started in 1991 to introduce the new form of *matura* in 1995—an external examination for students finishing 4-year secondary schools and intending to apply for entry to higher education.

9. Educational Assessment, Evaluation, and Research

Participation in comparative international projects, like those of the IEA (International Association for the Evaluation of Educational Achievement) and ETS (Lapointe et al. 1992a, 1992b), the "literacy study" by UNESCO, and the international baccalaureate has increased the awareness of assessment issues and also given rise to some controversies such as the autonomy of teachers and the importance of national goals versus outside criteria of achievement. Large evaluation studies, especially at the secondary level, were carried out in the 1980s and have influenced public opinion and the subsequent reform.

Similar research at the tertiary level is undertaken by the Center for Development at the University of Ljubljana. For example, the longitudinal study which followed a generation of students through 10 years (1976–86) revealed the low efficiency of the system (Stergar 1988).

Data on key educational indicators are collected regularly. These are especially concerned with the achievement of students and their progress through the system. In 1991, a national examination center was established, responsible for designing and delivering *matura*, for modernizing other forms of assessment, and for research and training in this area.

The educational research that is undertaken covers a wide range from developmental to theoretical studies. It is being undertaken by the Institute for Educational Research, the Departments of Education and Psychology at the University, teacher-training colleges, and other agencies. The scope of international projects, on a bilateral or multicultural basis, is increasing (e.g., with TEMPUS, ATEE, OECD/CERI, EC/CDCC, UNESCO, TAEP), including topics such as environmental education, civics education, European dimension of education, and teacher training.

Teachers themselves are now being given a more active part in developmental studies in the sense of action research methodology. This seems to be one answer to the perennial problem of bridging the gap between theory and practice.

10. Major Reforms in the 1980s and 1990s

The major (federal) reform in the 1980s aimed at establishing a comprehensive, vocationally oriented secondary school system. The deficiencies of this system led to the "reform of the reform" in 1990 which re-established the tripartite system of secondary education, as mentioned above. In secondary education, there are plans to have greater flexibility and diversification in terms of types of programs and schools, more paths to certain vocations, duration of schooling, etc.

There are plans to extend compulsory education to 9 years by making the school preparatory year obligatory. In the elementary school, more subject integration in the lower grades and diversification (electives, ability groupings, etc.) in the final grades are being planned. There is the intention to change the basic structure of elementary school from 4+4 to 3+3+3. In higher education, there are plans for student mobility and international compatability of programs by introducing a credit system and different forms of quality assessment.

In the field of teacher training, the task for the 1990s will be to find effective remedies for structural deficiencies in the scope and relations between academic–professional and theoretical–practical components. Furthermore, inservice training should increase in scope and quality, the aim for the 1990s being 30 hours per year for every teacher.

The 1990s will also see the expansion of private initiatives in schooling, especially in the sectors of special needs (problem children, the gifted, etc.). Another important task will be the creation of an efficient system of adult education.

11. Major Problems for the Year 2000

One of the major problems is the low efficiency of the system in terms of dropout and the repeating of grades. Among the official goals for the 1990s are: to include all elementary school leavers in one or another form of secondary schooling; to increase the proportion of those entering (and finishing) the tertiary education level; to enforce European standards of quality through an external examination system; to diversify educational offers for students with different abilities and interests through private initiative also; and to make education a lifelong process for the majority of the population (Nacionalni Program 1992). Effective strategies to implement international recommendations and conventions in the entire educational system (in terms of human rights, European citizenship, multiculturalism, etc.) will also have to be sought.

Another problem is how to adapt curricula and methods to the future of manifold (and unpredictable) social, economic, and technological changes and at the same time secure the survival of a small nation and its identity. The solution cannot be in simply adding new content and then "transmitting" it to the young. The search for new approaches in teaching and learning to develop autonomy and wisdom, rather than just a tendency to react to forthcoming changes, will be the major challenge for the 1990s.

References

Bevc M 1991 *Ekonomski pomen izobraževanja*. Didakta, Radovljica

Lapointe A E, Mead N A, Askew J M 1992a *Learning Mathematics*. ETS IAEP, Princeton, New Jersey

Lapointe A E, Mead N A, Askew J M 1992b *Learning Science*. ETS IAEP, Princeton, New Jersey

Marentič Požarnik B, Kotnik N 1988 Practical components in teacher-training programmes in Slovenia (Yugoslavia). *European Journal of Teacher Education*. 1: 41–48

Marentič Požarnik B 1991 Issues and trends in teacher education in Slovenia, Yugoslavia. *Action in Teacher Education* 3: 30–34

Ministry of Education and Sport 1993 *The Development of Education in the Republic of Slovenia 1992*. Ministry of Education and Sport, Board of Education and Sport, Ljubljana

Piciga D (ed.) 1992a *Znanstvene in strokovne podlage za prenovo osnovne šole*. Slovensko društvo raziskovalcev šolskega polja, Ljubljana

Piciga D 1992b *New Aims and Goals of the Slovenian Primary and Lower Secondary School (Age 6–15)*. CE, DECS/Rech (92)25. Council for Cultural Cooperation, Ljubljana

Stergar E (ed.) 1988 *Proučevanje študijske poti študentov v SRS: Generacija 1976. Zbornik* (with English summary). Center za razvoj univerze, Ljubljana

Tratnik M 1991 Presentation synopsis of education in Slovenia. Prepared for XXVII IIEP Annual Training program in Educational Planning and Administration 1991–92 at the International Institute for Educational Planning, UNESCO, Paris

Nacionalni program preduniverzitetnega izobraževanja v republiki Sloveniji 1992 *Okvirni program modernizacije vzgoje in izobraževanja v Republiki Sloveniji do leta 2000*. Ministrstvo za šolstvo in šport, Ljubljana

Further Reading

Lazarini F 1989 Development of education in the SFR of Yugoslavia 1986–1988. Report prepared for the 40th session of the International Conference on Education (UNESCO/BIE). Yugoslav Commission for UNESCO, Ljubljana–Belgrade

Leitner E, Marentič Požarnik B 1986 Curriculum research in Yugoslavia. In: Hameyer U, Frey K, Haft H, Kuebart F (eds.) 1986 *Curriculum Research in Europe*. Swets North America/Berwyn

Marentič Požarnik B 1989 Some data and reflections on research and development in higher education in Slovenia/Yugoslavia. *Zeitschrift fur Hochschuldidaktik* 3: 150–69

Rečnik F 1991 *Izobraževanje v Sloveniji za 21. stoletje. Globalna koncepcija razvoja vzgoje in izobraževanja v Republiki Sloveniji* (with summary in English). Zavod Republike Slovenije za šolstvo, Ljubljana

Publications of Zavod Republike Slovenije za statistiko

Šoljan N N (ed.) 1989 *Higher Education in Yugoslavia*. Andragoški centar, Zagreb

South Africa

M. J. Bondesio and S. J. Berkhout

1. General Background

South African society is in the process of extensive political and economic change. This process is moving at a rapid pace toward a nonracial democratic society. Structures and institutions are changing in terms of form, content, and functions in order to be able to reflect a new democratic value system. Constitutional negotiations are taking place at different levels and between the whole spectrum of participants. Education is on the agenda. The government's Educational Renewal Strategy document (Department of National Education 1991b), as well as, among others, the proposals of the African National Congress (1991), make it clear that fundamental changes in education are an important part of societal changes. This new, yet to be created education system must be generally acceptable, adaptable, and affordable. Within the framework of limited resources, and a growing demand for equal educational opportunities, it is evident that this description of the South African educational system could well become outdated by the mid-1990s.

The Republic of South Africa is located south of the Limpopo River at the southernmost tip of Africa. It has a surface area of 1,123,226 square kilometers. This excludes the landlocked, politically independent countries of Lesotho and Swaziland, as well as the so-called four TBVC states (the Transkei, Bophuthatswana, Venda, and Ciskei) which are not internationally acknowledged as independent. These four states, as well as six self-governing territories within South Africa (Lebowa, Kwazulu, Qwaqwa, Gazankulu, KwaNdebele, and KaNgwane), have the responsibility for providing their own education, but receive financial aid from South Africa.

The country is characterized by ethnic and cultural diversity. This is reflected in the number of languages spoken by the 30.8 million inhabitants (1990). The mother tongue of the majority of Whites is either Afrikaans (56%) or English (36%). Zulu-speaking peoples number some 7.6 million, the Xhosa-speaking some 3 million, the Sotho (including the North Sotho, South Sotho, and Tswana-speaking tribes) approximately 7.6 million, the Tsonga a little over 1.5 million, and the Venda about 200,000. The variety of ethnic and language groups forms one of the main problems for educational provision, and the medium of instruction is a hotly debated issue.

Much of the character of the South African education system has resulted from the philosophy of separate provision of education for the different ethnic groups ("apartheid"). This formally commenced after the Second World War with the creation of a separate department of education (that of Bantu Education) for Blacks. South Africa has largely separate schools for each of the four main population groups (Asians, Blacks, Coloreds, and Whites). The principle of separate schooling for the various race groups will be removed from the statute books. This is indicated by the annulment of several acts of parliament that formalized "apartheid," such as the Population Registration Act, the Land Act, and the Group Areas Act.

In 1990 South Africa had 30.8 million inhabitants, 956,000 of whom were Asian, 21 million Black, 3.2 million Colored, and 5 million White. The total population is growing at a rate of 2.07 percent per annum and is expected to reach 53.9 million (or between 64 and 65 million if the TBVC states are included) by the year 2010. The implication for education becomes clear when it is recognized that 49 percent of the population is under the age of 18.

In 1990, 55.9 percent of the population lived in urban centers. The recent abolition of influx control is placing additional demands on the provision of education. Some urban areas recorded a 100 percent growth rate in little more than 6 months, causing excessive growth in the number of students attending available schools.

South Africa's Gross National Product (GNP) in real terms (with 1985 as basic year) increased from R75 billion in 1970 to R119 billion in 1990. The contribution of agriculture and mining to the GNP decreased from 35 percent in 1946 to 15.8 percent in 1990. In 1990 net gold exports comprised R18 billion of the total exports of R72 billion, while imports amounted to R67 billion. Economically active South Africans increased from 4.6 million in 1951 to 10.9 million in 1989. During the same period the workforce in the agricultural sector decreased from 33 to 13.6 percent of the economically active population. The relative employment in the mining sector decreased from 16 to 8.5 percent of the total workforce. The remainder of the workforce is employed in sectors and industries such as manufacturing (15.9%); electricity, water, and gasworks (1.1%); construction (6.4%); transport and communication (4.8%); commercial (10.8%); financial (3.9%); and community, social, and personal services (22.6%). Approximately 11.1 percent of economically active inhabitants are employed in a professional, semiprofessional, technical, managerial, administrative, and executive capacity; and 21 percent of these are Blacks. The economic development reflected by these changes is creating an increasing demand for more varied, specialized, and vocationally orientated education.

In 1985, 9.2 percent of the economically active population held a postschool educational qualification (degree, diploma, certificate, or trade qualification), while 17.7 percent had no formal education. Those with incomplete primary and secondary education constitute 23.8 and 30.5 percent respectively of the economically active population, while those with complete primary and secondary education constitute 8.5 and 10.5 percent respectively.

Estimates of the total number of unemployed persons are close to 6 million. It is therefore expected that by the year 2000 some 10 million persons will be jobless. The stimulation of economic growth which will lead to the creation of more jobs features high on the priority list of the government which subscribes to a market-orientated philosophy. A number of economists and politicians, however, favor a more socialist philosophy and affirmative action to promote economic growth and to correct the existing inequalities. Pressure is consequently brought to bear on the education system to help effect a solution to these problems.

2. Politics and the Goals of the Education System

Since 1948 the political scene has been dominated by the ruling National Party of the White electorate. However, in 1990, the unbanning of organizations such as the African National Congress and the South African Communist Party, and the scrapping of discriminatory legislation such as the Separate Amenities Acts and the Population Registration Act to name but a few, has paved the way for negotiations and a more democratic society.

In 1980 the Human Sciences Research Council conducted at the request of the South African government an in-depth investigation into all facets of education in South Africa. This investigation resulted, among other things, in the formulation of 11 guiding principles of educational provision. Despite the fact that these principles are interpreted differently by various interest groups, they are still generally accepted as a common basis for the formulation of educational objectives and policies. The 11 principles are listed below:

(a) equal educational opportunities;

(b) a balance of commonality and diversity;

(c) freedom of choice;

(d) relevance;

(e) linkage between formal and nonformal education;

(f) state and parental responsibility for formal education;

(g) state and private sector responsibility for nonformal education;

(h) state support for private education;

(i) balance between administrative centralization and decentralization;

(j) professional status of educators;

(k) continuing research.

The implementation of these principles is limited by the present constitutional framework, government policies, and legislation. The basis on which the proposed positive recognition of diversity (principle b) was to be afforded, was racial, instead of educationally relevant, such as language, culture, or religion. The removal (lifting) of these constraints is essential as the implementation of the true spirit of the principles is dependent on the acceptance and involvement of all the participants—parents, teachers, and organized society—of the education system.

The broad objectives of the educational sectors are outlined by legislation. The emphasis is on providing relevant education for all, according to the needs of the individual (aptitude and interest), and those of the community (labor force demands).

In general it can be stated that during the primary phases of schooling, the emphasis is on the promotion of literacy, numeracy, and the general development and socialization of the child. As in other countries, broader economic and social objectives tend to become more significant at the upper-secondary and tertiary levels of the education system.

3. The Formal System of Education

3.1 Primary, Secondary, and Tertiary Education

Figure 1 presents an outline of the structure of the formal education system. Key statistics on enrollments and resources in the major education sectors can be observed in Table 1.

With the exception of Black children, school attendance is compulsory for children between the ages of 7 and 16. This includes the junior primary, senior primary, junior secondary (3 years each), and in most cases one year of the senior secondary phase. By way of 11 state departments of education, schooling is in general provided on a separate basis for the various population or ethnic groupings. Reform policy will, however, ensure that the legal separation in schools according to race is phased out (e.g., by means of a Bill of Human Rights and the annulment of the Population Registration Act). It was estimated that in 1988 about 22 percent of Black children between the ages of 6 and 14 were not attending school.

The formal education system provides for preprimary, primary, secondary, and tertiary institutions and is characterized by differentiation in terms of language and culture. The medium of instruction varies, but is usually mother tongue education. All children are taught the two official languages: Afrikaans and English. Both are compulsory for matriculation, with the exception of Blacks who can substitute an African language for either English or Afrikaans during the last three school years. In most Black schools the initial period of four years of instruction in the child's mother tongue is followed by instruction in English. Teachers in many cases, however, continue instruction in the relevant mother tongue.

Primary education usually commences at the age of 6 and lasts for 6 years. Apart from reading, writing, and arithmetic in the basis years, subjects such as health education, mathematics, environmental studies (or geography), science, music, arts and crafts, religious studies, physical training, and languages (mother tongue and English) are offered.

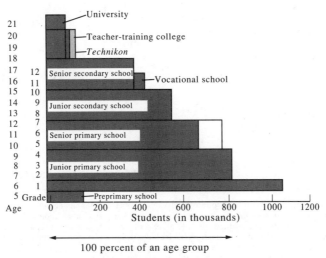

Figure 1
South Africa: Structure of the formal education system

The secondary school phase provides for differentiation but in comprehensive units, mainly focusing on broadening the general knowledge of the various academic subjects to prepare pupils for their choice of career or for further study. From Standard 7 onwards students choose, in addition to the compulsory official languages, four subjects from the following main streams: general, commercial, natural science, social science, technical, art, agricultural and domestic science. Most students, however, follow the general curriculum (more than 50% in 1984). In 1990 only about 1 percent of the school population attended technical colleges.

A new curriculum model for primary and secondary education was recommended in December 1991 that provides for earlier tracking into vocational training.

In 1985 approximately 600,000 (6.4%) Black pupils attended farm schools, each of which had, on average, less than 100 pupils. This requires teachers to teach simultaneously at different grade levels. These children therefore often experience problems in continuing with secondary education. The attrition rate for Black students is in general much higher than that for pupils of other groups. This is generally ascribed to the existing inequalities in educational provision. Approximately 30 percent of the teachers in Black

education are suitably qualified (i.e., having had 12 years of schooling followed by 3 years of teacher training). Pupil–teacher ratios are 41:1 (compared to 20:1 for those of White schools), and often overcrowded classrooms reflect this. During the 1980s Black schools have become increasingly politicized. Participation in strikes and other forms of disruptive behavior by pupils affect education.

The school year commences in January, usually consists of four quarters, and ends in early December. School hours, for 5 days per week, average 5.5 hours per day. The average number of school days per year is 200.

Tertiary education mainly takes place at *technikons*, teacher-training institutions (discussed in Sect. 6 below), and universities. By far the largest number of tertiary students attend universities. In 1990 the ratio of university to *technikon* students was 7:2. Although the natural sciences (including medicine and engineering) are offered at universities, most students enroll for courses in the social sciences. A gradual process of rationalization, which was introduced in the 1980s, has become imperative as a result of a decrease in state subsidies for universities. In some cases this has forced the amalgamation of disciplines offered by the 17 universities. The University of South Africa (with

Table 1
Enrollments and Resources in Formal Education, South Africa 1990

| | Comprehensive schools | | Tertiary education | |
	Primary section	Secondary section	Teacher-training *technikons*	Universities
Number of students[a]	5,263,129	2,254,927	133,508	286,910
Percentage of age group enrolled[b]				
Age 15–16	67.4%		—	—
17–18	42.9%		—	—
20–24	—		—	—
Number of institutions[c]	20,207		85	17
Average number of students per institution	372		1,570	1,687
Student–teacher ratio[d]	25.0:1		9.2:1	9.2:1
Expenditure per student[e]	R1,480[f]		R5,172	R7,890

a The school data include students enrolled in private schools and technical colleges. It includes teacher-training, *technikon*, and post-Standard 10 level technical college students. About 35 percent of university students are enrolled at distance learning centers (e.g., UNISA {120,000}, Vista)   b Statistics for universities not available   c Excludes special school education, but includes technical colleges and private schools   d Excludes special school personnel, but includes permanent personnel and/or full-time equivalent personnel   e The school data refer to the 1991–92 financial year and comprise estimates of government expenditure as supplied by Department of National Education. Amount of R5,172 is for *technikon* education only   f Figures are for the 1991–92 financial year

over 110,000 students) and Vista University offer higher education by means of correspondence courses. Labor shortages in certain job categories suggest that an imbalance exists between the number of universities and the more vocationally oriented *technikons*. The ratio of White to Black students enrolled at universities for 1990 was 10:1. The number of students enrolled at universities and *technikons* between 1970 and 1990 respectively increased from 82,909 to 286,910, and from 36,253 to 83,424. The minimum admission requirement for attending university is a matriculation exemption certificate. However, with regard to certain disciplines or fields, additional requirements exist at most universities. During 1991 more White male than female students attended universities (88,696 against 68,736). However, more Black female than male students (59,195 against 50,935) were enrolled at universities.

3.2 Preschool Education

The predominant aim of preschool education is to offer an enriched learning environment in order to prepare children for school. Although this kind of education is provided on a limited scale only, it has been recommended as a measure to ameliorate the present high attrition rate in Black education.

3.3 Special Education

Approximately 34,000 children attended 222 special schools in 1990, constituting about 0.01 percent of the total student population. A variety of institutions cater for the special needs of the physically and mentally handicapped such as those for autistic, deaf, hard of hearing, blind, partially sighted, epileptic, cerebral palsied, physically handicapped, and those for children with special learning disabilities. Mainstreaming has not yet been attempted. These institutions are mostly state-aided and have to make use of sponsors to generate sufficient or additional funding. They increasingly focus on vocational training. Advisory bodies exist to coordinate the transition or transfer from an institution to a suitable type of work.

3.4 Vocational, Technical, and Business Education

The low and occasionally negative economic growth rate since the late 1970s and the shortage of technically trained workers has resulted in an increasing interest in vocational and technical training, as well as in business-oriented courses. The *Raad vir Geesteswetenskaplike Navorsing* (1989) and *Departement van Onderwys en Kultuur* (1990) undertook important studies in this area. The 1991 Education Reform documents focused on labor force development, and there are indications that secondary education will be diversified to provide for more career-oriented training and education (see Sect. 10 below). Financial

limitations imposed by general economic conditions hamper the availability of funds for education, and the involvement to a much larger extent of the private sector seems unavoidable.

Apart from the *technikons* which more than doubled their enrollments in the 1980s, special "training boards" (accredited by the Registrar of Manpower Training) were established to oversee the development and provision of inservice and other special training courses for the different industries such as mining, building, printing, and so forth. A large variety of training programs, such as apprentice training and other training schemes, is made available in the many private, industrial, and other training centers. In 1990 these centers trained approximately 514,598 persons. The state provides a variety of financial incentive schemes for the training of workers.

3.5 Adult and Nonformal Education

Adult and nonformal education is provided by the government as well as by private organizations. The main objectives for government involvement are related to economic development needs—addressing the high number of unemployed and the high population growth rate, and eradicating illiteracy. It is, however, difficult to indicate the extent of these programs as formal data are not available. A special project was launched in 1988 to train the unemployed. According to the Department of Manpower, more than 610,000 people attended training courses under this initiative up to 1990.

Under the auspices of the Department of Health and Welfare, a population development program covering the essentials of birth control, health, and nutrition, is offered. Literacy programs for adults have also been developed. These are offered by the Department of Education and Training, among others, which is responsible for the education of Blacks.

A large number of parastatal and private organizations are involved in the development of human potential. Organizations such as the Development Bank of Southern Africa are increasingly becoming involved in the funding and development of human resources. The private sector established a council (the PRISEC) for the development of education and training programs. The Independent Development Trust, which received a grant of R500 million from the government for educational purposes, also develops and offers some educational programs.

Formal training institutions such as technical colleges are increasingly becoming involved in nonformal education, offering more flexible and adaptable training courses. These courses aim at satisfying short-term needs in specific areas.

4. Administrative and Supervisory Structure and Operation

In terms of the 1983 amendments to the South African Constitution, the education of each of the four population groups was described as "own affairs," and has subsequently become, in terms of its cultural and value framework, the responsibility of each relevant group. "Own affairs" administrations were made responsible for the provision of education, including responsibility for "their" respective universities and *technikons*. The Constitution provides for three departments of education and culture, which are responsible to the House of Assembly (Whites), the House of Representatives (Coloreds), and the House of Delegates (Asians). Separate departments of education exist for the self-governing Black states (KwaZulu, Lebowa, Gazankulu, Qwaqua, KwaNdebele, and KaNgwane). The central government provides for and controls education for all other Blacks living in South Africa through the Department of Education and Training.

The National Policy for General Education Affairs Act (Act 76 of 1984) defines the spheres and determines certain limits within which education must be provided by the various "own affairs" education departments. These include norms (criteria, rules, or prescriptions according to which action should be taken, and/or something/someone could be judged or compared), and standards for the financing of running costs and capital expenditure, salaries and conditions of employment for staff; the professional registration of teachers; norms and standards for syllabuses and examination, as well as those for certification of qualifications. The general education policy is determined by the Minister of National Education in consultation with all the ministers of education of the departments of state for education. In developing such policy, a number of statutory councils and committees assist the Minister in an advisory capacity.

Parliament approves the budget for education, for redistribution by the Minister of National Education. The budget allocated by Parliament for financial aid to the four TBVC states is the responsibility of the Minister of Foreign Affairs.

For administrative purposes, South Africa is divided into a number of regions. Sub-state departments were established to administer these regions. Figure 2 presents a schematic overview of the present educational administrative system.

The educational departments of the various population groups are responsible for matters such as the recruitment and appointment of teachers for public schools, the supply of buildings and land, the provision of equipment and materials, and within the bounds of general policy have responsibility for the curriculum. In the case of White schools, the four provinces of South Africa have considerable say in all matters pertaining to schooling. The functions of the former inspectorates have been changed, and are mainly advisory in nature, although the inspectorates still exert considerable influence.

Schools for Whites generally have elected management boards comprising parents, the school principal, and his deputy. Besides these, parent and parent–teacher associations exist to promote involvement of the community in school affairs. These associations assist schools in generating additional funds for the purpose of maintenance and the purchase of additional equipment and facilities, but have little or no effective decision-making authority. Such boards are becoming increasingly prevalent in schools catering for education to the other population groups.

In 1990 additional models for the administration of schools were developed by the Department of Education and Culture: House of Assembly. Schools have a choice to vote for three models: Model A, B, or C. The Model A school constitutes a private, but government subsidized school; Model B empowers a school to lay down rules in regard to school entrance; while Model C is a state-aided school. More than 200 schools have already opted for Model B and have opened their doors to students of other race groups.

Furthermore, in 1991, the government announced arrangements by which unutilized or underutilized schools for Whites could be used to provide education mainly for Blacks. These arrangements revolve around educational services rendered on an agency basis to other departments by the Department of Education and Culture: House of Assembly.

5. Educational Finance

The education budget as a proportion of the state budget increased from 16.2 percent in 1985–86 to 20.3 percent in 1990–91. The Department of National Education distributes funds according to set formulas to the other education departments. Of the 1989–90 education budget, 32 percent was allocated to the Department of Education and Culture: House of Assembly; 6 percent to the Department of Education and Culture: House of Delegates; 15 percent to the Department of Education and Culture: House of Representatives; and 34 percent to the Department of Education and Training and the self-governing states combined. Education in the TBVC states is financed through the Department of Foreign Affairs and is not included in the figures mentioned above. Although the education budget increased by 57 percent in nominal terms between 1987–88 and 1990–91, in real terms it represented a decrease of 6 percent. This was due mainly to an annual increase in pupils and students of about 4.4 percent during this period. In 1990–91 education expenditure amounted to approximately 5.5% of GNP.

Of the 1990–91 education budget 11.3 percent was allocated to universities, 2.7 percent to *technikons*, 0.5 percent to private ordinary schools, and 85.5 percent to the rest of the education sector. Approximately 70 percent of the total education expenditure is spent on the remuneration of teachers and lecturers, implying that in 1991 a 1 percent salary increase would cost the state about R15 million. There

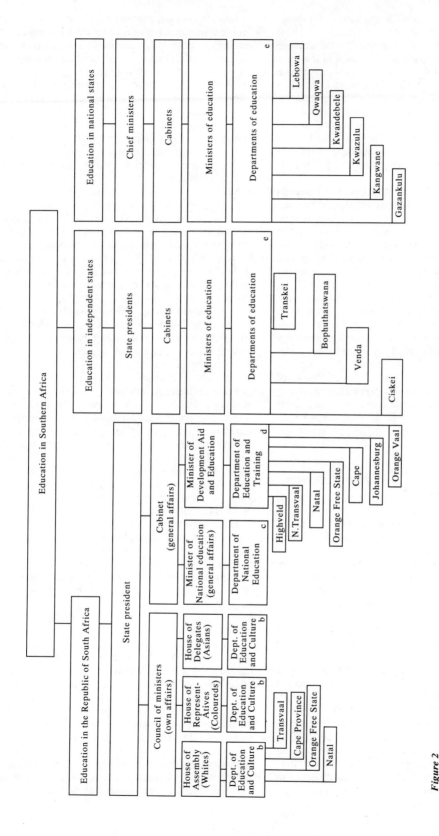

Figure 2
The decentralized educational administrative structure in South Africa[a]

Source: Du Pisani et al. 1991

a Uniform educational standards: except for the National States, as well as Bophuthatswana, Ciskei, and Venda, where pupils write the examinations set by the Department of Education and Training, all other departments have their own examining bodies. In order to provide for control over norms and standards of subject matter and examination, as well as awarding of certificates at the various exit points in school, technical college, and nonformal education, the South African Certification Council was founded according to Act 85 of 1986. The mission of the Council is to ensure that all certificates awarded by the Council at a specific exit point represent the same standard of education and examination.   b The administration of education for Whites, Coloreds, and Asians is considered to be an own affair and rests with separate departments of education for each of these population groups   c The Department of National Education is responsible for the formulation of educational policy in South Africa   d The Department of Education and Training administers the education of Blacks outside the National and Independent States   e Ten separate departments of education administer education for Blacks of the different ethnic groups in the independent (TBVC) and National States

are inequalities in per capita expenditure for public ordinary schools between the various population groups. In 1989 the per capita expenditure for college and school education amounted to R3,572 in the case of the Department of Education and Culture: House of Assembly; R927 for the Department of Education and Training; and R647 for the self-governing states. Calculations indicate that equalizing expenditure on the basis of the expenditure for White education will absorb more or less 48 percent of the total state budget for primary and secondary education alone. This will be a major problem for the development of the education system.

The Department of National Education recommends at least 0.5 percent of total expenditure should be used for adult and nonformal education. The 1980s has seen the growth of foreign financial assistance for education purposes, especially for Blacks, but the full extent of assistance is impossible to calculate. Private and parastatal organizations are increasing their support for specific educational projects.

In 1990, there were 384 private fee-paying schools. Since the early 1980s these schools have children from all population groups. In an effort to accommodate Black students in schools catering exclusively for White pupils, and possibly to ameliorate financial problems, the three additional models proposed by the Department of Education and Culture: House of Assembly provide for degrees of privatization.

Bursaries which are as a rule based on educational merits and type of study, as well as loans from banks and other institutions at moderate interest rates, are available to students.

6. Supplying Personnel for the Education System

In 1991 more than 256,000 (full-time equivalent) comprehensive school educators were employed in schools. A further 29,000 noneducators occupied administrative positions, and more than 35,000 employees worked as service workers. Nonteaching personnel thus totaled more than 63,000. Some 61 percent of school teachers are female. Although gender parity exists in all respects in education, men are still more likely than women to occupy senior administrative positions in schools.

Teacher shortages in especially the disadvantaged communities are common, and scholarships are offered for teacher training. The enrollment figures for Black pupils predict an increase of about 400,000 per year at the start of the 1990s, and this will increase to almost 700,000 per year by the turn of the century. It is estimated that the total pupil enrollment in South Africa (including the independent states) will be a staggering 9.9 million in 1991, and 14.7 million in 2001. This will require exceptional measures to ensure teacher supply. The shortages in subjects such as mathematics, biology, and the physical sciences are more acute in rural than in urban areas.

Education departments undertake annual studies to decide on the number of teacher trainees and practicing teachers required. The education departments recruit trainees by direct liaison with schools, and by offering financial assistance for teacher education purposes. In exceptional circumstances, departments may recruit from commerce and industry by offering special incentives. Practicing teachers and newly qualified teachers are invited to apply for vacancies which are published in official gazettes. Where there are special conditions (such as severe shortages), departments may try to recruit from society at large by, for instance, advertising in newspapers.

Normally, persons desiring to be appointed to teaching posts register with education departments. An education department may (sometimes after consulting the school concerned) place a person in a post. Posts are normally advertised, allowing aspirants to apply for posts which are filled by the department concerned at the recommendation of the school community concerned. Departments may transfer or second teachers already employed by them.

Government school teachers usually serve a one- or two-year probationary period during which teachers are assessed before receiving permanent employment. Private-school teachers are directly employed by the board of the school, and the requirements for permanent employment vary.

Teacher training occurs in universities, teacher-training colleges, and *technikons*. The various education departments are responsible for determining the standard of teacher qualifications. The normal length for the initial training of secondary teachers is four years, although some departments recognize three years. The course generally comprises either a three-year degree, during which a student majors in two subjects, followed by a one-year diploma in education, or an integrated four-year degree or diploma.

The primary-education teacher normally completes a three- or four-year diploma course. At some universities a four-year degree course for primary teachers and even a four-year degree course for preprimary education are offered. Many primary teachers with three-year diplomas later upgrade their qualifications by undertaking a one-year diploma course in areas such as remedial teaching, counseling, or education management.

The qualification level of teachers differs substantially and so does the interpretation of what could be regarded as a professionally qualified teacher. If the completion of 12 years of pretertiary training and 3 years of professional tertiary training is regarded as the minimum for qualified status, in 1991 47.2 percent of practicing teachers were unqualified and 52.8 percent qualified (Department of National Education 1991a).

Evidence of limited promotion opportunities, relatively low salaries, and unattractive and, in some areas, unsafe working conditions have contributed to the fact that the teaching profession has become unattractive as a career. Teachers' salaries are approximately 2 percent lower than those of persons occupying comparable posts in the public service. Salaries in the education sector are approximately 30 percent lower than those in the private sector. This poses problems for the recruitment and retention of staff.

There are attempts to improve working conditions and promotion opportunities. For promotion, demonstrated competence and qualifications are usually emphasized, and not seniority. Improving the situation is difficult because the growing education budget already taxes limited revenues.

Considerable effort is also being directed toward improving and adapting initial teacher as well as inservice training to meet the demands of a drastically changing, nonracial, multicultural society.

Retraining of inservice staff usually takes place when new subjects are added to the school curriculum, when the curriculum is substantively altered, or when subjects are removed from the curriculum. Such training takes the form of formal studies, leading to the awarding of degrees or diplomas or of in-house training sessions offered by departments such as seminars, orientation courses, or workshops. Continuing professional development by means of inservice training and distance education is encouraged. However, a comprehensive and coordinated program is needed to meet the growing and changing demands.

7. Curriculum Development and Teaching Methodology

The National Policy for General Education Affairs Act (Act 76 of 1984) accorded the Minister of National Education with the responsibility for determining general policy for formal, informal, and nonformal education in consultation with all the ministers of departments of state responsible for education. This includes norms and standards for syllabuses, examinations, and the certification of qualifications.

Framework committees under the auspices of the Committee of Heads of Education Departments were established to develop curricula. These committees consist of representatives of all the departments of education and, where necessary, subject experts from universities and relevant private-sector groups. These committees develop and design national curricula frameworks. These core curricula, comprising of aims, content, and evaluation guidelines, form the basis for the further development of syllabuses by the various departments and the management boards of private schools.

The need for a new national curriculum arose because of the diversity of what was taught in different schools and departments, as well as the demand for relevant curricula, especially in terms of vocational orientation.

Curricula for schools administered by the various education departments differ because the syllabuses used are developed by the department administering the schools. Teachers have considerable autonomy in deciding their own teaching methodology. Most teachers, however, feel more comfortable when they closely follow the contents of the textbooks supplied. They are generally more inclined to disseminate information than to utilize new experimental methods.

The curricula used in practically all primary schools expose students to reading and writing, as well as to mathematics, science (health education), social studies (history), expressive and performing arts, religion, physical education, and one additional language. Up to the fourth grade such subjects are taught by general classroom teachers. Thereafter specialists are employed.

Secondary schools provide for differentiation in subject areas, such as the natural or social sciences, commerce, business, home economics, agriculture, and technical subjects. These subjects can usually be taken at one of three levels of difficulty: lower, standard, or higher. University entrance requirements still tend to dominate the choice of subjects. A matter for concern is that relatively few Black pupils take courses in natural sciences and mathematics. In 1988, only 15, 32, and 0.3 percent of all Black pupils in Standard 10 respectively took physical science, mathematics, and technical drawing.

A key issue in curriculum development is the quest for relevant education, and the standardization of the large variety of curricula used by the various education departments with sufficient room being left for the accommodation of cultural diversity. A new curriculum model has been developed by the Committee of Heads of Education Departments which proposes earlier vocational training.

8. The System of Examinations, Promotions, and Certifications

Internal examinations determine the annual promotion of pupils from one school level to the next. At the end of the Standard 10, a public examination is taken. This examination is set by any one of nine examining bodies. The standards of the examining bodies have been coordinated and moderated by the Joint Matriculation Board in order to assure the equivalence of the various certificates. This role arose from the traditional function of the Joint Matriculation Board, a body established to regulate university entrance requirements.

In 1986 parliament established the South African Certification Council. This council was given the authority to establish national norms and standards for certification, and to appoint examining bodies. It is the curriculum determined by the Minister of National Education that will form the basis for the establishment of norms and standards for certification. Thus in future, all school-leaving certificates will be issued by the Council. The Committee of University Principals will establish minimum requirements for university entrance from the Matriculation Board. The examining function of the Joint Matriculation Board, which functions mainly for pupils from private schools, will most probably be taken over by the Independent Examination Board.

The most important problem facing the Certification Council will be the establishment of equivalence of standards for the various examining bodies. Research has already commenced. Research and assessment are undertaken by the Human Sciences Research Council as well as by special research units attached to the education departments.

9. Educational Assessment, Evaluation, and Research

During the 1980s many changes in educational evaluation and research took place, but no national assessment of educational achievement has yet been undertaken. In 1985 the Department of National Education assumed responsibility for the collection of data and the dissemination of information on the education system. This led to the development of an extensive data bank on the education system. Evaluation systems, especially in regard to the financial aspects of education, were developed.

The most prominent indicators on which data are published on a regular basis are: per capita expenditure, teacher–student ratios, the percentage of qualified (Standard 10 or N3 plus 3 years or more professional training) teaching personnel, the number of students aged 6 to 16 years attending school, Grade 1–Standard 10 ratios, population growth rate, and student–classroom ratios.

The Human Sciences Research Council, in conjunction with the various education authorities, also often undertakes and sponsors research projects on education. A question bank with standardized items for objective testing has been developed, and extensive research on cross-cultural assessment of achievement is regularly undertaken.

10. Major Reforms in the 1980s and 1990s

Since 1970, education in South Africa has been characterized by strife, protest, extensive inquiry, and several major reform proposals. Against the political fluidity of the late 1980s, several research projects resulting in reform proposals were undertaken. This process was initiated in 1981 by the Human Sciences Research Council's proposals for educational reform. Extensive proposals for reform were also published in June 1991 in the form of an Education Renewal Strategy, and in November 1991 in the form of a Curriculum Model by the Committee of Education Heads. These

reform proposals followed a functionalist approach based on identified major problem areas and after extensive consultation with expert and representative bodies reform strategies were proposed. The core of the problems were found to be: (a) backlogs in respect of teachers, classrooms, and other educational services, particularly for the schooling of Black pupils, owing to rapid population growth, recent large-scale population migration, and poor economic conditions; (b) the politically contentious nature of the education system as a result of its racial basis, which has inter alia led to conflict and resistance and even to the collapse of discipline and order in certain geographical areas; and (c) the exceptional problems associated with the provision of schooling in a society which is deeply divided on ethnic, cultural, and economic lines.

In a policy statement by the state president on February 1, 1991 a clear indication was given of the need for the educational system to change. The guidelines for a new education system must:

(a) be nondiscriminatory;

(b) offer equal educational opportunities;

(c) enjoy the acceptance and support of the majority of the people;

(d) leave room for community-based education for those who desire it.

A study of the reform proposals and those of other organizations leaves no doubt about the seriousness and complexity of the challenge to reform the education system in such a way as to contribute toward the future development of a prosperous, just, and democratic society in South Africa.

References

African National Congress (ANC) 1991 *Discussion Paper for the ANC on Education Policy.* (mimeo)

Department of National Education 1991a *Education Realities in South Africa, 1990* (NATED 02–300 {91/06}). Government Printer, Pretoria

Department of National Education 1991b *Education—Renewal Strategy: Discussion Document.* University of South Africa, Pretoria

Departement van Onderwys en Kultuur: Administrasie Volksraad 1990 *Die evaluering en bevordering van loopbaanonderwys.* Hoofverslag van die Komitee insake die evaluering en bevordering van loopbaanonderwys in die Departement van Onderwys en Kultuur, Administrasie Volksraad. Walters-verslag, Pretoria

Du Pisani T, Plekker S J, Dennis C R, Straus J P 1991 *Education and Manpower Development 1990, No. 11.* RIEP, University of the Orange Free State, Bloemfontein

Human Sciences Research Council 1981 *Provision of Education in the RSA.* Human Sciences Research Council, Pretoria

Raad vir Geesteswetenskaplike Navorsing 1989 *Die RGN/NOR Ondersoek na Vaardigheidsopleiding in die RSA*. Raad vir Geesteswetenskaplike Navorsing. Pittendrich-verslag, Pretoria

Further Reading

Behr A L 1988 *Education in South Africa. Origins, Issues and Trends: 1652–1988*. Academica, Cape Town
Central Statistical Service 1986 *Population Census: Report No. 02.85.07. Economic Characteristics: Statistics According to Occupation Industry and Identity of Employer* (DI D10). Government Printer, Pretoria
Christie P 1988 *The Right to Learn. The Struggle for Education in South Africa*, 4th edn. Sached Trust/Ravan Press Pty. Ltd., Braamfontein
Davenport T R H 1991 *South Africa: A Modern History*, 4th edn. Macmillan SA, Johannesburg

Department of National Education 1990 *Preliminary Education Statistics for 1990* (NATED 02–214 {90/08}). Government Printer, Pretoria
Heese C 1990 *Aspekte van die onderwys in Suid-Afrika*. Kernaantekeninge vir Vergelykende Opvoedkunde, Universiteit van Stellenbosch
Malherbe E G 1925 *Education in South Africa. Vol. 1: 1652–1922*. (Repr. 1975) Juta and Co. Ltd., Johannesburg
Malherbe E G 1977 *Education in South Africa. Vol. 2: 1923–75*. Juta and Co. Ltd., Johannesburg
Republic of South Africa 1990 *South African Statistics 1990*. (Compiled by the Central Statistical Service). Government Printer, Pretoria
Republic of South Africa 1991 *South African Labour Statistics 1991* (D1,D6). Central Statistical Service, Pretoria
Republic of South Africa 1991–92 *South Africa 1991–92. Official Yearbook*. South African Communication Service, Pretoria
South African Reserve Bank 1991 *Quarterly Bulletin* (June) No. 180. South African Reserve Bank, Pretoria

Spain

G. A. Gil

1. General Background

Spain is situated on the Iberian Peninsula in the southwest of the European continent. It essentially forms part of European history and culture, though its closeness to the African continent has facilitated contact with other cultures which established themselves in North Africa. Its geographical position and historical events have made Spain a crossroads at which many cultures have met. Its varied traditions and languages—Catalonian, Galician, Valencian, Basque, and Castilian which has traditionally been the official national language—have resulted from the mixture, integration, and coexistence of cultures. Furthermore, the historical part which Spain played in the discovery and colonization of America has conferred upon it a special role in liaison between European and American countries.

The country covers 504,782 square kilometers, the Balearic and Canary Islands accounting for 15 percent of this territory. It had a population of nearly 39.1 million inhabitants in 1992, and a population density of 77.7 inhabitants per square kilometer. Coastal areas are more populated than the interior regions, with the exception of the capital Madrid. Some 79 percent of all inhabitants lived in urban areas in 1991.

In the periods 1970–80 and 1980–91, the annual population growth rates were 1.0 and 0.4 percent respectively. The birth rate fell gradually from the 1960s, being 20, 15, and 9.9 births for every thousand inhabitants in 1970, 1980, and 1991, respectively. The fecundity rate decreased from 2.8 in 1970 to 1.3 in

1991. The death rate was around 8 people per every thousand inhabitants in 1970 and around 8.6 in 1991. The life expectancy in 1991 was 77 years.

A period of modernization and reintegration into the developed Western world was begun in the mid-1960s, a process which ended with the establishment of a democratic system similar to other Western countries in the mid-1970s and the incorporation of Spain into the European Community in the mid-1980s.

In the 1960s, there was major economic development in Spain, accompanied by large-scale internal migration and industrialization. The 1970s were marked by an economic crisis and a change in the political system, a new Constitution being passed in 1978 which established a democratic political system structured as a parliamentary monarchy with political parties. The 1980s were devoted to the strengthening of the political system and the accomplishment of sustained economic growth. The objective of all the policies was centered on Spain's integration into the European Community. For the 1990s, the major political objectives are to achieve more and better integration into Europe and the final implementation of the decentralized state system of autonomous communities.

The economic situation has not been very favorable since the crisis at the beginning of the 1970s, but the Spanish economy did grow at a faster rate than the average for the OECD countries in the 1980s, with investments in production increasing and the process of economic transformation speeding up. In 1991, the per capita Gross National Product (GNP) was US$12,460, but at the beginning of the 1990s there were the problems of inflation (around 6.5% in 1990, reducing progressively to 5.3% in 1992), unemployment (approximately 15% in 1990, increasing to around 18% in 1992), and a large foreign trade deficit. The economic crisis was becoming more acute in 1993 and 1994.

The process of rapid economic development which the country has undergone since the 1960s has led to major social changes—in the kinds of work undertaken, living standards, lifestyle (due to the gradual and large-scale incorporation of women into the labor market), and increased urbanization of the population. Changes in the occupational structure of the Spanish population, as presented in Table 1 show a constant and significant fall in the proportion of people working in the primary sector, while the proportion of people employed in the tertiary sector has increased very markedly.

At the end of the 1980s, a series of legal, social, political, and educational issues resulted in a proposed overall reform of the education system in terms of both structure and content. From a legal point of view, it was necessary to adapt both the content and formulation of the educational legislation to the new Constitution and to the new political and administrative structure of the state, whereby the legal powers in educational management were divided between the central government and the autonomous community governments. From a social point of view, the demand for education had increased in terms of quantity, variety of disciplines, content and methods. Furthermore, the widespread incorporation of women into the labor market had generated the need for earlier schooling. Economic development had led to a demand for more and higher social, technological, and vocational qualifications, which meant that the time spent in the education system, both before and after compulsory education, was becoming increasingly longer.

The process of integration into the European Community has broadened the future horizons of Spanish society and established new challenges for economic development and social welfare. These require an increase in the level of competitiveness associated with an improvement in the quality of the education system. In a similar way, the right of citizens

Table 1
Evolution of the occupational structure of the Spanish population by sectors from 1950 to 1991

Sectors	1950	1960	1970	1980	1990	1991
Primary (agriculture)	51	43	26	18	12	11
Secondary (industry)	23	28	36	35	33	33
Tertiary (services)	26	29	38	47	55	56

to move within the framework of a united Europe requires international equivalence to be established for educational and vocational training qualifications. Finally, from the educational point of view, it was necessary to rectify malfunctions and shortcomings in the system established in 1970. The most blatant of these were streaming within the education system at too early an age leading to two certificates, the failure to regulate infant education, curriculum rigidity, little school self-government, and the structural inadequacy of the university transition course. In addition, both grade repetition rates and dropout rates were too high. Consequently, the situation and problems of the Spanish educational system led to general reform of the structure, contents, and functioning of the system that is, in the 1990s, in a period of transition.

2. Politics and the Goals of the Education System

The socioeconomic and political changes that have taken place since the 1960s have had a significant impact on the educational system. The process of modernization in the 1960s led to the reform of the education system, the centerpiece of which was the 1970 General Education Act (LGE). This reform's major objective was to extend education to the whole population, based on the principle of equal opportunities. This law was in force until 1983 for higher education and 1990 for nonuniversity educational levels. Its structure and provisions will continue in operation until the new structure and regulations promulgated by the General Arrangement of Education System Act of October 1990 (LOGSE) have been gradually introduced, a process which, it is estimated, will take 10 years. The main purpose of this new law is to attain higher quality teaching levels, once the objective of providing at least eight-year schooling for the whole population has been achieved.

The 1978 Constitution defined the principles governing the management of education and established citizens' rights to education. Furthermore, it altered the regional organization of the state, starting a process of decentralization of a large number of its duties, at the end of which it is expected to have devolved a large number of governmental powers onto the 17 autonomous communities into which state territory has been divided, including the majority of the powers relating to education.

The general principles of educational policy are centered, first, on the basic right of all citizens to education (basic education being established as compulsory and free), to which end the public authorities are responsible for the general programming of education with the participation of all sectors of society, as well as for the inspection and approval of the educational system. Second, they focus on the objective of education being the full development of the human personality with respect for the democratic principles of coexistence and basic rights and freedom. Third, educational freedom, the freedom to set up private schools and assistance for those that meet the requirements established by law, as well as the right of parents to have their children receive the religious and moral education they wish, are recognized. Fourth, the participation of teachers, parents, and pupils in the control and running of state-funded schools is established; and finally, universities are granted self-government. Other major constitutional rights related to education are: ideological and religious freedom; children's and human rights in general, as laid down in international agreements; and especially the rights of the physically and mentally handicapped and people with sensory impairments. The 1983 University Reform Act (LRU), the 1985 Right to Education Act (LODE), and the 1990 General Arrangement of Education System Act (LOGSE) are the laws which have implemented the constitutional principles.

The ends that these legal dispositions are looking for, in the framework of the basic principle that the education has to be permanent, are the full development of the student's personality; the knowledge of basic rights and liberties exercised in tolerance and freedom within the democratic principles of coexistence; the acquisition of intellectual habits and working techniques, as well as scientific, technical, humanistic, historic, and aesthetic knowledge; the training for professional activities; the education concerning the linguistic and cultural plurality of Spain; the preparation for actively participating in social and cultural life; and the promotion of peace, cooperation, and solidarity between different parts of the country and between other countries.

The above mentioned goals have to be achieved taking into account the following principles of the educational system: the personalized training which shall provide an overall education of knowledge, skills, and moral values to students, in all areas of personal, family, social, and professional life; the involvement and cooperation of parents and tutors so that educational objectives have a better chance of success; the effective equality of rights between the sexes, rejection of all types of discrimination, and respect for all cultures; the development of creative abilities and the ability to make critical evaluations; the formation of democratic behavioral patterns; the pedagogic autonomy of schools with limits established by law; the research activity by teachers encompassed within their teaching practice; the availability of educational psychologists and educational and professional counseling; the use of an active methodology which positively involves the student in the teaching and learning process; the assessment of the teaching and learning process, of schools, and the evaluation of the different elements involved in the educational system; the relationship with the social, economic, and cultural environment; and the education for respect towards and preservation of the environment.

3. The Formal System of Education

The nonuniversity education system legally in force in Spain is the one established by the LOGSE in 1990, although this is still in the process of being introduced. This means that the system really existing in 1991, and on which data are available, is the one based on the old 1970 General Education Act (LGE).

Figure 1 presents an outline of the Spanish system of education as it was in 1991–92.

The LGE system had four educational levels: preschool education, general basic education (EGB), baccalaureate (BUP), and higher education. Despite its essential difference, vocational training also constituted an integral part of the system and, together with the baccalaureate, made up the stage which in Spain is referred to as *Enseñanzas Medias* (secondary education).

The 1970 Education Act also regulated other types and kinds of education, such as continuing adult education (EPA), special education, distance education, night school courses, or specialized education which are not integrated into the regular system levels. EPA can be completed in institutions set up especially for this purpose or in regular schools.

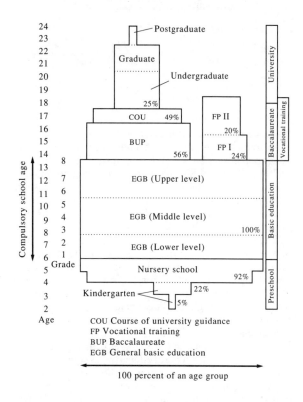

Figure 1

Spain: Structure of the formal education system 1991–92)[a]

a Based on the 1970 General Education Act (LGE)

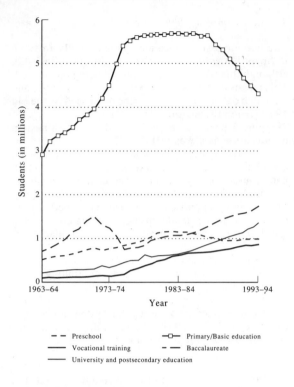

Students (in millions)

1963–64   1973–74   1983–84   1993–94

Year

- - Preschool   —□— Primary/Basic education
— Vocational training   - - Baccalaureate
— University and postsecondary education

Figure 2
Evolution of the size of the educational system (number of students
in the core structure of the system)[a]
a Data for 1992–93 and 1993–94 are estimates

The development of enrollments in the different
levels of education for the period 1963–64 to 1993–94
is presented in Figure 2. The trends in enrollment show
the expansion of basic schooling during the 1960s and
1970s up to 1986–87, the increase in postcompulsory
education during the 1980s and 1990s and a decrease in
enrollment in preschool education and in general basic
education from the mid-1980s onwards. This was due
to the fall in the birthrate.

The 1990 Educational Act (LOGSE) established a
new structure of education system, dividing education
into two groups: general-system education (infant
education, primary education, compulsory secondary
education, postcompulsory secondary education or
baccalaureate, higher-grade vocational training, and
higher education) and special-system education (arts
education—music and dancing, dramatic art and "3-
D" arts and design—and languages). In Figure 3, the
new structure of the general education system is shown.
The process of implementation of the new educational
system began in the academic year 1991–92 and it is
expected that it will be concluded in the year 2000–01.
Distance education, whose courses are nationwide,
is organized around the Distance University (UNED)
for university levels, the Center of Innovation and

Development of Distance Education (CIDEAD) for
nonuniversity levels that has been adapted in 1992 to
the new system of the LOGSE.

There are private as well as state schools, and the
former may be denominational or otherwise, and may
receive financial assistance from the state or other
sources. The contribution of the Catholic Church is
very important in the private education sector. In primary and secondary education, some 30 to 40 percent
of students are enrolled in private schools.

3.1 Primary, Secondary, and Tertiary Education

In the 1990 LGE system, the General Basic Education (EGB) which was comprehensive and equal for
all pupils, lasted eight years, and was divided into
three cycles (2+3+3): lower, intermediate, and higher.
The first two cycles were general and comprehensive education. Orientation towards separate subject
matter-teaching is begun in the last cycle. In sparsely
populated rural areas there are unitary (often one
classroom) schools in which just one teacher teaches
all of the pupils in different grades. The recommended
timetable for the EGB is 25 hours per week and the
academic year stretches from 15 September to 20 June.

In the academic year 1993–94, the first four years
of EGB have been already substituted by the first four
years of the new primary education and in 1997–98 the
EGB will be completely disappeared.

In the new system, primary education—from 6 to 12
years—and compulsory secondary education (ESO)—
from 12 to 16 years—will continue to constitute the ten
years of compulsory, comprehensive basic education.
Primary education will be made up of three two-year
cycles. Its purpose is to promote children's integration
into Spanish culture and provide them with basic
communication and cognitive skills. Subjects to be
covered include language and literature, mathematics,
knowledge of the social and natural environments, arts
education (music and "3-D" art), a foreign language
(starting at 8 years of age) and physical education.
Primary teachers will take charge of a group of pupils
throughout each cycle but may be helped by specialized
teachers in the areas of physical education, foreign
languages, and music.

In the old LGE system, the Unified Polyvalent
Baccalaureate (BUP) lasted three years. The Course of
University Guidance (COU) consists of a transitional
year, mainly aimed at preparation for higher education.
The timetables for BUP and COU are 29 and 26 hours
per week. The academic year begins on 1 October and
ends on 30 June.

The new compulsory secondary education (ESO) will
be divided, as primary education, into two cycles, each
lasting two years. Optional subjects will gradually be
added to core subjects for all pupils. Options will
amount to 10 percent of the total curriculum in the
first and 35 percent in the last year. Teachers will
be university graduates. Subjects will include natural
sciences, physical education, "2-D" and "3-D" expres-

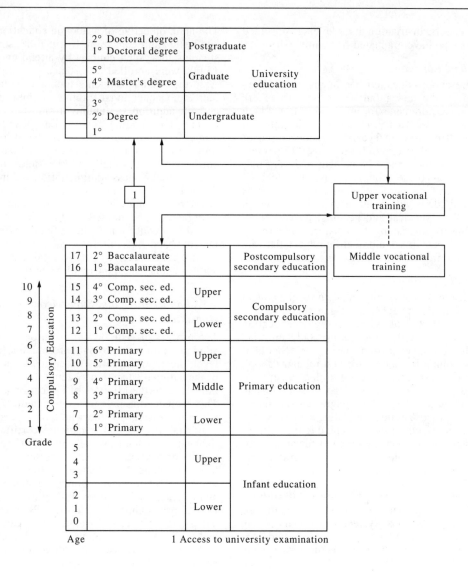

Figure 3
New structure of the general education system[a]
a Based on the 1990 General Arrangement of Education System Act (LOGSE). To be implemented by the year 2000

sion, geography, history and social sciences, foreign languages, language and literature, mathematics, music, and technology.

The are four possible kinds of baccalaureate: arts, natural sciences and health, humanities and social sciences, and technology. The specific purpose of the baccalaureate is to build on pupils' cultural, scientific and social education, and prepare them for higher education or higher vocational training. Baccalaureate teachers will be university licentiates. The subjects will be divided into three categories: core subjects, subjects related to the particular kind of baccalaureate and optional unrelated subjects

Higher education is structured on the basis of departments and can be completed in three kinds of institution: university schools, faculties, and higher technical schools. University schools offer one-cycle courses (2–3 years) and the faculties and higher technical schools offer courses of at least two cycles (normally 4–5 years). The third cycle provides for the completion of a doctorate (normally 2 years), with a basic orientation towards research. In 1993, there were 44 public universities and 7 private universities.

The pupil–teacher ratio is 27:1 in EGB, 17:1 in BUP, and COU, and 15:1 in FP. In higher education, it is 21:1 in faculties, 19:1 in university schools, and 11:1 in higher technical schools. Instruction at all levels is provided by teachers who have graduated from university.

3.2 Preschool Education

The old preschool education has in the 1990s been substituted by the new infant education. There are no admission requirements for infant education which admits children aged 0 to 6 years and is divided into two cycles (from 0 to 3 and 3 to 6 years). It is not compulsory, even though 100 percent of 5-year olds, 99.7 percent of 4- and 5-year olds, and 47.4 percent of 3-year olds were enrolled in these schools during the 1993–94 academic year. The purpose of infant education is to provide children with a set of experiences which encourage their physical and personal development, with the objective of making them mature for learning. Teachers are specialized and qualified specialists are also employed in the first cycle.

3.3 Special Education

The overall aim is to have students with special educational needs be able to achieve the general objectives established for all students within the regular education system. In other words, students are only enrolled in separate special education classes or schools if their needs cannot be catered for in a regular school. In 1988–89, 40,000 pupils were enrolled in separate special education schools (54% in private schools) and some 60,000 under the school integration scheme in regular schools (90% of these attending state schools). In special schools, education is adapted to the abilities of these pupils and is mainly oriented towards vocational training to enable them to be integrated into society and the labor market.

3.4 Vocational, Technical, and Business Education

In the 1970 LGE system which will gradually be replaced by the 1990 LOGSE system, vocational training (FP) is divided into two levels (2+2 or 2+3) and constitutes a bridge between the general education system and the world of work. Part of the training is carried out in companies by means of periods of practice, especially at the FP II level. Instruction is provided by university licentiates and master craftsmen. Timetables are 32 hours per week for FP I and 34 (plus 9 practice) hours per week for FP II. The academic year begins on 1 October and ends on 30 June.

In the new 1990 LOGSE system, vocational training will be directed towards practical training in an occupation, constituting a mechanism for linking schools and the work system. It will be made up of the intermediate and higher grades, divided into specific formative cycles, or vocational modules, of varying lengths. These cycles or modules will also serve continuing education and in the training of adult workers.

3.5 Adult and Nonformal Education

Adult education is organized around three kinds of instruction: academic, occupational, and sociocultural.

The main objective of academic education is literacy and basic adult education. In 1987–88, some 200,000 students took such courses by attending classes and 13,000 were enrolled in distance education schemes. A further 22,000 students took the distance baccalaureate. Occupational training is employment-based and, in addition to funding from state institutions, also receives funding from the European Social Fund. Some 275,000 adults received basic occupational training courses and another 200,000 participated in elite courses, especially in the fields of computer science and business administration and management. Sociocultural training is oriented towards the personal development of adults. On the whole, adult education is organized and funded in the public sector by six ministries (Education; Culture; Social Affairs; Justice; Defense; and Agriculture, Fisheries, and Food); and, in the private sector, by people's universities, people's adult schools, and the Catholic Church.

4. Administrative and Supervisory Structure and Operation

The process of state decentralization for educational administration operates at three levels. At the first level, the essential duties for ensuring the basic unity of the national education system fall to the central administration (the Ministry of Education and Science). This includes the overall arrangement of the regular education system for the whole nation, regulation of academic awards and vocational certificates, establishment of school and teaching staff requirements, regulation of Castilian teaching as the common official language, general inspection of the system, student grants and allowances policy, distance education, and international relations. In addition, the ministries of Defense, Labor, Agriculture, Fisheries and Food, Transport, Justice, and Health administer, supervise, and fund their own programs of education.

At the second level, the autonomous communities are responsible for the regulation and administration of all educational matters in their areas within the limits defined by the state. In particular, they are responsible for encouraging local culture, research, and where applicable, teaching of the autonomous community's own language. By 1994, seven autonomous communities (Andalusia, the Canary Islands, Catalonia, Galicia, the Basque Country, Valencia, and Navarre) had assumed full powers in education, constituting their own organizational structure and institutions (education departments) which vary from community to community. The remaining ten communities are in the process of assuming these powers, the Ministry of Education and Science provisionally taking charge of the major part of their management through the provincial head offices of education. It is planned that the process of transference of educational powers to these ten autonomous communities will be finalized by the year 1998.

At the third level, the local administrations (town councils) have a priority role in providing land for and maintaining/building state schools, as well as for collaborating in school life through participatory bodies and through the organization of complementary educational activities.

For the supervision of the system, both the central and the autonomous community administrations have implemented their respective technical inspection systems, the duties of which are to advise on and support the educational process, ensure that legislation is complied with, cooperate in the evaluation of the operation of the system, and establish communication between schools and the educational authorities and administrations.

The process of decentralizing state powers in matters of education also involves encouraging society to participate. The participatory bodies at the state level are the State Schools Board, the General Vocational Training Board, and the Universities Board. At the higher education level, the social council; the university staff meeting; the governing board; and the boards of faculties, higher technical schools, and university schools are the basic bodies of participation. The participatory bodies at publicly funded, nonuniversity institutions are the school board (made up of representatives of teachers, parents, pupils, auxiliary school staff, and the local community) and the staff meeting.

5. Educational Finance

Educational funding comes from public and private sources. Public funding is supplied by the central educational administration (mainly the Ministry of Education and Science and, to a lesser extent, by other ministries), the autonomous community, and local administrations. Public funds are earmarked both for the maintenance of state schools and the subsidization of private schools, as well as for student grants and allowances. Similarly, some private funds go to funding state education.

In state schools, education is completely free for the EGB / Primary, ESO, baccalaureate, and vocational training levels. Private schools may receive state subsidies mainly for the compulsory levels (EGB / Primary / ESO) and, in some special cases, for vocational training or may be funded exclusively by family contributions. At state universities, students have to pay for a small part of the costs of education, while at private universities the students cover all expenses. At all educational levels, families pay for school books and materials, as well as the cost of school meals, transport, and extra-curricular activities in both state and private schools.

Total expenditure on education in Spain was 2,717,817 million pesetas in 1990, which amounted to 5.4 percent of the Gross Domestic Product (GDP). In 1991, 4.95 percent of the national budget was earmarked for education. Of this amount, 80 percent came from the public purse (40% from the central administration, 35% from the autonomous communities, and 5% from local administrations) and the remaining 20 percent from families. The breakdown of expenditure by educational activities is shown in Table 2.

The state uses public funds to finance compulsory education in private schools which meet given requirements, such as free education; the establishment of a school board; voluntary religious practice; and the use of set criteria for pupil admission, teacher selection, pupil–teacher ratio, and also meeting given minimum requirements to guarantee teaching quality. This funding covers expenditure on teaching staff, administration and services, maintenance and upkeep of facilities, and investment.

The state also provides grants to students who have the aptitude but not the financial means to complete courses at the noncompulsory levels. Around 706,000 pupils benefited from such allowances in 1992–93, which amounted to around 70,000 million pesetas. At the compulsory levels, the state provides allowances toward covering the complementary costs of school meals and transport, and boarding school. In 1990–91, the cost for these complementary services amounted to 30,000 million pesetas, affecting more than 1 million students.

The funds allocated by families to education represent almost 2 percent of total private consumption. About 80 percent of this expenditure is for strictly educational activities and 20 percent for complementary activities and school materials.

6. Supplying Personnel for the Education System

In the 1991–92 academic year, there were more than 500,000 teachers in the education system: 281,766 in

Table 2
Breakdown of public spending on education, 1989

Categories	%
Educational activities	89.7
Preschool/EGB	38.1
BUP–COU–FP	22.1
Higher education	14.3
Special education	2.1
Other education	4.3
Occupational training	8.8
Additional activities	10.3
Administration	2.6
Grants and allowances	2.9
Complementary services	2.0
Teacher training	0.7
Other activities	2.1
Total public spending	100.0

preschool general basic education (EGB), and primary education; 99,650 in baccalaureate (BUP), compulsory secondary education (ESO), and university guidance course (COU); 67,992 in vocational training (FP); and 63,665 in higher education. Furthermore, 4,904 teachers are charged with special education and 14,008 are assigned to other kinds of education (applied arts and craftmenship, music, dramatic art and dancing, and foreign languages). The proportion of female teachers is 96 percent in preschool, 65 in EGB/primary education, 53 in BUP and COU, 42 in FP, 64 in special education, and 29 percent in higher education.

In order to be able to work as a teacher at any educational level, one must have a university degree (three years for EGB/primary education and five years for the others) as well as teacher training. An important change introduced by the 1990 Education Act is that teachers in preschool education must be qualified. Since 1990, primary school teacher training has been divided into seven specialization categories (infant, primary, foreign language, physical education, music, special, and hearing and language) and lasts three years. A state examination must be passed in order to teach in state schools. The admission procedure in private education is based on employment contracts.

Inservice teacher training is carried out by means of specialized courses or training at the workplace, and it is noncompulsory. A large part of inservice training is completed in teachers' centers (CEP) in the area administered by the Ministry of Education and Science, and in similar centers in the autonomous communities with devolved powers in education. During the 1990–91 academic year, 91,744 teachers participated in such training courses and 10,608 took part in training activities at the schools where they work. Educational administrations try to adjust their offer of inservice training courses to the new curriculum developed on the basis of the new 1990 LOGSE. Since the mid-1980s, emphasis has been placed on the areas of foreign language teaching, new technologies, health education, environmental education, cooeducation, adult, and compensatory education.

7. Curriculum Development and Teaching Methodology

One characteristic of the system introduced by the 1970 Education Act is that there is a core curriculum for the whole country defined by the central administration. The 1990 Act establishes the creation of a basic curriculum design which consists of a nationwide core curriculum in which the general objectives of each educational stage, the curriculum areas to be taught, the blocks of subject content, and the didactic and assessment guidelines are specified.

At the first level, the Ministry of Education and Science establishes an initial general curriculum (syllabus) which is the criterion of nationwide unity and to which the provisions of the autonomous communities are added for purposes of cultural pluralism. At the second level, schools develop a more specific curriculum, adapted to make it relevant with regard to the environment and suitable for the school's pupils. This school curriculum plan is drawn up by teams of teachers as a plan of didactic methods adapted to a particular background. At the third level, the teacher translates the school curriculum into particular programs for each class, and where applicable for each student, breaking down the content, activities, and assessment procedures into didactic units suited to the students. The curriculum allows for different kinds of adaptation and diversification to cater for the needs of students with different aptitudes and interests in different sociocultural circumstances and surroundings.

Table 3 presents the school timetable corresponding to the minimum teaching standards in the different levels of the new 1990 Spanish educational system. The LOGSE established that the minimum teaching standards in the different education levels will be 65 percent of the total school time for the autonomous communities without their own language and 55 percent in communities with their own language (Basque, Catalonian, Galician, and Valencian).

As regards teaching materials, the educational administrations provide guidelines for their development and the publishing houses write the books and supplementary materials. The educational administrations approve the materials for use. Teachers have a high degree of freedom to choose textbooks and materials for their pedagogical work.

8. The System of Examinations, Promotions, and Certifications

Assessment of the learning process in preschool and general basic education (EGB) is continuous, and upgrading is automatic at the preschool level. A maximum of only one year per cycle may be repeated in EGB until students reach 16 years of age. At the end of the compulsory stage in the 1970 LGE system, there are two certificates: the *Graduado Escolar* for pupils who complete this stage successfully (giving access to both the baccalaureate and to vocational training) and the *Certificado de Escolaridad* (which gives access only to vocational training).

Students who pass the all three years of the baccalaureate course receive the baccalaureate certificate without any final examination and, after having completed the course of university guidance (COU), can take the university entrance examination to go on to higher education.

In vocational training, students who pass the first grade (FPI) receive the Auxiliary Technician Certificate for their particular occupation. After completing further courses they can enter second-grade vocational

Table 3
School timetable corresponding to the millenium teaching standards in the different levels of the new 1990 Spanish educational system

Areas	Hours per year
Primary education	
First cycle	
Castilian (Spanish) language and literature	350
Mathematics	175
Knowledge of the natural, social and cultural environment	175
Arts education	140
Physical education	140
Religion/ethical education	105
Total	1,085
Second and third cycles	
Castilian (Spanish) language and literature	275
Mathematics	170
Knowledge of the natural, social and cultural environment	170
Foreign languages	170
Arts education	105
Physical education	105
Religion/ethical education	105
Total	1,100
Compulsory secondary education	
First cycle	
Castilian (Spanish) language and literature	210
Foreign languages	210
Mathematics	140
Social sciences, history and geography	140
Natural sciences	140
Technology	125
Religion/ethical education	105
Physical education	70
Plastic and visual arts education	70
Music	70
Total	1,280
Second cycle	
Castilian (Spanish) language and literature	240
Foreign languages	240
Mathematics	160
Social sciences, history and geography	160
Natural sciences	90
Technology	70
Religion/ethical education	105
Physical education	70
Physical and visual arts education	35
Music	35
Total	1,205
Baccalaureate	
Common subjects	Hours (2 years)
Castilian (Spanish) language and literature	210
Foreign languages	210
Philosophy	70
History	70
Religion/ethical education	70
Physical education	35
Total	665

Specific subjects[a]

Arts modality: Artistic Drawing, Technical Drawing, Volume, Arts History, Image, Foundations of Design, Graphic and Plastic Expression Techniques

Natural and health sciences modality: Mathematics, Physics, Chemistry, Technical Drawing, Biology, Geology, Earth and Environmental Sciences

Humanities and social sciences modality: Mathematics applied to the social sciences, Latin, Greek, Economy, History of the Contempoary World, Economy and Enterprise Organization, Geography, Art History, History of Philosophy

Technology modality: Mathematics, Industrial Technology, Physics, Chemistry, Technical Drawing, Electrotechnics, Mechanics

---

a Hours of specific subjects rank between 70 to 140 hours for the two-year baccalaureate

---

training (FPII) (as can those who have taken the baccalaureate), at the end of which they receive the Specialist Technician Certificate.

In higher education, university schools award the degrees of Diplomate, Architectural Technician, and Engineering Technician. The faculties and higher technical schools award the degrees of Graduate, Architect, or Engineer. Students who complete the first two cycles may enter the third cycle (Doctorate). After a course of adaptation, university school graduates may enter the second cycle at some faculties or higher technical schools.

Under the new 1990 Education Act, preschool assessment will still be continuous and upgrading automatic. There will be continuous assessment throughout primary and secondary education to gather knowledge on each student's development. The main methods of assessment will be monitoring pupils' activities; systematic observation; the analysis of work; and oral, written, or practical tests. Students will proceed to the next cycle upon the achievement of the objectives of the previous cycle. Students may repeat an additional year in a cycle if they have not achieved its objectives, although they may repeat no more than two years throughout compulsory education. Those who achieve all the objectives at the end of secondary school will be awarded the certificate of *Graduado en Educación Secundaria*, which will give them the right to enter baccalaureate or intermediate-grade vocational education. Students not receiving the certificate of *Graduado en Educación Secundaria* will receive a document from the school certifying the number of years completed and their marks.

Students with a positive assessment in all of the baccalaureate subjects will receive the Baccalaureate Certificate which allows them to enter the higher-grade vocational school or take the university entrance examination.

At the end of the vocational education stages, vocational training certificates will be awarded. Upon completion of the intermediate and higher-grade vocational schools, vocational certificates equivalent to Levels 2 and 3 of the European Union qualification will be awarded.

9. Educational Assessment, Evaluation, and Research

Educational research in Spain is mainly carried out at universities and at the Ministry of Education and Science's Center of Research, Documentation, and Evaluation (CIDE). CIDE is the main body funding research, earmarking around 400 million pesetas (US\$2.85 million) per year for some 100 research projects to be maintained annually. At the end of the 1980s, the most popular research themes were academic achievement and teaching methods, but with an increasing interest being shown in educational psychology, inequalities in education, curriculum matters, and teachers and teacher training.

The 1990 Education Act provides for general and nationwide evaluation studies of the system, schools, teachers, pupils, and educational administration. An Institute of Quality and Evaluation (INCE) was established in 1994 and charged with nationwide evaluation studies on the state and evolution of the quality of the system, in cooperation with the autonomous communities. The INCE will assess reforms and partial aspects of the education system and will also be responsible for the international evaluation studies carried out in cooperation with such bodies as the International Association for the Evaluation of Educational Achievement (IEA), the International Assessment of Educational Progress (IAEP), and the Organisation for Economic Cooperation and Development (OECD).

At the beginning of the 1990s, there was insufficient funding for research and a shortage of effective mechanisms for passing on general information to those responsible for formulating policies. In addition, the division of powers between the central administration and the autonomous community administrations as regards research and evaluation was notable. However, the establishment of the INCE, the continued improvement in the quality and relevance of research, the trend towards the internationalization of research and evaluation, and the increase in international cooperation in this area are positive features.

10. Major Reforms in the 1980s and 1990s

Any outline of the Spanish education system is necessarily a description of the many reform processes which have been undertaken—the whole Spanish education system having been completely reformed since the 1970s.

It is important to stress that the 1985 Education Act (LODE) established an integrated network of schools (state and private) that guaranteed the right to education and stated that the state would cater to the demand for schooling thus enabling a free choice of school for all on an equal footing. It also set up mechanisms for the community to participate in school life. The 1990 Education Act (LOGSE) reformed the legal structure for the educational system and, in particular, for curriculum renewal. It also created special regulations on the integration of students with special needs into regular primary schools; continuous teacher training, especially as regards the establishment of teacher centers; and the encouragement of psychopedagogical guidance in schools. All of these reforms have substantially changed nonuniversity education.

The 1983 University Reform Act (LRU) defined the division of governmental and administrative powers between the state administration, the autonomous communities, and the universities themselves. The Act reformed the organization and operation of the universities, strengthened the departmental structure, reshaped the structure of university teaching staff, and established new university curricula for a large number of degrees. All of this drastically changed the face of higher education.

11. Major Problems for the Year 2000

There are several challenges facing the education system up to the year 2000. The first is the implementation of the new system in terms of structure, content, and teaching methodologies. A lack of sufficient financial resources will be the main problem for this implementation. The increase in the quality of all levels of education will be the second most important goal. Another challenge is to improve the retraining and continuous training systems for practicing teachers. Yet a further problem will be the restructuring and

introduction of an effective vocational training system that provides real occupational skills, closely linked with company production systems, that satisfactorily plays its role in the transition from education to work, and is compatible with the qualification standards of the European Union. Another goal of main importance is to improve the administration of the schools by giving more power to the heads and directive teams of the schools at the same time as their autonomy is increased.

In higher education, there is a need to increase the quality and relevance of research work, improve relations with the international scientific community, to rationalize entry to the university teaching profession in order to ensure the quality of university lecturers' teaching and research work, and to introduce a new system of evaluation of the universities and teaching and research staff.

Finally, the achievement of a suitable balance between the process of decentralization of state powers in education to autonomous community governments, the simultaneous process of conferring qualifications in education in accord with the European Union requirements, and the establishment of priorities in an economic crisis period are the main political challenges facing Spanish educational policy.

Bibliography

CIDE 1992 *El Sistema Educativo Español. Informe Nacional para la Red Eurydice*. Ministerio de Educación y Ciencia, Madrid

Consejo de Universidades 1992 *Anuario de Estadística Universitaria 1992*. Ministerio de Educación y Ciencia, Madrid

El País 1994 *Anuario 1994*. El País, Madrid

Gil G A 1991 The reform of compulsory education. In: McNair J, Beattie N (eds.) 1991 *Education for the New Spain*. Centre for Community and Educational Policy Studies, Liverpool

McNair J 1984 *Education for a Changing Spain*. Manchester University Press, Manchester

McNair J, Beattie N (eds.) 1991 *Education for the New Spain*. Centre for Community and Educational Policy Studies, Liverpool

Ministerio de Educación y Ciencia 1973 *Ley General de Educación y Disposiciones Complementarias*. Ministerio de Educación y Ciencia, Madrid

Ministerio de Educación y Ciencia 1989 *Libro Blanco para la Reforma del Sistema Educativo*. Ministerio de Educación y Ciencia, Madrid

Ministerio de Educación y Ciencia 1992 *España. Informe Nacional de Educación. Conferencia Internacional de Educación, 43ª reunión, Ginebra, 1992*. Ministerio de Educación y Ciencia, Madrid

Múñoz-Repiso M et al. 1988 *El Sistema Educativo Español*. Ministerio de Educación y Ciencia, Madrid

Múñoz-Repiso M et al. 1992 *El Sistema Educativo Español 1991*. Ministerio de Educación y Ciencia, Madrid

OECD 1986 *Spain: Reviews of National Policies for Education*. OECD, Paris

Sri Lanka

A. M. Ranaweera

1. General Background

The Republic of Sri Lanka, a pear-shaped island measuring 435 kilometers from north to south and 225 kilometers from east to west with an area of 65,600 square kilometers, is located off the southeastern tip of the Indian subcontinent. The country has a typical tropical climate with heavy monsoon rains and average temperatures around 27°C in the lowlands and 10–20°C in the central highlands.

In 1990, the population was estimated to be nearly 17 million. The population growth rate declined from 1.9 in the 1960s to 1.5 in the 1990s, but the population is expected to be well beyond 20 million by the year 2000 and about 27 million by the 2040s. More than 75 percent of the population is rural. The fact that 35 percent of the population is below the age of 14 has significant implications for educational planning. Furthermore, the older age groups are becoming relatively larger than the younger ones due to the declining fertility level. This foretells a change in the demands made on the social infrastructure and consequently on education. The density of population varies widely from 2,909 per square kilometer (in the Colombo district—1989) to 36 (in the Mullaitivu district); the national average is 260 per square kilometer.

The Sinhalese comprise 74 percent of the population, Sri Lankan Tamils 12.6 percent, Indian Tamils 5.5 percent, Moors 7.1 percent, and others (Eurasians, Malays, etc.) 0.8 percent. About 69 percent of the people are Buddhists, 15.5 percent Hindus, 7.6 percent Muslims, and 7.5 percent Christians according to the 1981 census. Sinhala and Tamil are the two national languages and they are also the media of instruction, although English is a widely used second language. The multiracial, multilingual, multireligious character of the population has given rise to various types of socioeconomic problems (particularly in education) and has also been the cause of ethnic conflicts, mainly between the Sinhalese and the Tamils, which surfaced after Independence and escalated into armed confrontation in the 1980s. With the adoption of a free market economic policy in 1977 and the expansion of the modern sector of employment, there has been an increasing demand for English which is considered to be the key with which to gain access to that sector.

Sri Lanka is predominantly an agricultural country whose export income is mainly from tea, rubber, and coconut, which account for nearly 60 percent of export earnings and 26 percent of the Gross Domestic Product (GDP). The most important food crop is rice, which is also the staple food of the people. The industrial base of the economy is still weak, the main industries being cement, textiles, leather and rubber goods, paper, ceramics, and petroleum products. Nontraditional exports such as precious stones and garments are gaining in importance as foreign-exchange earners. The composition of the GDP in 1989 was: agriculture 26.0 percent; industry 25.6 percent; and services 48.4 percent. The Gross National Product (GNP) (at 1990 prices) was 284,553 million rupees, equivalent to US$7,103 million and a per capita GNP of US$418. Imports exceeded exports by about US$705 million in 1990.

Of those employed in 1991, most were in elementary occupations (39.5%) followed by skilled agricultural workers (25.2%) and crafts and related workers, machine operators, and so on (14.3%). Only about 12 percent were in senior or management level and professional occupations, or technical or similar occupations. Just over 50 percent of all working-age persons were reported to be economically active, but about 14 percent of this group were unemployed. Over 70 percent of the people between 20 and 34 years and 30 percent between 15 and 19 years of age were unemployed. Thus, there is a problem of unemployed youth, since the unemployed have a much higher educational profile than the employed.

The problem of abject poverty has driven children to work at various trades such as pavement hawkers, domestic labor, private bus conductors and criers, and in repair shops and small industries. These children are either early dropouts from school or those who were never enrolled.

Sri Lanka has been able to achieve considerable social progress despite low economic development, due to welfare measures taken by successive governments since Independence for meeting the basic needs of the people through such means as food subsidies, free education and healthcare, and nationalization of essential services. This is reflected in Sri Lanka being placed 75th in the Human Development Index (HDI) of 160 countries while its GNP rank is as low as 120 (UNDP 1991). Ironically, it is the disproportionate success of these services relative to economic development which has put inexorable pressures on the socioeconomic system of the country. Since 1989, the government has placed high priority on alleviation of poverty and launched a major trans-sectorial strategy known as the *Janasaviya* Program (JSP) aimed at combating income disparities, unemployment, landlessness, malnutrition, and the like.

With the expansion of economic activities the demand for trained personnel—especially in the fields of construction, industry, finance, tourism and other service sectors—has increased considerably. Also, increasing external demand, particularly from the Middle-East countries for skilled personnel in technical fields, further augments the necessity for trained personnel.

Sri Lanka can claim to have a satisfactory level of infrastructure for a developing country. The country has developed its electric power capacity mainly through hydro power and has a good public transport system providing access even to remote rural areas.

Sri Lanka has a well-developed health system in which both the Western and the traditional (*Ayurveda*) system function side by side focusing on primary healthcare resulting in a substantial lowering of death rates, infant and maternal mortality rates, and raised life expectancy levels.

Sri Lanka gained independence from British colonial rule in 1948 and adopted a parliamentary system of government. The country was declared a republic within the Commonwealth in 1972. Since 1987 there has been some devolution of powers from the national government to the provincial councils. The provincial council system was designed to decentralize the administration and, within the framework of a unitary state, to have a system of devolution of power. Education and education services are subjects that come within the purview of the provincial councils, which have limited and specified powers assigned to them in certain areas. The devolution of power has brought in a new dimension to educational planning and development in Sri Lanka, with implications in particular for curriculum development, teacher education, and evaluation and accreditation at the school level and for entry into tertiary-level education.

2. Politics and the Goals of the Education System

The traditional education base, which has evolved since the introduction of Buddhism in the third century BC, gradually eroded with the advent of the Western powers—the Portuguese, Dutch, and British—from the sixteenth to the twentieth centuries. Certain radical policy changes introduced in the 1940s constitute a landmark in the democratization of education. The most significant changes were the introduction, in 1945, of free education from kindergarten through to university and the adoption of the mother tongue of the child as the medium of instruction. These measures were expected to provide for greater equality of opportunity and social mobility. After Independence (1948), successive governments have declared their intention to continue with the policies of democratization of education, removal of elitism and privilege, and of providing equality of opportunity to all.

As the political pendulum swung with changes of government, each government attempted to introduce educational reforms to suit its political and socioeconomic ideologies, which contributed to a high degree of disorder in the system. A government that came into power with the support of the Sinhala–Buddhist majority introduced drastic changes to eradicate inequalities that stemmed from the existence of a Western-oriented English-educated elite and a privileged Christian denominational sector in the education system. In spite of these policy changes, most middle-class parents consider education to be the key to social mobility and demand a system which would enable their children to enter the prestigious professions in society such as medicine, engineering, accountancy, and law, or to qualify for lucrative jobs in a foreign land.

As a result, attempts to restructure the education system and make it more relevant to the socioeconomic needs and realities of the country have met with strong resistance from certain classes of parents. Such situations are invariably exploited by rival political parties to woo voters at general elections and offer professionally unsound counterproposals in their election manifestos.

The main political goals of the government in the 1990s are to eradicate poverty, to adopt a free market economic policy to encourage rapid economic growth, and to take appropriate measures to solve the ethnic conflict between the Sinhalese and Tamils and ensure national unity. The achievement of these goals would entail the modernization of the school curriculum giving special emphasis to science and technology, English and other foreign languages, multicultural understanding, and proficiency in the two national languages; strengthening nonformal basic education for the general population, and making structural changes in terms of the devolution of power to the provincial level and more effective management at the micro level.

3. The Formal System of Education

3.1 Primary, Secondary, and Tertiary Education

There are two categories of schools in Sri Lanka—government schools and nongovernment schools. The nongovernment schools consist of private schools, estate schools, *Pirivena* institutions, approved/certified schools, preschools, international schools, and special schools. *Pirivenas* are educational institutions attached to Buddhist temples catering primarily to the education of Buddhist monks and also conducting general education classes for lay students. In 1989 there were 9,805 government schools, 427 *Pirivenas*, 12 estate schools, and 37 private schools. Of these 4,430 are primary (or junior) schools having classes up to year 5 (or year 8), 3,511 up to year 11, and 1,864 up to year 13. More than 2,000 of the primary schools are considered to be "small schools" having fewer than 100 pupils and one or two teachers. There is a special category of about 30 very large prestigious schools called "national schools" having 3,000 to 6,000 pupils each.

Table 1
Enrollments and government expenditure on education 1989

Number of schools (government and private)	10,253
Number of schools (government)	9,805
Number of pupils:	
primary (years 1–5)	2,085,700
secondary (years 6–11)	1,783,200
collegiate (years 12–13)	188,800
Total	4,057,700
Number of teachers	151,434
Expenditure on general and higher education (in millions of rupees)	7,477
Education budget as a percentage of:	
total government expenditure	7.9
the GNP	3.36

Sources: *School Census*, Ministry of Education 1989; *Annual Reports*, Central Bank of Sri Lanka

Figure 1 outlines the structure of the formal school system. Key statistics on enrollments and resources in the major education sectors are given in Table 1. The flow through the system of a cohort of pupils entering Grade 1 is shown in Fig. 2. General education is

Table 2
Repetition and dropout rates 1987

School year	1	2	3	4	5	6	7	8	9
Repetition rate	8.0	9.6	9.4	9.7	8.5	6.4	6.6	4.6	3.6
Dropout rate	—	0.8	2.1	3.1	5.2	6.0	6.3	6.2	7.1

Source: Ministry of Education

divisible into four stages: primary (years 1–5), junior-secondary (years 6–8), senior-secondary (years 9–11), and collegiate (years 12–13).

Age of admission to school in year 1 is 5+ years and all children are expected to remain in school up to year 11 (age 15+), although there is no legal provision to enforce compulsory schooling.

There is a fairly high rate of dropout and grade repetition at different levels, as shown in Table 2. The enrollment ratios for 1986–88 as a percentage are: primary 100, secondary 71, and tertiary 4 (UNDP 1991). The school system has about 4.23 million pupils and about 180,000 teachers with a pupil–teacher ratio of 23:1 for the system and 32:1 for the primary level. There is no male–female gap either in terms of access or success in school education. In regard to enrollment, "female as a percentage to male" was 100

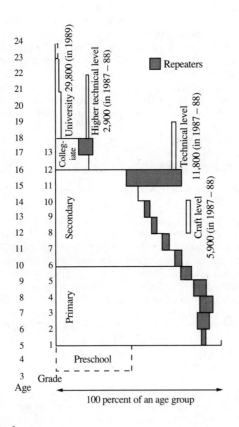

Figure 1
Sri Lanka: Structure of the formal education system 1991

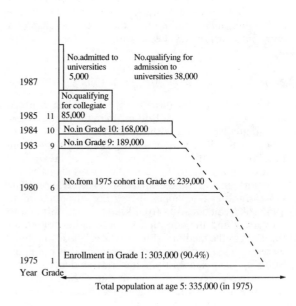

Figure 2
The flow through the formal system: Progress of an annual cohort by educational level 1975–87
Source: Based on data from the Ministry of Education School Census 1975–87

for the primary level and 109 for the secondary level in 1987–88.

Formal school education is free at all levels in all state and state-aided institutes (except in a few fee-levying private institutions) and the medium of instruction is the mother tongue of the pupil. The essential textbooks are provided free to all students up to the senior-secondary level (year 11). A scheme to provide a free mid-day meal to all has been in operation since 1989.

The school year lasts from January to December, with three terms separated by three holiday periods, and consists of a minimum of 190 school days per year. The lower-primary level (years 1–3) has 4 hours of work per day while the upper-primary, secondary, and collegiate levels have 5.5 hours of work per day.

Since the 1940s, university education has grown so rapidly that by 1989 there were 8 universities with a total enrollment of 29,800, 12,600 of whom were females. Sri Lanka also has an open university offering a variety of academic and professional courses through distance education.

In addition, there are 10 other institutes of higher education. Action was taken in 1992 to establish nine affiliated university colleges, one in each province, to provide higher education to a large number of students who are denied educational opportunities because of the lack of places in the national universities.

3.2 Preschool Education

Preschool education is not a component of state-managed general education. However, some preschool facilities are provided by local government authorities, nongovernmental organizations, and by the private sector on a fee-levying basis. It is estimated that about 50 percent of Sri Lankan children attend preschool for periods ranging from a few months to a year. Many pupils do not receive any systematic preschool education, especially in rural areas.

3.3 Special Education

Special education is provided through two types of programs: the integrated special education program under which handicapped children attend regular schools and learn with normal children; and the non integrated special schools program where handicapped children learn in special schools which are mostly residential. As a matter of policy, handicapped children are sent to regular schools under the integrated system wherever possible. Special education programs are available for the following categories: the visually handicapped; the hearing handicapped; the mentally handicapped; and crippled children and slow learners. The Ministry of Education has a special unit to implement the special education program and coordinate other related activities, such as those concerned with

health and employment, with the different ministries and departments.

3.4 Vocational, Technical, and Business Education

Vocational, technical, and business education covers a wide spectrum of vocational and technical levels and is administered by a variety of institutional arrangements under about 20 ministries and state agencies. The following are the main ministries: Education and Higher Education; Youth Affairs and Sports; Labor; Rural Industrial Development; Local Government, Housing, and Construction; Transport; and Fisheries and Health. Some private-sector institutions also offer industrial training courses catering to a small clientele.

In 1981, the government issued a white paper on educational proposals for reform which suggested several proposals for expanding and consolidating technical/vocational education both for school dropouts and those having completed general education. The main proposals consisted of: a technical stream parallel to the academic GCE (O-level) stream in years 9–11; artisan courses for school leavers at the junior-secondary level; an "Open School" providing a nonformal type of enrichment courses; technical, commerce, fine arts, and apprenticeship courses under a "Technical Education Authority"; open university courses; and professional colleges (at university level) providing courses for a wide range of established professions. Some of these proposals have yet to be implemented.

The existing technical/vocational education programs broadly fall into four categories: professional engineering education at university level; technical education at technician level; technical/vocational education at craft level; and vocational training courses, mostly short ones, for a wide range of skill levels. In addition, inservice training given by the employer and informal training provided in traditional guild form by trained craftsmen are also in existence.

Degree-level professional education is provided by the engineering faculties of two universities and the Open University. A total of 24 technical colleges and 5 affiliated units under the Ministry of Education and Higher Education offer diplomas and certificate-level courses in a wide range of fields including commerce, accountancy, stenography, and so on. In addition, full-time and part-time craft (trade) level courses are also offered by the colleges. The National Apprenticeship and Industrial Training Authority (NAITA) provides training in over 200 industrial establishments to more than 11,000 apprentices in about 150 categories of trades. These programs have a built-in linkage with industry and the employment market. The National Youth Services Council and the Ministry of Labor offer vocational training programs at different levels based on current market demands. The state and state-sponsored agencies bear the major burden of technical/vocational education and the participation of private enterprise is relatively small, generally being coordinated via NAITA. The state-sponsored programs are usually free. Apprentices of NAITA are financially supported by the state during training and absorbed into industrial ventures on completion of training. Voluntary organizations like *Sarvodaya* and some private agencies also offer vocational training programs.

Since a large number of governmental and nongovernmental agencies are involved in technical/vocational training, there is a lack of proper coordination between these programs as regards standardization and horizontal and vertical mobility, as well as higher marketability and productivity through quality improvement. In order to remedy this situation a Tertiary Vocational Education Commission (TVEC) was established.

With the expansion and modernization of the economy, new courses have been introduced and appropriate curriculum changes have been made, particularly in areas relevant to computers and informatics, tourism and the hotel industry, and the development of new nontraditional industries.

3.5 Adult and Nonformal Education

The educational needs of adults and out-of-school children did not receive high priority until the early 1980s when the Nonformal Education Division of the Ministry of Education was established and several projects launched. Nonformal education is now a part of accepted governmental policy. In 1992, there were four programs conducted by the Nonformal Education Division for children, youth, and adults: skills development programs for school leavers, literacy programs for nonschool-goers and primary-school dropouts, adult education/community education programs, and English-language classes for adults. Several new programs are being planned.

The nonformal education programs are supported by donor agencies such as UNICEF and SIDA. Existing infrastructure facilities of the formal sector are being used. A proposal to introduce an islandwide network of "open schools" to provide a variety of short-term courses for those who have left the formal school system or a more comprehensive "open learning system" is being considered in new educational reform projects. A Department of Nonformal Education has been set up at the National Institute of Education which is mainly concerned with research and development work in this field.

In the nongovernment sector, many social service and voluntary organizations conduct various types of nonformal education programs for adults and children, mainly in income generating activities such as handicrafts and farming.

4. Administrative and Supervisory Structure and Operation

The Ministry of Education and Higher Education (MOE&HE) (formerly two separate ministries, but amalgamated since 1990) is responsible for the design, implementation, control, and maintenance of general education, teacher education, higher education, and technical/vocational education in Sri Lanka. The Minister of Education and Higher Education who is the executive head of the Ministry is assisted by a State Minister of Education, a Project Minister of Education Services, and a Project Minister of Higher Education. The Secretary to the Ministry, who is also the Director General of Education, is the most senior public servant in the Ministry and is responsible for the supervision and management of the entire education system within the Ministry. An independent body named the "Education Service Committee" under the Public Service Commission is responsible for such functions as recruitment, promotions, and disciplinary matters of teachers and officers of the education service. The University Grants Commission deals with matters related to universities and other institutes of higher education. Certain functions which were formerly under the Ministry (e.g., curriculum development, research, distance education, management of the Staff College for Education Administration, etc.) have been transferred to the newly created National Institute of Education (NIE).

Educational structure and management in Sri Lanka was hitherto highly centralized. The situation has changed with the devolution of power to the provincial councils. The provincial councils have provincial ministries of education to deal with the powers and functions assigned to them by central government. Suitable organizational arrangements and appropriate structural changes in the central ministry are being worked out to ensure smooth coordination between the center, NIE, and the provincial councils.

The "school circuit" which formed the unit for administration and supervision under the Circuit Education Officer has been gradually giving way to a "school cluster system" since the early 1980s. The school clusters are managed by divisional education offices which are the subunits of the provincial education departments.

5. Educational Finance

The total government expenditure on education in 1989 was 7,477 million rupees, which was 7.9 percent of all government expenditure and 3.36 percent of the GNP. Expenditure on education has fluctuated since Independence, depending on the priorities of successive governments and their educational policies. Expenditure as a proportion of the GNP increased through the 1950s from 3 percent in 1952 to 4.8 percent in 1960. It rose to 4.9 percent in 1965 and remained between 4.0 to 4.9 up to 1972, showing a steady decline from 1973 (3.4%) to 2.8 percent in 1977 and 2.48 percent in 1984, with a gradual increase in the late 1980s to around 3 percent. Since 1983, about 37 million rupees per year were received as foreign aid. This was less than 1 percent of the recurrent expenditure on general education. About 80 percent of the education budget is spent on teachers' salaries. The distribution of current expenditure in 1990 among various levels was about 93 percent on first- and second-level education and ·7 percent on tertiary education. The total recurrent expenditure per pupil per year was 906 rupees (in 1985) while the nonsalary recurrent expenditure was 136 rupees.

Since the formal system is almost entirely a state system, capital and recurrent costs are borne by the state except in the case of a few fee-levying private institutions. Schools may levy a facilities fee from pupils to cover the cost of extracurricular activities such as sports. School development societies and alumni associations sometimes assist in providing facilities for schools.

Even though education is free from year 1 up to the first-degree level in the universities, pupils from low income families need financial assistance to sustain them in school. There are several support schemes to help pupils in need of such financial assistance. The year 5 scholarship test, conducted by the Ministry of Education, and a few other schemes offer bursaries to needy pupils. Bank loans and scholarships are also available for students in higher education institutions.

6. Supplying Personnel for the Education System

The total number of teachers in state schools in 1990 was estimated to be about 184,000, of whom only 106,000 were professionally trained. The number of teaching staff at universities was about 1,785 in 1988–89.

Teachers are recruited at two levels: university graduates and those possessing a minimum of passes in three subjects at the General Certificate of Education (Advanced level) which is the examination at the end of the collegiate level (year 13). The rapid expansion of education necessitated a large number of untrained teachers to be appointed to schools. In 1990, 42 percent of all teachers still had not received a professional training. In 1992 there were four systems of initial training: a three-year program in 16 teachers colleges for nongraduate inservice teachers; a three-year pre-service program in 7 colleges of education; a distance education program administered by the National Institute of Education (NIE), and a postgraduate Diploma in Education for graduate teachers conducted by the education faculties of three universities and also by the NIE. The teachers colleges and colleges of education are administered by the Ministry of Education.

As well as initial training, the NIE and the provincial departments of education conduct inservice education programs to re-orient the teachers to changes in the curriculum and methodology. A "Master Teacher Scheme" has been in operation for this purpose. There are several special projects to train teachers of English. The NIE conducts Bachelor of Education courses in selected areas of specialization. The Department of Education Management Development of the NIE has various programs to train principals and deputy principals of schools and administrators.

7. Curriculum Development and Teaching Methodology

For purposes of curriculum development, school education may be considered to consist of the four stages outlined in Sect. 3.1 above. There is a commonly prescribed national curriculum for years 1 to 11. The lower-primary stage is characterized by a highly integrated curriculum involving first language, mathematics, environmental studies, creative and aesthetic activities, and religion. In the upper-primary stage, the curriculum is semi-integrated with more emphasis on subject-bound competencies. A "Beginning Science" course and English-as-a-second-language are also introduced. At the secondary stage the curriculum consists of the following subjects, some of which are interdisciplinary in nature: religion, first language, English, mathematics, integrated science, social studies and history, aesthetic education, health, physical education, and life skills/technical subjects. Life skills is a subject in years 7 and 8, and in year 9 pupils select one out of 53 prevocational-type courses designed to cover a wide field of vocations. Pupils may choose a technical subject out of several options in years 10–11.

At the end of year 11, which is also the end of the span of general education for all, the General Certificate of Education Ordinary-level (GCE O-level) examination—a centrally planned national school leaving examination—is held. Only those who achieve certain prescribed standards at GCE O level are permitted to enter the collegiate stage (years 12–13). Generally about 25–30 percent qualify to enter the collegiate level. The curriculum of this stage is discipline oriented and consists of a wide choice of subjects classified under three streams—arts, science, and commerce. Pupils select four subjects within any one of the streams for which they are qualified to enter. At the end of this stage the General Certificate of Education Advanced-level (GCE A-level) is held. Schools with GCE A-level science streams have a course designed to provide computer literacy.

The National Institute of Education is responsible for the preparation of syllabuses of instructions, teachers' guides, and textbooks for the school curriculum. The curriculum teams consist of specialist officers from the NIE, teacher educators, and teachers seconded for service to the respective teams. The Education Publications Department is responsible for printing and distributing the textbooks.

The last major curriculum revision at the primary and secondary levels was effected in 1986 and that of the collegiate level in 1979. However, there is an on-going process of qualitative improvement of an informal nature to infuse important changes in both content and methodology and emerging current issues. But the actual curriculum, as transacted in the classroom, does not measure up to the expectations of the prescribed specifications. The teaching methodology still remains rather traditional and didactic in spite of efforts made to introduce activity-based learning rather than a teaching-oriented approach.

Educational radio and television programs have been developed to support the learning of science, mathematics, and English.

The lack of continuity in education policy has resulted in sudden changes in the curriculum causing hardships to teachers and pupils. The relevance and balance of the curriculum and its academic bias and lack of sufficient flexibility are often questioned by critics.

The problem of making the school curriculum relevant to the needs of both the minority, who wish to proceed to higher levels of specialization, as well as to the large majority, who fail or do not wish to do so, has hitherto remained unsolved. The examination-oriented rote-learning approach adopted by most teachers and pupils is also a major concern.

8. The System of Examinations, Promotions, and Certifications

A system of automatic promotion from one year to the next is practiced in principle, but there are exceptions as can be seen from the number of grade repeaters. The rule imposed in 1991 makes it compulsory for pupils to obtain the Junior Technical Certificate at year 9 to proceed further. The GCE O-level examination at the end of year 11 is the main national school leaving examination which also serves as the selection examination for the different streams of the collegiate stage. While the grades obtained at the GCE A level serve for certification, the aggregate marks are used to select students to the universities on an all-island merit basis as well as on a district quota basis.

Sri Lankan society places more faith in centrally controlled national examinations with identical criteria and standards for the entire country than on decentralized or school-based assessment procedures. School-based continuous assessment systems introduced at various times have met with strong opposition from parents and teachers and had to be abandoned. This has resulted in the classroom teaching–learning process becoming heavily examination-oriented to the neglect of more desirable objectives envisaged in the curriculum. National school examinations are conducted by the Department of Examinations.

9. Educational Assessment, Evaluation, and Research

The Research Division of NIE is mainly responsible for conducting and promoting research. Prior to the setting up of NIE, research and assessments were conducted in an ad hoc manner by various sections and individual officers of the Ministry. Research in universities was mainly confined to theses and dissertations submitted for graduate degrees. The Planning Division of the Ministry conducts a school census every year, processes the data and makes summary statistics available to policymakers. The Department of Examinations analyzes the results of national examinations GCE O and A levels, which provide some feedback to the system.

The Research Division of NIE has carried out or sponsored several studies on issues such as indicators of school effectiveness, management reforms, teacher requirements, school profiles, policy changes, pupil achievement, regional disparities, and so forth.

The main emphasis of research in the 1990s, as foreseen by NIE, is on problems and issues such as low achievement in certain subjects like mathematics, science, and English; establishing a minimum learning continuum for the primary level; nonformal approaches to basic education; the validity of the year 5 scholarship examination; experimental work in science; rehabilitation problems arising out of the ethnic conflict; devolution of power to the provincial councils; and quality improvement of teacher education.

There is no special allocation in the primary and secondary school budget for evaluation and research.

10. Major Reforms in the 1980s and 1990s

Reforms in education were initiated by the Education Reforms Committee (ERC) appointed in 1977. The ERC Report (1982) recommended certain reforms in the structure and content of the education system. The 1981 white paper on education (Ministry of Education 1981) provided a basic framework for reforms in the 1980s and was considered a major step in transforming school and technical/vocational education in Sri Lanka. The proposals were concerned with all aspects of the system and generated much public debate. Certain proposals, such as school clusters and continuous assessment, came in for public criticism. Some of these proposals were implemented, some tried out and abandoned, and some others remain to be implemented.

The government appointed a National Education Commission in 1991 to be an advisory body to the government in matters of reform and innovation, coordination, and the rationalization of educational policies. The attention of the Commission has been drawn to the need for diversifying the products of the system in close collaboration with employers and making it a multilayered and more efficient human resource development system.

11. Major Problems for the Year 2000

Sri Lanka has already advanced considerably insofar as quantitative progress in terms of participation and literacy rates is concerned. The challenge for the future is therefore to improve the quality and the internal efficiency of the system to meet the demands of a rapidly changing society, and to obtain a better return for the vast investment of resources made on education. The major problems in the above context are those concerned with the low internal efficiency of the system; inter-regional disparities; inter-racial harmony; lack of curriculum relevance; the backlog of untrained teachers; lack of accountability, effective supervision, monitoring, and evaluation; and failure to have national consensus and continuity in policies, which creates disorder in the system and lack of proper linkages and coordination both within and with other sectors outside the system.

Successive governments have been confronted with the problem of ensuring that the output from the educational system is capable of providing the knowledge, skills, attitudes, and values needed to improve the quality of life of the individual and to execute tasks required to achieve national goals. The "mass–elite gap" between the English-educated Western-oriented elites and the vernacular educated mostly rural masses poses major problems for policymakers and planners. The reluctance to break away from traditional models inherited from colonial times and those imposed more recently by the developed countries, and the resistance to change shown by the dominant elitist culture influenced by Eurocentric norms and biases makes the task of reform even more difficult. The overall challenge for the future is to break away from overdependence on the traditional formal system and evolve an innovative system integrating the formal, nonformal, and informal sectors and harnessing all settings for learning in society to achieve the goals of individual and national development.

References

ERC 1982 *Towards Relevance in Education: Report of the Education Reforms Committee 1979*. Ministry of Education, Colombo
Ministry of Education 1981 *White Paper on Education Proposals for Reform*. Ministry of Education, Colombo
Ministry of Education 1989 *School Census 1989*. Ministry of Education, Colombo
Sri Lanka 1990 *Annual Report for the Year 1990*. Central Bank of Sri Lanka, Colombo
UNDP 1991 *Human Development Report 1991*. Oxford University Press, New York

Further Reading

De Silva W A, Gunawardena C 1989 *Educational Policies and Change 1977–1986*. National Institute of Education, Maharagama
Gunawardena G B n.d. *A National Study on Secondary Education in Sri Lanka*. National Institute of Education, Maharagama
Herath J P 1991 *Sri Lanka Country Paper for SAARC Expert Group Meeting on Modernization of Curriculum*. National Institute of Education, Maharagama
Jayasuriya J E n.d. *Educational Policies and Progress during British Rule in Sri Lanka 1796–1948*. Associated Educational Publishers, Colombo
Jayaweera S 1988 *Educational Policies and Change from the Mid-twentieth Century to 1977*. National Institute of Education, Maharagama
Nyström K 1985 *Schooling and Disparities. A Study of Regional Differences in Sri Lanka*. Institute of International Education, University of Stockholm, Stockholm
Singhal R P et al. 1989 *Education and Training in Sri Lanka*, Vols 1–4. Educational Consultants India Ltd., New Delhi
Sri Lanka 1969 *Education in Ceylon (from the 6th Century to the Present Day): A Centenary Volume*, Vols 1–3. Ministry of Education and Cultural Affairs, Colombo
Sri Lanka 1990a *Report of the Presidential Commission on Youth*. Department of Government Printing, Colombo
Sri Lanka 1990b *Statistical Pocket Book of Sri Lanka 1990*. Department of Census and Statistics, Colombo
Sumathipala K H M 1968 *History of Education in Ceylon*. Tisara Prakasakayo, Dehiwala

Sudan

F. Leach

1. General Background

The Republic of Sudan is the largest country in Africa, with a surface area of 2.5 million square kilometers. It is situated in the northeast of the continent between latitudes 4 and 22 degrees north and longitudes 22 and 38 degrees east. The land ranges from desert in the north through rich grasslands in the center to thick jungle in the south. Only 12 percent of the land is currently cultivated, while 22 percent is forest. The climate is hot, reaching temperatures of 45 centigrade at times, being dry in the north with little seasonal rain, and tropical in the south. Sudan shares borders with nine countries: Egypt, Libya, Chad, Zaire, the

Central African Republic, Uganda, Kenya, Ethiopia, and Eritrea. Conflict and famine in the region have resulted in Sudan in the early 1990s playing host to well over one million refugees, predominantly from Eritrea, Ethiopia, and Chad, which puts great strain on its limited social welfare system.

The country is entirely landlocked, except for some 630 kilometers of coastline on the Red Sea, where the only port is situated. The capital, Khartoum (which is actually made up of the three towns of Khartoum, Omdurman, and North Khartoum), is situated some 1260 kilometers along the country's main highway from the coast, at the confluence of the Blue and the White Nile rivers. The size of the country, its widely scattered population, and the lack of an extensive transport network make communications difficult and impose obvious restrictions and costs on the provision of even the most basic goods and services.

In 1990 Sudan's population was estimated at just over 25 million, with 45 percent being under the age of 14. The annual population growth rate is estimated at 2.7 percent, having declined slightly from a high of 3 percent. The population has more than doubled in 30 years and is expected to reach over 33 million by the year 2000. Such a large increase puts an enormous strain on public services, in particular the provision of education and health care.

Sudan is one of the world's poorest and least developed countries. Life expectancy in 1990 stood at 50.4 years, having improved from an estimated 39 years in 1960. The infant mortality rate in the same year was 102.4 per 1000 inhabitants. While being a great improvement from a figure of 170 in 1960, this is still very high. Health care, like education, is unevenly distributed, with isolated and sparsely populated rural communities being particularly underresourced. Illiteracy is still very high, with the latest estimate being 72.9 percent of the population (in 1956 it was 86%); 88.3 percent of females are illiterate, whereas the figure for males is 57.3 percent.

In 1988 GNP per capita was US$380 per annum, having declined by 1.8 percent since 1980. The Sudan's external debt stands at US$15.3 billion, an enormous burden for such a poor country. However, it has experienced some economic growth since 1990.

Sudan's population is overwhelmingly rural, with two-thirds engaging in agricultural activity, most of it subsistence farming. Over 2 million people are estimated to be still entirely nomadic. Ninety-five percent of the country's exports are agricultural products. It has great scope for agricultural development as only 2 percent of its potential arable land is under irrigation.

The latest official estimate is that only 22 percent of the population is urbanized. However, unofficial squatter camps on the edge of major towns are likely to make the figure higher. Refugees from neighboring countries and large movements of Sudanese people during the 1984–5 drought brought an estimated 3 million people into the capital, Khartoum, swelling its population to 5 million (26% of the total population). This figure has decreased somewhat with the voluntary or enforced repatriation of some refugees.

Sudan's people are ethnically very diverse. The 1956 census identified 597 tribes, with 19 major tribal groupings. Arabs in the north form the largest group (40% of the total); the second largest group are the Dinka in the south (at 12%). Over 115 languages are spoken, 26 by more than 100,000 people. Approximately 60 percent of the population are Muslim, 4 percent are Christian (the majority in the south), and the remainder, mainly in the south and west, are animist. There has been a policy of progressive Islamicization of the population over the years. Arabic is the official language of the country, although in the south English is widely used as a *lingua franca*.

For 56 years, Sudan was the Anglo-Egyptian Condominium, in effect a British colony. Its borders were artificially drawn by the British to include Africans in the south and west, Arabs in the north, and Hamites in the east, the result being a nation of very diverse ethnic groupings sharing no common culture, language, or religious faith. However, the traditional division in the country has always been perceived as being between the dominant Muslim Arab north and the African, largely animist, south. Lack of contact between the two parts of the country and the development of separate political and social systems, which the British encouraged (until as late as 1944 education in the south was provided totally by Christian missions), was to contribute much to the later mistrust and lack of mutual interest between the two sides.

Even before Independence in 1956, the longstanding animosity between northerners and southerners, fuelled by the growing economic and political dominance of the north during the last years of British rule, was to erupt into a civil war which has engulfed the country for all but 11 years of its postindependence history. Although the 1972 Addis Ababa peace agreement gave a high degree of autonomy to the south, absorbed the region into formal political life, and allowed for some development to take place, Sudan returned to full-scale civil war in 1984 when President Numeiri introduced Islamic law (*Sharia*) throughout the country. The conflict has continued since then and has completely devastated the south, where 25 percent of the country's population used to live. Many have died from the fighting or from famine, while others have fled to northern Sudan or to neighboring countries. Public services including education have almost totally ceased to function outside the main towns. The war is estimated by the International Monetary Fund (IMF) to cost the government US$2 million a day, with 22 percent of the total government budget being allocated to defense. This has had an obvious negative impact on budgetary allocations to other sectors, including education.

In addition to the civil war, Sudan has experienced much political instability. There have been only three short-lived periods of democratically elected government. The remainder of the time the country has been under military rule. The longest, and with hindsight relatively peaceful, period of continuous government was the military dictatorship of Jaafar Numeiri (1969–84). The latest military regime took power in June 1989. It has pursued a radical Islamic social and economic policy, combined with liberalization of the economy. The nature of the regime and its support for Iraq during the Gulf War have led to the country's political and financial isolation from the majority of its former Arab and Western allies, who have cut off much of their aid. In addition, Sudan's inability at the present time to pay interest on its debts to the IMF means that it is unable to borrow further on the international finance markets.

Administratively, Sudan is divided into nine regions, one of which is the capital, Khartoum, and three of the regions are situated in the south. These nine regions are in turn divided into a total of 19 provinces. In 1991 the government introduced a federal system of government, with the regions becoming states, each with its appointed governor and regional ministers. In the south this has little meaning at the present time (1995).

In terms of skilled labor, the Sudan economy has suffered from a massive brain drain of skilled workers and professionals to the oil-rich Arab states starting in the mid-1970s, although many were obliged to return in the aftermath of the Gulf War. In 1983 the Food and Agriculture Organization (FAO) estimated that there were 350,000 Sudanese working abroad, with up to 50 percent of those trained in some professions having left the country. In education, very large numbers of teachers have gone abroad, in particular university lecturers and graduate teachers. While the brain drain has brought in badly needed hard currency remittances, the cost in terms of the loss of skilled personnel for the country's development effort has been incalculable.

Despite the generally pessimistic economic picture, the early 1990s government has launched an ambitious educational reform program aimed at achieving universal basic education by the year 2001, diversifying secondary education, and doubling the intake to higher education. The cost of the program is not known. Although economic performance has improved since 1990, it has grown from a very low base which was the result of declining performance during the 1980s. It is too early to judge how effective the recent economic liberalization program will be in increasing revenue. However, without very large and sustained economic growth, and a reversal of the sharp decline in public expenditure for education experienced during the late 1980s, the educational reforms cannot become a meaningful reality and can only result in existing resources being spread ever more thinly through an already chronically underfunded service. In the south, there will need to be a massive reconstruction and retraining program if education is to become a normal activity again.

2. Politics and the Goals of the Education System

The various governments of Sudan have all viewed education as playing an important role in the economic and social development of the country through meeting the requirements for educated and skilled workers. Until the mid-1980s they regularly apportioned 10–15 percent of the national budget to education. However, in response to public pressure, they have allowed secondary and higher education to expand at the expense of primary. Also, despite efforts to promote technical secondary education and nonarts-based higher studies according to declared policy, the trend has been overwhelmingly in favor of academic education. This has meant that there is an excess of arts graduates from both secondary and higher institutions, while there is still a serious shortage of middle-level technicians. At the same time, the whole educational system has expanded much more rapidly than the economy, with the result that there are large numbers of educated unemployed (one source estimates 20,000 unemployed university graduates).

With these imbalances in mind, the present government is seeking through its recent reforms to expand basic education and at the same time make it more terminal and more relevant to the economic needs of the country. It is also attempting to inject a greater degree

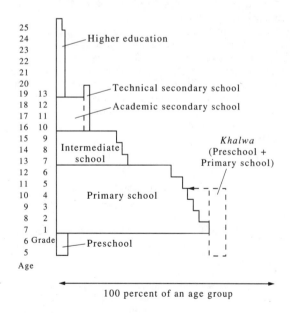

Figure 1
Sudan: Structure of the formal education system 1989 (Northern regions only)

of technical and vocational education into the secondary and tertiary levels, while allowing expansion to take place in the appropriate subject areas. Throughout, the curriculum is to be revised in order to better reflect national values and Islamic principles in line with the government's political and social ideology.

Limited political decentralization was introduced during the early 1980s, which included some devolution of educational responsibility to the regions. This has been taken much further by the recent introduction of a federal system of states. In education, all but major policy decisions will be taken at the state level.

3. The Formal System of Education

Figure 1 outlines the structure of the formal educational system as it existed in 1990. Key statistics are provided in Table 1.

3.1 Primary, Secondary, and Tertiary Education

Reforms to education at the primary to secondary levels were announced in 1991 as part of a ten-year plan for general education and took effect from the 1992–93 school year. At the tertiary level, reforms were announced in 1989 and took effect in 1991–92.

Under the previous system, which was introduced in 1970, primary education lasted for six years, intermediate for three years and secondary for a further three years (or four years in the case of technical schools), with entry at age 7 years. In southern Sudan, village schools, offering only the first four years of primary schooling, were also common. Entry to intermediate and secondary education was by competitive examination at the end of the preceding cycle. Pupils who achieved the highest grades in the intermediate school certificate were offered places in general (academic) secondary schools, while some of those with lower grades would find places in technical and commercial schools, or in primary teacher training institutes.

In 1990, 47 percent of primary schools were coeducational, but at the intermediate level fewer than 3 percent were. At the secondary level under 6 percent were coeducational, and these were either Catholic mission schools or southern schools. Government secondary schools in the north are all single sex.

An alternative, but less widely available, route through the educational system is offered by religious schools, with children attending primary level education in Islamic *khalwa* schools, then moving on to religious schools at the intermediate and secondary levels. However, there are only 37 schools at the intermediate level and 20 at the secondary level. Students in religious schools sit the same intermediate and secondary school-leaving examinations as those studying in the secular schools. Those with the highest grades can gain places at Islamic universities.

The 1991 reforms set out a radical restructuring and expansion program for schooling. The 6–3–3 system was replaced by eight years of basic education, followed by three years of secondary education, resulting in 11 instead of 12 or 13 years of formal schooling as the maximum available. The school entry age has also been lowered to 6 years. At the secondary level, academic and technical schools will be integrated, offering a mixture of academic and technical subjects alongside a core curriculum. For males who are eligible to proceed to higher education, a period of national service is now compulsory before they may continue their studies.

At the tertiary level, prior to the 1991 reforms, there were eight universities (the oldest being the University of Khartoum) and about ten specialist higher institutes in Sudan. All but two of these universities are situated in the capital, Khartoum. The University of Cairo runs a Khartoum branch, which is funded by the Egyptian Government and administered and staffed by the University of Cairo. There is also an Islamic University of Omdurman. The two regional universities specialize in rural-based studies, one in Gezira province and the other in Juba (the capital of the south). There are also two privately funded universities, Ahfad University for Women and Ahlia University. The Sudan's only

Table 1
The Sudan educational system 1990

Level	Enrolled	Numbers Male	Female	Institutions	Number of Teachers
Primary	2,026,519	1,146,263	880,256	7,939	60,048
Intermediate	413,321	224,944	188,377	2,421	23,654
Academic secondary	247,896	141,880	106,016	485	7,884
Technical secondary	23,003	16,430	6,573	72	1,103
Primary teacher training	5,328	2,452	2,876	16	683
Higher education	60,134	35,970	24,164	18	2,522
(1989) of which University	54,558	32,065	22,493	8	1,933

polytechnic became the Sudan University of Science and Technology in 1989. In 1989, 91 percent of higher education students were in universities.

The specialist higher education institutions include institutes of music and drama, physical education, hygiene, nursing, radiography, and mechanical engineering (in Atbara). There are also two graduate institutions within the University of Khartoum, the Institute of African and Asian Studies and the Development Studies Research Center.

Competition for places in higher education is fierce. Prior to the reforms, only about 7.5 percent of those sitting the secondary school leaving certificate could expect to find places in higher education. As a result, many young Sudanese were studying abroad and the government was obliged to provide them with hard currency at a subsidized rate. In 1992, an estimated 11,000 were studying abroad, representing some 22 percent of Sudanese undergraduates. In 1984, as many as 21,700 were studying abroad.

The 1991 Higher Education Act was aimed at increasing the annual intake, distributing it more evenly around the country, and increasing the numbers enrolled in nonarts-based courses. It was also hoped that this expansion would encourage those studying abroad to continue their studies at home. The initial aim was to increase the intake to higher education from 11,336 in 1989 to 22,716 in 1991. Of the eight universities created since 1991, six are situated in the regions. Two are intended for the south. However, the lack of security in the region will make it extremely difficult for these to become a functional reality in the foreseeable future. Indeed, the University of Juba has had to move to temporary premises in Khartoum because it became impossible to operate in a war zone.

In addition, eight new private institutions of higher education have been established. These will offer degree and diploma courses in subjects such as civil engineering, aviation, business administration, computer studies, and Islamic religion. There is also a distance education institution (Open University). These private institutions will receive some financial support from the government and will be supervised by a special committee of the National Council for Higher Education.

Schooling is not compulsory in Sudan and is by no means available to all those who wish to attend. At independence, educational provision was very limited, and during the 1960s and early 1970s, the country witnessed an enormous expansion in educational provision, in particular at the secondary and higher levels. During the 1960s school enrollments at all levels grew at a rate of around 10–11 percent annually. Between 1970 and 1981 primary enrollments doubled, intermediate and academic secondary grew sixfold while technical secondary grew ninefold. During the 1980s growth rates at all levels slowed down, but secondary enrollments doubled again between 1981 and 1991. As a result, at the primary level the gross enrollment ratio

increased from 30.5 percent of the 7–12 age group in 1970 to 38.8 percent in 1980 to 49.8 percent in 1985 to 58 percent in 1989 (the latter figure for the six northern regions only). At the intermediate level, the enrollment ratio increased from 26 percent of the 13–15 age group in 1981 to 28.2 percent in 1985, but this had dropped to 24 percent by 1989 (still an increase in total enrollments because of the growth in the size of the age group). At the secondary level, the enrollment ratio increased from 12.8 percent of the 16–18 age group in 1981 to 16.6 percent in 1985, but this had dropped to 15.8 percent by 1989. At the tertiary level, despite enormous growth, still only 2.9 percent of the 19–23 age group were able to find places in higher education in 1989.

These figures do not reflect the wide discrepancies in provison of education between regions, between urban and rural areas, and between males and females. Traditionally the greatest opportunity for education is found in the Khartoum area and in the northern and central regions (now states), while the least opportunity has always been in the south. For example, in northern Sudan primary enrollment ratios in 1989 were highest in the northern region, at 75 percent of the relevant age-group, and lowest in the eastern region, at 42.5 percent. At the intermediate level, they were highest in Khartoum at 32 percent, and lowest in Darfur region (in the west) at 12.6 percent. At secondary level the highest enrollment ratio was again in Khartoum, with 32 percent, and lowest in Darfur, at 3.8 percent. In the south the ratios are consistently lower than those in the north. For example, in 1986 (the last available such figures for the south) primary enrollments were highest in Equatoria region, at 40.2 percent, and lowest in Bahr-el-Ghazal region, at 9.5 percent. Given that, in the early 1990s, there is very little educational provision in the south outside the major towns, the current ratios would be even lower. However, some schools have relocated temporarily to Khartoum, where many of the southern refugees are to be found.

Likewise, urban areas have always been favored over rural areas and males over females. Girls have been traditionally underrepresented in education, largely for socioeconomic and cultural reasons, but the gap has been slowly narrowing. In 1989, 42.2 percent of primary school pupils were female (representing 52.6 percent of the relevant female age group, as compared to 62.8 percent of the male age group). At the intermediate level 44.7 percent of pupils were female, and at the secondary level, 42.7 percent. At the tertiary level, the figure is 40 percent. Although females are still underrepresented at all levels of education, the gap is much smaller than in many other African countries, especially in higher education.

The school day lasts six hours, six days per week, officially for 200 days in the year (but the real figure is likely to be much lower due to shortages of teachers, books, electricity, water, and other basic amenities). The average pupil–teacher ratio in 1990 was 34:1 at the primary level, 18:1 at intermediate, 31:1 at academic secondary, and 21:1 at technical secondary. However, actual class size frequently exceeds 60 at all levels and can reach 100. Dropout rates are relatively high: in 1989 only 80 percent of those who had entered Grade 1 reached Grade 6.

In the northern Sudan, the language of instruction throughout primary and secondary education is Arabic. At the tertiary level it was English until 1990. However a continuing decline in the standard of English among both students and lecturers, combined with a desire for greater national and cultural relevance, led the government to decree that Arabic was to become the language of instruction, albeit progressively. This has presented considerable difficulties due to the shortage of appropriate textbooks and materials in Arabic.

In the south, it has been customary for local languages to be used as the medium of instruction for the first three to four years of primary education, with English used at all subsequent levels. The future status of English in southern education is not clear, as Arabic is not widely spoken and its introduction would be culturally unacceptable.

Under the reforms, the 1991 first year intake to primary education of 61.2 percent of the age group is to be increased to 81 percent by 1994 and to 99 percent by the year 2000, making basic education available for all school-age children. This is a very ambitious target. With a projected primary school population of 5.4 million in the year 2000, this would require an absorption of at least 3 million children into basic education. The government itself has estimated that reducing the school entry age from 7 to 6 years alone will require places for an additional 960,000 children, constructing nearly 20,000 classrooms and engaging an additional 26,000 teachers.

A considerable number of schools in Sudan are nongovernmental. The highest proportion are academic secondary schools. Approximately 20 percent of intermediate schools and 50 percent of secondary schools are nongovernmental. However, few of these are elite private schools. These are only located in the major towns and charge high fees. Several of the elite schools are run by Catholic missions.

The majority of nongovernmental schools are schools which have been built through private donation or through community contributions on a self-help basis (*ahlia* schools). They charge low fees. These schools have been established largely in response to the enormous public demand for education which the government has been unable to satisfy. They are usually of poor quality with a high number of untrained teachers. There are also around 30 Egyptian schools staffed by Egyptian teachers and 30 Catholic mission schools (both types having a number of schools at each level).

In 1990 pupils in private schools accounted for less than 1 percent of all primary level enrollments, 11 percent of intermediate, 43 percent of academic secondary and 18 percent of technical secondary school enrollments. At the preschool level, almost all provision comes from outside the government system, either through private nursery schools or religious *khalwa* schools.

In higher education, as already mentioned, the government is encouraging the creation of private institutions, and government institutions are urged to seek ways of raising additional revenue from private sources.

3.2 Preschool Education

Approximately 6 percent of the 5–7 age group were in kindergarten in 1990. In addition an unknown number of preschool age children were among the 162,000 children attending some 3700 Islamic *khalwa* schools, where they learn to recite the Koran. Of children studying in *khalwas* 77 percent are boys. Many of the preprimary age children will transfer to state basic (exprimary) schools at the age of 6 (formerly 7), while a small minority will continue up the educational ladder through the parallel religious route.

Under the reforms, the aim is to provide preschool education for all 4–6-year olds by the year 2000. This is to be done, first by providing places automatically to children of preschool age as new *khalwas* are set up as part of the expansion program, second by opening nursery classes in existing primary schools, and third by encouraging the creation of private or community-run nursery schools.

3.3 Special Education

There is very limited provision of special education in the Sudan. There are seven institutions for the disabled, which cater for around 700 individuals (both children and adults); five of the institutions are based in the capital. Teachers are provided by the Ministry of Education and the Ministry of Social Welfare. In the late 1980s a vocational training center for the disabled was set up in Khartoum with ILO/World Bank support.

3.4 Vocational, Technical, and Business Education

Numerous public statements have been made over the years regarding Sudan's need for more technical education at secondary and higher levels, but a lack of planning and coordination, inadequate resources, and pressure from the public to expand academic education has meant that schooling in Sudan is still overwhelmingly of an academic nature. In particular the fact that half the academic secondary schools are in private hands has meant that much of the expansion has been carried out outside the government's control in a direction contrary to declared policy. Likewise at the tertiary level, over half the students prior to the expansion were at the University of Cairo, Khartoum branch, which offers predominantly courses in the arts, social sciences, and commerce, and which is also outside the control of the Sudan government.

In 1990 only 13 percent of Sudan's 557 secondary schools were technical (72 schools). Industrial and commercial courses dominated, with home economics also being available for girls. Usually places in technical schools were less sought after than those in the academic secondary schools, as technical jobs are much less well paid and considered to be of lower status than those open to academic school graduates.

Under the reforms, academic and technical secondary schools will be integrated to become diversified schools offering three streams of study (academic, technical, and religious). At the same time, the government aims eventually to increase the proportion of students studying technical subjects to 60 percent of the total (from 10% at the present time). Students taking technical subjects will be able to compete on equal terms with those taking academic subjects for entry to higher education. (Under the previous system graduates from technical secondary schools were usually limited to places in technical institutes and at Khartoum Polytechnic.)

In the new diversified schools, all streams will study religion, Arabic language, English language, elementary mathematics and a number of other subjects in their first year. In their second and third years they will specialize. The courses available for specialization include science, religion, industry, commerce, agriculture, animal welfare, and arts and letters. Schools are able to choose courses to suit their environment and to make a selection of the subjects offered within each course. However the shortage of teachers at the secondary level, especially in mathematics and science-related subjects, and the shortage of suitable textbooks and materials will constrain the options available to all but the most generously supported schools.

At the higher education level, there are opportunities at the Sudan University of Science and Technology to undertake vocational, technical, and business studies. Cairo University also has a large Faculty of Commerce and Ahfad University for Women offers a degree course in secretarial studies. Commercial and business studies are popular because of the higher salaries found in private enterprises. There are also a number of private institutes offering advanced secretarial studies.

Under the 1991 reforms many of the existing universities are to have new faculties or colleges added to them, in specialist areas such as environmental studies, business administration, computer studies, information technology, accountancy, and textile technology. Some of these have already opened but the lack of suitable buildings, specialist staff, and course materials and textbooks in Arabic, as well as financial constraints are likely to make it difficult to run a wide range of courses.

Opportunities also exist for technical and vocational training in the nonformal sector (see Sect. 3.5).

3.5 Adult and Nonformal Education

Several ministries, including the Ministries of Education, Labor, Youth, and Social Affairs are responsible for running programs in adult and nonformal education. During the 1980s the World Bank and a number of donors gave considerable support to nonformal programs.

In 1990 there were 59,000 registered students in adult education. The Ministry of Education was running 17 vocational training centers, with just over 2,000 students. These are open to those who have completed intermediate schooling and offer two to three year courses.

The Sudan Ministry of Youth also runs a number of Youth Training Centers which provide training in income-generating activities for uneducated or poorly educated youth from low-income families. Courses usually last for 2 years.

During the 1980s around 24 integrated rural education centers (IRECs) were set up around the Sudan with ILO/World Bank support. These were intended to serve as multipurpose educational establishments, combining formal primary schooling with rural-oriented adult education. However they no longer function as originally planned.

The National Council of Literacy, under the auspices of the Ministry of Education, has been running literacy campaigns since the early 1960s. This has been the major area of activity in nonformal adult education in the Sudan. In 1991 a new council was set up to run a national campaign providing classes in schools, clubs, workplaces, and mosques, with trade unions, political organizations and national service and popular defense personnel being involved in running classes.

The problems experienced by all nonformal programs in the Sudan are inadequate funding, lack of nationwide coherent organization, and lack of equipment, resources, and suitably trained personnel.

4. Administrative and Supervisory Structure and Operation

Under the new federal system of government set up in 1991 each of the nine former regions became states (only nominally so in the case of the three southern regions). Each state has its own minister of education and director-general of education. The administration of basic and secondary education are the responsibility of the states, the latter having been previously a central government responsibility. However, higher education remains the responsibility of the central government, which has also taken over teacher education, since this is now part of higher education (see below). Basic and secondary level teachers will continue to be recruited and administered by the individual states.

Inspectors will continue to be appointed by the central government. Major policy decisions relating to education will also continue to be made by the central government, but the administration of schools will, as before, be carried out at the district and provincial level under the authority of the individual state.

5. Educational Finance

Public education is nominally free at primary and secondary level. However, given inadequate government financing, parents are being increasingly obliged to make contributions towards building and recurrent costs and to provide textbooks and other materials for their children. Because of the huge demand for education which the government cannot meet, many schools have been built and furnished by local communities, but frequently the government has been unable to provide teachers for them.

All community-financed and private schools must follow Ministry of Education regulations concerning teachers' terms of service (including salaries), the curriculum and examinations.

In higher education institutions, student fees are levied for all but those from the poorest families. The level of fees is determined by the level of parental income. Students used to receive free board and accommodation (where appropriate) but this is being phased out.

During the 1960s and 1970s, between 12 and 19 percent of annual government expenditure was allocated to education. In 1974 education accounted for 14.8 percent of total government expenditure (and 5.5% of GNP) but by 1980 this figure had fallen to 9.1 percent (4.8% of GNP). It rose again to 15 percent (4% of GNP) in 1985 but has since declined rapidly to stand at only 1.7 percent in 1991. However, whereas in the past the bulk of the financing of education came from central government, a much greater share is now expected to be provided by the states. Only higher education will continue to be funded centrally (together with teacher education).

In 1990, expenditure per student was: SD 670 (US$51.6) per primary pupil, SD 1206 (US$92.9) per intermediate pupil and SD 1636 (US$126) per academic secondary pupil; 84.3 percent of the education budget went on salaries and wages.

6. Supplying Personnel for the Education System

In 1989 50 percent of primary teachers were female, as were 39 percent of intermediate teachers and 21 percent of secondary teachers. Only 16 percent of higher education teachers were female. At the preschool level, 100 percent of kindergarten teachers were female, but 95 percent of *khalwa* teachers were male.

At all levels there are shortages of trained and experienced teachers. In 1989, 23 percent of primary teachers, 32 percent of intermediate teachers and 53 percent of academic secondary teachers in government schools in the Northern regions were untrained. In community-financed schools, the figures would be even higher.

The rapid expansion of schooling at all levels has put great strain on teacher training facilities. In addition, the rapid decline in status and remuneration of teachers has also meant that large numbers of trained teachers have deserted the profession, or have sought more lucrative teaching posts abroad. The result is that many secondary school graduates have been recruited as primary and intermediate teachers without any initial training. The shortage of trained teachers has always been particularly acute in the south, where there were limited training facilities, general educational levels were considerably lower than in the north, and teachers were often not paid regularly.

Under the old system, primary teachers were trained in primary teacher training institutes (PTTIs). There were 16 such institutes in 1992 (although the three in the south were not functioning). The average annual intake of the PTTIs was 150, with 80 percent completing their training successfully. Students entered after completing intermediate schooling and underwent four years of training. Primary teachers taught all subjects at primary level.

Intermediate teachers were trained in intermediate teacher training institutes (ITTIs), of which there were eight in 1992. Two more are currently under construction. Only one is situated in the South (at Maridi). The intake for intermediate training was taken from secondary school graduates, who underwent two years of training. This two-year training period was reduced to one year during the 1980s to speed up the availability of trained teachers to meet the requirement of the rapidly expanding intermediate sector. This returned to two years at the end of the 1980s. The average intake is 100–150 per annum.

At the secondary level, teachers are university graduates. Usually they have received no special training. Although the three Faculties of Education (at Khartoum, Juba, and Wadi Nil Universities) produce graduates in education, almost all seek employment abroad or outside the education sector. Among secondary school teachers, there are particular shortages of teachers of science, mathematics, and English. In 1990 39 percent of mathematics teachers were neither subject specialists nor trained, as were 17 percent of science teachers and 13 percent of English teachers. This has led the Ministry of Education in the past to seek teachers of these subjects abroad. Science and mathematics teachers were usually recruited from Egypt and English teachers from the United Kingdom. Specialist training institutes exist for the teaching of English Language, Arabic, and Islamic religion.

To meet the growing need for trained teachers, an alternative training route was established in 1972, first for primary and then for intermediate teachers through the Inservice Educational Institute (ISETI), which trained practicing teachers in regional centers. The untrained teachers were released one and a half days per week over a two-year period to attend their nearest center. Since 1991 this function of ISETI has been dropped and the institute now concentrates on inservice courses for head teachers, inspectors, and for practicing teachers, in particular with regard to the new basic education system.

Under the new system, efforts are to be made to increase the number of graduate teachers. In 1991 six new faculties of education were established in the new universities for the training of secondary school graduates. The current output of the existing faculties is about 350 graduates per annum.

To meet the training requirements for the new basic education teachers, seven new colleges of education, to be affiliated to the faculties of education, will open during 1993. These will be created from the existing primary and intermediate training institutes. They will be the joint responsibility of the central Ministry of Education (for finance and administration) and the faculties of education (for academic and technical matters). They will take their recruits from the ranks of existing primary and intermediate teachers and from new secondary school graduates. Basic level teachers holding a teacher's certificate will have the opportunity to obtain graduate status by returning for BEd studies after a period of teaching in schools. The ultimate aim is to have an all-graduate teaching profession.

7. Curriculum Development and Teaching Methodology

A national compulsory curriculum exists at all levels of schooling. Curriculum development remains a central government responsibility and has traditionally been undertaken at Sudan's oldest teacher training institute at Bakht-er-Ruda, which recently became the National Center for Curriculum Development and Educational Research. Teaching materials are prepared there and tried out in local schools. Dissemination is undertaken by the central Ministry of Education. The syllabuses and course books for all subjects at the basic level are currently being rewritten, with the aim of increasing relevance of content and providing a better integration of course material. Extensive curriculum development is also taking place at the secondary level, where academic and technical education are being integrated.

In the north, under the old system, English was introduced as a compulsory subject in the first year of intermediate schooling and French was introduced as a compulsory subject in the first year of secondary school. The language competence of teachers of these two subjects is usually low.

The south has always followed its own development in syllabuses and course books, to reflect its different cultural background. English is both a taught subject and the medium of instruction from the fourth year of primary schooling.

Classroom methods are on the whole very traditional, with blackboard and chalk being the only teaching aids in many cases (and sometimes even these are absent). Severe shortages of trained teachers in the different subjects on the curriculum, and of textbooks, teacher's manuals and basic classroom equipment continue to undermine the quality of education in most schools.

8. The System of Examinations, Promotions, and Certifications

There is no official policy of automatic promotion from one grade to another in Sudanese schools. Pupils are expected to pass the end-of-term examinations, which are set and marked independently within each school (usually by the class teacher). At the end of each cycle (now only basic and secondary), the school-leaving examinations are the responsibility of the state education authorities. Under the old system, the secondary leaving certificate (the Sudan School Certificate) was the responsibility of the central authority, but this has now passed to the individual states. In 1990, 59.4 percent of those who sat the Sudan School Certificate examinations passed (a progressive decline from 67.1% in 1985).

9. Educational Assessment, Evaluation, and Research

These activities are very limited in scope. The traditional role of the inspector is to assess the teachers, largely on classroom performance. It is not usually seen as including an advisory or supportive role. However, the Inservice Educational Training Institute runs courses for inspectors to help them expand their role within the educational system.

Most educational research is carried out at Bakht-er-Ruda, although some education-related research is also done at the University of Khartoum (e.g., at the Development Studies Research Center and at the Faculty of Education) and also by the National Council for Research.

10. Major Reforms in the 1980s and 1990s

There were no major reforms to the educational system during the 1980s. The current reforms, initiated in 1989–91, which have already been discussed, are the most sweeping reforms for decades.

11. Major Problems for the Year 2000

The ambitious reforms set out above will require strenuous efforts at both the central and the state level if they are not to remain mere rhetoric. They are aimed at both very high rates of expansion at all levels and an improvement in quality and relevance. This will involve major construction work, training and retraining of large numbers of teachers, and competent curriculum development. Sudan in the early 1990s does not possess either a highly committed and motivated teaching force or an efficient bureaucracy, so that implementation of the reforms will be difficult. In par-

927

ticular, there will be a chronic shortage of competent teaching staff in the new specializations offered in higher education. Moreover, the reforms will require substantial increases of funding, which will only be forthcoming if there is considerable economic growth, which in turn is necessary if jobs are to be found for those who graduate from an expanded educational system.

References

Government of Sudan 1991a *Comprehensive National Strategy, Social Development Sector. The Ten-Year Plan for General Education*. General Education Committee, Khartoum
Government of Sudan 1991b *Comprehensive National Strategy Conference Report of the Higher Education Committee*. Higher Education Committee, Khartoum

Further Reading

Beshir M O 1969 *Educational Development in the Sudan 1898–1956*. Clarendon Press, Oxford

Brown G N, Hiskett M (eds.) *Conflict and Harmony in Education in Tropical Africa*. George Allen and Unwin, London
Daly M 1992 *Sudan*. Clio Press, Oxford
Economist Intelligence Unit 1993 *Sudan Country Profile 1992–3*. Economist Intelligence Unit, London
Griffiths V L 1975 *Teacher-Centred Quality in Sudan Primary Education 1930 to 1970*. Longman, London
Ministry of Education 1991 *Summary of Educational Statistics*. Educational Planning Secretariat, Section of Educational Statistics, Khartoum
Ministry of Education 1992 *Educational Statistics Academic Year 1989/90*. Educational Planning Secretariat, Section of Educational Statistics, Khartoum
Sanyal B C, Yacoub S A 1975 *Higher Education and Employment in the Sudan*. UNESCO IIEP, Paris
Sanyal B C, Yaici L, Mallasi I 1987 *From College to Work: the Case of the Sudan*. UNESCO IIEP, Paris
Twose N, Pogrund B 1988 *War Wounds: Development Costs of Conflict in Southern Sudan*. Panos, London
UNESCO 1991a *Development of Education in Africa: A Statistical Review*. Sixth Conference of Ministers of Education and Those Responsible for Economic Planning in African Member States, Dakar, July 1991. UNESCO, Section of Statistics on Education, Division of Statistics, Paris
UNESCO 1991b *Statistical Yearbook*. UNESCO, Paris
UNESCO 1991c *World Education Report*. UNESCO, Paris

Suriname

W. W. Dwarkasing

1. General Background

The Republic of Suriname, with an area of 164,000 square kilometers, is situated on the northeast coast of South America, bordered by Guyana, French Guiana, and Brazil. It is a former Dutch colony which became a constituent part of the Kingdom of the Netherlands in 1954 and attained political independence in 1975. The last census in 1980 recorded a population of 355,000, showing a 6.5 percent decrease from 1972 to 1980. The decrease was mainly due to emigration to the Netherlands immediately before and after Independence. Since 1980, after a military coup, there has again been a high emigration to the Netherlands, both recorded and unrecorded. Since 1986, when civil war activities started in the eastern and southern regions opposed to the military regime, a flight of refugees in significant numbers took place to French Guiana. Inward migration especially from Guyana has offset this emigration in recent years. In 1989 the population was estimated to be 403,000. The annual population growth rate was 2.1 percent between 1964 and 1972. In the 1980s the annual growth rate was estimated at 1.4 percent.

Almost 90 percent of the population resides on the coastal strip which is approximately 40 kilometers wide. Two-thirds of the population is concentrated in two of the ten districts—approximately 1 percent of the total area. The two districts, Paramaribo (the capital city with 205,000 inhabitants) and the district of Wanica (which surrounds the capital city with 70,000 residents) are forming a population conglomerate. Therefore, senior-secondary and higher level schools and most educational services are concentrated in and around the capital city. As the remaining population is scattered in the country, school mapping becomes critical since it takes much effort to bring schools and other education facilities to the sparsely populated and rural areas. Some 39 percent of the population are below the age of 15 and 53 percent below the age of 22.

Demographic conditions include ribbon developments in the rural areas and some tribe-based settlements in the interior along the rivers. The latter are populated by Bush Negroes—former slaves (40,000) —and Native Americans (6,000). Except for Native Americans, the citizens have their origins in several other parts of the world and belong to different ethnic groups, including Blacks and Creoles (Blacks mixed with others), Hindustanis, Indonesians, Chinese, and Europeans. All have lived in Suriname for generations but have still preserved much of their original cultures and languages. One-third of the population consists of

Blacks and Creoles, around a third are Hindustanis, and one-fifth Indonesians. Sranang Tongo (a mixture of English, different African languages, Dutch, and Portuguese) serves as a *lingua franca*. Dutch is the official language in government and education. For the vast majority, Dutch is a second and foreign language to be mastered in the early school grades. This bilingual characteristic of the different ethnic groups and the multilingual situation of the nation set extra requirements on the curriculum and instructional methods for the early years. One of the major objectives of preschool and early primary education is a sufficient command of Dutch to proceed in the school system where Dutch is the instructional language.

Between 1975 and 1980 the Gross Domestic Product (GDP) in real terms (constant 1975 guilders) grew at an average rate of 3.4 percent. This growth was due mainly to government investments from Dutch development aid funds and an extra bauxite levy. The 1980s, however, were difficult economic times. Growth of GDP was hampered by discontinuation of the flow of Dutch funds from 1983 onwards and the recession in the bauxite industry, followed by an upturn in the late 1980s. Sectorial contributions to GDP in 1989 were as follows: primary 19 percent, secondary 27 percent, and tertiary 54 percent. The bauxite industry contributes a third of government revenue. Government expenditure increased in size from 26 percent in 1975 to 41 percent in 1985. At the beginning of the 1990s it was running at a level some 35 percent above revenues. Per capita income in real terms (constant in 1980 guilders) in 1989 was G3,540 (US\$1=G1.77). Between 1980 and 1989, exports increased slightly from G888 million to 966 million, while imports decreased from G925 million to 791 million.

Some 20.5 percent of the population in 1989 was economically active. Employment distribution by sector is as follows: primary 7 percent, secondary 17 percent, and tertiary 76 percent (including government 50 percent). Labor surveys estimated unemployment to be 15.8 percent in 1986, 19.5 percent in 1987, and 18.1 percent in 1989.

The military coup of February 25, 1980 resulted in a radical change of the government structure. The parliament was abolished and a military authority (three members) together with a policy center (two military members and the civilian prime minister) became the principal authorities for legislation and policy-making. The President, the head of the state, was appointed by these bodies in consultation with functional organizations. The board of ministers consisted of civilian and military members. The judiciary remained independent while the Constitution was replaced by a decree including basic human rights. Following some unsuccessful counter coup attempts, military actions resulted in the killing of 15 prominent citizens including academics, lawyers, journalists, and union leaders in December 1982. The Dutch government, as a reaction to this traumatic event, stopped the flow of treaty funds, causing the national economy to deteriorate in the mid-1980s.

There was a growing dissatisfaction with the political situation and the military regime. Forced by external and internal opposition forces calling for the restoration of democracy, military leaders agreed to hold a general election in November 1987. This brought about a coalition government of the three major political parties. After a conflict with military leaders, the civilian government was again overthrown by a military coup in December 1990, and replaced by an interim government. The main task of the interim government was to organize general elections since the coup leaders were in favor of a new government. The election was held in May 1991. Delegations from interested democratic nations and international institutions were present for observation purposes. The same coalition with the addition of a fourth party won the election. A national assembly, consisting of 52 elected members, became responsible for legislation and elected the President who has executive power. The central government consists of 16 ministries including dependent directorates, each headed by a minister of cabinet rank.

One of the forces opposed to the military regime was the armed Jungle Commando. It started its guerrilla-like revolt against the military regime in 1986 in the eastern and southern parts of the country. The armed combat in these regions caused dramatic demographic movements: approximately 6,000 refugees moved to French Guiana. These refugees, including 2,000 children who were deprived of basic education, were still in French Guiana in 1991 awaiting arrangements for repatriation. Furthermore, around 5,000 Blacks and some Native Americans migrated to Paramaribo and are camped in extremely poor conditions on the outskirts of the city.

2. Politics and the Goals of the Education System

The main political goals of the Suriname government include: restoration of democracy and reinforcement of democratic institutions, recovery of production (agriculture and industry) and economic growth, expansion of employment (job creation), a fair share for all the people in prosperity and welfare, and improved participation of the people in socioeconomic development.

In consequence, efforts will be concentrated to improve the performance of the education system and to provide educational opportunities for all. This involves making the education system more life- and work-oriented than it is now. Vocational and, more particularly, technical education has become a sector of special interest. The goal is to achieve a better match with labor requirements. Due to the social and economic setback, school buildings and other facilities have deteriorated while teaching–learning materials have become scarce. The government is in search of external funds for the recovery of facilities and the supply of educational materials.

3. The Formal System of Education

3.1 Primary, Secondary, and Tertiary Education

Since 1876, primary education has been compulsory for children aged 6–12 years. Until 1950, there were three types of schools: the primary school offering elementary education (Grades 1 to 6), the extended primary school (Grades 1 to 8), and the more extended primary school (Grades 1 to 10). Children were entitled to enroll in each of these schools at age 6. Most primary schools had a kindergarten for children aged 5. For vocational and professional training, including teacher training, a few evening courses were offered.

The requirements of the economy and the growing demand for education have resulted in a tremendous increase in enrollment and the establishment of various types of school at the secondary level since 1950. Total school enrollment rose from 37,000 in 1950 to just over 135,000 in 1970 and 1975 and dropped thereafter. After an upturn around 1985, it dropped again to less than 118,000 in 1989 (see Fig. 1). This decrease was mainly due to migration to the Netherlands. The education system at the beginning of the 1990s (see Fig. 2) originated from, and is modeled on, that of the Netherlands. Enrollments and teacher statistics are presented in Table 1. Formal education at all levels became free upon Independence in 1975.

Primary education, lasting 6 years, is almost universal in the coastal areas where the participation rate is approximately 90 percent. A school year in preschool and primary education has around 200 days. A school day lasts for 3.5 hours of tuition in preschool and in primary Grades 1 and 2, and 4.5 hours in higher primary grades. Primary schools are distributed among almost all rural areas and settlements in the interior. A large number of these schools are very small and

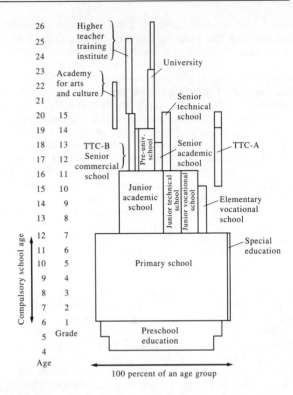

Figure 2
Suriname: Structure of the formal education system 1991

have a remote location. Staffing these remote schools and supplying them with the necessary material and supporting services puts a considerable strain on the administrative authorities. Nationwide, the number of government schools is almost the same as that of private schools at preschool and primary school level. The distribution of pupils and teachers among government and private schools is also equal at these levels.

Secondary education is offered in a wide variety of schools on two levels: junior and senior. Junior-secondary education is available for either 3 or 4 years. Three-year courses are offered as final schooling in a technical or service trade in elementary vocational schools. Approximately 90 percent of the pupils at this level are enrolled in four-year courses in either an academic type or a technical or vocational type of school. Graduates from these courses can enter the employment market or proceed with schooling at the senior level. At the junior level a school year consists of 200 days and a school day lasts 5 hours. The academic schools are distributed across all the districts, but the technical and vocational schools are, with a few exceptions, concentrated in the capital city. Enrollments in government schools and in private schools are equal, and participation of both sexes at this level is the same.

At the senior level there are also both types of courses: academic type (including preuniversity edu-

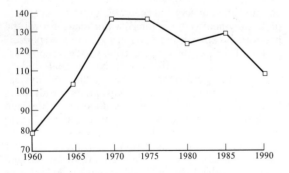

Figure 1
Total school enrollment 1960–89

cation) and technical and vocational schools. These courses vary in duration from 2 to 4 years. The academic and technical schools at this level have entry examinations for admission. Entry examinations are not required for admission to the teacher-training college and the senior commercial school. The senior technical school offers courses for the technician level in chemistry, mining, mechanics, electricity, and construction. A school year at senior level has 190 days and a school day consists of 5 hours of instruction. Surprisingly, participation of females at this level increased from 47 percent in 1981 to 62 percent in 1989. Except for one teacher-training college, all schools at the senior-secondary level are government schools.

There are three institutes for higher education, all located in Paramaribo: the University of Suriname, the Higher Institute for Teacher Training, and the Academy for Arts and Culture. The University, founded in 1968, has three faculties: medicine, social sciences, and technical sciences. Law and economics are included in the faculty of social sciences. With 2,164 students in 1989, enrollment had increased by almost 200 percent in ten years. The distribution of students among the faculties was as follows in 1989: 20 percent in medicine, 65 percent in social sciences, and 15 percent in technical sciences. Females constitute 44 percent of the student body. The Higher Institute for Teacher Training offers two- to five-year courses for teacher training for secondary education. Except for a few, most are part-time and evening courses. The upper-level secondary school certificate is required for admission. In 1989 approximately 90 percent of enrollment consisted of teachers already inservice but taking courses for upgrading purposes. Females constituted 65 percent of students and total enrollment was 1850 in 1989. The Academy for Arts and Culture established in 1985, has three faculties, each offering a wide variety of courses, and each of three years' duration. The faculties are: plastic arts, cultural education, and study of literature and com-

munication. Total enrollment in 1989 was 210, with a female participation rate of 70 percent.

3.2 Preschool Education

Preschool education is now included in almost all primary schools, and is offered to children aged 4 and 5. In the capital city Paramaribo, there are also a few private institutes offering only preschool programs, but on payment of fees. A growing portion of 4- and 5-year olds attend preschool programs before commencing primary education at the prescribed age of 6. In general the preschool programs focus on social learning and learning of the Dutch language through structured play. The enrollment rate in preschool was 82 percent in 1989.

3.3 Special Education

Special education programs are provided for children with physical, intellectual, and emotional disabilities. It is provided in special classes in some primary schools, and in special schools or institutes. In 1989 there were 18 special classes and 18 special schools, providing programs for about 2000 children, which is about 1.7 percent of total enrollment in formal education. Almost two-thirds of the total enrollment are male. There are two levels, an elementary level focusing on the "three R's" and an advanced level preparing for the world of work through training in a handicraft. Approximately 20 percent is enrolled in an advanced-level program. In 1989 the pupil–teacher ratio was 10.9:1. There were 180 teachers.

There are three special institutes in Paramaribo: an institute for the hearing impaired, one for the vision impaired, and one for the physically handicapped. There are also two institutes for severely intellectually retarded children in Paramaribo. These are all charity-based private institutes, but they are almost completely financed by the government.

Table 1
Student enrollments and teachers by level and type of education 1989

Level and type of education	Student enrollment	Percentage male	Teachers	Pupil-teacher ratio
Preschool	16,711	51	652	25.6:1
Primary	61,435	51	2,733	22.5:1
Junior-secondary	24,810	49	1,767	14.0:1
Senior-secondary	8,355	38	722	11.6:1
Higher education[a]	4,234	46	495	8.5:1
Special education	1,954	65	180	10.9:1
Total	117,489	50	6,549	17.9:1

Source: Ministry of Education, Department of Planning, 1991
a Higher education teachers include 412 part-time teachers

A department for special education named the Pedological Institute was founded in 1967 and provides the required support and counseling services in this sector. The services include testing, the placement and guidance of pupils in cooperation with other agents, curriculum development, and the inservice training of teachers.

3.4 Vocational, Technical, and Business Education

Vocational, technical, and business education is available in the formal system at the junior- and senior-secondary levels. Demand for this type of education is less than for the general or academic type of education. Total enrollment in vocational, technical, and business education amounts 40 to 45 percent of secondary school population. Allocation to the three types of courses is, in most cases, determined by the selective entry tests at both junior and senior level.

Evening schools offer a wide variety of technical and business courses with a duration of 1 to 4 years. Two evening senior technical schools provide four- to five-year courses for the training of technicians in the civil, mechanical, and electrical domains. One is administered by the Ministry of Education and the other by the Ministry of Public Works. All of these evening schools, including the evening senior business school, are government schools and free of fees. There are some private institutes that provide management training and accounting courses for a fee in the evening.

The Ministry of Labor has two training centers, each providing elementary craft training of 1 to 2 years' duration to the unemployed over 16 years of age. Each year approximately 150 students take a full-time course in a civil, mechanical, electrical, or related trade. Courses in fishery and agriculture extension services are provided by the Ministry of Agriculture. The Ministry of Home Affairs conducts inservice initial and upgrading courses for civil servants. An average of 300 to 400 civil servants are enrolled each year in these evening courses of 1 to 2 years' duration. A few private and semi-government business concerns have their own centers for inservice training of their employees. In addition, the two bauxite companies and the telephone company maintain their own apprentice training.

3.5 Adult and Nonformal Education

Nonformal education is provided by a wide variety of public and private sources. Government efforts in this field have been intensified since the late 1970s.

A nationwide literacy program was initiated in 1981 by the Ministry of Education targeting all illiterates above 12 years of age (19% of the population). As the results were not satisfactory, a more ambitious program, named Alfa '84, was launched in 1984 with technical assistance from UNESCO. Due to financial and organizational constraints Alfa '84 was not successful.

With technical assistance from the Regional Center of Adult Education and Literacy for Latin America and the Caribbean (CREFAL) a new literacy program was developed in 1987 by the Department of Adult Education. This program included the creation of a nationwide nonformal education mechanism with regional offices, to be established and administered in cooperation between government and nongovernment agencies. Classes in the regions were conducted by formal teachers in schools during out-of-school hours with teaching–learning materials developed centrally by the Department of Adult Education. After 3 to 4 years, illiterates can be awarded a certificate equivalent to a primary-school certificate. Due to lack of funds the program is presently being implemented on a very small scale, and only in a few regions. In 1991, a total of approximately 500 adults were enrolled in literacy classes.

Literacy programs in the tribe-based settlements in the interior are also provided by some religious foundations including the Summer Institute of Linguistics. The objective of these programs is, however, conversion to the Christian faith.

4. Administrative and Supervisory Structure and Operation

There are both public and private schools at primary and secondary levels. At the primary and junior-secondary levels some 50 percent of enrollments are in private schools, most being denominational and administered by a religious body (school board), that is, Catholic, Protestant, Hindu, or Moslem. At the senior-secondary level only about 10 percent of enrollments are in private schools. All higher education institutes are government-run.

Except for a very small portion of administrative costs, private schools are subsidized completely by the government. All schools, public and private, operate under the jurisdiction of the Ministry of Education and Community Development. This ministry (hereafter to be referred to as the Ministry of Education) is in charge of formulating educational policy and is headed by a minister of cabinet rank. Science, culture, and sports are also under the jurisdiction of this ministry. Except for having to meet prescribed minimum educational standards for registration and funding purposes, private schools are free from close government direction.

While private schools are staffed and administratively controlled by their respective boards, public schools are staffed and controlled by the Ministry of Education. The state inspectorate monitors all schools (both private and public). The Ministry has two administrative sections, the larger, education section and the culture section, each headed by a permanent secretary. The education section larger, comprises four divisions: supervision, finance and administrative services, technical services, and developmental services.

Each division is supervised by an assistant permanent secretary, reporting to the permanent secretary for education. Administrative control is centralized and all divisions operate from the capital city where the Ministry is located. Only the inspectorate is decentralized to the district level.

However, in addition to their monitoring role, district inspectors arrange for and coordinate all other services for schools in their areas. At primary and junior-secondary level the schools (public and private) are geographically grouped into school clusters (6 to 12 schools), allowing them to share facilities and services. Individual clusters form a network for communication, cooperative thinking, and collaborative work between teachers. School clusters are considered as target systems for the provision of supervision and consultancy services.

5. Educational Finance

Education, including private schools run by religious bodies, is almost entirely financed from the recurrent budget of the Ministry of Education. The technical ministries, the Ministry of Labor, and some private institutions and industries also provide training and education. It is difficult, however, to determine the educational expenditure of these agents.

Recurrent expenditure of the Ministry of Education has risen rapidly since Independence in 1975, increasing by a factor of 3.4 between 1977 and 1990. As a proportion of the total government budget there was an increase in this period from 12.4 to 22.4 percent. As a percentage of the GNP it rose from 5.9 to 9.1 percent. The budget of the Ministry was G72.4 million in 1977 and G249.5 million in 1990. In addition to inflation and higher unit costs at all levels, the increase resulted mainly from the linear expansion of the secondary system.

The breakdown of the 1990 budget of the Ministry of Education was: administration 7.5 percent, first level including preschool 47.6 percent, second level 30.8 percent, third level 8.8 percent, adult and nonformal education 0.6 percent, special education 0.2 percent, and scholarships 2.4 percent. The capital budget for education is not a part of the Ministry's budget. Instead, it is included in the budget of the Ministry of Public Works. Capital investments are financed mainly from Dutch, European, American, and international development funds.

6. Supplying Personnel for the Education System

At the first and second levels of schooling, the overall pupil–teacher ratio is relatively low (see Table 1). For these levels, the supply from teacher-training colleges is sufficient to keep up with the demand for new teachers and the replacement of the brain drain of qualified

teachers in the late 1980s. The teaching force at the preschool and primary levels is completely qualified. Some 95 percent of teachers are qualified at the junior-secondary level, but there is an enduring shortage of qualified teachers at senior-secondary and higher levels. At the senior-secondary level only one-fourth of the teaching force is completely qualified, half is partly qualified, and the remaining fourth is unqualified. The supply of teachers at these levels continues to come partially from external sources. In addition, in higher education a large proportion of teachers work part-time.

There are three types of teacher-training colleges: the A-level teacher-training college, the B-level teacher-training college, and the Higher Institute for Teacher Training.

The A-level teacher-training college offers a four-year course after 2–3 years' junior-secondary education, qualifying graduates for preschool and primary teaching (Grades 1 and 2). An optional one-year course qualifies graduates for supervision of a kindergarten. Although there are no formal restrictions for males, only female students enroll.

The B-level teacher-training college is also a four-year course. The certificate of four-year junior-secondary school (academic course) is required for entry. B-level teachers are qualified to teach in primary schools.

The Higher Institute for Teacher Training offers two- and five-year subject-oriented evening courses, which qualify teachers for the junior- and senior-secondary levels respectively. Courses for teaching in special education are also provided. Entry requirement is the B-level qualification or another senior-secondary certificate.

7. Curriculum Development and Teaching Methodology

With the establishment of the Ministry of Education's development services division (including a Curriculum Department) in 1980, an infrastructure was created for curriculum development and related services. The first step was taken for the development of a new nationwide common school curriculum. Disparity among the regions, and in many cases among schools, had caused a long-felt need for a new nationwide standard core curriculum for primary and secondary level. Core curricula and timetables are prescribed by central authorities of the Ministry of Education.

A major project for primary education curriculum reform launched in 1980 was near completion in 1990. With the exception of geography, curricula and teaching–learning materials were developed, piloted, and implemented for all subjects in all grades. Primary-school subjects are: language, reading, writing, arithmetic, geography, history, science, creative arts, and physical education. Except for girls, who can attend needlework classes in some schools, there are no electives in primary education. Denominational schools are entitled to provide religious education in addition to the core curriculum. In primary schools teachers are assigned to a specific grade and they teach all subjects involved.

The update and reform of curricula for the different types of secondary education started in the mid-1970s and continued in the 1980s. For some school types curriculum reform resulted in the extension of the cycle time with one year (i.e., junior technical and vocational schools). Subject matter qualification is required for teaching in secondary schools. English as a foreign language is compulsory in all secondary schools, while Spanish as a second foreign language is compulsory only in the junior academic school.

The development of curricula and teaching–learning materials is performed by a variety of agents including sections of the curriculum department, special committees and teams, subject matter specialists and experienced teachers, working either on a part-time or full-time basis. Once developed and approved, the curricula and materials are produced and distributed by the Ministry of Education. Dissemination of materials is performed by the Department of Educational Guidance through its network of guidance officers and school clusters. This department is also in charge of improving teaching methods and practices by means of classroom observation, consultation, and inservice training of teachers. State inspectors or supervisors ensure the proper implementation of prescribed curricula and teaching methods. In the early 1990s it is foreseen that all curricula and other quality-related activities will be concentrated into a Learning Resource Center.

8. The System of Examinations, Promotions, and Certifications

Admission to preschool and primary school is based on age, respectively 4 and 6 years. Promotion to subsequent grades in primary and secondary schools is based on internal assessment. Primary schools award a certificate upon successful completion, normally at the age of 12 years.

For most secondary schools, the primary school certificate together with a nationwide entry examination is required for admission. The examination is selective and this, in spite of some efforts to equalize schools, leads to stratification in the secondary-school system. Social demand for the academic types of schools is the highest. Promotion within schools takes place through internal assessment.

For diagnostic purposes a nationwide test is taken at the completion of Grade 5 in primary education. This test makes it possible to compare the achievements of individual pupils, groups of pupils, schools, and geographical areas. Following the comparison of these data, remedial and other corrective measures are taken for improvement.

Transition from junior- to senior-secondary schools varies. In some cases the certificate of the junior-level school is sufficient; in other cases an entry examination is required, and in still other cases both are needed. This entry examination, taken nationwide, is again a selective one, strengthening stratification of the system.

All nationwide entry examinations and the diagnostic test are developed and taken by the central Examination Office of the Ministry of Education. This office is also involved with the core portion of the terminal examination of most of the school types in the secondary system.

9. Educational Assessment, Evaluation, and Research

Rapid increase of education expenditure on the one hand, and dissatisfaction with the performance of the system on the other, have resulted in the need for assessment and evaluation of the system. In the 1980s several ad hoc attempts at assessment and evaluation were made. They were all undertaken by designated committees and focused on a particular sector or part of the education system. A mechanism for a thorough assessment of the educational system has not yet been established.

The outcomes of the annual nationwide entry examinations for secondary education at both junior and senior level and final school examinations are used as performance indicators of the system. As standardization of these examinations is not guaranteed, their validity and reliability are questionable. This is, however, the only evaluative information available. A Ministry-commissioned study of education expenditure in 1987 concluded that (a) the repetition rate decreased from an average of 25 percent in the 1960s to an average of 21 percent in the mid-1980s; and (b) entry examination results were very low with a high variability in the last 10 years; at junior-secondary level it varied between 35 and 46 percent and at senior level between 23 and 35 percent.

This information reflected a very low internal efficiency of the system. With regard to the external validity of the school programs, there is a general feeling of dissatisfaction, especially related to the vocational schools.

10. Major Reforms in the 1980s and 1990s

As a consequence of a study performed in cooperation with UNESCO (Rensch et al. 1979), a major project for primary education curriculum reform was launched in 1980. This project consisted of three programs: (a) inservice training of teachers and education officers (change agents), (b) development of new syllabuses through nationwide discussions with teachers, and (c) development of curricula and teaching–learning materials for all subject areas. The project was almost completely implemented by 1990.

The military coup of 1980 gave rise to many revolutionary ideas and evoked considerable changes in the early 1980s. Many were poorly prepared and the results failed to materialize. One of these attempts was the very ambitious literacy program (Alfa '84), which had to be changed in scope and pace in 1987.

In continuation of the primary-education curriculum reform project a more inclusive program for the improvement of the quality of primary education started in 1986. It will include the construction and furnishing of a Learning Resource Center which will have departments for curriculum development, educational guidance, educational assessment and research, planning, a central library, and the examination office. Training facilities will also become available in the Center. Total costs are estimated at US$10 million, 80 percent of which should come from a loan from the Inter-American Development Bank (IDB). The execution of the project, originally planned for 4 years, has been severely delayed and is now estimated to take 6 to 8 years.

There is a discrepancy between the output of the educational system and labor force requirements, quantitatively and qualitatively. Although there is a shortage of technically trained people, the labor market is oversupplied with people with a service type of education. The government, recognizing the importance of proper vocational education for the development of the economy, started a major project for improvement in 1990. With Dutch technical assistance, the project included changes in the education structure, its contents, and its administration so as to achieve a better match with the labor market.

11. Major Problems for the Year 2000

Rising educational costs in connection with the growing demand for senior-secondary and higher education will be a problem. In this context education cost analysis together with strategies and measures for improvement of the internal efficiency of the educational system will become a challenge in the 2000s. Development of an appropriate vocational and technical education sector will put an extra burden on scarce resources.

The pressure of the brain drain will increase in the future if social and economic conditions remain poor. The training of higher-level teachers and academics in key disciplines will remain an issue of vital importance. However, it will require much more effort to retain them in the country as Suriname moves toward a global market and global economy. The capability to cope with these issues will largely determine the quality of the nation's education and economy.

References

Rensch E S, Murdoch J P, Van Kemenade J A 1979 *Preparing for Change in Education. Draft policy document.* Minov/Paramaribo and UNESCO, Paris

Suriname, Ministry of Education 1987 *National Report on Progress and Achievements in the Framework of the Major Project in the Field of Education in Suriname.* Ministry of Education, Paramaribo

Further Reading

Dwarkasing W W 1976 *Development of an In-service Education System in Suriname: A Proposal.* UNESCO IIEP/IP76/4.1, Paris

Dwarkasing W W, Belfor F, Gulpen E, Tjon H 1987 *Eindverslag werkgroep: evaluatie onderwijsuitgaven.* Ministerie van Onderwijs, Paramaribo

Marshall E K 1975 The beginning of educational planning in Suriname. *J. Int. Soc. Educ. Planners* 3(4): 81–92

Mathijsen A, Pollen P, Dundas J, Roell S, Meijer M 1990 *Beroepsonderwijs en volwasseneducatie in Suriname. Voorstellen tot herstructurering.* Factfinding Mission, Amsterdam

Mys A A 1973 Onderwijs en ontwikkeling in Suriname. Doctoral thesis, University of Amsterdam, Amsterdam

Netherlands Universities Foundation for International Cooperation (NUFFIC) 1989 *Onderwijs in Suriname, verslag van de identificatiemissie technische samenwerking onderwijs.* NUFFIC, The Hague

Suriname 1991 *National Accounts Statistics.* General Bureau for Statistics, Paramaribo

Swaziland

E. Dlamini

1. General Background

The Kingdom of Swaziland is the smallest country in Southern Africa, covering an area of 17,364 square kilometers with a length of 193 kilometers north to south and a width of 145 kilometers east to west. The country is surrounded by the Transvaal and the Natal provinces of South Africa, except in the northeast, where the country borders on the Republic of Mozambique for a distance of 97 kilometers.

Swaziland's four geographical regions are the Highveld, the Middleveld, the Lowveld, and the Lubombo. These cover 29, 26, 37, and 8 percent respectively. The capital city of Mbabane is situated in the mountainous Highveld. The Middleveld and Lubombo are at somewhat lower altitudes (610 to 762 meters), and the Lowveld is a region of bush vegetation at altitudes from 152 to 305 meters. The climate is temperate in the highlands and subtropical in the lowlands. The population of the country was estimated at 681,000 persons in the period 1976–86 and the annual average population growth rate was estimated at 3.2 percent. Nearly half of the population lives in the Middleveld which has some of the best soils in Swaziland.

Swaziland became a British High Commission territory in 1907 and remained such until gaining Independence in 1968. Executive authority is vested in the king and exercised through a cabinet presided over by a prime minister. The country is divided into chieftaincies, each of which elects two members to the electoral college. In each of the nation's four regions, a council made up of members of the college is responsible for implementing government policies.

The nation's main economic base is agriculture, in which a high percentage of the labor force is engaged. The major crops for both export and consumption are sugar, maize, cotton, and pineapples. Cattle farming dominates the country's livestock sector, but there is rapid development in goats, sheep, poultry, and pigs. Other activities include forestry, mining construction, and manufacturing.

In religion and official language, the country reflects its colonial background. Around 60 percent of the population is Christian (Protestant and Roman Catholic), while the remainder adheres to traditional African beliefs. The official languages are English and Siswati, a Bantu language related to Zulu.

The King is Head of State and is advised by a cabinet of Ministers responsible to a two-chamber parliament. On the other hand, he is advised by the Supreme Council of State, which is traditionally responsible to the Swazi Nation Council made up of all Swazi adults. The political dualism created by the role of the monarchy has distinctly shaped the nation's administration and the way of life of the Swazi people and is thought to ensure a balance in the political power structure and also to prevent any rift between the modern (westernized) elite and the traditional (conservative) majority.

Western education was introduced in Swaziland around the beginning of the twentieth century by missionaries, with the colonial government later becoming involved. Schools were developed along ethnic lines, with separate schools for Africans, for Europeans, and for Euro-Africans. By mid-century a large number of the schools for Africans were limited to a four-year primary course, which later was extended to six years. Although enrollments grew over the decades, by the 1950s more than half of school-age African children still did not attend school, and more than half of

the teachers were untrained (Pott 1955). The period between the close of the Second World War and the attainment of independence witnessed a more rapid increase in educational opportunities. Whereas only 11,600 pupils attended 207 primary schools in 1945, there were 172,908 pupils in 1991 and this enrollment is projected to increase to nearly 200,000 by 1995. Over the same period, secondary school enrollment increased from 318 students to 44,085 students in 1991 and the projection for 1995 is 58,220.

2. Politics and the Goals of the Education System

Since independence, the government has had a goal of universal primary education. For primary education the aims are the development of children's moral, intellectual, cultural, spiritual, and aesthetic values in order to prepare them for life. For secondary education the aims are to develop the individual by building upon and strengthening the foundation that was laid in primary school, and to provide the type of education which will support the development of those qualities and skills that will be of benefit to the individual and society, through both academic and vocational streams. Higher education focuses on the production of high-level and middle-level personnel and on academic learning.

3. The Formal System of Education

Figure 1 presents the structure of the Swaziland system of education. The system consists of seven years of

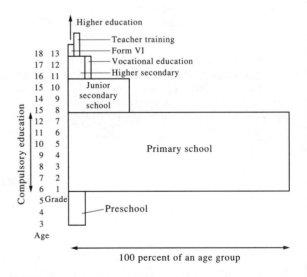

Figure 1
Swaziland: Structure of the formal education system

primary school, three years of junior secondary school and two years of senior secondary school.

3.1 Primary, Secondary, and Tertiary Education

The age of entry into primary school is 6 years and the cycle or duration is seven years, which means children theoretically finish when they are 12 years old after they have written an examination awarding the Swaziland Primary Certificate (SPC).

Secondary education is divided into two sublevels; the first is known as junior secondary. However, there are two schools in the country which go beyond these sublevels. The junior level has a duration of three years while the senior is two years and the two exceptional schools have one extra year.

The students who pass the junior level obtain a Junior Certificate and proceed to take the Cambridge O-level examination which offers a General Certificate of Education (GCE) for entry to tertiary institutions and to university, whereas the two schools beyond O level offer an A level. This latter certificate allows students to enter directly into the second year of a four-year course at the local university.

In 1993 there were not sufficient places at the secondary schools to permit all students to progress from primary to secondary schools, if they were all to pass the SPC examination. However, the ministry has taken steps to provide, as much as possible, the necessary facilities in the form of classrooms, teachers' houses and furniture at both the primary and the secondary levels. With the limited budget allocation, government together with community effort provide the facilities, but due to the high demand for education, this is not always sufficient to meet the annual requirements.

Table 1
Enrollment data at primary, secondary, and tertiary education for 1991, 1993[a], and 1995[a]

	1991	1993	1995
Primary			
Students	172,281	181,359	197,599
Teachers	5,584	6,133	7,059
Pupil–teacher ratio	32.3:1	29.6:1	28.0:1
Secondary[b]			
Students	44,085	50,662	58,220
Teachers	2,430	2,927	3,523
Pupil–teacher ratio	18.1:1	17.3:1	16.5:1
University[c]			
Agriculture	258	242	—
Education	138	165	—
Humanities	261	252	—
Science	300	298	—
Social science	778	773	—

a Projected values b Source: Ministry of Education c Source: University of Swaziland

The University of Swaziland is the only institution in the country offering degree programs and to which other tertiary institutions are affiliated. It offers degree and diploma programs in agriculture, education, natural sciences, humanities, and social sciences, and it also has an extramural services division that offers courses in adult education, management, and business studies. Table 1 presents enrollment data for selected years.

3.2 Preschool Education

Preschool education provides care for children between the ages of 3 and 5 years with emphasis on their socialization, development of their audio-sensorial skills, communication skills in Siswati and English, potential aptitudes, enhancement of their personality and character building, and preparation for entry into the school system.

While the country waits for preschool education to be universally available, primary schools are not allowed to consider preschool education as a prerequisite for entry into their first year. In 1993, some of these preschools were owned and run by communities, religious organizations, private individuals, and companies. In 1990, there were 260 preschools with an enrollment of 6,113 children.

3.3 Special Education

The purpose of special education is to provide educational opportunities to children with disabilities. These include the physically and mentally handicapped, and those with visual and hearing disabilities. In 1993 special education was offered at four centers or schools that offer formal courses of instruction, and suitable facilities for disabled students.

3.4 Vocational, Technical, and Business Education

In 1993 there were three colleges offering vocational education: (a) the Swaziland College of Technology which offers both vocational and technical programs with Junior Certificate and O-level admission requirements; (b) the Vocational and Commercial Training Institute (VOCTIM), with a minimum entry qualification of Junior Certificate, but also taking O-level graduates due to the competition for entry; and (c) the Manzini Industrial Training Center (MITC) which provides trades training for students who have not graduated from the regular school system and who do not have the prerequisites for admission to other vocational training institutions. MITC is run as a business with training occurring in tandem with repairs and production activities carried out by the students for outside clients. The goal of the administration of MITC is to become self-sufficient as a result of the proceeds of these businesses.

3.5 Adult and Nonformal Education

Adult education is intended to provide an opportunity to adults and youths who either had no formal education or who benefited little from their education. The aim is to educate and inculcate literacy and numeracy skills so that each individual can participate and contribute effectively both to his or her overall well-being and to society.

Adult education is offered on a nonformal basis through various institutes, rural education centers, agricultural and industrial training centers, and the Division of Extramural Services administered by the Faculty of Education at the University of Swaziland.

There is also a system of distance education, the purpose of which is to provide correspondence and continuing education and inservice correspondence education training. The students include those who have bypassed the formal school system as well as working youths and adults. The students who pass their examinations rejoin the formal school system or continue to further their education through correspondence. Inservice teacher education is also conducted through distance education.

4. Administrative and Supervisory Structure and Operation

All schools, colleges, and the university operate under the jurisdiction of the Ministry of Education, which is headed by a minister and deputy minister. Subordinate to these political appointees is a principal secretary, who is supported by a director of education, an undersecretary, and a research and planning unit; a chief inspector, subject inspectors, and regional education officers. The chief inspectors for primary schools and secondary schools direct the activities of the inspectors in individual subjects who visit the schools to monitor the quality of teaching.

5. Educational Finance

Of the state budget, 28.5 percent is spent on education. Of this, 37.2 percent is spent on primary education, 29.3 on secondary education, and 17.9 on higher education. The student unit costs are E 492 (US$180) at primary, E 1,577 (US$576) at secondary, and E 12,236 (US$4468) at tertiary.

Although universal primary education has been achieved, there are problems in having sufficient schools and classrooms to meet the demand in secondary education, and parents and communities are expected to help finance or build the classrooms needed.

6. Supplying Personnel for the Education System

There are three teacher training colleges: Nazarene Teachers' College and Ngwane Teachers' College,

both of which produce primary school teachers, and William Pitcher Teachers' Training College, which produces both primary and secondary school teachers. The training of primary school teachers is being phased out at this last college. All of these teacher training colleges have a three-year resident course. The minimum entrance requirement is O level.

Commercial and technical teachers are trained at the Swaziland College of Technology. The University of Swaziland also trains primary school teachers and secondary teachers, including specialization in agricultural education, prevocational agricultural education, and home economics. The Swaziland College of Technology offers a three-year program and the University of Swaziland offers a four-year degree program for secondary school teachers. The number of expatriates teaching in secondary schools has been reduced.

Inservice teacher training both at the university and through distance education is an important feature. Following independence, the nation was faced with a critical shortage of qualified teachers so that a large number of unqualified people had to be employed to staff primary school classrooms. However, by 1993, only 7 percent of primary school teachers were unqualified.

7. Curriculum Development and Teaching Methodology

The National Curriculum Center is responsible for curriculum development and coordination at the primary and secondary levels. The development of the primary school curriculum is well advanced; the center is planning to focus on strengthening its role in secondary curriculum development in the coming years. One of the center's main concerns is that the curriculum at one level should be linked to ensure a smooth transition to the next level because now it is being diversified to offer even more subjects. For example, practical arts subjects have been introduced in a number of schools in Grade 7. Hence, in Form I or Grade 8, the woodwork curriculum should begin at the point where the Grade 7 curriculum left off.

8. The System of Examinations, Promotions, and Certifications

Promotion from one grade to the next within the cycle of education is determined by the students' performance during the year. In order to ensure a continuous progression in the system, donor assistance has been obtained through the Education Policy Management and Technology Project (EPMT) for the development of methodologies and teacher training.

Assessment will be criterion-referenced, that is, pupils will attain skills to a specified standard at each stage of their education. All primary teachers will be trained in methodology and remedial approaches required to assist pupils in reaching the criteria. In the light of the introduction of continuous assessment and of examination system improvements, the examinations at the end of Grades 7 and 10 will be phased out and replaced by a system of diagnostic testing. The Education Testing, Guidance, and Psychological Services Section of the Ministry of Education is being strengthened in order to fulfill its task of assisting in continuous assessment and diagnostic testing. Its major tasks will include conducting diagnostic tests to detect learning strengths and weaknesses, administering a centralized continuous assessment system for the maintenance of uniform standards in the country, and identifying students' abilities, talents, and inclinations. Specific activities will include internships for local personnel in institutions abroad to provide training in testing and continuous assessment, in-country training for teachers and headmasters, long-term training to Master's degree level in guidance, and the production of test materials and the development of guidance strategies.

9. Educational Assessment, Evaluation, and Research

The Research and Planning Section of the Ministry of Education is responsible for the production of statistics about areas of concern in the education system. It is also responsible for evaluating and assessing the impact of educational projects that have been implemented. Research work conducted in the 1980s included tracer studies from school to work, school mapping exercises, wastage studies, and a preschool sector study as well as work for sector reviews.

Small scale research projects were also undertaken by the University and other institutions in the period 1990–93. These included: distribution of textbooks, skills for the future, a tracer study of prevocation students output, and auditing of school revenue and expenditure.

10. Major Reforms in the 1980s and 1990s

At the preschool level the reforms in the 1980s were the establishment of:

(a) qualified teacher leaders;

(b) health checks (i.e., immunization and other medical care);

(c) feeding schemes in some rural and urban schools;

(d) assistance in the form of grants from government and donor funds to preschools;

(e) parent/community involvement in the development of self-help schemes for preschools;

(f) administrative services of the ministry of education to strengthen preschool education at headquarters and at the regional level.

At the primary school level, universal primary education was achieved in 1985 and the curriculum has been diversified to some extent to include practical subjects. Proposals for a nine-year basic education were made and plans for developing the curriculum for both academic and prevocational education in secondary schools were begun. Finally, the introduction of master's programs at the university was initiated.

11. Major Problems for the Year 2000

The reforms of the education system will have serious cost implications in procuring and maintaining equipment for the prevocational stream. The inservice training of teachers to adapt to the above reforms will involve carefully planned training, both at home and abroad.

Many schools need to be upgraded and new ones need to be built.

The nationalizing and changing of the examination will bring about changes in the present system to which Swazis have been accustomed for quite some time. The introduction of new technologies will necessitate year-to-year inservice teacher programs.

Reference

Pott D 1955 *Swaziland: A General Survey*. South African Institute for Race Relations, Johannesburg

Further Reading

Government of Swaziland 1973 *Second National Development Plan 1973–77*. Government Printing Office, Mbabane

Government of Swaziland 1985 *National Review Commission Report*. Government Printing Office, Mbabane

Government of Swaziland 1991–92, 1992–93, 1993–94, 1994–95 *Rolling Development Plan*. Government Printing Office, Mbabane

Swaziland Ministry of Education 1986 *Wastage in the Education System*. Ministry of Education, Mbabane

Swaziland Ministry of Education 1990, 1991 *Education Statistics Reports*. Ministry of Education, Mbabane

Swaziland Ministry of Education 1992 *Education Preparatory Study*. Ministry of Education, Mbabane

Sweden

S. Marklund

1. General Background

Sweden is located in northern Europe and has an area of 450,000 square kilometers. Its length from north to south is 1,650 kilometers. The present borders were fixed in 1815. Sweden's population has increased from nearly 2.5 million inhabitants in 1800 to 5.1 million in 1900 and 8.4 million in 1992. The birthrate has been low since the 1920s. However, this has been counteracted by an increased average life expectancy and increased immigration. The population density is low, with only 20 inhabitants per square kilometer.

Ethnically, the population was homogeneous until the 1950s. Small national minorities include the Lapps in the north and a Finnish-speaking population along the northeastern borders. The remainder, excluding some small groups, form the Swedish majority population with Swedish as their national language. The dominant religion is that of the Lutheran State Church. Since 1950 immigration has exceeded emigration. Immigrants and their children now number 1 million and they live almost exclusively in the cities. This has considerably affected the school system. Swedish-as-a-foreign-language was introduced as a school subject in 1974. Nearly all immigrant students are also taught their mother tongue at school.

The economically active population numbered 4.7 million in 1990. The percentage breakdown by type of sectoral employment for 1992 is shown in Table 1. Since the early 1970s the number of employees in manufacturing and mining has slightly decreased and the number in health, social services, and education has increased. Government policies on labor, salaries, and general welfare have resulted in considerable equalization and overlapping of socioeconomic classes. The differences in disposable income and working conditions seem to be smaller than in any other country.

Sweden is a constitutional monarchy with a parliamentary representative democracy written into its constitution. Universal suffrage was introduced in 1908 for men and in 1919 for women. In local political elections, immigrants have the right to vote in the district in which they live. Elections are held every three years. A significant factor for reform activities in general has been Sweden's political stability. The dominant political party has been the Social Democrats. Between 1932 and 1976, they were in power practically without interruption. However, during 1976–82 Sweden had, and since 1991 has again had a right-wing liberal government. The same political situation has prevailed, by and large, in local government. Political stability has been paralleled by a comparatively conflict-free labor market.

An additional factor of importance has been the growth of material prosperity. Using the Gross Domestic Product (GDP) per capita as a yardstick, Sweden is usually ranked as one of the richest countries in the world. Through social welfare legislation, there are high standards for all in such matters as unemployment insurance, basic old-age and supplementary income-related pensions, public health and medical care, as well as child and housing allowances. The reforms in the educational system from preschool to higher education are part of this welfare program. It includes benefits for everyone, such as free schooling and higher education.

2. Politics and the Goals of the Education System

In 1950, Parliament decided upon a general strategy for the future development of the whole school system. The main objective was to raise the general level of education. The period of compulsory schooling had to be lengthened. At the same time, there was a desire to "democratize" the school system, by improving educational opportunities for previously underprivileged groups and by replacing the tripartite system of schools at secondary level with a comprehensive system, thereby creating greater equality of educational opportunity. Practical training was to receive equal status with theoretical ("academic") training. These objectives comprised both a social and an educational program.

After 12 years of experimental activities throughout the country, a new school structure was decided upon in 1962. In the school laws, statutes, and central curricular guidelines, the development of the individual student according to his or her inherent aptitudes was pronounced as the first and major goal of education. The second general goal put society at the center:

Table 1
Percentages of workers in types of industry 1992

	Percentage
Agriculture, forestry, fishing, and hunting	3.9
Mining, manufacturing, construction, electricity, gas, and water service	27.0
Wholesale and retail trade, restaurants, and hotels	14.6
Transport, storage, and communication	7.6
Finance and insurance	8.3
Services	38.4

school was to educate the individual for participation in the affairs of society for productivity and for social usefulness. The third goal concerned the handing down from the older to the younger generation of traditions and values—the cultural heritage. In interpreting these goals, equality and justice are the right of everyone, regardless of social, economic, ethnic, or geographical conditions.

3. The Formal System of Education

From 1962 to 1972, a nine-year compulsory comprehensive school (*grundskola*) was introduced all over the country. In 1971, an integrated upper-secondary school (*gymnasieskola*) was likewise introduced throughout the country, comprising academic, general and technical—vocational education within the same organization. The preschool structure was reorganized in 1967 and 1971, and higher education (universities and corresponding tertiary institutes) in 1975, 1977, and 1992.

Thus the traditional stages of preschool, primary school, and secondary and vocational school were restructured as precompulsory, compulsory, and postcompulsory (see Fig. 1). The inconspicuous part played by private schools is typical. The Education Act (1962) does not place any obstacles in the way of private persons or groups wishing to provide their

own education for their children. They can also receive the same state and municipal grants as the regular municipal schools, provided they follow the basic governmental school statutes.

Most children aged 7–16 years attend the *grundskola*. The private school population is only 2.5 percent. The school year starts in late August and ends in mid-June. It encompasses 40 weeks. The school year is basically the same for primary, secondary, and higher education. Until 1978 the maximum class size was 30. The average size was 22.6 in the compulsory schools and 24.0 in upper-secondary schools. In 1992 it was similar. However, as a result of increased possibilities for working with small groups or single individuals, the student–teacher ratio is much lower. Owing to this and other changes during the 1980s (mainly reduction of the teachers' annual tuition load) the compulsory school had 9 full-time teachers per 100 students in 1993. The corresponding figure for the upper-secondary school was 7.5.

The most important dividing line in Swedish public education is at age 16 when compulsory, full-time, and continuous schooling ends. Students then move to a postcompulsory school, not necessarily full-time and continuous, but often part-time and recurrent. The traditional upper-secondary school can be used in a more flexible way, as can higher education and various kinds of adult education to an even greater degree. Recurrent education can vary in timing, length, and content depending on how a single individual wishes to plan his or her studies and work.

3.1 Primary, Secondary, and Tertiary Education

Since 1972, there have been no separate official secondary schools before the postcompulsory stage. English is compulsory in Grades 4 to 9. Grades 1 to 6 usually have class teachers. Grades 7 to 9 have specialized teachers, most of them in two school subjects. In Grades 7 to 9, the students have a common course except for 10 to 15 percent of the time when they have elective subjects—either a second foreign language or extra courses in their general subjects. Regardless of electives, a complete nine-year school course qualifies students to study in the upper-secondary school.

As a consequence of the introduction of the nine-year comprehensive school a new type of postcompulsory upper-secondary school has developed. In 1971, all types of postcompulsory schools were brought together into an integrated upper-secondary school (*gymnasieskola*). As an official national school this seems to be unique in the world. An important aim was to give equal status to academic, general, and technical–vocational education at this level: general academic education should be "vocationalized" and technical–vocational education should be "generalized."

In principle, students enjoy a free choice of study routes in the upper-secondary school. The school has

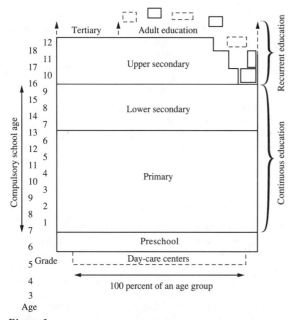

Figure 1

Sweden: Structure of the formal education system

places for all who finish the compulsory school, and more than 90 percent of them continue with upper-secondary training. Because of limited availability of places in certain programs, the students cannot always get their first choice. Whenever the number of applicants exceeds the supply of student places, admission preference is accorded on the basis of marks earned in comprehensive school and occasionally on other qualifications such as work experience. The students' preferences are strongly influenced by the labor market situation.

Dropout used to be a problem in the traditional Swedish secondary school. In the nine-year compulsory school this has now been eradicated, although it happens that a few students end with an "incomplete" final grade. In the integrated upper-secondary school, nearly a fifth "dropout" of their courses, but most of them return later to upper-secondary or adult education to complete these courses or take others. In the context of recurrent and lifelong learning the concept of "dropout" is now being redefined.

In 1975, Parliament approved general principles for a new higher education system. Undergraduate studies were organized into study programs grouped into five sectors (technical, administrative–economic–social welfare, medical–paramedical, teaching, and cultural–informational) as well as into single courses. Efforts to create greater diversity in available undergraduate programs were an important part of a policy which aimed at reaching new categories of students. Development of the content and structure of study programs was seen as a necessary complement to the new admission rules for reaching new categories of students.

For centuries Sweden had only two universities: Uppsala, founded in 1477, and Lund, founded in 1668. Institutes of higher studies in Stockholm and Göteborg were reorganized into universities during the 1950s and 1960s. An annex to Stockholm University was created at Linköping, one to Göteborg University at Karlstad, one to Uppsala at Örebro, and one to the University of Lund at Växjö. The most popular subjects within the faculties of humanities (social sciences and mathematics–natural sciences) were offered at the branch campuses. The university annex at Linköping was organized as an independent university in 1970.

Regional development policies were taken into account in planning higher education. North of Uppsala—within an area covering more than two-thirds of Sweden's total area—there were no resources for higher education and research. A university was established at Umeå in 1963, and an institute of higher education was also founded at Luleå to provide higher technical education and research.

Since 1977, higher education has included state-run institutes of higher education in 14 towns in addition to those 7 which had already been allotted resources. Most of these towns already had postsecondary schools

Table 2
Number of children in day homes and nursery schools

Age	Day homes[a]			Nursery schools[b]		
	1981	1990	1992	1981	1990	1992
0–4	87,800	162,000	160,000	2,300	1,600	1,700
5	27,500	49,400	51,300	14,300	11,000	10,900
6+	26,600	54,800	51,400	79,000	50,500	51,300
Total	141,900	266,200	262,700	95,600	63,100	63,900

a Full-time   b Some part-time

or professional colleges of various kinds. In 1990, the Swedish universities and other tertiary training institutes had 165,000 students, of whom 92,000 were women.

3.2 Preschool Education

The establishment of day homes, nursery schools, kindergartens, and corresponding preschool-care institutions has predominantly been seen as a social welfare enterprise. Centrally, and usually also locally, preschool institutions are managed by the boards of health and social welfare and not by the boards of education. Compulsory school does not start until the age of 7. An earlier start has long been discussed. In 1973, Parliament decided to retain the starting age of 7, but also decided that preschool should be available for all 6-year old children ("common preschool year"). However, an earlier school start is being reinvestigated by a governmental committee.

The treatment of preschool care and education as primarily a social question has given Swedish preschool institutions some unique features. They have a low child–adult ratio (seldom more than 5:1 or 6:1). They also have a special responsibility for children with difficulties and special needs, for instance, immigrant children. The statistics in Table 2 are from 1981 and 1990. These figures should be seen in relation to the birthrate in Sweden, which in the 1980s, was about 100,000 per year.

3.3 Special Education

Mentally retarded children are educated at special schools and training centers. Similarly, children who are blind, deaf, suffering from severe eyesight or hearing difficulties, or who have severe physical disabilities receive their schooling at special institutions. However, these students account for only 1 percent of the school-age population. Regular schools also provide special education. Such a provision has been developing since the late 1800s. Slow-learning stu-

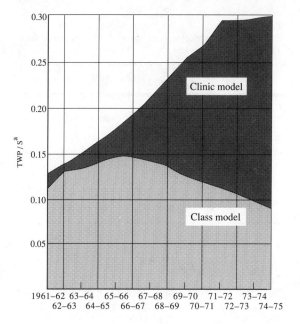

Figure 2
Development of special education in Swedish compulsory schools 1961/62–1974/75

a   Proportions of Teacher Weekly Periods per Student (TWP/S) in Class teaching (lower part) and Clinic teaching (upper part)

dents were taught in "help-classes." In 1942 these classes acquired their own structure when special training for their teachers started. In the nine-year compulsory *grundskola*, special classes were also organized for children judged as insufficiently mature to start schooling, as well as for children with reading disabilities and for students with social and emotional problems.

From the 1960s onward these special classes were gradually replaced by a system of special lessons for students taught individually or in small groups in so-called "clinics" parallel to teaching in special classes. Figure 2 indicates how the proportion of these two kinds of special education developed during the implementation of the new comprehensive school system. The total amount of special education doubled from 1961–62 to 1974–75, measured as the amount of "Teacher Weekly Periods per Student" (TWP/S) spent on special education. The lower part of the figure represents the amount of teaching in special classes, whereas the upper part represents special education in clinics, individually or in small groups. The clinic model increased from the mid-1960s at the same time as the class model decreased.

The proportions of the two models have generally remained unchanged since 1974–75. In 1972, an upper limit for special education was set at 0.30 TWP/S.

This meant that approximately every fifth teacher in *grundskola* was a special teacher. In 1978 this limit was abolished when special education became subject to decisions by local authorities, although still within the overall framework for state grants. There are no official statistics about special education since 1978.

3.4 Vocational, Technical, and Business Education

The integrated upper-secondary school has three main sectors of study: arts and social subjects, economics and commercial subjects, and scientific and technical subjects. In each one of these three sectors there are academic, general, and vocational courses. The majority of students have so far taken one of 25 tracks. These tracks have had a length of two to four years.

Vocational, technical, and business education has in this way been integrated with upper-secondary and higher education as parts of the municipal secondary and the governmental postsecondary education systems. Only a few schools and institutes for these purposes are now run on a nonpublic basis.

3.5 Adult and Nonformal Education

Adult and nonformal education in Sweden is of three kinds: popular-movement education, municipal adult education, and labor market training.

Popular-movement education is of two types: folk high schools and evening study circles. The first folk high schools were founded in 1868. In 1992, they numbered more than 100. They are run by county councils, and special organizations and associations. They provide a general civic education, mostly as two- or three-year full-time courses in boarding schools, with the aim of giving students an insight into their responsibilities as human beings and as members of society. Each school designs its own program. Folk high schools try to meet educational needs not fulfilled by the regular schools. The minimum age of eligibility is 18 years.

An evening study circle is a nonformal group of adults, usually 5 to 20, meeting for a minimum of 12 evenings over a period of at least 4 weeks. One of the members leads the circle. There are 11 nationwide adult education associations that operate folk high schools and study circles; all are entitled to state grants. These associations have links with various organizations, such as blue-collar and white-collar trade unions, political parties, and churches. The adult education associations collaborate with libraries and other cultural institutions. They cover a broad range of subjects varying from one association to another. In 1990, nearly two million people participated in study circles.

In 1967, Parliament decided that the local school authorities should also be responsible for providing opportunities for adult education. The number of adult students then grew quickly. During the 1970s and

1980s more than 200,000 people participated in such programs every year. This is as many as are trained in the regular upper-secondary schools. Municipal adult education aims at providing preparation for continued studies or for an occupation. About one-fourth took comprehensive-school courses. Nearly half were in upper-secondary courses, and almost one-third were in special vocationally oriented courses. Municipal adult education is provided within all of Sweden's 280 municipal districts.

Labor market training provides vocational education for those are unemployed or in danger of losing their jobs. It is paid for by the government and is conducted at special training centers and within the regular educational system. The main emphasis is on manufacturing operations. Participation in labor market training varies from year to year. In 1981 it had 40,000 trainees. In 1991 it had increased to 125,000.

4. *Administrative and Supervisory Structure and Operation*

Primary and secondary education (the latter including vocational and technical education) are subordinate to local school boards, one in each district. At the central level they are subordinate to the government, including the Ministry of Education. Until 1991, Sweden had a special administrative body—the National Board of Education (NBE)—corresponding to what in most other countries constitutes the administrative nonpolitical branch of the Ministry of Education. The NBE had a fairly free and independent position but was subordinate to the government as a whole and not just the Ministry of Education. Thus, for instance, the far-reaching school reform activities in the period 1950 to 1980 in compulsory and postcompulsory schools was led and executed by the NBE, within relatively general guidelines given by the government.

In 1991, the NBE was replaced by a smaller central authority called the Central Agency for Education (CAE). This change was a consequence of a far-reaching decentralization of responsibility for further development of the schools from the central government to local authorities. The local districts were made bigger and fewer (from approximately 2,500 in 1950 to 1,000 in 1953, 800 in 1962, and 280 in 1974).

A school inspectorate for upper-secondary education, attached to the NBE, was abolished in 1980. For compulsory education, a corresponding system of regionally attached inspectors was abolished in 1991. Their responsibilities were taken over by the local district boards and the heads of schools.

Universities and colleges have their own boards. At the central level, they are under the government and have long since been administered by a National Board of Universities and Colleges. In 1992 this board was replaced with four smaller administrative units.

Table 3
Primary and secondary school costs in selected years, with 1950–51 as a base year

	1950–51	1960–61	1970–71	1980–81	1989–90	1991–92
Costs						
Total	100	214	395	640	636	618
Per						
student	100	192	262	411	405	401
GDP	100	138	206	242	241	239
Costs as percentage of GDP						
State	1.3	2.1	2.8	3.5	2.9	2.8
Municipality	1.0	1.6	2.5	3.6	3.1	3.0
Total	2.3	3.7	5.3	7.1	6.0	5.8

5. *Educational Finance*

The extent to which school costs have increased can be seen in Table 3. For comparison purposes figures for 1950–51 have been put at 100. In 1989–90 (39 years later), costs in a fixed currency increased nearly 6 times (from 100 to 636). Per student costs increased from 100 to 405.

Since the 1950s, Sweden's material wealth also increased considerably (the GDP rose from 100 to 245). In 1950, some 2.3 percent of the GDP went to schools; 40 years later it was 6.0 percent. However, this increase seems to have stopped. According to World Bank statistics, Sweden, Denmark, and Norway seem to have the most expensive school systems in the world. The annual cost for a student in 1989–90 was US$7,600 in the compulsory comprehensive school and US$8,300 in the integrated upper-secondary school. These costs are shared roughly evenly by the state and the municipality.

6. *Supplying Personnel for the Education System*

Before 1968, the major part of teacher training was clearly divided into two levels. Primary teacher training was mostly conducted at the preuniversity level and was of an apprenticeship type, with training in academic subjects and teaching practice. Secondary academic teachers were trained at the postsecondary level, usually at universities and with a final preparatory pedagogical year (or half-year) to provide a formal qualification for teaching. Teachers in arts, music, home economics, physical education, or manual instruction had special kinds of training somewhere between these two types.

From 1968 onward different types of training (for primary, secondary academic, and secondary nonacademic teachers) were gradually placed in the tertiary education system. There have also been steps taken to equalize salaries and teaching conditions. Training has usually been two years for preprimary teachers, two and a half or three years for primary teachers, and four years (minimum) for secondary teachers. In 1988 the training of teachers for compulsory schools was extended to three and a half to four and a half years, depending on the type of specialization.

From 1952 to 1972, Sweden had a severe teacher shortage, due primarily to the introduction of extended compulsory education and a broadening of postcompulsory education. Since 1972, there has been a fair balance between supply and demand of teachers.

7. Curriculum Development

The major aim of the first six school years is to give the pupils basic skills in reading, writing, and arithmetic and a general social and science orientation. As early as Grade 3 a foreign language (English) is introduced as a compulsory subject. Since 1970, all primary teachers have been formally qualified to teach English.

A national curriculum for the compulsory school was introduced in 1962 with many electives in Grades 7–8 and 9 streams in Grade 9. In 1969 streaming was banned all through the compulsory school. Some 15 percent of instructional time in Grades 7 to 9 (lower-secondary) was allocated to electives where the student could choose between a second foreign language (German, French, or mother tongue for immigrants), technical subjects, economics, and art. In 1980, Parliament decided that the choice of postcompulsory training could be made independently of the choice of electives in the preceding compulsory education.

The upper-secondary curriculum is clearly tracked but all tracks include Swedish, civics, and physical education. A total of six tracks are predominantly academic with more than 10 subjects in each. However, as from 1993, the system of tracks with fixed combinations of subjects will be replaced by a system of 16 so-called "study programs," within which students will have some possibility for composing their own curricula. The central curricular guidelines for compulsory, as well as postcompulsory, schools were were being revised, again in 1992. The implementation of this revision was expected to take place sometime in the period 1993 to 1995.

8. The System of Examinations, Promotions, and Certifications

There are no final examinations in the compulsory comprehensive school (*grundskola*) and the integrated upper-secondary school (*gymnasieskola*). In the compulsory school the pass–fail concept was abolished. With few exceptions all students move to the next grade at the end of the school year.

In the compulsory school, students are awarded subject marks at the end of the Autumn and Spring terms in Grades 8 and 9. The latter make up the basis for further studies in postcompulsory schools. There the students receive marks in all subjects at the end of the Autumn and Spring terms. Marks are given on a five-point scale, where 1 is lowest and 5 highest. The basis for selection of students to higher education is the average mark in Grade 12 (and, for some kinds of higher education, in Grade 11).

Since 1977, admission to tertiary education can also be granted on the basis of a voluntary central entrance test of "suitability for higher studies." Around 40 percent of available training places are filled by persons having taken the entrance test, and around 60 percent on the basis of marks from preceding schools. In each case, the applicants must fulfill both general requirements and special requirements for admission. The former is usually the completion of secondary school, but can also be experience of other kinds. The latter are mostly secondary school marks in subjects relevant to the specific training for which application was made.

At the tertiary level most faculties and corresponding bodies set a basic exam (*högskoleexamen*), usually after three or four years of full-time studies. Some faculties also have a master's degree or a licentiate degree between this basic exam and the final doctoral degree. Exams are judged "well approved," "approved," or "not approved."

In Sweden, certification for a number of professions following tertiary studies has disappeared for many occupational areas. The medical and legal professions usually demand special certificates after fulfilled studies, but for most other professions tertiary examination in relevant subjects is usually enough.

9. Educational Assessment, Evaluation, and Research

In the "new" school as of 1962 it was said that assessment should be continuous, regardless of how often students received formal marks. Standardized central achievement tests had existed since 1944 in primary schools for reading, writing, and mathematics, and from 1959 for English. Tests in these subjects, plus physics, chemistry, German, and French (and for some time also in business economics and accountancy), were introduced in upper-secondary education.

The standardized tests for primary education were at first voluntary for teachers, but 90 to 95 percent used them. As from the 1980s the tests became compulsory but were restricted to Grades 8 and 9. In upper-secondary school the central tests became mandatory upon their introduction in 1971. The tests were constructed by a special department at the NBE, but from 1982 this task was decentralized to a number of educational research institutes. The main objective of these tests was to help teachers make students' marks comparable all over the country. The results were not registered in the students' final certificates.

Another kind of assessment is the National Evaluation of Compulsory Education, an on-going project started in 1989. It is based on a national sampling of classes in Grades 2, 5, and 9 every three years. Student achievements in all major school subjects are measured. Methods of how students work, learn, and communicate are also studied.

Since the 1960s, Sweden has also participated in international studies of student achievement. The largest project so far has been organized by the International Association for the Evaluation of Educational Achievement (IEA) for samples of 10-year old, 14-year old, and preuniversity-age students. In general, Sweden achieved average or above-average results.

In addition to achievement studies of this nature, the Swedish government has, since 1962, set aside special resources for educational research. These funds have been administered by the NBE, and from 1991 by its replacement, the CAE. During the first decade of activities, funds were predominantly used for so-called "development projects"; these included studies of methods and materials, and development of learning aids according to the "educational technology" of the time. Since then the scope of studies has broadened to include many other kinds of studies. The amount of funding increased until 1977–78, when the NBE provided resources equivalent to US$7.5 million for educational research and development. This was 0.4 percent of the government school budget. Since 1978 the annual sum has decreased to sums less than half of that amount.

10. Major Reforms in the 1980s and 1990s

Compared with the period 1950 to 1980, when the Swedish education system was almost totally reshaped, the 1980s became a period mostly characterized by quiet and stabilization. New national curricular guidelines for the compulsory school were established in 1980. The 1980s was also the decade of decentralization to local authorities of responsibility for the development of the school. State grants could, within a wide national framework, be used locally for varying organizational arrangements. Elective subjects in Grades 7 to 9 (lower secondary) could, from 1980, be extended courses in any of the school subjects in the curriculum, even in cross-disciplinary local subjects. Practical vocational orientation with local employers, previously restricted to 2 weeks in Grade 8, was extended to 6 to 10 weeks spread over Grades 1 to 9. It was broadened to "working life orientation" and was decided upon locally.

In the period 1985 to 1988 the upper-secondary school (Grades 10–12) was the focus of varying local experiments concerning internal study forms and external organizational structures. These experiences

became the starting point for later changes from the "track system" to the "study program system," to be introduced in the period 1993 to 1995.

In higher education the most far-reaching change will be the replacement of the five general "study lines" by more freely composed programs for professional training. This began in 1993.

11. Major Problems for the Year 2000

Prospective major questions will probably concern how to find a new and constructive balance of the two main forces in social and educational policy-making which have been operating since the 1950s. Left-wing forces, promoting a "democratized" education with extended schooling and delayed differentiation in comprehensive systems will, more than before, be counteracted by right-wing liberal forces demanding more freedom for "profiling" school and education independent of central policy-making.

Such a dialogue between forces and opinions will include general as well as specific issues such as the balance between educational policy-making and social welfare policy-making. One of the long-discussed but still unresolved questions is the transition of children from preschool to compulsory school. In 1993 the age of transition was 7 years. It might change to 6 in the year 2000 or even before that time.

Bibliography

Gurgsdies E 1975 *Schulreform und Chancengleichheit. Ergebnisse der schwedischen Gesamtschulreformen.* Dietz, Berlin

Hörner H 1970 *Demokratisierung der Schule in Schweden, Erziehungswissenschaftliche Forschungen*, Vol. 4. Beltz, Weinheim

Jüttner E 1970 *Der Kampf um die schwedische Schulreform.* Mannheim

Marklund S 1980 *The Democratization of Education in Sweden: A UNESCO Case Study*, Studies in Comparative and International Education, No. 2. Institute of International Education, Stockholm University, Stockholm

Marklund S 1980 The role of central government in educational development in Sweden. In: Hoyle E, Megarry J (eds.) 1980 *Professional Development of Teachers. World Yearbook of Education 1980.* Kogan Page, London

Marklund S 1981 Sweden: Setting up the comprehensive school. *Prospects* 11(2): 161–79

Marklund S 1984 Sweden. In: Hough J R (ed.) 1984 *Educational Policy: An International Survey.* Croom Helm, London

Marklund S 1984 Effects of educational research on educational policy-making: The case of Sweden. In: Husén T, Kogan M (eds.) 1984 *Educational Research and Policy. How Do They Relate?* Pergamon Press, Oxford

Marklund S, Bergendal G 1979 *Trends in Swedish Educational Policy*: The Swedish Institute, Stockholm

OECD 1981 *Educational Reforms in Sweden*, Reviews of National Policies for Education. OECD, Paris

Sweden, Ministry of Education and Cultural Affairs 1991 *"Growing with Knowledge." A Reform of Upper-Secondary and Municipal Education in Sweden. Government Bill and the Decisions of Parliament in June 1991*. Ministry of Education and Cultural Affairs, Stockholm

Sweden, Skolöverstyrelsen (various years) *Läroplan för grundskolan 1962, 1969 och 1980*. Skolöverstyrelsen, Stockholm

Sweden, Skolöverstyrelsen 1970 *Läroplan för gymnasieskolan 1970*. Skolöverstyrelsen, Stockholm

Sweden, Skolöverstyrelsen 1990 *Anslagsbetänkanden för åren 1950/51–1990/91*. Skolöverstyrelsen, Stockholm

Sweden, Statistiska Centralbyrån 1991 *Statistisk Årsbok, åren 1950–1991*. Statistiska Centralbyrån, Stockholm

Wieser K 1974 *Bildungspolitik und Gesellschaft in Schweden. Dargestellt unter besonderer Berücksichtigung der Einführung der Gymnasieschule als Berufsgrundschule*. Jobst Schultze, Hamburg

Switzerland

A. Gretler

1. General Background

Switzerland is a small country in the heart of Europe, covering an area of roughly 41,300 square kilometers or 15,945 square miles (about one-fourth of it being unproductive). Geographically, the country is made up of three main parts: the Jura, the Central Plain, and the Alps. Its rivers, which have their sources in the Alps, flow into the North Sea, the Mediterranean Sea, and the Black Sea. Founded in the year 1291 (with three cantons), Switzerland grew at different stages and found its present shape at the beginning of the nineteenth century, after the Napoleonic wars (25 cantons; a 26th canton was established in 1978).

In 1990, the population reached 6,751,000 inhabitants, 1,127,000 (16.7 percent) of whom were foreigners. With an average annual growth rate of 0.6 percent between 1980 and 1990, the total population is growing slowly. There are, however, significant changes in the age structure of the population: between 1950 and 1990, the age group 0–19 years has decreased from 30.6 to 23.4 percent, whereas the age group above 65 increased from 9.6 to 14.6 percent. This trend toward a society of more and more elderly people has important repercussions on the level and structure of qualifications and causes specific educational needs: since fewer new qualifications are brought to the active population by the young generation, updating and refreshing of the economically active people's qualifications by further training is gaining in importance. The average life expectancy still on the rise, is 80.8 years for women and 74.1 years for men. Due to its geographical situation (its neighbors being Germany, Austria, France, Italy, and Liechtenstein) and also to political will, Switzerland is a multicultural and multilingual country. Some 65 percent of the population speak German, 18.4 percent French, 9.8 percent Italian, and 0.8 percent Rhaeto-Romanic, the remainder being foreigners with other mother tongues. As to

religious denomination, 47.9 percent are Roman Catholics, 44.3 percent Protestants, 3.2 percent belong to other religions, and 4.9 percent are without professed religion.

Economically, Switzerland has followed the general evolution of European countries from an agrarian to an industrial and, finally, to a service-dominated economy. Whereas in 1800, roughly 65 percent of the active population worked in the primary sector, this figure diminished to 5.6 percent by 1990; the corresponding figures for the secondary sector are roughly 25 and 34.9 percent (with a peak of almost 50 percent around 1965), and for the still growing tertiary sector which was less than 10 percent in 1800 but was 59.5 percent in 1990. This change in the economic structure was accompanied by a process of urbanization: in 1990, 14.2 percent of the population was living in towns with more than 100,000 inhabitants, 28.5 percent in communities with 10,000–99,999 inhabitants, and 57.3 percent in small localities (sometimes suburban) with less than 10,000 inhabitants; on the whole, 59.8 percent of the population live in urban and 40.2 percent in rural settings. The Swiss economy depends heavily on exports, mainly of high-quality products (imports, however, normally exceed exports—in 1990, by 9.5%) and on a high proportion of foreign labor (26.8% in 1990). Women account for 37.5 percent of the total labor force. National income per inhabitant (nominal US$ 30,600 in 1990) is one of the highest in the world.

Politically and administratively, the country is structured into three main levels: the Confederation, the 26 cantons, and the 3,029 communes, each of which has its own legislative and executive political power. The modern state in its present form was founded on the basis of the Federal Constitution of 1848. The central government (Federal Council), formed by seven ministers, is a coalition representing the four most important political parties; it is characterized by great stability.

Legislative power at the federal level consists of two houses, the National Council (200 deputies representing 10 political parties) and the Council of States (46 deputies). Adopting a very simple right-center-left model, it can be said that, in 1990, 138 deputies of the National Council belonged to the center and the right, and the other 62 represented the left. Neutrality in foreign affairs (increasingly being questioned with the possibility of Switzerland joining the European Community), a free market economy, and increasing social security are some salient points of long-term government policy. Decreasing interest and participation in voting at elections is one of the contemporary problems of the Swiss democratic system.

2. Politics and Goals of the Education System

Formal schooling started in the monastery schools of the Middle Ages with the purpose of ensuring the supply of priests. From the twelfth century onwards, so-called "small schools" catered for the needs of the rising bourgeoisie, teaching languages, elementary mathematics, and geography. Schooling was intensified with the Reformation and Counter-Reformation, but the middle schools and Latin schools were limited to the cities, whereas schools in rural areas continued to be dominated by religious instruction. The Age of Enlightenment brought some liberation from this domination, and the teaching of mathematics and science was reinforced. In that period, Rousseau (1712–78), born in Geneva, developed his concept of education, and Pestalozzi (1746–1827), working as a practitioner and a theoretician of education, founded and directed his schools and wrote his books.

The nineteenth century—with the emergence of the modern state, the economic revolution, and the spread of new ideas—brought general compulsory schooling. It was recognized that the education of the young generation was one of the most important public goals to be achieved. The cantons created school laws, established primary schools, and founded cantonal secondary schools (*Kantonsschulen*). Both existing universities (Basle and Geneva) were reorganized, and new universities were founded. The public educational system as it still essentially exists today was created.

One of the pre-eminent features of Switzerland's political system is the permanent search for an equilibrium between federal and cantonal power. Education essentially lies within the competence of the cantons, the federal state having very little to say in this field; consequently there is no federal ministry of education. Attempts to give more power to the central state in educational matters failed in 1874, when the constitution was totally revised, and again in 1973, when a constitutional amendment was accepted by a small majority of the voters, but rejected by the smallest possible majority of cantons. These failures show that the cantons are very anxious to safeguard their almost exclusive authority in educational matters. Therefore, there is no Swiss system of education: there are 26 cantonal systems. The following description of the "Swiss system" tries to underline both the differences between and the features common to the cantonal systems.

As there is no central authority in education and therefore no real educational planning at national level, the goals of the educational system are not easy to define. Goals for compulsory schooling are defined in each of the 26 cantonal school laws; for upper secondary education, they are formulated in the federal law on vocational training and the federal maturity regulation. Generally, these goals cover three dimensions: (a) personal development; (b) socialization in the sense of integrating the young generations into the local, national, and to an increasing extent into the European and the global society by means of introducing them into the essential cultural and other values; (c) economic qualification.

3. The Formal System of Education

Figure 1 presents an overall picture of the Swiss system of education. There are, however, marked differences between the 26 cantonal systems both in structure and in the richness and variety of educational provision. Thus, the educational provision in some small rural cantons with low per capita income is sometimes limited to preschool education, compulsory including special education, and just one gymnasium and one vocational school at the upper-secondary level, there being no provision at all (apart from private adult education) at the tertiary level. At the other extreme, there are urban cantons with high per capita income, offering an extremely rich variety of educational institutions at the upper-secondary and the university and nonuniversity tertiary level. Given the short distances in a small country, attending higher education institutions in another canton constitutes no major problem for students of small rural cantons. A system of cantonal scholarships, subsidized by the national government, widely provides for educational opportunities for economically underprivileged students.

3.1 Primary, Secondary, and Tertiary Education

The duration of compulsory schooling, divided into primary and lower-secondary education, has gradually been extended; in 1992, it was 9 years in almost all cantons. The enrollment rate at this level is virtually 100 percent (see Fig. 1).

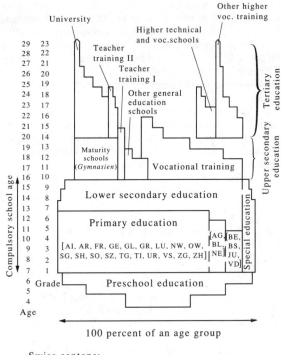

Figure 1
Switzerland: Structure of the formal education system 1990–91

Swiss cantons:

AG Aargau	NW Nidwalden
AI Appenzell(Inner-Rhoden)	OW Obwalden
AR Appenzell(Außer-Rhoden)	SG St Gall
BE Berne	SH Schaffhausen
BL Basel–Country	SO Solothurn
BS Basel–Town	SZ Schwyz
FR Fribourg	TG Thurgau
GE Geneva	TI Ticino
GL Glarus	UR Uri
GR Graubünden	VD Vaud
JU Jura	VS Valais
LU Lucerne	ZG Zug
NE Neuchâtel	ZH Zurich

Primary education, with all pupils in the same type of school, lasts 4 years in 4 cantons, 5 years in 3, and 6 years in the other 19 cantons (see Fig. 1). Since the end of primary education is the first point of selection in the system, there is a tendency in the first-mentioned cantons to prolong it by 1 or 2 years. From a curricular point of view, the period 1975 to 1990 was characterized by a reform of mathematics and the introduction of a foreign language as early as the fourth or fifth grade.

A feature of growing importance in the Swiss educational system is the high number of foreign pupils and students. As shown in Fig. 2, the proportion of foreign-origin and foreign-language schoolchildren in compulsory education varies between more than 40 percent in the canton of Geneva and less than 5 percent in the cantons of Nidwalden and Obwalden. The Swiss average is 17.5 percent. The Swiss Conference of Cantonal Ministers of Public Education has issued several recommendations concerning the schooling of foreign-language children. Roughly speaking the policy in this field can be characterized by three different stages: assimilation (in the 1960s), integration (in the 1970s and early 1980s), and intercultural education (from the mid-1980s onwards).

The average class size in 1990–91 was 19 pupils in primary education (with a minimum of 15.3 in the canton of Jura and a maximum of 21.4 in the canton of Thurgau) and 17.8 students in secondary education (with a minimum of 14.2 in Graubünden and a maximum of 19.9 in Ticino).

Lower-secondary education takes place in different types of school. Some cantons have organized their lower-secondary level in a comprehensive form; in others, the different types of schools may be classified into two groups: schools with basic requirements and schools with extended requirements. In 1991, 31.3 percent of the total number of pupils attended the first type and 68.7 percent the second type.

Upper-secondary education can be divided into four major types: *Maturitätsschulen*, designed for university entrance; other general education schools; teacher-training institutions; and vocational training institutions (see Sect. 3.4).

Unlike other schools, *Maturitätsschulen* are governed by a federal regulation. Originally, there were only two types of *Matura* (the final examination providing access to university): Type A (with emphasis on Greek and Latin) and Type B (Latin and modern languages). Type C (mathematics and science) was added in 1925 and Types D (modern languages) and E (economics) in 1972. In 1992, a proposed revision of this federal regulation was made in order to reduce the different types to just one, offering a great number of individual options. A decision will be taken after consultation with all interested parties.

Until the Second World War, *Maturitätsschulen* were reserved for a small elite; after the war, and particularly after 1960, enrollment increased spectacularly. It almost doubled between 1960 and 1970 and again between 1970 and 1980. In 1991 the total enrollment was 54,300. This increase was a response to two objectives of educational policy: to provide highly qualified personnel for the economy and to reduce inequality of educational opportunity by geographical region, social stratum, and sex. The means by which this increase took place were mainly decentralization of *Maturitätsschulen* and the development of the system of educational grants.

The other general education schools at this level (total enrollment in 1991: 12,000) prepare students primarily for certain nonuniversity professions (such as in the paramedical and social fields).

The main and traditional part of tertiary education is university education, but there is also a growing and increasingly diversified extra-university tertiary sector.

Academic education is provided for in the two federal institutes of technology (Zurich and Lausanne), in the seven cantonal universities: Basle (founded in 1460), Berne (1834), Freiburg (1889), Geneva (1559), Lausanne (1890), Neuchâtel (1909), and Zurich (1833), as well as in the School of Economics, Law, and Social Sciences of St Gallen. The increase in enrollment since 1960 has been spectacular and is expected to continue for some time to come. Thus, the total number of students in the above-mentioned university level institutions has grown as follows: 1960: 21,300; 1970: 42,200; 1980: 60,500; and 1991: 86,000.

The extra-university tertiary sector is characterized by diversity. This is not so much the result of a deliberate central policy as of a desire to provide pragmatic and specific answers to emerging needs. Admission normally depends on diplomas or certificates acquired in upper-secondary education. Six professional fields can be distinguished: (a) teaching; (b) higher technical and agricultural professions; (c) social work; (d) health professions; (e) commerce, traffic, administration, and communication; and (f) liberal arts. In addition to this, there are higher vocational courses and examinations in most of the trades which are accessed by apprenticeship. In 1990–91, a total of 52,000 students were enrolled in extra-university tertiary education, about two-thirds being part-time and the rest full-time students. In Switzerland, the extra-university tertiary enrollment as a proportion of total tertiary enrollment is higher than in most other countries. Of particular note are the higher technical institutes (*Höhere Technische Lehranstalt* or HTL) and the higher business and administration institutes (*Höhere Wirtschafts- und Verwaltungsschule* or HWV). There is general agreement that the engineers and middle-level staff trained in these institutes play an important role in the development of Swiss business and industry. In order to guarantee full international recognition of the diplomas conferred in the extra-university sector, tertiary teaching and training institutions providing a high quality education of at least three years' duration will obtain the status of specialized university institutes (*Fachhochschulen*).

3.2 Preschool Education

Normally, Swiss children spend one or two years in kindergarten before going to primary school. Preschool attendance in 1990–91 was 24.9 percent for 4-year olds, 75 percent for 5-year olds, and 98.4 percent for 6-year olds (this last figure representing, however, a mixture of preschool and school attendance). There are notable differences between urban and rural regions. Total enrollment in 1990–91 was 139,800; the enrollment rate has steadily increased and will probably continue to do so.

As these figures show, preschool attendance is not compulsory. It is considered to be complementary to family education. About two-thirds of the cantons have preschool regulations at the cantonal level; the most important public body in preschool education, however, is the commune. The trend is to leave preschool education as noncompulsory, but to offer parents, by cantonal legislation, the opportunity of a one- or two-year enrollment for every child. Special

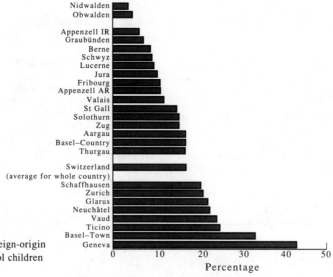

Figure 2
Compulsory schooling: foreign-origin and foreign-language school children by canton 1988–89

measures such as the setting up of peripatetic kindergartens are sometimes taken in rural regions. The
trend is also away from private to public preschool
institutions. However, the former still play an important part. Besides the traditional (in some areas often
church-run) private institutions, new forms of mostly
parent-run playgroups are growing in importance. Special attention is given to the transition from preschool
institutions to primary schooling.

As far as the philosophy and ideology of preschool
education are concerned, there is a difference between German-speaking Switzerland, whose system
is based on Fröbel (1782–1852), and the French- and
Italian-speaking parts of the country, whose system
is mainly based on Claparède (1873–1940), Ferrière
(1879–1960), and Montessori (1870–1952). This difference, however, seems to be on the decrease in
practice.

3.3 Special Education

For the duration of compulsory schooling, special
education is offered to handicapped children (total
enrollment in 1990–91: 36,000, which was 5% of
pupils in compulsory schooling). As in many other
countries, the development in this field was characterized by the separation versus integration debate in the
early 1990s. In order to keep the growing proportions
of children with learning difficulties within normal
classes, and also in order to reduce the class repetition
rates (14% of the children repeat a class in the course
of compulsory schooling), different forms of special
learning assistance (*Stütz- und Förderunterricht*) have
been developed and play an important role in a growing number of cantons.

3.4 Vocational, Technical, and Business Education

By far the largest proportion of the young (more
than 70% of an age group; total enrollment in 1991:
221,000) enter vocational training after compulsory
schooling (normally from about age 16 to about age
19). This is mostly in the form of apprenticeship,
consisting of two basic elements: practical training
on the job in an enterprise (3.5 to 4 days per week),
and theoretical and general instruction in a vocational
school (1 to 1.5 days per week). A third element, basic
courses in training centers, bringing together apprentices of the same craft or trade for some weeks, is
becoming more popular. Following a very old tradition
going back to pre-industrial times, apprenticeship is
regulated by a contract between master (employer) and
apprentice. Craft and trade associations play an important part in establishing job descriptions, training
programs, and examination rules. Vocational training
is regulated by federal law; responsibility in the central
administration is with the Federal Office of Industry,
Trades, and Labor in the Federal Department of Public

Economy. Leaving aside agriculture and public health,
there are recognized apprenticeships (of two to four
years' duration) in about 280 vocations in the fields
of industry, handicrafts, and different service sectors.
At the beginning of the 1970s, the vocational school
with an augmented curriculum (*Berufsmittelschule*)
was introduced for particularly gifted or ambitious
apprentices.

In relation to the transformation of the extra-
university tertiary institutes (*Fachhochschulen*, see
Sect. 3.1) and also influenced by the educational policy of the European Community (EC), an important reform will be introduced in the field of basic vocational
training: apprentices will be offered the opportunity
of additional general education (about 1,200 lessons)
resulting in an examination (*Berufsunatuvität*) offering access to the specialized university institutes in
the corresponding vocational field. On the other hand,
graduates from the upper-secondary general education
schools with an additional year of vocational practice
will also be admitted to these specialized university
institutes.

Two main types of higher vocational training can be
distinguished: higher technical and vocational schools
(mostly full-time, sometimes also part-time) and other
higher vocational training (mostly part-time, see Fig.
1). As explained above, most of the higher technical
and vocational schools (total enrollment in 1990–91:
15,000) will be transformed into specialized university
institutes (*Fachhochschulen*). However, this is not
the case for the so-called technicians' schools (total
enrollment in 1990–91: 5,000). Other higher vocational training (total enrollment in 1990–91: 32,000)
consists mainly of part-time courses preparing for
higher vocational examinations known as the master
examinations in the trades. Access is by successful
completion of an apprenticeship. The conferment of
a Master (*Meister*) title allows the holder to train
apprentices.

3.5 Adult and Nonformal Education

Adult education is almost completely a private matter.
On the vocational side, industry and other economic
sectors organize a wide range of further training
courses on an intra- or interfirm level, whereas general adult education is offered by a great number
of organizations and associations, sometimes on
ideological grounds and sometimes on a commercial
basis. About 90 of the most important associations
and institutions form the Swiss Federation for Adult
Education, founded in 1951. Courses organized by the
federation are attended by about 900,000 participants
each year, totalling about 17 million participant hours.
In vocational further training alone, the number of
participants per year is about 500,000, corresponding
to about 17 percent of the population in the 25–64
age group.

Participation in continuing education is very clearly

a function of the level of basic education: the higher it is, the higher the participation rate in continuing education. One third of the population with a university degree is active in continuing education, whereas the participation rate is only about one-tenth for persons without postcompulsory basic education.

4. Administrative and Supervisory Structure and Operation

As already mentioned, responsibility for education lies essentially with the cantons (for instance, they take decisions on the structure of the system, the curriculum, and the time spent on the various subjects at the various grade levels). Each canton has its own school law and its own system of education. Cantonal governments all have a department of education. In a number of cantons, the government is assisted by an elected consultative body in educational matters (*Erziehungsrat*). The next level of the supervisory structure in many cantons, but not in all, is the district (*Bezirksschulrat*). Local decisions are taken by the local educational authority (*Schulpflege* or *commission scolaire*), a body elected and formed by members of the communal population, in which the local teacher representatives have a consultative voice. Each teacher is supervised by an inspector. In some cantons, these are part-time fellow teachers or lay persons and in other cantons full-time staff of the department of education. As a result of this decentralized multilevel structure, the link between the population and its educational system is very close. On the other hand, since all important decisions are voted on by the population, changes in the system of education are normally very slow.

An educational system characterized by decentralization and by cantonal authority calls for harmonization and coordination. This is the main task of the Swiss Conference of Cantonal Directors of Education (SCCDE), which was founded in 1897, but which has significantly extended its activities since about 1970. Its main constituent bodies are the Concordat on School Coordination (dating from 1970), a number of commissions, and a few institutions. The Concordat stipulates the compulsory school-entrance age (6 years), the duration of compulsory schooling (at least 9 years), and the beginning of the school year. This last point has been widely discussed and put to the vote in a number of cantons (in some of them several times) over a period of more than 10 years. Since the cantons were unable to solve this organizational problem on their own, a popular initiative had finally to be voted on at federal level: by decision of the Swiss population, the school year in all cantons now starts between August and October.

More importantly the provisions of the Concordat aim at common principles for the programs, common

textbooks and manuals, and so on. Among the different coordinating bodies of the Conference, the Pedagogical Commission, founded in 1972 and responsible for compulsory school affairs, is probably the most important. Its activity is characterized by a close link between coordination and pedagogical reform.

The SCCDE has a permanent secretariat, and also four regional conferences with regional secretaries: French- and Italian-speaking Switzerland, northwestern, central, and eastern Switzerland (all three of them German speaking). These regions are culturally more homogeneous than the country as a whole and play an important role as an intermediate structure between the national level and the cantons. However, final decisions in most matters are taken by the cantons.

The SCCDE runs several national institutions: the Swiss Educational Documentation Center in Geneva, the Swiss Coordination Center for Research in Education in Aarau, and the Swiss Center for In-service Education of Secondary School Teachers in Lucerne. The first two are institutions common to the conference and the federal government; in this they are an expression of what is called cooperative federalism in education. The same is true for the Swiss University Council (*Schweizerische Hochschulkonferenz*), an intercantonal and federal planning and coordination body for university education. On the other hand, the federal government is assisted in scientific and educational affairs (as far as federal competence goes) by the Swiss Science Council, a consultative body.

5. Educational Finance

Of the total public expenditure for education and research for the year 1989, 53.2 percent of the funds went to compulsory education, 14.5 percent to vocational schools, 12.5 percent to upper-secondary education (other than vocational), 17.7 percent to universities and federal institutes of technology and research, and 2.1 percent to other educational matters. The classification by sources of funding, on the other hand, shows that 12 percent of total public expenditures for education and research were from the confederation, 53.8 percent from the cantons, and 34.2 percent from the communes.

Overall spending on education and research in 1989 was 14,560 million Swiss francs, corresponding to 18.6 percent of total public expenditure, making education the recipient of the highest percentage of public spending. Public expenditure on education as a percentage of gross domestic product was about 5 percent.

The financing of universities was originally completely a cantonal matter. The cantons were unable, however, to meet the increase in expenditure resulting from the fast-growing number of students after 1960.

In 1968, the federal law of subsidy to the cantonal universities (*Hochschulförderungsgesetz*) was implemented. When the Confederation's financial budget began to meet difficulties in the 1970s, the number of financial resources for the universities had to be enlarged again. Since students from all cantons are enrolled in the eight cantonal universities, the university cantons asked the nonuniversity cantons to contribute to the financing of the universities. In 1981 for the first time, the nonuniversity cantons paid a per capita contribution for each of their students to the university cantons.

Figure 3 shows the approximate public expenditure per pupil/student by educational levels. In 1988, public expenditure per pupil in compulsory schooling varied in the different cantons between 6,739 and 14,421 Swiss francs; 11 cantons spent less than 8,000, 10 cantons between 8,000 and 10,000, and 5 cantons more than 10,000 Swiss francs per pupil.

6. Supplying Personnel for the Education System

Despite the diversity of teacher-training institutions, two main types can be identified. The traditional one is the *Seminar*, starting after compulsory schooling and training teacher candidates in a program of typically four years' duration. There is no strict separation in the curriculum between general education and professional preparation. When, in the late 1960s and early 1970s, the *Seminar* became the object of growing criticism, its training being judged insufficient, two alternative solutions were put forward: (a) maintaining the structure of the *Seminar*, but extending the duration to five or six years, and (b) changing the

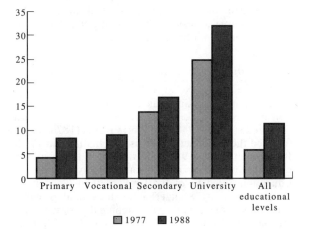

Figure 3
Approximate public expenditure per pupil by educational level (in thousands SF) 1977 and 1988

training to a type which already existed in Basle and Geneva. In this second type, candidates first finish upper-secondary education with a *Matura* certificate, thus consolidating their general education, and then undergo professional training of two years' duration at university or in an extra-university tertiary education institution such as a *Höhere Pädagogische Lehranstalt* (HPL). In the 1970s, there were reforms in a number of cantons, with a clear trend toward the second type, but the extended *Seminar* type nevertheless retained much of its traditional importance. For at least some time to come, the two types will probably coexist. The teachers trained in the above-mentioned institutions are certified for teaching in primary and, in some cases, lower-secondary education.

Teachers for upper-secondary education obtain their qualification on completion of full academic studies in the field in which they are going to teach. There is an almost general agreement that the professional aspect of their training (courses in pedagogy) should be strengthened. In the part-time vocational schools for apprentices there are different teachers for general education and for vocational specialization. Whereas the latter are normally master artisans with little teacher training, the former are now trained in the Swiss Institute for Vocational Education (*Schweizerisches Institut für Berufspädagogik*), created by the Confederation at the beginning of the 1970s. For all categories of teachers, further training is considered very important; it is partly voluntary and partly compulsory, partly organized by the educational authorities and partly by teacher associations on a cantonal, regional, or sometimes national, level. A few cantons have also created full-time further-training institutes to which teachers can return after a certain number of years of practical work. Such courses normally last six months, during which teachers receive their full salary.

Most teacher-training reforms are heavily influenced by the report "Teacher Training of Tomorrow" (*Lehrerbildung von morgen*), commissioned by the Swiss Conference of Cantonal Directors of Education and published in 1975. Its recommendations include detailed proposals for structure, curriculum, didactic principles, supervision at the beginning of professional activity, and further training. This basic study in teacher training has been completed by official national reports on teacher training for lower-secondary

Table 1
Estimate of teaching staff 1987–88

	Primary	Lower secondary
Total	27,000	19,000
Women	16,000	6,000
Men	11,000	13,000

education (1983), upper-secondary education (1989), and further teacher training (1991).

In 1990–91, 8,100 teacher students were trained in over 50 institutions at the upper-secondary level, and 3,900 were trained in around 120 institutions at the extra-university tertiary education level; the first figure has decreased (from 9,900), the second figure has increased (from 3,100) over the last ten years, thus confirming the trend toward tertiary level teacher training.

Teacher statistics at the national level still do not exist. Table 1 shows an estimate of total teaching staff for compulsory schooling; in primary education there are more women than men, whereas the opposite is true for lower-secondary education.

Compared with other countries, teacher salaries in Switzerland are among the highest: for the early 1990s, the average salary of a primary teacher having reached the top of his or her salary scale has been estimated at US$57,900. However, there is considerable variation between the different cantons.

Teacher assessment other than by the traditional inspectorate has become an issue in the early 1990s. Some cantons are likely to introduce salary effective assessment systems, one model being based on external evaluation, and the other more on self-evaluation.

7. Curriculum Development and Teaching Methodology

As with most functions of the educational system, curriculum development is a cantonal matter. Basically, each canton has its own curricula for compulsory schooling. In the 1970s and 1980s, almost all cantons revised their curricula. The development process normally involves a considerable number of cantonal commissions and working parties (overall, by level, and by subject matter) including relevant teacher participation. Two of the four educational regions have founded regional research and development institutions, the *Institut romand de recherches et de documentation pédagogiques (IRDP)* for French- and Italian-speaking Switzerland and the *Zentralschweizerischer Beratungsdienst für Schulfragen (ZBS)* for central Switzerland. Among other tasks, these institutes are in charge of developing common curricula for all of the cantons in their region. At the national level—but this only holds for mathematics and foreign language teaching—there is some curriculum coordination by general recommendations and so-called "meeting points" (setting subject standards which should be met at given levels of compulsory schooling).

At the level of upper-secondary education, there are centrally developed curricula for vocational training and, for the first time in the history of Swiss education, national curricula recommendations for *Maturitätsschulen*, published in 1992 (*Rahmenlehrpläne für Maturitätsschulen*).

In teaching methodology and instruction materials, the individual teacher usually has considerable freedom. In addition to a few compulsory textbooks (regulation varies from canton to canton), he or she can normally choose among a wide range of optional learning materials. There are many reform and development projects in the field of teaching methodology, with a general trend toward more group work and individualized learning (e.g., the important regional project "Enlarged learning forms" or *Erweiterte Lernformen* of the early 1990s in north-western Switzerland).

8. The System of Examinations, Promotions, and Certifications

One of the characteristics of the Swiss educational system underlined by the OECD (1991) in its review of the Swiss national policy for education is its selectivity. The first important and often decisive point of selection is the transition from primary to lower-secondary education. The decision whether a pupil will attend either the basic or extended lower-secondary education is normally taken (in varying ways in the different cantons) on the basis of school performance during the last year of primary education and/or a special examination and/or teachers' advice and/or parents' opinion, the latter two factors becoming more and more important. As far as promotion from one grade to the other is concerned, one out of six pupils misses promotion to the next grade at least once in the course of compulsory schooling; this means that he or she has to repeat that grade.

Normally there is no special examination and therefore no special certificate at the end of compulsory education, but at the end of upper secondary education there is one. Apprenticeship ends with a final examination (the same all over the country) and a certificate. *Maturitätsschulen* also end with a final examination according to national regulations; the *Matura* certificate gives free access (without additional admission examination) to all Swiss universities.

9. Educational Assessment, Evaluation, and Research

Research in education has a relatively long tradition in French-speaking Switzerland, where Edouard Claparède (1873–1940) and Pierre Bovet (1878–1965) founded the Jean-Jacques Rousseau Institute in 1912. Jean Piaget (1896–1980) also worked in this institute, which has now become the Faculty of Psychology and Education Sciences of the University of Geneva. In German-speaking Switzerland, educational research was almost exclusively philosophically based until the Second World War. Experimental and empirical research in education started with research institutes being founded in the late 1960s and the early 1970s (see Fig. 4). Three main types of institutions can be distinguished: (a) university institutes, mostly in

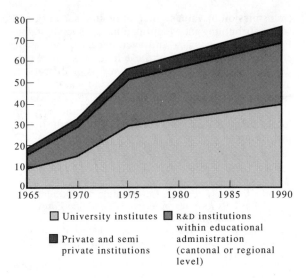

□ University institutes ■ R&D institutions
within educational
■ Private and semi administration
private institutions (cantonal or regional
level)

Figure 4
Quantitive evolution of R & D institutions in education 1965–90

the fields of education, psychology, or sociology; (b) institutions within the framework of educational administration at the cantonal or regional level (most of them with an emphasis on development activities); and (c) private and semipublic institutions. The importance of research in education was officially underlined by the Swiss Science Council on several occasions. In its 1973 report on urgent research needs, research in education was among the few disciplines to be given top priority.

The establishment, in 1971, of the Swiss Coordination Centre for Research in Education was a result of an initiative of the Science Council. This center, whose main task consists of promoting research and coordination between research, teaching practice, administration, and politics, publishes information on research and development projects. These continuing surveys show that research, on the whole, is still fairly scattered and dispersed, that small projects dominate, and that only a few institutions are able to work with effect and continuity.

There were and are three large nationwide projects. *Education et vie active* (Education and Active Life 1979–85) was a national research program, financed by the Swiss National Science Foundation. The program had three parts: (a) personality development and vocational training in the work situation, (b) organizational problems in vocational training institutions and the organization of teaching and learning processes, and (c) transition problems in careers and the life cycle. *Überprüfung der Situation der Primarschule* (General Review of the Situation of Primary Education, 1978–86) had four parts: (a) goals of primary education—claims and

reality, (b) functions and forms of pupil evaluation, (c) transition from preschool to primary education, and (d) cooperation between schools and parents. The National Research Program "The Efficiency of our Education and Training Systems," 1991–97, again financed by the Swiss National Science Foundation, aims at increasing the self-evaluation and innovation capacity of educational subsystems and institutions.

The increasing vitality of research in education in Switzerland and a growing consciousness of its importance are also demonstrated by the foundation, in 1975, of the Swiss Society for Research in Education (SSRE). The society publishes a scientific review called *Bildungsforschung und Bildungspraxis/Education et Recherche* (Research and Practice in Education), and in 1988, it presented a "Development Plan for Educational Research in Switzerland."

Since the end of the 1980s, Switzerland has also been participating in the international projects of the International Association for the Evaluation of Educational Achievement (IEA). In 1992, a National Coordination Conference for Educational Research Policy, involving the most important federal and cantonal authorities in this field, was founded.

10. Major Reforms in the 1980s and 1990s

The major reforms in the 1980s and 1990s were:

(a) earlier start of second language learning (fourth or fifth grade of primary education);

(b) curricula revision in mathematics as well as most other subjects of compulsory education;

(c) introduction of the computer into lower- and upper-secondary (and sometimes primary) education;

(d) measures aiming at closing the gap between general and vocational education at the upper-secondary level (introduction of a vocational *Matura* certificate);

(e) revision of the *Matura* examination regulations;

(f) restructuring of the extra-university tertiary level of education (*Fachhochschulen*);

(g) ongoing reform of basic and further teacher training.

11. Major Problems for the Year 2000

Any prognosis of future problems is partially subjective, the appraisal of the future depending, among other things, on value judgments which differ from political party to political party. Nonetheless, some of the major problems which may have to be faced by the Swiss educational system around the year 2000 are given below.

As in many other countries, Switzerland, in the first half of the 1990s, is suffering from financial restrictions in public expenditure, not excluding education. This might have an impact on the quality of education (i.e., teacher–student ratio, failure to create necessary new chairs at university level, postponement of planned reforms, etc.). Depending upon the economic development in the second half of the 1990s, relative lack of public financial resources for education might still be a major problem around the year 2000.

Given the fact that the Swiss system of education has a federal structure, one of its permanent problems—and this will be the same around the year 2000—is the search for the degree of coordination and harmonization at national level judged necessary even in a decentralized structure. With a more strongly integrated Europe—irrespective of whether Switzerland will be a member of the EC or not—and other factors, the trend seems to be toward strengthening coordination and harmonization and thereby also strengthening the national aspects of educational policy. To state it simply, the question is: will Switzerland—in spite of its federal structure—have a national policy of education or not?

Some limited progress has been made toward the equalization of educational opportunity. Nevertheless, socioeconomic origin, gender, and regional origin still play an important role in a school career. Thus, measures which favor equal educational opportunity will still be a major problem in the year 2000.

If one accepts the hypothesis that, on the one hand, the growing complexity of life calls for even more education in the future, and that, on the other hand, duration of initial formal education should not be further prolonged (the discrepancy between the biological and socioeconomic status of many young people being most probably one of the roots of youth unrest), then the challenge arises to provide more education without prolonging initial education. The solution to this problem may be sought among the principles of lifelong and recurrent education. This would require structural changes in tertiary and upper-secondary education and have an impact on the whole system of education. It could at the same time provide for an extension of adult education and its gradual integration into the system. Given the participation structure in further education, it will be difficult not to widen the gap between the relatively well-educated and the relatively poorly educated parts of the population.

Other structural reforms will probably focus on lower-secondary education in an attempt to reduce the qualitative differences between schools with basic and schools with extended requirements. Reforms of teacher training for this level of education will have to be introduced, along with structural reforms.

It may be assumed that education has the following fundamental functions: (a) development of the personality (in a broad sense); (b) qualification (in a restricted economic sense); (c) socialization (transmission of values, integration into society); and (d) distribution and legitimation of social status. For the coming years, and even decades, increasing conflicts between some of these functions can be predicted (personality development versus qualifications asked for by the economy, or social-status aspirations versus qualifications needed by the economy). Therefore, the search for an equilibrium between these functions is likely to be a problem in the near future.

References

Organisation for Economic Co-operation and Development (OECD) 1991 *Reviews of National Policies for Education: Switzerland.* OECD, Paris

Schweizerische Konferenz der kantonalen Erziehungs-direktoren (EDK) 1975 *Lehrerbildung von morgen.* EDK, Bern

Schweizerische Konferenz der kantonalen Erziehungs-direktoren (EDK) 1992 *Rahmenlehrpläne für die Maturitätsschulen.* EDK, Bern

Schweizerischer Nationalfonds zur Förderung der wissenschaftlichen Forschung (SNF) 1991 *Die Wirksamkeit unserer Bildungssysteme angesichts der demographischen und technologischen Entwicklung und angesichts der Probleme in der mehrsprachigen Schweiz.* Ausführungsplan zum Nationalen Forschungsprogramm 33, SNF, Bern

Swiss Co-ordination Centre for Research in Education *Permanent Inquiry into Educational Research.* Swiss Co-ordination Centre for Research in Education, Aarau

Further Reading

Bundesamt für Statistik (BFS) 1990 *Der Weiterbildungs-bereich—Entwicklung, Strukturen, Forschungsstand.* BFS, Bern

Bundesamt für Statistik (BFS), Schweizerische Konferenz der kantonalen Erziehungsdirektoren (EDK) 1993 *Bildungs-indikatoren Schweiz.* BFS, EDK, Bern

Federal Statistical Office, Federal Administration of Finances, CESDOC 1991 *The Swiss Educational Mosaic—A Study in Diversity.* Swiss Federal Statistical Office, Bern

Schweizerische Gesellschaft für Bildungsforschung (SGBF/SSRE) 1988 *Entwicklungsplan der schweizerischen Bildungsforschung. Sondernummer von Bildungsforschung und Bildungspraxis.* Schweizerische Koordinationsstelle für Bildungsforschung, Aarau

Schweizerische Konferenz der kantonalen Erziehungs-direktoren (EDK) 1983 *Die Ausbildung der Lehrer für die Sekundarstufe I.* EDK, Bern

Schweizerische Konferenz der kantonalen Erziehungs-direktoren (EDK) 1986 *Primarschule Schweiz. 22 Thesen zur Entwicklung der Primarschule.* EDK, Bern

Schweizerische Konferenz der kantonalen Erziehungs-direktoren (EDK) *Bildung in der Schweiz von morgen.* Literaturanalyse 1988, Expertenbefragung 1989, Schlussbericht 1990. EDK, Bern

Schweizerische Konferenz der kantonalen Erziehungs-direktoren (EDK) 1992 *Reform des Fremd-sprachenunterrichts in der obligatorischen Schule.* EDK, Bern

Syria

A. Gennaoui

1. General Background

Historically, "Syria" was the name of the fertile strip between the eastern Mediterranean coast and the desert of northern Arabia, covering almost all the present northern Arabic countries of the Middle East except for Iraq. In 1992, Syria is a relatively small country on the eastern side of the Mediterranean sea.

The geographical shape of the state was determined at the beginning of the French mandate in 1920. Syria is bordered by Turkey on the north, Iraq on the east, Jordan and Israel on the south, and Lebanon and the Mediterranean Sea on the west. Its total area is 185,180 square kilometers, of which eight million hectares are arable.

The principal result of the First World War for the Middle East was the termination of the Ottoman occupation of Syria which had lasted for four centuries (1516–1918), and the setting up of a Hashemite kingdom under King Faisal I. This lasted until July 1920, when Syria and Lebanon were occupied and controlled by France under a League of Nations mandate. The French forces left Syria in April 1946 and Independence was declared.

Between 1945 and 1958, a representative regime was installed; but it was frequently interrupted by military coup d'états. A political union with Egypt, under the name of the United Arab Republic, was declared in 1958; but this was terminated in September 1961. Since then, the country has been known as the Syrian Arab Republic. The regime installed by the military forces in 1961 was abolished by a second military coup in March 1963. Since 1963, the Baath Socialist Party has been in power.

The present constitution of Syria was approved and promulgated in 1973. It defines the Syrian Arab Republic as a democratic sovereign, and socialist state. The political regime can be viewed as a mixture of a presidential and a representative regime. It gives the president, the chief executive, the predominant share of power. The president, who is elected for a seven-year term, chooses the vice president, the prime minister, and the cabinet ministers. The legislative function is vested in the People's Assembly, which has grown to 250 members. The number of parties allowed to operate in Syria is limited. They recognize the leadership of the Baath Party and run under its umbrella. These parties are represented through the ruling National Progressive Front and the government.

The Front obtained two-thirds of the seats in the parliamentary election held in May 1990. Independents, of whom 21 are women, received the other third of the seats.

Arabic is the mother tongue of more than 80 percent of the Syrian population: estimated to be 12,116,000 in the middle of 1990. Arabic is also the official language and is spoken by all of the population. The other spoken languages are: Kurdish, Armenian, Turkish, Circassian, Syriac, and Hebrew. English and French are the main foreign languages taught in the schools.

The population is concentrated mainly along the coast and in the plain region parallel to the coast, with probably equal settlement in 1990 in rural and urban areas. The highest density of population is in western and southern regions. The overall density is relatively low: 66 inhabitants per square kilometer. The low density is due to two main factors: (a) an important part of the territory is desert; and (b) the country's historical background of being susceptible to invasion—an unfavorable condition for the settlement of people. The demographic growth, which is one of the highest rates in the world, increased from 3.28 percent per annum between 1960 and 1970 to 3.35 percent per annum between 1970 and 1981. It has remained at this high level. Thus, the age structure of the Syrian population is very young with more than 49 percent of the people below the age of 15.

The main demographic factors influencing education and development are:

(a) a high population growth rate;

(b) an increasing proportion of children below the age of 15 among the total population;

(c) an unequal distribution of population growth throughout the country: the rural—urban migration is declining but is still significant. (Urban areas are still growing at a higher rate than rural ones (3.9 vs. 2.9) due essentially to the migration from rural to urban areas.)

Historically, Syria's economy has been agriculturally based. However, industrialization campaigns since the early 1960s have built a good-sized industrial base. The Syrian economy showed slight changes in terms of the structure and distribution of employment in the 1980s.

Employment in agriculture accounted for about one-third of the labor force (16% of GDP in 1980). At the end of 1980s, it dropped to about one-fourth of the GDP, and remained approximately the same in 1990. Similarly, the industrial sector, which accounted for 28 percent of the labor force and 37 percent of the GDP in the early 1980s, showed little variation (one-third for employment) at the beginning of the 1990s due to stagnation in the economic situation during this period. In fact, the main changes in the structure and the distribution of employment were achieved in the 1970s.

Some 44 percent of the Syrian population is of working age; 15- to 59-years old. Only one-fourth of the total population comprised the labor force in 1990, of which 6 percent were unemployed. Female participation in the labor force was 16 percent. The dependence ratio is high as a result of the youthful concentration of the age structure and low female participation in the labor force. For the country as a whole, there are four dependents for each active person. Consequently, the rapid economic development is difficult to achieve, particularly when a significant level of investment is oriented to satisfy the basic social needs of the population (i.e., education, health).

On the other hand, the labor market shows sectoral imbalance between supply and demand (shortage, excess) in several jobs and specialties in the labor force.

Syria was the site of many great cultural centers in ancient times, with famous names like Ugarit, Mari, Elba, Palmira, Damascus, and Aleppo. The earliest known alphabet, dating back to the fourteenth century BC, was discovered in Ugarit.

During the Ottoman occupation (1516–1918), the schools' objective was to teach the Koran; the principles of religion; and the rudiments of reading, writing, and arithmetic. *Sharia* and language were taught to adults. Through contact with the West, the introduction of some educational reforms led gradually to the foundation of Ottoman state schools in the 1850s which prepared students to serve the ruling authorities. Education was extended outside the control of the Ottoman authorities by foreign mission schools and Christian communities with the protection of foreign powers. Only some of them taught Arabic. Thus, the model of the modern schools in terms of their content, methods, and materials appeared as both a revolutionary innovation and a rupture.

Syria had more state schools than other Arab provinces, but Ottoman expenditure on Syrian education was very limited. Most people remained illiterate. Education was restricted to the sons of famous people and civil servants, and Turkish was the medium of instruction.

The Arab State under King Faisal (1918–20) had a beneficial impact on education by initiating some important and symbolic educational projects. It made Arabic the instructional language; founded new schools based on the Occidental models; and established the Academy of Arabic, the Arab Scientific Society, the School of Law, and the Institute of Medicine.

The constitution of 1928, initiated under the French Mandate (1920–46), provided that:

(a) Education should be free and the primary level should be compulsory.

(b) Arabic should be the official language in the public sector.

(c) Technical education should be imposed as compulsory in order to meet the country's needs for technical personnel.

Only some of the above reforms were implemented before the mandate ended. The French authorities managed education according to their objectives. In 1945, only 5 percent of the state budget was allocated to education and the schools were located mainly in towns.

Soon after Independence, many decisions were taken, such as the opening of the Higher Teachers' College in 1946, the establishment of the National Cultural Committee for the Organization of Education, the Law on Vocational Training, the regulation for primary education in 1948, the standardization of textbooks in 1949, and so on. In 1947, the budget of the Ministry of Education rose to 16 percent of the state budget and the number of students increased by about 40 percent from the 1946 level. During the Period of Unity with Egypt (1958–61) the conversion from a five- to six-year primary school, with automatic promotion from grade to grade, was introduced. An attempt to unify primary and secondary schools curricula between the two countries was also undertaken.

2. Politics and the Goals of the Education System

Education was strongly supported by the government in the 1960s, particularly when the Baath Party came to power. However, the policy and the content of education were, to some extent, influenced by its principles and ideology.

The established educational and curriculum goals are stated in several articles in the 1973 Constitution:

> The educational and cultural system shall aim to bring up a national Arab generation who are socialist and scientific in their manner of thinking, attached to their land and history, proud of their heritage . . . The national socialist culture shall be the basis of building up the unified Arab society. It shall aim at enhancing moral values, realizing the ideals of the Arab Nation . . . Science, scientific research and all scientific achievements constitute a mean for the progress of Arab socialist society. The state shall give it full support. Education shall be a right guaranteed by the state. It shall be free at all stages and compulsory in the primary steps. The state shall endeavor to make other stages compulsory, shall supervize education, and direct it in a manner ensuring its adaptation to the needs of society and production.

These objectives can be best interpeted by taking them out of their general framework and making them the basis for the curriculum strategies.

3. The Formal System of Education

Figure 1 presents the formal system of education.

3.1 Primary, Secondary, and Tertiary Education

The education system of Syria consists of 1–3 years of preprimary education, 6 years of primary education, 3 years of lower-secondary and intermediate education, and 3 years of secondary education. Postsecondary education may be undertaken at a university, higher institute of technology, or an intermediate institute.

In 1990, school enrollment was close to 100 percent for boys and 95 percent for girls at the primary level. Before 1981, primary education was free but not compulsory. To achieve compulsory education, a large campaign was mounted to encourage parents to enroll all children of primary school age. Special measures were taken to enroll children between 10 and 12 years of age. A new Department for Compulsory Education was created in the Ministry for monitoring and evaluating school attendance. Despite this, some differences still exist among geographic regions and between the sexes. However, three Governorates (Deir Elzhor, Hama, and Rakkha) have an enrollment rate between 95 and 98 percent. The factors impeding complete enrollment are: nomadism, poverty, lack of facilities in some remote areas with small populations, and lack of coordination between official parties involved in the compulsory law.

The primary course lasts six years and children begin at the age of six. The primary school day normally

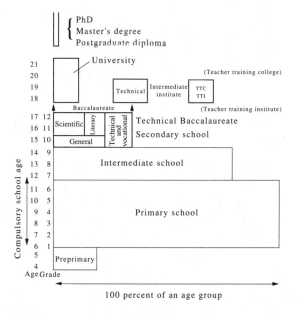

Figure 1
Syria: Structure of the formal education system

lasts for about 5 hours and the school year for around 200 days. Most schools are run by the government, but a small proportion (less than 3%) are private. UNRWA provides 2 percent. Both the private sector and UNRWA use the curriculum of the Ministry of Education (MOE). All pupils who have successfully completed the primary level can enter intermediate schools. Before 1970, there was an entrance examination for Grade 7 but this has been abolished.

The lower-secondary (or intermediate) level lasts 3 years and is free but not compulsory. The curriculum includes all the subjects taught at primary level, with the addition of English, French, and "female education." At the end of Grade 9, there is a examination for the Intermediate Level Diploma. In 1990, the enrollment rate in Grade 7 was close to 80 percent. The total enrollment in intermediate level was 631,000 pupils. Most schools are run by the government, but a small proportion (less than 4%) are private and 2 percent are provided by UNRWA. Both the private sector and UNRWA use the curriculum of the MOE. Since 1970, successive educational plans have included objectives to merge primary and intermediate levels (Grades 1 to 9) into a basic cycle and to extend compulsory education to cover it. This aim had not been achieved by 1992, but it can be achieved if the financial situation of the state improves. The upper-secondary level also lasts 3 years and is free of charge. It includes Grades 10 to 12. There are two types of upper-secondary schooling: general and technical. Entry is selective and based on the Intermediate Diploma examination at the end of Grade 9. Pupils who are 15-years old are free to choose either general or technical schools, but those beyond this age must enter technical schools. The total enrollment in secondary education in 1989–90 was 273,000.

The general school continues to be the most popular, accounting for 78 percent of the total secondary enrollment in 1990. The first year of the general program is an introductory one, after which pupils enter one of two streams: scientific or literary. About three-fourths of pupils opt for the scientific stream. Upon completion of the course, pupils sit for the Secondary Diploma (or baccalaureate). This diploma is the sole qualification to grant automatic entrance to higher education institutions. About 90 percent of general secondary schools are provided by the government and 10 percent are private.

Technical and vocational schools cover industrial, commercial, and agricultural specializations, as well as the "female" specializations of home economics and nursing. Their respective percentages within technical education in 1989–90 were 51, 22, 7, and 20. Technical secondary schools are run by the MOE, except for agriculture schools which are run by the Ministry of Agriculture. The 76 industrial schools give instruction in 10 engineering trades.

On the other hand, intermediate industrial and banking institutes also provide instruction in 17 engineering specializations. Timetables consist of 18 hours of instruction per week and 20 hours of practical training. Pupils who fail their practical examinations must repeat the grade. At the end of the course, students take the technical baccalaureate, but holders have only limited opportunities for further education. The top students proceed to university. The remainder can enroll in intermediate institutes belonging to the Ministry of Higher Education. The other specialization streams (agricultural and female education) do not lead to the baccalaureate examination.

Religious education is run by the *Awkaf* Ministry and provides a six-year course parallel to the intermediate and secondary cycles in the secular system. The number of pupils in religious schools is less than 1 percent of those in the secular schools. Curricula are substantially different from those drawn up by the MOE.

Higher education is comprised of universities, higher, and intermediate institutes. There are four universities (Damascus, Aleppo, Lattaquieh, and Homs), one Higher Institute for Political Science, one Higher Institute of Administrative Science, and 47 intermediate institutes with total enrollments of 138,700 and 44,200 for universities and institutes respectively in 1986. The growth of attendance has been very rapid since the early 1960s. The expansion has stabilized in the early 1990s. The University of Damascus is the oldest and largest university, having 15 faculties. Aleppo, Lattaquieh, and Homs universities now have 9, 7, and 6 faculties respectively. A significant proportion of university students study abroad. Some of them have scholarships, but the majority are studying at their own expense. The other type of higher education is the two-year postsecondary intermediate institute which provides training at technician level. These institutes are administered by technical ministries: Agriculture, Industry, Natural Resources, Public Works, and so forth. The Secondary Diploma is required for entry, and most courses last two years. Entry to those institutes controlled by the Ministry of Higher Education is limited to graduates of the general secondary schools. Those controlled by the Ministry of Education and other technical ministries are open to graduates of the technical and vocational secondary schools. The government hopes to accommodate an increasing percentage (almost 50) of technical–vocational secondary school graduates in this type of higher education.

The Law of Absorption, promulgated in 1973, gives the right to any student who passes the general secondary diploma to enter the university. However, in practice there is a *numerus clausus*. Only the previous year's secondary school graduates are admitted, and applicants are accepted according to their grades within the quotas specified for each subject by the Council of Higher Education. In general, holders of the technical secondary schools cannot apply for admission to university. The faculties of Medicine and Engineering require very high marks from their prospective students.

University education is free as long as the student passes his or her final examinations. Degree courses last between four and six years. At the graduate level, a diploma takes one year, a master's degree a further year after the diploma, and the PhD a further two years after the master's. However, few opportunities exist to study for a doctorate in Syria.

The medium of instruction in Syrian universities is Arabic. However, English is used as a medium of instruction in some subjects at both undergraduate and graduate level.

3.2 Preschool Education

Preprimary education is optional and is run on a fee-paying basis. It lasts 3 years (from age 3 to 5 years). However, it is provided on a limited scale and proposals for increased provision are being considered. Some classes are attached to public primary schools; others are run by private groups (for more than 60% of children) or by the General Union of Syrian Arab Women or by the Teacher's Union. In 1989–90, there were 84,800 children (about 5% of an age group) enrolled in preprimary, and 793 kindergardens and 2,711 teachers. Preprimary education was relatively neglected in the 1960s and 1970s. The state now supports the extension of this education due to the increasing percentage of working women. The 1928 Constitution included compulsory education as an aim for the primary level—it took more than half a century to achieve it.

3.3 Special Education

Reliable information concerning disabled persons is not available. Syria has started to include disability statistics in its population census. Pupils with mild difficulties attend ordinary schools. Their needs are generally unidentified and they tend to drop out at the primary level.

The notion of special education as a part of the educational system is unknown in Syria. Opinion is divided in the educational community between regular and special education. The Ministry of Social Affairs and Labor administers 20 centers for the social care of the deaf, dumb, and blind providing "special programs and services" for almost 2,500 disabled students. This represents less than 0.7 per 1,000 of the pre-university student population.

3.4 Vocational, Technical, and Business Education

The technical and vocational secondary school system, as well as the intermediate industrial schools, were dealt with in section 3.1 above. A great deal of trade training is undertaken under the umbrella of adult and nonformal education (see section 3.5 below).

3.5 Adult and Nonformal Education

There are two types of nonformal education. The first is literacy education, while the second covers a wide range of vocational and cultural activities.

In 1990, the literacy rate was estimated to be 70 percent. In 1972 and 1978, two literacy campaigns were undertaken under the supervision of the Higher Council for Literacy. The Ministry of Culture is in charge of coordinating all programs and administering literacy classes. Each Governorate also has its own regional literacy committee. The literacy curriculum comprises two parts: basic training lasting six months (360 hours) and a second three months devoted to integrated training. Other technical ministries and agencies involved in literacy training and functional projects are: the ministries of Social Affairs and Labor, Agriculture, and Industry; the General Federation of Women's Trade Unions; farmers; and students. The last campaign, which began in 1978, succeeded in eradicating the illiteracy of 434,511 persons by 1989.

The Ministry of Culture runs adult education centers and institutes of popular culture. These centers offer a number of part-time vocational courses (knitting, sewing, housekeeping, arts, music) throughout the day, for people who have completed primary schooling and are over 15 years of age. At the same time, the Ministry of Social Affairs provides craft centers which provide classes in the traditional skills of carpet weaving and rug making.

The Ministry of Social Affairs provides, through its community development centers, courses and activities such as home economics, nursing education, veterinary medicine, and film shows. The Ministry of Agriculture provides long- and short-term training courses for literate farmers above 16 years of age. Since 1975, farmer training has been the responsibility of the General Union of Peasants. This paragovernmental organization has training centers in each Governorate. These centers run courses in cooperative management every year.

The Ministry of Industry is in charge of several vocational training courses for literate adults. These include accelerated training for basic-entry-level job skills, long-term industrial apprenticeship courses preparing skilled workers of 15 to 18 years of age for public industries, a specialized training program for new skills, and on-the-job training to meet the needs of the public sector. There are two types of programs offered in factory schools or training centers respectively. These courses are open only to the employees of public enterprises who are preparatory school graduates. Training centers offer more general training in subjects like electronics, electricity, textiles, drafting, and so on. The Ministry of Public Works also operates several centers for accelerated training in the building and construction trades. Some other international nongovernmental agencies or organizations undertake nonformal education activities but they operate generally through national authorities. Almost all these activities and centers are financed by the central budget, but detailed statistics about them are not available.

4. Administrative and Supervisory Structure and Operation

Educational administration (and the overall administrative system) in Syria is very centralized. There are two levels in the administration of education: the central level and the local level. Education in Syria is primarily the responsibility of the central government. However, organizational changes instituting local administration took place in the 1970s and 1980s. The main philosophy of the reform is the centralization of conception and planning and the decentralization of implementation. The directorates of education in the Governorates create primary and secondary schools and decide on their location, as well as deciding pedagogical orientation within the region. They appoint teachers, distribute teaching materials, organize training programs, and manage primary schooling.

There are two ministries which are exclusively concerned with education: the Ministry of Education and the Ministry of Higher Education. However, other ministries are in charge of some vocational or technical education. UNRWA and the private sector have a limited role in this field. (More than 95% of enrollments are in the public sector.)

The Ministry of Education controls all preuniversity education (except for agricultural secondary schools which are under the Ministry of Agriculture) as well as some of the intermediate institutes training teachers for primary, intermediate, or technical schools, and for all levels in some specializations (music, handicrafts, physical education). The ministries define policy guidelines, carry out the major programs, and allocate resources to main subsectors and Governorates. The MOE designs teaching programs and textbooks. Implementation of programs, which are the same for the whole country, is maintained through inspectorates. The Ministry, through its Establishment for Schools Books, prints and distributes textbooks for all schools (these are free at the primary level only).

The Ministry of Higher Education controls and coordinates the four universities, the Higher Institute of Political Science, the Higher Institute of Administrative Sciences, and the other intermediate institutes. Coordination among these institutions is maintained through the Council of Higher Education which is the major executive body in higher education and is presided over by the Minister. This Council is also responsible for planning, policy guidelines, academic programs, funding, and entrance quotas.

In addition, there are several other ministries involved in different types of education and training (formal or nonformal): these include the ministries of Health, Planning, Information, Industry, and Agriculture—all of which control institutes designed to meet certain specific needs.

Communal and foreign schools were nationalized in 1967. Since then, private schools have been strictly controlled by the MOE, which appoints their principals.

However, due to the financial crisis and the international political evolution at the beginning of the 1990s, the educational authorities are beginning to realize the limits of the expansion of public education. It is therefore possible that a new orientation may appear gradually, granting greater recognition and autonomy to the private sector in the various educational levels. Thus, the private sector will probably be called upon to play a greater role in this field.

5. Educational Finance

It is difficult to compare, in absolute terms, the present budget with the budgets in the 1940s and 1950s since data in constant prices are not available. However, it can be said that the budgets of the 1970s and 1980s had nothing in common with the budget of 1946. In relative terms, the total budget (current and capital expenditure) of education (excluding the third level) between 1975 and 1987, as a percentage of the consolidated government expenditure, increased from 7.8 percent in 1975, to 11.8 percent in 1985, and to 14 percent in 1987. As a percentage of GDP, the evolution was 3.9 percent in 1975, 6.1 percent in 1985, and 4.7 percent in 1987. The percentage of the current education expenditure, in the consolidated government expenditure, was 12.6 percent in 1987, 11.4 percent in 1988, 12.1 percent, in 1989, and 12.7 percent in 1990. The corresponding percentages for higher education were: 2.95 in 1987, 3.2 in 1988, and 3.05 in 1989.

UNESCO figures concerning the evolution of public current and capital expenditure on education at constant prices (base year 1980) gave 96 for 1986 (57 in 1975). After substantial increases in current and capital expenditure on education between 1975 and 1985, the 1990 level is lower than it was in 1980. After 1986, the rate of inflation was generally higher than the annual rate of increase of public expenditure. On the other hand, the per pupil expenditure, expressed in units of GNP per capita, for all levels of education did not vary between 1980 and 1987, and at 0.14, is amongst the lowest in the region. This overall figure masks a decrease in higher education expenditure and a slight increase at the secondary and primary levels.

The 1990 education budget allocation was 81 percent for prehigher education and 19 percent for higher education. For the same year, the prehigher education funds were distributed as follows: 49 percent for primary and preprimary, 27 percent for intermediate and general secondary, 8 percent for technical secondary, 11 percent for school building projects, and 5 percent for others. It should be noted that local administration pays for part of primary school expenditures. The percentage of teaching materials and scholarships dropped from 5.9 and 2.5 percent respectively in 1975 to 2.6 and 0.6 percent in 1987. On the other hand, teachers salaries and emoluments account for more than 90 percent of total current expenditure.

Since other ministries are also involved in education, their expenditures must be added to the figures of the two ministries of education. Consequently, the percentages mentioned above must be considered as a minimum.

6. Supplying Personnel for the Education System

Nearly 145,000 teachers were employed in schools in 1990. About 92,000 teachers were employed in primary and preprimary schools and 51,000 in all types of secondary schools. Some 75 percent of primary school teachers are female.

Until the late 1980s, there were teacher shortages at all levels. Auxiliary teachers and contractual teachers (on temporary or part-time basis) were employed at that time. The implementation of compulsory education (and the extension of preprimary education) has created a continuous demand for teachers in the public sector. The main requirements for this level in the 1980s were met by employing female teachers. Their number increased by a factor of two between 1980 and 1990. The expected expansion of the preprimary level will create a demand for even more teachers. On the other hand, the number of teachers in the intermediate and secondary schools has decreased since 1986–87. In the intermediate schools, the enrollment has been almost static since 1986–87, whereas enrollment has been decreasing since 1988–89 for general education and since 1984–85 for technical education. However, enrollment in the vocational secondary schools has slightly increased since 1989. The pupil–teacher ratio has declined somewhat, but is still high: 31:1 in primary schools, 36:1 in intermediate schools, and 35:1 in secondary schools.

Primary teachers and intermediate school auxiliary teachers are trained in the 20 two-year postsecondary teacher-training colleges and 22 two-year postsecondary auxiliary teacher-training institutes (in those subjects for which there is a shortage of teachers) under the Ministry of Education. Intermediate and secondary school teachers may attend a one-year course at the Faculty of Education of Damascus following their university degree. However, this training is not obligatory. The universities and the intermediate institutes run by the MOE are the main sources of trained instructors and trainers for the technical and vocational secondary schools.

Regular inservice training is not common in Syria. In 1988, 24,097 persons (including administrative and pedagogical staff) were involved in different training courses managed by the training department of the MOE at all levels. Their number dropped to 6,000 in 1989.

7. Curriculum Development and Teaching Methodology

The curriculum is uniform and nationwide. A detailed syllabus is developed by the central authorities. The

Department of Curriculum and Research at the MOE is in charge of the development of courses, learning materials, and teaching methods. Additionally, it is responsible for trying out the learning materials at all preuniversity levels. In primary education, the curriculum includes Arabic, mathematics, religious instruction, elements of science and health education, social and national education, art, music, and physical education. Fewer than 300 primary schools provided four hours a week of rural education in Grades 4, 5, and 6 in 1989. In the intermediate and general secondary schools, the curriculum includes all of the subjects taught at the primary level with the addition of English or French and practical work and female education (rural education for boys). In the technical secondary schools, two-thirds of the curriculum is oriented towards scientific and practical training.

For many years, curriculum was characteristically traditional and theoretical, putting emphasis on the humanities and factual data rather than on scientific concepts, attitudes, skills, and values. The MOE intends to develop curricula by defining successively pedagogical objectives, content, teaching methods, and, finally the practical exercises for the evaluation of pupil achievement. At the end of the 1980s, various attempts at curriculum reform for primary and secondary schools and for teacher-training college were made. These aimed at introducing some practical aspects related to productive work, and nutritional, environmental, and population subjects. These reforms are on-going and no appraisal of how far they have been successful has yet been undertaken.

One experiment introduced foreign language teaching into Grades 5 and 6 in some primary schools. Again, the results of the experiment are not yet known.

The private sector is authorized to add a few hours of foreign language teaching to the official curriculum. In some areas, the directorate of education in the Governorates can decide to make additions to the intermediate school courses in agricultural subjects.

Teaching methods are rather didactic and verbal. Inservice and self-training have not yet developed to any degree in Syria. Some attempts are being made to introduce educational radio and television, especially in general and languages teaching, and cultural programs. An Educational Materials Production Center has been created by the Department of Materials and Equipment in the MOE. The authorities consider it to be a base for Arabic cooperation in the development of teaching materials and intend to promote it as such.

8. The System of Examinations, Promotions, and Certifications

There is automatic promotion based on age in primary education. However, in order to sit for the final grade, the pupils must score a 50 percent in Arabic and an overall average of 50 percent. Grading is left to the discretion of the teacher; there is no standardized national examination. At the end of the intermediate (Grade 9) and the secondary levels, there is a public nationwide examination for the intermediate and secondary diploma. At the end of the technical secondary school, students take the technical secondary diploma. Only the top students have access to the universities. The percentage of grade repeaters in the first and second levels declined from 10 and 16 percent respectively in 1975 to 7 and 13 percent in 1987.

Any student who passes the secondary diploma has the right to enter university, but there is a *numerus clausus* determined by the authorities. The diplomas awarded by universities are: the bachelor's degree, the master of arts or science, and the PhD in some fields such as law and Arabic literature.

University degrees, especially the highest (i.e. the PhD), have traditionally been held in great esteem. The social and economic value of these diplomas has decreased due to the increasing number of graduates coming from Eastern and Western countries and from Egypt.

Examinations in Syria are based on memorization and affirmative modes rather than ways of thinking, attitudes, and skills. The Syrian educational system relies on written or oral formative evaluation, on the one hand, and summative evaluation in the form of final examinations, formal teacher evaluation by inspectors, and comparisons of pupil performance on general examinations for school evaluation on the other. General examinations are still "considered as aims in themselves" and contribute to the rigidity of the curriculum. In fact valuable feedback is rarely provided to those developing curriculum.

9. Educational Assessment, Evaluation, and Research

In general, the main focus of the MOE—as a management structure—is on monitoring resource inputs rather than pupils outcomes. Evaluation and assessment are rarely applied. In practice, evaluation is perceived as a monitoring process and no clear criteria are identified for its implementation. At the preuniversity level, the Department of Planning and Statistics and the Department of Curriculum and Research are in charge of educational research and studies. The first conducts sectoral and diagnostic studies, whereas the second focuses on educational processes. The main studies which have been undertaken (the results of which are supposed to be used by the planning process and decision-making) are: (a) the introduction of environmental, population, and health education into school curriculum; (b) the introduction of basic education into the educational system; (c) the development and implementation of school mapping as a regional planning tool at secondary and university levels; (d) the development of computer data in managing the educational system and in research; (e) creating the conditions for teaching foreign languages at the primary level; (f) monitoring the impact of educational television programs; and,(g) monitoring some aspects of dropout in the educational system. Research at the university level is undertaken by faculties as a part of graduate programs.

10. Major Reforms in the 1980s and 1990s

Population education is being introduced into Syrian secondary schools. As an on-going reform, it consists of revising the curriculum at the secondary level and determining the concepts to be integrated. On the other hand, teaching materials are expected to be produced (teacher guide, reference book in population education). The project was initiated in 1986 and the second phase is expected to be achieved in 1994. Other reforms that have also been proposed include: the establishment of a Research Center for Pedagogical Development; the establishment of vocational courses lasting 1 to 3 years after basic education; the opening of channels or pathways between the technical secondary schools, intermediate institutes, and the related departments in the universities having the same specialization; the establishment of a special department for scientific research in each university with ad hoc financial resources; and, the establishment of basic compulsory education (from Grades 1 to 9).

11. Major Problems for the Year 2000

There are two problems that seem to be outstanding: the extension of compulsory school education to Grade 9 and improvement in the quality of education. The government is conscious of the limits of existing strategy, but the major constraint for the designing and implementation of the two reforms is financial. In fact, the two problems are interdependent. The first problem implies that, with the introduction of basic compulsory education, an in-depth revision of the present curriculum, the reform of teacher preservice and inservice training, and a redistribution of the main resources such as teachers and schools will be necessary. The second implies, among other things, revising the curriculum and pedagogical methods, introducing foreign languages, eliminating the multigrade teacher in the primary schools, and improving inservice teacher training.

In 1987 objectives were formulated to bring about: the orientation of 60 percent of the pupils, after basic education, towards the labor market and 40 percent towards the secondary schools at the beginning of the 1990s; and the orientation of 70 percent of the enrollment in secondary schools towards the technical and vocational secondary schools (60% vocational and 10% technical) and the remainder (30%) towards general secondary in 1995. The two reforms mentioned above should be considered as a means to implement these objectives.

Bibliography

Akrawi M 1967 *Arab Education During Fifty Years*. Amman
Alrabaa S 1985 Sex division of labor in Syrian school textbooks. *IRE* 31: 335–48
Azzam M 1985 Syria: system of education. In: Husén T, Postlethwaite TN (eds.) 1985 *International Encyclopedia of Education*, 1st edn. Pergamon Press, Oxford
British Council 1979 *Syria, Education Profile*. British Council, London
Central Bureau of Statistics 1991 *Syrian Arab Republic: Statistical Abstract 1991*. Central Bureau of Statistics, Damascus
Gennaoui A 1990 Etude régionale: Bilan et Perspective de la Planification et de la Gestion de l'Education dans les pays arabes. Congrès International de Mexico 1990. UNESCO, Paris
Ministère de l'éducation 1990 *Le Développement de l'Education en RAS 1989–1990, ICE 42ème session Genève*. Ministère de l'éducation, Damascus
Ministry of Education 1990 *Education in SAR for the school year 1989–1990*. Ministry of Education, Damascus (in arabic)
UNDP 1990 *Development Co-operation, Syrian Arab Republic. 1989 Report*. UNDP, Damascus
UNESCO 1991 *Statistical Yearbook 1991*. UNESCO, Paris

Tanzania

B. N. V. Buretta

1. General Background

Tanzania is a republic on the East Coast of Africa. It lies between latitudes 1 and 11 South and longitudes 30–40 East. It attained its Independence as Tanganyika in 1961 within the British Commonwealth of Nations and it declared complete Independence with republic status in 1962. In 1964, Tanganyika united with the then newly formed People's Republic of Zanzibar, an island off the coast of Tanganyika in the Indian Ocean, to form the United Republic of Tanzania. There is one union constitution although two governments operate, one in Zanzibar with autonomy over the internal affairs of Zanzibar. The Union government has overall responsibility for defence, home affairs, foreign affairs, and a number of other subsectors such as higher education, civil aviation, post, and telecommunications. Some other sectors, for example primary, secondary, and vocational education, agriculture, and industry are not Union concerns.

Tanzania covers an area of 945,087 square kilometers and is divided into 25 administrative regions. It has a population of about 25 million with an average growth rate of 2.8 percent. The economy is predominantly agricultural, although steady progress is being made toward industrialization.

2. Politics and the Goals of the Education System

Since the Arusha Declaration in 1967, Tanzania has followed an ideology of socialism and self-reliance, an ideology well-articulated in various documents including *Socialism and Rural Development* (1967) and *Freedom and Socialism* (1968). The goals and objectives aspire to achieve the building of a society in which all members have equal rights and equal opportunities, in which justice is observed and where exploitation is not tolerated. Up to 1992, the country had a one-party political system but in that year, the country opened the way for a multiparty system.

The country's education system is based on the *Education for Self-reliance* (1967) philosophy which is derived from the major policy of socialism and self-reliance. The philosophy propounds the merging of individuals and communities, a reflection of the idea of education and society being inseparable. It proposes a functional education combining skills and academic learning geared toward opening up the future for the individual learner.

Education in Tanzania is called upon to play an important role in producing the needed knowledge and skills for national development. The importance Tanzania places on education for every citizen cannot be overemphasized. The National Constitution (1977, amended in 1984) safeguards the right of the individual to learning opportunities. Education Act no. 25 of 1978 also stipulates that "every citizen of the United Republic of Tanzania shall be entitled to receive such category, nature and level of education as his ability may permit". Hence, equal opportunity exists for everyone to pursue one or other type of education.

The general aims and objectives of education can be summarized as follows:

(a) to provide all the population with the basic tools of education, namely reading, writing, and numeracy;

(b) to provide Tanzanians with such knowledge, skills, and attitudes as are appropriate and essential for development;

(c) to develop in each citizen an inquiring mind, self-confidence, creativity, and a scientific outlook necessary for an informed and rational choice of strategies needed to improve the quality of life;

(d) to enable learners to appreciate, emulate, and promote national, social, and cultural values.

3. The Formal System of Education

3.1 Primary, Secondary, and Tertiary Education

Primary education in Tanzania is a right for every child. The age of entry is 7 years and primary education lasts for seven years. In Zanzibar, the first cycle of school includes the seven years of primary education and three of secondary education. In mainland Tanzania the gross enrollment rate was 81.3 percent (1991); in Zanzibar it was 65.0. Pupils in mainland Tanzania are promoted to secondary education only after sitting for and passing a national examination set and administered under the supervision of the National Examinations Council of Tanzania (NECTA). Promotion to secondary school depends on the number of vacan-

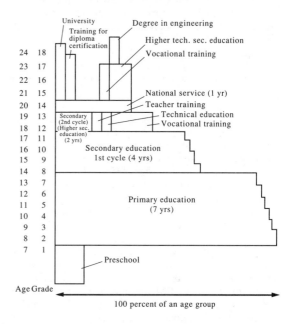

Figure 1

Tanzania: Structure of the formal education system

cies available and the level at which the pupil passed the examination. The transition rate from primary to secondary education was 15.4 percent in 1991.

The primary school curriculum consists of eight subjects, namely Kiswahili (the national language), English, mathematics, home economics, health, science, practical arts, and religious studies.

Most primary schools are owned by the local government. Some are owned and managed by nongovernment organizations and a few by the central government. Consequently, the teaching/learning materials and facilities are provided by the owners and managers of the schools. Staff for the schools are trained and allocated centrally by the central government.

Secondary education has two cycles. The first cycle consists of four years, at the end of which a national examination is taken. Promotion to the next two-year cycle depends on the number of available places and a student's performance in the national examination. After another final examination at the end of the second cycle, a student may secure entry into a university, other tertiary education colleges or vocational training colleges, or secure employment.

Secondary schools are owned by both the government (central and local), and nongovernmental organizations, and secondary education is not free of charge. There is a nominal fee determined by the government. In 1993 the fee was 5,000 Tanzania Sh (US$11.30) per year for a day student and 8,000 Sh (US$18.13) for a boarding student in a government-owned school. This fee, however, covers only a small part of the cost of providing education, which is about 186,000 Sh (US$426) for a day student and 242,000 Sh (US$554) for a boarder. The major part of the cost is funded by the government. The fee payable by students in nongovernment secondary schools is 35,000 Sh (US$80) for a day student and 45,000 Sh (US$103) for a boarder. The curriculum, as in primary education, is centrally controlled. Within the curriculum, students have to study seven core subjects, comprising Kiswahili, English, mathematics, unified science, social studies, computer literacy, and religious instruction. In addition, students are encouraged to study three more subjects from either the sciences or the arts or they can drop the combined course and opt for separate pure science or arts subjects (e.g., physics, chemistry, biology, geography, and history).

Tertiary education is provided in technical colleges and universities. In 1993 there were three advanced technical colleges situated in Dar es Salaam, Arusha, and Mbeya and three universities, namely the Sokoine University of Agriculture at Morogoro, the University of Dar es Salaam with its affiliate college, the Muhimbili College of Medical Sciences, and the Open University based in Dar es Salaam. All institutions offering higher education are government owned and are under the umbrella of the Ministry of Science, Technology, and Higher Education. The universities

are semiautonomous and manage their own affairs under the vice-chancellor, who is appointed by the President of Tanzania. However, their running costs are subsidized by the government.

3.2 Preschool Education

Prior to the 1980s, preschool institutions were managed by private institutions. There was no proper coordination and no clear curriculum. There are now clear policies on the care of children below age three (day care centers), and for the provision of education to children between ages 4 and 7 (preschool education). The Ministry of Education and Culture registers the schools, trains the teachers, supervises them, and develops the curriculum. The curriculum comprises activities in language, arithmetic, nature study, art, music, physical education, health education, good behavior, and character training. There were 134 preprimary schools in mainland Tanzania in 1991 while in Zanzibar there were 18 such government preschools (Ministry of Education and Culture 1992).

3.3 Special Education

In 1992 there were 118 educational institutions (government and nongovernment) catering for the education of disabled students. Of these, 100 provided primary education. The rest were at secondary and college level. Some of these schools were special in that they received pupils with special learning needs only. The children in these schools were isolated in terms of the nature of their handicap. In 1992 there were 14 such schools. The rest of the schools catering for the handicapped were ordinary integrated boarding and/or day schools. Most physically handicapped students and Albinos had access to education in the ordinary schools. This is to enhance interaction with other students and bring up the handicapped children in a natural environment. Emphasis tends to be on itinerant teaching programs rather than special schools.

All schools for handicapped students use the same syllabuses and textbooks as ordinary schools. However, the former employ additional specialized equipment and materials and have to teach extra learning skills depending on the nature of the handicap. Blind children are taught sense perception, braille reading and writing, typewriting, and mobility. In addition to the normal school subjects, deaf and partially hearing students are taught speech, lip-reading, auditory training, and vocational skills in agriculture, tailoring, and carpentry.

In contrast to the control and management of normal primary education which is concentrated at the regional level, special education is monitored and controlled at both the ministerial and regional levels. There is a unit at the Ministry of Education and Culture headquarters which directly coordinates efforts, both national and international, directed toward the improvement and expansion of special education.

3.4 Vocational, Technical, and Business Education

In Tanzania the learning of skills useful for life starts formally at the primary level. The curriculum requires that pupils learn skills such as agriculture, technical skills, home craft, and commerce so that after leaving school, they can be usefully employed. The secondary school curriculum also requires the student to study at least one vocational subject which will be accompanied by practical applications in the school setting. These subjects include agriculture, technical subjects, home economics, commerce, and accounts. These are taught at a level which will be of immediate use after school. Vocational training is offered after completion of any one level or cycle of formal education. There are vocational colleges/centers and institutes which train primary school leavers in various trades. Some of these centers are under the department of primary education of the Ministry of Education and Culture but the majority are under the Ministry of Labor and Community Development. A few others are managed by nongovernment organizations. Vocational training is not free. For government-owned centers a government-stipulated fee is paid, while for the other institutions a fee is charged for every subject or skill learnt, with rates being dependent on the market demand for the skills. Vocational training is also offered to young women and men who have completed the first and second cycles of secondary education; most institutions offering training at this level are run by the government under respective ministries.

Entry into these institutions is based on examination results, performance at work after secondary education, and individual preference for the course. Certification at the end of the course is either ministerial or national, that is, awarded by the National Examination Council of Tanzania (NECTA). Curriculum at these institutions is not centralized but its quality is controlled by the respective ministries.

Technical education starts at the first cycle of secondary education in some designated schools. Those performing well in this field at the end of the cycle are selected for further technical education and training in the technical colleges or at the Faculty of Engineering at the University of Dar es Salaam. A relatively small number of students sometimes pursue such studies at universities outside the country.

The curriculum in the technical colleges is centrally prescribed and examinations and certification are national. The technical colleges are multifaculty. Subjects and trades include electronics, electrical, mechanical, and structural engineering, plumbing, welding, woodwork, and foundry.

3.5 Adult and Nonformal Education

The objective of adult literacy is to help adults (especially in rural areas) to find solutions to problems like hunger, ignorance, and disease including malnutrition.

Programs include the provision of, among other things, functional literacy skills to adults in their respective communities; other skills include simple techniques in agriculture, rural construction, health education, home economics, and civics.

Adult literacy programs were initiated in 1968 on an experimental basis in four regions: Mara, Mwanza, Shinyanga, and Kagera. In 1970, a nationwide campaign against illiteracy was launched. The operational objectives of adult education were to create ideological awareness as well as imparting skills which would be functional and instrumental in improving the rural or agricultural settings in which the majority of the population live.

Several subprograms and projects have been initiated. In 1970, "The Choice is Yours" campaign was launched. This emphasized participative democracy in decision-making and development. The national literacy campaign, inspired by the functional literacy approach, was launched in 1972–75. In 1973 there was a campaign known as "Man is Health," which emphasized the need to observe good health habits for a prolonged lifespan, while in 1974 the "Agriculture for Life" campaign was launched. In these campaigns, important technical information about the respective themes was transmitted to the people.

There are three main categories of adult literacy classes. These are: (a) literacy classes which deal with reading, writing, and numeracy; (b) those for the retention of acquired literacy skills; and (c) those aimed at the application and extension of knowledge and skills.

Adult literacy programs are organized in eight stages. Stages 1–4 involve different categories of adults based on their ability to read and write and the utilization and/or comprehension of the literacy skills; stages 5–8 are for those adults who wish to continue after stage 4. Students in both literacy and postliteracy programs are provided with the necessary books and materials free of charge.

Apart from this formal program, there are supporting programs which offer services in the following domains:

(a) Education through radio; this keeps contact with learners every week.

(b) Folk development colleges (FDCs) which offer short courses of one to three weeks and long courses of up to two years in handicrafts, home economics, mechanics, and so on.

(c) Rural libraries, functioning in about a third of the villages in the country.

(d) Rural newspapers; these are published in each of the seven zones in the country and sold at low prices to postliteracy adult education students.

The management and coordination of adult education is the responsibility of the Department of Adult

Education at the Ministry of Education and Culture. Apart from the Department, there is an Institute of Adult Education, a semiautonomous public institution which is charged with the duty of providing continuing education to adults through short and long courses, workshops, seminars, and distance learning mainly by correspondence. An open university has been established through which adults can acquire university education through correspondence. Nonformal education has existed in Tanzania for years although without the guidance of any clearly defined policy. However, programs have been implicitly recognized through guidelines, statements, resolutions, and educational policies issued at different times since Independence in 1961.

Out-of-school education programs can be categorized according to the needs of the out-of-school population. These include semiscientific-oriented activities resulting in vocational training institutions, backyard garages, traditional tin-smithing, watch repair works and the like. Examples are:

(a) activities which deal with distributive business and community services, such as fishmongers, street vendors, and so on;

(b) small-scale farming including vegetable growing, poultry keeping, and pig keeping;

(c) dress making, cobbling, and handicrafts;

(d) professional-oriented activities, such as secretarial services and commercial consultancy services;

(e) cultural and recreational activities.

A common feature of these programs is that they are specific and need oriented. Categories of program include:

(a) those under industries, such as small-scale industry programs;

(b) programs under nongovernmental organizations including church organizations such as YMCA, YWCA, CARITAS, Tanzania Family Planning Association, and the Tanzania Red Cross Society;

(c) programs which are offered by private companies and individuals (e.g., computer distribution companies, secretarial services companies, and private garages).

The out-of-school programs are normally small in size, having about 10 to 60 students at a time. The clientele for the programs consists essentially of primary school leavers, school dropouts, and various target groups in search of continuing education or certain skills. Admission involves individuals' efforts to apply for a course and for most programs basic literacy is essential. In some programs, students are admitted on the basis of competitive examinations. The length of a course varies according to its objectives. Most of the prevocational programs range from six months to two years. Courses to upgrade the skills of those already employed vary from a few days to two years.

The financing of most programs, particularly those run by nongovernmental organizations, is through voluntary contributions. Privately owned institutions charge fees. Staffing is through the institution's own initiatives except for government-run programs where staffing is organized by government.

4. Administrative and Supervisory Structure and Operation

The Minister for Education and Culture is responsible for the development and implementation of all education plans in the country. The Minister is assisted by an Advisory Council. The Principal Secretary is the chief executive of the Ministry. Under the Principal Secretary, there are two Commissioners; the Commissioner for Education who is the chief advisor to the Minister on education policies and practices and the Commissioner for Culture who advises the Minister on cultural affairs and coordinates the departments and units involved in culture and sports.

The headquarters of the Ministry is organized into various departments: the departments of primary, secondary, teacher and adult education, educational planning, administration, and personnel. Others include the school inspectorate, arts, games and sports, and national museums. There are also units responsible for national antiquities and archives. The departments are headed by directors, who manage and coordinate the activities of the institutions in their respective levels of education. The day-to-day functions of the primary and adult education departments are decentralized and are administratively under the Ministry of Regional Administration and Local Government. The regional and district education officers are representatives of the Ministry of Education and Culture at the regional and district levels respectively.

In its efforts to ensure effective deployment of its specialist staff in the design and proper implementation and evaluation of educational programs, the Ministry established independent and semigovernmental institutes which perform specialist functions. The Institute of Curriculum Development (ICD) is responsible for the development of education content and instructional materials, while the Institute of Adult Education (IAE) ensures the development of programs for adult literacy and postliteracy education. The National Examination Council of Tanzania (NECTA) specializes in the design and administration of national examinations and the certification of candidates. These organizations work closely with the office of the Commissioner for Education. Other semigovernmental organizations include the Tanzania Library Services (TLS), which ensures the national readership and promotion of school libraries, and The Tanzania Elimu Supplies (TES) which deals with the distribution of educational materials countrywide.

The universities and higher technical colleges which were formerly under the Ministry of Education and Culture are now under the umbrella of the Ministry of Science, Technology, and Higher Education.

5. Educational Finance

Since Independence the financing of education has been largely the responsibility of the central government. Since the mid-1980s parents and owners of schools have been required to contribute more toward meeting the ever-increasing costs of education. During the 1970s, the government spent 15–20 percent of its total annual recurrent budget on education for most of the years. In 1980 to 1984 about 12 percent of the central government's budget was allocated to education. Since 1984–85 it has ranged between 4.8 percent and 7.9 percent. In 1990–91, it was 6.3 percent.

Part of this decline has been offset by cost-sharing initiatives. At the preschool level, privately owned kindergartens determine their own fees. Government-owned preschools do not charge fees but parents contribute toward the cost of school meals and play materials. The contributions range from 400 Sh (US$0.9) per child per year in rural schools to 12,000 Sh (US$27) per child per year in urban areas. At primary school level, the government requires parents to contribute 200 Sh (US$0.5) per child per year toward the cost of learning materials. In overall terms, the financing of primary education is low. In 1991, per capita expenditure was 3,200 Sh (US$7) per child while actual requirement stood at 17,000 Sh (US$39) per student per year.

Pupils in government-managed day secondary schools pay 5,000 Sh (US$11.3) per pupil per year while boarding pupils pay 8,000 Sh (US$18.13) each. A nongovernment secondary school pupil pays between 30,000 (US$69) and 46,000 Sh (US$105) depending on whether he or she is a day or boarding student in the first or second cycle of secondary education.

The cost of training teachers and that for providing adult education is the responsibility of the central government.

Up until 1991 costs of preparing examinations administration, supervision, and correction of scripts were covered by the government. Since then, every pupil sitting for the national examinations, except for primary school students, has to pay a small fee to subsidize the cost of materials and examination administration. Development projects in education are heavily dependent on external financing. Up to 75 percent of development projects funding is external.

6. Supplying Personnel for the Education System

The training of teachers is a central government responsibility. Student teachers for primary schools are recruited mainly from successful applicants from the first cycle of secondary education. These receive residential training in teachers colleges for two years and if they successfully complete the course they become Grade A teachers.

Similarly, applicants from the second cycle of secondary education receive training for two years to be awarded a Diploma in Education; they may teach in secondary forms 1–4 (the first cycle of secondary education).

Teachers trained at the university level teach in both cycles of secondary education and in teacher training colleges. Selection to teacher training is based on the prospective candidate's level of pass in the requisite examination, and vacancies for training available in the institutes or colleges. Each educational institution is headed by an education officer appointed by the Ministry. The appointment criteria are mainly academic merit, management, and leadership competence. Seniority may also contribute toward these appointments. Staffing and transfers of personnel are implemented by the ministries concerned. Discipline of staff is handled by the head of the school or college in collaboration with a school/college board. Staff discipline is also handled by the Ministry headquarters and the Teacher Service Commission (TSC). The commission is also charged with the responsibility of hiring teachers, and proposing teacher promotion, on behalf of the government. Heads of schools and colleges have no power to dismiss staff. Certification and registration of teachers is done by the Commissioner for Education.

7. Curriculum Development and Teaching Methodology

Curriculum development for kindergartens, schools, teacher training colleges, postprimary technical centers, and special education programs in mainland Tanzania is the responsibility of the Institute of Curriculum Development (ICD). It operates through a system of subject panels and curriculum boards.

A subject panel examines the selection and organization of the subject matter of a specific subject at the different levels of education and recommends the outcomes for approval and use in schools by the Commissioner for Education.

In the early 1990s, the ICD, in consultation with the Ministry of Education and Culture, proposed significant changes in the design of the curriculum offered at primary, secondary, and teacher training levels. The focus is mainly on the reduction of the number of subjects for easy management by students and teachers and on methods for improving instruction. As part of the curriculum reform, consideration was given to a number of key issues including:

(a) problems in the old curriculum package;

(b) educational demands by parents, students, teachers and employers;

(c) research findings;

(d) the philosophy, goals, and objectives of education in Tanzania as reflected in government policy and statements;

(e) trends of curriculum reforms which had been taking place globally in the 1980s;

(f) contemporary theories and practices in education;

(g) the need to balance theoretical content and practical skills and to diversify the provision of vocational and life skills in every school to give students a wider choice of subjects to pursue through a definition of core, obligatory choices, work-oriented and optional subjects.

Redefinition and streamlining of the curriculum package for teacher training programs has been made with more emphases on studies in the principles of education and teaching, educational psychology and counselling, and teaching methods in order to improve the quality of teachers.

In 1993, the ICD was revising syllabuses, instructional materials, equipment, charts, and other audio-visual aids. Induction and orientation into the new content and materials were planned for all teachers.

8. The System of Examinations, Promotions, and Certifications

At the end of every level of formal education there is a final examination which also determines whether a student is promoted to the next level or not. The examinations include national examinations at the end of primary Grades 4 and 7. Failure in the primary Grade 4 examination does not terminate a pupil's primary education but gives the educators information about the progress of the pupil. The Grade 7 examination is terminal. Those who do not gain access to secondary education enter the economy.

The examinations administered at secondary school level are: the National Form 2 (Grade 9) Examination,

the Certificate of Secondary Education Examination (CSEE) and the Advanced Certificate of Secondary Education Examination (ACSEE). While the last two are terminal, the Form 2 examination provides information about the learners' progress.

Teacher certification examinations are administered for trainees of various courses, namely Grade B, Grade A, and Diploma student courses.

9. Educational Assessment, Evaluation, and Research

Teachers assess their pupils both in their classroom work and also in practical skills as demonstrated by self-reliance activities, attitudes toward manual work, and commitment to community endeavors. In practice, however, teachers are able to assess factual knowledge only.

Educational administrators at ward, district, and regional level, heads of schools, subject teachers, the National Examinations Council of Tanzania (NECTA) and the Inspectorate are all involved in one way or another in the evaluation of education.

School inspectors evaluate the teaching of various subjects, the general administration of the educational institutions, financial management, and other matters relating to the organization of these institutions.

A coordinating unit for Educational Research and Evaluation has been established at the Ministry of Education and Culture headquarters. It conducts and supports the conduct of different types of small- or large-scale studies. Further, it renders advisory services to various researchers, facilitates research clearances, and organizes or takes part in collaborative research endeavors with other institutions. It plays a significant role in feeding planners with information about development trends in education so as to influence policy direction.

10. Major Reforms in the 1980s and 1990s

Major educational reforms in the 1980s and 1990s resulting from policy reviews included:

(a) The Special Education School Inspection Services, introduced in 1980.

(b) The first attempt in setting a direction for education toward the year 2000 by the Presidential Commission on Education.

(c) The National Conference on Education held in 1984 to discuss and adopt the recommendations of the 1982 Presidential Commission on Education report.

(d) The introduction of an Early Childhood Education Project following the resolutions and recommendations of the National Committee for the International Year of the Child. The project, which was launched on a pilot basis 1983 to 1985, continues to operate on a small scale but is expected to be integrated into the mainstream of the education system by July 1993.

(e) Increasing intersectoral collaboration in education. Health and environmental projects since 1985 included the following projects:

   (i) Child Survival Development Program;
   (ii) School Feeding Program;
   (iii) AIDS Education and Prevention;
   (iv) Health Education and Environmental Sanitation;
   (v) Family Life Education.

(f) Establishment of an open university to cater for the needs of the out-of-school population necessitated the appointment of a special committee in 1988 to undertake a needs assessment survey and make recommendations for action.

(g) The establishment of the Ministry of Science, Technology, and Higher Education in 1990 was prompted by the need for Tanzania to deal with the development of science and technology more effectively while the establishment of the Ministry of Community Development, Women's Affairs, and Children was promoted by the need for the country to deal with issues of gender and the rights of women and children more realistically.

(h) Review of the education system for the twenty-first century in the light of technological change was undertaken in 1992 with the ultimate goal of producing an education policy for mainland Tanzania.

(i) Revision of the curriculum and the introduction of the new curriculum package which includes science and technology, environmental education, cultural values, civics, and social studies.

(j) National inservice teacher workshops for primary teachers have continued under the "Mpango wa Tanzania/UNESCO/UNICEF" (MTUU) programs.

(k) A national Education Conference was held in 1991 as a follow-up to Jomtien Conference on Education for All.

(l) A survey on the needs of special education in Tanzania to cater for the disabled was begun in 1991.

(m) A national conference on special education was held with the purpose of expanding and promoting education so as to integrate disabled students into ordinary schools, and looking into possibilities of establishing a teacher training college.

(n) An early childhood education (ECE) workshop was held in 1991. It was organized by the Ministry of Education and Culture in collaboration with the Aga Khan Education Services Tanzania to revitalize ECE provision and to establish an ECE association.

(o) National, subregional, and regional workshops for inservice teachers were supported by the Australian government under the Education Program for Southern Africa (EPSA).

(p) Through the financial assistance of SIDA, short-term upgrading teachers courses and seminars were conducted to develop teachers' aptitudes, skills, and competence.

(q) There has been a re-structuring of the Ministry of Education, integrating it with culture with a purpose of promoting education for cultural development.

11. Major Problems for the Year 2000

As the year 2000 approaches the following major issues will have to be addressed:

(a) eradication of remaining illiteracy;

(b) ensuring full primary education for all school-age children;

(c) improving the quality of basic education;

(d) emphasizing science and technology.

References

Ministry of Education and Culture 1992 *National Report of the United Republic of Tanzania*. International Conference on Education, 43rd session, Geneva 1992. Ministry of Education and Culture, Dar es Salaam

Further Reading

Ministry of Education 1986 *National Report of the United Republic of Tanzania*. International Conference on Education, 40th Session Geneva 1986, Ministry of Education, Dar es Salaam

Ministry of Education 1989 *Education for All: Meeting Basic Learning Needs, to the Year 2000, Tanzania National Document*. Ministry of Education, Dar es Salaam

Ministry of Education 1990 *National Report of the United Republic of Tanzania*. International Conference on Education, 42nd session, Geneva 1990. Ministry of Education, Dar es Salaam

Ministry of Education and Culture 1992–93 *Budget speech*. Ministry of Education and Culture, Dar es Salaam

Thailand

T. Boonchuay and M. Siaroon

1. General Background

Thailand, formerly known as Siam, has an area of 513,511 square kilometers, the largest area of arable land of all Southeast Asian countries. Thailand has never been colonized by Western countries. Shaped like an axe, the country is geographically divided into five regions: the Central Plain, the North, the East, the Northeast, and the South. There are 76 provinces and Bangkok is the capital city.

Since 1961, Thailand has organized its development through "national development" plans. The National Education Development Plan has been an integral part of the National Economic and Social Development Plan. Each plan has a five-year span. At the time of writing this entry, the Seventh Plan (1992–96) is in force.

During the period of the First and the Second Plans (1961–71), the population growth rate was at 3.2 percent per annum. The first demographic planning was set forth in the Third Plan (1972–76) together with the launching of a family planning campaign project (Boonchuay 1991).

In 1993, Thailand had a population of 57.7 million with a growth rate of 1.4 percent per annum. The majority of the population is Thai but there are numerous other ethnic groups including Chinese, Indian, European, Vietnamese, and the hill tribes. The language of communication and instruction is Thai. Educational provision in some provinces is difficult because of the language problem, particularly in the border area of the South, the hill tribes' area in the North, and the remote rural areas in the Northeast. This problem is one of the factors influencing student learning outcomes. In 1991, 94 percent of the primary school age group was enrolled in school. The remaining 6 percent comprised the hill tribes, migrants, the disadvantaged, and the disabled (Office of the National Education Commission 1993).

In the period 1960–93 the Thai population could be categorized into two broad societies: the urban class-conscious society and the rural classless society. The Thai socioeconomic and cultural environment has changed drastically. People in the urban areas have a new lifestyle and place more emphasis on competition for personal achievement, and materialistic and luxurious consumption. People in rural areas still lack the advantages of technological advancement. Social disparities have become a crucial issue to be tackled by the Thai government.

In 1993, the national economic growth was 7.5 percent—higher than the 7.2 percent of the previous year. The overall imports amounted to 1,151,000 million Baht (25 Baht=US$1). This was an increase of 12.8 percent over the previous year. Exports amounted to 909,000 million Baht, an increase of 11.5 percent. With regard to domestic products, the agricultural sector contributed 97,700 million Baht and the nonagricultural sector contributed 691,000 million Baht (Bank of Thailand 1993).

The labor force aged 11 and over in 1990 numbered 31.7 million, but only 30.2 million were employed. Of this total, 60.9 percent was in the agricultural sector, 10.3 percent in the manufacturing sector, and the rest were in other sectors. There was also a shortage of skilled vocational/technical labor such as craftworkers and engineers, reflecting the presence of some qualitative mismatching between labor demand and supply.

With respect to educated unemployment, it was found that primary education or lower graduates were ranked highest, followed by vocational/technical, lower-secondary, upper-secondary, university, and teacher education graduates respectively (Office of the National Economic and Social Development Board 1990).

The Thai Government has always regarded education as an essential foundation for achieving national development goals. Since 1960 education has been considered a key instrument for the development of an independent economy and for creating social harmony in the nation. Education should also serve as a basis for earning and self-fulfillment. Education, has therefore, been closely linked to national economic and social development (Ministry of Education 1987).

In response to the World Declaration on Education for All Conference held at Jomtien, Thailand in 1990, a pilot project to expand basic education from 6 to 9 years was launched in primary and secondary schools in the academic year 1990. This was, of course, subject to sufficient teaching personnel and school facilities being made available (Office of the National Education Commission 1992).

Along with government efforts to universalize compulsory education and to expand basic education, the Office of the National Education Commission recommended a revised National Education Scheme 1992 to replace that of 1977. According to this scheme, quality improvement, self-discipline, values education, and national tradition, culture, and arts were to be emphasized from the preprimary level upward.

2. Politics and the Goals of the Education System

A national policy was perceived essential to guide and provide effective delivery of the educational system. This framework is called the National Education Scheme. The government goals on the Thai education system stated in the 1992 National Education Scheme emphasized four main characteristics: intellectual, spiritual, physical, and social development (Office of the National Education Commission 1992).

The concepts and innovations stated in the Scheme were operationalized in the National Education Development Plan. The major aims stated in this plan focused on the qualitative improvement of citizens' ethics, morality, intellects, health, and occupations. It seeks to improve their knowledge and skills so that they will be self-reliant, their ability to live a happy life under the constitutional monarchy, and their abilities to adjust themselves properly to any situation, to be creative, and to take initiative. Furthermore, it is expected that they will be able to support socioeconomic changes in a systematic and harmonious pattern, corresponding to the limitation of resources and the needs of individuals, communities, and societies.

3. The Formal System of Education

3.1 Primary, Secondary, and Tertiary Education

Formal education has four major sequential levels: preprimary, primary, secondary, and higher education.

With the implementation of the 1977 National Education Scheme the Thai educational system was changed from 4:3:3:2:4 to 6:3:3:4. A six-year primary schooling is compulsory, followed by lower- and upper-secondary schooling of three years each and four years or more for university undergraduate degrees.

Primary education lays the firm foundation for the overall growth of children through the development of basic skills, character development, and work-oriented subjects geared toward being a good member of the family and society. This level of education is compulsory and provided free of charge.

Secondary education is for the preadolescent and adolescent groups. Secondary education in Thailand is divided into three years of lower-secondary education and another three years of upper-secondary education. It adds to the general education of youth and provides some degree of vocational training. The students in the upper level are guided to concentrate more on areas of specialization needed for their chosen careers or occupation, while those in the lower-secondary level are equipped with the knowledge, skills, capability, and potential to acquire continuous learning and take part in the preservation of natural resources and the community's arts and culture.

Higher education includes undergraduate and graduate studies. It aims at the full development of the human being to intellectual maturity, in order to facilitate the advancement of knowledge and technology which will result in the production of a high-level academic and professional labor force for national development. Higher education is organized into colleges, universities, and institutions for specialized studies.

Thailand's first open university, Ramkamhaeng University, was established in 1971 in response to the national policy on human resource development and social demand for higher education, especially from secondary school graduates and working adults. However, this university still conducts lectures mainly on campus like other universities. This does not fulfill the most comprehensive concept of an open university. Therefore, in 1979, a new open university, Sukhothai Thammathirat Open University, was established. It aims at providing greater opportunity and access to higher education. This university utilizes distance learning, employing mass media such as television and radio, and correspondence courses together with textbooks, exercise sheets, and other supplementary educational materials. No class attendance is required. Figure 1 depicts the school structure and enrollment rates.

The private sector is encouraged to supplement the public sector in providing education at all levels and for all disciplines except teacher education which is conducted solely by government institutions. In 1991, government schools made up 86 percent of the national total and private schools 14 percent. The proportion of enrollment by level for government and private institutions respectively were reported as follows: preprimary, 75 and 25 percent; primary, 90 and 10 percent; lower-secondary, 90 and 10 percent; upper-secondary, 94 and 6 percent for the general program, 50 and 50 percent for the vocational program; and higher education, 64 and 36 percent (Office of the National Education Commission 1993). Most government and private schools are coeducational. There is no sex discrimination regarding access to education. There were

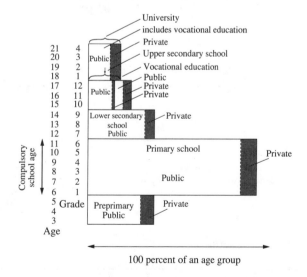

Figure 1

Thailand: Structure of the formal education system 1989

more students enrolled in rural communities than in urban areas since three-fourths of the Thai population reside in rural areas.

Educational institutions in the formal education system from preprimary to upper-secondary levels normally have 7 learning periods per school day and each period lasts 50 minutes. The school year consists of approximately 200 days. For higher education the daily hours of tuition are flexible to meet the needs of students. There are approximately 180 days in a school year. Some statistics on formal education in 1991 are provided in Table 1.

3.2 Preschool Education

Preschool education includes postnatal care as well as the nurture and education of children aged 3–5 years. It is accepted that a good part of children's education takes place in their early years. Emphasis, therefore, has been placed on discipline as the foundation of self-control, and on fostering cooperative habits and the enrichment of sensitivity through affection and trust. The principal agencies for providing care and development at this early stage are the home, community child development centers, nursery schools, and kindergartens.

3.3 Special Education

Children who possess individual differences in their physical, mental, emotional, or social development and are regarded as exceptional or atypical children require substantial modifications in their educational environment. Education for handicapped children must be attuned both to their basic needs as children and to their special needs as handicapped persons. The arrangements provided to meet their special needs is commonly known as "special education." In Thailand, education for this special group of children is provided in parallel with formal education from kindergarten upward through other levels of schooling. In 1991, schools, centers, and agencies working in the field of special education numbered 92. Of these, 39 were public organizations, and 53 were private or charity foundations. A large amount of donated funding is needed to help support such operations. There are four basic categories of handicap: mental, physical, emotional, and social disorders. Children are generally classified by their mental ability group as the gifted or talented, the normal or average, and the mentally retarded. Physical disorder is categorized into four groups: visual handicaps, crippling or orthopedic handicaps, aural handicaps, and oral handicaps. Socially and emotionally distressed children are also categorized as having special educational problems. Those who are moderately handicapped are now being placed in regular classroom environments alongside normal children in regular public schools. For severely handicapped children, who cannot attend school at all, short vocational courses are widely offered to suit their abilities, provided free of charge in public welfare centers, so that they may, whenever possible, be self-supporting or placed in remunerative employment. In 1991, there were 20,305 handicapped children enrolled in the preprimary, primary, and secondary levels.

3.4 Vocational and Technical Education

Vocational and technical education begins at the secondary education level and continues on to the postsecondary level in the formal system and is provided separately from the general education secondary school. Vocational education is offered by both the public and private sectors. The curriculum contains

Table 1
Statistics on formal education in Thailand 1991

| | | | Classified Level | | |
	Preprimary	Primary	Lower-secondary	Upper-secondary	University
Age group	3–5	6–11	12–14	15–17	18–21
Population (in millions)	3.6	7.4	3.7	3.7	8.5
Percentage of enrolled per population	42.66	93.62	41.87	23.55	5.66
Ratio of enrollment public–private institutions	75:25	90:10	90:10	94:6[a] 50:50[b]	64:36
Class size	20	26	40	36[a] 35[b]	—
Student–teacher ratio	23:1	22:1	17:1	18:1	12:1
Cost per head (Baht[c])	5,543			7,166[a] 16,198[b]	58,658

Source: NEC, Educational Information Division, 1991
a Upper-secondary school (general education)   b Upper-secondary school (vocational education)   c 25 Baht=US$1

four types of program: (a) the Vocational Education Certificate—a three-year course after Grade 9 (the equivalent to upper-secondary education level); (b) the Higher Vocational Education Certificate—a two-year course of postsecondary education equivalent to diploma level or an associate degree; (c) the Technical Certificate—a two-year program after completing Grade 12 from general secondary schools (equivalent to an associate degree); and (d) the bachelor's degree program of four years' duration.

The vocational programs provided at each level deal with five major areas: industry, agriculture, commerce, home economics, and arts and crafts. (In 1991, the number of students enrolled totaled 677,590, of which 448,010 were in vocational upper-secondary school programs and the rest [229,580] were enrolled in the postsecondary vocational education and undergraduate programs.) The five fields of study mentioned above are further subdivided into areas of specialization. For example, industry consists of such fields as electricity, electronics, sheet metal work and welding, auto mechanics, and so on. Likewise, other subject fields are composed of several specialized programs. Courses offered in these subject fields are revised at regular intervals in order to keep up with the development and introduction of new technologies or changes in occupational patterns in society.

The types and number of institutions offering vocational/technical education at postsecondary levels in 1991 were as follows:

(a)   The two-year postsecondary programs leading to the Diploma in Vocational/Technical Education and the Diploma in Technician Education. These are in institutions which provide an equivalent of the associate degree program leading to a diploma in vocational/technical education. Of these institutions, 205 colleges are under the Department of Vocational Education (DOVE) of the Ministry of Education (MOE). Rajamangala Institute of Technology (RIT) also belongs to the MOE, and offers two-year postsecondary programs in 28 campuses throughout the country. The King Mongkut Institute of Technology (KMIT), North Bangkok Campus, which is under the Ministry of University Affairs (MUA), also offers the same kind of programs. The remaining 341 private vocational/technical schools and colleges all provide postsecondary programs.

(b)   Undergraduate programs leading to the bachelor's degree are offered in various institutions. The eight campuses of RIT offer undergraduate programs in the areas of engineering technology, home economics, business administration, fine arts, and agriculture. The King Mongkut Institute of Technology offers both undergraduate and graduate programs at all three campuses. The undergraduate programs are open to holders of a Diploma in Vocational/Technical Education in

their respective fields who wish to continue their studies for two more years in order to obtain a bachelor's degree.

The duration of study in a diploma program in every area (industry, commerce, etc.) and every specialized subject is two years. Diploma graduates can terminate their study and apply for jobs as technicians in the labor market. If they wish to study further, the program also prepares them for a two-year degree-level program.

Vocational/technical teachers are trained in four major institutions: RIT, and the three independent campuses of the KMIT. Teachers of general subjects are trained in teachers' colleges and at both public and private universities.

Financial support of vocational/technical education has become a matter of national concern. The government subsidizes about 80 percent of the cost of public schools and colleges. Other sources are derived from tuition fees and private donations. A student pays a tuition fee of 800–2,600 Baht a year (25 Baht=US$1) in public institutions and 7,000–9,000 Baht a year in private colleges. Private colleges receive educational revenues only from students' tuition fees and donations. The rates of private college tuition fees are therefore three to five times higher than those in public colleges.

3.5 Adult and Nonformal Education

Nonformal education provides services to an ever-increasing number of Thai citizens. It has long played an important role in providing education to approximately 50 percent of the total Thai population.

The Department of Nonformal Education under the Ministry of Education is the main agency responsible for nonformal education. More than 50 private organizations and foundations also conduct nonformal education programs.

The main programs of nonformal education to supplement the formal school system and to promote lifelong learning opportunities are as follows:

(a)   Adult functional literacy, for example, literacy/numeracy and equivalency programs at Grades 6 and 9, and to a limited extent, Grade 12 levels.

(b)   Training in life experiences and vocational skills, for instance, short vocational courses, interest groups, and so on.

(c)   Access to current news and information, through community or village libraries, reading centers, educational/technical information broadcasting, and so on.

In the early 1990s numerous activities were undertaken: the expansion of nonformal education programs to reach educationally disadvantaged groups, diver-

975

sification of courses to respond more effectively to local needs and conditions, and integration with other development services to achieve a desirable impact.

In 1991, total enrollment according to the Department of Nonformal Education was 1,739,423. The first category, adult functional literacy, enrolled 736,872; the second category, training programs, enrolled 358,116 learners in short vocational courses; and the rest (644,435) were enrolled in the third category.

4. Administrative and Supervisory Structure and Operation

The educational administration system in Thailand parallels all other sectors of public administration. It follows a three level approach: the central or national level, the regional level, and the local level. The chief educational agencies in Thailand are four ministries. The Ministry of Education is responsible for primary and secondary education, teacher education, and vocational education. The Ministry is also responsible for the operation of private schools and colleges from preprimary to secondary levels, and to some extent postsecondary education. The Ministry of the Interior is responsible for Bangkok Metropolitan Administration (BMA) primary schools and also for municipal primary schools throughout the country. The Ministry of University Affairs is responsible for public and private universities and colleges. The Office of the National Education Commission attached to the Office of the Prime Minister is responsible for national education policy and the formulation of development plans.

5. Educational Finance

In the Seventh National Education Development Plan (1992–96), the amount appropriated for educational development in the public sector was 3.4 percent of the Gross Domestic Product (GDP). The highest proportion of the education budget (52%) was allocated for preprimary and primary education; 18 percent was allocated for secondary education, 14 percent for higher education, 6 percent for vocational/technical education, 2 percent for teacher education, 3 percent for nonformal education, and 5 percent for educational administration and promotion (Bureau of Budget 1992). The government also subsidizes private primary and secondary schools. Moreover, financial assistance for private universities/colleges' technical development was also granted. Per unit expenditures are presented in Table 1.

6. Supplying Personnel for the Education System

The training of teachers at the postsecondary and undergraduate (BEd) level in general subjects areas is the responsibility of the Department of Teacher Education via 36 teachers' colleges. Some 40 other colleges which also offer teacher training in specific disciplines (i.e., physical education, dramatic arts, fine arts, vocational and technical education, etc.) come under the Department of Physical Education, the Department of Fine Arts, and the RIT. All of these agencies are attached to the Ministry of Education. The Ministry of University Affairs offers teacher-training courses at the undergraduate and graduate levels through its 20 faculties of education in various public universities. In 1991, the number of students enrolled at teacher-training institutions totalled 46,983. Of these, 3,743 students were in undergraduate programs. More emphasis is placed on the training of teachers in specific subjects than teachers in general subject areas partly to avoid educated unemployment and partly to meet the needs for specific subject teachers.

Many teacher recruits are found to be insufficiently prepared for teaching in educational institutions as they still lack the knowledge, skills, and responsibilities required to be good teachers. There has been a growing recognition of the importance of staff development among educational institutions and a commitment to make staff development an on-going process.

Teacher training includes at least one semester of practice teaching as a requirement before graduation. The supervision of teaching is undertaken by teachers' college supervisors. Techniques adopted for monitoring and evaluating the performance of teacher trainees are based on the criterion-referenced method and focus on the candidates' competence, behavior, and determination. After beginning work, every teacher is evaluated in terms of working performance, desirable behavior, punctuality, and so on. This is done twice a year as a supplementary record for the administrator's consideration when deciding on yearly promotion.

7. Curriculum Development and Teaching Methodology

The evaluation of past experiences and needs assessment surveys are undertaken by special educational provision agencies. Information on the general success and failure of educational objectives together with a knowledge of the contexts of the educational system are essential inputs for curriculum development and revision.

At primary and secondary levels, curriculum development falls under the responsibility of the Department of Curriculum and Instruction Development (DCID) at the Ministry of Education, whereas for vocational/technical and higher-certificate level courses, it is under the Department of Vocational Education and Rajamangala Institute of Technology (RIT). At the university level, initiatives usually come from departments and progress through administrative channels, that is, faculties, university councils, and the Ministry of University Affairs (MUA). After the curriculum is approved by the Minister of University Affairs, the decision is made known to the Civil Service Commission so that accreditation and pay scales can be revised accordingly.

At the primary level, the core curriculum comprises five areas of learning experiences, namely:

(a) Area I: Skills and tool subjects, comprising Thai language and mathematics.

(b) Area II: Life experiences, dealing with the process of solving life problems and social problems, emphasizing scientific process skills for good living and good ways of life.

(c) Area III: Character development, dealing with activities relating to the enhancement of acceptable habits, moral values, attitudes, and behavior leading one to become a desirable citizen.

(d) Area IV: Work-oriented experiences, dealing with general work experiences and basic knowledge in carrying out honest occupations.

(e) Area V: Special experiences, dealing with activities in accordance with learner's interests.

At the lower-secondary level, there are 6 core subjects which encompass 57 learning units (credits) in Thai language, science, mathematics, social studies, health education, and art education. Moreover, there are 3 compulsory elective subjects of 18 units (social studies, health education, and work education) and 5 free elective subjects of 33 units comprising: (a) the language group (Thai language and foreign languages), (b) science/mathematics group (science and mathematics), (c) social studies group, (d) personality development group (health education and art education), and (e) work/career education.

At the upper-secondary level, there are 3 compulsory core subjects (Thai language, social studies, and health education), 3 compulsory elective subjects (health education, science and foundations of vocational education), and 5 free elective subject areas (Thai language and foreign languages, social studies personality development, health education and art education, science and mathematics, and career education).

Room is provided for educational establishments and local authorities to prepare and adjust compulsory electives and free elective courses in terms of their content to suit the local environment and learners' needs, but always on condition that they conform to the MOE's procedures. However, few schools take advantage of this, which may be attributed to the fact that external tests and assessment are conducted periodically by DCID at Grades 2, 4, and 6, and that the entrance examination and selection to the next cycle of education

tend to dictate what is taught in the lower levels.

The DCID also develops textbooks, manuals, and instructional materials. In the metropolitan area, the director-generals of the respective departments decide on the collection of curricular materials. In the regions, the heads of provincial education offices (HPEO) undertake the selection with the prior consent of the heads of regional education offices. Any schools wishing to use instructional materials different from those selected by HPEOs must seek approval from their respective director-generals or HPEOs.

In foreign language teaching, the new scheme of education introduced in 1992 states that it will increase opportunities in foreign language learning that contribute to national development. However, for historical and security reasons instruction of Chinese is not allowed at preprimary level and at Grades 5 and 6. Of all the foreign languages taught in Thailand, English is the most popular.

8. The System of Examinations, Promotions, and Certifications

It is clearly stated in the primary curriculum of 1978 that, in principle, individual schools operate their own year-end assessment except in Grade 6, the last year of primary level, where the responsibility lies with respective departments. Moreover, for progression purposes, students in Grades 1, 3, and 5 must have an 80 percent attendance rate and reach the 60 percent pass mark in every subject area. In Grades 2, 4, and 6 students must sit and pass examinations and have an attendance rate of 80 percent.

At the secondary level, assessment and evaluation criteria are to be decided by each school cluster comprised of 7 to 10 schools in the same vicinity. The awarding of certificates at Grades 6, 9, and 12 is the responsibility of school principals with prior consent from school clusters.

At the tertiary level, admission to state universities is highly competitive. Several studies on educational opportunity reveal that most successful university entrants are those from well-off, professional and managerial families. Measures redressing student social class imbalances have been implemented. These include the establishment of regional and open universities, and the introduction of special quotas for the economically and socially disadvantaged.

9. Educational Assessment, Evaluation, and Research

At the national policy level the NEC undertakes the monitoring and evaluation of the National Education Schemes and the National Education Development Plans. It also conducts research and studies on the current state of education to check on policy implementation and as a basis for proposing recommendations for approval to the cabinet and related educational agencies.

At the implementation and operational level, every related educational department conducts follow-up studies and evaluates its programs and projects. The DCID undertakes follow-up studies of curriculum implementation to monitor educational quality on a yearly basis. A collaborative effort of educational supervisors, teachers, and technical staff has been undertaken to construct: (a) an external school evaluation system; (b) seven achievement tests of which three focus on language, mathematics and science, and the rest involve critical thinking, problem solving, and general, vocational, and social development; and (c) guides for internal school evaluation.

Basic and applied research are equally stressed. Educational establishments within the MOE place more emphasis on research and development to raise the quality of life of the rural community whereas those under the MUA are engaged in basic research to develop a body of knowledge contributing to technological development and self-reliance. Resources allocated for research rose from 3 percent of the total educational budget in the period 1982–86 to 7 percent in the period 1987–91.

So far budget and resources for assessment and evaluation have not been specifically classified, but 0.2 percent of the total educational budget in the Seventh Plan was allocated to the DCID which may give a rough guide to the extent of resources used for this purpose.

10. Major Reforms in the 1980s and 1990s

In 1987 the NEC undertook an extensive study of the national education system. Several task forces and academic committees (e.g., on the roles of higher educational institutions and local wisdom for local community development and learning network development, etc.), were commissioned to explore future needs and new directions for educational development. It was envisaged that curriculum content, directives, and policy strategies presented in the 1977 Scheme would not be appropriate to respond to the drastic changes brought about by fast information and technological progress. An Educational Scheme Drafting Committee was appointed and the new scheme was introduced in 1992.

In addition, legal and structural reform are underway. Emphases are placed on the unity and consistency of policies and plans rather than on administration and decentralization of educational provision and decision-making processes to local authorities. Moreover, deregulation and liberalization of state universities to promote flexibility, academic excellence, and academic freedom is also underway.

11. Major Problems for the Year 2000

The year 2000 will see a large number of adjustments. The Thai bureaucracy, which is a major distributor of educational provision, will undergo structural and legal reform. The number of educational personnel must be decreased and made more effective and accountable by means of redeployment and retraining since the staff payroll occupies nearly 80 percent of the educational budget, leaving very little for extensive expansion of educational programs and quality development. The educational system will be faced with rising demands for an efficient and ethical labor force from both the bureaucracy itself, and the business and industrial sectors.

Urgent problems that need to be resolved are those concerning labor force development as it is a crucial foundation or springboard for national development and self-reliance. It is essential to expand basic education for all to nine years of schooling in order to produce an input for the next levels or cycles of education and, ultimately, for the learned society. It is anticipated that the Thai citizen will be able to make an active and fruitful contribution to the country's development. Concerted efforts from both the private and public are sought to realize this goal.

References

Bank of Thailand 1993 *Thailand: Economic Developments in 1993 and Outlook for 1994*, Special Supplement. Ministry of Finance, Bangkok
Boonchuay T 1991 *A Country Monograph on Vocational/Technical Education in Thailand*. International Institute for Education Planning (IIEP), Paris
Bureau of Budget 1993 *Budget Allocation Fiscal Year 1992–1994*. Office of the Prime Minister, Bangkok
Office of the National Economic and Social Development Board (NESDB) Human Resource Development Division Thailand Development Research Institute (TDRI) 1990 *Directions and Employment Opportunities During the Seventh Plan*. NESDB, Bangkok
Ministry of Education (MOE) 1987 *Ministry of Education, Thailand, 1987*. Amarin Printing Group Co., Ltd., Bangkok
Office of the National Education Commission (NEC) 1992 *An Effort to Raising Achievement Level in Primary School in Thailand*. A state-of-the-art review submitted to Southeast Asia Research Review and Advisory Group (SEARRAG). NEC, Malaysia
Office of the National Education Commission (NEC) 1993 *Annual Report on Thai Education 1991*. NEC, Bangkok

Further Reading

Department of Curriculum and Instruction Development, Ministry of Education 1987 Report on curriculum development by level and type (mimeo). MOE, Bangkok

Office of the Permanent Secretary, Ministry of Education 1988 *A Summary Report on Research for Planning Educational Resource Distribution.* Charoenpol Press, Bangkok

Office of the National Economic and Social Development Board (NESDB) 1991 *Summary: The Seventh National Economic and Social Development Plan.* Chumnoom Sahakorn Press, Bangkok

Office of the National Education Commission (NEC) 1987 *Vocational/Technical Education in Thailand.* A state-of-the-art review submitted to Southeast Asia Research Review and Advisory Group (SEARRAG). NEC,

Malaysia

Office of the National Education Commission (NEC) 1989 *Report on the Implementation of the National Education Scheme 1977.* Roongroengsan Press, Bangkok

Office of the National Education Commission (NEC) 1990 *School Management in Thailand.* A state-of-the-art review submitted to Southeast Asia Research Review and Advisory Group (SEARRAG). NEC, Malaysia

Office of the National Education Commission (NEC) 1991 *Teacher Education in Thailand.* A state-of-the-art review submitted to Southeast Asia Research Review and Advisory Group (SEARRAG). NEC, Malaysia

Togo

A. Mingat

1. General Background

The Republic of Togo gained independence in 1960. It is located on the west coast of Africa along the Bight of Benin in between Ghana and Benin. The country is relatively narrow, being only between 50 and 150 kilometers from east to west, and 600 kilometers from south to north (Burkina Faso border). The population (3.5 million in 1989) is concentrated more in the south of the country. Population density declines from south (Maritime region) to north (Savannah) where the population is relatively scattered.

In spite of the small size of the country, the population of Togo consists of over 20 ethnic groups, most of them being unable to communicate with each other. Historically, the population of the south has been open to accept the education offered by (German, then French) missionaries, while populations in the north have always been more reluctant to receive this type of education. In 1992, the official medium of instruction was French from primary to higher education, but national languages are also used at the primary level: Ewe in the south and Kabye in the north.

To some extent as a consequence of historical and geographical forces, regional differences exist in education, both in quantity (enrollment ratios are higher in the south than in the north) and in the conditions of schooling (the average class size is very large in cities of the south and relatively small in the rural north).

The country's socioeconomic characteristics affect the development of education. On the demographic side, the global rate of growth of the population has been estimated at 3.5 percent during the 1980s and is assumed to be around 3.3 percent in the 1990s. The school-age population is anticipated to grow at a rate of 3.6–3.7 percent between 1990 and the year 2000. The demographic burden is such that there are as many children under the age of 15 in the country as adults between the ages of 15 and 65. This structure will be stable at least up to the year 2005.

The primary sector of the economy predominates and about 8 percent of the active population has a job in the modern sector (70,000 in 1989). Within the modern sector itself, civil service and semipublic organizations represent the major share of employment, the private sector accounting for only 21,000 jobs (about 30 percent of the modern sector jobs). Since 1980, employment has declined in the various segments of the modern sector with a loss of about 20 percent in the civil service as well as in private firms. It is clear that, within this environment, graduates have experienced difficulties in finding jobs. Unemployment has developed at all levels of education.

The government in the early 1990s is making plans to overcome this bleak situation. Elements of privatization of the economy are being considered as well as changes to limit taxes for productive firms. However, these changes will take time to materialize and the creation of a steady flow of new jobs is yet to be observed. Furthermore, these jobs will not primarily concern the civil service and may be suitable mostly for those with relatively low levels of qualification.

These characteristics (demographic trends, availability of public resources, and demand for graduates from the economic sector) of the Togolese context have shaped the dynamics of the education sector since the early 1980s. They are likely to play a major role in the future in the absence of a new policy; discussions for a new policy are, however, under way in 1992.

2. Politics and the Goals of the Education System

As in most African countries, education plays an important role in Togolese society, and there are various ways in which education broadly relates to the political situation. One aspect concerns the public perception of education. Education is in general recognized as a necessary instrument toward upward social mobility and access to modern life. This makes education very attractive for most of the population but also makes part of the population reluctant to enroll their children. This duality is manifested in the policymakers of the system, with some seeing the goal of education to be related to modernization while others insist on the necessity that education meets local needs.

A second aspect concerns the use of languages. Togo is made of various population groups that cannot communicate with each other; in these circumstances, French, the official medium of teaching, plays a special role. However, French is considered a foreign language and there have always been arguments for developing the use of national languages. Two of them are used: Ewe in the south and Kabye in the north. While Ewe is widely spoken in the south of the country, Kabye is only one among the various languages spoken in the north; therefore, the use of Kabye is not completely accepted.

The third aspect of the relation between education and politics is the fact that teacher unions and higher education students are two very important vocal groups in the country, influencing not only educational matters but also other political issues. This situation does not necessarily lead to a balanced educational policy between the different levels of education, nor to a fair assessment of the needs of those who are not enrolled.

3. The Formal System of Education

3.1 Primary, Secondary, and Tertiary Education

Schools were opened by German missionaries before the First World War and education was subsequently developed under French colonial power. By the time of Independence, the percentage of an age-group enrolled in school was relatively limited. The country undertook to make education broadly available and to produce the qualified people needed for the development of the country. The shortage was particularly acute among higher education graduates.

As in most French-speaking countries, the structure of the system is quite similar to what is found in France: a six years primary cycle, followed by a four years *second degré* (lower secondary) and a three years *troisième degré* (upper secondary). Higher education is provided at the University of Benin in Lomé and in some higher professional schools. Table 1 provides the main quantitative characteristics of the system for the year 1989–90.

Figure 1 presents the pattern of year-specific enrollment ratios for the system. Only 76 percent of an age-group enter Grade 1. Of those who enter Grade 1, only 58 percent survive to Grade 6. Compounding these two figures, only 44 percent of an age-group get to the end of primary schooling. A similar pattern emerges both in lower and upper secondary education: a large proportion of those who enter the first year of the cycle do not remain in school to the end of the cycle.

As a consequence of budgetary constraints on the one hand and the demographic trends on the other, enrollment has not grown at a pace sufficient to keep up enrollment ratios at the levels observed in 1980. In primary education, the loss in the net enrollment ratio is as large as 15 percent. In lower secondary, the numbers of students enrolled is even lower in 1990 than it was 10 years before. In the period 1980–85 enrollments decreased dramatically at all levels (except higher education), but in the period 1985–90, these negative trends were reversed. The explanation for this change is not obvious, but it is clear that a recovery has occurred. This outcome has not been achieved through an increase in resources but through a decrease in spending per pupil. In 1980, 4,100 students were registered in Togolese higher education institutions and in 1990, 8,600. This increase was also achieved through a reduction in spending per student.

Differences in access and dropout between sexes are quite pronounced in Togo. While 89 percent of boys enter Grade 1, only 61 percent of girls do so. Girls, then,

Table 1
Main quantitative characteristics of the system[a] (1989–90)

	Primary	Lower Secondary	Upper Secondary	Higher
Students enrolled	598,895	103,521	19,481	8,577
Enrollment Ratio (%)				
Gross	101	33	10	3
Net	63	21	6	—
Pupils–teacher ratio	58:1	35:1	22:1	31:1
% of age-group				
Intake 1st year	76	31	8	3
End of cycle	44	16	4	1
% Survival in cycle	58	52	50	30
% Repeaters	35	32	na	na

a The table refers only to general education. Vocational education has only 1,500 students at the lower secondary level, and 4,400 students at the upper secondary level.

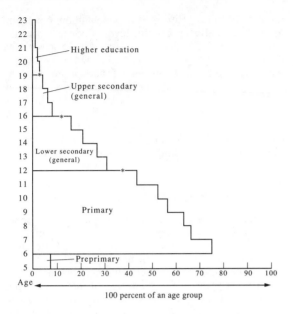

Figure 1
Togo: Structure of the formal education system 1990

tend to drop out more often than boys do during primary education (the survival rate is respectively 65 and 33 percent for boys and girls). The differences between boys and girls increase after primary education. At the end of lower secondary education, the enrollment ratio is 15 percent for boys and only 6 percent for girls; one year later, as a consequence of a difference in the pass rate at the lower secondary certificate, the girls enrolled in higher secondary represent only 1.9 percent of their age group while the corresponding figure is 6.8 percent for boys.

Differences also exist according to the socioeconomic status of the parents. Children of parents holding a job in the modern sector have better chances of entering school and of reaching higher levels of schooling. This is particularly true for survival in primary education and for the transition to lower secondary; later on, differences between groups increase but most of the differences are in place at this level. While representing 8 percent of the population, the proportion of children of modern-sector job holders is 13 percent among primary students, 32 percent among lower secondary students, and 37 percent among students both in upper secondary and higher education.

There are also urban–rural differences which are to some extent related to socioeconomic status circumstances. The net enrollment ratio is 74 percent in the Maritime region (with a long history of openness to education and high density of population) but only 30 percent in the Savannah where education is less in demand and the population relatively scattered. There are differences within regions; for example, within

the Kara region (where Kabyé is used as the national language), the net enrollment ratio is 74 percent in the Préfecture of Kozah (where Kabyé is the common language) but only 40 percent in the Préfecture of Bassar where a different language is spoken locally.

The average class size in primary schools is much larger in Grade 1 than in Grade 6 as a consequence of the dropping out process described earlier. In 1986, where the average figure for primary was 46:1, the average was 62:1 in Grade 1 but 24:1 in Grade 6. Within each grade, there are large differences across schools in class size; for example, in Grade 2 the range is as large as 15 to 130. Similarly, in primary schools there are teachers with only the primary certificate, while others have one year of higher education. The proportion of pupils with a reading book is 36 percent at the country level, but the figure varies across classes from virtually nothing to 100 percent.

3.2 Preschool Education

With only about 10,000 pupils, preschool education is developed mostly in urban areas and in particular in the city of Lomé. Private schools account for more than half of enrollment at this level. An important objective of these schools (apart from that of taking care of the children of working mothers) concerns the integration of children into a socialized environment. Direct cognitive aspects are limited and it has been shown that pupils who have attended preschool do not perform better in primary schooling than pupils who did not. Discussions are under way with respect to making preschool a preparatory course for primary schooling.

3.3 Vocational, Technical, and Business Education

Vocational and technical education is not well-developed in the country. Enrollments are only 1,500 at the lower secondary level (about 2 percent of the student body at this level). In upper secondary, about 5,000 students are enrolled in vocational public and private schools, accounting for over 20 percent of the students enrolled at this level of schooling. Clerical work and accounting accounts for two-thirds of the students, while mechanics, wood and metal work, electricity and a few other specialties enroll a small number of students. Unemployment of graduates from general education helped develop the political sense that the expansion of vocational education was to be given priority; this has been made concrete by the creation of a Ministry for Technical Education and Training.

In parallel to formal schools, Togo has a well-established tradition of apprenticeship. It concerns both small firms in the private sector and the informal sector. This flexible scheme seems to be well in tune with the needs of the country since a real market exists: employers give young people the opportunity to train while working in the shop, and individuals are willing to pay to get training that will help them to get jobs later on.

4. Administrative and Supervisory Structure and Operation

Education is centralized, with a common curriculum for all schools. The system is organized at the national level with the help of the Directorate of Planning, but major decisions are often influenced by political arguments more than by technical considerations.

The administrative structure comprises the national Directorates (pedagogical and planning) and regional directorates. Decentralization is limited and the latter have mainly a logistical role. The allocation of teachers and resources to schools (in particular at the secondary level) is made at the central level; the process is however far from perfect and there are substantial inconsistencies.

The pedagogical monitoring of the system, countrywide, is conducted by inspectors and pedagogical advisors. They control the pedagogical activities of teachers and schools, both in terms of curriculum and teaching methods.

5. Educational Finance

The Togolese system is almost completely financed by public funds: in public schools parents do contribute but the amount collected is very small in proportion to the total cost. Private schools also exist; they account for less than 25 percent at all levels except preprimary, and are mainly financed by government subsidies.

In 1990, Togo allocated about 20 percent of the government budget for the education sector, accounting for 5 percent of the country's gross national product (GNP); this proportion is above regional average (4%). Unit costs of education are relatively low in Togo compared with the average for sub-Saharan French-speaking countries. At the primary level, unit costs represent 0.13 units of GNP per capita while the corresponding figure is 0.19 units for comparable countries. For the secondary level as a whole, the unit cost in Togo is estimated at 0.50 units of GNP per capita and 0.90 units in other Francophone African countries. Unit cost derives mainly from the conjunction of three elements: the pupil–teacher ratio, teachers' salaries and the amount of subsidies (in kind and in money) given to the students.

At the primary level, and in comparison with the other French-speaking sub-Saharan African countries, Togo has both a higher pupil–teacher ratio (58:1 against 47:1) and lower teacher salaries (on average they amount to about 5 times the GNP per capita against 6.5). At the secondary level, the pupil–teacher ratio is around 30:1 (against an average of 27:1) and the average salary is about nine times the per capita GNP

(against 13 times). Bursaries represent about 6 percent of the budget allocated to this level of education while the corresponding figure is estimated at 15 percent in the countries under comparison. In higher education, bursaries represent, as in other Francophone African countries, a high proportion of the resources allocated at this level of education. The figure is as high as 50 percent, much the same as what is observed, on average, in Francophone African countries (51%) but much more than in Anglophone African countries (23%) or in low-income Asian countries (7%).

6. Supplying Personnel for the Education System

In primary education, about 20 percent of the teachers are *moniteurs*, who have not received any kind of preservice teacher training and, in general, do not hold the lower secondary certificate. Fifty-six percent are *instituteurs-adjoints* who generally hold the lower secondary certificate and a proportion of them have been exposed to a one-year teacher-training program (some others did not receive this preservice training, but have been upgraded via inservice activities). Finally, 24 percent are *instituteurs* who have either the upper secondary certificate plus one year of professional training, or the lower secondary certificate plus four years of teacher training college (*école normale*).

At the lower secondary level, about 40 percent of the teachers are qualified primary teachers (*instituteurs*), 30 percent have one year of higher education, and 30 percent have completed the "recommended" two-year program (DUEL or DUES). In upper secondary schools, most of the teachers have at least the *licence* (three years of higher education) and are considered qualified teachers.

Since 1980, the academic and administrative qualification of teachers has increased at all levels; in primary, the proportion of *moniteurs* declined from 44 to 20 percent while the proportion of *instituteurs* increased from 9 to 24 percent. In lower secondary, the proportion of primary teachers has declined from 75 to 40 percent. From a normative and pedagogical point of view, these changes tend to be considered as quality improvements. However, it is to be stressed that this view concerns an "input" perspective in the quality of education and that what is more important is the "output" perspective in which student learning is placed first.

In primary education, substantial differences are noted in the pedagogical efficiency of the various teachers; however, no difference is detected in student learning where the teacher is an *instituteur-adjoint* or a "full" *instituteur*. Since the salary gap is around 30 percent, the change incurred in promoting teacher qualification would have add-on cost consequences rather than a positive impact on student learning. In lower secondary education, *instituteurs* proved to be much more efficient than *instituteurs-adjoints*, but no different from the "real" lower secondary teachers. Again, the increase in teacher qualification may have had stronger negative consequences on costs than positive effects on student learning.

7. The System of Examinations, Promotions, and Certifications

Grade repetition is particularly frequent in Togolese education. At the primary level, the repeaters account for 35 percent, while the comparable figure is 24 percent on average in French-speaking sub-Saharan African countries, and only 10 percent in their English-speaking counterparts. Similarly, repeaters represent 32 percent at the secondary level in Togo but 21 and 2 percent respectively in the two corresponding groups of African countries.

The inspectors provide the schools for which they are responsible with common examinations that enable different schools to have more or less similar requirements for the promotion of pupils to the next grade. This procedure is clearly useful; there remains however a visible degree of inconsistency across schools in these decisions. Promotion from one grade to another is taken on this basis at the class level, but end-of-cycle certifications (primary certificate, lower secondary certificate and *baccalauréat*) that determine access to the next cycle are national examinations.

Most of the selection in the system takes place within and not between cycles. The role of end-of-cycle examinations is therefore limited despite the relatively low average pass-rate (66% for lower secondary certificate). Repetition is extensively used in case of failure at the examination and most students who have succeeded in reaching the last year of the cycle will eventually pass.

8. Educational Assessment, Evaluation, and Research

Neither educational assessment nor research is conducted in Togo; the system is managed on the input side and there is no factual assessment of student learning out of what is directly and subjectively observed by the inspectors. At the end of the 1980s, a research study was conducted on the factors accounting for student achievement in primary schooling (Grades 2 and 5). A Grade 5 test (designed with the help of Togolese inspectors and educators) was administered to a sample of students in French schools; the results showed that Togolese pupils do not perform as well as their counterparts in French schools. The discrepancy is particularly large in French (the Togolese average is 1.3 standard deviations below that of foreigners in French schools), but is relatively limited in mathematics wher the average difference is 0.8 of a standard

deviation with French nationals and 0.5 of a standard deviation with foreigners in French schools. In French, it is shown that the difficulties of the Togolese pupils are not in grammar but in those language competencies that are basically learned out of school in the French context.

9. Major Reforms in the 1980s and 1990s

A major educational reform had been proposed in 1976; the reform, designed in times when the country anticipated bright macroeconomic prospects as a consequence of the rise in international prices of phosphates, has not been implemented. Its implementation was in fact subject to budgetary circumstances that did not materialize. During the 1980s, economic conditions were very hard for Togo with a growth in GDP smaller than that of the population and even more so than that of the school-age population and as a consequence, educational policy has been very conservative.

At the beginning of the 1990s, political changes were under way with a lot of social difficulties for the country. In this atmosphere, Togo was seriously considering changes in its educational policy. The intention is to reduce the number of higher education students (mainly in humanities and law) and to promote the fields of studies for which there is a demand in the economy. These changes would help both to improve the quality of the studies and to increase the chances of graduates finding a job. To this end, short professional courses may be developed in order to establish a regulation of the flows at intermediate loci in the system, and to provide the students with practical knowledge that could help them to enter the labor market (for those who do not go on to the next cycle of studies). At the same time, and for equity reasons, the country also places a priority on the expansion of coverage (in particular for girls) and on quality improvements at the primary level.

Given the stringency of the budgetary constraints, the overall program would imply that substantial efficiency gains be achieved, and probably that extrabudgetary resources be mobilized. A reduction of the number of grade repetitions (at all levels) is being considered as well as cost-effective measures such as the use of multigrade teaching, the recruitment of *instituteurs-adjoints* (instead of *instituteurs*) and the availability of books for all pupils in primary education. It is also envisaged that external donors could participate in financing the major sectoral adjustment implied by the discussions under way, and that foreign aid be better targeted toward the new priorities of the system.

10. Major Problems for the Year 2000

A major and difficult problem concerns the overall regulation of student flows in the system: each level of education is considered as the gateway to access to the next level (the curricula of education at the different levels tend to support this view), and people tend to assume that only higher education is terminal. As a consequence those who leave the system at the end of primary or lower secondary are seen as wasting the system. Since a substantial proportion of higher education graduates have been experiencing unemployment, there is a risk that the trust of parents in education may diminish.

Bibliography

Cornavin R 1962 *Histoire du Togo*. Berger-Levrault, Paris
Dravie A, Dougna K 1991 *Coûts et financement de l'éducation au Togo*. Sigma-Etudes for DGPE/MEN, Lomé

Gbikpi-Benissan F, Dravie A, Gozo K, Nuakey Y 1991 *Adaptation du système éducatif à l'environnement socio-économique*. INSE, Lomé
Jarousse J P, Mingat A 1991 *Analyse des dotations à l'enseignement du second degreé*. DGPE/MEN, Lomé
Jarousse J P, Mingat A 1991 *Eléments pour une politique éducative nouvelle au Togo*. DGPE/MEN, Lomé
Jarousse J P, Mingat A 1992 *L'école primaire en Afrique: fonctionnement, qualité, produits: le cas du Togo*. Cahier de l'IREDU no. 52, Dijon
Kudjoh A, Mingat A 1993 Towards a better understanding of the functioning of school systems for better decision making: the case of primary schools in Togo. In: Chapman D, Mählck L (eds.) 1993 *Strategies for Improving Educational Efficiency Through Better Use of Information*. IEEE, Paris
SOTED-IREDU 1991 *Amélioration de l'efficacité interne du système éducatif*. DGPE/MEN, Lomé

Tonga

A. M. Taufe'ulungaki

1. General Background

The Kingdom of Tonga is an archipelago of 170 small islands, 36 of which are inhabited, with a total land area of 171,695 acres but occupying an ocean area of 140,000 square miles. From north to south, it is 450 miles long. Its nearest neighbors are Fiji to the northwest, Niue to the east, and Samoa to the northeast. The capital, Nuku'alofa, is located on the biggest island, Tongatapu (64,697 acres).

The Kingdom falls naturally into three main groups: the largest is the Tongatapu group in the south, which includes the island of 'Eua (21,604 acres); the northern Vava'u group (36,228 acres), which includes the two Niuas (17,072 acres), is the second largest; and the central Ha'apai group is the third largest (32,094 acres). Tonga often suffers from severe hurricanes and earthquakes.

Isolation, the scattered nature of the islands and the vast distances which separate them from each other, their smallness, and the dearth of natural resources profoundly influence educational policies and practices. Island schools are small and need multiple-class teachers. Staffing them poses problems as most schools lack staff housing and contacts are dependent on irregular and costly sea and air transport. Teachers posted to them are usually male, young, and inexperienced.

The 1986 census enumerated 94,649 persons for the whole of Tonga, of whom 47,611 were males and 47,038 were females. Some 98 percent of these were ethnic Tongans (95.5%) and part-Tongans (2.8%).

The Tongans are Polynesian by race, culture, and language. They speak Tongan, a member of the Polynesian languages group. The population distribution reflects perceived educational and economic advantages rather than available land area. A disproportionate 67.4 percent of the population reside on the main island of Tongatapu, with only 37.7 percent of the total land area; 16 percent in Vava'u, with 21.1 percent of the land area; 9.4 percent in Ha'apai, with 18.7 percent of the land area; 4.6 percent in 'Eua, with 12.6 percent of the land area; and only 2.5 percent in the two Niuas, with 9.9 percent of the land area.

The population grew at a decreasing rate from 1956 to 1986. Improved primary healthcare contributed significantly to a 36.2 percent intercensual growth between 1956 and 1966. However, it dropped to 16.4 percent between 1966 to 1976 and to 5.1 percent between 1976 and 1986. This means, assuming constant growth, that the population grew in the 1980s at a rate of 0.5 percent per annum, which is very low. The main contributing factor is migration. The birthrate for the same period was 30 per thousand population; the death rate was 6.5 per thousand; and, therefore, the rate of natural increase was 23.5 per thousand, which does not take account of migration but the rate of intercensual growth does, which means that the rate of net migration was about 18.5 per thousand.

The government responded to the unprecedented growth of the population in the 1950s and 1960s by assuming greater responsibility for primary education

from 52.5 percent in 1957 to 63.9 percent in 1970 and to 93.4 percent by 1980 and beyond. Primary enrollment increased from 15,816 in 1957 to 17,865 (13%) in 1970 and to 19,012 (6.4%) in 1980, but dropped to 16,655 in 1991 (−12.3%). Simultaneously, the churches relinquished their primary schools to concentrate on secondary education, with the consequence that secondary enrollment increased from 2,963 in 1957 to 10,057 in 1970 (239%), to 14,125 in 1980 (40.4%), and to 17,479 in 1984 (23.7%), its highest level yet. Government participation remained at a steady 10 percent from 1957 to 1980 and only increased to its early 1990s level of approximately 20 percent since 1987.

The slower population growth due to external migration means that enrollments at both primary and secondary levels have decreased every succeeding year since 1987. However, urban drifts for both educational and economic purposes have continued. The establishment of quality secondary schools in outer island groups and the upgrading of teacher training, facilities, and curricula are strategies that the government has adopted as countermeasures.

Before the advent of Europeans, Tongan society was monolingual and monocultural. The Tongan language did not possess a written form and education was purely informal. The first missionaries introduced Western education and a written form for the Tongan language. The aim was to enable the Tongans to read the Bible for themselves in their own language. Tongan was the medium of education, but the need to acquire a world language, especially the language of those who brought the new institutions of Christianity and education, soon arose, and English was taught as a subject. English is the medium of instruction at the secondary level, the dominant language in official communications, and the language of the elite and business communities. Concerns have been expressed about the ability of the Tongan language to survive the onslaught. In response, the Ministry of Education launched an integrated language program aimed at developing equal bilingual skills in Tongan and English in all Tongan students.

Tonga still has a basically subsistence economy, despite the efforts of the government since 1965 to diversify it and promote industrial and business developments. More than half of the population was classified by the 1986 census as "not economically active," which included women who were "housewives" but who might have been engaged in agricultural work or cottage industry. Of the economically active (43.2%), 39.3 percent were employed, of whom 46.5 percent were agricultural workers; 12.2 percent were professionals; 10.9 percent were in administration; and 12.9 percent were production workers. The differences in occupations between the 1976 and 1986 censuses were slight, but the main difference was a move away from agricultural (4%) to administrative and managerial occupations and the service sector, reflecting the importance of clerical and service-related jobs in government and in the tourist sector.

However, the primary sector remains the mainstay of the economy, although its output has not increased since the mid-1970s and its share in the gross domestic product (GDP) has declined from 50 percent (1974–75) to 30 percent (1988–89) mainly due to low productivity in traditional cash crops, such as bananas and copra, resulting from low export prices, labor shortages, and adverse weather conditions. However, growth was recorded in the other sectors, such as manufacturing from 3.6 percent (1982–83) to 4.8 percent (1988–89), mainly from the significant impacts of aid and remittances on domestic activities. Trade balances have been very much in favor of imports and trade deficits have increased from $T53.34m (US$35.56m) in 1986–87 to $T72.94m (US$48.62m) in 1990–91. Net private and net official transfers, however, were worth a total of $T54.83m and $T67.12m respectively for the same periods, which largely accounted for overall balances of $T11.86m (US$7.90m) and $T3.17m (US$2.11m) respectively for those years. The merchandise trade reflects the one-sided production structure of the economy. Export volumes account for less than 10 percent of GDP, with primary products comprising some 60 percent, but merchandise imports represent about 40 percent of GDP, with food and beverages accounting for nearly 30 percent.

The major objectives of development planning are to achieve sustainable economic growth conducive to a higher per capita income; to generate more employment opportunities; and to restore and control external financial balances. The task allocated to education is to ensure that the population is provided with the appropriate skills, knowledge, and attitudes it needs to achieve these objectives. Thus, at the same time, the education system is attempting to provide quality education at both primary and secondary levels, and in recent years and through into the 1990s its priority is and will continue to be postsecondary development, particularly skills training in areas which are urgently needed to generate employment opportunities and achieve sustainable economic growth.

Tonga's government structure is different from most countries in the Pacific region in that it is a Kingdom under an inherited constitutional monarch, but unlike the United Kingdom, all the members of its executive branch, the Cabinet and Privy Council, are appointed by the King and are only responsible to him. They also constitute more than one-third of the law enactment body (12 members), the Legislative Assembly. Another 9 members are elected from the hereditary chiefs (33), who are all appointed to their titles by the King, and only 9 are elected by the commoners, who constitute about 98 percent of the total population. The judiciary consists of the Court of Appeal, the Supreme Court and Magistrate's Court, and the Land Court. The Chief Justice and the other judges are all appointed by the King with the consent of Privy Council.

Tonga's political system began with the 1875 Constitution, which Tupou I granted to the people of Tonga. This was an unusual procedure as the emancipation of the common people was more commonly wrested by force by the people themselves from their rulers. However, since the people's representatives constitute less than a third of the law enactment body, decision-making in the nation is largely "declarative." It means that the three government bodies reserve the right to formulate and implement policies with or without the consent of the people. The schools and the education systems are expected to reinforce and maintain the status quo. Since the government does not educate all students at all levels, there is, in practice, a great deal of variation in educational philosophies, goals, and strategies. They do not necessarily conform to mainstream political aspirations.

2. Politics and the Goals of the Education System

Tonga's political system in both pre-European and in modern times is highly centralized. Most of the decisions relating to education are vested in the Minister of Education through the powers bestowed on him or her by the Education Act of 1974, from issues relating to educational aims and objectives, syllabuses, prescriptions, school curricula, examinations, teaching methods and contents, and evaluation procedures to regulations pertaining to teachers and their appointments.

The main educational objective since the government became involved in the formal education of Tongans has always been the training of skilled labor to meet the developmental needs of the government and the nation. The emphases for obvious reasons have changed over the years in response to evolving circumstances. In the period from 1828 to 1881, the focuses were on the acquisition of basic literacy, numeracy, and the skills and knowledge considered necessary by the missionaries for the appropriation of "civilized" habits. In the first half of the twentieth century, the emphases shifted to the provision of universal primary education, the development of secondary and vocational education, and the acquisition of English. In the second half of the century, with the achievement of universal primary education in the late 1950s and early 1960s, the needs of the economic sector became paramount and the education system was geared accordingly, although the need to upgrade primary education and to expand and upgrade secondary education were still considered priorities. However, from the mid-1980s when universal secondary education has been more or less achieved, there has been a gradual movement away from provision of basic education at the primary and secondary levels to increasing stress on postsecondary and tertiary education. As stated in the Sixth Development Plan 1991–1995, one of the major aims of education is to "expand post-secondary training programmes in areas that are important to the development of the country (e.g. technical skills, health, tourism, etc.)."

However, the eight nongovernment education systems (seven church and one independent organization) still provide 80 and 53 percent respectively of places at secondary and postsecondary levels. Government schools emphasize academic excellence and programs that promote economic well-being but nongovernment schools stress holistic development. In their view, government educational goals focus on economic growth and investment, resource utilization, corporate ownership, debt financing, and export expansion. Their own educational goals are people centered and people controlled, and are concerned with human well-being, self-reliance, internal market developments, meeting basic needs, environmental stewardship, and sustainable development. The application in either system is less dichotomous than in theory.

Since the government subsidizes nongovernment schools to the amount of only $T50.00 per student per year, it has to rely on the nongovernment education systems' goodwill rather than legislation and financial control to obtain their cooperation on the achievement of national educational goals. The nongovernment education systems have petitioned the government for greater financial assistance. The government could meet some of their needs in order to gain more control. If the government fails to meet their expectations, as is likely in the economic recession in the early 1990s, nongovernment education systems could capitalize on the issue to justify increasingly deviant educational developments.

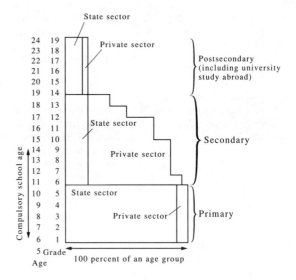

Figure 1

Tonga: Structure of the formal education system 1991

3. The Formal System of Education

Figure 1 represents the structure of the formal education system.

Education is free and compulsory from 6 to 14 years of age. It has been compulsory since the 1862 Code of Laws. Tonga's financial resources are severely limited and it has to prioritize its educational programs. It concentrates therefore on those educational activities which are considered essential for continuing national development, such as the provision of basic primary and secondary education and of requisite postsecondary educational programs.

3.1 Primary, Secondary, and Tertiary Education

Tonga has enjoyed universal primary education since the 1950s and universal secondary education since the late 1970s and early 1980s, despite the fact that all secondary schools, including those of the government, are fee paying. Primary education takes six years from Class 1 to Class 6 and entry to Class 1 is legally in the year when the child turns six. All schools are coeducational. The school day begins at 9.00 am and officially ends at 3.20 pm, with a one-and-a-half hour break for lunch to allow the children to return home. Each school year consists of three 14-week terms, and legislation requires that each school year must have at least 200 school days. In 1991, there were 115 primary schools in which were enrolled 16,655 children, of whom 15,380 (92.3%) were educated in 104 government primary schools and taught by 626 teachers. The remaining 1,275 (7.7%) pupils were educated in 11 church schools and taught by 63 teachers. Because of the isolated and scattered nature of the rural and island communities, most of their schools are composite or multiple class (73.3% in Vava'u and 84.2% in Ha'apai).

Entry into the secondary level is through the Secondary Entrance Examination (SEE), administered by the Ministry of Education, which is sat in Class 6. Each secondary school selects its entrants on the basis of their choice of schools and their performance in the examination. Secondary education takes six years from Form 1 to Form 6. However, most students leave school after sitting the Tonga School Certificate Examination (TSCE) at Form 5. Some church schools have a pre-Form 1 class called "Class 7" and a lower and an upper fifth class in Year 5. Some have a two-tier secondary system: middle schools consisting of Forms 1 and 2 and senior secondary schools consisting of Forms 3 to 6. Most schools have six hours of teaching per day and most follow the three 14-week terms of the government schools. All schools are required by the school examination regulations to have at least 200 days of schooling a year.

Comparison of school enrollment figures for 1986 with the 1986 census data show that essentially 100 percent of children attend school from 6 to 15 years of age. At 16, only 80 percent of the age cohort still attend school and only 61, 43, and 24 percent at 17, 18, and 19 respectively. Since the government has provided a primary school on every inhabited island and within walking distance of every child, there are no gender or rural–urban differences in primary school enrollment. However, at the secondary level, the 1991 enrollment figures show that by Form 4 girls outnumber boys (53%, 52%, and 50.2% for Forms 4, 5, and 6 respectively). In the Ha'apai group, the only group without a government high school and a Form 6 secondary school, a comparison of the 1989 enrollment figures with the projected estimated secondary-school population shows that Ha'apai secondary schools are educating a decreasing percentage of the secondary-school population (80% in 1984 but 39.6% in 1989). It appears that a significant number is migrating to Tongatapu for educational purposes.

In 1991, 13,839 students attended 40 secondary schools and were taught by 876 teachers, of whom 2,551 (18.4%) attended the 7 government high schools and were taught by 181 teachers and the remaining 11,288 (81.6%) attended 33 nongovernment schools and were taught by 695 teachers. With only three exceptions (one government school {boys} and two Free Wesleyan schools {one for boys, one for girls}), all schools are coeducational. A significant number of secondary schools have boarding facilities to cater for rural and island students. Most live with relatives while attending secondary schools on Tongatapu or in the main urban centers at Ha'apai and Vava'u.

A common phenomenon of postsecondary education in Tonga and other small countries of the region is the extent to which they rely on overseas funding, expertise, and institutions for the provision, externally and internally, of middle- and high-level labor force training. However, in 1985, the government established the Community Development and Training Centre (CDTC) to coordinate all training at this level and to rationalize the use of scarce human and material resources. The Centre promotes flexible, short but specific skills-based in-country postsecondary training programs, which are cost effective and relevant. It expanded technical training in mechanics, automotive engineering, building and construction, carpentry, plumbing, electricity and electronics, refrigeration, and computer engineering. Fees are charged for full-time courses and are usually recovered from the employers. Because of the increasingly high costs of external funding, the trend toward increasing in-country postsecondary training, even to university level, is likely to accelerate.

Before 1985, government postsecondary training was conducted by each ministry, such as the police training center, the school of nursing, and the primary teachers' college. Minimal entry qualification was the Tonga Higher Leaving Certificate Examination (Form 4 level). Nongovernment establishments included theological colleges, and technical, secretarial, and agricultural institutes. Enrollments in 1985 and 1989 were 1,224 and 1,840 respectively and did not include private and scholarship students in overseas institutions, which were estimated at twice these numbers.

The immediate effect of increased localization of postsecondary training was a dramatic expansion in the number of government trainees from 246 in 1985 to 867 in 1989 (252.4%), which increased its share of trainees at this level from 20.1 percent in 1985 to 47.1 percent in 1989 and there was also a rise in the number of part-time students (30.3%). Prerequisite qualifications for formal courses were upgraded. Certificate programs require the TSC (Year 5) as a minimal qualification and diploma programs require at least a Form 6 qualification. Programs of nongovernment institutions were rationalized to minimize overlaps and omissions. Inadvertently, postsecondary opportunities were mostly accessed by urban and male students since most of the courses were conducted in urban institutions and in areas that were traditionally male domains, such as technical and agricultural training. In 1989, females represented only 43.7 percent of postsecondary students.

Tonga has not established a national university, although there is one private one, 'Atenisi, which is not recognized by the government. The University of the South Pacific (USP) operates a center in Tonga which enrolls extension students for most nondegree and degree courses offered by the University. In 1990, 194 students were enrolled at the center, a dramatic drop from 800 in 1986, which reflects the improvements in civil servants' salaries. A common incentive for enrollment was the award of an increment in salary for every two degree papers completed.

Tonga still relies mostly on overseas university institutions in the region and in Australia and New Zealand to meet its high-level labor force training requirements. In 1990, largely with assistance from Australia and New Zealand, it had 153 scholarship students studying abroad. Only 53 were awarded to girls because technical and agricultural areas represented a high percentage of the awards.

3.2 Preschool Education

There are no official provisions for preschool or kindergarten, although there are plans for the establishment of a one-year teacher-training program for kindergarten teachers. However, kindergartens of various quality are found all over the Kingdom, but most of the quality establishments are located in the Nuku'alofa area and cater largely to the children of the elite. All these institutions are supported entirely by parents and communities and almost all charge fees.

3.3 Special Education

Tonga does not operate special schools for children with special needs, although nongovernment organi-

zations run centers for the severely physically and mentally handicapped.

However, within the formal school system, the Ministry of Education began in 1987 a special program at the primary level known as LINK, which is aimed at training preservice and inservice teachers and at developing special materials to assist children with learning difficulties.

3.4 Vocational, Technical, and Business Education

The provision of vocational, technical, and business education has always posed major problems for small countries with small populations and severely limited resources such as Tonga. It requires very expensive facilities and tools and specialist teachers. In the mid-1970s, Tonga, with other regional countries, implemented a vocational program of industrial arts, home economics, commercial studies, and agricultural science at the secondary level in an attempt to meet urgent technical training needs. The program was largely unsuccessful due to financial and staffing difficulties.

With the establishment of CDTC, the government's most recent strategy is to provide high-quality general education to the highest level affordable by the country in order to create a flexible workforce that can adapt readily to fast-changing technological advances. Isolation, smallness, and dearth of economic and human-skilled resources severely constrain Tonga's attempts to keep abreast of quantum leaps in world technological and scientific developments.

Since Tonga's business and industrial sectors are very much in their infancies, they have yet to play major roles in the development of vocational, technical, and business education.

4. Administrative and Supervisory Structure and Operation

The government system is centralized and the Ministry of Education recruits, appoints, pays, and dismisses all government teachers at all levels, subject to ministerial and cabinet approval, and provides buildings, materials, and equipment. Government secondary and postsecondary institutions are allowed greater latitude in the administration of their own budgets.

The eight nongovernment educational managing authorities are responsible to the Minister of Education for the management and administration of their institutions at all levels. The Advisory Council for Education, whose members are all appointed by the Minister, but in which all education systems are represented, facilitates communication and dialogue between the Ministry and nongovernment education systems. In practice, the Education Act is flexibly applied and nongovernment systems are more or less free to administer their institutions in their own way. The Free Wesleyan Church (FWS) is the largest nongovernment educational authority, and educated in 1991, 658 primary pupils (4%), 3,986 (28.8%) secondary students, and 145 (14.7%) postsecondary students. The Catholic Church (RC) and Latter Day Saints (LDS) educate similar numbers of secondary-school pupils as the government, and the Catholics administer the only business college in the Kingdom. 'Atenisi (AI), the only independent education system, operates a secondary school and a university institution.

The Ministry's inspectorate division is responsible for the monitoring of schools' and teachers' performance at primary and secondary levels. It was assisted until 1988 by inspectors from New Zealand, who were mainly concerned with the ability of Tongan secondary schools to meet the requirements of the then New Zealand-administered School Certificate and University Entrance Examinations in terms of quality teaching and qualified staff. The Curriculum Development Unit (CDU) monitors the trialing and implementation of curricular programs. Both groups service government and nongovernment education systems.

At the postsecondary level, Tonga is concerned with the international credibility of its training programs. External validators mainly from the University of the South Pacific (USP), New Zealand, and Australia assess most of the postsecondary programs. Such external validation is expected to become a permanent feature of postsecondary education and training to ensure that quality is comparable with standards obtaining in reputable institutions abroad. Although there is no national accreditation board, the Ministry of Education in collaboration with the Establishment Division of the Prime Minister's Office, which is responsible for the civil service, acts in that capacity for all training at this level. Plans, however, have been set in motion for the establishment of a national qualifications authority, which would be responsible for the certification of all formal and nonformal training.

Schools, whether government or nongovernment, are directly responsible to their managing authorities. They are administered by a principal, who is responsible to the director of education. In a few experimental cases at the secondary level, where the government established community high schools by absorbing existing church schools, a board of governors, reflecting such amalgamations, has been established to which the principal directly accounts. At the postsecondary level, most institutions are governed by boards. Those that are not are in the process of establishing them.

5. Educational Finance

The government's budgetary allocation to the education sector grew at an average rate of 14.6 percent at constant prices between the 1986–87 and 1990–91 financial years. The allocation for 1990–91 was $T8.593m (US$5.72m) or 17.9 percent of the total national budget. This fiscal year was exceptional as the recurrent expenditure allocated to the Department for that year was augmented by 40 percent at constant prices (as compared with 7.6% in 1989–90) as a result of a structural review and general increase of teachers' and other officers' salaries. This raised to a record 18 percent the proportion of government recurrent expenditure allocated to education (from 13.5% in 1989–90). Thus, the education sector receives the largest departmental allocation within the government's recurrent budget (for example, 65% more than the health sector, or 120% more than the public works portfolio).

Of the 1990–91 allocation, $T3.230m (US$2.15m) or 37.6 percent was allotted to primary education; $T1.588m (US$1.05m) or 18.5 percent was appropriated for secondary education; and $T2.149m (US$1.43m) (25%) was given to postsecondary education, which included contributions to regional institutions, such as USP, overseas scholarships, and in-country training. Government spending per student for each level (in-country training only) increased from $T93 (US$62) for the primary level in 1985–86 to $T139 (US$92.6) in 1989–90; for the secondary level from $T311 (US$207) in 1985–86 to $T325 (US$216.6) in 1989–90; but decreased in vocational and technical training respectively for the same periods from $T1,500 (US$1,000) to $T782 (US$521.3) and from $T2,176 (US$1,451) to $T862 (US$575). These figures do not include significant contributions from nongovernment sources, such as parents and ex-students. The difference in trends reflects increases in teachers' salaries at the lower levels.

There are no official figures on the finances of nongovernment education systems, but in 1990, nongovernment secondary schools reported a recurrent budget of $T5.138m and a total revenue of $T2.411m (US$1.6m), most of which was obtained from fees. The government subsidy to nongovernment schools, which began only in 1989, is $T50 (US$33.3) per head per year (raised from $T20 {US$13.3} per head) and was $T499,438 (US$332,958) in 1990. Capital development expenditure came to $T1.684m. From these figures, nongovernment expenditure per student was $T456 (US$304), which is higher than the government's for the same level for the same period. Nongovernment systems have petitioned the government, in the name of equity, to raise the subsidy to the same amount that the government spends per year per student in its own secondary schools, which in 1990–91 was estimated at $T607. This would mean significant increases in the education budget, which the government could not afford. The government also provides indirect assistance in the form of curriculum and examination materials, duty-free concessions on the importation of educational materials, and training opportunities for staff.

989

Tonga depends on external assistance for most of its developmental activities. In 1985–86, 82.5 percent of a $T4.5m developmental program was financed through foreign aid, which mainly supported vocational and technical education efforts, and in 1989–90, of the $T1.8m received from abroad, 98 percent served to finance overseas training. These amounts do not include foreign aid to nongovernment systems. It is estimated that the number of private students studying abroad far exceeds that of scholarship students who are all fully funded.

6. Supplying Personnel for the Education System

The pupil–teacher ratio for 1991 was 23:1 and 16:1 for the primary and secondary levels respectively. However, 10 percent of the primary-school teachers were untrained and another 9.5 percent were in the lowest professional category. The large number of composite schools (54%) requires a low pupil–teacher ratio to maintain quality education in small schools. At the secondary level, expatriate and untrained teachers constituted one-third (13.5% and 21% respectively) of the teaching force. Another 24 percent were trained as primary-school teachers.

The supply of primary-school teachers is satisfactory. By the end of 1992, the primary level had a fully trained teaching force. In 1987, the government introduced an integrated three-year diploma program for primary and secondary teachers. Students, after a first year of common core courses, select whether to specialize in primary or secondary teaching. Primary teachers can teach from Class 1 to Form 2 and secondary teachers can teach to Form 5 level. It is anticipated that the teacher-training needs of the secondary schools will be met by 1997. In 1994 it is planned to introduce one-year postprofessional training programs to meet more specialized needs. The programs would include counseling; teaching English as a second language; physical education and sports; educational administration, management, and planning; curriculum development and educational assessment; computer studies; and single-subject diplomas, such as physics and music. Since the 1989 salary review, better caliber trainees are increasingly being attracted into the general teaching service but senior secondary-school and postsecondary-school teaching services still have to compete with prestigious professions such as law and medicine for the best graduates. Grave shortages in the technical areas and the sciences will therefore be experienced for some time; as well as in accounting and economics, where the private sector tends to attract the best graduates.

Staffing the small schools in the remote islands will remain a major problem as most schools lack standard staff housing and social conventions prevent the posting of female staff to such posts. A major item in the Sixth Development Plan is the provision of standard staff housing to rural and island schools. Already a positive discrimination policy in the recruitment of teachers in favor of men ensures that at least 50 percent of new recruits are men, although in practice the better applicants are usually women. Even with such a policy, 68.9 percent of primary teachers are women. At the secondary level, women represent only 45 percent of the teaching force. All government teachers are required to teach for three years in an outer island school.

Serving teachers receive inservice training on a regular basis. The primary division is well-staffed by field officers who conduct in-school, district, and national workshops as the need arises. Inservice training for secondary teachers is normally undertaken by the CDU on new or upgrading programs and by the EU on new examination prescriptions and syllabuses. Tonga also benefits from workshops, seminars, and short training courses offered in-country, in the region, and in metropolitan countries by external organizations, such as AIDAB, NZODA, WHO, UNESCO, and USP.

Primary teachers trained at certificate level are required to sit professional examinations, which classifies them into three levels, Classes I to III, with Class I being the highest, and they are paid accordingly. All teachers are assessed annually on their performance on a 5-point scale, with 1 being the highest. Both scales are used in promotion exercises.

7. Curriculum Development and Teaching Methodology

The Minister of Education approves all school curricula and examination prescriptions and prescribes the core curriculum. The government curriculum development and examinations units develop the national school curricula and public examinations, with assistance from teachers and schools. However, nongovernment schools can pursue different programs with the approval of the Minister. With the exception of the independent schools which follow the New South Wales school and higher school certificate programs, all other schools follow the government programs. At the primary level, the core curriculum consists of Tongan and English, mathematics, and environmental science, an integrated science and social studies program. Music, physical education and sports, and Tongan culture are also compulsory but are nonexamination subjects. Tongan is the medium of instruction at this level with English being taught as a subject from Class 1. All primary schools follow a common timetable, which is developed centrally and distributed free of charge to schools. All students sit the SEE in four subjects: Tongan, English, environmental science, and mathematics, except for the only English-medium primary school, which follows a different program and has examinations in English, advanced English, mathematics, and general studies.

Teachers at this level are generalists but there are plans to train specialist teachers to teach only English and Tongan.

At the secondary level, specialization begins, which requires specialist teachers. The core curriculum at Forms 1 and 2 comprises Tongan and English, mathematics, science, social science, music, physical education, and health studies. The optional subjects are industrial arts, agricultural science, and home economics. At Forms 3 to 5, the only compulsory subjects are Tongan and English, although most schools also offer science and mathematics as core subjects. Students usually take eight to nine subjects at Forms 3 and 4, which are reduced to five or six at Form 5 level. The subjects include Tongan, English, accounting, economics, geography, history, science, mathematics, industrial arts, home economics, agricultural science, typing and shorthand, music, art, French, and Japanese. Most schools offer all these subjects, excepting Japanese and French, which are taught in only a few schools. The terminal examination for this level is the TSCE, the prescriptions and syllabuses for which are developed by the curriculum and examinations units, with inputs from teachers and schools.

Only nine subjects are commonly offered at Form 6 level: English, mathematics, physics, chemistry, biology, accounting, economics, geography, and history. The terminal examination at this level is the Pacific Senior School Certificate (PSSC), a regional examination, administered by the South Pacific Board for Educational Assessment (SPBEA), which has replaced the New Zealand University Entrance Examination. The prescriptions and syllabuses were developed with inputs from regional teachers and schools. The PSSC examination is a temporary measure only. A Form 7 program, based on the New Zealand Bursaries examination, was established in one national center in 1991 but will be implemented in the schools in 1996, thus replacing the PSSC program. After Form 5, there will be a two-year program leading to the Form 7 qualification, which is also expected in the long term to be fully localized when funds and expertise permit.

With assistance mainly from Australia and New Zealand, Tonga is undergoing major curriculum reviews and development. The main objectives are to develop appropriate and relevant quality curricula for both primary and secondary levels in key subject areas in order to upgrade basic literacy, numeracy, and scientific skills and knowledge. The subjects that have been identified for priority treatment within the lifetime of the $T1.5 million (US$1 million) project (1991–93) are Tongan, English, mathematics, and science from Class 1 at the primary level to Form 7 at the secondary level. A great deal of effort is directed at coordinating primary and secondary curricula programs and preservice and inservice teacher-training programs to ensure complementarity and to avoid overlaps and omissions. The general approach is child centered and enquiry based, with special emphases on skills and concept development.

Most nongovernment education systems supplement the national core programs with their own system-specific activities. Most schools, within the prescribed programs, also develop their own school-based curricula and assessment strategies and procedures. Fees are charged for the terminal examinations at the secondary level and for most secondary curricula materials.

8. The System of Examinations, Promotions, and Certifications

The general policy at the primary level is for students to be automatically promoted to each level. However, schools are allowed a great deal of discretion. Since the LINK program is still at an experimental stage, pupils are allowed to repeat a level, particularly Class 1, if the teachers feel that the child has not acquired the basic skills required for the next level. At the end of Class 6, all pupils sit the SEE. Entry to government schools is limited to students who have not reached age 12 in the year of the examination.

At the secondary level, most schools require students to attain certain school-determined minimal criteria for promotion to each succeeding level. Students either repeat the level when they do not meet the criteria, transfer to another school, or leave the education system. Public examinations are offered at Forms 2, 5, 6, and 7. The Examinations Unit (EU) administers the common Form 2 examination, whose main purpose is to monitor national performance at this level, and the TSCE at Form 5, which was formerly the New Zealand School Certificate Examination, and localized with its assistance. The SPBEA administers the PSSC at Form 6 for four countries of the region, namely, Tonga, Western Samoa, the Solomons, and Kiribati; and New Zealand allows Tongans to sit for the New Zealand Bursaries examination at Form 7. Some schools do the USP's foundation program as an alternative Form 7 program, but the foundation program is to be terminated at the end of 1992. Increasingly, internal assessment (IA) is assuming more importance. The EU is conducting research on the feasibility of introducing some IA components into the SEE. Most subjects of the TSCE, PSSC, and NZ Bursaries have some IA components. In Tonga, its use has been constrained by the teachers' and schools' inexperience in its administration but when teachers and schools have gained sufficient competence and confidence, school-based assessments could be used more extensively.

9. Educational Assessment, Evaluation, and Research

Like other parts of the world, Tonga has been concerned with the issue of upgrading students' performance, particularly in basic literacy and numeracy. Although no national tests have been developed to monitor achievements at the various levels, the SEE and the TSCE have been used to compare performance among students, subjects, schools, districts, and different years. The Planning Unit, EU, CDU, and the Inservice Division have also collected data, and conducted research and assessment exercises from time to time to evaluate the effectiveness of various educational programs. Tonga has also participated in similar regional exercises, the latest being the Pacific Islands Literacy Levels (PILL) conducted by UNESCO, which assessed the literacy and numeracy levels of nine Pacific countries (2,529 Class 6 students in 94 schools). As with similar studies in other parts of the world, it has generated some conflicts, but the general conclusions are positive in that many have achieved basic literacy and numeracy competence; about 75 percent have achieved basic competence in both of the two languages they sat; also, the study found that girls consistently outperform boys at all levels.

The main research emphases in the remainder of the decade will be at the postsecondary level. Tonga has recently joined other Pacific countries in the PEACESAT program, which will allow it to access information and data from the University of Hawaii and other mainland libraries and databases to which it has access.

10. Major Reforms in the 1980s and 1990s

The 1980s saw a number of major reforms in Tongan education. With universal primary and secondary education being achieved, the main emphases were no longer on increasing access but on quality basic education. The school curricula at both primary and secondary levels were made more relevant and appropriate. This process culminated in the establishment of the EU and the localization of the TSCE in 1987. The terminal examination was upgraded from the Tonga Higher Leaving Examination at Form 4 to the TSCE at Form 5.

The government expanded its secondary-school system to most outer island groups, excepting Ha'apai, which is expected to receive its new government high school by 1994. Postsecondary education was also expanded and preservice teacher training upgraded from a primary-only two-year certificate program to an integrated primary and secondary three-year diploma program in 1987. The CDTC was established in 1985. In 1988 Tonga cofounded the Consortium of Pacific Education (COPE) with American and Western Samoa and the Pacific International Center for High Technology Research (PICHTR), an organization that aims at assisting Pacific member countries to improve their scientific and technological capabilities.

The 1990s and beyond will see the consolidation as well as expansion of these activities. Tonga will

assume responsibility for the external examinations at Forms 6 and 7. Most senior secondary schools will become Forms 1 to 7 schools instead of Forms 1 to 6 schools. More in-country training will take place at the postsecondary level, even to degree and graduate levels, by capitalizing on Tonga's ready accessibility to the new information and communications technology. Applied research projects in priority areas such as marine science will be established. The Tonga Maritime Polytechnic Institute (TMPI), expanded with funds from the Federal Republic of Germany to cater for nonmaritime technical training and research, will become the new Institute of Science and Technology. Similarly, Australia is funding the upgrading and expansion of training offered by CDTC, which will see the establishment of three other institutions under the umbrella of CDTC: the Institute of Education (the present teacher-training college), the Institute of Health Studies, and the Institute of Higher Education. Tonga also hopes to derive full benefit from the opportunities offered by the newly established Commonwealth of Learning.

11. Major Problems for the Year 2000

Tonga's educational problems have always centered on two issues: lack of financial support and scarcity of skilled human resources. The educational developments at the postsecondary level will increase its pool of competent middle-level professionals and the scholarship program is similarly providing much needed high-level skilled labor. However, the economic situation remains uncertain. Tonga relies very heavily on external assistance for almost all educational developments. Inevitably, external aid agencies, regardless of disinterested benevolence, will exercise degrees of control on the philosophies and practices of education. If the ultimate aim of the country is to gain self-reliance, it has some very difficult choices to make: to curb educational developments to match its capability to control and direct them or to continue the present trends.

Bibliography

Biles J, Low B, Dunkley M (eds.) 1981 *Aims of Education for Tonga.* Pacific Programs, Macquarie University, Sydney
Government of Tonga 1956–91 *Report of the Ministry of Education for the Year 1956 {to 1991}.* Government Printer, Nuku'alofa
Government of Tonga 1956–1993 *Estimates of Revenue and Expenditure and the Development Estimates for the Year 1956/57 {to 1992/93}.* Government Printer, Nuku'alofa
Government of Tonga 1991a *Sixth Development Plan 1991–1995.* Government Printer, Nuku'alofa
Government of Tonga 1991b *Population Census.* Government Printer, Nuku'alofa
UNESCO 1992 *Pacific Islands Literacy Levels: A Criterion-referenced Study.* South Pacific Board for Educational Assessment, Suva, Fiji

Tunisia

H. Ben Jaballah and B. Lamine

1. General Background

Tunisia is a North African country located at the northern tip of the African continent, between the Western and the Eastern basins of the Mediterranean and has an area of 162,155 square kilometers. With a 1,298 kilometer-long coastline, Tunisia is also bordered by Algeria and Libya. The Tunisian landscape is mainly one of lowlands and its highest mountain is Mount Chambi (1,544m). Three regions can be identified according to climate and geographic location: the North, which is rainy and fertile, and has the highest concentration of population; the center, characterized by both low and high plains, it extends to the coastal area; the South: characterized by desert expanses punctuated with oases.

The Tunisian climate is moderate, with average temperatures ranging between 11.4 C in December and 29.3 in July. Rainfall is irregular and is mainly concentrated during the cold season (75% of the total). The average rainfall is above 1,500 millimeters in the North and less than 150 millimeters in the far South. Snow can sometimes fall on the Northern highlands.

Tunisia's largest cities are Tunis (capital city), Sfax, Sousse, Gabes, Nabeul, Kairouan, and Bizerta. With a total population of about 8.2 million in 1991, Tunisia is a middle-size nation whose urban population has grown to 52 percent. Approximately 40 percent of the total population are under 15 and life expectancy is around 65.7 for males and 66.9 for females. Population density was 47 inhabitants per square kilometer in 1988.

Tunisia has been a recognizable nation for over 3,000 years. Ancient Romans called it Africa, a name which extended in later years to the whole continent. The nation city of Carthage, founded in 814 BC, was to be in constant rivalry with the Roman Empire for the control over the Mediterranean sea. The Punic wars (264–146 BC) were to end with the total destruction of the city of Carthage. Rome's granary, Tunisia was to know unprecedented urbanization and prosperity during the Roman Era.

In the middle of the seventh century AD, Tunisia became part of the Islamic Empire and Kairouan was founded in 670 AD. Until the twelfth century the country went through a period of peace and prosperity. Subsequently, the Eastern coastline was occupied by the Normans. A dynasty from Morocco, the Almoravides, was to reconquer the country and take Tunis for their capital city from 1236 to 1574. This period is especially remembered for cultural revival embodied most characteristically in Ibn Khaldun, the founder of modern sociology.

The sixteenth century was characterized by rivalry between Spain and the Ottoman Empire and, in 1705, Hussein Ibn-Ali proclaimed independence from Turkey and became the first Bey of Tunis. The Husseinite Dynasty was to last until 1957 when the Republic was established.

The country was invaded by French troops in 1881. The Bey was then compelled to sign the Bardo Treaty by virtue of which Tunisia became a French protectorate. Soon, political movements were to stir public opinion against French occupation. In the mid-1930s, the Neo Destour (Constitutional) Party was to lead the country to Independence from the French in 1956.

In 1957, the Tunisian people deposed the beys and proclaimed a republic. Between 1957 and 1987, Tunisia was led by its founding father and first President of the Republic, Habib Bourguiba. In 1987, Tunisia inaugurated a new era with the access of President Zinel-Abidine Ben-Ali to the presidency in compliance with the Constitution.

Tunisia, according to the 1959 Constitution and as amended in 1987, is an independent, sovereign nation whose language is Arabic and whose religion is Islam.

Immediately after independence from France, the 1956 Constitution was promulgated defining the present political system in Tunisia, a presidential regime characterized by the segregation of the executive, legislative, and judiciary branches of government. The legislative branch consists of one chamber, called since 1976 the Chamber of Representatives, where 141 deputies of the nation are elected according to universal suffrage for a five-year mandate. The executive branch is headed by the head of state who is also the President of the Republic, and is elected for a five-year mandate, renewable twice. He is assisted by a government led by a prime minister. The Constitution provides for total independence of the judiciary from both the executive and the legislative branches of government.

The Tunisian economy is based on agriculture and tourism. Although still young, its diversified industry ranks third in the economic life of the country. With extremely modest natural resources, Tunisia has chosen to rely on its human resources and has granted priority to its educational system. Privatization of large sectors of hitherto public activities has called for private enterprise. Such an orientation does not mean, however, that the government has totally abandoned its role. The state still plays a major part in vital sectors such as education, health, and transportation. For all these reasons, Tunisia is reforming its educational system to address the needs of comprehensive development at all levels.

2. *Politics and the Goals of the Education System*

The Tunisian educational system was unified in 1958 with the promulgation of the 1958 Education Act. During the colonial period, the system of education was divided into three subsystems: (a) Zeitouni, traditional and Koranic; (b) colonial, French; and (c) Sadiqi, a blend of the virtues of tradition and the efficiency of modernity. After Independence, the Sadiqi system became the model for the unified national educational system which was both modern in its approach and also rooted in the cultural heritage of the nation. Publicly sponsored, the system was open to all children six years of age.

During the first decade of Independence, the teaching staff, which was mainly French, was gradually replaced by Tunisian teachers. By 1992, cooperation with France in this field was limited to a few teachers in higher education, mainly in science and technology.

The 1958 Reform, which was for all purposes a revolution, has provided the nation with scientific and technical qualifications which have ensured its social, intellectual, and economic advance. However, tossed by constant changes implemented by rapidly changing officials who were often incompetent, the Tunisian educational system was soon to lose some of its lustre, and it declined both in quantity and quality. In a country where leadership was lacking, at a time when the great leader Habib Bourguiba was feeling the burden of old age after a long militant past, education nearly fell into the hands of obscurantists from the mid-1970s to 1986. However, in 1987, the new president began to guide the country, which had gone through a long period of indecision, to a new policy where education holds a central position and is the spearhead of change.

This policy aimed at ensuring the comprehensive development of the country through two concurrent channels: democracy (political pluralism, the revival of associative life, wider consultation on all issues related to the life of the nation), and knowledge.

The New Education Act of 1990 reinforces the democratic dimension of the Tunisian educational system by stipulating that education is compulsory. The new Education Act also initiated basic education; Article 1 of the Act proclaimed that, within the framework of the identity of the Tunisian nation and its belonging to the Arab and Moslem sphere of civilization, the educational system is aimed at:

(a) providing the young from early childhood with the knowledge necessary to strengthen their awareness of the identity of the Tunisian nation, to develop their civic feeling and their sense of belonging to the Tunisian nation, to the Maghreb, to the Arab sphere and to Islamic culture, and to reinforce an open attitude to modernization and human civilization;

(b) educating the young to be faithful to Tunisia and loyal to it;

(c) preparing the young for a life where there is no room for any form of discrimination or segregation based on sex, social status, race, or religion;

(d) providing the young with a good grounding in the Arabic language, to enable them to use it in learning and in production, in the social sciences as well as in science and technology;

(e) providing for the students to acquire one foreign language at least to allow them to gain direct access to works of universal thought, technology, scientific theories, and human values and to prepare them to monitor their development so as to contribute to the culture of the nation and its interaction with universal human culture;

(f) encouraging students to build their own personality and assisting them in reaching maturity so that they are educated with respect to the values of tolerance and moderation;

(g) contributing to the promotion of students' personality and the development of their potential, promoting the development of their critical faculties and will-power so that they are gradually educated in rationality and moderation in judgment, self-confidence in attitude, initiative and creativity in work;

(h) striking a balance between the various topics of learning so that there is equal emphasis on the sciences, humanities, technology, and manual skills as well as cognitive, moral, affective, and practical education;

(i) providing the young with an opportunity for physical activities and sports as an integral part of their education;

(j) preparing the young for the future by training them throughout the various cycles of the educational system so that when they leave school they are able to keep up with a rapidly changing modern environment and contribute positively to its development;

(k) preparing students to have a positive attitude towards work and to consider its moral dimension and the effective role it plays in building the personality, in safeguarding the nation and in contributing to human civilization;

(l) ensuring that educational activity plays its role in the overall advance of the nation by training qualified and competent citizens capable of discharging the duties inherent to comprehensive development required by such an advance;

(m) throughout the various stages of the educational system, in both curricula and approaches, arousing awareness of citizenship and civic sense so that when students leave school, they became citizens for whom awareness of their rights is not separable from the discharge of their duties in a civil and institutional society based on the blending of freedom and responsibility.

The new impulse given to education in Tunisia was identified at the outcome of a two-year broad consultation. At the outcome of its work, which was made public, the Tunisian legislator translated all viewpoints on which there was a consensus into legislation which was first submitted to the High Council for Education, a legal body, and then to the Economic and Social Council, a constitutional body.

3. The Formal System of Education

The current education system in Tunisia is going through a period of transition where the old system is being phased out and a new system is being phased in after its initiation in 1989–90. The reform is to shift from a 6–(3–4) organization to a (6–3)–4 organization, that is, from a system where there was primary education for six years and a two-stage secondary education for seven years (lower secondary for three years and upper secondary for four years of specialized education), to a system where basic education lasts for nine years (six years of primary, three years preparatory) and then secondary education in four years with two stages (two years of general education and two years of prespecialized education).

This shift was dictated by two major factors: the demand to increase compulsory education and the fact that specialized education was deemed to be too early in the 9th grade and was thus postponed to the 11th grade. The first two years of secondary education will thus be used to reinforce general education. Simultaneously the baccalaureates, or final qualifications of secondary education had been extended by adding two new options to the existing three: arts, mathematics, sciences, technology, economy, and management.

As the new system is well advanced at both primary and secondary stages, the following will be a description of the system initiated in 1989.

3.1 Primary, Secondary, and Tertiary Education

Basic education which lasts nine years, is compulsory and state sponsored. The government, therefore, ensures that all children between the ages of 6 and 16 are schooled at no expense to their families.

Basic education is divided into two stages. The first lasts six years and aims at providing pupils with the instruments of knowledge acquisition: the basic mechanisms of reading, writing, and arithmetic (the three r's); as well as contributing to the development of their mind, their intelligence, their artistic sense, and their manual and physical potential, it endeavors to cultivate their religious and civic education. This stage is known as the primary education stage.

The second stage lasts three years and aims at consolidating the general training provided by the primary school, reinforcing the pupil's intellectual capabilities and developing practical skills. This is known as the preparatory stage. Basic education ends with a diploma in basic education which enables those who obtain it to gain access to secondary education.

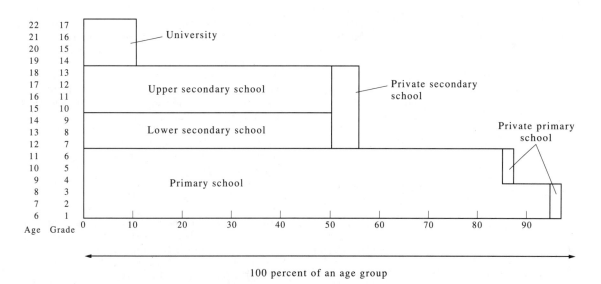

Figure 1
Tunisia: Structure of the formal education system

Table 1
Number of schools, pupils, classes, and teachers in primary education 1989–93

	1989–90	1990–91	1991–92	1992–93
Schools	3,774	3,941	4,040	4,044
Pupils	1,369,476	1,398,119	1,417,803	1,432,112
Classes	44,911	45,790	46,811	46,872
Teachers	46,077	50,280	53,652	54,740

In 1991–92, pupils registered in both primary and basic education schools accounted for 87.8 percent of the 6–13 age-group, a percentage which is slightly higher than for the previous school year. Female pupils accounted for about 46 percent of enrollment (54% in urban areas and 32% in rural areas).

Table 1 shows the development of basic and primary education from 1989 to 1993. In the 1992–93 school year, the pupil–teacher ratio was 26.2:1 compared to 27.8:1 in 1990–91.

Primary school efficiency has been improving over the years in that the pass rates at the end of primary school have risen from 40.2 percent in 1990 to 57.8 percent in 1992.

Available statistical data on secondary education exists only for the old organization, which still exists. However, data related to the lower secondary stage could be assumed to represent the data for the preparatory stage of basic education, and data for the upper secondary stage could be assumed to be representative of data on the new secondary system. Table 2 presents these data.

In 1991–92, there were 599 general education schools. If technical education schools are taken into account, there would be a total of 625 schools, six of which are "pilot schools." The pilot schools are restricted to brilliant students selected at the outcome of primary education. These schools are designed to provide students with optimal conditions to pursue secondary studies in the fields of science and technology, the arts and humanities, as well as sport.

In secondary education the student–teacher ratio was 21.6:1 in 1992–93. Of the 336 secondary schools there

Table 2
Enrollments in lower and upper secondary education 1990–93

	1990–91	1991–92	1992–93
Lower secondary	299,498	308,126	342,305
Upper secondary			
General education	166,855	189,462	197,850
Technical education	27,990	20,318	27,226
Total	194,845	209,780	225,076

are 22 private lower secondary schools and 28 upper secondary schools.

Secondary education finishes with a final exam: the baccalaureate. In 1992–93, the baccalaureate comprised: mathematics, experimental science, mathematics and technology, and the arts. The baccalaureate gives a student the right to enter the university. In 1991, the overall pass rate was 36.7 percent and in 1992 it was 41.1 percent.

Higher education is governed by the Education Act of 1989. It consists of 82 public institutions of higher education organized within six universities: Tunis University of the Arts and Humanities (Tunis I); Tunis University of Science, Technology, and Medicine (Tunis II); Tunis University of Law, Economics, and Management (Tunis III); Ezzitouna University (theology); Center University (multidisciplinary); and South University (multidisciplinary).

Higher education is open to all students holding the baccalaureate or an equivalent qualification. Under certain conditions, students who do not have the baccalaureate may have access to higher education.

Although there may be considerable variations from one branch of learning to the other, the overall organization of higher education is as follows:

(a) Short-term (2–3 years) training of technicians, paramedical staff, and teachers for primary schools;

(b) Medium-term (4 years) leading to the bachelor degree (*Maîtrise*) or a degree in practical engineering;

(c) Long-term (4 years or more) studies in subjects such as medicine, architecture, and engineering.

Graduate courses are provided in major subjects and are in the form of a two-year course, and research activities leading to a dissertation (*Thèse de 3ème cycle, Thèse d'Etat*).

Since the mid-1970s, higher education has undergone dramatic changes. The number of institutions of higher education and the number of students have quadrupled. In 1992, the coverage of the 20–24 age-group has reached 9.39 percent, compared to 3.58 percent in 1976. The number of female students is increasing, and accounts for more than 40 percent of all students. During the same period, the number of teachers trebled and there were 4,941 teachers in the 1991–92 academic year. The student–teacher ratio is around 16:1.

The efficiency of higher education has stagnated since the early 1980s. Out of every 100 first-year students enrolled in universities, approximately 40 to 45 students obtain a first degree (two years) or a second degree (4 years or more). Consequently, the number of graduates has evolved relatively slowly, with an overall increase of 43 percent from 1983 to 1993.

Higher education is free and sponsored by the public sector; its cost is mainly incurred by government expenditure. Given that operational costs, expressed in current terms, trebled in the 1980s, government expenditure has developed considerably. If capital expenditure was added, the share of higher education would account for 3–4 percent of total government expenditures. As a percentage of GNP, this share has varied between 1 and 1.3 percent.

3.2 Preschool Education

Preschool education is regulated under the Education Act of 1990 which organizes the educational system as a whole. The Tunisian government has a ministry concerned with children. Additionally, Tunisia ratified the International Agreement on the Rights of Children as an integral part of human rights.

A vast network of Kindergartens has been established everywhere in the country under the supervision of the Ministry of Youth and Children. These institutions are run either by private individuals or by local authorities (251 by municipalities, 164 by associations, and 315 by private institutions).

The kindergartens enrolled more than 47,500 children in 1991–92 which is a 5.5 percent coverage rate for the 3–6 age-group. There were 1,899 trainers, of whom only 740 were properly trained professionals.

The goals of preschool education are to provide children with an educational environment to allow for the development of their motor, linguistic, intellectual, and social functions. In 1993, a vast program was being developed to reinforce the promotion of infrastructure, curricula, and staff.

3.3 Special Education

The pilot schools in the secondary system have been set up to cater for the brightest students. At the other end, special arrangements were taken to provide for handicapped students. Since the early 1980s, the number of pilot schools increased from two to six and is expected to continue increasing in the 1990s. They cater for selected students who passed their primary school examination at the highest level and who are expected to do very well in education. The pilot schools that have already been set up may be general or specialized schools. Among the specialized institutions there is one where most teaching is in English and another specializes in sports and physical education.

The 1989 census indicated that the total handicapped population, as defined according to international standards, was 53,500. This can be broken down into the following categories: the blind (more than 50% are over 60 years of age); the deaf (8,800 out of 11,000 are under 15 years of age); and motor-deficient, of which 17 percent are under 15 years of age.

Within the educational system, various practical measures were taken by the Ministry of Education and Science to ensure adequate and efficient education for handicapped students:

(a) reinforcing and generalizing the preventive care infrastructure in close cooperation with medical authorities;

(b) reinforcing information on the rights of handicapped individuals, especially the right for equal opportunity and treatment within the educational institution at both primary and secondary levels;

(c) increasing the number of classes within primary and secondary schools;

(d) providing associations with teaching staff;

(e) providing students with an opportunity to pursue education until the legal age for employment;

(f) retraining of teachers specialized in teaching the handicapped;

(g) organizing within schools an individualized training program;

(h) ensuring that for national examinations and competitions, measures are taken to give the handicapped equal opportunity (time periods, premises, etc.).

Generally, Tunisia's policy in this field is aimed at integrating handicapped students into the general educational system. The effort already made is generous, but there is plenty left to do:

(a) addressing the increasing requirements of handicapped students;

(b) reinforcing the preventive care structure and improving resources and services;

(c) providing a larger number of integrated classes or specialized classes while ensuring a more equitable geographic distribution;

(d) improving teaching materials;

(e) reinforcing specialized staff in both quality and numbers.

3.4 Vocational, Technical, and Business Education

It has become increasingly apparent that a high quality basic education and initial vocational training, conducted if possible without interruption, are a fundamental condition for the introduction of young people into professional and economic life.

The concurrent implementation of the two reforms not only takes into account the implications of the reform of the educational system on the system of vocational training, but also aims at strengthening the relation between the two systems in such a way as to develop their coherence and shift to a situation where the student is "reoriented rather than excluded."

As far as the objectives of vocational training are concerned, it has become imperative to provide the country with a modern system allowing for improved occupational perspectives for the young. Training in this context is responsible at one end for providing the largest number possible with skills likely to help them sustain competition on a rapidly changing job market and, at the other end, for contributing to establish their own work environment.

During the 8th Plan (1992–97), it is expected that the national economy will generate 320,000 jobs in sectors other than agriculture. In addition, taking into account new staffing needs and the necessity for gradually improving technical skills, the demand of the economy for qualified personnel would be around 227,000 during the Plan period. Of these 145,000 will be trained in institutions and the rest will receive on-site training. Furthermore, 100,000 skilled workers, 27,000 technicians, and 13,000 employees will be trained in vocational training centers to address the needs of various sectors of the economy.

3.5 Adult and Nonformal Education

Following Independence, Tunisia made unlimited efforts to address illiteracy. The illiteracy eradication program which was initiated in 1958 provided for the establishment of literacy centers under the supervision of the Ministry of Education. In 1962, program supervision was transferred to the Ministry of Social Affairs which expanded the program to most provinces. A national center for the eradication of illiteracy was also set up to coordinate these activities and select teaching methods and materials. The National Program for the Eradication of Illiteracy was terminated in 1969 and its activities were transferred to the Social Development Department within the Ministry of Social Affairs. Overall, the program had very positive results. In 1989, the illiteracy rate was 37.2 percent as against 84.7 percent in 1956. However, illiteracy was not fully eradicated especially among women, rural populations and, to some extent, among the young.

In 1993, illiteracy eradication was integrated into social education activities which include: adult education (three levels); rehabilitation of primary school dropouts; and cultural education within vocational training. In 1990–91, 4,457 learners attended the program (i.e. 2 out of every 1,000). During that year, women accounted for 76 percent of all such learners. The program was staffed by 268 trainers covering 107 centers and was supervised by ministries, local authorities, and various other organizations.

Illiteracy rates are still very high, due to inadequate resources, low coverage, and low turnover: only 25 percent graduate from the program.

In 1992 the government initiated a new National Plan for the Eradication of Illiteracy. The first two years (1992–94) of this plan are to be used to undertake a major review of needs. During this stage, experts will collect the necessary data and design a work plan for the following stage. The second stage of the new Plan (1994–96), will be the implementation stage. The third and final stage will be for evaluation and follow-up activities.

4. Administrative and Supervisory Structure and Operation

The Ministry of Education and Science is the main government agent for education. However, other ministries also have a role to play at the various stages of the educational system. The Ministry of Agriculture has its own secondary schools and its own higher education institutions. The Ministry of Health has control over schools of medicine and schools for the training of nurses and other paramedical staff. The Ministry of Social Affairs is responsible for schools for the handicapped and higher education institutions. The Ministry of Culture is responsible for institutions of higher education in music, drama, and the fine arts. In most cases, especially for higher education, there is dual supervision of institutions by the relevant ministry and the Ministry of Education and Science. As the vast majority of educational activity is under the direct supervision of the Ministry of Education and Science, the following will be an account of the organizational structure of that ministry.

In November 1992, the organizational structure of the Ministry of Education and Science was reviewed and expanded to allow for proper supervision of an expanding sector. The new structure confirms the existence of one ministry for all three stages of education: basic, secondary, and tertiary. However, for practical purposes, the ministry is organized into two sections or departments, one for basic and secondary education and the other for higher education.

The Minister's Cabinet assists the minister and is responsible for centralizing and examining all matters submitted to the minister's approval, transmitting the minister's decisions, and ensuring that they are put into practice. The cabinet keeps the minister informed of the general activity in the department. It is also responsible for relations with other government agencies and national organizations.

The General Secretariat is responsible for the day-to-day management of the department, for giving the necessary impetus and for coordinating the department's activities. It ensures follow-up and coordination of the work undertaken by the various divisions as well as that of the agencies under the ministry's supervision. Various divisions report directly to the Secretary General. These are: human resources (education), finance (education), legal division (education), buildings and procurement (education), planning and statistics (education), archives (education), human resources (higher education), finance (higher education), planning and statistics (higher education), legal division (higher education), buildings and procurement (higher education), archives (higher education), methods and organization (education and higher education).

Basic and secondary education has divisions for secondary education, continuing education, examinations, general inspectorate for education, primary education, preparatory education, private education, curricula, cultural activities, and sports.

Higher Education has: general division for higher education, general division for projects, programs and pedagogy, division for student affairs, division for higher technological institutes, division for higher institutes for teacher training. There is one common division for international cooperation.

Basic and secondary education is supervised by 24 regional divisions which have a fair degree of autonomy in the day-to-day management of educational affairs (financial, administrative, and pedagogic).

Over the years, the administrative and supervisory structure of education in Tunisia has wavered between a complete split between primary and secondary education and higher education and a total merger between the two. The system in the early 1990s is a compromise whereby one minister supervises two major departments with different geographical locations and different organizational structures. This has allowed for increased coordination between the various stages and also for relative autonomy in day-to-day management.

5. Educational Finance

Ever since Independence, Tunisia has allocated a major part of its budget to education. This continued effort explains the exceptional development of all educational stages.

In the period 1962–71, the share of education in the national budget increased from 21.7 to 34.5 percent for current expenses and from 6.7 to 11.6 percent for capital expenses. As a share of the national income, educational expenses accounted for 4.7 percent in 1960 and for 10.5 percent in 1968.

In the period 1972–81 current expenses, after a record 34.5 percent in 1971, fell to a low 28.1 percent in 1975 and 24.5 in 1978. In 1979, they were a mere 23.3 percent. During this period, necessary cuts had to be made on management expenses and on social activities as it was not easy to cut on salaries or overheads.

In the period 1982–91 current expenses on education grew at an average annual rate of 7.4 percent with 90 percent of the Ministry's budget allocated to salaries. Under the pressure of demography and the influx of waves of new students (an increase of 53.6% in secondary education and over 78.7% in higher education), capital investment resumed at even higher levels than before.

Over the years the cost of education has been incurred almost exclusively by the national budget. Parent participation is minimal or nonexistent. In fact, the government sponsors and supports low-income students through a system of grants and subsidized services. One of the major objectives of the educational system is the democracy of education (the widest coverage possible), this tendency will continue in the future, although there are some signs that parents are incurring an increasing share of educational expenses by payment of fees to private educational institutions. The funding of education is however an issue which is being considered very seriously by public authorities and it is certainly one of the matters to be scrutinized during the 1990s.

6. Supplying Personnel for the Education System

At the eve of Independence, the Tunisian educational system was almost exclusively staffed by foreign teachers, mainly French. The growing number of students and schools was to be followed by an equal increase in the number of teachers. A teacher training policy was developed for the three stages of the educational system.

For a number of years, primary school teachers were recruited at the end of the secondary school system. Special secondary schools for the training of teachers were set up to train as quickly as possible the staff necessary for the education of the growing mass of primary school pupils. These schools accomplished an admirable effort by training thousands of teachers, but were unable to address the growing demand. During the early 1980s, primary schools had to recruit from among university dropouts to make up for the shortage.

With the new reform, the training of teachers for primary education was to undergo a major change in the late 1980s with the establishment of higher institutes for the training of teachers. The change was both in quality and in quantity. First, the new institutes started recruiting their students among baccalaureate holders, thus promoting teacher training from secondary to professionalized higher education. Second, the number of graduates from these institutes was such that they supplied the basic education system with enough teachers annually to meet demand and to make up for loss of staff through retirement. The qualification delivered by these institutes became the minimal qualification required of the potential teacher in primary education.

A vast effort is being made to retrain existing teachers through continuing (distance) education and through on-site training. To this effect, the new organizational structure of the Ministry of Education and Science provides for a general division for continued education. Additionally, Tunisia now has an Institute of Education and Continued Education which caters for primary and secondary school teachers.

The growth of higher education has included the training of teachers for the secondary school system. Overall, Tunisian universities were able to supply secondary schools with adequately qualified teachers in all fields. However, certain fields are still understaffed—especially mathematics.

It should also be noted that apart from one institution, secondary school teachers do not receive a specific training. Usually, they are university graduates in the arts and the sciences and have not received any special education in the teaching profession. Onsite training by a body of inspectors and pedagogic counsellors makes up for the shortage in training received before recruitment. Formal retraining through continued education is also provided to vast numbers of underqualified teachers.

Whereas for primary education the conversion of teaching staff from foreign to Tunisian was successful, the same is not true at the secondary level where this conversion was ill-prepared and sometimes demagogic. The new Tunisian teachers were not adequately trained either scientifically or pedagogically. Indeed, many among them did not have the university degree required for such a position. Furthermore they did not have the pedagogic training needed to deliver knowledge in the most efficient way. In 1993, there are still areas where secondary schools are staffed by underqualified teachers. This is particularly the case with mathematics and French. This explains the relative loss of prestige that the Tunisian secondary school system has experienced since the early 1980s. The new reform has endeavored to remedy this situation by developing a strategy for the training of teachers, especially in educational science, by sending a number of graduate students overseas to learn from prestigious centers of learning around the world. The objective is to ensure that by the year 2000 there will be no unqualified teachers.

At one time, most Tunisian higher education teachers were trained overseas, especially in France. These were mainly in the science and technology fields. By 1993, graduate studies staffed by Tunisian professors supplied the six Tunisian universities with adequately trained teachers in the various fields of learning. However, the government is still continuing a major effort for training students overseas especially in those subjects where opening graduate studies would not be cost-effective.

7. Curriculum Development and Teaching Methodology

Primary and secondary school curricula in Tunisia are developed at the central (ministry) level for both public and private schools.

Curriculum development is undertaken after wide consultation with professionals and nonprofessionals alike. A High Commission for the Reform of Education works hand in hand with sectorial committees and specialized committees. The first are organized according to 14 subjects taught in schools. The latter are responsible for reviewing technical matters in education such as weekly time periods, holidays, and teaching material.

The membership of such committees is composed of teachers, inspectors, educational advisors, and of nonprofessionals from various political, economic, social, and cultural organizations. These committees develop curricula, and teachers are consulted. These steps were taken to stop the negative trend, which had become rampant in education, of handbooks and curricula being changed as soon as a new minister was appointed. Previously, curricula were the Minister's sole decision; now they are published as an act of parliament which ensures more enduring curricula developed through a consensus of both professionals and concerned nonprofessionals.

Based on these curricula, school handbooks are developed either by competition organized by the Ministry and open to all teachers or through appointment, especially when time limits are too short or when there are not enough qualified teachers to allow for a competition. Textbooks are first evaluated by an ad hoc committee. If they are approved by this committee they are then authorized to be used temporarily in schools. The Ministry then calls for teacher comments and discussions. A final edition is developed which includes changes suggested by the concerned teachers and professionals. The textbooks thus developed also define the teaching methodology to be used. Basically, Tunisian manuals foster educational dialogue and active pedagogy where students are led to discover by themselves the meaning of the concepts that they are introduced to. In the sciences, the methodology is based on an alternation between theory and practice.

Although scientific equipment may be inadequate in most schools, there is usually a minimum of such equipment to allow for proper training in science and technology. This is however one of the priority areas to be addressed during the 1990s. There are teacher guides for all subjects at all levels. These guides are designed to help the less trained and/or isolated teachers discharge their duty in the best possible way.

8. The System of Examinations, Promotions, and Certifications

Examinations are an integral part of the evaluation process of the educational system. They are of two kinds: (a) end-of-year examinations organized within each school under the supervision of the headteacher; and (b) diploma examinations organized at the central level by the Ministry of Education. In this transitional period, the two national examinations left are the competition for access to secondary schools and the end of secondary school examination, or baccalaureate. In higher education, the same pattern prevails except that every university organizes its own examinations.

The new reform which initiated compulsory basic education from 6 to 16 provides for a smoother policy for promotion from primary to preparatory school. To this effect, the competition, the dread of all 12-year olds, is being phased out as a national examination. Soon, promotion from the primary to the preparatory level will be based on the pupil's results in the sixth grade and his or her results in a regionally organized and supervised examination. The basic education system will end with a centrally organized and supervised diploma which will allow successful students to enter secondary schools. Thus, what was considered a major filter or, according to some, a major obstacle has been delayed by three years. It will be organized for students who have reached an age where they can adequately face a major examination and where unsuccessful candidates can easily and legally access the job market.

In secondary education, the baccalaureate remains a major national option. It is perceived as a guarantee of quality for the educational system and is also considered as a major factor of equity and justice.

Tunisian examinations of all types are evaluated through a system of average marks expressed out of 20. The student obtaining an average mark of ten has obtained a pass. In some cases, students who obtain an average between nine and ten may be granted a pass. To allow for balanced education, the weights used to distinguish between subjects vary from one to three.

In higher education, a trend has been to provide for minimal coordination between universities teaching the same subjects. Although this coordination does not go as far as unified examinations, 80 percent of all subjects taught in a given field have been unified and students are now satisfied that they receive equal training wherever they are. This move has boosted regional universities. The remaining 20 percent is for the individual university to determine according to its circumstances and regional characteristics.

9. Educational Assessment, Evaluation, and Research

The 1990 Education Act stated that the educational system, its curricula and its methods be submitted to periodic evaluations to ensure continued improvement and adaptation to progress in learning and to improve efficiency in terms of knowledge, teaching methods, and output.

This kind of evaluation is continuously made by the Ministry of Education staff through surveys, seminars, and workshops attended by teachers, inspectors, educational advisors, and researchers. Another type of evaluation is made by non-Ministry professionals from Tunisia and from overseas. Evaluation is also undertaken by university researchers and academics who belong to two key institutions: the National Institute for Educational Science and the Department of Educational Science in the Center for Studies and Research in the Social Sciences. Generally, evaluation is concerned with the following aspects of educational activity:

(a) the functional adequacy of the overall system;

(b) the adequacy of curricula at a given level;

(c) the adequacy of teaching methods with reference to subject matter;

(d) student comprehension of subject matter;

(e) student flows within each level and from one level to the other;

(f) coverage of age-groups concerned;

(g) regional and gender differences in performance;

(h) coordination between education and the job market.

Evaluation of the educational system was not taken seriously and was not undertaken on a regular basis. The objectives enumerated above are essentially a new option rather than a firmly established tradition. Only in 1991–92 did the Ministry of Education envisage the initiation of a program for the formal training of specialists in educational science. These will be trained both in Tunisia and overseas to provide the Tunisian educational system with planners, evaluators, trainers, specialists in educational guidance, and so on. This new program completes an older, but much less ambitious program initiated in the teacher training schools.

10. Major Reforms in the 1980s and 1990s

After the major reform initiated by the 1958 Education Act and which was implemented during the 1960s, the Tunisian educational system was to go through a period not so much of stagnation but of rapid, badly prepared, and often demagogic reorientation. No major fully fledged reform was envisaged until the late 1980s when it became apparent that ad hoc adjustments were no longer sufficient. The reform which was first envisaged in 1987 came into effect in 1989. The major aspects of the reform include:

(a) reinforcing and expanding the democracy of education;

(b) initiating compulsory basic education from 6 to 16;

(c) increasing importance given to cultural extra-curricular activities;

(d) allowing for a smoother flow of students both within levels and from one level to the other;

(e) keeping students as long as possible within the educational system;

(f) opting for reorientation rather than exclusion;

(g) improving efficiency and output at all levels;

(h) increasing the number of centers of excellence in the secondary schools system;

(i) creating centers of excellence in higher education (engineering schools, applied advanced technology institutes) to minimize brain-drain;

(j) improving education–job market coordination;

(k) opening the university on its environment;

(l) shorter, more finalized, flexible technical higher education to supply adequately trained technicians to an emerging industry;

(m) promoting primary teacher training from secondary to higher education;

(n) continuing education for teaching staff;

(o) coordination between higher education institutions (up to 80% of common subjects);

(p) renovating higher education through a revision of graduate studies;

(q) more discipline in curriculum implementation by schools;

(r) one month more teaching time per year in most schools;

(s) availability of staff for guidance to students at the end of the secondary schools system.

11. Major Problems for the Year 2000

During the 1990s and until the year 2000 and beyond, Tunisia will face a number of momentous challenges, the most important being related to demography, although demographic growth is being checked, thanks to a rationally established family planning program.

By the year 2000, the number of students is expected to double and 14 percent of the 20–24 age-group will be covered. Additionally, this development will mainly concern the following fields: science and technology, law, economics, and management. To address these needs, a higher education map was developed providing for the establishment of two new university centers in the north west and south west regions. Furthermore, a wide reform has been initiated to improve the efficiency of higher education and to address the country's needs in qualified senior officers.

Basic education will probably be the least hit by demographic growth during the 1990s. The challenges will therefore be more qualitative than quantitative. Government's goal in this field is to improve coverage of the 6–12 year age-group from 89 percent in 1991 to 95 percent in 1996 and from 79 percent to 87 percent respectively for the 6–15 age-group. The strategy likely to be followed will be to allow for a smoother promotion of pupils from the primary to the preparatory level by dealing with the causes of educational failure (poverty, distance, etc.) and keeping unsuccessful students within the system by reorienting them to finalized practical studies. Another dramatic challenge at this level will be to provide all schools with the necessary equipment and teaching materials.

Secondary education in the 1990s will have to face the results of the post-Independence baby boom. It will also have to make room for the additional students promoted thanks to a smoother promotion policy between the primary and the preparatory levels. It is expected that the number of students at this stage will double between 1991–97. This dramatic expansion will entail even more effort in the training of teachers, building new schools, and providing more equipment. However the decrease in the population growth will probably alleviate the building aspect of this challenge since some primary schools can be turned into secondary schools in areas where the baby boom wave has already reached its peak for this age-group.

The baby boom population effect will be felt even more acutely in higher education than in secondary education. The number of students at this level is expected to double in the period 1991–2001. Already in a difficult situation as far as staffing is concerned, Tunisian universities will have to make an unprecedented effort in the training of trainers.

A new higher education map has already been developed to address the larger number of students and to bring higher education closer to the student. In the 1990s, higher education will also have to address issues such as student halls, restaurants, subsidized transportation, and so on. New funding solutions will have to be found. The trend of phasing out grants and phasing in loans will have to be reinforced. The private sector, which has just started showing interest in higher education, will have to be encouraged. For long almost a taboo subject, parent participation in financing will have to be envisaged.

Qualitatively, the Tunisian system of education is still faced with the issues of illiteracy, citizenship, and moderation. Compulsory education from 6 to 16 years should help to alleviate illiteracy rates in the country. It is, however, necessary to make additional efforts to keep Tunisians from lapsing into illiteracy after schooling. Also, Tunisian schools will have to consider that science and technology, although important, are not sufficient and they will also have to train students how to be good citizens and how to live in a civilized society. Finally, at all levels, Tunisia's educational system is called on to ward off obscurantism and fanaticism by establishing the virtues of tradition and opening vistas on the values of modern civilization: democracy, human rights, and moderation.

Bibliography

Abdessalem A 1975 *1875–1975 Sadiki et les Sadikiens.* Cerèsproductions, Tunis

Ben Jaballah H 1990 Rapport général des travaux de la Haute Commission de la Réforme du système éducatif. (Unpublished document) Ministère de l'Education et des Sciences, Tunis

Ben Jaballah H 1992 Réforme éducative et épopée des valeurs. *Le 7 novembre, la révolution paisible*

Ben Salem B 1991 *Enseignement Moderne et Politique d'Orientation Scolaire en Tunisie.* Tunis

Ben Salem L 1969 Démocratisation de l'enseignement en Tunisie: Essai d'analyse du milieu d'origine des étudiants tunisiens. *Revue Tunisienne des Sciences Sociales* 16: 81–135

Bousnina M 1991 *Développement Scolaire et Disparités Régionales.* Publications de l'Université Tunis I, Faculté des Sciences Humaines et Sociales, Tunis

Charfi M Réflexions et positions (Unpublished document). Ministère de l'Education et des Sciences, Tunis

Institut National des Sciences de l'Education 1991 *L'Evaluation dans le Domaine de l'Education.* L'Institut National des Sciences de l'Education, Tunis

Mahfoudh D, Dhahri N et al. 1976 Analyse critique des contenus des programmes scolaires de l'enseignement primaire eu égard aux objectifs définis par cet enseignement. *Revue Tunisienne des Sciences de l'Education* 2: 67–117

Messaâdi M 1958 Les nouveaux fondements du système éducatif. *El Amal (l'Action)* 17 septembre p. 3

Ministère de l'Education et des Sciences 1992 *Statistiques de l'Enseignement, 1992.* Ministère de l'Education et des Sciences, Tunis

Tlili B 1974 *Les rapports culturels et idéologiques entre l'Orient et l'Occident, en Tunisie, au XIXème siècle (1830–1880).* Publications de l'Université de Tunis, Tunis

Turkey

B. A. Öney

1. General Background

Turkey lies at the junction of Europe and Asia and is situated at the northeast of the Mediterranean. The total area of Turkey is 815,000 square kilometers, of which 97 percent lies in Asia, and the rest in Europe. The borders with neighboring countries are 2,753 kilometers long and the total length of the coastline is 8,333 kilometers. The coastal regions consist of the Black Sea, the Sea of Marmara, the Aegean, and the Mediterranean, while the inland regions consist of central, eastern, and southeastern Anatolia.

The Turkish Republic has a parliamentary system. With the proclamation of the Republic of Turkey in 1923, the first president, Kemal Atatürk, led the country in building a politically and economically independent, secular, and Western social state. In 1924, religious schools were closed, the Latin alphabet was adopted, and all schools were placed under the control of the Ministry of National Education.

The population of Turkey which was 13.6 million in 1927 increased almost 4 times to 57 million in 1990 (State Institute of Statistics 1990). Due to massive population losses following the First World War and the War of Independence (1919–23), there was a population policy encouraging high birthrates until 1965. The Population Planning Law which was passed in 1965 reflects an anti-natalist policy (UNICEF 1991). The population growth rate was 2.5 percent in 1990.

Over the years there have been structural changes in the composition of the society. Between 1935 and 1960 over three-fourths of Turkey's population was rural. The proportion of the rural population decreased in the 1950s and in 1991 it was 49 percent.

Turkey's population is a young one. In urban areas approximately one-third and, in rural areas, two-fifths of the population is under 15. The high population growth rate is regarded as one of the most important factors negatively affecting schooling rates and the quality of education (Baloğlu 1990).

There has been a continuing population flow from rural areas to commercial centers such as Istanbul, Adana, and Izmir, as well as to Ankara, the capital of Turkey. This has resulted in squatter areas around big cities. The population flow is heaviest from eastern and southeastern Anatolia to western Anatolia. Centers which receive these migrants are being challenged by increasing problems of providing sufficient infrastructure, education, and health services. Cities where urbanization rates are high are faced with educational problems such as large classrooms and double-shift schools.

There was also a considerable migration to Europe between 1960 and 1975. There are Turkish workers in North Africa, the Middle East, and the Arab Peninsula. Today, there are over 4.4 million Turkish citizens abroad, of which one-third are children. The Ministry of National Education, in cooperation with the host countries, sends Turkish teachers to the host countries for the education of workers' children. However, the student–teacher ratio seems to be 142:1 and the demand for such teachers far outstrips the supply. Ethnically, Turks form the majority of the population but there is also a Kurdish and Arabic population. Turkish is the mother tongue of the vast majority of the population, while Kurdish is spoken in some areas. At the beginning of the 1990s the non-Turkish-speaking population continued to be a challenge for the implementation of educational programs.

The Turkish Latin alphabet was adopted in 1928 to transcribe the Turkish language. This system, where the correspondence between letters and sounds is very high, has contributed to increasing literacy rates. Although regional and gender differences exist, literacy rates have continued to rise. By 1990, Turkey had achieved a 90 percent literacy rate in the 14–44-year old age group. A series of interventions, including the literacy campaign of 1982, helped increase the literacy rate from 72 percent in 1981 to 90 percent in 1990. Literacy rates are higher for men (96%) than for women (84%), and higher in developed regions than in less-developed regions. The more developed a region, the less the gap between male and female literacy rates.

The Turkish Republic which had taken over the economic inheritance of the Ottoman empire reflected a very different economic structure in 1923 than the beginning of the 1990s. The economy was agriculture based, the per capita income was low, and the labor force lacked sufficient education. Between 1923 and 1950 the main economic policy was statism, which may best be characterized by a reluctance to accept foreign investment and keeping a highly protected domestic industry. Since 1950, however, a liberal economic policy became increasingly dominant. The policies for the 1990s reflect efforts to strengthen a competitive economy, encourage private sector investments, and support and provide education for the social and economic well-being of the people.

Especially in the 1980s, the economy was marked by a high growth in agriculture, industry, and services. The structure of the labor force also changed considerably. In 1989 agriculture employed 50 percent of the labor force while 15 percent were employed in industry, and 35 percent in the service sector. The economy experienced an increase in the proportion of the population employed in industry and services. Thus, economic changes have created an increasing demand for vocational and technical education.

Employment rates vary according to educational level, gender, and geographic location. According to the 1988 census, 8.3 percent of the population was unemployed, and unemployment was higher in the rural areas than in urban areas (13.2 % vs. 5%). The highest rate of unemployment is found among secondary school graduates for both males and females. Nonformal education which is designed to provide new skills and knowledge has been regarded as one of the possible solutions for unemployment, especially in less-developed regions.

2. Politics and the Goals of the Education System

Since 1924, the Ministry of National Education has been responsible for the performance, supervision, and control of all educational services on behalf of the state. This constituted a major step in achieving unity in education. In 1973 the Fundamental Principles of National Education went into force. The general aims of the Principles are: (a) to bring up citizens in the spirit of Turkish nationalism with Atatürk's reforms and principles which are dedicated to preserving and developing the national, moral, human, and cultural values of the Turkish nation; (b) to develop interest, ability, and talent in citizens by supplying the required knowledge; and (c) raising Turkish citizens who support social and cultural development in national unity. The principles used for achieving these general goals are: (a) equality in education (educational institutions are open to all regardless of race, sex, or religion); (b) meeting individual and societal needs; (c) orientation (individuals are oriented toward programs or schools depending on their interests, talents, and abilities); (d) continuity (the state takes measures to ensure the continued education of adults); (e) Atatürk's reforms (Atatürk's reforms and principles are the basis of the curriculum at each level of the educational system); (f) secularism; (g) scientific norms in education; (h) co-education; (i) planning (national education is planned on the basis of economic, social, and cultural development); (j) cooperation between school and family; and (k) widespread education (MONE 1989).

The year 1983 marked the beginning of a series of reorganization efforts within the education system. Such reorganization affected the structure of the education system as well as the organization of the Ministry of National Education.

3. The Formal System of Education

3.1 Primary, Secondary, and Tertiary Education

Formal and nonformal education are organized, supervised, and controlled by the Ministry of National Education. While formal education covers preschool, primary, secondary, and higher education institutions, nonformal education is offered outside the school system. Figure 1 presents the structure of the formal education system.

Preschool education is voluntary and covers children who have not yet reached primary school age. Early childhood education is the responsibility of the Ministry of National Education and the General Directorate of Social Welfare and Child Protection

Agency. The Ministry of National Education provides education for children between the ages of 4 and 5.

The Ministry of National Education supervises private or institutional (workplace) kindergartens, sets up educational and health requirements, and establishes teachers' educational requirements. Preschool teachers are required to have completed a four-year university degree in early childhood education.

Primary education comprises the education of children in the 6 to 14 age group. This includes five years of primary schooling and three years of secondary schooling. Primary education is being restructured to increase compulsory education from five to eight years, and eight year compulsory education has started in some schools. Diplomas are given at the end of primary and secondary schools. Primary education is compulsory and is offered free of charge at public schools. Private schools also exist but they are supervised and controlled by the Ministry of National Education. In 1989 there were 7 million primary students and only 5 percent of them were enrolled in private schools. All public and private primary schools are coeducational. A primary school diploma can also be obtained by adults who take the prescribed exams. This was, in fact, a very popular method of adult education in the 1950s and 1960s.

In areas where the population is dispersed, schools may not be provided in each settlement. In such cases, several villages are grouped, and "regional primary schools" with boarding facilities are established.

A marked increase was observed in primary-school enrollment rates between 1924 and 1991. While the primary-school enrollment rate was only 22 percent in 1924, it increased to 86 percent in 1984 and to 94 percent in 1991. Although nearly full-capacity enrollment was realized in 1991, gender differences in enrollment rates exist. According to the 1985 census, while school enrollment rates for boys and girls were almost equal in developed provinces, they were 52 percent for girls and 72 percent for boys in less-developed rural areas. Furthermore, in less-developed areas, the chance of graduation is lower for girls then boys. Reasons for the low school attendance rates for girls include early marriages, limited means of transportation, and family attitudes to giving priority to boys for education.

The increasing number of students enrolled in primary education have necessitated double-shift schools in some regions. Double-shift schools constitute 71 percent of all primary schools in cities and 17 percent of schools in rural areas. The student–teacher ratio is 29:1 in rural areas and 33:1 in urban areas, but these figures also show regional variation. Cities which receive a large population influx may have classes with up to 60 or 70 students. Crowded classes are regarded as one of the most important factors adversely affecting the quality of primary education.

The length of the school year varies between rural and urban primary schools. In urban areas, the school year is 175 days while it is 155 days in rural areas. The primary school day consists of 5 hours of instruction.

Upon completion of primary school, students may either attend secondary schools which are independent schools giving three years of education, or if the student is enrolled in a basic education school, which is a combination of primary and secondary school, he or she may complete eight years of primary education in this school. About 10 percent of the secondary school students attend private schools or public "Anatolian *lycées*" which provide an additional year of preparatory classes designed for foreign language learning. The language of instruction in these schools is English, French, or German. Some private schools, and the Anatolian *lycées*, have strict entrance requirements, and student evaluation is based on a centralized entrance examination.

Secondary education covers general, vocational, and technical education institutions. The aim of secondary education is to prepare students for either higher education or for a vocation. Most institutions of secondary education are government schools which are free of charge while a small percentage are privately owned. The majority of secondary education institutions are coeducational. The school year in secondary education is 175 days, and the school day consists of 5 hours

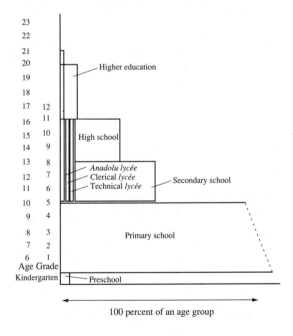

Figure 1

Turkey: Structure of the formal education system 1990[a]

a The fact that more than 100 percent of an age group is enrolled in some grades in primary school is because of grade repetition

of instruction in general high schools and 6 hours of instruction in technical schools.

Higher education covers all educational institutions which provide at least two years of education over and above secondary education. These institutions consist of universities, institutes, higher schools, conservatories, and higher vocational schools. Only around 23 percent of students graduating from secondary education institutions are able to pursue higher education. Entrance to higher education institutions is governed by the centralized University Entrance Examination. This is a competitive examination. In 1989, 824,000 students sat the University Entrance Examination and only 193,000 gained a place in an institution of higher education. Many students attend private courses which prepare students for the entrance examination. In 1991, 226,000 students attended private courses in order to prepare for the examination.

Higher education is provided by the government. A small tuition fee is levied. Scholarships are provided for academically successful, but economically disadvantaged students. Many universities offer graduate programs in various fields as well.

The number of universities increased from 19 in 1981 to 29 in 1991. The number of students attending institutions of higher education also increased dramatically. While in 1981 the number of students in higher education was 232,627, this number had increased to 434,748 by 1991. The total number of faculty members also increased from 20,917 in 1981 to 34,469 in 1991 (YÖK 1991). In 1991, the student–teacher ratio in higher education was 39:1.

3.2 Preschool Education

The aims of preschool education are to develop the physical, intellectual, and emotional abilities of children by preparing them for basic education and helping them acquire an adequate knowledge of the Turkish language, and by providing a common environment for children coming from deprived environments. Although the number of preschool centers have increased recently, existing centers are far from meeting the demand. Only about 5 percent of the 4- and 5-year olds were able to receive preschool education in 1990.

3.3 Special Education

Special education services are provided by the Directorate of Special Education and Counseling. These services were provided by the Ministry of National Health between 1924 and 1951. Special education programs are provided for students with visual, auditory, orthopedic, and mental disabilities. Some services are offered at special education schools, while some services are offered in special classes in regular schools. In line with an integration approach, some students with disabilities attend regular classes. A total of 19,000 students were receiving special education services in 1989. More than half of the existing special education classes are at the primary-school level.

Special education services are provided by the government. There are also a few private schools offering special education services. Courses are offered in universities to better equip teachers for dealing with students requiring special education.

3.4 Vocational and Technical Education

Vocational and technical education is provided by the 128 vocational higher education schools. Between 1989 and 1991, the number of vocational higher education schools doubled. A number of projects have been initiated with the purpose of increasing the quality of education in these schools.

3.5 Adult and Nonformal Education

Adult and nonformal education is offered outside the formal education system. The aim of adult and nonformal education is to provide individuals who have either never been to school or who have dropped out with new skills such as literacy, health education, and job training, all of which are believed to offer new opportunities in life.

These services are provided free of charge by the government. Tuition may be charged for some programs. Except for the literacy programs, 87 percent of the nonformal education students are young girls or women. This may be due to the fact that girls are not provided with the same formal education opportunities as boys, and they try to make up for this loss later in life.

Apprenticeship training is also offered under nonformal education. The apprenticeship training program was reorganized in 1986. The new program offers theoretical classes free of charge once a week. During the remaining four days of the week students practice their skills in appropriate workplaces.

4. Administrative and Supervisory Structure and Operation

The Ministry of National Education is responsible for planning, carrying out, following up, and supervising all educational services on behalf of the state. In 1983 the existing educational structure was reorganized and the present organization was established. Education at all levels depends on a centralized structure which is run by public funding. The Ministry of National Education opens or grants permission to open all institutions of formal or nonformal education. Since 1984, the Ministry of National Education has transferred the appointment of teachers and their promotion to provincial governments.

The inspectorate is also under the control of the Ministry of National Education. In fact, the inspectorate is one way of ensuring that government supervision over education is continued. In 1990, there were 365 ministerial inspectors and 1,763 primary education inspectors working under the Ministry of National Education.

The Board of Higher Education was established in 1981 as part of a reform movement in higher education. The planning, coordination, and control of higher education is the responsibility of the Council of Higher Education, which was also established under the Higher Education Law of 1981.

5. Educational Finance

Since 1970 the proportion of Gross Domestic Product (GDP) allocated to education has decreased continually. While in 1971 the share for education of the GDP was 4.4 percent, it dropped to 3.5 percent in 1977, and 2.77 percent in 1989. This decrease created substantial problems for educational institutions, along with problems related to the quality of education provided by these institutions. The share for education of the state budget also declined from 16.5 percent in 1975 to 12.2 percent in 1989.

Personnel costs constitute the largest expenditure item within education. Just over 59 percent of the educational budget was allocated to primary education.

Private funding for education has been increasing. The "Build Your Own School Campaign" initiated in 1981 helped to increase private participation in the costs of education. There are also several foundations which contribute to education by donating buildings and land, or by building dormitories and sports complexes, or by establishing scholarships for education in Turkey or abroad.

6. Supplying Personnel for the Education System

Teacher education is performed by three types of institutions: (a) higher schools of education which prepare primary education teachers, (b) faculties of education preparing secondary education teachers, and (c) faculties of science and literature offering programs in basic and social sciences. As of 1990–91, the higher schools of education which used to offer a two-year undergraduate program now provide a four-year program. Thus, teacher training now requires a minimum of four years of higher education. In 1989–90 there were 6,734 preschool, 224,382 primary, 47,239 secondary, and 105,700 high-school teachers working full-time in Turkey.

Low teacher salaries have meant that the attractiveness of teaching as a career has declined. Salaries at all levels of education decreased between 1980 and 1988. The average salary of a primary teacher decreased from US$171 per month in 1980, to US$157 in 1982, US$124 in 1984, and US$148 in 1988. A parallel decrease can also be observed in secondary education teachers'

salaries. The declining attractiveness of teaching as a career is reflected by the academic standards of students entering schools of education. Of the 17,984 students entering schools of education in 1986, none had grade-point averages above 80 over 100.

As the qualification requirements for teaching have increased over the years, inservice training programs and degree-completion programs for the graduates of the two-year programs have been offered. Furthermore, other inservice training programs offer training in computer skills, foreign languages, or other selected areas in order to upgrade the knowledge and skills of teachers at all levels.

7. Curriculum Development and Teaching Methodology

There is a set curriculum used across the country. At the primary education level all students follow basically the same curriculum. There are also very few elective classes in secondary education. There are efforts underway to increase the flexibility of the curriculum and provide students with a choice of classes, based on their interests and abilities. However, such changes have not yet been implemented.

Textbooks that are used at all levels of education are either prepared or approved by the Ministry of National Education. Schools are required to choose books from the list of books approved by the Ministry.

Foreign languages are taught in secondary education and the intensity of training depends on the type of secondary school. Some schools place a higher emphasis on foreign language learning and the language of instruction is primarily the foreign language. There are however, some classes that are required to be taught in Turkish. English is the most commonly taught foreign language, while there are some schools offering foreign language teaching in French and German as well.

8. The System of Examinations, Promotions, and Certifications

In all schools students are promoted between levels according to their academic performance. Students receive a certificate at the end of the fifth year of primary school. Students receive certificates upon the completion of secondary school and high school as well. There are no external examinations for certification.

9. Educational Assessment, Evaluation, and Research

Student assessment is not performed at the national or regional levels. However, the development of student assessment methods is among the plans of the Ministry of National Education.

Educational research is performed by the Ministry of National Education or in institutes of higher education.

Since 1984, the funds for research increased dramatically and allocation of research funds was based on peer review.

10. Major Reforms in the 1980s and 1990s

Many changes occurred in the education system in the 1980s. The most striking change was the extension of compulsory education from five to eight years. By 1991, this change was still in a transitional phase and eight-year primary education was only being provided in some experimental classrooms. The whole system will switch to eight years' compulsory education only when facilities have been provided and teacher training completed.

At the higher education level the establishment of the Board of Higher Education (YÖK) in 1981 marked one of the most important changes in the higher education system. This board was criticized for its efforts to standardize the higher education system in the country by centralizing all major academic decisions including faculty appointments. The fact that two-thirds of the board's members were appointed by the Ministry of Education and by the president, and only one-third was elected by the universities produced outcries from the universities of political meddling. (Most of these shortcomings were corrected in 1990.) Nevertheless, the board had some success in increasing the quality of education in some new universities founded in smaller cities in the country, and it generally increased the number of much-needed faculty members.

11. Major Problems for the Year 2000

The major obstacle for the education system in Turkey has been the steady population growth which has led to social demands which have not always been successfully met because of the increasing student population in the system. Thus, double-shift education, crowded classrooms, insufficient physical capacity, limitations of educational programs and educational materials, and most importantly, an insufficient number of teachers have become major problems facing the system of education in Turkey. Obviously, limited resources set aside for education constitute the common obstacle for all of these problems.

A further problem has been the growing tendency toward regional inequalities in education. Although providing equal educational opportunities for all is one of the important goals of national education, success rates for students from different geographical regions suggest that there have been diversions from this goal. Gender disparities in schooling rates also need to be addressed. It is in the interest of the whole society to meet the education demands of both boys and girls.

Restructuring of the education system in accordance to the social and economic demands of the community is needed and the Ministry of National Education has been showing some signs for these long-needed reforms.

References

Baloğlu Z 1990 *Turkiyede Eğitim: Sorunlar, ve Değisime Yapisal Uyum Önerileri.* Apa Press, Istanbul

MONE 1989 *1990–1992 Board of Education Work Plan* (in Turkish). Ministry of National Education Press, Ankara

State Institute of Statistics 1990 *General Population Census: Preliminary Results.* State Institute of Statistics, Ankara

UNICEF 1991 *The Situation Analysis of Mothers and Children in Turkey.* Yenicağ Printing House, Ankara

Yüksek Öğretim Kurulu (YÖK) 1991 *Türk Yüksek Öğretiminde On Yıl 1981–1991: 1981 Reformu ve Sonuçları.* Yüksek Öğretim Kurulu, Ankara

Tuvalu

J. N. Johnstone

1. General Background

The two Pacific island nations now called Kiribati and Tuvalu became independent after having been joined as a British colony called the Gilbert and Ellice Islands Protectorate since 1892. A referendum on separation of Tuvalu was held in 1974 and a separate dependency called Tuvalu was formed on 1 October 1975. Political independence from Britain for Tuvalu was declared on 1 October 1978.

Tuvalu consists of nine islands (the name implies only eight islands as the southernmost island was not included in naming the group) located between 5° and 10° latitude and 176° longitude. Six of the islands are built around lagoons and are atolls. There is some evidence that Tuvalu has been settled for nearly 2,000 years although little is known about any but the last 700 years.

The nine islands are all fairly small—total land area is 26 square kilometers —although they stretch over a distance of about 580 kilometers. The largest island is Vaitupu at 5.6 square kilometers. Their dispersion gives the country a reasonably large EEZ of nearly 1 million square kilometers. Most of the islands are less than 1.5 meters above sea level although one island has a point which is 4 meters above sea level. The capital is Funafuti.

There are about 9,500 people living in Tuvalu although the real number of Tuvaluans is probably closer to 10,000 because the census figure does not include Tuvalu nationals working at sea or in nearby Kiribati and Nauru. Given the small land area, the population density is high at about 900 people per square kilometer. Urbanization is about 30 percent. The literacy rate is estimated at about 96 percent. About 21 percent of the population have at least attended a secondary school with about 5 percent having attended a tertiary institution. Thirty-five of the resident population at the last census had a degree.

The Tuvaluans are Polynesian ethnically with strong ancestral links to Samoa and Tonga. In the northern islands, there are also strong Micronesian influences. The local language is Tuvaluan, and English is spoken in most areas. There are also a number of people who speak Gilbertese because of the original links with Kiribati.

Given the lack of natural resources, Tuvalu has great difficulty in developing its economy and its export industry. The GNP per capita is about US$550. The main industries are copra, coconut products, handicrafts, and fish and these, together with postage stamps, form the principal exports. About 70 percent of the economically active population are engaged in the traditional or subsistence sector.

Government in Tuvalu has been very stable. There are no political parties formally established. The present prime minister, Bikenibeu Paeniu, was elected in 1989. There is also a Governor General, Toaripi Lauti, who was appointed in 1990 and who had previously been prime minister from 1978 to 1981. There are four ministers, who take responsibility for several sectors each.

The economy was very dependent on the United Kingdom before Independence and has been aid-dependent since, because of the lack of opportunities for economic development. In 1988, for example, about 75 percent of government expenditure (capital and recurrent) was accounted for by foreign aid. To reduce that dependence, the Tuvalu government, through the leadership of its then finance minister, Henry Naisali, sought and successfully established a trust fund in the mid-1980s. That fund received contributions from various aid donors and forms an investment base. The interest from the Fund can then be used to fund recurrent costs of government.

The economy is also dependent on Tuvaluans working overseas and the remittances they send home. Such contracts are, however, intimately linked to conditions in those other countries. There are about 300 Tuvaluans working in the phosphate mining operations in Nauru but that operation is expected to close in 1996. There are also about 250 Tuvaluans working for international shipping companies although competition for such places is increasing, with declining numbers being employed.

2. Politics and the Goals of the Education System

In a small country such as Tuvalu, the question of the purpose of education is critical. It is not, however, a question which has been addressed directly with consequent policy support and action. Partly this shortcoming might be attributed to the significant impact of aid donors in all activities and the preferences they see (and often impose) for their aid contributions.

The education system in Tuvalu seeks to deliver quality education which is relevant to the nation's needs. Literacy is of course fundamental. The other basic need is the training of sailors who are able to work on merchant ships carrying any of several different flags.

The small scale of the country—and therefore of the education system—makes it essential to make special efforts for each student. The future of the country depends on each student enrolled. The size of the economy, however, constrains expenditure and forces teachers to improvise, especially with regard to teaching materials.

Demand for labor comes from four main sources: subsistence (72% of the workforce), government (12%), overseas employment (10%), and private and cooperative enterprises (6%).

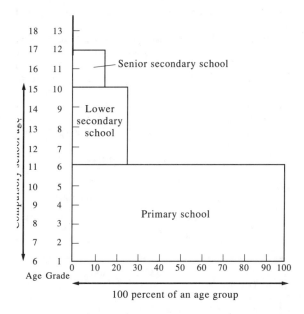

Figure 1

Tuvalu: Structure of the formal education system

3. The Formal System of Education

3.1 Primary, Secondary, and Tertiary Education

Figure 1 outlines the structure of the formal education in Tuvalu while the key statistics on enrollments and resources in the major education sectors are provided in Table 1.

Education is compulsory for all students aged 6 to 15 years. There are six years of primary education and six years of secondary education. There is a government-provided primary school on each island and three primary schools run by the Seventh Day Adventist Church. The number of students accommodated in primary schools has increased about 15 percent since the early 1980s.

At the end of primary school, there is a competitive examination (see Sect. 9) for entrance to the only secondary school in the country—Motufua—which is located on the island of Vaitupu. As only 25 percent of students are accepted into Motufua, many students must go overseas to undertake secondary education while others move to community training centers (see Sect. 3.4). Some students who fail to gain admission to Motufua can return to primary school to attempt a so-called Year 7 which provides the possibility of resitting the entrance examination. Few however are successful at their second attempt.

There has been discussion for several years on the possibility of the Church of Tuvalu opening another secondary school, provided that the government will accept responsibility for the recurrent costs. Such a move would significantly affect the primary–secondary transition rate. Agreement for the funding of such a school, which would involve significant government funds, has not yet been agreed (in 1993).

Students at Motufua have difficulties facing few secondary school students in other countries. Transport between islands is difficult and only by boat. Hence to visit home requires the single boat to time its departure from Vaitupu at the time when school closes, and its arrival when school reopens, given that its scheduled route on that voyage includes a student's home island. Most students are able to go home once a year given such constraints.

The nature of the primary school selective examina-tion has been questioned for several years. Its presence imposes an intense academic stream into a context which is that of a subsistence economy. There is thus a significant dysfunctionality of education provision for the majority of primary school students. This problem is compounded by the finding that transition rates are up to 60 percent higher in the Funafuti primary school than the national average. Parents are aware of this difference and hence urban drift is compounded. A more equitable distribution of resources and quality provision is urgently required.

There is no higher education in Tuvalu. There are however two avenues for postsecondary education. The major provision is the Tuvalu Maritime School on the island of Amatuku (near Funafuti). It provides a one-year course in basic seamanship for students between the ages of 17 and 22. Enrollment is presently about 40 students compared to a capacity of about 60 students. The other avenue for postsecondary education is the Tuvalu Extension Center of the University of the South Pacific. This center can offer most of the courses available from the USP in Fiji.

3.2 Preschool Education

A system of preschool education has been established, although it is outside the government sector. In 1993, there were 13 privately owned kindergartens throughout the islands.

3.3 Special Education

No provision is made for special education in Tuvalu.

3.4 Vocational, Technical, and Business Education

For children who cannot enter Motufua, the opportunity exists to enter a community training center. There is one center on each island. Courses are offered in a limited range of vocationally oriented subjects. These courses depend on availability of personnel; in 1993 there are no typing courses on offer in the country. Teachers come from the local communities and many do not have teaching experience. Discussion has been held about the possibility of developing quality modules which would form the basis of the courses.

The centers have considerable difficulties in achieving the aims established for them. By definition, they accept those students who failed to gain entrance to Motufua or who could not afford to study at the secondary level overseas. That immediately establishes an image problem which is reflected in high absentee rates and a fall in enrollments of nearly 10 percent in the late 1980s.

The Catholic Church has been planning for several years to open an education center, possibly combining secondary education and postschool training facilities. That would be in addition to the school proposed by the Church of Tuvalu (mentioned in Sect. 3.1).

In addition to these centers, the ILO (International

Table 1
Summary of basic education statistics, Tuvalu 1991

	Primary	Secondary	Technical/ Vocational
No. of Students	1,349	300	100
No. of Teachers	61	21	9
No. of Institutions	11	1	1
Expenditure per student (US$)	100	570	1,260

Labor Organization) and UNDP (United Nations Development Programme) conduct a series of modular-based training courses in selected trades areas. Students in these courses can then present themselves for competency-based examinations and, if successful, obtain formal certification.

Some trade training in fitting and welding, plumbing, carpentry, and electrical skills has also been arranged through the Fiji Institute of Technology in block courses. The advantage of these courses is that practical course attachments can generally be organized in Tuvalu, hence increasing its relevance. Normally such training is provided full-time in Fiji through aid-funded scholarships.

3.5 Adult and Nonformal Education

There are several sources for adult and nonformal education. The Government Business Development Advisory Bureau (the Development Bank as from July 1, 1993) offers various courses for people wishing to develop business skills to operate in the private sector. The University of the South Pacific also offers several courses through its extension center.

Other programs are also offered from time to time by nongovernment organizations. For example, the Save the Children Office provides workshops in such areas as family planning, nutrition, and sanitation. The Women's Council also offers a range of courses.

4. Administrative and Supervisory Structure and Operation

Education is administered as part of the responsibilities of the Department for Social Services. There is a Senior Education Officer who is responsible for primary education, while the Principal of Motufua and the Captain of the Maritime School report directly to the Secretary of the Department. There is hence a fragmentation of administrative and policy responsibility.

There is little decentralization of decision-making allowed despite the difficulties of communication with the outer islands. Even minor decisions about school operations must be referred to Funafuti.

5. Educational Finance

Finance for the education system comes from the Tuvalu government. The education system in 1993 accounts for about 18 percent of government expenditure. Families also make contributions in the form of fees to the private schools at home, to institutions overseas, and to cover boarding costs at Motufua.

6. Supplying Personnel for the Education System

Teachers are trained overseas for both the primary schools and Motufua, mainly at the University of the South Pacific in Fiji. Some teachers have received training elsewhere, such as New Zealand, Australia, or the United Kingdom. Funding for their scholarships is provided by aid funds. In addition, there is still some reliance on expatriate teachers for Motufua and the Maritime School.

Children on outer islands are often disadvantaged by the lack of adequate teacher provision. Teacher transfers are frequent and a number of posts are allowed to remain vacant for long periods. Teachers in charge of primary schools, with the exception of the person in charge of the Funafuti Primary School, do not receive any allowance for their extra responsibility. This lack also contributes to management and administrative difficulties.

7. Curriculum Development and Teaching Methodology

Efforts have been made to develop Tuvaluan curriculum to follow, at least to some extent, the Fiji and New Zealand curriculum. These developments have been useful in terms of increasing the relevance of materials especially to the Tuvalu context. As noted elsewhere, these changes have also incorporated a total change of emphasis during the last two years of the primary level where preparation for the Motufua entrance examination dominates the curriculum.

Teaching methodology is very conventional, with little reliance on modern teaching aids. Electrical power is very limited, if available, in all schools. Generators must be provided in each of the islands except Funafuti where there is only one power point in the primary school.

8. The System of Examinations, Promotions, and Certifications

As noted, there is a selective examination at the end of the primary school which allows about 25 percent of primary school students to enter Motufua for secondary education. That examination is set by the educational authorities in Tuvalu and covers English and mathematics only. It dominates the teaching during the last two grades of the primary cycle.

At the end of Year 10, students have sat for the Fiji Junior Certificate examination although changes to that examination to introduce school-based assessment practices have necessitated a change to a Tuvalu Year 10 Certificate. At the end of Year 12, students sit for the New Zealand School Certificate Examination. Similarly, changes to the regulations for that examination in New Zealand have required the Tuvalu Government to organize examinations for a Tuvalu School Certificate Examination. Assistance with quality control for that examination is being provided through the South Pacific Board for Education Assessment.

9. *Educational Assessment, Evaluation, and Research*

Tuvalu does not have any national assessment of its educational achievement or quality. The examinations conducted in association with Fiji and New Zealand did not permit such an analysis because of the very different nature and purpose of those examinations.

10. *Major Reforms in the 1980s and 1990s*

A number of reports have been prepared on Tuvalu education during the period since Independence. Responsibility for these reports has almost always been with an aid donor and sometimes there has been cooperation amongst donors. Except for slight modifications, however, little change in terms of real reform has been achieved. That is not to say that there has been no improvement as the system in the early 1990s is better than it was 10 years earlier. It is, however, basically the same system with the same kind of orientation and the same problems.

There have on occasions been differences accorded to certain activities by aid donors which have resulted in lack of action or counterproductive activities. The master plan activity scheduled for Motufua which was designed to rehabilitate and/or replace all facilities is one such example. Although 5 years old, it has not yet been acted upon and there is the possibility of yet another donor being involved in such a plan formulation in the future.

11. *Major Problems for the Year 2000*

The problem of providing relevant education for all children up to age 15 will continue to be the single greatest problem for Tuvalu education planners until the year 2000. The needs of the future citizens must be established clearly as there are few resources which can provide export income for the country. Human resources are therefore the major opportunity for economic development. The curriculum needs reform, especially in the later stages of primary school and more students need to receive secondary education which encompasses academic, technical, and vocational aspects. Furthermore the present community training centers need to be abolished.

Reforms are costly and political. A small country such as Tuvalu will find the above reforms possible but difficult although they are essential, and many advisers have suggested them or variations. The difficulties therefore need to be overcome when possible and in accordance with national priorities, which must include a level of economic activity, trust fund investment, and environmental issues.

Bibliography

Faaniu S et al. 1976 *Tuvalu: A History*. University of the South Pacific, Suva

Hancock G et al. 1988 *Education for Life: A Review of the Manpower, Education and Training Needs of Tuvalu*. A Report to the Government of Tuvalu, Government Printers, Funafuti

Uganda

C. F. Odaet

1. *General Background*

Uganda is located in the heart of Africa in the Western Rift Valley, astride the Equator. Uganda has a total land area of 241,139 square kilometers, of which 17 percent are swamp and water, and 12 percent are forest reserves and national parks. Of the remaining land, less than 10 percent is under cultivation. The country has good soil, which is suitable for farming. The country has a large expanse of savanna-type vegetation, that is, high grass mixed with trees. There are also thick natural forests mainly in the western region. Northeast Uganda (Karamoja) is mainly semidesert.

British protection commenced in Uganda in 1894 and remained in force until October 1962 when Uganda gained independence from Britain. The country inherited the colonial system of education, with voluntary agencies having a strong influence.

Throughout the colonial period in Uganda, African education was almost entirely in the hands of religious "voluntary agencies" under general direction of the government. The Church Missionary Society (CMS) and the White Fathers, whose representatives arrived in Uganda in 1877 and 1879 respectively, were primarily concerned with the furtherance of evangelism. To encourage this, literacy education was used to contribute significantly to the spread of Christianity. Muslim influences became strong in 1893. Various missions had complete liberty to initiate and develop schools in accordance with their varied, often conflicting, policies. The curriculum expanded to incorporate academic, practical, and vocational subjects.

In the mid-1920s, largely as a result of the Phelps–Stokes Commission Report (1924), but also due to the various developments in the country and a British White Paper on Education in Tropical Africa

(1925), it was realized that it was incumbent upon the government to take a more direct part in education. In that year, the government created the Department of Education for the formulation and direction of policy.

The Department of Education was intended to create an educational policy with a wider scope to cater for the increasing prosperity of the Protectorate, by expanding the aspirations and intelligence of the natives. It was also intended to develop and encourage missionary efforts by providing grants and carrying out inspection and supervision work in schools. This partnership between the missions and the government helped the education system to expand its curriculum from the "3Rs" to include a host of other subjects. It is this system which continued with modification until Independence and has since been subjected to criticism. With changing social and economic circumstances, it has attracted debate and reform.

In 1991, the population was 16.6 million, showing an intercensal growth rate of 2.5 percent from 1980 to 1991. This was down from the 2.8 percent recorded between 1969 and 1980 perhaps due to declining economic opportunities, internal conflict, outbound migration, and the increasing incidence of AIDS. Some important changes have taken place in the country's population composition since 1960: the sex ratio has declined from 101.8 in 1969 to 96.1 in 1991; the population of children aged 0–4 is almost half the total population (48%). There is, therefore, a high dependency ratio which has the effect of raising expenditure on social services like education and health. The total number of children and women in the reproductive age group constitutes more than half of the country's population. This forms the bulk of the most vulnerable group to whom due priority has to be accorded in education.

The country's rural and urban population is concentrated in the Lake Victoria crescent, which produces most of the country's coffee, sugar, some tea and livestock products, fish, and staple food products. The majority of the people reside in rural areas. If urban centers are defined as having a population of 2,000 or more, only 11 percent of the population are classified as living in urban centers. Nonetheless, most of the towns defined as urban do not show any indications of urban life-style. Only two towns, Kampala (the capital city, and a commercial and industrial center) and Jinja (an industrial center), can be considered as having an urban environment.

The population growth rate in the 1950s and 1960s was 4.6 percent, due partly to improved health facilities and partly to a large net inflow of people from the neighboring countries of Rwanda, Zaire, and Sudan as a result of the political instabilities then prevailing in those countries. In the 1970s, the population growth rate fell to 2.8 percent, and to 2.5 in 1991, due to a lowering of the standard of living and a rise in the mortality rate. There are a number of implications for education arising from population issues. There is an increasing recognition of the need for education to be more responsive to population needs. Population growth, even at the declining rate, implies a new addition to the vast pool of people that do not yet have access to education.

The Ugandan economy has always been dominated by agriculture, with 90 percent of the population dependent on agricultural and agro-based industries. The rural nature of the population implies that the major area of focus for education provision is the rural population. Apportionment of resources on the basis of equality of access to education resources would require a positive discrimination in favor of the female–child population (i.e., the larger sector of the population). In general, though, rural people remain economically and educationally disadvantaged in the country.

Other industries requiring a labor force which have developed are: forestry and fishing; mining and quarrying; manufacturing; electricity and water; construction; wholesale and retail trade; restaurants and hotels; transport, storage, and communication; finance; insurance and business services; public administration; educational services; medical, health-related, and veterinary services; and other social, community, and personal services.

Uganda, like several other developing countries in Africa, continues to suffer from a shortage of high-level skilled personnel. This has continued to be a major impediment to economic and social development. The reasons given for the existence of these vacancies in the indicated sectors were low salary, lack of a labor force, and low economic activities. The general political position is that participation in education and training needs to be increased, curricula need to be more relevant to national priorities, and that individuals should finance an increasing share of the costs of educational expansion. Curriculum policies are placing an increasing emphasis on practical skills, technology literacy, and the ability to work with others in groups.

Upon Independence in 1962, Uganda had a small but highly organized system of education, a situation which continued until the early 1970s. This system started to disentangle from the mid-1970s as a result of political turmoil and economic decline.

Until 1971, Uganda had one of the strongest and fastest growing economies in Sub-Saharan Africa. The Gross Domestic Product (GDP) grew at an average annual rate of 5 percent between 1960 and 1970. As a result, public sector employment during the same period increased by 42 percent, while that in the private sector grew by 23.5 percent. In addition, there was a well-developed social and physical infrastructure in the urban centers upon which future economic growth could be based. This pattern of growth came to a halt with the overthrow of the government in 1971. A severe economic crisis was precipitated by the expulsion from the country of the entrepreneur Asian business class in 1972. The economy was destroyed, physical capital was neglected and rapidly depreciated, and the social institutions declined.

Between 1972 and 1977, the GDP grew by only 0.5 percent as the socioeconomic situation was characterized by migration of employees out of the private to the public sector and from the formal sector to the informal sector during a series of political crises within the government and the country as a whole. High inflation meant that there was considerable erosion of real wages resulting in a high degree of under-employment, low productivity, and low incomes. The destruction which occurred during the 1979 liberation war further compounded the economic decline. Public facilities, including schools, were particularly hit by the war.

With peace and political stability restored in 1986, the NRM government's initial efforts were concentrated on halting and reversing economic decline. The guiding rationale was based on instituting macroeconomic policies in order to build an independent, integrated, and self-sustaining economy. In May 1987, a major economic adjustment and development program supported by the International Monetary Fund

(IMF) and the World Bank was initiated. As a result of these measures, the economic decline was reversed with GDP growing by 6 to 7 percent annually from 1987 onward. However, despite GDP increases, the balance of payment position continued to experience difficulties, due mainly to unfavorable external trade environments and the fall in the price of coffee, the country's main export crop. Debt burden and inflation have also remained high.

2. Politics and the Goals of the Education System

Governments in Uganda have played a dominant role in financing and administering education, so government education policies are of considerable importance. All governments have consistently underlined the centrality of education in Uganda as a foundation for economic growth and well-being of society as a whole. In the field of education and training, the main long-term objectives of the successive governments since Independence have been:

(a) to make primary education available to a fast-increasing proportion of school-age children until universal primary education is achieved, providing every individual with the basic skills and cultural awareness necessary for a full and productive life within a dynamic society;

(b) to provide sufficient personnel of the type and quality needed to meet the skill requirements of the expanding Uganda economy.

The very important role of education at all levels as a factor in the cultural and intellectual development of the Uganda community has continued to be recognized. To this end, government planning has paid close attention to the role of the schools in socioeconomic development.

The broad purposes of the educational sectors and institutions in Uganda are generally outlined in legislation or reflected in the major economic and social development plans of the government or the successive National Development Plans and Recovery Programs since Independence. The basic goals and principles which do emerge from these national policy documents are:

(a) forging national unity and harmony;

(b) evolving democratic institutions and practices in all sections of life;

(c) guaranteeing fundamental human rights, including personal security and property rights and the rule of law for all citizens;

(d) creating national wealth needed to enhance the

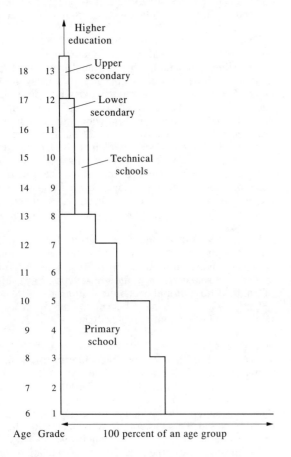

Figure 1
Uganda: Structure of the formal education system

quality of life and self-reliance;

(e) upholding and maintaining national independence and patriotic feeling;

(f) promoting moral and ethical values in citizens;

(g) promoting a feeling of humanitarianism and co-operation in citizens.

These broad goals of education differ in emphasis at each level. Lower down in the education system more emphasis is placed on the development of the individual and general socialization, while high in the system beginning at the upper-secondary level the emphasis is put on broader economic issues intended to enhance social goals.

3. The Formal System of Education

3.1 Primary, Secondary, and Tertiary Education

Figure 1 outlines the structure of the formal education

Table 1
Educational Statistics 1983–91

	1983	1984	1985	1986	1987	1988	1989	1990	1991
Number of institutions									
Primary schools	5,695	6,425	7,025	7,350	7,627	7,905	7,684	7,667	8,046
Secondary schools[a]	287	430	500	508	515	774	854	508	514
Teacher training colleges	55	68	73	73	92	94	68	—	71
Technical schools and institutes	36	47	52	56	55	52	52	52	52
Teacher colleges	4	4	10	10	10	10	10	10	10
Uganda technical colleges	1	9	5	5	5	5	5	5	—
Uganda commercial colleges	1	6	8	8	4	4	4	4	5
Other higher institutions[b]	—	—	—	—	3	3	3	3	3
Universities	1	1	1	1	2	3	3	3	3
Number of teachers, tutors, and lecturers									
Primary schools	49,206	57,078	61,424	66,101	72,970	75,561	81,418	81,590	78,259
Secondary schools	5,617	6,561	6,903	10,193	12,000	12,300	12,919	11,069	13,476
Teacher training colleges	558	743	906	1,105	1,105	1,429	1,429	—	1,338
Technical schools and institutes	407	436	443	649	649	649	278	667	787
Teacher colleges	138	151	163	176	276	276	331	234	548
Uganda technical colleges	173	240	367	561	79	140	128	124	—
Uganda commercial colleges	107	124	134	99	99	106	100	95	190
Other higher institutions[b]	—	—	—	—	400	411	200	215	455
Universities	369	390	435	485	558	558	573	579	579
Enrollment									
Primary schools	1,730,299	1,930,698	2,117,000	2,203,824	2,307,800	2,416,800	2,532,800	2,281,590	2,539,549
Secondary schools	117,087	144,527	159,702	196,010	224,375	238,111	238,467	223,498	235,245
Teacher training colleges[c]	11,314	11,382	11,229	12,551	13,179	13,173	15,166	—	15,980
Technical schools and institutes	4,995	6,079	6,932	6,491	6,548	6,556	3,804	8,094	8,579
Teacher colleges	1,175	1,670	1,650	1,674	1,412	1,819	3,008	3,464	4,178
Uganda technical colleges	669	1,368	1,505	435	635	723	342	328	—
Uganda commercial colleges	750	991	1,090	924	1,009	1,009	1,991	1,949	2,490
Other higher institutions[b]	—	—	—	1,681	2,111	2,088	2,521	2,422	3,219
Universities	4,854	5,042	5,271	5,390	5,533	5,565	5,405	5,746	7,468

Source: Planning Unit, Ministry of Education and Sports including some data from Establishment Survey in 1991
a 1988 and 1989 provisional figures include private schools   b Institute of Teacher Education, Kyambogo; Uganda Polytechnic, Kyambogo; National College of Business Studies, Nakawa   c Including service and ordinary intake

system, and key statistics on enrollments and resources in the major education sectors are provided in Table 1.

The structure of the education system has remained essentially unchanged since Independence and reflects its British heritage. It consists basically of four levels. Primary education has a seven-year cycle followed by a four-year lower-secondary cycle (UCE, or O-level) and a two-year senior-secondary cycle (UACE, or A-level). University education takes three to five years to complete. The Education Policy Review Commission (EPRC) Report has recommended extending the primary cycle and reducing the lower-secondary cycle by one year. Education is not compulsory at any level.

There are several options for the graduates of every level of the education system. Upon successful completion of primary education, graduates can either proceed to secondary schools or opt for three-year crafts courses in technical schools. However, only 25 percent of primary school graduates are absorbed into these two options, with the majority of pupils who complete primary education entering the labor market.

Four options exist for the successful graduates of the lower-secondary (UCE) level: proceeding into UACE, undertaking two-year advanced crafts courses in the technical institutes or two-year Grade III primary teacher training, or joining one of the government's departmental training programs. On successful completion of their courses, UACE graduates may go on to the University or undertake advanced courses at the national teachers colleges, Uganda colleges of commerce, Uganda technical colleges, the National College of Business Studies, and the Institute of Teacher Education, Kyambogo. They may also enter government departmental training programs. University graduates either enter government departments or the private sector, while a few proceed to graduate work and may later join the staff of the University and other institutions of higher learning or research.

Despite political disruption and the substantial decline in the economy, the education system grew dramatically during the 1980s. The growth in the number of primary schools in the face of turmoil is remarkable. Growth has occurred in an unplanned fashion, due almost entirely to the efforts of local communities. During the 1980s, the number of primary schools doubled, as did the number of primary school students, which rose to over 2.5 million students in 1989. The increase in the number of untrained teachers, which abetted such a rapid expansion, gives a first indication of the deterioration in quality that occurred during this period. While the number of teachers more than doubled, the percentage of untrained teachers in the teaching force rose from 35 percent in 1980 to 48 percent in 1989.

Although the growth rate of primary school enrollments has exceeded the rate of growth of the school-age population, a large proportion of the primary school-age cohort still receives no schooling. Gross enrollment ratios increased from about 50 percent in 1980 to about 70 percent in 1989. While net enrollment ratios are not known, it is estimated that about half the school-age population was not in primary school in 1989. In some regions, the gross enrollment ratio shows that fewer than one-fourth of the 6–12 year olds attend primary school. The dropout rate in the lower grades is about 8 percent, probably due both to the financial burden on parents of keeping children in school and the futility felt by parents in continuing to send their children to ineffective schools. The situation intensifies from P1 through the cycle of basic education (during which dropout rates increase, especially for girls). Of those who enter P1, only 32 percent complete the primary education cycle and can be said to have gained a basic education.

The secondary subsector is much smaller but has grown even more quickly in proportionate terms. The number of schools increased by four times and the enrollment by slightly over 227 percent. The teaching force officially increased by 260 percent, while the official student–teacher ratio decreased modestly from about 23:1 to 21:1 and to a regional average of 28:1. Of the students who successfully complete primary school, only about one-fourth pass their O levels (5% of population) and of these, only one in five (1%) completes their A levels. These dismal statistics reflect national averages; for disadvantaged groups such as females, migrants and nomadic ethnic groups, the poor, orphans, and the disabled, internal efficiency is much lower. There are also significant differences between regions of the country. An analysis of disparities at the district level showed representation indexes differing by a factor of more than five to one. It is believed that differences at the subdistrict level are even more dramatic.

The same analysis showed that of children entering P1, the probability of boys completing S4 was twice that of girls, with the probability of boys continuing on to the upper-secondary level being almost three times as high. The situation intensifies from P1 through all basic education. Dropout rates increase, especially for girls, as the child's education continues. Girls' persistence rate in primary schools is lower than that of boys. Though the pattern of dropping out has not been researched sufficiently, it is evident that by the time girls start secondary school, they make up about one-third of the total number of students (39%), while their number in the first grade of primary school is about the same as that of boys (46%).

Girls are disadvantaged largely due to a high economic emphasis being placed on the education of boys. Communities have also in the recent past felt that the place of girls was in the home. This is due to the social and cultural attitudes which have persisted. In addition, the high degree of poverty in communities has tended to dictate which sex of child is to continue with education; very often boys receive preferential treatment to continue with their education, while girls find themselves marrying early to raise families. This state of affairs certainly persists more in rural areas. However, the situation is being fought vigorously and some change of attitude is already evident. There is also a deliberate policy, especially in Makerere University, to give 1.5 points to each female student who qualifies to receive university education with a view to increasing her competitiveness to enter. This has helped the number of female students to rise on the campus.

Although average enrollment has continued to rise, schools in urban areas are very overcrowded, while in most rural schools the enrollment is extremely low. The reason for this is largely economic. Rural areas are extremely poor and are largely unaware of the value of education. There is, therefore, a greater number of school-age children not in school in rural areas. This is in addition to there being few schools available.

For many decades, Makerere University was Uganda's only university, but there are now four additional universities which are still very small. These comprise a second public university, the Mbarara University of Science and Technology in western Uganda; the private Islamic University in Uganda (sponsored by the Organization of Islamic Conferences, an international organization); Universities-Uganda Martyrs, a private institution, sponsored by the Catholic Church; and the Christian University of East Africa. The private universities offer degrees mainly in fields where the costs of instruction are relatively low, such as education, business, nursing, and religious studies. There are also numerous other tertiary education institutions which have helped to expand young people's access to higher education. In 1991, Makerere University accounted for 98 percent of public university enrollment, and 95 percent of total university enrollment.

Although disabled children make up an estimated 10 percent of the total population, there are only 61 special schools, with an average enrollment of 120 children each. Institutions for special education lack adequate physical facilities, transport, special instructional materials, and so on.

3.2 Preschool Education

There is a total lack of Government control of preprimary education in Uganda. Preschool education programs are provided by economically able individual and voluntary agencies on an almost commercial basis. These people and agencies have even gone as far as establishing boarding schools for preschool education. This has led to undesirable trends regarding the content and quality of the curriculum, teaching methods, facilities, age of entry, quality of teachers, school charges, and ultimately to widespread violation of pedagogical and sociopsychological principles of child development. As a result, the government discourages the establishment and operation of preprimary boarding schools for normal and underprivileged children.

The government has, however, agreed to undertake some control of and responsibility for the quality of preprimary education which will for the time being continue to be run primarily by the private sector.

3.3 Special Education

Special Education programs are provided for students with physical, intellectual, and emotional disabilities. The government has not yet assumed enough responsibility for special education, but voluntary organizations have made valuable contributions in supporting special education. However, the government does support special education programs, that is, the type of education which is designed specifically for the disabled (those with an objective deficiency of physical, sensory, or mental functions) such as the deaf, the blind, and the mentally handicapped.

The government is aware that institutions for special education are not only inadequate, but that they are also faced with the problem of lack of permanent and direct sources of income. To this end, the government is ready to give adequate support to all institutions offering special education to enable them to operate more effectively and efficiently.

3.4 Vocational, Technical, and Business Education

The industrial base in Uganda is small and industries have long played a relatively small part in employee training. Because of the urgent need to relate education to the labor market, there is an increasing focus on the provision of vocational, technical, and business education. Many secondary schools have broadened their curriculum since Independence and continue to do so in an attempt to make them more vocationally relevant. Similarly, tertiary institutions with a vocational bias have increased in type, level, and the number of student places has grown in subject areas that are in high labor market demand such as accountancy, technology, business, marketing, and even computing.

This type of education is provided within the structure of formal education and there is no explicit policy as to which students should receive vocational training; students choose freely and are admitted according to admission requirements. The increased emphasis on vocational, technical, and business education has substantial implications for the future of education–industry relations in Uganda.

3.5 Adult and Nonformal Education

The main purpose of adult and nonformal education in Uganda is to facilitate the personal development of youth and adults and prepare them for their social and economic roles in society. The overall goal is to improve the quality of life, both for individuals and for society as a whole.

Basic education in reading, writing, and arithmetic

is provided by the churches, local literacy associations, and the Ministry of Local Government. The government's Adult Literacy Campaign of 1964–65 had little success, but plans are in place to renew it.

The government also provides general education in hygiene, health precautions, nutrition, family welfare, agriculture and livestock farming, and trading. This is done by extension services and through radio and television.

Education for vocational, technical, and professional competence is provided by the government, the Young Women's Christian Association (YWCA), the Young Men's Christian Association (YMCA), the trade unions, and the churches. Education for civic, political, and community participation is provided by the government, the Makerere University's Institution of Adult and Continuing Education, the YWCA, the YMCA, the trade unions, and the NRM Government.

The work of certain institutions is of interest as they offer formal courses to adults. The Nakawa Vocational Institute, Kampala offers full-time courses of three months' duration for upgrading in motor-vehicle mechanics, electrical installations, electrical fittings, and industrial engineering. The Institute also offers six-month full-time courses for 16-year old school-leavers with a minimum educational standard of two years of secondary school. The national teachers colleges, the Institute of Teacher Education, Kyambogo, and Makerere University all have schemes through which adults can receive adult continuing education. To obtain national figures reflecting the map of adult and nonformal education is problematic. The government has decided to put in place a structure for coordination of adult and nonformal education, and it is hoped that this will facilitate the compilation of national figures.

4. Administrative and Supervisory Structure and Operation

The management and administration of the education system is officially centralized in the Ministry of Education and Sports. The management and administration arm is headed by the Commissioner for Education (Administration). In addition, a number of semi-autonomous institutions exist, including the Teaching Service Commission (TSC), a constitutional personnel management agency entrusted with the task of advising the President in matters affecting appointment, confirmation, promotion, and discipline "in respect of the offices of teachers;" the Uganda National Examination Board (UNEB), responsible for conducting various public examinations; and the Uganda National Curriculum Development Center (NCDC), responsible for curriculum development.

Despite the historically strong central role of the Ministry of Education and Sports, finances, communication, and staffing have reduced the effectiveness of headquarters in exercising control over the district- and school-level operations. This *de facto* decentralization is particularly prominent in the primary education subsector where the operation of the school is the responsibility of the headteacher and the School Management Committee in which the Ministry of Education and Sports exercises influence in a limited way by nominating their representatives. The School Management Committee, with the headteacher as the secretary, oversees school policy formulation and implementation. Its activities include supervising school budgets, reviewing educational performance, overseeing student and staff discipline, and making plans for school facilities expansion and repair.

At the secondary school level, the Board of Governors is responsible for policy formulation and implementation. Unfortunately much of the policy formulation concerns collection of funds for noninstructional purposes.

The Inspectorate is the principal arm of the Ministry of Education and Sports, responsible for monitoring educational system performance, including advising the Ministry of Education and Sports on ways to improve the quality of education. It is headed by the Commissioner for Education (Inspectorate). It should function in collaboration with the NCDC and the UNEB to ensure that the established education standards are observed. At the local level, each region is headed by a Regional Inspector of Schools with a staff of at least one Senior Inspector of Schools, District Inspector of Schools, and one or more Assistant Inspector, all of whom should be responsible for routinely visiting the schools. However, the Inspectorate has not been able to perform many of these functions due to lack of transportation, low motivation, lack of training, and a grossly insufficient number of staff.

In the higher education sector, institutions are operated by councils and, in some cases, boards of governors which have more exacting authority. Since the late 1980s, the need to reorganize and revamp the administration of the education system has been recognized. The existing administrative machinery has become inefficient and ineffective in performing its functions. The system suffers from a number of interrelated deficiencies, including poorly motivated staff, absence of guidelines and job descriptions for most of the posts, and delays in decision-making and the consequent poor results. Drastic measures are therefore called for, especially in view of the need for a strong administration that can plan and manage the implementation of various recommendations of the Education Policy Review Commission accepted by the government. In fact, there is a very strong move to decentralization — pushing most of the management, planning, and administration of education far down to the grassroots level.

5. Educational Finance

The government contribution is the main provider of resources for education, but the poor performance of the economy since the early 1970s has greatly affected the financing of education. While expanding quantitatively, the education sector has experienced severe resources constraints.

Both the recurrent and development–budgets have dropped from 25 percent in the early 1970s to 10 percent in 1990–91. In the 1980s, education's share of the recurrent budget declined by a factor of almost 2:1 and the overall level of aggregate resources and facilities declined drastically. In real terms, the 1988–89 education budget was 21.1 percent of the 1970–71 budget. In per capita terms, real expenditure declined to 13 percent of the 1970 period. The lasting effects of the economic war and years of declining real budgets plus quantitative expansion of enrollment have left resources spread thinly across both institutions and pupils; structures are badly depleted at all levels, and teachers' salaries are low. The education sector in 1991–92 was allocated 17.76 percent of the recurrent budget and 7.87 percent of the development budget. These percentages are almost unchanged from 1990–91 levels. Increases in the development budget as a whole meant an increase in real funding of 23 percent for development activities in the education sector.

The government has been meeting the full boarding, travel, and other living expenses of students at the tertiary level, and a substantial portion of the boarding expenses at the secondary level in the form of capitation grants. A good percentage of the scarce financial resources has therefore been used for nonpedagogical purposes, rather than for the important instructional costs which have remained unfulfilled, especially at the primary level.

Teachers' salaries have remained extremely low. As a result of this, many teachers have been forced to seek additional employment to supplement their incomes and this has affected adversely the quality of instruction in schools. The percentage of under-qualified and untrained teachers has remained high.

As a result of diminishing financial resources from the government, a situation has emerged where parents share a greater responsibility for resourcing primary and secondary education. The money so collected has been used for supplementing staff salaries, purchasing educational materials, and even building classrooms and teachers' houses. Parents who have been unable to give financial support to the Parent–Teacher Associations have had to withdraw their children from school, and regions which are economically backward have lagged far behind others. All this has increased and perpetuated inequalities of educational opportunity and hindered uniform social development in the country.

Parental responsibility has also emerged in tertiary education through cost-sharing policies and the institution of private students in university education. Financing private schools and colleges is done privately and through dues from fees. In fact, all private students at any level meet all their tuition fees and other dues.

6. Supplying Personnel for the Education System

In 1987, there were 289,528 persons employed in Uganda's civil service of which 57 percent were established staff and 47 percent group employees. The 1989 National Manpower Survey detailed exact deficiencies in human resources in the education sector and highlighted considerable gaps in staffing. The survey revealed that in 1989 the education/training institutions had only 52 percent of the teaching personnel they required. The largest number of vacancies was in the government education/training institutions where as many as 48 percent of the established posts were vacant. This critical situation, compounded by lack of input, bedevilled the system. The situation has not much improved since 1989.

Teachers in Uganda are trained at three levels: namely universities and the Institute of Teacher Education, Kyambogo(ITEK); the National Teachers Colleges (NTCs); and Grade III primary teachers colleges. The pupils who enter primary schooling expect to enter secondary where they are taught by teachers trained at the NTCs, the university, and, since 1987, the ITEK. The graduates of the secondary schools who wish to become primary teachers train in Grade III primary teachers colleges. The tutors in the primary teachers colleges are graduates of university Faculties of Education, ITEK and the NTCs; graduates other than those from the NTCs can become lecturers and undertake graduate work at the universities and ITEK. Through other established avenues, some of these teachers and teacher educators become managers, administrators, and supervisors of the education system. Teacher education was undergoing reform in the early 1990s for the purpose of improving the quality of education, particularly at the primary level.

7. Curriculum Development and Teaching Methodology

There is a common school curriculum across the country covering English language, mathematics, physics, chemistry, biology, history, and geography. The curriculum detail and scope are determined centrally. In primary schools, most subjects offered are taught by a general classroom teacher with specialization being introduced as one enters the upper primary levels; whereas in secondary schools various subject specialists are the teachers. All students in secondary schools have a good range of elective subjects at Uganda Certificate Level, whereas clear specialization emerges at A level in terms of either the sciences or the arts in preparation for tertiary education.

The National Curriculum Development Center (NCDC) is legally charged with the responsibility of developing curriculum for the whole national school system. All its work is conducted by subject panels consisting of teachers and representatives from the examining board, the teacher education institutions, the University, and the inspectorate. The panels decide, under the general aegis of the NCDC, on the syllabuses for each subject at each grade level, write the textbooks (or other materials) and teachers' guide, try them out, revise them, and print them. All curriculum syllabuses and materials are reviewed by national conferences on education or policy review commissions on education. This is primarily to ensure the economic, social, and political relevance of the curriculum.

After revision and printing, the curriculum for a subject or grade level, or cluster of subjects and grade levels, is implemented under the supervision of the inspectorate of the Ministry of Education and Sports.

Teacher-training college syllabuses are prepared by the ITEK and the universities.

Learning materials and tests are prepared by a variety of agents including the NCDC, academics, commercial publishers, individual teachers, and teachers' subject associations and groups. In the state of affairs extant in the early 1990s, schools and individual teachers have a great deal of independence in the selection of learning materials.

8. The System of Examinations, Promotions, and Certifications

In all schools students are supposed to be automatically promoted between year levels according to age. The first certificate is received at Year 12, the second at Year 16, and the third at Year 18 before entering the tertiary level. External examinations by UNEB determine entry from one level of education to the next.

Within the three levels of the education system, pupils have to sit class tests or examinations, the results of which are used by the schools or institutions to promote pupils to the next class.

Considerable debate and thought is being directed toward incorporating continuous assessment in order to facilitate promotion from one level to the next, as well as including it as a factor in the certification of students.

9. Educational Assessment, Evaluation, and Research

Little research has been developed. There is, however, discussion about educational assessment, evaluation, and research. The UNEB research department undertakes some of all these activities.

10. Major Reforms in the 1980s and 1990s

Despite political disruption and the substantial decline in the economy, the education system grew dramatically during the 1980s. One of the more notable changes

was the rise in the proportion of young people who entered primary schools and completed secondary education. This was reflected at the higher level through the impetus it had on the consequent expansion of tertiary education. This has stimulated far-reaching changes in curricula, assessment, and school structures as reflected in the Education Policy Review Commission Report. Reforms have been under consideration to attract and retain people in the teaching service. There is greater momentum for increased access to education for all. This in turn has gone hand in hand with increased involvement on the part of parents in financing the education of the Ugandan child at all levels.

11. Major Problems for the Year 2000

There is still unequal access to education in Uganda and its quality varies considerably between institutions. Finding the resources to support the continued expansion of education at all levels will be a problem. Already there is evidence of low enrollment in rural areas and overcrowding in urban areas as well as indications of looming shortages of teachers and academics in key discipline areas.

Education in Uganda is already seen as inefficient and of poor quality. This is reflected by high dropout rates, an outdated curriculum, weak examination and assessment results, inadequate teacher training, and poor terms and conditions of service. There is weak planning and poor management of the educational system. There is insufficient finance and a lack of sustainability of educational investments. Yet the educational demands of rapid social and economic change are unlikely to abate. It will be difficult to accommodate these demands without further burdening poor parents and the curriculum in the midst of this major challenge. Teachers will continue to be supplied and to acquire new skills and knowledge to assist their students to anticipate and control the pace of change. Developing mechanisms of rewarding career structures for teachers and academics in Uganda is likely to be a major problem.

In addition, the perennial problems of Ugandan education will certainly remain. It will be difficult to rebuild the system overnight. This, therefore, will affect the education of the Ugandan child.

Bibliography

Evans D R, Odaet C F 1991 *Teacher Education in Uganda 1990–2000: A Pre-investment Study*. A Report For The Ministry of Education
Fleuret A 1992 *Girls Persistence and Teacher Incentives in Primary Education.* USAID Study, Kampala
Ministry of Education 1989 *Education Policy Review Commission Report*. Ministry of Education, Kampala
Ministry of Education 1991 *Ugandan Five-year Education Sector Investment Program, 1992–93 to 1996–97*. Ministry of Education, Kampala

Ministry of Education and Sports 1992 *Government White Paper on National Integration and Development.* Ministry of Education and Sports, Kampala

Ministry of Finance and Economic Planning 1992a *Background To The Budget 1992/93.* Ministry of Finance and Economic Planning, Kampala

Ministry of Finance and Economic Planning 1992b *Uganda National Program of Action for Children: Priorities for Social Services Sector Development in the 1990s and Implementation Plan 1992–93 to 1994–95.* Ministry of Finance and Economic Planning, Kampala

Ministry of Finance and Economic Planning 1992c *Rehabilitation and Development Plan 1991–92 to 1994–95, Volume 1: Macroeconomic and Sectoral Policy.* Minis-try of Finance and Economic Planning, Kampala

United States Agency for International Development 1992 *Program Assistance Approval Document.* USAID, Washington, DC

World Bank 1985 *Uganda Progress Towards Recovery and Prospects for Development.* World Bank, Washington, DC

World Bank 1991 *Staff Appraisal Report, Uganda, Primary Education Development Project.* World Bank, Washington, DC

World Bank 1992 *Staff Appraisal Report, Republic of Uganda, Education Reconstruction and Development Project.* World Bank, Washington, DC

United Arab Emirates

M. A. Al-Nayadi

1. General Background

The United Arab Emirates (UAE) is a federation of seven Arab Gulf Emirates: Abu Dhabi, Dubai, Sharjah, Ras Al Khaimah, Umm Al Qaiwain, Fujairah, and Ajman. These emirates were formerly known as the Trucial States and, for much of the nineteenth and early twentieth centuries, were supervised and regulated by the United Kingdom. The UAE was proclaimed an independent state on the withdrawal of Britain from "East of Suez" in December 1971. The new country became the 132nd state of the United Nations and joined a number of regional organizations such as the Arab League and the Islamic charter organizations, and became a member of their specialized agencies. It is a founder member of the Gulf Cooperation Council (GCC).

The UAE stretches for 900 kilometers along the southern shore of the Arabian Gulf, plus 90 kilometers on the Gulf of Oman. It has a tropical arid climate with an annual rainfall of 6.5 centimeters mainly during November to April. The summer is very hot and humid. The UAE is bordered by the Arabian Gulf in the north and northwest, Qatar and Saudi Arabia in the west, and the Sultanate of Oman and Oman Gulf in the east.

The federal government is the central authority of the country, but each emirate still retains its own ruler and local government. The Supreme Council, which is composed of the rulers of the seven emirates, is the country's highest authority. The Council elects the president of the union from among its members and appoints the Cabinet of Ministers. The Council proposes laws for the elected 40 members of the Federal National Council.

All UAE nationals are Arab and Moslem. In 1992 the total population was estimated to be 1.8 million. Nearly 80 percent are non-UAE nationals. Intensive development plans and economic expansion has created,

since 1970, a large number of jobs, and hence the large number of non-nationals. Their presence does not pose any educational problem because the children of school age can either enter the national system schools or their own community schools in UAE. The expatriate population, mainly Asiatic, is predominantly male, young, and illiterate or with little schooling. These characteristics are reflected strongly in the overall population mix and consequently in several social and economic aspects. Some of the expatriates, however, especially in the oil industry, are very highly qualified and trained.

The economy of the United Arab Emirates is based largely on oil and its by-products. The production of oil, which was discovered in 1958, rose steadily during the 1960s and 1970s and by 1980 production reached 626,630,000 barrels. The oil industries alone employ about half of the total working force while the remaining 50 percent is employed in service industries, such as construction, business, education, local services, transport, and health. While agricultural activities, fisheries, and light industry constitute a reasonable portion of the economy, the country still has to import the bulk of its basic food supply from abroad.

2. Politics and the Goals of the Education System

Since the establishment of the federation in 1971, responsibility for education has rested in the hands of the UAE Ministry of Education. Hence, the national educational system is highly centralized. Article 17 of the UAE Constitution reads "Education is the basic right for the advancement of society. It is compulsory in the primary stage and free at all stages." To encourage citizens to attain a high educational level, higher education was also made free for all.

The broad purposes of education are "to create good citizens with a balanced personality . . . and to enable

1021

them to acquire and develop aptitudes, abilities, skills, values, and positive orientations that qualify them to participate in the national development of the UAE society in particular and the progress of humankind in general."

There are a number of private and community fee-paying schools in the UAE. They are free to adopt any curriculum but if they desire their certificates to be recognized and accredited by the Ministry of Education, they must teach some specific subjects, such as language and religion. Students may transfer from and to these schools providing they satisfy certain conditions.

3. The Formal System of Education

Education has become one of the top priorities in the government's overall plans and efforts for expansion, development, and modernization. Before 1953 the educational system in the UAE was characterized by two main attributes: (a) education was generally informal, and (b) most of it was conducted in *Kuttabs* based on religious teachings and memorization of the Koran along with basic arithmetic and language studies. The Sharjah Emirate took the lead and opened the first school for formal education on modern lines in 1953. Figure 1 presents the structure of the education system.

3.1 Primary, Secondary, and Tertiary Education

The UAE has a four-stage primary and secondary educational system (see Fig. 1). Kindergarten of two years duration is accessible to children from the age of

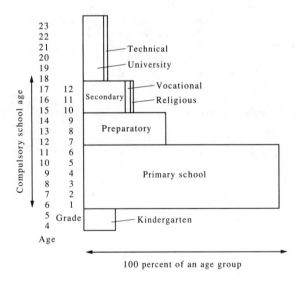

Figure 1
United Arab Emirates: Structure of the formal education system

four. Elementary (primary) lasts six years. Enrollment in 1990–91 was 154,548 primary students, of whom some were enrolled in private schools. In most government schools, at all stages, boys and girls are taught in separate schools but are given equal opportunities. The primary school day normally starts at 07:30 and ends at 13:30 and the school year comprises 200 teaching days.

The preparatory stage is of three years duration and students normally enroll at the age of 12 years. A number of preparatory students are enrolled in private schools. The school year is approximately 200 teaching days, with 7 hours of instruction per day.

The secondary stage has a duration of three years and students enroll at the age of 15 years. After the first year of core subjects, students branch into scientific and literary streams. In accordance with their choice and ability students may follow either of the two courses of study. At the end of the third year of the secondary stage, students in both sections take the General Secondary Certificate examination which entitles them to proceed to university and higher education.

The United Arab Emirates University at Al Ain was founded in 1976—only five years after Independence. The University has seven faculties: arts, sciences, education, administration and politics, agriculture, engineering, medicine and community health, and several research centers. Student enrollment rose from 502 in the foundation year to 9,564 students in 1990–91.

Higher education is also available in some other institutes and colleges which offer courses of three to six years duration in different disciplines. These include the higher colleges of technology for men and women (three-year course); the Dubai College of Medicine for women (six-year course); the Air College, Dubai (three-year course); and the Ajman College of Technology (five-year course). The total enrollment in the institutes is relatively small. This is due to the good opportunities for secondary school leavers to go to university or enter well-paid employment in the public and private sectors.

3.2 Preschool Education

In the main cities there are a number of nursery schools to cater, in particular, for children whose parents are both working. These schools are modern, privately owned and fee paying.

3.3 Special Education

Special education programs are provided for physically and emotionally handicapped children. The Ministry of Labor and Social Affairs—rather than the Ministry of Education—is responsible for these schools. The number and distribution of special schools in UAE covers the needs of parents who wish to give their children such education.

3.4 Vocational, Technical, and Business Education

Technical education was started in 1958 when the first school was founded in Sharjah. Two more such schools were added, the first at Dubai and the second in Ras Al Khaimah in 1969. All three are specialized schools which offer, respectively, a three-year course in commerce, technology, and agriculture. The final certificate awarded by these schools to successful students is accepted as a minimum requirement for entrance to the University of the UAE.

3.5 Adult and Nonformal Education

The Ministry of Education directly supervises the literacy and adult education programs. Evening education centers were opened by the Ministry for this purpose and are attended by groups of male and female nationals. There are at present 135 adult education centers with 19,209 participants. The course offered by these centers is the same as that of the primary school. Stage I covers the syllabus for Grades 1 and 2; Stage II covers that for Grades 3 and 4. On completion of Stage II participants join evening schools for the syllabus of Grades 5 and 6.

4. Administrative and Supervisory Structure and Operation

Education, except for special schools, is the responsibility of the Ministry of Education. The Ministry recruits and appoints teachers for government schools and is in charge of providing buildings, equipment, and materials. The organization of the Ministry of Education is both central and regional or zonal. Educational zones correspond to the boundaries between the different emirates.

The functions of the central Ministry of Education include: drawing up the overall educational plan, budget estimates, laying down the national curriculum, textbooks, controlling conditions for employment of teachers, and other basic functions and regulations which guarantee equal opportunities, and high standards of teaching and learning.

At the regional level there are six educational zones and two educational offices. Zones and offices are authorized to implement and follow up educational plans to supervise education in schools in their respective areas and to make suggestions for the further development of education. At the institute level schools receive their instructions and directions directly from the educational zones.

5. Educational Finance

The education budget is part of the national budget of the federation. Expenditure on education is increasing continuously. In 1989–90 Ministry of Education expenditure was UD2.03 billion (US$553 million) which represents 14.9 percent of total government expenditure. The greater part of this budget goes to the construction of schools for the benefit of children of the nationals and the expatriates living in the UAE. Private funding of education is mostly in the form of tuition fees paid by parents to private schools.

Figures regarding unit cost, expenditure on each level or sector etc. are not available. Instead, the breakdown is given under three headings, namely: Salaries, 80.4 percent; Services, 18.2 percent; and Special expenses 1.4 percent.

6. Supplying Personnel for the Education System

Personnel for the education system are of two main categories: nationals and expatriates. As the medium of instruction is Arabic the latter are recruited mainly from Arab countries and their number is much greater than that of national personnel. All expatriate staff are trained teachers and are carefully selected according to the needs of the system. Special attention is given to a balanced distribution by sex, specialization, and so on. As a result of the relatively generous terms of service, selection is very competitive and the teachers and supervisors employed are qualified and experienced.

In view of concentrated efforts in the field of preservice and inservice teacher training, the percentage of national staff in the educational system is rising steadily. Complete nationalization (i.e., employment of national teachers only) is envisaged in the near future. As a result, initial full-time teacher training at university level is given special attention, as is part-time inservice training for teachers already employed, whether male or female. In both cases teachers of mathematics, science, and computer studies are given priority. Requirements for the BEd degree from the UAE University stipulate that students should do adequate practical teaching in schools under the supervision of experienced teachers. The standard of school administration, supervision, inspection, and so on is being raised by conducting special short training programs for staff already in the service.

7. Curriculum Development and Teaching Methodology

All schools follow the national curriculum specified by the central authority. A special department in the Central Ministry of Education is in charge of curriculum development. Among the more important aims which the Department and its committees endeavor to achieve are:

(a) All students should achieve the highest possible level in reading, writing, mathematics, science, and the humanities.

(b) There should be a solid common core curriculum applicable to all areas and sectors of the federation.

(c) All schools should adopt similar teaching methods and achieve comparable results in national examinations.

(d) The study of languages (Arabic and English), science, mathematics, and computer science—which are considered important for oil industries—should be emphasized.

The National Textbook Committee undertakes the writing of all textbooks. The Committee is composed of experienced teachers chosen by the Directorate of Curriculum whose head is ex officio chair of the Committee. All books are formally approved by the minister of education.

8. The System of Examinations, Promotions, and Certifications

In primary, preparatory, and secondary education promotion from one year to the next is based on pupils' daily work as assessed by the class teacher and end of term or year final tests and examinations. Promotion from one level of schooling to another and branching into scientific and literary streams, on the other hand, is based on a final examination which is set and marked by the school in which a student is enrolled.

The final secondary examination, the basis for selection to higher education, is the same for all schools throughout the UAE. It is centrally controlled and is therefore considered a national examination. Such examinations are conducted in accordance with detailed regulations laid down by the central authority. This is deemed necessary for the recognition of certificates issued to successful students by any educational zone, by all the other zones, and also for the maintenance of a national standard of educational achievement.

Selection of students for the university, to institutes of technology, and for postsecondary employment is based (as far as academic achievement is concerned) on the students' results in the Secondary Certificate Examination. Not all subjects of the curriculum are given the same weight in final examinations. Languages, science, and mathematics are given more weight. Students who do not pass a paper, subject, or the whole examination are allowed to resit or they may be asked to repeat the year.

9. Educational Assessment, Evaluation, and Research

No national attempt has been made to conduct educational assessment and evaluation. The small total number of students, the very recent history of education, and the centrally controlled system of examinations do not warrant that priority be given to this aspect. However, the importance and necessity of such an attempt is fully recognized. Some international consultants have been employed from time to time by certain bodies to make a limited evaluation or assessment of certain aspects of student achievement, particularly in English, languages, science, and mathematics.

Educational research is increasing but is still mainly confined to the faculty of education of the University and is, in most cases, in the form of postgraduate work for MA, MEd, and PhD theses at home and abroad. Though relevant to problems of education in UAE such work does not form a coherent research program that is strongly related to the priorities of the educational system.

10. Major Reforms in the 1980s and 1990s

The UAE University and the Ministry of Education began to lay the foundations of joint work to improve the standard of primary school teaching, an aspect which is considered of the greatest importance. Work began on improving secondary education by reviewing the syllabus, as well as the detailed educational objectives and teaching–learning methods. The diversification of postsecondary education to satisfy human resource development and the labor market is an important aspect of the major reforms of the 1980s and 1990s.

11. Major Problems for the Year 2000

The UAE is a fast-developing country. The major problems of education reflect some of the major problems of the country at large. There is the need to nationalize the teaching force so that as far as teacher supply is concerned the country should be self-reliant. This should be achieved without detriment to standards and in the shortest possible time.

Eradication of illiteracy should be achieved by the year 2000 if not before. Follow-up work in this direction and, in particular, the establishment of lifelong education for the whole population (and not only for children) must be given adequate attention.

The voluntary demand for education should increase without the need for government incentives to individuals to enter schools and remain there until the end of the course.

An optimum balance should be reached between several sets of conditions, particularly: boys' and girls' education, sciences and arts at all levels, and formal and nonformal education.

Bibliography

Al-Nayadi M 1988 *Educators' Perceptions of the Teacher Evaluation System in* UAE. *(Unpublished doctoral thesis, George Washington University) Washington*, DC

Daa'ir S 1991 *Educational Change in the United Arab Emirates (1977–1987)*. The Cultural Foundation, Abu Dhabi

Garzarolli 1979 *Education at the Double*. UAE Ministry of Information and Culture, Abu Dhabi

Head B F 1982 *From Trucial States to United Arab Emirates. A Society in Transition*. Longman, London,

Khader F et al. 1986 *Educational System in the* UAE.

Alwataniyh Press, Dubai

Ministry of Education 1988 *Development of Education 1986–1988 National Report of United Arab Emirates*. Ministry of Education, Abu Dhabi

Ministry of Education 1991 *Educational Statistics*. Ministry of Education, Abu Dhabi

Ministry of Information and Culture 1981 UAE: *A Record of Achievement*. Ministry of Information and Culture, Abu Dhabi

Mursi A 1978 *The United Arab Emirates: A Modern History*. Croom Helm, London

Mustafa S, Najat A 1986 *Educational Administration*. Dar Al Qalam, Dubai

United Kingdom

W. D. Halls

1. General Background

The United Kingdom of Great Britain and Northern Ireland comprises England, Scotland, and Wales, together with part of the former province of Ulster known as Northern Ireland. The territory occupies most of the British Isles, and lies just west of the European mainland. Although this entry deals mainly with the educational system of England and Wales, reference is made wherever possible to Scotland and Northern Ireland.

The total population is about 56.8 million: 47.3 million in England, 5.1 million in Scotland, 2.8 million in Wales, and 1.6 million in Northern Ireland. England is divided into eight regions, three of which have a population larger than Scotland. Population density is greatest in the Southeast region. In 1988 the number of children aged 0–16 was 11.57 million, and it is estimated that there will be a rise of 0.8 percent per annum until 2003 and a small decline thereafter.

Historically, at least in England and Wales, state participation in education was minimal. The task was initially left to the Church. In 1870, when universal elementary education was introduced, local school boards were set up to supplement school provision by the churches, and central government financing was increased. In 1902 the boards were replaced by Local Education Authorities (LEAs). Since that time, these bodies have had the main responsibility for educational provision. The 1944 Education Act instituted secondary education for all. In 1947 the leaving age was raised to 16. A Secretary of State for Education was assigned the general supervision of the new system, exercising functions of "direction and control" through the LEAs. Since 1980 LEA responsibilities have progressively diminished.

The secretaries of state for Scotland, Wales, and Northern Ireland—all members of the British Government—exercise responsibility for all school and further education. Voluntary schools, largely run by religious bodies—Anglican, Roman Catholic, and Jewish—exist, and are mainly financed from public funds.

The 1944 Education Act stated the aim of the system as "to secure for children a happier childhood and a better start in life." The reforms that resulted were based on equality of opportunity. Until the early 1970s the concept of equity dominated education, seen by some as a tool for social engineering. Innovations such as the comprehensive secondary school, the phasing out of the 11+ secondary entrance examination, and mixed-ability teaching were introduced with this in mind. For primary education the influential Plowden Report (Department of Education and Science 1967)—*Children and Their Primary Schools*—set the seal of approval at that time on child-centered teaching and "progressive" methods. It also recommended "positive discrimination" favoring disadvantaged children, and the creation of "educational priority areas" (EPAs), where additional resources would be made available. The success of EPAs was patchy.

In the 1970s and 1980s a massive expansion in higher and further education occurred. More universities were created; 30 new institutions, known as polytechnics, were set up, as were additional colleges of education for the training of teachers (many of which were later closed or diversified into colleges of higher education); and there was an expansion of colleges of further education, largely offering part-time courses. In 1992 most of the institutions of higher education were upgraded to full university status.

The existence of four different governmental bodies for dealing with education in the different constituent parts of the United Kingdom makes central educational planning difficult, as did the strong local organisation of education (now considerably weakened).

2. Politics and the Goals of the Education System

The goals of the system are still broadly those laid down in the 1944 Education Act: children are to be educated according to their age, ability, and aptitude so as to further their spiritual, moral, mental, and physical development, and in accordance with parental wishes.

The 1980s were marked by public and political discontent, not with the purposes of the education system, but with how to realize them. Educational "theorists" were attacked. Parents felt that standards were low and they had too little say in their children's schooling. Politicians reacted accordingly, and also argued that higher and further education should be more vocationally oriented. "Consumer choice" became the watchword, so that by the end of the 1980s parents were given the right to choose between schools.

Until the mid-1980s, educational reforms have been proposed after independent committees set up by the government have considered some particular aspect of education. Their "reports" have been used as a basis for

reform, although some have merely been pigeonholed. The politicization of education has meant more direct intervention by central government, with the independent report system having fallen into disuse. The pace of reform has consequently quickened.

3. The Formal System of Education

3.1 Primary, Secondary, and Tertiary Education

Figure 1 gives the structure of the formal education system. Separate up-to-date figures for Scotland and Northern Ireland were not available. Tables 1 to 3 present enrollment figures. Education is compulsory from 5 to 16 years of age and attendance is virtually 100 percent in primary and secondary education.

Preschool education consists of nursery education from 2 to 5 years of age. The participation rate for under-5s in official nursery and primary schools was 46 percent in 1990, although this does not include a small number of 2-year olds, nor an additional 6.4 percent in private preschool classes. Attendance is usually part-time. In addition, there are a large number of creches and voluntary playgroups attached to business or industrial enterprises or run by parents. Playgroups may receive local authority financial support.

Primary education comprises an "infant" stage (5 to 7 years of age) and a junior stage (8 to 11/12). Primary schooling normally lasts 6 years, from ages 5 to 11. In 1990 there were 3.9 million pupils in official ("maintained") schools. To this must be added 191,700 pupils aged between 5 and 10 in private schools. Small schools were being amalgamated into larger units where feasible. The school day lasts from approximately 9 a.m. to 3.30–4 p.m. The teaching year for all schools consists of 195 days and teachers are contracted to work 1,265 hours in any year.

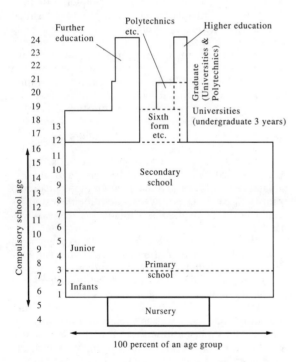

Figure 1
United Kingdom: Structure of the formal education system

Table 1
Numbers in education (in thousands)

Public sector schools	Students	Teachers	Ratio
Nursery	58.4	2.7	21.6:1
Primary	4,662.8	213.3	21.9:1
Secondary	3,551.7	237.0	15.0:1
Further education Colleges	4,175.0		
Higher education Universities	469.0		
Polytechnics and colleges	562.0		

Source: DES 1991

Table 2
Numbers of students aged 16 and over (in thousands)

	Under 21	21–24	25+	Total
School	509	0	0	509
Further education	1,094	495	2,035[a]	4,175
Higher education	376	236	343	956

Source: DES 1991
a Includes adult "leisure" classes

Under the 1964 and 1968 Education Acts, LEAs were allowed (but not obliged) to establish "Middle Schools" for the age group 10½ to 12/13. These may be classified as either primary or secondary.

Secondary education consists of a minimum five-year course (four years in Scotland), although a seven-year course (six in Scotland) is available. In 1990, 2.9 million pupils attended maintained (official) secondary schools. While a few grammar (more academic) schools and single-sex schools continue to exist, education at this level is generally comprehensive and coeducational. Some 20 percent stay on at school beyond the statutory leaving age, although another 33 percent of the age cohort 16–18 take up full-time courses in further education. Education for the 16–19 age group takes place in secondary schools (in what are known as "sixth forms"), as well as in special institutions ("sixth form colleges"), tertiary colleges, and colleges of further education.

Independent (private) schools account for an additional 313,000 pupils. There is a move toward coeducation, and away from boarding, in these once largely single-sex schools. Since 1984 the numbers in such schools (both secondary and primary) have risen by 8.5 percent. Private education accounted for 7.4 percent of all pupils in 1990. An official Assisted

Table 3
Participation rates as percentages of age groups[a]

	16–18	19–20	21–24
Schools	20	—	—
Further education	33	14	13
Higher education[b]	4	15	6

Source: DES 1991
a Nursery (as percentage of total of all 3–4-year olds=49.1 percent) b 46 percent of total in higher education were in universities; 54 percent were in polytechnics and colleges of higher education

Places Scheme finances some poorer pupils. About half of such places are taken up by pupils whose parents earn less than the average wage.

Since 1987, as part of the diversification mentioned above, 13 "City Colleges" directly controlled and mainly financed by the central authority, the Department for Education (DFE), and catering for the secondary age range, have been started. All colleges are located in urban areas and are of two kinds: City Technology Colleges (CTCs) and City Colleges for the Technology of the Arts (CCTAs). In the CTCs the emphasis is on science and technology; in the CCTAs it is on technology applied to the performing and creative arts.

In Scotland the staying-on rate in secondary schools in 1988–89 was 53.7 percent—much higher than in England. In Northern Ireland there are two types of grant-aided secondary schools: intermediate schools, giving an education up to age 16, and grammar schools, which provide a seven-year academic course. Selection for the latter type takes place at age 11 and is based on tests in English and mathematics.

The tertiary sector comprises universities, including the Open University; teacher-training colleges; and colleges of higher, technical, or further education. In 1989 some 9.6 million students were in postcompulsory official tertiary (16+) institutions: 74 percent in further (nonhigher) education, and 17 percent in higher education; 9 percent were still in school. In all, 73 percent of these were part-time, and 43 percent of the total were aged 25 or over.

3.2 Preschool Education

The aim of preprimary education is to prepare the child for formal full-time schooling. Activities are centered around directed play, socialization, and physical development, although, since nothing is officially prescribed, reading and writing are not necessarily discouraged.

3.3 Special Education

Children with special needs (defined as pupils with mental, emotional, or physical handicaps) are educated in special schools, although since 1981 the aim has been to integrate them into ordinary schools so far as possible. Some 2,000 special schools exist, often all-age, including some which are privately run. Approximately 1.4 percent of an age group are enrolled in such special schools, about a quarter of which offer boarding facilities. Children who are moderately or severely educationally subnormal make up two-thirds of the total enrollment, some 10 percent suffer from emotional maladjustment, and the remainder have a variety of physical handicaps. Additionally, ordinary schools may have special classes or units to deal with those with learning difficulties arising from mental, emotional, or physical maladjustment.

3.4 Vocational, Technical, and Business Education

Secondary technical schools existed under a former tripartite system; few now remain. However, in the 1980s and early 1990s the need for a more technically and vocationally oriented bias in secondary education was felt. Technology, including craft and design, has been made a compulsory "foundation" subject (see Sect. 7 below). More practically oriented courses are developing in schools, although at present most are offered in colleges of further education after the age of 16. The nature of some of these courses can best be described under the qualifications to which they lead (see Sect. 8 below).

The Enterprise and Education Directorate of the Department of the Environment funds projects to encourage vocational education. A Technical and Vocational Education Initiative (TVEI) scheme provides courses in schools concentrating on science, technology (including information technology), and languages for the 14–18 age group. A "Compacts" project consists of local partnerships between employers and inner-city schools to raise motivation and achievement. The Youth Training Scheme (YTS) is a two-year program outside schools, designed for school leavers and comprising vocational and some general education as well as work experience. The aim is to provide training for those who are neither continuing in education nor taking up employment immediately.

3.5 Adult and Nonformal Education

Adult education takes place in adult education centers in tertiary institutions, and through the Open University which runs courses at both degree and subdegree level. University external studies departments, working with voluntary bodies such as the Workers' Education Association, also provide courses.

Nonformal education is given in colleges of further education. About half a million adults attend leisure classes, mainly evening classes, in a wide variety of subjects.

4. Administrative and Supervisory Structure and Operation

The Department for Education (DFE) has overall responsibility for education in England. It is also responsible for all universities in the United Kingdom. Its minister, the Secretary of State for Education and Science, is assisted by ministers of state (also political appointments) and a staff of some 2,500 civil servants. Direct contact with schools is through an inspectorate drawn largely from professionals, but the day-to-day running of the schools and further education has generally been in the hands of the 104 Local Education Authorities (LEAs). Hence the description of the education system in the United Kingdom as being "national,

but locally administered." LEAs are responsible to local education committees, which consist of elected representatives of local councils and co-opted members.

A number of voluntary schools, usually provided by Anglican, Catholic, or Jewish denominations, exist. An aided voluntary school is one where the religious body controls the religious education program, admissions, and staff, receiving part of its maintenance costs from the LEA. A controlled voluntary school has all its costs financed by the LEA, though it still maintains a voice in the religious education program offered. Certain governors are designated as "foundation governors," whose duty is to preserve the school's religious character.

The Scottish Education Office is responsible for all education in Scotland, apart from universities, and is under the Secretary of State for Scotland, who deals with all Scottish affairs. (Similar arrangements apply for Wales.) Scotland is divided into nine regional and three island education authorities (EAs). An Act of 1980 consolidating previous arrangements for Scottish education legislated for three types of school: public (i.e., "maintained"), grant-aided, and independent. The Scottish Education Office prescribes regulations for the 12 EAs, provides for children with special educational needs, controls a Scottish Examination Board, and operates the machinery for deciding teacher's salaries.

Education in Northern Ireland is run by the Department of Education for Northern Ireland (DENI), part of the Northern Ireland Office. In 1947 a system resembling that set up in 1944 in England was established. A total of five education boards function at local level, but, unlike England, appointments to them are made by DENI. Clergymen customarily constitute one-fourth of the membership of these boards. There are four types of school: controlled, controlled-integrated, voluntary (maintained), and voluntary (nonmaintained). Controlled schools are run by the local education board through school governors and all costs are met by DENI. Controlled-integrated schools—integrated as regards religious denominations—also exist. Voluntary (maintained) schools, usually Catholic, receive 85 percent of capital expenditure from DENI, with current costs defrayed by the education board. Voluntary (nonmaintained) schools are principally grammar schools, and either Protestant or Catholic. Run by boards of governors, on which official representatives may serve, 85 percent of their capital expenditure is met by DENI, while the running costs are met partly by a central authority block grant and fees—although the latter are often paid by the education board.

In England and Wales, while greater control has passed to central government at the expense of the LEAs, there has been a move to give greater autonomy to schools. A 1977 report—*A New Partnership for Our Schools* (DES)—recommended that the management and governance of schools should be by a governing body on which parents (and where appropriate, pupils) and LEA nominees should be equally represented. The governing body would enjoy maximum autonomy from the LEA and in turn would delegate this to the headteacher. Governors would determine the school's aims and receive training. These recommendations, incorporated into earlier legislation, were considerably expanded in the 1988 Education Reform Act (see Sect. 10 below).

The headteacher is "responsible for the internal organization, management and control of the school." Every school must publish a "prospectus," available to present and potential parents of pupils, giving full details of the institution, including examination results. Accountability depends upon the kind of school. Thus, official ("maintained") schools generally are responsible to the LEA. (New "grant-maintained" schools established under the 1988 Act, however, are responsible directly to the DFE—see Sect. 10 below). Voluntary schools are accountable to the LEA and to the religious body which established the school. Certain aspects of independent schools are supervised by the DFE.

5. Educational Finance

Expenditure on education and science as a percentage of total government expenditure was estimated at 14.1 percent in 1990, exactly the same as a decade earlier. Expenditure on education was estimated at 4.5 percent of Gross Domestic Product (GDP). Although central government provides the bulk of resources, these resources are mainly spent by LEAs. The estimated total current expenditure by LEAs for 1990–91 in England stood at £17,272 million as compared with the central authority's spending of £3,647 million— 83 percent as against 17 percent.

The principal expense for schools is teachers' salaries, which account for some 70 percent of total expenditure. The central government funds all higher education. Former polytechnics (now universities) and colleges of higher education receive their money through the Polytechnics and Colleges Funding Council (PCFC). Funds for universities and research councils are channelled through the Universities Funding Council (UFC).

Grant-related inservice training (GRIST) for teachers is funded through an LEA training grants scheme, spent in accordance with what the DFE specifies as "national priority areas [of concern]" or what local authorities designate as "local priority areas." Special funds are available for providing extra training for teaching immigrants.

Total DFE and LEA expenditure on education is divided as follows: schools—61 percent; higher and further education—29 percent; research councils—4 percent; and administration—5.7 percent (based on 1989 figures). Spending per pupil in England and Wales is £1,200 per head, as compared with Scotland's £1,900 per head.

In 1991 a proposal was made to give all schools charitable status, already enjoyed by the new city technology colleges and the independent schools. This would enable them to acquire and enjoy assets free of tax. The Revenue Support Grant (RSG) is a general fund from central government to cover all services for which a local authority is responsible. The local authority also receives other grants from central government and a national nondomestic rate (a local tax). The total of these three elements, known as the Aggregate External Finance, is determined centrally for each individual authority. LEAs also derive income from various charges, such as fees for leisure classes. About half the total sum available to local authorities from all sources is spent by them on education, although the proportion is declining.

6. Supplying Personnel for the Education System

The Inspectorate (Her Majesty's Inspectors or "HMIs") is attached to the DFE and numbers about 500. Inspectors are largely recruited from serving teachers. They work mainly at local level, looking after a group of schools and colleges. Each is attached to a divisional inspector. Staff inspectors based at the DFE are responsible for particular facets of education, for instance, foreign-language teaching or special education. The senior chief inspector is in charge of seven chief inspectors, who coordinate the work of divisional inspectors. Scotland, Wales, and Northern Ireland have their own inspectorates.

This system is to undergo fundamental change in the 1990s. One proposal is to reduce the number of HMIs drastically and to set up teams of inspectors drawn not only from the profession, but also from laypeople. Under the supervision of an HMI, these teams would contract with LEAs to carry out school inspections. Each LEA has a chief education officer (usually an ex-teacher) responsible for the functioning of the local education system. He or she is assisted by professionals such as other ex-teachers, psychologists, careers officers, youth and community workers, and so on.

Schools have a headteacher, assisted by a deputy and class teachers, and ancillary staff. Pilot courses have been introduced for the training of headteachers, who are chosen from the ranks of their peers. Initial teacher training takes place in colleges of education (many of which are amalgamated with colleges of higher education), in polytechnics, and in university departments of education. Emphasis has been laid on "better" teacher training, interpreted as more practice and less theory (see Sect. 10 below). Thus, in the early 1980s, the DFE required teacher-training institutions to put more stress on subject teaching and classroom work. Colleges and university training departments responded to this by producing more school-oriented courses.

Since 1984 new teachers must possess a degree in a relevant school subject. The DFE has also introduced a system of "licensed" teachers. These must possess a relevant degree and have had work experience. Inservice training is generally not compulsory, although local circumstances may differ, and considerable pressure may be put on teachers to attend courses. They need not undergo a training course, but learn on the job. After two years they are recognized as qualified teachers. The hope is that this expedient will eventually alleviate present teacher shortages in such subjects as science; craft, design, and technology; and modern languages. In 1990 there were 44,771 students enrolled in education courses in higher education.

7. Curriculum Development

In 1988, for the first time, central government imposed a compulsory curriculum for all schools in England and Wales. The range and content of subjects to be studied are prescribed. This was a major departure from the 1944 Education Act which laid responsibility for the curriculum upon local education authorities (LEAs) and the schools themselves.

The national curriculum consists of "foundation" subjects, of which three—English, mathematics, and science—are "core" subjects. The other subjects are: foreign languages; history and geography; technology; art, music, drama, and design; and physical education. In primary schools the stress is on the core subjects, and no foreign language is studied (in Wales, however, Welsh may be a foundation subject and the curriculum studied through the medium of Welsh). In secondary schools, 30 to 40 percent of the time must be devoted to the core subjects, and 45 percent to the other foundation subjects. The rest of the time may be given over to nonfoundation subjects, at the school's choice. Secondary schools are required to emphasize science.

A new School Curriculum and Assessment authority, working through groups of teachers and academics, was at the time of writing this article revising the curriculum so that the concentration is on "core" subjects. Content of the curriculum is to be scaled down by September 1995. The new program will be less prescriptive. In addition, employment-related courses based on a General National Vocational Qualification are to be elaborated.

Curriculum standardization was generally welcomed by teachers and parents. It also provided central government with the raw data, through testing, for comparing nationally the performance of LEAs, schools, teachers, and pupils. The impact of introducing a national curriculum pattern has been both limited and radical. A 1987 survey showed that in the last two years of secondary schooling pupils were already spending, on average, 42 percent of their time on core subjects. In practice, external examination requirements determined the curriculum for these years and this is still the case.

The new prescribed curriculum had the effect of eliminating "hybrid" subjects, whose content was often devised by teachers locally, and which were interdisciplinary. It has also put pressure on "minority subjects" such as "rare" foreign languages—Russian or Latin, for example. A further consequence of prescribing compulsory subjects may be to check the marked tendency for boys to concentrate on the sciences and girls on the humanities. In primary schools it has meant a return to "basics" and an overhaul of teaching methods. The main effect, however, of the central authority stipulating the curriculum has been to curtail the power of the LEAs, which could control the curriculum directly, or obliquely by imposing staffing and resource requirements on schools.

In England a National Curriculum Council (in Wales, a Curriculum Council) was set up to supervise the new curriculum. In Scotland no national curriculum exists as such, although the Scottish Education Department commended proposals for one laid down in the Munn Report (Scottish Education Department 1977). In Northern Ireland, the curriculum pattern is broadly that followed in England and Wales. However, since the province has kept a selective secondary system, an attainment test based on the prescribed curriculum at age 11 will be of special importance.

8. The System of Examinations, Promotions, and Certifications

A series of national attainment tests are being introduced for all children aged 7, 11, 14, and 16. As a result of the trialing of tests for 7-year olds it was decided that only pencil-and-paper tests should be used. In 1992 the first national tests, lasting six hours, for 14-year old secondary pupils were taken in mathematics and science. There are four degrees of difficulty available and teachers can choose the appropriate level for their class. They mark their own pupils' work, and also give their own estimate of a pupil's level of ability, but external moderators monitor standards. From 1993, tests in English and technology were added to the tests in mathematics and science, and in 1994, tests in history and geography. Some idea of the scope of the operation can be gleaned from the fact that, for example, some half a million 14-year olds are due to be tested each year. Teachers' objections to testing, on educational grounds and because of workload, have meant tests have been scaled down, but as of 1994 the issue has not been totally resolved.

The final assessment of a pupil is given by tests taken at 16, at present after a two-year program ending in the examination for the General Certificate of Secondary Education (GCSE). This examination was first taken in 1988, and is used in England, Wales, and Northern Ireland. Intended for candidates of 16 or over, grading is on a seven-point scale. There is a formal examination, but marks are also awarded for coursework. The intention, however, is to reduce the percentage of marks awarded for the latter.

Two years after the GCSE pupils may sit for the General Certificate of Education Advanced Level (GCE A-level). This is an academic examination in two to four subjects (usually three) that can also be taken by students in further education colleges. Despite arguments going back more than a generation that the scope is too narrow, the pattern of this examination remains basically the same as when it was first introduced in 1951.

For prevocational and vocational education a wide variety—some 6,000—of qualifications are awarded by no less than 600 different bodies. The present policy is to rationalize this array of options. Many now come under a National Council for Vocational Qualifications (NCVQ). The City and Guilds of London Institute (CGLI) operates courses in some 200 "craft" subjects at three levels; the Royal Society of Arts (RSA) awards qualifications in commerce and languages; and the Business and Technical Educational Council (BTEC) offers three levels of training for technical and business qualifications. All three institutions encourage their prevocational and general qualifications to be taken in schools, but they are more usually taken in colleges of further education. In 1986 a Joint Board for Prevocational Education instituted a Certificate of Prevocational Education (CPVE) taken after the age of 16 in schools or colleges of further education. This consists mainly of basic subjects and vocational options, and can be taken after one year's study. The aim is to give a general preparation for working life. It may well supplant other qualifications.

In Scotland there have been since 1986 SCE Standard grade courses, with three levels of examination—Foundation, General, and Credit. After four years of secondary education pupils are given a profile of their abilities. To this extent the Scottish examination procedures differ from the GCSE. A further year of study leads on to the SCE Higher Grade examination, taken in four to five subjects. A year later still, at about the age of 18, pupils may sit for the Certificate of Sixth Year Studies (CSYS). The Scottish Vocational Education Council (SCOTVEC) awards a modular certificate, with courses to cover all forms of technical, vocational, and business education.

9. Education Assessment, Evaluation, and Research

The national tests mentioned above are supervised by a body controlled by the DFE entitled the School Examinations and Assessment Authority. Arrangements are also in hand for the systematic assessment of teacher performance as an adjunct to accountability. Provided such assessment is carried out by their peers, teachers' unions have generally welcomed this.

Economic conditions have affected resources available for educational research, which in any case never found much favor with the central authorities. Possibly less than 0.1 percent of the educational budget is spent directly on school research. Private funds from charitable foundations have also almost dried up. However, the National Foundation for Educational Research (NFER), partly funded by the LEAs, continues to carry out research and development studies. Instead of research-backed studies, the DFE would appear to rely on ad hoc committees, which survey a particular topic and then report back without carrying out detailed investigations.

10. Major Reforms in the 1980s and 1990s

Some major reforms of the 1980s and 1990s have already been referred to in previous sections. In fact, the 1980s saw the incipient implementation of more far-reaching reforms than in any decade since the 1950s. A number of bodies, under the direct authority of the Minister for Education have been established to deal with school programs, assessment, and standards. This has meant central government has much tighter control than hitherto.

Under legislation of 1986 and 1988, the DFE gave school governors responsibility for the local management of schools (LMS), thus effectively reducing the power of LEAs. Since 1986 the conduct of the individual school is the responsibility of a governing body composed of a minority of representatives appointed by the LEA, and a majority of parents (after an election among pupils' parents), teachers (elected by other teachers in the school), and a number of co-opted governors (including persons from the local business community). If there are sufficient pupils over 18, a student may also serve as a governor. Governors have responsibility for certain aspects of school finance as well as staffing. They are also responsible for seeing that the national curriculum is taught, overseeing arrangements for pupils with special educational needs, ensuring that sex education is given, guarding against political indoctrination of pupils, and reporting annually to parents. They may delegate some powers to the headteacher.

A similar law (1988) applying to Scotland stipulates that EAs must appoint school boards to promote involvement of parents and local communities. Thus parents, staff, and co-opted members constitute the school board, whose size depends upon pupil numbers. School boards are delegated some functions from the EA, but cannot deal with staffing, the curriculum, or admissions. They do, however, control the school capitation allowance (expenditure on books, etc.) The Department for Education for Northern Ireland has signified its intention of introducing similar provision.

Power has thus shifted toward the center and also to the school level, at the expense of LEAs, whose role has diminished. Schools of over 200 pupils, under local management schemes, may now apply to the DFE to "opt-out" completely of all LEA control. This arrangement effectively divides schools into two types: those that are local-authority controlled, and those that have opted-out and have become "grant-maintained" (i.e., receiving their finance direct from the DFE). Parents decide by ballot whether they wish to remove a school from local control. By early 1992, 285 schools had voted to opt-out.

If an application is approved, the governors of a school assume all powers previously assigned to the LEA, apart from a few residual powers that revert to the DFE. The most significant function assumed by the schools is overall responsibility, within strict limits, for their budgets. Thus "opted-out" schools deal with salaries and day-to-day running costs. Capital expenditure, on the other hand, is not the concern of the school.

Education, in the United Kingdom as elsewhere, has been seen as an integrating force in society. The problems posed by the influx of immigrants and the education of their children, particularly those of Afro-Caribbean origin and those from the Indian subcontinent (Pakistan and Bangladesh), have exercised successive governments. In the early 1980s there was much debate as to the policy to be followed regarding the education of children of immigrant origin. Policies such as "multiculturalism" and "assimilation" were postulated.

Two reports highlighted the underachievement of children of West Indian origin (Rampton 1981, Committee of Enquiry into the Education of Children from Ethnic Minority Groups 1985). One cause identified was racialism, often unintended but relating to "stereotyping" of pupils. Other causes were lack of preschool education, a mismatch between the curriculum and teaching methods and the needs of West Indian children, bias against the dialect of English used, and various socioeconomic factors. The remedy indicated was greater acceptance by the wider community of ethnic minorities and special training for teachers. Moreover, all children should be educated for life in a multicultural society. Expedients such as segregated schools and bilingual teaching for minority groups were rejected. However, the aim is not for total assimilation but for integration of minorities into the mainstream of society.

11. Major Problems for the Year 2000

Stricter immigration control and the fact that most children of immigrants are now British-born mean that educational problems that arose in the past will lessen. There is, however, a demand from some Islamic leaders for separate schools for Muslim children, particularly for the education of girls. Up to now this has been resisted on the grounds that coeducation is the norm. The existence of schools run by other religions is, however, put forward as an argument for Muslim schools.

The most pressing need, however, is for larger financial resources. Approximately one-third of all school buildings are not satisfactorily maintained—it is estimated that to bring them up to standard would require an outlay of £4 billion (1992 prices). Their renewal is therefore a high priority. At the same time it is argued that teachers' salaries must be improved in order to attract better recruits.

Associated with higher standards in teaching are problems relating to the standards of attainment and early leaving. Low achievement in the present mass education system, both at primary and secondary level, is a cause for concern. The majority of pupils leave full-time education for good at age 16—a phenomenon not found elsewhere in Western Europe. The general view is that this must be partially remedied by devising more relevant courses for the 16–19 age group. The perceived need is for relevant vocational courses devised in cooperation with industry, which may entail improved and enlarged apprenticeship schemes. Academic courses may be overhauled. Specialization may be replaced by more broadly based courses, with the emphasis not only on entrance to higher education but on future employment. Better curriculum development and a more rationalized and efficient examination system are prerequisites for accomplishing these desiderata.

Access to higher education, for which great expansion is planned, may be simplified. Since polytechnics acquired university status in 1993, the dual system in higher education has disappeared. It may well be that some universities will be designated as mainly research, and others as mainly teaching institutions. At the opposite end of the age range a first priority will be to ensure greater participation in preschool education, in which the United Kingdom lags behind most European Community countries.

A major task will be a review of teaching training, already under way. The concept of school-oriented training is being replaced by the more radical one of school-based training. One proposal is for graduates, who at present follow a one-year 36-week course, to undergo 80 percent of their training in the classroom. Similar arrangements may be made for teachers not educated in universities: the four-year (BEd) degree in education is to be cut to three, at least one year of which will be spent in classroom practice. The concept of designated "teaching schools," analogous to a system already used in the legal and medical professions, has been revived. How this may work in practice has not yet been elaborated. Certain schools will be designated as "internship schools," and trainees will be assigned to work under outstanding teachers.

Whereas the tendency in Europe is for teacher training to be integrated into universities, the moves in the United Kingdom represent a step away from this direction. While generally endorsing the concept of longer practice teaching, the University Council for the Education of Teachers (UCET), a quasi-governmental advisory body, has drawn attention to this anomaly, pointing out that the priority for school staff must be to teach pupils and not to train future teachers.

The governance of schools remains contentious, although it is likely that power will continue to shift from local to central government, which, while retaining control, will delegate authority to the school itself so far as it thinks fit.

Many of the above tasks seem to have gained a fragile political consensus, although views differ as to how to perform them. Progress depends upon the economic situation, but in any case a drive for cost-effectiveness will continue.

References

Committee of Enquiry into the Education of Children from Ethnic Minority Groups 1985 *Education for All* (The Swann Report). HMSO, London

Department of Education and Science 1967 *Children and Their Primary Schools* (The Plowden Report). HMSO, London

Department of Education and Science 1977 *A New Partnership for Our Schools*. HMSO, London

Rampton A 1981 *West Indian Children in Our Schools*. HMSO, London

Scottish Education Department Consultative Committee on the Curriculum 1977 *The Structure of the Curriculum in the Third and Fourth Years of Scottish Secondary School* (The Munn Report). HMSO, Edinburgh

Further Reading

Bowles G, Fidler B (eds.) 1989 *Effective Local Management of Schools: A Strategic Approach*. Longman, London

Brett M (ed.) 1988 *Education Yearbook, 1988*. Longman, Harlow

Department of Education and Science 1987 *Statistical Bulletin 10/87: The 1984 Secondary School Staffing Survey—Data on the Curriculum in Maintained Secondary Schools in England*. HMSO, London

Department of Education and Science 1991 *Statistical Bulletin 9/13: Education Statistics for the United Kingdom*, 1990 edn. HMSO, London

Husén T, Halls W D, Tuijnman A (eds.) 1992 *Schooling in Modern European Society*. Pergamon Press, Oxford

Statham J, Cathcart H, Mackinnon D 1989 *The Education Fact File. A Handbook of Education Information in the UK*. Hodder and Stoughton, London

Tomlinson J 1989 The Education Reform Bill—44 years of progress? *J. Educ. Policy* 4(3):275–79

The Treasury 1991 *The Government's Expenditure Plans, 1991–1992 to 1993–1994*. HMSO, London

United States

G. A. Valverde

1. General Background

The United States of America has an area of 9,847,305 square kilometers. Most of this area is located on the American continent between the international boundaries of Canada on the north and Mexico on the south. The Atlantic and Pacific Oceans are on the east and west respectively.

The country is divided into 50 states and several territories that include possessions in Polynesia and Micronesia (the islands of Guam and American Samoa, and the islands and atolls forming the Trust Territory of the Pacific Islands), as well as in the Caribbean (the island of Puerto Rico and the United States Virgin Islands).

In 1990, the population of the United States was 249,975,000 inhabitants. The population growth rate declined from 16.1 percent in 1960 to 10.1 percent in 1989. A large portion of population growth in the 1980s and 1990s was due to immigrants and refugees, the majority of whom arrived from Asia and Latin America. In 1989, 1,091,000 immigrants and 84,288

refugees arrived in the United States from all over the world.

Since the early 1960s the United States has become increasingly urbanized; 77.5 percent of the population lived in metropolitan areas in 1990. In that same year there were 23 cities with populations of over 500,000.

The United States is also extremely diverse in the racial and ethnic backgrounds of its citizens. In 1989 Whites made up 77.6 percent of the population, Blacks 11.4 percent, Native Americans and Alaskan Natives 0.7 percent, Asians and Pacific Islanders 2.7 percent, and Hispanics 7.6 percent.

The educational attainment of the different ethnic and racial groups in the United States varies substantially. For example, in 1989 78.8 percent of the White population aged 25 years and older had completed four or more years of high school (approximately 12 years of schooling overall). Only 67 percent of the Black population in this age group had completed the same amount of schooling.

In 1989 the incidence of poverty (defined as an average annual income of US$7,372 or less for a householder of 65 or younger) was about 12.8 percent. However, ethnic and racial minorities were by far the poorest citizens of the United States. Approximately 30.7 percent of all Blacks and 26.7 percent of all Hispanics were living below the poverty line in 1990, whereas only 10 percent of the White population was living in that condition. The incidence of poverty among children of 18 or younger is dissimilar for the different racial and ethnic groups in the United States. In 1989, it was 19 percent for the total population, but for Whites it was 14.1 percent, in contrast with 43.2 percent for Blacks and 35.5 percent for Hispanics.

In 1989 the mean number of years of schooling of the labor force was 12.8, with insignificant gender differences. Unemployment rates were highest for those with less education: 11.8 percent of the workers with one to three years of secondary school were unemployed, whereas the figure was only 2.2 percent for holders of college degrees.

The necessity to educate such a vast and diverse population in a climate of competing demands on limited public resources presents the United States with serious challenges. Thus, the subject of education has become a prominent theme on the national agenda.

2. Politics and the Goals of the Education System

A salient characteristic of education in the United States is that it is an extremely decentralized system. Federal, state, and local governments share varying degrees of responsibility for its administration and regulation.

The federal government of the United States has no general mandate for the control or provision of public education. This is because the issue of education was not addressed by the authors of the Constitution. (The authors of the Constitution stated that all powers not expressly given to the federal government belong to each state government.)

There are a variety of federal regulations concerning issues of access to education for racial minorities and the handicapped. The federal government also supports educational research. However, the United States has no centrally governed system of public education.

It is not the case, however, that the federal government exerts no influence in educational matters. In fact, all three branches (executive, legislative, and judicial) of the federal government have been extremely active, especially after the Second World War, in educational policy-making. The federal government has participated in efforts to racially desegregate schools, equalize school financial allocations, provide access to education for poor and handicapped children, and to satisfy new public pressures for increased quality and accountability in schools. This participation does not indicate the existence of a federal system.

It reveals, however, varying ways in which federal actions can influence educational policy.

Each of the 50 states in the Union is responsible for its own system of public instruction. State governments vary in the degree of centralized control that they attempt to exercise. The majority of them confer a large amount of control to local governing bodies known as "local school boards." These local school boards are the organizations that exercise direct jurisdiction over local school districts (geographical areas with one or more interrelated schools), either by directly operating public schools or, in rare cases, contracting for public school services. In 1990–91 there were 15,358 local school districts, each with its own board. Some states have a great many local school districts, such as California which has 1,076. At the other extreme, the state of Hawaii has only one regular school district.

Local school districts are in some ways so different that it might be said that the United States possesses 15,358 distinct school systems. The members of the school boards are usually elected democratically, but in some cases they are appointed. Some school boards are entrusted with the operation of a single school, others with the supervision of immense metropolitan school districts.

In addition to these local school boards that are in charge of public education, there are also many private schools in the United States. In 1987 there were 26,807 private schools, of which 17,807 were elementary schools, 2,423 were secondary schools, and 7,296 were combined primary–secondary schools.

3. The Formal System of Education

All states provide free and compulsory education. Most states provide education from the age of 6 or 7 to 16. There is some variation in the ages for compulsory school attendance among the different states. For example, in the state of Arizona the ages of compulsory attendance are from 8 to 16. In Wisconsin, compulsory attendance begins at age 6 and concludes at age 18. There is even some variation within states. The state of New York has established compulsory attendance between ages 6 and 16, but New York City and Buffalo have extended compulsory attendance to age 17.

The average length of the school year in the United States is 178 days. The average duration of the school day is 5.4 hours.

3.1 Primary, Secondary, and Tertiary Education

Figure 1 presents the structure of education in the United States.

Typically, primary schooling begins at the age of 6 and concludes at the age of 11. Important exceptions

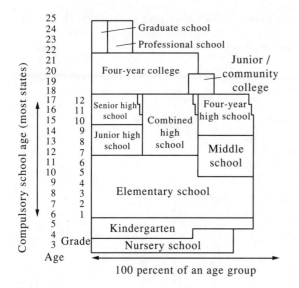

Figure 1

United States of America: Structure of the formal education system

structure as the other secondary schools in the same district. All of these types of secondary school typically award students a diploma after the completion of the twelfth grade.

High school graduation rates have increased steadily over the history of public instruction in the United States. In 1870, only 2 percent of the population of 17-year olds had graduated from high school. By 1950, 59 percent of this population had graduated from high school. The percentage of high school graduates in the 17-year old population peaked at 76.9 percent in 1970, declining to 71.4 percent in 1980. In 1989, 74.1 percent of the 17-year old population had graduated from regular day high school programs.

Early school leaving is now regarded as a measure of school failure. About 6 percent of 16- to 17-year olds drop out of high school every year. There are noteworthy ethnic and gender differences in this dropout rate, as depicted in Table 1. It will be noticed that 94 percent of an age group are enrolled in Grade 12, but only 74.1 percent of an age group graduates. The other 20 percent leave high school without graduating.

Total public elementary and secondary school enrollment declined during the 1970s and 1980s. This circumstance reflected a decrease in the number of 5- to 13-year olds in the general population from 33,516,000 in 1976 to 31,793,000 in 1989. A similar decline was experienced in 14- to 17-year olds from 17,119,000 in 1976 to 13,476,000 in 1989. These declines in the school-age population followed periods of high enrollment during the 1950s and 1960s. High enrollments during those two decades were associated with a period of very high birthrates in the United States following the Second World War. Enrollment figures for the 1990–91 school year are presented in Table 2.

Increased enrollments are expected in primary schools until the mid-1990s. The population of 5- to 13-year olds is expected to peak at approximately 33,854,000 in 1995, declining slightly toward the end of the century.

Enrollments in secondary schools are expected to rise steadily into the twenty-first century. This is due to the anticipated growth of the 14- to 17-year old population to 15,382,000 in the year 2001 (see Table 3).

The tertiary level of the formal educational system is composed of three types of institutions of higher education: junior or community colleges, vocational/technical institutions, and colleges and universities. Junior colleges, as well as vocational/technical institutions, usually offer two- to three-year programs that grant an associate degree or certificate, whereas four-year colleges and universities offer the four-year bachelor's degree. There is some movement of students transferring from two- to four-year institutions, but the precise numbers are uncertain. There are some states—such as Florida, New York, and California—

to this rule are those school districts that possess a middle school system. In such systems, students attend middle schools from about age 10 to 13. By age 6, 99.78 percent of all children in the United States have begun their formal schooling.

Some school districts divide secondary schooling into lower- and upper-secondary schools called "junior" and "senior" high schools respectively. Other systems have a single unified high school that covers all of the secondary grades. Still other systems have middle schools that lead to three- or four-year high schools. Vocational high schools (devoted to the teaching of trades) usually have the same grade

Table 1

Percentage of high school dropouts among persons 16- to 17-years old, by race, ethnicity, and gender, October 1989

All Races	6.0
Males	5.9
Females	5.8
White	6.1
Males	6.4
Females	5.7
Black	5.6
Males	4.1
Females	7.1
Hispanic	12.5
Males	9.6
Females	15.7

Source: National Center for Education Statistics 1990 Digest of Education Statistics. US Government Printing Office, Washington, DC

Table 2
United States: Age/grade enrollment table—number of students (in thousands) by age enrolled in Grades 1–12, 1990–91 school year

Age	1	2	3	4	5	Grades 6	7	8	9	10	11	12	Total	Population
5	159	10	0	0	0	0	0	0	0	0	0	0	169	3,792
6	2,886	164	11	0	0	0	0	0	0	0	0	0	3,061	3,679
7	855	2,604	218	18	11	0	0	0	0	0	0	0	3,706	3,744
8	47	834	2,491	191	11	9	0	0	0	0	0	0	3,583	3,592
9	3	80	886	2,462	208	17	1	0	0	0	0	0	3,660	3,676
10	6	10	112	843	2,416	205	12	6	0	0	0	0	3,610	3,627
11	2	2	18	114	940	2,278	217	14	12	0	0	0	3,597	3,611
12	4	3	5	16	112	822	2,158	212	8	5	0	0	3,345	3,354
13	3	1	2	6	17	156	933	2,157	197	9	1	0	3,482	3,499
14	2	1	0	1	3	26	187	844	2,028	183	6	4	3,285	3,299
15	0	0	0	0	0	0	35	154	842	2,008	210	15	3,264	3,321
16	0	0	0	0	0	0	8	4	216	765	1,968	178	3,139	3,294
17	0	0	0	0	0	0	0	0	48	171	741	1,827	2,788	3,297
18	0	0	0	0	0	0	0	0	18	38	148	603	807	3,419
19	0	0	0	0	0	0	0	0	6	7	38	166	217	3,645
20	0	0	0	0	0	0	0	0	4	2	1	39	46	3,649
Total	3,967	3,709	3,746	3,651	3,718	3,513	3,551	3,391	3,379	3,188	3,114	2,832	41,795	63,913

that possess highly integrated systems of two- and four-year institutions. In such states, movement of students from one type of institution to the other is much more frequent.

Higher education in the United States has undergone expansion since the Second World War. This trend began in 1944 with the enactment of the Servicemen's Readjustment Act (also known as the "GI Bill"). This law provided federal funds to subsidize the expenses of veterans who wished to attend college. As a result of this legislation, more than 2.2 million veterans attended colleges between 1944 and 1951. This enormous influx of students into the nation's colleges and universities began a trend of expansion in enrollments that has not yet ended.

College enrollment in the United States reached 13.8 million students in 1989, the highest level in national history. An important aspect of the expansion of this sector is the increased participation of older students. Enrollment among students of 24 or younger increased 24 percent between 1970 and 1989. However, the enrollment of students older than 24 increased 141 percent in the same period. Currently, enrollments of students of 24 and younger are projected to decline by approximately 2 percent by 1996. Yet, students older than 24 are projected to increase their participation in higher education programs by 8 percent.

3.2 Preschool Education

Preschool education—that is, education in the years preceding the age of compulsory school attendance—expanded between 1965 and 1989. Enrollment in preprimary programs before kindergarten increased from 27.1 percent of 3- to 5-year olds in 1965, to 54.6 percent in 1989. In 1990, approximately 37 percent of all children enrolled in preprimary programs attended school for a full day.

The 1991 National Household Education Survey (NHES) found that most school children in the United States attend kindergarten. Among children in the first and second grade only 2 percent had not attended kindergarten. Of those that attended kindergarten, 33 percent attended full-time public institutions.

Table 3
Enrollment and projected enrollments in United States elementary and secondary schools in selected years (in thousands)

	1976	1980	1985	1990	2000	2001
Total						
elementary	29,255	28,212	28,424	29,522	30,267	29,995
secondary	20,229	18,037	16,555	16,670	19,708	19,791
Public						
elementary	25,430	24,220	24,229	25,303	25,876	25,636
secondary	18,887	16,698	15,193	15,498	18,310	18,386
Private						
elementary	3,825	3,992	4,195	4,219	4,391	4,359
secondary	1,342	1,339	1,362	1,172	1,398	1,405

Source: National Center for Education Statistics 1990

3.3 Special Education

Special education became an issue of national political concern in the 1970s. In 1971, the District Court ordered schools in the state of Pennsylvania to provide education to mentally handicapped students between the ages of 4 and 21. Other judicial orders similar to this one followed in other states.

The Education for All Handicapped Children Act of 1975 marked the entry of the federal executive branch into the area of special education. This Law requires all states to identify children with one of seven conditions (speech impairment, learning disability, emotional disturbance, mental retardation, hearing impairment, vision impairment, and orthopedic/medical impairment) and provide them with special education services. Children with disabilities are to be educated, whenever possible, in regular classrooms without separation from their nonhandicapped peers. When disabled children cannot be educated with other children, they are to receive instruction in hospitals, their homes, or in other public or private institutions at no cost to their parents. This law also provides for medical and transportation support services for special education programs.

This legislation, by mandating that handicapped children be educated in the least restrictive environment possible, led to the practice of "mainstreaming." Mainstreaming refers to serving handicapped children within the regular school program, rather than placing them in special classes in isolation from their nonhandicapped peers.

There was a large increase in the number of special education students between 1978 and 1987 from 3.9 to 4.4 million. This rise is attributable to an increase in the number of students classified as "learning disabled." Children are diagnosed as learning disabled if they present disorders in language development and communication skills that are not related to impairments of vision, hearing, or motor functions; or to emotional disturbances or mental retardation. Thus, a learning disability includes such conditions as minimal brain damage, dyslexia, and perceptual disorders.

In 1990, about 11 percent of all public school students were enrolled in special education programs.

3.4 Vocational, Technical, and Business Education

The influence of the federal government on vocational education became significant with the passing of the Vocational Education Act (1963). This law requires every state to form a Board of Vocational Education to monitor and formulate state policy in this area. States receive federal money for these programs. Substantial quantities of funding were available in the 1960s and 1970s. However, since the Job Training Partnership Act (1983), the federal government has diminished assistance to vocational education. The federal government now requires all such programs to demonstrate their effectiveness in order to receive what funds are available.

Public high schools are the primary providers of secondary vocational programs in the United States. Both general vocational and occupational-specific programs are common.

In 1984, 56.9 percent of all high school students 16-years old or over had completed two years or more of industrial arts, shop, or home economics courses. An additional 41.8 percent of these students had received at least two years of business courses. This occurred even though there were only 225 high schools in the United States that were officially designated as "vocational" in 1984.

Relations between industry, business, and vocational education programs were addressed in the Carl D Perkins Vocational Education Act (1984), which provides financial incentives for states to include private sector members on their state councils for vocational education. This act also promotes cooperation between industry and schools in the development of curricula and degree programs.

Parallel to traditional educational institutions, a large proportion of vocational training programs are provided by private industry. In 1986, it was estimated that US$30 billion was spent on these programs, in which almost 37 million members of the workforce participated.

There is also a large quantity of proprietary institutions offering vocational, technical, and business education. In 1987, there were 8,956 noncollegiate institutions offering postsecondary vocational education, of which only 830 were public.

Business education is offered principally in universities and colleges. In 1987–88 a total of 1,312 institutions of higher education offered bachelor's degrees in Business and Management, 648 institutions offered master's degrees, and 101 offered doctorates. In that same year, 23.3 percent of all master's degrees awarded in the United States were awarded in the field of business. Only in education was a higher percentage of master's degrees awarded (26%).

3.5 Adult and Nonformal Education

The federal government was not an important actor in the area of adult education until the passage of Title III of the 1965 Elementary and Secondary School Act (ESEA). This title, called the "Adult Education Act," created a partnership between each state and the federal government. The purpose of this partnership is to originate adult education programs to help adult learners overcome English-language proficiency limitations and improve basic educational skills in preparation for occupational training, further education, or responsible citizenship.

Adult and nonformal educational initiatives are also coordinated through the 1991 National Literacy Act, which is also notable for its provision of a United

States national definition of "literacy" as the ability to read, write, and speak in English; and to compute and solve mathematical problems at levels of proficiency necessary to function on the job and in society, to achieve a person's goals, and to develop a person's knowledge and potential.

There are also a variety of public alternative schools in the United States that offer subject matter or employ pedagogical techniques that are not generally offered to students in traditional school settings. These alternative schools include "schools without walls," schools within schools, continuation schools, multicultural schools, and fundamental schools.

"Schools without walls" offer community-based programs in a variety of public and private buildings. Schools within schools are specialized programs within existing public elementary or secondary schools. Continuation schools offer programs especially designed to help public school dropouts, pregnant teenagers, teenage parents, and other high-risk students continue their educations. Multicultural schools offer programs that emphasize cultural pluralism and human relations. Fundamental schools offer conservative academic programs in contrast with the more liberal and experimental nature of most public alternative programs.

4. Administrative and Supervisory Structure and Operation

There is no dominant central educational authority. Federal, state, and local governments share responsibility in the administration and supervision of instruction.

The federal government does, nevertheless, have a department that represents it in educational policy. The Department of Education was established in 1867. It later became a small bureau within the Department of the Interior. It remained there until it was made an office of the Federal Security Agency in 1939. The Office of Education later came to form part of the Department of Health, Education, and Welfare.

In 1979, the Department of Education was reestablished and its secretary became a member of the President's Cabinet.

Other government departments also represent federal policy in education. These departments include the Department of Health and Human Services, the Department of Agriculture, the Department of Defense, the Department of Energy, the Department of Labor, and the National Science Foundation. These agencies contributed almost 50 percent of all federal funds for education in 1987.

5. Educational Finance

Traditionally, the federal government has maintained that the United States is among the countries that spend the most on students in the public education system. The figure most often cited to support this claim is the average expenditure per pupil, which has grown substantially since the 1950s, even adjusting for inflation. Expenditure per pupil tripled from 1950 to 1986. In 1988–89 prices, the average expenditure per pupil averaged US$1,504 in 1976. This sum rose to US$4,841 in 1990 and it is expected to grow to US$6,000 by the mid-1990s.

A dissenting opinion was voiced in 1990, however, by the Economic Policy Institute, which asserted that, when proper adjustments are made, United States public and private spending on the grades which comprise the period of compulsory schooling is less than all but 3 of 16 industrialized nations. When only public spending is compared to public spending in these 16 industrialized nations, the United States ranks 14th in expenditures on all levels of the educational system.

Between the 1920s and mid-1970s, most financial resources for education came from local governments. Since 1974, this level has declined to the 1990 level of 44 percent of all revenue. State governments, which contributed an average of 16.55 percent of all funds for schooling in 1974, contributed 50 percent in 1987. Federal funds, always less than 10 percent, were 6 percent in 1987.

Local school districts use local property taxes as the principal basis of revenue for schools. Such a scheme produces considerable inequities since property values are not equally distributed across the country. Hence, poor school districts are often able to levy only modest sums per pupil despite high property tax rates, whereas rich school districts are able to raise considerable sums per pupil despite low tax rates.

6. Supplying Personnel for the Education System

In 1990, there were 1,680,000 elementary school teachers and 1,072,000 secondary school teachers in the United States.

Licensing of teachers is a function of state governments. Each state has its own set of educational requirements for the awarding of teaching certificates. In addition, some states also have provisions for "emergency" or "alternate" certification schemes that permit people to practice the teaching profession without fulfilling standard certification requirements.

All states require the licensed teacher to have completed a bachelor's degree program that includes both subject-matter and pedagogical studies to obtain their initial credential. However, states vary considerably in their requirements for additional coursework. Completion of courses in special education, drug and alcohol abuse, as well as computer science, are among some additional requirements in particular states.

Many states award certification in stages. Typically, the first-stage teaching license is issued to individuals who have completed a bachelor's degree program in teaching. The second stage is often awarded after a master's degree is earned, or after a determined amount of semester hours of graduate education and years of teaching experience are completed. The third stage of certification is most often awarded upon completion of a determined amount of teaching hours after receipt of the second-stage license. Several states only require an initial teaching credential; others require a succession of nonrenewable phases of licenses. Most states also include the passage of written or performance examinations as a condition for either entering a teacher education program or for obtaining or retaining teaching certificates. Some states also have continuing education requirements.

States are also responsible for the certification of school administrative personnel such as principals and local school system superintendents. Requirements for these certificates vary widely. Some states issue a single credential for all supervisory and administrative positions, while others issue up to 12 different types of administrative licenses.

Since 1971 the pupil–teacher ratio in both public and private schools in the United States has declined (i.e., fewer pupils per teacher) by approximately 20 percent. In 1990, the pupil–teacher ratios in public elementary and secondary schools were 18.6:1 and 14.9:1 respectively. In private schools these ratios were 15.0:1 in elementary and 11.4:1 in secondary schools.

It is forecast that demand for new hiring of teachers will increase by over 35 percent by the mid-1990s. Most of this increased demand will be at the secondary school level. Complications in meeting this demand are anticipated. A survey of school principals reported severe difficulty in locating qualified teachers of physical sciences, languages, and mathematics. Rural schools have traditionally experienced the most problems in hiring and retaining qualified personnel.

Retention and recruitment of teachers has been adversely affected by the decrease in the purchasing power of teacher's salaries associated with economic inflation in the 1970s and recession in the 1980s. Recognition of this fact led to increases in teacher salaries. The 1989–90 average teacher's salary in the United States was US$31,300, representing a record high for the profession.

7. Curriculum Development and Teaching Methodology

A key feature of schooling in the United States is that students are separated into three distinct curricular tracks during their high school years. This practice, known as "streaming" or "tracking," hinges upon the preparation for college entry. One track is considered college preparatory; the second is generally more vocational in orientation. A third general track provides lower-level academic training and is being abandoned

by some school systems. Whether the practice of tracking can be considered to be voluntary, with children choosing one track over another according to their own expectations or life plans, or involuntary, with students being allocated into one track or another with little personal control over the process, is a matter of much debate in the United States. A notable feature about this phenomenon is the prevalence of this practice despite the lack of a national curriculum.

Curriculum policy is traditionally under the purview of each state and often each local school district or each individual school. Some states exercise a considerable amount of control over teaching content, whereas others permit greater freedom of decision to local communities and teachers.

In 1992, the National Council of Education Standards and Testing (a panel appointed by the Congress) called for voluntary national standards in mathematics, history, English, science, and geography. This idea has been endorsed by a variety of influential figures in educational policy including the president of the American Federation of Teachers, an important teacher's union. Notwithstanding, it is to be expected that the long tradition of state and local control in the United States will likely cause resistance to any movement that can be perceived as promoting the establishment of a national curriculum. On the other hand, growing national concern about international economic competitiveness and the quality of the labor force may provide impetus to move the educational system in that direction, at least to the point of more widespread acceptance of a set of general academic standards.

Textbooks are produced almost exclusively by commercial publishing houses, with 7 publishers controlling approximately 80 percent of the market in 1991. In that same year, 22 states had official adoption schemes in which lists of textbooks were approved for use by schools. Textbook approval boards approve lists of textbooks in cycles of approximately 5 years. The lists of approved texts are then made available to teachers in schools who select from them. In some states the textbook selection agency may operate at the state level, in others it functions at the local school district level. In still others, there exists a system of shared responsibilities between the two levels of governance. In the 28 states with no textbook adoption policies, each school, and sometimes each teacher, selects textbooks according to their own criteria.

8. The System of Examinations, Promotions, and Certifications

The United States has no official examination system to assess competency as a requirement for the high school diploma. Decisions concerning promotion of students from one grade to the next are made according to a variety of policies at the local school district level.

There are a variety of private examination companies that administer tests that aid some colleges and universities in the selection of high school graduates for admission. However, not all institutions rely on such examinations to the same degree, and some do not rely on them at all.

9. Educational Assessment, Evaluation, and Research

The federal government implemented a cross-sectional study of educational achievement, called the *National Assessment of Educational Progress* (NAEP) in 1969. That year, the NAEP assessed 9-, 13- and 17-year olds in the subjects of science, writing, and citizenship. Since that time, the NAEP has collected data biennially on selected levels of educational achievement in different subject areas across the country.

The purpose of NAEP is to study the knowledge, skills, and performance of schoolchildren in the United States. It is a cross-sectional study of samples of students in which scores for individual students do not exist. The data are intended to provide information on the system of education, not on individual students.

The subject matter that the NAEP studies varies from year to year according to changing policy priorities. Some of the subject areas receiving attention include reading, mathematics, science, computer competence, literature, career and occupational development, art, music, literature, and United States history.

In the early 1990s, the federal government increased the amount of money allocated to NAEP by 55 percent. This increased funding reflected the administration's interest in the extensive use of examinations as a means of improving instruction. In fact, it is thought by some that the NAEP may serve as the foundation of an eventual national examination system. It remains to be seen, however, whether this is possible given the long tradition of absence of centralized control over the curriculum in the United States.

The Office of Educational Research and Improvement (OERI) is in charge of the administration of federal educational research programs. Some of the agencies within OERI include the National Center for Education Statistics, Office of Research, Office for Programs for the Improvement of Practice, and the Office of Library Programs.

The National Center for Educational Statistics (NCES) surveys and compiles statistics on all levels of education throughout the United States. It collects data on enrollment, revenues, expenditures, quantity of schools, number of teachers and staff, graduation rates, and so forth. Each state education agency also reports to the NCES data on the educational systems that they are mandated to compile. Since each state varies in the type of data it requires its education agency to collect, the NCES must expend considerable effort in assuring comparability of statistics.

The Office of Research (OR) funds and coordinates educational research projects, as well as performing policy-oriented research with its own staff. Research topics of especial interest to OR include: teacher education, instructional leadership, postsecondary teaching, educational technology, student testing, and many others.

The Office for Programs for the Improvement of Practice (OPIP) is in charge of transmitting the results of research to teachers, school administrators, and other individuals and organizations involved in the practice of education. Through a variety of programs, this office attempts to ensure that practitioners become aware of new and effective instructional and administrative techniques.

The Office of Library Programs (OLP) is devoted to the enhancement of libraries and library services.

10. Major Reforms in the 1980s and 1990s

The declining quality of education in the United States became an important issue in the 1980s. Most evidence points to its remaining on the national agenda in the coming decades.

Primary factors in the activity that surrounds this issue are a series of reports on education in the United States that have been issued with a great deal of publicity since the early 1980s. Perhaps the most influential of these was the 1983 report of the National Commission on Excellence in Education entitled *A Nation at Risk*. This report found education in the United States in the midst of so dire a crisis that:

> If an unfriendly foreign power had attempted to impose on America the mediocre educational performance that exists today, we might well have viewed it as an act of war. As it stands, we have allowed this to happen to ourselves.

This report is similar to most others, including those of the Twentieth Century Fund Task Force on Federal Educational Policy and the Carnegie Foundation for the Advancement of Teaching, in concluding that education in the United States requires profound improvement.

Some reports lament the poor performance of students in the United States on international comparative tests of mathematics, science, and geography. Others consider the increased incidence of violence and unacceptably high dropout rates in the nation's urban school systems. All look at a variety of measures of school effectiveness and find the United States in serious need of comprehensive educational reform.

Reform initiatives in the United States have important common features. First, they presuppose that most policy-making should be made at the state and local levels. Few, if any, additional responsibilities are proposed for the federal government. Second, they advocate that educational quality be promoted by the setting of stringent standards for educational achievement. Third, such standards are to be closely monitored through mediums such as student examinations and strict adherence to teacher certification requirements. Fourth, they propose a reorganization of the administrative and supervisory structure within schools. These four points primarily propose reform of what takes place on the school site.

The federal government's role has been to disseminate the results of such reports. It has also sought to stimulate some reform initiatives by providing federal resources and through the formulation of national goals in education.

11. Major Problems for the Year 2000

In 1990 the President and the governors of each state jointly endorsed six national goals that are intended to guide educational policy in the United States to the end of the twentieth century. The national goals are:

(a) By the year 2000, all children in the United States will start school ready to learn.

(b) By the year 2000, the high school graduation rate will increase to at least 90 percent.

(c) By the year 2000, students in the United States will leave Grades 4, 8, and 12 having demonstrated competency in challenging subject matter including English, mathematics, science, history, and geography; and every school in the United States will ensure that all students learn to use their minds well, so they may be prepared for responsible citizenship, further learning, and productive employment in a modern economy.

(d) By the year 2000, students in the United States will be the first in the world in science and mathematics achievement.

(e) By the year 2000, every adult in the United States will be literate and will possess the knowledge and skills necessary to compete in a global economy and exercise the rights and responsibilities of citizenship.

(f) By the year 2000, every school in the United States will be free of drugs and violence and will offer a disciplined environment conducive to learning.

The reports and the formulation of national goals have resulted in a number of reform efforts at the level of states and local school districts. The reform efforts include such features as increments in teacher salaries; revision of teacher certification requirements and teacher education programs; reduction of teaching loads; establishment of a core curriculum in the sciences, mathematics, and language; mandatory examinations; provision of greater choice in public education; and increased involvement of parents and teachers in local school governance.

The results of these efforts remain to be seen. There are some who claim that institutional inertia in the United States is such that reform efforts are likely to do little to change the nature of schooling. Still others assert that the mediocrity of the outcomes of schooling have little to do with what happens in schools themselves, maintaining that a host of institutions and other characteristics of society must share the blame. Consequently, they conclude that the current reform movement, having centered its initiatives exclusively on the school and classroom, has little likelihood of succeeding. Data currently show no further decline in the achievement levels of students in the United States; however, they show no substantive improvement either.

Unemployment and recession have made the issue of the economic competitiveness of the United States labor force an extremely important political topic. Since many sectors of the country now believe that school reform is essential for the revitalization of the labor force (and therefore the economy), an increasing amount of private groups, including businesses, are likely to enter the educational policy debate. For the same reason, numerous experiments in educational reform are likely to be implemented by federal, state, and local authorities throughout the 1990s.

Bibliography

Bowles S, Gintis H 1976 *Schooling in Capitalist America: Educational Reform and the Contradictions of Economic Life.* Basic Books, New York

Cremin A 1988 *American Education: The Metropolitan Experience, 1876–1980.* Harper and Row, New York

Dacdalus—Journal of the American Academy of Arts and Sciences, Vol. 110, No. 3, 1981 America's Schools: Public and Private (special issue)

Kozol J 1985 *Illiterate America.* New American Library, New York

National Academy of Education 1991 *Research and the Renewal of Education.* A Report from the National Academy of Education, Stanford, California

National Association of State Directors of Teacher Education and Certification 1991 *Manual on Certification and Preparation of Educational Personnel in the United States.* Kendall/Hunt, Dubuque, Iowa

National Center for Education Statistics 1990 *Projections of Education Statistics to 2001: An Update.* US Government Printing Office, Washington, DC

National Commission for Excellence in Education 1984 *A Nation at Risk: The Full Account.* USA Research, Cambridge, Massachusetts

National Governors' Association Center for Policy Research and Analysis 1991 *Time for Results: The Governors' 1991 Report on Education.* National Governors' Association, Washington, DC

Tyack D B 1974 *The One Best System: A History of American Urban Education.* Harvard University Press, Cambridge, Massachusetts

US Bureau of the Census 1991 *Statistical Abstract of the United States: 1991.* US Government Printing Office, Washington, DC

Uruguay

M. T. Salvo Payssé and R. E. Cruz Cárdenas

1. General Background

The Republic of Uruguay occupies an area of 176,215 square kilometers on the east coast of the South American continent. It is bordered by Brazil and Argentina, and to the east is the Atlantic Ocean. Some 87 percent of its three million inhabitants live in cities, and nearly one-half live in Montevideo, the capital. The country's small size and the fact that such a large segment lives in cities have made educational facilities readily accessible to the majority of people and thus have enabled the country to achieve the highest literacy rate (95%) in Latin America.

Ethinically, the citizens of Uruguay are of Spanish or Italian origin, with a small portion of the population of mixed (*mestizo*) European–Indian–African stock. The society and its cultural tradition, like the national language, is Spanish. The prevailing religion is Roman Catholic. The population growth rate is low, partly as a result of emigrations in the 1970s. A total of 16 percent of the population is over the age of 60 and 31 percent is below the age of 18.

Although the national literacy rate is the highest in Latin America, it is lower among isolated rural groups and some persons from low social status groups. It is generally agreed that the grade repeating rate is too high (12.9%), as is the level of dropout before the end of schooling (15%).

The labor force constituted nearly 50 percent of the population in 1990. Of the labor force in urban areas, 3.9 percent were employed in the primary sector, 28.4 in the secondary, and 65.3 in the tertiary sector. The chief industry is meat packing and processing, and meat is a major export. Hydroelectric power is also increasing in volume as an export.

Uruguay became an independent country with a democratic government in 1830. However, from 1973 to 1985, there was a military dictatorship which resulted in an extremely bad economic situation. Since 1985, there has been a democratically elected government and all efforts are being made to resuscitate the economy.

Politics and Goals of the Education System

The democratic organization of the government has placed great importance on education for the development of persons as individuals and as responsible citizens, who are sufficiently knowledgeable for life in a democratic society. In order that education should play a greater role, the government is instituting certain changes which will affect all levels of education.

The improvement of the quality and equity of the services provided is the major goal for all levels of education. The management of education will also be improved by a certain degree of decentralization of the system. A further goal is to update the curriculum in the sense of making it more relevant for the lives of Uruguayans in the 1990s. Finally, a mechanism for compensatory education will be introduced.

3. The Formal System of Education

3.1 Primary, Secondary, and Tertiary Education

Figure 1 presents the structure and enrollment pattern of the Uruguayan educational system. Public education is nonreligious and free from kindergarten to

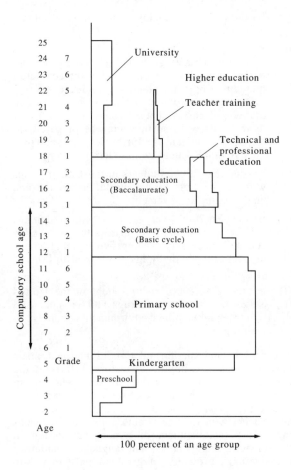

Figure 1

Uruguay: Structure of the formal education system

university. Compulsory education is from Grades 1 to 9. Children enter school when they are 6 years old. Primary school contains six grades. In urban areas, there are 4 hours of instruction per school day (i.e., 20 hours per week) and 180 school days per year. Some private schools teach more hours per day with a broader curriculum. In rural areas, children attend primary school for 25 hours per week and the teachers attempt to make the curriculum relevant to the particular rural environments in which they are teaching. Classes are coeducational and have a general classroom teacher for all subjects. In very small rural schools, there may be only one teacher for all six grades.

Some 81 percent of primary school pupils were, in 1990, in state schools and the remainder were in private schools. Of those in state schools, slightly more than 10 percent were in rural areas. There were 12,895 teachers in public primary schools and the pupil–teacher ratio was 27:1.

Lower-secondary school—known as the "basic cycle"—lasts for three years. Depending on grade, there are between 32 and 36 periods of instruction per week. There are 180 school days per year. The education offered is general but with some prevocational classes. Enrollment in the basic cycle quadrupled between 1945 and 1965, and in the period from 1982 to 1989 it rose by 25.6 percent. A total of 17 percent of students are in private schools at this level. It will be seen from Fig. 1 that there is a certain amount of dropout at each grade level. Following the basic cycle, pupils may enter a three-year upper-secondary education known as the "baccalaureate" or they may enter technical–professional schools. These latter schools prepare students for the labor market and for higher education. The baccalaureate school does the same and several types of courses are available. There is the more academic stream and the diversified stream. The numbers of students in the diversified stream increased by 57 percent in the period 1982 to 1989. Approximately 15 percent of baccalaureate students are in private schools.

Higher education consists of university and teacher-training colleges. The average length of higher education courses is from four to seven years. Entrance depends on having completed the baccalaureate school or technical education. There are no admission examinations to university. There are two universities: the University of the Republic and the Catholic University of Uruguay, Dámaso Antonio Larrañaga. In 1990, the Catholic University had an enrollment of 983 students in 2 faculties, whereas the University of the Republic had over 60,000 students in 12 faculties.

3.2 Preschool Education

In 1990, there were 65,800 children enrolled in kindergartens and kinder-classes. About one-third of these were enrolled in private institutions. In most cases, the children are from 3 to 5 years old. In some experimental situations, 2-year olds are also enrolled. Some of the kinder-classes are attached to primary schools.

The kindergartens provide a typical preschool course, but they are also there to help children from underprivileged homes (a type of compensatory education) and to allow working mothers a place to lodge their children. Some of the kindergartens are open for 40 hours per week and others for 20 hours. There were 1,479 teachers in preschool education in 1990; this was 11 percent of the whole number of primary school teachers.

3.3 Special Education

In 1990, there were nearly 9,000 students in schools for physically and mentally handicapped children. For children up to the age of 14, there are special schools parallel to the kindergartens and primary schools. Typically, these schools work a two-shift system. They are open 30–45 hours per week (Monday to Friday only). All efforts are made to have the children enter ordinary schools as soon as possible. The courses cover the learning of basic skills and, at the higher levels, occupational workshops are provided. Teachers are specialized in teaching children with specific types of handicap.

After the age of 13 years, there is a number of special schools for intellectually impaired students. These are known as "workshop schools for occupational recuperation." Basic courses are given to prepare these students for the labor market. In some cases, the students can continue to secondary technical schools where special courses are given for physically and mentally handicapped students, as well as for socially marginalized groups (prisoners, the elderly, or "at-risk" students). Special programs are devised based on the assessment of each student and it is the Council of Technical Education that supplies the teachers.

3.4 Vocational, Technical, and Business Education

The aims of technical–professional education, both in the basic cycle of secondary school and in upper-secondary school, include providing the knowledge to students to allow them to make an informed choice about the type of job they would like to have based on their aptitudes, skills, and wishes.

The National System of Vocational Orientation (NSVO) under the auspices of the National Administration of Public Education is responsible for this work. The major effort is directed toward teacher and technician training, and the development of the curriculum for the various courses from which the students can choose. The NSVO is also establishing a network of teachers to be able to reach all zones of the country.

3.5 Adult and Nonformal Education

These are courses for illiterate persons or those who do not complete primary education which enable them to continue their studies or prepare them for entry to the labor market. It is primarily workers who attend these classes after work. There are some adult institutions in nonformal education. For example, the CECAP (*Centro de Capacitación y Producción*) belongs to the Ministry of Education and Culture; its work is focused on young people (14–24 years old) who have dropped out of formal education. The COCAP (*Consejo de Capacitación Profesional*) trains adults from 18 years of age with a technical–professional education. Other organizations (state and private) offer training courses to workers to improve their knowledge and skills. It is also common for enterprises to provide their own training courses to help their workers improve their job skills and to achieve higher levels of education.

4. Administrative and Supervisory Structure and Operation

The Ministry of Education is responsible for giving the general directives of education. The Coordination Commission for Teaching is responsible for coordinating public education at all levels, including the university level. The National Administration of Education is an independent organization responsible for the day-to-day administration of education. It consists of a Central Directorate (Central Directive Council) and other councils for primary, secondary, and technical education. There are also regional offices responsible for the local administration and supervision of schools. The school principals and inspectors are responsible for the supervision of the teachers within their establishments. Each council also has its own inspectorate.

5. Educational Finance

Ever since the 1960s, the percentage of the state budget and the Gross Domestic Product (GDP) allocated to education has been decreasing. In 1991, it was 2 percent. For the period 1990 to 1995, it was anticipated that it would be 2.91 percent of GDP. In 1990, this amounted to 17.7 percent of the state budget. Only 8 percent of the education budget is allocated for capital expenditure, with the remainder being for recurrent costs. Nearly 35 percent is allocated to primary (and preprimary) education, 28 percent to secondary and technical, 23 percent to university education, and 14 percent for administration and other matters.

The per student unit costs decreased from 1973 to 1987 by 10 percent (primary), 14 percent (secondary), 33 percent (technical), and 30 percent (university). The nadir of government expenditure on education was 1984. However, for the same first three levels of education, the percentage increases in the period

1984 to 1987 were 32, 22, and 36 respectively, and 50 percent for the university level.

6. Supplying Personnel for the Education System

There are approximately 46,500 teachers. Of these, 17,000 are in basic education, 15,500 in secondary, 7,500 in technical, and 6,500 in higher education.

There are 22 teacher-training institutes for primary, secondary, and technical teachers, and the courses last four years and cover the appropriate content and practice of teaching. In 1990, over 2,000 students were enrolled for primary, nearly 4,000 for secondary teacher training, and nearly 200 for technical subjects. There was a decrease of 55 percent in enrollment in primary teacher-training institutes in the period 1972 to 1989. For entry, students must have completed the second level of secondary or technical education. All must follow a basic course according to the type of institute in which they will teach. Practice teaching is also conducted in the type of school they will enter. Assessment is undertaken at regular intervals throughout the course.

Further qualifications at the master's level can be acquired by attending courses at the Superior Magisterial Institute. This Institute also runs courses for the training of school principals, education officers, and inspectors.

The competitive (*concours*) type of examinations still exists for teachers to gain certain levels of qualification. Teachers' results in these examinations, as well as teaching experience and good assessments, are the key factors determining a teacher's place in the hierarchy.

Economic and social factors have caused a diminution in the attractiveness of the teaching profession. Enrollments in teacher-training institutes, especially, for primary schools, decreased in the period 1970 to 1990. There are shortages of teachers at the primary school and lower-secondary levels, as well as for certain subjects at the secondary (baccalaureate) level. Steps have been taken to offer teacher accommodation where possible and to allow teachers to teach in two schools up to a maximum of 40 hours teaching per week.

7. Curriculum Development and Teaching Methodology

There are syllabuses for each type of school. Within primary schools, there are two types of syllabus—one for urban schools and a second for rural schools. The former was revised in 1980 and the latter in 1987. The urban school syllabus includes mother tongue, mathematics, geography, history, moral and civic education, science, art, music, dance, rhythm, and physical exercise. The rural school syllabus is much the same as the urban one, particularly for mother tongue and mathematics, but lays much more emphasis on the practical application of such learning in rural life. State and private schools have the same syllabus. It is possible for a school to be authorized to have a different syllabus, but in this case the students must pass a state examination to enter secondary school.

Since 1987, secondary schools have also had separate urban and rural syllabuses. Technical education has separate syllabuses for each specific subject. The syllabuses are determined by commissions composed of subject matter specialists and teachers. Revisions are undertaken at regular intervals, and in 1991, there was renewed activity in the revision of syllabuses.

There is no special policy for books and learning materials. Generally, they are produced by private enterprises, which work with specialists and teachers. In some cases, the books are approved by the inspectorate or by the respective council.

Some innovations are worthy of mention. English as a foreign language is being introduced on an experimental basis in primary schools. English and French are elective subjects in lower-secondary schools and Italian is added to this in the upper-secondary school. With the possibility of much stronger regional cooperation between Argentina, Brazil, and Paraguay, introducing Portuguese as a foreign language is under consideration.

A more ecological component to the curriculum is deemed to be important, particularly for the development of values and attitudes. More resources will be required if individual learning approaches are to be increased.

8. The System of Examinations, Promotions, and Certifications

Promotion from grade to grade in primary school requires a teacher assessment of "good" and 80 percent attendance at school. At the end of primary school, the student obtains a certificate to indicate that primary school was satisfactorily completed. Without this certificate, a student cannot enter the basic cycle of secondary education. For adults who do not obtain the primary school certificate, it is possible to obtain it by taking a special test in which teachers can give some help. At the baccalaureaute part of secondary education, and in technical schools, promotion is based on the assessment made by the groups of teachers teaching the student. These teacher assessments are made three times per year. The scale used is from 1 to 12 for achievement, but the behavior of the student and his or her personality characteristics are also taken into account. To be

promoted, a scale score of 6 is required as well as 80 percent attendance. In some subjects in higher level schools, there are end-of-year examinations. In higher education, promotion is based on course examinations.

9. Educational Assessment, Evaluation. and Research

At the beginning of the 1960s, educational planning was undertaken in Uruguay. The types of indicators used for that diagnosis of the educational system are still used. However, it must be recalled that, between 1965 and 1985, no assessment, evaluation, or research was undertaken. Since 1985, however, various national studies were undertaken, especially in primary and the basic cycle of secondary education. Researchers and advisors, including CEPAL (*Comisión Económica para América Latina y el Caribe*), undertook research studies, the results of which are being used for the reform of different parts of the system. For example, some primary schools with special weekly timetables (8 hours of instruction per school day) and with social and educational resources have been created in order to decrease the number of school failures. Another technical initiative provides special attention to pupils from underprivileged urban areas. Teachers are taught how to give a compensatory education. Since 1991, a special plan has been developed during the summer holidays (January and February) for pupils in need of compensatory education. It includes sports, games, art, and also provides a meals service.

10. Major Reforms in the 1980s and 1990s

Until 1985, there had been no reforms in the 1980s. The era of reconstruction began in 1985 with a law delineating the structure of the system, the hierarchical and decentralized administration of the system, and the aims for each type of school.

Syllabuses were revised in 1986 and 1987. In 1985, new curricula were promulgated for teacher education. In addition the private Catholic university was formally recognized.

At the end of the 1980s and beginning of the 1990s, new courses were introduced at the universities and special measures to help preschool and primary education were introduced.

11. Major Problems for the Year 2000

Enrollment in secondary education is increasing. Material and human resources are required to meet this increased demand. Improving education to cope with increased demand, improving the quality of education, and providing competent workers for the labor market are three major challenges. Efforts will be needed to eradicate dropout. Preschool educational provision will have to be increased. Special programs will need to be developed to help the at-risk students to enter apprenticeship schemes. Standards will have to be improved, and much of this will depend on the educational budget being increased. Finally, as regional cooperation develops, adjustments will need to be made to come into line with a common regional policy for education.

Bibliography

Anuario Estadístico de Educación 1990 *Dirección de Educación del Ministerio de Educación y Cultura de la República Oriental del Uruguay.* Ministerio de Educación, Montevideo

Government of Uruguay (annual) *Anuario Estadístico de la Dirección General de Estadística y Censas-1986 a 1990.* Government of Uruguay, Montevideo

Gran Atlas SPES 1979 *Universal y de la República Oriental del Uruguay.* Bioliograf, Barcelona

Informe del Sistema Educativo Uruguayo 1990 *Elaborado en la Dirección de Educación del Ministerio de Educación y Cultura de la ROU 1990–1991.* Ministerio de Educación, Montevideo

Vanuatu

J. N. Johnstone

1. General Background

The independent Pacific Island country now called Vanuatu is located west of Fiji, southeast of the Solomon Islands, and northeast of New Caledonia. It consists of about 80 islands spread across an area of the western Pacific measuring about 900 by 500 kilometers. The 10 largest islands account for almost 90 percent of the total land area of 11,900 square kilometers. About half of the land area is potentially suitable for agriculture because the islands are very mountainous. Only one-sixth of the arable acreage is under cultivation.

By 1992, the population of Vanuatu exceeded 150,000 while the annual growth rate was about 2.5 percent. Just under 20 percent of ni-Vanuatu live in urban areas. The situation of significant growth is in marked contrast to the population decline of the late 1800s and early 1900s when epidemics and labor recruitment significantly reduced the numbers living in the islands.

In terms of ethnic composition, Vanuatu is 95 percent Melanesian with the remainder a mixture of other Pacific islanders, Chinese, Vietnamese, French, Australians, and British. The indigenous inhabitants who are distributed throughout the islands speak well over 100 Melanesian languages or vernaculars, none of which is used for general communication in the nation. For purposes of general communication and education, the three languages in popular use are English, French, and Bislama (a Pidgin English). The first two were the official languages for the two former colonial powers and were used for the administrative and legal systems, for trade in businesses run by each power's expatriate residents, and for education in the two systems of schooling set up by the English and French. Bislama is used extensively throughout the country and assists in unifying the diversity of people and their interests and objectives.

Vanuatu achieved its Independence in 1980. It had originally been called the New Hebrides and had been subject to a joint administration from both United Kingdom and France for nearly 100 years. That administration had imposed a dual system on the colony: two sets of laws, two sets of hospitals, two sets of police, two sets of schools, two sets of colonial attitudes and two official languages. There has been, and still is to some extent, competition between the Anglophone and Francophone influences. This competition affects education in particular and the way in which it is planned and administered. To some extent, Bislama helps to avoid the separate philosophies of the two excolonial rulers.

In 1992 the Gross National Product (GNP) was about US$780 per capita and was growing at about 0.7 percent per annum. The major exports are copra, beef, and cocoa while the major industries include foodstuffs, beverages, tobacco, and timber.

With the coming of independence, Vanuatu government officials wished to unify both school systems to produce one national system. Even in 1993, the literacy rate was estimated to be only about 53 percent. Their plan for unification faced several complications. One was the existence of an Anglican mission school system that received government grants but was largely autonomous in administration. Also in the Protestant sector there was a Seventh Day Adventist mission system that made up about 15 percent of the British schools but received no grants. The Catholic schools were in the French system. English-speaking primary schools took children from the age of 6 and their preschools were wholly fee-supported and entirely outside the government administration. The French-speaking system accepted children at the age of 3, free of cost to the parents.

2. Politics and the Goals of the Education System

From Independence to 1991, the ruling party was the Anglophone Vanuaaka party under the leadership of Walter Lini. Following a series of political difficulties and challenges, the Francophone-oriented party under the leadership of Maxime Carlot became the ruling party in 1992. The change is expected to reorient the directions taken in various aspects, especially the provision of education, over the term of the government.

The government is committed to improving access to education to all citizens and to improving the quality and relevance of education to the modern world. In this context, the Ministry of Education formulated its long-term objective of 10 years of high quality education for the majority of children. In the short to medium term, priority will be placed on the improvement of quality across all levels of education in Vanuatu while striving for a sustainable expansion of the education system.

3. The Formal System of Education

Figure 1 outlines the structure of the formal education in Vanuatu, while the key statistics on enrollments and resources in the major education sectors are provided in Table 1.

The Ministry of Education is responsible for formal education. Although there is a variety of nonformal education on offer, it is very diverse and consequently responsibility for it is scattered across a variety of government and nongovernment organizations. Most formal education is provided in public institutions, although there are a number of schools with religious affiliations and some schools are run by private organizations.

3.1 Primary, Secondary, and Tertiary Education

The Vanuatu education system provides six years of primary education, four years of junior secondary education, and two to three years of senior secondary education. The medium of instruction from primary to higher education levels is either English or French according to the school in which the student enrolls or to the stream within a school. As noted in Sect. 1, both English and French are the two official languages but neither language is the mother tongue of most ni-Vanuatu children. Some primary schools do use the national language and *lingua franca*—Bislama—in some classes but this practice is not official.

Schools are spread over more than 60 of the country's islands, almost all of which are only accessible by boat. Almost all ni-Vanuatu children have access to primary schools with more than 95 percent of 6-year olds enrolling in school. It is considered that most primary school children complete the primary stage, although reliable data are not available to confirm this. Repetition rates were high although they have been reduced since 1988 due to an enforced policy of automatic progression.

Demand for places in primary schools has increased due in part to the urban drift and also in part to the high birthrates. Intercensus data show that the urban population has grown at about 7.5 percent per year while the school-age population is growing at about 2.7 percent per year. In the main areas, therefore, the supply of places has not been sufficient to accommodate the demand and many schools in these areas are now requiring new primary entrants to have attended a preschool. Given the high fees, children of poor parents—especially those living in the main urban areas—are going to find it increasingly difficult to enroll in schools near their homes.

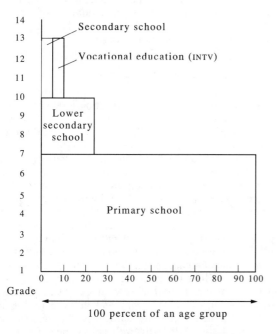

Figure 1
Vanuatu: Structure of the formal education system

Table 1
Summary of basic education statistics Vanuatu 1990

	Primary	Secondary	Technical/ Vocational
Number of students	26,267	3,799	400
Number of teachers	984	125	23
Number of institutions	78	14	1
Expenditure per student (US$)	170	500	—

Junior secondary education has increased significantly since Independence and most especially through a major expansion program in 1986. By 1993, the government would claim to provide junior secondary education in all but one local government area. Nevertheless only about 20–25 percent of primary graduates entered the junior secondary level. Repetition is only a minor problem but dropout rates still appear to be significant. To overcome their inability to enter junior secondary education, many young ni-Vanuatu children must go overseas to study as private students, probably equal to about 10 percent of the enrollment. Given the high cost of this option, a significant unmet demand is indicated.

In 1993, senior secondary education was provided in three schools: Malapoa College and the Lycee (both in Port Vila) and Matevulu College (on the island of Santo). At both Malapoa and Matevulu, instruction is in English and two years of education are provided. At the Lycee, instruction is in French. Two new schools have been completed at Rensarie and Tafea and they will also provide senior secondary education. Only 20–25 percent of year 10 graduates can access senior secondary education, although that percentage will increase when the two new schools become fully operational.

Girls have good access to education compared to many countries, although some room for further improvement still exists. About 53 percent of primary enrollments are boys while about 56 percent of lower secondary enrollments are boys. At the senior secondary level however, the percentage of boys enrolled has risen to 65 percent.

School construction is a problem, with many schools suffering from no or at best little maintenance. The two new schools and Matevulu have been built in remote areas which have no supportive infrastructure. As there is little budgetary allocation for maintenance, the conditions of these schools—built according to high cost metropolitan standards using World Bank and Australian aid funds—can be expected to deteriorate rapidly. That deterioration is already noticeable at Matevulu with two of three stages now complete.

There is no university in Vanuatu and so students must attend an overseas institution. The University of the South Pacific (USP) in Fiji has perhaps been the most popular choice although the numbers of students studying there in the late 1980s and early 1990s has declined. It has a campus now operating in Port Vila for both English-and French-speaking students. Students studying at the USP Vanuatu campus have different requirements and practices. French-speaking students come from the Lycee or the INTV (see Sect. 3.4) and follow a course which is designed and supervised in association with the *Université Française du Pacifique* (the French version of the USP). In contrast, English-speaking students have generally had to complete previous extension courses through the USP or received secondary education overseas. About 30 percent have come from year 13 at Malapoa College. These students follow the Foundation Year Studies program to gain university entrance, although that will be phased out in 1993.

Students who complete their studies to university entrance level can compete for scholarships to overseas universities. In each of the years 1990 and 1991, 21 students graduated at the bachelor level each year while 83 graduated over the 1987–91 period. This number is expected to increase to about 40 in a few years with an increasing number (from the 4 in 1991) of graduate degrees as well.

3.2 Preschool Education

Preschool education has developed due to the efforts of communities and individuals who have a strong commitment to that kind of educational provision. Most developments are now planned through the Vanuatu Preschool Association. Financing for each preschool is from private sources and that pattern is almost certain to continue although the government has now appointed a coordinator to assist the private efforts in this area.

Fees for attendance vary significantly according to the school and its location. In the capital—Port Vila—fees can be as high as 4,000–5,000 vatu each term (about US$35).

3.3 Special Education

There is no provision for special education in Vanuatu. Attempts have been made by a number of private groups to provide for some handicaps but these have not yet led to any formal response.

3.4 Vocational, Technical, and Business Education

There is one technical school—*Ecole Saint Michel* in Luganville—which offers secondary technical and vocational training. Enrollments are few and support for the school is limited. It is now under the Education Ministry.

The main responsibility for the delivery of vocational and technical education rests with the *Institut National Technique et Vocational de Vanuatu* (INTV). It accepts lower secondary school graduates, of whom about 40 percent enter the INTV. The INTV was a part of the French-speaking system until recently. Since providing some basic courses in the English language in 1988, the demand for English language technical courses has increased such that now about 25 percent of total enrollment is accounted for by such courses. In part the introduction of these courses was in response to falling enrollments—from 387 in 1985 to 160 in 1989. The change then saw enrollments increase again to about 400 in 1991, still well below the capacity of about 560 places. Courses at the institute cover most basic technical subjects although curricula are not always wholly appropriate. Considerable revision is, however, being undertaken. Some business training is also provided.

There are also some private or religious colleges offering vocational education courses, especially in the secretarial and basic trades areas. Demand for their courses is always high.

Other vocational courses are offered by several different government agencies. The Government Training Center, for example, offers a wide range of courses for government employees on a continuing and rotating basis. This Center has been supported through various aid grants which have not always allowed it to plan to cater for all demands. Another review of its operation is presently being undertaken.

Other agencies offering vocational courses include the Vanuatu Center for Nurse Education, the Tagabe Agriculture College, and the Police Training School. There are also rural training centers.

3.5 Adult and Nonformal Education

There are few opportunities to receive adult or nonformal education programs in Vanuatu. The main source is the USP campus which enables ni-Vanuatu students to enroll in various courses from the USP. Attached to that campus is the USP Extension Center which offers, from Fiji, a range of extension programs. Courses in these programs range from several days to months and they cover a wide variety of topics. Instruction combines written material, audiovisual materials and tutorials either face-to-face or via teleconferencing with Fiji.

4. Administrative and Supervisory Structure and Operation

The Ministry of Education has a senior minister who in turn appoints a director general to be the permanent head. There are then five principal education officers appointed to be in charge of the various major functions.

A second branch also exists in all Vanuatu ministries to parallel this cadre of civil servants. That branch is the political wing and it consists of three political secretaries whose ostensible function is to ensure party interests are being looked after. In contrast to the civil servants, the political secretaries may or may not be educators. It is therefore possible—and indeed not uncommon—for decisions made by professional educators to be overturned or at least delayed by the political secretaries.

A major advance, however, is that the administration of the education system is now unified. No longer are the two stands of schools catered for separately. Decentralization of certain management functions has therefore also become possible and 11 regional educa-

tion offices have been created.

A special system of primary advisers has also been established by the principal education officer (primary and secondary education) to complement the regional offices. This system covers the whole country although some schools are very much easier to access than others. The regional officers and advisers have the responsibility of visiting all schools at least twice each year to help teachers improve their teaching techniques and to implement curriculum changes. They conduct inservice courses in a variety of areas especially in methods of how to teach multigrade classes.

5. Educational Finance

The education sector is the Vanuatu government's first priority and receives the largest percentage of public expenditure. In 1986, education received 25 percent of total government expenditure although this percentage had decreased to 19 percent by 1991 and 1992. As the total budget had also decreased, this meant that the budget available to the Ministry of Education had contracted by about 27 percent, from about 1.395 billion vatu in 1986 to 950 million vatu in 1992. Real expenditure per primary school pupil fell from 30,000 vatu in 1987 to 20,000 vatu in 1991 (US$250 to US$170). Expenditure per secondary school student also fell from 109,000 vatu to 63,000 vatu over the same period (US$900 to US$500).

The Ministry has had to adopt special and severe strategies to accommodate these significant decreases. In particular, it has increased student–teacher ratios to about 30:1 in primary schools and increased average class sizes to about 30 in secondary schools. Both values could go even higher in the 1990s. It has also fully implemented a policy of automatic progression which means that there are few repeaters, except at the grade 6 level at the end of the primary level. Entrance to primary school has also been more closely observed, with children having to be 6 or 7 years of age. In a country such as Vanuatu, such a policy is difficult to enforce but it appears to have had an effect on new entrant numbers.

Unfortunately, support to schools has also had to be reduced. The greatest problem is that related to school building maintenance. This situation was already severe before the cuts, with an estimated need for 2 billion vatu to repair rural primary schools alone. The total primary maintenance budget in 1993 was, however, only about 25 million vatu.

6. Supplying Personnel for the Education System

At the time of Independence, there were about 400 ni-Vanuatu trained teachers in the Anglophone schools, more in the mission schools, and about 240 in the

Francophone schools. In addition there were about 300 untrained teachers.

The Vanuatu Teachers College was established to train teachers for both systems at the primary level. It is now essential to have a Certificate in Primary Education from the Teachers College or an adequate overseas qualification for employment as a primary teacher. Inservice training of primary teachers—sometimes in conjunction with the regional advisers—is also a major function of the Teachers College. The College has also run special courses from time to time to train secondary school teachers either inservice or preservice, the most recent courses being conducted over the 1990–93 period. These efforts to train teachers for the junior secondary level, together with students sent on scholarship overseas, have been in part oriented toward replacing expatriate teachers in the junior secondary schools. This localization program has had significant success with the percentage of ni-Vanuatu teachers increasing from 40 percent in 1985 to 70 percent in 1991. Unfortunately, the Teachers College does not have a coherent or ongoing plan to continue or even to build up its capacity to undertake this form of training. Hence training of these kinds of teachers will be a major problem to be confronted in the future.

At the senior secondary level, there is still a heavy reliance on expatriate teachers and significant levels of localization cannot be expected soon. Nevertheless as increased numbers of graduates return from overseas universities, some impact will be made, although there will be a strong attraction for new graduates to leave teaching for more attractive posts in the emerging private sector or elsewhere in the government service.

7. Curriculum Development and Teaching Methodology

The Vanuatu Institute of Education is responsible for both curriculum development and teacher education. There are two separate divisions within the Institute: the Curriculum Development Center and the Vanuatu Teachers College (see above). Prior to 1988, curriculum development had been the responsibility of a senior education officer but there had been no real center in which curriculum officers and the writers on the curriculum panels could work and interact continually. With the construction of a new building, such a focus was created.

The curricula for the English-speaking schools have been very different from those used in the French-speaking schools. Ministry officials have long seen this as an undesirable situation and in 1987 made the decision to rectify it. Plans were formulated to have a common primary curriculum developed and implemented in schools as soon as possible. An Australian aid project supported especially by a New Zealand aid commitment with some contribution from French aid was requested to complete the task. In 1993, common

curricula and materials should be introduced into Years 1 and 2 with the total primary curriculum converted by 1996. More materials will then be available for both teachers and students and the quality and relevance will also be greater. Plans are also prepared for a common curriculum through to Year 10. Work has also begun on most subjects but implementation is also unlikely to be completed before 1996.

Teaching methodology varies significantly between the two systems. In the English-speaking schools, the intended approach is on discovery and experiential activity with some rote learning. In the French-speaking schools, rote learning of facts is emphasized almost exclusively. A lot of that learning has, up to 1993, emphasized topics and facts which relate to France rather than to Vanuatu in particular or to the Pacific Islands in general. This distinction is a major issue in terms of attempting to unify the curriculum especially in the primary school grades.

The introduction of a new examination system—the Pacific Senior Secondary Certificate—is seen as possibly leading to a school-based program at the senior secondary level. By 1993, however, that system had not fully been introduced.

8. The System of Examinations, Promotions, and Certifications

Students cannot qualify for direct university entrance at the senior secondary schools in Vanuatu. Those in the English-speaking schools used to sit for the International General Certificate of Secondary Education in Year 12, although that certificate is really only a Year-11 examination. After that examination, both Malapoa College and Matevulu College offered an additional year of study which was equivalent to the Preliminary Studies year for the University of the South Pacific (in Fiji). Graduates from Year 13 would then proceed to the Foundation Year studies for the USP and thence, if successful, enter the University. For several years, the best students in Year 12 have gone to New Zealand to repeat that year and then move on to the New Zealand bursary year to enable them to gain direct access to a New Zealand university.

French-speaking students originally had the opportunity to present themselves for the *baccalauréat* examination from Paris. As no student had been successful for several years, the *lycee* was downgraded and students then sat for an internal Year-12 examination. The best students from this examination (or sometimes after Year 11) went to schools in Noumea.

Both the certificate examination (for English-speaking students) and the internal examination (for French-speaking students) will now be replaced by the Pacific Senior Secondary Certificate at the Year-12 level. This examination is an attempt to rationalize the senior secondary cycle as it will be introduced into both types of schools. It will be accepted as being equivalent to the University of the South Pacific preliminary studies examination and so students will still have one more year of Foundation Studies to complete before gaining admission to the University. The PSSC system requires Vanuatu to be a member of the South Pacific Board of Educational Assessment which is based in Suva. The actual Certificate examination is set on the Vanuatu curriculum but subject to a variety of moderation procedures to ensure that quality and equivalent standards are achieved with other Pacific Island countries. One advantage of the PSSC is that it will reduce the number of preuniversity years of study required from 14 to 13 and thus equate ni-Vanuatu students to students studying in other Pacific Island countries.

9. Educational Assessment, Evaluation, and Research

Little work has been undertaken to assess performance levels in Vanuatu or to evaluate the education system. One study was undertaken by UNESCO as part of its assessment of Pacific Islands literacy levels. That study showed that ni-Vanuatu children had literacy and numeracy levels equal to or higher than students in other Pacific Island countries. As that was only one study however, it is not possible to comment on whether change has taken place due to the considerable activity aimed at improving quality of provision.

10. Major Reforms in the 1980s and 1990s

The Second Development Plan emphasized the distinction between quality and quantity in planning the allocation of resources to education. It recommended that developments should emphasize quality over the Plan period. A considerable amount of external assistance, especially from the World Bank and Australian governments but also from the British, New Zealand, and French governments, has enabled the quality issue to be addressed and at the same time facilitated some quantitative expansion.

A major debate about quantity of junior secondary education in particular took place about 1985–87. In part, this debate resulted in the government placing in its government gazette, a notice officially establishing a number of new schools from that day onward. Buildings for most of these schools were not available and teachers were not in sufficient supply to staff all schools. Finally—partly due to pressure from aid donors concerned about quality considerations—the government capitulated and closed several.

11. Major Problems for the Year 2000

In view of such a multiplicity of ethnic backgrounds and of languages in the population, the task for ni-Vanuatu educators to provide a culturally unifying curriculum and a common instructional language for a newly unified school system is formidable indeed.

The educational complexities created by such cultural diversity and a previous condominium form of government cannot be overestimated.

The geographic characteristics of Vanuatu also pose problems for educational planners in terms of providing equal access to schooling for all pupils and of locating schools in the most suitable sites. The supply of teachers and schools to remote, sparsely populated regions and the need to communicate with such regions is particularly difficult.

There are four major problems to be confronted by education officials and planners in Vanuatu in the period leading to the year 2000. These problems are:

(a) The language issue is perhaps the most fundamental problem of all. A country the size of Vanuatu with its limited (and shrinking) financial resources cannot hope to cope alone with the demands of having dual language provision. For most students, the language of instruction is at best a second language and more commonly a third language. That places a considerable strain on them as they attempt to learn concepts and knowledge which are often very strange and alien. Even with the best of intentions, a developing country cannot provide sufficient materials in even one language to ensure some kind of equity of experience and provision. Vanuatu is nevertheless attempting to do that with as much support as it can attract from the aid community.

(b) The restriction on places at both the junior and senior secondary school levels places a major barrier on the development of the human resources for Vanuatu's own economic development. Already transition rates between levels are low but with rapidly increasing numbers of births, increased pressure is being placed on the system which cannot be met. Transition rates will therefore fall even further.

(c) The opportunity to train secondary school teachers is not provided. The demand for secondary school teachers will increase quite significantly in the 1990s. There is however no training course available to enable training to be conducted in Vanuatu. The present "crash-course" will not be an option because it is being entirely provided by expatriate lectures funded through an Australian aid project. Hence ni-Vanuatu, hoping to become secondary school teachers, will have to earn their degree through the scholarship program (where there is competition from a variety of other development sectors) or accept special awards to study abroad, possibly in Fiji or Papua New Guinea. All approaches are less appropriate than the development of a sound, cost-efficient course delivered in Vanuatu.

(d) Education facilities will continue to deteriorate if they are not maintained. Buildings and equipment are already in bad condition, especially those schools built to metropolitan standards, and the many pieces of equipment supplied by aid donors which have high demand for consumable parts. The academic environments in which children will be expected to learn and derive inspiration over the coming years are therefore likely to deteriorate to such an extent as to become negative influences militating against any desire to receive education within the country itself.

Venezuela

F. Reimers

1 General Background

Venezuela is located in the northern part of South America. Its total territory is 912,000 square kilometers. In 1811, it declared Independence from Spain, along with four other South American republics, under the leadership of Simón Bolívar.

Education has long been a policy priority of the Venezuelan government. Simón Bolívar used to refer to the importance of education in the establishment of the new republics; a well-known saying of his is "Morality and enlightenment are our prime needs." In 1870 president Guzman Blanco passed a law that made primary education free and compulsory.

The oil industry has shaped much of the economic and political landscape of contemporary Venezuela. Democracy was consolidated in 1958. Oil revenues fueled many of the aspirations of the emerging democracy, allowing the formation of a middle class, and the expansion of education, health, and social programs. They also contributed to a bloated government bureaucracy and to other distortions in the economy which virtually eliminated other sources of comparative advantage (Dutch disease).

Between 1930 and 1958 the Venezuelan economy shifted from being predominantly based on exports of agricultural goods to an industrial economy based on import substitution policies. The population became increasingly urban during this time. In 1989 only 6 percent of the Gross Domestic Product (GDP) came from agriculture, 46 percent came from industry (of which 40% came from nonmanufacturing activities), and 48 percent came from services.

The population grew from 4.2 million in 1945 to 19 million in 1989. In 1989, 85 percent of the population lived in urban areas and 21 percent in the capital city of Caracas. In 1945, only 35 percent of the population lived in urban areas. The population grew at 2.8 percent per year between 1980 and 1989, although this figure had declined from 3.5 percent between 1965 and 1980. There was a high dependency ratio as 39 percent of the population was younger than 14 years.

Venezuela's population is a racial mix of three dominant groups: the various tribes of the original inhabitants of the country, Blacks who were brought as slaves in colonial times, and the Spanish settlers. More recently, rapid economic growth and explicit government policies at different periods stimulated immigration from all corners of the world. Spanish is the prevalent language.

Gross National Product per capita in 1989 was US$2,450. In 1987, 51 percent of the household income was in the hands of 20 percent the population, and 34 percent of the income was in the hands of 10 percent of the population. At the same time, 40 percent of the population lived on only 14 percent of the income. According to government figures, in 1989, 22 percent of the population lived in extreme poverty and 31 percent lived in critical poverty.

During the 1980s Venezuela lived under an ever-increasing foreign debt crisis. This led to severe economic adjustments toward the end of the decade. Public and publicly guaranteed long-term debt increased from US$718 million in 1970 to US$25,339 million in 1989. In 1989 Venezuela's total external debt was US$33,144 million. As a percentage of exports, debt servicing was 25 percent in 1989 and interest payments were 20 percent.

2. Politics and the Goals of the Education System

Since 1958 Venezuela has been governed by two large parties who have alternated in the executive, sharing power in Congress with a number of smaller parties. Of the seven constitutional presidents since 1958, five have been from the social democratic party, *Acción Democrática*, and two from the Christian democratic party, COPEI.

Education has been an explicit priority of both parties controlling the executive, and of all represented in Congress. There are no obvious differences between the educational policies of the two main parties, both of which see education as an important component of the Venezuelan project of democratization.

With the advent of the new democracy, a new constitution was approved in 1960. This constitution states that all Venezuelans have the right to be educated and assigns the responsibility to the state for opening schools and education services to ensure free access to education. In the 1980s Congress passed a new Law of Education which expanded basic education from 6 to 9 years.

The arrival of democracy in 1958 expanded the education system at all levels. The annual growth of primary enrollments increased from 7 percent prior to democracy to over 20 percent in the years immediately following the establishment of the democratic regime. The rate of growth for secondary education also doubled in this period. Growth in university enrollments increased from 12 percent a year in the last year of the dictatorship to 60 percent in the first year of democracy. For the next 30 years, combined enrollments of primary and secondary education grew at an annual average of 4 percent and higher education at an annual average of 11 percent.

Overall enrollments have expanded drastically since 1960 but from 1970 to 1990 this expansion has concentrated on the higher levels of the education system. While in 1972 net enrollment ratios in primary school were 83 percent, and increased to 85 percent in 1989, net enrollments increased from 11 to 25 percent in higher education in the same period.

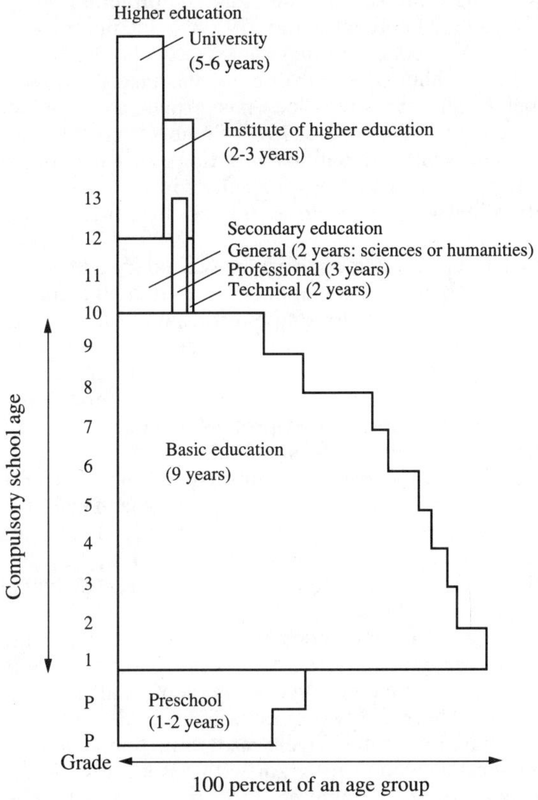

Table 1
Student enrollments in Venezuela 1990

	Basic	Secondary	University	Other
Public institutions				
No. of students	3,339,173	211,375	332,091	54,547
No. of teachers	151,152	22,647	25,295	5,046
No. of schools	13,270	763	16	36
Student–teacher ratio	22:1	9:1	13:1	11:1
Student–school ratio	252:1	277:1	20,756:1	1,515:1
Private institutions				
No. of students	531,867	68,367	59,654	82,181
No. of teachers	29,111	9,531	3,629	5,519
No. of schools	1,903	691	13	28
Student–teacher ratio	18:1	7:1	16:1	15:1
Student–school ratio	279:1	99:1	4,589:1	2,935:1

Source: Ministerio de Educación 1990

The control of educational administration by political parties and factions has led to severe discontinuities every time a government changes office, and sometimes even when ministers are changed within the same government. As the largest employer in the country, the education sector has been a prime target for patronage and political clientelism. More often than not, competency and professionalism have been sacrificed to having the right political connection for

Table 2
Net enrollment and expenditure per student in Venezuela 1990

	Net enrollment	Expenditure per student (Bs)[a]
Preschool		9,419
Basic	85	9,523
Secondary	19	16,666
General		15,114
Technical		22,600
Agriculture		27,512
Industry		27,680
Commercial		18,055
Social		42,477
Higher	25	77,985
University		83,864
Other		42,194
Ratio Secondary–Basic		2:1
Ratio Higher–Basic		8:1

Sources: Ministerio de Educación (1990); Schiefelbein and Heikkinen (1991); Fizsbein and Psacharopoulos (1991)
a In 1991 60 Bs = US$1

Figure 1
Venezuela: Structure of the formal education system 1991

appointment and promotion within the public education system.

3. The Formal System of Education

3.1 Primary, Secondary, and Tertiary Education

Public education is free at all levels and compulsory until Grade 9. All public schools are coeducational. Figure 1 and Tables 1 and 2 summarize basic statistics about the formal education system.

Until 1980, the formal education system comprised 6 years of primary education and 5 years of high school. A new Law of Education (*Ley Organica de Educación*) was then approved by Congress (Ministry of Education 1980). The Law established the following levels of education: preschool, basic, secondary, and higher. It also specified the following modalities: special education, arts education, military education, education for religious personnel, and adult education.

The 1980 Education Law rules that basic education should include the former primary level (Grades 1–6) plus junior high school (Grades 7–9), extending basic education from 6 to 9 years. As discussed below, a substantial part of this education reform has not been implemented. The official school year for basic education is 180 days and 1,500 hours of instruction, though in practice most schools rarely teach more than 5–6 hours per day and frequent teacher strikes reduce the length of the school year.

In 1990 there were 3,871,040 students in the nine grades of basic education in Venezuela, of which 14 percent were enrolled in private schools; 279,742 students were enrolled in senior high school of which 24 percent were enrolled in private schools; and 528,473 students were enrolled in higher education institutions of which 27 percent attended private institutions.

In basic education public schools fall under four kinds of authorities: national, state, municipal, and autonomous. In 1990 enrollments in basic education were distributed as follows: 67 percent in national schools, 29 percent in state schools, and 4 percent in municipal and autonomous schools.

There were, in 1990, 171,431 teachers of basic education, of which 17 percent taught in private schools. Of those in public schools, 71 percent teach in national schools, 26 percent in state schools, and 4 percent in municipal and autonomous schools.

There were 15,173 schools teaching all or some levels of basic education in 1990 (some schools share the same building in different school shifts; the number of school buildings is estimated to be 12,500).

In 1990, 85 percent of the students in the 6–14 age group were enrolled in school. Though most (95%) children enter primary school, many repeat and eventually dropout. An estimated 30 percent of all students in basic education were repeating a grade in 1989. Of all students who enroll in basic education, only

46 percent graduate from Grade 9, and 50 percent of them do it after repeating a grade three or more times (Schiefelbein and Heikkinen 1991 p. 6).

Entering and remaining in school is biased against the poorer children and those living in rural areas (World Bank 1991a). These access disparities, showing that the state has failed to provide equality of educational opportunity, are due to the fact that the poor, and especially the rural poor, receive educational services of inferior quality to that of the middle classes. While urban schools have one teacher per grade, multigrade teachers are common in rural areas. The educational level of teachers and the supervision and distribution of resources is also higher in urban as opposed to rural areas.

The low levels of efficiency of basic education are also observed in the low levels of learning achieved by students. In 1990, the Ministry of Education administered a test in basic subjects to a sample of 4,782 students beginning Grade 6. The results (Ministry of Education 1991) show low levels of student achievement, as well as the higher levels of those living in urban areas and those attending private schools. Only 23 percent of the students could correctly answer a multiple-choice question to a basic applied mathematics problem involving a sum and a subtraction.

In 1990, 24 percent of the 279,742 students enrolled in secondary education were in private schools. Private secondary education enrollment, the fastest growing level of private education, has grown at a rate of 1.8 percent annually since 1980. Some 99 percent of the students enrolled in public institutions were in national schools. There were 30,447 teachers in secondary education in 1990, of which 31 percent taught in private schools.

There are three modalities of secondary education; they can better be understood as part of the formal education system prior to the reform of 1980. Preceding the reform, secondary education had two cycles: basic and diversified (junior and senior high school). Diversified education was offered in 3 modalities: sciences, humanities, and professional; the first two prepared students to pursue studies at the university level, the third prepared students to enter the workforce while also granting a high-school diploma. Theoretically, however, the three branches of the diversified cycle allowed a student to pursue higher studies. Besides the diversified cycle there were several technical programs.

The three current modes of secondary education are a two-year general academic program in sciences or humanities, which enrolled 82 percent of all students in 1990. There are two options for technical secondary education: a three-year program, that combines a general academic program with a specialization in agriculture, art, commerce, industry, or social work, and which enrolled 13 percent of all students in 1990. There is also a two-year professional program in agriculture, art, commerce, industry, social work, and various technical occupations. Some 5 percent of all secondary students were enrolled in these programs in 1990 and of these only 8 percent were enrolled in private schools.

Though in theory the expected ages for students in secondary education would be 15–17, in practice they range from 13 to over 21 (this reflects the high rates of repetition at lower levels of the education system). In 1990 only 74 percent of all secondary-school students were aged between 15 and 17. While only 17 percent of all the students in this age group are enrolled in secondary school (19% of the 16–17 age group), a few more will eventually be enrolled at a later age. Gross enrollment rates are 23 percent (35% if computed only over the 16–17 population). Some 75 percent of all the students who enroll in secondary education graduate from that level.

Most students (95%) enrolled in secondary education live in urban areas. There are few schools offering secondary education in rural areas. While 58 percent of all the students aged 15–19 living in urban areas are enrolled in school, only 36 percent of the girls and 21 percent of the boys living in rural areas are enrolled in school (World Bank 1991a p. 185).

Students learn little in secondary education as suggested by a test administered in 1984 to high-school graduates. This test also showed differences in the ability of graduates from public or private schools and schools in rural and urban areas. Table 3 presents a summary of the results of this test.

The Venezuelan Higher Education System (VHES) comprises several types of institutions: universities, teacher-training institutes, polytechnics, institutes of technology, and community colleges, both public and private. Universities offer education leading to degrees at the bachelor and graduate levels. Traditionally, the first university degree in Venezuela, is a fairly specialized training in the professions (law, engineering, medicine), akin to a French *license*, rather than to the bachelor's degree in the United States. The other institutes of higher studies offer a variety of types of training, which include courses as long as 4 to 5 years, to shorter courses lasting 2 or 3 years. By design, the institutes are expected to be integrated with the universities, so that graduates from the institutes can later complete a university education. In practice this integration of the system has not been achieved

as many universities refuse to give credit for courses taken in the institutes.

The VHES has experienced accelerated growth since 1960. Enrollment has increased 30 times in this period. Until the beginning of this century the system was made up of only four public universities. By 1960 one public and two private universities and two public teacher-training institutes had been added. In 1989 the VHES included 93 institutions: 16 public and 13 private universities, and 36 public and 28 private institutes of higher studies.

Of the 528,473 students enrolled in higher education in 1990, 74 percent were enrolled in universities. Of these, 15 percent were in private universities. Among the students enrolled in institutions of higher education other than universities, more than 50 percent were in private institutions.

There were 39,489 faculty members in universities and other institutes of higher education. Some 65 percent of teachers in public institutions work full-time, but only 13 percent of those in private institutions do so.

Since 1979 high-school graduates take an examination to enter the higher education system, and indicate several options of study. Assignments to specific universities and departments are made on the basis of students' preferences, and their test results and high-school grades. Around 40 percent of those who take the test are admitted to pursue higher studies.

Students in the VHES still come disproportionately from the middle and upper classes. In 1986, while about 68 percent of the households in Venezuela were headed by workers, only 36 percent of the students entering the VHES came from such households. In all, 70 percent of VHES students came from the top 20 percent income households.

The VHES offers primarily undergraduate education, though graduate offerings have increased. However, the higher education system is inefficient. On average, only 26 percent of the students who enter a public university will graduate in 5 or 6 years, while 87 percent will finish in the same amount of time in private universities.

In 1974 the government set up a foundation (*Fundayacucho*) to finance students who wished to pursue higher education at the undergraduate and graduate levels in Venezuela and abroad. Until 1990,

Table 3
Average scores obtained by high-school graduates in a test in six basic subjects (scale 1 to 50)

	Science	Mathematics	Chemistry	Physics	Biology	Language
Public	5.53	3.93	6.60	10.19	9.06	32.22
Private	11.98	9.76	12.07	16.45	14.14	39.73

Source: OPSU-CENAMEC (1986)

Fundayacucho had awarded 43,910 scholarships (51% for study overseas) and 9,520 student loans (33% for study overseas).

3.2 Preschool Education

There are several modalities of early childhood education. One of them, an expanding community-based national program (*Hogares de Cuidado Diario*), emphasizes child care and nutrition and is run by a foundation (*Fundación del Niño*) and the Ministry of Family Affairs. The Ministry of Education is expanding enrollments in programs with an academic orientation. In 1989 there were 570,615 students enrolled in such preschool programs, of which 17 percent attended private preschools. The Ministry of Education directly administered 80 percent of the public preschools, while the rest were managed by the states and a small number by municipalities.

Since 1980, preschool education has been the fastest growing level of education as enrollments increased 35 percent in this period. In all, 40 percent of the 4–5 year olds and 49 percent of the 5-year olds are enrolled in preschool. Some 85 percent of the students enrolled in preschool live in urban areas. They range in age from 3 to 7, while 80 percent are 4 or 5 years old. In 1990 there were 34,450 teachers teaching preschool, of which 18 percent taught in private schools. Many of the 7,566 schools where preschool education is taught are attached to a primary school.

3.3 Special Education

There are special education programs for handicapped students. They all take place in special schools since there is no "mainstreaming" in Venezuela. In 1989, 132,250 students were enrolled in such programs in the government sector. There are also private institutions, but no reliable statistics are available.

3.4 Adult and Nonformal Education

Adult education is offered by the National Institute for Educational Cooperation (INCE), financed by a 2.5 percent tax on the payroll and by transfers from the Ministry of Education. In 1990 INCE trained 360,000 workers offering over 28,000 courses. INCE has its own staff of trainers that provide courses in the facilities of the institute in all states of the country, and also in the firms themselves. Courses are free to trainees. INCE offers courses ranging from basic education to technical courses.

In 1989, as a result of the perception that INCE training was largely irrelevant and outdated and that there were problems of mismanagement in the institution, the president of Venezuela appointed a senior executive of the human resources department of the largest oil company as president of INCE with the mandate to reorganize the institute. The new plans include promoting closer participation with the private sector in the provision of training, the rationalization and modernization of course offerings, the use of surveys to identify needs as perceived by employers, and the development of flexible modular training emphasizing skill development rather than credentialism.

In addition to INCE a number of public and private institutions offer primary and secondary courses for adults in evening classes. These are structured to cover the same curriculum in a smaller amount of time. In 1989, 372,963 students were enrolled in adult education classes.

4. Administrative and Supervisory Structure and Operation

The 20-story building which houses the Ministry of Education in the capital city of Caracas symbolizes the degree to which education is highly centralized in Venezuela. This building is the sanctuary of planning and research, budgeting, curriculum design, textbook selection, staffing, administration and record keeping, establishing the examination and evaluation system, and the repair and maintenance of all national schools (which account for 67% of enrollments in basic education and 99% of high-school enrollment). Private schools also have to teach the national curriculum and are registered and monitored by the national system of supervision.

The inefficiency of such a highly centralized education system has long been recognized in Venezuela, and the country has attempted several reforms to decentralize administration. In practice, most of them have failed due to the lack of policy continuity when governments change or when Ministers of Education change. At the time of writing the Ministry of Education was attempting yet another decentralization reform, although the specific activities to be decentralized and their sequencing had not been specified. It is believed that decentralization efforts will now have a better chance since the National Planning Office is helping implement the 1990 decentralization law that transfers competencies to the governors of the states.

School construction is managed by a national agency, the Ministry of Urban Development (MINDUR). School repair and maintenance is managed by a foundation of the Ministry of Education (FEDE), and by a directorate of the Ministry of Education. It is expected that both of these units will be integrated.

Curriculum is designed at the national level. The Ministry of Education also approves textbooks in accordance with the National Curriculum.

The 3,541 national supervisors have been organized in 23 national zones in the country (one in each state). The national zones are mini ministries of education that act as intermediaries between the schools in the zone and the Ministry of Education. They have no policy-making powers and very limited administrative discretion. They collect statistics (the form of which are referred to the Ministry of Education in Caracas), nominate candidates for appointment as teachers, establish priorities for school repairs, and prepare lists of recommendations that are sent to the Ministry for study and approval.

Municipal and state schools are under the jurisdiction of the secretaries of education. There is one secretary of education in each state, and their departments have a similar structure to the national zones. State secretaries have more administrative powers and flexibility than the head supervisors in the national zones because they are accountable to and have direct access to the governor of the state and to the executive offices of the state that can contribute to educational activities. For instance, the state secretary of construction allocates resources for school repair and construction in consultation with the state secretary of education.

Universities are managed by the National University Council, which also distributes the budget for all public higher education institutions. This council is presided over by the Minister of Education. All decisions of the council are voted for; each president of the autonomous universities has a vote, while the experimental and private universities have a total of three votes. Representatives of faculty, students, Congress, and the National Council for Science and Development have six additional votes.

5. *Educational Finance*

The Venezuelan state has assigned an increasing proportion of resources to education. Education as a percentage of government expenditures increased from 18 percent in 1965 to 21 percent in 1988. Education expenditures began to decline in real terms in 1983. As a percentage of the gross national product, education increased from 3.3 percent in 1970 to 4.5 percent in 1988.

Central Government funds account for 80 percent of public education expenditure, while the rest comes from state and municipal governments and autonomous agencies. The Ministry of Education administers 58 percent of all public education expenditures, higher education institutions administer 28 percent, and autonomous agencies (e.g., the National Library and INCE) another 10 percent. MINDUR and FEDE spend 6 percent of public education expenditure on school construction.

About one-third of all expenditures of the Ministry of Education are for planning and administrative support, and the remaining two-thirds are allocated directly to specific education levels. In 1988 current expenditures were distributed as follows: 24 percent for preprimary and basic education, 5 percent for secondary education, and 36 percent for higher education. This underestimates expenditures for higher education as it excludes *Fundayacucho* and CONICIT (the National Council for Science and Development) which funds research and advanced studies.

Financing of state and municipal schools is through transfers from the central government to the state government. The Ministry of Education subsidizes private schools that enroll poor students.

Private financing of education takes the form of tuition fees paid to private schools which vary widely. Some private schools run by the Catholic Church (*Fe y Alegría*) cater to poor children in urban marginal areas and charge no fees (they are subsidized by the government). Elite private schools charge as much as US$300 a year. Public universities charge only nominal fees. Private universities charge varying amounts which can be as high as US$600 a year. Public universities generate only 3 percent of their income from nominal tuition fees and services. The rest is from government financing.

6. *Supplying Personnel for the Education System*

In 1990 there were 24,696 preschool teachers, 180,263 teachers in basic education, 32,178 high-school teachers, and 39,892 university teachers. There were 37,112 additional staff working for the Ministry of Education (including 6,973 staff and instructors at the National Center for Educational Cooperation, INCE).

The New Education Law of 1980 increased the requirements for teacher training to a university degree. As a result, all teacher-training institutions are in the process of revising their programs and have been integrated into an umbrella pedagogic university. In all, 8,845 teachers graduated from the public pedagogic institutes and 199 from the private pedagogic institute in 1990 (the graduates of the faculties of education in some of the public and private universities are also qualified as teachers), so there is no quantitative shortfall of teacher supply to occupy new openings.

The major challenge is in upgrading the skills of the existing teaching force to comply with the new programs designed to respond to the education reform. There are 35,637 teachers of basic education and 5,706 high-school teachers in public and private schools who are untrained. An additional difficulty resulting from the upgrading of training requirements to university degrees is that university programs seem better targeted to train high-school teachers, neglecting abilities to teach basic skills such as reading, writing, and numeracy. There is the impression, among Venezuelan educators, of a growing problem in that children in the early grades of basic education are not learning to read. Teacher-training programs seem disconnected from the realities faced by teachers in schools. For instance, a number of courses teach prospective teachers how to develop curriculum, while no practicing teacher has the freedom to develop his or her own curriculum.

The lack of appropriate resources and programs to retrain the teachers in the implementation of the new programs designed as part of the 1980 education reform has resulted in very little impact of that reform being made in actual practices in schools and classrooms.

In 1991 the Ministry of Education approved a new teaching statute aimed at professionalizing the teaching profession by making promotion opportunities more transparent and less dependent on political recommendations.

Teachers at universities are university graduates themselves, who have had little training in teaching methods and only rarely in graduate education.

7. Curriculum Development and Teaching Methodology

For basic and secondary education there is a national curriculum with three variants for each of these areas: urban schools, rural schools, and schools for indigenous populations. The same curriculum is covered, although examples and exercises used aim to represent the differences between each of these zones.

Curriculum is developed in the Ministry of Education in Caracas. There is a special center mandated with the design and improvement of the mathematics and science curriculum (CENAMEC). The Ministry of Education prepares copies of the curriculum that have to be followed by all teachers and also approves textbooks (produced by private publishers) after inspecting them to determine the degree to which they cover the national curriculum. Regions and schools have no discretion regarding curriculum contents, although teachers can select among a number of suggested alternative activities to implement specific curriculum objectives. There are no elective subjects in the curriculum. English is taught as a foreign language in basic and secondary education. Some private schools offer other languages as well. Humanities students learn French and Latin in high school.

The 1980 reform made substantial changes to the curriculum, attempted to modernize it and to produce more integration between subjects and levels. Because of the fiscal crisis experienced by the education system during the 1980s, however, the Ministry had no resources to supply the manuals with the new curriculum to the teachers. Some teachers were trained and some teacher guides had been distributed early in the 1980s, but funds soon ran out and these programs stopped. Many teachers have never even seen what the new curriculum guides look like. A major challenge for the 1990s will be to implement the curriculum reform of the 1980s. This will require the design of dissemination strategies to acquaint teachers with the new curriculum, the simplification and distribution of curriculum materials, and the setting up of inservice training courses.

8. The System of Examinations, Promotions, and Certifications

Student promotion from one year to the next is based on obtaining a pass grade at the end of the school year. The final grade is computed on the basis of student performance throughout the year as assessed by each individual teacher in periodic exams.

Until 1986, this final grade in secondary education accounted for 60 percent of the total final grade, the remaining 40 percent resulting from a final examination covering all subjects. The Ministry of Education eliminated this final exam in 1986.

One of the main problems of the system is the high percentage of students who repeat grades in primary education. Since there is no uniform criteria to evaluate students' performance, and since teachers receive limited training in students assessment, the chances of being promoted to the next grade depend not only on student ability, but also on the criteria used by the teacher to decide how students should be promoted.

Entrance to university is based on a score which combines the student's cumulative performance in high school and his or her achievement in an examination covering basic subjects. Some 40 percent of the applicants are admitted to university.

9. Educational Assessment, Evaluation, and Research

Aside from the university entrance examination there is no national or regional assessment of student performance. Evaluation and research are relatively infrequent, unimportant activities of the Ministry of Education, and have no impact on policy or on the initiation or termination of programs.

The Statistics Division of the Ministry of Education routinely collects statistics, but these are not processed to inform policy decisions. Indicators routinely collected are enrollment by age and grade at the beginning and end of year, number of students promoted and repeaters, and the number of teachers. Several ratios are computed from these basic indicators. There are no outcome indicators routinely collected.

10. Major Reforms in the 1980s and 1990s

The New Education Law of 1980 was a major attempt to reform the education system. As a result, basic education would be extended from 6 to 9 years, teacher training would be raised to university level, and curricula would be modernized and integrated.

The curriculum of the 9 years of basic education would be organized in 3 cycles of 3 years each. The first cycle (instrumental) would have highly interrelated units, emphasize language and mathematics, and be taught by the same teacher. The second cycle (consolidation) would present more differentiated subjects, and each grade would have at least 6 teachers. Values education would be emphasized. The last cycle (independence) would emphasize sciences and work education, and curriculum units would be highly differentiated with a teacher specialist for each subject.

In practice, however, the economic crisis affecting the education sector and the country, and the inefficiencies of a highly politicized bureaucracy account for the fact that the spirit of the law has had little effect in the schools and classrooms.

The Ministry for the Development of Human Intelligence was created in 1979 to launch a series of programs aimed at expanding human potential. Some of these programs were implemented through schools on an experimental basis where a new subject was created to teach creative thinking skills based on various psychological theories. When the government changed hands at the beginning of 1984 the Ministry for the Development of Human Intelligence was shut down. Some of the programs were transferred to other social ministries, but funding was sharply cut. Very few of those programs are still in existence.

Social programs aimed at school-age children have increased in recent years as a means to alleviate the hardship caused by the economic adjustment program. The percentage of the education budget for these programs increased from 5 percent in 1988 to 25 percent in 1991; they include providing funds for food and school supplies to children in Grades 1–6.

Other educational reforms have responded to the government's concern about the lack of connection between education and the world of work. To this end, the president of the country appointed a high-level commission for the reform of technical education and also promoted the reorganization of INCE discussed earlier. As a means to encourage industries to train their workers, they are allowed to deduct up to 60 percent of their taxes for training activities.

After a period of diminished resources, *Fundayacucho* has increased its activities in the last few years, this time emphasizing student loans over scholarships and studies in Venezuela whenever possible. A new scholarship program (*Galileo*) is aimed at the development of exceptional talent. In 1991, 415 outstanding high-school graduates had scholarships to pursue college studies in any institution and country of their choice.

The proposed decentralization of educational management may, in fact, be supported by the broader political reforms (e.g., decentralization law and nominal election of state governors), which could give it a better fate than the previous attempts to decentralize which failed.

The Venezuelan government is currently negotiating large education loans to improve basic education quality and the physical condition of schools.

11. Major Problems for the Year 2000

The major challenges facing the education system are the low levels of efficiency at basic levels: students are learning too little, too many of them end up repeating grades, and teachers are not ready to implement the changes proposed in the curriculum designed ten years ago. In addition, the education system is failing to provide equality of educational opportunity as it is the children from more favored socioeconomic backgrounds that are also learning more.

The expansion of the education system has increased the average number of years of schooling of the labor force from 4.6 in 1975 to 7.7 in 1989. However, the education system is not providing all graduates with the skills needed to obtain productive employment. This challenge is perceived as a serious constraint to Venezuela's attempts to open up the economy and increase the international competitiveness of its industries.

The need to focus on primary and secondary education is suggested by the salary incentives with which the market responds to relative scarcities at these levels. In 1989 the earnings of primary-school graduates was double those of workers without schooling, graduates of technical high schools earned 22 percent more than graduates from general high schools. The social rates of return were 18 percent for primary, 9 percent for secondary general, 11 percent for secondary technical, and 7 percent for higher education (Fizsbein and Psacharopoulos 1991).

As economic adjustment continues, the challenge for educational managers and policymakers will be how to do more with less. Morale of teachers at all levels is lowering as they face how in real terms declining education budgets affect their own salaries and their working environment (e.g., libraries and materials).

In addition, in a highly politicized system where there are no traditions of technically based policies, the problems associated with resource constraints are compounded. It will be a real challenge in this scenario for the education system to implement education reforms or to attempt to provide equal educational opportunity to children of all social backgrounds.

References

Fizsbein A, Psacharopoulos G 1991 *A Cost Benefit Analysis of Educational Investment in Venezuela, 1989*. World Bank, Human Resources Division, Technical Department, Latin America and the Caribbean Region, Washington, DC

OPSU-CENAMEC 1986 *Diagnóstico del nivel de conocimientos en biología, matemáticas, química, física, ciencias de la tierra, y uso instrumental del lenguaje*. Ministerio de Educación, Caracas

Ministerio de Educación *Ley Orgánica de Educación*. Ministerio de Educación, Caracas

Ministerio de Educación 1990 *Memoria y Cuenta. 1990*. Ministerio de Educación, Caracas

Ministerio de Educación 1991 *Evaluación del Nivel de Educación Básica—Primera Fase*. Ministerio de

Educación, Caracas

Schiefelbein E, Heikkinen S 1991 Venezuela. Access, repetition and efficiency in primary education. (manuscript) OREALC-UNESCO, Santiago

World Bank 1991a *Venezuela Poverty Study: From Generalized Subsidies to Targeted Programs*. Latin America and the Caribbean Regional Office, Washington, DC

Further Reading

Hanson M 1986 *Educational Reform and Administrative Development. The Cases of Colombia and Venezuela*. Hoover Institution Press, Stanford, California

Reimers F 1990 *The Feasibility of Introducing Loan Schemes to Finance Higher Education in Latin America. The Case of Venezuela*. World Bank, Latin American and the Caribbean Technical Department, Washington, DC

Reimers F 1991a *Educación para todos en América Latina en el siglo XXI*. Cinterplan, Caracas

Reimers F 1991b The impact of economic stabilization and adjustment on education in Latin America. *Comp. Educ. Rev.* 35(2): 319–53

Rodriguez N 1989 *La Educación Básica en Venezuela*. Academia Nacional de la Historia, Caracas

Villegas-Reimers E 1992 *An Analysis of Teacher Training in Venezuela*. World Bank, Washington, DC

World Bank 1990 *Staff Appraisal Report. Venezuela Social Development Project*. World Bank, Washington, DC

World Bank 1991b *World Development Report 1991*. Oxford University Press, New York

Vietnam

D. C. Bernard and Le Thac Can

1. General Background

Vietnam in the 1990s is richly endowed in human and natural resources but has been constrained by almost a century of colonialism and 30 years of devastating war. It is now poised to begin to realize its potential. Encompassing the eastern coastline of Southeast Asia, it houses the basins of two of Southeast Asia's greatest rivers—the Red and the Mekong. The deltas of these two rivers irrigate some of the richest rice-growing areas on earth. Vietnam is already one of the world's top rice exporters. The 331,700 square kilometers of the country also contain large reserves of coal, bauxite, gemstones, and a sizeable forest cover. Petroleum and natural gas have been found off the coast and it is generally believed that the largest reserves are yet to be found.

Approximately 80 percent of the 64.4 million population of Vietnam is rural (52.4 million). Most people live in the river delta areas and along the coast. The largest cities are Hanoi (1.2 million) in the north and Ho Chi Minh City (3.2 million), formerly Saigon, in the south . Ethnically, the majority of the population (87 percent) are members of the Kinh tribe. Minority groups comprise 8.4 million members of the population, the largest groups being the Tay, Thai, Hoa, Kho Me, Muong, and Nung. There are more than 50 separate ethnic groups scattered throughout the country, but most live in the mountainous areas of the central plateau and the northern part of the country. The population growth rate slowed to 2.1 percent in 1991. Infant mortality in 1989 was 54 per 1000 and average life expectancy was 62.7 years.

Vietnam has had a turbulent history. For 11 centuries Vietnam was under Chinese domination, but its people continually fought against Chinese rule. In the sixth century AD independence was established with the founding of the state of Van Xuan, only for it to be overcome again by the Chinese Sui and Tang empires. In 938 AD, Vietnam again gained independence which lasted through the Ly (1009–1225) and Tran (1226–1400) dynasties until the Ho dynasty of the fifteenth century. Confucianism began to develop during this period in Vietnam.

Control by the Ming dynasty of China was overcome in the fifteenth century. From the fifteenth to the eighteenth centuries, Vietnam was governed by the Le Dynasty (1428–1788). In 1802, with the help of the French, the Nguyen Dynasty was established, as was the European presence. In 1857 the French decided to occupy Vietnam, but encountered strong resistance and were not successful until 1887. From this date, the Vietnamese people did not cease their fight for national independence. Many years of struggle finally led to the liberation of the country from French and Japanese occupation and the foundation of the Democratic Republic of Vietnam in 1945. After the Second World War, Vietnam again encountered French, then American, intervention until 1975 when the North and South of Vietnam were reunified into the Socialist Republic of Vietnam.

Upon reunification in 1975, Vietnam's initial development model was based upon a command economy and a highly centralized administration. The primarily rural agrarian economy of the country was collectivized and the country suffered economic stagnation and isolation from world and regional markets. Problems were recognized early and a gradual loosening of central control began. In the period 1980–85, a family-based contract system was introduced in agriculture. Production decisions and planning were decentralized to the local and enterprise levels. The next five-year plan (1986–90) incorporated additional measures. Internal trade barriers were reduced, longer term leases to family households were introduced in agriculture, and farmers were allowed to sell their produce at market prices and not necessarily to the state or to cooperatives. The most decisive phase of reform was initiated in 1989 when the government set out to establish a state-managed market economy with a socialist orientation.

2. Politics and the Goals of the Education System

The primary political goal of the government is economic growth and development through transition to a market economy. It is intended that market liberalization will take place within the existing socialist political structure. This structure, however, unlike some socialist countries, contains a high amount of decentralization. The government wants to continue and even improve this decentralization while maintaining authority over policy. Government policies have led to tremendous economic progress through the decontrol of prices, monetization of the wage system, abolition of mandatory targets and subsidies for state enterprises, encouragement of foreign investment, establishment of an open banking structure, and stabilization of the currency (the Dong). A number of serious constraints have yet to be overcome. Inflation remains a problem as well as inaccessibility to international funding agencies due to a United States embargo.

Education and the economy are viewed as linked in Vietnam. In accord with its socialist perspective and traditional cultural roots, Vietnam has always placed high priority on education. This has resulted in a comparatively well-educated population. The literacy rate, for example, is 86 percent, and according to the 1989 National Census only 12.3 percent of the population of 10 years and older has never attended school. The emphasis on economic growth and development, however, has placed new and more challenging demands on the education system. Improving the external efficiency of the education system with an emphasis on production of skilled, qualified, and productive graduates will be a priority. More flexibility and responsiveness to job market needs will be necessary for the education system. Improved education of managers and entrepreneurs is urgently required.

At the same time, the gains of the past cannot be lost. Socialism in Vietnam has led to a high level of equity in the education system and an emphasis on serving the needs of the less fortunate members of society. Transition to a market economy will put pressure on this orientation. Care must be taken to ensure that the education system continues to meet the needs of the disadvantaged and minority members of society, while at the same time fulfilling demands for the transition from an agrarian to an industrial society and for the production of a more skilled labor force.

3. The Formal System of Education

3.1 Primary, Secondary, and Tertiary Education

General education in Vietnam begins at the age of 6 and consists of 5 years of primary school, 4 years of lower-secondary school, 3 years of upper-secondary school, and 2 to 8 years of tertiary or professional education (see Fig. 1).

Education is compulsory through to lower-secondary school, but dropout rates are high and the transition rate from primary to lower-secondary school is low. In the past, an attempt was made to link primary and lower-secondary education into 9 years of basic education. A number of combined primary and secondary schools was built. The objective to make lower-secondary education compulsory has been postponed and concentration shifted to ensuring at least a primary education is received by the school-age population.

In 1990, there were 8.6 million students and 252,000 teachers at the primary level with a student–teacher ratio of 34:1. There are 2.7 million lower-secondary school students and 151,000 teachers (18:1), and 1,880 schools that are lower-secondary only. Combined primary/lower-secondary schools amount to 7,942 of the total of approximately 14,300 schools; 4,634 schools are primary only. Double shifting in schools is common

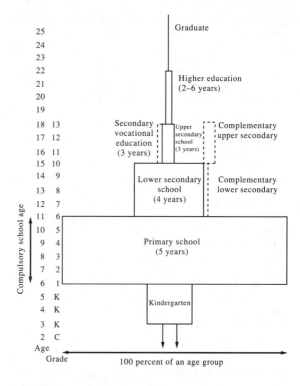

Figure 1
Vietnam: Structure of the formal education system

and triple shifting is not unknown. There are about 690,000 upper-secondary students, 41,000 teachers, and 1,078 schools. The student–teacher ratio is 17:1. Enrollments at both the lower-secondary and upper-secondary school levels have been decreasing. At the primary level, 448 students out of 1,000 complete 5 years of education. The average number of years for completion is 5.43 and the average dropout rate is 15 percent. Some 72 percent of the primary school students go on to lower-secondary and 30 percent of lower-secondary students move on to upper-secondary school. Dropout from lower-secondary school is 25 to 30 percent, and in upper-secondary it is 15 to 19 percent.

Higher education enrollments decreased from approximately 120,000 in 1980–81 to 86,000 full-time students in 1985–86, but then increased again to 93,000 full-time students in 1989–90. There is a total of 126,000 full-time, part-time, and inservice training students in 102 universities, colleges, junior colleges, and institutes. This represents 20 students per 10,000 inhabitants, which is relatively low compared with other Asian countries. Long- and short-term higher education courses offer diplomas in a range of programs from associate (3 years), bachelor's (4 to 5 years), and master's (2 years), to PhD (4 years).

3.2 Preschool Education

Vietnam has long considered preschool education to be important not only in the development of the child, but as preparation for further schooling. Although there is debate regarding the extent to which it should be emphasized, the 6,850 kindergartens throughout the country have a strong academic orientation. Approximately 1.6 million children aged 3 to 5 years are enrolled in kindergartens, a total that has remained relatively constant over a period of several years due to a lack of funds for expansion. There are also 13,000 creches providing early childhood care to children up to 3 years of age. The number of children in creches, however, has decreased substantially from 1.2 million children in 1985 to 550,000 in 1990. The bulk of the state budget for preschool education goes to kindergartens (5.3% for preschool, with 3.3% to kindergartens). It is considered that creches should be more reliant on parent and local community financing but this was less available in the early 1990s than in the 1980s.

There are 85,000 teachers in creches and 76,000 kindergarten teachers. The student–teacher ratios are 6.:15 and 21:1 respectively. The creches now serve only 13 percent of the age group and many are in more urban areas. Kindergartens serve 33.7 percent of the 3–5 age group.

3.3 Special Education

Approximately 2 percent of the population aged 9 to 13 years are handicapped. There are some special schools for handicapped children such as those in Hanoi and Ho Chi Minh City for blind and deaf/mute children, but their numbers are small and insufficient to meet the need.

3.4 Vocational, Technical, and Business Education

Vocational/technical training is provided at the secondary level in a variety of specialized and vocational secondary schools; through inservice training programs at regional centers, higher education institutions, and enterprises; and in professional programs at the secondary and tertiary level. A variety of government ministries and other agencies offer vocational and technical training. The system is highly complex and is in need of coordination.

Vocational education trade schools can be entered from lower-secondary school for a two-year program or upper-secondary school for a one and a half-year program. Enrollments decreased from 244,000 in 1980 to 100,000 in 1990. The number of schools also decreased from 313 in 1985 to 242 in 1990, of which 119 were centrally run and 123 locally administered. A total of seven areas of specialization are offered: agriculture/forestry/fisheries (20 schools), communication/postal (7 schools), construction (46 schools), machinery (49 schools), mechanics/electricity (71 schools), trade (30 schools), and other (19 schools).

Secondary professional education is offered in 270 institutions, of which 100 are centrally administered and 170 locally managed. A total of five major areas of specialization are offered: agriculture/forestry/fisheries (41), culture and art (75), economics (60), industry (38), and medicine/physical education/sport (47). A three-year course is offered to entrants from lower-secondary education and a two and a half-year course for upper-secondary graduates. Enrollment remained fairly steady in the 1980s and in 1990 it was 138,500 students.

Enrollments in short programs (not more than six months in duration) at approximately 200 vocational centers seem to have increased substantially since 1986, while inservice programs at higher education institutions have declined from 28,500 in 1986 to 53,600 in 1990. Enterprise-based inservice programs have also experienced decreasing enrollments.

3.5 Adult and Nonformal Education

Out-of-school programs for youths and adults can be categorized as literacy, complementary, inservice, vocational/technical, and social welfare education programs. They are administered by a number of ministries and agencies such as the Women's Union and Youth Union. Literacy programs received a special emphasis in the late 1970s and early 1980s and contributed to Vietnam's current high adult literacy rate of 86 percent. Enrollments in literacy programs declined in the late 1980s to about

189,000 in 1990 or about 35 percent of complementary education students. Overall complementary education enrollments have increased from approximately 399,000 in 1980 to 553,000 in 1990. Most of the increase in enrollments has come at the upper-secondary level which has risen from 184,000 in 1980 to 284,000 in 1990. Lower-secondary complementary education enrollments dropped during the 1980s.

Inservice and vocational/technical out-of-school programs have been mentioned above. Social welfare education includes a variety of programs with different objectives, levels of enrollment, and delivery methods. For example, education for health programs serve 1.6 million women with small children, while 276,000 women are enrolled in the education for improving incomes program. Some of these efforts receive assistance from nongovernmental organizations and international agencies, as well as funding through fees, work units, and communes. However, most of the financing comes from state sources.

4. Administrative and Supervisory Structure and Operation

Education policy is determined at the national level, but implementation and administration is the responsibility of the provincial level and below. Primary education is administered by the districts/communes and secondary education is the responsibility of the provincial education service. Some junior colleges are administered by the provinces, but higher education is, in general, the responsibility of the national level. As mentioned above, a variety of ministries and agencies oversee inservice, vocational/technical, and some social welfare education programs. Supervision, inspection, and funding of education are the joint responsibility of the central and local levels. The central government provides the funding for most salaries and scholarships, with the provinces, districts, and communes providing most other expenditures.

Before 1987 education activities at the national level were directed by four separate ministries. They were merged into two ministries in 1987: the Ministry of General Education and the Ministry of Higher, Technical, and Vocational Education. The two were combined into a single Ministry of Education and Training in 1990. The Ministry has 15 divisions, 2 national institutes, and a number of ministerial institutes. The divisions are: the office of the ministers, planning and finance, organization and personnel, international cooperation, science and technology, inspection, preschool education, general education, inservice and complementary education, technical and vocational education, higher education, graduate education, student affairs, teachers, and physical education and sport. The two national institutes are the National Institute for Educational Sciences and the National Institute for Higher and Professional Education. Provincial education services have five offices

for preschool education, general education, vocational education, complementary education, and finance and planning. District offices have two bureaus: inspection, and management and facilities.

5. Educational Finance

The allotment for education from the state budget increased from 6.9 percent in 1986 to 8.1 percent in 1989. This represents about 2 percent of the gross domestic product. Preprimary education received 5.3 percent, primary 50 percent, secondary 8.4 percent, and higher education 15 percent of the state education budget. The central government finances about 99 percent of the expenditures for higher and vocational education (with scholarships accounting for about one-fourth of this), but it finances only about 20 percent of the budget for general education. Overall, approximately 75 percent of the total budget for education is paid from local sources. The amount of local funding available for education varies from region to region.

Most teacher salaries are paid by the central government. Salaries of teachers and administrators comprise about 77 percent of the state education budget. Other expenditures for education are financed locally through local taxes, levies, contributions, or fees. Much of the support for construction, rehabilitation, and other important needs of the schools comes from the voluntary contribution of time and money by local communities.

The unit costs for primary education in Vietnamese Dong were about D38,000 (US$3.60) per student in the cities, D60,000 (US$5.60) in the mountainous areas, and D32,000 (US$3) for students in the midlands and plains areas. Lower-secondary unit costs averaged D50,000 (US$4.80) and upper-secondary about D85,000 (US$8). The standard for higher education was D1,000,000 (US$94), D700,000 (US$66) for secondary professional, and D720,000 (US$67.80) for vocational students. Primary schooling is free, but a Ministry survey in 1992 indicated that parents still pay about 26 percent of pupil costs. Parents are required to contribute a fee equivalent to about 1.5 kilograms of rice for lower-secondary and 3 kilograms for upper-secondary.

6. Supplying Personnel for the Education System

The state sector labor force is 3.7 million. Numbering 800,000, the teaching corps forms the largest professional group in this labor force. The government payroll covers 600,000 of these teachers. Teachers are highly respected in Vietnam, but their salaries are low. A primary teacher's salary averages 0.8 to 1.2 times the per capita gross national product compared to 2.6 in other Asian countries. Salaries have increased significantly but, due to inflation, the real purchasing value of the salary has declined. A university teacher's average salary in 1985 was equivalent to 87 kilograms of rice. By late 1991 it purchased only 34 kilograms. To complement their regular salaries many teachers hold outside jobs.

A large number of teachers at each level of the educational system are underqualified. Only 33 percent of the primary teachers have received the standard full-time preservice training. This was 48 percent of lower-secondary teachers and 90 percent of the upper-secondary teachers. The minimum qualification for primary teachers is three years' training after graduation from lower-secondary school or two years' after upper-secondary graduation. For lower-secondary teachers it is three years' after graduation from upper-secondary school.

Teacher training in Vietnam is decentralized, with 9 national teacher-training colleges, 8 national junior teacher-training colleges, and 30 provincial junior teacher-training colleges throughout the country. In 1989–90, these institutions enrolled 34,000 students or 36.7 percent of the total full-time higher education students. Inservice teacher-training programs are conducted using facilities of the provincial junior teacher-training colleges (often during the summer holidays), but the system is not extensive and is underfunded.

As in most developing countries, teachers are reluctant to take assignments in rural, remote, or disadvantaged areas. Not only are such postings uncomfortable, but they also may adversely affect promotion and career advancement prospects. Shortages of teachers are also encountered in certain subject specialities such as primary level music and art.

7. Curriculum Development and Teaching Methodology

In an effort to allow more children to complete primary education, Vietnam has established a three-tier curriculum: 160 weeks (full curriculum) for most students, 120 weeks for ethnic minority students, and 100 weeks for students in remote areas. The full primary curriculum requires five 165-day school years to complete. The standard number of hours for primary school is 24 per week, with the standard for lower-secondary being 26 to 28 hours per week and upper-secondary 30 to 32 hours per week.

The primary school curriculum consists of the following subjects: literature and Vietnamese language, mathematics, moral education, physical culture and military training, music, painting, and labor. Secondary school subjects include history, geography, civil education, foreign language, mathematics, literature and Vietnamese language, physics, chemistry, biology, technology, physical culture and military training, labor, and vocational training. The curriculum is revised on a 12-year cycle, one level per year. Teachers find

it difficult to cover the entire curriculum and tend to concentrate on language and mathematics which are the focus of the certifying examinations.

8. The System of Examinations, Promotions, and Certifications

Teachers make daily assessments of the performance of students, and term examinations help determine student scores. However, performance criteria are not standardized. Students desiring entry to higher education must sit for two tests, the secondary leaving examination and a university entrance examination. The relationship between the two tests is sometimes unclear.

Students are not automatically promoted. The repetition rates in primary school range from 4 to 14 percent. Many rural ethnic minority students are held back because of low ability in the language of instruction which is Kinh. Repetition in secondary school is approximately 12 percent. Some 72 percent of primary graduates go on to lower-secondary school, and 30 percent of lower-secondary school students move on to the upper-secondary level.

9. Educational Assessment, Evaluation, and Research

The decentralized nature of the education system and a lack of resources have constrained Vietnam's ability to develop a nationwide education assessment system. Therefore, no reliable measures for quality improvement or accountability are available. There is a unit for test development in the Department of General Education but the staff lacks resources and training.

Educational research is conducted by universities and the national institutes. The Institute for Educational Sciences and the Institute for Higher and Professional Education have produced over 500 research reports and papers since 1982. In 1991–92 a large-scale education and human resources sector review was conducted by the Ministry of Education and Training with the help of two institutes, UNESCO, and UNDP.

10. Major Reforms in the 1980s and 1990s

Since reunification in 1975, the Vietnamese government has emphasized literacy training and the expansion of basic and preschool education. A mass literacy program in the late 1970s and early 1980s raised the adult literacy rate to 86 percent by 1990.

At the same time, a major effort was made to encourage preschool education for children up to 5 years of age. Creches, which are run at the local levels by factories and communes to act as daycare centers as well as preschools, expanded quickly but enrollments declined toward the end of the 1980s. Kindergartens for older children expanded their enrollments and emphasized academic skills to prepare children for the first grade.

Prior to 1986, the government considered basic education to encompass primary education only. After this date, it was considered to include lower-secondary school as well. Many combined primary and secondary school facilities were established. This concept was adjusted in 1991 with acceptance of the goal of universal primary education. The combined schools have begun to break apart.

In 1990, there was a switch from a 4–3–3 system to a 5–4–3 system. An additional year (10th grade) was added to the lower-secondary schools located in the northern part of the country resulting in a large drop in upper-secondary enrollment for one year.

Administratively, much consolidation of education has taken place since 1975. The four ministries involved in the delivery of education services in the 1970s were reduced to one ministry covering all major subsectors of education. In 1992, there were several ministries providing out-of-school and vocational/technical training. Further consolidation may be expected in these areas.

11. Major Problems for the Year 2000

The strategy for socioeconomic stabilization and development for Vietnam up to the year 2000 defines the country's education and training objectives as: the development of human resources; the raising of the intellectual level of the people; the training of talented people; and the building of contingents of intellectuals, business-people, managers, technical experts, and highly skilled workers able to pave the way for the country to enter the twenty-first century. The education and training system is to be improved to achieve higher quality and practical efficiency, while the quantity of education and training will be expanded in keeping with the objectives of socioeconomic development.

In the area of general education, efforts will focus on implementation of the objectives of "education for all" and the universalization of primary education, the expansion of lower-secondary education, the eradication of illiteracy, the consolidation and improvement of preschool education, and the amelioration of adult education. Technical and vocational education will be developed through formal and nonformal delivery modes offering long- and short-term training courses organized by state-run schools as well as by collectives or private institutions.

The higher education system will be renovated through the determination of new objectives for education and training according to the socioeconomic and cultural environment, and by improvement of teaching content and methods. Higher education institutions and networks will be restructured to regroup and incorporate small segmented institutions into larger institutions with multidisciplinary programs of teaching and research at undergraduate and graduate levels. National and regional centers for scientific and cultural development will be established.

Development of education and training programs for minority ethnic groups and inhabitants of remote areas will be considered a national priority. Financial and other resources for education and training activities will be increased and diversified. Special attention will be paid to the improvement of the working conditions of teachers.

Bibliography

Communist Party of Vietnam 1991 *Seventh National Congress Documents*. Vietnam Foreign Languages Publishing House, Hanoi
Ministry of Education and Training 1991 *Education in Vietnam 1945–1991*. MOET, Hanoi
Ministry of Education and Training and UNESCO 1992 *The Socialist Republic of Vietnam: Education Sector Review and Human Resources Sector Analysis Draft Phase 1 Diagnosis Report*. MOET, Hanoi

Western Samoa

T. Esera

1. General Background

Western Samoa is a Pacific Island country situated between 13°–15° south and between 168°–75° west and is made up of a total of nine islands, four of which are inhabited. The total land area is 2,934 square kilometers within 120,000 square kilometers of ocean (economic zone). The total population is 165,000 (1992 census) and is Polynesian. The capital, Apia, on the island of Upolu, is the center of commerce. Its population is about 35,000.

Many Western Samoans live overseas, mostly in New Zealand, Australia, and America. The Rev. John Williams of the London Missionary Society arrived in Samoa in 1830 and established a mission station which was the beginning of pastors' schools in villages. Their main aim was to christianize Samoans. To do this, they educated Samoans to read their own language. An orthography of the Samoan language was soon developed and the Bible and other religious manuscripts were translated into Samoan.

The Malua Theological College was established in 1845 to train pastors. After training at the College, the pastors returned to the villages to set up schools which taught reading and writing in Samoan, as well as religious instruction, hymn singing, and basic arithmetic. The young men in these pastor schools were also taught some carpentry and agriculture. The pastors' wives trained the females in domestic skills.

In 1900, the Samoan islands were divided between two colonial powers. The western islands (Western Samoa) came under German rule and the eastern islands came under the United States. The German administration left the education of Samoans in the hands of the pastors but established a school, where German was the medium of instruction, for expatriates and half-caste or mixed-raced children in Apia.

With the advent of the First World War in 1914, New Zealand took over from Germany. At the end of the war, New Zealand was granted the administration of Western Samoa under a League of Nations mandate. In 1920, the New Zealand administration cooperated with the churches and shared the control and responsibility of village schools. Some pastors' schools were upgraded and turned into Grade 2 schools (Primer 1–Standard 2), modeled on the New Zealand school system. The Leifiifi School in Apia that took only expatriates and part-European students had classes up to Standard 6 and these students were able to sit the New Zealand Proficiency Examinations. Education policies were set and administered from New Zealand.

The continuing questioning of New Zealand's colonial rule in Samoa started with the Mau Movement during the 1920s and 1930s and this prompted the New Zealand authorities to reassess educational policy and practice in Western Samoa.

In 1945 the New Zealand Director General of Education, C. E. Beeby, took up with the New Zealand government, the educational direction required to produce future leaders of an independent Western Samoa. As a result of Beeby's mission, a scholarship scheme was borne under which young Samoans were sent to New Zealand for secondary schooling and higher education.

In 1953 the first secondary school, Samoa College was opened by Dr Beeby. It was "dedicated to the people of Western Samoa by the people of New Zealand in token of friendship and as a help toward self-government." In the mid-1960s, Avele College (in Upolu) and Vaipouli College (in Savaii) were upgraded to secondary schools to cater for those deserving further education but who had not gained entry to Samoa College. These school were almost entirely staffed by New Zealand teachers and were monitored by New Zealand school inspectors.

Western Samoa became an independent state on January 1st, 1962 but with a heritage of state apparatus bequeathed to them by the colonial administrations of Germany and New Zealand. By the end of the decade, dissatisfaction with the inherited educational structures was being expressed by educators, both local and foreign, and by politicians. Despite the large amount of resources used by the educational system, only about 80 percent of primary school-aged children were enrolled. The secondary schools could cope with only 50 percent of those graduating from primary schools; only 5 percent entered the last year of secondary schools and 1 percent entered tertiary education.

2. Politics and the Goals of the Education System

In June 1994, a law was enacted for compulsory education between the ages of 5 and 14 years. There had been no compulsory education prior to that date despite the fact that the majority of school-aged children did attend school.

The overall goal of education in Samoa is human resource development. In other words, "Education must focus on developing Samoans into productive cultural and social citizens who will be committed to developing the country's economy."

The following objectives are pursued in order to achieve the above general goal:

(a) to provide lifelong education from early childhood and preschool to adult education;

(b) to promote universalization of compulsory primary education;

(c) to provide a balanced program of education for the full development of children as individuals in a changing society, taking into account their abilities, interests, and attitudes;

(d) to create equal opportunities for learning from early primary to the end of secondary education;

(e) to broaden opportunities for senior and postsecondary education to provide an adequate resource pool for the workforce;

(f) to prepare the youth to cope with challenges and pressures of an increasingly modern society;

(g) to strengthen the organization and infrastructure of the educational support systems to achieve quality education.

3. The Formal System of Education

Both public (government) and private (nongovernment) institutions provide education for the popula-

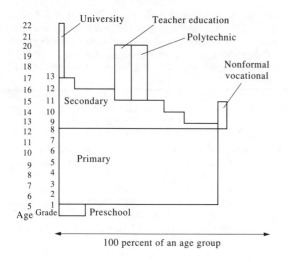

Figure 1
Western Samoa: Structure of the formal education system 1994

tion. Public schools range from primary schools to tertiary institutions. Private schools are mostly run by missions, for example, Catholic, Methodist, Latter Day Saints, Adventist, and Congregational Church. Nearly all schools are coeducational. Private schools also include preschools, primary schools, special education centers, and secondary schools. The structure of the formal education system is shown in Fig. 1; the enrollment is shown in Fig. 2.

3.1 Primary, Secondary, and Tertiary Education

The new reform structure implemented in 1987 removed one "year" from the previous nine-year primary school. Hence, primary school now consists of 8 grades, pupils entering school at the age of 5 years. In

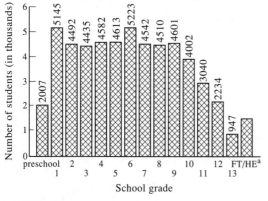

a FT/HE - Full-time higher education

Figure 2
Western Samoa: Enrollment figures 1992

1994, there were 141 government primary schools, 14 mission schools, and 2 private schools.

At the end of Grade 8 in the government primary school, students sit a national selection examination from which the top 12 percent of candidates go to the three government senior secondary colleges. The mission primary school pupils go to mission secondary schools. All Grade 8 candidates who do not go to the government senior college or mission schools enter the government junior secondary schools which run from Grade 9–Grade 11.

Secondary education consists of 5 years (Grades 9–13). Within the secondary level, there is a dual system. There are junior secondary schools and senior secondary schools. Junior secondary schools (JSS) run from Grade 9–Grade 11. Pupils who enroll at these schools are those not selected for senior secondary schools. There are 22 government junior secondary schools and 6 mission junior secondary schools. Senior secondary schools (SSS) run from Grade 9–Grade 13. There are 3 government senior secondary schools and 13 mission senior secondary schools. Out of a total of 206 schools, 169 are governmental and 37 nongovernmental.

There are three higher education institutions in the country: first, the Western Samoan Teachers' College (WSTC) (see Sect. 6); second, the Western Samoan Polytechnic (WSP); and third, the National University of Samoa (NUS). In 1993 the previous Western Samoa Technical Institute became the Western Samoa Polytechnic. In 1994, the total enrollment was 550 full-time students and some 400 part-time students. The major courses offered are as follows: secretarial studies; electrical; welding and fabrication; plumbing and gas fitting; carpentry, joinery, and construction; electronics; refrigeration; automotive; fitting and machinery. The courses have a duration of 2 years for a certificate and 3 years for a diploma. It is expected that the Polytechnic will also develop training programs at the trade certificate level given the strong demand for such courses and the national manpower needs for the types of skills embodied in such courses. For a summary of educational institutions from primary to tertiary, see Table 1.

The National University of Samoa opened in 1984. The main activity of the University has been the University Preparatory Year (UPY) course. In 1993 and 1994, about 30 percent of all students sitting the Pacific Senior Secondary Certificate (PSSC), once called the New Zealand University Entrance, were enrolled in the University Preparatory Year. The percentage of those enrolled who obtained certificates was just over 50 percent in the early 1990s. The other activities of the University were as follows: a BA degree course, mostly for primary and secondary school teachers studying on a part-time basis; part-time certificate and diploma courses in accounting; and a number of "public courses," such as introductory computing courses for which fees are paid. In 1991 and 1992, the number of persons enrolled in the BA courses were 107 and 232 respectively. In accounting, the enrollments were 232 and 250 in 1992 and 1993. However, the success rate in both the BA and accounting courses was low. There is also a Faculty of Nursing at the University which was once the School of Nursing under the jurisdiction of the Health Department.

3.2 Preschool Education

Preschooling in Western Samoa started in 1978 as a private venture for the 3- to 4-year olds. In 1988, there were 23 established preschools with enrollments ranging from 30 to 120 pupils each, totaling about 1,600 pupils in all. In 1994, 24 preschools were recorded with total preschool enrollments reaching just over 2,000 pupils.

Preschools in Western Samoa are administered mainly by village communities (though not attached to the village primary school) and church groups as well as some private operators. Government financial support was declared in 1989 to assist the administrative functions of preschools. The government financial grant is apportioned on a per capita basis. About 20 percent of the 3- to 4-year olds attend preschools.

3.3 Special Education

The Compulsory Act of 1992 makes it mandatory for the government to share some of the educational responsibility for special needs children. However, the Department of Education recognizes the valuable work being done collectively by parents and the community and in 1994 was able to propose that the government supplement and support what already exists.

In 1994 there were two special needs institutions: the "Fiamalamalama School," run by Western Samoa Society for the intellectually handicapped, with a school enrollment of around 40–45 pupils and 4 professional staff since 1989; and the "Loto Taumafai School," catering for the deaf, spastic, and cerebral palsied children, with a school enrollment of around 25–30 pupils and 4 professional and 2 assistant staff since 1988.

In the short term, the Education Department will fulfill its obligation under the Compulsory Education Act to special needs children by granting an agreed per capita grant to the existing institutions. Furthermore, the particular learning needs and residential locations of special needs children will be identified so that the establishment of special classes in existing "normal schools," where necessary, can be planned and implemented. In addition, the alternative for training special education teachers will be explored with the aim of producing and maintaining a body of skilled special needs educators in adequate numbers to staff all special education institutions.

3.4 Vocational, Technical, and Business Education

Applied "vocational" subjects are included in the junior secondary school level. This is justified by the relatively high participation in junior secondary education up to Grade 11. Vocational subjects in the junior secondary schools are: home economics, business studies, and industrial arts (technology).

Don Bosco Technical Institute (Catholic Institution) and Tuasivi Technical Institute (Congregational Church Institution) provide vocational education and training in basic trades for school leavers, mostly from the junior secondary level.

The bulk of vocational, technical, and business education is done by the Western Samoa Polytechnic. The majority of students are enrolled in trades skills culminating in the award of a certificate followed by about 18 months relevant industrial experience. There are also small enrollments in technician-level diploma programs. The Polytechnic also provides part-time courses for apprentices registered with the Apprenticeship Council under the Labor Department.

Table 1
Summary of educational institutions 1993

Level of schools	No. of schools	No. of teachers				No of students				Pupil–teacher ratio
		M	F	%F	Totals	M	F	%F	Total	
Primary	156	409	1,032	71.6	1,441	18,376	16,785	47.7	35,161	24
JSS	28	168	180	51.7	348	3,322	3,831	53.6	7,153	21
SSS	16	178	115	39.2	293	3,465	3,040	46.7	6,505	22
Vocational	2	32	1	3.0	33	199	33	14.2	232	7
Teacher education	1	13	15	53.6	28	129	169	56.7	298	11
Tertiary (polytechnic)	1	23	3	11.5	26	356	81	18.5	437	17
Special	2	1	9	90.0	10	25	40	61.5	65	10
Total	206	824	1,355	62.1	2,179	25,872	23,979	48.1	49,851	23

The National University of Samoa (NUS) also offers courses in business education qualifying with a diploma in accountancy or Certificate in Public Accounts (CPA).

3.5 Adult and Nonformal Education

Besides formal vocational training by the Polytechnic and others mentioned in Section 3.4 an increasing number of people who are not qualified for admission to the Polytechnic are being given basic skill training by various organizations such as the YMCA, the YWCA, the National Youth Council, and the Ministry of Youth, Sports, and Culture. The University of the South Pacific (USP) also has a center which offers a variety of courses of varying types and durations.

4. Adminstrative and Supervisory Structure and Operation

All government schools, the vocational schools, and the Teacher Training College are administered by a structure headed by the Director of Education. The Director is aided by the Deputy Director and four assistant directors along with professional staff located in the central office in the capital of Apia. The four assistant directors are in charge of curriculum and assessment, personnel and training, planning and research, and services. There are 22 school districts, each with an inspector who serves as a liaison officer for the central administration and as a professional consultant for the school principals and teachers. Decisions on policy are made by the Policy and Planning Committee which consists of the Director, Deputy Director, and the four assistant directors upon recommendations of subject committees.

Mission schools are administered under their own directors and church boards.

5. Educational Finance

The financing of public education is divided between villages and the central government. Traditionally, villages were responsible for providing their own school buildings and equipment and the government paid the salaries of teachers and administrators. However, in 1990, after one of the big hurricanes, the government funded repairing and rebuilding of primary schools with assistance from New Zealand and Australia. The New Zealand government rebuilt 19 junior secondary schools.

Mission schools have been supported by tuition fees and, in some cases, by grants from the local church organizations of churches overseas.

In 1993, the percentage of the state budget allocated to education was 15.80. This was the equivalent of 5.67 percent of the gross domestic product

(GDP). The education budget was subdivided into 52.68 percent for primary schooling, 17.90 percent for secondary schooling, 5.33 percent for the Polytechnic, 2.85 percent for the Teachers' College, and 6.32 for the National University of Samoa.

The unit costs were US$138 for primary education, US$151 for secondary education, and US$1,003 for higher education (see Table 2 for a breakdown of costs).

6. Supplying Personnel for the Education System

As previously mentioned there is only one teacher training college in Western Samoa and it is responsible to the Department of Education. There is a primary school division and a secondary school division; both courses last 3 years. To enter the primary school division, a student must have successfully completed either Grade 12 or Grade 13. To enter the secondary school division, a student must have successfully completed Grade 13.

The content and methodology of the courses were revised in 1991. More or less equal emphasis is given to subject matter knowledge and pedagogy. There is a minimum of 4 weeks supervised teaching practice per year. Each student must complete 42 credit hours over the three-year duration of their course.

Primary trainees cover all subjects in the primary curriculum while secondary trainees specialize in two major subject areas and one minor area.

In 1992 there was a total of 363 student teachers with 179 in the secondary division and 184 in the primary division. Secondary graduates supply the teaching force for the JSS and junior secondary classes in the senior secondary schools and primary graduates supply the teaching force for the primary school level. Teaching personnel for the senior secondary level are graduates from universities.

7. Curriculum Development and Teaching Methodology

Curriculum for primary and secondary school is a nationally prescribed one. There is a national curriculum

Table 2
Education budget 1994 (in WS tala)

Primary Schools	WS$9,871,518
Secondary Schools	WS$3,354,984
Teachers' College	WS$535,574
Central Administrations and General Services to Primary, Secondary, and Teachers' College	WS$2,791,652
Polytechnic	WS$1,000,000
National University	WS$1,184,409
Total	WS$18,738,137

unit within the Department of Education. This unit consists of curriculum writers, one for each of the subject areas. Each curriculum writer has a curriculum committee of eight to ten people (teachers) who discuss curriculum issues and assist in making recommendations to the Policy and Planning Committee of the Education Department that approves curriculum renewal, changes, and any other innovations.

The primary school curriculum covers Samoan studies, English, mathematics, science, social education, health and hygiene, expressive arts (crafts and music), and physical education. Much work has been done in curriculum development in recent years. Emphasis in the coming medium term, will be on consolidating existing curricula by improving the methods of delivery and strengthening literacy and numeracy skills.

The policy on the delivery of the curriculum is as follows:

Grades 1–2 — all teaching in Samoan
Grade 3 — teaching in Samoan with some oral English
Grades 4–6 — teaching in Samoan except English courses
Grades 7–8 — all teaching in English except Samoan studies

In the secondary school curriculum there is common core up to Grade 11. The subjects are Samoan studies, English, mathematics, science, social education, business studies, home economics and industrial arts (technology). In Grades 12 and 13, candidates must take Samoan and English and then choose at least four other subjects from a wide offering of options. Delivery of the secondary curriculum is all in English except for Samoan studies.

Provision is made for the regular review of curriculum coverage and sequence across all subject areas in the long term.

8. The System of Examinations, Promotions, and Certifications

Primary students are automatically promoted between levels until the last year of primary education (Grade 8) when they sit a selection of examinations for entry into the secondary school system. As a result of the Grade 8 examination, the most academically capable students are selected into the government's three senior secondary schools (Grades 9–13). Those who do not succeed in having a Grade 9 place in the government senior secondary schools or private/mission schools go to the government's 22 junior secondary schools (Grades 9–11). Pupils who have sat the Grade 8 examination receive a certificate indicating that they have completed 8 years of primary education.

In secondary schools, there is automatic promotion from Grade 9 until Grade 11 when there is a national examination at that level. The most academically able students, as assessed by the results of this national examination, are selected into Grade 12 in the senior secondary schools. Again, a certificate is issued to mark the end of 3 years of secondary schooling.

At Grade 12, there is a Western Samoa school certificate examination for selection into Grade 13, which is the final year of secondary education. The Western Samoa school certificate is the minimum entry qualification into the primary division of the Teachers' College and also into the Polytechnic.

In Grade 13, the Western Samoa students sit a regional examination called the Pacific Senior Secondary Certificate (PSSC) which selects candidates into the National University of Samoa (NUS) to do the University Preparatory Year course. The PSSC qualification is the entry requirement into the secondary division of the Teachers' College and also the Polytechnic.

9. Educational Assessment, Evaluation, and Research

Other than the Grade 8 national examination, there has been no mechanism in place to monitor national standards in primary schools.

At the end of 1993 the Examination Unit and the curriculum writers developed Samoan Primary Education Literacy Level (SPELL) tests which were put to the trial in June, 1994. There are two tests: SPELL 1, given in Grade 4, and SPELL 2, given in Grade 6. The results should give a better picture of how pupils are performing in Western Samoa.

National standardized tests are also being developed. In 1994, the Department of Education installed a research component in the Examination Unit which is focusing on assessment and monitoring.

10. Major Reforms in the 1980s and 1990s

In 1987 the eight-year primary level was implemented, effectively removing one year from the "old nine-year primary education." In 1985 the present junior secondary school curriculum was written and was, in 1994, under review. In 1989, the Western Samoa School Certificate was implemented for the first time, signaling the move away from complete dependence on New Zealand curriculum.

In 1990 the amalgamation took place of the Primary Teachers' College with the Secondary Teachers' College to form the Western Samoa Teachers' College.

In 1994 the Department of Education was working on strengthening the capacity of the secondary level so that in the long term (7–10 years), the secondary level will be one stream rather than the two JSS and SSS levels previously held by Western Samoa.

11. Major Problems for the Year 2000

Despite the economic constraints due to the major setbacks in 1990 and 1991 when two cyclones caused massive devastation, the following vision for the year 2000 will be pursued wherever and whenever possible:

(a) Equity: this requires that the education system will treat all individuals fairly and justly in the provision of educational opportunity. As far as it is practicable, policies and practices which give advantage to some social groups and disadvantage to others will be avoided. Those which address existing inequalities in educational access, treatment, and outcome between social groups will be promoted.

(b) Quality: educational quality is exemplified by high standards of academic achievement, cultural understanding, and social behavior. It results from a complex interplay of professional and technical factors, and social and cultural practices. Policies promoting all of these will be put in place. Their focus will be on the learning institution and specifically, day-to-day classroom practices.

(c) Relevance: a relevant education is one that is meaningful, recognized, applicable, and useful to one's life. It should enhance individual well-being, community well-being and ultimately national development, including the cultural, humanistic, and spiritual aspects of development. All policy decisions will address what is relevant to the individual learner, to the community, and to the nation.

(d) Efficiency: an efficient education system demonstrates effective management practices and provides evidence of the optimum use of resources (i.e., human, financial, and material) at all levels of the system. The prompt delivery of services, unhampered communication flows, and coordinated decision-making are all essential to the operation of an efficient system. Policies which establish the mechanisms for these practices, which monitor their effectiveness, and which account for the equitable use of resources will be a priority.

Bibliography

Back K 1993 *A Development Plan for the National University of Samoa*. Canberra Apia
Coxon E Report to the Churchill Trust on "Senior Secondary Education in the Pacific".
Rees T 1991 The First Decade 1980–90. South Pacific Board for Educational Assessment, Suva
Singh S 1988 *Development of Western Samoa Technical Institue (now Polytechnic)*
Government of Western Samoa 1993 Central Bank Bulletin. Government of Western Samoa, Apia
Department of Education 1986–93 *Annual Reports*. Government of Western Samoa, Apia
Department of Statistics 1991 *Census of Population and Housing*. Government of Western Samoa, Apia
Department of Statistics 1992 *Annual Report* and *Annual Statistical Abstract*. Government of Western Samoa, Apia
Government of Western Samoa 1992–94 *Seventh Development Plan*. Government of Western Samoa, Apia
Government of Western Samoa 1992 *Human Resource Plan*. Public Service Commission, Apia
World Bank 1992 Western Samoa—Rebuilding the education system. *Education Sector Review*. World Bank, Washington, DC

Yemen

M. M. Mottahar

1. General Background

The Republic of Yemen (ROY) is located on the southwestern part of the Arabian Peninsula, bordered to the north by Saudi Arabia and the Empty Quarter, to the south by the Gulf of Aden and the Arabian Sea, to the west by the Red Sea, and to the east by the Sultanate of Oman. The total land mass area (excluding the Empty Quarter) is 550,000 square kilometers and consists largely of plains especially on the coastal side, the fertile central highlands with inland valleys and plains, and the semidesert areas which lie to the east of the country.

The Republic of Yemen is a result of the reunification of the Yemen Arab Republic (YAR) and the People's Democratic Republic of Yemen (PDRY) in May 1990. Yemen was a united country until the mid eighteenth century, when Hadramout and, later, Lahj districts in the south, declared independence from the central government in Sana'a. The partition was further deepened by the British occupation of Aden in 1839. Later the British expanded their control to include all south Yemen which remained under British occupation until its Independence in November 1967.

The north was also exposed to foreign domination when in 1872 it fell under Turkish rule. The struggle against the Turks started in the late 1890s and continued until the North won Independence in 1918. During the rule of Imam Yahia (1904–48) and his son Ahmed (1948–62), North Yemen was largely isolated from foreign influences. It also lacked modern economic and education systems. The isolation ended with the outbreak of the 26th September Revolution in 1962 that ended the Hamidudin Dynasty (1891–1962) and proclaimed the Yemen Arab Republic. However, the YAR faced great difficulties in building modern economic and civil infrastructures including the introduction and expansion of modern schooling. These efforts were adversely affected by the outburst of the civil war (1962–69).

Before reunification the PDRY adopted scientific socialism in planning its social and economic development, whereas the YAR adopted the free-enterprise system. The two opposing political systems were at odds with each other and on at least two occasions in the 1970s they engaged in armed confrontation with each other. The failure of each system to absorb the other, scarce resources and formidable economic difficulties in the 1980s, and the collapse of the Eastern Block all played critical roles in achieving the unity of Yemen in May 1990.

The total population in 1990 was about 11.3 million and 12.5 million in 1991 due to the high annual growth rate of 3.1 percent and the return of about eight hundred thousand to one million Yemeni emigrants following the Gulf Crisis and the war in the Horn of Africa. This situation created a large burden on the country's limited resources and put considerable pressures on social services and particularly on education.

Less than one-fourth of the total population (21.4%) dwell in urban areas, the rest living in rural areas (78.6%). The bulk of the population lives in the low and central highlands and in the inland and coastal plains, whereas only a minority of the population live in the eastern semidesert plains. The population, however, is widely scattered in small settlements (more than 60,000) and the population density is 21 per square kilometer. This phenomenon puts considerable pressure on education to provide a large number of school buildings for small population settlements and for more teachers and administrative personnel. Population data show the preponderance of young people in the population. For example, 52.5 percent are under the age of 14, 44.2 percent are in the age group 15–64 years, and only 3.3 percent of the population are in the age group 65 years and over. Thus, Yemen's educational system has to deal with a large number of those eligible to enter school and this has consequences for the limited resources available to prepare and provide teachers, administrators, supervisors, educational materials, and school buildings.

The implications for the education system of the high annual growth rate, the widely scattered population settlements, the dominance of rural inhabitants, and the youthful age structure of the population are likely to continue in the 1990s. The outcome of this will be evident in continuous high growth of student enrollment at the expense of quality due to scarcity of human and financial resources and the need for the educational system to compete with other social services.

The people of Yemen are largely homogenous. They speak the Arabic language and believe in the faith of Islam. To a large extent Yemen is a traditional, largely rural society characterized by a strong tribal system, particularly in the northern and eastern parts of the country. Tribal rivalries and values, in addition to other social factors, have hampered, to some extent, the expansion of female education. They have also compelled authorities to build separate schools in nearby villages to avoid tribal conflicts, which have further aggravated the demand for educational personnel and school buildings.

Although various economic and social plans were implemented in both YAR and PDRY in the 1970s and 1980s, the economy remains traditional. Agriculture accounts for 62.9 percent of employment, construction 7.5 percent, trade and hotels 4 percent, transportation and communication 4 percent, manufacturing 3.9 percent, and public and private sectors 12.9 percent. The educational level of the labor force in Yemen is low. Only 3.8 percent of the labor force has secondary education and above. Among the 2.6 million workers in 1990, professional and technical workers represented only 3.1 percent, administrative 0.4 percent, clerical 3 percent, sales 4.9 percent, service 6.7 percent, agriculture 64.1 percent, production 16.3 percent, and others 1.5 percent.

The fact that Yemen is a poor country creates additional difficulty for the educational sector. There has been low economic growth since 1985. Agriculture's share of GDP decreased from 28.2 percent in 1985, in both YAR and PDRY, to 23.8 percent in 1989. Manufacturing and services, with shares of 13.7 percent and 56.7 percent respectively, remained almost unchanged. The only increase was in mining and quarrying in the former YAR which increased from 0.7 percent to 5.8 percent as a result of oil production. Moreover, a high budget deficit, unemployment, inflation, external debts, and low domestic saving and investment added further complications.

Stagnation and low productivity of the economy led to more awareness, on the part of the government, regarding the central importance of human resources and development. The government intends to increase its investment in education and training in general, with special emphasis on expanding the coverage of basic and secondary education, improving its quality, and linking it with the country's needs and priorities.

2. Politics and the Goals of the Education System

The new educational goals of the ROY represent a political compromise between the People's General

Congress that was the ruling party in the former YAR and the Yemeni Socialist Party that controlled the former PDRY. The new goals are included in the new Law of Education that was passed by parliament in summer 1992.

The Education Law specified the general goals of education in Yemen as well as the goals of each type and level of education. The Law emphasized the importance of Islamic principles and values in shaping the educational system's philosophy and goals. It also stressed the importance of providing students with comprehensive and integrated education, the need to recognize and satisfy students' needs and abilities, and in the meantime, working toward satisfying the country's needs for qualified human resources.

The Law adopted the 9-3 structure for basic and secondary education. Basic education intends to ingrain Islamic principles and values, promoting an understanding of the environment, and acquiring basic learning skills, especially in the Arabic language, English, and social and scientific knowledge. Secondary education intends to further students' skills and knowledge base and qualify them for entering the labor market or pursuing higher studies.

3. The Formal System of Education

Figure 1 outlines the structure of the formal education system. Key statistics on enrollments and resources in the major education sectors are provided in Table 1.

In 1993, there were two educational ladders: 6-3-3 in the northern governorates and 8-4 in the southern governorates, the difference reflecting the past parti-

Table 1
Enrollment and resources in formal education, Yemen 1990–91

	Basic education	Secondary education	Higher education
Enrollment			
Number of students	2,200,963	118,372	43,169
% of age groups			
6–15 years	59.4	—	—
16–18 years	—	13.3	—
19–22 years	—	—	5.9
Number of Schools	11,254	724	
Student–teacher ratio	37:1	23:1	
Resources			
Educational expenditure^a as % of:			
State budget (all levels)	17.2		
GNP	7.9		
GDP	7.7		

a of 1990 budget expenditure

tion of Yemen. Educational policy in the former YAR sought to achieve compulsory education for the 6–11 age group (primary school), and for the 7–14 age group (unity schools) in the former PDRY. Both systems of education have contributed significantly to increasing enrollment since the 1960s, but have failed to achieve compulsory education.

3.1 Primary, Secondary, and Tertiary Education

The new educational system, which is being partially implemented after unification, adopted a new ladder (9-3). It seeks to expand compulsory education to nine years (6–15 age group), followed by three years of secondary education (16–18 age group). Basic education in Yemen is compulsory and it covers the ages from 6–7 to 15. In 1991, 2.08 million students were registered in basic education, of whom 24.9 percent were females. The total enrollment represents 59.4 percent of the school age group 6–15, in which males represent 85.5 percent of the male age group, while females represent only 30.9 percent of the female age group. The low rate of female participation is due to the serious shortage of girls schools, especially in rural areas, and to the high dropout rate of females in the early years of schooling. It is to be noted that the 1991 enrollment in basic education represents an outstanding growth from 234,313 students in 1970–71, and 680,259 students in 1980–81, of whom females represented 15.5 percent and 18.9 percent respectively.

Secondary education, which accepts graduates of basic schools, lasts for three years. Upon successful completion of the first year of secondary education, students are expected to enroll either in the literary section or the scientific section for two more years. In 1991 enrollment reached 118,372, of whom only 15.9 percent were females. The figure represented 13.3 percent of the 16–18 age group, of whom the male age group represents 27.8 percent and the female age group is only 5.8 percent. These figures represent a tremendous increase from 3,846 in 1970–71 to 21,083 in 1980–81, in which females represent 14.4 percent and 24 percent respectively. The small number of students in secondary education is due to the high dropout rate in the first six grades of basic education reaching approximately 40 percent. Moreover, dropouts are more common among females than males because of social traditions of early marriages. The dropout rate, however, is lower in secondary education. Those who are able to reach secondary education are more likely to successfully graduate from secondary schools.

Higher education comprises community colleges, specialist postsecondary institutes, and university education. University education is provided by the University of Sana'a and the University of Aden. Established in the academic year 1970–71, the University of Sana'a offers a variety of specializations in eight colleges: Sharia'h (Islamic Law) and Law, Education,

Science, Arts, Commerce and Economics, Agriculture, Engineering, Medicine and Health Sciences. The University has also established colleges of education in six cities. Enrollment has increased dramatically since its establishment from 64 students in 1971 to 4,519 in 1981. The number increased to 37,754 in 1991. Aden University, which was established in 1970, offers university studies in the colleges of Economics, Law, Medicine, Agriculture, and the college of Education which has branches in three cities. Enrollment at Aden University rose from 103 in 1971 to 3,731 in 1981, and reached only 4,415 in 1991. The low enrollment at Aden University is due to its selective admission policy, unlike Sana'a University's open admission policy.

Community colleges are burgeoning structures in Yemen and are attached to the colleges of education in both Sana'a and Aden Universities. The number of community colleges is expected to increase

in enrollment and further diversification of their programs to meet society's need for middle-level professionals. Postsecondary institutes offer specialized courses for two years in the fields of public administration and accounting, health, irrigation engineering, and communication. Enrollment at these institutions, however, does not exceed 1,000 students.

Total higher education, which reached 43,169 in 1991 (17.2% females), is still modest, but it represents a tremendous growth in comparison to the 167 students in 1970–71. It represents 5.9 percent of the 19–22 age group (9.8% of the male and only 2% of the female age groups). The low representation of females in higher education enrollment is due to the small percentage of them who overcome social and economic constraints.

Enrollment is expected to continue to rise due to the increasing number of students who successfully complete secondary education. To meet such rising de-

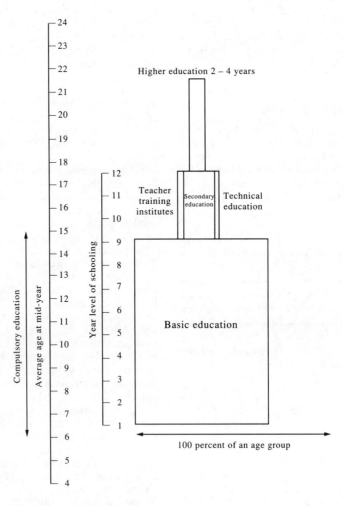

Figure 1
Yemen: Structure of the formal education system 1990–91

mand the Ministry of Higher Education and Scientific Research is planning to open two new universities in Taiz and Hadramout. Moreover, the Ministry intends to expand the community college system and diversify their programs in order to meet the country's critical needs for middle level technicians and to relieve the student demand on universities.

3.2 Preschool Education

A small number of kindergarten children (10,067) between the ages 4 to 5 years are enrolled in governmental and private preschool centers that exist in the main cities, particularly Sana'a, Aden, Taiz, and Hodeidah. Education policies intend to develop this type of education and relate it to the basic education stage. Moreover, since 1990 there has been a growing interest from the private sector in developing and proliferating preschool education, which may be expanded to include large numbers of the 4–5 years age group. The development of this stage is likely to be confined largely to urban areas which contain a large percentage of working mothers requiring this service. Parents in governmental preschool centers pay only a small portion of the cost, whereas in private centers they pay the full fees.

3.3 Special Education

There are no special education programs for those who enter basic and secondary education, but there are some special programs offered to a few handicapped students (less than 5,000 students) in the major cities. Tutoring is provided in separate locations such as centers for the blind, social guidance (delinquents), disabled, and the mentally retarded. All programs of special education are organized and supervised by the Ministry of Social Security and Social Affairs (MSSA) and funded by the Government. The slow development of special education is due to the lack of governmental policy and financial resources. The 1990s are expected to witness a growth in enrollment as a result of a new governmental policy to expand special education opportunities and to foster private sector interest in this area.

3.4 Vocational, Technical, and Business Education

Two different Vocational and Technical Education (VTE) systems existed in Yemen before reunification. The VTE system in the former YAR was supervised by the Ministry of Education, except for health education. Vocational training lasted for two years after the primary stage, whereas technical, commercial, agricultural, health, and veterinary education lasted for three years. After the preparatory stage, VTE in the former PDRY was supervised by the Ministries of Education, Labor, and Vocational Training. Entry to the VTE system starts after the Unification School (1–8 age group) and continues for 2–5 years.

The new public education policy intends to unify the entry level and diversify the system to meet public and private sector needs. Two years of vocational training start after the completion of basic education to qualify students to enter the labor market. Technical education graduates will, upon completion of three years of study, either enter the labor market or pursue higher study in their field of specialization. Governance of the new VTE system will be the responsibility of the MOE and the Ministry of Labor and Vocational Training (MOLVT). The development of the VTE system is hampered by the lack of financial resources and the lack of good linkage with public and private sectors.

3.5 Adult and Nonformal Education

Adult and nonformal education is limited to literacy and skill training programs organized mainly by the Ministry of Education through the Illiteracy and Adult Education Organization. Nonformal education programs are directed mainly toward illiterate males and females in urban and rural areas as well as those who dropped out of formal education before achieving literacy levels. In the early 1980s, enrollment began to increase reaching 110,000 in 1984. It decreased in 1988 to 75,677 but rose again to 122,500 in 1991. Female enrollment increased from 20 percent in 1984 to 50 percent in 1991. The majority (67%) of enrollment is registered in rural areas, in comparison to only 33 percent in urban areas.

Illiteracy and nonformal education is provided mainly through Literacy Training Centers and District Training Centers (DTCs). Literacy training is organized into two stages of two years each. The first stage aims at enabling learners to achieve fourth grade literacy level whereas the second stage seeks to advance the learner to the sixth grade level in basic education. District Training Center programs combine literacy education skills and training in the areas of electricity, mechanics, carpentry, and others.

The shortage of provision of adult education and job training remains of great concern, especially in a country that has a 55 percent illiteracy rate. Moreover, 67 percent of the labor force is illiterate and only 3.8 percent has secondary education or above. The number of illiteracy and adult education programs decreased at the end of the 1980s. Only 6.8 percent of the illiterate labor force were served in 1991, indicating low budgetary allocations. The MOE efforts combined with the prospective role of the new Ministry of Labor and Vocational Training as well as other ministries are expected to expand and diversify adult education programs in the 1990s.

4. Administrative and Supervisory Structure and Operation

Education is one of the major responsibilities of the state. The reunification of Yemen in 1990 has resulted in major changes in the governance of education. The educational system is currently administered by a number of ministries. The MOE is responsible for the administration of basic and secondary education. It is also responsible for enforcing teacher training, and improving the quality of teachers, supervisors, school administrators, and all educational leaders. At the central level, the MOE holds the major responsibilities, particularly of policy-making, planning, curricula development, teacher preparation, and distribution of human and financial resources. Educational authorities in the governorates supervise the implementation of policy in their regions, whereas schools seek to implement educational objectives, policies, and curricula. The participation of lower levels in policy-making and planning is not only limited, but almost nonexistent. Administration of nonformal education for youth and adults is shared between the MOE and the MOLVT. The MOLVT has been assigned the responsibility for nonformal education for preparing skilled and semi-skilled labor.

The establishment of the Ministry of Higher Education and Scientific Research in 1990 is expected to limit the degree of autonomy enjoyed by the two universities and affiliated community colleges. The ministry is expected to exercise more influence in planning and guiding the long-range growth of higher education and setting up admission policies, staff appraisal, and research activities. More control can also be expected in the field of developing and expanding the community colleges.

General government policy is for gradual decentralization. The MOE policy aims at delegating more responsibilities to the governorate and institutional level in matters related to supervision and evaluation. The private sector is also encouraged to join in the educational development either by supporting the establishment of public school buildings or establishing and running private schools of various types, including vocational, technical, and higher education institutions.

5. Educational Finance

The total financial allocation for education in 1990 was 6,190 million Yemeni Rials, which represented 17.2 percent of the state budget. This figure represents a big increase from 5.5 percent in 1970 to 12.7 percent in 1980, and from 14.2 percent in 1971 to 16.9 percent in 1980, for the YAR and PDRY respectively. The proportion of the GNP allocated to education increased from 6.2 percent in 1980 in both YAR and PDRY to 7.9 percent in 1990 in the unified Yemen. This growth reflects an increase in enrollment as well as an increase in teachers' and administrators' salaries.

The bulk of education expenditure in Yemen is provided by the government. The educational budget of 1990 was distributed approximately as follows:

65 percent for basic education, 12 percent for secondary education, 8 percent for teacher training, 2 percent for vocational and technical education, and 13 percent for higher education. Education is almost free from first grade to university. Students pay only nominal fees for registration, examinations, textbooks, and examination certificates. The total revenues from educational services represent only 1.5 percent of the 1990 budget. Moreover, the state provides private schools with supplementary resources to cover part of their teachers' salaries as part of a deliberate policy encouraging the private sector to invest in building and running schools. Enrollment and expenditure figures in private schools are not available but they are marginal. Their share of student enrollment and expenditure is expected to rise in the 1990s due to the burgeoning interest of the private sector which is fueled by the decreasing quality of public education.

Financial aid provided by Arab and foreign countries as well as from the World Bank in the form of loans and grants played an important role in enhancing educational development during the 1970s and the 1980s. Financial aid, however, began to decrease in the 1980s. Grants and loans provided by Arab countries, especially Kuwait, which was the major financier of Sana'a University, stopped completely after the Gulf Crisis in 1990.

6. Supplying Personnel for the Education System

The educational system employed 60,282 teachers in 1991, of which 55,011 were in basic education and 5,271 in secondary education. Yemeni teachers in basic education represent 53.7 percent and expatriate teachers 46.2 percent of all teachers. Yemeni teachers at the secondary stage represent 46.1 percent and non-Yemeni teachers represent 53.8 percent. The employment of 28,283 expatriate teachers indicates a shortage of qualified Yemeni teachers that should be attracted to and retained in the teaching profession. This shortage is due to the lack of sufficient financial incentives and inadequate school conditions, particularly in rural areas.

Teacher training occurs at various levels. Teachers of the first six grades of basic education are prepared by the secondary teacher-training institutes (STTI) as well as by the teachers' community colleges affiliated with colleges of education. Teachers for Grades 7–9 of basic education and secondary education receive a four-year training program at the colleges of education. The MOE intends to attract qualified students to the teaching profession and to improve the quality of teachers, curricula, teaching methods, and practice teaching of the STTIs, and the expansion of the two-year postsecondary teacher-training system.

Generally, inservice training receives little attention and support. It is optional and participants do not receive financial incentives to attend workshops and seminars to upgrade their knowledge and skills. Nevertheless, in 1990 the MOE established a training and qualifying sector chaired by a deputy minister in order to supervise and organize the preservice and inservice training of teachers as well as educational leaders, and especially school administrators. The training and qualifying sector is expected to develop and operate an effective inservice training program in the 1990s.

7. Curriculum Development and Teaching Methodology

School curriculum is unified across the country. At the basic education stage, particularly Grades 1–6, students are exposed to a general curriculum that covers the Arabic language, Islamic education, mathematics, social studies, science, and art education. Breadth and depth of studies are greater in Grades 7–9 of basic education. In addition to the above subjects, the program includes English language, which is compulsory, civics, geography, history, and physical education. All subjects in Grades 1–4 are taught by one teacher, whereas in Grades 5–9 subjects are taught by subject specialist teachers. Grade 10 remains common to all students who continue to study all previous subjects, but with more emphasis on physics, chemistry, and biology. Upon entering Grades 11–12 students can opt for either the literary or scientific sections. These sections have subjects in common: Islamic education, Arabic, English, arts, and physical education. The literary section includes history, geography, philosophy, logic, psychology, society and sociology, whereas the scientific section covers in greater depth mathematics, physics, chemistry, and biology. The majority of students select the scientific section because it offers wider options in postsecondary institutions in Yemen and abroad.

Prior to reunification, the curriculum in YAR was under the jurisdiction of the Department of Curricula, Books, and Educational Aids in the MOE, whereas in PDRY it was under the jurisdiction of the Educational Research Center. Following unification, curriculum development and the writing of learning materials became the responsibility of the Educational Research and Development Center affiliated to the MOE.

Key issues in the curriculum include the need to design and develop new curricula and textbooks that reflect the educational goals and aspirations of the Yemen people, the need for effective preparation of Yemeni youth to enter the labor market or to pursue higher education, and the establishment of systematic and practical methods to ensure continuous curriculum development.

8. The System of Examinations, Promotions, and Certifications

Students in Grades 1 and 2 are automatically promoted. Internal school examinations are used to promote students from one grade to the next. Within a cycle of education there are national examinations at the end of the primary, unity, preparatory, and secondary cycles. The new system of education which is being implemented requires external examinations only after nine years of basic and three years of secondary education. Upon passing the national examinations students receive a certificate of success from the MOE.

Students' success in internal school examinations is based on cumulative monthly examinations which receive a weight of 40 percent, with the other 60 percent based on the end of year examination. The national examinations, however, are common. In-school and national examinations are mainly of the essay type but they lack reliability and validity. The need to improve the examination system at the school, regional, and national levels has been recognized, but is hampered by the lack of funds to support the training of teachers in the testing and measurement of achievement.

9. Educational Assessment, Evaluation, and Research

Examinations are regarded by the MOE as an important means of measuring student achievement. However, the MOE has not conducted an objective assessment or evaluation of the country's educational state because most of the effort is absorbed in the process of managing the quantitative expansion of education, involving the preparation and recruitment of teachers and the provision of financial resources. The relation between educational inputs and outputs has not yet been tackled.

The Educational Research and Development Center (ERDC), established in 1982 by the MOE to help improve education through research and development, has been facing a number of difficulties. There is, for example, a lack of both sufficient resources and effective links with MOE policymakers. Such difficulties have hampered ERDC research plans. Research projects are mainly on demand and supply for teachers, school mapping, and factors influencing female enrollment. Future research projects are expected to include, in addition to the above, assessment and evaluation of education, quality improvement, and curriculum development.

Research, at the higher education level, is expected to gain momentum as a result of the establishment of the scientific research sector under the auspices of the Ministry of Higher Education. The sector is expected to identify critical research areas, fund individual and group research in the universities and research centers affiliated with some ministries, as well as providing resources to publish and disseminate research projects.

The expenditure on educational assessment, evaluation, and research was marginal in the 1980s due to the novelty of organized research and the lack of positive links between researchers, policymakers, and planners. Research funds, however, are expected to grow in the

1990s because of a rising awareness of the importance of research and the establishment of the scientific research sector in the Ministry of Higher Education.

10. Major Reforms in the 1980s and 1990s

The 1980s were characterized by unprecedented quantitative growth in student enrollments, but at the expense of the quality of education. Since the late 1980s the MOE has been working on a wide range of activities to prevent further deterioration of quality and to improve and upgrade the various components of the system. Special attention is being given to curricula, science education, teacher programs, postgraduate training for school administrators and supervisors, curriculum specialists, and counseling guidance specialists.

11. Major Problems for the Year 2000

The educational system of the Republic of Yemen is likely to continue to suffer from a shortage of financial resources to support and effectively sustain the enrollment growth in terms of buildings, equipment, and teachers. There is evidence that the school system is suffering from school overcrowding and low internal efficiency. Moreover, the system is hampered by a high degree of centralization, a shortage of qualified educational administrators, teachers, school principals, educational supervisors, and curriculum and evaluation specialists. The Government and MOE policy are attempting to increase the budget. Efforts are being made to encourage local community and private sector

investments in education, and to attract more grants and loans from Arab and foreign sources. Further, the MOE intends to rationalize the budget expenditure, and upgrade the national institutions to prepare qualified teachers and supporting staff.

Bibliography

Ghanim M, Mottahar M 1992 Population and education in the Republic of Yemen. *Proceedings of the First National Population Policy Conference (October 26–29)*. Central Statistical Organization, Sana'a

Ministry of Education 1990 *Education in the Republic of Yemen*. A report presented to the 42nd session of the International Conference of Education. National committee for Education, Culture and Science, Sana'a

Ministry of Education 1992 The education sector. A working paper presented to the Round Table Conference, Ministry of Education, Sana'a

Parliamentary Council 1993 The general law of education. *Democracy*. 1(6): 26–32 Sana'a

Pridham B R (ed.) 1984 *Contemporary Yemen: Politics and Historical Background*. Croom Helm, London

Pridham B R (ed.) 1985 *Economy, Society and Culture in Contemporary Yemen*. Croom Helm, London

Republic of Yemen, Ministry of Planning and Development 1992 *General Economic Memorandum: Round Table Conference, Geneva 30 June-1 July 1992*, 2 vols. Ministry of Planning and Development, Sana'a

Republic of Yemen, Ministry of Planning and Development 1992 *Statistical Year Book 1991*. Central Statistical Organisation, Sana'a

Republic of Yemen, Ministry of Planning and Development 1992 *Population and Development*. Central Statistical Organization, Sana'a

Zabarah M A 1982 *Yemen: Traditionalism versus Modernity*. Prager, New York

Zaire

M. Magabe

1. General Background

Zaire lies at the heart of Africa and covers a territory of 2,345,550 square kilometers. Its major river is the River Zaire, which has various tributaries. This large territory is divided into 11 regions and the capital, Kinshasa. Each region has different characteristics. There are geographic variations: mountainous regions with a cooler climate, valleys with equatorial forests in the center of the country, and some plateaus in the west of the country. There are several hundred tribes speaking more than 200 languages (Bantu and non-Bantu) which make for difficulties in teaching in the mother tongue. Nevertheless, the country has been divided into four large linguistic zones: Swahili,

Kikongo, Lingala, and Tshiluba. In primary schools, the vernacular languages are used as the media of instruction. Despite the large size of Zaire and the different regional characteristics, there is one nationwide educational program. This, on the one hand, helps to unify a nation, but, on the other hand, means that the curriculum often lacks direct relevance for some local areas.

From 1908 to 1960, Zaire was a Belgian colony. The year before independence Zaire had 14.5 million inhabitants (Tshibangu 1982). By 1979 this figure was 26.4 million. It is estimated that by 1994 the number will reach 42.5 million (Ngondo et al. 1992 pp. 17, 55). The annual average population growth rate is 3.29 percent (Ngondo et al. 1992 p. 18). However, there is variation and the large pockets of the population are in the east with different population growth rates ranging from 2.1 to 5.7 percent, the latter being in the capital city. Eleven percent of the population lives in Kinshasa. Fifty-two percent of the population is female. The two largest towns after the capital are Lubumbashi the copper town, and Kisangani in the northeast.

The country has many natural resources, including gold, copper, and diamonds. The soil is fertile, and 80 percent of the population lives in rural areas and works in agriculture. Since independence, Zairian policy has been to produce indigenous managers capable of occupying those posts previously reserved for Europeans. Schools were created everywhere and higher education institutions followed after 1970 (Magabe 1992). However, it must be noted that only a very small proportion of the active labor force is salaried. Increasingly it can be seen that there are distortions between the education system and the employment market. Higher education is often criticized as being a nursery of unemployment even though there are many serious problems in national life (health, infrastructure, agriculture, etc.). In the 1980s the economy deteriorated rapidly. Businesses have the problems of a lack of spare parts and materials and poor management; there is no longer any investment and the political problems of the early 1990s made an already alarming situation worse. Inflation in 1993 was at an all-time high: the zaire (national currency) in 1993 was worth US$0.0000604, whereas in 1967 it was worth US$2. Zairians in 1993 had to rely on subsistence agriculture (the informal sector, which was well developed), given the demise of the state economy.

In its short history, Zaire has known two political periods: the first republic (1960–1965) which was basically characterized by a decentralized political regime with a federalist orientation; and the second republic (1965–90) dominated by one party, the *Mouvement Populaire de la Révolution* (MPR) which was characterized by an excessive centralization of power. In both cases, the education system was controlled by the government, but in the first republic the private sector was more developed. The nationalization of schools (1974–77) under the second republic proved to be an unfortunate experience. Demand for education has increased. The Government organized many schools, but was unable to fund them fully. In the mid-1970s, private universities and higher education institutions were created and thought was being given to parents' paying toward their children's education.

2. Politics and the Goals of the Education System

In a highly centralized state system, the overall aims of education are decided at the central level. Educational policy is embedded in the constitution, ordinances, ministerial decrees, and other official instructions

and circulars. Although, in general, there have been no major changes, there have been slight shifts in orientation. In 1960 there was a drive to train many professionals, since the country had need of them after the departure of the Europeans. Efforts were made to create structures and curricula to allow as many as possible to be given a high-quality education of sufficient length. Two major goals were propounded: (a) to prepare the child to fulfill a useful role in the economy and society, and (b) to prepare those children capable of further study for higher education.

In 1961, following the Conference of Addis Ababa, thought was being given to developing primary and secondary education. In the years 1971–80, the general

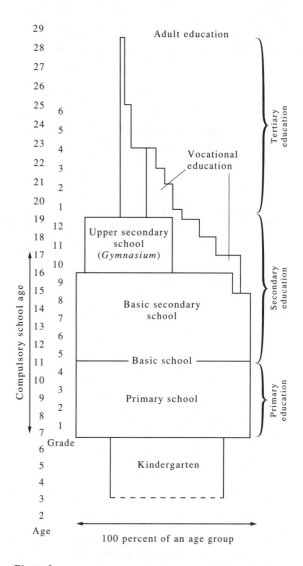

Figure 1
Zaire: Structure of the formal education system

philosophy was to produce authentic indigenous "Zairians" with their own value system. However, the operational definition of an authentic Zairian proved difficult.

In the 1990s the major objectives are based on the Law No. 86–005 of national education. It restates the need to train citizens who will be useful to their country and to develop a form of education responding to the socioeconomic needs of the country. The Sovereign National Council has proposed a national charter of education which describes the philosophy and future policy of national education and the profiles of those to be trained (e.g., productive citizens who are creative, cultured, and conscious of social values). At higher levels of education there is the same concern as before, namely that of producing persons capable of contributing to local and national development. The idea behind this social concept is based on a critical analysis of a dynamic educational system. It is to be hoped that it will materialize.

3. The Formal System of Education

Figure 1 presents the structure of the Zairian educational system.

3.1 Primary, Secondary, and Tertiary Education

There are four levels of education: preschool, primary, secondary, and higher.

Primary education begins at 6 years of age and lasts for six years. The age of entry is a matter of theory only because parents, who must pay something toward their children's schooling, have difficulty in raising the money. Nevertheless, there was great effort in the 1960s and 1970s—by the state, followed by the parents—to develop education. A 1991 study showed that the gross enrollment rate in 1987–88 was 79 percent.

Secondary school lasts for six years and is attended by those pupils having received a certificate of primary education. Until 1980 the first two years comprised a *cycle d'orientation*, but this ceased in 1980. However, no changes were made to the curriculum. There are three main tracks: general, technical, and short vocational courses. In theory, the general track prepares pupils for higher education and the technical track prepares pupils for a job, but in such a way that they could proceed to higher education should they wish to do so. There are 202 school days per year with approximately 6 hours of instruction per day. Class sizes are large, with an average of 60 pupils per class in Grade 7 and 45 in Grade 12. Schools in towns sometimes run a two-shift system because of the many people in urban areas. In the school year 1990–91, there were 5,704,646 pupils in primary and secondary school. Of these, 80 percent were in primary school.

Higher education consists of universities and institutes of higher education (Magabe 1992). In 1989–90,

the number of students enrolled in the 37 establishments of higher education was 66,617. Exactly 10 years earlier, this figure had been 26,508. Given that the population of Zaire in 1990 was 35,561,939, it can be said that 1 in 533 Zairians was a student.

The Zairian system of education is organized by the state and by private initiative. In many cases, state schools are run by the churches (Catholic, Protestant, and Kimbangu). In principle, private schools receive no subsidy from the state, but should they wish to have one, they must be inspected and follow the national curriculum. There is inefficiency in the system, as can be seen from the fact that out of four children who begin primary school, only one completes it. Despite the doubling of enrollment in higher education between 1985 and 1991, it is still a fact that only one out of four students receiving their state diploma at the end of secondary school actually enters higher education.

3.2 Preschool Education

Preschool education is for children from 3 to 5 years of age. This form of education takes place primarily in towns and cities and has not reached villages, where the extended family continues to play an important role in the raising of children. The number of students in preschool education is minimal. Such education is organized privately.

3.3 Special Education

Very little attention is given to special education. Except in rare cases, children suffering from a mental or physical handicap are left to their own devices. For example, in a region like Kivu, with 6 million inhabitants, there is no special education school. However, there are schools for blind and hearing-impaired students in Lubumbashi and Kinshasa.

3.4 Vocational, Technical, and Business Education

As already mentioned, the technical secondary schools prepare children for jobs, but in such a way that they can also enter higher education. At the end of secondary school, pupils sit for a national exam and, if successful, receive a state diploma which gives them access to higher education. Within technical studies, there are subdivisions of commerce and administration, agriculture, and industry (electricity, mechanics, etc.). The vocational schools, on the other hand, prepare children for a job without any possibility of entering a university. This type of education typically lasts four or five years. This is also the case for teacher training, car mechanics, nursing, and so on.

There are two major problems with this type of education. Links with industry are weak. The knowledge and skills of those produced by the system are often said to be irrelevant, and there is no way in which the employers can have a say in the content of the curriculum. To counteract this state of affairs, certain large companies develop their own training schools. The second problem is that many of those graduating from the technical secondary schools prefer to follow a university career rather than enter the labor market directly.

At the higher education level the vocationalization of studies was an important point in the 1971 reform. The idea was to give students skills to help them enter a particular job. This scheme was more successful in the higher institutions than in the universities.

3.5 Adult and Nonformal Education

In 1971 the *Centre Interdisciplinaire pour le Développement de l'Education Permanente* was created. The intention was to train adults for their vocational needs and to update their education in terms of technical progress. Unfortunately, with time this institute moved more to becoming a kind of university rather than helping employers have their needs satisfied. There is also a national institute for vocational training for workers who are employed for updating their knowledge and skills. A nonformal mechanism created by the *Organisme Non Gouvernemental de Développement* aims at training peasants, artisans, women, and so on. The number of adults attending these courses and the exact content of the courses differs from region to region and job to job. The overall aim for now, however, is to liberate the masses from inertia and exploitation and to resuscitate this vital and creative force among adults such that they can improve their own lots. There are also scattered literacy initiatives.

In short, the state does little for adult education. It should also be noted that parents show more interest in the education of boys than of girls and rural areas have lower enrollment in such courses than urban areas. There are also regional inequalities. Historically, the colonizers sited schools where they themselves were. Thus, the western regions have more schools than elsewhere. Despite efforts to reduce the inequality, there are many problems. Attempts were made to reduce regional inequalities in higher education by having a regional quota system (Isango 1980).

4. Administrative and Supervisory Structure and Operation

It is the state which decides on the objectives, length, and content of education. As already mentioned, the state nationalized higher education in 1971 and primary and secondary education in 1974. In this way, those schools run by the churches came under the control of the state and the daily management of the schools was given to persons designated by the state. At the primary and secondary level this decision was

contested and had to be withdrawn. In 1977 a "*convention de gestion des écoles nationales*" (Zaïre Afrique 1977) was signed and returned the control of the schools to their original managers. The law of 1986, apart from indicating the forms, content, management, and so forth of education, also stated that private persons could create private schools under certain conditions.

Hence, there are three types of schools: official, religious (*écoles conventionnées*), and private schools. The first two are state schools, with government financial support for teacher salaries and so forth. The only difference between the two is that the religious schools are run by the churches and it is the churches which recruit the teachers, appoint the directors, and organize the inspection of schools, but according to the state Ministry of Education norms. Private schools are dependent on funding from parents or from the owner. They must follow the state curriculum and satisfy ministry norms for equipment, supplies, qualifications of teachers, and so on. They respond to the inefficiencies experienced in the state system. The exact number of private schools is not known.

Administratively, the system is highly centralized. The central powers are the Ministry of Education and the General Inspectorate. Each of these is also represented at the provincial level. The first is responsible for the management and administrative control, whereas the second is responsible for the pedagogical aspects. From 1985 onward, there was a special unit (SECOPE) responsible for paying teachers. There are many misunderstandings among these three units.

Higher education is controlled centrally and is dependent on the ministry of national education and administrative council for higher education. However, in 1992 the *Conférence National Souveraine* enacted several amendments to allow universities and higher education institutions to obtain more regional power.

5. Educational Finance

Educational finance is difficult to describe accurately, mainly because private schools do not publish their accounts. What follows refers only to the official statistics of public education (i.e., state and religious).

Between 1970 and 1988, expenditures vacillated from 0.6 to 27.7 percent of the state budget. The high years were 1978 and 1979 with 12.83 and 27.7 percent respectively. The low years were in the time of the Shaba wars. By 1988, education had 7.6 percent of the state budget. In the 1980s it was political institutions and the army which received the highest share of the state budgets. This was the time when the MPR was at its height.

According to the report on human development of 1991, Zaire spent 2.4 percent of its Gross Domestic Product (GDP) on education; this had been 5.8 percent in 1980 and 0.4 percent in 1986. However, in 1988 just over 54 percent of all educational expenditure was allocated to primary schools. Bit by bit, the state has withdrawn from the financing of education, but still insists on controlling the content and staff. The drop in the price of copper, increased enrollment, and political expenditures no longer allow the government to reach the levels of education expenditure of the 1960s. It is also the case in higher education that there has been a diminution in money allocated for scholarships and the transport and health costs of students have been cut such that parents have been asked more and more to contribute to the costs of education.

6. Supplying Personnel for the Education System

National education is one of the better employers in Zaire. This sector employs not only teachers, but also supports personnel.

There are several ways in which teachers are trained. Primary school teachers are trained in secondary schools, either in four-year courses leading to a D4 diploma for teaching in the lower primary school, or in educational courses which at the end of secondary school result in a state diploma for teaching in the upper primary school. These courses combine general studies with educational studies and practice teaching experience. There is a trend for more students to enroll in the courses for upper than for lower primary school.

In 1975 there were 80,489 primary school teachers (Mulier and Mulier 1977) and in 1992 this number was 104,305, a production of about 1,400 teachers per year. Since there is one teacher per class, it is possible to deduce the number of primary school classes.

Secondary school teachers are trained in higher institutes of education where courses are offered for all subjects taught in secondary school. There are two parts to this training: the first part consists of three years of training at the end of which students are graduates; the second part is two years at the end of which, if the students are successful in a competitive examination, they receive a *licence*. Graduates teach in the first four years of secondary school, whereas the *licenciés* teach in the final years of secondary school. In 1990 there were 189,281 secondary school teachers in the 29,883 classes with an enrollment of 1,160,676 pupils. It was estimated (Amyot and Nzuzi 1988 p. 12) that approximately 23 percent of children aged 12 to 17 were enrolled in state secondary school.

In higher education there are scientific personnel and academic personnel. As a result of a 1971 law, the recruitment, promotion, and salaries are the same for all faculties. A professor must have a doctorate and must have successfully completed a six-month probationary period.

The status of teacher or professor at whatever level in the school system has decreased. Many teachers have left education for more lucrative employment either in the country or abroad. As an example, the

higher education institute in Bukavu produces about 100 graduates and *licenciés* per year who, as soon as they receive their certificate, depart for Rwanda and/or Burundi where, in 1993, they were able to earn 10 times more than they would earn in Zaire. Several university professors from Zaire are to be found in countries such as Gabon, the Congo, Algeria, and Cameroon. One of the consequences of this brain drain is a decrease in the quality of education. Schools are then forced to take on underqualified teachers at levels of education for which they are not legally qualified. In most rural secondary schools, for example, there are teachers who are not qualified to teach in secondary schools.

Apart from a few private initiatives, there is no form of inservice training in the country. Given the evolution of knowledge, particularly in the sciences, and in general of methods of teaching, there is a major problem that teachers not qualified for the level at which they teach cannot receive inservice training. There was a *Centre d'Animation Pédagogique*, funded by Belgium, which offered seminars to secondary school teachers. Unfortunately, this center ceased to exist when, in 1990, cooperation between Zaire and Belgium ceased.

7. Curriculum Development and Teaching Methodology

For each program or course there is a nationwide curriculum. No local modification is allowed.

At the primary school level, the curriculum includes arithmetic, French, geography, history, and natural sciences. In the lower primary school, the basic skills of reading, writing, and arithmetic are inculcated, whereas at the upper primary school, basic mathematic operations, reading and understanding in French (including conjugation, grammar, and vocabulary), are offered, and at the end of primary school, problem-solving and essay writing are emphasized. The only difference between the lower and upper primary levels is that of language. In the lower primary school, it is Swahili in east, Kikongo in the west, Tshiluba in the west-central, and Lingala in the north that are studied in parallel with French.

In secondary school, the curriculum varies by track. The most popular tracks are: arts, sciences (biology/chemistry or mathematics/physics), education, and technical (commerce, electricity, mechanics, agriculture, dressmaking, etc.). In all tracks the only foreign language introduced after French is English. The hours of instruction in English vary from one track to another, but are generally around five hours per week.

In the vocational courses, the curriculum is directly relevant to the specific skills being learned (auto mechanic, carpenter, teacher, etc.).

In higher education, the curriculum of the early 1990s stressed the vocational aspect of learning. This was the main theme of the 1971 reform. This vocationalization more or less succeeded in the higher institutes, but was difficult to achieve in the university faculties, because of insufficient means, and the concept, ever dominant, of "the university" (Isango 1980 p. 207–22).

8. *The System of Examinations, Promotions, and Certifications*

Promotion is based on school examinations given at the end of each grade. At the end of Grade 6, pupils receive, upon successful completion of the six years, a certificate of primary school study. This certificate gives the pupil the right to enter any secondary school. However, from the end of the 1980s onward it became increasingly common for secondary schools to set an examination to those pupils wishing to enter, so that the school only takes the best students in terms of the number of places available.

At the end of secondary school, external examinations (known as state examinations) are given. If successful, the student receives a state diploma. This type of diploma began in 1967 and serves not only as an evaluation tool, but also as a hurdle between school and higher education. The examination is marked by the inspectorate. The number of pupils taking the exam increased in the 1980s. In 1981, just over 24,000 students obtained a state diploma and in 1990, this number was 53,360.

Despite the fact that this system of examination has ended the hegemony debate among schools, the reliabilities of the state examinations have been criticized. The discrimination power of the examinations in order to differentiate better from poorer pupils has also been criticized on the grounds that too many poor candidates succeed in the examination who are incapable of taking any higher education course.

At the university level, practical work, quizzes, oral and written examinations are used to determine progress.

Finally, it should be said that teachers are being requested to learn evaluation techniques.

9. *Educational Assessment, Evaluation, and Research*

There is no formal structure for the evaluation of the school system as a whole. Since 1960, such evaluation has taken place at specially convened meetings. These meetings have always ended with qualitative evaluations, usually restating ideas put forward by those present at the meeting as well as things known to the public. It is difficult to base corrective action on such evaluations, since the explanatory factors are not arrived at scientifically.

Research study in education is usually the result of work by individual researchers. Sometimes these studies are students' theses or work carried out by assistant professors for promotion. Most higher education institutes have their own research centers. Some of the research studies have much merit, but are rarely concerned with the actual practice of education.

One of the major efforts to be undertaken in the 1990s is that of promoting research and researchers.

10. *Major Reforms in the 1980s and 1990s*

In 1981 the Central Committee of the Popular Movement of the Revolution firmly resolved to reform Zairian education to be relevant to the conditions of the country at that time. Various committees were charged with major aspects of reform, but produced very little. In primary and secondary education, the pre-1961 curriculum was readopted, national languages were used in the lower primary school, and the orientation cycle at the beginning of secondary school was abandoned. Indeed, although the names and the jargon changed, the content remained the same.

In higher education, the major reform was concerned with restructuring. The national university of Zaire with its various campuses and higher education institutions became decentralized and the universities and institutions acquired autonomy.

The demand for education has not ceased to increase; the quality of education has deteriorated, as has the infrastructure. On the other hand, a trend to more private provision of education can be noted at all levels. It is the era of liberalization. Hundreds of schools have sprung up in all areas, and the system is in need of reform.

11. *Major Problems for the Year 2000*

The financing of the system will determine the enrollments which will be possible given the increased demand for education. Indeed, it would appear that in the mid-1990s it will be important to put a brake on expanding enrollment and rather improve the quality of education. This will be difficult, because education is the only way to promotion in the system and therefore demand cannot be decreased.

At the same time, the quality of teaching should be improved and the adaptation of the outdated curriculum to the realities of life must be undertaken. At the university level, it is the 1978 curriculum that still prevails. The status of the teacher must be improved; it is often discussed, but nothing is achieved. Teachers' purchasing power has decreased and their social status has fallen. The system has begun to rely on unqualified teachers and this should not continue.

However, the flow to federalism will also affect education. More autonomy will be given to the provinces and more coordination will be undertaken with private initiatives. This, unfortunately, will not solve the problems of regional disparity, inequities, and inservice training.

References

Amyot M, Nzuzi P L 1988 *Prévision de la population d'âge scolaire et estimation des effectifs scolaires du Zaïre et de ses régions, 1986 à 2.000*. Direction de Planification et Statistiques, Kinshasa

Isango I W 1980 La politique d'éducation au Zaïre: Le cas de l'Université Nationale du Zaïre. Essai d'analyse des conditions d'adaptation de l'enseignement. (Doctoral thesis, University of Lubumbashi)

Magabe M 1992 Higher education in Zaïre. In: Clark B, Neave G (eds.) 1992 *The Encyclopedia of Higher Education*. Pergamon Press, Oxford

Mulier V, Mulier S 1977 Analyse et bilan de l'enseignement primaire 1965–75. *Cahiers de CRIDE* 17–18

Ngondo S, de Saint Moulin L, Tambashe B 1992 *Perspectives démographiques du Zaïre 1984–1999 et Population d'âge électoral en 1993 et 1994*. CEPAS, Kinshasa

Tshibangu T 1982 *La crise contemporaine; l'enjeu africain et l'université de l'an 2.000*. PUZ, Kinshasa

Zaïre Afrique 1977 Convention de gestion des écoles nationales 114: 245–49

Further Reading

Ministère de l'enseignement supérieur, universitaire et de la recherche scientifique 1991 *Projet de Nationalisation de l'Enseignement Supérieur et Universitaire*. Ministère de l'enseignement supérieur, Kinshasa

Vanderlinden J et al. 1981 *Du Congo au Zaïre 1960–1980: Essai de bilan*. CRISP, Brussels

Zimbabwe

B. S. M. Gatawa

1. General Background

Zimbabwe is situated in the southern part of Africa and is bordered by Mozambique to the east, South Africa to the south, Botswana to the west, and Zambia to the north and northwest. It has an area of 390,759 square kilometers and has a tropical continental climate moderated by altitude, especially over the Central Highveld and the Eastern Highlands. About 98 percent of the population is indigenous. The remainder comprises small European, Asian, and Colored communities. The country achieved Independence from the United Kingdom in 1980 after a long liberation struggle.

During the 90 years of colonization (1890–1980) Zimbabwe (which was then the Colony of Southern Rhodesia) was run by a settler European community which established a racially segregated education system. Education for the indigenous people was left largely to church organizations, while the education subsystem for Europeans, Asians, and Coloreds received substantial state support. Between 1980 and 1990 the government succeeded in bringing the two subsystems together, but their resource bases continue to be unequal.

Between 1969 and 1982 Zimbabwe's population grew from 5.1 million to 7.5 million, a growth rate of 2.9 percent per year. The total population in 1990 was estimated at 9,435,000 and at this rate of increase, it will double by the year 2009. Over 73 percent of the population lives in rural areas. Almost 40 percent of the population is of school-going age.

Outside the commercial farming areas, the rural areas are economically disadvantaged and have very low per capita incomes. These latter areas witnessed a spectacular expansion in educational provision between 1980 and 1990 as a result of a combination of government and community efforts. On the other hand, the economically more prosperous commercial farming areas still have the most inadequate educational infrastructure in the country.

English is the official language of Zimbabwe. Shona and Ndebele are the two major local languages and are spoken widely across the country. In addition, there are five minority languages which are taught in their localities up to the third year of schooling. The general government policy is to encourage nonindigenous Zimbabweans to learn one of the two major local languages.

Zimbabwe has a highly diversified economy whose foundation rests on rich mineral resources, a strong agricultural base, and a well-developed transport, commercial, and financial infrastructure. Within the economy, manufacturing accounts for 24 percent of Gross Domestic Product (GDP), followed by agriculture and distribution. In 1986, most people were employed in agriculture. In 1982 the labor force was about a third of the total population: three-fourths worked in rural areas and the rest in towns. With over 200,000 school leavers competing for less than 15,000 new jobs each year, both underemployment and unemployment are increasing. Given this scenario, curriculum policies have deliberately encouraged self-reliance through the promotion of technical–practical subjects, especially agriculture.

In 1982, 72 percent of males and 64 percent of females aged 5 to 19 years were enrolled in schools; 62 percent of the population over 15 years of age was literate. The illiteracy rate among adults is therefore significant. This prompted the launching of a national literacy campaign in 1982 to empower participants for effective involvement in the economy. It is accepted that education is the key to economic development and that it should provide answers to problems in the economy.

2. Politics and the Goals of the Education System

Although the majority of primary and secondary schools are owned by district council and church authorities, education policies are determined by central government because of its dominant role in financing and administering education. All teachers, with the exception of an insignificant percentage, are hired and paid by central government. In addition, central government gives additional support to education through a grants system for tuition and building. Since 1980, however, Zimbabwe has been governed by one political party. Opposition parties have been very weak with virtually no representation in Parliament. For this reason educational developments have not attracted political controversy.

Central to the goals of primary and secondary education since 1980 have been attempts to use school programs to promote national unity, establish a nonracial egalitarian society, and produce a productive and thinking citizenry. In this thrust, ideology was regarded to be as important as a curriculum based on science, mathematics, and technology. In practice, however, not much has been achieved in this direction since education in Zimbabwe continues to be highly academic because of the requirements of the British examinations boards.

The general mandate of the education sector is defined in the Education Act which is amended from time to time. Details relating to structures, aims, and objectives; school programs; and assessment and evaluation procedures are given, on an on-going basis,

in Ministry circulars. These documents reflect the centrality accorded labor force development in the overall development of the economy. This aspect is more pronounced in postsecondary levels of education.

3. The Formal System of Education

Figure 1 outlines the structure of the formal education system. Statistics on enrollments are provided in Table 1 for the years 1979 to 1990.

Officially, primary-school education is compulsory, but in practice the government has no mechanism to enforce attendance. Generally, children start primary school at the age of 7 years. In urban areas, a significant number of children attend preschool between the ages of 3 and 7 years. This facility is not readily available in rural areas although there has been a deliberate program to establish preschool centers in these areas since 1980. Preschool education is the responsibility of local communities. Government involvement takes the form of a small allowance to the teachers who work at these centers and meeting the cost of training, management, and supervision.

3.1 Primary, Secondary, and Tertiary Education

Primary education runs for seven years. In 1990 there were 4,559 primary schools with a total enrollment of 2,119,865 pupils. While urban and rural district council areas have an adequate primary-school infrastructure, the commercial farming areas are not so well provided. Between 1980 and 1991 primary-school education was tuition-free. In 1992, however, tuition fees were introduced as a cost-recovery measure but with different rates for different socioeconomic groups. The rural areas, which are largely disadvantaged, were completely exempted from primary-school tuition fees but parents contribute in other forms toward the

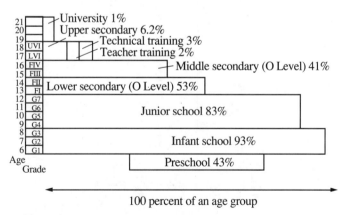

Figure 1
Zimbabwe: Structure of the formal education system

Table 1
Number of primary and secondary schools and enrollment figures 1979–89

	1979	1980	1981	1982	1983	1984	1985	1986	1987	1988	1989	1990
Primary												
No. of schools		2,401	3,161	3,698	3,880	3,960	4,161	4,234	4,297	4,339	4,471	4,504	4,559
Enrollment		819,586	1,235,984	1,715,163	1,907,225	2,044,487	2,130,487	2,216,878	2,265,053	2,251,319	2,212,103	2,214,939	2,119,865
Secondary												
No. of schools		177	197	694	738	790	1,182	1,215	1,276	1,395	1,484	1,506	1,512
Enrollment		66,215	74,321	148,690	227,047	316,348	416,413	482,000	537,427	606,652	641,005	678,615	676,884

Source: Annual Reports of the Secretary for Education 1979–89

development of schools. All primary schools are co-educational. The primary school day normally consists of 5 hours of tuition and three hours of structured out-of-classroom activities. The school year lasts for 188 days.

Secondary education is available for either four or six years depending on whether the student leaves the system after O-level examinations or proceeds to A-level studies which are a preparation for university work. The 1980s saw a marked increase in secondary schools and secondary-school enrollments. In 1979, there were 177 secondary schools but in 1990 the figure had increased to 1,512. Enrollment figures rose from 66,215 in 1979 to 676,884 in 1990. The secondary-school completion rate is higher for boys than for girls mainly because of parental attitudes which value the education of boys more than that of girls. All government secondary schools are coeducational, but a number of church schools are single sex. Boarding secondary schools are more popular because of their relatively superior performance in public examinations. The secondary-school day is made up of 8 hours of tuition. The school year lasts for 188 days.

Up to 1990, tertiary education comprised the University of Zimbabwe and colleges offering a wide range of programs. In 1990, two more universities were established: the National University of Science and Technology and a private university established by the United Methodist Church. In addition, the two major polytechnic colleges in the country offer bachelor's degrees in technology. The colleges provide a wide range of programs on a full-time or part-time basis covering the whole gamut of labor force needs of the economy. Teachers' colleges, both primary and secondary, have a special scheme of association with the University of Zimbabwe which enables them to offer university certificates to their graduates.

The basic entry requirements for college programs are five O-level credits of Grade C or more, including English language. For university studies, the minimum requirements are A-level passes in at least two subjects. Entry to college and university programs is highly competitive because of the large number of O- and A-level graduates. About 3 percent of O-level graduates enter college programs and 6.2 percent proceed to A-level studies. Of those who complete A level, 50 percent proceed to university studies at the local institutions. The remainder either take up college programs or enter the labor market or seek university education outside the country.

3.2 Special Education

Special education was accorded full recognition after 1980 and national, provincial, district, and school-level structures were created to facilitate its provision. It covers pupils with learning difficulties and those with hearing, sight, and physical impairments. The delivery system comprises both separate facilities for the

severely handicapped and integration into mainstream schools and classes for those with slight to moderate impairment. In a majority of cases, integration has not been more than coexistence within the same physical environment largely because teachers are not sufficiently trained to handle integrated classes. The trend, however, is toward integration and this is likely to become the norm in future as teachers' colleges increase their output of special education teachers.

3.3 Vocational, Technical, and Business Education

The low absorptive capacity of the economy in the 1980s and the large percentage of school-leaver unemployment emphasized the need for schools to impart technical–vocational skills which would enable school graduates to be self-reliant. The response of the education sector took a number of forms. First, the range of technical–practical subjects in the school curriculum was increased. Where workshop facilities were not available, technical subjects kits were provided. Second, vocational training at craft-certificate level was introduced on a pilot basis in schools as an extension of the general education curriculum. This has since been scaled down because it imposed heavy demands on students. Instead, technical–vocational foundation courses were introduced; they provide self-reliance skills and also lead to post O-level craft-certificate training. At the same time, business education was introduced as it was felt that productive skills were not enough. Students needed accounting and management skills to enable them to run their own enterprises.

At the tertiary level, technical colleges were built across the country with a college in each of the nine provinces offering vocational, technical, and business education programs. Linkages were established with industry to enable students to acquire "hands-on" experience in workplaces. In addition, industry contributes on a regular basis to a labor force development fund.

3.4 Adult and Nonformal Education

In the professions, adult participation in education is on the increase because of its links with increased levels of performance and promotion prospects. It is either sponsored by employers or as a result of individuals seeking self-fulfillment and takes the form of both college and university programs. The importance of further and higher qualifications became more pronounced in the 1980s following the flight of European expertise from the country.

Nonformal education in the Zimbabwean context refers to the out-of-school education provided through correspondence and study groups. The main providers are private correspondence colleges but government is also beginning to make an impact in this area. The programs followed are the same as for the formal school sector. The main participants are school drop-outs but there is a sizable number of adults on correspondence programs. Also, there is a national adult literacy program but its impact so far has been minimal. There are a number of nonaward interest-specific programs which are provided by the private sector and church organizations.

4. Administrative and Supervisory Structure and Operation

Education is the responsibility of national government and is administered by two ministries. The Ministry of Education and Culture is in charge of primary and secondary education while the Ministry of Higher Education administers tertiary education. There is also a Department of National Scholarships in the President's Office. The Ministry of Education and Culture appoints and pays teachers in both government and private schools. It supplies school buildings and instructional materials in government schools. In private schools, government support is in the form of tuition and building grants which are channeled through the relevant responsible authorities or school committees. The curriculum is centrally determined through subject panels. The functions of administration, staffing, and supervision are decentralized to regional, district, and school levels.

Most of the schools are privately owned and belong to an assortment of authorities which comprise churches, local government authorities, boards, committees, and individuals. The majority of these schools are owned by district councils which administer rural communal areas where most Zimbabweans live. While the largest percentage of teachers are civil servants paid by government, private schools are free to hire additional teachers to improve teacher–pupil ratios. The hiring of additional teachers is widespread in high fee-paying private schools patronized by the mostly White well-to-do population.

With the exception of a number of teacher-training and commercial and secretarial colleges, almost all tertiary institutions are run by the government which hires and pays lecturers. The universities are autonomous although they are run almost entirely on government funding. The government has substantial influence in the governance of these institutions.

Before 1980, successive colonial administrations exercised direct control over education. This tradition continued after independence. For this reason, decentralization has taken the form of dispersing functions while effective control remains anchored in Head Office. The curriculum has remained uniform throughout the system and this is likely to continue unchanged in the 1990s.

5. Educational Finance

Between 1980 and 1991 total financial outlays on education averaged 15 percent of annual state budgets.

In the 1990–91 financial year, government financial commitment to education was Z$1,628,315,000 (US$245,991,320) which represented 17.7 percent of the state budget. This large investment in education is a reflection of the pride of place accorded to labor force development in the overall development of the economy.

In 1990–91, Z$1,410,224,000 (US$213,044,080) went to schools and Z$218,091,000 (US$32,947,245) went to tertiary education. About 85 percent of this outlay went toward the payment of salaries. The remainder covered tuition and building grants.

Until 1992, primary education was tuition-free in both government and private schools. In private schools, however, parents paid building fees to supplement government building grants. In 1992, tuition fees for primary education were introduced in urban areas only but with arrangements which protected the disadvantaged. The largely poor rural areas were exempted. All children pay tuition fees in secondary schools, but the rate depends on the type of school. In private secondary schools, building fees are also levied.

In nongovernment primary and secondary schools, the government contributes tuition and building grants in addition to paying teachers' salaries. In the primary cycle the tuition grant per child ranges from Z$12–Z$25 (US$1.81–3.78) depending on the grade, while for the secondary cycle it is Z$15 (US$2.27) per child.

At the tertiary level, students are financed through a grant and loan system. The loan is repayable on commencement of work after completing the training program. Industry makes a modest contribution through the Zimbabwe Manpower Development Fund toward the cost of training in technical colleges.

6. Supplying Personnel for the Education System

The need for trained teachers increased with the growth of enrollments. At the primary level, the number of teachers increased from 28,500 in 1980 to 58,200 in 1989. At the secondary level, the number increased from 3,730 in 1980 to 25,030 in 1989. While only 3 percent were not trained in 1980, in 1989 about 49 percent were not trained.

Most teachers are civil servants and their salaries are paid by the government. Some private schools, however, hire extra teachers paid by school management committees. The official pupil–teacher ratios is 40:1 for all primary grades, 30:1 for Forms 1 to 4, and 20:1 for Forms 5 and 6.

The problem of untrained teachers is more pronounced in remote rural areas and in the science and mathematics and practical–technical subjects. There is also a high turnover of teaching staff. The government has tried to respond to these problems in a variety of ways—increasing teacher salaries, reducing the teacher training program from 4 to 3 years, using expatriate teachers, and introducing teacher-training and teacher-support systems based on distance education. The overall picture is one of the government trying very hard—but not fully succeeding—to improve both the quality and quantity of teachers in the school system.

Teacher training is the responsibility of colleges of education and the universities. For college–level teacher training, the academic requirements are five O-level credits of Grade C or more, including English language. The colleges of education are associate institutions of the University of Zimbabwe which is charged with the certification of college students. The university–level training program generally comprises a three-year degree in two major teaching subjects followed by a one-year graduate certificate in education. In addition, there are a number of specialist BEd and MEd programs at the universities.

Teachers serve a one-year probationary period before becoming eligible for permanent employment. They are supervised and supported by education officers based in district and regional offices in addition to school-level support from the headteacher.

For the 1990s, the problems of training teachers in sufficient numbers, reducing the rate of turnover among teachers through improved working conditions, and providing a meaningful teacher-support system will be the major teacher-related issues to be resolved.

7. *Curriculum Development and Teaching Methodology*

Zimbabwe has a common school curriculum. It is centrally determined by national subject panels composed of education officers, teachers, and representatives of interested bodies such as universities, churches, and the teachers' association. The work of these subject panels is coordinated by the Curriculum Development Unit, which is a department within the Ministry of Education and Culture. The primary-school curriculum comprises English, mathematics, environmental and agricultural science, social studies, physical education, art and craft, music, religious and moral education, and one of the local languages (Shona or Ndebele). (The local minority languages of Tonga, Venda, Kalanga, Shangaan, and Nambya are taught during the first three grades in areas where they are spoken.) In primary schools, these subjects are taught by a general classroom teacher, whereas in secondary schools various subject specialists are used.

At secondary-school level the situation is different. Up to O level, there is a compulsory core curriculum consisting of mathematics, science, and English. Outside this core, schools are free to choose from a specified range of electives depending on facilities available. The curriculum is more specialized at A level. A student can opt for either the sciences or the humanities, and within each of these two clusters a student or a school is free to choose any combination of three subjects. Subject combinations across the two clusters are possible depending on the school timetable.

Foreign languages are taught in some secondary schools. The most commonly taught foreign languages are French and Afrikaans. The French government has a program which seeks to promote the teaching of French through investment in teacher training at the university level. The program also provides for attachments to institutions in France.

Textbooks and other learning materials are prepared by the Curriculum Development Unit and private publishing houses. Most of these materials are, in fact, produced by publishing houses. The Curriculum Development Unit tends to concentrate more on controlling quality than developing materials. Schools are free to select any materials from the range of materials approved and recommended by the Curriculum Development Unit.

Efforts in the 1990s are likely to be directed toward creating a research-based curriculum development process, making more materials available at affordable prices, and making teachers more effective in using materials.

8. *The System of Examinations, Promotions, and Certifications*

The education system in Zimbabwe is examination-oriented. There is, however, automatic promotion from grade to grade between examinations. At the end of the seven-year primary cycle, there is a common national primary school-leaving examination in English, mathematics, Shona/Ndebele, and a general paper which covers all content subjects. The secondary segment has three examinations: the Zimbabwe Junior Certificate examinations at the end of the first two years of secondary education, the Cambridge O-level examinations after four years of secondary education, and the Cambridge A-level examinations which come after six years of secondary education and are an entry qualification for university studies.

The primary school-leaving examinations and the Zimbabwe Junior Certificate examinations are developed and administered locally. The O- and A-level Cambridge examinations are developed and administered jointly by the Zimbabwe Ministry of Education and the University of Cambridge Local Examinations Syndicate. Zimbabwe is, however, on a localization program which will lead to the establishment of a local examinations body.

9. *Educational Assessment, Evaluation, and Research*

The first ten years of Independence (1980–90) saw considerable research and evaluation activities in education. The government itself wanted to monitor and evaluate the impact of the large national resources which were being invested in education. At the same time, such major donors to the sector as the United Nations Children Fund (UNICEF), the Swedish International Development Agency (SIDA), and the United States Agency for International Development (USAID) used research and evaluation to monitor the use and effect of their contributions.

For the first eight years, the focus was on monitoring resource inputs. The Ministry's Policy Planning and Evaluation Unit undertook a number of evaluation exercises to determine whether the expansion program was on target, whether the necessary implementation capacity was there, whether the planned housing units were being built every year, and whether there were enough instructional materials in schools. The donor groups were concerned with whether the Ministry was implementing fully the projects they funded. UNICEF funded a distance-education based primary teacher-training program and a multifaceted project which sought to promote the survival and development of children. It commissioned research and evaluation studies to establish whether such resources as vehicles and printing machines were being used for the promotion of project objectives and whether supply was meeting demand.

SIDA and USAID commissioned a number of evaluation studies on the procurement, storage, and distribution of science and technical subjects kits which they funded. They were largely concerned with the capacity of the Ministry to implement the projects they funded.

Thus, both the Ministry and the donor groups were more concerned with monitoring resource inputs. The turning point occurred around 1988 when there was an observable concern with learning achievement. The donors extended their concern to the area of how materials provided were being used at the classroom level. Did teaching–learning become more effective as a result of donor intervention? Research assignments pertaining to appropriateness of curricula, the effect of untrained teachers on student achievements, and the importance of teacher motivation and gender issues began to be commissioned by both the Ministry and the donor groups. This slant in educational research and evaluation reached full expression in 1990 when the World Bank commissioned studies on factors which affected learning achievements. At about the same time, the Human Resources Centre of the Faculty of Education at the University of Zimbabwe began to explore similar issues and to encourage graduate students to research these issues. This trend is likely to continue in the 1990s and will be a welcome adjunct to the current Ministry efforts to improve the quality of education.

Consonant with this thrust was the establishment of the Research Council of Zimbabwe which, among other things, seeks to make research findings available to decision-makers and to use research as a tool for development.

10. Major Reforms in the 1980s and 1990s

The 1980s were a period of considerable reform in all aspects of education in Zimbabwe. Primary, secondary, and tertiary education expanded beyond recognition and experienced exponential enrollment figures.

Equally dramatic developments occurred in the area of curricula. The primary-school curriculum became a vehicle for imparting essential functional skills related to health, environment, and interpersonal relations in addition to innovative approaches to reading, writing, and numeracy.

At the secondary level, the issues of relevance and quality led to innovative methodologies in the teaching of science and technical subjects. To facilitate the teaching of those subjects in schools where there were no laboratories and workshops, kits and self-instructional materials were used as substitutes. This measure freed science and technical subjects teaching from a dependence on specialist rooms and therefore democratized access to these subjects. Attempts at vocationalization have not been fully successful and the search for a workable formula continues.

At the teacher-training level, the use of multimedia approaches which combine face-to-face contact, correspondence text, and radio broadcast has led to an increase in student–teacher intakes and made it possible for student teachers to take up full teaching loads in schools, thus reducing the number of untrained teachers in the system.

These innovative measures sought to bring about qualitative improvements in education thereby reducing the gap between quantity and quality that characterized the 1980s. This trend will be a feature of the education reform in the 1990s.

11. Major Problems for the Year 2000

The overarching problem for the year 2000 will be finding resources to bring about qualitative improvements in education. School infrastructures are still characterized by a widespread absence of essential facilities such as libraries, laboratories, workshops, and adequate classrooms. There is a critical shortage of basic textbooks and reference and supplementary materials in schools. In the remote rural areas, housing for teachers is a major problem which makes those areas fail to attract and retain trained teachers.

In addition, the twin problem of a large number of untrained teachers and poor teacher-support systems will still be around in the year 2000. The related problems of inadequate supervision, large turnover of teaching staff, and poor teacher motivation will continue to demand attention. The search for curricular strands which directly address economic problems will become more urgent as more and more school leavers continue to fail to find employment in the labor market.

Bibliography

Atkinson N 1972 *Teaching Rhodesians: A History of Educational Policy in Rhodesia*. Longman, London

Gatawa B S M 1990 The Zimbabwe Integrated National Teacher Education Course (ZINTEC). In: Koul B N, Jenkins J (eds.) 1990 *Distance Education: A Spectrum of Case Studies*. Kogan Page, London

Gatawa B S M in press *Quantity-Quality Dilemma in Education: The Zimbabwe Experience*. College Press, Harare

Ministry of Education 1980–89 *Annual Reports of the Secretary for Education 1980 to 1989*. Government Printer, Harare

Mothobi B D 1977 Technical training in Rhodesia for African workers in industry with particular reference to apprenticeship training. University of Zimbabwe Institute of Adult Education, Salisbury (mimeo)

World Bank 1990 *Zimbabwe: A Review of Primary and Secondary Education: From Successful Expansion to Equity of Learning Achievements*. World Bank, Harare

Zvobgo R J 1986 *Transforming Education: The Zimbabwe Experience*. College Press, Harare

List of Contributors

Contributors are listed in alphabetical order together with their affiliations. Titles of articles which they have authored follow in alphabetical order, along with the respective page numbers. Where articles are co-authored, this has been indicated by an asterisk preceding the article title.

ABDULLAH, D. H. A. (Ministry of Education, Bandar Seri Begawan, Brunei Darussalam)
Brunei Darussalam 134–41

AL-BAADI, H. M. (Ministry of Education, Riyadh, Saudi Arabia)
Saudi Arabia 836–44

ALI, M. M. (Ministry of Education, Dhaka, Bangladesh)
Bangladesh 70–77

ALMANNAI, L. (Ministry of Education, Manama, Bahrain)
Bahrain 64–70

ALMEIDA, C. (Department of Education, Macau)
Macau 583–89

ALMOTAWA, A. (Ministry of Education, Manama, Bahrain)
Bahrain 64–70

AL-NAYADI, M. A. (United Arab Emirates University, Abu Dhabi, United Arab Emirates)
United Arab Emirates 1021–25

AL-SHANFARI, A. M. (Ministry of Education, Muscat, Oman)
Oman 745–51

AL-SUBAIE, A. A. T. (Ministry of Education, Doha, Qatar)
Qatar 808–14

ALTRICHTER, H. (University of Innsbruck, Innsbruck, Austria)
Austria 48–58

ANT, M. (National Institute for the Development of Professional Training, Luxembourg)
Luxembourg 576–83

ATHERLEY, L. (UNESCO, Paris, France)
Barbados 77–85

AZIZ, A. A. (Ministry of Education, Kuala Lumpur, Malaysia)
Malaysia 601–08

AZIZ-ZADEH, H. (Tehran, Iran)
Iran 448–52

BARRINGTON, J. M. (Victoria University of Wellington, Wellington, New Zealand)
New Zealand 708–15

BÁTHORY, Z. (National Institute of Public Education, Budapest, Hungary)
Hungary 415–23

BEEN, V. R. (Ministry of Education, Kingston, Jamaica)
Jamaica 474–81

BELACHEW, M. (Addis Ababa University, Addis Ababa, Ethiopia)
Ethiopia 308–13

BELLI, H. (Ministry of Education, Managua, Nicaragua)
Nicaragua 716–21

BEN JABALLAH, H. (Ministry of Education, Tunis, Tunisia)
Tunisia 993–1003

BENNETT, J. A. (Ministry of Education, Belize City, Belize)
Belize 92–98

BERG, D. L. (Council of Ministers of Education, Toronto, Ontario, Canada)
Canada 180–89

BERGMANN, H. (German Institute for International Educational Research, Frankfurt, Germany)
Niger 721–29

BERKHOUT, S. J. (University of Pretoria, Pretoria, South Africa)
South Africa 891–901

BERMAMET, T. (Ministry of Education, Amman, Jordan)
Jordan 489–96

BERNARD, D. C. (UNESCO, Bangkok, Thailand)
Vietnam 1060–65

BJØRNDAL, I. R. (Østfold Board of Higher Education, Halden, Norway)
Norway 738–45

BONDESIO, M. J. (University of Pretoria, Pretoria, South Africa)
South Africa 891–901

BOONCHUAY, T. (Office of the National Education Commission, Bangkok, Thailand)
Thailand 972–79

BORDIA, A. (Lok Jumbish Parishad, Jaipur, India)
India 430–39

BRAY, M. (University of Hong Kong, Hong Kong)
Hong Kong 408–15; *Macau* 583–89

BURETTA, B. N. V. (Ministry of Education, Dar es Salaam, Tanzania)
Tanzania 964–71

CEESAY, M. (Ministry of Education, Youth Sports, and Culture, Banjul, The Gambia)
Gambia 339–45

CLASSEN-BAUER, I. (University of Lüneburg, Lüneburg, Germany)
Bolivia 109–17

COOLAHAN, J. (Maynooth University College, Maynooth, Republic of Ireland)
Ireland, Republic of 452–60

CRAELIUS, M. H. (Ministry of Education and Culture, Windhock, Namibia)
Namibia 684–91

CRELLIN, C. T. (Oxford, UK)
Bhutan 103–09; *Myanmar* 676–83

CRUZ CÁRDENAS, R. E. (Ministry of Education and Culture, Montevideo, Uruguay)
Uruguay 1042–46

DE VALLE, A. L. (Contiguo ESNACIFOR, Comayagua, Honduras)
Honduras 403–08

DIALLO, H. A. B. (Ministry of Education, Conakry, Republic of Guinea)
Guinea 385–90

DÍAZ DÍAZ, V. H. (Lima, Peru)
Peru 778–85

DJEFLAT, A. (Oran, Algeria)
Algeria 12–18

DLAMINI, E. (Ministry of Education, Mbabane, Swaziland)
Swaziland 935–39

DUBERG, R. (Research Development International, Stockholm, Sweden)
Laos 531–37; *Liberia* 558–63

DWARKASING, W. W. (Training Department Suralco, Paramaribo, Suriname)
Suriname 928–35

DWOMOH, Y. (Ministry of Education, Accra, Ghana)
Ghana 355–61

ESERA, T. (Ministry of Education, Apia, Western Samoa)
Western Samoa 1065–71

FAROOQ, R. A. (Ministry of Education, Islamabad, Pakistan)
*Pakistan 751–58

FARRUGIA, C. J. (University of Malta, Msida, Malta)
Malta 623–30

FAXAS, Y. F. (University of Havana, Havana, Cuba)
*Cuba 243–49

GANDÁSEGUI, M. A. (CELA, Panama City, Panama)
Panama 758–63

GATAWA, B. S. M. (Harare, Zimbabwe)
Zimbabwe 1084–91

GENNAOUI, A. (National Planning Office, Port Vila, Vanuatu)
Syria 957–64

GEZI, K. (California State University, Sacramento, California, USA)
Libya 563–69

GHAFOOR, A. (Ministry of Education, Islamabad, Pakistan)
*Pakistan 751–58

GIL, G. A. (Ministry of Education and Science, Madrid, Spain)
Spain 901–11

GOMES, C. A. C. (Catholic Integrated Colleges of Brasília, Brazil)
Brazil 127–34

GRETLER, A. (Swiss Coordination Center for Research in Education, Aarau, Switzerland)
Switzerland 947–56

GWANG-CHOL CHANG (International Institute for Educational Planning, Paris, France)
Korea, Democratic People's Republic of 509–14

HAKEEM, A. H. A. (Ministry of Education, Male, Republic of Maldives)
Maldives 609–14

HALLS, W. D. (University of Oxford, Oxford, UK)
United Kingdom 1025–33

HAQ, F. (Ministry of Education, Kabul, Afghanistan)
Afghanistan 1–7

HERRANEN, M. (Ministry of Education, Helsinki, Finland)
Finland 322–31

HOI, N. (Department of Education, Port Moresby, Papua New Guinea)
*Papua New Guinea 764–70

HUSAIN, M. A. (UNESCO, Paris)
Congo 220–27

HUSSEIN, M. G. (Ministry of Education, Kuwait, State of Kuwait)
Kuwait 524–31

JACKŪNAS, Z. (Vilnius, Lithuania)
*Lithuania 569–76

JANOWSKI, A. (Institute for Educational Research, Warsaw, Poland)
*Poland 794–801

JANSEN, M. (Danish National Institute for Educational Research, Copenhagen, Denmark)
*Denmark 266–74

JIYONO (Office of Education and Cultural Research and Development, Jakarta, Indonesia)
Indonesia 439–48

JOHNSTONE, J. N. (Australian Planning and Training Associates Pty Ltd, Sydney, New South Wales, Australia)
Kiribati 505–08; *Tuvalu* 1008–12; *Vanuatu* 1046–52

KALA, U. (Tallinn Pedagogical University, Tallinn, Estonia)
Estonia 302–07

KANAYA, T. (Sonoda Women's College, Amagasaki, Japan)
Japan 482–89

KANN, U. (Ministry of Education and Culture, Windhoek, Namibia)
Namibia 684–91

KARIUKI, M. (UNICEF, Nairobi, Kenya)
Kenya 496–504

KGOMANYANE, G. (Ministry of Education, Gaborone, Botswana)
Botswana 118–26

KHANIYA, T. R. (Ministry of Education and Culture, Kathmandu, Nepal)
Nepal 691–98

KIERNAN, M. A. (Ministry of Education and Culture, Kathmandu, Nepal)
Nepal 691–98

KNOWLES, J. (Ministry of Education, Culture and Youth Affairs, St John's, Antigua and Barbuda)
Antigua and Barbuda 27–33

KOKORA, P. D. (Georgetown University, Washington, DC, USA)
Côte d'Ivoire 235–43

KOMOROWSKA, H. (University of Warsaw, Warsaw, Poland)
Poland 794–801

KONTOGIANNOPOULOU-POLYDORIDES, G. (University of Patras, Patras, Greece)
Greece 362–70

KÕRGESAAR, J. (Tartu University, Tartu, Estonia)
Estonia 302–07

KOTÁSEK, J. (Charles University, Prague, Czech Republic)
Czech Republic 257–65

KREINER, S. (Danish National Institute for Educational Research, Copenhagen, Denmark)
Denmark 266–74

LAMBIN, R. (University of Hamburg, Hamburg, Germany)
Cambodia 161–70

LAMINE, B. (Ministry of Education, Tunis, Tunisia)
Tunisia 993–1003

LÁRUSSON, H. (Ministry of Culture and Education, Reykjavik, Iceland)
Iceland 424–30

LAYNE, A. (University of the West Indies, Cave Hill, Barbados)
Barbados 77–85

LE THAC CAN (Hanoi, Vietnam)
Vietnam 1060–65

LEACH, F. (University of London, London, UK)
Sudan 919–28

LEAL FILHO, W. D. S. (University of Bradford, Bradford, UK)
Guinea-Bissau 390–96

LEHMANN, R. H. (University of Hamburg, Hamburg, Germany)
Germany 346–55

LEYTON SOTO, M. (SIMAC, Guatemala City, Guatemala)
Guatemala 378–85

LIMBASSA, D. (University of Bangui, Bangui, Central African Republic)
Central African Republic 189–92

LUKŠIENÉ, M. (Vilnius, Lithuania)
*Lithuania 569–76

McKENZIE, P. A. (Australian Council for Educational Research, Hawthorn, Victoria, Australia)
Australia 40–48

McLEAN, M. (University of London, London, UK)
Bahamas 58–64

MAGABE, M. (Catholic University of Bukavu, Rwanda)
Zaire 1078–84

MAHROUSE, M. E. (Assiut University, Sohag City, Egypt)
Egypt 286–95

MAIMUNAH, S. (Ministry of Education, Kuala Lumpur, Malaysia)
*Malaysia 601–08

MANGUBHAI, F. (University of Southern Queensland, Toowoomba, Queensland, Australia)
Fiji 314–22

MARENTIČ POŽARNIK, B. (University of Ljubljana, Ljubljana, Slovenia)
Slovenia 883–91

MARKLUND, S. (University of Stockholm, Stockholm, Sweden)
Sweden 940–47

MARTIN E. (University of Havana, Havana, Cuba)
*Cuba 243–49

MASRI, M. (Ministry of Education, Amman, Jordan)
*Jordan 489–96

MATEEV, M. D. (University of Sofia, Sofia, Bulgaria)
Bulgaria 141–48

MICHEL, C. (University of California, Santa Barbara, California, USA)
*Guadeloupe and Martinique 370–78

MINGAT, A. (Institut de Recherche sur l'Economie de l'Education, Dijon, France)
Togo 979–84

MOADJIDIBAYE, T. D. (University of Chad, N'Djamena, Chad)
Chad 192–98

MOEGIADI (Office of Education and Cultural Research and Development, Jakarta, Indonesia)
*Indonesia 439–48

MONCHABLON, A. (Paris, France)
France 331–39

MORA, J. (Del Valle University, Cali, Colombia)
Colombia 212–20

MORRIS, R. R. (Ministry of Education, Kingston, Jamaica)
*Jamaica 474–81

MOTTAHAR, M. M. (University of Sana'a, Sana'a, Yemen)
Yemen 1071–78

MUKENDWA, M. J. (Ministry of Education and Culture, Windhock, Namibia)
*Namibia 684–91

MUNBODH, S. (Industrial and Vocational Training Board, Rose Hill, Mauritius)
Mauritius 635–43

MUST, O. (Tartu University, Tartu, Estonia)
*Estonia 302–07

MYLONAS, T. (University of Patras, Patras, Greece)
Greece 362–70

NDENGEJEHO, P. B. (National University of Rwanda, Ruhengeri, Rwanda)
Rwanda 828–35

NHAVOTTO, A. (Ministry of Education, Maputo, Mozambique)
Mozambique 669–76

NIKANDROV, N. D. (Russian Academy of Education, Moscow, Russia)
Russia 819–28

NOMBRE, J. D. (Ouagadougou, Burkina Faso)
Burkina Faso 148–52

NYIRENDA, S. (Ministry of Education and Culture, Lilongwe, Malawi)
Malawi 596–601

ODAET, C. F. (Makerere University, Kampala, Uganda)
Uganda 1012–21

ÖNEY, B. A. (Boğaziçi University, Istanbul, Turkey)
Turkey 1003–08

OUANE, A. (UNESCO Institute for Education, Hamburg, Germany)
Mali 615–22

OUEDRAOGO, N. M. (Ouagadougou, Burkina Faso)
Burkina Faso 148–52

OUSMANE, D. A. (Nouakchott, Mauritania)
Mauritania 630–35

PAPANASTASIOU, C. (University of Cyprus, Nicosia, Cyprus)
Cyprus 250–57

PETERS, M. E. (Dominica Teachers' Training College, Roseau, Dominica)
Dominica 274–80

PETTY, M. A. (Universidad Católica de Córdoba, Córdoba, Argentina)
Argentina 33–39

PHILIPPART, A. (Ministry of Education, Research, and Training, Brussels, Belgium)
Belgium 85–92

PIEBALGS, A. (Ministry of Education, Riga, Latvia)
Latvia 537–42

PIERRE-JACQUES, C. (University of Quebec at Montreal, Montreal, Quebec)
Haiti 397–403

PIGEON, G. (University of California, Santa Barbara, California, USA)
Guadeloupe and Martinique 370–78

POSCH, P. (University of Klagenfurt, Klagenfurt, Austria)
Austria 48–58

RADI, M. (Ministry of Education, Rabat, Morocco)
Morocco 664–69

RAKOTONDRAZAKA, R. (Ministry of Universities, Antananarivo, Madagascar)
Madagascar 589–96

RANAWEERA, A. M. (UNESCO, Hamburg, Germany)
Sri Lanka 912–19

RAU, J. M. (Ministry of Education, Lisbon, Portugal)
Portugal 801–08

REIMERS, F. (Harvard University, Cambridge, Massachusetts, USA)
Costa Rica 228–34; *Venezuela* 1052–60

REYES, M. E. (International Institute for Educational Planning, Paris, France)
Mexico 643–53

RIVAROLA, D. M. (Centro Paraguayo de Estudios Sociológicos, Asunción, Paraguay)
Paraguay 771–78

RODRÍGUEZ, C. (Santiago College, Santiago, Chile)
Chile 198–206

RUIZ-ESPARZA, R. (Albuquerque, New Mexico, USA)
El Salvador 295–302

RWEHERA, M. (Paris, France)
Burundi 152–60

SACK, R. (Paris, France)
Benin 98–102

SALVO PAYSSÉ, M. T. (Ministry of Education and Culture, Montevideo, Uruguay)
*Uruguay 1042–46

SAMANIEGO F., J. (Quito, Ecuador)
Ecuador 280–86

SEITLHEKO, A. N. (Ministry of Education, Maseru, Lesotho)
Lesotho 550–58

SESAY, A. B. (Ministry of Education, Youth and Sport, Freetown, Sierra Leone)
*Sierra Leone 857–864

SHAMLAYE, B. (Ministry of Education, Mont Fleuri, The Seychelles)
Seychelles 852–56

SHIN, SE-HO. (Korean Educational Development Institute, Seoul, Republic of Korea)
Korea, Republic of 515–24

SHMUELI, E. (Jerusalem, Israel)
Israel 461–66

SIAROON, M. (Office of the National Education Commission, Bangkok, Thailand)
*Thailand 972–79

SOLOMON, J. (University of Patras, Patras, Greece)
*Greece 362–70

SOW, M. (Ministry of National Education, Dakar, Senegal)
Senegal 845–52

SPAULDING, S. (University of Pittsburgh, Pittsburgh, Pennsylvania, USA)
Mongolia 653–64

SUTARIA, M. C. (SEAMEO/INNOTECH, Quezon City, The Philippines)
Philippines 785–93

ŠVECOVÁ, J. (Charles University, Prague, Czech Republic)
*Czech Republic 257–65

TAUFE'ULUNGAKI, A. M. (Ministry of Education, Nuku'alofa, Tonga)
Tonga 984–92

TAYLOR, W. A. (Ministry of Education, Youth and Sport, Freetown, Sierra Leone)
*Sierra Leone 857–864

TEMO, S. (Tirana, Albania)
Albania 7–12

TENG TENG (Chinese Academy of Social Sciences, Beijing, People's Republic of China)
China, People's Republic of 206–12

THOMAS, R. M. (University of California, Santa Barbara, California, USA)
American Samoa 19–27

VAIDEANU, G. (Bucharest, Romania)
Romania 814–19

VALVERDE, G. A. (Michigan State University, East Lansing, Michigan, USA)
United States 1033–41

VANTUCH, J. (Bratislava, Slovakia)
Slovak Republic 874–83

VERGIDIS, D. (University of Patras, Patras, Greece)
*Greece 362–70

VISALBERGHI, A. (University "La Sapienza," Rome, Italy)
Italy 466–74

VUYK, E. J. (Ministry of Education and Science, Zoetermeer, The Netherlands)
Netherlands 699–708

WAHBE, N. (Ministry of Education, Manama, Bahrain)
*Bahrain 64–70

WARI, P. (Department of Education, Port Moresby, Papua New Guinea)
*Papua New Guinea 764–70

YEMBE, O. W. (University of Yaounde, Yaounde, Cameroon)
Cameroon 170–80

YEOH, O. C. (National Institute of Nanyang Technological University, Singapore, Republic of Singapore)
Singapore 864–74

YOLOYE, E. A. (Amoye Institute for Educational Research and Development, Ibadan, Nigeria)
Nigeria 729–37

ZOUAIN, G. (UNESCO, Paris, France)
Lebanon 542–50

Name Index

The Name Index has been compiled so that the reader can proceed either directly to the page where an author's work is cited, or to the reference itself in the bibliography. For each name, the page numbers for the bibliographic citation are given first, followed by the page number(s) in parentheses where that reference is cited in text. Where a name is referred to only in text, and not in the bibliography, the page number appears only in parentheses.

The accuracy of the spelling of authors' names has been affected by the use of different initials by some authors, or a different spelling of their name in different papers or review articles (sometimes this may arise from a transliteration process), and by those journals which give only one initial to each author.